TROUBLESHOOTING
GUIDE TO RESIDENTIAL CONSTRUCTION

The Diagnosis and Prevention of Common Building Problems

From the Editors of The Journal of Light Construction

Cover Illustration: Tim Healey
Cover Photos: Carolyn Bates, Ron Whitaker

Editor: Steven Bliss
Production Editor: Josie Masterson-Glen
Article Editors: Sal Alfano, Ted Cushman, Clayton DeKorne, Dave Dobbs, Don Jackson, Carl Hagstrom

Production Manager: Theresa Emerson
Graphic Designer: Lyn Hoffelt
Illustrator: Tim Healey

International Standard Book Number: 0-9632268-9-4
Library of Congress Catalog Card Number: 96-079909
Printed in the United States of America

A Journal of Light Construction Book

The Journal of Light Construction is a tradename of Builderburg Group, Inc.

Builderburg Group Inc.
932 West Main Street
Richmond, VT 05477

INTRODUCTION

"If we learn so much from our mistakes, I must be a near genius by now." — unknown builder

In home building and remodeling, as in many other professions, the important lessons are learned on the job. To a great extent that means learning from our own mistakes — which is good up to a point. Some mistakes, however, we'd just as soon not experience personally. We don't want to crack a foundation, start an electrical fire, or drop a set of trusses, the learning experience notwithstanding. These are things we'd rather learn some other way — preferably from someone with solid, first-hand experience.

This book was put together in that spirit — to help readers tap into the vast pool of hard-won knowledge that exists on job sites across the country. To that end, we looked over the past ten years of *The Journal of Light Construction* and gleaned all the best material on product and material failures, structural trouble spots, and other problems that lead to customer complaints and callbacks. As in *The Journal*, you, the readers, are the primary source of the information; we just help put it to work.

We hope the book works for you and helps you prevent a significant building problem or solve one you already face. First-hand experience may in fact be the best teacher, but the experience of others can be a pretty close second if we pay attention — and it's a whole lot cheaper.

Steven Bliss
Editorial Director

TABLE OF CONTENTS

CHAPTER 1

FOUNDATIONS & SITEWORK

- Preventing Basement Leakage

- Foundation Settlement and Frost Heaves

- Building on Fill

- Controlling Cracks in Slabs

- Retaining Walls

- Septic Systems: Remodeler's Guide

PREVENTING BASEMENT LEAKAGE

Wet basements and crawlspaces are the most common problems I see as a consultant, followed by attic moisture problems. And sometimes the two are related. But there is no excuse for a wet foundation in a new house.

The marketplace is full of waterproofing systems, all of which are relatively expensive. But there is a system available to builders everywhere that is inexpensive, easy to apply, and foolproof. It requires no special skills, and causes no delays in delivery. It's simply a combination of standard materials, good sense, and careful drainage details.

The Usual Way

The excavation hole is usually backfilled with loose, disturbed material that will settle over time as water puddles on it. But where is this water to go once it reaches the bottom of the excavation? It's trapped between undisturbed soil and concrete.

Even if a perimeter drain has been provided and run to daylight or to a sump, it will soon silt up and become useless (Figure 1). Water will build up against the walls. If the drain has no outlet — as is too often the case — water will build up that much faster. When it does, the water pressure often finds relief through joints and cracks in the walls.

If the walls are reasonably watertight, the weight of saturated soil can crack and buckle the foundation. In very cold climates, this process is aggravated by frost.

Those who build in areas with coarse and sandy soils have an easier life — but not necessarily without problems. I have been called a number of times to diagnose buckling foundation walls in sandy areas. Every single case was caused by rain or melting snow — with temperatures near the freezing point during the day and below freezing at night. The sandy soil didn't have time to drain and the water froze, putting pressure on the foundation. Over the course of the winter, the situation got worse until finally the foundation gave way.

So how can these problems be prevented?

A Better Way

First, you need to build houses with foundations that stick up far enough above the natural grade to permit proper final grading that drops away from the house. For instance, if you now excavate about 8 feet deep so that your houses hug the ground when completed, try going down only 6 1/2 feet. You'll save on dozer time and won't have as much dirt to store and handle.

Next, if you build with poured foundations, you must ensure that the concrete cures properly. And, finally, you must carefully follow a strict procedure to build and protect the foundation drain, backfill, and final grade.

As soon as the wall forms come off, knock off the ties and cover the foundation walls — inside and out — with 6-mil clear plastic. Don't use black plastic except in winter pours, as it can cause the concrete to overheat.

Keep the number of joints in the poly to a minimum, overlap them substantially, and tape them with duct tape. Let the plastic drape over and cover the footings, and hold it in place with shovelfuls of crushed

Figure 1. Drain tile filled with roots (left) or silt (below) is worthless. The combination of a properly detailed gravel bed and filter fabric will keep out both.

stone. This will prevent dehydration of the concrete and thus allow complete curing, which takes 28 days. The end result will be rock-hard walls that are less prone to shrinkage cracks or water penetration.

Leave the outside plastic on permanently; you may remove the inside plastic after a month.

Footing Drains

If you plan on insulating the foundation from the outside — which I highly encourage — this is the time to do it. Then pin a strip of filter fabric (Typar, Mirafi, etc.) to the bank of the excavation (see Figure 2). Make sure the strip is wide enough to cover the entire perimeter drain that you are about to install.

The filter fabric must extend from the bottom of the trench all the way to the foundation wall with a few inches to spare. This will keep the footing drains from silting up. Don't be stingy; backfilling makes the fabric "shrink."

Spread a couple of inches of 1 1/2-inch crushed stone on the bottom of the trench outside the footings. Next, lay the perforated pipe (holes face down) around the perimeter on the crushed-stone bed. The pipe doesn't need to be sloped; sloping the pipe is impractical and could endanger the footing, since its lower end would have to be below the footing. Water rarely runs in the pipe, anyway. Except in flood-like conditions, the 2 inches of stone below the pipe will handle the water. (Sites that need to use the perforated pipe regularly should probably not have been developed in the first place.)

Now cover the pipe with enough crushed stone to cover the entire footing plus the bottom 4 to 6 inches of the foundation wall. Drape the filter fabric over the stones and turn it up the foundation wall. Then proceed carefully with backfilling.

Backfilling

Backfilling should be done only with coarse material such as bank-run gravel or coarse sand. Do not use silty or clayey soils, because they will quickly plug up the pores of the filter fabric and render the drain useless.

I strongly recommend that you backfill up to, or almost to, natural grade with this coarse material. This not only provides excellent percolation for any water that penetrates the surface, but also gives good protection against frost pressure. Also, the bank-run gravel or coarse sand is dense enough that it won't silt up from the topsoil.

Where the excavation trench around the foundation is quite wide, it is easy to reduce the amount of coarse material needed by gently dumping a band of it against the foundation and following with native soil pushed over the lip to even out the level. These procedures should be alternated until you reach the top.

You will now have about 2 feet of foundation sticking out of the ground. Use the native soil to build the grade up to several inches below the siding. The slope of this final grading is necessary to shed water away from the building; shoot for a slope of about 2 inches per foot. Generally, you will use most of the native soil to accomplish this, and will have to haul away little or none.

There's another advantage to this system. In subdivisions — or where

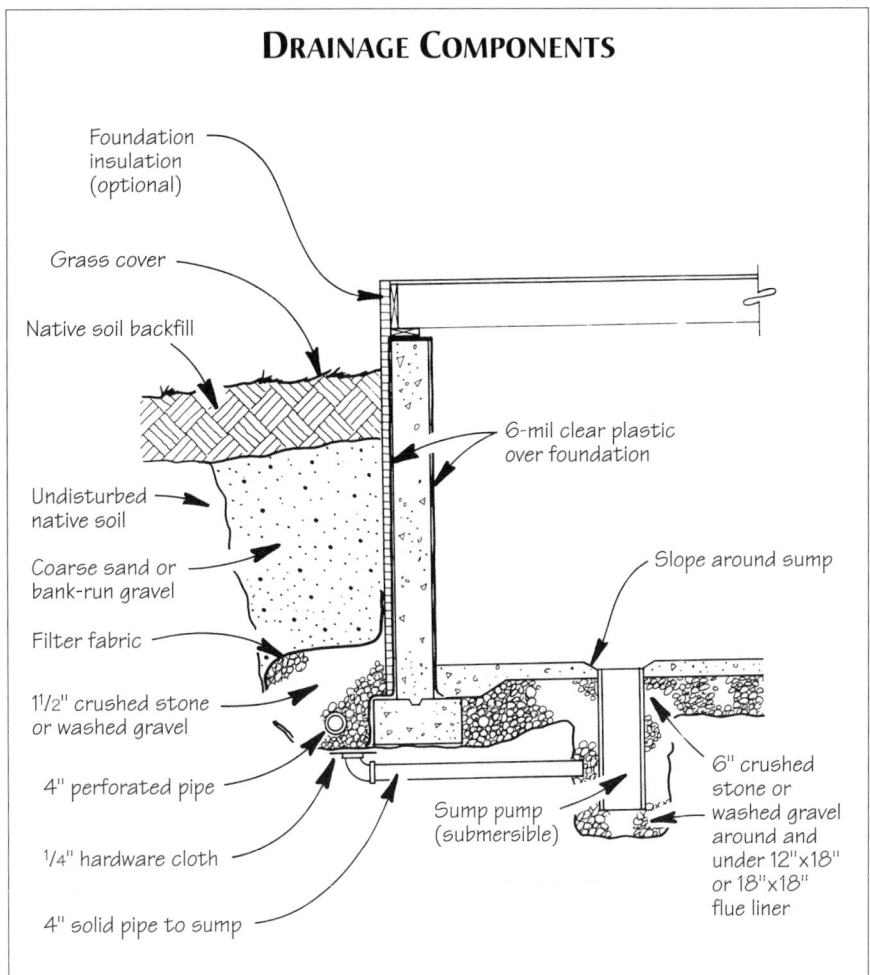

Figure 2. The gravel bed and footing drains remove subsurface water. The filter fabric keeps out silt, and the coarse sand keeps the filter fabric from clogging up. The sloped finish grade and grass keep most water out from the start.

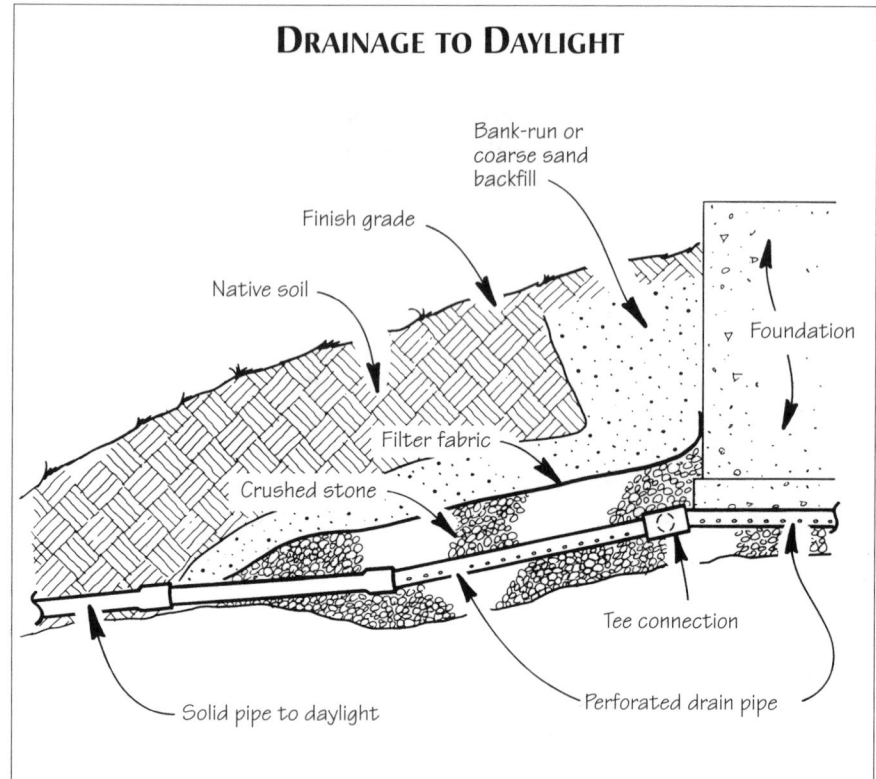

DRAINAGE TO DAYLIGHT

Bank-run or coarse sand backfill

Finish grade

Native soil

Foundation

Filter fabric

Crushed stone

Tee connection

Solid pipe to daylight

Perforated drain pipe

Figure 3. Run the footing drain to daylight, if possible. The outlet should be capped with hardware cloth to keep out rodents.

you build two or more houses on flat, contiguous lots — you can vary the grade and create interesting contours, while providing swales between houses that will conduct water to main disposal channels.

If you provide landscaping, don't stick shrubs or flower beds directly against the foundation (put them 4 to 6 feet away). Advise your customers that if placed closer these would trap water and could damage the waterproofing system. Instead, plant grass or lay sod around the foundation. Grass next to the foundation is one of the best insurance policies against water problems you can buy. It will shed a lot of water, and most of the rest will be caught in its deep root mat and re-evaporated.

To Sump or Daylight

If these steps are carefully followed, surface water should never reach the perimeter drain. In many areas, however, *subsurface* water might be a problem. To function properly in either case, the drain must have an outlet.

If you are building on a lot that permits the footing drain to flow to daylight, the following procedure is recommended. At the point where you tee the drain into the outlet, excavate a sloping (minimum 1 inch per foot) shelf that extends from the footing drain to 10 feet away. Connect a 5- to 10-foot section of perforated pipe to the tee, and lay it in a heavy bed of crushed stone that is covered with filter fabric (see Figure 3). Connect solid pipe to the single section of perforated pipe, and run solid pipe to daylight. This will allow water to drain away from the foundation perimeter into this collection basin and be carried away, thereby keeping the soil under the footing dry.

Cap the daylight outlet with removable hardware cloth to keep rodents from nesting inside this secure shelter, and build a loose-stone culvert around it to keep grass and soil from closing it up.

When building on a flat site, connect the perimeter drain to a solid pipe that goes under the footing to a sump inside the basement or crawlspace. The pipe should turn up and terminate level with the bottom of the footing, and be covered with hardware cloth to keep out the crushed stones. The sump should pump to the exterior, for example through a band joist, with a check valve at the base of the hose to prevent drain-back. The water should strike a splash block and drain away from the foundation on a sloping grade.

To handle a rising water table under the slab, spread 4 to 8 inches of crushed stone under it, and connect this stone layer to the exterior perimeter drain with a solid pipe that runs through the footing. In the case of a sump, surround the sump with crushed stones so the water can drain into it. I should mention that for a sump I always use — and recommend — a large clay flue-liner section that is set on and surrounded by 6 inches of crushed stone.

I use the term "crushed stone" for a reason. In some areas, gravel means washed round gravel, and it can be obtained in about 1½ inch diameter. But in other areas, gravel means bank or river gravel, which is not suitable for the fast movement of water. Crushed stone should go around the footing drains; bank-run gravel or coarse sand goes above.

Carefully follow this prescription and you'll have an inexpensive and effective — indeed, foolproof — foundation waterproofing system that will ensure crack-free walls and an unblemished reputation.

By Henri deMarne, a home inspector and nationally syndicated columnist from Waitsfield, Vt.

FOUNDATION SETTLEMENT AND FROST HEAVES

Most builders fail to recognize that the soil surrounding a foundation is responsible for the majority of foundation failures. Even foundations built with good materials and first-rate workmanship will fail if poor soil conditions are not considered.

The five leading causes of foundation callbacks in cold climates, listed in order from the most to the least frequent, are

1. Frost-related damage
2. Settlement problems
3. High water-table problems
4. Leaky basements
5. Soil contaminant problems

Preventing Frost-Damaged Foundations

Water expands in volume by about 10% when it freezes, and can exert pressures of up to 80,000 pounds per square foot as it expands. If wet soil below a footing is allowed to freeze, significant heaving will occur, causing damage to the structure above.

For frost heave to take place, three conditions must be present: a frost-susceptible soil, a source of water, and freezing temperatures. Eliminate any one of these conditions and you'll eliminate frostheave.

To avoid frostheave in colder climates, footings are placed below the frostline. But this alone doesn't prevent frost problems altogether.

Adfreezing

Severe damage to the foundation wall can result from adfreezing, or side grip, of the soil to the wall (Figure 4). This phenomenon happens much more frequently in unheated buildings, like garages (Figure 5). As the soil surrounding the wall freezes and expands, it exerts an upward thrust on the foundation walls, which can result in costly damage.

Since soils such as clay, fine sands, tills, and silts are susceptible to frost action, they should not be used to backfill around unheated structures.

A practical method that prevents adfreezing is to provide a "slip plane" at the surface of the foundation wall. Many builders create this slip plane by placing two or more layers of 6-mil construction-grade polyethylene between the soil and the surface of the wall. The durability of polyethylene has improved dramatically over the past few years, and the builders I've talked to have reported good results.

Pier or sonotube foundations are a cheaper alternative for seasonal homes in my area. Since these foundations are even more susceptible to adfreezing, it's critical that a slip plane be provided.

Uninsulated basements in heated buildings will typically leak enough heat to keep the surrounding soil from freezing. However, placing

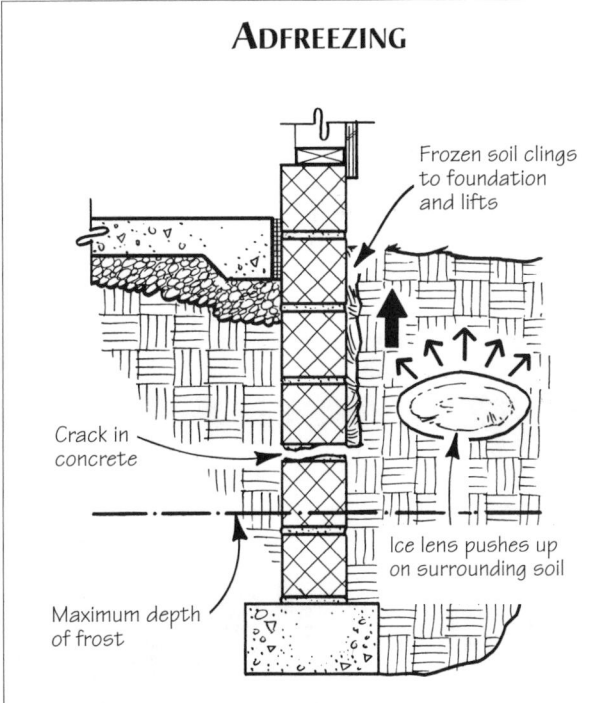

ADFREEZING

Frozen soil clings to foundation and lifts

Crack in concrete

Maximum depth of frost

Ice lens pushes up on surrounding soil

Figure 4. As the soil around an unheated building freezes and expands, it can "grip" the foundation and lift the wall apart (left). Although block walls are particularly susceptible, poured concrete walls can also be damaged (below).

insulation on the interior of basement walls will reduce this heat leakage and contribute to adfreezing. The only instances of this full basement adfreezing that I've observed have occurred where concrete block walls were used. Again, two layers of 6-mil poly on the exterior of interior-insulated foundation walls will prevent this type of adfreezing from occurring.

Other frost-related problems can occur when improper winter construction methods are used. If a foundation is built in subfreezing weather and the soil below the footings (or surrounding the walls) freezes, frost heave can effectively destroy the foundation. If you can't avoid building during winter conditions, be sure to protect the foundation and keep the temperature in the basement above 40°F.

Preventing Settlement Problems

Most settlement problems are caused by "problem" soils — soils that do not have the bearing capacity to carry structural loads without specialized engineering design (Figure 6). These soils are typically soft clays, including volatile, expansive, and lead clays.

If there are any doubts about the suitability of the soils where you intend to build, make a call to a geotechnical consultant. These experts are often aware of "problem pockets" in the region and can advise you how to proceed with a soils investigation. The Soil Conservation Service is another source for soils information.

Soft clays can often be recognized by probing with a piece of rebar: If soft clay is present, the rod will penetrate the soil easily. Builders should also note any unusual soil profiles or signs of soft clay uncovered during excavation. Keep in mind that in some cases the soil observed in the excavation may be adequate, while the underlying soil may be a soft clay or contain some other buried monster.

If a problem soil is discovered or suspected during excavation, have a soils engineer dig an auger test hole to check the underlying soil within the house excavation. A possible alternative to the auger test hole is to have a backhoe excavate outside the house foundation area. These tests can determine soil strength, which is critical for the proper design of your foundation.

Once the soil strength is determined, engineered footings and the foundation can be designed. Solutions may include a raft or pile foundation, preloading of the site to consolidate weaker soils, or the use of engineered fill.

These measures may add $4,000 to $5,000 to the cost of the foundation, but I consider that a good buy. I've seen situations where it cost more than $60,000 to repair improperly built foundations on problem soils.

Poorly Compacted Fill

Many foundation problems are due to improperly compacted fill material. Soil that is too wet or too dry will not compact properly. Builders should bring in a qualified engineer who will advise (and document) proper compaction techniques.

Be aware that when a foundation hole is "overdug" and excavated soil is returned to the foundation hole to raise the final level, the same compaction rules apply. Whenever possible, avoid using excavated material to raise the level of a foundation hole. By pouring thicker footings or building taller foundation walls, an engineered solution can sometimes be avoided.

High Water Tables

A high water table may result in insufficient foundation support. Excavations below the water table will create a wet hole, which will lead to poor-quality concrete in the footings. If gravel fill is used, the migration of fines will cause foundation settlement.

Figure 5. Unheated garages are prone to damage from adfreezing (left). Two layers of 6-mil polyethylene placed on both sides of the foundation wall provides a slip plane that prevents freezing soils from bonding to the foundation wall (right).

Figure 6. The foundation of this factory home (left) was built on unstable soil. Settlement caused extensive foundation damage (below), which required complete excavation and engineered underpinnings (bottom left and right).

To avoid the problem, check the local groundwater levels and always build above the groundwater table. If disturbance does occur in the foundation soil, do not dig deeper, as additional hydrostatic pressures will occur, causing further loosening of soil. In these cases, consult a geotechnical engineer.

Some areas have a seasonal water table that is highest in the spring and lowest in late summer. In these areas, it's important to establish an "average" water table, and base building decisions on that.

Get Accurate Information

The best no-cost measure for preventing foundation problems is to look at any available soils maps and to check with municipal planning/building departments before starting the job. On larger projects, seek out any geotechnical reports that may have been provided by the developer. The soil type and water table levels are usually analyzed before a subdivision goes in. Geotechnical consultants often have a database of local soils, including known problem areas. Look for a proven track record from the consultant and make sure he or she has liability insurance.

Make sure all geotechnical reports and foundation inspections are certified by a geotechnical engineer and in compliance with local codes. This can be valuable information to present to the home buyer.

In the absence of expert information (or in addition to it), local well drillers and — in more rural areas — farmers have a wealth of knowledge about local water table levels and soil types. The important point is to collect this information as early as possible in the building design process to avoid costly problems or delays.

By Rob Marshall, a civil engineer and building science specialist in Ontario, Canada. Photos courtesy of Ontario New Home Warranty Program.

BUILDING ON FILL

Few foundation topics generate as much confusion as does building on filled sites. Many homeowners and contractors — and even some engineers — assume that filled sites offer good foundation support, particularly for residential or light-commercial structures. The assumption is that if someone took the time to fill a site, it must be better than it was before. This contrasts sharply with my experience, so my first reaction to a filled site is generally, How bad is the problem?

When dealing with a filled site, a prospective developer or contractor should keep in mind the roadside signs that say "Clean Fill Wanted." These signs exemplify the uncertainties you face with a filled site: how was the site filled, and what happens when it is later developed?

There are probably as many different reasons for wanting fill as there are signs. The fill may be needed to provide a level area for parking cars or storing material, or to provide space for a garden or play area. In some instances, a site is filled to cover up a swampy depression or poor soil, such as peat. Some people mistakenly believe that hiding the problem solves it.

The range in the quality of fill is even wider. People take what they can get: loam, silt, wood, ash, building rubble from demolition projects — sometimes even sand and gravel! The homeowners, farmers, and others who do the filling are often unaware that engineering is required, or they are unwilling to spend the money to construct an engineered fill. At any rate, the result rarely conforms to good construction practice.

An Engineered Fill

What is an engineered fill? While each site and building must be assessed individually, when planning an engineered fill you should generally do the following:

• Have a geotechnical engineer assess the underlying soils.
• Know the nature of the structure to be built on top of the fill.
• Establish criteria for fill materials and the degree of compaction.
• Remove organic soils or other deleterious material before placing the fill.
• Place the fill on top of appropriate subgrade soils in thin lifts that are mechanically compacted to the specified densities.
• Have a geotechnical engineer monitor and test the fill materials and the degree of compaction.

Unfortunately, many people involved in filling undeveloped sites don't take these steps. The questions that then arise are:
1. What soils are present below the fill?
2. What fill materials were used?
3. Was the fill compacted?

First, determine *why* the area was filled. Poor quality soils frequently lie under the fill. So even if the fill satisfies all the other requirements of an engineered fill — a rare case — poor subgrade soils could still result in damage to the foundation.

In terms of fill quality, the terms "clean," "solid," or "good" are ambiguous and have no technical meaning. The developer should assess the quality of the material that was used. Trash, wood, stumps, cinders, and ash, for example, are not appropriate for use below structures, even if compacted.

A growing concern is whether environmentally hazardous materials are present in the fill. Contaminated soils may require removal at

POOR SUBGRADE SOIL BENEATH "GOOD" FILL

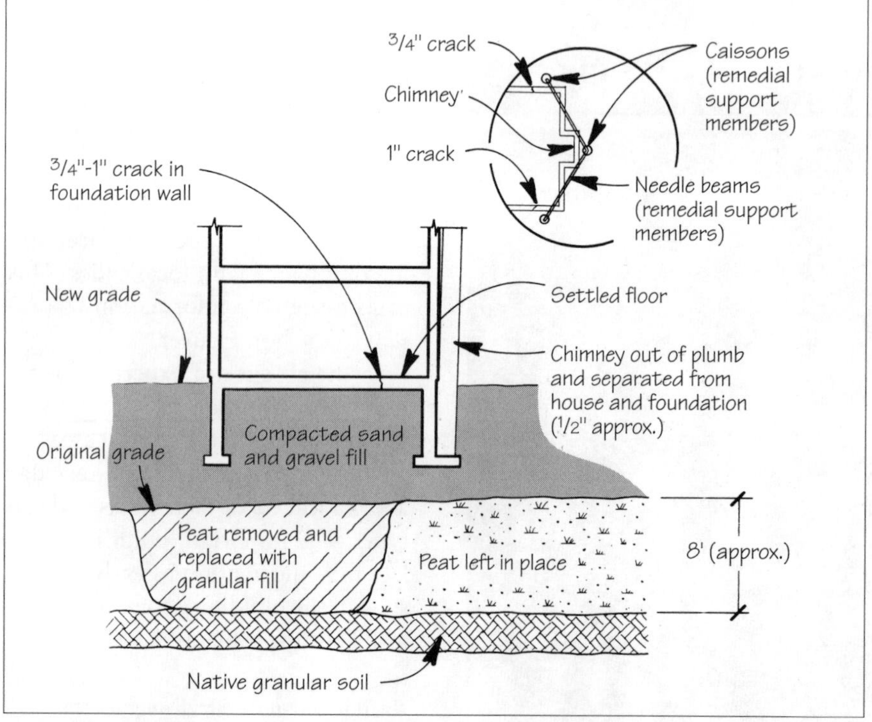

3/4" crack
Chimney
1" crack
Caissons (remedial support members)
Needle beams (remedial support members)
3/4"-1" crack in foundation wall
New grade
Settled floor
Chimney out of plumb and separated from house and foundation (1/2" approx.)
Original grade
Compacted sand and gravel fill
Peat removed and replaced with granular fill
Peat left in place
8' (approx.)
Native granular soil

Figure 7. "Good fill" hid a peat deposit up to 8 feet thick that supposedly had been removed from this site. But part of it remained and cracked the foundation, which later had to be stabilized with caissons and needle beams.

costs far greater than the value of the entire project. Prospective developers should test for hazardous materials when purchasing the property — and, in fact, many mortgage lenders now require this. "Clean fill" has begun to take on a whole new meaning.

Compaction

I am frequently asked, "The fill has been there for a year (or ten years): Is that enough compaction?" In almost all instances, the answer is no. Natural processes do not provide enough compaction for fill to support structures.

"Ponding" (or "flooding") the fill area is not a recommended method of compaction. This procedure cannot be systematically controlled, and its effectiveness is hard to gauge. Most fills have not been systematically compacted, and should be considered inadequate unless proved otherwise.

Assessing compaction *after* the fill has been placed is expensive and time-consuming. Moreover, it is fraught with unknowns because, under the best of circumstances, only a small fraction of the fill can be tested. There's no guarantee that the tested area represents the entire fill. And a small, uncompacted area can significantly damage a structure.

Unknown Fill

So far, this discussion has assumed that the prospective developer knows that the site was filled. Often, however, contractors are not aware that they are building over fill. In some cases, it is difficult to distinguish between fill soils and natural soils.

To guard against problems, you must research the site. Possible sources of information are old topographic site plans, USGS topographic maps, previous owners, neighbors, or local contractors.

Have a geotechnical engineer monitor explorations on all sites where fill is suspected. In fact, a pro-

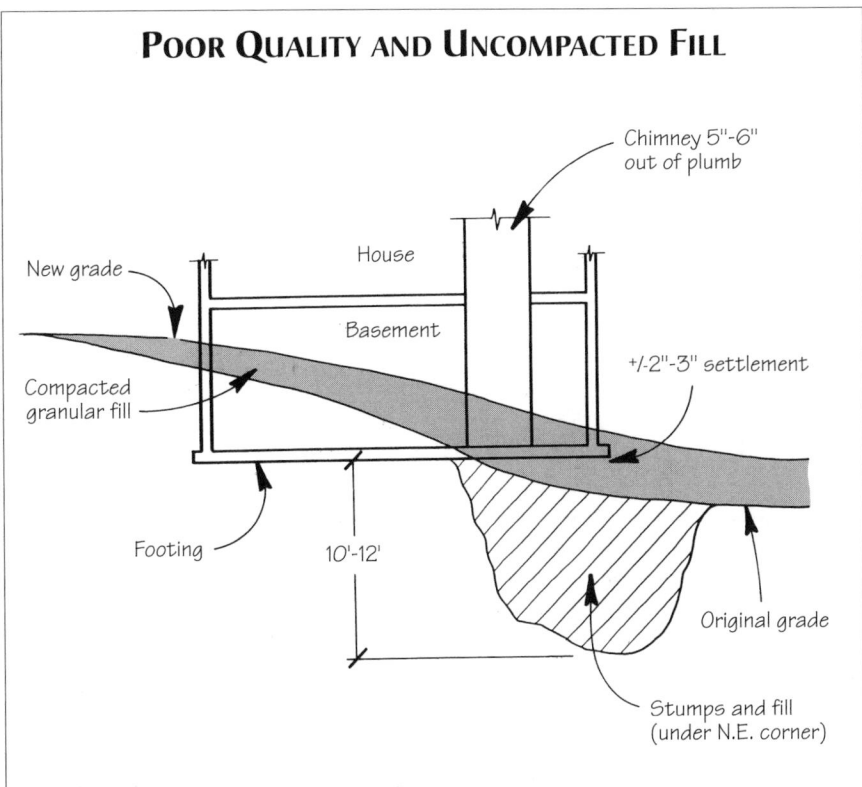

Figure 8. In leveling the site, the excavation contractor was told to bury the stumps at the far end of the lot. Unfortunately, they ended up under one corner of the house — cracking the foundation and shifting the chimney.

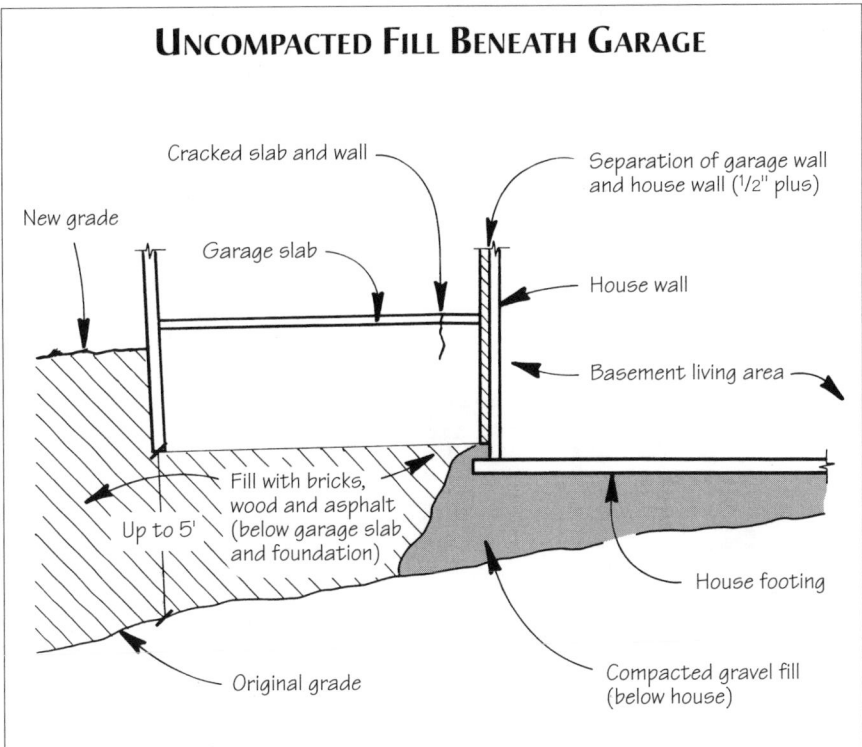

Figure 9. In leveling this site, fill material was properly placed and compacted under the house. But under the garage, the fill was sloppy. It later consolidated — and the slab and walls cracked.

fessional review of soil conditions is a good idea on all house sites — and is required by code in many areas.

Case Studies

A common attitude in residential construction is "It's *only* a house, with no real load on it." This is shortsightedness — particularly in filled sites.

The severity of the problems vary, but in all of the following cases it would have been cheaper to build the foundations right in the first place than it was to repair them later (and, in some cases, pay for the lawyers).

Case one. Compressible soils — frequently peat or other organic soils — that are left below fill are probably

the most common cause of problems on filled sites. The fill frequently appears to be good quality "gravel," which misleads the contractor into assuming that the bearing conditions are good. But the problem is still present *below* the foundation.

In this case, a peat deposit — 8 feet thick in places — was supposedly excavated from the site, and the exca-

---

GETTING GOOD COMPACTION

When a field test shows inadequate compaction, chances are good the problem is caused by soil gradation, poor compacting techniques, or moisture.

Choose the right soil. While every soil can be adequately compacted, the amount of effort

Figure A. Soil that's moist enough to compact well should hold shape when you ball it up in your hands. But the only sure way to determine optimum moisture content is to have the soil tested.

required varies greatly. Choose coarse, granular soils above silt and clay. Their moisture content is easier to manipulate, and they respond well to vibratory compactors. Given a choice, most earthwork contractors know instinctively that they would rather compact gravel than clay.

Between gravel and clay is a range of silt, silty sands and gravels, and clayey silts. Although silt is more permeable than clay, it's difficult to control the moisture content of both soil types. Generally speaking, the lower the percentage of silt and clay particles in the soil, the easier it will be to compact.

Under no circumstances should topsoil, roots, or other organic materials be incorporated into the fill. These materials will decay and decompose over time, eventually causing settling even in well-compacted soil.

Also be alert to changes in grain size in the fill material. If soil grada-

tion changes, so will the optimum dry density. In some cases, gradation changes will be visually obvious, but the tip-off is usually field test results that don't make sense.

Compact shallow lifts. You should compact soil in layers from 6 to 10 inches thick. Even heavy rollers don't have much effect at depths over a foot.

A common mistake in backfilling foundations is to place a 3- or 4-foot-thick layer and then try to salvage the situation by pounding on the surface until it looks great. This might compact the top 8 inches, but 18 or 24 inches down the percent compaction is still low. In this case, the fill will settle unless it is removed, and replaced and compacted in thin lifts.

Moisture matters. Moisture plays a major role in the compaction process. If the soil particles are absolutely dry, there's a lot of friction to overcome when trying to push the particles together, making the process difficult and inefficient. On the other hand, if the spaces between particles are full of water, the water absorbs some of the compaction energy — like a shock absorber. Then the soil particles don't get the full brunt of the compacting impact, and a lot of energy gets wasted.

Sand and gravel dry out quickly in hot weather. Before compacting this type of soil, it may be necessary to use hoses or a water truck to sprinkle the soil with water to increase the moisture content, bringing it closer to optimum.

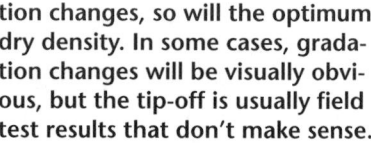

Figure B. The large surface area of a vibratory plate compactor works well with sand and gravel. Here a worker moistens dry sand to speed compaction.

vation was backfilled with sand and gravel fill (see Figure 7). The contractor had performed test borings before construction, and presumably verified that the peat had been removed. A shallow foundation was built bearing on the sand and gravel backfill.

Less than a year later, one end of the house had to be underpinned with caissons and needle beams to stabilize a 3/4-inch crack in the foundation. Although the footings were on the sand and gravel, peat still remained under part of the house. It is not known whether this problem resulted from improperly locating the house over the excavated area, or from inaccuracies in the boring logs.

Case two. Poor fill *material* can also cause settling in light structures.

On this site, the ground originally sloped 10 or 12 feet across the lot. To level the site, the lot was filled with material from nearby areas. In addition, the earthwork subcontractor was told to bury the stumps at the far end of the lot.

When the basement area was excavated, it extended into both natural soils and fill. Because the soils

---

On the other hand, prolonged, heavy rain can create a quagmire in less permeable silt and clay. Once these soils are saturated, it's pointless to attempt compaction. The result is usually surface weaving, rutting, and the kind of disturbance that loosens up even previously compacted soil. Waiting out the wet weather is usually the only answer. Eventually, the moisture will slowly percolate downward and, when the sun reappears, evaporate. Opening wet clay soil to aeration by discing will help speed up the drying process. To keep wet soil stable, you can sandwich in layers of dry sand or gravel.

To judge whether or not the soil you are using is near the optimum moisture content, try forming a handful into a ball (Figure A). If it crumbles easily, the soil is probably too dry; if moisture oozes out, it's too wet.

Avoid frozen soil. When temperatures dip below freezing, all bets are off. Frozen sand or gravel acts just like dry material because the moisture no longer acts to overcome friction. If there's enough moisture in the soil, it will freeze solid. The same is true for fine-grained soils. Once frozen, they can't be moved, let alone compacted. And when silt freezes, it can expand and heave, negating the effect of compaction.

Use the right equipment. Heavy drum rollers, rubber tire rollers, and sheepsfoot rollers work well when compacting clay. A jumping jack will also work in tight quarters. Vibratory rollers and plate compactors work best on sand and gravel (Figures B and C), although

rubber tire rollers and even loaded dump trucks can do the job.

A common error with hand-operated compactors is traveling too fast over an area and making too few passes. The more you pound on a particular spot, the better compacted it will be. The only way to be sure the soil is properly compacted is to test each lift.

Choosing the right equipment for a particular site and soil condition is important. Read the manufacturer's literature before you buy or rent a compactor. Discuss your needs with equipment suppliers and distributors. They usually have people on staff who can match the right machine to the problem at hand.

Test the soil. If you're placing more than a foot or two of fill that will support a structure or a slab, have it tested. First, get a sample of the proposed fill material to a testing lab (to find a lab, look in the Yellow Pages under "Laboratories — Testing" or "Engineers — Testing"). Have the lab perform a Proctor test (named after the engineer who introduced the concept of optimum dry density in the 1930s). The Proctor test subjects a sample of soil to a fixed compaction pressure at varying moisture contents and yields the optimum dry density, the benchmark against which to measure field compaction. Then have the in-place fill tested by someone from the testing lab or by an engineering firm. It's not an expensive process: $200 should cover the cost of a few hours on the job site plus the Proctor test.

If for some reason you can't test

Figure C. The small footprint of a jumping jack does a good job of compacting, particularly in tight spaces.

every lift, at least test compaction in the first lift so that if it's not right, you can adjust the compacting effort before it's too late. There's nothing more discouraging that finding out after 5 feet of fill is placed and compacted that the effort wasn't good enough. The only remedy at that point is to remove the fill and start over.

Keep a shovel handy during the field test. The technician should dig a few shallow test holes to verify that the fill matches the soil on which the Proctor was performed. Test holes are also a good way to check for organics, which should always be removed when detected.

By Roger Dorwart, P.E., president of Knight Consulting Engineers, Inc. in Williston, Vt.

were similar, the contractor didn't realize that part of the house was built on top of fill.

The result was substantial settling of the foundation and slab. The chimney separated from the house, and one corner of the house settled and cracked. Subsequent investigation revealed stumps below the corner of the house to depths of 10 to 12 feet. Figure 8 shows the soil profile below the house.

Case three. The final case shows what can happen when fills are not compacted.

A house and attached garage were located on a sloping site (Figure 9). According to the owner, the main area of the house was built partially on a granular fill that had been properly placed and compacted in thin lifts by the contractor.

The garage, however, was built over an uncompacted mixture of topsoil, subsoil, sand, silt, asphalt, and other materials. Later, the foundation walls and slab at the rear of the garage significantly settled and cracked, due to the consolidation of the uncompacted fill. Apparently, the contractor had considered the garage foundation less important than the main house foundation — but the owners didn't share this view.

Buyers Beware

In summary, prospective developers should approach filled sites with a skeptical and critical eye. A general recommendation is to avoid building on top of any fill that cannot be proved to be an engineered fill.

Beyond that, developers must be aware that the risk of finding hazardous wastes in soil or groundwater is real — and clearly greater in filled sites. This should be considered when evaluating the feasibility of a project.

Finally, these foundation problems on small construction projects demonstrate the fallacy of the "it's only a house" philosophy. Because a structure is small or lightly loaded does not mean that an engineering evaluation of a site is not warranted. An ounce of prevention, in these cases, could have saved pounds of costly callbacks.

By M. Daniel Gordon, a consulting geotechnical engineer from Newton, Mass.

CONTROLLING CRACKS IN SLABS

When it comes to concrete slabs, there is one fact that must be faced by homeowners, contractors, and concrete subs alike: Concrete will crack. Period. The challenge for the concrete sub is to work with the material and make it behave in a way that is acceptable to both the customer and the contractor. The key to success is to control where the concrete is going to crack, and prepare the customer for the inevitable.

Brittle Behavior

Concrete does its best work under compression. It's great for driving cars on, rolling shopping carts on, even for raising elephants on. But it doesn't have great tensile strength. Picture a glass table cover at a restaurant: It works fine when it's in full contact with the table top. You could probably dance on it without any damage to the glass. Your reputation might be shot, but the glass would be okay. But if you hold one edge of the glass off the table and apply pressure to it, the glass shatters.

Concrete behaves the same way. It's this lack of tensile strength, or brittleness, that most often causes the cracking found in residential slabs. A new slab shrinks as it cures, setting up tensile stresses throughout the slab. When the tensile stresses caused by the shrinkage exceed the tensile strength of the concrete, the concrete surrenders, and a crack appears.

And the cracking's not over when the slab is fully cured. A slab expands as the temperature rises and contracts as the temperature drops. This thermal fluctuation guarantees that the slab will always be subjected to tensile stresses.

Figure 10. To prevent settlement cracks, the subgrade must be compacted properly. Here, a worker uses a vibratory plate compactor to correctly prepare the subgrade.

There's not much you can do to control the shrinkage and external forces at work on the slab. But there are other causes of cracking that can and should be avoided.

Compact Before You Pour

Proper subgrade preparation is essential. If the subgrade isn't compacted properly, the slab will settle and sink. If the slab settles and sinks, you'll be asking it to perform like the glass table top that's extended over the edge of the table, and cracking will occur. To prevent a slab from settling, the subgrade should be a minimum of 4 to 6 inches of well-drained and uniformly compacted material (Figure 10).

Never pour concrete on a frozen or heavily frosted subgrade. Water expands as it freezes, and when a frozen subgrade thaws out, the slab will settle.

The problem with plastic. A plastic vapor barrier is often specced as part of the subgrade preparation. The plastic keeps ground moisture from coming back up through the slab and affecting floor coverings and creating damp conditions. That's the good side. But vapor barriers can also increase the amount of shrinkage cracking in a slab. That's bad.

Once the concrete is out of the truck and in place, the water in the mix starts to evaporate. If the concrete is poured directly over plastic, the water has just one avenue of escape — through the surface. Once the top of the slab has dried, this subsurface water will cause shrinkage cracking to occur as it forces its way through the surface of the concrete. Fortunately, most shrinkage cracks are more cosmetic than structural, so if the floor is going to be covered, some cracking may be acceptable.

To reduce the chances of shrinkage cracking, cover the vapor barrier with 3 inches of compacted sand before placing the slab. This sand

Figure 11. The best way to guarantee concrete slump at the site is to perform a cone slump test (left). The wetter the concrete, the higher the slump (right).

Figure 12. Here, 3-inch strips of asphalt-impregnated expansion board isolate a slab from wood framing. The flatworkers can also use the expansion board as a guide for finished slab height.

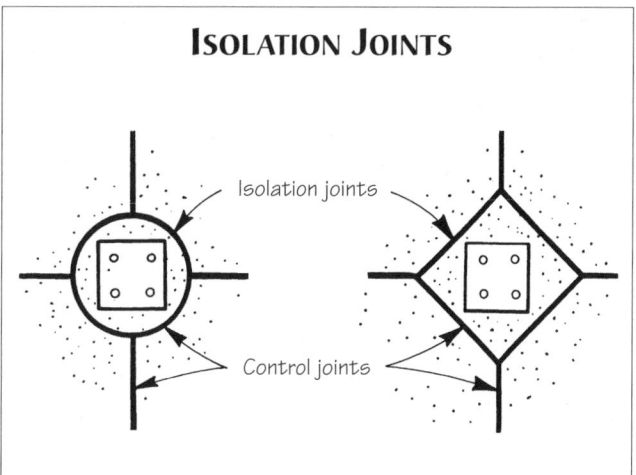

ISOLATION JOINTS

Isolation joints

Control joints

Figure 13. Columns should be isolated from the slab using blockouts. When forming square blockouts, the points of the square should be positioned to meet the control joints.

can be compacted by a thorough wetting the day before the pour.

Thickness, Strength, and Slump

Before you prepare the subgrade, you'll need to decide how thick the slab should be. The American

Figure 14. Sawn joints are cut with a power saw equipped with a diamond blade. They should be cut soon after the surface hardens.

Concrete Institute (ACI) has broken nonstructural concrete floors into five classes and lists design criteria for each class, including thickness, strength of the mix, and maximum slump (see the table, "Recommended Slab Thickness").

Concrete subcontractors should pay more attention to slump (Figure 11). It's controlled by the amount of water in the mix: The more water, the higher the slump and the weaker the concrete. When concrete is poured at a high slump because of excessive water in the mix, the ingredients in the mix don't stay together. The water and some of the cement go one direction, the sand and the rest of the cement go another direction, and the stones end up alone in their own pile. To produce strong, durable concrete, all of the ingredients need to be uniformly distributed so the concrete performs as a homogeneous material.

Exceeding the recommended slump can also result in excessive bleed water. Bleed water is the water in the mix that migrates to

the top of the slab immediately after placement. If this bleed water is not allowed to evaporate but is instead troweled back into the slab, it will create a weakened surface layer that will encourage shrinkage cracking, dusting, and possible crazing of the finish surface (see "The Finisher's Art").

Keeping it together. There is a very common misconception that the addition of wire mesh or rebar in the slab will eliminate cracking. It won't. Steel placed in the middle of the slab section will only limit the width of cracks, preventing them from opening up into canyons.

The highly touted fiber mesh that many concrete suppliers offer won't stop cracking, either. I once had an opportunity to pour two 40-yard slabs side by side, one with wire reinforcement and the other with fiber mesh added to the mix. The slab with the wire cracked where predicted, but the slab with the fiber mesh cracked randomly. (I think the mesh additive makes the concrete look stiffer as it comes

---

THE FINISHER'S ART

I have an immense amount of respect for good concrete finishers. Part athlete and part artisan, a finisher develops a sense of feel and timing that can only be gained by years and years of hard work and practice. I wager a claim that this is some of the toughest work in the trades. So it is only respectfully and carefully that I suggest some areas where finishing crews need to pay attention.

The water valve. Adding water to the concrete mix opens the door to problems. When a mix is designed, it is based on the relationship between the water and the cement, and the Portland Cement Association has established acceptable limits for this water/cement ratio. When water is added to the mix, strength and surface hardness decrease while shrinkage and crack-

ing increase. The bleed rate also increases and so does the chance for dusting and crazing. Concrete designed to be poured at a 4-inch slump should be poured at a 4-inch slump. If you are not familiar with what a 4-inch slump really looks like, I'll bet money that your ready-mix supplier would trip over himself to show you.

Bleed water. Troweling bleed water back into the concrete weakens the finished surface layer of the slab by raising the water/cement ratio. Since the very top of the slab gets all of the attention as well as all of the traffic, it should be as strong and durable as possible.

Air entrainment. In most areas of the country, if the concrete is expected to live outside, it's air entrained. Air entrainment creates billions and billions of microscopic

air bubbles in the mix. This gives moisture someplace to hang out during periods of freezing and thawing. Without air in the mix, the surface layer of concrete, which is exposed to cycles of freezing and thawing, will deteriorate much more quickly than air-entrained concrete. Be sure to ask if your supplier provides air entrainment.

Tools to avoid. I have yet to see a situation where a vibrator was needed when pouring a nonstructural slab. Likewise, the jitterbug should only be used on very low slump placements. The reason that it makes finishing easier is the same reason that it makes the surface much, much weaker: It pushes the large aggregate well below the surface and creates a weak plane where there needs to be a strong one. — D.G.

down the chute, so contractors often add additional water to compensate for what they think is an overly stiff mix.)

Isolation Joints

Since you can't prevent cracks altogether, the best approach is to control them with proper joint design and installation. There are two kinds of concrete joints: isolation, or expansion, joints and control joints.

Slabs are a bit antisocial — they don't interact well with the structural elements of a building. Nonstructural slabs must be allowed to expand, contract, and move up and down independent of surrounding walls and columns.

Installing expansion joint material where the slab meets adjoining walls effectively isolates the slab from the wall. Fastened to the wall before the pour, this material, typically an asphalt-covered fiber board, also serves to establish the finished concrete level (Figure 12).

Columns must also be blocked out and isolated from the rest of the slab. The blockouts at column bases should be round or square. If they're square, they should be positioned so that the points of the square meet the control joints (Figure 13).

Control Joints

This is where you step in and tell the slab where you want it to crack. If you don't, the concrete will crack at random. The most common types of control joints are sawn joints and tooled joints.

Sawn joints should be cut as soon as possible after the concrete hardens. This can be a real judgment call on the part of the finisher, but it's generally a few hours after the final finish has been applied (Figure 14). If stones pull out when sawing begins, you're too early. If random cracks begin to occur before sawing has begun, you're too late.

Tooled joints are formed using a hand-held grooving trowel and are "cut in" immediately after the bleed water has left the slab.

Plastic extrusions are pressed into the wet concrete as the pour progresses to form control joints. One of the most popular is the "zip strip" type, a two-piece tee-shaped extrusion. The 10-foot lengths are tapped into the slab with the butt of a hand float and the top portion of the tee is "zipped" off, leaving the remaining vertical section 1/8 inch below the surface of the slab (Figure 15). Check with your concrete supplier for availability in your area.

No matter which method you use to create control joints, you should follow a few rules of thumb:

- Control joints should be no less than one-fourth the thickness of the slab in depth. This ensures the concrete will crack where you put the joint.
- Joint spacing should equal slab width. Slabs that are rectangular in shape tend to crack in the middle (Figure 16).
- Maximum joint spacing for 4-inch slabs is between 12 and 18 feet (Figure 17).

Where random cracking is better. There are some situations where random cracking is actually preferred. If the slab is going to serve as the base for a tile floor, a random crack will

Figure 15. Two-piece plastic control joint materials are popular on residential sites. The tee-shaped extrusion is pressed into the wet concrete (left), then the top, horizontal piece is "zipped" off, leaving an invisible control joint (right).

RECOMMENDED SLAB THICKNESS

Floor Class	Application	Minimum Thickness	28-day Strength	Slump
1	Residential or tile covered	4"	3,000 psi	4"
2	Offices, churches, hospitals, schools, ornamental residential	4"	3,500 psi	4"
3	Drives, sidewalks for residences, garage floors	4"	3,500 psi	4"
4	Business or commercial walks	5"	3,500 psi	4"
5	Light industrial & commercial	5"	4,000 psi	3"

JIM ALLOR

Figure 16. Rectangular slabs tend to crack in the middle. Control joint spacing should equal slab width.

CONTROL JOINT SPACING

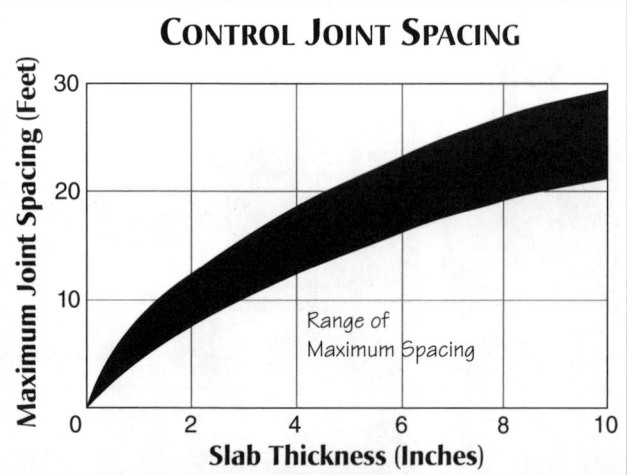

Range of Maximum Spacing

Maximum Joint Spacing (Feet)

Slab Thickness (Inches)

Figure 17. The maximum spacing for control joints depends on the thickness of the slab. The shaded area of the graph indicates the acceptable range.

Figure 18. These galvanized steel forming materials create a "keyed" control joint — essentially a tongue-and-groove — that helps keep adjacent slab sections in a flat, horizontal plane.

crack will appear above the strip. No gas-powered saws to worry about, no expensive diamond saw blades to fret over. During the pour, however, the crew has to realize that the keyway shouldn't be kicked, tripped over, smacked with a shovel, or otherwise moved.

Construction joints. All a construction joint actually does is draw the line where the concrete placement ended on a given day. For thin, lightly loaded floors, a straight-formed "butt joint" is adequate. For more heavily trafficked and loaded applications, a keyed joint may be more appropriate.

Cure It Before It Ails You

Proper curing is essential for controlling cracks as well as for producing strong concrete. Cement and water have a kind of love/hate relationship. When placing fresh concrete, too much water can cause a variety of problems. But once the slab is poured and finished, moisture should remain in the slab as long as possible.

The cement needs the water to complete the chemical process of hydration. If the water in the slab is allowed to evaporate too quickly, the rate of shrinkage — and shrinkage cracking — will increase. Curing is the process of ensuring that the water stays a part of this codependent relationship. It's important to plan on a method of curing before you pour.

If it sounds like a quality slab requires a whole lot of planning and a bushel of effort, you're right. Pouring a first-rate slab requires hard work and concentration from the time the project is conceived until the time that it becomes a rock-hard reality. But when the job is done properly, the rewards can last almost forever.

By Dennis Golden, a former concrete contractor and ready-mix quality control technician. He currently works for the Department of Public Works in Buckley, Wash.

often do less damage to the tile than a poorly aligned control joint. Ideally, a tile joint should fall directly over the control joint, but this is difficult to achieve in the real world.

Keyed Joints

This method is probably the most reliable jointing method for the conscientious concrete crew because it vertically aligns adjacent slab sections. These tongue-and-groove joints are most easily formed by using a manufactured galvanized piece of "keyway" material whose width matches the thickness of the slab (Figure 18). Most suppliers of forming accessories stock this item.

The galvanized strip is typically installed just below the surface of the slab. Once it's in, you're done — the

RETAINING WALLS

In most parts of the U.S. you don't have to look far to find failed or failing retaining walls. They can lead to callbacks, unhappy customers, and even worse, damage to property or even serious injury.

Catastrophic failure (walls tipping over completely) is unusual, partly because the process often progresses slowly and corrective action is usually taken before the catastrophe can occur. But that's not always true. One rainy afternoon in about 1960, the harmless-looking wall in Figure 19 suddenly and spontaneously tipped over. Fortunately my three sisters and I were inside playing Monopoly instead of out playing in the yard. The shock of the impact of five tons of masonry against our house, followed by twenty tons of mud, was something none of us will ever forget.

What made that wall tip, and why so suddenly? The answers are really pretty straightforward. First, the wall was a simple — and very poorly designed — gravity wall that had only a very small footing and no reinforcing steel. In short, it was not much different from a tall stack of blocks. During a period of prolonged heavy rains, the soil behind the wall soaked up a lot of water, and became heavier and more fluid, increasing the force behind the wall. At the same time the ground under and in front of the wall became soft and slippery, undermining the stability of the footing and offering little resistance to the tipping wall (Figure 20).

Clearly, water was the biggest factor in this failure. What could have been done differently? The single most important thing would have been to prevent the accumulation of water in the soil behind and beneath the wall. As the photograph in Figure 19 shows, there were occasional blocks placed sideways as well as gaps between blocks in the bottom course. These well-intended features, like the drain holes frequently seen in the face of retaining walls, were inadequate because water-retentive native soil was used as backfill.

Soils with more than a minimum of clay content (5% fines by weight) are generally water retentive and should not be used as backfill. Instead, place gravel or clean sand behind the wall, with footing drains

Figure 19. This block wall, which on its face looks sturdy and well-built, collapsed during heavy rains because it had no reinforcing, too small a footing, and was backfilled with native soil.

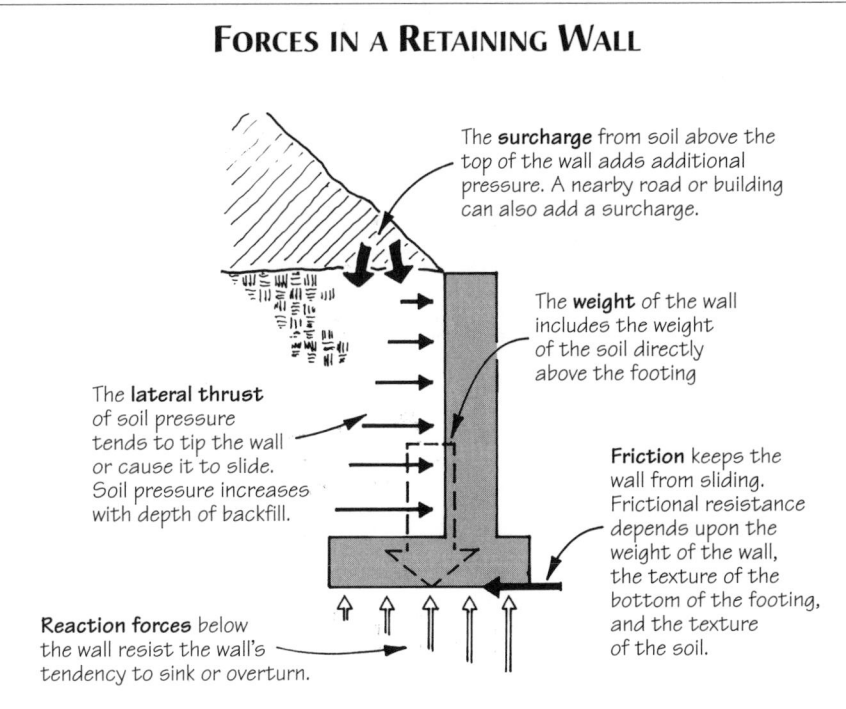

FORCES IN A RETAINING WALL

The **surcharge** from soil above the top of the wall adds additional pressure. A nearby road or building can also add a surcharge.

The **weight** of the wall includes the weight of the soil directly above the footing

The **lateral thrust** of soil pressure tends to tip the wall or cause it to slide. Soil pressure increases with depth of backfill.

Friction keeps the wall from sliding. Frictional resistance depends upon the weight of the wall, the texture of the bottom of the footing, and the texture of the soil.

Reaction forces below the wall resist the wall's tendency to sink or overturn.

Figure 20. The greater the depth of the wall, the greater the total lateral force of the soil. This exerts an overturning force that is resisted by the weight of the soil over the footing and the weight of the wall itself. Friction at the base of the footing keeps the wall from sliding.

MASONRY RETAINING WALL DETAILS

Concrete Block

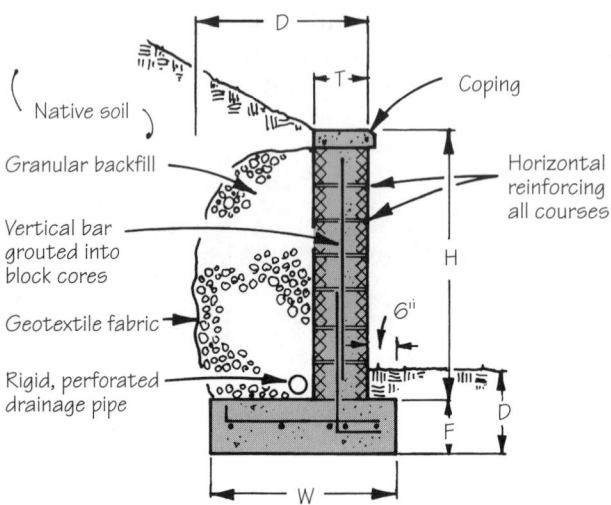

Poured Concrete

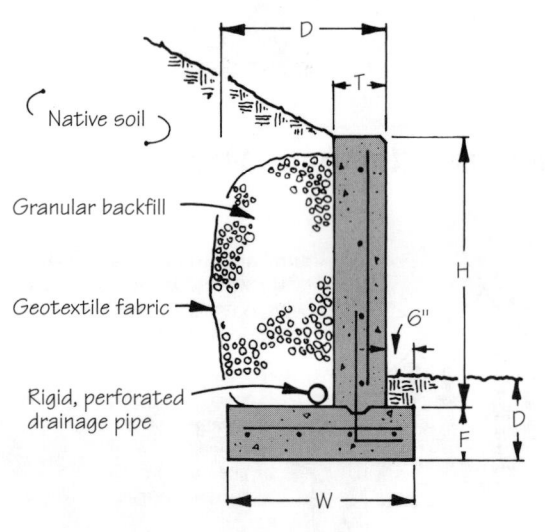

Mortared or Dry-Laid Stone

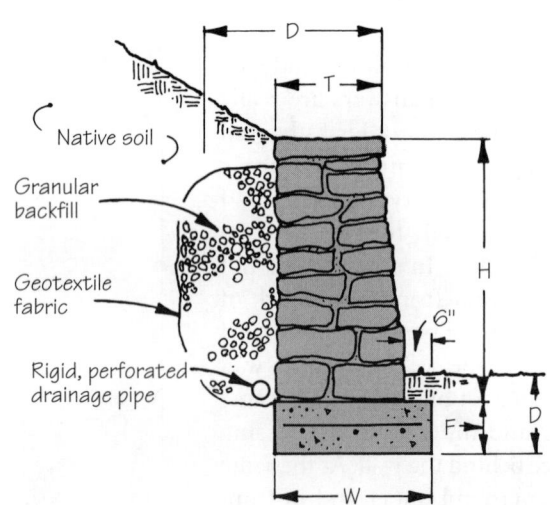

RECOMMENDED DIMENSIONS FOR LOW MASONRY RETAINING WALLS*

H	W	Steel Rebar	Bar Spacing	F	T	D
2'	20"	#3 ($3/8$")	2'-0" o.c.	9"	8"	Local
3'	25"	#4 ($1/2$")	2'-0" o.c.	10"	8"	frost
4'	32"	#5 ($5/8$")	2'-0" o.c.	11"	10"	depth or
5'	42"	#5 ($5/8$")	1'-6" o.c.	12"	12"	12"-18"

*Suggested details for walls no higher than 5 feet where dense, coarse-grain soil exists below footings. Not for loose or soft sand, peat, or clay.

similar to common foundation footing drains. Good practice is to separate the backfill from the native soil face of the excavation with geotextile fabric, often nothing more unusual than "weed mat."

Freeze Damage

The case described above was unusual in two regards: It ended in catastrophic failure, and the prime cause of failure was not freeze damage. In the northern half of the country at least, most retaining wall problems result from the expansion of wet soil when it freezes during cold weather. This type of failure is still an indirect result of backfilling with water-retentive soil and/or the lack of good drainage, but it is frost action that causes the damage.

Figure 21 shows retaining walls suffering from tipping brought on by frozen soil. This kind of damage often occurs over a period of years. With each freeze, the soil expands and pushes the wall outward a little bit. Then, as the soil thaws, it settles down to take up the extra space. I call this frost ratcheting, as it progresses in small increments, and never reverses itself.

The best solution for frost damage is to use gravel or sand backfill and footing drains. In some cases, you may be able to use 2-inch extruded polystyrene foam insulation to help retain ground heat and thereby prevent freezing. Put the foam directly against the back of the wall from the footing to just below grade at the top of the wall, and horizontally across the top of the granular backfill, again just below grade. This strategy is appropriate where a large amount of granular backfill cannot be accommodated, such as a tight site where excavation is limited. Consider foam insulation anywhere you don't have room to place backfill all the way to frost depth.

To paraphrase from an engineering text, the forces exerted by freez-

TIMBER RETAINING WALL DETAILS

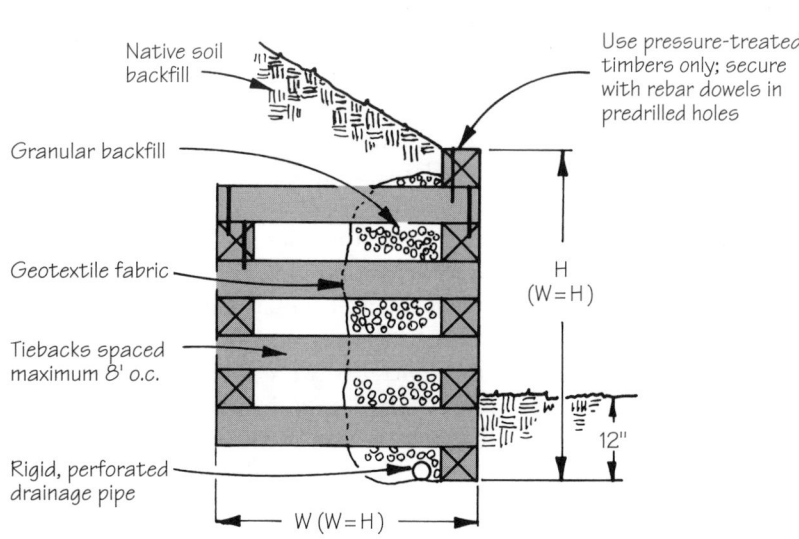

Native soil backfill

Use pressure-treated timbers only; secure with rebar dowels in predrilled holes

Granular backfill

Geotextile fabric

Tiebacks spaced maximum 8' o.c.

Rigid, perforated drainage pipe

H (W = H)

12"

W (W = H)

RECOMMENDED DIMENSIONS FOR LOW TIMBER CRIB WALLS*

Timber Size	Dowel Size	Spacing of Tiebacks
6x6	1/2" (#4 bar)**	6'-0" max
8x8	3/4" (#6 bar)**	8'-0" max

* Details apply to walls no higher than 5 feet.

** In acidic soils, increase by 1/4" or use hot-dipped galvanized.

Figure 21. In northern climates, the freeze-thaw cycle is the primary cause of retaining wall failure. Wet soil expands as it freezes, exerting enormous force against the wall, pushing it outward. As the soil thaws, it settles into the space against the wall and the cycle is set to begin again with the next frost. With poured concrete walls, the entire wall often tips as a whole (left). In the case of block walls (center) or mortared stone walls (right), cracks and bulges may appear as sections of the wall tip.

ing ground are too great to be resisted by any practical structural design. The only prevention is to eliminate the conditions which lead to freezing: water and cold.

Shear Failure

Figure 22 shows a relatively unusual condition known as shear failure. In this case, the upper part of the wall has managed to slide forward without tipping, along a failed mortar line. Mortar is not an effective glue; it usually fails under load unless there is a large compressive force such as the weight of a house sitting on it.

Sometimes the slippage occurs between the footing and the soil beneath (usually with clay soils), in which case the shear failure is also called a slipping failure. That's why you should always set footings 12 to 18 inches below grade and compact any fill between the toe of the footing and the footing excavation.

Other Problems

Look at Figure 23. Is this freeze damage or is it the tree? In a case like this it is hard to tell, because the forces exerted by growing tree roots

are nearly as irresistible as the force of freezing ground. Don't plant large or fast-growing trees near retaining walls.

Figure 24 illustrates classic bad design, frost damage, and material deterioration. How could anyone expect a stack of railroad ties spiked together to resist ground forces? The leaning end of the wall should have been secured to the corner of the foundation or anchored with timber or steel deadmen back into the earth behind. If that had been done, and properly drained backfill used, this wall would still be serviceable. The drainage would also have helped retard the decay visible in the top tie.

When building timber crib walls, dowel the timbers together with lengths of rebar. Driving spikes is ineffective and often splits the timbers, sometimes long after the wall is built. Instead, drill holes the same size as the rebar dowels you are using. Be sure to treat all cut ends and holes with a preservative.

How To Avoid Failures

Like anything else you build, to avoid failure in low retaining walls

you must design the wall right and build it accordingly. Here are the basic guidelines for walls no higher than 5 feet:

- Always use durable materials on sound footings. For poured concrete walls, use a 3,500 psi mix. For timber walls, use only pressure-treated timbers.
- Take into account local frost depth.
- Provide well-drained granular backfill with geotextile separation from native soil.
- Make the footings wide enough (see "Retaining Wall Details").
- Don't ever place footings on fill, no matter how much you compact it.
- Use proper reinforcement with masonry walls and tiebacks in the case of timber walls.
- Wherever you need to add fill in front of a footing, use good quality, compacted granular fill. This may help the footing resist slipping. However, to get any design "credit" for resisting slipping, you must pour the footing against the undisturbed face of the excavation trench.

Figure 22. Shear failure occurs when the force of the soil causes the retaining wall to slide along a mortar joint, but without tipping over.

Figure 23. Tree roots can cause retaining walls to lean; keep large or fast-growing trees away.

Figure 24. Railroad ties stacked and spiked together, but without tiebacks into the earth behind, cannot resist the force exerted by wet or frozen soil. Poor drainage also accelerates rotting.

Modular concrete an option. There are several excellent modular concrete block retaining wall systems that incorporate geogrid anchorage into the backfill, including Keystone (444 W. 78th St., Minneapolis, MN 55435; 800/747-8971), Unilock (287 Armstrong Ave., Georgetown, ON L7G 4X6, Canada; 905/873-0312); and Versa-Lok (6348 Highway 36, Suite 1, Oakdale, MN 55128; 612/770-3166). These products are similar in principle to the timber crib walls, and generally require more excavation and backfill than concrete walls. Where this can be accommodated, modular walls will probably be a competitive option. As with all retaining walls, success depends on good footings and drainage. Since they are unmortared, modular block walls are a little more forgiving than solid masonry to minor settlement or frost action.

By Robert Randall, P.E., a structural engineer in Mohegan Lake, N.Y.

SEPTIC SYSTEMS: REMODELER'S GUIDE

Many suburban or rural remodeling projects can involve a confrontation with a septic system when a contractor does any one of the following:
• increases the amount of sewage generated by changing the use of the building or adding facilities;
• changes the footprint of the building, interfering with the location of septic tanks, pipes, and absorption wells or fields;
• provides for delivery of materials or the passage of heavy construction equipment over a portion of a septic system.

In order to avoid problems, either with code violations or with septic system operation, it's wise to have a basic understanding of septic system fundamentals.

Sewerage systems were originally just holes in the ground that were blocked up with stones, bricks, blocks, wood, etc., to provide a cavity where all household waste could enter and be absorbed into the ground. When one of these *cesspools* failed, another one was usually added after it (Figure 25), and then another and so on. Then came the modern septic system, which generally consists of two basic components to handle household waste, a *septic tank* which acts as a settling and digestion chamber and a *leaching system* which returns

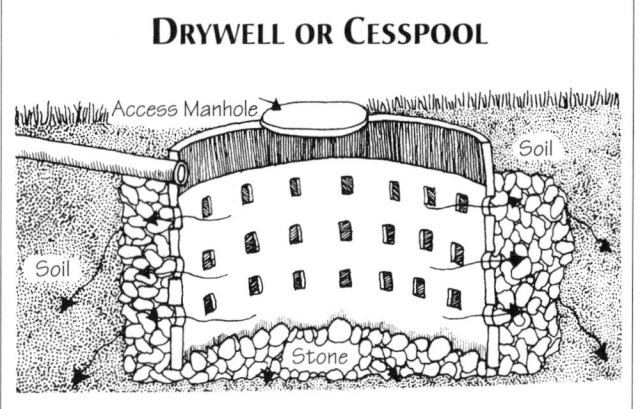

Figure 25. Cesspools and drywells are identical in construction. The only way to tell the difference is by what's going into it: fresh sewage (cesspool), or clarified effluent (drywell).

the *clarified effluent* to the ground.

In many states, the bottom of the leaching system must be located a minimum of 4 feet above the seasonal high groundwater level in an attempt to provide proper treatment of effluent before it reaches the water table. This requirement has resulted in the "elephant mounds" (raised leach beds) so common now on poor soils. It also often requires a *pumping station* to get the effluent up to the field. (Refer to the "Septic System Glossary," page 26, for explanations of septic system terminology.)

Let's look at some situations where septic systems should concern

a remodeling contractor and what he should to do save himself expense and aggravation.

Increasing Load

It is often necessary to demonstrate to code-enforcement people that an existing system is adequate to handle increased loads. In many states, verification of the existing system is required whenever the number of bedrooms (not bathrooms) in a dwelling is increased. Bedrooms rather than fixtures determine occupancy. Verification is also required when the use of a dwelling changes, such as from seasonal to

year-round use. If a system is shown to be inadequate for the increased flow (which is often the case), a new one will have to be designed, approved, and installed.

Adding a hot tub, a dish or clothes washer, or a garbage disposal onto an older system may *not* require a septic system upgrade by code. However, increased usage of a system built to handle the water consumption of 30 years ago will probably create a problem.

Solutions. Where it's permissible, I add a separate drywell or a leaching line for a washing machine or hot-tub drain to avoid introducing excessive soaps and bacteria-killing chemicals into an existing system. The *grey water* from these two fixtures is likely to cause more upset to a functioning system than any other wastewater we could add.

Dishwashers and garbage disposals can also cause problems. They should be discharged into septic tanks in order to separate and trap solids and greases, separating them from the wastewater. This protects the absorption surfaces of leach fields or drywells.

Although septic systems designed in recent years are *supposed* to be able to handle all of these appliances, many systems have proven marginal. Some states, such as New Hampshire, are starting to require larger septic tanks, or some means of reducing or separating kitchen-wastes input, whenever a garbage disposal is installed.

Low-volume appliances. Water conservation, where permitted, is a realistic option for offsetting increased demands on a septic system. Reducing the volume of water a flush toilet uses from over 5 gallons to less than $1\frac{1}{2}$ could make it possible to install other water-consuming fixtures or provide relief for a marginal system. Low-volume sink and shower aerators are also available. (Some states permit a considerable reduction in leach field size for such systems.)

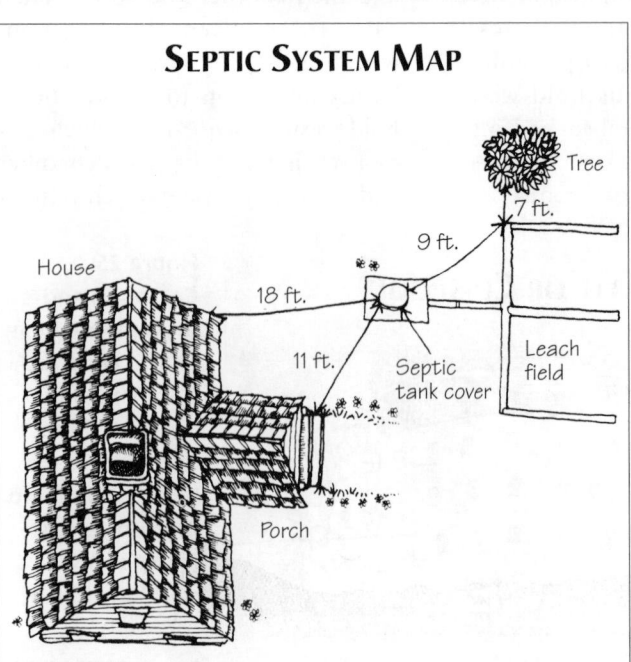

Figure 26. High-tech comes to the rescue. This hand-held wand can locate a small transmitting "mole" taped to the end of a snake. Here the snake is about to be inserted through the tank outlet to locate the leach field or drywell.

Figure 27. Map out the septic system before starting an addition or deck. Check clearances to basements and slabs allowed by code in your area.

In short, it's best to check with the appropriate state agency, the local building inspector, or a septic designer familiar with local codes to be sure that you are covering yourself for any of these upgrades. When working in an unfamiliar town, keep in mind that local codes can be more strict than state codes.

Changing Footprints

Many building codes ignore the existing septic system for any project that does not change use or flow as discussed above, even when plans involve adding onto the building. In these cases, it's completely up to a builder to locate and identify septic system components at the planning stage to avoid later conflict, either with the system or the owner. Special tools are available to help you locate underground components (Figure 26).

No one wants to have the top of their septic tank become the thermal mass of their new sunspace. Septic tanks generate offensive and explosive gasses during normal operation and can, in some cases, leak their contents into the surrounding ground. For this reason, codes require septic tanks and leach fields to be a safe distance from basements and slabs — typically 10 to 35 feet depending on the type of foundation and whether it has perimeter drains (Figure 27).

These and other distance requirements can be supplied by your designer or inspector. Some jurisdictions may grant waivers in certain cases where it is impossible to meet requirements and the solution is deemed appropriate.

Let's consider what we might do when it becomes impossible to construct an addition without interfering with some part of a septic system.

Moving or replacing a system. Surprisingly, it's not really difficult to move a concrete septic tank. Most septic tank companies should be willing to lift and reset a tank for $200 to $300 given reasonable access to the site and a tank that has been almost completely emptied and unearthed all the way to the bottom. Tanks over 1,000-gallon capacity may be a different story, as they are generally delivered in two halves (most septic truck hoists cannot lift an assembled 1,500-gallon tank), and once they are in place for some time they are hard to get apart. Fortunately, they aren't commonly used for most residences.

Moving a steel septic tank would be an unlikely consideration, as most steel tanks last 30 years at best, and should be replaced by concrete tanks when relocated. Don't plan to replace a 500-gallon steel tank with a 500-gallon concrete tank, however, even if code permits (which is unlikely) and the smaller tank is available. The cost difference between even a 750-gallon and a 1,000-gallon tank is only about $50. The larger tank is a better value because it does a better job.

Plastic tanks (a more recent innovation) would be well worth moving, especially because of their high cost (around twice that of concrete). Because of their ease of handling, they may provide a good replacement alternative for hard-to-reach sites. As for reusing fiberglass tanks, I've heard stories about them deteriorating, so I would assess the tank's condition before moving. In all cases, call a pumper to have the

---

THE SEPTIC TANK

Untreated household sewage will quickly clog all but the most porous gravel if released directly into the soil. The function of the septic tank is to condition the sewage so that it can percolate into the ground without clogging the soil. Within the tank, three important processes take place:

1. The heavier, solid particles in the sewage settle to the bottom of the tank forming a layer of sludge. Lighter materials, including fat and grease, float to the surface forming a "scum layer."

2. Bacteria living in the septic tank break down some of the organic solids into liquid components, helping to reduce the buildup of sludge in the tank.

3. Sludge and scum are stored within the septic tank rather than being allowed to flow out into the leaching system where they would quickly clog the soil.

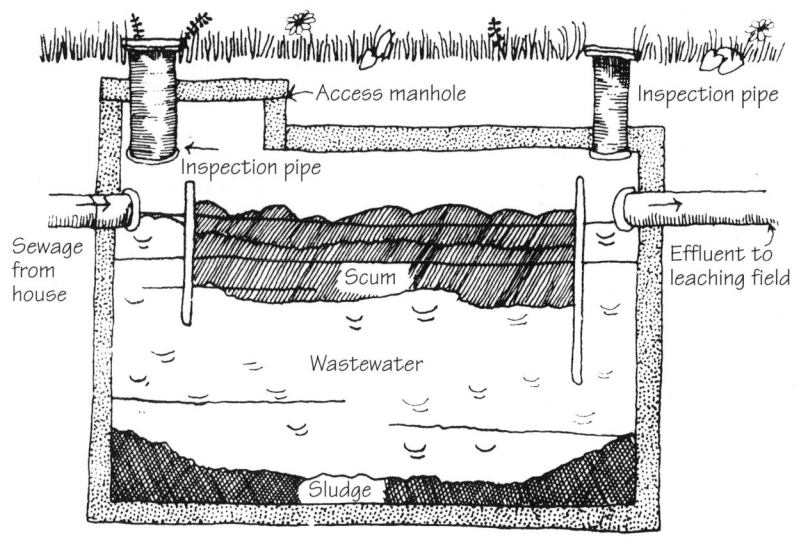

Access manhole · Inspection pipe · Inspection pipe · Sewage from house · Scum · Effluent to leaching field · Wastewater · Sludge

TROUBLESHOOTING NOTES

1. *Check lowest fixture or drain.* If problem is septic blockage, water should back up through any drain which is below level of toilet when flushed. Check washing machine outlet, floor drain, bathtub, downstairs apartment, or remove cleanout plug carefully (to avoid a flood). If not backup, problem is probably with toilet or other household plumbing only.

2. *D-Box problems.* If distribution box for side-hill trench system is out of level, one trench may be taking all water and "failing." Re-level pipes and block outlet to overload trench for several months. Roots may also be blocking one or more pipes. Remove roots and seal joints where roots enter if possible.

3. *Pumps and floats.* Exercise care handling pumps as they have 110- or 220-volt supply lines, which may not have GFIs. Some float systems (which turn pump and alarm on and off) may also contain full line voltage. Use insulating rubber gloves and follow procedures with a disinfecting hand wash for sanitation. Or call licensed plumber, if required by code.

4. *Snake safety.* Exercise care using snake in cleanouts or drains as some waterborne diseases can be transferred through contact. Use rubber gloves and surgical mask and follow with disinfecting wash. Stiff garden hose can sometimes be used in place of snake. Disinfect after use.

5. *Failed field.* Usually means soil plugged due to age, overuse, underdesign, lack of maintenance, or a combination of these. Requires field replacement or rest. (See "alternating fields" in Septic System Glossary.)

6. *Failed drywell.* Same reasons as (5) above. However, drywells can sometimes be excavated around and repacked with crushed stone to create a new soil surface for absorption. Check codes.

7. *Pipe problems.* Settling, breaking, crushing, pulling apart, and backsloping are installation related. Freezing, plugging at joints, and root plugging (though also caused by poor installation) can occur later. Insulating, replacing, releveling, sealing joints, and properly backfilling will resolve most problems.

8. *Find septic tank.* If homeowner does not know exact location of septic system or have accurate plan to follow, start looking for septic tank outside of house where waste pipe exits basement wall. (Note pipe direction through wall.) If plumbing exits below slab, check side of house with roof vent, especially if most of plumbing is on that side of house. Look for spot on the ground where snow melts first, grass turns brown, or there is a slight depression or mound. Steel tanks will sometimes bounce slightly when jumped on, but be careful, steel lids rust out!

A thin steel rod with a tee handle makes a handy probe. Drive probe until achieving several "hits" at the same depth to indicate tank top. A metal detector can help. Even concrete tanks and cesspool covers generally have steel reinforcing within. Another trick is to insert a snake in house cleanout and push it until it stops. Gently sliding snake against inlet baffle can often send a shock that can be heard and/or felt at ground surface by second person. (Note that sometimes a snake can curl up within a septic tank or, particularly, in a cesspool, sometimes making this technique useless.)

If snake hits obstruction but cannot be felt at surface, remove it from cleanout and measure its penetration. Draw an arc the distance of snake penetration from the house and try again with the probe. Remember that the pipe from the house may not be heading straight towards the tank.

If all else fails, locate and uncover the waste pipe where it leaves the house and again every few feet until the tank is located. Or ask previous owner, neighbor, or septic pumper who may have serviced the system in the past.

Note: Devices are available that transmit a radio signal along a snake or from a tiny "mole." Signal is traced by a receiver wand as snake is pushed through waste pipe.

9. *Determining the type of tank found.*
- *Primary/secondary septic tank.* Two or more tanks are used in some installations for better settling and detention of solids. First tank should have fresh waste entering directly from house. (Flush colored paper towel down toilet and watch it enter at inlet manhole.) Second tank should have a little floating grease and scum, with some settled sludge at bottom. Note that septic tank always has an outlet unless it is being used as a holding tank.
- *Cesspool or drywell.* Likely has no outlet and seldom has an inlet baffle. Liquid level could be low in a septic tank if tank is rusted out (steel tank) or if center seam leaks (concrete tank). If fresh waste is present, see Glossary, "cesspool." If no fresh waste is present, see Glossary, "drywell."
- *One of a series of cesspools* (see Glossary, "cesspool").
- *Greasetrap.* Found in restaurants, inns, markets, etc. (see Glossary).
- *Pump tank* (see Glossary). If water runs back into septic tank from the outlet pipe when the tank is pumped out, system has probably failed. See (5) or (6) above.

10. *Inlet/Outlet problems.* Plugging often occurs from scum buildup within baffles, roots entering through poorly sealed joints, tanks installed out-of-level or backwards, or pipes sticking into the tank too far and nearly hitting baffles, blocking waste. Correct as needed.

11. *Locating field or drywell.* Follow directions for finding septic tank (8), except start at septic tank outlet rather than at house. Snake will not hit a baffle within drywell as there is none. It may or may not hit side of D-Box but could pass through into one of outlet pipes.

SEPTIC SYSTEM TROUBLESHOOTING GUIDE

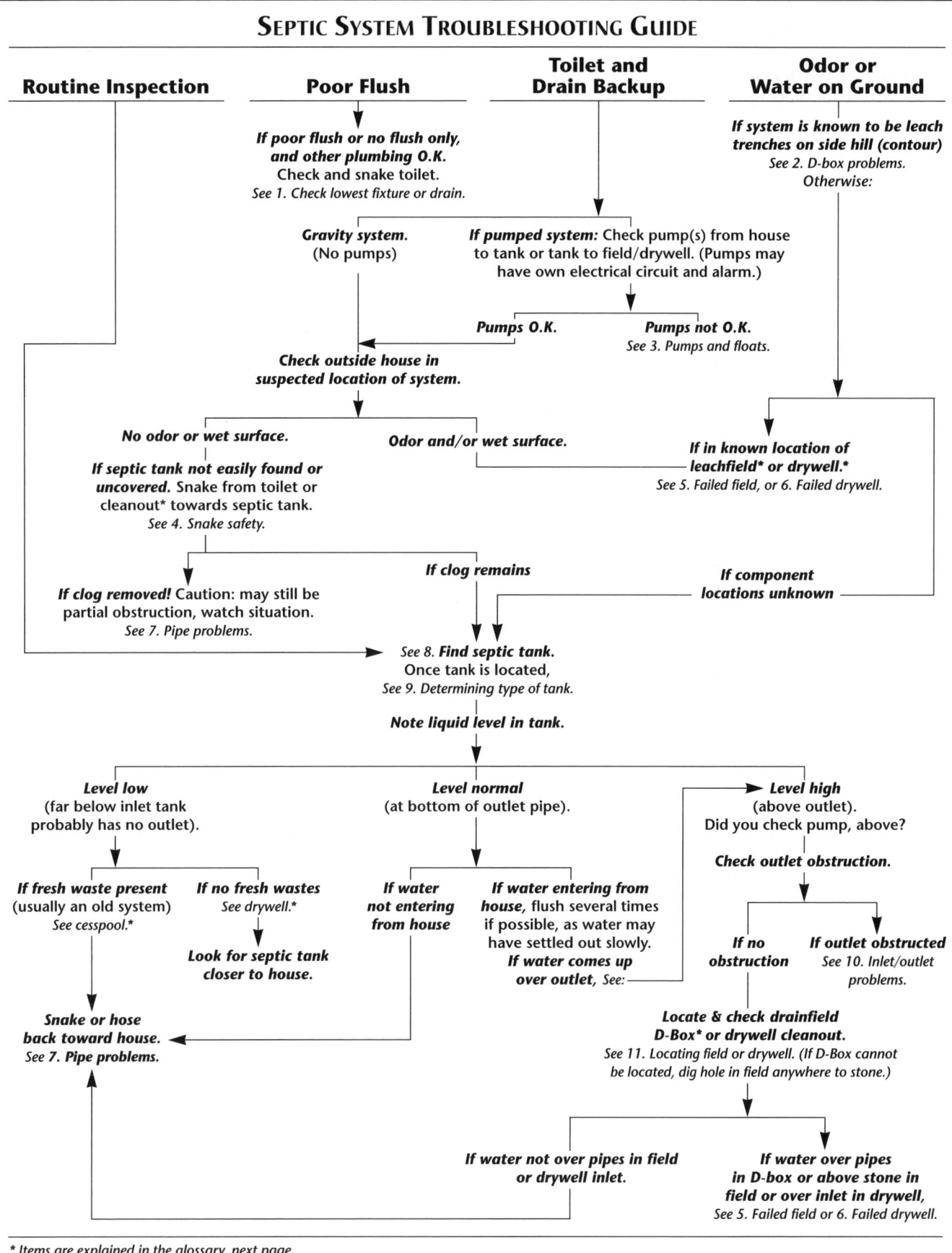

Routine Inspection

Poor Flush

If poor flush or no flush only, and other plumbing O.K. Check and snake toilet. *See 1. Check lowest fixture or drain.*

Toilet and Drain Backup

Odor or Water on Ground

If system is known to be leach trenches on side hill (contour) *See 2. D-box problems. Otherwise:*

Gravity system. (No pumps)

If pumped system: Check pump(s) from house to tank or tank to field/drywell. (Pumps may have own electrical circuit and alarm.)

Pumps O.K.

Pumps not O.K. *See 3. Pumps and floats.*

Check outside house in suspected location of system.

No odor or wet surface.

If septic tank not easily found or uncovered. Snake from toilet or cleanout* towards septic tank. *See 4. Snake safety.*

Odor and/or wet surface.

If in known location of leachfield or drywell.* *See 5. Failed field, or 6. Failed drywell.*

If clog removed! Caution: may still be partial obstruction, watch situation. *See 7. Pipe problems.*

If clog remains

If component locations unknown

See 8. Find septic tank. Once tank is located, *See 9. Determining type of tank.*

Note liquid level in tank.

Level low (far below inlet tank probably has no outlet).

Level normal (at bottom of outlet pipe).

Level high (above outlet). Did you check pump, above?

Check outlet obstruction.

If fresh waste present (usually an old system) *See cesspool.**

If no fresh wastes *See drywell.**

Look for septic tank closer to house.

If water not entering from house

If water entering from house, flush several times if possible, as water may have settled out slowly. *If water comes up over outlet, See:*

If no obstruction

If outlet obstructed *See 10. Inlet/outlet problems.*

Snake or hose back toward house. *See 7. Pipe problems.*

Locate & check drainfield D-Box* or drywell cleanout. *See 11. Locating field or drywell. (If D-Box cannot be located, dig hole in field anywhere to stone.)*

If water not over pipes in field or drywell inlet.

If water over pipes in D-box or above stone in field or over inlet in drywell, *See 5. Failed field or 6. Failed drywell.*

* Items are explained in the glossary, next page.
Numbered items are explained in accompanying notes.

tank cleaned out beforehand, both for ease of handling and for inspection of the tank and its baffles.

Moving a leach field is quite a different story. There is no practical way to reuse much of anything from an old leach field, except perhaps the distribution box (and I'm not sure that there are many folks who would want to handle a used "D-box"). Because of the life expectancy of an average leach field, it would probably be best to rebuild the field in a different location if it is over ten years old anyway, especially if the system has been poorly maintained.

I suspect that most states will require a new system approval if the leach field is being moved more than just a few feet or if it is within 75 feet of surface water or wells. If possible, eliminating a portion of the existing leach field to meet distance requirements and adding a second alternating leach field to fulfill size requirements would be best.

If a leach field or drywell must be replaced, the materials excavated from the old field or well will be quite offensive at first and should be handled with caution, but a few hours of good sunny weather will dispel the odors amazingly well, and the result-ing material spread out below a few inches of clean topsoil will provide a good base for a lawn. Keep this material 75 feet from water supplies, and the customer's and neighbors' wells. (Check your local codes, please!) If the old field or drywell has begun to fail, that is, wastewater is standing in the system, it is best to have it pumped out first. Try to find a patient and understanding licensed septic hauler to help you out.

Avoiding Vehicle Damage

It's prudent to know the exact location of a septic tank and other components if you are expecting the

---

SEPTIC SYSTEM GLOSSARY

Alarm: An electromechanical device that provides audible and visual indication that the water level in a pump or holding tank is above what it is supposed to be.

Alternating leach field: One of two or more leach fields designed to be used while the other(s) rest. They are generally fed via a manually operated diverter valve located in the line from the septic tank.

Baffles: Pipe tees or partitions within a septic tank, which reduce turbulence at the inlet and prevent floating greases and scum from escaping into the leaching system at the outlet. (They are usually the first part of a steel tank to rust away, leaving the leach field or dry-well unprotected from excessive solids overloading.)

Cesspool: The original type of sewerage system, often still in use in older homes. They were simply a single hole in the ground loosely blocked up with locally available materials — stone, brick, block, or railroad ties — and capped either with ties covered with a layer of old steel roofing or a cast-in-place concrete lid with a cleanout hole near the center. All

household wastewater entered and the liquid portion was absorbed into the ground. When the soil plugged, a new cesspool was added. Wiser installers placed an elbow, or better still, a tee in the outlet pipe from the first cesspool, creating a baffle to hold back the floating greases and scums (see *Baffles*).

In a sense, this created the first type of septic system, because the first cesspool in the line, sealed by its own demise, served as a septic tank and the subsequent tank provided a greater degree of set-tling and separation of soil-plug-ging solids and some absorption. (Owners often have the first tank pumped out to maintain system operation.)

Chambers or ameration chambers: Open-bottomed precast concrete or plastic structures, which are placed next to each other in an excavation to take the place of crushed stone in a leach field. Unlike leach fields, heavy-duty chambers can be driven over.

Cleanout: A removable plug in a "wye," or a "tee" in a sewer line, where a snake can be inserted to clear a blockage.

Distribution box or D-Box: Usually a small square concrete box within a leach field from which all pipes lead to disperse effluent within the field. Newer boxes should be marked at the surface to protect from vehicle traffic.

Drywell: Constructed identically to a cesspool and differs only in that the clarified effluent from a septic tank or the wastewater from a washing machine or other grey water may enter. Modern drywells are often precast perfo-rated rings surrounded by crushed stone to increase the absorption area.

Drywells are not commonly installed today because of laws requiring the bottom of a leach-ing system to be 4 feet above the seasonal high-water table.

Effluent: The liquid that flows out of the septic tank after the tank has "taken out the big pieces."

Grease trap: An in-ground cham-ber similar to a septic tank, usually used at restaurants, markets, and inns to trap grease from the kitchen wastewater before it reaches the septic tank. Unusual to find in private homes.

delivery of heavy materials or will be operating heavy equipment on site, even if only on the driveway. (I've seen more than one drywell or old steel septic tank under the middle of a driveway.) Because some tanks may weaken with age, and modern trucks and equipment are often much heavier than older models, it would be well to know what you are dealing with to avoid costly "pitfalls."

It may be possible to brace the lid of a tank that must be driven over with thick steel plates, railroad ties, or other materials once you know its location. A leach field should never be driven over and would be consid-erably more difficult to protect because of the greater area involved. Use good judgment, discuss liability with the owner, and perhaps seek the assistance of a local installer or pumper willing to help you assess the situation.

Building On Top

Setting a Sonotube on top of a concrete septic tank to support a deck would probably cause little harm as long as the inlet, cleanout, and outlet openings on top of the tank were not obstructed by either the tube or the deck. (Indeed, this footing would probably be the most substantial of the whole job.) Supporting a heavier load might warrant keeping a tube close to the edge of a tank unless it were a heavy-duty variety. The same principles would apply to drywells. (In all cases, check codes.)

Avoid setting anything on steel tanks because they cannot support much weight. If a steel tank is that close to an addition, it should be replaced while work is being done anyway because of its limited life expectancy and the possibility of reduced access to replace or main-tain it in the future.

As for setting a Sonotube or other building component over a leach

---

Grey water: All liquid wastewater except for the toilet wastes (sink, shower, washer, etc.).

Leaching system: The part of a septic system that returns water to the ground for reabsorption. Could be a drywell, leach field, trenches, chambers, etc.

Leach bed: A leaching system which consists of a continuous layer of crushed stone about a foot deep, usually in a rectangular layout, with perforated pipes laid level throughout to disperse efflu-ent as evenly as possible over the entire bed.

Leach field: Term often used to describe either a leach bed or leach trenches.

Leach trenches: Built essentially like beds, except that each pipe is in its own stone-filled level trench, usu-ally 3 feet wide. Each trench can be at a different level than the other trenches. Well suited to sloping ground.

Mound (or raised) system: A leach bed built on a mound of fine to medium-grained sand to elevate it above the seasonal high water table and/or to accommodate a system on a hillside.

Percolation test: A shallow, hand-dug hole saturated with water, per-formed as a part of a septic design to determine the soil's permeability — the rate at which water is absorbed by the soil — which dic-tates the system size.

Pump station, pump tank: A watertight container, usually (but not always) separate from the septic tank, into which effluent flows by gravity and is then ejected by a submersible electric pump through a pressure line to the leaching system. Pump tanks often are hooked to an alarm to warn of pump failure.

Seasonal high water table: The highest elevation that groundwa-ter reaches within the year (usually in the spring). Many states require the bottom of a leaching system to be at least 4 feet above this point.

Septic tank: A watertight chamber, which all household wastewater enters for settling and anaerobic digestion of greases and solids. Original tanks were made of asphalt-coated steel. Modern tanks are made of concrete, fiberglass, or plastic. All tanks should have a set of baffles, which are critical to their operation.

Most tanks have an inspection hatch at both the inlet and the outlet and some have a third hatch in between for pumping access. Locations of each of these should be recorded and/or marked. Steel tanks often have one round lid that covers the entire tank.

Septic tanks should be pumped every three years or so in normal operation. They should not be treated with any additives and should be protected from receiving any of the harmful chemicals used in many homes and commercial workshops. This includes disinfec-tants or bleaches, which can kill bacteria in the tank, and solvents, darkroom chemicals, or other materials that could pollute the water supply.

Septic design: Usually consists of a topographic survey, test pit, and perc test plus information about the water supply and subdivision and a filing fee to the state pre-pared by either a licensed designer or the owner.

Test pit: A hole dug to determine soil type, seasonal high water table, and depth to ledge. Some states require a test pit of specific depth (to determine that ledge is a minimum number of feet below bed bottom) while others require only a shallow pit to determine depth to hardpan soils.

field, most states do not permit anything to be built over the field except lawns and gardens (no trees or shrubs).

Note that decks installed over shallow septic tanks or pipes can create freezing problems by keeping the insulating layer of snow from reaching the ground. A couple of inches of extruded polystyrene over tanks and pipes can help prevent problems.

Documentation

Perhaps the easiest part of this whole task, yet the part that is most often overlooked, is making a record of the work for future reference. At the least, a customer should be provided with accurate measurements of all known parts of his system for maintenance needs and the dates when work was done. A simple plot plan hung on the cellar wall next to the plumbing can provide great assistance to a homeowner in a future emergency.

By Russ Lanoie, a licensed septic system designer and installer in New Hampshire.

CHAPTER 2

WOOD FRAMING

- Wall and Floor Framing

- Wood I-Joists

- Roof Framing

- Truss Bracing

- Shed Dormers

- Details for Wood Shrinkage

WALL AND FLOOR FRAMING

Over the past 17 years, first as a builder and then as a representative of the Western Wood Products Association, I have traveled extensively, talking to builders and code officials to see how framing is done throughout the country. While I've found regional differences, I've also found a few serious framing problems that tend to crop up everywhere, again and again.

All of these problems are covered by the model building codes. A given problem might occur because the builder doesn't know better, or because framers are paying more attention to other construction needs. Either way, these framing defects not only cause trouble with code officials, but cause problems big and small down the line.

Here are some of the most common framing errors I come across, along with code-approved, structurally sound solutions.

Framing Openings Cut in Floors

A common problem occurs with floors when subs cut through joists to make room for plumbing runs, hvac ductwork, or other mechanical elements. The loads these cut joists supported must be properly transferred to other joists. You can do this using header joists, end-nailed across the cut ends of the interrupted joists, to carry loads to the adjacent trimmer joists. Where the header has to span a space less than 4 feet wide, a single header end-nailed to the trimmer joists will do.

Things get more complicated if the header must span more than 4 feet, as in Figure 1. If that's the case, both header and trimmer joists should be doubled. The doubled trimmer joists must be nailed together properly (with spaced pairs of 16-penny nails every 16 inches) so that they act as beams. The header joists must be appropriately anchored to the trim-

mers. End nails will do for header spans up to 6 feet; beyond that, use hangers. Any tail joists over 12 feet should also be hangered.

When you're framing the floor, check the blueprints to see where any such openings might go, and header off any joists that might be in the way in advance. It's much easier than trying to work from underneath the subfloor later.

Holes and Notches

Whenever you cut a hole or notch in a joist, that joist is weakened. You (and your subs) should avoid this whenever possible. And when you absolutely have to cut or notch, you should know the rules for doing it in the least destructive manner.

Figure 2 shows proper guidelines for cutting holes and notches. Straying from these guidelines weakens the joists and risks a red tag from the building official. Trying to fix such problems can be very costly, since it usually involves redoing the plumbing and electrical work along with replacing or doubling the joists.

When Notch Becomes Rip

Occasionally, what might be thought of as a notch turns into a rip, such as when floor joists at the entry of a home are ripped down to allow underlayment for a tile floor (Figure 3). Unfortunately, ripping wide dimension lumber lowers the grade of the material, and is unacceptable under all building codes. You should frame these areas with narrow joists of a higher grade or stronger species, making sure they can carry the load.

Bearing Walls on Cantilevers

How far can a conventionally framed cantilever extend and still support a bearing wall?

Most of the confusion about how far a cantilever can extend beyond its support stems from an old rule of

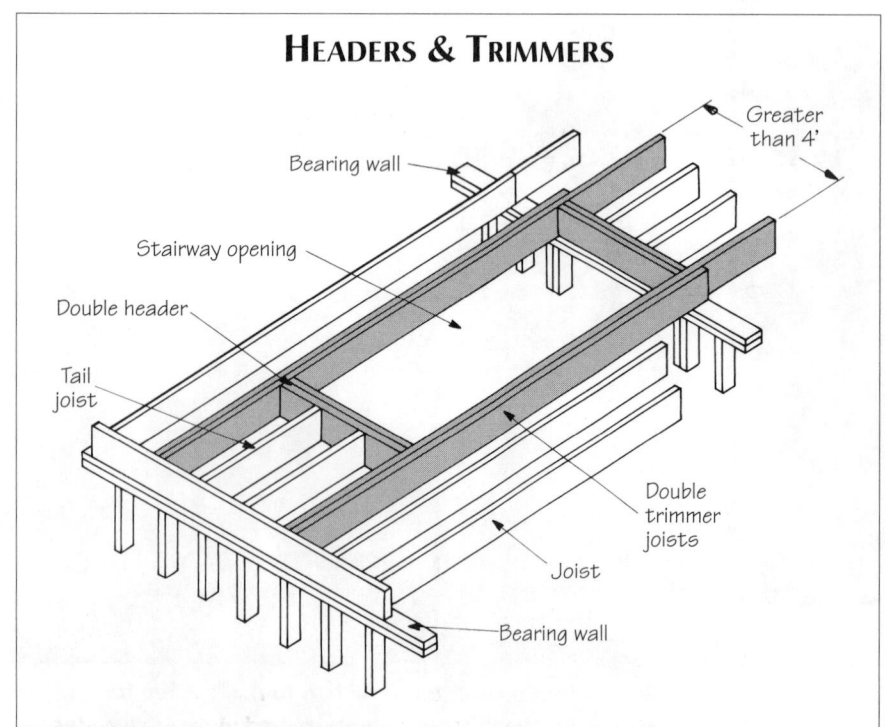

HEADERS & TRIMMERS

Bearing wall

Stairway opening

Double header

Tail joist

Greater than 4'

Double trimmer joists

Joist

Bearing wall

Figure 1. Head off interrupted joists to transfer their loads to adjacent joists. If the header spans more than 4 feet, it must be doubled and the loads transferred to double trimmer joists.

thumb used by builders and code officials alike: the rule of "one-to-three." This states that a joist should extend back inside the building at least three times the length of the cantilevered section — if the cantilevered section hangs 2 feet out, the joists should extend at least 6 feet in.

This rule works fine for nonbearing situations. But it does *not* apply to a cantilever that supports a bearing wall. In this situation, the maximum distance that joists can be cantilevered without engineering them is a distance equal to the depth of the joists, as in Figure 4. So if you are using 2x10 floor joists, the maximum cantilever for those joists supporting a bearing wall is 9¹/₄ inches. Beyond this distance, shear becomes a serious factor, as does the bending moment at the support. This combination could eventually cause splitting of the cantilevered joists. The only way to work around this problem is to have it engineered.

Broken Load Paths

A similar alignment problem relates to maintaining vertical load paths. All loads start at the roof and transfer vertically through the building to the foundation. If they aren't transferred properly, you can end up with cracking of interior finishes or sagging framing. Many cracking problems written off to "settling" are actually due to what might be called broken load paths — paths that end up putting loads on areas not meant to carry them. This is one of the most common framing errors I see, and one to which many building inspectors pay close attention.

Misaligned bearing walls. In other instances, loads carried by bearing walls or posts must be transferred through floor systems. If the bearing wall or post above doesn't line up closely enough with a bearing wall, post, or beam below, the floor joists in between can be overstressed, causing severe deflection. This can even-

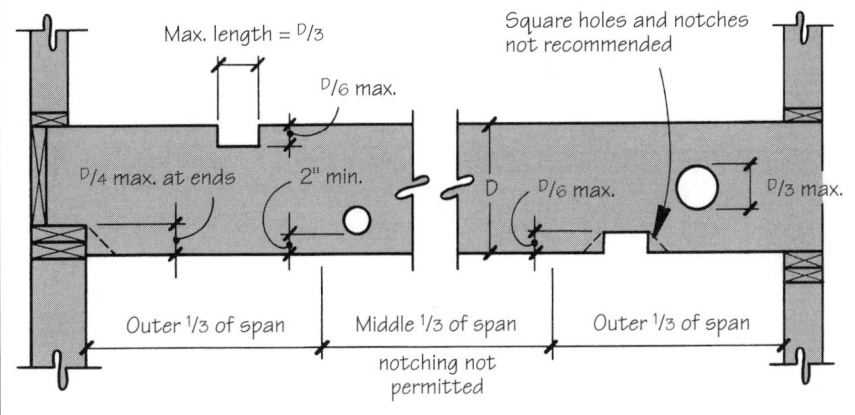

GUIDE FOR CUTTING, NOTCHING, AND BORING JOISTS

Joist Size	Maximum Hole	Maximum Notch Depth	Maximum End Notch
2 x 4	None	None	None
2 x 6	1¹/₂	⁷/₈	1³/₈
2 x 8	2³/₈	1¹/₄	1⁷/₈
2 x 10	3	1¹/₂	2³/₈
2 x 12	3³/₄	1⁷/₈	2⁷/₈

Max. length = D/3

Square holes and notches not recommended

D/6 max.

D/4 max. at ends   2" min.

D   D/6 max.   D/3 max.

Outer ¹/₃ of span   Middle ¹/₃ of span   Outer ¹/₃ of span

notching not permitted

Figure 2. In joists, never cut holes closer than 2 inches to joist edges, nor make them larger than one-third the depth of the joist. Don't notch the span's middle third where the bending forces are greatest. No notch should be deeper than one-sixth the depth of the joist, nor one-quarter the depth if the notch is at the end of the joist. Limit the length of notches to one-third of the joist's depth. Use actual, not nominal, dimensions.

Figure 3. Ripping long notches in floor joists, such as to make room for grouted entry floors, weakens the joists unacceptably and violates all codes. Instead, you need to use smaller dimension milled lumber of a higher grade, or set the joists closer together. If necessary, you can fur at the ends to bring non-grouted areas up to level.

tually split the joists, as well as cause finish cracking problems.

How closely must they align? Bearing walls supported by floor joists must be within the depth of the joist from their bearing support below (just as with cantilevers), as in Figure 5.

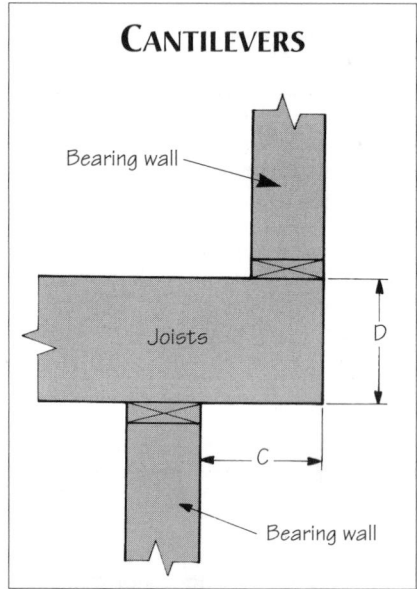

CANTILEVERS

Bearing wall

Joists

D

C

Bearing wall

Figure 4. When a cantilever supports a bearing wall, the distance it extends beyond its support (C) should not exceed the depth of the joist (D).

ALIGNING BEARING WALLS

D

D

This code requirement applies only to solid-sawn wood joists. Engineered products such as wood I-beams are required to have the loads line up *directly* over each other, and special blocking is required. Special engineering of either dimensional or engineered lumber may allow placing loads at other locations, but you shouldn't try it without consulting an engineer first.

Bringing columns to foundation properly. If you use a column to support a beam or other member, make sure it bears on something that can in turn support it. A common mistake is to rest one on the floor, without extra blocking or support beneath. Doing this can crush the underlying joists. Columns shouldn't rest on unsupported floor joists; they should run continuously to the foundation, or (if you must have a clear space beneath) to an engineered beam or header to transfer the load out to other columns or bearing members.

Columns shouldn't rest on rim joists either, for similar reasons. If you need to rest a column at the rim, add full-depth vertical blocking inside the rim joist the full depth and width of the column base, so

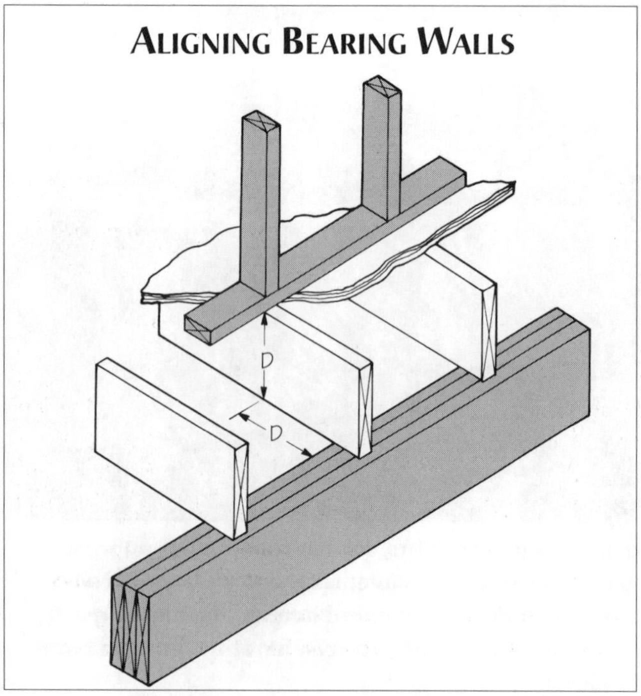

Figure 5. If a bearing wall doesn't line up with the support below, it should lie no farther away than the depth of the joists (D). If the joists are engineered lumber, the walls and support must align exactly.

that the load is transferred through the blocking to the foundation.

Puny Hangers

A simple but common framing error is hanging a three-member beam (such as three 2x10s nailed together) from a double joist hanger. This usually occurs because triple hangers are hard to find. But if only two of the three members are supported, then only two carry the load. The third member just goes along for the ride. Toe nails or end nails are not going to make it carry the load.

If you're going to use a hanger, use one that holds everything, and use the right size and the correct nails. Undersized hangers and inappropriate nails will weaken the system.

The correct hanger is necessary to carry the vertical load as well as to laterally support the member to prevent rotation. And without the correct nails, the hanger doesn't mean much. Eight-penny galvanized nails or roofing nails won't do. You can buy regular joist hanger nails that are heavy enough to handle the shear stress, yet only $1\frac{1}{2}$ inches long so that they won't go clear through the lumber and possibly cause a split.

Of course, the best way to support a beam is from beneath. When possible, use a beam pocket or a column directly under the end of the beam. Be sure the full bearing surface of the beam is supported clear to the foundation.

Tapering Beams and Joists

It's sometimes necessary (or at least convenient) to taper the ends of ceiling joists or beams to keep them under the plane of the roof, as in Figure 6. But by reducing the depth of the joist or beam, you reduce its load-carrying capacity.

If you must taper-cut the ends of ceiling joists, make sure the length of the taper cut does not exceed three times the depth of the member, and that the end of the joist or beam is at least one-half the member's original depth.

With taper-cut beams, you should also check the shear rating. If you can't meet this criteria, you'll probably have to lower the beam into a pocket so that enough cross-section can be left, after taper-cutting, to carry the applied load.

Raising the Rafters

Another way to add room for attic insulation at the eaves is to set the rafters atop a ledger board running perpendicular over the ceiling joists, as in Figure 7. Unfortunately, builders who do this often fail to put in a rim joist or block the ends of the joists to prevent them from rolling over. The resulting design creates, in essence, hinges at the top and bottom edge of each joist. With a strong enough lateral force, such as a high wind or a strong tremor, all the joists could rotate and fall over — bringing ledger, rafters, and roof crashing down onto the now-flat joists.

To prevent this, install full depth blocking between all joist ends or a rim joist nailed against the ends of the joists. Either solution will also provide a baffle to prevent air from penetrating the ends of the batts and keep the batts (or blown-in insulation) from creeping into the eaves.

Blocking is also a good idea where joists lap over a center girder at foundation level or over a support wall at second-story level. If the centers are unblocked, the job of keeping the joists upright falls to the nails holding the floor sheathing to the joists. These nails just aren't designed to resist the strong sideways forces created by wind or earthquake. Full-depth 2x blocking over center supports will prevent the joists from rotating in such an event. The blocking also stiffens the floor, since it stops the rotation caused by deflection of the joists under load.

What if a few of these blocks get knocked out by mechanical contractors putting in ductwork or plumb-

Figure 6. Overtapering joists to fit beneath roofs creates inadequate joist depth at the plate (left). A proper cut (below) leaves at least half the depth of the joist.

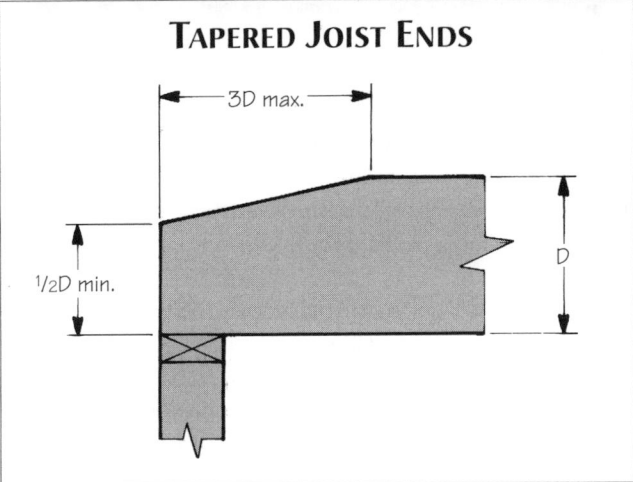

TAPERED JOIST ENDS

3D max.

1/2D min.

D

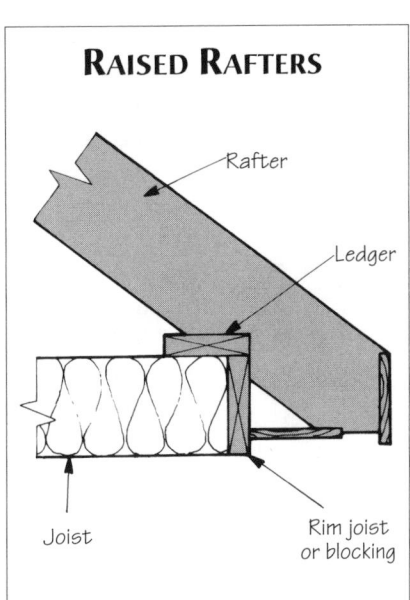

RAISED RAFTERS

Rafter

Ledger

Joist

Rim joist or blocking

Figure 7. When nailing rafters to a ledger over joists to make room for insulation, use a rim joist to keep the joists from rotating.

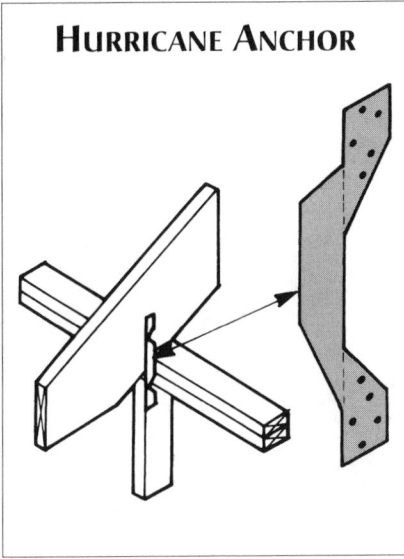

HURRICANE ANCHOR

Figure 8. Nailing rafters to plates, and plates to studs, is not always enough to resist high winds. Hurricane anchors at 4-foot intervals will securely tie rafters to studs.

ing? That's not usually a problem, as long as you don't remove consecutive blocks, so that each joist is blocked on at least one side.

Connecting Rafter to Wall

Conventional construction leaves too little connection between rafters and walls. Nails connect rafter to plate and plate to stud, but do nothing to connect the rafters to the wall itself. Such structures are subject to damage from the high, near-hurricane force winds that

sooner or later blow across virtually every roof.

As a result, the building codes are beginning to get more restrictive about how rafters and trusses are tied to the rest of the building. For example, the 1991 Uniform Building Code has added Appendix Chapter 25, which applies to high wind areas. Under its requirements, rafters or trusses must be tied not just to the top plate, but to the studs below at 4-foot intervals. This means using some kind of metal

connector to provide a positive tie to the studs.

The answer is the hurricane anchor (Figure 8). You don't need to face a hurricane to need it — winds of roof-damaging gale force blow in most parts of the country. If you build in an area subject to high winds (or seismic conditions), you should consider using these or other holddowns.

By David Utterback, a district manager for Western Wood Products Association and WWPA's designated code expert.

WOOD I-JOISTS

Builders who have used solid-wood 2x10s for 15 years know what they can and can't do; when they switch to wood I-joists, however, they're confronted with a relatively new product that has different structural characteristics. The product is often misapplied even by experienced builders.

Some of these errors are caused by poor design, while others are the work of subcontractors who alter the joists after they've been installed. Most of these mistakes could lead to squeaky or bouncy floors — problems that glue-nailed I-joist floors were specifically designed to solve. Other mistakes can cause more serious problems.

What follows are the most common problems I've encountered and ways to avoid them.

Misplaced Holes

The most common problem I see is misplaced and improperly sized holes in the web of the I-joist. With my company's I-joists, for example, you can cut holes up to 1 1/2 inches in diameter anywhere in the web, including right over a bearing point. Anything bigger than that risks compromising the web's shear capacity: The bigger the hole the bigger the problem, and the farther away from a bearing point it has to be.

Sometimes the problem is obvious. For instance, the hole cut for the ducts

in Figure 9 has completely destroyed the web, and with it the joist. (By the way, the problem was fixed by sliding a new I-joist next to the old and rerouting the ductwork.) Less obvious are properly sized holes drilled too close to the bearing point (Figure 10), which also compromises the strength of the joist. There's no need to guess about the location of holes in I-joists: Manufacturers supply hole charts with their I-joists. If you follow the chart, you'll avoid problems.

Hanger Problems

The next most common error is the improper use of joist hangers. The hanger in Figure 11 isn't tall enough to catch the I-joist's top flange. This leaves the top flange without lateral support, making it more likely to roll in the hanger. A worse problem is that the bottom flange had to be chiseled away to make it fit the seat of the hanger. This reduces the strength of the joist.

Sometimes I see hangers used that are wider than the joist flange. In this case, the carpenter has to nail across the gap between the hanger and the flange. If the joist ever moves at the bearing point, the nail will rub against the hanger and cause a squeak. Filling the space in the hanger with plywood blocking may

Figure 9. Routing five ducts through this I-joist meant removing the web, which effectively destroyed the joist.

stop the squeak, but hanger manufacturers say that this increases the stress on the hanger by loading it unevenly. The resulting deflection at the seat of the hanger could leave a void in the decking above and make a bulge in any drywall ceiling below. The bottom line is to use properly sized hangers.

Other common problems with I-joist hangers include:

- *No nails into joists.* I see plenty of hangers nailed to the supporting girder but not to the joist. The I-joist can then rub against the metal hanger and cause a squeak.
- *Too few nails into girder.* Face-mounted hangers need a nail in every hole, but sometimes installers leave some nails out. This greatly reduces the hanger's load-carrying capacity.
- *Wrong-size nails.* Hangers are typically nailed to I-joists by angling a nail down into the bottom flange. Though we recommend 1 1/2-inch-long, 10d nails for this, some installers use 2 1/2-inch-long nails, which go all the way through the flange, hit the bottom of the hanger, and curl under the joist. This can lift the joists slightly and cause a squeak.
- *Unnailed tabs.* Simpson hangers have tabs that bend over the top of the bottom flange to lock the joist to the hanger. It's very common for the nails to be left out of these; again, the penalty is a squeak.

The Two-By Rim

One of the main functions of a rim joist is to transfer loads from the wall above to the wall or foundation below. To accomplish this, the rim joist must be the same depth as the floor joists. A typical 2x10 is only 9 1/4 inches deep, so it doesn't match up well with a 9 1/2-inch I-joist. Using the 2-by as a rim joist leaves a gap at either the top or bottom (Figure 12). Some manufacturers make 9 1/4-inch I-joists, but even here a "matching" 2x10 won't do. The 2-by will shrink

Figure 10. These large holes are too close to the end bearing point, so they compromise the strength of the joists. Follow the I-joist manufacturer's hole charts to avoid problems.

Figure 11. Because this joist hanger isn't tall enough to catch the I-joist's top flange, the joist may roll in the hanger. Also, the builder chiseled away the bottom flange to make it fit in the hanger, weakening the joist.

Figure 12. A 2-by rim joist is usually shallower than the I-joists; even if it's not, it will eventually shrink and leave a gap. This concentrates the structural load on the narrow joist webs, which aren't designed to support concentrated loads.

and the I-joists won't, so you'll still end up with a gap.

The trouble with this gap is that it puts all the loads on the joists themselves; in fact, it concentrates the load at the points where the thin I-joist webs meet the flanges. Depending on the web and flange materials, this concentrated force may either crush the web or cause it to knife through

the flange. The same bearing problem occurs where the I-joists cross a girder and support a bearing wall; in this situation, the blocking between the I-joists must be full depth.

The solution, of course, is to use a full-depth rim joist. This can be another I-joist, ripped strips of 3/4-inch plywood, or an engineered rim joist. I usually recommend using engineered products because you can lag ledger boards for decks and porches into them without installing special blocking — something you can't easily do with I-joists or plywood. The two products I know of are Timberstrand LSL RimBoard (Trus Joist MacMillan, 200 E. Mallard Dr., Boise, ID 83706; 800/628-3997),

which is made from glued-up aspen chips, and Versa-Rim (Boise Cascade, P.O. Box 2400, White City, OR 97503; 800/232-0788), which is basically a 1-inch-thick LVL.

Joists Interrupted at Girder

Most I-joist systems are designed to run the entire width of the build-

ing, regardless of whether they cross an intermediate support. The main reason is performance: A 30-foot I-joist running continuously over an intermediate girder provides a stiffer floor than two 15-footers that break at the girder. This means that the floor in Figure 13 will be bouncier than it should be.

Ease of installation is also important: It takes less time to put up one set of 30-foot joists (a "continuous" span) than two sets of 15-foot joists (two "simple" spans). Using a single, continuous-span I-joist may also eliminate the blocking required where two simple-span I-joists meet above a bearing wall. (This blocking prevents the joist ends from rotating). Where there is a bearing wall above, however, full-depth blocking is always required to transfer the load to the girder.

An additional problem with Figure 13 is the nail in the I-joist's bottom flange. Because it was driven too close to the end of the flange, the nail caused a split. Splitting the flange reduces the allowable bearing stress because the web doesn't have as much flange to bear on; you need a minimum 1 3/4-inch bearing surface under I-joists. Nails should be no closer than 1 1/2 inches from the end.

Shear Destruction

Where I-joists meet rafters at an exterior wall, it's not uncommon for the joist bevels to be cut beyond the inside face of the bearing surface (Figure 14). Even with solid joists this isn't a good idea, because it reduces their effective depth.

Small loads and short spans are less worrisome than heavy loads and long spans, but other factors may contribute to the problem. Note, for example, the load-bearing wall on the left in Figure 14 — the exterior wall of a shed dormer. This wall raises the load on the already weakened joists, perhaps leading to a failure.

Our engineers fixed this problem by having the builder add plywood

Figure 13. Avoid breaking an I-joist at midspan over a girder, as the builder did here. Crossing the girder with a continuous-span I-joist will yield a stiffer floor. Note also the nail splitting the bottom flange, which reduces the joist's carrying capacity.

Figure 14. Beveling a joist beyond the inside of a bearing wall reduces its resistance to shear forces, which are greatest at the bearing. In this photo, the problem is made worse by the wall at the left, which rests on the joists with no bearing wall below.

Figure 15. Notching the flange of an I-joist seriously weakens it; the closer the notch is to the middle of the span, the worse the problem.

gussets to the webs. How far back these need to go depends on the situation and must be worked out by an engineer. It's better to avoid the problem altogether by designing the structure so that the rafter line is as high as possible, ensuring a small bevel cut on the joists.

Notched Flanges

It's not unusual for a plumber or hvac installer to notch part of a joist when installing pipes or heating ducts. With an I-joist, this might mean cutting the flange (Figure 15). I-joists have their highest-strength material in the top and bottom flanges. Cutting a flange seriously compromises the joist capacity and should be avoided at all costs.

The problem was fixed by cutting out the notched section and running a pair of headers between the two adjacent joists. Whether this would work in other cases depends on whether the two adjacent joists can handle the load. To find out, you'll need to go back to your designer or supplier so they can look at the original design. The best solution, of course, is to route mechanicals so as to avoid notching the joist in the first place.

Hollow Girder

Two I-joists that are doubled to serve as a header must be joined together with blocking at joist hanger locations. Without this blocking, one joist will have to support a load that should have been distributed between two (Figure 16). You could end up with a squeaky floor, or even with a lump in the floor. Where several I-joists are joined to form a girder, blocking between the members is even more important.

Attaching Sheathing

Most I-joist floors are covered with glue-nailed sheathing, and are designed to perform as a system. A bad sheathing job can cause squeaks and other problems. Common mis-

Figure 16. The absence of blocking here between the double joists means that the load at the joist hanger will be carried entirely by the I-joist it's attached to, instead of by the girder as a whole. The most likely result is a squeak or sag in the floor.

Figure 17. Notching an I-joist rafter over the inside edge of a wall leaves it bearing not on the heel, where it should, but on the toe. These rafters will split up the middle when loaded.

takes include the following:
- *Missed nails.* Often a nail will miss the joist and end up lying tightly against the side of the flange. When the sheathing moves up and down at that point, the nail rubs against the wood, causing a squeak.
- *Glue sets too soon.* Sheathing should be attached right after the glue is spread. Otherwise, the glue will set and the sheathing will not be properly attached. The problem here is not just squeaking. Most span charts assume that a floor is

properly glued and nailed. If it's not, it will have more bounce than it should.

Weakened Rafters

Toe-bearing is a common mistake with 2-by rafters, and I-joists are no exception. Never notch an I-joist rafter beyond the inside edge of the bearing wall: You risk splitting the web section of the rafter up its centerline (Figure 17).

Some roof framing problems are unique to I-joists (Figure 18). An I-

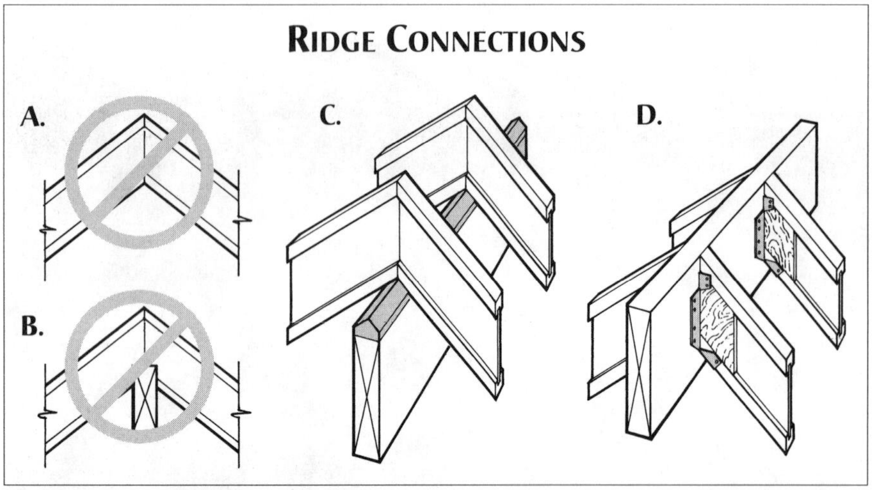

RIDGE CONNECTIONS

Figure 18. I-joist rafters can't be rested against each other at the ridge like 2-by rafters (A). Birdsmouths aren't permitted either (B). Instead, use a structural ridge and either rest the joists on a beveled plate (C) or hang them from the beam (D).

joist roof is like an I-joist floor in that it requires bearing at both ends. This means that you can't just bring the rafters together at the peak of the roof and expect them to hold each other up. To keep them from failing or sagging, you need to support the peak with a structural beam. You can't cut birdsmouths at the top of I-joist rafters, because this means cutting the bearing flanges. Instead, you'll need to either hang them off the face of the beam with joist hangers or cap the beam with a beveled plate and lay the rafters on top of this.

By Curtis Eck, P.E., a Seattle-based technical representative for Trus Joist MacMillan.

ROOF FRAMING

In recent years, houses have become larger and their roof systems more complicated. In light of this, it's worth revisiting the most common framing errors on both conventional and truss-framed roofs.

Toe-Bearing Rafters

A common error with low-slope rafters is excessive cutting of the rafter seat. This leaves the rafter bearing not on the heel of the seat cut, as it should, but on the toe. The seat cut may run straight from toe to heel, or there may be a deep birdsmouth at the inside edge of the wall — from a structural standpoint there's no difference.

There are two problems with this. One is that you no longer have the full width of the rafter to carry the load. Bearing on the toe effectively reduces the width of the entire rafter. The other problem is that the shear created by the flexing of the rafter can cause a split to start at the inside edge of the top plate. This is a particular problem with cathedral ceilings, where split rafters can lead to cracks in the ceiling drywall. The lumber's slope of grain will determine how likely it is to split, if at all.

But what if your roof is framed with 2x10s when, structurally, you only require 2x6s? Can't you safely overnotch the 2x10 to create an effective 2x6? The answer is no. For one thing, you still risk splitting the rafter. For another, lumber is graded to allow certain types of defects in certain parts of the lumber's cross-section. For instance, larger knots are allowed in 2x10s than in 2x6s. Turning a 2x10 into a 2x6 may put large knots close to the edge, ruining the board's structural integrity.

You can avoid all these problems by cutting the rafter so that it bears on the heel of the seat cut, rather than the toe. If that's not possible, try putting a ledger strip beneath the rafters to catch the heel, or support the rafters with joist hangers nailed into the top plates (Figure 19).

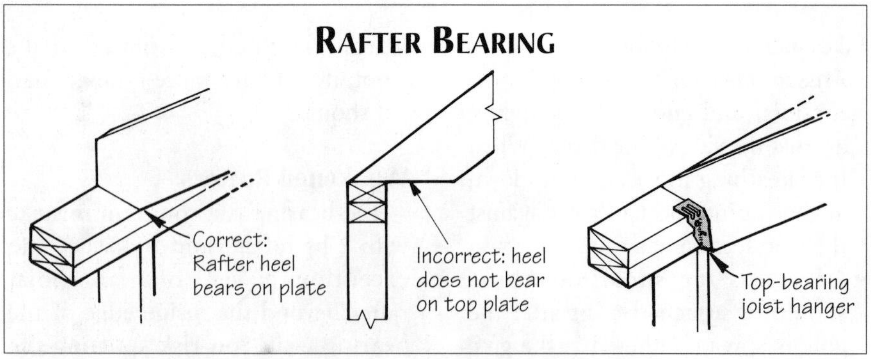

RAFTER BEARING

Correct:
Rafter heel
bears on plate

Incorrect: heel
does not bear
on top plate

Top-bearing
joist hanger

Figure 19. It's best to rest the rafter heel on the plate (left), not on the toe (center). Where this isn't possible, you can sometimes support it with a joist hanger (right). The joist hanger also keeps the rafter from rotating, a job that normally requires ceiling joists or solid blocking.

Transferred Loads

Another big problem with roof systems in today's large houses is load transfer. The complexity of some roof structures makes it hard to properly support some of the members. I see too many hips and valleys that are totally unsupported; sometimes these hips and valleys tie into lower ridges that are also unsupported.

Hip and valley rafters need to land on headers or doubled-up rafters sized to handle the loads. Headers around openings like skylights don't necessarily need to be plumb. But remember that the loads on a roof are vertical — not perpendicular to the rafters — and that lumber is strongest when placed on its edge. This means that, in most situations, the header should be put in plumb and its members stepped to follow the roof slope. A rule of thumb is that headers up to 4 feet long can be put in square with the rafters, while anything over 4 feet should be plumb. Header rafters more than 6 feet long should be supported by framing anchors.

Roof loads are also transferred by the purlins and struts used to break up rafter spans. Where I live, near Kansas City, every house has these — even inexpensive starter homes. Too often, the struts are not properly located. Diagonal struts must extend to bearing walls at less than a 45-degree angle from the horizontal. If the struts land on strongbacks set across undersized ceiling joists (Figure 20) or fall on nonbearing walls, the ceiling finish may crack or the doors in those nonbearing walls may bind and stick.

No Rafter Ties

Cathedral ceilings present special problems. If there are no ceiling joists, you must find another way to keep the rafters from pushing the exterior walls out. If not, symptoms can develop up to a year or two after the house has been built, and include cracks at the wall-ceiling intersection, cracks above headers, and walls

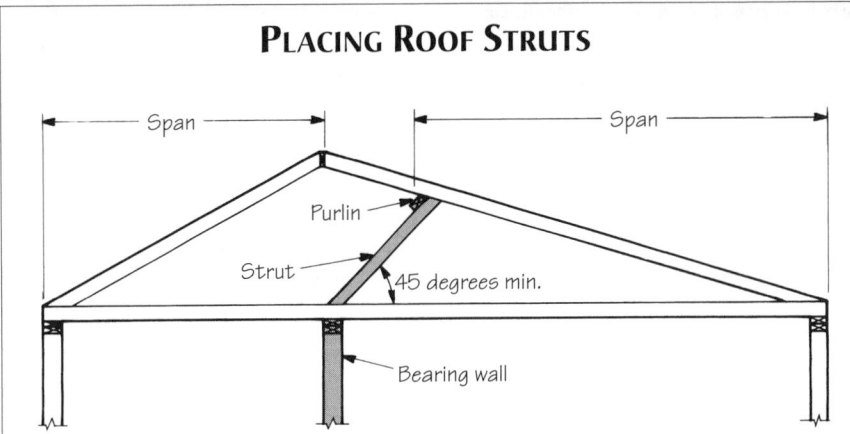

Figure 20. The rafters in this house (top) have been stiffened with a purlin that runs the length of the roof. Because the struts that hold the purlin bear on a set of unsupported ceiling joists, however, chances are that the ceiling will eventually crack. To properly support the roof, the braces need to go from the purlin to a bearing wall, and should not drop below a 45° angle as shown (above).

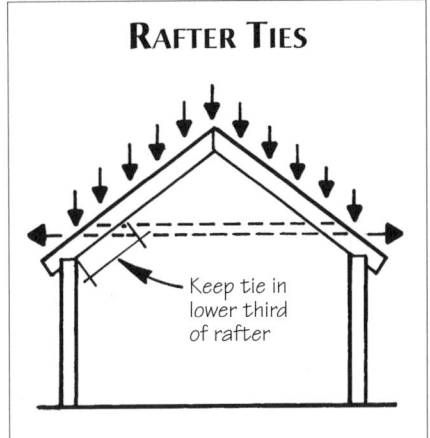

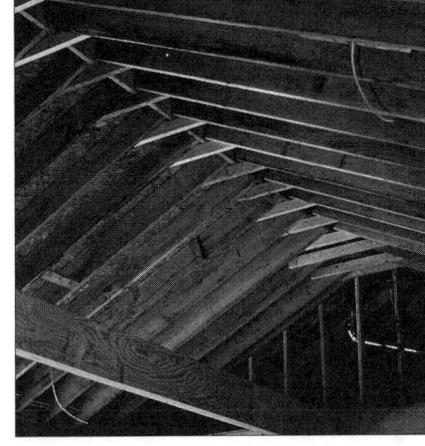

Figure 21. As rafters settle, their outward thrust pushes out on exterior walls. Rafter ties should be placed in the lower third of the rafter span (left) so they have enough leverage to resist this thrust. The ties in this photo (right) serve no structural purpose.

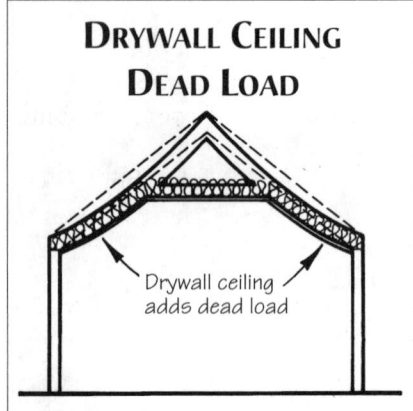

DRYWALL CEILING DEAD LOAD

Drywall ceiling adds dead load

Figure 22. Hanging a ceiling near the middle of the rafter span adds dead load to the rafter at its maximum bending point. Avoid this detail, or use a structural ridge to reduce the outward thrust of the rafters and design the rafters to support the additional dead load.

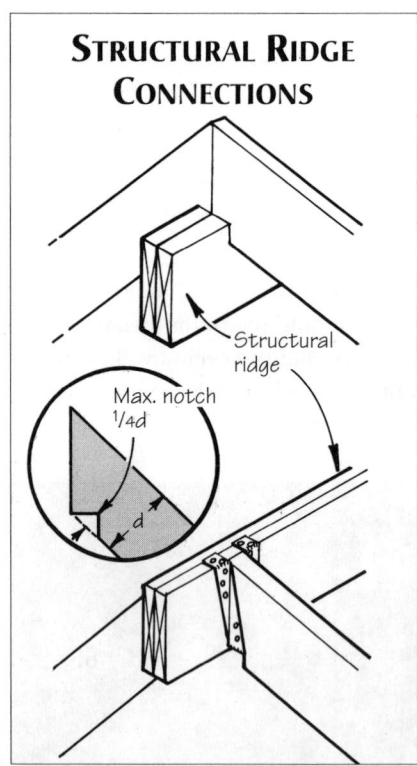

STRUCTURAL RIDGE CONNECTIONS

Structural ridge

Max. notch
$\frac{1}{4}d$

d

Figure 23. The most effective way to reduce outward roof thrust is to use a structural ridge beam. Either rest the rafters on top of a structural ridge (at top) or use joist hangers attached to the ridge beam (at bottom). The notch at the bottom of the plumb cut should be no deeper than one-fourth the rafter width.

that are greatly out of plumb. No builder needs callbacks on problems like these.

In rooms with attics above them, the ceiling joists or the bottom chords of the trusses create a tension tie between the outside walls. In a cathedral ceiling, open rafter ties can serve the same purpose if they're not placed too high. A good rule of thumb is that unless the roof structure has been specially engineered, don't place the rafter ties above the lower third of the rafter span (Figure 21); otherwise, they won't have enough leverage to resist the rafters' outward thrust.

You'll understand this if you think about the way a tree pruner works. Grabbing the handles at the end gives you plenty of leverage to cut off the limb; grabbing them near the cutter head makes the job considerably harder. Rafter ties do the same thing in reverse — instead of trying to squeeze the outside ends of the rafters together, the rafter ties keep them from moving farther apart. The closer the ties to the bottom of the rafter, the greater the leverage.

If you install ceiling joists near the center of a rafter span and hang drywall from them, you increase the dead load on the roof at the rafter's maximum bending point. This will cause the rafter to deflect and push out on the outside walls even more (Figure 22).

Ridge beams. You can also prevent cathedral ceiling rafters from pushing the walls out by using a structural ridge beam. By holding up the top of the rafters, a structural ridge lets the exterior walls carry the vertical loads applied to them by the rafters, but reduces the outward thrust. Keep in mind that a beam has to be sized to carry the load that will be imposed on it, and that the beam will have a limited span capability. It will also need proper supports at each end, and, if necessary, along its length. Too

often I see ridges that are neither properly sized nor properly supported. Many times the only thing holding up the ridge beam is the rafters themselves, which obviously defeats the purpose of the ridge beam. Designing a structural ridge is a bit complicated for the average builder, so get an engineer to do the calculations.

There are two ways to join rafters to a structural ridge: You can either butt the plumb cut to the ridge beam or you can cut a birdsmouth in the rafters and set them on top of the ridge. Either way is acceptable, as long as you follow the guidelines in Figure 23. A toe-nailed connection is not strong enough.

Trusses

As one would expect from engineered components, trusses present a different set of problems than solid lumber.

Field alteration. Don't try this on your own. Since trusses are engineered systems, they shouldn't be altered on the job site. To do so destroys the integrity of the truss. If you absolutely have to cut a truss, call the truss engineer.

Improper bearing. The average truss is designed to bear on the outside walls of a building and to clear-span everything between. One of the most frequent framing errors I see is nailing the bottom chords of roof trusses to interior partitions. A truss can be engineered with an additional bearing point along its bottom chord, but on the typical roof truss, creating an additional bearing point on the bottom chord will redistribute the loads through the truss. This can cause web members designed for tension to become compression members and vice versa. In extreme cases, the truss could fail.

Another problem with nailing to interior partitions is cracked drywall from truss movement. During the winter months, the uninsulated top chord picks up moisture from the air

Figure 24. Most roof trusses are designed to bear only at the exterior walls. Avoid nailing roof trusses to interior partitions (left); otherwise, as the bottom chord rises with changes in moisture content, it will move the wall with it and open up cracks in the ceiling drywall. Instead, use truss clips (bottom left), which allow the truss to move independently of the partition wall.

But once I tell them to measure the joists and check them for level, they find out that while the joists may contribute to the problem, something else is going on.

What can be done about rising trusses? First of all, don't shim under the wall. The trusses and the wall will nearly always come back down in the summer. If you try to prevent this from happening, you'll create that unwanted bearing point I mentioned earlier. You can also replace the nails holding the bottom chord to the wall with truss clips — metal connectors that let a truss move up and down without taking the wall with it (Figure 24). If you use truss clips, don't screw the ceiling drywall to the truss where it passes over the partition. Instead, hold your screws 12 to 14 inches back from the partition and screw the edge of the ceiling to 2-by nailers that have been fastened to the top plate between the trusses. This will let the drywall flex and prevent a crack from forming at the wall/ceiling intersection.

By David Utterback, a district manager for Western Wood Products Association and WWPA's designated code expert.

and expands. As it expands it arches, pulling the bottom chord up with it. If the bottom chord is nailed to an interior partition, either the nails will simply pull loose or the rising truss will pull the wall right off the floor, opening a gap below the baseboard. Most of the calls I get about this are complaints from builders that the floor joists are shrinking.

TRUSS BRACING

Using roof trusses lets you close in a building quickly and gives you flexibility in placing interior partitions. But except for some data published by the Truss Plate Institute (Madison, Wis.; 608/833-5900), there is little written information on how to install and brace trusses. The few books that do discuss the issue typically show the first truss located directly over the end wall and braced diagonally to stakes driven into the ground.

I can give three reasons why you should, or in one case must, support your trusses another way. First, depending on the building's height and the slope of the site, the length of a diagonal brace from the peak of a truss to the ground can measure more than 40 feet — too long a span for strong, rigid bracing. Second, in the case of a hip roof, the girder truss usually sits at least 12 feet inside the end wall, where it's impossible to brace it diagonally to the ground. Finally, braces running from the roof to the ground clutter the site, slowing the work and creating safety hazards.

A Different Approach

To avoid these problems, I use a different technique for installing roof trusses. First, I straighten and brace the exterior walls as usual. Then I beef up the bracing of one of the end walls — the end where I plan to start truss installation. But instead of starting directly above the end wall, I position the first truss 8 to 12 feet in, then brace it back to that wall (Figure 25). Here's how it works.

Before plunging into the stack of trusses, I mark the truss spacings (usually 2 feet on-center) on the top plates of the bearing walls. While I mark the layout, I have another carpenter prepare plenty of 2-by lateral braces by marking off the truss centers and starting a duplex nail at each mark.

Next, either with a crane or with lots of muscle, we raise the first truss and set it in position on the first layout mark farther from the end wall than the height of the truss. For example, for 7-foot-high trusses, we would position the first truss at the fifth layout mark (8 feet in for trusses 2 feet on-center). This ensures that all the braces from the top chord of the truss will be at less than a 45-degree angle, making them much stronger than braces at steeper angles.

Then, with the help of the crane or with braces from the end wall or the deck below, we hold the truss plumb while we position it exactly on the layout marks and toenail it to the plates.

At this point we pull a dry line from the front to the back plate and 6 inches in front of the truss. We position braces at 6- to 8-foot intervals from the top of the bottom chord to the top of the end wall. Depending on the distance between the end wall and the first truss, I've used almost everything from 2x4s to staging planks. *Never* use 1-inch stock for bracing.

We first spike each brace into the top of the bottom chord. Then, as one worker measures, his or her partner adjusts each brace and spikes it to the end wall when the truss's bottom chord is exactly 6 inches from the line.

Next, with either the crane or workers on the deck or end wall still steadying the truss, I climb an extension ladder to the peak and plumb the truss, using a 6-foot level and straightedge or a plumb bob. (For lower-pitch trusses, staging or a tall step or trestle ladder also works for getting to the peak.) When the truss is plumb, I nail a brace from the peak to the top of the end wall. Then I work down the top chord at 6- to 8-foot intervals, straightening and plumbing it, then bracing it back to the end wall.

The Rest Is Easy

With the first truss in place, straight and plumb, the rest of the trusses go more quickly. We nail the second truss in place; then, using the premarked lateral bracing, we secure it to the first truss.

For a standard house truss, say 24 to 36 feet long, we install at least one row of lateral bracing along the peak, one along the attic walkway, and one along the midpoint of each top chord. Larger trusses require more.

To be sure the trusses will withstand a windstorm, we connect all the trusses to one another with diagonal web bracing. We begin installing this as soon as the fourth truss is up.

Once we've set a dozen or so trusses, another crew can start the roof sheathing to help stiffen them. We keep the lowest lateral brace at least 5 feet up from the bottom edge of the truss so we don't have to remove it until the first row of plywood is nailed off. Meanwhile, the first crew continues across the building, setting trusses and installing the diagonal and lateral braces. When the entire roof assembly is anchored together, we nail two continuous 2x6

A PROVEN TRUSS TECHNIQUE

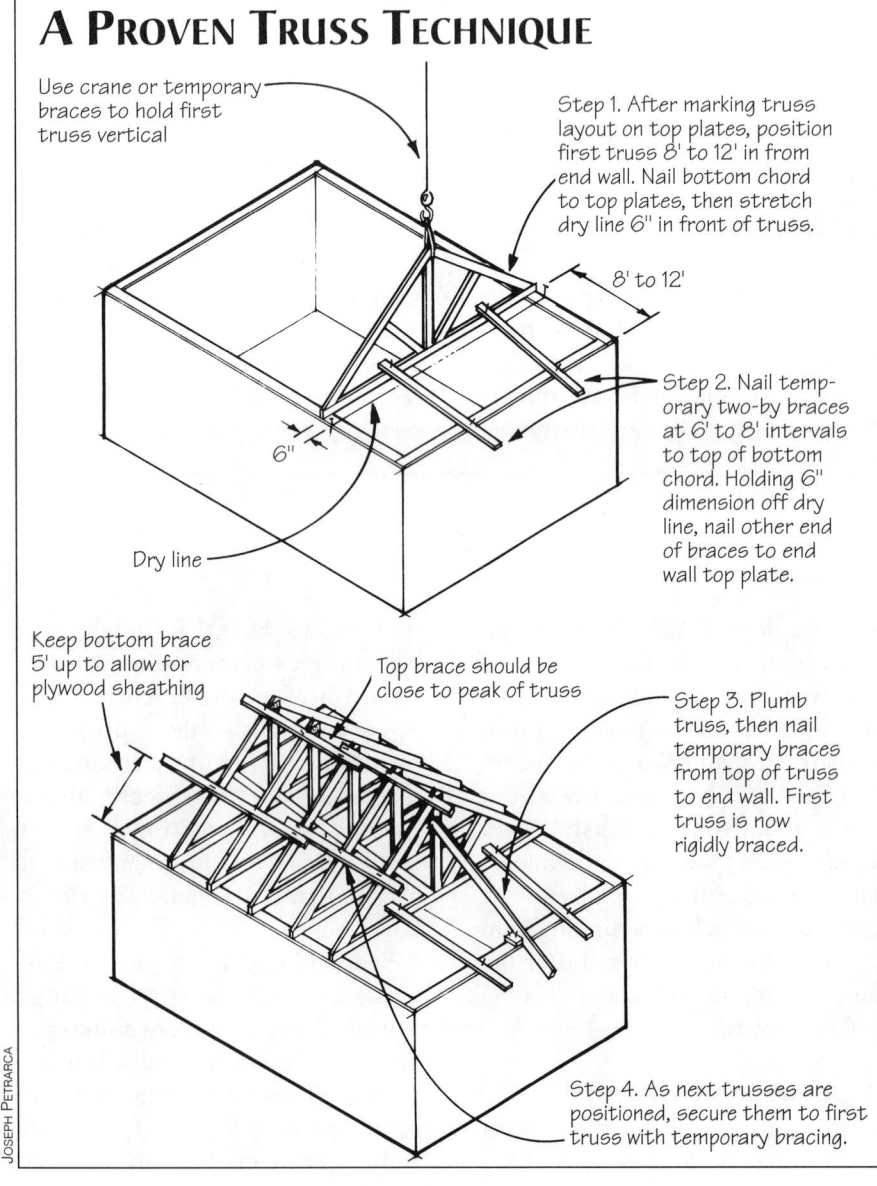

Use crane or temporary braces to hold first truss vertical

Step 1. After marking truss layout on top plates, position first truss 8' to 12' in from end wall. Nail bottom chord to top plates, then stretch dry line 6" in front of truss.

8' to 12'

6"

Dry line

Step 2. Nail temporary two-by braces at 6' to 8' intervals to top of bottom chord. Holding 6" dimension off dry line, nail other end of braces to end wall top plate.

Keep bottom brace 5' up to allow for plywood sheathing

Top brace should be close to peak of truss

Step 3. Plumb truss, then nail temporary braces from top of truss to end wall. First truss is now rigidly braced.

Step 4. As next trusses are positioned, secure them to first truss with temporary bracing.

JOSEPH PETRARCA

Figure 25. By starting truss installation several feet in from one end of the building and bracing back to the end wall, the author avoids using long bracing from the roof to the ground.

braces from the ridge to the floor in the form of an "X" or an "A."

To finish the roof, we remove the end wall braces to the first truss and work back to the end wall. Finally, we install the permanent bracing and metal tie-downs per the engineered bracing plan from the truss manufacturer.

By Paul De Baggis, an instructor at Minuteman Technical School in Lexington, Mass. and former builder.

SHED DORMERS

S hed dormers remain a popular remodeling project but they are often retrofitted without proper concern for whether the structure can handle the new loads. Below, we'll examine some of the structural concerns that must be considered before retrofitting a shed dormer to an existing roof. Of course, the same concerns and recommendations apply equally to new construction as well.

Shed Dormer Basics

Consider a basic frame roof, like the one in Figure 26. Assuming its members are correctly sized, this roof is a rigid triangle. The rafters lean against each other at the ridge with a force equal to their outward thrust, which is resisted by the ceiling joists. All vertical loads are transferred to the walls, which (we hope) safely carry them down to the foundation.

However, if you introduce a shed dormer on one side of this roof, you upset the balance of forces in this stable triangle. Unless proper precautions are taken, the roof will tend to deflect, as indicated by the dashed lines in Figure 26B. This kind of deflection is not usually apparent within weeks, or even months, of the completion of a shed dormer project. But my observations in the field have shown me

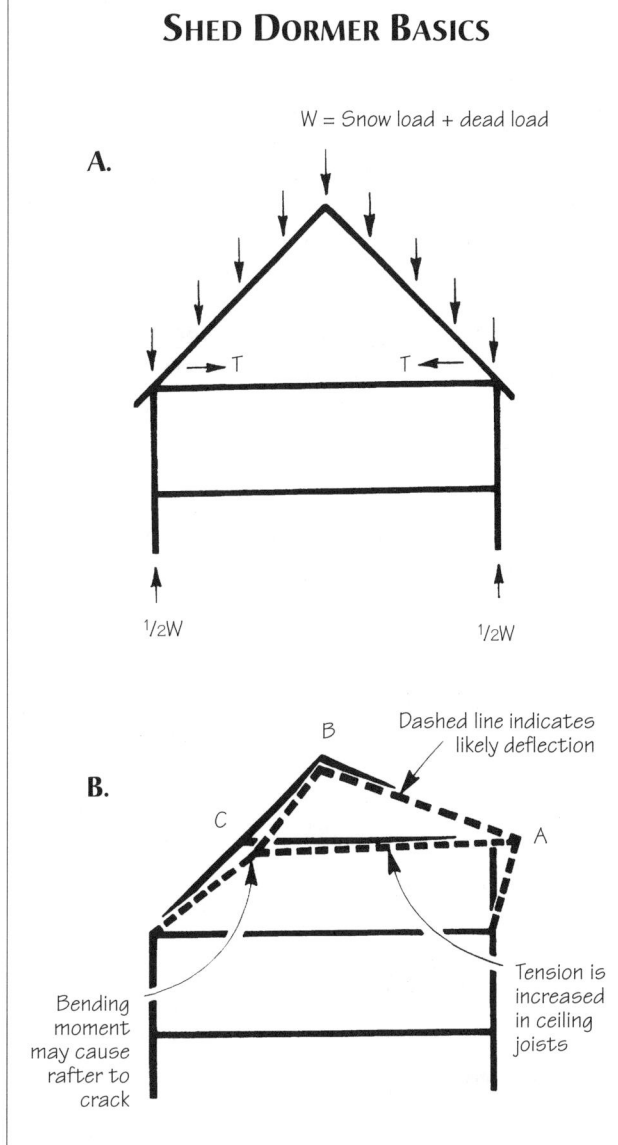

SHED DORMER BASICS

A.

W = Snow load + dead load

T T

$\frac{1}{2}W$ $\frac{1}{2}W$

B.

B

Dashed line indicates likely deflection

C

A

Bending moment may cause rafter to crack

Tension is increased in ceiling joists

Figure 26. A properly built gable roof is a stable triangle (A). The rafters lean against each other with a force equal to the tension, T, carried by the joists, which resist the tendency of the roof to spread. Install a shed dormer, though, and the stable triangle is upset (B). The tension in the dormer ceiling joists increases considerably, adding bending stress at the rafter/joist connections. In situations where the triangle ABC is less than 4 feet in height, the author recommends two 1/2-inch carriage bolts each at connections A and C.

that over many years houses will experience this kind of movement. In several cases, I've seen exterior walls leaning out by as much as $1^1/2$ inches, and in many cases I've seen sagging ridge lines that are noticeable from the street.

Undersized framing. There are several causes of deflection in shed dormers. A common one is that shed dormers are often added to roofs that already have undersized rafters. Many 19th-century capes — common choices for shed additions — have 4x4 rafters 3 or 4 feet on-center, often without a structural ridge beam. And many modern frame houses have 2x8 or even 2x6 rafters — where 2x10s or 2x12s should have been used.

In these situations, retrofitting a shed dormer without providing for the new loads is asking for trouble. These undersized rafters simply don't have any reserve strength to accommodate the bending loads which can be imposed by the dormer. Not only is a noticeable sag in the roof possible, but very high bending moments can create a real risk of cracking in the rafters.

Also, attic floor joists are usually sized smaller than main floor framing. With the addition of a shed dormer, the attic joists must support living space loads. And in many cases, the outside wall of the dormer

is set in from the outside wall of the house (Figure 27), bringing additional roof loads onto the joists. Often, a kneewall is incorporated somewhere near the eaves along the non-dormered side of the roof; this, too, transfers roof loads. All of these conditions can greatly increase bending loads on the attic floor joists, causing visible deflection — often as much as an inch — in the floor and the ceiling below.

Creeping deflection. Another reason that shed dormer roofs deflect is that creeping deflection takes place. Over the years the rafters develop a permanent sag from continued loading. This is especially true in snow climates. And since shed dormer roofs usually have a fairly shallow pitch, they tend to hold more snow.

Loosening connections. A third cause of deflection is that over time nails begin to slip and bend, loosening the connections. This is especially true of the ceiling joist/rafter connection at the shed dormer eaves.

Supporting Dormer Loads

There are some basic precautions you can take to make sure your shed dormer addition doesn't sag with time:
• Provide a continuous path to the foundation for all roof loads. This may mean adding structural elements.

• Use properly-sized framing members. For dormers where you're adding new loads onto existing framing, this may mean sistering new members to the old.
• Make strong connections. Adequate nailing, bolts, metal connectors, and plywood can all help here.

The simplest solution — on paper at least — is to fully support the new dormer loads all the way to the foundation. There are two common ways to do this: a structural ridge or a center bearing wall. Which you use depends on the design and layout of the particular house you are remodeling.

Structural ridge. Though they can be troublesome to retrofit, structural ridge beams can solve most of the loading problems associated with shed dormers (Figure 28). The structural ridge can either replace the existing ridge or be installed below it. The table in Figure 28 offers guidance in sizing structural ridges. The table is based on a 24-foot-wide house, with 30-psf snow loads.

Take special care to provide adequate support at ends of the structural ridge. In the case described in the table in Figure 28, two 2x4 studs in a plywood sheathed wall would adequately support each end of the ridge beam. Without the lateral support of plywood sheathing, however, more careful examination of stud buckling would be required. A triple 2x6 post, properly nailed, would suffice in any case. Be sure that the load path is continuous to foundation.

A structural ridge design requires nothing of ceiling joists, other than supporting the ceiling; they can be omitted if you like.

Center support wall. In many cases, interior support is provided by walls located at or near the center of the structure (Figure 29). The advantages are the same as for the structural ridge, but the need for a sturdy beam with double or triple 2x posts is eliminated.

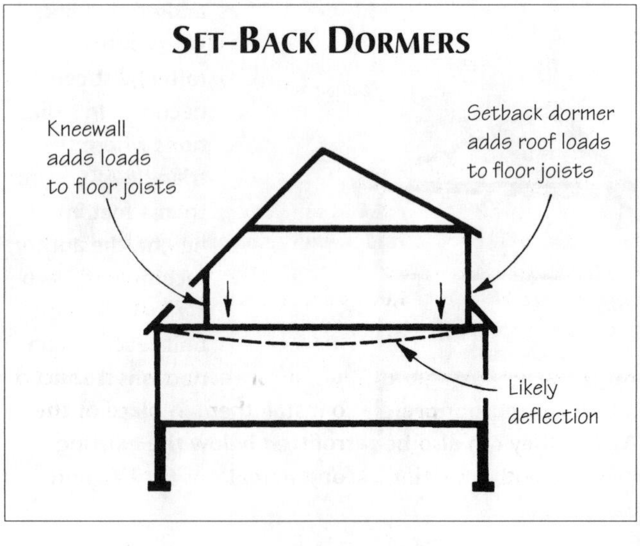

SET-BACK DORMERS

Kneewall adds loads to floor joists

Setback dormer adds roof loads to floor joists

Likely deflection

Figure 27. If you set back the front wall of a shed dormer for aesthetic reasons, make sure the floor joists can handle the additional roof loads. A kneewall on the non-dormered side of the roof shortens the rafter span but also adds roof loads to the floor.

As with the structural ridge design, continuity of load paths to the foundation is important. Ideally, the support wall should stand directly below the ridge line, and be in line with walls or girders all the way to the foundation. It's okay if the support wall is a few inches out of line with the wall below, but in this case you should align the studs over the floor joists or use a double sole plate. If the walls are more than a few inches out of alignment, have an engineer check the joists to avoid sagging and ceiling distress.

But Can I Do It Without Additional Support?

Admittedly, many shed dormers have been built in roofs without structural ridges or where no center support wall exists. And many of these dormers, which under engineering analysis with code loads would seem deficient, have fared well.

In many of these cases, the main factor that saves an otherwise troubled design is the relatively short length of the dormer (parallel to the ridge). Also, partition walls may provide some vertical support and even an existing ridge beam, if it's 2x8 or larger, may serve for spans between partitions of less than 12 feet. In general, a small shed dormer may work without a structural ridge or center bearing wall if the following conditions are met:

• Set the exterior wall of the shed dormer directly above the first-floor exterior wall (Figure 30). This ensures that at least half the dormer roof loads are carried safely to the foundation — assuming the wall below is well-built, with properly sized door and window headers.

• Include a kneewall at the rear (non-dormered side of the roof). This provides midspan support to the rafters on that side. Keep the horizontal distance between the

STRUCTURAL RIDGE

A.

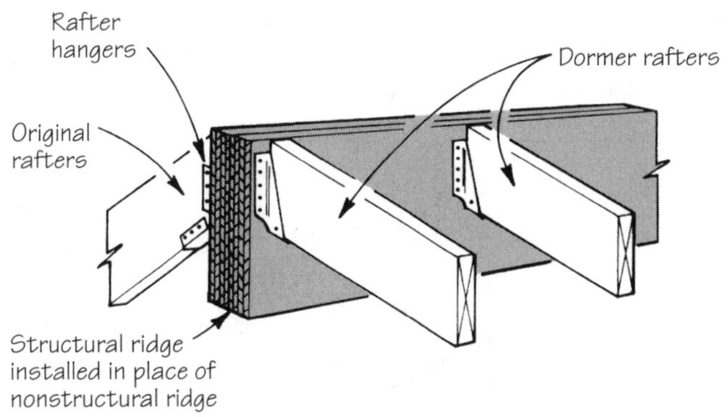

Rafter hangers

Original rafters

Dormer rafters

Structural ridge installed in place of nonstructural ridge

B.

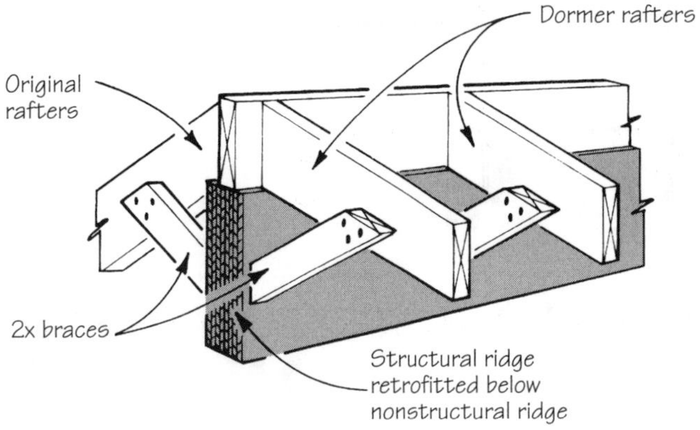

Dormer rafters

Original rafters

2x braces

Structural ridge retrofitted below nonstructural ridge

SIZING STRUCTURAL RIDGE BEAMS

Ridge length	LVL beam	2x beam*
8'	LVL 1³/₄ x 9¹/₂	(2) 2x10
9'	"	(3) 2x10, (2) 2x12
10'	LVL 1³/₄ x 11⁷/₈	"
11'	"	(2) 2x12
12'	"	(3) 2x12
13'	LVL 1³/₄ x 14	Not recommended
14'	"	"
15'	(2) LVL 1³/₄ x 14	"
16'	"	"

Note: This table is based on a sample house 24 feet wide (eaves to eaves), with design snow loads of 30 psf.
* Fb = 760 psi min. (new grading tables), or 1,000 psi with the old tables

Figure 28. Structural ridge beams are a good solution for the loads introduced by a shed dormer addition. The author prefers to install them in place of the nonstructural ridge (A), but they can also be retrofitted below the existing ridge (B). The table gives the author's sizing recommendations for LVL and laminated 2x ridge beams.

kneewall and the dormer's ceiling joist/rafter intersection to less than 4 feet, unless the rafters are 2x10s or larger. Also, make sure the floor joists below the kneewall are large enough — if less than 2x10, they will usually have to be sistered.

• The vertical distance between the ridge and the dormer ceiling should be 3 feet or more. The dormer ceiling joists act in tension to resist the roof spread. As they go higher, the tension increases, as does the bending moment at the connection. This increases the risk that the rafter will crack or that the connection will slip.

• Use perpendicular interior walls to brace the dormer's exterior wall against leaning out. This will not work well if the partitions are covered only with drywall. Sheathe these partitions with plywood and use strap ties to tie them to the top plate of the dormer's exterior wall, as shown in Figure 30.

• Use minimum 1/2-inch plywood roof sheathing, properly nailed, to develop diaphragm action in the dormer roof. Also, an existing ridge beam 2x8 or larger will help maintain ridge alignment.

Taken collectively, these features may prevent deflection problems, whereas any single feature would be inadequate.

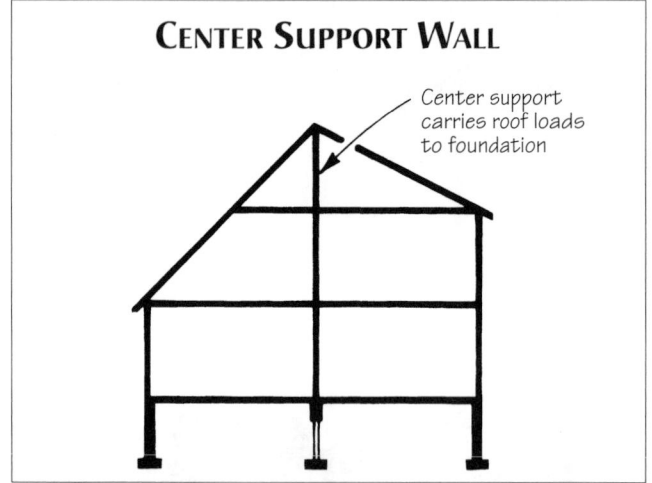

CENTER SUPPORT WALL

Center support carries roof loads to foundation

Figure 29. Center support walls are often the easiest way to handle shed dormer loads, but they must provide a continuous path to the foundation.

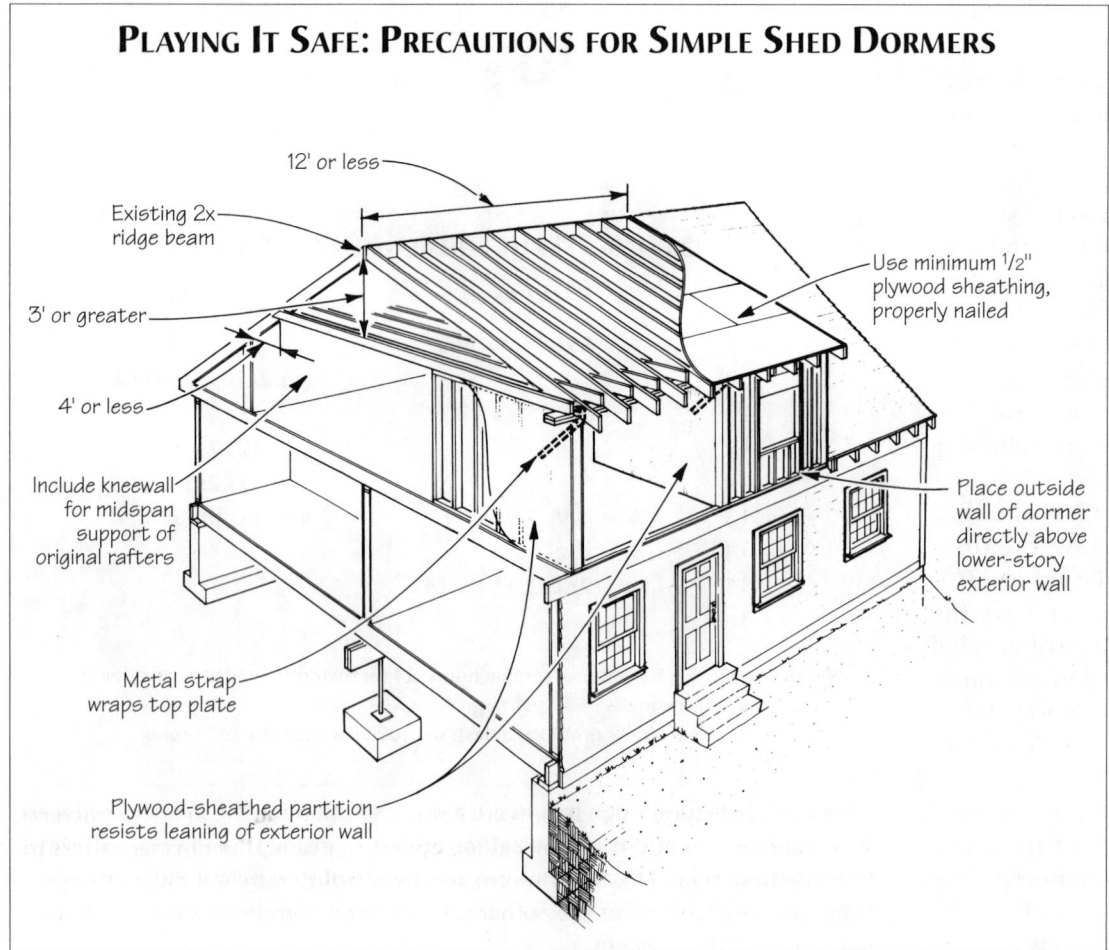

PLAYING IT SAFE: PRECAUTIONS FOR SIMPLE SHED DORMERS

12' or less

Existing 2x ridge beam

3' or greater

4' or less

Include kneewall for midspan support of original rafters

Metal strap wraps top plate

Plywood-sheathed partition resists leaning of exterior wall

Use minimum 1/2" plywood sheathing, properly nailed

Place outside wall of dormer directly above lower-story exterior wall

Figure 30. Although it's a safer practice to include a structural ridge or center support wall when retrofitting a shed dormer, it's possible to add a dormer without these structural elements as long as certain conditions are met, as shown here.

Other Design Considerations

There are many small variations on shed dormer design that have structural implications.

Supporting set-back dormers. As mentioned above, many dormer designs set the outside wall of the dormer back from the line of the main wall of the house for the sake of appearance. The problem common to these designs is the transfer of roof loads to the floor joists. Where the floor joists are 2x6s, this set-back design should not be considered without sistering the floor joists. Where 2x8 floor joists exist, a setback no greater than one foot is suggested. With 2x10 floor joists, a 2-foot setback is probably reasonable. (Have your design reviewed by a licensed engineer to verify these recommendations.) Where you have a structural ridge or a center support wall, the setback distances can be increased somewhat.

Drop-ridge dormers. If aesthetic considerations lead you to drop the shed dormer ridge (because practical considerations are not likely to!), then all the previous guidelines still apply. Where you have a structural ridge or center support, this detail is easy. Just tie the dormer rafters in at the ridge or center wall and finish the roof off with short nonstructural rafters above the shed (Figure 31).

If you're retrofitting a dormer where there's no structural ridge or center support wall and you want to drop the ridge, an added challenge lies in making careful connections at the ridge. I would recommend two ½-inch carriage bolts at each connection.

Except for very small dormers, I would not recommend using a header between doubled rafters to support the top of drop-ridge dormer rafters. Although this practice is common, these headers are usually undersized and a sagging roof or cracked rafters can result.

Dormers over half-walls. Often the existing construction has second-story half-walls, either balloon-

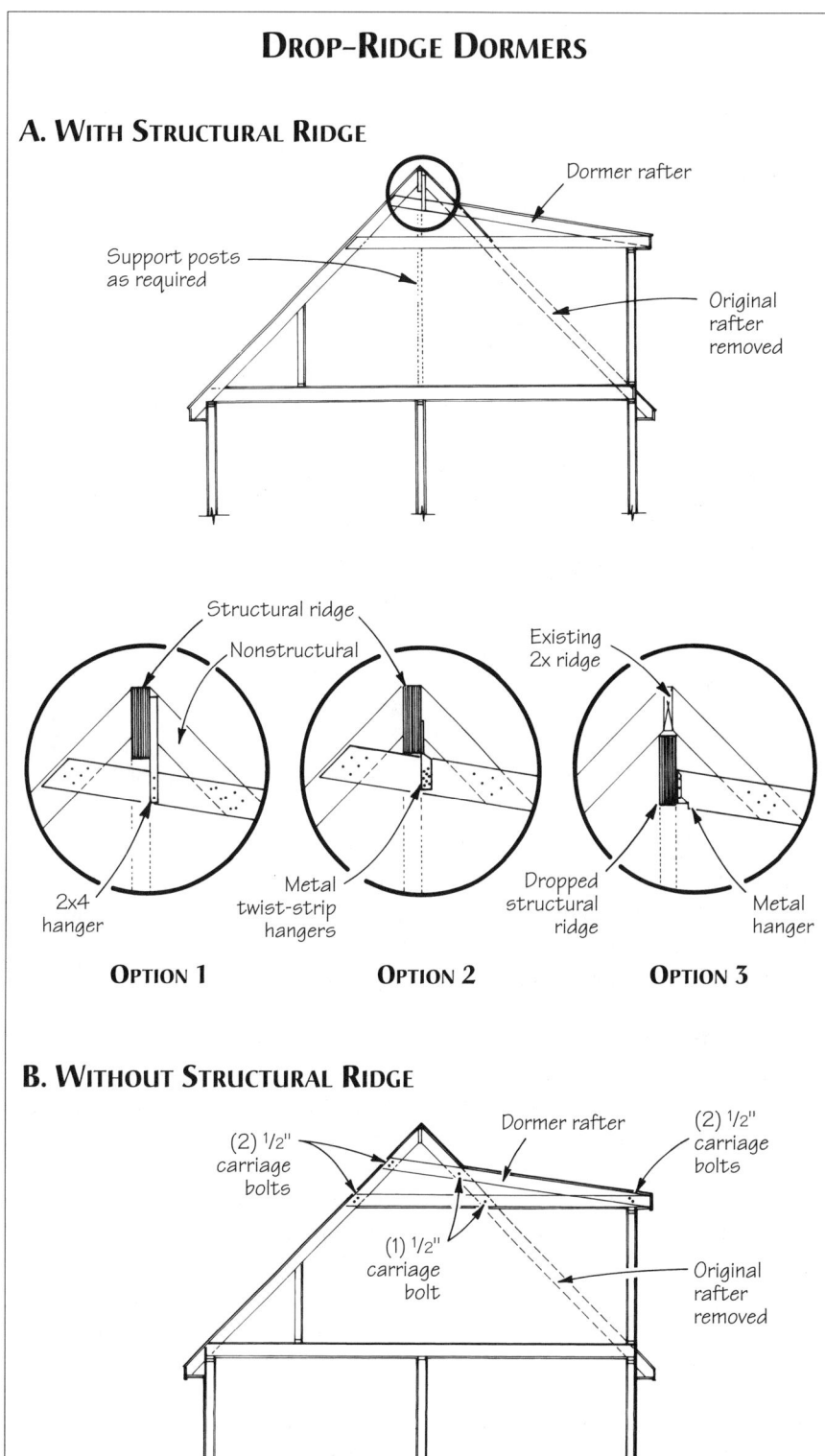

Figure 31. Shed dormer designs sometimes drop the shed ridge below the main ridge of the house. With a center bearing wall or structural ridge (A), this presents no problem; just tie in the dormer rafters and add short nonstructural rafters above. The drawing shows three options for tying the dormer rafters to the structural ridge. However, in situations without a structural ridge (B), special attention must be given to connecting the dormer rafters. The author recommends ½-inch carriage bolts at all connections.

BALLOON-FRAMED HALF-WALLS

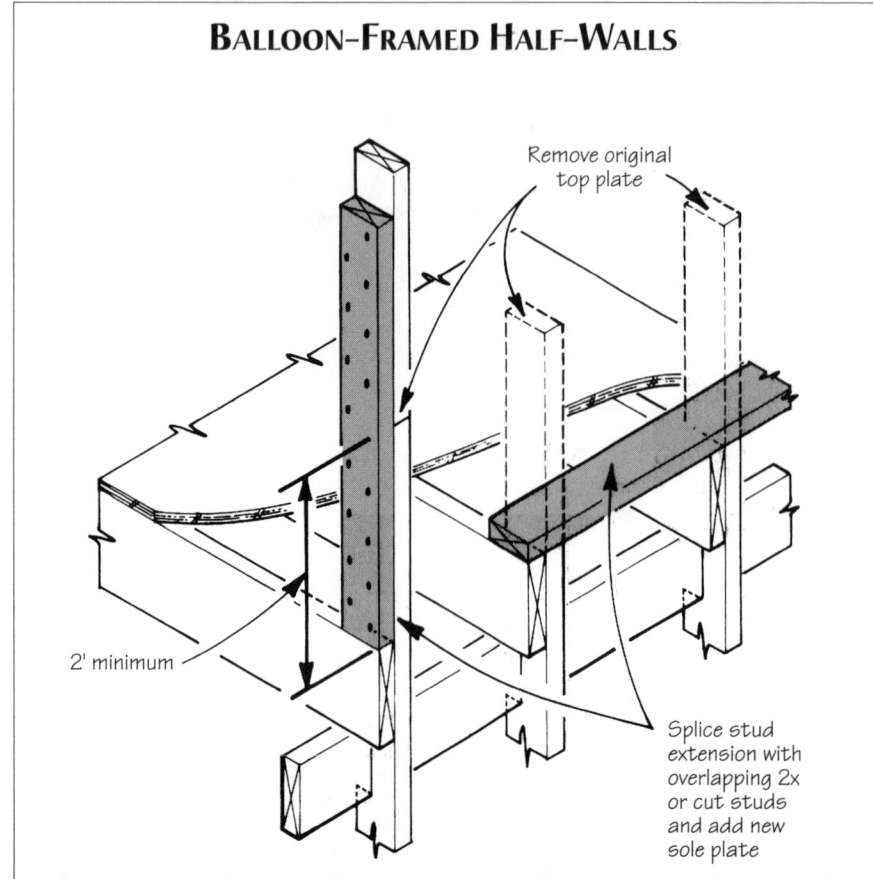

Remove original top plate

2' minimum

Splice stud extension with overlapping 2x or cut studs and add new sole plate

Figure 32. When adding a shed dormer above balloon-framed half-walls, don't build the wall extension directly on top of the balloon wall top plate. Instead, either remove the top plate and carefully splice on stud extensions or cut the balloon studs flush and build a new full-height stud wall.

framed or of platform construction (Figure 32). Resist the temptation to scab on to the half-wall when raising the shed roof — it's never a good idea to have a weak wall splice midway between floor and ceiling. Instead, remove the top plate of balloon-framed half-walls and add stud extensions, splicing them together with an overlapping 2x member. Or you can cut the balloon studs off flush with the floor deck and add a top plate, then build a new full-height stud wall on top. Remove platform-framed half-walls altogether and replace them with full-height stud walls.

There is another problem that can occur when a shed dormer is added over half-walls. Because a half-wall affords some access under the non-dormered side of the roof, the knee-wall on that side is often omitted,

leaving a clear-span roof and no load transfer to floor joists (good). Unfortunately, the resulting bending moments applied to rafters at ceiling joist connection points are likely to be unacceptable (very bad). In this situation it's best to provide a structural ridge or center bearing wall, or to seek the help of an engineer.

Hybrid dormers. In many cases, a long dormer may incorporate two or three of the basic designs described above, selected according to interior wall placement and available load paths below. There is really little to worry about with such combinations as long as each section, taken alone, is structurally adequate.

Final Precautions

Regardless of the type of dormer being built, it is important to verify

the strength of the existing framing beneath the new construction, and to consider flashing and ventilation details for the new roof:

- *Floor joists* may require sistering if the new construction adds significant bending loads to the floor. Two-by-sixes should always be sistered and 2x8s will often need to be. Two-by-tens may not need sistering if the new loads are not excessive.
- *Interior walls,* if used to carry vertical loads, should be inspected to make sure the headers are adequate. Check the alignment of support walls with walls and girders below. If more than a few inches of misalignment exists, seek professional review.
- *Girders* should be analyzed for the new loads. Examine them for signs of twisting, lateral instability, or excessive sagging or crushing of wood members at points of support.
- *Columns* should be checked for deformation at the top, for proper attachment, and for any settlement. Inspect steel columns for corrosion as well.
- *Footings* are usually adequate to carry additional loads, but should be inspected just in case they were poorly constructed in the first place.
- *Ventilation* may be needed where you're finishing previously unfinished attic space. Don't forget to pay proper attention to details of insulation and ventilation of the new roof.
- *Roofing* may require special thought, depending on the slope of the dormer roof. Shingles will not drain as well as they did on the original steeper roof. If the roof cannot be readily seen from the ground, or if the slope is less than 4:12, I recommend a single-ply material, such as modified bitumen. And regardless of the slope, you should incorporate an ice and water membrane for the first 36 inches of the roof above the eaves to avoid ice dams.

By Robert Randall, a structural engineer from Mohegan Lake, N.Y.

DETAILS FOR WOOD SHRINKAGE

Today, most builders frame with kiln-dried stock. But if you think that means you don't have to be concerned about wood shrinkage, think again: Kiln-dried lumber will definitely shrink. How much depends on its moisture content at the time of installation (see "Calculating Shrinkage," page 51). And as the lumber shrinks, it tends to twist and bow, causing humps and nail pops in walls, and bumpy, squeaky, out-of-level floors.

Understanding Wood Shrinkage

Moisture affects wood the same way it affects a sponge. If you take a sopping-wet sponge and wring it out, you'll remove some of the water, though not enough to change the sponge's size. But if you let the damp sponge dry out, it will shrink. And if you wet the dry sponge, it will swell back up until it reaches the point where it can't absorb any more water and can't get any larger.

In a piece of wood, moisture resides both in the cell cavities and in the cell walls. Green wood is like a sopping-wet sponge: As it dries, the moisture in the cavities is the first to go. But, as with the sponge, this doesn't cause the wood to shrink. The point at which there is moisture in cell walls, but not in cell cavities is called the *fiber saturation point*. Below this level, the wood (like the sponge) will shrink as it dries and swell as it absorbs moisture.

The amount of moisture in a piece of wood is referred to as its *moisture content* (MC). Moisture content is the ratio of the weight of the moisture in a piece of wood to the weight of the piece of wood if all of the moisture were removed. Because the water in a piece of green wood can easily outweigh the

wood fiber, wood can have a moisture content of more than 100%. The fiber saturation point of most wood species is 25% to 30% MC; kiln-dried framing lumber is supposed to have no more than 19% MC. Since this is well below the fiber saturation point, the wood will swell and shrink with changes in moisture content.

Wood stored at a constant humidity eventually reaches a stable MC, called the *equilibrium moisture content*. For most of the U.S., the

equilibrium MC of wood that's inside a building is around 8%. In arid climates like Arizona, it's closer to 6%, while in moist climates like Florida, it's closer to 11%. This means that a piece of kiln-dried lumber will lose 8% to 13% MC after installation.

Start With Dry Lumber

Kiln-dried framing lumber is stamped KD or S-DRY (surfaced dry). Lumber stamped S-GRN (surfaced green) has not been kiln dried.

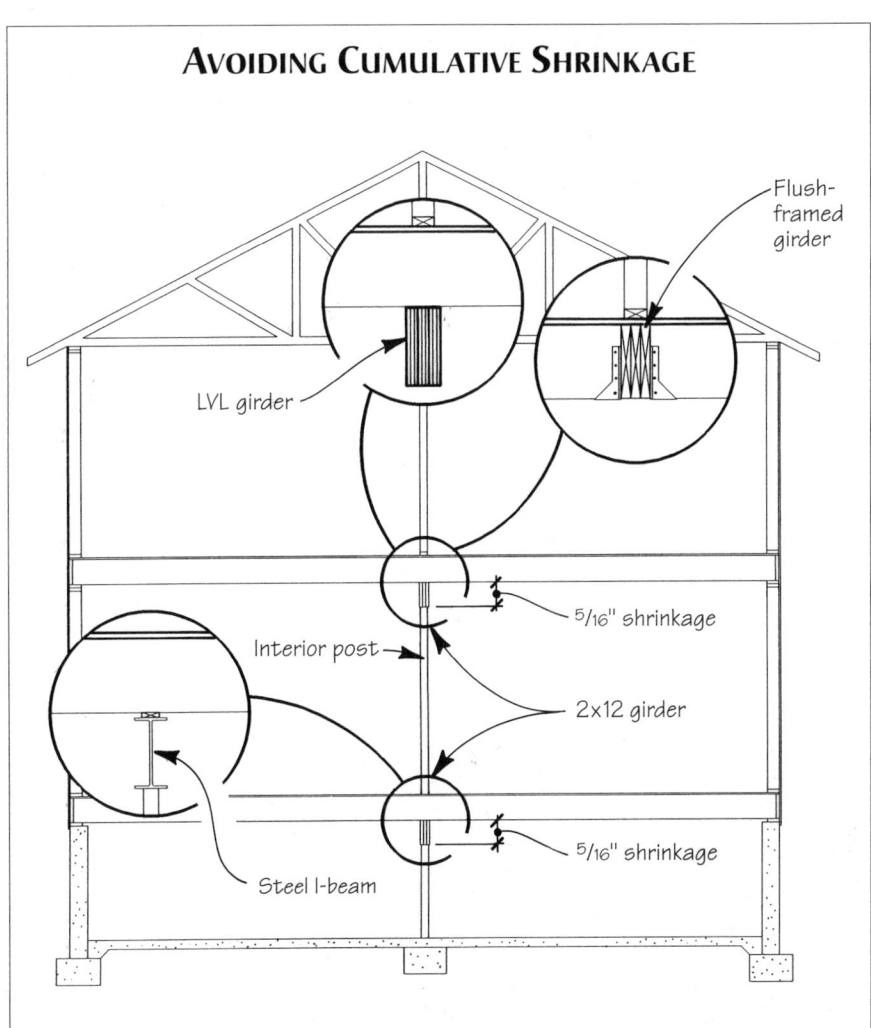

AVOIDING CUMULATIVE SHRINKAGE

Flush-framed girder

LVL girder

5/16" shrinkage

Interior post

2x12 girder

5/16" shrinkage

Steel I-beam

Figure 33. In the house shown here, the two built-up 2x12 girders will cause the center bearing wall to shrink much more than the exterior walls. This will result in a 1/2-inch drop at the second floor level — enough to cause nail pops and cracks in the finishes. Using a steel I-beam in the basement and engineered lumber or flush framing at the second floor will alleviate the problem.

Its MC was higher than 19% at the time it was milled — probably a lot higher. Avoid S-GRN lumber anywhere you're concerned about shrinkage. Also be aware that anything larger than a 4x4 isn't available in KD. The outside of these timbers may be somewhat dry, but assume that the inside is pretty green. When using a large solid beam, like a 6x6 or a 6x10, keep in mind that it will shrink a lot more than a comparable built-up beam made from kiln-dried stock.

You can minimize the effects of moisture swings by ensuring that all your framing lumber has the same MC. This means storing it up off the ground and protecting it from sun and rain with a tarp. It's just as bad to let the joists on top of the lift dry out in the sun as it is to let the bottom ones soak in a puddle. The idea is to make sure that all of the members in a given component — all of the joists in a floor, for instance — shrink the same amount.

Dry the Frame

Studs that are straight at 19% MC can do a lot of twisting and bowing as they dry to 8%. The U.S. Forest Products Lab (FPL) recommends that a frame be within 5% of its final moisture content before walls and ceilings are closed in. At the company I work for, we try to dry the frame to 10% or 12% MC before installing drywall or plaster. This gives us a chance to fix or replace any pieces that bow.

In cold weather, drying the frame may require some heat. A few winters back, I used a moisture meter to record how long it took the frame of a house I was working on to dry out. It was cold, but the humidity was low and the house was weathertight. After three weeks, most of the frame was stuck at 15%. We then set up an old gas furnace as a temporary heater. A week and half later, everything had dried to around 10%. Of course, it's not cheap to use heat to dry out a house. But if you're doing a high-end job, it beats coming back later to repair drywall, tile, and trim. And the heat doesn't have to be all that high. The FPL says that you need to keep the inside of the building only 10 to 15 degrees warmer than the outside.

Pay Attention to Framing Details

Even if you purchase high-quality framing lumber and protect it after it arrives, you still won't be able to prevent the wood from shrinking altogether. But if you use framing details that *allow* for the shrinkage, you will avoid most of the problems that can occur when the frame shrinks.

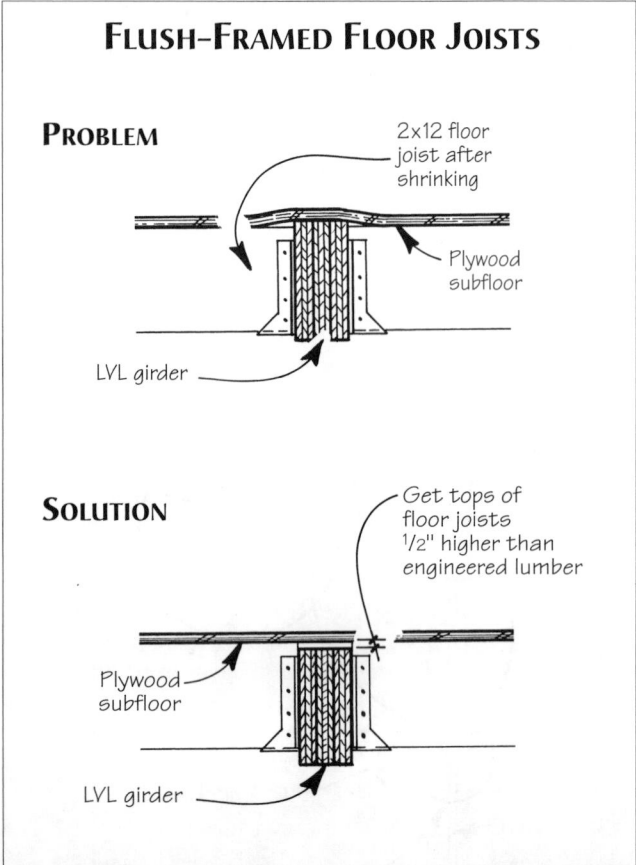

FLUSH-FRAMED FLOOR JOISTS

PROBLEM

2x12 floor joist after shrinking

Plywood subfloor

LVL girder

SOLUTION

Get tops of floor joists 1/2" higher than engineered lumber

Plywood subfloor

LVL girder

Figure 34. Floor joists laid flush with the top of engineered or steel beams will create a bump in the floor when they shrink. In these situations, install the joists 1/2 inch higher to accommodate the anticipated shrinkage (left). Where I-joists meet an engineered lumber beam (below), you can install them flush since shrinkage is not an issue with I-joists.

Problems occur when one side of the building has considerably more headers and plates than the other side, when there's an improper connection to masonry, or when solid lumber is mixed with steel or engineered lumber without compensating for the materials' different shrinkage rates. The symptoms include sloping floors, and lumps and dips in floors and walls. Although this sounds complicated, it's fairly easy to design a frame that will shrink evenly.

Avoid Lopsided Shrinkage

It's important to recognize situations when a structure will shrink unevenly. Look at the example in Figure 33. Here, the first-floor joists are supported by a built-up 2x12 girder. The upstairs features an open floor plan, with the second-floor joists also resting on a 2x12 girder.

The problem with this configuration is that the two girders may shrink as much as 5/16 inch each as the lumber dries from 19% moisture content to 8%. This is much more than the shrinkage that would occur in the exterior walls. The first-story ceiling and the second-story floor will then drop by 1/2 inch or more, wreaking havoc with the drywall finish and possibly leaving noticeable dips in the floor.

The solution is to use girder material that doesn't shrink — either steel or LVL — or to flush-frame the girders.

Whenever you're flush-framing a floor system where solid wood joists meet an engineered lumber or steel beam, don't set the tops of the joists exactly even with the top of the beam (Figure 34). Otherwise, when the joists shrink, they'll leave a bump in the floor. When I'm faced with this situation, I drop the beam approximately 1/2 inch in relation to the joists, so the joists can shrink without the top of the beam contacting the subfloor.

Foundation Details

Some designs call for the first-floor joists to bear on an interior foundation ledge, as in Figure 35. The problem here is that when the joists shrink, the ends pull away from the subfloor, leaving a slope at the exterior wall. I once installed a refrigerator in a kitchen that was framed this way; the floor sloped so badly that I couldn't level the refrigerator with the leveling feet.

A better detail is to keep the subfloor off the sill plate. When the floor joists shrink, the subfloor will move with them. When installing a wood floor, you can prevent a gap from opening beneath the baseboard

---

CALCULATING SHRINKAGE

Because wood shrinks and swells at a predictable rate, it's possible to calculate how much a building, or any part of a building, will shrink as it dries. Let's say we want to find out how much a kiln-dried Hem-Fir 2x12 at 19% MC will shrink if it's dried to 8% MC. We need something called the coefficient for dimensional change — the shrinkage coefficient — which expresses the percentage

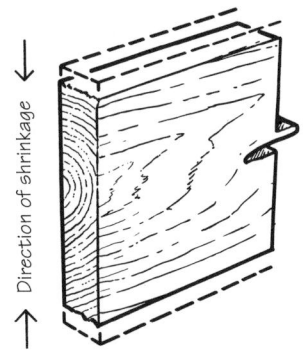

change in the size of a piece of wood for each percentage change in its MC. Although different wood species have slightly different shrinkage coefficients, an average number for flat-sawn framing lumber is .0025. You can safely use this to calculate the shrinkage for average 2-by stock.

With that in mind we can use the following formula:

Shrinkage (or swelling) =
Width of wood x change in MC
x Shrinkage Coefficient

So a typical 2x12 will shrink about 5/16 inch as it moves from 19% MC to 8% MC (11.25 inches x (19-8) x .0025). A 2x6 would shrink half as much (see chart, below). The formula can also be used to calculate how much wood swells as MC increases.

PREDICTED SHRINKAGE OF DIMENSION LUMBER

Lumber Size	Actual Width	Width @ 19% MC (at Delivery)	Width @ 11% MC (Humid Climates)	Width@ 8% MC (Average Climates)	Width @ 6% MC (Arid Climates)
2x4	3 1/2"	3 1/2"	3 7/16"	3 3/8"	3 3/8"
2x6	5 1/2"	5 1/2"	5 3/8"	5 5/16"	5 5/16"
2x8	7 1/2"	7 1/4"	7 1/8"	7 1/16"	7"
2x10	9 1/4"	9 1/4"	9 1/16"	9"	8 15/16"
2x12	11 1/4"	11 1/4"	11"	10 15/16"	10 7/8"

Note: Framing lumber shrinks primarily across its width; shrinkage along the lumber length is insignificant. Actual shrinkage varies depending on the lumber's moisture content when delivered and the area's climate.

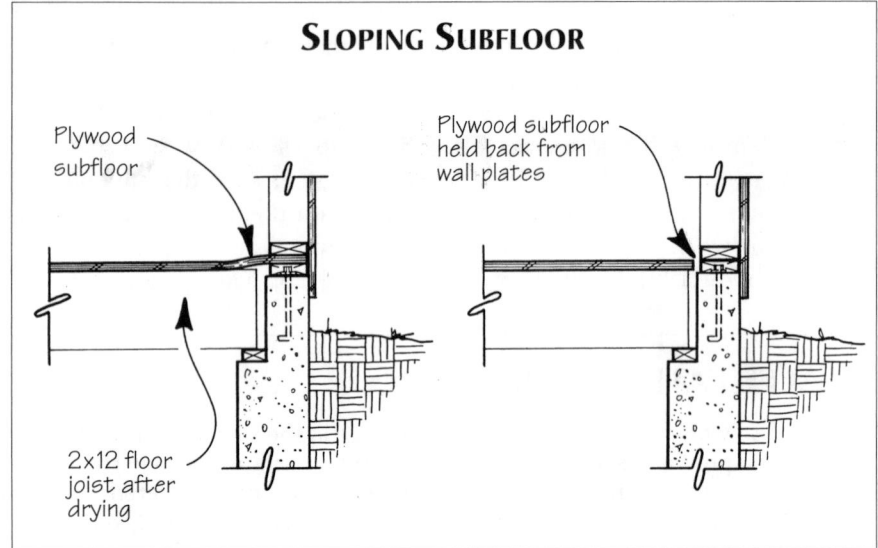

SLOPING SUBFLOOR

Plywood subfloor

Plywood subfloor held back from wall plates

2x12 floor joist after drying

Figure 35. Subflooring that is installed underneath the exterior wall framing (at left) will cause a slope as the floor joists shrink. Where floor joists bear on a foundation ledge, the subflooring should stop short of the exterior wall (at right). This allows the subfloor to move with the joists as they shrink.

by installing the flooring after the baseboard and using a shoe mold that's attached to the floor.

Where Wood Meets Masonry

If the framing isn't dry when a concrete hearth is poured, the framing will shrink so that the hardwood floor surface ends up slightly below the hearth. Because hearths are usually set late in the job, after the framing has had time to dry, this is seldom a problem. But if the hearth is set earlier — or if cold weather prevents the frame from drying — you should anticipate shrinkage and set the hearth a bit lower.

By David Frane, a contributing editor to The Journal of Light Construction *and* JLC's Tools of the Trade.

CHAPTER 3

WOOD & HARDBOARD SIDING

MAKING WALLS WATERTIGHT

I vividly remember the job where I learned that even properly installed siding isn't waterproof. It was a large, expensive gambrel on the peak of the highest hill in town. Start to finish, the job was a plum. The clients were overjoyed with my work and moved in ahead of schedule. But six months later, a wind-driven rain converted my plum into a prune. In a late-night phone call, the owner explained in detail how many drips-per-minute were falling from the head jamb of the east-facing double-mullion window.

I "fixed" the leak the next day, but it reoccurred once a year for three consecutive years. Each time there was a heavy east wind driving the rain directly against the window and the wall surrounding it. I caulked every joint and tightened every flashing connection on the east wall of the home in an effort to fix the leak, but with no luck.

When out of desperation I finally removed every course of bevel siding from the east wall, the problem was right in front of me. I had pre-wrapped the entire wall with 15-lb. felt and popped in the back-ordered window later. The problem was caused by the Z-flashing above the window head casing — I had attached the Z-flashing against the felt paper rather than tucking it under. Heavy winds forced rain water through the butt joints of the siding above the window, where it ran down the face of the felt paper, behind the window flashing and head casing, and dripped into the house.

Wind and rain can drive water through the smallest of cracks in any siding. All homes should have a second line of protection, especially those exposed to wind-driven rain (Figure 1). After investigating structural failures and repairing homes for many years, I have found that some failures are chronic. The details provided here will improve your chances of preventing leaks, even in severe conditions.

Housewraps

Too often, builders neglect to wrap houses with a water-resistant membrane before they apply siding.

Figure 1. To protect this oceanfront home from wind-driven rain and surf spray, the builder has covered the housewrap around doors and windows with a self-adhering bituminous membrane.

Figure 2. Water driven behind the siding can soak the sheathing and find its way into the house at gaps between upper and lower courses of housewrap (left), and at backwards overlaps (above).

This is especially true when the house will be sided with vinyl — many builders are convinced that nothing gets past vinyl siding. But vinyl siding isn't waterproof, as I learned while inspecting a house in frigid temperatures after a heavy, wind-driven rain. The sidewall had icicles protruding from beneath one section of the vinyl siding where rain had penetrated the siding and was frozen in its tracks trying to escape.

Patchwork. Poorly installed housewrap is just as bad as no housewrap. Figure 2 shows a combination of Tyvek and Typar on the same house. This is not a problem in itself, but the lack of consistency caught my eye. What concerns me is how the builder has cobbled together little scraps of housewrap; there are gaps, and in some cases the lower pieces overlap the upper pieces. If rain penetrates the siding on this house, it could easily find a path behind the housewrap.

Wrapping windows. Most builders wrap the entire house before installing windows or doors. In fact, manufacturers recommend wrapping over rough openings, then cutting an X into the window opening and folding the wrap inward. The windows are then installed over the housewrap. When I see this, I am always reminded of my leakage problem with the gambrel. When rain penetrates the siding on homes wrapped this way, it will find its way behind the window flashing and into the house.

Step flashing. Another problem area is a sloping roof that intersects a taller sidewall, as when the gable end of a garage is attached to the gable end of a two-story house. The garage roof shingles are usually step-flashed against the housewrap on the sidewall sheathing of the main house. But in cold climates, water from melting snowdrifts collects at this joint and will find its way through butt joints, knots, cracks, and other irregularities in the siding. The solution is to place the garage roof flashing directly against the bare house sheathing, then make sure the housewrap overlaps the step flashing.

Corners

Not all leaks result in water dripping on carpets in plain view of nervous clients; some leaks slowly compromise the structural integrity of a building. Rip off the corner boards of enough old houses and you will see your share of rotting corner posts. In general, corners of buildings experience the greatest effects of wind pressure, so you should take special care to protect this area from exposure to rain water.

Last month I visited the construction site of a very expensive new home. Overall, the quality of construction was excellent, but one detail troubled me. The 1-by wood corner boards were applied directly over the plywood sheathing, with no housewrap underneath. Over time, the corner boards and the wood siding will shrink and expand, giving rain water a path to the sheathing and framing.

Many builders caulk between corner boards and siding, assuming this creates a watertight joint. In wood-frame construction, however, the bond between most sealants and wood deteriorates within a few years, faster in severe exposures. In my opinion, caulking only makes matters worse by retarding the drying process when water penetrates the corner joints.

A more forgiving corner detail is to extend whatever type of housewrap you're using around the corner before installing the corner board. And because corners of houses are often dinged and damaged during construction, I would also recommend that a second vertical spline of felt paper or housewrap be applied over wrapped corners just before the corner boards go on.

Windows and Doors

One of my first assignments as an apprentice carpenter was wrapping

Housewrap Checklist
- Use housewrap or felt paper on all houses, no matter what kind of siding you're using.
- The wrap should be continuous; avoid a patchwork of small pieces.
- Provide an unrestricted path down and out of the space behind the siding. Wall membranes should overlap by 3 inches horizontally and 6 inches vertically. Tape all seams.
- Protect all pathways into the building envelope by lapping housewrap over flashings.

Corner Board Checklist
- Install felt paper or housewrap at all corners.
- Double-wrap corners by applying vertical felt or housewrap splines under the corner boards.
- Don't caulk the joint between the siding and corner board; caulk deteriorates over time, providing a pathway for water to get into the frame and preventing trapped water from escaping.

Window Flashing Checklist
- Protect the top of the window flashing with overlapping wrap.
- Double-overlap housewrap around nailing fins of vinyl and clad windows.
- At sills, splines must direct water over underlying housewrap.
- At head, leave a 1/4-inch gap between the window flashing and bottom edge of siding to prevent wicking of moisture.

Siding Checklist
- Don't install board siding on a diagonal.
- For horizontal board siding, use top-grade boards with no knots, splits, or other defects. Install T&G and shiplap siding so that the joints between boards drain away from the sheathing.
- For panel siding, use housewrap over studs. Housewrap should overlap Z-flashing at the joint between panel courses.
- Protect wall sheathing close to grade with bituminous membrane.
- Siding should overlap sill-to-foundation joints by at least 2 inches.

window and door jambs. I would unroll a length of felt on the deck, cut 1-foot-wide strips (a little longer than the window and door openings), then fasten these "splines" along the sides of the window and door rough openings (Figure 3). I was taught that splines protect the sheathing from any weather that might penetrate the joint between the siding and window casings.

This makes sense, but there is a little more to this detail. Don't bury the bottom of the splines beneath a layer of housewrap. The bottom of the spline should be lifted and placed over the felt or housewrap that runs horizontally beneath the window. This will guide any water that penetrates the joint down the spline and over the felt or wrap that covers the wall.

Windows with nailing fins (vinyl, clad, and metal) have nearly replaced traditional wood-cased units on most job sites. When these units are properly installed, they offer more protection against water infiltration than wood-cased units, because the housewrap membrane can be double-overlapped in a weather-tight detail (Figure 4).

Head flashing is critical for window installations. The top edge of the window fin or Z-flashing should be protected by an overlapping membrane (Figure 5). When using a housewrap like Tyvek or Typar, it is not as easy to weave the flashing under the wrap as it is with felt. When using these wraps, you can prewrap the entire house, install the windows and flashing, and then tape the top of the flashing to the housewrap with 3M contractors tape (3M Center, St. Paul, MN 55144-1000; 612/733-1110). You can also wrap the walls before the windows are installed and slice the wrap above the window so you can slide the top of the window flashing beneath the housewrap.

Whatever method you use, be sure the splines don't lead rain water beneath the housewrap in any way (Figure 6). Be very careful at the window head: On windy days, water that collects on top of the window flashing will be blown sideways and may leak when it reaches the window's edge. Nailing flanges on clad windows provide good protection when double-wrapped, but make sure that Z-flashing leads water over the housewrap at the ends of the window. This may require carefully patching in with pieces of housewrap or felt at windows.

Siding

Many books have been written about siding, so I won't explain again how to prevent siding failures. But I will provide a sampling of some failures I've investigated in recent months.

Diagonal board siding. I don't like board siding that is installed at a diagonal. On rainy days, windward walls are covered by a thin film of water that's looking for somewhere to go. Gravity may pull it down; wind may push it sideways, upward, or even inward through breaches in the siding. Eventually, most of the rain water finds its way into the seams between adjacent siding boards. These seams act like gutters, collecting and channeling the water downward at an angle. The water is forced against the sides of windows, doorways, corner

Figure 3. When water gets behind window and door casings, correctly installed felt-paper splines keep water from wetting the sheathing.

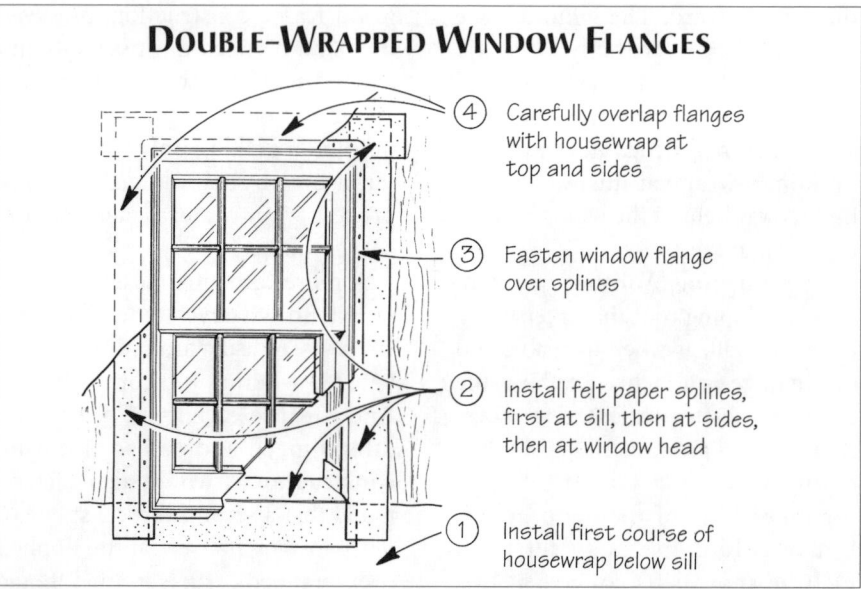

DOUBLE-WRAPPED WINDOW FLANGES

④ Carefully overlap flanges with housewrap at top and sides

③ Fasten window flange over splines

② Install felt paper splines, first at sill, then at sides, then at window head

① Install first course of housewrap below sill

Figure 4. Clad window flanges provide excellent protection against water penetration when double-wrapped with splines and housewrap. Make sure the upper course of housewrap overlaps the flanges at the top and sides of the window; at the sill, however, the spline and window flange should overlap the housewrap.

boards, and any vertical element that stands in its path. Without very careful detailing, the runoff will leak into the building at these points.

Horizontal boards. I'm not crazy for horizontal board siding in windy or exposed locations either. If the design calls for horizontally applied, tongue-and-groove or shiplap siding, be sure to install it with the tongues up so the joint will drain. Even when installed correctly, knots, splits, and other defects in the milled edges may allow water to pass through the siding, so good housewrapping details are critical.

Panel siding. Problems typically occur with plywood panel siding at the joints between upper and lower panels. Often, plywood panel siding like T1-11 is used to economize, so structural sheathing is not installed beneath the siding panels and neither is housewrap. Typically, either Z-flashing is installed at the top of the lower panel or the top and bottom edges of adjoining panels are beveled to "prevent" leakage. These connections, however, are not weather-tight. The safest practice is to apply housewrap before installing the lower course of panels. Then install Z-flashing at the top of the lower panels and overlap the Z-flashing with the upper course of housewrap (Figure 7). Be sure to leave at least a 1/4-inch gap between panels to prevent capillary suction.

Splashback. We've all noticed siding that is discolored just above grade. This heavy weathering is caused by splashback — water bouncing off the ground and splashing back onto the siding — and is unavoidable on most homes. Regardless of the type of siding, this part of the wall will experience heavy exposure to water, so the sheathing just above grade must be carefully protected with a continuous layer of housewrap. Installing a strip of bituminous membrane like Ice and Water Shield under the siding at the bottom of the wall

Figure 5. To prevent leaks at window heads, lap felt paper or housewrap over the cap flashing.

Figure 6. Because this carpenter has stretched the housewrap over the splines at the bottom of the window, wind-driven rain will be able to run down behind the housewrap onto the sheathing.

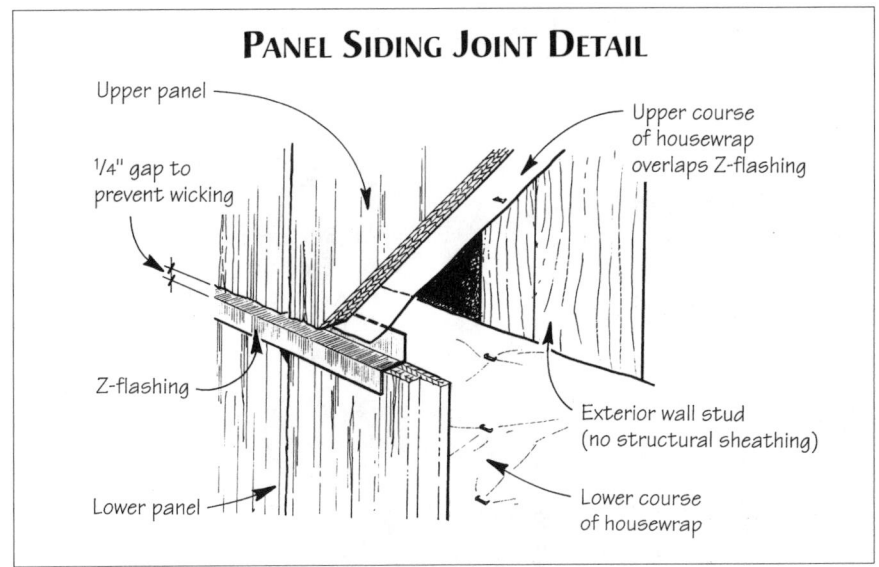

PANEL SIDING JOINT DETAIL

Upper panel

1/4" gap to prevent wicking

Z-flashing

Lower panel

Upper course of housewrap overlaps Z-flashing

Exterior wall stud (no structural sheathing)

Lower course of housewrap

Figure 7. Apply the lower course of panel siding over the housewrap, then overlap the Z-flashing with the upper course of housewrap before installing the upper panels. Leave at least a 1/4-inch gap between panels to prevent wicking.

may be a worthwhile investment.

The intersection of the sill to the foundation is critical. Be sure that water runs down the siding and is carried past this joint. Also make sure wind will not drive water under the sill — let the siding overlap the sill-foundation joint by at least 2 inches.

As is the case for all detailing, be conservative in your estimation of the

forces influencing your design. Plan on water penetrating your primary line of defense, and develop a plan that offers solid backup protection.

By Paul Fisette, a wood technologist and director of the Building Materials Technology and Management program at the University of Massachusetts in Amherst. Photos by author, except where noted.

WOOD SIDING

Many siding problems stem from selecting the wrong material for the job. Picking the wrong grade, size, or pattern can lead to a finished product that either doesn't look good, doesn't last long, or both.

Select a proper grade. Many siding problems occur because the grade is not adequate for the job. The chart "Standard Siding Grades" can guide you in speccing a suitable grade. If your lumberyard uses other terms for their siding grades, find out if they are equivalent to the standard grades established by industry trade associations shown in the chart.

Many mills or yards, for instance, use their own proprietary grades. And many use a hodgepodge of grades to compose their "knotty" grade of siding, also known as "STK"

or *select tight knotty.* Make sure any STK or knotty grade is composed of siding grades identified in the chart as acceptable for quality siding jobs. Otherwise you won't know what you're buying until it shows up on the job site. And if it turns out to be a pile of green wood with loose knots and a host of other defects, you'll have little recourse. You can't argue that it doesn't meet grade or request a reinspection if there are no written rules to be met.

Buying actual industry grades, such as "Select Knotty" or "Quality Knotty," is a lot safer. Another option is to use common board grades such as No. 2 or No. 3 Common, which give you the same knotty appearance and perform as well as siding.

Customers who want the highest quality appearance — and are willing to pay for it — will prefer the premium grades or some of the special cedar siding grades.

Don't forget moisture content. Nearly all wood siding shrinks somewhat after installation. If the wood's moisture content is too high when installed, shrinkage will be excessive and can lead to splitting, warping, or cupping, as well as paint checking. You can minimize these types of problems by specifying "S-Dry" material. S-Dry contains no more than 19% moisture. You should still stack the siding in a sheltered place on site for a week to ten days so it can acclimate to its surroundings. This will minimize the shrinkage after installation.

Premium grades are dried to MC 15, meaning that the wood has 15% moisture content or less (and that 85% of the pieces are dried to 12% or less). This wood should arrive at the site with close to its final installed moisture content.

"Alternate" grades follow standard grading rules but are unseasoned, with unknown moisture content. The same is true for ungraded sidings.

The importance of pattern. Many failures result from choosing the wrong pattern for the job. The least forgiving pattern is tongue and groove (T&G), because the pieces can come apart with relatively little shrinkage. Therefore T&G siding should be close to its final moisture content when installed and should be prefinished (see Figure 8).

As a rule of thumb, narrow patterns perform best because there is less movement from wet to dry periods, and from season to season. Thicker patterns are safer since they have less tendency to cup or split than thinner patterns. And the surface texture will affect how well the finish performs. Rough textures will

Figure 8. T&G is not a forgiving pattern. When installed green (left), it is bound to fail from excessive shrinkage. Even installed at 19% moisture content, the 1x10 siding (below left) opened at numerous joints. A better choice would have been 1x6s, acclimatized for at least a week before installation.

STANDARD SIDING GRADES

Product	Grade	Description	Moisture Content
Standard Clear Grades – Western Red Cedar			
Bevel Siding	Clear VG (vertical grain)	Free of knots and imperfections; for use where the highest quality appearance is desired.	MC-15 (15% or less — most pieces 12% or less)
	A Grade	Includes some mixed grain and minor growth characteristics.	
	B Grade	Includes mixed grain, limited characteristics and occasional cutouts in longer pieces.	
	Rustic	Similar to A grade, but graded from sawn face.	
	C Grade	Admits larger and more numerous characteristics than A or B grades.	
Boards (Finish, Trim)	Clear	Finest appearance with clear face, few minor characteristics.	MC-15 (15% or less — most pieces 12% or less)
	A Grade	Recommended for fine appearance. May include minor imperfections or growth characteristics.	
	B Grade	Permits larger and more characteristics, but may have short lengths of fine appearance.	
Standard Knotty Grades – Western Red Cedar			
Bevel Siding, Boards, Channel, T&G, etc.	Select Knotty	For fine knotty appearance.	19% or less
	Quality Knotty	Permits more pronounced characteristics and has occasional cutouts in longer pieces.	
Boards, Channel, T&G, etc.	Select Merchantable	Has fine appearance and includes knots and minor markings.	Unseasoned
	Construction	Limited characteristics allowed to assure high degree of serviceability.	
	Standard	Allows more characteristics than construction.	
Standard Softwood Grades (All species except redwood)			
All patterns	C select	Mixed grain, a few small knots allowed. For uses where a fine finished appearance is desired.	MC-15 (15% or less — most pieces 12% or less)
	D select	Mixed grain, slightly larger knots than allowed in C Select.	
All patterns	#2 common	Has fine appearance and includes knots and minor markings.	19% or less
	#3 common	Limited characteristics allowed to assure high degree of serviceability.	
	#4 common	Allows more characteristics than #3. Used chiefly for serviceability rather than appearance.	

Note: These grades apply to all lumber graded under the rules of Western Wood Products Assoc. (WWPA), West Coast Lumber Inspection Bureau (WCLIB), or National Lumber Grades Authority (NLGA) of Canada. The term "characteristics" refers to knots, wane, pitch pockets, irregular grain, etc.

typically hold a finish longer than smooth textures.

The chart "Wood Siding Patterns" suggests which products to use for various types of jobs and provides installation tips.

Pattern width. Finally, many of the problems we see are caused by siding that is too wide. Because wide pieces of siding move more, they are more prone to warp, cup, or cause checking in the finish. In general, patterns over 8 inches in width will probably cause you some problems.

In an effort to save time and money, many builders like wider patterns because they cover an area faster, thus reducing labor costs. But these savings are more often than not wiped out by callback problems later on. If you have experienced this problem, try using the same patterns, but in widths of 8 inches or less.

Putting It Up Right

Even if you start out with the right pattern, grade, and width, it will not perform well if you put it up wrong. The basics of siding installation are not complex, but following them is crucial.

Nailing. The most common problem is improper nailing. The chart "Wood Siding Patterns" gives nailing guidelines. One rule holds for any pattern and size: *Never double-nail solid wood siding.* That is, never nail through more than one layer of siding at a time. New siding is going to shrink as it acclimates to its new surroundings. If the siding is nailed at both the top and bottom edges (or left and right edge for vertical applications), the nails will restrict the movement of the siding and cause it to split (see Figure 9). With bevel siding, be sure that each nail is slightly above the top of the underlying piece.

Another common problem with bevel siding is overdriving. Drive the nails just flush. Overdriving can cause cupping or splitting.

Finally, make sure the siding nails hit solid wood, not just sheathing or air. On vertical siding, this means using horizontal blocking where two pieces meet (see Figure 10).

Proper overlap. A related problem stems from the amount of overlap. Some builders will use too wide a pattern for the amount of reveal they desire — say, a 6-inch-wide board when they want a 4-inch reveal. This leaves too much board under the overlapping board, forcing you either to double-nail (causing splitting) or to nail through the thin part of the board, causing cupping and

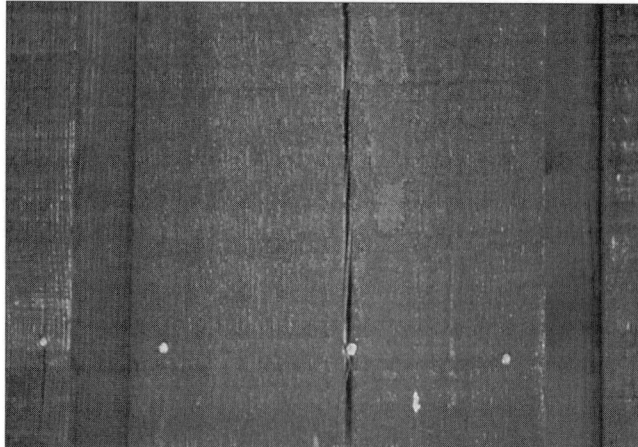

Figure 9. Nails at both edges and the middle of this wide piece of channel rustic (left) caused cracking. Two nails per board, 3 to 4 inches apart — with no nails through the overlap — is best. Bevel siding that is double-nailed is prone to cracking, particularly at the ends (below).

Figure 10. Use horizontal blocking at the joints in vertical siding. Otherwise, the end joints will pull loose and flap in the breeze — even with T&G, as shown here.

WOOD SIDING PATTERNS

Siding Patterns	Nominal sizes (thickness and width)	Nailing (Do not nail where siding pieces overlay)	
		6 in. and narrower	**8 in. and wider**
Bevel or Bungalow Bungalow (Colonial) is slightly thicker than Bevel. Either can be used with the smooth or rough-faced surface exposed. Patterns provide a traditional-style appearance. Horizontal applications only.	$1/2$ x 4 $1/2$ x 5 $1/2$ x 6 $5/8$ x 8 $5/8$ x 10 $3/4$ x 6 $3/4$ x 8 $3/4$ x 10	Recommend 1" overlap. One siding nail or box nail per bearing, just above the 1" overlap. Plain	Recommend 1" overlap. One siding nail or box nail per bearing, just above the 1" overlap. Plain
Tongue & Groove T&G siding is available in a variety of patterns. Vertical or horizontal applications.	1 x 4 1 x 6 1 x 8 1 x 10 Available with $1/4$", $3/8$", or $7/16$" tongues. For wider widths, specify the longer tongue.	Use one casing nail per bearing to blind nail. Plain	Use two siding nails or box nails 3" to 4" apart to face nail. Plain
Channel Rustic Channel Rustic has $1/2$" overlap and a 1" to $1 1/4$" channel when installed. The profile allows for maximum dimensional change without harming appearance. Available smooth, rough or saw-textured. Horizontal or vertical applications.	$3/4$ x 6 $3/4$ x 8 $3/4$ x 10	Use one siding nail or box nail to face nail once per bearing, 1" up from bottom edge.	Use two siding nails or box nails 3" to 4" apart per bearing.
Board-and-Batten Boards are surfaced smooth, rough or saw-textured. Rustic ranch-style appearance. Requires horizontal nailers. Vertical applications only.	($4/4$) 1 x 2 1 x 4 1 x 6 1 x 8 1 x 10 1 x 12 ($5/4$) $1 1/4$ x 6 $1 1/4$ x 8 $1 1/4$ x 10 $1 1/4$ x 12	Recommend $1/2$" overlap. One siding or box nail per bearing. $1/2$" Board and Batten	Increase overlap proportionately. Use two siding nails or box nails, 3" to 4" apart. Board and Batten Board on Board

possibly splitting (see Figure 11). You should buy bevel siding 3/4 to 1 inch wider than the reveal you want. If you want a 5-inch exposure, buy 6-inch siding, not 8-inch.

Metal studs. Another fastening problem arises when attaching wood siding to metal studs. In this case, builders often nail the siding into the plywood or OSB structural sheathing. While plywood is good for lateral wall bracing, it's a poor nail base for siding. For good performance, siding

must be nailed into 1 1/2 inches of solid wood. This is supported by all the model building codes.

The best way to achieve this is to attach 2x nailers at each metal stud. An alternative is to fasten directly to the metal studs with stainless-steel or galvanized screws. But I doubt there's much cost difference between this approach and using 2x blocking and regular siding nails.

Rusty nails. Another problem that rears its ugly head time after time is

rusting fasteners or rusty streaks draining from nail holes (see Figure 12). This is a great way to ruin a nice siding job. To avoid it, always use corrosion-resistant fasteners — typically hot-dipped, galvanized nails. More costly alternatives include stainless-steel and high-tensile-strength aluminum nails. Do not use the nails galvanized through an electrolytic process, as the zinc coating can crack during installation and the nails will rust.

Keeping the weather out. Siding is a weather barrier, but it is not waterproof. Water can and will find its way in behind the siding at times, and if nothing else is there to stop it, it may eventually work its way through the wall to the inside of the building (see Figure 13). Some sheathings claim to be waterproof and say you can put siding directly over them. However, the industry recommendation is to use a building paper or a house wrap over all types of sheathing before applying the siding. This is the real waterproofing of your wall. We've also

Figure 11. The carpenter nailed this bevel siding too high up, where the boards are thin and unsupported. This can cup and split the siding. The maximum overlap should be one inch.

NAILING KNOTTY-GRADE

The key to successful installation of knotty-grade siding is to use non-corrosive nails that are long enough to resist withdrawal, and to place them so they don't restrict the siding as it moves seasonally. It sounds simple, but the problems I see most often as a field rep are caused by failing to follow these recommendations.

Nails. I'm amazed at how many builders and remodelers try to save $30 or $40 on nails only to end up with a project that is ruined by streaking within weeks. And the only way you can correct the problem permanently at that point is to pull the siding.

My first choice is stainless-steel nails, but they are very expensive. On budget-minded jobs you might consider high-tensile-strength aluminum nails. Both are available with color coating to help hide them.

Hot-dipped galvanized (HDG) are okay with a heavy body stain or paint. The zinc on HDG nails isn't as vulnerable as electrogalvanized (EG) coatings, which chip when you're driving the nails, and wear off quickly. However, you might consider stainless-steel or aluminum nails if you're using a clear preservative — a few problems have been reported in the field when galvanized nails were used with some of these finishes.

For knotty siding which is prone to greater wood movement, consider using spiral or ringshank nails. These are required to penetrate 1 1/4 inches into solid wood (for smooth-shank nails it's 1 1/2 inches). "Solid wood" means any combination of framing lumber and sheathing. But don't just nail into the sheathing.

Nails should be box or siding nails (see illustration) with *blunt*

rather than *needle* points to cut down on splitting problems. It's tempting to use casing nails because of their low head profile, but these lead to problems with "pull through" when the siding cups. They are recommended for blind nailing tongue-and-groove siding, but that's not something you should be doing in knotty grades on the exterior.

Nailing. Although it takes longer, hand nailing has real quality advantages over pneumatic nailing. You aren't as likely to "overnail" clapboards or drive the head of the nail below the surface of the wood, and it's a lot more accurate in putting nails just where you want them. If you have to use a nail gun, make sure you keep the air pressure adjusted so you're not overnailing, and never use staples.

Vertical siding should be nailed at a maximum of 36 inches on-found that the siding itself performs better when installed this way.

The use of building paper or a house wrap is particularly important behind any vertical or horizontal patterns, since those installations don't shed water as well as overlapping horizontal installations. It's a good idea on vertical installations to scarf any butt joints to prevent water penetration at these points. Make sure, however, that the scarfed joints are angled so they drain toward the exterior of the building.

The biggest problem with diagonal siding is that it channels water directly into door jambs, window moldings, or other joinery details on a structure. This means flashing and caulking details are critical. The best approach is to flash each side of the window with a cap molding (like the one used over the head casing).

Finishing Problems

Finally, many problems stem from choosing the wrong finish or applying it incorrectly.

First things first: Backprime. On most jobs, siding is finished after it is installed, so only the exposed face gets sealed. The back does not. This allows the back of the siding to absorb more moisture than the front, leading to cupping, warping, or even paint failure as the moisture looks for a way to escape. Backpriming equalizes the flow of moisture into and out of the front and back of the siding, minimizing these problems. For this reason I highly recommend backpriming or

prefinishing siding before installing it. This one step would prevent a large percentage of siding callbacks.

Let it weather? Some people choose to let the siding weather naturally, expecting it to turn that light gray color they've seen in pictures of houses on Cape Cod. The problem is, most places don't have Cape Cod's salty air to discourage mildew growth, so the unfinished siding ends up uneven in color. It tends to blacken in areas exposed to high moisture, while

Figure 12. Rusting nails leave ugly streaks down the side of a building. The right nails are stainless steel or hot-dipped galvanized — not electrogalvanized.

center when face nailed, and 32 inches when blind nailed. (However, some building codes now require a 24-inch maximum spacing.) Horizontal siding can be nailed at a maximum of 24 inches on-center over sheathing, and 16 inches on-center without it.

But maybe the most critical rule is *never* nail through two courses of siding with a single nail, sometimes called "double nailing." On patterns 8 inches and up (except clapboards and Dolly Varden) you will need to drive two nails, spaced 3 to 4 inches apart, into each stud. But still, each piece is nailed independently of its neighbor.

Nailing two courses together may have developed in New England several centuries ago when the lower edge of a clapboard was nailed through the one below to help keep the wind out. Unfortunately, the practice is still common. Because of the void that is created when bevel siding is

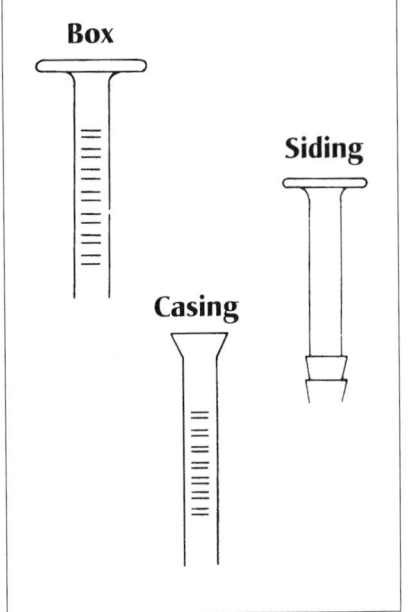

Box nails (left) and siding nails (right) will discourage the "pull through" common with casing nails (center), particularly with the wood movement common to knotty siding.

lapped, it's tempting to nail down toward the bottom edge where the lap makes it feel more solid. Although you may get away with this if you're using narrow, clear, vertical-grain siding in a climate that doesn't have a long drying season, you can end up with problems with knotty material.

All patterns should be fitted together without any gap or expansion space except board-and-batten, which calls for a 1/2-inch space between boards. Bevel siding (clapboards) should lap the previous course by only 1 inch so your nails don't end up going through the top of the course below. This means you'll get a 4 1/2-inch exposure from a 6-inch clapboard; if you want a narrower exposure, you'll need to rip the material down.

By Norm Sievert, Northwest field representative for the Western Wood Products Association.

protected areas, such as under eaves, remain the original color (see Figure 14). Some blackened areas eventually lighten up, but areas exposed to water splash stay dark for a long time.

To achieve that gray, weathered appearance quickly while adding some protection, use a bleaching oil. This preparation typically contains bleach as well as some light pigment

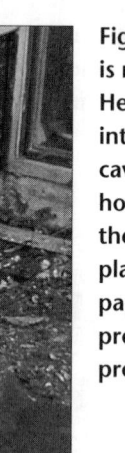

Figure 13. Siding is not waterproof. Here, water got into the wall cavity of a new home and rotted the studs and plates. Building paper would have prevented the problem.

Figure 14. The silver-gray, weathered look that some clients desire happens naturally only where there's plenty of sunlight and salty air to discourage mildew growth. Left untreated, cedar siding is more likely to end up dark and blotchy.

Figure 15. Solid-body stain applied directly to smooth siding has led to many failures. The solution: Use a primer first or put the rough side out. In either case, backbrush the finish if applied by spraying.

to help keep the coloring consistent.

Solid stains. Recently I have seen a number of problems with opaque stains when they were applied to smooth surfaces. These are sometimes called solid-color or heavy-body stains. Since they have more pigment than semitransparent stains, you might think of them as thin paints.

Since opaque stains form a thin film on the wood surface, they can flake and peel if the bond is poor (see Figure 15). Consequently these stains are not recommended directly over smooth surfaces. If you choose to use this type of finish on smooth siding, the wood should be primed first.

Brush it in. Speed is often the top priority when it comes to painting or staining siding. For this reason, many finishes are sprayed on. But spraying leaves the paint or stain sitting on the surface without penetrating into the wood. Eventually, it will start to flake off, even on a rough-textured surface. For that reason, spray-applied finishes should be backrolled or backbrushed to work them into the wood fibers.

The natural look. Many customers want their wood siding to look brand new and "natural" forever. Unfortunately, the natural process is for the wood surface to oxidize and break down. A number of clear finishes containing fungicides and mildewcides can delay the weathering process and keep the wood looking young for several years. But these generally require reapplication every year.

A better approach, I feel, is to apply a semitransparent oil-based stain with pigments that match the color of the natural wood. This allows the grain to show through, but keeps the color true. As the wood is periodically refinished, the color can be restored indefinitely.

By David Utterback, midwestern regional manager for the Western Wood Products Association.

WOOD SIDING OVER FOAM

As early as 1976, problems were reported with horizontal wood and hardboard siding applied over foam sheathing on the exterior of homes. Hardboard siding typically failed between nailing points, primarily because of expansion, which caused the boards to bow out. Wood siding, primarily redwood and cedar, failed because of cupping, which caused nails to pull out and boards to split.

The failures follow a fairly characteristic pattern. For all types of siding, failure is most severe on the east and south exposures of a building. Fewer problems exist on the west exposures, and almost none on north exposures.

For hardboard siding, the failures occur between the nails as the fibers expand and the siding buckles, creating a bowed-out "wave" pattern between each nailing point. Wood sidings generally cup and split — severely enough at times to cause siding boards to actually fall off.

The overall problem cannot be attributed to any single cause. Several factors — including the characteristics of rigid plastic foam itself, the wood siding involved, the use of sealers, the type of nails, and the method of installation — all play a role.

Characteristics of Rigid Plastic Foams

The same characteristics that make rigid plastic foams ideal for thermal insulation — their light weight, softness, and resistance to heat and moisture — can cause moisture problems when foams are used under wood sidings.

The softness of the foams increases the likelihood that the expansion and contraction of the wood, as well as the nailing of the siding, will dent the sheathing slightly and loosen the connection between the siding and the foam. This leaves larger gaps in which moisture can collect.

In addition, the foam provides less support for nails. Thus, as the siding expands and contracts longitudinally, the nails move back and forth and loosen.

The foam's resistance to heat and moisture also creates a moisture buildup between the foam and the siding. In fact, this moisture buildup on the back of the siding is considered the major contributor to the siding problems.

All sidings undergo a series of wet and dry cycles, during which the moisture within the wood as well as from the air is driven to the back side of the siding. At the same time that moisture is accumulating on the back side, the front of the siding is being dried by exposure to the sun and the air. These cycles are exacerbated by the presence of foam sheathing.

The more severe failures on east and south exposures of homes result partially from the increased drying of the siding exterior by the sun, and also partially from the heat of the early morning sun, which heats the space between the sheathing and the siding. This causes dew points to be reached and thus moisture to collect on the back of the siding. Again, the foam's resistance to heat and moisture intensifies the situation.

Type and Size of Wood Siding

The type and size of wood siding installed also affects the seriousness of the problem at the foam and siding interface.

Wood sidings that are thicker (greater than 1/2 inch) and narrower (6 inches or less wide), for example, better resist the wet-dry cycles and the resulting cupping failures. And shorter boards (that is, less than 6 feet long) show less longitudinal expansion and contraction and thus

Figure 16. The use of redwood siding and rigid plastic foam has spelled disaster for the owner of this home, which has been plagued with pulled-out nails and split and cupped siding.

cause less stress on nails.

Finally, of course, wood siding should be at a stable moisture content before installation. This always is a major factor to consider for wood siding, whether it is installed over foam sheathing or not.

For hardboard siding, the most critical material-related factor appears to be its density. The most dense sidings tend to resist breakdown from moisture better than the less dense ones.

Color and Sealers

Color and sealers also play a role in the problem. Darker colors attract more heat into siding and intensify the problem. The use of a lighter color can create a considerable difference in temperature.

It now is recommended that wood and hardboard sidings be treated with sealers on all sides — but especially on the back — before installation. A sealer certainly will make any siding more resistant to moisture. Over time, however, sealers also will fail under continued intense heat and wet-dry cycling.

Nail Type and Size

The type and size of nails also can have an impact on the problem. Manufacturers recommend the use of galvanized or stainless-steel nails with improved grip and the use of nails with a blunt point for wood siding.

In addition, a 1½-inch penetration into the wood stud is considered critical. For hardboard, a needle-point nail will reduce ripping as it passes through the back of the siding. While secure nailing is important for hardboard siding, it is not as likely as wood siding to fail at nailing points, so it is not as critical an item.

Recommendations

To minimize the chance of failure when installing wood siding over foam, follow closely all manufacturers' recommendations for installation as well as the following:

- Drive nails carefully to avoid denting the foam;
- Use thicker, narrower, and shorter siding pieces;
- Pay attention to the proper storage and stabilized moisture content of the wood;
- Select the proper type and size of nails;
- Apply sealers on all sides;
- Choose light-colored stains and paints;
- Choose proper locations for driving your nails; and
- Take care to achieve proper overall installation.

These recommendations, of course, treat the symptoms — moisture accumulation on the back of the siding — not the problem itself. The ultimate solution involves creating and venting a space between the sheathing and the siding in addition to following the above recommendations.

Furring strips to separate the foam sheathing and siding will allow the space to vent itself of heat and moisture and will reduce the heat and wet-dry cycles considerably. The space must be open at the top and bottom edges of the siding (insect screens are advised) to allow full movement of air.

By John Russo, an engineering consultant in Minneapolis, Minn.

HARDBOARD SIDING

Hardboard siding comes in forms imitating almost any other siding material you can think of. But most hardboard falls into two basic categories: lap and panel siding.

Lap and multilap. Lap and multilap siding, designed to look like

Figure 17. This hardboard has absorbed excessive moisture and expanded, causing buckling and bowing.

cedar, redwood, or fir clapboards, accounts for 60% of hardboard sales. It comes in sizes from 4-inch to 16-inch boards, and it is available in multilap versions that take care of several "rows" of siding at once to speed installation. Most lap siding is face nailed. Lap siding is especially prominent in the East, Midwest, and parts of the South — wherever clapboards are popular.

Panel siding. Hardboard siding also comes in 2x8-foot, 4x8-foot, and 4x9-foot panels. The panels imitate everything from board-and-batten construction and vertical rabbeted laps to stone and stucco. The large panels install quickly.

Panels are popular where the materials they imitate are common (stucco sells well in the Southwest, for instance) or where cutting costs is important, as in low-end mobile homes.

Different grades and thicknesses. Hardboard comes in five different grades and two basic thicknesses.

The better quality sidings are of "standard" or "tempered" grade. Tempered siding is impregnated with additives and/or heat treated to make it stiffer, harder, and more resistant to water and abrasion.

Siding comes in 7/16-inch and 1/2-inch thicknesses. Several of the builders and distributors I talked to said the 1/2-inch product performed significantly better than the thinner versions.

Unprimed, primed, or prefinished. Unprimed hardboard siding is a rarity these days, because most installers want to reduce finishing time. Primed siding, which accounts for most of the market, comes ready to paint or stain. Most manufacturer warranties require finishing within 30 to 90 days of installation. Two coats of an acrylic latex paint or acrylic stain are recommended for hardboard.

Prefinished sidings are taking a steadily increasing share of the market — 10% and growing, according to the American Hardboard Association (AHA). Though more expensive, prefinished siding offers the advantage of quicker job completion. Both manufacturers and distributors say the extra cost is usually less than that of paying someone to paint primed siding.

Most finish warranties are for five years. But a few newer lap products that have blind nailing (nails hidden under the lap above) offer warranties up to 15 years.

Performance Promises

Hardboard promises a lot: the look, solidity, and insulating qualities of natural wood; a wide variety of types and patterns; resistance to impact; and a reasonable price.

But whether or not it delivers on these promises depends on several critical factors. Moisture absorption tops the list, followed by quality of installation, paint performance, and manufacturer support.

Moisture is bad news to hardboard — even more than to regular wood.

Dobbin McNatt, who has researched hardboard at the U.S. Forest Products Laboratory in Madison, Wis., for almost 20 years, says that by its nature, hardboard is vulnerable to moisture.

"Hardboard, as it comes out of the factory, is pretty dry," says McNatt. "If it's not equilibrated before it's put up, it will pick up moisture and expand. Since it's homogenized wood, it expands more in length than a piece of solid wood siding will. And it will buckle if it's nailed down when it expands."

This expansion from moisture absorption lies behind most hardboard siding failures. The industry standard allows an expansion of 2.4 inches for every 50 feet of siding. That's enough to cause severe buckling of the board — enough to pull nail heads through the board as it bows away from the wall. This expansion is even enough to move studs out of line and cause cracking in interior surfaces.

Buckling and bending. Any break or weakness in hardboard's finish — an overdriven nail, an unpainted butt edge, an uncaulked seam — can lead to moisture problems (see Figure 17). Once moisture gets a toehold, a cycle sets in. Breaks in the finish caused by pulled nails, for instance, invite more moisture infiltration, causing more expansion and more pulled nails, and so on. Moisture can also speed paint degradation, and as the paint comes off, more moisture comes in.

Bad enough to quit. Problems like that are driving some hardboard dealers and installers out of the business. Minneapolis siding distributor Marty Bennis, for instance, has sold and installed hardboard siding for 20 years. In recent years, however, he has begun to phase the product out of his sales.

"A lot of hardboard is good product, but it's inconsistent," says Bennis. "You get what you pay for. We've just had too many problems over the years." Bennis says moisture "wicking" into the hardboard caused most of his problems, which included buckling boards and peeling paint (see Figure 18).

Tim Melgren, operations manager at Inner Mountain Lumber in Missoula, Mont., tells of similar problems.

"It's pretty dry here," says Melgren, "but we've still had expansion problems, swelling and shrinking. Where you have long runs on a wall, you get swaying and buckling. It'll pull nails and swell up over the heads. We've also had some shrinkage problems, where the gap opens and the caulk pops off."

Melgren blames some of these failures on builders who butt the boards too tightly or fail to caulk and paint adequately. But, he says, "We're seeing some problems even when people follow the installation guidelines strictly... and the problems are

Figure 18. Overdriving nails into hardboard siding invites trouble. The broken surface gives an inroad to moisture, leading to cracking and further moisture absorption. Overdriven nails should be caulked.

Figure 19. Undersized corner boards have aggravated the expansion problem on this installation by allowing moisture access to the ends of siding panels. Corner boards should fully cover the ends of the siding.

bad enough to discourage us from using it." As a result, says Melgren, he now sells hardboard "reluctantly." When possible, he steers his customers to the OSB product Inner-Seal made by Louisiana-Pacific instead.

It's not just the humidity, it's the heat. Hardboard fares worst in areas that have big swings in humidity and temperature and does best in areas that are dry year-round. Louis Wagner, technical director of the

American Hardboard Association (AHA), says "you'll very rarely see a rot or buckling problem in Arizona, but in Louisiana or Mississippi or across the South where you've got high summer temperatures and high humidity, you tend to see more problems with linear expansion. And in the North, where you get condensation from inside, you tend to get more problems with rot. There's a band in the central part of the country where you don't see problems very often."

Proper installation crucial. Along with weather, quality of installation is a crucial factor in hardboard's performance. To stray from the manufacturer's installation guidelines is to ask for trouble.

Installation guidelines vary only slightly from one manufacturer to another (see "Hardboard Do's and Don'ts"). Most companies void the warranty if certain guidelines aren't followed. Generally, key guidelines include:

HARDBOARD DO'S AND DON'TS

Always follow the manufacturer's recommendations for the specific hardboard product you use. Failing to do so risks product failure and voiding the warranty. Most manufacturers' guidelines are similar to the ones described here, which are compiled from American Hardboard Association (AHA) literature, manufacturers' instructions, and conversations with builders, suppliers, and researchers.

If the product doesn't come with instructions, call the manufacturer and have them send you a copy.

Pre-Application

Hardboard performs best if you take a few precautions and do a little planning before you install it.

Get it used to the place. It's best to get hardboard siding a week early and store it at the job site to let it adjust to the site's humidity. That should minimize expansion or shrinking after application. Store it flat on stickers in an unheated, covered building or under tarps. Keep it away from moisture.

Some manufacturers recommend "splintering" the bundles (breaking them up and restacking them with stickers placed between every few layers of siding) to help this stabilizing process. In fact, splintering is the only way to ensure the siding will reach the proper humidity level.

Let the place dry first. Don't install hardboard siding when a building's concrete foundation is

still drying. The moisture released by the foundation may condense on the back side of the hardboard. If you have no choice, says AHA technical director Louis Wagner, "Make sure that you find other ways to dispose of that water vapor — leave a window open — and make sure you're getting some outdoor air exchange." Leaving the interior unheated as long as possible will also help.

Installation

The instructions below are fairly representative, but you should follow your manufacturer's guidelines to protect your warranty.

Use a warm-side vapor barrier. The hardboard industry requires warm-side vapor barriers — if you don't use one and have problems, you'll probably strike out trying to get a warranty settlement.

Use a vapor retarder rated at one perm or less (this includes polyethylene film, kraft paper, or foil-backed gypsum board). Some manufacturers will accept foil-backed fiberglass batts.

These requirements generally apply to retrofit jobs, too. If you can't provide a suitable interior vapor barrier on a residing job, some manufacturers will accept exterior foam sheathing. Some will also accept an exterior vapor barrier with strapping between it and the hardboard; however, in cold climates, an exterior vapor barrier could trap moisture within the wall

cavity. Either solution may require you to extend the window and door trim as well.

Cut it correctly. Use a fine tooth saw. Always cut into the face of the board: that is, place boards face up when using a hand saw, face down when using a circular saw.

Stay clear of the ground and roofs. Don't install hardboard siding closer than 6 or 8 inches to the ground (many codes require an 8-inch clearance) or closer than 2 inches to roofs. If you're in an area where it snows a lot, you might want to leave a 4- or 6-inch gap above roofs.

Gap all butt ends. To allow for expansion, follow the manufacturer's recommendations for spacing between boards. Usually this is 1/16 inch or 1/8 inch; a few recommend 3/16; some recommend different gaps for board-to-board and board-to-trim spaces. If you use H-strips, you may need to leave an even bigger gap.

Seal the gaps. You can either caulk the gaps or install "H-strips" manufactured for sealing them. Use an acrylic or urethane-based caulk — silicone won't take paint. You'll need to leave a larger gap between boards — up to 1/2 inch — when using H-strips.

Builders are divided on whether caulk or H-strips perform better. Some feel the caulk makes for a smoother look; others feel that H-strips look okay and are worth the protection they give from caulk

- Installing a continuous warm-side vapor barrier.
- Leaving gaps of about 1/8 inch between butt ends of boards and between boards and trim. The gaps must be caulked or covered with a special "H-joint" (see Figure 19).
- Using only galvanized box nails driven flush with the board's surface.
- Finishing the siding within a certain period, usually 30 to 90 days after installation.

Leaving out any of these steps opens the door to moisture and expansion problems, and later to warranty disputes. So knowing and following the guidelines is crucial.

Unfortunately, not all manufacturers do a good job of getting these guidelines to builders. Builders unaware that special instructions exist might easily put the siding up incorrectly — only to run into problems with warranty claims later.

Paint: Another Sticky Subject

Hardboard's need for frequent painting is another source of complaint from builders and homeowners. Jim Adams, who used to use hardboard for the 400 homes his Good Value Homes builds in the Minneapolis area every year, quit using it primarily because it required painting so often.

"We just had too many claims from clients," he says. "The freeze/thaw cycle was rough on the paint, and it

bulging or falling out when boards expand and contract.

Use proper corner boards and trim. Corner boards and trim must be thick enough to completely cover the ends and edges of the siding. Leave a gap of about 1/8 inch between board and trim and caulk this (see illustration). Where boards run over the top of a door or window trim, use a proper flashing and caulk.

Use the right nails, and don't overdrive them. Use galvanized box nails of the recommended size; usually it's a 6d, 8d, or 10d nail. Nails should penetrate at least 1 1/2 inches into the studs.

Drive the nails just flush with the surface. An underdriven nail will loosen; an overdriven nail breaks the surface of the siding, opening an avenue for moisture infiltration. If you overdrive one, caulk the hole.

Finishing

To protect the wood and the warranty, you must finish with the thoroughness of a tax auditor.

Use the right primer and paint. Hardboard manufacturers leave the back side of their siding unprimed and unfinished, and they recommend that you do the same. According to AHA's Wagner, this is done to give moisture some means of escape.

For unprimed siding, use oil/alkyd primers. Over the primer or on primed siding, apply two coats of a high-quality acrylic latex paint or acrylic stain that is *recommended for use on hardboard*.

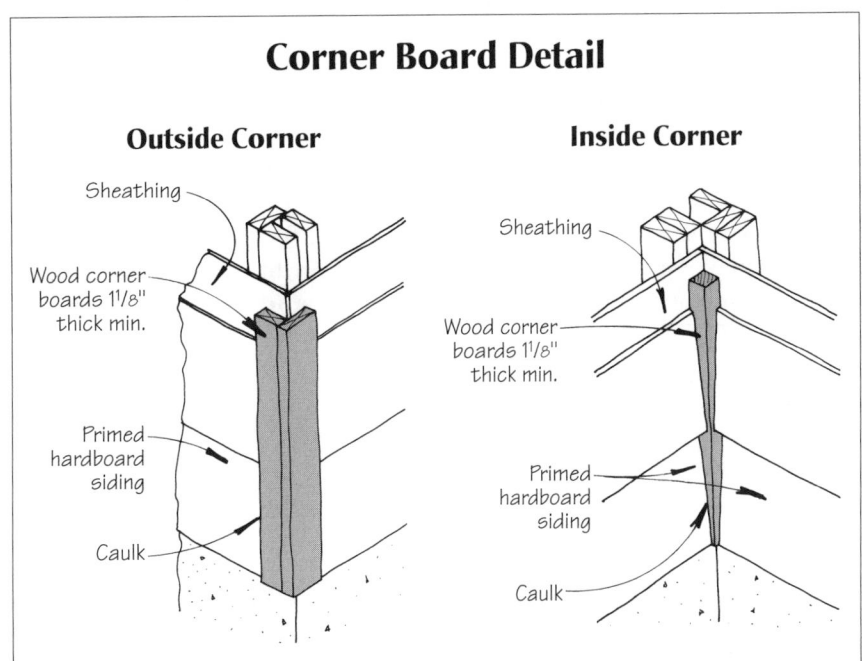

Corner Board Detail

Outside Corner

Sheathing

Wood corner boards 1 1/8" thick min.

Primed hardboard siding

Caulk

Inside Corner

Sheathing

Wood corner boards 1 1/8" thick min.

Primed hardboard siding

Caulk

Corner boards must be thick enough to cover ends or edges of siding, with a caulked gap of about 1/8 inch between boards and siding.

Products not recommended may not adhere as well or last as long. Don't skimp on the paint; if necessary remind your client that cheap paint will likely mean a new paint job a lot sooner.

It helps to use a paler color, preferably with a lot of white in it. "The whiter the color, usually, the longer it'll last," says Wagner. "There are some colors that don't last well at all — yellow, for example. Titanium dioxide makes a stable color, and will last longer than anything else." Titanium dioxide content is highest in white or off-white paints.

Don't take any "holidays." Painters call a missed spot a "holiday." Don't take any with hardboard siding. Hit every spot, paying special attention to the butt edges along the bottom of each board. This will mean getting down low to hit the bottoms of the lower boards, which will need protection the most.

Emphasize maintenance. Clients need to keep an eye on the siding and look for popped caulk, missing H-joints, or nail holes that open. These should be caulked and refinished immediately. — *D.D.*

would crack. You have to repaint every two or three years. Then we got a batch with some bad primer and the paint wouldn't stick, and that was the frosting on the cake for us."

According to construction consultant Paul Cove, Adams' problem with frequent painting isn't unusual. "Hardboard has to be painted more often than wood," he says, because cracked or peeling paint opens the way to moisture infiltration.

A few of the newer hardboard products address this issue, offering longer finish warranties. MacMillan-Bloedel, for instance, recently came out with a blind-nailed product that carries a 15-year finish warranty, and Masonite offers its blind-nailed "Colorlock" with a 15-year warranty.

Such products might ease many of the industry's problems. According to manufacturers, blind-nailing makes the product both more durable and more attractive. In face-nailed sidings, nail holes usually offer moisture its first entry; hiding the nail holes under the lap above removes this entryway. The absence of visible nails also gives the siding a much cleaner look.

By David Dobbs, a freelance writer from Montpelier, Vt.

GUIDE TO GALVANIZED NAILS

Builders typically use galvanized nails for framing decks, for applying wood siding, and for installing exterior trim. But not everyone knows that "galvanized" can have more than one meaning when you're talking about nails. All galvanized nails are made of steel and coated with zinc. The zinc coating is what protects the nail from rust. But how much zinc is on the nail, and how the zinc is applied, make a big difference in how well the nail will resist rust.

Hot-Dipping

The traditional way to coat steel nails with zinc is "hot-dipping." In the hot-dipping process, the nails are immersed in a bath of molten zinc, like french fries in a pot of oil. The intense heat of the zinc bath causes the zinc and the steel to bind together in an alloy layer that acts as a base for a heavy zinc coating and provides long-lasting protection against rust.

"Double hot-dipped" galvanized nails are actually dipped twice in molten zinc, and are processed for uniformity between dips. The second dip is designed to fill up any pinholes and adds thickness to the outer layer of zinc (Figure 20).

Electroplating

Steel nails are electroplated by immersing them in an electrolytic solution. An electric current in the bath deposits a thin film of zinc from a zinc anode onto the surface of the nails. With their smooth, shiny coating, electroplated nails work well as collated nails in mechanical nail guns — and they look beautiful when they're brand-new. But the thin zinc coating commonly applied to nails in commercial electroplating oxidizes away rapidly when exposed to weather, and the nails then begin to rust (Figure 21). Siding trade associations warn against using these nails in exterior applications.

Hot-Galvanizing

A lot of the galvanized nails sold in lumberyards are coated by "hot-galvanizing." Nails produced this way are labeled "HG," while nails produced by hot-dipping are labeled "HD." Because the labels are so similar, carpenters looking for hot-dipped galvanized nails are often sold hot-galvanized nails. But even though the terms sound similar, there is a significant difference in the nails. In hot-galvanizing, also known

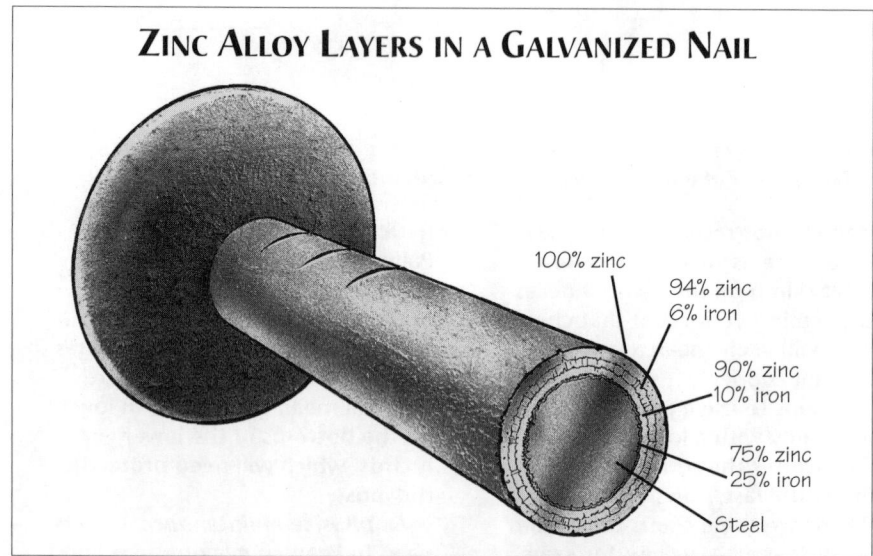

ZINC ALLOY LAYERS IN A GALVANIZED NAIL

100% zinc
94% zinc 6% iron
90% zinc 10% iron
75% zinc 25% iron
Steel

Figure 20. According to the American Galvanizers' Association in Aurora, Colo., hot-dip galvanizing creates a series of protective alloy layers around a steel nail. The outer layer is 100% zinc, while inner layers contain progressively less zinc and more steel. If the zinc and alloy layers are scratched and some steel is exposed, zinc in the outer layers will corrode before the steel does, preventing rust formation.

Extractive Bleeding & Wood Staining

Builders who install wood siding and leave it natural or use a clear finish frequently notice staining of the wood around nail heads. This staining is often blamed on the nails themselves. But if wood contains moisture when installed or gets wet after installation, stains often occur around nail heads even when the galvanized layer is still intact, and even when stainless-steel or aluminum nails are used. In these cases, the source of the problem is extractive bleeding.

All wood contains a certain amount of naturally occurring substances like pigments, tannins, oils, and resins. These substances are called extractives because they can be drawn from wood by various solvents, including water. The water-soluble extractives are sometimes brought to the surface of the wood by moisture inside the wood — whether from the wood's inherent moisture, from moisture inside a dwelling that migrates into the siding because there is no vapor barrier, or from moisture that penetrates the wood from outside. This migration of extractives is intensified by the "drawing effect" of the sun. Extractive bleeding often stains the wood, and can also discolor applied finishes, whether paint or stain. Extractive bleeding is a risk any time wood siding is used. Beautiful woods like cedar and redwood, which are durable because they contain the most extractives, have the highest risk of bleeding.

Extractive bleeding often occurs around nail holes. A poor-quality nail makes the problem worse because tannins react with unprotected iron to form a blue-black stain that spreads around and below the nail head.

To prevent extractive bleeding, pay close attention to construction details. Protect wood siding from water before, during, and after

"Extractive bleeding" has streaked these shingles below the nail holes (top). Iron in nails can react with natural wood tannins to make bleeding worse. Bleeding stains can also emerge from wood grain, even on stained or painted siding (middle). Bleeding is caused by exposure to water — note that the shingles protected by the eaves show less staining (bottom).

installation. Proper drying of lumber, moisture control within the building, effective finishing, and careful flashing and caulking are all important. And keep in mind that painted or stained siding requires periodic refinishing to retain its beauty. — *T.C.*

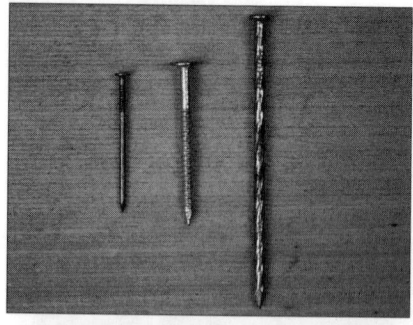
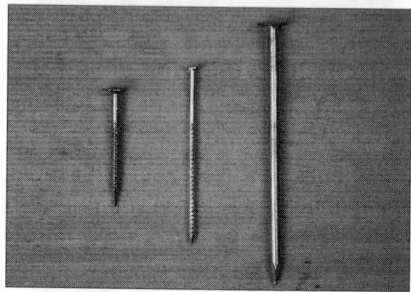

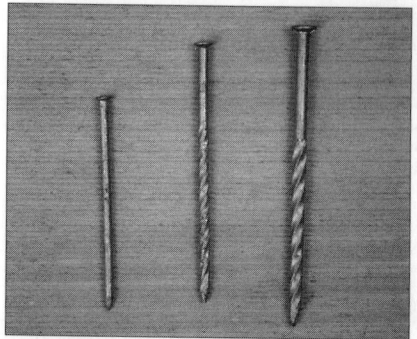

Figure 21. Electroplated nails (top) are bright and shiny, but have a relatively thin zinc coating. Peen-plated nails (second) also have a thin zinc coating. "Hot-galvanized" nails (third) are not hot-dipped, but coated with zinc chips in a hot tumbler, a process that can yield an uneven coating. Double hot-dipped galvanized nails (bottom) have a thick zinc alloy coating. High-quality hot-dipped nails outperform all other types of galvanized nails in exterior applications.

as "tumbler galvanizing," zinc chips are sprinkled on top of cold nails in a large barrel, then the barrel is rotated in a large furnace to melt and distribute the zinc. Like buttering popcorn, the results are uneven. Some nails receive too much zinc, and others not enough. It is hard to deposit enough zinc on and under the nail heads by this method, and globs of zinc tend to clog the threads of ring- and screw-shank nails.

Unlike hot-dipping, the hot-galvanizing process does not create a uniform alloy layer between the steel nail and the surface layer of pure zinc. Lacking this metallurgical bond between the nail and the coating, some percentage of hot-galvanized nails will be prone to rusting if used on the outside of a building. Often you can spot the rust on these nails in their shipping cartons, even before they are used.

Mechanical Plating

Mechanically plated nails are also called "peen-plated." In this relatively new process, the cold nails are rolled around in a drum containing zinc dust, tiny glass BBs, and an activator fluid. As the drum rotates, the BBs hammer, or "peen," the zinc dust onto the nails.

Mechanical plating works well for adding a zinc coating to screws or ring-shank nails, because the thin zinc coating applied does not clog the threads or rings. Mechanical plating is also commonly used to apply a zinc coating to hardened nails like the concrete fasteners used in powder-driven nail guns (hot-dipping is unsuitable for hardened nails because the intense heat of the molten zinc bath would soften the tempered nails). But mechanical-plated nails typically lack the thickness of zinc found on a hot-dipped nail, and they do not have the alloy layer that hot-dipped galvanized nails have. Most mechanically-plated screws or nails are less corrosion-resistant than hot-dipped nails.

Stainless Steel and Aluminum

Galvanized nails are not the only rust-resistant nails available. Stainless-steel nails are a more costly but very effective alternative. Stainless steel is a steel-nickel-chromium alloy that provides excellent rust protection, even when exposed to substances that might ultimately corrode a hot-dipped galvanized nail. Stainless-steel nails are definitely worth the extra expense in seashore environments, below-grade applications, or when cedar or redwood trim or siding is left natural or given a transparent finish.

Most stainless-steel nails found in lumberyards are labeled either "304" or "316." The 316 stainless nails contain higher levels of the alloy metals. You should use 316 stainless nails in rough environments like the seashore.

Aluminum nails are also available for use on exterior siding. They will not usually rust or corrode when exposed to the weather, but they may cause corrosion in other metals.

The Western Wood Products Association, the California Redwood Association, and the Western Red Cedar Lumber Association all recommend stainless-steel nails for installing natural wood siding on homes — especially in corrosive environments like coastal sites. But in most applications, all those associations agree that a galvanized nail can give excellent performance — as long as it is a high-quality, hot-dipped galvanized nail. Other methods of applying zinc to nails, they say, are not usually as resistant to corrosion.

By Ted Cushman, an associate editor at The Journal of Light Construction.

CHAPTER 4

BRICK, STUCCO & MASONRY

- Brick Veneer

- Brick Masonry Restoration

- Caulking Masonry Joints

- Leak-Proof Chimney Flashing

- Retrofit Chimney Flashing

- Patching Stucco

- EIFS Performance Review

BRICK VENEER

Many home buyers like the low maintenance and quality look of a brick veneer home. The veneer will never need painting; it will protect the house from wind (Figure 1); and if the work is done right, the veneer will last the lifetime of the house.

But contractors with a carpentry background may not understand the finer points of masonry-veneer construction. Mistakes made in foundation construction, in design, and even in homeowner maintenance can undermine long-term performance of brick veneer.

The brick veneer layer behaves differently than the structural wall behind it. Wood begins to shrink the moment a house is finished; concrete does too. But brick actually *expands* as it ages.

And unlike structural components, brick veneer can only support its own weight; in fact, *it* must be supported (Figure 2). Think of veneer as a stack of dominoes; the higher the stack, the more unstable it becomes. A stack on a slanted surface is extremely unstable.

Finally, the brick skin isn't completely waterproof. Water squeezes through small cracks in the mortar, and the brick itself can absorb water. Small amounts of water evaporate without causing problems, but if brick is exposed to a downpour or to water-saturated soil, it can be damaged.

Four simple concepts will help you avoid problems and help you understand the details that follow:
• Support the brick on a stiff, stable ledge.
• Tie the brick securely to its back-up.
• Leave room for expansion.
• Use flashing to keep water out.

Vertical Support

If you support brick veneer properly, you're off to a good start. The foundation, the brick ledges, and the lintels all have to support the brick without moving or deflecting.

Firm footings. Contractors know they should build on undisturbed soil. This minimizes building settlement. Settlement is not necessarily bad for a structure, however. If a building settles uniformly, you probably won't see cracks in brick veneer.

A major problem *will* show up if a building settles at different rates across its foundation area. If differential settlement occurs, step cracks will occur and will follow the mortar joints (Figure 3). The crack pattern will grow larger as it goes from the bottom to the top of the wall.

Even though uniform settlement probably won't hurt the wall, you don't want to take chances. The only way to guarantee that settlement won't damage the veneer is to make sure the underlying soil has been properly compacted. Don't throw in an extra shovelful of dirt just to save a little on concrete. In parts of the country where soil has a high expansive-clay content (like Texas), you may have to take special precautions. These can include subsoil foundation watering or foundation drainage systems.

Sometimes homeowner maintenance can cause problems with

Figure 1. A brick veneer goes right over insulating board and wood studs. The veneer protects the house from wind.

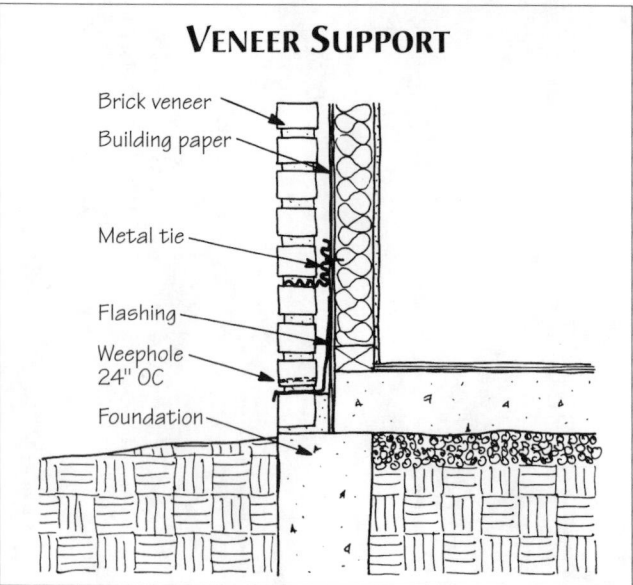

VENEER SUPPORT

Brick veneer
Building paper
Metal tie
Flashing
Weephole 24" OC
Foundation

Figure 2. The foundation supports the veneer. Elastomeric or metal flashing comes through the wall above the first brick joint. Metal ties connect the brick back to the structure.

veneer. If you're brought in to repoint a cracked veneer, you should look for the cause. Poor drainage of surface water away from the foundation can cause settling. More often the problem is caused by a downspout spilling water against the foundation wall (Figure 4).

Downspouts frequently end at the corner of the house. Water gathers around the foundation and percolates down to the footing or foundation slab. The moving water washes away fine particles of silt, creating voids in the soil and undermining the slab or foundation footing. Eventually, the weight of the house causes the soil to collapse, and a corner of the slab can crack off. In an extreme case, the foundation tips because the footing is undercut.

After you've repaired the damage, make sure you build up the soil level around the house so water drains away. Otherwise, you may be blamed if the crack opens again. Make sure all downspouts use extensions or splash pans.

Ledge. If you're sure the foundation's on solid footing, concentrate on getting a good brick ledge to support the veneer. The brick ledge should be large enough so that it will support two-thirds of the width of the brick.

Sometimes the contractor provides a 3¹/₂-inch ledge, thinking this is adequate for the masonry. However, the contractor may also install 1-inch rigid insulation, taking the ledge down to 2¹/₂ inches. The mason also needs finger room behind the brick. Without this finger room the mortar would push the veneer away from the wall. After taking away finger room, the mason is left with only 2 inches — less than the minimum needed. The mason's not going to stop work if you didn't leave enough room. He'll build it anyway. It's up to the general contractor to provide a minimum of 2¹/₂ inches *plus finger room* for the veneer.

Brick veneer can be added to an existing building — even if no brick

Figure 3. Spray-paint was used to highlight differential settlement cracks on the inside of this foundation. You can imagine what the brick outside looks like.

Figure 4. This conductor pipe spills water down the foundation wall and excavates a trench below the footing.

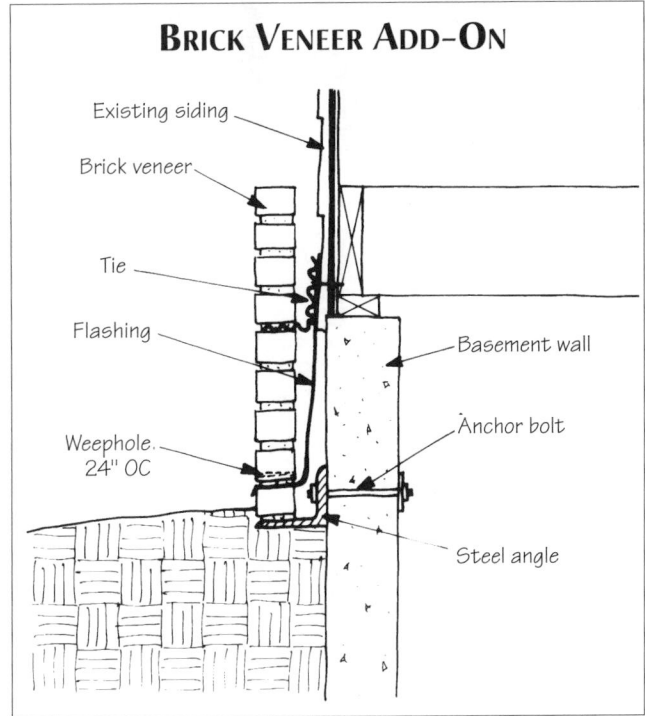

BRICK VENEER ADD-ON

Existing siding
Brick veneer
Tie
Flashing
Weephole 24" OC
Basement wall
Anchor bolt
Steel angle

Figure 5. When adding brick veneer to an existing building, the angle of the support shelf and the number of bolts tying it to the building must be figured by an engineer.

Figure 6. Deflection of a wood window frame caused the triangular chunk of brick above the window to drop. The brick was only supported by the window frame.

ledge was provided originally (Figure 5). But you will need to make a ledge from steel angle attached to the existing foundation. Place the angle at or below grade, and make sure it's corrosion-resistant. Also make sure you get an engineer to look at the angle size, foundation strength, and bolt size and spacing.

Lintels. Poor lintel design is common. Lintels over garage openings or wide windows should be designed to minimize deflection (Figure 6). With wood lintels, you should limit deflection to $1/600$ of the span length or a maximum of 0.3 inch. This will prevent cracking of the supported brick veneer. Or, use steel lintels for openings that exceed 8 feet. Make sure you leave extra room at the ends of the lintel where it is supported on the masonry. Steel expands, and you need to leave space for expansion. Otherwise the expanding steel will induce high stresses and cause the surrounding brick to spall (Figure 7).

For smaller openings, steel angles or reinforced-masonry lintels may be adequate. However, some builders leave out lintels over basement windows altogether. This is a poor practice that will lead to future window and veneer problems.

Tie It Tight

The brick veneer receives its vertical support from the foundation

BRICK VENEER DETAILS

Figure A. Because flashing was never installed below this window sill, the brick became saturated with water and efflorescence has occurred.

Figure B. This parapet wall, capped with numerous small bricks, created many joints and greater vulnerability to water damage. A better design would have used large stone, continuous metal, or glazed tile coping.

Of all the essentials of brick veneer construction, none is more important than proper detailing. Most problems involve wood shrinkage and inadequate flashing. Caulking and sealants for sills, jambs, shelf angles, lintels, and parapets also need special attention. If the detailing is well thought out and construction is done according to plans, the problems of efflorescence, water penetration, brick cracking and spalling, and wall bowing can be virtually eliminated.

Wood shrinkage. Wood shrinks far more along its width than it does along its length. Floor joists, for example, shrink more across their width than studs do along their length. With a two-story, split-level house, you may have as many as three platforms. If you're using a brick veneer, you need to allow for shrinkage of the wood and expansion of the brick.

For instance, problems often occur beneath windows. Leave room for the window to come down to the brick. If you don't take shrinkage into account, the window frame can come

or from stiff horizontal lintels. But the veneer must also be supported laterally. This is the job of the tie-support system. The wall ties transfer the horizontal wind loads on the building into the structural system and ultimately into the foundation. The ties must be strong enough to resist tensile and compressive forces.

Follow these rules of thumb in low-rise construction:

- Use one tie for every 3 1/4 square feet of wall area, with a maximum spacing of 24 inches on-center, or approximately one tie per stud every sixth or seventh course.
- For a concrete masonry back-up, use continuous horizontal joint-reinforcement with U-tabs or individual Z-ties.
- For wood framing, ties should

Figure 7. Expansion of the steel lintel caused this brick to spall.

be corrosion-resistant corrugated metal, at least 22-gauge, 7/8 inch wide, and 6 inches long.

Engrave these numbers in your mind — maximum spacing of *24 inches on-center*. Put a tie about

every *6th or 7th course*. You see a lot of veneer installed with no wall ties. The mason might tell you ties aren't needed for a one-story building, but they are. Winds whip across the prairie and along the coasts, and even an occasional high

---

down hard on the brick. The window will jam and become inoperable.

A similar problem occurs with half-height veneer on a single-story house. When the wood shrinks, the siding can come down tight onto the veneer. If the soldier course has been flashed, the flashing tips towards the house, causing water to drain towards the inside. Even if no flashing is used, the siding will frequently be so tight that it will begin to buckle or rot. To avoid this, leave room between the flashing and siding for shrinkage, but tuck metal flashing behind the siding so that the gap does not allow water to penetrate.

Depending on the height of the building, you could get as much as 1/2 to 1 1/2 inches of shrinkage in the wood frame. You can try to overcome the shrinkage problem by using balloon framing. If you do, however, make sure you also use balloon framing for interior walls as well.

Another way to tackle shrinkage on multi-story buildings is to support the veneer with shelf angle at each floor level. Leave an expansion joint below the shelf angle. Use a foam neoprene pad in the joint, and face the joint with backer rod and sealant.

Figure C. Be sure to seal the joints on a parapet wall. If sealant is not maintained, mortar deteriorates and efflorescence occurs.

Flashing problems. Brick needs flashing to stop the flow of water. In Figure A, flashing was left out below the sill. Notice the efflorescence. This is salt that rises to the surface as brick goes through wet/dry cycles. The surface efflorescence shows that water has entered the wall at the sill. Over time, through freezing and thawing, there is a good chance the brick will begin to spall.

Parapets are another place where it's easy for water to get in. Parapet design should be considered carefully before construction begins. Notice how the wall in Figure B was

capped. The numerous brick joints allow water to enter the wall. Instead, the wall should have been capped with large pieces of stone, continuous metal, or glazed terra-cotta tile coping. These materials create fewer joints and therefore fewer potential headaches. But remember to properly seal the coping joints with sealant. Figure C shows what happens if the sealant is inadequate or omitted. The mortar has begun to fall apart. Not only will wall damage eventually occur, but efflorescence will result as well. — *R.B. and R.R.*

wind can put unacceptable stress on a veneer wall.

Make sure the ties are *corrosion-resistant*, particularly in coastal climates or in areas where rainfall is high. Also, if you're building in winter, heat your water and materials instead of using an admixture. Admixtures can cause tie corrosion and veneer failure.

Leave Room for Expansion

Walls are subjected to movement. Thermal expansion and contraction, moisture absorption, material shrinkage, or building loads may cause movement of the building components. Provide room for this movement so it won't damage the veneer. The main way to handle movement is with expansion joints.

Expansion joints. Expansion joints look like long, vertical slices down a brick wall. You'll see them near corners of large buildings. Expansion joints are placed in brick masonry construction to prevent overstressing of the veneer. Expansion joints prevent cracking due to thermal movement, moisture-absorption, and load effects. Since the brick is exposed to the outside, temperature and moisture changes can be significant. A south-facing wall, for example, can experience temperature swings of 140°F in a day.

In residential construction, most walls are relatively short. Accumulated movements are usually not large

enough to warrant expansion joints. However, long walls — 75 feet or more — can have problems. Problems also occur where there are abrupt changes in wall geometry. If you're building a long ranch house, with the brick veneer facing the sun, you may need to use expansion joints.

The approximate amount of expansion from the various sources can be calculated by an engineer. When you build an expansion joint, however, you'd better make sure the joint is about twice as large as the anticipated movement because the mason will fill this joint with sealant. If you don't provide enough room for the volume of the sealant, it will squeeze out of the joint during maximum expansion, and the water seal may break. In repairing a wall that has cracked because of wall movement, you should never seal the crack with mortar. Always repair with a compressible sealant to prevent further distress.

Keep Water Out

The fourth concept is probably the hardest to accomplish in practice. That's because there are many ways for water to enter a veneer wall. And in residential construction, masons do not always follow recommended industry practice. For example, it's common for masons to leave out base flashing. But base flashing is one of the most important safeguards against water damage.

Flashing. Although many masons don't use base flashing, it's very important and *should be used*. Even when it is used, it is often torn or damaged during construction. Figure 8 shows how to do the job right. The bricklayer is lapping and sealing the flashing to ensure a continuous membrane. He has also extended the flashing beyond the exterior face of the brick. This will direct water that enters the wall to exit on the exterior face. Water won't accumulate in the cavity between the block and the veneer.

Weep holes. In case water should get into this cavity, the mason must provide channels for it to escape. Put weep holes every 24 inches on-center directly above all flashing. Some contractors incorrectly place weep holes several courses above the flashing. This can cause problems since it allows water to accumulate from the flashing up to the exit point. The water may freeze, and the resulting ice can put pressure on the brick, causing cracking or spalling.

Also, the mason should make sure the mortar droppings do not clog the weep holes. One way to keep weep holes free is to use short lengths of cotton sash cord. Place the cord where the weep holes should be, but make it long enough so it will stay above the mortar droppings. Water will wick out the sash cord. When the sash cord eventually rots, the weep hole will be free.

Another way to provide weep holes is to leave out every third brick in the base course. As the wall goes up, the brick mason can have a helper clean out the mortar droppings. When the wall is finished, the mason mortars in the missing brick, leaving out the head joint (the joint at the side of the brick). You'll have weep slots right where you need them.

The masonry contractor should also flash any horizontal brick ledge or surface. Suppose, for example, the brick veneer is only half the height of the wall. A flat soldier course will

Figure 8. The bricklayer laps the flashing and seals the joint. Loose bricks hold the flashing in place and ensure that it won't get bunched up in the wall or torn during construction.

collect water. The soldier course should either be flashed or sloped to shed water. It's best to avoid flat soldier courses altogether.

Mortar and brick quality. The quality of brick and mortar can affect how much water gets into a wall. On the one hand, porous brick absorbs water. On the other hand, very hard-fired brick may not bond as well with mortar. Without a good mortar joint, the wall may leak, even though the brick is not porous. Brick with about

6% to 9% water absorption by boiling (ask for bricks that conform to ASTM C216) provides good bonds.

Mortar quality is also critical. The mason should be using mortar made from portland cement and Type S (fully hydrated) lime. Cement makes the mortar strong, and lime makes the mortar "plastic." Lime mortars fill in small cracks that could otherwise allow water to penetrate the wall.

Make sure the temperature doesn't fall below freezing until the mortar

cures because ice crystals can form in mortar. The mortar may eventually cure, but the crystalline holes will be embedded in the joints. Even a normal rain will get through the joints and leak into the house.

By Robert J. Beiner, P.E., director of technical services for the International Masonry Institute in Washington, D.C., and by Robert Rhault, New England regional director of the International Masonry Institute.

BRICK MASONRY RESTORATION

The masonry rehab techniques described below are in compliance with the *Standards for Rehabilitation* approved by the National Park Service for projects seeking rehab tax credits. However, they are good

guidelines for any masonry rehab where high-quality, durable workmanship is desired.

Many projects have been denied rehab tax credits due to poor or inappropriate work — specifically

masonry work. This means: Do not sandblast masonry, replace waterstruck brick with extruded wire-cut units, or repoint with portland cement mortar and expect to get approval.

Why Repoint?

There are several possible reasons why any particular building needs to be repointed. These are listed with the most common reason first, the rarest last. If buildings were built and maintained better the sequence would be reversed:

Poor workmanship — past or current. Not only may past work be visually inappropriate, but it can actually speed up the deterioration

Figure 9. This brick was sandblasted and then repointed with hard portland-cement mortar. Deteriorating brick and protruding mortar joints resulted. Old soft brick and new portland cement mortar don't mix for reasons shown below.

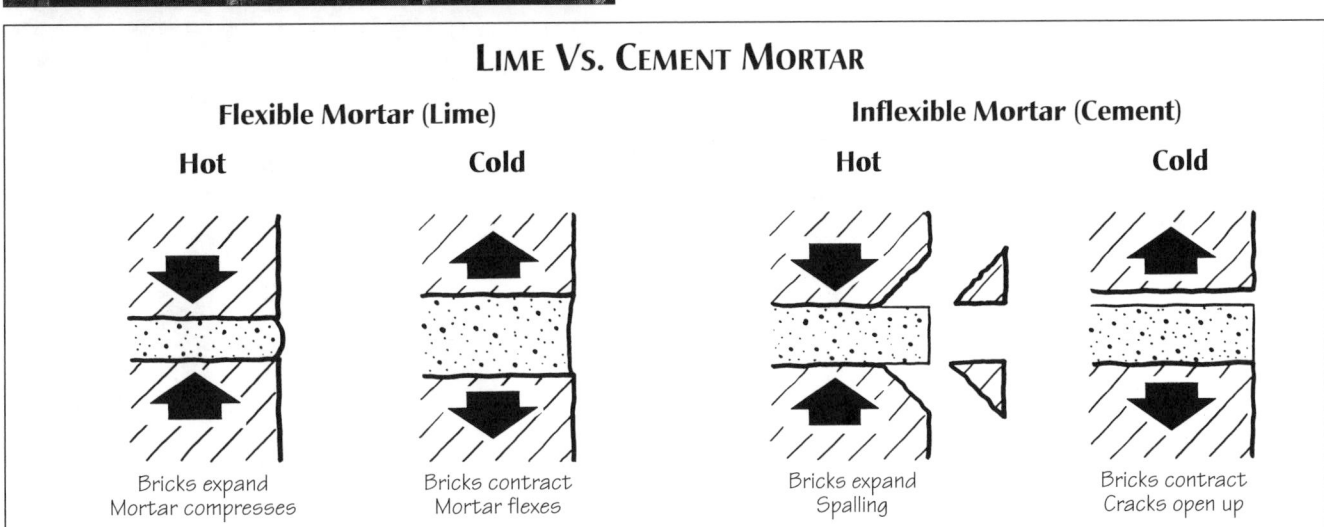

LIME VS. CEMENT MORTAR

Flexible Mortar (Lime) — Hot: Bricks expand Mortar compresses. Cold: Bricks contract Mortar flexes.

Inflexible Mortar (Cement) — Hot: Bricks expand Spalling. Cold: Bricks contract Cracks open up.

Figure 10. It makes no sense to bid a repointing job until the type and condition of mortar is known. Test patches yield this information along with data on how best to strip and clean. The brick under this deteriorated paint turned out to be in excellent condition.

of the brickwork. For example, sand-blasting can cause the masonry to crumble. The use of portland-rich mortar can lead to spalling brick and visually unacceptable patches (Figure 9). These problems are very costly to repair.

Work rejected by an owner or architect may also need to be redone — at substantial cost to the contractor or mason. Masonry work may be rejected because it is just plain bad work, but often it stems from inadequate specifications: the scope of work does not provide an adequate standard of reference for the job.

Structural deficiencies. Structural problems may be caused by faulty

DETAILS FOR GOOD JOINTS

A. REMOVAL OF OLD MORTAR

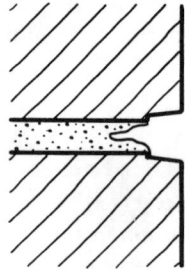

Incorrect
Mortar is not cleaned out to a uniform depth. Edges of brick are damaged by tool or grinder, which creates a wider joint.

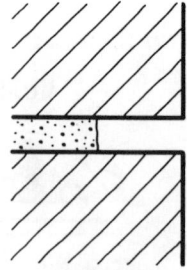

Correct
Mortar is cleaned out to a uniform depth — about 1" deep. Edges of brick are undamaged.

Old mortar should be removed to a minimum depth of two-and-a-half times the width of the joint — about 1 inch deep for most brick joints — to ensure an adequate bond (Figure A). Any loose or disintegrated mortar beyond this depth should also be removed. Joints should be cleaned with care since damage to the bricks can affect not only the appearance, but can also lead to accelerated weather damage.

Where existing mortar has been removed to a depth greater than 1 inch, these deeper areas should be filled first, compacting the new mortar in several 1/4-inch-thick layers to reduce overall shrinkage. It is important to allow each layer time to harden before applying the next layer, since most of the shrinkage occurs while the mortar hardens.

The rate of hardening can be controlled by dampening the brick

B.

construction (possibly altered during renovations), deteriorated structural members, or hydrostatic pressure. Whatever the case, a builder must determine if there is active movement. This will require evaluation — possibly by an engineer — to determine the cause, present activity, and corrective treatment needed. This may require substantial work before starting the masonry restoration.

Water damage. Change in grade, splashback, deteriorated flashing, missing gutters, colorless coatings, and sandblasted brick can all cause or contribute to water-related damage. Well-maintained masonry itself will seldom fail prematurely. If there is spalling, efflorescence, or mildew, suspect water as the culprit. Eliminate the source of damage before undertaking any masonry restoration.

To fix water-related damage may require a lot of related work: regrading, roofing, flashing, cornice repair, and new downspouts. Even if all of this is beyond the scope of your work, be certain to inform the owner/architect of these essentials. Otherwise your best work — backed by a guarantee — may prematurely fail through no fault of its own or yours.

Deteriorated masonry. This means the normal, anticipated erosion of mortar that is to be expected after about a hundred years. Under these conditions, work is typically limited in scope and should not require 100% repointing. In fact, the rule is to repoint only where required.

Putting Masonry to the Test

Too often, contractors are expected to bid on masonry repairs based on poorly developed specifications, no test patches, and materials defined by phrases like "or equal." In these instances, the burden falls on the contractor to do the impossible; for example, to "match existing" mortar that is obscured from vision.

The only way to develop meaningful specs is to test first. Initial testing should be done during a preliminary evaluation of existing conditions (Figure 10). The results

---

and old mortar before filling the joint, but avoid free water or excessive wetting. Too much water will delay the tooling or cause excessive shrinkage; too little water will reduce bond strength.

When the final layer of mortar is thumb-print hard, the joint should be tooled to match the historic joint (Figure B). Proper timing of the tooling is important for uniform color and appearance. If tooled too soft, the color will be lighter than expected, and hairline cracks may occur. If tooled too hard, there may be dark streaks called "tool burning," and you won't get good closure of the mortar against the brick.

If the old bricks have worn, rounded edges, it is usually best to recess the final mortar slightly from the face of the bricks. This will help avoid a joint wider than the actual joint width, which would change the character of the original brickwork. It will also avoid the creation of a large, thin feathered edge that is easily damaged (Figure C).

If the repointing work is done carefully, the only cleaning required will be a small amount of mortar brushed from the edge of the joint with a stiff bristle brush following tooling. This is done after the

mortar has dried, but before it is fully hardened (one to two hours). Mortar that has hardened can usually be removed with a wooden paddle or, if necessary, a chisel. Further cleaning is best accomplished with plain water and bristle brushes.

New construction "bloom" or efflorescence occasionally appears within the first few months after repointing and usually disappears through the normal weathering process. If the efflorescence is not

removed by natural processes, the safest way to remove it is by dry brushing with stiff natural or nylon-bristle brushes and water. Muriatic acid is generally ineffective and should be avoided. In fact, it can deposit salts which can lead to additional efflorescence.

Adapted with permission from Preservation Brief 2: Repointing Mortar Joints in Historic Buildings, *published by the National Park Service, Preservation Assistance Division.*

C. TOOLING THE JOINT

Incorrect
Joints are filled too full. Wide feather edge is susceptible to spalling.

Correct
Joints are slightly recessed, which makes a durable joint.

should be incorporated into the specifications for the scope of work, materials, and methods. These specs must be available to the contractor at the time of the walk-through prior to bidding the project.

After the initial scope of work is established, it may need to be updated as more information becomes available during the course of the project. For example, the degree of repointing needed on painted or badly stained masonry cannot be determined until the entire building is stripped or

cleaned. The contractor should make allowances in the contract for the additional work anticipated and allow time in the schedule to complete the work.

Testing includes test patches on the building, mock-up panels, and work samples. By testing we mean *non-destructive* testing. There have been a number of cases where poorly executed test patches posed more problems than the surrounding work. For example, sandblasting to remove paint, or using electric grinders to remove mortar profiles can cause more damage in

one hour than a building has sustained in 100 years.

Matching Materials

Repair work may require several ranges of brick from various manufacturers (if existing bricks are no longer made); mortar ingredients from different lime/cement companies; a range of sand aggregate for color and texture; and two or three mortar colorings to properly "age" the new to look old. Also, the use of properly slaked quick-lime is worth considering on brick structures built before 1850 where the mortar

JOINT PREPARATION: A JOB FOR PNEUMATICS

Proper joint preparation is at least as important as the actual repointing work. Joint preparation consists of carefully removing deteriorated or inappropriate mortar from between the masonry or stone units. Deteriorated mortar, by nature, is not difficult to remove: The challenge is to remove it *carefully* to a sufficient depth. Inappropriate mortar, on the other hand, is typically hard portland-rich mortar, which can cause irreversible damage to the surrounding masonry.

There are two prevalent methods of raking out mortar joints: the hand method and the use of electric grinders. You would do well to consider a third option: We've had great success with certain pneumatic carving tools described below.

Hand tools. Many contractors consider the use of hand tools — a mason's hammer and chisel — the best way to remove mortar. If you are among those, you'll have plenty of time to consider other options while using this slow, imprecise method. Laborious hand tooling is not only a matter of time and expense, but also of worker fatigue. A weary body and mind are prone to mistakes, here in the form of irreversible damage.

Electric grinders. At this point, electric grinders might seem a viable option. Perhaps they are, but

only on moderately wide horizontal joints that are uninterrupted by decorative elements such as brick window lintels or decorative terra cotta. And only if you have the skill to match the power of this tool.

Rotary electric grinders are frequently dangerous to both the building and the builder. Work cannot be properly viewed under the clouds of dust and fast-moving debris generated by a blade spinning at speeds as high as 6,000 rpm.

A major limitation of electric grinders is that they tend to overcut into neighboring courses when used on vertical mortar joints. Also the depth of removal is limited by the working radius of the blade. A 4-inch blade offers only $1^1/2$ inches maximum raking depth. Yes, grinders have their place, but only in conjunction with the preferred methods described below.

Pneumatic tools. The use of pneumatic tools has had a tremendous impact on historic masonry restoration. Why? Exactly because of the precise manner and controlled impact of these air-powered instruments. They remove mortar by causing it to crumble and fall.

We're not talking about the implements used to remove mufflers from cars, or to drill post holes into sidewalks for "no parking" signs. These pneumatic tools are

totally unacceptable for any restoration work.

The tool we're describing is made by the Trow and Holden Company, a firm that has specialized in tools for the stone industry since 1890. Trow and Holden's pneumatic carving tool was designed as a precision sculpting instrument and has been used by the arts and industry since 1890. If the tool is precise enough to sculpt the face of Abraham Lincoln, why shouldn't it be able to rake out loose mortar from masonry?

Unlike the "muffler remover," the Trow and Holden tool has neither a retainer nor a throttle. This unconventional design provides for some unique control characteristics.

For instance, this tool has a chisel with a round shank, hand-held in place in the carving tool. A round shank permits the chisel blade to be oriented independent of the tool, an essential feature that is impossible with square-shank tools. The absence of a retainer, or any mechanical connection, enables the mason to defeat the power of the tool immediately by simply pulling the chisel away from the piston. One hand operates the tool while the other controls the chisel.

The chisel blades are tempered and available with carbide tips. They can be custom-made to any length or width. Even very thin

contains lime specks.

For matching mortar, dozens of samples may be needed to match the structural properties and texture of the original joints. Ingredients will include various aggregates, mortar dyes, cement, and lime. Do not use ready-mixed mortar, latex additives, or anti-freezing agents. Each sample should be carefully labeled, accurately proportioned by volume (coffee cans work well), and documented. These must be allowed to dry naturally before a perfect match for color and texture can be achieved.

A single building can have substantial differences in mortar from elevation to elevation. Over a dozen different mortar mixes may be required on one side of a two-story house. We know of one project, however, where the test results for two mortar samples served as the basis for restoring mortar on a 200,000-square-foot mill constructed over a period of 50 years.

Raking Out Mortar

There are several techniques for raking out mortar and removing masonry units. What is excellent for one job, however, can be disastrous for another. The methods include:
- Hand raking (hammer and chisel)
- Mechanical/electrical raking (tuck-point grinders)
- Mechanical/pneumatic raking (small grinders, reciprocating hammers)

In many cases, a combination of techniques is useful. For example, most historic masonry with soft lime mortar will require a combination of hand and mechanical/pneumatic techniques. On newer structures — with hard portland mortar —

The Trow and Holden pneumatic chisel was developed for sculptors (left), but can also remove old mortar quickly and with little fatigue to the worker. The worker maintains precise control by manipulating the loose-fitting chisel (center), and controlling the pneumatic back-pressure with his other hand. Vertical joints are easily cleaned (right), without harming adjacent brick — a real problem with grinding equipment.

"butter" joints can be cleaned, and a joint whose width is the distance between the lines on this page can be easily raked out. As with other raking tools, the width of the chisel should not exceed three-quarters of the width of the mortar joint.

Once mortar joints have been carefully raked out, any remaining debris can be easily cleaned with a regulated, light application of compressed air.

The Trow and Holden pneumatic carving tool is about three times faster than hand raking in removing loose mortar, hard mortar, and damaged bricks. Keep in mind that the object of masonry restoration is to restore only that material which actually requires work, with as little "intervention" as possible.

As with any instrument, it takes time and practice to master the correct use of this tool and its potential. For product and technical information, contact: Trow and Holden Company, Inc., 45 South Main Street, Barre, VT 05641; 800/451-4349 (out of state), or 802/476-7221. — *M.W. and P.M.*

grinders are predominantly employed but the fine work is done using pneumatics.

Proper selection and testing of tools will also help you match the original mortar-joint condition and depth of joint. The right tool can also make a major difference in efficiency (see "Joint Preparation," previous page).

Repointing Techniques

Aside from matching the color, texture, and physical properties of the mortar, the application, tooling, and cleaning all must be done correctly to match the original work. This will often involve a study of the joint profile to determine the original — and present — tooling. If the original tool is no longer manufactured, this might require making a special tool.

The time allowed between tuck-pointing and tooling (dwell time) is critical. This will affect how deep the tool penetrates, and the mortar's viscosity and density. It also affects the texturing techniques used at the end (for example, brushing, burlapping, or water/air spraying).

Final cleaning must be done carefully and, again, after testing. Various materials react differently with a common chemical. Improper cleaning can lead to problems such as efflorescence, erosion, and burning of the mortar joint.

New Materials

The need to match the original materials exactly is the single most overlooked element of masonry restoration. With the range of materials available today — cement, lime, aggregate, dyes, brick, and stone — you can meet almost any job requirements. These elements, in the hands of a skilled individual, can produce work that's virtually impossible to tell apart from the original.

By Michael J. Watson, owner of Green Mountain Restoration Company in Shaftsbury, Vt., and by Philip C. Marshall, an architectural masonry conservator and an associate professor in the historic preservation program at Roger Williams University's School of Architecture in Bristol, R.I. Photos by Philip C. Marshall.

CAULKING MASONRY JOINTS

When it's done skillfully, caulking — or joint sealing — is almost invisible on a masonry exterior. But when it's botched, it can create a real eyesore. Worse, a poor caulking job can allow water into a building — with resultant damage, callbacks, lost time and money, and poor customer relations.

Masonry joint sealants are called for in three situations: in an expansion or control joint, in a joint between dissimilar materials, and at the perimeter of an opening in the masonry surface (Figure 11).

For the small general contractor, a single-family home or remodeling job that involves exterior masonry probably won't require enough caulking and sealing to make it worth hiring a specialty sub. But any joints, such as window and door perimeters or seams where brick meets wood siding, should be correctly sealed against water penetration. At least one person on your crew should understand the fundamentals of caulking.

While face brick is probably the most common masonry finish the caulker encounters, the same principles and similar procedures will apply for sealing joints in other materials — block, precast concrete, stone, stucco, and EIFS (exterior insulation and finish systems).

Size and Shape

A very tight joint — say, a joint less than 1/4 inch wide — is fairly easy to caulk, especially if it's a right-angle joint. This is usually the case with a window in a masonry opening. You are simply gunning the sealant and tooling it into a corner. The two perpendicular surfaces will guide the tip of your gun and your finishing tool.

However, because tight tolerances are hard to achieve in masonry work, you will typically encounter joints that are 1/2 inch wide or greater. And because a control or expansion joint needs to be fairly wide in order to tolerate the expansion, contraction, and movement in the masonry wall, it's not uncommon to come up against joints 3/4 inch, 1 inch, or even 1 1/2 inches wide. It's a real challenge to make a larger joint look good and provide a good seal.

The design of details should take joint sealants into account. If two dissimilar materials meet, there needs to be enough length of parallel return inside the joint so that backer rod will stay in place (more on backer rod below) and so that the joint sealant will have sufficient bonding surface.

Joint Prep

To achieve proper bonding on the two sides of the joint, some surface preparation may be necessary. Joint surfaces should be dry, sound, and free of dust, dirt, and loose or foreign material. Be prepared to scrape, chip, and dust the inside of the joint or even blow it out with compressed air. Depending on the conditions and the manufacturer's instructions, you may have to clean the joint with solvent or apply a primer.

If you have the unenviable job of recaulking an older building, you will need to check with the sealant manufacturer for special procedures to thoroughly cut out the old caulk. Old caulk can be pretty stubborn stuff, so you may need a special saw and a machine grinder. You also might have to prime every surface to be sealed.

Joint Sealants

The joint sealants that are most often specified for construction work are polyurethanes, silicones, and polysulfides. Silicones usually come in tubes. Polyurethanes and polysulfides can come packaged in tubes or in bulk. All joint sealants should be finished with a steel tool.

If you're a beginning caulker, tube caulk is much easier to work with. Keep in mind, though, that masonry caulking can use up a large number of tubes. For a $1/4$-inch or $3/4$-inch joint you may only get about 10 feet per 10.5-ounce tube. Also, tube sealants are air-cured and can take a week or longer to cure.

Bulk sealants are mixed with an activator before application, so they are chemically cured and can cure in a day or two. To work with bulk materials, you'll need a bulk gun, a large drill (at least $1/2$ inch), and a special mixing paddle (Figure 12). Once you get it down, you can do a lot more caulking and save money on materials using bulk sealant. But you'll have a messier job and more cleanup, and you'll have to work with some unpleasant solvents.

Joint sealants come in a variety of standard colors. It's even possible to have the factory make up custom colors. Color decisions should be made well ahead of time, as some colors are hard to get and have to be special-ordered.

For a light-colored surface, I like a lighter sealant color; a darker surface calls for a still darker sealant color. For example, on a regular reddish brown brick wall, I often use a somewhat darker "Redwood Tan" sealant color to good effect. On a light gray block wall, a lighter "Off-White" looks good.

With this kind of scheme, the caulk line doesn't stand out so much.

Backer Rod

Backer rod is made out of foam and looks like long strings of spaghetti. It comes in sizes as thin as $1/4$ inch and as thick as 2 inches and up. If you choose backer rod that's just a little larger than the joint you have to caulk, you can insert it under a slight compression so it will stay in place and allow you to control the depth of the sealant.

The main purpose of backer rod is to keep sealant off the back of the joint, thus preventing back-bonding, or three-sided bonding. To properly expand and compress, the joint sealant should be bonded to only two sides of the joint. If the joint is too shallow to fit backer rod, you can apply bond-breaker tape to the back of the joint to prevent back-bond-

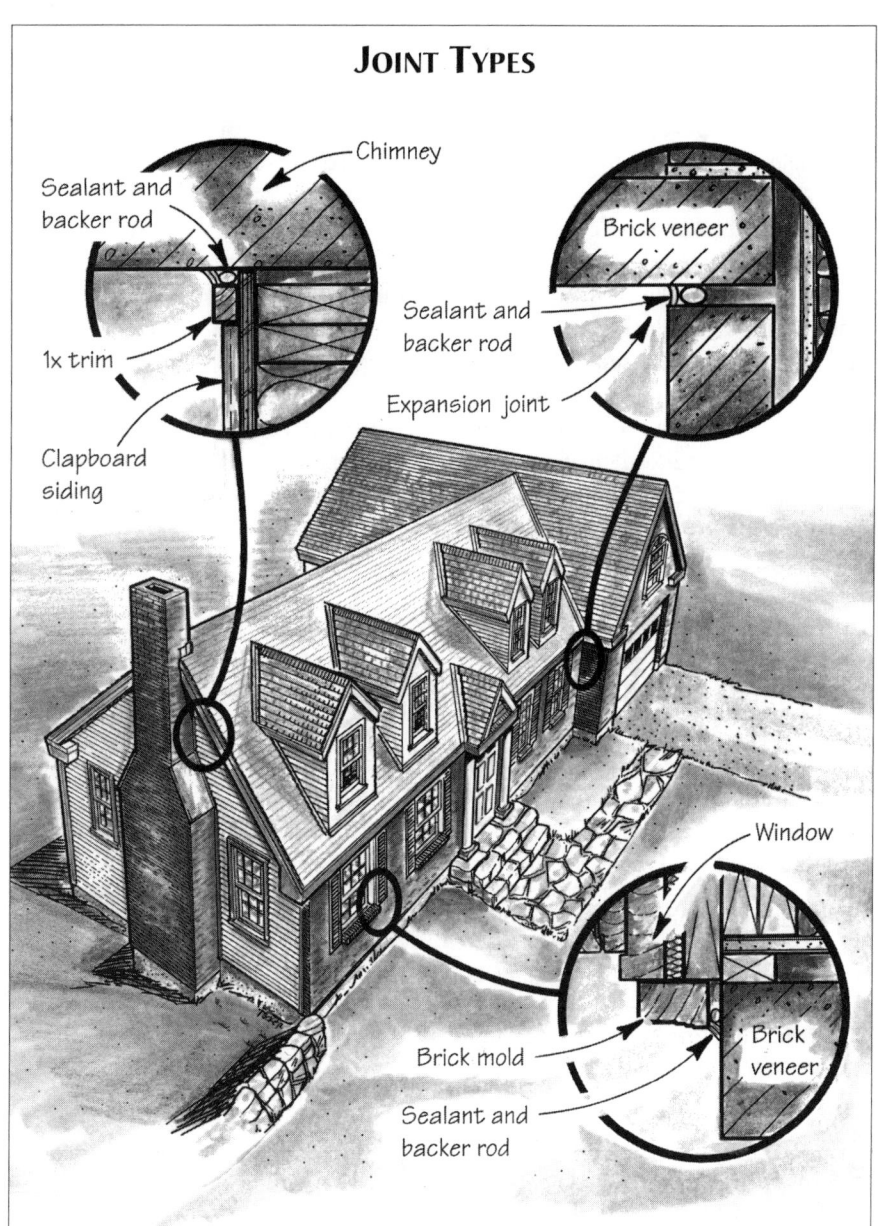

Figure 11. To create longlasting joints in masonry, use the tools and materials found in commercial work, such as backer rod and polyurethane, silicone, or polysulfide sealants. Three typical joint types found in residential work are shown.

Figure 12. Two-part bulk sealants have to be mixed with a drill and paddle (left). Using a bulk caulking gun (center and right) allows you to do high-volume caulking more cost-effectively, but is messy.

ing. Bond-breaker tape comes on a roll and looks like cellophane tape.

You can buy backer rod from joint sealant suppliers. Backer rod comes in open cell and closed cell form. Open cell compresses more and is easier to work with. However, some architects don't like it because it's like a sponge and can absorb water, while closed-cell backer rod is impervious to water.

Whichever type you're using, push the backer rod into the joint gently, using a blunt tool that won't pierce or tear it (Figure 13). A piece of wood shingle makes a good backer rod tool.

Applying Joint Sealants

Joint sealants have both a functional and an aesthetic purpose. In sealing a joint, you are trying to provide a seal against penetration by

water and air, and you are applying a finish detail. The aesthetic aspect is affected mostly by your tooling method, but several factors will affect the water-tightness of a joint.

In sealing joints, don't think of yourself as just filling a crack. Be aware that you are providing a flexible seal between the surfaces of two independent building components, which move and shift in relation to

---

Caulking Tips

Good caulking requires a great deal of skill and a certain amount of artistry. I've found that not just anyone can be trained to do caulking. You need aesthetic sense, patience, an eye for detail, and a real concern for the integrity and appearance of the finished product.

Here are some little tricks that might help improve your sealant work.

Tube caulking. Cut the nozzle of your tube at an angle and slightly smaller than the size of the joint. If the joint size varies, have two or three tubes going at the same time, each with the nozzle cut at a different size.

Cold weather. Keep your material warm. You can even buy an electric heat chest to keep your tubes or bucket in. Use gloves with the fin-

gers cut off to keep your dexterity.

Steel tooling. Use long, steady strokes. Attempt to tool every run only once rather than dabbing at it repeatedly. Rather than tooling towards your previous work (as if you were painting), pull away from the last section you tooled. Press the sealant firmly, so that it fills the joint and bonds to the sides.

Spatula. Provide yourself with a selection of various sizes. For any given run, choose a spatula slightly smaller than the width of the joint.

Keeping your tool clean. At the beginning of your work day, take a newspaper and rip it into pieces about 4x4 inches. Use these pieces to keep your tool clean.

Tools. Wear a tool belt or nail apron to carry your various spatulas, scrapers, other tools, and your

pieces of newspaper. Don't use your favorite carpenter tool belt for caulking, as it will get pretty messy.

Sturdy caulking gun. Get a good sturdy caulking gun made for production work. Get a hook attachment so you can hang it on the staging or ladder. Use a gun with a release, so you can stop the flow of sealant quickly.

Backer rod. Rather than struggling to cram large backer rod into a small joint, keep a variety of sizes on hand for different sizes of joints.

Annoying details. When you're working on a section of a building, take note of things that weren't ready to be caulked the first time you went through. Have a plan for getting back to them later, especially if they are high up, hard to get to, and easily overlooked. — *A.B.*

Figure 13. Compressible foam backer rod fills the back of a joint and helps the caulk perform properly. Use a size slightly thicker than the crack and insert it gently with a blunt tool.

Figure 14. Caulk should be applied to a joint in a smooth, even bead. When applying tube caulk to a joint whose thickness varies, carry several tubes with various size openings.

Figure 15. To properly finish a joint, smooth it in a continuous motion with a steel caulking tool or spatula. The author sometimes custom-fabricates a tool from a wooden tongue depressor.

one another. The dimensions of that seal must be carefully controlled. It can't be just a thin skin, but neither can it be a thick gob.

If your joint sealant is not applied properly, it will not expand and compress with the movement of the joint. Instead, it may split or rip away from one of the two joint surfaces.

Most polyurethane joint sealants are designed to tolerate up to 40% extension and 25% compression. However, they will not achieve that degree of movement if the joint is too deep. For example, for a joint 1/2 inch to 2 inches wide, one sealant manufacturer requires that the joint depth be no more than 1/2 inch.

When gunning sealant into the joint, try to achieve a smooth, even flow (Figure 14). Don't try to just zip down a skin. Fill — but don't overfill — the joint, placing sufficient sealant to achieve proper joint depth.

Tooling

Correct tooling is critical to creating a sealant joint that's tight and looks good (Figure 15). The best tool is a steel spatula or sculptor's tool that is slightly smaller than the width of the joint. Try to achieve a smooth, even appearance, without squeeze-out on the sides. Good tooling takes a lot of practice.

For special circumstances, I have on occasion made a custom-sized wooden tool by whittling down a tongue depressor. I have also seen plastic joint tools. Unless the joint is very small, don't try to tool with your finger. It slows you down and makes a mess. Also, manufacturers' instructions usually discourage using water or solvent to tool a joint.

Planning a Caulking Job

On the surface, caulking can seem pretty simple. It's rarely on the "critical path" of a project plan. However, one key aspect of joint sealing guarantees complications: Often, the sealant is being used to treat the joint between two dissimilar materials, and these materials are often installed by different trades and at different times.

If the caulking work is to be done off the staging, make sure that it will be left up long enough. Because staging is often rented, there's a lot of pressure to get it off the job quickly.

Don't forget conditions on the ground. How steep is the grade — not the finished grade, but the grade as it will be when you're doing the caulking? Will it be safe for a ladder? Will a boom lift be able to operate

in the area? Keep in mind that a boom lift won't work if the grade is too steep.

Identify the scope of work. What gets caulked and what doesn't? Will one party be responsible for all caulking on the job? Or will each trade be responsible for caulking its own work? (This is a strategy that often yields poor results, in my experience.)

Weather and temperature affect caulking work. You can't caulk a wet surface, so allow flexibility in the schedule. And, although you can caulk in cold weather (check the manufacturer's limitations), sometimes ice or frost will collect in a joint and can be very hard to detect.

The application of joint sealants is a little-known construction specialty. But it can make a big difference in the integrity and life span of a masonry building. If you take care to apply the materials properly and give attention to detail, this is a trade that can add to your profits — and give the satisfaction that comes with doing fine work.

By Al Bredenberg, of Cornwall, Conn., a former contractor who writes frequently on construction topics. Photos by Carolyn Bates.

LEAK-PROOF CHIMNEY FLASHING

What is a flashing job required to do? The obvious requirement is to seal the opening around the chimney where it goes through the roof. Second, the flashing should provide a sliding connection that will allow the building to move independently of the chimney. The third, not so obvious requirement is to prevent the transfer of water, absorbed by the masonry above the roof, into the masonry below the roof. The flashing should meet these requirements for the life of the chimney.

Most of the masons I've seen lately prefer to use lead flashing in their masonry. Lead is the easiest metal to work, which makes up for its higher cost over aluminum and galvanized metal in time saved. Copper is the most expensive flashing, but it will probably last longer than lead. Since it too is difficult to form, copper flashing has to be formed in a metal shop. This shop work adds to the cost, so you usually see copper only on more expensive homes where it is specified by the architect.

On the average home, the mason sticks the ends of the lead an inch or so into the mortar joint and leaves it hanging down around the chimney. The roofers arrive, shingle up to the chimney, fold the flashing down between shingle courses, and nail the ends to the roof. If they are more conscientious than usual, they may slap some tar on the end of the flashing before they lay the next shingle.

The above scenario creates a number of problems. All wooden structures shrink in height as they age and shift slightly with seasonal changes. The chimney, however, does not move. The shifting and shrinkage of the frame structure stresses the flashing, causing the ends of the shingles to lift, breaking the tar seal and eventually tearing the flashing. Sooner or later, but usually within the first ten years, leaks will begin around the chimney. Also, since the problem of water transfer through the masonry units was not addressed

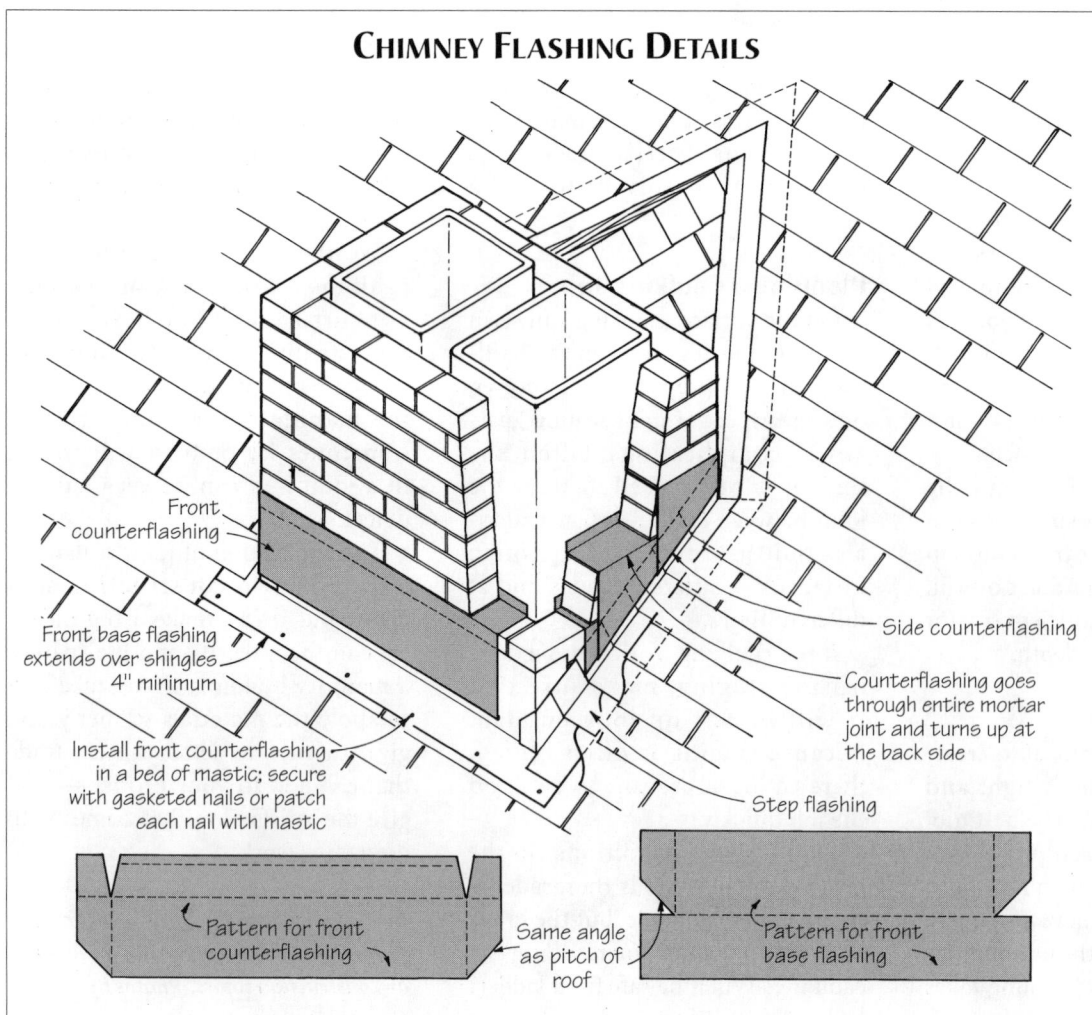

CHIMNEY FLASHING DETAILS

Front counterflashing

Front base flashing extends over shingles 4" minimum

Install front counterflashing in a bed of mastic; secure with gasketed nails or patch each nail with mastic

Pattern for front counterflashing

Same angle as pitch of roof

Side counterflashing

Counterflashing goes through entire mortar joint and turns up at the back side

Step flashing

Pattern for front base flashing

Figure 16. When flashing a chimney, never attach a flashing to both the chimney and the roof. The base flashings are attached to the roof only, the counterflashings to the chimney only. This creates a slip membrane, allowing the house to move independently of the chimney.

at all, the chimney begins transferring moisture into the house with the first good rain. This is because masonry units, whether brick, block, or stone, are not waterproof or even water-resistant; they can transfer gallons of water into a house. Doing the job right in the beginning can save the builder the headache of trying to fix a "leak" that no amount of tarring or reflashing can solve.

Three Trades Involved

Flashing a chimney involves workers from three trades: Usually at least one, and sometimes all of them, does not do the job correctly.

The carpenter. A good flashing job begins with the carpenter who makes the opening in the roof. If you're the carpenter on a chimney job, you must find out, preferably from the mason, the exact dimensions of the chimney at the point where it exits the roof. Codes usually require that the framing for the opening be kept 2 inches away from the masonry. If the roof sheathing is extended into the opening 1 1/2 inches on all sides (leaving a hole 1 inch larger than the dimensions of the chimney) the mason can then drop plumb lines from the corners to position the chimney at its base. You must also make sure that the roof opening lines up with the openings for the chimney in any floors or ceilings below and that the opening size is corrected for the roof pitch. These things may seem obvious, but mistakes are common.

The next step is to build the cricket. All chimneys, even small ones, should have a cricket unless they go through the roof directly at the ridge. The cricket should be no wider than the up-roof dimension of the chimney and should be constructed like the roof of a small dormer, with both sides the same pitch as the main roof. If the chimney is close to the ridge, the pitch of the sides may have to be less than the roof pitch to avoid extending the cricket above the ridge.

Tack the completed cricket to the roof in its intended location. (The mason may want to move it to facilitate his work, but he will need the completed cricket to correctly position the flashing in the masonry.)

The mason. Preventing the water transfer problem mentioned above is the responsibility of the mason. If you are the mason building the chimney, you may have to make a minor, but very important, change in the way you place the flashing pieces in the chimney. Instead of sticking them into the mortar joints only an inch or so, you must place the flashing so it passes completely through the mortar joint and turns up on the back of the masonry unit. This does not weaken the chimney because the flashing goes in at different levels of mortar joints as it follows the pitch of the roof. If you place the flashing this way, there will be no transfer of water into the house through the masonry units.

The roofer. The roofer's part of the job requires the most attention. If you are roofing around a chimney, a critical point to keep in mind is that you must *never* fasten any flashing connected to the chimney to the roof. The job goes as follows:

• On the down-roof side, or front, of the chimney, nail a continuous piece of flashing over the last shingle course and bend it up against the chimney to a height of about 3 inches. Take care to form this front flashing so that the first step flashing on each side can bend around it to prevent water from being funnelled into the building at this point (Figure 16). You may want to try Flash-Rite Corner Shingles (P.O. Box 23, Grabill, IN 46741; 219/627-3086) to give added protection at the corners. These are inexpensive prebent corner flashings, made of corrugated aluminum, that can be shaped to match your roof pitch (Figure 17).

• Next, beginning at the bottom and working up, install the step flashings where the end of each shingle course abuts the chimney.

• When you reach the up-roof side, or back, of the chimney, nail the cricket in place and shingle it as if it were a dormer roof, again using step flashings where the shingle courses abut the back of the chimney (Figure 18). It is usually easier to cover a small cricket with lead flashing rather than shingles. The step flashings may be lead, too, but on a large chimney it is easier

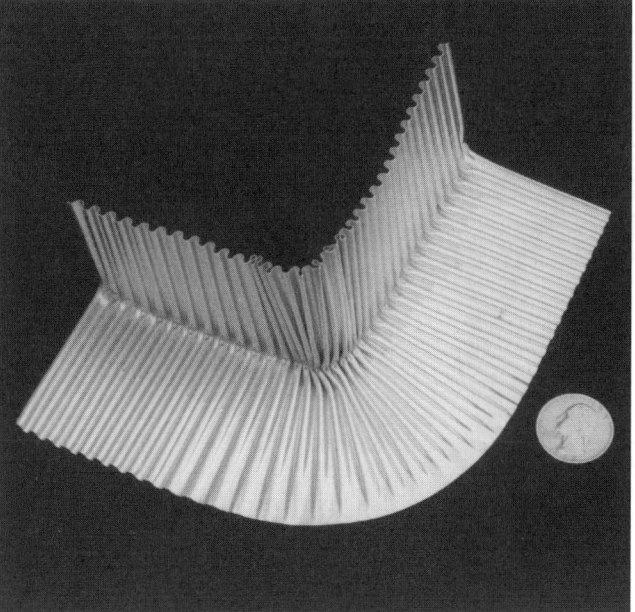

Figure 17. Install Flash-Rite corner shingles between base and counterflashings to protect the vulnerable spot at chimney corners. The corner shingles cost less than $2 each.

FLASHING THE CRICKET

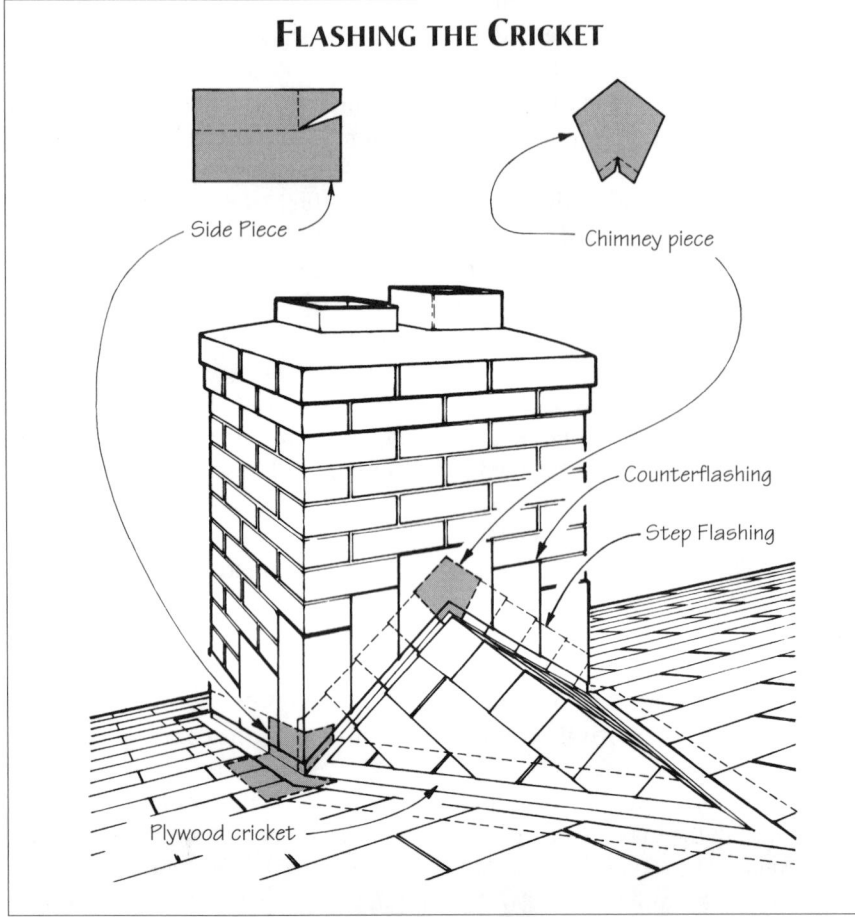

Side Piece

Chimney piece

Counterflashing

Step Flashing

Plywood cricket

Figure 18. You can build the cricket from plywood and cover it with shingles or metal flashing (for a small chimney). The joint at the cricket is step-flashed and counter flashed like the rest of the chimney.

and quicker to use standard 5x7-inch preformed aluminum step flashings.

• To complete the job, fold the flashings attached to the chimney down over the step flashings and cut the ends in line with and slightly above the bends in the step flashing. As you fold down each piece, cement it to the previous piece at the vertical joint, using clear silicone caulk for mastic. The caulk will prevent a high wind from lifting the flashings and allowing water in. Also be careful not to cement the step flashings to the chimney or the counterflashing to the step flashing. You should not need mastic anywhere else.

When the flashing job is done this way it will last many decades and the builder will have no call-backs. Also, when the time comes to reroof, it is easy to remove the old shingles and install new ones, reusing the flashing embedded in the mortar.

By Peter Scripture, a builder of 30 years who specializes in building, repairing, lining, and cleaning chimneys.

RETROFIT CHIMNEY FLASHING

To prepare an existing chimney for counterflashing, a mason cuts a 1¹/4-inch groove in the mortar joints using a gas-powered concrete saw.

Many contractors make the mistake of fastening the counterflashing to the side of the chimney, using masonry screws to secure the flashing to the side of the chimney, then applying a bead of caulk at the top edge of the flashing (Figure 19). As daily temperature changes cause the flashing to expand and contract, the adhesive bond of the caulk joint is constantly stressed. This type of flashing detail will fail — sometimes in less than a year. Roofing cement doesn't last any longer.

Properly installed counterflashing is "let in" to a groove in the chimney and overlaps the upturned

sides of the base flashing. No fasteners are required. I've used these methods for both aluminum and copper flashing.

If you're working on an existing chimney, you've got no choice but to get out your goggles and dust mask and saw the joints in the chimney. You can use a circular saw equipped with a masonry blade, a heavy-duty concrete saw, or a hand-held grinder equipped with a diamond blade. The groove should be 1¹/4 inches deep and the width of a saw kerf (Figure 20). Make sure you do your cutting before the new shingles are installed. Otherwise, you'll be cleaning masonry dust off the newly installed

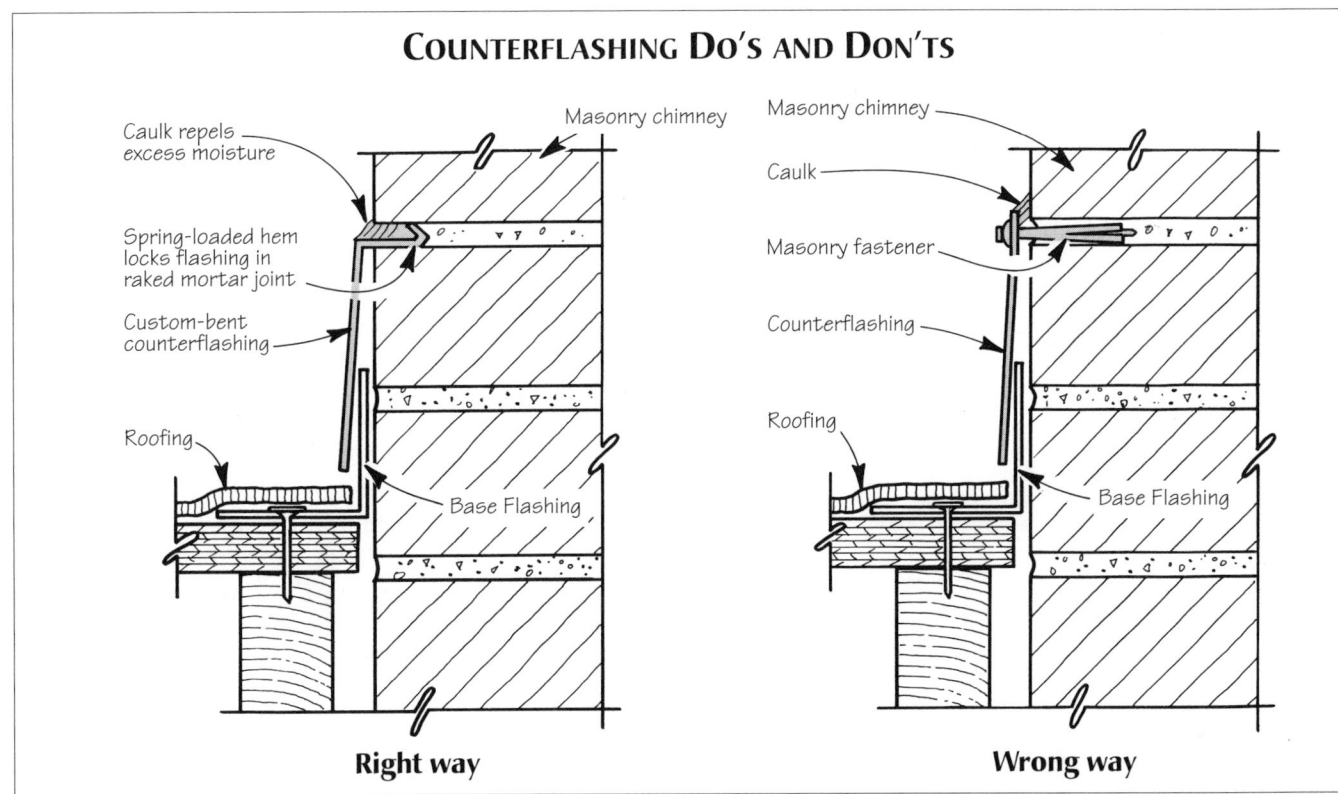

COUNTERFLASHING DO'S AND DON'TS

Right way

Caulk repels excess moisture

Spring-loaded hem locks flashing in raked mortar joint

Custom-bent counterflashing

Roofing

Masonry chimney

Base Flashing

Wrong way

Masonry chimney

Caulk

Masonry fastener

Counterflashing

Roofing

Base Flashing

Figure 19. The proper way to counterflash a chimney is to insert the counterflashing into a raked joint (at left). A small bend in the horizontal leg of the flashing ensures that no water can run behind the flashing. Caulk provides a secondary line of defense against moisture intrusion. Flashing fastened directly to the face of the chimney relies entirely on caulk to maintain a watertight joint (at right); in time, the caulk will fail, allowing water to penetrate the house.

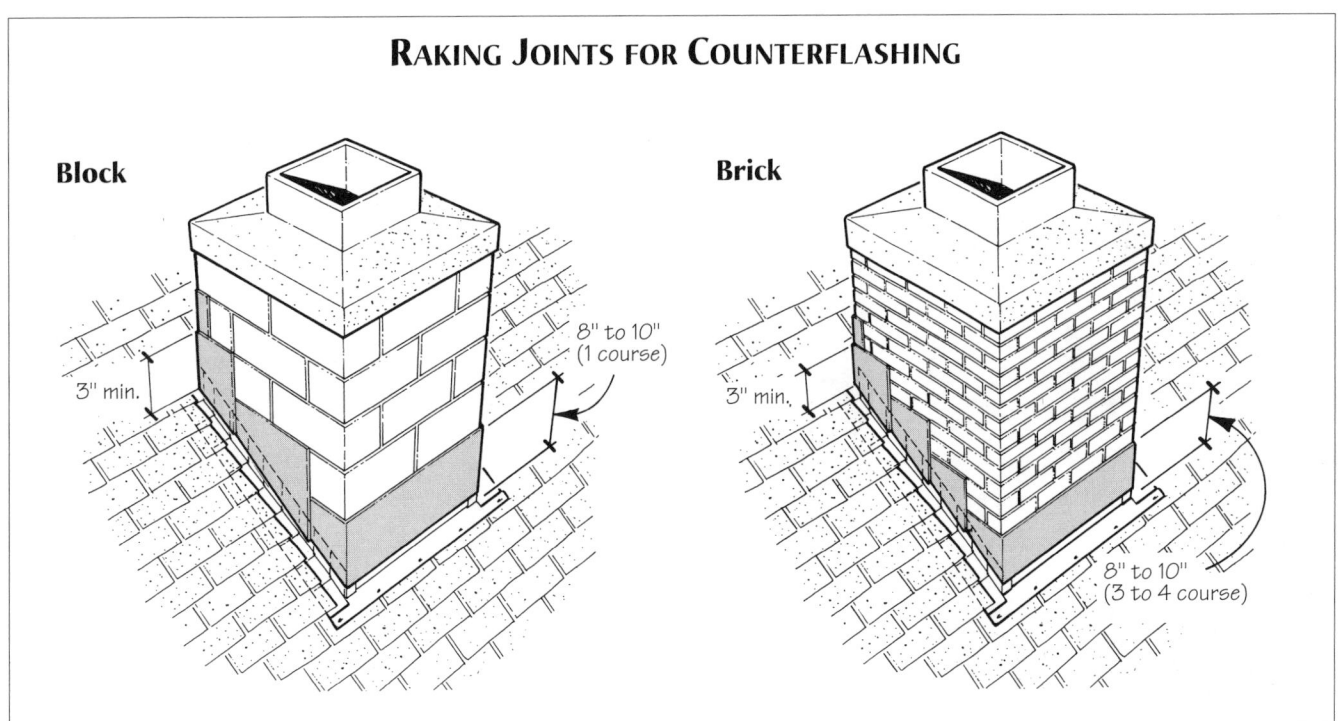

RAKING JOINTS FOR COUNTERFLASHING

Block

8" to 10" (1 course)

3" min.

Brick

3" min.

8" to 10" (3 to 4 course)

Figure 20. Rake the mortar joints to leave a 1¹/₄-inch-deep groove for the counterflashing. On the down-slope side of the chimney, choose a joint that is 8 to 10 inches above the roof deck (one course for block chimneys; three to four courses for brick). Rake the joint along the side of the chimney until the joint is about 3 inches above the roof deck.

Figure 21. The author cuts the upper and lower pieces of counterflashing from painted-aluminum coil stock (.019 inches thick). The tapered cuts match the roof pitch; layout lines mark the folds at the chimney corners.

THREE-STEP LOCKING BEND

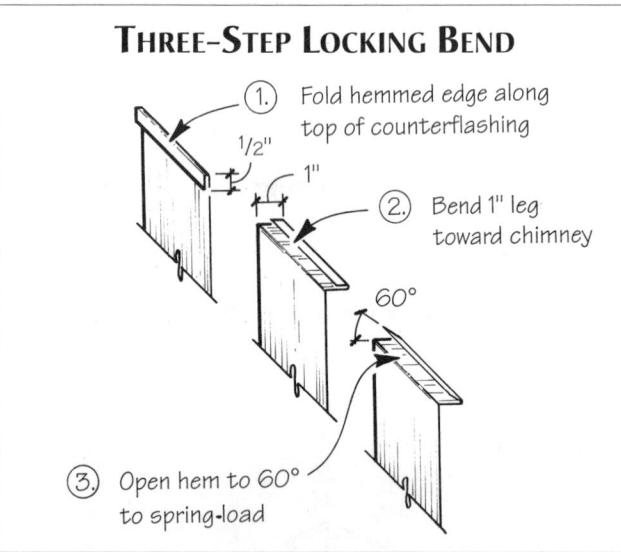

1. Fold hemmed edge along top of counterflashing

1/2"   1"

2. Bend 1" leg toward chimney

60°

3. Open hem to 60° to spring-load

Figure 22. First, make two simple bends along the top edge of the counterflashing, then pry open the hem to "spring-load" it: The V-shape will form a strong mechanical "lock" in the raked joint.

roof — a tough chore when working with dark-colored shingles.

Custom Counterflashing

For counterflashing, I like to use painted aluminum coil stock (.019 inches thick). If you have access to a break, forming the metal will be easier, but I've shaped flashing for more than one chimney using a 2x6 and a brick hammer.

To prepare the flashing, follow these steps:

• *Lay out the dimensions on the flashing stock and cut to size* before making any bends (Figure 21). Be sure to mark the fold lines where the counterflashing will turn the corner of the chimney.

• *Fold a 1/2-inch hem, then a 1-inch leg,* along the top edge of the counterflashing (Figure 22). Cut away a pie-shaped piece where the flashing must wrap around a corner of the chimney (Figure 23).

• *Pry open the hem to "spring-load" it.* This creates both a water stop and a mechanical "lock" that holds the flashing in place. Test-fit the flashing before opening the hem; removing the flashing once it's locked in place can be difficult.

Before inserting the counterflashing, make sure the groove is free of debris, and is cut or raked out at least 1/4 inch deeper then the length of the angled leg. Then insert the V-shaped edge formed by the leg and the open hem into the groove (Figure 24) and seal the joint with caulk. I use Sikaflex-1a, a high-quality one-component polyurethane sealant available from Resource Conservation Technology (2633 N. Calvert St., Baltimore, MD 21218; 410/366-1146). It's gummy stuff, but forms a tenacious bond with masonry. Since the joint is watertight, the caulk serves to keep out excess moisture and wind-driven rain.

By Tom Brewer, a roofing contractor from northeast Pennsylvania.

Figure 23. The author cuts pie-shaped pieces in the folded hem so that the counterflashing can be bent around the chimney corner.

Figure 24. In this mock-up, the V-shaped leg of both the upper and lower pieces of counterflashing is locked into the joint between chimney blocks. A bead of caulk in the joint will keep out excess water and wind-driven rain.

PATCHING STUCCO

Stucco, when applied correctly in the first place, will not one day decide to fail of its own volition. Still, it's likely that all stucco homes will eventually require patching for one reason or another, whether to cover holes bored by blown insulation installers, or to repair heavy-handed demolition work done by carpenters adding onto the house.

The primary aim when patching stucco is to restore the integrity of the exterior cladding system — but that's the easy part. The challenge is to have the patch blend in well, rather than stick out like a sore thumb. It's a rare situation where you can make the patch truly invisible.

Novice attempts by homeowners or handymen to patch stucco are not only ugly to look at, but often compromise the structure's weather-resistance. In my work, I've seen patches done with everything from spackle and paint to Thorite, which has a compressive strength approaching that of stainless steel. I've seen cracks around windows filled in with what must have been dozens of tubes of caulk. These "bubblegum patches" look abysmal and have to be removed for a professional job to be done.

What follows is a description of how to patch the stucco in a wall where a window or door has been removed.

Preparing The Substrate

After adding the necessary studs, install new sheathing flush with the plane of the old sheathing. Carefully remove a swath of the existing stucco around the infill area, leaving at least 6 inches of the existing wire and paper intact. Saw cuts are not encouraged because they cut the wire, as well as leave a sharp edge that is difficult to transi-

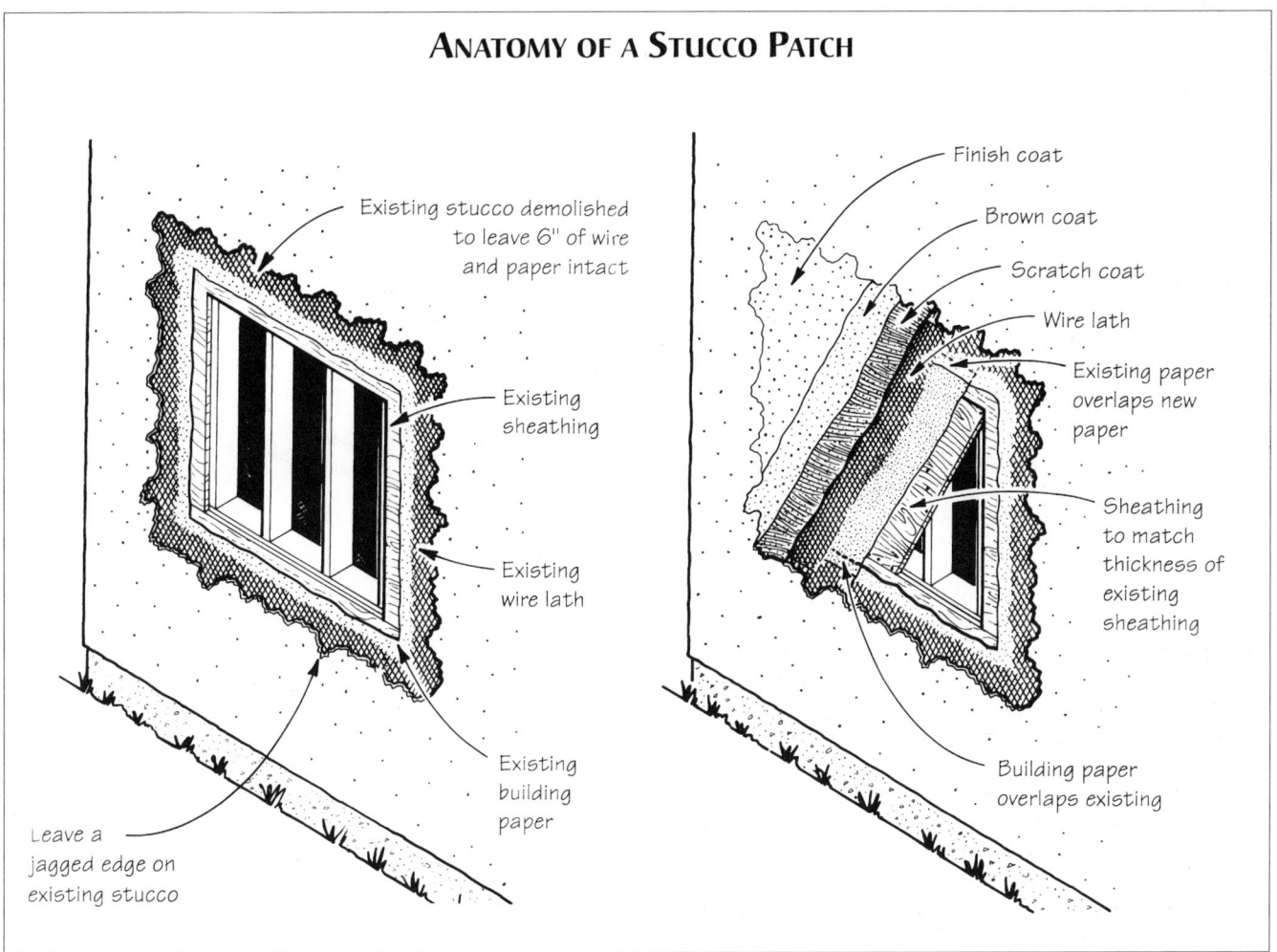

ANATOMY OF A STUCCO PATCH

Existing stucco demolished to leave 6" of wire and paper intact

Existing sheathing

Existing wire lath

Leave a jagged edge on existing stucco

Existing building paper

Finish coat

Brown coat

Scratch coat

Wire lath

Existing paper overlaps new paper

Sheathing to match thickness of existing sheathing

Building paper overlaps existing

Figure 25. When patching stucco, leave at least 6 inches of the existing lath and building paper exposed around the edge of the patch (left). The existing stucco should have a jagged edge, to create a less noticeable transition to the new stucco. Match the thickness of the existing sheathing (right), and make sure to lap the new building paper correctly — this guarantees a waterproof patch.

tion into. A jagged stucco edge is best (Figure 25).

Building paper. Next, cut a piece of asphaltic sheathing paper — Class D or better — that's slightly larger than the patch area. Carefully slip it behind the existing paper by at least one inch at the top and sides, and let it extend over the old paper at the bottom of the patched area. Remember that this paper protects the wall from the weather; lap it accordingly. Where the existing paper edges are destroyed, you can use duct tape to seal old to new. All stucco patches develop hairline shrinkage cracks around the perimeter, so great pains should be taken to ensure the paper is lapped adequately.

Lath. Cut the lath to completely fill the area to be patched. Remember that stucco requires a means of attachment to stay in place, and the grip the scratch coat gets on the lath is critical to a durable patch job. Use staples or galvanized roofing nails of sufficient length to get a good "bite" into the plywood or OSB sheathing. If you're installing the lath over foam sheathing, use longer nails and make sure you hit the studs.

The Mix

I can speak only for our company, but here in central Ohio, we use white waterproof cement, lime, bagged silica sand, and water. For our finish, we add iron-oxide pigment to achieve colors. We use bagged silica to ensure that there are no iron particles mixed in (from being loaded by a front loader which has been parked in the rain for three days), or rivets and nail heads found

---

FILLING STUCCO CRACKS

When asked to patch cracks in stucco, I often advise the homeowner to do the work himself using caulk, not stucco.

Houses are built primarily of wood. Wood is subject to expansion, contraction, racking, shifting, etc. The bulk of this movement occurs during the first couple of years after construction, as the house attempts to reach some kind of equilibrium.

Cement is intolerant of movement, which results in cracks. These cracks, ranging from hairline to 3/16 inch wide, are usually cosmetic only. If the building paper has been installed correctly, the house is protected from water damage.

If stucco is used to fill these cracks, not only will you be left with an expensive paint job, but the material will most likely crumble out as the building continues to shift.

For cracks 1/16 to 3/16 inch wide (leave hairline cracks alone), filling the crack with a caulk that matches the color of the wall is the best solution. Ohio Sealants Inc. (7405 Production Dr., Mentor, OH 44060; 216/255-8900), among others, makes a surprisingly wide palette of caulking colors. Have the homeowner determine which color most closely matches their stucco. Don't use silicone-based caulk, which will not hold paint.

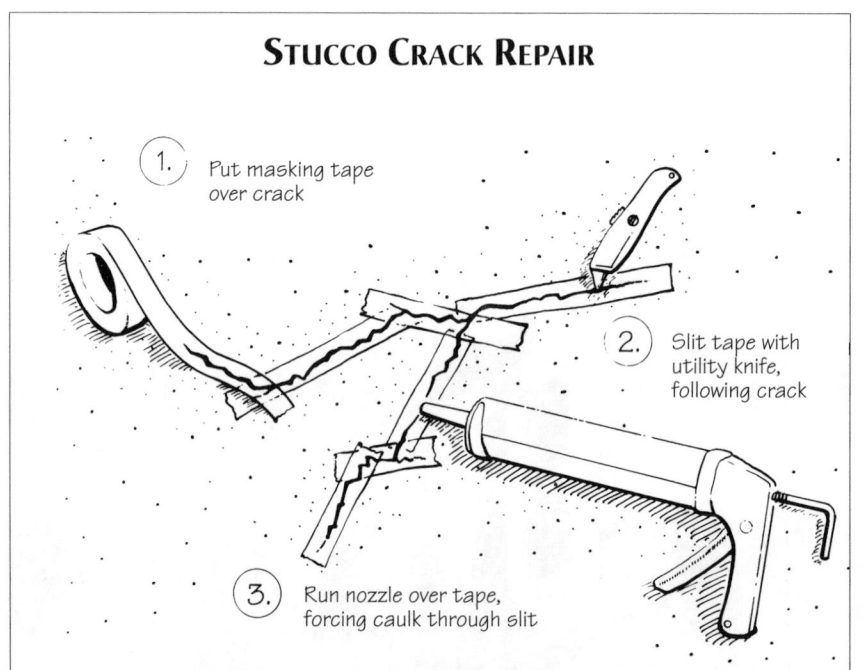

STUCCO CRACK REPAIR

1. Put masking tape over crack

2. Slit tape with utility knife, following crack

3. Run nozzle over tape, forcing caulk through slit

To fill a stucco crack with color-matching caulk, first cover the crack with masking tape, then slit the tape with a utility knife. Apply the caulk through the slit and remove the tape before the caulk sets up.

Don't open up or expand the width of the crack. Place masking tape over the length of the crack, then use a utility knife or razor blade to slit the tape, following the crack. Apply the caulk by running the nozzle over the slit, forcing the caulk through the tape into the crack. Finally, strip the tape before the caulk sets up. This approach keeps most of the caulk where you want it.

We've had good results with this technique. It makes a successful seal because the inherent flexibility of the caulk is able to tolerate later movement of the building. The customers make the decision on color, and their investment is minimal. They end up thinking we're heroes for giving them good advice and helping them to save money. — *S.T.*

in the less expensive "yard sand" available locally. We use the more expensive pigments because they won't fade in a couple of years like the cheaper pigments.

The American Society of Testing and Materials (ASTM) has published guidelines on what mixtures to use for various applications. This is a generic menu that will perform well in most situations. They also offer specific direction on lathing and its attachment, control joint placement, and other aspects of stucco work. This advice — however accurate or well intentioned — is routinely overridden at the field level because local contractors know what works best in their area. Stucco work routinely performed on the West Coast, for instance, has to stand up to seismic activity and therefore is different from work performed here in the Midwest.

The Scratch Coat

The first coat of "mud" is called the scratch coat, characterized by the marks left by the square-tooth trowel when it's applied. The scratch coat should be approximately $3/8$ inch thick. Its job is to get a grip on the wire.

The scratch coat is composed of cement, lime, and washed mason's sand. The thickness of the mud should just cover the wire. Stucco (like concrete) derives its strength as a result of two factors: the relative strength of the mix and its drying time. A wet mixture will result in excessive shrinkage (often called checking), and a dry mixture or a stucco patch completed in very hot weather will dry rapidly and create a weak bond. If it's hot or the wind is blowing, you should lightly mist the walls a few times to retard the drying and produce a stronger first coat. If possible, avoid doing your work in direct sunlight.

The Brown Coat

The following coat, which is called a brown coat for some

unknown reason, is applied the day after the scratch coat. The brown coat is actually gray in color, but is composed of slightly more sand than the scratch coat mixture and is therefore a more manageable but a slightly weaker mix. It should be applied $3/8$ inch thick, and if space permits, straight-edged and floated to ensure a flat plane held approximately $1/8$ inch below the finished surface of the adjacent stucco. A pointer trowel should be used to work the stucco into the cracks where the new stucco meets the existing. You can lay a 2x4 or other straight edge across the patch (resting it on the existing wall surface) to measure the required thickness of the finish coat.

It's important that the brown coat be both flat and uniformly depressed below the level of the surrounding finish coat. An uneven brown coat will lead to an inconsistent thickness in the finish coat that will cause some areas of the finish coat to dry before other areas. If this happens, the finish coat will have color variations and excessive cracking. The result, if the finish coat is applied with pigment, will be splotchy or "mottled." If the finish coat is to be painted, there might be cracks that won't paint over easily.

The Finish Coat

How successfully the finish coat matches the existing depends largely upon the quality of the brown coat. Matching texture, and in the case of a pigmented finish coat, matching the color, are very difficult to accomplish. The mixture, drying conditions, and application method of the existing finish coat are all unknown. In the field you're left to your best judgment, but you'll almost never produce a perfect match.

The final coat is usually floated on, except in the case of machine-textured finishes. Most small patch jobs don't warrant the cost of bring-

ing a hoppergun and compressor onto the job site, when a skilled worker can apply a machinelike texture with a hand-thrown dash.

Sometimes a paint brush dipped in water is used to smooth the transition between a patch and the existing stucco. This helps to eliminate the sharp line between the two different textures. When painted, the seam between the new and existing is less noticeable.

There are products available for the purpose of strengthening the bond between the new and used stucco. These syruplike, brightly colored materials are expensive, and in our experience have done little to prevent cracking between the new and existing stucco. If the substrate is installed correctly, this will help keep cracking to a minimum. If the substrate isn't installed correctly, the movement in the wall will not be held back by a stucco bonding agent.

One-Coat Stucco

When a stucco patch is small and the homeowner wants to avoid the labor costs of three trips, a one-coat stucco material can be used. One-coat stucco, like standard stucco, is applied over paper and wire. These mixes are quite a bit more expensive, so they aren't cost-effective on larger jobs. We use Parex's *Monocouche* and *Greycouche* products (Parex Inc., P.O. Box 189, Redan, GA 30074; 800/537-2739), which are applied up to a 7/8-inch thickness according to manufacturer's instructions. Monocouche is white cement-based, and may be tinted using the same iron oxides used for stucco. Less expensive is the Greycouche, which is gray in color and suitable for patchwork if you're confident the area will eventually receive paint.

Besides the advantage of the single trip application, this "just-add-water" one-coat stucco shrinks less than standard stucco. But adhere to the manufacturer's temperature warnings when using these products.

Painting Stucco

When faced with a large patch like a patio door infill in a two-story, 40-foot-long wall, you have a problem: If the existing wall is composed of pigmented stucco, chances are very high that both the color and texture of the new stucco will not match. Regrettably, this patch occurs at eye level. One solution might be to rebrown and refinish the entire wall plane, which will render the patch invisible, but the job then lurches from a 42-square-foot patch to a 720-square-foot job requiring scaffolding, a lot more cement, lime, sand, etc. Plus, you'll need a mixer instead of a wheelbarrow.

My recommendation is to paint. Painting stucco is not only possible, but often advantageous to assure uniformity of color. It focuses the stucco worker on the goal of tying together the texture and plane of the new and the existing, and it's very likely that the paint will make the wall uniform in color.

Here are three tips on painting stucco:
• Newly applied stucco should be allowed about 30 days to cure, depending on the weather conditions.
• Existing stucco surfaces should be power-washed and allowed to thoroughly dry before painting. Do not use a water blaster, as its excessive pressure can do severe damage to the stucco.
• Stucco should only be painted with acrylic-based paints with adequate vapor transmission characteristics, so as not to create new moisture-related problems within the house. Oil-based, rubber-based, and latex paints all have their places, but none of them were intended for exterior stucco.

Client Expectations

When writing a quote for stucco work involving patching, I typically use phrases like: "In spite of our best efforts, this area will likely appear patched," or "Due to weathering of adjacent stucco surfaces, precise color and texture matching may not be achievable." These phrases are not meant to serve as escape clauses to condone bad work, but rather to alert the homeowner or contractor to the realities of stucco patchwork. We do occasionally hit it right on the head and achieve a perfect color and texture match, but this is the exception, not the rule.

The man who does our patch work (jobs less than 100 square feet) has been with us for 17 years. His dad worked here for 40 years. He still "misses" hitting a perfect match in most cases. One way I convey to clients the difficulty of the task at hand is with a clothing analogy: Imagine cutting a 4-inch-square patch out of one of your favorite shirts and then sewing it back in place. While it's exactly the same fabric filling in the exact hole from which it was cut, it will still be apparent as a patch, and not part of the undisturbed cloth surrounding it. The same is true of stucco patching.

By Steve Thomas, general sales manager for Reitter Stucco, in Columbus, Ohio.

EIFS PERFORMANCE REVIEW

The use of exterior insulation finish systems (EIFS) has grown dramatically in recent years, in both commercial and residential markets, accounting for more than 200 million square feet of building exteriors in 1991. The systems, sometimes called "synthetic stucco," are economical and give designers a lot of flexibility with colors and architectural details (Figure 26). In addition, they provide good insulation without thermal gaps and greatly reduce air infiltration.

Of the two generic types of EIFS, polymer-based (PB) and polymer-modified (PM), the PB systems are by far the more commonly used in the U.S. today. PB systems, some-times called "soft-coat," are typically thin (approximately 1/8 inch total thickness), adhesively attached, and flexible, and they require few control joints. They cannot tolerate prolonged wetting.

PM systems, on the other hand, are typically greater than 1/4 inch in total thickness, mechanically attached, rigid, and insensitive to moisture, and they require frequent control joints, similar to cement stucco. Sometimes called "hard-coat," PM systems do offer several significant advantages:
• They are mechanically attached, so 15-pound felt or similar moisture protection can be placed over the sheathing. This prevents any water that enters the system from damaging the sheathing and studs.
• They have greater puncture and abrasion resistance and better tolerate abuse from traffic at grade.
• They are more resistant to damage from internal moisture.
• They use metal or vinyl casing beads, which provide a more durable substrate for sealants.

PB systems, however, are far more popular, primarily because they cost less, allow for greater design freedom (because fewer control joints are needed), and have been marketed more aggressively by manufacturers. In fact, PB systems account for approximately 80% of the current

EIFS market. Because of its wide use, we will address only the PB type of system below.

The HUD Experience

Unfortunately, the increased use of EIFS has been accompanied by an increase in problems and failed applications. The U.S. Department of Housing and Urban Development (HUD) owns a large number of buildings finished with EIFS that have required extensive repairs or total replacement within ten years of installation. This high rate of early failure has caused HUD to reevaluate the acceptability of EIFS for use on HUD-funded construction. In the past, HUD required little more than a 20-year warranty and compliance with manufacturer specifications. Because of the high failure rate, however, HUD is in the process of reviewing the material and may establish new criteria for EIF systems.

As part of an ongoing study being conducted with the coopera-

Figure 26. Soft-coat synthetic stucco gives designers a lot of flexibility with colors and architectural details.

Figure 27. Mesh that's exposed on the surface of the base coat is likely to get wet and lose tensile strength. Once weakened, it will not provide adequate impact resistance.

EIFS Lawsuits Leading to Change

In 1995 a number of lawsuits were filed in North Carolina and South Carolina against EIFS manufacturers. The class-action suits claim that the systems are inherently defective, primarily because they do not allow water to escape once it penetrates behind the exterior skin.

In theory, water can penetrate an EIFS either by entering through the exterior skin or around it at openings and where the EIFS abuts other materials. However, our review of over 200 homes that had the EIFS removed revealed that — especially in coastal areas — water is penetrating via abutting components, not through the skin. The main causes of water penetration we observed in the Carolinas are described below:

Lack of sealant at window openings. Over 50% of the dwellings,

even those at the ocean front, did not have any sealant between the edge of the EIFS and the window system. This was a major source of water penetration.

Roof/wall flashing. The flashing at the wall/roof intersection (step flashing) was, in most cases, installed so the flashing terminated behind the EIFS. Water that accumulated on the flashing was directed behind the protective skin of the EIFS. In some subdivisions, over 90% of the homes had this problem.

Window systems. We observed water penetration where window units were mulled together and where brick molds (locally manufactured) were used with wood windows. Water penetrated at center mullions, between the brick mold and sill, or between the brick mold and stile. Where

two-piece sills were used, water penetrated into the EIFS once the sills split.

Recommendations. The state of North Carolina now requires that EIFS used with wood-frame construction have sealants at window and door openings, a secondary water barrier, and a positive method for draining water to the exterior. Based upon our involvement with EIFS and wood-frame construction over many years, we recommend that a secondary moisture barrier, such as 15-lb. building paper or membrane flashing, be used at all window openings, and that proper window flashing be required for EIFS and all types of wall cladding when used with wood framing and moisture-sensitive sheathing. One model code agency is considering similar requirements. — R.K.

Figure 28. The sealant at this control joint failed within six months of installation, allowing water into the system. To prevent this, use a low-modulus sealant and apply it to the base coat, not the finish coat.

tion of HUD's Washington Office of Materials and Standards and the HUD area offices in Boston, Kansas City, and Pittsburgh, we reviewed a random selection of more than 30 buildings with EIFS exteriors, ranging from jobs under construction to buildings twelve years old. None of the buildings included in the study were known to have EIFS problems. The review included visual inspection, non-destructive moisture readings at random locations, and test cuts at a few buildings. The results to date strongly support

A BETTER EIFS

Despite the problems, we believe PB EIF systems can be modified to provide good durability and service life. The modified systems cost more than most current systems, yet still compare favorably with other exterior wall materials. The following requirements are, in our opinion, the minimum necessary to assure good durability, and they have been used successfully on a number of recent projects:

- The substrate should be masonry, concrete, or cement fiberboard. Gypsum sheathing has been a contributing factor in the failure of many applications. When water enters the system for whatever reason, it is absorbed by the sheathing, and when gypsum sheathing is kept moist (20% or more water by weight), the paper facing delaminates from the gypsum core, debonding the system. At approximately 30% moisture, the gypsum core deteriorates and wood studs can rot. These problems can occur with relatively small amounts of water penetration, minor cracking, and no water leakage into the building interior.

  One alternative is Georgia Pacific's Dens Glass (ASTM C1177). This product is significantly more water resistant than standard gypsum sheathing, although more testing and field experience are necessary to determine its long-term durability.

- The expanded polystyrene (EPS) insulation board must have good bead fusion to resist the passage of water when the surface is damaged. You can check for bead fusion by snapping a piece of board. At least 50% of the beads should break in two, rather than pull apart and remain whole.

- EPS board joints must not align with door and window openings and must be offset from sheathing joints (see illustration). Board joints aligned with openings are a

INSULATION BOARD LAYOUT AROUND WINDOWS

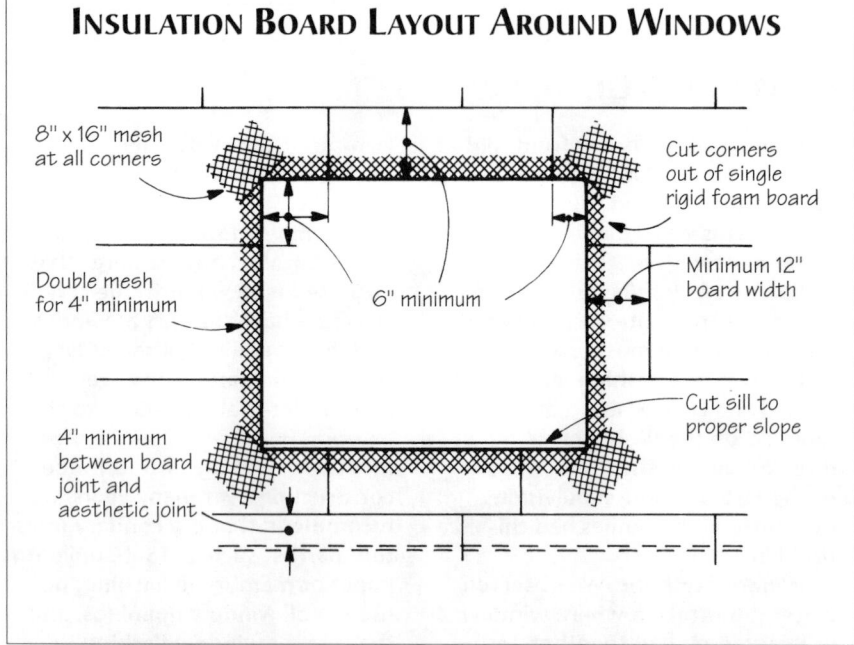

8" x 16" mesh at all corners

Cut corners out of single rigid foam board

Double mesh for 4" minimum

6" minimum

Minimum 12" board width

Cut sill to proper slope

4" minimum between board joint and aesthetic joint

Insulation board joints aligned with door and window openings are a common cause of cracks. To prevent problems, joints must be offset from the openings and the corners reinforced with diagonal mesh. In addition, decorative joints should not align with board joints or openings; board joints should not align with sheathing joints; and laps in the mesh should be offset from the edges of openings, grooves, and corners.

HUD's desire to improve the quality standards for EIFS materials and application.

Common Problems

The most common deficiencies found were caused by poor workmanship and were evident on the majority of projects reviewed.

Thin base coat. Applications with base coats thinner than the manufacturer's required thickness were very common.

Exposed mesh. Many jobs had exposed mesh at joint edges and at terminations (Figure 27). We observed mesh on the surface of the base coat on some jobs under construction, and we could see mesh patterns through the finish coat on a few jobs. These are signs of thin base coats and mesh that is not adequately embedded in the base coat.

Mesh that's not fully embedded is exposed to moisture and won't provide good impact resistance. Moisture alone can reduce the tensile strength of reinforcing mesh, and it is well known that moisture combined with alkalinity (from the cement) speeds the strength reduction of the mesh.

Sealant failure. The majority of projects, including some less than six months old, had some sealant failure. Failures at EIFS field joints were more common than at perimeter joints (Figure 28). The typical failure was a *cohesive* failure of the finish coat. This means that the sealant didn't pull away from the finish coat; rather, the finish coat itself pulled apart. This is because some acrylic finish coats

---

common cause of cracks. When V-grooves align with board joints at openings, cracking is very common.

- Decorative grooves must not align with EPS board joints or openings, and their use should be held to a minimum. Rounded grooves are preferable to V-grooves.
- The base coat should have no more than 33% cement by weight. Many U.S. products currently use 50% cement. The main problem is that the high alkalinity of the cementitious base coats weakens the fiberglass reinforcing mesh. Although mesh has an alkali-resistant coating, the quality and quantity of the coating is inconsistent, and the amount of coating on U.S. mesh is substantially less than on European mesh. In addition, base coats with higher amounts of cement are less flexible and can become brittle with age.
- The base coat should be applied in two layers with at least 24 hours between applications. This has several distinct advantages over a single application. In this system, the mesh is troweled onto the surface of the first layer, and the second application then fully covers the mesh. No mesh or mesh pattern is visible.

Because the polymer-modified base material is more "sticky" than traditional cement stucco, it is difficult to apply in thick layers. With a double-layer application, however, the typical installer can get adequate thickness and fully cover the mesh.

- The minimum base-coat thickness should be $3/32$ inch. This is the actual minimum allowed at any location, not an average or nominal thickness. Thinner base coats do not adequately protect the mesh from moisture and have inadequate impact resistance.
- No mesh or mesh pattern should be visible at any surface, including corners and joints. Corners and surfaces that will receive sealant are especially critical because thin base coats provide a weak substrate for sealants, and exposed mesh will wick moisture into the system. A third application of base material is often necessary to touch up corners and joints.
- Cementitious base coats must be primed before the finish is applied. The acrylic primers improve the water resistance of the base coat and provide a surface with uniform suction to receive the finish. Some newer non-cementitious base coats are being developed that may not require primer.
- Failed elastomeric sealant joints are a major cause of water entry in EIF systems. To prevent these failures, the sealant must be applied to the primed base coat, not to the finish coat, which can soften when wet. And because EIFS is a relatively weak substrate

for elastomeric sealants, you must choose a *low-modulus* sealant that maintains its low-modulus over the life of the sealant. (When a low-modulus sealant stretches, it exerts less stress on a joint.)

Ideally, the sealant should last as long as the system, because it is difficult to remove and replace sealant without damaging the thin layers. In general, silicone sealants are less affected by aging and cold temperatures than urethane sealants. Dow 790 Silicone Sealant is the recommended sealant for most EIFS applications, although its appearance may be an issue with some designers.

- Window sills, parapet tops, and similar sloped surfaces should be protected with metal flashing. EIFS is not an acceptable roofing material, even for very small "roofs." The manufacturers' requirements for a 1:2 pitch is not adequate to shed snow and prevent lengthy wetting. A minimum 1:1 (45-degree) pitch is preferred when it is not possible to properly flash the surface.

The only PB EIF systems currently marketed in the U.S. that meet all these criteria are Premium Cementitious System 3 and Premium Full Synthetic System 3 by Parex Inc. (Redan, Ga.). We have successfully used other systems, however, when they have been modified to meet our criteria. — *R. P. & R. K.*

Figure 29. V-grooves, added for decorative effect, should never line up with window or door openings. This one cracked, was recoated with the manufacturer's elastomeric coating, and cracked again within a year.

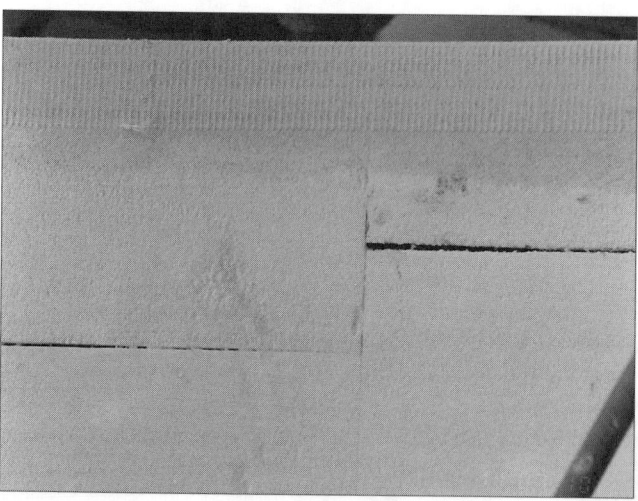

Figure 30. Gaps between EPS insulation boards are a common cause of cracks. To prevent problems, fill any cracks with insulation slivers.

soften when kept damp and therefore do not generally provide a durable surface for elastomeric sealants. Nevertheless, most EIFS and sealant manufacturers still either require or recommend sealants to be applied to the finish.

Cracking in V-grooves. V-grooves are sometimes added for decorative effects. Approximately one half of all projects with V-grooves had some cracking in the grooves sufficient to allow water penetration. Cracking is most common when the V-groove falls on an insulation board joint beneath (Figure 29).

Cracking at openings. Approximately one third of all projects had some cracking at the corners of windows and similar openings. These cracks are caused by stresses at the reentrant (inside) corners. Almost all projects with vertical V-grooves extending from window to window, in line with the jambs, had some cracks in these grooves, and many cracks were continuous the full height of the V-groove.

Cracking at board joints. More than 10% of all projects had some cracking not associated with openings or joints. These cracks mostly occur over the gaps between insulation boards (Figure 30) and grow worse as the reinforcing mesh loses tensile strength from exposure to moisture and alkalinity.

Workmanship Falls Short

We observed three projects while the EIFS was being applied. In one of these, mediocre workmanship resulted in gaps between insulation boards and poorly embedded mesh at sealant joints. A few V-grooves had already cracked before the job was completed.

On the second project, workmanship was poor, resulting in large gaps between boards, exposed mesh at joints, and a thin base coat. The third project showed very poor workmanship, resulting in a thin, brittle base coat, large areas of exposed mesh, inadequate board adhesion, and other serious violations of the manufacturer's standards.

On three other projects, prefabricated panels were adhesively applied to either precast concrete or gypsum sheathing. Two of these buildings had been occupied for less than six months and one for 18 months. The latter project had many failed sealant joints, V-groove cracking, exposed mesh at joints, a thin base coat, and water weeping out of the system in a few locations. The first two projects showed failed sealant joints, exposed mesh, a thin base coat, and V-groove cracking. Several panels had blown off the most recently completed project.

In summary, less than half of the buildings more than seven years old were in good condition, and none over two years old were without visible deficiencies.

This survey suggests that the high rate of EIFS failure on HUD-funded buildings is primarily due to improper application. It also suggests that improved standards for materials and application are critical if PB EIF systems are to provide a reasonable service life without extensive maintenance and early repair.

Gypsum Sheathing Vulnerable

Most of the cracks and sealant failures we saw in the survey were sufficient to allow water to enter the EIF system. From our earlier investigations of several hundred EIFS buildings, we know that such leaks can lead to water damage of the gypsum sheathing underneath (Figure 31). When wet, the sheathing is prone to deterioration and delamination. Water also tends to collect at horizontal terminations and joints that are "back-wrapped" with mesh. The water often collects well below the point of entry, and it can cause the gypsum sheathing to delaminate and the sealant joints to fail.

Because EIFS — as typically applied — often cracks and allows water penetration, we believe that EIFS should not be adhesively applied to gypsum sheathing (ASTM C79). The fact that the current systems continue to be adhesively applied to gypsum sheathing on high-rise buildings in locations exposed to high winds and heavy rains is hard to understand or justify. Projects with masonry, concrete, or cement fiberboard substrates are less vulnerable to water penetration.

Figure 31. Moderate wetting will cause the facing of gypsum sheathing to delaminate. With increased wetting, the core will deteriorate, as seen in this cut-away section.

Figure 32. Areas near walkways face greater wear and tear. Use high-impact mesh in these locations.

Application

For EIF systems to last, quality workmanship is critical. Good materials and details, alone, will not guarantee a durable finish. The work must be inspected during installation by those knowledgeable about EIFS. Unfortunately, such knowledge is not commonplace in the architectural and construction industry today, which results in a large number of EIFS applications failing to meet the manufacturers' minimum requirements. The major concerns during installation are:

- *Board application.* Provide good adhesion between the insulation board and substrate. Offset board joints from sheathing joints and door and window openings. Also, offset them from any decorative V-grooves. Fill any gaps larger than 1/16 inch between boards with insulation. Rasp all insulation surfaces to rough them up and remove weathered material before applying the finish.

- *Base coat.* Make the base coat at least 3/32 inch thick, and apply it in two layers. Use primer on all cementitious base coat surfaces.
- *Mesh.* Offset any laps in the mesh from edges of openings, grooves, and corners. Use diagonal mesh for reinforcing at door or window (reentrant) corners. Use a double layer of mesh, lapped at least 4 inches, at all outside and inside corners. Fully embed the mesh, leaving no mesh ends or mesh pattern visible. Use high-impact (heavyweight) mesh at all surfaces near grade or near balconies or walkways, where they will face additional wear and tear (Figure 32).
- *Sealant joints.* Provide smooth, straight, sound surfaces to receive sealants, with no mesh or mesh pattern visible. Allow adequate

joint width for the expected movement. Use primer on all surfaces to receive sealant. Apply sealant to the base coat only, never to the finish coat, and tool all sealant joints.

Properly detailed and applied, PB EIFS can provide durable, cost-effective exterior walls with a service life of 20 to 30 years. Improperly designed and applied systems, on the other hand, will have a greatly reduced useful life, and many will require extensive repairs or early replacement.

By Richard Piper and Russell Kenney, of R.J. Kenney Assoc. Inc. in Plainville, Mass. Piper and Kenney consult on building exteriors and have conducted extensive research on the performance of EIF systems.

SOURCES OF SUPPLY

Caulking Guns and Tools

Albion Engineering Co.
2080A Wheatsheaf Ln.
Philadelphia, PA 19124
215/535-3476

Joint Sealants

Dow Corning Corp.
P.O. Box 994
Midland, MI 48686
517/496-6000

Sika Chemical Corp.
201 Polito
Lindhurst, NJ 07071
800/933-7452

GE Silicones
260 Hudson River Rd.
Waterford, NY 12188
800/255-8886

Tremco Inc.
3735 Green Rd.
Beechwood, OH 44122
216/292-5000

Joint Sealants and Water Repellents

ChemRex Inc.
Sonneborn Building Products
889 Valley Park Dr.
Shakopee, MN 55379
612/496-6000

Pecora Corp.
165 Wambold Rd.
Harleysville, PA 19438
215/723-6051

CHAPTER 5

ROOFING

- Asphalt Shingle Failures

- Shallow Roof Details

- Restoring Wood Shakes and Shingles

- Preventing Ice Dams

- Slate Roof Repairs

- Tricky Flashing Details

ASPHALT SHINGLE FAILURES

The most common residential roofing material applied in the U.S. today is fiberglass asphalt shingles. Since they were introduced in the late 1970s, fiberglass shingles have come to dominate the market, accounting for nearly 90% of all shingles installed today. In fact, the original "organic felt" shingles are now hard to find in many areas.

Evaluating the quality of organic shingles has always been pretty straightforward: In general, the heavier the shingle, the longer it will last on the roof. Fiberglass shingles, on the other hand, have a different composition and cannot be easily evaluated based on weight. This has made it more complicated for builders to choose a shingle. And recent reports of some fiberglass shingles failing prematurely have made the choice even tougher.

Anatomy of a Shingle

All asphalt shingles consist of a fiber mat coated with asphalt (Figure 1). The fiber mat, which gives the shingle most of its strength, is made either from an organic cellulose material (derived from wood or recycled paper) or from the newer and more popular fiberglass. The organic mats, sometimes called "felt" mats, are similar to ordinary roofing felt. They are saturated with a soft, pure asphalt to form a sturdy, pliable base. Fiberglass mats are much thinner, and are not saturated with asphalt.

Both types of mat are surface-coated on both sides with a layer of hard asphalt that has been "stabilized" with inexpensive mineral fillers, such as finely ground limestone or slate. The filler adds bulk and helps to make the shingles more

fire resistant. The top coating of asphalt also holds a layer of small granules of rock, usually colored with a ceramic coating, that protect the asphalt from damaging sunlight. The back surface of the shingle is covered with a fine mineral dust, such as talc, sand, or mica, to keep the shingles from sticking together and from staining each other in the package.

Worth Its Weight?

All of these components add to the weight of a shingle, but only some add strength and durability. Heavier stone, for example, can add weight without increasing shingle life. Similarly, in a high-profile "architectural" shingle, the added weight of the extra layer of stabilized asphalt contributes little to shingle strength unless it's applied to a thicker mat.

Despite this, the quality of organic asphalt shingles can still be reliably judged from their weight — when comparing shingles of the same brand and type. This is because the additional weight of the heavier shingle is mostly accounted for by a thicker mat with more soft asphalt saturant — factors that add strength and durability as well as weight. The pure asphalt typically adds 25 or 30 pounds per square.

But weight is generally not a good basis for comparison of fiberglass shingles. The additional weight of a heavier fiberglass shingle is accounted for primarily by additional hard, stabilized asphalt — a component that adds weight but not necessarily strength or durability. In fact, if too much mineral filler is used in the hard coating asphalt, it can make the shingle brittle and more likely to crack, despite the added weight.

As for the fiberglass mat, a better mat will make a stronger shingle. But it is the type of binder, strand

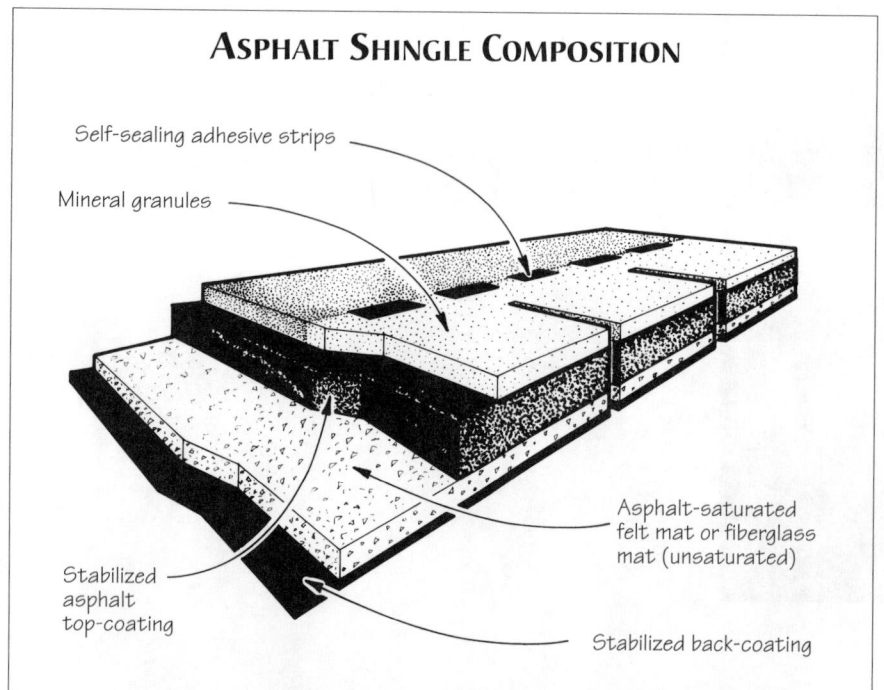

ASPHALT SHINGLE COMPOSITION

Self-sealing adhesive strips

Mineral granules

Asphalt-saturated felt mat or fiberglass mat (unsaturated)

Stabilized asphalt top-coating

Stabilized back-coating

Figure 1. All asphalt shingles are built around a mat of either organic felt or fiberglass. The organic mats are thicker and are saturated with soft, pliable asphalt. Both types of shingles have a top layer of harder, stabilized asphalt topped with colored stone to protect against UV light. On the bottom, all shingles have a thin coating of asphalt coated with talc, sand, or mica to keep the shingles from sticking together in the package.

orientation, and other components of the base material that make a better fiberglass mat, not necessarily the thickness or weight. Also, a heavier fiberglass mat adds only a pound or two per square, so it barely registers anyway.

Warranty Woes

Since you can't use shingle weight as a standard for choosing fiberglass shingles, a lot of roofers look at the manufacturer's warranty to gauge quality. This has traditionally worked for organic shingles, since the heavier, longer-lasting shingles usually carry a longer warranty. But the warranty periods of fiberglass shingles — typically expressed as 20-year, 25-year, and 30-year — do not necessarily correspond with shingle quality. In some cases you are simply paying more for a longer warranty.

The warranties differ from company to company, but none gives the installer full coverage. According to the terms of most warranties, for example, the manufacturer agrees to pay only the depreciated cost of the roofing material, and none of the labor to install it or the cost to dispose of the old shingles, which are two of the biggest expenses for roofers. Also, most shingle warranties aren't transferable when the home is sold. Since the average American homeowner sells after about six years, shingle companies are not liable even if their product doesn't perform as advertised. The builder's reputation, however, is still at risk if the roof fails, no matter who owns the house.

Even though warranties don't necessarily predict shingle life, it's still worth comparing coverage among the different roof manufacturers. Some warranties, like CertainTeed's, include payment of labor costs and provide 100% coverage for the first five years. BPCO, a Canadian manufacturer of organic shingles, provides similar "up front" coverage in a warranty that is transferable to subsequent owners of the home.

Another key to warranty protection is installation: If you want to ensure coverage, you have to install the roofing properly. And for warranty purposes, the "right" way is the way the package says to do it. Bear in mind, also, that no matter how the shingles are installed, the warranty could be voided if the roof framing, sheathing, or ventilation is determined by the manufacturer to be substandard.

Shingle Failure

In past years, warranties weren't much of a concern because the organic felt shingles usually lasted longer than the 15 or 20 years for which they were guaranteed. Some organic shingles on roofs today have seen 30 years and are still hanging on.

Many roofs with fiberglass shingles, however, aren't faring as well. Several roofing contractor associations have heard complaints from their members that some fiberglass shingles are failing within ten years — and sometimes as early as six months — into the warranty period.

When fiberglass shingles were first introduced, their biggest problem was with blow-offs. Manufacturers responded by improving the adhesive in the shingle sealant strip. The more recent failures usually involve cracking, which can occur vertically up the roof over many courses of shingles, horizontally across tabs, or diagonally (Figure 2). No one has fully documented how common the problems are, but industry experts feel they are fairly widespread.

The causes are also difficult to pin down, but appear to involve a combination of weak fiberglass mats, thin and inflexible asphalt, and the effects of thermal expansion and contraction. Some shingles crack because they can't adjust to movement in the roof substructure. More commonly, however, cracks are caused by dimensional changes in the shingles themselves as they respond to temperature changes. Shingles expand in the heat and contract in the cold, but because they're pinned to the roof by nails and stuck

Figure 2. Fiberglass shingles that fail early usually crack, either vertically up the roof over many courses of shingles, or horizontally and diagonally across tabs.

to each other by their own adhesive strips, the shingles rip themselves apart. Ironically, manufacturers' efforts to solve the blow-off problem by improving seal strip adhesion may have made the cracking problems worse.

Aging is also a factor in early failure. Over time, the volatile elements in the asphalt cook off, reducing the tensile strength and flexibility of the shingles. So roofs that get a lot of sun or are not well ventilated may fail sooner.

According to Don Berg, of the National Roofing Contractors Association's (NRCA) technical department, the cracking is "not limited to one or two brands, or one or two types or qualities of shingle. It has occurred in the commodity-grade and the architect-grade shingles." Berg has received reports of the problem "from generally around the country" but says NRCA "doesn't really have a handle on how widespread it is."

The Midwest Roofing Contractors Association (MRCA), another trade organization, has also received reports from their members of early failure of fiberglass shingles. And the president of Western States Roofing Contractors Association (WSRCA), Don Bosnick of Bosnick Roofing in Tacoma, Wash., says his organization has looked at samples of failed shingles "from Connecticut

to California," mostly in the 20-year three-tab type.

The Asphalt Roofing Manufacturers Association (ARMA) is also aware of the problem, and responding in part to WSRCA test results, has recently formed a task force to study it and find solutions. According to Joe Jones, a retired senior technical executive at Owens Corning, who heads the ARMA task force, "The cracking problem occurs in a number of different types of shingles, from a number of different manufacturers, in many parts of the country." Jones emphasizes, however, that the number of homes reporting cracking problem "is miniscule compared with the number of shingles sold."

Tear Strength

There is growing evidence that a shingle's tear strength is a good indicator of its resistance to cracking. The American Society of Testing and Materials (ASTM) has a minimum standard for tear strength, included in ASTM D3462. The standard establishes that, using an Elmendorf tear tester, it should take at least 1,700 grams (3 3/4 pounds) of force to tear a shingle that already has a notch in it. Although the tear test does not directly relate to cracking of shingles, high test results indicate a strong fiber mat. This standard was

adopted in 1976 when fiberglass shingles were first introduced, and was based on the lightest organic shingle known to have performed acceptably. Most organic felt shingles still available today have tear strengths of over 2,250 grams, and some as high as 3,500 grams.

Compliance with ASTM D3462 is voluntary, and ASTM does not check whether manufacturers who claim their shingles meet the standard actually comply. In fact, many don't. In tear strength tests conducted in early 1992 by two independent laboratories at the request of WSRCA, 22 of 24 fiberglass shingle samples (two each from 12 manufacturers) tested below the 1,700-gram standard.

Underwriters Laboratories recently announced that it would independently check tear test results, so you can start looking for UL certification of ASTM D3462 in a special box on the shingle wrapper. So far, only CertainTeed has received such certification, but a spokesman for UL says several other companies are expected to receive certification soon.

Manufacturers Respond

According to Jones, head of the ARMA task force, most manufacturers have already taken steps to eliminate the cracking. Some have gone to a heavier fiberglass mat; others have changed their asphalt formulation.

San Francisco-based WSRCA is also continuing to work on the problem. WSRCA's Bosnick says the association is looking at several different characteristics of new fiberglass shingles, including tensile strength, flexibility or pliability, and response to thermal shock. In February 1992, WSRCA started a comprehensive testing program on actual shingle samples from failed roofs, hoping to determine exactly why the shingles have cracked.

An ASTM subcommittee, which includes representatives from industry and the trades as well as consultants, architects, and academics, has

SHINGLE INSTALLER'S DISCLAIMER

The roofing contractor and materials supplier have no control over the production quality of shingles or the length of time the manufacturer claims they will last. The manufacturer has the sole liability for these properties of the shingle.

In your case, the name of the manufacturer of the product being applied is _____ and the type of shingle is _____.

Contractor's sole liability is limited to the warranty in the contract. This is in lieu of all other warranties, express or implied.

Figure 3. WSRCA has distributed this disclaimer to its members so they don't unintentionally warrant the roofing materials they install. Roofers give the disclaimer to homeowners along with the roofing manufacturer's warranty.

also been trying to develop a new standard. But since ASTM subcommittees make decisions by consensus, new ASTM standards may be slow in coming.

Choosing A Shingle

Until new standards are set and enforced, contractors need to be careful when choosing a shingle. One option is to avoid fiberglass and use organic felt shingles, which have not shown any premature cracking problems. Some organic shingles have been reported to "blister" and "curl," but the problem is not as widespread as the cracking of fiberglass shingles, and rarely results in leaks or blow-offs. Organic shingles have higher tear strength, good flexibility, and a high resistance to nail pull-through. They usually cost more than fiberglass shingles, primarily because their heavier weight makes them more expensive to ship.

If you use fiberglass shingles, consider stepping up to a longer warranty period. This may reduce the chances of a roofing failure, because the cracking problem seems to occur mostly among the 20-year fiberglass shingles. But you still can't be sure, because 25-year and 30-year fiberglass shingles have failed prematurely, too.

Also be careful how you guarantee your work. WSRCA has distributed a standard disclaimer to their members to be given to customers along with a copy of the manufacturer's warranty (see Figure 3). The disclaimer states that the contractor guarantees his workmanship, not the shingles; the shingles are covered only by the manufacturer's warranty. If you say something vague to the customer like "this is a 20-year roof" or "these shingles will last 25 years," you may be held to that promise even though the shingle warranty doesn't really say that.

By Ted Cushman, an associate editor with The Journal of Light Construction.

SHALLOW ROOF DETAILS

Asphalt shingles, clay and cement tiles, and wood shingles and shakes work well on steep slopes, where rain and melting snow drain rapidly. On shallow slopes, however, wind-driven rain and ice dams at the eaves can cause water to back up under the roofing and find its way into the house. That's why single-ply roofing materials, such as EPDM and modified bitumen, are a better choice for shallow slopes.

But in many cases, putting a single-ply material on a shallow roof — a porch or a shed dormer, for example — clashes with the shingles used on steeper roof planes on the same house. Builders who want to use shingles on a shallow roof, need to take extra precautions against leaks.

How Low Can You Go?

Building codes are not much help when it comes to shallow slopes. CABO's *One and Two Family Dwelling Code*, for example, sets a minimum slope of 3-in-12 for tiles, 2-in-12 for asphalt shingles, and 3-in-12 for wood shakes and shingles. Roofs below these minimums are not permitted without approval of the building inspector.

There are two problems with these code minimums. First, porch roofs and shed dormers are often shallower than code minimums, but the code leaves it up to the builder to devise a roofing application that will meet approval. Second, depending on what part of the country you work in, the code recommendations for underlayment may not provide sufficient protection, even at permitted minimum slopes.

Underlayment. The most important factor in devising a watertight

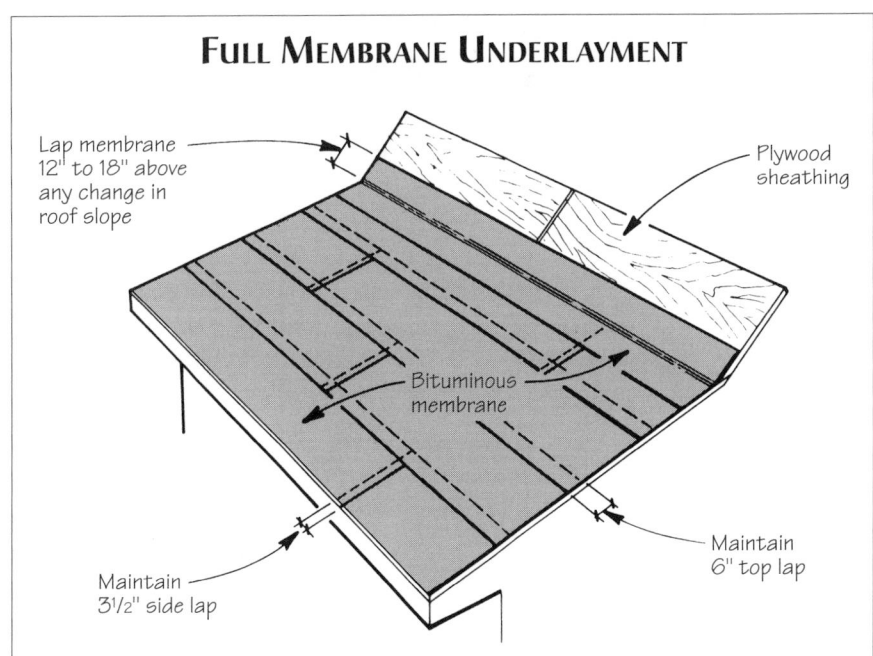

FULL MEMBRANE UNDERLAYMENT

Lap membrane 12" to 18" above any change in roof slope

Plywood sheathing

Bituminous membrane

Maintain 6" top lap

Maintain 3½" side lap

Figure 4. On shallow slopes, lay a bituminous membrane from the eaves to the ridge, or from the eaves to a point 12 to 18 inches above any change in slope.

roof at shallow slopes is the type of underlayment you use. An underlayment is a backup watershed installed beneath the shingles that prevents water from reaching the sheathing. On a shallow roof, it's wise to lavish some extra care on this part of the job.

The most current (1989) edition of the *Steep Roof Manual*, published by the NRCA (National Roofing Contractors Association, 10255 W. Higgins Rd., Suite 600, Rosemont, IL 60018; 847/299-9070) recommends two layers of 15-pound, asphalt-saturated felt glued together with plastic asphalt cement. To keep water from seeping between the layers, the cement must be spread uniformly with a comb trowel, at a rate of two gallons per 100 square feet, so that the two layers of felt don't touch at any point.

This method, however, is messy and time-consuming, and the final quality depends heavily on workmanship. And because the two layers of felt are glued to each other but not to the roof sheathing, any water that does get beneath the membrane can travel to other parts of the roof.

All of the roofers I've spoken with agree that the best underlayment is a self-adhering bituminous membrane, like Grace's Ice and Water Shield — a 4-mil polyethylene film backed by a 36-mil layer of rubberized asphalt adhesive. At about 60¢ to 80¢ per square foot installed, bituminous membranes are fast becoming standard fare for lining valleys and eaves, but they're also good for shallow roofs.

Compared to felt-based systems, membranes are easier to install and are relatively foolproof. They're also self-healing in that they automatically seal nail penetrations. And because membranes are fully adhered, water can't travel beneath them, so any leaks remain localized.

In fact, NRCA Deputy Director of Research and Technology Mark Graham says that a revised manual due out later this year will add bituminous membranes as a second underlayment option. (By the way, the association won't be recommending single-ply roofing membranes, like EPDM rubber, for roof underlayment. Those membranes are cumbersome to work with — if you want them fully adhered, you have to use messy adhesives — and they're not self-healing.)

Roofers who start using bituminous membranes are easily hooked. "We cover the entire roof with Ice and Water Shield whenever the slope is 5-in-12 or below," notes Joe Cazeault, a Weymouth, Mass., roofing contractor with 30 years in the

Figure 5. Workers place self-adhering bituminous membrane at the edge of a shallow-pitched roof. The membrane is installed by unrolling it across the roof while peeling off the backing paper. The job requires at least two sets of hands — one to hold the roll and another to smooth out the wrinkles.

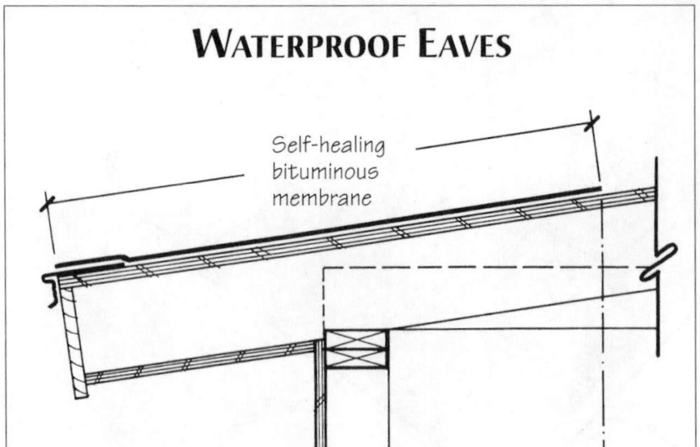

WATERPROOF EAVES

Self-healing bituminous membrane

24" min.

Figure 6. To prevent water backed up behind an ice dam from entering the building, place a self-adhering bituminous membrane from the edge of the roof to a point 24 inches inside the living space. Install metal dripedge on top of the membrane.

business. It may not be required by code, he says, but there's just too much chance that snow will back up under the shingles. Cazeault recommends laying the membrane from the edge of the roof to the ridge or to a point 12 to 18 inches above a change to a steeper pitch (Figure 4).

Membrane Tips

Properly installing self-adhering membranes takes practice. First, roll the membrane out and cut it into 10-foot to 15-foot lengths, then reroll it. Sweep the roof clean and apply the membrane by peeling off the paper while unrolling the membrane across the roof. This takes at least two sets of hands: one to work the roll, and a second to smooth the membrane onto the roof (Figure 5). The membrane should be applied with a 6-inch top lap (the amount of each course that's covered by the succeeding course) and a 3½-inch side lap (the amount adjacent sheets overlap at the ends). Peel-and-stick membranes are slippery, so they're more dangerous to walk on than felt systems. Rubber-soled shoes are a good idea.

Wrinkles. A big problem with membranes installed by inexperienced workers is excessive wrinkling. "It's like putting up wallpaper for the first time," says Larry Shapiro, a product manager at Grace. The membrane sticks to the sheathing on contact, so there's little room for error. A nail driven through a wrinkle won't seal properly and may leak. Wrinkles can be repaired by cutting them away with a utility knife, then patching them with a small piece of membrane.

Temperature. Shapiro stresses the need to follow the manufacturer's application instructions, especially the minimum installation temperatures. Membranes don't stick well below 40°F, making them more vulnerable to leaks. Some products may also have upper temperature limits, above which the adhesive tends to

melt. In the worst cases, says Shapiro, a gooey mess can seep out from beneath the membrane at the eaves. To prevent seepage during peak summer temperatures, make sure the product you choose is rated for at least 180°F.

UV damage. Membranes are also subject to damage from the sun's ultraviolet rays. While short-term exposure to the sun — up to several months, depending on the product — doesn't harm them, long exposure can cause the polyethylene film to become brittle and crack. Some brands of membrane last longer in the sun than others, but none is designed as a finish roof material. Of course, a membrane used as an underlayment is protected by the finish roof.

Nailing. The self-healing properties of bituminous membranes effectively seal smooth-shank roofing nails, but you'll need to be more careful with other types of fasteners. Ring-shank nails, for example, may tear the membrane instead of slicing cleanly through it. The result is a slew of isolated leaks.

Ventilation. Membrane manufacturers also caution that their products should be installed over a well-ventilated roof deck. On inadequately ventilated roofs, a membrane acts as a cold-side vapor barrier, making it more apt to trap heat and moisture. In the worst cases, this results in damage to the roof sheathing and framing.

Shallow Slope Roof Details

Whether you use felt paper or a bituminous membrane, shallow slope roofs require special care.

Asphalt shingles. CABO sets the minimum slope for asphalt shingles at 2-in-12, and requires that any roof below 4-in-12 be covered first with a double layer of building paper. The eaves must also be protected with underlayment, whether lapped-and-glued felt or a bituminous membrane.

Although codes allow a double layer of cemented saturated felt at the eaves, bituminous membranes offer the best eaves protection. Manufacturers recommend placing the membrane from the edge of the sheathing to a point at least 24 inches, measured horizontally, inside the living space (Figure 6). Where metal dripedge is used, place it on top of the membrane.

Wood shingles and shakes. CABO sets a minimum slope of 3-in-12 for wood shingles and shakes. At those slopes, however, you'll have to reduce the weather exposure according to the length of the shake or shingle (Figure 7). And remember that decreasing exposure increases the number of shingles needed to cover a square of roof area.

For slopes below these minimums, NRCA and the Cedar Shake and Shingle Bureau (515 116th Ave. NE, Suite 275, Bellevue, WA 98004; 206/453-1323) recommend installing wood roofing on a latticelike framework of strapping over a

MAXIMUM EXPOSURES FOR WOOD ROOFS

Length of Shingles/Shakes	Shingles (3:12 min. slope)	Shakes (4:12 min. slope)
16"	3 3/4"	—
18"	4 1/4"	7 1/2"
24"	5 3/4"	10 "

Figure 7. These exposures will work at slopes below 3:12 for wood shingles and 4:12 for shakes, but only in conjunction with a watertight subroof and a double-strapping system.

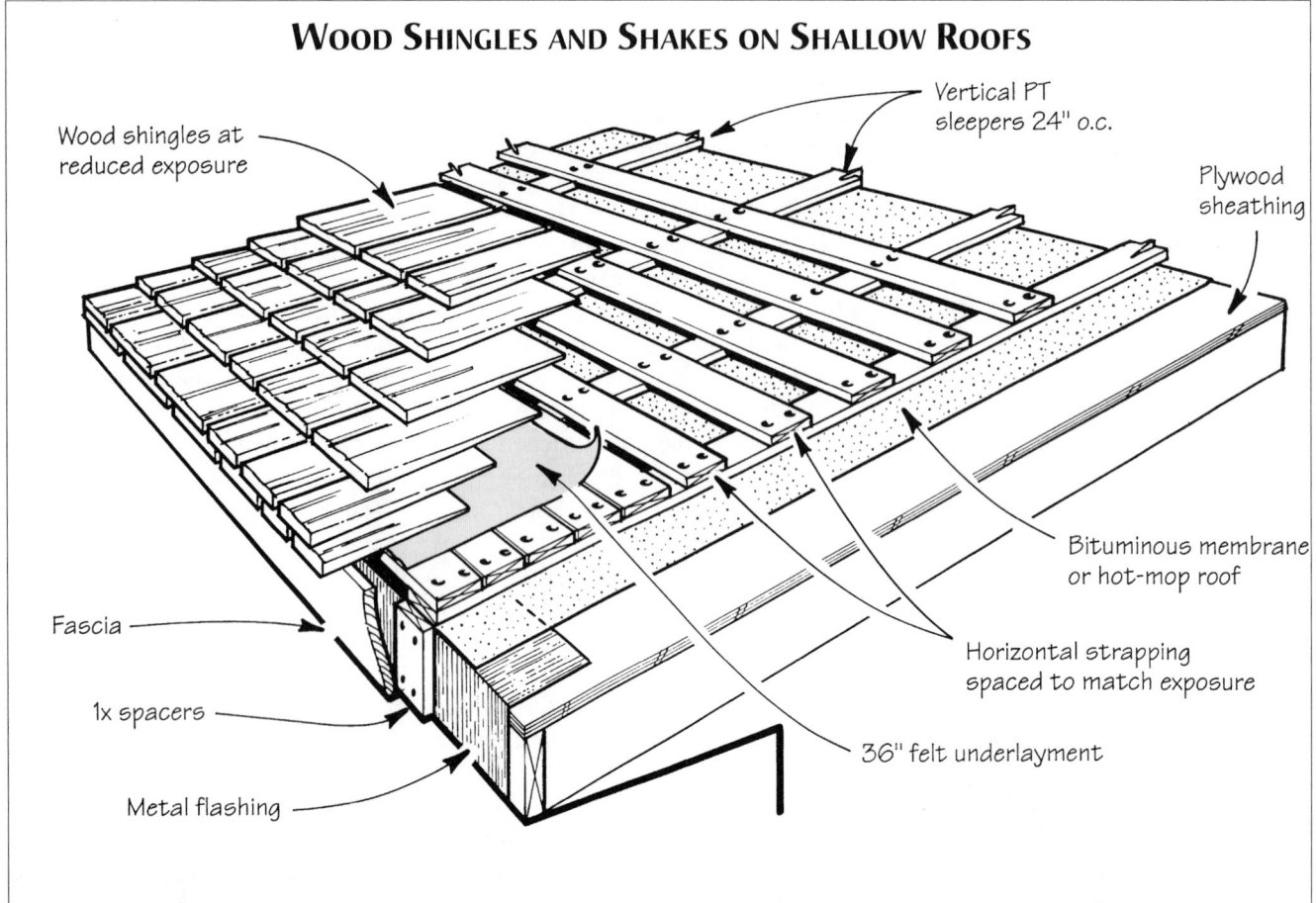

WOOD SHINGLES AND SHAKES ON SHALLOW ROOFS

Wood shingles at reduced exposure

Vertical PT sleepers 24" o.c.

Plywood sheathing

Fascia

1x spacers

Metal flashing

Bituminous membrane or hot-mop roof

Horizontal strapping spaced to match exposure

36" felt underlayment

Figure 8. On shallow slopes, install wood shingles and shakes over a watertight subroof and a framework of pressure-treated strapping. The fascia is spaced out from the metal flashing at the eaves to allow any water that gets under the roofing to drain from the subroof.

watertight membrane (Figure 8). First, install the membrane over solid sheathing, making sure that water will drain freely over the drip edge. Next, lay 1x2 pressure-treated strapping from the eaves to the ridge, spaced at 24 inches on-center. Over this, install a layer of horizontal strapping, spaced to ensure proper shingle exposure. The wood roof does most of the water-shedding and protects the membrane from UV degradation. The double strapping provides air circulation and permits free drainage of any water that does get beneath the shingles.

Slate, clay, and concrete tile. The minimum slope CABO allows for flat concrete, slate, and clay tile is 3-in-12, but in snow country, some manufacturers won't guarantee their tiles below 4-in-12.

As a general rule for shallow slopes, install the tiles with a minimum 4-inch top lap on the same type of double strapping and waterproof membrane system used for wood roofs. The tiles function like shingles and shakes, shedding most, if not all, of the water and protecting the membrane from damage.

In coastal regions and other windy areas, you'll need to nail all the tiles, and you may need to place hurricane clips along the eaves. In most other parts of the country, the first three tiles or courses should be nailed at eaves, rakes, valleys, and hips. On the rest of the roof, the tile's head lug grabs the batten to keep the tile from sliding down the roof, while the weight of the tiles themselves hold them down. Details should be available from the tile manufacturer.

Flashings

Whatever the roofing surface, remember that flashings are a weak link, especially on shallow roofs. A good flashing job takes time, so you can expect to pay your roofing sub a little extra for this part of the job.

For a watertight subroof, the flashing should be installed before the roofing goes down, and the joints should be soldered. Use at least 28-gauge galvanized steel or an equivalent noncorrosive, nonstaining material, such as lead or aluminum. Copper is an excellent flashing material, but water runoff from copper can leave stains on the house siding. Lead-coated copper has the advantages of copper, but doesn't cause stains.

By Charles Wardell, a contractor and freelance writer from Edgartown, Mass.

RESTORING WOOD SHAKES AND SHINGLES

Cedar shakes and shingles offer strength, durability, insulation, and beauty to our homes. A wood roof imparts a look of quality that few other roof coverings can match. Only a few years of exposure to the weather, however, can drastically change this "quality" roofing. Sunlight and rain can cause cedar shakes and shingles to lose virtually all their natural preservatives in as short a time as five years. Around this age, most cedar roofs begin to show signs of cupping, curling, splitting, and decay.

Unlike most roofing materials, however, cedar shingles and shakes can be restored and maintained through proper care and treatment, often doubling or tripling their remaining service life (Figure 9).

Why Wood Roofs Weather

Western red cedar is an extremely durable material even under adverse conditions, but its useful life depends upon the environment. If left unprotected it can suffer photodegradation from ultraviolet light (sunlight), leaching, hydrolysis, shrinking and swelling from water exposure, and discoloration and degradation from decay microorganisms.

Photodegradation by sunlight. Solar radiation is the most damaging component of the outdoor environment. Photodegradation due to sunlight occurs fairly rapidly on the exposed shingle surface. The initial color change from the golden, orange-brown color to gray is related to the decomposition of lignin in the surface wood cells. (Lignin is Mother Nature's way of holding wood cells together.) The wood cells at the shingle surface lose their strength and eventually are washed away by rainwater. In addition, microscopic cracks and checks develop, allowing deeper water penetration.

Degradation by moisture. Accompanying this loss of wood fiber at the shingle surface are the shrinking and swelling stresses set up by fluctuations in moisture content. These stresses cause deeper checks and splits to develop. The result: shakes and shingles begin to cup, curl, split, and check at an accelerated rate.

Degradation by wood-destroying fungi. The natural decay resistance of western red cedar is due to its heartwood extractive, including the *thujaplicins* and a variety of *phenolic compounds.* The thujaplicins contribute to the decay resistance of red cedar while the phenolic compounds and resins give cedar its ability to repel water and its *lubricity* (slippery surface).

Since the natural preservatives in cedar are somewhat water soluble, they can be depleted in service. In roof exposure, extractives may leach out in a relatively short time and allow colonization by wood-inhabiting fungi. Aided by favorable climatic conditions, these in turn allow the growth of wood destroying fungi, which ultimately cause the early failure of a roof (Figure 10). The wood becomes soft and spongy, stringy, pitted, and cracked or crumbly. This usually occurs first at the butt region of the shingles where they overlap.

An added factor is that more shakes and shingles are being manufactured today from younger, less decay-resistant cedar since old, high-thujaplicin-content logs are no longer readily available. This shortens the roof's life expectancy even more.

How fast a wood roof weathers is a function of slope, direction, and shading. The more shallow a roof is, the more likely it is to suffer decay from fungi. South-facing slopes suffer because they experience the greatest swings in temperature and humidity — leading to more splits and other degradation. Shade is also a concern. Wood roofs shaded by trees are more likely to develop mold, mildew, and decay than unshaded roofs.

Shake and Shingle Quality

In the past, Grade No. 1 (Blue Label) shingles and shakes were cut from 100% clear, vertical-grain heartwood. However, grading stan-

Figure 9. After power washing and repairing this red-cedar roof, a worker applies a wood preservative, which will keep it free of mold, lichen, and decay for up to five years.

dards have been relaxed over the years allowing more flat-grain and defects. These shakes and shingles are particularly susceptible to cupping, curling, and splitting. Improper nailing, nailing too high or too far in from the edge, only worsens the problem.

To Repair or Not

The older the roof, the more difficult it is to repair satisfactorily (see "Repair Procedures"). Although you can salvage a roof that requires as many as 30 repairs per square, it may not be cost-effective. A good rule of thumb is that shingle roofs older than 20 years, and shake roofs older than 25 years, will be extremely diffi-

cult, if not impossible, to repair satisfactorily (Figure 11). In some geographic areas such as the Gulf States, repairs on shingle roofs over 10 years old and shake roofs over 15 years old should not be attempted. Foot traffic on these roofs will cause considerable breakage and dislodging of shingles.

The final decision to repair, clean, and treat with preservatives a wood roof is going to be a subjective one. There are no iron-clad rules. But don't go ahead with restoration if the benefits are questionable.

Cleaning With Bleach

Depending on the condition of the wood roof, there are two methods of cleaning prior to treatment:

chemical cleaning (bleaching) and power washing. In many areas of the country, wood roofs are discolored primarily by sunlight and surface mildews or algae. These roofs can be cleaned quite easily and effectively with bleaching agents such as sodium hypochlorite (household bleach) or calcium hypochlorite (swimming-pool chlorine) mixed in tapwater. These chlorine solutions quickly remove the oxidized wood fibers on the shingle surface as well as kill surface mildews and algae. The roof is transformed from its initial dirty gray color to a "buff" or buckskin tan color.

To use liquid chlorine (Purex, Chlorox, etc.), mix one gallon of liquid bleach (5% sodium hypochlorite) with one gallon of water to remove mold, mildew, and the gray color. Higher concentrations of bleach (12% to 15% sodium hypochlorite) are available through commercial cleaning-supply companies. They can be diluted with water or used up to "full strength" if necessary to remove discoloration.

Stronger, more cost-effective chlorine solutions can be formulated using granular chlorine (calcium hypochlorite) mixed at a ratio of 2 to 4 ounces per gallon of water. The type found at swimming pool supply companies (65% available chlorine) does a very good job of removing mildew and discoloration due to weathering. Bleach solutions are not effective, however, in removing dirt, rust stains, extractive stains, heavy moss, or lichen growth.

Whichever type of chlorine you use, you can apply the solution of chlorine and water to the roof using a typical garden-pump sprayer. Scrubbing or brushing is not necessary. Let the chemical do the work. The recommended coverage is 1 to 1¹/₂ gallons per 100 square feet of roof area. Leave the solution on the roof for 15 to 30 minutes, then rinse thoroughly with a high-pressure power washer or a garden hose. The

Figure 10. These 14-year-old untreated shingles (top) in the humid Houston area show severe decay, splitting, and heavy accumulations of moss and lichen. Organic debris left on the roof (above) traps moisture and hastens decay.

high-pressure rinsing gives more dramatic results and aids in removing the oxidized roof fibers, plant organisms, and leaf debris from the roof.

Take care not to spray vegetation. If this does happen, rinse the plants thoroughly with water. Also, chlorine solutions are corrosive and should be applied using commercial spray equipment with stainless-steel or plastic internal parts. Pump-up garden sprayers work fine for small roofs but are too slow and cumbersome for large jobs or commercial applications. High-pressure spray rigs or airless sprayers are not necessary to effectively bleach the wood. Pressures of 100 to 125 psi are adequate with flow rates of a half gallon to 1 gallon per minute. To minimize any possible damage to shrubbery

Figure 11. Any wood roof that requires more than 30 repairs per square, such as this one, is probably not worth restoring. Shingle roofs over 20 years old and shake roofs over 30 may be too far gone.

REPAIR PROCEDURES

One common way to spot-repair damaged or decayed shingles is merely to replace them with new ones. All you need are a roofing hammer, metal hacksaw blade or heavy wire cutters, a wood block, nail set, shingle nails (hot-dipped galvanized), and new No. 1 grade shingles or shakes.

The replacement of a shingle or shake can be completed in seven easy steps:

1. Split the old shingle using the blade end of the roofing hammer, in line with the original attachment nails.
2. Then remove the broken shingle with the serrated head of the roofing hammer.
3. Saw or clip off the nail heads left just under the butt of the overlapping shingle.
4. Then drive a new shingle into the void until the butt is within approximately 1 inch of the butt line of the adjacent shingles.
5. At this point, toenail two nails (which should be about 1/2 inch longer than the original nails) through the shingle up under the overlapping shingle at a 45-degree angle.

6. Finish driving the nails, using the nailset to avoid damaging the shingles.
7. After setting the nails, drive the shingle in by striking the wood block held against the butt of the shingle, until the butt of the new shingle is even with the shingle course line.

The entire process generally takes about five minutes to complete. *Under no circumstances should new shingles be "face nailed" leaving the nailheads exposed.* When face nailing, the nails tend to extrude and the shingles tend to crack through fastener holes in the weathered surface.

Repeated wetting of shingles causes them to swell, grabbing the nails and raising them. As the shingles dry, the wood shrinks, leaving the nails elevated. Over time, this can cause loose shingles and lost nails. In addition, as the wood ages, it tends to shrink, causing holes to enlarge, and leaving the nails loose in the nail holes.

One problem with removing damaged or decayed shingles is

that surrounding shingles can be loosened or broken.

Undershimming. Another method of spot repair, especially on older and more weathered roofs, is "undershimming." Undershimming involves placing a waterproof shim under the damaged shingle. Recommended shimming materials are heavy 45-pound roofing felt, aluminum, or galvanized sheet metal.

Undershimming is easily accomplished. With a claw hammer, the shingle is raised, and a 4x8-inch shim is slipped in under the shingle. Friction between the wood and the asphalt-impregnated felt is sufficient to hold the shim in place. Metal shims have either a rough burr on the surface, or the lower corners can be bent down to bite into the wood to hold the shim in place. The shim should not be visible after installation. Obviously this technique is only suitable when the shingles or shakes are split and not decayed or loose. This technique is faster and less expensive than replacing individual shingles and it doesn't disturb surrounding shingles. — *B.B.*

and grass, the area should be sprayed with water thoroughly before, during, and after bleaching. This eliminates the need to cover the shrubbery with plastic tarps.

Power Washing

Because certain forms of algae, moss, and lichen are unaffected by chlorine solutions, they must be mechanically removed using a high-pressure washer, similar to those used to clean automobiles. Power washing of wood roofs works quite well and is used extensively on the West Coast (Figure 12). Power washing essentially removes the top layer of wood fibers from the shingles much the same way sandblasters remove rust from metal. Take care not to damage the shingles by using too high a pressure. Pressures of 1,000 to 1,500 psi are generally adequate to clean the roof quickly and efficiently. Although power washing is slow and dirty work, the results are truly remarkable with the roof returning to its original cedar-brown color.

Power washers can be rented through local equipment rental companies or paint stores such as Sherwin Williams for $50 to $75 per day. If you purchase a power washer, you should choose a gasoline or diesel-powered unit with 1,500 to 3,000 pounds of pressure, and a flow rate of 4 to 6 gallons per minute.

Power washing roofs is fairly straightforward. Always work from the top of the roof down, keeping your feet on the dry portion of the roof. Keep the spray wand moving a distance of 8 to 12 feet from the shingle surface. Use cold fresh water. Hot water washing or the use of strong soaps or cleaners is unnecessary. Experiment with various tip sizes to get the best results. A 15-degree spray fan is recommended.

Preservative Treatments

Until recently, it made little sense to preservative-treat an existing wood roof because of the low cost to replace. But as replacement costs have increased, the economics of preservative treatment look much better. One roofer's advertisement reads, "Why worry about a dirty roof? Because a clean and preserved roof looks a lot better than a re-roofer's bill!"

The high replacement costs of wood roofs and the development of new preservative finishes that are cheaper, less toxic, and more durable has made treating wood roofs feasible and desirable.

In 1975 the Texas Forest Service (Forest Products Laboratory) began evaluating preservative treatments for wood shakes and shingles.

Figure 12. Power washing with water (top), popular in California, restores cedar roofs to their original brown color (above), even if they are covered with bleach-resistant lichen and algae. Power washers can be rented at many paint stores. Roofs that are merely discolored can be bleached instead, which is easier on the wood.

Results from both accelerated and long-term outdoor exposure tests indicate that a number of both water-borne and oil-borne treatments are quite effective in controlling the effects of weathering and decay for up to five years. The most effective products are those that contain one or more of the following:

- Copper octoate (1% metal content)
- Copper naphthenate (1% metal content)
- Zinc naphthenate (3% to 4% zinc metal content)
- Busan 1009 or Busan 1025 (2% to 5% TCMTB)
- Polyphase (.5% to 1% 3-iodo-2-propynyl butyl carbamate)

The following is a more detailed examination of these preservatives, their cost, availability, and use. They are ranked in order of overall performance. This ranking is based upon actual long-term outdoor exposure tests on wood roofing in East Texas.

Water-Borne Preservatives

For maximum mildew and decay resistance in a water-borne treatment, *Cunapsol 5* is recommended. Cunapsol 5 (cut 1:4 with water) is quite popular with roof applicators in northern California and the Pacific Northwest because of its low cost and effectiveness in controlling moss and lichen growth. Because Cunapsol contains copper naphthenate, it imparts an initial green color to the wood. If allowed to weather naturally, the color changes to a pleasing cedar brown. To hide the initial bright green color, you can pigment the Cunapsol solution with Presco Cedar Brown Pigment or Millbrite 582 Pigment. Cunapsol 5 and the pigments are available from ISK Biosciences (6075 Poplar Ave., Suite 306, Memphis, TN 38119; 800/238-2523). Cunapsol 5 provides excellent mold, mildew, and decay resistance for up to five years or longer (Figure 13). But like other water-borne preservatives, it has *little effect* on cupping, curling, or splitting of the wood. The cost per gallon of a pigmented, ready-to-use solution is approximately $2.50 to $3.50. Cunapsol is available in both concentrate and ready-to-use form in 5- and 55-gallon quantities.

Busan 1009 (TCMTB) is a liquid microbicide which, when mixed with water at a 2% to 5% concentration, provides effective mold and mildew control for up to three years. Outdoor exposure tests now in progress show Busan 1009 superior to zinc naphthenate in controlling surface discoloration due to molds and mildew. How well the Busan 1009 formulations will do over a five-year period remains to be seen. Current results lead me to recommend Busan 1009 at a 5% to 9% concentration as a suitable alternative to zinc.

Busan 1009 is available in concentrate form from Buckman Laboratories (1256 N. McLean Blvd., Memphis, TN 38108; 901/278-0330). A 5% concentration of Busan 1009 in water will cost approximately $2 to $2.50 per gallon.

Oil-Borne Preservatives

One of the main drawbacks of waterborne treatments is they do very little to control the drying effects of the sun and subsequent cupping, curling, splitting, and surface checking. A durable oil-borne preservative containing a suitable naphthenic or paraffinic oil will replenish the wood with oils that have been lost by sun and rainfall (Figure 14). Both naphthenic and paraffinic oils (when applicable) are resistant to oxidation by sunlight, do not contribute to the flammability of the treated wood, and are reasonable in price. Care should be taken to choose only those oils *not* restricted by OSHA's Standard 29 CFR Part 1910.1200, which became effective in 1985. In essence, it states that certain oils manufactured today have been tested and concluded to be carcinogenic. As of 1985 these oils and any products that contain them require special labeling. Please check with the oil supplier for clarification on this. Examples of good naphthenic oils are Chevron's Shingle and Floor Oil and Sun Oil Company's Sunthene 410.

Copper octoate has shown great promise not only in controlling mildew and decay, but also in giving "life" back to aged wood when combined with a suitable naphthenic oil. A 10% concentrate of copper octoate must be diluted 1:9 with

Figure 13. In a side-by-side test, cedar shingles treated with Cunapsol when new (at right) outshine untreated shingles (at left) after four years of exposure in the humid Gulf Coast region.

Figure 14. These 12-year-old shingles from an arid climate suffer more from sunlight than wood decay: the UV breaks down the wood, leading to cupping, curling, and splitting. Oil-borne treatments are needed to fight these drying stresses.

Figure 15. Small commercial applicators can purchase spray equipment for bleach or preservatives from lawncare or golf course suppliers. This unit is the Suburban Sprayer from Weatherguard Systems, Inc., in Marshall, Texas.

naphthenic oil. Like Cunapsol, the preservative is green in color and therefore must be pigmented to provide natural-looking finishes for wood roofs. It's available in 55-gallon drums only. The cost per gallon of a ready-to-use solution (with pigment) is $5 to $6.

Oil-soluble copper naphthenates are an alternative to copper octoate and are available from many suppliers, including OMG America (2301 Scranton Rd., Cleveland, OH 44113;

216/781-8383) and Continental Products (1150 E. 222nd St., Euclid, OH 44117; 216/531-0710). Pound for pound, copper naphthenate and copper octoate are equal in performance. However, the copper octoate is available in higher concentrations than copper naphthenate so it's more cost-effective to large-volume users. In addition, there is less odor with the copper octoate. Prices for 1% copper naphthenate solutions can vary from $3 to $6 a gallon. Copper naphthenate solutions will be green in color but can be pigmented.

Zinc naphthenates in oil are readily available and in use in many areas of the country, but I cannot recommend them at concentrations lower than 3% to 4%. In mildew-prone areas, particularly in the South, 1% to 2% zinc naphthenate solutions are poor performers over time (they have some merit in areas not prone to mildew and decay). Price per gallon of 3% zinc naphthenate solutions will vary from $4 to $7 per gallon. Zinc naphthenate is available from manufacturers such as OMG America (MGARD S-150).

Because many of the preservative suppliers cannot or will not sell their

products in small quantities (less than 5 gallons), the applicator should consider the following ready-to-use treatments because of their availability, price, and performance:

- Natural Seal X-100 (American Building Restoration Chemicals, Inc., 9720 So. 60th St., Franklin, WI 53132; 414/421-4127)
- Seal Treat II (W.M. Barr, Co., 2105 Channel Ave., Memphis, TN 38113; 901/775-0100)
- TWP Roof and Deck Coat (Amteco, P.O. Box 9, Pacific, MO 63069; 314/271-1300)

The Texas Forest Products Laboratory is continually searching for new and effective finishes for wood roofing. The recommendations given in this report are based solely upon tests performed here in East Texas. The opinions given here are just that — opinions — and by no means should be interpreted as an official endorsement by the Texas Forest Service.

Equipment Needed for Roof Restoration

There are as many different designs for spray equipment as there are people who sell it. Because of its low cost and availability, the common garden sprayer is an easy and effective way of applying bleach solutions, water-borne preservatives, and preservatives in light solvent. It is not suited, however, for the naphthenate-oil treatments. Also note that this is a slow and cumbersome way to apply chemicals to the roof.

Many commercial applicators choose an airless sprayer such as those manufactured by Graco, Binks, or Hero. These are excellent choices but are quite expensive and "overqualified" for roof restoration work.

A much cheaper and more reliable sprayer can be made with a diaphragm pump (Figure 15). Twin diaphragm pumps, such as those available from Hypro Company, are an excellent choice for wood restoration work. They are economical, dependable, long-lived, and highly adaptable. They are capable of delivering oil- or water-borne chemicals to the roof with plenty of pressure and volume. Diaphragm pumps are superior to gear and piston pumps in handling the abrasiveness of preservative solutions, particularly those containing pigments or mildewcides.

For information on quality diaphragm sprayers, contact manufacturers that supply the lawn, turf, and pest control industry, such as the Broyhill Company or Oldham

Chemicals Company. Both provide complete sprayer packages including diaphragm pumps, storage tanks, hose reels, and spray guns. Most complete spray packages sell for under $2,000.

Sprayers can be truck-mounted or totally portable depending on personal preference. Truck-mounted units eliminate the need to continually move the sprayer around the job site. Everything is self-contained on the truck bed. Usually 300 feet of hose is adequate to reach most roofs. Manual or electric hose reels are advisable when using over 100 feet of hose. Pumps are usually driven by gasoline or diesel engines.

Spray guns can be purchased from companies such as Spraying Systems. They should be the high-pressure type (800 to 3,000 psi capacity) with spray tips of .015 to .040 orifice and a 15- to 65-degree fan. Attaching a 10-inch extension wand to the gun makes the coating process less tiring. Longer wands up to 64 inches can provide greater reach but can be heavy. They are very useful where foot traffic on the roof is limited or dangerous.

By Brian Buchanan, a forest products researcher and consultant in Lufkin, Texas and former wood technologist for the Forest Products Laboratory.

PREVENTING ICE DAMS

Ice dams are not peculiar to northern regions: They can and do occur in any area of the U.S. with a total mean snowfall of 6 or more inches annually — which is nearly three-fourths of the continental United States, according to U.S. Weather Bureau data.

Most of us are familiar with how ice dams form, and the damage they can cause. But few of us seem to know how to prevent them or even how to limit their damage.

Ice Dam Basics

For those unschooled in the mechanics of ice dams, a quick review may be helpful. On the roof of an *unheated* building, snow will melt gradually from the perimeter first, while slowly sinking over the entire blanket. On a *heated* building, the snow will melt in the same pattern if the roof is properly designed and built. On a roof with ice-dam problems, however, the snow will soon take the shape of a wedge. It is paper-thin at the top where it melts faster from warmed attic air that has risen to the peak, and thickest at the eaves, where it

ends in a ridge of ice. In old houses that have little or no attic insulation, the roof above the attic will soon be bare but snow and ice will cling to the overhangs.

Most roofs, unfortunately, have too little insulation for the climate or insulation that was installed sloppily. In addition, few roofs have adequate ventilation, and many have none at all.

Heat from the living quarters works its way through the ceiling insulation or convects into the attic (or rafter spaces in a cathedral ceiling) through unsealed openings around chimneys, bathroom fans, recessed light fixtures, plumbing vents, electrical wires, or attic hatches. This warms the attic air and the roof sheathing to temperatures above the freezing point. The snow blanket begins to melt and the melted water runs down the roof where it freezes as it reaches the end of the insulating snow blanket or a cold eaves. Ice begins to build up and can get as thick as a foot or more. Once this happens, run-off from the melting snow begins to pond behind the ice curb and finds

its way under the roof shingles and into the building.

In houses with overhangs and steep roofs, water penetration may end there. In shallower roofs or during winters of heavy snowfall, however, water may penetrate the attic and walls and even the inside finishes, particularly at door and window heads where the leakage is often first noticed.

Regardless of the type of construction of a house, ice dams and the water damage they cause can be avoided. What are the solutions?

Shoveling all the snow off the roof or building the roof so that it will shed its snow cover after each snowfall are two very effective ways to prevent ice dams. However, the former is not too practical, hard on the roof covering, and dangerous to life and limb.

Removing the snow partially from the bottom of the roof by means of a snow rake, while standing on the ground or on a ladder, only results in a secondary ice dam forming higher up the roof at the bottom of the snow blanket. All that this accomplishes is to shift the water leakage higher where it can create more havoc with the ceiling insulation and finish.

Every fall, hardware stores heavily advertise electric roof cables as a sure means of solving the ice dam problem. Instructions recommend their installation in a zigzag pattern at the eaves of the roof and in valleys, gutters, and downspouts. Secondary ice dams form just out of reach of the tape and the situation is further aggravated by the fact that you now have "V"s of ice catching the water.

Metal ice belts are very commonly used in heavy snow areas and many contractors swear by them. They are certainly more effective at eliminating leakage than the previously mentioned methods, but are no panacea.

Secondary ice dams form at the upper edge of the metal band after it has shed the ice that formed on it. And do you really want a roof with a 3-foot (or wider) metal edge if you can avoid it? Why do so many contractors still install these unsightly devices when far better means are available?

W.R. Grace, the pioneer of the now widely used bitumen membrane, came out several years ago with its Bituthene Ice and Water Shield. There are now several competitors on the market. The material comes in a 3-foot-wide roll and is self-adhering to clean roof sheathing. It is applied at the eaves, in valleys, and around skylights — wherever the possibility of water ponding behind

ice dams exists. In houses with wide overhangs and shallow roofs, it may be advisable to use more than one strip at the eaves in order to obtain at least 2 feet of coverage above the line of the wall plate.

The roof covering is simply nailed right through the membrane, which seals around the nails much like a puncture-proof tire does.

But as effective as this underlaid membrane is, you should use it only where you can't *design in* the best solution: a combination of adequate insulation and ventilation.

Design Solutions

With what we know today, ice dams are inexcusable in new houses.

ICE DAMS BELOW SKYLIGHTS

Heat loss around a skylight is usually greater than on other parts of a roof, causing melting and subsequent ice buildup below the skylight — even on a well-ventilated roof. In extremely cold temperatures, melted water from around the skylight can get trapped between the cold, vented roof and the snowpack on the roof, freezing almost immediately. A thick sheet of ice can form between the skylight and the eaves causing water to back up into the building.

Since there is no way to prevent the melting altogether, I recommend the following procedure, even on cold roofs.

After the skylight is installed, but before the counterflashing is in place, cover the area around and below the skylight with a self-adhering bituminous membrane, such as Ice and Water Shield (W.R. Grace Construction Products, 62 Whittemore Ave., Cambridge, MA 02140; 617/876-1400). Begin at the eaves, and lay the membrane so that it extends 3 feet above the skylight as well. To prevent water from leaking into the skylight, roll strips of membrane up the sides of the curb, lapping the main

membrane by 6 inches. Finally, apply the skylight counterflashing and roofing in the normal manner.

While you may not need this kind of protection every year, the

extra cost of the protective membrane layer is a small price to pay for peace of mind. And it's a lot easier than standing at the top of a ladder, chipping away at an ice dam. — *H.D.*

PROTECTING SKYLIGHT WITH MEMBRANE

When ice dams can't be prevented, protect against leaks with a continuous bituminous membrane applied before the skylight counterflashing. Extend the membrane 3 feet on all sides of the skylight, and run it all the way down to the eaves.

First, the designer should avoid roof details that make good ventilation difficult or impossible.

Valleys are one of the worst offenders. If dormers are necessary, use shed dormers instead of "A" roofs, which converge the snow into the valleys. Avoid secondary gables as decorations over front doors or half circle windows. Get rid of valleys and you are well on the way to preventing the problem, if you follow it up with the right combination of insulation and ventilation.

The goals are to:

• reduce heat loss to the attic by using ample insulation that's properly installed

• carefully seal all ceiling air leaks mentioned earlier by means of foaming urethane, packed mineral wool, caulking, weatherstripping, or sheet metal, as appropriate

• install an effective air-vapor retarder on the winter-warm side of the ceiling and walls

• provide ample and effective attic ventilation to quickly remove from the attic whatever heat gets through the insulation before it has a chance to warm the sheathing

Particularly vulnerable areas are the wall platelines. Standard construction generally leaves very little space for insulation over the top plate. And often, insulation over the plate blocks any air passage from soffits to attic space. In new construction, however, it's easy to allow space for both the full thickness of insulation and adequate ventilation at the plates.

Raised Heels

If you're using trusses, order them with an elevated seat (Figure 16). Otherwise, set a secondary 2x4 plate on top of the ceiling joists at the eaves and set the rafters on top of it instead of next to the joists (Figure 17). Use metal fasteners to tie rafter ends to the plate and

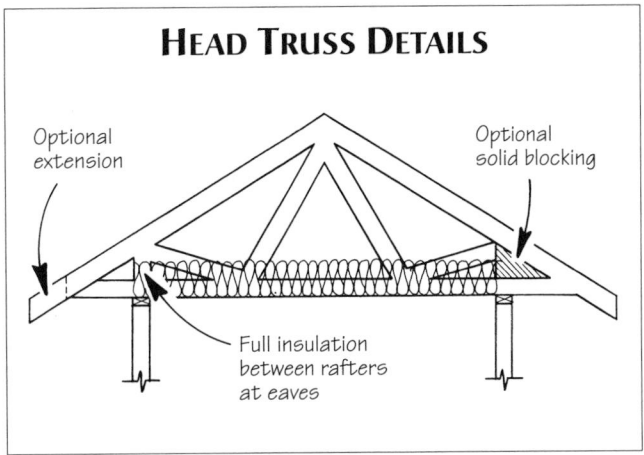

HEAD TRUSS DETAILS

Optional extension

Optional solid blocking

Full insulation between rafters at eaves

Figure 16. If you use trusses, order them with an elevated seat to accommodate a full thickness of insulation at the eaves. Note the vertical support at the bearing point.

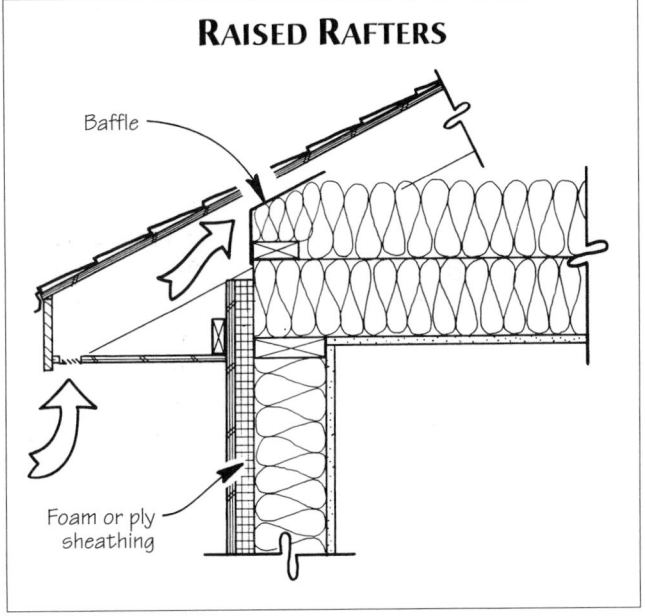

RAISED RAFTERS

Baffle

Foam or ply sheathing

Figure 17. To get extra room for insulation with conventional rafters, you can set a second top plate above the ceiling joists. You may want to tie rafter to joist with metal connectors.

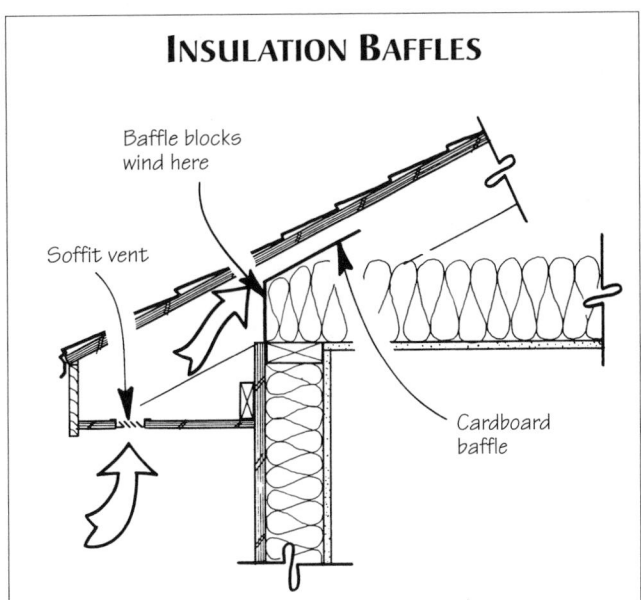

INSULATION BAFFLES

Baffle blocks wind here

Soffit vent

Cardboard baffle

Figure 18. Cardboard baffles have stapling flanges for easy installation. They also have the advantage of folding over the end of the insulation to block out wind penetration.

joists if you need stronger anchoring here.

In order to ensure that the air channels at the eaves remain unblocked as the insulation fluffs up, use insulation baffles. Molded-polystyrene baffles do not cover the vulnerable lower ends of the insulation batt, have rather shallow air slots, and do not ventilate the entire width of the rafter bay. Condensation can occur in the remaining unventilated area.

Cardboard baffles are preferable since they can be easily altered to fit any insulation thickness (Figure 18). One manufacturer of a HUD-approved baffle is Edwil Manufac-

turing (10223 Timber Ridge Dr., Ashland, VA 23005; 804/550-2800). The cardboard baffles have the advantage of providing a pocket that seals the lower end of the insulation, preventing soffit air from washing through and reducing its R-factor. Another strategy with elevated rafter seats is to carry the foam or plywood sheathing all the way to the rafters thus sealing the ends of the insulation as shown in Figure 17. For retrofits, you can use a site-built plywood baffle with extended arms for slipping it into place (Figure 19).

The depth of the air space generally recommended is 1 1/2 inches.

Provide more wherever possible, as cold winter air is very heavy and sluggish. The insulation thickness at the eaves should be at least R-38 for northern regions.

Adequate Ventilation

HUD's minimum property standards offer guidance on how much ventilation to have. The standards call for 1 square foot of net-free (unobstructed) vent area for every 150 square feet of attic floor area, or for every 300 square feet if the ceiling has a vapor barrier. But I have seen problem-free roofs with far less than the recommended ventilation levels, while others that appeared to meet the standards have had horrendous ice problems. Therefore, be guided by the commonsense rule that says there is no such thing as too much ventilation in an attic.

We still find many technical writers advocating the use of gable vents. However, anyone who has studied the subject should know that no ventilation system, except for continuous soffit and ridge vents, does a complete job of venting an attic.

Gable louvers function only when the wind is blowing against them, and then they ventilate only partially. Combined with soffit vents, their performance is not much better.

Other types of vents, such as cupolas, roof vents and fans, turbines, or soffit vents alone, do not do a thorough job. There are always large areas of the sheathing that do not get ventilated.

On the other hand, a balanced combination of soffit and ridge vents encourages a continuous air wash of every square inch of sheathing where condensation is most likely to occur.

All Vents Not Equal

But not all ridge vents are created equal. The only type that should be used is a *baffled* ridge

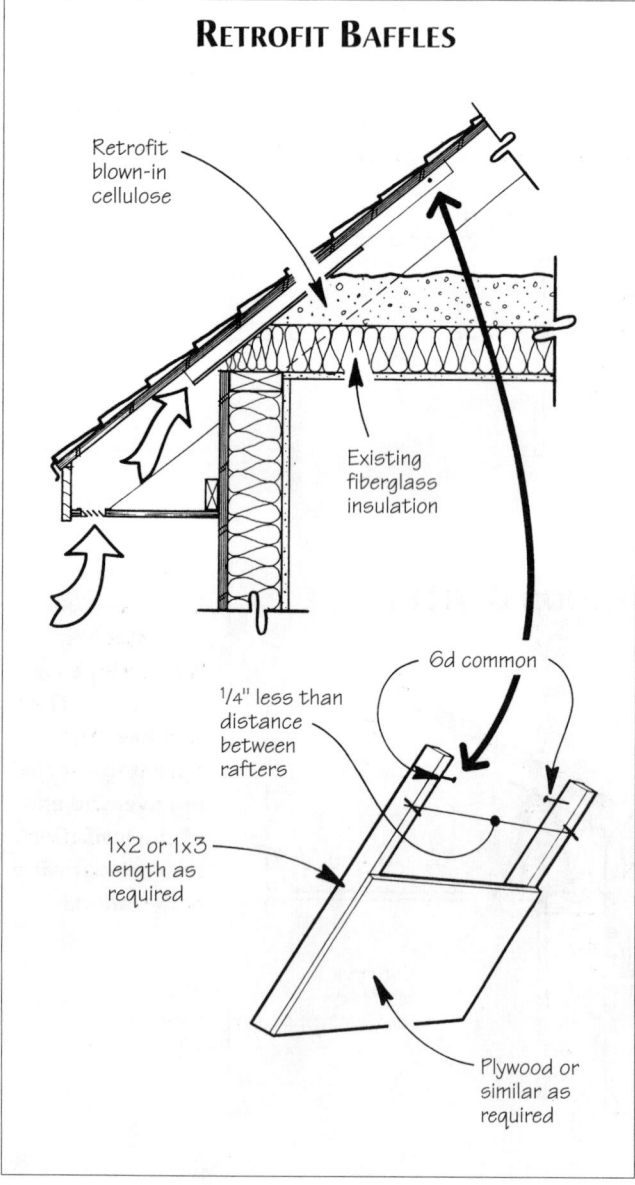

RETROFIT BAFFLES

Retrofit blown-in cellulose

Existing fiberglass insulation

6d common

1/4" less than distance between rafters

1x2 or 1x3 length as required

Plywood or similar as required

Figure 19. For retrofits, you can fashion baffles from strapping and thin plywood. The strapping extensions form handles to slip the baffle in place, and provide a convenient place to nail.

vent. The baffle deflects wind blowing up on the roof. This both increases the airflow from the attic (due to the *venturi* effect), and prevents the penetration of water and snow. Conversely, ridge vents without baffles can admit water and snow in large quantities, wetting insulation and ruining ceilings.

The better ridge vents are made of metal and have an integral metal baffle. (Do not accept accessory plastic wind baffles.) In heavy snow regions, however, even the best aluminum ridge vents can collapse from the weight of a deep, wet dump. To prevent this, order enough joint blocks so that you can insert one

every 24 inches maximum into the ridge-vent sections before installation.

Most metal ridge vents available commercially are manufactured for shallow to medium-pitch roofs. When used on steeper roofs, they must be bent to fit the pitch. This closes their throats and reduces the air flow, while also exposing the lou-

---

CATHEDRAL CEILING RETROFIT

The roof panels of this pre-cut house in northern Vermont were panelized and built of 2x4s, 16 inches on-center, with a plastic vapor retarder towards the inside, R-11 fiberglass batts, and plywood glued and nailed to both faces. This formed a cathedral roof that was covered with cedar shakes with felt strips interlaid. The ice-dam problem was very serious and eventually the eaves rotted.

The roof was retrofitted by the addition of 1-inch extruded polystyrene over the old sheathing. Two-by-three sleepers were fastened on edge over the rigid insulation from eaves to ridge but extending 3 inches past the old fascia. New sheathing was nailed over the sleepers and covered with new fiberglass shingles. Continuous soffit venting was installed under the projection of the sleepers as was a new fascia. Ridge venting was also installed. In the last four winters not a sign of ice damming was seen. This same system can be used to retrofit uninsulated cathedral ceilings with exposed wood decking (see illustration).

With cathedral ceilings, it is important to pay close attention to design and workmanship. You must take great care to seal all possible paths of convection of moist, heated air from the living spaces into the rafter spaces and to provide the best possible air-vapor retarder. Recessed lights are out.

The amount of insulation is limited by the depth of the rafters and the ventilation space. The pre-

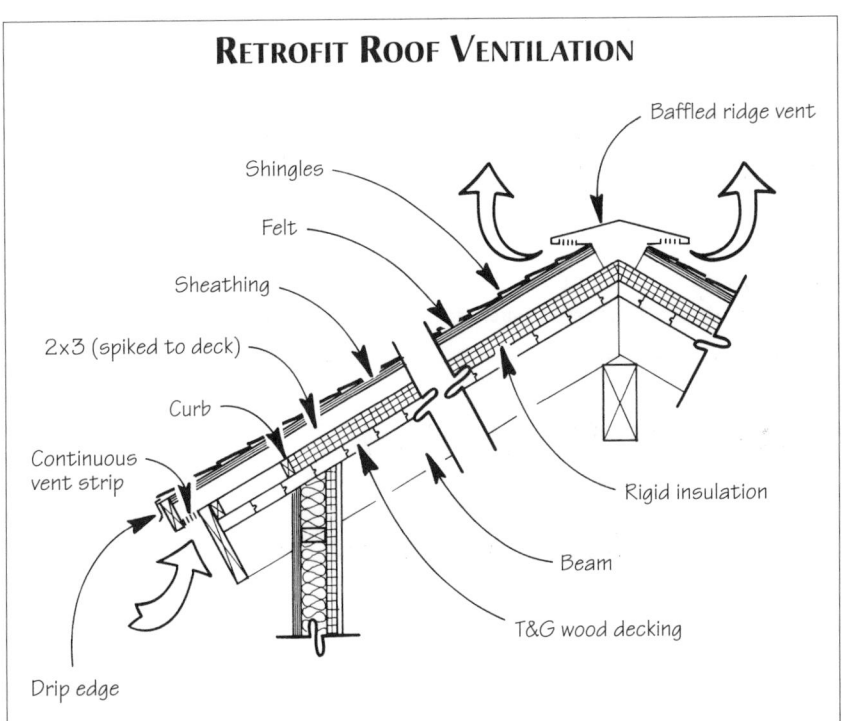

RETROFIT ROOF VENTILATION

Baffled ridge vent

Shingles

Felt

Sheathing

2x3 (spiked to deck)

Curb

Continuous vent strip

Drip edge

Rigid insulation

Beam

T&G wood decking

To retrofit insulation into a cathedral ceiling with exposed wood decking (common on log homes and vacation homes), insulation and ventilation must go on top.

ferred system, in my opinion, is to allow a 2-inch minimum air space under the sheathing, fill the rest of the rafter spaces with fiberglass insulation, and fasten rigid insulation below the rafters.

Now, what will assure that the 2-inch air space will not be restricted by the fiberglass insulation, which might fluff up? Instead of the molded polystyrene vents discussed above, I would suggest tightly stapling nylon cord in a zigzag pattern to the sides of the rafters no less than 2 inches below the sheathing. Preferably use two

staples at each point and drive them in with a follow-up blow if necessary.

Wherever the levels of insulation and ventilation can be improved enough to reach this goal, that is what should be done. But where this is not possible, the next best alternative is to install a product such as W.R. Grace's Ice & Water Shield at the eaves and at all other leak-prone points of the roof.

No other procedure, except building a metal roof steep enough to shed snow, is truly safe or foolproof. — *H.D.*

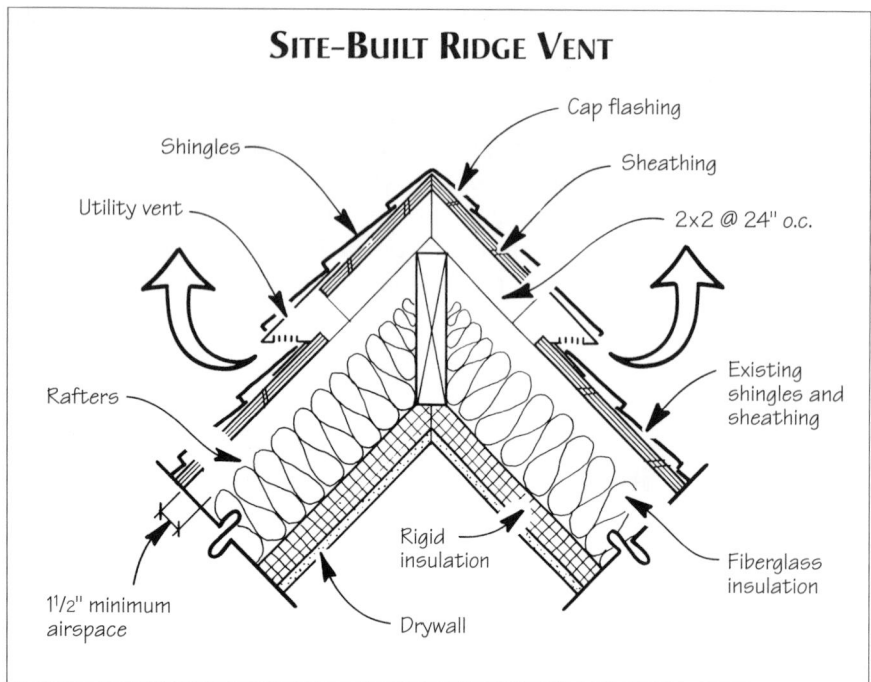

Figure 20. A standard baffle won't work well on steep pitches. A simple site-built vent with two half vents (such as Air Vent's Utility Vent) does the trick.

vered sections to wind-driven snow and rain (since the louvers are now above the baffle). Ridge vents should not be used when they need to be deformed to fit.

Some manufacturers make a version of their standard ridge vent for steeper roofs, or recommend installing a wedge under the base of the vent to reduce the pitch of the roof. Neither of these suggestions work as well as a site-built vent that makes use of a product called the Utility Vent (Air Vent, Inc., 7700 Parker Dr., Suite B, Peoria Heights, IL 61615; 800/247-8368). The utility vent is nothing more than a half ridge vent (see Figure 20 for installation procedure).

By Henri deMarne, a home inspector and nationally syndicated columnist from Waitsfield, Vt.

SLATE ROOF REPAIRS

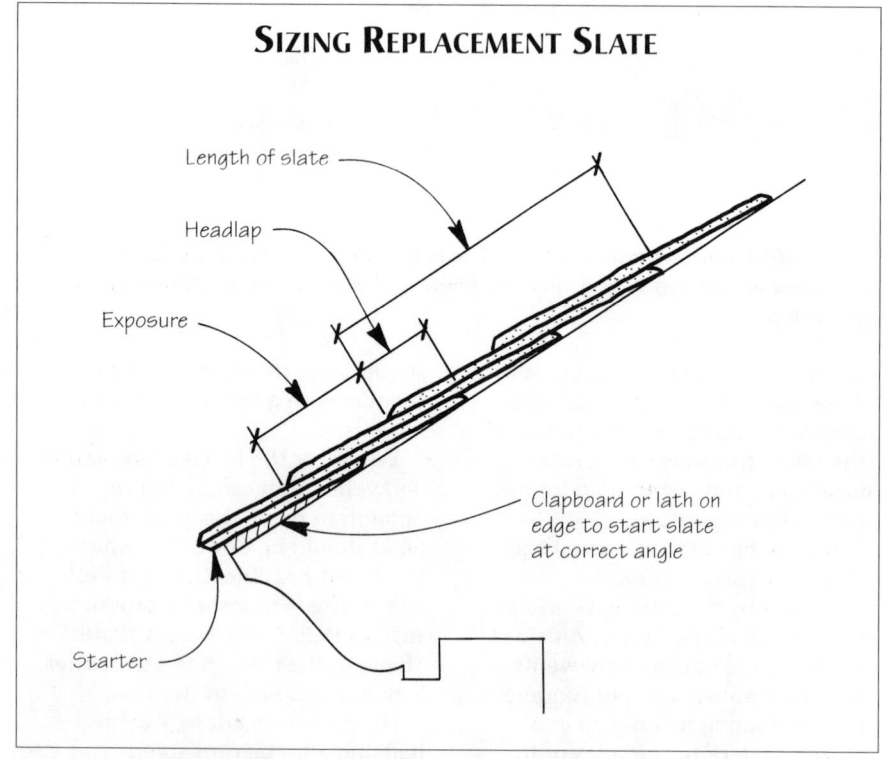

Figure 21. To find the size of the replacement slate, multiply the exposure by two, and add 3 inches for the headlap. Then round up to 12, 14, or 16 inches — the standard sizes of slates.

Slate is a very desirable roofing material. Once the hard, dense stone is properly laid, it will require little maintenance to keep it in prime condition. And as a product of nature, a slate roof will permanently add to the appearance and character of a building.

Houses are sometimes enlarged or remodeled, however, requiring slates to be removed and replaced. Or slates are sometimes broken by various causes (including careless workers). When replacing a slate, it's absolutely essential that you use the right size and that you match the existing roof in both shade and texture.

The Right Size

The width of the replacement slates should be obvious. But be observant. Some slates may be wider than the rest, such as along the rake or gable edge, or for use in the valleys. The roof may also have random-width slate with as many as five or six different widths.

To find the proper length, it may be possible to measure the slate along a gable end or some other place where the underside of the slate is exposed. If this is not possible, you can calculate the length from the amount of the slate exposed to the weather (Figure 21).

Measure the exposure, then multiply by two, and add 3 inches for the *headlap* — the area covered by three shingle layers. Bear in mind two factors: Slate comes in even lengths only — 12, 14, 16 inches and so on — so you may have to round up. Also, steeper roofs such as mansards, or improperly laid roofs, may have only 2 inches of headlap.

Matching Color

Slate color depends on chemical and mineral makeup, and can vary drastically from quarry to quarry. The grey and black slate quarried in Pennsylvania is very common in some areas. Many times it can be identified by obvious streaks or ribbons. A higher quality slate from Virginia is blue-grey to black in color. This is a very tough and durable slate. An equally durable slate is that quarried along the Vermont-New York border. It comes in a wide variety of colors including grey, green, purple, and red.

Color is further qualified as either unfading (permanent) or weathering. The former will not change in color over the years, whereas the weathering type may change to a brown, rust, or grey. This change occurs for the most part only on the exposed surface, so by looking at the underside or the inside of the broken slate you can ascertain the original color. If you are still in doubt as to the color or origin of the slate, send a sample to one of the slate companies listed at the end of this chapter.

Rippers and Hooks

First, all remnants of the original slates need to be removed along

Figure 22. To remove the damaged slate, first hook the ripper (top) on one of the two nails holding the slate. Then hammer downward on the ripper (middle) to cut or pull the nail. Next drive in a slate hook (above) to hold the replacement slate.

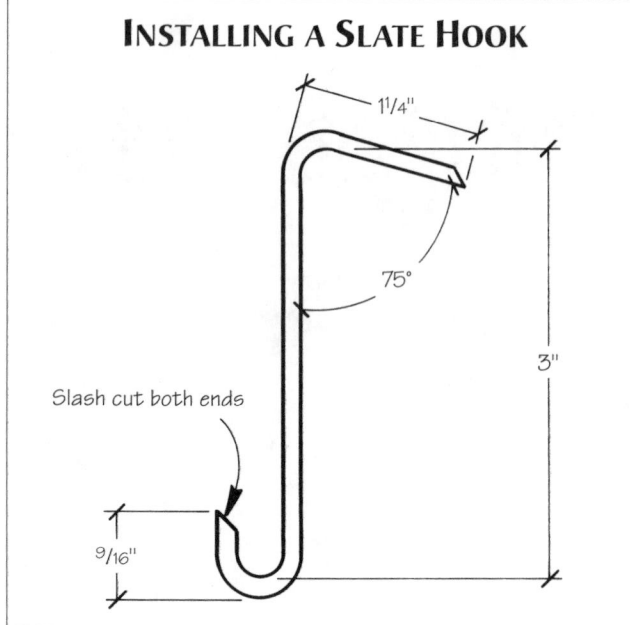

INSTALLING A SLATE HOOK

1¹/₄"

75°

3"

Slash cut both ends

⁹/₁₆"

Figure 23. A slate hook is driven into the sheathing in the joint under the replacement slate. Use copper or stainless steel for a permanent repair.

with the nails that held them in. This first step is done with a tool called a ripper (Figure 22). Use the ripper carefully. It's very important that when you slide it under a slate, you exert very little upward pressure on the slate above the broken one. Since slates will break very easily, you could end up with two slates to replace.

By sliding the ripper under the slate that is to be removed you can hook the ripper on one of the two nails that hold it. Then hammer downward on the ripper — you will either cut or pull the nail out. (You may wish to use a rubber mallet so your ripper will last longer.) Repeat this procedure on the other nail.

The broken slate will now slide out. (Note: Some larger slates such as 24x14-inch and larger have four nails holding them.) After all of the slates are removed, install a *slate hook* (Figure 23). The slate hook is installed in the joint underneath the slate that is being replaced. Drive the 3-inch shaft of the hook into the roof above the headlap of the slate below it. Then simply slide the replacement slate up into the area once occupied by the broken slate. The slate is pushed up past the hook

— then pulled down (usually with the ripper).

Slate hooks are available at some lumberyards, but these are usually galvanized. These will start to rust after only a couple of years and can fail completely after 40 to 50 years. For a more permanent installation, you can buy copper or stainless-steel hooks through the slate quarries in Vermont and New York (see "Sources of Supply" at end of this chapter).

Stagings

How do you get out onto the field of a slate roof to repair a slate or two? Many people work off a rope. This is economical, but in the end may cost you more, since you can easily break more slates than you set out to fix. To spread your weight around, you can pad the area where you are working with rigid foam insulation or plywood.

If practical, you can set up standard triangular roof brackets, but only after removing a slate where the bracket is to be nailed. Broken or missing slates offer good spots to place brackets.

The method we prefer in most cases is to work off a ladder with a ladder hook attached. As with plywood, this puts the pressure on a

large portion of the roof rather than in one spot. But each case should be examined individually, and a bit of ingenuity is often required.

Larger Repairs

If a larger area has to be removed — whether for an addition, dormer, or skylight — the same principles can be applied. Starting at the uppermost spot to be stripped, you can remove these slates using the ripper. From that point on, many of the slates can be taken off simply by pulling the nails with a hammer, with some help from the ripper.

When it's time to reinstall the slates, two preliminary steps are necessary: You must cut the slates to size and make nail holes.

There are two ways to cut slate. The old-fashioned, but still acceptable way, is with a slater's stake and slate hammer. A somewhat easier method for a novice would be to use a slate cutter. These tools are available through most slate quarries.

To make nail holes, you can either punch them with a slate hammer (one end of the slate hammer comes to a point that is designed for this very use), or use a drill. A ³/₁₆-inch masonry drill does very nicely. Punch or drill the holes, one-quarter to one-third the length of the slate from the upper end, and approximately 2 inches from the edge. On slates larger than 14x24 inches, a second course of nails is recommended 2 inches above the regular holes.

As you reinstall the slates, work them back into the areas that remain open, cutting them to fit where necessary. The joints in each course should be well broken with those below. They should never be any closer than 3 inches from the joint above or below.

Nail the slates so the nail heads just touch the slate. Do not drive them home or draw the slate into the roof. Rather, the slate should just hang on the nails. For a better quality job, you may want to use copper or stainless-steel slating nails instead of galvanized.

If the new slate roofing comes up to a vertical wall or a skylight, you'll have to use step flashing. If only half of the upper portion of a slate is exposed for nailing, you can either use a slate hook or use two nails on that side of the slate. Space the two nails as far apart as you can along the edge of the slate in the upper half, and these two nails will hold the slate firmly in place.

By Les Gove, owner of Middlebury Slate Company located in Montgomery Center, Vt. Gove specializes in the repair and restoration of slate roofs.

TRICKY FLASHING DETAILS

Flashing often gets too little attention in the design process, particularly in residential work. Blueprints end up vague on the flashing details, and contractors end up doing a make-shift job with roll stock and roofing cement.

But that's asking for trouble. You can do beautiful work on the big expanses of siding or roofing, but water is going to get in where things intersect. And the designs today aren't short on intersecting planes.

The only way to make sure the structure is weathertight, and will remain that way, is to take the time to review tricky flashing situations on a job-by-job basis. Here are four tough areas we see often, and the way we flash them.

Garage/House Corner

Where the roof on a one-story attached garage butts into a two-story

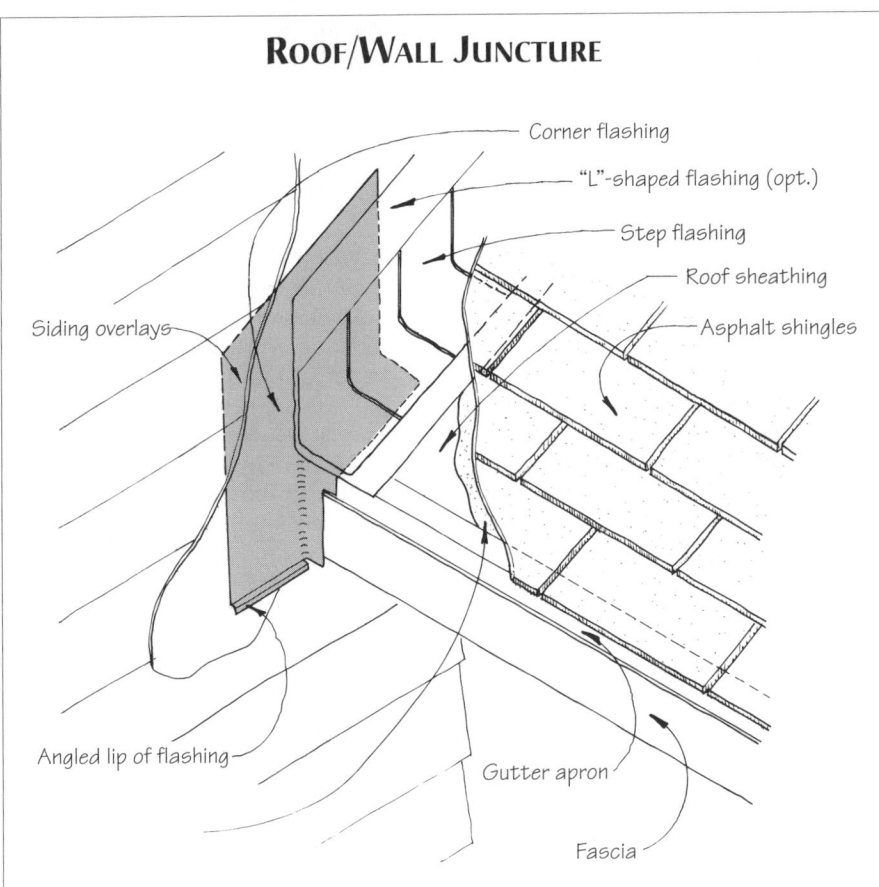

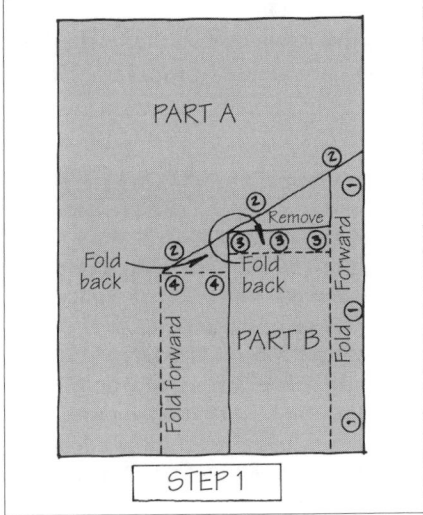

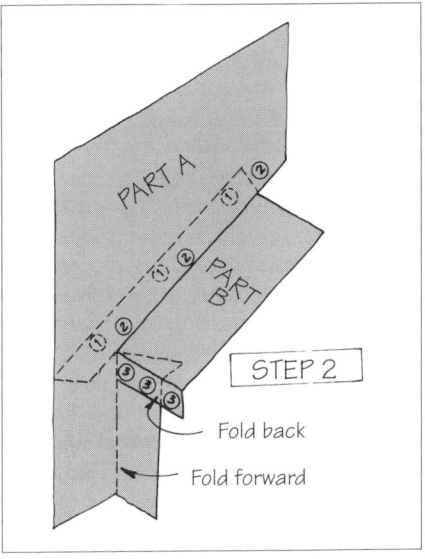

Figure 24. Where a one-story roof butts into a two-story wall, start with a custom-fabricated corner flashing (above). Then add L-shaped pieces up the slope, and step flash the rest as usual. The corner flashing can be made out of a square piece of heavy-gauge metal, cut into two pieces — Part A and Part B (at right). Cut along solid lines and bend along dotted lines on a metal brake. Solder parts A and B at the overlapping flaps.

wall, you'll need more than a straight flashing running from the garage's eaves to ridge. Where water running down the garage roof spills off the edge, it damages the siding and saturates the wall behind it. Even gutters don't always intercept the flow, particularly if the gutter is clogged.

The best solution is to have a sheet-metal or roofing contractor make up a flashing to fit this corner, or if you own a sheet-metal brake, you can try it yourself (Figure 24). Use a heavy gauge metal, such as 16-ounce copper or baked-enamel galvanized sheet metal.

The corner flashing, which is the piece you install first, is cut from a square piece of metal as shown in Figure 24. The square is cut into two pieces which you solder together to form the flashing.

At the job site, make one change from your standard procedure. Use a simple gutter apron, rather than a style-D drip edge. Place the corner flashing on top of your gutter apron and black paper. Make sure you're using nails compatible with your flashing. Galvanized nails will corrode copper flashing, though they are fine if you're using galvanized flashing. Also, get your step flashing in the same metal as the back-up flashing. Flashing is always going to be damp or wet, and electrolytic action between different metals will create pin holes in no time.

You can install the corner flashing behind the fascia, or the corner flashing can overlap the fascia if it's already in place. Overlapping the fascia, as shown in Figure 24, looks best if you use a baked-enamel galvanized flashing because you can match the paint color.

Let the bottom edge of the corner flashing run long until you see where your siding falls, then trim the bottom edge, and create a narrow, angled lip with a hand brake. Place the flashing over the lower piece of siding, then install the siding over it. This routes any water that gets into this area to the outside.

If you want a little extra protection behind your step shingles (which you might, if you use an off-the-shelf step shingle), put in pieces of L-shaped back-up flashing that are 8 to 10 inches high. Each length of L-flashing should overlap the preceding piece by 8 to 10 inches. The L-flashing is formed on a metal brake.

Now you're ready for step flashing. I prefer a 5-inch-high by 4-inch-out shingle for the extra protection it gives, and you could leave out the L-shaped flashing if you use these larger step shingles.

FLASHING MATERIAL OPTIONS

Flashing should last at least as long as the roof covering, preferably longer. In the long run, it doesn't pay to skimp on quality materials. Upgrading from lead to copper, for example, will only add $50 to the cost of the average chimney, but the flashing will last as long as the building. And on a big job like a chimney pan, most of the cost is for labor anyway.

Before putting different types of metals together (say, aluminum and copper or lead), make sure you understand the galvanic series, which classifies metals by how chemically active they are (see illustration, facing page). The gist of it is that when two dissimilar metals come into contact in the presence of moisture, the more active metal corrodes by transferring ions to the more passive; the more passive metal remains unharmed. The farther apart the metals are on the list, the faster the ion exchange, and the greater the corrosion. (This same process is used to advantage to pro-tect steel by galvanizing: The zinc coating on a piece of galvanized steel corrodes instead of the under-lying steel.) The best way to prevent galvanic corrosion is to not use dissimilar metals in the same place; if that's impossible, combine only those metals that are close together on the list. Painting the metal surfaces with a primer may help, but I typically separate dissimilar metals with a piece of eaves membrane.

Here is a rundown of the main choices for flashing materials:

Galvanized steel is probably the least expensive flashing material, but I rarely use it because it will eventually rust. If you've ever seen a metal roof on an old shed, you know that once the protective zinc coating corrodes, the underlying steel is left bare to the elements. The rust stains will then run down the siding.

Zinc is also common in my area. I never use zinc, however, because it becomes pitted when exposed to salt or acid. This includes acid rain and chimney exhaust from an oil burner or wood stove.

Aluminum is widely used for step flashings, which are generally covered by roofing and siding. But I don't recommend aluminum in other areas. For one thing, it can't be soldered by normal means. For another, it tends to pit and oxidize, especially in salty or polluted air. If you must use aluminum in these environments, the .032-inch thickness will last substantially longer. Anodized or painted aluminum is less prone to oxidation, but remember that a cut edge will eventually deteriorate.

Aluminum is also inappropriate around masonry, because the lime and acids in the masonry will eat the aluminum. If you must put aluminum flashing against masonry, either paint the flashing or separate the flashing from the masonry with a membrane.

Copper flashings can be fabricated from either cold-rolled or soft copper. Soft copper is easily

Metal Valleys

Contractors often call asking for "valley aluminum." This is very lightweight roll aluminum, about .015 inch thick, but it is much too thin to last in a valley. Lightweight aluminum will wrinkle. If it does wrinkle it will break from thermal expansion and contraction. Leaks start wherever kinks or buckles occur.

If we do a job with metal valleys, we use .032- or .040-inch aluminum and cut it to 8- or 10-foot lengths (the thicker aluminum comes in a sheet, not a roll). Or we use 16-ounce copper or .015-inch stainless steel.

Depending on the slope, we overlap the valley sections 8 to 12 inches, with less overlap on steeper slopes (Figure 25). On steeper slopes we don't seal the overlap to allow expansion and contraction of the metal, but on lower slopes (5/12 or

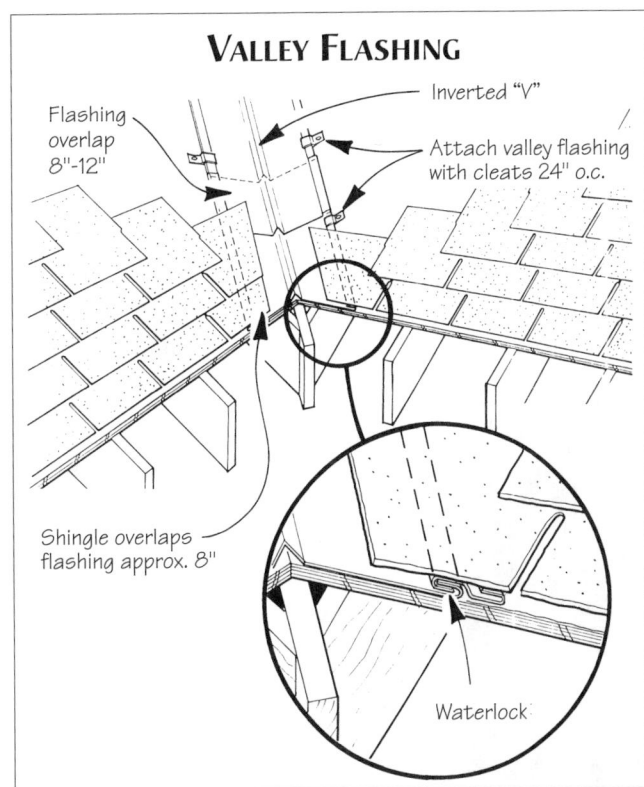

VALLEY FLASHING

Flashing overlap 8"–12"

Inverted "V"

Attach valley flashing with cleats 24" o.c.

Shingle overlaps flashing approx. 8"

Waterlock

Figure 25. An inverted "V" in the middle of the valley makes the flashing stronger and keeps water from rushing up the opposite slope. Fastening with cleats allows for expansion and contraction and keeps the flashing free of nail holes. On shake, tile, or slate, you'll also need a waterlock at the edges (inset).

worked, making it useful for decorative jobs, as well as for complicated shapes like the tops of valleys, where malleability is a real asset. Cold-rolled copper is harder to work with, but it's far stronger.

The green patina that eventually appears on copper can stain trim and shingles when rain runs off it. Even new copper isn't immune, as its surface is etched by acid. The main symptoms are bright red streaks on the roof and green stains on the siding.

Lead is durable and malleable, making it a favorite for cap flashing. It's also very common at the tops of valleys or at the bases of dormers and chimneys. Lead won't stain and is paintable. Before painting lead, let it weather for a bit, then scrub it with a good household cleaner to remove any oily film. Lead is a good choice for use in industrial environments.

The main problem with lead is the very softness that makes it popular. Lead tears easily, making it a poor choice for places where workers might walk at some point. Lead

GALVANIC SCALE

Active

Zinc
Aluminum
Steel
Cast Iron
Lead
Tin
Copper

Passive

When two dissimilar metals come together in the presence of moisture, the more "active" metal will corrode — a process called galvanic corrosion. The farther apart the metals are on the galvanic series, the greater the corrosion. To prevent galvanic corrosion, don't put dissimilar metals together, or — if you must — separate them with building paper or a bituminous membrane.

is also more durable if left hanging fairly free, as on a apron; when fastened on all sides, it will fatigue from movement.

Lead-coated copper is my first choice for most jobs, since it combines copper's durability with lead's resistance to staining. It consists of a sheet of 6-ounce cold-rolled copper with a coating of lead on each side. It has the same working properties as cold-rolled copper.

For added insurance, I install metal flashing over a self-adhering bituminous membrane, which serves as a backup watershed if the flashing develops any leaks. Membranes are easy to install and are relatively foolproof. They're also self-healing, which means that they automatically seal nail penetrations and the laps between sheets. And they're fully adhered, so water can't travel beneath them. Any leaks will remain localized. This prevents any water that gets under the roofing from reaching the sheathing.

By Joseph Cazeault, a roofer and metalworker from Edgartown, Mass.

INTERSECTION DETAILS

Valleys meeting at top. One place to avoid a soldered joint is where two valleys meet at the peak of a roof. Some builders cap the valleys with the same metal they use in the valley, and solder the valleys to the cap. But expansion and contraction of the valley will eventually break the soldered joint. The solution is to lap the cap over the valley as much as possible. I use lead flashing for this application (Figure A). If the overlap is sufficient, it will keep out windblown water without soldering. Six inches overlay is usually sufficient on a valley.

Shed dormers. Another problem area is where the sidewall of a shed dormer dies into the main roof, since snow can pile up at the intersection and water can blow up under the dormer's eaves. The cheek of the dormer is generally lined with step flashings, so the solution is to install taller step flashings along the top few feet of the dormer, and to fold these over the top of the roof sheathing (Figure B). The intersection where the dormer roof and sidewall meet the main roof is then covered with a continuous sheet of lead (which can be molded to fit the intersection) and isolated from the step flashings with a bituminous membrane. This takes some extra planning on the part of the builder, since the tall step flashing must be installed before the rake boards on the dormer. But it can save a callback down the road.

Cross gables. Where a pair of cross gables meet at an outside corner, drainage can be a headache. Since there's no place to put a gutter here, water is usually left to dump on the ground. But this invites water to puddle up against the foundation, and can soak the siding. The traditional way to drain these trouble spots was with a conductor head — a cylindrical catch basin poised at the top of a downspout. But if the downspout gets clogged, the conductor head can fill up with water and freeze. This can break it apart at the seams and cause water to back up under the roof.

A better solution is to use a cone-shaped scupper (Figure C). If the downspout stops up, the scupper's cone shape lets excess water spill over the sides instead of backing up under the roof; if it freezes, the ice will push itself up out of the cone, rather than pushing the cone apart.

Recessed windows. A tough flashing job which I occasionally

Figure A. A soldered joint at the top of a valley will break when the valley expands and contracts. Instead, the author laps a lead cap over the top of the valley flashing.

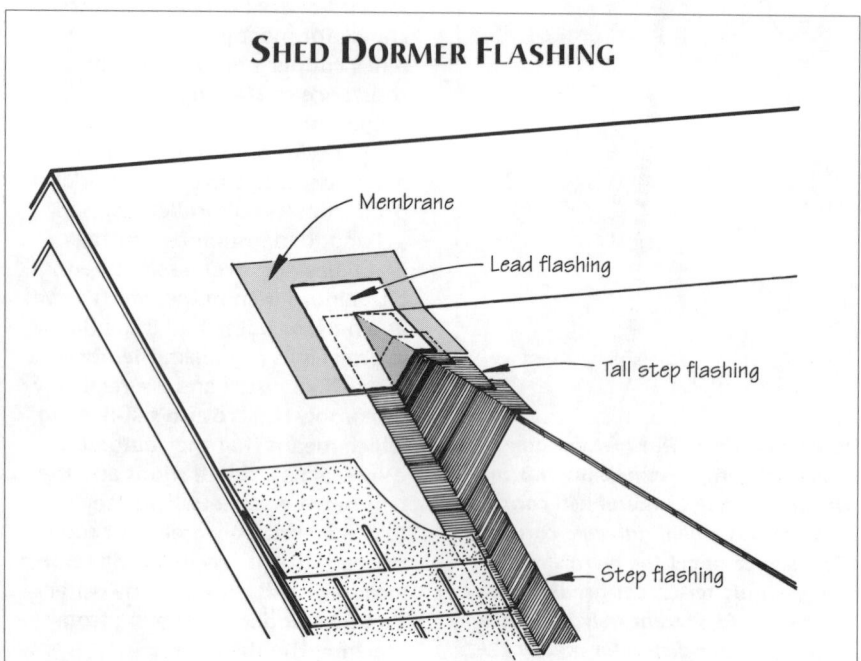

SHED DORMER FLASHING

Membrane

Lead flashing

Tall step flashing

Step flashing

Figure B. Using taller step flashings along the top few feet of a shed dormer will keep melting snow and windblown water out of the intersection.

Figure C. The author catches water at the junction of two cross gables with a soldered, cone-shaped scupper. Besides being attractive, the cone lets excess water spill over rather than backing up beneath the roof.

encounter is second-story windows recessed into a sloped roof — an application where sloppy flashings could spell disaster. Framing is important in these windows. I've seen recessed windows that sit right on the floor of the recess — a mistake that practically begs melting snow to seep under the sill. To prevent this, I typically ask the framer to step the rough sill at least 4 inches up from the recess. It's also good practice to slope the recess away from the window and toward the edge of the roof; the more slope, the better.

After lining the opening with a membrane, I solder together a lead-coated copper pan that covers the rough sill and the floor of the recess, as well as bending about 8 inches onto the shed roof (Figure D). The asphalt roof shingles later tuck beneath this bend. I then set the pan in place and carefully solder on a series of counterflashing pieces, making the flashing along the sides of the recess wide enough to extend a few inches beneath the roofing. The pan is left free-floating so that expansion and contraction doesn't break the solder joint. To keep out drafts and windblown rain, I set the window in a thick bead of caulk, holding the bead 1½ inches back from the sides of the opening to allow for drainage.

Crickets. Chimneys aren't the only places that need crickets. You need a cricket anywhere a roof slope runs into a vertical surface — such as the small towers that commonly break the roof line in Victorian houses (Figure E). A cricket should be a single piece of metal, whether bent in the shop or soldered together on site. The cricket needs firm support underneath, usually a base made of plywood.

Since a cricket is typically a large sheet of metal, it shouldn't be locked in place with nails, which will restrict expansion and contraction. Instead, it should be held with cleats like a valley flashing.

By Joseph Cazeault, a roofer and metalworker from Edgartown, Mass.

Figure D. To protect recessed windows, the author first covers the sloping shelf with bituminous eaves membrane, then covers the membrane with a one-piece soldered pan. Counterflashings are soldered on as needed.

Figure E. A cricket should be a single piece of metal, whether shop-fabricated or soldered together on site (left). To permit expansion and contraction, attach a cricket with cleats (below).

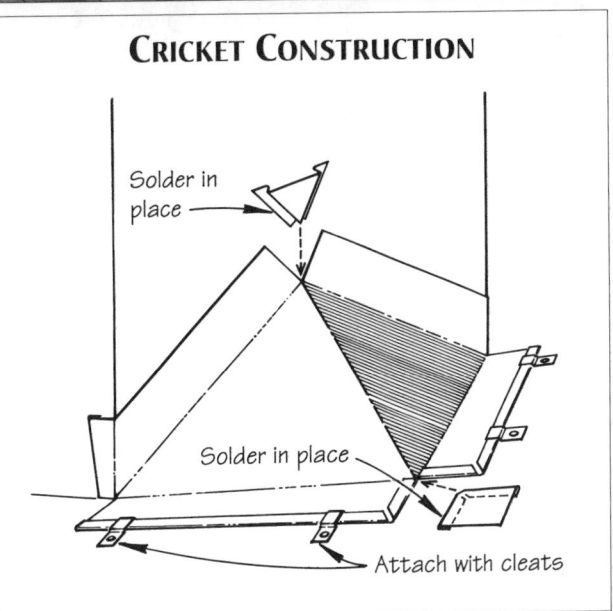

CRICKET CONSTRUCTION

Solder in place

Solder in place

Attach with cleats

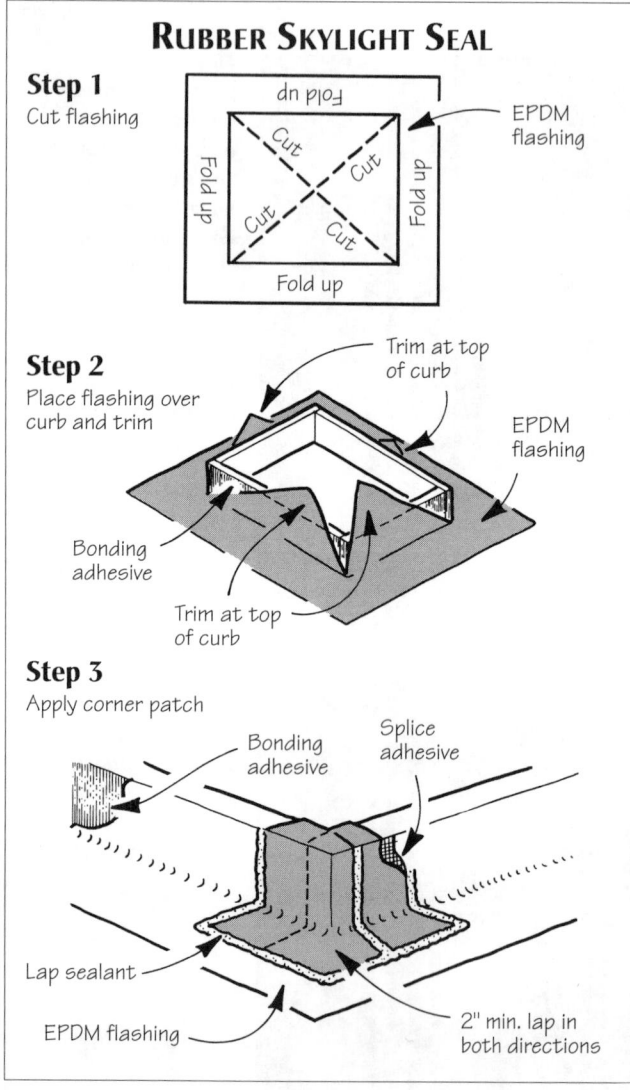

Rubber Skylight Seal

Step 1
Cut flashing

Fold up · Cut · Cut · Fold up · Fold up · Cut · Cut · Fold up · Fold up

EPDM flashing

Fold up

Step 2
Place flashing over curb and trim

Trim at top of curb

EPDM flashing

Bonding adhesive

Trim at top of curb

Step 3
Apply corner patch

Bonding adhesive

Splice adhesive

Lap sealant

EPDM flashing

2" min. lap in both directions

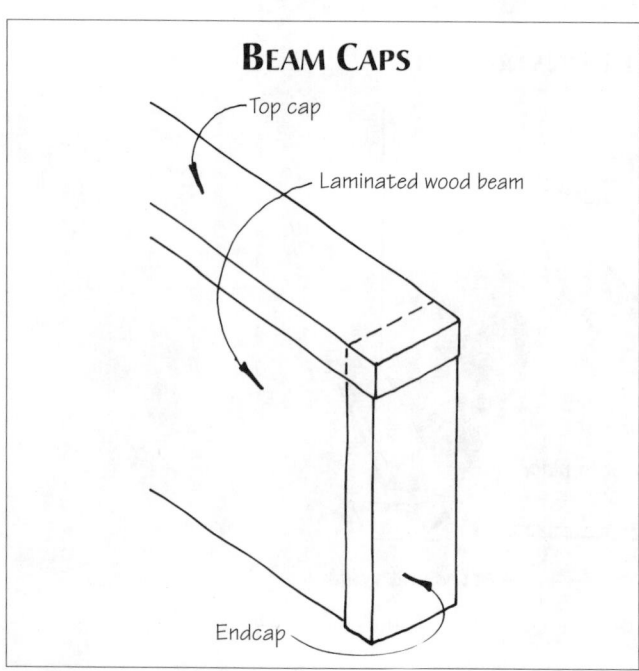

Beam Caps

Top cap

Laminated wood beam

Endcap

Figure 26. Cut a square of EPDM flashing to fit around the skylight. Trim the triangular flaps flush with the top of the curb. Bonding adhesive holds the EPDM rubber to the curb. The material is flexible enough to patch the corners as shown. Use splice adhesive where pieces of EPDM overlap.

Figure 27. Cover the ends and tops of laminated beams with flashing to prevent delamination.

less) we use a silicone sealant to keep blowing rain or snow out.

How far we extend the flashing under the shingles has a lot to do with the slope of the roof, but in general, we shoot for 24-inch-wide flashing. This gives us 12 inches up each slope. At the top of the valley, the shingles overlap the flashing 10 inches on each side, leaving 4 inches of valley flashing exposed. We plan our valleys so more of the valley is exposed as we get closer to the eaves. We need more exposure near the eaves because the valley carries more water lower on the roof. Besides, a slightly tapered valley looks better.

To give a valley greater strength and to keep water from rushing down one slope and up the other, we often form an inverted "V" in the center of the flashing. You can have a sheet metal shop form this "V" on a brake. This knocks about an inch off the flashing width, so you have to start with wider flashing. You always want shingles to overlap the flashing by about 8 inches.

On a slate, tile, wood shake, or concrete-tile roof, you should always use the "V." You also have to use flashing with a *water lock* — the edge on each side of the valley is folded back to stop the water. Also, cleats slip over the water-lock edges, and your nails go through the cleats, not the flashing. This makes your valley a trough to contain any water flowing into it.

Skylights

Flashing skylights can be a big headache, particularly if the skylight is attached to a curb. The traditional way to flash skylights is to use a metal flashing, but lately I've been using a synthetic rubber (EPDM) flashing, and I've found it a lot less expensive and more reliable.

I think an EPDM flashing beats metal for reliability, and it costs less too. For flashing, you'll want to use *uncured* EPDM, which is material intended to take a shape. Cured EPDM sheets lay flat and are used for large, flat roofs. If you go to a local roofing company and ask for a scrap piece of uncured EPDM flashing and a small quantity of the bonding adhesives, you'll be in business. The four major manufacturers of EPDM roofing market under many trade names, but if you use the generic name "uncured EPDM flashing," you should be able to buy what you need. The EPDM carries a 20-year warranty, and the material costs less than copper flashing.

Synthetic rubber is very simple to work with. You can take a large square of rubber, your shears, and adhesive (bonding adhesive, splice adhesive, and lap sealant) and carry them up to the roof. Sitting on the roof, you cut the rubber into pieces, brush on the bonding adhesive, and make up a fully waterproof skylight flashing. With metal, I have to measure the job, go back to the shop to make up the flashing, then go back and install it.

Use bonding adhesive to stick the EPDM to a 3 1/2- or 7 1/2-inch-high wood curb, but don't glue it down to the roof deck. Run the EPDM flashing 12 inches out under the shingles, on top of your black paper. At the corners, where you're bonding EPDM to itself, use splice adhesive (Figure 26). It's as easy as patching an inner tube, and if you make a mistake, you can always repair it. When you're done, run a bead of lap sealant along all the patched seams.

Nail shanks from the roofing nails can go through EPDM without causing leaks. I favor rubber for wood shingle or shake roofs because they're hard to flash with metal. You can't use EPDM over skip sheathing, but many shake, shingle, and tile roofs are installed over solid sheathing.

Projections

Any wood member that projects from the house should be flashed. Cornice returns, glulam beams, and balconies should be protected with flashing.

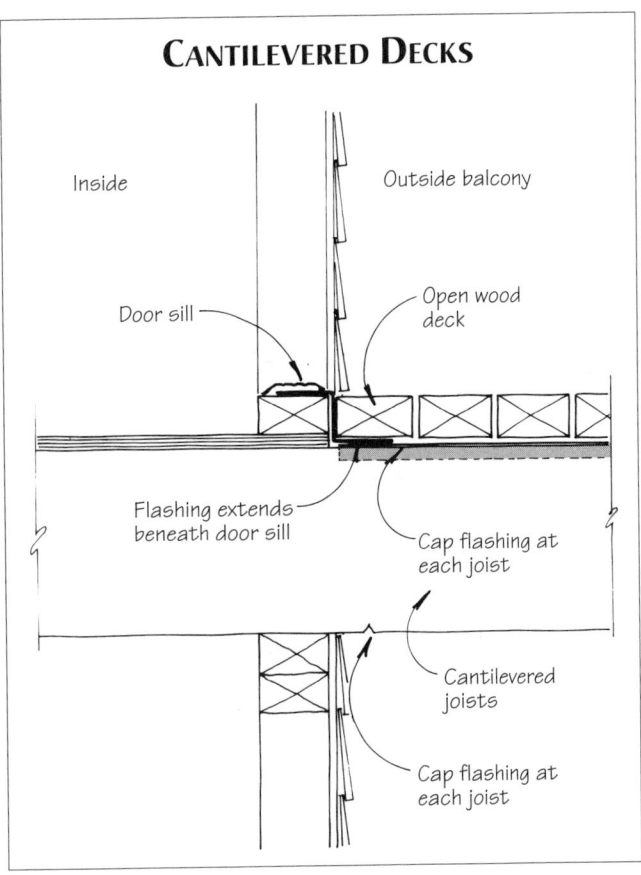

CANTILEVERED DECKS

Inside / Outside balcony / Door sill / Open wood deck / Flashing extends beneath door sill / Cap flashing at each joist / Cantilevered joists / Cap flashing at each joist

Figure 28. Flash cantilevered balcony joists and where the deck meets the wall. Run the flashing underneath the door sill and up the walls on either side of the door. A saw cut or bead of caulk on the underside of the joists about 2 inches from the siding will make water drip off the beam rather than run into the building.

Glulam or heavy timber beams projecting from the peak or eaves should be capped with metal. Turn down the metal an inch around the sides. You need flashing over the ends of glulam beams to keep the laminations from separating (Figure 27).

Balconies aren't immune to water damage, even when you build with pressure-treated wood. Water can run back into the house and damage untreated wood. Also, pressure-treated wood eventually decays. We're seeing many relatively new apartment buildings with cantilevered balconies that are rotting off. You can always replace a deck if it decays, but replacing the cantilevered joists is an expensive proposition.

You need to handle balcony flashing carefully because water or snow can pile up on the balcony and creep in under the sill of a sliding door. Water can also run back into the house from dripping balcony joists.

Bring your flashing under the door sill, and if the door is on the same level as the balcony, caulk between the sill and the flashing (Figure 28). You should also flash the wall where the balcony deck joins the house. Use the same flashing detail where the deck meets the wall, only run your flashing up under the siding.

It's also a good idea to top off your balcony joists with a 2 1/2-inch-wide piece of metal flashing running the length of the joist. Make it U-shaped so it slips down half an inch on both sides.

To keep water from running off the bottom of the joists, we make a saw mark across the bottom of the joists a couple of inches from the house, or we run a bead of caulk an inch from the wall if the client objects to the saw mark. This break causes water to drip off and keeps it from crawling inside.

By Lloyd Hitchins, president of Hitchins Roofing in Urbana, Ill., and a roofer of 45 years.

SOURCES OF SUPPLY

Slate Suppliers

Buckingham Virginia Slate Corp.
P.O. Box 8
Arvonia, VA 23004
804/581-1131

Structural Slate Company
222 E. Main St.
Pen Argyl, PA 18072
610/863-4141

Evergreen Slate Company
P.O. Box 248
Granville, NY 12832
518/642-2530

Vermont Structural Slate Company, Inc.
P.O. Box 98
Fair Haven, VT 05743
802/265-4933

Organic Felt Asphalt Shingles

BPCO Inc.
2850 Dollard Ave.
Lasalle, Quebec H8N 2V2
800/361-3656

Globe Building Materials Inc.
2230 Indianapolis Blvd.
Whiting, IN 46394
219/473-4500

Organic Felt Asphalt & Fiberglass Asphalt Shingles

Celotex Corp.
1 Metro Center
4010 Boy Scout Blvd.
Tampa, FL 33607
800/331-7451

GAF Building Materials Corp.
Residential Roofing Products
1361 Alps Rd.
Wayne, NJ 07470
201/628-3000

IKO Chicago Inc.
8725 W. Higgins Rd.
Suite 585
Chicago, IL 60631
708/496-2800

CertainTeed Corp.
Roofing Products Group
P.O. Box 1100
Blue Bell, PA 19422-0761
800/345-1145

Georgia-Pacific Corp.
133 Peachtree St. NE
Atlanta, GA 30303
404/652-4000

Tamko Asphalt Products Inc.
220 W. Fourth St.
Joplin, MO 64802
800/641-4691

Bituminous Membranes

Bird Inc.
1077 Pleasant St.
Norwood, MA 02062
617/551-0656
Ice and Water Barrier

CertainTeed Corp.
P.O. Box 1100
Blue Bell, PA 19422-0761
800/345-1145
Winter Guard

Protecto Wrap Co.
2255 S. Delaware St.
Denver, CO 80223
303/777-3001
Ice and Water Guard

Celotex Corp.
996 Old Eagle School Rd.
Wayne, PA 19087
610/964-8047
Celoguard

GAF Building Materials Corp.
1861 Alps Rd.
Wayne, NJ 07470
201/628-3000
Weather Watch

W.R. Grace & Co.
62 Whittemore Ave.
Cambridge, MA 02140
800/354-5414
Ice and Water Shield

CHAPTER 6

PAINTS AND COATINGS

- Painting Failures: Case Studies

- The New Water-Based Paints

- Clear Finishes for Wood Siding

- Problem-Free Floor Finishes

- Remodelers and Lead Paint

PAINTING FAILURES: CASE STUDIES

Case One: Yellowing Enamel

Project: White oil enamel on the interior trim in high-end condos in southern California.

The problem. The building interiors were specced out in straight white, both walls and trim. The plan called for a good oil enamel on the baseboards and a lot of other interior trim that normally doesn't get a gloss finish. The walls were flat latex. And within six months, the trim in some of those houses was almost a mustard color next to the white walls. The enamel had yellowed, but the flat latex remained white.

The builder tired to correct the problem by painting again with another batch of white oil enamel, but it yellowed too.

What the painting contractor Mark Robson had run into was a two-fold problem: a regional decorating trend calling for straight white enamels on trim surfaces; and new environmental regulations that have compromised the fade resistance of those same oil-based enamels.

All oil-alkyd resin materials yellow. But they yellow more now than in the past because of the higher resin content in the low-VOC

paints. The yellowing effects can be dramatic in as little as three months. And it's especially noticeable with extremely light colors like pure whites and near whites.

Robson found that the degree of yellowing varied with exposure to sunlight. Surfaces that got little or no sunlight yellowed faster than those that were well-lit. Sunny living rooms might not have a noticeable problem, while a closet or the interior of a cabinet would have mustard-colored trim.

The fix. One option is to use latex. But latex has its own problems. It doesn't stand up to abrasion and

THE IMPORTANCE OF PREP WORK

Applying a top coat on bare wood without first brushing the dust off and priming is a frequent source of early peeling on new houses. Experienced painters carry a dust brush in their overalls pocket and brush all areas to be painted.

On already-painted buildings, paint failure can be caused by:
• Applying a new coat over chalky, dusty, oily, or dirty paint.
• Painting over mildew.

Backed-up water from ice dams can wreck both interior and exterior finishes — including paint on the soffit, fascia, and siding.

No primer was used here and the result was poor adhesion and wholesale peeling to bare wood. One telltale sign was the absence of any white pigment on the wood or the back of the paint chips.

• Painting over shiny paint.
• Applying oil-based paint on a surface not thoroughly dry.

Some of the remedies should be self-evident, but others aren't. How should a surface be prepared to ensure a longlasting job?

Bare wood should first be brushed dry and then be primed with an oil-based primer; it has a greater penetration of the wood-fiber surface than latex.

It's best to brush the bare wood as you go along and prime only an area you can handle in a day. Try to do only one side of the house or stop at logical spots where picking up later will not show. Then, applying a finish coat over the day's primer coat within 48 hours, if possible. The longer you wait the weaker the bond is going to be, since the surface of the primer is increasingly compromised by dust and weather.

Previously painted surfaces should also be brushed clean and even washed if dirt, chalk, mildew, or other impurities are present. Rub your hand on the wood to determine chalkiness, a self-cleaning feature of many oil paints. Wash a small test area with detergent

washing as well as oil does, and it doesn't stick to previously painted surfaces as well unless you really prep the surface. It can freeze windows shut and stick other surfaces together, though latexes are better about that than they used to be. Sometimes it doesn't cover as well as oil material would, on both old and new work. But mostly, you just cannot get the appearance, feel, and hard durability of oil from a latex enamel.

Another option is to change the color of off-whites — since these tend to be yellow-gray to begin with — so the discoloration will be less noticeable. Use something as dark as a Navajo White and you're probably not going to have problems with the homeowner. Lighter than that, though, and you're taking chances if you're using oil.

Case Two: Slippery Stucco

Project: Exterior woodwork on a 40-house subdivision in southern California. The siding material was spray-on stucco, a plaster material.

Where painting contractor Mark Robson paints, in southern California, spray-on stucco — actually a plaster material — is a popular exterior treatment. But Robson has found that the prep work done by stucco subs can foul things up for the painters.

The problem. Robson's crew painted the woodwork on an entire 40-house subdivision. It looked fine when they finished, but the paint on the exterior of the window frames peeled off in less than three or four months. It was the worst nearest the glass, but it peeled away from the glass as well.

With a little detective work Robson discovered that the plasterers, who sprayed the stucco over the outside walls, had sprayed an oily solution over all the windows. Like greasing a frying pan, this lets any stucco that hits the glass come off easily. Unfortunately, this solution hit the frames as well as the windows, causing the paint to peel.

In the end, Robson had to go back to the site, scrape all the peeling paint off the window frames to expose bare wood, wash the wood with solvent,

(trisodium phosphate works best) and water to determine if the blotchy look is caused by dirt, mildew, or both. Dirt will come off but mildew spores will not be affected.

Mildew, however, will respond immediately to the bleach test; put a small amount of fresh bleach in a glass container, add the same amount of water, and rub the suspected spots with a white cloth dipped in the mixture. Rubber gloves and eye protection are advised as well as old clothing. If the spots yellow and disappear before your eyes, mildew is the culprit and must be entirely removed before painting (or staining, for that matter).

A good way to clean a chalky, oily, or dirty surface while killing mildew spores is to wash it with a mixture of one cup of trisodium phosphate (TSP), one quart fresh bleach, and three quarts of warm water (do not mix any products containing ammonia with bleach as the resulting gas is deadly). Use a scrub brush. Rinse thoroughly with fresh water.

If mildew is a severe problem, follow the above treatment by scrubbing with a solution of 50 percent fresh bleach and 50 percent water but, this time, do not rinse. Let dry and follow immediately

Make sure you prep and paint the butt edges and butt joints to prevent this type of water penetration and peeling. Also avoid painting when the wood is swollen with moisture lest it shrink and crack the paint at joints — especially if you're using oil-based paint, which is less flexible than latex.

with painting before airborne spores of mildew are deposited again. (Water-based paints can be applied while the surface is damp but not wet.)

Mildew, however, is likely to recur. The spores are everywhere in the air and will take hold and develop wherever the conditions are propitious: warmth, humidity, and lack of sun. A mildewcide added to the paint should delay new growth for a while.

Before repainting, remove all peeling paint, feather the edges of any paint still adhering, prime the bare wood, and apply a new coat over all. A word of caution here: If the remaining coats of paint are thick, adding another on top may create more problems. It would be better to only spot-paint the bare, primed areas — even though the house may look like it has a rash or jaundice — unless you want to sand down or remove the areas of thick paint.

The only reason to paint over an existing coat in good shape is to change color. If the paint is still shiny, it will have to be roughed up with sandpaper and brushed clean to form a good bond with the new coat.

By Henri deMarne, a consultant, home inspector, and nationally syndicated columnist from Waitsfield, Vt.

and reprime and repaint. (The builder paid for it all.) But even with these steps, the longevity of the finish coat will be compromised.

To avoid this problem, have the plasterers mask the windows; leave the window casings off until after the plasterers are gone; or have the painters come out ahead of the plasterers and prime the windows. Of these, priming is the least effective, since the oil will still stick to the primer, which will require cleaning afterward. Keeping the oily solution from ever hitting the window frames in the first place is the best prevention and keeps painting costs down.

Case Three: Mildew on New Home Siding

Project: White oil-based paint on the wood siding of a custom home in Illinois.

The problem. This was a large new house built in 1989 for a retiree. The owner wanted oil paint, so the contractor Margaret Clifton specced top-of-the-line oil. The owner also insisted that the painter use up a few gallons of 8- to 10-year-old Sears oil paint he had in the basement.

A year later, the owner asked Clifton to stop by and showed her that the expensive oil-based paint had turned gray on every side of the house with mildew (Figure 1). However, the old Sears paint, which they had used on the garage, remained sparkling white.

The rep from the paint company came to the site and confirmed that it was mildew caused, in part, by the cool, damp spring.

But why did the porch with the old Sears paint look so good? As it turns out, the older paint had mercury in it as a mildewcide, while the newer paint didn't. The company had removed mercury from all its formulations because of the impending ban on mercury. The new mildewcides, the rep said, are not as effective, and furthermore, mildew feeds on the oil in oil-based paints.

The fix. The rep's suggestion was to wash the house with a mixture of one part chlorine bleach to three parts water and one part trisodium phosphate. That, he said, would remove the mildew but it wouldn't prevent the mildew from coming back.

For that, they would need to repaint the house with latex — after sanding the entire house to rough up the nice glossy finish of the oil paint.

Case Four: Cool, Wet Weather Peels Paint

Project: A repaint of a large 150-year-old colonial in northern Vermont.

The problem. In Vermont, where painting contractor Jay Bowen is based, the painting season is short, and summertime brings heavy use of the second homes and resort sites that make up much of his work. So Bowen must often paint exteriors in early spring or late fall, when cold evening temperatures can bring heavy dew. Under some conditions,

Figure 1. Mildew appeared on this house (top) in Momence, Ill., within a year of repainting. The contractor traced the problem to new blends of oil-based paint that don't contain mercury mildewcides. Where a ten-year-old Sears paint was used on a porch (above), the walls were still gleaming white.

dew can take new paint off the same day it's applied.

In this case, the house needed major prep work: scraping and sanding right down to the wood. Then Bowen's crew applied an oil primer and two coats of white latex finish on both the clapboards and trim. This was in late September.

They finished brushing the second coat on a nice fall day with the temperatures in the 60s. They worked until late in the afternoon, and as they were putting away their brushes it got cooler and damp. It didn't start raining, but a mist developed as it got dark. It stayed foggy all night. Most of the paint had tacked up nicely before they left.

When they went back the next day to hang the shutters, they found the paint on two sides of the house was completely wet — as if they'd just brushed it on.

The fix. Because the paint was still so wet, they were able to brush out what was on there, using a can of paint to keep the brushes wet. Had the paint been oil, a skin would have formed, and the water from the dew would have discolored everything. Then they would have had to let it dry, sand it, and repaint. With the latex, there was no skin and they could pick up where they left off.

They were also fortunate that they

PAINT PROBLEMS

Cross-grain cracking and alligatoring are frequently found on older houses that have been painted many times over the years, and often before a new coat of paint was due. These problems occur because the paint becomes too thick to flex with the seasonal movement of the wood.

The paint principally cracks perpendicular to the brush strokes, which generally follow the grain of the wood. Hence the term "cross-grain cracking." The phenomenon is also known as "alligatoring" because the cracking paint mimics the pattern of the skin of that amphibian.

If this is the paint condition, all paint should be removed down to bare wood by scraping, sanding, or heat gun (never a torch). Painting over alligatoring is a waste of energy and money.

Blistering can also occur when a second coat of oil-based paint is applied before the first one is thoroughly dry. In this case, paint thinner instead of water vaporizes under the influence of the sun and causes the paint to blister.

Bleed-through can be caused by certain natural wood products. Redwood and cedar contain a pigment which is dissolved by moisture and leaches out onto painted surfaces through cracks in the paint surface. Resolving the moisture problem, whether it is through leaks from the outside or from internal moisture pressure, then letting the wood dry

over several months of summer and fall, is the solution.

The remaining stains can be washed off with a mixture of 50% denatured alcohol and 50% water after the failed paint has been removed. The edges of the sound paint should be feathered and the wood primed.

Hardboard siding has similar problems. Bleed-through is caused by some of the products used in its manufacture — including wax. The treatment is similar to that for redwood and cedar; the composition siding must be allowed to dry and the reason for its wetness removed. Hardboard siding is more prone to problems caused by internal moisture pressure because it does not have the moisture storage ability that wood has.

Some species of wood exude resin at knots. This may be a tricky problem to resolve. The excess resin should be removed with a sharp knife or chisel and the knot treated with a stain killer such as B.I.N. This treatment may not be successful at first. It may have to be repeated until most of the resin has oozed out.

Nailhead staining is caused by rusting nails. (Using hot-dipped galvanized nails in new construction will prevent this.) Where encountered, the rust should be removed by sanding, wirebrushing, or the application of a liquid rust remover. The coated nail should be slightly countersunk and primed. The hole should be filled

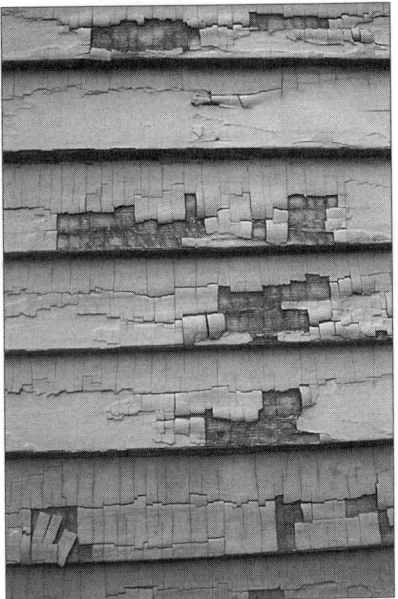

Painting too often causes alligatoring and cross-grain cracking. These problems are most common on areas sheltered from the weather where the paint is put on but never wears off. Painting every 5 to 10 years is best.

with caulk which can be painted when dry.

Obtaining a successful and lasting paint job requires proper preparation of the surface, good application procedures, and quality products. Where failures occurred in the past, you'll need to find and resolve the underlying problems if you want the new coat to last.

By Henri deMarne, a consultant, home inspector, and nationally syndicated columnist from Waitsfield, Vt.

arrived on the job early in the day, because if they had waited until afternoon, the drips would have hardened, and they would have had to scrape or sand. It also happened to be a good sunny day, so by the afternoon the backbrushing work had set up nicely. Six years later the paint job still looks great.

The moral of this story, says Bowen, is that with a high dew point (high relative humidity and cooler night-time temperatures) and a short day, you can get into trouble. In fall and spring he now pays atten-

tion to weather forecasts to find out whether the overnight low is expected to dip below the dew point. Then he keeps an eye on the afternoon weather so he can leave the paint sufficient time to dry. If there's any chance that they might get a big enough drop in temperature to cross the dew point, says Bowen, they knock off with a couple of hours of daylight left.

Case Five: Two Coats in One Day

Project: Solid oil-based stain on new cedar siding in Vermont.

The problem. Painter Jay Bowen was called in to diagnose and correct a problem on a new house in Vermont that had been sided in cedar and stained just four months earlier. Two coats of oil-based solid stain had been applied and both coats were bubbling right off the surface. This was on two or three areas of the house — the back, and two areas on one side. So Bowen suspected an application problem rather than a problem with the wood or stain.

The factory rep from the stain manufacturer was called in to take a look, and his best guess was that the first coat hadn't been allowed to fully cure before the second coat was put on. At that point the owner recalled that the shaded front of the house — which was the side in best shape — had been first-coated one afternoon and top-coated the next. The problem sides, on the other hand, got two coats in one day, and got a lot of midday sun.

This is actually a fairly easy mistake to make with solid stains, says Bowen, because they can appear dry on the surface but still be damp underneath. If you put on a second coat at that point, the solvent in the first coat won't be able to evaporate, and it'll bubble the stain. In this case, the sides in question were exposed to the sun, so after a first coat in the morning, the painters probably checked it at lunch and found it dry to the touch. But underneath, the first coat hadn't cured.

The same thing can happen with an oil-based paint, since oil-based coatings can't breathe. It's less dangerous with a latex.

The fix. For this reason, Bowen likes to let all oil-based coatings cure for at least 24 hours before recoating, while he'll recoat latexes after only 12 hours.

As for the bubbled stain job, Bowen had to scrape the problem areas off and repaint. That was most of the material on those two walls

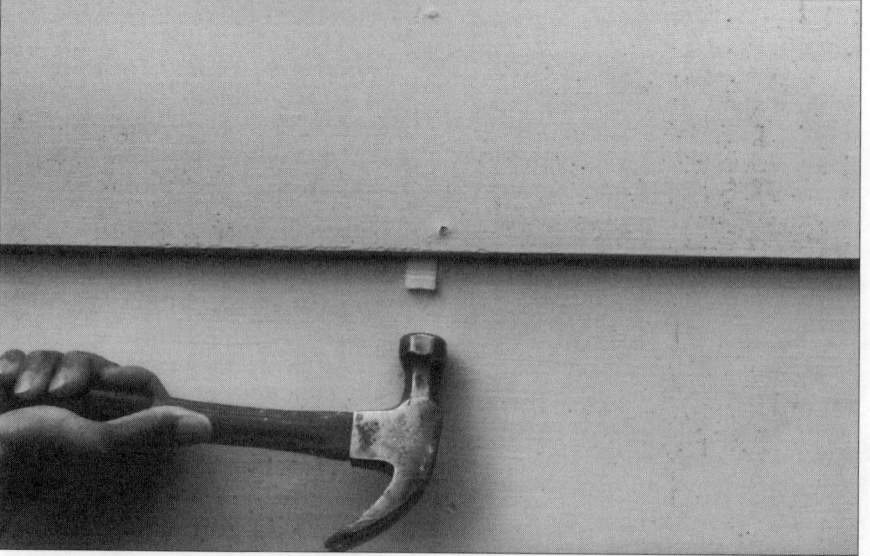

Figure 2. No vapor barrier and high indoor humidity caused the paint to peel on this building (top). The painting contractor found that driving small wedges (above) under every sixth row of siding, 3 or 4 feet apart, allowed the moisture to escape and solved the problem.

which came off with one pass of a sharp scraper.

After scraping he left the surface bare for two or three days to let it dry, then resealed it with another linseed-oil-based solid stain. He let that dry for another three days, then put on the second coat. The house didn't have any more problems.

Case Six: Missing Vapor Barrier

Project: A large wood-frame commercial building in Vermont with wood siding that needed frequent repainting.

The problem. One of the most common causes of paint failure is moisture being pushed through the siding from behind, due to high indoor humidity and the lack of a good air and vapor barrier. The ideal solution for this problem is to install vapor barriers indoors, ventilate bathrooms and kitchens, and back-prime the siding. A house wrap can

also help by keeping moist interior air from getting to the back of the siding. But owners may balk at the expense of these retrofitting measures. Painter Jay Bowen found an innovative way to increase paint longevity on a building he was repainting every two years.

It was a big clapboard building near a river, with shops downstairs and apartments upstairs. It was about 150 years old. Every year the whole thing would peel, despite the fact that they would do a high-quality job — scraping it down to the wood, putting on an oil-based primer and two coats of good latex.

The side that peeled the most faced the river, but it also got a lot of sun in the afternoon. So it tended to pick up moisture at night and dry in the day. But the main problem was from within. The worst peeling came from exactly where the bathrooms and kitchens were.

The fix. Since Bowen couldn't keep the moisture inside, he decided to let it get out easier so it wouldn't peel the paint. His solution was to tap wedges under every sixth row or so of clapboards, spaced about 3 or 4 feet apart (Figure 2). The tiny wedges were just big enough to leave a fingernail-sized gap. He also put a few round, 1-inch vents into the walls, and primed the whole building with Zinsser's Bull's-Eye (William Zinsser & Co. Inc., 39 Belmont Dr., Somerset, NJ 08875; 201/469-8100), which is designed to prevent cedar and knot bleed, and followed that with two coats of latex.

There were no further serious problems. There were still small areas that would peel every few years, but these were easy to repair.

David Dobbs is a freelance writer from Montpelier, Vt.

THE NEW WATER-BASED PAINTS

The paint industry is changing fast these days. As coatings manufacturers reformulate their products to adhere to stricter air pollution standards, they are altering the way paints and other finishes behave, both on the brush and on the finished surface.

The move to water-based paints (often generically called "latex" paints, though latex is no longer an ingredient) is being driven by a growing body of state and city regulations that limit the amount of VOCs — volatile organic compounds — allowed in paints. When VOCs are released into the air, they react with other elements and with sunlight to form ozone. Ozone is desirable in the upper atmosphere, where it filters sunlight; at ground level, though, it's a harmful pollutant and the main ingredient in smog.

Because traditional oil-based

paints contain very high levels of VOCs (about 5 to 10 times higher than water-based coatings), manufacturers have had to radically change their formulations. This has reduced the workability of oil-based paints, radically lengthened drying time, and produced enamels that lose their gloss or discolor within months of application. The problems have proved so difficult to solve that most paint professionals believe that oil-based paints are on their way out, except for specialized uses.

Because I share this opinion, I've made a conscious effort to move gradually toward the use of water-based paints in almost all applications.

Water-Based Advantages

Today's best water-based paints have several advantages over reformulated oil-based finishes, and man-

ufacturers are rapidly solving the remaining deficiencies.

Water-based coatings generally apply more easily and retain both color and sheen better than the new oil-based paints do. Dark colors fade less, whites stay white longer, clears are clearer. Water-based paints, which use acrylic or vinyl-acrylic binders, flex and stretch more readily, allowing them to withstand wood movement. They dry faster, too, which can sometimes cause problems but usually proves an asset because it speeds the job.

Water-based paints present fewer problems in humid or damp weather; you can even paint over slightly damp surfaces, because the more open chemical structure of water-based paint lets moisture out. Water-based paints resist mildew better than oil-based paints do. And of course, water-based paints are less messy to apply, easier to clean up, and don't smell as strong as oil-based paints.

Application Tips

With water-based coatings, attention to quality products and good technique are more important than ever.

Buy the good stuff. Most contractors already know that the best latex paints are the "all acrylics" — those in which the binders are 100% acrylic, which is more durable than the vinyl used in early latex paints and in some bargain paints today.

I use different brands of paints for different applications, but if I have a favorite overall brand, it's Miracle Adhesives (Pratt & Lambert Specialty Products, P.O. Box 1505, Buffalo, NY 14240; 800/876-7005). Pratt & Lambert offers good quality across its entire product line, and their technical assistance has been excellent. Benjamin Moore (Benjamin Moore & Co., 51 Chestnut Ridge Rd., Montvale, NJ 07645; 201/573-9600) is another brand with high quality across its entire line. I also like Sherwin-Williams (The Sherwin-Williams Co., 101 Prospect Ave. NW, Cleveland, OH 44115; 216/566-2000) because they have such a wide selection, particularly in speciality products like sign paint and primers for metal surfaces.

Whatever brand you choose, buy at or near the top of the line. It's also important to read the label directions and any supplementary literature the manufacturer offers. And don't be shy about calling the company's technical staff with specific questions. These people often possess recently acquired information that has not yet found its way onto the paint can.

For instance, I once called Sikkens (AKZO Nobel Coatings, Inc., 1845 Maxwell St., Troy, MI 48084; 800/833-7288) because I was having problems getting a semi-transparent finish to adhere to some cedar benches and decks. The Sikkens people told me that the "mill glaze" on the new lumber was probably repelling the stain and suggested I wash the wood before finishing it. I did, and the stain adhered beautifully. This was a few years ago, at a time when mill glaze was a new problem, and the tech people were just learning how to deal with it. Such current information is particularly helpful today, when product manufacturers are in the middle of a learning curve themselves.

Be prepared. Water-based finishes require more thorough surface preparation, cleaning, and careful application than oil-based finishes. Remove any loose paint, and clean any dirty or oily surfaces. For most surfaces, I use Spic-and-Span powder; on a very oily surface, I use painter's naptha.

Put it on right. Applying water-based paints is different from applying oil-based paints. Spraying water-based paints, for instance, often produces an orange-peel texture. Sometimes you can solve this problem by adding thinner — water in the case of water-based paints — though too much thinner degrades the paint film. You might also try using larger or smaller spray tips. As a last resort, have a second person brush or roll right behind the sprayer. Paint manufacturers are making progress on this problem, but brands vary, so it pays to experiment a bit.

Also take care not to spray too thick a coat, because water-based paints have a greater tendency to run and sag. To prevent this, don't linger with the nozzle and avoid lapping passes, both on flat surfaces and in corners. And stay alert: Because

Figure 3. Because water-based paints dry quickly, it's easy to over-brush — leaving visible brush marks in the finished surface (left). Likewise, with latex stains, lapping marks result when a second coat is applied over partially dried stain (below). Avoid laps by brushing or spraying small areas at a time and keeping a wet edge.

water-based paints dry so quickly, you have only a few minutes — often less than 20 — to go back and brush or roll out any sags or runs. Brushing requires similar cautions. It's a good idea, whether brushing, rolling, or spraying, to keep a wet edge. This may mean painting smaller areas at a time (Figure 3).

Interior latex enamels are even more demanding. The best new interior acrylic enamels level fairly well with a high-quality paintbrush — but you should brush less than you would with oil-based paints. It takes practice not to leave fine brush marks in high-gloss latex paints. Use long, fairly rapid strokes, taking care not to abruptly dive in or pull off with the brush at the beginning or end of a stroke. Use as few strokes as required to produce an even coat, then leave it alone — you'll leave a brush mark if you try to touch up when the paint is half-dry.

Finally, use the best brush you can buy. This should be standard practice by now, but I'm still surprised at how many contractors try to save money on paintbrushes. I like brushes made by Purdy, which are widely available.

Inside Jobs

Here's how I handle the peculiarities and limitations of water-based finishes in different interior situations.

Walls. Since most people already use latex interior wall paint, I'll limit myself here to a summary of the different finishes and their uses. Different paint makers use varying nomenclatures, but most make three wall finishes: flat; eggshell (slight sheen); and semi-gloss, or satin. I use flat for most walls, though I often use eggshell in closets, because glare is not a problem and the sheen makes the wall more cleanable. I use eggshell or satin for bathrooms or kitchen walls that will receive some splash or dirt (Figure 4).

For priming walls before wallpapering, oil-base primers have long

been standard, and many wall covering manufacturers still specify it. However, I successfully use Zinsser's Shieldz (Wm. Zinsser & Co., 173 Belmont Dr., Somerset, NJ 08875; 908/469-8100).

Trim: the last frontier. By "trim" I mean doors, door and window casings, baseboards and other moldings, and cabinet work. The finish on these areas will receive close scrutiny, so you want an attractive and smooth, easy-to-clean surface. Trim paint must be durable, for it will be touched, bumped, banged, and brushed against. The paint surface will have to stand up to chemicals (oils from hands on door jambs, chemical cleaners mopped up against baseboards) and abrasion.

At present, oil-based enamels still

excel in providing most of these qualities — particularly the smooth, lustrous sheen — and trim is thus one of the few areas where I still routinely use oil-based paints. (Where I live, you can still buy the older formulas.) I've already used a latex enamel, however — Sherwin-Williams Super Paint — on a couple of small jobs, and it's worked pretty well. I had difficulty preventing sags and runs when spraying, though I worked that out, and the paint lacked the luster that oil paints have when they dry. But the owner was pleased and the job is holding up well.

Water-based enamels are catching up with oil-based, and I expect to switch over within a few years.

Primers for trim. I may be slower to switch to water-based interior

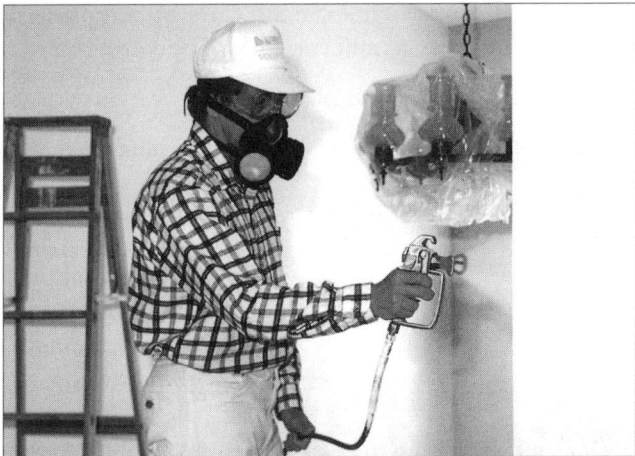
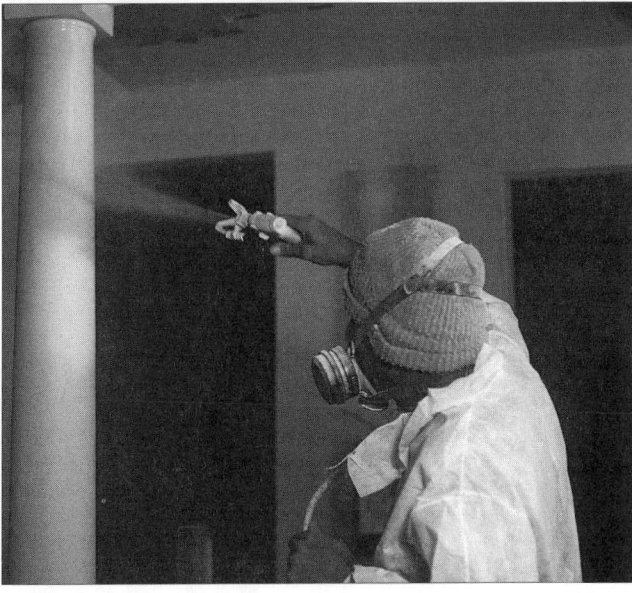

Figure 4. The author uses water-based paints for interior walls and ceilings (left), though he prefers oil-based paints, which are glossier, for interior trim (below).

primers for trim — this seems to be an area where water-based products still lag significantly. To produce a really smooth surface for enamel finishes on trim, I often extensively sand the primer (which itself needs to lay on smoothly), but the water-based primers I've tried so far don't sand well. Their "gummy" nature clogs the paper, and the rubberlike surface often stretches and tears rather than powdering. What's worse, the water in water-based primers can raise the wood's grain, thus requiring even more sanding. Between the raised grain and the difficulty with sanding — and the severe degree to which these problems compromise the final finish — I find it better to stick to oil-based primers for now.

Even here, though, there are signs of promise. For instance, the Hydrocote Co. (P.O. Box 160, Tennent, NJ 07763; 800/229-4937) makes a water-based sanding sealer, a protective clear coat you put on wood — cabinets, for instance — before painting, and it sands beautifully. I would never have dreamed a water-based finish could sand so well. I don't know how this quality is achieved, but it bodes well for the sandability of future paints and primers.

Interior stains. With the old oil-based stains I once used, I could put a beginner on a job and end up with a good finish. With water-based stains I've used, any place you overlap or brush twice — such as at a corner — will be twice as dark as the places you brush just once. And the quick drying time leaves little opportunity to go back and level out thick spots. The stains perform well, however, if you spread them evenly, don't overlap, and make sure you produce a uniform thickness. In other words, use an extra measure of the same good technique that all water-based products require.

Interior clear finishes. I started using Hydrocote for floors and other interior clear finishes about six years ago, and I have stuck with it. Most of the major brands make similar products now. These new products behave differently from their oil-based cousins, and you have to get the hang of using them. For instance, the labels on Hydrocote products warn of a temporary purplish cast on the drying finish, but on those first couple of jobs, I still got nervous waiting for that loud purple sheen to clear up. The color disappeared, however, and the finishes have held up well.

On the Outside

Outdoors, I use water-based paints for almost everything except priming tricky spots or tannin-heavy wood species.

Walls. Latex paints are more flexible, breathable, weather-durable, and mildew-resistant than oil-based paints are — all the qualities we look for in an exterior paint. The only place an oil-based topcoat might hold a marginal advantage is for frequently handled surfaces such as doors or handrails.

For routine outdoor priming, including priming the backs and ends of new siding (a must with today's finicky lumber), I use latex primers; they apply easily, hold up well, and their quick drying time lets me get to the topcoats more quickly. There are two exterior conditions, however, in which I still prefer oil.

Priming those iffy spots. I don't do too many exterior repaint jobs, but when I do, I still use oil primers where the paint is chalky, oily, or poorly adhered (Figure 5). Ideally, such areas should be sanded to bare wood before priming; but where budget restrictions prevent such preparation, an oil-based primer will provide the most secure base for the finish coat. Some of the new water-based acrylic

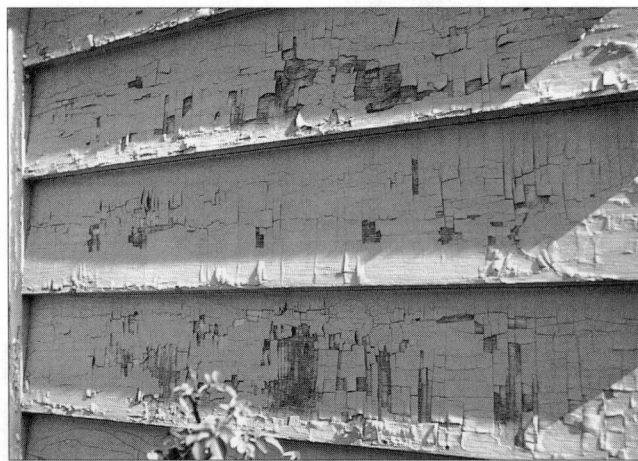

Figure 5. For exterior jobs, the author uses an oil-based primer on woods that are prone to staining, such as redwood and cedar, and on any previously painted surfaces where the paint has failed. Examples include cross-grain cracking, which results from excessive paint buildup (above), and intercoat peeling, which is caused by poor surface preparation (left).

primers, such as Zinsser's 1-2-3, are closing this gap. This is an area in which I'm experimenting, but for now I tend to go with oil-based primers.

Priming tannin-heavy woods. The other place most water-based primers presently fall short is in blocking the tannin stains characteristic of cedar and redwood. Some of the new "stain killing" water-based primers may do the job, but they usually require two coats. If I just need to seal a few knot-holes, that's okay. But if I need to block tannin stains in an entire siding job, as with redwood or cedar, priming twice costs too much — I'd lose the bid. So I still use oil-based primers for priming redwood or cedar; then I follow with a topcoat of high-quality acrylic.

Exterior stains and clears. Outside, I still use oil-based stains and clear finishes, usually Sikkens or Penofin (Performance Coatings, P.O. Box 1569, Ukiah, CA 95482; 800/736-6346). These look great, though they require washing and recoating every year or two. I haven't found any exterior stain or clear finish, either oil- or water-based, that will hold up longer than that. For a clear finish on cedar siding, you might also consider Flood's CWF — a petroleum-distillate-based product that usually costs less than many oil-based formulas (The Flood Co., P.O. Box 2535, Hudson, OH 44236; 800/321-3444).

As far as water-based stains go, the ones I've used so far don't penetrate well and look kind of muddy. If you use a water-based exterior stain, take care to apply a consistent coat and minimize overlaps so as not to produce uneven color.

Adapting to Change

When change is unavoidable, as it is now with paints, smart painters and contractors will embrace it slowly rather than all at once. You can't just bring in a whole new line of paints on a big job and expect to dodge major trouble. It's better to change proven methods and products gradually, experimenting when time permits, working out the bugs one at a time. That way, you will avoid major disruptions in your schedule and maintain the quality of work you are known for.

By Byron Papa, a custom builder and remodeler in Durham, N.C.

CLEAR FINISHES FOR WOOD SIDING

In siding, the "natural" look is in vogue these days, with many customers wanting to preserve the color of new redwood or cedar siding without painting or staining. However, keeping the natural look requires unnatural finishes to block the action of moisture and sun.

Wood siding turns gray because of two factors: the degradation by sun and water of the outermost layer of wood cells, which turn gray as their natural oils dry out; and the growth of tiny mildew spores on the wood's surface. Preventing this graying while retaining a natural look is the job of the current generation of clear and natural-tone tinted finishes. These coatings are formulated to protect the wood from graying with a combination of replenishing oils (which are essentially the same as in any other oil-based stain) and what the industry calls "UV blockers."

Clear Vs. Tinted

Clear finishes, having no pigment, attempt to block the sun's effect solely with UV blockers. These come in two basic types, either or both of which might be present in a given clear finish. (Manufacturers are fairly secretive about their formulas.) One type is an inorganic "reflector," made of transparent iron-oxide pigments that let visible light through, but which block UV light. The other type is the "absorber," composed of organic chemicals that protect the wood by absorbing UV rays.

These UV blockers are similar to skin sunscreens: They block and/or absorb the sun's UV rays, but only for a while. Given exposure to sun and water, they eventually wear off (in the case of the "reflecting" clear pigments) or wear out (in the case of UV absorbers). This usually happens within a year or two. At that point, they must be replenished if the skin of the building is to remain protected. If they're not, the siding gets its version of sunburn — it turns gray.

A *tinted* finish — that is, one lightly pigmented to a wood tone such as cedar or redwood — is often a better choice than a clean finish when a client or builder wants to preserve and enhance the natural tones of new cedar or redwood siding; that is, they want the siding to retain its original honey or reddish tone and not turn gray. While a tinted finish won't substantially change the appearance of the wood (other than heightening the grain and deepening the tones), its pigments will protect the wood longer than a clear finish will — perhaps for three to five years instead of one to two years.

However, there are cases where a clear finish is called for: When the client wants already-weathered siding to retain its gray or pewter tones or when an owner has new siding treated to turn the wood gray, for a weathered appearance. In some cases, the siding will have taken on some other color tone, either through age or previous stain, that the owner likes and wants to preserve.

In these cases, a clear finish can preserve the wood's appearance while helping to protect it from further weathering or degradation. But it will need to be reapplied every year or two to remain effective.

Finding a Good Product

Whether you want clear or tinted, you'll find many finishes to choose from. Over the last 20 years, I've used many of the available products. I've found quite a few clear finishes that would protect siding for a year or so, and many tinted finishes that would work for two to three years. But over the years I've settled on two products that roughly double these figures and outperform anything else I've tried: Amteco's Total Wood Preservative (TWP), and Flood's Clear Wood Finish, or CWF.

These products have several important similarities and a few differences. They are both oil-based products with paraffin added for water protection. Both come in clear and wood-tone tinted versions. In both cases, the clear finishes will turn wood slightly darker on application; but that will lighten up in a few days or weeks to return to the original new-wood tone. In the tinted versions, the pigments add depth and color to the grain of the wood, and they may even out variations in the natural wood's tone. But they won't change the wood's basic color.

Amteco

Amteco's clear and tinted products are known in the trade as TWP — the clear finishes as TWP 100, the tinted versions (redwood and cedar) as TWP 101 (Amteco Inc., P.O. Box 9, Pacific, MO 63069; 800/969-4811). TWP stands for different things in the older, non-VOC-compliant and newer, compliant versions. The non-compliant version — still available in places without VOC regulations — is known as Total Wood Preservative. The compliant version, available mainly in regulated areas, is called Total Wood Protectant.

I've used the older, non-VOC-compliant formulas for 12 years. In the past few years, I've switched mainly to the new compliant versions. These have a higher solids content than the older formula (about 90%) and so take longer to

MAKING OLD WOOD LOOK NEW

There are three common types of siding restoration jobs:
- a homeowner wants his old, gray siding to have that "new-wood" look (which he'll then preserve with a clear or tinted finish)
- the older, weathered siding on an existing home needs to be restored so it can match the new siding on an addition or section of replaced siding
- clear-finished siding has been left to weather too long between coats, and needs to be reconditioned before refinishing

In any of these cases, the task is the same: restore the weathered

siding to an even, "new-wood" appearance so that it can then be protected with a clear or tinted finish. This involves cleaning the mildew, algae, fungus, and dirt off the siding. You might also need to replace a few pieces of far-gone siding or trim here and there.

Match the Cure to the Disease

In most cases, the best way to clean mildew and dirt from siding is with a solution of sodium hypochlorite (bleach) in water. Some sources recommend equal parts bleach, water, and trisodium phosphate, but I never found that TSP added anything.

Before:
Unfinished siding exposed to sun and rain eventually darkens as the surface degrades, turning gray and providing a habitat for mildew.

Because I use large quantities, I buy my sodium hypochlorite in commercial tubs and dilute it in my sprayer tanks. But for smaller jobs, household bleach works fine. (We used to use it, until we found ourselves cleaning out stores' entire stocks — several grocery carts full of bleach.) Depending on the job, you might use anywhere from 1 part bleach to 8 parts water (2 cups for every gallon) to 1 part bleach to 1 part water. Occasionally you might need to use straight bleach, which is about a 4% sodium hypochlorite solution.

How concentrated a solution you need will depend on how much mildew you're dealing with. This, in turn, will depend on how much sun and (especially) moisture the siding has been exposed to, and for how long. I've had to hit ten-year-old, exposed, untreated wood in Baton Rouge, La., with three coats of straight bleach, while in Chicago I usually find a 1:2 solution handles the toughest jobs.

To find out what's necessary on a given job, experiment with a few different concentrations. One

dry. But since they soak into the wood, this doesn't pose a serious problem; if anything, it gives you a little more leeway when trying to get a wet-on-wet application.

It's too soon to tell if the new versions will last as long as the old versions — up to two years for the clear finishes, four to five for the tinted. But I've used a similar Amteco product — Shake and Shingle Sealant — in a VOC-compliant version for about four years, and it has performed quite well.

Amteco's clear TWP 100 lasts as long as any clear finish I've used. With a single coat on most surfaces and a double coat on southern or southwestern surfaces, it can last up to two years before graying starts. (Amteco's basic recommendation is

for one coat; but with all these products, we've found a second coat increases longevity.) After that, exposed wood will begin to gray, turning completely gray by the end of the third year. Like other Amteco products, TWP 100 applies easily and doesn't tend to "lap" — that is, reasonable variations in spraying thickness don't produce uneven tones.

Amteco's tinted products are also highly durable. Generally, TWP 101 applied at 150 square feet per gallon (one coat on most surfaces, two on southern exposures) will last about 36 to 40 months; sometime in the fourth year, the wood will begin to turn brownish. At this point, a cleaning with a bleach solution (see "Making Old Wood Look New") will

remove mildew and dirt, and another coat of TWP will reestablish that new-wood look for another three to four years. (TWP's tinted products can also be used for roof and deck surfaces, on which they will generally last for about two to three years.)

Flood's

Flood's CWF (P.O. Box 2535, Hudson, OH 44236; 800/321-3444) also comes in both VOC-compliant and non-VOC-compliant versions; the compliant version, out for about a year and a half now, is labeled CWF/UV. I've found that CWF's tinted finishes wear out about a year earlier than Amteco's — lasting about three to four years. But they, too, are easy to recoat, requiring little

---

coat will do its work in 10 to 15 minutes, after which you can see whether you need a stronger solution or another coat. For environmental and health reasons, I like to use the lowest concentration possible.

Use plastic containers for mixing the solution, since sodium hypochlorite corrodes metal. And always wear gloves, long sleeves, goggles, and masks when spraying bleach solution.

If the wood has algae along with mildew, we've found a 10% solution of calcium hypochlorite works better than sodium hypochlorite. Sodium hypochlorite remains active for only about 10 minutes, whereas calcium hypochlorite works for 24 hours. Calcium hypochlorite, commonly known as HTH, is a 70% granular chlorine available at most pool chemical companies.

Applying The Cleaner

Rate of delivery isn't as crucial with cleaner as with finishes, so you can spray with anything from a pump-up garden sprayer to a gas-driven pump. Smaller sprayers with aluminum parts, however, will be destroyed by the bleach. Don't

spray at over 1,500 psi, or you may gouge the wood.

Start at the gables or fascia, and let the water cascade down the siding as you work your way down. The solution itself should kill and clean the mildew. If a second application doesn't wash the mildew and dirt off, you may want to hit it with a long-handled scrub brush while the solution is still fresh.

Watch Those Plants

You'll need to protect any plants below your work. To do so, saturate the ground around the roots and soak all the leaves with water. Then cover the plants with woven poly tarps; these will shed

the bleach solution, but let the plants "breathe" more than ordinary plastic will. You should also cover any brass, copper, or aluminum fixtures so they're not corroded by the bleach, and any stained or painted wood, such as window frames, casing, or other trim, that you don't want to bleach.

When you're done, rinse everything (including the windows and woodwork) thoroughly with water, and uncover the plants so they don't overheat under the tarps. Replace any rotten or damaged siding with fresh stock, let everything dry a couple of days, and you're ready to apply the clear finish. — A.R.

After: Cleaning with a bleach solution, however, can remove the mildew and brighten the wood to close to its original tone. It can then be protected with a clear or tinted finish.

prep as long as the client doesn't wait too long. You can tell it's time to recoat when the siding shows the usual graying. With Flood's you might also see some light flakes on the surface that can easily be rubbed off with your hand.

You can clean the siding of both mildew and the CWF flakes by spraying with a bleach solution. At that point you can repeat your original application, except that, as mentioned above, you probably need only one coat (at 150 sq.ft./gal) rather than the two coats Flood's recommends for a first application. You would, however, need to apply two coats if the siding has turned completely gray.

If you're applying only one coat of CWF, you must take care to produce an even coating; if you lap the brush or spray strokes too heavily, you can produce the uneven tone called "lapping." If this happens, however, a second coat will usually make it disappear.

Application Fundamentals

Most general contractors sub out their finishes. But for those who do their own, or who do the occasional small job, a few application basics will help the job go smoothly — or help you keep tabs on the sub.

Open the grain. Any penetrating finish works best if it's applied to wood that is relatively free of moisture and excess oils and extractives, so that the finish can soak in. Old wood is almost always this way, but new wood often needs help. One approach is to let new wood siding age in the sun and rain. But that degrades the wood's outer layer and grays it.

A quicker way, and one that doesn't degrade the wood, is to spray the new siding with a solution of household bleach — one cup to a gallon of water — and then power rinse. The bleach removes any surface oil, extractives, and mill glaze, and the wetting and drying helps to open the wood's grain. Make sure you wait at least two days after rinsing (or any rain) before applying the finish so the wood can dry. Sun or wind, of course, can accelerate this schedule a bit.

No discussion of opening grain would be complete without a reference to the perennial question of whether the siding should be rough-side out or smooth-side out. Like any penetrating finish, a clear or tinted finish works best if applied to the rough side of siding. The more open grain of the rough side absorbs more of the finish, giving the siding more protection. Smooth sides should be reserved for paint jobs.

What to spray it with. The easiest way to apply these finishes is with sprayers (Figure 6). I use sprayers from the Wagner 8000 to 8500 series (Wagner Spray Tech, 1770 Fernbrook Ln., Plymouth, MN 55447; 612/553-0759). These are gas-powered, airless, diaphragm-type sprayers capable of delivering constant pressure up to 2,500 pounds per square inch. We tend to spray around 800 psi, which delivers at a good rate but prevents overspraying.

These Wagner sprayers can pump from $1/2$ to $1^1/2$ gallons per minute, supplying up to three hoses. We generally leave the pump on a trailer pulling either a 200-gallon or 500-gallon tank, and run long hoses from there. We use about 200 feet of hose per gun. Each gun has a Graco Reverse-A-Clean IV 517 nozzle, which has a .017-inch opening and a 10-inch fan to spread the finish.

This, of course, is expensive equipment, appropriate only for big operations like ours. Wagner (and other companies) also sell smaller, electric airless units, complete with guns and one- to five-gallon hoppers, for under $500. You might consider buying or renting one. (Bleach will destroy these pumps, however, so on a small job just use a garden-type pump sprayer for bleach.)

How many times to spray? On most jobs, I apply one coat on the whole house and add a second coat to southern and southwestern exposures.

Figure 6. High-volume painting contractors require sprayers with a large tank and a heavy-duty airless pump. For smaller operations, rented pumps and small buckets or tanks will suffice.

We generally let any side we're going to recoat soak up the first coat for an hour or two before hitting it with the second. My feeling is that you might get a little extra wear if you waited until the next day for the second coat. But those extra few months aren't worth the considerable cost of setting up and taking down everything a second time.

Sometimes more coats are appropriate. For instance, in sun-intensive places, where wood takes an extra beating, a second coat all over, and a third on the most exposed areas, can significantly increase the value of the job, particularly if you can do them all in one day, as is often possible.

How to spray. For the first coat, we generally spray clear and tinted finishes at a rate of 150 square feet per gallon. On the second coat, we go slightly lighter, at 200 square feet per gallon. If a budget is extra tight, we might make our second southern-exposure coat just a mist coat to save materials.

Start spraying at the top of the wall, and work your way down in long side-to-side sweeps. Spray just enough to saturate the wall — enough, in other words, so that the preservative slightly runs down the wall, or "curtains," as the trade calls it.

You can also pace yourself if you know the delivery rate of your sprayer and the area of the walls you're covering: If you're spraying a gallon a minute, for instance, you'll want to take about one minute to cover a 15-foot stretch of 10-foot-high wall.

In general, you want to spray from about a foot away, making horizontal passes with the tip turned vertically to the siding. A 3-foot pole is the best general-use extension pole; it will keep you out of the spray but still reach the eaves. Some pros use a 6-foot pole, which can be a little unwieldy and takes some practice.

By Al Rubin, a finishing contractor from St. Louis, Mo.

PROBLEM-FREE FLOOR FINISHES

The performance demanded of finishes for wood flooring makes this the most critical coating application in the entire house. But as we all know, typical job-site conditions are much less stable than finishing-room conditions. Good floor finishers have learned how to make the best of these less-than-ideal conditions, but there's generally plenty that a GC can do to improve the situation. It helps to understand how temperature and humidity affect finishes, and to learn how to prepare for the finishing process.

Drying Vs. Curing

The question a flooring contractor hears most often is "When will the floor be dry enough to walk on?" The question betrays the common misconception that once a coating is dry, it is ready to be put into full service. Following the application of the floor finish, there is usually a flurry of activity at the job site. Punch lists, final inspections, walk-throughs — the list goes on. If everything is in order, the owner is backing trailers up to the door and unloading furnishings or the real estate agent is

tying balloons to a sign in the yard that invites the free world inside to buy the house of their dreams.

Unfortunately, the fact that the finish is dry to the touch simply means that it's no longer tacky and will not stick to your hand or shoe. But only when the coating is fully *cured* will it reach maximum hardness. Until then, the finish is susceptible to scratching, abrasion, and chemical damage.

The curing of a floor finish is like the curing of concrete: It's a chemical process that continues for days after the floor finish is dry, until the finish

Figure 7. To ensure proper curing of oil- or water-based finishes, keep the site warm, dry, and traffic-free.

Figure 8. Hidden source of moisture. Think twice before setting up a portable combustion heater to warm the site for floor finishing. For every 28,000 Btus such heaters produce, they release 1½ pints of water as a byproduct of combustion. Use them only in conjunction with a dehumidifier.

is as hard as it's going to get. With concrete, moisture drives the process; with flooring finishes, oxygen is typically the crucial ingredient.

Until the curing process is complete, all activity on the surface should be minimal (Figure 7). Depending on the product, *drying time* can vary from two to eight hours. However, *curing* can take from five to thirty days, depending on the product. And these figures are for ideal conditions — the type seldom found at the job site. As the conditions become less than ideal, the curing times will be extended.

Effects of Excessive Humidity

There are two basic variables that can extend the drying and curing time of finishes and coatings. One is *moisture,* which includes the relative humidity in the air and the moisture content of the wood being finished. The second is *temperature,* which includes the temperature of both the air and the wood being finished.

Excessive humidity on a job site slows down the drying and curing of coatings; this is the single greatest threat to proper finishing. As floor coatings dry, the solvents escape and fill up microscopic voids in the sur-

rounding air. As humidity increases, the air becomes "crowded" with particles of water and will not allow the solvents to evaporate, or "flash off." Solvent that does not flash off the coating just sits there.

Since drying occurs from the top down, any solvents left in the product are released at a much slower rate. Combine this with the fact that you are usually applying more than one coat and you begin to see how excess humidity can prolong drying.

Theoretically, as the coating cures, all the solvents should percolate through the various layers and eventually make their way out of the coating and into the air. The key word here is "eventually." When the curing process is delayed from too much humidity, the coating will remain soft for a much longer time.

If humidity levels exceed 75%, the curing time can easily be doubled. The real danger with extended curing times is the damage that can — and will — occur to the soft finish if normal construction activities are allowed to take place. (In fact, according to a staff chemist at one of the finish manufacturers, if curing is extended over too long a time, the finish may *never* reach its maximum hardness.)

Thick vs. thin coats. There are a number of application devices that allow a finisher to apply a thicker coat of finish. The desired final thickness can be achieved in fewer applications, saving time for the finisher. But if curing is slowed by excessive humidity, thicker coats of finish will produce greater amounts of solvent that will take even longer to flash off. This approach saves time for the finisher but increases drying and curing time.

Watch out for stains. Stains applied before the final finish are also affected by excessive humidity. Even under ideal conditions, many popular brands of stains actually have longer drying times than the coatings applied on top of them.

Also, if the solvent base of the finish and the stain are the same (oil-based, for example), you are walking on thin ice if you apply finish to stain that has not dried. In areas where the stain has not dried completely, the finish coat will not bond properly to the flooring. But if the solvent bases are different (water-borne finish over oil-based stain, for example), you're going right through that thin ice and will most likely see a complete failure of the coating to adhere to the stain. The irony is that the failure is usually blamed on the products, when the real problem is the failure to provide the right conditions for drying and curing.

Recognizing Sources of Moisture

With the emphasis on building tighter homes, controlling humidity at the job site has become a much more important issue. In older, drafty homes, humidity introduced by job-site activities is quickly reduced by rapid air exchanges. In tighter homes, however, this humidity will remain. Before you can hope to control humidity at the job site, you must first learn to recognize the sources of moisture that will raise humidity levels.

There are two main moisture sources: activity-induced and site-induced. Site-induced moisture could come from a damp basement, lack of gutters, or poor grading and drainage. These sources tend to be more of a problem during periods of high rainfall.

Activity-induced moisture most often comes from trade activities that take place before and, in some cases, during the floor finishing process. The most common sources are drywall mud and latex paints. Water-based replacements for petroleum-based adhesives and mastics are another source of job-site moisture. Recently completed tile and masonry work — a tile floor over a mud bed or a recently poured base-

EDGE-BONDING: YOU HAVE TO SEE IT TO BELIEVE IT

Water-based floor finishes have a number of advantages over oil-based finishes: They dry quickly, release less toxic vapors as they dry, and form a stronger bond to the wood flooring. But as with many new products, unpleasant side effects are often discovered as they are used more extensively in the field.

Last year, I agreed to install 350 square feet of ash flooring in a 100-year-old home. Since the house was occupied during the installation, I made every effort to keep the dust down and arranged to have the flooring presanded. My floor finishing contractor and I both agreed to finish the floor with a water-based product, since it would produce less objectionable fumes.

The floor turned out beautifully, the customer was satisfied, and I went on my way. About eight months later, though, I received a call from the customer, complaining that cracks were appearing in the flooring, so I stopped by to take a look. What I found was not a pretty picture.

The joint between every sixth or seventh course of flooring had opened up, in some cases as much as 5/16 inch. In certain places, the actual ash board had split, creating large, unsightly cracks (see photo).

After a few days of phone calls, I found out that this floor was a victim of edge-bonding. When edge-bonding occurs, the floor finish acts like an adhesive, effectively gluing the boards together. In December, well into the heating season, the humidity in the house had dropped significantly, and the flooring was adjusting to this change by shrinking. Typically, each individual floor board would shrink between 1/32 and 1/16 of an inch. In this case, however, the entire floor was behaving like a glued-up panel and was trying to absorb more than 3 inches of combined shrinkage. As the staples resisted this movement, the flooring broke into smaller "panels" of six or seven courses.

My floor finisher had used this

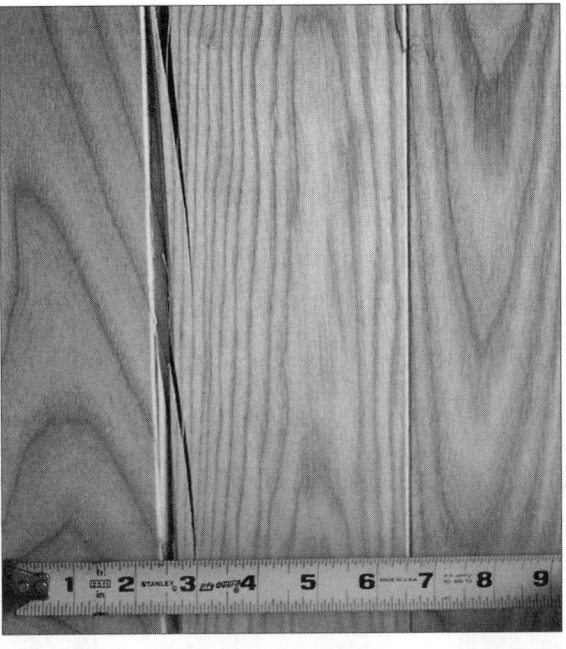

The edges of these ash floor boards were effectively glued together by the flooring finish. As the floor shrank in the winter, large gaps and splits occurred every six to seven courses.

product on more than a hundred floors and never encountered the problem. So what caused edge-bonding to occur in this situation?

The only reference material I found on the subject was from the National Oak Flooring Manufacturers Association (NOFMA), which prefaced its explanation of edge-bonding by stating that the phenomenon is not fully understood. When I questioned a technical representative at NOFMA, he explained that a "latex filler" should be troweled into the joints of the flooring to prevent edge-bonding. (There was no mention of this procedure, or edge-bonding in general, on the instructions found on the finish container.)

After reviewing what little available information there was and describing the event to product representatives and other tradespeople, I concluded that three circumstances contributed to the edge-bonding.

Presanded flooring. Because the flooring was presanded, the sanding fines that would normally sift between floor boards and discourage the finish from bonding to the edge of the boards were absent.

Eased edging. The flooring was machined with an eased edge. The resulting small V-groove probably had a funneling effect, directing additional finish into the joint.

Ambient humidity. The flooring was installed in late spring, when humidity levels were high, so the moisture content of the flooring increased after it was installed. The slight swelling caused by the increase in moisture content produced a clamping effect that forced the floor boards together immediately after the finish was applied.

The outcome? The NOFMA reference offered some hope. It mentioned that with time, many floors affected by edge-bonding tend to release at the joints, thus spreading the effect of shrinkage more evenly among more joints. In some cases, the finish will release its grip as the flooring expands and contracts through the annual heating and cooling cycle. At this point, the clients and I are waiting to see what happens; with any luck, I may have to replace only a few boards.

By Carl Hagstrom, an associate editor with The Journal of Light Construction.

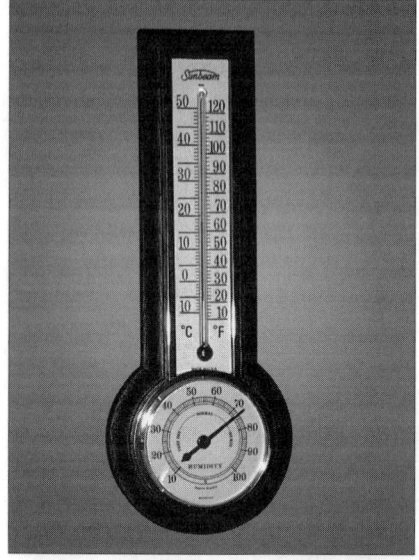

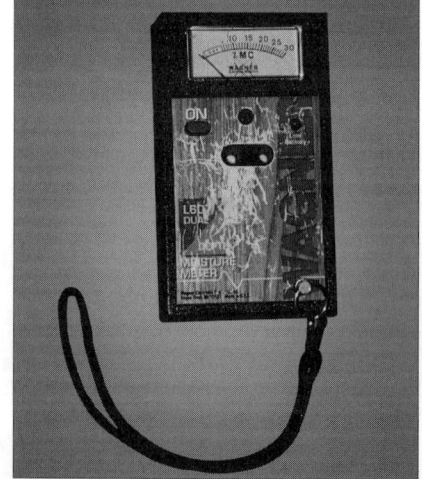

Figure 9. Tools of the finisher's trade. The author uses two diagnostic tools on every job: a combination thermometer/hygrometer (top) and a moisture meter (above) to measure the wood flooring's moisture content. If conditions are not within the proper range, the finish may fail.

ment slab — will also release large amounts of moisture as they cure. The moisture generated by these products means there is less "room" in the air for the floor finish to dry.

You Can't Beat Heat

Lack of heat has similar consequences for drying and curing: The lower the temperature, the longer it takes for an application of finish to dry. This tends to be less of a problem than excessive humidity, since

job sites are usually kept at a reasonable temperature range for the comfort of the workers. But when temperatures fall below 60°F, drying time increases significantly. I remember a project where temperatures fell below 50°F during the evenings, and I had to wait *four days* for each coat of finish to dry.

As temperatures decrease, air density increases, and the solvents escaping from the floor finish have fewer places to go. When what little air space there is becomes filled, all drying and curing of the finish stops.

Beware combustion heaters. When the temperature drops, many builders bring out a kerosene "torpedo" heater or a propane "salamander" heater. This seems like a good idea, except that a typical 150,000-Btu kerosene or liquid propane heater produces about a gallon of water per hour as a byproduct of combustion (Figure 8). So instead of improving drying conditions, these heaters can actually make matters worse by significantly raising the relative humidity at the site! If you must use this type of heater, use it only in conjunction with a dehumidifier. A better choice is to use an electric heater, which adds no humidity to the air.

Air conditioning. In summer, when outside temperatures and humidity are high, crank up the A/C if possible. That will dry the air and keep the temperature in a workable range. High temperatures (above 85°F) cause the finish to dry so quickly that it doesn't flow and level as well. If there's no air conditioner, apply finish early in the morning when the temperatures are lower.

Simple Precautions

As complicated as this may sound, there are some simple steps you can take to ensure proper conditions for floor finishing.

• The surest approach is to have all hvac systems operational and running three to four weeks before any finishing work begins. This will

help keep excessive humidity in check and prevent unfinished wood from absorbing any moisture from the surrounding air.

• Many contractors and homeowners object to the use of the heating system during construction out of fear that the duct system will become contaminated with dust. If a forced-air heating system is being used, place prefilters on all air return vents, and change the furnace filters regularly during sanding and screening operations. I use a paper towel over the air return vents and I have never stressed a heating system yet.

• If your only source of heat is a torpedo heater, be sure you have a simple dehumidifier on the project to remove the moisture that the heater introduces. The dehumidifier should be in place when the flooring is installed. Unfinished wood flooring acts like a sponge;, it will absorb any excess moisture when humidity levels are high.

• Purchase a good moisture meter and use it (Figure 9). Mine goes with me everywhere; I am constantly taking readings. If the cost seems high ($200 to $300), just think how much you'll lose going back to correct mistakes. A moisture meter is worth every penny.

• Monitor the temperature and humidity levels. You'll need a hygrometer to measure the relative humidity. The ideal range for drying and curing coatings is between 45% and 75% RH at 65°F to 85°F.

Controlling job-site conditions will always be a challenge. But the next time your flooring finisher makes some special demands, don't just assume he's a whining pain-in-the-neck. Remember, it's your product and your reputation he's protecting.

By Michael Purser, a second-generation wood flooring contractor in Atlanta, Ga. Purser owns and operates the Rosebud Company.

REMODELERS AND LEAD PAINT

Lead paint has garnered lots of media attention in recent years, and there are valid reasons for the concern. Not only can lead poison children, but it can also poison adults — namely, your crew and your clients. Common symptoms of lead poisoning include loss of appetite, stomach cramps, nausea, constipation, decreased sex drive, difficulty sleeping, moodiness, headache, joint and muscle aches, even anemia.

How Big a Hazard?

Lead used to be added to paint to make the pigments brighter and more durable. By 1978, dangerous lead levels were banned from paints, furniture, and toys by the Consumer Product Safety Commission. (This ban specifies concentrations of .06% of lead by weight or higher, so paint, toys, and furniture aren't always completely lead free.) But because vendors were allowed to sell existing paint inventories, any work performed on houses built prior to 1980 has the potential for exposing workers to lead. In fact, 75% of the housing built before 1980 still contains some lead-based paint, and the older a house is, the more likely it is to have lead: 80% of the housing built between 1940 and 1959 contains lead paint, and 90% of housing built before 1940 contains lead paint. Older homes are also more likely to have been remodeled, and to continue to need remodeling. This all adds up to a significant risk for remodeling contractors, their crews, and the homeowners.

The two major routes of exposure to lead are inhalation and ingestion. Exposure by inhalation can be caused by any activity that creates dust and fumes — scraping and sanding, for example, or using a heat gun to soften paint. Exposure to fumes can be caused by operations such as torch cutting, burning paint, even smoking.

Unlike children, who are often attracted to the sweet taste of lead paint, adults rarely ingest lead on purpose. Still, it is not uncommon for dust or chips to make their way into food, beverages, and cigarettes, or for workers to forget to wash their hands before eating, drinking, or smoking.

Abatement Vs. Remodeling

To control lead hazards, the federal and state governments have instituted several regulations, some of which apply to residential remodelers (see "Contractors and the Law," page 153). But many remodelers think that lead paint regulations don't apply unless they're purposefully removing lead paint. Remodelers also wrongly assume that only "lead abatement" contractors need to be concerned about lead paint hazards.

However, renovators and remodelers perform many of the same activities that lead abatement contractors perform: removing paint; removing and demolishing painted plaster, concrete, and wood surfaces; and

WILLIAMSPORT PRESERVATION TRAINING CENTER, NPS

Figure 10. Chemically stripping painted woodwork (left) is a safer alternative than sanding. If you must sand, wet the woodwork to keep dust levels down (below), then repaint with a high-quality oil/alkyd for maximum protection.

Figure 11. Using a stripper with a paper cover, remodelers safely strip lead paint. The lead-laden residue adheres to the paper after the stripper has softened the paint.

Neil Sandler/NIBS

Figure 12. When sanding or water blasting a house exterior, shroud the scaffolding with plastic or tarps to contain dust and over-spray.

covering over, encapsulating, or otherwise enclosing painted materials. In fact, any activity that disturbs painted surfaces in older homes can create hazardous conditions that might cause lead poisoning. The only real difference between an abatement contractor and a remodeler is the purpose each one has for doing the work. Remodelers need to approach their work just as responsibly as abatement contractors do to prevent exposing those around them to lead hazards on site.

Plan Your Work

At the beginning of every remodeling job, it is imperative that you first find out if lead-based paint is present on site (see "Testing for Lead," page 155). If any lead-based paint is found, then you must take certain steps to protect your crew and your customers.

Keep in mind that the quickest way to spread a lead hazard is to disturb lead-painted surfaces by creating a lot of dust or fumes. Dust and fumes are much harder to contain than large pieces of painted material. When evaluating the scope of the work, consider the options you have to reduce dust and fumes. Rather than sanding down a piece of existing woodwork, for example, you might consider removing or replacing it.

Of course, a contractor doesn't always have absolute control over how a job will be done. If a homeowner has strong preferences or a constrained budget that you'll have to work around, explore alternatives. If the customer wants to keep the woodwork, consider chemical stripping on site (see "Sources of Supply" at end of chapter). Another alternative is to have the components dip-stripped off site. Yet another option is to wet scrape and sand (Figure 10).

A fourth alternative is to remove the woodwork and scrape or sand it outside where there is more ventilation. When working outdoors, however, take precautions against contaminating the yard, especially if children play in or around the area. Lay down 6-mil poly to collect the dust and chips and to prevent them from spreading through the grass and into neighboring yards. When you pick up the plastic, make a concerted effort to contain the paint chips. Some dust will inevitably escape, either tracked away from the work area or blown into the air. But use common sense: Avoid working if there's a stiff breeze. And don't leave piles of paint chips in the grass, where they will draw kids' attention after you have left the job.

Similarly, if you are removing lead-based paint from the outside of a building by scraping, water blasting, or stripping (Figure 11), it's important that you not let stray dust and particles contaminate the ground around the house and neighboring homes. Precautions include covering the ground, and shrouding scaffolding with plastic or tarps to contain the dust and overspray (Figure 12).

Engineering Controls

You may hear lead abatement professionals talk about "engineering controls." This is a fancy way of describing tools and equipment used to control dust and fumes. For example, if the homeowner insists on sanding, use a tool-mounted dust shroud connected to a high-efficiency particulate air (HEPA) vacuum to capture the dust. A HEPA vacuum filter will capture micron-sized particles that contain lead.

One of the most important steps in any renovation job is to seal off the work area to restrict entry and to prevent contamination throughout the entire house. During work operations, the work area should be off-limits to nonessential workers and to visitors, especially children and pregnant women. To segregate the area, use 6-mil poly taped on all edges.

Don't forget to seal hot-air registers, air conditioners, and baseboard

---

CONTRACTORS AND THE LAW

Title X, Residential Lead-Based Paint Hazard Reduction Act of 1992, pertains to virtually every type of construction, including residential remodeling. Several government agencies — the Environmental Protection Agency (EPA), Housing and Urban Development (HUD), Health and Human Services (HHS), Occupational Safety and Health Administration (OSHA), and others — are responsible for gathering information and enforcing the provisions of Title X.

OSHA requirements. Section 1031 of Title X directs OSHA to issue safety standards to address lead hazards for construction. OSHA's rule, published in May 1993, sets requirements for contractors to assess exposures to lead, provide respiratory protection and protective work clothes, install work-site facilities for cleanup and clothes changing, provide safety training, and pay for periodic blood testing. For a copy of the OSHA standard, *Lead in Construction,* contact the Government Printing Office (202/219-4667) or your local OSHA office.

Occupant awareness. Title X also requires remodeling contractors to provide the owner and occupant with printed information about lead paint before starting work on any house or apartment built prior to 1978. The EPA, HUD, and HHS shared the responsibility for writing and distributing a pamphlet, which includes information about the health risks of exposure to lead, the risks of renovation, methods to evaluate and reduce lead-based paint hazards, and a discussion about the effectiveness of these methods. You can obtain a copy of this pamphlet and a copy of the proposed rule by contacting the National Lead Information Clearinghouse (800/424-5323).

Disclosure. One of the provisions of Title X includes mandatory disclosure in all real estate transactions. If you know about any lead hazard on the premises, you will be required to disclose this knowledge before selling, leasing, or renting the property. If you do not know, you must allow the buyer time to find out before closing the deal. While no requirements to correct a problem will be placed upon the property owner, this is a hotly contested law, pitting the real estate industry against lending institutions that handle mortgages. For more infor-mation on this rule, contact the National Lead Information Clearinghouse at the phone number printed above.

Certification. Another seriously debated issue concerns contractor certification. Under Title X, the EPA will issue a federal certification program that will go into effect in 1997, except where a state has instituted its own program. Anyone *abating* lead from a building will have to be certified under the program; at this point, the EPA is still leaning towards exempting anyone *remodeling* buildings.

But there is mounting evidence that remodeling activities have a greater effect on children in terms of lead poisonings than was previously assumed. In New York state, for example, recent data have revealed that almost 10% of children with elevated blood lead levels were poisoned by some type of remodeling work. In some cases the work was performed by homeowners; in others, by professional contractors.

Such data underscore the fact that everyone must take precautions during any remodeling project to avoid contaminating the environment. — *E.F.*

convectors. After the work is complete and these hvac systems are put back in service, any lead-laden dust that settled in them could be spewed into the air, poisoning the homeowners and their children.

Before starting a job, remove furniture, carpeting, food, clothing, and toys from the area. If these items can't be removed, cover them with 6-mil poly to keep lead dust from settling on them. Cover floors with poly, taped continuously to the perimeter baseboards or walls. Then lay down hardboard or thin plywood to protect the poly and create a less slippery work surface. Taping the sheets together will prevent this surface from shifting over the poly as you work on it.

Also, provide additional ventilation, such as a window fan blowing outward, to depressurize the work area. This will help keep dust from getting blown through the plastic barriers into other parts of the house. The idea here is to get air moving out of the work area; you're not trying to suck up clouds of dust and push them outside.

Clean Up Daily

Give the work area a good cleaning at the end of each day to assure that no dust or paint chips are left behind. Perform another thorough cleaning at the end of the job.

To clean up properly, use a lead-specific cleaning product (Figure 13) and a HEPA vacuum (a vacuum that does not have a HEPA filter may actually put lead dust *into* the air through the exhaust port). Lead-specific cleaners contain phosphates or EDTA (ethylenediaminetetraacetic acid), both of which bind with lead, so they clean up the hazard better than other cleaners. If the label doesn't list EDTA or phosphates, consult the Material Safety Data Sheet (MSDS), which lists the active contents. (Manufacturers are required to provide an MSDS, and OSHA requires contractors to keep an MSDS for all materials used on site.) TSP (trisodium phosphate) is a widely available cleaner, although it is banned in some states. Many automatic dishwasher detergents also contain phosphates, and can be used if no other cleaning products with phosphates or EDTA are available.

Disposal. All debris should be disposed of properly at the end of a job. Most states have specific guidelines for disposing of lead-laden debris; check with the public health department. Don't just take the lead hazard from inside the job and move it to the outside of the building. If lead-coated materials or dust and debris are left on the curb for pickup, children could play in and around the area and become poisoned. All lead-covered components — such as painted trim, flooring, and old plas-

ter and lath — should be wrapped in 6-mil poly to keep them from contaminating the area.

Respirators

In addition to working responsibly to protect clients and their neighborhood, you need to take measures to protect yourself and your crew. Again, substituting a less hazardous method or using engineering controls should be the first alternatives you consider. But workers who are continually exposed to the hazard inside the work area need additional protection.

A respirator is the most important personal protective device a worker can wear — but it must be the right respirator. If a worker wears the wrong type of respirator or one that does not fit properly, it is actually worse than not wearing one at all because workers may take unnecessary chances, thinking they are well protected.

HEPA filters. The minimum level of respiratory protection is a half- or full-face HEPA-filtered respirator. As levels of dust and fumes increase, other protective measures, such as air-purifying or continuous-flow respirators, may be needed. Regardless of the manufacturer, you can always recognize HEPA filters by the bright pink cartridges or the bright pink label.

Proper sizing. Before passing out respirators, make sure your workers are examined by a physician to assure that they are capable of wearing a respirator safely. Also insist on buying respirators that are sized to fit each worker.

Every time a worker puts on a respirator, he or she must perform a "fit check." A fit check involves covering the exhalation valve and breathing out, then covering the cartridges and breathing in. In both cases, no air should leak in or out from any part of the respirator.

Also remember that if the respirator is taken off for lunch or break

Figure 13. Job-site cleanup includes washing down walls and woodwork with a phosphate solution, such as TSP, or a detergent containing EDTA.

TESTING FOR LEAD

Before making any decisions about the costs, scheduling, and scope of a remodeling job, a contractor must find out if there's any lead paint on site. There are three test methods available: X-ray fluorescence, laboratory analysis, and chemical spot tests.

XRF. A portable X-ray fluorescence (XRF) analyzer measures a concentration of lead on a painted surface (in milligrams per square centimeter). These instruments give instant results, so a large number of surfaces can be sampled in a short time. Also, XRF machines read through many layers of paint without marring or discoloring the surface.

Unfortunately, XRF can't tell you which layer of paint contains lead, and the instruments often give inaccurate readings on samples that contain low levels of lead. Dense substrates such as concrete and metal may affect the accuracy of measurements as well. Also, the instrument must be held against a flat surface — readings taken from curved, molded, or textured surfaces may be too high or too low, depending on the material and the shape of the surface.

Finally, XRF is expensive. The instruments themselves cost from $4,000 to $40,000. The cost to hire someone to test the house for you is a few hundred dollars, depending on where you live.

AAS. Laboratory analysis — technically known as Atomic Absorption Spectrophotometry (AAS) — is widely regarded as the most accurate test method for lead. AAS results are given as a percentage of lead by weight, and are very precise (anything at 0.5% or higher is considered a hazard).

The accuracy of AAS depends on how well the sample is taken. For a testable sample, you need about a teaspoonful of flakes, or several large chips, from one area. The object is to get all the layers of paint in each chip but none of the underlying substrate. This requires a steady hand with a sharp chisel or utility knife. Put the flakes in a resealable plastic bag labeled with the location of the sample surface (for example, "upper bedroom, north windowsill"), and your name, address, and phone number.

It's important to take a sample from each surface that will be disturbed in the course of work. In the case of a gut remodel, for instance, you would need to take a sample from the floor, baseboards, wall, windowsills, casing, crown molding, and ceiling of each affected room. And don't assume the paint is the same in every room — different-colored paints may have different quantities of lead in them.

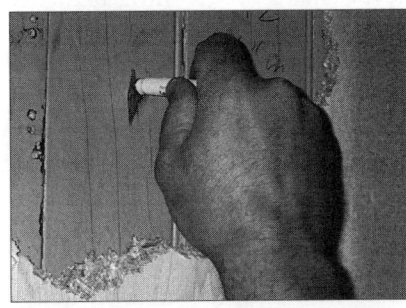

This test swab contains rhodizonate, a chemical that reacts with lead and turns pink if the paint contains around 0.5% or more lead by weight.

The author uses an XRF machine to test the paint on a door for lead paint. XRF gives instant results and will read through all layers of paint without marring the surface.

Test labs (call the Public Health Department or consult the Yellow Pages under "Laboratories — Testing") typically charge between $20 and $30 per sample. A standard turnaround time is usually a week to 10 days. If you want faster results, you may have to pay more. A 48-hour turnaround can cost double the standard fee; 24-hour turnaround may be four times the original fee.

Spot testing. A third type of test for lead uses chemical test kits, which are available from local paint or hardware stores. These typically include a swab or dropper that allows you to apply a chemical reagent that reacts to lead and changes color if the paint contains approximately 0.5% or more lead by weight. One of two reagents is used — rhodizonate turns pink, sodium sulfide turns gray or black.

Chemical spot tests give instant results, but the reagent only reacts with lead on the surface. So it's important to cut, scrape, or sand the paint to expose all layers.

Spot tests are inexpensive — 14¢ to $6 per test — and the kits have a long shelf life, so you can keep them on hand to use as needed.

Combine tests. You can use chemical test swabs to scope out a job. But if the results show up positive for lead, send the samples to a lab to get accurate, quantitative AAS results before deciding on the level of precaution you should take. Make sure to double check any negative spot-test results to be sure there are no dangerous levels of lead.

If you have room in the budget and need to take many samples over a wide area, or if you are especially concerned about not marring surfaces, use XRF. But if the surfaces you are testing are uneven, or the substrate is questionable, follow the XRF with AAS analysis to accurately nail down the extent of the hazard and the exact layer of paint where the lead is found.

— Eileen Franko and Kevin Sheehan

and left lying around, there is a good chance lead dust will settle inside the mask. When the worker puts it back on and breathes in, he or she may inhale dust from inside the respirator. Respirators should be stored in plastic bags, cleaned regularly (use nonalcohol cleaning wipes available from safety supply houses), and checked for broken or damaged parts.

Habits Count

Next time you have a morning cup of coffee with your crew on site, notice how the plastic lids are neatly folded back to allow dust and chips in the coffee. This is one of the most common ways workers accidentally ingest lead dust and chips. The same holds true for food that is stored or eaten in the work area. Anything that falls onto the food or is on the worker's hands can end up being ingested. Cigarettes can easily become contaminated with lead dust, either from a worker's hands or when stored filter up in a worker's chest pocket.

The best way to prevent these exposures from ingestion and inhalation is to not eat, drink, smoke, or store any of these items in the work area. Keep them in the truck, prefer-ably in a covered lunch box or cooler. And always wash your hands prior to eating, drinking, or smoking.

Work clothing. Improper handling or laundering of work clothing can expose you and your family to high levels of lead. Change your clothing and shoes before you head home from work, especially if you have young children. Any lead dust on clothes and shoes can come off as you walk in the house. A child crawling on the floor may get this dust on her hands, then put them into her mouth, ingesting the lead.

Launder all work clothing contaminated with lead separately from the rest of the family's laundry. Never shake the clothing prior to washing; this will only create a cloud of dust. You might consider disposable clothing, such as a Tyvek suit, for working on site. If you do use these, be sure to replace them anytime they rip or start to fall apart.

Clean truck policy. It's also important not to take any of the lead home with you in your work vehicle. If you have a dedicated work vehicle, do not give your children rides in this vehicle or let them play in it or with any of your tools. If you do not have a dedicated work vehi-cle, make sure you change your clothes and shoes prior to getting into your vehicle. At a minimum, wash your hands and face and never let your children play with any of your work equipment.

Employee Blood Tests

Any worker who is exposed to lead should have periodic blood tests to assure that engineering controls and personal protective equipment used on the job are sufficient to keep their exposure to lead at acceptable levels.

OSHA's *Lead in Construction* standard requires blood tests every two months for the first six months of a job involving lead, then every six months thereafter until the end of the job. Based on the varied exposures remodeling contractors and their crews face, it's important to get blood tests as frequently as possible. Use the OSHA requirements as a minimum so that elevated blood lead levels do not go undetected.

By Eileen M. Franko, M.S., a research scientist and industrial hygienist at the New York State Bureau of Commercial Sanitation and Food Protection, in Albany, N.Y.

SOURCES OF SUPPLY

Lead Paint Test Kits

Accu-Test
P.O Box 143
East Weymouth, MA 02189
617/337-5546

Know Lead
Carolina Environment
P.O. Box 26661
Charlotte, NC 28221
800/448-5323

LeadCheck Swabs
HyBrivet Systems Inc.
P.O. Box 1210
Framingham, MA 01701
800/262-5323

The Lead Detective
Innovative Synthesis Corp.
2143 Commonwealth Ave.
Newton, MA 02166
617/965-5653

Lead Zone
Enzone
P.O. Box 290480
Davie, FL 33329
800/448-0535

Chemical Strippers

Dumond Chemicals Inc.
1501 Broadway
New York, NY 10036
212/869-6350

Fiberlock Technologies Inc.
630 Putnam Ave.
Cambridge, MA 02139
800/342-3755

Nutec East
31 Buena Vista Rd.
Arlington, MA 02174
800/274-7650

INSULATION & AIR SEALING

- Hidden Heat Leaks

- Air-Sealing One-and-a-Half Story Homes

- Problem-Free Cathedral Ceilings

HIDDEN HEAT LEAKS

For ten years researchers at Princeton University looked at where and how most buildings lose energy. Studying hundreds of buildings under real-life conditions, the researchers found many ways that heat escapes by *bypassing* the usual weatherization measures of weatherstripping and caulking (see "Common Thermal Bypasses," page 160). These thermal bypasses can greatly compromise a home's comfort, contribute to moisture problems, and add significantly to energy bills.

The benefits of fixing these bypasses vary greatly from building to building; Princeton researchers found a 15% to 20% average annual energy savings. In some buildings the problem areas are inaccessible or just too difficult to identify. However, many problems can be found and corrected with simple measures, reaping significant energy savings, clearing up moisture problems, and — perhaps the biggest benefit to consumers — increasing comfort.

In existing houses, these gaps are usually hidden behind walls and can be hard to see and get to — thus the fancy diagnostic equipment. In new construction, however, they are easy to see and fix. Either way, they are

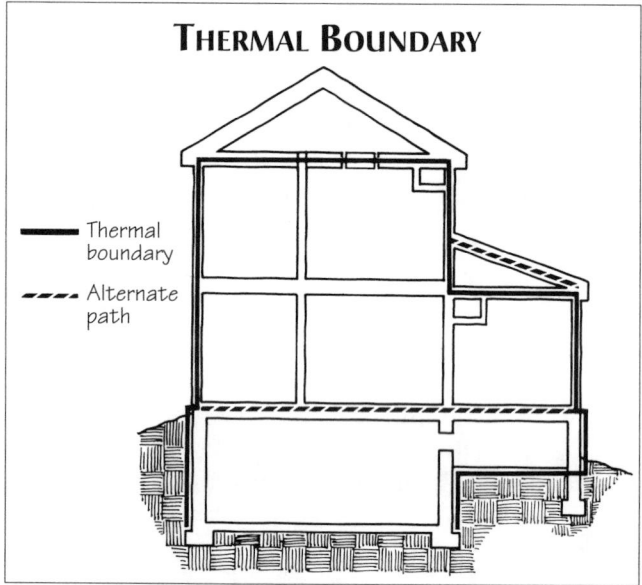

THERMAL BOUNDARY

——— Thermal boundary

‐ ‐ ‐ Alternate path

Figure 1. The thermal boundary divides conditioned indoor space from unconditioned space. The boundary needs to be continuous and should follow the shortest, most compact route. Heating equipment and other utilities should lie inside the thermal boundary.

PLUGGING THE GAP: A CASE STUDY

Imagine an apartment conversion of a 1920s three-story brick school building, with a corridor down the middle and high-ceilinged classrooms on each side. The contractor blew insulation into the exterior walls and installed new windows and mechanical systems; it was a quality project. All in all, everyone did their jobs competently, but the thermal boundary got lost because no one was in charge of thinking about it. This scenario often happens.

In this case, each apartment had two zones. Zone 1 was living room and bedrooms, which had the existing high ceilings. Zone 2 had dropped ceilings over entry, kitchen, bath, and mechanical rooms — several different ceiling heights, some made of drywall, some of dropped-in tile. Open-backed walls framed with steel studs joined the staggered ceilings. Through these and other chases ran the wires, plumbing lines and vents, AC ducts, refrigerant lines, and kitchen and bath exhausts, with lots of fiberglass laid over the ceilings and tucked down along the adjoining walls for insulation.

Now try to imagine the thermal boundary in this building. It's difficult, right? That's because there wasn't any. A three-dimensional maze of air passages had been created from the building's top to bottom. In places, it would have been possible to raise a ceiling tile and release a bird that could then find its way to the open attic without encountering any barrier.

Plenty of cold air could travel the same path downward. This would have caused a disaster from burst water lines alone, but fortunately it was October and not January when the owner, on a hunch, called the house doctors. It took two crews (six of us) about three weeks to set things right.

Zone 1 was fine because the insulation had been laid over the existing plaster, as in any house attic. In Zone 2, we didn't even try to follow and fix every zig and zag. Instead, we established a new boundary by putting a simple cap over the whole thing. We removed all the batts, constructed an auxiliary 2x6 frame at a higher level, laid polyethylene over this, carefully stapling seams and edges, and then laid the insulation on top of that. The only other item was the stairs to the attic, which we covered with an insulated flap. — *T. B.*

easier to find and fix if you know where to look, which is where a knowledge of common problem spots comes into play.

A Few Fundamentals

Knowledge of a few crucial concepts can help builders and remodelers diagnose or prevent most thermal leaks.

The thermal boundary. This is the boundary between the cold and windy outside and the inside, which we want to keep warm and draft-free (Figure 1). This seems obvious. However, many buildings have compromised thermal boundaries where cold air gets in the spaces and hollows behind finishes and in floors, walls, and ceilings. If buildings were made of solid concrete, the only problems would be cracks and imperfect joints. But as we know, most buildings in North America are assembled out of thousands of little sticks and layers of sheet material laced with holes for pipes, wires, and mechanicals.

Infiltration. Infiltration occurs when outside air enters the building envelope; an equal amount exits elsewhere (Figure 2). This often occurs at doors and windows, but other places are often more important to examine for leaks.

Convective loops. A convective loop begins when warm interior air loses heat to a cold surface, such as a cold attic hatch or an open-block party wall (Figure 3). As the air loses heat, it drops, making room for more warm air to move into place, thus setting up a circular pattern of movement. With a convective loop, the home's interior air temperature drops, even though air isn't penetrating the thermal boundary — only heat is passing through.

Gaps between insulation and air seal. Insulation suppresses heat flow not with the insulation material, but with the air it traps. If air is moving through the material, it

doesn't insulate. (Fiberglass, for instance, is often used as a filter material.) So unless the insulation is up against the air seal — typically the poly vapor barrier — it doesn't do its job well. Rigid board insulations do, of course, form their own air seal when properly sealed at the edges.

Air seals on the inside. Buildings should be sealed at the inside finish surface (that is, on the warm side of

the insulation), and there should be no gaps between the insulation and the air seal. The more snugly the insulation fits against this barrier the better, because air movement is discouraged. On the outside of the insulation layer there needs to be an escape for any moisture that does penetrate the finish. Thus it is useless, and can even be detrimental, to deal with infiltration through a frame wall by caulking the exterior,

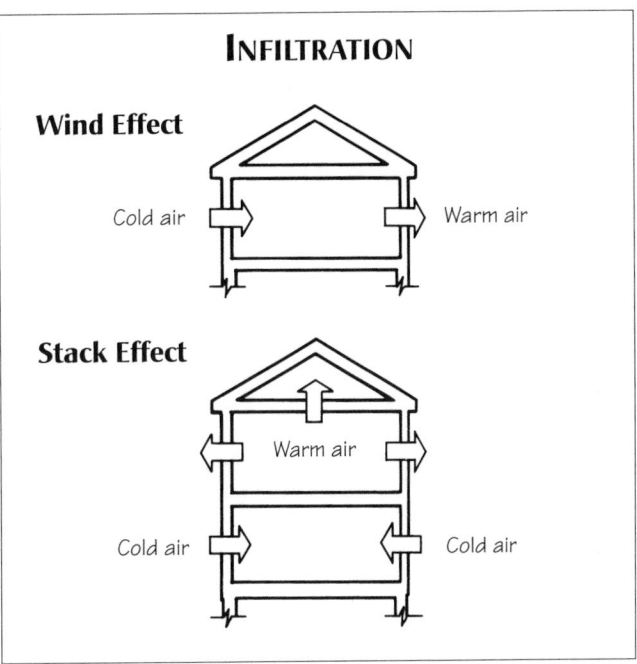

Figure 2. Infiltration occurs when outside air enters the building through an opening in the thermal boundary. An equal amount of inside air will always exit elsewhere. Infiltration occurs because of wind (at top) and the stack effect (at bottom).

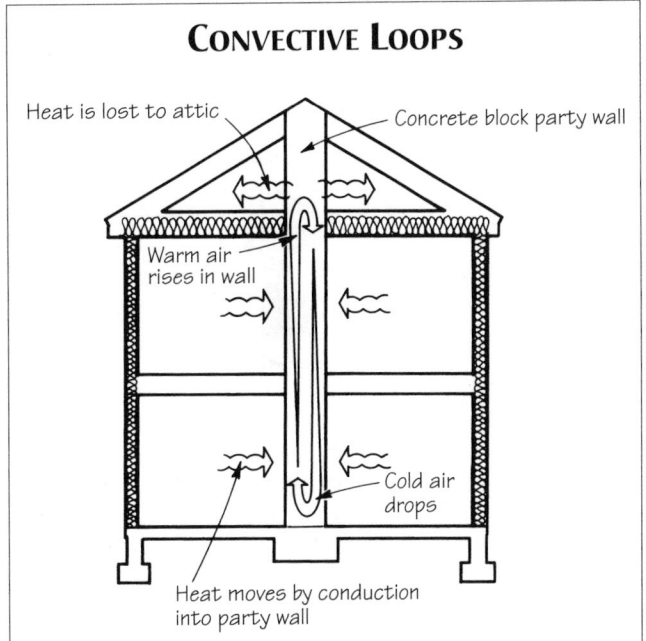

Figure 3. Convective loops occur when warm inside air loses heat to a cold surface, such as a party wall that bleeds heat into an unheated attic. No air exchange takes place; only the heat leaves the building.

which should be done only for the purpose of keeping rain out.

Stopping the Gaps

The illustrations in the box below show some good examples of thermal bypasses. In a building under construction, you can watch out for these bypasses and fix them while it's easy, before the drywall goes up.

Search for the symptoms. In an existing building, however, you'll most often find thermal bypasses by identifying their symptoms. A cold corner at a partition wall or wall-ceiling intersection, for instance, may reveal itself through mildew that has formed on its cold surface. A draft from an outlet might suggest that the wall is serving as a conduit for cold air coming all the way down from the attic. Cold floorboards on the second floor of a garrison might suggest air is leaking in through unblocked cantilevered framing. And a blast of cold air from the cabinet under the sink might suggest that cold air from the soffit is entering the stud space.

Without a knowledge of where bypasses occur, these symptoms are just mysteries. But if you know enough to make an educated guess as to where the cold air is coming from, you can often track down the cause.

In all cases, it is a matter of thinking about how air moves. Air, being a

COMMON THERMAL BYPASSES

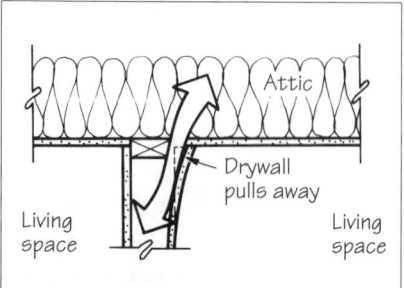

Leaks at wall-ceiling intersection.
If the top plate shrinks and pulls away from the drywall, cold air will enter the partition and then the living space through openings such as electrical boxes. Prevent this by caulking the top plate or laying poly beneath the insulation batts in the ceiling. The same problem can also occur where a partition wall joins an exterior wall.

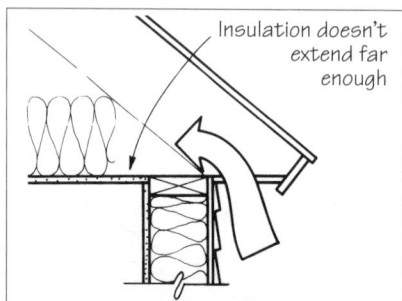

Cold wall-ceiling intersection at eaves; may have mildew from condensation. This occurs when insulation doesn't extend deeply enough into the eaves. Fix by extending batt far enough to completely cover the living space, but make sure to leave ventilation space below the roof sheathing.

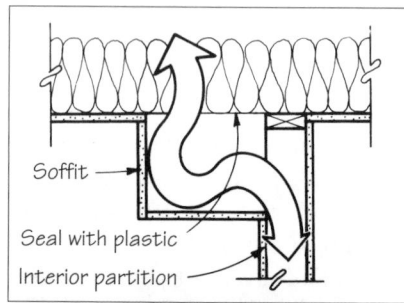

Unsealed kitchen or bath soffit.
This happens all the time. A soffit is hung from the framing with no wallboard at ceiling level to seal the insulation. Cold air filters down through the insulation and into the partition wall. Seal with plastic under the ceiling insulation. This may be hard to retrofit, but it's a major problem.

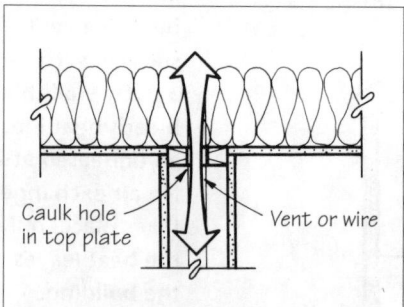

Leaks around plumbing vents and wiring. This is one of the most frequent problems. Fix by caulking or foaming around openings in the top plate or using rubber boots that slip around pipes or chases.

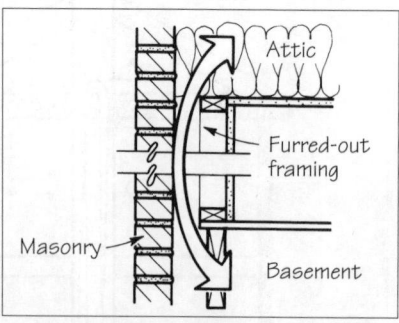

Furred-out masonry. Cold air winds its way between masonry wall and stud wall, resulting in both convective loss and infiltration. Seal the top of the space with caulked rigid foam.

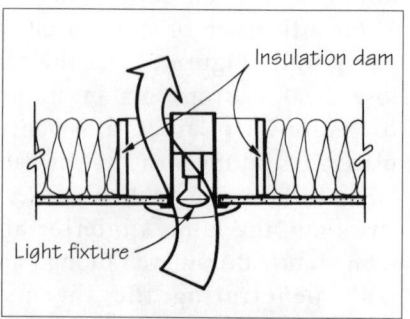

Recessed ceiling lights. These are tough to deal with, though some models now offer good air sealing. Reduce use of recessed cans as much as possible.

gas, obeys the laws of physics, moving in response to differences in pressure and temperature; humidity plays a role, too. But I find it helps to think of cold air as smart and resourceful — assume it will find a house's weak spots and get in. The stack effect — cold air entering the basement, moving up through the house, and out the attic — spurs much of the leakage. This makes the attic the most important place to look for leaks. The basement is second in importance, but don't tighten the basement so much that the heating unit can't draw enough combustion air.

House doctoring on a budget. If you want to get into professional house doctoring, you can spend quite a bit of money. A late-model Agema hand-held infrared scanner that can detect even slight temperature differences behind walls can cost about $25,000. A blower door with accessories is a bit more rea-sonable at around $2,000, but that's still more than most builders/remodelers want to pay for use on the occasional house-doctoring day. But you can diagnose many of the problems illustrated here by digging around and spotting the signs of infiltration already mentioned, such as moisture. This is something akin to the family doctor diagnosing ills by poking, prodding, and asking questions, rather than by putting the patient

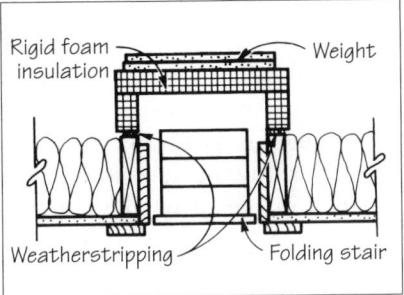

No seal or insulation over folding attic stair. The best solution is a box made of rigid foam with a little weight on top (wallboard works well), with weatherstripping to seal it.

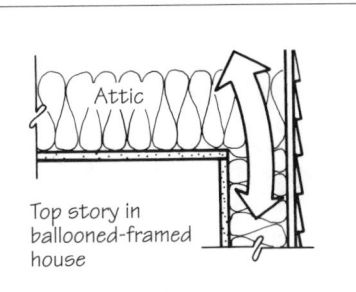

Unblocked stud bay in balloon framing. Whether in partitions or outside walls, the stud bay needs a cap at attic level even if the wall is insulated. Use rigid foam and caulk.

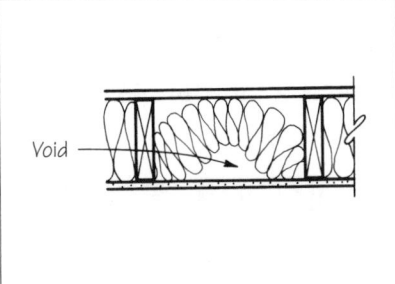

Insulation installed with voids allows small convective loops to form, lowering the insulation's R-value. Prevent or fix by cutting and installing insulation accurately.

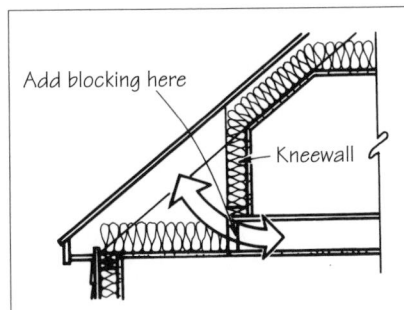

Gap below kneewall in Cape Cod second story. Unless the joist space is blocked below the kneewall, cold air enters the joist space. Block with rigid foam sealed with caulk.

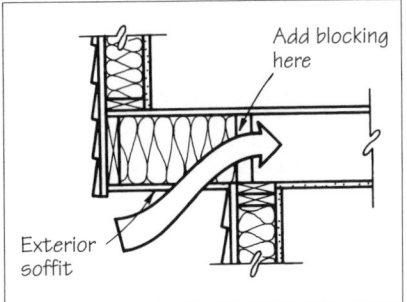

Unblocked joist space behind over-hang. In garrison and other can-tilevered designs, soffits are almost never well sealed. To fix, block the joist space just over the plate with rigid foam sealed with caulk.

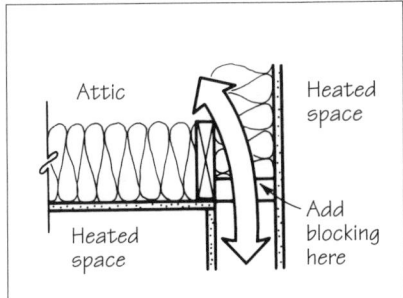

Unblocked stud bay to attic in split-levels. Similar to the problem in balloon framing, this happens where stud bays continue past ceil-ing joists to the attic. Block with rigid foam.

through a battery of high-tech tests. In most cases, it will work.

Actually fixing the thermal breaks once you find them requires relatively inexpensive materials and tools — mostly insulation scraps, poly, and caulk and sealants. Blockers and hatch covers can be made from 3/4- or 1-inch foil-faced rigid insulation. The type of foil-faced duct board used to fabricate insulated ducts works, too. By joining the duct board into a box with foil-faced tape, you can make a nice hatch over folding stair units; flat doors over stairs need an insulated door made of hardboard, rigid foam, and 1x framing.

For blocking stud cavities, use waxed cardboard (such as that used for eaves ventilation chutes), duct board, or scraps of rigid foam cut to fit. Seal cracks with acrylic-latex or siliconized acrylic caulk. (Use acrylic-latex for any surfaces to be painted, as siliconized caulks won't take paint.)

Another good material for cracks is the foam backer rod used to back caulk joints in masonry. Backer rod comes in various diameters. Another option for such cracks, or for the spaces around window or door frames, is the foam insulation that comes in pressurized cans; the cans come in various sizes with hoses and nozzles. Get the nonexpanding kind if possible, as the expanding type can get out of control and sometimes bulge window or door frames. It takes some practice to be able to dispense neatly — be careful what you get it on, as it never comes off. (Gloves and coveralls are definitely required; I've ruined lots of clothes with that stuff.)

Despite the low cost of these materials, fixing thermal gaps can be expensive in existing homes if you have to tear away and replace existing finishes — walls and ceilings, most commonly — to get to the trouble spots. But often enough there is a way. In new homes, it's simply a matter of sealing the area in question before the wallboard goes up.

MECHANICAL SYSTEM
Problems and Solutions

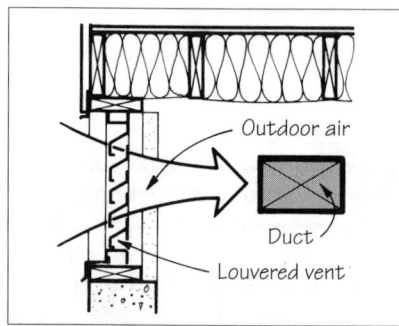

Pipes and ducts in unheated spaces. Either insulate them or include them in the thermal boundary by insulating the basement or crawlspace.

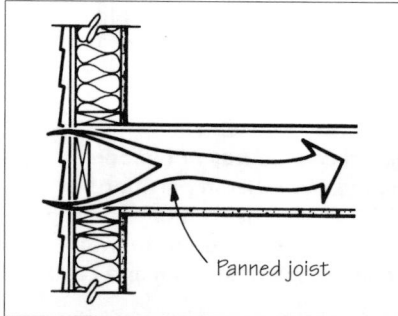

Return air plenum pulls outside air. This occurs when a joist bay is used as a return air plenum. Block and caulk at the inside of the band joist.

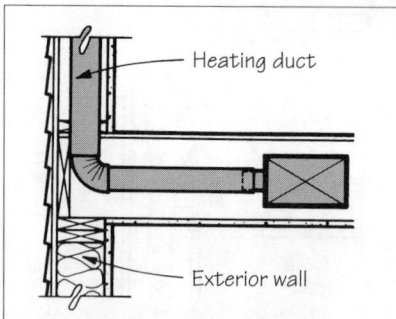

Ducts in outside walls lose heat, both by radiant loss and by leaks through untaped seams. This is a tough one to solve; the options include using insulated duct, moving the duct, or adding exterior rigid foam.

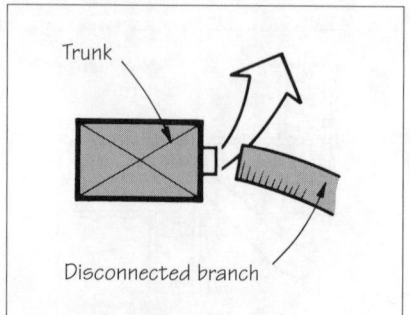

Are ducts connected? If the hot-air furnace isn't blowing well or warmly enough, perhaps the ducts aren't well-connected. Check all connections and tape any seams.

Don't Forget the Basics

When combing a house for cracks, crevices, unblocked stud and joist spaces, and other thermal bypasses, don't neglect the more fundamental issues of temperature and air control. Doors and windows should close well and have good weatherstripping. Hvac systems should be well-tuned and in good working condition, with any ductwork sealed and checked. The house should have high-quality, properly vented bathroom and kitchen exhaust fans to expel moisture. Eaves and ridge vents should be properly sized and clear of obstruction. Any dirt crawlspaces or basement floors should be covered with 6-mil poly to prevent moisture infiltration.

By Thomas Blandy, an architect in Troy, N.Y. Blandy operated a house doctoring company in the early 1980s and currently specializes in the adaptive reuse of older buildings.

AIR-SEALING ONE-AND-A-HALF STORY HOMES

One of the toughest styles of houses to insulate and seal is, surprisingly, one that is visually very simple — the cape. The architectural details that make cape homes popular and attractive — the cozy upstairs rooms with knee walls, the affordable "expansion" shed dormers — can also make them big energy losers. Another style that creates problems is the Colonial with an overhanging upper story.

Using blower doors, infrared imaging cameras, and pressure gauges, weatherizers have identified the main structural areas in wood-frame homes that cause heat to bleed away. We call these critical framing points the "key junctures" in a house. Over the years, we've learned to cut energy losses in existing homes by attacking these key junctures in order of importance. The bulk of energy savings is often achieved by plugging a few big leaks.

Unfortunately, however, the big leaks aren't always accessible. That's why it's most cost-effective to seal up a frame house while you're building it, rather than coming back later to crawl around under the eaves plugging leaks.

The Five Key Junctures

Five main framing details cause most of the energy problems in wood-frame houses (Figure 4):
• floor-knee wall transitions
• eyebrow roofs
• cantilevered floors
• balloon-framed gable ends
• balloon-framed shed dormers

Unless these five areas are carefully sealed and insulated, the building will have one of two problems, and probably both. In the simplest cases, heated air will escape from the house completely, with cold makeup air finding its way in somewhere else. But often, even when house air

can't actually leave the building, convection currents will move air around or through insulation, so that either cold air contacts a warm surface or warm air contacts a cold surface. The result is often not only heat loss, but condensation on roof or wall sheathing, which can lead to mildew and rot.

Floor-Knee Wall Transitions

Knee walls can cause big energy losses, even in a tight house. Usually, the problem is that the insulation (thermal boundary) and the air barrier (sometimes called the "pressure boundary") are not located in the same place. The key to insulating this area successfully is to make sure that there is a continuous thermal boundary and a continuous air barrier, and that both are in the same place.

There are two common ways to insulate the knee wall area. Some builders install fiberglass batts in the crawlspace floor, in the knee wall, and in the ceiling rafter bays. This creates a thermal boundary in the floor and the wall. Others simply install batts between the rafters all the way down to the exterior wall top plates. In the latter case, the thermal boundary follows the roof.

But either way you do it, you must make sure that the air barrier will follow the insulation (Figure 5). If you install the insulation in the floor and the knee wall, you must also install a continuous poly air barrier on the inside face of the knee wall, and on the ceiling below the insulation. In addition, you have to block air movement through the joist bays by installing solid wood blocking,

LEAKAGE TROUBLE SPOTS

Figure 4. Five "key junctures" account for most of the energy leaks in wood-frame houses. Taking the trouble to seal and insulate each of these spots will pay off in lower energy bills and improved comfort for your customers.

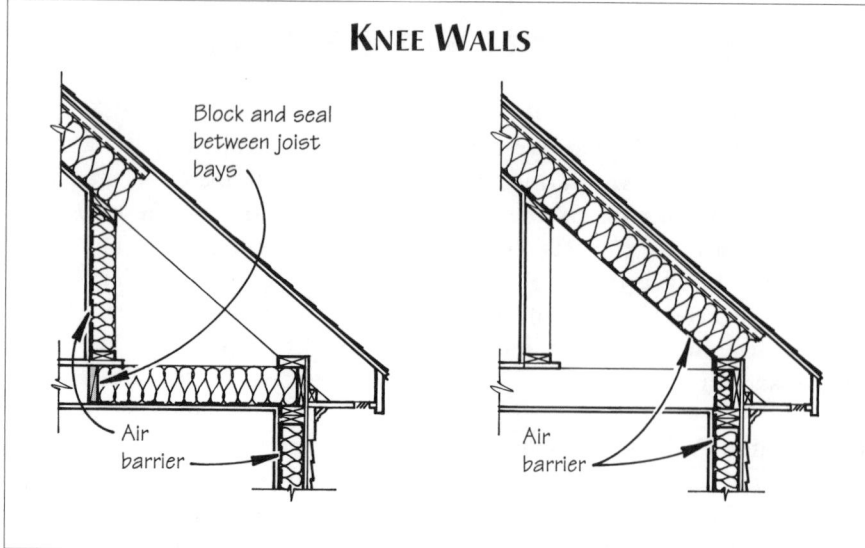

KNEE WALLS

Block and seal between joist bays

Air barrier

Air barrier

Figure 5. When building knee walls, make sure that you place an effective air barrier on the warm side of the insulation. When the thermal boundary follows the knee wall — a trickier detail to get right — it's especially important to install an air block between the joists directly below the knee wall (at left). The author prefers to insulate between the rafters all the way to the outside walls, then install a continuous air barrier on the inside face of the rafters (at right).

Figure 6. In existing structures, foil-faced foam provides an effective air barrier behind knee walls. Here, spray foam seals the gaps left where the foam board has been installed over unfaced batts between the rafters.

Figure 7. In new construction, rigid foam can easily provide an air block below an upper-story knee wall. Gaps are sealed with spray foam and the ceiling air/vapor barrier is taped to the foil face of the foam board.

waxed cardboard, or rigid foam, then caulking or foaming the joints.

If you choose to install your insulation in the rafter bays, you need to put the air barrier on the bottom side of the rafters, facing the heated space. A continuous poly barrier is fine, but it should be sealed to the framing at the bottom with tape. In retrofits, we usually attach 4x8-foot sheets of rigid foil-faced foam insulation to the rafters, sealing the edges and joints with expanding foam (Figure 6).

Often, builders staple Kraft-faced fiberglass batts up to the rafters inside the knee wall crawlspace. If you then cover the insulation with drywall and seal the edges, that can make an effective air barrier. But Kraft-faced insulation by itself, with nothing covering it, is ineffective as an air barrier. I recall one particularly bad case of a cape with Kraft-faced insulation between the rafters. The occupants were extremely uncomfortable because the air was always very dry in the winter, despite a humidifier that ran constantly. The humidified air easily bypassed the insulation batts in the knee wall area, and the moisture condensed on the underside of the roof sheathing. That house was very expensive to heat, very uncomfortable, and the roof sheathing was a fungal jungle. But curiously, it had a pretty low blower-door reading because it was a reasonably tight house. The problem was that the effective air barrier formed by the roof sheathing was on the cold side of the insulation. To prevent condensation and heat loss, the air barrier has to be continuous and be on the warm face of the insulation.

The most common mistake builders make is not providing an air barrier between the joists below a knee wall. Fiberglass batts between the joists, by themselves, will not stop air movement. Without an air barrier, warm air in the joist bays between the first and second stories will flow through the fiberglass into the cold crawlspace, contacting the roof sheathing or even making its way into the attic and outside. If the first-floor ceilings are strapped for drywall, which they often are, the strapping provides a further channel for airflow, and effectively connects just about every framing void in the building to the attic.

Figure 7 shows an effective air barrier and insulation combination for the knee wall-floor area in a new cape. The poly air barrier on the outside walls continues up onto the ceiling of the first floor. The plastic is taped to rigid foil-faced foam insulation installed between the floor joists. The joist cavities are insulated with R-30 fiberglass batts. When insulation and a poly air barrier are installed in the knee wall directly above, there will be a continuous pressure and thermal boundary between the heated space and the cold space, ensuring a snug house.

Eyebrow Roofs

Depending on how they are framed, these small decorative roofs, usually attached to shed dormers, can cause significant problems. In retrofits, we've often found that sealing up the floor-knee wall transition on one side of the house has no effect until major leaks in the eyebrow roof area are plugged.

I often see eyebrow roofs that have no insulation at all — I suppose because the builders don't think they're important. But if air from the house can get into the small eaves area, it is often able to move along to the end of the building and flow up the gable-end rafter cavities into the attic. That kind of large leak is quite costly.

In retrofits, we try to find a way to pack the whole eyebrow roof space with dense-blown cellulose. (To provide an air barrier, cellulose has to be installed at a density of 3.5 pounds per cubic foot. This requires a powerful blower in good working order.)

How we gain access to the space depends upon the framing details. Usually we have to drill a hole for the blower hose through either the soffit or the roof sheathing, then patch and seal the hole.

In new construction, it's important to concentrate on stopping the airflow. It helps to sheathe the wall before you frame the eyebrow roof, attaching the small rafters to a ledger board nailed over the sheathing (Figure 8). If you frame the eyebrow roof by nailing small rafter-tail pieces onto the sides of second-floor wall studs, it will be hard to seal and insulate the area — you'll create a lot of small, irregular voids.

Cantilevered Floors

Many Colonial-style houses have a section of second floor cantilevered over the first-story wall. Without proper attention, this area can lose a lot of heat.

Typically, builders jam a fiberglass batt into the space between the joists where it extends past the wall (that is, if they insulate it at all). Often it's an R-19 batt that doesn't completely fill the space, so that air movement is not impeded at all. Even if it's a bigger batt and it's carefully installed, fiberglass is still not a good air barrier, and convection currents will bring warm air from between the floors in contact with the building's skin.

To compound the problem, baseboard heating units in second-floor rooms are often directly above this cold between-floor space. We can observe the continuous energy loss from a setup like that from either inside or outside the house with an infrared scanner.

During construction, you can treat cantilevered floors like the floor-knee wall transition, but the vapor barrier goes on the subfloor of the second floor rather than on the ceiling of the first floor (Figure 9). Where the poly air barrier on the wall meets the floor, tape the

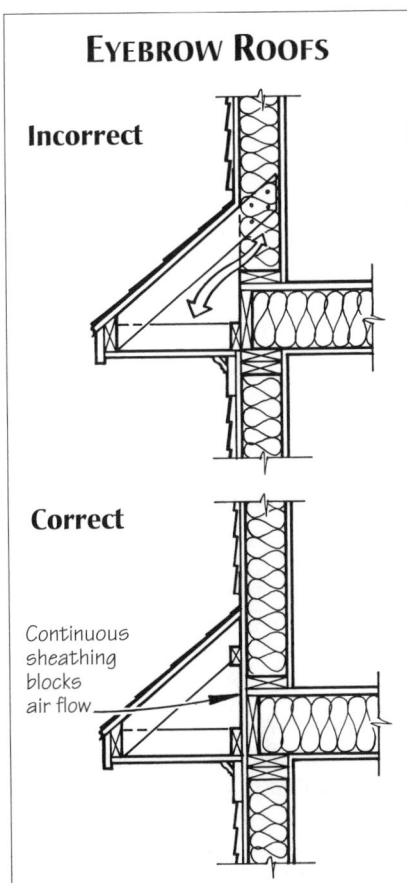

Figure 8. Eyebrow roofs, if built wrong (at top), allow cold air to penetrate exterior walls and leak out the ends of the building. To build one correctly, sheathe the exterior wall first, then attach the rafter tails to a ledger (above).

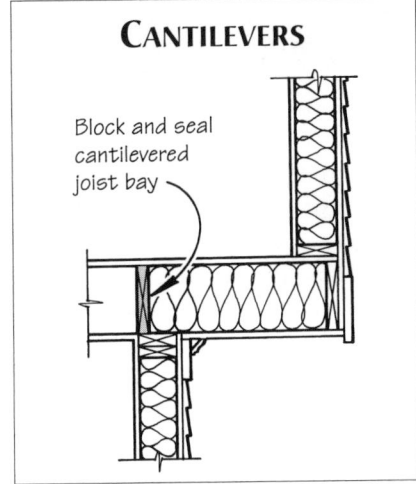

Figure 9. Cantilevers can cause convective heat loss unless an air block is added in the joist bay above the first-story top plate.

BALLOON-FRAMED GABLES

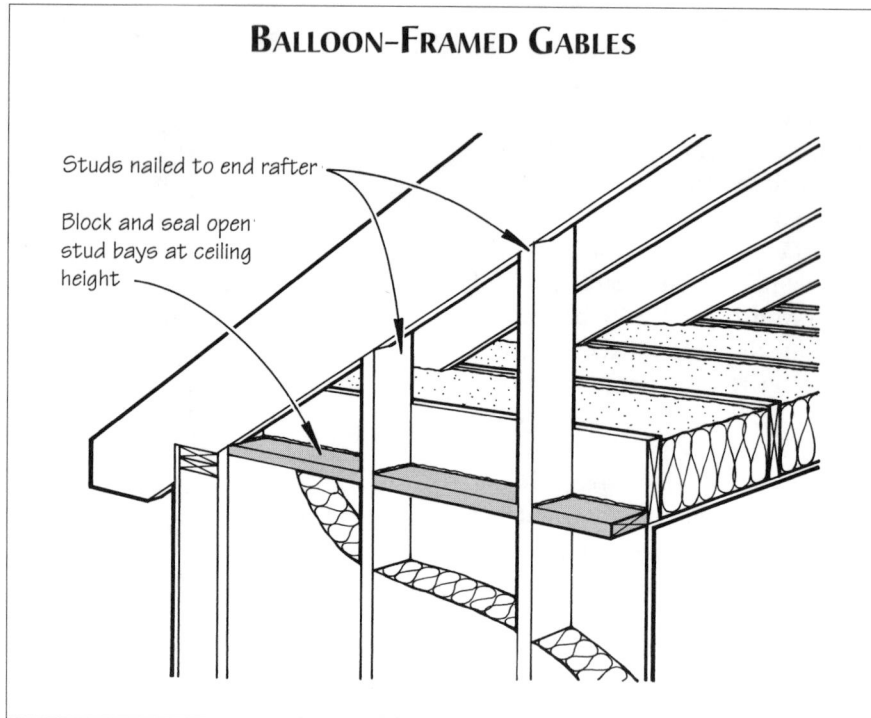

Studs nailed to end rafter

Block and seal open stud bays at ceiling height

Figure 10. Balloon-framed walls should always be blocked to prevent convective air movement into the attic.

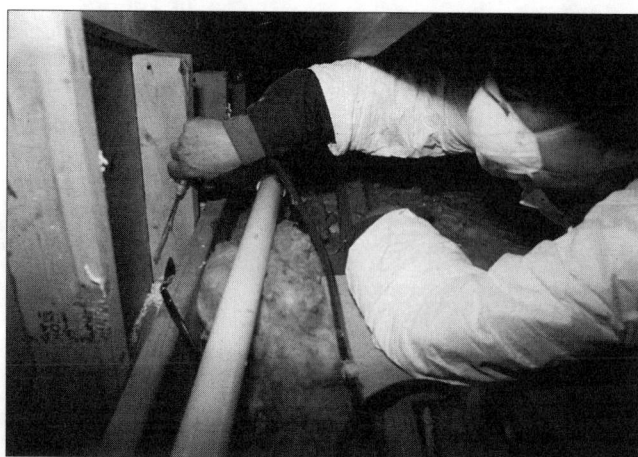

Figure 11. It's much easier to seal balloon-framed stud bays during framing than to have to do it later. Here, a weatherization worker foams a cardboard baffle into place where a gable-end stud bay passes into the attic.

Sometimes heated air enters the wall through a penetration, like an electrical outlet or even a crack around the baseboard and drywall at the bottom of the wall. The warm air rises in the stud cavity like smoke in a chimney, escaping into the cold attic and exiting through the roof vents. But even where there is no penetration in the wall, cold air from the attic will drop into the stud cavity, where it is warmed by the wall and rises back into the attic. This kind of convection loop carries heat out of the house.

Fiberglass insulation works well as long as the stud cavities are sealed. In retrofits, we crawl into the attic and seal the top of stud bays with waxed cardboard, stapled in place and sealed with a bead of expanding foam (Figure 11).

In new construction, you should block off the top of open stud bays at ceiling height with cardboard, rigid foam, 2-by blocking, or spray foam. Seal the blocking with caulk or expanding foam. Another option is to insulate the wall with dense-blown cellulose.

Balloon-Framed Shed Dormers

Shed dormers on many capes are framed like the gable ends, with the sidewall studs attached directly to the rafters, so that open stud bays run past the ceiling, and air can pass freely into the attic. These walls lose heat the same way the gable walls do: Either hot air enters wall penetrations and escapes into the attic, or convection currents carry heat away. The solution is the same as in the gable ends: Close off the tops of the stud cavities, or use an insulating material that is also an air barrier, such as dense-blown cellulose. The simplest option, of course, is to frame dormer side-walls with top plates in the first place.

By David Legg, an energy-efficiency consultant from Auburn, Mass.

plastic to the plywood. Then seal all the seams in the plywood subfloor with tape or caulk — that way, the plywood will function as an effective air barrier on the warm side of the insulation. Between the cantilevered floor joists, fill the voids completely with fiberglass or cellulose insulation, then install rigid foil-faced foam insulation in the bays where the joists bear on the first-floor wall and seal the edges where the foam meets the framing with caulk or foam. Tape the joint

where the poly on the first-floor wall face meets the foam between the joists.

Balloon-Framed Gable Ends

Often, builders frame gable ends by nailing end-wall studs directly to the end rafter, or to a plate attached to that rafter (Figure 10). The end ceiling joist is then nailed to the gable-wall studs. This means that there is no top plate at ceiling height, and air can move freely between the stud cavity and the attic space.

PROBLEM-FREE CATHEDRAL CEILINGS

For a cathedral ceiling to perform well and not collect moisture, the rest of the house must also work to keep dampness out. No ceiling ventilation scheme can compensate for big influxes of moisture. Adequate gutters, good site drainage, and foundation drain tile will keep water away from the house, while sealed poly, rigid foam, and pea gravel under and around the basement floor and foundation walls will keep the house from sucking up moisture from the ground. Without such control of moisture sources, no cathedral ceiling will perform well. With proper control and a good air barrier, such ceilings can work beautifully even when unventilated.

Sealing the Interior

The tighter you build a house, the higher the indoor moisture levels typically are. In an airtight home, you can maintain this high moisture level without doing damage to the structure. But if moist indoor air finds a leak in the air barrier — even of a few square inches — you can expect to find damp insulation in the attic and condensation stains on the ceiling. A larger leak may cause it to "rain" inside. This is one reason I use an exhaust-only ventilation system in most of my houses; the slight negative pressure it creates inside the house tends to reverse the air flow through any small leaks in the building shell, reducing the likelihood that excessive moisture will be forced into the ceiling.

For the same reason, I try to seal the inside surfaces of the house as tightly as possible. To achieve this, we use the Airtight Drywall Approach (ADA), taping all drywall carefully, sealing switch and outlet openings, and installing rubber gaskets around the top plates to make the drywall system airtight (Figure 12). Other alternatives for airtight walls include sealed layers of rigid foam or sealed sheets of polyethylene.

Any of these air-barrier systems, if applied diligently, can keep moisture out of ceilings and walls. Roof ventilation then becomes unimportant. In fact, I have so much confidence in my airtight drywall system that in many cathedral ceilings, I use no ventilation at all.

Tape, gaskets, and blocking. In our airtight drywall system, we seal the tops of the drywall to the edge of the top plate with 3/8 x 3/8-inch saturated urethane "Sure-Seal" gaskets from Denarco Inc. (301 Industrial Drive, Constantine, MI 49042; 616/435-8404). EPDM rubber gaskets from Resource Conservation Technology (2633 N. Calvert Street, Baltimore, MD 21218; 410/366-1146) also work

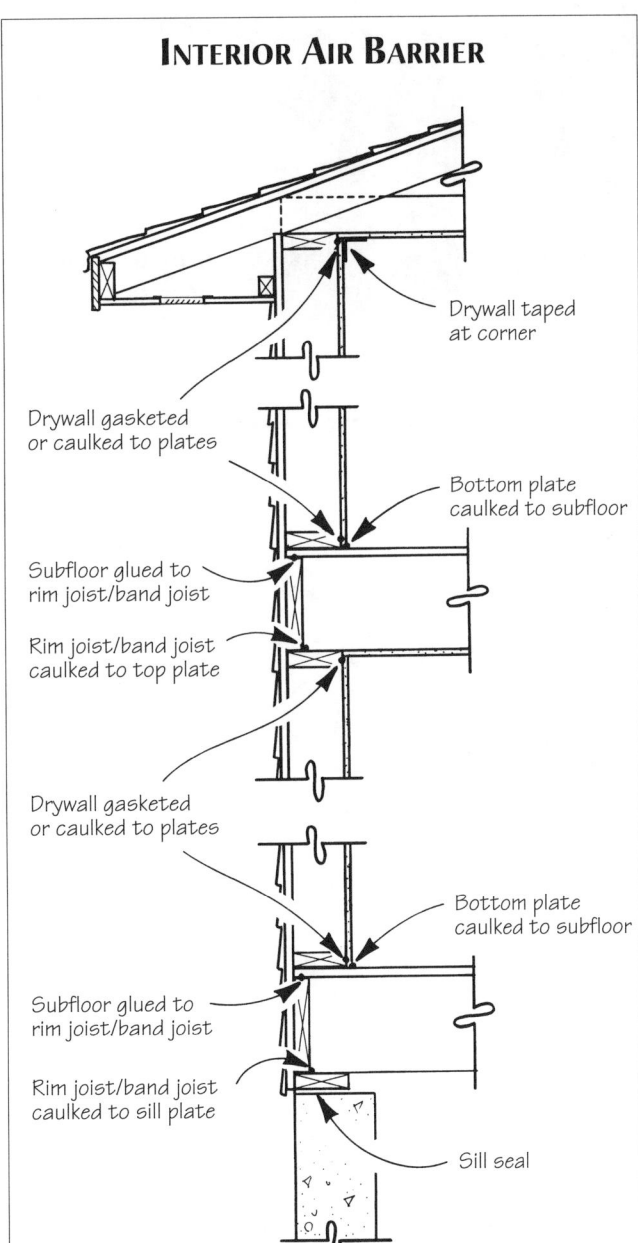

INTERIOR AIR BARRIER

Drywall taped at corner

Drywall gasketed or caulked to plates

Bottom plate caulked to subfloor

Subfloor glued to rim joist/band joist

Rim joist/band joist caulked to top plate

Drywall gasketed or caulked to plates

Bottom plate caulked to subfloor

Subfloor glued to rim joist/band joist

Rim joist/band joist caulked to sill plate

Sill seal

Figure 12. Cathedral ceiling moisture problems are caused when moist indoor air leaks through walls and ceilings into roof cavities. To prevent problems, tightly seal all interior surfaces using the Airtight Drywall approach, shown here, or with polyethylene.

well. Such gaskets cost 10¢ to 15¢ per lineal foot. We apply them around the perimeter of the ceiling on the top plate or on the drywall backing, then lay the wallboard over them so that it compresses them; this ensures a tight seal between the wallboard and the top plate, preventing any moisture within the wall cavity from finding its way to the ceiling space.

As for interior walls that meet the cathedral ceiling, we always install and seal the ceiling before building those walls so there's no internal connection.

We also carefully seal all penetrations in the outside wall top plates. Foam sealants work best for larger gaps around pipes or wires, while flexible caulks or acoustic sealants

Figure 13. Foam blocks at the bottom of a rafter-framed cathedral ceiling will prevent cold air intrusion into the insulation near the eaves. The blocks should be caulked in place to ensure a good seal.

work for smaller cracks. For larger pipes you can also use rubber boots like the ones used on roofs for plumbing vents.

Sealing light fixtures. Recessed lights in cathedral ceilings also present problems. Standard units are very leaky and are responsible for a number of moisture problems. However some of the new units rated for insulation contact (IC) are well sealed. We use the X18 Series made by Scientific Component Systems (2651 Dow Ave., Tustin, CA 92680; 712/730-3555).

Another option is the recessed compact fluorescent, by Scientific Components Systems. It has a low wattage (two 7-watt bulbs), low operating temperature, and high lumen output, yet it costs about the same as a standard recessed fixture, and it is airtight. Its only drawback is that you can't use a dimmer switch with it, and trim choices are limited.

Standard light openings are relatively easy to seal. Bring the light wire through a solid 2x4 block, seal the wire with a foam sealant, and then use a shallow, surface-mounted metal rough-in box after the drywall is hung. Another way is to use a poly pan rough-in box (from Lessco, 990 Mink Lane, Campbellsport, WI 53010; 414/533-8690) and seal the poly air barrier to it. Yet another method uses a special ceiling box (model BX-OCT-F) made by Nutek Plastics, a Canadian company, and available from Columbia International (800 Beriault Street, Longueuil, Quebec, J4G 1R8 Canada; 514/677-2841). Nutek's product has a recessed flange that makes it easy to seal the drywall barrier or poly air barrier to it. The poly pans cost about $2 to $2.50 each, and the Nutek boxes cost about $4.

Dealing with skylights. To reduce condensation potential and save energy, I use the highest R-value skylight my budget allows — at minimum, a double-glazed, low-E, R-3 model. I carefully gasket between the

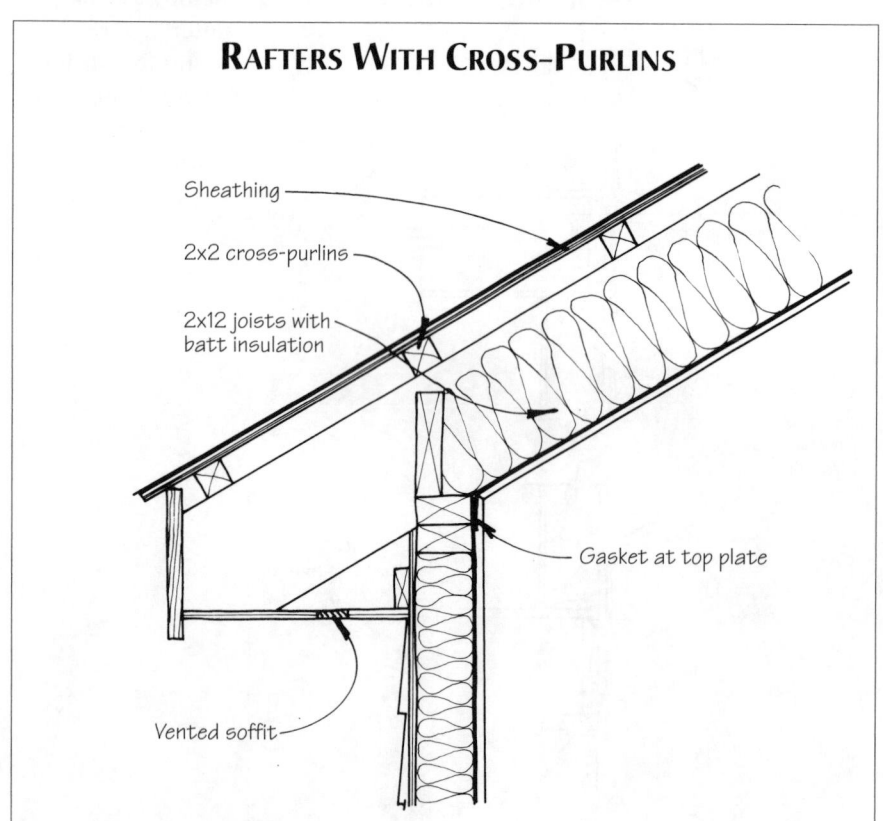

RAFTERS WITH CROSS-PURLINS

Sheathing

2x2 cross-purlins

2x12 joists with batt insulation

Gasket at top plate

Vented soffit

Figure 14. On a rafter-framed cathedral ceiling, cross-purlins provide good air movement under the sheathing, even where there are obstructions such as skylights.

skylight's jams and the framing to prevent air leaks around its frame. To provide ventilation in the rafter space below and above the unit, I either notch the top edges of the rafter below and above the skylight or install cross-purlins over the rafters to provide lateral flow (more on that later).

Framing and Insulating

We have two basic ways of framing and insulating vaulted ceilings. Where budgets are tight, we go with a 12-inch-thick, R-38 rafter system insulated with fiberglass batts. When we can spend more, we use 16- to 18-inch parallel-chord trusses with blown or batt insulation and end up with an R-55 system.

Ventilation an option. For both systems, we consider ceiling ventilation optional for most jobs. As explained earlier, that's one of the beauties of creating a tight air barrier — it does more than just keep the house warm, it can actually eliminate the need for ventilation.

Nevertheless, I've included ventilation details in this section for those times when sealing problems, code requirements, client insistence, or other factors make ventilation necessary.

Shallow systems. For the 12-inch system, we use ordinary 2x12 rafters and insulate with fiberglass batts. To keep the batts from sliding into the soffit space and to prevent undue airflow through the batts, we install scraps of foam or wood blocking vertically at the bottom of the rafter spaces, leaving a 1½- to 2-inch space above the blocking if we want to ventilate (Figure 13). This is a good place to use up your scrap pieces of foam sheathing. You can cut them snug between the trusses and caulk them in place, or you can leave your exterior wall sheathing one inch short of the top of the wall and nail the infiltration stops in when the soffit is installed. After the blocking is in and as the ceiling goes up, we lay in the

batts (either one 12-inch layer or two 6-inch layers), taking care that we don't leave any gaps or spaces.

When I want to ventilate a rafter system, I add a 2x2 nailer along the top edge of each rafter (to allow an air space above 12 inches of insulation), then nail 2x2 cross-purlins perpendicular to those. This arrangement allows air to flow freely over the entire roof system regardless of obstructions such as skylights (Figure 14).

We prefer standard continuous soffit vents and a ridge vent when ventilating. I prefer vents made by Air Vent (7700 Harker Dr., Suite B, Peoria Heights, IL 61615; 309/688-5020).

Finally, to prevent the batts from piling or fluffing up to block the vent opening over the eaves blocking described earlier, I first attach a plastic air chute made by ADO Products (21800 129th Ave. N., Rogers, MN 55374; 800/666-8191) to the sheathing just above the eaves. The chute is

about 4 feet long and slides down to the space over the blocking and then staples to the sheathing to make sure the ventilation path doesn't get clogged by insulation. We've found these plastic chutes much more durable than similar cardboard and foam chutes.

Bigger budget, deeper ceilings. For our deeper ceilings we usually use parallel-chord trusses 16 to 18 inches deep. Parallel-chord trusses can either sit atop the exterior wall or butt against it. In either case, the top chord extends out to form an overhang (Figure 15). If you set the truss atop the plate, you will need to seal at the eaves with foam or wood blocks as shown in Figures 13 and 14.

If a truss roof has a fairly shallow pitch — 6/12 or less — we blow in loose fill insulation, leaving enough space (1½ to 2 inches) above the fill to provide air flow along the sheathing. Steeper pitched roofs will

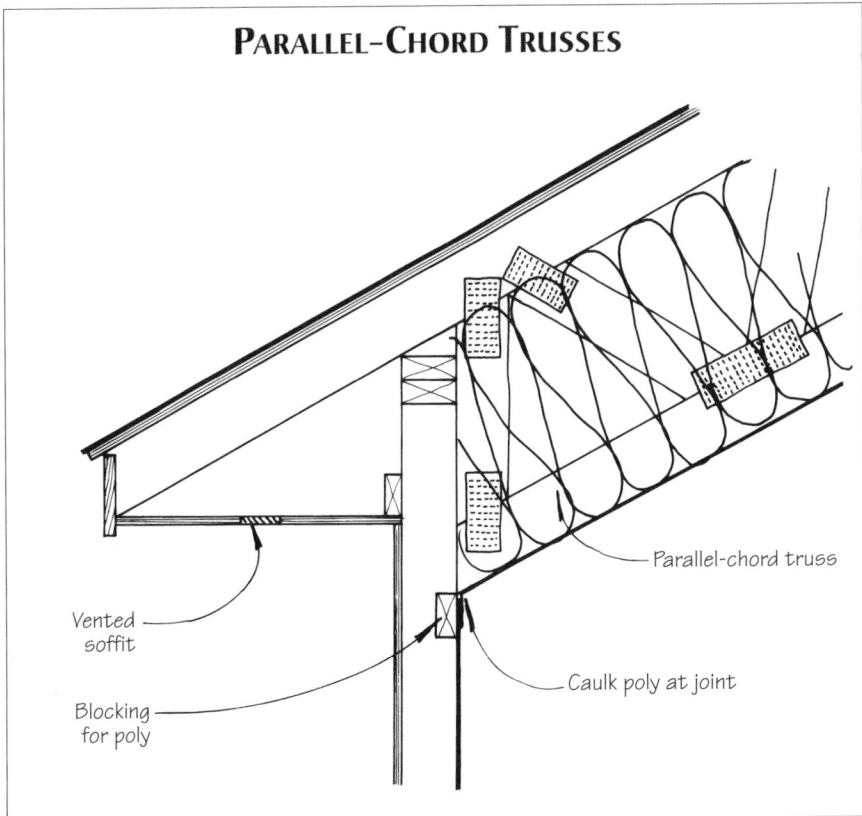

PARALLEL-CHORD TRUSSES

Parallel-chord truss

Caulk poly at joint

Vented soffit

Blocking for poly

Figure 15. Parallel-chord trusses can butt into the exterior wall as shown, or sit atop the top plate. In either case, the top chord extends outward, providing an overhang.

encourage the loose fill to collect down toward the eaves, however, so for those roofs we go with batt insulation, choosing thicknesses that will bring the insulation to within a couple of inches of the sheathing. Whenever possible we get batts as wide as the on-center truss spacings — for instance, a full 24 inches instead of 22 inches for trusses 24 inches on-center — so that the batts will expand sideways to fill the spaces between the webs.

Ventilating a truss roof system is fairly simple: you adjust the thickness of insulation to leave a space (1^1/$_2$ to 2 inches) on the sheathing's underside, and provide for air intake and outflow by installing continuous soffit and ridge vents.

Worth the Headaches

Building a cathedral ceiling that works requires constant attention to detail — one or two oversights and you can run into some serious problems down the line. But it's worth the trouble. The visual excitement and sense of space a cathedral ceiling generates make the client's home a greater asset almost instantly. And that, in turn, translates into the builder's greatest asset, which is another satisfied client.

By Bill Eich, a builder and the owner of Bill Eich Construction Company in Spirit Lake, Iowa.

CHAPTER 8

HVAC SYSTEMS

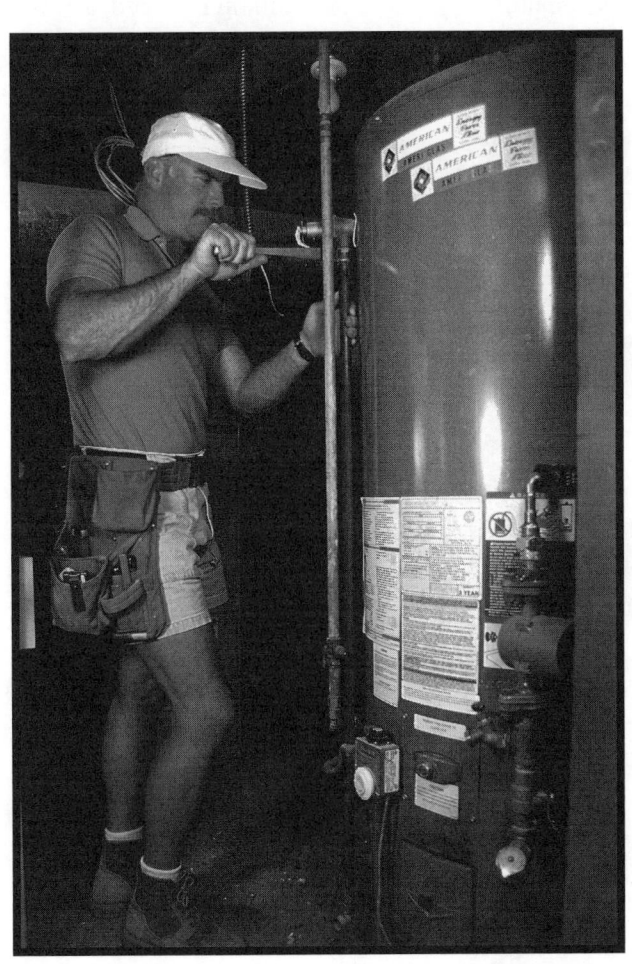

- Heating System Tuneups & Upgrades

- High-Efficiency HVAC

- Mechanical Cooling Systems

- Water Heaters

- Simple Ventilation for Tight Houses

- Flue and Chimney Safety

- Backdrafting Causes and Cures

HEATING SYSTEM TUNEUPS & UPGRADES

Heating systems more than three to five years old can usually be improved through add-ons, modifications, or improved maintenance. Most combustion units are oversized, for instance — particularly if the house has had insulation added since the unit was installed — and most have unsophisticated control systems. In addition, heat distribution systems can usually be improved through adjustment, new products, or in the case of air systems, tightening of the ductwork.

The options presented here are among the most promising and practical, and should apply to the 65% of our nation's homes that are heated by forced hot air and the 10% heated by forced hot water. Remodeling contractors who educate themselves about these options have an opportunity to give clients a valuable service. These modifications may well result in fuel savings that will help pay for more remodeling work; in many cases, an upgrade will give you the extra heating capacity you need to heat any space you add.

All Systems

We'll consider forced-air and hydronic systems separately, but there are some steps you can take that apply to both types of heating systems.

Cleaning and tuneups. Routine maintenance is the homeowner's job, but it won't hurt for you to point out the importance of regular tuneups (yearly for oil-fired systems, every two years for gas). These should include combustion and flame checks, draining hot water systems of sediment and bleeding them of air, checking air ducts for leaks, and so on. Table A lists routine maintenance for forced hot air and forced hot water or steam systems; these steps alone will promote better performance and longer life in nine out of ten systems.

Upgrade thermostats. Another way to quickly improve virtually any hvac system is to upgrade its brain — the thermostat. Compared with "clock" thermostats first introduced in the 1970s, today's microprocessor-controlled setback thermostats are more sophisticated but easier to install and use (Figure 1). An investment of $30 to $100 will buy a computerized thermostat that can improve system efficiency from 7% to 10%.

Some setback thermostats have two cycles, one for weekdays and one for the weekend; the better ones have

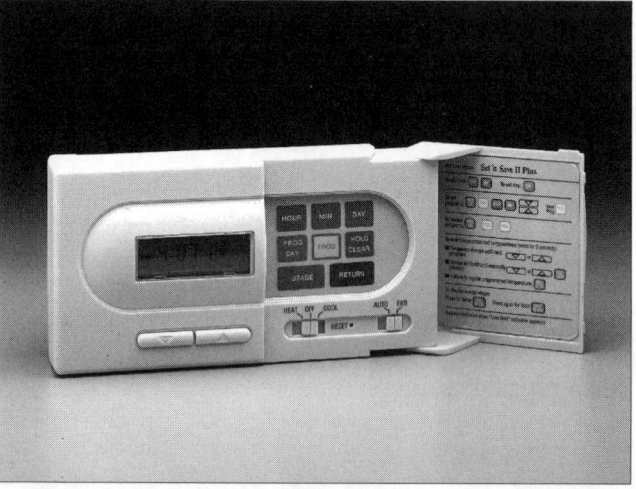

Figure 1. A programmable thermostat, such as the Set 'n Save II Plus (Hunter Fan Co., 2500 Frisco Ave., Memphis, TN 38114; 800/971-3267), saves on fuel by automatically lowering the temperature setting when the house is unoccupied.

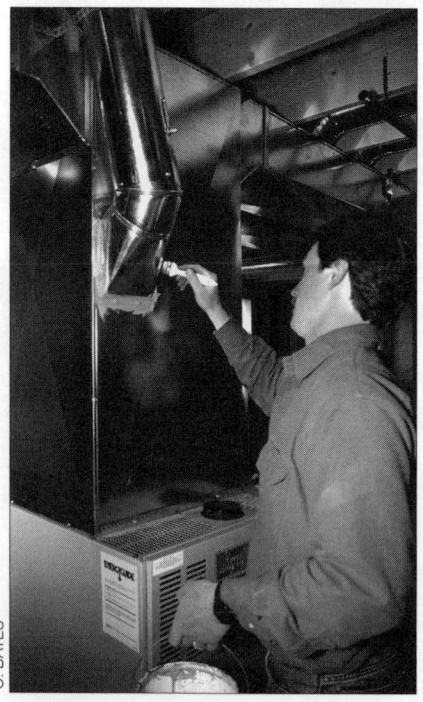

Figure 2. Nearly 11% of all heat loss in forced-air systems comes from leaky ducts. Replace duct tape at joints and seams with a high-quality mastic.

Figure 3. Pay close attention to sealing cracks where ductwork penetrates unconditioned spaces such as attics or basements.

seven-day cycles, for people who want to be able to program each day of the week individually. Almost any unit allows a user to temporarily override the programmed settings. If you avoid the bottom of the line, you'll usually get a unit that's easier to program. I've found that the more buttons a thermostat has, the simpler it is to use, since you don't have to figure out how to make buttons serve multiple tasks.

Hot Air Systems

These modifications apply primarily to forced hot air systems — those with a fan that drives the air through the house. But many (particularly those concerning ductwork) also apply to passive, or "gravity-fed," hot air systems.

Focus first on flow. Assuming the basic layout of the air distribution system is sound, you need to check the condition of the ductwork itself. Unfortunately, loose ductwork is the rule: One study found that the average home with forced hot air heat lost 11% of its heat through leaky ductwork. The cost of fixing these leaks can run anywhere from the price of a few hours of labor and some mastic to hundreds of dollars for a ductwork overhaul. But any repairs *should* bring immediate returns in comfort, and most will provide a payback of no more than two to five years.

The three most common leak sites are in the return air plenum, at joints between branch ducts and the main trunk line, and where ducts attach to room outlets (see "Mechanical Cooling Systems," Figure 12, page 182). Ideally, you should seal all seams and joints that appear loose or that are sealed with duct tape, which will degrade within a few years. Tear off the duct tape (even the stuff that looks okay) and seal the seams and cracks with mesh tape and a high-quality mastic (Figure 2), such as Uni-Mastic or Seal-N-Save (United McGill Corp., P.O. Box 820, Columbus, OH 43216; 800/624-5535). Use a flexible caulk to seal penetrations where the ductwork passes through to the exterior or to unconditioned spaces such as attics or basements (Figure 3). Make sure ducts are clean near their terminal ends and that the registers aren't covered or blocked by furniture or rugs and such. Finally, insulate any ductwork running through unconditioned spaces with R-11 fiberglass blankets.

Do the balancing act. One potential drawback of forced-air systems is that they can cause pressure differences throughout a house. If the system isn't properly designed or if someone messes with the control dampers, some rooms will be pressurized and some depressurized, leading to unwanted temperature discrepancies within zones. Pressurized rooms are poorly heated because new air can't get in. In depressurized areas, infiltration of outside air causes drafts and dryness, and raises fuel consumption. This is more than an occasional problem: The Electric Power Research Institute found that,

---

TABLE A.
RECOMMENDED MAINTENANCE FOR GAS AND OIL-FIRED SYSTEMS

All Furnaces and Boilers
- Clean burner and combustion chamber.
- Run combustion test to check furnace or boiler efficiency and preclude any danger of backdraft.
- Check for fuel-line leaks.
- Check and calibrate thermostat.
- Change oil filter.*

Forced-Air Systems
- Test airflow.
- Check for duct leaks and make needed repairs.
- Check fan belts for snugness and wear.
- Clean or replace air filter.
- Clean fan.
- Lubricate fan motors.
- Adjust fan switch.
- Make sure registers are properly oriented and free of obstructions.
- Vacuum ducts.
- Check, repair, and improve duct insulation.
- Clean humidifier (if present).

Hot Water or Steam Systems
- Clean or replace fuel nozzle.
- Insulate pipes with compressed fiberglass.
- Keep radiators clean and free of obstructions.
- Manually adjust aquastat.
- Bleed air out of system.
- Lubricate motor and pumps.
- Drain expansion tank.
- Drain sediment from boiler.
- Clean or replace clogged radiator vents.**
- Replace bad steam trap.***
- Check system for proper amount of water.

---

*   Oil-fired systems only.

**   One-pipe steam system only.

*** Two-pipe steam system only.

Note: The maintenance steps listed here should be performed yearly for oil-fired systems and every two years for gas systems.

on average, household infiltration rates are 15% to 36% higher in forced hot air homes than in others.

The way to avoid pressure differentials — to "balance" the system — is to match supply and return air capacity and, just as important, to provide low-resistance return air paths between every room and the return air register or registers. Giving every room its own ducted return register solves this challenge but is expensive. Instead, most homes have one or two centrally located return registers to which return air must flow. The problem comes when something — usually a closed door — blocks the free flow of air to this central return register from individual rooms.

It takes a sharp hvac contractor with a blower-door test kit to eval-uate and fix a system where the supply and return capacities are badly out of balance. But there are some simple things a GC can do to improve return airflow. You can undercut the doors to bedrooms and other isolated rooms 1½ to 2 inches, or you can install transom grilles. Unfortunately, both of these easy solutions badly compromise privacy. A more discreet solution is

TABLE B. EFFICIENCY UPGRADE

Upgrade	Cost	Estimated Fuel Savings	Comments
Forced-Air Furnace			
Replace fuel nozzle with a smaller one	Up to $60	2% to 10%	More expensive with gas furnaces; may be free with oil furnace tuneup.
Flame-retention head oil burner	$250-$600	10% to 25%	Oil furnaces only; may require downsizing the combustion chamber.
Replace pilot light with electric ignition	$150-$300	5% to 10%	Gas furnaces only.
Install automatic vent damper	$250-$400	3% to 15%	Closes flue to reduce standby heat loss up chimney. Savings usually greater with oil furnace than with gas.
Install a setback thermostat	$40-$280	7% to 10%	Lowers the temperature setting automatically while occupants are sleeping or away from home.
Install power burner	$400-$600	10% to 20%	Converts old oil and coal systems to gas.
Boiler			
Install thermostatic radiator valve (TRV)	$200 per unit	10% to 15%	Do-it-yourself project on one-pipe steam system will cost $35 to $75 per radiator.
Weather-responsive control (outdoor reset control)	$300-$1,000	5% to 25%	Hot water boilers only. Adjusts boiler water temperature according to outdoor temperature. Savings highest when used with setback thermostat and TRVs.
Replace fuel nozzle with a smaller one	Up to $60	2% to 10%	Hot water systems only. More expensive with gas boilers; may be free with oil boiler tuneups.
Flame-retention head oil burner	$250-$600	10% to 25%	Oil-fired boilers only. A better but more expensive option than downsizing the nozzle.
Replace pilot light with electric ignition	$150-$300	5% to 10%	Gas boilers only.
Install automatic vent damper	$250-$400	3% to 15%	Closes flue to reduce standby heat loss up chimney. Savings usually greater with oil than with gas.
Install setback thermostat	$40-$280	10% to 20%	Lowers temperature setting automatically while occupants are sleeping or away from home.
Install gas power burner	$400-$600	10% to 20%	Converts old oil and coal systems to gas.
Radiator reflectors	$10-$100	Varies	Galvanized sheet metal, aluminum foil, foil-faced insulation, or metalized film mounted to the walls behind radiators reduce heat loss through walls.

Note: Most furnaces five years old or older will benefit from one or more of these upgrades. Estimated savings are not cumulative, however. On older furnaces, consult with your hvac sub or energy auditor about the cost effectiveness of modifying the furnace versus installing a new one.

to install "transfer" grilles high on one side of a stud bay and low on the other side, connecting an airway to rooms on both sides of the wall. For yet more privacy, create a "jumper duct" by putting a ceiling grille in the isolated room and connecting it via a short run of duct to the open space nearest the main return register.

Keep in mind, however, that you shouldn't make these modifications unless you have good reason (such as a blower-door test) to believe you've got blocked return air paths.

Consider adding zones. In houses so badly out of balance or so spread out that the above steps won't work, extra ductwork may be required to balance the system. If that's the case, consider having an hvac contractor create some zones in the existing system. This usually involves installing a thermostat for each new zone, new ductwork or modifications to existing ductwork to create the new zones, and a few tweaks and add-ons to the furnace (a good control electrician or manufacturer's tech consultant can help here). A new zone can often be created by putting in "variable air volume" or "flow control" dampers in existing duct runs. These dampers, which include some innovative products such as pneumatically-controlled dampers, respond to the thermostat setting by automatically opening or closing to allow more or less treated air into the zone.

It can run from $1,200 to $1,500 to add a second zone to a one-zone system; installing a variable air volume system could cost twice that. Again, this should be done only by hvac contractors with lots of experience in FHA design and with training from the system's designers, because it's easy to mess up. But if it's done right, zoning will deliver a huge increase in the flexibility, comfort, and efficiency you can get out of an existing forced hot air system.

Tweak the furnace. Table B lists several modifications you can make to forced hot air furnaces. All bring real savings quickly, and most pay for themselves in one or two heating seasons. While these changes won't get a standard five- to ten-year-old system up into the 85% efficiency range of today's new units, they can take a furnace that is running at about 55% or 60% efficiency and bring it up to 70% or 75%.

One furnace modification not listed in the table is a variable speed blower, which kicks on and off gradually to reduce noise and also varies its speed depending on the heating or cooling load. These blowers are a nice improvement found in many new systems, and in theory they should make a sensible retrofit. But putting one into an existing furnace and blower unit is tricky and likely to lead to problems and expense, so I don't recommend them as a retrofit option.

Hydronic Systems

I like hydronic systems because they're less finicky than forced hot air systems and because they offer many options for increasing control of where, when, and how much heat is delivered. Many of the patches and modifications I will mention have

been developed in just the last few years, offering new opportunities to improve even old steam radiator systems. And most of these modifications are fairly easy to make.

Table A shows the routine maintenance every hydronic system needs; as with forced hot air systems, these should be the first line of attack in any evaluation or overhaul. Table B shows options for upgrading or modifying hydronic systems, with rough estimates for both costs and benefits of each upgrade.

Most of these options are straightforward, but a few, particularly the newer ones, are worth describing in some detail.

TRVs. Thermostatic radiator valves (TRVs) have been used for decades in Europe, but have become more readily available in the U.S. over the past ten years or so. TRVs mounted on individual steam or hot-water radiators control the flow of hot water (or venting air in steam radiators), acting as thermostats for those individual radiators. TRVs allow the occupant to tailor the amount of heat delivered to different radiators within a single zone. On a second floor, for instance, an infant's bedroom can be kept at a toasty 70°F degrees all night, the parents' at 60°F, and the spare bedroom at 55°F. Depending on the household,

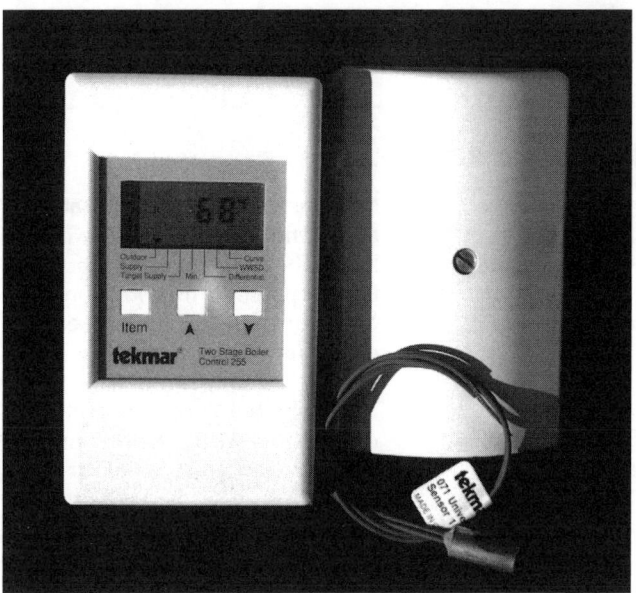

Figure 4. Weather-responsive boiler controls like this one from Tekmar adjust the temperature of boiler water to match changes in outdoor temperature. This increases system efficiency because the boiler never heats the water more than is necessary to keep the house at the desired temperature.

the increased convenience and comfort comes with considerable energy savings.

Weather-responsive controls. A fairly recent development for hot water (but not steam) systems is the weather-responsive boiler control (also known as "modulating aquastats," or "reset controls"). A weather-responsive boiler control works by constantly sensing the outdoor temperature and adjusting the boiler water temperature accordingly via the aquastat (Figure 4). Thus, when it's 0°F out, the boiler will heat the water to maximum temperature (usually around 180°F); if it's around 30°F out-

side, the boiler might heat the hot water to only 135°F. The system never heats the water any more than necessary to keep the house at the desired temperature. For every 3°F that you can lower the boiler water temperature and still heat the building, you save 1% in fuel. This increased efficiency can cut a home's heating bill by 15% to 25%. Good models include those from Honeywell (1985 Douglas Dr. North, Golden Valley, MN 55422; 800/328-5111), Stadler (3 Alfred Circle, Bedford, MA 01730; 800/370-3122, and Tekmar Control (4611 23rd St., Vernon, BC V1T 4K7, Canada; 604/545-7749).

Weather-responsive controls aren't cheap — the control itself runs about $300 and takes an hvac contractor a half day or so to install. These controls also can't be used with a tankless boiler system unless you install a four-way mixing valve, which gets a bit more complicated and pricey. These aren't reasons to avoid weather-responsive controls; they're simply factors that an experienced hvac or plumbing-heating contractor should evaluate before going ahead.

By Richard Trethewey, an hvac contractor and consultant from Dedham, Mass.

HIGH-EFFICIENCY HVAC

Some residential hvac appliances have enjoyed a relatively trouble-free evolution to higher efficiencies. Heat pumps and air conditioners, for example, have not been radically modified to increase efficiency. No new major components have been added and the newest units are not generally more complex or more difficult to install than older, lower-efficiency models.

Gas furnaces, on the other hand, have had a long and bumpy journey to high efficiency. Several new major components have been added, including secondary heat exchang-

ers, draft inducers, and electric ignition (Figure 5). Some of the mechanical components in early models were poorly designed and failed regularly. A few models, such as the Amana Energy Command and Lennox Pulse used totally new technology with almost no resemblance to "conventional" furnaces.

The Amana unit, which used water and glycol heat transfer fluid, is one of only two furnaces that can heat domestic water (the other is Glowcore). However, it ran into a string of problems, including glycol leakage in early units. In 1990,

Amana brought out a new and less expensive condensing gas furnace using more conventional technology.

The Lennox unit pioneered "pulse combustion," and after early problems with noise, turned out to be one of the biggest success stories in high-efficiency hvac (Figure 6). The first ten years of development, from 1980 to 1990, were fraught with factory recalls, contractor callbacks, and dissatisfied consumers who complained of nuisance shutdowns, noise problems, and poor comfort. Some homeowners even (unfairly) blamed their high-efficiency furnaces for moisture and indoor air quality problems.

Things got so bad that in 1985 a group of contractors at the Air Conditioning Contractors of America annual meeting offered a resolution stating that they had suffered "unacceptable loss of time, money, and reputation due to multiple failures of new high-efficiency equipment."

The good news is that after a number of years of trial and error combined with applied research, most of the design problems appear to be fixed. But there is still one

AVOIDING CORROSION PROBLEMS

To minimize corrosion problems with high-efficiency furnaces and boilers, follow these recommendations:
• Use only outdoor air for combustion.
• Locate air intake away from potential outdoor chloride sources such as swimming pools and dryer exhaust vents. If necessary, run the air intake through the roof rather than a sidewall.

• Make sure the furnace is installed level. If not, condensate may collect in the heat exchanger, increasing the potential for corrosion.
• Never use an installed high efficiency furnace as a construction heater. Not only is this likely to contaminate the furnace and duct system with construction dust (true for any type of furnace), but sealers and adhesives can quickly damage the heat exchanger surfaces.

catch. Unlike automobiles, which are fully preassembled and ready to drive, hvac must be properly installed. High-efficiency equipment, particularly condensing furnaces and boilers, is generally less forgiving of installation error than older equipment. A few basic guidelines and specifications must be followed to ensure good performance and trouble-free, long-lasting service.

Corrosion in Condensing Gas Furnaces

The Arkla Recuperative Plus gas furnace was introduced in 1982 and recalled in 1984 after more than 2,000 reported claims of heat exchanger corrosion and carbon monoxide problems. The same furnace was also sold under different names by GE, Trane, and SnyderGeneral. This was the beginning of the worst problem to plague high-efficiency gas furnaces. The next five years saw recalls of Heil, Whirlpool, and Coleman condensing gas furnaces — all for heat exchanger corrosion.

The situation has been vastly improved, but not completely fixed. After extensive research at Battelle Laboratory and the American Gas Association Laboratories, manufacturers now use corrosion-resistant materials for heat exchangers and other components. Most use a special stainless-steel alloy called AL29-4C for the secondary heat exchanger (Figure 7), although some have tried different approaches with varying success. For example, Heil tried a ceramic-lined heat exchanger that had to be recalled due to scaling problems, while Carrier uses a plastic-lined heat exchanger, which seems to be working well.

Chloride a problem. Regardless of the type of heat exchanger, high-efficiency furnaces can and do still rust badly if the combustion air contains high levels of chlorides. The chloride combines with water vapor in the flue gases to form a corrosive condensate that attacks metal parts in the heat

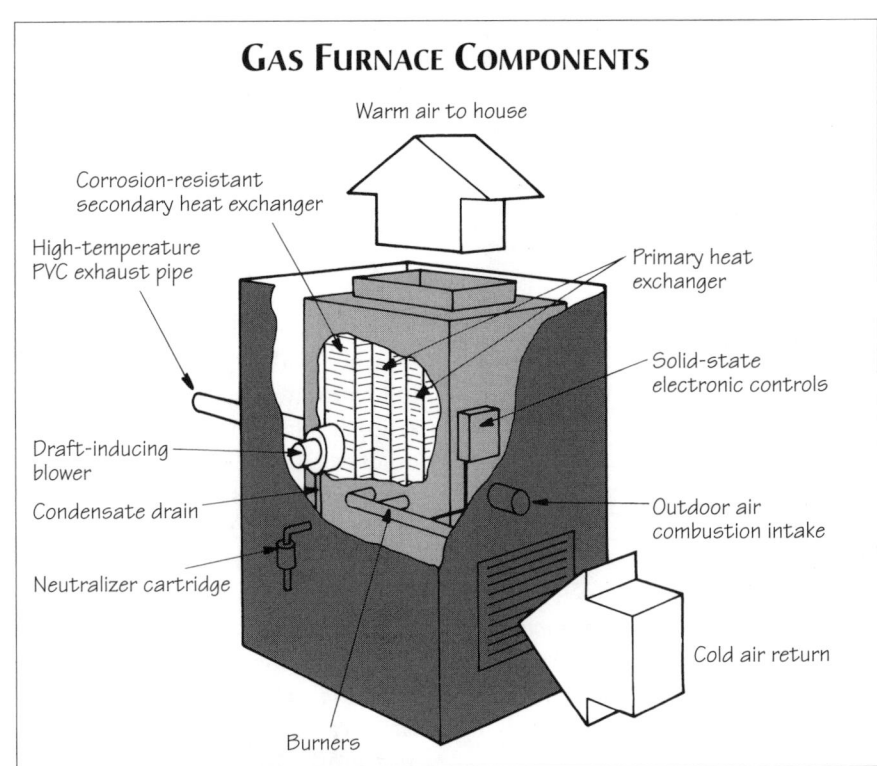

GAS FURNACE COMPONENTS

Warm air to house

Corrosion-resistant secondary heat exchanger
High-temperature PVC exhaust pipe
Primary heat exchanger
Solid-state electronic controls
Draft-inducing blower
Condensate drain
Outdoor air combustion intake
Neutralizer cartridge
Cold air return
Burners

Figure 5. Look inside a high-efficiency furnace and you'll see components not found in low- and mid-efficiency models. The draft-inducing blower plays a key role, drawing air into the combustion chamber for more efficient controlled combustion, then forcing the hot air through the primary and secondary heat exchangers for maximum heat transfer. As the combustion air passes through the secondary heat exchanger, it cools to the point where moisture condenses, releasing another burst of heat.

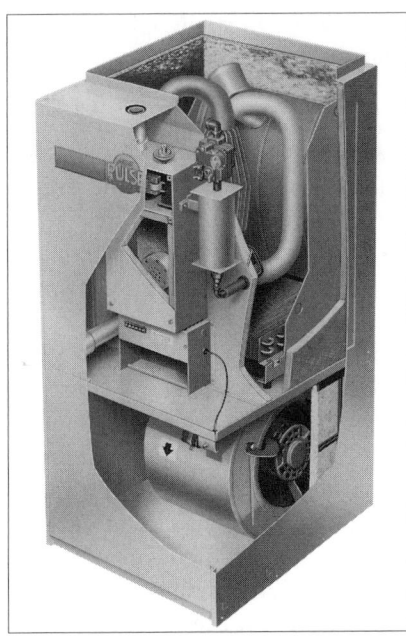

Figure 6. After early problems with noise, the Lennox Pulse turned out to be one of the biggest success stories in high-efficiency hvac.

Figure 7. The Yukon oil furnace, one of only two condensing oil furnaces on the market, uses highly resistant (and very expensive) AL29-4C stainless steel for the secondary heat exchanger and 301 stainless steel for the primary.

177

Figure 8. The Hydropulse is the first and only residential pulse boiler. Like its furnace cousin, the Lennox Pulse, it has enjoyed a relatively trouble-free history.

Figure 9. To prevent corrosion in a high-efficiency boiler, such as the Weil McLain GV model shown here, the venting system must be Ultravent or Plexvent high-temperature plastic vent pipe (the black pipe). Made of GE Ultem plastic, these vent systems can withstand temperatures up to 480°F. The white pipe is the fresh air intake, which is made of ordinary Schedule 40 PVC.

exchanger and exhaust system. Bard Manufacturing Company voids its lifetime warranty if a heat exchanger in one of its gas furnaces is corroded from "contaminated air."

Unfortunately, indoor air often contains large amounts of chloride compounds, especially in basements and near laundry rooms. It comes from chlorinated tap water, chlorine bleaches, and a host of other household products such as paint, paint stripper, and adhesives. The results of an extensive testing of 572 houses conducted by Battelle Laboratory indicated that 1 in 10 homes has indoor air chloride concentrations high enough to produce corrosive flue-gas condensate.

Even outdoor air sometimes contains high chloride levels, particularly near swimming pools, hot tubs, and clothes dryer exhausts. One horror story is told by David Hahn, a training specialist at Wisconsin Natural Gas who has inspected hundreds of failed systems.

Hahn was called in to inspect a Lennox Pulse furnace with corrosion problems. The house was located near a road-salt storage depot and the road was usually covered with spilled salt. The chloride concentration in the outdoor air was so high that the furnace rusted out completely in only eight months! The solution, according to Hahn, was to install a new furnace with the combustion air intake at the back side of the house, away from the road.

Venting Problems

Venting high-efficiency condensing furnaces (those in the 83% to 97% AFUE, or *annual fuel utilization efficiency*, range) is actually easier and less problematic than venting mid-efficiency furnaces (78% to 83% AFUE). But despite their apparent simplicity, these vent systems have had problems.

Nuisance shutdowns. A 600-house Canadian study of high-efficiency gas furnaces found that 16%

of the installations suffered frequent shutdown due to improper vent installation. These "nuisance shutdowns" are most likely to occur if the vent system is too long or improperly sloped. Some building codes prohibit venting a furnace in the direction of neighboring houses. To comply with this restriction, contractors sometimes install long horizontal runs to reach the back or front of the house. The long pipe creates high static pressure. A wind against the termination may then be all that is needed to raise the back pressure above the setpoint of the safety pressure switch, which then shuts down the system. (This typically occurs around midnight on Christmas eve.)

Annoying fumes. Flue gases from condensing furnaces are not terribly toxic, but they do contain slightly acidic vapors, considerable moisture, and trace amounts of pollutants. They are also accompanied by noise. Improperly positioned exhaust vents can kill bushes, steam up windows, and annoy neighbors. In one installation in Madison, Wis., a contractor put the exhaust vent directly over the outdoor air conditioner unit. Dripping condensate corroded the air conditioner casing and eventually penetrated into the outdoor coil, causing the air conditioner to fail.

In another installation, a dripping roof vent termination rusted out the metal rain gutters. And one disgruntled homeowner in Arlington, Mass., had her contractor move the vent termination for her Glowcore furnace because of the unsightly "steam" visible through the living room picture window.

Noise. High-efficiency gas furnaces are generally noisier than low-efficiency units because the main blowers are bigger and because they have an additional draft-inducing blower that is not used in low-efficiency furnaces. The original Lennox Pulse furnace was terribly noisy, especially when not installed properly. (Lots of jokes were made about small outboard motors in the basement.)

The best news regarding noise is the development of variable-speed furnaces by Carrier and Trane, both of which are so quiet that it is hard to tell they are operating when standing 2 feet away. And Lennox has significantly reduced sound levels from the Pulse furnace.

Boilers

Despite some radical departures from conventional design, high-efficiency boilers have been relatively trouble free (Figure 8). One nagging problem that plagued the first high-efficiency systems was condensate formation in the heat exchangers and flue pipes.

To protect the heat exchangers, all high-efficiency boilers now have thermostatic bypass valves which shunt supply water back to the heat exchanger to prevent flue gas condensation. Unfortunately, nothing is foolproof. In one case, a contractor in Springfield, Mass., neglected to install the bypass valve on a Heatmaker boiler. With no temperature control, the boiler ran too cool, resulting in serious condensate damage to the heat exchanger.

To eliminate flue corrosion, literally every manufacturer now recommends high-temperature plastic flue pipe made of GE "Ultem" resin (Figure 9). Some manufacturers also allow Type 301 stainless steel, which is almost as resistant to corrosion, but much more difficult to work with.

One problem with mid-efficiency (83% to 88% AFUE) boilers has to do with condensation in masonry chimneys, particularly with chimneys located on outside walls. The corrosive condensate can attack mortar joints in unlined chimneys and can even cause damage in chimneys with clay liners. If possible, mid-efficiency boilers should be

Venting Guidelines

- Keep vent runs as short as possible. Never exceed manufacturers' guidelines (typically 30 to 40 feet with two elbows).
- On horizontal runs, the vent pipe must slope toward the furnace, allowing condensate to drain back into the furnace.
- Keep the exhaust termination 10 inches from the wall to reduce icing on the wall and to prevent paint damage. If the vent faces prevailing winds, install a protective plate around the termination to protect the wall.
- Maintain about a 2-foot clearance from shrubbery.
- Never use a "U" termination on a roof vent. Dripping condensate can damage roofing and gutters. The roof vent should be a straight vertical pipe. Rain will not be a problem since it will drain through the condensate drain.
- Insulate any section of vent pipe that passes through unheated spaces or extends more than 3 feet outdoors. The vent pipe should also be insulated if an exterior masonry chimney is used as a chase.
- Do not install exhaust vents over anything that cannot tolerate dripping condensate. This

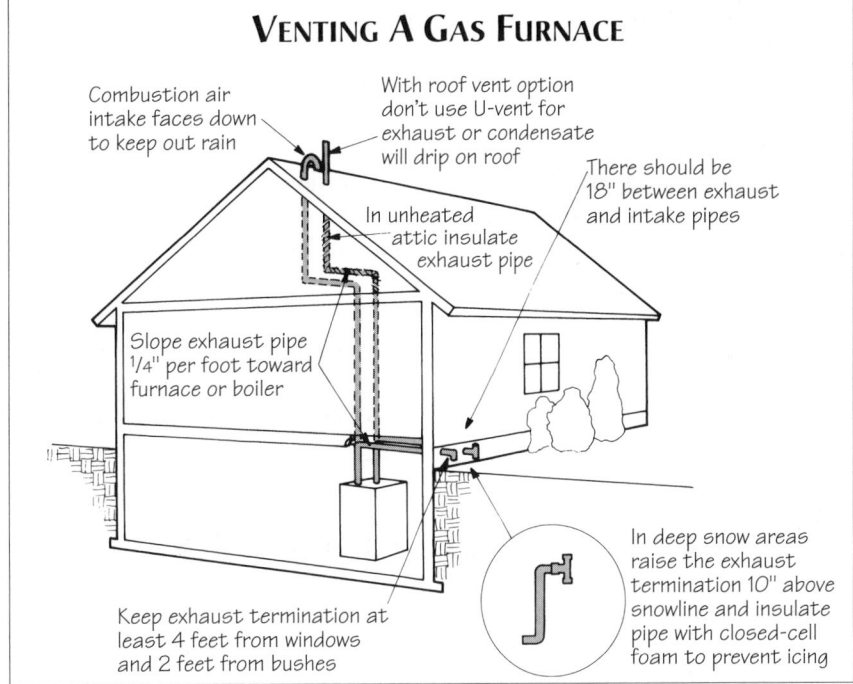

By following a few basic guidelines, most of the annoying problems associated with venting high-efficiency furnaces and boilers can be eliminated.

includes walkways, windows, air conditioners, gas meters, etc.
- Do not install the exhaust vent near any air intakes or under windows. Aside from the obvious hazard of drawing exhaust gases into the house, rising water vapor will be visible through windows and can even condense moisture on the glass surface.
- Locate the vent terminal so that the noise will be directed toward open space or through the roof rather than toward a neighboring house which could echo the sound (and annoy the neighbor).

Figure 10. The new Copeland Compliant Scroll compressor is more efficient and reliable than conventional piston compressors. Most major heat pump manufacturers now sell models equipped with scroll compressors.

side-vented using stainless-steel or high-temperature plastic vent pipe.

Air Conditioners and Heat Pumps

High-efficiency air conditioners and heat pumps have not suffered any notable problems other than those normally associated with compressor technology. If anything, the new high-efficiency air conditioners and heat pumps are more reliable than older equipment.

The most noteworthy development was the scroll compressor (Figure 10), which was first intro-duced by Lennox in 1987 in its HP-20 heat pump. Most of the other major equipment manufacturers quickly followed. Using far fewer parts than conventional piston-type compressors, scroll compressors are not only more efficient, they also are quieter and more durable.

One problem with high-efficiency cooling equipment is its generally lower dehumidification capacity. During very humid weather, these units sometimes reduce indoor temperature without removing sufficient humidity — the so-called "cool but clammy" effect.

Manufacturers have effectively addressed this problem with variable-speed (Carrier and Trane) and two-speed (Lennox) equipment that has variable dehumidification capacity. Contractors can also help the problem by not installing oversized equipment, which naturally tends to cycle more frequently. Since dehumidification is lowest during startup, frequent cycling causes poor dehumidification.

Federal Regs

High-efficiency heating and cooling equipment has captured a significant share of the residential market since the new federal minimum efficiency standards took effect in 1992.

These federal regulations completely eliminated low-efficiency furnaces, boilers, and air conditioners from the marketplace. Given the relatively small price differential between the remaining mid- and high-efficiency models, the buying public tends to skip to top-of-the line models. So it makes sense to familiarize yourself with the new technology.

Training available. When Weil McLain introduced its new GV series boiler, it also produced an excellent training video and workbook that explains exactly how and why the system works and then shows detailed step-by-step installation procedures. Carrier, Trane, and Lennox all produce comprehensive training materials and seminars. In addition, the installation manuals that accompany all appliances usually (but unfortunately not always) include most of the recommendations and guidelines given here, along with all the necessary details for proper installation and startup.

By J.D. Ned Nisson, president of Energy Design Associates Inc., a New York City-based building systems consulting firm, and editor of Energy Design Update.

MECHANICAL COOLING SYSTEMS

Field studies across the nation indicate that residential air conditioners are running far below their rated efficiencies because of poor installation. One extensive study found that duct leakage alone raised the average cooling load in new homes by about 23%. Duct leakage is the largest loss, followed by improper charge, air flow problems, and oversizing.

The time to fix these problems is during design and construction, when small improvements will yield big payoffs in efficiency. Retrofitting at a later date, however, when many of the problems are buried behind drywall and finished floors means less gain for more money. In addition to saving the homeowner a lot of money, a better job up front means fewer callbacks for the contractor — for the electric bill that's "twice as high as my neighbor's" or the unit that won't stop running but still leaves the owners uncomfortable.

Duct Leakage

Because of standard installation practices, duct leakage plagues almost all forced-air heating and cooling systems. While only 10% to 15% of the total air leakage in a home is located in the duct system, duct leaks are under pressures 10 to 20 times higher than other building leaks whenever the air handler runs. The result is that when the air handler is running, duct leaks can double or triple the total air leakage in a home. And this typically happens when you least want it — at the hottest or coldest times of the year.

So where do the leaks occur? Disconnected ducts and framing cavities are the most common leakage sites (Figure 11). It is not unusual to find ducts that have either been accidentally disconnected by another trade or that were never connected in the first place. The take-offs and collars where branch lines exit the trunk are notoriously leaky (Figure 12). Basically, there are leaks wherever there is a joint or a seam in the system (one exception is the snap-lock joints along the length of a straight section of duct). Even the cabinets that house the units are leaky.

Another big problem is the widespread use of framing cavities as part of the air supply and return system. This includes platform plenums, and panned joist and stud cavities (Figure 13). Typically, the hvac contractor says it's the contractor's, drywaller's, or framer's responsibility to seal up framing cavities; whereas the contractor points the finger at the hvac sub. Even if the contractor does a thorough job of sealing these cavities, they may not survive the work of plumbers and electricians. Regardless, most framing lumber shrinks as it dries and new cracks will appear. Our conclusion is that the building industry must get away from using building cavities as part of the air distribution system.

If you are skeptical, we suggest you examine one of your duct systems as it is being installed. Pop off a return grille on a panned joist return and scrutinize all the seams. Examine where supply lines branch from trunk lines. If you have the opportunity, look down a trunk line while it is being installed. You will most likely see light coming in every 48 inches where the sections connect. A flashlight and an inspection mirror are handy for this.

Sealing the ducts. Fortunately, duct leakage is simple to eliminate during

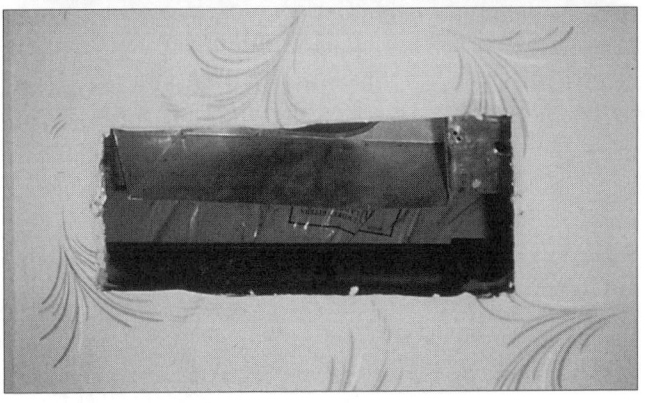

Figure 11. Prime leakage sites include: connections where flex ducts join junction boxes (top), disconnected ductwork (center), and poorly installed boots at grilles and registers (bottom). Leaky ductwork can spoil the performance of an otherwise tight, well-insulated home.

new construction if you know where to look for leaks and how to seal them. Depending on the complexity of the system, sealing can cost from $150 to $350. Research has shown that the payback period on this added cost ranges from less than a year to about three years. And there are important health and safety benefits as well.

The product of choice for duct sealing is water-based mastic accompanied by a fiberglass mesh on larger holes. Two good duct mastics are Glencoat (I.M. Distributors, 8541 23rd Ave., Sacramento, CA 95826;

916/381-1800) and RCD #6 (RCD, P.O. Box 1020, Eustis, FL 32727-1020; 800/854-7494). These mastics have the consistency of mashed potatoes and can be easily spread over joints in the ductwork with an inexpensive paint brush or one's gloved hand. On cracks and gaps wider than 1/4 inch, place a section of 2-inch-wide fiberglass mesh tape in the bed of mastic to reinforce the seal. The beauty of water-based mastic is that it provides a long-term durable seal and cleans up with water.

The traditional duct tape approach doesn't work. Because of

the extreme temperature conditions that ducts are subjected to, the tape eventually fails. Mastic is actually less labor intensive than a "good" taping job (Figure 14).

The last step in the sealing procedure is to test to make sure your hvac contractor got it right. You can use either a blower door and flow hood or the newest arrival — the Duct Blaster (The Energy Conservatory, 5158 Bloomington Ave. S., Minneapolis, MN 55417; 612/827-1117). With proper training, these diagnostic tools are fairly simple to use (Figure 15). The goal is to have no more than 25 cfm of leakage at .10 inches of water column in smaller homes and no more than 50 cfm leakage in larger homes. This is achievable, but it takes a lot more attention to detail than most hvac contractors are accustomed to.

The testing has several benefits. First, when an hvac contractor knows his work will be tested, he's more likely to get it right the first time. Second, diagnostic tools turn up leaks that are virtually undetectable

by visual inspection. And third, the test teaches the participants where to seal better next time, as well as making believers out of skeptics.

Improper Charge

The second most important problem with mechanical cooling systems involves the refrigerant charge. Over half the homes we evaluated in one study had the wrong charge. For the most common systems (capillary tube), a 10% overcharge results in a 10% loss in efficiency. When undercharged by 20%, the same system loses 16% of its designed efficiency. Incorrect charge also reduces capacity and may shorten compressor life.

An undercharge causes the compressor to run longer and hotter, while an overcharge causes the compressor to work harder and can lead to compressor failure. In the case of an undercharge, less heat is removed from the indoor air as it passes through the coil, so the unit has to run longer.

Technicians typically use guesswork to determine if the charge is

correct. One common but unreliable technique is to feel the suction line. If the temperature to the compressor "feels right," then the charge is assumed to be correct. The accurate way to check the charge is straightforward for a trained person and takes less than an hour. The process involves first checking the air flow and then either the *superheat* or *subcooling*, depending on system design.

Low Air Flow

The third major problem with mechanical cooling is low air flow over the indoor coil. The indoor coil, or evaporator, is where heat and moisture are removed from warm indoor air. Most manufacturers recommend that air flow across the coil should be 400 cfm per ton. When the air flow drops below 350 cfm, the unit's efficiency drops off.

In simple terms, lower air flow means less heat is transferred to the refrigerant, so the unit has to run longer to remove the same amount of heat. Another effect of low air flow is that the coil may begin to freeze,

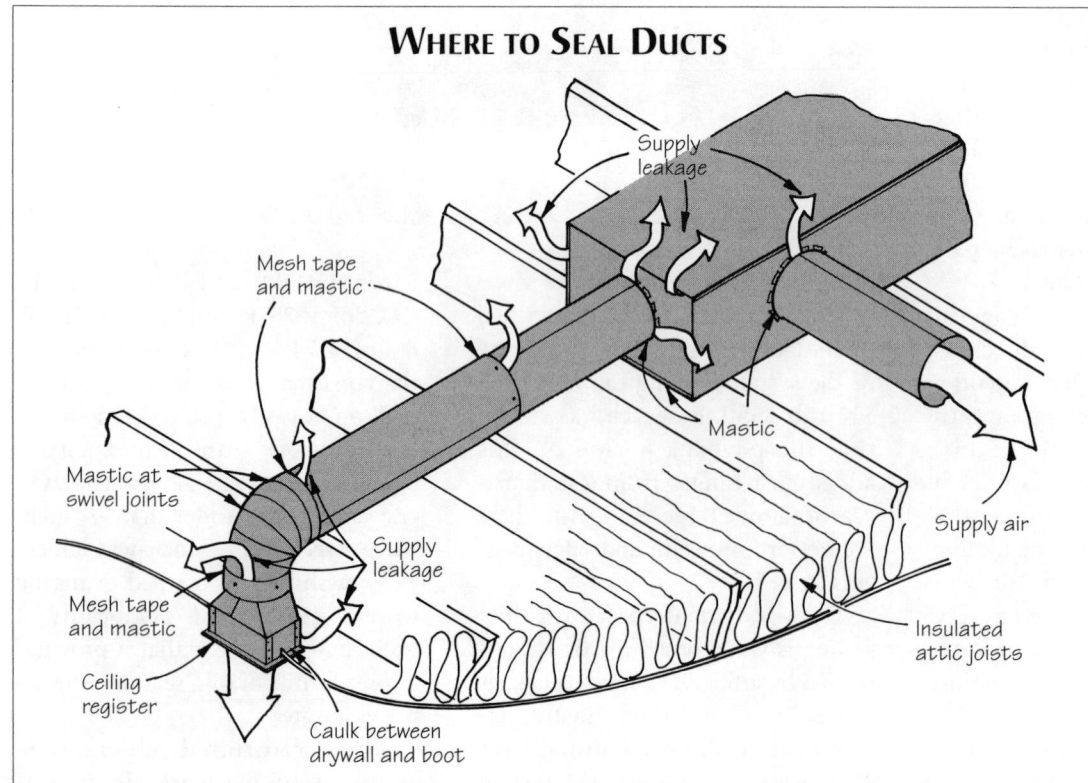

WHERE TO SEAL DUCTS

Supply leakage

Mesh tape and mastic

Mastic

Mastic at swivel joints

Supply leakage

Mesh tape and mastic

Ceiling register

Caulk between drywall and boot

Supply air

Insulated attic joists

Figure 12. To control metal duct leaks in attics and other unconditioned spaces, seal all joints with mastic except lengthwise snap-lock joints, which are relatively tight. With flex duct, seal the inside liner to the metal collar with a plastic tie, then apply mastic and fibermesh.

which further reduces efficiency and can cause the compressor to fail.

A study we conducted of 175 newer homes revealed that 24% of the homes had air flow of 350 cfm per ton or less, some as low as 196 cfm per ton. The average efficiency loss was 8%.

Reduced air flow has many causes. The most common cause is poor duct design and installation (Figure 16). Closed registers also reduce the air flow. If the air distribution system relies on a filter grille at the return, return leaks can suck dust and insulation into the duct system, which accumulates on the coils and reduces air flow. A dirty air filter has a similar effect. Even without duct problems, it is important to inspect both the indoor coil and air filter on a regular basis.

Unfortunately, the indoor coil is often installed in an inaccessible location. If the supply plenum has to be dismantled to gain access to the coil, chances are it will never be inspected. If, on the other hand, an access panel is incorporated into the supply riser and only a handful of sheet metal screws have to be backed out, the service technician can make a visual inspection as part of the annual service.

The best way to measure air flow is with the Duct Blaster, described above. For efficient performance, the flow should be within 5% of manufacturer's specs.

Oversizing

The majority of air conditioners are oversized by 25% or more. When duct leakage, low air flow, and improper charge have been addressed, this oversizing becomes apparent. An oversized unit is more expensive to run, compromises comfort, and can be a source of callbacks. Once again, the penalty for this problem involves more than just a higher utility bill.

An oversized system will "short cycle," meaning the unit cycles on and off rapidly instead of running steadily. A capillary tube system takes over five minutes to reach 95% of its operating capacity. Short cycles never allow the equipment to perform to its designed capacity.

Oversizing can also degrade comfort in hot, humid climates, because the unit's ability to dehumidify (latent cooling) is reduced. The unit cools the air so quickly that it kicks off before the indoor coil removes an

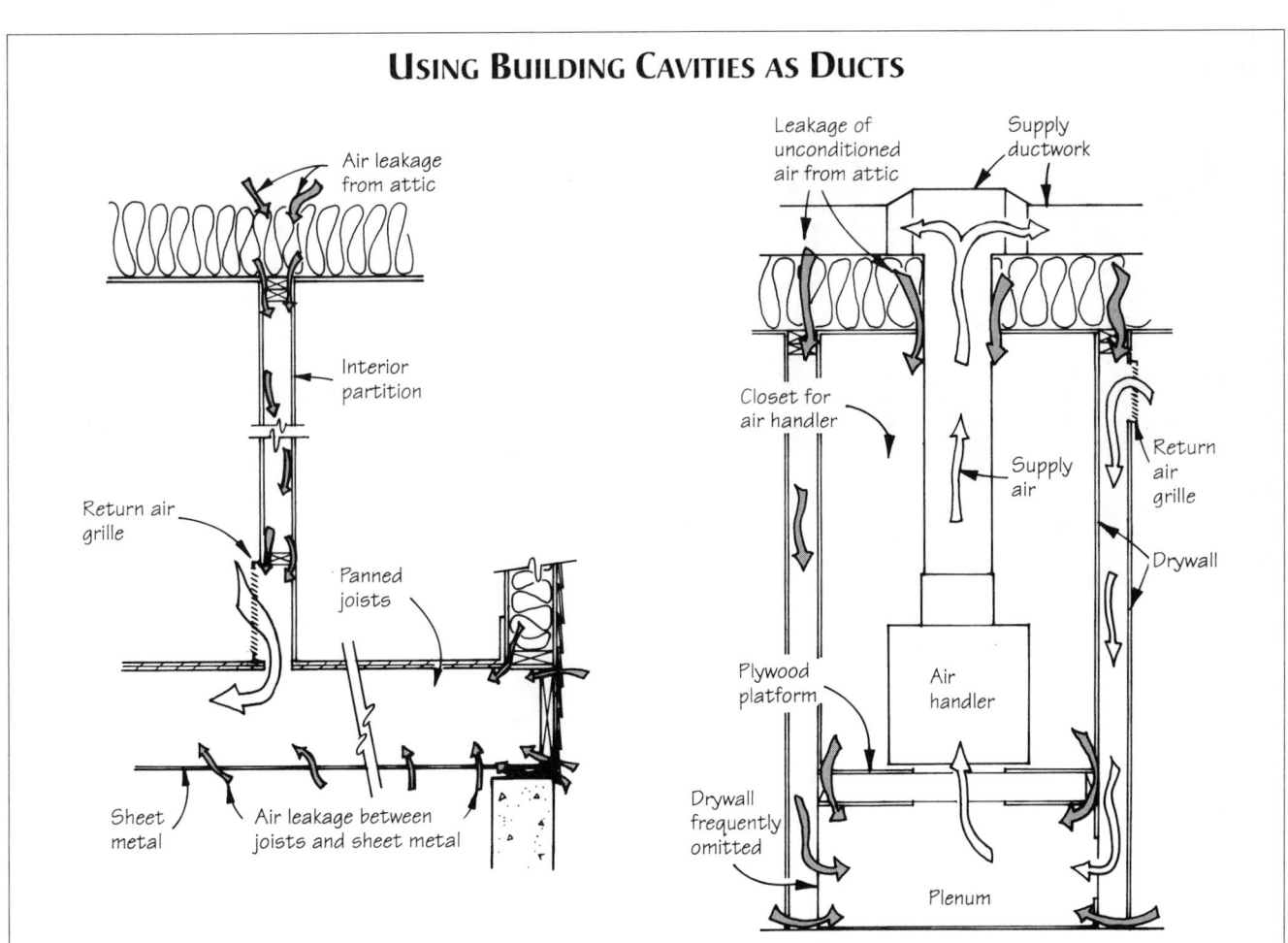

USING BUILDING CAVITIES AS DUCTS

Figure 13. Stud and joist bays make handy return ducts, but are a major source of leakage (left). Air handlers set on raised platforms (right) suffer from similar leaks. The author's recommendation: Use ductwork instead of building cavities.

Figure 14. Throw away your duct tape and smear on water-based mastic instead, if you want a long-lasting seal against duct leakage. Duct mastic has the consistency of mashed potatoes and is applied by hand or with a cheap paint brush.

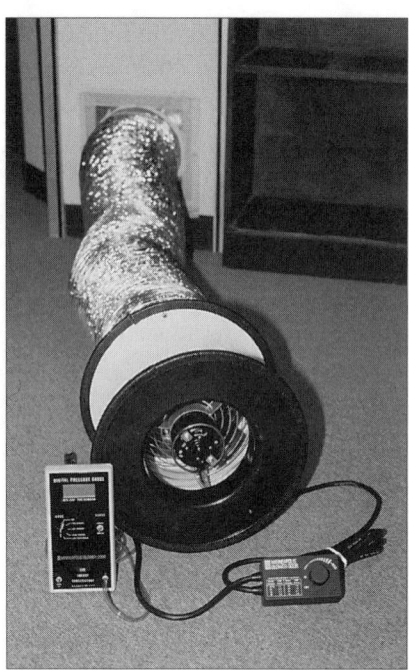

Figure 15. Measuring duct leakage takes under half an hour using the Duct Blaster, a portable calibrated fan. Used as a powered flow hood, it can also accurately measure air flow through the duct system.

Figure 16. Too many twists and turns in the duct runs create excess resistance to flow. This lowers system performance and can freeze up the evaporator coil.

adequate amount of moisture. The indoor humidity remains high, preventing a person's body from keeping cool through natural evaporation from the skin.

The result is that the air ends up cool and clammy, and occupants respond by turning down the thermostat further, driving up energy use. For example, turning the thermostat down from 75°F to 70°F can easily increase the cooling load by 25%.

Ask your hvac contractor how he sizes equipment. Most rely on rules of thumb based on the square footage of the house. Window orientation, levels of conservation, and occupant load are often not taken into consideration.

The solution is Manual J, which is a simple method for sizing heating and cooling loads. Manual J becomes fairly easy to navigate once you've waded through it a couple of times. A companion manual, Manual D, is for sizing duct work. The manuals cost $24 each from the Air Conditioner Contractors Association, (1513 16th St. NW, Washington, DC 20036). Both procedures are also available on computer software called Wright J and Wright D (Wright Associates, 394 Lowell St., Lexington, MA 02173). With the software, an experienced estimator can do a run on a simple 1,800-square-foot home in about an hour — compared to about three hours manually.

The time it takes to correctly size a cooling system is well spent. A properly sized unit will often reduce the initial cost of the system, run more efficiently, last longer, and enhance the comfort level in the home. If your hvac contractor isn't already sizing systems correctly, encourage him to learn how to use Manual J and Manual D.

Summary

It's safe to say that over 95% of new air-conditioned homes being built today will suffer from one or more of the problems discussed here: duct leakage, low air flow, improper refrigerant charge, and oversizing. To correct these problems, builders and designers need to start using detailed specifications that require quality installations. The payback period for eliminating these problems is typically less than three years, not counting the benefits of better comfort and indoor air quality, as well as fewer callbacks.

For More Information

Professional training in duct doctoring is offered by the Florida Solar Energy Center (1679 Clearlake Rd., Cocoa, FL 32922; 407/638-1000).

By Michael Uniacke, a building science educator and consultant in Prescott Valley, Ariz. And by John Proctor, P.E., of Proctor Engineering Group in Corte Madera, Calif., a consultant and researcher on hvac and building shell efficiency.

WATER HEATERS

Many times, the failure to recognize a small, easy-to-repair problem leads to an expensive — and unnecessary — replacement. Recently, for instance, a client who wasn't getting enough hot water "solved" the problem by purchasing a bigger water heater. When he called us in to hook it up, we found that his cold water dip tube had broken off, so cold water had been entering at the top, diluting the hot water. A little troubleshooting could have solved this problem with a $5 replacement part.

Maintenance is the best way to avoid problems (see "Maintaining Water Heaters," next page). When troubles do arise (short of a leaking tank), it helps to be familiar with a heater's parts (Figure 17). Good troubleshooting may prevent the need for heater replacement.

Before you start. Always turn off the power before troubleshooting an electric water heater (assuming you've determined that the problem isn't electrical). For gas heaters, it's usually sufficient to turn the control valve down to the "pilot" setting.

Next, shut off the water supply to the water heater; you can turn it back on later if you need to perform a test. Most installers provide a shut-off at the cold water supply inlet; otherwise, use the main house shut-off. To remove any pressure buildup in the tank, open a hot water faucet at any fixture in the house. Finally, hook up a hose to the drain valve on the bottom. (When it's time to refill the tank, leave the house faucet open until all of the air is out of the system.)

Now you're ready to explore the symptoms of trouble.

No Hot Water

Only two things cause no hot water: Either the energy supply has

INSIDE A WATER HEATER

Electric

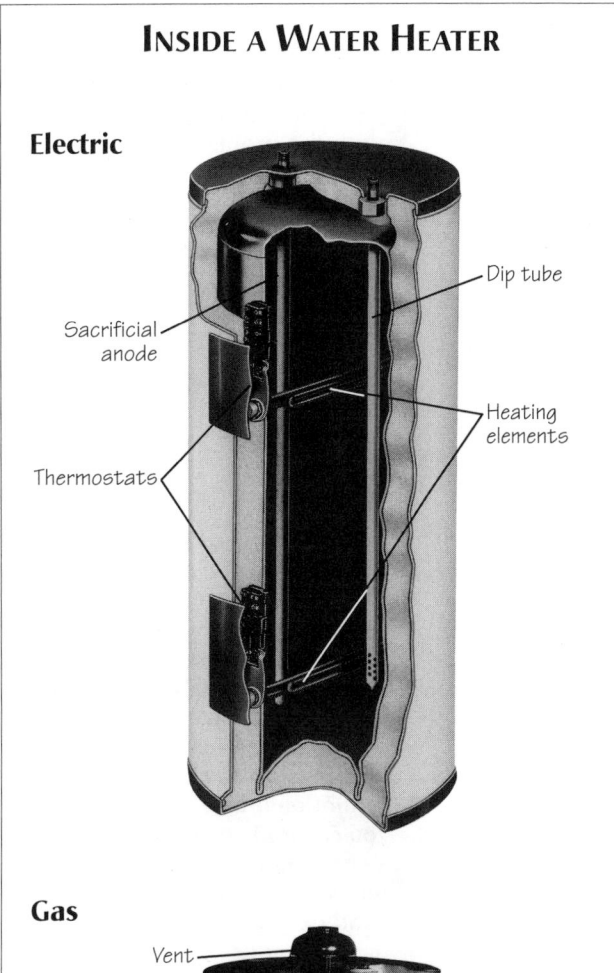

Sacrificial anode

Thermostats

Dip tube

Heating elements

Gas

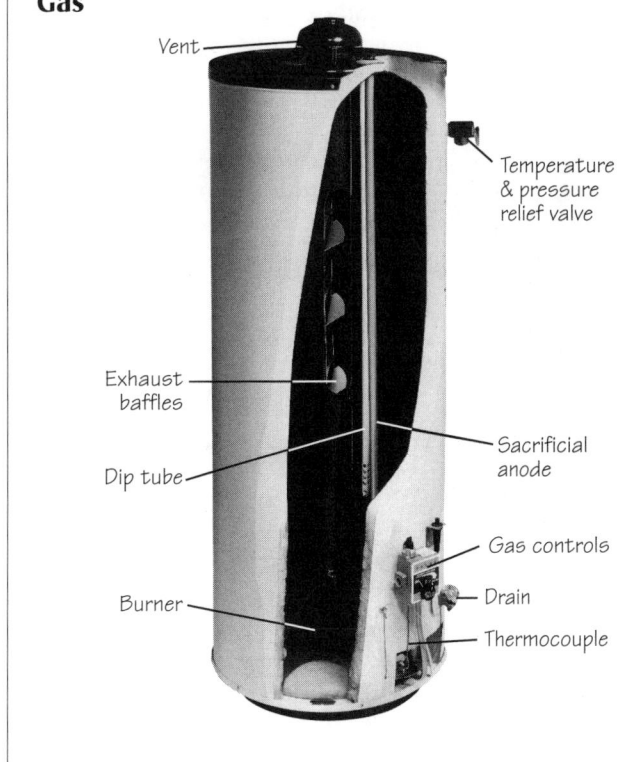

Vent

Temperature & pressure relief valve

Exhaust baffles

Dip tube

Sacrificial anode

Gas controls

Drain

Burner

Thermocouple

Figure 17. Electric heaters (left) have one or two immersed electric elements and thermostats; in gas models (below), the water is heated from the bottom and by flue gases traveling through the baffled center vent. In both types of heaters, a supply connection on top delivers cold water to the bottom of the tank through a plastic dip tube; a sacrificial metal anode prevents rust.

been interrupted, or there's a control problem.

Electric heaters. If an electric heater has no hot water, look first at the upper thermostat (Figure 18). Use a volt-ohm meter or a "pigtail" tester to check for power at the top two screw connections. If you find no power at these screws, there's no power getting to the heater: The problem is somewhere between the water heater and the main panel.

If you do have power at these two screws, but not at the two screws just below the red reset button, then the high-limit switch has turned the power off. If the red button clicks when you press it, power will be restored.

A tripped high-limit switch, however, is a symptom of very high temperatures, and unless the culprit is found, the problem will recur. One possible cause is fusing of the contacts in either the upper or lower thermostat. This prevents the heating elements from shutting off and leads to overheating. Also, a thermostat that is not mounted firmly against the tank wall, or one that is missing its insulation cover, may not read temperature correctly.

If there is no hot water in a dual element heater, the upper element may be burned out, preventing power from being switched to the lower element (which does most of the heating). With the power off and one wire disconnected, use a volt-ohm meter to check for continuity in the suspect element. Replacing the bad element will restore hot water.

Gas heaters. In gas heaters, the problem is usually either a worn-

MAINTAINING WATER HEATERS

Like all heavily used appliances, water heaters need maintenance. You can often spot early signs of trouble simply by looking at the tank. A great ooze of calcium and other scale debris piling up on top of the heater (Figure A) usually signals leaky connections in the plumbing overhead.

Some maintenance items, however, are less obvious. Here's a list of simple checks to encourage homeowners to become involved with.

Check the Anode

All glass-lined tanks come with a sacrificial anode rod which is usu-ally screwed into a separate port at the top of the heater (Figure B). The anode is about 3/4 inch in diameter and formed around a steel wire that extends down nearly to the tank's bottom. Other tanks do not have separate anodes but combine their anode with the hot outlet. If the original anode cannot be found or unscrewed, you can add an anode by screwing a combination-type anode into the hot water outlet port. Where overhead clearance is restricted, flexible-link anodes can be bent and "snaked in." The lower rod in Figure B is a link-type combination anode.

The magnesium or aluminum anode rods are meant to corrode slowly as part of an electrochemical reaction that prevents rusting in the tank, and which in turn prevents leaks. We prefer to use magnesium anodes, especially until aluminum is proven innocent of contributing to Alzheimer's Disease. (You can tell these metals apart by bending the anode: Aluminum is soft, while magnesium is somewhat springy.)

Anode replacement. You need the right tool to get the anode out. Usually, a 12-point socket on a breaker bar will do; other times you'll need a 6-point socket and a torque multiplier to free stubborn anodes.

It's best to find a source for replacement anodes before open-

Figure A. Leaking at unions in the overhead plumbing caused this scale to accumulate on top of the water heater. Because the leaks went unnoticed for several years, the heater rusted through from the outside in and had to be replaced.

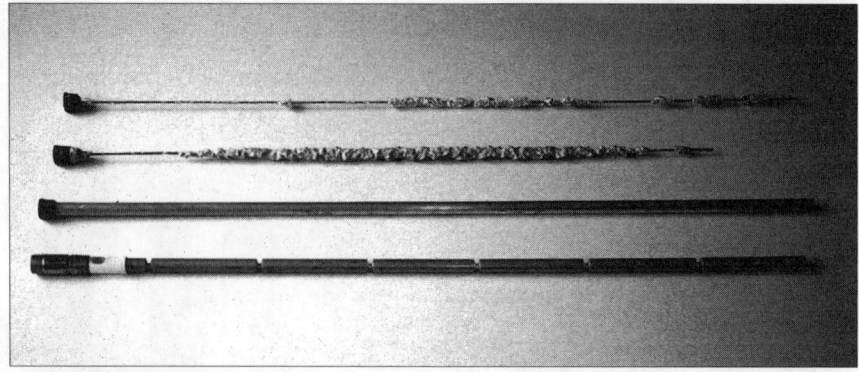

Figure B. The slow corrosion of a magnesium or aluminum anode rod protects glass-lined tanks from rust. Check the anode every few years and replace it if 6 inches or more of the steel core wire is exposed, or if the rod is coated over with a brittle scale. Use a flexible-link rod where overhead clearance is restricted.

out thermocouple or a faulty gas control (Figure 19). First, look to see if the pilot flame actually touches the end of the thermocouple, as it's supposed to. Then check to see that the thermocouple is firmly screwed into the control. If you have doubts about this connection, unscrew the thermocouple, use extra-fine sandpaper or a knife to polish the contact point, and re-install. Special thermocouple testers are also available, but it may be easier (and cheaper) to replace the thermocouple and see if that

revives the heater. (A thermocouple costs about $15 and takes ten minutes to replace.)

If the heater was supplying very hot water before there was no hot water, the energy cutoff switch, which is built into the gas control, was probably activated. With modern heaters, once this has tripped, the control valve must be replaced (about $80 plus installation).

Insufficient Hot Water

When there's not enough hot water, first check to see if the heater

is correctly sized for its demand. A heater should deliver about 75% of its volume as hot water. You can measure flow at fixtures such as the showerhead to determine how much the tank is capable of delivering. (Empty five-gallon drywall buckets work well for this test: Count the number of buckets you can fill with hot water, then compare the result with the tank's capacity.)

Cross connections. If the tank is not overtaxed, check for cross connections. Turn off the water supply

---

ing up your tank. While hardware stores seldom stock anodes, plumbing supply houses have them for $18 to $45.

It's time for anode replacement when 6 inches of the steel core wire is exposed, or if the rod is coated over with a brittle scale. Check anodes every three to four years (more often if you have hard, softened, or acidic water).

Control Sediment

Sediment is the curse of water heaters. Accumulated sediment slows heat transfer in gas heaters, and the elevated temperatures weaken the steel and dissolve the glass lining. Sediment also provides a breeding ground for bacteria. In gas heaters, sediment can cause annoying noise, and in electric heaters it can cause the lower element to burn out.

Getting rid of sediment. You can remove sediment by dissolving, vacuuming, or flushing it out of the tank. If you decide to try dissolving, do not use compounds containing lye. It's very dangerous. Instead, use a citric acid product such as Mag-Erad. The process takes several hours and may need to be repeated if not initially effective.

We like to vacuum sediment using a tool we developed called the Muck-Vac, which pulls water and sediment off the bottom and returns filtered water to the tank

(Figure C). In electric heaters, you can pull out the bulk of the sediment using a wet/dry shop vac with a piece of 3/4-inch pipe for a nozzle. Go in through the element port after draining the tank.

The third method, flushing, is effective only if water pressure and flow are good, and the sediment buildup is not too heavy. For flushing to work, a heater must have a ball-valve drain and a dip tube with a curve on the end. Some heaters come from the factory with curved dip tubes already installed; if not, you can replace a straight tube with a curved one on standard tanks.

To flush the tank, attach a hose to the drain, open the ball valve, and let water run out full force for three to five minutes. The curved dip tube creates a swirling action in the tank that stirs up sediment and rinses it out the drain.

Prevent sediment buildup. Softening the water helps to reduce sediment accumulation, as does lowering the water pressure; high pressure tends to cause more sediment. If you can adjust the gas pressure to the main burner of your gas heater, turn it down: The smaller flame will slow sediment buildup.

Inspect Relief Valves

The temperature and pressure (T&P) relief valve kicks in at temperatures over 210°F and pressures of more than about 150 psi. If the valve

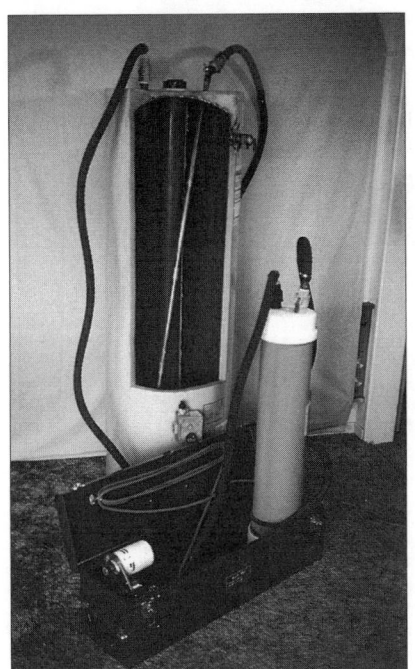

Figure C. The authors designed the Muck-Vac to pull sediment off the bottom of the tank, filter it, and return clean water to the heater.

is blocked with scale or rust, neither water nor steam will be able to escape, and you'll have a very dangerous problem. The valve should be checked every six months.

Checking the T&P operation is easy. Lift the lever on the valve. Be sure there is good water flow and that it shuts off when you let the lever flip back down. If it drips or doesn't reseat, replace it.

— L.W. & S.W.

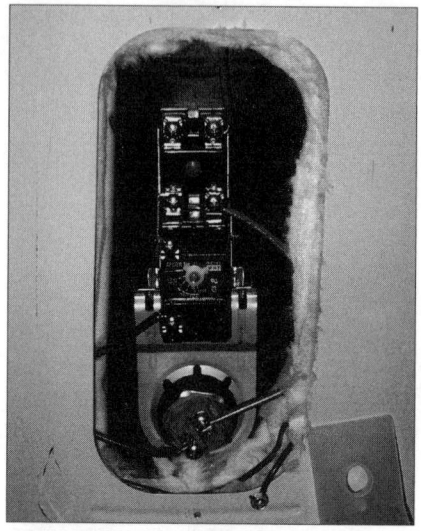

Figure 18. Lack of hot water from an electric water heater is often caused by a failed upper element. Use a volt-ohm meter or pigtail tester to check for power at the two pairs of screws above and below the red reset button.

to the heater and turn on any hot tap. If you continue to get a flow of water, there is a cross-connection somewhere between the hot and cold plumbing. Cross connections can be found in clothes washers, tempering valves, and many single-handle faucets and shower valves.

Sometimes hot and cold lines are inadvertently switched at the water heater when it is hooked up. This delivers cold water to the top of the tank and causes warm water to be drawn through the dip tube from the bottom.

Faulty dip tube. Split, broken, or missing dip tubes may allow cold incoming water to mix with hot water at the top of the tank. To check the condition of the dip tube, undo the cold inlet and remove the pipe nipple from the tank. Insert a straight pliers handle or a wooden

dowel into the dip tube and, using a circular motion, pull up and "walk" the dip tube up high enough to grasp. Pull it out to check for damage. Replace it, if needed, with another plastic dip tube (a copper tube will increase corrosion).

Gas supply and controls. Gas heaters may not produce enough hot water because of gas supply or control problems. Start your diagnosis by watching the main burner in operation. Is the flame sooty or too small? Poor draft, inadequate combustion, or low gas pressure may be at fault. If the temperature of the water leaving the tank varies widely, the on and off set points in the control may have drifted; a new control may be needed. Another possibility is that heavy sediment buildup in the tank is covering the control's probe and slowing response time.

TROUBLESHOOTING CHECKLIST

No Hot Water

Cause: Faulty electric thermostat; faulty electric heating element

Remedy: Check power to thermostat; if okay, trace power back to panel. Replace thermostat or element.

Cause: Inoperative gas thermocouple; failed gas control valve

Remedy: Reposition, tighten, or replace thermocouple. Replace controls.

Rumbling or Popping Noise (gas heaters)

Cause: Sediment buildup
Remedy: Remove sediment.

"Singing" (electric heaters)

Cause: Scale buildup on elements
Remedy: Clean scale from tank and elements; install low-watt density element.

Not Enough Hot Water

Cause: Damaged dip tube
Remedy: Replace dip tube.

Cause: Incorrect plumbing
Remedy: Eliminate cross connections at faucets and water heater. Check operation of tempering valve.

Cause: Check-valve on recirculating line is missing or stuck open
Remedy: Repair or replace check valve (use a spring-loaded valve on pumped systems).

Rusty Water

Cause: Glass lining is failing
Remedy: Replace sacrificial anode; test water for iron content.

Sulfur Oder

Cause: Bacteria, which thrives in sediment
Remedy: Flush sediment; treat tank and water lines with hydrogen peroxide solution; use zinc-alloy anode.

Water on Floor Near Heater

Cause: T&P valve leak due to excessive pressure
Remedy: Install T&P on house side of pressure reducer (set to release at 20 pounds higher than pressure reducer). Install expansion tank.

Cause: T&P valve leak due to overheating
Remedy: Adjust or replace thermostat. Lower thermostat setting to prevent overheating from frequent small draws.

Cause: T&P valve leak due to stuck valve
Remedy: Operate valve to flush debris. Replace valve if leak persists.

Cause: T&P valve leak due to surge from washing machine or dishwasher
Remedy: Install water hammer arrestor.

Heating element and thermostat. Not enough hot water in electric heaters is usually caused by problems with the lower element or either thermostat. Use a volt-ohm meter or pigtail to check for power at the element. If there's power, then check for continuity. A burned-out lower element was probably buried in sediment and overheated. Remove the sediment before installing a new element. Consider using a low-watt density element in hard-water areas to slow sediment buildup.

If the element is good, check the upper thermostat as described earlier. If it tests okay, lower the setting until it's below the water temperature (about 130°F). At that point, the thermostat should switch power to the lower thermostat. If it doesn't, the upper thermostat is bad and needs to be replaced. If power does switch but the lower element still isn't getting juice, replace the lower thermostat.

Subtle Symptoms

Some water heater problems are less obvious, but can cause everything from mild annoyance to panic when they are finally discovered.

Water on the floor. This symptom may be reason for panic, but only after ruling out several simple problems. With a gas heater, the water you see on the floor may only be condensation. Water is one of the main byproducts of combustion, and it will condense out of the flue gases if the tank is cold, especially after a heavy hot water demand.

If there's always a puddle, check for leaks in the line running from the temperature and pressure (T&P) relief valve. A faulty valve may be constantly dripping water that then runs down the pipe alongside the tank, creating the puddle.

If neither of these is the problem, look at every threaded fitting on the tank, especially the plastic drain valve. Don't rule out overhead

plumbing: Flex-line connections and packing nuts on gate valves are notorious seepers. (If you tighten up flex-line unions when they are about six months old, you'll head off trouble.) In electric tanks, check for leaks where the elements attach to the tank wall.

If you still haven't uncovered a problem, go ahead and panic. With a little contortion and a dental-type mirror, you can look up through the combustion chamber to the bottom of the tank and the base of the flue. If you see any water marking or heavy rusting, or if you find water inside the combustion chamber, start shopping for a new tank. If the combustion chamber is dry, it has to be a fitting or tank leak. Recheck those fittings.

Sulfur odor. The rotten egg odor that some heaters develop occurs when hydrogen gas generated by the action of the anode feeds anaerobic bacteria in the tank. The bacteria take up residence in the sediment, where the warmth of the water encourages growth. Both aggressive and artificially softened water will speed anode consumption and generate even more hydrogen. Things get really bad when the tank sits unused for any length of time.

The cure lies in making the tank less hospitable for the bacteria. First, flush out any sediment to remove the breeding ground. Then oxygenate the water with hydrogen peroxide (one or two pints of 3% peroxide per 40 gallons of water) to kill off the remaining bacteria in the tank. Also, run some of the treated water into the plumbing to clean the pipes. Allow the hydrogen peroxide solution to sit for at least one hour in both the tank and the pipes. This treatment is nontoxic and does not require rinsing the way bleach does.

If the odor returns, replace the anode with one that contains a small percentage of zinc. Turning the heat down or off when the tank is unused

Figure 19. In a gas water heater, the burner will not operate unless the pilot flame is touching the thermocouple. To operate properly, the thermocouple must also be firmly screwed into the gas control.

will also help. Should the problem persist after all this, then a plastic-lined tank (which has no anode) or an instantaneous heater are the only options.

Bothersome noises. A rumbling or popping noise can occur in gas heaters when sediment builds up on the bottom. This sediment slows heat transfer from flame to water, causing overheating of the bottom. Overheating causes boiling and the noise you hear. Every time hot water is used, water pressure is lowered; this allows boiling to occur more readily, and the noise begins to sound like a bowling alley. Getting rid of the sediment is the key.

For many of us, water heaters are memorable for all the wrong reasons, but it doesn't have to be that way. Given a little attention from time to time, water heaters will give dependable service without complaint for decades.

By Larry and Suzanne Weingarten, partners in Elemental Enterprises, a Monterey, Calif., company that services conventional and solar water heaters.

SIMPLE VENTILATION FOR TIGHT HOUSES

Today's builders, seeking to save energy, are building homes significantly tighter than those built 20 or even 10 years ago. This is admirable. But too often neither builder nor owner recognizes that these tight homes need controlled ventilation.

Historically, natural air leakage (infiltration) has ventilated our homes and controlled moisture levels, odors, and indoor air pollutants. The tradeoff has been that we've had to accept cold drafts and excessive heat loss. To get the best of both worlds, we need tight houses that have *controlled* ventilation systems, so that we, and not the weather, determine where, when, and how much ventilation occurs.

How Much Ventilation Is Enough?

ASHRAE publishes ventilation standards based on house volume, but requiring no less than 15 cfm air change per hour per person. But because sizing by house volume can lead to overventilation in a large home and underventilation in a small home, I prefer to design my ventilation systems based on number of bedrooms. This keeps the ventilation needs in line with the number of occupants the house is likely to hold, rather than square footage.

I also slightly oversize the system, and I provide a speed control that lets the occupants turn the system down below maximum capacity. Oversizing accomplishes several things: It provides extra capacity in case ductwork or other calculations aren't perfect; it may provide enough capacity for more ductwork if the house is expanded; and since the oversized fan will usually be run at less than peak capacity, the system runs quietly. The extra cost for the added capacity is usually quite small, adding less than 5% to the system's cost.

So how much is enough? A good rule of thumb is to provide exhaust capacity of 100 cubic feet per minute (cfm) in a two-bedroom unit and 150 cfm in a three-bedroom unit. The fan control should be either two-speed or, preferably, variable speed so that these peak capacities can be reduced when occupants are few or moisture levels are low. If a house is bigger than 2,500 square feet and four or five bedrooms, I usually go to a 200 cfm fan, which is large enough for all but the biggest abodes.

Ventilation Basics

A ventilation system needs both an exhaust system and a fresh air supply. Stale air should be exhausted from rooms likely to have high moisture or odor content, such as the kitchen, bathrooms, laundry, or special-use rooms such as darkrooms. Fresh air should be supplied to the bedrooms and living areas where people spend most of their time. The goal in locating inlets and exhaust grilles is to create airflow paths from inlet to exhaust that will ensure good distribution of fresh air throughout the habitable areas of the home (Figure 20).

You can do this with an air-to-air heat exchanger (with both intake and exhaust fans). That can be a good choice when the budget allows it and heating fuel cost is high. But buying a heat exchanger is an economic decision, rather than one of occupant health or building durability. You can effectively ventilate a tight house with a modest amount of heat loss with any of several whole-house ventilation systems that use exhaust fans only. This article describes how to create such a system and what the options are for fresh air intake and stale air exhaust.

Breathing In

In exhaust-only systems, fresh air supply is passive, meaning that it is provided by adjustable holes through which air is drawn as the fan-driven exhaust system removes stale air from the home. There are at least three variations of this method.

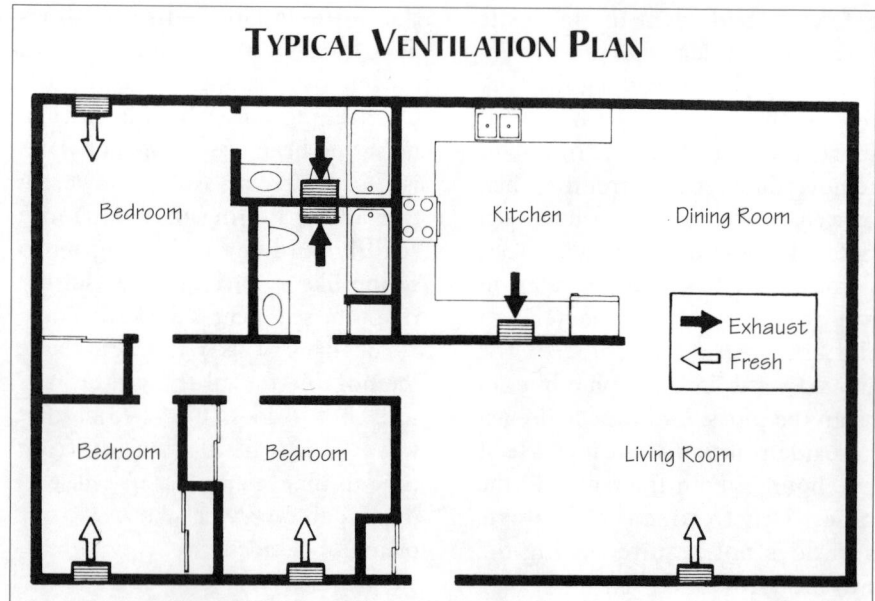

TYPICAL VENTILATION PLAN

Bedroom
Kitchen
Dining Room

➡ Exhaust
⬅ Fresh

Bedroom
Bedroom
Living Room

Figure 20. Fan-driven exhaust vents pull moisture, pollutants, and odors from kitchens and baths, while passive inlets in bedrooms and living room provide fresh air.

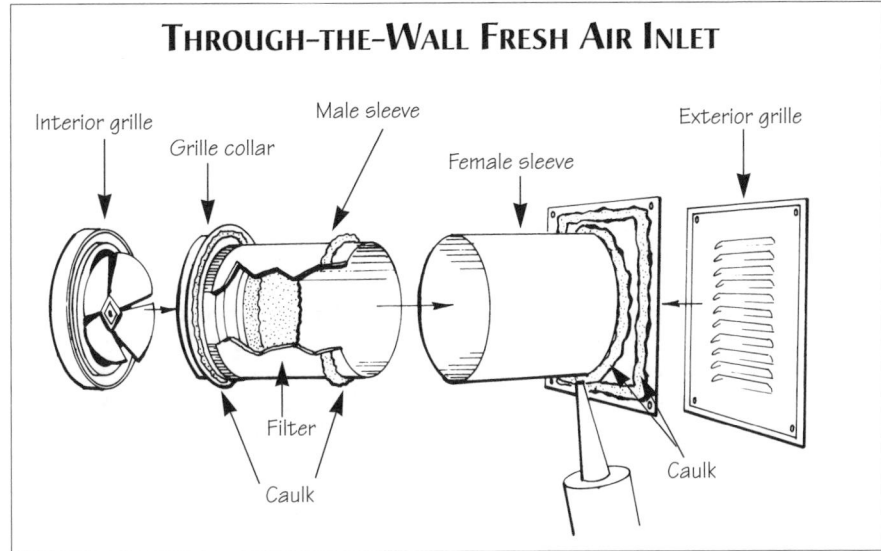

THROUGH-THE-WALL FRESH AIR INLET

Interior grille

Grille collar

Male sleeve

Female sleeve

Exterior grille

Filter

Caulk

Caulk

Figure 21. What looks like a closet light is actually a through-the-wall fresh air inlet. The pull cord opens and closes the vent as needed for intake control. Other models offer adjustable intakes operated either manually or by humidity sensors.

Through-the-wall vents (sold by American Aldes, 4537 Northgate Ct., Sarasota, FL 34234; 941/351-3441, and Therma-Stor Products Group, P.O. Box 8050, Madison, WI 53708; 800/533-7533) offer the simplest, lowest-cost solution. These have adjustable openings designed to admit from 5 to 20 cfm quietly and without drafts. Some have humidity sensors that increase the airflow opening as indoor humidity rises. In most cases, through-the-wall vents offer the most cost-effective fresh air intake.

A second option is a ducted system with a single inlet from outdoors supplying ductwork that carries fresh air to selected rooms. These ducts carry cold air, and therefore should have insulation and an exterior vapor barrier to keep moisture from condensing on the outside of the duct-work. This method costs more than the through-the-wall vents, but provides the future option of converting the entire ventilation system to a balanced heat recovery system with an air-to-air heat exchanger.

Houses with forced-hot-air heating present a third option: duct the fresh air from a single dampered outdoor inlet to the heating system's return duct. This is a tricky system to spec correctly, however. More

details on this system, and an excellent treatment of non-heat-recovery ventilation systems in general, can be found in a videotape and instruction book, *Installing Non-Heat Recovery Ventilation Systems,* available from the Extension Energy Program, Oregon State University, Batcheller Hall 344, Corvallis, OR 97331-2405; 541/737-3004.

In most cases, I recommend through-the-wall vents, unless the owner is serious about later adding a heat exchanger. But whichever fresh air supply method I choose, I site the inlet point(s) away from outdoor pollution sources such as garages, chimneys, and plumbing vents. In addition, even though incoming air mixes with room air quickly, I site the intake points to minimize drafts — preferably high on a wall and at least 4 feet from any seating areas. Bedroom closets (Figure 21) make ideal sites as long as any solid doors are undercut at least 3/4 inch.

Exhausting Possibilities

The exhaust side of the ventilation system is powered by a fan. There are three approaches you may take, depending on house size, budget, and how important you find the convenience of a packaged system:

upgraded range hoods or bath fans; an in-line fan system you put together yourself; or a multiport system that comes complete from the manufacturer.

Upgrading the Range or Bath Fan

This least-cost approach works best in homes of not more than 1,500 square feet. In many homes, range and/or bath fans already exist to provide spot ventilation, so all that's needed to create a whole-house fan is to upgrade to a fan of higher capacity and lower noise level.

Such fans must be rated for continuous service — this means high-quality bearings with permanent lubrication. Sound level ratings should be no more than 5.5 sones for the range hood, 2.5 sones for the bath fan.

Range hoods. A range hood serving as a whole-house fan should have a capacity of 200 to 350 cfm and a solid-state, infinitely variable speed control, so it can be turned down to barely audible ventilation flowrate levels of 50 to 100 cfm. Sears and Broan (Broan Mfg. Co. Inc., 926 W. State St., Hartford, WI 53027; 414/673-4340) both make this type of range hood, which costs

DUCTWORK AND FAN INSTALLATION

Multiport systems come with full sets of ductwork, hanging hardware, and instructions. In a single-port in-line system, however, you need to put the pieces together yourself. Installation is mainly a matter of hanging ductwork and fans from framing members and installing grilles in walls — pretty basic hvac procedures. Following a few rules of thumb can make the installation go smoother and help you maximize the system's performance.

Installing ductwork and fans. Maximize airflow by making ductwork runs as short and straight as you can, with as few elbows and fit-

tings as possible. To keep the ductwork simple, I like to make the plumbing wall 2x8, stack the baths, and serve both baths with one 6-inch thinwall sewer and drain PVC duct run up through the plumbing wall. I usually use PVC instead of galvanized duct because it goes in quickly, seals easily with PVC cement, and won't rust if bathroom moisture condenses inside. The PVC hangs easily from joists or other framing with metal straps placed at roughly 10-foot intervals. Some installers may prefer to use regular galvanized hvac ductwork for its familiarity. (If you do this, make sure to tape all

seams, transverse and longitudinal, with tape meeting UL 181A-P requirements; I like Nashua 324A, available from Grainger.) I often use both rectangular and round duct, joining them with transitional galvanized boots readily available at hvac suppliers. The schematic drawing (Figure A) shows such a system.

I recently came across a product that looks promising: galvanized oval ductwork made by Southwark Metal (1600 Washington Ave., Philadelphia, PA 19146; 800/523-1052). It comes in what the company calls 5-inch, 6-inch, and 7-inch sizes; these are basically what you'd

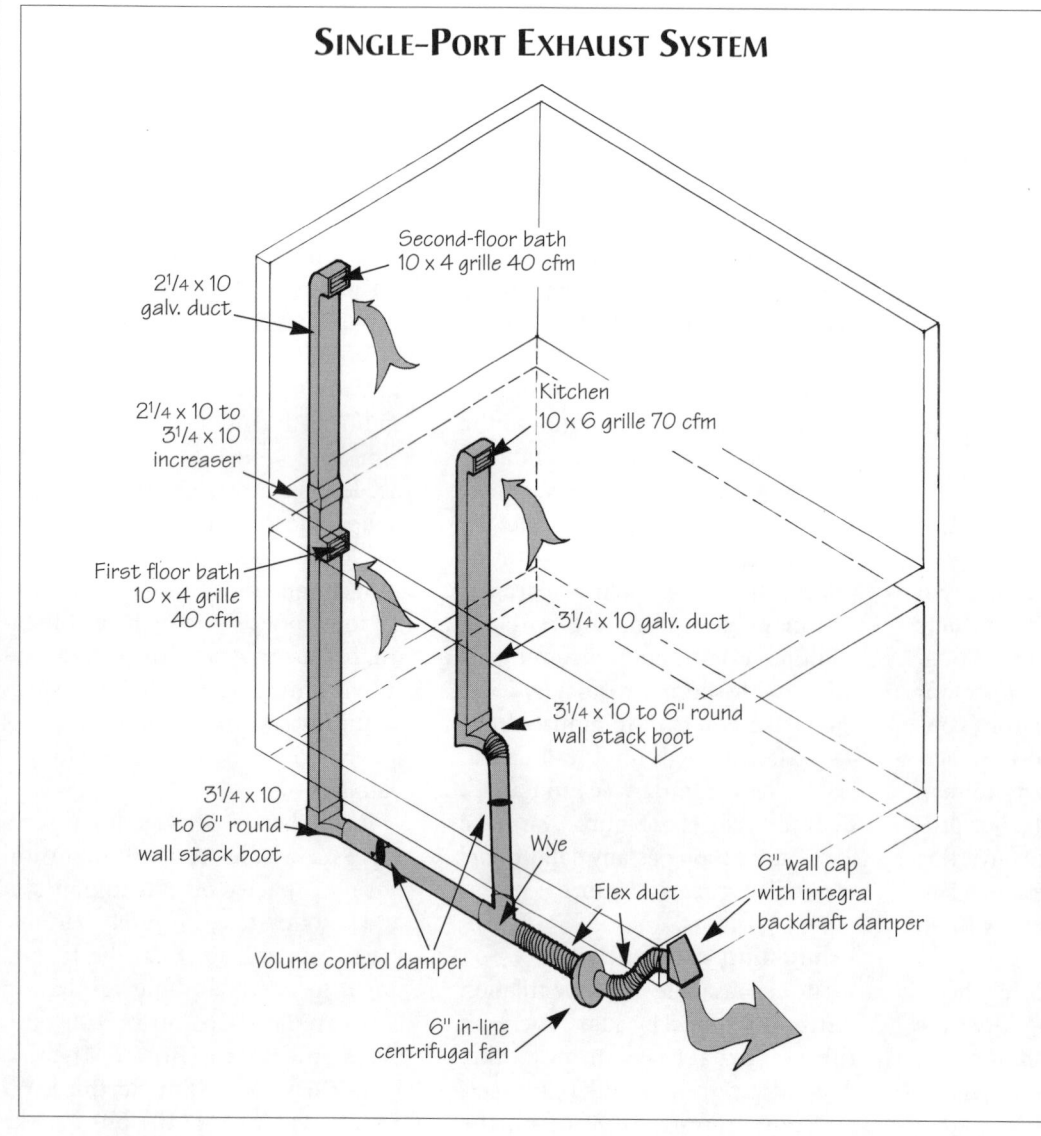

SINGLE-PORT EXHAUST SYSTEM

Second-floor bath
10 x 4 grille 40 cfm

2¼ x 10 galv. duct

2¼ x 10 to 3¼ x 10 increaser

Kitchen
10 x 6 grille 70 cfm

First floor bath
10 x 4 grille
40 cfm

3¼ x 10 galv. duct

3¼ x 10 to 6" round wall stack boot

3¼ x 10 to 6" round wall stack boot

Wye

Flex duct

6" wall cap with integral backdraft damper

Volume control damper

6" in-line centrifugal fan

Figure A. In a single-port ducted exhaust system, a single rectangular duct exhausts the stacked baths; a boot at the bottom of its vertical run makes the transition from rectangular to 6-inch round duct. A separate, larger duct exhausts the kitchen. Both runs of duct have volume control dampers for fine-tuning the system after installation.

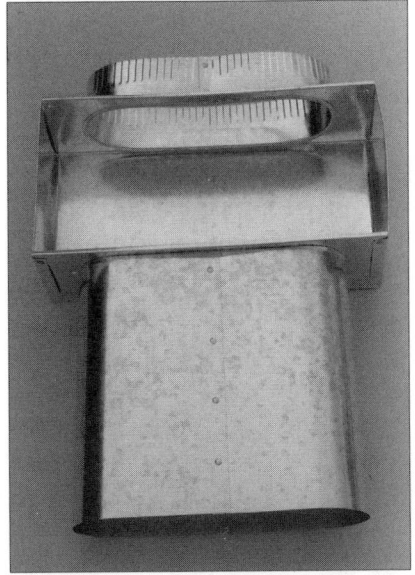

Figure B. *This stackhead with collar, made by Southwark, allows you to vent stacked baths with a single duct run.*

Figure C. *Putting four to six feet of flexible duct on either side of the in-line fan minimizes fan noise and can help reduce sharp bends in the exhaust line.*

get if you slightly flattened round ductwork of those same dimensions to fit them into a 2x4 wall. This flattening somewhat reduces the cross section and flow capacity.

The company also makes fittings that make putting a ductwork system together easier. Their No. 150 stackhead with collar, for instance, enables you to easily vent two stacked baths with one riser (Figure B). For faster assembly, the ductwork comes in 100-inch lengths (as opposed to the 30-inch lengths common in rectangular ductwork).

There are two basic options to mounting the fan: You can attach it to plywood lagged to a concrete wall; or you can suspend it from framing, with ductwork runs on either side (Figure C). I usually do the latter. The important thing is to isolate the fan's vibration from the building's structure and the ductwork.

Rubber boots help reduce vibration and noise when attaching PVC pipe to fan housings. They are available from major suppliers, and come in sizes that let you step up or down from one duct diameter to

another. They attach with standard hose clamps.

Transmitted fan noise can be a problem in very short duct runs. In these situations I like to use 4 to 6 feet of insulated flexible duct — called "flex duct" — on either side of the fan. This really quiets a system down. Be careful to hang flex duct so that it doesn't have any kinks, which drastically reduce airflow.

If you use flex duct, you might want to opt for a fan that has hanging brackets attached; this will make it easier to hang the fan. But you can still use one of the round, in-line centrifugal fans (such as a Rosenberg or Fantech), attaching the fan to the joists with plastic or rubber straps.

Sizing ductwork. Size the ductwork according to the airflow it will carry. The table at left shows my rules of thumb for ductwork as well as for stale air grilles.

If you have trouble deciding between two sizes, use the larger one, as it will permit higher airflow. If your duct runs are long (over 40 feet or so), have more than two turns in them, or number more than three, it might be worthwhile to hire an engineer or systems designer to make sure everything is sized correctly. — *M.R.*

SIZING DUCTS AND GRILLES

Expected Airflow	Less than 50 cfm	50-100 cfm	100-150 cfm
Duct Type			
Round PVC or metal	4-5 in.	6 in.	7 in.
Round flex duct	5 in.	6-7 in.	8 in.
Rectangular metal	2$\frac{1}{4}$ x 10 in.	3$\frac{1}{4}$ x 10 in.	3$\frac{1}{4}$ x 14 in.
Southwark oval	5 in.	7 in.	N/A
Grille Type			
Rectangular	10 x 4 in.	10 x 6 in.	14 x 6 in.
Round	6 in.	6 in.	8 in.

about $225. Using the range hood as the whole-house ventilator has the advantage that the kitchen is the best location to use if only one exhaust pickup is provided. You should still have a bath fan in the bathroom for spot ventilation.

If you use an upgraded bath fan for the whole-house fan, use one that has the capacity you need (100 to 200 cfm, at 0.3 inch of water, depending on house size). Typical upgraded bath fans, costing about $80 to $100, are the Nutone QT series (NuTone Inc., Madison & Red Bank Rds., Cincinnati, OH 45227; 513/527-

5100), the Broan Lo-Sone fans, and the Penn Zephyr series (Penn Ventilator Co. Inc., 9995 Gantry Rd., Philadelphia, PA 19115; 215/464-8900). To ventilate the whole house, the bathroom door must be undercut by at least one inch to allow the fan to draw air from the rest of the house. If there is more than one bath, put the whole-house fan in the one nearest the kitchen.

Single-Port, In-Line Systems

The next step up in cost and performance is a central, single-port, in-line centrifugal fan. This will cost

about $125 for the fan and another $150 to $400 for the ductwork and grilles. This is my preferred choice in the typical three-bedroom, two-bath home. Such a system can effectively ventilate houses up to around 3,500 square feet, provided the ductwork runs aren't too long or convoluted (see "Ductwork and Fan Installation," previous page). The housings of these centrifugal fans, which are manufactured by companies including Kanalflakt (1712 Northgate Blvd., Sarasota, FL 34234; 941/359-3267) and Fantech (1712 Northgate Blvd., Sarasota, FL 34234; 941/351-2947) mount easily in line with round ducts (typically 6-inch-diameter, although sizes are available to fit duct diameters from 4 to 16 inches).

In these systems, the single fan is hung from joists in the basement (Figure 22), crawlspace, or (as a last resort) attic. The fan is fed by a single duct into which are channeled stale air ducts from the kitchen, all baths, the laundry, and any other odor or moisture producing rooms. The fan pulls exhaust air from these rooms and ejects it through a wall terminal equipped with a backdraft damper. I avoid attic locations whenever possible, because the chimney effect sends warm house air up the ducts, and also because frost may form in the frigid attic ductwork.

This single remote fan replaces any individual bath fans, but does not replace the kitchen range hood, which is still needed. Its principal advantage over the range hood or upgraded bath fan is that the remote mounting results in a quieter system, and one fan can serve multiple bathrooms. If the fan is adequately oversized, it can also handle a bath or laundry added later. The only additional cost would be for ductwork and a grille.

These systems, along with through-the-wall vents or other fresh-air intake, can provide integrated, controlled whole-house ventilation for moderately sized houses — say, 1,500 to 3,500 square feet. They require

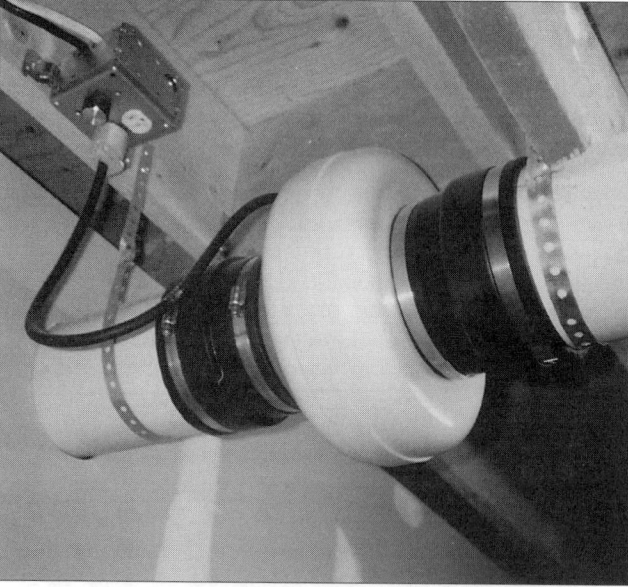

Figure 22. This single-port in-line fan, made by Fantech, is quiet, fairly inexpensive, and powerful enough to exhaust most three-bedroom, two-bathroom houses. The rubber boots on either side dampen the fan noise; the fan is light enough that simple metal straps easily support it from the joists.

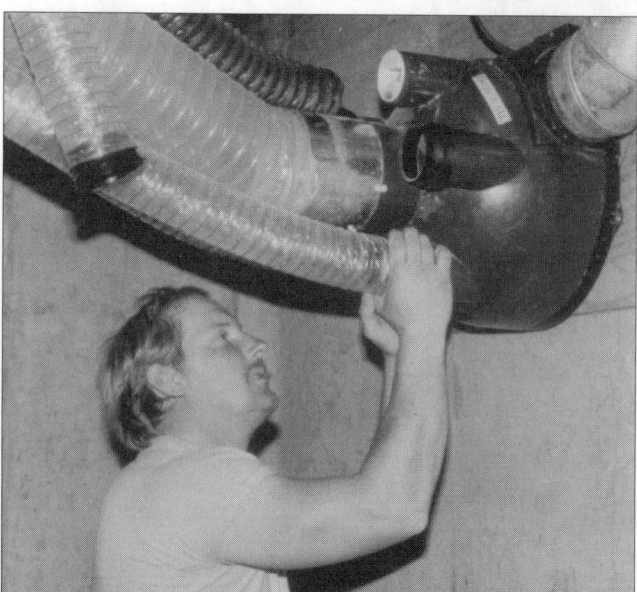

Figure 23. This Aldes multiport fan is lagged to concrete. Large flexible ducting completes the kitchen run; the smaller ones come from baths. The galvanized duct is the exhaust to outdoors. Such systems, which can exhaust several rooms, can also be suspended by wire in either attic or basement installations.

sound planning and some running around to collect materials and components. But since the materials are fairly inexpensive as long as the ductwork is not too complex, the installed cost is usually lower than the third option, a multiport exhaust fan package complete from the manufacturer.

Central, Multiport Systems

These fan systems can be mounted in the basement, crawlspace, or attic. The multiple stale air connections typically include a 6-inch connection for the kitchen and 3-inch or 4-inch ones for the baths and laundry (Figure 23). Most have two-speed fans and integrally mounted controls. Often the low speed is continuous or timer-controlled, and the high speed is an occupant-selected boost to clear the kitchen or bath. American Aldes, Fantech, and Therma-Stor Products all sell complete systems, including fans, controls, some ductwork, grilles, and wall jacks.

The fans alone are $200 to $300; complete systems start at around $500 (materials only). You pay more for one of these systems, but if you want to save the time of rounding up separate components, want to have the assurance of manufacturer support, or need to vent more than three or four spaces, it may be your best option.

Maintaining Control

A ventilation system's controls should be readily accessible and easily understood. Multiport systems come with their own controls, some with on-demand switches as well as 24-hour or even seven-day timers, so that occupants can coordinate ventilation rates with the house's use.

For range, bath, and single-port ducted systems, I usually recommend, at minimum, variable speed controls with manual on-off switches. Range fans can have these on the unit, since the kitchen is centrally located, but bath or remote ducted fans should have controls mounted in a central location. For added flexibility, you can wire any of these controls to a 24-hour or seven-day automatic timer. The timer will provide regular intervals of venting which can be overridden by the manual on-off switch.

Finally, you should provide each bathroom with a 15- or 30-minute crank timer or time delay switch. This timer should be wired in parallel to the central control so the bathroom's occupant can select ventilation as needed.

Most of these control devices, as well as many of the fans and accessories, can be obtained from W.W. Grainger (6335 N. Basin Ave., Portland, OR 97217; 503/283-0366).

You can also control ventilation systems automatically with a dehumidistat (instead of a timer). In theory, this is an excellent way to control ventilation, except in very dry regions, where the ventilation will seldom come on. But dehumidistats have fallen somewhat into disfavor because field results show that few people understand how to use a dehumidistat or what a desirable humidity level is (usually around 40%), and so use them incorrectly.

Finally, I like to label all controls clearly and provide for the owner a "user's manual" that explains the operation of the system and the function and importance of the various components.

Operating Costs

Operating costs for these systems consist of fan operating costs of about $7 to $20 per year, plus the cost of heating the fresh air intake. The added heating load (compared to an unventilated tight house) is surprisingly low, about $20 to $100 per year for a 1,500- to 2,500-square-foot house, depending on fuel costs.

A Note on Backdrafting

Powerful exhaust-only ventilation systems can reverse the flow of combustion gases in chimneys, creating a potentially lethal hazard. For this reason, I insist that any fuel-burning appliances be sealed combustion models, which have their own air intake and exhaust systems. This completely decouples the combustion process from the house air pressure levels and prevents backdrafting.

By Marc Rosenbaum, P.E., a designer and engineer of solar and low-energy-use homes in Meriden, N.H.

FLUE AND CHIMNEY SAFETY

Every remodeler will eventually be asked, "Can we use this chimney?" Obviously, if the exterior masonry is cracked, bricks are loose, and mortar is falling from the joints, you have to assess the integrity of the chimney structure. But usually evaluating an old chimney comes down to evaluating the flue, and matching a new liner with the combustion appliances you will hook up to it. The following information will help you make the right choices.

Avoid Tile Liners

If an old chimney has a liner, it will most likely be clay tile. Most codes allow tile liners for use with virtually all appliances. But code assumes proper installation, and in my experience, that's a bad assumption. In the thousands of chimneys I have inspected or taken apart, I have never found a chimney (not one!) in which the tile liner was properly installed.

The biggest problem is that masons always cement the tiles into

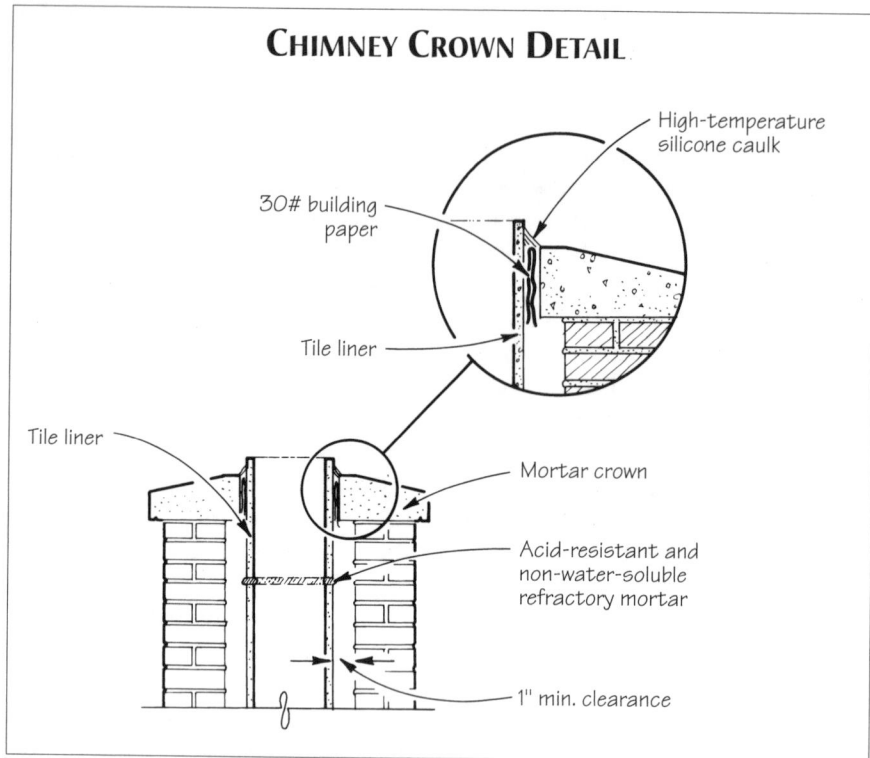

CHIMNEY CROWN DETAIL

High-temperature silicone caulk

30# building paper

Tile liner

Tile liner

Mortar crown

Acid-resistant and non-water-soluble refractory mortar

1" min. clearance

Figure 24. A proper crown installation requires a bond-breaker such as 30# felt between the tile and the crown. After the mortar crown has set up, cut back the building paper just below the surface of the concrete and apply a bead of high-temperature silicone caulk. This creates a slip joint, which allows the chimney to expand upward when it is hot.

place, usually by grouting around them at the bottom and top of the chimney. Sometimes the space around the entire length of the liner is filled with mortar. This prevents the liner from moving freely as it expands and contracts with normal use.

Tile expansion. Tile expands a lot when it gets hot. I have seen tile liners that have expanded 4 to 5 inches upward when heated by a chimney fire. An inch or two is not unusual under normal conditions. This movement is particularly noticeable at the crown, which cracks almost as soon as it is installed because the liner pushes up when it gets hot. A chimney crown must have a bond-breaker between the flue and mortar (Figure 24).

Corrosion. Even when installed correctly, there's ample evidence that tile does not perform well. Tile is very susceptible to corrosion from moisture and other compounds in flue gases. If the chimney gets cool enough, the vapor

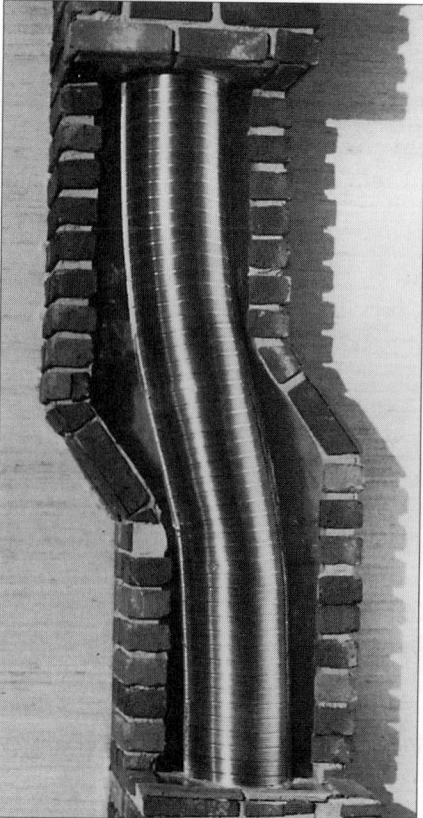

Figure 25. Flexible stainless-steel pipe is a good choice for lining an old masonry chimney (far left). It comes in several alloys to match different fuel types, and it easily installs in any chimney configuration, even one with an offset (left).

Z-Flex

condenses on the inside of the chimney as a very acidic solution. Consequently, most codes require acid- and water-resistant refractory cement in tile joints. Yet this is rarely done in new chimneys, and was never done in older chimneys. The acidic water rapidly eats away the tile joints, exposing the unglazed ends of the clay tile and the masonry of the chimney, which will then rapidly degrade.

If there is enough moisture, it will be absorbed into the masonry. At excess levels, it can cause water staining and paint blistering inside the house. When this problem begins to show up, most people think they have a roof leak, but no amount of tar slapped over the chimney flashing will cure the problem.

More typically, the moisture absorbed by the tile and masonry freezes, causing the tile to break up and collapse inside the chimney. Sometimes the masonry of the outer chimney will also crack. If freezing occurs only rarely, it can take years for problems to appear. In northern climates, however, problems can surface very quickly.

Code exception. To meet code, every lining material *except clay tile* must have a UL 1777 listing. Tile has been grandfathered in, even though it failed heat shock resistance and heat transfer tests conducted by the National Bureau of Standards in 1949. In tests similar to those required for the UL standards, 21 masonry chimneys were subjected to 200 test procedures using coal, wood, and gas fuels. After the fires, examination showed that all the tiles were cracked, a few were badly broken, but all remained in place. Also, all the chimney walls were cracked, and in 24 cases, the wooden test structure caught fire. I have found no evidence to show that clay tiles are any better now than they were then.

Hopefully, you get the idea that tile is not a good choice for a chim-

ney liner. But if you must use tile liner, try to limit its use to fireplaces or oil-burning appliances. Gas causes too much corrosion (see "Match the Liner to the Appliance," next page). Make sure the chimney is inspected by a chimney expert before installing the appliance. To find one, look in the yellow pages under "Chimneys, Cleaning and Repair." In most parts of the country you will find someone who offers *Chim-Scan* inspections. A Chim-Scan is a video camera that can be moved up and down inside the chimney, plus a monitor to view what the camera sees. With this instrument, an inspector can literally see if the chimney is safe to use. If the tile liner is not safe, it should be removed and a new, better liner installed.

Stainless-Steel Liners

Stainless-steel pipe is a much better choice than tile for a chimney liner. Stainless-steel liner is available in almost any size or shape, and in either flexible (Figure 25) or rigid form. Stainless steel is made in many types, depending on the alloys used, and the type must be matched with the intended use (see table, below).

All stainless-steel liners require insulation, which reduces creosote buildup and condensation by keeping flue gases warm (Figure 26). In addition, every liner, regardless of

the material, requires a cap to meet code. The cap keeps out rain and snow, and reduces the chance of downdrafts from wind and low pressure, which can block the draft. However, many installers do not include a cap in their bids. Do not accept a bid without one.

Insulation critical. The most common installation problems I have found with stainless-steel liners relate to insulation systems. The type of insulation and how it should be applied is specified in each liner manufacturer's manual. Most liner insulation comes in foil-faced sleeves that are secured by a stainless-steel mesh. Using an insulation system approved by one manufacturer with liner pipe produced by another violates the UL listing and may be unsafe. And under no circumstances should a loose insulation be poured into the chimney around the liner pipe. I have found vermiculite, perlite, fiberglass, and even cellulose. None of these is approved for use by any manufacturer, and all can create a dangerous chimney.

All masonry absorbs water when it rains or snows. If loose-fill insulation fills the cavity between the chimney and flue, water is transferred through the insulation from the masonry to the hot flue pipe, creating steam. I have seen chimneys literally hopping up and down on the roof, "burping" steam with each

STAINLESS-STEEL LINER TYPES

Combustion Appliance	Stainless-Steel Liner
Wood	Type 304
Pellet	Type 304
Coal	Type 316 or 321
Oil (noncondensing)	Type 304
Mid-efficiency gas (noncondensing)	AL 29-4C

Note: Do not use stainless-steel liners with any condensing gas appliance. Use only high-temperature plastic vent.

MATCH THE LINER TO THE APPLIANCE

Different residential appliances have varying flue requirements, both in size and material. Here's a look at the common types, starting with fireplaces.

Fireplaces

A properly-sized fireplace flue will go a long way towards assuring that the new fireplace will draw well and not leak smoke into the home. The size (cross-sectional area) of the flue and its height above the damper determine the size of the fireplace opening. For a conventional style fireplace (one in which the opening is wider than it is high), follow the sizing rules shown in the chart below. If you are considering a Rumford fireplace, the flue size should be even larger, as shown.

Gas Appliances

Gas-burning appliances vary widely in their venting needs, depending on how efficiently they produce heat. Old-style furnaces (less than 78% AFUE) send so much heat up the flue that there is rarely a problem, because the exhaust gases stay hot until they are safely past the flue cap. But as furnaces have improved, more heat goes into the house and less goes up the flue. If the flue gases cool below about 130°F before they leave the flue, the water vapor that is a natural product of combustion will condense in the flue.

High-efficiency furnaces. These run at 83% to 97% AFUE and always condense. They should never be hooked up to a conventional chimney. Instead they must be direct-vented through a special noncorrosive plastic vent pipe made with GE Ultem plastic. Two brands are available — Plexvent (Plexco, 1050 Illinois Route 83, Suite 200, Bensonville, IL 60106; 630/350-3700) and Ultravent (Hart and Cooley, 500 E. 8th St., Holland, MI 49423; 616/392-7855). These vents must have a drain line to carry the acidic condensate to a floor drain.

Mid-efficiency furnaces. Like most of the high-efficiency models, any mid-efficiency (78% to 83% AFUE) boiler or furnace must have a fan-induced draft to drive the cooler combustion gases up the vent. These also have a tendency to condense and may require high-temperature plastic vents. Follow the manufacturer's recommendations closely.

This is not to say that furnaces designated "noncondensing" can't cause condensation in the chimney. In fact, damage from condensation is the most common problem I see in chimneys with mid-efficiency furnaces connected to them. If you add a new gas furnace to an existing tile flue, you're likely to see flue damage within a couple of years.

Proper vent sizing is the most important way to ensure that combustion gases stay warm. If the vent is too big, the combustion gases won't be able to warm the large column of cold air in the flue and will condense immediately. Familiarize yourself with the new sizing tables in the National Fuel Gas Code (available for $22 from the American Gas Association, 1515 Wilson Blvd., Arlington, VA 22209, or the National Fire Protection Association, 1 Battery March Park, Quincy, MA 02269). This code, which is referenced as NFPA 54 ANSI Z223.1, includes new vent

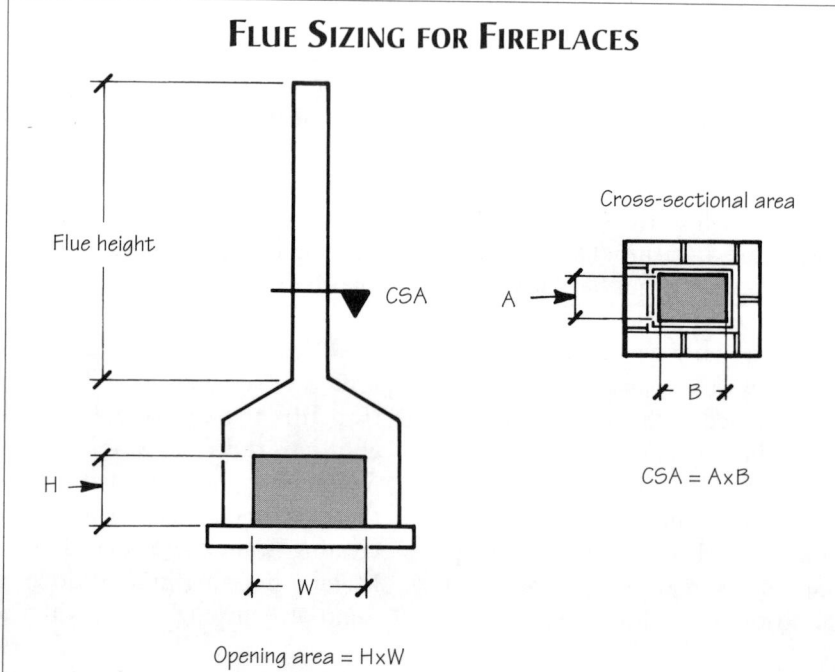

FLUE SIZING FOR FIREPLACES

Flue height

CSA

Cross-sectional area

A

B

CSA = AxB

H

W

Opening area = HxW

	Flue height		
	11 to 15 ft.	15 to 25 ft.	25 ft. or more
Conventional fireplace	CSA = $1/10$ opening area	CSA = $1/12$ opening area	CSA = $1/14$ opening area
Rumford fireplace	CSA = $1/8$ opening area	CSA = $1/10$ opening area	CSA = $1/12$ opening area

In determining the size of a fireplace flue, the cross-sectional area (CSA) of the flue must be proportional to the area of the fireplace opening. The proportion varies with flue height. Note that the proportions differ for Rumford fireplaces.

sizing tables. To make sense of these in "real world" vent configurations, get a copy of Simpson DuraVent's Sizing Handbook (see "Sources of Supply" at the end of this chapter).

If your client has an outside chimney, lives in a very cold climate, or heats the house only intermittently, the chances are high that the gases from a natural-draft appliance will condense. Where the possibility of condensation exists, use Al 20-4C stainless steel or one of the cementitious liners. Be aware, however, that recent evidence indicates that even A1 20-4C may not resist corrosion well if the furnace draws chlorine vapor in its combustion air (as may occur if the laundry area is near the furnace). The chlorine and water vapor produce hydrochloric acid, so even the slightest wetting of the flue liner leads quickly to corrosion.

Oil Appliances

In general, oil-fired appliances have fewer flue problems, because flue temperatures are higher and the exhaust gases contain less water vapor. Type 304 stainless steel is suitable for noncondensing oil-fired appliances. Nevertheless, the safest liner choice is A1 20-4C stainless steel or one of the cementitious liners. Oil soot contains sulfur, which combines with water to make highly corrosive sulfuric acid. To avoid this, do not vent a gas water heater into the same flue with an oil-fired furnace. Also have the chimney cleaned before hooking up a new gas appliance to a flue that used to vent an oil-fired appliance. Even if you stick with oil, the chimney should be inspected and cleaned yearly.

Solid-Fuel Appliances

Solid-fuel appliances include wood, coal, and pellet-burning stoves and furnaces.

Wood. Any cementitious liner or Type 304 stainless steel is suitable for use with wood or pellet fuels. However, the flue must be cleaned regularly.

Most wood furnaces regulate heat output by damping down the fire. This causes inefficient combustion, which creates a lot of creosote in the chimney flue, particularly if the flue is too large. A heavy creosote accumulation in a flue is a significant fire hazard. The chimney should be cleaned to remove this creosote whenever the deposits inside the flue reach $1/4$ inch in thickness. Since this amount can form in a few weeks (or sometimes in a few days), any homeowner planning to use a wood furnace should be prepared to inspect and clean the chimney often. If the chimney is not cleaned, the accumulating creosote will eventually cause a chimney fire.

Wood stove flue requirements are similar to those for wood furnaces. Wood stoves are the most common type of heating appliance I see in my area and they have the most problems, chiefly because the draft required for combustion is directly regulated by the owner.

In general, wood should always be burned in a flaming fire, not a smoldering fire. If more than a few wisps of smoke are visible coming out of the chimney, wood heat is being wasted. If less heat is required, the owner should put less wood in the stove instead of reducing the draft.

Pellet. In some areas, pellets are the cheapest fuel available on a heat output basis. Pellet fuels look like feed-grain pellets and are produced with similar equipment. They are made from various organic materials, usually considered waste, that are high in cellulose. These materials include lumber mill trimmings and sawdust, used cardboard, corn cobs, and shells from pecans and walnuts. Pellet furnaces require a small flue, usually 4 to 6 inches in diameter. Combustion residue in the flue consists of a fine noncombustible ash, which accumulates quite slowly.

Coal. Unless you go with a cementitious liner, Type 316 or 321 stainless steel is required for coal. Coal combustion produces considerable ash and some of it collects inside the flue. This ash has a lot of sulfur in it and is hydroscopic, drawing moisture out of the air when the furnace is not operating. This creates sulfuric acid, which attacks the mortar joints between flue tiles and will rapidly destroy the vent pipe on a furnace as it sits idle for the summer in a damp basement.

Coal stoves, in common with coal furnaces, require very precise draft regulation to operate properly. But stoves tend to have more draft problems because they are usually not installed by professionals. Coal stoves require a barometric damper in the vent pipe; this damper must be adjusted with a draft gauge when the stove is operating. In my experience this is usually not done, and creates incomplete combustion with its attendant problems.

Combining Appliances

The National Fuel Gas Code prohibits mixing the combustion gases from any solid-fuel appliance with any gas appliance. If a client wants to hook up a wood stove to a chimney that vents a gas furnace, for example, each appliance should have its own properly-sized flue. If you need two flues, say for a wood stove and a gas furnace, and the existing chimney is not large enough for both, the safest choice may be to replace the furnace with a direct-vented model. Then line the chimney to accommodate the wood stove.

The code does allow mixing gases from oil and gas appliances in the same flue, provided the flue is sized and connected properly. But while this practice is legal, I don't think it's wise. By introducing the "wet" gases from a gas-burning water heater into a flue that vents an oil furnace, for example, you are increasing the risk of creating a highly-acidic condensation that will degrade a chimney rapidly.

In general, I don't recommend combining the combustion gases from two different fuels in one flue. However, if you must, mixing oil and wood is the least likely to cause problems. And, of course, it's all right to vent the gases from like fuels — a gas water heater and a gas furnace, for example — provided the flue is big enough to handle both appliances. — *P.S.*

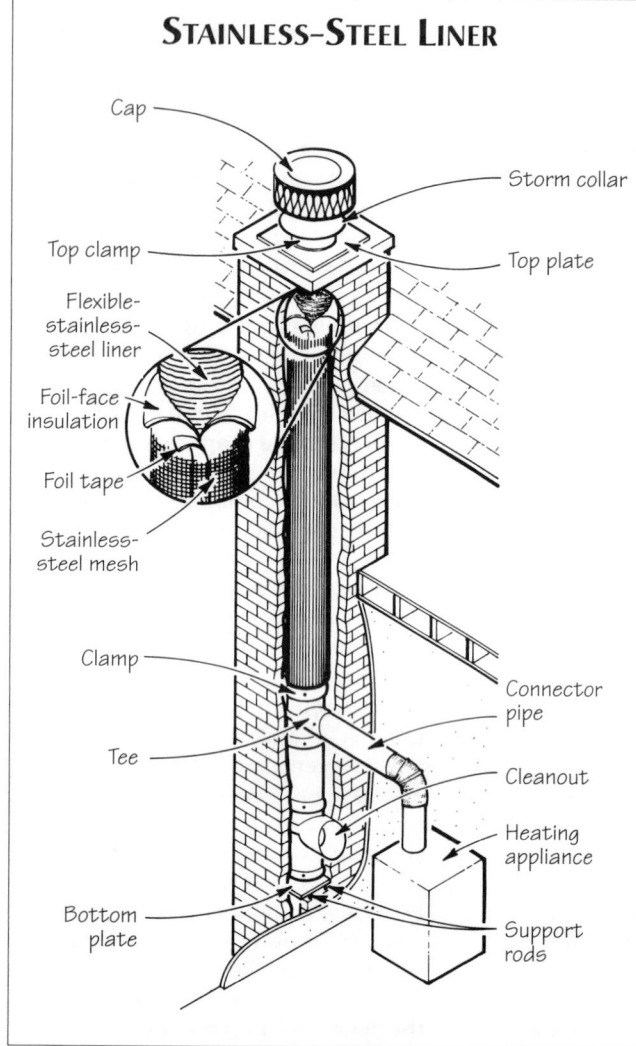

Stainless-Steel Liner

- Cap
- Storm collar
- Top clamp
- Top plate
- Flexible-stainless-steel liner
- Foil-face insulation
- Foil tape
- Stainless-steel mesh
- Clamp
- Tee
- Bottom plate
- Connector pipe
- Cleanout
- Heating appliance
- Support rods

Figure 26. All stainless-steel chimney liners must have insulation to meet UL standards. The insulation jacket prevents flue gases from condensing inside the flue. Also, every liner, regardless of the material it is made from, must have a cap to meet code. The cap keeps out rain and snow and reduces the chance of downdrafts that can block the draft.

Figure 27. A Class A chimney is suitable for all fuel types, but it works better as a free-standing chimney than as a liner for an existing masonry chimney. The sections can be installed only in a straight chimney, and are extremely heavy, requiring a power winch and cable to lower them into place.

hop, during normal operation of a wood stove. If a chimney fire occurs in this situation, the release of steam can be explosive.

If properly installed, however, a tested and listed liner can usually contain a chimney fire. But after the fire the liner must be replaced, even if it looks undamaged. Most fire codes require this, and for good reasons. When stainless steel is overheated (generally above 800°F to 900°F), it loses its corrosion-resistance, and can develop holes after only a few months of continued use. Overheated liner pipe can also become very brittle. I have seen pieces of 24-gauge stainless steel that you could snap as easily as a potato chip.

Class A and B Chimneys

Aluminum and galvanized-steel liners — sometimes referred to as factory-built chimneys — are sometimes used as liners, but are more appropriate for free-standing chimneys or vents inside a wooden chase.

Class A chimneys — often referred to in the field by the tradename *Metalbestos* — can be used with all fuels (Figure 27). These are made in two types: solid-pack-insulated double-wall pipe and air-insulated triple-wall pipe. The chief problem in using factory-built chimney sections as liners is that the old chimney is usually not large enough to allow for their installation. Also, you can use these sections only in a straight chimney, and they are extremely heavy — you'll need a power winch and cable to lower one into a chimney. For this reason, the installed cost of a retrofit job is often much higher than that of an insulated stainless-steel liner.

Class B (double-wall air-insulated) chimneys — commonly called *B-vent* — are designed for venting noncondensing gas appliances only. Typically, these have an aluminum liner inside a galvanized steel sleeve. Although usually installed inside a wooden chase, this type of vent can be installed as a liner in a masonry chimney if space allows. B-vent is much lighter than a Class A chimney, and so is much easier to install.

No factory-built chimney has a zero-clearance listing, so all Class A and Class B chimneys must be installed with the clearances specified by the manufacturer. Most of the builder installations I see violate these clearances.

Cast Liners

From my experience, cementitious, cast-in-place liners are the best choice for all fuels. In general, the insulation properties and moisture resistance of these lining systems are superior. This means they are more resistant to heat shock and condensation problems and therefore offer the longest expected lifetimes. They are often the most expensive option, but not by a lot. Material costs vary by the amount of cement required. An 8x8 chimney with a 6-inch flue, for example, doesn't require a lot of cement, and so can be a less expensive option than an insulated stainless-steel liner, depending on conditions.

The most common brand names are Ahrens, Golden/Flue, National Supaflu, and Solid/Flue (see "Sources of Supply" at the end of the chapter). All of these products, except Ahrens, are installed in a similar manner (Figure 28). A rubber "tube form" is inserted and centered in the chimney, then inflated to the diameter of the flue required by the appliance being installed. A "gate form" is positioned in the thimble opening (where the vent pipe connects), then the liner material is mixed and pumped into the chimney. In general, these liner materials should not be bucketed and dumped in the chimney. Bucketing is slow and can cause

cold joints in the concrete and consequent damage to the liner.

Ahrens uses a different installation method. A vibrating steel bell of the correct flue size is suspended in the chimney. Then a very stiff liner mix is dumped into the chimney while the bell is winched to the top. This vibrating bell compacts the mix and forms the flue opening.

Look for UL rating. Most cast liners are tested and UL-listed. The exception is Insulcrete. If you run across someone who installs this brand, be warned that this product is not tested and listed.

To pass the test for a UL 1777 listing, a liner must survive a series of

high-temperature burns (with flue gas temperatures ranging from 1,000°F to 2,100°F). The test procedures monitor the liner for resistance to *heat shock damage* and *resistance to heat transfer* (see "Common Chimney Terms," next page) to make sure that liners can withstand even the worst chimney fire without causing a fire in the building. All listed products have passed these tests with a 1-inch air space around the chimney. However, chimney liner installers wanted the products to be tested to zero-clearance standards, since few chimneys outside the laboratory have an air space around them. UL devised an

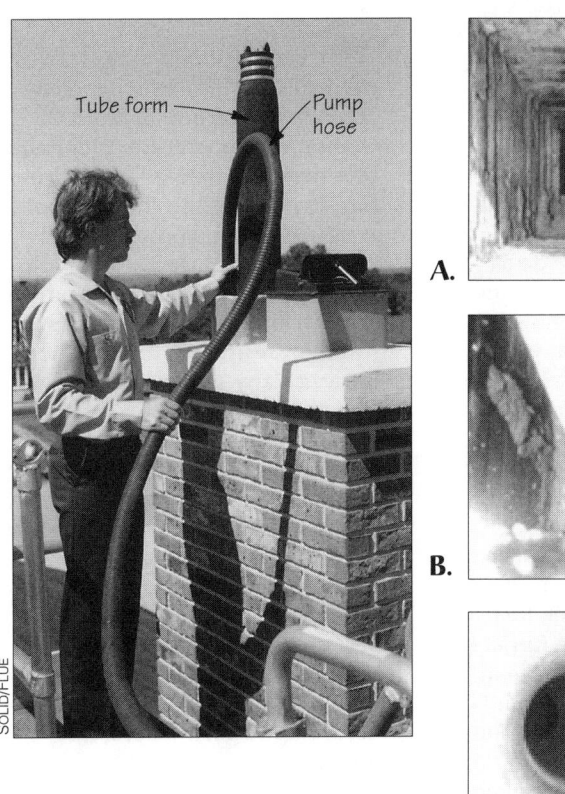

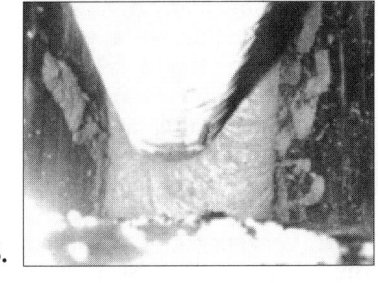
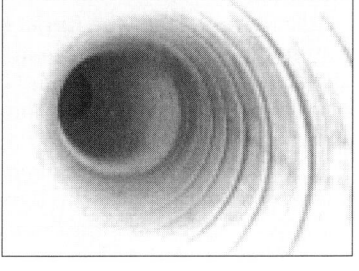

Figure 28. Starting with an unlined chimney (A), a rubber tube form is inflated with air, then centered between the chimney walls. Next, the liner material is mixed and pumped into the chimney (B). After the mix sets up, the tube is deflated and removed, creating a flue (C). Depending on the fuel to be burned by the appliance, the flue may have to be sealed.

optional, second series of tests, but only Solid/Flue passed the original tests for a zero-clearance listing. Manufacturers then lobbied UL to reduce the burn times. Now all the cast liners have a zero-clearance listing.

Conflicting requirements. To pass the tests, cast liners must have a low coefficient of expansion (to prevent heat shock that will crack the material when heated). But they must also insulate well (to prevent heat transfer to the structure) and be lightweight (so the wet mix will not push the chimney outward when it's installed). These requirements call for a low-density cement with a lightweight, insulating aggregate. But

resistance to abrasion, high strength, and low water-absorption are also required, and for these you really need a heavy, dense cement.

Different manufacturers solve these conflicting requirements in different ways. To meet the heat transfer requirements, different brands require various minimum thicknesses. For the 1-inch clearance requirement, Solid/Flue requires only 3/4 inch of material. The other brands require 1 inch to meet the revised UL 1777 zero-clearance standard. Because of the testing expense, Ahrens and Solid/Flue have not been tested to the new standard and still require 1 1/2 inches for a zero-clearance listing.

These differences in thickness may seem small, but they can be very important. Suppose the furnace you need to connect has a 7-inch-diameter outlet pipe. The lined flue in this case would need to be 7 inches in diameter, too. If the existing brick chimney has a typical interior dimension of 8 1/2x12 1/2 inches, only Solid/Flue could line this chimney and meet code. (Ahrens could do it too, if an oval bell 5 1/2x9 1/2 inches were available, but to my knowledge the smallest oval bell is larger than that.)

To pass the strength requirements, manufacturers vary the compressive strengths of the concrete mixes. Compressive strengths range from a

COMMON CHIMNEY TERMS

Chimney and flue: The terms "chimney" and "flue" are often used interchangeably, but this is incorrect. A *flue* is a shaft designed to vent the products of combustion from a stove, furnace, or water heater to the outside air. The *chimney* surrounds and supports the flue. Many chimneys have just one flue. But a chimney can have more than one flue, such as a colonial center chimney with flues for several fireplaces, or a wooden condo chimney with several metal chimney flues inside.

Draft, buoyancy, and flue sizing: The tendency of hot air to rise is called the *buoyancy* of air. In a flue, hot air venting from the furnace is confined by the flue and "floats" upward, allowing the surrounding air to flow into the furnace. This is what we know as *draft*.

From this you can see the importance of proper *flue sizing*. If a small amount of hot gas venting from a furnace mixes with a large amount of cool air in an oversized flue, the gas will cool rapidly and reduce the draft. If the flue gas cools to the temperature of the surrounding air, the draft stops altogether.

Heat shock: This occurs when a cold liner undergoes a rapid change in temperature. When outside temperatures are below freezing, any part of the chimney not enclosed by the house will be frozen, too. So just building a rip-roaring fire in the fireplace can crack a liner. Tile, which is not UL listed for resistance to heat shock, is particularly susceptible.

Heat transfer: This is simply the insulation value of the liner material, and is important since virtually all old houses, and some new ones, have framing that touches the chimney. Therefore it is very important that the liner you choose has passed the UL zero-clearance test, and even more important that the liner is installed according to the manufacturer's instructions.

Liner: This term is often interchangeably with "flue." This is okay, though the term *liner,* when correctly used, refers to the material that the flue is made of, while "flue" denotes the space inside the liner. An *unlined chimney* is a chimney without a flue, which is not

suitable for any use. Using an unlined chimney to vent any type of combustion appliance is a violation of all fire codes. But just because a chimney has a liner does not automatically make it suitable for all uses.

Pyrolization: During a chimney fire, temperatures inside a flue can exceed 2,000°F. This will heat the outside of the chimney to extremely high temperatures, causing combustibles such as framing or lath that touch the chimney to catch fire. Wood normally combusts at just over 400°F. But if chimney fires have occurred in the past, the combustion point of the surrounding wood can be much lower. Repeatedly heating wood to temperatures near its combustion point causes a chemical change called *pyrolization*. This change can cause the wood to combust at temperatures below 200°F.

Vent: The term *vent* is commonly used to refer to a flue of any type, but in the official language of building codes, it specifically refers to a flue for a gas-burning appliance. — *P.S.*

low of 693 psi for National Supaflu to a high of 2,090 psi for Solid/Flue. A high-strength mix allows you to save an old chimney made with soft bricks and weak mortar joints. A chimney like this may require temporary support while it is being lined, but once lined, the liner material in effect supports the chimney.

Finally, cementitious materials must have good resistance to water absorption. Ahrens requires coating the inside of the cast liner with a sealer before using the flue for any type of fuel. Some of the other brands require a coating only when using gas-burning appliances. All of these coatings must be redone periodically to maintain the service life of the flue — except Solid/Flue, which does not require a coating for any fuel.

New Liners

There are also a few brands of tile liner, usually imported, that are very different from common clay tile. For example, Ahrens produces a ceramic liner called Ceramu-Flue, which can be lowered into a chimney in sections. It seems equivalent in durability to the best of the cast-in-place liners, but can be used only in a straight chimney without any offsets.

Solid/Flue has a similar product on the drawing boards. In general, these products promise to handle much like tile liners, but without all of their attendant problems.

By Peter Scripture, a builder who has specialized in building, repairing, lining, and cleaning chimneys for the last 16 years.

BACKDRAFTING CAUSES AND CURES

If there were universal laws to describe ventilation, the first might be: *Air out equals air in.* This means that all of the air exhausted from fans and chimneys in a house is immediately replaced — somehow. Either it is forced into the house by a fan, or the indoor air pressures drop until outdoor pressures are strong enough to push replacement air through leaks and holes in the structure.

This works fine up to a point. But when indoor negative pressures overcome the natural buoyancy of warm gas in chimney or furnace flues, they can reverse the upward flow of combustion gases and draw them back down into the house. When this happens, you have *backdrafting*: the pressure-induced spillage of exhaust gases into the house's living space.

Backdrafting is a health, safety, and comfort concern. To prevent it you must either build a house without a chimney, or balance all the ventilation systems to prevent indoor-outdoor pressure differentials. In short, houses need to inhale as easily as they exhale.

Tighter Houses
Part of the Problem

Backdrafting has always been a problem. But several recent trends in construction have narrowed the margin of safety for houses with unbalanced ventilation systems.

Tight houses. We're building tighter houses than ever. Tight houses are more prone to backdrafting problems because you can't rely on air leaks to balance sudden surges in "exhalation" from a powerful stovetop, bathroom, or dryer fan. As the shift to tight housing continues, builders will have to counter the backdrafting potential created by airtight construction.

More powerful exhaust fans. Today's more numerous and powerful local exhaust fans also contribute to backdrafting. Downdraft cooktops pose the biggest problem, because their make-up air requirements (the amount of air they draw) are extraordinary. Sometimes it is as much as 1,000 cubic feet per minute (cfm). I've visited many houses where the chimney backdrafts virtually every time the cooktop fan is operated.

I'm also seeing more powerful overhead range hoods. And some

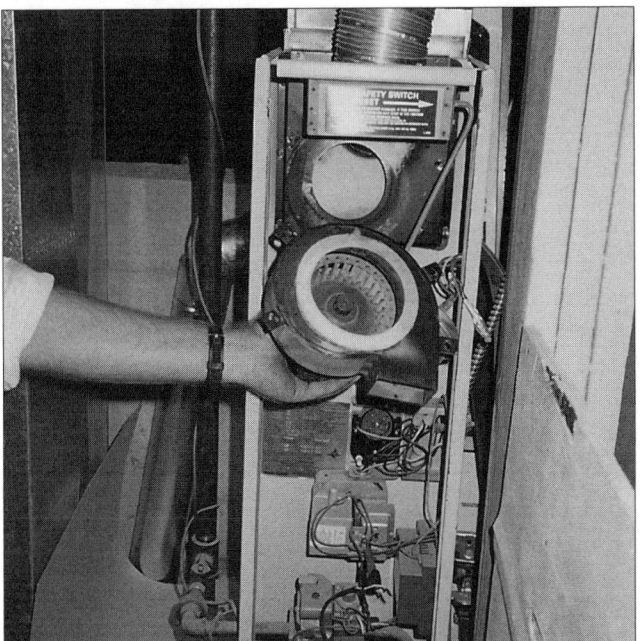

Figure 29. Induced-draft furnaces, such as this one, are not safe from backdrafting as is commonly thought. In this case, because of a misaligned blower gasket (at center) and unsealed flue collar, gases high in carbon monoxide were spilling into the house.

new clothes dryers exhaust at 250 cfm. That's about twice the previous norm! Unless a house is built like a sieve, the make-up air demands of such fans can be met only by a forced make-up air supply.

Exhaust-only ventilation systems. Finally, the increasing reliance upon exhaust-only whole-house ventilation systems poses a backdrafting threat. Until recently, the few whole-house exhaust fans in use were unlikely to exhaust more than half their specified capacity. However, the recent introduction of highly effective exhaust ventilators changed that. In combination with more powerful local exhaust fans and tighter building envelopes, the backdrafting effect of these whole-house exhaust fans can be deadly.

Gas Furnace Problems

A 1984 survey of hundreds of houses suggested that 10% to 15% experienced furnace spillage at least once per year. Oil-fired systems spilled most frequently, but only for 15 seconds or so at the start-up of each operating cycle. Gas-fired systems spilled less frequently, but often for the entire five or six minutes of the cycle.

Gas furnace spillage. Fortunately, spillage from gas-fired furnaces or water heaters rarely poses a serious health hazard. In tighter houses, spillage raises humidity and carbon dioxide (CO_2) levels above the norms recommended for indoor air, but seldom above what might be considered a health limit.

Natural gas combustion exhaust can contain nitrogen oxides, such as nitrogen dioxide gas (NO_2), which can damage lungs. Fortunately, NO_2 is unstable and is usually neutralized or diluted before it pollutes living areas. A gas range actually poses a much greater NO_2 pollution risk than a gas furnace, since people will be close to the source and exhaust hoods seldom capture more than 50% of stovetop exhaust.

The biggest spillage concern with natural gas furnaces is carbon monoxide (CO). This is rare but worrisome. A poorly tuned, broken, or dirty gas furnace *can* produce lots of CO (Figure 29). But even poor installation and maintenance won't ordinarily affect air quality unless spillage problems are also present. This is an unusual combination that can be avoided through regular maintenance, such as a furnace tune-up and spillage check every two to five years by qualified service people.

For most homeowners, then, the risk of backdrafting doesn't warrant major investments in elaborate ventilation systems; maintenance and safety tests will usually take care of the problem as long as the house does not get severely depressurized.

To give a little extra piece of mind, you can invest in a gas detector or CO alarm. A "dot" detector, such as that made by Aptech Detectors (515 Princess Louise, Orleans, ON K4A 1Y2, Canada; 613/837-4470), installs near likely spillage sites on furnaces or water heaters and changes colors when exposed to hot gases — usually from 138° to 160°F. These require frequent checking to be of any value.

Good CO alarms — either battery-operated, plug-in, or hard-wired — are readily available from several manufacturers. These use a loud blare to warn homeowners of

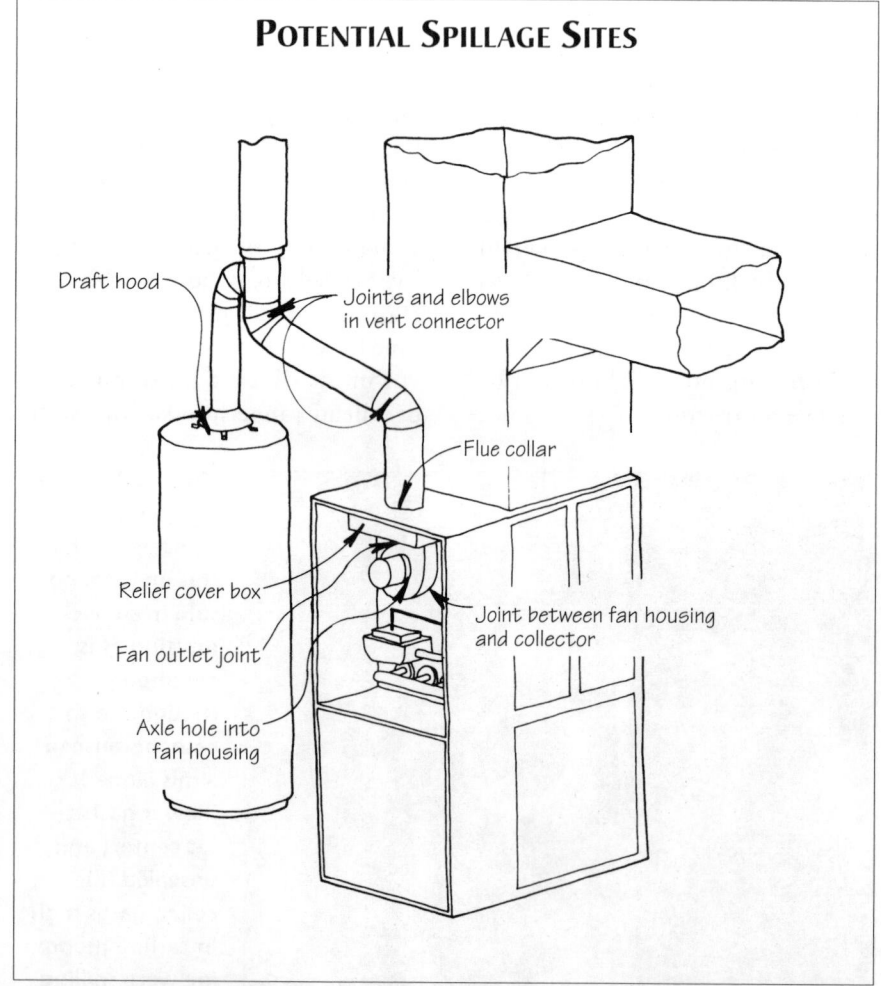

POTENTIAL SPILLAGE SITES

Draft hood

Joints and elbows in vent connector

Flue collar

Relief cover box

Joint between fan housing and collector

Fan outlet joint

Axle hole into fan housing

Figure 30. Even induced-draft furnaces have a surprising number of potential spillage sites. The so-called "spillage switches" on these units will shut off the furnace if the chimney is completely plugged, but they generally fail to detect the backdrafting or spillage common in normal use.

high concentrations of this dangerous gas. Make sure you get units that are certified by UL or the Canadian Gas Associations (see "Sources of Supply" at the end of the chapter).

Gas Furnace Solutions – Good and Bad

Eventually, changes to gas furnace design will probably solve the problem of spillage. So far, however, the more expensive alternatives have been disappointing.

Induced-draft furnaces. Also called ID or mid-efficiency furnaces, these appliances hold some promise. However, because of the way they are typically manufactured and installed, they offer little improvement over natural-draft appliances with regard to backdrafting.

An ID furnace has a little fan in the flue that induces a small draft to overcome the resistance of the more efficient heat exchanger. Theoretically, these furnaces should be able to withstand a normal range of house depressurization — up to about 20 pascals. (A pascal is a unit of pressure equal to $1/250$ of the pressure exerted by a 1-inch-deep column of water. For example, a 20-knot wind exerts about 10 pascals of pressure on the side of a house; on a very cold day, the warm air in your attic pushes through the cracks at about 3 pascals; hot chimneys usually have drafts of 20 to 30 pascals.)

Unfortunately, ID furnaces are not designed to resist the negative pressures found in many new homes. Flue gasses can spill out of leaky B-vents or around the blower housing (Figure 30). Where the furnace shares a common vent with a water heater, as is often the case, gasses will spill out of the water heater's flue pipe. Unless the manufacturer provides proof of increased resistance to negative pressures, it is wise to assume that an ID appliance is just as prone to spillage as a conventional one.

Water heaters are a concern, as well. Induced-draft models have all the same problems as ID furnaces.

Sealed combustion and condensing units. These days, many installers opt for sealed-combustion furnaces. These are virtually immune to spillage problems if properly installed, even with house depressurization as high as 50 pascals.

Sealed-combustion units are a good choice for new homes with down-draft grills or other big exhaust appliances, or for retrofits with chronic backdrafting problems.

Sealed-combustion water heaters are also available, as well as sealed-

---

A SIMPLE CHIMNEY BACKDRAFTING TEST

In general, houses with chimneys or furnace flues should avoid depressurization in excess of five pascals. To measure the amount of depressurization that will occur under "worst case" situations in a given house, follow the checklist below. You will need a "magnahelic" pressure gauge accurate within a low range and with a resolution of one pascal or less. Several companies make such pressure gauges, including Dwyer Instruments (P.O. Box 373, Michigan City, IN 46361; 219/872-9141), which has models of this type starting at $43.

For a more complete description of this test, obtain a draft copy of the Canadian General Standards Board Standard 51.71, available from Canadian General Standards Board (222 Queen St., Suite 1402, Ottawa, ON K1A 1G6, Canada; 613/941-8709).

(1) Prepare and calibrate the equipment.

- Turn off all fans.
- Turn off furnace and water heater.
- Close windows and exterior doors.
- Close interior doors leading to perimeter and basement rooms.
- Close fireplaces and wood stoves.
- Set up pressure gauge close to the chimney or flue you are concerned about.
- As per the gauge manufacturer's instructions, extend a hose to a sheltered position outdoors to get a pressure sampling there.
- "Zero" the pressure gauge.
- Observe normal fluctuations in pressure due to wind. If they are greater than two pascals, wait for a calmer period to do the test.

(2) Conduct the test and record pressure drop.

- Operate all exhaust fans (as well as any interlocked supply air systems), one at a time.

- Record level of house depressurization as measured on gauge.
- Operate any other fans that may be imbalanced, such as heat recovery ventilators, furnace blowers, etc.
- Record those levels of house depressurizations.

This will give you the basic depressurization levels you need. If a depressurization exists, you can try to locate the site of any spillage using the following test:

- Operate all the vented combustion appliances one at a time. While you have this depressurization in effect, check for flue gas spillage near the furnace, using either a smoke tube that creates "cool" colored smoke or a CO_2 gas analyzer.
- Return house to condition in which it was found — reset thermostats, turn off hot water taps if running, switch off furnace blowers and exhaust fans, etc.

—S.M.

combustion combo units that supply both hot water and space heating. Either option offers good protection against spillage.

Power venters can be a better option. An alternative in retrofits to installing an induced-draft or sealed-combustion furnace unit is to install a conventional unit and vent it with a "power venter kit." Such a kit lets you vent the furnace through any convenient external wall rather than a vertical chimney flue (Figure 31). For instance, it can be a horizontal "flue" of ductwork that exits a basement wall.

The units cost between $200 and $400 and come as a kit with controls

and color-coded wiring included. The average gas fitter can install one without previous training. Two companies make them: Field Controls Company (2308 Airport Road, Kinston, NC 28504; 919/522-3031) and Tjernlund Products Inc. (1601 9th St., White Bear Lake, MN 55110; 612/426-2993). Field makes a unit that mounts outside the house; the external location ensures that any leakage from around the fan housing can't spill indoors.

Backdrafting in Oil Furnaces

The most toxic by-product of oil combustion is sulfur dioxide (SO_2) which, like the NO_2 from gas fur-

naces, is an acid gas that damages lungs. Fortunately, SO_2, unlike NO_2, carries a strong odor that makes even small quantities easily detected.

To protect against spillage from a conventional oil burner, the burner should be fitted with a "delayed action solenoid valve." This delays the flow of oil to the combustion chamber for about three to six seconds after ignition, giving the airflow within the burner time to set up a draft. This ensures that the oil is burned more completely, which reduces sooting and backdrafting, and also increases efficiency.

Delayed action solenoid valves cost under $100, and the increase in

TESTING FOR TIGHTNESS

Despite the growing importance of house airtightness, few builders actually know how tight they are building their houses. Until recently, the building community has tended to rely on subjective estimates of airtightness. Unfortunately, it is impossible to accurately estimate the tightness

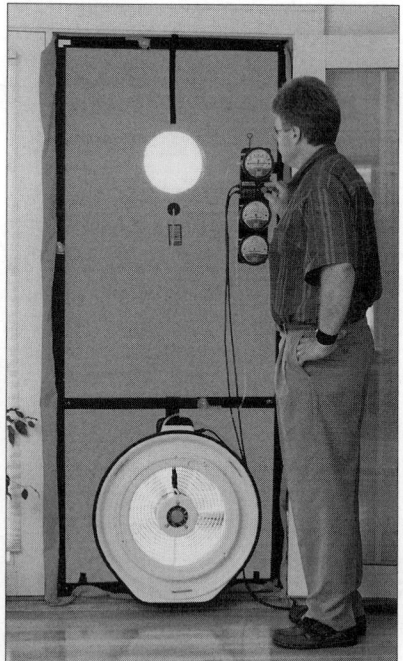

A blower door operator adjusts the fan speed to maintain a house depressurization of 50 pascals.

level of houses by visual inspection alone. And without knowing house airtightness, it is difficult to assess the need for, or to design an effective approach to, ventilation for good indoor air quality.

When discussing these issues, it is important to distinguish between two terms — *airtightness and natural ventilation.* The airtightness of a house is related directly to the cumulative size of all the holes and penetrations in the exterior building envelope. The natural ventilation rate is determined by the forces driving air in or out through the leaks in the envelope.

The easiest way to measure house airtightness is with a diagnostic tool called a blower door. This device consists of a powerful, calibrated fan that is temporarily sealed into an exterior doorway of a house. The fan blows air out of the house to create a slight pressure difference between the inside and outside. House airtightness is determined by the amount of air flow that it takes to maintain a 50 pascal (0.2 inches of water column) depressurization of the house. The tighter the house, the less air you need to exhaust in order to maintain the pressure.

It takes about 20 minutes to set

up a blower door and do a test to document the airtightness of the building envelope. An experienced operator can use the blower door to get other important information about a house, such as an estimate of duct leakage or leakage between the living space and an unconditioned attic, as well as the location of air leaks in the building envelope. This information can help you assess the potential for backdrafting caused by exhaust fans.

In addition to knowing the airtightness of the envelope, it's also good to know the natural ventilation rate, because this is what determines how much indoor pollutants are diluted. While it doesn't measure this directly, the blower door test provides us with a measure of the total hole size in the exterior envelope. And that information can be used along with a simple mathematical model to provide useful estimates of the average annual natural infiltration rate of the house. This ventilation estimate can then be compared with published ventilation guidelines to help determine if additional mechanical ventilation may be needed.

— *Gary Nelson, Robert Nevitt, and Gary Anderson*

efficiency will pay for them within a couple of years. The flue pipe should have a high-quality barometric damper that is balanced and lubricated every year. Since even the best dampers leak, you should mount a smoke alarm on the ceiling directly over the damper to give warning if gases do spill for more than a few seconds at start-up.

A better approach is to forsake the conventional oil burner for a *high-pressure* oil burner. A high-pressure oil burner forces combustion air into the combustion chamber under pressure, so that the furnace burns with less excess air. This allows you to have a smaller chimney with less heat loss and higher efficiency. These units also withstand pressure changes up to ten pascals, and this prevents backdrafting and blow-outs within a normal range of chimney pressure fluctuations. They don't cost much more than conventional systems, and they eliminate the need for a barometric damper altogether. They also burn very cleanly. I've checked chimneys on these furnaces four years after installation and found them perfectly clean. Make sure to seal both the furnace or boiler and the flue pipe airtight at all joints.

Fireplaces

Fireplaces number fewer than furnaces, but their backdrafting record is worse. My 1986 field monitoring of fireplaces indicated that virtually every fireplace backdrafts or spills at least once per year, and that the typical unit spills for 1% to 2% of its operating time. This will happen most commonly at start-up and during stoking, and less often as the fire burns down. (This is less true for wood stoves, because their smaller, better-insulated flues are more resistant to pressure-induced spillage.)

Since fireplace spillage contains poisonous gases such as CO and cancer-causing substances such as benzene, backdrafting *always* poses a serious health hazard. CO concentrations in fireplace combustion gases run far above health limits, and they get worse at the end of burn, when backdrafting is most likely. From a rational point of view, the conventional fireplace doesn't belong in a modern home.

Of course, decisions about fireplaces are seldom rational. Since you can't know whether occupants will use a fireplace every day or only on Christmas, you must account for the worst case scenario, which is constant use.

Airtights not the answer. "Airtight" fireplaces — with airtight doors to the indoors and make-up air supplied directly from outdoors to the firebox — sound promising. Unfortunately, these designs depend heavily on the tightness of the fireplace doors, which fireplace manufacturers have yet to make airtight. As a result, when a house is depressurized by an exhaust fan or other force, these fireplaces act essentially as big make-up air ducts: air comes from the outdoor fireplace supply, through the fireplace, and into the house, bringing the toxic combustion gases with it.

Dual air supply even worse. Fireplaces designed to provide both outside and household air to the firebox pose a worse threat. The indoor supply, which is usually a vent beneath or alongside the doors, makes it even easier for the entire unit to act as a make-up air duct when the house is depressurized. These units pose a serious threat in any house that experiences even minor depressurizations.

Gas fireplaces. Note that the newly popular vent-free gas fireplaces effectively have a spillage rate of 100%, far outweighing the occasional spillage from most water heaters or furnaces. The latest versions are protected by an oxygen-depletion switch designed to guard against CO emissions. However, these still emit flue gases into the air, and are therefore banned in Canada and a number of municipalities in the U.S. and do not belong in a modern, tight home.

Many manufacturers now offer sealed-combustion gas fireplaces as an alternative. These are a good choice if house depressurization is a problem.

An alarm for every hearth. Given these hazards, a homeowner who plans to use a fireplace frequently should not only make sure the house has balanced ventilation, but should also install a CO alarm and a smoke alarm in the same room as the fireplace. If the alarms sound frequently, occupants will quickly learn to change their habits, or install a reliable ventilation system such as the one described below. For minor

Figure 31. Add-on power venters can help prevent backdrafting by pulling furnace or water heater exhausts out of the house. The Field Controls model, shown at left, typically vents out a side wall.

backdrafting problems, cracking a window may be a solution.

Testing for and Preventing Backdrafting

With airtight furnaces and fireplaces so elusive, what can you do to prevent backdrafting?

The best approach is to keep ventilation systems balanced and thereby avoid pressure-induced spillage: Design a house that lets fresh air intake match peak forced exhaust, and you'll avoid backdrafting.

When to ventilate. As a rule of thumb, you should provide additional fresh air intake to balance any single exhaust fan that blows more than one-half air change per hour. For example, in a 12,000-cubic-foot house (a 1,500-square-foot house with 8-foot ceilings), a 100-cfm exhaust fan would be the maximum unbalanced exhaust permitted, because such a fan blows 6,000 cubic feet per hour (100 cfm x 60 minutes). You can roughly figure a house's area by multiplying its square footage by 8, assuming the

ceilings are about 8 feet high.

The main problem with this method is that predicting the actual air-flow from exhaust fans is almost as tricky as guessing how tight a house will be. Manufacturers provide air delivery ratings, but actual flows vary depending on how much restriction is created by ducts, grilles, screens, and louvers. We tested all the ventilation devices in 200 houses; the measured air-flows generally ran at about half the ratings. So you can usually figure that an exhaust fan actually moves

---

EXHAUST FANS AND DEPRESSURIZATION: CRUNCHING THE NUMBERS

Exhaust fans, such as those found in bathrooms and above kitchen ranges, blow air out of the house. This can have the effect of depressurizing the house relative to the outside. Small bath fans — those in the 50- to 75-cfm range — are turned on for short periods of time and generally cause no problems. However, some range hoods — those with 200-cfm or larger blowers — may cause problems.

The level of negative pressure in a house is usually the main factor that causes backdrafting in natural-draft combustion appliances. Studies done for the Canadian Mortgage and Housing Corporation (CMHC) have found that typical natural-draft furnaces, boilers, and water heaters begin to have venting problems if negative pressures exceed about 5 to 7 pascals. (A pascal is a measure of air pressure equal to 0.004 inches of water column as measured by a manometer. A pascal is equal to about .02 pounds per square feet.) Conventional fireplaces were found to start having problems at only 3 pascals. In the summer, we see problems with backdrafting on natural-draft appliances at negative pressures of 3 pascals.

How much negative pressure is caused by exhaust equipment, such as kitchen and bath exhaust fans, depends on the tightness of the envelope and the flow rate of the fan. The graph (opposite) is a useful tool for understanding the relation-

ships between house pressure, tightness, and flow rate. The horizontal axis gives house pressure in cfm^{50}, as determined by a blower door. This is the flow rate, in cubic feet per minute, necessary to depressurize the house by a pressure of 50 pascals, and is a common standard for blower door testing. The vertical axis gives exhaust fan flow in cfm. The diagonal lines represent various levels of house depressurization measured in pascals.

Suppose we have a well-insulated new house that has been measured with a blower door to have a cfm^{50} value of 1,200 (including leakage through the code-required combustion air inlet). This is about average for a typical new Minnesota house. We want to know if there might be a problem with the natural-draft gas water heater if we install a downdraft kitchen range fan rated at 350 cfm. We draw a vertical line up from 1,200 cfm^{50} and a horizontal line from 350 cfm on the fan flow scale (in a solid rule on the chart). The diagonal line closest to the intersection of these two lines gives the depressurization level that would be caused by the operation of the downdraft exhaust fan in this particular house. In this case, we get about 8 pascals of depressurization — clearly a problem for the operation of the water heater, according to the work by CMHC. If some interior doors are closed, the part of the house that is open to the exhaust

fan could be depressurized even more.

We can also calculate the size of the fresh air inlet hole that would be necessary to limit depressurization to, say, 5 pascals, a level we might feel comfortable with. Starting at the intersection of the 5 pascal line and the 1,200 cfm^{50} vertical line, draw a horizontal line (in a dotted rule on the chart) over to the fan flow scale. This tells us that at 5 pascals of depressurization, this house would leak at about 260 cfm. Therefore, in order to maintain 5 pascals' depressurization while the exhaust fan is operating, we would have to add 90 cfm of makeup air (350 – 260 = 90).

It turns out that an unrestricted hole between the outside and inside will leak at a rate in cfm approximately equal to the area of the hole in square inches times the square root of the pressure difference (in pascals). So

$$90 = \text{Area of vent} \times \sqrt{5}$$

$$\text{Area of vent} = 90 \div \sqrt{5} = 40 \text{ sq. in.}$$

This means that you would have to cut a 7-inch-diameter hole in the house to provide makeup air for the exhaust fan — hardly a practical solution. A better solution is to install a draft-assist fan on the water heater.

By Gary Nelson, Robert Nevitt, and Gary Anderson

about half its advertised rate.

Combined use of two or more smaller exhaust fans can cause problems. For example, a range hood, bathroom fan, and clothes dryer operating at the same time can produce up to 285 cfm in exhaust and a depressurization of 5 pascals or more. But these events are infrequent and of short duration, so they can usually be tolerated.

The "Chimney Backdraft Test." After construction you can run a more exact test to see if balanced ventilation is required. This test is described in "A Simple Chimney Backdrafting Test" (page 205). It takes only a few minutes and gives you hard information on which to base your ventilation decisions.

Supplying More Air

How do you meet the need for increased air supply? If you choose a balanced ventilation system such as a heat recovery ventilator instead of traditional exhaust fans, you may never have a depressurization problem. However, these systems are expensive to install and not really designed to provide makeup air, when needed.

Another option is to interlock an air supply fan to any exhaust fan(s) likely to depressurize the house so that whenever the exhaust fan comes on, the supply fan is switched on. The Air In-Forcer from Tjernlund or A Fan in a Can from Field Controls are packaged systems which accomplish this.

A simpler variation is to interlock the exhaust fan(s) with the thermo-

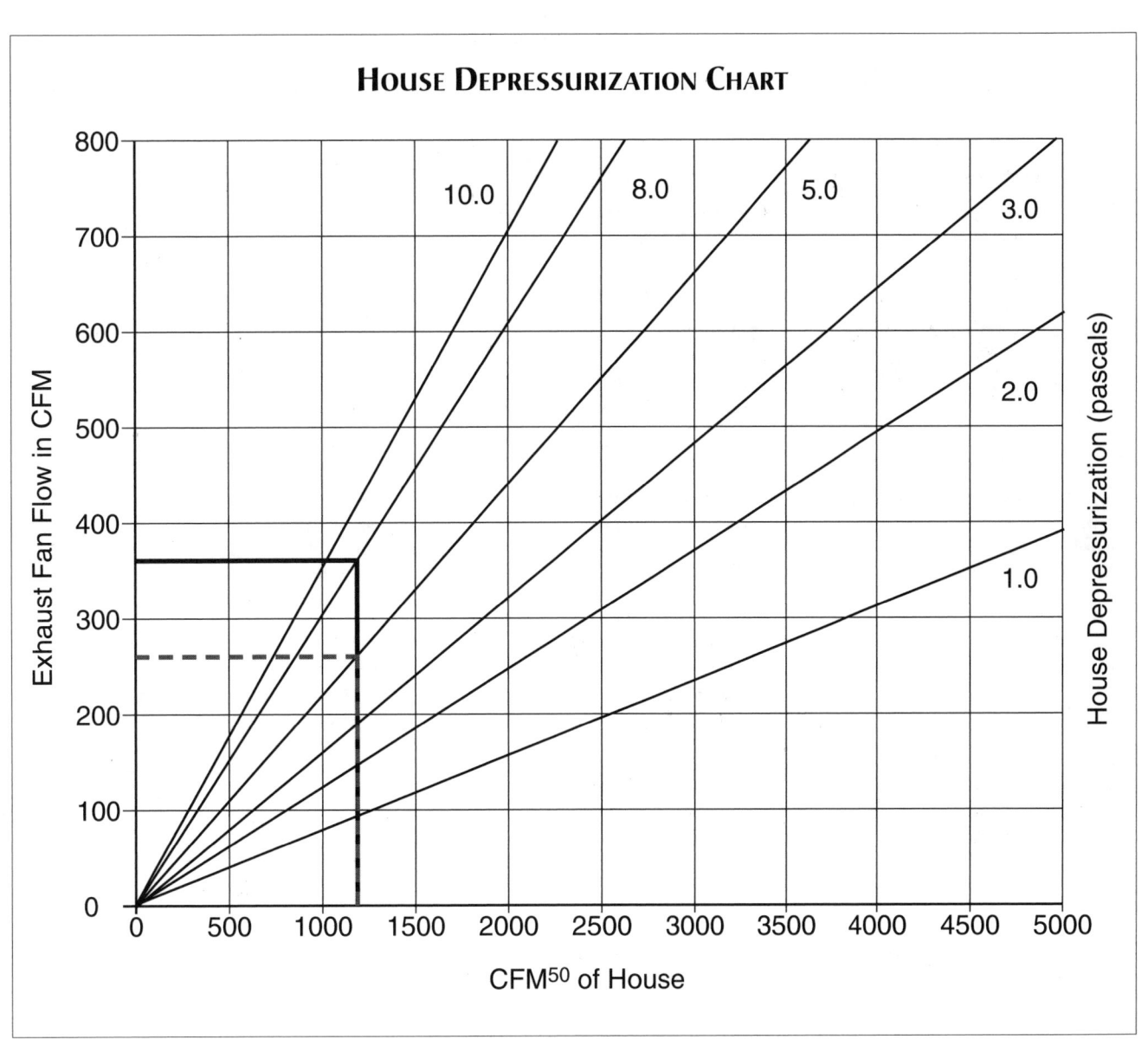

stat so that the furnace is switched off whenever the exhaust fan is on. Although such interlock systems are technically feasible, they are not widely used.

The folly of more passive supply. One seemingly obvious solution to increasing air supply is to install a larger make-up air opening or another "combustion-air" duct. Unfortunately, passive air supply rarely does the job; or rather, it does it too crudely. For the typical house with an exhaust flow of 235 cfm, you would need an opening of 93 square inches to avoid excess home depressurization. Double that size if, as is almost certain, you'll be using a screened and louvered inlet. Such

massive openings inevitably get covered up by the house's chilly, incredulous occupants.

Connecting the make-up air supply to a return air plenum leading directly to the furnace may avoid such tampering, but this leads to a slew of other problems: high heating costs, cool drafts, condensation on furnace heat exchangers, and even frosty door hardware in freezing weather. (Using a motorized damper on make-up air openings can avoid some of these problems and reduce air entry into the house when the furnace is off.)

Despite these drawbacks, codes often require some type of passive air opening to supply combustion

air. But in limiting their attention to combustion air rather than total make-up air requirements, the codes miss the point. Almost any furnace will be able to draw sufficient combustion air through leaks, even in tight houses. The issue that should be addressed is not whether appliances have sufficient combustion air, but whether a house has sufficient make-up air to prevent back-drafting.

By Sebastian Moffatt, owner and manager of Sheltair Scientific Ltd., a Vancouver-based company that specializes in developing technology and testing buildings for health, safety, comfort, and energy efficiency.

SOURCES OF SUPPLY

Cast Chimney Liners

Ahrens Chimney Technique
2000 Industrial Ave.
Sioux Falls, SD 57104
800/843-4417

National Supaflu Systems
5 Holly St.
Scarborough, ME 04074
800/788-7636

Golden's Chimney Lining
19061 Shumans Rd.
Rutherglen, VA 22546
804/994-5522

Solid/Flue
4937 Starr St.
Grand Rapids, MI 49546
800/444-3583

Metal Chimney Liners

Copperfield Chimney Supply
304 S. 20th St.
Fairfield, IA 52556
515/472-4126

Heat Fab
38 Haywood St.
Greenfield, MA 01301
800/772-0739
413/774-2356 (in Mass.)

Metal-Fab
P.O. Box 1138
Wichita, KS 67201
800/835-2830
316/943-2351 (in Kan.)

Michigan Chim Flex
1584 Dickerson Rd.
Gaylord, MI 49735
800/289-2446

ProTech Systems
26 Ganesvoort St.
Albany, NY 12202
518/463-7284

Selkirk Metalbestos
1820 E. Fargo Ave.
Nampa, ID 83651
800/635-6507

Simpson Duravent
877 Cotting Ct.
Vacaville, CA 95688
800/227-8446
800/922-1611 (in Calif.)

Z-Flex
P.O. Box 4035
20 Commerce Park North
Bedford, NH 03110
800/654-5600

CO Detectors

American Sensors Electronics
100 Tempo Ave.
Toronto, ON M2H 3S5 Canada
416/496-5900

Quantum Group, Inc.
11211 Sorrento Valley Rd.
San Diego, CA 92121
619/457-3048

CHAPTER 9

MOISTURE DAMAGE

- Mold, Mildew and Wood Decay

- Moisture in Wall Cavities: Case Studies

- Interior Moisture Problems: Case Studies

- A Rotting Timber Frame

- Wood Moisture Content & Interior Finishes

- Moisture Problems from "Dry Basements"

- Using Moisture Meters

MOLD, MILDEW AND WOOD DECAY

More than 5% of all construction lumber manufactured in the U.S. each year is used to replace wood that has decayed in existing structures. This need not be the case. Damage to wood-frame buildings by mildew, mold, staining, and decay is entirely preventable. Their presence points to design flaws, poor workmanship, and neglected maintenance.

The Culprits: Microorganisms

The microscopic organisms that cause mildew, mold, staining, and decay in wood belong to a huge group of primitive plants known as fungi. Unable to produce their own food, fungi feed instead on natural substances that make up organic materials such as leather, cloth, rattan, paper, and wood.

Mushrooms that spring from lawns and tree trunks are fungal "fruits." They release millions of dust-size "seeds" called spores that are scattered helter-skelter by wind. When conditions are right on the surfaces where they eventually settle, the spores germinate, sending out thread-like filaments called hyphae. Enzymes secreted by *hyphae* break down organic matter so fungi can use it for food.

Before fungi can colonize wood, four requirements must be met: an oxygen supply, temperature in the 40°F to 100°F range, sufficient moisture, and a food source (wood). Infection can be prevented by eliminating any one of the requirements. Obviously, it's hard to limit oxygen. Temperature control is tough too, since most living things thrive in this range. And even at subfreezing temperatures, many fungi don't die; they just go dormant.

Since you can usually control moisture to some extent, the most effective way to prevent fungal deterioration of wood is to keep it dry. Most fungi need a wood moisture content of at least 20% to grow. Since the moisture content of interior wood throughout most of the U.S. fluctuates between 6% and 16%, it's usually too dry for most microorganisms to get started.

In exterior or other situations where wood can't be kept dry, you can use naturally rot-resistant woods like western red cedar and redwood. Nature has partially protected these woods from fungi by depositing toxic extractives in their heartwood. But the supplies of naturally durable woods are shrinking, so to meet the demand, less naturally durable woods are impregnated with pesticides like CCA (chromated copper arsenate) that extend their service life by 30 to 50 years or longer.

Mildew

Mildew grows both inside and outside houses. Most mildews are black, but reds, greens, blues, and browns are possible. The familiar gray color of weathered wood is the work of mildew.

Masses of dark spores and hyphae give mildews their characteristic splotchy look. But although they discolor the surface they grow on, mildews have no appreciable effect on wood itself. Some mildews that feed on airborne organic matter can even grow on inorganic vinyl and aluminum sidings. Dew and rain supply the needed moisture.

Exterior mildew. Outside, mildews appear most often on unheated, projecting parts of buildings that cool quickly after sunset, like eaves, decks, and porch ceilings. North-facing walls and walls shaded by trees and other obstructions that restrict sunlight and airflow are also candidates. You often find mildew in the same places where dew forms. While mildew won't grow where siding crosses studs and other thermal bridges, mildew may thrive over the cooler, insulated bays between studs, where the dew persists to provide the needed moisture.

Interior mildew. Mildew occurs indoors most frequently in baths, basements, and other areas prone to high relative humidity. It also shows up in places with poor air circulation, such as behind furniture against exterior walls, and in closets and closed-off rooms. Mildew can form whenever the relative humidity of air near a surface exceeds 70%. This can happen when warm air near the ceiling cools as it flows down colder wall surfaces. The relative humidity of 70°F air, for example, rises from 40% to 70% when it's cooled to about 52°F.

Thermal bridges that lead to "hot spots" outside create "cold spots" inside where mildew can form. Exterior corners are notoriously mildew-prone because of poor air circulation inside and heat-robbing wind outside. In summer, water vapor from warm, humid air entering crawlspaces and basements below air-conditioned rooms may condense on cooler joists and subflooring, creating good conditions for mildew, as well as mold, stain, and decay. Moisture condensed as ice from heated air leaking into attics in winter likewise wets rafters and sheathing when it melts.

Stopping mildew. Not only is mildew unsightly, its spores and odors indoors can trigger allergic reactions. Fortunately, ridding wood of mildew is easy. But first, do a simple test to see if the splotches are mildew or just plain dirt. Place a drop of fresh household bleach containing sodium hypochlorite on the suspected area. The dark color of mildew will fade in a minute or two, while dirt is unchanged.

Once you've determined the stain is mildew, clean it by brushing or sponging the surface with a solution of one-third cup household detergent, one to two quarts household bleach, and two to three quarts of warm water. Or use commercial cleaners. Wear eye protection and gloves, and rinse surfaces with water.

Virtually all exterior finishes — paints, solid color and semitransparent stains, and water repellents alike — are susceptible to mildew. Oil-based formulations, especially those with linseed oil, are particularly vulnerable. Among water-based coatings, acrylic latexes have proven the most mildew-resistant. Defend against mildew on siding and trim by using only primers and topcoats that contain mildewcide, or by mixing in the add-it-yourself types that paint shops sell. Finishes with zinc oxide pigments also deter mildew. But beware: Finishes applied over mildewed surfaces that are recoated without first killing the fungus will soon discolor.

The amount of moisture generated inside a home may be beyond your control, but you can encourage use of the bath exhaust fan, for example, by wiring it to the room light switch or to a timer. Install louvered doors to ensure airflow in closets. Use a soil cover and vent and/or insulate crawlspaces as site and climatic conditions dictate. Always install a vapor retarder and use plenty of insulation in walls and attics, and provide adequate roof ventilation.

Molds

Molds need a wood surface moisture content of about 20% to get started. To provide that, simply surround wood with air at 90% relative humidity at any temperature from 40°F to 100°F, and presto! That's why

mold and mildew sometimes suddenly appear on furniture during the dog days of summer.

While most molds are green, black and orange molds are not uncommon. The color comes from spores strewn across the surface. Though hyphae reach deeper into wood, discoloration in softwoods tends to be limited to the surface of the sapwood. It can usually be planed, sanded, or even brushed off. Brown, gray, or black patches penetrate more deeply into hardwoods and can't be machined away. Discoloration aside, molds generally have little effect on wood's integrity.

Some molds are surprisingly tolerant of wood preservatives. This explains the fuzzy growths occasionally found between boards in banded

DETECTING DECAY

I use several methods when looking for decay in wood. When wood is suspiciously wet or discolored, but otherwise looks okay, I first determine its subsurface

moisture content with a moisture meter. If it's 20% or below, I know that there's no active decay present. If it's between 20% and 28%, existing decay can continue mer-

rily on its way. If it's over 28%, conditions are ripe for fungi to get started.

The pick test is also useful (see photos). I judge the soundness of the wood from the way a large splinter breaks when I pry it with an awl or ice pick. Sound wood emits a sharp crack as the splinter is pried up. The splinter is typically long, with one end still attached to the wood. Sometimes it breaks in the middle over the tool, but the fracture will still be splintery.

A splinter pried from wood with incipient decay lifts quietly from the surface and almost always fails directly over the tool, with both ends still anchored to the wood.

The pick test is highly subjective; natural characteristics of sound wood can produce misleading results. Accurate interpretation comes only with experience and consideration of other clues.

To find decay hidden inside timbers, I take a small-diameter boring and examine the shavings. Discolored, wet, and musty shavings signal decay. I always plug the hole with a preservative-treated dowel. — S.S.

Pick test. A short splinter pried from decayed wood (left) typically breaks quietly over the tool with both ends still anchored. When pried from sound wood (below), the splinter cracks sharply, is longer, and remains attached at one end only.

FUNGI FIELD GUIDE — A GUIDE TO FUNGUS IDENTIFICATION AND HABITAT

White Rot

Most common in hardwoods, giving them a whitish, gray, or yellow bleached appearance. Turns wood spongy and stringy.

Partially decayed, or "spalted," rock maple. Spalted maple is prized by woodworkers for its figure.

Staining Fungi

Discoloration of wood in logs or freshly sawn lumber, primarily softwood. Can also occur on pine windows wet from condensation. Steel-gray to blue-black color, commonly called blue stain. Stain is indelible.

Eastern white pine lumber, sawn green during humid summer months, discolored by blue stain.

> **Note:** All case studies photographed in southern New England.

Mold

Green, black, or orange discoloration on surface of wood. Can penetrate below the surface of hardwoods and cause permanent stain. Needs a surface moisture content of 20% to get started.

Location: *Douglas-fir floor joists in basement.*
Cause: *High humidity in basement.*

Mildew

Dark stains, usually black, on surface of wood. Needs 70% relative humidity at surface to grow. Primarily a visual problem. Will lighten from bleaching.

Location: *Cedar siding on shady side of house.*
Cause: *Persistent wetting from dew.*

Location: *Bottom side of roof sheathing, new home.*
Cause: *Dryer vented into attic.*

Brown Rot
The most common decay fungi in softwoods. Requires 28% moisture content to start, but once established, needs only 20%. Turns wood brown and crumbly, with cross-grain and cubical checking. May sprout cottony mycelia and mushroomlike fruiting bodies.

Location: *Sill in direct contact with concrete in 5-year-old home.*
Cause: *Untreated wood on concrete slab-on-grade.*

Location: *Behind shower stall in 22-year-old home.*
Cause: *No vapor retarder, no bath exhaust, cold outside wall corner.*

Location: *Crawlspace of 20-year-old apartment building.*
Cause: *Standing water and poor ventilation. Note mycelia (top) and fruiting bodies (above).*

Location: *Trim at entrance to 3-year-old home.*
Cause: *Splashing water from unguttered eaves two stories above. Exposed endgrain sitting on metal flashing.*

shipments of CCA-treated southern yellow pine. Molds die once lumber dries, but can be washed off beforehand with the same solution used for mildew.

Preventing mold. Flourishing in damp crawlspaces and basements and in poorly vented attics, molds form a living veneer on framing and sheathing. Prevention lies wholly in controlling air moisture levels and condensation potential through proper site drainage and dampproofing, and again, the proper use of soil covers, vapor retarders, insulation, and ventilation as required in your area.

Staining Fungi

Discoloration of wood by staining fungi happens almost exclusively in logs and freshly sawn lumber. As a precaution, rough lumber is often dipped in a fungicidal bath immediately after sawing.

Also called sap stains, these fungi are most troublesome in softwoods, where they cause a steel-gray to blue-black color commonly called blue stain. In hardwoods, staining fungi may create blue or brown hues. The stains result from dark hyphae that permeate sapwood in search of stored starches and sugars. You can often spot inactive blue stain in doors, millwork, and other pine products. Active staining fungi sometimes discolor the bottom rails and corners of pine windows that are kept wet by condensation. These stains are indelible and will not wash off.

In their search for food, staining fungi destroy certain wood cells. As a result, the wood becomes more permeable, and more susceptible to decay. Its strength and toughness are slightly reduced as well.

Decay Fungi

While discoloration by mildew, mold, and staining fungi is only an appearance problem, decay fungi threaten the structural integrity of wood. Aptly termed the "slow fire," these fungi eat the very cellulose and lignin of which wood cells are made.

Moisture content is the critical factor that makes wood susceptible to decay. It must exceed 28%, and liquid water must be present in cell cavities before decay fungi can gain a toehold. Once established, some fungi can carry on their destruction at a moisture content as low as 20%. When moisture content falls below this level, all fungal activity ceases. That's one reason why framing lumber is dried to 19% moisture content or less.

In its early, or incipient, stages, decay can be difficult to detect, even with a microscope, yet strength loss can still be appreciable. As the slow fire advances, wood's luster fades. Surfaces become dull and discolored, and a musty odor is often present. The rate at which decay progresses depends on moisture content, temperature, and the specific fungus.

It doesn't take a trained eye to recognize decay in its advanced stages. Wood is visibly discolored, spongy, and musty. Surfaces may be stringy, shrunken, or split across the grain. Cottony masses of hyphae called mycelia, as well as fruiting bodies, may be present. Decay extends deep into wood; strength loss is significant.

Brown rots and white rots. Decay fungi fall into three major groups: brown rots, white rots, and soft rots. Soft rots are rarely found inside homes, though they occasionally degrade wood shakes and shingles on heavily shaded roofs in wet climates.

Brown rots are so-named because infected wood turns dark brown. They usually colonize softwoods, consuming cellulose but hardly touching the darker lignin, which is the natural glue that holds wood cells together. Mycelia appear as white growths, either sheetlike or fluffy, on the wood's surface. Brown-rotted wood shrinks excessively and splits across the grain as it dries. The surface becomes friable and crumbly, and shows cubical checking.

Water-conducting fungi are a special type of brown rot that show up infrequently in the Southeast, Northeast, and Pacific Northwest. These fungi are unique in their ability to pipe moisture from the soil over long distances. They do this through rootlike fusions of hyphae called *rhizomorphs*, wetting otherwise dry wood in advance of their attack. Water-conducting fungi are sometimes called dry rot fungi. Unfortunately, this name suggests that dry wood can decay. Dry wood can't decay, period! What builders, inspectors, and homeowners alike routinely mislabel as dry rot is almost always, in reality, wood that got wet, rotted, and dried out before discovery.

Water-conducting fungi infect both softwoods and hardwoods. Their light-colored mycelia look like large, papery, fan-shaped sheets. Damp crawlspaces and wood in contact with the ground are avenues for entry.

White rots give wood a white, gray-white, yellow-white, or otherwise bleached appearance. They most often infect hardwoods, feeding on both cellulose and lignin. In advanced stages of decay, white-rotted wood is spongy, has a stringy texture, and lacks the cubical checking of brown-rotted wood. A thin black line often marks the advancing edge of incipient white rot in hardwoods. Ironically, this partially decayed, or *spalted*, wood is coveted by woodworkers for its unique figure.

Dealing With Decay

Like mold, mildew, and staining, existing decay can be stopped by drying up the moisture. But remember that to make the remedy permanent, you've got to cure the disease (water infiltration) not just treat the symptoms (mildew, mold, and decay).

Stopping decay. The first and most important step when you find decay is to figure out where the water is coming from. Check for the obvious — roof and plumbing leaks, and missing or punctured flashing. Look for stains and drip tracks caused by ice dams. Are the eaves wide enough to prevent water from cascading down sidewalls? Are gutters poorly maintained or missing? Do finish grades slope towards the foundation? Are foundation cracks admitting water? Is untreated wood in direct contact with concrete, masonry, or soil?

Check to see if crawlspaces have soil covers and if venting and/or insulation is adequate and properly installed. Look for adequate attic ventilation as well.

Peeling and blistering paint often signal inadequate interior ventilation or a missing vapor retarder. Water stains on framing and sheathing inside walls suggest condensation from excessive indoor humidity.

Once the source of water has been shut off, remove as much decayed wood as is practical and economical. Decayed wood absorbs and holds water more readily than sound wood, inviting further decay and insect attack. This is especially important with girders, columns, and other critical members whose load-carrying ability may have been compromised. There's no known way to accurately determine the remaining strength of decayed wood left in place. Cut back rotted members to sound wood, keeping in mind that difficult-to-detect incipient decay can extend well beyond visibly rotted areas.

When a partially decayed structural member can't be replaced, reinforce it with a sister anchored to sound wood. Let any rotted areas you don't remove dry out before making repairs. Otherwise, you're just adding fuel to the slow fire.

In damp crawlspaces or other places where water is likely to reappear, replace decayed members with preservative-treated wood. The major model building code agencies — BOCA, ICBO, and SBCCI — require that treated wood be used for sills and sleepers on concrete or masonry in contact with the ground, for joists within 18 inches of the ground, for girders within 12 inches of the ground, and for columns embedded in the ground that support permanent structures.

Borates. Dormant fungi can be reactivated when dry, infected wood is rewetted. Consider treating infected but otherwise serviceable wood left in place with a water-borne borax-based preservative that will not only kill active fungi, but will guard against future infection as well (see "Sources of Supply" at end of chapter). Borates have low toxicity to humans and are even approved for interior use in food processing plants. They don't affect wood's strength, color, or finishability, don't corrode fasteners, and don't outgas vapors. Widely used in treating new timbers for log homes, they're the preservative of choice for remedial treatment of wood in service. Because of the decay hazard posed whenever wood bears on concrete or masonry, solid borate rods are often inserted into holes bored near contact areas. Should wood ever get wet, the rods dissolve and ward off infection.

Epoxy. Sometimes replacing rotted wood isn't an option. In conserving historic buildings, for example, the goal is to preserve as much of the original "architectural fabric" as possible. Stabilizing deteriorated wood with epoxy is often the only choice. Epoxies consist of resin and hardener that are mixed just before use. Liquids for injection and spatula-applied pastes are available. After curing, epoxy-stabilized wood can be shaped with regular woodworking tools and painted. Epoxies are useful for consolidating rotted wood, restoring lost portions of moldings and carvings, and for strengthening weakened structural members. In the last case, they're used to bond concealed metal reinforcement inside holes or channels cut into hidden timber faces. Epoxies aren't preservatives and won't stop existing decay or prevent future infection. They can also be tricky to use; follow the manufacturer's mixing, application, and safety instructions to the letter.

By Stephen Smulski, president of Wood Science Specialists Inc., in Shutesbury, Mass., a consulting firm specializing in wood performance problems in light-frame structures.

MOISTURE IN WALL CAVITIES: CASE STUDIES

Moisture is one of the worst enemies of wood-framed buildings. The trend toward tighter, more energy-efficient houses has made it important for builders to understand how moisture behaves and to plan ways for the house to handle moisture. Increased insulation levels and better air-sealing techniques have lengthened the time needed for the air in these homes to be replaced by natural infiltration. As a result, water vapor from showering, cooking, plants, people, and pets lingers indoors longer than it does in older, leakier homes, while the moisture trapped in new framing lumber escapes more slowly. This paves the way for mildew, mold, decay fungi, and insects.

You can avoid these problems by using kiln-dried framing lumber and mechanically venting water vapor directly to the outside before it does any damage. As these three case studies show, failure to do so can lead to disaster.

Case 1: Indoor Humidity Causes Exterior Stains

A contractor was living with his family in an unsold spec house he had built ten months before. When numerous red-brown streaks appeared at random on the home's white siding in February, he complained to his supplier that the siding was defective. The streaks appeared on all sides of the house, but were worse around the windows and outside the master bath.

The contractor had sided the home with 1x6 clear heart, vertical-grain western red cedar bevel siding. The siding had been machine-primed on all sides with a stain-blocking primer and field-coated with two topcoats of a solid color exterior white stain. The wall construction was typical of a modern energy-efficient home: gypsum wallboard, a polyethylene vapor retarder, unfaced fiberglass batt insulation between 2x6 studs, ply-wood sheathing, an exterior air infiltration barrier, and the siding.

The dark streaks were what most contractors call "cedar bleed," though a more accurate term is "run-down extractive staining." It's a problem with redwood and red cedar, and shows up occasionally on Douglas fir and southern pine as well. Happening commonly during late winter, run-down staining occurs when liquid water — in this case water vapor from inside the home that leaked through wall cavities and condensed on the cold siding — wets the back of the siding for a prolonged period. Eventually, the water penetrates the primer, causing the wood's water-soluble extractives to leach out. The dark brown solution then seeps out from behind the siding through the overlap between courses, dripping down and discoloring the face of the courses below.

During my inspection, I found live mold on some joists and stair stringers in the basement. I wasn't too surprised, given the fact that basement relative humidity and wood moisture content (62% and 12%, respectively) were more typical of June than February. Relative humidity on the first and second floors (46%), was also much higher than the 25% to 35% typical for this time of year.

When I removed the siding in a heavily stained area, I found liquid water and extractive staining on its backside (Figure 1). Water also saturated the plywood sheathing behind the wet and stained air infiltration barrier. Siding, sheathing, and framing checked in at 33%, 50%, and 30% moisture content, respectively, instead of the 12% to 15% that I would have expected. Though I found no decay, conditions were ripe for rot. The reason rot hadn't yet taken hold was that it was simply too cold outside.

The cause of the wet siding was excessive indoor humidity. Sources included a humidifier on each of the

Figure 1. Water vapor from inside this new house (left) — caused in part by a humidifier on the forced-hot-air heating system, a dryer vented directly into the basement, and green framing lumber — leaked through the walls and caused extractive staining on the primed and painted siding (below).

home's two forced-hot-air heating systems, a clothes dryer vented into the basement, four bathroom exhaust fans vented into the attic, a recirculating-type kitchen range fan and, as shown by the S-GRN grade stamps, green framing lumber. Despite the weight of this evidence, the contractor insisted that the water vapor from inside his "tight" house couldn't be leaking through the walls. Not until I pointed out that there was no staining whatsoever on the attached garage did he finally come around.

The solution to the staining problem was simple: lower the indoor relative humidity. To do so, I recommended that the builder disconnect the humidifiers and vent the clothes dryer, bath exhaust fans and kitchen range directly to the outside. Stains could be removed later by washing the siding with a dilute solution of oxalic acid (available from paint or hardware stores) once the framing, sheathing, and siding had dried to below 19% moisture content. Repainting with a stain-resistant primer would complete the job.

Case 2: Bathroom Moisture Recipe for Decay

While renovating a bathroom in their 22-year-old home, the owners were shocked to find wet insulation, severely decayed framing and sheathing, and live carpenter ants behind the tiled shower stall (Figure 2). Tucked into an outside corner, two sides of the stall were against exterior walls. The walls consisted of floor-to-ceiling ceramic tiles set on mortar and metal lath, standard gypsum wallboard, unfaced fiberglass batt insulation between 2x4 studs, plywood sheathing, and wood shingles. The bathroom had a window, but no exhaust fan.

The shower pan and drain tested leakfree, and the owners recalled that the tiles and grout had only a few cracks. This told me that the cause of the problem was not liquid water

leaking into the walls. Instead, a construction error — omission of a vapor retarder behind the wallboard — had let water vapor diffuse into the wall cavity. Lack of an exhaust fan also allowed water vapor and liquid condensation generated by showering to persist in the bathroom. This increased the chance that the moisture would get into the walls

through hidden air leakage paths, then condense and freeze on the cold sheathing. When it melted in warmer weather, the liquid water increased the moisture content of framing and sheathing to the 28% threshold required for decay. Carpenter ants followed.

My diagnosis was confirmed by the run-down staining on the home's

Figure 2. The framing behind this shower stall (left) rotted because bathroom moisture leaked into the walls. The excess moisture also caused extractive staining on the home's siding (below). The solution was to add a bath fan that vented moisture directly to the outside.

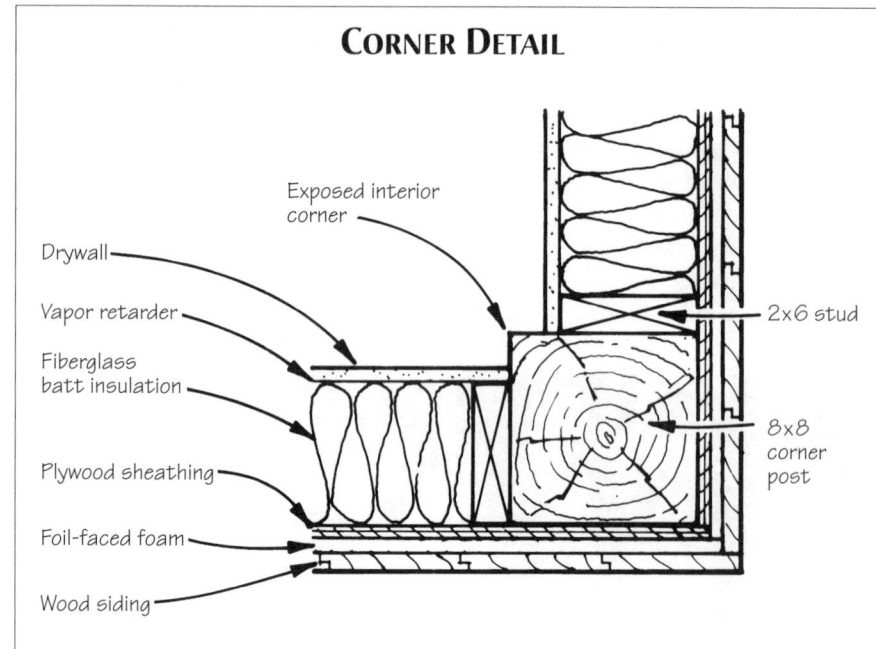

Figure 3. While remodeling their six-year-old timber-frame home, the owners found that the corner posts had decayed along the outside edge. The builder had boxed in the green timbers with framing and sheathing, holding the wood at a decay-susceptible moisture content for years after closing-in. Drying could only take place through the one exposed corner.

when green (about 97% moisture content). When it eventually dries to the 12% moisture content typical of framing in heated buildings, it will contain about one gallon of water. The other eight gallons will have been released into the air or the surrounding materials. The total water given off by a green frame counts in the hundreds of gallons, with the greatest release occurring during the first heating season. In fact, the owners of this home recalled a "Niagara Falls" of window condensation that damaged sashes, sills, and walls for the first three winters of occupancy. They actually put towels on the window sills to sop up the flow.

Fortunately, enough of the corner posts' cross-section was still sound enough to make reinforcement or replacement unnecessary. Following my recommendations, the builder replaced the decayed studs and sheathing, and treated the timbers with a waterborne borate preservative to kill existing decay and prevent future infection.

This problem could have been avoided. One option would have been to use partially air-dried timbers or to use salvaged timbers that had dried in place years before. Another would have been to use naturally decay-resistant timbers. Hemlock and red oak have no resistance to decay; white oak has very high natural resistance; eastern white pine has moderate resistance. You can virtually eliminate the decay risk of any species by applying foam-core stress-skin panels to the outside of the timber frame. This leaves three faces exposed on the inside, which provides an escape route for water and promotes faster drying.

By Stephen Smulski, president of Wood Science Specialists Inc., in Shutesbury, Mass., a consulting firm specializing in wood performance problems in light-frame structures.

white shingles outside and below the second floor bathroom. The owners remarked that despite washing the streaks off each summer, they always reappeared the following spring.

To prevent future problems, I recommended that they add a vapor retarder to the warm side of the exterior wall and install a bath exhaust fan vented directly to the outside. Running the fan would reduce the amount of moisture infiltrating into the wall to a negligible amount.

Case 3: Green Timbers Spawn Decay

While adding a porch to their six-year-old hemlock timber-frame home, the owners found extensive decay in the corner posts. After removing more siding and trim, they found at least minor decay wherever the timbers contacted studs and sheathing.

The builder had framed conventional 2x6 walls between the posts and sheathed them with plywood.

From inside to outside, the walls consisted of gypsum wallboard, a polyethylene vapor retarder, unfaced fiberglass batt insulation, plywood sheathing, rigid foam insulation, and wood siding. The studs were fastened directly to the faces of the posts.

Built-in during construction, the source of the decay-causing moisture was the huge gallonage of water trapped in the green (water-saturated) timbers. In an effort to make the house energy-efficient, the builder had boxed the timbers in on three faces with studs, sheathing, and rigid foam (Figure 3). This had severely retarded the drying of the timbers. As a result, the wood stayed at a decay-susceptible moisture content for years after closing-in. The timbers were forced to dry through the one face exposed inside the home. Corner posts were especially slow to dry because of the tiny exposed surface area.

An 8-foot-long hemlock 8x8 contains about nine gallons of water

INTERIOR MOISTURE PROBLEMS: CASE STUDIES

Moisture problems are caused by two culprits: a source of excess moisture and a cold surface. Solving the problem is just as logical: Identify and remove (or reduce) the moisture source, and warm the cold surface.

Most homeowners recognize that taking a long, hot shower is contributing moisture to the house, but there are lots of other sources that even many builders don't recognize. Big contributors include:

• firewood stored indoors
• unvented gas ranges
• power humidifiers
• cooking
• laundering and cleaning
• houseplants and aquariums
• poorly-drained foundations
• downspouts that are tied into footing tile
• capillary action through basement floors and walls
• uncovered or loosely covered dirt crawlspaces (1,000 square feet of uncovered earth in a crawlspace

can generate as much moisture as five power humidifiers, even if the ground appears dry!)

Moisture can enter wall and ceiling cavities through a number of air leakage points in conventional construction (Figure 4). Once inside the cavities, there are many cold surfaces on which the moisture can condense.

Cold interior surfaces generally have fewer causes: wind blowing through the insulation (windwashing), or misplaced and missing insulation (Figure 5). If indoor humidity is high, these cold spots will breed mold and mildew growth on the drywall or wallpaper.

In hopes of alerting builders who aren't up to speed on moisture control, here are three examples from

When double-glazed windows show this much condensation, humidity levels are too high and should be corrected by eliminating moisture sources and increasing ventilation.

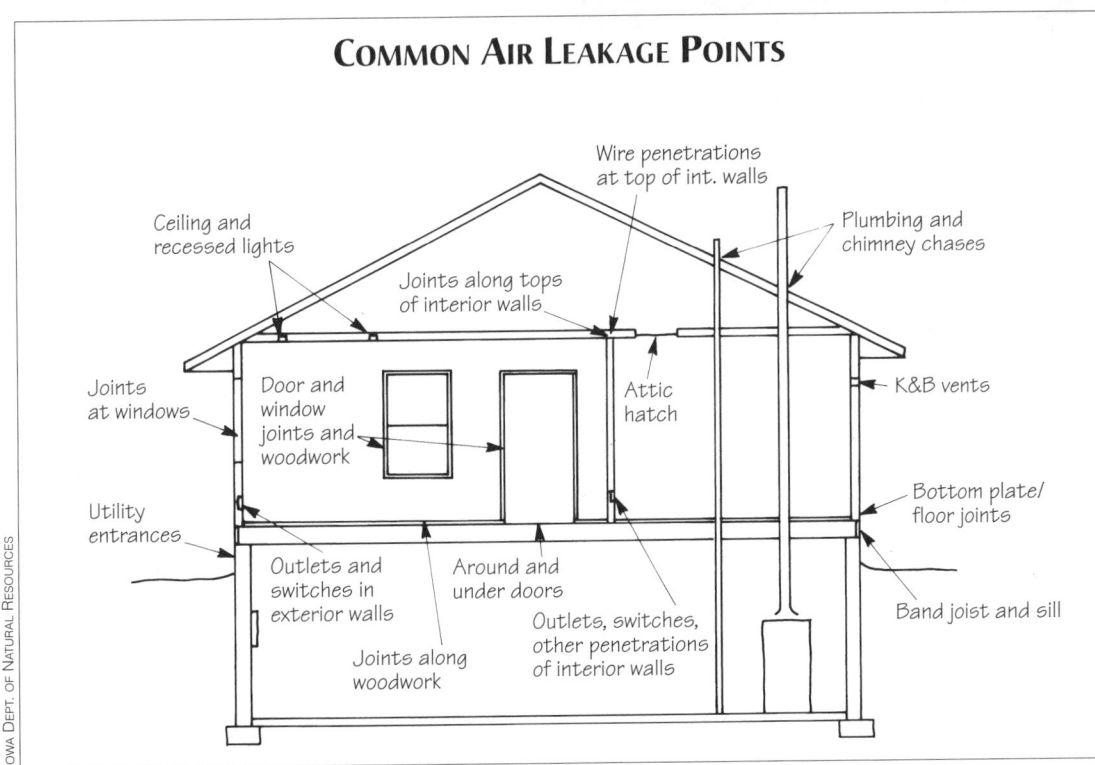

COMMON AIR LEAKAGE POINTS

Figure 4. Moist interior air can enter wall and ceiling cavities through these common leaks in conventionally built buildings. The moisture can then condense and, in extreme cases, lead to structural decay.

IOWA DEPT. OF NATURAL RESOURCES

COLD SURFACE CAUSES

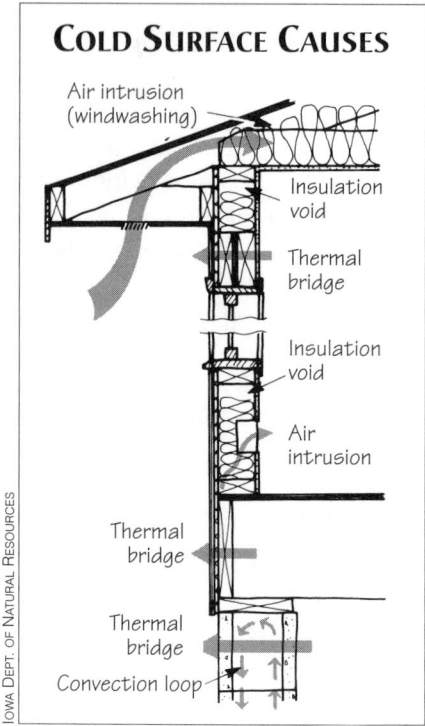

Figure 5. Insulation defects can cause cold spots on the interior surfaces of a home. Moist interior air can condense on these cold surfaces, causing mildew growth or rot.

CORRECT BAFFLE PLACEMENT

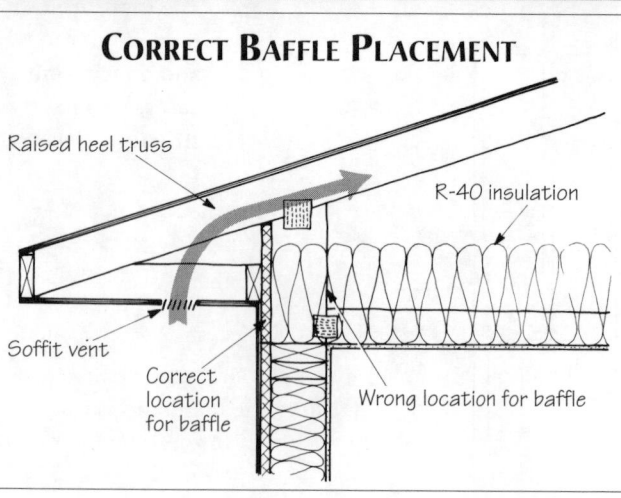

my consulting work. If you're still building with yesterday's technology, you may find yourself or a client in one of the following situations.

Case 1: Multifamily With Multi-Problems

My client was an apartment developer in a Midwest college town. He owned six identical, three-story apartment buildings each with 30 units. All had been built by the same builder using the same subcontractors. The three buildings that went up three years earlier had no problems, but the other three, built the previous year, were a mess.

There was mold growing on ceilings, walls, and sash, and the windows showed heavy condensation. As far as the owner was concerned, the culprit was a loose-fit poly vapor retarder on the ceilings — the only difference he could identify between the newer and older buildings. (It's pretty common for old-line builders to blame moisture problems on the presence or

Figure 6. These insulation baffles (left) are ineffective since they are misplaced and damaged from heavy condensation. The baffles should be rigid and placed as shown (below) to keep wind from blowing under the insulation — windwashing — and causing condensation, mold, and mildew at the ceiling corners.

absence of poly in the ceiling.)

I found that all six buildings had a great deal of air leakage between units and between floors. The units with the highest moisture readings — 50% to 70% relative humidity in February — were mainly third floor apartments, indicating a strong stack effect.

The older apartments without problems were occupied by young working singles. They didn't cook much and seldom used the shower more than once a day. The attic insulation above these units was blown fiberglass.

The newer apartments with the problems were occupied by college students — two or three to a unit — who cooked at home and took several showers per day per unit. The range hoods in these units weren't ducted, and the bath exhaust fans weren't very effective. Aquariums were in style and every third unit had one.

The attics were insulated with blown-in cellulose, which forms a better air barrier than fiberglass. However, the insulating was poorly done since many of the infiltration stops (baffles) were improperly located flush with the inside of the wall (Figure 6). This created a cold ceiling corner and defeated the purpose of using raised-heel "energy trusses."

Most of the bath exhaust ducting in these "problem apartments" was exposed and uninsulated, and large chunks of ice blocked many ducts. Several birds were nesting in the wall grilles of the lower level bath exhausts. The new buildings pressure-tested 25% tighter than the older ones — indicating that the builder and subcontractors had progressed somewhat on the learning curve of energy-efficient building. But they had neglected to account for moisture.

The exterior walls consisted of steel siding, gyp board sheathing, 6-inch batt insulation, a loose-fit vapor barrier, and ½-inch drywall. After seeing icicles forming on the siding,

I was sure enough of what was happening in the walls that I cut a hole in the drywall from the inside of a third-floor unit and invited the owner to reach inside this exterior wall. He pulled out a handful of wet insulation.

An attic inspection showed that the stack effect had driven so much moisture up there that you could see the outline of the interior walls from above where the insulation had become soaked and had settled. So much for loose-fit ceiling vapor barriers.

The real impact of the moisture generated by cooking and showering wasn't apparent until the early evening hours when everyone got back from home and began showering and cooking in earnest. So I chose this time period to demonstrate to the owner how increasing the ventilation would solve the problem. Using the three existing 1,000-cfm attic exhaust fans, I opened the attic scuttles in the common hallways and stood back. Despite my 3,000-cfm ventilating effort, the moisture level rose 10%.

It was obvious that the building was tight enough that it needed continuous ventilation in each unit. Sure enough, a survey of the occupants revealed that over half rated their apartment air quality fair to poor.

My recommendations included correcting the obvious insulation and bath venting problems, as well as ventilating all third-floor units continuously with a 60-cfm roof-mounted exhaust fan. To reduce the stack effect, I suggested two American Aldes, humidity-controlled fresh-air inlets for each unit, and a time-delay switch on all bath exhaust fans that kept them running 15 minutes after the lights were switched off.

Case 2: Basement Moisture Causes Ceiling Stains

This was a two-year-old ranch house with a partial basement and partial crawlspace. It had a full brick exterior, 2x6 walls, foam sheathing, Tyvek, low-e windows, a loose-fit vapor barrier, and a high-efficiency furnace. The nicest home in town, it was built by a conscientious builder using conventional building techniques.

The owner called me in because he was concerned about ceiling stains around the three bath exhaust fans, and heavy condensation on the high-performance glass. To the owner's dismay, the first place I went was the basement and crawlspace. "My problem is in the attic," he said.

After noting a loose-fitting vapor barrier on the crawlspace floor, I removed one of the fiberglass insulation batts at the band (rim) joist. When the owner saw it was black with mold, he knew the attic was the least of his problems (Figure 7).

The home was pressure-tested at 2½ air changes per hour at 50 pascals with a blower door; pretty tight for a conventional builder. At two air changes or better I usually recommend continuous ventilation. At three to four air changes per hour, intermittent ventilation is usually sufficient. But this home was carrying 60% to 70% relative humidity in January, and the bathroom exhaust fans were all ducted into the attic. In addition, the homeowners had a large collection of house plants and a large aquarium. I recommended central ventilation, a sealed poly ground cover in the crawlspace, an air barrier at the band joist, and exterior ducting for the bathroom exhaust fans.

As it turned out, we solved another problem at the same time. Out of curiosity, I did a radon test before we started. The home had a radon level of 32 picocuries per liter (pCi/l) on top of the moisture problem. With the central ventilation and basement sealing, we were able to lower the radon level to an acceptable 4 pCi/l.

When we cut the hole through the wall to install the heat exchang-

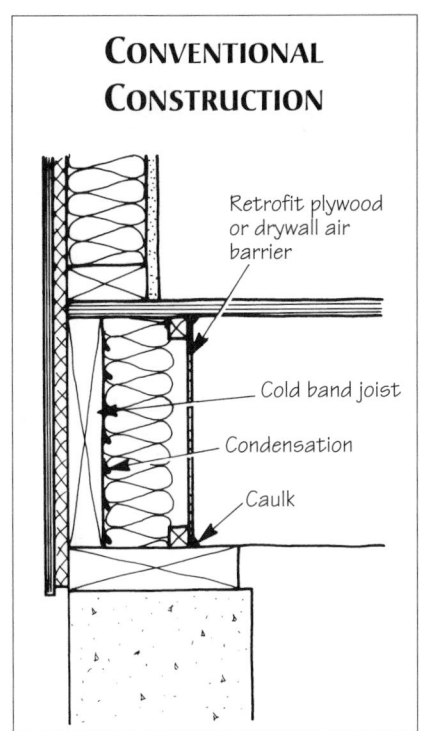

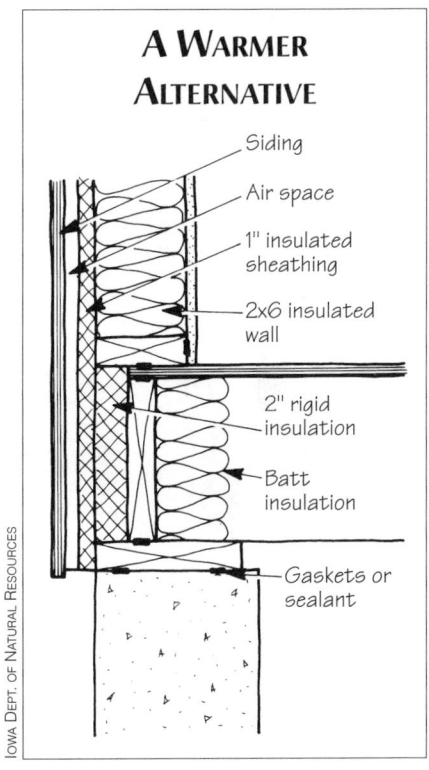

Iowa Dept. of Natural Resources

Figure 7. Conventional band or rim joists have cold interior surfaces that can condense moisture. The solution: Carefully retrofit airtight blocking between the joists (top) to keep moist air out. In new construction, insulate the band joist on the exterior (above) to keep the band joist warm.

HOUSEHOLD HUMIDITY SOURCES

Moisture Source	Estimated Amount (measured in pints)
Bathing *(excludes towels & spillage)*	
Bath	0.12/standard size bath
Shower	0.52/5-minute shower
Clothes Drying	
Vented outside	0+/load *(usually nil)*
Not vented	4.68 to 6.18/load *(more if gas dryer)*
Combustion *(unvented kerosene heater)*	7.6/gallon of kerosene burned
Cooking *(family of four)*	
Lunch	0.53 *(plus 0.68 if gas stove)*
Dinner	1.22 *(plus 1.58 if gas stove)*
Boiling — *10 minutes, 6" pan (plus gas)*	0.48 covered; 0.57 uncovered
Dishwashing by hand	
Dinner	0.68/family of four
Firewood storage	
Cord of green wood	400 to 800/6 months
Floor mopping	0.03/square foot
Gas range pilot light *(each)*	0.37-/day
House plants	
5 to 7 average size	0.86 to 0.96/day
Human respiration/perspiration	0.44/hour *(family of four)*
Saunas, steambaths, whirlpools	0 to 2.7+/hour
Ground moisture migration	
1,000 sq. ft. basement	0 to 105/day

Source: William Angell and Wanda Olsen, Cold Climate Housing Info. Ctr., Univ. of Minn.

er's air intake, we noted that the wall cavity was also saturated with moisture. With the full brick veneer and the vinyl-clad windows, the owner might not have known there was a problem until the walls began to fall apart from rot in five to ten years.

Case 3: New Furnace Catalyst Not Cause

This homeowner replaced his old fuel oil furnace with a new high-efficiency gas model. The first spring after it was installed, the paint on the exterior of the 27-year-old house began to peel and the windows were heavy with condensation. The homeowner filed suit against the mechanical contractor and the furnace manufacturer. The owner was convinced that the new furnace was "pumping moisture" into his home because he could see the water flowing out of the condensation line.

The insurance company hired me to sort out the facts and analyze the problem. I looked at a lot more than the furnace (Figure 8). I found poor site drainage away from the foundation, a sagging and leaking rain

Figure 8. These sources of excess moisture — a shower without an exhaust fan (left) and a bathroom exhaust vented into the attic (right) — are easy to fix if the homeowner and builder are aware of the damage they can cause.

gutter, a heavily used basement shower with no exhaust fan, a main-floor exhaust fan ducting into the attic, lots of house plants, a family with both a teenager and a baby (lots of showers and lots of laundry), and a clothesline full of wash hanging out to dry in the basement (they were proud of how much energy they saved by not using the dryer).

All of these moisture generating sources were in the home prior to the installation of the high-efficiency furnace, and the homeowner admitted that "the house never did quite dry out in the winter." But the old conventional furnace flue had been providing enough ventilation to partially relieve the problem. (A conventional furnace flue exhausts about 70 cfm continuously from a home, even when the furnace is not running).

A blower door test revealed that the house had 5.5. air changes per hour at 50 pascals pressure with the conventional furnace flue in place. The reading was 4.0 air changes at 50 pascals with the flue sealed. This difference in ventilation rates brought the relative humidity up to 68% — which was the primary cause of the paint peeling and blistering. Contributing causes were wind-driven rain that penetrated the siding, and deteriorating putty around the windows.

In this case, I suggested improving the site grading, repairing gutters and downspouts, adding an exhaust fan for the basement bath, and cutting down the basement clothesline.

These suggestions should also bring the humidity down to a level where the house can dry out season-ally, eliminating the flywheel effect of increasing the moisture each year by building on the previous one. The house was already experiencing a moisture problem; the new furnace merely accelerated it, making it surface sooner. As is often the case, the "last guy in" got the blame.

There's some truth to the old saying "They don't build 'em the way they used to." In fact, homes today are built much better, but that means less margin for error. Proper moisture control, good air barriers, and adequate ventilation are the keys to houses that are more comfortable and durable as well as cleaner, quieter, and healthier to live in.

By Bill Eich, a contractor who builds energy-efficient houses in Spirit Lake, Iowa.

A ROTTING TIMBER FRAME

"If you don't put in a vapor barrier, your house is going to rot away." You've heard this many times, but it's not so simple.

Thousands of insulated houses with no vapor barriers (or lousy vapor barriers such as kraft paper) have not rotted away. Furthermore, installing a sheet of poly in the wall is no guarantee against problems. Take for example, this rotting timber-frame house in southern Vermont.

The 1,800-square-foot, one-and-a-half-story Cape was four years old. The walls were framed with 8x8 timbers, which are exposed on the interior of the house. Between the 8x8s, the builder framed in with 2x4s to provide nailing and a place for fiberglass insulation. The frame was sheathed with 1-inch boards, then wrapped with 1-inch-thick, foil-faced isocyanurate, which was taped and caulked. Clapboard siding was installed over kraft paper.

Rotting Beams

The owner discovered the problem when a renovation contractor opened up the south side of the

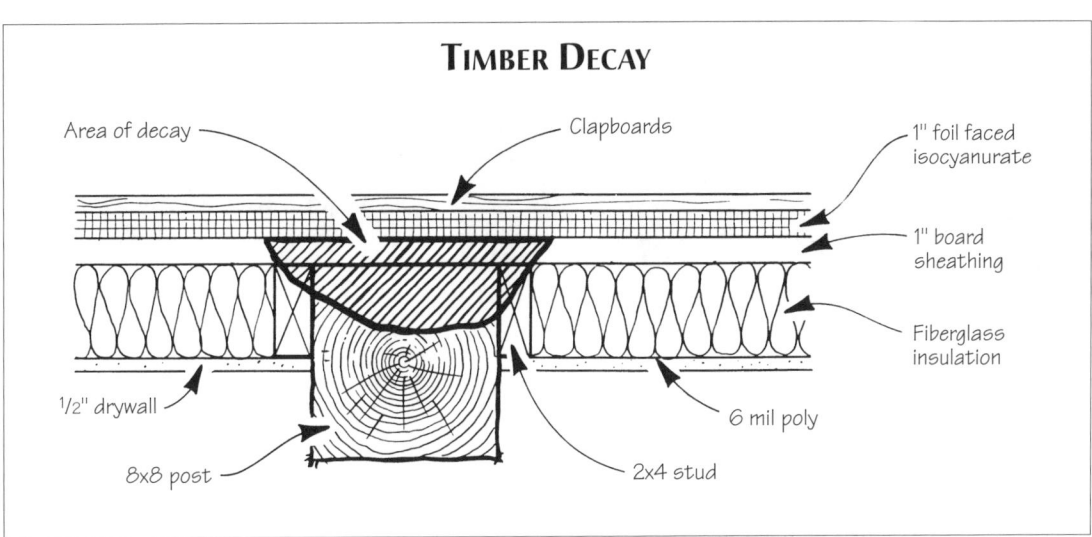

TIMBER DECAY

Area of decay

Clapboards

1" foil faced isocyanurate

1" board sheathing

Fiberglass insulation

½" drywall

8x8 post

2x4 stud

6 mil poly

Figure 9. Decay was concentrated on the outer portion of the timbers and the nearby sheathing and studs, as shown in the darkened area.

house in order to add a sunspace. He found extensive decay in and around the timbers. The rot occurred on the outer face of the timbers — up to 2 inches deep in some sections — and in the sheathing and 2x4s wherever they touched the timbers (Figure 9).

To learn more, the owner cut out sections of siding and sheathing on all sides of the house and found decayed wood on the north, south,

and west sides (Figure 10). Only one hole was cut on the east side, and showed only minor damage.

There was decay on nearly all the beams looked at — high and low, on vertical posts, and on horizontal beams. Rot also occurred in the 2x4s that were directly nailed to the beams, and in the 1x pine sheathing where it touched the beams. No decay was found in the wall sections between the beams, or elsewhere —

although a thorough search was not made of all areas.

Looking Further

When I visited the house in November, I looked for evidence of high moisture levels. It was a sunny day in the 40s — too warm for condensation to form on the windows. But all the second-floor windows — and most on the first floor — were badly stained from pooling condensation.

The owner confirmed that condensation covered most of the windows for most of the winter. The sources of moisture were many. For the first two years, the house had a wet basement each spring. (This was finally cured by regrading around the foundation.) There were no bathroom or kitchen fans, and the dryer vented indoors. The house was heated mostly by a wood-fired furnace in the basement, which tended to keep the basement warm and drive any moisture upstairs. To this day, the basement houses wet firewood.

Up in the attic, the owner and I found black mold covering the underside of the sheathing on the north side. The wood felt wet.

What let moisture *into* the attic were eight recessed lights, along with the usual wiring, plumbing, and framing holes. The attic was vented with two large gable-end vents. Judging by the mold, however, the vents could not handle the excessive moisture load.

Surprisingly, the home's interior had no musty smell, and no obvious signs of water damage other than on the window sash. All the damage was "safely" hidden from view.

The Diagnosis

So what caused the problem? In short, a combination of green wood, a moist house, a cold-side vapor barrier, and a cold climate. The timber-frame, built of 8x8 hemlock beams, had been assembled green in the fall

Figure 10. The west face of the house (top) was cut open in four spots, all revealing severe decay of the timber frame and adjoining wood (above left). The southwest corner (above right) is shown up close.

and was closed in the next spring. Since wood does not dry well in the cold, it was probably still quite wet when wrapped in foam the following spring. The water in the green wood gave the decay fungi a head start the first year.

Why didn't the beams dry toward the inside of the house over the summer? They did — at least near the inside faces, which became severely checked. But when winter came, the high moisture levels in the house drove the moisture back into the beams toward the sheathing, where it condensed.

The large gaps in the 8x8s provided an easy path for moisture into the wood, which is quite permeable anyway. Moisture could also penetrate the wall along the sides of the beams. Other interruptions in the vapor barrier — at floors, ceilings, and electrical outlets — let more moisture into the wall cavities. The inside face of the foam was below the dew point of the moist interior air throughout much of the winter.

The exposed inside sections of the beams dried, but the wet outer sections festered. Enough water got into the wood each winter so that each spring temperatures caused decay before the wood could dry out. The foam kept the wood from drying outward, and kept the sun from drying the wood inward. By mid-summer, perhaps, the wood fell below saturation levels, stifling decay

WHERE DOES THE DEW DROP?

To figure out how much insulating foam sheathing you should install on the exterior of a building, you need to know the dew point of the interior air during winter.

First look at the chart to figure out what the dew point is for a given air temperature and relative humidity. Say you have an indoor relative humidity of 50% at 70°F. On the horizontal scale, locate the temperature and move up to the curve that represents 50% relative humidity, as shown. Then move left to the saturation curve, and down to find the dew point temperature — 50°F in this case.

Moisture must condense on a solid surface (it won't condense in midair and is unlikely to condense in fiberglass), and the inside surface of the sheathing is where the condensation is most likely to occur. The objective is to put enough foam on the wall so its inside surface remains above the dew point (in this case, above 50°F) for the average winter temperature at the site.

You can find the temperature at any point inside the wall if you know the R-values of the wall insulations you are using. The temperature change through the wall is in direct proportion to that R-value. For example, for an average outdoor winter temperature of 32°F, the temperature inside the 1-inch foam sheathing in Wall A will

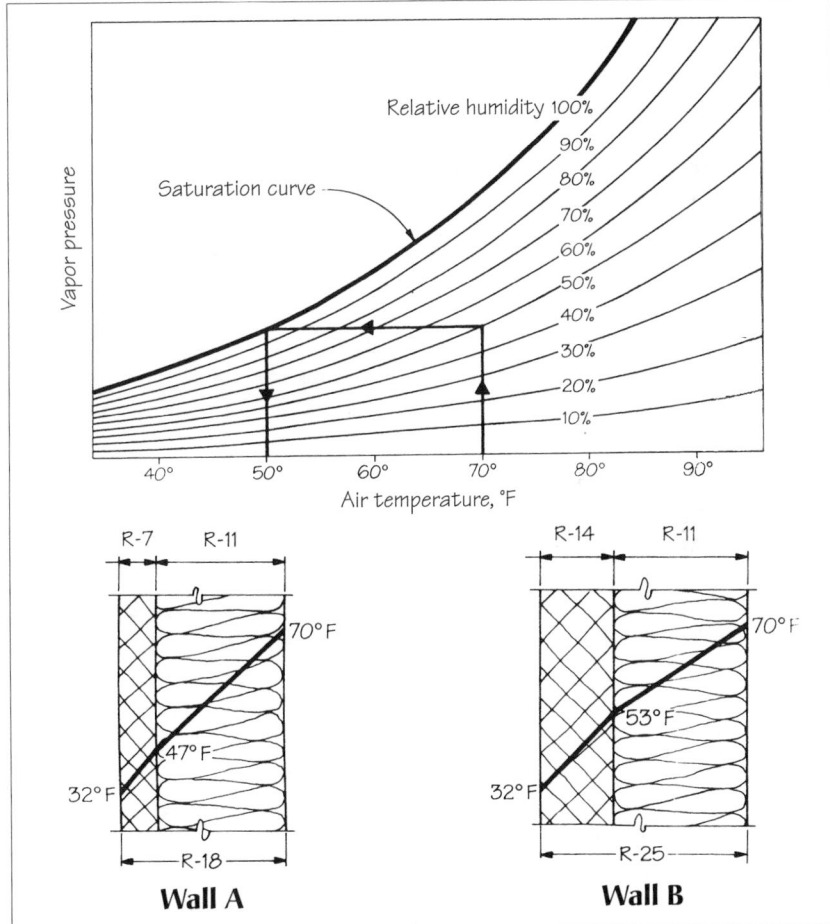

be $7/18$ (R-7 over R-18) of the way from 32°F to 70°F, or 47°F. This is below the dew point, so condensation is likely to form on the inside of the foam sheathing.

In Wall B, with 2 inches of foam, the temperature at the inside sheathing surface is $14/25$ of the way, or 53°F — safely above the dew point. This thicker insulating sheathing would be your safest bet in climates with an average winter temperature of 32°F or less.

growth. But the next winter the cycle would repeat.

The Treatment

To prevent further deterioration, the wood must be kept dry. A building consultant, Bill Lotz, recommended a three-pronged approach:

1. Keep household moisture levels down by adding fans and venting the clothes dryer outdoors.
2. Seal the checking in the beams and the gaps around the beams with caulking. Then seal the beams with a clear finish.
3. Replace the foil-faced sheathing at the beams with beadboard to allow some drying at these points.

It is possible that just reducing the moisture level would do the trick. In fact, most of the damage may have occurred in the first two years when household and wood moisture levels were highest. But several layers of defense is the best approach.

Conclusions

Up to a point, wood-frame houses are forgiving; they can safely store winter condensation and get rid of it in the spring. But if you push things too far, watch out.

This house violated too many rules. It combined too much moisture with too little ventilation, too cold a condensing surface, and too few opportunities for the wood to dry out. The moisture balance was tipped the wrong way, and the consequences were severe. But how far is too far? What precautions should you take?

If you like to live dangerously, you — or an engineer — can make an educated guess about how wet a given wall system will get in a given climate, and how fast it will dry. But there are always unknowns.

To play it safe and allow for a margin of error, you should design for dry wall and ceiling cavities. Keep the following points in mind:

• You can't control how a homeowner will run a house, but you can reduce the likelihood of high moisture levels. At a minimum, install kitchen and bath fans, continuous soffit and ridge vents, and build a dry foundation. Inform the customers that if they have condensation all winter long on double-glazed windows, they need to reduce moisture levels.

• A vapor barrier with gaping holes (like the beams and recessed lights) is no barrier at all. To keep moisture out of the walls and ceiling, seal all significant seams and holes in the air/vapor barrier. If you use recessed lights, put them in a dropped ceiling or use IC-type units.

• In cold climates, keep the exterior of the wall more permeable than the interior, or keep the sheathing temperature warm enough that condensation there is rare. In practice, this means don't use foil-faced exterior insulation at all, or use a lot of it — at least 2 inches. Better yet, put it on the inside.

• And for remodelers: Don't weatherize a house without solving moisture problems first.

By Steven Bliss, co-publisher and editorial director of The Journal of Light Construction.

WOOD MOISTURE CONTENT & INTERIOR FINISHES

Complaints about misaligned wood moldings, floor squeaks, and drywall cracks are like fingernails on a blackboard to a builder's ears. Callbacks can lead to customer dissatisfaction that will threaten a builder's reputation. Regardless of how you resolve these problems, you can always count on one thing: The cure will cost you money. Prevention is always the least expensive and most effective remedy.

Here is a selection of callback complaints that builders face over and over again. Each time the questions remain the same: What is causing this problem and how can it be prevented?

Gaps in the Floor Boards

Six months after a new home is occupied, large gaps may open up between the floor boards. The gaps are rarely uniform. Usually several individual boards appear to have shrunk significantly while large areas of flooring remain tight. The separations run in a connecting zig-zag pattern across the room.

Cause: Fluctuation in relative humidity causes wood to absorb and lose moisture and, consequently, to expand and contract. Wood shrinks and swells the most in the direction tangent to the growth rings (across a typical flat-grained board) and about half as much perpendicular to them.

Shrinking and swelling along the length of a board are insignificant.

Even if the flooring is delivered at a low moisture content and installed correctly, and the indoor humidity at the time of installation is kept at a reasonable level (between 40% and 60%), moisture can still be a problem. The floor can absorb moisture from the basement slab, fresh paint, and curing drywall mud. The wood expands as it takes on this moisture and the edges of the boards press against each other and compress. As indoor humidity drops, the boards shrink to a size smaller than their installed size — a condition known as compression set. Furthermore, polyurethane finish drips between the floor boards during finishing, gluing portions together, so areas of the floor shrink as a monolith. When this happens, it appears that only a few boards have shrunk, when in reality all the boards have swelled and then shrunk.

Cure: Contrary to conventional wisdom, leaving a 3/4-inch gap around the perimeter of the room does not solve the problem. Flooring nails would have to be sheared off or pulled out of the subfloor in order for flooring to fill the recommended 3/4-inch perimeter gap.

In this case, the only cure is prevention. Relaying the floor is the only fix.

To avoid similar problems with a new floor, only install wood flooring that has equalized to its in-use moisture content (see "Acclimating Wood"). Ideally, according to the National Oak Flooring Manufacturers Association, you should buy wood flooring at 6% to 9% moisture content. But even if the flooring arrives at the job site at 10% to 12% moisture content, it should still acclimate to job-site conditions in a few days, as long as indoor humidity at the site is controlled by mechanical ventilation and, if necessary, dehumidifiers. The floor may take on additional moisture from curing construction materials after you have left the job, but at least the chances for compression set are reduced. Advise your customers that continual ventilation during the first year after construction will reduce the swelling as long as no large sources of moisture are introduced into the home. Keep records showing the moisture content of the wood when it arrived and what the humidity conditions in the home were during storage and installation. Good recordkeeping will help reduce your liability when problems arise.

Miters Open Up

Often the miters on window and door casings are tight when you install them, but they open up at either the long point or the short point after you leave the job, so the angles look as if they were miscut.

Cause: A dry piece of wood casing, tightly mitered and installed during the winter months, can look much different during the summer months as the humidity in the home rises. Indoor relative humidity can drop to 20% during cold periods and rise above 75% during humid summer months. Under these conditions, the moisture content of the wood casings can swing from 4% to as much as 16%. A 6-inch-wide casing can expand more than 1/8 inch. Because wood swells by different amounts in each direction, mitered connections remain tight at the bottom, but separate at the top as the casing swells. Similarly, the miters open near the short points as the wood shrinks (Figure 11).

Cure: To prevent miters from opening up, first install high-quality wood casing that has an 8% to 12% moisture content. The easiest way to check the moisture content is with a moisture meter (see "Moisture Meter Basics," page 232). At the very least, acclimate the casing material to indoor humidity conditions. You

ACCLIMATING WOOD

The moisture content in woodwork is directly related to the relative humidity level inside a home. If the relative humidity rises, the wood will absorb water and swell. If the relative humidity drops, the wood will lose water and shrink. If the air remains at a fixed humidity level, the amount of moisture bound in the wood eventually stabilizes. At this point, the wood has reached its *equilibrium moisture content.*

The trick to keeping joints tight in finish woodwork is to use wood that has acclimated to indoor humidity levels. Finish stock should be brought into the house and stickered up to allow air to circulate around it. Wood that is brought from the lumberyard at an 8% to 12% moisture content should acclimate to job-site conditions in a few days. If the wood is at 15% to 18% moisture content, allow at least a week. To be sure, check the wood with a moisture meter periodically until it reaches its equilibrium moisture content. The table below shows typical equilibrium moisture contents over a range of indoor humidity levels.

Once the wood has acclimated, make every effort to stabilize the relative humidity level in the building, at least until you've applied a finish. — *P. F.*

INDOOR HUMIDITY VS. WOOD MOISTURE CONTENT

Relative humidity (%)	Equilibrium moisture content (%)
10	2.5
20	4.5
30	6.2
40	7.7
50	9.5
60	11.0
70	13.1
80	16.0
90	20.5

Note: The equilibrium moisture contents shown here are typical for most softwoods at 70°F. The moisture levels will fluctuate slightly, depending on wood species and temperature.

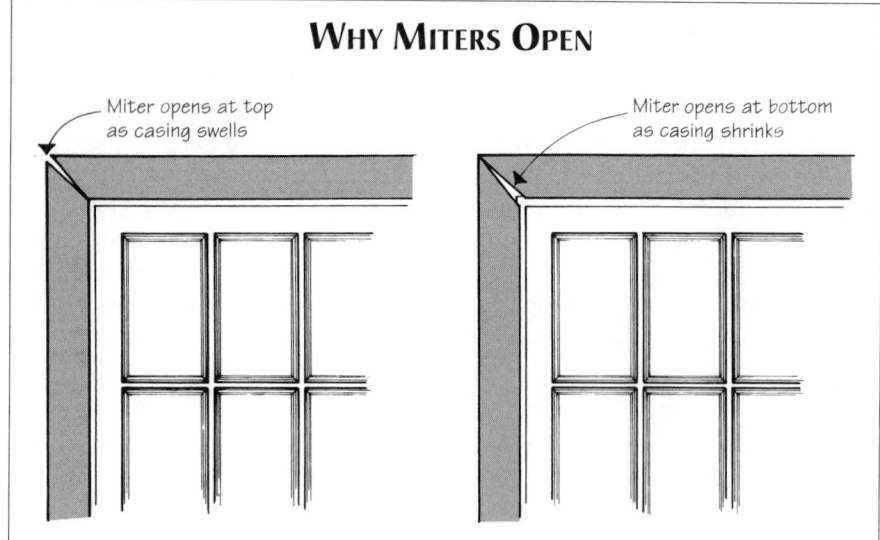

WHY MITERS OPEN

Miter opens at top as casing swells

Miter opens at bottom as casing shrinks

Figure 11. As indoor humidity fluctuates, wood casings shrink and swell, causing miters to open up. As the casing swells, miters separate at the top but remain tight at the bottom (left). As the wood shrinks, the opposite occurs (right).

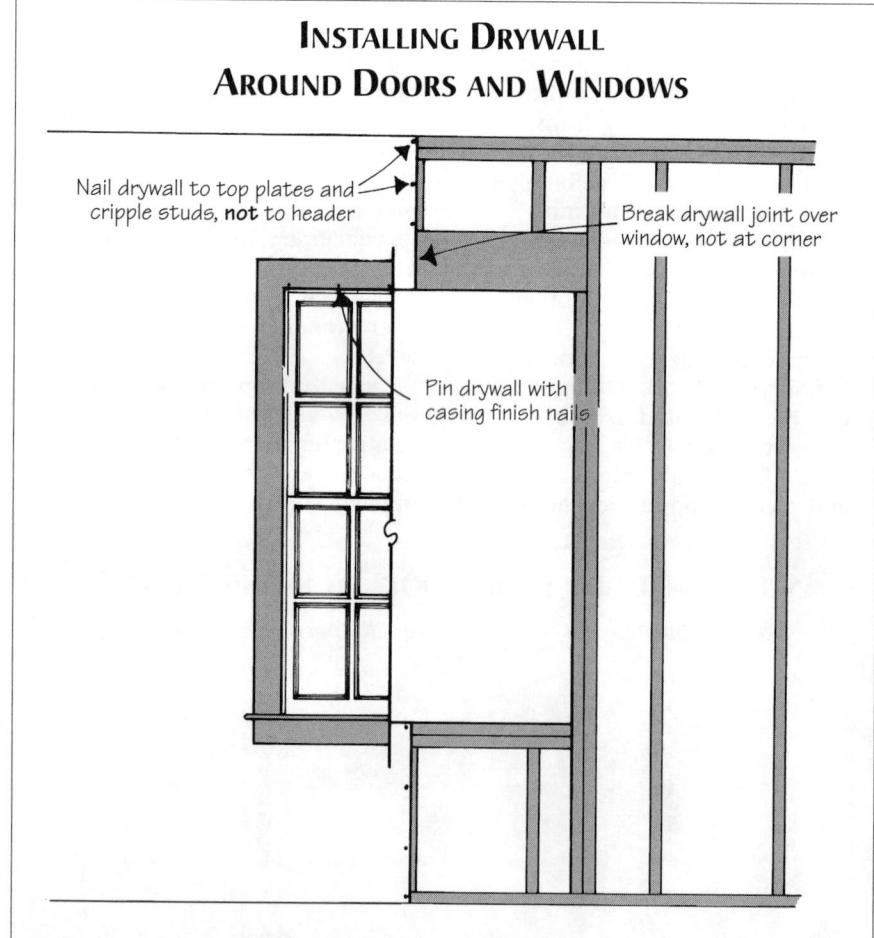

INSTALLING DRYWALL AROUND DOORS AND WINDOWS

Nail drywall to top plates and cripple studs, **not** to header

Break drywall joint over window, not at corner

Pin drywall with casing finish nails

Figure 12. To prevent drywall joints from cracking at the corners of windows and doors, place the sheet so the joint falls in the center of the opening, and then cut out the waste. Also, do not fasten the drywall to the header, but use the interior casing to secure the loose edge of the drywall.

might try using biscuits at the joint. But beware that if the indoor humidity fluctuates too much, the wood will have to move somewhere. If the miters are held rigid, the casing may pull away from the window stool, warp, or, in extreme cases, split.

The best prevention is to educate your customers about controlling indoor humidity. Encourage them to maintain indoor humidity levels between 40% and 60% year-round. This range is healthy and will help keep your work looking good. Finally, be sure to lead your customer on a careful walk-through after the job is complete and point out the level of craftsmanship. Again, record and document humidity levels in the home and the moisture content of the trim stock during storage and installation.

Squeaky Floors

Squeaky floors rank high in nuisance value. Customers usually hold their complaints until the squeak has frayed their nerve endings. Then, when you attempt to fix it, they watch you like a hawk.

Cause: Squeaks result from wood rubbing against wood. Often the squeak occurs when a floor joist shrinks after it is installed. A space develops between the subfloor and the top of the floor joist, and when the homeowner walks over this spot, the subfloor moves against the joist and squeaks.

Cure: The best cure for floor squeaks is prevention. Use dry wood, keep it dry, and apply construction adhesive between all wooden surfaces. Also, use screws — not nails — to fasten subfloors and underlayment.

In theory, fixing floor squeaks is simple — stop the movement of the wood. But accomplishing this is often difficult.

If the squeaks are located in the first floor, you're in luck because you can usually get at the floor frame from the basement or crawlspace. One cure is to sister a length of 1x3 to the side of the offending floor joist. Holding it tight to the underside of the subfloor, attach the strip along the top edge of the joist using screws and glue. Make sure you also spread adhesive between the top of the 1x3 strip and the subfloor. The adhesive will help prevent future rubbing.

The solution is not so simple when the squeak is located on an upper level of a home. To fix these, you must add the extra step of opening and repatching the finished ceiling.

Cracked Drywall

Drywall cracks when the framing moves. This happens most often at the upper corners of windows and doors.

Cause: If the drywall joints fall at the edges of a window, the finished joint will crack when the header shrinks. Headers with a moisture content of 19% can shrink 1/4 inch across their width.

Cure: Don't break drywall sheets at the corners of an opening. Instead, lap the sheet over the corner so the joint falls in the center of the window or door span, and then cut out the opening (Figure 12). Also, do not fasten the drywall to the header. Screw the drywall into the cripples and wall plate above the headers. This lets the wallboard float down over the header. Use the interior window casing to hold the loose edge of the drywall secure.

Faux Truss Uplift

Have you ever seen drywall cracks at a ceiling corner or a center partition separate from the ceiling? This is often caused by truss uplift, but not always.

Cause: In many cases, the triple-2x12 girder in the basement that supports the floor joists is the cause (Figure 13). Since the beam is located directly beneath the center partitions and the partition sole plates are nailed securely to the deck, shrinkage of this beam can pull the partitions down-

ward, opening a crack at the ceiling. This happens frequently with lumber that is grade-stamped "S-DRY," meaning that it was surfaced at a moisture content of 19% or lower. Yet once the house is occupied and heated, the moisture content of the girder, joists, and partition studs can fall to 11%. The cumulative shrinkage of all these members can easily equal 3/8 inch.

Cure: While the cause is not true truss uplift, the effect is the same. Fasten trusses to partitions with hardware such as the Truss-Float-R (Stud Claw USA, 5370 Chestnut Ridge Rd., Orchard Park, NY 14127-3298; 716/662-7877), which allows the ceiling drywall and wall partition to float independently. Use dry framing lumber, especially for girders. Lumber stamped "MC 15" is a good choice.

The fix is the same as with truss uplift. Install a molding in the corner at the ceiling. Attach the molding to the ceiling only, allowing the wall to move.

By the way, this problem can occur in houses without roof trusses, too. To prevent this, break ceiling joists over a center bearing partition. As the partition settles, this break will act like a hinge, allowing the ceiling to drop as the center bearing shrinks.

Interior Doors Won't Close

The doors closed properly when they were installed, but after a couple of months the doors began to rub against the strike jamb and now they are too wide to be forced closed.

Cause: The doors have absorbed moisture, but to find the exact source requires a bit of investigation. Determine whether all doors have swollen or if just certain ones have, like the bathroom or basement doors. Isolated swelling suggests local humidity problems.

Cure: Wood doors should be delivered and installed at a moisture

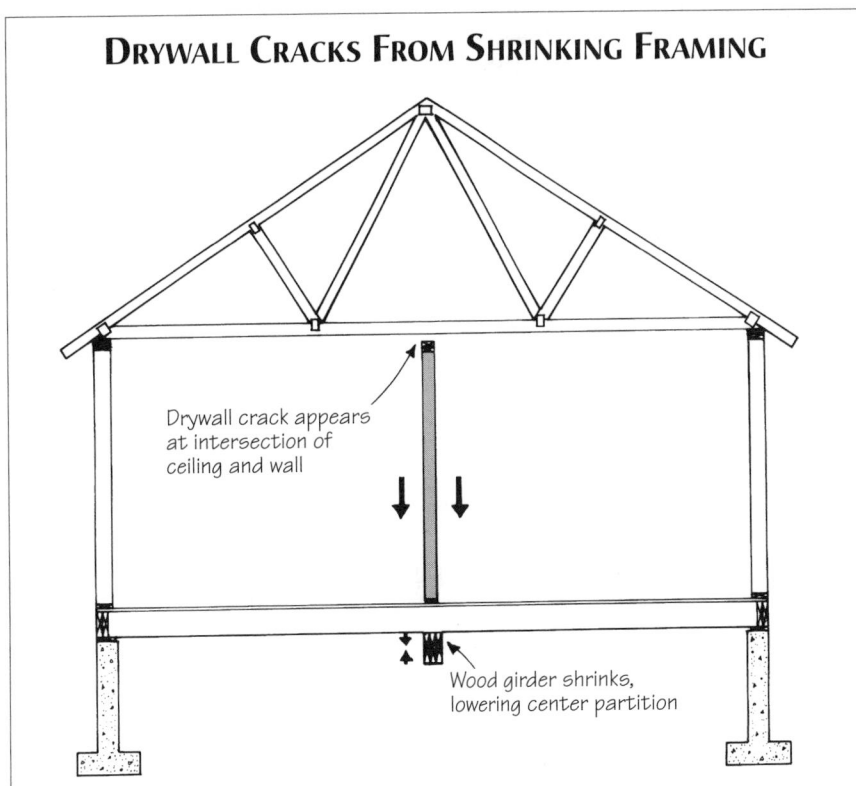

DRYWALL CRACKS FROM SHRINKING FRAMING

Drywall crack appears at intersection of ceiling and wall

Wood girder shrinks, lowering center partition

Figure 13. Drywall cracks at the ceiling can open up when the basement girder shrinks and pulls the partition downward. The only fix is to install crown molding over the crack. Attach the molding to the ceiling but not to the wall.

content between 6% and 12%. But even those doors can become unstable in houses with fluctuating humidity levels. For best results, doors should be sealed as soon as they are delivered (right after they are made would be even better). If the doors are prehung units, remove all the hardware and seal the undercut edge and all hardware cutouts, including hinge mortises and the inside of lock bores. Endgrain is very absorbent. An unsealed edge will suck up moisture rapidly under humid conditions. If doors arrive at the job site unsealed, check the moisture content by inserting the probes of a moisture meter into the endgrain. Then seal it when conditions are right.

To solve the immediate problem, plane the door to size and reseal the edges. Also, as with all wood movement problems, control the indoor humidity.

By Paul Fisette, a wood technologist and director of the Building Materials Technology and Management program at the University of Massachusetts in Amherst.

MOISTURE PROBLEMS FROM "DRY BASEMENTS"

We've known for a long time that much of the moisture that condenses on windows in winter, or promotes mold growth in summer, comes from damp basements or crawlspaces. With many indoor moisture problems, however, the source of the moisture is not so obvious. New research indicates that in many cases the basement or crawlspace is still at fault even though it appears to be dry.

Below-Grade Moisture Diffusion

At the University of Minnesota Underground Space Center research-

ers showed that "dry" basements can, in fact, contribute significant amounts of soil moisture to a home. Both surface water and deep ground water are sources of this moisture, which rises up by capillarity and evaporation into the sandy soil and then diffuses into the basement through the concrete walls and floor. The study also showed exterior wall waterproofing alone is only marginally effective at solving the problem.

The researchers built four test basements in a well-drained sandy site and over four months measured 36 and 50 gallons of moisture entry though a block foundation and a poured foundation, respectively. (Why more water entered through the poured concrete than the block in this test is unclear.)

The scientists installed 2 inches of Styrofoam on the outside of one of the foundations to test the effectiveness of exterior wall waterproofing. Contrary to expectations, the Styrofoam only slightly reduced moisture entry, from 36 to 30 gallons. An identical basement with *interior* foam insulation showed significantly better moisture control, with only 14 gallons measured.

The explanation, according to Minnesota researcher Louis Goldberg, is that much of the moisture enters up through the footings (Figure 14). Since interior wall waterproofing is inside the footings, it isolates the basement interior from the footings and the moisture. Exterior wall waterproofing, on the other hand, is outside the footings. For truly effective wall waterproofing, the footings must also be waterproofed. More on that later.

Below-Grade Moist Air Leakage

Underground air leakage into houses has become an important issue since radon was discovered in homes. But radon is just one component of soil gas. During winter, soil gas is usually saturated (100% relative humidity) with *water vapor*. Whenever a basement is at a lower atmospheric pressure than the surrounding soil (caused by exhaust fans, combustion appliances, or the "stack effect"), soil gas enters through cracks and penetra-

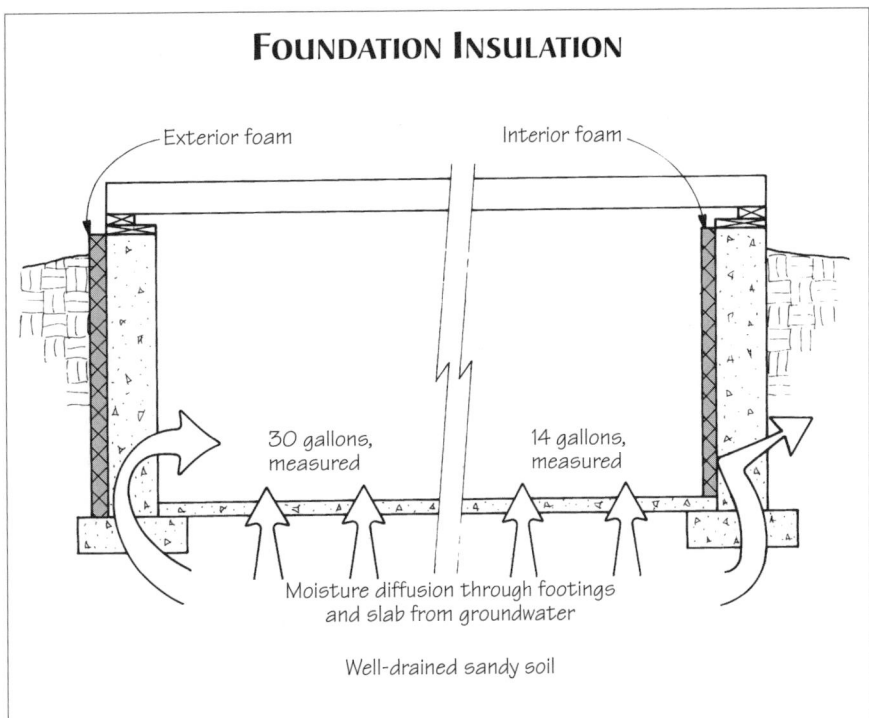

FOUNDATION INSULATION

Exterior foam — Interior foam —

30 gallons, measured — 14 gallons, measured

Moisture diffusion through footings and slab from groundwater

Well-drained sandy soil

Figure 14. Researchers at the University of Minnesota discovered that significant amounts of moisture rise up into the wall through the footings. So placing the insulation on the interior surface is far more effective than on the exterior since the footings are then outside the waterproof layer.

tions and carries moisture into the basement.

In two Canadian test houses, 7.5 and almost 10 gallons of water per day, respectively, were drawn in through basement air leakage when the houses were depressurized with small (125-cfm) exhaust fans. These results indicate that foundations must be properly sealed against air leakage as well as moisture diffusion. Fortunately, many of the techniques used to seal a basement against radon, such as caulked control joints in slabs and airtight sump covers, will also help control water vapor.

Practical Underground Air and Vapor Barriers

As with above-grade air and vapor retarders, proper design is mostly common sense. The vapor retarder should be a durable, low-permeable material that covers most of the foundation on either the inner or outer surface. Neither concrete nor block is a good vapor

retarder. Some type of membrane or parging must be applied.

The air barrier, on the other hand, should be continuous over the entire foundation. Concrete is a suitable air barrier as long as it isn't cracked and all seams and penetrations are sealed.

As with above-grade air and vapor barriers, a single material component, like sealed polyethylene sheeting or rigid foam, can serve as both an air and a vapor barrier. If poly is used on the foundation exterior, the plastic should be heavy-duty (minimum 6-mil) and preferably made for below-grade use. Recommended products include *Cross-Tuff* (Manufactured Plastics and Distribution, 10367 W. Centennial Rd., Littleton, CO 80127; 303/972-0123), *Dura-Tuff* (Yunker Plastics, P.O. Box 190, Lake Geneva, WI 53147; 800/236-3328), and *Tu-Tuff* (StoCote Products, P.O. Box 310, Richmond, IL 60071; 800/435-2621). Another option is to build a stud wall on the interior and

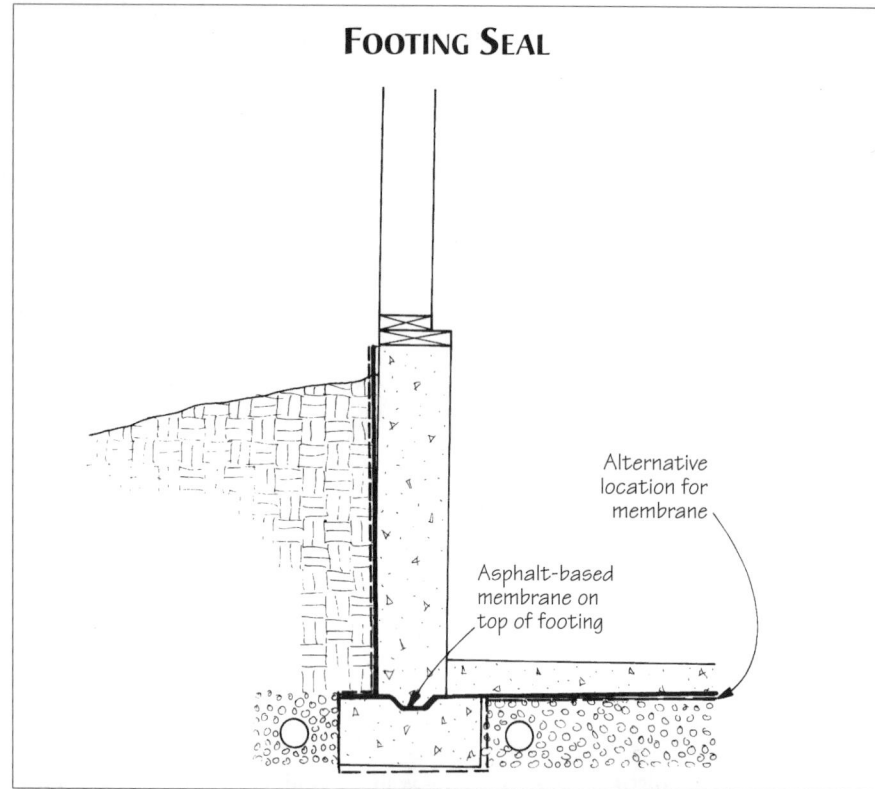

FOOTING SEAL

Alternative
location for
membrane

Asphalt-based
membrane on
top of footing

Figure 15. The best foundation air/vapor barrier is a continuous long-lasting membrane installed under the slab, over the footing, and up the exterior wall surface. An alternative is to install the membrane around the outside of the footing.

important to seal them against air and moisture leakage.

The Footings Question

The Minnesota research clearly suggests that homes can be kept drier by installing a waterproof layer either on top of or underneath the footings. One option commonly used by Swedish builders is to place the high-density polystyrene foam either on top of or underneath footings for thermal and moisture protection.

Despite engineering assurances and Swedish documentation, however, most U.S. builders will be reluctant to build a house on rigid foam. A more palatable alternative is a durable waterproofing membrane. W.R. Meadows, Inc. (P.O. Box 2284, York, PA 17405; 800/342-5976) sells a line of specially reinforced asphaltic membranes for foundation moisture. The company recommends that the membrane be installed over the top of the footing and lapped up the exterior wall surface (Figure 15), but it can also wrap around the bottom of the footing.

By J.D. Ned Nisson, president of Energy Design Associates, a building systems consulting firm in N.Y.C., and editor of Energy Design Update *of Arlington, Mass.*

place the poly under the drywall as you would in a typical outside wall.

Block Foundations

Block foundations are more prone to moisture intrusion than poured foundations. Air circulation within the cores distributes moisture over the entire wall area. Blocks are also very porous to air. You can literally blow through most concrete blocks, so it is especially

USING MOISTURE METERS

I learned about wood moisture content the hard way. One hot, humid New England summer we laid down an absolutely gorgeous solid-cherry plank floor. But after just one winter's worth of dry central heating, the entire floor surface turned into a maze of ugly cracks and wide gaps between the boards. The client's response was none too pretty, either. In another home I worked on around that time, we installed an oak floor over a newly laid plywood substrate. Less than a month later we came back to a rip-

pled floor surface that resembled a mill pond on a breezy autumn day.

The demons that visited those projects were not hidden in the methods we used to put down the floor. Our installation techniques were fine. Nor can I pin the blame upon the woods themselves. Cherry and oak are generally well-mannered species. The fault lay in my ignorance of how wood moves in relation to moisture content, and in not having a couple of crucial instruments: an electronic moisture meter and low-cost digital hygrometer.

Identifying the Problems

In the case of the cherry flooring, although it was kiln-dried, it had probably soaked up a considerable amount of moisture between the time we had it delivered to the site and when we installed it (we stacked it in the client's garage over the summer). The moisture content of the floor boards likely grew to 12% or more, consequently expanding them in width and thickness. Once the floor was laid, the boards had no choice but to shrink and crack over the next winter as the home's heat-

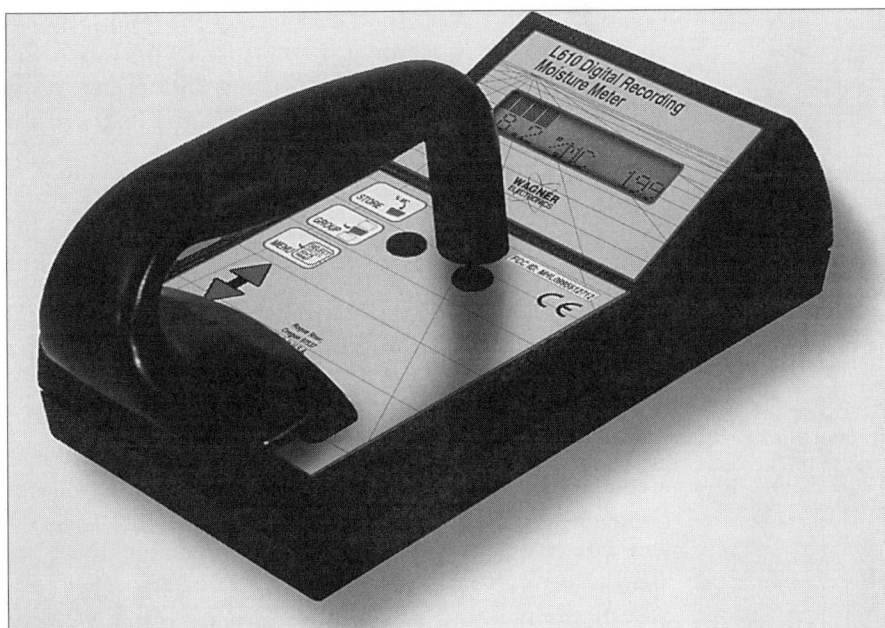
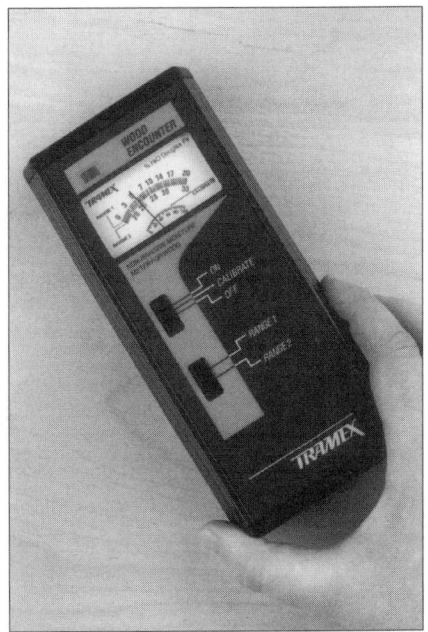

Figure 16. Dielectric meters don't require pushing pins in the material. Instead, you simply pass the meter over the surface. The section of material measured, however, must be at least as wide and thick as the electromagnetic field that the instrument emits.

ing system sucked the moisture out of the wood.

The rippling of the oak flooring, on the other hand, was a result of expansion. If I had the foresight (and the tools) to check the moisture content of the plywood subfloor, which I suspected may have been rained on, I probably would have discovered a level of 15% to 18% — not something I should have put dry wood on. It was only a matter of time before the drier oak sponged up some of this moisture (yes, even through the plastic vapor barrier) and cupped upward as the edges pushed hard against one another.

These days, I never lay down a wood floor without first using a meter to check the amount of moisture in the flooring and sub-flooring.

Meter Types

There are two main types of moisture meters: resistance meters and dielectric meters.

Resistance meters. Resistance-type moisture meters have two sharp metal prongs that pass a low-voltage electric current between them. The wetter a material is, the less resistance that material has to conducting the electric current. Thus, this type of moisture meter is similar to an ohm meter, yet it's calibrated to read a material's resistance as a percentage of moisture content. The range for most meters extends from 6% moisture content (fully seasoned wood in an arid climate) to 36% (unseasoned "green" wood).

To take a reading with a resistance meter, you insert its two electrodes (sharp pins) into the material and read the percentage of moisture content shown on the meter (or series of LED lights). Generally speaking, the deeper you insert the pins, the more accurate the reading will be. Don't prolong taking the reading with a resistance meter, however. As the current passes through the wood, a small amount of electrolysis begins to occur, which sometimes can create an artificially low reading.

Dielectric meters. Dielectric-type meters do not require you to push pins into the material (Figure 16). Instead, these instruments irradiate the material with a low-power (harmless) electromagnetic field that reads the apparent density of the material. Unlike resistance-type meters, which read the moisture of only the wettest fibers lying along a straight line between the two electrodes, the dielectric analyzes a broader area. While this helps ensure a more accurate reading, it can also work against you in some situations. A dielectric meter needs to be held to a mass at least as large in area as the electromagnetic field that the instrument emits. (The field of the Wagner L606, for example, is about $1^3/4$ inches wide by $2^1/2$ inches long by $^3/4$ inches deep.) Resistance meters, on the other hand, can take a reading in nearly any size or configuration of material — you just need enough surface area to push in the two pins.

Using Moisture Meters

There are some tricks when using moisture meters to ensure that you get accurate, consistent readings. First, never be satisfied with a single reading on a board — you could be measuring a dry or wet pocket. Instead, always read a number of

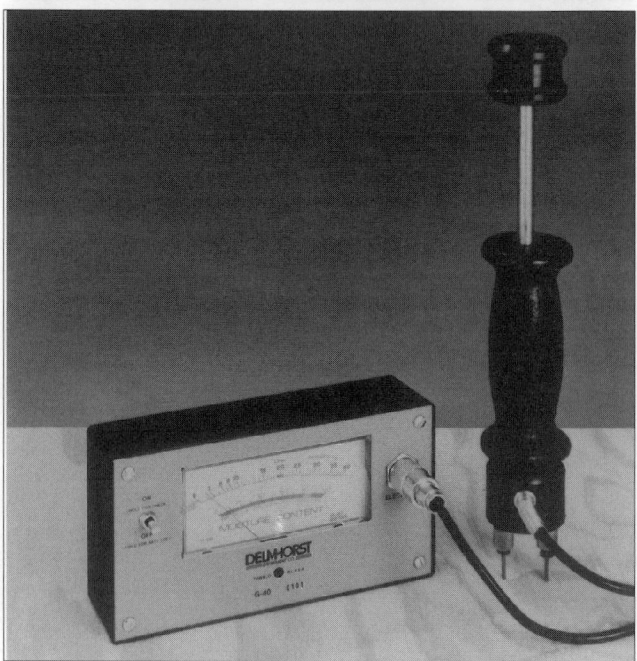

Figure 17. With an inexpensive resistance meter that has short prongs, you will need to make a fresh cut at least 1¹/₂ inches in from one end (top). Or, drive a pair of finish nails to extend the prongs (center). Higher-cost resistance meters often have remote electrodes with interchangeable, insulated pins (bottom).

spots and average the results. It does not usually matter, by the way, if you take the readings with or across the grain. However, it may matter if the wood is rough-sawn — the up-raised fibers tend to dry out or absorb water more quickly than the fibers along a smoothed surface. Whether rough or smooth, always wipe away any standing surface moisture before taking a reading, and if possible, wait to allow the surface of the board to dry.

Measure at the core. If the board is thicker than 1 inch, you should take a reading at the core to see if it is substantially wetter than the surfaces.

With a resistance meter, you can do this in two ways: The first is to make a fresh crosscut to expose the interior of the board, then push the pins into the end grain. Unless the board has been exposed to rain, you need not make the cut more than 3 inches in from the rough end to get an accurate reading. The other option is to drive the electrodes through the face into the core of the board. If your meter has only short electrodes, you can drive a pair of finish nails into the core (set them in at the pin spacing) and take a reading off their heads (Figure 17). You should paint the nail shanks so the meter's current passes between the tips. The shanks of long-pin electrodes are usually insulated.

Because the field depth of most dielectric meters is about 1 inch, they automatically read to the core of a 2-inch-thick board. You'll need to measure off a fresh end grain cut if the board is thicker.

Taking readings of thin boards can be tricky with any type of moisture meter. Dielectrics cannot, for example, read any material less than about ¹/₂ inch thick. Even at this dimension you must be sure nothing sits directly behind the wood, as any type of material (especially metal) can throw off the reading. The trick to reading thin stock with dielectrics is to gather up enough stock to make a stack about 3/4 inch high. The reading then automatically averages the moisture content of all the pieces.

Watch the variables. To ensure an accurate reading, you must take several variables into account (see "Getting Accurate Moisture Readings"). Most resistance meters are calibrated to a certain temperature setting and to one species (or to be more precise, to the specific gravity of that species). You then have to calculate the true reading by multiplying the number shown on the meter by an adjustment percentile taken from a chart to correct for temperature and species. Top-of-the-line resistance meters (such as Lignomat's Mini-Master and Lignomaster series) use microprocessors to automatically calculate these adjustments for you, once you've punched in numbers for the correct species and temperature.

Dielectric instruments are unaffected by temperature or humidity, which is a distinct advantage over resistance meters. But you must still make corrections from a chart for species (the Wagner models, for example, are calibrated to Douglas fir).

Measuring the moisture in plywood. Taking moisture content readings of plywood or other manmade wood products containing glues and compressed wood fibers is problematic. While many meter manufacturers can provide you with calibration tables for some of these materials, you might consider this simple, but accurate, approach instead: Measure a sample that you've thoroughly dried in an oven (you'll know it's dry when no more weight is lost after about 24 hours in a 220°F oven). The meter should read zero. If it doesn't, record the reading and add this number to correct each reading.

If you suspect that your meter is consistently taking untrue readings — or if a bone-dry sample doesn't read zero — you may need to send the instrument back to the manufacturer for recalibration. But first check the zero adjustment of the needle, the condition of the battery, and the cleanliness of the electrodes or sensor pad.

Measuring Moisture in the Air

For first-rate finish work, it's often not enough to just monitor the moisture in the wood, then slap the boards down when they've reached a suitable moisture content. You also have to make some attempt to monitor the moisture in the air on site while the wood is in storage awaiting installation.

To measure the moisture content of the surrounding air (the humidity level), I use a low-cost digital hygrometer. This tool can tell me what will happen to the wood when

---

GETTING ACCURATE MOISTURE READINGS

To ensure accurate readings in wood, watch out for these variables:

- *Species.* With either simple dielectric or resistance meters, you have to correct for the wood species. Simple resistance meters are calibrated to one species (typically Doug fir). For any other species, you have to calculate a true reading by multiplying by a number shown on a chart to correct for that species.
- *Temperature.* With resistance meters you also have to correct for temperature, using a similar chart. Dielectric meters are not as sensitive to different temperatures. However, if the wood temperature is below freezing, a dielectric meter may give a reading that erroneously adds 15% to the apparent moisture content.
- *Wild grain or knots.* Dielectrics are particularly affected by

anomalous changes in the wood's density. Try to avoid knots and wild grain.

- *Surface moisture.* Always wipe the surface off and allow it to dry if possible. This is more of a problem with inexpensive resistance meters with short, uninsulated pins, because the meter will read the path of least resistance — in this case, saturated surface fibers. Better resistance meters (the Delmhorst with a 26 ES electrode, for example) have long insulated pins that eliminate this problem. Also, if wood is rough-sawn, the raised fibers absorb or lose moisture more readily than a smooth-surface board, producing untrue readings near the surface with resistance meters.
- *Finishes.* Some finishes and preservatives contain salts that can affect resistance meters. (Dielectric meters are unaf-

fected by these salts.) To check if a finish is affecting the reading, dry a finished sample in the oven and then check it with the meter. If it reads wet, the finish has salt in it, so you won't be able to rely on a resistance meter.

- *Microenvironments.* Avoid taking readings of installed components — like flooring — in areas subjected to direct sun, heat outlets, or excessive dampness.
- *Readouts.* Resistance-type meters with LED readouts may be affected by ambient static electricity or electromagnetic fields. Near motors or wires carrying current, readings may fluctuate or two lights may come on at the same time. Move the wood away from the affected area and try again. Dielectric meters are unaffected by stray electromagnetic fields.

— J.T.

LOW-COST HUMIDITY METERS

Problem scenario: Homeowner calls builder, complaining of condensation dripping from "those crummy windows." Builder asks homeowner what the humidity in the house is. Homeowner reads 30% relative humidity from the brass dial humidity meter on the wall. So begins another moisture callback.

Since one primary cause of moisture problems is high indoor relative humidity, and since most "hardware store" humidity meters are notoriously inaccurate, the first step to resolve this problem should be a visit to the home with an accurate portable hygrometer. The problem is finding one.

Digital meters. A recent research project by Canada Mortgage and Housing Corporation (CMHC) showed that those digital units cannot always be relied on for accuracy.

CMHC tested three different brands: Bionaire, Micronta (made by Radio Shack), and Thermo-Hygro (made by Airguide, and sold under many other brand names). When placed in a calibration cham-ber, the Bionaire and Micronta units were accurate to within 5% of the humidity range from about 25% to 80%. But the Thermo-Hygro read up to 20% too high over the entire range.

According to an environmental consultant who has extensively studied these meters, most of the low-cost digital hygrometers, including all three in the CMHC tests, are produced by the same company. All three use the same *Shinyei* humidity sensor. The only difference between the various models is the packaging of the electronics.

In general, the Shinyei sensor is fairly accurate and reliable. The problem is in occasional manufacturing inconsistencies — now and then, you will get one that is way off. If you buy just one of these meters, there is no guarantee that it's accurate.

There are two solutions to this problem. The first is to have the meter checked against a calibrated hygrometer. The other is to test several units and look for agree-ment. If they all agree, they are probably accurate.

Mechanical meters. When all is said and done, a simple mechanical meter may be a builder's best bet. According to CMHC researchers, if you use a simple calibration procedure to verify the accuracy of a dial hygrometer, you have the best chance for getting an accurate reading.

The calibration procedure goes like this: Mix $1/2$ cup of table salt (sodium chloride) with $1/4$ cup water in a coffee cup. The salt doesn't have to dissolve, it just needs to be stirred so the water covers the salt. Then put this mixture with the dial meter in a Zip-lock bag (an airtight environment) and let it sit for about 8 hours so the temperatures of the mixture and the meter equalize. The salt mixture will create a climate with 75% relative humidity inside the bag.

If the meter does not read 75%, you can reset the dial position by either giving the indicator a delicate twist, or by adjusting a screw, if it has one. Some dial-type humidity meters have fancy cases that prevent you from moving the needle. So if a model doesn't have the screw adjust, it's better to steer clear of it.

This procedure will calibrate most mechanical meters to within ±5%, which is an acceptable degree of accuracy for most builders. The only meter the CMHC team was unable to accurately calibrate was the Taylor 6567. This model had problems below 40% relative humidity.

When reading the humidity level, according to CMHC, a builder is looking for broad differences — those between 20%, 40%, and 75%. Properly calibrated, a mechanical humidity meter will do this for you.

Adapted with permission from Energy Design Update, published monthly by Cutter Information Corp. of Arlington, Mass.

Digital hygrometer. *A simple electronic hygrometer can measure the relative humidity on site where trim stock is stored. Not all meters read accurately, however. Compare the meter to several others of the same make, or to a calibrated mechanical model, to make sure it reads accurately.*

it's placed in a certain environment. It's also useful as a troubleshooting tool in new and old houses, but you need to make sure you get an accurate one (see "Low-Cost Humidity Meters").

When measuring the humidity in the storage area, you want a relative humidity that's similar to what's inside the house — anything in the range of 30% to 50%. Most of all I want to avoid storing dry wood in a humid environment, or installing dry wood in an abnormally moist interior climate. If the wood measures 7% to 8% moisture content at 70°F on the moisture meter, for example, it will be perfectly stable in an environment that maintains this temperature at a relative humidity level of 35%. If the hygrometer reads a higher humidity level in the storage area or room in which the wood is to be installed, I can be sure that the wood will suck in some moisture and expand (and I can tell my client that). Changes in ambient relative humidity have a much greater effect on the moisture content in the wood than changes in temperature alone. On more than one occasion, my use of the humidity meter along with my moisture meter has nipped a potential problem in the bud — or explained the flowering of another.

By Jim Tolpin, a finish carpenter in Port Townsend, Wash.

SOURCES OF SUPPLY

Epoxy Resins

Abatron Inc.
5501 95th Ave.
Kenosha, WI 53144
800/445-1754
LiquidWood, WoodEpox

Sika Corp.
201 Polito Ave.
Lyndhurst, NJ 07071
800/933-7452
Colma-Dur Gel, Sikadur Hi-Mod

Borax-Based Wood Preservatives

Bethel Products Inc.
P.O. Box 176
New Carlisle, OH 45344
513/845-2380
AquaBor

Nisus Corp.
215 Duravent Dr.
Rockford, TN 37853
800/264-0870
Bora-Care, Impel Rods

Chemical Specialties Inc.
One Woodlawn Green, Suite 250
200 E. Woodlawn Rd.
Charlotte, NC 28217
704/522-0825
Impel Rods

U.S. Borax, Inc.
26877 Tourney Rd.
Valencia, CA 91355-1847
805/287-5400
Tim-Bor

Moisture Meters

Delmhorst Instrument Co.
51 Indian Ln. East
Towaco, NJ 07082
201/334-2557

SDS Company
P.O. Box 844
Paso Robles, CA 93447
805/238-3229

Wagner Electronic Products
326 Pine Grove Rd.
Rogue River, OR 97537
800/944-7078

Lignomat USA
P.O. Box 30145
Portland, OR 97294
800/227-2105

Veritas
12 E. River St.
Ogdensburg, NY 13669
613/596-1922

Humidity Meters

Bionaire
2000 32nd Ave.
Lachine, Quebec H8T 3H7
800/253-2764

Radio Shack
P.O. Box 1052
Fort Worth, TX 76102
817/390-3011
(or check the Yellow Pages for local listings)

Sonin
670 White Plains Rd.
Scarsdale, NY 10583
800/223-7511

CHAPTER 10

INSECT DAMAGE

- Wood-Destroying Insects

- Controlling Termites and
  Carpenter Ants with Borates

- Controlling Subterranean Termites

WOOD-DESTROYING INSECTS

One and one-half billion dollars is spent annually in the U.S. to treat, repair, and replace wood in buildings that has been damaged by wood-destroying insects. Recognizing damage is usually pretty easy, but figuring out who's responsible can be tricky. Since selection of the right remedial treatment depends on knowing who's responsible, it's important to identify the offenders.

With this primer on some of wood's six-legged pests, you should be able to figure out who's been eating you and your customers out of house and home.

Termites

With two thirds of the total annual infestation control bill spent on this insect alone, termites are by far the most economically damaging pest plaguing wood structures. Though more than 50 species of termites live in the U.S., about 95% of all damage is done by subterranean termites, which nest underground. Other termites of local significance include drywood termites found along America's southern border from California to Florida, dampwood termites of the coastal Pacific Northwest, and a recent exotic arrival in several Gulf states, the Formosan termite.

Lacking the natural antifreeze of other insects, subterranean termites cannot hibernate during freezing weather and must remain active year-round. Concentrated in the Southeast, they have expanded northward only since the early 1900s with the widespread adoption of central heating. These soil-dwellers live in large colonies whose six-legged citizenry is divided into castes of kings and queens, workers, and soldiers. Responsible for reproduction, kings and queens are black or brown, up to 1/2 inch long, and winged. Sterile, eyeless, and wingless, workers are white and 1/4 inch long (Figure 1). Rarely seen because they avoid light, workers maintain the nest and, in foraging for food, destroy wood. Some metamorphose into soldiers who fend off invaders with menacing mandibles.

After several years of colony growth, swarms of winged reproductives will emerge from the soil in spring, usually in daylight and after a rain, and fly off to establish a new colony. Termites stake out new territories based on their need for high soil moisture and a readily available source of wood from which they derive their diet of cellulose. Once a suitable site is found, reproductives shed their wings and reenter the ground.

In nature, termites feast on downed and dead trees and stumps

Figure 1. Termite workers (top left) are 1/4 inch long and wingless. They avoid light and thus are rarely seen. After several years of colony growth, winged adults (top right) emerge briefly and swarm to establish new colonies. Termites will tunnel in all wood products, except for PT, and can cause serious structural damage (above) — typically hidden below an unbroken wood surface.

and may forage for food 100 feet or so from their underground headquarters. In buildings, termites will attack virtually all wood- and cellulose-based building materials. In addition to structural lumber, plywood, flooring, and siding, I've found their damage in woodfiber insulation board sheathing, cardboard forming tubes, wastepaper-based cellulose insulation, and even the paper faces of gypsum wallboard. Though attracted to odors given off by moist or decaying wood,

termites will attack wood at a moisture content as low as 8%, which is typical of the year-round average moisture content of indoor wood across most of the U.S. No species of untreated wood is immune from attack, but wood pressure-impregnated with CCA (chromated copper arsenate) preservative is an effective deterrent.

Termites usually enter structures through existing gaps at or below grade. If they can't find shrinkage and settlement cracks in foundations

and slabs or gaps at electrical, plumbing, and septic penetrations, they build shelter tubes of soil and digested wood up the sides of exposed foundations to reach the wood above. Contrary to popular belief, metal shields inserted between foundation and sill won't stop termites from entering, as these beasties will simply build shelter tubes up and over such inconveniences. Shields, however, do force shelter tubes to be built where they are more easily visible, prevent termites

WOOD-DESTROYING INSECTS AT A GLANCE

	Preferred Wood Type	Preferred Wood Moisture Content	Emergence/ Bore Holes	Galleries and Frass	Possible Reinfestation	Typical Source of Infestation	Remarks
Termite	Softwood, hardwood, sapwood, heartwood, old wood, new wood*	>8%	Seldom seen; uses existing gaps, cracks	Messy, packed with excrema, soil, wood fragments	Yes	Enters heated buildings from soil	Seldom seen except when swarming; discarded wings indicate presence
Carpenter Ant	Softwood, hardwood, sapwood, heartwood, old wood, new wood*	>15%	Seldom seen; uses existing gaps, cracks	Clean with "sandpapered" walls; insect parts and shredded wood near nest	Yes	Enters heated and unheated buildings from soil	Often seen foraging in building though nest is in nearby tree or stump
True Powderpost Beetle	Hardwood, sapwood, new wood*	6% to 30%	Round, 1/32" to 1/8"	Loosely packed with very fine powder	Yes	Brought into buildings in infected furniture, flooring, firewood, etc.	Hardwoods coated with film-forming finishes safe from attack
Old House Borer	Softwood, sapwood, new wood*	10% to 30%	Oval, 1/4" to 3/8"	Tightly packed with fine powder and tiny pellets; walls with ripple-marks	Yes	Brought into buildings in infected new and salvaged lumber; can enter from outside	Larvae in wood make rasping, ticking, or clicking sound
Anobiid Beetle	Softwood, hardwood, sapwood, old wood, new wood*	13% to 30%	Round, 1/16" to 1/8"	Loosely packed with fine powder and tiny pellets	Yes	Enters damp areas like crawlspaces and basements from outside	Infestations develop slowly; 30 holes per sq. ft. indicates well established infestation

* "New wood" is less than ten years old; "old wood" is more than ten years old.

from entering sills directly through hollow masonry block foundations, and provide a capillary break between concrete and wood.

Poor building practices that invite termites include burying stumps, cutoffs, and other wood debris during backfilling, failing to remove

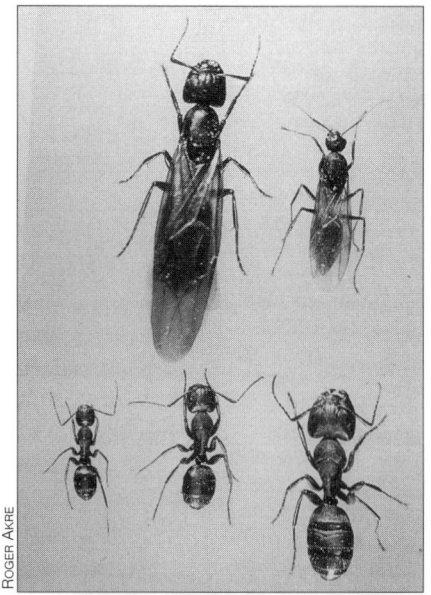

ROGER AKRE

DON JACKSON

Figure 2. Carpenter ant queens and males are winged and up to an inch long. Workers range from 1/8 to 1/2 inch long (top). Carpenter ants don't eat wood, but carve tunnels for nesting — preferring moist decayed wood or foam insulation. Tunnels in wood (above) run parallel to the grain.

wood or cardboard concrete forms, using untreated wood in ground contact, extending siding and trim to 6 inches above grade or below, and leaving soil exposed in crawlspaces. Termites' high soil-moisture needs can be met by omitting gutters and downspouts, backfilling with poor-draining soils, or failing to provide adequate foundation and site drainage.

Undetected, termite damage can lead to serious structural damage and even collapse. Because termites hollow out the interiors of wood members without breaking through the surface, there are few visible signs of their presence. Symptoms include blistered or puckered wood surfaces, crushed and collapsed wood at framing bearing points, and fine soil lining the edges of cracks in concrete and masonry. Termite-damaged wood resounds with a dull thud when tapped with a hammer. When broken open, termite galleries (tunnels) are characteristically messy and often filled with a mixture of fecal matter, soil, and chewed wood that looks like dried oatmeal. Because they prefer to tunnel parallel to the grain in the softer early wood portion of growth rings, damaged wood may appear as a series of concentric shells of late wood. In the absence of live insects, there are a few clues that reveal whether termite damage is ongoing. Clouds of swarming insects and piles of shed wings nearby strongly suggest it; shelter tubes that reappear after being destroyed confirm it.

Creating a toxic moat around your customer's castle by treating soil with a pesticide before footings, foundation, and slab are poured is the best defense against termite invasion in new construction. Infestations in existing buildings can be treated by pressure-inject-ing pesticide into the soil surrounding the foundation and beneath the slab. Though over-the-counter termiticides are available, treating

for termites is best left to reputable professionals.

Carpenter Ants

Carpenter ants, though found throughout the U.S., are primarily a problem in the Northeast and Northwest. Like termites, these colonial insects live mainly underground. Unlike termites, carpenter ants don't actually eat wood, but tunnel in it only as a place to live. The distinction may seem trivial, but it's not. CCA-treated wood, for example, while immune to termite attack, is still susceptible to carpenter ant destruction because they don't ingest the tainted wood.

Most of the many kinds of native carpenter ants are black or black and dark red. Kings and queens (reproductives) are winged and up to one inch long. Wingless workers are 1/8 to 1/2 inch long (Figure 2). Carpenter ants may nest underground, in live and dead trees, in stumps, in stored lumber and firewood, and inside wood buildings. Those nesting outdoors hibernate during freezing weather, while ants cozying up inside heated buildings may be active all year. Workers forage for food up to 150 feet from their nest. Plant juices, "honeydew" secreted by aphids, insects, and household food scraps make up the menu.

Winged carpenter ants swarm from mature nests in spring to establish new colonies, shedding their wings before nesting anew. Often mistaken for termites, and vice versa, it's easy to tell the two apart. Carpenter ants have two pairs of wings of unequal length, a con-stricted, hourglass waist, and "elbowed" antennae. Both pairs of termites' wings are the same length, and their waists and antennae straight. Color alone tells you that so-called "white ants" are actually worker termites.

Ants enter buildings via the same routes as termites, but they don't build shelter tubes. No untreated wood (not even CCA-treated wood) is safe from ant attack. These hexapods prefer wood whose moisture content is 15% or higher and are especially attracted to decayed wood. As owners of stressed-skin panel homes have learned, carpenter ants will also tunnel in the panels' foam cores. Panel makers now treat the foam with a pesticide and recommend that panel edges near grade be capped with a metal shield.

Carpenter ants excavate an irregular maze of tunnels in wood parallel to the grain, often following softer early wood. Fastidious in habit, their galleries are free of debris, with signature "sandpapered" walls. Extensive tunneling can weaken structural members, but ant infestations are usually detected long before damage becomes serious. A sure sign of activity is the coarse shreds of wood called frass, and occasionally insect parts, that workers dispose of through joints and cracks outside the nests as they tidy their tunnels. In established infestations, ants can sometimes be heard gnawing on wood.

Live ants seen inside a home may or may not mean the building is infested. If, for example, only a few ants show up each day and it's late spring or summer, they're probably workers on a foraging expedition from a nest in a nearby tree or stump. Don't overlook the possibility of ants escaping from firewood brought inside. However, if more than a few are appearing inside daily while the ground is still cold, then a nest hidden in a wall may have gotten the late winter sun's wakeup call. Consistently large numbers of ants seen inside during the winter or winged ants seen inside any time of year are sure signs of an indoor nest.

Inviting trouble spots include eaves and walls wetted by roof leaks, ice dams, condensation, and overflowing or leaky gutters. Plumbing leaks and within-wall condensation can raise wood moisture content to

ant-attractive levels. Exposed soil, wood in ground contact, inadequate ventilation, and poor foundation and site drainage create crawlspace and basement moisture conditions that attract ants. Homeowners can attract ants by leaving crumbs about or by putting pet food in bowls outdoors.

Once a carpenter ant nest has been located, usually by observing the path by which foraging workers travel, it can be easily treated. When a nest behind a wall can't be precisely located, professional exterminators may resort to a "shotgun" approach, spraying pesticide through bored holes in hopes of hitting the hideaway.

Old House Borers

One type of long-horned beetle common in the mid-Atlantic states, the misnamed "old house borer," primarily infests wood that has been in service for ten years or less. This brownish-black 1/2- to 1-inch-long beetle has lengthy antennae and twin bumps on its thorax. But it's in the worm-like larval stage that this bugger does damage to attic framing, floor joists over crawlspaces and

basements, and other softwood structural members (Figure 3).

After larvae emerge from eggs deposited in drying checks or joints between framing members, they immediately bore into wood. Homeowners may hear the faint ticking sound these white, up to 1 1/4-inch-long larvae make when tunneling. Though their attack is limited to

Figure 3. Old house borer larvae (at right) attack the sapwood of structural members. They may feed for three to seven years before emerging from 1/4- to 3/8-inch exit holes as adult beetles (at left).

Figure 4. Powderpost beetles (left) are no more than 1/4 inch long, and are reddish-brown to black. The larvae attack only the sapwood of porous hardwoods, like oak, ash, and elm. Fresh frass the color of new wood indicates an active infestation (right).

USDA

STEPHEN SMULSKI

Figure 5. Anobiid beetles (top) are $^1/_8$ to $^1/_4$ inch long. Attracted by moist conditions, they fly into the house and lay eggs in cracks and checks in wood (center). The larvae attack the sapwood of hardwood or softwood for three or more years, then emerge as adult beetles from $^1/_{16}$- to $^1/_8$-inch round exit holes (above).

the sapwood, it is so thorough that the wood beneath a thin, intact surface layer may be completely pulverized. Oval larval tunnels, running parallel to the grain and up to $^3/_8$ inch wide, are tightly packed with fine powder and rod-shaped fecal pellets. Walls are characteristically ripple-marked, looking like sand that's been lapped by waves. Larvae feed in wood for three to seven years before emerging as adult beetles sometime between July and October. Adults leave wood through $^1/_4$- to $^3/_8$-inch oval exit holes previously made by larvae. Occasionally exit holes are chewed through the materials covering infested lumber — wood sheathing, siding, flooring, and even gypsum wallboard. Exit holes are often the first and only sign of infestation seen by homeowners. Fortunately, the majority of infestations die out once adults emerge.

Most old house borer infestations are caused during construction of new homes when softwood lumber infected during drying or storage or salvaged wood is used. Beetles can infest or reinfest wood older than ten years, providing its nutritional content is still high and its moisture content exceeds 10%. Even professionals find it difficult to determine whether an old house borer infestation is active. Two sure signs of ongoing activity are the sounds made by tunneling larvae and the reappearance of fresh frass on cleaned surfaces. In the absence of exit holes, bulging or blistered wood surfaces over powder-packed tunnels indicate activity.

True Powderpost Beetles

Three distinct insects, true powderpost beetles, false powderpost beetles, and anobiid beetles, are collectively called powderpost beetles, because each reduces wood to a fine powdery frass. Of these, true powderpost beetles and anobiids are the more common.

True powderpost beetles occur throughout the U.S. and are second

only to termites in the dollar damage done. From residences in dead trees, they routinely infest hardwood logs and lumber at sawmills and storage yards. Reddish-brown to black, and at most $^1/_4$ inch long, occasionally-seen adults lay eggs only in the large early wood pores of ring-porous hardwoods, like oak, ash, and elm, that are less than ten years old (Figure 4).

After hatching, these larvae limit their attack to sapwood with a moisture content of 6% to 30%, where they tunnel extensively in search of stored starch. Hidden under a veneer of unaffected wood, galleries are loosely packed with talcum powder-like frass that sifts from drying checks and $^1/_{32}$- to $^1/_8$-inch round bore holes. Adults emerge from wood between April and September after one to two years. Infestations tend to die out naturally as the carbohydrate content of wood drops over the first few years, but reinfestation can occur if favorable food and moisture conditions persist.

True powderpost beetles most commonly enter homes as eggs or larvae in new hardwood flooring, furniture, and millwork. Tropical hardwood products are frequently a source of infestation because of inadequate wood storage and drying practices in the countries of origin. They may lurk in firewood, antique furniture, and tools recovered from unheated buildings. Hardwoods coated with film-forming finishes are safe from attack, as the coating clogs pores where adults lay eggs. In many cases, damage is limited to a single piece of flooring or trim, so removal of the affected item solves the problem. Adults and larvae can be killed by freezing or by heat-sterilizing wood at 135°F. If exit holes or adult beetles aren't seen within five years after a home has been built, chances are they'll never show up.

Again, it's difficult to gauge whether or not true powderpost beetle activity is ongoing. One way is to vacuum up all frass and mark existing bore holes. The reappearance of frass and new holes over the next few months confirms activity. Fresh frass is bright and cream-colored like new wood; old frass sifting from an inactive infestation is yellow or brown.

Anobiid Beetles

Anobiids, such as the common furniture beetle and the deathwatch beetle, also make their natural home in dead trees. While concentrated in the Southeast, their handiwork can be found in homes in the northeastern, north-central, and Pacific coastal states as well. The least discriminating of the powderpost beetles, anobiids attack the sapwood of softwoods and hardwoods, regardless of age. Attracted to wood with a 13% to 30% moisture content as well as decayed wood, anobiids most often infest framing in damp crawlspaces and basements.

Rarely seen, adults are $1/8$ to $1/4$ inch long and reddish-black to black (Figure 5). Eggs are deposited in drying checks, on rough-sawn lumber surfaces, and in joints. Tunnels excavated by larvae are loosely packed with fine powder and lemon-shaped fecal pellets that feel gritty when rubbed between the fingers. Adults emerge after three or more years from $1/16$- to $1/8$-inch round exit holes from which frass freely sifts. Anobiid infestations develop so slowly that the few exit holes present may go unnoticed for ten or more years. Thirty or more holes per square foot indicates a well-established infestation. Reinfestation is routine.

Unlike true powderpost beetles, anobiids rarely enter homes via infected wood. Adults fly in directly from the outside, invited by the moist conditions found in crawlspaces and basements lacking soil covers, proper ventilation, and foundation and site drainage. The same techniques for detecting and treating true powderpost beetle infestations are used for anobiids.

By Dr. Stephen Smulski, president of Wood Science Specialists Inc., in Shutesbury, Mass., a consulting firm specializing in wood performance problems in light-frame structures.

CONTROLLING TERMITES AND CARPENTER ANTS WITH BORATES

Borates are an ideal material for protecting buildings from carpenter ants, termites, and other wood-damaging pests. They are effective against a broad spectrum of pests and decay fungi, have no odor, do not discolor wood, and are no more toxic to humans than common table salt.

They also offer deep penetration of dry wood compared to other insecticides and are readily available from a network of pesticide formulators and distributors. Because they are so effective and so benign to the environment, the use of borates is growing rapidly.

Treated Wood Popular Abroad

If you were a builder in New Zealand, you would be legally required to use borate-treated wood for the house framework — a technique used successfully there since 1955. Framing lumber pressure-treated with borate is also readily available to builders in Hawaii and the U.S. Virgin Islands.

On the mainland U.S., however, borate-treated wood is available from only a handful of lumber companies around the country, primarily suppliers to the log-home industry.

Where borate-treated lumber is not available, another approach is to apply borates in the field during construction. This option is growing in use by licensed pest control operators (PCOs), largely due to the environmental concerns PCOs face regarding more toxic chemicals.

Common Uses of Borates

Borate is a generic term for compounds containing the elements boron and oxygen. Examples of borates include boric acid, borax, and disodium octaborate tetrahydrate (DOT). Boron compounds are pervasive in our daily lives. The average person consumes about 25 mg every day if following a balanced diet containing fruits and vegetables. Trace amounts of borates occur in eye washes, cosmetics, and mouth washes; large quantities are found in washing powders (20 Mule-Team Borax), and fire retardants.

Some people may be familiar with boron's pesticidal properties from their experience with various cockroach control products, which are essentially just boric acid. Mention Bora-care or Tim-bor, however, and a blank look results. EPA registration was granted for Bora-care, a glycol/borate formulation containing DOT, as an insecticide and preservative in 1989. Tim-bor, a brand name for DOT, was registered as a preservative in 1973 and as an insecticide in 1990.

How Do Borates Kill Insects?

Research suggests that borates inhibit enzymes that aid food breakdown in the gut of insects. In most cases, insects must ingest some boron from food or from cleansing themselves to be killed.

While a tiny amount of boron can kill individual termites, to repel them you need at least 1,500 ppm (about 0.9% boric acid on a weight to weight basis in wood). Minimizing damage from Formosan termites (found in Hawaii and Southern coastal regions) requires 3,500 ppm (2.0% boric acid).

Worker termites eating a small amount of boron live long enough to transfer boron-tainted food to other colony members by feeding soldiers, young, and reproductives. In this way the boron acts as a slow-acting toxic "bait," often eliminating most or all of a colony.

Thus, borates offer the same capability as the new termite baiting systems now being widely promoted without requiring expensive monitoring and repeat applications. In fact, a one-time application of borates to structures may permanently repel attacks by termites, wood-destroying beetles, and decay fungi as long as the borates are not subjected to persistent exposure to water.

How Do Borates Penetrate Wood?

Field-applied borates penetrate wood by a combination of absorption and diffusion. In diffusion, the chemical moves through the water in the wood from a high concentration on the surface to a lower concentration within. For effective diffusion to occur, the wood must be above the fiber-saturation point (about 25% moisture content). Complete, rapid penetration by diffusion requires unseasoned wood with 40%, and preferably higher, moisture content and several weeks of storage where drying of wood is restricted (such as tarping). Some borates also enter by absorption of water into the surface of the wood.

In new construction treated on site, borates will typically penetrate $1/8$ to $3/8$ inch beneath treated surfaces. Penetration will be somewhat deeper if the wood has higher than average moisture levels. Even without completely penetrating wood, borates may still effectively prevent insect attacks. Here's why.

The amount of boron in the outer layer of treated wood typically ranges from about 1,500 to 2,500 ppm — well above the levels needed to kill insects. Also, boron will continue to slowly penetrate the wood by diffusion, absorption, or movement across the wood surface (when wetted from condensation). The high humidity typically found in new homes the first year can work to your advantage here. Data also show that ends and backsides of studs may obtain borate even when not directly treated, although it is best not to cut any wood after treatment, since untreated ends would be exposed.

Borates also uniquely exploit termite feeding and foraging habits. Subterranean termites typically build tubes of soil to the wood being attacked. Because the termites keep the tubes and wood moist with water from the soil, borates quickly diffuse into the damaged wood and tubes.

WHERE TO TREAT WITH BORATES

For Carpenter Ants or Drywood Termites

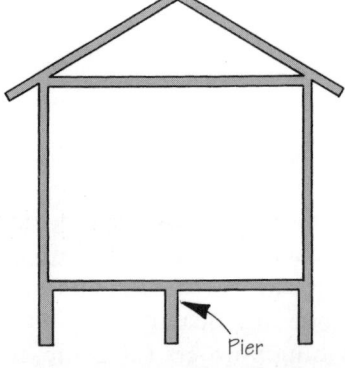

All exposed wood on interior and exterior walls, partition walls, crawlspace, and attic

Subterranean Termites (with Tim-bor)

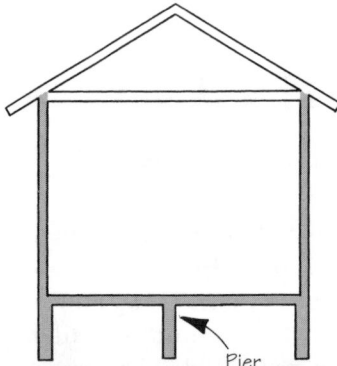

All exposed wood on interior and exterior walls, partition walls, and crawlspace

Subterranean Termites (with Bora-Care)

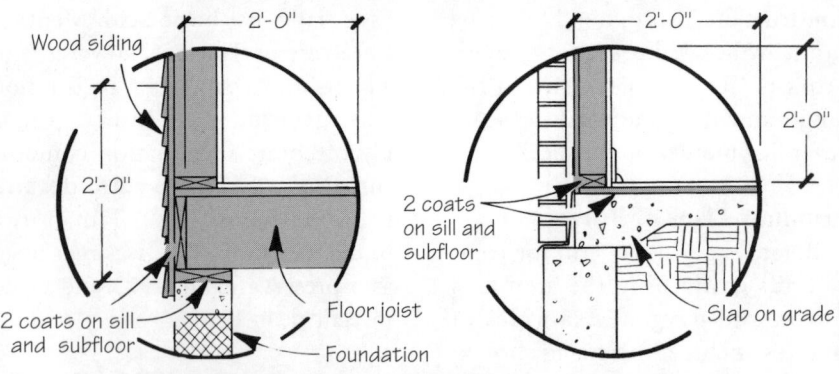

A 2-foot uninterrupted band above sills around perimeter walls; all wood 2 feet in from foundation wall or crawlspace perimeter; 2 feet around all piers, utility openings, fireplaces, and connections to porches and garages

Thus, many termites contact boron and are discouraged from building more tubes or feeding.

Limitations of Borates

One concern with borates is that they are soluble in water and can, therefore, leach out if moisture is present. This characteristic can be an advantage up to a point in that it helps you achieve better treatment of building timbers. However, it limits the usefulness of borates for exterior uses because extensive leaching would occur within a few years. Therefore borates should not be applied to exterior wood unless it is subsequently coated with paint, water repellent, or other covering. And although borates can be effectively injected in timbers with ground contact, they do not last long in that application.

The key uncertainty concerning borate treatment in new construction is how well it controls subterranean termites over the long term. Although testing and field experience over the past five to ten years is very positive, it does not go back far enough to be conclusive. However, with many documented failures of traditional soil treatments, many PCOs believe that the best approach available today is borate treatment of wood as a supplement to soil treatment with termiticide.

Borates are also proving themselves effective as a stand-alone pretreatment in new construction. If field experience with borates shows continuing success, increasing consumer demand may permanently change the traditional approach to termite prevention.

Regulations

The federal EPA requires that anyone who provides services or products which claim to prevent or control pests must use EPA-registered products or face stiff fines. Every EPA-registered product carries a label that specifies the pest and application site, and PCOs are required to follow that label.

While some borate compounds are labelled for use against termites, other institutional barriers to their use exist. For example, in most Southern states and many other areas, certified termite treatment by PCOs is required to get building permits and financing from a bank. Termite treatments are inspected and enforced by structural pest control officials in about 35 states. In most cases, these regulators require soil treatment with termiticide around and beneath the foundation, as has been done for 50 years.

If code or loan officials in your area are uncertain about borates, you may sway them with the following facts:

- Bora-care literature states that it is "recognized by EPA as a primary termiticide treatment for both eliminating existing infestations and preventing future infestations."
- Tim-bor literature reports that it is used as a preventive treatment by PCOs.
- Traditional termiticide soil barrier treatments are frequently failing partly because termites can transport untreated soil to build "bridges" across these barriers. This has been verified by PCOs, regulators, and government researchers.
- Many PCOs currently supplement soil treatments with borate wood treatments.

Even with official approval, concerns about property value and potential liability will deter most builders in termite-prone areas from treating houses solely with borates. However, readers who live where termite-control regulations are limited or where carpenter ants cause more damage than termites should consider borates as a viable option. Anyone can use labeled or unlabeled products, including borates, to treat houses they are building for them-

selves or existing houses they own (see "Sources of Supply" at end of chapter).

Preventive Treatment of New Construction

I strongly recommend carefully reading labels and company literature for the major EPA-labeled borate pesticides whether you're hiring a PCO or applying the product yourself. Why? The labels and literature, especially from Nisus Corp., provide many details about the insects and their treatment. These

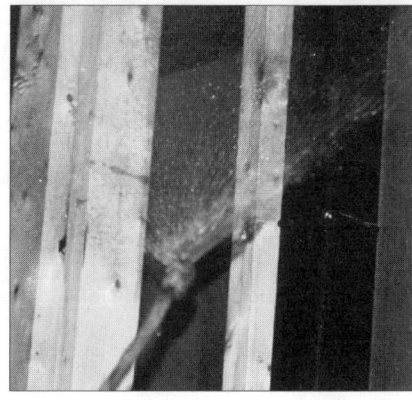

Figure 6. For an effective treatment against termites and carpenter ants, PCOs spray all framing and sheathing surfaces with a borate solution at the "dried-in" stage of construction (top). The low-pressure sprayer uses a wide nozzle to deliver a fan-shaped spray (above).

details cannot be adequately covered here and application directions differ for different products. Effective, long-lasting control of both carpenter ants and termites requires more than just spraying all exposed wood with borate.

Both ant and termite treatments should be done at the "dried-in" stage of construction when all structural wood and sheathing is installed and the roof is on, but before instal-lation of drywall, insulation, mechanical systems, and electrical wiring (Figure 6).

In general, all exposed wood, exterior and interior, should be treated with borate solution until thoroughly wetted, using a low pressure sprayer. Tim-bor should be applied to all exposed wood for both ants and termites using a 15% solution (1¹/₂ pounds of powder per gallon of water). Bora-care is applied at a 1:1 dilution of the supplied concentrate with water for termites, and at a 2:1 dilution rate for ants.

Bora-care can be applied more selectively, according to research, because of its greater toxicity. Applications for termites can be limited to the lower 2 to 3 feet of walls and a 2- to 3-foot-wide strip around the perimeter of crawlspaces and basement foundations and around piers (see "Where To Treat With Borates," page 248).

Both borate products should be applied twice to surfaces of wood members that are critical areas for termite attack and can only be treated on one side — such as band joists, box sills, sill plates, and girders (Figure 7). For slabs and basements, the soil around utility pipes and expansion joints must be treated with termiticide (Figure 8).

Dusts can also be used for pretreatment, but these don't coat all wood surfaces as well as solutions, and tend to cake and lose effectiveness over time. A product such as Niban FG is better than straight boric acid, because it is coated for better moisture resistance. In general, dusts are better suited for treatment of ants in existing construction.

Builders and owners should work together for effective control of carpenter ants. Ants often have colonies outdoors and will forage into a house for food via openings around plumbing or wiring and will travel along these materials within houses thus avoiding treated wood. Therefore, effective control often requires bait applications to reduce outdoor populations. The product of choice is Niban Granular Bait which should be broadcast in a 2- to 4-foot band around the perimeter of the house and around all logs, stumps, etc. (Figure 9). This product contains food attractive to ants and is coated to withstand up to 2 inches of water before losing effectiveness.

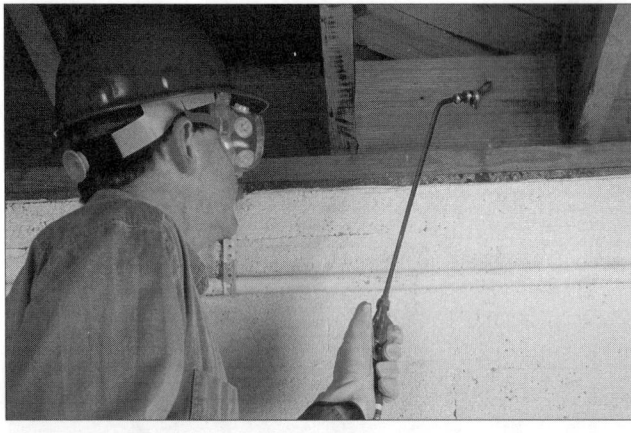

Figure 7. Areas prone to termite entry that can only be treated from one side — such as this band joist — should get two borate applications.

Figure 8. Borate treatment of the wood near these utility pipes provides extra protection. Traditional soil treatments are also recommended around such slab penetrations.

Figure 9. To control outdoor populations of carpenter ants, broadcast bait around the perimeter of the building, and around nearby trees, stumps, and firewood piles.

Use in Existing Construction

PCOs have started using borates widely in existing homes over the past six to eight years and have generally given them favorable reports. Borates can often provide control when other treatments are not effective or are too costly.

In existing construction, PCOs can typically do a better job than contractors or homeowners because of their specialized equipment and familiarity with insect behavior. Application methods include sprays, injections, dusts, fogging, ultra-low volume mists, and in-foam carriers.

For example, PCOs can deliver borates in a foam carrier to treat otherwise inaccessible areas beneath beetle-infested hardwood flooring or drywood termite-infested window and door frames. For deep-seated termite or beetle infestations in large timbers, borate can be injected into holes drilled in the timbers. This technique is used with log homes where the timbers are too wet or too large for effective fumigation.

PCOs can also inject borates into posts, piers, and pilings with untreated centers which are vulnerable to termite damage. Untreated centers often result when large timbers are pressure-treated with preservatives such as CCA or creosote.

While surface treatments with borates are generally effective, they will not protect the interiors of wood pieces from the aggressive Formosan termite. Many PCOs also report better control of active infestations of termites with the borate/glycol formulation Bora-care than with water-based solutions, possibly because of the better coating of dry wood surfaces and the higher toxicity compared to pure DOT.

By Lonnie Williams, owner of Rich Mountain Wood Protection Services in Gulfport, Miss., and former research entomologist at the USDA Forest Service Wood Products Insect Research Laboratory.

CONTROLLING SUBTERRANEAN TERMITES

Subterranean termites are the most widespread and destructive termite group in North America. They are so-named because they excavate through the soil to reach wood in contact with the ground. To reach material above ground, they either move through connecting wood, or through earthen "shelter tubes" which they build over concrete, masonry, or other materials. Given the choice, subterranean termites will usually access above-ground wood through protected cracks and cavities, such as in concrete slabs and foundations.

Subterranean termites normally return to the soil periodically for moisture. However, if the moisture content of wood above ground level is high enough, they can survive and multiply indefinitely with no ground contact.

Eliminating conditions favorable to termites is an essential first step in long-term control. This entails reducing termites' access to food (wood), moisture, and shelter, which they need for their survival. The best time to address these concerns is during planning and con-

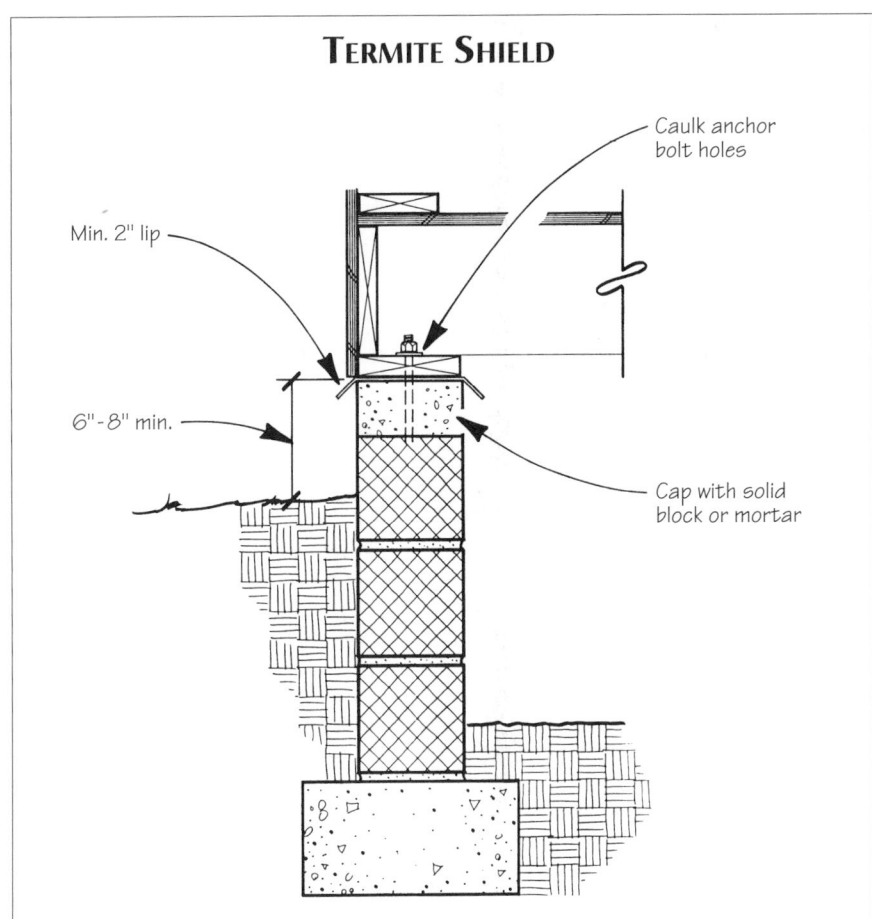

Figure 10. Metal shields force subterranean termites to build their tubes where they can readily be seen, but do not prevent infestations. To be effective, all joints and penetrations in the shield must be well sealed.

struction (see "Termite-Resistant Details," page 254).

Termite Shields

Metal termite shields are perhaps the oldest type of termite barrier and are widely used in the tropics and the southern U.S. The metal strips are installed on foundations, piers, pipes, and similar avenues of termite entry (Figure 10). They do not prevent termites from entering, but can be helpful in detecting infestations. Properly designed, installed, and maintained, shields force subterranean termites to build their tubes around the protruding edge and over the top of the shield where they can readily be seen.

To be effective, the ends of the metal strips must be firmly joined, either by soldering or by an interlocking mechanical joint. Some typical defects found in the shields include:

• Loose joints between metal sections
• Improperly cut and soldered corners where walls intersect
• Anchor bolt holes not sealed
• Insufficient clearance between the

outer edge of the shield and adjacent woodwork or piping
• Shields less than 12 inches above grade
• Projecting edges that are bent, torn, corroded, or flattened against foundation
• High-risk areas such as filled porches left unprotected

Sand Barriers

About 40 years ago, researchers discovered that subterranean termites were unable to tunnel through sand if the particles were too large for termites to move with their mandibles, but small enough that termites could not crawl between them — in the range of 2.0 to 2.8 mm for most subterranean termites.

Sand and basaltic rock barriers are now routinely installed on new buildings and utility poles in Hawaii and Australia. Only a handful of U.S. companies outside Hawaii (mainly in California) are currently providing such treatments. Most of the jobs in California to date have been retro-

fits in crawlspace homes.

Typically, a 4-inch-thick, 20-inch-wide layer of sand is blown inside the crawlspace along the foundation, and around piers and plumbing entries. Areas outside the foundation, under slabs, and within construction voids are still treated with conventional termiticide. Preliminary field trials have been encouraging but widespread use may not be practical in the U.S.

Barrier Treatment with Termiticide

Liquid termiticides have been the mainstay of subterranean termite control for more than 40 years. The goal of this approach is to provide a continuous chemical barrier in the soil surrounding and beneath a structure (Figure 11). Termites attempting to penetrate through treated soil are either killed or repelled.

Continuous coverage requires both horizontal and vertical barriers. Horizontal barriers are created under slabs, garages, patios, sidewalks, and other slabs abutting the

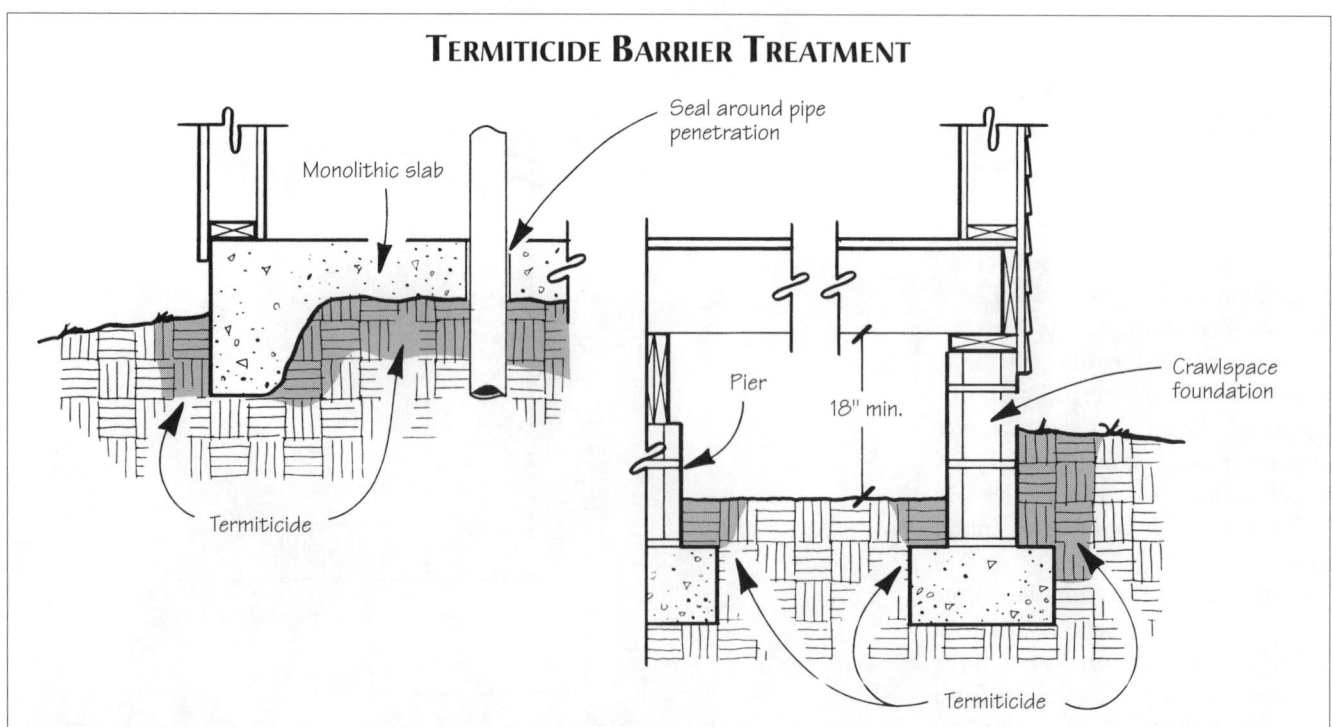

TERMITICIDE BARRIER TREATMENT

Seal around pipe penetration

Monolithic slab

Termiticide

Pier

18" min.

Crawlspace foundation

Termiticide

Figure 11. The goal in soil treatment is to establish an unbroken barrier around the structure. Horizontal barriers are created under slabs, garages, patios, driveways, and other slabs abutting the structure. Vertical barriers are required around foundation walls, piers, posts, etc., down to the footings.

structure. Vertical barriers are required around foundation piers, posts, filled porches, and chimneys down to their footings. The termiticide must be of sufficient concentration, applied at the proper rate (gallonage), and strategically placed to block all potential entry routes.

Comprehensive instructions for treating different types of construction can be found in the Approved Reference Procedures for Subterranean Termite Control (NPCA 1991, 8100 Oak St., Dunn Loring, VA 22027; 703/573-8330) and by referring to the directions on termiticide labels.

Pretreatment Vs. Retrofit

The most effective and economical time to apply a soil treatment is during construction — when termiticide can be precisely placed where it is needed below slabs, around pipes and utility conduits and along all sides of foundations and piers. A subsequent treatment along the foundation is needed after the final backfilling and grading.

Postconstruction treatment is complicated by many factors, including poor soil absorption, inaccessible areas, and a general inability to see where the termiticide is flowing. Many of the potential termite entry points are hidden behind walls, floor coverings, tubs, and other obstructions. The risk of puncturing and contaminating ducts, drains, and wells also increases with postconstruction applications. Due to all these factors, many more untreated gaps occur in the soil barriers — increasing the likelihood and need for retreatment.

Concrete Slabs

Concrete slabs present a number of challenges for treatment and have produced the greatest number of retreatments and damage-related claims for the industry. Termites enter slab-on-ground buildings through expansion joints, settlement cracks, posts, forms and grade stakes embedded in the slab, and around

utility penetrations. Many of the interior entry points are hidden by floor coverings and other obstructions. Termites can also gain hidden entry by tunneling up the foundation under stucco, brick veneer, or wood siding at or below ground level.

Slab-related termite problems would rank even higher if "attached slabs" such as porches, stoops, garages, and additions were included in this assessment. Filled porches (raised slabs) are an especially common source of termite problems and a challenge to treat. Form boards, scrap lumber, paper, and other construction debris are often discarded here before the slab is poured. Besides being an attraction to termites, the hidden debris can obstruct the flow of termiticide.

The New Termiticides

For more than 40 years, the standard method of controlling subterranean termites was soil barrier treatment — Chlordane and Heptachlor were the dominant products for years until they were withdrawn from the market in 1987. USDA tests showed these compounds to last for more than 35 years in the soil. This characteristic

made them very effective but was viewed negatively by environmental groups and regulatory agencies. Furthermore, the chemicals had been labeled possible carcinogens (based on lab experiments with mice) and often left detectable odors in houses that persisted for years.

The current generation of termiticide products are more expensive, shorter lived, and perceived by many to be less reliable than their predecessors. Presently nine products are being marketed for soil barrier treatments around and beneath structures. Six of these products are different types of synthetic pyrethroids, two are organophosphates, and the last and most recent (imidacloprid) is from a new chemical class called the chloronicotinyls. Other new products are undergoing tests throughout the country.

Some of the new products have lower acute toxicity to mammals than others, or are less likely to irritate the skin of applicators. Most have extremely low vapor pressures, resulting in virtually no indoor odors. All can be normally cleansed from surfaces with detergent and water. Because these products are relatively insoluble in water, they can

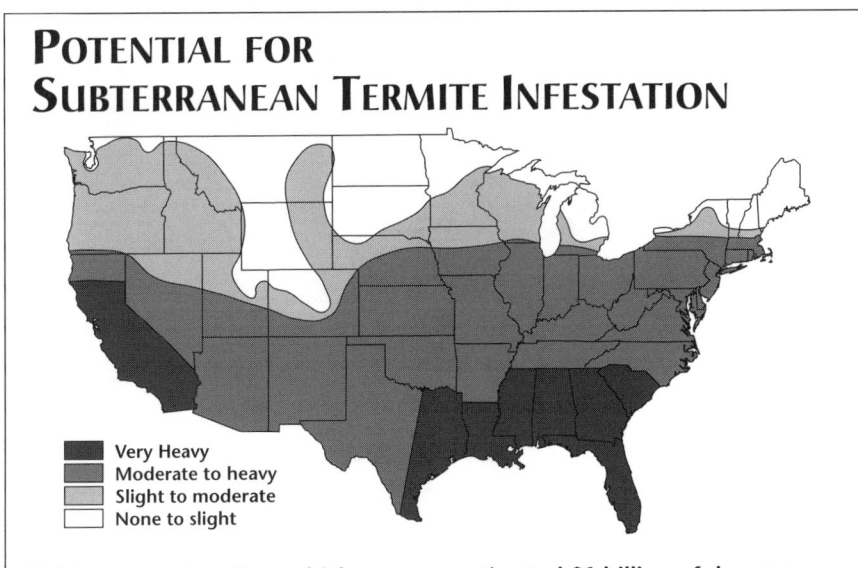

POTENTIAL FOR SUBTERRANEAN TERMITE INFESTATION

- ■ Very Heavy
- ■ Moderate to heavy
- ■ Slight to moderate
- □ None to slight

Subterranean termites, which cause an estimated $1 billion of damage annually to U.S. homes, are found from New England to Florida in the East and from Washington to the Gulf of Mexico in the West.

CABO

be expected to remain largely in place in the soil following application. Although the new chemicals pose no known significant hazard to humans or pets, many are toxic to fish, necessitating extra care when treating structures adjacent to water.

Despite the handling and safety benefits, adjusting to the post-Chlordane termiticides has been a trying experience for many pest control companies. In comparison to Chlordane, the current products are more expensive to apply, yet less persistent in the soil. USDA studies suggest that these products should control termites for at least five years if they are applied at label concentra-tions. The actual length of control will depend on such factors as thoroughness of application, foraging intensity, and conducive conditions. Moreover, soil and climatic factors appear to have a much greater influence on the longevity of these products. What works well in one area may be an inferior product in another.

Application techniques. With any of the current chemicals, a continuous barrier is the key to long-term control. Once a group of foraging termites finds a gap of untreated soil and tunnels upward into the structure, other nest mates will follow their scented trail. One way to reduce untreated gaps is to use as many gal-lons of termiticide as the label and soil will allow. In one New England survey, researchers found that houses treated with over 200 gallons required far fewer retreatments than those that received less than 100 gallons. It is also important that the current termiticides be applied at their full labeled concentrations. Of course, high gallonage and concentrations are of little value if critical entry areas for termites are missed.

Use of foams. The most difficult area to accurately place termiticide is under slabs, which have historically produced the greatest number of retreatments and damage claims for the pest control industry. Liquid

---

TERMITE-RESISTANT DETAILS

Although there is currently no method to make a building "termite-proof," there are ways to make structures less vulnerable to termite attack.

Wood-to-ground contact. It has been estimated that 90% of structural termite infestations are the result of wood coming into contact with the ground. Keep wood siding, lattice work, door frames, and trim at least 6 inches above grade; 18 inches for horizontal structural members (24-30 inches in humid areas). Wood posts, stair carriages, etc., should never penetrate concrete floors. Set outdoor wood porches and steps on a concrete base at least 6 inches above grade (Figure A).

Where wood-to-soil contact cannot be eliminated, use preservative-treated wood. However, be aware that termites can still enter the wood through cut ends and cracks and may also build tunnels over the surface.

Debris and vegetation. Remove cellulose materials such as stumps, scrap wood, form boards and grade stakes from under and around the building. Keep firewood and compost piles, as well as dense vegetation away from the foundation. Decorative wood chips and mulch should never contact wood siding or trim.

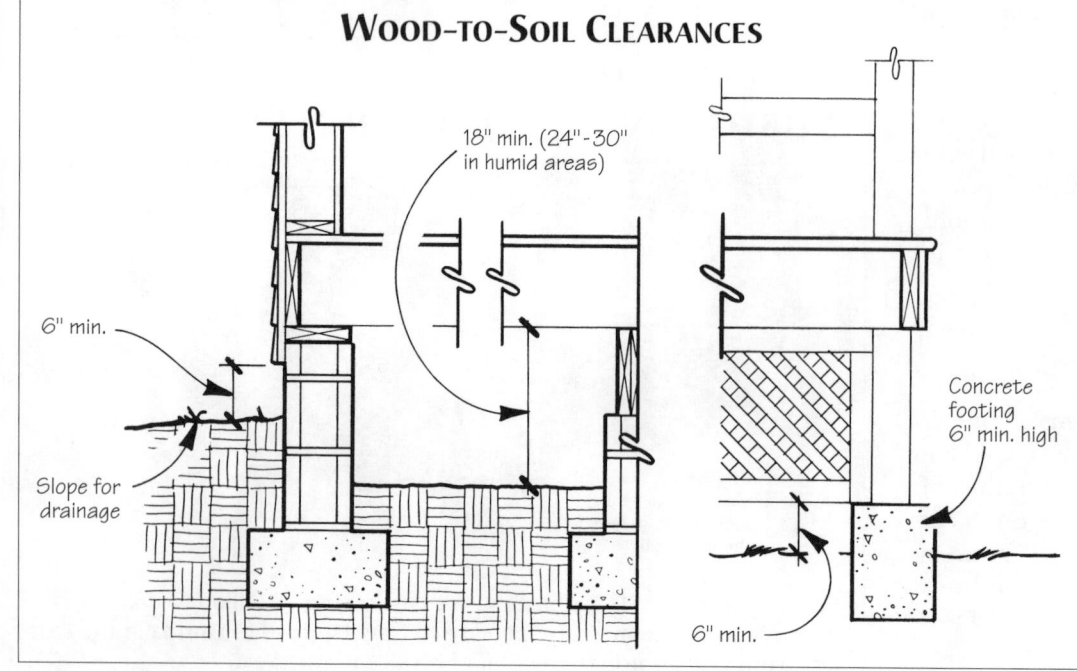

WOOD-TO-SOIL CLEARANCES

18" min. (24"-30" in humid areas)

6" min.

Slope for drainage

Concrete footing 6" min. high

6" min.

Figure A. Keep wood siding, lattice work, door frames, and trim at least 6 inches above grade; 18 inches for horizontal structural members (24-30 inches in humid areas). Wood posts, stair carriages, etc., should never penetrate concrete floors. Set outdoor wood porches and steps on a concrete base at least 6 inches above grade.

dilutions tend to disperse randomly under slabs resulting in inconsistent coverage.

One approach is to apply the termiticide as foam, which serves as a carrier to disperse termiticide laterally in the space that often exists between the bottom of the slab and the fill. Foam has proven useful in stopping termites from tunneling along the underside of slabs, within voids of concrete block or stone foundations, and behind brick veneer.

While it is not a panacea, foam can help deliver termiticide to hard-to-reach areas and has proven very effective in retreating chronically infected structures.

Wood Treatments

Wood can be treated for termites either as a preventive measure or to eliminate existing infestations. The best approach, where feasible, is to use preservative-treated lumber. Most termiticides used for soil treatment can also be applied to wood either by spraying, brushing, or injecting into voids and galleries of infested wood.

Products containing borates have certain advantages (see "Controlling Termites and Carpenter Ants with Borates," page 247). They are toxic to many species of wood destroying insects and fungi, and unless exposed to constant rewetting, maintain their preservative qualities for decades. In addition, they are nonstaining, odorless, and low in toxicity to mammals (about the same as table salt), making them especially attractive for remedial treatment of wood inside homes.

Research and practical experience suggest that borate-treated wood is protected from subterranean termite attack, provided sufficient boron concentrations are achieved in areas where termites are feeding.

Termite Baits

Regardless of the amount of termiticide used, barrier treatments do little to reduce colonies in the surrounding soil. Termite baits are a whole different concept. With baits,

Moisture-related conditions. Termites are more likely to infest a structure if wood or surrounding soil is consistently moist. Slope finish grade, walkways, patios, etc., away from the building, and install and maintain gutters, downspouts, and splash blocks.

Moist crawlspaces also promote termite problems. To reduce humidity levels, cover the exposed soil with polyethylene or heavy roofing paper and install adequate foundation vents.

Problem building details. Certain construction details are conducive to termites. Dirt-filled porches, steps, patios, and similar raised attachments are responsible for a large percentage of termite infestations (Figure B).

Stucco extending below grade is another common source of hidden termite entry into buildings, especially in the South (Figure C). When stucco separates from the foundation wall, termites can tunnel upward undetected.

Foam insulation. When foam board insulation is installed below grade, termites may tunnel undetected through or behind it into the structure. The foam is of no nutritional value to termites, but apparently offers ideal nesting and tunneling conditions. Liquid termiticide cannot be applied remedially because the foam panels resist wetting. In light of these difficulties, many pest control companies refuse to treat structures with foam insulation or provide no guarantee. — *M.P.*

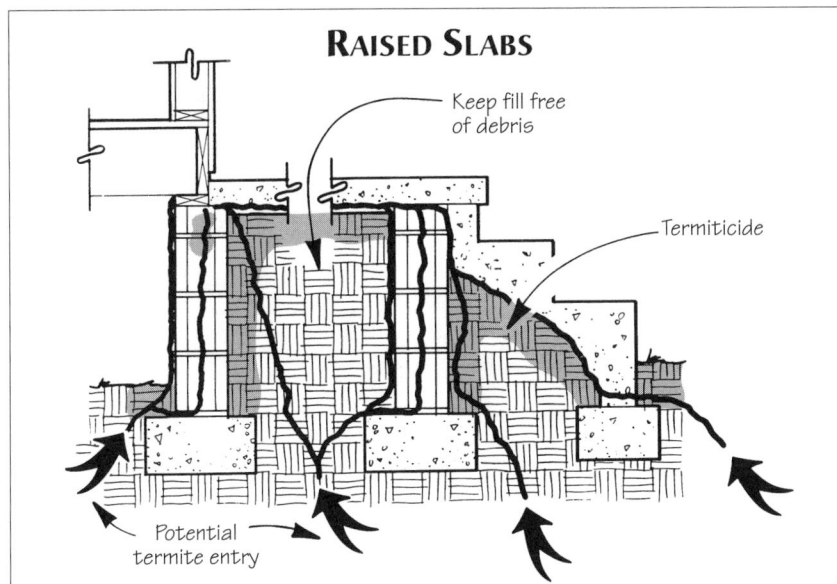

Figure B. Termites frequently enter buildings where porches, steps, or other raised slabs are attached. If such details can't be avoided, make sure all fill is free of debris and that soil and foundation voids are pretreated with termiticide.

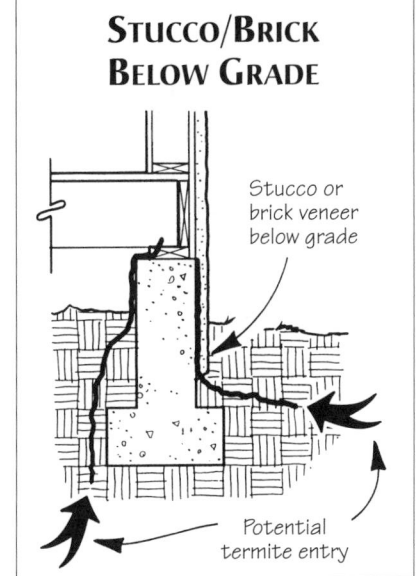

Figure C. Stucco or brick extending below grade is another common source of hidden termite entry.

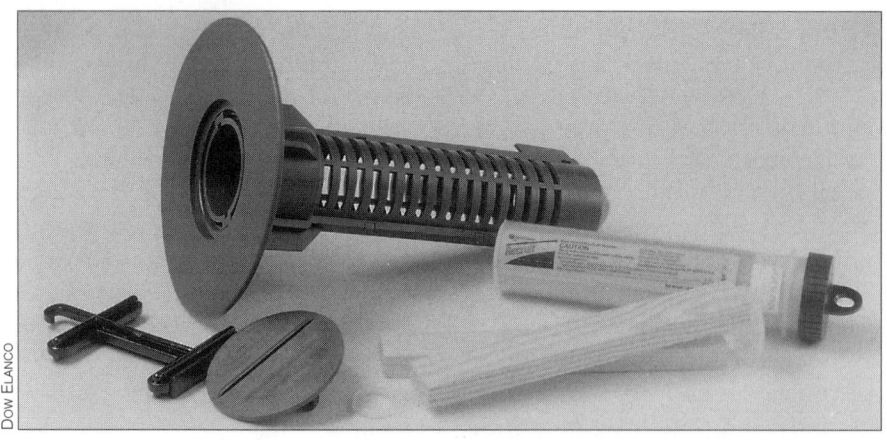

DOW ELANCO

Figure 12. The new baiting systems coming on the market use slow-acting toxicants, which spread among termites by feeding and grooming. The Sentricon system shown above uses plastic monitoring stations (at left in photo) inserted in the soil — first with wood to lure termites, then with toxicant-laced baits (at right) formulated to eliminate entire colonies.

minuscule amounts of material are deployed like edible "smart missiles" to knock out groups of foraging termites. An aggressive baiting program seeks to achieve a termite-free zone around the structure through ongoing monitoring and rebaiting as needed.

Baits are being developed for both exterior and interior use, both below and above ground. Some may be used as comprehensive, stand-alone treatments. Others will be better suited for spot treatments of active infestations. While debates exist over which compounds and strategies are most effective, a variety of systems are now coming on the market. By the end of the decade, there could be almost as many termite baits as conventional termiticides.

Below-ground baits work by luring termites to feed on wooden stakes or other cellulose materials placed around the structure and/or around wood piles, stumps, moist areas, and adjacent to damage. Since termites cannot see or smell the bait, getting termites to find it requires planning and persistence, and can be a lengthy process.

One commercial system, called Senitron (DowElanco, Indianapolis, Ind.), uses a three-step process involving initial monitoring, delivery of the bait, and subsequent monitoring at three- to four-month intervals to guard against reinfestation (Figure 12). A portable computer and barcode scanner are used to input data at the job site. Researchers have confirmed the effectiveness of this type of system, but emphasize the importance of continued monitoring.

Baits are especially useful in chronic retreatment situations and where contamination is a risk. Difficult construction features, such as wells, plenums, sub-slab heating ducts, inaccessible crawlspaces, rigid foam insulation, stucco below grade, and rubble foundations, can all be treated with baits. As versatile as baits can be, however, they will not work by simply hammering a few into the ground and walking away. Success requires a thoughtful approach with diligent monitoring by crews knowledgeable about termite biology.

By Dr. Michael F. Potter, an urban extension entomologist at the University of Kentucky College of Agriculture in Lexington, Ky. Adapted from the eighth edition of The Handbook of Pest Control, published by G.I.E. Publishing, Inc., Cleveland, Ohio.

SOURCES OF SUPPLY

The following listing provides sources of borate products EPA-labelled for beetles, carpenter ants, and termites. To obtain Bora-care and Tim-bor, the two major products, call the manufacturer's 800 number to find a local distributor.

Nisus Corporation
215 Dunavant Dr.
Rockford, TN 37853
800/264-0870
Bora-care, Niban Granular Bait, Jecta Diffusible Boracide

Perma-Chink Systems, Inc.
1605 Prosser Rd.
Knoxville, TN 37914
800/548-3554
Shellguard Guardian

Sashco
10300 E. 107th Place
Brighton, CO 80601
800/767-5656
Penetreat Impel Rods

U.S. Borax
26877 Tourney Rd.
Valencia, CA 91355
800/984-6267
Tim-Bor Insecticide

NOTE: Two unlabeled products, chemically identical to Tim-bor Insecticide but less costly, are Solubor, a fertilizer-grade borate available from agricultural supply centers and Tim-bor DPT, available from Sashco. With either, follow label directions for Tim-bor Insecticide. Another option is mixing 1.2 parts borax and 1 part boric acid, yielding a similar compound.

CHAPTER 11

PLUMBING

- Plumbing Pitfalls for Remodelers

- Common Plumbing Service Calls

PLUMBING PITFALLS FOR REMODELERS

Relocating and adding to plumbing systems can be very expensive on a remodeling job. Since plumbing codes are stringent and complicated, it's always best to call in a professional plumber before giving a final estimate. Still, there are many red flags you can learn to recognize on an initial visit to a site. Sizing up the system can help you and your client plan well and avoid surprises.

For any plumbing system you should ask four basic questions:
• Has the existing plumbing caused hidden damage you will be responsible for once the job is started?
• Will your plumber be able to work with the existing plumbing, or will it be impractical to connect the new to the old?
• Will the existing system handle the increased demands of your remodeling work?

• Are there existing code violations your plumber will have to correct in performing the desired work?

All of these questions must be answered before you can compile accurate cost projections.

Hidden Damage

Water is a powerful force; it can carve rock, erode the earth, and destroy your remodeling budget. If you fail to disclaim unseen damage or don't notice evidence pointing to a problem, you could lose serious money.

In bathrooms, look for places where water may be getting behind and underneath fixtures (Figure 1). Check to see that the trim plates around faucets, drains, and overflow outlets are well-sealed with plumber's putty. Look at the caulking around tubs and showers; if it's dried and cracking, you may have rotted lumber in the walls or floors. Check around the base of the toilet. Water damage can be caused by faulty wax seals or condensation dripping off the tank — particularly where cold well water is used.

In the kitchen inspect every area you can gain access to. Whenever possible, go below all the plumbing fixtures and inspect the structure supporting them. This will often reveal subfloor stained by water.

Remove the access panel of the dishwasher if there is one and look under the appliance. Refrigerators with ice makers can leak and rot the floor underneath. Look also for any water heaters, washing machines, and well and water conditioning equipment that might be installed in the living areas of the house.

Assessing Existing Supply Lines

One of the main things to look out for, especially with an older home, is the type of water supply lines.

Figure 1. Water will penetrate the wall at the faucet handles (left) whenever the shower is used. The holes should have been covered with trim plates sealed with plumber's putty. The curling and torn linoleum around the toilet (below) indicates water damage to the underlayment, probably from a faulty toilet seal.

Galvanized. Galvanized water pipes are commonly found in older homes. Get rid of them; if you don't, you're asking for trouble (Figure 2). Galvanized pipe will gradually close up with rust and mineral deposits until, ultimately, pressure is reduced to a trickle.

Worn threads on galvanized fittings are a frequent cause of leaks. When working around old galvanized fittings, any significant jarring or vibration can cause the fittings to let go at any moment. If this happens to a riser hidden in a wall, it will cause a lot of trouble and expense to fix.

When tying into old galvanized pipe, you may want to protect yourself in the contract. If the client doesn't want to replace the galvanized piping and you have to tie into it, your plumber may have to remove several sections to find solid pipe to make a good connection. This will increase your costs unless your contract has a clause disclaiming responsibility for the condition of existing piping.

CPVC. Another type to watch out for is CPVC plastic water pipe. It's fragile and hard to work with. Also, do-it-yourself types like CPVC because it does not require soldering skills. They can cut it with a hacksaw and glue it together. If I see CPVC in a house my crew has to work on, I automatically increase the expected labor to allow for potential problems.

Polybutylene. This pipe is gray and very pliable, but unlike CPVC, "polybute" is very rugged. In freezing temperatures, it will expand to reduce the risk of splitting. When polybute was first introduced, there were problems with faulty connections, so you need to watch out for these. Remodeling plumbers like polybute because it can be snaked through walls without any concealed joints.

PVC. If you find PVC supply pipe, you'd better talk with your plumber. Most codes limit the use of PVC water distribution pipe to cold water. The code generally requires your cold water piping to be of the same material as the hot water pipe, and since PVC cannot be used for hot water, it's not suitable for residential use.

Copper. If you find copper supply line you're probably in good shape. It's easy to repair, add on to, and install.

Main shut-off. Locate and test the main water shut-off valve to see if it works properly. If water leaks past the valve, the plumber will have trouble soldering copper connections (the water turns to steam and causes voids in the solder joint). With CPVC pipe, water will prevent the glue from setting up properly. With polybutylene connections, a small amount of water will have no adverse effects on the connection.

Accessibility. Keep in mind that the plumber not only has to be able to see the plumbing, he will need room to work with it. In general, if you can easily put your hand around the water pipes, the plumber will be able to do his job. But if the pipes are tight against the subfloor, or notched into the top of floor joists, you may have to remove the floor to make a connection.

Placement of lines. In cold climates, pipes in attics, crawlspaces, and outside walls may freeze and burst if not insulated properly. In some cases, pipes in an outside wall may have been saved from freezing only because there was *no* insulation in the wall. In a house where you encounter distribution lines in an outside wall, make sure that you don't isolate the pipe by insulating on the wrong side — the insulation must not be between the pipe and the heated space.

Assessing Existing Drainage

Residential drains are typically installed with a grade of $1/4$ inch per foot, and you'll have to maintain this pitch with any new lines. Make sure that any new drain pipe will not be lower than the existing pipe when it reaches the point of connection — an installed, sewage-ejector system can cost in excess of $1,000.

The plumber will need 18 to 24 inches of straight pipe to work with to cut a new fitting into the existing drain line. Also, make sure he has the room to install any new pipe and traps that may be necessary.

Cast-iron drain lines. Most of the main drain lines in older homes are cast iron, usually 3 to 4 inches in diameter. As long as these pipes are properly graded, they will give years of good service. Cast iron is generally easy to tie into, using a rubber coupling with stainless-steel hose clamps.

However, because cast iron can rust, the interior of the pipe becomes rough and can catch hair, grease, and other objects. Cast iron can also rust through from the inside. Rust stains on the outside of the pipe are reason for some concern.

Galvanized and lead drain lines. Galvanized and lead drain pipe are the ones to watch out for. Galvanized pipe is a metallic color, with heavy fittings at the connections. It was used as recently as 20

Figure 2. Galvanized supply lines should be replaced when found in older homes. The threads rust, causing leaks, and can eventually break off altogether if the pipe is jarred.

years ago for sink, shower, and tub connections (it's still code-approved for drainage). Over the years, it becomes restricted with rust and accumulated buildup of hair and grease (Figure 3).

As with galvanized supply lines, galvanized drains are prone to leaking because of rusted threads. This can cause water damage as well as health hazards, since sewer gas can escape. If the connections show a buildup of rust or a white efflorescence around the threads, the pipe will probably leak in the near future. Or the threads may simply break off when worked with. It's best to replace galvanized drain pipe.

In very old homes, you might find lead pipe and traps. These will be a dull gray color and very soft. The drains will rarely be straight and properly graded. When lead is bent, it creases and cracks and will leak. If the pipe runs through a spongy area of the floor, the effects of walking across the floor can take its toll on the soft material. When you see lead plumbing, plan to replace it.

Copper. You may find copper in the drain/waste/vent (DWV) system. Copper drains usually work very well and cause few problems, re-

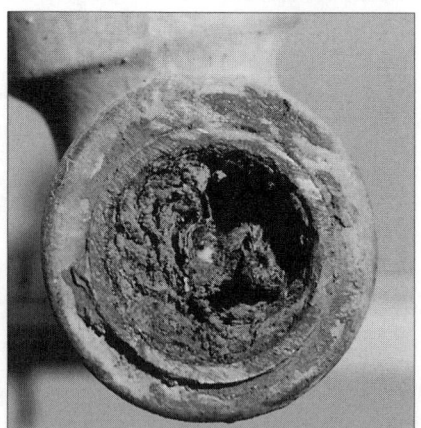

Figure 3. Rust, grease, and hair completely clogged this galvanized drain pipe. The author attempted to unclog the pipe with a snake, but succeeded only in punching a hole through the blockage.

maining smooth and blockage-free. Except for rare circumstances, there will be no reason to replace a copper DWV system.

Plastic. Schedule 40 plastic pipe — either PVC or ABS — is now the most commonly used DWV material. Your plumber should have no problems tying into a correctly installed plastic DWV system.

Fixtures

It is not unusual to find odd-sized bathtubs and sinks. Trying to find a modern unit with comparable measurements may be impossible. If you have to alter the opening for a bathtub, it is best to know it before you submit your proposal.

When choosing a location for tubs or showers, provide an access wall for the faucet in case it ever needs to be replaced. Also, if you are replacing a bathtub with a shower, you'll need to increase the size of the drain. Bathtubs, even those with showers, require a $1^1/_2$-inch trap and drain. Shower stalls, though, require a 2-inch trap and drain. This conversion may require removing the bathroom floor, or the ceiling below the floor.

If the customer wants to replace a lavatory or vanity with a pedestal sink, you'll have to relocate the plumbing; pedestal sinks require special spacing on the waste and water lines.

Assessing the Demand: Water Distribution

Undersized water pipe is a common problem. It was not unusual in the past for plumbers to install $1/_2$-inch pipe throughout a house. Unfortunately, this is not in keeping with current codes and creates problems. In a house with all $1/_2$-inch pipe, if someone is taking a shower when another fixture is turned on, they get drenched with cold or hot water. Adding another bathroom can make the water pressure even worse.

If you are unable to see what size the water pipe is, run a test. Turn the water on at full volume in the tub and notice the pressure. With the tub running, have someone turn on the kitchen sink. Then flush the toilet near the tub. Watch the pressure at the tub. If the house has more than one bathroom, try the test with both tubs running at full capacity. You may find some extreme differences between an upstairs and downstairs bath.

Sizing distribution lines. You should never have more than two fixtures being fed by a single $1/_2$-inch pipe. There should be at least a $3/_4$-inch line up until the point of the last two fixtures. With a $3/_4$-inch water service, most houses will have adequate pressure and be in code compliance.

Assessing the Demand: Drainage

The size of a house's building drain will be determined by the number of fixtures it handles. Most codes will not allow more than two toilets or bathrooms grouped on a 3-inch drain. A 4-inch drain can handle all ordinary residential demands.

Slow drains. When your work involves tying into the existing DWV system, you may become responsible for slow or clogged drains. Kitchen remodeling, for instance, may include the addition of a garbage disposal. When this device is installed, the existing kitchen drain may no longer be adequate.

To test a kitchen drain, fill the sink to the flood rim with water. If it is double-bowl, fill both sides. Release all the water at the same time. Repeat this procedure two or three times. Occasionally, if there is a clog down the line, a single bowl of water may appear to drain fine, even with the clog. By draining several bowls of water quickly, though, you'll discover the problem.

Check any fixtures your work may involve. Flush the toilet, fill and drain the tub, and test the lavatory. Follow this rule: If it has a drain, test it.

The absence of a vent can cause a drain to operate slowly. If you have a fixture that drains, but does so without force, it may need a vent. In any case, note existing drain problems and have the customer acknowledge the condition before you begin work.

Code Violations

Beware of existing code violations. If you alter existing plumbing, you may be required to correct all code deficiencies. Remodeling can expose all types of plumbing code violations.

Undersized distribution pipe. Undersized water distribution pipe is a common code problem. If the whole house is piped in 1/2-inch pipe, the plumber may connect to it, in most cases, without changing the existing pipe. However, if there is larger pipe available in an accessible location, the plumber will be required to make his connections to the larger pipe. This can mean running pipe for a much longer distance than you planned.

Unvented fixtures. Unvented fixtures are a frequent problem with older homes (most states require every fixture drain to be vented). If the drain goes straight down through the floor, the fixture is not properly vented and your plumber will have to install a vent for the new fixture being installed. Under remodeling conditions, you may be able to use a mechanical vent, a small plastic device that screws into a female fitting installed in the fixture drain line. Check with the local code official to see if mechanical vents are allowed.

Illegal traps. If the drain comes out of the wall into a "P" trap, you should be okay. If the drain comes straight up through the floor to an "S" trap, you have a code violation.

Drum traps, typically installed below the floor, are also prohibited in most states (Figure 4).

Illegal drains. Sink drains dumping into a sump-pump pit are in violation of code. If this condition exists, your plumber will have to tie the drain into the sanitary drainage system. This could result in additional costs of several hundred dollars.

Space requirements. If you are doing an extensive bathroom remodel, you may have to expand the size of the bathroom to meet modern code requirements. For example, the center of the toilet drain must have

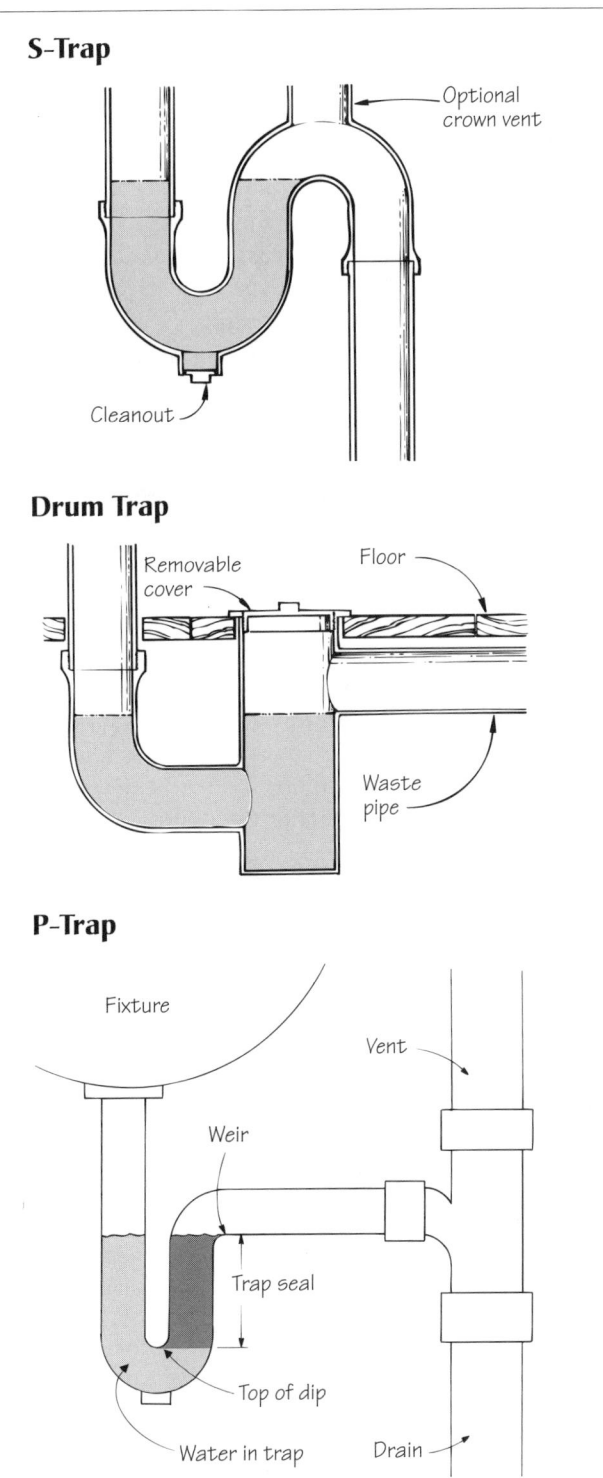

Figure 4. The S-trap (top) does not meet code. Because it is unvented and has only a 2-inch water seal, it is likely to fail and release sewer gases into the home — even with the addition of a crown vent. The drum trap (middle) has a deeper water seal than the S-trap, but is still prohibited in most states. The modern vented P-trap (bottom) creates an effective seal to block gases from entering the home.

261

15 inches of clear space on each side and 18 inches of clear space in front.

Septic capacity. Another issue to consider, if you are adding space to a home, is whether the existing septic system will be adequate. Adding bedrooms may necessitate enlarging the septic system, which can cost several thousand dollars, depending on the soil type and the local code requirements. Locate and inspect the septic system. If you find the leach field to be soggy and saturated with liquid, the system may be defective. Strong odor in the air is another warning of a failed system.

Conclusion

Even if the plumbing you anticipate seems trivial, give the entire system a full inspection. A checklist is helpful. After a general walk-through, go back over the specific plumbing you plan to deal with. With the expense of plumbing work, this phase of your estimate deserves your concentrated attention.

By Dodge Woodson, a master plumber and general contractor in Topsham, Maine.

COMMON PLUMBING SERVICE CALLS

Over the years I have spent thousands of hours troubleshooting plumbing problems — everything from burst water mains to clogged stack vents on the roof. The problems are varied, and some are seasonal. But there are many that simply occur over and over. Here are a dozen of the most common ones.

Leaks Under the Kitchen Sink

Kitchen sink drain lines are arguably the most ill-conceived systems in American plumbing — they are simply designed to leak. Everything is held together with slip joints — those hand-tightened connections that come loose every time they're bumped. And since all the traps and drain lines are placed right up front, you can't help but bump them every time you reach into the cabinet (Figure 5). I would wager that at least 60% of those reading this book currently have a leak under the kitchen sink.

I used to hate working under the kitchen sink. I would fuss until I got the right no-leak combination, call it a day, and then someone would bump the trap or drainpipe and the leaks would start again. But that has all changed, ever since I figured out a drain-line configuration that works. Now remedying undersink problems has become a high-profit part of my business.

Strainers. Many leaks come from cheap strainers: The water leaks under the strainer's lip right down onto the outside of the drain lines. The fix is simple: I replace cheap strainers with high-quality ones — usually the Kohler 8801-CP Duostrainer, which is chrome-plated solid brass and has an O-ring on the strainer insert (Figure 6). The Duostrainer also has *cut* threads, like a threaded steel pipe, as opposed to the leak-prone rolled threads on cheap strainers. I also install my strainers with a Dow Corning 100% clear silicon sealant — never plumbers putty. (Even so-called nonhardening plumbers putty hardens and cracks.)

New drain lines. Under the sink, I throw away all the existing drain lines, all the way to the schedule-40 main drainpipe coming through the wall or floor. As a replacement, I use one of several methods, depending on the budget.

The best (and most costly) method is to move the trap and waste arm to the back wall of the sink cabinet so they won't get bumped (Figure 7).

Figure 5. A typical kitchen sink drain assembly, with its leak-prone slip fittings, leaves a lot to be desired. This two-sink setup has no less than six slip connections.

Figure 6. The author likes the Kohler Duostrainer for kitchen sinks — its cut threads are less likely to leak than the rolled threads on cheaper strainers.

Figure 7. For a leakproof drain and trap assembly, the author uses glued plastic fittings and places the pipes at the back of the sink cabinet. The rubber 90-degree elbows, attached with hose clamps, allow for quick disassembly.

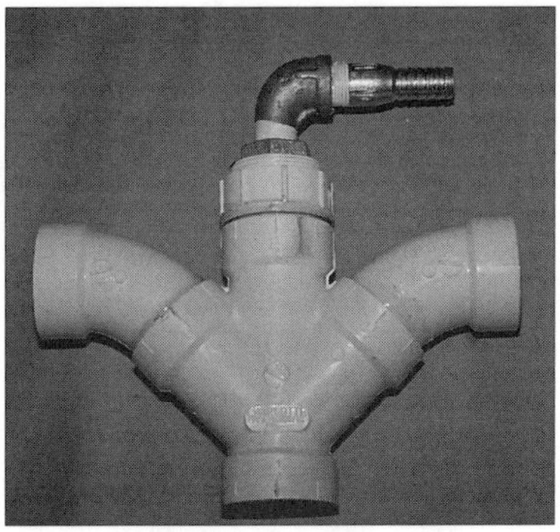

Figure 8. For connecting a dishwasher, a double-Y fitting with a galvanized reducer in the center hub works well.

This only works in installations where the water lines are not in the way and the drain line is towards the back of the cabinet. Instead of thin-wall metal waste lines and slip fittings, I use 1¹/₂-inch glue-type schedule-40 plastic traps, pipe, and fittings (either ABS or PVC). I make an immediate right turn below each strainer with a flexible PVC 90-degree elbow (more on flexible PVC later) pointed towards the back wall. At the back wall I glue a 90 on each arm and connect the two waste arms together with schedule-40 plastic pipe and a 1¹/₂-inch double L, then drop straight down into a schedule-40 trap. (A trap with a built-in cleanout at the bottom is best.) If I'm slightly off-line entering the main drain, I'll use a 1¹/₂-inch flexible coupling.

Connecting the dishwasher drain. Whenever the under-sink lines need to accommodate a dishwasher drain hose, I use a double T or Y in place of the double L (Figure 8). Besides having drain inputs on both sides for the sink waste arms, these fittings have a center hub that points straight up. Here I glue a plastic threaded reducing bushing. I screw a galvanized reducing bushing into the plastic bushing, then a galvanized street 90, and finally a barbed fitting for the dishwasher hose to connect to.

Low-budget option. For a faster and less costly method, I use a waste

assembly system that attaches straight to the strainers (Figure 9). This way I avoid those idiotic standpipes that place the drain lines and P-trap so low that they are assured of being constantly in the way. This assembly also has an attachment point for the dishwasher so I don't have to have another fitting, cutting out two more potential leak points. To minimize leaky slip joints and keep the P-trap off to one side, out of the way, I always use an end-outlet waste assembly as opposed to the more common center-waste.

Leaky traps. If I can't stop a trap from leaking, I replace it with a flexible PVC trap that fastens with stainless steel clamps. If I can't stop a leak from around the strainers threads, I install a flexible trap adapter. I also use the flexible drain and trap con-

nector to connect onto the main drainpipe whenever the pipes are slightly out of alignment. These flexible PVC fittings are a little more expensive than rigid plastic, but they install quickly and are easy to disassemble if needed. I buy fittings made by Fernco (300 S. Dayton St., Davison, MI 48423; 810/653-9626). These should be available at most professional plumbing supply shops. Another brand is available by mail-order from Barnet Brass & Copper, 3333 Lenox Ave., Jacksonville, FL 32254; 800/288-2000.

Clogged Kitchen Drain

Unlike in the TV commercials, my kitchen drain problems are always in the drain line and rarely in the trap. Sometimes kitchens are located on the opposite end of the house from

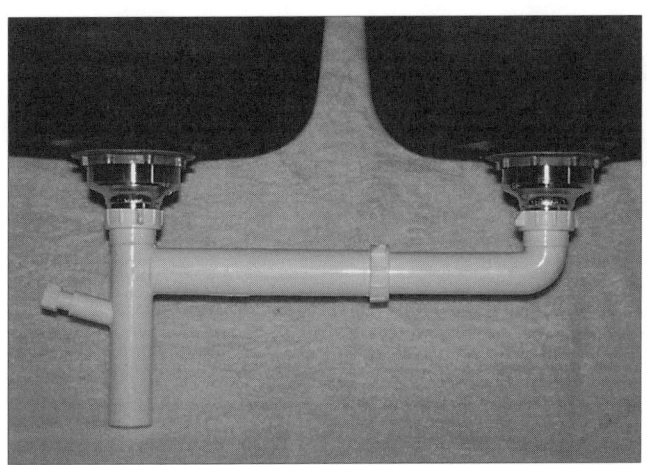

Figure 9. This less costly but improved drain configuration replaces the typical vertical standpipes — as well as their slip fittings — with screw-on elbows attached directly to the strainers. The only slip fitting is in a horizontal position, so it is less likely to leak.

the rest of the plumbing, resulting in a long kitchen drain line. If a shallow slope ($1/8$ inch per foot) has been used with $11/4$- or $11/2$-inch drainpipe, it's only a matter of time until the drain will become totally clogged. In this case, it's actually much faster to replace the drain line than to try to clean out a 40-foot run of totally plugged pipe. I normally replace it with a 2-inch, or preferably, 3-inch drain with an increased slope ($1/4$ inch per foot minimum).

Slow Drain

Here the complaint is, "My kitchen sink takes forever to drain!" Again, if the pipe is almost totally clogged for a long length, I replace the entire pipe with a larger one. But sometimes there's a blockage at some point along the line. To diagnose an isolated blockage, there's a simple test that often works. First, drain all the water out of the sink and the

drain lines. Then run hot water into a bucket until the water coming out of the faucet is extremely hot. Once hot, let the water run into the sink drain until it backs up into the sink. Shut off the water and run your hand along the drain line. You'll feel the hot water (especially noticeable on metal drain lines) until you come to the clog — at that spot the pipe will feel cold. Cut the line there and clean it. Once it's clean, I install a cleanout at the cut.

Toilet Never Stops Running

There are three common problems that can cause a toilet to "run."

Refill valve. First is a faulty refill valve (Figure 10). The refill valve controls the flow of water entering the tank. Waterborne trash — such as powdered granite from drilling the well, pieces of rust flaking off galvanized pipes, or gravel from a water-main break — can get into the

turn-off mechanism and prevent the valve from turning off. Or the valve can simply wear out.

It will be obvious if the refill valve is faulty, because the water in the toilet tank will be flowing into the overflow tube — that 1-inch tube that sticks up in the center of the tank. I either replace the seals on the refill valve (Figure 11), assuming parts are locally available, or I replace the entire assembly — the more common fix.

You'll notice a small flexible pipe running from the refill valve into the overflow tube. This is called the refill tube — it puts water back into the bowl during the refill cycle. Make sure that this small pipe is not broken off and that it runs into the overflow tube.

Overflow tube. A second common problem, especially on older units, is the overflow tube itself. If the tube is brass, it may have corroded at the threads where it screws into the tank. Plastic tubes, on the other hand, sometimes crack along the side. If the overflow tube is damaged in any way, water will constantly flow through it into the bowl. A damaged overflow tube will have to be replaced.

Flush valve. A third possibility is that water is leaking out of the tank because of a faulty flush valve — the stopper that keeps the water inside the tank until the toilet is flushed. Replacing the flush valve, normally a rubber flapper or ball, will usually fix the problem. However, if the seat area under the flush valve has jagged edges, a new rubber flapper alone will not stop the problem. Instead, you'll have to use a special replacement unit with a putty seal that covers the rough seat area (Figure 12).

A minor but annoying problem is a flush valve stuck in the open position, so that you have to jiggle the handle to get the rubber seal to fall back into place. To solve this, readjust the linkage from the flush valve to the flush handle arm as necessary. Also check to see that nothing

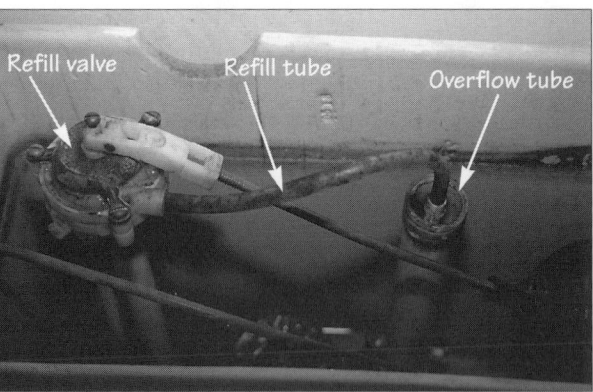

Figure 10. The refill valve opens when the toilet tank empties. The refill tube shunts water back into the bowl via the overflow tube.

Figure 11. Sometimes replacing the seal in the refill valve can remedy a running toilet. More often, though, the entire assembly must be replaced.

is catching the flush valve and keeping it from dropping into place.

Water or Sewer Gas Leaking Around Toilet

If water or sewer gas is leaking out at the base of the toilet, it means the wax ring is not sealing the joint between the toilet "horn" and the toilet flange. In this case, I have to replace the wax ring, but I also have to figure out why the seal has failed; otherwise, the problem is likely to recur.

For instance, if the toilet rocks back and forth on the floor, the wax ring will compress, leaving a gap that water and sewer gas can escape through. Often, the toilet's attachment bolts have come loose or rusted through. Or sometimes the floor has rotted, causing the toilet to tilt to one side. I also often see closet flanges installed too low. The flange is suppose to be installed *on top of the finished floor* — not level with it (Figure 13). If the flange is too low, I may have to install two wax rings, one on top of the other, to obtain a good seal.

There are two types of wax rings (Figure 14). I use the type that has a built-in plastic funnel that goes down into the flange. The cheaper type is a simple wax ring. I never use this ring by itself — I've seen too many leaks with these. When extra height is needed, however, I'll use a plain ring in conjunction with the funnel type.

If the floor is rotted out, it has to be rebuilt. But before I remove a toilet to replace a seal, I always make sure that the water around it is not coming from condensation or a leaky water pipe.

Toilet Won't Drain or Drains Slowly

This is caused either by mineral buildup in the toilet itself or by an obstruction in the toilet or drain line. If the toilet is old and the problem has been getting worse over the years, it's probably from mineral buildup. In that case, a new toilet

will be needed. As for obstructions, I've pulled toys, wire baskets, plastic cups, toothbrushes, and other things too numerous to mention out of toilets. I've used everything from wire grippers and a closet auger to clothes hangers to fish things out.

If a toilet flushes fine for two or three times and then starts to have problems, there is probably a restriction in the sewer line. This could be caused by tree roots, foreign matter, or a shift in the sewer pipes in the ground. The solution can involve anything from cleaning the lines with a snake to digging up the yard and replacing old drain lines.

No Hot Water

This can be the result of a tripped breaker or blown fuse, a bad heating element, a faulty thermostat, or the

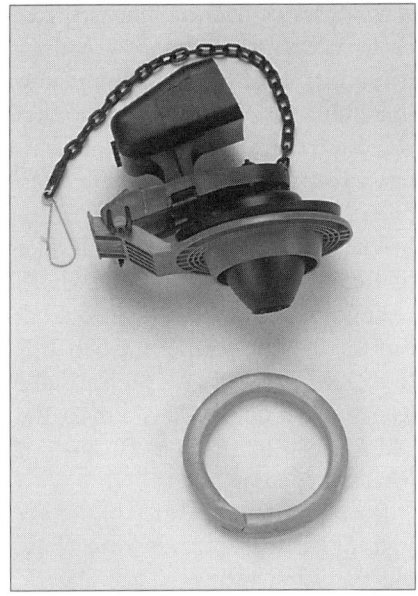

Figure 12. This flapper replacement kit comes with a putty ring for cushioning jagged edges in the outlet of the toilet tank, ensuring a good seal.

Figure 13. For a tight seal, the closet flange must be installed on top of the finished floor — not level with it, as is often the case.

Figure 14. When setting toilets, the author always uses a wax ring with a built-in funnel (left). A plain wax ring (right) may eventually leak.

water heater's overload switch. The problem with water heaters is not figuring out what happened, but *why* something happened. What happened will be obvious to a good plumber — but it may take a Sherlock Holmes to find out why.

As a remodeler, you can waste a lot of time trying to figure out what's wrong with a water heater. I wouldn't bother — call your plumber. But there are a couple of preliminary tests you can do before you make the call to give the plumber an idea of what's happening.

Look around the water heater for signs of leakage. Also, determine how old the water heater is. For electric heaters, check the breaker. If the breaker's tripped, reset it and see whether it trips again. If so, you may have an electrical problem. If the breaker's still open, find out whether there's no hot water at all, or only a

limited amount — a sign that the bottom heating element may be worn out while the top one is still working. Another quick test you can do is to raise the setting on the thermostat to see whether the heating elements come on. If they don't, it may mean the thermostat has worn out.

Beyond that, it's best to call a plumber.

Leaky Copper Pipes

Sulfur and excessive oxygen in the water can cause copper pipes to fail prematurely. Pinholes will appear, with a resulting spray of water. Installing a union or coupling at the hole will temporarily fix the problem, but the rest of the pipes will eventually fail. All the pipes should be replaced and water conditioning installed to prevent the corrosion from recurring. With really aggressive water, I usually rec-

ommend plastic (CPVC) or polybutylene supply lines rather than water conditioning.

Water Hammer

"It sounds like there's a jackhammer in the walls!" — a common complaint whenever metal supply pipes are installed along with fast-closing faucets and valves. Whenever any faucet, valve, or solenoid opens, the water rushes through the pipes to the outlet. Then, when the valve closes quickly, all that fast rushing water slams to a stop. But its energy is transferred into the metal pipes. From there it reverses itself and hits the opposite end of the water lines, then comes back again. The noise sounds as if someone is hitting the pipes with a hammer.

A common solution is to install an air column — a vertical pipe with a cushion of air in it — to dissipate the pressure of the rebounding water. This is not a good long-term solution, however, because the air that provides the cushion will eventually dissolve into the water and the problem will return. Special shock absorbers made by Sioux Chief Manufacturing (P.O. Box 397, Peculiar, MO 64078; 800/821-3944) are designed just to prevent this problem and should be installed at point of use and at the end of the plumbing line. Called the Mini-Rester, this patented shock absorber comes in many configurations for a variety of installations (Figure 15).

Leaky Faucets

Leaky faucets seem more common today than in the past. I suspect this is because there's an overabundance of cheap fixtures available in do-it-yourself stores. But if your customers pay their water bill on a per gallon basis, and especially if their sewer bill is based on water consumption, a small drip can be very expensive.

Some single-lever faucet designs use springs to help close the valve — the springs press little rubber seals

Figure 15. Water hammer arrestors — not simply vertical pipes filled with air — are the best way to prevent water hammer.

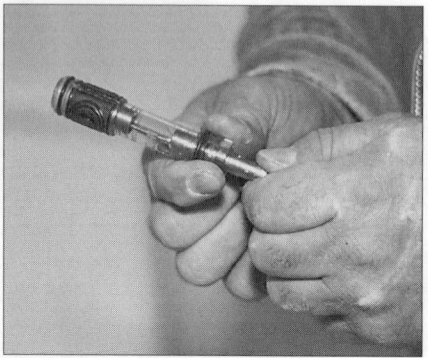

Figure 16. This Delta single-lever faucet repair kit includes new springs and gaskets (left); for other faucet designs, such as the Moen, the entire cartridge is replaced (right).

against a plastic seat (Figure 16). If the springs lose their tension over a period of time, or if they rust or get cut by debris in the water, they'll typically need to be replaced (as a temporary fix, I have been known to restretch the springs by simply pulling them apart with a pair of needle-nose pliers).

If the faucet is the type with a plastic ball — a poor design that never worked well — replace it with a stainless-steel one, which should be available at a plumbing supply house (Figure 17). If the faucet has a worn-out cartridge, replace that. If the faucet leaks around the handle only when the faucet is turned on, replace the appropriate gasket or O-ring. (If it's a cheap faucet, I simply replace it with a high-quality one. It costs more to maintain a cheap faucet than it does to install a good one.)

Older-style faucets have many replaceable parts — the stem assembly, the washer, and the seat itself. The stem assembly removes with a socket or crescent wrench, the washer with a screwdriver, and the seat with a hex wrench. Between all the old and new designs, no one can keep all the parts in stock. Therefore, when you can't find the part you need, you'll have to replace the faucet. Be sure to install one from a company that has been around a long time and has easily obtainable parts.

Low Water Pressure

When low pressure is the complaint, I ask several questions: Is the problem throughout the house, or only at one or two faucets? Or, is there a problem only on the higher floors of the house? Also, is the problem in both the hot and cold lines?

The most common complaint is low pressure on both the hot and cold sides at only one faucet. Usually the faucet screens are clogged with silt or sediment, although sometimes trash gets caught in the faucet body itself or at the stop valve beneath the sink. If the problem is throughout

the house, don't forget the obvious — is there an in-line cartridge filter that is clogged with trash?

If the customer is on city water, I check the water pressure from the utility by cutting into the line where it enters the house and hooking up a pressure gauge. If the pressure is good coming into the house, then the problem must be within the pipes. I first check the faucet closest to the incoming main to verify its pressure, then work from there. In old homes, the galvanized lines are commonly choked with rust. New homes suffer more from incorrect supply line design, or from debris lodged in the lines.

When the pressure problem is only on the top floor, the house pressure must be raised. For city dwellers, I install a booster pump. In homes with wells, I simply raise the setting on the water tank's pressure switch and increase the air pressure within the tank (Figure 18).

Frozen Water Lines

If a water line freezes, it usually means the line was installed improperly. After thawing a supply line, I prefer to relocate it to within the heated space of the house. If the customer doesn't want to pay for that, I will install a UL-approved low-wattage heat tape.

If a drain line freezes, it's because it wasn't pitched properly. Water

should never be in a drain line except when it's flowing through to the septic tank or sewer main. I have seen drain lines pitched uphill on which the owners installed heat tape to prevent freezing. Eventually, though, PVC or ABS drain pipe will start to deform and sag because of the heat.

Never use a welder when thawing metal water lines — it's a dangerous tool that can cause fires. For metal pipes, use a torch; for plastic pipes, a hair dryer will have to do. (Whenever I use a torch in a "tight" location, I always use a fiberglass fireproof backstop to prevent a house fire.) A sometimes faster

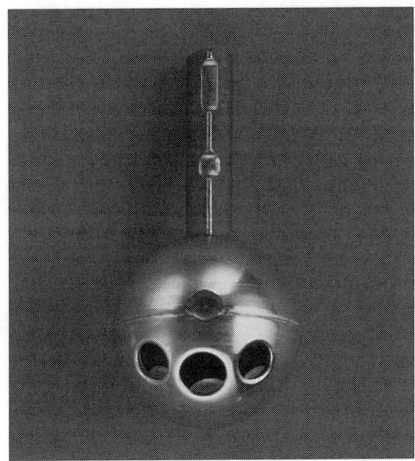

Figure 17. Some inexpensive single-lever faucets use a plastic ball to control water flow. This should be replaced with a stainless-steel ball like the one shown here.

Figure 18. There are two screws on a water tank's pressure switch. Turning the tall screw clockwise raises both the high and low cut-off pressures; turning the shorter screw clockwise raises only the high cut-off pressure.

option is to cut the frozen areas out and either replace them or take the iced-up pipe into the house and let it thaw out.

Different types of pipes respond differently to freezing. Galvanized pipe splits, and copper will either split or change diameter. With copper, I often have to cut away large sections of pipe to find a section that's not too deformed to accept a fitting. On occasion, I have had to use my flaring tool and squeeze a small section of copper pipe back to its original diameter so I could slip a fitting on. Plastic pipe cracks in long sections, while polybutylene normally expands. Polybutylene will occasionally break, but freezing problems are minimal compared with other types of pipe. Polybutylene is also flexible enough that I can use pliers and gently squeeze the pipe to find the frozen areas — the pipe, which will normally compress when squeezed, remains inflexible when frozen. I find the frozen sections this way, and simply cut them out and replace them.

By Rex Cauldwell, a master plumber in Copper Hill, Va.

CHAPTER 12

ELECTRICAL

- Electrical Planning for Remodelers

- Rewiring Tips

- Common Electrical Inspection Failures

- GFCI Circuits

- Plug-In Electrical Testers

ELECTRICAL PLANNING FOR REMODELERS

Because most remodeling contractors are not electricians, this is an area where it's easy to overlook potential problems. By anticipating these problems, a contractor can avoid underbidding and, in some cases, simplify the work for the electrician. Below I'll look at some common problem areas where contractors typically underbid.

If the remodel requires any electrical add-ons, you should first look at the main service panel. Identify any existing problems within the panel and determine how much room is available for additional circuits. These panels will either be fuse boxes, circuit breakers, or a combination.

Fuse Boxes

If the main service panel is an old 60-amp fuse box, additional circuits probably should not be wired into it.

Although you may be adding a few receptacle outlets to an existing circuit, it's possible the additional load will be enough to overload the time-worn fuse box and cause a fire. Even if the fuse panel is 100 amps or more, it should be scrutinized thoroughly before any additional loads are added. Look for the following:

• Is there room for more circuits? Look for empty screws adjacent to the glass fuses. If there aren't enough empty circuits, an expensive service upgrade may be required. If there are empty screws, check the voltage on the screw terminals to verify that full voltage is present for the new circuits. Old fuse boxes are famous for loose, corroded connections, which allow only partial voltage to be available. This may be why there isn't a circuit presently using that connection.

• Are there two or more wires (circuits) under one screw and using one fuse? This situation normally occurs when a circuit is added to a panel that is already completely full, or when a circuit within the panel fails and a working circuit is doubled up to compensate. This is never allowed by code.

• Is the fuse amperage already exceeding the circuit maximum? For example, suppose a 30-amp glass fuse (colored green) is installed into a circuit wired with 12-gauge wire. The fuse won't open until 30 amps is exceeded, but the wiring starts overheating and burning at 20 amps. This commonly happens when circuits are overloaded and homeowners keep increasing the fuse size until the fuse finally holds. Watch out for this situation; it's a fire waiting to happen.

• Are there any hot spots on the fuse box that have melted and then solidified, or any discoloration due to overheating? Pull the main cartridge fuses out and the check the main prongs and the fuse itself for discoloration due to overheating. The plastic on the old fuse panels doesn't hold up well to heat. The most common problem in fuse panels next to oversizing fuses is meltdown.

Replacement is the best option. If budget permits, it's a good idea to recommend replacement of all older fuse panels with new circuit breaker panels. If you don't do this, you must assure yourself of the following: (1) that the fuse panel isn't already overloaded, (2) that it's in satisfactory condition for additional loads, and (3) that there is room for the additional circuits required for the remodel. Note any problems before work begins and add in the necessary extra money on the contract. Otherwise you may have to absorb the extra cost of correcting them

Figure 1. On its face the circuit-breaker panel seems to have room for extra circuits (left). Inside, though, the author found the panel completely full (right).

after the work begins. Whatever you do, don't ignore problems with the panel or you may end up in court.

Circuit Breaker Panels

Circuit breaker panels must also be carefully checked. You cannot tell if a service panel is full by observing the cover. There might be several blank knock-outs on the cover, but inside no empty slots for the breakers (Figure 1). Remove the cover to see if there is room for additional breakers. Also, look for damage to the hot buss. For example, either lightning or arcing in the box (from loose circuit breakers) can burn and deform the buss, making it physically impossible to pop in a new breaker.

Expensive breakers. Make note of the brand of service panel. Some manufacturers have gone out of business, which makes their breakers hard to find and very expensive. If you need a considerable number of these hard-to-find breakers, it could be less expensive to change out the panel to one that has readily available breakers.

Load Calculation

Once you have verified that the new circuits can be inserted into the panel, you must determine that the additional loads of these new circuits won't exceed the maximum load allowed for the service panel, main breaker, and service entrance wire. Just because there are physical openings for additional breakers doesn't mean the code allows them to be added.

Sometimes it is obvious that additional loads can be added. For example, a 200-amp box may have only one or two low-amperage double-pole breakers with a few 15 or 20 single-pole breakers. However, many times it is not so obvious. A 200-amp panel may hold up to a maximum of 40 circuits and have only 10 in it. Yet these 10 circuits could be pulling all the current the main breaker can hold.

To be absolutely certain, a house load calculation must be done. Page 761 of the 1990 National Electrical Code (NEC) or page 1103 of the NEC Handbook describes in detail how to do this. See also Sections 220-31, 220-30, and 220-35 of the NEC. Do not shy away from doing the load calculation. As a contractor you should know how to do it. If it seems overwhelming, hire a competent licensed electrician.

If the main panel has no main breaker, have a certified electrician verify the size of the service entrance wire and current rating of the service panel itself (the current rating for the panel will be indicated on a sticker inside the panel). Base the load maximum on that current figure (the lesser of the two if they differ).

Tying Into Existing Circuits

If you are adding only square footage without any fixed loads, and you intend to tie into an existing branch circuit, you must consider three items:

• First, what is the condition of the old wiring? Is it old knob-and-tube wiring, installed in the 1920s? Or ungrounded wiring, installed during the post-war building boom? In any case, if the existing wiring is ungrounded, the new wiring should run all the way back to the main panel to obtain a ground. Use a plug-in analyzer on a receptacle of the circuit that you are tapping into to verify that the existing wiring on that circuit is wired properly (Figure 2). Also, verify that the service has a service ground other than the house metal pipes. If none exists or the ground rod or ground connection is corroded beyond repair, a new house grounding system will need to be installed.

• Second, verify that the wire you are tapping into is of the proper gauge. If your renovation requires a 20-amp circuit, physically check the old wiring to make sure it is not 14 gauge (15-amp wire).

• Third, the load of the house increases by the additional square footage multiplied by 3 watts per square foot (NEC Section 220-3d). The increased house load must not exceed the house service load. Loads for additional circuits without any structural add-ons are also covered in the same section.

The bottom line here is not to tie into the existing house wiring unless you verify its gauge, that you are not placing too many receptacle outlets on one branch circuit, and that the existing wiring is in good condition and grounded. Be sure to add the new loads to the house load calculation to verify that the current is still under the amount allowed by the main service.

Service Main Panels Used as Subpanels

In the midst of renovation, it is not uncommon to change the existing service panel to a subpanel as a new and larger main service is installed. This situation is considerably more expensive than most contractors are led to believe.

You normally cannot use the existing three-wire service entrance

Figure 2. This three-prong outlet looks like it's on a grounded circuit, but when he used a simple plug-in analyzer the author found there was no ground wire present.

cable as the feed to the old panel. The feed from the new service entrance panel to the old main (now a subpanel) must be a four-conductor (or three-conductor with metal raceway) feeder (hot, hot, neutral, ground). The ground wire connecting the old panel to earth ground (ground rods, structural steel, etc.) as well as any ground wire to metallic plumbing pipes, must be disconnected from the old panel and run to the new one. In addition, as a newly created subpanel, it must have the neutrals (white wires) separated from both the equipment grounding wires (the bare wires coming into the box within the NM wire) and the box (the panel itself). All of these problems can translate into a significant cost.

Moving the Service Entrance Panel

If the service entrance panel needs to be moved away from the power company's meter base, the electrical inspector may require you to add an additional disconnect to the system immediately adjacent to the meter base. This is easy to overlook, but is costly to correct. The logic here is that it is dangerous to have the service panel too far from the meter base since the service entrance (SE) cable is not fused until it gets to the service panel. If a nail is driven into the SE cable between the meter base and the service entrance panel, it can cause a fire since there is no fusing to open the circuit. Therefore many inspectors require a disconnect immediately adjacent to the meter base. The cost is significant, so be sure to add it to the contract if the inspector in your area requires it.

Baseboard Heating

Baseboard heaters are normally installed whenever low initial costs are being considered. Because they are moderate in price and install quickly, they fit a limited budget. But

you need to watch out for some items that, if overlooked, can cause labor and material costs to skyrocket.

- Baseboard heaters cannot be placed under an electrical outlet. Lamp cords draped over the top of the heater could burn. In such locations, two smaller heaters may have to be placed on both sides of the outlet, staying several inches away from the receptacle. This small but significant problem increases material costs and may more than double the installation time. An alternative solution is to obtain baseboard heaters that have the outlets built in. However, you cannot use the 240-volt line that powers the baseboard for the 120-volt outlet. For that, a second cable or circuit will have to be installed. All existing receptacles immediately above the proposed heaters must be removed and blank plates installed.

- Baseboard heaters place heavy current loads on the service panel; 250 watts or approximately 1 amp per foot is typical for 240-volt heaters. Several baseboard units can create such a heavy load that the contractor must be certain that the service panel can handle it. A load calculation may be required for this situation to determine if an expensive service upgrade is required. Do not make the mistake of saying to yourself "that this little extra load doesn't matter since I am only adding one or two heaters." If the panel is already overloaded, the extra load that you add may be the straw that breaks the camel's back.

- Baseboard heaters install quickly only if the thermostats are located in the unit itself. If the owner wants the thermostats in the walls, labor and material increase tremendously. If the walls are plaster-on-lath, the thermostats should remain in the heaters or be wired using conduit. Cutting holes

in such walls risks cracking the plaster for several feet horizontally in both directions. Unless you have developed a method of sawing plaster-on-lath walls without cracking the adjacent plaster, I cannot emphasize too strongly not to try it.

HVAC

The most common electrical problem in hvac installations is overloading of the service entrance panel. As previously mentioned, just because there is room for the breaker doesn't mean the panel won't be overloaded when it's installed. If the service entrance is a 60- or 100-amp panel, it's probably not large enough. Be sure to allow enough money in the contract for the service upgrade. In addition, do not assume a 200-amp panel is large enough for the system, especially if an electric backup system is attached to the hvac unit. A load calculation should be done to verify that there is room for the extra load.

Though hvac units normally have the fusing requirements printed right on them, even experienced electricians can miscalculate hvac loads. For example, does the compressor run all the time the electric backup heat is running, or does it automatically shut off? The compressor can add 20 to 30 amps to the house load, but can be overlooked in the load calculation. If the load calculations are already close to the maximum the service panel will allow, the extra load from the compressor may trip the breaker.

Wherever the hvac unit is installed, code now requires switched lighting at the point of entrance. Don't forget to add it to the estimate. And make sure that you do not split the 240 volts supplied for the hvac system for the required 120-volt lighting (against code). Tap into another 120-volt line in the immediate area or run a separate circuit.

Kitchens and Dining Areas

The kitchen is usually the most miswired room in a house. A kitchen requires several circuits; if you're doing a kitchen remodel, make sure the service panel has room enough for any additional circuits you may need.

The NEC codes that apply to the kitchen also apply to the dining room, breakfast room, and pantry. If any renovation is to be done, the local inspector may require updating the wiring to current codes. This is extremely expensive as there are many code articles that apply. As a reminder:

- A minimum of two circuits (20-amp, 12-AWG wire) must feed the countertop receptacle outlets. The outlets must be no farther apart than 4 feet. I normally use the kitchen sink as a reference: to the left, one circuit; to the right, the second.
- All receptacle outlets within 6 feet of the kitchen sink (straight line distance) must have GFCIs (ground fault circuit interrupters).
- The lights must not be on same circuit as the kitchen/dining/pantry receptacle outlets. In addition, it is not good practice, and most of the time against code, to install the lights on the same circuit as the undercounter appliances.
- Additional circuits must be brought into the kitchen to power the fixed appliances such as the dishwasher, garbage disposal, compactor, etc., since these appliances cannot be powered by the kitchen/dining room/pantry receptacle outlets. Usually these appliances require their own separate circuits; be sure to read the instructions.
- An island is required to have receptacle outlets, and getting the wire there is sometimes labor intensive. How and where to place the receptacle without having a drawer slide into it is always a problem.

- The most common kitchen wiring error is installing the microwave on one of the kitchen receptacle circuits. The NEC doesn't specifically mention the microwave, but it does state that you must follow manufacturer's recommendations. Most manufacturers of medium and large microwave appliances require them to be put on a separate circuit. Read the instructions!

Porches

Open porches do not count in house loading, but specific codes do apply to special applications. If the owner wants electrical service on the porch area, and the porch is at or close to ground level, the receptacle outlets must have expensive GFCI protection. As before, verify that the branch circuit you are tapping into doesn't exceed the maximum number of allowed receptacle outlets, and that the house wiring is grounded and in good condition. In addition, if a door was added to the house to obtain entrance to the porch, a switched light must be added at the point of entrance. Walls that are to be removed normally have electrical wires inside, so be sure to allow finances to cover their splicing and relocation.

Garages

Do not make the error of bidding on a garage without the bid price reflecting the increased cost of GFCIs, which are required for general purpose outlets in garages. Dedicated and inaccessible receptacle outlets, however, are exempt; for example, receptacles for garage door openers, freezers, refrigerators, fans, etc.

If standard household receptacles are installed in the garage, be prepared for complaints. These receptacles are fine as long as heavy duty grounded cords aren't plugged in and out on a daily basis. Being made out of a brittle plastic, the grounding plug will break them apart in short

order if they are wiggled up and down as they are inserted and withdrawn. For such locations, it would be best to recommend to the owner the use of receptacles made out of nylon (about $6 apiece). If he refuses, he can't later complain to you about breakage.

Miscellaneous

Suppose your customers want to add one or two bedrooms to their house. Besides the required carpentry work, there are some code-required electricals that they'll have to have. Here are some items to watch for.

Smoke alarms. The new bedrooms will need hard-wired smoke alarms in the adjacent hallway. These can no longer be powered by batteries alone; I use hard-wired with a battery backup. If the bedrooms share the same hallway and are reasonably close to each other, one smoke alarm will normally suffice. However, if the renovation requires bedrooms that are separated from each other, you will need alarms for each. Further, the alarms will all have to be wired together so that when one sounds they all sound. Labor, as well as the wire itself, is not cheap. Don't be forced to "eat it" because you forget to "add it."

Closets. Closets are always problem areas. Closet lighting requirements (NEC Section 410-8) are extremely strict in the type and placement of the lights. Low-cost, bare incandescent bulbs can no longer be installed in closets. If the bulb is broken, the hot filament can fall on top of clothes or storage items and start a fire. Incandescent bulbs must be totally enclosed and be mounted at least 12 inches away from all clothes and storage items.

If fluorescent lights are to be installed in the closet, be sure the owner knows that these fixtures normally emit a 60-cycle hum. Also, NEC Section 410-8 applies severe restrictions to fluorescent lights as

Figure 3. When bidding a paddle fan installation, remember to include the cost of the extension pipe and a UL-approved electrical box to support the weight of the fan.

well. This article is far too complex to detail here, but it is imperative that it be understood by the contractor.

Recessed lighting. If the owner wants recessed lighting in the ceiling, be careful. Some recessed fixtures, especially the high wattage ones, cannot be placed next to insulation. Unless the light is rated "IC" (insulated ceiling) or equivalent, all insulation must be removed from the area determined by the requirements of that specific fixture. This means that if loose insulation is in the attic, barriers may have to be built around

the light to keep the insulation away from the fixture. Failure to do so may cause a fire. If you have to keep costs down, a low-voltage, battery-operated light fixture can be installed.

Switches. Be sure to ask how the client wants the lights switched. Switched outlets and three-way switching are much more expensive and labor intensive than standard switched lighting. You may assume the owners want a switched overhead light when what they really wanted was switched outlets. Do not put yourself in the position of having to pay for the increased cost of the latter because you didn't think to ask.

Dimmer controls. If the owner wants dimmer controls on his trac lighting, outside lighting, chandeliers, or any other heavily loaded lighting system, be wary. A standard low-cost dimmer is rated for only 600 watts. This limits the lighting to no more than four 150-watt bulbs. And there is no way to limit the amount of lights installed on a trac. Also, low-cost dimmers get hot with only a minimum load applied.

Don't assume you can use $5 dimmer controls and then find out later you really needed $50 high-wattage units. Question the owners to determine if they plan to add additional lamps at some time in the future. If you install the trac lighting with four 150-watt lights controlled

by a 600-watt dimmer and later the owners add a few more trac lights, the dimmer control could overheat and cause a fire. A 1,000-watt or larger dimmer has a heatsink located outside the wall which dissipates the heat and provides protection. But even with the expensive, high-wattage dimmers, the contractor should specify in the contract the maximum number of trac lights or floods allowed on the circuit if a dimmer is installed.

Ceiling fans. If the owners want one or more paddle fans, the contractor should realize that only UL-listed boxes may now be used for hanging them. These boxes are expensive, so be sure to include the extra cost (Figure 3). If the owner wants the fans on a variable speed control, make sure you use one that doesn't "sing," or complaints will follow. In addition, if the fan is hanging on a vaulted ceiling, an expensive extension pipe will be required to lower the fan so the blades won't hit the ceiling.

Splicing. When tying into existing circuits, splices cannot be covered up and left inside walls. All in-house splices are considered maintainable items, and access must be allowed. Splices are normally put in standard receptacle boxes with a blank plate.

By Rex Cauldwell, a master electrician and owner of Little Mountain Electric in Copper Hill, Va.

REWIRING TIPS

Rewiring old houses is not just a skill — it's an art. You have to be part electrician, part carpenter, part plasterer, and part magician. And like most magic, it's all an illusion. We can't always get wires to where we need them without disturbing the existing walls. The trick is knowing how to make it look like we weren't there.

Pulling Wires

To snake wires from one part of the house to another, I use 1/8-inch-wide metal fish tape. It's stiff enough that I can shove it through some obstructions (like plaster buildup) and flexible enough to detour around others (such as blocking and cleats). It's usually easiest to pull the wires through the wall cavity in the

same direction that you fed the snake in. Since snakes come in 50- or 100-foot lengths, I often cut them shorter to avoid having to pull all of it up on a shorter pull. I recommend getting the longest snaking jobs done first in case you have to cut the snake shorter for another pull.

I store my snakes coiled up, so I have to straighten them before I start work. If the snake is still coiled, it will coil up inside the wall cavity.

On each end of the snake I bend a hook approximately 1 inch long and about 1/4 inch across. To attach three-wire Romex to a snake, cut through two of the wires at a 45-degree angle about 5 inches from the end (Figure 4). Bend the third wire through the hook on the end of the snake. Tape everything shut to avoid snagging inside the wall. If a pull is long or there is likely to be a lot of friction to fight, twist the wire around itself a few times before you tape it.

String. In straight chases or in balloon-framed buildings, it's often easiest to use a string and a slim weight. I can usually get the string to the bottom with just a couple of shakes. In difficult areas, it's a good idea to pull an extra string when you pull the wires — you may need it later.

Snake Grabber

With a little patience and finesse, one person with a "snake grabber" can do some of those difficult snaking jobs that usually take two people. This is a tool that I make from BX cable, aircraft cable, and a short length of fish tape (Figure 5).

To use the snake grabber, slide the cable end into a 3/8- to 3/4-inch-diameter hole, making sure the cable feeds into the wall. Pull the piece of fish tape toward you while holding the handle still, then twist the tape half a turn. The cables will now fill most of the bay.

Now stick your snake into the bay with an open hook on the end. Push the snake up and down in the bay until you hook the grabber. Pull the handle gently back to the end and gently guide the cable that is hooked on the snake out through the hole, pulling the snake out with it. (If your hole is bigger than 3/4 inch, be careful not to pull the grabber into the wall.)

The snake grabber obviously works better in an uninsulated wall, but I have had some success with it in insulated walls, too.

Using a Tone Generator

Sometimes when I am having difficulty locating a snake, I use my tone generator (Figure 6), which can locate a conductor or other metal object. To use the tone generator, I clip one of its leads to a snake I have fished up a wall. The tone generator causes the snake to emit an electronic tone that can be picked up by the tone amplifier. (An AM radio will also work adequately instead of a tone amplifier; for best results, tune the radio so that it's not on a station.) Hold the amplifier or radio near the area of the wall where you think the snake is. The tone will get louder as the receiver gets closer to the snake.

To help locate a wall from the cellar, I bend a piece of Romex in the shape of a T and clip the leads onto two conductors of the Romex. I place the T against the baseboard at the spot I want to locate. From the cellar I then use a tone amplifier to locate the T.

From the Cellar

Once you determine which walls you want the wires to run through, the next job is to find places in the cellar where you can drill access holes. Finding these walls can sometimes be a challenge, but there are usually clues — like pipes, heating ducts, and other wires — to lead you in the right direction.

When you're ready to drill, it's a good idea to post a "spotter" upstairs. The spotter rests a hand on the floor and baseboard near where you're aiming. If you miss the wall and the bit starts chewing into the baseboard, the spotter will feel the difference in the vibration and tell you to stop before you do any serious damage. Remember to drill slowly to give your spotter time to

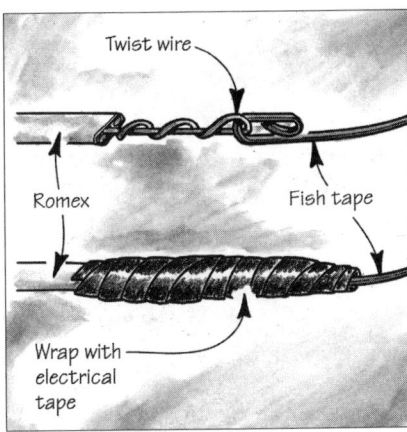

Figure 4. When attaching Romex to a snake for a long pull, the author makes a strong, twisted loop, as shown, and wraps the whole connection in electrical tape.

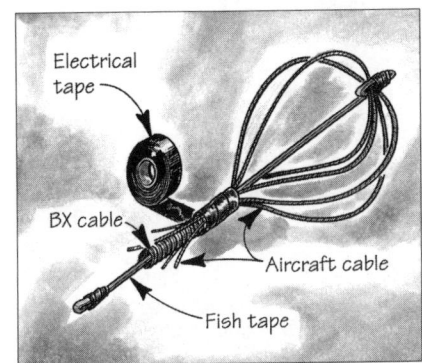

Figure 5. The author's homemade "snake grabber" uses aircraft cable inside a stud bay to help hook a snake that is probing the wall.

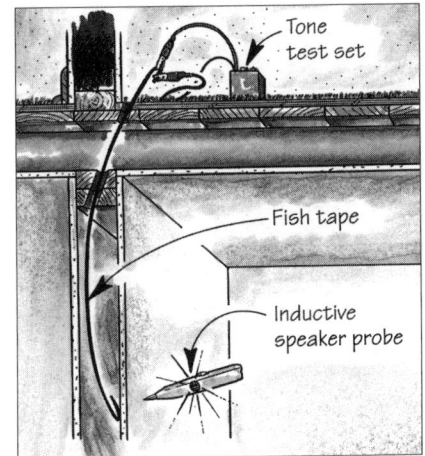

Figure 6. A tone generator turns a fish tape into a transmitter. Using a speaker probe (or radio tuned between stations), you can locate the tape inside a finished wall.

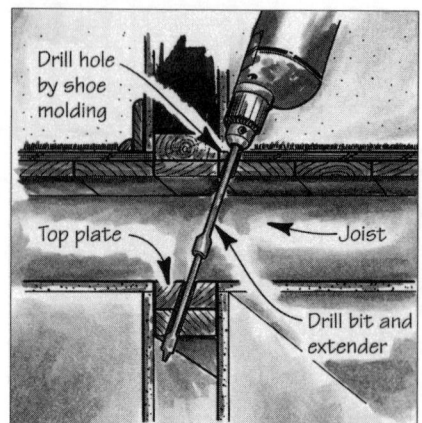

Figure 7. By removing the shoe molding at the edge of a carpeted room, you can drill an inconspicuous hole through the floor.

Figure 8. When an old sill is deeper than the wall, use a bit extender and drill at a shallow angle.

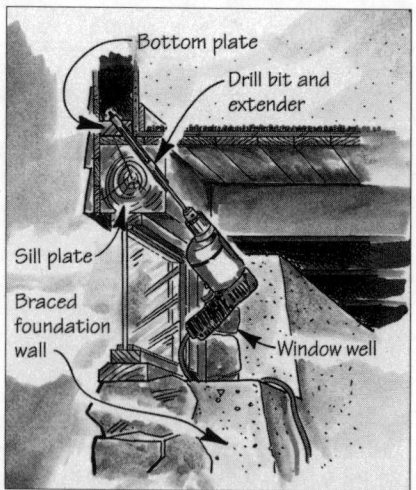

Figure 9. For old foundation walls that have been reinforced with concrete, a window well sometimes provides enough room for drilling.

react. If the wall cavity you're aiming for is near a doorway, the spotter can often feel both sides of the wall. Otherwise, I have the spotter feel the side that would be the most trouble to fix.

When a floor is going to be carpeted or covered with linoleum or tile, you can sometimes cut a hole in the floor to help gain access to an area. If a room already has carpeting, you can sometimes drill carefully at the edge of the carpet with a small feeler bit. Be extra careful not to snag a carpet thread while drilling. You can unravel a large section of carpet in just a few seconds if you don't pay close attention.

If the baseboard sits off the wall a little, you can sometimes drill a hole behind it with a small feeler bit to help locate the wall. You can also lift shoe moldings and carpet strips and drill where the hole won't be seen (Figure 7).

On an old wood floor that has not been refinished recently, there is sometimes a small crack between the boards that you can fit a small drill bit in to give you a reference point to help find the wall. Always remember to patch these small holes into the cellar. You don't want to create a draft.

Sill Drilling

It's easier to locate exterior walls, but before drilling, remember to take into account the width of the sill and the depth of the wall. In old buildings, the sills tend to be 6 to 8 inches wide, while the walls are typically 3½ inches deep. So you have to drill at an angle through the sill to get inside the wall (Figure 8). Often, the easiest way to figure the angle is to find a wire or pipe already drilled at the necessary angle and try to duplicate the angle.

To further complicate the situation, many old foundations are made of stone. The stones protrude at irregular intervals, making it difficult to drill exactly where you wish. Also,

many old foundations have been braced by having another foundation poured inside the old one; this makes the foundation even deeper and more impossible to drill. When faced with this situation, you may be able to drill up at the window wells (Figure 9). This is very restrictive, but can sometimes solve the problem in a pinch.

Feeds to the Attic

Plumbing chases and chimney chases are the first places to look when trying to find a route for feeds to the attic. When these don't work, you should check to see if any closets line up from one floor to the next. You may be able to run a piece of pipe in the corner of the closet to pull your feeds through.

If there is an obvious way to get wires to the attic (such as a chimney chase or plumbing chase), I usually pull a few up there, then work down into the walls. It's also easier to find walls from the attic because they were often framed before the ceiling was covered. All you have to do is lift the insulation and look (Figure 10).

Notching

It's often necessary to make notches in the wall and ceiling to get around framing members. These should be as small and neat as possible.

The most common place I have to notch is where the wall meets the ceiling (Figure 11). Say I'm running a wire from a wall switch to a ceiling light. The goal is to get a wire from the wall bay up into the joist bay. Using a ½-inch spade bit, I start at the corner and drill to find the bottom edge of the top plate. I then drill up from the corner through the plate into the joist bay.

You may also have to make notches to get from one stud (or joist) bay into the next. After finding the stud, I drill a 1-inch-deep hole in its center. I then drill at a tight angle

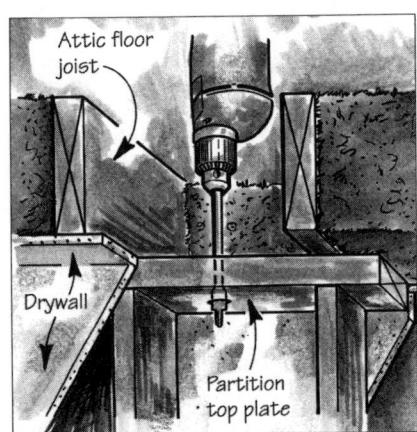

Figure 10. Finding partition walls from the attic is usually easy — just lift the insulation and look for the top plates.

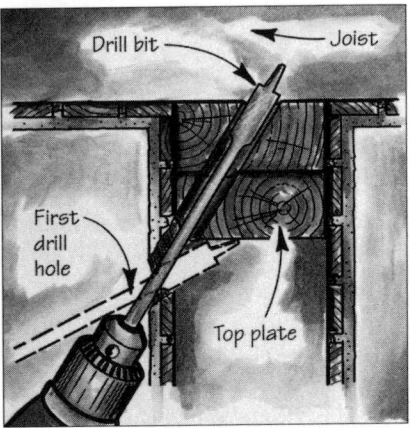

Figure 11. After drilling one hole to find the bottom edge of the top plate, you can drill at an angle that will pop the bit through the center of the wall in the attic.

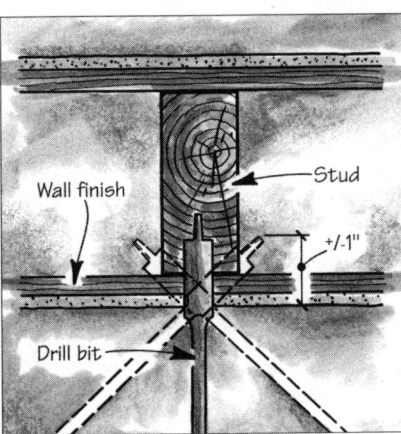

Figure 12. To run a wire across a stud or joist, the author drills three holes: one straight in, and one each at a tight angle into each bay.

in both directions to get access into both bays (Figure 12). This leaves only a small hole to patch.

Cutting in Boxes

After establishing where I want a box to be (Remember: Measure to the height of the other *boxes* in the room, not the cover plates!), I trace the outline of the box onto the wall. Then, depending on the wall finish, I often scribe the outline of the box with a razor knife. With wood paneling, scribing prevents splintering; if the wall is wallpapered, it prevents tearing. On a skim-coat plaster wall, scribing with a razor knife prevents the plaster edge from splitting and peeling away from the blueboard. Next, using a 3/8-inch spade bit, I drill out the corners of the box, then cut it out with a cordless jigsaw.

I carry two hole saws for cutting in round boxes: a dull one for cutting through plaster and a sharp one for cutting through wood and wood lath.

Plaster and Lath

Cutting rectangular boxes into true plaster and lath requires a little more work. After determining the approximate location of the box, I drill 1/8-inch holes about 1/4 inch

apart until I find the space between two pieces of lath. I work my way up until I find the next space, then I center the box on the piece of lath before tracing the outline of the box.

I drill out the corners, then I use the razor knife to scribe and completely remove the plaster. I like the cordless jigsaw for cutting lath because it vibrates the wall less than a keyhole saw. A recip saw or corded jigsaw will shake the wall to pieces. When using the cordless jigsaw, I never let the shoe touch the plaster. Any vibration will turn the plaster to dust.

To finish the cut, slide a screwdriver behind the middle piece of lath and hold the lath firmly between your thumb and the screwdriver. Then cut the lath on one side, leaving 1/4 inch uncut. This helps keep the lath from vibrating while you cut the other side.

After removing the middle piece, you can grab hold of the top and bottom pieces while cutting them out.

Metal Lath

My first impulse when I find out that a job has metal lath walls is to run away. After my heart stops pounding, I pull out my jigsaw with as many metal blades as I can find — I often go through two blades for

each box I cut in. The lath will also destroy a drill bit after a couple of boxes.

Another thing that makes working with metal lath walls more difficult is that you can't use a tone generator. If the energized snake touches the metal lath, the lath will become energized, making an accurate reading impossible.

Patching

Patching your holes may be the most important part of the job. A good patching job creates the illusion that you were never there. I like to patch holes as I go so I have time for another coat before going home. Go light on the spackle to avoid sanding.

For small holes, I use Onetime, a lightweight spackle from Red Devil that dries so quickly I can get a second or third coat on in the same day. For larger holes, I'll use a quick-drying mix-up powder like Durabond. This dries even harder and faster than spackle, giving me a solid base coat in a short time. The stuff dries in about 15 minutes, so mix up only what you can use quickly.

By Sean Kenney, a master electrician from Amesbury, Mass.

COMMON ELECTRICAL INSPECTION FAILURES

The *National Electrical Code* (NEC) says, "Electrical equipment shall be installed in a neat and workmanlike manner." This regulation is open to interpretation, and it means that, technically, the inspector can fail a job simply because the work looks sloppy. When asked about the first thing they look for when they inspect a job, most of the inspectors said the same thing: Neatness. In fact, sloppy work is a tipoff that the whole job needs some extra scrutiny (Figure 13).

Many electricians never realize how important neatness is because they aren't cited directly for a workmanship violation. Enforcing a workmanship violation can be difficult, but if the work is messy, inspectors say they usually have no trouble finding plenty of other violations to enforce.

Although neatness is subjective, there are certain guidelines to follow:

• Wires should be run in straight lines that are level and plumb.
• Romex should be unwound so it will lie flat without any twists.
• All electrical equipment should be installed level and plumb.

Keep Informed

Most code violations are caused by ignorance of the *NEC* or blatant disregard of the code. In many cases, it's a little of both.

The *NEC* is updated every three years, and it's difficult to keep up with all the changes. Many states require electricians to stay current by taking an update course during each code cycle. Many electricians don't bother to take the update course, however, until near the end of the cycle. By the time they learn about current changes, the code is about to change again.

Tub or Hot Tub?

Hydromassage bathtubs are a common source of code misinterpretations, because they are often confused with hot tubs. The rules for grounding and locating outlets and switches around hot tubs are much stricter than those dealing with hydromassage bathtubs.

According to the current *NEC*, "a hydromassage bathtub is designed so it can accept, circulate, and discharge water upon each use," and a "spa or hot tub is not designed or intended to have its contents drained or discharged after each use."

A bathtub with massage jets is clearly not a hot tub, yet many inspectors will require one to be wired as if it was. You won't achieve much, however, by waving the *NEC* in your inspector's face and arguing the point. Just find out what the inspector requires before you do the job.

"Accessible Outlet" Confusion

In garages, all receptacles on the ground level must be GFCI-protected — with two exceptions. No GFCI protection is required on "receptacles that are not readily accessible," or on a receptacle that is "located within dedicated space" and intended for use only with a single appliance.

The confusion lies in the phrase "readily accessible." If a receptacle cannot be reached without a ladder, few people would consider it readily accessible. Many inspectors, however, will require a GFCI-protected receptacle for a garage door opener receptacle because this is

Figure 13. Sloppy wiring like this is an invitation to an inspector to check the job very carefully for further violations.

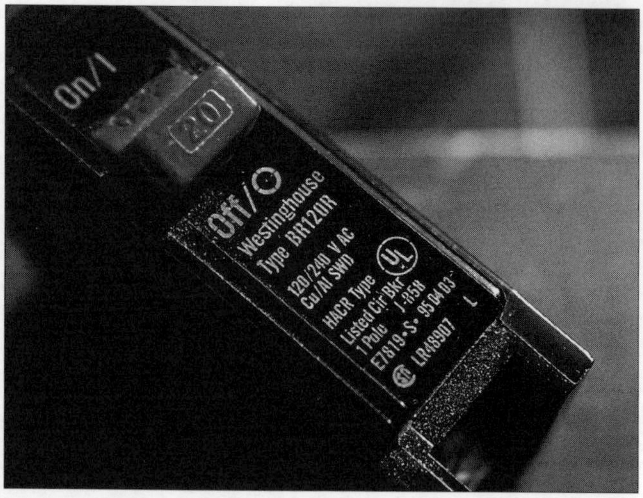

Figure 14. An approval from Underwriters Laboratory is the accepted industry standard for materials used in electrical installations. But keep your eyes open — lots of home centers sell non-UL-listed equipment because it's cheaper.

often the "most accessible" outlet in the garage. Other inspectors consider it a dedicated, single-appliance receptacle and don't require a GFCI.

Using Improper Equipment

Listing services like Underwriters Laboratory (UL) examine and test electrical equipment to be sure it complies with the *NEC* and other appropriate standards. Violations having to do with product listings come in two categories: using unlisted products, and not using a product according to its listing.

Unlisted products. Keep your eyes open. Many supply houses and home centers carry products that are not listed by UL or other listing services (Figure 14). These products usually don't meet the standards set by the *NEC*. Their selling point is that they are usually much cheaper than their listed counterparts. These unlisted products most often turn up in very competitive markets where price is always a big issue.

These products can show up in a project for a variety of reasons. Sometimes it's just because the electrician didn't check the stock carefully; sometimes UL-listed stock is unavailable and the job needs to be finished. And occasionally an electrician will use unlisted products because of the cheaper price.

Many inspectors in my area keep an eye out for these unlisted materi-

---

FREQUENT VIOLATIONS

Stapling Romex. Romex must be secured within 12 inches of the box and every 4¹/2 feet thereafter. Not securing Romex properly is one of the most obvious code violations. It's one of those "neat and workmanlike" violations that tip off an inspector to check everything carefully.

Outside receptacle. In new construction, some electricians will wire the outside receptacle from the kitchen appliance circuit. This is a clear violation of the 1996 *NEC*. The outdoor circuit can come off of any other nearby circuit or be a homerun back to the panel.

Underground service riser. When running wires underground, many electricians forget to put clips on the conduit riser that houses the wire from the ground up to the meter socket. The riser must be secured within 3 feet of the meter socket. Some inspectors will pass a riser that's buried at least 2 feet deep — but some won't. The *NEC* says that you must clip the pipe to the house.

Many municipalities also require an expansion fitting on the PVC riser where it comes out of the ground to protect against ground movement damaging the equipment (Figure A).

Subpanels. Most electricians know that a subpanel must be wired using a four-wire feed rather than a three-wire feed, but many are still confused about where to connect the wires in the subpanel.

In the main panel, the ground and the neutral wires from each circuit are tied into a single neutral/ground bar. The subpanel has separate ground and neutral bars.

The ground bar must be bonded to the subpanel and the neutral bar must be isolated from the subpanel. The ground wire coming from the main panel will go to the ground bar and the neutral wire will go to neutral bar. All branch circuits will be tied in with the ground wires on the ground bar and the neutral wires on the neutral bar.

Circuits labels. The *NEC* says "All panelboard circuits and circuit modifications shall be legibly identified as to purpose or use on a circuit directory located on the face or inside of the panel doors." Many electricians fail to mark the circuit breakers after doing work.

Changeover fittings. When you switch from one wiring method to another, you must use a changeover fitting. The most common place this violation occurs is in the cellar. When using a piece of pipe as a sleeve for Romex, many electricians do not use a combination connector (changeover fitting) at the top of the pipe to secure the Romex to the pipe (Figure B). — *S.K.*

Figure A. The PVC riser that carries the main service feed to a house's electric meter needs an expansion fitting near the ground. Without it, the movement from the freezing and thawing of the soil could crack the pipe.

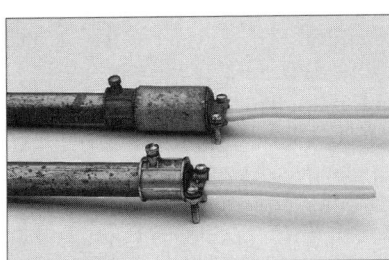

Figure B. When switching from one wiring method to another, code requires a changeover fitting (at bottom) or a similar transition fitting made from standard parts (at top).

als and require the electrician to replace them with listed materials.

Ground clamps are a good example of an unlisted product which is inferior to its listed counterpart. UL-listed ground clamps are made of brass, while unlisted ground clamps are usually made of cast aluminum. If you tighten an aluminum ground clamp firmly, it can break later, even if everything looks okay when you install it.

Follow listing instructions. The *NEC* says, "... equipment shall be installed, used or both, in accordance with any instructions included in the listing or labeling."

The most common violation of this type has to do with circuit breakers. Many brands of circuit breakers are physically interchangeable, but don't be fooled: Just because it fits doesn't mean you can use it. The model number on the circuit breaker must be printed on the circuit breaker panel cover. Usually breaker panels will only accept breakers of the same brand.

Permits and Licensing

Some electricians will perform work without pulling the necessary permits. If the inspector discovers this, he will shut down the job and often fine the electrician. In many areas the electrician will have to pay double for the permit if he is caught working without one.

Most states also require one licensed electrician for every helper on the job; some require a master electrician to be present if there is more than one journeyman on the job.

Another common problem crops up when electrical work is performed by someone without an electrician's license, such as other tradespeople. Hvac contractors, remodelers, and alarm installers will sometimes do their own electrical work to save time and money. While nonelectrician tradespeople may know how to make something work electrically, they seldom know the codes involved. This can lead to some dangerous installations.

By Sean Kenney, a master electrician from Amesbury, Mass.

GFCI Circuits

Whenever a customer asks me to defend the need for GFCIs (ground-fault circuit interrupters), I recount the old movie scene where the radio falls — or is thrown — into a water-filled bathtub, swiftly electrocuting the unfortunate bather. I then explain that if the radio had been plugged into a GFCI receptacle, the bather would still be alive. This leads us to the ultimate purpose of GFCIs — the protection of life.

Do GFCIs work? Absolutely. These devices have saved countless lives and provide much needed protection for both the tradesman and homeowner.

If you are ever unlucky enough to receive an electrical shock, but lucky enough to have a GFCI in the line, it will feel like you're being stuck with a needle, then the GFCI will trip and open the circuit, stopping the current.

How GFCIs Work

In ordinary 125-volt residential circuits using NM (non-metallic sheath) wire, the amperage leaving the panel, usually through a black wire, must equal the amperage returning to the panel through a neutral, or white, wire.

A GFCI continually monitors the amount of current going to the load and compares it to that coming back. As long as the two are equal, the electricity is doing its work properly. However, if some of the electrons are missing and the current coming back from the load is less than that going to it, the GFCI will trip the circuit. The logic of GFCI design is that if the current is not coming back via the wiring, it must be going somewhere else. Often this "somewhere else" is to earth (ground) through a person holding a tool or appliance.

Here's an example from my own experience. I was using a drill that was plugged into an extension cord that, in turn, was plugged into a GFCI receptacle in my garage. The drill was old and the shell made out of solid metal. While I was using it, one of the wires inside the drill shorted to the metal case, which made it electrically hot. Since electricity can cause mus-

cles to contract, my hand tightened around the metal handle so that I could not release it. The current was now leaving the service panel, traveling through the black wire of the house wiring to the GFCI, then through the extension cord into the drill. From the drill, the current was flowing through me to ground. This was a classic ground fault: The electrical short within the drill caused the current to pass through me to ground, rather than flowing back to the service panel via the white wire. The GFCI detected this imbalance and opened the circuit immediately, saving my life. My only discomfort was the pin prick feeling.

Split-second response. The time it takes for a GFCI to open a circuit will vary from manufacturer to manufacturer, but it should be no more than $1/30$ of a second to comply with UL standards. The actual amount of current imbalance that the GFCI must detect before it trips is four to six milliamps (thousandths of an amp), also a UL standard. Theoretically, the average person can tolerate four to six milliamps of current for 1/30 of a second before his or her heart goes into fibrillation. (Fibrillation means that the heart goes out of sync; the result can be death.) With GFCI protection, you may still get a shock, but its duration will be limited to 1/30 of a second.

Why doesn't the circuit breaker trip? Most circuit breakers controlling general purpose receptacles will not trip until at least 15 or 20 amps of current flow has been exceeded. This amount of current is normally fatal. In order to protect against fatal shocks, you need a device on line, like the GFCI, that will trip before the circuit breaker can trip.

Common sense. Just because you are plugged into a GFCI doesn't mean that you can cast all common sense to the wind. You can still die if your body — your heart in particular — is placed between the incoming black wire and the outgoing white wire. In this case, your body is in series with the electrical current, just like a light bulb. As long as your body isn't grounded, you are no different to the GFCI than a normal working load (Figure 15). If you get caught in this situation, the GFCI will not trip because there is no current leakage to ground to create an imbalance...and you could be killed.

GFCI Types

For residences, GFCIs come in two types (Figure 16). One type looks like a receptacle. It has a test button on it and sometimes a light. The second type looks like a 15- or 20-amp circuit breaker with a test button on it. In both designs, the purpose of the test button is, when pressed, to place a current imbalance on the circuit. The GFCI should then trip if it is working properly.

Circuit breaker GFCIs. Use a GFCI circuit breaker only if all receptacles on the circuit require ground-fault protection. It fits into the service panel like a standard breaker but wires a little differently. Circuit

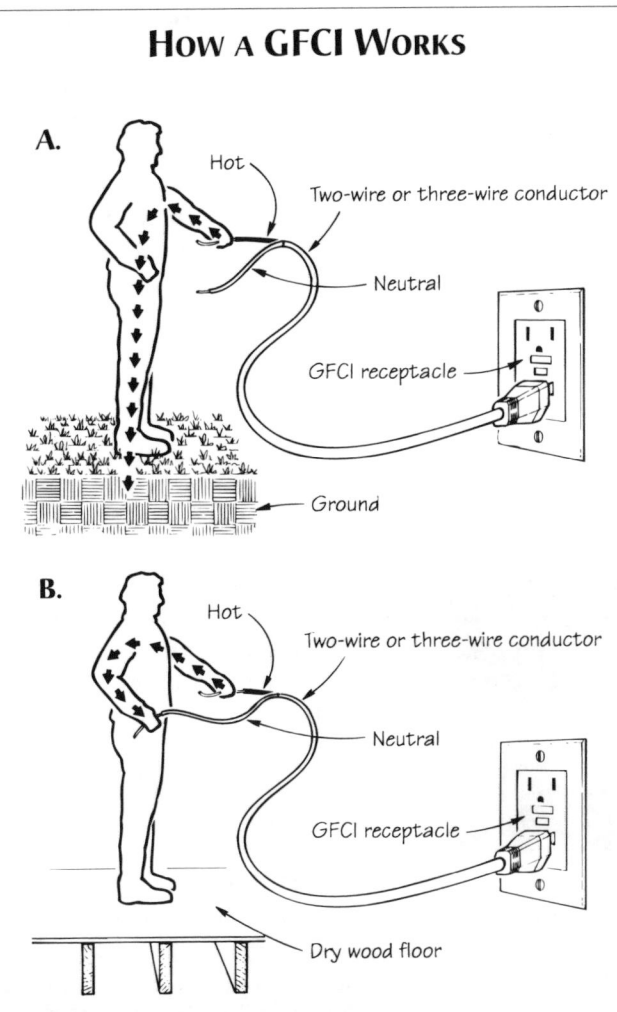

How a GFCI Works

Figure 15. A GFCI trips when it senses a current imbalance, protecting you from shock if you accidentally contact a hot conductor while you are grounded (A). If you come between a black and white conductor and are not grounded, however, a GFCI may not protect you (B), since there will be no current imbalance.

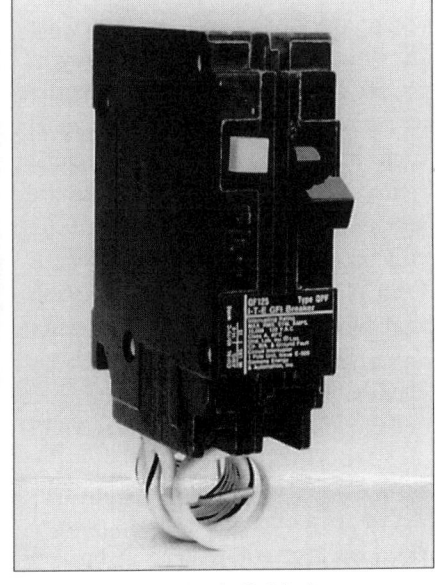

Figure 16. Residential ground-fault circuit interrupters are available in two types. Use receptacle-style GFCIs where possible for convenient resetting at the point of use (left). GFCI circuit breakers (right) protect an entire circuit but must be reset at the panel.

281

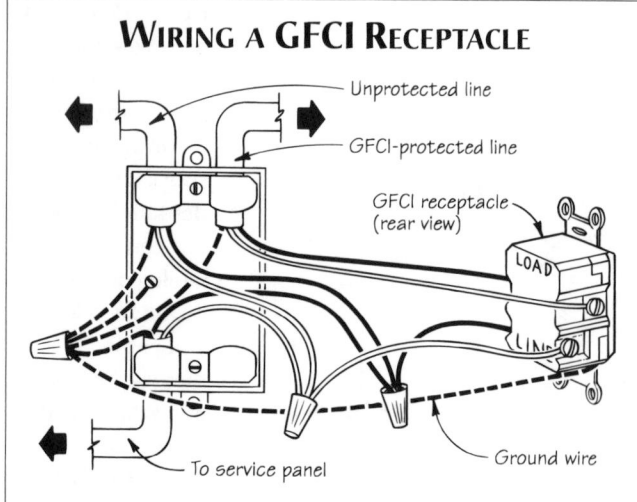

WIRING A GFCI RECEPTACLE

Unprotected line

GFCI-protected line

GFCI receptacle (rear view)

LOAD

LINE

To service panel

Ground wire

Figure 17. To give ground-fault protection to downstream receptacles, you must wire them off the load side of the GFCI.

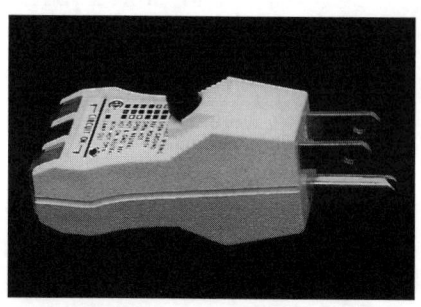

Figure 18. This plug-in tester can test a GFCI receptacle and any downstream receptacles it protects, but only in a grounded circuit.

breaker GFCIs have two main disadvantages: They cost more than receptacle GFCIs and are somewhat inconvenient. Because they're located in the service panel, the homeowner has to walk to the panel each time the GFCI trips the circuit.

Receptacle GFCIs are fed from the service panel through a standard circuit breaker. The GFCI receptacle is then placed at the point of use so that when it trips, the homeowner can immediately reset it without leaving the room.

I recommend using GFCI receptacles wherever possible inside the house, both for cost and convenience. However, the cost can escalate far above the cost of a circuit-breaker GFCI if you install them at several locations on a single circuit.

To power outdoor receptacles, however, I definitely recommend using a

GFCI circuit breaker. Experience has shown that GFCI receptacles can have a short life span when located outside, even in watertight boxes. The boxes and lids may be watertight but they are not vapor tight. The water vapor seems to shorten the life of the electronics within.

Incorrect Wiring of GFCIs

A GFCI receptacle may be wired incorrectly by a homeowner or novice electrician. GFCI receptacles have a "line," or input, side and a "load," or output, side. The line side must be connected to the wiring that originates at the service panel. The load side must be connected to any downside receptacles that are to be protected (Figure 17).

Often a receptacle GFCI is wired incorrectly by pigtailing the downstream receptacles off the line side. These receptacles are now in parallel with the GFCI and are not ground-fault protected. Only those receptacles feeding out of the load side will be protected.

Remember to label any downstream receptacles as ground-fault protected. Use the stickers supplied with the receptacle expressly for this purpose. Inspectors often overlook this, but be sure to do it anyway. Without the label, the homeowner has no way of knowing that a particular outlet is protected.

It is also possible to wire a circuit-breaker GFCI incorrectly. However, the incorrect hookup would be immediately apparent if the "test" button doesn't trip the device. Under test, this type of device typically places an eight milliamp ground-fault on the circuit.

Testing

Always test GFCIs (using the test button located on the GFCI) immediately after installation. If you are at a site where you will be using a pre-existing GFCI to power your tools, always test it first to verify that the ground-fault protection is still working. It's possible to obtain 125 volts from a GFCI receptacle without its ground-fault protection working. Manufacturers normally request monthly testing of GFCIs.

Plug-in tester. Do not test a GFCI by shorting across the hot-to-neutral slots in the receptacle. This will not test the GFCI and may cause damage. Three-prong plug-in testers with a push button are specifically designed for the testing of GFCIs and are commonly available at most electrical supply houses. This type of tester typically places a .0068-amp current imbalance on the line to trip the GFCI. All electricians, contractors, and inspectors should carry and use these little testers (Figure 18).

You can also use a plug-in tester to test a GFCI that has several receptacles on its load side. First test the actual GFCI receptacle or GFCI circuit breaker. Then test the most distant receptacle working off its load side. The GFCI should trip when you push the button on the tester.

Testing GFCIs in an ungrounded circuit. Plug-in testers create an actual fault to the ground wire in a three-wire circuit, causing the GFCI to trip if it is working properly. However, this can lead to uncertain test results for a GFCI installed in an ungrounded (two-wire) circuit. The GFCI may actually work fine, but it will not respond to the tester since there is no ground wire to short to.

However, for UL-approved receptacle GFCIs, the test button on the device itself will still yield an accurate test. This is because the built-in test device works by taking some of the current from the black wire on the load side of the GFCI and shunting it back to the white wire on the line side to unbalance the circuit. This is, in effect, a ground-fault simulation rather than a true ground fault, but the imbalance effect is the same.

Code Requirements

The National Electric Code (NEC) defines where and how GFCIs should be used. Here are some of the more common regulations affecting residences. (Unless otherwise stated, "receptacle" refers to a 125-volt, single-phase, 15-amp or 20-amp standard residential receptacle.)

Kitchen. All countertop receptacles within a 6-foot straight-line distance from the kitchen sink must have GFCI protection. Since, according to code, two separate circuits must feed the countertop receptacles, I normally wire my kitchens with one GFCI circuit to the left of the sink and one GFCI circuit to the right (assuming the sink is in the center of the countertop). This normally separates the load evenly and, if I come back ten years later to troubleshoot a problem, I know exactly how the circuits are wired. I use GFCI receptacles, as opposed to circuit breaker GFCIs, since the former can be reset at the point-of-use in the kitchen. Countertop receptacles beyond the 6-foot limit, as well as other general use kitchen, dining, and pantry receptacles, can be wired into the line, or unprotected, side of the GFCI.

Bathroom. All receptacles installed in bathrooms must have GFCI protection. I always use receptacle GFCIs for reset convenience.

Garage. Every receptacle in a garage must have GFCI protection

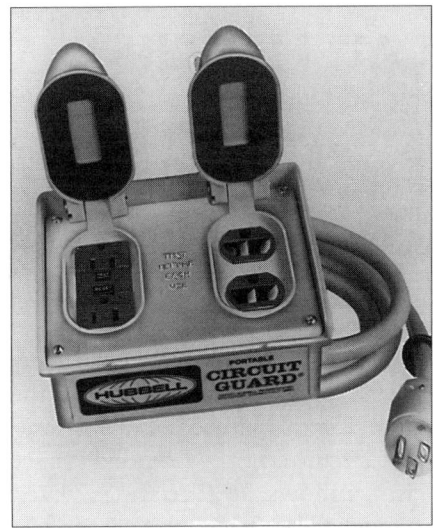 

Figure 19. GFCI-protected extension cords are recommended by OSHA for power tool use in outdoor or damp locations (at left). Another option is a portable plug-in GFCI (at right).

unless it is not readily accessible, such as a receptacle located on the ceiling for a garage door opener, or one serving a plug-in appliance occupying dedicated space, such as a freezer. Any 230-volt outlet is exempt, as is the laundry circuit.

Outdoors. All receptacles installed outdoors that are readily accessible and within 6 feet 6 inches of grade level must have ground-fault protection.

Unfinished basements and crawlspaces at or below grade level. All receptacles installed in these locations must have ground-fault protection, except for:
- A single (not duplex or triplex) receptacle supplied by a dedicated branch circuit for a plug-in appliance such as a freezer or refrigerator
- A laundry circuit
- A single receptacle supplying a permanently installed sump pump

Job-site protection. In most areas of the country, builders are required to use a GFCI-protected temporary panel. This type of panel normally protects single-phase, 125-volt, 15-amp and 20-amp receptacle outlets. If you use a generator of five kilowatts or less, you may be exempt. (See Section 305(6)(a) of the NEC

for more information.) Extension cords with built-in GFCI protection are also available for job-site use and are recommended by OSHA (Figure 19).

Where Not to Use GFCIs

Even though it isn't against code, room lights should not be placed on a GFCI unless there is a specific need for doing so. The reason is simple: If the GFCI trips, you don't want to be left in the dark trying to find your way out of the room — especially in the bathroom, where the floor might be wet and slippery, with many objects to bump against or trip over.

Avoid this by wiring only the receptacles in the room, if you want them protected, off the load side of the GFCI, but put the lights on the line side.

Also, unless there is a specific reason, don't use a GFCI for equipment and appliances that cannot go without power for an extended time, such as a freezer or sump pump, since GFCIs are sensitive and are subject to nuisance tripping.

By Rex Cauldwell, a master electrician and owner of Little Mountain Electric in Copper Hill, Va.

PLUG-IN ELECTRICAL TESTERS

Plug-in testers are a safe, inexpensive way to troubleshoot 120-volt household circuits. By simply plugging in the tester, you get the results of a variety of tests, indicated by a series of three lights on the front of the unit. A key on the tester tells you what each particular combination of lights means.

Plug-in testers will work only with 120-volt receptacles. If a receptacle is incorrectly wired with 240 volts, the unit will be destroyed when it's plugged in. Most plug-in testers perform several standard tests; the most common are described below.

1. Correct Wiring

There's not a lot to say here — obviously, this is the reading you want — but there is one point that I can't stress enough. When wiring a receptacle, never use the push-in type connections that come on the backs of some receptacles. These are not reliable; they may work loose over time. Always use the screws; otherwise, a "Correct Wiring" indication one month may result in a dangerous situation the next month.

Loop the stripped end of the wire around the screw and tighten it snugly. Make sure you loop the wire so that it gets tighter, not looser, as you tighten the screw.

2. Reversed Polarity

I've been asked why this matters. "What difference does it make if you plug in a lamp and the current goes in the neutral leg and comes out the hot leg? The light bulb still comes on, doesn't it?"

Not long ago, a little girl in my home state put her tongue into the round metal bulb holder of a decorative electric candle — the kind you see in windows at Christmas. Even though the switch was off, the girl was electrocuted because the fixture had been wired backwards and the round cylinder that holds the bulb was hot.

On a recent service call, I was working on a pump in an underground concrete enclosure. The owner had switched off the power; I measured 0 volts from hot to neutral. But when I touched the neutral, I got a nasty shock that caused my elbow to smash into the concrete wall. Remeasuring, I read 120 volts from neutral to earth. On troubleshooting, I found that the receptacle the pump was plugged into was wired in reverse, so the neutral was hot. I went home with a sore, bruised elbow, but the situation could have been lethal.

If a branch circuit is wired backward, the same situation exists every time an appliance or light fixture is plugged in. Unfortunately, this is more common than you might think. In some cases, I have seen entire houses wired in reverse. The only remedy is to rewire.

3. Open Neutral

If the neutral is open, a plugged-in tool or appliance should not work. This presents no danger unless the user attempts to work on the tool or appliance while it is still plugged in. Since the hot is still connected, the user could provide a neutral path and get a severe shock. The same applies inside the receptacle — turn off the power at the panel before rewiring.

If you check the receptacle and the neutral is properly connected, you'll need to trace the wire back toward the panel, looking for a loose connection or a nail that has cut the wire. A loose or partially severed wire can cause a fire. Always leave the power off until you find and fix the problem.

4. Open Hot

An open hot is immediately obvious: None of the display lights on the tester will light. Turn the circuit off as soon as you've finished making the test; a loose or broken hot can start a fire.

If there is nothing obviously wrong inside the box, you'll have to look for a loose connection or severed wire somewhere in the circuit.

5. Open Ground

In this case, there is no ground connection at the receptacle, perhaps because it's a two-wire circuit, or because the ground wire has come loose, or because the installer cut the ground wire too short to make the connection. (Sometimes this is done on purpose because an untrained installer doesn't know what to do with the wire.)

An open ground gives the illusion of safety when actually there is grave danger. People see the three-prong

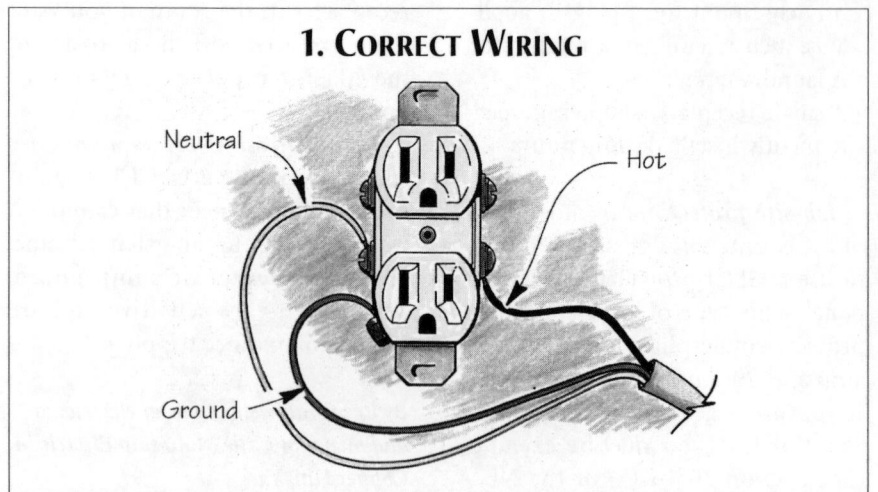

1. CORRECT WIRING

Neutral

Hot

Ground

receptacle and assume there's a proper ground. If a tool or appliance plugged into that receptacle develops a hot-to-ground fault, the user can get shocked and possibly electrocuted.

If in fact there is no ground on a circuit, the proper procedure is to use an older-type two-prong receptacle; that way, no one is misled into assuming there's a ground when there isn't. (Code also allows the use of GFCIs in this situation, though I don't like to use them without an actual ground connection.) If the ground wire was cut, you should rewire the receptacle with a properly connected ground.

6. Hot and Ground Reversed

An installer would have to be drunk to do this. This could only happen on a circuit with just one receptacle; otherwise, the breaker would immediately trip. Assuming the one receptacle, it's a potentially lethal situation. If an appliance like a clothes washer or electric drill is plugged in, its frame will be hot and will shock anyone that touches it.

7. Hot on Neutral With Open Hot

I've never encountered this situation and probably never will. It's basically a reversed polarity situation where the neutral has come loose. Even though the hot is on the neutral side, there is no return path to

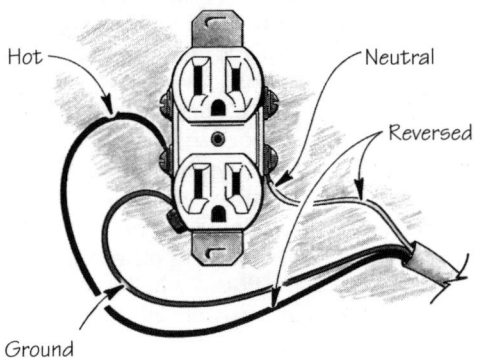

2. REVERSED POLARITY

Hot
Neutral
Reversed
Ground

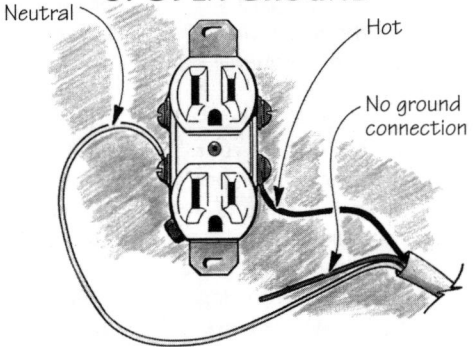

5. OPEN GROUND

Neutral
Hot
No ground connection

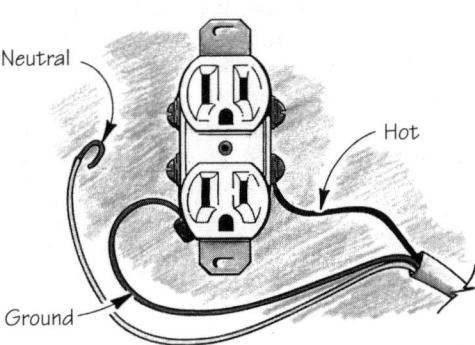

3. OPEN NEUTRAL

Neutral
Hot
Ground

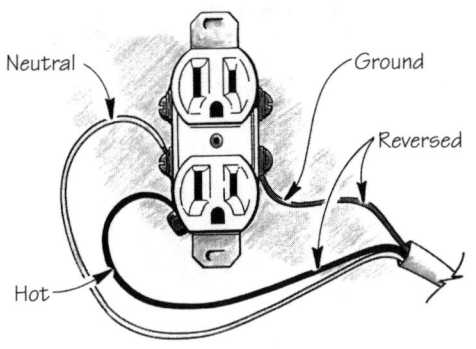

6. HOT AND GROUND REVERSED

Neutral
Ground
Reversed
Hot

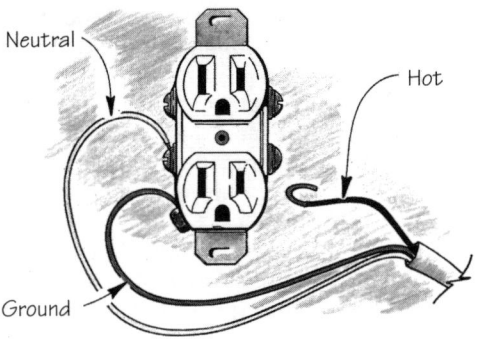

4. OPEN HOT

Neutral
Hot
Ground

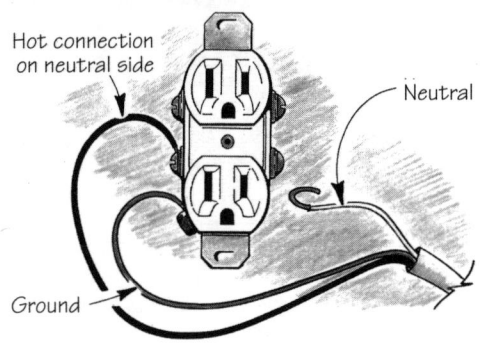

7. HOT ON NEUTRAL WITH OPEN HOT

Hot connection on neutral side
Neutral
Ground

ADVANCED PLUG-IN TESTER

Industrial Commercial Electronics has taken the plug-in tester concept to a new level of sophistication with its SureTest line of "branch circuit analyzers." Besides the usual checks that common plug-in testers do, the SureTest ST-1D (the model we tested) will check for a bootleg ground, read line voltage, check for voltage drop, measure the load on the circuit between the receptacle and the panel, and measure the impedance of the building's grounding path. Considering the cost — less than $300 — the tool is great for anyone who needs to quickly and safely check a circuit.

Say, for instance, that you're adding on a home office for your client, and that the office will be stuffed with expensive, state-of-the-art electronic equipment — computer, fax machine, copier, etc. Despite assurances from the electrician, and despite the presence of plug-in surge protector strips at every receptacle, your client still wants evidence that the equipment is protected against power surges (either from the utility or lightning), and that neither noise in the lines nor power fluctuations will garble data. Unfortunately, there is no way for you to guaran-

tee protection against lightning — the voltage from a near or direct hit is massive; and it's up to the power company to deliver continuous, good-quality electricity. But with the SureTest, you can be reasonably certain of the power quality within the house itself.

So you pull out the SureTest and plug it in a receptacle. The green lights tell you the receptacle is wired correctly; the digital display confirms that you've got 120 volts present from the utility. (Wild fluctuations in the reading would indicate that the utility is delivering poor-quality power.) You push the "display advance" button, and you get the voltage drop on that receptacle under 15-amp load (given as a percentage of 120 volts). Push the button again and you get voltage drop under 20-amp load.

For either size circuit, any drop under 5% is okay; above that, you may have a problem. Besides causing equipment problems, excessive voltage drop causes heat buildup in the wire and at connections, and can be a fire hazard.

Let's say you get a reading above 5%. Maybe this is because you've pulled the wiring for the addition off a lightly loaded preexisting bed-

room circuit, but the extra length of wire is creating too much resistance. So you rewire the circuit as a "homerun" back to the panel. Or maybe there's a bad connection at the receptacle that's causing the resistance. Either way, you locate the problem, fix it, and test again.

The next test is for excessive voltage between ground and neutral — an indication of how much noise is in the lines from the operation of other appliances on the circuit. For computer operation, a few volts is okay; for dedicated lines for faxes or copiers, no more than a few millivolts should be present. With this test, it's best to leave the SureTest plugged in overnight, or even for a few days. It will hold the peak reading that develops. That way, you can figure out how the intermittent operation of other appliances on the line — a hairdryer, a television, or a vacuum cleaner — might affect the circuit.

Push the advance button again and you get a reading of the load on that circuit, in amps, back to the panel (it's best to take this reading from the last receptacle on the circuit). This is a good way to check a dedicated circuit; if you get any reading at all, it may mean that the circuit shares a neutral. Again, the SureTest allows you to test for load over an extended period; just leave the device plugged in and it will record the peak reading.

A final test measures the resistance of the ground path in ohms — a very important test when it comes to sensitive electronic equipment. A low reading, preferably below .25 ohms, helps assure that excessive voltages that may develop in the line (from lightning or a power spike, for example) will be safely returned to ground at the panel without destroying equipment.

For more information on the SureTest ST-1D or other less expensive models, contact ICE (2421 Harlem Rd., Buffalo, NY 14225; 800/442-3462). — R.C.

This branch circuit analyzer performs more sophisticated tests than a common plug-in tester. For example, it can check for false grounds and measure voltage and voltage drops.

complete the circuit. Appliances won't work when plugged into a receptacle wired this way.

GFCI Button

Many testers also have a GFCI test button. When the button is pressed, a simulated ground fault is placed on the line. A properly working GFCI will trip (assuming it's on a grounded circuit). You can also test GFCI-protected receptacles wired downstream from a GFCI receptacle (or circuit breaker). The simulated ground fault at the downstream receptacle should trip the GFCI receptacle.

Although GFCI receptacles will work on two-wire circuits, they can't be tested with plug-in testers, which work by creating an actual fault to ground. On two-wire circuits you have to use the test button on the GFCI receptacle itself.

Plug-In Tester Limitations

Be aware of what these testers cannot test for:

• *False, or "bootleg," ground:* This is where some idiot has jumped the neutral onto the ground connection of the receptacle (see illustration, above right). Why? Who knows? It might be an effort to fool an inspector into thinking a circuit is grounded when it's not. This is a very dangerous connection and can be life-threatening. Assuming something is plugged into that receptacle and turned on, this puts current on the grounding circuit in parallel with the neutral. That means anyone using an appliance anywhere on that branch would be in danger of shock.

• *Ground and neutral reversed:* This is rare because most people wiring a receptacle know that the ground wire is the bare wire. If it should happen, an appliance plugged into that receptacle will put current flow through the grounding wire instead of the neutral. This can endanger anyone who operates an appliance anywhere on that branch circuit. (It also endangers an electrician who is troubleshooting the circuit.)

• *Quality of ground:* This is a test to verify that the ground resistance path from the receptacle to the main panel is not only intact but is also a low-resistance path. This can only be done with a more elaborate plug-in tester (see "Advanced Plug-In Tester").

• *Any combination of defects:* If two of the tests share the same indicator light — for example, the open neutral test and the open hot test — you might think there is only

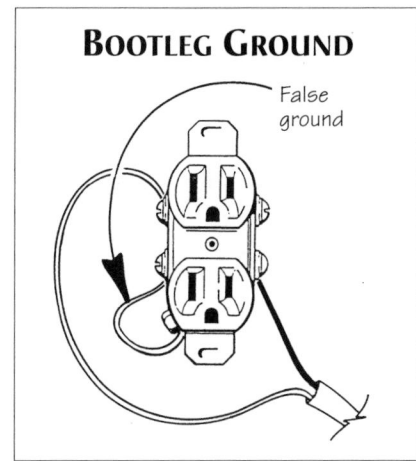

BOOTLEG GROUND

False ground

an open hot when the neutral is also open. Since the power is off to the receptacle (because of the open hot), there is no way for the tester to light the indicator for the open neutral. The solution is to remedy the open hot, then retest for other faults.

• *Check a standard two-prong ungrounded receptacle:* For this, you will need a more expensive test device, one with a retractable ground prong.

• *Check for voltage drop on the line:* Again, this is a job for the professional tester.

By Rex Cauldwell, a master electrician and owner of Little Mountain Electric in Copper Hill, Va.

INDEX

OTHER TITLES FROM BUILDERBURG GROUP, INC.

Builderburg Group, Inc. publishes *The Journal of Light Construction*, the building industry's leading technical magazine. For subscription information, call **800-859-3669**.

The Lead Carpenter Handbook: The Complete, Hands-On Guide to Successful Job-Site Management
The practical guide to understanding, developing, and implementing this powerful job-site management system. It allows a remodeling or custom building company to grow and increase profits while maintaining the quality and attention to detail that small contractors take pride in. Written for both contractors and lead carpenters, you get practical step-by-step advice, plus numerous field-tested forms and checklists.
196 pages, 7x10, softcover — #TLF98: $29.95

The Contractor's Legal Kit
Written in plain English by construction attorney and contractor Gary Ransone, this user-friendly guide gives you a proven approach to running a more profitable business. Includes all the forms, contracts, and practical techniques you need to take control of your jobs from the first client meeting to collecting the last check. All forms and contracts included on IBM-compatible (DOS/WINDOWS) computer disk.
344 pages, 8^{1}/2x11, softcover — #LB001: $59.95

Managing the Small Construction Business: A Hands-On Guide
An outstanding resource for the builder or remodeler who came up through the trades and is now running his own business — or would like to. With over 50 business articles from *The Journal of Light Construction*, it provides detailed solutions to all the problems and challenges a residential contractor faces.
244 pages, 8^{1}/2x11, softcover — #MS362: $27.95

Kitchens & Baths: A Builder's Guide to Design and Construction
An excellent reference for any professional involved in the remodeling, construction, or design of kitchens and baths, this book contains over 50 *Journal of Light Construction* articles on every phase of K&B design and construction, plus up-to-date material on codes, safety, and space planning. Over 400 photos and illustrations.
256 pages, 8^{1}/2x11, softcover — #KB300: $34.95

Advanced Framing: Techniques, Troubleshooting and Structural Design
How far can I safely cantilever the floor joists? How many collar ties can I remove before the roof sags? You'll find answers to these and hundreds of other questions about residential framing in this best-selling volume from *The Journal*. Over 46 articles with over 250 photos and illustrations.
288 pages, 8^{1}/2x11, softcover — #AF002: $27.95

To order a book or obtain a copy of our full bookstore catalog, please call **800-859-3669**
($3.50 shipping and handling for book orders in continental U.S.)

Publisher Provided Course Homepage

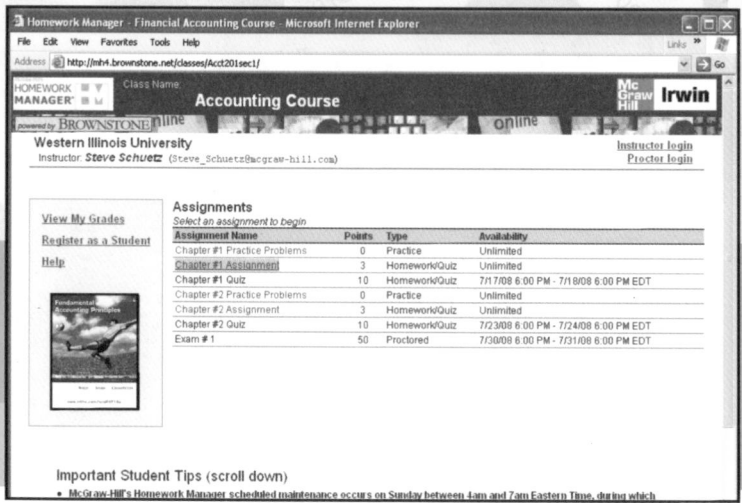

McGraw-Hill's **HOMEWORK MANAGER PLUS** HM
THE COMPLETE SOLUTION

Wild/Shaw/Chiappetta
Fundamental Accounting
Principles, 19e
978-0-07-7336623-4

2 TERM

Easily Assign Online Homework

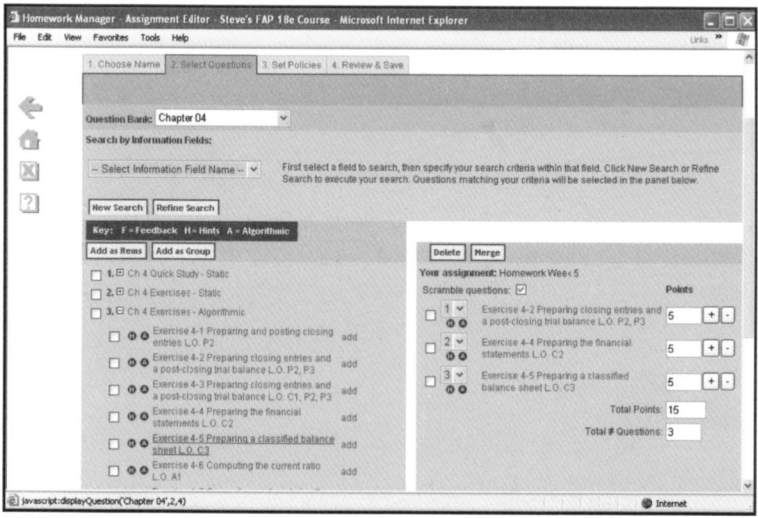

Track Student Results

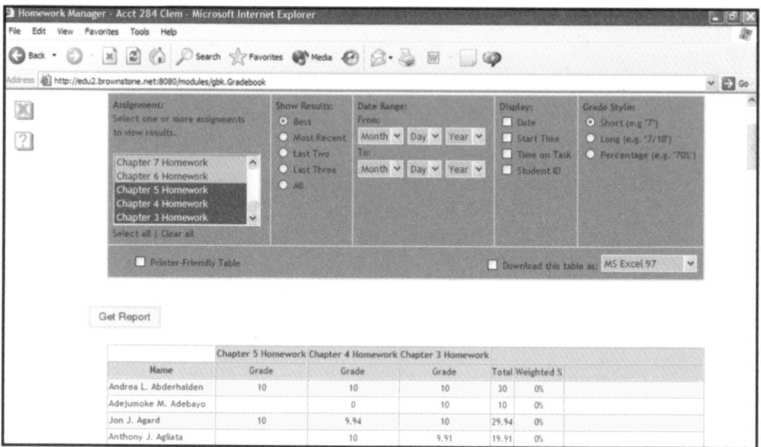

It's that easy.

Continuously Improving!

McGraw-Hill is committed to listening to our customers and making changes based on our customer desires; hence we are updating our system to bring you the following new features:

- Single Entry Point, Single Registration, Single Sign-on
- Local Time Zone Support
- Enhanced Grade Book Reporting Capabilities
  - Run reports on multiple sections at once
  - Export reports to WebCT and BlackBoard
- Enhanced Question Selection
  - Select by learning objective, AACSB Accreditation Criteria
- Enhanced Assignment Policies
- Enhanced eBook*
- Integrated eBook – Simple Toggle (no secondary log-in)
  - Topic Search
  - Adjustable text size
  - Jump to Page #
  - Print by Section
- Student Assignment Preview for Instructors

study on the go
THIS TEXT IS Media Integrated

It provides students with
portable educational content

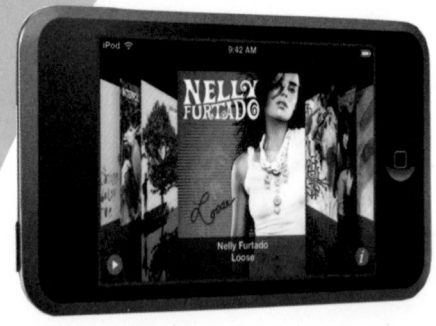

Based on research and feedback, we realize the study habits of today's students are changing. Students want the option to study when and where it's most convenient to them. They are asking for more than the traditional textbook to keep them motivated and to make course content more relevant. McGraw-Hill listened to these requests and is proud to bring you this **Media Integrated** textbook.

This Media Integrated edition adds new downloadable content for the Apple iPods® and most other MP3/MP4 devices. iPod icons appear throughout the text pointing students to related audio and video presentations, quizzes and other related content that correlate to the text. iPod content can be purchased and quickly downloaded online from the text website.

This iPod content gives students a strong set of educational materials that will help them learn by listening and/or watching them on their iPod.

Look for this iPod icon throughout the text.
Icons connect textbook content to your iPod or other MP3 device.

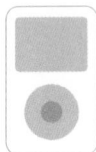

Content includes:
- Lecture presentations
  Audio and video
  Audio only
  Video only
- Demonstration problems+
- Interactive self quizzes*
- Accounting videos+

+Available with some textbooks

* Available for certain iPod models only.

Don't have an iPod? Content
can be viewed on any computer! Visit the text website for directions.

Want to see iPod in action?
Visit **www.mhhe.com/ipod** to view a demonstration of our iPod® content.

19 edition

Fundamental Accounting Principles

John J. Wild
University of Wisconsin at Madison

Ken W. Shaw
University of Missouri at Columbia

Barbara Chiappetta
Nassau Community College

McGraw-Hill
Irwin

Boston   Burr Ridge, IL   Dubuque, IA   New York
San Francisco   St. Louis   Bangkok   Bogotá   Caracas   Kuala Lumpur
Lisbon   London   Madrid   Mexico City   Milan   Montreal   New Delhi
Santiago   Seoul   Singapore   Sydney   Taipei   Toronto

To my wife **Gail** and children, **Kimberly, Jonathan, Stephanie,** and **Trevor.**
To my wife **Linda** and children, **Erin, Emily,** and **Jacob.**
To my husband **Bob,** my sons **Michael** and **David,** and my **mother.**

**McGraw-Hill
Irwin**

FUNDAMENTAL ACCOUNTING PRINCIPLES

Published by McGraw-Hill/Irwin, a business unit of The McGraw-Hill Companies, Inc., 1221 Avenue of the Americas, New York, NY, 10020. Copyright © 2009, 2007, 2005, 2002, 1999, 1996, 1993, 1990, 1987, 1984, 1981, 1978, 1975, 1972, 1969, 1966, 1963, 1959, 1955 by The McGraw-Hill Companies, Inc. All rights reserved. No part of this publication may be reproduced or distributed in any form or by any means, or stored in a database or retrieval system, without the prior written consent of The McGraw-Hill Companies, Inc., including, but not limited to, in any network or other electronic storage or transmission, or broadcast for distance learning.

Some ancillaries, including electronic and print components, may not be available to customers outside the United States.

This book is printed on acid-free paper.

1 2 3 4 5 6 7 8 9 0 DOW/DOW 0 9 8

ISBN-13: 978-0-07-337954-8 (combined edition)
ISBN-10: 0-07-337954-9 (combined edition)
ISBN-13: 978-0-07-336629-6 (volume 1, chapters 1–12)
ISBN-10: 0-07-336629-3 (volume 1, chapters 1–12)
ISBN-13: 978-0-07-336628-9 (volume 2, chapters 12–25)
ISBN-10: 0-07-336628-5 (volume 2, chapters 12–25)
ISBN-13: 978-0-07-336630-2 (with working papers volume 1, chapters 1–12)
ISBN-10: 0-07-336630-7 (with working papers volume 1, chapters 1–12)
ISBN-13: 978-0-07-336631-9 (with working papers volume 2, chapters 12–25)
ISBN-10: 0-07-336631-5 (with working papers volume 2, chapters 12–25)
ISBN-13: 978-0-07-336627-2 (principles, chapters 1–17)
ISBN-10: 0-07-336627-7 (principles, chapters 1–17)

Vice president and editor-in-chief: *Brent Gordon*
Editorial director: *Stewart Mattson*
Publisher: *Tim Vertovec*
Executive editor: *Steve Schuetz*
Senior developmental editor: *Christina A. Sanders*
Executive marketing manager: *Sankha Basu*
Managing editor: *Lori Koetters*
Full service project manager: *Sharon Monday, Aptara®, Inc.*
Lead production supervisor: *Carol A. Bielski*

Lead designer: *Matthew Baldwin*
Senior photo research coordinator: *Lori Kramer*
Photo researcher: *Sarah Evertson*
Lead media project manager: *Brian Nacik*
Cover and interior design: *Matthew Baldwin*
Cover photo: © *Photolibrary*
Typeface: *10.5/12 Times Roman*
Compositor: *Aptara®, Inc.*
Printer: *R. R. Donnelley*

Library of Congress Cataloging-in-Publication Data

Wild, John J.
  Fundamental accounting principles / John J. Wild, Ken W. Shaw, Barbara Chiappetta.—19 ed.
    p. cm.
  Includes index.
  ISBN-13: 978-0-07-337954-8 (combined edition : alk. paper)
  ISBN-10: 0-07-337954-9 (combined edition : alk. paper)
  ISBN-13: 978-0-07-336629-6 (volume 1 ch. 1–12 : alk. paper)
  ISBN-10: 0-07-336629-3 (volume 1 ch. 1–12 : alk. paper)
  [etc.]
  1. Accounting. I. Shaw, Ken W. II. Chiappetta, Barbara. III. Title.
HF5635.P975 2009
657—dc22

2008035921

www.mhhe.com

Dear Colleagues/Friends,

As we roll out the new edition of *Fundamental Accounting Principles*, we thank each of you who provided suggestions to enrich this textbook. As teachers, we know how important it is to select the right book for our course. This new edition reflects the advice and wisdom of many dedicated reviewers, focus group participants, students, and instructors. Our book consistently rates number one in customer loyalty because of you. Together, we have created the most readable, concise, current, accurate, and innovative accounting book available today.

We are thrilled to welcome Ken Shaw to the *Fundamental Accounting Principles* team with this edition. Ken's teaching and work experience, along with his enthusiasm and dedication to students, fit nicely with our continuing commitment to develop cutting–edge classroom materials for instructors and students.

Throughout the writing process, we steered this book in the manner you directed. This path of development enhanced this book's technology and content, and guided its clear and concise writing.

Reviewers, instructors, and students say this book's enhanced technology caters to different learning styles and helps students better understand accounting. *Homework Manager Plus* offers new features to improve student learning and to assist instructor grading. Our *iPod* content lets students study on the go, while our *Algorithmic Test Bank* provides an infinite variety of exam problems. You and your students will find all these tools easy to apply.

We owe the success of this book to our colleagues who graciously took time to help us focus on the changing needs of today's instructors and students. We feel fortunate to have witnessed our profession's extraordinary devotion to teaching. Your feedback and suggestions are reflected in everything we write. Please accept our heartfelt thanks for your dedication in helping today's students understand and appreciate accounting.

With kindest regards,

John J. Wild   Ken W. Shaw   Barbara Chiappetta

#1 with Customers

Fundamental Accounting Principles rates #1 in Instructor and Student satisfaction over the prior three editions, and we are now proud to report that both independent research and development reviews show that *Fundamental Accounting Principles* is now #1 in customer loyalty!

#1 CUSTOMER LOYALTY

#1 in Accuracy **#1 in Assignments**

#1 in Topic Coverage **#1 in Supplements**

#1 in Readability **#1 in Organization**

#1 in Overall Textbook Satisfaction

With ratings such as these, it is no surprise that *Fundamental Accounting Principles* is the fastest growing textbook in the accounting principles market. Take a look at **what instructors are saying** about *Fundamental Accounting Principles*.

Ken Coffey, Johnson County Community College

"There is nothing about this text that I do not like. We have been using it since I started teaching the course in 1971. We switched texts three times, but always went back to this one and I do not think we will try anything else."

Linda Rose, Westwood College

"Very thorough, readable, and graphically pleasant! Engages students in a variety of activities that create learning opportunities and [...link] materials to real-work scenarios and situations. End-of-chapter materials are engaging learning tools and broaden the learner's opportunity to practice and enhance retention of the chapter content."

Shafi Ullah, Broward CC

"The book contains detailed information with alternative exercises, problems, and cases with 'Beyond the Numbers'."

Gloria Worthy, Southwest Tennessee CC

"FAP is a very good text and it is also good for our students because it addresses a variety of learning styles"

Marilyn Cilolino, Delgado CC

"I have always been a big fan of this book and praise it every chance I get. The authors are great people and are really concerned with their product. They listened to the instructors and take our comments and suggestions seriously. And they are always ready to help or answer any questions one might have."

Phillip Lee, Nashville State Tech CC

"The Wild text packs more useful material into fewer pages than other principles of accounting textbooks."

John J. Wild is a distinguished professor of accounting at the University of Wisconsin at Madison. He previously held appointments at Michigan State University and the University of Manchester in England. He received his BBA, MS, and PhD from the University of Wisconsin.

Professor Wild teaches accounting courses at both the undergraduate and graduate levels. He has received numerous teaching honors, including the Mabel W. Chipman Excellence-in-Teaching Award, the departmental Excellence-in-Teaching Award, and the Teaching Excellence Award from the 2003 and 2005 business graduates at the University of Wisconsin. He also received the Beta Alpha Psi and Roland F. Salmonson Excellence-in-Teaching Award from Michigan State University. Professor Wild has received several research honors and is a past KPMG Peat Marwick National Fellow and is a recipient of fellowships from the American Accounting Association and the Ernst and Young Foundation.

Professor Wild is an active member of the American Accounting Association and its sections. He has served on several committees of these organizations, including the Outstanding Accounting Educator Award, Wildman Award, National Program Advisory, Publications, and Research Committees. Professor Wild is author of *Financial Accounting, Managerial Accounting,* and *College Accounting,* each published by McGraw-Hill/Irwin. His research articles on accounting and analysis appear in The Accounting Review, Journal of Accounting Research, Journal of Accounting and Economics, Contemporary Accounting Research, Journal of Accounting, Auditing and Finance, Journal of Accounting and Public Policy, and other journals. He is past associate editor of Contemporary Accounting Research and has served on several editorial boards including The Accounting Review.

Professor Wild, his wife, and four children enjoy travel, music, sports, and community activities.

Ken W. Shaw is an associate professor of accounting and the CBIZ/MHM Scholar at the University of Missouri. He previously was on the faculty at the University of Maryland at College Park. He received an accounting degree from Bradley University and an MBA and PhD from the University of Wisconsin. He is a Certified Public Accountant with work experience in public accounting.

Professor Shaw teaches financial accounting at the undergraduate and graduate levels. He received the Wiliams Keepers LLC Teaching Excellence award in 2007, was voted the "Most Influential Professor" by the 2005 and 2006 School of Accountancy graduating classes, and is a two-time recipient of the O'Brien Excellence in Teaching Award. He is the advisor to his School's chapter of Beta Alpha Psi, a national accounting fraternity.

Professor Shaw is an active member of the American Accounting Association and its sections. He has served on many committees of these organizations and presented his research papers at national and regional meetings. Professor Shaw's research appears in the Journal of Accounting Research; Contemporary Accounting Research; Journal of Financial and Quantitative Analysis; Journal of the American Taxation Association; Journal of Accounting, Auditing, and Finance; Journal of Financial Research; Research in Accounting Regulation; and other journals. He has served on the editorial boards of Issues in Accounting Education and the Journal of Business Research, and is treasurer of the American Accounting Association's FARS. Professor Shaw is co-author of *Financial and Managerial Accounting* and *College Accounting,* both published by McGraw-Hill.

In his leisure time, Professor Shaw enjoys tennis, cycling, music, and coaching his children's sports teams.

Barbara Chiappetta received her BBA in Accountancy and MS in Education from Hofstra University and is a tenured full professor at Nassau Community College. For the past two decades, she has been an active executive board member of the Teachers of Accounting at Two-Year Colleges (TACTYC), serving 10 years as vice president and as president from 1993 through 1999. As an active member of the American Accounting Association, she has served on the Northeast Regional Steering Committee, chaired the Curriculum Revision Committee of the Two-Year Section, and participated in numerous national committees.

Professor Chiappetta has been inducted into the American Accounting Association Hall of Fame for the Northeast Region. She had also received the Nassau Community College dean of instruction's Faculty Distinguished Achievement Award. Professor Chiappetta was honored with the State University of New York Chancellor's Award for Teaching Excellence in 1997. As a confirmed believer in the benefits of the active learning pedagogy, Professor Chiappetta has authored *Student Learning Tools,* an active learning workbook for a first-year accounting course, published by McGraw-Hill/Irwin.

In her leisure time, Professor Chiappetta enjoys tennis and participates on a U.S.T.A. team. She also enjoys the challenge of bridge. Her husband, Robert, is an entrepreneur in the leisure sport industry. She has two sons—Michael, a lawyer, specializing in intellectual property law in New York, and David, a composer, pursuing a career in music for film in Los Angeles.

Helping students achieve their goal!

Fundamental Accounting Principles 19e

Assist your students in achieving their goals by giving them what they need to succeed in today's accounting principles course.

Whether the goal is to become an accountant or a businessperson, or even just gain an understanding of the principles of accounting, *Fundamental Accounting Principles* (FAP) has helped generations of students succeed by giving them the support in the form of leading-edge accounting content that engages students, with state-of-the-art technology.

With FAP on your team, you'll be passed **engaging content** and a **motivating style** to help students see the relevance of accounting. Students are motivated when reading materials that are clear and relevant. FAP runs ahead of the field in engaging students. Its chapter-opening vignettes showcase dynamic, successful entrepreneurial individuals and companies guaranteed **to interest and excite students.** This edition's featured companies—Best Buy, Circuit City, RadioShack, and Apple—engage students with their annual reports, which are a pathway for learning financial statements. Further, this book's coverage of the accounting cycle fundamentals is widely praised for its clarity and effectiveness.

FAP also delivers innovative technology to help students succeed. **Homework Manager** provides students with instant grading and feedback for assignments that are completed online. **Homework Manager Plus** integrates an online version of the textbook with Homework Manager. Our algorithmic test bank in Homework Manager offers infinite variations of numerical test bank questions. FAP also offers students portable **iPod-ready content** to help students study and raise their scores.

We're confident you'll agree that **FAP will help your students achieve their goal**.

Engaging Content

FAP content continues to set the standard in the principles course. Take a look at Chapters 1, 2 and 3 and you'll see how *FAP* leads with the best coverage of the accounting cycle. We are the first book to cover equity transactions the way most instructors teach it and students learn it—by introducing the separate equity accounts upfront and not waiting until a chapter or two later. Chapter 2 has the time-tested 4-step approach to analyzing transactions: [1] Identify, [2] Analyze, [3] Record, and [4] Post. And Chapter 3 offers a new 3-step process to simplify adjusting accounts. *FAP* also motivates students with engaging chapter openers. Students identify with them and can even picture themselves as future entrepreneurs. Each book includes the financial statements of Best Buy, Circuit City, RadioShack, and Apple to further engage students.

State-of-the-Art Technology

FAP offers the most advanced and comprehensive technology on the market in a seamless, easy-to-use platform. As students learn in different ways, *FAP* provides a technology smorgasbord that helps students learn more effectively and efficiently. Homework Manager, eBook options, and iPod content are some of the options. Homework Manager Plus takes learning to another level by integrating an online version of the book with all the power of Homework Manager. Technology offerings follow:

- Homework Manager
- Homework Manager Plus
- iPod content
- Algorithmic Test Bank

- Online Learning Center
- Carol Yacht's General Ledger
- ALEKS for the Accounting Cycle
- ALEKS for Financial Accounting

Premier Support

McGraw-Hill/Irwin has mobilized a new force of specialists committed to training and supporting the technology we offer. Our commitment to instructor service and support is top notch and leads the industry. Our new "McGraw-Hill Cares" program provides you with the fastest answers to your questions or solutions to your training needs. Ask your McGraw-Hill sales rep about our Key Media Support Plan and the McGraw-Hill Cares Program.

Through contemporary and engaging content, state-of-the-art technology, and committed service and support, *FAP* provides you and your students everything you need to achieve your goals!

How Technology helps

What Can McGraw-Hill Technology Offer You?

Whether you are just getting started with technology in your course, or you are ready to embrace the latest advances in electronic content delivery and course management, McGraw-Hill/Irwin has the technology you need, and provides training and support that will help you every step of the way.

Our most popular technologies, Homework Manager and Homework Manager Plus, are optional online Homework Management systems that will allow you to assign problems and exercises from the text for your students to work out in an online format. Student results are automatically graded, and the students receive instant feedback on their work. Homework Manager Plus adds an online version of the book.

Students can also use the Online Learning Center associated with this book to enhance their knowledge of accounting. Plus we now offer iPod content for students who want to study on the go.

For instructors, we provide all of the crucial instructor supplements on one easy to use Instructor CD-ROM; we can help build a custom class Website for your course using PageOut; we can deliver an online course cartridge for you to use in Blackboard, WebCT, or eCollege; and we have a technical support team that will provide training and support for our key technology products.

How Can Students Study on the Go Using Their iPod?

iPod Content

Harness the power of one of the most popular technology tools students use today–the Apple iPod. Our innovative approach allows students to download audio and video presentations right into their iPod and take learning materials with them wherever they go. Students just need to visit the Online Learning Center at **www.mhhe.com/wildFAP19e** to download our iPod content. For each chapter of the book they will be able to download audio narrated lecture presentations and financial accounting videos for use on various versions of iPods. iPod Touch users can even access self-quizzes.

It makes review and study time as easy as putting in headphones.

How Can My Students Use the Web to Complete Their Homework?

McGraw-Hill's Homework Manager®
is a Web-based supplement that duplicates problem structures directly from the end-of-chapter material in your textbook, using algorithms to provide a limitless supply of online self-graded assignments that can be used for student practice, homework, or testing. Each assignment has a unique solution. Say goodbye to cheating in your classroom; say hello to the power and flexibility you've been waiting for in creating assignments. Most Quick Studies, Exercises, and Problems are available with Homework Manager.

McGraw-Hill's Homework Manager is also a useful grading tool. All assignments can be delivered over the Web and are graded automatically, with the results stored in your private grade book. Detailed results let you see at a glance how each student does on an assignment or an individual problem—you can even see how many tries it took them to solve it.

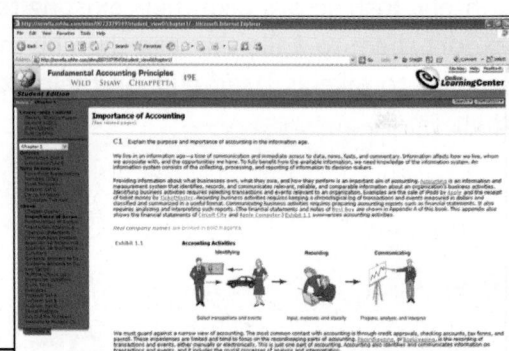

Barbara Gershowitz, Nashville State Technical Community College

"Very thorough . . . and there is a wide variety of supplemental materials that can be used by students. Homework Manager is a real time saver for instructors . . . as it provides immediate feedback to the students and gives them the opportunity to rework problems so that if they did not understand the concept the first time, they can repeat several times until they get it. Homework Manager Plus has worked very well for us. The instructors like it and I have lots of positive feedback from students."

Homework Manager Plus
is an extension of McGraw-Hill's popular Homework Manager System. With Homework Manager Plus you get all of the power of Homework Manager plus an integrated online version of the book. Students simply receive one single access code which provides access to all of the resources available through Homework Manager Plus.

Paula Ratliff, Arkansas State University
"I like the idea that there are online assignments that change algorithmically so that students can practice with them."

When students find themselves needing to reference the textbook to complete their homework, they can now simply click on hints and link directly to the most relevant materials associated with the problem or exercise they are working on.

Use EZ Test Online with Apple iPod® iQuiz to help students succeed.

Using our EZ Test Online you can make test and quiz content available for a student's Apple iPod®.

Students must purchase the iQuiz game application from Apple for 99¢ to use the iQuiz content. It works on the iPod fifth generation iPods and better.

Instructors only need EZ Test Online to produce iQuiz-ready content. Instructors take their existing tests and quizzes and export them to a file that can then be made available to the student to take as a self-quiz on their iPods. It's as simple as that.

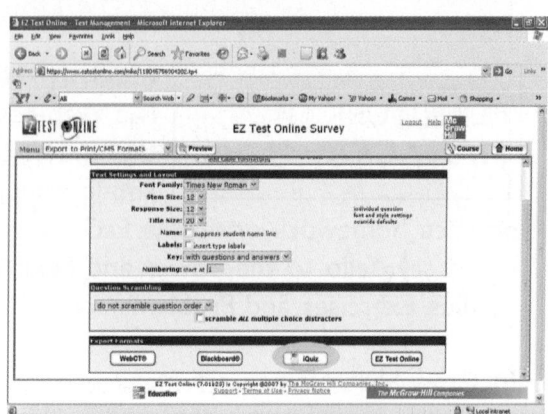

How Can Text-Related Web Resources Enhance My Course?

Online Learning Center (OLC)

We offer an Online Learning Center (OLC) that follows *Fundamental Accounting Principles* chapter by chapter. It doesn't require any building or maintenance on your part. It's ready to go the moment you and your students type in the URL: **www.mhhe.com/wildFAP19e**.

As students study and learn from *Fundamental Accounting Principles*, they can visit the Student Edition of the OLC Website to work with a multitude of helpful tools:

- Generic Template Working Papers
- Chapter Learning Objectives
- Interactive Chapter Quizzes
- PowerPoint® Presentations
- Problem Set C
- Narrated PowerPoint® Presentations

- Video Library
- Excel Template Assignments
- Animated Demonstration Problems
- iPod Content
- Peachtree Templates

A secured Instructor Edition stores essential course materials to save you prep time before class. Everything you need to run a lively classroom and an efficient course is included. All resources available to students, plus . . .

- General Ledger and Peachtree Solution Files
- Problem Set C Solutions
- Instructor's Manual

- Solutions Manual
- Solutions to Excel Template Assignments
- Test Bank

The OLC Website also serves as a doorway to other technology solutions, like course management systems.

> **Lillian Grose**, Delgado CC
> "Logical, concise, comprehensive with excellent publisher support material."

Save money. Go green. McGraw-Hill eBooks.

Green…it's on everybody's mind these days. It's not only about saving trees, it's also about saving money. At 55% of the bookstore price, McGraw-Hill eBooks are an eco-friendly and cost-saving alternative to the traditional printed textbook. So, do some good for the environment…and do some good for your wallet.

CourseSmart
CourseSmart is a new way to find and buy eTextbooks. CourseSmart has the largest selection of eTextbooks available anywhere, offering thousands of the most commonly adopted textbooks from a wide variety of higher education publishers. CourseSmart eTextbooks are available in one standard online reader with full text search, notes, and highlighting, and email tools for sharing between classmates. Visit **www.CourseSmart.com** for more information on ordering.

McGraw-Hill's Homework Manager Plus
If you use Homework Manager in your course, your students can purchase McGraw-Hill's Homework Manager Plus for *FAP* 19e.

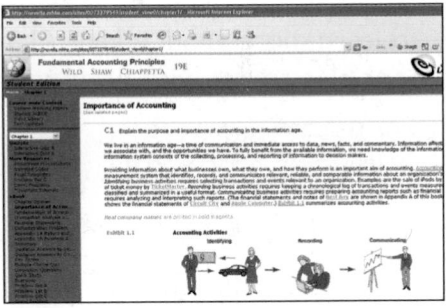

Homework Manager Plus gives students direct access to an online edition of the text while working assignments within Homework Manager. If you get stuck working a problem, simply click the "Hint" link and jump directly to relevant content in the online edition of the text.

Visit the Online Learning Center at www.mhhe.com/wildFAP19e to purchase McGraw-Hill's Homework Manager Plus.

McGraw-Hill/Irwin CARES

At McGraw-Hill/Irwin, we understand that getting the most from new technology can be challenging. That's why our services don't stop after you purchase our book. You can e-mail our Product Specialists 24 hours a day, get product training online, or search our knowledge bank of Frequently Asked Questions on our support Website.

McGraw-Hill/Irwin Customer Care Contact Information

For all Customer Support call **(800) 331-5094**
Email **be_support@mcgraw-hill.com**
Or visit **www.mhhe.com/support**
One of our Technical Support Analysts will be able to assist you in a timely fashion.

How Can McGraw-Hill Help Me Teach My Course Online?

ALEKS®

ALEKS® for the Accounting Cycle and ALEKS® for Financial Accounting
Available from McGraw-Hill over the World Wide Web, ALEKS (Assessment and LEarning in Knowledge Spaces) provides precise assessment and individualized instruction in the fundamental skills your students need to succeed in accounting.

ALEKS motivates your students because ALEKS can tell what a student knows, doesn't know, and is most ready to learn next. ALEKS does this using the ALEKS Assessment and Knowledge Space Theory as an artificial intelligence engine to exactly identify a student's knowledge of accounting. When students focus on precisely what they are ready to learn, they build the confidence and learning momentum that fuel success.

To learn more about adding ALEKS to your principles course, visit www.business.aleks.com.

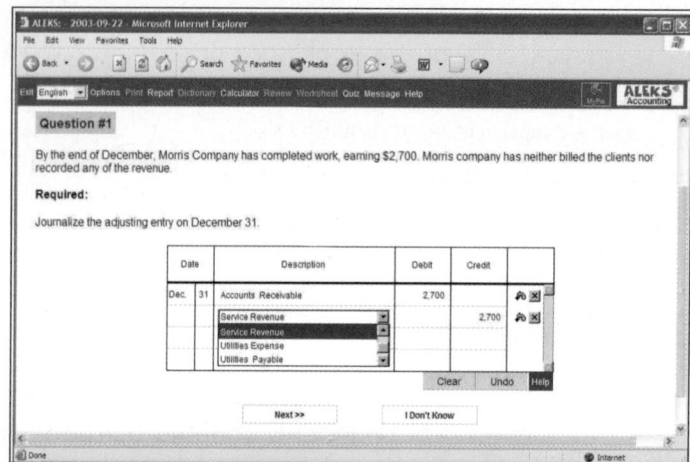

> **Janice Stoudemire**, Midlands Technical College
> "The supplemental material that this principles accounting text provides is impressive: homework manager, the extensive online learning center, general ledger application software, as well as ALEKS."

How Can I Make My Classroom Discussions More Interactive?

CPS Classroom Performance System
This is a revolutionary system that brings ultimate interactivity to the classroom. CPS is a wireless response system that gives you immediate feedback from every student in the class. CPS units include easy-to-use software for creating and delivering questions and assessments to your class. With CPS you can ask subjective and objective questions. Then every student simply responds with their individual, wireless response pad, providing instant results. CPS is the perfect tool for engaging students while gathering important assessment data.

eInstruction®

> **Liz Ott**, Casper College
> "I originally adopted the book because of the tools that accompanied it: Homework Manager, ALEKS, CPS."

Online Course Management

No matter what online course management system you use (WebCT, BlackBoard, or eCollege), we have a course content ePack available for *FAP* 19e. Our new ePacks are specifically designed to make it easy for students to navigate and access content online. They are easier than ever to install on the latest version of the course management system available today.

Don't forget that you can count on the highest level of service from McGraw-Hill. Our online course management specialists are ready to assist you with your online course needs. They provide training and will answer any questions you have throughout the life of your adoption. So try our new ePack for *FAP* 19e and make online course content delivery easy and fun.

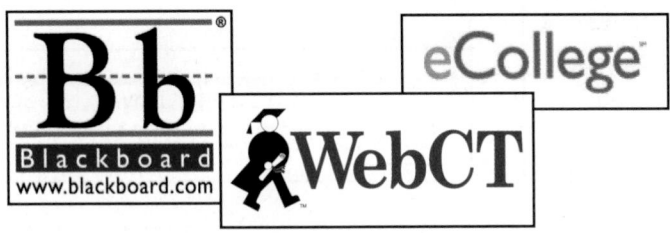

PageOut: McGraw-Hill's Course Management System

PageOut is the easiest way to create a Website for your accounting course. There is no need for HTML coding, graphic design, or a thick how-to book. Just fill in a series of boxes with simple English and click on one of our professional designs. In no time, your course is online with a Website that contains your syllabus!

Should you need assistance in preparing your Website, we can help. Our team of product specialists is ready to take your course materials and build a custom Website to your specifications. You simply need to call a McGraw-Hill/Irwin PageOut specialist to start the process. To learn more, please visit www.pageout.net and see "PageOut & Service" below.

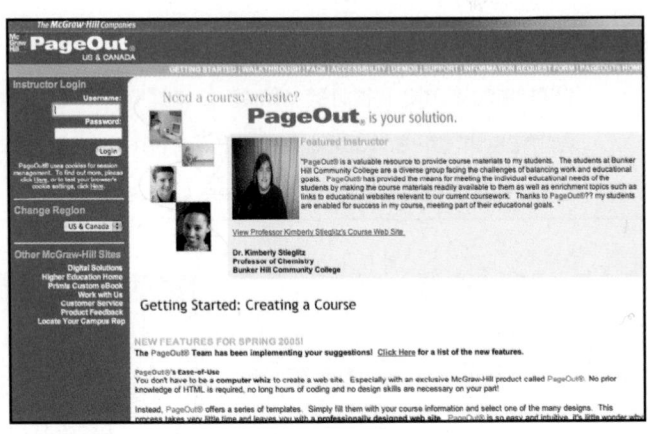

Best of all, PageOut is free when you adopt *Fundamental Accounting Principles*!

PageOut Service

Our team of product specialists is happy to help you design your own course Website. Just call 1-800-634-3963, press 0, and ask to speak with a PageOut specialist. You will be asked to send in your course materials and then participate in a brief telephone consultation. Once we have your information, we build your Website for you, from scratch.

Decision Center

Whether we prepare, analyze, or apply accounting information, one skill remains essential: decision-making. To help develop good decision-making habits and to illustrate the relevance of accounting, *Fundamental Accounting Principles* 19e uses a unique pedagogical framework called the Decision Center. This framework is comprised of a variety of approaches and subject areas, giving students insight into every aspect of business decision-making. Answers to Decision Maker and Ethics boxes are at the end of each chapter.

Decision Insight

IFRSs IFRSs require that companies report the following four financial statements with explanatory notes:
—Balance sheet   —Statement of changes in equity (or statement of recognized revenue and expense)
—Income statement   —Statement of cash flows
IFRSs do not prescribe specific formats; and comparative information is required for the preceding period only.

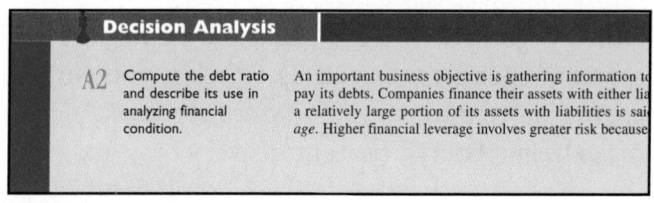

Decision Analysis

A2 Compute the debt ratio and describe its use in analyzing financial condition.

An important business objective is gathering information to pay its debts. Companies finance their assets with either lia a relatively large portion of its assets with liabilities is sai *age.* Higher financial leverage involves greater risk because

Decision Ethics

Credit Manager As a new credit manager, you are being trained by the outgoing manager. She explains that the system prepares checks for amounts net of favorable cash discounts, and the checks are dated the last day of the discount period. She also tells you that checks are not mailed until five days later, adding that "the company gets free use of cash for an extra five days, and our department looks better. When a supplier complains, we blame the computer system and the mailroom." Do you continue this payment policy? [Answer—p. 203]

Decision Maker

Entrepreneur You open a wholesale business selling entertainment equipment to retail outlets. You find that most of your customers demand to buy on credit. How can you use the balance sheets of these customers to decide which ones to extend credit to? [Answer—p. 71]

"This text has the best introductions of any text that I have reviewed or used. Some texts simply summarize the chapter, which is boring to students. Research indicates that material needs to be written in an 'engaging manner.' That's what these vignettes do—they get the students interested."
Clarice McCoy, Brookhaven College

CAP Model

The Conceptual/Analytical/Procedural (CAP) Model allows courses to be specially designed to meet your teaching needs or those of a diverse faculty. This model identifies learning objectives, textual materials, assignments, and test items by C, A, or P, allowing different instructors to teach from the same materials, yet easily customize their courses toward a conceptual, analytical, or procedural approach (or a combination thereof) based on personal preferences.

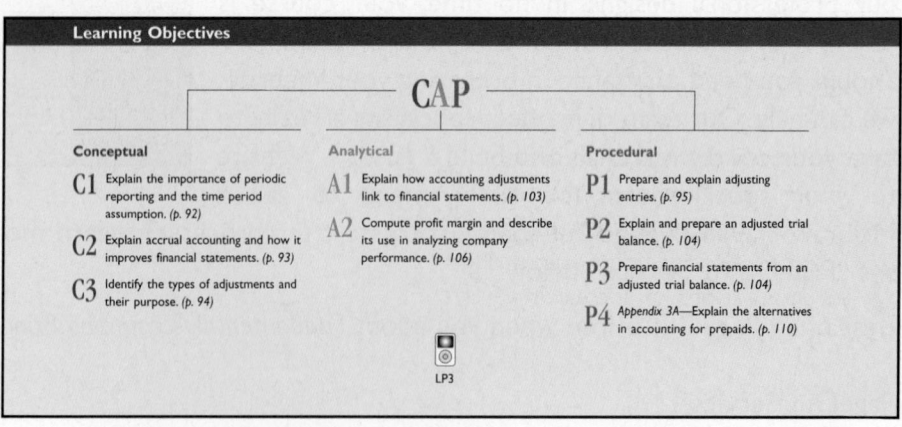

Learning Objectives

CAP

Conceptual

C1 Explain the importance of periodic reporting and the time period assumption. (p. 92)

C2 Explain accrual accounting and how it improves financial statements. (p. 93)

C3 Identify the types of adjustments and their purpose. (p. 94)

Analytical

A1 Explain how accounting adjustments link to financial statements. (p. 103)

A2 Compute profit margin and describe its use in analyzing company performance. (p. 106)

Procedural

P1 Prepare and explain adjusting entries. (p. 95)

P2 Explain and prepare an adjusted trial balance. (p. 104)

P3 Prepare financial statements from an adjusted trial balance. (p. 104)

P4 Appendix 3A—Explain the alternatives in accounting for prepaids. (p. 110)

LP3

Chapter Preview with Flow Chart

This feature provides a handy textual/visual guide at the start of every chapter. Students can now begin their reading with a clear understanding of what they will learn and when, allowing them to stay more focused and organized along the way.

Buyers of merchandise expect many products, discount prices, inventory on demand, and high quality. This chapter introduces the accounting practices used by companies engaged in merchandising. We show how financial statements reflect merchandising activities and explain the new financial statement items created by merchandising activities. We also analyze and record merchandise purchases and sales, and explain the adjustments and the closing process for these companies.

Accounting for Merchandising Operations

Merchandising Activities	Merchandising Purchases	Merchandising Sales	Accounting Cycle	Financial Statement Formats
• Reporting income • Reporting inventory • Operating cycles • Inventory systems	• Purchase discounts • Purchase returns and allowances • Transportation costs	• Sales of merchandise • Sales discounts • Sales returns and allowances	• Adjusting entries • Preparing financial statements • Closing entries	• Multiple-step income statement • Single-step income statement • Classified balance sheet

Quick Check

These short question/answer features reinforce the material immediately preceding them. They allow the reader to pause and reflect on the topics described, then receive immediate feedback before going on to new topics. Answers are provided at the end of each chapter.

Quick Check
Answers—p. 204

4. How long are the credit and discount periods when credit terms are 2/10, n/60?

5. Identify which items are subtracted from the *list* amount and not recorded when computing purchase price: (*a*) freight-in; (*b*) trade discount; (*c*) purchase discount; (*d*) purchase return.

6. What does *FOB* mean? What does *FOB destination* mean?

"(This book is) visually friendly with many illustrations. Good balance sheet presentation in margin."

Joan Cook, Milwaukee Area Technical College

Marginal Student Annotations

These annotations provide students with additional hints, tips, and examples to help them more fully understand the concepts and retain what they have learned. The annotations also include notes on global implications of accounting and further examples.

ransactions is to post journal entries to dger is up-to-date, entries are posted as time permits. All entries must be posted to ensure that account balances are up- ts in journal entries are transferred into

Point: Computerized systems often provide a code beside a balance such as *dr.* or *cr.* to identify its balance. Posting is automatic and immediate with accounting software.

FastForward

FastForward is a case that takes students through the Accounting Cycle, chapters 1-4. The FastForward icon is placed in the margin when this case is discussed.

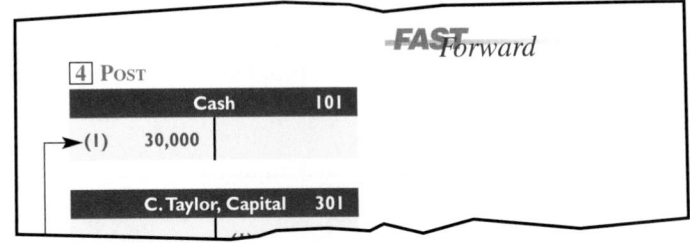

How are chapter concepts

Once a student has finished reading the chapter, how well he or she retains the material can depend greatly on the questions, exercises, and problems that reinforce it. This book leads the way in comprehensive, accurate assignments.

Demonstration Problems present both a problem and a complete solution, allowing students to review the entire problem-solving process and achieve success.

Chapter Summaries provide students with a review organized by learning objectives. Chapter Summaries are a component of the CAP model (see page xiv), which recaps each conceptual, analytical, and procedural objective.

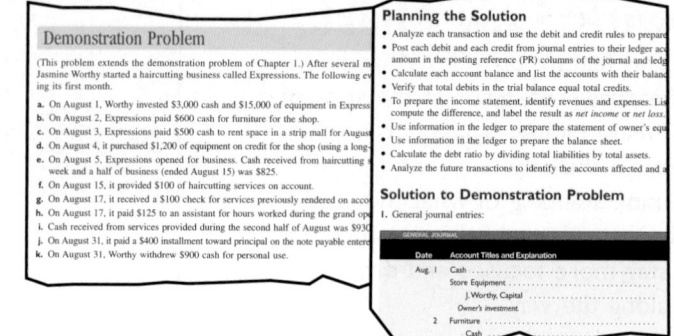

Key Terms are bolded in the text and repeated at the end of the chapter with page numbers indicating their location. The book also includes a complete Glossary of Key Terms.

Multiple Choice Questions Multiple Choice Questions quickly test chapter knowledge before a student moves on to complete Quick Studies, Exercises, and Problems.

Quick Study assignments are short exercises that often focus on one learning objective. All are included in Homework Manager. There are usually 8-10 Quick Study assignments per chapter.

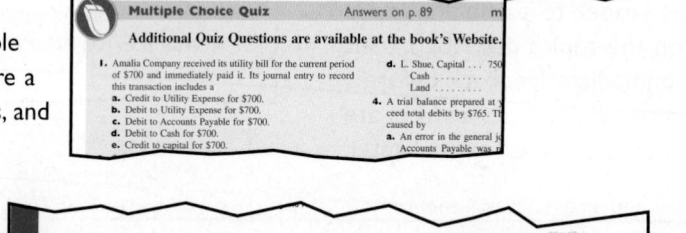

Exercises are one of this book's many strengths and a competitive advantage. There are about 10-15 per chapter and all are included in Homework Manager.

Problem Sets A & B are proven problems that can be assigned as homework or for in-class projects. Problem Set C is available on the book's Website. All problems are coded according to the CAP model (see page xiv), and Set A is included in Homework Manager.

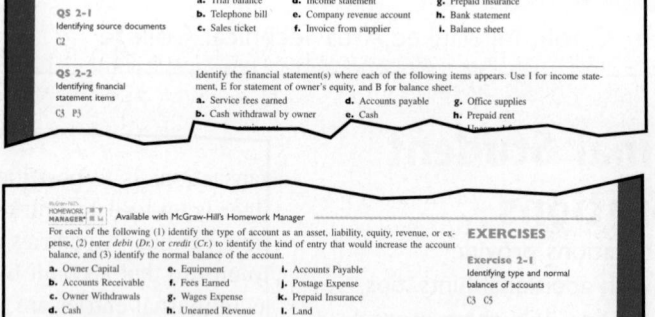

"One of the best features in FAP is the Serial Problem. I find the continuation of a company from a service to a merchandiser, to a manufacturing, and from a sole proprietorship form or business to a corporation, provides the student a real picture of a company's development. It also provides a consistency from one lesson to another."

Barbara Marotta, Northern Virginia Community College, Woodbridge

Beyond the Numbers exercises ask students to use accounting figures and understand their meaning. Students also learn how accounting applies to a variety of business situations. These creative and fun exercises are all new or updated, and are divided into sections:

- Reporting in Action
- Comparative Analysis
- Ethics Challenge
- Communicating in Practice
- Taking It To The Net
- Teamwork in Action
- Hitting the Road
- Entrepreneurial Decision
- Global Decision

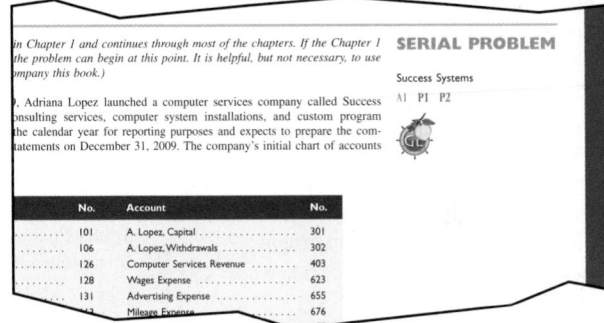

BEYOND THE NUMBERS

REPORTING IN ACTION
A1 A2

BTN 2-1 Refer to Best Buy's financial statements in Appendix

Required

1. What amount of total liabilities does it report for each of the fisca and March 3, 2007?
2. What amount of total assets does it report for each of the fiscal ye March 3, 2007?
3. Compute its debt ratio for each of the fiscal years ended February
4. In which fiscal year did it employ more financial leverage (Februa Explain.

Serial Problem uses a continuous running case study to illustrate chapter concepts in a familiar context. The Serial Problem can be followed continuously from the first chapter or picked up at any later point in the book; enough information is provided to ensure students can get right to work.

SERIAL PROBLEM

in Chapter 1 and continues through most of the chapters. If the Chapter 1 the problem can begin at this point. It is helpful, but not necessary, to use ompany this book.)

Success Systems

A1 P1 P2

, Adriana Lopez launched a computer services company called Success onsulting services, computer system installations, and custom program he calendar year for reporting purposes and expects to prepare the com-tatements on December 31, 2009. The company's initial chart of accounts

No.	Account	No.
101	A. Lopez, Capital	301
106	A. Lopez, Withdrawals	302
126	Computer Services Revenue	403
128	Wages Expense	623
131	Advertising Expense	655
	Mileage Expense	676

> "The best feature of this book is the use of real (financial) information in the Beyond the Numbers section. This is something that I do on my own, which can be very time consuming. I also like the Entrepreneurial questions, which are not even addressed in most textbooks."
>
> **Cindy Navaroli,** Chaffey Community College

The End of the Chapter Is Only the Beginning

Our valuable and proven assignments aren't just confined to the book. From problems that require technological solutions to materials found exclusively online, this book's end-of-chapter material is fully integrated with its technology package.

- Quick Studies, Exercises, and Problems available on Homework Manager (see page ix) are marked with an icon.

- Problems supported by the General Ledger Application Software or Peachtree are marked with an icon.

- Online Learning Center (OLC) includes Interactive Quizzes, Excel template assignments, and more.

mhhe.com/wildFAP19e

- Problems supported with Microsoft Excel template assignments are marked with an icon.

- Material that receives additional coverage (slide shows, videos, audio, etc.) available in iPod ready format are marked with an icon.

Put Away Your Red Pen

We pride ourselves on the accuracy of this book's assignment materials. Independent research reports that instructors and reviewers point to the accuracy of this book's assignment materials as one of its key competitive advantages.

The authors extend a special thanks to accuracy checkers Barbara Schnathorst, The Write Solution, Inc.; Helen Roybark, Radford University; Beth Woods, CPA, Accuracy Counts; David Krug, Johnson Community College; ANSR Source; David Burba, Bowling Green State University; and Marilyn Sagrillo, University of Wisconsin - Green Bay.

This edition's revisions are driven by feedback from instructors and students. Many of the revisions are summarized here. Feedback suggests that this is the book instructors want to teach from and students want to learn from. General revisions include:

- Revised and updated assignments throughout
- Updated ratio analyses for each chapter
- New material on International Financial Reporting Standards (IFRSs) in most chapters
- New and revised entrepreneurial elements
- Revised serial problem through nearly all chapters

- New art program, visual graphics, and text layout
- New Best Buy Annual Report with comparisons to Circuit City, RadioShack, Apple, and DSG (UK) with new assignments
- New graphics added to each chapter's analysis section
- New iPod content integrated and referenced in book

Chapter 1

Life is Good NEW opener with new entrepreneurial assignment

Revised section on accounting principles and assumptions

New visual layout on building blocks for GAAP

New graphic listing recent publicized accounting scandals

Transaction analysis with expanded accounting equation

Updated compensation data in exhibit

New discussion of conceptual framework linked to IFRSs

Chapter 2

SPANX NEW opener with new entrepreneurial assignment

New 4-step process to learn accounting for transactions: Identify, Analyze, Record, and Post

New sequential art layout for visualizing transaction accounting

New arrow lines link journal entries to the ledger

New material on financial statements related to IFRSs

Chapter 3

PopCap Games NEW opener with new entrepreneurial assignment

New 3-step process for accounting adjustments: (1) Determine what is, (2) Determine what should be, (3) Record adjustment

New summary tables show the accounting adjustment AND account balances before and after adjustment

New adjustment tables for prepaid expenses, including insurance, supplies, and depreciation

New adjustment tables for unearned revenue, accrued expenses, and accrued revenues

Chapter 4

Kathryn Kerrigan NEW opener with new entrepreneurial assignment

New graphic for learning the 4-step closing process

New graphic to aid learning of accounting cycle

Streamlined presentation of classified balance sheet

Chapter 5

BigBadToyStore NEW opener with new entrepreneurial assignment

Enhanced discussions on purchase allowances and purchase returns

Revised discussions on sales returns and sales allowances

Streamlined 4-step process for merchandisers' closing entries

New material on income statement formats for U.S. GAAP vis-à-vis IFRSs

Chapter 6

Beauty Encounter NEW opener with new entrepreneurial assignment

Specific Identification explanation revised for additional clarity

New explanation added to First-in, First-Out

Enhanced explanation to Last-in, First-Out

New description of weighted average

Enhanced explanations for LCM

New material on inventory methods for U.S. GAAP vis-à-vis IFRSs

Illustration of inventory errors is revised and enhanced

Revised exhibit on inventory errors for balance sheet

Appendix 6A, enhanced discussion of periodic inventory

Appendix 6A, expanded explanations of periodic FIFO, LIFO, and weighted average

Chapter 7

TerraCycle NEW opener with new entrepreneurial assignment

Enhanced exhibits for special journals and ledgers

New explanations for controlling and subsidiary ledgers

Updated discussion of enterprise resource planning

Chapter 8

Dylan's Candy Bar NEW opener with new entrepreneurial assignment

New material added on Sarbanes-Oxley and internal controls required

New section on cash management

Additional description of electronic funds transfer

Enhanced explanation of bank reconciliation with new assignments

New discussion of internal controls for IFRSs conversion

Chapter 9

Under Armor NEW opener with new entrepreneurial assignment

Reorganized sections on valuing accounts receivable

Enhanced explanation of recovering a bad debt

New material on assessing the direct write-off method

Reorganized section on estimating bad debts using percent of receivables

New enhanced summary Exhibit 9.13 on methods to estimate bad debts

Added new exercises on bad debts estimation

Chapter 10

Sambazon NEW opener with new entrepreneurial assignment

Updated all real world examples and graphics

Enhanced explanations on declining-balance and impairments

New description of ordinary repairs and its journal entry

Reorganized discussion of betterments and extraordinary repairs

New material on depreciation estimates for U.S. GAAP vis-à-vis IFRSs

Enhanced illustration for depletion including journal entry

Reorganized section on types of intangibles

Enhanced material related to franchises, licenses, trademarks and other intangibles

Enhanced explanation of exchanging plant assets

Chapter 11

Feed Granola Company NEW opener with new entrepreneurial assignment

Updated real world examples including those for Univision, Six Flags, AMF, and K2

New material on contingent liabilities for U.S. GAAP vis-à-vis IFRSs

Updated tax illustrations and assignments using the most recent rates

New section on "Who Pays What Payroll Taxes and Benefits"

Chapter 12

Samanta Shoes NEW opener with new entrepreneurial assignment

Updated real world examples including those for Macadamia Orchards and Big River

Productions

New example of partnership accounting using Trump Entertainment Resorts

Streamlined explanation of partnership liquidation

Chapter 13

Inogen NEW opener with new entrepreneurial assignment

New info graphic on subcategories of authorized stock

Updated many real world examples

New info graphic on stock splits

New material on preferred stock classification for U.S. GAAP vis-à-vis IFRSs

Additional explanation on closing process for corporations

Updated statement of stockholders' equity using Apple

Chapter 14

Rap Snacks NEW opener with new entrepreneurial assignment

Enhanced graphic and explanation of determining bond discount and premium

Revised bond illustration to use a 4-period bond

Streamlined bond illustration to show entire amortization process from issuance to maturity

Streamlined bond illustration for effective interest amortization

New material on bond interest computation for U.S. GAAP vis-à-vis IFRSs

Added new assignments that require accounting for bonds given an amortization table

Chapter 15

Tibi NEW opener with new entrepreneurial assignment

Updated real world examples and graphics including those for Gap, Pfizer, Starbucks, and Brunswick

Enhanced summary graphic on accounting for securities

Updated discussion related to FAS 157 and 159

New material on consolidation per U.S. GAAP vis-à-vis IFRSs

Chapter 16

Jungle Jim's NEW opener with new entrepreneurial assignment

Updated graphics for operating, investing and financing cash flows

Enhanced steps 1 through 5 for preparing the statement of cash flows

Simplified summary Exhibit 16.12 for indirect adjustments

Updated real world examples and graphics including that for Harley, Starbucks, and Nike

New info on indirect vs direct method for U.S. GAAP vis-à-vis IFRSs

Chapter 17

The Motley Fool REVISED opener with new entrepreneurial assignment

New Best Buy, Circuit City and RadioShack data throughout chapter, exhibits, and illustrations with comparative analysis

Enhanced presentation on comparative financial statements

Chapter 18

Kernel Season's NEW opener with new entrepreneurial assignment

New section on fraud and the role of ethics in managerial accounting

Added discussion on Institute of Management Accountants and its road-map for resolving ethical dilemmas

Updated real-world examples including that for Apple

Added balance sheet to exhibits that show cost flows across accounting reports

New discussion on role of nonfinancial information

Chapter 19

Sprinturf NEW opener with new entrepreneurial assignment

New info on custom design involving Nike

Enhanced exhibit on job order production activities

Added discussion linking accurate overhead application for jobs to both product pricing and performance evaluation

Streamlined explanation of closing over- and underapplied overhead

New discussion of employee payroll fraud schemes

Chapter 20

Hood River Juice Company NEW opener with new entrepreneurial assignment

New discussion on impact of automation for quality control and overhead application

Added explanation for use of a process cost summary in product pricing

Chapter 21

RockBottomGolf.com NEW opener with new entrepreneurial assignment

Enhanced explanation of evaluating investment center performance with financial measures

New discussion of residual income

Added explanation of economic value added

New section on evaluating investment center performance with nonfinancial measures including balanced scorecard

New Appendix 21A on transfer pricing

Decision Analysis: new explanation of investment center profit margin and investment turnover with new assignments

Chapter 22

Moe's Southwest Grill NEW opener with new entrepreneurial assignment

New section on working with changes in estimates for CVP analysis

New graphics illustrating how changes in estimates impact break-even analysis

New discussion on weighted average contribution margin in multiple product CVP analysis

New Appendix 22A on using Excel to estimate least squares regression

New assignments on break-even and changes in estimates

Chapter 23

Jibbitz NEW opener with new entrepreneurial assignment

Enhanced discussion of master budgets

New assignments on preparing budgets and budgeted financial statements

Chapter 24

Martin Guitar NEW opener with new entrepreneurial assignment

Reorganized discussion of overhead variance analysis

Revised graphics on framework for understanding overhead variances

New discussion of increased automation for overhead application

Revised explanation of journal entries for standard costing

Simplified discussion of closing variance accounts

New assignments on variance analysis

Added journal entries to chapter demonstration problem

Chapter 25

Prairie Sticks Bat Company NEW opener with new entrepreneurial assignment

New info graphic on cost of capital estimates across industries

Added discussion and example on use of profitability index to compare projects

New discussion on incorporating inflation in net present value calculations

Added explanation on conflicts between meeting analysts' forecasts and choosing profitable long-term projects

New Appendix 25A on using Excel to compute net present value and internal rate of return

New assignments on profitability index

Assurance of Learning Ready

Assurance of learning is an important element of many accreditation standards. *Fundamental Accounting Principles* 19e is designed specifically to support your assurance of learning initiatives.

Each chapter in the book begins with a list of numbered learning objectives which appear throughout the chapter, as well as in the end-of-chapter problems and exercises. Every test bank question is also linked to one of these objectives, in addition to level of difficulty, AICPA skill area, and AACSB skill area. EZ Test, McGraw-Hill's easy-to-use test bank software, can search the test bank by these and other categories, providing an engine for targeted Assurance of Learning analysis and assessment.

AACSB Statement

The McGraw-Hill Companies is a proud corporate member of AACSB International. Understanding the importance and value of AACSB accreditation, *Fundamental Accounting Principles* 19e has sought to recognize the curricula guidelines detailed in the AACSB standards for business accreditation by connecting selected questions in the test bank to the general knowledge and skill guidelines found in the AACSB standards.

The statements contained in *Fundamental Accounting Principles* 19e are provided only as a guide for the users of this text. The AACSB leaves content coverage and assessment within the purview of individual schools, the mission of the school, and the faculty. While *Fundamental Accounting Principles* 19e and the teaching package make no claim of any specific AACSB qualification or evaluation, we have, within the *Fundamental Accounting Principles* 19e test bank labeled questions according to the six general knowledge and skills areas.

Instructor's Resource CD-ROM

FAP 19e, Chapters 1-25
ISBN13: 9780073366456
ISBN10: 0073366455

This is your all-in-one resource. It allows you to create custom presentations from your own materials or from the following text-specific materials provided in the CD's asset library:

- Instructor's Resource Manual
  Written by Barbara Chiappetta, Nassau Community College, and Patricia Walczak, Lansing Community College.
  This manual contains (for each chapter) a Lecture Outline, a chart linking all assignment materials to Learning Objectives, a list of relevant active learning activities, and additional visuals with transparency masters.

- Solutions Manual
- Test Bank, Computerized Test Bank
- PowerPoint® Presentations
  Prepared by Jon Booker, Charles Caldwell, and Susan Galbreth. Presentations allow for revision of lecture slides, and includes a viewer, allowing screens to be shown with or without the software.
- Link to PageOut

Test Bank

Vol. 1, Chapters 1-12
ISBN13: 9780073366524
ISBN10: 0073366528

Vol. 2, Chapters 13-25
ISBN13: 9780073366487
ISBN10: 007336648X

Revised by Barbara Gershowitz and Laurie Swanson of Nashville State Technical Community College.

Algorithmic Test Bank

ISBN13: 9780073366395
ISBN10: 0073366390

Solutions Manual

Vol. 1, Chapters 1-12
ISBN13: 9780073366517
ISBN10: 007336651X

Vol. 2, Chapters 13-25
ISBN13: 9780073366470
ISBN10: 0073366471

Written by John J. Wild, Ken W. Shaw, and Marilyn Sagrillo.

Geoffrey Heriot, Greenville Technical College

"The text is well presented and has excellent materials for both students and instructors. It is certainly one of the top texts in an entry level principles of accounting marketplace."

Excel Working Papers CD *(Chapters 1-25)*

ISBN13: 9780073366371
ISBN10: 0073366374

Written by John J. Wild.

Working Papers delivered in Excel spreadsheets. These Excel Working Papers are available on CD-ROM and can be bundled with the printed Working Papers; see your representative for information.

Working Papers

Vol. 1, Chapters 1-12
ISBN13: 9780077289515
ISBN10: 007728951X

Vol. 2, Chapters 12-25
ISBN13: 9780073366364
ISBN10: 0073366366

PFA, Chapters 1-17
ISBN13: 9780073366340
ISBN10: 007336634X

Written by John J. Wild.

Study Guide

Vol. 1, Chapters 1-12
ISBN13: 9780073366388
ISBN10: 0073366382

Vol. 2, Chapters 12-25
ISBN13: 9780073366357
ISBN10: 0073366358

Written by Barbara Chiappetta, Nassau Community College, and Patricia Walczak, Lansing Community College.

Covers each chapter and appendix with reviews of the learning objectives, outlines of the chapters, summaries of chapter materials, and additional problems with solutions.

Carol Yacht's General Ledger CD-ROM

ISBN13: 9780073366401
ISBN10: 0073366404

The CD-ROM includes fully functioning versions of McGraw-Hill's own General Ledger Application software. Problem templates prepared by Carol Yacht and student user guides are included that allow you to assign text problems for working in Yacht's General Ledger or Peachtree.

Contributing Author
The authors and book team wish to thank Marilyn Sagrillo for her excellent contributions.

Marilyn Sagrillo is an associate professor at the University of Wisconsin at Green Bay. She received her BA and MS from Northern Illinois University and her PhD from the University of Wisconsin at Madison. Her scholarly articles are published in *Accounting Enquiries, Journal of Accounting Case Research*, and the *Missouri Society of CPAs Casebook*. She is a member of the American Accounting Association and the Institute of Management Accountants. She previously received the UWGB Founder's Association Faculty Award for Excellence in Teaching. Professor Sagrillo is an active volunteer for the Midwest Renewable Energy Association. She also enjoys reading, traveling, and hiking.

Acknowledgments

John J. Wild, Ken W. Shaw, Barbara Chiappetta, and McGraw-Hill/Irwin would like to recognize the following instructors for their valuable feedback and involvement in the development of *Fundamental Accounting Principles* 19e. We are thankful for their suggestions, counsel, and encouragement.

Janet Adeyiga, Hampton University

Audrey Agnello, Niagara County Community College

John Ahmad, Northern Virginia Community College

Sylvia Allen, Los Angeles Valley College

Donna Altepeter, University of North Dakota

Juanita Ardavany, Los Angeles Valley College

Charles Baird, University of Wisconsin-Stout

Scott Barhight, Northampton Community College

Richard Barnhart, Grand Rapids Community College

Mary Barnum, Grand Rapids Community College

Allen Bealle, Delgado Community College

Susan Beasley, Community College of Baltimore County-Catonsville

Beverly Beatty, Anne Arundel Community College

Irene Bembenista, Davenport University

Laurel Berry, Bryant and Stratton College

Jaswinder Bhangal, Chabot College

Rick Bowden, Oakland Community College-Auburn Hills

Deborah Boyce, Mohawk Valley Community College

Nancy Boyd, Middle Tennessee State University

Debbie Branch, Surry Community College

Karen Brayden, Front Range Community College-Fort Collins

Nat Briscoe, Northwestern State University

Linda Bruff, Strayer University

Scott Butterfield, University of Colorado-Colorado Springs

James Capone, Kean University

Roy Carson, Anne Arundel Community College

Trudy Chiaravelli, Lansing Community College

Siu Chung, Los Angeles Valley College

Marilyn Ciolino, Delgado Community College

Ken Coffey, Johnson County Community College

Edwin Cohen, DePaul University

Kerry Colton, Aims Community College-Main Campus

James Cosby, John Tyler Community College

Kenneth Couvillion, San Joaquin Delta College

Ana Cruz, Miami-Dade College-Wolfson

Walter DeAguero, Saddleback College

Suryekaent Desai, Cedar Valley College-Lancaster

Mike Deschamps, Chaffey College

Susan Dickey, Motlow State Community College

Beth Dietz, South Texas College

Andy Dressler, Walla Walla College

Betty Driver, Murray State University

Michael Farina, Cerritos College

Jeannie Folk, College of DuPage

Jim Formosa, Nashville State Technical College

Ron Dustin, Fresno City College

Anthony Espisito, Community College of Baltimore County-Essex

Steve Fabian, Hudson County Community College

Patricia Feller, Nashville State Technical Community College

Anna Fitzpatrick, Gloucester City College

John Gabelman, Columbus State Community College

Dan Galvin, Diablo Valley College

Barbara Gershowitz, Nashville State Technical Community College

Lillian Grose, Delgado Community College

Betty Habershon, Prince George's Community College

Patricia Halliday, Santa Monica College

Jeff Hamm, University of Arkansas-Little Rock

John Hancock, University of California Davis

Jeannie Harrington, Middle Tennessee State University

Sara Harris, Arapahoe Community College

Laurie Hays, Western Michigan University-Kalamazoo

Kathy Hill, Leeward Community College

Patricia Holmes, Des Moines Area Community College

Constance Hylton, George Mason University

Vincent Huygen, North Greenville University

Bill Johnstone, Montgomery College

Jeffery Jones, Community College of Southern Nevada

Richard Irvine, Pensacola Jr. College

Irv Jason, Southwest Tennessee Community College-Macon Campus

Frank Jordan, Erie Community College South Campus-Orchard Park

Thomas Kam, Hawaii Pacific University

John Karbens, Hawaii Pacific University

George Katzt, Phillips College

Charles Kee, Kingsborough Community College

Howard Keller, Indiana University/Purdue University Indiana

Monique Kelly (Byrd), Fresno City College

Chula King, University of West Florida

Debra Kiss, Davenport University

Shirley Kleiner, Johnson County Community College

Robert Koch, St. Peter's College

Jerry Kreuze, Western Michigan University

David Krug, Johnson County Community College

Tara Laken, Joliet Junior College

Michael Landers, Middlesex County Community College

Sherman Layell, Surry Community College

Philip Lee, Nashville State Technical Community College

Paul Lee, Cleveland State University

Natasha Librizzi, Milwaukee Area Technical College

Danny Litt, University of California-Los Angeles

Steve Ludwig, Northwest Missouri State University

Maria Mari, Miami Dade College

Diane Marker, University of Toledo-Scott Park

Barbara Marotta, Northern Virginia Community College-Woodbridge

Brenda Mattison, Tri-County Technical College

Lynn Mazzola, Nassau County Community College

Cynthia McCall, Des Moines Area Community College

Patricia McClure, Springfield Technical Community College

Robert Mcwhorter, Northwest Vista College

Audrey Morrison, Pensacola Junior College

Andrea Murowski, Brookdale Community College

Tim Murphy, Diablo Valley College

Joe Nicassio, Westmoreland County Community College

Jamie O'Brien, South Dakota State University

Kathleen O'Donnell, Onondaga Community College

Ralph Ostrowski, Illinois Central College

Shelley Ota, Lee Ward Community College

Susan Pallas, Southeast Community College

Thomas Parker, Surry Community College

Ash Patel, Normandale Community College

Anahid Petrosian, South Texas College

Yvonne Phang, Boro of Manhattan Community College

Mary Phillips, Middle Tennessee State University

Gary Pieroni, Diablo Valley College

Greg Prescott, University of Southern Alabama

Paula Ratliff, Arkansas State University-State University

David Ravetch, University of California-Los Angeles

Jenny Resnick, Santa Monica College

Jim Riley, Palo Alto College

Richard Roding, Red Rocks Community College

Linda Rose, Westwood College

Al Ruggiero, Suffolk County Community College-Selden

Roger Sands, Milwaukee Area Tech-Milwaukee

Marilyn Sagrillo, University of Wisconsin-Green Bay

Richard Sarkisian, Camden County College

Wallace Satchell, St. Phillips College

Christine Schalow, University of Wisconsin-Stevens Point

William Schmalz, Sanford Brown College

Brad Smith, Des Moines Area Community College

Nancy Snow, University of Toledo

Laura Solano, Pueblo Community College

Charles Spector, State University of New York-Oswego

Gene Sullivan, Liberty University

Laurie Swanson, Nashville State Technical Community College

Larry Swisher, Muskegon County Community College

Margaret Tanner, University of Arkansas-Fort Smith

Domenico Tavella, Pittsburgh Technical Institute

Thomas G. Thompson, Madison Area Technical College

Debra Tyson, Bryant & Stratton College

Shafi Ullah, Broward Community College

Bob Urell, Irvine Valley College

Patricia Walczak, Lansing Community College

Valerie Walmsley, South Texas College

Keith Weidkamp, Sierra College

Dale Westfall, Midland College

Gloria Worthy, Southwest Tennessee Community College

Ray Wurzburger, New River Community College

Lynnette Yerbury, St. Louis Community College

Judith Zander, Grossmont College

In addition to the helpful and generous colleagues listed above, we thank the entire McGraw-Hill/Irwin *Fundamental Accounting Principles* 19e team, including Stewart Mattson, Tim Vertovec, Steve Schuetz, Christina Sanders, Sharon Monday of Aptara, Lori Koetters, Matthew Baldwin, Carol Bielski, and Brian Nacik. We also thank the great marketing and sales support staff, including Krista Bettino, Sankha Basu, and Randy Sealy. Many talented educators and professionals worked hard to create the supplements for this book, and for their efforts we're grateful. Finally, many more people we either did not meet or whose efforts we did not personally witness nevertheless helped to make this book everything that it is, and we thank them all.

John J. Wild   Ken W. Shaw   Barbara Chiappetta

Brief Contents

Contents

Fundamental
Accounting
Principles

A Look at This Chapter

Accounting is crucial in our information age. In this chapter, we discuss the importance of accounting to different types of organizations and describe its many users and uses. We explain that ethics are essential to accounting. We also explain business transactions and how they are reflected in financial statements.

A Look Ahead

Chapter 2 describes and analyzes business transactions. We explain the analysis and recording of transactions, the ledger and trial balance, and the double-entry system. More generally, Chapters 2 through 4 show (via the accounting cycle) how financial statements reflect business activities.

Accounting in Business

Chapter

Learning Objectives

Learning Objectives are classified as conceptual, analytical, or procedural.

CAP

Conceptual

C1 Explain the purpose and importance of accounting in the information age. *(p. 4)*

C2 Identify users and uses of accounting. *(p. 5)*

C3 Identify opportunities in accounting and related fields. *(p. 6)*

C4 Explain why ethics are crucial to accounting. *(p. 8)*

C5 Explain generally accepted accounting principles and define and apply several accounting principles. *(p. 9)*

C6 *Appendix 1B*—Identify and describe the three major activities of organizations. *(p. 24)*

Analytical

A1 Define and interpret the accounting equation and each of its components. *(p. 12)*

A2 Analyze business transactions using the accounting equation. *(p. 13)*

A3 Compute and interpret return on assets. *(p. 20)*

A4 *Appendix 1A*—Explain the relation between return and risk. *(p. 23)*

LP1

Procedural

P1 Identify and prepare basic financial statements and explain how they interrelate. *(p. 17)*

*A **Decision Feature** launches each chapter showing the relevance of accounting for a real entrepreneur. An **Entrepreneurial Decision** problem at the end of the assignments returns to this feature with a mini-case.*

Life Is Good

BOSTON—Bert and John Jacobs launched their T-shirt company, **Life is good**® (**Lifeisgood.com**), with "nothing in our bank account and $78 in cash," explains Bert. Sales activities involved peddling T-shirts on college campuses and at street fairs. Although they lived and slept in their van and made only enough to pay for food and gas, they stayed the course. Then, Bert says, "We created Jake, and he showed us the way!"

Jake is the smiling stick figure that now adorns their products. Bert and John first drew Jake on their apartment wall and then printed him on a batch of T-shirts that sold within an hour at a Cambridge street fair. "It scared the hell out of us," says Bert. "We looked at each other and said, 'Oh my God, what do we have here?'" What they had was a Hollywood story in the making. Within a few years, Jake was adorning T-shirts, sweatshirts, and headwear and was producing millions in sales.

Bert and John have integrated their fun and quirky style into their business. A walk through the Life is good factory reveals blaring music, popcorn machines, free-roaming dogs, and giant murals on bright-colored

"People are drawn to Jake usually with a grin or a big laugh... Jake rules!" — Bert Jacobs

walls. "We take our inspiration from Dr. Seuss," insists Bert. "We like to feel that in our own way we're having a positive impact ... and having a lot of fun along the way." The brothers have successfully organized their business, set up accounting systems, learned to prepare and read financial reports, and apply financial analysis. Adds John, "Consistent performance is what has enhanced and strengthened [our products]."

The brothers' accounting system tracks all transactions, and they regularly prepare financial reports when making business decisions. Those accounting realities have been creatively merged with their fun-loving approach. In recent years, Life is good has held a factory talent show, bowling tournament, and watermelon seed–spitting contest. The brothers exude positive thinking. "The foundation of our brand is optimism," explains Bert, "and optimism is timeless."

[Sources: *Life is good Website,* January 2009; *SGB,* January 2006; *Boston Common,* Winter 2006; *Worthwhile Magazine,* 2005; *American Executive,* August 2005; *Inc.,* October 2006; *Entrepreneur,* May 2007]

← *A **Preview** opens each chapter with a summary of topics covered.*

Today's world is one of information—its preparation, communication, analysis, and use. Accounting is at the core of this information age. Knowledge of accounting gives us career opportunities and the insight to take advantage of them. This book introduces concepts, procedures, and analyses that help us make better decisions, including career choices. In this chapter we describe accounting, the users and uses of accounting information, the forms and activities of organizations, and several accounting principles. We also introduce transaction analysis and financial statements.

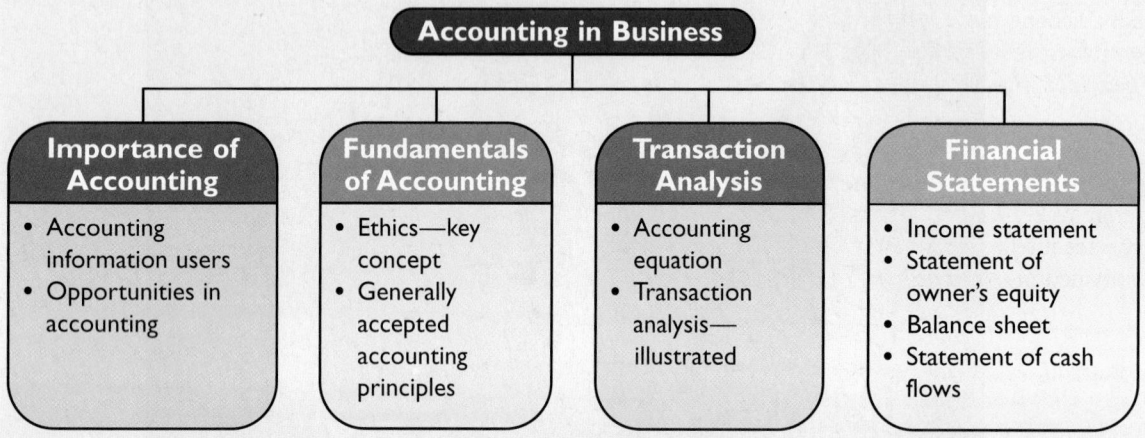

Accounting in Business

Importance of Accounting	Fundamentals of Accounting	Transaction Analysis	Financial Statements
• Accounting information users • Opportunities in accounting	• Ethics—key concept • Generally accepted accounting principles	• Accounting equation • Transaction analysis—illustrated	• Income statement • Statement of owner's equity • Balance sheet • Statement of cash flows

Importance of Accounting

C1 Explain the purpose and importance of accounting in the information age.

Video1.1

Real company names are printed in bold magenta.

Why is accounting so popular on campuses? Why are there so many accounting jobs for graduates? Why is accounting so important to companies? Why do politicians and business leaders focus on accounting regulations? The answer is that we live in an information age, where that information, and its reliability, impacts the financial well-being of us all.

Accounting is an information and measurement system that identifies, records, and communicates relevant, reliable, and comparable information about an organization's business activities. *Identifying* business activities requires selecting transactions and events relevant to an organization. Examples are the sale of iPods by **Apple** and the receipt of ticket money by **TicketMaster**. *Recording* business activities requires keeping a chronological log of transactions and events measured in dollars and classified and summarized in a useful format. *Communicating* business activities requires preparing accounting reports such as financial statements. It also requires analyzing and interpreting such reports. (The financial statements and notes of **Best Buy** are shown in Appendix A of this book. This appendix also shows the financial statements of **Circuit City**, **RadioShack**, and **Apple**.) Exhibit 1.1 summarizes accounting activities.

We must guard against a narrow view of accounting. The most common contact with accounting is through credit approvals, checking accounts, tax forms, and payroll. These experiences are limited and tend to focus on the recordkeeping parts of accounting. **Recordkeeping,** or **bookkeeping,** is the recording of transactions and events, either manually or electronically. This

EXHIBIT 1.1

Accounting Activities

Identifying	Recording	Communicating
Select transactions and events	Input, measure, and classify	Prepare, analyze, and interpret

is just one part of accounting. Accounting also identifies and communicates information on transactions and events, and it includes the crucial processes of analysis and interpretation.

Technology is a key part of modern business and plays a major role in accounting. Technology reduces the time, effort, and cost of recordkeeping while improving clerical accuracy. Some small organizations continue to perform various accounting tasks manually, but even they are impacted by technology. As technology has changed the way we store, process, and summarize masses of data, accounting has been freed to expand. Consulting, planning, and other financial services are now closely linked to accounting. These services require sorting through data, interpreting their meaning, identifying key factors, and analyzing their implications.

Users of Accounting Information

Accounting is often called the *language of business* because all organizations set up an accounting information system to communicate data to help people make better decisions. Exhibit 1.2 shows that the accounting information system serves many kinds of users (this is a partial listing) who can be divided into two groups: external users and internal users.

Margin notes further enhance the textual material.

Point: Technology is only as useful as the accounting data available, and users' decisions are only as good as their understanding of accounting. The best software and recordkeeping cannot make up for lack of accounting knowledge.

External users

- Lenders
- Shareholders
- Governments
- Consumer groups
- External auditors
- Customers

Internal users

- Officers
- Managers
- Internal auditors
- Sales staff
- Budget officers
- Controllers

EXHIBIT 1.2

Users of Accounting Information

Infographics reinforce key concepts through visual learning.

External Information Users **External users** of accounting information are *not* directly involved in running the organization. They include shareholders (investors), lenders, directors, customers, suppliers, regulators, lawyers, brokers, and the press. External users have limited access to an organization's information. Yet their business decisions depend on information that is reliable, relevant, and comparable.

Financial accounting is the area of accounting aimed at serving external users by providing them with *general-purpose financial statements*. The term *general-purpose* refers to the broad range of purposes for which external users rely on these statements.

Each external user has special information needs depending on the types of decisions to be made. *Lenders* (creditors) loan money or other resources to an organization. Banks, savings and loans, co-ops, and mortgage and finance companies are lenders. Lenders look for information to help them assess whether an organization is likely to repay its loans with interest. *Shareholders* (investors) are the owners of a corporation. They use accounting reports in deciding whether to buy, hold, or sell stock. Shareholders typically elect a *board of directors* to oversee their interests in an organization. Since directors are responsible to shareholders, their information needs are similar. *External* (independent) *auditors* examine financial statements to verify that they are prepared according to generally accepted accounting principles. *Employees* and *labor unions* use financial statements to judge the fairness of wages, assess job prospects, and bargain for better wages. *Regulators* often have legal authority over certain activities of organizations. For example, the Internal Revenue Service (IRS) and other tax authorities require organizations to file accounting reports in computing taxes. Other regulators include utility boards that use accounting information to set utility rates and securities regulators that require reports for companies that sell their stock to the public.

Accounting serves the needs of many other external users. *Voters, legislators,* and *government officials* use accounting information to monitor and evaluate government receipts and

C2 Identify users and uses of accounting.

expenses. *Contributors* to nonprofit organizations use accounting information to evaluate the use and impact of their donations. *Suppliers* use accounting information to judge the soundness of a customer before making sales on credit, and *customers* use financial reports to assess the staying power of potential suppliers.

Internal Information Users   **Internal users** of accounting information are those directly involved in managing and operating an organization. They use the information to help improve the efficiency and effectiveness of an organization. **Managerial accounting** is the area of accounting that serves the decision-making needs of internal users. Internal reports are not subject to the same rules as external reports and instead are designed with the special needs of internal users in mind.

There are several types of internal users, and many are managers of key operating activities. *Research and development managers* need information about projected costs and revenues of any proposed changes in products and services. *Purchasing managers* need to know what, when, and how much to purchase. *Human resource managers* need information about employees' payroll, benefits, performance, and compensation. *Production managers* depend on information to monitor costs and ensure quality. *Distribution managers* need reports for timely, accurate, and efficient delivery of products and services. *Marketing managers* use reports about sales and costs to target consumers, set prices, and monitor consumer needs, tastes, and price concerns. *Service managers* require information on the costs and benefits of looking after products and services. Decisions of these and other internal users depend on accounting reports.

Both internal and external users rely on internal controls to monitor and control company activities. *Internal controls* are procedures set up to protect company property and equipment, ensure reliable accounting reports, promote efficiency, and encourage adherence to company policies. Examples are good records, physical controls (locks, passwords, guards), and independent reviews.

Decision Insight boxes highlight relevant items from practice.

Decision Insight

They Fought the Law   Our economic and social welfare depends on reliable accounting information. A few managers forgot that and are now paying their dues. They include L. Dennis Kozlowski (in photo) of **Tyco**, convicted of falsifying accounting records; Bernard Ebbers of **WorldCom**, convicted of an $11 billion accounting scandal, Andrew Fastow of **Enron**, guilty of hiding debt and inflating income, and Joe Nacchio of **Qwest**, accused of falsely reporting sales.

Opportunities in Accounting

Accounting information affects many aspects of our lives. When we earn money, pay taxes, invest savings, budget earnings, and plan for the future, we are influenced by accounting. Accounting has four broad areas of opportunities: financial, managerial, taxation, and accounting-related. Exhibit 1.3 lists selected opportunities in each area.

C3   Identify opportunities in accounting and related fields.

EXHIBIT 1.3

Accounting Opportunities

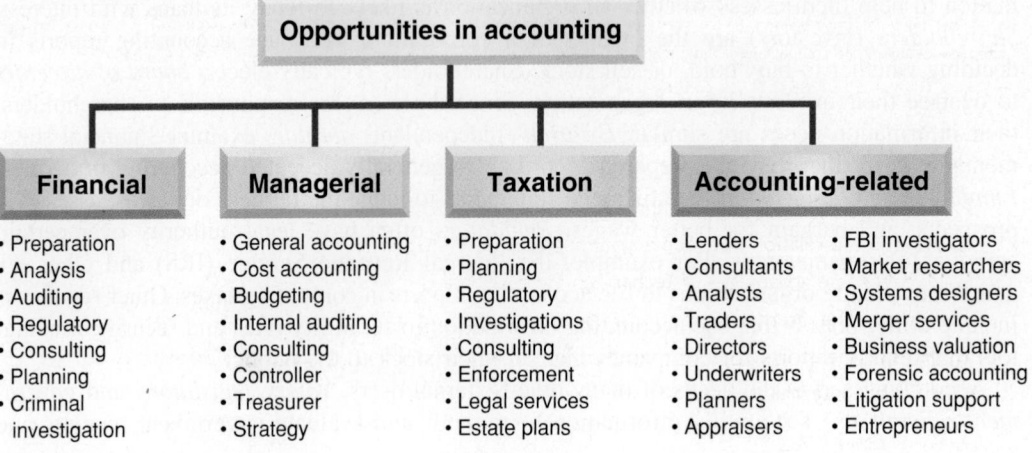

Opportunities in accounting			
Financial	**Managerial**	**Taxation**	**Accounting-related**	
• Preparation	• General accounting	• Preparation	• Lenders	• FBI investigators
• Analysis	• Cost accounting	• Planning	• Consultants	• Market researchers
• Auditing	• Budgeting	• Regulatory	• Analysts	• Systems designers
• Regulatory	• Internal auditing	• Investigations	• Traders	• Merger services
• Consulting	• Consulting	• Consulting	• Directors	• Business valuation
• Planning	• Controller	• Enforcement	• Underwriters	• Forensic accounting
• Criminal investigation	• Treasurer	• Legal services	• Planners	• Litigation support
	• Strategy	• Estate plans	• Appraisers	• Entrepreneurs

The majority of accounting opportunities are in *private accounting,* as shown in Exhibit 1.4. *Public accounting* offers the next largest number of opportunities. Still other opportunities exist in government (and not-for-profit) agencies, including business regulation and investigation of law violations.

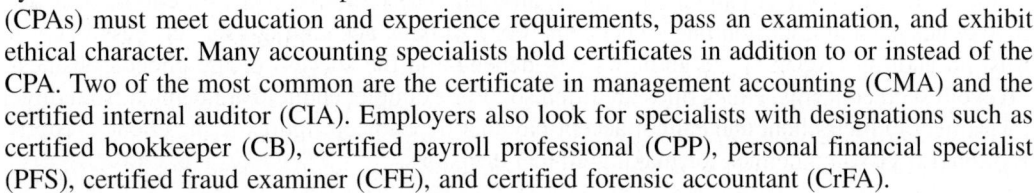

EXHIBIT 1.4

Accounting Jobs by Area

Accounting specialists are highly regarded. Their professional standing often is denoted by a certificate. Certified public accountants (CPAs) must meet education and experience requirements, pass an examination, and exhibit ethical character. Many accounting specialists hold certificates in addition to or instead of the CPA. Two of the most common are the certificate in management accounting (CMA) and the certified internal auditor (CIA). Employers also look for specialists with designations such as certified bookkeeper (CB), certified payroll professional (CPP), personal financial specialist (PFS), certified fraud examiner (CFE), and certified forensic accountant (CrFA).

Point: The largest accounting firms are Deloitte & Touche, Ernst & Young, PricewaterhouseCoopers, and KPMG.

Individuals with accounting knowledge are always in demand as they can help with financial analysis, strategic planning, e-commerce, product feasibility analysis, information technology, and financial management. Benefit packages can include flexible work schedules, telecommuting options, career path alternatives, casual work environments, extended vacation time, and child and elder care.

Demand for accounting specialists is booming. Exhibit 1.5 reports average annual salaries for several accounting positions. Salary variation depends on location, company size, professional designation, experience, and other factors. For example, salaries for chief financial officers (CFO) range from under $75,000 to more than $1 million per year. Likewise, salaries for bookkeepers range from under $30,000 to more than $80,000.

Point: Census Bureau (2007) reports that for workers 18 and over, higher education yields higher average pay:
Advanced degree $79,946
Bachelor's degree 54,689
High school degree 29,448
No high school degree 19,915

Field	Title (experience)	2007 Salary	2012 Estimate*
Public Accounting	Partner.	$190,000	$242,500
	Manager (6–8 years)	94,500	120,500
	Senior (3–5 years).	72,000	92,000
	Junior (0–2 years)	51,500	65,500
Private Accounting	CFO.	232,000	296,000
	Controller/Treasurer	147,500	188,000
	Manager (6–8 years)	87,500	111,500
	Senior (3–5 years).	72,500	92,500
	Junior (0–2 years)	49,000	62,500
Recordkeeping	Full-charge bookkeeper	57,500	73,500
	Accounts manager.	51,000	65,000
	Payroll manager.	54,500	69,500
	Accounting clerk (0–2 years)	37,500	48,000

EXHIBIT 1.5

Accounting Salaries for Selected Fields

* Estimates assume a 5% compounded annual increase over current levels.

Point: For updated salary information:
www.AICPA.org
Abbott-Langer.com
Kforce.com

Quick Check

Answers—p. 26

1. What is the purpose of accounting?
2. What is the relation between accounting and recordkeeping?
3. Identify some advantages of technology for accounting.
4. Who are the internal and external users of accounting information?
5. Identify at least five types of managers who are internal users of accounting information.
6. What are internal controls and why are they important?

Quick Check is a chance to stop and reflect on key points.

Fundamentals of Accounting

Accounting is guided by principles, standards, concepts, and assumptions. This section describes several of these key fundamentals of accounting.

Ethics—A Key Concept

C4 Explain why ethics are crucial to accounting.

The goal of accounting is to provide useful information for decisions. For information to be useful, it must be trusted. This demands ethics in accounting. **Ethics** are beliefs that distinguish right from wrong. They are accepted standards of good and bad behavior.

Identifying the ethical path is sometimes difficult. The preferred path is a course of action that avoids casting doubt on one's decisions. For example, accounting users are less likely to trust an auditor's report if the auditor's pay depends on the success of the client's business. To avoid such concerns, ethics rules are often set. For example, auditors are banned from direct investment in their client and cannot accept pay that depends on figures in the client's reports. Exhibit 1.6 gives guidelines for making ethical decisions.

Point: Sarbanes-Oxley Act requires each issuer of securities to disclose whether it has adopted a code of ethics for its senior financial officers and the contents of that code.

EXHIBIT 1.6

Guidelines for Ethical Decision Making

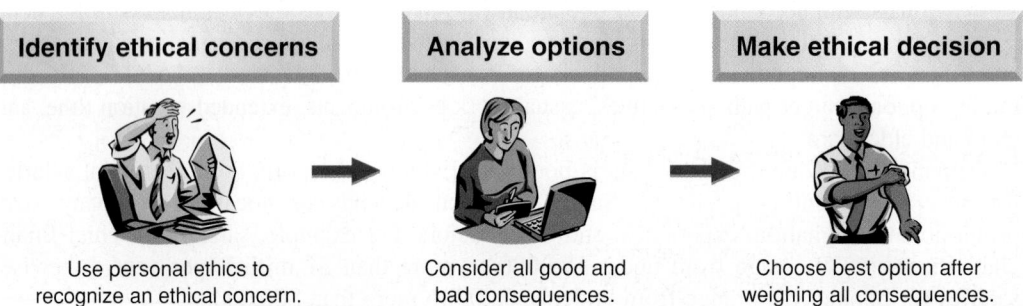

Identify ethical concerns	Analyze options	Make ethical decision
Use personal ethics to recognize an ethical concern.	Consider all good and bad consequences.	Choose best option after weighing all consequences.

Providers of accounting information often face ethical choices as they prepare financial reports. These choices can affect the price a buyer pays and the wages paid to workers. They can even affect the success of products and services. Misleading information can lead to a wrongful closing of a division that harms workers, customers, and suppliers. There is an old saying: *Good ethics are good business.*

Some people extend ethics to *social responsibility,* which refers to a concern for the impact of actions on society. An organization's social responsibility can include donations to hospitals, colleges, community programs, and law enforcement. It also can include programs to reduce pollution, increase product safety, improve worker conditions, and support continuing education. These programs are not limited to large companies. For example, many small businesses offer discounts to students and senior citizens. Still others help sponsor events such as the Special Olympics and summer reading programs.

Point: The American Institute of Certified Public Accountants' *Code of Professional Conduct* is available at **www.AICPA.org**.

Decision Insight

Virtuous Returns Virtue is not always its own reward. Compare the S&P 500 with the Domini Social Index (DSI), which covers 400 companies that have especially good records of social responsibility. We see that returns for companies with socially responsible behavior are at least as high as those of the S&P 500.

Copyright © 2007 by KLD Research & Analytics, Inc. The "Domini 400 Social Index."

Graphical displays are often used to illustrate key points. ———————————➤

Generally Accepted Accounting Principles

Financial accounting practice is governed by concepts and rules known as **generally accepted accounting principles (GAAP).** To use and interpret financial statements effectively, we need to understand these principles, which can change over time in response to the demands of users. GAAP aims to make information in financial statements *relevant, reliable,* and *comparable.* Relevant information affects the decisions of its users. Reliable information is trusted by users. Comparable information is helpful in contrasting organizations.

C5 Explain generally accepted accounting principles and define and apply several accounting principles.

Setting Accounting Principles   Two main groups establish generally accepted accounting principles in the United States. The **Financial Accounting Standards Board (FASB)** is the private group that sets both broad and specific principles. The **Securities and Exchange Commission (SEC)** is the government group that establishes reporting requirements for companies that issue stock to the public.

In today's global economy, there is increased demand by external users for comparability in accounting reports. This often arises when companies wish to raise money from lenders and investors in different countries. To that end, the **International Accounting Standards Board (IASB)** issues *International Financial Reporting Standards (IFRS)* that identify preferred accounting practices. The IASB hopes to create more harmony among accounting practices of different countries. If standards are harmonized, one company can potentially use a single set of financial statements in all financial markets. Many countries' standard setters support the IASB, and differences between U.S. GAAP and IASB's practices are fading. Yet, the IASB does not have authority to impose its standards on companies.

Point: State ethics codes require CPAs who audit financial statements to disclose areas where those statements fail to comply with GAAP. If CPAs fail to report noncompliance, they can lose their licenses and be subject to criminal and civil actions and fines.

Decision Insight

Principles and Scruples   Auditors, directors, and lawyers are using principles to improve accounting reports. Examples include accounting restatements at **Navistar,** financial restatements at **Nortel,** accounting reviews at **Echostar,** and expense adjustments at **Electronic Data Systems.** Principles-based accounting has led accounting firms to drop clients deemed too risky. Examples include **Grant Thornton**'s resignation as auditor of **Fremont General** due to alleged failures in providing information when promised, and **Ernst and Young**'s resignation as auditor of **Catalina Marketing** due to alleged accounting errors.

Principles and Assumptions of Accounting   Accounting principles (and assumptions) are of two types. *General principles* are the basic assumptions, concepts, and guidelines for preparing financial statements. *Specific principles* are detailed rules used in reporting business transactions and events. General principles stem from long-used accounting practices. Specific principles arise more often from the rulings of authoritative groups.

We need to understand both general and specific principles to effectively use accounting information. Several general principles are described in this section that are relied on in later chapters. General principles (in red font) and assumptions (in yellow font) are portrayed as building blocks of GAAP in Exhibit 1.7. The specific principles are described as we encounter them in the book.

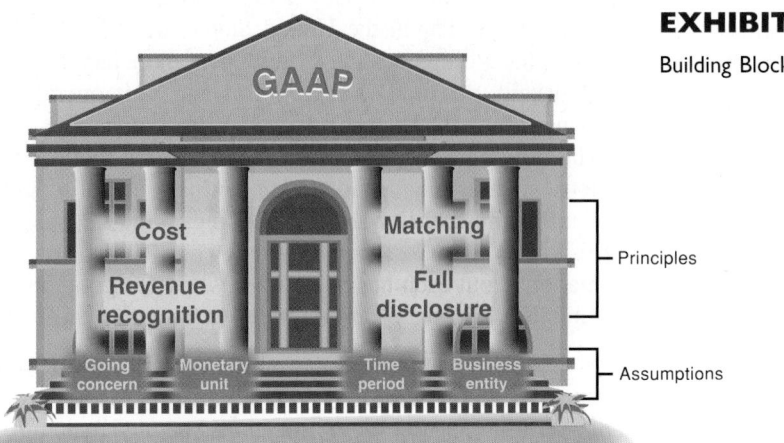

EXHIBIT 1.7

Building Blocks for GAAP

Accounting Principles   General principles consist of at least four basic principles, four assumptions, and certain constraints. The **cost principle** means that accounting information is based on actual cost. Cost is measured on a cash or equal-to-cash basis. This means if cash is given for a service, its cost is measured as the amount of cash paid. If something besides cash is exchanged

Point: The cost principle is also called the *historical cost principle.*

(such as a car traded for a truck), cost is measured as the cash value of what is given up or received. The cost principle emphasizes reliability and verifiability, and information based on cost is considered objective. *Objectivity* means that information is supported by independent, unbiased evidence; it demands more than a person's opinion. To illustrate, suppose a company pays $5,000 for equipment. The cost principle requires that this purchase be recorded at a cost of $5,000. It makes no difference if the owner thinks this equipment is worth $7,000.

Revenue (sales) is the amount received from selling products and services. The **revenue recognition principle** provides guidance on when a company must recognize revenue. To *recognize* means to record it. If revenue is recognized too early, a company would look more profitable than it is. If revenue is recognized too late, a company would look less profitable than it is.

Three concepts are important to revenue recognition. (1) *Revenue is recognized when earned.* The earnings process is normally complete when services are performed or a seller transfers ownership of products to the buyer. (2) *Proceeds from selling products and services need not be in cash.* A common noncash proceed received by a seller is a customer's promise to pay at a future date, called *credit sales.* (3) *Revenue is measured by the cash received plus the cash value of any other items received.*

The **matching principle** prescribes that a company must record its expenses incurred to generate the revenue reported. The **full disclosure principle** requires a company to report the details behind financial statements that would impact users' decisions. Those disclosures are often in footnotes to the statements.

Example: When a bookstore sells a textbook on credit is its earnings process complete? *Answer:* A bookstore can record sales for these books minus an amount expected for returns.

Decision Insight

Revenues for the **San Diego Chargers** football team include ticket sales, television and cable broadcasts, radio rights, concessions, and advertising. Revenues from ticket sales are earned when the Chargers play each game. Advance ticket sales are not revenues; instead, they represent a liability until the Chargers play the game for which the ticket was sold. At that point, the liability is removed and revenues are reported.

Accounting Assumptions   There are four accounting assumptions. The **going-concern assumption** means that accounting information reflects a presumption that the business will continue operating instead of being closed or sold. This implies, for example, that property is reported at cost instead of, say, liquidation values that assume closure.

The **monetary unit assumption** means that we can express transactions and events in monetary, or money, units. Money is the common denominator in business. Examples of monetary units are the dollar in the United States, Canada, Australia, and Singapore; and the peso in Mexico, the Philippines, and Chile. The monetary unit a company uses in its accounting reports usually depends on the country where it operates, but many companies today are expressing reports in more than one monetary unit.

Point: For currency conversion: cnnfn.com/markets/currencies

The **time period assumption** presumes that the life of a company can be divided into time periods, such as months and years, and that useful reports can be prepared for those periods.

The **business entity assumption** means that a business is accounted for separately from other business entities, including its owner. The reason for this assumption is that separate information about each business is necessary for good decisions. A business entity can take one of three legal forms: *proprietorship, partnership,* or *corporation.*

Point: Abuse of the entity assumption was a main culprit in **Enron's** collapse.

1. A **sole proprietorship,** or simply **proprietorship,** is a business owned by one person. No special legal requirements must be met to start a proprietorship. It is a separate entity for accounting purposes, but it is *not* a separate legal entity from its owner. This means, for example, that a court can order an owner to sell personal belongings to pay a proprietorship's debt. This *unlimited liability* of a proprietorship is a disadvantage. However, an advantage is that a proprietorship's income is not subject to a business income tax but is instead reported and taxed on the owner's personal income tax return. Proprietorship characteristics are summarized in Exhibit 1.8, including those for partnerships and corporations.

2. A **partnership** is a business owned by two or more people, called *partners.* Like a proprietorship, no special legal requirements must be met in starting a partnership. The only

Characteristic	Proprietorship	Partnership	Corporation
Business entity	yes	yes	yes
Legal entity	no	no	yes
Limited liability	no*	no*	yes
Unlimited life	no	no	yes
Business taxed	no	no	yes
One owner allowed	yes	no	yes

EXHIBIT 1.8

Characteristics of Businesses

* Proprietorships and partnerships that are set up as LLCs provide limited liability.

·requirement is an agreement between partners to run a business together. The agreement can be either oral or written and usually indicates how income and losses are to be shared. A partnership, like a proprietorship, is *not* legally separate from its owners. This means that each partner's share of profits is reported and taxed on that partner's tax return. It also means *unlimited liability* for its partners. However, at least three types of partnerships limit liability. A *limited partnership* (*LP*) includes a general partner(s) with unlimited liability and a limited partner(s) with liability restricted to the amount invested. A *limited liability partnership* (*LLP*) restricts partners' liabilities to their own acts and the acts of individuals under their control. This protects an innocent partner from the negligence of another partner, yet all partners remain responsible for partnership debts. A *limited liability company* (*LLC*) offers the limited liability of a corporation and the tax treatment of a partnership (and proprietorship). Most proprietorships and partnerships are now organized as LLCs.

Point: Proprietorships and partnerships are usually managed by their owners. In a corporation, the owners (shareholders) elect a board of directors who appoint managers to run the business.

3. A **corporation** is a business legally separate from its owners, meaning it is responsible for its own acts and its own debts. Separate legal status means that a corporation can conduct business with the rights, duties, and responsibilities of a person. A corporation acts through its managers, who are its legal agents. Separate legal status also means that its owners, who are called **shareholders** (or **stockholders**), are not personally liable for corporate acts and debts. This limited liability is its main advantage. A main disadvantage is what's called *double taxation*—meaning that (1) the corporation income is taxed and (2) any distribution of income to its owners through dividends is taxed as part of the owners' personal income, usually at the 15% rate. (For lower income taxpayers, the dividend tax is less than 15%, and in some cases zero.) An *S corporation,* a corporation with special characteristics, does not owe corporate income tax. Owners of S corporations report their share of corporate income with their personal income. Ownership of all corporations is divided into units called **shares** or **stock.** When a corporation issues only one class of stock, we call it **common stock** (or *capital stock*).

Decision Ethics boxes are role-playing exercises that stress ethics in accounting and business.

Decision Ethics

Entrepreneur   You and a friend develop a new design for in-line skates that improves speed by 25% to 30%. You plan to form a business to manufacture and market those skates. You and your friend want to minimize taxes, but your prime concern is potential lawsuits from individuals who might be injured on these skates. What form of organization do you set up? [Answer—p. 25]

Sarbanes–Oxley (SOX)

Congress passed the **Sarbanes–Oxley Act,** also called *SOX,* to help curb financial abuses at companies that issue their stock to the public. SOX requires that these public companies apply both accounting oversight and stringent internal controls. The desired results include more transparency, accountability, and truthfulness in reporting transactions.

Compliance with SOX requires documentation and verification of internal controls and increased emphasis on internal control effectiveness. Failure to comply can yield financial penalties, stock market delisting, and criminal prosecution of executives. Management must issue a report stating that internal controls are effective. CEOs and CFOs who knowingly sign off on bogus accounting reports risk millions of dollars in fines and years in prison. **Auditors** also must verify the effectiveness of internal controls.

Point: An **audit** examines whether financial statements are prepared using GAAP. It does *not* attest to absolute accuracy of the statements.

Point: *BusinessWeek* reports that external audit costs run about $35,000 for startups, up from $15,000 pre-SOX.

A listing of some of the more publicized accounting scandals in recent years follows.

Company	Alleged Accounting Abuses
Enron	Inflated income, hid debt, and bribed officials
WorldCom	Understated expenses to inflate income and hid debt
Fannie Mae	Inflated income
Adelphia Communications	Understated expenses to inflate income and hid debt
AOL Time Warner	Inflated revenues and income
Xerox	Inflated income
Bristol-Myers Squibb	Inflated revenues and income
Nortel Networks	Understated expenses to inflate income
Global Crossing	Inflated revenues and income
Tyco	Hid debt, and CEO evaded taxes
Halliburton	Inflated revenues and income
Qwest Communications	Inflated revenues and income

To reduce the risk of accounting fraud, companies set up *governance systems.* A company's governance system includes its owners, managers, employees, board of directors, and other important stakeholders, who work together to reduce the risk of accounting fraud and increase confidence in accounting reports.

The impact of SOX regulations for accounting and business is discussed throughout this book. Ethics and investor confidence are key to company success. Lack of confidence in accounting numbers impacts company value as evidenced by huge stock price declines for **Enron**, **WorldCom**, **Tyco**, and **ImClone** after accounting misconduct was uncovered.

Decision Insight

IFRSs Like the FASB, the IASB uses a conceptual framework to aid in drafting standards. However, unlike the FASB, the IASB's conceptual framework is used as a reference when specific guidance is lacking. Also unlike the FASB, the IASB requires that transactions be accounted for according to their substance (not only their legal form).

Quick Check
Answers—p. 26

7. What three-step guidelines can help people make ethical decisions?
8. Why are ethics and social responsibility valuable to organizations?
9. Why are ethics crucial in accounting?
10. Who sets U.S. accounting rules?
11. How are U.S. companies affected by international accounting standards?
12. How are the objectivity concept and cost principle related?
13. Why is the business entity assumption important?
14. Why is the revenue recognition principle important?
15. What are the three basic forms of business organization?
16. Identify the owners of corporations and the terminology for ownership units.

Transaction Analysis and the Accounting Equation

To understand accounting information, we need to know how an accounting system captures relevant data about transactions, and then classifies, records, and reports data.

Accounting Equation

A1 Define and interpret the accounting equation and each of its components.

The accounting system reflects two basic aspects of a company: what it owns and what it owes. **Assets** are resources with future benefits that are owned or controlled by a company. Examples are cash, supplies, equipment, and land. The claims on a company's assets—what it owes—are separated into owner and nonowner claims. **Liabilities** are what a company owes its nonowners (creditors) in future payments, products, or services. **Equity** (also called owner's equity or capital) refers to the claims of its owner(s). Together, liabilities and equity are the source of funds to acquire assets. The relation of assets, liabilities, and equity is reflected in the following **accounting equation:**

Assets = Liabilities + Equity

> **Assets = Liabilities + Equity**

Liabilities are usually shown before equity in this equation because creditors' claims must be paid before the claims of owners. (The terms in this equation can be rearranged; for example, Assets − Liabilities = Equity.) The accounting equation applies to all transactions and events, to all companies and forms of organization, and to all points in time. For example, **Best Buy**'s assets equal $13,570, its liabilities equal $7,369, and its equity equals $6,201 ($ in millions). Let's now look at the accounting equation in more detail.

Videos1.1&1.2

Assets   **Assets** are resources owned or controlled by a company. These resources are expected to yield future benefits. Examples are Web servers for an online services company, musical instruments for a rock band, and land for a vegetable grower. The term *receivable* is used to refer to an asset that promises a future inflow of resources. A company that provides a service or product on credit is said to have an account receivable from that customer.

Point: The phrases "on credit" and "on account" imply that cash payment will occur at a future date.

Liabilities   **Liabilities** are creditors' claims on assets. These claims reflect company obligations to provide assets, products or services to others. The term *payable* refers to a liability that promises a future outflow of resources. Examples are wages payable to workers, accounts payable to suppliers, notes payable to banks, and taxes payable to the government.

Equity   **Equity** is the owner's claim on assets. Equity is equal to assets minus liabilities. This is the reason equity is also called *net assets* or *residual equity*.

Equity for a noncorporate entity—commonly called owner's equity—increases and decreases as follows: owner investments and revenues *increase* equity, whereas owner withdrawals and expenses *decrease* equity. **Owner investments** are assets an owner puts into the company and are included under the generic account **Owner, Capital. Revenues** increase equity and are the assets earned from a company's earnings activities. Examples are consulting services provided, sales of products, facilities rented to others, and commissions from services. **Owner withdrawals** are assets an owner takes from the company for personal use. **Expenses** decrease equity and are the cost of assets or services used to earn revenues. Examples are costs of employee time, use of supplies, and advertising, utilities, and insurance services from others. In sum, equity is the accumulated revenues and owner investments less the accumulated expenses and withdrawals since the company began. This breakdown of equity yields the following **expanded accounting equation.**

*Key **terms** are printed in bold and defined again in the end-of-book **glossary.***

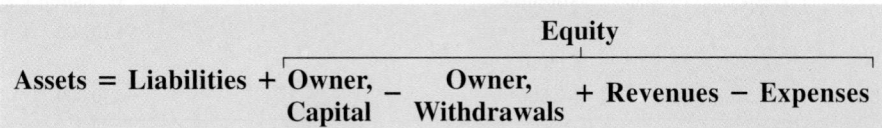

$$\text{Assets} = \text{Liabilities} + \overbrace{\underset{\text{Capital}}{\text{Owner,}} - \underset{\text{Withdrawals}}{\text{Owner,}} + \text{Revenues} - \text{Expenses}}^{\text{Equity}}$$

Net income occurs when revenues exceed expenses. Net income increases equity. A **net loss** occurs when expenses exceed revenues, which decreases equity.

Decision Insight

Web Info   Most organizations maintain Websites that include accounting data—see **Best Buy** (**BestBuy.com**) as an example. The SEC keeps an online database called **EDGAR** (**www.sec.gov/edgar.shtml**), which has accounting information for thousands of companies that issue stock to the public. Information services such as **Finance.Google.com** and **Finance.Yahoo.com** offer additional online data and analysis.

Transaction Analysis

Business activities can be described in terms of transactions and events. **External transactions** are exchanges of value between two entities, which yield changes in the accounting equation. **Internal transactions** are exchanges within an entity; they can also affect the accounting equation. An example is a company's use of its supplies, which are reported as expenses when used.

 A2   Analyze business transactions using the accounting equation.

Events refer to happenings that affect an entity's accounting equation *and* can be reliably measured. They include business events such as changes in the market value of certain assets and liabilities, and natural events such as floods and fires that destroy assets and create losses. They do not include, for example, the signing of service or product contracts, which by themselves do not impact the accounting equation.

This section uses the accounting equation to analyze 11 selected transactions and events of FastForward, a start-up consulting (service) business, in its first month of operations. Remember that each transaction and event leaves the equation in balance and that assets *always* equal the sum of liabilities and equity.

Transaction 1: Investment by Owner   On December 1, Chuck Taylor forms a consulting business focused on assessing the performance of athletic footwear and accessories, which he names FastForward. He sets it up as a proprietorship. Taylor owns and manages the business. The marketing plan for the business is to focus primarily on consulting with sports clubs, amateur athletes, and others who place orders for athletic footwear and accessories with manufacturers. Taylor personally invests $30,000 cash in the new company and deposits the cash in a bank account opened under the name of FastForward. After this transaction, the cash (an asset) and the owner's equity each equal $30,000. The source of increase in equity is the owner's investment, which is included in the column titled C. Taylor, Capital. (Owner investments are always included under the title *'Owner name,' Capital.*) The effect of this transaction on FastForward is reflected in the accounting equation as follows:

Point: There are 3 basic types of company operations: (1) **Services**—providing customer services for profit, (2) **Merchandisers**—buying products and re-selling them for profit, and (3) **Manufacturers**—creating products and selling them for profit.

	Assets	=	Liabilities	+	Equity
	Cash	=			C. Taylor, Capital
(1)	+$30,000	=			+$30,000

Transaction 2: Purchase Supplies for Cash   FastForward uses $2,500 of its cash to buy supplies of brand name athletic footwear for performance testing over the next few months. This transaction is an exchange of cash, an asset, for another kind of asset, supplies. It merely changes the form of assets from cash to supplies. The decrease in cash is exactly equal to the increase in supplies. The supplies of athletic footwear are assets because of the expected future benefits from the test results of their performance. This transaction is reflected in the accounting equation as follows:

	Assets			=	Liabilities	+	Equity
	Cash	+	Supplies	=			C. Taylor, Capital
Old Bal.	$30,000			=			$30,000
(2)	−2,500	+	$2,500				
New Bal.	$27,500	+	$ 2,500	=			$30,000
		$30,000				$30,000	

Transaction 3: Purchase Equipment for Cash   FastForward spends $26,000 to acquire equipment for testing athletic footwear. Like transaction 2, transaction 3 is an exchange of one asset, cash, for another asset, equipment. The equipment is an asset because of its expected future benefits from testing athletic footwear. This purchase changes the makeup of assets but does not change the asset total. The accounting equation remains in balance.

	Assets					=	Liabilities	+	Equity
	Cash	+	Supplies	+	Equipment	=			C. Taylor, Capital
Old Bal.	$27,500	+	$2,500			=			$30,000
(3)	−26,000			+	$26,000				
New Bal.	$ 1,500	+	$2,500	+	$ 26,000	=			$30,000
			$30,000					$30,000	

Transaction 4: Purchase Supplies on Credit   Taylor decides he needs more supplies of athletic footwear and accessories. These additional supplies total $7,100, but as we see from the accounting equation in transaction 3, FastForward has only $1,500 in cash. Taylor

arranges to purchase them on credit from CalTech Supply Company. Thus, FastForward acquires supplies in exchange for a promise to pay for them later. This purchase increases assets by $7,100 in supplies, and liabilities (called *accounts payable* to CalTech Supply) increase by the same amount. The effects of this purchase follow:

Example: If FastForward pays $500 cash in transaction 4, how does this partial payment affect the liability to CalTech? What would be FastForward's cash balance? *Answers:* The liability to CalTech would be reduced to $6,600 and the cash balance would be reduced to $1,000.

	Assets					=	Liabilities	+	Equity
	Cash	+	Supplies	+	Equipment	=	Accounts Payable	+	C. Taylor, Capital
Old Bal.	$1,500	+	$2,500	+	$26,000	=			$30,000
(4)		+	7,100				+$7,100		
New Bal.	$1,500	+	$9,600	+	$26,000	=	$ 7,100	+	$30,000
			$37,100					$37,100	

Transaction 5: Provide Services for Cash

FastForward earns revenues by consulting with clients about test results on athletic footwear and accessories. It earns net income only if its revenues are greater than its expenses incurred in earning them. In one of its first jobs, FastForward provides consulting services to an athletic club and immediately collects $4,200 cash. The accounting equation reflects this increase in cash of $4,200 and in equity of $4,200. This increase in equity is identified in the far right column under Revenues because the cash received is earned by providing consulting services.

	Assets					=	Liabilities	+		Equity		
	Cash	+	Supplies	+	Equipment	=	Accounts Payable	+	C. Taylor, Capital	+	Revenues
Old Bal.	$1,500	+	$9,600	+	$26,000	=	$7,100	+	$30,000		
(5)	+4,200									+	$4,200
New Bal.	$5,700	+	$9,600	+	$26,000	=	$7,100	+	$30,000	+	$ 4,200
			$41,300						$41,300		

Transactions 6 and 7: Payment of Expenses in Cash

FastForward pays $1,000 rent to the landlord of the building where its facilities are located. Paying this amount allows FastForward to occupy the space for the month of December. The rental payment is reflected in the following accounting equation as transaction 6. FastForward also pays the biweekly $700 salary of the company's only employee. This is reflected in the accounting equation as transaction 7. Both transactions 6 and 7 are December expenses for FastForward. The costs of both rent and salary are expenses, as opposed to assets, because their benefits are used in December (they have no future benefits after December). These transactions also use up an asset (cash) in carrying out FastForward's operations. The accounting equation shows that both transactions reduce cash and equity. The far right column identifies these decreases as Expenses.

By definition, increases in expenses yield decreases in equity.

	Assets					=	Liabilities	+		Equity				
	Cash	+	Supplies	+	Equipment	=	Accounts Payable	+	C. Taylor, Capital	+	Revenues	–	Expenses
Old Bal.	$5,700	+	$9,600	+	$26,000	=	$7,100	+	$30,000	+	$4,200		
(6)	−1,000											–	$1,000
Bal.	4,700	+	9,600	+	26,000	=	7,100	+	30,000	+	4,200	–	1,000
(7)	− 700											–	700
New Bal.	$4,000	+	$9,600	+	$26,000	=	$7,100	+	$30,000	+	$4,200	–	$ 1,700
			$39,600						$39,600				

Transaction 8: Provide Services and Facilities for Credit

FastForward provides consulting services of $1,600 and rents its test facilities for $300 to an amateur sports club. The rental involves allowing club members to try recommended footwear and accessories at FastForward's testing area. The sports club is billed for the $1,900 total. This transaction results in a new asset, called *accounts receivable,* from this client. It also yields an increase in equity from the two revenue components reflected in the Revenues column of the accounting equation:

	Assets						=	Liabilities	+			Equity			
	Cash	+	Accounts Receivable	+	Supplies	+	Equipment	=	Accounts Payable	+	C. Taylor, Capital	+	Revenues	–	Expenses
Old Bal.	$4,000	+		+	$9,600	+	$26,000	=	$7,100	+	$30,000	+	$4,200	–	$1,700
(8)		+	$1,900									+	1,600		
												+	300		
New Bal.	$4,000	+	$ 1,900	+	$9,600	+	$26,000	=	$7,100	+	$30,000	+	$6,100	–	$1,700
			$41,500									$41,500				

Transaction 9: Receipt of Cash from Accounts Receivable

Point: Receipt of cash is not always a revenue.

The client in transaction 8 (the amateur sports club) pays $1,900 to FastForward 10 days after it is billed for consulting services. This transaction 9 does not change the total amount of assets and does not affect liabilities or equity. It converts the receivable (an asset) to cash (another asset). It does not create new revenue. Revenue was recognized when FastForward rendered the services in transaction 8, not when the cash is now collected. This emphasis on the earnings process instead of cash flows is a goal of the revenue recognition principle and yields useful information to users. The new balances follow:

	Assets						=	Liabilities	+			Equity			
	Cash	+	Accounts Receivable	+	Supplies	+	Equipment	=	Accounts Payable	+	C. Taylor, Capital	+	Revenues	–	Expenses
Old Bal.	$4,000	+	$1,900	+	$9,600	+	$26,000	=	$7,100	+	$30,000	+	$6,100	–	$1,700
(9)	+1,900	–	1,900												
New Bal.	$5,900	+	$ 0	+	$9,600	+	$26,000	=	$7,100	+	$30,000	+	$6,100	–	$1,700
			$41,500									$41,500				

Transaction 10: Payment of Accounts Payable

FastForward pays CalTech Supply $900 cash as partial payment for its earlier $7,100 purchase of supplies (transaction 4), leaving $6,200 unpaid. The accounting equation shows that this transaction decreases FastForward's cash by $900 and decreases its liability to CalTech Supply by $900. Equity does not change. This event does not create an expense even though cash flows out of FastForward (instead the expense is recorded when FastForward derives the benefits from these supplies).

	Assets						=	Liabilities	+			Equity			
	Cash	+	Accounts Receivable	+	Supplies	+	Equipment	=	Accounts Payable	+	C. Taylor, Capital	+	Revenues	–	Expenses
Old Bal.	$5,900	+	$ 0	+	$9,600	+	$26,000	=	$7,100	+	$30,000	+	$6,100	–	$1,700
(10)	– 900								– 900						
New Bal.	$5,000	+	$ 0	+	$9,600	+	$26,000	=	$6,200	+	$30,000	+	$6,100	–	$1,700
			$40,600									$40,600				

Transaction 11: Withdrawal of Cash by Owner

By definition, increases in withdrawals yield decreases in equity.

The owner of FastForward withdraws $200 cash for personal use. Withdrawals (decreases in equity) are not reported as expenses because they are not part of the company's earnings process. Since withdrawals are not company expenses, they are not used in computing net income.

	Assets						=	Liabilities	+			Equity					
	Cash	+	Accounts Receivable	+	Supplies	+	Equipment	=	Accounts Payable	+	C. Taylor, Capital	–	C. Taylor, Withdrawals	+	Revenues	–	Expenses
Old Bal.	$5,000	+	$ 0	+	$9,600	+	$26,000	=	$6,200	+	$30,000			+	$6,100	–	$1,700
(11)	– 200											–	$200				
New Bal.	$4,800	+	$ 0	+	$9,600	+	$26,000	=	$6,200	+	$30,000	–	$200	+	$6,100	–	$1,700
			$40,400										$40,400				

Summary of Transactions

We summarize in Exhibit 1.9 the effects of these 11 transactions of FastForward using the accounting equation. First, we see that the accounting equation remains in balance after each transaction. Second, transactions can be analyzed by their effects on components of the accounting equation. For example, in transactions 2, 3, and 9, one asset increased while another asset decreased by equal amounts.

Point: Knowing how financial statements are prepared improves our analysis of them. We develop the skills for analysis of financial statements throughout the book. Chapter 17 focuses on financial statement analysis.

EXHIBIT 1.9

Summary of Transactions Using the Accounting Equation

	Assets				=	Liabilities	+	Equity			
	Cash	+ Accounts Receivable	+ Supplies	+ Equipment	=	Accounts Payable	+ C. Taylor, Capital	− C. Taylor, Withdrawals	+ Revenues	− Expenses
(1)	$30,000				=		$30,000			
(2)	− 2,500		+ $2,500							
Bal.	27,500		+ 2,500		=		30,000			
(3)	−26,000			+ $26,000						
Bal.	1,500		+ 2,500	+ 26,000	=		30,000			
(4)			+ 7,100			+$7,100				
Bal.	1,500		+ 9,600	+ 26,000	=	7,100	+ 30,000			
(5)	+ 4,200								+ $4,200	
Bal.	5,700		+ 9,600	+ 26,000	=	7,100	+ 30,000		+ 4,200	
(6)	− 1,000									− $1,000
Bal.	4,700		+ 9,600	+ 26,000	=	7,100	+ 30,000		+ 4,200	− 1,000
(7)	− 700									− 700
Bal.	4,000		+ 9,600	+ 26,000	=	7,100	+ 30,000		+ 4,200	− 1,700
(8)		+ $1,900							+ 1,600	
									+ 300	
Bal.	4,000	+ 1,900	+ 9,600	+ 26,000	=	7,100	+ 30,000		+ 6,100	− 1,700
(9)	+ 1,900	− 1,900								
Bal.	5,900 +	0	+ 9,600	+ 26,000	=	7,100	+ 30,000		+ 6,100	− 1,700
(10)	− 900					− 900				
Bal.	5,000 +	0	+ 9,600	+ 26,000	=	6,200	+ 30,000		+ 6,100	− 1,700
(11)	− 200							− $200		
Bal.	$ 4,800 +	$ 0	+ $ 9,600	+ $ 26,000	=	$ 6,200	+ $ 30,000	− $ 200	+ $6,100	− $ 1,700

Quick Check

Answers—p. 26

17. When is the accounting equation in balance, and what does that mean?
18. How can a transaction not affect any liability and equity accounts?
19. Describe a transaction increasing equity and one decreasing it.
20. Identify a transaction that decreases both assets and liabilities.

Financial Statements

This section introduces us to how financial statements are prepared from the analysis of business transactions. The four financial statements and their purposes are:

P1 Identify and prepare basic financial statements and explain how they interrelate.

1. **Income statement**—describes a company's revenues and expenses along with the resulting net income or loss over a period of time due to earnings activities.
2. **Statement of owner's equity**—explains changes in equity from net income (or loss) and from any owner investments and withdrawals over a period of time.

3. **Balance sheet**—describes a company's financial position (types and amounts of assets, liabilities, and equity) at a point in time.

4. **Statement of cash flows**—identifies cash inflows (receipts) and cash outflows (payments) over a period of time.

We prepare these financial statements using the 11 selected transactions of FastForward. (These statements are technically called *unadjusted*—we explain this in Chapters 2 and 3.)

Income Statement

FastForward's income statement for December is shown at the top of Exhibit 1.10. Information about revenues and expenses is conveniently taken from the Equity columns of Exhibit 1.9. Revenues are reported first on the income statement. They include consulting revenues of $5,800 from transactions 5 and 8 and rental revenue of $300 from transaction 8. Expenses are reported after revenues. (For convenience in this chapter, we list larger amounts first, but we can sort expenses in different ways.) Rent and salary expenses are from transactions 6 and 7. Expenses reflect the costs to generate the revenues reported. Net income (or loss) is reported at the bottom of the statement and is the amount earned in December. Owner's investments and withdrawals are *not* part of income.

> **Point:** Net income is sometimes called *earnings* or *profit*.

Statement of Owner's Equity

> **Point:** The statement of owner's equity is also called the *statement of changes in owner's equity*. Note: Beg. Capital + Net Income − Withdrawals = Ending Capital

The statement of owner's equity reports information about how equity changes over the reporting period. This statement shows beginning capital, events that increase it (owner investments and net income), and events that decrease it (withdrawals and net loss). Ending capital is computed in this statement and is carried over and reported on the balance sheet. FastForward's statement of owner's equity is the second report in Exhibit 1.10. The beginning capital balance is measured as of the start of business on December 1. It is zero because FastForward did not exist before then. An existing business reports a beginning balance equal to that as of the end of the prior reporting period (such as from November 30). FastForward's statement of owner's equity shows that Taylor's initial investment created $30,000 of equity. It also shows the $4,400 of net income earned during the period. This links the income statement to the statement of owner's equity (see line ①). The statement also reports Taylor's $200 cash withdrawal and FastForward's end-of-period capital balance.

Balance Sheet

FastForward's balance sheet is the third report in Exhibit 1.10. This statement refers to FastForward's financial condition at the close of business on December 31. The left side of the balance sheet lists FastForward's assets: cash, supplies, and equipment. The upper right side of the balance sheet shows that FastForward owes $6,200 to creditors. Any other liabilities (such as a bank loan) would be listed here. The equity (capital) balance is $34,200. Line ② shows the link between the ending balance of the statement of owner's equity and the equity balance on the balance sheet. (This presentation of the balance sheet is called the *account form:* assets on the left and liabilities and equity on the right. Another presentation is the *report form:* assets on top, followed by liabilities and then equity at the bottom. Either presentation is acceptable.)

> *Decision Maker boxes are role-playing exercises that stress the relevance of accounting.*

Decision Maker

Retailer   You open a wholesale business selling entertainment equipment to retail outlets. You find that most of your customers demand to buy on credit. How can you use the balance sheets of these customers to help you decide which ones to extend credit to? [Answer—p. 26]

> **Point:** Statement of cash flows has three main sections: operating, investing, and financing.

> **Point:** Payment for supplies is an operating activity because supplies are expected to be used up in short-term operations (typically less than one year).

Statement of Cash Flows

FastForward's statement of cash flows is the final report in Exhibit 1.10. The first section reports cash flows from *operating activities*. It shows the $6,100 cash received from clients and the $5,100 cash paid for supplies, rent, and employee salaries. Outflows are in parentheses to denote subtraction. Net cash provided by operating activities for December is $1,000. If cash paid exceeded the $5,100 cash received, we would call it "cash used by operating activities." The second section

EXHIBIT 1.10

Financial Statements and
Their Links

FASTFORWARD
Income Statement
For Month Ended December 31, 2009

Revenues

Consulting revenue ($4,200 + $1,600)	$ 5,800	
Rental revenue	300	
Total revenues		$ 6,100
Expenses		
Rent expense	1,000	
Salaries expense	700	
Total expenses		1,700
Net income		$ 4,400

Point: A statement's heading identifies the company, the statement title, and the date or time period.

FASTFORWARD
Statement of Owner's Equity
For Month Ended December 31, 2009

C. Taylor, Capital, December 1, 2009		$ 0
Plus: Investments by owner	$30,000	
Net income	4,400	34,400
		34,400
Less: Withdrawals by owner		200
C. Taylor, Capital, December 31, 2009		$34,200

Point: Arrow lines show how the statements are linked. ① Net income is used to compute equity. ② Owner capital is used to prepare the balance sheet. ③ Cash from the balance sheet is used to reconcile the statement of cash flows.

FASTFORWARD
Balance Sheet
December 31, 2009

Assets		Liabilities	
Cash	$ 4,800	Accounts payable	$ 6,200
Supplies	9,600	Total liabilities	6,200
Equipment	26,000		
		Equity	
		C. Taylor, Capital	34,200
Total assets	$40,400	Total liabilities and equity	$ 40,400

Point: The income statement, the statement of owner's equity, and the statement of cash flows are prepared for a *period* of time. The balance sheet is prepared as of a *point* in time.

FASTFORWARD
Statement of Cash Flows
For Month Ended December 31, 2009

Cash flows from operating activities		
Cash received from clients ($4,200 + $1,900)	$ 6,100	
Cash paid for supplies ($2,500 + $900)	(3,400)	
Cash paid for rent	(1,000)	
Cash paid to employee	(700)	
Net cash provided by operating activities		$ 1,000
Cash flows from investing activities		
Purchase of equipment	(26,000)	
Net cash used by investing activities		(26,000)
Cash flows from financing activities		
Investments by owner	30,000	
Withdrawals by owner	(200)	
Net cash provided by financing activities		29,800
Net increase in cash		$ 4,800
Cash balance, December 1, 2009		0
Cash balance, December 31, 2009		$ 4,800

Point: A single ruled line denotes an addition or subtraction. Final totals are double underlined. Negative amounts are often in parentheses.

Point: Investing activities refer to long-term asset investments by the company, *not* to owner investments.

reports *investing activities,* which involve buying and selling assets such as land and equipment that are held for *long-term use* (typically more than one year). The only investing activity is the $26,000 purchase of equipment. The third section shows cash flows from *financing activities,* which include the *long-term* borrowing and repaying of cash from lenders and the cash investments from, and withdrawals by, the owner. FastForward reports $30,000 from the owner's initial investment and the $200 cash withdrawal. The net cash effect of all financing transactions is a $29,800 cash inflow. The final part of the statement shows FastForward increased its cash balance by $4,800 in December. Since it started with no cash, the ending balance is also $4,800—see line ③.

Quick Check   Answers—p. 26

21. Explain the link between the income statement and the statement of owner's equity.

22. Describe the link between the balance sheet and the statement of owner's equity.

23. Discuss the three major sections of the statement of cash flows.

Decision Analysis (a section at the end of each chapter) introduces and explains ratios helpful in decision making using real company data. Instructors can skip this section and cover all ratios in Chapter 17.

Decision Analysis   **Return on Assets**

A3 Compute and interpret return on assets.

A *Decision Analysis* section at the end of each chapter is devoted to financial statement analysis. We organize financial statement analysis into four areas: (1) liquidity and efficiency, (2) solvency, (3) profitability, and (4) market prospects—Chapter 17 has a ratio listing with definitions and groupings by area. When analyzing ratios, we need benchmarks to identify good, bad, or average levels. Common benchmarks include the company's prior levels and those of its competitors.

This chapter presents a profitability measure: return on assets. Return on assets is useful in evaluating management, analyzing and forecasting profits, and planning activities. **Dell** has its marketing department compute return on assets for *every* order. **Return on assets (ROA),** also called *return on investment (ROI),* is defined in Exhibit 1.11.

EXHIBIT 1.11

Return on Assets

$$\text{Return on assets} = \frac{\text{Net income}}{\text{Average total assets}}$$

Net income is from the annual income statement, and average total assets is computed by adding the beginning and ending amounts for that same period and dividing by 2. To illustrate, **Best Buy** reports net income of $1,377 million in 2007. At the beginning of fiscal 2007, its total assets are $11,864 million and at the end of fiscal 2007, they total $13,570 million. Best Buy's return on assets for 2007 is:

$$\text{Return on assets} = \frac{\$1,377 \text{ million}}{(\$11,864 \text{ million} + \$13,570 \text{ million})/2} = 10.8\%$$

Is a 10.8% return on assets good or bad for Best Buy? To help answer this question, we compare (benchmark) Best Buy's return with its prior performance, the returns of competitors (such as **Circuit City**, **RadioShack**, and **CompUSA**), and the returns from alternative investments. Best Buy's return for each of the prior five years is in the second column of Exhibit 1.12, which ranges from 1.3% to 10.8%.

EXHIBIT 1.12

Best Buy, Circuit City, and Industry Returns

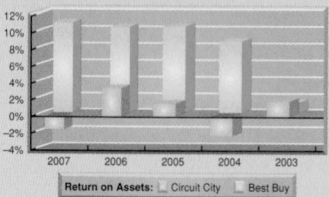

		Return on Assets	
Fiscal Year	**Best Buy**	**Circuit City**	**Industry**
2007	10.8%	(1.9)%	3.5%
2006	10.3	3.5	3.3
2005	10.4	1.6	3.2
2004	8.6	(2.3)	3.1
2003	1.3	1.9	3.0

Best Buy's returns show an increase in its productive use of assets in recent years. We also compute Circuit City's returns in the third column of Exhibit 1.12. In four of the five years, Best Buy's return exceeds Circuit City's, and its average return is higher for this period. We also compare Best Buy's return to the normal return for similar merchandisers of electronic products (fourth column). Industry averages are available from services such as **Dun & Bradstreet**'s *Industry Norms and Key Ratios* and **Robert Morris Associates**' *Annual Statement Studies*. When compared to the industry, Best Buy performs well.

Each Decision Analysis section ends with a role-playing scenario to show the usefulness of ratios.

Decision Maker

Business Owner   You own a small winter ski resort that earns a 21% return on its assets. An opportunity to purchase a winter ski equipment manufacturer is offered to you. This manufacturer earns a 19% return on its assets. The industry return for this manufacturer is 14%. Do you purchase this manufacturer? [Answer—p. 26]

*The **Demonstration Problem** is a review of key chapter content. The* Planning the Solution *offers strategies in solving the problem.*

Demonstration Problem

After several months of planning, Jasmine Worthy started a haircutting business called Expressions. The following events occurred during its first month of business.

DP1

a. On August 1, Worthy invested $3,000 cash and $15,000 of equipment in Expressions.
b. On August 2, Expressions paid $600 cash for furniture for the shop.
c. On August 3, Expressions paid $500 cash to rent space in a strip mall for August.
d. On August 4, it purchased $1,200 of equipment on credit for the shop (using a long-term note payable).
e. On August 5, Expressions opened for business. Cash received from haircutting services in the first week and a half of business (ended August 15) was $825.
f. On August 15, it provided $100 of haircutting services on account.
g. On August 17, it received a $100 check for services previously rendered on account.
h. On August 17, it paid $125 cash to an assistant for hours worked during the grand opening.
i. Cash received from services provided during the second half of August was $930.
j. On August 31, it paid a $400 installment toward principal on the note payable entered into on August 4.
k. On August 31, Worthy made a $900 cash withdrawal from the company for personal use.

Required

1. Arrange the following asset, liability, and equity titles in a table similar to the one in Exhibit 1.9: Cash; Accounts Receivable; Furniture; Store Equipment; Note Payable; J. Worthy, Capital; J. Worthy, Withdrawals; Revenues; and Expenses. Show the effects of each transaction using the accounting equation.
2. Prepare an income statement for August.
3. Prepare a statement of owner's equity for August.
4. Prepare a balance sheet as of August 31.
5. Prepare a statement of cash flows for August.
6. Determine the return on assets ratio for August.

Planning the Solution

- Set up a table like Exhibit 1.9 with the appropriate columns for accounts.
- Analyze each transaction and show its effects as increases or decreases in the appropriate columns. Be sure the accounting equation remains in balance after each transaction.
- Prepare the income statement, and identify revenues and expenses. List those items on the statement, compute the difference, and label the result as *net income* or *net loss*.
- Use information in the Equity columns to prepare the statement of owner's equity.
- Use information in the last row of the transactions table to prepare the balance sheet.
- Prepare the statement of cash flows; include all events listed in the Cash column of the transactions table. Classify each cash flow as operating, investing, or financing.
- Calculate return on assets by dividing net income by average assets.

Solution to Demonstration Problem

1.

	Cash	+	Accounts Receivable	+	Furniture	+	Store Equipment	=	Note Payable	+	J. Worthy, Capital	−	J. Worthy, Withdrawals	+	Revenues	−	Expenses
a.	$3,000						$15,000				$18,000						
b.	− 600			+	$600												
Bal.	2,400	+		+	600	+	15,000	=			18,000						
c.	− 500															−	$500
Bal.	1,900	+		+	600	+	15,000	=			18,000					−	500
d.						+	1,200		+$1,200								
Bal.	1,900	+		+	600	+	16,200	=	1,200	+	18,000					−	500
e.	+ 825													+	$ 825		
Bal.	2,725	+		+	600	+	16,200	=	1,200	+	18,000			+	825	−	500
f.		+	$100											+	100		
Bal.	2,725	+	100	+	600	+	16,200	=	1,200	+	18,000			+	925	−	500
g.	+ 100	−	100														
Bal.	2,825	+	0	+	600	+	16,200	=	1,200	+	18,000			+	925	−	500
h.	− 125															−	125
Bal.	2,700	+	0	+	600	+	16,200	=	1,200	+	18,000			+	925	−	625
i.	+ 930													+	930		
Bal.	3,630	+	0	+	600	+	16,200	=	1,200	+	18,000			+	1,855	−	625
j.	− 400								− 400								
Bal.	3,230	+	0	+	600	+	16,200	=	800	+	18,000			+	1,855	−	625
k.	− 900											−	$900				
Bal.	$ 2,330	+	0	+	$600	+	$ 16,200	=	$ 800	+	$ 18,000	−	$900	+	$1,855	−	$625

2.

EXPRESSIONS
Income Statement
For Month Ended August 31

Revenues		
Haircutting services revenue		$1,855
Expenses		
Rent expense	$500	
Wages expense	125	
Total expenses		625
Net Income		$1,230

3.

EXPRESSIONS
Statement of Owner's Equity
For Month Ended August 31

J. Worthy, Capital, August 1*		$ 0
Plus: Investments by owner	$18,000	
Net income	1,230	19,230
		19,230
Less: Withdrawals by owner		900
J. Worthy, Capital, August 31		$18,330

* If Expressions had been an existing business from a prior period, the beginning capital balance would equal the Capital account balance from the end of the prior period.

4.

EXPRESSIONS
Balance Sheet
August 31

Assets		**Liabilities**	
Cash	$ 2,330	Note payable	$ 800
Furniture	600	**Equity**	
Store equipment	16,200	J. Worthy, Capital	18,330
Total assets	$19,130	Total liabilities and equity	$19,130

5.

EXPRESSIONS
Statement of Cash Flows
For Month Ended August 31

Cash flows from operating activities		
Cash received from customers	$1,855	
Cash paid for rent	(500)	
Cash paid for wages	(125)	
Net cash provided by operating activities		$1,230
Cash flows from investing activities		
Cash paid for furniture		(600)
Cash flows from financing activities		
Cash investments by owner	3,000	
Cash withdrawals by owner	(900)	
Partial repayment of (long-term) note payable	(400)	
Net cash provided by financing activities		1,700
Net increase in cash		$2,330
Cash balance, August 1		0
Cash balance, August 31		$2,330

6. $\text{Return on assets} = \dfrac{\text{Net income}}{\text{Average assets}} = \dfrac{\$1,230}{(\$18,000^* + \$19,130)/2} = \dfrac{\$1,230}{\$18,565} = \textbf{6.63\%}$

* Uses the initial \$18,000 investment as the beginning balance for the startup period only.

APPENDIX

Return and Risk Analysis

This appendix explains return and risk analysis and its role in business and accounting.

    Net income is often linked to **return.** Return on assets (ROA) is stated in ratio form as income divided by assets invested. For example, banks report return from a savings account in the form of an interest return such as 4%. If we invest in a savings account or in U.S. Treasury bills, we expect a return of around 2% to 7%. We could also invest in a company's stock, or even start our own business. How do we decide among these investment options? The answer depends on our trade-off between return and risk.

A4   Explain the relation between return and risk.

Risk is the uncertainty about the return we will earn. All business investments involve risk, but some investments involve more risk than others. The lower the risk of an investment, the lower is our expected return. The reason that savings accounts pay such a low return is the low risk of not being repaid with interest (the government guarantees most savings accounts from default). If we buy a share of eBay or any other company, we might obtain a large return. However, we have no guarantee of any return; there is even the risk of loss.

EXHIBIT 1A.1

Average Returns for Bonds with Different Risks

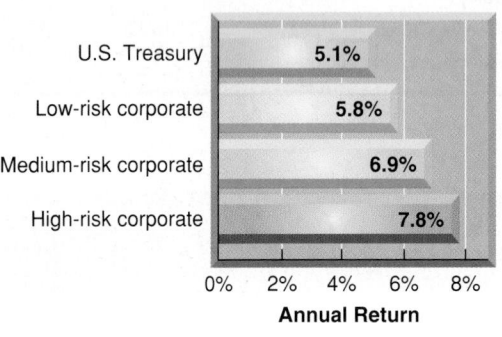

The bar graph in Exhibit 1A.1 shows recent returns for 30-year bonds with different risks. *Bonds* are written promises by organizations to repay amounts loaned with interest. U.S. Treasury bonds provide a low expected return, but they also offer low risk since they are backed by the U.S. government. High-risk corporate bonds offer a much larger potential return but with much higher risk.

The trade-off between return and risk is a normal part of business. Higher risk implies higher, but riskier, expected returns. To help us make better decisions, we use accounting information to assess both return and risk.

1B Business Activities and the Accounting Equation

C6	Identify and describe the three major activities of organizations.

This appendix explains how the accounting equation is derived from business activities.

There are three major types of business activities: financing, investing, and operating. Each of these requires planning. *Planning* involves defining an organization's ideas, goals, and actions. Most public corporations use the *Management Discussion and Analysis* section in their annual reports to communicate plans. However, planning is not cast in stone. This adds *risk* to both setting plans and analyzing them.

Point: Management must understand accounting data to set financial goals, make financing and investing decisions, and evaluate operating performance.

Financing   *Financing activities* provide the means organizations use to pay for resources such as land, buildings, and equipment to carry out plans. Organizations are careful in acquiring and managing financing activities because they can determine success or failure. The two sources of financing are owner and nonowner. *Owner financing* refers to resources contributed by the owner along with any income the owner leaves in the organization. *Nonowner* (or *creditor*) *financing* refers to resources contributed by creditors (lenders). *Financial management* is the task of planning how to obtain these resources and to set the right mix between owner and creditor financing.

Investing   *Investing activities* are the acquiring and disposing of resources (assets) that an organization uses to acquire and sell its products or services. Assets are funded by an organization's financing. Organizations differ on the amount and makeup of assets. Some require land and factories to operate. Others need only an office. Determining the amount and type of assets for operations is called *asset management*.

Point: Investing (assets) and financing (liabilities plus equity) totals are *always* equal.

Invested amounts are referred to as *assets*. Financing is made up of creditor and owner financing, which hold claims on assets. Creditors' claims are called *liabilities*, and the owner's claim is called *equity*. This basic equality is called the *accounting equation* and can be written as: Assets = Liabilities + Equity.

Operating   *Operating activities* involve using resources to research, develop, purchase, produce, distribute, and market products and services. Sales and revenues are the inflow of assets from selling products and services. Costs and expenses are the outflow of assets to support operating activities. *Strategic management* is the process of determining the right mix of operating activities for the type of organization, its plans, and its market.

Exhibit 1B.1 summarizes business activities. Planning is part of each activity and gives them meaning and focus. Investing (assets) and financing (liabilities and equity) are set opposite each other to stress their balance. Operating activities are below investing and financing activities to show that operating activities are the result of investing and financing.

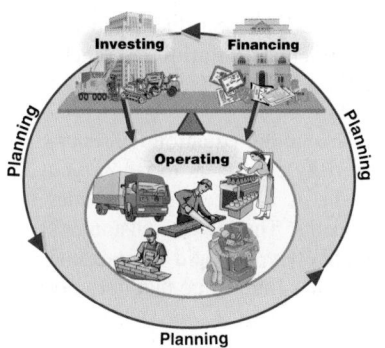

EXHIBIT 1B.1

Activities of Organizations

*— A **Summary** organized by learning objectives concludes each chapter.*

Summary

C1 **Explain the purpose and importance of accounting in the information age.** Accounting is an information and measurement system that aims to identify, record, and communicate relevant, reliable, and comparable information about business activities. It helps assess opportunities, products, investments, and social and community responsibilities.

C2 **Identify users and uses of accounting.** Users of accounting are both internal and external. Some users and uses of accounting include (a) managers in controlling, monitoring, and planning; (b) lenders for measuring the risk and return of loans; (c) shareholders for assessing the return and risk of stock; (d) directors for overseeing management; and (e) employees for judging employment opportunities.

C3 **Identify opportunities in accounting and related fields.** Opportunities in accounting include financial, managerial, and tax accounting. They also include accounting-related fields such as lending, consulting, managing, and planning.

C4 **Explain why ethics are crucial to accounting.** The goal of accounting is to provide useful information for decision making. For information to be useful, it must be trusted. This demands ethical behavior in accounting.

C5 **Explain generally accepted accounting principles and define and apply several accounting principles.** Generally accepted accounting principles are a common set of standards applied by accountants. Accounting principles aid in producing relevant, reliable, and comparable information. Four principles underlying financial statements were introduced: cost, revenue recognition, matching, and full disclosure. Financial statements also reflect four assumptions: going-concern, monetary unit, time period, and business entity.

C6[B] **Identify and describe the three major activities of organizations.** Organizations carry out three major activities:

financing, investing, and operating. Financing is the means used to pay for resources such as land, buildings, and machines. Investing refers to the buying and selling of resources used in acquiring and selling products and services. Operating activities are those necessary for carrying out the organization's plans.

A1 **Define and interpret the accounting equation and each of its components.** The accounting equation is: Assets = Liabilities + Equity. Assets are resources owned by a company. Liabilities are creditors' claims on assets. Equity is the owner's claim on assets (*the residual*). The expanded accounting equation is: Assets = Liabilities + [Owner Capital − Owner Withdrawals + Revenues − Expenses].

A2 **Analyze business transactions using the accounting equation.** A *transaction* is an exchange of economic consideration between two parties. Examples include exchanges of products, services, money, and rights to collect money. Transactions always have at least two effects on one or more components of the accounting equation. This equation is always in balance.

A3 **Compute and interpret return on assets.** Return on assets is computed as net income divided by average assets. For example, if we have an average balance of $100 in a savings account and it earns $5 interest for the year, the return on assets is $5/$100, or 5%.

A4[A] **Explain the relation between return and risk.** *Return* refers to income, and *risk* is the uncertainty about the return we hope to make. All investments involve risk. The lower the risk of an investment, the lower is its expected return. Higher risk implies higher, but riskier, expected return.

P1 **Identify and prepare basic financial statements and explain how they interrelate.** Four financial statements report on an organization's activities: balance sheet, income statement, statement of owner's equity, and statement of cash flows.

Guidance Answers to **Decision Maker** and **Decision Ethics**

Entrepreneur (p. 11) You should probably form the business as a corporation if potential lawsuits are of prime concern. The corporate form of organization protects your personal property from lawsuits directed at the business and places only the corporation's

resources at risk. A downside of the corporate form is double taxation: The corporation must pay taxes on its income, and you normally must pay taxes on any money distributed to you from the business (even though the corporation already paid taxes on this money). You should also examine the ethical and socially responsible aspects of starting a business in which you anticipate injuries to others. Formation as an LLC or S corp. should also be explored.

Retailer (p. 18) You can use the accounting equation (Assets = Liabilities + Equity) to help identify risky customers to whom you would likely not want to extend credit. A balance sheet provides amounts for each of these key components. The lower a customer's equity is relative to liabilities, the less likely you would be to extend credit. A low equity means the business has little value that does not already have creditor claims to it.

Business Owner (p. 21) The 19% return on assets for the manufacturer exceeds the 14% industry return (and many others). This is a positive factor for a potential purchase. Also, the purchase of this manufacturer is an opportunity to spread your risk over two businesses as opposed to one. Still, you should hesitate to purchase a business whose return of 19% is lower than your current resort's return of 21%. You are probably better off directing efforts to increase investment in your resort, assuming you can continue to earn a 21% return.

Guidance Answers to **Quick Checks**

1. Accounting is an information and measurement system that identifies, records, and communicates relevant information to help people make better decisions.

2. Recordkeeping, also called *bookkeeping,* is the recording of financial transactions and events, either manually or electronically. Recordkeeping is essential to data reliability; but accounting is this and much more. Accounting includes identifying, measuring, recording, reporting, and analyzing business events and transactions.

3. Technology offers increased accuracy, speed, efficiency, and convenience in accounting.

4. External users of accounting include lenders, shareholders, directors, customers, suppliers, regulators, lawyers, brokers, and the press. Internal users of accounting include managers, officers, and other internal decision makers involved with strategic and operating decisions.

5. Internal users (managers) include those from research and development, purchasing, human resources, production, distribution, marketing, and servicing.

6. Internal controls are procedures set up to protect assets, ensure reliable accounting reports, promote efficiency, and encourage adherence to company policies. Internal controls are crucial for relevant and reliable information.

7. Ethical guidelines are threefold: (1) identify ethical concerns using personal ethics, (2) analyze options considering all good and bad consequences, and (3) make ethical decisions after weighing all consequences.

8. Ethics and social responsibility yield good behavior, and they often result in higher income and a better working environment.

9. For accounting to provide useful information for decisions, it must be trusted. Trust requires ethics in accounting.

10. Two major participants in setting rules include the SEC and the FASB. (*Note:* Accounting rules reflect society's needs, not those of accountants or any other single constituency.)

11. Most U.S. companies are not directly affected by international accounting standards. International standards are put forth as preferred accounting practices. However, stock exchanges and other parties are increasing the pressure to narrow differences in worldwide accounting practices. International accounting standards are playing an important role in that process.

12. The objectivity concept and cost principle are related in that most users consider information based on cost as objective. Information prepared using both is considered highly reliable and often relevant.

13. Users desire information about the performance of a specific entity. If information is mixed between two or more entities, its usefulness decreases.

14. The revenue recognition principle gives preparers guidelines on when to recognize (record) revenue. This is important; for example, if revenue is recognized too early, the statements report revenue sooner than it should and the business looks more profitable than it is. The reverse is also true.

15. The three basic forms of business organization are sole proprietorships, partnerships, and corporations.

16. Owners of corporations are called *shareholders* (or *stockholders*). Corporate ownership is divided into units called *shares* (or *stock*). The most basic of corporate shares is common stock (or capital stock).

17. The accounting equation is: Assets = Liabilities + Equity. This equation is always in balance, both before and after each transaction.

18. A transaction that changes the makeup of assets would not affect liability and equity accounts. FastForward's transactions 2 and 3 are examples. Each exchanges one asset for another.

19. Earning revenue by performing services, as in FastForward's transaction 5, increases equity (and assets). Incurring expenses while servicing clients, such as in transactions 6 and 7, decreases equity (and assets). Other examples include owner investments that increase equity and withdrawals that decrease equity.

20. Paying a liability with an asset reduces both asset and liability totals. One example is FastForward's transaction 10 that reduces a payable by paying cash.

21. An income statement reports a company's revenues and expenses along with the resulting net income or loss. A statement of owner's equity shows changes in equity, including that from net income or loss. Both statements report transactions occurring over a period of time.

22. The balance sheet describes a company's financial position (assets, liabilities, and equity) at a point in time. The equity amount in the balance sheet is obtained from the statement of owner's equity.

23. Cash flows from operating activities report cash receipts and payments from the primary business the company engages in. Cash flows from investing activities involve cash transactions from buying and selling long-term assets. Cash flows from financing activities include long-term cash borrowings and repayments to lenders and the cash investments from and withdrawals by the owner.

A list of key terms with page references concludes each chapter (a complete glossary is at the end of the book and also on the book's Website).

Key Terms   mhhe.com/wildFAP19e

Key Terms are available at the book's Website for learning and testing in an online Flashcard Format.

Accounting (p. 4)
Accounting equation (p. 13)
Assets (p. 12)
Auditors (p. 11)
Balance sheet (p. 18)
Bookkeeping (p. 4)
Business entity assumption (p. 10)
Common stock (p. 11)
Corporation (p. 11)
Cost principle (p. 9)
Equity (p. 12)
Ethics (p. 8)
Events (p. 14)
Expanded accounting equation (p. 13)
Expenses (p. 13)
External transactions (p. 13)
External users (p. 5)
Financial accounting (p. 5)
Financial Accounting Standards Board (FASB) (p. 9)

Full disclosure principle (p. 10)
Generally Accepted Accounting Principles (GAAP) (p. 8)
Going-concern assumption (p. 10)
Income statement (p. 17)
Internal transactions (p. 13)
Internal users (p. 6)
International Accounting Standards Board (IASB) (p. 9)
Liabilities (p. 12)
Managerial accounting (p. 6)
Matching principle (p. 10)
Monetary unit assumption (p. 10)
Net income (p. 13)
Net loss (p. 13)
Owner, Capital (p. 13)
Owner investment (p. 13)
Owner withdrawals (p. 13)
Partnership (p. 10)
Proprietorship (p. 10)

Recordkeeping (p. 4)
Return (p. 23)
Return on assets (p. 20)
Revenue recognition principle (p. 10)
Revenues (p. 13)
Risk (p. 24)
Sarbanes–Oxley Act (p. 11)
Securities and Exchange Commission (SEC) (p. 9)
Shareholders (p. 11)
Shares (p. 11)
Sole proprietorship (p. 10)
Statement of cash flows (p. 18)
Statement of owner's equity (p. 17)
Stock (p. 11)
Stockholders (p. 11)
Time period assumption (p. 10)
Withdrawals (p. 13)

Multiple Choice Quiz   Answers on p. 45   mhhe.com/wildFAP19e

Additional Quiz Questions are available at the book's Website.

Quiz1

1. A building is offered for sale at $500,000 but is currently assessed at $400,000. The purchaser of the building believes the building is worth $475,000, but ultimately purchases the building for $450,000. The purchaser records the building at:
   a. $50,000
   b. $400,000
   c. $450,000
   d. $475,000
   e. $500,000

2. On December 30, 2008, KPMG signs a $150,000 contract to provide accounting services to one of its clients in 2009. KPMG has a December 31 year-end. Which accounting principle or assumption requires KPMG to record the accounting services revenue from this client in 2009 and not 2008?
   a. Business entity assumption
   b. Revenue recognition principle
   c. Monetary unit assumption
   d. Cost principle
   e. Going-concern assumption

3. If the assets of a company increase by $100,000 during the year and its liabilities increase by $35,000 during the same year, then the change in equity of the company during the year must have been:
   a. An increase of $135,000.
   b. A decrease of $135,000.
   c. A decrease of $65,000.

   d. An increase of $65,000.
   e. An increase of $100,000.

4. Brunswick borrows $50,000 cash from Third National Bank. How does this transaction affect the accounting equation for Brunswick?
   a. Assets increase by $50,000; liabilities increase by $50,000; no effect on equity.
   b. Assets increase by $50,000; no effect on liabilities; equity increases by $50,000.
   c. Assets increase by $50,000; liabilities decrease by $50,000; no effect on equity.
   d. No effect on assets; liabilities increase by $50,000; equity increases by $50,000.
   e. No effect on assets; liabilities increase by $50,000; equity decreases by $50,000.

5. Geek Squad performs services for a customer and bills the customer for $500. How would Geek Squad record this transaction?
   a. Accounts receivable increase by $500; revenues increase by $500.
   b. Cash increases by $500; revenues increase by $500.
   c. Accounts receivable increase by $500; revenues decrease by $500.
   d. Accounts receivable increase by $500; accounts payable increase by $500.
   e. Accounts payable increase by $500; revenues increase by $500.

Superscript letter ^{A} (^{B}) denotes assignments based on Appendix 1A (1B).

Discussion Questions

1. What is the purpose of accounting in society?

2. Technology is increasingly used to process accounting data. Why then must we study and understand accounting?

3. ♟ Identify four kinds of external users and describe how they use accounting information.

4. ♟ What are at least three questions business owners and managers might be able to answer by looking at accounting information?

5. Identify three actual businesses that offer services and three actual businesses that offer products.

6. ♟ Describe the internal role of accounting for organizations.

7. Identify three types of services typically offered by accounting professionals.

8. ♟ What type of accounting information might be useful to the marketing managers of a business?

9. Why is accounting described as a service activity?

10. What are some accounting-related professions?

11. How do ethics rules affect auditors' choice of clients?

12. What work do tax accounting professionals perform in addition to preparing tax returns?

13. What does the concept of *objectivity* imply for information reported in financial statements? Why?

14. A business reports its own office stationery on the balance sheet at its $400 cost, although it cannot be sold for more than $10 as scrap paper. Which accounting principle and/or assumption justifies this treatment?

15. Why is the revenue recognition principle needed? What does it demand?

16. Describe the three basic forms of business organization and their key characteristics.

17. Define (*a*) *assets,* (*b*) *liabilities,* (*c*) *equity,* and (*d*) *net assets.*

18. What events or transactions change equity?

19. Identify the two main categories of accounting principles.

20. What do accountants mean by the term *revenue?*

21. Define *net income* and explain its computation.

22. Identify the four basic financial statements of a business.

23. ♟ What information is reported in an income statement?

24. Give two examples of expenses a business might incur.

25. What is the purpose of the statement of owner's equity?

26. ♟ What information is reported in a balance sheet?

27. The statement of cash flows reports on what major activities?

28. ♟ Define and explain return on assets.

29.^{A}♟ Define return and risk. Discuss the trade-off between them.

30.^{B}Describe the three major business activities in organizations.

31.^{B}Explain why investing (assets) and financing (liabilities and equity) totals are always equal.

32. Refer to the financial statements of **Best Buy** in Appendix A near the end of the book. To what level of significance are dollar amounts rounded? What time period does its income statement cover?

33. Refer to **Circuit City**'s balance sheet in Appendix A near the end of the book. Confirm that its total assets equal its total liabilities plus total equity.

34. Identify the dollar amounts of **Radio-Shack**'s 2006 assets, liabilities, and equity as reported in its statements in Appendix A near the end of the book.

35. ♟ Access the SEC EDGAR database (www.sec.gov) and retrieve **Apple**'s 2006 10-K (filed 12-29-2006). Identify its auditor. What responsibility does its independent auditor claim regarding Apple's financial statements?

♟ **Denotes Discussion Questions that involve decision making.**

Quick Study exercises give readers a brief test of key elements.

Homework Manager repeats assignments on the book's Website, which allows instructors to monitor, promote, and assess student learning. It can be used in practice, homework, or exam mode.

Available with McGraw-Hill's Homework Manager   McGraw-Hill's HOMEWORK MANAGER®

QUICK STUDY

QS 1-1
Identifying accounting users
C2

Identify the following users as either external users (E) or internal users (I).

a. Shareholders	**d.** FBI and IRS	**g.** Customers	**j.** Business press
b. Lenders	**e.** Consumer group	**h.** Suppliers	**k.** Managers
c. Controllers	**f.** Sales staff	**i.** Brokers	**l.** District attorney

---

QS 1-2
Identifying accounting terms
C1

Reading and interpreting accounting reports requires some knowledge of accounting terminology. (*a*) Identify the meaning of these accounting-related acronyms: GAAP, SEC, FASB and IASB. (*b*) Briefly explain the importance of the knowledge base or organization that is referred to for each of the accounting-related acronyms.

QS 1-3
Accounting opportunities
C3

There are many job opportunities for those with accounting knowledge. Identify at least three main areas of opportunities for accounting professionals. For each area, identify at least three job possibilities linked to accounting.

An important responsibility of many accounting professionals is to design and implement internal control procedures for organizations. Explain the purpose of internal control procedures. Provide two examples of internal controls applied by companies.

QS 1-4
Explaining internal control
C1

Identify which accounting principle or assumption best describes each of the following practices:

a. In December 2009, Ace Landscaping received a customer's order and cash prepayment to install sod at a new house that would not be ready for installation until March 2010. Ace should record the revenue from the customer order in March 2010, not in December 2009.

b. If $51,000 cash is paid to buy land, the land is reported on the buyer's balance sheet at $51,000.

c. Jay Keren owns both Sailing Passions and Dockside Supplies. In preparing financial statements for Dockside Supplies, Keren makes sure that the expense transactions of Sailing Passions are kept separate from Dockside's statements.

QS 1-5
Identifying accounting principles
This icon highlights assignments that enhance decision-making skills.
C5

Accounting professionals must sometimes choose between two or more acceptable methods of accounting for business transactions and events. Explain why these situations can involve difficult matters of ethical concern.

QS 1-6
Identifying ethical concerns
C4

Use the accounting equation to compute the missing financial statement amounts (*a*), (*b*), and (*c*).

Company	Assets	=	Liabilities	+	Equity
1	$375,000		$ (a)		$250,000
2	$ (b)		$90,000		$160,000
3	$185,000		$60,000		$ (c)

QS 1-7
Applying the accounting equation
A1

---

a. Total assets of Charter Company equal $500,000 and its equity is $320,000. What is the amount of its liabilities?

b. Total assets of Golfland equal $900,000 and its liabilities and equity amounts are equal to each other. What is the amount of its liabilities? What is the amount of its equity?

QS 1-8
Applying the accounting equation
A1

Use **Apple**'s September 30, 2006, financial statements, in Appendix A near the end of the book, to answer the following:

a. Identify the dollar amounts of Apple's 2006 (1) assets, (2) liabilities, and (3) equity.

b. Using Apple's amounts from part *a*, verify that Assets = Liabilities + Equity.

QS 1-9
Identifying and computing assets, liabilities, and equity
A2

Accounting provides information about an organization's business transactions and events that both affect the accounting equation and can be reliably measured. Identify at least two examples of both (*a*) business transactions and (*b*) business events that meet these requirements.

QS 1-10
Identifying transactions and events
A2

Indicate in which financial statement each item would most likely appear: income statement (I), balance sheet (B), statement of owner's equity (OE), or statement of cash flows (CF).

a. Equipment   **d.** Net decrease (or increase) in cash   **g.** Assets

b. Expenses   **e.** Revenues   **h.** Cash from operating activities

c. Liabilities   **f.** Total liabilities and equity   **i.** Withdrawals

QS 1-11
Identifying items with financial statements
P1

In a recent year's financial statements, **Home Depot** reported the following results. Compute and interpret Home Depot's return on assets (assume competitors average a 12% return on assets).

Sales	$90,837 million
Net income	5,761 million
Average total assets	48,334 million

QS 1-12
Computing and interpreting return on assets
A3

EXERCISES

Exercise 1-1
Identifying accounting users and uses

C2

Much of accounting is directed at servicing the information needs of those users that are external to an organization. (*a*) Identify at least three external users of accounting information and indicate two questions they might seek to answer through their use of accounting information. (*b*) Identify at least three internal users of accounting information and describe how each might use accounting information in their jobs.

Exercise 1-2
Describing accounting responsibilities

C2 C3

Many accounting professionals work in one of the following three areas:

A. Financial accounting   **B.** Managerial accounting   **C.** Tax accounting

Identify the area of accounting that is most involved in each of the following responsibilities:

_____ **1.** Investigating violations of tax laws.   _____ **5.** Internal auditing.
_____ **2.** Planning transactions to minimize taxes.   _____ **6.** External auditing.
_____ **3.** Preparing external financial statements.   _____ **7.** Cost accounting.
_____ **4.** Reviewing reports for SEC compliance.   _____ **8.** Budgeting.

Exercise 1-3
Identifying ethical concerns

C4

Assume the following role and describe a situation in which ethical considerations play an important part in guiding your decisions and actions:

a. You are an accounting professional with audit clients that are competitors in business.
b. You are an accounting professional preparing tax returns for clients.
c. You are a manager with responsibility for several employees.
d. You are a student in an introductory accounting course.

Exercise 1-4
Identifying accounting principles and assumptions

C5

Match each of the numbered descriptions with the principle or assumption it best reflects. Enter the letter for the appropriate principle or assumption in the blank space next to each description.

A. General accounting principle   **E.** Specific accounting principle
B. Cost principle   **F.** Full disclosure principle
C. Business entity assumption   **G.** Going-concern assumption
D. Revenue recognition principle   **H.** Matching principle

_____ **1.** Usually created by a pronouncement from an authoritative body.
_____ **2.** Financial statements reflect the assumption that the business continues operating.
_____ **3.** Derived from long-used and generally accepted accounting practices.
_____ **4.** Every business is accounted for separately from its owner or owners.
_____ **5.** Revenue is recorded only when the earnings process is complete.
_____ **6.** Information is based on actual costs incurred in transactions.
_____ **7.** A company reports details behind financial statements that would impact users' decisions.
_____ **8.** A company records the expenses incurred to generate the revenues reported.

Exercise 1-5
Distinguishing business organizations

C5

The following describe several different business organizations. Determine whether the description refers to a sole proprietorship, partnership, or corporation.

a. Wallingford is owned by Gary Malone, who is personally liable for the company's debts.
b. Ava Fong and Elijah Logan own Financial Services, a financial services provider. Neither Fong nor Logan has personal responsibility for the debts of Financial Services.
c. IBC Services does not have separate legal existence apart from the one person who owns it.
d. Computing Services pays its own income taxes and has two owners.
e. Ownership of Zander Company is divided into 1,000 shares of stock.
f. Emma Bailey and Dylan Kay own Speedy Packages, a courier service. Both are personally liable for the debts of the business.
g. Physio Products does not pay income taxes and has one owner.

Determine the missing amount from each of the separate situations *a*, *b*, and *c* below.

Assets	=	Liabilities	+	Equity
a. ?	=	$164,000	+	$16,000
b. $ 90,000	=	$ 39,000	+	?
c. $201,000	=	?	+	$62,000

Match each of the numbered descriptions with the term or phrase it best reflects. Indicate your answer by writing the letter for the term or phrase in the blank provided.

A. Audit   **C.** Ethics   **E.** SEC   **G.** Net income

B. GAAP   **D.** Tax accounting   **F.** Public accountants   **H.** IASB

_____ **1.** An accounting area that includes planning future transactions to minimize taxes paid.

_____ **2.** Amount a business earns after paying all expenses and costs associated with its sales and revenues.

_____ **3.** Principles that determine whether an action is right or wrong.

_____ **4.** Accounting professionals who provide services to many clients.

_____ **5.** An examination of an organization's accounting system and records that adds credibility to financial statements.

Answer the following questions. (*Hint:* Use the accounting equation.)

a. Office Supplies has assets equal to $137,000 and liabilities equal to $110,000 at year-end. What is the total equity for Office Supplies at year-end?

b. At the beginning of the year, Addison Company's assets are $259,000 and its equity is $194,250. During the year, assets increase $80,000 and liabilities increase $52,643. What is the equity at the end of the year?

c. At the beginning of the year, Quasar Company's liabilities equal $57,000. During the year, assets increase by $60,000, and at year-end assets equal $190,000. Liabilities decrease $16,000 during the year. What are the beginning and ending amounts of equity?

Check   (c) Beg. equity, $73,000

Provide an example of a transaction that creates the described effects for the separate cases *a* through *g*.

a. Increases an asset and increases a liability.

b. Decreases a liability and increases a liability.

c. Decreases an asset and decreases a liability.

d. Increases an asset and decreases an asset.

e. Increases a liability and decreases equity.

f. Increases an asset and increases equity.

g. Decreases an asset and decreases equity.

Zen began a new consulting firm on January 5. The accounting equation showed the following balances after each of the company's first five transactions. Analyze the accounting equation for each transaction and describe each of the five transactions with their amounts.

	Assets				=	Liabilities	+		Equity	
Trans-action	Cash	+	Accounts Receiv-able	+	Office Sup-plies	+	Office Furni-ture	=	Accounts Payable	+	Zen, Capital	+	Revenues
a.	$20,000	+	$ 0	+	$ 0	+	$ 0	=	$ 0	+	$20,000	+	$ 0
b.	18,000	+	0	+	3,000	+	0	=	1,000	+	20,000	+	0
c.	10,000	+	0	+	3,000	+	8,000	=	1,000	+	20,000	+	0
d.	10,000	+	6,000	+	3,000	+	8,000	=	1,000	+	20,000	+	6,000
e.	11,000	+	6,000	+	3,000	+	8,000	=	1,000	+	20,000	+	7,000

Exercise 1-11

Identifying effects of transactions on accounting equation

A1 A2 ♟

The following table shows the effects of five transactions (*a* through *e*) on the assets, liabilities, and equity of Trista's Boutique. Write short descriptions of the probable nature of each transaction.

	Assets					=	Liabilities	+	Equity		
	Cash	+	Accounts Receivable	+	Office Supplies	+	Land	=	Accounts Payable	+	Trista, Capital	+	Revenues

	Cash	+	Accounts Receivable	+	Office Supplies	+	Land	=	Accounts Payable	+	Trista, Capital	+	Revenues
	$ 21,000	+	$ 0	+	$3,000	+	$ 19,000	=	$ 0	+	$43,000	+	$ 0
a.	− 4,000					+	4,000						
b.					+ 1,000				+1,000				
c.		+	1,900									+	1,900
d.	− 1,000								−1,000				
e.	+ 1,900	−	1,900										
	$ 17,900	+	$ 0	+	$4,000	+	$ 23,000	=	$ 0	+	$43,000	+	$1,900

Exercise 1-12

Identifying effects of transactions using the accounting equation

A1 A2 ♟

Leora Diamond began a professional practice on June 1 and plans to prepare financial statements at the end of each month. During June, Diamond (the owner) completed these transactions:

a. Owner invested $70,000 cash in the company along with equipment that had a $20,000 market value.

b. The company paid $2,000 cash for rent of office space for the month.

c. The company purchased $25,000 of additional equipment on credit (payment due within 30 days).

d. The company completed work for a client and immediately collected the $3,000 cash earned.

e. The company completed work for a client and sent a bill for $9,500 to be received within 30 days.

f. The company purchased additional equipment for $5,000 cash.

g. The company paid an assistant $3,500 cash as wages for the month.

h. The company collected $6,500 cash as a partial payment for the amount owed by the client in transaction *e*.

i. The company paid $25,000 cash to settle the liability created in transaction *c*.

j. Owner withdrew $1,500 cash from the company for personal use.

Required

Check Net income, $7,000

Create a table like the one in Exhibit 1.9, using the following headings for columns: Cash; Accounts Receivable; Equipment; Accounts Payable; L. Diamond, Capital; L. Diamond, Withdrawals; Revenues; and Expenses. Then use additions and subtractions to show the effects of the transactions on individual items of the accounting equation. Show new balances after each transaction.

Exercise 1-13

Preparing an income statement

P1

On October 1, Keisha King organized Real Answers, a new consulting firm. On October 31, the company's records show the following items and amounts. Use this information to prepare an October income statement for the business.

Cash	$11,500	Cash withdrawals by owner	$ 2,000
Accounts receivable	12,000	Consulting fees earned	14,000
Office supplies	24,437	Rent expense	2,520
Land	46,000	Salaries expense	5,600
Office equipment	18,000	Telephone expense	760
Accounts payable	25,037	Miscellaneous expenses	580
Owner investments	84,360		

Check Net income, $4,540

Exercise 1-14

Preparing a statement of owner's equity P1

Use the information in Exercise 1-13 to prepare an October statement of owner's equity for Real Answers.

Exercise 1-15

Preparing a balance sheet P1

Use the information in Exercise 1-13 (if completed, you can also use your solution to Exercise 1-14) to prepare an October 31 balance sheet for Real Answers.

Use the information in Exercise 1-13 to prepare an October 31 statement of cash flows for Real Answers. Also assume the following:

a. The owner's initial investment consists of $38,360 cash and $46,000 in land.

b. The company's $18,000 equipment purchase is paid in cash.

c. The accounts payable balance of $25,037 consists of the $24,437 office supplies purchase and $600 in employee salaries yet to be paid.

d. The company's rent, telephone, and miscellaneous expenses are paid in cash.

e. $2,000 has been collected on the $14,000 consulting fees earned.

Exercise 1-16
Preparing a statement of cash flows

P1

Check   Net increase in cash, $11,500

Indicate the section where each of the following would appear on the statement of cash flows.

O. Cash flows from operating activity

I. Cash flows from investing activity

F. Cash flows from financing activity

_____ **1.** Cash paid for rent   _____ **5.** Cash paid for advertising

_____ **2.** Cash paid on an account payable   _____ **6.** Cash paid for wages

_____ **3.** Cash investment by owner   _____ **7.** Cash withdrawal by owner

_____ **4.** Cash received from clients   _____ **8.** Cash purchase of equipment

Exercise 1-17
Identifying sections of the statement of cash flows

P1

Iowa Group reports net income of $36,000 for 2009. At the beginning of 2009, Iowa Group had $135,000 in assets. By the end of 2009, assets had grown to $185,000. What is Iowa Group's 2009 return on assets? How would you assess its performance if competitors average a 10% return on assets?

Exercise 1-18
Analysis of return on assets

A3

Match each transaction or event to one of the following activities of an organization: financing activities (F), investing activities (I), or operating activities (O).

a. _____ An organization purchases equipment.

b. _____ An organization advertises a new product.

c. _____ The organization borrows money from a bank.

d. _____ An owner contributes resources to the business.

e. _____ An organization sells some of its land.

Exercise 1-19^B
Identifying business activities

C6

Problem Set B located at the end of Problem Set A is provided for each problem to reinforce the learning process.

McGraw-Hill's
HOMEWORK MANAGER®   Available with McGraw-Hill's Homework Manager

The following financial statement information is from five separate companies:

PROBLEM SET A

Problem 1-1A
Computing missing information using accounting knowledge

A1   A2

	Company A	Company B	Company C	Company D	Company E
December 31, 2008					
Assets	$33,000	$25,740	$21,120	$58,740	$90,090
Liabilities	27,060	18,018	11,404	40,530	?
December 31, 2009					
Assets	36,000	25,920	?	65,520	99,360
Liabilities	?	17,625	11,818	31,449	78,494
During year 2009					
Owner investments	6,000	1,400	9,750	?	6,500
Net income (loss)	7,760	?	(1,289)	8,861	7,348
Owner cash withdrawals	3,500	2,000	5,875	0	11,000

Required

1. Answer the following questions about Company A:

    a. What is the amount of equity on December 31, 2008?

    b. What is the amount of equity on December 31, 2009?

    c. What is the amount of liabilities on December 31, 2009?

2. Answer the following questions about Company B:

    a. What is the amount of equity on December 31, 2008?

    b. What is the amount of equity on December 31, 2009?

    c. What is net income for year 2009?

3. Calculate the amount of assets for Company C on December 31, 2009.

4. Calculate the amount of owner investments for Company D during year 2009.

5. Calculate the amount of liabilities for Company E on December 31, 2008.

Problem 1-2A

Identifying effects of transactions on financial statements

A1 A2

Identify how each of the following separate transactions affects financial statements. For the balance sheet, identify how each transaction affects total assets, total liabilities, and total equity. For the income statement, identify how each transaction affects net income. For the statement of cash flows, identify how each transaction affects cash flows from operating activities, cash flows from financing activities, and cash flows from investing activities. For increases, place a "+" in the column or columns. For decreases, place a "−" in the column or columns. If both an increase and a decrease occur, place a "+/−" in the column or columns. The first transaction is completed as an example.

		Balance Sheet			Income Statement	Statement of Cash Flows		
	Transaction	**Total Assets**	**Total Liab.**	**Total Equity**	**Net Income**	**Operating Activities**	**Financing Activities**	**Investing Activities**
1	Owner invests cash in business	+		+			+	
2	Receives cash for services provided							
3	Pays cash for employee wages							
4	Incurs legal costs on credit							
5	Borrows cash by signing long-term note payable							
6	Buys land by signing note payable							
7	Provides services on credit							
8	Buys office equipment for cash							
9	Collects cash on receivable from (7)							
10	Owner withdraws cash							

Problem 1-3A

Preparing an income statement

P1

The following is selected financial information for Elko Energy Company for the year ended December 31, 2009: revenues, $66,000; expenses, $51,348; net income, $14,652.

Required

Prepare the 2009 calendar-year income statement for Elko Energy Company.

Problem 1-4A

Preparing a balance sheet

P1

The following is selected financial information for Amity Company as of December 31, 2009: liabilities, $54,244; equity, $87,756; assets, $142,000.

Required

Prepare the balance sheet for Amity Company as of December 31, 2009.

Following is selected financial information of Fortune Co. for the year ended December 31, 2009.

Cash used by investing activities	$(3,250)
Net increase in cash	750
Cash used by financing activities	(4,050)
Cash from operating activities	8,050
Cash, December 31, 2008	4,100

Problem 1-5A
Preparing a statement of cash flows

P1

Check   Cash balance, Dec. 31, 2009, $4,850

Required

Prepare the 2009 statement of cash flows for Fortune Company.

Following is selected financial information for Atlee Co. for the year ended December 31, 2009.

A. Atlee, Capital, Dec. 31, 2009	$16,750	A. Atlee, Withdrawals	$ 2,000
Net income	7,750	A. Atlee, Capital, Dec. 31, 2008	11,000

Problem 1-6A
Preparing a statement of owner's equity

P1

Required

Prepare the 2009 statement of owner's equity for Atlee Company.

Holden Graham started The Graham Co., a new business that began operations on May 1. The Graham Co. completed the following transactions during its first month of operations.

May 1   H. Graham invested $43,000 cash in the company.
     1   The company rented a furnished office and paid $2,200 cash for May's rent.
     3   The company purchased $1,940 of office equipment on credit.
     5   The company paid $750 cash for this month's cleaning services.
     8   The company provided consulting services for a client and immediately collected $5,800 cash.
    12   The company provided $2,800 of consulting services for a client on credit.
    15   The company paid $850 cash for an assistant's salary for the first half of this month.
    20   The company received $2,800 cash payment for the services provided on May 12.
    22   The company provided $4,000 of consulting services on credit.
    25   The company received $4,000 cash payment for the services provided on May 22.
    26   The company paid $1,940 cash for the office equipment purchased on May 3.
    27   The company purchased $85 of advertising in this month's (May) local paper on credit; cash payment is due June 1.
    28   The company paid $850 cash for an assistant's salary for the second half of this month.
    30   The company paid $400 cash for this month's telephone bill.
    30   The company paid $260 cash for this month's utilities.
    31   H. Graham withdrew $2,000 cash from the company for personal use.

Problem 1-7A
Analyzing transactions and preparing financial statements

C5 A2 P1

mhhe.com/wildFAP19e

Required

1. Arrange the following asset, liability, and equity titles in a table like Exhibit 1.9: Cash; Accounts Receivable; Office Equipment; Accounts Payable; H. Graham, Capital; H. Graham, Withdrawals; Revenues; and Expenses.

2. Show effects of the transactions on the accounts of the accounting equation by recording increases and decreases in the appropriate columns. Do not determine new account balances after each transaction. Determine the final total for each account and verify that the equation is in balance.

3. Prepare an income statement for May, a statement of owner's equity for May, a May 31 balance sheet, and a statement of cash flows for May.

Check   (2) Ending balances: Cash, $46,350; Expenses, $5,395

(3) Net income, $7,205; Total assets, $48,290

Problem 1-8A

Analyzing transactions and
preparing financial statements

C5   A2   P1

mhhe.com/wildFAP19e

Helga Anderson started a new business and completed these transactions during December.

Dec. 1	Helga Anderson transferred $68,800 cash from a personal savings account to a checking account in the name of Anderson Electric.
2	The company rented office space and paid $1,800 cash for the December rent.
3	The company purchased $13,000 of electrical equipment by paying $4,800 cash and agreeing to pay the $8,200 balance in 30 days.
5	The company purchased office supplies by paying $1,000 cash.
6	The company completed electrical work and immediately collected $1,600 cash for these services.
8	The company purchased $2,680 of office equipment on credit.
15	The company completed electrical work on credit in the amount of $6,000.
18	The company purchased $360 of office supplies on credit.
20	The company paid $2,680 cash for the office equipment purchased on December 8.
24	The company billed a client $1,000 for electrical work completed; the balance is due in 30 days.
28	The company received $6,000 cash for the work completed on December 15.
29	The company paid the assistant's salary of $1,500 cash for this month.
30	The company paid $570 cash for this month's utility bill.
31	H. Anderson withdrew $900 cash from the company for personal use.

Required

1. Arrange the following asset, liability, and equity titles in a table like Exhibit 1.9: Cash; Accounts Receivable; Office Supplies; Office Equipment; Electrical Equipment; Accounts Payable; H. Anderson, Capital; H. Anderson, Withdrawals; Revenues; and Expenses.

2. Use additions and subtractions to show the effects of each transaction on the accounts in the accounting equation. Show new balances after each transaction.

3. Use the increases and decreases in the columns of the table from part 2 to prepare an income statement, a statement of owner's equity, and a statement of cash flows—each of these for the current month. Also prepare a balance sheet as of the end of the month.

Analysis Component

4. Assume that the owner investment transaction on December 1 was $49,000 cash instead of $68,800 and that Anderson Electric obtained another $19,800 in cash by borrowing it from a bank. Explain the effect of this change on total assets, total liabilities, and total equity.

Check   (2) Ending balances: Cash,
$63,150, Accounts Payable, $8,560

(3) Net income, $4,730;
Total assets, $81,190

Problem 1-9A

Analyzing effects of transactions

C5   P1   A1   A2

Inez Lopez started Wiz Consulting, a new business, and completed the following transactions during its first year of operations.

a. I. Lopez invests $67,000 cash and office equipment valued at $11,000 in the company.

b. The company purchased a $144,000 building to use as an office. Wiz paid $15,000 in cash and signed a note payable promising to pay the $129,000 balance over the next ten years.

c. The company purchased office equipment for $12,000 cash.

d. The company purchased $1,000 of office supplies and $1,700 of office equipment on credit.

e. The company paid a local newspaper $460 cash for printing an announcement of the office's opening.

f. The company completed a financial plan for a client and billed that client $2,400 for the service.

g. The company designed a financial plan for another client and immediately collected a $4,000 cash fee.

h. I. Lopez withdrew $3,025 cash from the company for personal use.

i. The company received $1,800 cash as partial payment from the client described in transaction *f*.

j. The company made a partial payment of $500 cash on the equipment purchased in transaction *d*.

k. The company paid $1,800 cash for the office secretary's wages for this period.

Required

1. Create a table like the one in Exhibit 1.9, using the following headings for the columns: Cash; Accounts Receivable; Office Supplies; Office Equipment; Building; Accounts Payable; Notes Payable; I. Lopez, Capital; I. Lopez, Withdrawals; Revenues; and Expenses.

2. Use additions and subtractions within the table created in part *1* to show the dollar effects of each transaction on individual items of the accounting equation. Show new balances after each transaction.

3. Once you have completed the table, determine the company's net income.

Check   (2) Ending balances: Cash,
$40,015; Expenses, $2,260; Notes
Payable, $129,000

(3) Net income, $4,140

Coca-Cola and PepsiCo both produce and market beverages that are direct competitors. Key financial figures (in $ millions) for these businesses over the past year follow.

Key Figures ($ millions)	Coca-Cola	PepsiCo
Sales	$24,088	$35,187
Net income	5,080	5,642
Average assets	29,695	30,829

Problem 1-10A
Computing and interpreting return on assets

A3

Required

1. Compute return on assets for (a) Coca-Cola and (b) PepsiCo.

2. Which company is more successful in its total amount of sales to consumers?

3. Which company is more successful in returning net income from its assets invested?

Check (1a) 17.1%; (1b) 18.3%

Analysis Component

4. Write a one-paragraph memorandum explaining which company you would invest your money in and why. (Limit your explanation to the information provided.)

Notaro manufactures, markets, and sells cellular telephones. The average total assets for Notaro is $250,000. In its most recent year, Notaro reported net income of $64,000 on revenues of $468,000.

Problem 1-11A
Determining expenses, liabilities, equity, and return on assets

A1 A3

Required

1. What is Notaro's return on assets?

2. Does return on assets seem satisfactory for Notaro given that its competitors average a 9.5% return on assets?

3. What are total expenses for Notaro in its most recent year?

4. What is the average total amount of liabilities plus equity for Notaro?

Check (3) $404,000
(4) $250,000

All business decisions involve aspects of risk and return.

Problem 1-12A^A
Identifying risk and return

A4

Required

Identify both the risk and the return in each of the following activities:

1. Investing $10,000 in Yahoo! stock.

2. Placing a $2,500 bet on your favorite sports team.

3. Investing $2,000 in a 5% savings account.

4. Taking out a $7,500 college loan to earn an accounting degree.

A start-up company often engages in the following transactions in its first year of operations. Classify those transactions in one of the three major categories of an organization's business activities.

F. Financing   **I.** Investing   **O.** Operating

___ **1.** Purchasing equipment.
___ **2.** Selling and distributing products.
___ **3.** Paying for advertising.
___ **4.** Paying employee wages.
___ **5.** Owner investing land in business.
___ **6.** Purchasing a building.
___ **7.** Purchasing land.
___ **8.** Borrowing cash from a bank.

Problem 1-13A^B
Describing organizational activities

C6

An organization undertakes various activities in pursuit of business success. Identify an organization's three major business activities, and describe each activity.

Problem 1-14A^B
Describing organizational activities C6

PROBLEM SET B

Problem 1-1B
Computing missing information using accounting knowledge

A1 A2

The following financial statement information is from five separate companies.

	Company V	Company W	Company X	Company Y	Company Z
December 31, 2008					
Assets	$36,000	$ 28,080	$23,040	$64,080	$ 98,280
Liabilities	29,520	19,656	12,441	44,215	?
December 31, 2009					
Assets	39,000	28,080	26,130	?	107,640
Liabilities	21,450	?	12,803	34,070	85,035
During year 2009					
Owner investments	6,000	1,400	?	7,000	6,500
Net income or (loss)	?	1,162	(1,147)	10,045	7,449
Owner cash withdrawals	3,500	2,000	5,875	0	11,000

Required

1. Answer the following questions about Company V:
  a. What is the amount of equity on December 31, 2008?

Check (1b) $17,550

  b. What is the amount of equity on December 31, 2009?
  c. What is the net income or loss for the year 2009?
2. Answer the following questions about Company W:
  a. What is the amount of equity on December 31, 2008?
  b. What is the amount of equity on December 31, 2009?

(2c) $19,094

  c. What is the amount of liabilities on December 31, 2009?
3. Calculate the amount of owner investments for Company X during 2009.

(4) $70,980

4. Calculate the amount of assets for Company Y on December 31, 2009.
5. Calculate the amount of liabilities for Company Z on December 31, 2008.

Problem 1-2B
Identifying effects of transactions on financial statements

A1 A2

Identify how each of the following separate transactions affects financial statements. For the balance sheet, identify how each transaction affects total assets, total liabilities, and total equity. For the income statement, identify how each transaction affects net income. For the statement of cash flows, identify how each transaction affects cash flows from operating activities, cash flows from financing activities, and cash flows from investing activities. For increases, place a "+" in the column or columns. For decreases, place a "−" in the column or columns. If both an increase and a decrease occur, place "+/−" in the column or columns. The first transaction is completed as an example.

		Balance Sheet			Income Statement	Statement of Cash Flows		
	Transaction	Total Assets	Total Liab.	Total Equity	Net Income	Operating Activities	Financing Activities	Investing Activities
1	Owner invests cash in business	+		+			+	
2	Buys building by signing note payable							
3	Pays cash for salaries incurred							
4	Provides services for cash							
5	Pays cash for rent incurred							
6	Incurs utilities costs on credit							
7	Buys store equipment for cash							
8	Provides services on credit							
9	Collects cash on receivable from (8)							
10	Owner withdraws cash							

Selected financial information for Onshore Co. for the year ended December 31, 2009, follows.

| Revenues . . . . | $69,000 | Expenses . . . . | $53,682 | Net income . . . . | $15,318 |

Problem 1-3B
Preparing an income statement
P1

Required

Prepare the 2009 income statement for Onshore Company.

The following is selected financial information for NuTech Company as of December 31, 2009.

| Liabilities . . . . | $46,222 | Equity . . . . | $74,778 | Assets . . . . | $121,000 |

Problem 1-4B
Preparing a balance sheet
P1

Required

Prepare the balance sheet for NuTech Company as of December 31, 2009.

Selected financial information of HalfLife Co. for the year ended December 31, 2009, follows.

Cash used by investing activities	$(3,750)
Net increase in cash	250
Cash used by financing activities	(4,550)
Cash from operating activities	8,550
Cash, December 31, 2008	3,700

Problem 1-5B
Preparing a statement of cash flows
P1

Required

Prepare the 2009 statement of cash flows for HalfLife Company.

Following is selected financial information of Act First for the year ended December 31, 2009.

| I. Firstact, Capital, Dec. 31, 2009 . . . . | $10,500 | I. Firstact, Withdrawals . . . . | $ 2,000 |
| Net income . . . . | 7,000 | I. Firstact, Capital, Dec. 31, 2008 . . . . | 5,500 |

Problem 1-6B
Preparing a statement of owner's equity
P1

Required

Prepare the 2009 statement of owner's equity for Act First.

Nikolas Benton launched a new business, Benton's Maintenance Co., that began operations on June 1. The following transactions were completed by the company during that first month.

June 1 N. Benton invested $41,000 cash in the company.
2 The company rented a furnished office and paid $2,200 cash for June's rent.
4 The company purchased $1,860 of equipment on credit.
6 The company paid $780 cash for this month's advertising of the opening of the business.
8 The company completed maintenance services for a customer and immediately collected $5,700 cash.
14 The company completed $2,400 of maintenance services for City Center on credit.
16 The company paid $810 cash for an assistant's salary for the first half of the month.
20 The company received $2,400 cash payment for services completed for City Center on June 14.
24 The company completed $3,300 of maintenance services for Build-It Coop on credit.
25 The company received $3,300 cash payment from Build-It Coop for the work completed on June 24.
26 The company made payment of $1,860 cash for the equipment purchased on June 4.
27 The company purchased $80 of product advertising in this month's (June) local newspaper on credit; cash payment is due July 1.
28 The company paid $810 cash for an assistant's salary for the second half of this month.
29 N. Benton withdrew $1,600 cash from the company for personal use.
30 The company paid $250 cash for this month's telephone bill.
30 The company paid $300 cash for this month's utilities.

Problem 1-7B
Analyzing transactions and preparing financial statements
C5 A2 P1

Required

1. Arrange the following asset, liability, and equity titles in a table like Exhibit 1.9: Cash; Accounts Receivable; Equipment; Accounts Payable; N. Benton, Capital; N. Benton, Withdrawals; Revenues; and Expenses.

2. Show the effects of the transactions on the accounts of the accounting equation by recording increases and decreases in the appropriate columns. Do not determine new account balances after each transaction. Determine the final total for each account and verify that the equation is in balance.

3. Prepare a June income statement, a June statement of owner's equity, a June 30 balance sheet, and a June statement of cash flows.

Problem 1-8B
Analyzing transactions and preparing financial statements

C5   A2   P1

Truro Excavating Co., owned by Raul Truro, began operations in July and completed these transactions during that first month of operations.

July 1   R. Truro invested $68,600 cash in the company.
   2   The company rented office space and paid $1,300 cash for the July rent.
   3   The company purchased excavating equipment for $14,600 by paying $6,400 cash and agreeing to pay the $8,200 balance in 30 days.
   6   The company purchased office supplies for $900 cash.
   8   The company completed work for a customer and immediately collected $2,000 cash for the work.
  10   The company purchased $2,720 of office equipment on credit.
  15   The company completed work for a customer on credit in the amount of $4,300.
  17   The company purchased $350 of office supplies on credit.
  23   The company paid $2,720 cash for the office equipment purchased on July 10.
  25   The company billed a customer $1,000 for work completed; the balance is due in 30 days.
  28   The company received $4,300 cash for the work completed on July 15.
  30   The company paid an assistant's salary of $1,900 cash for this month.
  31   The company paid $590 cash for this month's utility bill.
  31   R. Truro withdrew $900 cash from the company for personal use.

Required

1. Arrange the following asset, liability, and equity titles in a table like Exhibit 1.9: Cash; Accounts Receivable; Office Supplies; Office Equipment; Excavating Equipment; Accounts Payable; R. Truro, Capital; R. Truro, Withdrawals; Revenues; and Expenses.

2. Use additions and subtractions to show the effects of each transaction on the accounts in the accounting equation. Show new balances after each transaction.

3. Use the increases and decreases in the columns of the table from part 2 to prepare an income statement, a statement of owner's equity, and a statement of cash flows—each of these for the current month. Also prepare a balance sheet as of the end of the month.

Analysis Component

4. Assume that the $14,600 purchase of excavating equipment on July 3 was financed from an owner investment of another $14,600 cash in the business (instead of the purchase conditions described in the transaction). Explain the effect of this change on total assets, total liabilities, and total equity.

Problem 1-9B
Analyzing effects of transactions

C5   P1   A1   A2

Nico Mitchell started a new business, Financial Management, and completed the following transactions during its first year of operations.

a. N. Mitchell invests $70,000 cash and office equipment valued at $12,000 in the company.
b. The company purchased a $141,000 building to use as an office. It paid $15,000 in cash and signed a note payable promising to pay the $126,000 balance over the next ten years.
c. The company purchased office equipment for $11,000 cash.
d. The company purchased $600 of office supplies and $1,300 of office equipment on credit.
e. The company paid a local newspaper $500 cash for printing an announcement of the office's opening.
f. The company completed a financial plan for a client and billed that client $2,400 for the service.
g. The company designed a financial plan for another client and immediately collected a $4,000 cash fee.

h. N. Mitchell withdrew $3,325 cash from the company for personal use.

i. The company received $1,750 cash as a partial payment from the client described in transaction *f.*

j. The company made a partial payment of $700 cash on the equipment purchased in transaction *d.*

k. The company paid $1,750 cash for the office secretary's wages.

Required

1. Create a table like the one in Exhibit 1.9, using the following headings for the columns: Cash; Accounts Receivable; Office Supplies; Office Equipment; Building; Accounts Payable; Notes Payable; N. Mitchell, Capital; N. Mitchell, Withdrawals; Revenues; and Expenses.

2. Use additions and subtractions within the table created in part *1* to show the dollar effects of each transaction on individual items of the accounting equation. Show new balances after each transaction.

3. Once you have completed the table, determine the company's net income.

Check   (2) Ending balances: Cash, $43,475; Expenses, $2,250; Notes Payable, $126,000

(3) Net income, $4,150

AT&T and Verizon produce and market telecommunications products and are competitors. Key financial figures (in $ millions) for these businesses over the past year follow.

Problem 1-10B
Computing and interpreting return on assets

A3

Key Figures ($ millions)	AT&T	Verizon
Sales	$ 63,055	$ 84,144
Net income	7,356	6,197
Average assets	208,133	178,467

Required

1. Compute return on assets for (*a*) AT&T and (*b*) Verizon.

2. Which company is more successful in the total amount of sales to consumers?

3. Which company is more successful in returning net income from its assets invested?

Check   (1*a*) 3.5%; (1*b*) 3.5%

Analysis Component

4. Write a one-paragraph memorandum explaining which company you would invest your money in and why. (Limit your explanation to the information provided.)

Carbondale Company manufactures, markets, and sells ATV and snowmobile equipment and accessories. The average total assets for Carbondale is $243,000. In its most recent year, Carbondale reported net income of $62,500 on revenues of $473,000.

Problem 1-11B
Determining expenses, liabilities, equity, and return on assets

A1   A3

Required

1. What is Carbondale Company's return on assets?

2. Does return on assets seem satisfactory for Carbondale given that its competitors average a 10% return on assets?

3. What are the total expenses for Carbondale Company in its most recent year?

4. What is the average total amount of liabilities plus equity for Carbondale Company?

Check   (3) $410,500

(4) $243,000

All business decisions involve aspects of risk and return.

Problem 1-12B[A]
Identifying risk and return

A4

Required

Identify both the risk and the return in each of the following activities:

1. Investing $20,000 in Nike stock.

2. Placing a $250 bet on a horse running in the Kentucky Derby.

3. Stashing $500 cash under your mattress.

4. Investing $35,000 in U.S. Savings Bonds.

Problem 1-13B^B

Describing organizational
activities

C6

A start-up company often engages in the following activities during its first year of operations. Classify
each of the following activities into one of the three major activities of an organization.

F. Financing   **I.** Investing   **O.** Operating

_____ **1.** Supervising workers.   _____ **5.** Providing client services.

_____ **2.** Owner investing money in business.   _____ **6.** Obtaining a bank loan.

_____ **3.** Renting office space.   _____ **7.** Purchasing machinery.

_____ **4.** Paying utilities expenses.   _____ **8.** Research for its products.

Problem 1-14B^B

Describing organizational
activities   C6

Identify in outline format the three major business activities of an organization. For each of these activities, identify at least two specific transactions or events normally undertaken by the business's owners
or its managers.

---

*This serial problem starts in this chapter and continues throughout most chapters of the book. It is most
readily solved if you use the Working Papers that accompany this book.*

SERIAL PROBLEM

Success Systems

SP 1   On October 1, 2009, Adriana Lopez launched a computer services company, **Success Systems,**
that is organized as a proprietorship and provides consulting services, computer system installations, and
custom program development. Lopez adopts the calendar year for reporting purposes and expects to prepare the company's first set of financial statements on December 31, 2009.

Required

Create a table like the one in Exhibit 1.9 using the following headings for columns: Cash; Accounts
Receivable; Computer Supplies; Computer System; Office Equipment; Accounts Payable; A. Lopez,
Capital; A. Lopez, Withdrawals; Revenues; and Expenses. Then use additions and subtractions within
the table created to show the dollar effects for each of the following October transactions for Success
Systems on the individual items of the accounting equation. Show new balances after each transaction.

Oct.   1   Adriana Lopez invested $55,000 cash, a $20,000 computer system, and $8,000 of office equip-
           ment in the company.
       3   The company purchased $1,420 of computer supplies on credit from Harris Office Products.
       6   The company billed Easy Leasing $4,800 for services performed in installing a new Web server.
       8   The company paid $1,420 cash for the computer supplies purchased from Harris Office Products
           on October 3.
      10   The company hired Lyn Addie as a part-time assistant for $125 per day, as needed.
      12   The company billed Easy Leasing another $1,400 for services performed.
      15   The company received $4,800 cash from Easy Leasing as partial payment toward its account.
      17   The company paid $805 cash to repair computer equipment damaged when moving it.
      20   The company paid $1,940 cash for an advertisement in the local newspaper.
      22   The company received $1,400 cash from Easy Leasing toward its account.
      28   The company billed IFM Company $5,208 for services performed.
      31   The company paid $875 cash for Lyn Addie's wages for seven days of work this month.
      31   A. Lopez withdrew $3,600 cash from the company for personal use.

Check Ending balances: Cash,
$52,560; Revenues, $11,408; Expenses,
$3,620

---

*Beyond the Numbers (BTN) is a special problem section aimed to refine communication, conceptual,
analysis, and research skills. It includes many activities helpful in developing an active learning environment.*

BEYOND THE NUMBERS

**REPORTING IN
ACTION**

A1   A3   A4

BTN 1-1   Key financial figures for **Best Buy's** fiscal year ended March 3, 2007, follow.

Key Figure	In Millions
Liabilities + Equity	$13,570
Net income	1,377
Revenues	35,934

Required

1. What is the total amount of assets invested in Best Buy?

2. What is Best Buy's return on assets? Its assets at February 25, 2006, equal $11,864 (in millions).   **Check** (2) 10.8%

3. How much are total expenses for Best Buy for the year ended March 3, 2007?

4. Does Best Buy's return on assets seem satisfactory if competitors average an 8.1% return?

Fast Forward

5. Access Best Buy's financial statements (Form 10-K) for fiscal years ending after March 3, 2007, from its Website (BestBuy.com) or from the SEC Website (www.sec.gov) and compute its return on assets for those fiscal years. Compare the March 3, 2007, fiscal year-end return on assets to any subsequent years' returns you are able to compute, and interpret the results.

BTN 1-2 Key comparative figures ($ millions) for both Best Buy and RadioShack follow.

Key Figure	Best Buy	RadioShack
Liabilities + Equity	$13,570	$2,070
Net income	1,377	73
Revenues and sales	35,934	4,778

Required

1. What is the total amount of assets invested in (*a*) Best Buy and (*b*) RadioShack?

2. What is the return on assets for (*a*) Best Buy and (*b*) RadioShack? Best Buy's beginning-year assets   **Check** (2b) 3.4%
equal $11,864 (in millions) and RadioShack's beginning-year assets equal $2,205 (in millions).

3. How much are expenses for (*a*) Best Buy and (*b*) RadioShack?

4. Is return on assets satisfactory for (*a*) Best Buy and (*b*) RadioShack? (Assume competitors average an 8.1% return.)

5. What can you conclude about Best Buy and RadioShack from these computations?

BTN 1-3 Liz Thorne works in a public accounting firm and hopes to eventually be a partner. The management of Allnet Company invites Thorne to prepare a bid to audit Allnet's financial statements. In discussing the audit fee, Allnet's management suggests a fee range in which the amount depends on the reported profit of Allnet. The higher its profit, the higher will be the audit fee paid to Thorne's firm.

Required

1. Identify the parties potentially affected by this audit and the fee plan proposed.

2. What are the ethical factors in this situation? Explain.

3. Would you recommend that Thorne accept this audit fee arrangement? Why or why not?

4. Describe some ethical considerations guiding your recommendation.

BTN 1-4 Refer to this chapter's opening feature about Life is good.® Assume that Bert and John Jacobs desire to expand their manufacturing facilities to meet customer demand. They decide to meet with their banker to discuss a loan to allow them to expand.

Required

1. Prepare a half-page report outlining the information you would request from the Jacobs brothers if you were the loan officer.

2. Indicate whether the information you request and your loan decision are affected by the form of business organization for Life is good.

TAKING IT TO THE NET

A3

BTN 1-5 Visit the EDGAR database at (www.sec.gov). Access the Form 10-K report of Rocky Mountain Chocolate Factory (ticker RMCF) filed on May 14, 2007, covering its 2007 fiscal year.

Required

1. Item 6 of the 10-K report provides comparative financial highlights of RMCF for the years 2004–2007. How would you describe the revenue trend for RMCF over this four-year period?
2. Has RMCF been profitable (see net income) over this four-year period? Support your answer.

TEAMWORK IN ACTION

C1

BTN 1-6 Teamwork is important in today's business world. Successful teams schedule convenient meetings, maintain regular communications, and cooperate with and support their members. This assignment aims to establish support/learning teams, initiate discussions, and set meeting times.

Required

1. Form teams and open a team discussion to determine a regular time and place for your team to meet between each scheduled class meeting. Notify your instructor via a memorandum or e-mail message as to when and where your team will hold regularly scheduled meetings.
2. Develop a list of telephone numbers and/or e-mail addresses of your teammates.

ENTREPRENEURIAL DECISION

A1 A2

BTN 1-7 Refer to this chapter's opening feature about Life is good. Assume that Bert and John Jacobs decide to open a new manufacturing facility to produce sunscreen. This new company will be called LifeScreen Manufacturing Company.

Required

1. LifeScreen Manufacturing obtains a $500,000 loan and the Jacobs brothers contribute $250,000 of their own assets in the new company.
   a. What is the new company's total amount of liabilities plus equity?
   b. What is the new company's total amount of assets?

Check (2) 10.7%

2. If the new company earns $80,000 in net income in the first year of operation, compute its return on asset (assume average assets equal $750,000). Assess its performance if competitors average a 10% return.

HITTING THE ROAD

C2

BTN 1-8 You are to interview a local business owner. (This can be a friend or relative.) Opening lines of communication with members of the business community can provide personal benefits of business networking. If you do not know the owner, you should call ahead to introduce yourself and explain your position as a student and your assignment requirements. You should request a thirty minute appointment for a face-to-face or phone interview to discuss the form of organization and operations of the business. Be prepared to make a good impression.

Required

1. Identify and describe the main operating activities and the form of organization for this business.
2. Determine and explain why the owner(s) chose this particular form of organization.
3. Identify any special advantages and/or disadvantages the owner(s) experiences in operating with this form of business organization.

BTN 1-9 DSG international plc (www.DSGiplc.com) is the leading European retailer of consumer electronics and competes with both **Best Buy** and **RadioShack**. Key financial figures for DSG follow.

Key Figure*	Pounds in Millions
Average assets	£4,048
Net income	207
Revenues	7,930
Return on assets	5.2%

* Figures prepared in accordance with International Financial Reporting Standards.

GLOBAL DECISION

A1 A3 A4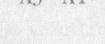

Required

1. Identify any concerns you have in comparing DSG's income and revenue figures to those of Best Buy and RadioShack (in BTN 1-2) for purposes of making business decisions.

2. Identify any concerns you have in comparing DSG's return on assets ratio to those of Best Buy and RadioShack (computed for BTN 1-2) for purposes of making business decisions.

ANSWERS TO MULTIPLE CHOICE QUIZ

1. c; $450,000 is the actual cost incurred.
2. b; revenue is recorded when earned.
3. d;

Assets	=	Liabilities	+	Equity
+$100,000	=	+35,000	+	?

Change in equity = $100,000 − $35,000 = $65,000

4. a
5. a

A Look Back

Chapter 1 defined accounting and introduced financial statements. We described forms of organizations and identified users and uses of accounting. We defined the accounting equation and applied it to transaction analysis.

 A Look at This Chapter

This chapter focuses on the accounting process. We describe transactions and source documents, and we explain the analysis and recording of transactions. The accounting equation, T-account, general ledger, trial balance, and debits and credits are key tools in the accounting process.

A Look Ahead

Chapter 3 extends our focus on processing information. We explain the importance of adjusting accounts and the procedures in preparing financial statements.

Analyzing and Recording Transactions

Chapter

Learning Objectives

CAP

Conceptual

C1 Explain the steps in processing transactions. *(p. 48)*

C2 Describe source documents and their purpose. *(p. 48)*

C3 Describe an account and its use in recording transactions. *(p. 49)*

C4 Describe a ledger and a chart of accounts. *(p. 52)*

C5 Define *debits* and *credits* and explain double-entry accounting. *(p. 53)*

Analytical

A1 Analyze the impact of transactions on accounts and financial statements. *(p. 57)*

A2 Compute the debt ratio and describe its use in analyzing financial condition. *(p. 66)*

LP2

Procedural

P1 Record transactions in a journal and post entries to a ledger. *(p. 54)*

P2 Prepare and explain the use of a trial balance. *(p. 63)*

P3 Prepare financial statements from business transactions. *(p. 64)*

The Bottom Line

"It has been a dream come true" — Sara Blakely

ATLANTA—"Working as a sales trainer by day and performing stand-up comedy at night, I didn't know the first thing about the pantyhose industry," admits Sara Blakely. "Except, I dreaded wearing most pantyhose." One night Sara cut the feet out of her pantyhose to wear with white pants and open-toed shoes, and at that moment, Sara knew she had a unique idea. Sara took $5,000 in savings and launched **SPANX (Spanx.com),** a manufacturer of footless pantyhose, slimming intimates, hosiery, and other women's apparel.

To pursue her business ambitions, Sara studied business activities and learned the value of accounting information. She established recordkeeping processes, transaction analysis, inventory accounting, and financial statement reporting. I had to get a handle on my financial situation, says Sara, as I wanted to remain self-funded. To this day, Sara remains self-funded and has a reliable accounting system to help her make good business decisions.

I had to account for product costs, office expenses, supplier payments, patent fees, and other expenses, says Sara. At the same time, Sara expanded sales and struggled to stay profitable. "I had no money to advertise, so I hit the road," laughs Sara. "For the entire first year, I did in-store rallies . . . staying all day introducing customers to Spanx."

In her first three months, Sara sold over 50,000 pairs of footless pantyhose. Today, just seven short years from her launch, Sara reports over $150 million in retail sales. "We are still a small company of women," claims Sara, "obsessed with inventing and improving comfortable undergarments." Sara continues to track and account for all revenues and expenses. She maintains that success requires proper accounting for and analysis of the financial side.

The bigger message of Spanx, says Sara, is promoting comfort and confidence for women. Insists Sara, "We believe all women deserve the opportunity to make the most of their assets!"

[Sources: *SPANX Website,* January 2009; *Entrepreneur,* May 2007; *Smart Money,* September 2002; *TV Guide,* July 2007; *Financial Times,* 2006; *ABC Television,* 2007]

Financial statements report on the financial performance and condition of an organization. Knowledge of their preparation, organization, and analysis is important. A main goal of this chapter is to illustrate how transactions are recorded, how they are reflected in financial statements, and how they impact analysis of financial statements. Debits and credits are introduced and identified as a tool in helping analyze and process transactions.

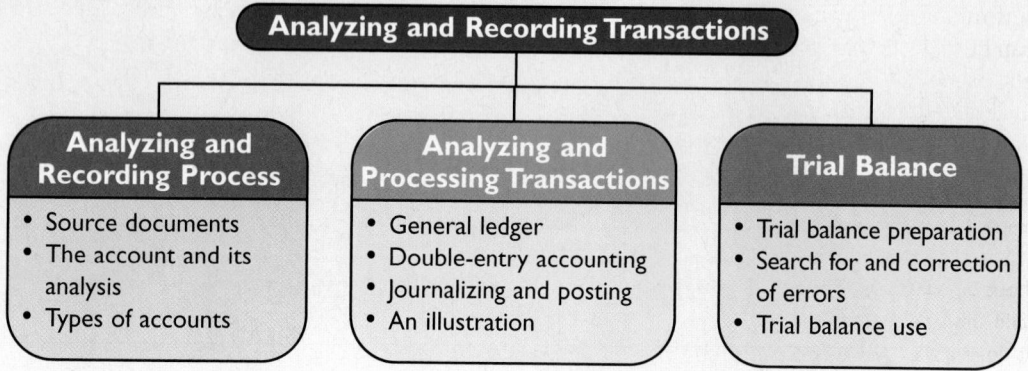

Analyzing and Recording Transactions		
Analyzing and Recording Process	**Analyzing and Processing Transactions**	**Trial Balance**
• Source documents • The account and its analysis • Types of accounts	• General ledger • Double-entry accounting • Journalizing and posting • An illustration	• Trial balance preparation • Search for and correction of errors • Trial balance use

Analyzing and Recording Process

C1 Explain the steps in processing transactions.

The accounting process identifies business transactions and events, analyzes and records their effects, and summarizes and presents information in reports and financial statements. These reports and statements are used for making investing, lending, and other business decisions. The steps in the accounting process that focus on *analyzing and recording* transactions and events are shown in Exhibit 2.1.

EXHIBIT 2.1

The Analyzing and Recording Process

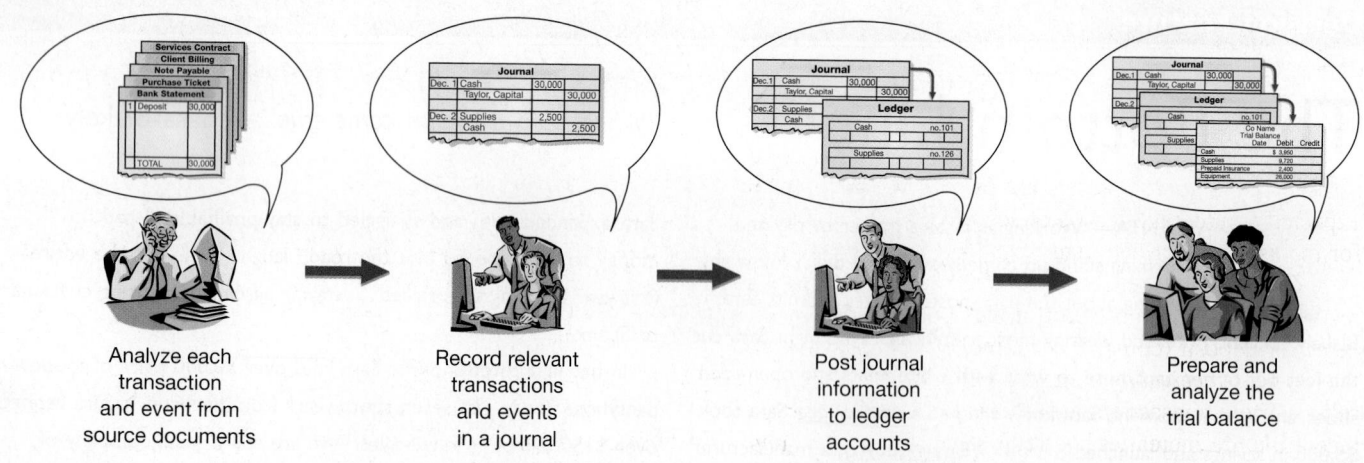

| Analyze each transaction and event from source documents | Record relevant transactions and events in a journal | Post journal information to ledger accounts | Prepare and analyze the trial balance |

Business transactions and events are the starting points. Relying on source documents, the transactions and events are analyzed using the accounting equation to understand how they affect company performance and financial position. These effects are recorded in accounting records, informally referred to as the *accounting books,* or simply the *books.* Additional steps such as posting and then preparing a trial balance help summarize and classify the effects of transactions and events. Ultimately, the accounting process provides information in useful reports or financial statements to decision makers.

Source Documents

C2 Describe source documents and their purpose.

Source documents identify and describe transactions and events entering the accounting process. They are the sources of accounting information and can be in either hard copy or electronic form. Examples are sales tickets, checks, purchase orders, bills from suppliers, employee earnings records, and bank statements. To illustrate, when an item is purchased on credit, the seller usually prepares at least two copies of a sales invoice. One copy is given to the buyer. Another copy, often sent electronically, results in an entry in the seller's information system to record the sale. Sellers use invoices for recording sales and for control; buyers use them for recording purchases and for monitoring purchasing activity. Many cash registers record information for each sale on a tape or electronic file locked inside the register. This record can be used as a source document for recording sales in the accounting records. Source documents, especially if obtained from outside the organization, provide objective and reliable evidence about transactions and events and their amounts.

Point: To ensure that all sales are rung up on the register, most sellers require customers to have their receipts to exchange or return purchased items.

Decision Ethics

Cashier Your manager requires that you, as cashier, immediately enter each sale. Recently, lunch hour traffic has increased and the assistant manager asks you to avoid delays by taking customers' cash and making change without entering sales. The assistant manager says she will add up cash and enter sales after lunch. She says that, in this way, the register will always match the cash amount when the manager arrives at three o'clock. What do you do? [Answer—p. 71]

The Account and Its Analysis

An **account** is a record of increases and decreases in a specific asset, liability, equity, revenue, or expense item. Information from an account is analyzed, summarized, and presented in reports and financial statements. The **general ledger,** or simply **ledger,** is a record containing all accounts used by a company. The ledger is often in electronic form. While most companies' ledgers contain similar accounts, a company often uses one or more unique accounts because of its type of operations. Accounts are arranged into three general categories (based on the accounting equation), as shown in Exhibit 2.2.

C3 Describe an account and its use in recording transactions.

EXHIBIT 2.2

Accounts Organized by the Accounting Equation

Asset Accounts   Assets are resources owned or controlled by a company and that have expected future benefits. Most accounting systems include (at a minimum) separate accounts for the assets described here.

A *Cash* account reflects a company's cash balance. All increases and decreases in cash are recorded in the Cash account. It includes money and any medium of exchange that a bank accepts for deposit (coins, checks, money orders, and checking account balances).

Accounts receivable are held by a seller and refer to promises of payment from customers to sellers. These transactions are often called *credit sales* or *sales on account* (or *on credit*). Accounts receivable are increased by credit sales and are decreased by customer payments. A company needs a separate record for each customer, but for now, we use the simpler practice of recording all increases and decreases in receivables in a single account called Accounts Receivable.

A *note receivable,* or promissory note, is a written promise of another entity to pay a definite sum of money on a specified future date to the holder of the note. A company holding a promissory note signed by another entity has an asset that is recorded in a Note (or Notes) Receivable account.

Prepaid accounts (also called *prepaid expenses*) are assets that represent prepayments of future expenses (*not* current expenses). When the expenses are later incurred, the amounts in prepaid accounts are transferred to expense accounts. Common examples of prepaid accounts include prepaid insurance, prepaid rent, and prepaid services (such as club memberships). Prepaid accounts expire with the passage of time (such as with rent) or through use (such as with prepaid meal tickets). When financial statements are prepared, prepaid accounts are adjusted so that (1) all expired and used prepaid accounts are recorded as regular expenses and (2) all unexpired and unused prepaid accounts are recorded as assets (reflecting future use in

Point: Customers and others who owe a company are called its **debtors.**

Point: A college parking fee is a prepaid account from the student's standpoint. At the beginning of the term, it represents an asset that entitles a student to park on or near campus. The benefits of the parking fee expire as the term progresses. At term-end, prepaid parking (asset) equals zero as it has been entirely recorded as parking expense.

Point: Prepaid accounts that apply to current and future periods are assets. These assets are adjusted at the end of each period to reflect only those amounts that have not yet expired, and to record as expenses those amounts that have expired.

future periods). To illustrate, when an insurance fee, called a *premium,* is paid in advance, the cost is typically recorded in the asset account Prepaid Insurance. Over time, the expiring portion of the insurance cost is removed from this asset account and reported in expenses on the income statement. Any unexpired portion remains in Prepaid Insurance and is reported on the balance sheet as an asset. (An exception exists for prepaid accounts that will expire or be used before the end of the current accounting period when financial statements are prepared. In this case, the prepayments *can* be recorded immediately as expenses.)

Supplies are assets until they are used. When they are used up, their costs are reported as expenses. The costs of unused supplies are recorded in a Supplies asset account. Supplies are often grouped by purpose—for example, office supplies and store supplies. *Office supplies* include stationery, paper, toner, and pens. *Store supplies* include packaging materials, plastic and paper bags, gift boxes and cartons, and cleaning materials. The costs of these unused supplies can be recorded in an Office Supplies or a Store Supplies asset account. When supplies are used, their costs are transferred from the asset accounts to expense accounts.

Equipment is an asset. When equipment is used and gets worn down, its cost is gradually reported as an expense (called depreciation). Equipment is often grouped by its purpose—for example, office equipment and store equipment. *Office equipment* includes computers, printers, desks, chairs, and shelves. Costs incurred for these items are recorded in an Office Equipment asset account. The Store Equipment account includes the costs of assets used in a store, such as counters, showcases, ladders, hoists, and cash registers.

Point: Some assets are described as *intangible* because they do not have physical existence or their benefits are highly uncertain. A recent balance sheet for **Coca-Cola Company** shows nearly $1 billion in intangible assets.

Buildings such as stores, offices, warehouses, and factories are assets because they provide expected future benefits to those who control or own them. Their costs are recorded in a Buildings asset account. When several buildings are owned, separate accounts are sometimes kept for each of them.

The cost of *land* owned by a business is recorded in a Land account. The cost of buildings located on the land is separately recorded in one or more building accounts.

Decision Insight

Women Entrepreneurs   The Center for Women's Business Research reports that women-owned businesses, such as **SPANX**, are growing and that they

- Total approximately 11 million and employ nearly 20 million workers.
- Generate $2.5 trillion in annual sales and tend to embrace technology.
- Are philanthropic—70% of owners volunteer at least once per month.
- Are more likely funded by individual investors (73%) than venture firms (15%).

Liability Accounts   Liabilities are claims (by creditors) against assets, which means they are obligations to transfer assets or provide products or services to other entities. **Creditors** are individuals and organizations that own the right to receive payments from a company. If a company fails to pay its obligations, the law gives creditors a right to force the sale of that company's assets to obtain the money to meet creditors' claims. When assets are sold under these conditions, creditors are paid first, but only up to the amount of their claims. Any remaining money, the residual, goes to the owners of the company. Creditors often use a balance sheet to help decide whether to loan money to a company. A loan is less risky if the borrower's liabilities are small in comparison to assets because this means there are more resources than claims on resources. Common liability accounts are described here.

Point: Accounts Payable are also called *Trade Payables.*

Accounts payable refer to oral or implied promises to pay later, which usually arise from purchases of merchandise. Payables can also arise from purchases of supplies, equipment, and services. Accounting systems keep separate records about each creditor. We describe these individual records in Chapter 5.

A *note payable* refers to a formal promise, usually denoted by the signing of a promissory note, to pay a future amount. It is recorded in either a short-term Note Payable account or a long-term Note Payable account, depending on when it must be repaid. We explain details of short- and long-term classification in Chapter 3.

Unearned Revenue refers to a liability that is settled in the future when a company delivers its products or services. When customers pay in advance for products or services (before revenue is earned), the revenue recognition principle requires that the seller consider this payment as unearned revenue. Examples of unearned revenue include magazine subscriptions collected in advance by a publisher, sales of gift certificates by stores, and season ticket sales by sports teams. The seller would record these in liability accounts such as Unearned Subscriptions, Unearned Store Sales, and Unearned Ticket Revenue. When products and services are later delivered, the earned portion of the unearned revenue is transferred to revenue accounts such as Subscription Fees, Store Sales, and Ticket Sales.[1]

Point: If a subscription is canceled, the publisher is expected to refund the unused portion to the subscriber.

Accrued liabilities are amounts owed that are not yet paid. Examples are wages payable, taxes payable, and interest payable. These are often recorded in separate liability accounts by the same title. If they are not large in amount, one or more ledger accounts can be added and reported as a single amount on the balance sheet. (Financial statements often have amounts reported that are a summation of several ledger accounts.)

Decision Insight

Revenue Spread   The **Chicago Bears** have *Unearned Revenues* of about $60 million in advance ticket sales. When the team plays its home games, it settles this liability to its ticket holders and then transfers the amount earned to *Ticket Revenues*.

Equity Accounts   The owner's claim on a company's assets is called *equity* or *owner's equity*. Equity is the owner's *residual interest* in the assets of a business after deducting liabilities. Equity is impacted by four types of accounts: owner's capital, owner's withdrawals, revenues, and expenses. We show this visually in Exhibit 2.3 by expanding the accounting equation.

Point: Equity is also called *net assets*.

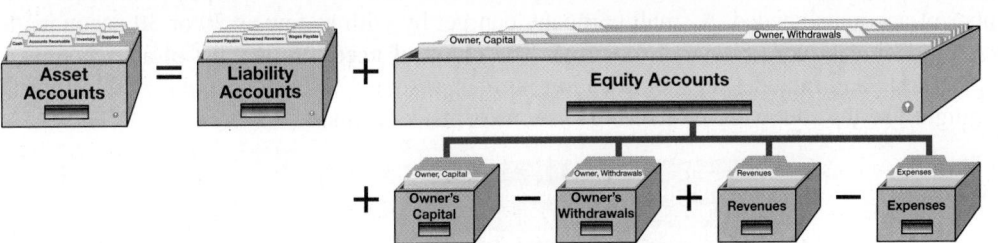

EXHIBIT 2.3

Expanded Accounting Equation

When an owner invests in a company, the invested amount is recorded in an account titled **Owner, Capital** (where the owner's name is inserted in place of "owner"). The account titled *C. Taylor, Capital* is used for FastForward. Any further owner investments are recorded in this account. When an owner withdraws assets for personal use it decreases both company assets and total equity. Withdrawals are not expenses of the business; they are simply the opposite of owner investments. The **Owner, Withdrawals** account is used to record asset distributions to the owner. The account titled *C. Taylor, Withdrawals* is used for FastForward. (Owners of proprietorships cannot receive company salaries because they are not legally separate from their companies; and they cannot enter into company contracts with themselves.)

Point: The Owner's Withdrawals account is a *contra equity* account because it reduces the normal balance of equity.

Point: The withdrawal of assets by the owners of a corporation is called a *dividend*.

Revenues and expenses also impact equity. Examples of revenue accounts are Sales, Commissions Earned, Professional Fees Earned, Rent Earned, and Interest Revenue. *Revenues increase equity* and result from products and services provided to customers. Examples of expense accounts are Advertising Expense, Store Supplies Expense, Office Salaries Expense, Office Supplies Expense, Rent Expense, Utilities Expense, and Insurance Expense. *Expenses decrease equity* and result from assets and services used in a company's operations. The variety of revenues and expenses can be seen by looking at the *chart of accounts* that follows the index

---

[1] In practice, account titles vary. As one example, Subscription Fees is sometimes called Subscription Fees Revenue, Subscription Fees Earned, or Earned Subscription Fees. As another example, Rent Earned is sometimes called Rent Revenue, Rental Revenue, or Earned Rent Revenue. We must use good judgment when reading financial statements because titles can differ even within the same industry. For example, product sales are called *revenue* at **Best Buy**, but *net sales and operating revenues* at **Circuit City**. Generally, the term *revenues* or *fees* is more commonly used with service businesses, and *net sales* or *sales* with product businesses.

at the back of this book. (Different companies sometimes use different account titles than those in this book's chart of accounts. For example, some might use Interest Revenue instead of Interest Earned, or Rental Expense instead of Rent Expense. It is important only that an account title describe the item it represents.)

Decision Insight

Sporting Accounts The **San Antonio Spurs** have the following major revenue and expense accounts:

Revenues	Expenses
Basketball ticket sales	Team salaries
TV & radio broadcast fees	Game costs
Advertising revenues	NBA franchise costs
Basketball playoff receipts	Promotional costs

Analyzing and Processing Transactions

This section explains several tools and processes that comprise an accounting system. These include a ledger, T-account, debits and credits, double-entry accounting, journalizing, and posting.

Ledger and Chart of Accounts

C4 Describe a ledger and a chart of accounts.

The collection of all accounts for an information system is called a *ledger* (or *general ledger*). If accounts are in files on a hard drive, the sum of those files is the ledger. If the accounts are pages in a file, that file is the ledger. A company's size and diversity of operations affect the number of accounts needed. A small company can get by with as few as 20 or 30 accounts; a large company can require several thousand. The **chart of accounts** is a list of all accounts a company uses and includes an identification number assigned to each account. A small business might use the following numbering system for its accounts:

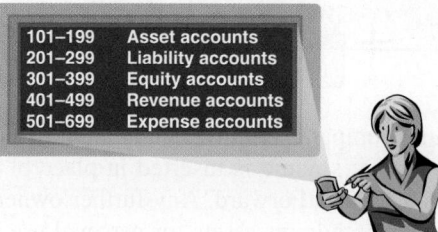

101–199	Asset accounts
201–299	Liability accounts
301–399	Equity accounts
401–499	Revenue accounts
501–699	Expense accounts

These numbers provide a three-digit code that is useful in recordkeeping. In this case, the first digit assigned to asset accounts is a 1, the first digit assigned to liability accounts is a 2, and so on. The second and third digits relate to the accounts' subcategories. Exhibit 2.4 shows a partial chart of accounts for FastForward, the focus company of Chapter 1. (Please review the more complete chart of accounts that follows the index at the back of this book.)

EXHIBIT 2.4

Partial Chart of Accounts for FastForward

Account Number	Account Name	Account Number	Account Name
101	Cash	301	C. Taylor, Capital
106	Accounts receivable	302	C. Taylor, Withdrawals
126	Supplies	403	Consulting revenue
128	Prepaid insurance	406	Rental revenue
167	Equipment	622	Salaries expense
201	Accounts payable	637	Insurance expense
236	Unearned consulting revenue	640	Rent expense
		652	Supplies expense
		690	Utilities expense

Debits and Credits

A **T-account** represents a ledger account and is a tool used to understand the effects of one or more transactions. Its name comes from its shape like the letter **T**. The layout of a T-account, shown in Exhibit 2.5, is (1) the account title on top, (2) a left, or debit side, and (3) a right, or credit, side.

C5   Define *debits* and *credits* and explain double-entry accounting.

The left side of an account is called the **debit** side, often abbreviated *Dr.* The right side is called the **credit** side, abbreviated *Cr.*[2] To enter amounts on the left side of an account is to *debit* the account. To enter amounts on the

Account Title	
(Left side)	(Right side)
Debit	*Credit*

EXHIBIT 2.5

The T-Account

right side is to *credit* the account. Do not make the error of thinking that the terms *debit* and *credit* mean increase or decrease. Whether a debit or a credit is an increase or decrease depends on the account. For an account where a debit is an increase, the credit is a decrease; for an account where a debit is a decrease, the credit is an increase. The difference between total debits and total credits for an account, including any beginning balance, is the **account balance.** When the sum of debits exceeds the sum of credits, the account has a *debit balance*. It has a *credit balance* when the sum of credits exceeds the sum of debits. When the sum of debits equals the sum of credits, the account has a *zero balance*.

Point: Think of *debit* and *credit* as accounting directions for left and right.

Double-Entry Accounting

Double-entry accounting requires that each transaction affect, and be recorded in, at least two accounts. It also means the *total amount debited must equal the total amount credited* for each transaction. Thus, the sum of the debits for all entries must equal the sum of the credits for all entries, and the sum of debit account balances in the ledger must equal the sum of credit account balances.

The system for recording debits and credits follows from the usual accounting equation—see Exhibit 2.6. Two points are important here. First, like any simple mathematical relation, net increases or decreases on one side have equal net effects on the other side. For example, a net increase in assets must be accompanied by an identical net increase on the liabilities and

"Total debits equal total credits for each entry."

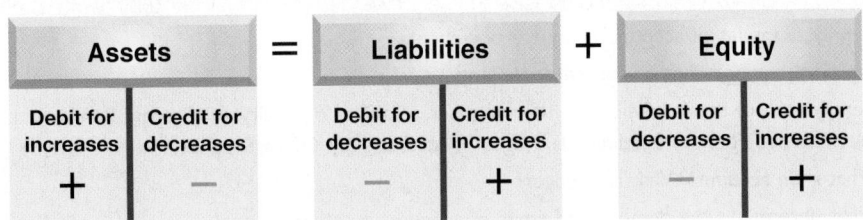

EXHIBIT 2.6

Debits and Credits in the Accounting Equation

equity side. Recall that some transactions affect only one side of the equation, meaning that two or more accounts on one side are affected, but their net effect on this one side is zero. Second, the left side is the *normal balance* side for assets, and the right side is the *normal balance* side for liabilities and equity. This matches their layout in the accounting equation where assets are on the left side of this equation, and liabilities and equity are on the right.

Recall that equity increases from revenues and owner investments and it decreases from expenses and owner withdrawals. These important equity relations are conveyed by expanding the accounting equation to include debits and credits in double-entry form as shown in Exhibit 2.7.

Increases (credits) to owner's capital and revenues *increase* equity; increases (debits) to withdrawals and expenses *decrease* equity. The normal balance of each account (asset, liability, capital, withdrawals, revenue, or expense) refers to the left or right (debit or credit) side where *increases* are recorded. Understanding these diagrams and rules is required to prepare, analyze, and interpret financial statements.

Point: Debits and credits do not mean favorable or unfavorable. A debit to an asset increases it, as does a debit to an expense. A credit to a liability increases it, as does a credit to a revenue.

---

[2] These abbreviations are remnants of 18th-century English recordkeeping practices where the terms *debitor* and *creditor* were used instead of *debit* and *credit*. The abbreviations use the first and last letters of these terms, just as we still do for Saint (St.) and Doctor (Dr.).

EXHIBIT 2.7

Debit and Credit Effects for Component Accounts

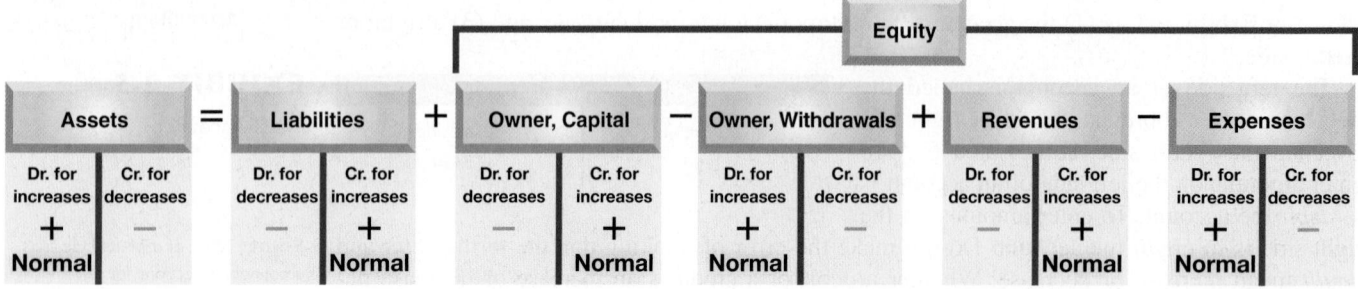

The T-account for FastForward's Cash account, reflecting its first 11 transactions (from Exhibit 1.9), is shown in Exhibit 2.8. The total increases in its Cash account are $36,100, the total decreases are $31,300, and the account's debit balance is $4,800. (We illustrate use of T-accounts later in this chapter.)

EXHIBIT 2.8

Computing the Balance for a T-Account

Cash			
Investment by owner	30,000	Purchase of supplies	2,500
Consulting services revenue earned	4,200	Purchase of equipment	26,000
Collection of account receivable	1,900	Payment of rent	1,000
		Payment of salary	700
		Payment of account payable	900
		Withdrawal by owner	200
Balance	4,800		

Point: The ending balance is on the side with the larger dollar amount.

Quick Check

Answers—p. 72

1. Identify examples of accounting source documents.
2. Explain the importance of source documents.
3. Identify each of the following as either an asset, a liability, or equity: (*a*) Prepaid Rent, (*b*) Unearned Fees, (*c*) Building, (*d*) Wages Payable, and (*e*) Office Supplies.
4. What is an account? What is a ledger?
5. What determines the number and types of accounts a company uses?
6. Does *debit* always mean increase and *credit* always mean decrease?
7. Describe a chart of accounts.

Journalizing and Posting Transactions

P1 Record transactions in a journal and post entries to a ledger.

Processing transactions is a crucial part of accounting. The four usual steps of this process are depicted in Exhibit 2.9. Steps 1 and 2—involving transaction analysis and double-entry accounting—were introduced in prior sections. This section extends that discussion and focuses on steps 3 and 4 of the accounting process. Step 3 is to record each transaction in a journal. A **journal** gives a complete record of each transaction in one place. It also shows debits and credits for each transaction. The process of recording transactions in a journal is called **journalizing.** Step 4 is to transfer (or *post*) entries from the journal to the ledger. The process of transferring journal entry information to the ledger is called **posting.**

Journalizing Transactions   The process of journalizing transactions requires an understanding of a journal. While companies can use various journals, every company uses a **general journal.** It can be used to record any transaction and includes the following information about each transaction: (1) date of transaction, (2) titles of affected accounts, (3) dollar amount of each

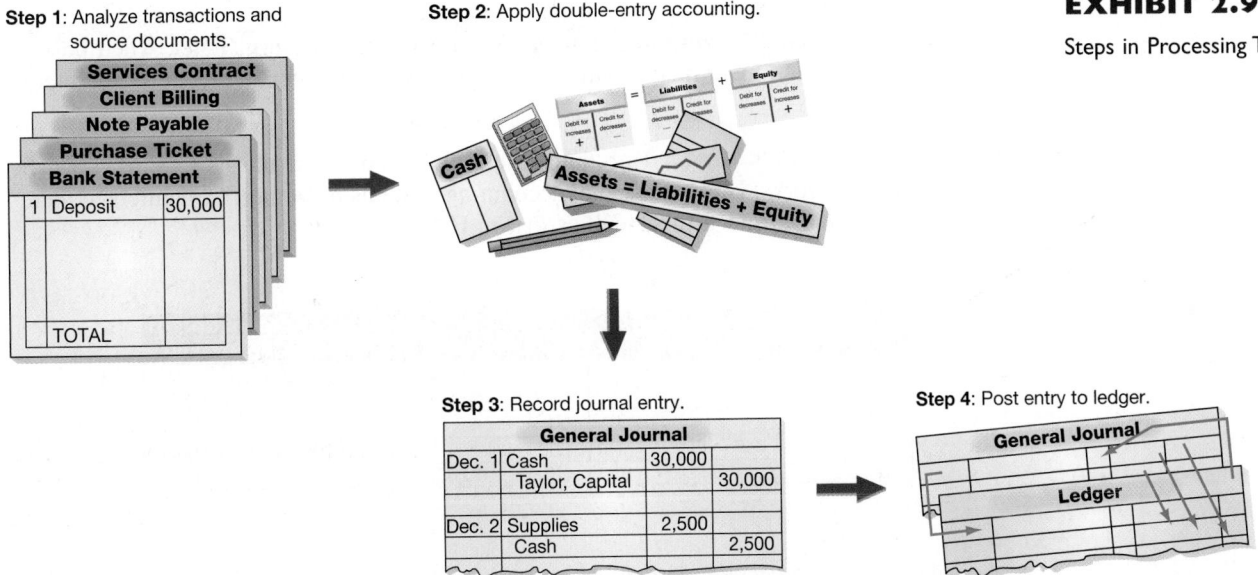

EXHIBIT 2.9

Steps in Processing Transactions

debit and credit, and (4) explanation of the transaction. Exhibit 2.10 shows how the first two transactions of FastForward are recorded in a general journal. This process is similar for manual and computerized systems. Computerized journals are often designed to look like a manual journal page, and also include error-checking routines that ensure debits equal credits for each entry. Shortcuts allow recordkeepers to select account names and numbers from pull-down menus.

EXHIBIT 2.10

Partial General Journal for FastForward

GENERAL JOURNAL				Page 1
Date	Account Titles and Explanation	PR	Debit	Credit
2009 Dec. 1	Cash		30,000	
	C. Taylor, Capital			30,000
	Investment by owner.			
Dec. 2	Supplies		2,500	
	Cash			2,500
	Purchased supplies for cash.			

To record entries in a general journal, apply these steps; refer to the entries in Exhibit 2.10 when reviewing these steps. ① Date the transaction: Enter the year at the top of the first column and the month and day on the first line of each journal entry. ② Enter titles of accounts debited and then enter amounts in the Debit column on the same line. Account titles are taken from the chart of accounts and are aligned with the left margin of the Account Titles and Explanation column. ③ Enter titles of accounts credited and then enter amounts in the Credit column on the same line. Account titles are from the chart of accounts and are indented from the left margin of the Account Titles and Explanation column to distinguish them from debited accounts. ④ Enter a brief explanation of the transaction on the line below the entry (it often references a source document). This explanation is indented about half as far as the credited account titles to avoid confusing it with accounts, and it is italicized.

Point: There are no exact rules for writing journal entry explanations. An explanation should be short yet describe why an entry is made.

Decision Insight

IFRSs   IFRSs require that companies report the following four financial statements with explanatory notes:
—Balance sheet   —Statement of changes in equity (or statement of recognized revenue and expense)
—Income statement   —Statement of cash flows
IFRSs do not prescribe specific formats; and comparative information is required for the preceding period only.

A blank line is left between each journal entry for clarity. When a transaction is first recorded, the **posting reference (PR) column** is left blank (in a manual system). Later, when posting entries to the ledger, the identification numbers of the individual ledger accounts are entered in the PR column.

Balance Column Account   T-accounts are simple and direct means to show how the accounting process works. However, actual accounting systems need more structure and therefore use **balance column accounts,** such as that in Exhibit 2.11.

EXHIBIT 2.11

Cash Account in Balance
Column Format

Date	Explanation	PR	Debit	Credit	Balance
Cash					Account No. 101
2009					
Dec. 1		G1	30,000		30,000
Dec. 2		G1		2,500	27,500
Dec. 3		G1		26,000	1,500
Dec. 10		G1	4,200		5,700

The balance column account format is similar to a T-account in having columns for debits and credits. It is different in including transaction date and explanation columns. It also has a column with the balance of the account after each entry is recorded. To illustrate, FastForward's Cash account in Exhibit 2.11 is debited on December 1 for the $30,000 owner investment, yielding a $30,000 debit balance. The account is credited on December 2 for $2,500, yielding a $27,500 debit balance. On December 3, it is credited again, this time for $26,000, and its debit balance is reduced to $1,500. The Cash account is debited for $4,200 on December 10, and its debit balance increases to $5,700; and so on.

Point: Explanations are typically included in ledger accounts only for unusual transactions or events.

The heading of the Balance column does not show whether it is a debit or credit balance. Instead, an account is assumed to have a *normal balance*. Unusual events can sometimes

EXHIBIT 2.12

Posting an Entry to the Ledger

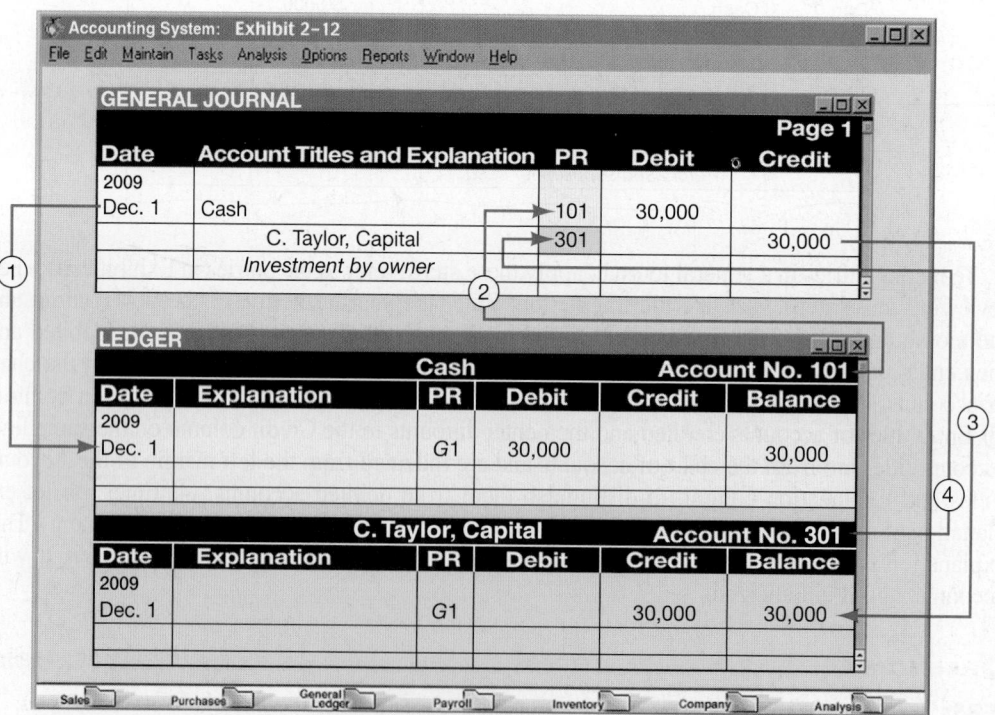

Point: The fundamental concepts of a manual (pencil-and-paper) system are identical to those of a computerized information system.

Key: ① Identify debit account in Ledger: enter date, journal page, amount, and balance.
   ② Enter the debit account number from the Ledger in the PR column of the journal.
   ③ Identify credit account in Ledger: enter date, journal page, amount, and balance.
   ④ Enter the credit account number from the Ledger in the PR column of the journal.

temporarily give an account an abnormal balance. An *abnormal balance* refers to a balance on the side where decreases are recorded. For example, a customer might mistakenly overpay a bill. This gives that customer's account receivable an abnormal (credit) balance. An abnormal balance is often identified by circling it or by entering it in red or some other unusual color. A zero balance for an account is usually shown by writing zeros or a dash in the Balance column to avoid confusion between a zero balance and one omitted in error.

Posting Journal Entries Step 4 of processing transactions is to post journal entries to ledger accounts (see Exhibit 2.9). To ensure that the ledger is up-to-date, entries are posted as soon as possible. This might be daily, weekly, or when time permits. All entries must be posted to the ledger before financial statements are prepared to ensure that account balances are up-to-date. When entries are posted to the ledger, the debits in journal entries are transferred into ledger accounts as debits, and credits are transferred into ledger accounts as credits. Exhibit 2.12 shows the *four steps to post a journal entry*. First, identify the ledger account that is debited in the entry; then, in the ledger, enter the entry date, the journal and page in its PR column, the debit amount, and the new balance of the ledger account. (The letter *G* shows it came from the General Journal.) Second, enter the ledger account number in the PR column of the journal. Steps 3 and 4 repeat the first two steps for credit entries and amounts. The posting process creates a link between the ledger and the journal entry. This link is a useful cross-reference for tracing an amount from one record to another.

Point: Computerized systems often provide a code beside a balance such as *dr.* or *cr.* to identify its balance. Posting is automatic and immediate with accounting software.

Point: A journal is often referred to as the *book of original entry*. The ledger is referred to as the *book of final entry* because financial statements are prepared from it.

Analyzing Transactions—An Illustration

We return to the activities of FastForward to show how double-entry accounting is useful in analyzing and processing transactions. Analysis of each transaction follows the four steps of Exhibit 2.9. First, we review the transaction and any source documents. Second, we analyze the transaction using the accounting equation. Third, we use double-entry accounting to record the transaction in journal entry form. Fourth, the entry is posted (for simplicity, we use T-accounts to represent ledger accounts). Study each transaction thoroughly before proceeding to the next. The first 11 transactions are from Chapter 1, and we analyze five additional December transactions of FastForward (numbered 12 through 16) that were omitted earlier.

A1 Analyze the impact of transactions on accounts and financial statements.

1. Investment by Owner

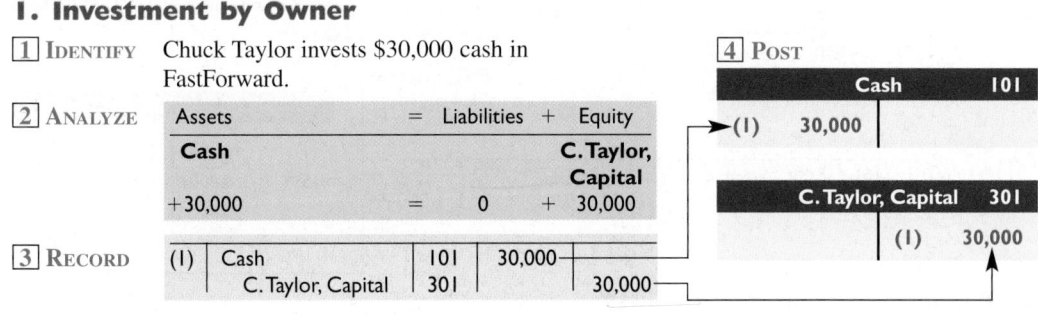

2. Purchase Supplies for Cash

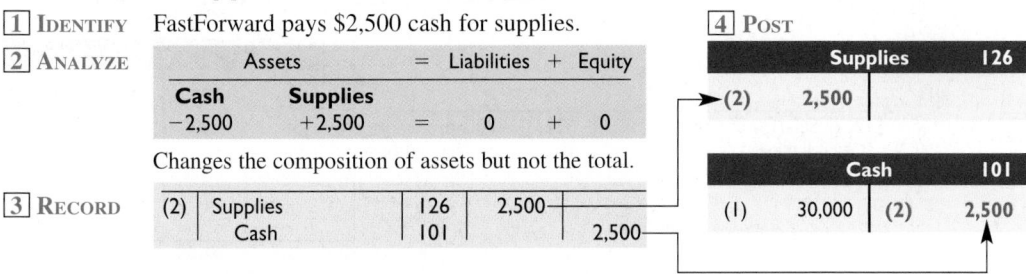

3. Purchase Equipment for Cash

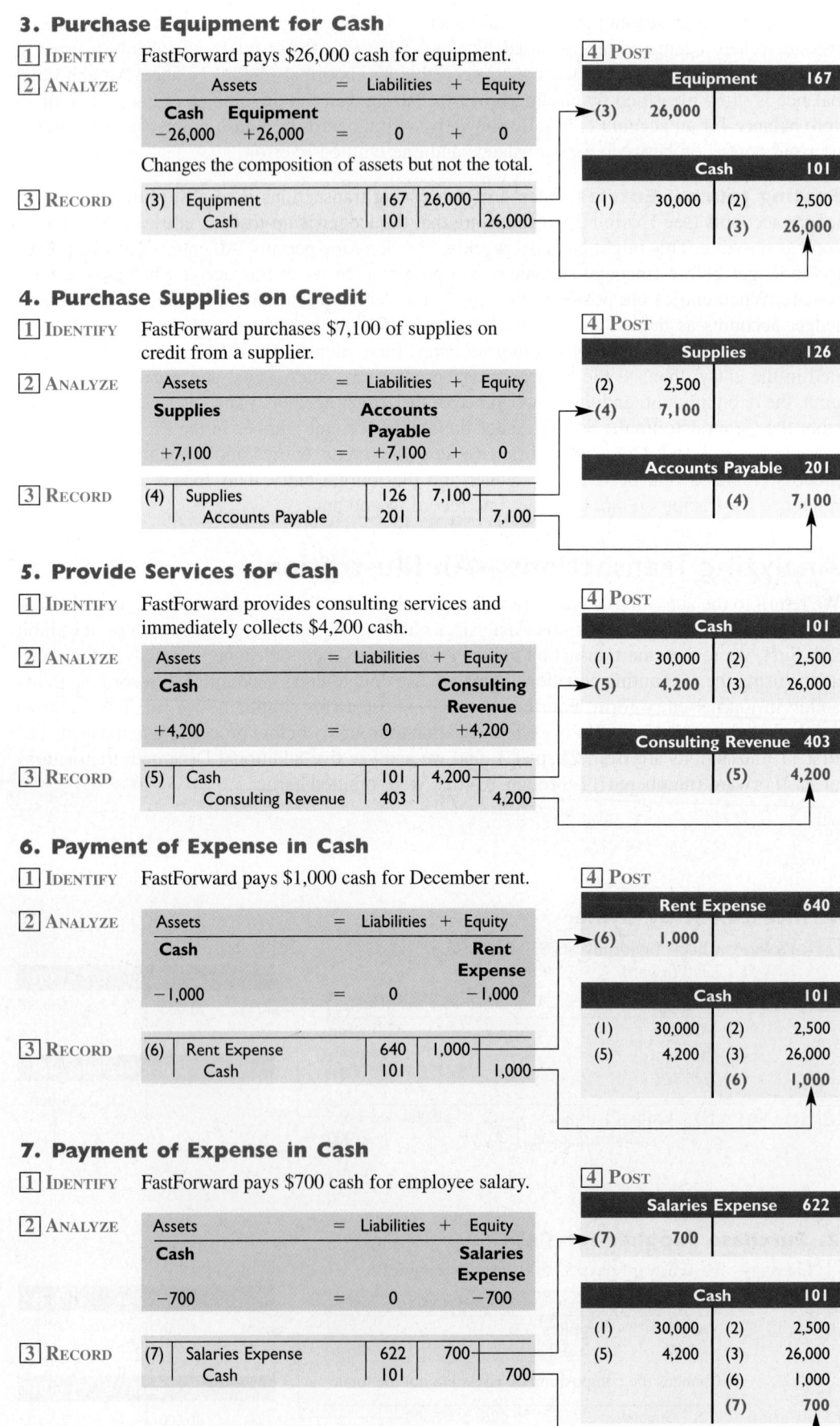

1 IDENTIFY   FastForward pays $26,000 cash for equipment.

2 ANALYZE

Assets		=	Liabilities	+	Equity
Cash	Equipment				
−26,000	+26,000	=	0	+	0

Changes the composition of assets but not the total.

3 RECORD

(3)	Equipment	167	26,000	
	Cash	101		26,000

4 POST

Equipment		167
(3)	26,000	

Cash		101
(1)	30,000	(2)	2,500
		(3)	26,000

4. Purchase Supplies on Credit

1 IDENTIFY   FastForward purchases $7,100 of supplies on credit from a supplier.

2 ANALYZE

Assets	=	Liabilities	+	Equity
Supplies		Accounts Payable		
+7,100	=	+7,100	+	0

3 RECORD

(4)	Supplies	126	7,100	
	Accounts Payable	201		7,100

4 POST

Supplies		126
(2)	2,500	
(4)	7,100	

Accounts Payable		201
		(4)	7,100

5. Provide Services for Cash

1 IDENTIFY   FastForward provides consulting services and immediately collects $4,200 cash.

2 ANALYZE

Assets	=	Liabilities	+	Equity
Cash				Consulting Revenue
+4,200	=	0		+4,200

3 RECORD

(5)	Cash	101	4,200	
	Consulting Revenue	403		4,200

4 POST

Cash		101
(1)	30,000	(2)	2,500
(5)	4,200	(3)	26,000

Consulting Revenue		403
		(5)	4,200

6. Payment of Expense in Cash

1 IDENTIFY   FastForward pays $1,000 cash for December rent.

2 ANALYZE

Assets	=	Liabilities	+	Equity
Cash				Rent Expense
−1,000	=	0		−1,000

3 RECORD

(6)	Rent Expense	640	1,000	
	Cash	101		1,000

4 POST

Rent Expense		640
(6)	1,000	

Cash		101
(1)	30,000	(2)	2,500
(5)	4,200	(3)	26,000
		(6)	1,000

7. Payment of Expense in Cash

Point: *Salary* usually refers to compensation for an employee who receives a fixed amount for a given time period, whereas *wages* usually refers to compensation based on time worked.

1 IDENTIFY   FastForward pays $700 cash for employee salary.

2 ANALYZE

Assets	=	Liabilities	+	Equity
Cash				Salaries Expense
−700	=	0		−700

3 RECORD

(7)	Salaries Expense	622	700	
	Cash	101		700

4 POST

Salaries Expense		622
(7)	700	

Cash		101
(1)	30,000	(2)	2,500
(5)	4,200	(3)	26,000
		(6)	1,000
		(7)	700

8. Provide Consulting and Rental Services on Credit

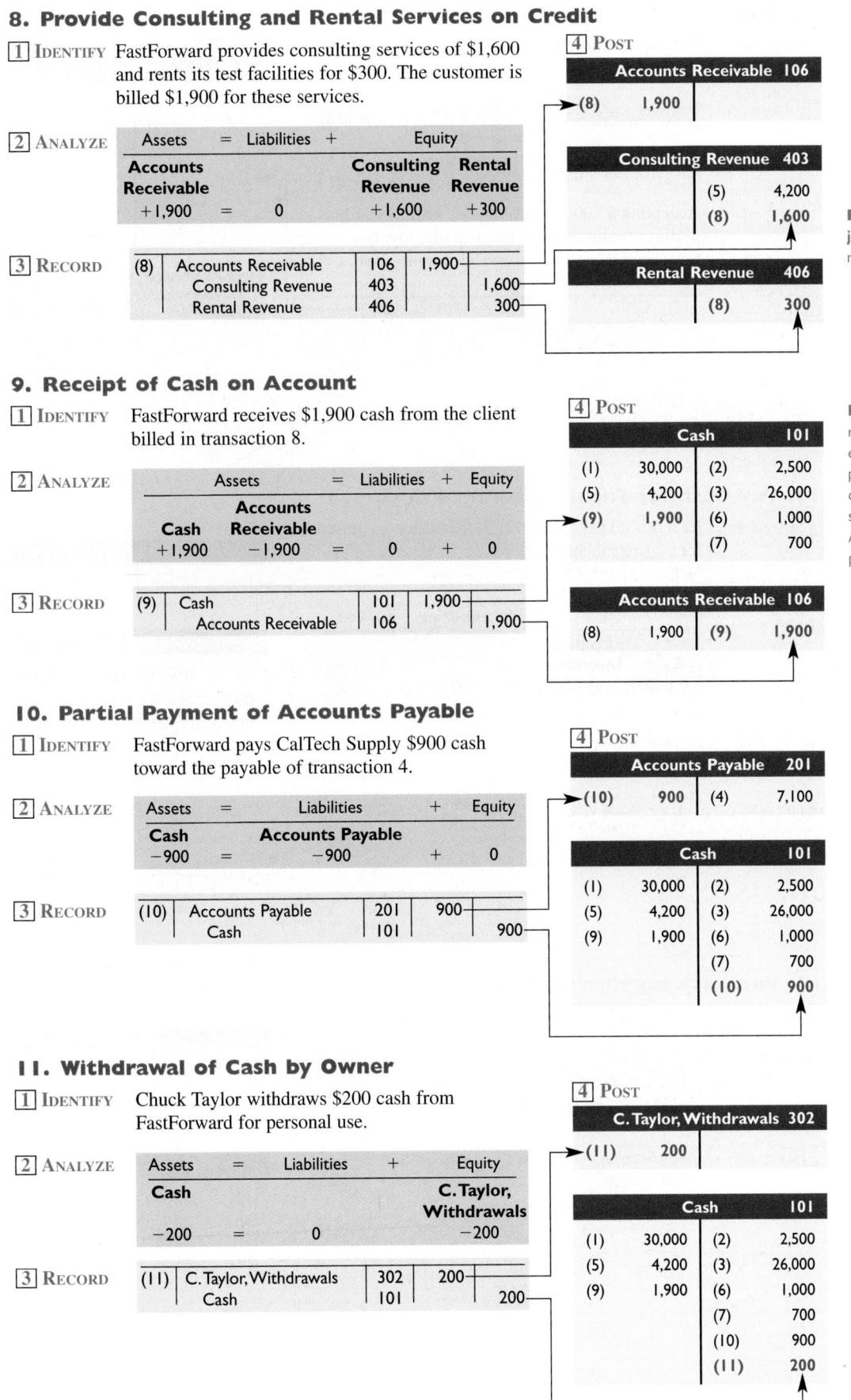

1 IDENTIFY   FastForward provides consulting services of $1,600 and rents its test facilities for $300. The customer is billed $1,900 for these services.

2 ANALYZE

Assets	=	Liabilities	+		Equity
Accounts Receivable				**Consulting Revenue**	**Rental Revenue**
+1,900	=	0		+1,600	+300

3 RECORD

(8)	Accounts Receivable	106	1,900	
	Consulting Revenue	403		1,600
	Rental Revenue	406		300

4 POST

Accounts Receivable 106

(8)	1,900	

Consulting Revenue 403

		(5)	4,200
		(8)	1,600

Point: Transaction 8 is a **compound journal entry,** which affects three or more accounts.

Rental Revenue 406

		(8)	300

9. Receipt of Cash on Account

1 IDENTIFY   FastForward receives $1,900 cash from the client billed in transaction 8.

2 ANALYZE

Assets		=	Liabilities	+	Equity
Cash	**Accounts Receivable**				
+1,900	−1,900	=	0	+	0

3 RECORD

(9)	Cash	101	1,900	
	Accounts Receivable	106		1,900

4 POST

Cash 101

(1)	30,000	(2)	2,500
(5)	4,200	(3)	26,000
(9)	1,900	(6)	1,000
		(7)	700

Accounts Receivable 106

(8)	1,900	(9)	1,900

Point: The *revenue recognition principle* requires revenue to be recognized when earned, which is when the company provides products and services to a customer. This is not necessarily the same time that the customer pays. A customer can pay before or after products or services are provided.

10. Partial Payment of Accounts Payable

1 IDENTIFY   FastForward pays CalTech Supply $900 cash toward the payable of transaction 4.

2 ANALYZE

Assets	=	Liabilities	+	Equity
Cash		**Accounts Payable**		
−900	=	−900	+	0

3 RECORD

(10)	Accounts Payable	201	900	
	Cash	101		900

4 POST

Accounts Payable 201

(10)	900	(4)	7,100

Cash 101

(1)	30,000	(2)	2,500
(5)	4,200	(3)	26,000
(9)	1,900	(6)	1,000
		(7)	700
		(10)	900

11. Withdrawal of Cash by Owner

1 IDENTIFY   Chuck Taylor withdraws $200 cash from FastForward for personal use.

2 ANALYZE

Assets	=	Liabilities	+	Equity
Cash				**C. Taylor, Withdrawals**
−200	=	0		−200

3 RECORD

(11)	C. Taylor, Withdrawals	302	200	
	Cash	101		200

4 POST

C. Taylor, Withdrawals 302

(11)	200	

Cash 101

(1)	30,000	(2)	2,500
(5)	4,200	(3)	26,000
(9)	1,900	(6)	1,000
		(7)	700
		(10)	900
		(11)	200

12. Receipt of Cash for Future Services

1 IDENTIFY   FastForward receives $3,000 cash in advance of providing consulting services to a customer.

2 ANALYZE

Assets	=	Liabilities	+	Equity
		Unearned		
Cash		**Consulting Revenue**		
+3,000	=	+3,000	+	0

Accepting $3,000 cash obligates FastForward to perform future services and is a liability. No revenue is earned until services are provided.

3 RECORD

| (12) | Cash | 101 | 3,000 | |
| | Unearned Consulting Revenue | 236 | | 3,000 |

4 POST

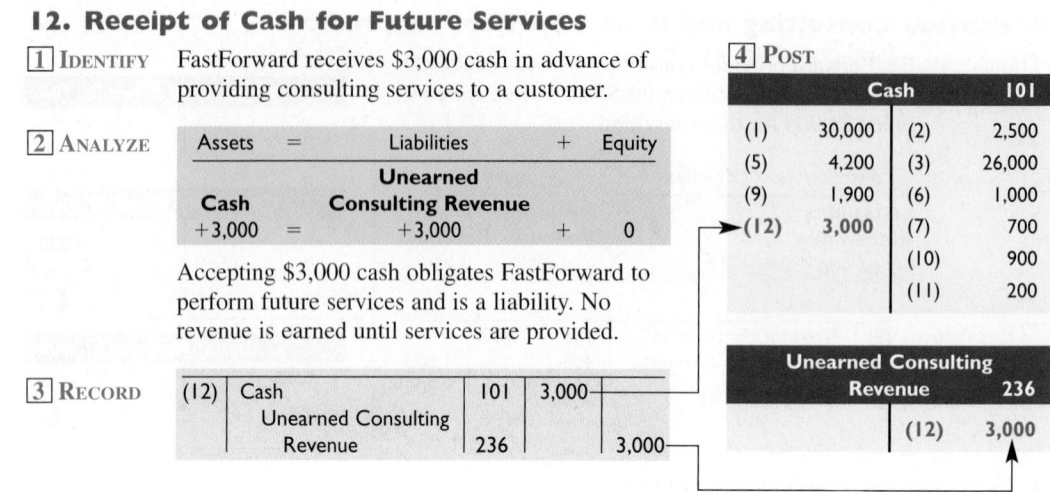

Cash		101	
(1)	30,000	(2)	2,500
(5)	4,200	(3)	26,000
(9)	1,900	(6)	1,000
(12)	3,000	(7)	700
		(10)	900
		(11)	200

Unearned Consulting Revenue		236
	(12)	3,000

13. Pay Cash for Future Insurance Coverage

1 IDENTIFY   FastForward pays $2,400 cash (insurance premium) for a 24-month insurance policy. Coverage begins on December 1.

2 ANALYZE

Assets		=	Liabilities	+	Equity
	Prepaid				
Cash	**Insurance**				
−2,400	+2,400	=	0	+	0

Changes the composition of assets from cash to prepaid insurance. Expense is incurred as insurance coverage expires.

3 RECORD

| (13) | Prepaid Insurance | 128 | 2,400 | |
| | Cash | 101 | | 2,400 |

4 POST

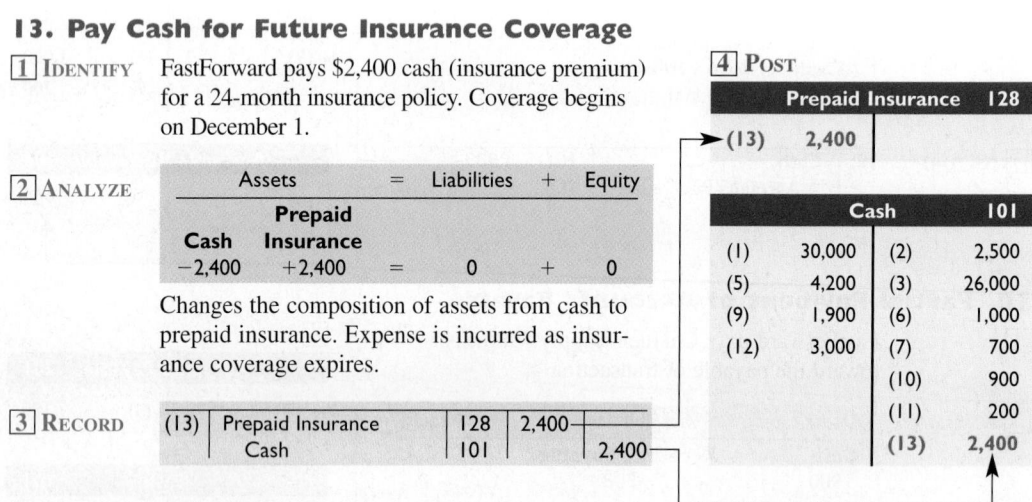

Prepaid Insurance		128
(13)	2,400	

Cash		101	
(1)	30,000	(2)	2,500
(5)	4,200	(3)	26,000
(9)	1,900	(6)	1,000
(12)	3,000	(7)	700
		(10)	900
		(11)	200
		(13)	2,400

14. Purchase Supplies for Cash

1 IDENTIFY   FastForward pays $120 cash for supplies.

2 ANALYZE

Assets		=	Liabilities	+	Equity
Cash	**Supplies**				
−120	+120	=	0	+	0

3 RECORD

| (14) | Supplies | 126 | 120 | |
| | Cash | 101 | | 120 |

4 POST

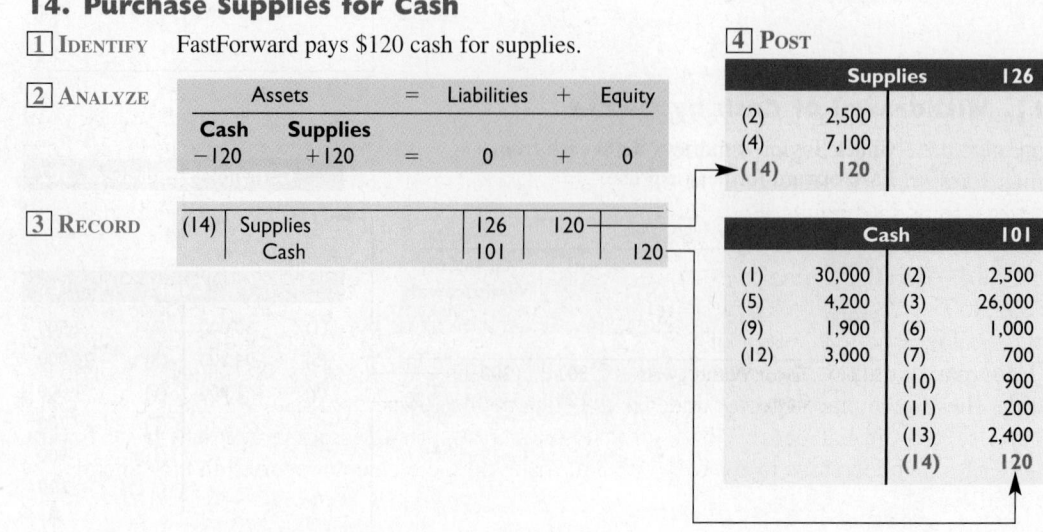

Supplies		126
(2)	2,500	
(4)	7,100	
(14)	120	

Cash		101	
(1)	30,000	(2)	2,500
(5)	4,200	(3)	26,000
(9)	1,900	(6)	1,000
(12)	3,000	(7)	700
		(10)	900
		(11)	200
		(13)	2,400
		(14)	120

15. Payment of Expense in Cash

1 IDENTIFY FastForward pays $230 cash for December utilities expense.

2 ANALYZE

3 RECORD

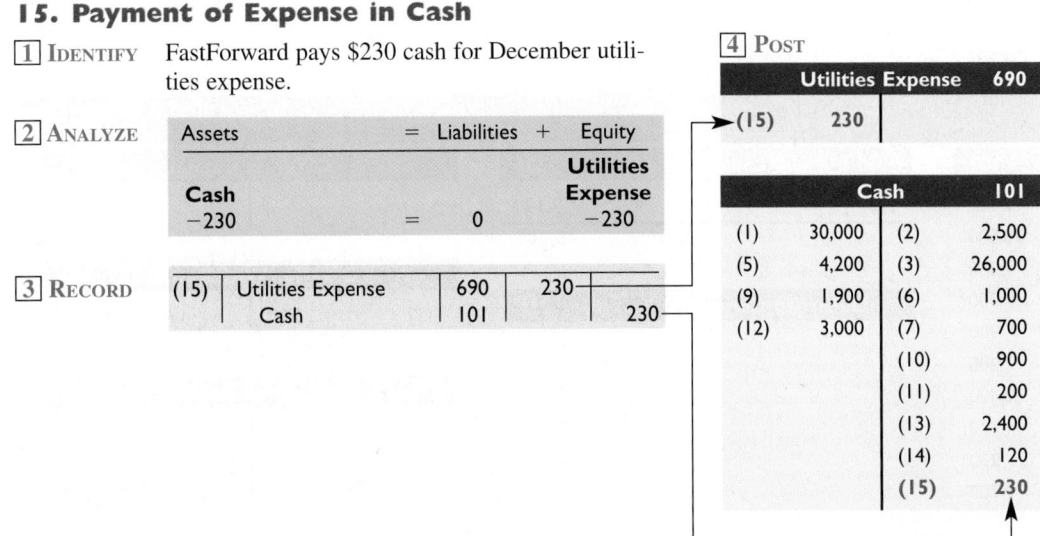

16. Payment of Expense in Cash

1 IDENTIFY FastForward pays $700 cash in employee salary for work performed in the latter part of December.

2 ANALYZE

3 RECORD

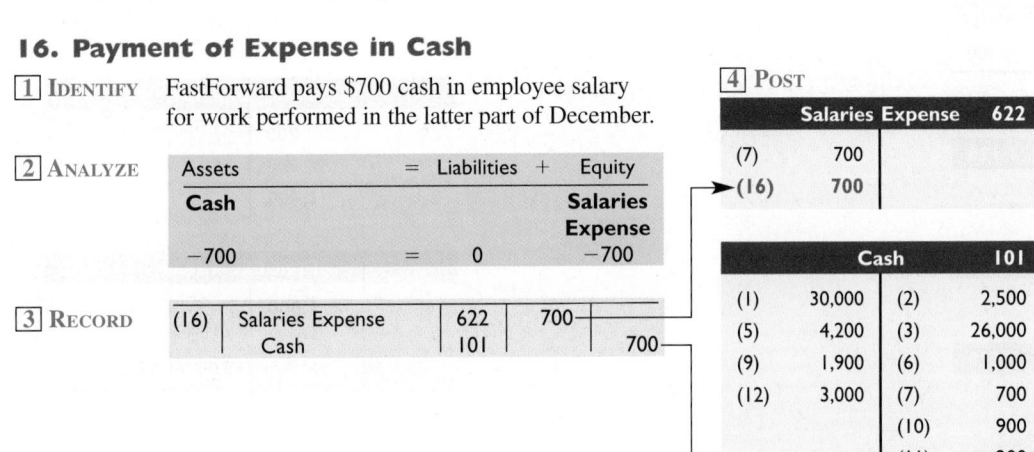

Point: We could merge transactions 15 and 16 into one *compound entry.*

Accounting Equation Analysis

Exhibit 2.13 shows the ledger accounts (in T-account form) of FastForward after all 16 transactions are recorded and posted and the balances computed. The accounts are grouped into three major columns corresponding to the accounting equation: assets, liabilities, and equity. Note several important points. First, as with each transaction, the totals for the three columns must obey the accounting equation. Specifically, assets equal $42,470 ($4,350 + $0 + $9,720 + $2,400 + $26,000); liabilities equal $9,200 ($6,200 + $3,000); and equity equals $33,270 ($30,000 − $200 + $5,800 + $300 − $1,400 − $1,000 − $230). These numbers prove the accounting equation: Assets of $42,470 = Liabilities of $9,200 + Equity of $33,270. Second, the capital, withdrawals, revenue, and expense accounts reflect the transactions that change equity. These account categories underlie the statement of owner's equity. Third, the revenue and expense account balances will be summarized and reported in the income statement. Fourth, increases and decreases in the cash account make up the elements reported in the statement of cash flows.

Point: Technology does not provide the judgment required to analyze most business transactions. Analysis requires the expertise of skilled and ethical professionals.

EXHIBIT 2.13

Ledger for FastForward (in T-Account Form)

Assets				=	Liabilities				+	Equity			

Assets

Cash   101

(1)	30,000	(2)	2,500
(5)	4,200	(3)	26,000
(9)	1,900	(6)	1,000
(12)	3,000	(7)	700
		(10)	900
		(11)	200
		(13)	2,400
		(14)	120
		(15)	230
		(16)	700
Balance	4,350		

Accounts Receivable   106

(8)	1,900	(9)	1,900
Balance	0		

Supplies   126

(2)	2,500		
(4)	7,100		
(14)	120		
Balance	9,720		

Prepaid Insurance   128

(13)	2,400		

Equipment   167

(3)	26,000		

Liabilities

Accounts Payable   201

(10)	900	(4)	7,100
		Balance	6,200

Unearned Consulting Revenue   236

		(12)	3,000

Equity

C. Taylor, Capital   301

		(1)	30,000

C. Taylor, Withdrawals   302

(11)	200		

Consulting Revenue   403

		(5)	4,200
		(8)	1,600
		Balance	5,800

Rental Revenue   406

		(8)	300

Salaries Expense   622

(7)	700		
(16)	700		
Balance	1,400		

Rent Expense   640

(6)	1,000		

Utilities Expense   690

(15)	230		

Accounts in this white area reflect those reported on the income statement.

$42,470	=	$9,200	+	$33,270

Quick Check

Answers—p. 72

8. What types of transactions increase equity? What types decrease equity?

9. Why are accounting systems called *double-entry*?

10. For each transaction, double-entry accounting requires which of the following? (*a*) Debits to asset accounts must create credits to liability or equity accounts, (*b*) a debit to a liability account must create a credit to an asset account, or (*c*) total debits must equal total credits.

11. An owner invests $15,000 cash along with equipment having a market value of $23,000 in a company. Prepare the necessary journal entry.

12. Explain what a compound journal entry is.

13. Why are posting reference numbers entered in the journal when entries are posted to ledger accounts?

Trial Balance

Double-entry accounting requires the sum of debit account balances to equal the sum of credit account balances. A trial balance is used to verify this. A **trial balance** is a list of accounts and their balances at a point in time. Account balances are reported in the appropriate debit or credit column of a trial balance. Exhibit 2.14 shows the trial balance for FastForward after its 16 entries have been posted to the ledger. (This is an *unadjusted* trial balance—Chapter 3 explains the necessary adjustments.)

Video2.1

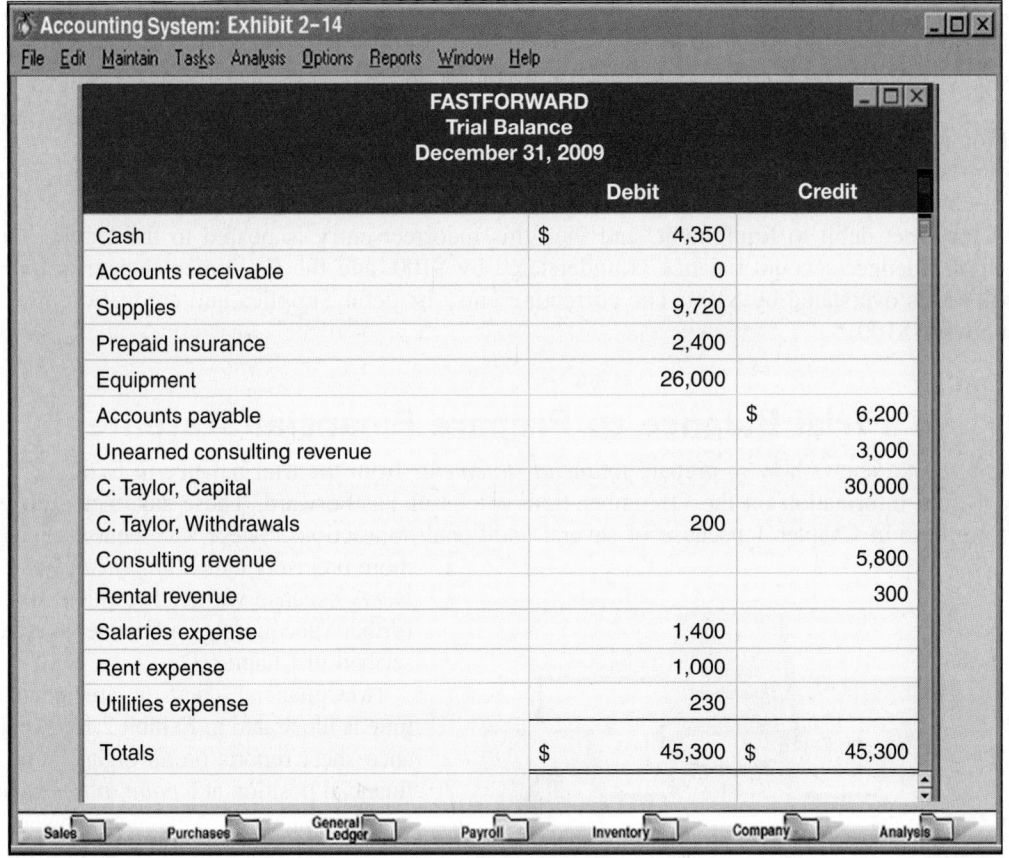

EXHIBIT 2.14

Trial Balance (Unadjusted)

FASTFORWARD
Trial Balance
December 31, 2009

	Debit	Credit
Cash	$ 4,350	
Accounts receivable	0	
Supplies	9,720	
Prepaid insurance	2,400	
Equipment	26,000	
Accounts payable		$ 6,200
Unearned consulting revenue		3,000
C. Taylor, Capital		30,000
C. Taylor, Withdrawals	200	
Consulting revenue		5,800
Rental revenue		300
Salaries expense	1,400	
Rent expense	1,000	
Utilities expense	230	
Totals	$ 45,300	$ 45,300

Point: The ordering of accounts in a trial balance typically follows their identification number from the chart of accounts.

Preparing a Trial Balance

Preparing a trial balance involves three steps:

P2 Prepare and explain the use of a trial balance.

1. List each account title and its amount (from ledger) in the trial balance. If an account has a zero balance, list it with a zero in its normal balance column (or omit it entirely).
2. Compute the total of debit balances and the total of credit balances.
3. Verify (*prove*) total debit balances equal total credit balances.

The total of debit balances equals the total of credit balances for the trial balance in Exhibit 2.14. Equality of these two totals does not guarantee that no errors were made. For example, the column totals still will be equal when a debit or credit of a correct amount is made to a wrong account. Another error that does not cause unequal column totals is when equal debits and credits of an incorrect amount are entered.

Searching for and Correcting Errors   If the trial balance does not balance (when its columns are not equal), the error (or errors) must be found and corrected. An efficient

Point: A trial balance is *not* a financial statement but a mechanism for checking equality of debits and credits in the ledger. Financial statements do not have debit and credit columns.

way to search for an error is to check the journalizing, posting, and trial balance preparation in *reverse order.* Step 1 is to verify that the trial balance columns are correctly added. If step 1 fails to find the error, step 2 is to verify that account balances are accurately entered from the ledger. Step 3 is to see whether a debit (or credit) balance is mistakenly listed in the trial balance as a credit (or debit). A clue to this error is when the difference between total debits and total credits equals twice the amount of the incorrect account balance. If the error is still undiscovered, Step 4 is to recompute each account balance in the ledger. Step 5 is to verify that each journal entry is properly posted. Step 6 is to verify that the original journal entry has equal debits and credits. At this point, the errors should be uncovered.[3]

If an error in a journal entry is discovered before the error is posted, it can be corrected in a manual system by drawing a line through the incorrect information. The correct information is written above it to create a record of change for the auditor. Many computerized systems allow the operator to replace the incorrect information directly.

If an error in a journal entry is not discovered until after it is posted, we do not strike through both erroneous entries in the journal and ledger. Instead, we correct this error by creating a *correcting entry* that removes the amount from the wrong account and records it to the correct account. As an example, suppose a $100 purchase of supplies is journalized with an incorrect debit to Equipment, and then this incorrect entry is posted to the ledger. The Supplies ledger account balance is understated by $100, and the Equipment ledger account balance is overstated by $100. The correcting entry is: debit Supplies and credit Equipment (both for $100).

Using a Trial Balance to Prepare Financial Statements

This section shows how to prepare *financial statements* from the trial balance in Exhibit 2.14 and from information on the December transactions of FastForward. These statements differ from those in Chapter 1 because of several additional transactions. These statements are also more precisely called *unadjusted statements* because we need to make some further accounting adjustments (described in Chapter 3).

EXHIBIT 2.15

Links between Financial Statements across Time

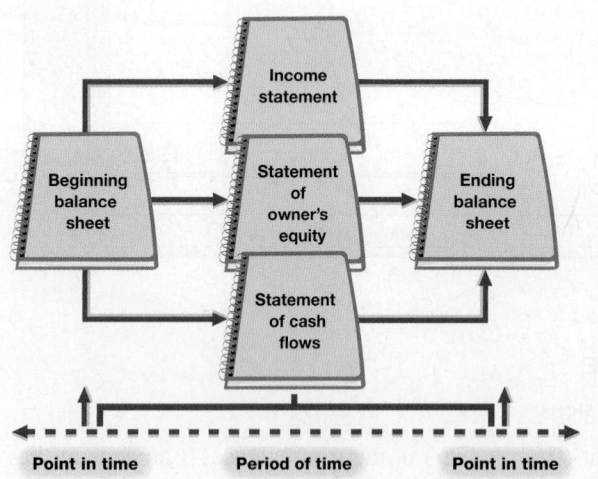

How financial statements are linked in time is illustrated in Exhibit 2.15. A balance sheet reports on an organization's financial position at a *point in time.* The income statement, statement of owner's equity, and statement of cash flows report on financial performance over a *period of time.* The three statements in the middle column of Exhibit 2.15 link balance sheets from the beginning to the end of a reporting period. They explain how financial position changes from one point to another.

---

[3] *Transposition* occurs when two digits are switched, or transposed, within a number. If transposition is the only error, it yields a difference between the two trial balance totals that is evenly divisible by 9. For example, assume that a $691 debit in an entry is incorrectly posted to the ledger as $619. Total credits in the trial balance are then larger than total debits by $72 ($691 − $619). The $72 error is *evenly* divisible by 9 (72/9 = 8). The first digit of the quotient (in our example it is 8) equals the difference between the digits of the two transposed numbers (the 9 and the 1). The number of digits in the quotient also tells the location of the transposition, starting from the right. The quotient in our example had only one digit (8), so it tells us the transposition is in the first digit. Consider another example where a transposition error involves posting $961 instead of the correct $691. The difference in these numbers is $270, and its quotient is 30 (270/9). The quotient has two digits, so it tells us to check the second digit from the right for a transposition of two numbers that have a difference of 3.

Preparers and users (including regulatory agencies) determine the length of the reporting period. A one-year, or annual, reporting period is common, as are semiannual, quarterly, and monthly periods. The one-year reporting period is known as the *accounting, or fiscal, year*. Businesses whose accounting year begins on January 1 and ends on December 31 are known as *calendar-year* companies. Many companies choose a fiscal year ending on a date other than December 31. **Best Buy** is a *noncalendar-year* company as reflected in the headings of its March 3 year-end financial statements in Appendix A near the end of the book.

Income Statement An income statement reports the revenues earned less the expenses incurred by a business over a period of time. FastForward's income statement for December is shown at the top of Exhibit 2.16. Information about revenues and expenses is conveniently taken from the trial balance in Exhibit 2.14. Net income of $3,470 is reported at the bottom of the statement. Owner investments and withdrawals are *not* part of income.

Statement of Owner's Equity The statement of owner's equity reports information about how equity changes over the reporting period. FastForward's statement of owner's

EXHIBIT 2.16

Financial Statements and Their Links

FASTFORWARD Income Statement For Month Ended December 31, 2009		
Revenues		
Consulting revenue ($4,200 + $1,600)	$ 5,800	
Rental revenue	300	
Total revenues		$ 6,100
Expenses		
Rent expense	1,000	
Salaries expense	1,400	
Utilities expense	230	
Total expenses		2,630
Net income		$ 3,470

FASTFORWARD Statement of Owner's Equity For Month Ended December 31, 2009		
C. Taylor, Capital, December 1, 2009		$ 0
Plus: Investments by owner	$30,000	
Net income	3,470	33,470
		33,470
Less: Withdrawals by owner		200
C. Taylor, Capital, December 31, 2009		$33,270

FASTFORWARD Balance Sheet December 31, 2009			
Assets		**Liabilities**	
Cash	$ 4,350	Accounts payable	$ 6,200
Supplies	9,720	Unearned revenue	3,000
Prepaid insurance . .	2,400	Total liabilities	9,200
Equipment	26,000	**Equity**	
		C. Taylor, Capital	33,270
Total assets	$42,470	Total liabilities and equity .	$ 42,470

equity is the second report in Exhibit 2.16. It shows the $30,000 owner investment, the $3,470 of net income, the $200 withdrawal, and the $33,270 end-of-period (capital) balance. (The beginning balance in the statement of owner's equity is rarely zero; an exception is for the first period of operations. The beginning capital balance in January 2010 is $33,270, which is December's ending balance.)

<aside>**Point:** An income statement is also called an *earnings statement, a statement of operations,* or a *P&L* (profit and loss) *statement.* A balance sheet is also called a *statement of financial position.*</aside>

<aside>**Point:** While revenues increase equity, and expenses decrease equity, the amounts are not reported in detail in the statement of owner's equity. Instead, their effects are reflected through net income.</aside>

Balance Sheet   The balance sheet reports the financial position of a company at a point in time, usually at the end of a month, quarter, or year. FastForward's balance sheet is the third report in Exhibit 2.16. This statement refers to financial condition at the close of business on December 31. The left side of the balance sheet lists its assets: cash, supplies, prepaid insurance, and equipment. The upper right side of the balance sheet shows that it owes $6,200 to creditors and $3,000 in services to customers who paid in advance. The equity section shows an ending balance of $33,270. Note the link between the ending balance of the statement of owner's equity and the capital balance here. (Recall that this presentation of the balance sheet is called the *account form:* assets on the left and liabilities and equity on the right. Another presentation is the *report form:* assets on top, followed by liabilities and then equity. Either presentation is acceptable.)

♟ Decision Maker

Entrepreneur   You open a wholesale business selling entertainment equipment to retail outlets. You find that most of your customers demand to buy on credit. How can you use the balance sheets of these customers to decide which ones to extend credit to? [Answer—p. 71]

<aside>**Point:** Knowing how financial statements are prepared improves our analysis of them.</aside>

Presentation Issues   Dollar signs are not used in journals and ledgers. They do appear in financial statements and other reports such as trial balances. The usual practice is to put dollar signs beside only the first and last numbers in a column. **Best Buy**'s financial statements in Appendix A show this. When amounts are entered in a journal, ledger, or trial balance, commas are optional to indicate thousands, millions, and so forth. However, commas are always used in financial statements. Companies also commonly round amounts in reports to the nearest dollar, or even to a higher level. Best Buy is typical of many companies in that it rounds its financial statement amounts to the nearest million. This decision is based on the perceived impact of rounding for users' business decisions.

Quick Check   Answers—p. 72

14. Where are dollar signs typically entered in financial statements?
15. If a $4,000 debit to Equipment in a journal entry is incorrectly posted to the ledger as a $4,000 credit, and the ledger account has a resulting debit balance of $20,000, what is the effect of this error on the Trial Balance column totals?
16. Describe the link between the income statement and the statement of owner's equity.
17. Explain the link between the balance sheet and the statement of owner's equity.
18. Define and describe revenues and expenses.
19. Define and describe assets, liabilities, and equity.

♟ Decision Analysis   Debt Ratio

A2 Compute the debt ratio and describe its use in analyzing financial condition.

An important business objective is gathering information to help assess a company's risk of failing to pay its debts. Companies finance their assets with either liabilities or equity. A company that finances a relatively large portion of its assets with liabilities is said to have a high degree of *financial leverage.* Higher financial leverage involves greater risk because liabilities must be repaid and often require regular interest payments (equity financing does not). The risk that a company might not be able to meet such required payments is higher if it has more liabilities (is more highly leveraged). One way to assess the risk associated with a company's use of liabilities is to compute the **debt ratio** as in Exhibit 2.17.

$$\text{Debt ratio} = \frac{\text{Total liabilities}}{\text{Total assets}}$$

EXHIBIT 2.17

Debt Ratio

To see how to apply the debt ratio, let's look at Skechers's liabilities and assets. The company designs, markets, and sells footwear for men, women, and children under the Skechers brand. Exhibit 2.18 computes and reports its debt ratio at the end of each year from 2002 to 2006.

Point: Compare the equity amount to the liability amount to assess the extent of owner versus nonowner financing.

EXHIBIT 2.18

Computation and Analysis of Debt Ratio

$ in millions	2006	2005	2004	2003	2002
Total liabilities	$288	$238	$224	$211	$224
Total assets	$737	$582	$519	$467	$483
Debt ratio	0.39	0.41	0.43	0.45	0.46
Industry debt ratio	0.48	0.47	0.48	0.46	0.45

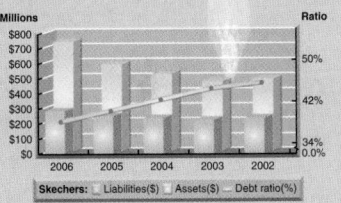

Skechers's debt ratio ranges from a low of 0.39 to a high of 0.46—also, see graph in margin. Its ratio is slightly lower, and has been declining, compared with the industry ratio. This analysis implies a low risk from its financial leverage. Is financial leverage good or bad for Skechers? To answer that question we need to compare the company's return on the borrowed money to the rate it is paying creditors. If the company's return is higher, it is successfully borrowing money to make more money. A company's success with making money from borrowed money can quickly turn unprofitable if its own return drops below the rate it is paying creditors.

Decision Maker

Investor You consider buying stock in Converse. As part of your analysis, you compute its debt ratio for 2006, 2007, and 2008 as: 0.35, 0.74, and 0.94, respectively. Based on the debt ratio, is Converse a low-risk investment? Has the risk of buying Converse stock changed over this period? (The industry debt ratio averages 0.40.) [Answer—p. 71]

Demonstration Problem

(This problem extends the demonstration problem of Chapter 1.) After several months of planning, Jasmine Worthy started a haircutting business called Expressions. The following events occurred during its first month.

DP2

a. On August 1, Worthy invested $3,000 cash and $15,000 of equipment in Expressions.
b. On August 2, Expressions paid $600 cash for furniture for the shop.
c. On August 3, Expressions paid $500 cash to rent space in a strip mall for August.
d. On August 4, it purchased $1,200 of equipment on credit for the shop (using a long-term note payable).
e. On August 5, Expressions opened for business. Cash received from haircutting services in the first week and a half of business (ended August 15) was $825.
f. On August 15, it provided $100 of haircutting services on account.
g. On August 17, it received a $100 check for services previously rendered on account.
h. On August 17, it paid $125 to an assistant for hours worked during the grand opening.
i. Cash received from services provided during the second half of August was $930.
j. On August 31, it paid a $400 installment toward principal on the note payable entered into on August 4.
k. On August 31, Worthy withdrew $900 cash for personal use.

Required

1. Open the following ledger accounts in balance column format (account numbers are in parentheses): Cash (101); Accounts Receivable (102); Furniture (161); Store Equipment (165); Note Payable (240); J. Worthy, Capital (301); J. Worthy, Withdrawals (302); Haircutting Services Revenue (403); Wages Expense (623); and Rent Expense (640). Prepare general journal entries for the transactions.

2. Post the journal entries from (1) to the ledger accounts.

3. Prepare a trial balance as of August 31.

4. Prepare an income statement for August.

5. Prepare a statement of owner's equity for August.

6. Prepare a balance sheet as of August 31.

7. Determine the debt ratio as of August 31.

Extended Analysis

8. In the coming months, Expressions will experience a greater variety of business transactions. Identify which accounts are debited and which are credited for the following transactions. (*Hint:* We must use some accounts not opened in part 1.)

    a. Purchase supplies with cash.

    b. Pay cash for future insurance coverage.

    c. Receive cash for services to be provided in the future.

    d. Purchase supplies on account.

Planning the Solution

- Analyze each transaction and use the debit and credit rules to prepare a journal entry for each.
- Post each debit and each credit from journal entries to their ledger accounts and cross-reference each amount in the posting reference (PR) columns of the journal and ledger.
- Calculate each account balance and list the accounts with their balances on a trial balance.
- Verify that total debits in the trial balance equal total credits.
- To prepare the income statement, identify revenues and expenses. List those items on the statement, compute the difference, and label the result as *net income* or *net loss*.
- Use information in the ledger to prepare the statement of owner's equity.
- Use information in the ledger to prepare the balance sheet.
- Calculate the debt ratio by dividing total liabilities by total assets.
- Analyze the future transactions to identify the accounts affected and apply debit and credit rules.

Solution to Demonstration Problem

1. General journal entries:

GENERAL JOURNAL   Page 1

Date	Account Titles and Explanation	PR	Debit	Credit
Aug. 1	Cash	101	3,000	
	Store Equipment	165	15,000	
	J. Worthy, Capital	301		18,000
	Owner's investment.			
2	Furniture	161	600	
	Cash	101		600
	Purchased furniture for cash.			
3	Rent Expense	640	500	
	Cash	101		500
	Paid rent for August.			
4	Store Equipment	165	1,200	
	Note Payable	240		1,200
	Purchased additional equipment on credit.			

[continued on next page]

[continued from previous page]

Date	Account	PR	Debit	Credit
15	Cash	101	825	
	Haircutting Services Revenue	403		825
	Cash receipts from first half of August.			
15	Accounts Receivable	102	100	
	Haircutting Services Revenue	403		100
	To record revenue for services provided on account.			
17	Cash	101	100	
	Accounts Receivable	102		100
	To record cash received as payment on account.			
17	Wages Expense	623	125	
	Cash	101		125
	Paid wages to assistant.			
31	Cash	101	930	
	Haircutting Services Revenue	403		930
	Cash receipts from second half of August.			
31	Note Payable	240	400	
	Cash	101		400
	Paid an installment on the note payable.			
31	J. Worthy, Withdrawals	302	900	
	Cash	101		900
	Cash withdrawal by owner.			

2. Post journal entries from part 1 to the ledger accounts:

General Ledger

Cash — Account No. 101

Date	PR	Debit	Credit	Balance
Aug. 1	G1	3,000		3,000
2	G1		600	2,400
3	G1		500	1,900
15	G1	825		2,725
17	G1	100		2,825
17	G1		125	2,700
31	G1	930		3,630
31	G1		400	3,230
31	G1		900	2,330

Accounts Receivable — Account No. 102

Date	PR	Debit	Credit	Balance
Aug. 15	G1	100		100
17	G1		100	0

Furniture — Account No. 161

Date	PR	Debit	Credit	Balance
Aug. 2	G1	600		600

Store Equipment — Account No. 165

Date	PR	Debit	Credit	Balance
Aug. 1	G1	15,000		15,000
4	G1	1,200		16,200

Note Payable — Account No. 240

Date	PR	Debit	Credit	Balance
Aug. 4	G1		1,200	1,200
31	G1	400		800

J. Worthy, Capital — Account No. 301

Date	PR	Debit	Credit	Balance
Aug. 1	G1		18,000	18,000

J. Worthy, Withdrawals — Account No. 302

Date	PR	Debit	Credit	Balance
Aug. 31	G1	900		900

Haircutting Services Revenue — Account No. 403

Date	PR	Debit	Credit	Balance
Aug. 15	G1		825	825
15	G1		100	925
31	G1		930	1,855

Wages Expense — Account No. 623

Date	PR	Debit	Credit	Balance
Aug. 17	G1	125		125

Rent Expense — Account No. 640

Date	PR	Debit	Credit	Balance
Aug. 3	G1	500		500

3. Prepare a trial balance from the ledger:

EXPRESSIONS
Trial Balance
August 31

	Debit	Credit
Cash	$ 2,330	
Accounts receivable	0	
Furniture	600	
Store equipment	16,200	
Note payable		$ 800
J. Worthy, Capital		18,000
J. Worthy, Withdrawals	900	
Haircutting services revenue		1,855
Wages expense	125	
Rent expense	500	
Totals	$20,655	$20,655

4.

EXPRESSIONS
Income Statement
For Month Ended August 31

Revenues		
Haircutting services revenue		$1,855
Operating expenses		
Rent expense	$500	
Wages expense	125	
Total operating expenses		625
Net income		$1,230

5.

EXPRESSIONS
Statement of Owner's Equity
For Month Ended August 31

J. Worthy, Capital, August 1		$ 0
Plus: Investments by owner	$18,000	
Net income	1,230	19,230
		19,230
Less: Withdrawals by owner		900
J. Worthy, Capital, August 31		$18,330

6.

EXPRESSIONS
Balance Sheet
August 31

Assets		Liabilities	
Cash	$ 2,330	Note payable	$ 800
Furniture	600	**Equity**	
Store equipment	16,200	J. Worthy, Capital	18,330
Total assets	$19,130	Total liabilities and equity	$19,130

7. Debt ratio $= \dfrac{\text{Total liabilities}}{\text{Total assets}} = \dfrac{\$800}{\$19,130} = \underline{\underline{\mathbf{4.18}\%}}$

8a. Supplies *debited*
　　　Cash *credited*

8b. Prepaid Insurance *debited*
　　　Cash *credited*

8c. Cash *debited*
　　　Unearned Services Revenue *credited*

8d. Supplies *debited*
　　　Accounts Payable *credited*

Summary

C1 Explain the steps in processing transactions. The accounting process identifies business transactions and events, analyzes and records their effects, and summarizes and prepares information useful in making decisions. Transactions and events are the starting points in the accounting process. Source documents help in their analysis. The effects of transactions and events are recorded in journals. Posting along with a trial balance helps summarize and classify these effects.

C2 Describe source documents and their purpose. Source documents identify and describe transactions and events. Examples are sales tickets, checks, purchase orders, bills, and bank statements. Source documents provide objective and reliable evidence, making information more useful.

C3 Describe an account and its use in recording transactions. An account is a detailed record of increases and decreases in a specific asset, liability, equity, revenue, or expense. Information from accounts is analyzed, summarized, and presented in reports and financial statements for decision makers.

C4 Describe a ledger and a chart of accounts. The ledger (or general ledger) is a record containing all accounts used by a company and their balances. It is referred to as the *books*. The chart of accounts is a list of all accounts and usually includes an identification number assigned to each account.

C5 Define *debits* and *credits* and explain double-entry accounting. *Debit* refers to left, and *credit* refers to right. Debits increase assets, expenses, and withdrawals while credits decrease them. Credits increase liabilities, owner capital, and revenues; debits decrease them. Double-entry accounting means each transaction affects at least two accounts and has at least one debit and one credit. The system for recording debits and credits follows from the accounting equation. The left side of an account is the normal balance for assets, withdrawals, and expenses, and the right side is the normal balance for liabilities, capital, and revenues.

A1 Analyze the impact of transactions on accounts and financial statements. We analyze transactions using concepts of double-entry accounting. This analysis is performed by determining a transaction's effects on accounts. These effects are recorded in journals and posted to ledgers.

A2 Compute the debt ratio and describe its use in analyzing financial condition. A company's debt ratio is computed as total liabilities divided by total assets. It reveals how much of the assets are financed by creditor (nonowner) financing. The higher this ratio, the more risk a company faces because liabilities must be repaid at specific dates.

P1 Record transactions in a journal and post entries to a ledger. Transactions are recorded in a journal. Each entry in a journal is posted to the accounts in the ledger. This provides information that is used to produce financial statements. Balance column accounts are widely used and include columns for debits, credits, and the account balance.

P2 Prepare and explain the use of a trial balance. A trial balance is a list of accounts from the ledger showing their debit or credit balances in separate columns. The trial balance is a summary of the ledger's contents and is useful in preparing financial statements and in revealing recordkeeping errors.

P3 Prepare financial statements from business transactions. The balance sheet, the statement of owner's equity, the income statement, and the statement of cash flows use data from the trial balance (and other financial statements) for their preparation.

Guidance Answers to **Decision Maker** and **Decision Ethics**

Cashier The advantages to the process proposed by the assistant manager include improved customer service, fewer delays, and less work for you. However, you should have serious concerns about internal control and the potential for fraud. In particular, the assistant manager could steal cash and simply enter fewer sales to match the remaining cash. You should reject her suggestion without the manager's approval. Moreover, you should have an ethical concern about the assistant manager's suggestion to ignore store policy.

Entrepreneur We can use the accounting equation (Assets = Liabilities + Equity) to help us identify risky customers to whom we would likely not want to extend credit. A balance sheet provides amounts for each of these key components. The lower a customer's equity is relative to liabilities, the less likely you would extend credit. A low equity means the business has little value that does not already have creditor claims to it.

Investor The debt ratio suggests the stock of Converse is of higher risk than normal and that this risk is rising. The average industry ratio of 0.40 further supports this conclusion. The 2008 debt ratio for Converse is twice the industry norm. Also, a debt ratio approaching 1.0 indicates little to no equity.

Guidance Answers to **Quick Checks**

1. Examples of source documents are sales tickets, checks, purchase orders, charges to customers, bills from suppliers, employee earnings records, and bank statements.

2. Source documents serve many purposes, including record-keeping and internal control. Source documents, especially if obtained from outside the organization, provide objective and reliable evidence about transactions and their amounts.

3.

Assets	Liabilities	Equity
a,c,e	b,d	—

4. An account is a record in an accounting system that records and stores the increases and decreases in a specific asset, liability, equity, revenue, or expense. The ledger is a collection of all the accounts of a company.

5. A company's size and diversity affect the number of accounts in its accounting system. The types of accounts depend on information the company needs to both effectively operate and report its activities in financial statements.

6. No. Debit and credit both can mean increase or decrease. The particular meaning in a circumstance depends on the *type of account*. For example, a debit increases the balance of asset, withdrawals, and expense accounts, but it decreases the balance of liability, capital, and revenue accounts.

7. A chart of accounts is a list of all of a company's accounts and their identification numbers.

8. Equity is increased by revenues and by owner investments. Equity is decreased by expenses and owner withdrawals.

9. The name *double-entry* is used because all transactions affect at least two accounts. There must be at least one debit in one account and at least one credit in another account.

10. The answer is (c).

11.

Cash	15,000	
Equipment	23,000	
Owner, Capital		38,000
Investment by owner of cash and equipment.		

12. A compound journal entry affects three or more accounts.

13. Posting reference numbers are entered in the journal when posting to the ledger as a cross-reference that allows the record-keeper or auditor to trace debits and credits from one record to another.

14. At a minimum, dollar signs are placed beside the first and last numbers in a column. It is also common to place dollar signs beside any amount that appears after a ruled line to indicate that an addition or subtraction has occurred.

15. The Equipment account balance is incorrectly reported at $20,000—it should be $28,000. The effect of this error understates the trial balance's Debit column total by $8,000. This results in an $8,000 difference between the column totals.

16. An income statement reports a company's revenues and expenses along with the resulting net income or loss. A statement of owner's equity reports changes in equity, including that from net income or loss. Both statements report transactions occurring over a period of time.

17. The balance sheet describes a company's financial position (assets, liabilities, and equity) at a point in time. The capital amount in the balance sheet is obtained from the statement of owner's equity.

18. Revenues are inflows of assets in exchange for products or services provided to customers as part of the main operations of a business. Expenses are outflows or the using up of assets that result from providing products or services to customers.

19. Assets are the resources a business owns or controls that carry expected future benefits. Liabilities are the obligations of a business, representing the claims of others against the assets of a business. Equity reflects the owner's claims on the assets of the business after deducting liabilities.

Key Terms

mhhe.com/wildFAP19e

Key Terms are available at the book's Website for learning and testing in an online Flashcard Format.

Account (p. 49)

Account balance (p. 53)

Balance column account (p. 56)

Chart of accounts (p. 52)

Compound journal entry (p. 59)

Credit (p. 53)

Creditors (p. 50)

Debit (p. 53)

Debtors (p. 49)

Debt ratio (p. 67)

Double-entry accounting (p. 53)

General journal (p. 54)

General ledger (p. 49)

Journal (p. 54)

Journalizing (p. 54)

Ledger (p. 49)

Posting (p. 54)

Posting reference (PR) column (p. 56)

Source documents (p. 48)

T-account (p. 53)

Trial balance (p. 63)

Unearned revenue (p. 50)

Multiple Choice Quiz   Answers on p. 89   **mhhe.com/wildFAP19e**

Additional Quiz Questions are available at the book's Website.

Quiz2

1. Amalia Company received its utility bill for the current period of $700 and immediately paid it. Its journal entry to record this transaction includes a
  a. Credit to Utility Expense for $700.
  b. Debit to Utility Expense for $700.
  c. Debit to Accounts Payable for $700.
  d. Debit to Cash for $700.
  e. Credit to capital for $700.

2. On May 1, Mattingly Lawn Service collected $2,500 cash from a customer in advance of five months of lawn service. Mattingly's journal entry to record this transaction includes a
  a. Credit to Unearned Lawn Service Fees for $2,500.
  b. Debit to Lawn Service Fees Earned for $2,500.
  c. Credit to Cash for $2,500.
  d. Debit to Unearned Lawn Service Fees for $2,500.
  e. Credit to capital for $2,500.

3. Liang Shue contributed $250,000 cash and land worth $500,000 to open his new business, Shue Consulting. Which of the following journal entries does Shue Consulting make to record this transaction?
  a. Cash Assets 750,000
      L. Shue, Capital   750,000
  b. L. Shue, Capital 750,000
      Assets   750,000
  c. Cash 250,000
      Land 500,000
      L. Shue, Capital   750,000

  d. L. Shue, Capital . . . 750,000
      Cash   250,000
      Land   500,000

4. A trial balance prepared at year-end shows total credits exceed total debits by $765. This discrepancy could have been caused by
  a. An error in the general journal where a $765 increase in Accounts Payable was recorded as a $765 decrease in Accounts Payable.
  b. The ledger balance for Accounts Payable of $7,650 being entered in the trial balance as $765.
  c. A general journal error where a $765 increase in Accounts Receivable was recorded as a $765 increase in Cash.
  d. The ledger balance of $850 in Accounts Receivable was entered in the trial balance as $85.
  e. An error in recording a $765 increase in Cash as a credit.

5. Bonaventure Company has total assets of $1,000,000, liabilities of $400,000, and equity of $600,000. What is its debt ratio (rounded to a whole percent)?
  a. 250%
  b. 167%
  c. 67%
  d. 150%
  e. 40%

Discussion Questions

1. Provide the names of two (*a*) asset accounts, (*b*) liability accounts, and (*c*) equity accounts.

2. What is the difference between a note payable and an account payable?

3. ♟ Discuss the steps in processing business transactions.

4. What kinds of transactions can be recorded in a general journal?

5. Are debits or credits typically listed first in general journal entries? Are the debits or the credits indented?

6. If assets are valuable resources and asset accounts have debit balances, why do expense accounts also have debit balances?

7. Should a transaction be recorded first in a journal or the ledger? Why?

8. ♟ Why does the recordkeeper prepare a trial balance?

9. If an incorrect amount is journalized and posted to the accounts, how should the error be corrected?

10. Identify the four financial statements of a business.

11. ♟ What information is reported in an income statement?

12. ♟ Why does the user of an income statement need to know the time period that it covers?

13. ♟ What information is reported in a balance sheet?

14. Define (*a*) *assets,* (*b*) *liabilities,* (*c*) *equity,* and (*d*) *net assets.*

15. Which financial statement is sometimes called the *statement of financial position?*

16. ♟ Review the Best Buy balance sheet in Appendix A. Identify three accounts on its balance sheet that carry debit balances and three accounts on its balance sheet that carry credit balances.

17. Refer to Circuit City's balance sheet in Appendix A. What does Circuit City title its current liability for the purchase of merchandise?

18. Review the RadioShack balance sheet in Appendix A. Identify an asset with the word *receivable* in its account title and a liability with the word *payable* in its account title.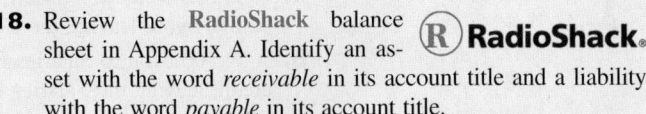

19. Locate Apple's income statement in Appendix A. What is the title of its revenue account?

♟ *Denotes Discussion Questions that involve decision making.*

QUICK STUDY

QS 2-1

Identifying source documents

C2

Identify the items from the following list that are likely to serve as source documents.

a. Trial balance   **d.** Income statement   **g.** Prepaid insurance

b. Telephone bill   **e.** Company revenue account **h.** Bank statement

c. Sales ticket   **f.** Invoice from supplier   **i.** Balance sheet

---

QS 2-2

Identifying financial statement items

C3 P3

Identify the financial statement(s) where each of the following items appears. Use I for income statement, E for statement of owner's equity, and B for balance sheet.

a. Service fees earned   **d.** Accounts payable   **g.** Office supplies

b. Cash withdrawal by owner **e.** Cash   **h.** Prepaid rent

c. Office equipment   **f.** Utilities expenses   **i.** Unearned fees

---

QS 2-3

Identifying normal balance

C5

Identify the normal balance (debit or credit) for each of the following accounts.

a. Office supplies   **d.** Wages Expense   **g.** Wages Payable

b. Owner Withdrawals   **e.** Cash   **h.** Building

c. Fees Earned   **f.** Prepaid Insurance **i.** Owner Capital

---

QS 2-4

Linking debit or credit with normal balance

C5

Indicate whether a debit or credit *decreases* the normal balance of each of the following accounts.

a. Repair Services Revenue **e.** Owner Capital   **i.** Owner Withdrawals

b. Interest Payable   **f.** Prepaid Insurance   **j.** Unearned Revenue

c. Accounts Receivable   **g.** Buildings   **k.** Accounts Payable

d. Salaries Expense   **h.** Interest Revenue   **l.** Office Supplies

---

QS 2-5

Analyzing debit or credit by account

C5 A1

Identify whether a debit or credit yields the indicated change for each of the following accounts.

a. To increase Land   **f.** To decrease Prepaid Insurance

b. To decrease Cash   **g.** To increase Notes Payable

c. To increase Utilities Expense **h.** To decrease Accounts Receivable

d. To increase Fees Earned   **i.** To increase Owner Capital

e. To decrease Unearned Revenue **j.** To increase Store Equipment

---

QS 2-6

Preparing journal entries

P1

Prepare journal entries for each of the following selected transactions.

a. On January 13, DeShawn Tyler opens a landscaping company called Elegant Lawns by investing $80,000 cash along with equipment having a $30,000 value.

b. On January 21, Elegant Lawns purchases office supplies on credit for $820.

c. On January 29, Elegant Lawns receives $8,700 cash for performing landscaping services.

d. On January 30, Elegant Lawns receives $4,000 cash in advance of providing landscaping services to a customer.

QS 2-7

Identifying a posting error

P2

A trial balance has total debits of $20,000 and total credits of $24,500. Which one of the following errors would create this imbalance? Explain.

a. A $2,250 credit to Consulting Fees Earned in a journal entry is incorrectly posted to the ledger as a $2,250 debit, leaving the Consulting Fees Earned account with a $6,300 credit balance.

b. A $4,500 debit to Salaries Expense in a journal entry is incorrectly posted to the ledger as a $4,500 credit, leaving the Salaries Expense account with a $750 debit balance.

c. A $2,250 debit to Rent Expense in a journal entry is incorrectly posted to the ledger as a $2,250 credit, leaving the Rent Expense account with a $3,000 debit balance.

d. A $2,250 debit posting to Accounts Receivable was posted mistakenly to Cash.

e. A $4,500 debit posting to Equipment was posted mistakenly to Supplies.

f. An entry debiting Cash and crediting Notes Payable for $4,500 was mistakenly not posted.

Indicate the financial statement on which each of the following items appears. Use I for income statement, E for statement of owner's equity, and B for balance sheet.

a. Rental Revenue
b. Insurance Expense
c. Services Revenue
d. Interest Payable
e. Accounts Receivable
f. Salaries Expense
g. Equipment
h. Prepaid Insurance
i. Buildings
j. Interest Revenue
k. Owner Withdrawals
l. Office Supplies

QS 2-8
Classifying accounts in financial statements

P3

McGraw-Hill's HOMEWORK MANAGER® Available with McGraw-Hill's Homework Manager

For each of the following (1) identify the type of account as an asset, liability, equity, revenue, or expense, (2) enter *debit (Dr.)* or *credit (Cr.)* to identify the kind of entry that would increase the account balance, and (3) identify the normal balance of the account.

a. Owner Capital
b. Accounts Receivable
c. Owner Withdrawals
d. Cash
e. Equipment
f. Fees Earned
g. Wages Expense
h. Unearned Revenue
i. Accounts Payable
j. Postage Expense
k. Prepaid Insurance
l. Land

EXERCISES

Exercise 2-1
Identifying type and normal balances of accounts

C3 C5

Use the information in each of the following separate cases to calculate the unknown amount.

a. During October, Alcorn Company had $104,750 of cash receipts and $101,607 of cash disbursements. The October 31 Cash balance was $17,069. Determine how much cash the company had at the close of business on September 30.

b. On September 30, Mordish Co. had a $83,250 balance in Accounts Receivable. During October, the company collected $75,924 from its credit customers. The October 31 balance in Accounts Receivable was $85,830. Determine the amount of sales on account that occurred in October.

c. Strong Co. had $148,000 of accounts payable on September 30 and $137,492 on October 31. Total purchases on account during October were $271,876. Determine how much cash was paid on accounts payable during October.

Exercise 2-2
Analyzing account entries and balances

A1

Nology Co. bills a client $65,000 for services provided and agrees to accept the following three items in full payment: (1) $12,000 cash, (2) computer equipment worth $90,000, and (3) to assume responsibility for a $37,000 note payable related to the computer equipment. The entry Nology makes to record this transaction includes which one or more of the following?

a. $37,000 increase in a liability account
b. $12,000 increase in the Cash account
c. $12,000 increase in a revenue account
d. $65,000 increase in an asset account
e. $65,000 increase in a revenue account
f. $37,000 increase in an equity account

Exercise 2-3
Analyzing effects of transactions on accounts

A1

Prepare general journal entries for the following transactions of a new company called Special Pics.

Aug. 1 Madison Harris, the owner, invested $14,250 cash and $61,275 of photography equipment in the company.
2 The company paid $3,300 cash for an insurance policy covering the next 24 months.
5 The company purchased office supplies for $2,707 cash.
20 The company received $3,250 cash in photography fees earned.
31 The company paid $871 cash for August utilities.

Exercise 2-4
Preparing general journal entries

A1 P1

Use the information in Exercise 2-4 to prepare an August 31 trial balance for Special Pics. Begin by opening these T-accounts: Cash; Office Supplies; Prepaid Insurance; Photography Equipment; M. Harris, Capital; Photography Fees Earned; and Utilities Expense. Then, post the general journal entries to these T-accounts (which will serve as the ledger), and prepare the trial balance.

Exercise 2-5
Preparing T-accounts (ledger) and a trial balance

C3 P2

Exercise 2-6

Recording effects of transactions in T-accounts

C5 A1

Record the transactions below for Amena Company by recording the debit and credit entries directly in the following T-accounts: Cash; Accounts Receivable; Office Supplies; Office Equipment; Accounts Payable; S. Amena, Capital; S. Amena, Withdrawals; Fees Earned; and Rent Expense. Use the letters beside each transaction to identify entries. Determine the ending balance of each T-account.

a. Sergey Amena, owner, invested $14,000 cash in the company.

b. The company purchased office supplies for $406 cash.

c. The company purchased $7,742 of office equipment on credit.

d. The company received $1,652 cash as fees for services provided to a customer.

e. The company paid $7,742 cash to settle the payable for the office equipment purchased in transaction *c*.

f. The company billed a customer $2,968 as fees for services provided.

g. The company paid $510 cash for the monthly rent.

h. The company collected $1,246 cash as partial payment for the account receivable created in transaction *f*.

Check Cash ending balance, $7,040

i. S. Amena withdrew $1,200 cash from the company for personal use.

Exercise 2-7

Preparing a trial balance   P2

After recording the transactions of Exercise 2-6 in T-accounts and calculating the balance of each account, prepare a trial balance. Use May 31, 2009, as its report date.

Exercise 2-8

Analyzing and journalizing expense transactions

A1 P1

Examine the following transactions and identify those that create expenses for Thomas Services. Prepare general journal entries to record those expense transactions and explain why the other transactions did not create expenses.

a. The company paid $12,200 cash for office supplies that were purchased more than 1 year ago.

b. The company paid $1,233 cash for the just completed two-week salary of the receptionist.

c. The company paid $39,200 cash for equipment purchased.

d. The company paid $870 cash for this month's utilities.

e. Owner (Thomas) withdrew $4,500 cash from the company for personal use.

Exercise 2-9

Analyzing and journalizing revenue transactions

A1 P1

Examine the following transactions and identify those that create revenues for Thomas Services, a company owned by Brina Thomas. Prepare general journal entries to record those revenue transactions and explain why the other transactions did not create revenues.

a. Brina Thomas invests $39,350 cash in the company.

b. The company provided $2,300 of services on credit.

c. The company provided services to a client and immediately received $875 cash.

d. The company received $10,200 cash from a client in payment for services to be provided next year.

e. The company received $3,500 cash from a client in partial payment of an account receivable.

f. The company borrowed $120,000 cash from the bank by signing a promissory note.

Exercise 2-10

Preparing an income statement

C4 P3

On October 1, Diondre Shabazz organized a new consulting firm called Tech Talk. On October 31, the company's records show the following accounts and amounts. Use this information to prepare an October income statement for the business.

Cash	$ 12,614	D. Shabazz, Withdrawals	$ 2,000
Accounts receivable	25,648	Consulting fees earned	25,620
Office supplies	4,903	Rent expense	6,859
Land	69,388	Salaries expense	12,405
Office equipment	27,147	Telephone expense	560
Accounts payable	12,070	Miscellaneous expenses	280
D. Shabazz, Capital	124,114		

Check Net income, $5,516

Exercise 2-11

Preparing a statement of owner's equity   P3

Use the information in Exercise 2-10 to prepare an October statement of owner's equity for Tech Talk. (The owner invested $124,114 to launch the company.)

Exercise 2-12

Preparing a balance sheet   P3

Use the information in Exercise 2-10 (if completed, you can also use your solution to Exercise 2-11) to prepare an October 31 balance sheet for Tech Talk.

A company had the following assets and liabilities at the beginning and end of a recent year.

Exercise 2-13
Computing net income
A1   P3

	Assets	Liabilities
Beginning of the year	$131,000	$56,159
End of the year	180,000	72,900

Determine the net income earned or net loss incurred by the business during the year for each of the following *separate* cases:

a. Owner made no investments in the business and no withdrawals were made during the year.

b. Owner made no investments in the business but withdrew $650 cash per month for personal use.

c. No withdrawals were made during the year but the owner invested an additional $45,000 cash.

d. Withdrew $650 cash per month for personal use and the owner invested an additional $25,000 cash.

Compute the missing amount in each of the following separate companies *a* through *d*.

Exercise 2-14
Analyzing changes in a
company's equity
C5   P3

	File Edit View Insert Format Tools Data Window Help			
		(a)	**(b)**	**(c)**	**(d)**
2	Equity, December 31, 2008	$ 0	$ 0	$ 0	$ 0
3	Owner investments during the year	112,500	?	85,347	201,871
4	Owner withdrawals during the year	?	(51,000)	(8,000)	(53,000)
5	Net income (loss) for the year	27,000	78,000	(6,000)	?
6	Equity, December 31, 2009	94,500	91,665	?	101,871

Assume the following T-accounts reflect Belle Co.'s general ledger and that seven transactions *a* through *g* are posted to them. Provide a short description of each transaction. Include the amounts in your descriptions.

Exercise 2-15
Interpreting and describing
transactions from T-accounts
C1   A1

Cash			
(a)	12,000	(b)	4,800
(e)	9,000	(c)	2,000
		(f)	4,600
		(g)	820

Office Supplies	
(c)	2,000
(d)	300

Prepaid Insurance	
(b)	4,800

Equipment	
(a)	15,200
(d)	9,700

Automobiles	
(a)	24,000

Accounts Payable			
(f)	4,600	(d)	10,000

D. Belle, Capital			
		(a)	51,200

Delivery Services Revenue			
		(e)	9,000

Gas and Oil Expense	
(g)	820

Use information from the T-accounts in Exercise 2-15 to prepare general journal entries for each of the seven transactions *a* through *g*.

Exercise 2-16
Preparing general
journal entries   A1   P1

Several posting errors are identified in the following table. In column (1), enter the amount of the difference between the two trial balance columns (debit and credit) due to the error. In column (2), identify the trial balance column (debit or credit) with the larger amount if they are not equal. In column (3), identify the account(s) affected by the error. In column (4), indicate the amount by which the account(s) in column (3) is under- or overstated. Item (a) is completed as an example.

Exercise 2-17
Identifying effects of
posting errors on the
trial balance   A1   P2

	Description of Posting Error	(1) Difference between Debit and Credit Columns	(2) Column with the Larger Total	(3) Identify Account(s) Incorrectly Stated	(4) Amount that Account(s) is Over- or Understated
a.	$1,870 debit to Rent Expense is posted as a $1,780 debit.	$90	Credit	Rent Expense	Rent Expense understated $90
b.	$3,560 credit to Cash is posted twice as two credits to Cash.				
c.	$7,120 debit to the Withdrawals account is debited to Owner's Capital.				
d.	$1,630 debit to Prepaid Insurance is posted as a debit to Insurance Expense.				
e.	$31,150 debit to Machinery is posted as a debit to Accounts Payable.				
f.	$4,460 credit to Services Revenue is posted as a $446 credit.				
g.	$820 debit to Store Supplies is not posted.				

Exercise 2-18
Analyzing a trial
balance error

A1 P2

You are told the column totals in a trial balance are not equal. After careful analysis, you discover only one error. Specifically, a correctly journalized credit purchase of a computer for $11,250 is posted from the journal to the ledger with a $11,250 debit to Office Equipment and another $11,250 debit to Accounts Payable. The Office Equipment account has a debit balance of $26,663 on the trial balance. Answer each of the following questions and compute the dollar amount of any misstatement.

a. Is the debit column total of the trial balance overstated, understated, or correctly stated?

b. Is the credit column total of the trial balance overstated, understated, or correctly stated?

c. Is the Office Equipment account balance overstated, understated, or correctly stated in the trial balance?

d. Is the Accounts Payable account balance overstated, understated, or correctly stated in the trial balance?

e. If the debit column total of the trial balance is $236,250 before correcting the error, what is the total of the credit column before correction?

Exercise 2-19
Interpreting the debt ratio
and return on assets

A2

a. Calculate the debt ratio and the return on assets using the year-end information for each of the following six separate companies ($ thousands).

	Case	Assets	Liabilities	Average Assets	Net Income
2	Company 3	$ 90,500	$ 12,000	$ 100,000	$ 20,000
3	Company 5	64,000	47,000	40,000	3,800
4	Company 6	32,500	26,500	50,000	660
5	Company 1	147,000	56,000	200,000	21,000
6	Company 4	92,000	31,000	40,000	7,500
7	Company 2	104,500	51,500	70,000	12,000

b. Of the six companies, which business relies most heavily on creditor financing?

c. Of the six companies, which business relies most heavily on equity financing?

d. Which two companies indicate the greatest risk?

e. Which two companies earn the highest return on assets?

f. Which one company would investors likely prefer based on the risk–return relation?

Available with McGraw-Hill's Homework Manager

Lancet Engineering completed the following transactions in the month of June.

a. Jenna Lancet, the owner, invested $195,000 cash, office equipment with a value of $8,200, and $80,000 of drafting equipment to launch the company.

b. The company purchased land worth $52,000 for an office by paying $8,900 cash and signing a long-term note payable for $43,100.

c. The company purchased a portable building with $55,000 cash and moved it onto the land acquired in *b*.

d. The company paid $2,300 cash for the premium on an 18-month insurance policy.

e. The company completed and delivered a set of plans for a client and collected $6,600 cash.

f. The company purchased $24,000 of additional drafting equipment by paying $9,600 cash and signing a long-term note payable for $14,400.

g. The company completed $14,500 of engineering services for a client. This amount is to be received in 30 days.

h. The company purchased $1,100 of additional office equipment on credit.

i. The company completed engineering services for $23,000 on credit.

j. The company received a bill for rent of equipment that was used on a recently completed job. The $1,410 rent cost must be paid within 30 days.

k. The company collected $8,000 cash in partial payment from the client described in transaction *g*.

l. The company paid $2,500 cash for wages to a drafting assistant.

m. The company paid $1,100 cash to settle the account payable created in transaction *h*.

n. The company paid $970 cash for minor maintenance of its drafting equipment.

o. J. Lancet withdrew $10,450 cash from the company for personal use.

p. The company paid $2,000 cash for wages to a drafting assistant.

q. The company paid $2,400 cash for advertisements in the local newspaper during June.

Required

1. Prepare general journal entries to record these transactions (use the account titles listed in part 2).

2. Open the following ledger accounts—their account numbers are in parentheses (use the balance column format): Cash (101); Accounts Receivable (106); Prepaid Insurance (108); Office Equipment (163); Drafting Equipment (164); Building (170); Land (172); Accounts Payable (201); Notes Payable (250); J. Lancet, Capital (301); J. Lancet, Withdrawals (302); Engineering Fees Earned (402); Wages Expense (601); Equipment Rental Expense (602); Advertising Expense (603); and Repairs Expense (604). Post the journal entries from part 1 to the accounts and enter the balance after each posting.

3. Prepare a trial balance as of the end of June.

PROBLEM SET A

Problem 2-1A
Preparing and posting journal entries; preparing a trial balance

C4 C5 A1 P1 P2

Check (2) Ending balances: Cash, $114,380; Accounts Receivable, $29,500; Accounts Payable, $1,410

(3) Trial balance totals, $386,210

Denzel Brooks opens a Web consulting business called Venture Consultants and completes the following transactions in March.

March 1 Brooks invested $180,000 cash along with $30,000 of office equipment in the company.
2 The company prepaid $8,000 cash for six months' rent for an office. (*Hint:* Debit Prepaid Rent for $8,000.)
3 The company made credit purchases of office equipment for $3,300 and office supplies for $1,400. Payment is due within 10 days.
6 The company completed services for a client and immediately received $6,000 cash.
9 The company completed a $9,200 project for a client, who must pay within 30 days.
12 The company paid $4,700 cash to settle the account payable created on March 3.
19 The company paid $7,500 cash for the premium on a 12-month insurance policy.
22 The company received $4,300 cash as partial payment for the work completed on March 9.
25 The company completed work for another client for $3,590 on credit.
29 Brooks withdrew $4,900 cash from the company for personal use.
30 The company purchased $1,700 of additional office supplies on credit.
31 The company paid $500 cash for this month's utility bill.

Problem 2-2A
Preparing and posting journal entries; preparing a trial balance

C4 C5 A1 P1 P2

mhhe.com/wildFAP19e

Required

1. Prepare general journal entries to record these transactions (use the account titles listed in part 2).

2. Open the following ledger accounts—their account numbers are in parentheses (use the balance column format): Cash (101); Accounts Receivable (106); Office Supplies (124); Prepaid Insurance (128); Prepaid Rent (131); Office Equipment (163); Accounts Payable (201); D. Brooks, Capital (301); D. Brooks, Withdrawals (302); Services Revenue (403); and Utilities Expense (690). Post the journal entries from part 1 to the ledger accounts and enter the balance after each posting.

3. Prepare a trial balance as of the end of March.

Problem 2-3A
Preparing and posting journal entries; preparing a trial balance

C4   C5   A1   P1   P2

Jayden Lanelle opens a computer consulting business called Viva Consultants and completes the following transactions in its first month of operations.

April 1   Lanelle invests $95,000 cash along with office equipment valued at $22,800 in the company.
    2   The company prepaid $7,200 cash for twelve months' rent for office space. (*Hint:* Debit Prepaid Rent for $7,200.)
    3   The company made credit purchases for $11,400 in office equipment and $2,280 in office supplies. Payment is due within 10 days.
    6   The company completed services for a client and immediately received $2,000 cash.
    9   The company completed a $7,600 project for a client, who must pay within 30 days.
  13   The company paid $13,680 cash to settle the account payable created on April 3.
  19   The company paid $6,000 cash for the premium on a 12-month insurance policy. (*Hint:* Debit Prepaid Insurance for $6,000.)
  22   The company received $6,080 cash as partial payment for the work completed on April 9.
  25   The company completed work for another client for $2,640 on credit.
  28   Lanelle withdrew $6,200 cash from the company for personal use.
  29   The company purchased $760 of additional office supplies on credit.
  30   The company paid $700 cash for this month's utility bill.

Required

1. Prepare general journal entries to record these transactions (use account titles listed in part 2).

2. Open the following ledger accounts—their account numbers are in parentheses (use the balance column format): Cash (101); Accounts Receivable (106); Office Supplies (124); Prepaid Insurance (128); Prepaid Rent (131); Office Equipment (163); Accounts Payable (201); J. Lanelle, Capital (301); J. Lanelle, Withdrawals (302); Services Revenue (403); and Utilities Expense (690). Post journal entries from part 1 to the ledger accounts and enter the balance after each posting.

3. Prepare a trial balance as of April 30.

Problem 2-4A
Computing net income from equity analysis, preparing a balance sheet, and computing the debt ratio

C3   A1   A2   P3

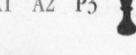

The accounting records of Faviana Shipping show the following assets and liabilities as of December 31, 2008 and 2009.

December 31	2008	2009
Cash	$ 47,867	$ 8,154
Accounts receivable	25,983	20,370
Office supplies	4,098	3,002
Office equipment	125,816	134,018
Trucks	49,236	58,236
Building	0	164,124
Land	0	40,956
Accounts payable	68,310	33,879
Note payable	0	85,080

Late in December 2009, the business purchased a small office building and land for $205,080. It paid $120,000 cash toward the purchase and an $85,080 note payable was signed for the balance. Ms. Faviana had to invest $34,000 cash in the business to enable it to pay the $120,000 cash. The owner withdraws $2,400 cash per month for personal use.

Required

1. Prepare balance sheets for the business as of December 31, 2008 and 2009. (*Hint:* Report only total equity on the balance sheet and remember that total equity equals the difference between assets and liabilities.)

2. By comparing equity amounts from the balance sheets and using the additional information presented in this problem, prepare a calculation to show how much net income was earned by the business during 2009.

Check   (2) Net income, $120,011

3. Compute the 2009 year-end debt ratio for the business.

(3) Debt ratio, 27.7%

Yi Min started an engineering firm called Min Engineering. He began operations and completed seven transactions in May, which included his initial investment of $18,000 cash. After those seven transactions, the ledger included the following accounts with normal balances.

Problem 2-5A
Analyzing account balances and reconstructing transactions

C1   C4   A1   P2

Cash	$44,132
Office supplies	1,090
Prepaid insurance	4,700
Office equipment	11,200
Accounts payable	11,200
Y. Min, Capital	18,000
Y. Min, Withdrawals	4,328
Engineering fees earned	44,000
Rent expense	7,750

Required

1. Prepare a trial balance for this business as of the end of May.

Check   (1) Trial balance totals, $73,200

Analysis Components

2. Analyze the accounts and their balances and prepare a list that describes each of the seven most likely transactions and their amounts.

3. Prepare a report of cash received and cash paid showing how the seven transactions in part 2 yield the $44,132 ending Cash balance.

(3) Cash paid, $17,868

Business transactions completed by Alanna Emitt during the month of September are as follows.

a. Emitt invested $82,000 cash along with office equipment valued at $22,000 in a new company named AE Consulting.

b. The company purchased land valued at $40,000 and a building valued at $165,000. The purchase is paid with $25,000 cash and a long-term note payable for $180,000.

c. The company purchased $1,700 of office supplies on credit.

d. Emitt invested her personal automobile in the company. The automobile has a value of $16,800 and is to be used exclusively in the business.

e. The company purchased $5,900 of additional office equipment on credit.

f. The company paid $1,500 cash salary to an assistant.

g. The company provided services to a client and collected $7,600 cash.

h. The company paid $630 cash for this month's utilities.

i. The company paid $1,700 cash to settle the account payable created in transaction *c*.

Problem 2-6A
Recording transactions; posting to ledger; preparing a trial balance

C4   A1   P1   P2

j. The company purchased $20,200 of new office equipment by paying $20,200 cash.

k. The company completed $6,750 of services for a client, who must pay within 30 days.

l. The company paid $2,000 cash salary to an assistant.

m. The company received $4,000 cash in partial payment on the receivable created in transaction *k*.

n. Emitt withdrew $2,900 cash from the company for personal use.

Required

1. Prepare general journal entries to record these transactions (use account titles listed in part 2).

Check (2) Ending balances: Cash, $39,670; Office Equipment, $48,100

2. Open the following ledger accounts—their account numbers are in parentheses (use the balance column format): Cash (101); Accounts Receivable (106); Office Supplies (108); Office Equipment (163); Automobiles (164); Building (170); Land (172); Accounts Payable (201); Notes Payable (250); A. Emitt, Capital (301); A. Emitt, Withdrawals (302); Fees Earned (402); Salaries Expense (601); and Utilities Expense (602). Post the journal entries from part 1 to the ledger accounts and enter the balance after each posting.

(3) Trial balance totals, $321,050

3. Prepare a trial balance as of the end of September.

PROBLEM SET B

Problem 2-1B
Preparing and posting journal entries; preparing a trial balance

C4 C5 A1 P1 P2

At the beginning of April, Vanessa Wende launched a custom computer solutions company called Softworks. The company had the following transactions during April.

a. Vanessa Wende invested $155,000 cash, office equipment with a value of $5,100, and $78,000 of computer equipment in the company.

b. The company purchased land worth $55,000 for an office by paying $8,700 cash and signing a long-term note payable for $46,300.

c. The company purchased a portable building with $59,000 cash and moved it onto the land acquired in *b*.

d. The company paid $3,500 cash for the premium on a two-year insurance policy.

e. The company provided services to a client and immediately collected $7,000 cash.

f. The company purchased $26,000 of additional computer equipment by paying $11,800 cash and signing a long-term note payable for $14,200.

g. The company completed $16,500 of services for a client. This amount is to be received within 30 days.

h. The company purchased $1,800 of additional office equipment on credit.

i. The company completed client services for $28,000 on credit.

j. The company received a bill for rent of a computer testing device that was used on a recently completed job. The $1,685 rent cost must be paid within 30 days.

k. The company collected $10,000 cash in partial payment from the client described in transaction *i*.

l. The company paid $1,300 cash for wages to an assistant.

m. The company paid $1,800 cash to settle the payable created in transaction *h*.

n. The company paid $985 cash for minor maintenance of the company's computer equipment.

o. V. Wende withdrew $10,230 cash from the company for personal use.

p. The company paid $1,300 cash for wages to an assistant.

q. The company paid $4,300 cash for advertisements in the local newspaper during April.

Required

1. Prepare general journal entries to record these transactions (use account titles listed in part 2).

Check (2) Ending balances: Cash, $69,085; Accounts Receivable, $34,500; Accounts Payable, $1,685

2. Open the following ledger accounts—their account numbers are in parentheses (use the balance column format): Cash (101); Accounts Receivable (106); Prepaid Insurance (108); Office Equipment (163); Computer Equipment (164); Building (170); Land (172); Accounts Payable (201); Notes Payable (250); V. Wende, Capital (301); V. Wende, Withdrawals (302); Fees Earned (402); Wages Expense (601); Computer Rental Expense (602); Advertising Expense (603); and Repairs Expense (604). Post the journal entries from part 1 to the accounts and enter the balance after each posting.

(3) Trial balance totals, $351,785

3. Prepare a trial balance as of the end of April.

Kylan Management Services opens for business and completes these transactions in November.

Nov. 1   Rollie Kylan, the owner, invested $190,000 cash along with $29,000 of office equipment in the company.
2   The company prepaid $10,000 cash for six months' rent for an office. (*Hint:* Debit Prepaid Rent for $10,000.)
4   The company made credit purchases of office equipment for $4,300 and of office supplies for $2,100. Payment is due within 10 days.
8   The company completed work for a client and immediately received $7,000 cash.
12   The company completed a $9,200 project for a client, who must pay within 30 days.
13   The company paid $6,400 cash to settle the payable created on November 4.
19   The company paid $4,100 cash for the premium on a 24-month insurance policy.
22   The company received $3,700 cash as partial payment for the work completed on November 12.
24   The company completed work for another client for $4,010 on credit.
28   R. Kylan withdrew $6,300 cash from the company for personal use.
29   The company purchased $1,200 of additional office supplies on credit.
30   The company paid $1,100 cash for this month's utility bill.

Required

1. Prepare general journal entries to record these transactions (use account titles listed in part 2).
2. Open the following ledger accounts—their account numbers are in parentheses (use the balance column format): Cash (101); Accounts Receivable (106); Office Supplies (124); Prepaid Insurance (128); Prepaid Rent (131); Office Equipment (163); Accounts Payable (201); R. Kylan, Capital (301); R. Kylan, Withdrawals (302); Services Revenue (403); and Utilities Expense (690). Post the journal entries from part 1 to the ledger accounts and enter the balance after each posting.
3. Prepare a trial balance as of the end of November.

Problem 2-2B
Preparing and posting journal entries; preparing a trial balance
C4 C5 A1 P1 P2

Check (2) Ending balances: Cash, $172,800; Accounts Receivable, $9,510; Accounts Payable, $1,200

(3) Total debits, $240,410

Hassan Management Services opens for business and completes these transactions in September.

Sept. 1   Jamal Hassan, the owner, invests $130,000 cash along with office equipment valued at $31,200 in the company.
2   The company prepaid $7,200 cash for 12 months' rent for office space. (*Hint:* Debit Prepaid Rent for $7,200.)
4   The company made credit purchases for $15,600 in office equipment and $3,120 in office supplies. Payment is due within 10 days.
8   The company completed work for a client and immediately received $2,000 cash.
12   The company completed a $10,400 project for a client, who must pay within 30 days.
13   The company paid $18,720 cash to settle the payable created on September 4.
19   The company paid $6,000 cash for the premium on an 18-month insurance policy. (*Hint:* Debit Prepaid Insurance for $6,000.)
22   The company received $8,320 cash as partial payment for the work completed on September 12.
24   The company completed work for another client for $2,640 on credit.
28   J. Hassan withdrew $6,200 cash from the company for personal use.
29   The company purchased $1,040 of additional office supplies on credit.
30   The company paid $700 cash for this month's utility bill.

Required

1. Prepare general journal entries to record these transactions (use account titles listed in part 2).
2. Open the following ledger accounts—their account numbers are in parentheses (use the balance column format): Cash (101); Accounts Receivable (106); Office Supplies (124); Prepaid Insurance (128); Prepaid Rent (131); Office Equipment (163); Accounts Payable (201); J. Hassan, Capital (301); J. Hassan, Withdrawals (302); Service Fees Earned (401); and Utilities Expense (690). Post journal entries from part 1 to the ledger accounts and enter the balance after each posting.
3. Prepare a trial balance as of the end of September.

Problem 2-3B
Preparing and posting journal entries; preparing a trial balance
C4 C5 A1 P1 P2

Check (2) Ending balances: Cash, $101,500; Accounts Receivable, $4,720; Accounts Payable, $1,040

(3) Total debits, $177,280

Problem 2-4B

Computing net income from equity analysis, preparing a balance sheet, and computing the debt ratio

C3   A1   A2   P3

The accounting records of Trinity Co. show the following assets and liabilities as of December 31, 2008 and 2009.

December 31	2008	2009
Cash	$ 54,773	$ 10,629
Accounts receivable	29,731	23,309
Office supplies	4,689	3,435
Office equipment	$143,968	153,353
Machinery	56,339	65,339
Building	0	187,802
Land	0	46,864
Accounts payable	78,165	38,767
Note payable	0	114,666

Late in December 2009, the business purchased a small office building and land for $234,666. It paid $120,000 cash toward the purchase and a $114,666 note payable was signed for the balance. Ms. Trinity, the owner, had to invest an additional $35,000 cash to enable it to pay the $120,000 cash toward the purchase. The owner withdraws $4,000 cash per month for personal use.

Required

1. Prepare balance sheets for the business as of December 31, 2008 and 2009. (*Hint:* Report only total equity on the balance sheet and remember that total equity equals the difference between assets and liabilities.)

Check   (2) Net income, $138,963

2. By comparing equity amounts from the balance sheets and using the additional information presented in the problem, prepare a calculation to show how much net income was earned by the business during 2009.

(3) Debt ratio, 31.3%

3. Calculate the December 31, 2009, debt ratio for the business.

Problem 2-5B

Analyzing account balances and reconstructing transactions

C1   C4   A1   P2

Roshaun Gould started a Web consulting firm called Gould Solutions. He began operations and completed seven transactions in April that resulted in the following accounts, which all have normal balances.

Cash	$46,518
Office supplies	850
Prepaid rent	4,700
Office equipment	11,300
Accounts payable	11,300
R. Gould, Capital	22,500
R. Gould, Withdrawals	4,172
Consulting fees earned	43,000
Operating expenses	9,260

Required

Check   (1) Trial balance total, $76,800

1. Prepare a trial balance for this business as of the end of April.

Analysis Component

2. Analyze the accounts and their balances and prepare a list that describes each of the seven most likely transactions and their amounts.

(3) Cash paid, $18,982

3. Prepare a report of cash received and cash paid showing how the seven transactions in part 2 yield the $46,518 ending Cash balance.

Witter Consulting completed the following transactions during June.

a. D. Witter, the owner, invested $82,000 cash along with office equipment valued at $23,000 in the new company.

b. The company purchased land valued at $50,000 and a building valued at $165,000. The purchase is paid with $30,000 cash and a long-term note payable for $185,000.

c. The company purchased $2,200 of office supplies on credit.

d. D. Witter invested his personal automobile in the company. The automobile has a value of $16,800 and is to be used exclusively in the business.

e. The company purchased $5,100 of additional office equipment on credit.

f. The company paid $1,500 cash salary to an assistant.

g. The company provided services to a client and collected $8,000 cash.

h. The company paid $630 cash for this month's utilities.

i. The company paid $2,200 cash to settle the payable created in transaction *c*.

j. The company purchased $20,400 of new office equipment by paying $20,400 cash.

k. The company completed $6,500 of services for a client, who must pay within 30 days.

l. The company paid $2,000 cash salary to an assistant.

m. The company received $4,000 cash in partial payment on the receivable created in transaction *k*.

n. D. Witter withdrew $2,700 cash from the company for personal use.

Required

1. Prepare general journal entries to record these transactions (use account titles listed in part 2).

2. Open the following ledger accounts—their account numbers are in parentheses (use the balance column format): Cash (101); Accounts Receivable (106); Office Supplies (108); Office Equipment (163); Automobiles (164); Building (170); Land (172); Accounts Payable (201); Notes Payable (250); D. Witter, Capital (301); D. Witter, Withdrawals (302); Fees Earned (402); Salaries Expense (601); and Utilities Expense (602). Post the journal entries from part 1 to the ledger accounts and enter the balance after each posting.

3. Prepare a trial balance as of the end of June.

Problem 2-6B
Recording transactions; posting to ledger; preparing a trial balance

C4 A1 P1 P2

Check (2) Ending balances: Cash, $34,570; Office Equipment, $48,500

(3) Trial balance totals, $326,400

(This serial problem started in Chapter 1 and continues through most of the chapters. If the Chapter 1 segment was not completed, the problem can begin at this point. It is helpful, but not necessary, to use the Working Papers that accompany this book.)

SERIAL PROBLEM

Success Systems

A1 P1 P2

SP 2 On October 1, 2009, Adriana Lopez launched a computer services company called Success Systems, which provides consulting services, computer system installations, and custom program development. Lopez adopts the calendar year for reporting purposes and expects to prepare the company's first set of financial statements on December 31, 2009. The company's initial chart of accounts follows.

Account	No.	Account	No.
Cash	101	A. Lopez, Capital	301
Accounts Receivable	106	A. Lopez, Withdrawals	302
Computer Supplies	126	Computer Services Revenue	403
Prepaid Insurance	128	Wages Expense	623
Prepaid Rent	131	Advertising Expense	655
Office Equipment	163	Mileage Expense	676
Computer Equipment	167	Miscellaneous Expenses	677
Accounts Payable	201	Repairs Expense—Computer	684

Required

I. Prepare journal entries to record each of the following transactions for Success Systems.

Oct.   1   Lopez invested $55,000 cash, a $20,000 computer system, and $8,000 of office equipment in the company.
       2   The company paid $3,300 cash for four months' rent. (*Hint:* Debit Prepaid Rent for $3,300.)
       3   The company purchased $1,420 of computer supplies on credit from Harris Office Products.
       5   The company paid $2,220 cash for one year's premium on a property and liability insurance policy. (*Hint:* Debit Prepaid Insurance for $2,220.)
       6   The company billed Easy Leasing $4,800 for services performed in installing a new Web server.
       8   The company paid $1,420 cash for the computer supplies purchased from Harris Office Products on October 3.
      10   The company hired Lyn Addie as a part-time assistant for $125 per day, as needed.
      12   The company billed Easy Leasing another $1,400 for services performed.
      15   The company received $4,800 cash from Easy Leasing as partial payment on its account.
      17   The company paid $805 cash to repair computer equipment that was damaged when moving it.
      20   The company paid $1,940 cash for an advertisement in the local newspaper.
      22   The company received $1,400 cash from Easy Leasing on its account.
      28   The company billed IFM Company $5,208 for services performed.
      31   The company paid $875 cash for Lyn Addie's wages for seven days' work.
      31   A. Lopez withdrew $3,600 cash from the company for personal use.
Nov.   1   The company reimbursed Lopez in cash for business automobile mileage allowance (Lopez logged 1,000 miles at $0.32 per mile).
       2   The company received $4,633 cash from Liu Corporation for computer services performed.
       5   The company purchased computer supplies for $1,125 cash from Harris Office Products.
       8   The company billed Gomez Co. $5,668 for services performed.
      13   The company received notification from Alex's Engineering Co. that Success Systems' bid of $3,950 for an upcoming project is accepted.
      18   The company received $2,208 cash from IFM Company as partial payment of the October 28 bill.
      22   The company donated $250 cash to the United Way in the company's name.
      24   The company completed work for Alex's Engineering Co. and sent it a bill for $3,950.
      25   The company sent another bill to IFM Company for the past-due amount of $3,000.
      28   The company reimbursed Lopez in cash for business automobile mileage (1,200 miles at $0.32 per mile).
      30   The company paid $1,750 cash for Lyn Addie's wages for 14 days' work.
      30   A. Lopez withdrew $2,000 cash from the company for personal use.

Check   (2) Cash, Nov. 30 bal., $48,052

(3) Trial bal. totals, $108,659

2. Open ledger accounts (in balance column format) and post the journal entries from part 1 to them.

3. Prepare a trial balance as of the end of November.

BEYOND THE NUMBERS

BTN 2-1   Refer to Best Buy's financial statements in Appendix A for the following questions.

Required

I. What amount of total liabilities does it report for each of the fiscal years ended February 25, 2006, and March 3, 2007?

2. What amount of total assets does it report for each of the fiscal years ended February 25, 2006, and March 3, 2007?

3. Compute its debt ratio for each of the fiscal years ended February 25, 2006, and March 3, 2007.

4. In which fiscal year did it employ more financial leverage (February 25, 2006, or March 3, 2007)? Explain.

Fast Forward

5. Access its financial statements (10-K report) for a fiscal year ending after March 3, 2007, from its Website (BestBuy.com) or the SEC's EDGAR database (www.sec.gov). Recompute its debt ratio for any subsequent year's data and compare it with the February 25, 2006, debt ratio.

BTN 2-2 Key comparative figures for Best Buy, Circuit City, and RadioShack follow.

($ millions)	Best Buy Current Year	Best Buy Prior Year	Circuit City Current Year	Circuit City Prior Year	RadioShack Current Year	RadioShack Prior Year
Total liabilities	$ 7,369	$ 6,607	$2,216	$2,114	$1,416	$1,616
Total assets	13,570	11,864	4,007	4,069	2,070	2,205

COMPARATIVE ANALYSIS

A1 A2

1. What is the debt ratio for Best Buy in the current year and for the prior year?
2. What is the debt ratio for Circuit City in the current year and for the prior year?
3. What is the debt ratio for RadioShack in the current year and for the prior year?
4. Which of the three companies has the highest degree of financial leverage? What does this imply?

BTN 2-3 Review the *Decision Ethics* case from the first part of this chapter involving the cashier. The guidance answer suggests that you should not comply with the assistant manager's request.

ETHICS CHALLENGE

C1 C2

Required

Propose and evaluate two other courses of action you might consider, and explain why.

BTN 2-4 Mora Stanley is an aspiring entrepreneur and your friend. She is having difficulty understanding the purposes of financial statements and how they fit together across time.

COMMUNICATING IN PRACTICE

C1 C3 A1 P3

Required

Write a one-page memorandum to Stanley explaining the purposes of the four financial statements and how they are linked across time.

BTN 2-5 Access EDGAR online (www.sec.gov) and locate the 2006 year 10-K report of Amazon.com (ticker AMZN) filed on February 16, 2007. Review its financial statements reported for years ended 2006, 2005, and 2004 to answer the following questions.

TAKING IT TO THE NET

A1

Required

1. What are the amounts of its net income or net loss reported for each of these three years?
2. Do Amazon's operations provide cash or use cash for each of these three years?
3. If Amazon has a 2005 net income, how is it possible that its cash balance at December 31, 2005, shows a decrease relative to its balance at December 31, 2004?

BTN 2-6 The expanded accounting equation consists of assets, liabilities, capital, withdrawals, revenues, and expenses. It can be used to reveal insights into changes in a company's financial position.

TEAMWORK IN ACTION

C1 C3 C5 A1

Required

1. Form *learning teams* of six (or more) members. Each team member must select one of the six components and each team must have at least one expert on each component: (*a*) assets, (*b*) liabilities, (*c*) capital, (*d*) withdrawals, (*e*) revenues, and (*f*) expenses.

2. Form *expert teams* of individuals who selected the same component in part 1. Expert teams are to draft a report that each expert will present to his or her learning team addressing the following:

    a. Identify for its component the (i) increase and decrease side of the account and (ii) normal balance side of the account.

    b. Describe a transaction, with amounts, that increases its component.

    c. Using the transaction and amounts in (*b*), verify the equality of the accounting equation and then explain any effects on the income statement and statement of cash flows.

    d. Describe a transaction, with amounts, that decreases its component.

    e. Using the transaction and amounts in (*d*), verify the equality of the accounting equation and then explain any effects on the income statement and statement of cash flows.

3. Each expert should return to his/her learning team. In rotation, each member presents his/her expert team's report to the learning team. Team discussion is encouraged.

ENTREPRENEURIAL DECISION

A1   A2   P3

BTN 2-7   Angel Fender is a young entrepreneur who operates Fender Music Services, offering singing lessons and instruction on musical instruments. Fender wishes to expand but needs a $30,000 loan. The bank requests Fender to prepare a balance sheet and key financial ratios. Fender has not kept formal records but is able to provide the following accounts and their amounts as of December 31, 2009.

Cash	$ 3,600	Accounts Receivable . . .	$ 9,600	Prepaid Insurance	$ 1,500
Prepaid Rent	9,400	Store Supplies	6,600	Equipment	50,000
Accounts Payable	2,200	Unearned Lesson Fees . .	15,600	Total Equity*	62,900
Annual net income	40,000				

* The total equity amount reflects all owner investments, withdrawals, revenues, and expenses as of December 31, 2009.

Required

1. Prepare a balance sheet as of December 31, 2009, for Fender Music Services. (Report only the total equity amount on the balance sheet.)

2. Compute Fender's debt ratio and its return on assets (the latter ratio is defined in Chapter 1). Assume average assets equal its ending balance.

3. Do you believe the prospects of a $30,000 bank loan are good? Why or why not?

A1   A2   P3

BTN 2-8   Assume Sara Blakely of **SPANX** plans on expanding her business to accommodate more product lines. She is considering financing her expansion in one of two ways: (1) contributing more of her own funds to the business or (2) borrowing the funds from a bank.

Required

Identify the issues that Blakely should consider when trying to decide on the method for financing her expansion.

HITTING THE ROAD

C1

BTN 2-9   Obtain a recent copy of the most prominent newspaper distributed in your area. Research the classified section and prepare a report answering the following questions (attach relevant classified clippings to your report). Alternatively, you may want to search the Web for the required information. One suitable Website is **CareerOneStop** (www.CareerOneStop.org). For documentation, you should print copies of Websites accessed.

1. Identify the number of listings for accounting positions and the various accounting job titles.

2. Identify the number of listings for other job titles, with examples, that require or prefer accounting knowledge/experience but are not specifically accounting positions.

3. Specify the salary range for the accounting and accounting-related positions if provided.

4. Indicate the job that appeals to you, the reason for its appeal, and its requirements.

BTN 2-10 DSG international plc (www.DSGiplc.com) competes with several companies, including **Best Buy** and **RadioShack**. Key financial ratios for the current fiscal year follow.

Key Figure	DSG	Best Buy	RadioShack
Return on assets	5.2%	10.8%	3.4%
Debt ratio	67.2%	54.3%	68.4%

Required

1. Which company is most profitable according to its return on assets?
2. Which company is most risky according to the debt ratio?
3. Which company deserves increased investment based on a joint analysis of return on assets and the debt ratio? Explain.

ANSWERS TO MULTIPLE CHOICE QUIZ

1. b; debit Utility Expense for $700, and credit Cash for $700.
2. a; debit Cash for $2,500, and credit Unearned Lawn Service Fees for $2,500.
3. c; debit Cash for $250,000, debit Land for $500,000, and credit L. Shue, Capital for $750,000.

4. d
5. e; Debt ratio = $400,000/$1,000,000 = 40%

A Look Back

Chapter 2 explained the analysis and recording of transactions. We showed how to apply and interpret company accounts, T-accounts, double-entry accounting, ledgers, postings, and trial balances.

A Look at This Chapter

This chapter explains the timing of reports and the need to adjust accounts. Adjusting accounts is important for recognizing revenues and expenses in the proper period. We describe the adjusted trial balance and how it is used to prepare financial statements.

A Look Ahead

Chapter 4 highlights the completion of the accounting cycle. We explain the important final steps in the accounting process. These include closing procedures, the post-closing trial balance, and reversing entries.

Adjusting Accounts and Preparing Financial Statements

Chapter

Learning Objectives

CAP

Conceptual

C1 Explain the importance of periodic reporting and the time period assumption. *(p. 92)*

C2 Explain accrual accounting and how it improves financial statements. *(p. 93)*

C3 Identify the types of adjustments and their purpose. *(p. 94)*

Analytical

A1 Explain how accounting adjustments link to financial statements. *(p. 103)*

A2 Compute profit margin and describe its use in analyzing company performance. *(p. 106)*

Procedural

P1 Prepare and explain adjusting entries. *(p. 95)*

P2 Explain and prepare an adjusted trial balance. *(p. 104)*

P3 Prepare financial statements from an adjusted trial balance. *(p. 104)*

P4 *Appendix 3A*—Explain the alternatives in accounting for prepaids. *(p. 110)*

LP3

High Score

SEATTLE—Jason Kapalka met John Vechey and Brian Feite, both 19 at the time, after the two had created an online game. "We hit it off really well," explains Jason. "We were all a little unhappy with our jobs. We thought, 'Hey, we could start our own company.'" Their startup company, **PopCap Games** (**PopCap.com**)**,** is a creator and provider of downloadable games. Jason recalls that their friends considered them crazy.

Undaunted, the three scraped together the little cash they had. Jason explains that each worked out of their respective apartments to save money. "We survived," admits Jason, "because we didn't have many expenses." The young trio quickly developed a system to account for everything, including cash, revenues, receivables and payables. They also adjusted to the deferral and accrual of revenues and expenses. Setting up a good accounting system is an important part of success, explains Jason. "Don't wait until . . . everything is a big mess."

Most of PopCap's sales are paid for in advance of game delivery. This means few uncollectible accounts. The team also defers payment

"Get a good accountant"—Jason Kapalka (from left: John Vechey, Brian Feite, Jason Kapalka)

of their expenses to the time permitted—which is good management. "We're trying to keep a very simple business model," insists Jason. The team continues to fine-tune their accounting system as they remain focused on revenues, income, assets, and liabilities. "No matter what you do," argues Jason, "there's always something that you haven't done."

Financial statements preparation and analysis are a process that the three continue to work on. Although they insist on timely and accurate accounting reports, Jason says "it really helped us to keep things simple." To help make it simple, they took time to understand accounting adjustments and their effects. It is part of the larger picture. "You're not going to get breaks unless you're working hard."

Today, PopCap is a success story. "Now we can afford Mac and Cheese, and the occasional bottle of water," laughs Jason. "Life is good!"

[Sources: *PopCap Website,* January 2009; *Entrepreneur,* February 2008; *Wired,* March 2008; *2o2p Magazine,* September 2006; *Washington Post,* March 2008]

Financial statements reflect revenues when earned and expenses when incurred. This is known as *accrual accounting,* which was the focus of Chapter 2. We showed how companies use accounting systems to collect information about *external* transactions and events. We also explained how journals, ledgers, and other tools are useful in preparing financial statements. This chapter describes the accounting process for producing useful information involving *internal* transactions and events. An important part of this process is adjusting the account balances so that financial statements at the end of a reporting period reflect the effects of all transactions. We then explain the important steps in preparing financial statements.

Adjusting Accounts and Preparing Financial Statements

Timing and Reporting

- Accounting period
- Accrual versus cash
- Recognition of revenues and expenses

Adjusting Accounts

- Prepaid expenses
- Unearned revenues
- Accrued expenses
- Accrued revenues
- Adjusted trial balance

Preparing Financial Statements

- Income statement
- Statement of owner's equity
- Balance sheet

Timing and Reporting

This section describes the importance of reporting accounting information at regular intervals and its impact for recording revenues and expenses.

The Accounting Period

C1 Explain the importance of periodic reporting and the time period assumption.

Video3.1

"Best Buy announces income of . . ."

The value of information is often linked to its timeliness. Useful information must reach decision makers frequently and promptly. To provide timely information, accounting systems prepare reports at regular intervals. This results in an accounting process impacted by the time period (or periodicity) assumption. The **time period assumption** presumes that an organization's activities can be divided into specific time periods such as a month, a three-month quarter, a six-month interval, or a year. Exhibit 3.1 shows various **accounting,** or *reporting,* **periods.** Most organizations use a year as their primary accounting period. Reports covering a one-year period are known as **annual financial statements.** Many organizations also prepare **interim financial statements** covering one, three, or six months of activity.

EXHIBIT 3.1

Accounting Periods

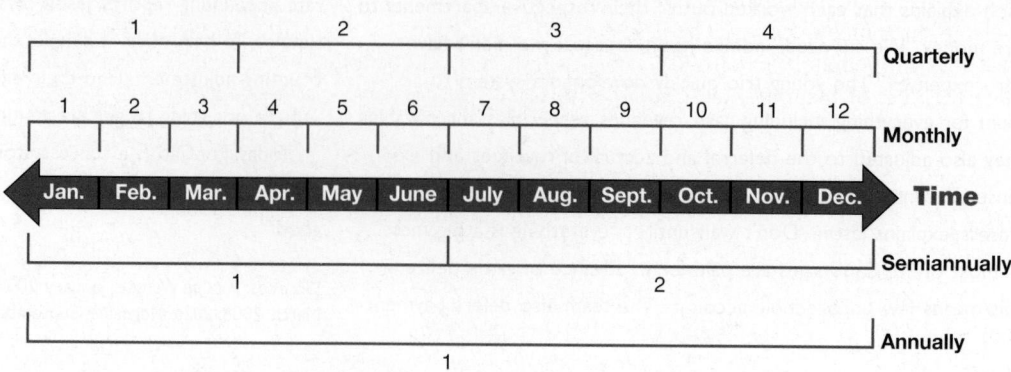

The annual reporting period is not always a calendar year ending on December 31. An organization can adopt a **fiscal year** consisting of any 12 consecutive months. It is also acceptable to adopt an annual reporting period of 52 weeks. For example, Gap's fiscal year consistently ends the final week of January or the first week of February each year.

Companies with little seasonal variation in sales often choose the calendar year as their fiscal year. For example, the financial statements of Marvel Enterprises (the company that controls characters such as Spider-Man, Fantastic Four, and Shang-Chi) reflect a fiscal year that ends on December 31. Companies experiencing seasonal variations in sales often choose a **natural business year** end, which is when sales activities are at their lowest level for the year. The natural business year for retailers such as Wal-Mart, Target, and Macy's usually ends around January 31, after the holiday season.

Accrual Basis versus Cash Basis

After external transactions and events are recorded, several accounts still need adjustments before their balances appear in financial statements. This need arises because internal transactions and events remain unrecorded. **Accrual basis accounting** uses the adjusting process to recognize revenues when earned and expenses when incurred (matched with revenues).

Cash basis accounting recognizes revenues when cash is received and records expenses when cash is paid. This means that cash basis net income for a period is the difference between cash receipts and cash payments. Cash basis accounting is not consistent with generally accepted accounting principles.

It is commonly held that accrual accounting better reflects business performance than information about cash receipts and payments. Accrual accounting also increases the *comparability* of financial statements from one period to another. Yet cash basis accounting is useful for several business decisions—which is the reason companies must report a statement of cash flows.

To see the difference between these two accounting systems, let's consider FastForward's Prepaid Insurance account. FastForward paid $2,400 for 24 months of insurance coverage beginning on December 1, 2009. Accrual accounting requires that $100 of insurance expense be reported on December 2009's income statement. Another $1,200 of expense is reported in year 2010, and the remaining $1,100 is reported as expense in the first 11 months of 2011. Exhibit 3.2 illustrates this allocation of insurance cost across these three years. The accrual basis balance sheet reports any unexpired premium as a Prepaid Insurance asset.

C2	Explain accrual accounting and how it improves financial statements.

EXHIBIT 3.2

Accrual Accounting for Allocating Prepaid Insurance to Expense

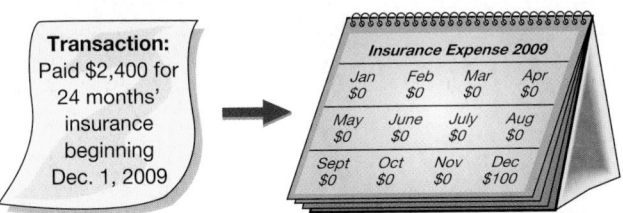

Alternatively, a cash basis income statement for December 2009 reports insurance expense of $2,400, as shown in Exhibit 3.3. The cash basis income statements for years 2010 and 2011 report no insurance expense. The cash basis balance sheet never reports an insurance asset because it is immediately expensed. This shows that cash basis income for 2009–2011 fails to match the cost of insurance with the insurance benefits received for those years and months.

EXHIBIT 3.3

Cash Accounting for Allocating Prepaid Insurance to Expense

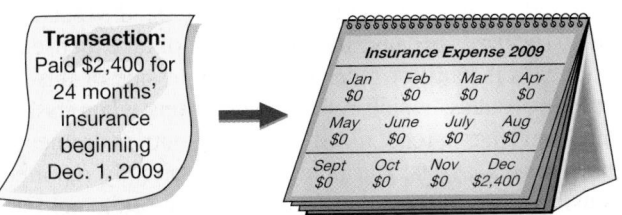
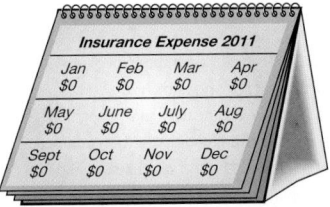

Recognizing Revenues and Expenses

We use the time period assumption to divide a company's activities into specific time periods, but not all activities are complete when financial statements are prepared. Thus, adjustments often are required to get correct account balances.

We rely on two principles in the adjusting process: revenue recognition and matching. Chapter 1 explained that the *revenue recognition principle* requires that revenue be recorded when earned, not before and not after. Most companies earn revenue when they provide services and products to customers. A major goal of the adjusting process is to have revenue recognized (reported) in the time period when it is earned. The **matching principle** aims to record expenses in the same accounting period as the revenues that are earned as a result of those expenses. This matching of expenses with the revenue benefits is a major part of the adjusting process.

Matching expenses with revenues often requires us to predict certain events. When we use financial statements, we must understand that they require estimates and therefore include measures that are not precise. **Walt Disney**'s annual report explains that its production costs from movies, such as *Pirates of the Caribbean,* are matched to revenues based on a ratio of current revenues from the movie divided by its predicted total revenues.

Decision Insight

Improper Adjustments   Revenue recognition and expense matching are key to recording account-ing adjustments. Good adjustments require good management judgment. Failure in judgment led to im-proper adjustments at **Fannie Mae, AOL Time Warner, WorldCom,** and **Xerox.**

Quick Check
Answers—p. 113

1. Describe a company's annual reporting period.
2. Why do companies prepare interim financial statements?
3. What two accounting principles most directly drive the adjusting process?
4. Is cash basis accounting consistent with the matching principle? Why or why not?
5. If your company pays a $4,800 premium on April 1, 2009, for two years' insurance coverage, how much insurance expense is reported in 2010 using cash basis accounting?

Adjusting Accounts

Adjusting accounts is a 3-step process:

Step 1:   Determine the current account balance.

Step 2:   Determine what the current account balance *should be.*

Step 3:   Record an adjusting entry to get from step *1* to step *2*.

Framework for Adjustments

Adjustments are necessary for transactions and events that extend over more than one period. It is helpful to group adjustments by the timing of cash receipt or cash payment in relation to the recognition of the related revenues or expenses. Exhibit 3.4 identifies four types of adjustments.

The left side of this exhibit shows prepaid expenses (including depreciation) and unearned revenues, which reflect transactions when cash is paid or received *before* a related expense or revenue is recognized. They are also called *deferrals* because the recognition of an expense (or revenue) is *deferred* until after the related cash is paid (or received). The right side of this exhibit shows accrued expenses and accrued revenues, which reflect transactions when cash is paid or received *after* a related expense or revenue is recognized. Adjusting entries are neces-sary for each of these so that revenues, expenses, assets, and liabilities are correctly reported. It is helpful to remember that each adjusting entry affects one or more income statement ac-counts *and* one or more balance sheet accounts (but never the Cash account).

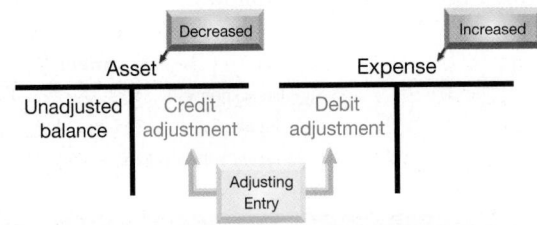

EXHIBIT 3.4

Types of Adjustments

*Includes depreciation.

Prepaid (Deferred) Expenses

Prepaid expenses refer to items *paid for* in advance of receiving their benefits. Prepaid expenses are assets. When these assets are used, their costs become expenses. Adjusting entries for prepaids increase expenses and decrease assets as shown in the T-accounts of Exhibit 3.5. Such adjustments reflect transactions and events that use up prepaid expenses (including passage of time). To illustrate the accounting for prepaid expenses, we look at prepaid insurance, supplies, and depreciation.

P1 Prepare and explain adjusting entries.

EXHIBIT 3.5

Adjusting for Prepaid Expenses

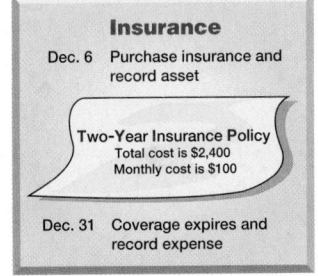

Prepaid Insurance We use our 3-step process for this and all accounting adjustments.

Step 1: We determine the current balance of FastForward's prepaid insurance to be equal to its payment of $2,400 for 24 months of insurance benefits beginning on December 1, 2009.

Step 2: With the passage of time, the benefits of the insurance gradually expire and a portion of the Prepaid Insurance asset becomes expense. For instance, one month's insurance coverage expires by December 31, 2009. This expense is $100, or 1/24 of $2,400.

Step 3: The adjusting entry to record this expense and reduce the asset, along with T-account postings, follows:

Insurance

Dec. 6 Purchase insurance and record asset

Two-Year Insurance Policy
Total cost is $2,400
Monthly cost is $100

Dec. 31 Coverage expires and record expense

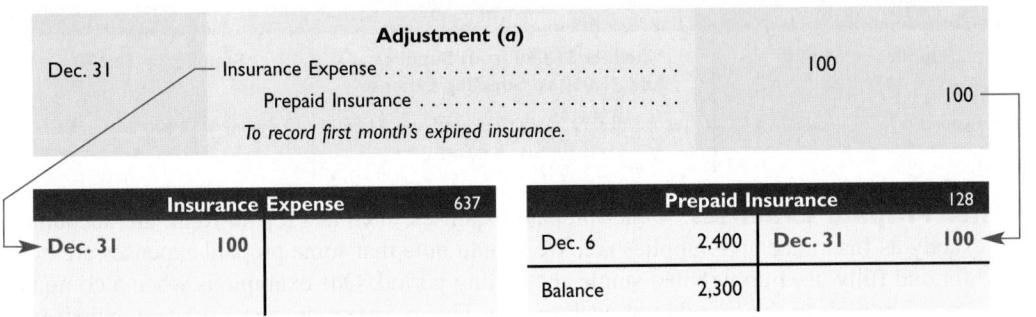

Assets = Liabilities + Equity
−100   −100

Explanation After adjusting and posting, the $100 balance in Insurance Expense and the $2,300 balance in Prepaid Insurance are ready for reporting in financial statements. *Not* making the adjustment on or before December 31 would (1) understate expenses by $100 and overstate net income by $100 for the December income statement and (2) overstate both prepaid insurance (assets) and equity (because of net income) by $100 in the December 31 balance sheet. Exhibit 3.2 showed that 2010's adjustments must transfer a total of $1,200 from Prepaid Insurance to Insurance Expense, and 2011's adjustments must transfer the remaining $1,100 to Insurance Expense. The following table highlights the December 31 adjustment for prepaid insurance.

Point: Many companies record adjusting entries only at the end of each year because of the time and cost necessary.

Before Adjustment	Adjustment	After Adjustment
Prepaid Insurance = $2,400	**Deduct $100 from Prepaid Insurance** **Add $100 to Insurance Expense**	**Prepaid Insurance = $2,300**
Reports $2,400 policy for 24-months' coverage.	Record current month's $100 insurance expense and $100 reduction in prepaid amount.	Reports $2,300 in coverage for remaining 23 months.

Supplies   Supplies are a prepaid expense requiring adjustment.

Supplies

Dec. 2,6,26   Purchase supplies
and record asset

Dec. 31   Supplies used and
record expense

Step 1:   Recall that FastForward purchased $9,720 of supplies in December and used some of them. When financial statements are prepared at December 31, the cost of supplies used during December must be recognized.

Step 2:   When FastForward computes (takes physical count of) its remaining unused supplies at December 31, it finds $8,670 of supplies remaining of the $9,720 total supplies. The $1,050 difference between these two amounts is December's supplies expense.

Step 3:   The adjusting entry to record this expense and reduce the Supplies asset account, along with T-account postings, follows:

Assets = Liabilities + Equity
−1,050   −1,050

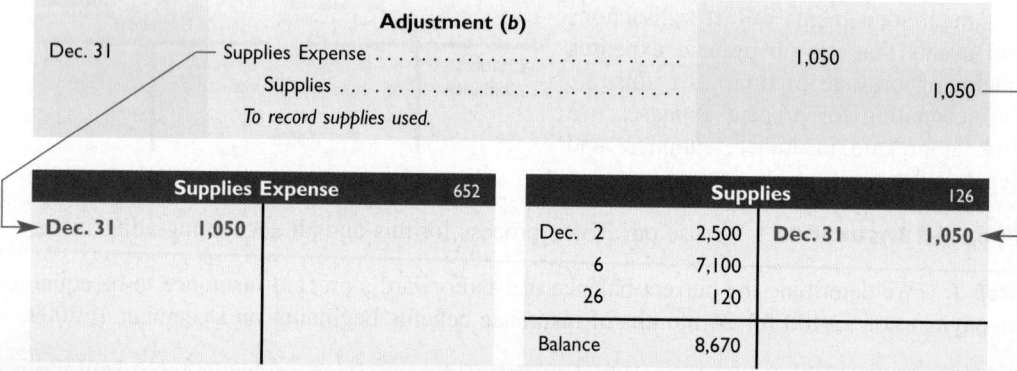

Adjustment (b)

Dec. 31	Supplies Expense	1,050	
	Supplies		1,050
	To record supplies used.		

Supplies Expense	652
Dec. 31	1,050

Supplies			126
Dec. 2	2,500	Dec. 31	1,050
6	7,100		
26	120		
Balance	8,670		

Explanation   The balance of the Supplies account is $8,670 after posting—equaling the cost of the remaining supplies. *Not* making the adjustment on or before December 31 would (1) understate expenses by $1,050 and overstate net income by $1,050 for the December income statement and (2) overstate both supplies and equity (because of net income) by $1,050 in the December 31 balance sheet. The following table highlights the adjustment for supplies.

Before Adjustment	Adjustment	After Adjustment
Supplies = $9,720	**Deduct $1,050 from Supplies** **Add $1,050 to Supplies Expense**	**Supplies = $8,670**
Reports $9,720 in supplies.	Record $1,050 in supplies used and $1,050 as supplies expense.	Reports $8,670 in supplies.

Point: We assume that prepaid and unearned items are recorded in balance sheet accounts. An alternative is to record them in income statement accounts; Appendix 3A discusses this alternative. The adjusted financial statements are identical.

Other Prepaid Expenses   Other prepaid expenses, such as Prepaid Rent, are accounted for exactly as Insurance and Supplies are. We should note that some prepaid expenses are both paid for and fully used up within a single accounting period. One example is when a company pays monthly rent on the first day of each month. This payment creates a prepaid expense on the first day of each month that fully expires by the end of the month. In these special cases, we can record the cash paid with a debit to an expense account instead of an asset account. This practice is described more completely later in the chapter.

 Decision Maker

Investor   A small publishing company signs a well-known athlete to write a book. The company pays the athlete $500,000 to sign plus future book royalties. A note to the company's financial statements says that "prepaid expenses include $500,000 in author signing fees to be matched against future expected sales." Is this accounting for the signing bonus acceptable? How does it affect your analysis? [Answer—p. 112]

Depreciation A special category of prepaid expenses is **plant assets,** which refers to long-term tangible assets used to produce and sell products and services. Plant assets are expected to provide benefits for more than one period. Examples of plant assets are buildings, machines, vehicles, and fixtures. All plant assets, with a general exception for land, eventually wear out or decline in usefulness. The costs of these assets are deferred but are gradually reported as expenses in the income statement over the assets' useful lives (benefit periods). **Depreciation** is the process of allocating the costs of these assets over their expected useful lives. Depreciation expense is recorded with an adjusting entry similar to that for other prepaid expenses.

Point: Depreciation does not necessarily measure decline in market value.

Point: An asset's expected value at the end of its useful life is called *salvage value.*

Step 1: Recall that FastForward purchased equipment for $26,000 in early December to use in earning revenue. This equipment's cost must be depreciated.

Step 2: The equipment is expected to have a useful life (benefit period) of four years and to be worth about $8,000 at the end of four years. This means the *net* cost of this equipment over its useful life is $18,000 ($26,000 − $8,000). We can use any of several methods to allocate this $18,000 net cost to expense. FastForward uses a method called **straight-line depreciation,** which allocates equal amounts of the asset's net cost to depreciation during its useful life. Dividing the $18,000 net cost by the 48 months in the asset's useful life gives a monthly cost of $375 ($18,000/48).

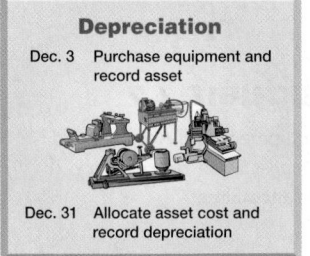

Step 3: The adjusting entry to record monthly depreciation expense, along with T-account postings, follows:

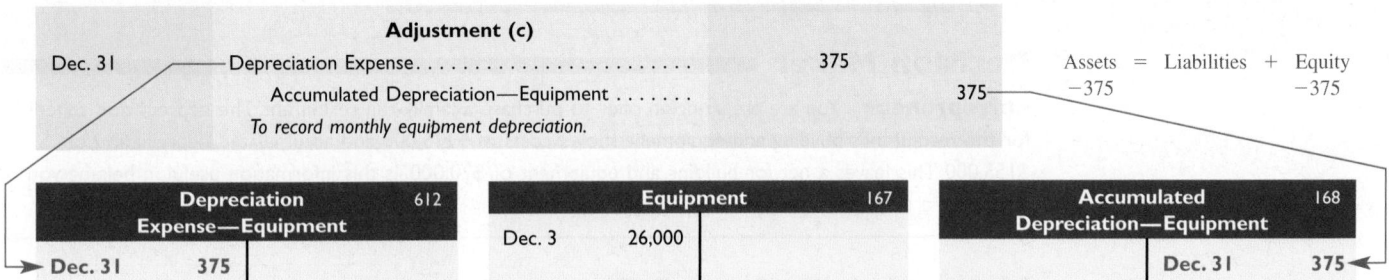

Explanation After posting the adjustment, the Equipment account ($26,000) less its Accumulated Depreciation ($375) account equals the $25,625 net cost of the 47 remaining months in the benefit period. The $375 balance in the Depreciation Expense account is reported in the December income statement. *Not* making the adjustment at December 31 would (1) understate expenses by $375 and overstate net income by $375 for the December income statement and (2) overstate both assets and equity (because of income) by $375 in the December 31 balance sheet. The following table highlights the adjustment for depreciation.

Before Adjustment	Adjustment	After Adjustment
Equipment, net = $26,000	Deduct $375 from Equipment, net Add $375 to Depreciation Expense	Equipment, net = $25,625
Reports $26,000 in equipment.	Record $375 in depreciation and $375 as accumulated depreciation, which is deducted from equipment.	Reports $25,625 in equipment, net of accumulated depreciation.

Accumulated depreciation is kept in a separate contra account. A **contra account** is an account linked with another account, it has an opposite normal balance, and it is reported as a subtraction from that other account's balance. For instance, FastForward's contra account of Accumulated Depreciation—Equipment is subtracted from the Equipment account in the balance sheet (see Exhibit 3.7). This contra account allows balance sheet readers to know both the full costs of assets and the total depreciation.

The title of the contra account, *Accumulated Depreciation,* indicates that this account includes total depreciation expense for all prior periods for which the asset was used. To illustrate, the Equipment and the Accumulated Depreciation accounts appear as in Exhibit 3.6 on February 28, 2010, after three months of adjusting entries. The $1,125 balance in the accumulated depreciation account can be subtracted from its related $26,000 asset cost. The difference ($24,875) between these two balances is the cost of the asset that has not yet been

Point: The cost principle requires an asset to be initially recorded at acquisition cost. Depreciation causes the asset's book value (cost less accumulated depreciation) to decline over time.

EXHIBIT 3.6

Accounts after Three Months of Depreciation Adjustments

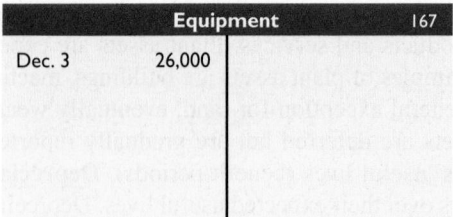

Equipment		167
Dec. 3 26,000		

Accumulated Depreciation—Equipment		168
	Dec. 31	375
	Jan. 31	375
	Feb. 28	375
	Balance	1,125

Point: The net cost of equipment is also called the *depreciable basis*.

depreciated. This difference is called the **book value**, or the *net amount*, which equals the asset's costs less its accumulated depreciation.

These account balances are reported in the assets section of the February 28 balance sheet in Exhibit 3.7.

EXHIBIT 3.7

Equipment and Accumulated Depreciation on February 28 Balance Sheet

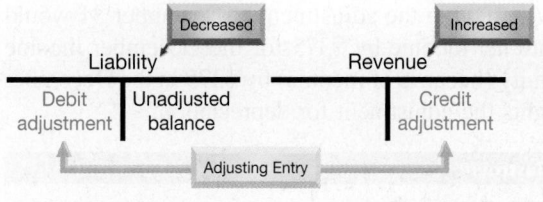

Assets (at February 28, 2010)		
Cash		$ ____
⋮		
Equipment	$26,000	
Less accumulated depreciation	1,125	24,875
Total Assets		$ ____

Commonly titled *Equipment, net*

 Decision Maker

Entrepreneur   You are preparing an offer to purchase a family-run restaurant. The depreciation schedule for the restaurant's building and equipment shows costs of $175,000 and accumulated depreciation of $155,000. This leaves a net for building and equipment of $20,000. Is this information useful in helping you decide on a purchase offer? [Answer—p. 113]

Unearned (Deferred) Revenues

The term **unearned revenues** refers to cash received in advance of providing products and services. Unearned revenues, also called *deferred revenues,* are liabilities. When cash

EXHIBIT 3.8

Adjusting for Unearned Revenues

Liability		Revenue	
	Decreased		Increased
Debit adjustment	Unadjusted balance		Credit adjustment
	Adjusting Entry		

is accepted, an obligation to provide products or services is accepted. As products or services are provided, the unearned revenues become *earned* revenues. Adjusting entries for unearned revenues involve increasing revenues and decreasing unearned revenues, as shown in Exhibit 3.8.

Point: To *defer* is to postpone. We postpone reporting amounts received as revenues until they are earned.

An example of unearned revenues is from **The New York Times Company**, which reports unexpired (unearned) subscriptions of nearly $80 million: "Proceeds from . . . subscriptions are deferred at the time of sale and are recognized in earnings on a pro rata basis over the terms of the subscriptions." Unearned revenues are nearly 10% of the current liabilities for the Times. Another example comes from the **Boston Celtics**. When the Celtics receive cash from advance ticket sales and broadcast fees, they record it in an unearned revenue account called *Deferred Game Revenues.* The Celtics recognize this unearned revenue with adjusting entries on a game-by-game basis. Since the NBA regular season begins in October and ends in April, revenue recognition is mainly limited to this period. For a recent season, the Celtics' quarterly revenues were $0 million for July–September; $34 million for October–December; $48 million for January–March; and $17 million for April–June.

FastForward has unearned revenues. It agreed on December 26 to provide consulting services to a client for a fixed fee of $3,000 for 60 days.

Unearned Revenues

Dec. 26   Cash received in advance and record liability

Thanks for cash in advance. I'll work now through Feb. 24

Dec. 31   Provided services and record revenue

Step 1:   On December 26, the client paid the 60-day fee in advance, covering the period December 27 to February 24. The entry to record the cash received in advance is

Dec. 26	Cash	3,000	
	Unearned Consulting Revenue		3,000
	Received advance payment for services over the		
	next 60 days.		

Assets = Liabilities + Equity
+3,000   +3,000

This advance payment increases cash and creates an obligation to do consulting work over the next 60 days.

Step 2:   As time passes, FastForward earns this payment through consulting. By December 31, it has provided five days' service and earned 5/60 of the $3,000 unearned revenue. This amounts to $250 ($3,000 × 5/60). The *revenue recognition principle* implies that $250 of unearned revenue must be reported as revenue on the December income statement.

Step 3:   The adjusting entry to reduce the liability account and recognize earned revenue, along with T-account postings, follows:

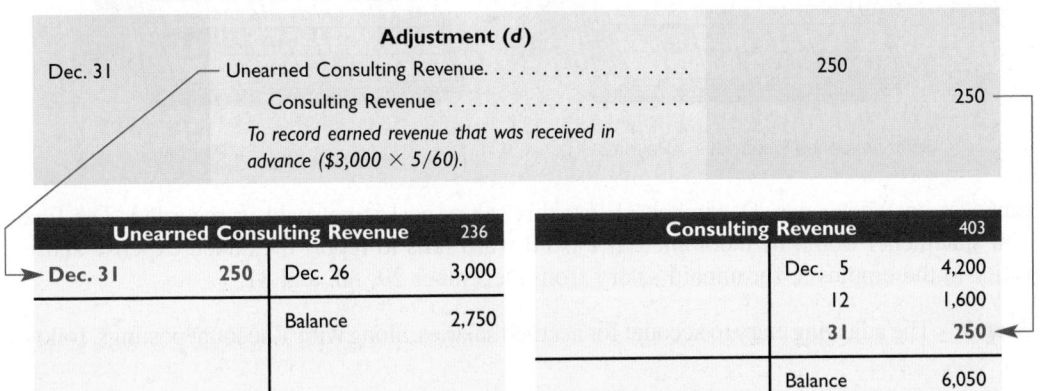

Adjustment (d)

Dec. 31	Unearned Consulting Revenue.	250	
	Consulting Revenue		250
	To record earned revenue that was received in		
	advance ($3,000 × 5/60).		

Assets = Liabilities + Equity
              −250   +250

Unearned Consulting Revenue		236		**Consulting Revenue**		403
Dec. 31	250	Dec. 26	3,000		Dec. 5	4,200
					12	1,600
		Balance	2,750		31	250
					Balance	6,050

Explanation   The adjusting entry transfers $250 from unearned revenue (a liability account) to a revenue account. *Not* making the adjustment (1) understates revenue and net income by $250 in the December income statement and (2) overstates unearned revenue and understates equity by $250 on the December 31 balance sheet. The following highlights the adjustment for unearned revenue.

Before Adjustment	**Adjustment**	**After Adjustment**
Unearned Consulting Revenue = $3,000	**Deduct $250 from Unearned Consulting Revenue Add $250 to Consulting Revenue**	**Unearned Consulting Revenue = $2,750**
Reports $3,000 in unearned revenue for consulting services promised for 60 days.	Record 5 days of earned consulting revenue, which is 5/60 of unearned amount.	Reports $2,750 in unearned revenue for consulting services owed over next 55 days.

Accounting for unearned revenues is crucial to many companies. For example, the **National Retail Federation** reports that gift card sales, which are unearned revenues for sellers, exceed $20 billion annually. Gift cards are now the top selling holiday gift.

Accrued Expenses

Accrued expenses refer to costs that are incurred in a period but are both unpaid and unrecorded. Accrued expenses must be reported on the income statement of the period when incurred. Adjusting entries for recording accrued expenses involves increasing expenses and increasing liabilities as shown in Exhibit 3.9. This adjustment recognizes expenses incurred in a period but not yet paid. Common examples of accrued expenses are salaries, interest,

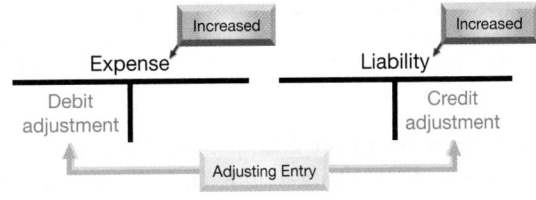

EXHIBIT 3.9

Adjusting for Accrued Expenses

Point: Accrued expenses are also called accrued liabilities.

rent, and taxes. We use salaries and interest to show how to adjust accounts for accrued expenses.

Accrued Salaries Expense   FastForward's employee earns $70 per day, or $350 for a five-day workweek beginning on Monday and ending on Friday.

Step 1:   Its employee is paid every two weeks on Friday. On December 12 and 26, the wages are paid, recorded in the journal, and posted to the ledger.

Step 2:   The calendar in Exhibit 3.10 shows three working days after the December 26 payday (29, 30, and 31). This means the employee has earned three days' salary by the close of

EXHIBIT 3.10

Salary Accrual and Paydays

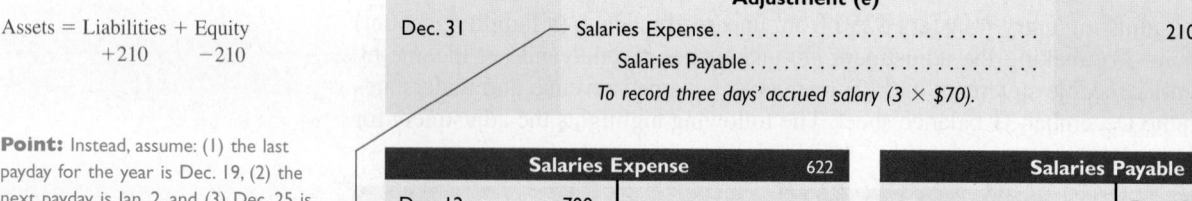

Pay period begins

Salary expense incurred   Payday   Payday

business on Wednesday, December 31, yet this salary cost is not paid or recorded. The financial statements would be incomplete if FastForward fails to report the added expense and liability to the employee for unpaid salary from December 29, 30, and 31.

Step 3:   The adjusting entry to account for accrued salaries, along with T-account postings, follows:

Assets = Liabilities + Equity
          +210   −210

Adjustment (e)		
Dec. 31 Salaries Expense	210	
Salaries Payable		210
To record three days' accrued salary (3 × $70).		

Salaries Expense		622
Dec. 12	700	
26	700	
31	210	
Balance	1,610	

Salaries Payable		209
	Dec. 31	210

Explanation   Salaries expense of $1,610 is reported on the December income statement and $210 of salaries payable (liability) is reported in the balance sheet. *Not* making the adjustment (1) understates salaries expense and overstates net income by $210 in the December income statement and (2) understates salaries payable (liabilities) and overstates equity by $210 on the December 31 balance sheet. The following highlights the adjustment for salaries incurred.

Before Adjustment	Adjustment	After Adjustment
Salaries Payable = $0	Add $210 to Salaries Payable Add $210 to Salaries Expense	Salaries Payable = $210
Reports $0 from employee salaries incurred but not yet paid in cash.	Record 3 days' salaries owed to employee, but not yet paid, at $70 per day.	Reports $210 salaries payable to employee but not yet paid.

Accrued Interest Expense   Companies commonly have accrued interest expense on notes payable and other long-term liabilities at the end of a period. Interest expense is incurred with the passage of time. Unless interest is paid on the last day of an accounting period, we need to adjust for interest expense incurred but not yet paid. This means we must accrue interest cost from the most recent payment date up to the end of the period. The formula for computing accrued interest is:

Principal amount owed × Annual interest rate × Fraction of year since last payment date.

To illustrate, if a company has a $6,000 loan from a bank at 6% annual interest, then 30 days' accrued interest expense is $30—computed as $6,000 × 0.06 × 30/360. The adjusting entry would be to debit Interest Expense for $30 and credit Interest Payable for $30.

Point: Interest computations assume a 360-day year; known as the *bankers' rule.*

Future Payment of Accrued Expenses Adjusting entries for accrued expenses foretell cash transactions in future periods. Specifically, accrued expenses at the end of one accounting period result in *cash payment* in a *future period*(s). To illustrate, recall that FastForward recorded accrued salaries of $210. On January 9, the first payday of the next period, the following entry settles the accrued liability (salaries payable) and records salaries expense for seven days of work in January:

Jan. 9	Salaries Payable (3 days at $70 per day)............	210	
	Salaries Expense (7 days at $70 per day)..........	490	
	Cash		700
	Paid two weeks' salary including three days		
	accrued in December.		

Assets = Liabilities + Equity
−700   −210   −490

The $210 debit reflects the payment of the liability for the three days' salary accrued on December 31. The $490 debit records the salary for January's first seven working days (including the New Year's Day holiday) as an expense of the new accounting period. The $700 credit records the total amount of cash paid to the employee.

Accrued Revenues

The term **accrued revenues** refers to revenues earned in a period that are both unrecorded and not yet received in cash (or other assets). An example is a technician who bills customers only when the job is done. If one-third of a job is complete by the end of a period, then the technician must record one-third of the expected billing as revenue in that period—even though there is no billing or collection. The adjusting entries for accrued revenues increase assets and increase revenues as shown in Exhibit 3.11. Accrued revenues commonly arise from services, products, interest, and rent. We use service fees and interest to show how to adjust for accrued revenues.

Point: Accrued revenues are also called *accrued assets.*

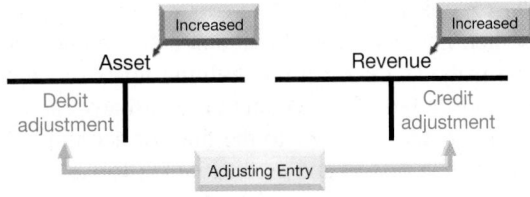

EXHIBIT 3.11

Adjusting for Accrued Revenues

Accrued Services Revenue Accrued revenues are not recorded until adjusting entries are made at the end of the accounting period. These accrued revenues are earned but unrecorded because either the buyer has not yet paid for them or the seller has not yet billed the buyer. FastForward provides an example.

Step 1: In the second week of December, it agreed to provide 30 days of consulting services to a local sports club for a fixed fee of $2,700. The terms of the initial agreement call for FastForward to provide services from December 12, 2009, through January 10, 2010, or 30 days of service. The club agrees to pay FastForward $2,700 on January 10, 2010, when the service period is complete.

Step 2: At December 31, 2009, 20 days of services have already been provided. Since the contracted services are not yet entirely provided, FastForward has neither billed the club nor recorded the services already provided. Still, FastForward has earned two-thirds of the 30-day

Accrued Revenues

Dec. 31 Record revenue and receivable for services provided but unbilled

Pay me next month

Jan. 10 Receive cash and reduce receivable

fee, or $1,800 ($2,700 × 20/30). The *revenue recognition principle* implies that it must report the $1,800 on the December income statement. The balance sheet also must report that the club owes FastForward $1,800.

Step 3: The year-end adjusting entry to account for accrued services revenue is

Assets = Liabilities + Equity
+1,800   +1,800

	Adjustment (f)		
Dec. 31	Accounts Receivable...........................	1,800	
	Consulting Revenue.......................		1,800
	To record 20 days' accrued revenue.		

Accounts Receivable				106
Dec. 12	1,900	Dec. 22	1,900	
31	1,800			
Balance	1,800			

Consulting Revenue		403
Dec. 5	4,200
12	1,600
31	250
31	1,800
Balance	7,850

Example: What is the adjusting entry if the 30-day consulting period began on December 22? *Answer:* One-third of the fee is earned:
Accounts Receivable... 900
   Consulting Revenue... 900

Explanation Accounts receivable are reported on the balance sheet at $1,800, and the $7,850 total of consulting revenue is reported on the income statement. *Not* making the adjustment would understate (1) both consulting revenue and net income by $1,800 in the December income statement and (2) both accounts receivable (assets) and equity by $1,800 on the December 31 balance sheet. The following table highlights the adjustment for accrued revenue.

Before Adjustment	Adjustment	After Adjustment
Accounts Receivable = $0	**Add $1,800 to Accounts Receivable** **Add $1,800 to Consulting Revenue**	**Accounts Receivable = $1,800**
Reports $0 from revenue earned but not yet received in cash.	Record 20 days of earned consulting revenue, which is 20/30 of total contract amount.	Reports $1,800 in accounts receivable from consulting services provided.

Accrued Interest Revenue In addition to the accrued interest expense we described earlier, interest can yield an accrued revenue when a debtor owes money (or other assets) to a company. If a company is holding notes or accounts receivable that produce interest revenue, we must adjust the accounts to record any earned and yet uncollected interest revenue. The adjusting entry is similar to the one for accruing services revenue. Specifically, we debit Interest Receivable (asset) and credit Interest Revenue.

Future Receipt of Accrued Revenues Accrued revenues at the end of one accounting period result in *cash receipts* in a *future period*(s). To illustrate, recall that FastForward made an adjusting entry for $1,800 to record 20 days' accrued revenue earned from its consulting contract. When FastForward receives $2,700 cash on January 10 for the entire contract amount, it makes the following entry to remove the accrued asset (accounts receivable) and recognize the revenue earned in January. The $2,700 debit reflects the cash received. The $1,800 credit reflects the removal of the receivable, and the $900 credit records the revenue earned in January.

Assets = Liabilities + Equity
+2,700   +900
−1,800

Jan. 10	Cash	2,700	
	Accounts Receivable (20 days at $90 per day)		1,800
	Consulting Revenue (10 days at $90 per day)		900
	Received cash for the accrued asset and recorded *earned consulting revenue for January.*		

Decision Maker ▬▬▬▬▬▬▬▬▬▬▬▬▬▬▬▬▬▬▬▬▬▬▬▬▬▬▬

Loan Officer   The owner of an electronics store applies for a business loan. The store's financial statements reveal large increases in current-year revenues and income. Analysis shows that these increases are due to a promotion that let consumers buy now and pay nothing until January 1 of next year. The store recorded these sales as accrued revenue. Does your analysis raise any concerns? [Answer—p. 113]

Links to Financial Statements

The process of adjusting accounts is intended to bring an asset or liability account balance to its correct amount. It also updates a related expense or revenue account. These adjustments are necessary for transactions and events that extend over more than one period. (Adjusting entries are posted like any other entry.)

Exhibit 3.12 summarizes the four types of transactions requiring adjustment. Understanding this exhibit is important to understanding the adjusting process and its importance to financial statements. Remember that each adjusting entry affects one or more income statement accounts *and* one or more balance sheet accounts (but never cash).

A1	Explain how accounting adjustments link to financial statements.

EXHIBIT 3.12

Summary of Adjustments and Financial Statement Links

Category	BEFORE Adjusting		Adjusting Entry
	Balance Sheet	Income Statement	
Prepaid expenses†	Asset overstated	Expense understated	**Dr. Expense**
	Equity overstated		**Cr. Asset***
Unearned revenues†	Liability overstated	Revenue understated	Dr. Liability
	Equity understated		Cr. Revenue
Accrued expenses	Liability understated	Expense understated	**Dr. Expense**
	Equity overstated		**Cr. Liability**
Accrued revenues	Asset understated	Revenue understated	Dr. Asset
	Equity understated		Cr. Revenue

* For depreciation, the credit is to Accumulated Depreciation (contra asset).

† Exhibit assumes that prepaid expenses are initially recorded as assets and that unearned revenues are initially recorded as liabilities.

Information about some adjustments is not always available until several days or even weeks after the period-end. This means that some adjusting and closing entries are recorded later than, but dated as of, the last day of the period. One example is a company that receives a utility bill on January 10 for costs incurred for the month of December. When it receives the bill, the company records the expense and the payable as of December 31. Other examples include long-distance phone usage and costs of many Web billings. The December income statement reflects these additional expenses incurred, and the December 31 balance sheet includes these payables, although the amounts were not actually known on December 31.

Decision Ethics ▬▬▬▬▬▬▬▬▬▬▬▬▬▬▬▬▬▬▬▬▬▬▬▬

Financial Officer   At year-end, the president instructs you, the financial officer, not to record accrued expenses until next year because they will not be paid until then. The president also directs you to record in current-year sales a recent purchase order from a customer that requires merchandise to be delivered two weeks after the year-end. Your company would report a net income instead of a net loss if you carry out these instructions. What do you do? [Answer—p. 113]

Quick Check   Answers—p. 113

6. If an adjusting entry for accrued revenues of $200 at year-end is omitted, what is this error's effect on the year-end income statement and balance sheet?

7. What is a contra account? Explain its purpose.

8. What is an accrued expense? Give an example.

9. Describe how an unearned revenue arises. Give an example.

Adjusted Trial Balance

P2   Explain and prepare an adjusted trial balance.

An **unadjusted trial balance** is a list of accounts and balances prepared *before* adjustments are recorded. An **adjusted trial balance** is a list of accounts and balances prepared *after* adjusting entries have been recorded and posted to the ledger.

Exhibit 3.13 shows both the unadjusted and the adjusted trial balances for FastForward at December 31, 2009. The order of accounts in the trial balance is usually set up to match the order in the chart of accounts. Several new accounts arise from the adjusting entries.

EXHIBIT 3.13

Unadjusted and Adjusted Trial Balances

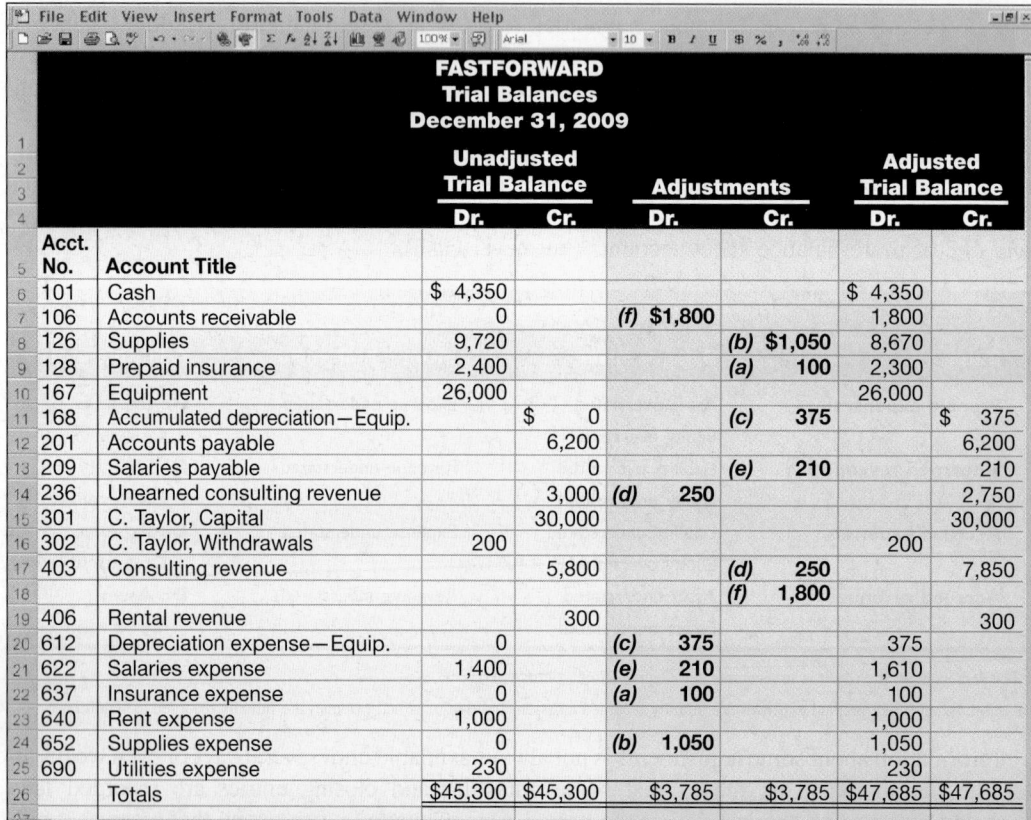

FASTFORWARD
Trial Balances
December 31, 2009

Acct. No.	Account Title	Unadjusted Trial Balance Dr.	Cr.	Adjustments Dr.	Cr.	Adjusted Trial Balance Dr.	Cr.
101	Cash	$ 4,350				$ 4,350	
106	Accounts receivable	0		(f) $1,800		1,800	
126	Supplies	9,720			(b) $1,050	8,670	
128	Prepaid insurance	2,400			(a) 100	2,300	
167	Equipment	26,000				26,000	
168	Accumulated depreciation—Equip.		$ 0		(c) 375		$ 375
201	Accounts payable		6,200				6,200
209	Salaries payable		0		(e) 210		210
236	Unearned consulting revenue		3,000	(d) 250			2,750
301	C. Taylor, Capital		30,000				30,000
302	C. Taylor, Withdrawals	200				200	
403	Consulting revenue		5,800		(d) 250		7,850
					(f) 1,800		
406	Rental revenue		300				300
612	Depreciation expense—Equip.	0		(c) 375		375	
622	Salaries expense	1,400		(e) 210		1,610	
637	Insurance expense	0		(a) 100		100	
640	Rent expense	1,000				1,000	
652	Supplies expense	0		(b) 1,050		1,050	
690	Utilities expense	230				230	
	Totals	$45,300	$45,300	$3,785	$3,785	$47,685	$47,685

Each adjustment (see middle columns) is identified by a letter in parentheses that links it to an adjusting entry explained earlier. Each amount in the Adjusted Trial Balance columns is computed by taking that account's amount from the Unadjusted Trial Balance columns and adding or subtracting any adjustment(s). To illustrate, Supplies has a $9,720 Dr. balance in the unadjusted columns. Subtracting the $1,050 Cr. amount shown in the adjustments columns yields an adjusted $8,670 Dr. balance for Supplies. An account can have more than one adjustment, such as for Consulting Revenue. Also, some accounts might not require adjustment for this period, such as Accounts Payable.

Preparing Financial Statements

P3   Prepare financial statements from an adjusted trial balance.

Point: Sarbanes-Oxley Act requires that financial statements filed with the SEC be certified by the CEO and CFO, including a declaration that the statements fairly present the issuer's operations and financial condition. Violators can receive fines and/or prison terms.

We can prepare financial statements directly from information in the *adjusted* trial balance. An adjusted trial balance (see the right-most columns in Exhibit 3.13) includes all accounts and balances appearing in financial statements, and is easier to work from than the entire ledger when preparing financial statements.

Exhibit 3.14 shows how revenue and expense balances are transferred from the adjusted trial balance to the income statement (red lines). The net income and the withdrawals amount are then used to prepare the statement of owner's equity (black lines). Asset and liability balances on the adjusted trial balance are then transferred to the balance sheet (blue lines). The ending capital is determined on the statement of owner's equity and transferred to the balance sheet (green lines).

EXHIBIT 3.14

Preparing Financial Statements (Adjusted Trial Balance from Exhibit 3.13)

FASTFORWARD
Adjusted Trial Balance
December 31, 2009

Acct. No.	Account Title	Debit	Credit
101	Cash	$ 4,350	
106	Accounts receivable	1,800	
126	Supplies	8,670	
128	Prepaid insurance	2,300	
167	Equipment	26,000	
168	Accumulated depreciation—Equip.		$ 375
201	Accounts payable		6,200
209	Salaries payable		210
236	Unearned consulting revenue		2,750
301	C. Taylor, Capital		30,000
302	C. Taylor, Withdrawals	200	
403	Consulting revenue		7,850
406	Rental revenue		300
612	Depreciation expense—Equip.	375	
622	Salaries expense	1,610	
637	Insurance expense	100	
640	Rent expense	1,000	
652	Supplies expense	1,050	
690	Utilities expense	230	
	Totals	$47,685	$47,685

Step 3 Prepare balance sheet

FASTFORWARD
Balance Sheet
December 31, 2009

Assets

Cash		$ 4,350
Accounts receivable		1,800
Supplies		8,670
Prepaid insurance		2,300
Equipment	$26,000	
Less accumulated depreciation	375	25,625
Total assets		$ 42,745

Liabilities

Accounts payable	$ 6,200
Salaries payable	210
Unearned consulting revenue	2,750
Total liabilities	9,160

Equity

C. Taylor, Capital	33,585
Total liabilities and equity	$ 42,745

Step 2 Prepare statement of owner's equity

FASTFORWARD
Statement of Owner's Equity
For Month Ended December 31, 2009

C. Taylor, Capital, December 1		$ 0
Plus: Investments by owner	$30,000	
Net income	3,785	
		33,785
Less: Withdrawals by owner		200
C. Taylor, Capital, December 31		$33,585

Step 1 Prepare income statement

FASTFORWARD
Income Statement
For Month Ended December 31, 2009

Revenues		
Consulting revenue	$7,850	
Rental revenue	300	
Total revenues		$8,150
Expenses		
Depreciation expense—Equip.	375	
Salaries expense	1,610	
Insurance expense	100	
Rent expense	1,000	
Supplies expense	1,050	
Utilities expense	230	
Total expenses		4,365
Net income		$3,785

We usually prepare financial statements in the following order: income statement, statement of owner's equity, and balance sheet. This order makes sense because the balance sheet uses information from the statement of owner's equity, which in turn uses information from the income statement. The statement of cash flows is usually the final statement prepared.

Quick Check

Answers—p. 113

10. Music-Mart records $1,000 of accrued salaries on December 31. Five days later, on January 5 (the next payday), salaries of $7,000 are paid. What is the January 5 entry?

11. Jordan Air has the following information in its unadjusted and adjusted trial balances. What are the adjusting entries that Jordan Air likely recorded?

	Unadjusted		Adjusted	
	Debit	Credit	Debit	Credit
Prepaid insurance	$6,200		$5,900	
Salaries payable		$ 0		$1,400

12. What accounts are taken from the adjusted trial balance to prepare an income statement?

13. In preparing financial statements from an adjusted trial balance, what statement is usually prepared second?

Decision Analysis   Profit Margin

A2　Compute profit margin and describe its use in analyzing company performance.

A useful measure of a company's operating results is the ratio of its net income to net sales. This ratio is called **profit margin,** or *return on sales,* and is computed as in Exhibit 3.15.

EXHIBIT 3.15

Profit Margin

$$\text{Profit margin} = \frac{\text{Net income}}{\text{Net sales}}$$

This ratio is interpreted as reflecting the percent of profit in each dollar of sales. To illustrate how we compute and use profit margin, let's look at the results of Limited Brands, Inc., in Exhibit 3.16 for the period 2004 through 2007.

EXHIBIT 3.16

Limited Brands' Profit Margin

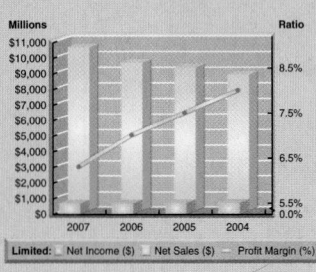

$ in millions	2007	2006	2005	2004
Net income	$ 676	$ 683	$ 705	$ 717
Net sales	$10,671	$9,699	$9,408	$8,934
Profit margin	6.3%	7.0%	7.5%	8.0%
Industry profit margin	1.6%	1.5%	1.4%	1.5%

The Limited's average profit margin is 7.2% during this period. This favorably compares to the average industry profit margin of 1.5%. However, Limited's profit margin has declined in recent years—from 8.0% in 2004 to 6.3% in 2007 (see margin graph). Future success depends on Limited maintaining and preferably increasing its profit margin.

Demonstration Problem 1

DP3

The following information relates to Fanning's Electronics on December 31, 2009. The company, which uses the calendar year as its annual reporting period, initially records prepaid and unearned items in balance sheet accounts (assets and liabilities, respectively).

a. The company's weekly payroll is $8,750, paid each Friday for a five-day workweek. Assume December 31, 2009, falls on a Monday, but the employees will not be paid their wages until Friday, January 4, 2010.

b. Eighteen months earlier, on July 1, 2008, the company purchased equipment that cost $20,000. Its useful life is predicted to be five years, at which time the equipment is expected to be worthless (zero salvage value).

c. On October 1, 2009, the company agreed to work on a new housing development. The company is paid $120,000 on October 1 in advance of future installation of similar alarm systems in 24 new homes. That amount was credited to the Unearned Services Revenue account. Between October 1 and December 31, work on 20 homes was completed.

d. On September 1, 2009, the company purchased a 12-month insurance policy for $1,800. The transaction was recorded with an $1,800 debit to Prepaid Insurance.

e. On December 29, 2009, the company completed a $7,000 service that has not been billed and not recorded as of December 31, 2009.

Required

1. Prepare any necessary adjusting entries on December 31, 2009, in relation to transactions and events *a* through *e*.

2. Prepare T-accounts for the accounts affected by adjusting entries, and post the adjusting entries. Determine the adjusted balances for the Unearned Revenue and the Prepaid Insurance accounts.

3. Complete the following table and determine the amounts and effects of your adjusting entries on the year 2009 income statement and the December 31, 2009, balance sheet. Use up (down) arrows to indicate an increase (decrease) in the Effect columns.

Entry	Amount in the Entry	Effect on Net Income	Effect on Total Assets	Effect on Total Liabilities	Effect on Total Equity

Planning the Solution

- Analyze each situation to determine which accounts need to be updated with an adjustment.
- Calculate the amount of each adjustment and prepare the necessary journal entries.
- Show the amount of each adjustment in the designated accounts, determine the adjusted balance, and identify the balance sheet classification of the account.
- Determine each entry's effect on net income for the year and on total assets, total liabilities, and total equity at the end of the year.

Solution to Demonstration Problem 1

1. Adjusting journal entries.

(a) Dec. 31	Wages Expense	1,750	
	Wages Payable		1,750
	To accrue wages for the last day of the year ($8,750 × 1/5).		
(b) Dec. 31	Depreciation Expense—Equipment	4,000	
	Accumulated Depreciation—Equipment		4,000
	To record depreciation expense for the year ($20,000/5 years = $4,000 per year).		
(c) Dec. 31	Unearned Services Revenue	100,000	
	Services Revenue		100,000
	To recognize services revenue earned ($120,000 × 20/24).		
(d) Dec. 31	Insurance Expense	600	
	Prepaid Insurance		600
	To adjust for expired portion of insurance ($1,800 × 4/12).		
(e) Dec. 31	Accounts Receivable......................	7,000	
	Services Revenue		7,000
	To record services revenue earned.		

2. T-accounts for adjusting journal entries *a* through *e*.

Wages Expense			
(a)	1,750		

Wages Payable			
		(a)	1,750

Depreciation Expense—Equipment	
(b)	4,000

Accumulated Depreciation—Equipment			
		(b)	4,000

Unearned Revenue			
		Unadj. Bal.	120,000
(c)	100,000		
		Adj. Bal.	20,000

Services Revenue			
		(c)	100,000
		(e)	7,000
		Adj. Bal.	107,000

Insurance Expense	
(d)	600

Prepaid Insurance			
Unadj. Bal.	1,800		
		(d)	600
Adj. Bal.	1,200		

Accounts Receivable	
(e)	7,000

3. Financial statement effects of adjusting journal entries.

Entry	Amount in the Entry	Effect on Net Income	Effect on Total Assets	Effect on Total Liabilities	Effect on Total Equity
a	$ 1,750	$ 1,750 ↓	No effect	$ 1,750 ↑	$ 1,750 ↓
b	4,000	4,000 ↓	$4,000 ↓	No effect	4,000 ↓
c	100,000	100,000 ↑	No effect	$100,000 ↓	100,000 ↑
d	600	600 ↓	$ 600 ↓	No effect	600 ↓
e	7,000	7,000 ↑	$7,000 ↑	No effect	7,000 ↑

Demonstration Problem 2

Use the following adjusted trial balance to answer questions 1–3.

CHOI COMPANY Adjusted Trial Balance December 31		
	Debit	Credit
Cash	$ 3,050	
Accounts receivable	400	
Prepaid insurance	830	
Supplies	80	
Equipment	217,200	
Accumulated depreciation—Equipment		$ 29,100
Wages payable		880

[continued on next page]

[continued from previous page]

Interest payable		3,600
Unearned rent		460
Long-term notes payable		150,000
M. Choi, Capital		40,340
M. Choi, Withdrawals	21,000	
Rent earned		57,500
Wages expense	25,000	
Utilities expense	1,900	
Insurance expense	3,200	
Supplies expense	250	
Depreciation expense—Equipment	5,970	
Interest expense	3,000	
Totals	$281,880	$281,880

1. Prepare the annual income statement from the adjusted trial balance of Choi Company.

Answer:

CHOI COMPANY		
Income Statement		
For Year Ended December 31		
Revenues		
Rent earned		$57,500
Expenses		
Wages expense	$25,000	
Utilities expense	1,900	
Insurance expense	3,200	
Supplies expense	250	
Depreciation expense—Equipment	5,970	
Interest expense	3,000	
Total expenses		39,320
Net income		$18,180

2. Prepare a statement of owner's equity from the adjusted trial balance of Choi Company. Choi's capital account balance of $40,340 consists of a $30,340 balance from the prior year-end, plus a $10,000 owner investment during the current year.

Answer:

CHOI COMPANY		
Statement of Owner's Equity		
For Year Ended December 31		
M. Choi, Capital, December 31 prior year-end		$30,340
Plus: Owner investments	$10,000	
Net income	18,180	28,180
....		58,520
Less: Withdrawals by owner		21,000
M. Choi, Capital, December 31 current year-end		$37,520

3. Prepare a balance sheet from the adjusted trial balance of Choi Company.

Answer:

CHOI COMPANY Balance Sheet December 31		
Assets		
Cash		$ 3,050
Accounts receivable		400
Prepaid insurance		830
Supplies		80
Equipment	$217,200	
Less accumulated depreciation	29,100	188,100
Total assets		$192,460
Liabilities		
Wages payable		$ 880
Interest payable		3,600
Unearned rent		460
Long-term notes payable		150,000
Total liabilities		154,940
Equity		
M. Choi, Capital		37,520
Total liabilities and equity		$192,460

APPENDIX

3A Alternative Accounting for Prepayments

This appendix explains an alternative in accounting for prepaid expenses and unearned revenues.

Recording the Prepayment of Expenses in Expense Accounts

P4 Explain the alternatives in accounting for prepaids.

An alternative method is to record *all* prepaid expenses with debits to expense accounts. If any prepaids remain unused or unexpired at the end of an accounting period, then adjusting entries must transfer the cost of the unused portions from expense accounts to prepaid expense (asset) accounts. This alternative method is acceptable. The financial statements are identical under either method, but the adjusting entries are different. To illustrate the differences between these two methods, let's look at FastForward's cash payment of December 6 for 24 months of insurance coverage beginning on December 1. FastForward recorded that payment with a debit to an asset account, but it could have recorded a debit to an expense account. These alternatives are shown in Exhibit 3A.1.

EXHIBIT 3A.1

Alternative Initial Entries for Prepaid Expenses

			Payment Recorded as Asset	Payment Recorded as Expense
Dec. 6	Prepaid Insurance		2,400	
	Cash			2,400	
Dec. 6	Insurance Expense			2,400
	Cash				2,400

At the end of its accounting period on December 31, insurance protection for one month has expired. This means $100 ($2,400/24) of insurance coverage expired and is an expense for December. The adjusting entry depends on how the original payment was recorded. This is shown in Exhibit 3A.2.

EXHIBIT 3A.2

Adjusting Entry for Prepaid Expenses for the Two Alternatives

		Payment Recorded as Asset	Payment Recorded as Expense
Dec. 31	Insurance Expense	100	
	Prepaid Insurance	100	
Dec. 31	Prepaid Insurance		2,300
	Insurance Expense		2,300

When these entries are posted to the accounts in the ledger, we can see that these two methods give identical results. The December 31 adjusted account balances in Exhibit 3A.3 show Prepaid Insurance of $2,300 and Insurance Expense of $100 for both methods.

EXHIBIT 3A.3

Account Balances under Two Alternatives for Recording Prepaid Expenses

Payment Recorded as Asset

Prepaid Insurance			128
Dec. 6	2,400	Dec. 31	100
Balance	2,300		

Insurance Expense			637
Dec. 31	100		

Payment Recorded as Expense

Prepaid Insurance			128
Dec. 31	2,300		

Insurance Expense			637
Dec. 6	2,400	Dec. 31	2,300
Balance	100		

Recording the Prepayment of Revenues in Revenue Accounts

As with prepaid expenses, an alternative method is to record *all* unearned revenues with credits to revenue accounts. If any revenues are unearned at the end of an accounting period, then adjusting entries must transfer the unearned portions from revenue accounts to unearned revenue (liability) accounts. This alternative method is acceptable. The adjusting entries are different for these two alternatives, but the financial statements are identical. To illustrate the accounting differences between these two methods, let's look at FastForward's December 26 receipt of $3,000 for consulting services covering the period December 27 to February 24. FastForward recorded this transaction with a credit to a liability account. The alternative is to record it with a credit to a revenue account, as shown in Exhibit 3A.4.

EXHIBIT 3A.4

Alternative Initial Entries for Unearned Revenues

		Receipt Recorded as Liability	Receipt Recorded as Revenue
Dec. 26	Cash	3,000	
	Unearned Consulting Revenue	3,000	
Dec. 26	Cash		3,000
	Consulting Revenue		3,000

By the end of its accounting period on December 31, FastForward has earned $250 of this revenue. This means $250 of the liability has been satisfied. Depending on how the initial receipt is recorded, the adjusting entry is as shown in Exhibit 3A.5.

EXHIBIT 3A.5

Adjusting Entry for Unearned Revenues for the Two Alternatives

		Receipt Recorded as Liability	Receipt Recorded as Revenue
Dec. 31	Unearned Consulting Revenue	250	
	Consulting Revenue	250	
Dec. 31	Consulting Revenue		2,750
	Unearned Consulting Revenue		2,750

After adjusting entries are posted, the two alternatives give identical results. The December 31 adjusted account balances in Exhibit 3A.6 show unearned consulting revenue of $2,750 and consulting revenue of $250 for both methods.

EXHIBIT 3A.6

Account Balances under Two Alternatives for Recording Unearned Revenues

Receipt Recorded as Liability			
Unearned Consulting Revenue			**236**
Dec. 31	250	Dec. 26	3,000
		Balance	2,750

Receipt Recorded as Revenue			
Unearned Consulting Revenue			**236**
		Dec. 31	2,750

Consulting Revenue			**403**
		Dec. 31	250

Consulting Revenue			**403**
Dec. 31	2,750	Dec. 26	3,000
		Balance	250

Summary

C1 Explain the importance of periodic reporting and the time period assumption. The value of information is often linked to its timeliness. To provide timely information, accounting systems prepare periodic reports at regular intervals. The time period assumption presumes that an organization's activities can be divided into specific time periods for periodic reporting.

C2 Explain accrual accounting and how it improves financial statements. Accrual accounting recognizes revenue when earned and expenses when incurred—not necessarily when cash inflows and outflows occur. This information is valuable in assessing a company's financial position and performance.

C3 Identify the types of adjustments and their purpose. Adjustments can be grouped according to the timing of cash receipts and cash payments relative to when they are recognized as revenues or expenses as follows: prepaid expenses, unearned revenues, accrued expenses, and accrued revenues. Adjusting entries are necessary so that revenues, expenses, assets, and liabilities are correctly reported.

A1 Explain how accounting adjustments link to financial statements. Accounting adjustments bring an asset or liability account balance to its correct amount. They also update related expense or revenue accounts. Every adjusting entry affects one or more income statement accounts *and* one or more balance sheet accounts. An adjusting entry never affects cash.

A2 Compute profit margin and describe its use in analyzing company performance. *Profit margin* is defined as the reporting period's net income divided by its net sales. Profit margin reflects on a company's earnings activities by showing how much income is in each dollar of sales.

P1 Prepare and explain adjusting entries. *Prepaid expenses* refer to items paid for in advance of receiving their benefits.

Prepaid expenses are assets. Adjusting entries for prepaids involve increasing (debiting) expenses and decreasing (crediting) assets. *Unearned* (or *prepaid*) *revenues* refer to cash received in advance of providing products and services. Unearned revenues are liabilities. Adjusting entries for unearned revenues involves increasing (crediting) revenues and decreasing (debiting) unearned revenues. *Accrued expenses* refer to costs incurred in a period that are both unpaid and unrecorded. Adjusting entries for recording accrued expenses involve increasing (debiting) expenses and increasing (crediting) liabilities. *Accrued revenues* refer to revenues earned in a period that are both unrecorded and not yet received in cash. Adjusting entries for recording accrued revenues involve increasing (debiting) assets and increasing (crediting) revenues.

P2 Explain and prepare an adjusted trial balance. An adjusted trial balance is a list of accounts and balances prepared after recording and posting adjusting entries. Financial statements are often prepared from the adjusted trial balance.

P3 Prepare financial statements from an adjusted trial balance. Revenue and expense balances are reported on the income statement. Asset, liability, and equity balances are reported on the balance sheet. We usually prepare statements in the following order: income statement, statement of owner's equity, balance sheet, and statement of cash flows.

P4ᴬ Explain the alternatives in accounting for prepaids. Charging all prepaid expenses to expense accounts when they are purchased is acceptable. When this is done, adjusting entries must transfer any unexpired amounts from expense accounts to asset accounts. Crediting all unearned revenues to revenue accounts when cash is received is also acceptable. In this case, the adjusting entries must transfer any unearned amounts from revenue accounts to unearned revenue accounts.

Guidance Answers to **Decision Maker** and **Decision Ethics**

Investor Prepaid expenses are items paid for in advance of receiving their benefits. They are assets and are expensed as they are used up. The publishing company's treatment of the signing bonus is

acceptable provided future book sales can at least match the $500,000 expense. As an investor, you are concerned about the risk of future book sales. The riskier the likelihood of future book sales is, the more likely your analysis is to treat the $500,000, or a portion of it, as an expense, not a prepaid expense (asset).

Entrepreneur   Depreciation is a process of cost allocation, not asset valuation. Knowing the depreciation schedule is not especially useful in your estimation of what the building and equipment are currently worth. Your own assessment of the age, quality, and usefulness of the building and equipment is more important.

Loan Officer   Your concern in lending to this store arises from analysis of current-year sales. While increased revenues and income are fine, your concern is with collectibility of these promotional sales. If the owner sold products to customers with poor records of paying

bills, then collectibility of these sales is low. Your analysis must assess this possibility and recognize any expected losses.

Financial Officer   Omitting accrued expenses and recognizing revenue early can mislead financial statement users. One action is to request a second meeting with the president so you can explain that accruing expenses when incurred and recognizing revenue when earned are required practices. If the president persists, you might discuss the situation with legal counsel and any auditors involved. Your ethical action might cost you this job, but the potential pitfalls for falsification of statements, reputation and personal integrity loss, and other costs are too great.

Guidance Answers to **Quick Checks**

1. An annual reporting (or accounting) period covers one year and refers to the preparation of annual financial statements. The annual reporting period is not always a calendar year that ends on December 31. An organization can adopt a fiscal year consisting of any consecutive 12 months or 52 weeks.

2. Interim financial statements (covering less than one year) are prepared to provide timely information to decision makers.

3. The revenue recognition principle and the matching principle lead most directly to the adjusting process.

4. No. Cash basis accounting is not consistent with the matching principle because it reports revenue when received, not necessarily when earned, and expenses when paid, not necessarily in the period when the expenses were incurred as a result of the revenues earned.

5. No expense is reported in 2010. Under cash basis accounting, the entire $4,800 is reported as an expense in April 2009 when the premium is paid.

6. If the accrued revenues adjustment of $200 is not made, then both revenues and net income are understated by $200 on the current year's income statement, and both assets and equity are understated by $200 on the balance sheet.

7. A contra account is an account that is subtracted from the balance of a related account. Use of a contra account provides more information than simply reporting a net amount.

8. An accrued expense is a cost incurred in a period that is both unpaid and unrecorded prior to adjusting entries. One example is salaries earned but not yet paid at period-end.

9. An unearned revenue arises when a firm receives cash (or other assets) from a customer before providing the services or products to the customer. A magazine subscription paid in advance is one example; season ticket sales is another.

10.
Salaries Payable	1,000	
Salaries Expense	6,000	
Cash		7,000

Paid salary including accrual from December.

11. The probable adjusting entries of Jordan Air are:

Insurance Expense	300	
Prepaid Insurance		300

To record insurance expired.

Salaries Expense	1,400	
Salaries Payable		1,400

To record accrued salaries.

12. Revenue accounts and expense accounts.

13. Statement of owner's equity.

Key Terms
mhhe.com/wildFAP19e

Key Terms are available at the book's Website for learning and testing in an online Flashcard Format.

Accounting period (p. 92)
Accrual basis accounting (p. 93)
Accrued expenses (p. 99)
Accrued revenues (p. 101)
Adjusted trial balance (p. 104)
Adjusting entry (p. 94)
Annual financial statements (p. 92)
Book value (p. 98)

Cash basis accounting (p. 93)
Contra account (p. 97)
Depreciation (p. 97)
Fiscal year (p. 93)
Interim financial statements (p. 92)
Matching principle (p. 94)
Natural business year (p. 93)
Plant assets (p. 97)

Prepaid expenses (p. 95)
Profit margin (p. 106)
Straight-line depreciation method (p. 97)
Time period assumption (p. 92)
Unadjusted trial balance (p. 104)
Unearned revenues (p. 98)

Multiple Choice Quiz   Answers on p. 133   mhhe.com/wildFAP19e

Additional Quiz Questions are available at the book's Website.

Quiz3

1. A company forgot to record accrued and unpaid employee wages of $350,000 at period-end. This oversight would
   a. Understate net income by $350,000.
   b. Overstate net income by $350,000.
   c. Have no effect on net income.
   d. Overstate assets by $350,000.
   e. Understate assets by $350,000.

2. Prior to recording adjusting entries, the Supplies account has a $450 debit balance. A physical count of supplies shows $125 of unused supplies still available. The required adjusting entry is:
   a. Debit Supplies $125; Credit Supplies Expense $125.
   b. Debit Supplies $325; Credit Supplies Expense $325.
   c. Debit Supplies Expense $325; Credit Supplies $325.
   d. Debit Supplies Expense $325; Credit Supplies $125.
   e. Debit Supplies Expense $125; Credit Supplies $125.

3. On May 1, 2009, a two-year insurance policy was purchased for $24,000 with coverage to begin immediately. What is the amount of insurance expense that appears on the company's income statement for the year ended December 31, 2009?
   a. $4,000
   b. $8,000

c. $12,000
d. $20,000
e. $24,000

4. On November 1, 2009, Stockton Co. receives $3,600 cash from Hans Co. for consulting services to be provided evenly over the period November 1, 2009, to April 30, 2010—at which time Stockton credited $3,600 to Unearned Consulting Fees. The adjusting entry on December 31, 2009 (Stockton's year-end) would include a
   a. Debit to Unearned Consulting Fees for $1,200.
   b. Debit to Unearned Consulting Fees for $2,400.
   c. Credit to Consulting Fees Earned for $2,400.
   d. Debit to Consulting Fees Earned for $1,200.
   e. Credit to Cash for $3,600.

5. If a company had $15,000 in net income for the year, and its sales were $300,000 for the same year, what is its profit margin?
   a. 20%
   b. 2,000%
   c. $285,000
   d. $315,000
   e. 5%

Superscript letter ^A denotes assignments based on Appendix 3A.

Discussion Questions

1. What is the difference between the cash basis and the accrual basis of accounting?
2. Why is the accrual basis of accounting generally preferred over the cash basis?
3. What type of business is most likely to select a fiscal year that corresponds to its natural business year instead of the calendar year?
4. What is a prepaid expense and where is it reported in the financial statements?
5. What type of assets require adjusting entries to record depreciation?
6. What contra account is used when recording and reporting the effects of depreciation? Why is it used?
7. What is unearned revenue and where is it reported in financial statements?
8. What is an accrued revenue? Give an example.
9.^AIf a company initially records prepaid expenses with debits to expense accounts, what type of account is debited in the adjusting entries for those prepaid expenses?

10. Review the balance sheet of **Best Buy** in Appendix A. Identify the asset accounts that require adjustment before annual financial statements can be prepared. What would be the effect on the income statement if these asset accounts were not adjusted?
11. Review the balance sheet of **Circuit City** in Appendix A. In addition to Prepayments, identify two accounts (either assets or liabilities) requiring adjusting entries.
12. Refer to **RadioShack**'s balance sheet in Appendix A. What year-end adjusting entry is necessary for accrued interest earned from its notes receivable listed under current assets? **(R) RadioShack.**
13. Refer to **Apple**'s balance sheet in Appendix A. If it made an adjustment for unpaid wages at year-end, where would the accrued wages expense be reported on its balance sheet?

Denotes Discussion Questions that involve decision making.

Available with McGraw-Hill's Homework Manager

In its first year of operations, Case Co. earned $60,000 in revenues and received $52,000 cash from these customers. The company incurred expenses of $37,500 but had not paid $6,000 of them at year-end. The company also prepaid $3,250 cash for expenses that would be incurred the next year. Calculate the first year's net income under both the cash basis and the accrual basis of accounting.

QUICK STUDY

QS 3-1
Computing accrual and cash income

P1   C2

Classify the following adjusting entries as involving prepaid expenses (PE), unearned revenues (UR), accrued expenses (AE), or accrued revenues (AR).

a. _____ To record wages expense incurred but not yet paid (nor recorded).

b. _____ To record expiration of prepaid insurance.

c. _____ To record revenue earned that was previously received as cash in advance.

d. _____ To record annual depreciation expense.

e. _____ To record revenue earned but not yet billed (nor recorded).

QS 3-2
Identifying accounting adjustments

P1

Adjusting entries affect at least one balance sheet account and at least one income statement account. For the following entries, identify the account to be debited and the account to be credited. Indicate which of the accounts is the income statement account and which is the balance sheet account.

a. Entry to record revenue earned that was previously received as cash in advance.

b. Entry to record wage expenses incurred but not yet paid (nor recorded).

c. Entry to record revenue earned but not yet billed (nor recorded).

d. Entry to record expiration of prepaid insurance.

e. Entry to record annual depreciation expense.

QS 3-3
Recording and analyzing adjusting entries

A1

---

a. On July 1, 2009, Rendex Company paid $3,000 for six months of insurance coverage. No adjustments have been made to the Prepaid Insurance account, and it is now December 31, 2009. Prepare the journal entry to reflect expiration of the insurance as of December 31, 2009.

b. Indus Company has a Supplies account balance of $900 on January 1, 2009. During 2009, it purchased $4,000 of supplies. As of December 31, 2009, a supplies inventory shows $750 of supplies available. Prepare the adjusting journal entry to correctly report the balance of the Supplies account and the Supplies Expense account as of December 31, 2009.

QS 3-4
Adjusting prepaid expenses

P1

---

a. Andrews Company purchases $45,000 of equipment on January 1, 2009. The equipment is expected to last five years and be worth $3,000 at the end of that time. Prepare the entry to record one year's depreciation expense of $8,400 for the equipment as of December 31, 2009.

b. Fortel Company purchases $40,000 of land on January 1, 2009. The land is expected to last indefinitely. What depreciation adjustment, if any, should be made with respect to the Land account as of December 31, 2009?

QS 3-5
Adjusting for depreciation

P1

Lakia Rowell employs one college student every summer in her coffee shop. The student works the five weekdays and is paid on the following Monday. (For example, a student who works Monday through Friday, June 1 through June 5, is paid for that work on Monday, June 8.) Rowell adjusts her books monthly, if needed, to show salaries earned but unpaid at month-end. The student works the last week of July—Friday is August 1. If the student earns $100 per day, what adjusting entry must Rowell make on July 31 to correctly record accrued salaries expense for July?

QS 3-6
Accruing salaries

A1   P1

---

a. Fortune Co. receives $30,000 cash in advance for 4 months of legal services on October 1, 2009, and records it by debiting Cash and crediting Unearned Revenue both for $30,000. It is now December 31, 2009, and Fortune has provided legal services as planned. What adjusting entry should Fortune make to account for the work performed from October 1 through December 31, 2009?

b. Warner Co. started a new publication called *Contest News*. Its subscribers pay $24 to receive 12 issues. With every new subscriber, Warner debits Cash and credits Unearned Subscription Revenue for

QS 3-7
Adjusting for unearned revenues

A1   P1

the amounts received. The company has 100 new subscribers as of July 1, 2009. It sends *Contest News* to each of these subscribers every month from July through December. Assuming no changes in subscribers, prepare the journal entry that Warner must make as of December 31, 2009, to adjust the Subscription Revenue account and the Unearned Subscription Revenue account.

QS 3-8

Preparing adjusting entries

C3 P1

During the year, Sonoma Co. recorded prepayments of expenses in asset accounts, and cash receipts of unearned revenues in liability accounts. At the end of its annual accounting period, the company must make three adjusting entries: (1) accrue salaries expense, (2) adjust the Unearned Services Revenue account to recognize earned revenue, and (3) record services revenue earned for which cash will be received the following period. For each of these adjusting entries (1), (2), and (3), indicate the account from *a* through *i* to be debited and the account to be credited.

a. Unearned Services Revenue   **d.** Prepaid Salaries   **g.** Salaries Payable

b. Accounts Receivable   **e.** Salaries Expense   **h.** Equipment

c. Accounts Payable   **f.** Services Revenue   **i.** Cash

QS 3-9

Interpreting adjusting entries

C2 P2

The following information is taken from Booker Company's unadjusted and adjusted trial balances.

	Unadjusted		Adjusted	
	Debit	Credit	Debit	Credit
Prepaid insurance	$4,100		$3,700	
Interest payable		$ 0		$800

Given this information, which of the following is likely included among its adjusting entries?

a. A $400 debit to Insurance Expense and an $800 debit to Interest Expense.

b. A $400 debit to Insurance Expense and an $800 debit to Interest Payable.

c. A $400 credit to Prepaid Insurance and an $800 debit to Interest Payable.

QS 3-10

Determining effects of adjusting entries

C3 A1

In making adjusting entries at the end of its accounting period, Chao Consulting failed to record $1,600 of insurance coverage that had expired. This $1,600 cost had been initially debited to the Prepaid Insurance account. The company also failed to record accrued salaries expense of $1,000. As a result of these two oversights, the financial statements for the reporting period will [choose one] (1) understate assets by $1,600; (2) understate expenses by $2,600; (3) understate net income by $1,000; or (4) overstate liabilities by $1,000.

QS 3-11

Analyzing profit margin

A2

Miller Company reported net income of $78,750 and net sales of $630,000 for the current year. Calculate the company's profit margin and interpret the result. Assume that its competitors earn an average profit margin of 15%.

QS 3-12ᴬ

Preparing adjusting entries

C3 P4

Bevin Consulting initially records prepaid and unearned items in income statement accounts. Given this company's accounting practices, which of the following applies to the preparation of adjusting entries at the end of its first accounting period?

a. Unpaid salaries are recorded with a debit to Prepaid Salaries and a credit to Salaries Expense.

b. The cost of unused office supplies is recorded with a debit to Supplies Expense and a credit to Office Supplies.

c. Unearned fees (on which cash was received in advance earlier in the period) are recorded with a debit to Consulting Fees Earned and a credit to Unearned Consulting Fees.

d. Earned but unbilled (and unrecorded) consulting fees are recorded with a debit to Unearned Consulting Fees and a credit to Consulting Fees Earned.

McGraw-Hill's
HOMEWORK
MANAGER®   Available with McGraw-Hill's Homework Manager

In the blank space beside each adjusting entry, enter the letter of the explanation A through F that most closely describes the entry.

A. To record accrued interest revenue.
B. To record accrued interest expense.
C. To record the earning of previously unearned income.
D. To record this period's depreciation expense.
E. To record accrued salaries expense.
F. To record this period's use of a prepaid expense.

EXERCISES

Exercise 3-1
Classifying adjusting entries
C3

___	1.	Interest Expense	2,208
		Interest Payable	2,208
___	2.	Insurance Expense	3,180
		Prepaid Insurance	3,180
___	3.	Unearned Professional Fees	19,250
		Professional Fees Earned	19,250
___	4.	Interest Receivable	3,300
		Interest Revenue	3,300
___	5.	Depreciation Expense	38,217
		Accumulated Depreciation	38,217
___	6.	Salaries Expense	13,280
		Salaries Payable	13,280

Prepare adjusting journal entries for the year ended (date of) December 31, 2009, for each of these separate situations. Assume that prepaid expenses are initially recorded in asset accounts. Also assume that fees collected in advance of work are initially recorded as liabilities.

a. Depreciation on the company's equipment for 2009 is computed to be $16,000.

b. The Prepaid Insurance account had a $6,000 debit balance at December 31, 2009, before adjusting for the costs of any expired coverage. An analysis of the company's insurance policies showed that $640 of unexpired insurance coverage remains.

c. The Office Supplies account had a $325 debit balance on December 31, 2008; and $3,480 of office supplies were purchased during the year. The December 31, 2009, physical count showed $383 of supplies available.

d. One-fifth of the work related to $15,000 of cash received in advance was performed this period.

e. The Prepaid Insurance account had a $6,800 debit balance at December 31, 2009, before adjusting for the costs of any expired coverage. An analysis of insurance policies showed that $6,160 of coverage had expired.

f. Wage expenses of $2,700 have been incurred but are not paid as of December 31, 2009.

Exercise 3-2
Preparing adjusting entries
P1

Check (c) Dr. Office Supplies Expense, $3,422; (e) Dr. Insurance Expense, $6,160

For each of the following separate cases, prepare adjusting entries required of financial statements for the year ended (date of) December 31, 2009. (Assume that prepaid expenses are initially recorded in asset accounts and that fees collected in advance of work are initially recorded as liabilities.)

a. One-third of the work related to $15,000 cash received in advance is performed this period.

b. Wages of $7,500 are earned by workers but not paid as of December 31, 2009.

c. Depreciation on the company's equipment for 2009 is $17,251.

d. The Office Supplies account had a $240 debit balance on December 31, 2008. During 2009, $6,102 of office supplies are purchased. A physical count of supplies at December 31, 2009, shows $660 of supplies available.

e. The Prepaid Insurance account had a $4,000 balance on December 31, 2008. An analysis of insurance policies shows that $1,300 of unexpired insurance benefits remain at December 31, 2009.

f. The company has earned (but not recorded) $1,400 of interest from investments in CDs for the year ended December 31, 2009. The interest revenue will be received on January 10, 2010.

g. The company has a bank loan and has incurred (but not recorded) interest expense of $2,000 for the year ended December 31, 2009. The company must pay the interest on January 2, 2010.

Exercise 3-3
Preparing adjusting entries
P1

Check (e) Dr. Insurance Expense, $2,700; (f) Cr. Interest Revenue, $1,400

Exercise 3-4
Adjusting and paying accrued wages

C1 P1

Arton Management has five part-time employees, each of whom earns $165 per day. They are normally paid on Fridays for work completed Monday through Friday of the same week. They were paid in full on Friday, December 28, 2009. The next week, the five employees worked only four days because New Year's Day was an unpaid holiday. Show (*a*) the adjusting entry that would be recorded on Monday, December 31, 2009, and (*b*) the journal entry that would be made to record payment of the employees' wages on Friday, January 4, 2010.

Exercise 3-5
Determining cost flows through accounts

C1 A1 P1

Determine the missing amounts in each of these four separate situations *a* through *d*.

	a	b	c	d
Supplies available—prior year-end	$ 350	$1,855	$ 1,576	?
Supplies purchased during the current year	2,450	6,307	?	$6,907
Supplies available—current year-end	800	?	2,056	800
Supplies expense for the current year	?	1,555	11,507	7,482

Exercise 3-6
Adjusting and paying accrued expenses

A1 P1

Check (*b*) May 20 Dr. Interest Expense, $3,800

The following three separate situations require adjusting journal entries to prepare financial statements as of April 30. For each situation, present both the April 30 adjusting entry and the subsequent entry during May to record the payment of the accrued expenses.

a. On April 1, the company retained an attorney at a flat monthly fee of $4,500. This amount is payable on the 12th of the following month.

b. A $760,000 note payable requires $5,700 of interest to be paid at the 20th day of each month. The interest was last paid on April 20 and the next payment is due on May 20. As of April 30, $1,900 of interest expense has accrued.

c. Total weekly salaries expense for all employees is $12,000. This amount is paid at the end of the day on Friday of each five-day workweek. April 30 falls on Tuesday of this year, which means that the employees had worked two days since the last payday. The next payday is May 3.

Exercise 3-7
Determining assets and expenses for accrual and cash accounting

C2

On November 1, 2007, a company paid a $15,300 premium on a 36-month insurance policy for coverage beginning on that date. Refer to that policy and fill in the blanks in the following table.

Balance Sheet Prepaid Insurance Asset Using				Insurance Expense Using		
	Accrual Basis	Cash Basis			Accrual Basis	Cash Basis
Dec. 31, 2007	$_____	$_____		2007	$_____	$_____
Dec. 31, 2008	_____	_____		2008	_____	_____
Dec. 31, 2009	_____	_____		2009	_____	_____
Dec. 31, 2010	_____	_____		2010	_____	_____
				Total	$_____	$_____

Check 2009 insurance expense: Accrual, $5,100; Cash, $0. Dec. 31, 2009, asset: Accrual, $4,250; Cash, $0.

Exercise 3-8
Analyzing and preparing adjusting entries

A1 P1 P3

Following are two income statements for Vix Co. for the year ended December 31. The left column is prepared before any adjusting entries are recorded, and the right column includes the effects of adjusting entries. The company records cash receipts and payments related to unearned and prepaid items in balance sheet accounts. Analyze the statements and prepare the ten adjusting entries that likely were recorded. (*Note:* 30% of the $6,600 adjustment for Fees Earned has been earned but not billed, and the other 70% has been earned by performing services that were paid for in advance.)

VIX CO. Income Statements For Year Ended December 31	Unadjusted	Adjusted
Revenues		
Fees earned	$24,000	$30,600
Commissions earned	36,500	36,500
Total revenues	$60,500	67,100
Expenses		
Depreciation expense—Computers	0	1,650
Depreciation expense—Office furniture	0	1,925
Salaries expense	12,500	15,195
Insurance expense	0	1,430
Rent expense	3,800	4,500
Office supplies expense	0	528
Advertising expense	2,500	3,000
Utilities expense	1,250	1,327
Total expenses	20,050	29,555
Net income	$40,450	$37,545

Use the following information to compute profit margin for each separate company a through e.

	Net Income	Net Sales			Net Income	Net Sales
a.	$ 6,039	$ 52,970		**d.**	$67,140	$1,721,520
b.	100,890	471,430		**e.**	84,780	513,800
c.	106,880	301,920				

Which of the five companies is the most profitable according to the profit margin ratio? Interpret that company's profit margin ratio.

Exercise 3-9
Computing and interpreting profit margin

A2

Lowes Construction began operations on December 1. In setting up its accounting procedures, the company decided to debit expense accounts when it prepays its expenses and to credit revenue accounts when customers pay for services in advance. Prepare journal entries for items a through d and the adjusting entries as of its December 31 period-end for items e through g.

a. Supplies are purchased on December 1 for $2,000 cash.

b. The company prepaid its insurance premiums for $1,540 cash on December 2.

c. On December 15, the company receives an advance payment of $13,000 cash from a customer for remodeling work.

d. On December 28, the company receives $3,700 cash from another customer for remodeling work to be performed in January.

e. A physical count on December 31 indicates that Lowes has $1,840 of supplies available.

f. An analysis of the insurance policies in effect on December 31 shows that $340 of insurance coverage had expired.

g. As of December 31, only one remodeling project has been worked on and completed. The $5,570 fee for this project had been received in advance.

Exercise 3-10^A
Adjusting for prepaids recorded as expenses and unearned revenues recorded as revenues

P4

Check (f) Cr. Insurance Expense, $1,200; (g) Dr. Remodeling Fees Earned, $11,130

Colgate Company experienced the following events and transactions during July.

July 1 Received $2,800 cash in advance of performing work for Vivian Solana.
     6 Received $8,100 cash in advance of performing work for Iris Haru.
    12 Completed the job for Solana.
    18 Received $7,300 cash in advance of performing work for Amina Jordan.
    27 Completed the job for Haru.
    31 None of the work for Jordan has been performed.

Exercise 3-11^A
Recording and reporting revenues received in advance

P4

a. Prepare journal entries (including any adjusting entries as of the end of the month) to record these events using the procedure of initially crediting the Unearned Fees account when payment is received from a customer in advance of performing services.

b. Prepare journal entries (including any adjusting entries as of the end of the month) to record these events using the procedure of initially crediting the Fees Earned account when payment is received from a customer in advance of performing services.

Check   (c) Fees Earned, $10,900

c. Under each method, determine the amount of earned fees reported on the income statement for July and the amount of unearned fees reported on the balance sheet as of July 31.

Available with McGraw-Hill's Homework Manager

PROBLEM SET A

Problem 3-1A

Identifying adjusting entries with explanations

C3 P1

For each of the following entries, enter the letter of the explanation that most closely describes it in the space beside each entry. (You can use letters more than once.)

A. To record an accrued revenue.

B. To record this period's use of a prepaid expense.

C. To record payment of a prepaid expense.

D. To record this period's depreciation expense.

E. To record receipt of unearned revenue.

F. To record this period's earning of prior unearned revenue.

G. To record payment of an accrued expense.

H. To record receipt of an accrued revenue.

I. To record an accrued expense.

_____	1.	Interest Expense	1,000
		Interest Payable	1,000
_____	2.	Depreciation Expense	4,000
		Accumulated Depreciation	4,000
_____	3.	Unearned Professional Fees	3,000
		Professional Fees Earned	3,000
_____	4.	Insurance Expense	4,200
		Prepaid Insurance	4,200
_____	5.	Salaries Payable	1,400
		Cash	1,400
_____	6.	Prepaid Rent	4,500
		Cash	4,500
_____	7.	Salaries Expense	6,000
		Salaries Payable	6,000
_____	8.	Interest Receivable	5,000
		Interest Revenue	5,000
_____	9.	Cash	9,000
		Accounts Receivable (from consulting)	9,000
_____	10.	Cash	7,500
		Unearned Professional Fees	7,500
_____	11.	Cash	2,000
		Interest Receivable	2,000
_____	12.	Rent Expense	2,000
		Prepaid Rent	2,000

Problem 3-2A

Preparing adjusting and subsequent journal entries

C1 A1 P1

Hormel Co. follows the practice of recording prepaid expenses and unearned revenues in balance sheet accounts. The company's annual accounting period ends on December 31, 2009. The following information concerns the adjusting entries to be recorded as of that date.

a. The Office Supplies account started the year with a $2,900 balance. During 2009, the company purchased supplies for $11,977, which was added to the Office Supplies account. The inventory of supplies available at December 31, 2009, totaled $2,552.

b. An analysis of the company's insurance policies provided the following facts.

Policy	Date of Purchase	Months of Coverage	Cost
A	April 1, 2008	24	$11,640
B	April 1, 2009	36	10,440
C	August 1, 2009	12	9,240

The total premium for each policy was paid in full (for all months) at the purchase date, and the Prepaid Insurance account was debited for the full cost. (Year-end adjusting entries for Prepaid Insurance were properly recorded in all prior years.)

c. The company has 15 employees, who earn a total of $1,830 in salaries each working day. They are paid each Monday for their work in the five-day workweek ending on the previous Friday. Assume that December 31, 2009, is a Tuesday, and all 15 employees worked the first two days of that week. Because New Year's Day is a paid holiday, they will be paid salaries for five full days on Monday, January 6, 2010.

d. The company purchased a building on January 1, 2009. It cost $800,000 and is expected to have a $45,000 salvage value at the end of its predicted 40-year life. Annual depreciation is $18,875.

e. Since the company is not large enough to occupy the entire building it owns, it rented space to a tenant at $3,000 per month, starting on November 1, 2009. The rent was paid on time on November 1, and the amount received was credited to the Rent Earned account. However, the tenant has not paid the December rent. The company has worked out an agreement with the tenant, who has promised to pay both December and January rent in full on January 15. The tenant has agreed not to fall behind again.

f. On November 1, the company rented space to another tenant for $2,718 per month. The tenant paid five months' rent in advance on that date. The payment was recorded with a credit to the Unearned Rent account.

Required

1. Use the information to prepare adjusting entries as of December 31, 2009.

2. Prepare journal entries to record the first subsequent cash transaction in 2010 for parts *c* and *e*.

Check   (1*b*) Dr. Insurance Expense, $12,280 (1*d*) Dr. Depreciation Expense, $18,875

Wells Teaching Institute (WTI), a school owned by Tracey Wells, provides training to individuals who pay tuition directly to the school. WTI also offers training to groups in off-site locations. Its unadjusted trial balance as of December 31, 2009, follows. WTI initially records prepaid expenses and unearned revenues in balance sheet accounts. Descriptions of items *a* through *h* that require adjusting entries on December 31, 2009, follow.

Problem 3-3A
Preparing adjusting entries, adjusted trial balance, and financial statements

A1 P1 P2 P3

mhhe.com/wildFAP19e

Additional Information Items

a. An analysis of the school's insurance policies shows that $3,000 of coverage has expired.

b. An inventory count shows that teaching supplies costing $2,000 are available at year-end 2009.

c. Annual depreciation on the equipment is $10,000.

d. Annual depreciation on the professional library is $5,000.

e. On November 1, the school agreed to do a special six-month course (starting immediately) for a client. The contract calls for a monthly fee of $2,500, and the client paid the first five months' fees in advance. When the cash was received, the Unearned Training Fees account was credited. The fee for the sixth month will be recorded when it is collected in 2010.

f. On October 15, the school agreed to teach a four-month class (beginning immediately) for an individual for $1,600 tuition per month payable at the end of the class. The services are being provided as agreed, and no payment has yet been received.

g. The school's two employees are paid weekly. As of the end of the year, two days' salaries have accrued at the rate of $120 per day for each employee.

h. The balance in the Prepaid Rent account represents rent for December.

	WELLS TEACHING INSTITUTE Unadjusted Trial Balance December 31, 2009		
		Debit	**Credit**
3	Cash	$ 28,064	
4	Accounts receivable	0	
5	Teaching supplies	11,000	
6	Prepaid insurance	16,000	
7	Prepaid rent	2,178	
8	Professional library	33,000	
9	Accumulated depreciation—Professional library		$ 10,000
10	Equipment	75,800	
11	Accumulated depreciation—Equipment		15,000
12	Accounts payable		39,500
13	Salaries payable		0
14	Unearned training fees		12,500
15	T. Wells, Capital		71,000
16	T. Wells, Withdrawals	44,000	
17	Tuition fees earned		111,000
18	Training fees earned		41,000
19	Depreciation expense—Professional library	0	
20	Depreciation expense—Equipment	0	
21	Salaries expense	52,000	
22	Insurance expense	0	
23	Rent expense	23,958	
24	Teaching supplies expense	0	
25	Advertising expense	8,000	
26	Utilities expense	6,000	
27	Totals	$ 300,000	$ 300,000

Required

Check (2e) Cr. Training Fees Earned, $5,000; (2f) Cr. Tuition Fees Earned, $4,000; (3) Adj. Trial balance totals, $319,480; (4) Net income, $41,384; Ending T. Wells, Capital $68,384

1. Prepare T-accounts (representing the ledger) with balances from the unadjusted trial balance.
2. Prepare the necessary adjusting journal entries for items *a* through *h* and post them to the T-accounts. Assume that adjusting entries are made only at year-end.
3. Update balances in the T-accounts for the adjusting entries and prepare an adjusted trial balance.
4. Prepare Wells Teaching Institute's income statement and statement of owner's equity for the year 2009 and prepare its balance sheet as of December 31, 2009.

Problem 3-4A

Interpreting unadjusted and adjusted trial balances, and preparing financial statements

C3 A1 P1 P2 P3

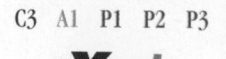

mhhe.com/wildFAP19e

A six-column table for KLJ Company follows. The first two columns contain the unadjusted trial balance for the company as of July 31, 2009. The last two columns contain the adjusted trial balance as of the same date.

Required

Analysis Component

1. Analyze the differences between the unadjusted and adjusted trial balances to determine the eight adjustments that likely were made. Show the results of your analysis by inserting these adjustment amounts in the table's two middle columns. Label each adjustment with a letter *a* through *h* and provide a short description of it at the bottom of the table.

Preparation Component

Check (2) Net income, $34,460; K. Jenkins, Capital (7/31/2009), $70,460; Total assets, $178,960

2. Use the information in the adjusted trial balance to prepare the company's (*a*) income statement and its statement of owner's equity for the year ended July 31, 2009 (*note:* K. Jenkins, Capital at July 31, 2008, was $46,000, and the current-year withdrawals were $10,000), and (*b*) the balance sheet as of July 31, 2009.

	Unadjusted Trial Balance		Adjustments		Adjusted Trial Balance	
Cash	$ 86,000				$ 86,000	
Accounts receivable	15,000				19,000	
Office supplies	17,800				9,000	
Prepaid insurance	6,040				3,960	
Office equipment	87,000				87,000	
Accum. depreciation— Office equip.		$ 24,000				$ 26,000
Accounts payable		9,100				24,000
Interest payable		0				2,500
Salaries payable		0				15,000
Unearned consulting fees		20,000				13,000
Long-term notes payable		54,000				54,000
K. Jenkins, Capital		46,000				46,000
K. Jenkins, Withdrawals	10,000				10,000	
Consulting fees earned		165,000				176,000
Depreciation expense— Office equip.	0				2,000	
Salaries expense	67,990				82,990	
Interest expense	1,270				3,770	
Insurance expense	0				2,080	
Rent expense	14,540				14,540	
Office supplies expense	0				8,800	
Advertising expense	12,460				27,360	
Totals	$318,100	$318,100			$356,500	$356,500

The adjusted trial balance for Clarita Company as of December 31, 2009, follows.

Problem 3-5A
Preparing financial statements from the adjusted trial balance and calculating profit margin

P3 A1 A2

	Debit	Credit
Cash	$149,000	
Accounts receivable	50,000	
Interest receivable	22,600	
Notes receivable (due in 90 days)	171,500	
Office supplies	16,000	
Automobiles	171,000	
Accumulated depreciation—Automobiles		$ 75,000
Equipment	146,000	
Accumulated depreciation—Equipment		23,000
Land	79,000	
Accounts payable		101,000
Interest payable		20,000
Salaries payable		42,000
Unearned fees		36,000
Long-term notes payable		140,000
S. Clarita, Capital		295,800
S. Clarita, Withdrawals	47,000	
Fees earned		534,000
Interest earned		20,000

[continued on next page]

[continued from previous page]

Depreciation expense—Automobiles	26,500	
Depreciation expense—Equipment	19,500	
Salaries expense	184,000	
Wages expense	43,000	
Interest expense	35,600	
Office supplies expense	33,800	
Advertising expense	65,500	
Repairs expense—Automobiles	26,800	
Totals	$1,286,800	$1,286,800

Required

Check (1) Total assets, $707,100

1. Use the information in the adjusted trial balance to prepare (*a*) the income statement for the year ended December 31, 2009; (*b*) the statement of owner's equity for the year ended December 31, 2009; and (*c*) the balance sheet as of December 31, 2009.

2. Calculate the profit margin for year 2009.

Problem 3-6A[A]

Recording prepaid expenses and unearned revenues

P1 P4

Riso Co. had the following transactions in the last two months of its year ended December 31.

Nov. 1 Paid $2,000 cash for future newspaper advertising.
      1 Paid $2,466 cash for 12 months of insurance through October 31 of the next year.
     30 Received $4,200 cash for future services to be provided to a customer.
Dec. 1 Paid $2,400 cash for a consultant's services to be received over the next three months.
     15 Received $7,250 cash for future services to be provided to a customer.
     31 Of the advertising paid for on November 1, $1,300 worth is not yet used.
     31 A portion of the insurance paid for on November 1 has expired. No adjustment was made in November to Prepaid Insurance.
     31 Services worth $1,600 are not yet provided to the customer who paid on November 30.
     31 One-third of the consulting services paid for on December 1 have been received.
     31 The company has performed $4,350 of services that the customer paid for on December 15.

Required

1. Prepare entries for these transactions under the method that records prepaid expenses as assets and records unearned revenues as liabilities. Also prepare adjusting entries at the end of the year.

2. Prepare entries for these transactions under the method that records prepaid expenses as expenses and records unearned revenues as revenues. Also prepare adjusting entries at the end of the year.

Analysis Component

3. Explain why the alternative sets of entries in requirements 1 and 2 do not result in different financial statement amounts.

PROBLEM SET B

Problem 3-1B

Identifying adjusting entries with explanations

C3 P1

For each of the following entries, enter the letter of the explanation that most closely describes it in the space beside each entry. (You can use letters more than once.)

A. To record this period's earning of prior unearned revenue.

B. To record an accrued expense.

C. To record payment of an accrued expense.

D. To record an accrued revenue.

E. To record receipt of accrued revenue.

F. To record payment of a prepaid expense.

G. To record this period's use of a prepaid expense.

H. To record this period's depreciation expense.

I. To record receipt of unearned revenue.

___	1.	Interest Receivable	3,500	
		Interest Revenue		3,500
___	2.	Salaries Payable	9,000	
		Cash		9,000
___	3.	Depreciation Expense	8,000	
		Accumulated Depreciation		8,000
___	4.	Cash	9,000	
		Unearned Professional Fees		9,000
___	5.	Insurance Expense	4,000	
		Prepaid Insurance		4,000
___	6.	Interest Expense	5,000	
		Interest Payable		5,000
___	7.	Cash	1,500	
		Accounts Receivable (from services)		1,500
___	8.	Salaries Expense	7,000	
		Salaries Payable		7,000
___	9.	Cash	1,000	
		Interest Receivable		1,000
___	10.	Prepaid Rent	3,000	
		Cash		3,000
___	11.	Rent Expense	7,500	
		Prepaid Rent		7,500
___	12.	Unearned Professional Fees	6,000	
		Professional Fees Earned		6,000

Wu-Tang Co. follows the practice of recording prepaid expenses and unearned revenues in balance sheet accounts. The company's annual accounting period ends on October 31, 2009. The following information concerns the adjusting entries that need to be recorded as of that date.

Problem 3-2B
Preparing adjusting and subsequent journal entries

C1 A1 P1

a. The Office Supplies account started the fiscal year with a $3,950 balance. During the fiscal year, the company purchased supplies for $16,313, which was added to the Office Supplies account. The supplies available at October 31, 2009, totaled $3,476.

b. An analysis of the company's insurance policies provided the following facts.

Policy	Date of Purchase	Months of Coverage	Cost
A	April 1, 2008	24	$10,824
B	April 1, 2009	36	9,540
C	August 1, 2009	12	8,424

The total premium for each policy was paid in full (for all months) at the purchase date, and the Prepaid Insurance account was debited for the full cost. (Year-end adjusting entries for Prepaid Insurance were properly recorded in all prior fiscal years.)

c. The company has 15 employees, who earn a total of $2,610 for each workday. They are paid each Monday for their work in the five-day workweek ending on the previous Friday. Assume that October 31, 2009, is a Tuesday, and all five employees worked the first day of that week. They will be paid salaries for five full days on Monday, November 7, 2009.

d. The company purchased a building on November 1, 2008, that cost $695,000 and is expected to have a $41,000 salvage value at the end of its predicted 30-year life. Annual depreciation is $21,800.

e. Since the company does not occupy the entire building it owns, it rented space to a tenant at $3,200 per month, starting on September 1, 2009. The rent was paid on time on September 1, and the amount received was credited to the Rent Earned account. However, the October rent has not been paid. The company has worked out an agreement with the tenant, who has promised to pay both October and November rent in full on November 15. The tenant has agreed not to fall behind again.

f. On September 1, the company rented space to another tenant for $2,899 per month. The tenant paid five months' rent in advance on that date. The payment was recorded with a credit to the Unearned Rent account.

Required

Check (1b) Dr. Insurance Expense, $9,373; (1d) Dr. Depreciation Expense, $21,800.

1. Use the information to prepare adjusting entries as of October 31, 2009.

2. Prepare journal entries to record the first subsequent cash transaction in November 2009 for parts c and e.

Problem 3-3B

Preparing adjusting entries, adjusted trial balance, and financial statements

A1 P1 P2 P3

Following is the unadjusted trial balance for Augustus Institute as of December 31, 2009, which initially records prepaid expenses and unearned revenues in balance sheet accounts. The Institute provides one-on-one training to individuals who pay tuition directly to the business and offers extension training to groups in off-site locations. Shown after the trial balance are items a through h that require adjusting entries as of December 31, 2009.

AUGUSTUS INSTITUTE
Unadjusted Trial Balance
December 31, 2009

	Debit	Credit
Cash	$ 27,000	
Accounts receivable	0	
Teaching supplies	10,000	
Prepaid insurance	16,000	
Prepaid rent	2,073	
Professional library	31,000	
Accumulated depreciation—Professional library		$ 9,000
Equipment	72,719	
Accumulated depreciation—Equipment		17,000
Accounts payable		35,600
Salaries payable		0
Unearned training fees		13,000
C. Augustus, Capital		66,000
C. Augustus, Withdrawals	41,000	
Tuition fees earned		106,000
Training fees earned		39,000
Depreciation expense—Professional library	0	
Depreciation expense—Equipment	0	
Salaries expense	50,000	
Insurance expense	0	
Rent expense	22,808	
Teaching supplies expense	0	
Advertising expense	7,000	
Utilities expense	6,000	
Totals	$ 285,600	$ 285,600

Additional Information Items

a. An analysis of the Institute's insurance policies shows that $3,000 of coverage has expired.

b. An inventory count shows that teaching supplies costing $3,000 are available at year-end 2009.

c. Annual depreciation on the equipment is $17,000.

d. Annual depreciation on the professional library is $6,000.

e. On November 1, the Institute agreed to do a special six-month course (starting immediately) for a client. The contract calls for a $2,600 monthly fee, and the client paid the first five months' fees in advance. When the cash was received, the Unearned Training Fees account was credited. The last one month's fees will be recorded when collected in 2010.

f. On October 15, the Institute agreed to teach a four-month class (beginning immediately) to an individual for $3,900 tuition per month payable at the end of the class. The class started on October 15, but no payment has yet been received.

g. The Institute's only employee is paid weekly. As of the end of the year, two days' wages have accrued at the rate of $170 per day.

h. The balance in the Prepaid Rent account represents rent for December.

Required

1. Prepare T-accounts (representing the ledger) with balances from the unadjusted trial balance.

2. Prepare the necessary adjusting journal entries for items *a* through *h*, and post them to the T-accounts. Assume that adjusting entries are made only at year-end.

3. Update balances in the T-accounts for the adjusting entries and prepare an adjusted trial balance.

4. Prepare the company's income statement and statement of owner's equity for the year 2009, and prepare its balance sheet as of December 31, 2009.

Check   (2e) Cr. Training Fees Earned, $5,200; (2f) Cr. Tuition Fees Earned, $9,750; (3) Adj. trial balance totals, $318,690; (4) Net income, $38,729; Ending C. Augustus, Capital, $63,729

A six-column table for Fresno Consulting Company follows. The first two columns contain the unadjusted trial balance for the company as of December 31, 2009, and the last two columns contain the adjusted trial balance as of the same date.

Problem 3-4B
Interpreting unadjusted and adjusted trial balances, and preparing financial statements

C3 A1 P1 P2 P3

	Unadjusted Trial Balance		Adjustments		Adjusted Trial Balance	
Cash	$106,890				$106,890	
Accounts receivable	9,000				18,500	
Office supplies	16,600				9,000	
Prepaid insurance	9,040				3,960	
Office equipment	85,000				85,000	
Accumulated depreciation—						
Office equip.		$ 24,000				$ 34,000
Accounts payable		11,100				22,000
Interest payable		0				1,500
Salaries payable		0				9,000
Unearned consulting fees		22,000				18,000
Long-term notes payable		56,000				56,000
Y. Fresno, Capital		54,000				54,000
Y. Fresno, Withdrawals	7,500				7,500	
Consulting fees earned		162,000				175,500
Depreciation expense—						
Office equip.	0				10,000	
Salaries expense	67,070				76,070	
Interest expense	1,230				2,730	
Insurance expense	0				5,080	
Rent expense	14,620				14,620	
Office supplies expense	0				7,600	
Advertising expense	12,150				23,050	
Totals	$329,100	$329,100			$370,000	$370,000

Required

Analysis Component

1. Analyze the differences between the unadjusted and adjusted trial balances to determine the eight adjustments that likely were made. Show the results of your analysis by inserting these adjustment amounts in the table's two middle columns. Label each adjustment with a letter *a* through *h* and provide a short description of it at the bottom of the table.

Preparation Component

2. Use the information in the adjusted trial balance to prepare this company's (*a*) income statement and its statement of owner's equity for the year ended December 31, 2009 (*note:* Y. Fresno, Capital at December 31, 2008, was $54,000, and the current-year withdrawals were $7,500), and (*b*) the balance sheet as of December 31, 2009.

Problem 3-5B

Preparing financial statements from the adjusted trial balance and calculating profit margin

P3   A1   A2

The adjusted trial balance for Rapid Courier as of December 31, 2009, follows.

	Debit	Credit
Cash	$109,000	
Accounts receivable	55,000	
Interest receivable	23,000	
Notes receivable (due in 90 days)	171,000	
Office supplies	16,000	
Trucks	174,000	
Accumulated depreciation—Trucks		$ 80,000
Equipment	144,000	
Accumulated depreciation—Equipment		44,000
Land	81,000	
Accounts payable		98,000
Interest payable		20,000
Salaries payable		22,000
Unearned delivery fees		32,000
Long-term notes payable		156,000
R. Rapid, Capital		311,800
R. Rapid, Withdrawals	55,000	
Delivery fees earned		474,000
Interest earned		32,000
Depreciation expense—Trucks	25,500	
Depreciation expense—Equipment	22,000	
Salaries expense	187,000	
Wages expense	43,000	
Interest expense	36,200	
Office supplies expense	35,600	
Advertising expense	63,500	
Repairs expense—Trucks	29,000	
Totals	$1,269,800	$1,269,800

Required

1. Use the information in the adjusted trial balance to prepare (*a*) the income statement for the year ended December 31, 2009, (*b*) the statement of owner's equity for the year ended December 31, 2009, and (*c*) the balance sheet as of December 31, 2009.

2. Calculate the profit margin for year 2009.

Problem 3-6B[A]

Recording prepaid expenses and unearned revenues

P1   P4

Jazz Co. had the following transactions in the last two months of its fiscal year ended May 31.

Apr. 1 Paid $2,600 cash to an accounting firm for future consulting services.
       1 Paid $2,484 cash for 12 months of insurance through March 31 of the next year.
      30 Received $4,600 cash for future services to be provided to a customer.
May   1 Paid $2,700 cash for future newspaper advertising.
      23 Received $7,450 cash for future services to be provided to a customer.

31 Of the consulting services paid for on April 1, $1,700 worth has been received.
31 A portion of the insurance paid for on April 1 has expired. No adjustment was made in April to Prepaid Insurance.
31 Services worth $1,400 are not yet provided to the customer who paid on April 30.
31 One-third the advertising paid for on May 1 has not yet been provided.
31 The company has performed $3,000 of services that the customer paid for on May 23.

Required

1. Prepare entries for these transactions under the method that records prepaid expenses and unearned revenues in balance sheet accounts. Also prepare adjusting entries at the end of the year.

2. Prepare entries for these transactions under the method that records prepaid expenses and unearned revenues in income statement accounts. Also prepare adjusting entries at the end of the year.

Analysis Component

3. Explain why the alternative sets of entries in parts 1 and 2 do not result in different financial statement amounts.

This serial problem began in Chapter 1 and continues through most of the book. If previous chapter segments were not completed, the serial problem can still begin at this point. It is helpful, but not necessary, to use the Working Papers that accompany the book.

SERIAL PROBLEM

Success Systems

SP 3 After the success of the company's first two months, Adriana Lopez continues to operate Success Systems. (Transactions for the first two months are described in the serial problem of Chapter 2.) The November 30, 2009, unadjusted trial balance of Success Systems (reflecting its transactions for October and November of 2009) follows.

No.	Account Title	Debit	Credit
101	Cash	$ 48,052	
106	Accounts receivable	12,618	
126	Computer supplies	2,545	
128	Prepaid insurance	2,220	
131	Prepaid rent	3,300	
163	Office equipment	8,000	
164	Accumulated depreciation—Office equipment		$ 0
167	Computer equipment	20,000	
168	Accumulated depreciation—Computer equipment		0
201	Accounts payable		0
210	Wages payable		0
236	Unearned computer services revenue		0
301	A. Lopez, Capital		83,000
302	A. Lopez, Withdrawals	5,600	
403	Computer services revenue		25,659
612	Depreciation expense—Office equipment	0	
613	Depreciation expense—Computer equipment	0	
623	Wages expense	2,625	
637	Insurance expense	0	
640	Rent expense	0	
652	Computer supplies expense	0	
655	Advertising expense	1,940	
676	Mileage expense	704	
677	Miscellaneous expenses	250	
684	Repairs expense—Computer	805	
	Totals	$108,659	$108,659

Success Systems had the following transactions and events in December 2009.

Dec. 2 Paid $1,025 cash to Hillside Mall for Success Systems' share of mall advertising costs.
      3 Paid $500 cash for minor repairs to the company's computer.
      4 Received $3,950 cash from Alex's Engineering Co. for the receivable from November.
     10 Paid cash to Lyn Addie for six days of work at the rate of $125 per day.
     14 Notified by Alex's Engineering Co. that Success's bid of $7,000 on a proposed project has
         been accepted. Alex's paid a $1,500 cash advance to Success Systems.
     15 Purchased $1,100 of computer supplies on credit from Harris Office Products.
     16 Sent a reminder to Gomez Co. to pay the fee for services recorded on November 8.
     20 Completed a project for Liu Corporation and received $5,625 cash.
  22–26 Took the week off for the holidays.
     28 Received $3,000 cash from Gomez Co. on its receivable.
     29 Reimbursed Lopez's business automobile mileage (600 miles at $0.32 per mile).
     31 A. Lopez withdrew $1,500 cash from the company for personal use.

The following additional facts are collected for use in making adjusting entries prior to preparing financial statements for the company's first three months:

a. The December 31 inventory count of computer supplies shows $580 still available.

b. Three months have expired since the 12-month insurance premium was paid in advance.

c. As of December 31, Lyn Addie has not been paid for four days of work at $125 per day.

d. The company's computer is expected to have a four-year life with no salvage value.

e. The office equipment is expected to have a five-year life with no salvage value.

f. Three of the four months' prepaid rent has expired.

Required

1. Prepare journal entries to record each of the December transactions and events for Success Systems. Post those entries to the accounts in the ledger.

2. Prepare adjusting entries to reflect *a* through *f*. Post those entries to the accounts in the ledger.

Check (3) Adjusted trial balance totals, $119,034

3. Prepare an adjusted trial balance as of December 31, 2009.

4. Prepare an income statement for the three months ended December 31, 2009.

5. Prepare a statement of owner's equity for the three months ended December 31, 2009.

(6) Total assets, $93,248

6. Prepare a balance sheet as of December 31, 2009.

BEYOND THE NUMBERS

REPORTING IN ACTION

C1 C2 A1 A2 ♟

BTN 3-1 Refer to Best Buy's financial statements in Appendix A to answer the following.

1. Identify and write down the revenue recognition principle as explained in the chapter.

2. Research Best Buy's footnotes to discover how it applies the revenue recognition principle. Report what you discover.

3. What is Best Buy's profit margin for fiscal years ended March 3, 2007, and February 25, 2006.

Fast Forward

4. Access Best Buy's financial statements (10-K) for fiscal years ending after March 3, 2007, at its Website (BestBuy.com) or the SEC's EDGAR database (www.sec.gov). Compare the March 3, 2007, fiscal year profit margin to any subsequent year's profit margin that you are able to calculate.

COMPARATIVE ANALYSIS

A2 ♟

 RadioShack.

BTN 3-2 Key figures for the recent two years of both Best Buy and RadioShack follow.

Key Figures ($ millions)	Best Buy		RadioShack	
	Current Year	Prior Year	Current Year	Prior Year
Net income	$ 1,377	$ 1,140	$ 73	$ 270
Net sales	35,934	30,848	4,778	5,082

Required

1. Compute profit margins for (*a*) Best Buy and (*b*) RadioShack for the two years of data shown.

2. Which company is more successful on the basis of profit margin? Explain.

BTN 3-3   Jerome Boland works for Sea Biscuit Co. He and Farah Smith, his manager, are preparing adjusting entries for annual financial statements. Boland computes depreciation and records it as

ETHICS CHALLENGE

C1 C2 A1 ♟

Depreciation Expense—Equipment	123,000	
Accumulated Depreciation—Equipment		123,000

Smith agrees with his computation but says the credit entry should be directly to the Equipment account. She argues that while accumulated depreciation is technically correct, "it is less hassle not to use a contra account and just credit the Equipment account directly. And besides, the balance sheet shows the same amount for total assets under either method."

Required

1. How should depreciation be recorded? Do you support Boland or Smith?

2. Evaluate the strengths and weaknesses of Smith's reasons for preferring her method.

3. Indicate whether the situation Boland faces is an ethical problem. Explain.

BTN 3-4   The class should be divided into teams. Teams are to select an industry (such as automobile manufacturing, airlines, defense contractors), and each team member is to select a different company in that industry. Each team member is to acquire the annual report of the company selected. Annual reports can be downloaded from company Websites or from the SEC's EDGAR database at (www.sec.gov).

COMMUNICATING IN PRACTICE

C1 A2 ♟

Required

1. Use the annual report to compute the return on assets, debt ratio, and profit margin.

2. Communicate with team members via a meeting, e-mail, or telephone to discuss the meaning of the ratios, how different companies compare to each other, and the industry norm. The team must prepare a single memo reporting the ratios for each company and identifying the conclusions or consensus of opinion reached during the team's discussion. The memo is to be copied and distributed to the instructor and all classmates.

BTN 3-5   Access the Gap's Website (GapInc.com) to answer the following requirements.

TAKING IT TO THE NET

C1 A2 ♟ 🖱

Required

1. What are Gap's main brands?

2. Access Gap's 2007 annual report (10-K) either at the company's Website or at www.sec.gov. What is Gap's fiscal year-end?

3. What is Gap's net sales for the period ended February 2, 2008?

4. What is Gap's net income for the period ended February 2, 2008?

5. Compute Gap's profit margin for the year ended February 2, 2008.

6. Do you believe Gap's decision to use a year-end of early February or late January relates to its natural business year? Explain.

TEAMWORK IN ACTION

C3 A1 P1

BTN 3-6 Four types of adjustments are described in the chapter: (1) prepaid expenses, (2) unearned revenues, (3) accrued expenses, and (4) accrued revenues.

Required

1. Form *learning teams* of four (or more) members. Each team member must select one of the four adjustments as an area of expertise (each team must have at least one expert in each area).
2. Form *expert teams* from the individuals who have selected the same area of expertise. Expert teams are to discuss and write a report that each expert will present to his or her learning team addressing the following:
   a. Description of the adjustment and why it's necessary.
   b. Example of a transaction or event, with dates and amounts, that requires adjustment.
   c. Adjusting entry(ies) for the example in requirement *b*.
   d. Status of the affected account(s) before and after the adjustment in requirement *c*.
   e. Effects on financial statements of not making the adjustment.
3. Each expert should return to his or her learning team. In rotation, each member should present his or her expert team's report to the learning team. Team discussion is encouraged.

ENTREPRENEURIAL DECISION

A2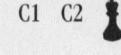

BTN 3-7 Review the opening feature of this chapter dealing with **PopCap Games**.

Required

1. Assume that PopCap sells a $300 gift certificate to a customer, collecting the $300 cash in advance. Prepare the journal entry for the (*a*) collection of the cash for delivery of the gift certificate to the customer and (*b*) revenue from the subsequent delivery of games when the gift certificate is used.
2. How can keeping no inventories help to improve PopCap profit margin?
3. PopCap understands that many companies carry inventories, and the owners are thinking of carrying an inventory of games on CDs. The owners desire your advice on the pros and cons of carrying such inventory. Provide at least one reason for and one reason against carrying inventories.

HITTING THE ROAD

C1

BTN 3-8 Visit the Website of a major company that interests you. Use the Investor Relations link at the Website to obtain the toll-free telephone number of the Investor Relations Department. Call the company, ask to speak to Investor Relations, and request a copy of the company's most recent annual report. You should receive the requested report within one to two weeks. Once you have received your report, use it throughout the term to see that the principles you are learning in class are being applied in practice.

GLOBAL DECISION

A2 C1 C2

DSG

BTN 3-9 **DSG international plc** is the United Kingdom's largest retailer of consumer electronics. Access its financial statements for the year ended April 28, 2007, at the company's Website (www.DSGiplc.com).

Required

1. Locate the notes to its financial statements, and read note *1.3 Revenue*. When is sales revenue recognized by DSG?
2. What is DSG's profit margin for the year ended April 28, 2007?
3. Compute DSG's current ratio for both the current year and the prior year. (DSG's balance sheet is in a slightly different format than the examples in the text: current assets follow fixed assets, and current liabilities follow current assets.)

ANSWERS TO MULTIPLE CHOICE QUIZ

1. b; the forgotten adjusting entry is: *dr.* Wages Expense, *cr.* Wages Payable.
2. c; Supplies used = $450 − $125 = $325
3. b; Insurance expense = $24,000 × (8/24) = $8,000; adjusting entry is: *dr.* Insurance Expense for $8,000, *cr.* Prepaid Insurance for $8,000.

4. a; Consulting fees earned = $3,600 × (2/6) = $1,200; adjusting entry is: *dr.* Unearned Consulting Fee for $1,200, *cr.* Consulting Fees Earned for $1,200.
5. e; Profit margin = $15,000/$300,000 = 5%

A Look Back

Chapter 3 explained the timing of reports. We described why adjusting accounts is key for recognizing revenues and expenses in the proper period. We prepared an adjusted trial balance and used it to prepare financial statements.

 A Look at This Chapter

This chapter emphasizes the final steps in the accounting process and reviews the entire accounting cycle. We explain the closing process, including accounting procedures and the use of a post-closing trial balance. We show how a work sheet aids in preparing financial statements.

A Look Ahead

Chapter 5 looks at accounting for merchandising activities. We describe the sale and purchase of merchandise and their implications for preparing and analyzing financial statements.

Completing the Accounting Cycle

Chapter

Learning Objectives

CAP

Conceptual

C1 Explain why temporary accounts are closed each period. (p. 140)

C2 Identify steps in the accounting cycle. (p. 144)

C3 Explain and prepare a classified balance sheet. (p. 145)

Analytical

A1 Compute the current ratio and describe what it reveals about a company's financial condition. (p. 147)

LP4

Procedural

P1 Prepare a work sheet and explain its usefulness. (p. 136)

P2 Describe and prepare closing entries. (p. 141)

P3 Explain and prepare a post-closing trial balance. (p. 142)

P4 *Appendix 4A*—Prepare reversing entries and explain their purpose. (p. 153)

Walk in Her Shoes

"Stay true to your vision and your mission"
—Kathryn Kerrigan

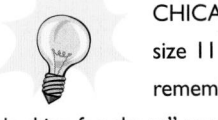

CHICAGO—As a teenager, Kathryn Kerrigan wore a size 11 shoe and found shopping for shoes grueling. "I remember driving with my dad to every shopping mall looking for shoes," recalls Kathryn. "It's embarrassing and it doesn't have to be." Kathryn decided to do something about it. She wrote a business plan for a college project and executed that plan with her dad's encouragement. Her start-up company, **Kathryn Kerrigan (KathrynKerrigan.com),** now provides stylish women's shoes through size 14.

Success, however, requires Kathryn to monitor costs. "We had to create the molds for every shoe size," explains Kathryn. "These cost about $2,000 each." She set up an accounting system to track revenues and control costs, but it is a constant struggle as her business grows. Kathryn says that properly applying the accounting cycle, preparing classified financial statements, and acting on that information increase the odds of success. However, at times, admits Kathryn, "I had to find humility and ask for help."

Kathryn has successfully controlled materials costs while monitoring both revenues and customer needs. She uses the accounting system and closing entries to help identify and match costs with revenues for specific time periods. Kathryn says she relies on classified balance sheets to know when to pay bills. But what pulls her through, admits Kathryn, is knowing that "we're putting out a product that's missing in the marketplace."

Kathryn is on a mission. "What keeps me going," explains Kathryn, "are all the women who keep coming up to me . . . asking for shoes that fit." To make that happen, she tracks the accounting numbers to be sure it is a money-making venture. "It's important for entrepreneurs to be realistic," insists Kathryn. Yet she adds, "A great pair of shoes can make all the difference!"

[Sources: *Kathryn Kerrigan Website,* January 2009; *Success Magazine,* February 2008; *Inc.com,* July 2007; *Beep,* October 2007; *Chicago Sun-Times,* February 2008]

Many of the important steps leading to financial statements were explained in earlier chapters. We described how transactions and events are analyzed, journalized, and posted. This chapter explains the closing process that readies revenue, expense, and withdrawal accounts for the next reporting period and updates the capital account. A work sheet is shown to be a useful tool for these final steps and in preparing financial statements. It also explains how accounts are classified on a balance sheet to increase their usefulness to decision makers.

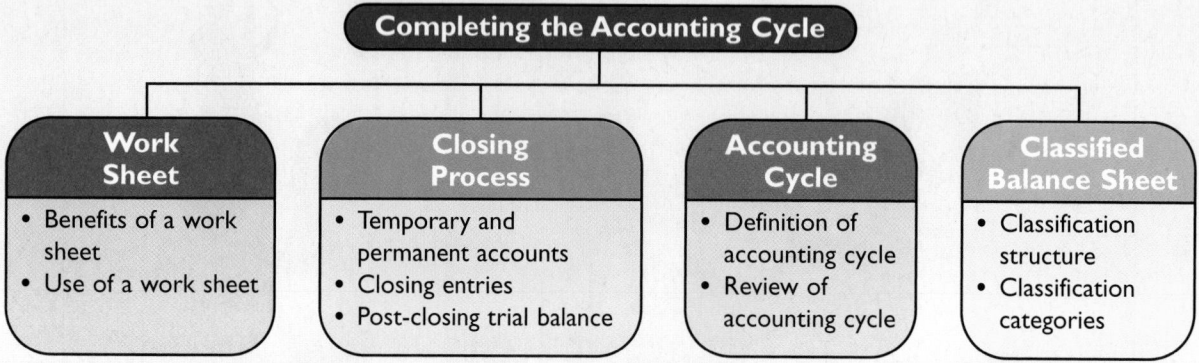

Work Sheet as a Tool

Information preparers use various analyses and internal documents when organizing information for internal and external decision makers. Internal documents are often called **working papers.** One widely used working paper is the **work sheet,** which is a useful tool for preparers in working with accounting information. It is usually not available to external decision makers.

Benefits of a Work Sheet

P1 Prepare a work sheet and explain its usefulness.

A work sheet is *not* a required report, yet using a manual or electronic work sheet has several potential benefits. Specifically, a work sheet

- Aids the preparation of financial statements.
- Reduces the possibility of errors when working with many accounts and adjustments.
- Links accounts and adjustments to their impacts in financial statements.
- Assists in planning and organizing an audit of financial statements—as it can be used to reflect any adjustments necessary.
- Helps in preparing interim (monthly and quarterly) financial statements when the journalizing and posting of adjusting entries are postponed until year-end.
- Shows the effects of proposed or "what-if" transactions.

Decision Insight

High-Tech Work Sheet An electronic work sheet using spreadsheet software such as Excel allows us to easily change numbers, assess the impact of alternative strategies, and quickly prepare financial statements at less cost. It can also increase the available time for analysis and interpretation.

Use of a Work Sheet

Point: Since a work sheet is *not* a required report or an accounting record, its format is flexible and can be modified by its user to fit his/her preferences.

When a work sheet is used to prepare financial statements, it is constructed at the end of a period before the adjusting process. The complete work sheet includes a list of the accounts, their balances and adjustments, and their sorting into financial statement columns. It provides two columns each for the unadjusted trial balance, the adjustments, the adjusted trial balance, the income statement, and the balance sheet (including the statement of owner's equity). To describe and interpret the work sheet, we use the information from FastForward. Preparing the work sheet has five important steps. Each step, 1 through 5, is color-coded and explained with reference to Exhibits 4.1 and 4.2.

① Step 1. Enter Unadjusted Trial Balance

Refer to Exhibit 4.1. The first step in preparing a work sheet is to list the title of every account and its account number that is expected to appear on its financial statements. This includes all accounts in the ledger plus any new ones from adjusting entries. Most adjusting entries— including expenses from salaries, supplies, depreciation, and insurance—are predictable and recurring. The unadjusted balance for each account is then entered in the appropriate Debit or Credit column of the unadjusted trial balance columns. The totals of these two columns must be equal. Exhibit 4.1 shows FastForward's work sheet after completing this first step. Sometimes blank lines are left on the work sheet based on past experience to indicate where lines will be needed for adjustments to certain accounts. Exhibit 4.1 shows Consulting Revenue as one example. An alternative is to squeeze adjustments on one line or to combine the effects of two or more adjustments in one amount. In the unusual case when an account is not predicted, we can add a new line for such an account following the *Totals* line.

② Step 2. Enter Adjustments

Refer to Exhibit 4.1a (turn over first transparency). The second step in preparing a work sheet is to enter adjustments in the Adjustments columns. The adjustments shown are the same ones shown in Exhibit 3.13. An identifying letter links the debit and credit of each adjusting entry. This is called *keying* the adjustments. After preparing a work sheet, adjusting entries must still be entered in the journal and posted to the ledger. The Adjustments columns provide the information for those entries.

Point: A recordkeeper often can complete the procedural task of journalizing and posting adjusting entries by using a work sheet and the guidance that *keying* provides.

③ Step 3. Prepare Adjusted Trial Balance

Refer to Exhibit 4.1b (turn over second transparency). The adjusted trial balance is prepared by combining the adjustments with the unadjusted balances for each account. As an example, the Prepaid Insurance account has a $2,400 debit balance in the Unadjusted Trial Balance columns. This $2,400 debit is combined with the $100 credit in the Adjustments columns to give Prepaid Insurance a $2,300 debit in the Adjusted Trial Balance columns. The totals of the Adjusted Trial Balance columns confirm the equality of debits and credits.

Point: To avoid omitting the transfer of an account balance, start with the first line (cash) and continue in account order.

④ Step 4. Sort Adjusted Trial Balance Amounts to Financial Statements

Refer to Exhibit 4.1c (turn over third transparency). This step involves sorting account balances from the adjusted trial balance to their proper financial statement columns. Expenses go to the Income Statement Debit column and revenues to the Income Statement Credit column. Assets and withdrawals go to the Balance Sheet & Statement of Owner's Equity Debit column. Liabilities and owner's capital go to the Balance Sheet & Statement of Owner's Equity Credit column.

⑤ Step 5. Total Statement Columns, Compute Income or Loss, and Balance Columns

Refer to Exhibit 4.1d (turn over fourth transparency). Each financial statement column (from Step 4) is totaled. The difference between the totals of the Income Statement columns is net income or net loss. This occurs because revenues are entered in the Credit column and expenses in the Debit column. If the Credit total exceeds the Debit total, there is net income. If the Debit total exceeds the Credit total, there is a net loss. For FastForward, the Credit total exceeds the Debit total, giving a $3,785 net income.

The net income from the Income Statement columns is then entered in the Balance Sheet & Statement of Owner's Equity Credit column. Adding net income to the last Credit column implies that it is to be added to owner's capital. If a loss occurs, it is added to the Debit column. This implies that it is to be subtracted from owner's capital. The ending balance of owner's capital does not appear in the last two columns as a single amount, but it is computed in the

[continued on p. 140]

EXHIBIT 4.1

Work Sheet with Unadjusted Trial Balance

	File Edit View Insert Format Tools Data Window Help

FastForward
Work Sheet
For Month Ended December 31, 2009

No.	Account	Unadjusted Trial Balance Dr.	Unadjusted Trial Balance Cr.	Adjustments Dr.	Adjustments Cr.	Adjusted Trial Balance Dr.	Adjusted Trial Balance Cr.	Income Statement Dr.	Income Statement Cr.	Balance Sheet & Statement of Owner's Equity Dr.	Balance Sheet & Statement of Owner's Equity Cr.
101	Cash	4,350									
106	Accounts receivable	0									
126	Supplies	9,720									
128	Prepaid insurance	2,400									
167	Equipment	26,000									
168	Accumulated depreciation—Equip.		0								
201	Accounts payable		6,200								
209	Salaries payable		0								
236	Unearned consulting revenue		3,000								
301	C. Taylor, Capital		30,000								
302	C. Taylor, Withdrawals	200									
403	Consulting revenue		5,800								
406	Rental revenue		300								
612	Depreciation expense—Equip.	0									
622	Salaries expense	1,400									
637	Insurance expense	0									
640	Rent expense	1,000									
652	Supplies expense	0									
690	Utilities expense	230									
	Totals	45,300	45,300								

List all accounts from the ledger and those expected to arise from adjusting entries.

A work sheet collects and summarizes information used to prepare adjusting entries, financial statements, and closing entries.

Enter all amounts available from ledger accounts. Column totals must be equal.

describe and interpret the work sheet, we use the information from FastForward. Preparing the work sheet has five important steps. Each step, 1 through 5, is color-coded and explained with reference to Exhibits 4.1 and 4.2.

① Step 1. Enter Unadjusted Trial Balance

Refer to Exhibit 4.1. The first step in preparing a work sheet is to list the title of every account and its account number that is expected to appear on its financial statements. This includes all accounts in the ledger plus any new ones from adjusting entries. Most adjusting entries—including expenses from salaries, supplies, depreciation, and insurance—are predictable and recurring. The unadjusted balance for each account is then entered in the appropriate Debit or Credit column of the unadjusted trial balance columns. The totals of these two columns must be equal. Exhibit 4.1 shows FastForward's work sheet after completing this first step. Sometimes blank lines are left on the work sheet based on past experience to indicate where lines will be needed for adjustments to certain accounts. Exhibit 4.1 shows Consulting Revenue as one example. An alternative is to squeeze adjustments on one line or to combine the effects of two or more adjustments in one amount. In the unusual case when an account is not predicted, we can add a new line for such an account following the *Totals* line.

② Step 2. Enter Adjustments

Refer to Exhibit 4.1a (turn over first transparency). The second step in preparing a work sheet is to enter adjustments in the Adjustments columns. The adjustments shown are the same ones shown in Exhibit 3.13. An identifying letter links the debit and credit of each adjusting entry. This is called *keying* the adjustments. After preparing a work sheet, adjusting entries must still be entered in the journal and posted to the ledger. The Adjustments columns provide the information for those entries.

Point: A recordkeeper often can complete the procedural task of journalizing and posting adjusting entries by using a work sheet and the guidance that *keying* provides.

③ Step 3. Prepare Adjusted Trial Balance

Refer to Exhibit 4.1b (turn over second transparency). The adjusted trial balance is prepared by combining the adjustments with the unadjusted balances for each account. As an example, the Prepaid Insurance account has a $2,400 debit balance in the Unadjusted Trial Balance columns. This $2,400 debit is combined with the $100 credit in the Adjustments columns to give Prepaid Insurance a $2,300 debit in the Adjusted Trial Balance columns. The totals of the Adjusted Trial Balance columns confirm the equality of debits and credits.

Point: To avoid omitting the transfer of an account balance, start with the first line (cash) and continue in account order.

④ Step 4. Sort Adjusted Trial Balance Amounts to Financial Statements

Refer to Exhibit 4.1c (turn over third transparency). This step involves sorting account balances from the adjusted trial balance to their proper financial statement columns. Expenses go to the Income Statement Debit column and revenues to the Income Statement Credit column. Assets and withdrawals go to the Balance Sheet & Statement of Owner's Equity Debit column. Liabilities and owner's capital go to the Balance Sheet & Statement of Owner's Equity Credit column.

⑤ Step 5. Total Statement Columns, Compute Income or Loss, and Balance Columns

Refer to Exhibit 4.1d (turn over fourth transparency). Each financial statement column (from Step 4) is totaled. The difference between the totals of the Income Statement columns is net income or net loss. This occurs because revenues are entered in the Credit column and expenses in the Debit column. If the Credit total exceeds the Debit total, there is net income. If the Debit total exceeds the Credit total, there is a net loss. For FastForward, the Credit total exceeds the Debit total, giving a $3,785 net income.

The net income from the Income Statement columns is then entered in the Balance Sheet & Statement of Owner's Equity Credit column. Adding net income to the last Credit column implies that it is to be added to owner's capital. If a loss occurs, it is added to the Debit column. This implies that it is to be subtracted from owner's capital. The ending balance of owner's capital does not appear in the last two columns as a single amount, but it is computed in the

[continued on p. 140]

EXHIBIT 4.1

Work Sheet with Unadjusted Trial Balance

File   Edit   View   Insert   Format   Tools   Data   Window   Help

	No.	Account	Unadjusted Trial Balance		Adjustments		Adjusted Trial Balance		Income Statement		Balance Sheet & Statement of Owner's Equity	
			Dr.	Cr.	Dr.	Cr.	Dr.	Cr.	Dr.	Cr.	Dr.	Cr.
7	101	Cash	4,350									
8	106	Accounts receivable	0									
9	126	Supplies	9,720									
10	128	Prepaid insurance	2,400									
11	167	Equipment	26,000									
12	168	Accumulated depreciation—Equip.		0								
13	201	Accounts payable		6,200								
14	209	Salaries payable		0								
15	236	Unearned consulting revenue		3,000								
16	301	C. Taylor, Capital		30,000								
17	302	C. Taylor, Withdrawals	200									
18	403	Consulting revenue		5,800								
19												
20	406	Rental revenue		300								
21	612	Depreciation expense—Equip.	0									
22	622	Salaries expense	1,400									
23	637	Insurance expense	0									
24	640	Rent expense	1,000									
25	652	Supplies expense	0									
26	690	Utilities expense	230									
27		Totals	45,300	45,300								

FastForward
Work Sheet
For Month Ended December 31, 2009

List all accounts from the ledger and those expected to arise from adjusting entries.

Enter all amounts available from ledger accounts.
Column totals must be equal.

A work sheet collects and summarizes information used to prepare adjusting entries, financial statements, and closing entries.

EXHIBIT 4.2

Financial Statements Prepared from the Work Sheet

FASTFORWARD
Income Statement
For Month Ended December 31, 2009

Revenues		
Consulting revenue	$ 7,850	
Rental revenue	300	
Total revenues		$ 8,150
Expenses		
Depreciation expense—Equipment	375	
Salaries expense	1,610	
Insurance expense	100	
Rent expense	1,000	
Supplies expense	1,050	
Utilities expense	230	
Total expenses		4,365
Net income		$ 3,785

FASTFORWARD
Statement of Owner's Equity
For Month Ended December 31, 2009

C. Taylor, Capital, December 1		$ 0
Add: Investment by owner	$30,000	
Net income	3,785	33,785
		33,785
Less: Withdrawals by owner		200
C. Taylor, Capital, December 31		$33,585

FASTFORWARD
Balance Sheet
December 31, 2009

Assets		
Cash		$ 4,350
Accounts receivable		1,800
Supplies		8,670
Prepaid insurance		2,300
Equipment	$26,000	
Accumulated depreciation—Equipment	(375)	25,625
Total assets		$42,745

Liabilities		
Accounts payable		$ 6,200
Salaries payable		210
Unearned consulting revenue		2,750
Total liabilities		9,160

Equity		
C. Taylor, Capital		33,585
Total liabilities and equity		$42,745

statement of owner's equity using these account balances. When net income or net loss is added to the proper Balance Sheet & Statement of Owner's Equity column, the totals of the last two columns must balance. If they do not, one or more errors have been made. The error can either be mathematical or involve sorting one or more amounts to incorrect columns.

 Decision Maker ▬▬▬▬▬▬▬▬▬▬▬▬▬▬▬▬▬▬▬▬▬▬▬

Entrepreneur   You make a printout of the electronic work sheet used to prepare financial statements. There is no depreciation adjustment, yet you own a large amount of equipment. Does the absence of depreciation adjustment concern you? [Answer—p. 153]

Work Sheet Applications and Analysis

A work sheet does not substitute for financial statements. It is a tool we can use at the end of an accounting period to help organize data and prepare financial statements. FastForward's financial statements are shown in Exhibit 4.2. Its income statement amounts are taken from the Income Statement columns of the work sheet. Similarly, amounts for its balance sheet and its statement of owner's equity are taken from the Balance Sheet & Statement of Owner's Equity columns of the work sheet.

Information from the Adjustments columns of a work sheet can be used to journalize adjusting entries. It is important to remember that a work sheet is not a journal. This means that even when a work sheet is prepared, it is necessary to both journalize adjustments and post them to the ledger.

Work sheets are also useful in analyzing the effects of proposed, or what-if, transactions. This is done by entering financial statement amounts in the Unadjusted (what-if) columns. Proposed transactions are then entered in the Adjustments columns. We then compute "adjusted" amounts from these proposed transactions. The extended amounts in the financial statement columns show the effects of these proposed transactions. These financial statement columns yield **pro forma financial statements** because they show the statements *as if* the proposed transactions occurred.

Video4.1

Quick Check   Answers—p. 154

1. Where do we get the amounts to enter in the Unadjusted Trial Balance columns of a work sheet?
2. What are the advantages of using a work sheet to help prepare adjusting entries?
3. What are the overall benefits of a work sheet?

Closing Process

C1 Explain why temporary accounts are closed each period.

Temporary Accounts
Revenues
Expenses
Owner Withdrawals
Income Summary

Permanent Accounts
Assets
Liabilities
Owner Capital

The **closing process** is an important step at the end of an accounting period *after* financial statements have been completed. It prepares accounts for recording the transactions and the events of the *next* period. In the closing process we must (1) identify accounts for closing, (2) record and post the closing entries, and (3) prepare a post-closing trial balance. The purpose of the closing process is twofold. First, it resets revenue, expense, and withdrawals account balances to zero at the end of each period. This is done so that these accounts can properly measure income and withdrawals for the next period. Second, it helps in summarizing a period's revenues and expenses. This section explains the closing process.

Temporary and Permanent Accounts

Temporary (or *nominal*) **accounts** accumulate data related to one accounting period. They include all income statement accounts, the withdrawals account, and the Income Summary account. They are temporary because the accounts are opened at the beginning of a period, used to record transactions and events for that period, and then closed at the end of the period. *The closing process applies only to temporary accounts.* **Permanent** (or *real*) **accounts** report on activities related to one or more future accounting periods. They carry their ending balances into the next period and generally consist of all balance sheet accounts. These asset, liability, and equity accounts are not closed.

Recording Closing Entries

To record and post **closing entries** is to transfer the end-of-period balances in revenue, expense, and withdrawals accounts to the permanent capital account. Closing entries are necessary at the end of each period after financial statements are prepared because

■ Revenue, expense, and withdrawals accounts must begin each period with zero balances.

■ Owner's capital must reflect prior periods' revenues, expenses, and withdrawals.

An income statement aims to report revenues and expenses for a *specific accounting period.* The statement of owner's equity reports similar information, including withdrawals. Since revenue, expense, and withdrawals accounts must accumulate information separately for each period, they must start each period with zero balances. To close these accounts, we transfer their balances first to an account called *Income Summary.* **Income Summary** is a temporary account (only used for the closing process) that contains a credit for the sum of all revenues (and gains) and a debit for the sum of all expenses (and losses). Its balance equals net income or net loss and it is transferred to the capital account. Next the withdrawals account balance is transferred to the capital account. After these closing entries are posted, the revenue, expense, withdrawals, and Income Summary accounts have zero balances. These accounts are then said to be *closed* or *cleared.*

Exhibit 4.3 uses the adjusted account balances of FastForward (from the Adjusted Trial Balance columns of Exhibit 4.1 or from the left side of Exhibit 4.4) to show the four steps necessary to close its temporary accounts. We explain each step.

Point: To understand the closing process, focus on its *outcomes*—updating the capital account balance to its proper ending balance, and getting *temporary accounts* to show *zero balances* for purposes of accumulating data for the next period.

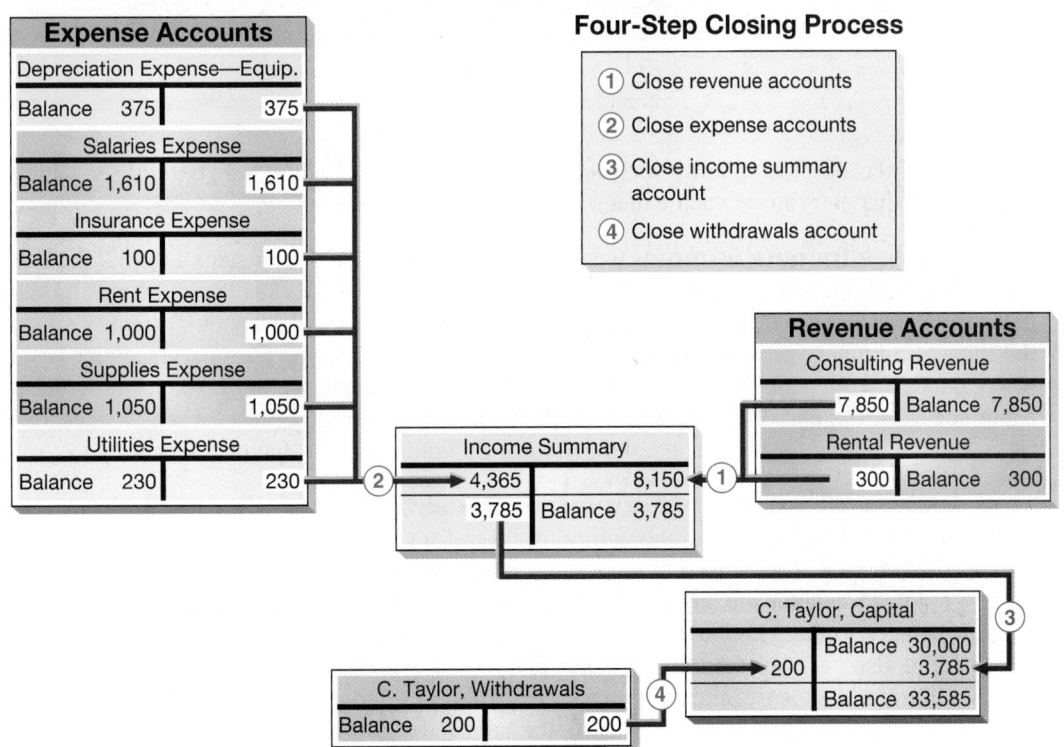

EXHIBIT 4.3

Four-Step Closing Process

Point: C. Taylor, Capital is the only *permanent account* in Exhibit 4.3.

Step 1: Close Credit Balances in Revenue Accounts to Income Summary The first closing entry transfers credit balances in revenue (and gain) accounts to the Income Summary account. We bring accounts with credit balances to zero by debiting them. For FastForward, this journal entry is step 1 in Exhibit 4.4. This entry closes revenue accounts and leaves them with zero balances. The accounts are now ready to record revenues when they occur in the next period. The $8,150 credit entry to Income Summary equals total revenues for the period.

P2 Describe and prepare closing entries.

Step 2: Close Debit Balances in Expense Accounts to Income Summary The second closing entry transfers debit balances in expense (and loss) accounts to the Income Summary account. We bring expense accounts' debit balances to zero by crediting them. With a balance of zero, these accounts are ready to accumulate a record of expenses for the next

Point: It is possible to close revenue and expense accounts directly to owner's capital. Computerized accounting systems do this.

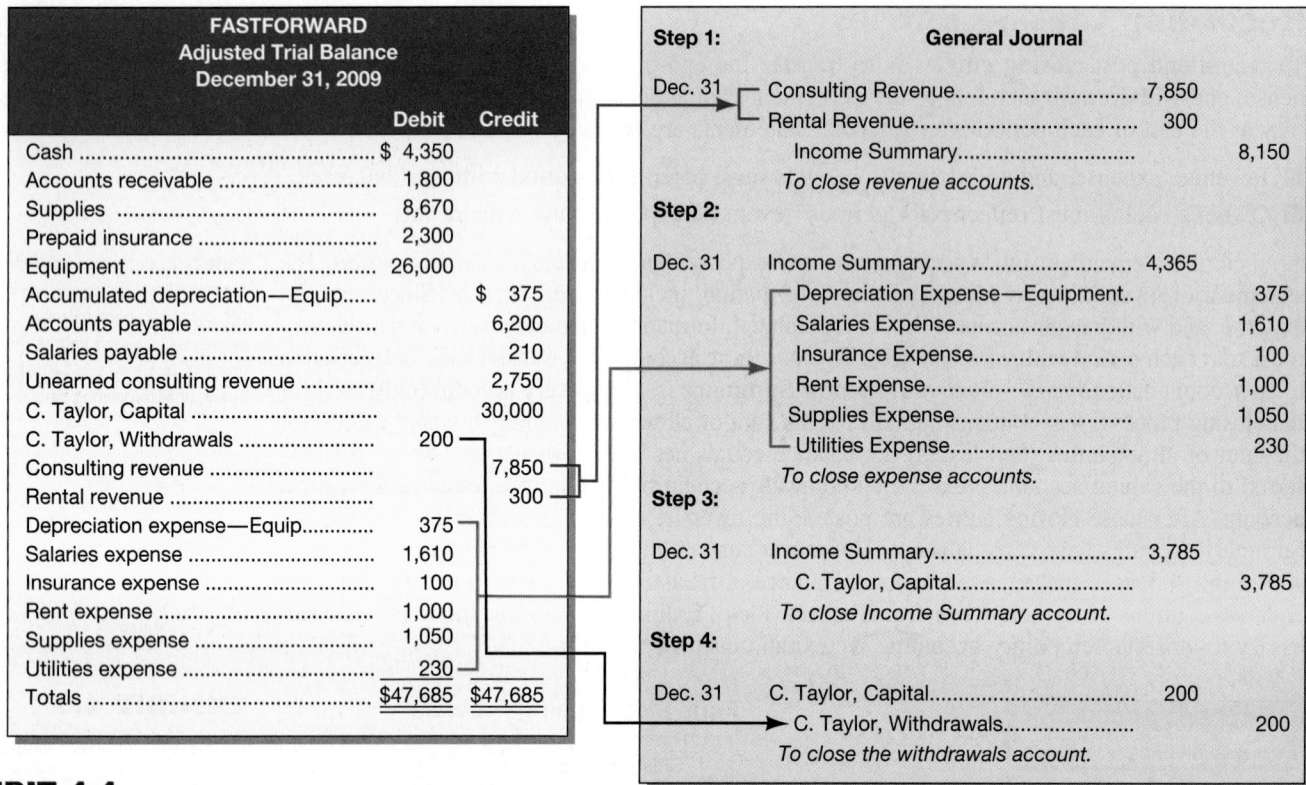

EXHIBIT 4.4

Preparing Closing Entries

period. This second closing entry for FastForward is step 2 in Exhibit 4.4. Exhibit 4.3 shows that posting this entry gives each expense account a zero balance.

Step 3: Close Income Summary to Owner's Capital   After steps 1 and 2, the balance of Income Summary is equal to December's net income of $3,785. The third closing entry transfers the balance of the Income Summary account to the capital account. This entry closes the Income Summary account–see step 3 in Exhibit 4.4. The Income Summary account has a zero balance after posting this entry. It continues to have a zero balance until the closing process again occurs at the end of the next period. (If a net loss occurred because expenses exceeded revenues, the third entry is reversed: debit Owner Capital and credit Income Summary.)

Step 4: Close Withdrawals Account to Owner's Capital   The fourth closing entry transfers any debit balance in the withdrawals account to the owner's capital account—see step 4 in Exhibit 4.4. This entry gives the withdrawals account a zero balance, and the account is now ready to accumulate next period's withdrawals. This entry also reduces the capital account balance to the $33,585 amount reported on the balance sheet.

We could also have selected the accounts and amounts needing to be closed by identifying individual revenue, expense, and withdrawals accounts in the ledger. This is illustrated in Exhibit 4.4 where we prepare closing entries using the adjusted trial balance.[1] (Information for closing entries is also in the financial statement columns of a work sheet.)

Post-Closing Trial Balance

P3   Explain and prepare a post-closing trial balance.

Exhibit 4.5 shows the entire ledger of FastForward as of December 31 after adjusting and closing entries are posted. (The transaction and adjusting entries are in Chapters 2 and 3.) The temporary accounts (revenues, expenses, and withdrawals) have ending balances equal to zero.

---

[1] The closing process has focused on proprietorships. It is identical for partnerships with the exception that each owner has separate capital and withdrawals accounts (for steps 3 and 4). The closing process for a corporation is similar with the exception that it uses a Retained Earnings account instead of a Capital account, and a Dividend account instead of a Withdrawals account.

EXHIBIT 4.5

General Ledger after the Closing Process for FastForward

Asset Accounts

Cash — Acct. No. 101

Date	Explan.	PR	Debit	Credit	Balance
2009					
Dec. 1		G1	30,000		30,000
2		G1		2,500	27,500
3		G1		26,000	1,500
5		G1	4,200		5,700
6		G1		2,400	3,300
12		G1		1,000	2,300
12		G1		700	1,600
22		G1	1,900		3,500
24		G1		900	2,600
24		G1		200	2,400
26		G1	3,000		5,400
26		G1		120	5,280
26		G1		230	5,050
26		G1		700	4,350

Accounts Receivable — Acct. No. 106

Date	Explan.	PR	Debit	Credit	Balance
2009					
Dec. 12		G1	1,900		1,900
22		G1		1,900	0
31	Adj.	G1	1,800		1,800

Supplies — Acct. No. 126

Date	Explan.	PR	Debit	Credit	Balance
2009					
Dec. 2		G1	2,500		2,500
6		G1	7,100		9,600
26		G1	120		9,720
31	Adj.	G1		1,050	8,670

Prepaid Insurance — Acct. No. 128

Date	Explan.	PR	Debit	Credit	Balance
2009					
Dec. 6		G1	2,400		2,400
31	Adj.	G1		100	2,300

Equipment — Acct. No. 167

Date	Explan.	PR	Debit	Credit	Balance
2009					
Dec. 3		G1	26,000		26,000

Accumulated Depreciation—Equipment — Acct. No. 168

Date	Explan.	PR	Debit	Credit	Balance
2009					
Dec. 31	Adj.	G1		375	375

Liability and Equity Accounts

Accounts Payable — Acct. No. 201

Date	Explan.	PR	Debit	Credit	Balance
2009					
Dec. 6		G1		7,100	7,100
24		G1	900		6,200

Salaries Payable — Acct. No. 209

Date	Explan.	PR	Debit	Credit	Balance
2009					
Dec. 31	Adj	G1		210	210

Unearned Consulting Revenue — Acct. No. 236

Date	Explan.	PR	Debit	Credit	Balance
2009					
Dec. 26		G1		3,000	3,000
31	Adj.	G1	250		2,750

C. Taylor, Capital — Acct. No. 301

Date	Explan.	PR	Debit	Credit	Balance
2009					
Dec. 1		G1		30,000	30,000
31	Closing	G1		3,785	33,785
31	Closing	G1	200		33,585

C. Taylor, Withdrawals — Acct. No. 302

Date	Explan.	PR	Debit	Credit	Balance
2009					
Dec. 24		G1	200		200
31	Closing	G1		200	0

Revenue and Expense Accounts (Including Income Summary)

Consulting Revenue — Acct. No. 403

Date	Explan.	PR	Debit	Credit	Balance
2009					
Dec. 5		G1		4,200	4,200
12		G1		1,600	5,800
31	Adj.	G1		250	6,050
31	Adj.	G1		1,800	7,850
31	Closing	G1	7,850		0

Rental Revenue — Acct. No. 406

Date	Explan.	PR	Debit	Credit	Balance
2009					
Dec. 12		G1		300	300
31	Closing	G1	300		0

Depreciation Expense—Equipment — Acct. No. 612

Date	Explan.	PR	Debit	Credit	Balance
2009					
Dec. 31	Adj.	G1	375		375
31	Closing	G1		375	0

Salaries Expense — Acct. No. 622

Date	Explan.	PR	Debit	Credit	Balance
2009					
Dec. 12		G1	700		700
26		G1	700		1,400
31	Adj.	G1	210		1,610
31	Closing	G1		1,610	0

Insurance Expense — Acct. No. 637

Date	Explan.	PR	Debit	Credit	Balance
2009					
Dec. 31	Adj.	G1	100		100
31	Closing	G1		100	0

Rent Expense — Acct. No. 640

Date	Explan.	PR	Debit	Credit	Balance
2009					
Dec. 12		G1	1,000		1,000
31	Closing	G1		1,000	0

Supplies Expense — Acct. No. 652

Date	Explan.	PR	Debit	Credit	Balance
2009					
Dec. 31	Adj.	G1	1,050		1,050
31	Closing	G1		1,050	0

Utilities Expense — Acct. No. 690

Date	Explan.	PR	Debit	Credit	Balance
2009					
Dec. 26		G1	230		230
31	Closing	G1		230	0

Income Summary — Acct. No. 901

Date	Explan.	PR	Debit	Credit	Balance
2009					
Dec. 31	Closing	G1		8,150	8,150
31	Closing	G1	4,365		3,785
31	Closing	G1	3,785		0

A **post-closing trial balance** is a list of permanent accounts and their balances from the ledger after all closing entries have been journalized and posted. It lists the balances for all accounts not closed. These accounts comprise a company's assets, liabilities, and equity, which are identical to those in the balance sheet. The aim of a post-closing trial balance is to verify that (1) total debits equal total credits for permanent accounts and (2) all temporary accounts have zero balances. FastForward's post-closing trial balance is shown in Exhibit 4.6. The post-closing trial balance usually is the last step in the accounting process.

EXHIBIT 4.6

Post-Closing Trial Balance

FASTFORWARD Post-Closing Trial Balance December 31, 2009		
	Debit	**Credit**
Cash	$ 4,350	
Accounts receivable	1,800	
Supplies	8,670	
Prepaid insurance	2,300	
Equipment	26,000	
Accumulated depreciation—Equipment		$ 375
Accounts payable		6,200
Salaries payable		210
Unearned consulting revenue		2,750
C. Taylor, Capital		33,585
Totals	$43,120	$43,120

Accounting Cycle

C2 Identify steps in the accounting cycle.

The term **accounting cycle** refers to the steps in preparing financial statements. It is called a *cycle* because the steps are repeated each reporting period. Exhibit 4.7 shows the 10 steps in the cycle, beginning with analyzing transactions and ending with a post-closing trial balance

EXHIBIT 4.7

Steps in the Accounting Cycle*

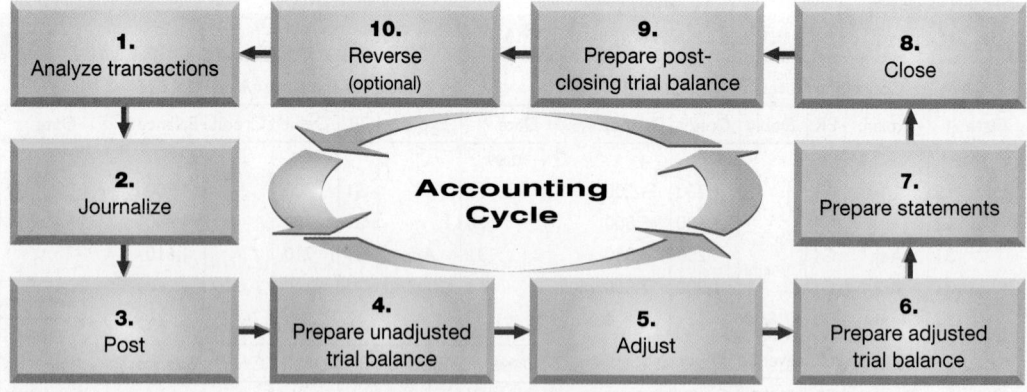

Video4.1

Explanations

1. Analyze transactions	Analyze transactions to prepare for journalizing.
2. Journalize	Record accounts, including debits and credits, in a journal.
3. Post	Transfer debits and credits from the journal to the ledger.
4. Prepare unadjusted trial balance	Summarize unadjusted ledger accounts and amounts.
5. Adjust	Record adjustments to bring account balances up to date; journalize and post adjustments.
6. Prepare adjusted trial balance	Summarize adjusted ledger accounts and amounts.
7. Prepare statements	Use adjusted trial balance to prepare financial statements.
8. Close	Journalize and post entries to close temporary accounts.
9. Prepare post-closing trial balance	Test clerical accuracy of the closing procedures.
10. Reverse (optional)	Reverse certain adjustments in the next period—optional step; see Appendix 4A.

* Steps 4, 6, and 9 can be done on a work sheet. A work sheet is useful in planning adjustments, but adjustments (step 5) must always be journalized and posted. Steps 3, 4, 6, and 9 are automatic with a computerized system.

or reversing entries. Steps 1 through 3 usually occur regularly as a company enters into transactions. Steps 4 through 9 are done at the end of a period. *Reversing entries* in step 10 are optional and are explained in Appendix 4A.

Quick Check
Answers—p. 154

4. What are the major steps in preparing closing entries?

5. Why are revenue and expense accounts called *temporary?* Identify and list the types of temporary accounts.

6. What accounts are listed on the post-closing trial balance?

Classified Balance Sheet

Our discussion to this point has been limited to unclassified financial statements. This section describes a classified balance sheet. The next chapter describes a classified income statement. An **unclassified balance sheet** is one whose items are broadly grouped into assets, liabilities, and equity. One example is FastForward's balance sheet in Exhibit 4.2. A **classified balance sheet** organizes assets and liabilities into important subgroups that provide more information to decision makers.

C3 Explain and prepare a classified balance sheet.

Classification Structure

A classified balance sheet has no required layout, but it usually contains the categories in Exhibit 4.8. One of the more important classifications is the separation between current and noncurrent items for both assets and liabilities. Current items are those expected to come due (either collected or owed) within one year or the company's operating cycle, whichever is longer. The **operating cycle** is the time span from when *cash is used* to acquire goods and services until *cash is received* from the sale of goods and services. "Operating" refers to company operations and "cycle" refers to the circular flow of cash used for company inputs and then cash received from its outputs. The length of a company's operating cycle depends on its activities. For a service company, the operating cycle is the time span between (1) paying employees who perform the services and (2) receiving cash from customers. For a merchandiser selling products, the operating cycle is the time span between (1) paying suppliers for merchandise and (2) receiving cash from customers.

Video4.1

Assets	Liabilities and Equity
Current assets	Current liabilities
Noncurrent assets	Noncurrent liabilities
Long-term investments	Equity
Plant assets	
Intangible assets	

EXHIBIT 4.8

Typical Categories in a Classified Balance Sheet

Most operating cycles are less than one year. This means most companies use a one-year period in deciding which assets and liabilities are current. A few companies have an operating cycle longer than one year. For instance, producers of certain beverages (wine) and products (ginseng) that require aging for several years have operating cycles longer than one year. A balance sheet lists current assets before noncurrent assets and current liabilities before noncurrent liabilities. This consistency in presentation allows users to quickly identify current assets that are most easily converted to cash and current liabilities that are shortly coming due. Items in current assets and current liabilities are listed in the order of how quickly they will be converted to, or paid in, cash.

Classification Categories

This section describes the most common categories in a classified balance sheet. The balance sheet for Snowboarding Components in Exhibit 4.9 shows the typical categories. Its assets are

EXHIBIT 4.9

Example of a Classified
Balance Sheet

SNOWBOARDING COMPONENTS		
Balance Sheet		
January 31, 2009		
Assets		
Current assets		
Cash	$ 6,500	
Short-term investments	2,100	
Accounts receivable, net	4,400	
Merchandise inventory	27,500	
Prepaid expenses	2,400	
Total current assets		$ 42,900
Long-term investments		
Notes receivable	1,500	
Investments in stocks and bonds	18,000	
Land held for future expansion	48,000	
Total long-term investments		67,500
Plant assets		
Equipment and buildings	203,200	
Less accumulated depreciation	53,000	150,200
Land		73,200
Total plant assets		223,400
Intangible assets		10,000
Total assets		$343,800
Liabilities		
Current liabilities		
Accounts payable	$ 15,300	
Wages payable	3,200	
Notes payable	3,000	
Current portion of long-term liabilities	7,500	
Total current liabilities		$ 29,000
Long-term liabilities (net of current portion)		150,000
Total liabilities		179,000
Equity		
T. Hawk, Capital		164,800
Total liabilities and equity		$343,800

classified as either current or noncurrent. Its noncurrent assets include three main categories: long-term investments, plant assets, and intangible assets. Its liabilities are classified as either current or long-term. Not all companies use the same categories of assets and liabilities for their balance sheets. K2 Inc.'s balance sheet lists only three asset classes: current assets; property, plant and equipment; and other assets.

Current Assets   Current assets are cash and other resources that are expected to be sold, collected, or used within one year or the company's operating cycle, whichever is longer. Examples are cash, short-term investments, accounts receivable, short-term notes receivable, goods for sale (called *merchandise* or *inventory*), and prepaid expenses. The individual prepaid expenses of a company are usually small in amount compared to many other assets and are often combined and shown as a single item. The prepaid expenses in Exhibit 4.9 likely include items such as prepaid insurance, prepaid rent, office supplies, and store supplies. Prepaid expenses are usually listed last because they will not be converted to cash (instead, they are used).

Point: Current is also called *short-term*, and noncurrent is also called *long-term*.

Long-Term Investments   A second major balance sheet classification is **long-term** (or *noncurrent*) **investments.** Notes receivable and investments in stocks and bonds are long-term assets when they are expected to be held for more than the longer of one year or the operating cycle. Land held for future expansion is a long-term investment because it is *not* used in operations.

Plant Assets   Plant assets are tangible assets that are both *long-lived* and *used to produce* or *sell products and services.* Examples are equipment, machinery, buildings, and land that are used to produce or sell products and services. The order listing for plant assets is usually from most liquid to least liquid such as equipment and machinery to buildings and land.

Point: Plant assets are also called *fixed assets; property, plant and equipment;* or *long-lived assets.*

Intangible Assets   **Intangible assets** are long-term resources that benefit business operations, usually lack physical form, and have uncertain benefits. Examples are patents, trademarks, copyrights, franchises, and goodwill. Their value comes from the privileges or rights granted to or held by the owner. **K2, Inc.,** reports intangible assets of $228 million, which is nearly 20 percent of its total assets. Its intangibles include trademarks, patents, and licensing agreements.

Current Liabilities   **Current liabilities** are obligations due to be paid or settled within one year or the operating cycle, whichever is longer. They are usually settled by paying out current assets such as cash. Current liabilities often include accounts payable, notes payable, wages payable, taxes payable, interest payable, and unearned revenues. Also, any portion of a long-term liability due to be paid within one year or the operating cycle, whichever is longer, is a current liability. Unearned revenues are current liabilities when they will be settled by delivering products or services within one year or the operating cycle, whichever is longer. Current liabilities are reported in the order of those to be settled first.

Point: Many financial ratios are distorted if accounts are not classified correctly.

Long-Term Liabilities   **Long-term liabilities** are obligations *not* due within one year or the operating cycle, whichever is longer. Notes payable, mortgages payable, bonds payable, and lease obligations are common long-term liabilities. If a company has both short- and long-term items in each of these categories, they are commonly separated into two accounts in the ledger.

Equity   Equity is the owner's claim on assets. For a proprietorship, this claim is reported in the equity section with an owner's capital account. (For a partnership, the equity section reports a capital account for each partner. For a corporation, the equity section is divided into two main subsections, common stock and retained earnings.)

Quick Check
Answers—p. 154

7. Classify the following assets as (1) current assets, (2) plant assets, or (3) intangible assets:
   (a) land used in operations, (b) office supplies, (c) receivables from customers due in 10 months, (d) insurance protection for the next 9 months, (e) trucks used to provide services to customers, (f) trademarks.
8. Cite two examples of assets classified as investments on the balance sheet.
9. Explain the operating cycle for a service company.

Current Ratio   Decision Analysis

An important use of financial statements is to help assess a company's ability to pay its debts in the near future. Such analysis affects decisions by suppliers when allowing a company to buy on credit. It also affects decisions by creditors when lending money to a company, including loan terms such as interest rate, due date, and collateral requirements. It can also affect a manager's decisions about using cash to pay debts when they come due. The **current ratio** is one measure of a company's ability

A1   Compute the current ratio and describe what it reveals about a company's financial condition.

to pay its short-term obligations. It is defined in Exhibit 4.10 as current assets divided by current liabilities.

EXHIBIT 4.10
Current Ratio

$$\text{Current ratio} = \frac{\text{Current assets}}{\text{Current liabilities}}$$

Using financial information from Limited Brands, Inc., we compute its current ratio for the recent four-year period. The results are in Exhibit 4.11.

EXHIBIT 4.11
Limited Brands' Current Ratio

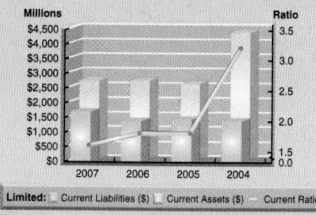

$ in millions	2007	2006	2005	2004
Current assets	$2,771	$2,784	$2,684	$4,433
Current liabilities	$1,709	$1,575	$1,451	$1,388
Current ratio	1.6	1.8	1.8	3.2
Industry current ratio	2.3	2.4	2.5	2.7

Limited Brands' current ratio averaged 2.1 for 2004 through 2007. The current ratio for each of these years suggests that the company's short-term obligations can be covered with its short-term assets. However, if its ratio would approach 1.0, Limited would expect to face challenges in covering liabilities. If the ratio were *less* than 1.0, current liabilities would exceed current assets, and the company's ability to pay short-term obligations could be in doubt.

 Decision Maker

Analyst   You are analyzing the financial condition of a company to assess its ability to meet upcoming loan payments. You compute its current ratio as 1.2. You also find that a major portion of accounts receivable is due from one client who has not made any payments in the past 12 months. Removing this receivable from current assets lowers the current ratio to 0.7. What do you conclude? [Answer—p. 153]

Demonstration Problem

DP4

The partial work sheet of Midtown Repair Company at December 31, 2009, follows.

	Adjusted Trial Balance		Income Statement		Balance Sheet and Statement of Owner's Equity	
	Debit	Credit	Debit	Credit	Debit	Credit
Cash	95,600					
Notes receivable (current)	50,000					
Prepaid insurance	16,000					
Prepaid rent	4,000					
Equipment	170,000					
Accumulated depreciation—Equipment		57,000				
Accounts payable		52,000				
Long-term notes payable		63,000				
C. Trout, Capital		178,500				
C. Trout, Withdrawals	30,000					
Repair services revenue		180,800				
Interest revenue		7,500				
Depreciation expense—Equipment	28,500					
Wages expense	85,000					
Rent expense	48,000					
Insurance expense	6,000					
Interest expense	5,700					
Totals	538,800	538,800				

Required

1. Complete the work sheet by extending the adjusted trial balance totals to the appropriate financial statement columns.
2. Prepare closing entries for Midtown Repair Company.
3. Set up the Income Summary and the C. Trout, Capital account in the general ledger (in balance column format) and post the closing entries to these accounts.
4. Determine the balance of the C. Trout, Capital account to be reported on the December 31, 2009, balance sheet.
5. Prepare an income statement, statement of owner's equity, and classified balance sheet (in report form) as of December 31, 2009.

Planning the Solution

- Extend the adjusted trial balance account balances to the appropriate financial statement columns.
- Prepare entries to close the revenue accounts to Income Summary, to close the expense accounts to Income Summary, to close Income Summary to the capital account, and to close the withdrawals account to the capital account.
- Post the first and second closing entries to the Income Summary account. Examine the balance of income summary and verify that it agrees with the net income shown on the work sheet.
- Post the third and fourth closing entries to the capital account.
- Use the work sheet's two right-most columns and your answer in part 4 to prepare the classified balance sheet.

Solution to Demonstration Problem

1. Completing the work sheet.

	Adjusted Trial Balance Debit	Adjusted Trial Balance Credit	Income Statement Debit	Income Statement Credit	Balance Sheet and Statement of Owner's Equity Debit	Balance Sheet and Statement of Owner's Equity Credit
Cash	95,600				95,600	
Notes receivable (current)	50,000				50,000	
Prepaid insurance	16,000				16,000	
Prepaid rent	4,000				4,000	
Equipment	170,000				170,000	
Accumulated depreciation—Equipment		57,000				57,000
Accounts payable		52,000				52,000
Long-term notes payable		63,000				63,000
C. Trout, Capital		178,500				178,500
C. Trout, Withdrawals	30,000				30,000	
Repair services revenue		180,800		180,800		
Interest revenue		7,500		7,500		
Depreciation expense—Equipment	28,500		28,500			
Wages expense	85,000		85,000			
Rent expense	48,000		48,000			
Insurance expense	6,000		6,000			
Interest expense	5,700		5,700			
Totals	538,800	538,800	173,200	188,300	365,600	350,500
Net income			15,100			15,100
Totals			188,300	188,300	365,600	365,600

2. Closing entries.

Dec. 31	Repair Services Revenue............	180,800	
	Interest Revenue............	7,500	
	Income Summary............		188,300
	To close revenue accounts.		

[continued on next page]

[continued from previous page]

Dec. 31	Income Summary..........................	173,200	
	Depreciation Expense—Equipment...........		28,500
	Wages Expense..........................		85,000
	Rent Expense...........................		48,000
	Insurance Expense.......................		6,000
	Interest Expense........................		5,700
	To close expense accounts.		
Dec. 31	Income Summary..........................	15,100	
	C. Trout, Capital.......................		15,100
	To close the Income Summary account.		
Dec. 31	C. Trout, Capital.........................	30,000	
	C. Trout, Withdrawals		30,000
	To close the withdrawals account.		

3. Set up the Income Summary and the capital ledger accounts and post the closing entries.

	Income Summary				Account No. 901
Date	**Explanation**	**PR**	**Debit**	**Credit**	**Balance**
2009					
Jan. 1	Beginning balance				0
Dec. 31	Close revenue accounts...........			188,300	188,300
31	Close expense accounts		173,200		15,100
31	Close income summary		15,100		0

	C. Trout, Capital				Account No. 301
Date	**Explanation**	**PR**	**Debit**	**Credit**	**Balance**
2009					
Jan. 1	Beginning balance				178,500
Dec. 31	Close Income Summary			15,100	193,600
31	Close C. Trout, Withdrawals		30,000		163,600

4. The final capital balance of $163,600 (from part 3) will be reported on the December 31, 2009, balance sheet. The final capital balance reflects the increase due to the net income earned during the year and the decrease for the owner's withdrawals during the year.

5.

MIDTOWN REPAIR COMPANY		
Income Statement		
For Year Ended December 31, 2009		
Revenues		
Repair services revenue	$180,800	
Interest revenue	7,500	
Total revenues		$188,300
Expenses		
Depreciation expense—Equipment	28,500	
Wages expense	85,000	
Rent expense	48,000	
Insurance expense	6,000	
Interest expense	5,700	
Total expenses		173,200
Net income		$ 15,100

MIDTOWN REPAIR COMPANY
Statement of Owner's Equity
For Year Ended December 31, 2009

C. Trout, Capital, December 31, 2008		$178,500
Add: Investment by owner	$ 0	
Net income	15,100	15,100
		193,600
Less: Withdrawals by owner		30,000
C. Trout, Capital, December 31, 2009		$163,600

MIDTOWN REPAIR COMPANY
Balance Sheet
December 31, 2009

Assets

Current assets		
Cash		$ 95,600
Notes receivable		50,000
Prepaid insurance		16,000
Prepaid rent		4,000
Total current assets		165,600
Plant assets		
Equipment	$170,000	
Less: Accumulated depreciation—Equipment	(57,000)	
Total plant assets		113,000
Total assets		$278,600

Liabilities

Current liabilities		
Accounts payable		$ 52,000
Long-term liabilities		
Long-term notes payable		63,000
Total liabilities		115,000

Equity

C. Trout, Capital		163,600
Total liabilities and equity		$278,600

APPENDIX

Reversing Entries

4A

Reversing entries are optional. They are recorded in response to accrued assets and accrued liabilities that were created by adjusting entries at the end of a reporting period. The purpose of reversing entries is to simplify a company's recordkeeping. Exhibit 4A.1 shows an example of FastForward's reversing entries. The top of the exhibit shows the adjusting entry FastForward recorded on December 31 for its employee's earned but unpaid salary. The entry recorded three days' salary of $210, which increased December's total salary expense to $1,610. The entry also recognized a liability of $210. The expense is reported on December's income statement. The expense account is then closed. The ledger on January 1,

Point: As a general rule, adjusting entries that create new asset or liability accounts are likely candidates for reversing.

EXHIBIT 4A.1

Reversing Entries for an
Accrued Expense

Accrue salaries expense on December 31, 2009

Salaries Expense 210
    Salaries Payable 210

Salaries Expense

Date	Expl.	Debit	Credit	Balance
2009				
Dec. 12	(7)	700		700
26	(16)	700		1,400
31	(e)	210		1,610

Salaries Payable

Date	Expl.	Debit	Credit	Balance
2009				
Dec. 31	(e)		210	210

— OR —

*No reversing entry recorded on
January 1, 2010*

NO ENTRY

Salaries Expense

Date	Expl.	Debit	Credit	Balance
2010				

Salaries Payable

Date	Expl.	Debit	Credit	Balance
2009				
Dec. 31	(e)		210	210
2010				

*Reversing entry recorded on
January 1, 2010*

Salaries Payable 210
    Salaries Expense 210

Salaries Expense*

Date	Expl.	Debit	Credit	Balance
2010				
Jan. 1			210	(210)

Salaries Payable

Date	Expl.	Debit	Credit	Balance
2009				
Dec. 31	(e)		210	210
2010				
Jan. 1		210		0

Pay the accrued and current salaries on January 9, the first payday in 2010

Salaries Expense 490
Salaries Payable 210
    Cash 700

Salaries Expense

Date	Expl.	Debit	Credit	Balance
2010				
Jan. 9		490		490

Salaries Payable

Date	Expl.	Debit	Credit	Balance
2009				
Dec. 31	(e)		210	210
2010				
Jan. 9		210		0

Salaries Expense 700
    Cash 700

Salaries Expense*

Date	Expl.	Debit	Credit	Balance
2010				
Jan. 1			210	(210)
Jan. 9		700		490

Salaries Payable

Date	Expl.	Debit	Credit	Balance
2009				
Dec. 31	(e)		210	210
2010				
Jan. 1		210		0

Under both approaches, the expense and liability accounts have
identical balances after the cash payment on January 9.

Salaries Expense $490
Salaries Payable .... $ 0

*Circled numbers in the *Balance* column indicate abnormal balances.

2010, shows a $210 liability and a zero balance in the Salaries Expense account. At this point, the choice is made between using or not using reversing entries.

Accounting *without* Reversing Entries

The path down the left side of Exhibit 4A.1 is described in the chapter. To summarize here, when the next payday occurs on January 9, we record payment with a compound entry that debits both the expense and liability accounts and credits Cash. Posting that entry creates a $490 balance in the expense account and reduces the liability account balance to zero because the debt has been settled. The disadvantage of this approach is the slightly more complex entry required on January 9. Paying the accrued liability means that this entry differs from the routine entries made on all other paydays. To construct the proper entry on January 9, we must recall the effect of the December 31 adjusting entry. Reversing entries overcome this disadvantage.

Accounting *with* Reversing Entries

The right side of Exhibit 4A.1 shows how a reversing entry on January 1 overcomes the disadvantage of the January 9 entry when not using reversing entries. A reversing entry is the exact opposite of an adjusting entry. For FastForward, the Salaries Payable liability account is debited for $210, meaning that this account now has a zero balance after the entry is posted. The Salaries Payable account temporarily understates the liability, but this is not a problem since financial statements are not prepared before the liability is settled on January 9. The credit to the Salaries Expense account is unusual because it gives the account an *abnormal credit balance*. We highlight an abnormal balance by circling it. Because of the reversing entry, the January 9 entry to record payment is straightforward. This entry debits the Salaries Expense account and credits Cash for the full $700 paid. It is the same as all other entries made to record 10 days' salary for the employee. Notice that after the payment entry is posted, the Salaries Expense account has a $490 balance that reflects seven days' salary of $70 per day (see the lower right side of Exhibit 4A.1). The zero balance in the Salaries Payable account is now correct. The lower section of Exhibit 4A.1 shows that the expense and liability accounts have exactly the same balances whether reversing entries are used or not. This means that both approaches yield identical results.

> **P4** Prepare reversing entries and explain their purpose.

Summary

C1 Explain why temporary accounts are closed each period. Temporary accounts are closed at the end of each accounting period for two main reasons. First, the closing process updates the capital account to include the effects of all transactions and events recorded for the period. Second, it prepares revenue, expense, and withdrawals accounts for the next reporting period by giving them zero balances.

C2 Identify steps in the accounting cycle. The accounting cycle consists of 10 steps: (1) analyze transactions, (2) journalize, (3) post, (4) prepare an unadjusted trial balance, (5) adjust accounts, (6) prepare an adjusted trial balance, (7) prepare statements, (8) close, (9) prepare a post-closing trial balance, and (10) prepare (optional) reversing entries.

C3 Explain and prepare a classified balance sheet. Classified balance sheets report assets and liabilities in two categories: current and noncurrent. Noncurrent assets often include long-term investments, plant assets, and intangible assets. Owner's equity for proprietorships (and partnerships) report the capital account balance. A corporation separates equity into common stock and retained earnings.

A1 Compute the current ratio and describe what it reveals about a company's financial condition. A company's current ratio is defined as current assets divided by current liabilities. We use it to evaluate a company's ability to pay its current liabilities out of current assets.

P1 Prepare a work sheet and explain its usefulness. A work sheet can be a useful tool in preparing and analyzing financial statements. It is helpful at the end of a period in preparing adjusting entries, an adjusted trial balance, and financial statements. A work sheet usually contains five pairs of columns: Unadjusted Trial Balance, Adjustments, Adjusted Trial Balance, Income Statement, and Balance Sheet & Statement of Owner's Equity.

P2 Describe and prepare closing entries. Closing entries involve four steps: (1) close credit balances in revenue (and gain) accounts to Income Summary, (2) close debit balances in expense (and loss) accounts to Income Summary, (3) close Income Summary to the capital account, and (4) close withdrawals account to owner's capital.

P3 Explain and prepare a post-closing trial balance. A post-closing trial balance is a list of permanent accounts and their balances after all closing entries have been journalized and posted. Its purpose is to verify that (1) total debits equal total credits for permanent accounts and (2) all temporary accounts have zero balances.

P4^{A} Prepare reversing entries and explain their purpose. Reversing entries are an optional step. They are applied to accrued expenses and revenues. The purpose of reversing entries is to simplify subsequent journal entries. Financial statements are unaffected by the choice to use or not use reversing entries.

Guidance Answers to **Decision Maker** and **Decision Ethics**

Entrepreneur   Yes, you are concerned about the absence of a depreciation adjustment. Equipment does depreciate, and financial statements must recognize this occurrence. Its absence suggests an error or a misrepresentation (there is also the possibility that equipment is fully depreciated).

Analyst   A current ratio of 1.2 suggests that current assets are sufficient to cover current liabilities, but it implies a minimal buffer in case of errors in measuring current assets or current liabilities. Removing the past due receivable reduces the current ratio to 0.7. Your assessment is that the company will have some difficulty meeting its loan payments.

Guidance Answers to **Quick Checks**

1. Amounts in the Unadjusted Trial Balance columns are taken from current account balances in the ledger. The balances for new accounts expected to arise from adjusted entries can be left blank or set at zero.

2. A work sheet offers the advantage of listing on one page all necessary information to make adjusting entries.

3. A work sheet can help in (a) accounting efficiency and avoiding errors, (b) linking transactions and events to their effects in financial statements, (c) showing adjustments for audit purposes, (d) preparing interim financial statements, and (e) showing effects from proposed, or what-if, transactions.

4. The major steps in preparing closing entries are to close (1) credit balances in revenue accounts to Income Summary, (2) debit balances in expense accounts to Income Summary, (3) Income Summary to owner's capital, and (4) any withdrawals account to owner's capital.

5. Revenue (and gain) and expense (and loss) accounts are called *temporary* because they are opened and closed each period. The Income Summary and owner's withdrawals accounts are also temporary.

6. Permanent accounts make up the post-closing trial balance, which consist of asset, liability, and equity accounts.

7. Current assets: (b), (c), (d). Plant assets: (a), (e). Item (f) is an intangible asset.

8. Investment in common stock, investment in bonds, and land held for future expansion.

9. For a service company, the operating cycle is the usual time between (1) paying employees who do the services and (2) receiving cash from customers for services provided.

Key Terms   mhhe.com/wildFAP19e

Key Terms are available at the book's Website for learning and testing in an online Flashcard Format.

Accounting cycle (p. 144) | Income Summary (p. 141) | Pro forma financial statements (p. 140)
Classified balance sheet (p. 145) | Intangible assets (p. 147) | Reversing entries (p. 151)
Closing entries (p. 141) | Long-term investments (p. 147) | Temporary accounts (p. 140)
Closing process (p. 140) | Long-term liabilities (p. 147) | Unclassified balance sheet (p. 145)
Current assets (p. 146) | Operating cycle (p. 145) | Working papers (p. 136)
Current liabilities (p. 147) | Permanent accounts (p. 140) | Work sheet (p. 136)
Current ratio (p. 147) | Post-closing trial balance (p. 144)

Multiple Choice Quiz   Answers on p. 175   mhhe.com/wildFAP19e

Additional Quiz Questions are available at the book's Website.

1. G. Venda, owner of Venda Services, withdrew $25,000 from the business during the current year. The entry to close the withdrawals account at the end of the year is:

a. G. Venda, Withdrawals 25,000
   G. Venda, Capital 25,000
b. Income Summary 25,000
   G. Venda, Capital 25,000
c. G. Venda, Withdrawals 25,000
   Cash 25,000
d. G. Venda, Capital 25,000
   Salary Expense 25,000
e. G. Venda, Capital 25,000
   G. Venda, Withdrawals 25,000

2. The following information is available for the R. Kandamil Company before closing the accounts. After all of the closing entries are made, what will be the balance in the R. Kandamil, Capital account?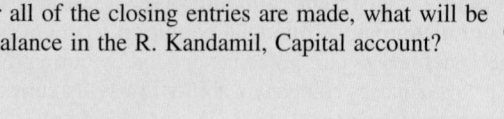

Total revenues $300,000
Total expenses 195,000
R. Kandamil, Capital 100,000
R. Kandamil, Withdrawals 45,000

a. $360,000   d. $150,000
b. $250,000   e. $60,000
c. $160,000

3. Which of the following errors would cause the balance sheet and statement of owner's equity columns of a work sheet to be out of balance?
    a. Entering a revenue amount in the balance sheet and statement of owner's equity debit column.
    b. Entering a liability amount in the balance sheet and statement of owner's equity credit column.
    c. Entering an expense account in the balance sheet and statement of owner's equity debit column.
    d. Entering an asset account in the income statement debit column.
    e. Entering a liability amount in the income statement credit column.

4. The temporary account used only in the closing process to hold the amounts of revenues and expenses before the net difference is added or subtracted from the owner's capital account is called the
    a. Closing account.
    b. Nominal account.
    c. Income Summary account.
    d. Balance Column account.
    e. Contra account.

5. Based on the following information from Repicor Company's balance sheet, what is Repicor Company's current ratio?

Current assets	$ 75,000
Investments	30,000
Plant assets	300,000
Current liabilities	50,000
Long-term liabilities	60,000
D. Repicor, Capital	295,000

a. 2.10   d. 0.95
b. 1.50   e. 0.67
c. 1.00

Superscript letter ᴬ denotes assignments based on Appendix 4A.

Discussion Questions

1. What accounts are affected by closing entries? What accounts are not affected?
2. What two purposes are accomplished by recording closing entries?
3. What are the steps in recording closing entries?
4. What is the purpose of the Income Summary account?
5. Explain whether an error has occurred if a post-closing trial balance includes a Depreciation Expense account.
6. What tasks are aided by a work sheet?
7. Why are the debit and credit entries in the Adjustments columns of the work sheet identified with letters?
8. What is a company's operating cycle?
9. What classes of assets and liabilities are shown on a typical classified balance sheet?
10. How is unearned revenue classified on the balance sheet?
11. What are the characteristics of plant assets?

12.ᴬHow do reversing entries simplify recordkeeping?
13.ᴬIf a company recorded accrued salaries expense of $500 at the end of its fiscal year, what reversing entry could be made? When would it be made?
14. Refer to the balance sheet for **Best Buy** in Appendix A. What five noncurrent asset categories are used on its classified balance sheet?
15. Refer to **Circuit City**'s balance sheet in Appendix A. Identify the accounts listed as current liabilities.
16. Refer to **RadioShack**'s balance sheet in Appendix A. Identify the accounts listed as current assets.
17. Refer to **Apple**'s financial statements in Appendix A. What journal entry was likely recorded as of September 30, 2006, to close its Income Summary account?

Denotes Discussion Questions that involve decision making.

McGraw-Hill's HOMEWORK MANAGER® ▪ Available with McGraw-Hill's Homework Manager

Irvine Company began the current period with a $35,000 credit balance in the M. Irvine, Capital account. At the end of the period, the company's adjusted account balances include the following temporary accounts with normal balances.

Service fees earned	$42,000	Interest revenue	$8,000
Salaries expense	31,000	M. Irvine, Withdrawals	9,200
Depreciation expense	11,000	Utilities expense	5,000

QUICK STUDY

QS 4-1
Determining effects of closing entries
C1 P2

After closing the revenue and expense accounts, what will be the balance of the Income Summary account? After all closing entries are journalized and posted, what will be the balance of the M. Irvine, Capital account?

QS 4-2

Identifying the accounting cycle

C2

List the following steps of the accounting cycle in their proper order.

a. Preparing the financial statements.

b. Preparing the unadjusted trial balance.

c. Journalizing transactions and events.

d. Preparing the post-closing trial balance.

e. Posting the journal entries.

f. Journalizing and posting adjusting entries.

g. Preparing the adjusted trial balance.

h. Journalizing and posting closing entries.

i. Analyzing transactions and events.

QS 4-3

Classifying balance sheet items

C3

The following are common categories on a classified balance sheet.

A. Current assets   **D.** Intangible assets

B. Long-term investments   **E.** Current liabilities

C. Plant assets   **F.** Long-term liabilities

For each of the following items, select the letter that identifies the balance sheet category where the item typically would appear.

_____ **1.** Accounts payable

_____ **2.** Store equipment

_____ **3.** Wages payable

_____ **4.** Cash

_____ **5.** Land not currently used in operations

_____ **6.** Notes payable (due in three years)

_____ **7.** Accounts receivable

_____ **8.** Trademarks

QS 4-4

Identifying current accounts and computing the current ratio

C3   A1

Compute Palmolive Company's current ratio using the following information.

Accounts receivable	$18,000	Long-term notes payable	$21,000
Accounts payable	11,000	Office supplies	2,860
Buildings	45,000	Prepaid insurance	3,500
Cash	7,000	Unearned services revenue	3,000

QS 4-5

Interpreting a work sheet

P1

The following selected information is taken from the work sheet for Fischer Company as of December 31, 2009. Using this information, determine the amount for J. Fischer, Capital, that should be reported on its December 31, 2009, balance sheet.

	Income Statement		Balance Sheet and Statement of Owner's Equity	
	Dr.	Cr.	Dr.	Cr.
J. Fischer, Capital				36,000
J. Fischer, Withdrawals			18,000	
Totals	61,000	90,000		

QS 4-6

Applying a work sheet

P1

In preparing a work sheet, indicate the financial statement Debit column to which a normal balance in the following accounts should be extended. Use I for the Income Statement Debit column and B for the Balance Sheet and Statement of Owner's Equity Debit column.

_____ **a.** Depreciation expense—Equipment

_____ **b.** Accounts receivable

_____ **c.** Insurance expense

_____ **d.** Equipment

_____ **e.** Owner, Withdrawals

_____ **f.** Prepaid rent

List the following steps in preparing a work sheet in their proper order by writing numbers 1–5 in the blank spaces provided.

a. _____ Prepare an unadjusted trial balance on the work sheet.

b. _____ Prepare an adjusted trial balance on the work sheet.

c. _____ Enter adjustments data on the work sheet.

d. _____ Total the statement columns, compute net income (loss), and complete work sheet.

e. _____ Extend adjusted balances to appropriate financial statement columns.

QS 4-7
Ordering work sheet steps
P1

The ledger of Edgardo Company includes the following unadjusted normal balances: Prepaid Rent $4,000, Services Revenue $65,000, and Wages Expense $30,000. Adjusting entries are required for (a) prepaid rent expense expired, $800; (b) accrued services revenue $950; and (c) accrued wages expense $750. Enter these unadjusted balances and the necessary adjustments on a work sheet and complete the work sheet for these accounts. *Note:* Also include the following accounts: Accounts Receivable, Wages Payable, and Rent Expense.

QS 4-8
Preparing a partial work sheet
P1

The ledger of Simms Company includes the following accounts with normal balances: P. Simms, Capital $18,000; P. Simms, Withdrawals $1,600; Services Revenue $26,000; Wages Expense $16,800; and Rent Expense $3,200. Prepare the necessary closing entries from the available information at December 31.

QS 4-9
Prepare closing entries from the ledger   P2

Identify the accounts listed in QS 4-9 that would be included in a post-closing trial balance.

QS 4-10
Identify post-closing accounts   P3

On December 31, 2008, Yates Co. prepared an adjusting entry for $24,000 of earned but unrecorded management fees. On January 16, 2009, Yates received $37,500 cash in management fees, which included the accrued fees earned in 2008. Assuming the company uses reversing entries, prepare the January 1, 2009, reversing entry and the January 16, 2009, cash receipt entry.

QS 4-11^A
Reversing entries
P4

McGraw-Hill's
HOMEWORK
MANAGER®   Available with McGraw-Hill's Homework Manager

Use the March 31 fiscal year-end information from the following ledger accounts (assume that all accounts have normal balances) to prepare closing journal entries and then post those entries to the appropriate ledger accounts.

EXERCISES

Exercise 4-1
Preparing and posting closing entries
P2

General Ledger				

R. Cruz, Capital   Acct. No. 301

Date	PR	Debit	Credit	Balance
Mar. 31	G2			65,000

R. Cruz, Withdrawals   Acct. No. 302

Date	PR	Debit	Credit	Balance
Mar. 31	G2			46,770

Services Revenue   Acct. No. 401

Date	PR	Debit	Credit	Balance
Mar. 31	G2			114,530

Depreciation Expense   Acct. No. 603

Date	PR	Debit	Credit	Balance
Mar. 31	G2			17,000

Salaries Expense   Acct. No. 622

Date	PR	Debit	Credit	Balance
Mar. 31	G2			32,500

Insurance Expense   Acct. No. 637

Date	PR	Debit	Credit	Balance
Mar. 31	G2			4,420

Rent Expense   Acct. No. 640

Date	PR	Debit	Credit	Balance
Mar. 31	G2			9,440

Income Summary   Acct. No. 901

Date	PR	Debit	Credit	Balance

Check   R. Cruz, Capital (ending balance), $69,400

Exercise 4-2

Preparing closing entries and a post-closing trial balance

P2   P3

The adjusted trial balance for Santara Marketing Co. follows. Complete the four right-most columns of the table by first entering information for the four closing entries (keyed *1* through *4*) and second by completing the post-closing trial balance.

No.	Account Title	Adjusted Trial Balance Dr.	Adjusted Trial Balance Cr.	Closing Entry Information Dr.	Closing Entry Information Cr.	Post-Closing Trial Balance Dr.	Post-Closing Trial Balance Cr.
101	Cash	$ 11,900					
106	Accounts receivable	24,000					
153	Equipment	41,000					
154	Accumulated depreciation—Equipment		$ 16,500				
193	Franchise	30,000					
201	Accounts payable		14,000				
209	Salaries payable		3,200				
233	Unearned fees		2,600				
301	T. Santara, Capital		66,701				
302	T. Santara, Withdrawals	14,400					
401	Marketing fees earned		83,000				
611	Depreciation expense—Equipment	11,000					
622	Salaries expense	33,034					
640	Rent expense	12,616					
677	Miscellaneous expenses	8,051					
901	Income summary						
	Totals	$186,001	$186,001				

Exercise 4-3

Preparing closing entries and a post-closing trial balance

C1   P2   P3

The following adjusted trial balance contains the accounts and balances of Ferrara Company as of December 31, 2009, the end of its fiscal year. (1) Prepare the December 31, 2009, closing entries for Ferrara Company. (2) Prepare the December 31, 2009, post-closing trial balance for Ferrara Company.

No.	Account Title	Debit	Credit
101	Cash	$18,000	
126	Supplies	13,900	
128	Prepaid insurance	2,000	
167	Equipment	23,000	
168	Accumulated depreciation—Equipment		$ 6,500
301	N. Ferrara, Capital		48,168
302	N. Ferrara, Withdrawals	6,000	
404	Services revenue		37,200
612	Depreciation expense—Equipment	2,000	
622	Salaries expense	21,687	
637	Insurance expense	1,562	
640	Rent expense	2,492	
652	Supplies expense	1,227	
	Totals	$91,868	$91,868

Check   (2) N. Ferrara, Capital (ending), $50,400; Total debits, $56,900

Use the following adjusted trial balance of Resource Trucking Company to prepare the (1) income statement, and (2) statement of owner's equity, for the year ended December 31, 2009. The J. Reso, Capital account balance is $161,901 at December 31, 2008.

Exercise 4-4
Preparing the financial statements
C2

Account Title	Debit	Credit
Cash	$ 5,800	
Accounts receivable	17,500	
Office supplies	3,000	
Trucks	156,000	
Accumulated depreciation—Trucks		$ 32,136
Land	85,000	
Accounts payable		9,800
Interest payable		4,000
Long-term notes payable		53,000
J. Reso, Capital		161,901
J. Reso, Withdrawals	20,000	
Trucking fees earned		121,000
Depreciation expense—Trucks	20,727	
Salaries expense	56,749	
Office supplies expense	6,655	
Repairs expense—Trucks	10,406	
Totals	$381,837	$381,837

Use the information in the adjusted trial balance reported in Exercise 4-4 to prepare Resource Trucking Company's classified balance sheet as of December 31, 2009.

Exercise 4-5
Preparing a classified balance sheet   C3
Check   Total assets, $235,164; J. Reso, Capital, $168,364

Use the information in the adjusted trial balance reported in Exercise 4-4 to compute the current ratio as of the balance sheet date (round the ratio to one decimal). Interpret the current ratio for the Resource Trucking Company. (Assume that the industry average for the current ratio is 1.5.)

Exercise 4-6
Computing the current ratio
A1

Calculate the current ratio in each of the following separate cases (round the ratio to two decimals). Identify the company case with the strongest liquidity position. (These cases represent competing companies in the same industry.)

Exercise 4-7
Computing and analyzing the current ratio
A1

	Current Assets	Current Liabilities
Case 1	$ 76,000	$26,666
Case 2	101,080	64,351
Case 3	42,863	41,204
Case 4	82,308	69,156
Case 5	58,444	84,638

Use the following information from the Adjustments columns of a 10-column work sheet to prepare the necessary adjusting journal entries (a) through (e).

Exercise 4-8
Preparing adjusting entries from a work sheet
P1

		Adjustments	
No.	Account Title	Debit	Credit
109	Interest receivable	(d) $ 636	
124	Office supplies		(b) $1,729
128	Prepaid insurance		(a) 979

[continued on next page]

[continued from previous page]

No.	Account			
164	Accumulated depreciation—Office equipment			(c) 3,300
209	Salaries payable			(e) 716
409	Interest revenue			(d) 636
612	Depreciation expense—Office equipment	(c) 3,300		
620	Office salaries expense	(e) 716		
636	Insurance expense—Office equipment	(a) 470		
637	Insurance expense—Store equipment	(a) 509		
650	Office supplies expense	(b) 1,729		
	Totals	$7,360		$7,360

Exercise 4-9

Extending adjusted account balances on a work sheet

P1

These 16 accounts are from the Adjusted Trial Balance columns of a company's 10-column work sheet. In the blank space beside each account, write the letter of the appropriate financial statement column (A, B, C, or D) to which a normal account balance is extended.

A. Debit column for the Income Statement columns.

B. Credit column for the Income Statement columns.

C. Debit column for the Balance Sheet and Statement of Owner's Equity columns.

D. Credit column for the Balance Sheet and Statement of Owner's Equity columns.

_____ **1.** Accounts Receivable   _____ **9.** Interest Revenue

_____ **2.** Accumulated Depreciation   _____ **10.** Machinery

_____ **3.** Office Supplies   _____ **11.** Owner, Withdrawals

_____ **4.** Insurance Expense   _____ **12.** Depreciation Expense

_____ **5.** Interest Receivable   _____ **13.** Accounts Payable

_____ **6.** Cash   _____ **14.** Service Fees Revenue

_____ **7.** Rent Expense   _____ **15.** Owner, Capital

_____ **8.** Wages Payable   _____ **16.** Interest Expense

Exercise 4-10

Extending accounts in a work sheet

P1

The Adjusted Trial Balance columns of a 10-column work sheet for Linn Company follow. Complete the work sheet by extending the account balances into the appropriate financial statement columns and by entering the amount of net income for the reporting period.

No.	Account Title	Debit	Credit
101	Cash	$ 8,200	
106	Accounts receivable	35,834	
153	Trucks	41,500	
154	Accumulated depreciation—Trucks		$ 16,683
183	Land	30,000	
201	Accounts payable		19,106
209	Salaries payable		4,370
233	Unearned fees		3,770
301	D. Linn, Capital		69,012
302	D. Linn, Withdrawals	15,534	
401	Plumbing fees earned		84,000
611	Depreciation expense—Trucks	5,561	
622	Salaries expense	39,312	
640	Rent expense	12,768	
677	Miscellaneous expenses	8,232	
	Totals	$196,941	$196,941

Check Net income, $18,127

These partially completed Income Statement columns from a 10-column work sheet are for Johnson's Bike Rental Company. (1) Use the information to determine the amount that should be entered on the net income line of the work sheet. (2) Prepare the company's closing entries. The owner, C. Johnson, did not make any withdrawals this period.

Exercise 4-11
Completing the income statement columns and preparing closing entries
P1   P2

Account Title	Debit	Credit
Rent earned		90,000
Salaries expense	39,960	
Insurance expense	5,670	
Office supplies expense	13,230	
Bike repair expense	2,790	
Depreciation expense—Bikes	17,190	
Totals		
Net income		
Totals		

Check   Net income, $11,160

The following unadjusted trial balance contains the accounts and balances of Santaga Delivery Company as of December 31, 2009, its first year of operations.

(1) Use the following information about the company's adjustments to complete a 10-column work sheet for Dylan.

a. Unrecorded depreciation on the trucks at the end of the year is $16,000.

b. The total amount of accrued interest expense at year-end is $8,000.

c. The cost of unused office supplies still available at the year-end is $500.

(2) Prepare the year-end closing entries for this company, and determine the capital amount to be reported on its year-end balance sheet.

Exercise 4-12
Preparing a work sheet and recording closing entries
P1   P2

Microsoft Excel - Book1
File Edit View Insert Format Tools Data Accounting Window Help
100%   Arial   10   B I U

Account Title	Debit	Credit
Cash	$ 15,000	
Accounts receivable	33,000	
Office supplies	4,000	
Trucks	340,000	
Accumulated depreciation—Trucks		$112,000
Land	150,000	
Accounts payable		23,550
Interest payable		6,000
Long-term notes payable		104,000
D. Santaga, Capital		272,770
D. Santaga, Withdrawals	38,000	
Delivery fees earned		274,350
Depreciation expense—Truck	48,000	
Salaries expense	128,670	
Office supplies expense	14,000	
Interest expense	6,000	
Repairs expense—trucks	16,000	
Totals	$792,670	$792,670

Sheet1 / Sheet2 / Sheet3 /

Check   Adj. trial balance totals, $810,670; Net income, $40,180

The following two events occurred for Tankwell Co. on October 31, 2009, the end of its fiscal year.

a. Tankwell rents a building from its owner for $3,300 per month. By a prearrangement, the company delayed paying October's rent until November 5. On this date, the company paid the rent for both October and November.

Exercise 4-13[A]
Preparing reversing entries
P4

b. Tankwell rents space in a building it owns to a tenant for $1,050 per month. By prearrangement, the tenant delayed paying the October rent until November 8. On this date, the tenant paid the rent for both October and November.

Required

1. Prepare adjusting entries that the company must record for these events as of October 31.

2. Assuming Tankwell does *not* use reversing entries, prepare journal entries to record Tankwell's payment of rent on November 5 and the collection of rent on November 8 from Tankwell's tenant.

3. Assuming that the company uses reversing entries, prepare reversing entries on November 1 and the journal entries to record Tankwell's payment of rent on November 5 and the collection of rent on November 8 from Tankwell's tenant.

Exercise 4-14^A
Preparing reversing entries
P4

Scholl Company records prepaid assets and unearned revenues in balance sheet accounts. The following information was used to prepare adjusting entries for the company as of August 31, the end of the company's fiscal year.

a. The company has earned $4,500 in unrecorded service fees.

b. The expired portion of prepaid insurance is $3,750.

c. The company has earned $2,100 of its Unearned Service Fees account balance.

d. Depreciation expense for office equipment is $2,600.

e. Employees have earned but have not been paid salaries of $2,700.

Prepare any necessary reversing entries for the accounting adjustments *a* through *e* assuming that the company uses reversing entries in its accounting system.

Available with McGraw-Hill's Homework Manager

PROBLEM SET A

Problem 4-1A
Determining balance sheet classifications
C3

In the blank space beside each numbered balance sheet item, enter the letter of its balance sheet classification. If the item should not appear on the balance sheet, enter a Z in the blank.

A. Current assets
B. Long-term investments
C. Plant assets
D. Intangible assets
E. Current liabilities
F. Long-term liabilities
G. Equity

_____ **1.** Accumulated depreciation—Trucks
_____ **2.** Cash
_____ **3.** Buildings
_____ **4.** Store supplies
_____ **5.** Office equipment
_____ **6.** Land (used in operations)
_____ **7.** Repairs expense
_____ **8.** Office supplies
_____ **9.** Current portion of long-term note payable

_____ **10.** Unearned services revenue
_____ **11.** Long-term investment in stock
_____ **12.** Depreciation expense—Building
_____ **13.** Prepaid rent
_____ **14.** Interest receivable
_____ **15.** Taxes payable
_____ **16.** Automobiles
_____ **17.** Notes payable (due in 3 years)
_____ **18.** Accounts payable
_____ **19.** Prepaid insurance
_____ **20.** Owner, Capital

Problem 4-2A
Applying the accounting cycle
C1 C2 P2 P3

mhhe.com/wildFAP19e

On April 1, 2009, Jiro Nozomi created a new travel agency, Adventure Travel. The following transactions occurred during the company's first month.

April 1 Nozomi invested $32,000 cash and computer equipment worth $26,000 in the company.
2 The company rented furnished office space by paying $1,300 cash for the first month's (April) rent.
3 The company purchased $2,500 of office supplies for cash.
10 The company paid $2,502 cash for the premium on a 12-month insurance policy. Coverage begins on April 11.
14 The company paid $2,300 cash for two weeks' salaries earned by employees.
24 The company collected $16,000 cash on commissions from airlines on tickets obtained for customers.
28 The company paid $2,400 cash for two weeks' salaries earned by employees.
29 The company paid $750 cash for minor repairs to the company's computer.
30 The company paid $550 cash for this month's telephone bill.
30 Nozomi withdrew $1,200 cash from the company for personal use.

The company's chart of accounts follows:

No.	Account	No.	Account
101	Cash	405	Commissions Earned
106	Accounts Receivable	612	Depreciation Expense—Computer Equip.
124	Office Supplies	622	Salaries Expense
128	Prepaid Insurance	637	Insurance Expense
167	Computer Equipment	640	Rent Expense
168	Accumulated Depreciation—Computer Equip.	650	Office Supplies Expense
209	Salaries Payable	684	Repairs Expense
301	J. Nozomi, Capital	688	Telephone Expense
302	J. Nozomi, Withdrawals	901	Income Summary

Required

1. Use the balance column format to set up each ledger account listed in its chart of accounts.

2. Prepare journal entries to record the transactions for April and post them to the ledger accounts. The company records prepaid and unearned items in balance sheet accounts.

3. Prepare an unadjusted trial balance as of April 30.

4. Use the following information to journalize and post adjusting entries for the month:

   a. Two-thirds of one month's insurance coverage has expired.

   b. At the end of the month, $700 of office supplies are still available.

   c. This month's depreciation on the computer equipment is $500.

   d. Employees earned $720 of unpaid and unrecorded salaries as of month-end.

   e. The company earned $3,050 of commissions that are not yet billed at month-end.

5. Prepare the income statement and the statement of owner's equity for the month of April and the balance sheet at April 30, 2009.

6. Prepare journal entries to close the temporary accounts and post these entries to the ledger.

7. Prepare a post-closing trial balance.

Check (3) Unadj. trial balance totals, $74,000

(4a) Dr. Insurance Expense, $139

(5) Net income, $8,591; J. Nozomi, Capital (4/30/2009), $65,391; Total assets, $66,111

(7) P-C trial balance totals, $66,611

The adjusted trial balance of Charon Repairs on December 31, 2009, follows.

Problem 4-3A
Preparing trial balances, closing entries, and financial statements

C3 P2 P3

mhhe.com/wildFAP19e

	CHARON REPAIRS		
	Adjusted Trial Balance		
	December 31, 2009		
No.	**Account Title**	**Debit**	**Credit**
101	Cash	$ 16,100	
124	Office supplies	1,300	
128	Prepaid insurance	2,800	
167	Equipment	50,000	
168	Accumulated depreciation—Equipment		$ 5,000
201	Accounts payable		12,000
210	Wages payable		1,400
301	L. Charon, Capital		33,000
302	L. Charon, Withdrawals	16,000	
401	Repair fees earned		98,600
612	Depreciation expense—Equipment	5,000	
623	Wages expense	39,000	
637	Insurance expense	800	
640	Rent expense	13,000	
650	Office supplies expense	3,100	
690	Utilities expense	2,900	
	Totals	$150,000	$150,000

Required

1. Prepare an income statement and a statement of owner's equity for the year 2009, and a classified balance sheet at December 31, 2009. There are no owner investments in 2009.

2. Enter the adjusted trial balance in the first two columns of a six-column table. Use columns three and four for closing entry information and the last two columns for a post-closing trial balance. Insert an Income Summary account as the last item in the trial balance.

3. Enter closing entry information in the six-column table and prepare journal entries for it.

Analysis Component

4. Assume for this part only that

    a. None of the $800 insurance expense had expired during the year. Instead, assume it is a prepayment of the next period's insurance protection.

    b. There are no earned and unpaid wages at the end of the year. (*Hint:* Reverse the $1,400 wages payable accrual.)

    Describe the financial statement changes that would result from these two assumptions.

Problem 4-4A

Preparing closing entries, financial statements, and ratios

C3 A1 P2

The adjusted trial balance for Tamar Construction as of December 31, 2009, follows.

No.	Account Title	Debit	Credit
	TAMAR CONSTRUCTION **Adjusted Trial Balance** **December 31, 2009**		
101	Cash	$ 7,000	
104	Short-term investments	23,500	
126	Supplies	8,200	
128	Prepaid insurance	7,500	
167	Equipment	45,000	
168	Accumulated depreciation—Equipment		$ 22,500
173	Building	162,000	
174	Accumulated depreciation—Building		54,000
183	Land	66,770	
201	Accounts payable		17,000
203	Interest payable		2,900
208	Rent payable		3,500
210	Wages payable		2,100
213	Property taxes payable		900
233	Unearned professional fees		7,100
251	Long-term notes payable		66,000
301	E. Tamar, Capital		131,700
302	E. Tamar, Withdrawals	11,000	
401	Professional fees earned		102,000
406	Rent earned		15,000
407	Dividends earned		3,000
409	Interest earned		2,200
606	Depreciation expense—Building	11,880	
612	Depreciation expense—Equipment	6,750	
623	Wages expense	30,500	
633	Interest expense	4,700	
637	Insurance expense	8,900	
640	Rent expense	10,900	
652	Supplies expense	5,500	
682	Postage expense	2,500	
683	Property taxes expense	5,000	
684	Repairs expense	6,200	
688	Telephone expense	3,100	
690	Utilities expense	3,000	
	Totals	$429,900	$429,900

E. Tamar invested $7,000 cash in the business during year 2009 (the December 31, 2008, credit balance of the E. Tamar, Capital account was $124,700). Tamar Construction is required to make a $7,500 payment on its long-term notes payable during 2010.

Required

1. Prepare the income statement and the statement of owner's equity for the calendar year 2009 and the classified balance sheet at December 31, 2009.

2. Prepare the necessary closing entries at December 31, 2009.

3. Use the information in the financial statements to compute these ratios: (*a*) return on assets (total assets at December 31, 2008, was $200,000), (*b*) debt ratio, (*c*) profit margin ratio (use total revenues as the denominator), and (*d*) current ratio.

Check (1) Total assets (12/31/2009), $243,470; Net income, $23,270

The following unadjusted trial balance is for Archer Construction Co. as of the end of its 2009 fiscal year. The June 30, 2008, credit balance of the owner's capital account was $55,800, and the owner invested $27,000 cash in the company during the 2009 fiscal year.

Problem 4-5A
Preparing a work sheet, adjusting and closing entries, and financial statements

C3 P1 P2

File Edit View Insert Format Tools Data Window Help			
	ARCHER CONSTRUCTION CO. Unadjusted Trial Balance June 30, 2009		
No.	**Account Title**	**Debit**	**Credit**
101	Cash	$ 17,000	
126	Supplies	7,000	
128	Prepaid insurance	5,500	
167	Equipment	149,200	
168	Accumulated depreciation—Equipment		$ 25,500
201	Accounts payable		5,200
203	Interest payable		0
208	Rent payable		0
210	Wages payable		0
213	Property taxes payable		0
251	Long-term notes payable		20,000
301	G. Archer, Capital		82,800
302	G. Archer, Withdrawals	31,500	
401	Construction fees earned		141,000
612	Depreciation expense—Equipment	0	
623	Wages expense	40,000	
633	Interest expense	2,200	
637	Insurance expense	0	
640	Rent expense	11,000	
652	Supplies expense	0	
683	Property taxes expense	4,900	
684	Repairs expense	2,900	
690	Utilities expense	3,300	
	Totals	$ 274,500	$ 274,500

Required

1. Prepare a 10-column work sheet for fiscal year 2009, starting with the unadjusted trial balance and including adjustments based on these additional facts.

   a. The supplies available at the end of fiscal year 2009 had a cost of $2,520.

   b. The cost of expired insurance for the fiscal year is $3,465.

   c. Annual depreciation on equipment is $8,300.

   d. The June utilities expense of $560 is not included in the unadjusted trial balance because the bill arrived after the trial balance was prepared. The $560 amount owed needs to be recorded.

   e. The company's employees have earned $1,900 of accrued wages at fiscal year-end.

   f. The rent expense incurred and not yet paid or recorded at fiscal year-end is $500.

   g. Additional property taxes of $700 have been assessed for this fiscal year but have not been paid or recorded in the accounts.

h. The long-term note payable bears interest at 12% per year. The unadjusted Interest Expense account equals the amount paid for the first 11 months of the 2009 fiscal year. The $200 accrued interest for June has not yet been paid or recorded. (Note that the company is required to make a $4,500 payment toward the note payable during the 2010 fiscal year.)

2. Use the work sheet to enter the adjusting and closing entries; then journalize them.

Check (3) Total assets, $136,955; Current liabilities, $13,560; Net income, $56,595

3. Prepare the income statement and the statement of owner's equity for the year ended June 30 and the classified balance sheet at June 30, 2009.

Analysis Component

4. Analyze the following separate errors and describe how each would affect the 10-column work sheet. Explain whether the error is likely to be discovered in completing the work sheet and, if not, the effect of the error on the financial statements.

    a. Assume that the adjustment for supplies used consisted of a credit to Supplies for $2,520 and a debit for $2,520 to Supplies Expense.

    b. When the adjusted trial balance in the work sheet is completed, assume that the $17,000 Cash balance is incorrectly entered in the Credit column.

Problem 4-6A^A

Preparing adjusting, reversing, and next period entries

P4

The following six-column table for Hunter Golf Range includes the unadjusted trial balance as of December 31, 2009.

	HUNTER GOLF RANGE December 31, 2009					
	Unadjusted Trial Balance		Adjustments		Adjusted Trial Balance	
Account Title	Dr.	Cr.	Dr.	Cr.	Dr.	Cr.
Cash	$ 10,000					
Accounts receivable	0					
Supplies	4,230					
Equipment	102,000					
Accumulated depreciation— Equipment		$ 19,584				
Interest payable		0				
Salaries payable		0				
Unearned member fees		10,770				
Notes payable		57,000				
A. J. Hunter, Capital		28,893				
A. J. Hunter, Withdrawals	15,000					
Member fees earned		40,800				
Depreciation expense— Equipment	0					
Salaries expense	21,542					
Interest expense	4,275					
Supplies expense	0					
Totals	$157,047	$157,047				

Required

1. Complete the six-column table by entering adjustments that reflect the following information.

    a. As of December 31, 2009, employees had earned $689 of unpaid and unrecorded salaries. The next payday is January 4, at which time $1,226 of salaries will be paid.

    b. The cost of supplies still available at December 31, 2009, is $2,076.

    c. The notes payable requires an interest payment to be made every three months. The amount of unrecorded accrued interest at December 31, 2009, is $1,425. The next interest payment, at an amount of $1,710, is due on January 15, 2010.

    d. Analysis of the unearned member fees account shows $4,308 remaining unearned at December 31, 2009.

e. In addition to the member fees included in the revenue account balance, the company has earned another $6,936 in unrecorded fees that will be collected on January 31, 2010. The company is also expected to collect $8,000 on that same day for new fees earned in January 2010.

f. Depreciation expense for the year is $9,792.

2. Prepare journal entries for the adjustments entered in the six-column table for part 1.

3. Prepare journal entries to reverse the effects of the adjusting entries that involve accruals.

4. Prepare journal entries to record the cash payments and cash collections described for January.

Check (1) Adjusted trial balance totals, $175,889

In the blank space beside each numbered balance sheet item, enter the letter of its balance sheet classification. If the item should not appear on the balance sheet, enter a Z in the blank.

A. Current assets   **E.** Current liabilities
B. Long-term investments   **F.** Long-term liabilities
C. Plant assets   **G.** Equity
D. Intangible assets

_____ **1.** Rent receivable
_____ **2.** Salaries payable
_____ **3.** Income taxes payable
_____ **4.** Owner, Capital
_____ **5.** Office supplies
_____ **6.** Interest payable
_____ **7.** Rent revenue
_____ **8.** Notes receivable (due in 120 days)
_____ **9.** Land (used in operations)
_____ **10.** Depreciation expense—Trucks
_____ **11.** Commissions earned

_____ **12.** Interest receivable
_____ **13.** Long-term investment in stock
_____ **14.** Prepaid insurance
_____ **15.** Machinery
_____ **16.** Notes payable (due in 15 years)
_____ **17.** Copyrights
_____ **18.** Current portion of long-term note payable
_____ **19.** Accumulated depreciation—Trucks
_____ **20.** Office equipment

PROBLEM SET B

Problem 4-1B
Determining balance sheet classifications

C3

On July 1, 2009, Carl Park created a new self-storage business, Safe Storage Co. The following transactions occurred during the company's first month.

July 1 Park invested $34,000 cash and buildings worth $175,000 in the company.
      2 The company rented equipment by paying $1,500 cash for the first month's (July) rent.
      5 The company purchased $1,300 of office supplies for cash.
     10 The company paid $3,600 cash for the premium on a 12-month insurance policy. Coverage begins on July 11.
     14 The company paid an employee $1,280 cash for two weeks' salary earned.
     24 The company collected $11,500 cash for storage fees from customers.
     28 The company paid $1,320 cash for two weeks' salary earned by an employee.
     29 The company paid $250 cash for minor repairs to a leaking roof.
     30 The company paid $850 cash for this month's telephone bill.
     31 Park withdrew $2,400 cash from the company for personal use.

Problem 4-2B
Applying the accounting cycle

C1 C2 P2 P3

The company's chart of accounts follows:

101	Cash	401	Storage Fees Earned
106	Accounts Receivable	606	Depreciation Expense—Buildings
124	Office Supplies	622	Salaries Expense
128	Prepaid Insurance	637	Insurance Expense
173	Buildings	640	Rent Expense
174	Accumulated Depreciation—Buildings	650	Office Supplies Expense
209	Salaries Payable	684	Repairs Expense
301	C. Park, Capital	688	Telephone Expense
302	C. Park, Withdrawals	901	Income Summary

Required

1. Use the balance column format to set up each ledger account listed in its chart of accounts.

2. Prepare journal entries to record the transactions for July and post them to the ledger accounts. Record prepaid and unearned items in balance sheet accounts.

3. Prepare an unadjusted trial balance as of July 31.

4. Use the following information to journalize and post adjusting entries for the month:

   a. Two-thirds of one month's insurance coverage has expired.

   b. At the end of the month, $800 of office supplies are still available.

   c. This month's depreciation on the buildings is $1,750.

   d. An employee earned $570 of unpaid and unrecorded salary as of month-end.

   e. The company earned $2,350 of storage fees that are not yet billed at month-end.

5. Prepare the income statement and the statement of owner's equity for the month of July and the balance sheet at July 31, 2009.

6. Prepare journal entries to close the temporary accounts and post these entries to the ledger.

7. Prepare a post-closing trial balance.

Problem 4-3B

Preparing trial balances, closing entries, and financial statements

C3 P2 P3

Goldsmith Company's adjusted trial balance on December 31, 2009, follows.

No.	Account Title	Debit	Credit
	GOLDSMITH COMPANY **Adjusted Trial Balance** **December 31, 2009**		
101	Cash	$ 10,300	
125	Store supplies	1,400	
128	Prepaid insurance	2,200	
167	Equipment	52,000	
168	Accumulated depreciation—Equipment		$ 9,000
201	Accounts payable		17,000
210	Wages payable		1,300
301	N. Goldsmith, Capital		33,400
302	N. Goldsmith, Withdrawals	16,500	
401	Repair fees earned		91,500
612	Depreciation expense—Equipment	8,500	
623	Wages expense	41,500	
637	Insurance expense	1,000	
640	Rent expense	11,400	
651	Store supplies expense	4,400	
690	Utilities expense	3,000	
	Totals	$152,200	$152,200

Required

1. Prepare an income statement and a statement of owner's equity for the year 2009, and a classified balance sheet at December 31, 2009. There are no owner investments in 2009.

2. Enter the adjusted trial balance in the first two columns of a six-column table. Use the middle two columns for closing entry information and the last two columns for a post-closing trial balance. Insert an Income Summary account (No. 901) as the last item in the trial balance.

3. Enter closing entry information in the six-column table and prepare journal entries for it.

Analysis Component

4. Assume for this part only that

   a. None of the $1,000 insurance expense had expired during the year. Instead, assume it is a prepayment of the next period's insurance protection.

   b. There are no earned and unpaid wages at the end of the year. (*Hint:* Reverse the $1,300 wages payable accrual.)

Describe the financial statement changes that would result from these two assumptions.

The adjusted trial balance for Myra Co. as of December 31, 2009, follows.

Problem 4-4B
Preparing closing entries, financial statements, and ratios

C3 A1 P2

MYRA COMPANY
Adjusted Trial Balance
December 31, 2009

No.	Account Title	Debit	Credit
101	Cash	$ 7,500	
104	Short-term investments	23,500	
126	Supplies	8,100	
128	Prepaid insurance	8,600	
167	Equipment	40,000	
168	Accumulated depreciation—Equipment		$ 20,000
173	Building	177,000	
174	Accumulated depreciation—Building		59,000
183	Land	68,120	
201	Accounts payable		17,000
203	Interest payable		3,000
208	Rent payable		3,500
210	Wages payable		2,500
213	Property taxes payable		1,300
233	Unearned professional fees		7,900
251	Long-term notes payable		64,500
301	S. Myra, Capital		132,600
302	S. Myra, Withdrawals	10,300	
401	Professional fees earned		104,000
406	Rent earned		18,000
407	Dividends earned		2,500
409	Interest earned		2,300
606	Depreciation expense—Building	12,980	
612	Depreciation expense—Equipment	6,000	
623	Wages expense	27,500	
633	Interest expense	3,800	
637	Insurance expense	7,700	
640	Rent expense	11,300	
652	Supplies expense	6,100	
682	Postage expense	2,800	
683	Property taxes expense	3,400	
684	Repairs expense	6,900	
688	Telephone expense	3,200	
690	Utilities expense	3,300	
	Totals	$438,100	$438,100

S. Myra invested $7,500 cash in the business during year 2009 (the December 31, 2008, credit balance of the S. Myra, Capital account was $125,100). Myra Company is required to make a $6,000 payment on its long-term notes payable during 2010.

Required

1. Prepare the income statement and the statement of owner's equity for the calendar year 2009 and the classified balance sheet at December 31, 2009.
2. Prepare the necessary closing entries at December 31, 2009.
3. Use the information in the financial statements to calculate these ratios: (a) return on assets (total assets at December 31, 2008, were $200,000), (b) debt ratio, (c) profit margin ratio (use total revenues as the denominator), and (d) current ratio.

Check (1) Total assets (12/31/2009), $253,820; Net income, $31,820

Problem 4-5B

Preparing a work sheet, adjusting and closing entries, and financial statements

C3 P1 P2

The following unadjusted trial balance is for Brawn Demolition Company as of the end of its April 30, 2009, fiscal year. The April 30, 2008, credit balance of the owner's capital account was $51,610, and the owner invested $30,000 cash in the company during the 2009 fiscal year.

File Edit View Insert Format Tools Data Window Help		
BRAWN DEMOLITION COMPANY		
Unadjusted Trial Balance		
April 30, 2009		

No.	Account Title	Debit	Credit
101	Cash	$ 17,000	
126	Supplies	9,500	
128	Prepaid insurance	6,500	
167	Equipment	140,460	
168	Accumulated depreciation—Equipment		$ 22,000
201	Accounts payable		6,000
203	Interest payable		0
208	Rent payable		0
210	Wages payable		0
213	Property taxes payable		0
251	Long-term notes payable		25,000
301	J. Brawn, Capital		81,610
302	J. Brawn, Withdrawals	25,500	
401	Demolition fees earned		140,000
612	Depreciation expense—Equipment	0	
623	Wages expense	48,000	
633	Interest expense	2,750	
637	Insurance expense	0	
640	Rent expense	15,400	
652	Supplies expense	0	
683	Property taxes expense	4,400	
684	Repairs expense	2,100	
690	Utilities expense	3,000	
	Totals	$ 274,610	$ 274,610

Sheet1 / Sheet2 / Sheet3 /

Required

1. Prepare a 10-column work sheet for fiscal year 2009, starting with the unadjusted trial balance and including adjustments based on these additional facts.

   a. The supplies available at the end of fiscal year 2009 had a cost of $3,420.

   b. The cost of expired insurance for the fiscal year is $4,095.

   c. Annual depreciation on equipment is $11,000.

   d. The April utilities expense of $580 is not included in the unadjusted trial balance because the bill arrived after the trial balance was prepared. The $580 amount owed needs to be recorded.

   e. The company's employees have earned $1,500 of accrued wages at fiscal year-end.

   f. The rent expense incurred and not yet paid or recorded at fiscal year-end is $1,400.

   g. Additional property taxes of $500 have been assessed for this fiscal year but have not been paid or recorded in the accounts.

   h. The long-term note payable bears interest at 12% per year. The unadjusted Interest Expense account equals the amount paid for the first 11 months of the 2009 fiscal year. The $250 accrued interest for April has not yet been paid or recorded. (Note that the company is required to make a $5,000 payment toward the note payable during the 2010 fiscal year.)

2. Enter the adjusting and closing entry information in the work sheet; then journalize it.

Check (3) Total assets, $130,285; current liabilities, $15,230; Net income, $38,945

3. Prepare the income statement and the statement of owner's equity for the year ended April 30 and the classified balance sheet at April 30, 2009.

Analysis Component

4. Analyze the following separate errors and describe how each would affect the 10-column work sheet. Explain whether the error is likely to be discovered in completing the work sheet and, if not, the effect of the error on the financial statements.

a. Assume the adjustment for expiration of the insurance coverage consisted of a credit to Prepaid Insurance for $2,405 and a debit for $2,405 to Insurance Expense.

b. When the adjusted trial balance in the work sheet is completed, assume that the $2,100 Repairs Expense account balance is extended to the Debit column of the balance sheet columns.

The following six-column table for Oberst Co. includes the unadjusted trial balance as of December 31, 2009.

Problem 4-6B^A
Preparing adjusting, reversing, and next period entries

P4

Account Title	Unadjusted Trial Balance Dr.	Unadjusted Trial Balance Cr.	Adjustments Dr.	Adjustments Cr.	Adjusted Trial Balance Dr.	Adjusted Trial Balance Cr.
OBERST COMPANY December 31, 2009						
Cash	$ 18,500					
Accounts receivable	0					
Supplies	7,825					
Machinery	188,700					
Accumulated depreciation— Machinery		$ 36,230				
Interest payable		0				
Salaries payable		0				
Unearned rental fees		19,924				
Notes payable		54,000				
B. Oberst, Capital		101,044				
B. Oberst, Withdrawals	27,750					
Rental fees earned		75,480				
Depreciation expense— Machinery	0					
Salaries expense	39,853					
Interest expense	4,050					
Supplies expense	0					
Totals	$286,678	$286,678				

Required

1. Complete the six-column table by entering adjustments that reflect the following information:

a. As of December 31, 2009, employees had earned $1,275 of unpaid and unrecorded wages. The next payday is January 4, at which time $2,269 in wages will be paid.

b. The cost of supplies still available at December 31, 2009, is $3,842.

c. The notes payable requires an interest payment to be made every three months. The amount of unrecorded accrued interest at December 31, 2009, is $1,350. The next interest payment, at an amount of $1,620, is due on January 15, 2010.

d. Analysis of the unearned rental fees shows that $7,969 remains unearned at December 31, 2009.

e. In addition to the machinery rental fees included in the revenue account balance, the company has earned another $12,831 in unrecorded fees that will be collected on January 31, 2010. The company is also expected to collect $8,000 on that same day for new fees earned in January 2010.

f. Depreciation expense for the year is $18,115.

Check (1) Adjusted trial balance totals, $320,249

2. Prepare journal entries for the adjustments entered in the six-column table for part 1.

3. Prepare journal entries to reverse the effects of the adjusting entries that involve accruals.

4. Prepare journal entries to record the cash payments and cash collections described for January.

SERIAL PROBLEM

Success Systems   P2   P3

(This serial problem began in Chapter 1 and continues through most of the book. If previous chapter segments were not completed, the serial problem can begin at this point. It is helpful, but not necessary, to use the Working Papers that accompany the book.)

SP 4   The December 31, 2009, adjusted trial balance of Success Systems (reflecting its transactions from October through December of 2009) follows.

No.	Account Title	Debit	Credit
101	Cash	$ 58,160	
106	Accounts receivable	5,668	
126	Computer supplies	580	
128	Prepaid insurance	1,665	
131	Prepaid rent	825	
163	Office equipment	8,000	
164	Accumulated depreciation—Office equipment		$ 400
167	Computer equipment	20,000	
168	Accumulated depreciation—Computer equipment		1,250
201	Accounts payable		1,100
210	Wages payable		500
236	Unearned computer services revenue		1,500
301	A. Lopez, Capital		83,000
302	A. Lopez, Withdrawals	7,100	
403	Computer services revenue		31,284
612	Depreciation expense—Office equipment	400	
613	Depreciation expense—Computer equipment	1,250	
623	Wages expense	3,875	
637	Insurance expense	555	
640	Rent expense	2,475	
652	Computer supplies expense	3,065	
655	Advertising expense	2,965	
676	Mileage expense	896	
677	Miscellaneous expenses	250	
684	Repairs expense—Computer	1,305	
901	Income summary		0
	Totals	$119,034	$119,034

Check   Post-closing trial balance totals, $94,898

Required

1. Record and post the necessary closing entries for Success Systems.

2. Prepare a post-closing trial balance as of December 31, 2009.

BEYOND THE NUMBERS

REPORTING IN ACTION

C1   P2 

BTN 4-1   Refer to Best Buy's financial statements in Appendix A to answer the following.

Required

1. For the fiscal year ended March 3, 2007, what amount is credited to Income Summary to summarize its revenues earned?

2. For the fiscal year ended March 3, 2007, what amount is debited to Income Summary to summarize its expenses incurred?

3. For the fiscal year ended March 3, 2007, what is the balance of its Income Summary account before it is closed?

4. In its statement of cash flows for the year ended March 3, 2007, what amount of cash is paid in dividends to common stockholders?

Fast Forward

5. Access Best Buy's annual report for fiscal years ending after March 3, 2007, at its Website (BestBuy.com) or the SEC's EDGAR database (www.sec.gov). How has the amount of net income closed to Income Summary changed in the fiscal years ending after March 3, 2007? How has the amount of cash paid as dividends changed in the fiscal years ending after March 3, 2007?

BTN 4-2   Key figures for the recent two years of Best Buy and RadioShack follow.

COMPARATIVE ANALYSIS

A1

Key Figures ($ thousands)	Best Buy		RadioShack	
	Current Year	Prior Year	Current Year	Prior Year
Current assets	$9,081	$7,985	$1,600	$1,627
Current liabilities	6,301	6,056	984	986

Required

1. Compute the current ratio for both years for both companies.

2. Which company has the better ability to pay short-term obligations according to the current ratio?

3. Analyze and comment on each company's current ratios for the past two years.

4. How do Best Buy's and RadioShack's current ratios compare to their industry average ratio of 1.6?

BTN 4-3   On January 20, 2009, Tamira Nelson, the accountant for Picton Enterprises, is feeling pressure to complete the annual financial statements. The company president has said he needs up-to-date financial statements to share with the bank on January 21 at a dinner meeting that has been called to discuss Picton's obtaining loan financing for a special building project. Tamira knows that she will not be able to gather all the needed information in the next 24 hours to prepare the entire set of adjusting entries that must be posted before the financial statements accurately portray the company's performance and financial position for the fiscal period ended December 31, 2008. Tamira ultimately decides to estimate several expense accruals at the last minute. When deciding on estimates for the expenses, she uses low estimates because she does not want to make the financial statements look worse than they are. Tamira finishes the financial statements before the deadline and gives them to the president without mentioning that several account balances are estimates that she provided.

ETHICS CHALLENGE

C2

Required

1. Identify several courses of action that Tamira could have taken instead of the one she took.

2. If you were in Tamira's situation, what would you have done? Briefly justify your response.

BTN 4-4   Assume that one of your classmates states that a company's books should be ongoing and therefore not closed until that business is terminated. Write a half-page memo to this classmate explaining the concept of the closing process by drawing analogies between (1) a scoreboard for an athletic event and the revenue and expense accounts of a business or (2) a sports team's record book and the capital account. (*Hint:* Think about what would happen if the scoreboard is not cleared before the start of a new game.)

COMMUNICATING IN PRACTICE

C1   P2

TAKING IT TO THE NET

A1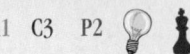

BTN 4-5   Access Motley Fool's discussion of the current ratio at Fool.com/School/Valuation/CurrentAndQuickRatio.htm. (If the page changed, search that site for the *current ratio*.)

Required

1. What level for the current ratio is generally regarded as sufficient to meet near-term operating needs?
2. Once you have calculated the current ratio for a company, what should you compare it against?
3. What are the implications for a company that has a current ratio that is too high?

TEAMWORK IN ACTION

P1 P2 P3

BTN 4-6   The unadjusted trial balance and information for the accounting adjustments of Noseworthy Investigators follow. Each team member involved in this project is to assume one of the four responsibilities listed. After completing each of these responsibilities, the team should work together to prove the accounting equation utilizing information from teammates (1 and 4). If your equation does not balance, you are to work as a team to resolve the error. The team's goal is to complete the task as quickly and accurately as possible.

Unadjusted Trial Balance		
Account Title	Debit	Credit
Cash	$16,000	
Supplies	12,000	
Prepaid insurance	3,000	
Equipment	25,000	
Accumulated depreciation—Equipment		$ 7,000
Accounts payable		3,000
D. Noseworthy, Capital		34,000
D. Noseworthy, Withdrawals	6,000	
Investigation fees earned		33,000
Rent expense	15,000	
Totals	$77,000	$77,000

Additional Year-End Information

a. Insurance that expired in the current period amounts to $2,200.
b. Equipment depreciation for the period is $4,000.
c. Unused supplies total $5,000 at period-end.
d. Services in the amount of $800 have been provided but have not been billed or collected.

Responsibilities for Individual Team Members

1. Determine the accounts and adjusted balances to be extended to the balance sheet columns of the work sheet for Noseworthy. Also determine total assets and total liabilities.
2. Determine the adjusted revenue account balance and prepare the entry to close this account.
3. Determine the adjusted account balances for expenses and prepare the entry to close these accounts.
4. Prepare T-accounts for both D. Noseworthy, Capital (reflecting the unadjusted trial balance amount) and Income Summary. Prepare the third and fourth closing entries. Ask teammates assigned to parts 2 and 3 for the postings for Income Summary. Obtain amounts to complete the third closing entry and post both the third and fourth closing entries. Provide the team with the ending capital account balance.
5. The entire team should prove the accounting equation using post-closing balances.

ENTREPRENEURIAL DECISION

A1 C3 P2

BTN 4-7   Review this chapter's opening feature involving Kathryn Kerrigan and her shoe business.

1. Explain how a classified balance sheet can help Kathryn Kerrigan know what bills are due when, and whether she has the resources to pay those bills.

2. Why is it important for Kathryn Kerrigan to match costs and revenues in a specific time period? How do closing entries help her in this regard?

3. What objectives are met when Kathryn Kerrigan applies closing procedures each fiscal year-end?

BTN 4-8   Select a company that you can visit in person or interview on the telephone. Call ahead to the company to arrange a time when you can interview an employee (preferably an accountant) who helps prepare the annual financial statements. Inquire about the following aspects of its *accounting cycle:*

HITTING THE ROAD

C2

1. Does the company prepare interim financial statements? What time period(s) is used for interim statements?

2. Does the company use the cash or accrual basis of accounting?

3. Does the company use a work sheet in preparing financial statements? Why or why not?

4. Does the company use a spreadsheet program? If so, which software program is used?

5. How long does it take after the end of its reporting period to complete annual statements?

BTN 4-9   DSG international plc is the United Kingdom's largest retailer of consumer electronics. Access its financial statements for the year ended April 28, 2007, at the company's Website (www.DSGiplc.com). The following selected information is available from DSG's financial statements.

GLOBAL DECISION

A1

DSG

(£ millions)	Current Year	Prior Year
Current assets	£2,067	£2,094
Current liabilities	1,869	1,749

Required

1. Compute DSG's current ratio for both the current year and the prior year.

2. Comment on any change from the prior year to the current year for the current ratio.

ANSWERS TO MULTIPLE CHOICE QUIZ

1. e

2. c

3. a

4. c

5. b

A Look Back

Chapters 3 and 4 focused on the final steps of the accounting process. We explained the importance of proper revenue and expense recognition and described the adjusting and closing processes. We also prepared financial statements.

A Look at This Chapter

This chapter emphasizes merchandising activities. We explain how reporting merchandising activities differs from reporting service activities. We also analyze and record merchandise purchases and sales transactions, and explain the adjustments and closing process for merchandisers.

A Look Ahead

Chapter 6 extends our analysis of merchandising activities and focuses on the valuation of inventory. Topics include the items in inventory, costs assigned, costing methods used, and inventory estimation techniques.

Accounting for Merchandising Operations

Chapter

Learning Objectives

CAP

Conceptual

C1 Describe merchandising activities and identify income components for a merchandising company. (p. 178)

C2 Identify and explain the inventory asset of a merchandising company. (p. 179)

C3 Describe both perpetual and periodic inventory systems. (p. 179)

C4 Analyze and interpret cost flows and operating activities of a merchandising company. (p. 187)

Analytical

A1 Compute the acid-test ratio and explain its use to assess liquidity. (p. 193)

A2 Compute the gross margin ratio and explain its use to assess profitability. (p. 193)

Procedural

P1 Analyze and record transactions for merchandise purchases using a perpetual system. (p. 180)

P2 Analyze and record transactions for merchandise sales using a perpetual system. (p. 185)

P3 Prepare adjustments and close accounts for a merchandising company. (p. 188)

P4 Define and prepare multiple-step and single-step income statements. (p. 191)

P5 *Appendix 5A*—Record and compare merchandising transactions using both periodic and perpetual inventory systems. (p. 198)

LP5

New Nightmare Freddy

Toy Story

"I've always been a gambler... but we were also growing exponentially the first few years" — Joel Boblit

SOMERSET, WI—Joel Boblit says his first and greatest business challenge was "being teased by my friends." But now Joel is having the time of his life. His retail business, BigBadToyStore (**BigBadToyStore.com**), deals in new and old action figures. Launched from his parents' basement, the store now projects over $4 million in annual sales.

But the early years were not easy. "I mortgaged everything I owned for the first two years," explains Joel. The business required a merchandising accounting system that Joel says needed to account for purchases and sales transactions. Inventory was especially important to account for. "Many of the store's customers offered inventory suggestions," explains Joel.

To succeed, Joel needed to make smart business decisions. He set up an accounting system to capture and communicate costs and sales information. Tracking merchandising activities was necessary to set prices and to manage discounts, allowances, and returns of both sales and purchases. A perpetual inventory system enabled Joel to stock the right type and amount of merchandise and to avoid the costs of out-of-stock and excess inventory. "We're [now] able to make much more efficient use of the space we have," recounts Joel.

Mastering accounting for merchandising is a means to an end for Joel. He says he loves his business and enjoys the nostalgia of childhood toys. Joel insists, however, that he will continue to take risks. "I've always been a gambler," insists Joel, and "I've always [believed] . . . that the harder you work, the more you'll be paid."

[Sources: *BigBadToyStore Website*, January 2009; *Entrepreneur*, December and October 2005; *St. Croix Chronicle*, March–April 2005; *Alma Matters*, Fall 2005; *YouMakeMillions.blogspot.com*, May 2007]

Buyers of merchandise expect many products, discount prices, inventory on demand, and high quality. This chapter introduces the accounting practices used by companies engaged in merchandising. We show how financial statements reflect merchandising activities and explain the new financial statement items created by merchandising activities. We also analyze and record merchandise purchases and sales, and explain the adjustments and the closing process for these companies.

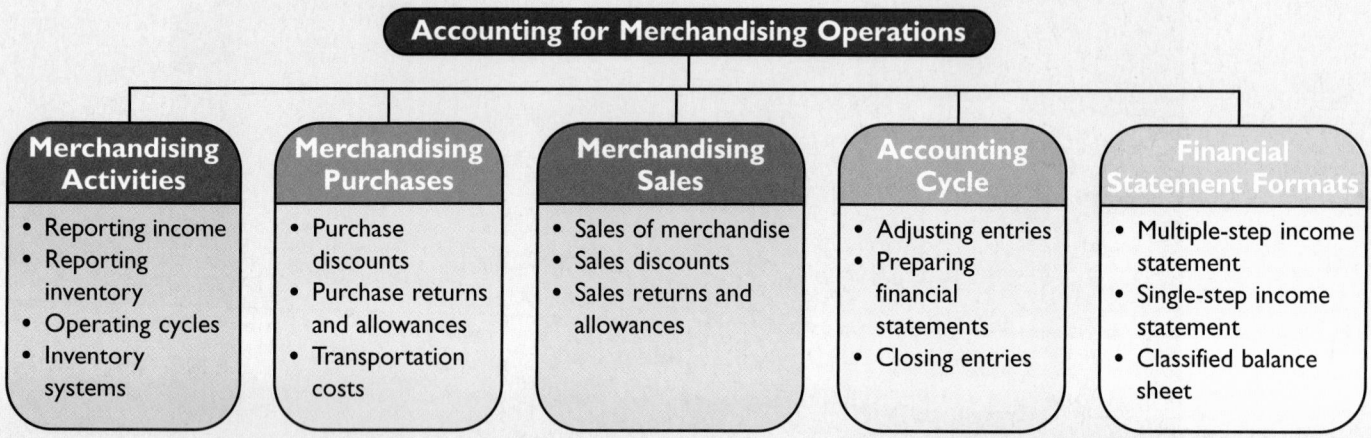

Accounting for Merchandising Operations

Merchandising Activities	Merchandising Purchases	Merchandising Sales	Accounting Cycle	Financial Statement Formats
• Reporting income • Reporting inventory • Operating cycles • Inventory systems	• Purchase discounts • Purchase returns and allowances • Transportation costs	• Sales of merchandise • Sales discounts • Sales returns and allowances	• Adjusting entries • Preparing financial statements • Closing entries	• Multiple-step income statement • Single-step income statement • Classified balance sheet

Merchandising Activities

C1 Describe merchandising activities and identify income components for a merchandising company.

Video5.1

Previous chapters emphasized the accounting and reporting activities of service companies. A merchandising company's activities differ from those of a service company. **Merchandise** consists of products, also called *goods,* that a company acquires to resell to customers. A **merchandiser** earns net income by buying and selling merchandise. Merchandisers are often identified as either wholesalers or retailers. A **wholesaler** is an *intermediary* that buys products from manufacturers or other wholesalers and sells them to retailers or other wholesalers. A **retailer** is an intermediary that buys products from manufacturers or wholesalers and sells them to consumers. Many retailers sell both products and services.

Reporting Income for a Merchandiser

Net income for a merchandiser equals revenues from selling merchandise minus both the cost of merchandise sold to customers and the cost of other expenses for the period, see Exhibit 5.1.

EXHIBIT 5.1

Computing Income for a Merchandising Company versus a Service Company

Service Company

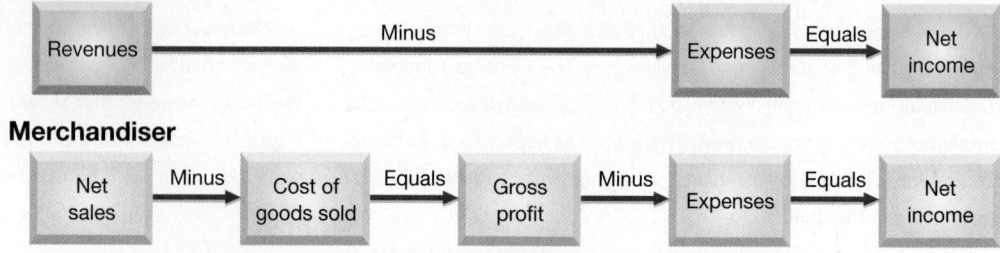

Merchandiser

The usual accounting term for revenues from selling merchandise is *sales,* and the term used for the expense of buying and preparing the merchandise is **cost of goods sold.** (Some service companies use the term *sales* instead of revenues; and cost of goods sold is also called *cost of sales.*)

The income statement for Z-Mart in Exhibit 5.2 illustrates these key components of a merchandiser's net income. The first two lines show that products are acquired at a cost of $230,400 and sold for $314,700. The third line shows an $84,300 **gross profit,** also called

Point: Fleming, SuperValu, and **SYSCO** are wholesalers. **Gap, Oakley, Target,** and **Wal-Mart** are retailers.

EXHIBIT 5.2

Merchandiser's Income Statement

Z-MART Income Statement For Year Ended December 31, 2009	
Net sales	$314,700
Cost of goods sold	230,400
Gross profit	84,300
Expenses	71,400
Net income	$ 12,900

Point: Analysis of gross profit is important to effective business decisions, and is described later in the chapter.

gross margin, which equals net sales less cost of goods sold. Additional expenses of $71,400 are reported, which leaves $12,900 in net income.

Reporting Inventory for a Merchandiser

A merchandiser's balance sheet includes a current asset called *merchandise inventory,* an item not on a service company's balance sheet. **Merchandise inventory,** or simply *inventory,* refers to products that a company owns and intends to sell. The cost of this asset includes the cost incurred to buy the goods, ship them to the store, and make them ready for sale.

C2 Identify and explain the inventory asset of a merchandising company.

Operating Cycle for a Merchandiser

A merchandising company's operating cycle begins by purchasing merchandise and ends by collecting cash from selling the merchandise. The length of an operating cycle differs across the types of businesses. Department stores often have operating cycles of two to five months. Operating cycles for grocery merchants usually range from two to eight weeks.

Exhibit 5.3 illustrates an operating cycle for a merchandiser with credit sales. The cycle moves from (*a*) cash purchases of merchandise to (*b*) inventory for sale to (*c*) credit sales to (*d*) accounts receivable to (*e*) cash. Companies try to keep their operating cycles short because assets tied up in inventory and receivables are not productive. Cash sales shorten operating cycles.

EXHIBIT 5.3

Merchandiser's Operating Cycle

Inventory Systems

Cost of goods sold is the cost of merchandise sold to customers during a period. It is often the largest single expense on a merchandiser's income statement. **Inventory** refers to products a company owns and expects to sell in its normal operations. Exhibit 5.4 shows that a company's merchandise available for sale consists of what it begins with (beginning

C3 Describe both perpetual and periodic inventory systems.

EXHIBIT 5.4

Merchandiser's Cost Flow for a Single Time Period

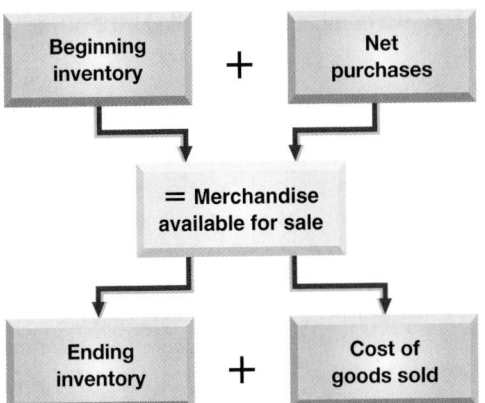

inventory) and what it purchases (net purchases). The merchandise available is either sold (cost of goods sold) or kept for future sales (ending inventory).

Two alternative inventory accounting systems can be used to collect information about cost of goods sold and cost of inventory: *perpetual system* or *periodic system*. The **perpetual inventory system** continually updates accounting records for merchandising transactions—specifically, for those records of inventory available for sale and inventory sold. The **periodic inventory system** updates the accounting records for merchandise transactions only at the *end of a period*. Technological advances and competitive pressures have dramatically increased the use of the perpetual system. (Some companies use a *hybrid* system where the perpetual system is used for tracking units available and the periodic system is used to compute cost of sales.)

Point: Growth of superstores such as Costco and Sam's is fueled by efficient use of perpetual inventory.

Quick Check
Answers—p. 204

1. Describe a merchandiser's cost of goods sold.
2. What is gross profit for a merchandising company?
3. Explain why use of the perpetual inventory system has dramatically increased.

The following sections on purchasing, selling, and adjusting merchandise use the perpetual system. Appendix 5A uses the periodic system (with the perpetual results on the side). An instructor can choose to cover either one or both inventory systems.

Accounting for Merchandise Purchases

P1 Analyze and record transactions for merchandise purchases using a perpetual system.

The cost of merchandise purchased for resale is recorded in the Merchandise Inventory asset account. To illustrate, Z-Mart records a $1,200 cash purchase of merchandise on November 2 as follows:

Assets = Liabilities + Equity
+1,200
−1,200

Nov. 2	Merchandise Inventory	1,200	
	Cash		1,200
	Purchased merchandise for cash.		

The invoice for this merchandise is shown in Exhibit 5.5. The buyer usually receives the original invoice, and the seller keeps a copy. This *source document* serves as the purchase invoice of Z-Mart (buyer) and the sales invoice for Trex (seller). The amount recorded for merchandise inventory includes its purchase cost, shipping fees, taxes, and any other costs necessary to make it ready for sale. This section explains how we compute the recorded cost of merchandise purchases.

Point: The Merchandise Inventory account reflects the cost of goods available for resale.

Decision Insight

Trade Discounts When a manufacturer or wholesaler prepares a catalog of items it has for sale, it usually gives each item a **list price,** also called a *catalog price.* However, an item's intended *selling price* equals list price minus a given percent called a **trade discount.** The amount of trade discount usually depends on whether a buyer is a wholesaler, retailer, or final consumer. A wholesaler buying in large quantities is often granted a larger discount than a retailer buying in smaller quantities. A buyer records the net amount of list price minus trade discount. For example, in the November 2 purchase of merchandise by Z-Mart, the merchandise was listed in the seller's catalog at $2,000 and Z-Mart received a 40% trade discount. This meant that Z-Mart's purchase price was $1,200, computed as $2,000 − (40% × $2,000).

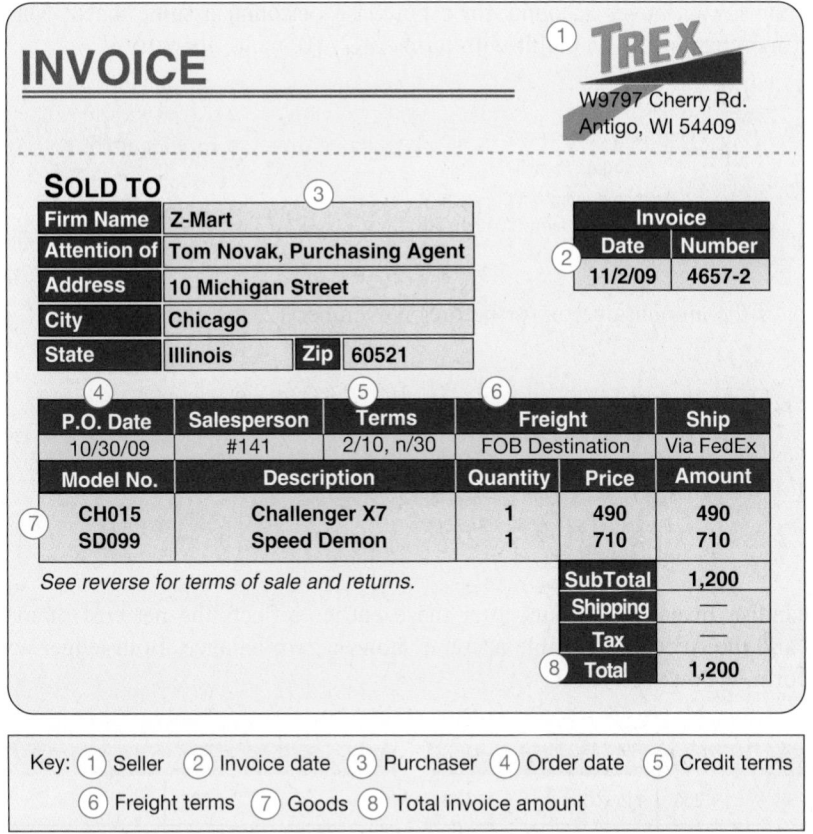

EXHIBIT 5.5

Invoice

Purchase Discounts

The purchase of goods on credit requires a clear statement of expected future payments and dates to avoid misunderstandings. **Credit terms** for a purchase include the amounts and timing of payments from a buyer to a seller. Credit terms usually reflect an industry's practices. To illustrate, when sellers require payment within 10 days after the end of the month of the invoice date, the invoice will show credit terms as "n/10 EOM," which stands for net 10 days after end of month (**EOM**). When sellers require payment within 30 days after the invoice date, the invoice shows credit terms of "n/30," which stands for *net 30 days.*

Exhibit 5.6 portrays credit terms. The amount of time allowed before full payment is due is called the **credit period.** Sellers can grant a **cash discount** to encourage buyers to pay earlier. A buyer views a cash discount as a **purchase discount.** A seller views a cash discount as a **sales discount.** Any cash discounts are described in the credit terms on the invoice. For example, credit terms of "2/10, n/60" mean that full payment is due within a 60-day credit period, but the buyer can deduct 2% of the invoice amount if payment is made within 10 days of the invoice date. This reduced payment applies only for the **discount period.**

Point: Since both the buyer and seller know the invoice date, this date is used in setting the discount and credit periods.

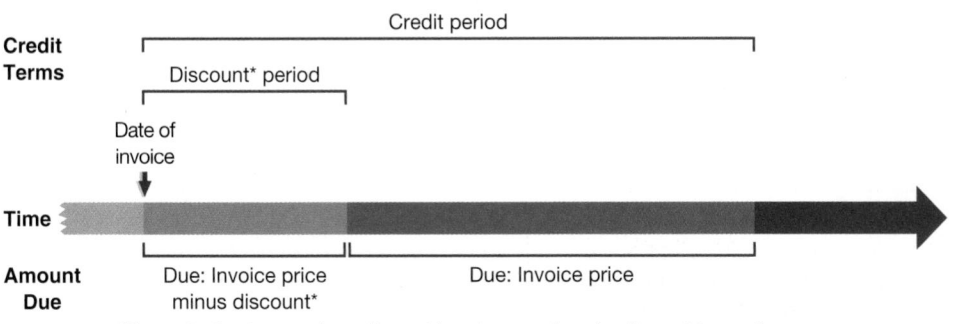

EXHIBIT 5.6

Credit Terms

To illustrate how a buyer accounts for a purchase discount, assume that Z-Mart's $1,200 purchase of merchandise is on credit with terms of 2/10, n/30. Its entry is

Assets = Liabilities + Equity
+1,200   +1,200

(a) Nov. 2	Merchandise Inventory	1,200	
	Accounts Payable		1,200
	Purchased merchandise on credit, invoice		
	dated Nov. 2, terms 2/10, n/30.		

If Z-Mart pays the amount due on (or before) November 12, the entry is

Assets = Liabilities + Equity
−24   −1,200
−1,176

(b) Nov. 12	Accounts Payable.	1,200	
	Merchandise Inventory		24
	Cash		1,176
	Paid for the $1,200 purchase of Nov. 2 less the		
	discount of $24 (2% × $1,200).		

The Merchandise Inventory account after these entries reflects the net cost of merchandise purchased, and the Accounts Payable account shows a zero balance. Both ledger accounts, in T-account form, follow:

Merchandise Inventory			
Nov. 2	1,200	Nov. 12	24
Balance	1,176		

Accounts Payable			
Nov. 12	1,200	Nov. 2	1,200
		Balance	0

A buyer's failure to pay within a discount period can be expensive. To illustrate, if Z-Mart does not pay within the 10-day 2% discount period, it can delay payment by 20 more days. This delay costs Z-Mart $24, computed as 2% × $1,200. Most buyers take advantage of a purchase discount because of the usually high interest rate implied from not taking it.[1] Also, good cash management means that no invoice is paid until the last day of the discount or credit period.

Decision Maker

Entrepreneur   You purchase a batch of products on terms of 3/10, n/90, but your company has limited cash and you must borrow funds at an 11% annual rate if you are to pay within the discount period. Do you take advantage of the purchase discount? [Answer—p. 203]

Purchase Returns and Allowances

Purchase returns refer to merchandise a buyer acquires but then returns to the seller. A *purchase allowance* is a reduction in the cost of defective or unacceptable merchandise that a buyer acquires. Buyers often keep defective but still marketable merchandise if the seller grants an acceptable allowance. When a buyer returns or takes an allowance on merchandise, the buyer issues a **debit memorandum** to inform the seller of a debit made to the seller's account in the buyer's records.

---

[1] The *implied annual interest rate* formula is:

$$(365 \text{ days} \div [\text{Credit period} - \text{Discount period}]) \times \text{Cash discount rate.}$$

For terms of 2/10, n/30, missing the 2% discount for an additional 20 days is equal to an annual interest rate of 36.5%, computed as (365 days/[30 days − 10 days]) × 2% discount rate. *Favorable purchase discounts* are those with implied annual interest rates that exceed the purchaser's annual rate for borrowing money.

Purchase Allowances   To illustrate purchase allowances, assume that on November 15, Z-Mart (buyer) issues a $300 debit memorandum for an allowance from Trex for defective merchandise. Z-Mart's November 15 entry to update its Merchandise Inventory account to reflect the purchase allowance is

(c) Nov. 15	Accounts Payable............................	300	
	Merchandise Inventory....................		300
	Allowance for defective merchandise.		

Assets = Liabilities + Equity
−300   −300

The buyer's allowance for defective merchandise is usually offset against the buyer's current account payable balance to the seller. When cash is refunded, the Cash account is debited instead of Accounts Payable.

Purchase Returns   Returns are recorded at the net costs charged to buyers. To illustrate the accounting for returns, suppose Z-Mart purchases $1,000 of merchandise on June 1 with terms 2/10, n/60. Two days later, Z-Mart returns $100 of goods before paying the invoice. When Z-Mart later pays on June 11, it takes the 2% discount only on the $900 remaining balance. When goods are returned, a buyer can take a purchase discount on only the remaining balance of the invoice. The resulting discount is $18 (2% × $900) and the cash payment is $882 ($900 − $18). The following entries reflect this illustration.

June 1	Merchandise Inventory......................	1,000	
	Accounts Payable		1,000
	Purchased merchandise, invoice dated June 1, terms 2/10, n/60.		
June 3	Accounts Payable...........................	100	
	Merchandise Inventory....................		100
	Returned merchandise to seller.		
June 11	Accounts Payable...........................	900	
	Merchandise Inventory	18	
	Cash		882
	Paid for $900 merchandise ($1,000 − $100) less $18 discount (2% × $900).		

Example: Assume Z-Mart pays $980 cash for $1,000 of merchandise purchased within its 2% discount period. Later, it returns $100 of the original $1,000 merchandise. The return entry is
Cash 98
  Merchandise Inventory ... 98

Decision Ethics

Credit Manager   As a new credit manager, you are being trained by the outgoing manager. She explains that the system prepares checks for amounts net of favorable cash discounts, and the checks are dated the last day of the discount period. She also tells you that checks are not mailed until five days later, adding that "the company gets free use of cash for an extra five days, and our department looks better. When a supplier complains, we blame the computer system and the mailroom." Do you continue this payment policy? [Answer—p. 203]

Transportation Costs and Ownership Transfer

The buyer and seller must agree on who is responsible for paying any freight costs and who bears the risk of loss during transit for merchandising transactions. This is essentially the same as asking at what point ownership transfers from the seller to the buyer. The point of transfer is called the **FOB** (*free on board*) point, which determines who pays transportation costs (and often other incidental costs of transit such as insurance).

Exhibit 5.7 identifies two alternative points of transfer. (1) *FOB shipping point,* also called *FOB factory,* means the buyer accepts ownership when the goods depart the seller's place of business. The buyer is then responsible for paying shipping costs and bearing the risk of damage or loss when goods are in transit. The goods are part of the buyer's inventory when they are in transit since ownership has transferred to the buyer. **Cannondale**, a bike manufacturer,

EXHIBIT 5.7

Ownership Transfer and
Transportation Costs

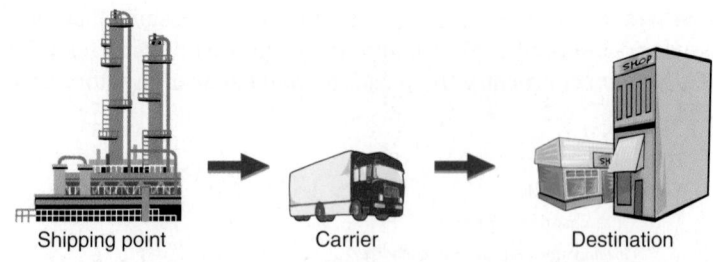

Shipping point	Carrier	Destination

	Ownership Transfers when Goods Passed to	Transportation Costs Paid by
FOB shipping point	Carrier	Buyer
FOB destination	Buyer	Seller

Point: The party not responsible for shipping costs sometimes pays the carrier. In these cases, the party paying these costs either bills the party responsible or, more commonly, adjusts its account payable or account receivable with the other party. For example, a buyer paying a carrier when terms are FOB destination can decrease its account payable to the seller by the amount of shipping cost.

uses FOB shipping point. (2) *FOB destination* means ownership of goods transfers to the buyer when the goods arrive at the buyer's place of business. The seller is responsible for paying shipping charges and bears the risk of damage or loss in transit. The seller does not record revenue from this sale until the goods arrive at the destination because this transaction is not complete before that point.

Z-Mart's $1,200 purchase on November 2 is on terms of FOB destination. This means Z-Mart is not responsible for paying transportation costs. When a buyer is responsible for paying transportation costs, the payment is made to a carrier or directly to the seller depending on the agreement. The cost principle requires that any necessary transportation costs of a buyer (often called *transportation-in* or *freight-in*) be included as part of the cost of purchased merchandise. To illustrate, Z-Mart's entry to record a $75 freight charge from an independent carrier for merchandise purchased FOB shipping point is

Assets = Liabilities + Equity
+75
−75

(d) Nov. 24	Merchandise Inventory	75	
	Cash		75
	Paid freight costs on purchased merchandise.		

A seller records the costs of shipping goods to customers in a Delivery Expense account when the seller is responsible for these costs. Delivery Expense, also called *transportation-out* or *freight-out,* is reported as a selling expense in the seller's income statement.

In summary, purchases are recorded as debits to Merchandise Inventory. Any later purchase discounts, returns, and allowances are credited (decreases) to Merchandise Inventory. Transportation-in is debited (added) to Merchandise Inventory. Z-Mart's itemized costs of merchandise purchases for year 2009 are in Exhibit 5.8.

EXHIBIT 5.8

Itemized Costs of
Merchandise Purchases

Z-MART Itemized Costs of Merchandise Purchases For Year Ended December 31, 2009	
Invoice cost of merchandise purchases	$ 235,800
Less: Purchase discounts received	(4,200)
Purchase returns and allowances	(1,500)
Add: Costs of transportation-in	2,300
Total cost of merchandise purchases	$232,400

Point: Some companies have separate accounts for purchase discounts, returns and allowances, and transportation-in. These accounts are then transferred to Merchandise Inventory at period-end. This is a *hybrid system* of perpetual and periodic. That is, Merchandise Inventory is updated on a perpetual basis but only for purchases and cost of goods sold.

The accounting system described here does not provide separate records (accounts) for total purchases, total purchase discounts, total purchase returns and allowances, and total transportation-in. Yet nearly all companies collect this information in supplementary records because managers need this information to evaluate and control each of these cost elements. **Supplementary records,** also called *supplemental records,* refer to information outside the usual general ledger accounts.

Accounting for Merchandise Sales

Merchandising companies also must account for sales, sales discounts, sales returns and allowances, and cost of goods sold. A merchandising company such as Z-Mart reflects these items in its gross profit computation, as shown in Exhibit 5.9. This section explains how this information is derived from transactions.

EXHIBIT 5.9

Gross Profit Computation

Z-MART Computation of Gross Profit For Year Ended December 31, 2009		
Sales		$321,000
Less: Sales discounts	$4,300	
Sales returns and allowances	2,000	6,300
Net sales		314,700
Cost of goods sold		230,400
Gross profit		$ 84,300

Sales of Merchandise

Each sales transaction for a seller of merchandise involves two parts. One part is the revenue received in the form of an asset from a customer. The second part is the recognition of the cost of merchandise sold to a customer. Accounting for a sales transaction under the perpetual system requires recording information about both parts. This means that each sales transaction for merchandisers, whether for cash or on credit, requires two entries: one for revenue and one for cost. To illustrate, Z-Mart sold $2,400 of merchandise on credit on November 3. The revenue part of this transaction is recorded as

P2 Analyze and record transactions for merchandise sales using a perpetual system.

(e) Nov. 3	Accounts Receivable.	2,400	
	Sales.		2,400
	Sold merchandise on credit.		

Assets = Liabilities + Equity
+2,400   +2,400

This entry reflects an increase in Z-Mart's assets in the form of an accounts receivable. It also shows the increase in revenue (Sales). If the sale is for cash, the debit is to Cash instead of Accounts Receivable.

The cost part of each sales transaction ensures that the Merchandise Inventory account under a perpetual inventory system reflects the updated cost of the merchandise available for sale. For example, the cost of the merchandise Z-Mart sold on November 3 is $1,600, and the entry to record the cost part of this sales transaction is

(e) Nov. 3	Cost of Goods Sold	1,600	
	Merchandise Inventory.		1,600
	To record the cost of Nov. 3 sale.		

Assets = Liabilities + Equity
−1,600   −1,600

Decision Insight

Suppliers and Demands Large merchandising companies often bombard suppliers with demands. These include discounts for bar coding and technology support systems, and fines for shipping errors. Merchandisers' goals are to reduce inventories, shorten lead times, and eliminate errors.

Sales Discounts

Sales discounts on credit sales can benefit a seller by decreasing the delay in receiving cash and reducing future collection efforts. At the time of a credit sale, a seller does not know whether a customer will pay within the discount period and take advantage of a discount. This means the seller usually does not record a sales discount until a customer actually pays within the discount period. To illustrate, Z-Mart completes a credit sale for $1,000 on November 12 with terms of 2/10, n/60. The entry to record the revenue part of this sale is

Assets = Liabilities + Equity
+1,000   +1,000

Nov. 12	Accounts Receivable........................	1,000	
	Sales....................................		1,000
	Sold merchandise under terms of 2/10, n/60.		

This entry records the receivable and the revenue as if the customer will pay the full amount. The customer has two options, however. One option is to wait 60 days until January 11 and pay the full $1,000. In this case, Z-Mart records that payment as

Assets = Liabilities + Equity
+1,000
−1,000

Jan. 11	Cash..	1,000	
	Accounts Receivable		1,000
	Received payment for Nov. 12 sale.		

The customer's second option is to pay $980 within a 10-day period ending November 22. If the customer pays on (or before) November 22, Z-Mart records the payment as

Assets = Liabilities + Equity
+980   −20
−1,000

Nov. 22	Cash..	980	
	Sales Discounts	20	
	Accounts Receivable		1,000
	Received payment for Nov. 12 sale less discount.		

Sales Discounts is a contra revenue account, meaning the Sales Discounts account is deducted from the Sales account when computing a company's net sales (see Exhibit 5.9). Management monitors Sales Discounts to assess the effectiveness and cost of its discount policy.

Sales Returns and Allowances

Point: Published income statements rarely disclose sales discounts, returns and allowances.

Sales returns refer to merchandise that customers return to the seller after a sale. Many companies allow customers to return merchandise for a full refund. *Sales allowances* refer to reductions in the selling price of merchandise sold to customers. This can occur with damaged or defective merchandise that a customer is willing to purchase with a decrease in selling price. Sales returns and allowances usually involve dissatisfied customers and the possibility of lost future sales, and managers monitor information about returns and allowances.

Sales Returns   To illustrate, recall Z-Mart's sale of merchandise on November 3 for $2,400 that had cost $1,600. Assume that the customer returns part of the merchandise on November 6, and the returned items sell for $800 and cost $600. The revenue part of this transaction must reflect the decrease in sales from the customer's return of merchandise as follows:

Assets = Liabilities + Equity
−800   −800

(f) Nov. 6	Sales Returns and Allowances	800	
	Accounts Receivable		800
	Customer returns merchandise of Nov. 3 sale.		

If the merchandise returned to Z-Mart is not defective and can be resold to another customer, Z-Mart returns these goods to its inventory. The entry to restore the cost of such goods to the Merchandise Inventory account is

Nov. 6	Merchandise Inventory	600	
	Cost of Goods Sold		600
	Returned goods added to inventory.		

Assets = Liabilities + Equity
+600   +600

This entry changes if the goods returned are defective. In this case the returned inventory is recorded at its estimated value, not its cost. To illustrate, if the goods (costing $600) returned to Z-Mart are defective and estimated to be worth $150, the following entry is made: Dr. Merchandise Inventory for $150, Dr. Loss from Defective Merchandise for $450, and Cr. Cost of Goods Sold for $600.

Decision Insight

Return to Sender Book merchandisers such as **Barnes & Noble, Borders Books, Books-A-Million**, and **Waldenbooks** can return unsold books to publishers at purchase price. Publishers say returns of new hardcover books run between 35% and 50%.

Sales Allowances To illustrate sales allowances, assume that $800 of the merchandise Z-Mart sold on November 3 is defective but the buyer decides to keep it because Z-Mart offers a $100 price reduction. Z-Mart records this allowance as follows:

Nov. 6	Sales Returns and Allowances	100	
	Accounts Receivable		100
	To record sales allowance on Nov. 3 sale.		

Assets = Liabilities + Equity
−100   −100

The seller usually prepares a credit memorandum to confirm a buyer's return or allowance. A seller's **credit memorandum** informs a buyer of the seller's credit to the buyer's Account Receivable (on the seller's books).

Point: The sender (maker) of a credit memorandum will *credit* the account of the receiver. The receiver of a credit memorandum will *debit* the sender's account.

Quick Check   Answers—p. 204

7. Why are sales discounts and sales returns and allowances recorded in contra revenue accounts instead of directly in the Sales account?

8. Under what conditions are two entries necessary to record a sales return?

9. When merchandise is sold on credit and the seller notifies the buyer of a price allowance, does the seller create and send a credit memorandum or a debit memorandum?

Completing the Accounting Cycle

Exhibit 5.10 shows the flow of merchandising costs during a period and where these costs are reported at period-end. Specifically, beginning inventory plus the net cost of purchases is the merchandise available for sale. As inventory is sold, its cost is recorded in cost of goods sold on the income statement; what remains is ending inventory on the balance sheet. A period's ending inventory is the next period's beginning inventory.

C4 Analyze and interpret cost flows and operating activities of a merchandising company.

EXHIBIT 5.10

Merchandising Cost Flow in the
Accounting Cycle

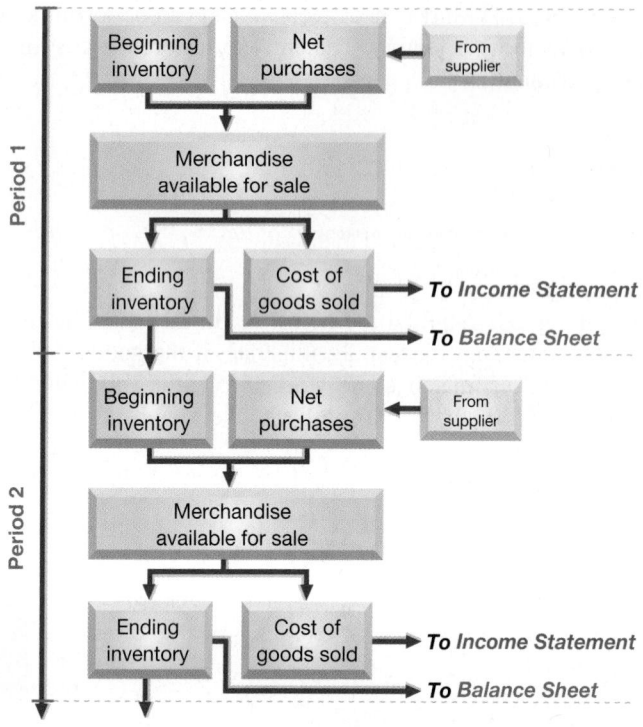

Adjusting Entries for Merchandisers

P3 Prepare adjustments and close accounts for a merchandising company.

Each of the steps in the accounting cycle described in the prior chapter for a service company applies to a merchandiser. This section and the next two further explain three steps of the accounting cycle for a merchandiser—adjustments, statement preparation, and closing.

Adjusting entries are generally the same for merchandising companies and service companies, including those for prepaid expenses (including depreciation), accrued expenses, unearned revenues, and accrued revenues. However, a merchandiser using a perpetual inventory system is usually required to make another adjustment to update the Merchandise Inventory account to reflect any loss of merchandise, including theft and deterioration. **Shrinkage** is the term used to refer to the loss of inventory and it is computed by comparing a physical count of inventory with recorded amounts. A physical count is usually performed at least once annually.

Point: About two-thirds of shoplifting losses are thefts by employees.

To illustrate, Z-Mart's Merchandise Inventory account at the end of year 2009 has a balance of $21,250, but a physical count reveals that only $21,000 of inventory exists. The adjusting entry to record this $250 shrinkage is

Assets = Liabilities + Equity
−250   −250

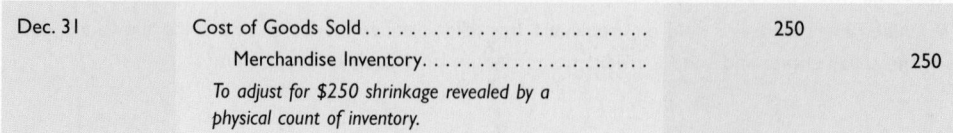

Dec. 31	Cost of Goods Sold.	250	
	Merchandise Inventory.		250
	To adjust for $250 shrinkage revealed by a		
	physical count of inventory.		

Preparing Financial Statements

The financial statements of a merchandiser, and their preparation, are similar to those for a service company described in Chapters 2 through 4. The income statement mainly differs by the inclusion of *cost of goods sold* and *gross profit*. Also, net sales is affected by discounts, returns, and allowances, and some additional expenses are possible such as delivery expense and loss from defective merchandise. The balance sheet mainly differs by the inclusion of *merchandise inventory* as part of current assets. The statement of owner's equity is unchanged. A work sheet can be used to help prepare these statements, and one is illustrated in Appendix 5B for Z-Mart.

Point: Staples's costs of shipping merchandise to its stores is included in its costs of inventories as required by the cost principle.

Closing Entries for Merchandisers

Closing entries are similar for service companies and merchandising companies using a perpetual system. The difference is that we must close some new temporary accounts that arise from merchandising activities. Z-Mart has several temporary accounts unique to merchandisers: Sales (of goods), Sales Discounts, Sales Returns and Allowances, and Cost of Goods Sold. Their existence in the ledger means that the first two closing entries for a merchandiser are slightly different from the ones described in the prior chapter for a service company. These differences are set in **red boldface** in the closing entries of Exhibit 5.11.

Point: The Inventory account is not affected by the closing process under a perpetual system.

EXHIBIT 5.11

Closing Entries for a Merchandiser

Step 1: Close Credit Balances in Temporary Accounts to Income Summary.

Dec. 31	Sales	321,000	
	Income Summary		321,000
	To close credit balances in temporary accounts.		

Step 2: Close Debit Balances in Temporary Accounts to Income Summary.

Dec. 31	Income Summary	308,100	
	Sales Discounts		4,300
	Sales Returns and Allowances		2,000
	Cost of Goods Sold		230,400
	Depreciation Expense		3,700
	Salaries Expense		43,800
	Insurance Expense		600
	Rent Expense		9,000
	Supplies Expense		3,000
	Advertising Expense		11,300
	To close debit balances in temporary accounts.		

Step 3: Close Income Summary to Owner's Capital.

The third closing entry is identical for a merchandising company and a service company. The $12,900 amount is net income reported on the income statement.

Dec. 31	Income Summary	12,900	
	K. Marty, Capital		12,900
	To close the Income Summary account.		

Step 4: Close Withdrawals Account to Owner's Capital.

The fourth closing entry is identical for a merchandising company and a service company. It closes the Withdrawals account and adjusts the Owner's Capital account to the amount shown on the balance sheet.

Dec. 31	K. Marty, Capital	4,000	
	K. Marty, Withdrawals		4,000
	To close the Withdrawals account.		

Summary of Merchandising Entries

Exhibit 5.12 summarizes the key adjusting and closing entries of a merchandiser (using a perpetual inventory system) that are different from those of a service company described in prior chapters (the Demonstration Problem 2 illustrates these merchandising entries).

EXHIBIT 5.12

Summary of Merchandising
Entries

	Merchandising Transactions	Merchandising Entries	Dr.	Cr.
Purchases	Purchasing merchandise for resale.	Merchandise Inventory . . . . Cash or Accounts Payable	#	#
	Paying freight costs on purchases; FOB shipping point.	Merchandise Inventory . . . . Cash	#	#
	Paying within discount period.	Accounts Payable . . . . Merchandise Inventory . . . . Cash	#	# #
	Recording purchase returns or allowances.	Cash or Accounts Payable . . . . Merchandise Inventory	#	#
Sales	Selling merchandise.	Cash or Accounts Receivable . . . . Sales	#	#
		Cost of Goods Sold . . . . Merchandise Inventory	#	#
	Receiving payment within discount period.	Cash . . . . Sales Discounts . . . . Accounts Receivable	# #	#
	Granting sales returns or allowances.	Sales Returns and Allowances . . . . Cash or Accounts Receivable	#	#
		Merchandise Inventory . . . . Cost of Goods Sold	#	#
	Paying freight costs on sales; FOB destination.	Delivery Expense . . . . Cash	#	#

	Merchandising Events	Adjusting and Closing Entries		
Adjusting	Adjusting due to shrinkage (occurs when recorded amount larger than physical inventory).	Cost of Goods Sold . . . . Merchandise Inventory	#	#
Closing	Closing temporary accounts with credit balances.	Sales . . . . Income Summary	#	#
	Closing temporary accounts with debit balances.	Income Summary . . . . Sales Returns and Allowances . . . . . . Sales Discounts . . . . Cost of Goods Sold . . . . Delivery Expense . . . . "Other Expenses"	#	# # # # #

Quick Check
Answers—p. 204

10. When a merchandiser uses a perpetual inventory system, why is it sometimes necessary to adjust the Merchandise Inventory balance with an adjusting entry?

11. What temporary accounts do you expect to find in a merchandising business but not in a service business?

12. Describe the closing entries normally made by a merchandising company.

Financial Statement Formats

Generally accepted accounting principles do not require companies to use any one presentation format for financial statements so we see many different formats in practice. This section describes two common income statement formats: multiple-step and single-step. The classified balance sheet of a merchandiser is also explained.

Multiple-Step Income Statement

A **multiple-step income statement** format shows detailed computations of net sales and other costs and expenses, and reports subtotals for various classes of items. Exhibit 5.13 shows a multiple-step income statement for Z-Mart. The statement has three main parts: (1) *gross profit,* determined by net sales less cost of goods sold, (2) *income from operations,* determined by gross profit less operating expenses, and (3) *net income,* determined by income from operations adjusted for nonoperating items.

P4 Define and prepare multiple-step and single-step income statements.

EXHIBIT 5.13

Multiple-Step Income Statement

Z-MART
Income Statement
For Year Ended December 31, 2009

Sales		$321,000
Less: Sales discounts	$ 4,300	
Sales returns and allowances	2,000	6,300
Net sales		314,700
Cost of goods sold		230,400
Gross profit		84,300
Operating Expenses		
Selling expenses		
Depreciation expense—Store equipment	3,000	
Sales salaries expense	18,500	
Rent expense—Selling space	8,100	
Store supplies expense	1,200	
Advertising expense	11,300	
Total selling expenses	42,100	
General and administrative expenses		
Depreciation expense—Office equipment	700	
Office salaries expense	25,300	
Insurance expense	600	
Rent expense—Office space	900	
Office supplies expense	1,800	
Total general and administrative expenses	29,300	
Total operating expenses		71,400
Income from operations		12,900
Other revenues and gains (expenses and losses)		
Interest revenue	1,000	
Gain on sale of building	2,500	
Interest expense	(1,500)	
Total other revenue and gains (expenses and losses)		2,000
Net income		$ 14,900

Gross profit computation

Income from operations computation

Nonoperating activities computation

Operating expenses are classified into two sections. **Selling expenses** include the expenses of promoting sales by displaying and advertising merchandise, making sales, and delivering goods to customers. **General and administrative expenses** support a company's overall operations and include expenses related to accounting, human resource management, and financial management. Expenses are allocated between sections when they contribute to more than one. Z-Mart allocates rent expense of $9,000 from its store building between two sections: $8,100 to selling expense and $900 to general and administrative expense.

Nonoperating activities consist of other expenses, revenues, losses, and gains that are unrelated to a company's operations. *Other revenues and gains* commonly include interest revenue, dividend revenue, rent revenue, and gains from asset disposals. *Other expenses and losses* commonly include interest expense, losses from asset disposals, and casualty losses. When a company has no reportable nonoperating activities, its income from operations is simply labeled net income.

Point: Z-Mart did not have any nonoperating activities; however, Exhibit 5.13 includes some for illustrative purposes.

Single-Step Income Statement

Point: Many companies report interest expense and interest revenue in separate categories after operating income and before subtracting income tax expense. As one example, see **Circuit City**'s income statement in Appendix A.

A **single-step income statement** is another widely used format, and is shown in Exhibit 5.14 for Z-Mart. It lists cost of goods sold as another expense and shows only one subtotal for total expenses. Expenses are grouped into very few, if any, categories. Many companies use formats that combine features of both the single- and multiple-step statements. Provided that income statement items are shown sensibly, management can choose the format. (In later chapters, we describe some items, such as extraordinary gains and losses, that must be reported in certain locations on the income statement.) Similar presentation options are available for the statement of owner's equity and statement of cash flows.

EXHIBIT 5.14

Single-Step Income Statement

Z-MART Income Statement For Year Ended December 31, 2009		
Revenues		
Net sales		$314,700
Interest revenue		1,000
Gain on sale of building		2,500
Total revenues		318,200
Expenses		
Cost of goods sold	$230,400	
Selling expenses	42,100	
General and administrative expenses	29,300	
Interest expense	1,500	
Total expenses		303,300
Net income		$ 14,900

Classified Balance Sheet

The merchandiser's classified balance sheet reports merchandise inventory as a current asset, usually after accounts receivable according to an asset's nearness to liquidity. Inventory is usually less liquid than accounts receivable because inventory must first be sold before cash can be received; but it is more liquid than supplies and prepaid expenses. Exhibit 5.15 shows the current asset section of Z-Mart's classified balance sheet (other sections are as shown in Chapter 4).

EXHIBIT 5.15

Classified Balance Sheet (partial) of a Merchandiser

Z-MART Balance Sheet (partial) December 31, 2009	
Assets	
Cash	$ 8,200
Accounts receivable	11,200
Merchandise inventory	21,000
Office supplies	550
Store supplies	250
Prepaid insurance	300
Total current assets	$ 41,500

Decision Insight

IFRSs There is no prescribed format for the income statement under IFRSs. This differs from the U.S. in that SEC regulations prescribe a basic format. IFRSs also prescribe that expenses be identified by their nature or function on the income statement. U.S. SEC regulations have no such requirement. IFRSs also allow alternative measures of income on the income statement. U.S. standards prohibit disclosure of alternative income measures in financial statements.

Acid-Test and Gross Margin Ratios

Decision Analysis

Acid-Test Ratio

For many merchandisers, inventory makes up a large portion of current assets. Inventory must be sold and any resulting accounts receivable must be collected before cash is available. Chapter 4 explained that the current ratio, defined as current assets divided by current liabilities, is useful in assessing a company's ability to pay current liabilities. Since it is sometimes unreasonable to assume that inventories are a source of payment for current liabilities, we look to other measures.

One measure of a merchandiser's ability to pay its current liabilities (referred to as its *liquidity*) is the acid-test ratio. It differs from the current ratio by excluding less liquid current assets such as inventory and prepaid expenses that take longer to be converted to cash. The **acid-test ratio,** also called *quick ratio*, is defined as *quick assets* (cash, short-term investments, and current receivables) divided by current liabilities—see Exhibit 5.16.

A1 Compute the acid-test ratio and explain its use to assess liquidity.

$$\text{Acid-test ratio} = \frac{\text{Cash and cash equivalents} + \text{Short-term investments} + \text{Current receivables}}{\text{Current liabilities}}$$

EXHIBIT 5.16

Acid-Test (Quick) Ratio

Exhibit 5.17 shows both the acid-test and current ratios of retailer **JCPenney** for fiscal years 2005 through 2007—also see margin graph. JCPenney's acid-test ratio reveals a general decrease from 2005 through 2007 that exceeds the industry average. Further, JCPenney's current ratio (never less than 1.9) suggests that its short-term obligations can be confidently covered with short-term assets.

EXHIBIT 5.17

JCPenney's Acid-Test and Current Ratios

($ millions)	2007	2006	2005
Total quick assets	$3,010	$3,286	$4,923
Total current assets	$6,648	$6,702	$8,232
Total current liabilities	$3,492	$2,762	$3,297
Acid-test ratio	0.86	1.19	1.49
Current ratio	1.90	2.43	2.50
Industry acid-test ratio	0.56	0.61	0.66
Industry current ratio	2.43	2.55	2.67

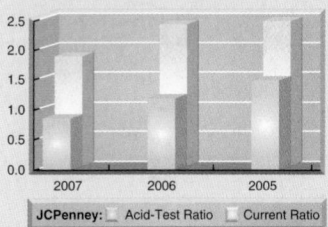

JCPenney: Acid-Test Ratio Current Ratio

An acid-test ratio less than 1.0 means that current liabilities exceed quick assets. A rule of thumb is that the acid-test ratio should have a value near, or higher than, 1.0 to conclude that a company is unlikely to face near-term liquidity problems. A value much less than 1.0 raises liquidity concerns unless a company can generate enough cash from inventory sales or if much of its liabilities are not due until late in the next period. Similarly, a value slightly larger than 1.0 can hide a liquidity problem if payables are due shortly and receivables are not collected until late in the next period. Analysis of JCPenney reveals a slight concern with its liquidity in 2007. However, in all years, JCPenney's acid-test ratios exceed the norm and are at reasonable levels (and its inventory is fairly liquid).

Point: Successful use of a just-in-time inventory system can narrow the gap between the acid-test ratio and the current ratio.

Decision Maker

Supplier A retailer requests to purchase supplies on credit from your company. You have no prior experience with this retailer. The retailer's current ratio is 2.1, its acid-test ratio is 0.5, and inventory makes up most of its current assets. Do you extend credit? [Answer—p. 203]

Gross Margin Ratio

The cost of goods sold makes up much of a merchandiser's expenses. Without sufficient gross profit, a merchandiser will likely fail. Users often compute the gross margin ratio to help understand this relation. It differs from the profit margin ratio in that it excludes all costs except cost of goods sold. The **gross margin ratio** (also called *gross profit ratio*) is defined as *gross margin* (net sales minus cost of goods sold) divided by net sales—see Exhibit 5.18.

A2 Compute the gross margin ratio and explain its use to assess profitability.

$$\text{Gross margin ratio} = \frac{\text{Net sales} - \text{Cost of goods sold}}{\text{Net sales}}$$

EXHIBIT 5.18

Gross Margin Ratio

Exhibit 5.19 shows the gross margin ratio of **JCPenney** for fiscal years 2005 through 2007. For JCPenney, each $1 of sales in 2007 yielded about 39¢ in gross margin to cover all other expenses and still produce a net income. This 39¢ margin is up from 37.5¢ in 2005. This increase is an important (and positive) development. Success for merchandisers such as JCPenney depends on adequate gross margin.

EXHIBIT 5.19

JCPenney's Gross Margin Ratio

($ millions)	2007	2006	2005
Gross margin	$ 7,825	$ 7,191	$ 6,792
Net sales	$19,903	$18,781	$18,096
Gross margin ratio	39.3%	38.3%	37.5%

Decision Maker

Financial Officer   Your company has a 36% gross margin ratio and a 17% net profit margin ratio. Industry averages are 44% for gross margin and 16% for net profit margin. Do these comparative results concern you? [Answer—p. 204]

Demonstration Problem 1

DP5

Use the following adjusted trial balance and additional information to complete the requirements.

KC ANTIQUES
Adjusted Trial Balance
December 31, 2009

	Debit	Credit
Cash	$ 7,000	
Accounts receivable	13,000	
Merchandise inventory	60,000	
Store supplies	1,500	
Equipment	45,600	
Accumulated depreciation—Equipment		$ 16,600
Accounts payable		9,000
Salaries payable		2,000
K. Carter, Capital		79,000
K. Carter, Withdrawals	10,000	
Sales		343,250
Sales discounts	5,000	
Sales returns and allowances	6,000	
Cost of goods sold	159,900	
Depreciation expense—Store equipment	4,100	
Depreciation expense—Office equipment	1,600	
Sales salaries expense	30,000	
Office salaries expense	34,000	
Insurance expense	11,000	
Rent expense (70% is store, 30% is office)	24,000	
Store supplies expense	5,750	
Advertising expense	31,400	
Totals	$449,850	$449,850

KC Antiques' *supplementary records* for 2009 reveal the following itemized costs for merchandising activities:

Invoice cost of merchandise purchases	$150,000
Purchase discounts received	2,500
Purchase returns and allowances	2,700
Cost of transportation-in	5,000

Required

1. Use the supplementary records to compute the total cost of merchandise purchases for 2009.
2. Prepare a 2009 multiple-step income statement. (Inventory at December 31, 2008, is $70,100.)
3. Prepare a single-step income statement for 2009.
4. Prepare closing entries for KC Antiques at December 31, 2009.
5. Compute the acid-test ratio and the gross margin ratio. Explain the meaning of each ratio and interpret them for KC Antiques.

Planning the Solution

- Compute the total cost of merchandise purchases for 2009.
- To prepare the multiple-step statement, first compute net sales. Then, to compute cost of goods sold, add the net cost of merchandise purchases for the year to beginning inventory and subtract the cost of ending inventory. Subtract cost of goods sold from net sales to get gross profit. Then classify expenses as selling expenses or general and administrative expenses.
- To prepare the single-step income statement, begin with net sales. Then list and subtract the expenses.
- The first closing entry debits all temporary accounts with credit balances and opens the Income Summary account. The second closing entry credits all temporary accounts with debit balances. The third entry closes the Income Summary account to the capital account, and the fourth entry closes the withdrawals account to the capital account.
- Identify the quick assets on the adjusted trial balance. Compute the acid-test ratio by dividing quick assets by current liabilities. Compute the gross margin ratio by dividing gross profit by net sales.

Solution to Demonstration Problem I

1.

Invoice cost of merchandise purchases	$150,000
Less: Purchases discounts received	2,500
Purchase returns and allowances	2,700
Add: Cost of transportation-in	5,000
Total cost of merchandise purchases	$149,800

2. Multiple-step income statement

KC ANTIQUES Income Statement For Year Ended December 31, 2009			
Sales			$343,250
Less: Sales discounts	$ 5,000		
Sales returns and allowances	6,000	11,000	
Net sales		332,250	
Cost of goods sold*		159,900	
Gross profit		172,350	
Expenses			
Selling expenses			
Depreciation expense—Store equipment	4,100		
Sales salaries expense	30,000		
Rent expense—Selling space	16,800		
Store supplies expense	5,750		
Advertising expense	31,400		
Total selling expenses	88,050		

[continued on next page]

[continued from previous page]

General and administrative expenses			
Depreciation expense—Office equipment	1,600		
Office salaries expense	34,000		
Insurance expense	11,000		
Rent expense—Office space	7,200		
Total general and administrative expenses	53,800		
Total operating expenses		141,850	
Net income		$ 30,500	

* Cost of goods sold can also be directly computed (applying concepts from Exhibit 5.4):

Merchandise inventory, December 31, 2008	$ 70,100
Total cost of merchandise purchases (from part 1)	149,800
Goods available for sale	219,900
Merchandise inventory, December 31, 2009	60,000
Cost of goods sold	$159,900

3. Single-step income statement

KC ANTIQUES
Income Statement
For Year Ended December 31, 2009

Net sales		$332,250
Expenses		
Cost of goods sold	$159,900	
Selling expenses	88,050	
General and administrative expenses	53,800	
Total expenses		301,750
Net income		$ 30,500

4.

Dec. 31	Sales	343,250	
	Income Summary		343,250
	To close credit balances in temporary accounts.		
Dec. 31	Income Summary	312,750	
	Sales Discounts		5,000
	Sales Returns and Allowances		6,000
	Cost of Goods Sold		159,900
	Depreciation Expense—Store Equipment		4,100
	Depreciation Expense—Office Equipment		1,600
	Sales Salaries Expense		30,000
	Office Salaries Expense		34,000
	Insurance Expense		11,000
	Rent Expense		24,000
	Store Supplies Expense		5,750
	Advertising Expense		31,400
	To close debit balances in temporary accounts.		
Dec. 31	Income Summary	30,500	
	K. Carter, Capital		30,500
	To close the Income Summary account.		
Dec. 31	K. Carter, Capital	10,000	
	K. Carter, Withdrawals		10,000
	To close the Withdrawals account.		

5. Acid-test ratio = (Cash and equivalents + Short-term investments + Current receivables)/
     Current liabilities

= (Cash + Accounts receivable/(Accounts payable + Salaries payable)

= ($7,000 + $13,000)/($9,000 + $2,000) = $20,000/$11,000 = 1.82

Gross margin ratio = Gross profit/Net sales = $172,350/$332,250 = 0.52 (or 52%)

KC Antiques has a healthy acid-test ratio of 1.82. This means it has more than $1.80 in liquid assets to satisfy each $1.00 in current liabilities. The gross margin of 0.52 shows that KC Antiques spends 48¢ ($1.00 − $0.52) of every dollar of net sales on the costs of acquiring the merchandise it sells. This leaves 52¢ of every dollar of net sales to cover other expenses incurred in the business and to provide a net profit.

Demonstration Problem 2

Prepare journal entries to record the following merchandising transactions for both the seller (BMX) and buyer (Sanuk).

May 4   BMX sold $1,500 of merchandise on account to Sanuk, terms FOB shipping point, n/45, invoice dated May 4. The cost of the merchandise was $900.

May 6   Sanuk paid transportation charges of $30 on the May 4 purchase from BMX.

May 8   BMX sold $1,000 of merchandise on account to Sanuk, terms FOB destination, n/30, invoice dated May 8. The cost of the merchandise was $700.

May 10   BMX paid transportation costs of $50 for delivery of merchandise sold to Sanuk on May 8.

May 16   BMX issued Sanuk a $200 credit memorandum for merchandise returned. The merchandise was purchased by Sanuk on account on May 8. The cost of the merchandise returned was $140.

May 18   BMX received payment from Sanuk for purchase of May 8.

May 21   BMX sold $2,400 of merchandise on account to Sanuk, terms FOB shipping point, 2/10, n/EOM. BMX prepaid transportation costs of $100, which were added to the invoice. The cost of the merchandise was $1,440.

May 31   BMX received payment from Sanuk for purchase of May 21, less discount (2% × $2,400).

Solution to Demonstration Problem 2

	BMX (Seller)			Sanuk (Buyer)		
May 4	Accounts Receivable—Sanuk	1,500		Merchandise Inventory	1,500	
	Sales		1,500	Accounts Payable—BMX		1,500
	Cost of Goods Sold	900				
	Merchandise Inventory		900			
6	No entry.			Merchandise Inventory	30	
				Cash		30
8	Accounts Receivable—Sanuk	1,000		Merchandise Inventory	1,000	
	Sales		1,000	Accounts Payable—BMX		1,000
	Cost of Goods Sold	700				
	Merchandise Inventory		700			
10	Delivery Expense	50		No entry.		
	Cash		50			
16	Sales Returns & Allowances	200		Accounts Payable—BMX	200	
	Accounts Receivable—Sanuk		200	Merchandise Inventory		200
	Merchandise Inventory	140				
	Cost of Goods Sold		140			
18	Cash	800		Accounts Payable—BMX	800	
	Accounts Receivable—Sanuk		800	Cash		800
21	Accounts Receivable—Sanuk	2,400		Merchandise Inventory	2,500	
	Sales		2,400	Accounts Payable—BMX		2,500
	Accounts Receivable—Sanuk	100				
	Cash		100			
	Cost of Goods Sold	1,440				
	Merchandise Inventory		1,440			
31	Cash	2,452		Accounts Payable—BMX	2,500	
	Sales Discounts	48		Merchandise Inventory		48
	Accounts Receivable—Sanuk		2,500	Cash		2,452

APPENDIX

5A Periodic Inventory System

A **periodic inventory system** requires updating the inventory account only at the *end of a period* to reflect the quantity and cost of both the goods available and the goods sold. Thus, during the period, the Merchandise Inventory balance remains unchanged. It reflects the beginning inventory balance until it is updated at the end of the period. During the period the cost of merchandise is recorded in a temporary *Purchases* account. When a company sells merchandise, it records revenue **but not the cost of the goods sold.** At the end of the period when a company prepares financial statements, it takes a *physical count of inventory* by counting the quantities and costs of merchandise available. The cost of goods sold is then computed by subtracting the ending inventory amount from the cost of merchandise available for sale.

Recording Merchandise Transactions

P5   Record and compare merchandising transactions using both periodic and perpetual inventory systems.

Under a periodic system, purchases, purchase returns and allowances, purchase discounts, and transportation-in transactions are recorded in separate temporary accounts. At period-end, each of these temporary accounts is closed and the Merchandise Inventory account is updated. To illustrate, journal entries under the periodic inventory system are shown for the most common transactions (codes *a* through *f* link these transactions to those in the chapter, and we drop explanations for simplicity). For comparison, perpetual system journal entries are shown to the right of each periodic entry, where differences are in gray font.

Purchases   The periodic system uses a temporary *Purchases* account that accumulates the cost of all purchase transactions during each period. Z-Mart's November 2 entry to record the purchase of merchandise for $1,200 on credit with terms of 2/10, n/30 is

(a)

Periodic		
Purchases	1,200	
Accounts Payable		1,200

Perpetual		
Merchandise Inventory	1,200	
Accounts Payable		1,200

Purchase Discounts   The periodic system uses a temporary *Purchase Discounts* account that accumulates discounts taken on purchase transactions during the period. If payment in (*a*) is delayed until after the discount period expires, the entry is to debit Accounts Payable and credit Cash for $1,200 each. However, if Z-Mart pays the supplier for the previous purchase in (*a*) within the discount period, the required payment is $1,176 ($1,200 × 98%) and is recorded as

(b)

Periodic		
Accounts Payable	1,200	
Purchase Discounts		24
Cash		1,176

Perpetual		
Accounts Payable	1,200	
Merchandise Inventory		24
Cash		1,176

Purchase Returns and Allowances   Z-Mart returned merchandise purchased on November 2 because of defects. In the periodic system, the temporary *Purchase Returns and Allowances* account accumulates the cost of all returns and allowances during a period. The recorded cost (including discounts) of the defective merchandise is $300, and Z-Mart records the November 15 return with this entry:

(c)

Periodic		
Accounts Payable	300	
Purchase Returns		
and Allowances		300

Perpetual		
Accounts Payable	300	
Merchandise Inventory		300

Transportation-In   Z-Mart paid a $75 freight charge to transport merchandise to its store. In the periodic system, this cost is charged to a temporary *Transportation-In* account.

(d)

Periodic			Perpetual		
Transportation-In	75		Merchandise Inventory	75	
Cash		75	Cash		75

Sales   Under the periodic system, the cost of goods sold is *not* recorded at the time of each sale. (We later show how to compute total cost of goods sold at the end of a period.) Z-Mart's November 3 entry to record sales of $2,400 in merchandise on credit (when its cost is $1,600) is:

(e)

Periodic			Perpetual		
Accounts Receivable	2,400		Accounts Receivable	2,400	
Sales		2,400	Sales		2,400
			Cost of Goods Sold	1,600	
			Merchandise Inventory		1,600

Sales Returns   A customer returned part of the merchandise from the transaction in (*e*), where the returned items sell for $800 and cost $600. (*Recall:* The periodic system records only the revenue effect, not the cost effect, for sales transactions.) Z-Mart restores the merchandise to inventory and records the November 6 return as

(f)

Periodic			Perpetual		
Sales Returns and			Sales Returns and		
Allowances	800		Allowances	800	
Accounts Receivable ...		800	Accounts Receivable		800
			Merchandise Inventory	600	
			Cost of Goods Sold		600

Sales Discounts   To illustrate sales discounts, assume that the remaining $1,600 of receivables (computed as $2,400 from *e* less $800 for *f*) has credit terms of 3/10, n/90 and that customers all pay within the discount period. Z-Mart records this payment as

Periodic			Perpetual		
Cash	1,552		Cash	1,552	
Sales Discounts ($1,600 × .03)	48		Sales Discounts ($1,600 × .03) ..	48	
Accounts Receivable ...		1,600	Accounts Receivable		1,600

Adjusting and Closing Entries

The periodic and perpetual inventory systems have slight differences in adjusting and closing entries. The period-end Merchandise Inventory balance (unadjusted) is $19,000 under the periodic system and $21,250 under the perpetual system. Since the periodic system does not update the Merchandise Inventory balance during the period, the $19,000 amount is the beginning inventory. However, the $21,250 balance under the perpetual system is the recorded ending inventory before adjusting for any inventory shrinkage.

A physical count of inventory taken at the end of the period reveals $21,000 of merchandise available. The adjusting and closing entries for the two systems are shown in Exhibit 5A.1. The periodic system records the ending inventory of $21,000 in the Merchandise Inventory account (which includes

EXHIBIT 5A.1

Comparison of Adjusting and Closing Entries—Periodic and Perpetual

PERIODIC			PERPETUAL		
Adjusting Entry—Shrinkage			**Adjusting Entry—Shrinkage**		
None			Cost of Goods Sold	250	
			Merchandise Inventory		250

[continued on next page]

[continued from previous page]

PERIODIC		
Closing Entries		
(1) Sales	321,000	
Merchandise Inventory	21,000	
Purchase Discounts	4,200	
Purchase Returns and Allowances	1,500	
Income Summary		347,700
(2) Income Summary	334,800	
Sales Discounts		4,300
Sales Returns and Allowances		2,000
Merchandise Inventory		19,000
Purchases		235,800
Transportation-In		2,300
Depreciation Expense		3,700
Salaries Expense		43,800
Insurance Expense		600
Rent Expense		9,000
Supplies Expense		3,000
Advertising Expense		11,300
(3) Income Summary	12,900	
K. Marty, Capital		12,900
(4) K. Marty, Capital	4,000	
K. Marty, Withdrawals		4,000

PERPETUAL		
Closing Entries		
(1) Sales	321,000	
Income Summary		321,000
(2) Income Summary	308,100	
Sales Discounts		4,300
Sales Returns and Allowances		2,000
Cost of Goods Sold		230,400
Depreciation Expense		3,700
Salaries Expense		43,800
Insurance Expense		600
Rent Expense		9,000
Supplies Expense		3,000
Advertising Expense		11,300
(3) Income Summary	12,900	
K. Marty, Capital		12,900
(4) K. Marty, Capital	4,000	
K. Marty, Withdrawals		4,000

shrinkage) in the first closing entry and removes the $19,000 beginning inventory balance from the account in the second closing entry.[2]

By updating Merchandise Inventory and closing Purchases, Purchase Discounts, Purchase Returns and Allowances, and Transportation-In, the periodic system transfers the cost of goods sold amount to Income Summary. Review the periodic side of Exhibit 5A.1 and notice that the **boldface** items affect Income Summary as follows.

Credit to Income Summary in the first closing entry includes amounts from:		
Merchandise inventory (ending)	$	21,000
Purchase discounts		4,200
Purchase returns and allowances		1,500
Debit to Income Summary in the second closing entry includes amounts from:		
Merchandise inventory (beginning)		(19,000)
Purchases		(235,800)
Transportation-in		(2,300)
Net effect on Income Summary		**$(230,400)**

This $230,400 effect on Income Summary is the cost of goods sold amount. The periodic system transfers cost of goods sold to the Income Summary account but without using a Cost of Goods Sold account. Also, the periodic system does not separately measure shrinkage. Instead, it computes cost of goods

---

[2] This approach is called the *closing entry method*. An alternative approach, referred to as the *adjusting entry method*, would not make any entries to Merchandise Inventory in the closing entries of Exhibit 5A.1, but instead would make two adjusting entries. Using Z-Mart data, the two adjusting entries would be: (1) Dr. Income Summary and Cr. Merchandise Inventory for $19,000 each, and (2) Dr. Merchandise Inventory and Cr. Income Summary for $21,000 each. The first entry removes the beginning balance of Merchandise Inventory, and the second entry records the actual ending balance.

available for sale, subtracts the cost of ending inventory, and defines the difference as cost of goods sold, which includes shrinkage.

Preparing Financial Statements

The financial statements of a merchandiser using the periodic system are similar to those for a service company described in prior chapters. The income statement mainly differs by the inclusion of *cost of goods sold* and *gross profit*—of course, net sales is affected by discounts, returns, and allowances. The cost of goods sold section under the periodic system follows

Calculation of Cost of Goods Sold For Year Ended December 31, 2009	
Beginning inventory	$ 19,000
Cost of goods purchased	232,400
Cost of goods available for sale	251,400
Less ending inventory	21,000
Cost of goods sold	$230,400

The balance sheet mainly differs by the inclusion of *merchandise inventory* in current assets—see Exhibit 5.15. The statement of owner's equity is unchanged. A work sheet can be used to help prepare these statements. The only differences under the periodic system from the work sheet illustrated in Appendix 5B using the perpetual system are highlighted as follows in blue boldface font.

File Edit View Insert Format Tools Data Accounting Window Help

	No.	Account	Unadjusted Trial Balance Dr.	Cr.	Adjustments Dr.	Cr.	Adjusted Trial Balance Dr.	Cr.	Income Statement Dr.	Cr.	Balance Sheet Dr.	Cr.
3	101	Cash	8,200				8,200				8,200	
4	106	Accounts receivable	11,200				11,200				11,200	
5	119	Merchandise Inventory	19,000				19,000		19,000	21,000	21,000	
6	126	Supplies	3,800			(b) 3,000	800				800	
7	128	Prepaid insurance	900			(a) 600	300				300	
8	167	Equipment	34,200				34,200				34,200	
9	168	Accumulated depr.—Equip.		3,700		(c) 3,700		7,400				7,400
10	201	Accounts payable		16,000				16,000				16,000
11	209	Salaries payable				(d) 800		800				800
12	301	K. Marty, Capital		42,600				42,600				42,600
13	302	K. Marty, Withdrawals	4,000				4,000				4,000	
14	413	Sales		321,000				321,000		321,000		
15	414	Sales returns and allowances	2,000				2,000		2,000			
16a	415	Sales discounts	4,300				4,300		4,300			
16b	505	Purchases	235,800				235,800		235,800			
16c	506	Purchases returns & allowance		1,500				1,500		1,500		
16d	507	Purchases discounts		4,200				4,200		4,200		
17	508	Transportation-in	2,300				2,300		2,300			
18	612	Depreciation expense—Equip.			(c) 3,700		3,700		3,700			
19	622	Salaries expense	43,000		(d) 800		43,800		43,800			
20	637	Insurance expense			(a) 600		600		600			
21	640	Rent expense	9,000				9,000		9,000			
22	652	Supplies expense			(b) 3,000		3,000		3,000			
23	655	Advertising expense	11,300				11,300		11,300			
24		Totals	389,000	389,000	8,100	8,100	393,500	393,500	334,800	347,700	79,700	66,800
25		Net income							12,900			12,900
26		Totals							347,700	347,700	79,700	79,700

Sheet1 Sheet2 Sheet3

APPENDIX

Work Sheet—Perpetual System

Exhibit 5B.1 shows the work sheet for preparing financial statements of a merchandiser. It differs slightly from the work sheet layout in Chapter 4—the differences are in **red boldface**. Also, the adjustments in the work sheet reflect the following: (a) Expiration of $600 of prepaid insurance. (b) Use of $3,000 of supplies. (c) Depreciation of $3,700 for equipment. (d) Accrual of $800 of unpaid salaries. (e) Inventory shrinkage of $250. Once the adjusted amounts are extended into the financial statement columns, the information is used to develop financial statements.

EXHIBIT 5B.1

Work Sheet for Merchandiser (using a perpetual system)

No.	Account	Unadjusted Trial Balance Dr.	Cr.	Adjustments Dr.	Cr.	Adjusted Trial Balance Dr.	Cr.	Income Statement Dr.	Cr.	Balance Sheet Dr.	Cr.
101	Cash	8,200				8,200				8,200	
106	Accounts receivable	11,200				11,200				11,200	
119	Merchandise Inventory	21,250			(g) 250	21,000				21,000	
126	Supplies	3,800			(b) 3,000	800				800	
128	Prepaid insurance	900			(a) 600	300				300	
167	Equipment	34,200				34,200				34,200	
168	Accumulated depr.—Equip.		3,700		(c) 3,700		7,400				7,400
201	Accounts payable		16,000				16,000				16,000
209	Salaries payable				(d) 800		800				800
301	K. Marty, Capital		42,600				42,600				42,600
302	K. Marty, Withdrawals	4,000				4,000				4,000	
413	Sales		321,000				321,000		321,000		
414	Sales returns and allowances	2,000				2,000		2,000			
415	Sales discounts	4,300				4,300		4,300			
502	Cost of goods sold	230,150		(g) 250		230,400		230,400			
612	Depreciation expense—Equip.			(c) 3,700		3,700		3,700			
622	Salaries expense	43,000		(d) 800		43,800		43,800			
637	Insurance expense			(a) 600		600		600			
640	Rent expense	9,000				9,000		9,000			
652	Supplies expense			(b) 3,000		3,000		3,000			
655	Advertising expense	11,300				11,300		11,300			
	Totals	383,300	383,300	8,350	8,350	387,800	387,800	308,100	321,000	79,700	66,800
	Net income							12,900			12,900
	Totals							321,000	321,000	79,700	79,700

Summary

C1 **Describe merchandising activities and identify income components for a merchandising company.** Merchandisers buy products and resell them. Examples of merchandisers include Wal-Mart, Home Depot, The Limited, and Barnes & Noble. A merchandiser's costs on the income statement include an amount for cost of goods sold. Gross profit, or gross margin, equals sales minus cost of goods sold.

C2 **Identify and explain the inventory asset of a merchandising company.** The current asset section of a merchandising company's balance sheet includes *merchandise inventory,* which refers to the products a merchandiser sells and are available for sale at the balance sheet date.

C3 **Describe both perpetual and periodic inventory systems.** A perpetual inventory system continuously tracks the cost of goods available for sale and the cost of goods sold. A periodic system accumulates the cost of goods purchased during the period and does not compute the amount of inventory or the cost of goods sold until the end of a period.

C4 **Analyze and interpret cost flows and operating activities of a merchandising company.** Cost of merchandise purchases flows into Merchandise Inventory and from there to Cost of Goods Sold on the income statement. Any remaining inventory is reported as a current asset on the balance sheet.

A1 **Compute the acid-test ratio and explain its use to assess liquidity.** The acid-test ratio is computed as quick assets (cash, short-term investments, and current receivables) divided by current liabilities. It indicates a company's ability to pay its current liabilities with its existing quick assets. An acid-test ratio equal to or greater than 1.0 is often adequate.

A2 **Compute the gross margin ratio and explain its use to assess profitability.** The gross margin ratio is computed as gross margin (net sales minus cost of goods sold) divided by net sales. It indicates a company's profitability before considering other expenses.

P1 **Analyze and record transactions for merchandise purchases using a perpetual system.** For a perpetual inventory

system, purchases of inventory (net of trade discounts) are added to the Merchandise Inventory account. Purchase discounts and purchase returns and allowances are subtracted from Merchandise Inventory, and transportation-in costs are added to Merchandise Inventory.

P2 **Analyze and record transactions for merchandise sales using a perpetual system.** A merchandiser records sales at list price less any trade discounts. The cost of items sold is transferred from Merchandise Inventory to Cost of Goods Sold. Refunds or credits given to customers for unsatisfactory merchandise are recorded in Sales Returns and Allowances, a contra account to Sales. If merchandise is returned and restored to inventory, the cost of this merchandise is removed from Cost of Goods Sold and transferred back to Merchandise Inventory. When cash discounts from the sales price are offered and customers pay within the discount period, the seller records Sales Discounts, a contra account to Sales.

P3 **Prepare adjustments and close accounts for a merchandising company.** With a perpetual system, it is often necessary to make an adjustment for inventory shrinkage. This is computed by comparing a physical count of inventory with the Merchandise Inventory balance. Shrinkage is normally charged to Cost of Goods Sold. Temporary accounts closed to Income Summary for a merchandiser include Sales, Sales Discounts, Sales Returns and Allowances, and Cost of Goods Sold.

P4 **Define and prepare multiple-step and single-step income statements.** Multiple-step income statements include greater detail for sales and expenses than do single-step income statements. They also show details of net sales and report expenses in categories reflecting different activities.

P5^A **Record and compare merchandising transactions using both periodic and perpetual inventory systems.** Transactions involving the sale and purchase of merchandise are recorded and analyzed under both the periodic and perpetual inventory systems. Adjusting and closing entries for both inventory systems are illustrated and explained.

Guidance Answers to **Decision Maker** and **Decision Ethics**

Entrepreneur   For terms of 3/10, n/90, missing the 3% discount for an additional 80 days equals an implied annual interest rate of 13.69%, computed as (365 days ÷ 80 days) × 3%. Since you can borrow funds at 11% (assuming no other processing costs), it is better to borrow and pay within the discount period. You save 2.69% (13.69% − 11%) in interest costs by paying early.

Credit Manager   Your decision is whether to comply with prior policy or to create a new policy and not abuse discounts offered by suppliers. Your first step should be to meet with your superior to find out if the late payment policy is the actual policy and, if so, its rationale. If it is the policy to pay late, you must apply your own sense of ethics. One point of view is that the late payment policy is unethical. A deliberate plan to make late payments means the company lies when it pretends to make payment within the discount period. Another

view is that the late payment policy is acceptable. In some markets, attempts to take discounts through late payments are accepted as a continued phase of "price negotiation." Also, your company's suppliers can respond by billing your company for the discounts not accepted because of late payments. However, this is a dubious viewpoint, especially since the prior manager proposes that you dishonestly explain late payments as computer or mail problems and since some suppliers have complained.

Supplier   A current ratio of 2.1 suggests sufficient current assets to cover current liabilities. An acid-test ratio of 0.5 suggests, however, that quick assets can cover only about one-half of current liabilities. This implies that the retailer depends on money from sales of inventory to pay current liabilities. If sales of inventory decline or profit margins decrease, the likelihood that this retailer will default on its payments increases. Your decision is probably not to extend credit. If you do extend credit, you are likely to closely monitor the retailer's financial condition. (It is better to hold unsold inventory than uncollectible receivables.)

Financial Officer   Your company's net profit margin is about equal to the industry average and suggests typical industry perform-

ance. However, gross margin reveals that your company is paying far more in cost of goods sold or receiving far less in sales price than competitors. Your attention must be directed to finding the problem with cost of goods sold, sales, or both. One positive note is that your company's expenses make up 19% of sales (36% − 17%). This favorably compares with competitors' expenses that make up 28% of sales (44% − 16%).

Guidance Answers to **Quick Checks**

1. Cost of goods sold is the cost of merchandise purchased from a supplier that is sold to customers during a specific period.

2. Gross profit (or gross margin) is the difference between net sales and cost of goods sold.

3. Widespread use of computing and related technology has dramatically increased the use of the perpetual inventory system.

4. Under credit terms of 2/10, n/60, the credit period is 60 days and the discount period is 10 days.

5. (*b*) trade discount.

6. *FOB* means "free on board." It is used in identifying the point when ownership transfers from seller to buyer. *FOB destination* means that the seller transfers ownership of goods to the buyer when they arrive at the buyer's place of business. It also means that the seller is responsible for paying shipping charges and bears the risk of damage or loss during shipment.

7. Recording sales discounts and sales returns and allowances separately from sales gives useful information to managers for internal monitoring and decision making.

8. When a customer returns merchandise *and* the seller restores the merchandise to inventory, two entries are necessary. One entry

records the decrease in revenue and credits the customer's account. The second entry debits inventory and reduces cost of goods sold.

9. Credit memorandum—seller credits accounts receivable from buyer.

10. Merchandise Inventory may need adjusting to reflect shrinkage.

11. Sales (of goods), Sales Discounts, Sales Returns and Allowances, and Cost of Goods Sold (and maybe Delivery Expense).

12. Four closing entries: (1) close credit balances in temporary accounts to Income Summary, (2) close debit balances in temporary accounts to Income Summary, (3) close Income Summary to owner's capital, and (4) close withdrawals account to owner's capital.

13. Cost of Goods Sold.

14. (*b*) Purchases and (*c*) Transportation-In.

15. Under a periodic inventory system, the cost of goods sold is determined at the end of an accounting period by adding the net cost of goods purchased to the beginning inventory and subtracting the ending inventory.

16. Both methods report the same ending inventory and income.

Key Terms   mhhe.com/wildFAP19e

Key Terms are available at the book's Website for learning and testing in an online Flashcard Format.

Acid-test ratio (p. 193)

Cash discount (p. 181)

Cost of goods sold (p. 178)

Credit memorandum (p. 187)

Credit period (p. 181)

Credit terms (p. 181)

Debit memorandum (p. 182)

Discount period (p. 181)

EOM (p. 181)

FOB (p. 183)

General and administrative expenses (p. 191)

Gross margin (p. 179)

Gross margin ratio (p. 193)

Gross profit (p. 178)

Inventory (p. 179)

List price (p. 180)

Merchandise (p. 178)

Merchandise inventory (p. 179)

Merchandiser (p. 178)

Multiple-step income statement (p. 191)

Periodic inventory system (pp. 180, 198)

Perpetual inventory system (p. 180)

Purchase discount (p. 181)

Retailer (p. 178)

Sales discount (p. 181)

Selling expenses (p. 191)

Shrinkage (p. 188)

Single-step income statement (p. 192)

Supplementary records (p. 184)

Trade discount (p. 180)

Wholesaler (p. 178)

Multiple Choice Quiz   Answers on p. 221   mhhe.com/wildFAP19e

Additional Quiz Questions are available at the book's Website.

Quiz5

1. A company has $550,000 in net sales and $193,000 in gross profit. This means its cost of goods sold equals
 a. $743,000
 b. $550,000
 c. $357,000
 d. $193,000
 e. $(193,000)

2. A company purchased $4,500 of merchandise on May 1 with terms of 2/10, n/30. On May 6, it returned $250 of that merchandise. On May 8, it paid the balance owed for merchandise, taking any discount it is entitled to. The cash paid on May 8 is
 a. $4,500
 b. $4,250
 c. $4,160
 d. $4,165
 e. $4,410

3. A company has cash sales of $75,000, credit sales of $320,000, sales returns and allowances of $13,700, and sales discounts of $6,000. Its net sales equal
 a. $395,000
 b. $375,300

 c. $300,300
 d. $339,700
 e. $414,700

4. A company's quick assets are $37,500, its current assets are $80,000, and its current liabilities are $50,000. Its acid-test ratio equals
 a. 1.600
 b. 0.750
 c. 0.625
 d. 1.333
 e. 0.469

5. A company's net sales are $675,000, its costs of goods sold are $459,000, and its net income is $74,250. Its gross margin ratio equals
 a. 32%
 b. 68%
 c. 47%
 d. 11%
 e. 34%

Superscript letter ^{A} (^{B}) denotes assignments based on Appendix 5A (5B).

Discussion Questions

1. In comparing the accounts of a merchandising company with those of a service company, what additional accounts would the merchandising company likely use, assuming it employs a perpetual inventory system?

2. What items appear in financial statements of merchandising companies but not in the statements of service companies?

3. ♟ Explain how a business can earn a positive gross profit on its sales and still have a net loss.

4. ♟ Why do companies offer a cash discount?

5. How does a company that uses a perpetual inventory system determine the amount of inventory shrinkage?

6. Distinguish between cash discounts and trade discounts. Is the amount of a trade discount on purchased merchandise recorded in the accounts?

7. What is the difference between a sales discount and a purchase discount?

8. ♟ Why would a company's manager be concerned about the quantity of its purchase returns if its suppliers allow unlimited returns?

9. Does the sender (maker) of a debit memorandum record a debit or a credit in the recipient's account? What entry (debit or credit) does the recipient record?

10. What is the difference between the single-step and multiple-step income statement formats?

11. ♟ Refer to the balance sheet and income statement for **Best Buy** in Appendix A. What does the company title its inventory account? Does the company present a detailed calculation of its cost of goods sold?

12. Refer to **Circuit City**'s balance sheet in Appendix A. What title does it use for cost of goods sold?

13. Refer to the income statement for **RadioShack** in Appendix A. What does RadioShack title its cost of goods sold account?

14. Refer to the income statement of **Apple** in Appendix A. Does its income statement report a gross profit figure? If yes, what is the amount?

15. ♟ Buyers negotiate purchase contracts with suppliers. What type of shipping terms should a buyer attempt to negotiate to minimize freight-in costs?

 Denotes Discussion Questions that involve decision making.

QUICK STUDY

QS 5-1

Recording purchases—
perpetual system   P1

Prepare journal entries to record each of the following purchases transactions of a merchandising company. Show supporting calculations and assume a perpetual inventory system.

Mar. 5   Purchased 1,000 units of product at a cost of $12 per unit. Terms of the sale are 2/10, n/60; the invoice is dated March 5.

Mar. 7   Returned 50 defective units from the March 5 purchase and received full credit.

Mar. 15   Paid the amount due from the March 5 purchase, less the return on March 7.

QS 5-2

Recording sales—
perpetual system

P2

Prepare journal entries to record each of the following sales transactions of a merchandising company. Show supporting calculations and assume a perpetual inventory system.

Apr. 1   Sold merchandise for $5,000, granting the customer terms of 2/10, EOM; invoice dated April 1. The cost of the merchandise is $3,000.

Apr. 4   The customer in the April 1 sale returned merchandise and received credit for $1,000. The merchandise, which had cost $600, is returned to inventory.

Apr. 11   Received payment for the amount due from the April 1 sale less the return on April 4.

QS 5-3

Computing and analyzing
gross margin

C1   A2

Compute net sales, gross profit, and the gross margin ratio for each separate case a through d. Interpret the gross margin ratio for case a.

	a	b	c	d
Sales	$140,000	$378,000	$42,500	$593,000
Sales discounts	1,700	6,000	400	2,500
Sales returns and allowances	9,000	17,000	3,400	15,300
Cost of goods sold	82,493	222,230	28,676	451,532

QS 5-4

Accounting for shrinkage—
perpetual system

P3

Crystal Company's ledger on July 31, its fiscal year-end, includes the following selected accounts that have normal balances (Crystal uses the perpetual inventory system).

Merchandise inventory	$ 42,000	Sales returns and allowances	$ 7,600
B. Crystal, Capital	124,900	Cost of goods sold	115,000
Sales	275,300	Depreciation expense	12,000
Sales discounts	5,200	Salaries expense	45,000
		Miscellaneous expenses	7,000

A physical count of its July 31 year-end inventory discloses that the cost of the merchandise inventory still available is $40,600. Prepare the entry to record any inventory shrinkage.

QS 5-5

Closing entries   P3

Refer to QS 5-4 and prepare journal entries to close the balances in temporary revenue and expense accounts. Remember to consider the entry for shrinkage that is made to solve QS 5-4.

QS 5-6

Computing and interpreting
acid-test ratio

A1

Use the following information on current assets and current liabilities to compute and interpret the acid-test ratio. Explain what the acid-test ratio of a company measures.

Cash	$ 3,000	Prepaid expenses	$ 1,400
Accounts receivable	5,580	Accounts payable	11,500
Inventory	12,000	Other current liabilities	1,700

QS 5-7

Contrasting liquidity ratios   A1

Identify similarities and differences between the acid-test ratio and the current ratio. Compare and describe how the two ratios reflect a company's ability to meet its current obligations.

QS 5-8^A

Contrasting periodic and
perpetual systems

C3

Identify whether each description best applies to a periodic or a perpetual inventory system.

a. Requires an adjusting entry to record inventory shrinkage.

b. Markedly increased in frequency and popularity in business within the past decade.

c. Provides more timely information to managers.

d. Records cost of goods sold each time a sales transaction occurs.

e. Updates the inventory account only at period-end.

Refer to QS 5-1 and prepare journal entries to record each of the merchandising transactions assuming that the periodic inventory system is used.

QS 5-9ᴬ
Recording purchases—
periodic system   P5

Refer to QS 5-2 and prepare journal entries to record each of the merchandising transactions assuming that the periodic inventory system is used.

QS 5-10ᴬ
Recording purchases—
periodic system   P5

McGraw-Hill's
HOMEWORK
MANAGER®   Available with McGraw-Hill's Homework Manager

EXERCISES

Prepare journal entries to record the following transactions for a retail store. Assume a perpetual inventory system.

Apr. 2   Purchased merchandise from Johns Company under the following terms: $5,900 price, invoice dated April 2, credit terms of 2/15, n/60, and FOB shipping point.
      3   Paid $330 for shipping charges on the April 2 purchase.
      4   Returned to Johns Company unacceptable merchandise that had an invoice price of $900.
     17   Sent a check to Johns Company for the April 2 purchase, net of the discount and the returned merchandise.
     18   Purchased merchandise from William Corp. under the following terms: $12,250 price, invoice dated April 18, credit terms of 2/10, n/30, and FOB destination.
     21   After negotiations, received from William a $3,250 allowance on the April 18 purchase.
     28   Sent check to William paying for the April 18 purchase, net of the discount and allowance.

Exercise 5-1
Recording entries for
merchandise purchases

P1

Check April 28, Cr. Cash $8,820

Fortuna Company purchased merchandise for resale from Lemar Company with an invoice price of $30,000 and credit terms of 2/10, n/60. The merchandise had cost Lemar $20,100. Fortuna paid within the discount period. Assume that both buyer and seller use a perpetual inventory system.

1. Prepare entries that the buyer should record for (a) the purchase and (b) the cash payment.
2. Prepare entries that the seller should record for (a) the sale and (b) the cash collection.
3. Assume that the buyer borrowed enough cash to pay the balance on the last day of the discount period at an annual interest rate of 8% and paid it back on the last day of the credit period. Compute how much the buyer saved by following this strategy. (Assume a 365-day year and round dollar amounts to the nearest cent.)

Exercise 5-2
Analyzing and recording
merchandise transactions—
both buyer and seller

P1 P2

Check (3) $278 savings (rounded)

Enter the letter for each term in the blank space beside the definition that it most closely matches.

A. Cash discount   **E.** FOB shipping point   **H.** Purchase discount
B. Credit period   **F.** Gross profit   **I.** Sales discount
C. Discount period   **G.** Merchandise inventory   **J.** Trade discount
D. FOB destination

Exercise 5-3
Applying merchandising terms

C1

_____ **1.** Time period in which a cash discount is available.
_____ **2.** Reduction below list or catalog price that is negotiated in setting the price of goods.
_____ **3.** Reduction in a receivable or payable if it is paid within the discount period.
_____ **4.** Time period that can pass before a customer's payment is due.
_____ **5.** Difference between net sales and the cost of goods sold.
_____ **6.** Ownership of goods is transferred when the seller delivers goods to the carrier.
_____ **7.** Ownership of goods is transferred when delivered to the buyer's place of business.
_____ **8.** Goods a company owns and expects to sell to its customers.
_____ **9.** Purchaser's description of a cash discount received from a supplier of goods.
_____ **10.** Seller's description of a cash discount granted to buyers in return for early payment.

Mechanic Parts was organized on May 1, 2009, and made its first purchase of merchandise on May 3. The purchase was for 1,200 units at a price of $7 per unit. On May 5, Mechanic Parts sold 720 of the units for $11 per unit to Radica Co. Terms of the sale were 2/10, n/60. Prepare entries for Mechanic Parts

Exercise 5-4
Recording sales returns and
allowances   P2

to record the May 5 sale and each of the following separate transactions *a* through *c* using a perpetual inventory system.

a. On May 7, Radica returns 251 units because they did not fit the customer's needs. Mechanic Parts restores the units to its inventory.

b. On May 8, Radica discovers that 60 units are damaged but are still of some use and, therefore, keeps the units. Mechanic Parts sends Radica a credit memorandum for $180 to compensate for the damage.

Check (c) Dr. Sales Returns and Allowances $411

c. On May 15, Radica discovers that 72 units are the wrong color. Radica keeps 43 of these units because Mechanic sends a $92 credit memorandum to compensate. However, Radica returns the remaining 29 units to Mechanic. Mechanic restores the 29 returned units to its inventory.

Exercise 5-5

Recording purchase returns and allowances P1

Refer to Exercise 5-4 and prepare the appropriate journal entries for Radica Co. to record the May 5 purchase and each of the three separate transactions *a* through *c*. Radica is a retailer that uses a perpetual inventory system and purchases these units for resale.

Exercise 5-6

Analyzing and recording merchandise transactions— both buyer and seller

P1 P2

On May 11, York Co. accepts delivery of $38,000 of merchandise it purchases for resale from Troy Corporation. With the merchandise is an invoice dated May 11, with terms of 3/10, n/90, FOB shipping point. The goods cost Troy $25,460. When the goods are delivered, York pays $520 to Express Shipping for delivery charges on the merchandise. On May 12, York returns $2,000 of goods to Troy, who receives them one day later and restores them to inventory. The returned goods had cost Troy $1,393. On May 20, York mails a check to Troy Corporation for the amount owed. Troy receives it the following day. (Both York and Troy use a perpetual inventory system.)

Check (1) May 20, Cr. Cash $34,920

1. Prepare journal entries that York Co. records for these transactions.

2. Prepare journal entries that Troy Corporation records for these transactions.

Exercise 5-7

Sales returns and allowances

C1 P2

Business decision makers desire information on sales returns and allowances. (1) Explain why a company's manager wants the accounting system to record customers' returns of unsatisfactory goods in the Sales Returns and Allowances account instead of the Sales account. (2) Explain whether this information would be useful for external decision makers.

Exercise 5-8

Computing revenues, expenses, and income

C1 C4

Using your accounting knowledge, fill in the blanks in the following separate income statements *a* through *e*. Identify any negative amount by putting it in parentheses.

	a	b	c	d	e
Sales	$82,800	$58,622	$50,094	$?	$32,540
Cost of goods sold					
Merchandise inventory (beginning)	7,866	3,507	10,519	9,902	3,351
Total cost of merchandise purchases	35,439	?	?	45,252	7,439
Merchandise inventory (ending)	?	(3,714)	(12,019)	(9,527)	?
Cost of goods sold	34,950	21,932	?	?	8,359
Gross profit	?	?	4,606	62,013	?
Expenses	9,000	10,650	14,923	32,600	6,100
Net income (loss)	$?	$26,040	$(10,317)	$29,413	$?

Exercise 5-9

Recording effects of merchandising activities

C4

The following supplementary records summarize Tandy Company's merchandising activities for year 2009. Set up T-accounts for Merchandise Inventory and Cost of Goods Sold. Then record the summarized activities in those T-accounts and compute account balances.

Cost of merchandise sold to customers in sales transactions	$296,000
Merchandise inventory, December 31, 2008	42,979
Invoice cost of merchandise purchases	303,459
Shrinkage determined on December 31, 2009	790
Cost of transportation-in	3,034
Cost of merchandise returned by customers and restored to inventory	2,700
Purchase discounts received	2,427
Purchase returns and allowances	3,900

Check Merchandise Inventory Dec. 31, $49,055

The following list includes selected permanent accounts and all of the temporary accounts from the December 31, 2009, unadjusted trial balance of Yamiko Co., a business owned by Kumi Yamiko. Use these account balances along with the additional information to journalize (*a*) adjusting entries and (*b*) closing entries. Yamiko Co. uses a perpetual inventory system.

Exercise 5-10
Preparing adjusting and closing entries for a merchandiser

P3

	Debit	Credit
Merchandise inventory	$ 30,200	
Prepaid selling expenses	4,000	
K. Yamiko, Withdrawals	1,600	
Sales		$543,600
Sales returns and allowances	20,656	
Sales discounts	5,783	
Cost of goods sold	267,451	
Sales salaries expense	59,796	
Utilities expense	17,395	
Selling expenses	46,749	
Administrative expenses	120,135	

Additional Information

Accrued sales salaries amount to $1,700. Prepaid selling expenses of $1,600 have expired. A physical count of year-end merchandise inventory shows $29,626 of goods still available.

Check Entry to close Income Summary: Cr. K. Yamiko, Capital $1,761

A retail company recently completed a physical count of ending merchandise inventory to use in preparing adjusting entries. In determining the cost of the counted inventory, company employees failed to consider that $5,000 of incoming goods had been shipped by a supplier on December 31 under an FOB shipping point agreement. These goods had been recorded in Merchandise Inventory as a purchase, but they were not included in the physical count because they were in transit. Explain how this overlooked fact affects the company's financial statements and the following ratios: return on assets, debt ratio, current ratio, profit margin ratio, and acid-test ratio.

Exercise 5-11
Interpreting a physical count error as inventory shrinkage

A1   A2   P3

Compute the current ratio and acid-test ratio for each of the following separate cases. Which company case is in the best position to meet short-term obligations? Explain.

Exercise 5-12
Computing and analyzing acid-test and current ratios

A1

	Case X	Case Y	Case Z
Cash	$ 920	$ 1,046	$1,220
Short-term investments	0	0	500
Current receivables	0	1,126	890
Inventory	2,300	1,136	4,600
Prepaid expenses	1,200	679	900
Total current assets	$4,420	$3,987	$8,110
Current liabilities	$2,563	$1,281	$4,254

Journalize the following merchandising transactions for Chiller Systems assuming it uses a perpetual inventory system.

Exercise 5-13
Preparing journal entries—perpetual system

P1   P2

1. On November 1, Chiller Systems purchases merchandise for $2,800 on credit with terms of 2/5, n/30, FOB shipping point; invoice dated November 1.

2. On November 5, Chiller Systems pays cash for the November 1 purchase.

3. On November 7, Chiller Systems discovers and returns $100 of defective merchandise purchased on November 1 for a cash refund.

4. On November 10, Chiller Systems pays $140 cash for transportation costs with the November 1 purchase.

5. On November 13, Chiller Systems sells merchandise for $3,024 on credit. The cost of the merchandise is $1,512.

6. On November 16, the customer returns merchandise from the November 13 transaction. The returned items sell for $205 and cost $115.

Exercise 5-14^A
Recording purchases—
periodic system   P5

Refer to Exercise 5-1 and prepare journal entries to record each of the merchandising transactions assuming that the periodic inventory system is used.

Exercise 5-15^A
Recording purchases and
sales—periodic system   P5

Refer to Exercise 5-2 and prepare journal entries to record each of the merchandising transactions assuming that the periodic inventory system is used by both the buyer and the seller. (Skip the part 3 requirement.)

Exercise 5-16^A
Buyer and seller transactions—
periodic system   P5

Refer to Exercise 5-6 and prepare journal entries to record each of the merchandising transactions assuming that the periodic inventory system is used by both the buyer and the seller.

Exercise 5-17^A
Recording purchases—
periodic system   P5

Refer to Exercise 5-13 and prepare journal entries to record each of the merchandising transactions assuming that the periodic inventory system is used.

PROBLEM SET A

Problem 5-1A

Preparing journal entries for
merchandising activities—
perpetual system

P1   P2

Check July 12, Dr. Cash $891
July 16, Cr. Cash $6,336

July 24, Cr. Cash $1,980
July 30, Dr. Cash $990

Prepare journal entries to record the following merchandising transactions of Flora Company, which applies the perpetual inventory system. (*Hint:* It will help to identify each receivable and payable; for example, record the purchase on July 1 in Accounts Payable—Arch.)

July 1 Purchased merchandise from Arch Company for $6,400 under credit terms of 1/15, n/30, FOB shipping point, invoice dated July 1.
      2 Sold merchandise to Driver Co. for $900 under credit terms of 1/10, n/60, FOB shipping point, invoice dated July 2. The merchandise had cost $533.
      3 Paid $130 cash for freight charges on the purchase of July 1.
      8 Sold merchandise that had cost $1,700 for $2,100 cash.
      9 Purchased merchandise from Kew Co. for $2,200 under credit terms of 1/15, n/60, FOB destination, invoice dated July 9.
     11 Received a $200 credit memorandum from Kew Co. for the return of part of the merchandise purchased on July 9.
     12 Received the balance due from Driver Co. for the invoice dated July 2, net of the discount.
     16 Paid the balance due to Arch Company within the discount period.
     19 Sold merchandise that cost $800 to Surtis Co. for $1,200 under credit terms of 1/15, n/60, FOB shipping point, invoice dated July 19.
     21 Issued a $200 credit memorandum to Surtis Co. for an allowance on goods sold on July 19.
     24 Paid Kew Co. the balance due after deducting the discount.
     30 Received the balance due from Surtis Co. for the invoice dated July 19, net of discount.
     31 Sold merchandise that cost $5,200 to Driver Co. for $6,900 under credit terms of 1/10, n/60, FOB shipping point, invoice dated July 31.

Problem 5-2A

Preparing journal entries for
merchandising activities—
perpetual system

P1   P2

Check Aug. 9, Dr. Delivery
Expense, $120

Prepare journal entries to record the following merchandising transactions of Gore Company, which applies the perpetual inventory system. (*Hint:* It will help to identify each receivable and payable; for example, record the purchase on August 1 in Accounts Payable—Arotek.)

Aug. 1 Purchased merchandise from Arotek Company for $7,800 under credit terms of 1/10, n/30, FOB destination, invoice dated August 1.
      4 At Arotek's request, Gore paid $270 cash for freight charges on the August 1 purchase, reducing the amount owed to Arotek.
      5 Sold merchandise to Larton Corp. for $5,460 under credit terms of 2/10, n/60, FOB destination, invoice dated August 5. The merchandise had cost $3,898.
      8 Purchased merchandise from Frees Corporation for $7,100 under credit terms of 1/10, n/45, FOB shipping point, invoice dated August 8. The invoice showed that at Gore's request, Frees paid the $240 shipping charges and added that amount to the bill. (*Hint:* Discounts are not applied to freight and shipping charges.)
      9 Paid $120 cash for shipping charges related to the August 5 sale to Larton Corp.
     10 Larton returned merchandise from the August 5 sale that had cost Gore $649 and been sold for $910. The merchandise was restored to inventory.

12 After negotiations with Frees Corporation concerning problems with the merchandise purchased on August 8, Gore received a credit memorandum from Frees granting a price reduction of $1,100.

15 Received balance due from Larton Corp. for the August 5 sale less the return on August 10.

18 Paid the amount due Frees Corporation for the August 8 purchase less the price reduction granted.

Aug. 18, Cr. Cash $6,180

19 Sold merchandise to Jones Co. for $4,680 under credit terms of 1/10, n/30, FOB shipping point, invoice dated August 19. The merchandise had cost $3,247.

22 Jones requested a price reduction on the August 19 sale because the merchandise did not meet specifications. Gore sent Jones a $780 credit memorandum to resolve the issue.

29 Received Jones's cash payment for the amount due from the August 19 sale.

Aug. 29, Dr. Cash $3,861

30 Paid Arotek Company the amount due from the August 1 purchase.

The following unadjusted trial balance is prepared at fiscal year-end for Helix Company.

Problem 5-3A

Preparing adjusting entries and income statements; and computing gross margin, acid-test, and current ratios

A1 A2 P3 P4

mhhe.com/wildFAP19e

File Edit View Insert Format Tools Data Accounting Window Help			
Σ ƒ ↓ ↓ 100% ▾ Arial ▾ 10 ▾ B I U $ %			
HELIX COMPANY			
Unadjusted Trial Balance			
January 31, 2009			
		Debit	**Credit**
2	Cash	$ 28,750	
3	Merchandise inventory	13,000	
4	Store supplies	5,500	
5	Prepaid insurance	2,400	
6	Store equipment	42,600	
7	Accumulated depreciation—Store equipment		$ 19,750
8	Accounts payable		14,000
9	A. Helix, Capital		39,000
10	A. Helix, Withdrawals	2,000	
11	Sales		115,800
12	Sales discounts	1,900	
13	Sales returns and allowances	2,300	
14	Cost of good sold	38,000	
15	Depreciation expense—Store equipment	0	
16	Salaries expense	27,400	
17	Insurance expense	0	
18	Rent expense	15,000	
19	Store supplies expense	0	
20	Advertising expense	9,700	
21	Totals	$ 188,550	$ 188,550

Sheet1 / Sheet2 / Sheet3 /

Rent expense and salaries expense are equally divided between selling activities and the general and administrative activities. Helix Company uses a perpetual inventory system.

Required

1. Prepare adjusting journal entries to reflect each of the following:

  a. Store supplies still available at fiscal year-end amount to $2,550.

  b. Expired insurance, an administrative expense, for the fiscal year is $1,450.

  c. Depreciation expense on store equipment, a selling expense, is $1,975 for the fiscal year.

  d. To estimate shrinkage, a physical count of ending merchandise inventory is taken. It shows $10,300 of inventory is still available at fiscal year-end.

2. Prepare a multiple-step income statement for fiscal year 2009.

3. Prepare a single-step income statement for fiscal year 2009.

4. Compute the current ratio, acid-test ratio, and gross margin ratio as of January 31, 2009.

Check (2) Gross profit, $70,900;
(3) Total expenses, $99,175; Net income, $12,425

Problem 5-4A
Computing merchandising
amounts and formatting
income statements

C4   P4

Rusio Company's adjusted trial balance on August 31, 2009, its fiscal year-end, follows.

	Debit	Credit
Merchandise inventory	$ 43,500	
Other (noninventory) assets	174,000	
Total liabilities		$ 50,242
C. Rusio, Capital		142,036
C. Rusio, Withdrawals	8,000	
Sales		297,540
Sales discounts	4,552	
Sales returns and allowances	19,637	
Cost of goods sold	114,571	
Sales salaries expense	40,762	
Rent expense—Selling space	13,984	
Store supplies expense	3,570	
Advertising expense	25,290	
Office salaries expense	37,192	
Rent expense—Office space	3,570	
Office supplies expense	1,190	
Totals	$489,818	$489,818

On August 31, 2008, merchandise inventory was $35,104. Supplementary records of merchandising activities for the year ended August 31, 2009, reveal the following itemized costs.

Invoice cost of merchandise purchases	$127,890
Purchase discounts received	2,685
Purchase returns and allowances	6.138
Costs of transportation-in	3,900

Required

1. Compute the company's net sales for the year.

Check (2) $122,967;

(3) Gross profit, $158,780;
Net income, $33,222;

(4) Total expenses, $240,129

2. Compute the company's total cost of merchandise purchased for the year.
3. Prepare a multiple-step income statement that includes separate categories for selling expenses and for general and administrative expenses.
4. Prepare a single-step income statement that includes these expense categories: cost of goods sold, selling expenses, and general and administrative expenses.

Problem 5-5A
Preparing closing entries and
interpreting information about
discounts and returns

C4   P3

Check (1) $33,222 Dr. to close
Income Summary

(3) Current-year rate, 6.6%

Use the data for Rusio Company in Problem 5-4A to complete the following requirements.

Required

1. Prepare closing entries as of August 31, 2009 (the perpetual inventory system is used).

Analysis Component

2. The company makes all purchases on credit, and its suppliers uniformly offer a 3% sales discount. Does it appear that the company's cash management system is accomplishing the goal of taking all available discounts? Explain.
3. In prior years, the company experienced a 4% returns and allowance rate on its sales, which means approximately 4% of its gross sales were eventually returned outright or caused the company to grant allowances to customers. How do this year's results compare to prior years' results?

Refer to the data and information in Problem 5-3A.

Problem 5-6A[B]
Preparing a work sheet for
a merchandiser

Required

Prepare and complete the entire 10-column work sheet for Helix Company. Follow the structure of Exhibit 5B.1 in Appendix 5B.

P3

Prepare journal entries to record the following merchandising transactions of Yarvelle Company, which applies the perpetual inventory system. (*Hint:* It will help to identify each receivable and payable; for example, record the purchase on May 2 in Accounts Payable—Pearl.)

PROBLEM SET B

Problem 5-1B
Preparing journal entries for
merchandising activities—
perpetual system

P1 P2

May	2	Purchased merchandise from Pearl Co. for $6,600 under credit terms of 3/15, n/30, FOB shipping point, invoice dated May 2.
	4	Sold merchandise to Miller Co. for $1,000 under credit terms of 3/10, n/60, FOB shipping point, invoice dated May 4. The merchandise had cost $550.
	5	Paid $120 cash for freight charges on the purchase of May 2.
	9	Sold merchandise that had cost $1,900 for $2,300 cash.
	10	Purchased merchandise from Verte Co. for $2,500 under credit terms of 3/15, n/60, FOB destination, invoice dated May 10.
	12	Received a $500 credit memorandum from Verte Co. for the return of part of the merchandise purchased on May 10.
	14	Received the balance due from Miller Co. for the invoice dated May 4, net of the discount.
	17	Paid the balance due to Pearl Co. within the discount period.
	20	Sold merchandise that cost $800 to Stephen Co. for $1,200 under credit terms of 3/15, n/60, FOB shipping point, invoice dated May 20.
	22	Issued a $100 credit memorandum to Stephen Co. for an allowance on goods sold from May 20.
	25	Paid Verte Co. the balance due after deducting the discount.
	30	Received the balance due from Stephen Co. for the invoice dated May 20, net of discount and allowance.
	31	Sold merchandise that cost $5,400 to Miller Co. for $7,100 under credit terms of 3/10, n/60, FOB shipping point, invoice dated May 31.

Check May 14, Dr. Cash $970
May 17, Cr. Cash $6,402

May 30, Dr. Cash $1,067

Prepare journal entries to record the following merchandising transactions of Allou Company, which applies the perpetual inventory system. (*Hint:* It will help to identify each receivable and payable; for example, record the purchase on July 3 in Accounts Payable—Magar.)

Problem 5-2B
Preparing journal entries for
merchandising activities—
perpetual system

P1 P2

July	3	Purchased merchandise from Magar Corp. for $4,100 under credit terms of 1/10, n/30, FOB destination, invoice dated July 3.
	4	At Magar's request, Allou paid $500 cash for freight charges on the July 3 purchase, reducing the amount owed to Magar.
	7	Sold merchandise to Konop Co. for $2,870 under credit terms of 2/10, n/60, FOB destination, invoice dated July 7. The merchandise had cost $2,049.
	10	Purchased merchandise from Payak Corporation for $3,400 under credit terms of 1/10, n/45, FOB shipping point, invoice dated July 10. The invoice showed that at Allou's request, Payak paid the $240 shipping charges and added that amount to the bill. (*Hint:* Discounts are not applied to freight and shipping charges.)
	11	Paid $120 cash for shipping charges related to the July 7 sale to Konop Co.
	12	Konop returned merchandise from the July 7 sale that had cost Allou $341 and been sold for $470. The merchandise was restored to inventory.
	14	After negotiations with Payak Corporation concerning problems with the merchandise purchased on July 10, Allou received a credit memorandum from Payak granting a price reduction of $500.
	17	Received balance due from Konop Co. for the July 7 sale less the return on July 12.
	20	Paid the amount due Payak Corporation for the July 10 purchase less the price reduction granted.
	21	Sold merchandise to Vescio for $2,460 under credit terms of 1/10, n/30, FOB shipping point, invoice dated July 21. The merchandise had cost $1,707.
	24	Vescio requested a price reduction on the July 21 sale because the merchandise did not meet specifications. Allou sent Vescio a credit memorandum for $360 to resolve the issue.
	30	Received Vescio's cash payment for the amount due from the July 21 sale.
	31	Paid Magar Corp. the amount due from the July 3 purchase.

Check July 17, Dr. Cash $2,344
July 20, Cr. Cash $3,111

July 30, Dr. Cash $2,029

Problem 5-3B

Preparing adjusting entries and
income statements; and
computing gross margin,
acid-test, and current ratios

A1 A2 P3 P4

The following unadjusted trial balance is prepared at fiscal year-end for Giaccio Products Company.

	File Edit View Insert Format Tools Data Accounting Window Help	_|8|x
	🗋 🖾 🖩 🖨 🗅 ❤	∽ ∼	🍇 🥋 Σ *fx* ⅛↓ ⅞↓ 🏢 🤎 ⅘ 100% ▾ 🔊 ‖ Arial ▾ 10 ▾ B I U $ % , ⅞⅞ ⅜⅜	

	GIACCIO PRODUCTS COMPANY Unadjusted Trial Balance October 31, 2009		
1		**Debit**	**Credit**
2	Cash	$ 30,150	
3	Merchandise inventory	13,000	
4	Store supplies	5,300	
5	Prepaid insurance	2,700	
6	Store equipment	42,900	
7	Accumulated depreciation—Store equipment		$ 19,900
8	Accounts payable		15,000
9	G. Giaccio, Capital		38,000
10	G. Giaccio, Withdrawals	2,050	
11	Sales		116,250
12	Sales discounts	1,950	
13	Sales returns and allowances	2,300	
14	Cost of goods sold	39,000	
15	Depreciation expense—Store equipment	0	
16	Salaries expense	26,000	
17	Insurance expense	0	
18	Rent expense	14,000	
19	Store supplies expense	0	
20	Advertising expense	9,800	
21	Totals	$ 189,150	$ 189,150
22			
	◄ ◄ ► ►| Sheet1 ⟨ Sheet2 ⟨ Sheet3 ⟩		

Rent expense and salaries expense are equally divided between selling activities and the general and administrative activities. Giaccio Products Company uses a perpetual inventory system.

Required

1. Prepare adjusting journal entries to reflect each of the following.
   a. Store supplies still available at fiscal year-end amount to $1,650.
   b. Expired insurance, an administrative expense, for the fiscal year is $1,300.
   c. Depreciation expense on store equipment, a selling expense, is $1,990 for the fiscal year.
   d. To estimate shrinkage, a physical count of ending merchandise inventory is taken. It shows $11,600 of inventory is still available at fiscal year-end.

Check (2) Gross profit, $71,600;
(3) Total expenses, $97,140;
Net income, $14,860

2. Prepare a multiple-step income statement for fiscal year 2009.
3. Prepare a single-step income statement for fiscal year 2009.
4. Compute the current ratio, acid-test ratio, and gross margin ratio as of October 31, 2009.

Problem 5-4B

Computing merchandising
amounts and formatting
income statements

C1 C4 P4

Frisco Company's adjusted trial balance on March 31, 2009, its fiscal year-end, follows.

	Debit	Credit
Merchandise inventory	$ 34,500	
Other (noninventory) assets	138,000	
Total liabilities		$ 39,847
N. Frisco, Capital		115,110
N. Frisco, Withdrawals	8,000	

[continued on next page]

[continued from previous page]

Sales		235,980
Sales discounts	3,610	
Sales returns and allowances	15,574	
Cost of goods sold	91,673	
Sales salaries expense	32,329	
Rent expense—Selling space	11,091	
Store supplies expense	2,831	
Advertising expense	20,058	
Office salaries expense	29,497	
Rent expense—Office space	2,831	
Office supplies expense	943	
Totals	$390,937	$390,937

On March 31, 2008, merchandise inventory was $27,841. Supplementary records of merchandising activities for the year ended March 31, 2009, reveal the following itemized costs.

Invoice cost of merchandise purchases	$101,430
Purchase discounts received	2,130
Purchase returns and allowances	4,868
Costs of transportation-in	3,900

Required

1. Calculate the company's net sales for the year.
2. Calculate the company's total cost of merchandise purchased for the year.
3. Prepare a multiple-step income statement that includes separate categories for selling expenses and for general and administrative expenses.
4. Prepare a single-step income statement that includes these expense categories: cost of goods sold, selling expenses, and general and administrative expenses.

Check (2) $98,332;

(3) Gross profit, $125,123; Net income, $25,543;

(4) Total expenses, $191,253

Use the data for Frisco Company in Problem 5-4B to complete the following requirements.

Required

1. Prepare closing entries as of March 31, 2009 (the perpetual inventory system is used).

Analysis Component

2. The company makes all purchases on credit, and its suppliers uniformly offer a 3% sales discount. Does it appear that the company's cash management system is accomplishing the goal of taking all available discounts? Explain.
3. In prior years, the company experienced a 5% returns and allowance rate on its sales, which means approximately 5% of its gross sales were eventually returned outright or caused the company to grant allowances to customers. How do this year's results compare to prior years' results?

Problem 5-5B
Preparing closing entries and interpreting information about discounts and returns

C4 P3

Check (1) $25,543 Dr. to close Income Summary

(3) Current-year rate, 6.6%

Refer to the data and information in Problem 5-3B.

Required

Prepare and complete the entire 10-column work sheet for Giaccio Products Company. Follow the structure of Exhibit 5B.1 in Appendix 5B.

Problem 5-6B[B]
Preparing a work sheet for a merchandiser

P3

SERIAL PROBLEM

Success Systems

(This serial problem began in Chapter 1 and continues through most of the book. If previous chapter segments were not completed, the serial problem can begin at this point. It is helpful, but not necessary, to use the Working Papers that accompany the book.)

SP 5   Adriana Lopez created Success Systems on October 1, 2009. The company has been successful, and its list of customers has grown. To accommodate the growth, the accounting system is modified to set up separate accounts for each customer. The following chart of accounts includes the account number used for each account and any balance as of December 31, 2009. Lopez decided to add a fourth digit with a decimal point to the 106 account number that had been used for the single Accounts Receivable account. This change allows the company to continue using the existing chart of accounts.

No.	Account Title	Dr.	Cr.
101	Cash	$58,160	
106.1	Alex's Engineering Co.	0	
106.2	Wildcat Services	0	
106.3	Easy Leasing	0	
106.4	IFM Co.	3,000	
106.5	Liu Corp.	0	
106.6	Gomez Co.	2,668	
106.7	Delta Co.	0	
106.8	KC, Inc.	0	
106.9	Dream, Inc.	0	
119	Merchandise inventory	0	
126	Computer supplies	580	
128	Prepaid insurance	1,665	
131	Prepaid rent	825	
163	Office equipment	8,000	
164	Accumulated depreciation—Office equipment		400
167	Computer equipment	20,000	
168	Accumulated depreciation—Computer equipment		1,250
201	Accounts payable		1,100

No.	Account Title	Dr.	Cr.
210	Wages payable		500
236	Unearned computer services revenue		1,500
301	A. Lopez, Capital		90,148
302	A. Lopez, Withdrawals	0	
403	Computer services revenue		0
413	Sales		0
414	Sales returns and allowances	0	
415	Sales discounts	0	
502	Cost of goods sold	0	
612	Depreciation expense—Office equipment	0	
613	Depreciation expense—Computer equipment	0	
623	Wages expense	0	
637	Insurance expense	0	
640	Rent expense	0	
652	Computer supplies expense	0	
655	Advertising expense	0	
676	Mileage expense	0	
677	Miscellaneous expenses	0	
684	Repairs expense—Computer	0	

In response to requests from customers, Lopez will begin selling computer software. The company will extend credit terms of 1/10, n/30, FOB shipping point, to all customers who purchase this merchandise. However, no cash discount is available on consulting fees. Additional accounts (Nos. 119, 413, 414, 415, and 502) are added to its general ledger to accommodate the company's new merchandising activities. Also, Success Systems does not use reversing entries and, therefore, all revenue and expense accounts have zero beginning balances as of January 1, 2010. Its transactions for January through March follow:

Jan. 4 The company paid cash to Lyn Addie for five days' work at the rate of $125 per day. Four of the five days relate to wages payable that were accrued in the prior year.

5 Adriana Lopez invested an additional $25,000 cash in the company.

7 The company purchased $5,800 of merchandise from Kansas Corp. with terms of 1/10, n/30, FOB shipping point, invoice dated January 7.

9 The company received $2,668 cash from Gomez Co. as full payment on its account.

Check Jan. 11, Dr. Unearned Computer Services Revenue $1,500

11 The company completed a five-day project for Alex's Engineering Co. and billed it $5,500, which is the total price of $7,000 less the advance payment of $1,500.

13 The company sold merchandise with a retail value of $5,200 and a cost of $3,560 to Liu Corp., invoice dated January 13.

15 The company paid $600 cash for freight charges on the merchandise purchased on January 7.

16   The company received $4,000 cash from Delta Co. for computer services provided.

17   The company paid Kansas Corp. for the invoice dated January 7, net of the discount.

20   Liu Corp. returned $500 of defective merchandise from its invoice dated January 13. The re-   **Check**   Jan. 20, No entry to Cost of
turned merchandise, which had a $320 cost, is discarded. (The policy of Success Systems is   Goods Sold
to leave the cost of defective products in cost of goods sold.)

22   The company received the balance due from Liu Corp., net of both the discount and the credit
for the returned merchandise.

24   The company returned defective merchandise to Kansas Corp. and accepted a credit against
future purchases. The defective merchandise invoice cost, net of the discount, was $496.

26   The company purchased $9,000 of merchandise from Kansas Corp. with terms of 1/10, n/30,
FOB destination, invoice dated January 26.

26   The company sold merchandise with a $4,640 cost for $5,800 on credit to KC, Inc., invoice
dated January 26.

29   The company received a $496 credit memorandum from Kansas Corp. concerning the mer-
chandise returned on January 24.

31   The company paid cash to Lyn Addie for 10 days' work at $125 per day.

Feb. 1   The company paid $2,475 cash to Hillside Mall for another three months' rent in advance.

3   The company paid Kansas Corp. for the balance due, net of the cash discount, less the $496
amount in the credit memorandum.

5   The company paid $600 cash to the local newspaper for an advertising insert in today's paper.

11   The company received the balance due from Alex's Engineering Co. for fees billed on January 11.

15   Adriana Lopez withdrew $4,800 cash from the company for personal use.

23   The company sold merchandise with a $2,660 cost for $3,220 on credit to Delta Co., invoice
dated February 23.

26   The company paid cash to Lyn Addie for eight days' work at $125 per day.

27   The company reimbursed Adriana Lopez for business automobile mileage (600 miles at $0.32
per mile).

Mar. 8   The company purchased $2,730 of computer supplies from Harris Office Products on credit,
invoice dated March 8.

9   The company received the balance due from Delta Co. for merchandise sold on February 23.

11   The company paid $960 cash for minor repairs to the company's computer.

16   The company received $5,260 cash from Dream, Inc., for computing services provided.

19   The company paid the full amount due to Harris Office Products, consisting of amounts created on December 15 (of $1,100) and March 8.

24   The company billed Easy Leasing for $8,900 of computing services provided.

25   The company sold merchandise with a $2,002 cost for $2,800 on credit to Wildcat Services,
invoice dated March 25.

30   The company sold merchandise with a $1,100 cost for $2,220 on credit to IFM Company, invoice dated March 30.

31   The company reimbursed Adriana Lopez for business automobile mileage (400 miles at $0.32
per mile).

The following additional facts are available for preparing adjustments on March 31 prior to financial
statement preparation:

a. The March 31 amount of computer supplies still available totals $2,005.

b. Three more months have expired since the company purchased its annual insurance policy at a $2,220
cost for 12 months of coverage.

c. Lyn Addie has not been paid for seven days of work at the rate of $125 per day.

d. Three months have passed since any prepaid rent has been transferred to expense. The monthly rent
expense is $825.

e. Depreciation on the computer equipment for January 1 through March 31 is $1,250.

f. Depreciation on the office equipment for January 1 through March 31 is $400.

g. The March 31 amount of merchandise inventory still available totals $704.

Required

1. Prepare journal entries to record each of the January through March transactions.

2. Post the journal entries in part 1 to the accounts in the company's general ledger. (*Note:* Begin with   **Check**   (2) Ending balances: Cash,
the ledger's post-closing adjusted balances as of December 31, 2009.) $77,845; Sales, $19,240;

(3) Unadj. totals, $161,198;
    Adj. totals, $163,723;

3. Prepare a partial work sheet consisting of the first six columns (similar to the one shown in Exhibit 5B.1) that includes the unadjusted trial balance, the March 31 adjustments (*a*) through (*g*), and the adjusted trial balance. Do not prepare closing entries and do not journalize the adjustments or post them to the ledger.

(4) Net income, $18,686;

4. Prepare an income statement (from the adjusted trial balance in part 3) for the three months ended March 31, 2010. Use a single-step format. List all expenses without differentiating between selling expenses and general and administrative expenses.

(5) A. Lopez, Capital
    (3/31/10), $129,034;

5. Prepare a statement of owner's equity (from the adjusted trial balance in part 3) for the three months ended March 31, 2010.

(6) Total assets, $129,909

6. Prepare a classified balance sheet (from the adjusted trial balance) as of March 31, 2010.

BEYOND THE NUMBERS

REPORTING IN ACTION

C4 A1

BTN 5-1   Refer to Best Buy's financial statements in Appendix A to answer the following.

Required

1. Assume that the amounts reported for inventories and cost of sales reflect items purchased in a form ready for resale. Compute the net cost of goods purchased for the fiscal year ended March 3, 2007.

2. Compute the current ratio and acid-test ratio as of March 3, 2007, and February 25, 2006. Interpret and comment on the ratio results. How does Best Buy compare to the industry average of 1.6 for the current ratio and 0.7 for the acid-test ratio?

Fast Forward

3. Access Best Buy's financial statements (form 10-K) for fiscal years ending after March 3, 2007, from its Website (BestBuy.com) or the SEC's EDGAR database (www.SEC.gov). Recompute and interpret the current ratio and acid-test ratio for these current fiscal years.

COMPARATIVE ANALYSIS

A2

BTN 5-2   Key comparative figures for both Best Buy, Circuit City, and RadioShack follow.

($ millions)	Best Buy		Circuit City		RadioShack	
	Current Year	Prior Year	Current Year	Prior Year	Current Year	Prior Year
Revenues (net sales)	$35,934	$30,848	$12,430	$11,514	$4,778	$5,082
Cost of sales	27,165	23,122	9,501	8,704	2,544	2,706

Required

1. Compute the dollar amount of gross margin and the gross margin ratio for the two years shown for each of these companies.

2. Which company earns more in gross margin for each dollar of net sales? How do they compare to the industry average of 27.5%?

3. Did the gross margin ratio improve or decline for these companies?

ETHICS CHALLENGE

C1 P2

BTN 5-3   Ashton Martin is a student who plans to attend approximately four professional events a year at her college. Each event necessitates a financial outlay of $100 to $200 for a new suit and accessories. After incurring a major hit to her savings for the first event, Ashton developed a different approach. She buys the suit on credit the week before the event, wears it to the event, and returns it the next week to the store for a full refund on her charge card.

Required

1. Comment on the ethics exhibited by Ashton and possible consequences of her actions.

2. How does the merchandising company account for the suits that Ashton returns?

BTN 5-4   You are the financial officer for Music Plus, a retailer that sells goods for home entertainment needs. The business owner, Jamie Madsen, recently reviewed the annual financial statements you prepared and sent you an e-mail stating that he thinks you overstated net income. He explains that although he has invested a great deal in security, he is sure shoplifting and other forms of inventory shrinkage have occurred, but he does not see any deduction for shrinkage on the income statement. The store uses a perpetual inventory system.

COMMUNICATING IN PRACTICE

C3 C4 P3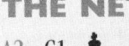

Required

Prepare a brief memorandum that responds to the owner's concerns.

BTN 5-5   Access the SEC's EDGAR database (www.sec.gov) and obtain the April 19, 2007, filing of its fiscal 2007 10-K report (for year ended February 3, 2007) for J. Crew Group, Inc.

TAKING IT TO THE NET

A2 C1

Required

Prepare a table that reports the gross margin ratios for J. Crew using the revenues and cost of goods sold data from J. Crew's income statement for each of its most recent three years. Analyze and comment on the trend in its gross margin ratio.

BTN 5-6   Best Brands' general ledger and supplementary records at the end of its current period reveal the following.

TEAMWORK IN ACTION

C1 C4

Sales	$600,000	Merchandise inventory (beginning of period)	$ 98,000
Sales returns	20,000	Invoice cost of merchandise purchases	360,000
Sales discounts	13,000	Purchase discounts received	9,000
Cost of transportation-in	22,000	Purchase returns and allowances	11,000
Operating expenses	50,000	Merchandise inventory (end of period)	84,000

Required

1. *Each* member of the team is to assume responsibility for computing *one* of the following items. You are not to duplicate your teammates' work. Get any necessary amounts to compute your item from the appropriate teammate. Each member is to explain his or her computation to the team in preparation for reporting to the class.

   a. Net sales   **d.** Gross profit

   b. Total cost of merchandise purchases   **e.** Net income

   c. Cost of goods sold

Point: In teams of four, assign the same student *a* and *e*. Rotate teams for reporting on a different computation and the analysis in step 3.

2. Check your net income with the instructor. If correct, proceed to step 3.

3. Assume that a physical inventory count finds that actual ending inventory is $76,000. Discuss how this affects previously computed amounts in step 1.

**ENTREPRENEURIAL
DECISION**

C1 C4 P4

BTN 5-7   Refer to the opening feature about BigBadToyStore. Assume that Joel Boblit reports current annual sales at approximately $10 million and discloses the following income statement.

BigBadToyStore Income Statement For Year Ended January 31, 2008	
Net sales	$10,000,000
Cost of sales	6,100,000
Expenses (other than cost of sales)	2,000,000
Net income	$ 1,900,000

Joel Boblit sells to various individuals and retailers, ranging from small shops to large chains. Assume that Joel currently offers credit terms of 1/15, n/60, and ships FOB destination. To improve his cash flow, Joel is considering changing his credit terms to 3/10, n/30. In addition, he proposes to change his shipping terms to FOB shipping point. He expects that the increase in discount rate will increase his net sales by 9%, but his gross margin ratio (and ratio of cost of sales divided by net sales) is expected to remain unchanged. He also expects that his delivery expenses will be zero under this proposal; thus, his expenses other than cost of sales are expected to increase only 6%.

Required

1. Prepare a forecasted income statement for the year ended January 31, 2009, based on the proposal.
2. Based on the forecasted income statement alone (from your part 1 solution), do you recommend that Joel implement the new sales policies? Explain.
3. What else should Joel consider before he decides whether or not to implement the new policies? Explain.

HITTING THE ROAD

C1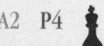

Point: This activity complements the Ethics Challenge assignment.

BTN 5-8   Arrange an interview (in person or by phone) with the manager of a retail shop in a mall or in the downtown area of your community. Explain to the manager that you are a student studying merchandising activities and the accounting for sales returns and sales allowances. Ask the manager what the store policy is regarding returns. Also find out if sales allowances are ever negotiated with customers. Inquire whether management perceives that customers are abusing return policies and what actions management takes to counter potential abuses. Be prepared to discuss your findings in class.

GLOBAL DECISION

A2 P4

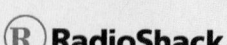

BTN 5-9   DSG (www.DSGiplc.com), Best Buy, Circuit City, and RadioShack are all competitors in the global marketplace. Key comparative figures for each company follow.

	Net Sales	Cost of Sales
DSG*	£ 7,930	£ 7,285
Best Buy†	$35,934	$27,165
Circuit City†	$12,430	$ 9,501
RadioShack†	$ 4,778	$ 2,544

* £ millions for DSG.

† $ millions for Best Buy, Circuit City, and RadioShack.

Required

1. Rank the four companies (highest to lowest) based on the gross margin ratio.
2. Which of the companies uses a multiple-step income statement format? (Access DSG's annual report from its Website to answer this; the other three companies' reports are in Appendix A.)
3. Which company's income statement would likely be most easily interpreted by potential investors? Provide a brief justification for your choice.

ANSWERS TO MULTIPLE CHOICE QUIZ

1. c; Gross profit = $550,000 − $193,000 = $357,000

2. d; ($4,500 − $250) × (100% − 2%) = $4,165

3. b; Net sales = $75,000 + $320,000 − $13,700 − $6,000 = $375,300

4. b; Acid-test ratio = $37,500/$50,000 = 0.750

5. a; Gross margin ratio = ($675,000 − $459,000)/$675,000 = 32%

A Look Back

Chapter 5 focused on merchandising activities and how they are reported. We analyzed and recorded purchases and sales and explained accounting adjustments and closing for merchandisers.

 A Look at This Chapter

This chapter emphasizes accounting for inventory. We describe methods for assigning costs to inventory and we explain the items and costs making up merchandise inventory. We also discuss methods of estimating and measuring inventory.

A Look Ahead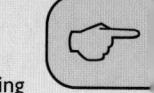

Chapter 7 emphasizes accounting information systems. We describe system principles, the system components, use of special journals and subsidiary ledgers, and technology-based systems.

6

Chapter

Inventories and Cost of Sales

Learning Objectives

CAP

Conceptual

C1 Identify the items making up merchandise inventory. (p. 224)

C2 Identify the costs of merchandise inventory. (p. 225)

Analytical

A1 Analyze the effects of inventory methods for both financial and tax reporting. (p. 232)

A2 Analyze the effects of inventory errors on current and future financial statements. (p. 235)

A3 Assess inventory management using both inventory turnover and days' sales in inventory. (p. 236)

LP6

Procedural

P1 Compute inventory in a perpetual system using the methods of specific identification, FIFO, LIFO, and weighted average. (p. 226)

P2 Compute the lower of cost or market amount of inventory. (p. 233)

P3 *Appendix 6A*—Compute inventory in a periodic system using the methods of specific identification, FIFO, LIFO, and weighted average. (p. 242)

P4 *Appendix 6B*—Apply both the retail inventory and gross profit methods to estimate inventory. (p. 247)

Scent of Success

"Believe in yourself, your product and services"
—Jacquelyn Tran

HUNTINGTON BEACH, CA—As U.S. immigrants, Jacquelyn Tran and her family had no money and did not speak English. "They [her family] took the risk," explains Jacquelyn, in the hope of opportunity. A few years passed and Jacquelyn caught a glimpse of her future. "I saw an opportunity to take . . . the retail perfume business to the next level." She launched **Beauty Encounter (BeautyEncounter.com)** to provide perfume and beauty products to consumers.

The entrepreneurial road was rough at times. Jacquelyn struggled with inventory and sales, and had to deal with discounts, returns, and allowances. A major challenge was maintaining appropriate inventories while controlling costs. "I made plenty of mistakes," admits Jacquelyn. "I just had to throw myself in there and learn."

Learn she did. Applying modern inventory management, and trial and error, Jacquelyn learned to fill orders, collect money, and stock the right inventory. "We have something for everyone," explains Jacquelyn, and her perpetual inventory system accounts for inventory sales and purchases in real time. "It's really important for customers to be able to find products . . . [and for me] to give them what they want."

But business success requires more than good products and perpetual inventory management, insists Jacquelyn. "[It] requires a lot of patience, energy and faith." We focus on customer satisfaction, says Jacquelyn. As a result, "we have very loyal customers."

Although Jacquelyn continues to measure, monitor, and manage inventories and costs, her success and growth are pushing her to a more managerial role. "We are moving into a larger warehouse, allowing us to expand our selection," explains Jacquelyn. Her inventory procedures contribute to her success and allow her customers to know which products are hot. "I never imagined I would be where I am today," says Jacquelyn. "It is really cool."

[Sources: *Beauty Encounter Website,* January 2009; *USA Today,* April 2008; *CNN Money,* June 2005; *Inc.com,* July 2007; *Entrepreneur,* December 2007; *MyWomanOwnedBusiness.com,* August 2007]

Merchandisers' activities include the purchasing and reselling of merchandise. We explained accounting for merchandisers in Chapter 5, including that for purchases and sales. In this chapter, we extend the study and analysis of inventory by explaining the methods used to assign costs to merchandise inventory *and* to cost of goods sold. Retailers, wholesalers, and other merchandising companies that purchase products for resale use the principles and methods described here. Understanding inventory accounting helps in the analysis and interpretation of financial statements and helps people run their businesses.

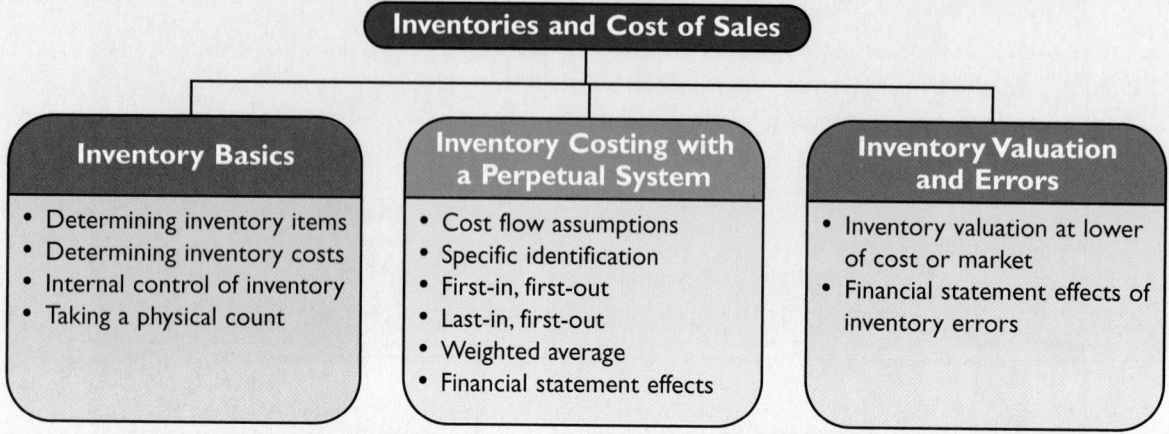

Inventory Basics

This section identifies the items and costs making up merchandise inventory. It also describes the importance of internal controls in taking a physical count of inventory.

Determining Inventory Items

C1 Identify the items making up merchandise inventory.

Merchandise inventory includes all goods that a company owns and holds for sale. This rule holds regardless of where the goods are located when inventory is counted. Certain inventory items require special attention, including goods in transit, goods on consignment, and goods that are damaged or obsolete.

Goods in Transit Does a purchaser's inventory include goods in transit from a supplier? The answer is that if ownership has passed to the purchaser, the goods are included in the purchaser's inventory. We determine this by reviewing the shipping terms: *FOB destination* or *FOB shipping point*. If the purchaser is responsible for paying freight, ownership passes when goods are loaded on the transport vehicle. If the seller is responsible for paying freight, ownership passes when goods arrive at their destination.

Goods on Consignment Goods on consignment are goods shipped by the owner, called the **consignor,** to another party, the **consignee.** A consignee sells goods for the owner. The consignor continues to own the consigned goods and reports them in its inventory. **Upper Deck,** for instance, pays sports celebrities such as Tiger Woods to sign memorabilia, which are offered to shopping networks on consignment. Upper Deck, the consignor, must report these items in its inventory until sold.

Goods Damaged or Obsolete Damaged and obsolete (and deteriorated) goods are not counted in inventory if they cannot be sold. If these goods can be sold at a reduced price, they are included in inventory at a conservative estimate of their **net realizable value.** Net realizable value is sales price minus the cost of making the sale. The period when damage or obsolescence (or deterioration) occurs is the period when the loss in value is reported.

Decision Insight

A wireless portable device with a two-way radio allows clerks to quickly record inventory by scanning bar codes and to instantly send and receive inventory data. It gives managers access to up-to-date information on inventory and its location.

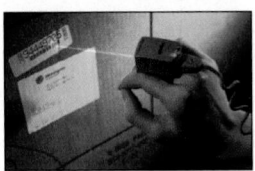

Determining Inventory Costs

Merchandise inventory includes costs of expenditures necessary, directly or indirectly, to bring an item to a salable condition and location. This means that the cost of an inventory item includes its invoice cost minus any discount, and plus any incidental costs necessary to put it in a place and condition for sale. Incidental costs can include import duties, freight, storage, insurance, and costs incurred in an aging process (for example, aging wine or cheese).

   Accounting principles prescribe that incidental costs be added to inventory. Also, the *matching principle* states that inventory costs should be recorded against revenue in the period when inventory is sold. However, some companies use the *materiality constraint (cost-to-benefit constraint)* to avoid assigning some incidental costs of acquiring merchandise to inventory. Instead, they expense them when incurred. These companies argue either that those incidental costs are immaterial or that the effort in assigning them outweighs the benefit.

> **C2**   Identify the costs of merchandise inventory.

Internal Controls and Taking a Physical Count

The Inventory account under a perpetual system is updated for each purchase and sale, but events can cause the Inventory account balance to differ from the actual inventory available. Such events include theft, loss, damage, and errors. Thus, nearly all companies take a *physical count of inventory* at least once each year—informally called *taking an inventory*. This often occurs at the end of a fiscal year or when inventory amounts are low. This physical count is used to adjust the Inventory account balance to the actual inventory available.

   A company applies internal controls when taking a physical count of inventory that usually includes the following:

- *Prenumbered inventory tickets* are prepared and distributed to the *counters*—each ticket must be accounted for.
- Counters of inventory are assigned and do not include those responsible for inventory.
- Counters confirm the validity of inventory, including its existence, amount, and quality.
- A second count is taken by a different counter.
- A manager confirms that all inventories are ticketed once, and only once.

> **Point:** The Inventory account is a controlling account for the inventory subsidiary ledger. This *subsidiary ledger* contains a separate record (units and costs) for each separate product, and it can be in electronic or paper form. Subsidiary records assist managers in planning and monitoring inventory.

Quick Check   Answers—p. 250

1. What accounting principle most guides the allocation of cost of goods available for sale between ending inventory and cost of goods sold?

2. If Skechers sells goods to Target with terms FOB shipping point, which company reports these goods in its inventory while they are in transit?

3. An art gallery purchases a painting for $11,400 on terms FOB shipping point. Additional costs in obtaining and offering the artwork for sale include $130 for transportation in, $150 for import duties, $100 for insurance during shipment, $180 for advertising, $400 for framing, and $800 for office salaries. For computing inventory, what cost is assigned to the painting?

Inventory Costing Under a Perpetual System

Accounting for inventory affects both the balance sheet and the income statement. A major goal in accounting for inventory is to properly match costs with sales. We use the *matching principle* to decide how much of the cost of the goods available for sale is deducted from sales and how much is carried forward as inventory and matched against future sales.

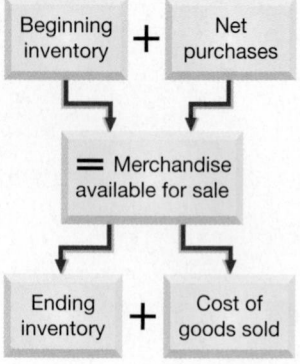

Video6.1

Management decisions in accounting for inventory involve the following:

- Items included in inventory and their costs.
- Costing method (specific identification, FIFO, LIFO, or weighted average).
- Inventory system (perpetual or periodic).
- Use of market values or other estimates.

The first point was explained on the prior two pages. The second and third points will be addressed now. The fourth point is the focus at the end of this chapter. Decisions on these points affect the reported amounts for inventory, cost of goods sold, gross profit, income, current assets, and other accounts.

One of the most important issues in accounting for inventory is determining the per unit costs assigned to inventory items. When all units are purchased at the same unit cost, this process is simple. When identical items are purchased at different costs, however, a question arises as to which amounts to record in cost of goods sold and which amounts remain in inventory.

Four methods are commonly used to assign costs to inventory and to cost of goods sold: (1) specific identification; (2) first-in, first-out; (3) last-in, first-out; and (4) weighted average. Exhibit 6.1 shows the frequency in the use of these methods.

EXHIBIT 6.1

Frequency in Use of Inventory Methods

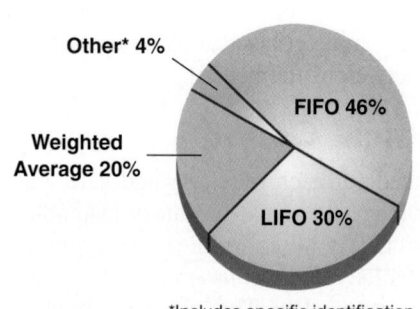

Other* 4%
FIFO 46%
Weighted Average 20%
LIFO 30%

*Includes specific identification.

Each method assumes a particular pattern for how costs flow through inventory. Each of these four methods is acceptable whether or not the actual physical flow of goods follows the cost flow assumption. Physical flow of goods depends on the type of product and the way it is stored. (Perishable goods such as fresh fruit demand that a business attempt to sell them in a first-in, first-out physical flow. Other products such as crude oil and minerals such as coal, gold, and decorative stone can be sold in a last-in, first-out physical flow.) **Physical flow and cost flow need not be the same.**

Inventory Cost Flow Assumption

P1 Compute inventory in a perpetual system using the methods of specific identification, FIFO, LIFO, and weighted average.

Point: It is helpful to recall the cost flow of inventory from Exhibit 5.4.

Beginning inventory + Net purchases

= Merchandise available for sale

Ending inventory + Cost of goods sold

This section introduces inventory cost flow assumptions. For this purpose, assume that three identical units are purchased separately at the following three dates and costs: May 1 at $45, May 3 at $65, and May 6 at $70. One unit is then sold on May 7 for $100. Exhibit 6.2 gives a visual layout of the flow of costs to either the gross profit section of the income statement or the inventory reported on the balance sheet for FIFO, LIFO, and weighted average.

(1) *FIFO assumes costs flow in the order incurred.* The unit purchased on May 1 for $45 is the earliest cost incurred—it is sent to cost of goods sold on the income statement first. The remaining two units ($65 and $70) are reported in inventory on the balance sheet.

(2) *LIFO assumes costs flow in the reverse order incurred.* The unit purchased on May 6 for $70 is the most recent cost incurred—it is sent to cost of goods sold on the income statement. The remaining two units ($45 and $65) are reported in inventory on the balance sheet.

(3) *Weighted average assumes costs flow at an average of the costs available.* The units available at the May 7 sale average $60 in cost, computed as ($45 + $65 + $70)/3. One unit's $60 average cost is sent to cost of goods sold on the income statement. The remaining two units' average costs are reported in inventory at $120 on the balance sheet.

Cost flow assumptions can markedly impact gross profit and inventory numbers. Exhibit 6.2 shows that gross profit as a percent of net sales ranges from 30% to 55% due to nothing else but the cost flow assumption.

The following sections on inventory costing use the perpetual system. Appendix 6A uses the periodic system. An instructor can choose to cover either one or both systems. If the perpetual system is skipped, then read Appendix 6A and return to the section (seven pages ahead) titled "Valuing Inventory at LCM and ..."

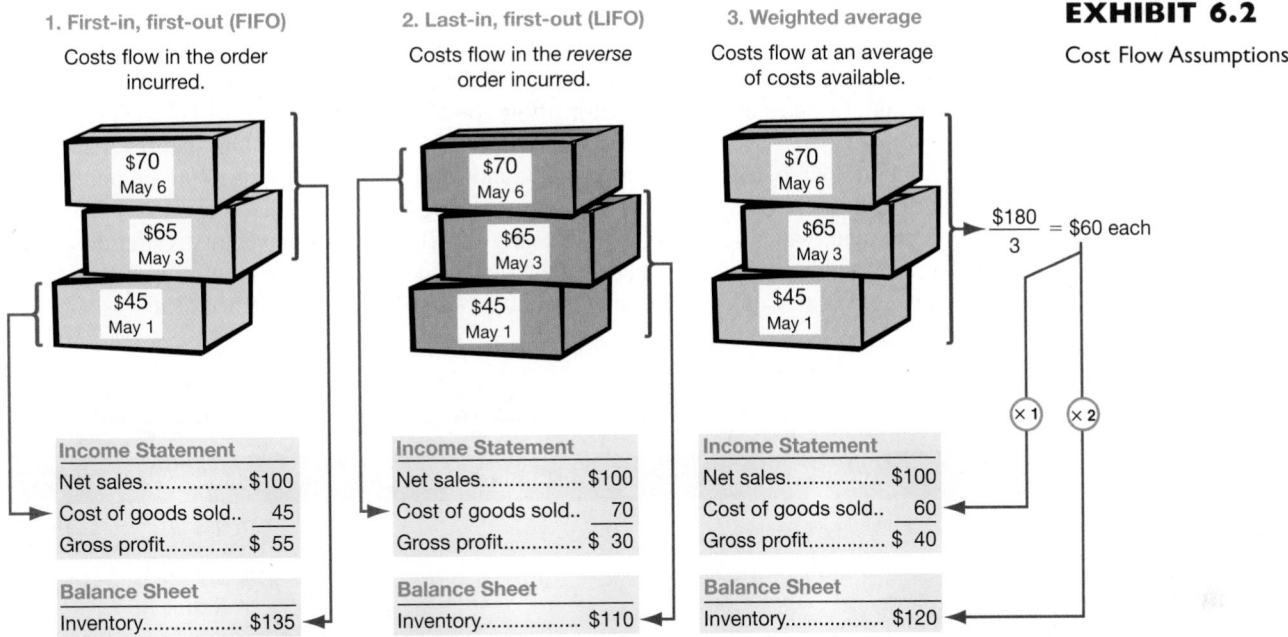

EXHIBIT 6.2

Cost Flow Assumptions

Inventory Costing Illustration

This section provides a comprehensive illustration of inventory costing methods. We use information from Trekking, a sporting goods store. Among its many products, Trekking carries one type of mountain bike whose sales are directed at resorts that provide inexpensive mountain bikes for complimentary guest use. Its customers usually purchase in amounts of 10 or more bikes. We use Trekking's data from August. Its mountain bike (unit) inventory at the beginning of August and its purchases and sales during August are shown in Exhibit 6.3. It ends August with 12 bikes remaining in inventory.

Date	Activity	Units Acquired at Cost	Units Sold at Retail	Unit Inventory
Aug. 1	Beginning inventory	10 units @ $ 91 = $ 910		10 units
Aug. 3	Purchases	15 units @ $106 = $1,590		25 units
Aug. 14	Sales		20 units @ $130	5 units
Aug. 17	Purchases	20 units @ $115 = $2,300		25 units
Aug. 28	Purchases	10 units @ $119 = $1,190		35 units
Aug. 31	Sales		23 units @ $150	12 units
	Totals	55 units $5,990	43 units	

EXHIBIT 6.3

Purchases and Sales of Goods

Trekking uses the perpetual inventory system, which means that its merchandise inventory account is continually updated to reflect purchases and sales. (**Appendix 6A describes the assignment of costs to inventory using a periodic system.**) Regardless of what inventory method or system is used, cost of goods available for sale must be allocated between cost of goods sold and ending inventory.

Point: The perpetual inventory system is now the most dominant system for U.S. businesses.

Point: Cost of goods sold plus ending inventory equals cost of goods available for sale.

Specific Identification

When each item in inventory can be identified with a specific purchase and invoice, we can use **specific identification** (also called *specific invoice inventory pricing*) to assign costs. We also need sales records that identify exactly which items were sold and when. Trekking's internal documents reveal the following specific unit sales:

August 14   Sold 8 bikes costing $91 each and 12 bikes costing $106 each
August 31   Sold 2 bikes costing $91 each, 3 bikes costing $106 each, 15 bikes
             costing $115 each, and 3 bikes costing $119 each

Point: Three key variables determine the dollar value of ending inventory: (1) inventory quantity, (2) costs of inventory, and (3) cost flow assumption.

Applying specific identification, and using the information above and from Exhibit 6.3, we prepare Exhibit 6.4. This exhibit starts with 10 bikes at $91 each in beginning inventory. On August 3, 15 more bikes are purchased at $106 each for $1,590. Inventory available now consists of 10 bikes at $91 each and 15 bikes at $106 each, for a total of $2,500. On August 14 (see sales above), 20 bikes costing $2,000 are sold—leaving 5 bikes costing $500 in inventory. On August 17, 20 bikes costing $2,300 are purchased, and on August 28, another 10 bikes costing $1,190 are purchased, for a total of 35 bikes costing $3,990 in inventory. On August 31 (see sales above), 23 bikes costing $2,582 are sold, which leaves 12 bikes costing $1,408 in ending inventory. Carefully study this exhibit and the boxed explanations to see the flow of costs both in and out of inventory. Each unit, whether sold or remaining in inventory, has its own specific cost attached to it.

EXHIBIT 6.4

Specific Identification Computations

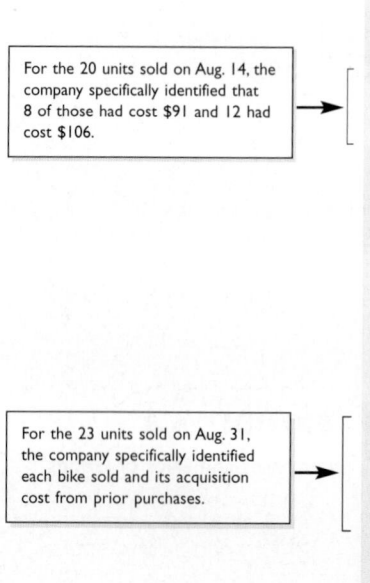

For the 20 units sold on Aug. 14, the company specifically identified that 8 of those had cost $91 and 12 had cost $106.

For the 23 units sold on Aug. 31, the company specifically identified each bike sold and its acquisition cost from prior purchases.

"goods in"   "goods out"   "what's left"

Date	Goods Purchased	Cost of Goods Sold	Inventory Balance
Aug. 1	Beginning balance		10 @ $ 91 = $ 910
Aug. 3	15 @ $106 = $1,590		10 @ $ 91 ⎫ = $2,500 15 @ $106 ⎭
Aug. 14		8 @ $ 91 = $ 728 ⎫ = $2,000* 12 @ $106 = $1,272 ⎭	2 @ $ 91 ⎫ = $ 500 3 @ $106 ⎭
Aug. 17	20 @ $115 = $2,300		2 @ $ 91 ⎫ 3 @ $106 ⎬ = $2,800 20 @ $115 ⎭
Aug. 28	10 @ $119 = $1,190		2 @ $ 91 ⎫ 3 @ $106 ⎪ 20 @ $115 ⎬ = $3,990 10 @ $119 ⎭
Aug. 31		2 @ $ 91 = $ 182 ⎫ 3 @ $106 = $ 318 ⎪ = $2,582* 15 @ $115 = $1,725 ⎬ 3 @ $119 = $ 357 ⎭	5 @ $115 ⎫ = $1,408 7 @ $119 ⎭
		$4,582	

* Identification of items sold (and their costs) is obtained from internal documents that track each unit from its purchase to its sale.

When using specific identification, Trekking's cost of goods sold reported on the income statement totals **$4,582**, the sum of $2,000 and $2,582 from the third column of Exhibit 6.4. Trekking's ending inventory reported on the balance sheet is **$1,408**, which is the final inventory balance from the fourth column of Exhibit 6.4.

The purchases and sales entries for Exhibit 6.4 follow (the colored boldface numbers are those impacted by the cost flow assumption).

Point: Specific identification is usually practical only for companies with expensive, custom-made inventory.

Purchases		
Aug. 3	Merchandise Inventory	1,590
	Accounts Payable	1,590
17	Merchandise Inventory	2,300
	Accounts Payable	2,300
28	Merchandise Inventory	1,190
	Accounts Payable	1,190

Sales		
Aug. 14	Accounts Receivable	2,600
	Sales	2,600
14	Cost of Goods Sold	**2,000**
	Merchandise Inventory	2,000
31	Accounts Receivable	3,450
	Sales	3,450
31	Cost of Goods Sold	**2,582**
	Merchandise Inventory	2,582

First-In, First-Out

The **first-in, first-out (FIFO)** method of assigning costs to both inventory and cost of goods sold assumes that inventory items are sold in the order acquired. When sales occur, the costs of the earliest units acquired are charged to cost of goods sold. This leaves the costs from the most recent purchases in ending inventory. Use of FIFO for computing the cost of inventory and cost of goods sold is shown in Exhibit 6.5.

Point: The "Goods Purchased" column is identical for all methods. Data are taken from Exhibit 6.3.

This exhibit starts with beginning inventory of 10 bikes at $91 each. On August 3, 15 more bikes costing $106 each are bought for $1,590. Inventory now consists of 10 bikes at $91 each and 15 bikes at $106 each, for a total of $2,500. On August 14, 20 bikes are sold—applying FIFO, the first 10 sold cost $91 each and the next 10 sold cost $106 each, for a total cost of $1,970. This leaves 5 bikes costing $106 each, or $530, in inventory. On August 17, 20 bikes costing $2,300 are purchased, and on August 28, another 10 bikes costing $1,190 are purchased, for a total of 35 bikes costing $4,020 in inventory. On August 31, 23 bikes are sold—applying FIFO, the first 5 bikes sold cost $530 and the next 18 sold cost $2,070, which leaves 12 bikes costing $1,420 in ending inventory.

Date	Goods Purchased	Cost of Goods Sold	Inventory Balance
Aug. 1	Beginning balance		10 @ $ 91 = $ 910
Aug. 3	15 @ $106 = $1,590		10 @ $ 91 / 15 @ $106 } = $2,500
Aug. 14		10 @ $ 91 = $ 910 / 10 @ $106 = $1,060 } = $1,970	5 @ $106 = $ 530
Aug. 17	20 @ $115 = $2,300		5 @ $106 / 20 @ $115 } = $2,830
Aug. 28	10 @ $119 = $1,190		5 @ $106 / 20 @ $115 / 10 @ $119 } = $4,020
Aug. 31		5 @ $106 = $ 530 / 18 @ $115 = $2,070 } = $2,600	2 @ $115 / 10 @ $119 } = $1,420
		$4,570	

EXHIBIT 6.5

FIFO Computations—
Perpetual System

> For the 20 units sold on Aug. 14, the first 10 sold are assigned the earliest cost of $91 (from beg. bal.). The next 10 sold are assigned the next earliest cost of $106.

> For the 23 units sold on Aug. 31, the first 5 sold are assigned the earliest available cost of $106 (from Aug. 3 purchase). The next 18 sold are assigned the next earliest cost of $115 (from Aug. 17 purchase).

Trekking's FIFO cost of goods sold reported on its income statement (reflecting the 43 units sold) is **$4,570** ($1,970 + $2,600), and its ending inventory reported on the balance sheet (reflecting the 12 units unsold) is **$1,420**.

Point: Under FIFO, a unit sold is assigned the earliest (oldest) cost from inventory. This leaves the most recent costs in ending inventory.

The purchases and sales entries for Exhibit 6.5 follow (the colored boldface numbers are those affected by the cost flow assumption).

Purchases		
Aug. 3 Merchandise Inventory	1,590	
Accounts Payable		1,590
17 Merchandise Inventory	2,300	
Accounts Payable		2,300
28 Merchandise Inventory	1,190	
Accounts Payable		1,190

Sales		
Aug. 14 Accounts Receivable	2,600	
Sales		2,600
14 Cost of Goods Sold	1,970	
Merchandise Inventory		1,970
31 Accounts Receivable	3,450	
Sales		3,450
31 Cost of Goods Sold	2,600	
Merchandise Inventory		2,600

Last-In, First-Out

The **last-in, first-out (LIFO)** method of assigning costs assumes that the most recent purchases are sold first. These more recent costs are charged to the goods sold, and the costs of the earliest purchases are assigned to inventory. As with other methods, LIFO is acceptable even when the physical flow of goods does not follow a last-in, first-out pattern. One appeal of LIFO is that by assigning costs from the most recent purchases to cost of goods sold, LIFO comes closest to matching current costs of goods sold with revenues (compared to FIFO or weighted average).

Exhibit 6.6 shows the LIFO computations. It starts with beginning inventory of 10 bikes at $91 each. On August 3, 15 more bikes costing $106 each are bought for $1,590. Inventory now consists of 10 bikes at $91 each and 15 bikes at $106 each, for a total of $2,500. On August 14, 20 bikes are sold—applying LIFO, the first 15 sold are from the most recent purchase costing $106 each, and the next 5 sold are from the next most recent purchase costing $91 each, for a total cost of $2,045. This leaves 5 bikes costing $91 each, or $455, in inventory. On August 17, 20 bikes costing $2,300 are purchased, and on August 28, another 10 bikes costing $1,190 are purchased, for a total of 35 bikes costing $3,945 in inventory. On August 31, 23 bikes are sold—applying LIFO, the first 10 bikes sold are from the most recent purchase costing $1,190, and the next 13 sold are from the next most recent purchase costing $1,495, which leaves 12 bikes costing $1,260 in ending inventory.

EXHIBIT 6.6

LIFO Computations— Perpetual System

For the 20 units sold on Aug. 14, the first 15 sold are assigned the most recent cost of $106. The next 5 sold are assigned the next most recent cost of $91.

For the 23 units sold on Aug. 31, the first 10 sold are assigned the most recent cost of $119. The next 13 sold are assigned the next most recent cost of $115.

Date	Goods Purchased	Cost of Goods Sold	Inventory Balance
Aug. 1	Beginning balance		10 @ $91 = $ 910
Aug. 3	15 @ $106 = $1,590		10 @ $91 } = $2,500 15 @ $106 }
Aug. 14		15 @ $106 = $1,590 } = $2,045 5 @ $91 = $ 455 }	5 @ $91 = $ 455
Aug. 17	20 @ $115 = $2,300		5 @ $91 } = $2,755 20 @ $115 }
Aug. 28	10 @ $119 = $1,190		5 @ $91 } 20 @ $115 } = $3,945 10 @ $119 }
Aug. 31		10 @ $119 = $1,190 } = $2,685 13 @ $115 = $1,495 } $4,730	5 @ $91 } = $1,260 7 @ $115 }

Trekking's LIFO cost of goods sold reported on the income statement is **$4,730** ($2,045 + $2,685), and its ending inventory reported on the balance sheet is **$1,260**.

The purchases and sales entries for Exhibit 6.6 follow (the colored boldface numbers are those affected by the cost flow assumption).

Purchases

Aug. 3	Merchandise Inventory	1,590
	Accounts Payable	1,590
17	Merchandise Inventory	2,300
	Accounts Payable	2,300
28	Merchandise Inventory	1,190
	Accounts Payable	1,190

Sales

Aug. 14	Accounts Receivable	2,600
	Sales	2,600
14	Cost of Goods Sold	2,045
	Merchandise Inventory	2,045
31	Accounts Receivable	3,450
	Sales	3,450
31	Cost of Goods Sold	2,685
	Merchandise Inventory	2,685

Weighted Average

The **weighted average** (also called **average cost**) method of assigning cost requires that we use the weighted average cost per unit of inventory at the time of each sale. Weighted average cost per unit at the time of each sale equals the cost of goods available for sale divided by the units available. The results using weighted average (WA) for Trekking are shown in Exhibit 6.7.

This exhibit starts with beginning inventory of 10 bikes at $91 each. On August 3, 15 more bikes costing $106 each are bought for $1,590. Inventory now consists of 10 bikes at $91 each and 15 bikes at $106 each, for a total of $2,500. The average cost per bike for that inventory

EXHIBIT 6.7

Weighted Average
Computations—Perpetual System

Date	Goods Purchased	Cost of Goods Sold	Inventory Balance
Aug. 1	Beginning balance		10 @ $ 91 = $ 910
Aug. 3	15 @ $106 = $1,590		10 @ $ 91 } 15 @ $106 } = $2,500 (or $100 per unit)[a]
Aug. 14		20 @ $100 = $2,000	5 @ $100 = $ 500 (or $100 per unit)[b]
Aug. 17	20 @ $115 = $2,300		5 @ $100 } 20 @ $115 } = $2,800 (or $112 per unit)[c]
Aug. 28	10 @ $119 = $1,190		5 @ $100 } 20 @ $115 } = $3,990 (or $114 per unit)[d] 10 @ $119 }
Aug. 31		23 @ $114 = $2,622	12 @ $114 = $1,368 (or $114 per unit)[e]
		$4,622	

> For the 20 units sold on Aug. 14, the cost assigned is the $100 *average cost* per unit from the inventory balance column at the time of sale.

> For the 23 units sold on Aug. 31, the cost assigned is the $114 *average cost* per unit from the inventory balance column at the time of sale.

[a] $100 per unit = ($2,500 inventory balance ÷ 25 units in inventory).
[b] $100 per unit = ($500 inventory balance ÷ 5 units in inventory).
[c] $112 per unit = ($2,800 inventory balance ÷ 25 units in inventory).
[d] $114 per unit = ($3,990 inventory balance ÷ 35 units in inventory).
[e] $114 per unit = ($1,368 inventory balance ÷ 12 units in inventory).

is $100, computed as $2,500/(10 bikes + 15 bikes). On August 14, 20 bikes are sold—applying WA, the 20 sold are assigned the $100 average cost, for a total cost of $2,000. This leaves 5 bikes with an average cost of $100 each, or $500, in inventory. On August 17, 20 bikes costing $2,300 are purchased, and on August 28, another 10 bikes costing $1,190 are purchased, for a total of 35 bikes costing $3,990 in inventory at August 28. The average cost per bike for the August 28 inventory is $114, computed as $3,990/(5 bikes + 20 bikes + 10 bikes). On August 31, 23 bikes are sold—applying WA, the 23 sold are assigned the $114 average cost, for a total cost of $2,622. This leaves 12 bikes costing $1,368 in ending inventory.

Trekking's cost of goods sold reported on the income statement (reflecting the 43 units sold) is **$4,622** ($2,000 + $2,622), and its ending inventory reported on the balance sheet (reflecting the 12 units unsold) is **$1,368**.

Point: Under weighted average, a unit sold is assigned the average cost of all items currently available for sale at the date of each sale.

The purchases and sales entries for Exhibit 6.7 follow (the colored boldface numbers are those affected by the cost flow assumption).

	Purchases		
Aug. 3	Merchandise Inventory	1,590	
	Accounts Payable		1,590
17	Merchandise Inventory	2,300	
	Accounts Payable		2,300
28	Merchandise Inventory	1,190	
	Accounts Payable		1,190

	Sales		
Aug. 14	Accounts Receivable.	2,600	
	Sales		2,600
14	Cost of Goods Sold.	2,000	
	Merchandise Inventory		2,000
31	Accounts Receivable.	3,450	
	Sales		3,450
31	Cost of Goods Sold.	2,622	
	Merchandise Inventory		2,622

Advances in technology have greatly reduced the cost of a perpetual inventory system. Many companies are now asking whether they can afford *not* to have a perpetual inventory system because timely access to inventory information is a competitive advantage and it can help reduce the level of inventory, which reduces costs.

Decision Insight

Inventory Control SOX demands that companies safeguard inventory and properly report it. Safeguards include restricted access, use of authorized requisitions, security measures, and controlled environments to prevent damage. Proper accounting includes matching inventory received with purchase order terms and quality requirements, preventing misstatements, and controlling access to inventory records.

Financial Statement Effects of Costing Methods

A1   Analyze the effects of inventory methods for both financial and tax reporting.

When purchase prices do not change, each inventory costing method assigns the same cost amounts to inventory and to cost of goods sold. When purchase prices are different, however, the methods nearly always assign different cost amounts. We show these differences in Exhibit 6.8 using Trekking's data.

EXHIBIT 6.8

Financial Statement Effects of Inventory Costing Methods

TREKKING COMPANY				
For Month Ended August 31				
	Specific Identification	FIFO	LIFO	Weighted Average
Income Statement				
Sales	$6,050	$6,050	$6,050	$6,050
Cost of goods sold	4,582	4,570	4,730	4,622
Gross profit	1,468	1,480	1,320	1,428
Expenses	450	450	450	450
Income before taxes	1,018	1,030	870	978
Income tax expense (30%)	305	309	261	293
Net income	$ 713	$ 721	$ 609	$ 685
Balance Sheet				
Inventory	$1,408	$1,420	$1,260	$1,368

This exhibit reveals two important results. First, when purchase costs *regularly rise,* as in Trekking's case, the following occurs:

■ FIFO assigns the lowest amount to cost of goods sold—yielding the highest gross profit and net income.

Point: FIFO is preferred when costs are rising *and* managers have incentives to report higher income for reasons such as bonus plans, job security, and reputation.

■ LIFO assigns the highest amount to cost of goods sold—yielding the lowest gross profit and net income, which also yields a temporary tax advantage by postponing payment of some income tax.

■ Weighted average yields results between FIFO and LIFO.

■ Specific identification always yields results that depend on which units are sold.

Point: LIFO inventory is often less than the inventory's replacement cost because LIFO inventory is valued using the oldest inventory purchase costs.

Second, when costs *regularly decline,* the reverse occurs for FIFO and LIFO. Namely, FIFO gives the highest cost of goods sold—yielding the lowest gross profit and income. However, LIFO then gives the lowest cost of goods sold—yielding the highest gross profit and income.

All four inventory costing methods are acceptable. However, a company must disclose the inventory method it uses in its financial statements or notes. Each method offers certain advantages as follows:

■ FIFO assigns an amount to inventory on the balance sheet that approximates its current cost; it also mimics the actual flow of goods for most businesses.

■ LIFO assigns an amount to cost of goods sold on the income statement that approximates its current cost; it also better matches current costs with revenues in computing gross profit.

■ Weighted average tends to smooth out erratic changes in costs.

■ Specific identification exactly matches the costs of items with the revenues they generate.

 Decision Maker ▮▮▮▮▮▮▮▮▮▮▮▮▮▮▮▮▮▮▮▮▮

Financial Planner   One of your clients asks if the inventory account of a company using FIFO needs any "adjustments" for analysis purposes in light of recent inflation. What is your advice? Does your advice depend on changes in the costs of these inventories? [Answer—p. 249]

Tax Effects of Costing Methods   Trekking's segment income statement in Exhibit 6.8 includes income tax expense (at a rate of 30%) because it was formed as a corporation. Since inventory costs affect net income, they have potential tax effects. Trekking gains a temporary tax advantage by using LIFO. Many companies use LIFO for this reason.

Companies can and often do use different costing methods for financial reporting and tax reporting. *The only exception is when LIFO is used for tax reporting; in this case, the IRS requires that it also be used in financial statements*—called the LIFO conformity rule.

Consistency in Using Costing Methods

The **consistency concept** prescribes that a company use the same accounting methods period after period so that financial statements are comparable across periods—the only exception is when a change from one method to another will improve its financial reporting. The *full-disclosure principle* prescribes that the notes to the statements report this type of change, its justification, and its effect on income.

The consistency concept does *not* require a company to use one method exclusively. For example, it can use different methods to value different categories of inventory.

Decision Ethics

Inventory Manager   Your compensation as inventory manager includes a bonus plan based on gross profit. Your superior asks your opinion on changing the inventory costing method from FIFO to LIFO. Since costs are expected to continue to rise, your superior predicts that LIFO would match higher current costs against sales, thereby lowering taxable income (and gross profit). What do you recommend? [Answer—p. 249]

Quick Check   Answers—p. 250

4. Describe one advantage for each of the inventory costing methods: specific identification, FIFO, LIFO, and weighted average.
5. When costs are rising, which method reports higher net income—LIFO or FIFO?
6. When costs are rising, what effect does LIFO have on a balance sheet compared to FIFO?
7. A company takes a physical count of inventory at the end of 2009 and finds that ending inventory is understated by $10,000. Would this error cause cost of goods sold to be overstated or understated in 2009? In year 2010? If so, by how much?

Valuing Inventory at LCM and the Effects of Inventory Errors

This section examines the role of market costs in determining inventory on the balance sheet and also the financial statement effects of inventory errors.

Lower of Cost or Market

We explained how to assign costs to ending inventory and cost of goods sold using one of four costing methods (FIFO, LIFO, weighted average, or specific identification). However, *accounting principles require that inventory be reported at the market value (cost) of replacing inventory when market value is lower than cost.* Merchandise inventory is then said to be reported on the balance sheet at the **lower of cost or market (LCM).**

P2 Compute the lower of cost or market amount of inventory.

Computing the Lower of Cost or Market   *Market* in the term *LCM* is defined as the current replacement cost of purchasing the same inventory items in the usual manner. A decline in replacement cost reflects a loss of value in inventory. When the recorded cost of inventory is higher than the replacement cost, a loss is recognized. When the recorded cost is lower, no adjustment is made.

LCM is applied in one of three ways: (1) to each individual item separately, (2) to major categories of items, or (3) to the whole of inventory. The less similar the items that make up inventory, the more likely companies are to apply LCM to individual items or categories. To illustrate, we apply LCM to the ending inventory of a motorsports retailer in Exhibit 6.9.

Video6.1

LCM to Whole   When LCM is applied to the *whole* inventory, it is determined from *one* comparison. We compare the $295,000 total from the Total Cost column with the $287,000 total from the Total Market column and select the lower amount. This yields a $287,000 reported inventory on the balance sheet.

EXHIBIT 6.9

Lower of Cost or Market
Computations

Items: $140,000 is the lower of
$160,000 or $140,000

Categories: $200,000 is the lower
of $210,000 or $200,000

Whole: $287,000 is the lower of
$295,000 or $287,000

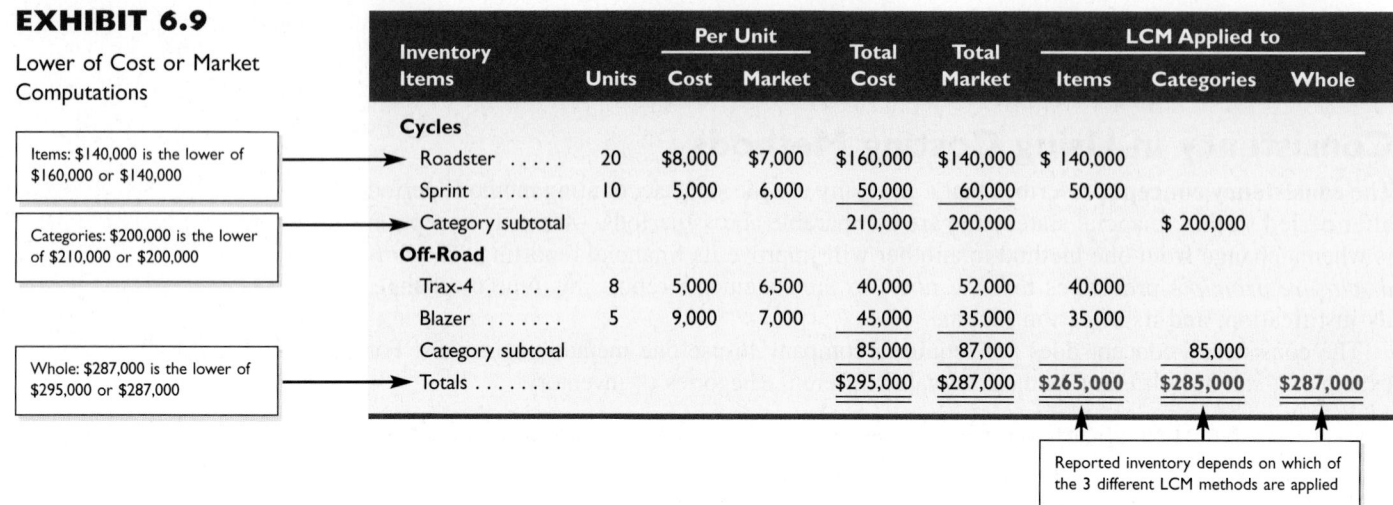

Inventory Items	Units	Per Unit Cost	Per Unit Market	Total Cost	Total Market	LCM Applied to Items	LCM Applied to Categories	LCM Applied to Whole
Cycles								
Roadster	20	$8,000	$7,000	$160,000	$140,000	$ 140,000		
Sprint	10	5,000	6,000	50,000	60,000	50,000		
Category subtotal				210,000	200,000		$ 200,000	
Off-Road								
Trax-4	8	5,000	6,500	40,000	52,000	40,000		
Blazer	5	9,000	7,000	45,000	35,000	35,000		
Category subtotal				85,000	87,000		85,000	
Totals				$295,000	$287,000	$265,000	$285,000	$287,000

Reported inventory depends on which of the 3 different LCM methods are applied

LCM to Categories   When LCM is applied to the major *categories* of inventory, it is computed from two comparisons, where the number of comparisons equals the number of categories. First, for cycles, $200,000 is the lower of the $210,000 cost and the $200,000 market. Second, for off-road, $85,000 is the lower of the $85,000 cost and the $87,000 market. This yields a $285,000 reported inventory, computed from $200,000 for category one plus $85,000 for category two.

LCM to Items   When LCM is applied to individual *items* of inventory, the number of comparisons equals the number of items. For Roadster, $140,000 is the lower of the $160,000 cost and the $140,000 market. For Sprint, $50,000 is the lower of the $50,000 cost and the $60,000 market. For Trax-4, $40,000 is the lower of the $40,000 cost and the $52,000 market. For Blazer, $35,000 is the lower of the $45,000 cost and the $35,000 market. This yields a $265,000 reported inventory, computed from $140,000 for Roadster plus $50,000 for Sprint plus $40,000 for Trax-4 plus $35,000 for Blazer.

Point: Advances in technology encourage the individual-item approach for LCM.

Any one of these three applications of LCM is acceptable. The retailer **Best Buy** applies LCM and reports that its "merchandise inventories are recorded at the lower of average cost or market."

Recording the Lower of Cost or Market   Inventory must be adjusted downward when market is less than cost. To illustrate, if LCM is applied to the individual items of inventory in Exhibit 6.9, the Merchandise Inventory account must be adjusted from the $295,000 recorded cost down to the $265,000 market amount as follows.

Cost of Goods Sold.	30,000	
Merchandise Inventory.		30,000
To adjust inventory cost to market.		

Accounting rules require that inventory be adjusted to market when market is less than cost, but inventory normally cannot be written up to market when market exceeds cost. If recording inventory down to market is acceptable, why are companies not allowed to record inventory up to market? One view is that a gain from a market increase should not be realized until a sales transaction verifies the gain. However, this problem also applies when market is less than cost. A second and primary reason is the **conservatism constraint,** which prescribes the use of the less optimistic amount when more than one estimate of the amount to be received or paid exists and these estimates are about equally likely.

Decision Insight

IFRSs   Use of the LIFO method is prohibited under IFRSs. Also under IFRSs, if inventory that previously had been written down to market subsequently increases in value, the write-down is reversed.

Financial Statement Effects of Inventory Errors

Companies must take care in both taking a physical count of inventory and in assigning a cost to it. An inventory error causes misstatements in cost of goods sold, gross profit, net income, current assets, and equity. It also causes misstatements in the next period's statements because ending inventory of one period is the beginning inventory of the next. As we consider the financial statement effects in this section, it is helpful if we recall the following *inventory relation.*

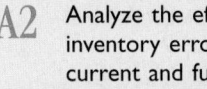

Analyze the effects of inventory errors on current and future financial statements.

Income Statement Effects   Exhibit 6.10 shows the effects of inventory errors on key amounts in the current and next periods' income statements. Let's look at row 1 and year 1. We see that understating ending inventory overstates cost of goods sold. This can be seen from the above inventory relation where we subtract a smaller ending inventory amount in computing cost of goods sold. Then a higher cost of goods sold yields a lower income.

To understand year 2 of row 1, remember that an understated ending inventory for year 1 becomes an understated beginning inventory for year 2. Using the above inventory relation, we see that if beginning inventory is understated, then cost of goods sold is understated (because we are starting with a smaller amount). A lower cost of goods sold yields a higher income.

Turning to overstatements, let's look at row 2 and year 1. If ending inventory is overstated, we use the inventory relation to see that cost of goods sold is understated. A lower cost of goods sold yields a higher income.

For year 2 of row 2, we again recall that an overstated ending inventory for year 1 becomes an overstated beginning inventory for year 2. If beginning inventory is overstated, we use the inventory relation to see that cost of goods sold is overstated. A higher cost of goods sold yields a lower income.

EXHIBIT 6.10

Effects of Inventory Errors on the Income Statement

	Year 1		Year 2	
Ending Inventory	**Cost of Goods Sold**	**Net Income**	**Cost of Goods Sold**	**Net Income**
Understated	Overstated	Understated	Understated	Overstated
Overstated*	Understated	Overstated	Overstated	Understated

* This error is less likely under a perpetual system because it implies more inventory than is recorded (or less shrinkage than expected). Management will normally follow up and discover and correct this error before it impacts any accounts.

To illustrate, consider an inventory error for a company with $100,000 in sales for each of the years 2008, 2009, and 2010. If this company maintains a steady $20,000 inventory level during this period and makes $60,000 in purchases in each of these years, its cost of goods sold is $60,000 and its gross profit is $40,000 each year.

Ending Inventory Understated—Year 1   Assume that this company errs in computing its 2008 ending inventory and reports $16,000 instead of the correct amount of $20,000. The effects of this error are shown in Exhibit 6.11. The $4,000 understatement of 2008 ending inventory causes a $4,000 overstatement in 2008 cost of goods sold and a $4,000 understatement in both gross profit and net income for 2008. We see that these effects match the effects predicted in Exhibit 6.10.

Ending Inventory Understated—Year 2   The 2008 understated ending inventory becomes the 2009 understated *beginning* inventory. We see in Exhibit 6.11 that this error causes an understatement in 2009 cost of goods sold and a $4,000 overstatement in both gross profit and net income for 2009.

Ending Inventory Understated—Year 3   Exhibit 6.11 shows that the 2008 ending inventory error affects only that period and the next. It does not affect 2010 results or any period thereafter. An inventory error is said to be *self-correcting* because it always yields an offsetting error in the next period. This does not reduce the severity of inventory errors. Managers, lenders, owners, and others make important decisions from analysis of income and costs.

Point: A former internal auditor at **Coca-Cola** alleges that just before midnight at the 2002 period-end, fully loaded Coke trucks were ordered to drive about 2 feet away from the loading dock so that Coke could record millions of dollars in extra sales.

EXHIBIT 6.11

Effects of Inventory Errors on Three Periods' Income Statements

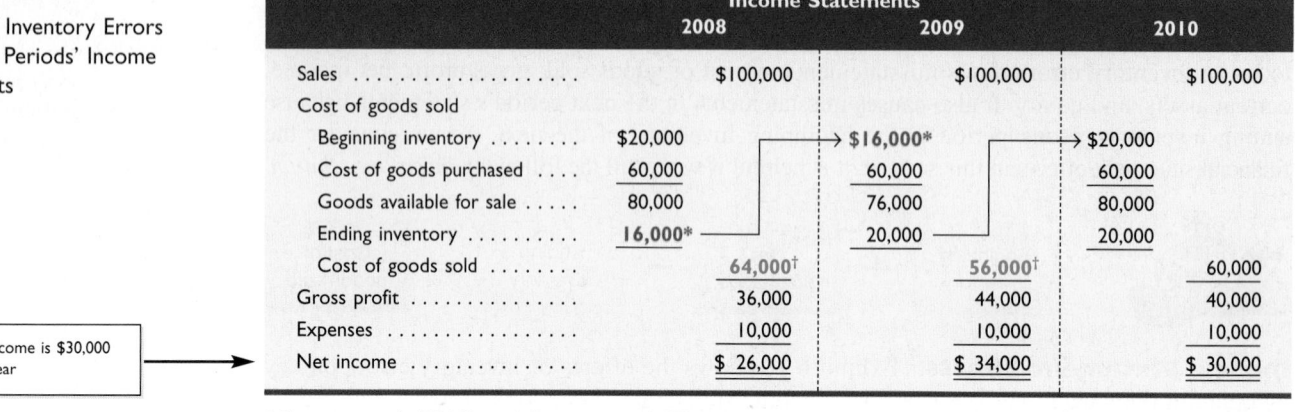

	Income Statements		
	2008	**2009**	**2010**
Sales	$100,000	$100,000	$100,000
Cost of goods sold			
Beginning inventory	$20,000	→ $16,000*	→ $20,000
Cost of goods purchased	60,000	60,000	60,000
Goods available for sale	80,000	76,000	80,000
Ending inventory	16,000*	20,000	20,000
Cost of goods sold	64,000†	56,000†	60,000
Gross profit	36,000	44,000	40,000
Expenses	10,000	10,000	10,000
Net income	$ 26,000	$ 34,000	$ 30,000

Correct income is $30,000 for each year

* Correct amount is $20,000.   † Correct amount is $60,000.

Example: If 2008 ending inventory in Exhibit 6.11 is overstated by $3,000 (not understated by $4,000), what is the effect on cost of goods sold, gross profit, assets, and equity? *Answer:* Cost of goods sold is understated by $3,000 in 2008 and overstated by $3,000 in 2009. Gross profit and net income are overstated in 2008 and understated in 2009. Assets and equity are overstated in 2008.

We can also do an analysis of beginning inventory errors. The income statement effects are the opposite of those for ending inventory.

Balance Sheet Effects   Balance sheet effects of an inventory error can be seen by considering the accounting equation: Assets = Liabilities + Equity. For example, understating ending inventory understates both current and total assets. An understatement in ending inventory also yields an understatement in equity because of the understatement in net income. Exhibit 6.12 shows the effects of inventory errors on the current period's balance sheet amounts. Errors in *beginning* inventory do not yield misstatements in the end-of-period balance sheet, but they do affect that current period's income statement.

EXHIBIT 6.12

Effects of Inventory Errors on Current Period's Balance Sheet

Ending Inventory	Assets	Equity
Understated	Understated	Understated
Overstated	Overstated	Overstated

Quick Check

Answers—p. 250

8. Use LCM applied separately to the following individual items to compute ending inventory.

Product	Units	Unit Recorded Cost	Unit Market Cost
A	20	$ 6	$ 5
B	40	9	8
C	10	12	15

Decision Analysis   Inventory Turnover and Days' Sales in Inventory

Inventory Turnover

A3 Assess inventory management using both inventory turnover and days' sales in inventory.

Earlier chapters described two important ratios useful in evaluating a company's short-term liquidity: current ratio and acid-test ratio. A merchandiser's ability to pay its short-term obligations also depends on how quickly it sells its merchandise inventory. **Inventory turnover,** also called *merchandise inventory turnover,* is one ratio used to assess this and is defined in Exhibit 6.13.

EXHIBIT 6.13

Inventory Turnover

$$\text{Inventory turnover} = \frac{\text{Cost of goods sold}}{\text{Average inventory}}$$

This ratio reveals how many *times* a company turns over (sells) its inventory during a period. If a company's inventory greatly varies within a year, average inventory amounts can be computed from interim periods such as quarters or months.

Users apply inventory turnover to help analyze short-term liquidity and to assess whether management is doing a good job controlling the amount of inventory available. A low ratio compared to that of competitors suggests inefficient use of assets. The company may be holding more inventory than it needs to support its sales volume. Similarly, a very high ratio compared to that of competitors suggests inventory might be too low. This can cause lost sales if customers must back-order merchandise. Inventory turnover has no simple rule except to say *a high ratio is preferable provided inventory is adequate to meet demand.*

Point: We must take care when comparing turnover ratios across companies that use different costing methods (such as FIFO and LIFO).

Days' Sales in Inventory

To better interpret inventory turnover, many users measure the adequacy of inventory to meet sales demand. **Days' sales in inventory,** also called *days' stock on hand,* is a ratio that reveals how much inventory is available in terms of the number of days' sales. It can be interpreted as the number of days one can sell from inventory if no new items are purchased. This ratio is often viewed as a measure of the buffer against out-of-stock inventory and is useful in evaluating liquidity of inventory. It is defined in Exhibit 6.14.

Point: Inventory turnover is higher and days' sales in inventory is lower for industries such as foods and other perishable products. The reverse holds for nonperishable product industries.

$$\text{Days' sales in inventory} = \frac{\text{Ending inventory}}{\text{Cost of goods sold}} \times 365$$

EXHIBIT 6.14

Days' Sales in Inventory

Days' sales in inventory focuses on ending inventory and it estimates how many days it will take to convert inventory at the end of a period into accounts receivable or cash. Days' sales in inventory focuses on *ending* inventory whereas inventory turnover focuses on *average* inventory.

Point: Days' sales in inventory for many Ford models has risen: Freestyle, 122 days; Montego, 109 days; Five Hundred, 118 days. The industry average is 73 days. (*BusinessWeek* 2005)

Decision Insight

Dell-ocity From its roots in a college dorm room, **Dell** now sells over 50 million dollars' worth of computers each day from its Website. The speed of Web technology has allowed Dell to slash inventories. Dell's inventory turnover is 88 and its days' sales in inventory is 5 days. Michael Dell asserts, "Speed is everything in this business."

Analysis of Inventory Management

Inventory management is a major emphasis for merchandisers. They must both plan and control inventory purchases and sales. **Toys "R" Us** is one of those merchandisers. Its inventory in fiscal year 2007 was $1,690 million. This inventory constituted 59% of its current assets and 20% of its total assets. We apply the analysis tools in this section to Toys "R" Us, as shown in Exhibit 6.15—also see margin graph.

EXHIBIT 6.15

Inventory Turnover and Days' Sales in Inventory for Toys "R" Us

($ millions)	2007	2006	2005	2004
Cost of goods sold	$8,638	$7,652	$7,506	$7,646
Ending inventory	$1,690	$1,488	$1,884	$2,094
Inventory turnover	5.4 times	4.5 times	3.8 times	3.6 times
Industry inventory turnover	3.0 times	2.8 times	2.6 times	2.6 times
Days' sales in inventory	71 days	71 days	92 days	100 days
Industry days' sales in inventory	129 days	135 days	139 days	141 days

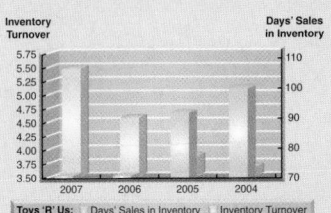

Its 2007 inventory turnover of 5.4 times means that Toys "R" Us turned over its inventory 5.4 times per year, or once every 68 days (365 days ÷ 5.4). We prefer inventory turnover to be high provided inventory is not out of stock and the company is not losing customers. The 2007 days' sales in inventory of 71 days reveals that it was carrying 71 days of sales in inventory. This inventory buffer seems more than adequate. Toys "R" Us would benefit from further management efforts to increase inventory turnover and reduce inventory levels.

Decision Maker

Entrepreneur Analysis of your retail store yields an inventory turnover of 5.0 and a days' sales in inventory of 73 days. The industry norm for inventory turnover is 4.4 and for days' sales in inventory is 74 days. What is your assessment of inventory management? [Answer—p. 249]

DILBERT reprinted by permission of United Feature Syndicate, Inc.

Demonstration Problem

DP6

Craig Company uses a perpetual inventory system for its one product. Its beginning inventory, purchases, and sales during calendar year 2009 follow.

Date	Activity	Units Acquired at Cost	Units Sold at Retail	Unit Inventory
Jan. 1	Beg. Inventory ..	400 units @ $14 = $ 5,600		400 units
Jan. 15	Sale		200 units @ $30	200 units
March 10	Purchase	200 units @ $15 = $ 3,000		400 units
April 1	Sale		200 units @ $30	200 units
May 9	Purchase	300 units @ $16 = $ 4,800		500 units
Sept. 22	Purchase	250 units @ $20 = $ 5,000		750 units
Nov. 1	Sale		300 units @ $35	450 units
Nov. 28	Purchase	100 units @ $21 = $ 2,100		550 units
	Totals	1,250 units $20,500	700 units	

Additional tracking data for specific identification: (1) January 15 sale—200 units @ $14, (2) April 1 sale—200 units @ $15, and (3) November 1 sale—200 units @ $14 and 100 units @ $20.

Required

1. Calculate the cost of goods available for sale.
2. Apply the four different methods of inventory costing (FIFO, LIFO, weighted average, and specific identification) to calculate ending inventory and cost of goods sold under each method.
3. Compute gross profit earned by the company for each of the four costing methods in part 2. Also, report the inventory amount reported on the balance sheet for each of the four methods.
4. In preparing financial statements for year 2009, the financial officer was instructed to use FIFO but failed to do so and instead computed cost of goods sold according to LIFO. Determine the impact on year 2009's income from the error. Also determine the effect of this error on year 2010's income. Assume no income taxes.
5. Management wants a report that shows how changing from FIFO to another method would change net income. Prepare a table showing (1) the cost of goods sold amount under each of the four methods, (2) the amount by which each cost of goods sold total is different from the FIFO cost of goods sold, and (3) the effect on net income if another method is used instead of FIFO.

Planning the Solution

- Compute cost of goods available for sale by multiplying the units of beginning inventory and each purchase by their unit costs to determine the total cost of goods available for sale.
- Prepare a perpetual FIFO table starting with beginning inventory and showing how inventory changes after each purchase and after each sale (see Exhibit 6.5).
- Prepare a perpetual LIFO table starting with beginning inventory and showing how inventory changes after each purchase and after each sale (see Exhibit 6.6).
- Make a table of purchases and sales recalculating the average cost of inventory prior to each sale to arrive at the weighted average cost of ending inventory. Total the average costs associated with each sale to determine cost of goods sold (see Exhibit 6.7).
- Prepare a table showing the computation of cost of goods sold and ending inventory using the specific identification method (see Exhibit 6.4).
- Compare the year-end 2009 inventory amounts under FIFO and LIFO to determine the misstatement of year 2009 income that results from using LIFO. The errors for year 2009 and 2010 are equal in amount but opposite in effect.
- Create a table showing cost of goods sold under each method and how net income would differ from FIFO net income if an alternate method is adopted.

Solution to Demonstration Problem

1. Cost of goods available for sale (this amount is the same for all methods).

Date		Units	Unit Cost	Cost
Jan. 1	Beg. Inventory	400	$14	$ 5,600
March 10	Purchase	200	15	3,000
May 9	Purchase	300	16	4,800
Sept. 22	Purchase	250	20	5,000
Nov. 28	Purchase	100	21	2,100
Total goods available for sale		1,250		$20,500

2a. FIFO perpetual method.

Date	Goods Purchased	Cost of Goods Sold	Inventory Balance
Jan. 1	Beginning balance		400 @ $14 = $ 5,600
Jan. 15		200 @ $14 = $2,800	200 @ $14 = $ 2,800
Mar. 10	200 @ $15 = $3,000		200 @ $14 } = $ 5,800 200 @ $15 }
April 1		200 @ $14 = $2,800	200 @ $15 = $ 3,000
May 9	300 @ $16 = $4,800		200 @ $15 } = $ 7,800 300 @ $16 }
Sept. 22	250 @ $20 = $5,000		200 @ $15 } 300 @ $16 } = $12,800 250 @ $20 }
Nov. 1		200 @ $15 = $3,000 100 @ $16 = $1,600	200 @ $16 } = $ 8,200 250 @ $20 }
Nov. 28	100 @ $21 = $2,100		200 @ $16 } 250 @ $20 } = $10,300 100 @ $21 }
Total cost of goods sold		$10,200	

Note to students: **In a classroom situation,** once we compute cost of goods available for sale, we can compute the amount for either cost of goods sold or ending inventory—it is a matter of preference. **In practice,** the costs of items sold are identified as sales are made and immediately transferred from the inventory account to the cost of goods sold account. The previous solution showing the line-by-line approach illustrates actual application in practice. The following alternate solutions illustrate that, once the concepts are understood, other solution approaches are available. Although this is only shown for FIFO, it could be shown for all methods.

Alternate Methods to Compute FIFO Perpetual Numbers

[FIFO Alternate No. 1: Computing cost of goods sold first]

Cost of goods available for sale (from part 1)			$ 20,500
Cost of goods sold			
Jan. 15 Sold (200 @ $14)	$2,800		
April 1 Sold (200 @ $14)	2,800		
Nov. 1 Sold (200 @ $15 and 100 @ $16)	4,600	10,200	
Ending inventory		$10,300	

[FIFO Alternate No. 2: Computing ending inventory first]

Cost of goods available for sale (from part 1)			$ 20,500
Ending inventory*			
Nov. 28 Purchase (100 @ $21)	$2,100		
Sept. 22 Purchase (250 @ $20)	5,000		
May 9 Purchase (200 @ $16)	3,200		
Ending inventory		10,300	
Cost of goods sold		$10,200	

* Since FIFO assumes that the earlier costs are the first to flow out, we determine ending inventory by assigning the most recent costs to the remaining items.

2b. LIFO perpetual method.

Date	Goods Purchased	Cost of Goods Sold	Inventory Balance
Jan. 1	Beginning balance		400 @ $14 = $ 5,600
Jan. 15		200 @ $14 = $2,800	200 @ $14 = $ 2,800
Mar. 10	200 @ $15 = $3,000		200 @ $14 200 @ $15 } = $ 5,800
April 1		200 @ $15 = $3,000	200 @ $14 = $ 2,800
May 9	300 @ $16 = $4,800		200 @ $14 300 @ $16 } = $ 7,600
Sept. 22	250 @ $20 = $5,000		200 @ $14 300 @ $16 250 @ $20 } = $12,600
Nov. 1		250 @ $20 = $5,000 50 @ $16 = $ 800	200 @ $14 250 @ $16 } = $ 6,800
Nov. 28	100 @ $21 = $2,100		200 @ $14 250 @ $16 100 @ $21 } = $ 8,900
Total cost of goods sold		**$11,600**	

2c. Weighted average perpetual method.

Date	Goods Purchased	Cost of Goods Sold	Inventory Balance
Jan. 1	Beginning balance		400 @ $14 = $ 5,600
Jan. 15		200 @ $14 = $2,800	200 @ $14 = $ 2,800
Mar. 10	200 @ $15 = $3,000		200 @ $14 ⎱ = $ 5,800 200 @ $15 ⎰ (avg. cost is $14.5)
April 1		200 @ $14.5 = $2,900	200 @ $14.5 = $ 2,900
May 9	300 @ $16 = $4,800		200 @ $14.5 ⎱ = $ 7,700 300 @ $16 ⎰ (avg. cost is $15.4)
Sept. 22	250 @ $20 = $5,000		200 @ $14.5 ⎱ 300 @ $16 ⎰ = $ 12,700 250 @ $20 (avg. cost is $16.93)
Nov. 1		300 @ $16.93 = $5,079	450 @ $16.93 = $ 7,618.5
Nov. 28	100 @ $21 = $2,100		450 @ $16.93 ⎱ = **$9,718.5** 100 @ $21 ⎰
Total cost of goods sold*		**$10,779**	

* The cost of goods sold ($10,779) plus ending inventory ($9,718.5) is $2.5 less than the cost of goods available for sale ($20,500) due to rounding.

2d. Specific identification method.

Date	Goods Purchased	Cost of Goods Sold	Inventory Balance
Jan. 1	Beginning balance		400 @ $14 = $ 5,600
Jan. 15		200 @ $14 = $2,800	200 @ $14 = $ 2,800
Mar. 10	200 @ $15 = $3,000		200 @ $14 ⎱ = $ 5,800 200 @ $15 ⎰
April 1		200 @ $15 = $3,000	200 @ $14 = $ 2,800
May 9	300 @ $16 = $4,800		200 @ $14 ⎱ = $ 7,600 300 @ $16 ⎰
Sept. 22	250 @ $20 = $5,000		200 @ $14 ⎱ 300 @ $16 ⎰ = $12,600 250 @ $20
Nov. 1		200 @ $14 = $2,800 100 @ $20 = $2,000	300 @ $16 ⎱ = $ 7,800 150 @ $20 ⎰
Nov. 28	100 @ $21 = $2,100		300 @ $16 ⎱ 150 @ $20 ⎰ = **$ 9,900** 100 @ $21
Total cost of goods sold		**$10,600**	

3.

	FIFO	LIFO	Weighted Average	Specific Identification
Income Statement				
Sales*	$ 22,500	$22,500	$ 22,500	$22,500
Cost of goods sold	10,200	11,600	10,779	10,600
Gross profit	$ 12,300	$10,900	$ 11,721	$11,900
Balance Sheet				
Inventory	$10,300	$ 8,900	$9,718.5	$ 9,900

* Sales = (200 units × $30) + (200 units × $30) + (300 units × $35) = $22,500

4. Mistakenly using LIFO when FIFO should have been used overstates cost of goods sold in year 2009 by $1,400, which is the difference between the FIFO and LIFO amounts of ending inventory. It understates income in 2009 by $1,400. In year 2010, income is overstated by $1,400 because of the understatement in beginning inventory.

5. Analysis of the effects of alternative inventory methods.

	Cost of Goods Sold	Difference from FIFO Cost of Goods Sold	Effect on Net Income If Adopted Instead of FIFO
FIFO	$10,200	—	—
LIFO	11,600	+$1,400	$1,400 lower
Weighted average	10,779	+ 579	579 lower
Specific identification	10,600	+ 400	400 lower

6A Inventory Costing Under a Periodic System

P3 Compute inventory in a periodic system using the methods of specific identification, FIFO, LIFO, and weighted average.

The basic aim of the periodic system and the perpetual system is the same: to assign costs to inventory and cost of goods sold. The same four methods are used to assign costs under both systems: specific identification; first-in, first-out; last-in, first-out; and weighted average. We use information from Trekking to show how to assign costs using these four methods with a periodic system. Data for sales and purchases are in Exhibit 6A.1. Also, recall that we explained the accounting entries under a periodic system in Appendix 5A.

EXHIBIT 6A.1

Purchases and Sales of Goods

Date	Activity	Units Acquired at Cost	Units Sold at Retail	Unit Inventory
Aug. 1	Beginning inventory	10 units @ $ 91 = $ 910		10 units
Aug. 3	Purchases	15 units @ $106 = $ 1,590		25 units
Aug. 14	Sales		20 units @ $130	5 units
Aug. 17	Purchases	20 units @ $115 = $ 2,300		25 units
Aug. 28	Purchases	10 units @ $119 = $ 1,190		35 units
Aug. 31	Sales		23 units @ $150	12 units
	Totals	55 units $5,990	43 units	

Specific Identification

We use the above sales and purchases information and the specific identification method to assign costs to ending inventory and units sold. Trekking's internal data reveal the following specific unit sales:

August 14   Sold 8 bikes costing $91 each and 12 bikes costing $106 each

August 31   Sold 2 bikes costing $91 each, 3 bikes costing $106 each, 15 bikes costing $115 each, and 3 bikes costing $119 each

Applying specific identification and using the information above, we prepare Exhibit 6A.2. This exhibit starts with 10 bikes at $91 each in beginning inventory. On August 3, 15 more bikes are purchased at $106 each for $1,590. Inventory available now consists of 10 bikes at $91 each and 15 bikes at $106 each, for a total of $2,500. On August 14 (see specific sales data above), 20 bikes costing $2,000 are sold—leaving 5 bikes costing $500 in inventory. On August 17, 20 bikes costing $2,300 are purchased, and on August 28, another 10 bikes costing $1,190 are purchased, for a total of 35 bikes costing $3,990 in inventory. On August 31 (see specific sales above), 23 bikes costing $2,582 are sold, which leaves 12 bikes costing $1,408 in ending inventory. Carefully study Exhibit 6A.2 to see the flow of costs both in and out of inventory. Each unit, whether sold or remaining in inventory, has its own specific cost attached to it.

EXHIBIT 6A.2

Specific Identification Computations

Date	Goods Purchased ("goods in")	Cost of Goods Sold ("goods out")	Inventory Balance ("what's left")
Aug. 1	Beginning balance		10 @ $91 = $910
Aug. 3	15 @ $106 = $1,590		10 @ $91, 15 @ $106 = $2,500
Aug. 14		8 @ $91 = $728, 12 @ $106 = $1,272 = $2,000*	2 @ $91, 3 @ $106 = $500
Aug. 17	20 @ $115 = $2,300		2 @ $91, 3 @ $106, 20 @ $115 = $2,800
Aug. 28	10 @ $119 = $1,190		2 @ $91, 3 @ $106, 20 @ $115, 10 @ $119 = $3,990
Aug. 31		2 @ $91 = $182, 3 @ $106 = $318, 15 @ $115 = $1,725, 3 @ $119 = $357 = $2,582*	5 @ $115, 7 @ $119 = $1,408
		$4,582	

For the 20 units sold on Aug. 14, the company specifically identified that 8 of those had cost $91 and 12 had cost $106.

For the 23 units sold on Aug. 31, the company specifically identified each bike sold and its acquisition cost from prior purchases.

* Identification of items sold (and their costs) is obtained from internal documents that track each unit from its purchase to its sale.

When using specific identification, Trekking's cost of goods sold reported on the income statement totals **$4,582**, the sum of $2,000 and $2,582 from the third column of Exhibit 6A.2. Trekking's ending inventory reported on the balance sheet is **$1,408**, which is the final inventory balance from the fourth column. The purchases and sales entries for Exhibit 6A.2 follow (the colored boldface numbers are those affected by the cost flow assumption).

Point: The assignment of costs to the goods sold and to inventory using specific identification is the same for both the perpetual and periodic systems.

Purchases

Aug. 3	Purchases	1,590	
	Accounts Payable		1,590
17	Purchases	2,300	
	Accounts Payable		2,300
28	Purchases	1,190	
	Accounts Payable		1,190

Sales

Aug. 14	Accounts Receivable	2,600	
	Sales		2,600
31	Accounts Receivable	3,450	
	Sales		3,450

Adjusting Entry

31	Merchandise Inventory	1,408	
	Income Summary		498
	Merchandise Inventory		910

First-In, First-Out

The first-in, first-out (FIFO) method of assigning costs to inventory assumes that inventory items are sold in the order acquired. When sales occur, the costs of the earliest units acquired are charged to cost of goods sold. This leaves the costs from the most recent purchases in ending inventory. Use of FIFO for computing the cost of inventory and cost of goods sold is shown in Exhibit 6A.3.

This exhibit starts with computing $5,990 in total units available for sale—this is given to us at the start of this appendix. Applying FIFO, we know that the 12 units in ending inventory will be reported at the cost of the most recent 12 purchases. Reviewing purchases in reverse order, we assign costs to the 12 bikes in ending inventory as follows: $119 cost to 10 bikes and $115 cost to 2 bikes. This yields 12 bikes costing $1,420 in ending inventory. We then subtract this $1,420 in ending inventory from $5,990 in cost of goods available to get $4,570 in cost of goods sold.

EXHIBIT 6A.3

FIFO Computations—
Periodic System

Exhibit 6A.1 shows that the 12 units in ending inventory consist of 10 units from the latest purchase on Aug. 28 and 2 units from the next latest purchase on Aug. 17.

Total cost of 55 units available for sale (from Exhibit 6A.1)		$5,990
Less ending inventory priced using FIFO		
10 units from August 28 purchase at $119 each	$1,190	
2 units from August 17 purchase at $115 each	230	
Ending inventory		1,420
Cost of goods sold		$4,570

Point: The assignment of costs to the goods sold and to inventory using FIFO is the same for both the perpetual and periodic systems.

Trekking's ending inventory reported on the balance sheet is **$1,420**, and its cost of goods sold reported on the income statement is **$4,570**. These amounts are the same as those computed using the perpetual system. This always occurs because the most recent purchases are in ending inventory under both systems. The purchases and sales entries for Exhibit 6A.3 follow (the colored boldface numbers are those affected by the cost flow assumption).

Purchases

Aug. 3	Purchases	1,590	
	Accounts Payable		1,590
17	Purchases	2,300	
	Accounts Payable		2,300
28	Purchases	1,190	
	Accounts Payable		1,190

Sales

Aug. 14	Accounts Receivable	2,600	
	Sales		2,600
31	Accounts Receivable	3,450	
	Sales		3,450
	Adjusting Entry		
31	Merchandise Inventory	1,420	
	Income Summary		510
	Merchandise Inventory		910

Last-In, First-Out

The last-in, first-out (LIFO) method of assigning costs assumes that the most recent purchases are sold first. These more recent costs are charged to the goods sold, and the costs of the earliest purchases are assigned to inventory. LIFO results in costs of the most recent purchases being assigned to cost of goods sold, which means that LIFO comes close to matching current costs of goods sold with revenues. Use of LIFO for computing cost of inventory and cost of goods sold is shown in Exhibit 6A.4.

This exhibit starts with computing $5,990 in total units available for sale—this is given to us at the start of this appendix. Applying LIFO, we know that the 12 units in ending inventory will be reported at the cost of the earliest 12 purchases. Reviewing the earliest purchases in order, we assign costs to the 12 bikes in ending inventory as follows: $91 cost to 10 bikes and $106 cost to 2 bikes. This yields 12 bikes costing $1,122 in ending inventory. We then subtract this $1,122 in ending inventory from $5,990 in cost of goods available to get $4,868 in cost of goods sold.

EXHIBIT 6A.4

LIFO Computations—Periodic System

Total cost of 55 units available for sale (from Exhibit 6A.1)		$5,990
Less ending inventory priced using LIFO		
10 units in beginning inventory at $91 each	$910	
2 units from August 3 purchase at $106 each	212	
Ending inventory		1,122
Cost of goods sold		$4,868

> Exhibit 6A.1 shows that the 12 units in ending inventory consist of 10 units from the earliest purchase (beg. inv.) and 2 units from the next earliest purchase on Aug. 3.

Trekking's ending inventory reported on the balance sheet is **$1,122**, and its cost of goods sold reported on the income statement is **$4,868**. When LIFO is used with the periodic system, cost of goods sold is assigned costs from the most recent purchases for the period. With a perpetual system, cost of goods sold is assigned costs from the most recent purchases at the point of *each sale*. The purchases and sales entries for Exhibit 6A.4 follow (the colored boldface numbers are those affected by the cost flow assumption).

Purchases				**Sales**		
Aug. 3	Purchases	1,590		Aug. 14	Accounts Receivable	2,600
	Accounts Payable		1,590		Sales	2,600
17	Purchases	2,300		31	Accounts Receivable	3,450
	Accounts Payable		2,300		Sales	3,450
28	Purchases	1,190			**Adjusting Entry**	
	Accounts Payable		1,190	31	Merchandise Inventory	1,122
					Income Summary	212
					Merchandise Inventory	910

Weighted Average

The **weighted average** or **WA** (also called **average cost**) method of assigning cost requires that we use the average cost per unit of inventory at the end of the period. Weighted average cost per unit equals the cost of goods available for sale divided by the units available. The weighted average method of assigning cost involves three important steps. The first two steps are shown in Exhibit 6A.5. First, multiply the per unit cost for beginning inventory and each particular purchase by the corresponding number of units (from Exhibit 6A.1). Second, add these amounts and divide by the total number of units available for sale to find the weighted average cost per unit.

EXHIBIT 6A.5

Weighted Average Cost per Unit

Example: In Exhibit 6A.5, if 5 more units had been purchased at $120 each, what would be the weighted average cost per unit? *Answer:* $109.83 ($6,590/60)

Step 1:	10 units @ $ 91 = $ 910
	15 units @ $106 = 1,590
	20 units @ $115 = 2,300
	10 units @ $119 = 1,190
	55 $5,990
Step 2:	$5,990/55 units = **$108.91** weighted average cost per unit

The third step is to use the weighted average cost per unit to assign costs to inventory and to the units sold as shown in Exhibit 6A.6.

EXHIBIT 6A.6

Weighted Average Computations—Periodic

Step 3:	Total cost of 55 units available for sale (from Exhibit 6A.1)	$ 5,990
	Less **ending inventory** priced on a weighted average cost basis: 12 units at $108.91 each (from Exhibit 6A.5)	1,307
	Cost of goods sold	$4,683

Trekking's ending inventory reported on the balance sheet is **$1,307**, and its cost of goods sold reported on the income statement is **$4,683** when using the weighted average (periodic) method. The purchases

Point: Weighted average usually yields different results for the perpetual and the periodic systems because under a perpetual system it recomputes the per unit cost prior to each sale, whereas under a periodic system, the per unit cost is computed only at the end of a period.

and sales entries for Exhibit 6A.6 follow (the colored boldface numbers are those affected by the cost flow assumption).

Purchases		
Aug. 3	Purchases	1,590
	Accounts Payable	1,590
17	Purchases	2,300
	Accounts Payable	2,300
28	Purchases	1,190
	Accounts Payable	1,190

Sales		
Aug. 14	Accounts Receivable	2,600
	Sales	2,600
31	Accounts Receivable	3,450
	Sales	3,450
	Adjusting Entry	
31	Merchandise Inventory........	1,307
	Income Summary	397
	Merchandise Inventory	910

Financial Statement Effects

Point: LIFO inventory is often less than the inventory's replacement cost because LIFO inventory is valued using the oldest inventory purchase costs.

When purchase prices do not change, each inventory costing method assigns the same cost amounts to inventory and to cost of goods sold. When purchase prices are different, however, the methods nearly always assign different cost amounts. We show these differences in Exhibit 6A.7 using Trekking's data.

EXHIBIT 6A.7

Financial Statement Effects of Inventory Costing Methods

TREKKING COMPANY **For Month Ended August 31**				
	Specific Identification	FIFO	LIFO	Weighted Average
Income Statement				
Sales	$ 6,050	$ 6,050	$ 6,050	$ 6,050
Cost of goods sold	4,582	4,570	4,868	4,683
Gross profit	1,468	1,480	1,182	1,367
Expenses	450	450	450	450
Income before taxes	1,018	1,030	732	917
Income tax expense (30%)	305	309	220	275
Net income	$ 713	$ 721	$ 512	$ 642
Balance Sheet				
Inventory	$1,408	$1,420	$1,122	$1,307

This exhibit reveals two important results. First, when purchase costs *regularly rise,* as in Trekking's case, observe the following:

■ FIFO assigns the lowest amount to cost of goods sold—yielding the highest gross profit and net income.

■ LIFO assigns the highest amount to cost of goods sold—yielding the lowest gross profit and net income, which also yields a temporary tax advantage by postponing payment of some income tax.

■ Weighted average yields results between FIFO and LIFO.

■ Specific identification always yields results that depend on which units are sold.

Second, when costs *regularly decline,* the reverse occurs for FIFO and LIFO. FIFO gives the highest cost of goods sold—yielding the lowest gross profit and income. And LIFO gives the lowest cost of goods sold—yielding the highest gross profit and income.

All four inventory costing methods are acceptable in practice. A company must disclose the inventory method it uses. Each method offers certain advantages as follows:

■ FIFO assigns an amount to inventory on the balance sheet that approximates its current cost; it also mimics the actual flow of goods for most businesses.

■ LIFO assigns an amount to cost of goods sold on the income statement that approximates its current cost; it also better matches current costs with revenues in computing gross profit.

■ Weighted average tends to smooth out erratic changes in costs.

■ Specific identification exactly matches the costs of items with the revenues they generate.

Quick Check Answers—p. 250

9. A company reports the following beginning inventory and purchases, and it ends the period with 30 units in inventory.

Beginning inventory	100 units at $10 cost per unit
Purchase 1	40 units at $12 cost per unit
Purchase 2	20 units at $14 cost per unit

a. Compute ending inventory using the FIFO periodic system.

b. Compute cost of goods sold using the LIFO periodic system.

APPENDIX

Inventory Estimation Methods

6B

Inventory sometimes requires estimation for two reasons. First, companies often require **interim statements** (financial statements prepared for periods of less than one year), but they only annually take a physical count of inventory. Second, companies may require an inventory estimate if some casualty such as fire or flood makes taking a physical count impossible. Estimates are usually only required for companies that use the periodic system. Companies using a perpetual system would presumably have updated inventory data.

This appendix describes two methods to estimate inventory.

P4 Apply both the retail inventory and gross profit methods to estimate inventory.

Retail Inventory Method

To avoid the time-consuming and expensive process of taking a physical inventory each month or quarter, some companies use the **retail inventory method** to estimate cost of goods sold and ending inventory. Some companies even use the retail inventory method to prepare the annual statements. **Home Depot**, for instance, says in its annual report: "Inventories are stated at the lower of cost (first-in, first-out) or market, as determined by the retail inventory method." A company may also estimate inventory for audit purposes or when inventory is damaged or destroyed.

The retail inventory method uses a three-step process to estimate ending inventory. We need to know the amount of inventory a company had at the beginning of the period in both *cost* and *retail* amounts. We already explained how to compute the cost of inventory. The *retail amount of inventory* refers to its dollar amount measured using selling prices of inventory items. We also need to know the net

Point: When a retailer takes a physical inventory, it can restate the retail value of inventory to a cost basis by applying the cost-to-retail ratio. It can also estimate the amount of shrinkage by comparing the inventory computed with the amount from a physical inventory.

amount of goods purchased (minus returns, allowances, and discounts) in the period, both at cost and at retail. The amount of net sales at retail is also needed. The process is shown in Exhibit 6B.1.

The reasoning behind the retail inventory method is that if we can get a good estimate of the cost-to-retail ratio, we can multiply ending inventory at retail by this ratio to estimate ending inventory at cost. We show in Exhibit 6B.2 how these steps are applied to estimate ending inventory for a typical company. First, we find that

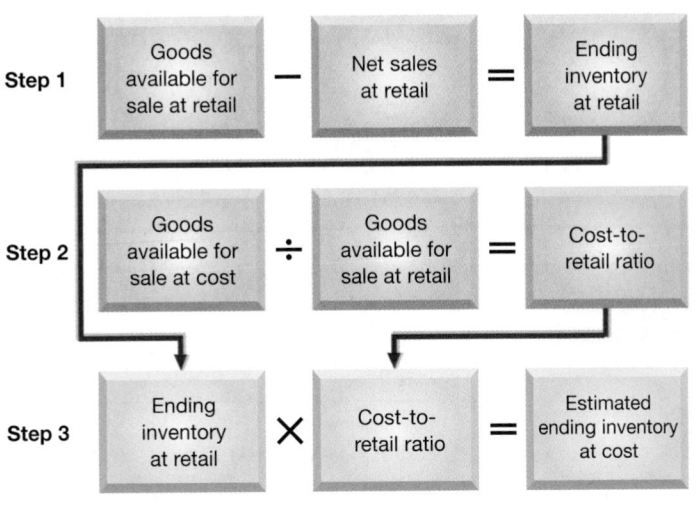

EXHIBIT 6B.1

Retail Inventory Method of Inventory Estimation

EXHIBIT 6B.2

Estimated Inventory Using the
Retail Inventory Method

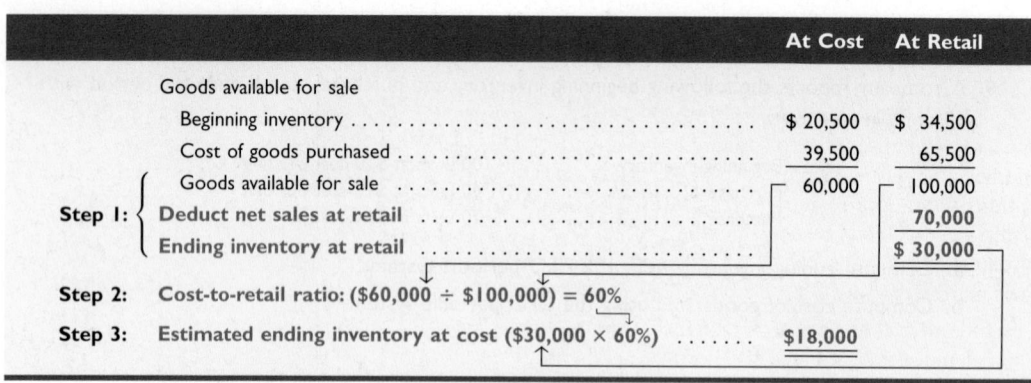

	At Cost	At Retail
Goods available for sale		
Beginning inventory	$ 20,500	$ 34,500
Cost of goods purchased	39,500	65,500
Step 1: Goods available for sale	60,000	100,000
Deduct net sales at retail		70,000
Ending inventory at retail		$ 30,000
Step 2: Cost-to-retail ratio: ($60,000 ÷ $100,000) = 60%		
Step 3: Estimated ending inventory at cost ($30,000 × 60%)	$18,000	

Example: What is the cost of ending inventory in Exhibit 6B.2 if the cost of beginning inventory is $22,500 and its retail value is $34,500? *Answer:* $30,000 × 62% = $18,600

$100,000 of goods (at retail selling prices) were available for sale. We see that $70,000 of these goods were sold, leaving $30,000 (retail value) of merchandise in ending inventory. Second, the cost of these goods is 60% of the $100,000 retail value. Third, since cost for these goods is 60% of retail, the estimated cost of ending inventory is $18,000.

Gross Profit Method

The **gross profit method** estimates the cost of ending inventory by applying the gross profit ratio to net sales (at retail). This type of estimate often is needed when inventory is destroyed, lost, or stolen. These cases require an inventory estimate so that a company can file a claim with its insurer. Users also apply this method to see whether inventory amounts from a physical count are reasonable. This method uses

EXHIBIT 6B.3

Gross Profit Method of
Inventory Estimation

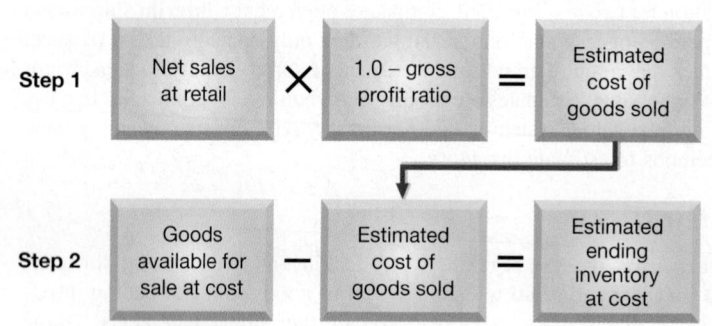

the historical relation between cost of goods sold and net sales to estimate the proportion of cost of goods sold making up current sales. This cost of goods sold estimate is then subtracted from cost of goods available for sale to estimate the ending inventory at cost. These two steps are shown in Exhibit 6B.3.

To illustrate, assume that a company's inventory is destroyed by fire in March 2009. When the fire occurs, the company's accounts show the following balances for January through March: sales, $31,500; sales returns, $1,500; inventory (January 1, 2009), $12,000; and cost of goods purchased, $20,500. If this company's gross profit ratio is 30%, then 30% of each net sales dollar is gross profit and 70% is cost of goods sold. We show in Exhibit 6B.4 how this 70% is used to estimate lost inventory of $11,500. To understand this exhibit, think of subtracting the cost of goods sold from the goods available for sale to get the ending inventory.

Point: A fire or other catastrophe can result in an insurance claim for lost inventory or income. Backup and off-site storage of data help ensure coverage for such losses.

Point: Reliability of the gross profit method depends on a good estimate of the gross profit ratio.

EXHIBIT 6B.4

Estimated Inventory Using the
Gross Profit Method

Goods available for sale		
Inventory, January 1, 2009	$12,000	
Cost of goods purchased	20,500	
Goods available for sale (at cost)	32,500	
Net sales at retail ($31,500 − $1,500)		$30,000
Step 1: Estimated cost of goods sold ($30,000 × 70%)	(21,000)	× 0.70
Step 2: Estimated March inventory at cost	$11,500	

Quick Check   Answer—p. 250

10. Using the retail method and the following data, estimate the cost of ending inventory.

	Cost	Retail
Beginning inventory	$324,000	$530,000
Cost of goods purchased	195,000	335,000
Net sales		320,000

Summary

C1 Identify the items making up merchandise inventory. Merchandise inventory refers to goods owned by a company and held for resale. Three special cases merit our attention. Goods in transit are reported in inventory of the company that holds ownership rights. Goods on consignment are reported in the consignor's inventory. Goods damaged or obsolete are reported in inventory at their net realizable value.

C2 Identify the costs of merchandise inventory. Costs of merchandise inventory include expenditures necessary to bring an item to a salable condition and location. This includes its invoice cost minus any discount plus any added or incidental costs necessary to put it in a place and condition for sale.

A1 Analyze the effects of inventory methods for both financial and tax reporting. When purchase costs are rising or falling, the inventory costing methods are likely to assign different costs to inventory. Specific identification exactly matches costs and revenues. Weighted average smooths out cost changes. FIFO assigns an amount to inventory closely approximating current replacement cost. LIFO assigns the most recent costs incurred to cost of goods sold and likely better matches current costs with revenues.

A2 Analyze the effects of inventory errors on current and future financial statements. An error in the amount of ending inventory affects assets (inventory), net income (cost of goods sold), and equity for that period. Since ending inventory is next period's beginning inventory, an error in ending inventory affects next period's cost of goods sold and net income. Inventory errors in one period are offset in the next period.

A3 Assess inventory management using both inventory turnover and days' sales in inventory. We prefer a high inventory turnover, provided that goods are not out of stock and customers are not turned away. We use days' sales in inventory to assess the likelihood of goods being out of stock. We prefer a small number of days' sales in inventory if we can serve customer needs and provide a buffer for uncertainties.

P1 Compute inventory in a perpetual system using the methods of specific identification, FIFO, LIFO, and weighted average. Costs are assigned to the cost of goods sold account *each time* a sale occurs in a perpetual system. Specific identification assigns a cost to each item sold by referring to its actual cost (for example, its net invoice cost). Weighted average assigns a cost to items sold by dividing the current balance in the inventory account by the total items available for sale to determine cost per unit. We then multiply the number of units sold by this cost per unit to get the cost of each sale. FIFO assigns cost to items sold assuming that the earliest units purchased are the first units sold. LIFO assigns cost to items sold assuming that the most recent units purchased are the first units sold.

P2 Compute the lower of cost or market amount of inventory. Inventory is reported at market cost when market is *lower* than recorded cost, called the *lower of cost or market* (*LCM*) *inventory*. Market is typically measured as replacement cost. Lower of cost or market can be applied separately to each item, to major categories of items, or to the entire inventory.

P3^A Compute inventory in a periodic system using the methods of specific identification, FIFO, LIFO, and weighted average. Periodic inventory systems allocate the cost of goods available for sale between cost of goods sold and ending inventory *at the end of a period*. Specific identification and FIFO give identical results whether the periodic or perpetual system is used. LIFO assigns costs to cost of goods sold assuming the last units purchased for the period are the first units sold. The weighted average cost per unit is computed by dividing the total cost of beginning inventory and net purchases for the period by the total number of units available. Then, it multiplies cost per unit by the number of units sold to give cost of goods sold.

P4^B Apply both the retail inventory and gross profit methods to estimate inventory. The retail inventory method involves three steps: (1) goods available at retail minus net sales at retail equals ending inventory at retail, (2) goods available at cost divided by goods available at retail equals the cost-to-retail ratio, and (3) ending inventory at retail multiplied by the cost-to-retail ratio equals estimated ending inventory at cost. The gross profit method involves two steps: (1) net sales at retail multiplied by 1 minus the gross profit ratio equals estimated cost of goods sold, and (2) goods available at cost minus estimated cost of goods sold equals estimated ending inventory at cost.

Guidance Answers to **Decision Maker** and **Decision Ethics**

Financial Planner The FIFO method implies that the oldest costs are the first ones assigned to cost of goods sold. This leaves the most recent costs in ending inventory. You report this to your client and note that in most cases, the ending inventory of a company using FIFO is reported at or near its replacement cost. This means that your client need not in most cases adjust the reported value of inventory. Your answer changes only if there are major increases in replacement cost compared to the cost of recent purchases reported in inventory. When major increases in costs occur, your client might wish to adjust inventory (for internal reports) for the difference between the reported cost of inventory and its replacement cost. (*Note:* Decreases in costs of purchases are recognized under the lower of cost or market adjustment.)

Inventory Manager It seems your company can save (or at least postpone) taxes by switching to LIFO, but the switch is likely to reduce bonus money that you think you have earned and deserve. Since the U.S. tax code requires companies that use LIFO for tax reporting also to use it for financial reporting, your options are further constrained. Your best decision is to tell your superior about the tax savings with LIFO. You also should discuss your bonus plan and how this is likely to hurt you unfairly. You might propose to compute inventory under the LIFO method for reporting purposes but use the FIFO method for your bonus calculations. Another solution is to revise the bonus plan to reflect the company's use of the LIFO method.

Entrepreneur Your inventory turnover is markedly higher than the norm, whereas days' sales in inventory approximates the norm. Since your turnover is already 14% better than average, you are probably best served by directing attention to days' sales in inventory. You should see whether you can reduce the level of inventory while maintaining service to customers. Given your higher turnover, you should be able to hold less inventory.

Guidance Answers to Quick Checks

1. The matching principle.

2. Target reports these goods in its inventory.

3. Total cost assigned to the painting is $12,180, computed as $11,400 + $130 + $150 + $100 + $400.

4. Specific identification exactly matches costs and revenues. Weighted average tends to smooth out cost changes. FIFO assigns an amount to inventory that closely approximates current replacement cost. LIFO assigns the most recent costs incurred to cost of goods sold and likely better matches current costs with revenues.

5. FIFO—it gives a lower cost of goods sold, a higher gross profit, and a higher net income when costs are rising.

6. When costs are rising, LIFO gives a lower inventory figure on the balance sheet as compared to FIFO. FIFO's inventory amount approximates current replacement costs.

7. Cost of goods sold would be overstated by $10,000 in 2009 and understated by $10,000 in year 2010.

8. The reported LCM inventory amount (using items) is $540, computed as $[(20 \times \$5) + (40 \times \$8) + (10 \times \$12)]$.

9.[A]a. FIFO periodic inventory $= (20 \times \$14) + (10 \times \$12)$
$$= \$400$$

   b. LIFO periodic cost of goods sold
$$= (20 \times \$14) + (40 \times \$12) + (70 \times \$10)$$
$$= \$1,460$$

10.[B] Estimated ending inventory (at cost) is $327,000. It is computed as follows:

Step 1: $(\$530,000 + \$335,000) - \$320,000 = \$545,000$

Step 2: $\dfrac{\$324,000 + \$195,000}{\$530,000 + \$335,000} = 60\%$

Step 3: $\$545,000 \times 60\% = \underline{\underline{\$327,000}}$

Key Terms   mhhe.com/wildFAP19e

Key Terms are available at the book's Website for learning and testing in an online Flashcard Format.

Average cost (pp. 230, 245)
Conservatism constraint (p. 234)
Consignee (p. 224)
Consignor (p. 224)
Consistency concept (p. 233)
Days' sales in inventory (p. 237)

First-in, first-out (FIFO) (p. 229)
Gross profit method (p. 248)
Interim statements (p. 247)
Inventory turnover (p. 236)
Last-in, first-out (LIFO) (p. 229)
Lower of cost or market (LCM) (p. 233)

Net realizable value (p. 224)
Retail inventory method (p. 247)
Specific identification (p. 227)
Weighted average (pp. 230, 245)

Multiple Choice Quiz   Answers on p. 265   mhhe.com/wildFAP19e

Additional Quiz Questions are available at the book's Website.

Use the following information from Marvel Company for the month of July to answer questions 1 through 4.

July 1	Beginning inventory	75 units @ $25 each
July 3	Purchase	348 units @ $27 each
July 8	Sale	300 units
July 15	Purchase	257 units @ $28 each
July 23	Sale	275 units

1. Assume that Marvel uses a perpetual FIFO inventory system. What is the dollar value of its ending inventory?
    a. $2,940   d. $2,852
    b. $2,685   e. $2,705
    c. $2,625

2. Assume that Marvel uses a perpetual LIFO inventory system. What is the dollar value of its ending inventory?
    a. $2,940   d. $2,852
    b. $2,685   e. $2,705
    c. $2,625

3. Assume that Marvel uses a perpetual specific identification inventory system. Its ending inventory consists of 20 units from beginning inventory, 40 units from the July 3 purchase, and 45 units from the July 15 purchase. What is the dollar value of its ending inventory?
    a. $2,940   d. $2,852
    b. $2,685   e. $2,840
    c. $2,625

4.[A] Assume that Marvel uses a *periodic* FIFO inventory system. What is the dollar value of its ending inventory?
    a. $2,940   d. $2,852
    b. $2,685   e. $2,705
    c. $2,625

5. A company has cost of goods sold of $85,000 and ending inventory of $18,000. Its days' sales in inventory equals:
    a. 49.32 days   d. 77.29 days
    b. 0.21 days   e. 1,723.61 days
    c. 4.72 days

Superscript letter ᴬ *(ᴮ) denotes assignments based on Appendix 6A (6B).*

Discussion Questions

1. Describe how costs flow from inventory to cost of goods sold for the following methods: (*a*) FIFO and (*b*) LIFO.

2. Where is the amount of merchandise inventory disclosed in the financial statements?

3. Why are incidental costs sometimes ignored in inventory costing? Under what accounting constraint is this permitted?

4. ♟ If costs are declining, will the LIFO or FIFO method of inventory valuation yield the lower cost of goods sold? Why?

5. What does the full-disclosure principle prescribe if a company changes from one acceptable accounting method to another?

6. Can a company change its inventory method each accounting period? Explain.

7. ♟ Does the accounting concept of consistency preclude any changes from one accounting method to another?

8. ♟ If inventory errors are said to correct themselves, why are accounting users concerned when such errors are made?

9. Explain the following statement: "Inventory errors correct themselves."

10. What is the meaning of *market* as it is used in determining the lower of cost or market for inventory?

11. ♟ What guidance does the accounting constraint of conservatism offer?

12. What factors contribute to (or cause) inventory shrinkage?

13.ᴬWhat accounts are used in a periodic inventory system but not in a perpetual inventory system?

14. Refer to **Best Buy**'s financial statements in Appendix A. On March 3, 2007, what percent of current assets is represented by inventory?

15. Refer to **Circuit City**'s financial statements in Appendix A. Compute its cost of goods available for sale for the year ended February 28, 2007.

16. Refer to **RadioShack**'s financial statements in Appendix A and compute its cost of goods available for sale for the year ended December 31, 2006.

17. Refer to **Apple**'s financial statements in Appendix A. What percent of its current assets are inventory as of September 30, 2006, and as of September 24, 2005?

18.ᴮWhen preparing interim financial statements, what two methods can companies utilize to estimate cost of goods sold and ending inventory?

♟ **Denotes Discussion Questions that involve decision making.**

McGraw-Hill's
HOMEWORK
MANAGER®   Available with McGraw-Hill's Homework Manager

A company reports the following beginning inventory and purchases for the month of January. On January 26, the company sells 360 units. What is the cost of the 155 units that remain in ending inventory at January 31, assuming costs are assigned based on a perpetual inventory system and use of (*a*) FIFO, (*b*) LIFO, and (*c*) weighted average? (Round per unit costs to three decimals, but inventory balances to the dollar.)

	Units	Unit Cost
Beginning inventory on January 1	320	$6.00
Purchase on January 9	85	6.40
Purchase on January 25	110	6.60

QUICK STUDY

QS 6-1
Inventory costing methods—perpetual system
P1

Check (c) $960

Rosen Company reports beginning inventory of 10 units at $28 each. Every week for four weeks it purchases an additional 10 units at respective costs of $30, $31, $32, and $34 per unit for weeks 1 through 4. Calculate the cost of goods available for sale and the units available for sale for this four-week period. Assume that no sales occur during those four weeks.

QS 6-2
Computing goods available for sale
P1

Mercedes Brown starts a merchandising business on December 1 and enters into three inventory purchases:

December 7	10 units @ $ 9 cost
December 14	20 units @ $10 cost
December 21	15 units @ $12 cost

QS 6-3
Assigning costs to inventory—perpetual system
P1

Brown sells 18 units for $35 each on December 15. Seven of the sold units are from the December 7 purchase and eleven are from the December 14 purchase. Brown uses a perpetual inventory system. Determine the costs assigned to the December 31 ending inventory based on (*a*) FIFO, (*b*) LIFO, (*c*) weighted average, and (*d*) specific identification. (Round per unit costs to three decimals, but inventory balances to the dollar.)

Check (c) $296

QS 6-4

Contrasting inventory
costing methods

A1

Identify the inventory costing method best described by each of the following separate statements. Assume a period of increasing costs.

1. Results in a balance sheet inventory amount approximating replacement cost.

2. The preferred method when each unit of product has unique features that markedly affect cost.

3. Matches recent costs against net sales.

4. Yields a balance sheet inventory amount often markedly less than its replacement cost.

5. Provides a tax advantage (deferral) to a corporation when costs are rising.

QS 6-5

Inventory ownership

C1

Homestead Crafts, a distributor of handmade gifts, operates out of owner Emma Flynn's house. At the end of the current period, Emma reports she has 800 units (products) in her basement, 10 of which were damaged by water and cannot be sold. She also has another 400 units in her van, ready to deliver per a customer order, terms FOB destination, and another 100 units out on consignment to a friend who owns a retail store. How many units should Emma include in her company's period-end inventory?

QS 6-6

Inventory ownership

C1

1. Jabar Company has shipped $600 of goods to Chi Co., and Chi Co. has arranged to sell the goods for Jabar. Identify the consignor and the consignee. Which company should include any unsold goods as part of its inventory?

2. At year-end, Liu Co. had shipped $750 of merchandise FOB destination to Kwon Co. Which company should include the $750 of merchandise in transit as part of its year-end inventory?

QS 6-7

Inventory costs

C2

Rivers Associates, antique dealers, purchased the contents of an estate for $75,000. Terms of the purchase were FOB shipping point, and the cost of transporting the goods to Rivers Associates' warehouse was $1,800. Rivers Associates insured the shipment at a cost of $300. Prior to putting the goods up for sale, they cleaned and refurbished them at a cost of $1,750. Determine the cost of the inventory acquired from the estate.

QS 6-8

Inventory costs

C2

A car dealer acquires a used car for $17,500, terms FOB shipping point. Additional costs in obtaining and offering the car for sale include $300 for transportation-in, $1,000 for import duties, $250 for insurance during shipment, $400 for advertising, and $3,000 for sales staff salaries. For computing inventory, what cost is assigned to the used car?

QS 6-9

Applying LCM to inventories

P2

Paoli Trading Co. has the following products in its ending inventory. Compute lower of cost or market for inventory (*a*) as a whole and (*b*) applied separately to each product.

Product	Quantity	Cost per Unit	Market per Unit
Mountain bikes	20	$650	$500
Skateboards	22	400	450
Gliders	40	850	790

QS 6-10

Inventory errors

A2

In taking a physical inventory at the end of year 2009, Peña Company erroneously forgot to count certain units. Explain how this error affects the following: (*a*) 2009 cost of goods sold, (*b*) 2009 gross profit, (*c*) 2009 net income, (*d*) 2010 net income, (*e*) the combined two-year income, and (*f*) income for years after 2010.

QS 6-11

Analyzing inventory   A3

Civic Company begins the year with $75,075 of goods in inventory. At year-end, the amount in inventory has increased to $89,925. Cost of goods sold for the year is $602,250. Compute Civic's inventory turnover and days' sales in inventory. Assume that there are 365 days in the year.

QS 6-12^A

Costing methods—
periodic system   P3

Refer to QS 6-1 and assume the periodic inventory system is used. Determine the costs assigned to the ending inventory when costs are assigned based on (*a*) FIFO, (*b*) LIFO, and (*c*) weighted average. (Round per unit costs to three decimals, but inventory balances to the dollar.)

QS 6-13^A

Costing methods—
periodic system   P3

Refer to QS 6-3 and assume the periodic inventory system is used. Determine the costs assigned to the December 31 ending inventory when costs are assigned based on (*a*) FIFO, (*b*) LIFO, (*c*) weighted average, and (*d*) specific identification. (Round per unit costs to three decimals, but inventory balances to the dollar.)

Kaysee Store's inventory is destroyed by a fire on September 5, 2009. The following data for year 2009 are available from the accounting records. Estimate the cost of the inventory destroyed.

Jan. 1 inventory	$230,000
Jan. 1 through Sept. 5 purchases (net)	$492,000
Jan. 1 through Sept. 5 sales (net)	$850,000
Year 2009 estimated gross profit rate	37%

QS 6-14[B]

Estimating inventories—gross profit method

P4

McGraw-Hill's
HOMEWORK
MANAGER®

Available with McGraw-Hill's Homework Manager

Liberty Company reported the following January purchases and sales data for its only product.

EXERCISES

Exercise 6-1

Inventory costing methods—perpetual

P1

Date	Activities	Units Acquired at Cost	Units Sold at Retail
Jan. 1	Beginning inventory	140 units @ $7.00 = $ 980	
Jan. 10	Sales		90 units @ $15
Jan. 20	Purchase	220 units @ $6.00 = 1,320	
Jan. 25	Sales		145 units @ $15
Jan. 30	Purchase	100 units @ $5.00 = 500	
	Totals	460 units $2,800	235 units

Liberty uses a perpetual inventory system. Ending inventory consists of 225 units, 100 from the January 30 purchase, 80 from the January 20 purchase, and 45 from beginning inventory. Determine the cost assigned to ending inventory and to cost of goods sold using (*a*) specific identification, (*b*) weighted average, (*c*) FIFO, and (*d*) LIFO. (Round per unit costs to three decimals, but inventory balances to the dollar.)

Check Ending inventory: LIFO, $1,300; WA, $1,273

Use the data in Exercise 6-1 to prepare comparative income statements for the month of January for Liberty Company similar to those shown in Exhibit 6.8 for the four inventory methods. Assume expenses are $1,250, and that the applicable income tax rate is 30%.

1. Which method yields the highest net income?

2. Does net income using weighted average fall between that using FIFO and LIFO?

3. If costs were rising instead of falling, which method would yield the highest net income?

Exercise 6-2

Income effects of inventory methods

A1

Harper Co. reported the following current-year purchases and sales data for its only product.

Exercise 6-3

Inventory costing methods (perpetual)—FIFO and LIFO

P1

Date	Activities	Units Acquired at Cost	Units Sold at Retail
Jan. 1	Beginning inventory	126 units @ $8 = $ 1,008	
Jan. 10	Sales		113 units @ $40
Mar. 14	Purchase	315 units @ $13 = 4,095	
Mar. 15	Sales		180 units @ $40
July 30	Purchase	250 units @ $18 = 4,500	
Oct. 5	Sales		378 units @ $40
Oct. 26	Purchase	50 units @ $23 = 1,150	
	Totals	741 units $10,753	671 units

Harper uses a perpetual inventory system. Determine the costs assigned to ending inventory and to cost of goods sold using (*a*) FIFO and (*b*) LIFO. Compute the gross margin for each method.

Check Ending inventory: LIFO, $1,345

Refer to the data in Exercise 6-3. Assume that ending inventory is made up of 5 units from the March 14 purchase, 15 units from the July 30 purchase, and all the units of the October 26 purchase. Using the specific identification method, calculate (*a*) the cost of goods sold and (*b*) the gross profit.

Exercise 6-4

Specific identification   P1

Exercise 6-5
Lower of cost or market   P2

Maya Company's ending inventory includes the following items. Compute the lower of cost or market for ending inventory (*a*) as a whole and (*b*) applied separately to each product.

Product	Units	Per Unit Cost	Per Unit Market
Helmets	19	$45	$49
Bats	12	73	67
Shoes	33	90	86
Uniforms	37	31	31

Check (*b*) $5,644

Exercise 6-6
Analysis of inventory errors

A2

Check 2008 reported gross profit, $382,000

Abco Company had $1,100,000 of sales in each of three consecutive years 2008–2010, and it purchased merchandise costing $700,000 in each of those years. It also maintained a $280,000 physical inventory from the beginning to the end of that three-year period. In accounting for inventory, it made an error at the end of year 2008 that caused its year-end 2008 inventory to appear on its statements as $262,000 rather than the correct $280,000.

1. Determine the correct amount of the company's gross profit in each of the years 2008–2010.

2. Prepare comparative income statements as in Exhibit 6.11 to show the effect of this error on the company's cost of goods sold and gross profit for each of the years 2008–2010.

Exercise 6-7
Inventory turnover and days' sales in inventory

A3

Use the following information for Palmer Co. to compute inventory turnover for 2009 and 2008, and its days' sales in inventory at December 31, 2009 and 2008. (Round answers to one decimal.) Comment on Palmer's efficiency in using its assets to increase sales from 2008 to 2009.

	2009	2008	2007
Cost of goods sold	$667,134	$442,104	$405,600
Ending inventory	92,232	87,840	97,600

Exercise 6-8
Comparing LIFO numbers to FIFO numbers; ratio analysis

A1 A3

Cook Company uses LIFO for inventory costing and reports the following financial data. It also recomputed inventory and cost of goods sold using FIFO for comparison purposes.

	2009	2008
LIFO inventory	$110	$177
LIFO cost of goods sold	760	828
FIFO inventory	270	457
FIFO cost of goods sold	680	645
Current assets (using LIFO)	250	200
Current liabilities	225	180

Check (1) FIFO: Current ratio, 1.8; Inventory turnover, 1.9 times

1. Compute its current ratio, inventory turnover, and days' sales in inventory for 2009 using (*a*) LIFO numbers and (*b*) FIFO numbers. (Round answers to one decimal.)

2. Comment on and interpret the results of part 1.

Exercise 6-9^A
Inventory costing— periodic system   P3

Refer to Exercise 6-1 and assume the periodic inventory system is used. Determine the costs assigned to ending inventory and to cost of goods sold using (*a*) specific identification, (*b*) weighted average, (*c*) FIFO, and (*d*) LIFO. (Round per unit costs to three decimals, but inventory balances to the dollar.)

Exercise 6-10^A
Inventory costing— periodic system   P3

Refer to Exercise 6-3 and assume the periodic inventory system is used. Determine the costs assigned to ending inventory and to cost of goods sold using (*a*) FIFO and (*b*) LIFO. Compute the gross margin for each method.

Martinez Co. reported the following current-year data for its only product. The company uses a periodic inventory system, and its ending inventory consists of 405 units—135 from each of the last three purchases. Determine the cost assigned to ending inventory and to cost of goods sold using (a) specific identification, (b) weighted average, (c) FIFO, and (d) LIFO. (Round per unit costs to three decimals, but inventory balances to the dollar.) Which method yields the highest net income?

Exercise 6-11[A]

Alternative cost flow assumptions—periodic

P3

Jan. 1	Beginning inventory	270 units @ $1.90 = $ 513
Mar. 7	Purchase	540 units @ $2.05 = 1,107
July 28	Purchase	1,350 units @ $2.30 = 3,105
Oct. 3	Purchase	1,230 units @ $2.60 = 3,198
Dec. 19	Purchase	390 units @ $2.70 = 1,053
	Totals	3,780 units $8,976

Check   Inventory; LIFO, $790; FIFO, $1,092

Genesis Gifts reported the following current-year data for its only product. The company uses a periodic inventory system, and its ending inventory consists of 360 units—120 from each of the last three purchases. Determine the cost assigned to ending inventory and to cost of goods sold using (a) specific identification, (b) weighted average, (c) FIFO, and (d) LIFO. (Round per unit costs to three decimals, but inventory balances to the dollar.) Which method yields the lowest net income?

Exercise 6-12[A]

Alternative cost flow assumptions—periodic

P3

Jan. 1	Beginning inventory	290 units @ $2.80 = $ 812
Mar. 7	Purchase	610 units @ $2.70 = 1,647
July 28	Purchase	810 units @ $2.40 = 1,944
Oct. 3	Purchase	1,110 units @ $2.20 = 2,442
Dec. 19	Purchase	260 units @ $1.90 = 494
	Totals	3,080 units $7,339

Check   Inventory: LIFO, $1,001; FIFO, $714

In 2009, Dakota Company had net sales (at retail) of $219,800. The following additional information is available from its records at the end of 2009. Use the retail inventory method to estimate Dakota's 2009 ending inventory at cost.

Exercise 6-13[B]

Estimating ending inventory—retail method

P4

	At Cost	At Retail
Beginning inventory	$ 57,100	$108,200
Cost of goods purchased	97,740	168,300

Check   End. Inventory, $31,752

On January 1, Java Shop had $360,000 of inventory at cost. In the first quarter of the year, it purchased $1,267,200 of merchandise, returned $11,450, and paid freight charges of $18,100 on purchased merchandise, terms FOB shipping point. The company's gross profit averages 34%, and the store had $1,594,800 of net sales (at retail) in the first quarter of the year. Use the gross profit method to estimate its cost of inventory at the end of the first quarter.

Exercise 6-14[B]

Estimating ending inventory—gross profit method

P4

McGraw-Hill's
HOMEWORK
MANAGER®   Available with McGraw-Hill's Homework Manager

Ammons Company uses a perpetual inventory system. It entered into the following purchases and sales transactions for January.

PROBLEM SET A

Problem 6-1A
Alternative cost flows—perpetual

P1

Date	Activities	Units Acquired at Cost	Units Sold at Retail
Jan. 1	Beginning inventory	5 units @ $500/unit	
Jan. 5	Purchase	20 units @ $550/unit	
Jan. 9	Sales		21 units @ $850/unit
Jan. 18	Purchase	6 units @ $600/unit	
Jan. 25	Purchase	10 units @ $620/unit	
Jan. 29	Sales		8 units @ $950/unit
	Totals	41 units	29 units

Required

1. Compute cost of goods available for sale and the number of units available for sale.

2. Compute the number of units in ending inventory.

3. Compute the cost assigned to ending inventory using (*a*) FIFO, (*b*) LIFO, (*c*) weighted average, and (*d*) specific identification. (Round per unit costs to three decimals, but inventory balances to the dollar.) For specific identification, the January 9 sale consisted of 4 units from beginning inventory and 17 units from the January 5 purchase; the January 29 sale consisted of 2 units from the January 18 purchase and 6 units from the January 25 purchase.

4. Compute gross profit earned by the company for each of the four costing methods in part 3.

Check (3) Ending Inventory: FIFO, $7,400; LIFO, $6,840, WA, $7,176

(4) LIFO gross profit, $8,990

Problem 6-2A
Alternative cost flows—perpetual

P1

Marlow Company uses a perpetual inventory system. It entered into the following calendar-year 2009 purchases and sales transactions.

Date	Activities	Units Acquired at Cost	Units Sold at Retail
Jan. 1	Beginning inventory	770 units @ $50/unit	
Feb. 10	Purchase	420 units @ $41/unit	
Mar. 13	Purchase	260 units @ $25/unit	
Mar. 15	Sales		770 units @ $75/unit
Aug. 21	Purchase	180 units @ $49/unit	
Sept. 5	Purchase	585 units @ $42/unit	
Sept. 10	Sales		650 units @ $75/unit
	Totals	2,215 units	1,420 units

Required

1. Compute cost of goods available for sale and the number of units available for sale.

2. Compute the number of units in ending inventory.

3. Compute the cost assigned to ending inventory using (*a*) FIFO, (*b*) LIFO, (*c*) specific identification— units sold consist of 95 units from beginning inventory, 175 from the February 10 purchase, 70 from the March 13 purchase, and 455 from the September 5 purchase, and (*d*) weighted average. (Round per unit costs to three decimals, but inventory balances to the dollar.)

4. Compute gross profit earned by the company for each of the four costing methods in part 3.

Check (3) Ending inventory: FIFO, $34,140; LIFO, $39,635; WA, $34,424;

(4) LIFO gross profit, $50,525

Analysis Component

5. If the company's manager earns a bonus based on a percent of gross profit, which method of inventory costing will the manager likely prefer?

Problem 6-3A
Lower of cost or market

P2

A physical inventory of SoundLand Company taken at December 31 reveals the following.

			Per Unit	
Item	Units		Cost	Market
Audio equipment				
Receivers	343		$ 88	$ 96
CD players	255		109	98
MP3 players	323		84	93
Speakers	198		50	39
Video equipment				
Handheld LCDs	481		148	123
VCRs	288		91	82
Camcorders	206		308	320
Car audio equipment				
Satellite radios	179		68	82
CD/MP3 radios	164		95	103

Required

Calculate the lower of cost or market for the inventory (*a*) as a whole, (*b*) by major category, and (*c*) applied separately to each item.

Check (*b*) $271,462; (*c*) $264,007

Nikita Company's financial statements show the following. The company recently discovered that in making physical counts of inventory, it had made the following errors: Inventory on December 31, 2008, is understated by $56,000, and inventory on December 31, 2009, is overstated by $25,000.

Problem 6-4A
Analysis of inventory errors

A2

mhhe.com/wildFAP19e

For Year Ended December 31		2008	2009	2010
(a)	Cost of goods sold	$ 623,000	$ 955,000	$ 780,000
(b)	Net income	230,000	275,000	250,000
(c)	Total current assets	1,247,000	1,360,000	1,230,000
(d)	Total equity	1,387,000	1,580,000	1,245,000

Required

1. For each key financial statement figure—(*a*), (*b*), (*c*), and (*d*) above—prepare a table similar to the following to show the adjustments necessary to correct the reported amounts.

Figure: _____	2008	2009	2010
Reported amount			
Adjustments for: 12/31/2008 error			
12/31/2009 error			
Corrected amount			

Check (1) Corrected net income:
2008, $286,000; 2009, $194,000;
2010, $275,000

Analysis Component

2. What is the error in total net income for the combined three-year period resulting from the inventory errors? Explain.

3. Explain why the understatement of inventory by $56,000 at the end of 2008 results in an understatement of equity by the same amount in that year.

Austin Company began year 2009 with 33,000 units of product in its January 1 inventory costing $17 each. It made successive purchases of its product in year 2009 as follows. The company uses a periodic inventory system. On December 31, 2009, a physical count reveals that 40,000 units of its product remain in inventory.

Problem 6-5A[A]
Alternative cost flows—periodic

P3

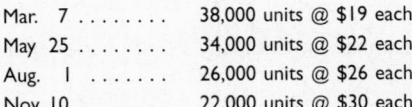

Mar. 7 . . . . 38,000 units @ $19 each
May 25 . . . . 34,000 units @ $22 each
Aug. I . . . . 26,000 units @ $26 each
Nov. 10 . . . . 22,000 units @ $30 each

Required

1. Compute the number and total cost of the units available for sale in year 2009.

2. Compute the amounts assigned to the 2009 ending inventory and the cost of goods sold using (*a*) FIFO, (*b*) LIFO, and (*c*) weighted average. (Round per unit costs to three decimals, but inventory balances to the dollar.)

Check (2) Cost of goods sold: FIFO,
$2,239,000; LIFO, $2,673,000; WA,
$2,486,720

Bay Corp. sold 6,500 units of its product at $50 per unit in year 2009 and incurred operating expenses of $5 per unit in selling the units. It began the year with 900 units in inventory and made successive purchases of its product as follows.

Problem 6-6A[A]
Income comparisons and cost flows—periodic

A1 P3

Jan. I   Beginning inventory . . . .   900 units @ $21 per unit
Feb. 20   Purchase . . . . 1,950 units @ $22 per unit
May 16   Purchase . . . . 1,050 units @ $25 per unit
Oct. 3   Purchase . . . .   700 units @ $26 per unit
Dec. 11   Purchase . . . . 2,750 units @ $27 per unit
         Total . . . . 7,350 units

Required

1. Prepare comparative income statements similar to Exhibit 6.8 for the three inventory costing methods of FIFO, LIFO, and weighted average. (Round per unit costs to three decimals, but inventory balances to the dollar.) Include a detailed cost of goods sold section as part of each statement. The company uses a periodic inventory system, and its income tax rate is 40%.

2. How would the financial results from using the three alternative inventory costing methods change if Bay had been experiencing declining costs in its purchases of inventory?

3. What advantages and disadvantages are offered by using (a) LIFO and (b) FIFO? Assume the continuing trend of increasing costs.

Problem 6-7A^B

Retail inventory method

P4

mhhe.com/wildFAP19e

The records of Ultra Company provide the following information for the year ended December 31.

	At Cost	At Retail
January 1 beginning inventory	$ 476,600	$ 927,950
Cost of goods purchased	3,481,060	6,401,050
Sales		5,565,800
Sales returns		49,800

Required

1. Use the retail inventory method to estimate the company's year-end inventory at cost.

2. A year-end physical inventory at retail prices yields a total inventory of $1,710,900. Prepare a calculation showing the company's loss from shrinkage at cost and at retail.

Problem 6-8A^B

Gross profit method

P4

Optek Company wants to prepare interim financial statements for the first quarter. The company wishes to avoid making a physical count of inventory. Optek's gross profit rate averages 39%. The following information for the first quarter is available from its records.

January 1 beginning inventory	$ 312,580
Cost of goods purchased	944,040
Sales	1,391,160
Sales returns	8,760

Required

Use the gross profit method to estimate the company's first-quarter ending inventory.

PROBLEM SET B

Sheila Company uses a perpetual inventory system. It entered into the following purchases and sales transactions for May.

Problem 6-1B

Alternative cost flows—perpetual

P1

Date	Activities	Units Acquired at Cost	Units Sold at Retail
May 1	Beginning inventory	150 units @ $300/unit	
May 6	Purchase	350 units @ $350/unit	
May 9	Sales		180 units @ $1,200/unit
May 17	Purchase	80 units @ $450/unit	
May 25	Purchase	100 units @ $458/unit	
May 30	Sales		300 units @ $1,400/unit
	Total	690 units	480 units

Required

1. Compute cost of goods available for sale and the number of units available for sale.

2. Compute the number of units in ending inventory.

3. Compute the cost assigned to ending inventory using (*a*) FIFO, (*b*) LIFO, (*c*) weighted average, and (*d*) specific identification. (Round per unit costs to three decimals, but inventory balances to the dollar.) For specific identification, the May 9 sale consisted of 80 units from beginning inventory and 100 units from the May 6 purchase; the May 30 sale consisted of 200 units from the May 6 purchase and 100 units from the May 25 purchase.

4. Compute gross profit earned by the company for each of the four costing methods in part 3.

Check   (3) Ending inventory: FIFO, $88,800; LIFO, $62,500; WA, $75,600;

(4) LIFO gross profit, $449,200

Hawaii Pacific Company uses a perpetual inventory system. It entered into the following calendar-year 2009 purchases and sales transactions.

Problem 6-2B
Alternative cost flows—perpetual

P1

Date	Activities	Units Acquired at Cost	Units Sold at Retail
Jan. 1	Beginning inventory	520 units @ $45/unit	
Jan. 10	Purchase	350 units @ $50/unit	
Feb. 13	Purchase	200 units @ $51/unit	
Feb. 15	Sales		620 units @ $75/unit
July 21	Purchase	260 units @ $52/unit	
Aug. 5	Purchase	595 units @ $53/unit	
Aug. 10	Sales		660 units @ $75/unit
	Total	1,925 units	1,280 units

Required

1. Compute cost of goods available for sale and the number of units available for sale.

2. Compute the number of units in ending inventory.

3. Compute the cost assigned to ending inventory using (*a*) FIFO, (*b*) LIFO, (*c*) specific identification— units sold consist of 105 units from beginning inventory, 140 units from the January 10 purchase, 105 units from the February 13 purchase, 50 units from the July 21 purchase, and 245 units from the August 5 purchase, and (*d*) weighted average. (Round per unit costs to three decimals, but inventory balances to the dollar.)

4. Compute gross profit earned by the company for each of the four costing methods in part 3.

Check   (3) Ending inventory: FIFO, $34,135; LIFO, $30,390; WA, $32,890;

(4) LIFO gross profit, $30,235

Analysis Component

5. If the company's manager earns a bonus based on a percent of gross profit, which method of inventory costing will the manager likely prefer?

A physical inventory of Office Mart taken at December 31 reveals the following.

Problem 6-3B
Lower of cost or market

P2

		Per Unit	
Item	**Units**	**Cost**	**Market**
Office furniture			
Desks	376	$231	$239
Credenzas	280	198	207
Chairs	725	36	33
Bookshelves	218	103	99
Filing cabinets			
Two-drawer	136	85	82
Four-drawer	317	129	126
Lateral	92	114	118
Office equipment			
Fax machines	352	55	65
Copiers	430	405	396
Telephones	515	63	61

Required

Compute the lower of cost or market for the inventory (*a*) as a whole, (*b*) by major category, and (*c*) applied separately to each item.

Check   (b) $477,375; (c) $470,440

Problem 6-4B
Analysis of inventory errors

A2

Watson Company's financial statements show the following. The company recently discovered that in making physical counts of inventory, it had made the following errors: Inventory on December 31, 2008, is overstated by $64,000, and inventory on December 31, 2009, is understated by $35,000.

For Year Ended December 31		2008	2009	2010
(a)	Cost of goods sold	$ 615,000	$ 957,000	$ 786,000
(b)	Net income	225,000	285,000	244,000
(c)	Total current assets	1,251,000	1,360,000	1,265,000
(d)	Total equity	1,387,000	1,520,000	1,250,000

Required

1. For each key financial statement figure—(a), (b), (c), and (d) above—prepare a table similar to the following to show the adjustments necessary to correct the reported amounts.

Figure: _____	2008	2009	2010
Reported amount			
Adjustments for: 12/31/2008 error			
12/31/2009 error			
Corrected amount			

Check (1) Corrected net income:
2008, $161,000; 2009, $384,000;
2010, $209,000

Analysis Component

2. What is the error in total net income for the combined three-year period resulting from the inventory errors? Explain.

3. Explain why the overstatement of inventory by $64,000 at the end of 2008 results in an overstatement of equity by the same amount in that year.

Problem 6-5B^A
Alternative cost flows—periodic

P3

Solaris Co. began year 2009 with 39,000 units of product in its January 1 inventory costing $21 each. It made successive purchases of its product in year 2009 as follows. The company uses a periodic inventory system. On December 31, 2009, a physical count reveals that 40,000 units of its product remain in inventory.

Jan. 4	....	34,000 units @ $20 each
May 18	....	32,000 units @ $19 each
July 9	....	18,000 units @ $16 each
Nov. 21	....	36,000 units @ $14 each

Required

1. Compute the number and total cost of the units available for sale in year 2009.

Check (2) Cost of goods sold:
FIFO, $2,331,000; LIFO, $2,060,000;
WA, $2,169,680

2. Compute the amounts assigned to the 2009 ending inventory and the cost of goods sold using (a) FIFO, (b) LIFO, and (c) weighted average. (Round per unit costs to three decimals, but inventory balances to the dollar.)

Problem 6-6B^A
Income comparisons and cost flows—periodic

A1   P3

Shasta Company sold 6,850 units of its product at $63 per unit in year 2009 and incurred operating expenses of $5 per unit in selling the units. It began the year with 1,100 units in inventory and made successive purchases of its product as follows.

Jan. 1	Beginning inventory	....	1,100 units @ $23 per unit
April 2	Purchase	....	2,100 units @ $24 per unit
June 14	Purchase	....	1,250 units @ $25 per unit
Aug. 29	Purchase	....	1,200 units @ $27 per unit
Nov. 18	Purchase	....	2,250 units @ $29 per unit
	Total	....	7,900 units

Required

1. Prepare comparative income statements similar to Exhibit 6.8 for the three inventory costing methods of FIFO, LIFO, and weighted average. (Round per unit costs to three decimals, but inventory balances to the dollar.) Include a detailed cost of goods sold section as part of each statement. The company uses a periodic inventory system, and its income tax rate is 30%.

2. How would the financial results from using the three alternative inventory costing methods change if the company had been experiencing decreasing prices in its purchases of inventory?

3. What advantages and disadvantages are offered by using (*a*) LIFO and (*b*) FIFO? Assume the continuing trend of increasing costs.

The records of Mercury Co. provide the following information for the year ended December 31.

	At Cost	At Retail
January 1 beginning inventory	$ 468,010	$ 934,950
Cost of goods purchased	3,383,110	6,471,050
Sales		5,573,800
Sales returns		48,800

Required

1. Use the retail inventory method to estimate the company's year-end inventory.

2. A year-end physical inventory at retail prices yields a total inventory of $1,701,900. Prepare a calculation showing the company's loss from shrinkage at cost and at retail.

Tacita Equipment Co. wants to prepare interim financial statements for the first quarter. The company wishes to avoid making a physical count of inventory. Tacita's gross profit rate averages 40%. The following information for the first quarter is available from its records.

January 1 beginning inventory	$ 301,580
Cost of goods purchased	941,040
Sales	1,401,160
Sales returns	9,100

Required

Use the gross profit method to estimate the company's first quarter ending inventory.

(This serial problem began in Chapter 1 and continues through most of the book. If previous chapter segments were not completed, the serial problem can begin at this point.)

SERIAL PROBLEM

Success Systems

SP 6
Part A

Adriana Lopez of Success Systems is evaluating her inventory to determine whether it must be adjusted based on lower of cost or market rules. Lopez has three different types of software in her inventory and the following information is available for each.

		Per Unit	
Inventory Items	Units	Cost	Market
Office productivity	3	$ 76	$ 74
Desktop publishing	2	103	100
Accounting	3	90	96

Required

1. Compute the lower of cost or market for ending inventory assuming Lopez applies the lower of cost or market rule to inventory as a whole. Must Lopez adjust the reported inventory value? Explain.

2. Assume that Lopez had instead applied the lower of cost or market rule to each product in inventory. Under this assumption, must Lopez adjust the reported inventory value? Explain.

Part *B*

Selected accounts and balances for the three months ended March 31, 2010, for Success Systems follow.

January 1 beginning inventory	$ 0
Cost of goods sold	14,052
March 31 ending inventory	704

Required

1. Compute inventory turnover and days' sales in inventory for the three months ended March 31, 2010.

2. Assess the company's performance if competitors average 10 times for inventory turnover and 29 days for days' sales in inventory.

BEYOND THE NUMBERS

REPORTING IN ACTION

C2 A3

BTN 6-1   Refer to Best Buy's financial statements in Appendix A to answer the following.

Required

1. What amount of inventories did Best Buy report as a current asset on March 3, 2007? On February 25, 2006?

2. Inventories represent what percent of total assets on March 3, 2007? On February 25, 2006?

3. Comment on the relative size of Best Buy's inventories compared to its other types of assets.

4. What accounting method did Best Buy use to compute inventory amounts on its balance sheet?

5. Compute inventory turnover for fiscal year ended March 3, 2007, and days' sales in inventory as of March 3, 2007.

Fast Forward

6. Access Best Buy's financial statements for fiscal years ended after March 3, 2007, from its Website (BestBuy.com) or the SEC's EDGAR database (www.SEC.gov). Answer questions 1 through 5 using the current Best Buy information and compare results to those prior years.

COMPARATIVE ANALYSIS

A3

BTN 6-2   Comparative figures for Best Buy, Circuit City, and RadioShack follow.

($ millions)	Best Buy			Circuit City			RadioShack		
	Current Year	One Year Prior	Two Years Prior	Current Year	One Year Prior	Two Years Prior	Current Year	One Year Prior	Two Years Prior
Inventory	$ 4,028	$ 3,338	$ 2,851	$1,637	$1,698	$1,455	$ 752	$ 965	$1,004
Cost of sales ...	27,165	23,122	20,938	9,501	8,704	7,861	2,544	2,706	2,407

Required

1. Compute inventory turnover for each company for the most recent two years shown.

2. Compute days' sales in inventory for each company for the three years shown.

3. Comment on and interpret your findings from parts 1 and 2. Assume an industry average for inventory turnover of 6.3.

BTN 6-3 Golf Depot is a retail sports store carrying golf apparel and equipment. The store is at the end of its second year of operation and is struggling. A major problem is that its cost of inventory has continually increased in the past two years. In the first year of operations, the store assigned inventory costs using LIFO. A loan agreement the store has with its bank, its prime source of financing, requires the store to maintain a certain profit margin and current ratio. The store's owner is currently looking over Golf Depot's preliminary financial statements for its second year. The numbers are not favorable. The only way the store can meet the required financial ratios agreed on with the bank is to change from LIFO to FIFO. The store originally decided on LIFO because of its tax advantages. The owner recalculates ending inventory using FIFO and submits those numbers and statements to the loan officer at the bank for the required bank review. The owner thankfully reflects on the available latitude in choosing the inventory costing method.

ETHICS CHALLENGE

A1

Required

1. How does Golf Depot's use of FIFO improve its net profit margin and current ratio?

2. Is the action by Golf Depot's owner ethical? Explain.

BTN 6-4 You are a financial adviser with a client in the wholesale produce business that just completed its first year of operations. Due to weather conditions, the cost of acquiring produce to resell has escalated during the later part of this period. Your client, Javonte Cruz, mentions that because her business sells perishable goods, she has striven to maintain a FIFO flow of goods. Although sales are good, the increasing cost of inventory has put the business in a tight cash position. Cruz has expressed concern regarding the ability of the business to meet income tax obligations.

COMMUNICATING IN PRACTICE

A1

Required

Prepare a memorandum that identifies, explains, and justifies the inventory method you recommend your client, Ms. Cruz, adopt.

BTN 6-5 Access the 2006 annual 10-K report for **Oakley, Inc.** (Ticker OO), filed on March 9, 2007, from the EDGAR filings at www.sec.gov.

TAKING IT TO THE NET

A3

Required

1. What product does Oakley sell that is especially popular with college students?

2. What inventory method does Oakley use? (*Hint:* See the notes to its financial statements.)

3. Compute Oakley's gross margin and gross margin ratio for the 2006 calendar year. Comment on your computations—assume an industry average of 35% for the gross margin ratio.

4. Compute Oakley's inventory turnover and days' sales in inventory for the year ended December 31, 2006. Comment on your computations—assume an industry average of 3.9 for inventory turnover.

BTN 6-6 Each team member has the responsibility to become an expert on an inventory method. This expertise will be used to facilitate teammates' understanding of the concepts relevant to that method.

1. Each learning team member should select an area for expertise by choosing one of the following inventory methods: specific identification, LIFO, FIFO, or weighted average.

2. Form expert teams made up of students who have selected the same area of expertise. The instructor will identify where each expert team will meet.

3. Using the following data, each expert team must collaborate to develop a presentation that illustrates the relevant concepts and procedures for its inventory method. Each team member must write the presentation in a format that can be shown to the learning team.

TEAMWORK IN ACTION

A1 P1

Point: Step 1 allows four choices or areas for expertise. Larger teams will have some duplication of choice, but the specific identification method should not be duplicated.

Data

The company uses a perpetual inventory system. It had the following beginning inventory and current year purchases of its product.

Jan.	1	Beginning inventory	50 units @ $100 =	$ 5,000
Jan.	14	Purchase	150 units @ $120 =	18,000
Apr.	30	Purchase	200 units @ $150 =	30,000
Sept.	26	Purchase	300 units @ $200 =	60,000

The company transacted sales on the following dates at a $350 per unit sales price.

Jan. 10	30 units	(specific cost: 30 @ $100)
Feb. 15	100 units	(specific cost: 100 @ $120)
Oct. 5	350 units	(specific cost: 100 @ $150 and 250 @ $200)

Concepts and Procedures to Illustrate in Expert Presentation

a. Identify and compute the costs to assign to the units sold. (Round per unit costs to three decimals.)

b. Identify and compute the costs to assign to the units in ending inventory. (Round inventory balances to the dollar.)

c. How likely is it that this inventory costing method will reflect the actual physical flow of goods? How relevant is that factor in determining whether this is an acceptable method to use?

d. What is the impact of this method versus others in determining net income and income taxes?

e. How closely does the ending inventory amount reflect replacement cost?

4. Re-form learning teams. In rotation, each expert is to present to the team the presentation developed in part 3. Experts are to encourage and respond to questions.

ENTREPRENEURIAL DECISION

A3

BTN 6-7 Review the chapter's opening feature highlighting Jacquelyn Tran and her company, **Beauty Encounter**. Assume that Beauty Encounter consistently maintains an inventory level of $300,000, meaning that its average and ending inventory levels are the same. Also assume its annual cost of sales is $1,200,000. To cut costs, Jacquelyn proposes to slash inventory to a constant level of $150,000 with no impact on cost of sales. She plans to work with suppliers to get quicker deliveries and to order smaller quantities more often.

Required

1. Compute the company's inventory turnover and its days' sales in inventory under (*a*) current conditions and (*b*) proposed conditions.

2. Evaluate and comment on the merits of Jacquelyn's proposal given your analysis for part 1. Identify any concerns you might have about the proposal.

HITTING THE ROAD

C1 C2

BTN 6-8 Visit four retail stores with another classmate. In each store, identify whether the store uses a bar-coding system to help manage its inventory. Try to find at least one store that does not use bar-coding. If a store does not use bar-coding, ask the store's manager or clerk whether he or she knows which type of inventory method the store employs. Create a table that shows columns for the name of store visited, type of merchandise sold, use or nonuse of bar-coding, and the inventory method used if bar-coding is not employed. You might also inquire as to what the store's inventory turnover is and how often physical inventory is taken.

BTN 6-9 Key figures (£ millions) for **DSG international plc** (www.DSGiplc.com) follow.

£ Millions	Current Year	One Year Prior	Two Years Prior
Inventory	1,031	873	811
Cost of sales	7,285	6,379	6,325

Required

1. Use these data and those from BTN 6-2 to compute (*a*) inventory turnover and (*b*) days' sales in inventory for the most recent two years shown for **DSG**, **Best Buy**, **Circuit City**, and **RadioShack**.

2. Comment on and interpret your findings from part 1.

ANSWERS TO MULTIPLE CHOICE QUIZ

1. a; FIFO perpetual

Date	Goods Purchased	Cost of Goods Sold	Inventory Balance
July 1			75 units @ $25 = $ 1,875
July 3	348 units @ $27 = $9,396		75 units @ $25 ⎱ = $ 11,271 348 units @ $27 ⎰
July 8		75 units @ $25 ⎱ 225 units @ $27 ⎰ = $ 7,950	123 units @ $27 = $ 3,321
July 15	257 units @ $28 = $7,196		123 units @ $27 ⎱ = $ 10,517 257 units @ $28 ⎰
July 23		123 units @ $27 ⎱ 152 units @ $28 ⎰ = $ 7,577 $15,527	105 units @ $28 = $ 2,940

2. b; LIFO perpetual

Date	Goods Purchased	Cost of Goods Sold	Inventory Balance
July 1			75 units @ $25 = $ 1,875
July 3	348 units @ $27 = $9,396		75 units @ $25 ⎱ = $ 11,271 348 units @ $27 ⎰
July 8		300 units @ $27 = $ 8,100	75 units @ $25 ⎱ = $ 3,171 48 units @ $27 ⎰
July 15	257 units @ $28 = $7,196		75 units @ $25 ⎱ 48 units @ $27 ⎬ = $ 10,367 257 units @ $28 ⎰
July 23		257 units @ $28 ⎱ 18 units @ $27 ⎰ = $ 7,682 $15,782	75 units @ $25 ⎱ = $ 2,685 30 units @ $27 ⎰

3. e; Specific identification perpetual—Ending inventory computation.

20 units @ $25	$ 500	
40 units @ $27	1,080	
45 units @ $28	1,260	
105 units	$2,840	

4. a; FIFO periodic—Ending inventory computation.

105 units @ $28 each = $2,940; The FIFO periodic inventory computation is identical to the FIFO perpetual inventory computation (see question 1).

5. d; Days' sales in inventory = (Ending inventory/Cost of goods sold × 365)
= ($18,000/$85,000) × 365 = 77.29 days

A Look Back

Chapters 5 and 6 focused on merchandising activities and accounting for inventory. We explained inventory systems, accounting for inventory transactions, and assigning costs to inventory.

 A Look at This Chapter

This chapter emphasizes accounting information systems. We describe fundamental system principles, the system's components, use of special journals and subsidiary ledgers, and technology-based systems.

A Look Ahead

Chapter 8 focuses on internal controls and accounting for cash and cash equivalents. We explain good internal control procedures and their importance.

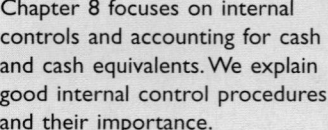

7

Accounting Information Systems

Chapter

Learning Objectives

CAP

Conceptual

C1 Identify fundamental principles of accounting information systems. *(p. 268)*

C2 Identify components of accounting information systems. *(p. 269)*

C3 Explain the goals and uses of special journals. *(p. 271)*

C4 Describe the use of controlling accounts and subsidiary ledgers. *(p. 272)*

C5 Explain how technology-based information systems impact accounting. *(p. 282)*

Analytical

A1 Compute segment return on assets and use it to evaluate segment performance. *(p. 284)*

Procedural

P1 Journalize and post transactions using special journals. *(p. 274)*

P2 Prepare and prove the accuracy of subsidiary ledgers. *(p. 275)*

P3 *Appendix 7A*—Journalize and post transactions using special journals in a periodic inventory system. *(p. 288)*

LP7

Trash to Treasure

"Push the envelope beyond the expected"—Tom Szaky

TRENTON, NJ—Tom Szaky could not shake the idea of making a product from trash. His dream product was biological waste, or what Tom affectionately calls "worm poop," which he would package in used soda bottles. Consumers would then apply it to their plants as liquid fertilizer. His start-up company, TerraCycle (**TerraCycle.net**), is successfully applying what Tom refers to as "upcycling," which is using existing recyclables in a saleable product.

Tom collects his bottling recyclables from dorms, schools, and even agreeable manufacturers. He also uses company rejects and over-runs for everything from cardboard boxes to trigger spray tops. In the process, Tom set up accounting systems to measure, track, summarize, and report on operations. "There are so many areas in which you need to make good decisions," explains Tom. "The scary thing is you are always making decisions without knowing the future. Should we invest in more machinery, or stay with more labor? Should we build a large inventory, or try to fill re-orders as they come in?" These business decisions fundamentally shape Tom's accounting system.

"I've always learned on-the-job," says Tom. That on-the-job learning includes applying internal controls, special journals, accounting ledgers, and systems technology. TerraCycle maintains special journals for its sales, cash receipts, purchases, and cash disbursements. Its purchases system is especially unique in that it uses others' trash and, in some cases, gets paid for it. "It's a total paradigm shift," explains Tom. "You get paid for your raw materials and then you're paid for your finished product." Developing his accounting system to capture those operations is no easy task, but well worth the effort. "If people are willing to pay us for our raw materials," insists Tom, "there's really no limit to what TerraCycle can do. Garbage is just something we hadn't been creative enough to solve yet."

Tom's company is riding high with the right systems and operations for long run success. "I love being an entrepreneur . . . hunker down, work very hard, and wish for a little luck," advises Tom. "That luck has come our way every time!"

[Sources: *TerraCycle Website,* January 2009; *Enterprising Solutions,* July 2008; *Inc.com,* July 2007; *Brand Packaging,* June 2008; *Peregrin Pages,* June 2008]

With increases in the number and complexity of business activities, the demands placed on accounting information systems increase. Accounting information systems must meet this challenge in an efficient and effective manner. In this chapter, we learn about fundamental principles guiding information systems, and we study components making up these systems. We also explain procedures that use special journals and subsidiary ledgers to make accounting information systems more efficient. An understanding of the details of accounting reports makes us better decision makers when using financial information, and it improves our ability to analyze and interpret financial statements.

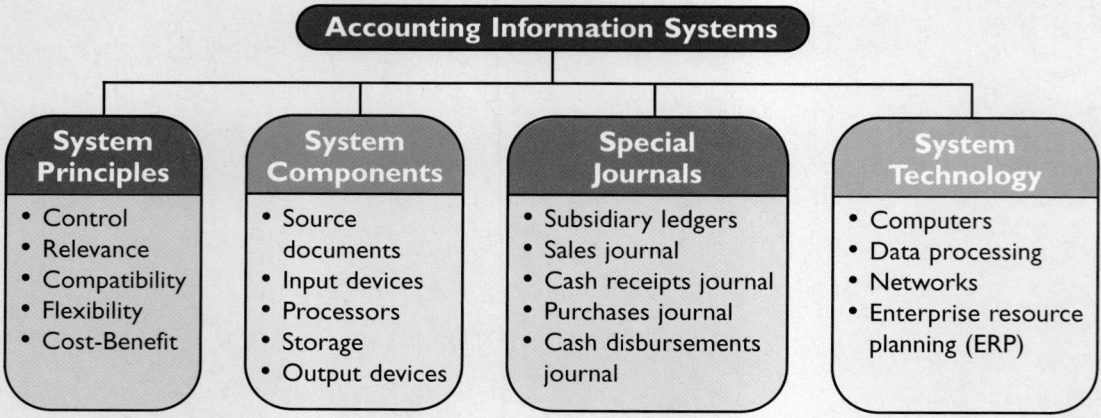

Accounting Information Systems

System Principles	System Components	Special Journals	System Technology
• Control • Relevance • Compatibility • Flexibility • Cost-Benefit	• Source documents • Input devices • Processors • Storage • Output devices	• Subsidiary ledgers • Sales journal • Cash receipts journal • Purchases journal • Cash disbursements journal	• Computers • Data processing • Networks • Enterprise resource planning (ERP)

Fundamental System Principles

C1 Identify fundamental principles of accounting information systems.

Accounting information systems collect and process data from transactions and events, organize them in useful reports, and communicate results to decision makers. With the increasing complexity of business and the growing need for information, accounting information systems are more important than ever. All decision makers need to have a basic knowledge of how accounting information systems work. This knowledge gives decision makers a competitive edge as they gain a better understanding of information constraints, measurement limitations, and potential applications. It allows them to make more informed decisions and to better balance the risks and returns of different strategies. This section explains five basic principles of accounting information systems, shown in Exhibit 7.1.

EXHIBIT 7.1

System Principles

Control Principle

Managers need to control and monitor business activities. The **control principle** prescribes that an accounting information system have internal controls. **Internal controls** are methods and procedures allowing managers to control and monitor business activities. They include policies to direct operations toward common goals, procedures to ensure reliable financial reports, safeguards to protect company assets, and methods to achieve compliance with laws and regulations.

Point: A hacker stole 300,000 credit card numbers from online music retailer CDUniverse due to internal control failure.

Relevance Principle

Decision makers need relevant information to make informed decisions. The **relevance principle** prescribes that an accounting information system report useful, understandable, timely, and pertinent information for effective decision making. The system must be designed to capture data that make a difference in decisions. To ensure this, we must consider all decision makers when identifying relevant information for disclosure.

Compatibility Principle

Accounting information systems must be consistent with the aims of a company. The **compatibility principle** prescribes that an accounting information system conform with a company's activities, personnel, and structure. It also must adapt to a company's unique characteristics. The system must not be intrusive but must work in harmony with and be driven by company goals. Most start-up entrepreneurs require only a simple information system. Harley-Davidson, on the other hand, demands both a merchandising and a manufacturing information system able to assemble data from its global operations.

Flexibility Principle

Accounting information systems must be able to adjust to changes. The **flexibility principle** prescribes that an accounting information system be able to adapt to changes in the company, business environment, and needs of decisions makers. Technological advances, competitive pressures, consumer tastes, regulations, and company activities constantly evolve. A system must be designed to adapt to these changes.

Cost-Benefit Principle

The **cost-benefit principle** prescribes that the benefits from an activity in an accounting information system outweigh the costs of that activity. The costs and benefits of an activity such as producing a specific report will impact the decisions of both external and internal users. Decisions regarding other systems principles (control, relevance, compatibility, and flexibility) are also affected by the cost-benefit principle.

Point: Law requires that *all* employers destroy credit-check and other employee records *before* tossing them. A cross-cut shredder is the tool of choice.

Decision Insight

Digital Is Forever   E-communications have helped bring down many employees, including the CEO of Boeing. To comply with Sarbanes-Oxley, more and more companies now archive and monitor e-mails, instant messages, blog postings, and Net-based phone calls. Using natural-language software, companies sift through digital communications in milliseconds, checking for trade secrets, bad language, porn, and pirated files.

Components of Accounting Systems

Accounting information systems consist of people, records, methods, and equipment. The systems are designed to capture information about a company's transactions and to provide output including financial, managerial, and tax reports. All accounting information systems have these same goals, and thus share some basic components. These components apply whether or not a system is heavily computerized, yet the components of computerized systems usually provide more accuracy, speed, efficiency, and convenience than those of manual systems.

The five basic **components of accounting systems** are source documents, input devices, information processors, information storage, and output devices. Exhibit 7.2 shows these components as a series of steps, yet we know that much two-way communication occurs between many of these components. We briefly describe each of these key components in this section.

C2 Identify components of accounting information systems.

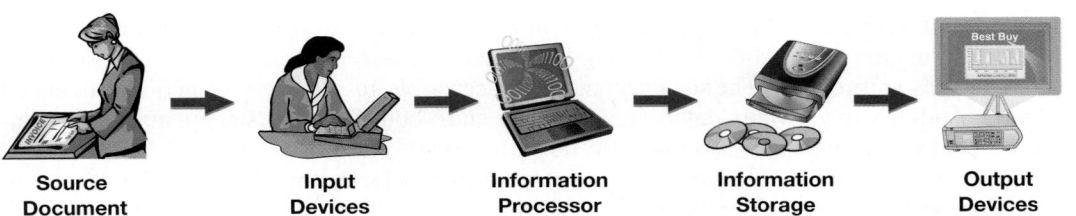

| Source Document | Input Devices | Information Processor | Information Storage | Output Devices |

EXHIBIT 7.2

Accounting System Components

Source Documents

We introduced source documents in Chapters 1 and 2 and explained their importance for both business transactions and information collection. Source documents provide the basic information processed by an accounting system. Examples of source documents include bank statements and checks, invoices from suppliers, billings to customers, cash register files, and employee earnings records. Source documents can be paper, although they increasingly are taking the form of electronic files and Web communications. A growing number of companies are sending documents directly from their systems to their customers' and suppliers' systems. The Web is playing a major role in this transformation from paper-based to *paperless* systems.

Accurate source documents are crucial to accounting information systems. Input of faulty or incomplete information seriously impairs the reliability and relevance of the information system. We commonly refer to this as "garbage in, garbage out." Information systems are set up with attention on control procedures to limit the possibility of entering faulty data in the system.

Input Devices

Input devices capture information from source documents and enable its transfer to the system's information processing component. These devices often involve converting data on source documents from written or electronic form to a form usable for the system. Journal entries, both electronic and paper based, are a type of input device. Keyboards, scanners, and modems are some of the most common input devices in practice today. For example, bar code readers capture code numbers and transfer them to the organization's computer for processing. Moreover, a scanner can capture writing samples and other input directly from source documents.

Controls are used to ensure that only authorized individuals input data to the system. Controls increase the system's reliability and allow information to be traced back to its source.

Decision Insight

Geek Chic   Cyberfashion pioneers are creating geek chic, a kind of wearable computer. Cyberfashion draws on digital cellular phones, lithium batteries, and miniature monitors. Special thread is woven into clothing to carry low-voltage signals from one part of the system to another, and fabric keyboards are sewn into clothes. These creations give new meaning to the term *software*.

Information Processors

Information processors are systems that interpret, transform, and summarize information for use in analysis and reporting. An important part of an information processor in accounting systems is professional judgment. Accounting principles are never so structured that they limit the need for professional judgment. Other parts of an information processor include journals, ledgers, working papers, and posting procedures. Each assists in transforming raw data to useful information.

Increasingly, computer technology (both computing hardware and software) is assisting manual information processors. This assistance is freeing accounting professionals to take on increased analysis, interpretive, and managerial roles. Web-based application service providers (ASPs) offer another type of information processor.

Information Storage

Information storage is the accounting system component that keeps data in a form accessible to information processors. After being input and processed, data are stored for use in future analyses and reports. The database must be accessible to preparers of periodic financial reports. Auditors rely on this database when they audit both financial statements and a company's controls. Companies also maintain files of source documents.

Older systems consisted almost exclusively of paper documents, but most modern systems depend on electronic storage devices. Advances in information storage enable accounting systems to increasingly store more detailed data. This means managers have more data to access and work with in planning and controlling business activities. Information storage can be online, meaning that data can be accessed whenever, and from wherever, it is needed. Off-line storage means access often requires assistance and authorization. Information storage is increasingly augmented by Web sources such as SEC databases, benchmarking services, and financial and product markets.

Decision Insight

Direct Output A screenless computer display, called *virtual retinal display* (VRD), scans rows of pixels directly onto the user's retina by means of a laser. VRDs can simulate three-dimensional virtual worlds, including 3D financial graphics.

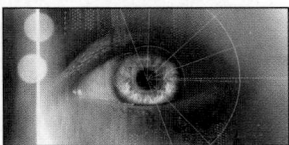

Output Devices

Output devices are the means to take information out of an accounting system and make it available to users. Common output devices are printers, monitors, LCD projectors, and Web communications. Output devices provide users a variety of items including graphics, analysis reports, bills to customers, checks to suppliers, employee paychecks, financial statements, and internal reports. When requests for output occur, an information processor takes the needed data from a database and prepares the necessary report, which is then sent to an output device. A special type of output is an electronic funds transfer (EFT). One example is the transfer of payroll from the company's bank account to its employees' bank accounts. This requires an interface to allow a company's accounting system to send payroll data directly to the bank's accounting system. This interface can involve a company recording its payroll data on CD and forwarding it to the bank. The bank then uses this output to transfer wages earned to employees' accounts.

Decision Ethics

Accountant Your client requests advice in purchasing software for its accounting system. You have been offered a 10% commission by a software company for each purchase of its system by one of your clients. Does this commission arrangement affect your evaluation of software? Do you tell your client about the commission arrangement? [Answer—p. 293]

Quick Check   Answers—p. 293

1. Identify the five primary components of an accounting information system.
2. What is the aim of information processors in an accounting system?
3. How are data in the information storage component of an accounting system used?

Special Journals in Accounting

This section describes the underlying records of accounting information systems. Designed correctly, these records support efficiency in processing transactions and events. They are part of all systems in various forms and are increasingly electronic. Even in technologically advanced systems, a basic understanding of the records we describe in this section aids in using, interpreting, and applying accounting information. It also improves our knowledge of computer-based systems. Remember that all accounting systems have common purposes and internal workings whether or not they depend on technology.

This section focuses on special journals and subsidiary ledgers that are an important part of accounting systems. We describe how special journals are used to capture transactions, and we explain how subsidiary ledgers are set up to capture details of accounts. This section uses a

C3 Explain the goals and uses of special journals.

perpetual inventory system, and the special journals are set up using this system. Appendix 7A describes the change in special journals required for a *periodic* system. We also include a note at the bottom of each of the special journals explaining the change required if a company uses a periodic system.

Basics of Special Journals

A **general journal** is an all-purpose journal in which we can record any transaction. Use of a general journal for all transactions is usually more costly for a business *and* is a less effective control procedure. Moreover, for less technologically advanced systems, use of a general journal requires that each debit and each credit entered be individually posted to its respective ledger account. To enhance internal control and reduce costs, transactions are organized into common groups. A **special journal** is used to record and post transactions of similar type. Most transactions of a merchandiser, for instance, can be categorized into the journals shown in Exhibit 7.3. This section assumes the use of these four special journals along with the general journal. The general journal continues to be used for transactions not covered by special journals and for adjusting, closing, and correcting entries. We show in the following discussion that special journals are *efficient tools in helping journalize and post transactions.* This is done, for instance, by accumulating debits and credits of similar transactions, which allows posting of amounts as column *totals* rather than as individual amounts. The advantage of this system increases as the number of transactions increases. Special journals allow an *efficient division of labor,* which is also an effective control procedure.

Point: Companies can use as many special journals as necessary given their unique business activities.

Point: A specific transaction is recorded in only *one* journal.

EXHIBIT 7.3

Using Special Journals with a General Journal

It is important to note that special journals and subsidiary ledgers *are designed in a manner that is best suited for each business.* The most likely candidates for special journal status are recurring transactions—for many businesses those are sales, cash receipts, purchases, and cash disbursements. However, good systems design for a business could involve collapsing sales and cash receipts in one journal, or purchases and cash disbursement in another. It could also involve adding more special journals or additional subsidiary ledgers for other recurring transactions. This design decision extends to journal and ledger format. That is, the selection on number of columns, column headings, and so forth is based on what is best suited for each business. Thus, read the following sections as one example of a common systems design, but not the only design.

Subsidiary Ledgers

C4 Describe the use of controlling accounts and subsidiary ledgers.

To understand special journals, it is necessary to understand the workings of a **subsidiary ledger,** which is a list of individual accounts with a common characteristic. A subsidiary ledger contains detailed information on specific accounts in the general ledger. Information systems often include several subsidiary ledgers. Two of the most important are:

■ *Accounts receivable ledger*—stores transaction data of individual customers.
■ *Accounts payable ledger*—stores transaction data of individual suppliers.

Individual accounts in subsidiary ledgers are often arranged alphabetically, which is the approach taken here. We describe accounts receivable and accounts payable ledgers in this section. Our discussion of special journals uses these ledgers.

Accounts Receivable Ledger   When we recorded credit sales in prior chapters, we debited (increased) Accounts Receivable. When a company has more than one credit customer, the accounts receivable records must show how much *each* customer purchased, paid, and has yet to pay. This information is collected by keeping a separate account receivable for each credit customer. A separate account for each customer *could* be kept in the general ledger with the other financial statement accounts, but this is uncommon. Instead, the general ledger usually has a single Accounts Receivable account, and a *subsidiary ledger* is set up to keep a separate account for each customer. This subsidiary ledger is called the **accounts receivable ledger** (also called *accounts receivable subsidiary ledger* or *customers ledger*), and it can exist in electronic or paper form.

Exhibit 7.4 shows the relation between the Accounts Receivable account and its individual accounts in the subsidiary ledger. After all items are posted, the balance in the Accounts Receivable account must equal the sum of all balances of its customers' accounts. The Accounts Receivable account is said to control the accounts receivable ledger and is called a **controlling account.** Since the accounts receivable ledger is a supplementary record controlled by an account in the general ledger, it is called a *subsidiary* ledger.

Point: When a general ledger account has a subsidiary ledger, any transaction that impacts one of them also impacts the other—some refer to this as *general and subsidiary ledgers kept in tandem.*

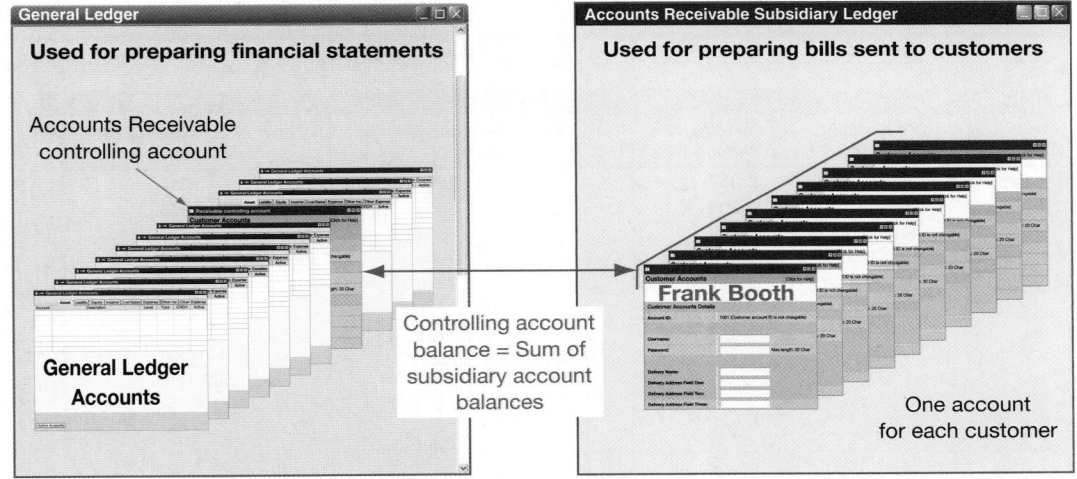

EXHIBIT 7.4

Accounts Receivable Controlling Account and Its Subsidiary Ledger

Accounts Payable Ledger   There are other controlling accounts and subsidiary ledgers. We know, for example, that many companies buy on credit from several suppliers. This means that companies must keep a separate account for each supplier by keeping an Accounts Payable controlling account in the general ledger and a separate account for each supplier (creditor) in an **accounts payable ledger** (also called *accounts payable subsidiary ledger* or *creditors ledger*).

Point: Subsidiary ledgers: (1) remove excessive details from general ledger, (2) provide up-to-date info on customer or other specific account balances, (3) aid in error identification for individual accounts, and (4) help with division of labor (recordkeeping tasks).

Other Subsidiary Ledgers   Subsidiary ledgers are common for several other accounts. A company with many classes of equipment, for example, might keep only one Equipment account in its general ledger, but its Equipment account would control a subsidiary ledger in which each class of equipment is recorded in a separate account. Similar treatment is common for investments, inventory, and any accounts needing separate detailed records. **Brunswick** reports sales information by product line in its annual report. Yet its accounting system keeps much more detailed sales records. Brunswick, for instance, sells hundreds of different products and must be able to analyze the sales performance of each. This detail can be captured by many different general ledger sales accounts but is instead captured by using supplementary records that function like subsidiary ledgers. Overall, subsidiary ledgers are applied in many different ways to ensure that the accounting system captures sufficient details to support analyses that decision makers need.

Sales Journal

P1 Journalize and post transactions using special journals.

A typical **sales journal** is used to record sales of inventory *on credit*. Sales of inventory for cash are not recorded in a sales journal but in a cash receipts journal. Sales of noninventory assets on credit are recorded in the general journal.

Journalizing   Credit sale transactions are recorded with information about each sale entered separately in a sales journal. This information is often taken from a copy of the sales ticket or invoice prepared at the time of sale. The top portion of Exhibit 7.5 shows a typical sales journal from a merchandiser. It has columns for recording the date, customer's name, invoice number, posting reference, and the retail and cost amounts of each credit sale. The sales journal in this exhibit is called a **columnar journal,** which is any journal with more than one column.

Each transaction recorded in the sales journal yields an entry in the "Accounts Receivable Dr., Sales Cr." column. We usually need only one column for these two accounts. (An exception is when managers need more information about taxes, returns, and other sales details.) Each transaction in the sales journal also yields an entry in the "Cost of Goods Sold Dr., Inventory Cr." column. This entry reflects the perpetual inventory system of tracking costs with each sale. To illustrate, on February 2, this company sold merchandise on account to Jason Henry for $450. The invoice number is 307, and the cost of this merchandise is $315. This information is captured on

Point: Each transaction in the sales journal includes a debit to accounts receivable and a credit to sales.

EXHIBIT 7.5

Sales Journal with Posting*

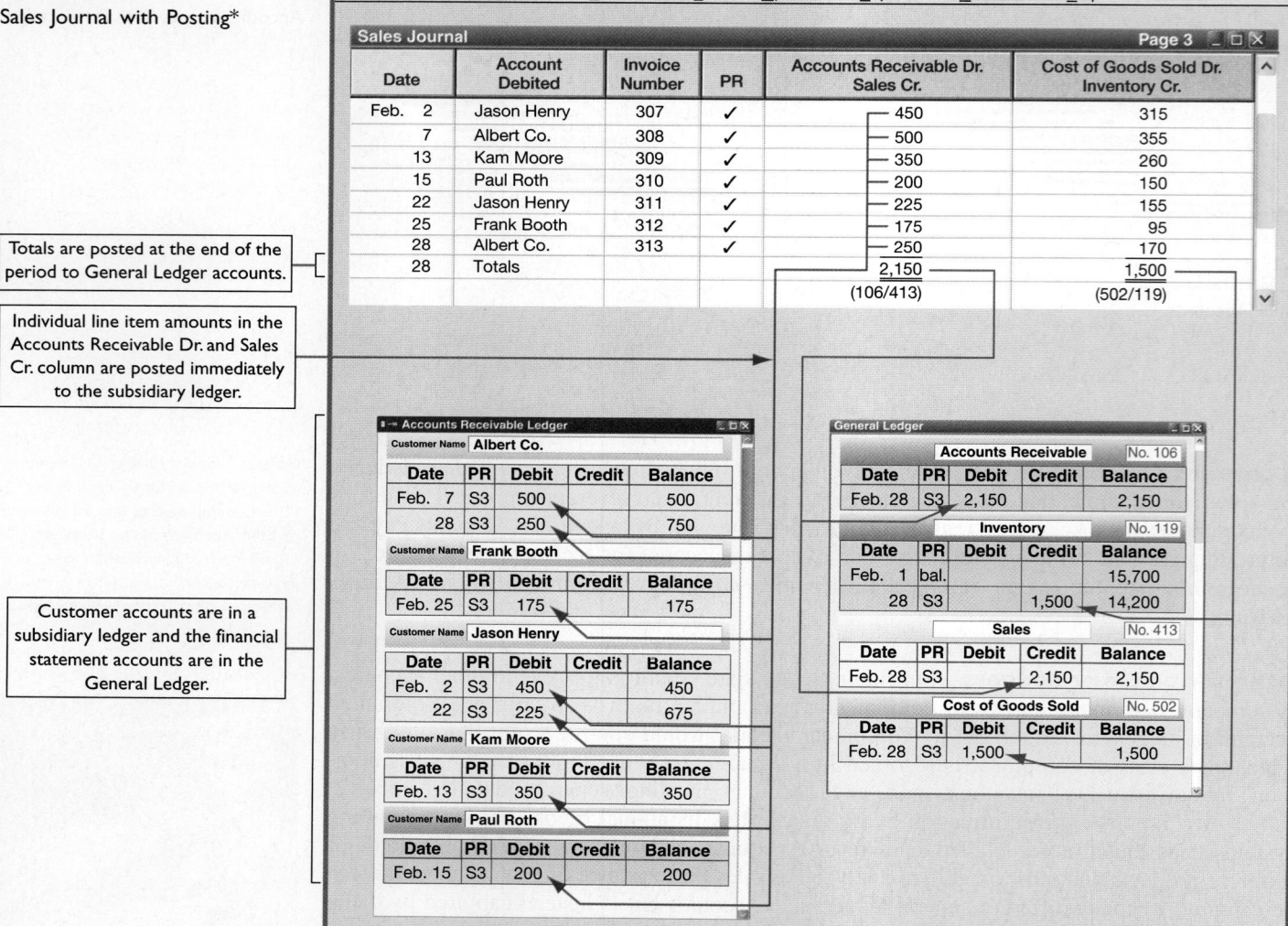

Totals are posted at the end of the period to General Ledger accounts.

Individual line item amounts in the Accounts Receivable Dr. and Sales Cr. column are posted immediately to the subsidiary ledger.

Customer accounts are in a subsidiary ledger and the financial statement accounts are in the General Ledger.

*The Sales Journal in a *periodic* system would exclude the column on the far right titled "Cost of Goods Sold Dr., Inventory Cr." (see Exhibit 7A.1).

one line in the sales journal. No further explanations or entries are necessary, saving time and effort. Moreover, this sales journal is consistent with most inventory systems that use bar codes to record both sales and costs with each sale transaction. Note that the Posting Reference (PR) column is not used when entering transactions but instead is used when posting.

Point: Continuously updated customer accounts provide timely information for customer inquiries on those accounts and on current amounts owed.

Posting   A sales journal is posted as reflected in the arrow lines of Exhibit 7.5. Two types of posting can be identified: (1) posting to the subsidiary ledger(s) and (2) posting to the general ledger.

Posting to subsidiary ledger.   Individual transactions in the sales journal are posted regularly (typically concurrently) to customer accounts in the accounts receivable ledger. These postings keep customer accounts up-to-date, which is important for the person granting credit to customers. When sales recorded in the sales journal are individually posted to customer accounts in the accounts receivable ledger, check marks are entered in the sales journal's PR column. Check marks are used rather than account numbers because customer accounts usually are arranged alphabetically in the accounts receivable ledger. Note that posting debits to Accounts Receivable twice—once to Accounts Receivable and once to the customer's subsidiary account—does not violate the accounting equation of debits equal credits. The equality of debits and credits is always maintained in the general ledger.

Point: PR column is only checked *after* the amount(s) is posted.

Posting to general ledger.   The sales journal's account columns are totaled at the end of each period (the month of February in this case). For the "sales" column, the $2,150 total is debited to Accounts Receivable and credited to Sales in the general ledger (see Exhibit 7.5). For the "cost" column, the $1,500 total is debited to Cost of Goods Sold and credited to Inventory in the general ledger. When totals are posted to accounts in the general ledger, the account numbers are entered below the column total in the sales journal for tracking. For example, we enter (106/413) below the total in the sales column after this amount is posted to account number 106 (Accounts Receivable) and account number 413 (Sales).

Point: Postings are automatic in a computerized system.

A company identifies in the PR column of its subsidiary ledgers the journal and page number from which an amount is taken. We identify a journal by using an initial. Items posted from the sales journal carry the initial *S* before their journal page numbers in a PR column. Likewise, items from the cash receipts journal carry the initial *R*; items from the cash disbursements journal carry the initial *D*; items from the purchases journal carry the initial *P*; and items from the general journal carry the initial *G*.

Proving the Ledgers   Account balances in the general ledger and subsidiary ledgers are periodically proved (or reviewed) for accuracy after posting. To do this we first prepare a trial balance of the general ledger to confirm that debits equal credits. Second, we test a subsidiary ledger by preparing a *schedule* of individual accounts and amounts. A **schedule of accounts receivable** lists each customer and the balance owed. If this total equals the balance of the Accounts Receivable controlling account, the accounts in the accounts receivable ledger are assumed correct. Exhibit 7.6 shows a schedule of accounts receivable drawn from the accounts receivable ledger of Exhibit 7.5.

P2 Prepare and prove the accuracy of subsidiary ledgers.

Schedule of Accounts Receivable February 28	
Albert Co.	$ 750
Frank Booth	175
Jason Henry	675
Kam Moore	350
Paul Roth	200
Total accounts receivable	$2,150

EXHIBIT 7.6

Schedule of Accounts Receivable

Additional Issues   We consider three additional issues with the sales journal: (1) recording sales taxes, (2) recording sales returns and allowances, and (3) using actual sales invoices as a journal.

Point: In accounting, the word *schedule* generally means a list.

Sales taxes.   Governmental agencies such as cities and states often require sellers to collect sales taxes from customers and to periodically send these taxes to the appropriate agency. When using a columnar sales journal, we can keep a record of taxes collected by adding a Sales Taxes Payable column as follows.

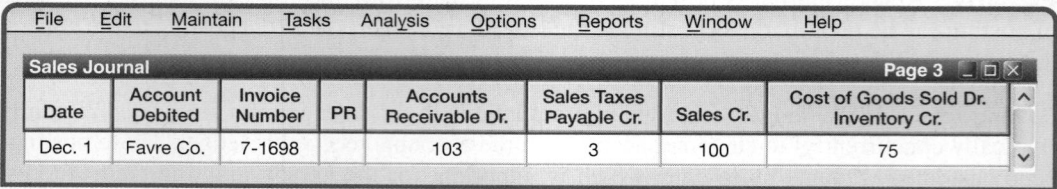

File	Edit	Maintain	Tasks	Analysis	Options	Reports	Window	Help

Sales Journal   Page 3 🔲☐⊠

Date	Account Debited	Invoice Number	PR	Accounts Receivable Dr.	Sales Taxes Payable Cr.	Sales Cr.	Cost of Goods Sold Dr. Inventory Cr.	
Dec. 1	Favre Co.	7-1698		103	3	100	75	

Individual amounts in the Accounts Receivable column would continue to be posted immediately to customer accounts in the accounts receivable ledger. Individual amounts in the Sales Taxes Payable and Sales columns are not posted. Column totals would continue to be posted as usual. (A company that collects sales taxes on its cash sales can also use a Sales Taxes Payable column in its cash receipts journal.)

Sales returns and allowances.   A company with only a few sales returns and allowances can record them in a general journal with an entry such as the following:

<table>
<tr><td rowspan="3">Assets = Liabilities + Equity
−175   −175</td></tr>
</table>

May 17	Sales Returns and Allowances	414	175	
	Accounts Receivable—Ray Ball	106/✓		175
	Customer returned merchandise.			

The debit in this entry is posted to the Sales Returns and Allowances account (no. 414). The credit is posted to both the Accounts Receivable controlling account (no. 106) and to the customer's account. When we enter the account number and the check mark, 106/✓, in the PR column on the credit line, this means both the Accounts Receivable controlling account in the general ledger and the Ray Ball account in the accounts receivable ledger are credited for $175. [*Note:* If the returned goods can be resold to another customer, the company would debit (increase) the Inventory account and credit (decrease) the Cost of Goods Sold account. If the returned goods are defective (worthless), the company could simply leave their costs in the Cost of Goods Sold account (see Chapter 5).] A company with a large number of sales returns and allowances can save time by recording them in a separate sales returns and allowances journal.

Sales invoices as a sales journal.   To save costs, some small companies avoid using a sales journal for credit sales and instead post each sales invoice amount directly to the customer's account in the accounts receivable ledger. They then put copies of invoices in a file. At the end of the period, they total all invoices for that period and make a general journal entry to debit Accounts Receivable and credit Sales for the total amount. The file of invoice copies acts as a sales journal. This is called *direct posting of sales invoices.*

Quick Check   Answers—p. 294

   4. When special journals are used, where are cash payments by check recorded?

   5. How does a columnar journal save posting time and effort?

   6. How do debits and credits remain equal when credit sales are posted twice (once to Accounts Receivable and once to the customer's subsidiary account)?

   7. How do we identify the journal from which an amount in a ledger account was posted?

   8. How are sales taxes recorded in the context of special journals?

   9. What is direct posting of sales invoices?

Cash Receipts Journal

A **cash receipts journal** is typically used to record all receipts of cash. Exhibit 7.7 shows one common form of the cash receipts journal.

Journalizing and Posting   Cash receipts can be separated into one of three types: (1) cash from credit customers in payment of their accounts, (2) cash from cash sales, and

EXHIBIT 7.7

Cash Receipts Journal with Posting*

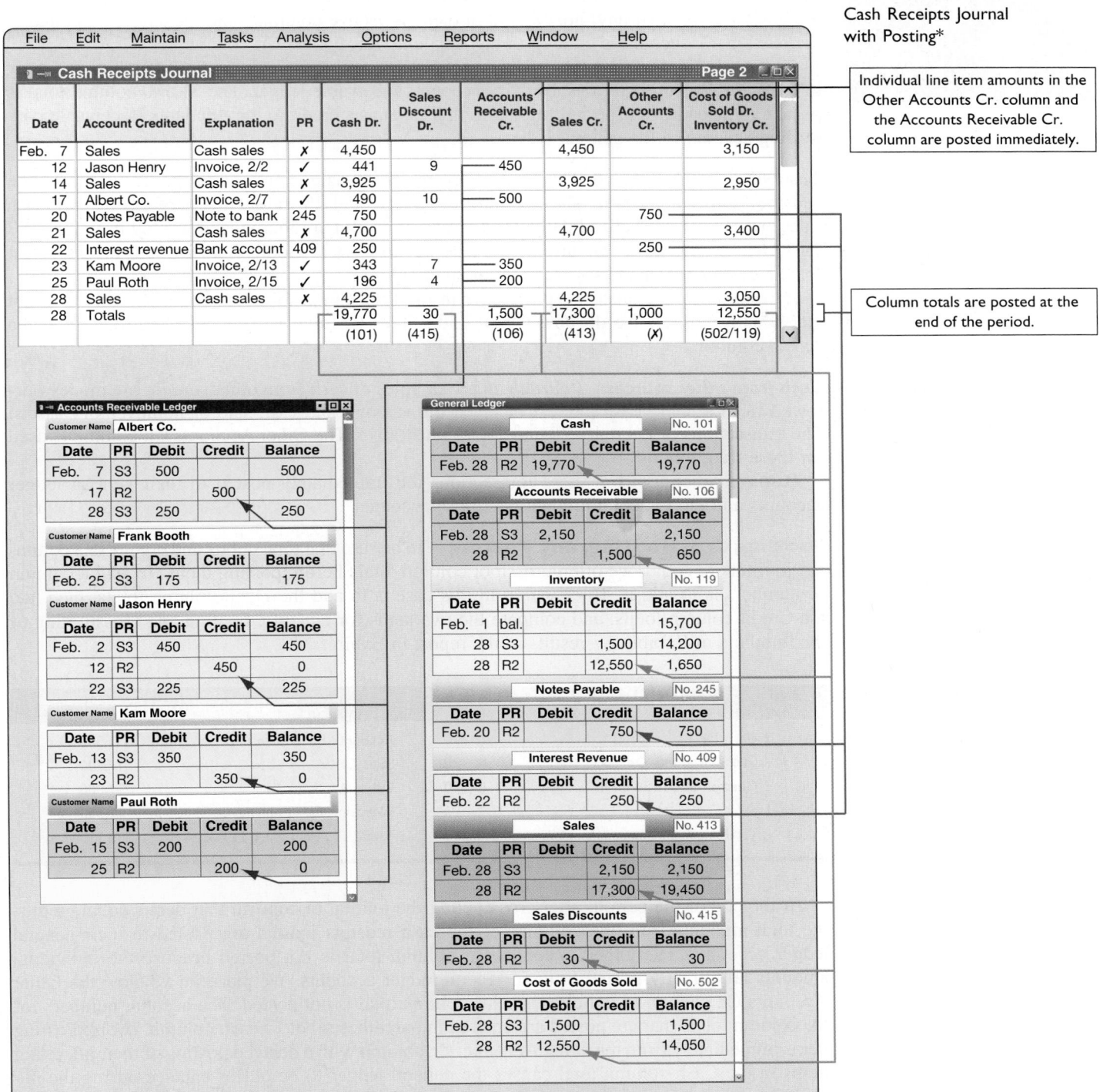

Individual line item amounts in the Other Accounts Cr. column and the Accounts Receivable Cr. column are posted immediately.

Column totals are posted at the end of the period.

*The Cash Receipts Journal in a *periodic* system would exclude the column on the far right titled "Cost of Goods Sold Dr., Inventory Cr." (see Exhibit 7A.2).

Point: Each transaction in the cash receipts journal involves a debit to Cash. Credit accounts will vary.

Point: Some software packages put cash sales in the sales journal.

Example: Record in the cash receipts journal a $700 cash sale of land when the land carries a $700 original cost. *Answer:* Debit the Cash column for $700, and credit the Other Accounts column for $700 (the account credited is Land).

Point: Subsidiary ledgers and their controlling accounts are *in balance* only after all posting is complete.

(3) cash from other sources. The cash receipts journal in Exhibit 7.7 has a separate credit column for each of these three sources. We describe how to journalize transactions from each of these three sources. (An Explanation column is included in the cash receipts journal to identify the source.)

Cash from credit customers. *Journalizing.* To record cash received in payment of a customer's account, the customer's name is first entered in the Account Credited column—see transactions dated February 12, 17, 23, and 25. Then the amounts debited to both Cash and the Sales Discount (if any) are entered in their respective columns, and the amount credited to the customer's account is entered in the Accounts Receivable Cr. column.

Posting. Individual amounts in the Accounts Receivable Cr. column are posted immediately to customer accounts in the subsidiary accounts receivable ledger. The $1,500 column total is posted at the end of the period (month in this case) as a credit to the Accounts Receivable controlling account in the general ledger.

Cash sales. *Journalizing.* The amount for each cash sale is entered in the Cash Dr. column and the Sales Cr. column. The February 7, 14, 21, and 28 transactions are examples. (Cash sales are usually journalized daily or at point of sale, but are journalized weekly in Exhibit 7.7 for brevity.) Each cash sale also yields an entry to Cost of Goods Sold Dr. and Inventory Cr. for the cost of merchandise—see the far right column.

Posting. For cash sales, we place an *x* in the PR column to indicate that its amount is not individually posted. We do post the $17,300 Sales Cr. total and the $12,550 total from the "cost" column.

Cash from other sources. *Journalizing.* Examples of cash from other sources are money borrowed from a bank, cash interest received on account, and cash sale of noninventory assets. The transactions of February 20 and 22 are illustrative. The Other Accounts Cr. column is used for these transactions.

Posting. Amounts from these transactions are immediately posted to their general ledger accounts and the PR column identifies those accounts.

Footing, Crossfooting, and Posting   To be sure that total debits and credits in a columnar journal are equal, we often crossfoot column totals before posting them. To *foot* a column of numbers is to add it. To *crossfoot* in this case is to add the Debit column totals, then add the Credit column totals, and compare the two sums for equality. Footing and crossfooting of the numbers in Exhibit 7.7 results in the report in Exhibit 7.8.

EXHIBIT 7.8

Footing and Crossfooting Journal Totals

Debit Columns		Credit Columns	
Cash Dr.	$19,770	Accounts Receivable Cr.	$ 1,500
Sales Discounts Dr.	30	Sales Cr.	17,300
Cost of Goods Sold Dr.	12,550	Other Accounts Cr.	1,000
		Inventory Cr.	12,550
Total	$32,350	Total	$32,350

At the end of the period, after crossfooting the journal to confirm that debits equal credits, the total amounts from the columns of the cash receipts journal are posted to their general ledger accounts. The Other Accounts Cr. column total is not posted because the individual amounts are directly posted to their general ledger accounts. We place an *x* below the Other Accounts Cr. column to indicate that this column total is not posted. The account numbers for the column totals that are posted are entered in parentheses below each column. (*Note:* Posting items immediately from the Other Accounts Cr. column with a delayed posting of their offsetting items in the Cash column total causes the general ledger to be out of balance during the period. Posting the Cash Dr. column total at the end of the period corrects this imbalance in the general ledger before the trial balance and financial statements are prepared.)

Decision Maker

Entrepreneur   You want to know how promptly customers are paying their bills. This information can help you decide whether to extend credit and to plan your cash payments. Where do you find this information? [Answer—p. 293]

Purchases Journal

A **purchases journal** is typically used to record all credit purchases, including those for inventory. Purchases for cash are recorded in the Cash Disbursements Journal.

Journalizing   Entries in the purchases journal in Exhibit 7.9 reflect purchase invoices or other source documents. We use the invoice date and terms to compute the date when payment for each purchase is due. The Accounts Payable Cr. column is used to record the amounts owed to each creditor. Inventory purchases are recorded in the Inventory Dr. column.

To illustrate, inventory costing $200 is purchased from Ace Manufacturing on February 5. The creditor's name (Ace) is entered in the Account column, the invoice date is entered in the Date of Invoice column, the purchase terms are entered in the Terms column, and the $200 amount is entered in the Accounts Payable Cr. and the Inventory Dr. columns. When a purchase involves an amount recorded in the Other Accounts Dr. column, we use the Account column to identify the general ledger account debited. For example, the February 28 transaction

Point: The number of special journals and the design of each are based on a company's specific needs.

Point: Each transaction in the purchases journal has a credit to Accounts Payable. Debit accounts will vary.

EXHIBIT 7.9

Purchases Journal with Posting*

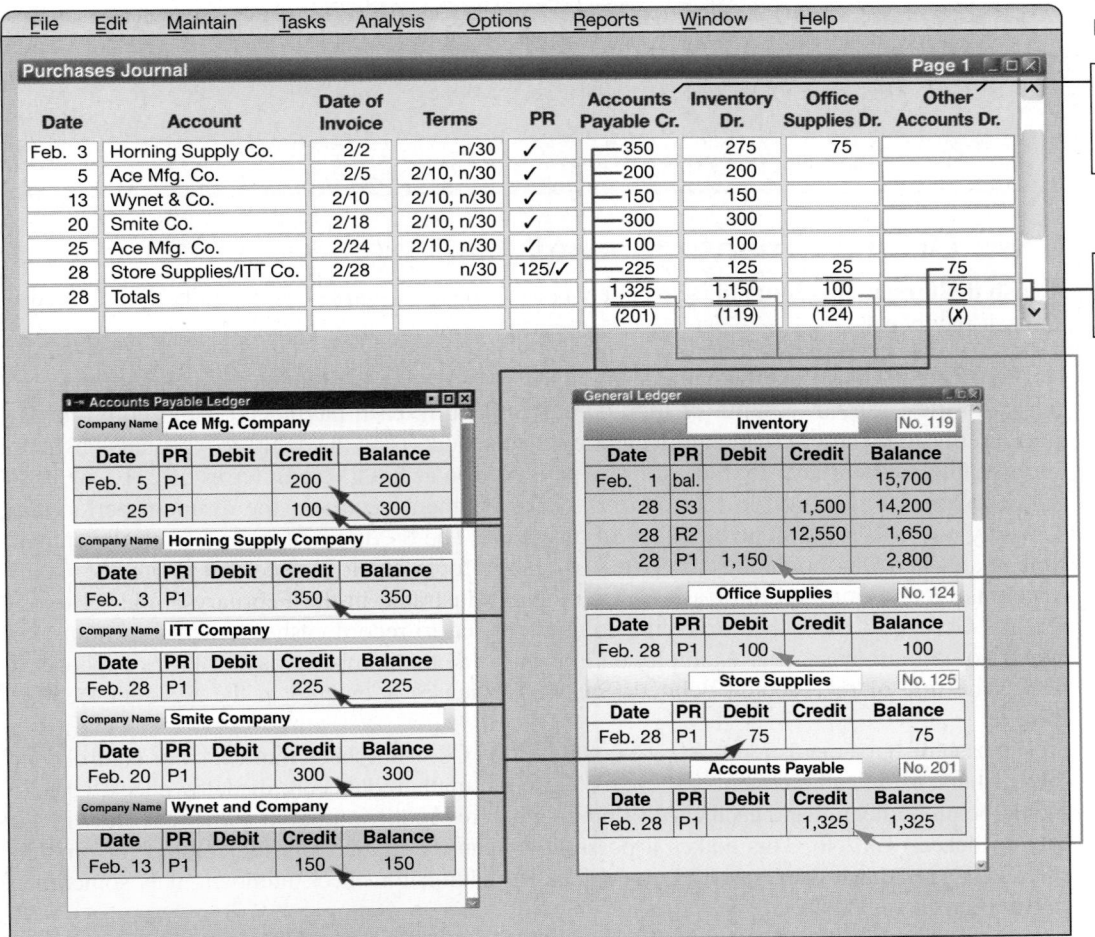

Individual amounts in the Other Accounts Dr. column and the Accounts Payable Cr. column are posted immediately.

Column totals, except for Other Accounts Dr. column, are posted at the end of the period.

*The Purchases Journal in a *periodic* system replaces "Inventory Dr." with "Purchases Dr." (see Exhibit 7A.3).

involves purchases of inventory, office supplies, and store supplies from ITT. The journal has no column for store supplies, so the Other Accounts Dr. column is used. In this case, Store Supplies is entered in the Account column along with the creditor's name (ITT). This purchases journal also includes a separate column for credit purchases of office supplies. A separate column such as this is useful when several transactions involve debits to the same account. Each company uses its own judgment in deciding on the number of separate columns necessary.

Posting The amounts in the Accounts Payable Cr. column are immediately posted to individual creditor accounts in the accounts payable subsidiary ledger. Individual amounts in the Other Accounts Dr. column are immediately posted to their general ledger accounts. At the end of the period, all column totals except the Other Accounts Dr. column are posted to their general ledger accounts.

Proving the Ledger Accounts payable balances in the subsidiary ledger are proved after posting the purchases journal. We prove the subsidiary ledger by preparing a **schedule of accounts payable,** which is a list of accounts from the accounts payable ledger with their balances and the total. If this total equals the balance of the Accounts Payable controlling account, the accounts in the accounts payable ledger are assumed correct. Exhibit 7.10 shows a schedule of accounts payable drawn from the accounts payable ledger of Exhibit 7.9.

EXHIBIT 7.10

Schedule of Accounts Payable

Schedule of Accounts Payable February 28	
Ace Mfg. Company	$ 300
Horning Supply Company	350
ITT Company	225
Smite Company	300
Wynet & Company	150
Total accounts payable	$1,325

Cash Disbursements Journal

A **cash disbursements journal,** also called a *cash payments journal,* is typically used to record all cash payments.

Journalizing The cash disbursements journal shown in Exhibit 7.11 illustrates repetitive entries to the Cash Cr. column of this journal (reflecting cash payments). Also note the frequent credits to Inventory (which reflect purchase discounts) and the debits to Accounts Payable. For example, on February 15, the company pays Ace on account (credit terms of 2/10, n/30—see February 5 transaction in Exhibit 7.9). Since payment occurs in the discount period, the company pays $196 ($200 invoice less $4 discount). The $4 discount is credited to Inventory. Note that when this company purchases inventory for cash, it is recorded using the Other Accounts Dr. column and the Cash Cr. column as illustrated in the February 3 and 12 transactions. Generally, the Other Accounts column is used to record cash payments on items for which no column exists. For example, on February 15, the company pays salaries expense of $250. The title of the account debited (Salaries Expense) is entered in the Account Debited column.

The cash disbursements journal has a column titled Ck. No. (check number). For control over cash disbursements, all payments except for those of small amounts are made by check. Checks should be prenumbered and each check's number entered in the journal in numerical order in the column headed Ck. No. This makes it possible to scan the numbers in the column for omitted checks. When a cash disbursements journal has a column for check numbers, it is sometimes called a **check register.**

Posting Individual amounts in the Other Accounts Dr. column of a cash disbursements journal are immediately posted to their general ledger accounts. Individual amounts in the Accounts

EXHIBIT 7.11

Cash Disbursements Journal with Posting*

File	Edit	Maintain	Tasks	Analysis	Options	Reports	Window	Help

Cash Disbursements Journal   Page 2

	Date	Ck. No.	Payee	Account Debited	PR	Cash Cr.	Inventory Cr.	Other Accounts Dr.	Accounts Payable Dr.
	Feb. 3	105	L. & N. Railroad	Inventory	119	15		15	
	12	106	East Sales Co.	Inventory	119	25		25	
	15	107	Ace Mfg. Co.	Ace Mfg. Co.	✓	196	4		200
	15	108	Jerry Hale	Salaries Expense	622	250		250	
	20	109	Wynet & Co.	Wynet & Co.	✓	147	3		150
	28	110	Smite Co.	Smite Co.	✓	294	6		300
	28		Totals			927	13	290	650
						(101)	(119)	(X)	(201)

Individual amounts in the Other Accounts Dr. column and the Accounts Payable Dr. column are posted immediately.

Column totals, except for Other Accounts column, are posted at the end of the period.

General Ledger

Cash   No. 101

Date	PR	Debit	Credit	Balance
Feb. 28	R2	19,770		19,770
28	D2		927	18,843

Inventory   No. 119

Date	PR	Debit	Credit	Balance
Feb. 1	bal.			15,700
3	D2	15		15,715
12	D2	25		15,740
28	S3		1,500	14,240
28	R2		12,550	1,690
28	P1	1,150		2,840
28	D2		13	2,827

Accounts Payable   No. 201

Date	PR	Debit	Credit	Balance
Feb. 28	P1		1,325	1,325
28	D2	650		675

Salaries Expense   No. 622

Date	PR	Debit	Credit	Balance
Feb. 15	D2	250		250

Accounts Payable Ledger

Company Name **Ace Mfg. Company**

Date	PR	Debit	Credit	Balance
Feb. 5	P1		200	200
15	D2	200		0
25	P1		100	100

Company Name **Horning Supply Company**

Date	PR	Debit	Credit	Balance
Feb. 3	P1		350	350

Company Name **ITT Company**

Date	PR	Debit	Credit	Balance
Feb. 28	P1		225	225

Company Name **Smite Company**

Date	PR	Debit	Credit	Balance
Feb. 20	P1		300	300
28	D2	300		0

Company Name **Wynet & Company**

Date	PR	Debit	Credit	Balance
Feb. 13	P1		150	150
20	D2	150		0

*The Cash Disbursements Journal in a *periodic* system replaces "Inventory Cr." with "Purchases Discounts Cr." (see Exhibit 7A.4).

Payable Dr. column are also immediately posted to creditors' accounts in the subsidiary Accounts Payable ledger. At the end of the period, we crossfoot column totals and post the Accounts Payable Dr. column total to the Accounts Payable controlling account. Also, the Inventory Cr. column total is posted to the Inventory account, and the Cash Cr. column total is posted to the Cash account.

Decision Maker

Controller   You wish to analyze your company's cash payments to suppliers and its purchases discounts. Where do you find this information? [Answer—p. 293]

General Journal Transactions

When special journals are used, we still need a general journal for adjusting, closing, and any other transactions for which no special journal has been set up. Examples of these other transactions might include purchases returns and allowances, purchases of plant assets by issuing a note payable, sales returns if a sales returns and allowances journal is not used, and receipt of a note receivable from a customer. We described the recording of transactions in a general journal in Chapters 2 and 3.

10. What are the normal recording and posting procedures when using special journals and controlling accounts with subsidiary ledgers?
11. What is the process for posting to a subsidiary ledger and its controlling account?
12. How do we prove the accuracy of account balances in the general ledger and subsidiary ledgers after posting?
13. Why does a company need a general journal when using special journals for sales, purchases, cash receipts, and cash disbursements?

Technology-Based Accounting Systems

C5 Explain how technology-based information systems impact accounting.

Accounting information systems are supported with technology, which can range from simple calculators to advanced computerized systems. Since technology is increasingly important in accounting information systems, we discuss the impact of computer technology, how data processing works with accounting data, and the role of computer networks.

Computer Technology in Accounting

Computer technology provides accuracy, speed, efficiency, and convenience in performing accounting tasks. A program can be written, for instance, to process customers' merchandise orders. Multipurpose off-the-shelf software applications exist for a variety of business operations. These include familiar accounting programs such as Peachtree® and QuickBooks®. Off-the-shelf programs are designed to be user friendly and menu driven, and many operate more efficiently as *integrated* systems. In an integrated system, actions taken in one part of the system automatically affect related parts. When a credit sale is recorded in an integrated system, for instance, several parts of the system are automatically updated, such as posting.

Point: Companies that have reported missing or stolen employee data such as Social Security numbers include Time Warner, Polo Ralph Lauren, Lexis/Nexis, ChoicePoint, and DSW Shoes.

Computer technology can dramatically reduce the time and effort devoted to recordkeeping. Less effort spent on recordkeeping means more time for accounting professionals to concentrate on analysis and managerial decision making. These advances have created a greater demand for accounting professionals who understand financial reports and can draw insights and information from mountains of processed data. Accounting professionals have expertise in determining relevant and reliable information for decision making. They also can assess the effects of transactions and events on a company and its financial statements.

Decision Insight

Middleware is software allowing different computer programs in a company or across companies to work together. It allows transfer of purchase orders, invoices, and other electronic documents between accounting systems. For example, suppliers can monitor inventory levels of their buyers for production and shipping purposes.

Data Processing in Accounting

Accounting systems differ with regard to how input is entered and processed. **Online processing** enters and processes data as soon as source documents are available. This means that databases are immediately updated. **Batch processing** accumulates source documents for a period of time and then processes them all at once such as daily, weekly, or monthly. The advantage of online processing is timeliness. This often requires additional costs related to both software and hardware requirements. Companies such as Intuit (Intuit.com) are making online processing of accounting data a reality for many businesses. The advantage of batch processing is that it requires only periodic updating of databases. Records used to send bills to customers, for instance, might require updating only once a month. The disadvantage of batch processing is the lack of updated databases for management to use when making business decisions.

Computer Networks in Accounting

Networking, or linking computers with each other, can create information advantages (and cost efficiencies). **Computer networks** are links among computers giving different users and different computers access to common databases, programs, and hardware. Many college computer labs, for instance, are networked. A small computer network is called a *local area network (LAN);* it links machines with *hard-wire* hookups. Large computer networks extending over long distances often rely on *modem* or *wireless* communication.

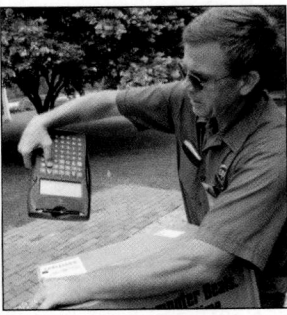

Demand for information sometimes requires advanced networks such as the systems Federal Express and UPS use to track packages and bill customers and the system Wal-Mart uses to monitor inventory levels in its stores. These networks include many computers and satellite communications to gather information and to provide ready access to its databases from all locations.

Enterprise Resource Planning Software

Enterprise resource planning (ERP) software includes the programs that manage a company's vital operations. They extend from order taking to manufacturing to accounting. When working properly, these integrated programs can speed decision making, identify costs for reduction, and give managers control over operations with the click of a mouse. For many managers, ERP software allows them to scrutinize business, identify where inventories are piling up, and see what plants are most efficient. The software is designed to link every part of a company's operations. This software allowed Monsanto to slash production planning from six weeks to three, trim its inventories, and increase its bargaining power with suppliers. Monsanto estimates that this software saves the company $200 million per year.

ERP has several suppliers. SAP leads the market, with Oracle, which gobbled up PeopleSoft and J. D. Edwards, a distant second (*AMR Research*). SAP software is used by more than half of the world's 500 largest companies. It links ordering, inventory, production, purchasing, planning, tracking, and human resources. A transaction or event triggers an immediate chain reaction of events throughout the enterprise. It is making companies more efficient and profitable.

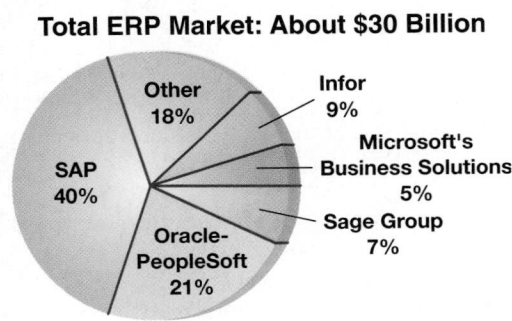

Total ERP Market: About $30 Billion

- Other 18%
- Infor 9%
- Microsoft's Business Solutions 5%
- SAP 40%
- Sage Group 7%
- Oracle-PeopleSoft 21%

ERP is pushing into cyberspace and customer relationship management (CRM). Now companies can share data with customers and suppliers. Applesauce maker Mott's is using SAP so that distributors can check the status of orders and place them over the Net, and the Coca-Cola Company uses it to ship soda on time. ERP is also increasingly used by small business. For example, NetSuite's accounting services to small and medium businesses are powered by Oracle's system.

Decision Insight ▬▬▬▬▬▬▬

A new generation of accounting support is available. With the touch of a key, users can create real-time inventory reports showing all payments, charges, and credit limits at any point in the accounting cycle. Many services also include "alert signals" notifying the company when, for example, a large order exceeds a customer's credit limit or when purchases need to be made or when a bank balance is running low. These alerts occur via e-mail, fax, PDA, or phone.

Decision Analysis   Segment Return on Assets

A1 Compute segment return on assets and use it to evaluate segment performance.

Good accounting information systems collect financial data for a company's various segments. A *segment* refers to a part of a company that is separately identified by its products or services, or by the geographic market it serves. **Harley-Davidson** reports that it operates in two business segments: (1) motorcycles and (2) financial services. Users of financial statements are especially interested in segment information to better understand a company's activities because segments often vary on profitability, risk, and growth.

Companies must report segment information, including their sales, operating income, identifiable assets, capital expenditures, and depreciation. However, managers are reluctant to release information that can harm competitive position. Exhibit 7.12 shows survey results on the number of companies with different (reported) segments.

EXHIBIT 7.12

Companies Reporting Operations by These Segments*

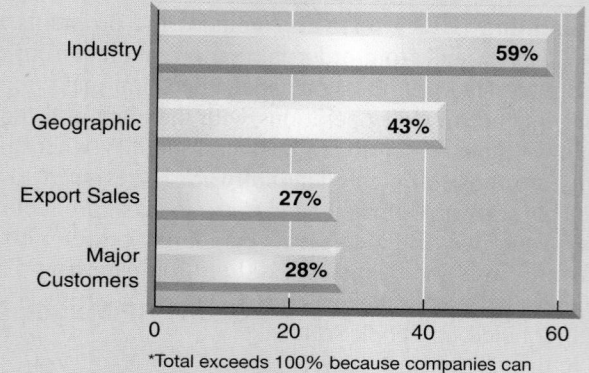

*Total exceeds 100% because companies can report more than one type of segment.

One measure of success for business segments is the **segment return on assets** ratio defined as follows.

$$\text{Segment return on assets} = \frac{\text{Segment operating income}}{\text{Segment average assets}}$$

This ratio reflects on the profitability of a segment. Exhibit 7.13 shows the segments' operating income, average assets, and return on assets for Harley-Davidson.

EXHIBIT 7.13

Harley-Davidson's Segment Return on Assets ($ millions)

Segment*	2006			2005			2004
	Operating Income	Average Assets	Return on Assets	Operating Income	Average Assets	Return on Assets	Return on Assets
Motorcycles	$1,414	$1,765	80%	$1,300	$1,746	74%	70%
Financial services	211	2,658	8%	192	2,294	8%	9%

* A segment's operating income is usually measured as income before taxes, and assets is usually measured as identifiable assets.

The trend in Harley's segment return on assets is increasing for its motorcycle segment, but not for its financial services segment. Also, its motorcycle segment is much more profitable (80%) than its financial services (8%) segment. Harley should consider further investment in its motorcycle segment if such returns can be sustained. Analysis can also be extended to geographical segments and any other segments that companies report.

Decision Maker

Banker A bicycle merchandiser requests a loan from you to expand operations. Its net income is $220,000, reflecting a 10% increase over the prior year. You ask about segment results. The owner reports that $160,000 of net income is from Cuban operations, reflecting a 60% increase over the prior year. The remaining $60,000 of net income is from U.S. operations, reflecting a 40% decrease. Does this segment information impact your loan decision? [Answer—p. 293]

Demonstration Problem—Perpetual System

Pepper Company completed the following selected transactions and events during March of this year. (Terms of all credit sales for the company are 2/10, n/30.)

DP7

Mar. 4   Sold merchandise on credit to Jennifer Nelson, Invoice No. 954, for $16,800 (cost is $12,200).

     6   Purchased $1,220 of office supplies on credit from Mack Company. Invoice dated March 3, terms n/30.

     6   Sold merchandise on credit to Dennie Hoskins, Invoice No. 955, for $10,200 (cost is $8,100).

   11   Purchased $52,600 of merchandise, invoice dated March 6, terms 2/10, n/30, from Defore Industries.

   12   Borrowed $26,000 cash by giving Commerce Bank a long-term promissory note payable.

   14   Received cash payment from Jennifer Nelson for the March 4 sale less the discount (Invoice No. 954).

   16   Received a $200 credit memorandum from Defore Industries for unsatisfactory merchandise Pepper purchased on March 11 and later returned.

   16   Received cash payment from Dennie Hoskins for the March 6 sale less the discount (Invoice No. 955).

   18   Purchased $22,850 of store equipment on credit from Schmidt Supply, invoice dated March 15, terms n/30.

   20   Sold merchandise on credit to Marjorie Allen, Invoice No. 956, for $5,600 (cost is $3,800).

   21   Sent Defore Industries Check No. 516 in payment of its March 6 dated invoice less the return and the discount.

   22   Purchased $41,625 of merchandise, invoice dated March 18, terms 2/10, n/30, from Welch Company.

   26   Issued a $600 credit memorandum to Marjorie Allen for defective merchandise Pepper sold on March 20 and Allen later returned.

   31   Issued Check No. 517, payable to Payroll, in payment of $15,900 sales salaries for the month. Cashed the check and paid the employees.

   31   Cash sales for the month are $134,680 (cost is $67,340). (Cash sales are recorded daily but are recorded only once here to reduce repetitive entries.)

Required

1. Open the following selected general ledger accounts: Cash (101), Accounts Receivable (106) Inventory (119), Office Supplies (124), Store Equipment (165), Accounts Payable (201), Long-Term Notes Payable (251), Sales (413), Sales Returns and Allowances (414), Sales Discounts (415), Cost of Goods Sold (502), and Sales Salaries Expense (621). Open the following accounts receivable ledger accounts: Marjorie Allen, Dennie Hoskins, and Jennifer Nelson. Open the following accounts payable ledger accounts: Defore Industries, Mack Company, Schmidt Supply, and Welch Company.

2. Enter the transactions using a sales journal, a purchases journal, a cash receipts journal, a cash disbursements journal, and a general journal similar to the ones illustrated in the chapter. Regularly post to the individual customer and creditor accounts. Also, post any amounts that should be posted as individual amounts to general ledger accounts. Foot and crossfoot the journals and make the month-end postings. *Pepper Co. uses the perpetual inventory system.*

3. Prepare a trial balance for the selected general ledger accounts in part 1 and prove the accuracy of subsidiary ledgers by preparing schedules of accounts receivable and accounts payable.

Planning the Solution

• Set up the required general ledger, the subsidiary ledger accounts, and the five required journals as illustrated in the chapter.

- Read and analyze each transaction and decide in which special journal (or general journal) the transaction is recorded.
- Record each transaction in the proper journal (and post the appropriate individual amounts).
- Once you have recorded all transactions, total the journal columns. Post from each journal to the appropriate ledger accounts.
- Prepare a trial balance to prove the equality of the debit and credit balances in your general ledger.
- Prepare schedules of accounts receivable and accounts payable. Compare the totals of these schedules to the Accounts Receivable and Accounts Payable controlling account balances, making sure that they agree.

Solution to Demonstration Problem — Perpetual System

Sales Journal   Page 2

Date	Account Debited	Invoice Number	PR	Accounts Receivable Dr. Sales Cr.	Cost of Goods Sold Dr. Inventory Cr.
Mar. 4	Jennifer Nelson	954	✓	16,800	12,200
6	Dennie Hoskins	955	✓	10,200	8,100
20	Marjorie Allen	956	✓	5,600	3,800
31	Totals			32,600	24,100
				(106/413)	(502/119)

Cash Receipts Journal   Page 3

Date	Account Credited	Explanation	PR	Cash Dr.	Sales Discount Dr.	Accounts Receivable Cr.	Sales Cr.	Other Accounts Cr.	Cost of Goods Sold Dr. Inventory Cr.
Mar. 12	L.T. Notes Payable	Note to bank	251	26,000				26,000	
14	Jennifer Nelson	Invoice 954, 3/4	✓	16,464	336	16,800			
16	Dennie Hoskins	Invoice 955, 3/6	✓	9,996	204	10,200			
31	Sales	Cash sales	x	134,680			134,680		67,340
31	Totals			187,140	540	27,000	134,680	26,000	67,340
				(101)	(415)	(106)	(413)	(x)	(502/119)

Purchases Journal   Page 3

Date	Account	Date of Invoice	Terms	PR	Accounts Payable Cr.	Inventory Dr.	Office Supplies Dr.	Other Accounts Dr.
Mar. 6	Office Supplies/Mack Co	3/3	n/30	✓	1,220		1,220	
11	Defore Industries	3/6	2/10, n/30	✓	52,600	52,600		
18	Store Equipment/Schmidt Supp	3/15	n/30	165/✓	22,850			22,850
22	Welch Company	3/18	2/10, n/30	✓	41,625	41,625		
31	Totals				118,295	94,225	1,220	22,850
					(201)	(119)	(124)	(x)

Cash Disbursements Journal   Page 3

Date	Ck. No.	Payee	Account Debited	PR	Cash Cr.	Inventory Cr.	Other Accounts Dr.	Accounts Payable Dr.
Mar. 21	516	Defore Industries	Defore Industries	✓	51,352	1,048		52,400
31	517	Payroll	Sales Salaries Expense	621	15,900		15,900	
31		Totals			67,252	1,048	15,900	52,400
					(101)	(119)	(x)	(201)

General Journal   Page 2

Mar. 16	Accounts Payable—Defore Industries	201/✓	200	
	Inventory	119		200
	To record credit memorandum received.			
26	Sales Returns and Allowances	414	600	
	Accounts Receivable—Marjorie Allen	106/✓		600
	To record credit memorandum issued.			

Accounts Receivable Ledger

Marjorie Allen

Date	PR	Debit	Credit	Balance
Mar. 20	S2	5,600		5,600
26	G2		600	5,000

Dennie Hoskins

Date	PR	Debit	Credit	Balance
Mar. 6	S2	10,200		10,200
16	R3		10,200	0

Jennifer Nelson

Date	PR	Debit	Credit	Balance
Mar. 4	S2	16,800		16,800
14	R3		16,800	0

Accounts Payable Ledger

Defore Industries

Date	PR	Debit	Credit	Balance
Mar. 11	P3		52,600	52,600
16	G2	200		52,400
21	D3	52,400		0

Mack Company

Date	PR	Debit	Credit	Balance
Mar. 6	P3		1,220	1,220

Schmidt Supply

Date	PR	Debit	Credit	Balance
Mar. 18	P3		22,850	22,850

Welch Company

Date	PR	Debit	Credit	Balance
Mar. 22	P3		41,625	41,625

General Ledger (Partial Listing)

Cash   Acct. No. 101

Date	PR	Debit	Credit	Balance
Mar. 31	R3	187,140		187,140
31	D3		67,252	119,888

Accounts Receivable   Acct. No. 106

Date	PR	Debit	Credit	Balance
Mar. 26	G2		600	(600)
31	S2	32,600		32,000
31	R3		27,000	5,000

Inventory   Acct. No. 119

Date	PR	Debit	Credit	Balance
Mar. 16	G2		200	(200)
21	D3		1,048	(1,248)
31	P3	94,225		92,977
31	S2		24,100	68,877
31	R3		67,340	1,537

Office Supplies   Acct. No. 124

Date	PR	Debit	Credit	Balance
Mar. 31	P3	1,220		1,220

Store Equipment   Acct. No. 165

Date	PR	Debit	Credit	Balance
Mar. 18	P3	22,850		22,850

Accounts Payable   Acct. No. 201

Date	PR	Debit	Credit	Balance
Mar. 16	G2	200		(200)
31	P3		118,295	118,095
31	D3	52,400		65,695

Long-Term Notes Payable   Acct. No. 251

Date	PR	Debit	Credit	Balance
Mar. 12	R3		26,000	26,000

Sales   Acct. No. 413

Date	PR	Debit	Credit	Balance
Mar. 31	S2		32,600	32,600
31	R3		134,680	167,280

Sales Returns and Allowances   Acct. No. 414

Date	PR	Debit	Credit	Balance
Mar. 26	G2	600		600

Sales Discounts   Acct. No. 415

Date	PR	Debit	Credit	Balance
Mar. 31	R3	540		540

Cost of Goods Sold   Acct. No. 502

Date	PR	Debit	Credit	Balance
Mar. 31	R3	67,340		67,340
31	S2	24,100		91,440

Sales Salaries Expense   Acct. No. 621

Date	PR	Debit	Credit	Balance
Mar. 31	D3	15,900		15,900

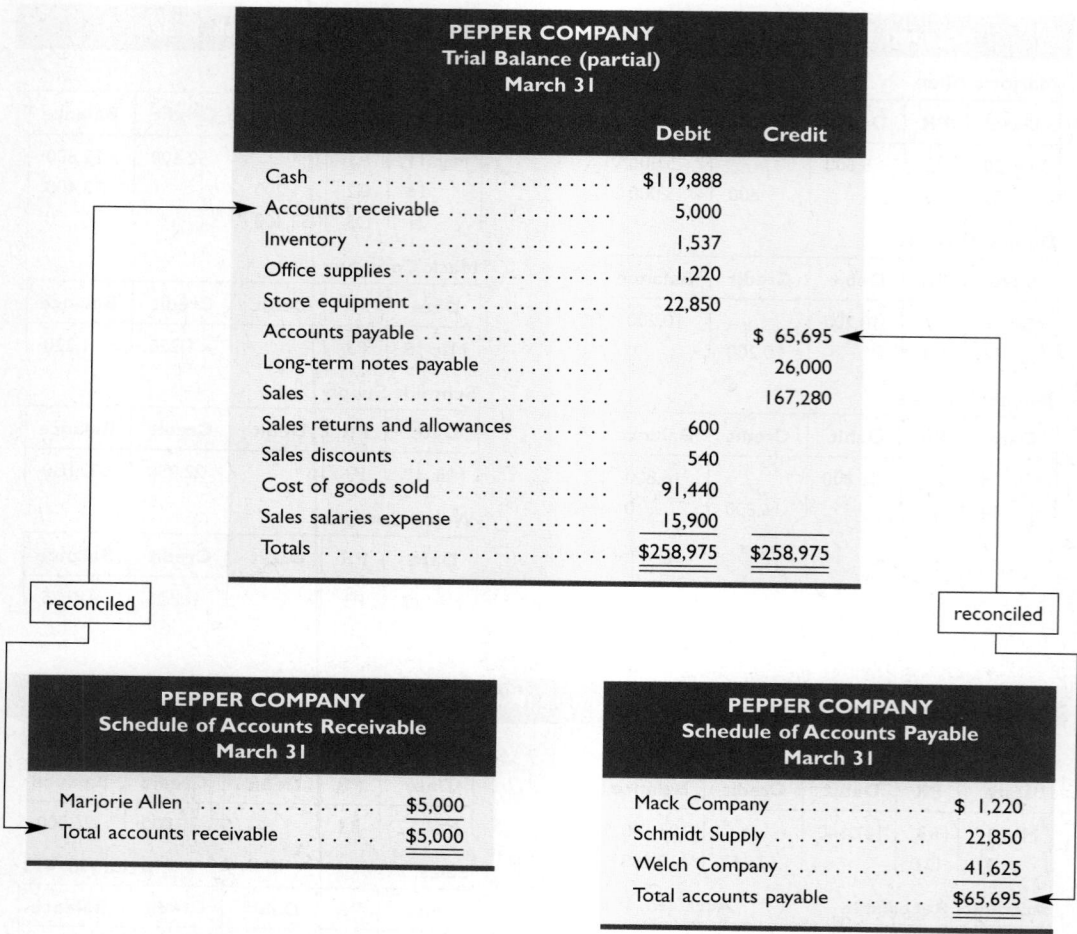

PEPPER COMPANY
Trial Balance (partial)
March 31

	Debit	Credit
Cash	$119,888	
Accounts receivable	5,000	
Inventory	1,537	
Office supplies	1,220	
Store equipment	22,850	
Accounts payable		$ 65,695
Long-term notes payable		26,000
Sales		167,280
Sales returns and allowances	600	
Sales discounts	540	
Cost of goods sold	91,440	
Sales salaries expense	15,900	
Totals	$258,975	$258,975

reconciled

reconciled

PEPPER COMPANY
Schedule of Accounts Receivable
March 31

Marjorie Allen	$5,000
Total accounts receivable	$5,000

PEPPER COMPANY
Schedule of Accounts Payable
March 31

Mack Company	$ 1,220
Schmidt Supply	22,850
Welch Company	41,625
Total accounts payable	$65,695

APPENDIX

7A   Special Journals under a Periodic System

P3
Journalize and post transactions using special journals in a periodic inventory system.

This appendix describes special journals under a periodic inventory system. Each journal is slightly impacted. The sales journal and the cash receipts journal both require one less column (namely that of Cost of Goods Sold Dr., Inventory Cr.). The Purchases Journal replaces the Inventory Dr. column with a Purchases Dr. column in a periodic system. The cash disbursements journal replaces the Inventory Cr. column with a Purchases Discounts Cr. column in a periodic system. These changes are illustrated.

Sales Journal

The sales journal using the periodic inventory system is shown in Exhibit 7A.1. The difference in the sales journal between the perpetual and periodic system is the exclusion of the column to record cost of goods sold and inventory amounts for each sale. The periodic system does *not* record the increase in cost of goods sold and the decrease in inventory at the time of each sale.

Sales Journal — Page 3

Date	Account Debited	Invoice Number	PR	Accounts Receivable Dr. Sales Cr.
Feb. 2	Jason Henry	307	✓	450
7	Albert Co.	308	✓	500
13	Kam Moore	309	✓	350
15	Paul Roth	310	✓	200
22	Jason Henry	311	✓	225
25	Frank Booth	312	✓	175
28	Albert Co.	313	✓	250
28	Total			2,150
				(106/413)

EXHIBIT 7A.1

Sales Journal—Periodic System

Cash Receipts Journal

The cash receipts journal using the periodic system is shown in Exhibit 7A.2. Note the absence of the column on the far right side to record debits to Cost of Goods Sold and credits to Inventory for the cost of merchandise sold (seen under the perpetual system). Consistent with the cash receipts journal shown in Exhibit 7.7, we show only the weekly (summary) cash sale entries.

EXHIBIT 7A.2

Cash Receipts Journal—Periodic System

Cash Receipts Journal — Page 2

Date	Account Credited	Explanation	PR	Cash Dr.	Sales Discount Dr.	Accounts Receivable Cr.	Sales Cr.	Other Accounts Cr.
Feb. 7	Sales	Cash sales	x	4,450			4,450	
12	Jason Henry	Invoice 307, 2/2	✓	441	9	450		
14	Sales	Cash sales	x	3,925			3,925	
17	Albert Co.	Invoice 308, 2/7	✓	490	10	500		
20	Notes Payable	Note to bank	245	750				750
21	Sales	Cash sales	x	4,700			4,700	
22	Interest revenue	Bank account	409	250				250
23	Kam Moore	Invoice 309, 2/13	✓	343	7	350		
25	Paul Roth	Invoice 310, 2/15	✓	196	4	200		
28	Sales	Cash sales	x	4,225			4,225	
28	Totals			19,770	30	1,500	17,300	1,000
				(101)	(415)	(106)	(413)	(x)

Purchases Journal

The purchases journal using the periodic system is shown in Exhibit 7A.3. This journal under a perpetual system included an Inventory column where the periodic system now has a Purchases column.

EXHIBIT 7A.3

Purchases Journal—Periodic System

Purchases Journal — Page 1

Date	Account	Date of Invoice	Terms	PR	Accounts Payable Cr.	Purchases Dr.	Office Supplies Dr.	Other Accounts Dr.
Feb. 3	Horning Supply Co.	2/2	n/30	✓	350	275	75	
5	Ace Mfg. Co.	2/5	2/10, n/30	✓	200	200		
13	Wynet and Co.	2/10	2/10, n/30	✓	150	150		
20	Smite Co.	2/18	2/10, n/30	✓	300	300		
25	Ace Mfg. Co.	2/24	2/10, n/30	✓	100	100		
28	Store Supplies/ITT Co.	2/28	n/30	125/✓	225	125	25	75
28	Totals				1,325	1,150	100	75
					(201)	(505)	(124)	(x)

Cash Disbursements Journal

The cash disbursements journal using a periodic system is shown in Exhibit 7A.4. This journal under the perpetual system included an Inventory column where the periodic system now has the Purchases Discounts column.

EXHIBIT 7A.4

Cash Disbursements Journal—Periodic System

	Cash Disbursements Journal								Page 2
	Date	Ck. No.	Payee	Account Debited	PR	Cash Cr.	Purchases Discounts Cr.	Other Accounts Dr.	Accounts Payable Dr.
	Feb. 3	105	L. and N. Railroad	Purchases	505	15		15	
	12	106	East Sales Co.	Purchases	505	25		25	
	15	107	Ace Mfg. Co.	Ace Mfg. Co.	✓	196	4		200
	15	108	Jerry Hale	Salaries Expense	622	250		250	
	20	109	Wynet and Co.	Wynet and Co.	✓	147	3		150
	28	110	Smite Co.	Smite Co.	✓	294	6		300
	28		Totals			927	13	290	650
						(101)	(507)	(x)	(201)

Demonstration Problem—Periodic System

Refer to Pepper Company's selected transactions described under the Demonstration Problem—Perpetual System to fulfill the following requirements.

Required

1. Open the following selected general ledger accounts: Cash (101), Accounts Receivable (106), Office Supplies (124), Store Equipment (165), Accounts Payable (201), Long-Term Notes Payable (251), Sales (413), Sales Returns and Allowances (414), Sales Discounts (415), Purchases (505), Purchases Returns and Allowances (506), Purchases Discounts (507), and Sales Salaries Expense (621). Open the following accounts receivable ledger accounts: Marjorie Allen, Dennie Hoskins, and Jennifer Nelson. Open the following accounts payable ledger accounts: Defore Industries, Mack Company, Schmidt Supply, and Welch Company.

2. Enter the transactions using a sales journal, a purchases journal, a cash receipts journal, a cash disbursements journal, and a general journal similar to the ones illustrated in Appendix 7A. Regularly post to the individual customer and creditor accounts. Also, post any amounts that should be posted as individual amounts to general ledger accounts. Foot and crossfoot the journals and make the month-end postings. *Pepper Co. uses the periodic inventory system in this problem.*

3. Prepare a trial balance for the selected general ledger accounts in part 1 and prove the accuracy of subsidiary ledgers by preparing schedules of accounts receivable and accounts payable.

Solution to Demonstration Problem—Periodic System

	Sales Journal				Page 2
	Date	Account Debited	Invoice Number	PR	Accounts Receivable Dr. Sales Cr.
	Mar. 4	Jennifer Nelson	954	✓	16,800
	6	Dennie Hoskins	955	✓	10,200
	20	Marjorie Allen	956	✓	5,600
	31	Totals			32,600
					(106/413)

	Cash Receipts Journal								Page 3
	Date	Account Credited	Explanation	PR	Cash Dr.	Sales Discount Dr.	Accounts Receivable Cr.	Sales Cr.	Other Accounts Cr.
	Mar. 12	L.T. Notes Payable	Note to bank	251	26,000				26,000
	14	Jennifer Nelson	Invoice 954, 3/4	✓	16,464	336	16,800		
	16	Dennie Hoskins	Invoice 955, 3/6	✓	9,996	204	10,200		
	31	Sales	Cash sales	x	134,680			134,680	
	31	Totals			187,140	540	27,000	134,680	26,000
					(101)	(415)	(106)	(413)	(x)

Purchases Journal   Page 3 ⬛

Date	Account	Date of Invoice	Terms	PR	Accounts Payable Cr.	Purchases Dr.	Office Supplies Dr.	Other Accounts Dr.
Mar. 6	Office Supplies/Mack Co	3/3	n/30	✓	1,220		1,220	
11	Defore Industries	3/6	2/10, n/30	✓	52,600	52,600		
18	Store Equipment/Schmidt Supp	3/15	n/30	165/✓	22,850			22,850
22	Welch Company	3/18	2/10, n/30	✓	41,625	41,625		
31	Totals				118,295	94,225	1,220	22,850
					(201)	(505)	(124)	(x)

Cash Disbursements Journal   Page 3 ⬛

	Date	Ck. No.	Payee	Account Debited	PR	Cash Cr.	Purchases Discount Cr.	Other Accounts Dr.	Accounts Payable Dr.
	Mar. 21	516	Defore Industries	Defore Industries	✓	51,352	1,048		52,400
	31	517	Payroll	Sales Salaries Expense	621	15,900		15,900	
	31		Totals			67,252	1,048	15,900	52,400
						(101)	(507)	(x)	(201)

General Journal   Page 2

Mar. 16	Accounts Payable—Defore Industries	201/✓	200	
	Purchases Returns and Allowances	506		200
	To record credit memorandum received.			
26	Sales Returns and Allowances	414	600	
	Accounts Receivable—Marjorie Allen	106/✓		600
	To record credit memorandum issued.			

Accounts Receivable Ledger

Marjorie Allen

Date	PR	Debit	Credit	Balance
Mar. 20	S2	5,600		5,600
26	G2		600	5,000

Dennie Hoskins

Date	PR	Debit	Credit	Balance
Mar. 6	S2	10,200		10,200
16	R3		10,200	0

Jennifer Nelson

Date	PR	Debit	Credit	Balance
Mar. 4	S2	16,800		16,800
14	R3		16,800	0

Accounts Payable Ledger

Defore Industries

Date	PR	Debit	Credit	Balance
Mar. 11	P3		52,600	52,600
16	G2	200		52,400
21	D3	52,400		0

Mack Company

Date	PR	Debit	Credit	Balance
Mar. 6	P3		1,220	1,220

Schmidt Supply

Date	PR	Debit	Credit	Balance
Mar. 18	P3		22,850	22,850

Welch Company

Date	PR	Debit	Credit	Balance
Mar. 22	P3		41,625	41,625

General Ledger (Partial Listing)

Cash   Acct. No. 101

Date	PR	Debit	Credit	Balance
Mar. 31	R3	187,140		187,140
31	D3		67,252	119,888

Accounts Receivable   Acct. No. 106

Date	PR	Debit	Credit	Balance
Mar. 26	G2		600	(600)
31	S2	32,600		32,000
31	R3		27,000	5,000

Office Supplies   Acct. No. 124

Date	PR	Debit	Credit	Balance
Mar. 31	P3	1,220		1,220

Store Equipment   Acct. No. 165

Date	PR	Debit	Credit	Balance
Mar. 18	P3	22,850		22,850

Accounts Payable   Acct. No. 201

Date	PR	Debit	Credit	Balance
Mar. 16	G2	200		(200)
31	P3		118,295	118,095
31	D3	52,400		65,695

Long-Term Notes Payable   Acct. No. 251

Date	PR	Debit	Credit	Balance
Mar. 12	R3		26,000	26,000

Sales   Acct. No. 413

Date	PR	Debit	Credit	Balance
Mar. 31	S2		32,600	32,600
31	R3		134,680	167,280

Sales Returns and Allowances   Acct. No. 414

Date	PR	Debit	Credit	Balance
Mar. 26	G2	600		600

Sales Discounts   Acct. No. 415

Date	PR	Debit	Credit	Balance
Mar. 31	R3	540		540

Purchases   Acct. No. 505

Date	PR	Debit	Credit	Balance
Mar. 31	P3	94,225		94,225

Purchases Returns and Allowances   Acct. No. 506

Date	PR	Debit	Credit	Balance
Mar. 16	G2		200	200

Purchases Discounts   Acct. No. 507

Date	PR	Debit	Credit	Balance
Mar. 31	D3		1,048	1,048

Sales Salaries Expense   Acct. No. 621

Date	PR	Debit	Credit	Balance
Mar. 31	D3	15,900		15,900

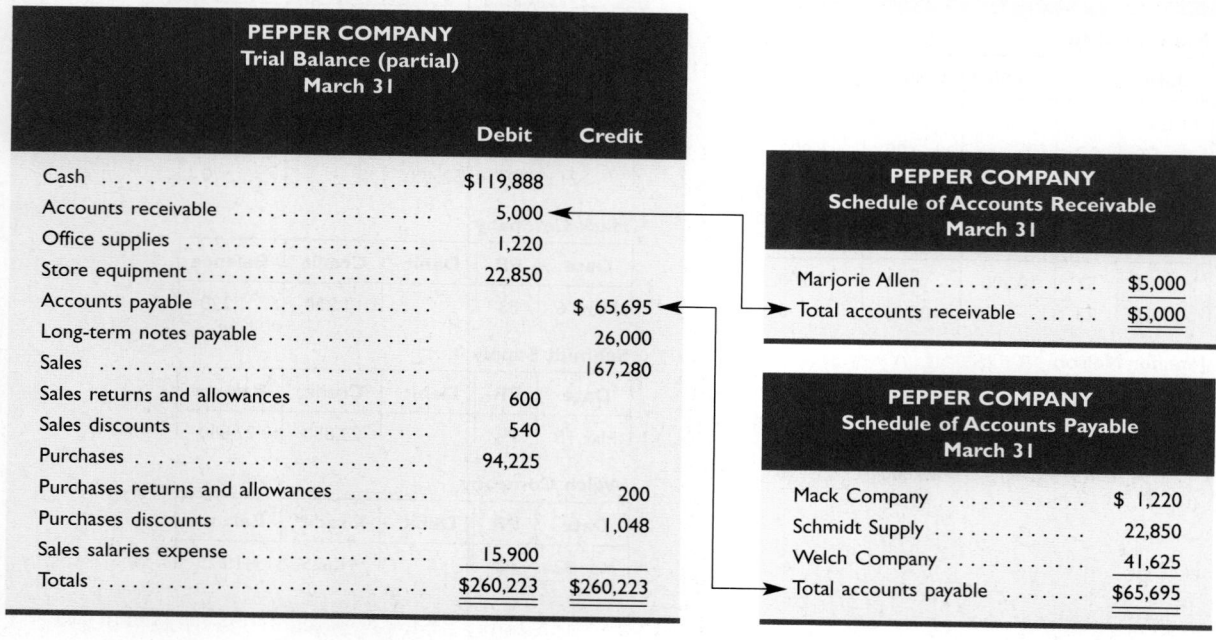

PEPPER COMPANY
Trial Balance (partial)
March 31

	Debit	Credit
Cash	$119,888	
Accounts receivable	5,000	
Office supplies	1,220	
Store equipment	22,850	
Accounts payable		$ 65,695
Long-term notes payable		26,000
Sales		167,280
Sales returns and allowances	600	
Sales discounts	540	
Purchases	94,225	
Purchases returns and allowances		200
Purchases discounts		1,048
Sales salaries expense	15,900	
Totals	$260,223	$260,223

PEPPER COMPANY
Schedule of Accounts Receivable
March 31

Marjorie Allen	$5,000
Total accounts receivable	$5,000

PEPPER COMPANY
Schedule of Accounts Payable
March 31

Mack Company	$ 1,220
Schmidt Supply	22,850
Welch Company	41,625
Total accounts payable	$65,695

Summary

C1 Identify fundamental principles of accounting information systems. Accounting information systems are governed by five fundamental principles: control, relevance, compatibility, flexibility, and cost-benefit.

C2 Identify components of accounting information systems. The five basic components of an accounting information system are source documents, input devices, information processors, information storage, and output devices.

C3 Explain the goals and uses of special journals. Special journals are used for recording transactions of similar type, each meant to cover one kind of transaction. Four of the most common special journals are the sales journal, cash receipts journal, purchases journal, and cash disbursements journal. Special journals are efficient and cost-effective tools in the journalizing and posting processes.

C4 Describe the use of controlling accounts and subsidiary ledgers. A general ledger keeps controlling accounts such as Accounts Receivable and Accounts Payable, but details on individual accounts making up the controlling account are kept in subsidiary ledgers (such as an accounts receivable ledger). The balance in a controlling account must equal the sum of its subsidiary account balances after posting is complete.

C5 Explain how technology-based information systems impact accounting. Technology-based information systems aim to increase the accuracy, speed, efficiency, and convenience of accounting procedures.

A1 Compute segment return on assets and use it to evaluate segment performance. A business segment is a part of a company that is separately identified by its products or services or by the geographic market it serves. Analysis of a company's segments is aided by the segment return on assets (segment operating income divided by segment average assets).

P1 Journalize and post transactions using special journals. Each special journal is devoted to similar kinds of transactions. Transactions are journalized on one line of a special journal, with columns devoted to specific accounts, dates, names, posting references, explanations, and other necessary information. Posting is threefold: (1) individual amounts in the Other Accounts column are posted to their general ledger accounts on a regular (daily) basis, (2) individual amounts in a column whose total is *not* posted to a controlling account at the end of a period (month) are posted regularly (daily) to their general ledger accounts, and (3) total amounts for all columns except the Other Accounts column are posted at the end of a period (month) to their column's account title in the general ledger.

P2 Prepare and prove the accuracy of subsidiary ledgers. Account balances in the general ledger and its subsidiary ledgers are tested for accuracy after posting is complete. This procedure is twofold: (1) prepare a trial balance of the general ledger to confirm that debits equal credits and (2) prepare a schedule to confirm that the controlling account's balance equals the subsidiary ledger's balance.

P3^A Journalize and post transactions using special journals in a periodic inventory system. Transactions are journalized and posted using special journals in a periodic system. The methods are similar to those in a perpetual system; the primary difference is that both cost of goods sold and inventory are not adjusted at the time of each sale. This usually results in the deletion (or renaming) of one or more columns devoted to these accounts in each special journal.

Guidance Answers to **Decision Maker** and **Decision Ethics**

Accountant The main issue is whether commissions have an actual or perceived impact on the integrity and objectivity of your advice. You probably should not accept a commission arrangement (the AICPA Code of Ethics prohibits it when you perform the audit or a review). In any event, you should tell the client of your commission arrangement. Also, you need to seriously examine the merits of agreeing to a commission arrangement when you are in a position to exploit it.

Entrepreneur The accounts receivable ledger has much of the information you need. It lists detailed information for each customer's account, including the amounts, dates for transactions, and dates of payments. It can be reorganized into an "aging schedule" to show how long customers wait before paying their bills.

Controller Much of the information you need is in the accounts payable ledger. It contains information for each supplier, the amounts due, and when payments are made. This subsidiary ledger along with information on credit terms should enable you to conduct your analyses.

Banker This merchandiser's segment information is likely to greatly impact your loan decision. The risks associated with the company's two sources of net income are quite different. While net income is up by 10%, U.S. operations are performing poorly and Cuban operations are subject to many uncertainties. These uncertainties depend on political events, legal issues, business relationships, Cuban economic conditions, and a host of other risks. Overall, net income results suggested a low-risk loan opportunity, but the segment information reveals a high-risk situation.

Guidance Answers to **Quick Checks**

1. The five components are source documents, input devices, information processors, information storage, and output devices.

2. Information processors interpret, transform, and summarize the recorded accounting information so that it can be used in analysis, interpretation, and decision making.

3. Data saved in information storage are used to prepare periodic financial reports and special-purpose internal reports as well as source documentation for auditors.

4. All cash payments by check are recorded in the cash disbursements journal.

5. Columnar journals allow us to accumulate repetitive debits and credits and post them as column totals rather than as individual amounts from each entry.

6. The equality of debits and credits is kept within the general ledger. The subsidiary ledger keeps the customer's individual account and is used only for supplementary information.

7. An initial and the page number of the journal from which the amount was posted are entered in the PR column next to the amount.

8. A separate column for Sales Taxes Payable can be included in both the cash receipts journal and the sales journal.

9. This refers to a procedure of using copies of sales invoices as a sales journal. Each invoice amount is posted directly to the customer's account. All invoices are totaled at period-end for posting to the general ledger accounts.

10. The normal recording and posting procedures are threefold. First, transactions are entered in a special journal if applicable. Second, individual amounts are posted to any subsidiary ledger accounts. Third, column totals are posted to general ledger accounts if not already individually posted.

11. Controlling accounts are debited periodically for an amount or amounts equal to the sum of their respective debits in the subsidiary ledgers (equals journal column totals), and they are credited periodically for an amount or amounts equal to the sum of their respective credits in the subsidiary ledgers (from journal column totals).

12. Tests for accuracy of account balances in the general ledger and subsidiary ledgers are twofold. First, we prepare a trial balance of the general ledger to confirm that debits equal credits. Second, we prove the subsidiary ledgers by preparing schedules of accounts receivable and accounts payable.

13. The general journal is still needed for adjusting, closing, and correcting entries and for special transactions such as sales returns, purchases returns, and certain asset purchases.

14. Integrated systems can save time and minimize errors. This is so because actions taken in one part of the system automatically affect and update related parts.

15. Computer systems offer increased accuracy, speed, efficiency, and convenience.

16. Computer networks can create advantages by linking computers, and giving different users and different computers access to common databases, programs, and hardware.

17. ERP software involves integrated programs, from order taking to manufacturing to accounting. It can speed decision making, help identify costs for reduction, and aid managers in controlling operations.

Key Terms
mhhe.com/wildFAP19e

Key Terms are available at the book's Website for learning and testing in an online Flashcard Format.

Accounting information systems (p. 268)
Accounts payable ledger (p. 273)
Accounts receivable ledger (p. 273)
Batch processing (p. 282)
Cash disbursements journal (p. 280)
Cash receipts journal (p. 277)
Check register (p. 280)
Columnar journal (p. 274)
Compatibility principle (p. 269)
Components of accounting systems (p. 269)

Computer networks (p. 283)
Controlling account (p. 273)
Control principle (p. 268)
Cost-benefit principle (p. 269)
Enterprise resource planning (ERP) software (p. 283)
Flexibility principle (p. 269)
General journal (p. 272)
Information processors (p. 270)
Information storage (p. 270)
Input devices (p. 270)

Internal controls (p. 268)
Online processing (p. 282)
Output devices (p. 271)
Purchases journal (p. 279)
Relevance principle (p. 268)
Sales journal (p. 274)
Schedule of accounts payable (p. 280)
Schedule of accounts receivable (p. 275)
Segment return on assets (p. 284)
Special journal (p. 272)
Subsidiary ledger (p. 272)

Multiple Choice Quiz
Answers on p. 311　　mhhe.com/wildFAP19e

Additional Quiz Questions are available at the book's Website.

1. The sales journal is used to record
   a. Credit sales
   b. Cash sales
   c. Cash receipts
   d. Cash purchases
   e. Credit purchases

2. The purchases journal is used to record
   a. Credit sales
   b. Cash sales
   c. Cash receipts
   d. Cash purchases
   e. Credit purchases

3. The ledger that contains the financial statement accounts of a company is the
   a. General journal
   b. Column balance journal
   c. Special ledger
   d. General ledger
   e. Special journal

4. A subsidiary ledger that contains a separate account for each supplier (creditor) to the company is the
   a. Controlling account
   b. Accounts payable ledger

   c. Accounts receivable ledger
   d. General ledger
   e. Special journal

5. Enterprise resource planning software
   a. Refers to programs that help manage company operations.
   b. Is another name for spreadsheet programs.
   c. Uses batch processing of business information.
   d. Is substantially declining in use.
   e. Is another name for database programs.

Superscript letter ^A *denotes assignments based on Appendix 7A.*

Discussion Questions

1. What are the five fundamental principles of accounting information systems?

2. What are five basic components of an accounting system?

3. What are source documents? Give two examples.

4. What is the purpose of an input device? Give examples of input devices for computer systems.

5. What is the difference between data that are stored off-line and data that are stored online?

6. What purpose is served by the output devices of an accounting system?

7. When special journals are used, they are usually used to record each of four different types of transactions. What are these four types of transactions?

8. What notations are entered into the Posting Reference column of a ledger account?

9. ♟ When a general journal entry is used to record sales returns, the credit of the entry must be posted twice. Does this cause the trial balance to be out of balance? Explain.

10. Describe the procedures involving the use of copies of a company's sales invoices as a sales journal.

11. Credits to customer accounts and credits to Other Accounts are individually posted from a cash receipts journal such as the one in Exhibit 7.7. Why not put both types of credits in the same column and save journal space?

12. ♟ Why should sales to and receipts of cash from credit customers be recorded and posted immediately?

13. ♟ Locate the note that discusses **Best Buy**'s operations by segments in Appendix A. In what two segments does it predominantly operate? **BEST BUY**

14. ♟ Does the income statement of **Circuit City** in Appendix A indicate the net income earned by its business segments? If so, list them. **circuit CITY**

15. Locate the note that discusses **RadioShack**'s segments from its 2006 annual report on its Website. What two reportable segments does RadioShack have? **ⓡ RadioShack®**

16. ♟ Does the balance sheet of **Apple** in Appendix A indicate the identifiable assets owned by its business segments? If so, list them.

♟ **Denotes Discussion Questions that involve decision making.**

McGraw-Hill's
**HOMEWORK
MANAGER®**   Available with McGraw-Hill's Homework Manager

For account titles and numbers, use the Chart of Accounts at the end of the book.

QUICK STUDY

QS 7-1
Accounting information
system principles

C1

Enter the letter of each system principle in the blank next to its best description.

A. Flexibility principle   **D.** Relevance principle
B. Cost-benefit principle   **E.** Compatibility principle
C. Control principle

1. _____ The principle prescribes the accounting information system to help monitor activities.

2. _____ The principle prescribes the accounting information system to adapt to the unique characteristics of the company.

3. _____ The principle prescribes the accounting information system to change in response to technological advances and competitive pressures.

4. _____ The principle that affects all other accounting information system principles.

5. _____ The principle prescribes the accounting information system to provide timely information for effective decision making.

QS 7-2
Accounting information system
C2

Fill in the blanks to complete the following descriptions.
1. With _____ processing, source documents are accumulated for a period and then processed all at the same time, such as once a day, week, or month.
2. A computer _____ allows different computer users to share access to data and programs.
3. A _____ is an input device that captures writing and other input directly from source documents.
4. _____ _____ _____ software comprises programs that help manage a company's vital operations, from manufacturing to accounting.

QS 7-3
Accounting information
system components
C2

Identify the most likely role in an accounting system played by each of the numbered items 1 through 12 by assigning a letter from the list A through E on the left.

A. Source documents
B. Input devices
C. Information processors
D. Information storage
E. Output devices

_____ **1.** Bar code reader
_____ **2.** Digital camera
_____ **3.** Invoice from a supplier
_____ **4.** Zip drive
_____ **5.** Computer scanner
_____ **6.** Filing cabinet
_____ **7.** Computer keyboard
_____ **8.** Computer printer
_____ **9.** Computer monitor
_____ **10.** MP3 player
_____ **11.** Bank statement
_____ **12.** Computer software

QS 7-4
Identifying the special journal
of entry
C3

Weber Electronics uses a sales journal, a purchases journal, a cash receipts journal, a cash disbursements journal, and a general journal as illustrated in this chapter. Weber recently completed the following transactions *a* through *h*. Identify the journal in which each transaction should be recorded.

a. Sold merchandise for cash.
b. Purchased merchandise on credit.
c. Purchased inventory for cash.
d. Paid cash to a creditor.
e. Sold merchandise on credit.
f. Purchased shop supplies on credit.
g. Paid an employee's salary in cash.
h. Borrowed cash from the bank.

QS 7-5
Entries in the general journal
C3

Adrian Gifts uses a sales journal, a purchases journal, a cash receipts journal, a cash disbursements journal, and a general journal as illustrated in this chapter. Journalize its November transactions that should be recorded in the general journal. For those not recorded in the general journal, identify the special journal where each should be recorded.

Nov. 2 The company purchased $2,600 of merchandise on credit from the Midwest Co., terms 2/10, n/30.
     12 The owner, R. Adrian, contributed an automobile worth $17,000 to the company.
     16 The company sold $1,200 of merchandise (cost is $800) on credit to L. Norton, terms n/30.
     19 L. Norton returned $175 of (worthless) merchandise to the company originally purchased on November 16 (assume the cost of this merchandise is left in cost of goods sold).

QS 7-6
Analyzing segment reports
A1

Apple reports the following income (and average assets in parentheses) for each of its geographic segments—$ millions: Americas, $1,665 ($800); Europe, $607 ($380); and Japan, $201 ($173). Apple also reports the following sales (only) by product segments: iPod, $7,676; Desktops, $3,319; Portables, $4,056; Other, $1,885. Compute Apple's return on assets for each of its geographic segments, and assess the relative performance of these segments. Compute the percentage of total sales for each of its four product segments.

For account titles and numbers, use the Chart of Accounts at the end of the book.

EXERCISES

Levine Company uses a sales journal, a purchases journal, a cash receipts journal, a cash disbursement journal, and a general journal. The following transactions occur in the month of March.

Exercise 7-1
Sales journal—perpetual

P1

Mar. 2   Sold merchandise costing $450 to R. Nagy for $675 cash, invoice no. 5703.
5   Purchased $3,000 of merchandise on credit from Central Corp.
7   Sold merchandise costing $1,215 to K. Anklam for $1,700, terms 2/10, n/30, invoice no. 5704.
8   Borrowed $8,000 cash by signing a note payable to the bank.
12   Sold merchandise costing $303 to B. Swanson for $484, terms n/30, invoice no. 5705.
16   Received $1,666 cash from K. Anklam to pay for the purchase of March 7.
19   Sold used store equipment for $900 cash to Algoma, Inc.
25   Sold merchandise costing $500 to F. Sayers for $785, terms n/30, invoice no. 5706.

Prepare headings for a sales journal like the one in Exhibit 7.5. Journalize the March transactions that should be recorded in this sales journal.

Refer to Exercise 7-1 and for each of the March transactions identify the journal in which it would be recorded. Assume the company uses a sales journal, purchases journal, cash receipts journal, cash disbursements journal, and general journal as illustrated in this chapter.

Exercise 7-2
Identifying journal of entry

C3

Prepare headings for a sales journal like the one in Exhibit 7A.1. Journalize the March transactions shown in Exercise 7-1 that should be recorded in the sales journal assuming that the periodic inventory system is used.

Exercise 7-3^A
Sales journal—periodic

P3

Mizuno Co. uses a sales journal, a purchases journal, a cash receipts journal, a cash disbursements journal, and a general journal. The following transactions occur in the month of November.

Exercise 7-4
Cash receipts journal—perpetual

P1

Nov. 3   The company purchased $3,500 of merchandise on credit from Abbott Co., terms n/20.
7   The company sold merchandise costing $923 on credit to E. Han for $1,015, subject to a $20 sales discount if paid by the end of the month.
9   The company borrowed $3,375 cash by signing a note payable to the bank.
13   I. Uno, the owner, contributed $4,675 cash to the company.
18   The company sold merchandise costing $147 to C. Knapp for $261 cash.
22   The company paid Abbott Co. $3,500 cash for the merchandise purchased on November 3.
27   The company received $995 cash from E. Han in payment of the November 7 purchase.
30   The company paid salaries of $1,750 in cash.

Prepare headings for a cash receipts journal like the one in Exhibit 7.7. Journalize the November transactions that should be recorded in the cash receipts journal.

Refer to Exercise 7-4 and for each of the November transactions identify the journal in which it would be recorded. Assume the company uses a sales journal, purchases journal, cash receipts journal, cash disbursements journal, and general journal as illustrated in this chapter.

Exercise 7-5
Identifying journal of entry

C3

Prepare headings for a cash receipts journal like the one in Exhibit 7A.2. Journalize the November transactions shown in Exercise 7-4 that should be recorded in the cash receipts journal assuming that the periodic inventory system is used.

Exercise 7-6^A
Cash receipts journal—periodic

P3

Exercise 7-7
Purchases journal—perpetual
P1

Altan Company uses a sales journal, a purchases journal, a cash receipts journal, a cash disbursements journal, and a general journal. The following transactions occur in the month of June.

June 1   Purchased $5,400 of merchandise on credit from Krause, Inc., terms n/30.
      8   Sold merchandise costing $720 on credit to G. Seles for $1,080 subject to a $21 sales discount if paid by the end of the month.
     14   Purchased $460 of store supplies from Chang Company on credit, terms n/30.
     17   Purchased $480 of office supplies on credit from Monder Company, terms n/30.
     24   Sold merchandise costing $272 to D. Lee for $432 cash.
     28   Purchased store supplies from Porter's for $72 cash.
     29   Paid Krause, Inc., $5,400 cash for the merchandise purchased on June 1.

Prepare headings for a purchases journal like the one in Exhibit 7.9. Journalize the June transactions that should be recorded in the purchases journal.

Exercise 7-8
Identifying journal of entry
C3

Refer to Exercise 7-7 and for each of the June transactions identify the journal in which it would be recorded. Assume the company uses a sales journal, purchases journal, cash receipts journal, cash disbursements journal, and general journal as illustrated in this chapter.

Exercise 7-9ᴬ
Purchases journal—periodic
P3

Prepare headings for a purchases journal like the one in Exhibit 7A.3. Journalize the June transactions from Exercise 7-7 that should be recorded in the purchases journal assuming the periodic inventory system is used.

Exercise 7-10
Cash disbursements journal—perpetual
P1

Louder Supply uses a sales journal, a purchases journal, a cash receipts journal, a cash disbursements journal, and a general journal. The following transactions occur in the month of April.

Apr. 3   Purchased merchandise for $2,700 on credit from Acco, Inc., terms 1/10, n/30.
      9   Issued check no. 210 to Major Corp. to buy store supplies for $436.
     12   Sold merchandise costing $486 on credit to N. Rogers for $816, terms n/30.
     17   Issued check no. 211 for $1,500 to pay off a note payable to City Bank.
     20   Purchased merchandise for $3,300 on credit from Factow, terms 1/10, n/30.
     28   Issued check no. 212 to Factow to pay the amount due for the purchase of April 20, less the discount.
     29   Paid salary of $1,675 to M. Robbins by issuing check no. 213.
     30   Issued check no. 214 to Acco, Inc., to pay the amount due for the purchase of April 3.

Prepare headings for a cash disbursements journal like the one in Exhibit 7.11. Journalize the April transactions that should be recorded in the cash disbursements journal.

Exercise 7-11
Identifying journal of entry
C3

Refer to Exercise 7-10 and for each of the April transactions identify the journal in which it would be recorded. Assume the company uses a sales journal, purchases journal, cash receipts journal, cash disbursements journal, and general journal as illustrated in this chapter.

Exercise 7-12ᴬ
Cash disbursements journal—periodic   P3

Prepare headings for a cash disbursements journal like the one in Exhibit 7A.4. Journalize the April transactions from Exercise 7-10 that should be recorded in the cash disbursements journal assuming that the periodic inventory system is used.

Exercise 7-13
Special journal transactions and error discovery
P1

Haver Pharmacy uses the following journals: sales journal, purchases journal, cash receipts journal, cash disbursements journal, and general journal. On June 5, Haver purchased merchandise priced at $14,000, subject to credit terms of 2/10, n/30. On June 14, the pharmacy paid the net amount due for the merchandise. In journalizing the payment, the pharmacy debited Accounts Payable for $14,000 but failed to record the cash discount on the purchases. Cash was properly credited for the actual $13,720 paid. (*a*) In what journals would the June 5 and the June 14 transactions be recorded? (*b*) What procedure is likely to discover the error in journalizing the June 14 transaction?

At the end of May, the sales journal of River View appears as follows.

Exercise 7-14
Posting to subsidiary ledger
accounts; preparing a schedule of
accounts receivable

P1 P2

Sales Journal						Page 2 _ □ ☒
Date	**Account Debited**	**Invoice Number**	**PR**	**Accounts Receivable Dr. Sales Cr.**	**Cost of Goods Sold Dr. Inventory Cr.**	^
May 6	Aaron Reckers	190		3,550	2,698	
10	Sara Reed	191		2,610	2,153	
17	Anna Page	192		1,161	682	
25	Sara Reed	193		464	272	
31	Totals			7,785	5,805	v

River View also recorded the return of defective merchandise with the following entry.

May 20	Sales Returns and Allowances	500	
	Accounts Receivable—Anna Page		500
	Customer returned (worthless) merchandise.		

Required

1. Open an accounts receivable subsidiary ledger that has a T-account for each customer listed in the sales journal. Post to the customer accounts the entries in the sales journal and any portion of the general journal entry that affects a customer's account.
2. Open a general ledger that has T-accounts for Accounts Receivable, Inventory, Sales, Sales Returns and Allowances, and Cost of Goods Sold. Post the sales journal and any portion of the general journal entry that affects these accounts.
3. Prepare a schedule of accounts receivable and prove that its total equals the balance in the Accounts Receivable controlling account.

Check (3) Ending Accounts
Receivable, $7,285

Boyar Company posts its sales invoices directly and then binds them into a Sales Journal. Boyar had the following credit sales to these customers during June.

Exercise 7-15
Accounts receivable ledger;
posting from sales journal

P1 P2

June 2	Joe Mack	$ 4,100
8	Eric Horner	6,929
10	Tess Wilson	15,252
14	Hong Jiang	23,329
20	Tess Wilson	11,400
29	Joe Mack	7,432
	Total credit sales	$68,442

Required

1. Open an accounts receivable subsidiary ledger having a T-account for each customer. Post the invoices to the subsidiary ledger.
2. Open an Accounts Receivable controlling T-account and a Sales T-account to reflect general ledger accounts. Post the end-of-month total from the sales journal to these accounts.
3. Prepare a schedule of accounts receivable and prove that its total equals the Accounts Receivable controlling account balance.

A company that records credit purchases in a purchases journal and records purchases returns in a general journal made the following errors. Indicate when each error should be discovered.

Exercise 7-16
Purchases journal and
error identification

P1 ♟

1. Made an addition error in determining the balance of a creditor's subsidiary account.
2. Made an addition error in totaling the Office Supplies column of the purchases journal.
3. Posted a purchases return to the Accounts Payable account and to the creditor's subsidiary account but did not post the purchases return to the Inventory account.
4. Posted a purchases return to the Inventory account and to the Accounts Payable account but did not post to the creditor's subsidiary account.
5. Correctly recorded a $4,000 purchase in the purchases journal but posted it to the creditor's subsidiary account as a $400 purchase.

Exercise 7-17

Computing and analyzing segment return on assets

A1

Refer to Exhibit 7.13 and complete the segment return on assets table for Triton Company. Analyze your findings and identify the segment with the highest, and that with the lowest, segment return on assets.

Segment	Segment Operating Income (in $ mil.)		Segment Assets (in $ mil.)		Segment Return on Assets
	2009	2008	2009	2008	2009
Specialty					
Skiing Group	$ 53	$ 47	$ 539	$398	
Skating Group	7	4	48	35	
Specialty Footwear	18	15	143	106	
Other Specialty	9	3	32	23	
Subtotal	87	69	762	562	
General Merchandise					
South America	26	29	281	207	
United States	6	6	45	33	
Europe	4	2	15	11	
Subtotal	36	37	341	251	
Total	$123	$106	$1,103	$813	

Check Europe segment return, 30.8%

PROBLEM SET A

Problem 7-1A

Special journals, subsidiary ledgers, and schedule of accounts receivable—perpetual

C4 P1 P2

Available with McGraw-Hill's Homework Manager

McGraw-Hill's
HOMEWORK
MANAGER

For account titles and numbers, use the Chart of Accounts at the end of the book.

Moore Company completes these transactions during April of the current year (the terms of all its credit sales are 2/10, n/30).

Apr. 2 Purchased $14,200 of merchandise on credit from Newt Company, invoice dated April 2, terms 2/10, n/60.

     3 Sold merchandise on credit to Ty Afton, Invoice No. 760, for $5,200 (cost is $2,100).

     3 Purchased $1,530 of office supplies on credit from Cray, Inc. Invoice dated April 2, terms n/10 EOM.

     4 Issued Check No. 587 to *World View* for advertising expense, $879.

     5 Sold merchandise on credit to Debra Kohn, Invoice No. 761, for $9,300 (cost is $7,600).

     6 Received a $70 credit memorandum from Cray, Inc., for the return of some of the office supplies received on April 3.

     9 Purchased $11,435 of store equipment on credit from Hafman Supply, invoice dated April 9, terms n/10 EOM.

   11 Sold merchandise on credit to Pat Orlof, Invoice No 762, for $12,300 (cost is $7,300).

   12 Issued Check No. 588 to Newt Company in payment of its April 2 invoice, less the discount.

   13 Received payment from Ty Afton for the April 3 sale, less the discount.

   13 Sold $6,900 of merchandise on credit to Ty Afton (cost is $3,600), Invoice No. 763.

   14 Received payment from Debra Kohn for the April 5 sale, less the discount.

   16 Issued Check No. 589, payable to Payroll, in payment of sales salaries expense for the first half of the month, $11,300. Cashed the check and paid employees.

   16 Cash sales for the first half of the month are $54,240 (cost is $42,400). (Cash sales are recorded daily from cash register data but are recorded only twice in this problem to reduce repetitive entries.)

   17 Purchased $12,850 of merchandise on credit from Dann Company, invoice dated April 17, terms 2/10, n/30.

   18 Borrowed $55,000 cash from First State Bank by signing a long-term note payable.

   20 Received payment from Pat Orlof for the April 11 sale, less the discount.

   20 Purchased $1,000 of store supplies on credit from Hafman Supply, invoice dated April 19, terms n/10 EOM.

   23 Received a $900 credit memorandum from Dann Company for the return of defective merchandise received on April 17.

   23 Received payment from Ty Afton for the April 13 sale, less the discount.

   25 Purchased $11,465 of merchandise on credit from Newt Company, invoice dated April 24, terms 2/10, n/60.

26 Issued Check No. 590 to Dann Company in payment of its April 17 invoice, less the return and the discount.

27 Sold $3,460 of merchandise on credit to Debra Kohn, Invoice No. 764 (cost is $2,470).

27 Sold $7,100 of merchandise on credit to Pat Orlof, Invoice No. 765 (cost is $4,895).

30 Issued Check No. 591, payable to Payroll, in payment of the sales salaries expense for the last half of the month, $11,000.

30 Cash sales for the last half of the month are $72,100 (cost is $61,500).

Required

1. Prepare a sales journal like that in Exhibit 7.5 and a cash receipts journal like that in Exhibit 7.7. Number both journal pages as page 3. Then review the transactions of Moore Company and enter those that should be journalized in the sales journal and those that should be journalized in the cash receipts journal. Ignore any transactions that should be journalized in a purchases journal, a cash disbursements journal, or a general journal.

2. Open the following general ledger accounts: Cash, Accounts Receivable, Inventory, Long-Term Notes Payable, Cost of Goods Sold, Sales, and Sales Discounts. Enter the March 31 balances for Cash ($85,000), Inventory ($152,000), Long-Term Notes Payable ($137,000), and B. Moore, Capital ($100,000). Also open accounts receivable subsidiary ledger accounts for Debra Kohn, Ty Afton, and Pat Orlof.

3. Verify that amounts that should be posted as individual amounts from the journals have been posted. (Such items are immediately posted.) Foot and crossfoot the journals and make the month-end postings.

4. Prepare a trial balance of the general ledger and prove the accuracy of the subsidiary ledger by preparing a schedule of accounts receivable.

Check Trial balance totals, $462,600

Analysis Component

5. Assume that the total for the schedule of Accounts Receivable does not equal the balance of the controlling account in the general ledger. Describe steps you would take to discover the error(s).

Assume that Moore Co. in Problem 7-1A uses the periodic inventory system.

Required

1. Prepare headings for a sales journal like the one in Exhibit 7A.1. Prepare headings for a cash receipts journal like the one in Exhibit 7A.2. Journalize the April transactions shown in Problem 7-1A that should be recorded in the sales journal and the cash receipts journal assuming the *periodic* inventory system is used.

2. Open the general ledger accounts with balances as shown in Problem 7-1A (do not open a Cost of Goods Sold ledger account). Also open accounts receivable subsidiary ledger accounts for Ty Afton, Debra Kohn, and Pat Orlof. Under the periodic system, an Inventory account exists but is inactive until its balance is updated to the correct inventory balance at year-end. In this problem, the Inventory account remains inactive but must be included to correctly complete the trial balance.

3. Complete parts 3, 4, and 5 of Problem 7-1A using the results of parts 1 and 2 of this problem.

Problem 7-2A^A

Special journals, subsidiary ledgers, and schedule of accounts receivable—periodic

C4 P2 P3

Check Trial balance totals, $462,600

The April transactions of Moore Company are described in Problem 7-1A.

Required

1. Prepare a general journal, a purchases journal like that in Exhibit 7.9, and a cash disbursements journal like that in Exhibit 7.11. Number all journal pages as page 3. Review the April transactions of Moore Company and enter those transactions that should be journalized in the general journal, the purchases journal, or the cash disbursements journal. Ignore any transactions that should be journalized in a sales journal or cash receipts journal.

2. Open the following general ledger accounts: Cash, Inventory, Office Supplies, Store Supplies, Store Equipment, Accounts Payable, Long-Term Notes Payable, Sales Salaries Expense, and Advertising Expense. Enter the March 31 balances of Cash ($85,000), Inventory ($152,000), Long-Term Notes Payable ($137,000), and B. Moore, Capital ($100,000). Also open accounts payable subsidiary ledger accounts for Hafman Supply, Newt Company, Dann Company, and Cray, Inc.

Problem 7-3A

Special journals, subsidiary ledgers, and schedule of accounts payable—perpetual

C4 P1 P2

3. Verify that amounts that should be posted as individual amounts from the journals have been posted. (Such items are immediately posted.) Foot and crossfoot the journals and make the month-end postings.

Check Trial balance totals, $262,360

4. Prepare a trial balance of the general ledger and a schedule of accounts payable.

Problem 7-4A^A

Special journals, subsidiary ledgers, and schedule of accounts payable—periodic

C4 P2 P3

Refer to Problem 7-1A and assume that Moore Co. uses the periodic inventory system.

Required

1. Prepare a general journal, a purchases journal like that in Exhibit 7A.3, and a cash disbursements journal like that in Exhibit 7A.4. Number all journal pages as page 3. Review the April transactions of Moore Company (Problem 7-1A) and enter those transactions that should be journalized in the general journal, the purchases journal, or the cash disbursements journal. Ignore any transaction that should be journalized in a sales journal or cash receipts journal.

2. Open the following general ledger accounts: Cash, Inventory, Office Supplies, Store Supplies, Store Equipment, Accounts Payable, Long-Term Notes Payable, Purchases, Purchases Returns and Allowances, Purchases Discounts, Sales Salaries Expense, and Advertising Expense. Enter the March 31 balances of Cash ($85,000), Inventory ($152,000), Long-Term Notes Payable ($137,000), and B. Moore, Capital ($100,000). Also open accounts payable subsidiary ledger accounts for Hafman Supply, Newt Company, Dann Company, and Cray, Inc.

Check Trial balance totals, $263,783

3. Complete parts 3 and 4 of Problem 7-3A using the results of parts 1 and 2 of this problem.

Problem 7-5A

Special journals, subsidiary ledgers, trial balance—perpetual

C4 P1 P2

mhhe.com/wildFAP19e

Crystal Company completes these transactions and events during March of the current year (terms for all its credit sales are 2/10, n/30).

Mar. 1   Purchased $43,300 of merchandise from Value Industries, invoice dated March 1, terms 2/15, n/30.
      2   Sold merchandise on credit to Chao Chu, Invoice No. 854, for $16,000 (cost is $8,050).
      3   Purchased $1,300 of office supplies on credit from Glen Company, invoice dated March 3, terms n/10 EOM.
      3   Sold merchandise on credit to Lance Wern, Invoice No. 855, for $9,500 (cost is $4,760).
      6   Borrowed $72,000 cash from Federal Bank by signing a long-term note payable.
      9   Purchased $21,000 of office equipment on credit from Simon Supply, invoice dated March 9, terms n/10 EOM.
      10 Sold merchandise on credit to Jovita Altern, Invoice No. 856, for $4,700 (cost is $2,380).
      12 Received payment from Chao Chu for the March 2 sale less the discount.
      13 Sent Value Industries Check No. 416 in payment of the March 1 invoice less the discount.
      13 Received payment from Lance Wern for the March 3 sale less the discount.
      14 Purchased $32,200 of merchandise from the AJ Company, invoice dated March 13, terms 2/10, n/30.
      15 Issued Check No. 417, payable to Payroll, in payment of sales salaries expense for the first half of the month, $17,700. Cashed the check and paid the employees.
      15 Cash sales for the first half of the month are $67,570 (cost is $39,080). (Cash sales are recorded daily, but are recorded only twice here to reduce repetitive entries.)
      16 Purchased $1,820 of store supplies on credit from Glen Company, invoice dated March 16, terms n/10 EOM.
      17 Received a $2,500 credit memorandum from AJ Company for the return of unsatisfactory merchandise purchased on March 14.
      19 Received a $630 credit memorandum from Simon Supply for office equipment received on March 9 and returned for credit.
      20 Received payment from Jovita Altern for the sale of March 10 less the discount.
      23 Issued Check No. 418 to AJ Company in payment of the invoice of March 13 less the March 17 return and the discount.
      27 Sold merchandise on credit to Jovita Altern, Invoice No. 857, for $14,300 (cost is $6,285).
      28 Sold merchandise on credit to Lance Wern, Invoice No. 858, for $5,400 (cost is $2,300).

31 Issued Check No. 419, payable to Payroll, in payment of sales salaries expense for the last half of the month, $17,700. Cashed the check and paid the employees.

31 Cash sales for the last half of the month are $77,625 (cost is $40,510).

31 Verify that amounts impacting customer and creditor accounts were posted and that any amounts that should have been posted as individual amounts to the general ledger accounts were posted. Foot and crossfoot the journals and make the month-end postings.

Required

1. Open the following general ledger accounts: Cash; Accounts Receivable; Inventory (March 1 beg. bal. is $50,000); Office Supplies; Store Supplies; Office Equipment; Accounts Payable; Long-Term Notes Payable; Z. Crystal, Capital (March 1 beg. bal. is $50,000); Sales; Sales Discounts; Cost of Goods Sold; and Sales Salaries Expense. Open the following accounts receivable subsidiary ledger accounts: Jovita Altern, Chao Chu, and Lance Wern. Open the following accounts payable subsidiary ledger accounts: Glen Company, Value Industries, Simon Supply, and AJ Company.

2. Enter these transactions in a sales journal like Exhibit 7.5, a purchases journal like Exhibit 7.9, a cash receipts journal like Exhibit 7.7, a cash disbursements journal like Exhibit 7.11, or a general journal. Number all journal pages as page 2.

3. Prepare a trial balance of the general ledger and prove the accuracy of the subsidiary ledgers by preparing schedules of both accounts receivable and accounts payable.

Check Trial balance totals, $340,585

Assume that Crystal Company in Problem 7-5A uses the periodic inventory system.

Problem 7-6A[A]

Special journals, subsidiary ledgers, trial balance—periodic

C4 P2 P3

mhhe.com/wildFAP19e

Required

1. Open the following general ledger accounts: Cash; Accounts Receivable; Inventory (March 1 beg. bal. is $50,000); Office Supplies; Store Supplies; Office Equipment; Accounts Payable; Long-Term Notes Payable; Z. Crystal, Capital (March 1 beg. bal. is $50,000); Sales; Sales Discounts; Purchases; Purchases Returns and Allowances; Purchases Discounts; and Sales Salaries Expense. Open the following accounts receivable subsidiary ledger accounts: Jovita Altern, Chao Chu, and Lance Wern. Open the following Accounts Payable subsidiary ledger accounts: Glen Company, Value Industries, Simon Supply, and AJ Company.

2. Enter the transactions from Problem 7-5A in a sales journal like that in Exhibit 7A.1, a purchases journal like that in Exhibit 7A.3, a cash receipts journal like that in Exhibit 7A.2, a cash disbursements journal like that in Exhibit 7A.4, or a general journal. Number journal pages as page 2.

3. Prepare a trial balance of the general ledger and prove the accuracy of the subsidiary ledgers by preparing schedules of both accounts receivable and accounts payable.

Check Trial balance totals, $344,545

For account titles and numbers, use the Chart of Accounts at the end of the book.

PROBLEM SET B

Problem 7-1B
Special journals, subsidiary ledgers, schedule of accounts receivable—perpetual

C4 P1 P2

Burns Industries completes these transactions during July of the current year (the terms of all its credit sales are 2/10, n/30).

July 1 Purchased $15,200 of merchandise on credit from Tryon Company, invoice dated June 30, terms 2/10, n/60.

3 Issued Check No. 300 to *The Weekly* for advertising expense, $890.

5 Sold merchandise on credit to Karen Noyes, Invoice No. 918, for $4,100 (cost is $3,300).

6 Sold merchandise on credit to Meg Azura, Invoice No. 919, for $9,200 (cost is $7,500).

7 Purchased $1,580 of store supplies on credit from Patton, Inc., invoice dated July 7, terms n/10 EOM.

8 Received a $90 credit memorandum from Patton, Inc., for the return of store supplies received on July 7.

9 Purchased $11,155 of store equipment on credit from Cheever Supply, invoice dated July 8, terms n/10 EOM.

10 Issued Check No. 301 to Tryon Company in payment of its June 30 invoice, less the discount.

13 Sold merchandise on credit to Tom Murphy, Invoice No. 920, for $13,600 (cost is $7,100).

14 Sold merchandise on credit to Karen Noyes, Invoice No. 921, for $6,500 (cost is $4,700).

15   Received payment from Karen Noyes for the July 5 sale, less the discount.

15   Issued Check No. 302, payable to Payroll, in payment of sales salaries expense for the first half of the month, $39,250. Cashed the check and paid employees.

15   Cash sales for the first half of the month are $59,920 (cost is $42,900). (Cash sales are recorded daily using data from the cash registers but are recorded only twice in this problem to reduce repetitive entries.)

16   Received payment from Meg Azura for the July 6 sale, less the discount.

17   Purchased $12,650 of merchandise on credit from Dart Company, invoice dated July 17, terms 2/10, n/30.

20   Purchased $1,050 of office supplies on credit from Cheever Supply, invoice dated July 19, terms n/10 EOM.

21   Borrowed $74,000 cash from College Bank by signing a long-term note payable.

23   Received payment from Tom Murphy for the July 13 sale, less the discount.

24   Received payment from Karen Noyes for the July 14 sale, less the discount.

24   Received a $1,050 credit memorandum from Dart Company for the return of defective merchandise received on July 17.

26   Purchased $11,635 of merchandise on credit from Tryon Company, invoice dated July 26, terms 2/10, n/60.

27   Issued Check No. 303 to Dart Company in payment of its July 17 invoice, less the return and the discount.

29   Sold merchandise on credit to Meg Azura, Invoice No. 922, for $3,340 (cost is $2,580).

30   Sold merchandise on credit to Tom Murphy, Invoice No. 923, for $6,200 (cost is $4,480).

31   Issued Check No. 304, payable to Payroll, in payment of the sales salaries expense for the last half of the month, $39,250.

31   Cash sales for the last half of the month are $74,200 (cost is $67,400).

Required

1. Prepare a sales journal like that in Exhibit 7.5 and a cash receipts journal like that in Exhibit 7.7. Number both journals as page 3. Then review the transactions of Burns Industries and enter those transactions that should be journalized in the sales journal and those that should be journalized in the cash receipts journal. Ignore any transactions that should be journalized in a purchases journal, a cash disbursements journal, or a general journal.

2. Open the following general ledger accounts: Cash, Accounts Receivable, Inventory, Long-Term Notes Payable, Cost of Goods Sold, Sales, and Sales Discounts. Enter the June 30 balances for Cash ($116,000), Inventory ($150,000), Long-Term Notes Payable ($166,000), and R. Burns, Capital ($100,000). Also open accounts receivable subsidiary ledger accounts for Karen Noyes, Tom Murphy, and Meg Azura.

3. Verify that amounts that should be posted as individual amounts from the journals have been posted. (Such items are immediately posted.) Foot and crossfoot the journals and make the month-end postings.

Check   Trial balance totals, $517,060

4. Prepare a trial balance of the general ledger and prove the accuracy of the subsidiary ledger by preparing a schedule of accounts receivable.

Analysis Component

5. Assume that the total for the schedule of Accounts Receivable does not equal the balance of the controlling account in the general ledger. Describe steps you would take to discover the error(s).

Problem 7-2B^A

Special journals, subsidiary ledgers, and schedule of accounts receivable—periodic

C4   P2   P3

Assume that Burns Industries in Problem 7-1B uses the periodic inventory system.

Required

1. Prepare headings for a sales journal like the one in Exhibit 7A.1. Prepare headings for a cash receipts journal like the one in Exhibit 7A.2. Journalize the July transactions shown in Problem 7-1B that should be recorded in the sales journal and the cash receipts journal assuming the periodic inventory system is used.

2. Open the general ledger accounts with balances as shown in Problem 7-1B (do not open a Cost of Goods Sold ledger account). Also open accounts receivable subsidiary ledger accounts for Meg Azura, Tom Murphy, and Karen Noyes. Under the periodic system, an Inventory account exists but is inactive

until its balance is updated to the correct inventory balance at year-end. In this problem, the Inventory account remains inactive but must be included to correctly complete the trial balance.

3. Complete parts 3, 4, and 5 of Problem 7-1B using the results of parts 1 and 2 of this problem.

Check   Trial balance totals, $517,060

The July transactions of Burns Industries are described in Problem 7-1B.

Problem 7-3B
Special journals, subsidiary ledgers, and schedule of accounts payable—perpetual

C4 P1 P2

Required

1. Prepare a general journal, a purchases journal like that in Exhibit 7.9, and a cash disbursements journal like that in Exhibit 7.11. Number all journal pages as page 3. Review the July transactions of Burns Industries and enter those transactions that should be journalized in the general journal, the purchases journal, or the cash disbursements journal. Ignore any transactions that should be journalized in a sales journal or cash receipts journal.

2. Open the following general ledger accounts: Cash, Inventory, Office Supplies, Store Supplies, Store Equipment, Accounts Payable, Long-Term Notes Payable, Sales Salaries Expense, and Advertising Expense. Enter the June 30 balances of Cash ($116,000), Inventory ($150,000), Long-Term Notes Payable ($166,000), and R. Burns, Capital ($100,000). Also open accounts payable subsidiary ledger accounts for Cheever Supply, Tryon Company, Dart Company, and Patton, Inc.

3. Verify that amounts that should be posted as individual amounts from the journals have been posted. (Such items are immediately posted.) Foot and crossfoot the journals and make the month-end postings.

4. Prepare a trial balance of the general ledger and a schedule of accounts payable.

Check   Trial balance totals, $291,330

Refer to Problem 7-1B and assume that Burns uses the periodic inventory system.

Problem 7-4B^A
Special journals, subsidiary ledgers, and schedule of accounts payable—periodic

C4 P2 P3

Required

1. Prepare a general journal, a purchases journal like that in Exhibit 7A.3, and a cash disbursements journal like that in Exhibit 7A.4. Number all journal pages as page 3. Review the July transactions of Burns Company (Problem 7-1B) and enter those transactions that should be journalized in the general journal, the purchases journal, or the cash disbursements journal. Ignore any transaction that should be journalized in a sales journal or cash receipts journal.

2. Open the following general ledger accounts: Cash, Inventory, Office Supplies, Store Supplies, Store Equipment, Accounts Payable, Long-Term Notes Payable, Purchases, Purchases Returns and Allowances, Purchases Discounts, Sales Salaries Expense, and Advertising Expense. Enter the June 30 balances of Cash ($116,000), Inventory ($150,000), Long-Term Notes Payable ($166,000), and R. Burns, Capital ($100,000). Also open accounts payable subsidiary ledger accounts for Tryon Company, Patton, Inc., Cheever Supply, and Dart Company.

3. Complete parts 3 and 4 of Problem 7-3B using the results of parts 1 and 2 of this problem.

Check   Trial balance totals, $292,916

Madison Company completes these transactions during November of the current year (terms for all its credit sales are 2/10, n/30).

Problem 7-5B
Special journals, subsidiary ledgers, trial balance—perpetual

C4 P2 P3

Nov. 1 Purchased $1,353 of office equipment on credit from Baxter Supply, invoice dated November 1, terms n/10 EOM.
  2 Borrowed $72,000 cash from Wisconsin Bank by signing a long-term note payable.
  4 Purchased $45,100 of merchandise from BLR Industries, invoice dated November 3, terms 2/15, n/30.
  5 Purchased $21,874 of store supplies on credit from Gorton Company, invoice dated November 5, terms n/10 EOM.
  8 Sold merchandise on credit to Cyd Ryan, Invoice No. 439, for $16,500 (cost is $8,340).
  10 Sold merchandise on credit to Carlos Mantel, Invoice No. 440, for $9,900 (cost is $4,960).
  11 Purchased $33,509 of merchandise from Ling Company, invoice dated November 10, terms 2/10, n/30.

12   Sent BLR Industries Check No. 633 in payment of its November 3 invoice less the discount.
15   Issued Check No. 634, payable to Payroll, in payment of sales salaries expense for the first half of the month, $13,900. Cashed the check and paid the employees.
15   Cash sales for the first half of the month are $174,537 (cost is $144,866). (Cash sales are recorded daily but are recorded only twice in this problem to reduce repetitive entries.)
15   Sold merchandise on credit to Tonya Will, Invoice No. 441, for $4,900 (cost is $2,480).
16   Purchased $1,873 of office supplies on credit from Gorton Company, invoice dated November 16, terms n/10 EOM.
17   Received a $2,659 credit memorandum from Ling Company for the return of unsatisfactory merchandise purchased on November 11.
18   Received payment from Cyd Ryan for the November 8 sale less the discount.
19   Received payment from Carlos Mantel for the November 10 sale less the discount.
19   Issued Check No. 635 to Ling Company in payment of its invoice of November 10 less the return and the discount.
22   Sold merchandise on credit to Carlos Mantel, Invoice No. 442, for $14,800 (cost is $6,540).
24   Sold merchandise on credit to Tonya Will, Invoice No. 443, for $5,600 (cost is $2,420).
25   Received payment from Tonya Will for the sale of November 15 less the discount.
26   Received a $256 credit memorandum from Baxter Supply for the return of office equipment purchased on November 1.
30   Issued Check No. 636, payable to Payroll, in payment of sales salaries expense for the last half of the month, $13,900. Cashed the check and paid the employees.
30   Cash sales for the last half of the month are $185,009 (cost is $111,398).
30   Verify that amounts impacting customer and creditor accounts were posted and that any amounts that should have been posted as individual amounts to the general ledger accounts were posted. Foot and crossfoot the journals and make the month-end postings.

Required

1. Open the following general ledger accounts: Cash; Accounts Receivable; Inventory (November 1 beg. bal. is $300,000); Office Supplies; Store Supplies; Office Equipment; Accounts Payable; Long-Term Notes Payable; O. Madison, Capital (Nov. 1 beg. bal. is $300,000); Sales; Sales Discounts; Cost of Goods Sold; and Sales Salaries Expense. Open the following accounts receivable subsidiary ledger accounts: Carlos Mantel, Tonya Will, and Cyd Ryan. Open the following accounts payable subsidiary ledger accounts: Gorton Company, BLR Industries, Baxter Supply, and Ling Company.
2. Enter these transactions in a sales journal like that in Exhibit 7.5, a purchases journal like that in Exhibit 7.9, a cash receipts journal like that in Exhibit 7.7, a cash disbursements journal like that in Exhibit 7.11, or a general journal. Number all journal pages as page 2.

Check Trial balance totals, $808,090

3. Prepare a trial balance of the general ledger and prove the accuracy of the subsidiary ledgers by preparing schedules of both accounts receivable and accounts payable.

Problem 7-6B^A
Special journals, subsidiary ledgers, trial balance—periodic

C4 P2 P3

Assume that Madison Company in Problem 7-5B uses the periodic inventory system.

Required

1. Open the following general ledger accounts: Cash; Accounts Receivable; Inventory (November 1 beg. bal. is $300,000); Office Supplies; Store Supplies; Office Equipment; Accounts Payable; Long-Term Notes Payable; O. Madison, Capital (Nov. 1 beg. bal. is $300,000); Sales; Sales Discounts; Purchases; Purchases Returns and Allowances; Purchases Discounts; and Sales Salaries Expense. Open the following accounts receivable subsidiary ledger accounts: Carlos Mantel, Tonya Will, and Cyd Ryan. Open the following accounts payable subsidiary ledger accounts: Gorton Company, BLR Industries, Baxter Supply, and Ling Company.
2. Enter the transactions from Problem 7-5B in a sales journal like that in Exhibit 7A.1, a purchases journal like that in Exhibit 7A.3, a cash receipts journal like that in Exhibit 7A.2, a cash disbursements journal like that in Exhibit 7A.4, or a general journal. Number journal pages as page 2.

Check Trial balance totals, $812,268

3. Prepare a trial balance of the general ledger and prove the accuracy of the subsidiary ledgers by preparing schedules of both accounts receivable and accounts payable.

(This serial problem began in Chapter 1 and continues through most of the book. If previous chapter segments were not completed, the serial problem can begin at this point. It is helpful, but not necessary, to use the Working Papers that accompany the book.)

SP 7   Assume that A. Lopez expands Success Systems' accounting system to include special journals.

Required

1. Locate the transactions related to January through March 2010 for Success Systems in Chapter 5.

2. Enter the Success Systems transactions for January through March in a sales journal like that in Exhibit 7.5 (insert "n/a" in the Invoice column), a cash receipts journal like that in Exhibit 7.7, a purchases journal like that in Exhibit 7.9 (use Computer Supplies heading instead of Office Supplies), and a cash disbursements journal like that in Exhibit 7.11 (insert "n/a" in the Check Number column), or a general journal. Number journal pages as page 2. If the transaction does not specify the name of the payee, state "not specified" in the Payee column of the cash disbursements journal.

3. The transactions on the following dates should be journalized in the general journal: January 5, 11, 20, 24, and 29 (no entry required) and March 24. Do not record and post the adjusting entries for the end of March.

(If the Working Papers that accompany this book are not available, omit this comprehensive problem.) Assume it is Monday, May 1, the first business day of the month, and you have just been hired as the accountant for Eureka Company, which operates with monthly accounting periods. All of the company's accounting work is completed through the end of April and its ledgers show April 30 balances. During your first month on the job, the company experiences the following transactions and events (terms for all its credit sales are 2/10, n/30 unless stated differently):

May 1   Issued Check No. 3410 to J&K Management Co. in payment of the May rent, $3,710. (Use two lines to record the transaction. Charge 80% of the rent to Rent Expense—Selling Space and the balance to Rent Expense—Office Space.)

   2   Sold merchandise on credit to Bowman Company, Invoice No. 8785, for $6,100 (cost is $4,100).

   2   Issued a $175 credit memorandum to Knott Co., for defective (worthless) merchandise sold on April 28 and returned for credit. The total selling price (gross) was $4,725.

   3   Received a $798 credit memorandum from Parker Products for the return of merchandise purchased on April 29.

   4   Purchased the following on credit from Gates Supply Co.: merchandise, $37,072; store supplies, $574; and office supplies, $83. Invoice dated May 4, terms n/10 EOM.

   5   Received payment from Knott Co., for the balance from the April 28 sale less the May 2 return and the discount.

   8   Issued Check No. 3411 to Parker Products to pay for the $7,098 of merchandise purchased on April 29 less the May 3 return and a 2% discount.

   9   Sold store supplies to the merchant next door at their cost of $350 cash.

  10   Purchased $4,074 of office equipment on credit from Gates Supply Co., invoice dated May 10, terms n/10 EOM.

  11   Received payment from Bowman Company for the May 2 sale less the discount.

  11   Purchased $8,800 of merchandise from Gatsby, Inc., invoice dated May 10, terms 2/10, n/30.

  12   Received an $854 credit memorandum from Gates Supply Co. for the return of defective office equipment received on May 10.

  15   Issued Check No. 3412, payable to Payroll, in payment of sales salaries, $5,470, and office salaries, $3,000. Cashed the check and paid the employees.

  15   Cash sales for the first half of the month are $55,220 (cost is $33,200). (Cash sales are recorded daily but are recorded only twice here to reduce repetitive entries.)

  15   Post to the customer and creditor accounts. Also post individual items that are not included in column totals at the end of the month to the general ledger accounts. (Such items are posted daily but are posted only twice each month because they are few in number.)

16   Sold merchandise on credit to Bowman Company, Invoice No. 8786, for $3,990 (cost is $1,890).

17   Purchased $13,650 of merchandise from Joey Corp., invoice dated May 14, terms 2/10, n/60.

19   Issued Check No. 3413 to Gatsby, Inc., in payment of its May 10 invoice less the discount.

22   Sold merchandise to Karim Services, Invoice No. 8787, for $6,850 (cost is $4,990), terms 2/10, n/60.

23   Issued Check No. 3414 to Joey Corp. in payment of its May 14 invoice less the discount.

24   Purchased the following on credit from Gates Supply Co.: merchandise, $8,120; store supplies, $630; and office supplies, $280. Invoice dated May 24, terms n/10 EOM.

25   Purchased $3,080 of merchandise from Parker Products, invoice dated May 23, terms 2/10, n/30.

26   Sold merchandise on credit to Dexter Corp., Invoice No. 8788, for $14,210 (cost is $8,230).

26   Issued Check No. 3415 to Trinity Power in payment of the May electric bill, $1,283.

29   The owner of Eureka Company, Emlyn Eureka, used Check No. 3416 to withdraw $2,000 cash from the business for personal use.

30   Received payment from Karim Services for the May 22 sale less the discount.

30   Issued Check No. 3417, payable to Payroll, in payment of sales salaries, $5,320, and office salaries, $3,150. Cashed the check and paid the employees.

31   Cash sales for the last half of the month are $70,052 (cost is $45,500).

31   Post to the customer and creditor accounts. Also post individual items that are not included in column totals at the end of the month to the general ledger accounts. Foot and crossfoot the journals and make the month-end postings.

Required

1. Enter these transactions in a sales journal, a purchases journal, a cash receipts journal, a cash disbursements journal, or a general journal as illustrated in this chapter (number all journal pages as page 2). Post when instructed to do so. Assume a perpetual inventory system.

Check (2) Unadjusted trial balance totals, $545,020; Adjustments column totals, $2,657

2. Prepare a trial balance in the Trial Balance columns of the work sheet form provided with the working papers. Complete the work sheet using the following information for accounting adjustments.

a. Expired insurance, $403.

b. Ending store supplies inventory, $2,232.

c. Ending office supplies inventory, $504.

d. Depreciation of store equipment, $567.

e. Depreciation of office equipment, $329.

Prepare and post adjusting and closing entries.

(3) Net income, $33,397; Total assets, $392,541

3. Prepare a May 2010 multiple-step income statement, a May 2010 statement of owner's equity, and a May 31, 2010, classified balance sheet.

4. Prepare a post-closing trial balance. Also prove the accuracy of subsidiary ledgers by preparing schedules of both accounts receivable and accounts payable.

BEYOND THE NUMBERS

REPORTING IN ACTION

A1 ♟

BTN 7-1   Refer to Best Buy's financial statements in Appendix A to answer the following.

1. Identify the note that reports on Best Buy's business segments.

2. Describe the focus and activities of each of Best Buy's business segments.

Fast Forward

3. Access Best Buy's annual report for fiscal years ending after March 3, 2007, from its Website (BestBuy.com) or the SEC's EDGAR database (www.sec.gov). Has Best Buy changed its reporting policy regarding segment information? Explain.

BTN 7-2   Key figures for **Best Buy** and **Circuit City** follow ($ millions).

Best Buy Segment	Current Year Segment Income	Current Year Segment Assets	One Year Prior Segment Income	One Year Prior Segment Assets	Two Years Prior Segment Income	Two Years Prior Segment Assets
Domestic	$1,889	$10,614	$1,588	$9,722	$1,393	$8,372
International	110	2,956	56	2,142	49	1,922

Circuit City Segment	Current Year Segment Income	Current Year Segment Assets	One Year Prior Segment Income	One Year Prior Segment Assets	Two Years Prior Segment Income	Two Years Prior Segment Assets
Domestic	$ 97	$3,658	$155	$3,594	$41	$3,405
International	(107)	350	(7)	475	16	435

Required

1. Compute the segment return on assets for each of the segments of Best Buy and Circuit City for each of the two most recent years shown.
2. Interpret and comment on your results of part 1.

BTN 7-3   Erica Gray, CPA, is a sole practitioner. She has been practicing as an auditor for 10 years. Recently a long-standing audit client asked Gray to design and implement an integrated computer-based accounting information system. The fees associated with this additional engagement with the client are very attractive. However, Gray wonders if she can remain objective on subsequent audits in her evaluation of the client's accounting system and its records if she was responsible for its design and implementation. Gray knows that professional auditing standards require her to remain independent in fact and appearance from her auditing clients.

Required

1. What do you believe auditing standards are mainly concerned with when they require independence in fact? In appearance?
2. Why is it important that auditors remain independent of their clients?
3. Do you think Gray can accept this engagement and remain independent? Justify your response.

BTN 7-4   Your friend, Wendy Geiger, owns a small retail store that sells candies and nuts. Geiger acquires her goods from a few select vendors. She generally makes purchase orders by phone and on credit. Sales are primarily for cash. Geiger keeps her own manual accounting system using a general journal and a general ledger. At the end of each business day, she records one summary entry for cash sales. Geiger recently began offering items in creative gift packages. This has increased sales substantially, and she is now receiving orders from corporate and other clients who order large quantities and prefer to buy on credit. As a result of increased credit transactions in both purchases and sales, keeping the accounting records has become extremely time consuming. Geiger wants to continue to maintain her own manual system and calls you for advice. Write a memo to her advising how she might modify her current manual accounting system to accommodate the expanded business activities. Geiger is accustomed to checking her ledger by using a trial balance. Your memo should explain the advantages of what you propose and of any other verification techniques you recommend.

**TAKING IT TO
THE NET**

A1 ♟ 🖱

BTN 7-5   Access the October 30, 2007, filing of the fiscal 2007 10-K report for **Dell** (ticker DELL) at www.sec.gov. Read its Note 10 that details Dell's segment information and answer the following.

1. Dell's operations are divided among which three geographic segments?

2. In fiscal year 2007, which geographic segment had the largest dollar amount of operating income? Which had the largest amount of assets?

3. Compute the return on assets for each segment for fiscal year 2007. Use operating income and average total assets by segment for your calculation. Which segment has the highest return on assets?

4. For what product groups does Dell provide segment data? What percent of Dell's net revenue is earned by each product group?

**TEAMWORK IN
ACTION**

C4 P1 P2

BTN 7-6   Each member of the team is to assume responsibility for one of the following tasks:
a. Journalizing in the purchases journal.
b. Journalizing in the cash disbursements journal.
c. Maintaining and verifying the Accounts Payable ledger.
d. Journalizing in the sales journal and the general journal.
e. Journalizing in the cash receipts journal.
f. Maintaining and verifying the Accounts Receivable ledger.
The team should abide by the following procedures in carrying out responsibilities.

Required

1. After tasks *a–f* are assigned, each team member is to quickly read the list of transactions in Problem 7-5A, identifying with initials the journal in which each transaction is to be recorded. Upon completion, the team leader is to read transaction dates, and the appropriate team member is to vocalize responsibility. Any disagreement between teammates must be resolved.

2. Journalize and continually update subsidiary ledgers. Journal recorders should alert teammates assigned to subsidiary ledgers when an entry must be posted to their subsidiary.

3. Team members responsible for tasks *a, b, d,* and *e* are to summarize and prove journals; members responsible for tasks *c* and *f* are to prepare both payables and receivables schedules.

4. The team leader is to take charge of the general ledger, rotating team members to obtain amounts to be posted. The person responsible for a journal must complete posting references in that journal. Other team members should verify the accuracy of account balance computations. To avoid any abnormal account balances, post in the following order: P, S, G, R, D. (*Note:* Posting any necessary individual general ledger amounts is also done at this time.)

5. The team leader is to read out general ledger account balances while another team member fills in the trial balance form. Concurrently, one member should keep a running balance of debit account balance totals and another credit account balance totals. Verify the final total of the trial balance and the schedules. If necessary, the team must resolve any errors. Turn in the trial balance and schedules to the instructor.

**ENTREPRENEURIAL
DECISION**

P1 ♟ 🖱

BTN 7-7   Refer to the chapter's opening feature about Tom Szaky and his company, **TerraCycle**. His small manufacturing company deals with numerous suppliers and customers.

Required

1. Identify the special journals that TerraCycle would be likely to use in its operations. Also identify any subsidiary ledgers that TerraCycle would likely use.

2. TerraCycle hopes to double yearly sales within five years hence from its current $3 million annual amount. Assume that TerraCycle's sales growth projections are as follows.

Year	One Year Hence	Two Years Hence	Three Years Hence	Four Years Hence	Five Years Hence
Projected growth in sales	0%	20%	15%	25%	20%

Estimate TerraCycle's projected sales for each year (round to the nearest dollar). If this pattern of sales growth holds, will TerraCycle achieve its goal of doubling sales in five years?

BTN 7-8 Access and refer to the April 28, 2007 annual report for DSG international plc at www.DSGiplc.com.

GLOBAL DECISION

A1

DSG

Required

1. Identify its Note 2 (Segmental Analysis) to its financial statements and locate its information relating to DSG's geographic segments. Identify those four segments.

2. What financial figures does it disclose for each geographic segment?

3. Does DSG have a dominant segment? Explain.

ANSWERS TO MULTIPLE CHOICE QUIZ

1. a

2. e

3. d

4. b

5. a

A Look Back

Chapter 7 focused on accounting information systems. We explained the principles and components of information systems, the use of special journals and subsidiary ledgers, and technology-based systems.

A Look at This Chapter

This chapter extends our study of accounting to internal control and the analysis of cash. We describe procedures that are good for internal control. We also explain the control of and the accounting for cash, including control features of banking activities.

A Look Ahead

Chapter 9 focuses on receivables. We explain how to account and report on receivables and their related accounts. This includes estimating uncollectible receivables and computing interest earned.

Cash and Internal Controls

Chapter

Learning Objectives

CAP

Conceptual

C1 Define internal control and identify its purpose and principles. *(p. 314)*

C2 Define cash and cash equivalents and explain how to report them. *(p. 319)*

C3 Identify control features of banking activities. *(p. 326)*

Analytical

A1 Compute the days' sales uncollected ratio and use it to assess liquidity. *(p. 332)*

LP8

Procedural

P1 Apply internal control to cash receipts and disbursements. *(p. 320)*

P2 Explain and record petty cash fund transactions. *(p. 323)*

P3 Prepare a bank reconciliation. *(p. 329)*

P4 *Appendix 8A*—Describe the use of documentation and verification to control cash disbursements. *(p. 335)*

P5 *Appendix 8B*—Apply the net method to control purchase discounts. *(p. 338)*

Sweet Success

"It's a creative outlet for me ... it doesn't feel like work"—Dylan Lauren (Jeff Rubin on left)

NEW YORK—A 10-foot chocolate bunny named Jeffrey greets you as you enter the store—that should be warning enough! This elite designer candy store, christened **Dylan's Candy Bar (<u>DylansCandyBar.com</u>),** is the brainchild of co-founders Dylan Lauren and Jeff Rubin (the bunny is named for him). This sweet-lovers heaven offers more than 5,000 different choices of sweets from all over the world. It has become a hip hangout for locals and tourists—and it has made candy cool. Says Lauren, "Park Avenue women come in, and the first thing they ask for is Gummi bears. They love that it's very childhood, nostalgic."

Although marketing is an important part of its success, Lauren and Rubin's management of internal controls and cash is equally impressive. Several control procedures monitor its business activities and safeguard its assets. An example is the biometric time and attendance control system using fingerprint characteristics. Says Rubin, "There's no fooling the system! It is going to help us remotely manage our employees while eliminating human error and dishonesty. [It] is a cost-effective and important business management tool." Similar controls are applied throughout the store. Rubin asserts that such controls raise productivity and cut expenses.

The store's cash management practices are equally impressive, including controls over cash receipts, disbursements, and petty cash. The use of bank reconciliations further helps with the store's control and management of cash.

Internal controls are crucial when on a busy day its store brings in more than a thousand customers, and their cash. Moreover, expansion is already underway in Orlando and Houston. Through it all, Lauren says it is "totally fun."

[Sources: *Dylan's Candy Bar Website,* January 2009; *Entrepreneur,* June 2005; *USA Today,* October 26, 2001; *Duke Magazine,* January–February 2004; *CNN.com,* November 2005; *CandyAddict.com,* June 2007]

We all are aware of theft and fraud. They affect us in several ways: We lock doors, chain bikes, review sales receipts, and acquire alarm systems. A company also takes actions to safeguard, control, and manage what it owns. Experience tells us that small companies are most vulnerable, usually due to weak internal controls. It is management's responsibility to set up policies and procedures to safeguard a company's assets, especially cash. To do so, management *and* employees must understand and apply principles of internal control. This chapter describes these principles and how to apply them. It focuses special attention on cash because it is easily transferable and is often at high risk of loss.

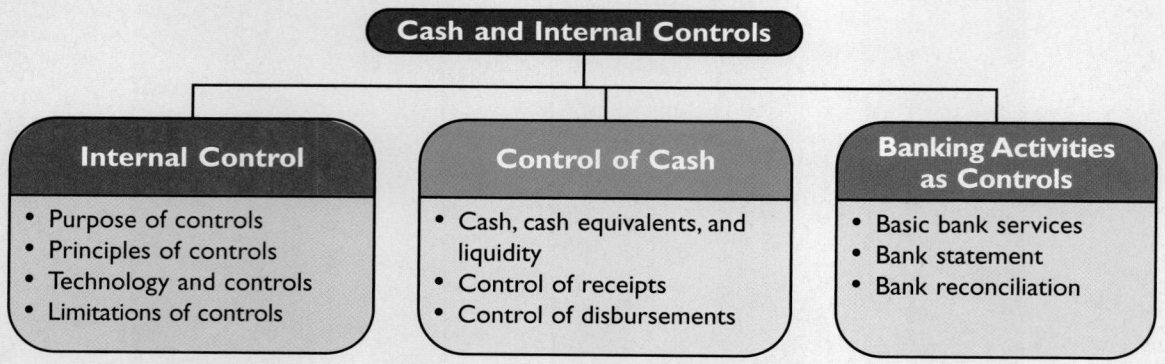

Cash and Internal Controls

Internal Control
- Purpose of controls
- Principles of controls
- Technology and controls
- Limitations of controls

Control of Cash
- Cash, cash equivalents, and liquidity
- Control of receipts
- Control of disbursements

Banking Activities as Controls
- Basic bank services
- Bank statement
- Bank reconciliation

Internal Control

This section describes internal control and its fundamental principles. We also discuss the impact of technology on internal control and the limitations of control procedures.

Purpose of Internal Control

C1 Define internal control and identify its purpose and principles.

Managers (or owners) of small businesses often control the entire operation. These managers usually purchase all assets, hire and manage employees, negotiate all contracts, and sign all checks. They know from personal contact and observation whether the business is actually receiving the assets and services paid for. Most companies, however, cannot maintain this close personal supervision. They must delegate responsibilities and rely on formal procedures rather than personal contact in controlling business activities.

Managers use an internal control system to monitor and control business activities. An **internal control system** consists of the policies and procedures managers use to

- ■ Protect assets.
- ■ Ensure reliable accounting.
- ■ Promote efficient operations.
- ■ Urge adherence to company policies.

Video8.1

A properly designed internal control system is a key part of systems design, analysis, and performance. Managers place a high priority on internal control systems because they can prevent avoidable losses, help managers plan operations, and monitor company and employee performance. Internal controls do not provide guarantees, but they lower the company's risk of loss.

The **Sarbanes-Oxley Act (SOX)** requires the managers and auditors of companies whose stock is traded on an exchange (called *public companies*) to document and certify the system of internal controls. Following are some of the specific requirements:

- ■ Auditors must evaluate internal controls and issue an internal control report.
- ■ Auditors of a client are restricted as to what consulting services they can provide that client.
- ■ The person leading an audit can serve no more than seven years without a two-year break.
- ■ Auditors' work is overseen by the *Public Company Accounting Oversight Board* (PCAOB).
- ■ Harsh penalties exist for violators—sentences up to 25 years in prison with severe fines.

SOX has markedly impacted companies, and the costs of its implementation are high. The benefits include greater confidence in accounting systems and their related reports. However, the public continues to debate the costs versus the benefits of SOX as nearly all business activities of these companies are impacted by SOX.

Principles of Internal Control

Internal control policies and procedures vary from company to company according to such factors as the nature of the business and its size. Certain fundamental internal control principles apply to all companies. The **principles of internal control** are to

1. Establish responsibilities.
2. Maintain adequate records.
3. Insure assets and bond key employees.
4. Separate recordkeeping from custody of assets.
5. Divide responsibility for related transactions.
6. Apply technological controls.
7. Perform regular and independent reviews.

This section explains these seven principles and describes how internal control procedures minimize the risk of fraud and theft. These procedures also increase the reliability and accuracy of accounting records.

Establish Responsibilities Proper internal control means that responsibility for a task is clearly established and assigned to one person. When a problem occurs in a company where responsibility is not identified, determining who is at fault is difficult. For instance, if two sales-clerks share the same cash register and there is a cash shortage, neither clerk can be held accountable. To prevent this problem, one clerk might be given responsibility for handling all cash sales. Alternately, a company can use a register with separate cash drawers for each clerk. Most of us have waited at a retail counter during a shift change while employees swap cash drawers.

Maintain Adequate Records Good recordkeeping is part of an internal control system. It helps protect assets and ensures that employees use prescribed procedures. Reliable records are also a source of information that managers use to monitor company activities. When detailed records of equipment are kept, for instance, items are unlikely to be lost or stolen without detection. Similarly, transactions are less likely to be entered in wrong accounts if a chart of accounts is set up and carefully used. Many preprinted forms and internal documents are also designed for use in a good internal control system. When sales slips are properly designed, for instance, sales personnel can record needed information efficiently with less chance of errors or delays to customers. When sales slips are prenumbered and controlled, each one issued is the responsibility of one salesperson, preventing the salesperson from pocketing cash by making a sale and destroying the sales slip. Computerized point-of-sale systems achieve the same control results.

Insure Assets and Bond Key Employees Good internal control means that assets are adequately insured against casualty and that employees handling large amounts of cash and easily transferable assets are bonded. An employee is *bonded* when a company purchases an insurance policy, or a bond, against losses from theft by that employee. Bonding reduces the risk of loss. It also discourages theft because bonded employees know an independent bonding company will be involved when theft is uncovered and is unlikely to be sympathetic with an employee involved in theft.

Point: Sarbanes-Oxley Act (SOX) requires that each annual report contain an *internal control report*, which must: (1) state managers' responsibility for establishing and maintaining adequate internal controls for financial reporting; and (2) assess the effectiveness of those controls.

Point: Many companies have a mandatory vacation policy for employees who handle cash. When another employee must cover for the one on vacation, it is more difficult to hide cash frauds.

Point: The Association of Certified Fraud Examiners (**cfenet.com**) estimates that employee fraud costs small companies more than $100,000 per incident.

Decision Insight

Tag Control A novel technique exists for marking physical assets. It involves embedding a less than one-inch-square tag of fibers that creates a unique optical signature recordable by scanners. Manufacturers hope to embed tags in everything from compact discs and credit cards to designer clothes for purposes of internal control and efficiency.

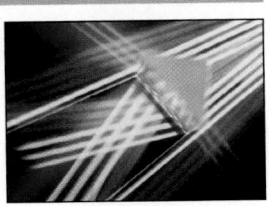

Separate Recordkeeping from Custody of Assets   A person who controls or has access to an asset must not keep that asset's accounting records. This principle reduces the risk of theft or waste of an asset because the person with control over it knows that another person keeps its records. Also, a recordkeeper who does not have access to the asset has no reason to falsify records. This means that to steal an asset and hide the theft from the records, two or more people must *collude*—or agree in secret to commit the fraud.

Divide Responsibility for Related Transactions   Good internal control divides responsibility for a transaction or a series of related transactions between two or more individuals or departments. This is to ensure that the work of one individual acts as a check on the other. This principle, often called *separation of duties,* is not a call for duplication of work. Each employee or department should perform unduplicated effort. Examples of transactions with divided responsibility are placing purchase orders, receiving merchandise, and paying vendors. These tasks should not be given to one individual or department. Assigning responsibility for two or more of these tasks to one party increases mistakes and perhaps fraud. Having an independent person, for example, check incoming goods for quality and quantity encourages more care and attention to detail than having the person who placed the order do the checking. Added protection can result from identifying a third person to approve payment of the invoice. A company can even designate a fourth person with authority to write checks as another protective measure.

Apply Technological Controls   Cash registers, check protectors, time clocks, and personal identification scanners are examples of devices that can improve internal control. Technology often improves the effectiveness of controls. A cash register with a locked-in tape or electronic file makes a record of each cash sale. A check protector perforates the amount of a check into its face and makes it difficult to alter the amount. A time clock registers the exact time an employee both arrives at and departs from the job. Mechanical change and currency counters quickly and accurately count amounts, and personal scanners limit access to only authorized individuals. Each of these and other technological controls are an effective part of many internal control systems.

Decision Insight

About Face   Face-recognition software snaps a digital picture of the face and converts key facial features—say, the distance between the eyes—into a series of numerical values. These can be stored on an ID or ATM card as a simple bar code to prohibit unauthorized access.

Perform Regular and Independent Reviews   Changes in personnel, stress of time pressures, and technological advances present opportunities for shortcuts and lapses. To counter these factors, regular reviews of internal control systems are needed to ensure that procedures are followed. These reviews are preferably done by internal auditors not directly involved in the activities. Their impartial perspective encourages an evaluation of the efficiency as well as the effectiveness of the internal control system. Many companies also pay for audits by independent, external auditors. These external auditors test the company's financial records to give an opinion as to whether its financial statements are presented fairly. Before external auditors decide on how much testing is needed, they evaluate the effectiveness of the internal control system. This evaluation is often helpful to a client.

Decision Maker

Entrepreneur   As owner of a start-up information services company, you hire a systems analyst. One of her first recommendations is to require all employees to take at least one week of vacation per year. Why would she recommend a "forced vacation" policy? [Answer—p. 340]

Technology and Internal Control

The fundamental principles of internal control are relevant no matter what the technological state of the accounting system, from purely manual to fully automated systems. Technology impacts an internal control system in several important ways. Perhaps the most obvious is that technology allows us quicker access to databases and information. Used effectively, technology

Point: There's a new security device—a person's ECG (electrocardiogram) reading—that is as unique as a fingerprint and a lot harder to lose or steal than a PIN. ECGs can be read through fingertip touches. An ECG also shows that a living person is actually there, whereas fingerprint and facial recognition software can be fooled.

Point: Information on Internet fraud can be found at these Websites: sec.gov/investor/pubs/cyberfraud.htm ftc.gov/bcp/consumer.shtm www.fraud.org

greatly improves managers' abilities to monitor and control business activities. This section describes some technological impacts we must be alert to.

Reduced Processing Errors   Technologically advanced systems reduce the number of errors in processing information. Provided the software and data entry are correct, the risk of mechanical and mathematical errors is nearly eliminated. However, we must remember that erroneous software or data entry does exist. Also, less human involvement in data processing can cause data entry errors to go undiscovered. Moreover, errors in software can produce consistent but erroneous processing of transactions. Continually checking and monitoring all types of systems are important.

Point: Evidence of any internal control failure for a company reduces user confidence in its financial statements.

More Extensive Testing of Records   A company's review and audit of electronic records can include more extensive testing when information is easily and rapidly accessed. When accounting records are kept manually, auditors and others likely select only small samples of data to test. When data are accessible with computer technology, however, auditors can quickly analyze large samples or even the entire database.

Limited Evidence of Processing   Many data processing steps are increasingly done by computer. Accordingly, fewer hard-copy items of documentary evidence are available for review. Yet technologically advanced systems can provide new evidence. They can, for instance, record who made the entries, the date and time, the source of the entry, and so on. Technology can also be designed to require the use of passwords or other identification before access to the system is granted. This means that internal control depends more on the design and operation of the information system and less on the analysis of its resulting documents.

Point: We look to several sources when assessing a company's internal controls. Sources include the auditor's report, management report on controls (if available), management discussion and analysis, and financial press.

Crucial Separation of Duties   Technological advances in accounting information systems often yield some job eliminations or consolidations. While those who remain have the special skills necessary to operate advanced programs and equipment, a company with a reduced workforce risks losing its crucial separation of duties. The company must establish ways to control and monitor employees to minimize risk of error and fraud. For instance, the person who designs and programs the information system must not be the one who operates it. The company must also separate control over programs and files from the activities related to cash receipts and disbursements. For instance, a computer operator should not control check-writing activities. Achieving acceptable separation of duties can be especially difficult and costly in small companies with few employees.

Increased E-Commerce   Technology has encouraged the growth of e-commerce. **Amazon.com** and **eBay** are examples of companies that have successfully exploited e-commerce. Most companies have some e-commerce transactions. All such transactions involve at least three risks. (1) *Credit card number theft* is a risk of using, transmitting, and storing such data online. This increases the cost of e-commerce. (2) *Computer viruses* are malicious programs that attach themselves to innocent files for purposes of infecting and harming other files and programs. (3) *Impersonation* online can result in charges of sales to bogus accounts, purchases of inappropriate materials, and the unknowing giving up of confidential information to hackers. Companies use both firewalls and encryption to combat some of these risks—firewalls are points of entry to a system that require passwords to continue, and encryption is a mathematical process to rearrange contents that cannot be read without the process code. Nearly 5% of Americans already report being victims of identity theft, and roughly 10 million say their privacy has been compromised.

"Worst case of identity theft I've ever seen!"

Copyright 2004 by Randy Glasbergen. www.glasbergen.com

Decision Insight

Cheery Fraud Victim   Certified Fraud Examiners Website reports the following: Andrew Cameron stole Jacqueline Boanson's credit card. Cameron headed to the racetrack and promptly charged two bets for $150 on the credit card—winning $400. Unfortunately for Cameron the racetrack refused to pay him cash as its internal control policy is to credit winnings from bets made on a credit card to that same card. Cameron was later nabbed; and the racetrack let Ms. Boanson keep the winnings.

Limitations of Internal Control

All internal control policies and procedures have limitations that usually arise from either (1) the human element or (2) the cost–benefit principle.

Internal control policies and procedures are applied by people. This human element creates several potential limitations that we can categorize as either (1) human error or (2) human fraud. *Human error* can occur from negligence, fatigue, misjudgment, or confusion. *Human fraud* involves intent by people to defeat internal controls, such as *management override,* for personal gain. Fraud also includes collusion to thwart the separation of duties. The human element highlights the importance of establishing an *internal control environment* to convey management's commitment to internal control policies and procedures.

The second major limitation on internal control is the *cost–benefit principle,* which dictates that the costs of internal controls must not exceed their benefits. Analysis of costs and benefits must consider all factors, including the impact on morale. Most companies, for instance, have a legal right to read employees' e-mails, yet companies seldom exercise that right unless they are confronted with evidence of potential harm to the company. The same holds for drug testing, phone tapping, and hidden cameras. The bottom line is that managers must establish internal control policies and procedures with a net benefit to the company.

Point: Cybercrime.gov pursues computer and intellectual property crimes, including that of e-commerce.

Hacker's Guide to Cyberspace

Pharming Viruses attached to e-mails and Websites load software onto your PC that monitors keystrokes; when you sign on to financial Websites, it steals your passwords.

Phishing Hackers send e-mails to you posing as banks; you are asked for information using fake Websites where they reel in your passwords and personal data.

WI-Phishing Cybercrooks set up wireless networks hoping you use them to connect to the Web; your passwords and data are stolen as you use their network.

Bot-Networking Hackers send remote-control programs to your PC that take control to send out spam and viruses; they even rent your bot to other cybercrooks.

Typo-Squatting Hackers set up Websites with addresses similar to legit outfits; when you make a typo and hit their sites, they infect your PC with viruses or take them over as bots.

Quick Check
Answers—p. 340

1. Principles of internal control suggest that (choose one): (*a*) Responsibility for a series of related transactions (such as placing orders, receiving and paying for merchandise) should be assigned to one employee; (*b*) Responsibility for individual tasks should be shared by more than one employee so that one serves as a check on the other; or (*c*) Employees who handle considerable cash and easily transferable assets should be bonded.

2. What are some impacts of computing technology on internal control?

Control of Cash

Cash is a necessary asset of every company. Most companies also own *cash equivalents* (defined below), which are assets similar to cash. Cash and cash equivalents are the most liquid of all assets and are easily hidden and moved. An effective system of internal controls protects these assets and it should meet three basic guidelines:

1. Handling cash is separate from recordkeeping of cash.
2. Cash receipts are promptly deposited in a bank.
3. Cash disbursements are made by check.

Video8.1

The first guideline applies separation of duties to minimize errors and fraud. When duties are separated, two or more people must collude to steal cash and conceal this action in the accounting records. The second guideline uses immediate (say, daily) deposits of all cash receipts to produce a timely independent record of the cash received. It also reduces the likelihood of cash theft (or loss) and the risk that an employee could personally use the money before depositing it. The third guideline uses payments by check to develop an independent bank record of cash disbursements. This guideline also reduces the risk of cash theft (or loss).

This section begins with definitions of cash and cash equivalents. Discussion then focuses on controls and accounting for both cash receipts and disbursements. The exact procedures used to achieve control over cash vary across companies. They depend on factors such as company size, number of employees, volume of cash transactions, and sources of cash.

Cash, Cash Equivalents, and Liquidity

Good accounting systems help in managing the amount of cash and controlling who has access to it. Cash is the usual means of payment when paying for assets, services, or liabilities. **Liquidity** refers to a company's ability to pay for its near-term obligations. Cash and similar assets are called **liquid assets** because they can be readily used to settle such obligations. A company needs liquid assets to effectively operate.

Cash includes currency and coins along with the amounts on deposit in bank accounts, checking accounts (called *demand deposits*), and many savings accounts (called *time deposits*). Cash also includes items that are acceptable for deposit in these accounts such as customer checks, cashier checks, certified checks, and money orders. **Cash equivalents** are short-term, highly liquid investment assets meeting two criteria: (1) readily convertible to a known cash amount and (2) sufficiently close to their due date so that their market value is not sensitive to interest rate changes. Only investments purchased within three months of their due date usually satisfy these criteria. Examples of cash equivalents are short-term investments in assets such as U.S. Treasury bills and money market funds. To increase their return, many companies invest idle cash in cash equivalents. Most companies combine cash equivalents with cash as a single item on the balance sheet.

C2 Define cash and cash equivalents and explain how to report them.

Point: The most liquid assets are usually reported first on a balance sheet; the least liquid assets are reported last.

Point: Google reports cash and cash equivalents of $3,544 million in its balance sheet. This amount makes up nearly 20% of its total assets.

Cash Management

When companies fail, one of the most common causes is their inability to manage cash. Companies must plan both cash receipts and cash payments. The goals of cash management are twofold:

1. Plan cash receipts to meet cash payments when due.
2. Keep a minimum level of cash necessary to operate.

The *treasurer* of the company is responsible for cash management. Effective cash management involves applying the following cash management principles.

- **Encourage collection of receivables.** The more quickly customers and others pay the company, the more quickly that company can use the money. Some companies have cash-only sales policies. Others might offer discounts for payments received early.
- **Delay payment of liabilities.** The more delayed a company is in paying others, the more time it has to use the money. Some companies regularly wait until the last possible day required to pay its bills—although, a company must take care not to hurt its credit standing.
- **Keep only necessary levels of assets.** The less money tied up in idle assets, the more money to invest in productive assets. Some companies maintain *just-in-time* inventory; meaning they plan inventory to be available at the same time orders are filled. Others might lease out excess warehouse space or rent equipment instead of buying it.
- **Plan expenditures.** Money should be spent only when it is available. Companies must look at seasonal and business cycles to plan expenditures.
- **Invest excess cash.** Excess cash earns no return and should be invested. Excess cash from seasonal cycles can be placed in a bank account or other short-term investment for income. Excess cash beyond what's needed for regular business should be invested in productive assets like factories and inventories.

Days' Cash Expense Coverage The ratio of *cash (and cash equivalents) to average daily cash expenses* indicates the number of days a company can operate without additional cash inflows. It reflects on company liquidity and on the potential of excess cash.

Control of Cash Receipts

P1 Apply internal control to cash receipts and disbursements.

Internal control of cash receipts ensures that cash received is properly recorded and deposited. Cash receipts can arise from transactions such as cash sales, collections of customer accounts, receipts of interest earned, bank loans, sales of assets, and owner investments. This section explains internal control over two important types of cash receipts: over-the-counter and by mail.

Over-the-Counter Cash Receipts For purposes of internal control, over-the-counter cash receipts from sales should be recorded on a cash register at the time of each sale. To help ensure that correct amounts are entered, each register should be located so customers can read the amounts entered. Clerks also should be required to enter each sale before wrapping merchandise and to give the customer a receipt for each sale. The design of each cash register should provide a permanent, locked-in record of each transaction. In many systems, the register is directly linked with computing and accounting services. Less advanced registers simply print a record of each transaction on a paper tape or electronic file locked inside the register.

Proper internal control prescribes that custody over cash should be separate from its record-keeping. For over-the-counter cash receipts, this separation begins with the cash sale. The clerk who has access to cash in the register should not have access to its locked-in record. At the end of the clerk's work period, the clerk should count the cash in the register, record the amount, and turn over the cash and a record of its amount to the company cashier. The cashier, like the clerk, has access to the cash but should not have access to accounting records (or the register tape or file). A third employee, often a supervisor, compares the record of total register transactions (or the register tape or file) with the cash receipts reported by the cashier. This record is the basis for a journal entry recording over-the-counter cash receipts. The third employee has access to the records for cash but not to the actual cash. The clerk and the cashier have access to cash but not to the accounting records. None of them can make a mistake or divert cash without the difference being revealed—see the following diagram.

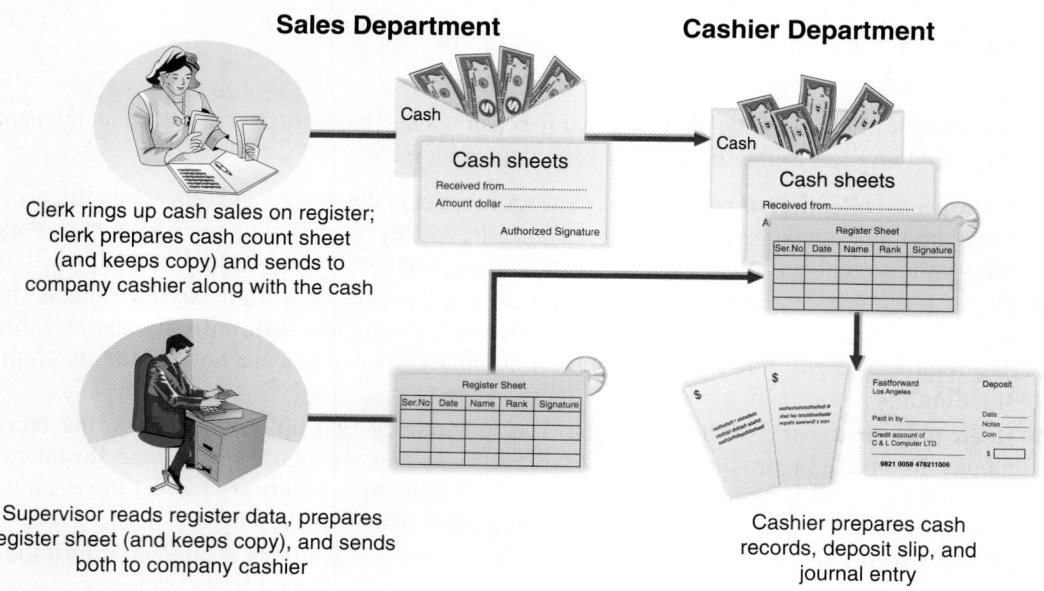

Clerk rings up cash sales on register; clerk prepares cash count sheet (and keeps copy) and sends to company cashier along with the cash

Supervisor reads register data, prepares register sheet (and keeps copy), and sends both to company cashier

Cashier prepares cash records, deposit slip, and journal entry

Point: Retailers often require cashiers to restrictively endorse checks immediately on receipt by stamping them "For deposit only."

Cash over and short. Sometimes errors in making change are discovered from differences between the cash in a cash register and the record of the amount of cash receipts. Although a clerk is careful, one or more customers can be given too much or too little change. This means that at the end of a work period, the cash in a cash register might not equal the record of cash receipts. This difference is reported in the **Cash Over and Short** account, also called *Cash Short and Over,* which is an income statement account recording the income effects of cash overages and cash shortages. To illustrate, if a cash register's record shows $550 but the count of cash in the register is $555, the entry to record cash sales and its overage is

Cash..	555	
Cash Over and Short.................		5
Sales		550
To record cash sales and a cash overage.		

Assets = Liabilities + Equity
+555   +   5
                                  +550

On the other hand, if a cash register's record shows $625 but the count of cash in the register is $621, the entry to record cash sales and its shortage is

Cash.....................................	621	
Cash Over and Short.....................	4	
Sales...................................		625
To record cash sales and a cash shortage.		

Assets = Liabilities + Equity
+621   −   4
                                  +625

Since customers are more likely to dispute being shortchanged than being given too much change, the Cash Over and Short account usually has a debit balance at the end of an accounting period. A debit balance reflects an expense. It is reported on the income statement as part of general and administrative expenses. (Since the amount is usually small, it is often combined with other small expenses and reported as part of *miscellaneous expenses*—or as part of *miscellaneous revenues* if it has a credit balance.)

Point: Merchants begin a business day with a *change fund* in their cash register. The accounting for a change fund is similar to that for petty cash, including that for cash shortages or overages.

Cash Receipts by Mail   Control of cash receipts that arrive through the mail starts with the person who opens the mail. Preferably, two people are assigned the task of, and are present for, opening the mail. In this case, theft of cash receipts by mail requires collusion between these two employees. Specifically, the person(s) opening the mail enters a list (in triplicate) of money received. This list should contain a record of each sender's name, the amount, and an explanation of why the money is sent. The first copy is sent with the money to the cashier. A second copy is sent to the recordkeeper in the accounting area. A third copy is kept by the clerk(s) who opened the mail. The cashier deposits the money in a bank, and the recordkeeper records the amounts received in the accounting records.

Point: Collusion implies that two or more individuals are knowledgeable or involved with the activities of the other(s).

This process reflects good internal control. That is, when the bank balance is reconciled by another person (explained later in the chapter), errors or acts of fraud by the mail clerks, the cashier, or the recordkeeper are revealed. They are revealed because the bank's record of cash deposited must agree with the records from each of the three. Moreover, if the mail clerks do not report all receipts correctly, customers will question their account balances. If the cashier does not deposit all receipts, the bank balance does not agree with the recordkeeper's cash balance. The recordkeeper and the person who reconciles the bank balance do not have access to cash and therefore have no opportunity to divert cash to themselves. This system makes errors and fraud highly unlikely. The exception is employee collusion.

Decision Insight

Perpetual Accounting   **Wal-Mart** uses a network of information links with its point-of-sale cash registers to coordinate sales, purchases, and distribution. Its supercenters, for instance, ring up 15,000 separate sales on heavy days. By using cash register information, the company can fix pricing mistakes quickly and capitalize on sales trends.

Control of Cash Disbursements

Control of cash disbursements is especially important as most large thefts occur from payment of fictitious invoices. One key to controlling cash disbursements is to require all expenditures to be made by check. The only exception is small payments made from petty cash. Another key is to deny access to the accounting records to anyone other than the owner who has the authority to sign checks. A small business owner often signs checks and knows from personal contact that the items being paid for are actually received. This arrangement is impossible in large businesses. Instead, internal control procedures must be substituted for personal contact. Such procedures are designed to assure the check signer that the obligations recorded are properly incurred and should be paid. This section describes these and other internal control procedures, including the voucher system and petty cash system. A method for management of cash disbursements for purchases is described in Appendix 8B.

Decision Insight

Cash Budget   Projected cash receipts and cash disbursements are often summarized in a *cash budget*. Provided that sufficient cash exists for effective operations, companies wish to minimize the cash they hold because of its risk of theft and its low return versus other investment opportunities.

Voucher System of Control   A **voucher system** is a set of procedures and approvals designed to control cash disbursements and the acceptance of obligations. The voucher system of control establishes procedures for

- Verifying, approving, and recording obligations for eventual cash disbursement.
- Issuing checks for payment of verified, approved, and recorded obligations.

A reliable voucher system follows standard procedures for every transaction. This applies even when multiple purchases are made from the same supplier.

A voucher system's control over cash disbursements begins when a company incurs an obligation that will result in payment of cash. A key factor in this system is that only approved departments and individuals are authorized to incur such obligations. The system often limits the type of obligations that a department or individual can incur. In a large retail store, for instance, only a purchasing department should be authorized to incur obligations for merchandise inventory. Another key factor is that procedures for purchasing, receiving, and paying for merchandise are divided among several departments (or individuals). These departments include the one requesting the purchase, the purchasing department, the receiving department, and the accounting department. To coordinate and control responsibilities of these departments, a company uses several different business documents. Exhibit 8.1 shows how documents are accumulated in a **voucher,** which is an internal document (or file) used

Point: MCI, formerly **WorldCom,** paid a whopping $500 million in SEC fines for accounting fraud. Among the charges were that it inflated earnings by as much as $10 billion. Its CEO, Bernard Ebbers, was sentenced to 25 years.

EXHIBIT 8.1

Document Flow in a Voucher System

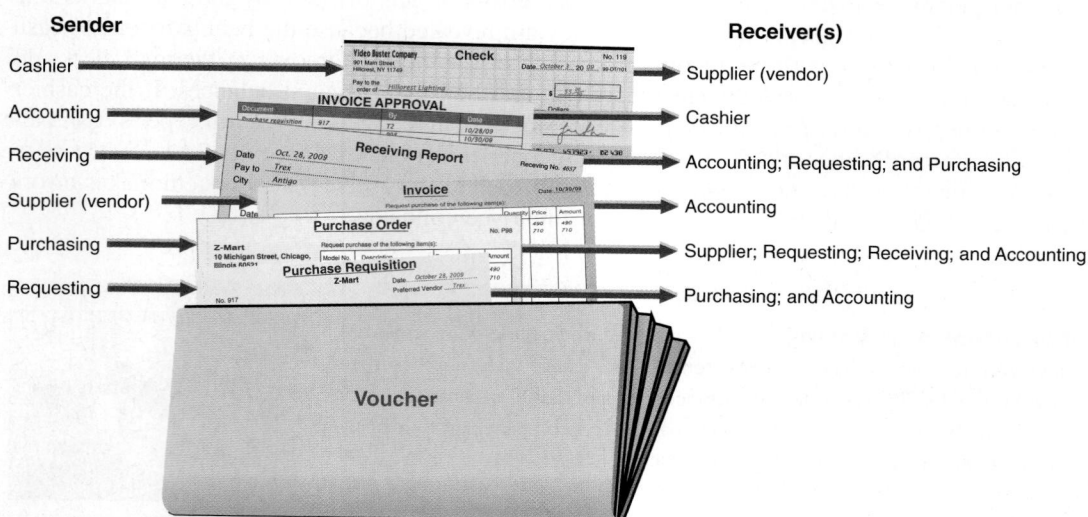

Sender	Receiver(s)
Cashier	Supplier (vendor)
Accounting	Cashier
Receiving	Accounting; Requesting; and Purchasing
Supplier (vendor)	Accounting
Purchasing	Supplier; Requesting; Receiving; and Accounting
Requesting	Purchasing; and Accounting

to accumulate information to control cash disbursements and to ensure that a transaction is properly recorded. This specific example begins with a *purchase requisition* and concludes with a *check* drawn against cash. Appendix 8A describes the documentation and verification necessary for a voucher system of control. It also describes the internal control objective served by each document.

A voucher system should be applied not only to purchases of inventory but to all expenditures. To illustrate, when a company receives a monthly telephone bill, it should review and verify the charges, prepare a voucher (file), and insert the bill. This transaction is then recorded with a journal entry. If the amount is currently due, a check is issued. If not, the voucher is filed for payment on its due date. If no voucher is prepared, verifying the invoice and its amount after several days or weeks can be difficult. Also, without records, a dishonest employee could collude with a dishonest supplier to get more than one payment for an obligation, payment for excessive amounts, or payment for goods and services not received. An effective voucher system helps prevent such frauds.

Point: A *voucher* is an internal document (or file).

Point: The basic purposes of paper and electronic documents are similar. However, the internal control system must change to reflect different risks, including confidential and competitive-sensitive information that is at greater risk in electronic systems.

Decision Insight

Cyber Setup The FTC is on the cutting edge of cybersleuthing. Opportunists in search of easy money are lured to **WeMarket4U.net/netops.** Take the bait and you get warned—and possibly targeted. The top 4 fraud complaints as compiled by the Internet Crime Complaint Center are shown to the right.

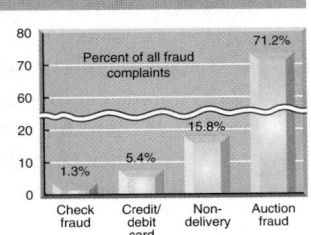

Quick Check   Answers—p. 340

3. Why must a company hold liquid assets?

4. Why does a company hold cash equivalent assets in addition to cash?

5. Identify at least two assets that are classified as cash equivalents.

6. Good internal control procedures for cash include which of the following? (*a*) All cash disbursements, other than those for very small amounts, are made by check; (*b*) One employee counts cash received from sales and promptly deposits cash receipts; or (*c*) Cash receipts by mail are opened by one employee who is then responsible for recording and depositing them.

7. Should all companies require a voucher system? At what point in a company's growth would you recommend a voucher system?

Petty Cash System of Control A basic principle for controlling cash disbursements is that all payments must be made by check. An exception to this rule is made for *petty cash disbursements,* which are the small payments required for items such as postage, courier fees, minor repairs, and low-cost supplies. To avoid the time and cost of writing checks for small amounts, a company sets up a petty cash fund to make small payments. (**Petty cash** activities are part of an *imprest system,* which designates advance money to establish the fund, to withdraw from the fund, and to reimburse the fund.)

P2 Explain and record petty cash fund transactions.

Operating a petty cash fund. Establishing a petty cash fund requires estimating the total amount of small payments likely to be made during a short period such as a week or month. A check is then drawn by the company cashier for an amount slightly in excess of this estimate. This check is recorded with a debit to the Petty Cash account (an asset) and a credit to Cash. The check is cashed, and the currency is given to an employee designated as the *petty cashier* or *petty cash custodian.* The petty cashier is responsible for keeping this cash safe, making payments from the fund, and keeping records of it in a secure place referred to as the *petty cashbox.*

Point: A petty cash fund is used only for business expenses.

When each cash disbursement is made, the person receiving payment should sign a prenumbered *petty cash receipt,* also called *petty cash ticket*—see Exhibit 8.2. The petty cash receipt is then placed in the petty cashbox with the remaining money. Under this system, the sum of all receipts plus the remaining cash equals the total fund amount. A $100 petty cash fund, for instance, contains any combination of cash and petty cash receipts that totals $100 (examples are $80 cash plus $20 in receipts, or $10 cash plus $90 in receipts). Each disbursement reduces cash and increases the amount of receipts in the petty cashbox.

EXHIBIT 8.2

Petty Cash Receipt

Z-Mart	No. 9
PETTY CASH RECEIPT	
For *Freight charges*	
Date *November 5, 2009*	Approved by
Charge to *Merchandise Inventory*	
Amount *$6.75*	Received by

Point: Petty cash receipts with either no signature or a forged signature usually indicate misuse of petty cash. Companies respond with surprise petty cash counts for verification.

The petty cash fund should be reimbursed when it is nearing zero and at the end of an accounting period when financial statements are prepared. For this purpose, the petty cashier sorts the paid receipts by the type of expense or account and then totals the receipts. The petty cashier presents all paid receipts to the company cashier, who stamps all receipts *paid* so they cannot be reused, files them for recordkeeping, and gives the petty cashier a check for their sum. When this check is cashed and the money placed in the cashbox, the total money in the cashbox is restored to its original amount. The fund is now ready for a new cycle of petty cash payments.

Illustrating a petty cash fund.   To illustrate, assume Z-Mart establishes a petty cash fund on November 1 and designates one of its office employees as the petty cashier. A $75 check is drawn, cashed, and the proceeds given to the petty cashier. The entry to record the setup of this petty cash fund is

Assets = Liabilities + Equity
+75
−75

Nov. 1	Petty Cash	75	
	Cash		75
	To establish a petty cash fund.		

Point: Reducing or eliminating a petty cash fund requires a credit to Petty Cash.
Point: Although *individual* petty cash disbursements are not evidenced by a check, the initial petty cash fund is evidenced by a check, and later petty cash expenditures are evidenced by a check to replenish them *in total.*

After the petty cash fund is established, the Petty Cash account is not debited or credited again unless the amount of the fund is changed. (A fund should be increased if it requires reimbursement too frequently. On the other hand, if the fund is too large, some of its money should be redeposited in the Cash account.)

Next, assume that Z-Mart's petty cashier makes several November payments from petty cash. Each person who received payment is required to sign a receipt. On November 27, after making a $26.50 cash payment for tile cleaning, only $3.70 cash remains in the fund. The petty cashier then summarizes and totals the petty cash receipts as shown in Exhibit 8.3.

EXHIBIT 8.3

Petty Cash Payments Report

Z-MART			
Petty Cash Payments Report			
Miscellaneous Expenses			
Nov. 2	Cleaning of LCD panels	$20.00	
Nov. 27	Tile cleaning	26.50	$ 46.50
Merchandise Inventory (transportation-in)			
Nov. 5	Transport of merchandise purchased	6.75	
Nov. 20	Transport of merchandise purchased	8.30	15.05
Delivery Expense			
Nov. 18	Customer's package delivered		5.00
Office Supplies Expense			
Nov. 15	Purchase of office supplies immediately used		4.75
Total			**$71.30**

Point: This report can also include receipt number and names of those who approved and received cash payment (see Demo Problem 2).

The petty cash payments report and all receipts are given to the company cashier in exchange for a $71.30 check to reimburse the fund. The petty cashier cashes the check and puts the $71.30 cash in the petty cashbox. The company records this reimbursement as follows.

Nov. 27	Miscellaneous Expenses	46.50	
	Merchandise Inventory	15.05	
	Delivery Expense	5.00	
	Office Supplies Expense	4.75	
	Cash		71.30
	To reimburse petty cash.		

Assets = Liabilities + Equity
−71.30   −46.50
                            −15.05
                            − 5.00
                            − 4.75

A petty cash fund is usually reimbursed at the end of an accounting period so that expenses are recorded in the proper period, even if the fund is not low on money. If the fund is not reimbursed at the end of a period, the financial statements would show both an overstated cash asset and understated expenses (or assets) that were paid out of petty cash. Some companies do not reimburse the petty cash fund at the end of each period under the notion that this amount is immaterial to users of financial statements.

Point: To avoid errors in recording petty cash reimbursement, follow these steps: (1) prepare payments report, (2) compute cash needed by subtracting cash remaining from total fund amount, (3) record entry, and (4) check "Dr. = Cr." in entry. Any difference is Cash Over and Short.

Increasing or decreasing a petty cash fund. A decision to increase or decrease a petty cash fund is often made when reimbursing it. To illustrate, assume Z-Mart decides to *increase* its petty cash fund from $75 to $100 on November 27 when it reimburses the fund. The entries required are to (1) reimburse the fund as usual (see the preceding November 27 entry) and (2) increase the fund amount as follows.

Nov. 27	Petty Cash	25	
	Cash		25
	To increase the petty cash fund amount.		

Event	Petty Cash	Cash	Expenses
Set up fund	Dr.	Cr.	—
Reimburse fund .	—	Cr.	Dr.
Increase fund . . .	Dr.	Cr.	—
Decrease fund . .	Cr.	Dr.	—

Alternatively, if Z-Mart *decreases* the petty cash fund from $75 to $55 on November 27, the entry is to (1) credit Petty Cash for $20 (decreasing the fund from $75 to $55) and (2) debit Cash for $20 (reflecting the $20 transfer from Petty Cash to Cash).

Cash over and short. Sometimes a petty cashier fails to get a receipt for payment or overpays for the amount due. When this occurs and the fund is later reimbursed, the petty cash payments report plus the cash remaining will not total to the fund balance. This mistake causes the fund to be *short*. This shortage is recorded as an expense in the reimbursing entry with a debit to the Cash Over and Short account. (An overage in the petty cash fund is recorded with a credit to Cash Over and Short in the reimbursing entry.) To illustrate, prepare the June 1 entry to reimburse a $200 petty cash fund when its payments report shows $178 in miscellaneous expenses and $15 cash remains.

$200 Petty Cash Fund

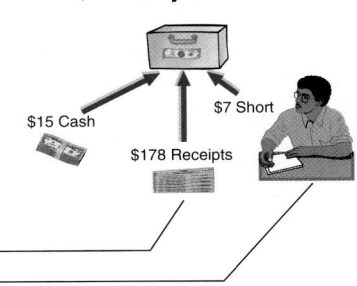

$15 Cash $7 Short

$178 Receipts

June 1	Miscellaneous Expenses	178 ◄	
	Cash Over and Short	7 ◄	
	Cash		185
	To reimburse petty cash.		

Decision Insight

Warning Signs There are clues to internal control violations. Warning signs from accounting include (1) an increase in customer refunds—could be fake, (2) missing documents—could be used for fraud, (3) differences between bank deposits and cash receipts—could be cash embezzled, and (4) delayed recording—could reflect fraudulent records. Warning signs from employees include (1) lifestyle change—could be embezzlement, (2) too close with suppliers—could signal fraudulent transactions, and (3) failure to leave job, even for vacations—could conceal fraudulent activities.

Quick Check Answers—p. 340

8. Why are some cash payments made from a petty cash fund and not by check?
9. Why should a petty cash fund be reimbursed at the end of an accounting period?
10. Identify at least two results of reimbursing a petty cash fund.

Banking Activities as Controls

Banks (and other financial institutions) provide many services, including helping companies control cash. Banks safeguard cash, provide detailed and independent records of cash transactions, and are a source of cash financing. This section describes these services and the documents provided by banking activities that increase managers' control over cash.

Basic Bank Services

C3 Identify control features of banking activities.

This section explains basic bank services—such as the bank account, the bank deposit, and checking—that contribute to the control of cash.

Bank Account, Deposit, and Check A *bank account* is a record set up by a bank for a customer. It permits a customer to deposit money for safekeeping and helps control withdrawals. To limit access to a bank account, all persons authorized to write checks on the account must sign a **signature card,** which bank employees use to verify signatures on checks. Many companies have more than one bank account to serve different needs and to handle special transactions such as payroll.

Each bank deposit is supported by a **deposit ticket,** which lists items such as currency, coins, and checks deposited along with their corresponding dollar amounts. The bank gives the customer a copy of the deposit ticket or a deposit receipt as proof of the deposit. Exhibit 8.4 shows one type of deposit ticket.

Point: Online banking services include the ability to stop payment on a check, move money between accounts, get up-to-date balances, and identify cleared checks and deposits.

EXHIBIT 8.4

Deposit Ticket

Front

Back

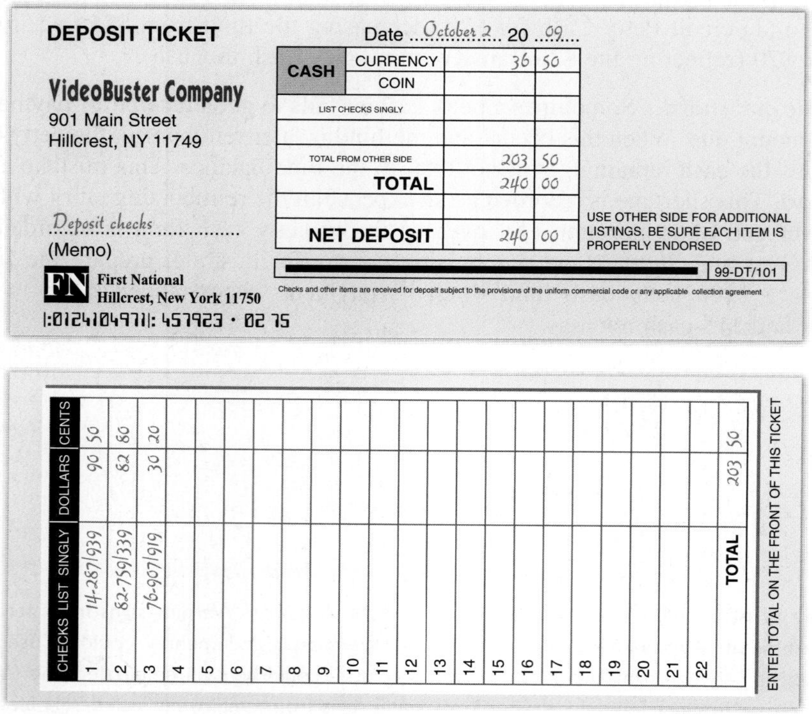
DEPOSIT TICKET

Date October 2 20 09

VideoBuster Company
901 Main Street
Hillcrest, NY 11749

CASH	CURRENCY	36	50
	COIN		
LIST CHECKS SINGLY			
TOTAL FROM OTHER SIDE		203	50
TOTAL		240	00
NET DEPOSIT		240	00

Deposit checks (Memo)

USE OTHER SIDE FOR ADDITIONAL LISTINGS. BE SURE EACH ITEM IS PROPERLY ENDORSED

99-DT/101

First National Hillcrest, New York 11750

Checks and other items are received for deposit subject to the provisions of the uniform commercial code or any applicable collection agreement

|:012410497|: 457923 · 02 75

CHECKS LIST SINGLY		DOLLARS	CENTS
1	14-287/939	90	50
2	82-759/339	82	60
3	76-907/919	30	20
4			
5			
6			
7			
8			
9			
10			
11			
12			
13			
14			
15			
16			
17			
18			
19			
20			
21			
22			
TOTAL		203	50

ENTER TOTAL ON THE FRONT OF THIS TICKET

To withdraw money from an account, the depositor can use a **check,** which is a document signed by the depositor instructing the bank to pay a specified amount of money to a designated recipient. A check involves three parties: a *maker* who signs the check, a *payee* who is the recipient, and a *bank* (or *payer*) on which the check is drawn. The bank provides a depositor the checks that are serially numbered and imprinted with the name and address of both the depositor and bank. Both checks and deposit tickets are imprinted with identification codes in magnetic ink for computer processing. Exhibit 8.5 shows one type of check. It is accompanied with an optional *remittance advice* explaining the payment. When a remittance advice is unavailable, the *memo* line is often used for a brief explanation.

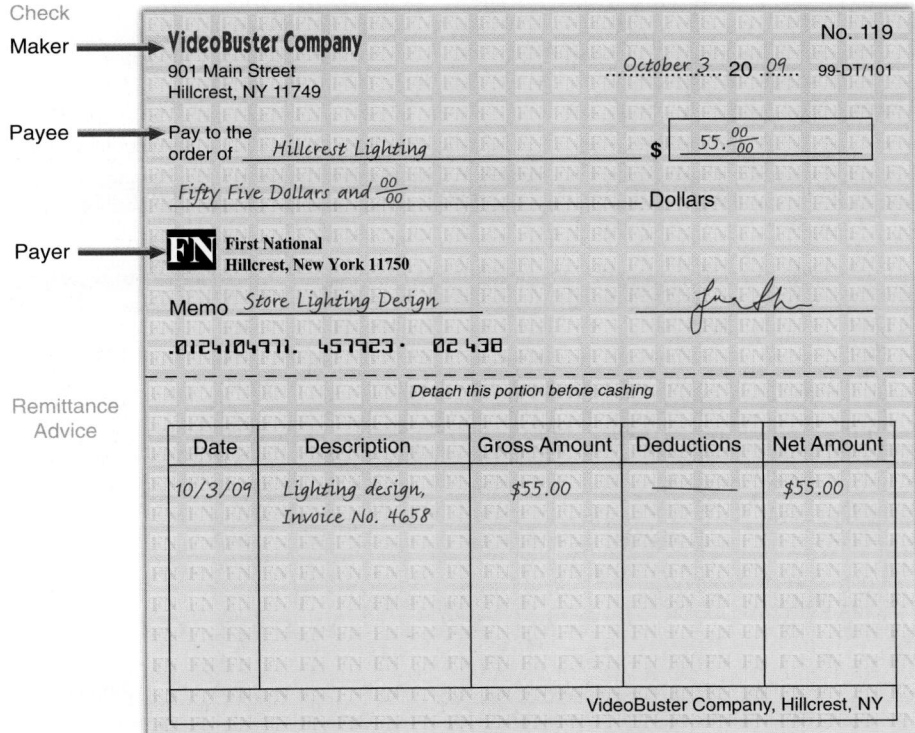

EXHIBIT 8.5

Check with Remittance Advice

Electronic Funds Transfer   **Electronic funds transfer (EFT)** is the electronic transfer of cash from one party to another. No paper documents are necessary. Banks simply transfer cash from one account to another with a journal entry. Companies are increasingly using EFT because of its convenience and low cost. For instance, it can cost up to 50 cents to process a check through the banking system, whereas EFT cost is near zero. We now commonly see items such as payroll, rent, utilities, insurance, and interest payments being handled by EFT. The bank statement lists cash withdrawals by EFT with the checks and other deductions. Cash receipts by EFT are listed with deposits and other additions. A bank statement is sometimes a depositor's only notice of an EFT. *Automated teller machines (ATMs)* are one form of EFT, which allows bank customers to deposit, withdraw, and transfer cash.

Bank Statement

Usually once a month, the bank sends each depositor a **bank statement** showing the activity in the account. Although a monthly statement is common, companies often regularly access information on its banking transactions. (Companies can choose to record any accounting adjustments required from the bank statement immediately or later, say, at the end of each day, week, month, or when reconciling a bank statement.) Different banks use different formats for their bank statements, but all of them include the following items of information:

1. Beginning-of-period balance of the depositor's account.
2. Checks and other debits decreasing the account during the period.
3. Deposits and other credits increasing the account during the period.
4. End-of-period balance of the depositor's account.

Point: Good internal control is to deposit all cash receipts daily and make all payments for goods and services by check. This controls access to cash and creates an independent record of all cash activities.

This information reflects the bank's records. Exhibit 8.6 shows one type of bank statement. Identify each of these four items in that statement. Part Ⓐ of Exhibit 8.6 summarizes changes in the account. Part Ⓑ lists paid checks along with other debits. Part Ⓒ lists deposits and credits to the account, and part Ⓓ shows the daily account balances.

EXHIBIT 8.6

Bank Statement

	FN First National Hillcrest, New York 11750			Bank Statement

Member FDIC

VideoBuster Company
901 Main Street
Hillcrest, NY 11749

October 31, 2009
Statement Date

494 504 2
Account Number

Ⓐ

Previous Balance	Total Checks and Debits	Total Deposits and Credits	Current Balance
1,609.58	723.00	1,163.42	2,050.00

Ⓑ Checks and Debits			Ⓒ Deposits and Credits		Ⓓ Daily Balance	
Date	No.	Amount	Date	Amount	Date	Amount
10/03	119	55.00	10/02	240.00	10/01	1,609.58
10/09	120	200.00	10/09	180.00	10/02	1,849.58
10/10	121	120.00	10/15	100.00	10/03	1,794.58
10/12		23.00 DM	10/16	150.00	10/09	1,774.58
10/14	122	70.00	10/23	485.00 CM	10/10	1,654.58
10/16	123	25.00	10/31	8.42 IN	10/12	1,631.58
10/23	125	15.00			10/14	1,561.58
10/25		20.00 NSF			10/15	1,661.58
		10.00 DM			10/16	1,786.58
10/26	127	50.00			10/23	2,256.58
10/29	128	135.00			10/25	2,226.58
					10/26	2,176.58
					10/29	2,041.58
					10/31	2,050.00

Symbols: **CM**–Credit Memo   **EC**–Error Correction   **NSF**–Non-Sufficient Funds   **SC**–Service Charge
DM–Debit Memo   **IN**–Interest Earned   **EFT**–Electronic Funds Transfer   **OD**–Overdraft

< Reconcile the account immediately. >

Point: Many banks separately report other debits and credits apart from checks and deposits.

In reading a bank statement note that a depositor's account is a liability on the bank's records. This is so because the money belongs to the depositor, not the bank. When a depositor increases the account balance, the bank records it with a *credit* to that liability account. This means that debit memos from the bank produce *credits* on the depositor's books, and credit memos from the bank produce *debits* on the depositor's books.

Enclosed with a bank statement is a list of the depositor's canceled checks (or the actual canceled checks) along with any debit or credit memoranda affecting the account. Increasingly, banks are showing canceled checks electronically via online access to accounts. **Canceled checks** are checks the bank has paid and deducted from the customer's account during the period. Other deductions that can appear on a bank statement include (1) service charges and fees assessed by the bank, (2) checks deposited that are uncollectible, (3) corrections of previous errors, (4) withdrawals through automated teller machines (ATMs), and (5) periodic payments arranged in advance by a depositor. (Most company checking accounts do not allow ATM withdrawals because of the company's desire to make all disbursements by check.) Except for service charges, the bank notifies the depositor of each deduction with a debit memorandum when the bank reduces the balance. A copy of each debit memorandum is usually sent with the statement (again, this information is often available earlier via online access and notifications).

Transactions that increase the depositor's account include amounts the bank collects on behalf of the depositor and the corrections of previous errors. Credit memoranda notify the

Global: If cash is in more than one currency, a company usually translates these amounts into U.S. dollars using the exchange rate as of the balance sheet date. Also, a company must disclose any restrictions on cash accounts located outside the U.S.

depositor of all increases when they are recorded. A copy of each credit memorandum is often sent with the bank statement. Banks that pay interest on checking accounts often compute the amount of interest earned on the average cash balance and credit it to the depositor's account each period. In Exhibit 8.6, the bank credits $8.42 of interest to the account.

Bank Reconciliation

When a company deposits all cash receipts and makes all cash payments (except petty cash) by check, it can use the bank statement for proving the accuracy of its cash records. This is done using a **bank reconciliation,** which is a report explaining any differences between the checking account balance according to the depositor's records and the balance reported on the bank statement.

Purpose of Bank Reconciliation   The balance of a checking account reported on the bank statement rarely equals the balance in the depositor's accounting records. This is usually due to information that one party has that the other does not. We must therefore prove the accuracy of both the depositor's records and those of the bank. This means we must *reconcile* the two balances and explain or account for any differences in them. Among the factors causing the bank statement balance to differ from the depositor's book balance are these:

■ **Outstanding checks. Outstanding checks** are checks written (or drawn) by the depositor, deducted on the depositor's records, and sent to the payees but not yet received by the bank for payment at the bank statement date.

■ **Deposits in transit** (also called **outstanding deposits**). **Deposits in transit** are deposits made and recorded by the depositor but not yet recorded on the bank statement. For example, companies can make deposits (in the night depository) at the end of a business day after the bank is closed. If such a deposit occurred on a bank statement date, it would not appear on this period's statement. The bank would record such a deposit on the next business day, and it would appear on the next period's bank statement. Deposits mailed to the bank near the end of a period also can be in transit and unrecorded when the statement is prepared.

■ **Deductions for uncollectible items and for services.** A company sometimes deposits another party's check that is uncollectible (usually meaning the balance in that party's account is not large enough to cover the check). This check is called a *non-sufficient funds (NSF)* check. The bank would have initially credited the depositor's account for the amount of the check. When the bank learns the check is uncollectible, it debits (reduces) the depositor's account for the amount of that check. The bank may also charge the depositor a fee for processing an uncollectible check and notify the depositor of the deduction by sending a debit memorandum. The depositor should record each deduction when a debit memorandum is received, but an entry is sometimes not made until the bank reconciliation is prepared. Other possible bank charges to a depositor's account that are first reported on a bank statement include printing new checks and service fees.

■ **Additions for collections and for interest.** Banks sometimes act as collection agents for their depositors by collecting notes and other items. Banks can also receive electronic funds transfers to the depositor's account. When a bank collects an item, it is added to the depositor's account, less any service fee. The bank also sends a credit memorandum to notify the depositor of the transaction. When the memorandum is received, the depositor should record it; yet it sometimes remains unrecorded until the bank reconciliation is prepared. The bank statement also includes a credit for any interest earned.

■ **Errors.** Both banks and depositors can make errors. Bank errors might not be discovered until the depositor prepares the bank reconciliation. Also, depositor errors are sometimes discovered when the bank balance is reconciled. Error testing includes: (a) comparing deposits on the bank statement with deposits in the accounting records and (b) comparing canceled checks on the bank statement with checks recorded in the accounting records.

P3   Prepare a bank reconciliation.

Forms of Check Fraud (CkFraud.org)
- Forged signatures—legitimate blank checks with fake payer signature
- Forged endorsements—stolen check that is endorsed and cashed by someone other than the payee
- Counterfeit checks—fraudulent checks with fake payer signature
- Altered checks—legitimate check altered (such as changed payee or amount) to benefit perpetrator
- Check kiting—deposit check from one bank account (without sufficient funds) into a second bank account

Point: Small businesses with few employees often allow recordkeepers to both write checks and keep the general ledger. If this is done, it is essential that the owner do the bank reconciliation.

Point: The person preparing the bank reconciliation should not be responsible for processing cash receipts, managing checks, or maintaining cash records.

EXHIBIT 8.7

Bank Reconciliation

Illustration of a Bank Reconciliation   We follow nine steps in preparing the bank reconciliation. It is helpful to refer to the bank reconciliation in Exhibit 8.7 when studying steps ① through ⑨.

	VIDEOBUSTER						
	Bank Reconciliation						
	October 31, 2009						
①	Bank statement balance		$ 2,050.00	⑤	Book balance		$ 1,404.58
②	Add			⑥	Add		
	Deposit of Oct. 31 in transit . . .		145.00		Collect $500 note less $15 fee . . .	$485.00	
			2,195.00		Interest earned	8.42	493.42
③	Deduct						1,898.00
	Outstanding checks			⑦	Deduct		
	No. 124	$150.00			Check printing charge	23.00	
	No. 126	200.00	350.00		NSF check plus service fee	30.00	53.00
④	**Adjusted bank balance**		**$1,845.00**	⑧	**Adjusted book balance**		**$1,845.00**

⑨ Balances are equal (reconciled)

① Identify the bank statement balance of the cash account (*balance per bank*). VideoBuster's bank balance is $2,050.

② Identify and list any unrecorded deposits and any bank errors understating the bank balance. Add them to the bank balance. VideoBuster's $145 deposit placed in the bank's night depository on October 31 is not recorded on its bank statement.

③ Identify and list any outstanding checks and any bank errors overstating the bank balance. Deduct them from the bank balance. VideoBuster's comparison of canceled checks with its books shows two checks outstanding: No. 124 for $150 and No. 126 for $200.

④ Compute the *adjusted bank balance,* also called the *corrected* or *reconciled balance.*

⑤ Identify the company's book balance of the cash account (*balance per book*). VideoBuster's book balance is $1,404.58.

⑥ Identify and list any unrecorded credit memoranda from the bank, any interest earned, and errors understating the book balance. Add them to the book balance. VideoBuster's bank statement includes a credit memorandum showing the bank collected a note receivable for the company on October 23. The note's proceeds of $500 (minus a $15 collection fee) are credited to the company's account. VideoBuster's bank statement also shows a credit of $8.42 for interest earned on the average cash balance. There was no prior notification of this item, and it is not yet recorded.

⑦ Identify and list any unrecorded debit memoranda from the bank, any service charges, and errors overstating the book balance. Deduct them from the book balance. Debits on VideoBuster's bank statement that are not yet recorded include (a) a $23 charge for check printing and (b) an NSF check for $20 plus a related $10 processing fee. (The NSF check is dated October 16 and was included in the book balance.)

⑧ Compute the *adjusted book balance,* also called *corrected* or *reconciled balance.*

⑨ Verify that the two adjusted balances from steps 4 and 8 are equal. If so, they are reconciled. If not, check for accuracy and missing data to achieve reconciliation.

Point: Outstanding checks are identified by comparing canceled checks on the bank statement with checks recorded. This includes identifying any outstanding checks listed on the *previous* period's bank reconciliation that are not included in the canceled checks on this period's bank statement.

Point: Adjusting entries can be combined into one compound entry.

Adjusting Entries from a Bank Reconciliation   A bank reconciliation often identifies unrecorded items that need recording by the company. In VideoBuster's reconciliation, the adjusted balance of $1,845 is the correct balance as of October 31. But the company's accounting records show a $1,404.58 balance. We must prepare journal entries to adjust the book balance to the correct balance. It is important to remember that only the items reconciling the *book balance* require adjustment. A review of Exhibit 8.7 indicates that four entries are required for VideoBuster.

Collection of note.   The first entry is to record the proceeds of its note receivable collected by the bank less the expense of having the bank perform that service.

Oct. 31	Cash	485	
	Collection Expense.	15	
	Notes Receivable		500
	To record the collection fee and proceeds		
	for a note collected by the bank.		

Assets = Liabilities + Equity
+485   −15
−500

Interest earned.   The second entry records interest credited to its account by the bank.

Oct. 31	Cash	8.42	
	Interest Revenue.		8.42
	To record interest earned on the cash		
	balance in the checking account.		

Assets = Liabilities + Equity
+8.42   +8.42

Check printing.   The third entry records expenses for the check printing charge.

Oct. 31	Miscellaneous Expenses	23	
	Cash		23
	Check printing charge.		

Assets = Liabilities + Equity
−23   −23

NSF check.   The fourth entry records the NSF check that is returned as uncollectible. The $20 check was originally received from T. Woods in payment of his account and then deposited. The bank charged $10 for handling the NSF check and deducted $30 total from VideoBuster's account. This means the entry must reverse the effects of the original entry made when the check was received and must record (add) the $10 bank fee.

Point: The company will try to collect the entire NSF amount of $30.

Oct. 31	Accounts Receivable—T. Woods.	30	
	Cash		30
	To charge Woods' account for $20 NSF check		
	and $10 bank fee.		

Assets = Liabilities + Equity
+30
−30

After these four entries are recorded, the book balance of cash is adjusted to the correct amount of $1,845 (computed as $1,404.58 + $485 + $8.42 − $23 − $30). The Cash T-account to the side shows the same computation, where entries are keyed to the numerical codes in Exhibit 8.7.

Cash			
Unadj. bal.	1,404.58		
⑥	485.00	⑦	23.00
⑥	8.42	⑦	30.00
Adj. bal.	1,845.00		

Point: The Demo Problem 1 shows an adjusting entry for an error correction.

Decision Insight

IFRSs   Internal controls are crucial to companies that convert from U.S. GAAP to IFRSs. Major risks include misstatement of financial information and fraud. Other risks are ineffective communication of the impact of this change for investors, creditors and others, and management's inability to certify the effectiveness of controls over financial reporting.

Quick Check   Answers—pp. 340–341

11. What is a bank statement?
12. What is the meaning of the phrase *to reconcile a bank balance?*
13. Why do we reconcile the bank statement balance of cash and the depositor's book balance of cash?
14. List at least two items affecting the bank balance side of a bank reconciliation and indicate whether the items are added or subtracted.
15. List at least three items affecting the book balance side of a bank reconciliation and indicate whether the items are added or subtracted.

A1   Compute the days' sales uncollected ratio and use it to assess liquidity.

An important part of cash management is monitoring the receipt of cash from receivables. If customers and others who owe money to a company are delayed in payment, then that company can find it difficult to pay its obligations when they are due. A company's customers are crucial partners in its cash management. Many companies attract customers by selling to them on credit. This means that cash receipts from customers are delayed until accounts receivable are collected.

One measure of how quickly a company can convert its accounts receivable into cash is the **days' sales uncollected,** also called *days' sales in receivables*. This measure is computed by dividing the current balance of receivables by net credit sales over the year just completed and then multiplying by 365 (number of days in a year). Since net credit sales usually are not reported to external users, the net sales (or revenues) figure is commonly used in the computation as in Exhibit 8.8.

EXHIBIT 8.8

Days' Sales Uncollected

$$\text{Days' sales uncollected} = \frac{\text{Accounts receivable}}{\text{Net sales}} \times 365$$

We use days' sales uncollected to estimate how much time is likely to pass before the current amount of accounts receivable is received in cash. For evaluation purposes, we need to compare this estimate to that for other companies in the same industry. We also make comparisons between current and prior periods.

To illustrate, we select data from the annual reports of two toy manufacturers, **Hasbro** and **Mattel**. Their days' sales uncollected figures are shown in Exhibit 8.9.

EXHIBIT 8.9

Analysis Using Days' Sales Uncollected

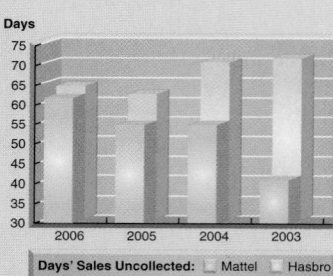

Company	Figure ($ millions)	2006	2005	2004	2003
Hasbro	Accounts receivable	$556	$523	$579	$608
	Net sales	$3,151	$3,088	$2,998	$3,139
	Days' sales uncollected	64 days	62 days	70 days	71 days
Mattel	Accounts receivable	$944	$761	$759	$544
	Net sales	$5,650	$5,179	$5,103	$4,960
	Days' sales uncollected	61 days	54 days	54 days	40 days

Days' sales uncollected for Hasbro in 2006 is computed as ($556/$3,151) × 365 days = 64 days. This means that it will take about 64 days to collect cash from ending accounts receivable. This number reflects one or more of the following factors: a company's ability to collect receivables, customer financial health, customer payment strategies, and discount terms. To further assess days' sales uncollected for Hasbro, we compare it to three prior years and to those of Mattel. We see that Hasbro's days' sales uncollected has generally improved over the past 4 years—from 71 days down to 64 days. In comparison, Mattel worsened on days' sales uncollected for each of those years—from 40 days to 61 days. Yet, for all years, Mattel is superior to Hasbro on this measure of cash management. The less time that money is tied up in receivables often translates into increased profitability.

 Decision Maker

Sales Representative   The sales staff is told to take action to help reduce days' sales uncollected for cash management purposes. What can you, a salesperson, do to reduce days' sales uncollected? [Answer—p. 340]

Demonstration Problem 1

Prepare a bank reconciliation for Jamboree Enterprises for the month ended November 30, 2009. The following information is available to reconcile Jamboree Enterprises' book balance of cash with its bank statement balance as of November 30, 2009:

a. After all posting is complete on November 30, the company's book balance of Cash has a $16,380 debit balance, but its bank statement shows a $38,520 balance.

b. Checks No. 2024 for $4,810 and No. 2026 for $5,000 are outstanding.

c. In comparing the canceled checks on the bank statement with the entries in the accounting records, it is found that Check No. 2025 in payment of rent is correctly drawn for $1,000 but is erroneously entered in the accounting records as $880.

d. The November 30 deposit of $17,150 was placed in the night depository after banking hours on that date, and this amount does not appear on the bank statement.

e. In reviewing the bank statement, a check written by Jumbo Enterprises in the amount of $160 was erroneously drawn against Jamboree's account.

f. A credit memorandum enclosed with the bank statement indicates that the bank collected a $30,000 note and $900 of related interest on Jamboree's behalf. This transaction was not recorded by Jamboree prior to receiving the statement.

g. A debit memorandum for $1,100 lists a $1,100 NSF check received from a customer, Marilyn Welch. Jamboree had not recorded the return of this check before receiving the statement.

h. Bank service charges for November total $40. These charges were not recorded by Jamboree before receiving the statement.

Planning the Solution

- Set up a bank reconciliation with a bank side and a book side (as in Exhibit 8.7). Leave room to both add and deduct items. Each column will result in a reconciled, equal balance.
- Examine each item *a* through *h* to determine whether it affects the book or the bank balance and whether it should be added or deducted from the bank or book balance.
- After all items are analyzed, complete the reconciliation and arrive at a reconciled balance between the bank side and the book side.
- For each reconciling item on the book side, prepare an adjusting entry. Additions to the book side require an adjusting entry that debits Cash. Deductions on the book side require an adjusting entry that credits Cash.

Solution to Demonstration Problem 1

JAMBOREE ENTERPRISES
Bank Reconciliation
November 30, 2009

Bank statement balance		$ 38,520	Book balance		$ 16,380
Add			Add		
Deposit of Nov. 30	$17,150		Collection of note	$30,000	
Bank error (Jumbo)	160	17,310	Interest earned	900	30,900
		55,830			47,280
Deduct			Deduct		
Outstanding checks			NSF check (M. Welch) . . .	1,100	
No. 2024	4,810		Recording error (# 2025) .	120	
No. 2026	5,000	9,810	Service charge	40	1,260
Adjusted bank balance . . .		**$46,020**	**Adjusted book balance** . .		**$46,020**

Required Adjusting Entries for Jamboree

Nov. 30	Cash	30,900	
	Notes Receivable		30,000
	Interest Earned		900
	To record collection of note with interest.		
Nov. 30	Accounts Receivable—M. Welch	1,100	
	Cash		1,100
	To reinstate account due from an NSF check.		
Nov. 30	Rent Expense	120	
	Cash		120
	To correct recording error on check no. 2025.		

[continued on next page]

[continued from previous page]

Nov. 30	Bank Service Charges........................	40	
	Cash		40
	To record bank service charges.		

Demonstration Problem 2

Bacardi Company established a $150 petty cash fund with Dean Martin as the petty cashier. When the fund balance reached $19 cash, Martin prepared a petty cash payment report, which follows.

Petty Cash Payments Report				
Receipt No.	Account Charged		Approved by	Received by
12	Delivery Expense	$ 29	Martin	A. Smirnoff
13	Merchandise Inventory	18	Martin	J. Daniels
15	(Omitted)	32	Martin	C. Carlsberg
16	Miscellaneous Expense	41	(Omitted)	J. Walker
	Total	$120		

Required

1. Identify four internal control weaknesses from the payment report.
2. Prepare general journal entries to record:
   a. Establishment of the petty cash fund.
   b. Reimbursement of the fund. (Assume for this part only that petty cash receipt no. 15 was issued for miscellaneous expenses.)
3. What is the Petty Cash account balance immediately before reimbursement? Immediately after reimbursement?

Solution to Demonstration Problem 2

1. Four internal control weaknesses are
   a. Petty cash ticket no. 14 is missing. Its omission raises questions about the petty cashier's management of the fund.
   b. The $19 cash balance means that $131 has been withdrawn ($150 − $19 = $131). However, the total amount of the petty cash receipts is only $120 ($29 + $18 + $32 + $41). The fund is $11 short of cash ($131 − $120 = $11). Was petty cash receipt no. 14 issued for $11? Management should investigate.
   c. The petty cashier (Martin) did not sign petty cash receipt no. 16. This omission could have been an oversight on his part or he might not have authorized the payment. Management should investigate.
   d. Petty cash receipt no. 15 does not indicate which account to charge. This omission could have been an oversight on the petty cashier's part. Management could check with C. Carlsberg and the petty cashier (Martin) about the transaction. Without further information, debit Miscellaneous Expense.
2. Petty cash general journal entries.
   a. Entry to establish the petty cash fund.   b. Entry to reimburse the fund.

Petty Cash	150	
Cash		150

Delivery Expense	29	
Merchandise Inventory	18	
Miscellaneous Expense ($41 + $32)	73	
Cash Over and Short	11	
Cash		131

3. The Petty Cash account balance *always* equals its fund balance, in this case $150. This account balance does not change unless the fund is increased or decreased.

Documentation and Verification

8A

This appendix describes the important business documents of a voucher system of control.

Purchase Requisition   Department managers are usually not allowed to place orders directly with suppliers for control purposes. Instead, a department manager must inform the purchasing department of its needs by preparing and signing a **purchase requisition,** which lists the merchandise needed and requests that it be purchased—see Exhibit 8A.1. Two copies of the purchase requisition are sent to the purchasing department, which then sends one copy to the accounting department. When the accounting department receives a purchase requisition, it creates and maintains a voucher for this transaction. The requesting department keeps the third copy.

P4 Describe the use of documentation and verification to control cash disbursements.

EXHIBIT 8A.1

Purchase Requisition

Z-Mart

PURCHASE REQUISITION   No. 917

From _Sporting Goods Department_   **Date** _October 28, 2009_
To _Purchasing Department_   **Preferred Vendor** _Trex_

Request purchase of the following item(s):

MODEL NO.	DESCRIPTION	QUANTITY
CH 015	Challenger X7	1
SD 099	SpeedDemon	1

Reason for Request _Replenish inventory_
Approval for Request _T.Z._

For Purchasing Department use only: Order Date _10/30/09_   P.O. No. _P98_

Purchase Order   A **purchase order** is a document the purchasing department uses to place an order with a **vendor** (seller or supplier). A purchase order authorizes a vendor to ship ordered merchandise at the stated price and terms—see Exhibit 8A.2. When the purchasing department receives a purchase requisition, it prepares at least five copies of a purchase order. The copies are distributed as follows: *copy 1* to the vendor as a purchase request and as authority to ship merchandise; *copy 2,* along with a copy of the purchase requisition, to the accounting department, where it is entered in the voucher and used in approving payment of the invoice; *copy 3* to the requesting department to inform its manager that action is being taken; *copy 4* to the receiving department without order quantity so it can compare with goods received and provide independent count of goods received; and *copy 5* retained on file by the purchasing department.

Invoice   An **invoice** is an itemized statement of goods prepared by the vendor listing the customer's name, items sold, sales prices, and terms of sale. An invoice is also a bill sent to the buyer from the supplier. From the vendor's point of view, it is a *sales invoice.* The buyer, or **vendee,** treats it as a *purchase invoice.* When receiving a purchase order, the vendor ships the ordered merchandise to the buyer and includes or mails a copy of the invoice covering the shipment to the buyer. The invoice is sent to the buyer's accounting department where it is placed in the voucher. (Refer back to Exhibit 5.5, which shows Z-Mart's purchase invoice.)

Point: It is important to note that a voucher system is designed to uniquely meet the needs of a specific business. Thus, you should read this appendix as one example of a common voucher system design, but *not* the only design.

Z-Mart
10 Michigan Street
Chicago, Illinois 60521

PURCHASE ORDER

No. P98

Date	10/30/09
FOB	Destination
Ship by	As soon as possible
Terms	2/15, n/30

To: Trex
W9797 Cherry Road
Antigo, Wisconsin 54409

Request shipment of the following item(s):

Model No.	Description	Quantity	Price	Amount	
CH 015	Challenger X7	1	490	490	
SD 099	SpeedDemon	1	710	710	

All shipments and invoices must include purchase order number

J.W.

ORDERED BY

Receiving Report   Many companies maintain a separate department to receive all merchandise and purchased assets. When each shipment arrives, this receiving department counts the goods and checks them for damage and agreement with the purchase order. It then prepares four or more copies of a **receiving report,** which is used within the company to notify the appropriate persons that ordered goods have been received and to describe the quantities and condition of the goods. One copy is sent to accounting and placed in the voucher. Copies are also sent to the requesting department and the purchasing department to notify them that the goods have arrived. The receiving department retains a copy in its files.

Invoice Approval   When a receiving report arrives, the accounting department should have copies of the following documents in the voucher: purchase requisition, purchase order, and invoice. With the information in these documents, the accounting department can record the purchase and approve its payment. In approving an invoice for payment, it checks and compares information across all documents. To facilitate this checking and to ensure that no step is omitted, it often uses an **invoice approval,** also called *check authorization*—see Exhibit 8A.3. An invoice approval is a checklist of steps necessary for approving an invoice for recording and payment. It is a separate document either filed in the voucher or preprinted (or stamped) on the voucher.

INVOICE APPROVAL

DOCUMENT		BY	DATE
Purchase requisition	917	TZ	10/28/09
Purchase order	P98	JW	10/30/09
Receiving report	R85	SK	11/03/09
Invoice:	4657		11/12/09
Price		JK	11/12/09
Calculations		JK	11/12/09
Terms		JK	11/12/09
Approved for payment		BC	

As each step in the checklist is approved, the person initials the invoice approval and records the current date. Final approval implies the following steps have occurred:

1. **Requisition check:** Items on invoice are requested per purchase requisition.
2. **Purchase order check:** Items on invoice are ordered per purchase order.
3. **Receiving report check:** Items on invoice are received per receiving report.
4. **Invoice check: Price:** Invoice prices are as agreed with the vendor.
   Calculations: Invoice has no mathematical errors.
   Terms: Terms are as agreed with the vendor.

Point: Recording a purchase is initiated by an invoice approval, not an invoice. An invoice approval verifies that the amount is consistent with that requested, ordered, and received. This controls and verifies purchases and related liabilities.

Voucher   Once an invoice has been checked and approved, the voucher is complete. A complete voucher is a record summarizing a transaction. Once the voucher certifies a transaction, it authorizes recording an obligation. A voucher also contains approval for paying the obligation on an appropriate date. The physical form of a voucher varies across companies. Many are designed so that the invoice and other related source documents are placed inside the voucher, which can be a folder.

Completion of a voucher usually requires a person to enter certain information on both the inside and outside of the voucher. Typical information required on the inside of a voucher is shown in Exhibit 8A.4, and that for the outside is shown in Exhibit 8A.5. This information is taken from the invoice and the supporting documents filed in the voucher. A complete voucher is sent to an authorized individual (often called an *auditor*). This person performs a final review, approves the accounts and amounts for debiting (called the *accounting distribution*), and authorizes recording of the voucher.

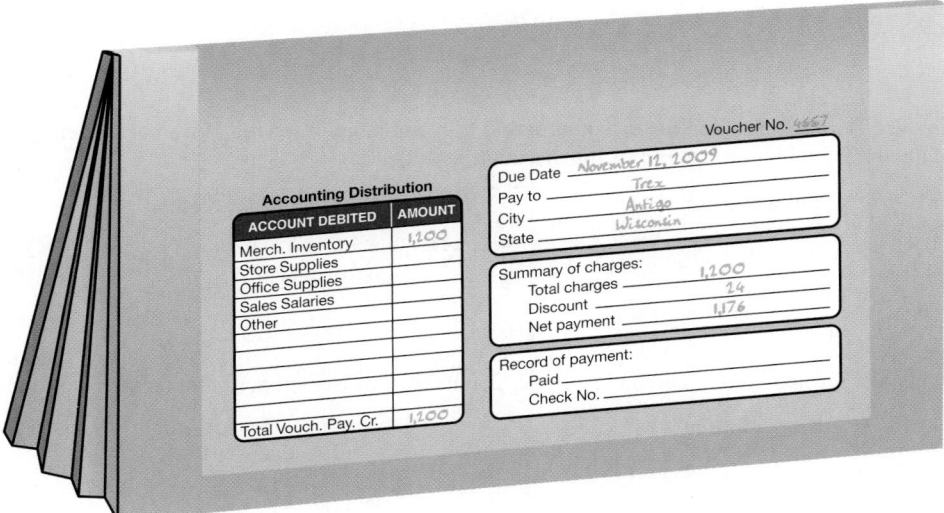

EXHIBIT 8A.4

Inside of a Voucher

After a voucher is approved and recorded (in a journal called a **voucher register**), it is filed by its due date. A check is then sent on the payment date from the cashier, the voucher is marked "paid," and the voucher is sent to the accounting department and recorded (in a journal called the **check register**). The person issuing checks relies on the approved voucher and its signed supporting documents as proof that an obligation has been incurred and must be paid. The purchase requisition and purchase order confirm the purchase was authorized. The receiving report shows that items have been received, and the invoice approval form verifies that the invoice has been checked for errors. There is little chance for error and even less chance for fraud without collusion unless all the documents and signatures are forged.

EXHIBIT 8A.5

Outside of a Voucher

8B Control of Purchase Discounts

P5   Apply the net method to control purchase discounts.

This appendix explains how a company can better control its cash *disbursements* to take advantage of favorable purchases discounts. Chapter 5 described the entries to record the receipt and payment of an invoice for a merchandise purchase with and without discount terms. Those entries were prepared under what is called the **gross method** of recording purchases, which initially records the invoice at its *gross* amount ignoring any cash discount.

The **net method** is another means of recording purchases, which initially records the invoice at its *net* amount of any cash discount. The net method gives management an advantage in controlling and monitoring cash payments involving purchase discounts.

To explain, when invoices are recorded at *gross* amounts, the amount of any discounts taken is deducted from the balance of the Merchandise Inventory account when cash payment is made. This means that the amount of any discounts lost is not reported in any account or on the income statement. Lost discounts recorded in this way are unlikely to come to the attention of management. When purchases are recorded at *net* amounts, a **Discounts Lost** expense account is recorded and brought to management's attention. Management can then seek to identify the reason for discounts lost such as oversight, carelessness, or unfavorable terms. (Chapter 5 explains how managers assess whether a discount is favorable or not.)

Perpetual Inventory System   To illustrate, assume that a company purchases merchandise on November 2 at a $1,200 invoice price with terms of 2/10, n/30. Its November 2 entries under the gross and net methods are

Gross Method			Net Method		
Merchandise Inventory	1,200		Merchandise Inventory	1,176	
Accounts Payable		1,200	Accounts Payable		1,176

If the invoice is paid on November 12 within the discount period, it records the following:

Gross Method			Net Method		
Accounts Payable	1,200		Accounts Payable	1,176	
Merchandise Inventory		24	Cash		1,176
Cash		1,176			

If the invoice is *not* paid within the discount period, it records the following November 12 entry (which is the date corresponding to the end of the discount period):

Gross Method			Net Method		
No entry			Discounts Lost	24	
			Accounts Payable		24

Then, when the invoice is later paid on December 2, outside the discount period, it records the following:

Gross Method			Net Method		
Accounts Payable	1,200		Accounts Payable	1,200	
Cash		1,200	Cash		1,200

(The discount lost can be recorded when the cash payment is made with a single entry. However, in this case, when financial statements are prepared after a discount is lost and before the cash payment is made, an adjusting entry is required to recognize any unrecorded discount lost in the period when incurred.)

Periodic Inventory System   The preceding entries assume a perpetual inventory system. If a company is using a *periodic system,* its November 2 entries under the gross and net methods are

Gross Method—Periodic		
Purchases	1,200	
Accounts Payable		1,200

Net Method—Periodic		
Purchases	1,176	
Accounts Payable		1,176

If the invoice is paid on November 12 within the discount period, it records the following:

Gross Method—Periodic		
Accounts Payable	1,200	
Purchases Discounts		24
Cash		1,176

Net Method—Periodic		
Accounts Payable	1,176	
Cash		1,176

If the invoice is *not* paid within the discount period, it records the following November 12 entry:

Gross Method—Periodic
No entry

Net Method—Periodic		
Discounts Lost	24	
Accounts Payable		24

Then, when the invoice is later paid on December 2, outside the discount period, it records the following:

Gross Method—Periodic		
Accounts Payable	1,200	
Cash		1,200

Net Method—Periodic		
Accounts Payable	1,200	
Cash		1,200

Summary

C1   Define internal control and identify its purpose and principles. An internal control system consists of the policies and procedures managers use to protect assets, ensure reliable accounting, promote efficient operations, and urge adherence to company policies. It can prevent avoidable losses and help managers both plan operations and monitor company and human performance. Principles of good internal control include establishing responsibilities, maintaining adequate records, insuring assets and bonding employees, separating recordkeeping from custody of assets, dividing responsibilities for related transactions, applying technological controls, and performing regular independent reviews.

C2   Define cash and cash equivalents and explain how to report them. Cash includes currency, coins, and amounts on (or acceptable for) deposit in checking and savings accounts. Cash equivalents are short-term, highly liquid investment assets readily convertible to a known cash amount and sufficiently close to their maturity date so that market value is not sensitive to interest rate changes. Cash and cash equivalents are liquid assets because they

are readily converted into other assets or can be used to pay for goods, services, or liabilities.

C3   Identify control features of banking activities. Banks offer several services that promote the control and safeguarding of cash. A bank account is a record set up by a bank permitting a customer to deposit money for safekeeping and to draw checks on it. A bank deposit is money contributed to the account with a deposit ticket as proof. A check is a document signed by the depositor instructing the bank to pay a specified amount of money to a designated recipient.

A1   Compute the days' sales uncollected ratio and use it to assess liquidity. Many companies attract customers by selling to them on credit. This means that cash receipts from customers are delayed until accounts receivable are collected. Users want to know how quickly a company can convert its accounts receivable into cash. The days' sales uncollected ratio, one measure reflecting company liquidity, is computed by dividing the ending balance of receivables by annual net sales, and then multiplying by 365.

P1   **Apply internal control to cash receipts and disbursements.** Internal control of cash receipts ensures that all cash received is properly recorded and deposited. Attention focuses on two important types of cash receipts: over-the-counter and by mail. Good internal control for over-the-counter cash receipts includes use of a cash register, customer review, use of receipts, a permanent transaction record, and separation of the custody of cash from its recordkeeping. Good internal control for cash receipts by mail includes at least two people assigned to open mail and a listing of each sender's name, amount, and explanation.

P2   **Explain and record petty cash fund transactions.** Petty cash disbursements are payments of small amounts for items such as postage, courier fees, minor repairs, and supplies. A company usually sets up one or more petty cash funds. A petty fund cashier is responsible for safekeeping the cash, making payments from this fund, and keeping receipts and records. A Petty Cash account is debited only when the fund is established or increased in amount. When the fund is replenished, petty cash disbursements are recorded with debits to expense (or asset) accounts and a credit to cash.

P3   **Prepare a bank reconciliation.** A bank reconciliation proves the accuracy of the depositor's and the bank's records. The bank statement balance is adjusted for items such as outstanding checks and unrecorded deposits made on or before the bank statement date but not reflected on the statement. The book balance is adjusted for items such as service charges, bank collections for the depositor, and interest earned on the account.

P4ᴬ   **Describe the use of documentation and verification to control cash disbursements.** A voucher system is a set of procedures and approvals designed to control cash disbursements and acceptance of obligations. The voucher system of control relies on several important documents, including the voucher and its supporting files. A key factor in this system is that only approved departments and individuals are authorized to incur certain obligations.

P5ᴮ   **Apply the net method to control purchase discounts.** The net method aids management in monitoring and controlling purchase discounts. When invoices are recorded at gross amounts, the amount of discounts taken is deducted from the balance of the Inventory account. This means that the amount of any discounts lost is not reported in any account and is unlikely to come to the attention of management. When purchases are recorded at net amounts, a Discounts Lost account is brought to management's attention as an operating expense. Management can then seek to identify the reason for discounts lost, such as oversight, carelessness, or unfavorable terms.

Guidance Answers to **Decision Maker** and **Decision Ethics**

Entrepreneur   A forced vacation policy is part of a good system of internal controls. When employees are forced to take vacations, their ability to hide any fraudulent behavior decreases because others must perform the vacationers' duties. A replacement employee potentially can uncover fraudulent behavior or falsified records. A forced vacation policy is especially important for employees in sensitive positions of handling money or in control of easily transferable assets.

Sales Representative   A salesperson can take several steps to reduce days' sales uncollected. These include (1) decreasing the ratio of sales on account to total sales by encouraging more cash sales, (2) identifying customers most delayed in their payments and encouraging earlier payments or cash sales, and (3) applying stricter credit policies to eliminate credit sales to customers that never pay.

Guidance Answers to **Quick Checks**

1. (c)
2. Technology reduces processing errors. It also allows more extensive testing of records, limits the amount of hard evidence, and highlights the importance of separation of duties.
3. A company holds liquid assets so that it can purchase other assets, buy services, and pay obligations.
4. It owns cash equivalents because they yield a return greater than what cash earns (and are readily exchanged for cash).
5. Examples of cash equivalents are 90-day (or less) U.S. Treasury bills, money market funds, and commercial paper (notes).
6. (a)
7. A voucher system is used when an owner/manager can no longer control purchasing procedures through personal supervision and direct participation.
8. If all cash payments are made by check, numerous checks for small amounts must be written. Since this practice is expensive and time-consuming, a petty cash fund is often established for making small (immaterial) cash payments.

9. If the petty cash fund is not reimbursed at the end of an accounting period, the transactions involving petty cash are not yet recorded and the petty cash asset is overstated.
10. First, petty cash transactions are recorded when the petty cash fund is reimbursed. Second, reimbursement provides cash to allow the fund to continue being used. Third, reimbursement identifies any cash shortage or overage in the fund.
11. A bank statement is a report prepared by the bank describing the activities in a depositor's account.
12. To reconcile a bank balance means to explain the difference between the cash balance in the depositor's accounting records and the cash balance on the bank statement.

13. The purpose of the bank reconciliation is to determine whether the bank or the depositor has made any errors and whether the bank has entered any transactions affecting the account that the depositor has not recorded.

14. Unrecorded deposits—added
Outstanding checks—subtracted

15. Interest earned—added   Debit memos—subtracted
Credit memos—added   NSF checks—subtracted
                                       Bank service charges—subtracted

Key Terms   mhhe.com/wildFAP19e

Key Terms are available at the book's Website for learning and testing in an online Flashcard Format.

Bank reconciliation (p. 329)	**Discounts lost** (p. 338)	**Principles of internal control** (p. 315)
Bank statement (p. 327)	**Electronic funds transfer (EFT)** (p. 327)	**Purchase order** (p. 335)
Canceled checks (p. 328)	**Gross method** (p. 338)	**Purchase requisition** (p. 335)
Cash (p. 319)	**Internal control system** (p. 314)	**Receiving report** (p. 336)
Cash equivalents (p. 319)	**Invoice** (p. 335)	**Sarbanes-Oxley Act** (p. 314)
Cash Over and Short (p. 321)	**Invoice approval** (p. 336)	**Signature card** (p. 326)
Check (p. 326)	**Liquid assets** (p. 319)	**Vendee** (p. 335)
Check register (p. 337)	**Liquidity** (p. 319)	**Vendor** (p. 335)
Days' sales uncollected (p. 332)	**Net method** (p. 338)	**Voucher** (p. 322)
Deposit ticket (p. 326)	**Outstanding checks** (p. 329)	**Voucher register** (p. 337)
Deposits in transit (p. 329)	**Petty cash** (p. 323)	**Voucher system** (p. 322)

Multiple Choice Quiz   Answers on p. 355   mhhe.com/wildFAP19e

Additional Quiz Questions are available at the book's Website.

Quiz8

1. A company needs to replenish its $500 petty cash fund. Its petty cash box has $75 cash and petty cash receipts of $420. The journal entry to replenish the fund includes
a. A debit to Cash for $75.
b. A credit to Cash for $75.
c. A credit to Petty Cash for $420.
d. A credit to Cash Over and Short for $5.
e. A debit to Cash Over and Short for $5.

2. The following information is available for Hapley Company:
• The November 30 bank statement shows a $1,895 balance.
• The general ledger shows a $1,742 balance at November 30.
• A $795 deposit placed in the bank's night depository on November 30 does not appear on the November 30 bank statement.
• Outstanding checks amount to $638 at November 30.
• A customer's $335 note was collected by the bank in November. A collection fee of $15 was deducted by the bank and the difference deposited in Hapley's account.
• A bank service charge of $10 is deducted by the bank and appears on the November 30 bank statement.

How will the customer's note appear on Hapley's November 30 bank reconciliation?
a. $320 appears as an addition to the book balance of cash.
b. $320 appears as a deduction from the book balance of cash.
c. $320 appears as an addition to the bank balance of cash.
d. $320 appears as a deduction from the bank balance of cash.
e. $335 appears as an addition to the bank balance of cash.

3. Using the information from question 2, what is the reconciled balance on Hapley's November 30 bank reconciliation?
a. $2,052
b. $1,895
c. $1,742
d. $2,201
e. $1,184

4. A company had net sales of $84,000 and accounts receivable of $6,720. Its days' sales uncollected is
a. 3.2 days
b. 18.4 days
c. 230.0 days
d. 29.2 days
e. 12.5 days

5.[B] A company records its purchases using the net method. On August 1, it purchases merchandise on account for $6,000 with terms of 2/10, n/30. The August 1 journal entry to record this transaction includes a
a. Debit to Merchandise Inventory for $6,000.
b. Debit to Merchandise Inventory for $5,880.
c. Debit to Merchandise Inventory for $120.
d. Debit to Accounts Payable for $5,880.
e. Credit to Accounts Payable for $6,000.

Superscript letter ^{A} (^{B}) denotes assignments based on Appendix 8A (8B).

Discussion Questions

I. List the seven broad principles of internal control.

2. Internal control procedures are important in every business, but at what stage in the development of a business do they become especially critical?

3. Why should responsibility for related transactions be divided among different departments or individuals?

4. Why should the person who keeps the records of an asset not be the person responsible for its custody?

5. When a store purchases merchandise, why are individual departments not allowed to directly deal with suppliers?

6. What are the limitations of internal controls?

7. Which of the following assets is most liquid? Which is least liquid? Inventory, building, accounts receivable, or cash.

8. What is a petty cash receipt? Who should sign it?

9. Why should cash receipts be deposited on the day of receipt?

10. Best Buy's statement of cash flows in Appendix A describes changes in cash and cash equivalents for

the year ended March 3, 2007. What amount is provided (used) by investing activities? What amount is provided (used) by financing activities?

I I. Refer to **Circuit City**'s balance sheet in Appendix A. How does its cash compare with its other current assets (in both amount and percent) as of February 28, 2007? Compare and assess the cash amount at February 28, 2007, with its amount at February 28, 2006.

12. Refer to **RadioShack**'s financial statements in Appendix A. RadioShack's net income for the year ended December 31, 2006, was $73,400,000. Is its net income equal to the increase in cash and cash equivalents for the year? Explain the difference between net income and the increase in cash and cash equivalents.

13. **Apple**'s balance sheet in Appendix A reports that cash and equivalents increased during the fiscal year ended September 30, 2006. Identify at least three major causes of this change in cash and equivalents.

Denotes Discussion Questions that involve decision making.

Available with McGraw-Hill's Homework Manager

QUICK STUDY

QS 8-1
Internal control objectives

C1

An internal control system consists of all policies and procedures used to protect assets, ensure reliable accounting, promote efficient operations, and urge adherence to company policies.

I. What is the main objective of internal control procedures? How is that objective achieved?

2. Why should recordkeeping for assets be separated from custody over those assets?

3. Why should the responsibility for a transaction be divided between two or more individuals or departments?

QS 8-2
Cash and equivalents

C2

Good accounting systems help in managing cash and controlling who has access to it.

I. What items are included in the category of cash?

2. What items are included in the category of cash equivalents?

3. What does the term *liquidity* refer to?

QS 8-3
Cash, liquidity, and return

C1 C2

Good accounting systems help with the management and control of cash and cash equivalents.

I. Define and contrast the terms *liquid asset* and *cash equivalent*.

2. Why would companies invest their idle cash in cash equivalents?

3. Identify five principles of effective cash management.

QS 8-4
Internal control for cash

P1

A good system of internal control for cash provides adequate procedures for protecting both cash receipts and cash disbursements.

I. What are three basic guidelines that help achieve this protection?

2. Identify two control systems or procedures for cash disbursements.

QS 8-5
Petty cash accounting

P2

I. The petty cash fund of the Kaley Agency is established at $75. At the end of the current period, the fund contained $8.18 and had the following receipts: film rentals, $26.50, refreshments for meetings, $32.17 (both expenditures to be classified as Entertainment Expense); postage, $5.15; and printing, $3. Prepare journal entries to record (*a*) establishment of the fund and (*b*) reimbursement of the fund at the end of the current period.

2. Identify the two events that cause a Petty Cash account to be credited in a journal entry.

1. For each of the following items, indicate whether its amount (i) affects the bank or book side of a bank reconciliation and (ii) represents an addition or a subtraction in a bank reconciliation.

    a. Unrecorded deposits   **d.** Debit memos   **g.** NSF checks

    b. Interest on cash balance   **e.** Outstanding checks

    c. Bank service charges   **f.** Credit memos

2. Which of the items in part 1 require an adjusting journal entry?

Madison Company deposits all cash receipts on the day when they are received and it makes all cash payments by check. At the close of business on July 31, 2009, its Cash account shows a $2,025 debit balance. Madison's July 31 bank statement shows $1,800 on deposit in the bank. Prepare a bank reconciliation for Madison Company using the following information.

a. The July 31 bank statement included a $30 debit memorandum for bank services; Madison has not yet recorded the cost of these services.

b. In reviewing the bank statement, a $90 check written by Madsen Company was mistakenly drawn against Madison's account.

c. July 31 cash receipts of $210 were placed in the bank's night depository after banking hours and were not recorded on the July 31 bank statement.

d. Outstanding checks as of July 31 total $100.

e. The bank statement included a $30 credit for interest earned on the cash in the bank.

The following annual account balances are taken from Mizuno Sports at December 31.

	2009	2008
Accounts receivable	$ 93,700	$ 90,450
Net sales	1,357,600	1,259,680

What is the change in the number of days' sales uncollected between years 2008 and 2009? According to this analysis, is the company's collection of receivables improving? Explain.

Management uses a voucher system to help control and monitor cash disbursements. Identify and describe at least four key documents that are part of a voucher system of control.

An important part of cash management is knowing when, and if, to take purchase discounts.

a. Which accounting method uses a Discounts Lost account?

b. What is the advantage of this method for management?

McGraw-Hill's
**HOMEWORK
MANAGER®**   Available with McGraw-Hill's Homework Manager

Pacific Company is a rapidly growing start-up business. Its recordkeeper, who was hired one year ago, left town after the company's manager discovered that a large sum of money had disappeared over the past six months. An audit disclosed that the recordkeeper had written and signed several checks made payable to her fiancé and then recorded the checks as salaries expense. The fiancé, who cashed the checks but never worked for the company, left town with the recordkeeper. As a result, the company incurred an uninsured loss of $184,000. Evaluate Pacific's internal control system and indicate which principles of internal control appear to have been ignored.

Some of Chapman Company's cash receipts from customers are received by the company with the regular mail. Chapman's recordkeeper opens these letters and deposits the cash received each day. (*a*) Identify any internal control problem(s) in this arrangement. (*b*) What changes to its internal control system do you recommend?

What internal control procedures would you recommend in each of the following situations?

1. A concession company has one employee who sells sunscreen, T-shirts, and sunglasses at the beach. Each day, the employee is given enough sunscreen, shirts, and sunglasses to last through the day and enough cash to make change. The money is kept in a box at the stand.

2. An antique store has one employee who is given cash and sent to garage sales each weekend. The employee pays cash for any merchandise acquired that the antique store resells.

Exercise 8-4
Petty cash fund accounting

P2

Check   (2) Cr. Cash $210

Fresno Co. establishes a $350 petty cash fund on January 1. On January 8, the fund shows $140 in cash along with receipts for the following expenditures: postage, $67; transportation-in, $35; delivery expenses, $52; and miscellaneous expenses, $56. Fresno uses the perpetual system in accounting for merchandise inventory. Prepare journal entries to (1) establish the fund on January 1, (2) reimburse it on January 8, and (3) both reimburse the fund and increase it to $550 on January 8, assuming no entry in part 2. (*Hint*: Make two separate entries for part 3.)

Exercise 8-5
Petty cash fund with a shortage

P2

Check   (2) Cr. Cash $216 and (3) Cr. Cash $50

Reichard Company establishes a $250 petty cash fund on September 9. On September 30, the fund shows $34 in cash along with receipts for the following expenditures: transportation-in, $47; postage expenses, $62; and miscellaneous expenses, $103. The petty cashier could not account for a $4 shortage in the fund. Reichard uses the perpetual system in accounting for merchandise inventory. Prepare (1) the September 9 entry to establish the fund, (2) the September 30 entry to reimburse the fund, and (3) an October 1 entry to increase the fund to $300.

Exercise 8-6
Bank reconciliation and adjusting entries

P3

Prepare a table with the following headings for a monthly bank reconciliation dated September 30.

Bank Balance		Book Balance			Not Shown on the Reconciliation
Add	Deduct	Add	Deduct	Adjust	

For each item 1 through 12, place an *x* in the appropriate column to indicate whether the item should be added to or deducted from the book or bank balance, or whether it should not appear on the reconciliation. If the book balance is to be adjusted, place a *Dr.* or *Cr.* in the Adjust column to indicate whether the Cash balance should be debited or credited. At the left side of your table, number the items to correspond to the following list.

1. NSF check from customer is returned on September 25 but not yet recorded by this company.
2. Interest earned on the September cash balance in the bank.
3. Deposit made on September 5 and processed by the bank on September 6.
4. Checks written by another depositor but charged against this company's account.
5. Bank service charge for September.
6. Checks outstanding on August 31 that cleared the bank in September.
7. Check written against the company's account and cleared by the bank; erroneously not recorded by the company's recordkeeper.
8. Principal and interest on a note receivable to this company is collected by the bank but not yet recorded by the company.
9. Checks written and mailed to payees on October 2.
10. Checks written by the company and mailed to payees on September 30.
11. Night deposit made on September 30 after the bank closed.
12. Special bank charge for collection of note in part 8 on this company's behalf.

Exercise 8-7
Voucher system

P1

The voucher system of control is designed to control cash disbursements and the acceptance of obligations.
1. The voucher system of control establishes procedures for what two processes?
2. What types of expenditures should be overseen by a voucher system of control?
3. When is the voucher initially prepared? Explain.

Exercise 8-8
Bank reconciliation

P3

Austin Clinic deposits all cash receipts on the day when they are received and it makes all cash payments by check. At the close of business on June 30, 2009, its Cash account shows a $15,671 debit balance. Austin Clinic's June 30 bank statement shows $15,382 on deposit in the bank. Prepare a bank reconciliation for Austin Clinic using the following information:
a. Outstanding checks as of June 30 total $2,700.
b. The June 30 bank statement included a $65 debit memorandum for bank services.

c. Check No. 919, listed with the canceled checks, was correctly drawn for $489 in payment of a utility bill on June 15. Austin Clinic mistakenly recorded it with a debit to Utilities Expense and a credit to Cash in the amount of $498.

d. The June 30 cash receipts of $2,933 were placed in the bank's night depository after banking hours and were not recorded on the June 30 bank statement.

Check Reconciled bal., $15,615

Exercise 8-9
Adjusting entries from bank reconciliation P3

Prepare the adjusting journal entries that Austin Clinic must record as a result of preparing the bank reconciliation in Exercise 8-8.

Exercise 8-10
Bank reconciliation
P3

Walsh Company deposits all cash receipts on the day when they are received and it makes all cash payments by check. At the close of business on May 31, 2009, its Cash account shows a $7,750 debit balance. Walsh's May 31 bank statement shows $6,900 on deposit in the bank. Prepare a bank reconciliation for Walsh Company using the following information.

a. May 31 cash receipts of $1,100 were placed in the bank's night depository after banking hours and were not recorded on the May 31 bank statement.

b. Outstanding checks as of May 31 total $800.

c. The May 31 bank statement included a $50 debit memorandum for bank services; Walsh has not yet recorded the cost of these services.

d. In reviewing the bank statement, a $200 check written by Wald Company was mistakenly drawn against Walsh's account.

e. A debit memorandum for $300 refers to a $300 NSF check from a customer; Walsh has not yet recorded this NSF check.

Check Reconciled bal., $7,400

Exercise 8-11
Liquid assets and accounts receivable
A1

Todd Co. reported annual net sales for 2008 and 2009 of $664,000 and $746,000, respectively. Its year-end balances of accounts receivable follow: December 31, 2008, $65,000; and December 31, 2009, $93,000. (*a*) Calculate its days' sales uncollected at the end of each year. (*b*) Evaluate and comment on any changes in the amount of liquid assets tied up in receivables.

Exercise 8-12^A
Documents in a voucher system
P4

Match each document in a voucher system in column one with its description in column two.

Document

1. Purchase requisition
2. Purchase order
3. Invoice
4. Receiving report
5. Invoice approval
6. Voucher

Description

A. An itemized statement of goods prepared by the vendor listing the customer's name, items sold, sales prices, and terms of sale.

B. An internal file used to store documents and information to control cash disbursements and to ensure that a transaction is properly authorized and recorded.

C. A document used to place an order with a vendor that authorizes the vendor to ship ordered merchandise at the stated price and terms.

D. A checklist of steps necessary for the approval of an invoice for recording and payment; also known as a check authorization.

E. A document used by department managers to inform the purchasing department to place an order with a vendor.

F. A document used to notify the appropriate persons that ordered goods have arrived, including a description of the quantities and condition of goods.

Exercise 8-13^B
Record invoices at gross or net amounts
P5

World Imports uses the perpetual system in accounting for merchandise inventory and had the following transactions during the month of October. Prepare entries to record these transactions assuming that World Imports records invoices (*a*) at gross amounts and (*b*) at net amounts.

Oct. 2 Purchased merchandise at a $5,600 price, invoice dated October 2, terms 1/10, n/30.
10 Received a $900 credit memorandum (at full invoice price) for the return of merchandise that it purchased on October 2.
17 Purchased merchandise at a $5,950 price, invoice dated October 16, terms 2/10, n/30.
26 Paid for the merchandise purchased on October 17, less the discount.
31 Paid for the merchandise purchased on October 2. Payment was delayed because the invoice was mistakenly filed for payment today. This error caused the discount to be lost.

PROBLEM SET A

Problem 8-1A
Analyzing internal control

C1

For each of these five separate cases, identify the principle(s) of internal control that is violated. Recommend what the business should do to ensure adherence to principles of internal control.

1. Chi Han records all incoming customer cash receipts for his employer and posts the customer payments to their respective accounts.
2. At Tico Company, Jenn and Kirsten alternate lunch hours. Jenn is the petty cash custodian, but if someone needs petty cash when she is at lunch, Kirsten fills in as custodian.
3. Nori Nozumi posts all patient charges and payments at the Hopeville Medical Clinic. Each night Nori backs up the computerized accounting system to a tape and stores the tape in a locked file at her desk.
4. Sanjay Shales prides himself on hiring quality workers who require little supervision. As office manager, Sanjay gives his employees full discretion over their tasks and for years has seen no reason to perform independent reviews of their work.
5. Cala Farah's manager has told her to reduce costs. Cala decides to raise the deductible on the plant's property insurance from $5,000 to $10,000. This cuts the property insurance premium in half. In a related move, she decides that bonding the plant's employees is a waste of money since the company has not experienced any losses due to employee theft. Cala saves the entire amount of the bonding insurance premium by dropping the bonding insurance.

Problem 8-2A
Establish, reimburse, and increase petty cash

P2

Beard Gallery had the following petty cash transactions in February of the current year.

Feb. 2   Wrote a $300 check, cashed it, and gave the proceeds and the petty cashbox to Reggie Gore, the petty cashier.
     5   Purchased bond paper for the copier for $14.55 that is immediately used.
     9   Paid $32.50 COD shipping charges on merchandise purchased for resale, terms FOB shipping point. Beard uses the perpetual system to account for merchandise inventory.
    12   Paid $7.85 postage to express mail a contract to a client.
    14   Reimbursed Jonny Carr, the manager, $66 for business mileage on her car.
    20   Purchased stationery for $67.67 that is immediately used.
    23   Paid a courier $23 to deliver merchandise sold to a customer, terms FOB destination.
    25   Paid $10.30 COD shipping charges on merchandise purchased for resale, terms FOB shipping point.
    27   Paid $55 for postage expenses.
    28   The fund had $20.82 remaining in the petty cash box. Sorted the petty cash receipts by accounts affected and exchanged them for a check to reimburse the fund for expenditures.
    28   The petty cash fund amount is increased by $100 to a total of $400.

Required

1. Prepare the journal entry to establish the petty cash fund.
2. Prepare a petty cash payments report for February with these categories: delivery expense, mileage expense, postage expense, merchandise inventory (for transportation-in), and office supplies expense. Sort the payments into the appropriate categories and total the expenditures in each category.

Check   (3a) Cr. Cash $279.18

3. Prepare the journal entries for part 2 to both (*a*) reimburse and (*b*) increase the fund amount.

Problem 8-3A
Establish, reimburse, and adjust petty cash

P2

Dylan Co. set up a petty cash fund for payments of small amounts. The following transactions involving the petty cash fund occurred in May (the last month of the company's fiscal year).

May 1   Prepared a company check for $350 to establish the petty cash fund.
    15   Prepared a company check to replenish the fund for the following expenditures made since May 1.
       a.   Paid $109.20 for janitorial services.
       b.   Paid $89.15 for miscellaneous expenses.
       c.   Paid postage expenses of $60.90.
       d.   Paid $80.01 to *The County Gazette* (the local newspaper) for an advertisement.
       e.   Counted $16.84 remaining in the petty cash box.

16   Prepared a company check for $200 to increase the fund to $550.

31   The petty cashier reports that $390.27 cash remains in the fund. A company check is drawn to replenish the fund for the following expenditures made since May 15.

    f.   Paid postage expenses of $59.10.

    g.   Reimbursed the office manager for business mileage, $47.05.

    h.   Paid $48.58 to deliver merchandise to a customer, terms FOB destination.

31   The company decides that the May 16 increase in the fund was too large. It reduces the fund by $50, leaving a total of $500.

Required

1. Prepare journal entries to establish the fund on May 1, to replenish it on May 15 and on May 31, and to reflect any increase or decrease in the fund balance on May 16 and May 31.

Check   (1) Cr. to Cash: May 15, $333.16; May 16, $200

Analysis Component

2. Explain how the company's financial statements are affected if the petty cash fund is not replenished and no entry is made on May 31.

The following information is available to reconcile Hamilton Company's book balance of cash with its bank statement cash balance as of July 31, 2009.

a. On July 31, the company's Cash account has a $25,862 debit balance, but its July bank statement shows a $28,575 cash balance.

b. Check No. 3031 for $1,670 and Check No. 3040 for $827 were outstanding on the June 30 bank reconciliation. Check No. 3040 is listed with the July canceled checks, but Check No. 3031 is not. Also, Check No. 3065 for $611 and Check No. 3069 for $2,438, both written in July, are not among the canceled checks on the July 31 statement.

c. In comparing the canceled checks on the bank statement with the entries in the accounting records, it is found that Check No. 3056 for July rent was correctly written and drawn for $1,250 but was erroneously entered in the accounting records as $1,240.

d. A credit memorandum enclosed with the July bank statement indicates the bank collected $6,000 cash on a non-interest-bearing note for Hamilton, deducted a $30 collection fee, and credited the remainder to its account. Hamilton had not recorded this event before receiving the statement.

e. A debit memorandum for $805 lists a $795 NSF check plus a $10 NSF charge. The check had been received from a customer, Evan Shaw. Hamilton has not yet recorded this check as NSF.

f. Enclosed with the July statement is a $9 debit memorandum for bank services. It has not yet been recorded because no previous notification had been received.

g. Hamilton's July 31 daily cash receipts of $7,152 were placed in the bank's night depository on that date, but do not appear on the July 31 bank statement.

Problem 8-4A

Prepare a bank reconciliation and record adjustments

P3

mhhe.com/wildFAP19e

Required

1. Prepare the bank reconciliation for this company as of July 31, 2009.

2. Prepare the journal entries necessary to bring the company's book balance of cash into conformity with the reconciled cash balance as of July 31, 2009.

Check   (1) Reconciled balance, $31,008; (2) Cr. Note Receivable $6,000

Analysis Component

3. Assume that the July 31, 2009, bank reconciliation for this company is prepared and some items are treated incorrectly. For each of the following errors, explain the effect of the error on (i) the adjusted bank statement cash balance and (ii) the adjusted cash account book balance.

    a. The company's unadjusted cash account balance of $25,862 is listed on the reconciliation as $25,682.

    b. The bank's collection of the $6,000 note less the $30 collection fee is added to the bank statement cash balance on the reconciliation.

Problem 8-5A

Prepare a bank reconciliation and record adjustments

P3

mhhe.com/wildFAP19e

Madison Company most recently reconciled its bank statement and book balances of cash on August 31 and it reported two checks outstanding, No. 5888 for $1,089 and No. 5893 for $542. The following information is available for its September 30, 2009, reconciliation.

From the September 30 Bank Statement

PREVIOUS BALANCE	TOTAL CHECKS AND DEBITS	TOTAL DEPOSITS AND CREDITS	CURRENT BALANCE
18,500	9,799	11,463	20,164

CHECKS AND DEBITS			DEPOSITS AND CREDITS		DAILY BALANCE	
Date	No.	Amount	Date	Amount	Date	Amount
09/03	5888	1,089	09/05	1,145	08/31	18,500
09/04	5902	711	09/12	2,282	09/03	17,411
09/07	5901	1,805	09/21	4,072	09/04	16,700
09/17		631 NSF	09/25	2,323	09/05	17,845
09/20	5905	986	09/30	23 IN	09/07	16,040
09/22	5903	402	09/30	1,618 CM	09/12	18,322
09/22	5904	2,073			09/17	17,691
09/28	5907	213			09/20	16,705
09/29	5909	1,889			09/21	20,777
					09/22	18,302
					09/25	20,625
					09/28	20,412
					09/29	18,523
					09/30	20,164

From Madison Company's Accounting Records

Cash Receipts Deposited				Cash Disbursements		
Date		Cash Debit		Check No.		Cash Credit
Sept.	5	1,145		5901		1,805
	12	2,282		5902		711
	21	4,072		5903		402
	25	2,323		5904		2,037
	30	1,753		5905		986
		11,575		5906		1,003
				5907		213
				5908		378
				5909		1,889
						9,424

Cash						Acct. No. 101
Date		Explanation	PR	Debit	Credit	Balance
Aug.	31	Balance				16,869
Sept.	30	Total receipts	R12	11,575		28,444
	30	Total disbursements	D23		9,424	19,020

Additional Information

Check No. 5904 is correctly drawn for $2,073 to pay for computer equipment; however, the recordkeeper misread the amount and entered it in the accounting records with a debit to Computer Equipment and a credit to Cash of $2,037. The NSF check shown in the statement was originally received from a customer, S. Nilson, in payment of her account. Its return has not yet been recorded by the company. The credit memorandum is from the collection of a $1,640 note for Madison Company by the bank. The bank deducted a $22 collection fee. The collection and fee are not yet recorded.

Required

1. Prepare the September 30, 2009, bank reconciliation for this company.

2. Prepare the journal entries to adjust the book balance of cash to the reconciled balance.

Analysis Component

3. The bank statement reveals that some of the prenumbered checks in the sequence are missing. Describe three situations that could explain this.

Check   (1) Reconciled balance, $19,994 (2) Cr. Note Receivable $1,640

For each of these five separate cases, identify the principle(s) of internal control that is violated. Recommend what the business should do to ensure adherence to principles of internal control.

1. Latisha Tally is the company's computer specialist and oversees its computerized payroll system. Her boss recently asked her to put password protection on all office computers. Latisha has put a password in place that allows only the boss access to the file where pay rates are changed and personnel are added or deleted from the payroll.

2. Marker Theater has a computerized order-taking system for its tickets. The system is active all week and backed up every Friday night.

3. Sutton Company has two employees handling acquisitions of inventory. One employee places purchase orders and pays vendors. The second employee receives the merchandise.

4. The owner of Super Pharmacy uses a check protector to perforate checks, making it difficult for anyone to alter the amount of the check. The check protector is on the owner's desk in an office that contains company checks and is normally unlocked.

5. Lavina Company is a small business that has separated the duties of cash receipts and cash disbursements. The employee responsible for cash disbursements reconciles the bank account monthly.

PROBLEM SET B

Problem 8-1B
Analyzing internal control

C1

Music City Center had the following petty cash transactions in March of the current year.

March	5	Wrote a $300 check, cashed it, and gave the proceeds and the petty cashbox to Abby Rode, the petty cashier.
	6	Paid $16.75 COD shipping charges on merchandise purchased for resale, terms FOB shipping point. Music City uses the perpetual system to account for merchandise inventory.
	11	Paid $44.50 delivery charges on merchandise sold to a customer, terms FOB destination.
	12	Purchased file folders for $7.95 that are immediately used.
	14	Reimbursed Alys Mingle, the manager, $68 for office supplies purchased and used.
	18	Purchased printer paper for $20 that is immediately used.
	27	Paid $11.60 COD shipping charges on merchandise purchased for resale, terms FOB shipping point.
	28	Paid postage expenses of $60.
	30	Reimbursed Mingle $56.80 for business car mileage.
	31	Cash of $16.81 remained in the fund. Sorted the petty cash receipts by accounts affected and exchanged them for a check to reimburse the fund for expenditures.
	31	The petty cash fund amount is increased by $50 to a total of $350.

Problem 8-2B
Establish, reimburse, and increase petty cash

P2

Required

1. Prepare the journal entry to establish the petty cash fund.

2. Prepare a petty cash payments report for March with these categories: delivery expense, mileage expense, postage expense, merchandise inventory (for transportation-in), and office supplies expense. Sort the payments into the appropriate categories and total the expenses in each category.

3. Prepare the journal entries for part 2 to both (*a*) reimburse and (*b*) increase the fund amount.

Check   (2) Total expenses $285.60

(3a) Cr. Cash $283.19

Problem 8-3B

Establishing, reimbursing, and adjusting petty cash

P2

Lansing Co. establishes a petty cash fund for payments of small amounts. The following transactions involving the petty cash fund occurred in January (the last month of the company's fiscal year).

Jan. 3   A company check for $150 is written and made payable to the petty cashier to establish the petty cash fund.

14   A company check is written to replenish the fund for the following expenditures made since January 3.

    a.   Purchased office supplies for $17.52 that are immediately used up.

    b.   Paid $20.50 COD shipping charges on merchandise purchased for resale, terms FOB shipping point. Lansing uses the perpetual system to account for inventory.

    c.   Paid $55.30 to All-Tech for minor repairs to a computer.

    d.   Paid $19.63 for items classified as miscellaneous expenses.

    e.   Counted $35.05 remaining in the petty cash box.

15   Prepared a company check for $50 to increase the fund to $200.

31   The petty cashier reports that $29.57 remains in the fund. A company check is written to replenish the fund for the following expenditures made since January 14.

    f.   Paid $52 to *The Smart Shopper* for an advertisement in January's newsletter.

    g.   Paid $55.61 for postage expenses.

    h.   Paid $65 to FedEx for delivery of merchandise, terms FOB destination.

31   The company decides that the January 15 increase in the fund was too little. It increases the fund by another $50, leaving a total of $250.

Required

Check   (1) Cr. to Cash: Jan. 14, $114.95; Jan. 15, $50

1. Prepare journal entries to establish the fund on January 3, to replenish it on January 14 and January 31, and to reflect any increase or decrease in the fund balance on January 15 and 31.

Analysis Component

2. Explain how the company's financial statements are affected if the petty cash fund is not replenished and no entry is made on January 31.

Problem 8-4B

Prepare a bank reconciliation and record adjustments

P3

The following information is available to reconcile Gardenia Co.'s book balance of cash with its bank statement cash balance as of December 31, 2009.

a. The December 31 cash balance according to the accounting records is $13,599, and the bank statement cash balance for that date is $26,379.

b. Check No. 1273 for $1,800 and Check No. 1282 for $892, both written and entered in the accounting records in December, are not among the canceled checks. Two checks, No. 1231 for $676 and No. 1242 for $2,568, were outstanding on the most recent November 30 reconciliation. Check No. 1231 is listed with the December canceled checks, but Check No. 1242 is not.

c. When the December checks are compared with entries in the accounting records, it is found that Check No. 1267 had been correctly drawn for $1,230 to pay for office supplies but was erroneously entered in the accounting records as $1,320.

d. Two debit memoranda are enclosed with the statement and are unrecorded at the time of the reconciliation. One debit memorandum is for $805 and dealt with an NSF check for $795 received from a customer, Millard Industries, in payment of its account. The bank assessed a $10 fee for processing it. The second debit memorandum is a $99.00 charge for check printing. Gardenia did not record these transactions before receiving the statement.

e. A credit memorandum indicates that the bank collected $19,000 cash on a note receivable for the company, deducted a $14 collection fee, and credited the balance to the company's Cash account. Gardenia did not record this transaction before receiving the statement.

f. Gardenia's December 31 daily cash receipts of $10,652 were placed in the bank's night depository on that date, but do not appear on the December 31 bank statement.

Required

Check   (1) Reconciled balance, $31,771; (2) Cr. Note Receivable $19,000

1. Prepare the bank reconciliation for this company as of December 31, 2009.

2. Prepare the journal entries necessary to bring the company's book balance of cash into conformity with the reconciled cash balance as of December 31, 2009.

Analysis Component

3. Explain the nature of the communications conveyed by a bank when the bank sends the depositor (*a*) a debit memorandum and (*b*) a credit memorandum.

Tamzen Systems most recently reconciled its bank balance on April 30 and reported two checks outstanding at that time, No. 1771 for $1,037 and No. 1780 for $516. The following information is available for its May 31, 2009, reconciliation.

Problem 8-5B
Prepare a bank reconciliation and
record adjustments

P3

From the May 31 Bank Statement

PREVIOUS BALANCE	TOTAL CHECKS AND DEBITS	TOTAL DEPOSITS AND CREDITS	CURRENT BALANCE
18,500	8,041	11,611	22,070

CHECKS AND DEBITS			DEPOSITS AND CREDITS		DAILY BALANCE	
Date	No.	Amount	Date	Amount	Date	Amount
05/01	1771	1,037	05/04	1,109	04/30	18,500
05/02	1783	782	05/14	2,280	05/01	17,463
05/04	1782	1,801	05/22	4,304	05/02	16,681
05/11	1784	424	05/25	1,520 CM	05/04	15,989
05/18		688 NSF	05/26	2,398	05/11	15,565
05/25	1787	993			05/14	17,845
05/26	1785	2,056			05/18	17,157
05/29	1788	238			05/22	21,461
05/31		22 SC			05/25	21,998
					05/26	23,330
					05/29	22,092
					05/31	22,070

From Tamzen Systems' Accounting Records

Cash Receipts Deposited			
Date			Cash Debit
May	4		1,109
	14		2,280
	22		4,304
	26		2,398
	31		1,716
			11,807

Cash Disbursements		
Check No.		Cash Credit
1782		1,801
1783		782
1784		424
1785		2,056
1786		935
1787		993
1788		228
1789		371
		7,590

Cash					Acct. No. 101	
Date		Explanation	PR	Debit	Credit	Balance
Apr.	30	Balance				16,947
May	31	Total receipts	R2	11,807		28,754
	31	Total disbursements	D23		7,590	21,164

Additional Information

Check No. 1788 is correctly drawn for $238 to pay for May utilities; however, the recordkeeper misread the amount and entered it in the accounting records with a debit to Utilities Expense and a credit to Cash for $228. The bank paid and deducted the correct amount. The NSF check shown in the statement was originally received from a customer, W. Sox, in payment of her account. The company has not yet recorded its return. The credit memorandum is from a $1,540 note that the bank collected for the company. The bank deducted a $20 collection fee and deposited the remainder in the company's account. The collection and fee have not yet been recorded.

Required

Check (1) Reconciled balance, $21,964; (2) Cr. Note Receivable $1,540

1. Prepare the May 31, 2009, bank reconciliation for Tamzen Systems.

2. Prepare the journal entries to adjust the book balance of cash to the reconciled balance.

Analysis Component

3. The bank statement reveals that some of the prenumbered checks in the sequence are missing. Describe three possible situations to explain this.

SERIAL PROBLEM

Success Systems

P3

(This serial problem began in Chapter 1 and continues through most of the book. If previous chapter segments were not completed, the serial problem can begin at this point. It is helpful, but not necessary, to use the Working Papers that accompany the book.)

SP 8   Adriana Lopez receives the March bank statement for Success Systems on April 11, 2010. The March 31 bank statement shows an ending cash balance of $77,354. A comparison of the bank statement with the general ledger Cash account, No. 101, reveals the following.

a. Lopez notices that the bank erroneously cleared a $500 check against her account in March that she did not issue. The check documentation included with the bank statement shows that this check was actually issued by a company named Sierra Systems.

b. On March 25, the bank issued a $50 debit memorandum for the safety deposit box that Success Systems agreed to rent from the bank beginning March 25.

c. On March 26, the bank issued a $102 debit memorandum for printed checks that Success Systems ordered from the bank.

d. On March 31, the bank issued a credit memorandum for $33 interest earned on Success Systems' checking account for the month of March.

e. Lopez notices that the check she issued for $128 on March 31, 2010, has not yet cleared the bank.

f. Lopez verifies that all deposits made in March do appear on the March bank statement.

g. The general ledger Cash account, No. 101, shows an ending cash balance per books of $77,845 as of March 31 (prior to any reconciliation).

Required

Check (1) Adj. bank bal. $77,726

1. Prepare a bank reconciliation for Success Systems for the month ended March 31, 2010.

2. Prepare any necessary adjusting entries. Use Miscellaneous Expenses, No. 677, for any bank charges. Use Interest Revenue, No. 404, for any interest earned on the checking account for the month of March.

BEYOND THE NUMBERS

REPORTING IN ACTION

C2 A1

BTN 8-1   Refer to Best Buy's financial statements in Appendix A to answer the following.

1. For both fiscal year-ends March 3, 2007, and February 25, 2006, identify the total amount of cash and cash equivalents. Determine the percent this amount represents of total current assets, total current liabilities, total shareholders' equity, and total assets for both years. Comment on any trends.

2. For fiscal years ended March 3, 2007, and February 25, 2006, use the information in the statement of cash flows to determine the percent change between the beginning and ending year amounts of cash and cash equivalents.

3. Compute the days' sales uncollected as of March 3, 2007, and February 25, 2006. Has the collection of receivables improved? Are accounts receivable an important asset for Best Buy? Explain.

Fast Forward

4. Access Best Buy's financial statements for fiscal years ending after March 3, 2007, from its Website (BestBuy.com) or the SEC's EDGAR database (www.sec.gov). Recompute its days' sales uncollected for fiscal years ending after March 3, 2007. Compare this to the days' sales uncollected for 2007 and 2006.

BTN 8-2 Key comparative figures for **Best Buy**, **Circuit City**, and **RadioShack** follow.

($ millions)	Best Buy Current Year	Best Buy Prior Year	Circuit City Current Year	Circuit City Prior Year	RadioShack Current Year	RadioShack Prior Year
Accounts receivable	$ 548	$ 449	$ 383	$ 221	$ 248	$ 309
Net sales	35,934	30,848	12,430	11,514	4,778	5,082

COMPARATIVE ANALYSIS A1

Required

Compute days' sales uncollected for these companies for each of the two years shown. Comment on any trends for the companies. Which company has the largest percent change in days' sales uncollected?

BTN 8-3 Harriet Knox, Ralph Patton, and Marcia Diamond work for a family physician, Dr. Gwen Conrad, who is in private practice. Dr. Conrad is knowledgeable about office management practices and has segregated the cash receipt duties as follows. Knox opens the mail and prepares a triplicate list of money received. She sends one copy of the list to Patton, the cashier, who deposits the receipts daily in the bank. Diamond, the recordkeeper, receives a copy of the list and posts payments to patients' accounts. About once a month the office clerks have an expensive lunch they pay for as follows. First, Patton endorses a patient's check in Dr. Conrad's name and cashes it at the bank. Knox then destroys the remittance advice accompanying the check. Finally, Diamond posts payment to the customer's account as a miscellaneous credit. The three justify their actions by their relatively low pay and knowledge that Dr. Conrad will likely never miss the money.

ETHICS CHALLENGE C1

Required

1. Who is the best person in Dr. Conrad's office to reconcile the bank statement?
2. Would a bank reconciliation uncover this office fraud?
3. What are some procedures to detect this type of fraud?
4. Suggest additional internal controls that Dr. Conrad could implement.

BTN 8-4[B] Assume you are a business consultant. The owner of a company sends you an e-mail expressing concern that the company is not taking advantage of its discounts offered by vendors. The company currently uses the gross method of recording purchases. The owner is considering a review of all invoices and payments from the previous period. Due to the volume of purchases, however, the owner recognizes that this is time-consuming and costly. The owner seeks your advice about monitoring purchase discounts in the future. Provide a response in memorandum form.

COMMUNICATING IN PRACTICE P5

BTN 8-5 Visit the Association of Certified Fraud Examiners Website at **cfenet.com**. Find and open the file "2006 Report to the Nation." Read the two-page Executive Summary and fill in the following blanks. (The report is under its *Fraud Resource Center* tab or under its *About ACFE* tab [under Press Room and under Fraud Statistics]; we can also use the *Search* tab.)

TAKING IT TO THE NET C1 P1

1. The median loss caused by occupational frauds was $_____.
2. Nearly _____ of fraud cases caused at least $1 million in losses.
3. Companies lose __% of their annual revenues to fraud; this figure translates to $____ billion in fraud losses.
4. The median length of fraud schemes was ___ months from the time the fraud began until it was detected.
5. Companies with anonymous fraud hotlines suffered a median loss of $_____, whereas those without hotlines had a median loss of $_____.

6. The median loss suffered by companies with fewer than 100 employees was $_____ per scheme.

7. The most common frauds in small businesses involve employees _____, _____, and _____.

8. Fewer than ___% of small businesses had anonymous fraud reporting systems, and less than ___% had internal audit departments, conducted surprise audits, or conducted fraud training.

9. Fewer than ___% of the perpetrators had convictions prior to committing their frauds.

TEAMWORK IN ACTION

C1

BTN 8-6   Organize the class into teams. Each team must prepare a list of 10 internal controls a consumer could observe in a typical retail department store. When called upon, the team's spokesperson must be prepared to share controls identified by the team that have not been shared by another team's spokesperson.

ENTREPRENEURIAL DECISION

C1   P1

BTN 8-7   Review the opening feature of this chapter that highlights Dylan Lauren and Jeff Rubin, and their company **Dylan's Candy Bar.**

Required

1. List the seven principles of internal control and explain how Dylan and Jeff could implement each of them in their retail stores.

2. Do you believe that they will need to add controls as their business expands? Explain.

HITTING THE ROAD

C1

BTN 8-8   Visit an area of your college that serves the student community with either products or services. Some examples are food services, libraries, and bookstores. Identify and describe between four and eight internal controls being implemented.

GLOBAL DECISION

C2   A1

DSG

BTN 8-9   The following information is from **DSG international plc** (www.DSGiplc.com) financial statements.

(£ millions)	Current Year	Prior Year
Cash	441	618
Accounts receivable	393	370
Current assets	2,067	2,094
Total assets	3,977	4,120
Current liabilities	1,869	1,749
Shareholders' equity	1,304	1,424
Net sales	7,930	6,984

Required

1. For each year, compute the percentages that cash represents of current assets, total assets, current liabilities, and shareholders' equity. Comment on any trends in these percentages.

2. Determine the percentage change between the current and prior year cash balances.

3. Compute the days' sales uncollected at the end of both the current year and the prior year. Has the collection of receivables improved? Explain.

ANSWERS TO MULTIPLE CHOICE QUIZ

1. e; The entry follows.

Debits to expenses (or assets)	420
Cash Over and Short	5
Cash	425

2. a; recognizes cash collection of note by bank.

3. a; the bank reconciliation follows.

Bank Reconciliation November 30			
Balance per bank statement	$1,895	Balance per books	$1,742
Add: Deposit in transit	795	Add: Note collected less fee	320
Deduct: Outstanding checks	(638)	Deduct: Service charge	(10)
Reconciled balance	$2,052	Reconciled balance	$2,052

4. d; ($6,720/$84,000) × 365 = 29.2 days

5. b; The entry follows.

Merchandise Inventory*	5,880
Accounts Payable	5,880

*$6,000 × 98%

A Look Back

Chapter 8 focused on internal control and reporting for cash. We described internal control procedures and the accounting for and management of cash.

A Look at This Chapter

This chapter emphasizes receivables. We explain that they are liquid assets and describe how companies account for and report them. We also discuss the importance of estimating uncollectibles.

A Look Ahead

Chapter 10 focuses on plant assets, natural resources, and intangible assets. We explain how to account for, report, and analyze these long-term assets.

Accounting for Receivables

Chapter

Learning Objectives

CAP

Conceptual

C1 Describe accounts receivable and how they occur and are recorded. *(p. 358)*

C2 Describe a note receivable and the computation of its maturity date and interest. *(p. 368)*

C3 Explain how receivables can be converted to cash before maturity. *(p. 371)*

Analytical

A1 Compute accounts receivable turnover and use it to help assess financial condition. *(p. 372)*

LP9

Procedural

P1 Apply the direct write-off and allowance methods to account for accounts receivable. *(p. 361)*

P2 Estimate uncollectibles using methods based on sales and accounts receivable. *(p. 364)*

P3 Record the receipt of a note receivable. *(p. 369)*

P4 Record the honoring and dishonoring of a note and adjustments for interest. *(p. 370)*

Sweat Equity

"Create what the industry is missing . . . it is worth the hardships"—Kevin Plank (center)

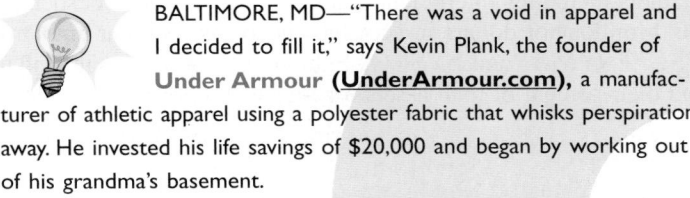 BALTIMORE, MD—"There was a void in apparel and I decided to fill it," says Kevin Plank, the founder of **Under Armour (UnderArmour.com),** a manufacturer of athletic apparel using a polyester fabric that whisks perspiration away. He invested his life savings of $20,000 and began by working out of his grandma's basement.

As sales grew, Kevin partnered with a factory in Ohio and hit it off with the factory manager, Sal Fasciana. Sal spent many evenings and weekends teaching Kevin about accounting and costs. "I said, 'OK, kid. This is the way it's going to be done,'" recalls Sal. Attention to details carried over to where Kevin learned to monitor receivables. Decisions on credit sales and policies for extending credit can make or break a start-up.

Kevin applied well what Sal taught him. He ensured that credit sales were extended to customers in good credit standing. Kevin knows his customers, including who pays and when. Says Kevin, we understand our customers—inside and out—including cash payment patterns that allow us to estimate uncollectibles and minimize bad debts. His financial report says, "We make ongoing estimates relating to the collectibility of our accounts receivable and maintain a reserve for estimated losses resulting from the inability of our customers to make required payments."

A commitment to quality customers is propelling Under Armour's sales and shattering Kevin's most optimistic goals. "It's about educating consumers . . . investing in the product." Kevin has also issued notes receivable to select employees. Both accounts and notes receivables receive his attention. His financial report states that they "review the allowance for doubtful accounts monthly."

"When I first started . . . I was a young punk who thought he knew everything," explains Kevin. Although he admits that insight and ingenuity are vital, he knows accounting reports must show profits for long-term success. "Most people out there are saying we're going to trip up at some point," says Kevin. "Our job is to prove them wrong." He might also prove Thomas Edison right: genius is 99 percent perspiration and 1 percent inspiration.

[Sources: *Under Armour Website,* January 2009; *Under Armour 10-K Report,* Filed February 2007; *Entrepreneur,* November 2003; *FastCompany,* 2005 and 2002; *USA Today,* December 2004; *Inc.com,* 2003 and 2004; *All Headline News,* August 2005; *Entrepreneur's Journey,* November 2007]

This chapter focuses on accounts receivable and short-term notes receivable. We describe each of these assets, their uses, and how they are accounted for and reported in financial statements. This knowledge helps us use accounting information to make better business decisions. It can also help in predicting future company performance and financial condition as well as in managing one's own business.

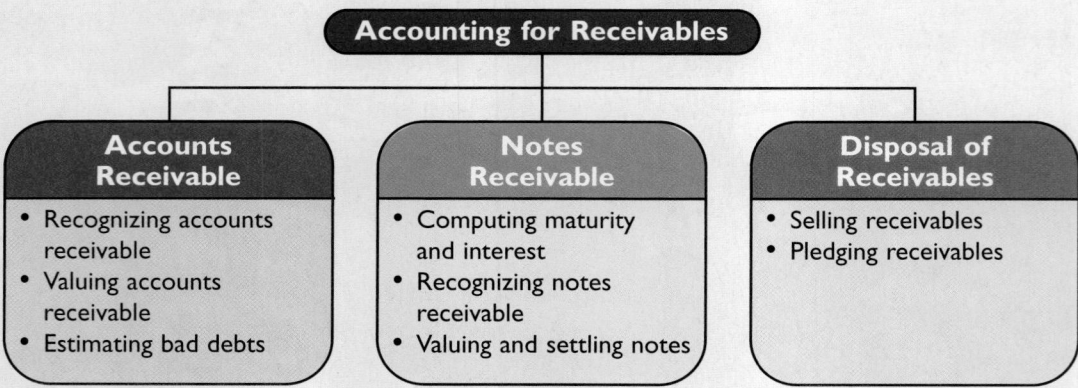

Accounting for Receivables

Accounts Receivable	Notes Receivable	Disposal of Receivables
• Recognizing accounts receivable • Valuing accounts receivable • Estimating bad debts	• Computing maturity and interest • Recognizing notes receivable • Valuing and settling notes	• Selling receivables • Pledging receivables

Accounts Receivable

Video9.1

A *receivable* is an amount due from another party. The two most common receivables are accounts receivable and notes receivable. Other receivables include interest receivable, rent receivable, tax refund receivable, and receivables from employees. **Accounts receivable** are amounts due from customers for credit sales. This section begins by describing how accounts receivable occur. It includes receivables that occur when customers use credit cards issued by third parties and when a company gives credit directly to customers. When a company does extend credit directly to customers, it (1) maintains a separate account receivable for each customer and (2) accounts for bad debts from credit sales.

Recognizing Accounts Receivable

C1 Describe accounts receivable and how they occur and are recorded.

Accounts receivable occur from credit sales to customers. The amount of credit sales has increased in recent years, reflecting several factors including an efficient financial system. Retailers such as **Limited Brands** and **Best Buy** hold millions of dollars in accounts receivable. Similar amounts are held by wholesalers such as **SUPERVALU** and **SYSCO**. Exhibit 9.1 shows recent dollar amounts of accounts receivable and their percent of total assets for four well-known companies.

EXHIBIT 9.1

Accounts Receivable for Selected Companies

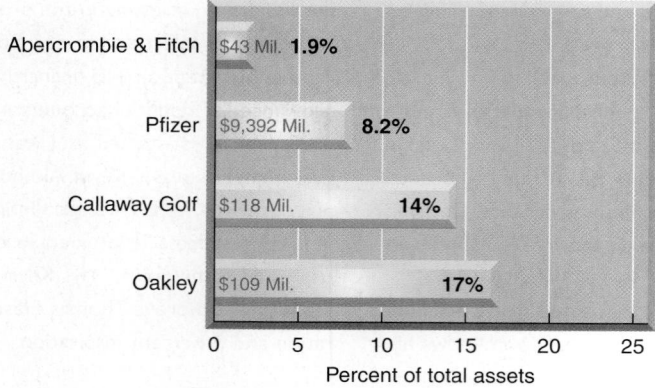

Sales on Credit   Credit sales are recorded by increasing (debiting) Accounts Receivable. A company must also maintain a separate account for each customer that tracks how much that customer purchases, has already paid, and still owes. This information provides the basis for sending bills to customers and for other business analyses. To maintain this information, companies that extend credit directly to their customers keep a separate account receivable for each one of them.

The general ledger continues to have a single Accounts Receivable account along with the other financial statement accounts, but a supplementary record is created to maintain a separate account for each customer. This supplementary record is called the *accounts receivable ledger*.

Exhibit 9.2 shows the relation between the Accounts Receivable account in the general ledger and its individual customer accounts in the accounts receivable ledger for TechCom, a small electronics wholesaler. This exhibit reports a $3,000 ending balance of TechCom's accounts receivable for June 30. TechCom's transactions are mainly in cash, but it has two major credit customers: CompStore and RDA Electronics. Its *schedule of accounts receivable* shows that the $3,000 balance of the Accounts Receivable account in the general ledger equals the total of its two customers' balances in the accounts receivable ledger.

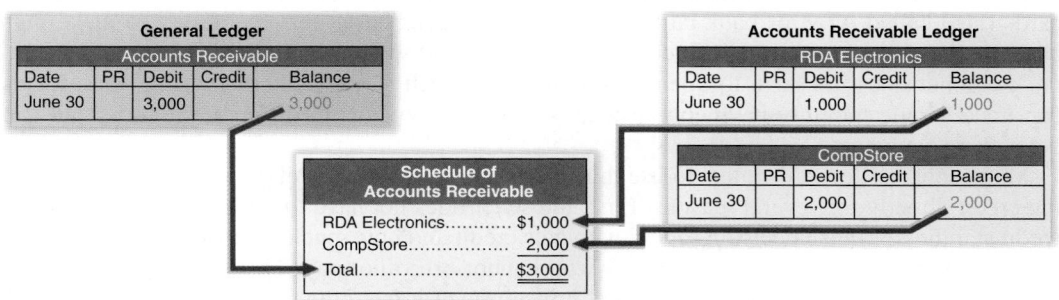

EXHIBIT 9.2

General Ledger and the Accounts Receivable Ledger (before July 1 transactions)

To see how accounts receivable from credit sales are recognized in the accounting records, we look at two transactions on July 1 between TechCom and its credit customers—see Exhibit 9.3. The first is a credit sale of $950 to CompStore. A credit sale is posted with both a debit to the Accounts Receivable account in the general ledger and a debit to the customer account in the accounts receivable ledger. The second transaction is a collection of $720 from RDA Electronics from a prior credit sale. Cash receipts from a credit customer are posted with a credit to the Accounts Receivable account in the general ledger and flow through to credit the customer account in the accounts receivable ledger. (Posting debits or credits to Accounts Receivable in two separate ledgers does not violate the requirement that debits equal credits. The equality of debits and credits is maintained in the general ledger. The accounts receivable ledger is a *supplementary* record providing information on each customer.)

EXHIBIT 9.3

Accounts Receivable Transactions

July 1	Accounts Receivable—CompStore	950	
	Sales.		950
	To record credit sales*		
July 1	Cash	720	
	Accounts Receivable—RDA Electronics		720
	To record collection of credit sales.		

Assets = Liabilities + Equity
+ 950   +950

Assets = Liabilities + Equity
+720
−720

* We omit the entry to Dr. Cost of Sales and Cr. Merchandise Inventory to focus on sales and receivables.

Exhibit 9.4 shows the general ledger and the accounts receivable ledger after recording the two July 1 transactions. The general ledger shows the effects of the sale, the collection, and the resulting balance of $3,230. These events are also reflected in the individual customer accounts: RDA Electronics has an ending balance of $280, and CompStore's ending balance is

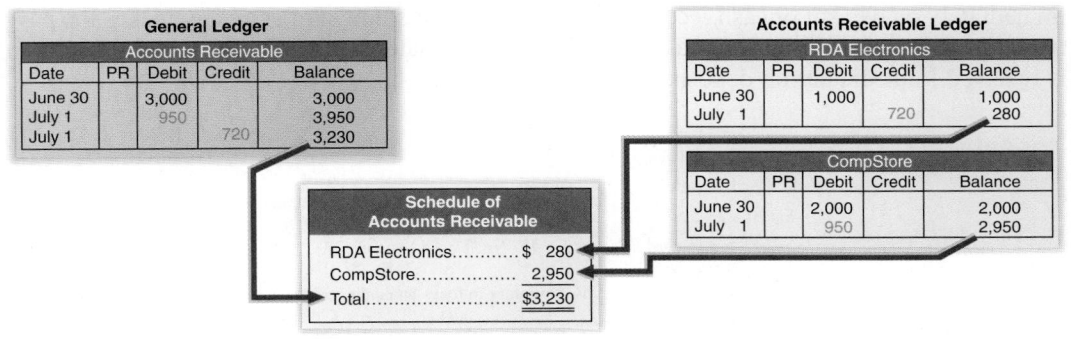

EXHIBIT 9.4

General Ledger and the Accounts Receivable Ledger (after July 1 transactions)

$2,950. The $3,230 sum of the individual accounts equals the debit balance of the Accounts Receivable account in the general ledger.

Like TechCom, many large retailers such as **Sears** and **JCPenney** sell on credit. Many also maintain their own credit cards to grant credit to approved customers and to earn interest on any balance not paid within a specified period of time. This allows them to avoid the fee charged by credit card companies. The entries in this case are the same as those for TechCom except for the possibility of added interest revenue. If a customer owes interest on a bill, we debit Interest Receivable and credit Interest Revenue for that amount.

Credit Card Sales   Many companies allow their customers to pay for products and services using third-party credit cards such as **Visa**, **MasterCard**, or **American Express**, and debit cards (also called ATM or bank cards). This practice gives customers the ability to make purchases without cash or checks. Once credit is established with a credit card company or bank, the customer does not have to open an account with each store. Customers using these cards can make single monthly payments instead of several payments to different creditors and can defer their payments.

Point: Visa USA now transacts more than $1 trillion from its credit, debit, and prepaid cards.

Many sellers allow customers to use third-party credit cards and debit cards instead of granting credit directly for several reasons. First, the seller does not have to evaluate each customer's credit standing or make decisions about who gets credit and how much. Second, the seller avoids the risk of extending credit to customers who cannot or do not pay. This risk is transferred to the card company. Third, the seller typically receives cash from the card company sooner than had it granted credit directly to customers. Fourth, a variety of credit options for customers offers a potential increase in sales volume. **Sears** historically offered credit only to customers using a Sears card but later changed its policy to permit customers to charge purchases to third-party credit card companies in a desire to increase sales. It reported: "SearsCharge increased its share of Sears retail sales even as the company expanded the payment options available to its customers with the acceptance . . . of Visa, MasterCard, and American Express in addition to the [Sears] Card."

There are guidelines in how companies account for credit card and debit card sales. Some credit cards, but mostly debit cards, credit a seller's Cash account immediately upon deposit. In this case the seller deposits a copy of each card sales receipt in its bank account just as it deposits a customer's check. Some other cards require the seller to remit a copy (often electronically) of each receipt to the card company. Until payment is received, the seller has an account receivable from the card company. In both cases, the seller pays a fee for services provided by the card company, often ranging from 1% to 5% of card sales. This charge is deducted from the credit to the seller's account or the cash payment to the seller.

Decision Insight

Debit Card vs. Credit Card   A buyer's debit card purchase reduces the buyer's cash account balance at the card company, which is often a bank. Since the buyer's cash account balance is a liability (with a credit balance) for the card company to the buyer, the card company would debit that account for a buyer's purchase—hence, the term *debit card*. A credit card reflects authorization by the card company of a line of credit for the buyer with preset interest rates and payment terms—hence, the term *credit card*. Most card companies waive interest charges if the buyer pays its balance each month.

Point: Web merchants pay twice as much in credit card association fees as other retailers because they suffer 10 times as much fraud.

The procedures used in accounting for credit card sales depend on whether cash is received immediately on deposit or cash receipt is delayed until the credit card company makes the payment. To illustrate, if TechCom has $100 of credit card sales with a 4% fee, and its $96 cash is received immediately on deposit, the entry is

Assets = Liabilities + Equity
+96   +100
                        −4

July 15	Cash	96	
	Credit Card Expense	4	
	Sales		100
	*To record credit card sales less a 4% credit card expense.**		

* We omit the entry to Dr. Cost of Sales and Cr. Merchandise Inventory to focus on credit card expense.

However, if instead TechCom must remit electronically the credit card sales receipts to the credit card company and wait for the $96 cash payment, the entry on the date of sale is

July 15	Accounts Receivable—Credit Card Co.	96	
	Credit Card Expense	4	
	Sales		100
	*To record credit card sales less 4% credit card expense.**		

Assets = Liabilities + Equity
+96   +100
                              −4

* We omit the entry to Dr. Cost of Sales and Cr. Merchandise Inventory to focus on credit card expense.

When cash is later received from the credit card company, usually through electronic funds transfer, the entry is

July 20	Cash	96	
	Accounts Receivable—Credit Card Co.		96
	To record cash receipt.		

Assets = Liabilities + Equity
+96
−96

Some firms report credit card expense in the income statement as a type of discount deducted from sales to get net sales. Other companies classify it as a selling expense or even as an administrative expense. Arguments can be made for each approach.

Point: Third-party credit card costs can be large. JCPenney recently reported third-party credit card costs exceeding $10 million.

Installment Sales and Receivables Many companies allow their credit customers to make periodic payments over several months. For example, **Ford Motor Company** reports more than $70 billion in installment receivables. The seller refers to such assets as *installment accounts receivable,* which are amounts owed by customers from credit sales for which payment is required in periodic amounts over an extended time period. Source documents for installment accounts receivable include sales slips or invoices describing the sales transactions. The customer is usually charged interest. Although installment accounts receivable can have credit periods of more than one year, they are classified as current assets if the seller regularly offers customers such terms.

Decision Maker

Entrepreneur As a small retailer, you are considering allowing customers to buy merchandise using credit cards. Until now, your store accepted only cash and checks. What analysis do you use to make this decision? [Answer—p. 376]

Quick Check
Answers—p. 376

1. In recording credit card sales, when do you debit Accounts Receivable and when do you debit Cash?
2. A company accumulates sales receipts and remits them to the credit card company for payment. When are the credit card expenses recorded? When are these expenses incurred?

Valuing Accounts Receivable—Direct Write-Off Method

When a company directly grants credit to its customers, it expects that some customers will not pay what they promised. The accounts of these customers are *uncollectible accounts,* commonly called **bad debts.** The total amount of uncollectible accounts is an expense of selling on credit. Why do companies sell on credit if they expect some accounts to be uncollectible? The answer is that companies believe that granting credit will increase total sales and net income enough to offset bad debts. Companies use two methods to account for uncollectible accounts: (1) direct write-off method and (2) allowance method. We describe both.

P1 Apply the direct write-off and allowance methods to account for accounts receivable.

Recording and Writing Off Bad Debts The **direct write-off method** of accounting for bad debts records the loss from an uncollectible account receivable when it is determined to be uncollectible. No attempt is made to predict bad debts expense. To illustrate, if TechCom

Point: Managers realize that some portion of credit sales will be uncollectible, but which credit sales are uncollectible is unknown.

determines on January 23 that it cannot collect $520 owed to it by its customer J. Kent, it recognizes the loss using the direct write-off method as follows:

Assets = Liabilities + Equity		
−520		−520

Jan. 23	Bad Debts Expense	520	
	Accounts Receivable—J. Kent		520
	To write off an uncollectible account.		

The debit in this entry charges the uncollectible amount directly to the current period's Bad Debts Expense account. The credit removes its balance from the Accounts Receivable account in the general ledger (and its subsidiary ledger).

Point: If a customer fails to pay within the credit period, most companies send out repeated billings and make other efforts to collect.

Recovering a Bad Debt   Although uncommon, sometimes an account written off is later collected. This can be due to factors such as continual collection efforts or a customer's good fortune. If the account of J. Kent that was written off directly to Bad Debts Expense is later collected in full, the following two entries record this recovery.

Assets = Liabilities + Equity		
+520		+520

Assets = Liabilities + Equity		
+520		+520
−520		

Mar. 11	Accounts Receivable—J. Kent	520	
	Bad Debts Expense		520
	To reinstate account previously written off.		
Mar. 11	Cash	520	
	Accounts Receivable—J. Kent		520
	To record full payment of account.		

Assessing the Direct Write-Off Method   Examples of companies that use the direct write-off method include **Rand Medical Billing**, **Gateway Distributors**, **Microwave Satellite Technologies**, **Frebon International**, **Slater Dome Properties**, **Interscope Technologies**, **On Line Payroll Services**, and **Sub Surface Waste Management**. The following disclosure by **Pharma-Bio Serv** is typical of the justification for this method: Bad debts are accounted for using the direct write-off method whereby an expense is recognized only when a specific account is determined to be uncollectible. The effect of using this method approximates that of the allowance method. Companies must weigh at least two accounting concepts when considering the use of the direct write-off method: the (1) matching principle and (2) materiality constraint.

Matching principle applied to bad debts.   The **matching principle** requires expenses to be reported in the same accounting period as the sales they helped produce. This means that if extending credit to customers helped produce sales, the bad debts expense linked to those sales is matched and reported in the same period. The direct write-off method usually does *not* best match sales and expenses because bad debts expense is not recorded until an account becomes uncollectible, which often occurs in a period after that of the credit sale. To match bad debts expense with the sales it produces therefore requires a company to estimate future uncollectibles.

Point: Oakley reports $15 million of bad debts expense matched against $762 million of sales in a recent year.

Materiality constraint applied to bad debts.   The **materiality constraint** states that an amount can be ignored if its effect on the financial statements is unimportant to users' business decisions. The materiality constraint permits the use of the direct write-off method when bad debts expenses are very small in relation to a company's other financial statement items such as sales and net income.

Valuing Accounts Receivable—Allowance Method

Point: Under direct write-off, expense is recorded each time an account is written off. Under the allowance method, expense is recorded with an adjusting entry equal to the total estimated uncollectibles for that period's sales.

The **allowance method** of accounting for bad debts matches the *estimated* loss from uncollectible accounts receivable against the sales they helped produce. We must use estimated losses because when sales occur, management does not know which customers will not pay their bills. This means that at the end of each period, the allowance method requires an estimate of the total bad debts expected to result from that period's sales. This method has two advantages over the direct write-off method: (1) it records estimated bad debts expense in the period when the related sales are recorded and (2) it reports accounts receivable on the balance sheet at the estimated amount of cash to be collected.

Recording Bad Debts Expense The allowance method estimates bad debts expense at the end of each accounting period and records it with an adjusting entry. TechCom, for instance, had credit sales of $300,000 during its first year of operations. At the end of the first year, $20,000 of credit sales remained uncollected. Based on the experience of similar businesses, TechCom estimated that $1,500 of its accounts receivable would be uncollectible. This estimated expense is recorded with the following adjusting entry.

Dec. 31	Bad Debts Expense	1,500	
	Allowance for Doubtful Accounts.		1,500
	To record estimated bad debts.		

Assets = Liabilities + Equity
−1,500   −1,500

The estimated Bad Debts Expense of $1,500 is reported on the income statement (as either a selling expense or an administrative expense) and offsets the $300,000 credit sales it helped produce. The **Allowance for Doubtful Accounts** is a contra asset account. A contra account is used instead of reducing accounts receivable directly because at the time of the adjusting entry, the company does not know which customers will not pay. After the bad debts adjusting entry is posted, TechCom's account balances (in T-account form) for Accounts Receivable and its Allowance for Doubtful Accounts are as shown in Exhibit 9.5.

Point: Credit approval is usually not assigned to the selling dept. because its goal is to increase sales, and it may approve customers at the cost of increased bad debts. Instead, approval is assigned to a separate credit-granting or administrative dept.

Accounts Receivable			Allowance for Doubtful Accounts		
Dec. 31	20,000			Dec. 31	1,500

EXHIBIT 9.5

General Ledger Entries after Bad Debts Adjusting Entry

The Allowance for Doubtful Accounts credit balance of $1,500 has the effect of reducing accounts receivable to its estimated realizable value. **Realizable value** refers to the expected proceeds from converting an asset into cash. Although credit customers owe $20,000 to TechCom, only $18,500 is expected to be realized in cash collections from these customers. In the balance sheet, the Allowance for Doubtful Accounts is subtracted from Accounts Receivable and is often reported as shown in Exhibit 9.6.

Point: Bad Debts Expense is also called *Uncollectible Accounts Expense.* The Allowance for Doubtful Accounts is also called *Allowance for Uncollectible Accounts.*

Current assets		
Accounts receivable	$20,000	
Less allowance for doubtful accounts	1,500	$18,500

EXHIBIT 9.6

Balance Sheet Presentation of the Allowance for Doubtful Accounts

Sometimes the Allowance for Doubtful Accounts is not reported separately. This alternative presentation is shown in Exhibit 9.7 (also see Appendix A).

Current assets	
Accounts receivable (net of $1,500 doubtful accounts)	$18,500

EXHIBIT 9.7

Alternative Presentation of the Allowance for Doubtful Accounts

Writing Off a Bad Debt When specific accounts are identified as uncollectible, they are written off against the Allowance for Doubtful Accounts. To illustrate, TechCom decides that J. Kent's $520 account is uncollectible and makes the following entry to write it off.

Jan. 23	Allowance for Doubtful Accounts	520	
	Accounts Receivable—J. Kent		520
	To write off an uncollectible account.		

Assets = Liabilities + Equity
+520
−520

Posting this write-off entry to the Accounts Receivable account removes the amount of the bad debt from the general ledger (it is also posted to the accounts receivable subsidiary ledger). The general ledger accounts now appear as in Exhibit 9.8 (assuming no other transactions affecting these accounts).

Point: The Bad Debts Expense account is not debited in the write-off entry because it was recorded in the period when sales occurred.

Accounts Receivable				Allowance for Doubtful Accounts			
Dec. 31	20,000					Dec. 31	1,500
		Jan. 23	520	Jan. 23	520		

EXHIBIT 9.8

General Ledger Entries after Write-Off

Point: In posting a write-off, the ledger's Explanation column indicates the reason for this credit so it is not misinterpreted as payment in full.

EXHIBIT 9.9

Realizable Value before and after Write-Off of a Bad Debt

The write-off does *not* affect the realizable value of accounts receivable as shown in Exhibit 9.9. Neither total assets nor net income is affected by the write-off of a specific account. Instead, both assets and net income are affected in the period when bad debts expense is predicted and recorded with an adjusting entry.

	Before Write-Off	After Write-Off
Accounts receivable	$ 20,000	$ 19,480
Less allowance for doubtful accounts	1,500	980
Estimated realizable accounts receivable	**$18,500**	**$18,500**

Recovering a Bad Debt   When a customer fails to pay and the account is written off as uncollectible, his or her credit standing is jeopardized. To help restore credit standing, a customer sometimes volunteers to pay all or part of the amount owed. A company makes two entries when collecting an account previously written off by the allowance method. The first is to reverse the write-off and reinstate the customer's account. The second entry records the collection of the reinstated account. To illustrate, if on March 11 Kent pays in full his account previously written off, the entries are

Assets = Liabilities + Equity
+520
−520

Mar. 11	Accounts Receivable—J. Kent..............	520	
	Allowance for Doubtful Accounts...........		520
	To reinstate account previously written off.		

Assets = Liabilities + Equity
+520
−520

Mar. 11	Cash......................	520	
	Accounts Receivable—J. Kent...........		520
	To record full payment of account.		

Example: If TechCom used a collection agency and paid a 35% commission on $520 collected from Kent, how is this recorded? *Answer:*
Cash 338
Collection Expense 182
  Accts. Recble.—J. Kent 520

In this illustration, Kent paid the entire amount previously written off, but sometimes a customer pays only a portion of the amount owed. A question then arises as to whether the entire balance of the account or just the amount paid is returned to accounts receivable. This is a matter of judgment. If we believe this customer will later pay in full, we return the entire amount owed to accounts receivable, but if we expect no further collection, we return only the amount paid.

Decision Insight

PayPal   PayPal is legally just a money transfer agent, but it is increasingly challenging big credit card brands—see chart. PayPal is successful because: (1) online credit card processing fees often exceed $0.15 per dollar, but PayPal's fees are under $0.10 per dollar. (2) PayPal's merchant fraud losses are under 0.2% of revenues, which compares to 1.8% for online merchants using credit cards.

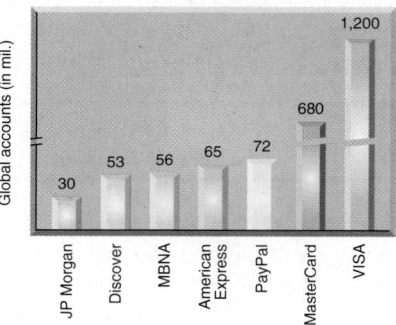

Estimating Bad Debts—Percent of Sales Method

P2 Estimate uncollectibles using methods based on sales and accounts receivable.

The allowance method requires an estimate of bad debts expense to prepare an adjusting entry at the end of each accounting period. There are two common methods. One is based on the income statement relation between bad debts expense and sales. The second is based on the balance sheet relation between accounts receivable and the allowance for doubtful accounts.

   The *percent of sales method,* also referred to as the *income statement method,* is based on the idea that a given percent of a company's credit sales for the period are uncollectible. To illustrate, assume that Musicland has credit sales of $400,000 in year 2009. Based on past experience,

Musicland estimates 0.6% of credit sales to be uncollectible. This implies that Musicland expects $2,400 of bad debts expense from its sales (computed as $400,000 × 0.006). The adjusting entry to record this estimated expense is

Point: Focus is on *credit* sales because cash sales do not produce bad debts. If cash sales are a small or stable percent of credit sales, total sales can be used.

Dec. 31	Bad Debts Expense	2,400	
	Allowance for Doubtful Accounts.		2,400
	To record estimated bad debts.		

Assets = Liabilities + Equity
−2,400   −2,400

The allowance account ending balance on the balance sheet for this method would rarely equal the bad debts expense on the income statement. This is so because unless a company is in its first period of operations, its allowance account has a zero balance only if the prior amounts written off as uncollectible *exactly* equal the prior estimated bad debts expenses. (When computing bad debts expense as a percent of sales, managers monitor and adjust the percent so it is not too high or too low.)

Point: When using the *percent of sales method* for estimating uncollectibles, the estimate of bad debts is the number used in the adjusting entry.

Estimating Bad Debts—Percent of Receivables Method

The *accounts receivable methods,* also referred to as *balance sheet methods,* use balance sheet relations to estimate bad debts—mainly the relation between accounts receivable and the allowance amount. The goal of the bad debts adjusting entry for these methods is to make the Allowance for Doubtful Accounts balance equal to the portion of accounts receivable that is estimated to be uncollectible. The estimated balance for the allowance account is obtained in one of two ways: (1) computing the percent uncollectible from the total accounts receivable or (2) aging accounts receivable.

The *percent of accounts receivable method* assumes that a given percent of a company's receivables is uncollectible. This percent is based on past experience and is impacted by current conditions such as economic trends and customer difficulties. The total dollar amount of all receivables is multiplied by this percent to get the estimated dollar amount of uncollectible accounts—reported in the balance sheet as the Allowance for Doubtful Accounts.

To illustrate, assume that Musicland has $50,000 of accounts receivable on December 31, 2009. Experience suggests 5% of its receivables are uncollectible. This means that *after* the adjusting entry is posted, we want the Allowance for Doubtful Accounts to show a $2,500 credit balance (5% of $50,000). We are also told that its beginning balance is $2,200, which is 5% of the $44,000 accounts receivable on December 31, 2008—see Exhibit 9.10.

Point: When using an accounts receivable method for estimating uncollectibles, the allowance account balance is adjusted to equal the estimate of uncollectibles.

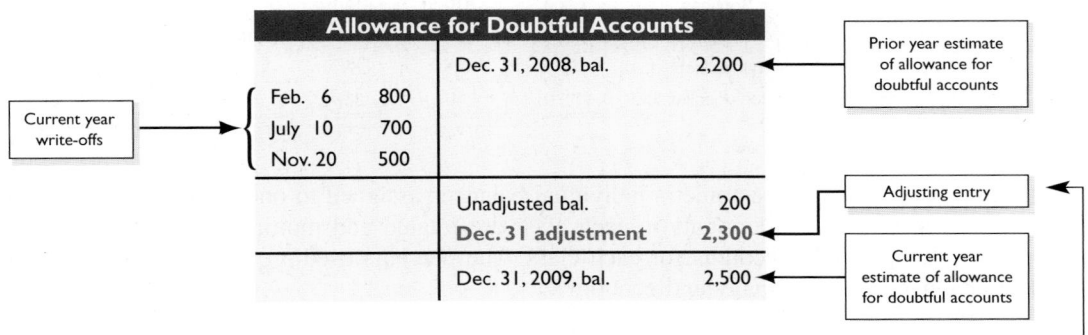

EXHIBIT 9.10

Allowance for Doubtful Accounts after Bad Debts Adjusting Entry

During 2009, accounts of customers are written off on February 6, July 10, and November 20. Thus, the account has a $200 credit balance *before* the December 31, 2009, adjustment. The adjusting entry to give the allowance account the estimated $2,500 balance is

Dec. 31	Bad Debts Expense	2,300	
	Allowance for Doubtful Accounts.		2,300
	To record estimated bad debts.		

Assets = Liabilities + Equity
−2,300   −2,300

Decision Insight

Aging Pains Experience shows that the longer a receivable is past due, the lower is the likelihood of its collection. An *aging schedule* uses this knowledge to estimate bad debts. The chart here is from a survey that reported estimates of bad debts for receivables grouped by how long they were past their due dates. Each company sets its own estimates based on its customers and its experiences with those customers' payment patterns.

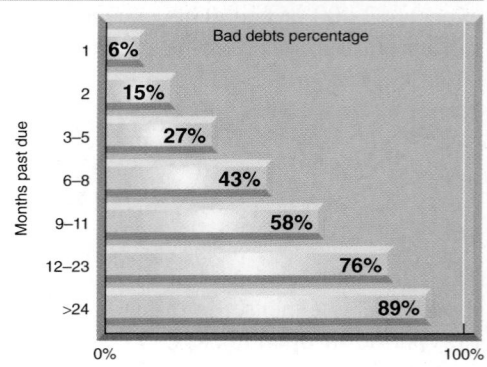

Estimating Bad Debts—Aging of Receivables Method

The **aging of accounts receivable** method uses both past and current receivables information to estimate the allowance amount. Specifically, each receivable is classified by how long it is past its due date. Then estimates of uncollectible amounts are made assuming that the longer an amount is past due, the more likely it is to be uncollectible. Classifications are often based on 30-day periods. After the amounts are classified (or aged), experience is used to estimate the percent of each uncollectible class. These percents are applied to the amounts in each class and then totaled to get the estimated balance of the Allowance for Doubtful Accounts. This computation is performed by setting up a schedule such as Exhibit 9.11.

EXHIBIT 9.11

Aging of Accounts Receivable

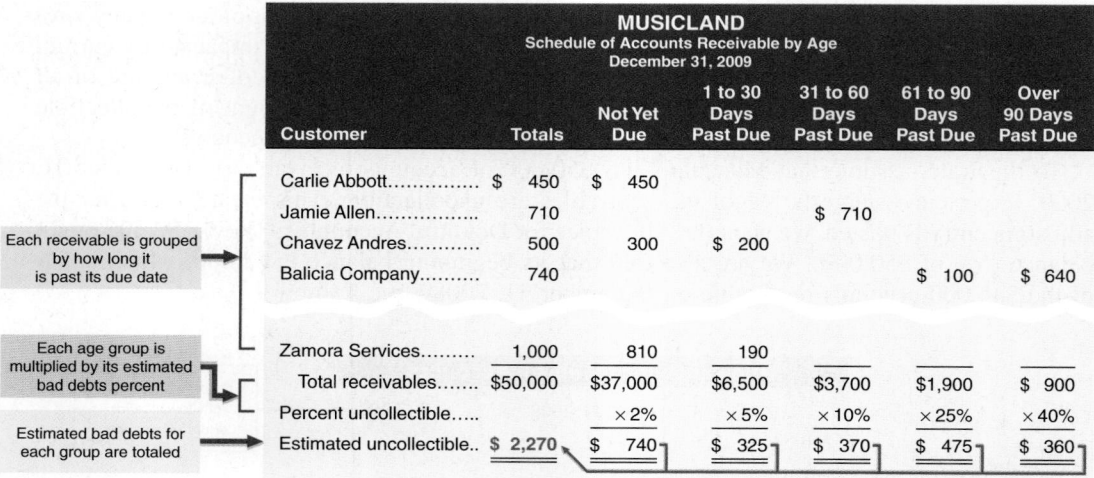

Exhibit 9.11 lists each customer's individual balances assigned to one of five classes based on its days past due. The amounts in each class are totaled and multiplied by the estimated percent of uncollectible accounts for each class. The percents used are regularly reviewed to reflect changes in the company and economy.

To explain, Musicland has $3,700 in accounts receivable that are 31 to 60 days past due. Its management estimates 10% of the amounts in this age class are uncollectible, or a total of $370 (computed as $3,700 × 10%). Similar analysis is done for each of the other four classes. The final total of $2,270 ($740 + $325 + 370 + $475 + $360) shown in the first column is the estimated balance for the Allowance for Doubtful Accounts. Exhibit 9.12 shows that since the allowance

EXHIBIT 9.12

Computation of the Required Adjustment for the Accounts Receivable Method

Unadjusted balance	$ 200 credit
Estimated balance	2,270 credit
Required adjustment	**$2,070 credit**

account has an unadjusted credit balance of $200, the required adjustment to the Allowance for Doubtful Accounts is $2,070. This yields the following end-of-period adjusting entry.

Dec. 31	Bad Debts Expense	2,070	
	Allowance for Doubtful Accounts.		2,070
	To record estimated bad debts.		

Assets = Liabilities + Equity
−2,070   −2,070

Alternatively, if the allowance account had an unadjusted *debit* balance of $500 (instead of the $200 credit balance), its required adjustment would be computed as follows.

Adjusting entry amount

Unadjusted balance	$ 500 debit
Estimated balance	2,270 credit
Required adjustment	**$ 2,770 credit**

Current year estimate of allowance for doubtful accounts

The entry to record the end-of-period adjustment for this alternative case is

Dec. 31	Bad Debts Expense	2,770	
	Allowance for Doubtful Accounts.		2,770
	To record estimated bad debts.		

Assets = Liabilities + Equity
−2,770   −2,770

The aging of accounts receivable method is an examination of specific accounts and is usually the most reliable of the estimation methods.

Estimating Bad Debts—Summary of Methods   Exhibit 9.13 summarizes the principles guiding all three estimation methods and their focus of analysis. Percent of sales, with its income statement focus, does a good job at matching bad debts expense with sales. The accounts receivable methods, with their balance sheet focus, do a better job at reporting accounts receivable at realizable value.

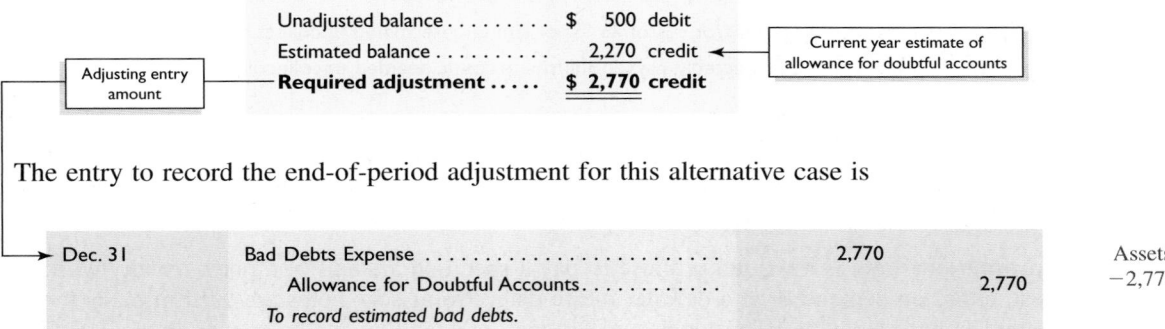

EXHIBIT 9.13

Methods to Estimate Bad Debts

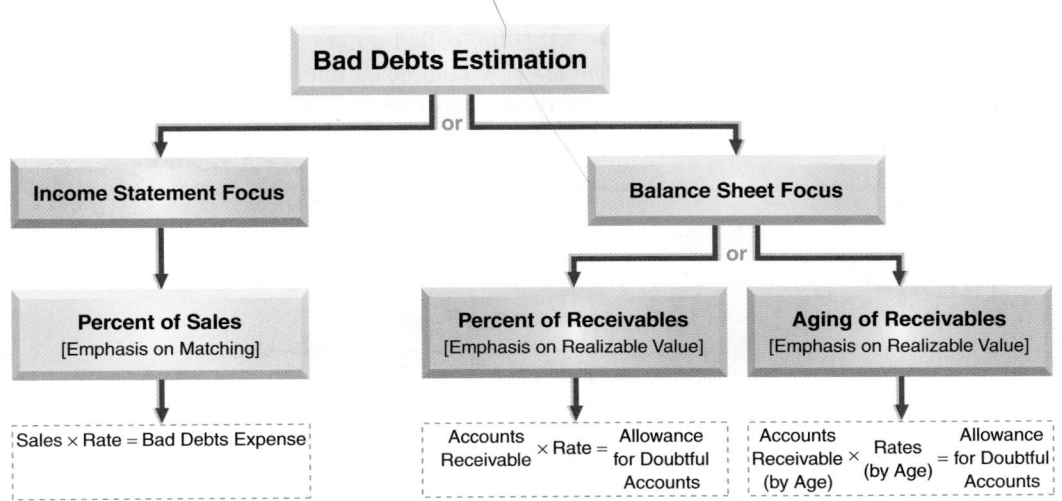

Decision Maker

Labor Union Chief   One week prior to labor contract negotiations, financial statements are released showing no income growth. A 10% growth was predicted. Your analysis finds that the company increased its allowance for uncollectibles from 1.5% to 4.5% of receivables. Without this change, income would show a 9% growth. Does this analysis impact negotiations? [Answer—p. 376]

Answers—p. 376
Quick Check

3. Why must bad debts expense be estimated if such an estimate is possible?

4. What term describes the balance sheet valuation of Accounts Receivable less the Allowance for Doubtful Accounts?

5. Why is estimated bad debts expense credited to a contra account (Allowance for Doubtful Accounts) rather than to the Accounts Receivable account?

6. SnoBoard Company's year-end balance in its Allowance for Doubtful Accounts is a credit of $440. By aging accounts receivable, it estimates that $6,142 is uncollectible. Prepare SnoBoard's year-end adjusting entry for bad debts.

7. Record entries for these transactions assuming the allowance method is used:

Jan. 10   The $300 account of customer Cool Jam is determined uncollectible.

April 12   Cool Jam unexpectedly pays in full the account deemed uncollectible on Jan. 10.

Notes Receivable

C2 Describe a note receivable and the computation of its maturity date and interest.

A **promissory note** is a written promise to pay a specified amount of money, usually with interest, either on demand or at a definite future date. Promissory notes are used in many transactions, including paying for products and services, and lending and borrowing money. Sellers sometimes ask for a note to replace an account receivable when a customer requests additional time to pay a past-due account. For legal reasons, sellers generally prefer to receive notes when the credit period is long and when the receivable is for a large amount. If a lawsuit is needed to collect from a customer, a note is the buyer's written acknowledgment of the debt, its amount, and its terms.

Exhibit 9.14 shows a simple promissory note dated July 10, 2009. For this note, Julia Browne promises to pay TechCom or to its order (according to TechCom's instructions) a specified amount of money ($1,000), called the **principal of a note,** at a definite future date (October 8, 2009). As the one who signed the note and promised to pay it at maturity, Browne is the **maker of the note.** As the person to whom the note is payable, TechCom is the **payee of the note.** To Browne, the note is a liability called a *note payable.* To TechCom, the same note is an asset called a *note receivable.* This note bears interest at 12%, as written on the note. **Interest** is the charge for using the money until its due date. To a borrower, interest is an expense. To a lender, it is revenue.

EXHIBIT 9.14

Promissory Note

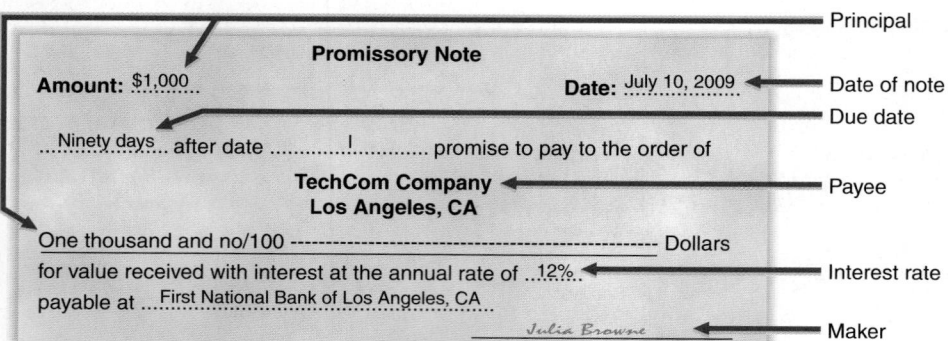

Computing Maturity and Interest

This section describes key computations for notes including the determination of maturity date, period covered, and interest computation.

Maturity Date and Period   The **maturity date of a note** is the day the note (principal and interest) must be repaid. The *period* of a note is the time from the note's (contract) date to its maturity date. Many notes mature in less than a full year, and the period they cover is often expressed in days. When the time of a note is expressed in days, its maturity date is the specified number of days after the note's date. As an example, a five-day note dated June 15 matures and is due on June 20. A 90-day note dated July 10 matures on October 8. This October 8 due date is computed as shown in Exhibit 9.15. The period of a note is sometimes expressed in months or years. When months are used, the note matures and is payable in the month of its maturity on the *same day of the month* as its original date. A nine-month note dated July 10, for instance, is payable on April 10. The same analysis applies when years are used.

Video9.1

Days in July	31
Minus the date of the note	10
Days remaining in July	21 ← July 11–31
Add days in August	31 ← Aug. 1–31
Add days in September	30 ← Sept. 1–30
Days to equal 90 days, or **maturity date of October 8**	8 ← Oct. 1–8
Period of the note in days	90

EXHIBIT 9.15

Maturity Date Computation

Interest Computation   *Interest* is the cost of borrowing money for the borrower or, alternatively, the profit from lending money for the lender. Unless otherwise stated, the rate of interest on a note is the rate charged for the use of the principal for one year. The formula for computing interest on a note is shown in Exhibit 9.16.

$$\begin{array}{ccc}\textbf{Principal}\\\textbf{of the note}\end{array} \times \begin{array}{c}\textbf{Annual}\\\textbf{interest rate}\end{array} \times \begin{array}{c}\textbf{Time expressed}\\\textbf{in years}\end{array} = \textbf{Interest}$$

EXHIBIT 9.16

Computation of Interest Formula

To simplify interest computations, a year is commonly treated as having 360 days (called the *banker's rule* in the business world and widely used in commercial transactions). **We treat a year as having 360 days for interest computations in the examples and assignments.** Using the promissory note in Exhibit 9.14 where we have a 90-day, 12%, $1,000 note, the total interest is computed as follows.

$$\$1{,}000 \times 12\% \times \frac{90}{360} = \$1{,}000 \times 0.12 \times 0.25 = \$30$$

Recognizing Notes Receivable

Notes receivable are usually recorded in a single Notes Receivable account to simplify record-keeping. The original notes are kept on file, including information on the maker, rate of interest, and due date. (When a company holds a large number of notes, it sometimes sets up a controlling account and a subsidiary ledger for notes. This is similar to the handling of accounts receivable.) To illustrate the recording for the receipt of a note, we use the $1,000, 90-day, 12% promissory note in Exhibit 9.14. TechCom received this note at the time of a product sale to Julia Browne. This transaction is recorded as follows.

P3 Record the receipt of a note receivable.

July 10*	Notes Receivable..........................	1,000	
	Sales...................................		1,000
	Sold goods in exchange for a 90-day, 12% note.		

Assets = Liabilities + Equity
+1,000   +1,000

* We omit the entry to Dr. Cost of Sales and Cr. Merchandise Inventory to focus on sales and receivables.

When a seller accepts a note from an overdue customer as a way to grant a time extension on a past-due account receivable, it will often collect part of the past-due balance in cash. This partial payment forces a concession from the customer, reduces the customer's debt (and the seller's risk), and produces a note for a smaller amount. To illustrate, assume that TechCom agreed to accept $232 in cash along with a $600, 60-day, 15% note from Jo Cook to settle

Point: Notes receivable often are a major part of a company's assets. Likewise, notes payable often are a large part of a company's liabilities.

her $832 past-due account. TechCom made the following entry to record receipt of this cash and note.

Assets = Liabilities + Equity
+232
+600
−832

Oct. 5	Cash..	232	
	Notes Receivable.............................	600	
	Accounts Receivable—J. Cook..............		832
	Received cash and note to settle account.		

Valuing and Settling Notes

P4 Record the honoring and dishonoring of a note and adjustments for interest.

Recording an Honored Note   The principal and interest of a note are due on its maturity date. The maker of the note usually *honors* the note and pays it in full. To illustrate, when J. Cook pays the note above on its due date, TechCom records it as follows.

Assets = Liabilities + Equity
+615   +15
−600

Dec. 4	Cash..	615	
	Notes Receivable		600
	Interest Revenue.............................		15
	Collect note with interest of $600 × 15% × 60/360.		

Interest Revenue, also called *Interest Earned,* is reported on the income statement.

Recording a Dishonored Note   When a note's maker is unable or refuses to pay at maturity, the note is *dishonored.* The act of dishonoring a note does not relieve the maker of the obligation to pay. The payee should use every legitimate means to collect. How do companies report this event? The balance of the Notes Receivable account should include only those notes that have not matured. Thus, when a note is dishonored, we remove the amount of this note from the Notes Receivable account and charge it back to an account receivable from its maker. To illustrate, TechCom holds an $800, 12%, 60-day note of Greg Hart. At maturity, Hart dishonors the note. TechCom records this dishonoring of the note as follows.

Point: When posting a dishonored note to a customer's account, an explanation is included so as not to misinterpret the debit as a sale on account.

Assets = Liabilities + Equity
+816   +16
−800

Oct. 14	Accounts Receivable—G. Hart	816	
	Interest Revenue.............................		16
	Notes Receivable		800
	To charge account of G. Hart for a dishonored note and interest of $800 × 12% × 60/360.		

Point: Reporting the details of notes is consistent with the **full disclosure principle,** which requires financial statements (including footnotes) to report all relevant information.

Charging a dishonored note back to the account of its maker serves two purposes. First, it removes the amount of the note from the Notes Receivable account and records the dishonored note in the maker's account. Second, and more important, if the maker of the dishonored note applies for credit in the future, his or her account will reveal all past dealings, including the dishonored note. Restoring the account also reminds the company to continue collection efforts from Hart for both principal and interest. The entry records the full amount, including interest, to ensure that it is included in collection efforts.

Recording End-of-Period Interest Adjustment   When notes receivable are outstanding at the end of a period, any accrued interest earned is computed and recorded. To illustrate, on December 16, TechCom accepts a $3,000, 60-day, 12% note from a customer in granting an extension on a past-due account. When TechCom's accounting period ends on December 31, $15 of interest has accrued on this note ($3,000 × 12% × 15/360). The following adjusting entry records this revenue.

Assets = Liabilities + Equity
+15   +15

Dec. 31	Interest Receivable..........................	15	
	Interest Revenue.............................		15
	To record accrued interest earned.		

Interest Revenue appears on the income statement, and Interest Receivable appears on the balance sheet as a current asset. When the December 16 note is collected on February 14, TechCom's entry to record the cash receipt is

Feb. 14	Cash	3,060	
	Interest Revenue		45
	Interest Receivable		15
	Notes Receivable		3,000
	Received payment of note and its interest.		

Assets = Liabilities + Equity
+3,060 +45
−15
−3,000

Total interest earned on the 60-day note is $60. The $15 credit to Interest Receivable on February 14 reflects the collection of the interest accrued from the December 31 adjusting entry. The $45 interest earned reflects TechCom's revenue from holding the note from January 1 to February 14 of the current period.

Quick Check
Answers—p. 376

8. Irwin purchases $7,000 of merchandise from Stamford on December 16, 2008. Stamford accepts Irwin's $7,000, 90-day, 12% note as payment. Stamford's accounting period ends on December 31, and it does not make reversing entries. Prepare entries for Stamford on December 16, 2008, and December 31, 2008.

9. Using the information in Quick Check 8, prepare Stamford's March 16, 2009, entry if Irwin dishonors the note.

Disposing of Receivables

Companies can convert receivables to cash before they are due. Reasons for this include the need for cash or the desire not to be involved in collection activities. Converting receivables is usually done either by (1) selling them or (2) using them as security for a loan. A recent survey shows that about 20% of companies obtain cash from either selling receivables or pledging them as security. In some industries such as textiles, apparel and furniture, this is common practice.

Selling Receivables

A company can sell all or a portion of its receivables to a finance company or bank. The buyer, called a *factor,* charges the seller a *factoring fee* and then the buyer takes ownership of the receivables and receives cash when they come due. By incurring a factoring fee, the seller receives cash earlier and can pass the risk of bad debts to the factor. The seller can also choose to avoid costs of billing and accounting for the receivables. To illustrate, if TechCom sells $20,000 of its accounts receivable and is charged a 4% factoring fee, it records this sale as follows.

C3 Explain how receivables can be converted to cash before maturity.

Global: Firms in export sales increasingly sell their receivables to factors.

Aug. 15	Cash	19,200	
	Factoring Fee Expense	800	
	Accounts Receivable		20,000
	Sold accounts receivable for cash, less 4% fee.		

Assets = Liabilities + Equity
+19,200 −800
−20,000

The accounting for sales of notes receivable is similar to that for accounts receivable. The detailed entries are covered in advanced courses.

Pledging Receivables

A company can raise cash by borrowing money and *pledging* its receivables as security for the loan. Pledging receivables does not transfer the risk of bad debts to the lender because the borrower retains ownership of the receivables. If the borrower defaults on the loan, the lender has a right to be paid from the cash receipts of the receivable when collected. To illustrate, when TechCom borrows $35,000 and pledges its receivables as security, it records this transaction as follows.

Assets = Liabilities + Equity
+35,000   +35,000

Aug. 20	Cash.......................................	35,000	
	Notes Payable		35,000
	Borrowed money with a note secured by pledging receivables.		

Since pledged receivables are committed as security for a specific loan, the borrower's financial statements disclose the pledging of them. TechCom, for instance, includes the following note with its statements: Accounts receivable of $40,000 are pledged as security for a $35,000 note payable.

Decision Insight

What's the Proper Allowance? How can we assess whether a company has properly estimated its allowance for uncollectibles? One way is to compute the ratio of the allowance account to the gross accounts receivable. When this ratio is analyzed over several consecutive periods, trends often emerge that reflect on the adequacy of the allowance amount.

Decision Analysis | Accounts Receivable Turnover

A1 | Compute accounts receivable turnover and use it to help assess financial condition.

For a company selling on credit, we want to assess both the quality and liquidity of its accounts receivable. *Quality* of receivables refers to the likelihood of collection without loss. Experience shows that the longer receivables are outstanding beyond their due date, the lower the likelihood of collection. *Liquidity* of receivables refers to the speed of collection. **Accounts receivable turnover** is a measure of both the quality and liquidity of accounts receivable. It indicates how often, on average, receivables are received and collected during the period. The formula for this ratio is shown in Exhibit 9.17.

EXHIBIT 9.17

Accounts Receivable Turnover

Video9.1

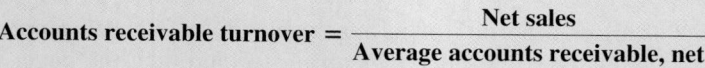
$$\text{Accounts receivable turnover} = \frac{\text{Net sales}}{\text{Average accounts receivable, net}}$$

We prefer to use net *credit* sales in the numerator because cash sales do not create receivables. However, since financial statements rarely report net credit sales, our analysis uses net sales. The denominator is the *average* accounts receivable balance, computed as (Beginning balance + Ending balance) ÷ 2. TechCom has an accounts receivable turnover of 5.1. This indicates its average accounts receivable balance is converted into cash 5.1 times during the period. Exhibit 9.18 shows graphically this turnover activity for TechCom.

EXHIBIT 9.18

Rate of Accounts Receivable Turnover for TechCom

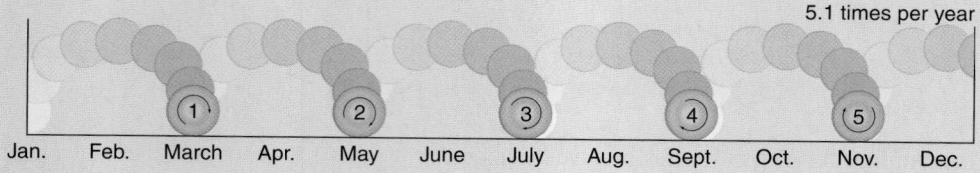

Point: Credit risk ratio is computed by dividing the Allowance for Doubtful Accounts by Accounts Receivable. The higher this ratio, the higher is credit risk.

Accounts receivable turnover also reflects how well management is doing in granting credit to customers in a desire to increase sales. A high turnover in comparison with competitors suggests that management should consider using more liberal credit terms to increase sales. A low turnover suggests management should consider stricter credit terms and more aggressive collection efforts to avoid having its resources tied up in accounts receivable.

To illustrate, we take data from two competitors: Dell and Apple. Exhibit 9.19 shows accounts receivable turnover for both companies.

Company	Figure ($ millions)	2006	2005	2004	2003
Dell	Net sales	$57,420	$55,788	$49,121	$41,327
	Average accounts receivable, net	$ 4,352	$ 3,826	$ 4,025	$ 3,111
	Accounts receivable turnover	13.2	14.6	12.2	13.3
Apple	Net sales	$19,315	$13,931	$ 8,279	$ 6,207
	Average accounts receivable, net	$ 1,074	$ 835	$ 770	$ 666
	Accounts receivable turnover	18.0	16.7	10.8	9.3

EXHIBIT 9.19

Analysis Using Accounts Receivable Turnover

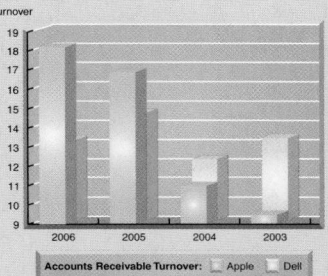

Dell's 2006 turnover is computed ($ millions) as $57,420/$4,352 = 13.2. This means that Dell's average accounts receivable balance was converted into cash 13.2 times in 2006. Its turnover declined in 2006, but is higher than that for 2004. Apple's turnover exceeds that for Dell in each of the past two years. Is either company's turnover too high? Since sales are markedly growing over this time period, each company's turnover rate does not appear to be too high. Instead, both Dell and Apple seem to be doing well in managing receivables. Turnover for competitors is generally in the range of 7 to 12 for this same period.[1]

Decision Maker

Family Physician   Your medical practice is barely profitable, so you hire a health care analyst. The analyst highlights several points including the following: *"Accounts receivable turnover is too low. Tighter credit policies are recommended along with discontinuing service to those most delayed in payments."* How do you interpret these recommendations? What actions do you take? [Answer—p. 376]

Demonstration Problem

Clayco Company completes the following selected transactions during year 2009.

DP9

July 14   Writes off a $750 account receivable arising from a sale to Briggs Company that dates to 10 months ago. (Clayco Company uses the allowance method.)

30   Clayco Company receives a $1,000, 90-day, 10% note in exchange for merchandise sold to Sumrell Company (the merchandise cost $600).

Aug. 15   Receives $2,000 cash plus a $10,000 note from JT Co. in exchange for merchandise that sells for $12,000 (its cost is $8,000). The note is dated August 15, bears 12% interest, and matures in 120 days.

Nov. 1   Completed a $200 credit card sale with a 4% fee (the cost of sales is $150). The cash is received immediately from the credit card company.

3   Sumrell Company refuses to pay the note that was due to Clayco Company on October 28. Prepare the journal entry to charge the dishonored note plus accrued interest to Sumrell Company's accounts receivable.

5   Completed a $500 credit card sale with a 5% fee (the cost of sales is $300). The payment from the credit card company is received on Nov. 9.

15   Received the full amount of $750 from Briggs Company that was previously written off on July 14. Record the bad debts recovery.

Dec. 13   Received payment of principal plus interest from JT for the August 15 note.

Required

1. Prepare journal entries to record these transactions on Clayco Company's books.

2. Prepare an adjusting journal entry as of December 31, 2009, assuming the following:
   a. Bad debts are estimated to be $20,400 by aging accounts receivable. The unadjusted balance of the Allowance for Doubtful Accounts is $1,000 debit.

---

[1] As an estimate of *average days' sales uncollected,* we compute how many days (*on average*) it takes to collect receivables as follows: 365 days ÷ accounts receivable turnover. An increase in this *average collection period* can signal a decline in customers' financial condition.

b. Alternatively, assume that bad debts are estimated using the percent of sales method. The Allowance for Doubtful Accounts had a $1,000 debit balance before adjustment, and the company estimates bad debts to be 1% of its credit sales of $2,000,000.

Planning the Solution

- Examine each transaction to determine the accounts affected, and then record the entries.
- For the year-end adjustment, record the bad debts expense for the two approaches.

Solution to Demonstration Problem

1.

Date	Account	Debit	Credit
July 14	Allowance for Doubtful Accounts	750	
	Accounts Receivable—Briggs Co.		750
	Wrote off an uncollectible account.		
July 30	Notes Receivable—Sumrell Co.	1,000	
	Sales.		1,000
	Sold merchandise for a 90-day, 10% note.		
July 30	Cost of Goods Sold.	600	
	Merchandise Inventory.		600
	To record the cost of July 30 sale.		
Aug. 15	Cash	2,000	
	Notes Receivable—JT Co.	10,000	
	Sales.		12,000
	Sold merchandise to customer for $2,000 cash and $10,000 note.		
Aug. 15	Cost of Goods Sold	8,000	
	Merchandise Inventory.		8,000
	To record the cost of Aug. 15 sale.		
Nov. 1	Cash	192	
	Credit Card Expense	8	
	Sales.		200
	To record credit card sale less a 4% credit card expense.		
Nov. 1	Cost of Goods Sold	150	
	Merchandise Inventory.		150
	To record the cost of Nov. 1 sale.		
Nov. 3	Accounts Receivable—Sumrell Co.	1,025	
	Interest Revenue.		25
	Notes Receivable—Sumrell Co.		1,000
	To charge account of Sumrell Company for a $1,000 dishonored note and interest of $1,000 × 10% × 90/360.		
Nov. 5	Accounts Receivable—Credit Card Co.	475	
	Credit Card Expense	25	
	Sales.		500
	To record credit card sale less a 5% credit card expense.		
Nov. 5	Cost of Goods Sold.	300	
	Merchandise Inventory.		300
	To record the cost of Nov. 5 sale.		
Nov. 9	Cash	475	
	Accounts Receivable—Credit Card Co.		475
	To record cash receipt from Nov. 5 sale.		
Nov. 15	Accounts Receivable—Briggs Co.	750	
	Allowance for Doubtful Accounts.		750
	To reinstate the account of Briggs Company previously written off.		

[continued on next page]

[continued from previous page]

Nov. 15	Cash	750	
	Accounts Receivable—Briggs Co.		750
	Cash received in full payment of account.		
Dec. 13	Cash	10,400	
	Interest Revenue.		400
	Note Receivable—JT Co.		10,000
	Collect note with interest of		
	$10,000 × 12% × 120/360.		

2a. Aging of accounts receivable method.

Dec. 31	Bad Debts Expense	21,400	
	Allowance for Doubtful Accounts.		21,400
	To adjust allowance account from a $1,000		
	debit balance to a $20,400 credit balance.		

2b. Percent of sales method.*

Dec. 31	Bad Debts Expense	20,000	
	Allowance for Doubtful Accounts.		20,000
	To provide for bad debts as 1% × $2,000,000		
	in credit sales.		

* For the income statement approach, which requires estimating bad debts as a percent of sales or credit sales, the Allowance account balance is *not* considered when making the adjusting entry.

Summary

C1 **Describe accounts receivable and how they occur and are recorded.** Accounts receivable are amounts due from customers for credit sales. A subsidiary ledger lists amounts owed by each customer. Credit sales arise from at least two sources: (1) sales on credit and (2) credit card sales. *Sales on credit* refers to a company's granting credit directly to customers. Credit card sales involve customers' use of third-party credit cards.

C2 **Describe a note receivable and the computation of its maturity date and interest.** A note receivable is a written promise to pay a specified amount of money at a definite future date. The maturity date is the day the note (principal and interest) must be repaid. Interest rates are normally stated in annual terms. The amount of interest on the note is computed by expressing time as a fraction of one year and multiplying the note's principal by this fraction and the annual interest rate.

C3 **Explain how receivables can be converted to cash before maturity.** Receivables can be converted to cash before maturity in three ways. First, a company can sell accounts receivable to a factor, who charges a factoring fee. Second, a company can borrow money by signing a note payable that is secured by pledging the accounts receivable. Third, notes receivable can be discounted at (sold to) a financial institution.

A1 **Compute accounts receivable turnover and use it to help assess financial condition.** Accounts receivable turnover is a measure of both the quality and liquidity of accounts receivable. The accounts receivable turnover measure indicates how often, on average, receivables are received and collected during the period. Accounts receivable turnover is computed as net sales divided by average accounts receivable.

P1 **Apply the direct write-off and allowance methods to account for accounts receivable.** The direct write-off method charges Bad Debts Expense when accounts are written off as uncollectible. This method is acceptable only when the amount of bad debts expense is immaterial. Under the allowance method, bad debts expense is recorded with an adjustment at the end of each accounting period that debits the Bad Debts Expense account and credits the Allowance for Doubtful Accounts. The uncollectible accounts are later written off with a debit to the Allowance for Doubtful Accounts.

P2 **Estimate uncollectibles using methods based on sales and accounts receivable.** Uncollectibles are estimated by focusing on either (1) the income statement relation between bad debts expense and credit sales or (2) the balance sheet relation between accounts receivable and the allowance for doubtful accounts. The first approach emphasizes the matching principle using the income statement. The second approach emphasizes realizable value of accounts receivable using the balance sheet.

P3 **Record the receipt of a note receivable.** A note received is recorded at its principal amount by debiting the Notes Receivable account. The credit amount is to the asset, product, or service provided in return for the note.

P4 **Record the honoring and dishonoring of a note and adjustments for interest.** When a note is honored, the payee debits the money received and credits both Notes Receivable and Interest Revenue. Dishonored notes are credited to Notes Receivable and debited to Accounts Receivable (to the account of the maker in an attempt to collect), and Interest Revenue is recorded for interest earned for the time the note is held.

Guidance Answers to **Decision Maker** and **Decision Ethics**

Entrepreneur   Analysis of credit card sales should weigh the benefits against the costs. The primary benefit is the potential to increase sales by attracting customers who prefer the convenience of credit cards. The primary cost is the fee charged by the credit card company for providing this service. Analysis should therefore estimate the expected increase in dollar sales from allowing credit card sales and then subtract (1) the normal costs and expenses and (2) the credit card fees associated with this expected increase in dollar sales. If your analysis shows an increase in profit from allowing credit card sales, your store should probably accept them.

Labor Union Chief   Yes, this information is likely to impact your negotiations. The obvious question is why the company markedly increased this allowance. The large increase in this allowance means a substantial increase in bad debts expense *and* a decrease in earnings. This change (coming immediately prior to labor contract discussions) also raises concerns since it reduces

the union's bargaining power for increased compensation. You want to ask management for supporting documentation justifying this increase. You also want data for two or three prior years and similar data from competitors. These data should give you some sense of whether the change in the allowance for uncollectibles is justified.

Family Physician   The recommendations are twofold. First, the analyst suggests more stringent screening of patients' credit standing. Second, the analyst suggests dropping patients who are most overdue in payments. You are likely bothered by both suggestions. They are probably financially wise recommendations, but you are troubled by eliminating services to those less able to pay. One alternative is to follow the recommendations while implementing a care program directed at patients less able to pay for services. This allows you to continue services to patients less able to pay and lets you discontinue services to patients able but unwilling to pay.

Guidance Answers to **Quick Checks**

1. If cash is immediately received when credit card sales receipts are deposited, the company debits Cash at the time of sale. If the company does not receive payment until after it submits receipts to the credit card company, it debits Accounts Receivable at the time of sale. (Cash is later debited when payment is received from the credit card company.)

2. Credit card expenses are usually *recorded* and *incurred* at the time of their related sales, not when cash is received from the credit card company.

3. If possible, bad debts expense must be matched with the sales that gave rise to the accounts receivable. This requires that companies estimate future bad debts at the end of each period before they learn which accounts are uncollectible.

4. Realizable value (also called *net realizable value*).

5. The estimated amount of bad debts expense cannot be credited to the Accounts Receivable account because the specific customer accounts that will prove uncollectible cannot yet be identified and removed from the accounts receivable subsidiary ledger. Moreover, if only the Accounts Receivable account is credited, its balance would not equal the sum of its subsidiary account balances.

6.

Dec. 31	Bad Debts Expense	5,702	
	Allowance for Doubtful Accounts		5,702

7.

Jan. 10	Allowance for Doubtful Accounts	300	
	Accounts Receivable—Cool Jam		300
Apr. 12	Accounts Receivable—Cool Jam	300	
	Allowance for Doubtful Accounts		300
Apr. 12	Cash	300	
	Accounts Receivable—Cool Jam		300

8.

Dec. 16	Note Receivable—Irwin	7,000	
	Sales		7,000
Dec. 31	Interest Receivable	35	
	Interest Revenue		35
	($7,000 × 12% × 15/360)		

9.

Mar. 16	Accounts Receivable—Irwin	7,210	
	Interest Revenue		175
	Interest Receivable		35
	Notes Receivable—Irwin		7,000

Key Terms

Key Terms are available at the book's Website for learning and testing in an online Flashcard Format.

Accounts receivable (p. 358)
Accounts receivable turnover (p. 372)
Aging of accounts receivable (p. 366)
Allowance for Doubtful Accounts (p. 363)
Allowance method (p. 362)
Bad debts (p. 361)

Direct write-off method (p. 361)
Interest (p. 368)
Maker of the note (p. 368)
Matching principle (p. 362)
Materiality constraint (p. 362)
Maturity date of a note (p. 368)

Payee of the note (p. 368)
Principal of a note (p. 368)
Promissory note (or **note**) (p. 368)
Realizable value (p. 363)

Multiple Choice Quiz   Answers on p. 389   **mhhe.com/wildFAP19e**

Additional Quiz Questions are available at the book's Website.

1. A company's Accounts Receivable balance at its December 31 year-end is $125,650, and its Allowance for Doubtful Accounts has a credit balance of $328 before year-end adjustment. Its net sales are $572,300. It estimates that 4% of outstanding accounts receivable are uncollectible. What amount of Bad Debts Expense is recorded at December 31?
  a. $5,354
  b. $328
  c. $5,026
  d. $4,698
  e. $34,338

2. A company's Accounts Receivable balance at its December 31 year-end is $489,300, and its Allowance for Doubtful Accounts has a debit balance of $554 before year-end adjustment. Its net sales are $1,300,000. It estimates that 6% of outstanding accounts receivable are uncollectible. What amount of Bad Debts Expense is recorded at December 31?
  a. $29,912
  b. $28,804
  c. $78,000
  d. $29,358
  e. $554

3. Total interest to be earned on a $7,500, 5%, 90-day note is
  a. $93.75
  b. $375.00
  c. $1,125.00
  d. $31.25
  e. $125.00

Quiz9

4. A company receives a $9,000, 8%, 60-day note. The maturity value of the note is
  a. $120
  b. $9,000
  c. $9,120
  d. $720
  e. $9,720

5. A company has net sales of $489,600 and average accounts receivable of $40,800. What is its accounts receivable turnover?
  a. 0.08
  b. 30.41
  c. 1,341.00
  d. 12.00
  e. 111.78

Discussion Questions

1. How do sellers benefit from allowing their customers to use credit cards?

2. Why does the direct write-off method of accounting for bad debts usually fail to match revenues and expenses?

3. Explain the accounting constraint of materiality.

4. Explain why writing off a bad debt against the Allowance for Doubtful Accounts does not reduce the estimated realizable value of a company's accounts receivable.

5. Why does the Bad Debts Expense account usually not have the same adjusted balance as the Allowance for Doubtful Accounts?

6. Why might a business prefer a note receivable to an account receivable?

7. Refer to the financial statements of **Best Buy** in Appendix A. In its presentation of accounts receivable, Best Buy does not mention uncollectible accounts, nor does it list its receivables as "net." Why do you believe that Best Buy does not include information about uncollectible accounts?

8. Refer to the balance sheet of **Circuit City** in Appendix A. Does it use the direct write-off method or allowance method to account for doubtful accounts? What is the realizable value of its accounts receivable as of February 28, 2007?

9. Refer to the financial statements of **Apple** in Appendix A. What are Apple's gross accounts receivable at September 30, 2006? What percentage of its accounts receivable does Apple believe to be uncollectible at September 30, 2006?

Denotes Discussion Questions that involve decision making.

McGraw-Hill's
HOMEWORK MANAGER®   Available with McGraw-Hill's Homework Manager

Prepare journal entries for the following credit card sales transactions (the company uses the perpetual inventory system).

1. Sold $16,000 of merchandise, that cost $7,000, on MasterCard credit cards. The net cash receipts from sales are immediately deposited in the seller's bank account. MasterCard charges a 4% fee.

2. Sold $18,000 of merchandise, that cost $7,800, on an assortment of credit cards. Net cash receipts are received 5 days later, and a 3% fee is charged.

QUICK STUDY

QS 9-1
Credit card sales

C1

QS 9-2
Allowance method for bad debts
P1

Kordas Corp. uses the allowance method to account for uncollectibles. On October 31, it wrote off a $750 account of a customer, D. Elwick. On December 9, it receives a $400 payment from Elwick.

1. Prepare the journal entry or entries for October 31.

2. Prepare the journal entry or entries for December 9; assume no additional money is expected from Elwick.

QS 9-3
Percent of accounts receivable method
P1

Darius Company's year-end unadjusted trial balance shows accounts receivable of $95,000, allowance for doubtful accounts of $550 (credit), and sales of $350,000. Uncollectibles are estimated to be 1.5% of accounts receivable.

1. Prepare the December 31 year-end adjusting entry for uncollectibles.

2. What amount would have been used in the year-end adjusting entry if the allowance account had a year-end unadjusted debit balance of $150?

QS 9-4
Percent of sales method   P2

Assume the same facts as in QS 9-3, except that Darius estimates uncollectibles as 0.5% of sales. Prepare the December 31 year-end adjusting entry for uncollectibles.

QS 9-5
Note receivable
P3 P4

On August 2, 2009, Passat Co. receives a $9,000, 90-day, 6% note from customer Dee Kissick as payment on her $9,000 account. Prepare Passat's journal entries for August 2 and for the note's maturity date assuming the note is honored by Kissick.

QS 9-6
Note receivable
C2 P4

Marlin Company's December 31 year-end unadjusted trial balance shows a $24,000 balance in Notes Receivable. This balance is from one 6% note dated December 1, with a period of 45 days. Prepare any necessary journal entries for December 31 and for the note's maturity date assuming it is honored.

QS 9-7
Accounts receivable turnover

A1

The following data are taken from the comparative balance sheets of Despina Company. Compute and interpret its accounts receivable turnover for year 2009 (competitors average a turnover of 7.5).

	2009	2008
Accounts receivable, net	$138,500	$153,400
Net sales	910,600	854,200

Available with McGraw-Hill's Homework Manager   McGraw-Hill's HOMEWORK MANAGER®

EXERCISES

Exercise 9-1
Accounting for credit card sales
C1

Hue Company uses the perpetual inventory system and allows customers to use two credit cards in charging purchases. With the Omni Bank Card, Hue receives an immediate credit to its account when it deposits sales receipts. Omni assesses a 4% service charge for credit card sales. The second credit card that Hue accepts is the Continental Card. Hue sends its accumulated receipts to Continental on a weekly basis and is paid by Continental about a week later. Continental assesses a 2.5% charge on sales for using its card. Prepare journal entries to record the following selected credit card transactions of Hue Company.

Apr. 8 Sold merchandise for $5,600 (that had cost $4,138) and accepted the customer's Omni Bank Card. The Omni receipts are immediately deposited in Hue's bank account.
    12 Sold merchandise for $6,000 (that had cost $4,400) and accepted the customer's Continental Card. Transferred $6,000 of credit card receipts to Continental, requesting payment.
    20 Received Continental's check for the April 12 billing, less the service charge.

Exercise 9-2
Accounts receivable subsidiary ledger; schedule of accounts receivable
C1

Beachum Company recorded the following selected transactions during November 2009.

Nov. 5	Accounts Receivable—Ski Shop	5,817	
	Sales.		5,817
10	Accounts Receivable—Welcome Enterprises	1,774	
	Sales.		1,774
13	Accounts Receivable—Kit Ronin.	1,040	
	Sales.		1,040
21	Sales Returns and Allowances	268	
	Accounts Receivable—Kit Ronin		268
30	Accounts Receivable—Ski Shop	3,698	
	Sales.		3,698

1. Open a general ledger having T-accounts for Accounts Receivable, Sales, and Sales Returns and Allowances. Also open an accounts receivable subsidiary ledger having a T-account for each customer. Post these entries to both the general ledger and the accounts receivable ledger.

2. Prepare a schedule of accounts receivable (see Exhibit 9.4) and compare its total with the balance of the Accounts Receivable controlling account as of November 30.

Check   Accounts Receivable ending balance, $12,061

At year-end (December 31), Terner Company estimates its bad debts as 0.6% of its annual credit sales of $858,000. Terner records its Bad Debts Expense for that estimate. On the following February 1, Terner decides that the $429 account of D. Fidel is uncollectible and writes it off as a bad debt. On June 5, Fidel unexpectedly pays the amount previously written off. Prepare the journal entries of Terner to record these transactions and events of December 31, February 1, and June 5.

Exercise 9-3
Percent of sales method; write-off

P1 P2

At each calendar year-end, Rivka Supply Co. uses the percent of accounts receivable method to estimate bad debts. On December 31, 2009, it has outstanding accounts receivable of $139,500, and it estimates that 2% will be uncollectible. Prepare the adjusting entry to record bad debts expense for year 2009 under the assumption that the Allowance for Doubtful Accounts has (*a*) a $2,371 credit balance before the adjustment and (*b*) a $487 debit balance before the adjustment.

Exercise 9-4
Percent of accounts receivable method

P1 P2

Paloma Company estimates uncollectible accounts using the allowance method at December 31. It prepared the following aging of receivables analysis.

Exercise 9-5
Aging of receivables method

P1 P2

	Total	0	1 to 30	31 to 60	61 to 90	Over 90
				Days Past Due		
Accounts receivable	$95,000	$66,000	$15,000	$6,000	$3,000	$5,000
Percent uncollectible		1%	2%	4%	7%	12%

a. Estimate the balance of the Allowance for Doubtful Accounts using the aging of accounts receivable method.

b. Prepare the adjusting entry to record Bad Debts Expense using the estimate from part *a*. Assume the unadjusted balance in the Allowance for Doubtful Accounts is a $300 debit.

c. Prepare the adjusting entry to record Bad Debts Expense using the estimate from part *a*. Assume the unadjusted balance in the Allowance for Doubtful Accounts is a $200 credit.

Refer to the information in Exercise 9-5 to complete the following requirements.

a. Estimate the balance of the Allowance for Doubtful Accounts assuming the company uses 2% of total accounts receivable to estimate uncollectibles, instead of the aging of receivables method.

b. Prepare the adjusting entry to record Bad Debts Expense using the estimate from part *a*. Assume the unadjusted balance in the Allowance for Doubtful Accounts is a $300 debit.

c. Prepare the adjusting entry to record Bad Debts Expense using the estimate from part *a*. Assume the unadjusted balance in the Allowance for Doubtful Accounts is a $200 credit.

Exercise 9-6
Percent of receivables method

P1 P2

Refer to the information in Exercise 9-5 to complete the following requirements.

a. On February 1 of the next period, the company determined that $950 in customer accounts is uncollectible; specifically, $200 for Laguna Co. and $750 for Malibu Co. Prepare the journal entry to write off those accounts.

b. On June 5 of that next period, the company unexpectedly received a $200 payment on a customer account, Laguna Company, that had previously been written off in part *a*. Prepare the entries necessary to reinstate the account and to record the cash received.

Exercise 9-7
Writing off receivables

P1 P2

At December 31, Bowie Company reports the following results for its calendar-year.

Exercise 9-8
Estimating bad debts

P1 P2

Cash sales	$400,000
Credit sales	300,000

Its year-end unadjusted trial balance includes the following items.

Accounts receivable	$65,000 debit
Allowance for doubtful accounts	1,000 debit

Check   Dr. Bad Debts Expense:
(a) $6,000

a. Prepare the adjusting entry to record Bad Debts Expense assuming uncollectibles are estimated to be 2% of credit sales.

b. Prepare the adjusting entry to record Bad Debts Expense assuming uncollectibles are estimated to be 1% of total sales.

(c) $6,200

c. Prepare the adjusting entry to record Bad Debts Expense assuming uncollectibles are estimated to be 8% of year-end accounts receivable.

Exercise 9-9
Selling and pledging accounts receivable

C3

On June 30, Twain Co. has $145,600 of accounts receivable. Prepare journal entries to record the following selected July transactions. Also prepare any footnotes to the July 31 financial statements that result from these transactions. (The company uses the perpetual inventory system.)

July	4	Sold $7,160 of merchandise (that had cost $4,582) to customers on credit.
	9	Sold $20,300 of accounts receivable to Main Bank. Main charges a 5% factoring fee.
	17	Received $3,938 cash from customers in payment on their accounts.
	27	Borrowed $11,000 cash from Main Bank, pledging $14,700 of accounts receivable as security for the loan.

Exercise 9-10
Honoring a note

P4

Prepare journal entries to record these selected transactions for Alvarez Company.

Nov.	1	Accepted a $15,000, 180-day, 7% note dated November 1 from Carlos Cruz in granting a time extension on his past-due account receivable.
Dec.	31	Adjusted the year-end accounts for the accrued interest earned on the Cruz note.
Apr.	30	Cruz honors his note when presented for payment; February has 28 days for the current year.

Exercise 9-11
Dishonoring a note

P4

Prepare journal entries to record the following selected transactions of Calio Company.

Mar.	21	Accepted a $17,200, 180-day, 7% note dated March 21 from James Penn in granting a time extension on his past-due account receivable.
Sept.	17	Penn dishonors his note when it is presented for payment.
Dec.	31	After exhausting all legal means of collection, Calio Company writes off Penn's account against the Allowance for Doubtful Accounts.

Exercise 9-12
Notes receivable transactions and entries

C2 P3 P4

Check   Dec. 31, Cr. Interest
Revenue $63

Feb. 11, Dr. Cash $14,210

June 1, Dr. Cash $10,225

Prepare journal entries for the following selected transactions of Hirona Company.

2008

Dec.	13	Accepted a $14,000, 60-day, 9% note dated December 13 in granting Allie Sumera a time extension on her past-due account receivable.
	31	Prepared an adjusting entry to record the accrued interest on the Sumera note.

2009

Feb.	11	Received Sumera's payment for principal and interest on the note dated December 13.
Mar.	3	Accepted a $10,000, 9%, 90-day note dated March 3 in granting a time extension on the past-due account receivable of Kudak Company.
	17	Accepted a $9,000, 30-day, 8% note dated March 17 in granting Rod Burgess a time extension on his past-due account receivable.
Apr.	16	Burgess dishonors his note when presented for payment.
May	1	Wrote off the Burgess account against the Allowance for Doubtful Accounts.
June	1	Received the Kudak payment for principal and interest on the note dated March 3.

The following information is from the annual financial statements of Lucilla Company. Compute its accounts receivable turnover for 2008 and 2009. Compare the two years results and give a possible explanation for any change (competitors average a turnover of 7).

Exercise 9-13
Accounts receivable turnover

A1

	2009	2008	2007
Net sales	$262,000	$193,000	$245,000
Accounts receivable, net (year-end)	42,700	40,500	37,200

McGraw-Hill's
HOMEWORK
MANAGER®   Available with McGraw-Hill's Homework Manager

PROBLEM SET A

Bantay Co. allows select customers to make purchases on credit. Its other customers can use either of two credit cards: Zisa or Access. Zisa deducts a 3.5% service charge for sales on its credit card and credits the bank account of Bantay immediately when credit card receipts are deposited. Bantay deposits the Zisa credit card receipts each business day. When customers use Access credit cards, Bantay accumulates the receipts for several days before submitting them to Access for payment. Access deducts a 2.5% service charge and usually pays within one week of being billed. Bantay completes the following transactions in June. (The terms of all credit sales are 2/15, n/30, and all sales are recorded at the gross price.)

Problem 9-1A
Sales on account and credit card sales

C1

June 4 Sold $700 of merchandise (that had cost $220) on credit to Alfredia Bullaro.
5 Sold $8,400 of merchandise (that had cost $4,300) to customers who used their Zisa cards.
6 Sold $6,000 of merchandise (that had cost $3,680) to customers who used their Access cards.
8 Sold $4,480 of merchandise (that had cost $2,600) to customers who used their Access cards.
10 Submitted Access card receipts accumulated since June 6 to the credit card company for payment.
13 Wrote off the account of Trenton Wanek against the Allowance for Doubtful Accounts. The $467 balance in Wanek's account stemmed from a credit sale in October of last year.
17 Received the amount due from Access.
18 Received Bullaro's check in full payment for the purchase of June 4.

Check June 17, Dr. Cash $10,218

Required

Prepare journal entries to record the preceding transactions and events. (The company uses the perpetual inventory system. Round amounts to the nearest dollar.)

Ming Company began operations on January 1, 2008. During its first two years, the company completed a number of transactions involving sales on credit, accounts receivable collections, and bad debts. These transactions are summarized as follows.

Problem 9-2A
Accounts receivable transactions and bad debts adjustments

C1 P1 P2

2008

a. Sold $1,347,700 of merchandise (that had cost $982,500) on credit, terms n/30.
b. Wrote off $20,676 of uncollectible accounts receivable.
c. Received $671,100 cash in payment of accounts receivable.
d. In adjusting the accounts on December 31, the company estimated that 1.3% of accounts receivable will be uncollectible.

Check (d) Dr. Bad Debts Expense $29,203

2009

e. Sold $1,517,800 of merchandise (that had cost $1,302,200) on credit, terms n/30.
f. Wrote off $32,624 of uncollectible accounts receivable.
g. Received $1,118,100 cash in payment of accounts receivable.
h. In adjusting the accounts on December 31, the company estimated that 1.3% of accounts receivable will be uncollectible.

(h) Dr. Bad Debts Expense $37,396

Required

Prepare journal entries to record Ming's 2008 and 2009 summarized transactions and its year-end adjustments to record bad debts expense. (The company uses the perpetual inventory system. Round amounts to the nearest dollar.)

Problem 9-3A
Estimating and reporting bad debts

P1   P2

At December 31, 2009, Vizarro Company reports the following results for its calendar-year.

Cash sales	$2,184,700
Credit sales	3,720,000

In addition, its unadjusted trial balance includes the following items.

Accounts receivable	$1,127,500 debit
Allowance for doubtful accounts	29,030 debit

Required

1. Prepare the adjusting entry for Vizarro Co. to recognize bad debts under each of the following independent assumptions.

   a. Bad debts are estimated to be 1.5% of credit sales.

   b. Bad debts are estimated to be 1% of total sales.

   c. An aging analysis estimates that 3% of year-end accounts receivable are uncollectible.

2. Show how Accounts Receivable and the Allowance for Doubtful Accounts appear on its December 31, 2009, balance sheet given the facts in part 1a.

3. Show how Accounts Receivable and the Allowance for Doubtful Accounts appear on its December 31, 2009, balance sheet given the facts in part 1c.

Check   Bad Debts Expense:
(1a) $55,800, (1c) $62,855

Problem 9-4A
Aging accounts receivable and accounting for bad debts

P1   P2

Ghosh Company has credit sales of $2.8 million for year 2009. On December 31, 2009, the company's Allowance for Doubtful Accounts has an unadjusted credit balance of $22,800. Ghosh prepares a schedule of its December 31, 2009, accounts receivable by age. On the basis of past experience, it estimates the percent of receivables in each age category that will become uncollectible. This information is summarized here.

File   Edit   View   Insert   Format   Tools   Data   Accounting   Window   Help

December 31, 2009 Accounts Receivable	Age of Accounts Receivable	Expected Percent Uncollectible
$784,000	Not yet due	1.25%
380,200	1 to 30 days past due	2.00
81,800	31 to 60 days past due	6.50
52,000	61 to 90 days past due	32.75
13,000	Over 90 days past due	68.00

Required

1. Estimate the required balance of the Allowance for Doubtful Accounts at December 31, 2009, using the aging of accounts receivable method.

2. Prepare the adjusting entry to record bad debts expense at December 31, 2009.

Check   (2) Dr. Bad Debts Expense $25,791

Analysis Component

3. On June 30, 2010, Ghosh Company concludes that a customer's $4,750 receivable (created in 2009) is uncollectible and that the account should be written off. What effect will this action have on Ghosh's 2010 net income? Explain.

Problem 9-5A
Analyzing and journalizing notes receivable transactions

C2   C3   P3   P4

The following selected transactions are from Chantay Company.

2008

Dec. 16   Accepted a $14,400, 60-day, 8% note dated this day in granting Adam Bakko a time extension on his past-due account receivable.

    31   Made an adjusting entry to record the accrued interest on the Bakko note.

2009

Feb.	14	Received Bakko's payment of principal and interest on the note dated December 16.	
Mar.	2	Accepted an $8,000, 9%, 90-day note dated this day in granting a time extension on the past-due account receivable from Mayday Co.	
	17	Accepted a $2,200, 30-day, 6% note dated this day in granting Carrie Kadin a time extension on her past-due account receivable.	
Apr.	16	Kadin dishonored her note when presented for payment.	
June	2	Mayday Co. refuses to pay the note that was due to Chantay Co. on May 31. Prepare the journal entry to charge the dishonored note plus accrued interest to Mayday Co.'s accounts receivable.	
July	17	Received payment from Mayday Co. for the maturity value of its dishonored note plus interest for 46 days beyond maturity at 9%.	
Aug.	7	Accepted an $8,400, 90-day, 12% note dated this day in granting a time extension on the past-due account receivable of Trenton Co.	
Sept.	3	Accepted a $3,335, 60-day, 9% note dated this day in granting Collin Marin a time extension on his past-due account receivable.	
Nov.	2	Received payment of principal plus interest from Marin for the September 3 note.	
Nov.	5	Received payment of principal plus interest from Trenton for the August 7 note.	
Dec.	1	Wrote off the Carrie Kadin account against Allowance for Doubtful Accounts.	

Check Feb. 14, Cr. Interest
Revenue $144

June 2, Cr. Interest
Revenue $180

Nov. 2, Cr. Interest
Revenue $50

Required

1. Prepare journal entries to record these transactions and events. (Round amounts to the nearest dollar.)

Analysis Component

2. What reporting is necessary when a business pledges receivables as security for a loan and the loan is still outstanding at the end of the period? Explain the reason for this requirement and the accounting principle being satisfied.

Marbus Co. allows select customers to make purchases on credit. Its other customers can use either of two credit cards: Commerce Bank or Aztec. Commerce Bank deducts a 2% service charge for sales on its credit card and immediately credits the bank account of Marbus when credit card receipts are deposited. Marbus deposits the Commerce Bank credit card receipts each business day. When customers use the Aztec card, Marbus accumulates the receipts for several days and then submits them to Aztec for payment. Aztec deducts a 1% service charge and usually pays within one week of being billed. Marbus completed the following transactions in August (terms of all credit sales are 2/15, n/30; and all sales are recorded at the gross price).

PROBLEM SET B

Problem 9-1B
Sales on account and credit card sales

C1

Aug.	4	Sold $600 of merchandise (that had cost $470) on credit to Kirby Carpen.
	10	Sold $6,100 of merchandise (that had cost $5,100) to customers who used their Commerce Bank credit cards.
	11	Sold $7,200 of merchandise (that had cost $6,150) to customers who used their Aztec cards.
	14	Received Carpen's check in full payment for the purchase of August 4.
	15	Sold $4,900 of merchandise (that had cost $3,500) to customers who used their Aztec cards.
	18	Submitted Aztec card receipts accumulated since August 11 to the credit card company for payment.
	22	Wrote off the account of Rayvac Co. against the Allowance for Doubtful Accounts. The $568 balance in Rayvac's account stemmed from a credit sale in November of last year.
	25	Received the amount due from Aztec.

Check Aug. 25, Dr. Cash $11,979

Required

Prepare journal entries to record the preceding transactions and events. (The company uses the perpetual inventory system. Round amounts to the nearest dollar.)

Freeman Co. began operations on January 1, 2008, and completed several transactions during 2008 and 2009 that involved sales on credit, accounts receivable collections, and bad debts. These transactions are summarized as follows.

Problem 9-2B
Accounts receivable transactions and bad debts adjustments

C1 P1 P2

2008

a. Sold $1,346,800 of merchandise (that had cost $980,300) on credit, terms n/30.

b. Received $666,300 cash in payment of accounts receivable.

c. Wrote off $21,000 of uncollectible accounts receivable.

Check (d) Dr. Bad Debts Expense
$28,914

d. In adjusting the accounts on December 31, the company estimated that 1.2% of accounts receivable will be uncollectible.

2009

e. Sold $1,562,400 of merchandise (that had cost $1,339,300) on credit, terms n/30.

f. Received $1,168,400 cash in payment of accounts receivable.

g. Wrote off $30,400 of uncollectible accounts receivable.

(h) Dr. Bad Debts Expense
$34,763

h. In adjusting the accounts on December 31, the company estimated that 1.2% of accounts receivable will be uncollectible.

Required

Prepare journal entries to record Freeman's 2008 and 2009 summarized transactions and its year-end adjusting entry to record bad debts expense. (The company uses the perpetual inventory system. Round amounts to the nearest dollar.)

Problem 9-3B

Estimating and reporting bad debts

P1 P2

At December 31, 2009, Tobie Company reports the following results for the year.

Cash sales	$1,600,000
Credit sales	2,926,000

In addition, its unadjusted trial balance includes the following items.

Accounts receivable	$886,000 debit
Allowance for doubtful accounts	2,300 credit

Required

1. Prepare the adjusting entry for Tobie Co. to recognize bad debts under each of the following independent assumptions.

   a. Bad debts are estimated to be 1.2% of credit sales.

Check Bad debts expense:
(1b) $31,682, (1c) $42,000

   b. Bad debts are estimated to be 0.7% of total sales.

   c. An aging analysis estimates that 5% of year-end accounts receivable are uncollectible.

2. Show how Accounts Receivable and the Allowance for Doubtful Accounts appear on its December 31, 2009, balance sheet given the facts in part 1a.

3. Show how Accounts Receivable and the Allowance for Doubtful Accounts appear on its December 31, 2009, balance sheet given the facts in part 1c.

Problem 9-4B

Aging accounts receivable and accounting for bad debts

P1 P2

Margrett Company has credit sales of $2.2 million for year 2009. At December 31, 2009, the company's Allowance for Doubtful Accounts has an unadjusted debit balance of $2,800. Margrett prepares a schedule of its December 31, 2009, accounts receivable by age. On the basis of past experience, it estimates the percent of receivables in each age category that will become uncollectible. This information is summarized here.

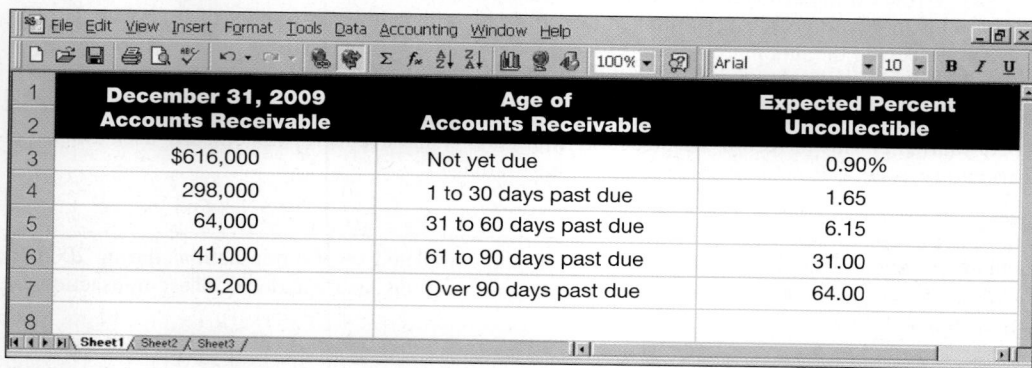

December 31, 2009 Accounts Receivable	Age of Accounts Receivable	Expected Percent Uncollectible
$616,000	Not yet due	0.90%
298,000	1 to 30 days past due	1.65
64,000	31 to 60 days past due	6.15
41,000	61 to 90 days past due	31.00
9,200	Over 90 days past due	64.00

Required

1. Compute the required balance of the Allowance for Doubtful Accounts at December 31, 2009, using the aging of accounts receivable method.

2. Prepare the adjusting entry to record bad debts expense at December 31, 2009.

Check (2) Dr. Bad Debts Expense $35,795

Analysis Component

3. On July 31, 2010, Margrett concludes that a customer's $3,455 receivable (created in 2009) is uncollectible and that the account should be written off. What effect will this action have on Margrett's 2010 net income? Explain.

The following selected transactions are from Castella Company.

Problem 9-5B
Analyzing and journalizing notes receivable transactions

C2 C3 P3 P4

2008

Nov. 1   Accepted a $13,560, 90-day, 10% note dated this day in granting Eric Merklin a time extension on his past-due account receivable.

Dec. 31   Made an adjusting entry to record the accrued interest on the Merklin note.

2009

Jan. 30   Received Merklin's payment for principal and interest on the note dated November 1.

Mar. 1   Accepted a $6,000, 8%, 30-day note dated this day in granting a time extension on the past-due account receivable from Zada Co.

Mar. 2   Accepted a $4,080, 60-day, 5% note dated this day in granting Shane Patru a time extension on his past-due account receivable.

       30   The Zada Co. dishonored its note when presented for payment.

May   1   Received payment of principal plus interest from S. Patru for the March 2 note.

June 15   Accepted a $9,000, 60-day, 11% note dated this day in granting a time extension on the past-due account receivable of Mary Braff.

       21   Accepted a $3,160, 90-day, 10% note dated this day in granting Harris Guam a time extension on his past-due account receivable.

Aug. 14   Received payment of principal plus interest from M. Braff for the note of June 15.

Sep. 19   Received payment of principal plus interest from H. Guam for the June 21 note.

Nov. 30   Wrote off Zada Co.'s account against Allowance for Doubtful Accounts.

Check Jan. 30, Cr. Interest Revenue $113

May 1, Cr. Interest Revenue $34

Sep. 19, Cr. Interest Revenue $79

Required

1. Prepare journal entries to record these transactions and events. (Round amounts to the nearest dollar.)

Analysis Component

2. What reporting is necessary when a business pledges receivables as security for a loan and the loan is still outstanding at the end of the period? Explain the reason for this requirement and the accounting principle being satisfied.

(This serial problem began in Chapter 1 and continues through most of the book. If previous chapter segments were not completed, the serial problem can begin at this point. It is helpful, but not necessary, to use the Working Papers that accompany the book.)

SERIAL PROBLEM

Success Systems

SP 9   Adriana Lopez, owner of Success Systems, realizes that she needs to begin accounting for bad debts expense. Assume that Success Systems has total revenues of $43,853 during the first three months of 2010, and that the Accounts Receivable balance on March 31, 2010, is $22,720.

Required

1. Prepare the adjusting entry needed for Success Systems to recognize bad debts expense on March 31, 2010, under each of the following independent assumptions (assume a zero unadjusted balance in the Allowance for Doubtful Accounts at March 31).

    a. Bad debts are estimated to be 1% of total revenues. (Round amounts to the dollar.)

    b. Bad debts are estimated to be 2% of accounts receivable. (Round amounts to the dollar.)

Check (2) Bad Debts Expense, $51

2. Assume that Success Systems' Accounts Receivable balance at June 30, 2010, is $20,250 and that one account of $100 has been written off against the Allowance for Doubtful Accounts since March 31, 2010. If Lopez uses the method prescribed in Part 1*b*, what adjusting journal entry must be made to recognize bad debts expense on June 30, 2010?

3. Should Lopez consider adopting the direct write-off method of accounting for bad debts expense rather than one of the allowance methods considered in part 1? Explain.

BEYOND THE NUMBERS

REPORTING IN ACTION

A1

BTN 9-1   Refer to Best Buy's financial statements in Appendix A to answer the following.

1. What is the amount of Best Buy's accounts receivable as of March 3, 2007?
2. Compute Best Buy's accounts receivable turnover as of March 3, 2007.
3. How long does it take, *on average,* for Best Buy to collect receivables? Why is this period so short? Do you believe that customers actually pay the amounts due within this short period? Explain.
4. Best Buy's most liquid assets include (*a*) cash and cash equivalents, (*b*) short-term investments, and (*c*) receivables. Compute the percentage that these liquid assets make up of current liabilities as of March 3, 2007. Do the same computations for February 25, 2006. Comment on the company's ability to satisfy its current liabilities at the 2007 fiscal year-end compared to the 2006 fiscal year-end.
5. What criteria did Best Buy use to classify items as cash equivalents?

Fast Forward

6. Access Best Buy's financial statements for fiscal years after March 3, 2007, at its Website (www.BestBuy.com) or the SEC's EDGAR database (www.sec.gov). Recompute parts 2 and 4 and comment on any changes since March 3, 2007.

COMPARATIVE ANALYSIS

A1 P2

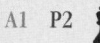

BTN 9-2   Comparative figures for Best Buy, Circuit City, and RadioShack follow.

($ millions)	Best Buy			Circuit City			RadioShack		
	Current Year	One Year Prior	Two Years Prior	Current Year	One Year Prior	Two Years Prior	Current Year	One Year Prior	Two Years Prior
Accounts receivable, net ...	$ 548	$ 449	$ 375	$ 383	$ 221	$ 231	$ 248	$ 309	$ 241
Net sales	35,934	30,848	27,433	12,430	11,514	10,414	4,778	5,082	4,841

Required

1. Compute the accounts receivable turnover for Best Buy, Circuit City, and RadioShack for each of the two most recent years using the data shown.

Hint: Average collection period equals 365 divided by the accounts receivable turnover.

2. Using results from part 1, compute how many days it takes each company, *on average,* to collect receivables. Why are these periods so short? Do you believe that receivables are actually collected this quickly? Explain.

3. Which company is more efficient in collecting its accounts receivable? Explain.

BTN 9-3   Astin Blair is the manager of a medium-size company. A few years ago, Blair persuaded the owner to base a part of his compensation on the net income the company earns each year. Each December he estimates year-end financial figures in anticipation of the bonus he will receive. If the bonus is not as high as he would like, he offers several recommendations to the accountant for year-end adjustments. One of his favorite recommendations is for the controller to reduce the estimate of doubtful accounts.

ETHICS CHALLENGE

P1   P2

Required

1. What effect does lowering the estimate for doubtful accounts have on the income statement and balance sheet?

2. Do you believe Blair's recommendation to adjust the allowance for doubtful accounts is within his right as manager, or do you believe this action is an ethics violation? Justify your response.

3. What type of internal control(s) might be useful for this company in overseeing the manager's recommendations for accounting changes?

BTN 9-4   As the accountant for Pure-Air Distributing, you attend a sales managers' meeting devoted to a discussion of credit policies. At the meeting, you report that bad debts expense is estimated to be $59,000 and accounts receivable at year-end amount to $1,750,000 less a $43,000 allowance for doubtful accounts. Sid Omar, a sales manager, expresses confusion over why bad debts expense and the allowance for doubtful accounts are different amounts. Write a one-page memorandum to him explaining why a difference in bad debts expense and the allowance for doubtful accounts is not unusual. The company estimates bad debts expense as 2% of sales.

COMMUNICATING IN PRACTICE

P1   P2

BTN 9-5   Access eBay's, February 28, 2007, filing of its 10-K report for the year ended December 31, 2006, at www.sec.gov.

TAKING IT TO THE NET

C1

Required

1. What is the amount of eBay's net accounts receivable at December 31, 2006, and at December 31, 2005?

2. Note 7 to its financial statements lists eBay's gross accounts receivable, allowance for doubtful accounts, allowance for authorized credits, and net accounts receivable. For the two years ended December 31, 2006 and 2005, compute its allowance for doubtful accounts as a percent of gross accounts receivable.

3. Do you believe that these percentages are reasonable based on what you know about eBay? Explain.

BTN 9-6   Each member of a team is to participate in estimating uncollectibles using the aging schedule and percents shown in Problem 9-4A. The division of labor is up to the team. Your goal is to accurately complete this task as soon as possible. After estimating uncollectibles, check your estimate with the instructor. If the estimate is correct, the team then should prepare the adjusting entry and the presentation of accounts receivable (net) for the December 31, 2009, balance sheet.

TEAMWORK IN ACTION

P2

ENTREPRENEURIAL DECISION

C1

BTN 9-7   Kevin Plank of **Under Armour** is introduced in the chapter's opening feature. Kevin currently sells his products through multiple outlets. Assume that he is considering two new selling options.

Plan A. Under Armour would begin selling products online directly to customers. Online customers would use their credit cards. It currently has the capability of selling through its Website with no additional investment in hardware or software. Credit sales are expected to increase by $250,000 per year. Costs associated with this plan are: cost of these sales will be $135,500, credit card fees will be 4.75% of sales, and additional recordkeeping and shipping costs will be 6% of sales. These online sales will reduce the sales to stores by $35,000 because some customers will now purchase items online. Sales to stores have a 25% gross margin percentage.

Plan B. Under Armour would expand its market to more stores. It would make additional credit sales of $500,000 to those stores. Costs associated with those sales are: cost of sales will be $375,000, additional recordkeeping and shipping will be 4% of sales, and uncollectible accounts will be 6.2% of sales.

Required

Check   (1b) Net income, $74,000

1. Compute the additional annual net income or loss expected under (a) Plan A and (b) Plan B.
2. Should Under Armour pursue either plan? Discuss both the financial and nonfinancial factors relevant to this decision.

HITTING THE ROAD

C1

BTN 9-8   Many commercials include comments similar to the following: "We accept **VISA**" or "We do not accept **American Express**." Conduct your own research by contacting at least five companies via interviews, phone calls, or the Internet to determine the reason(s) companies discriminate in their use of credit cards. Collect information on the fees charged by the different cards for the companies contacted. (The instructor can assign this as a team activity.)

GLOBAL DECISION

C1   P1   **DSG**

BTN 9-9   Key information from **DSG international plc** (**DSGiplc.com**) follows.

(£ millions)	Current Year	Prior Year
Accounts receivable, net	£ 393	£ 370
Sales	7,930	6,984

1. Compute the accounts receivable turnover for the current year.
2. How long does it take on average for DSG to collect receivables?
3. Refer to BTN 9-2. How does DSG compare to Best Buy, Circuit City, and RadioShack in terms of its accounts receivable turnover and its collection period?

ANSWERS TO MULTIPLE CHOICE QUIZ

1. d; Desired balance in Allowance for Doubtful Accounts = $ 5,026 cr.
($125,650 × 0.04)

Current balance in Allowance for Doubtful Accounts = _____(328) cr.

Bad Debts Expense to be recorded = $ 4,698

2. a; Desired balance in Allowance for Doubtful Accounts = $29,358 cr.
($489,300 × 0.06)

Current balance in Allowance for Doubtful Accounts = _____554 dr.

Bad Debts Expense to be recorded = $29,912

3. a; $7,500 × 0.05 × 90/360 = $93.75

4. c; Principal amount $9,000
Interest accrued . . . .   _____120 ($9,000 × 0.08 × 60/360)
Maturity value $9,120

5. d; $489,600/$40,800 = 12

A Look Back

Chapters 8 and 9 focused on short-term assets: cash, cash equivalents, and receivables. We explained why they are known as liquid assets and described how companies account and report for them.

A Look at This Chapter

This chapter introduces us to long-term assets. We explain how to account for a long-term asset's cost, the allocation of an asset's cost to periods benefiting from it, the recording of additional costs after an asset is purchased, and the disposal of an asset.

A Look Ahead

Chapter 11 focuses on current liabilities. We explain how they are computed, recorded, and reported in financial statements. We also explain the accounting for company payroll and contingencies.

Chapter

Plant Assets, Natural Resources, and Intangibles

Learning Objectives

CAP

Conceptual

C1 Describe plant assets and issues in accounting for them. *(p. 392)*

C2 Explain depreciation and the factors affecting its computation. *(p. 395)*

C3 Explain depreciation for partial years and changes in estimates. *(p. 400)*

Analytical

A1 Compare and analyze alternative depreciation methods. *(p. 399)*

A2 Compute total asset turnover and apply it to analyze a company's use of assets. *(p. 410)*

Procedural

P1 Apply the cost principle to compute the cost of plant assets. *(p. 393)*

P2 Compute and record depreciation using the straight-line, units-of-production, and declining-balance methods. *(p. 396)*

P3 Distinguish between revenue and capital expenditures, and account for them. *(p. 402)*

P4 Account for asset disposal through discarding or selling an asset. *(p. 404)*

P5 Account for natural resource assets and their depletion. *(p. 406)*

P6 Account for intangible assets. *(p. 407)*

P7 *Appendix 10A*—Account for asset exchanges. *(p. 413)*

Fruitful Assets

"The best way to predict the future is to create it"
—Jeremy Black (from left: E. Nichols, R. Black,
T. Baumgardner, J. Black)

SAN CLEMENTE, CA—Surfing is the common bond for Ryan Black, Ed Nichols, and Jeremy Black. It also was the driving force for an excursion to ride the waves of Brazil. But what they encountered would change their lives forever.

The three surfers discovered beachgoers eating a purple berry called *acai* (ah-sigh-ee). "We too fell in love with it," says Ed. "We didn't want to leave Brazil without it." Adds Jeremy, "When people start eating acai, they want it . . . every day."

The three decided to become business missionaries and introduce acai to the masses. They launched Sambazon (**Sambazon.com**), short for Sustainable Management of the Brazilian Amazon, to manu-facture and distribute acai. Scraping up just enough money, they started operations. Says Jeremy, "Financing our equipment, machinery, and other assets was a struggle as our operating cycle is long. We must pay cash to Brazilian acai growers, then pay for processing and shipping, and finally package and distribute acai products to buyers."

The power of the wave was with them. Sambazon now employs 120 workers, churns out numerous acai products, and generates nearly $20 million in annual sales. A continuing challenge is maintaining the right kind and amount of plant assets to meet demand and be profitable. Explains Jeremy, "Sambazon's success depends on monitor-ing and controlling plant asset costs, which range from bottling and packaging equipment to delivery vehicles, plant facilities, and land."

Sambazon must account for, manage, and recover all costs of long-term assets. "We built Sambazon on a triple bottom line business model . . . economic, environmental, and social," says Ryan. "[And we] recognize some things that are not just on our balance sheet."

Their success in asset management permits them to pursue other passions. "We've been given this incredible opportunity to make a lot of positive change with this berry," declares Jeremy. "It's not just a job . . . it's a mission!"

[Sources: *Sambazon Website,* January 2009; *The Wall Street Journal,* March 2007; *San Clemente Times,* March 2006; *CU Business Portfolio,* Spring 2007; *Entrepreneur,* November 2007]

This chapter focuses on long-term assets, which can be grouped into plant assets, natural resource assets, and intangible assets. Plant assets make up a large part of assets on most balance sheets, and they yield depreciation, often one of the largest expenses on income statements. The acquisition or building of a plant asset is often referred to as a *capital expenditure*. Capital expenditures are important events because they impact both the short- and long-term success of a company. Natural resource assets and intangible assets have similar impacts. This chapter describes the purchase and use of these assets. We also explain what distinguishes these assets from other types of assets, how to determine their cost, how to allocate their costs to periods benefiting from their use, and how to dispose of them.

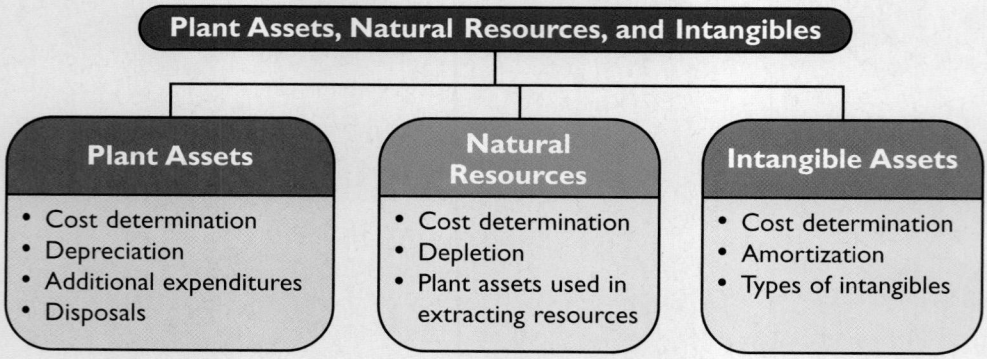

Plant Assets	Natural Resources	Intangible Assets
• Cost determination • Depreciation • Additional expenditures • Disposals	• Cost determination • Depletion • Plant assets used in extracting resources	• Cost determination • Amortization • Types of intangibles

Section 1—Plant Assets

Plant assets are tangible assets used in a company's operations that have a useful life of more than one accounting period. Plant assets are also called *plant and equipment; property, plant, and equipment;* or *fixed assets.* For many companies, plant assets make up the single largest class of assets they own. Exhibit 10.1 shows plant assets as a percent of total assets for several companies. Not only do they make up a large percent of these companies' assets, but their dollar values are large. **McDonald's** plant assets, for instance, are reported at more than $20 billion, and **Wal-Mart** reports plant assets of more than $85 billion.

EXHIBIT 10.1

Plant Assets of Selected Companies

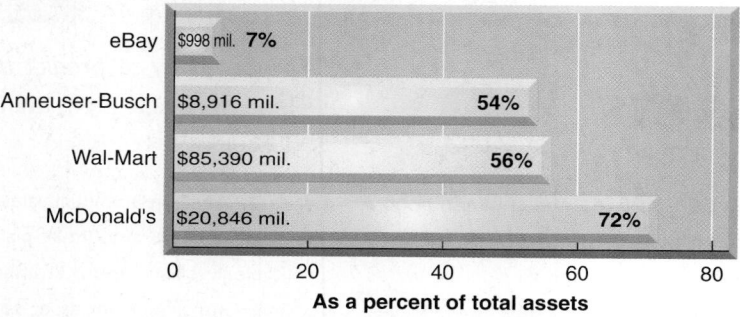

eBay $998 mil. **7%**

Anheuser-Busch $8,916 mil. **54%**

Wal-Mart $85,390 mil. **56%**

McDonald's $20,846 mil. **72%**

0   20   40   60   80

As a percent of total assets

C1 Describe plant assets and issues in accounting for them.

Plant assets are set apart from other assets by two important features. First, *plant assets are used in operations.* This makes them different from, for instance, inventory that is held for sale and not used in operations. The distinctive feature here is use, not type of asset. A company that purchases a computer to resell it reports it on the balance sheet as inventory. If the same company purchases this computer to use in operations, however, it is a plant asset. Another example is land held for future expansion, which is reported as a long-term investment. However, if this land holds a factory used in operations, the land is part of plant assets. Another example is equipment held for use in the event of a breakdown or for peak periods of production, which is reported in plant assets. If this same equipment is removed from use and held for sale, however, it is not reported in plant assets.

The second important feature is that *plant assets have useful lives extending over more than one accounting period.* This makes plant assets different from current assets such as supplies that are normally consumed in a short time period after they are placed in use.

The accounting for plant assets reflects these two features. Since plant assets are used in operations, we try to match their costs against the revenues they generate. Also, since their useful lives extend over more than one period, our matching of costs and revenues must extend over several periods. Specifically, we value plant assets (balance sheet effect) and then, for many of them, we allocate their costs to periods benefiting from their use (income statement effect). An important exception is land; land cost is not allocated to expense when we expect it to have an indefinite life.

Exhibit 10.2 shows four main issues in accounting for plant assets: (1) computing the costs of plant assets, (2) allocating the costs of most plant assets (less any salvage amounts) against revenues for the periods they benefit, (3) accounting for expenditures such as repairs and improvements to plant assets, and (4) recording the disposal of plant assets. The following sections discuss these issues.

Point: It can help to view plant assets as prepaid expenses that benefit several future accounting periods.

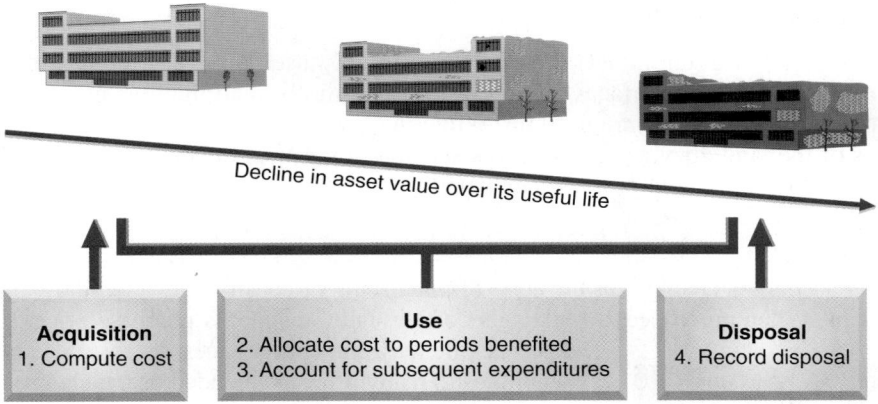

Decline in asset value over its useful life

Acquisition	**Use**	**Disposal**
1. Compute cost	2. Allocate cost to periods benefited 3. Account for subsequent expenditures	4. Record disposal

EXHIBIT 10.2

Issues in Accounting for Plant Assets

Cost Determination

Plant assets are recorded at cost when acquired. This is consistent with the *cost principle.* **Cost** includes all normal and reasonable expenditures necessary to get the asset in place and ready for its intended use. The cost of a factory machine, for instance, includes its invoice cost less any cash discount for early payment, plus any necessary freight, unpacking, assembling, installing, and testing costs. Examples are the costs of building a base or foundation for a machine, providing electrical hookups, and testing the asset before using it in operations.

To be recorded as part of the cost of a plant asset, an expenditure must be normal, reasonable, and necessary in preparing it for its intended use. If an asset is damaged during unpacking, the repairs are not added to its cost. Instead, they are charged to an expense account. Nor is a paid traffic fine for moving heavy machinery on city streets without a proper permit part of the machinery's cost; but payment for a proper permit is included in the cost of machinery. Charges are sometimes incurred to modify or customize a new plant asset. These charges are added to the asset's cost. We explain in this section how to determine the cost of plant assets for each of its four major classes.

Video 10.1

Land

When land is purchased for a building site, its cost includes the total amount paid for the land, including any real estate commissions, title insurance fees, legal fees, and any accrued property taxes paid by the purchaser. Payments for surveying, clearing, grading, and draining also are included in the cost of land. Other costs include government assessments, whether incurred at the time of purchase or later, for items such as public roadways, sewers, and sidewalks. These assessments are included because they permanently add to the land's value. Land purchased as a building site sometimes includes structures that must be removed. In such cases, the total purchase price is charged to the Land account as is the cost of removing the structures, less any amounts recovered through sale of salvaged materials. To illustrate, assume that **Starbucks** paid $167,000 cash to acquire land for a retail store.

P1 Apply the cost principle to compute the cost of plant assets.

Cash price of land	$ 167,000
Net cost of garage removal	13,000
Closing costs	10,000
Cost of land	**$190,000**

This land had an old service garage that was removed at a net cost of $13,000 ($15,000 in costs less $2,000 proceeds from salvaged materials). Additional closing costs total $10,000, consisting of brokerage fees ($8,000), legal fees ($1,500), and title costs ($500). The cost of this land to Starbucks is $190,000 and is computed as shown in Exhibit 10.3.

Land Improvements

Land has an indefinite (unlimited) life and is not usually used up over time. **Land improvements** such as parking lot surfaces, driveways, fences, shrubs, and lighting systems, however, have limited useful lives and are used up. While the costs of these improvements increase the usefulness of the land, they are charged to a separate Land Improvement account so that their costs can be allocated to the periods they benefit.

Buildings

A Building account is charged for the costs of purchasing or constructing a building that is used in operations. When purchased, a building's costs usually include its purchase price, brokerage  fees, taxes, title fees, and attorney fees. Its costs also include all expenditures to ready it for its intended use, including any necessary repairs or renovations such as wiring, lighting, flooring, and wall coverings. When a company constructs a building or any plant asset for its own use, its costs include materials and labor plus a reasonable amount of indirect overhead cost. Overhead includes the costs of items such as heat, lighting, power, and depreciation on machinery used to construct the asset. Costs of construction also include design fees, building permits, and insurance during construction. However, costs such as insurance to cover the asset *after* it is placed in use are operating expenses.

Machinery and Equipment

The costs of machinery and equipment consist of all costs normal and necessary to purchase them and prepare them for their intended use. These include the purchase price, taxes, transportation charges, insurance while in transit, and the installing, assembling, and testing of the machinery and equipment.

Lump-Sum Purchase

Plant assets sometimes are purchased as a group in a single transaction for a lump-sum price. This transaction is called a *lump-sum purchase,* or *group, bulk,* or *basket purchase.* When this occurs, we allocate the cost of the purchase among the different types of assets acquired based on their *relative market values,* which can be estimated by appraisal or by using the tax-assessed valuations of the assets. To illustrate, assume **Oakley** paid $90,000 cash to acquire a group of items consisting of land appraised at $30,000, land improvements appraised at $10,000, and a building appraised at $60,000. The $90,000 cost is allocated on the basis of these appraised values as shown in Exhibit 10.4.

	Appraised Value	Percent of Total	Apportioned Cost
Land	$ 30,000	30% ($30,000/$100,000)	$27,000 ($90,000 × 30%)
Land improvements	10,000	10 ($10,000/$100,000)	9,000 ($90,000 × 10%)
Building	60,000	60 ($60,000/$100,000)	54,000 ($90,000 × 60%)
Totals	$100,000	100%	$ 90,000

Depreciation

Depreciation is the process of allocating the cost of a plant asset to expense in the accounting periods benefiting from its use. Depreciation does not measure the decline in the asset's market value each period, nor does it measure the asset's physical deterioration. Since depreciation reflects the cost of using a plant asset, depreciation charges are only recorded when the asset is actually in service. This section describes the factors we must consider in computing depreciation, the depreciation methods used, revisions in depreciation, and depreciation for partial periods.

Video 10.1

Factors in Computing Depreciation

Factors that determine depreciation are (1) cost, (2) salvage value, and (3) useful life.

C2 Explain depreciation and the factors affecting its computation.

Cost   The **cost** of a plant asset consists of all necessary and reasonable expenditures to acquire it and to prepare it for its intended use.

Salvage Value   The total amount of depreciation to be charged off over an asset's benefit period equals the asset's cost minus its salvage value. **Salvage value,** also called *residual value* or *scrap value,* is an estimate of the asset's value at the end of its benefit period. This is the amount the owner expects to receive from disposing of the asset at the end of its benefit period. If the asset is expected to be traded in on a new asset, its salvage value is the expected trade-in value.

Point: If we expect additional costs in preparing a plant asset for disposal, the salvage value equals the expected amount from disposal less any disposal costs.

Useful Life   The **useful life** of a plant asset is the length of time it is productively used in a company's operations. Useful life, also called *service life,* might not be as long as the asset's total productive life. For example, the productive life of a computer can be eight years or more. Some companies, however, trade in old computers for new ones every two years. In this case, these computers have a two-year useful life, meaning the cost of these computers (less their expected trade-in values) is charged to depreciation expense over a two-year period.

Point: Useful life and salvage value are estimates. Estimates require judgment based on all available information.

Several variables often make the useful life of a plant asset difficult to predict. A major variable is the wear and tear from use in operations. Two other variables, inadequacy and obsolescence, also require consideration. **Inadequacy** refers to the insufficient capacity of a company's plant assets to meet its growing productive demands. **Obsolescence** refers to a plant asset that is no longer useful in producing goods or services with a competitive advantage because of new inventions and improvements. Both inadequacy and obsolescence are difficult to predict because of demand changes, new inventions, and improvements. A company usually disposes of an inadequate or obsolete asset before it wears out.

A company is often able to better predict a new asset's useful life when it has past experience with a similar asset. When it has no such experience, a company relies on the experience of others or on engineering studies and judgment. In note 1 of its annual report, **Tootsie Roll**, a snack food manufacturer, reports the following useful lives:

Buildings	20–35 years
Machinery and Equipment	5–20 years

Life Line   Life expectancy of plant assets is often in the eye of the beholder. For instance, **Hershey Foods** and **Tootsie Roll** are competitors and apply similar manufacturing processes, yet their equipment's life expectancies are different. Hershey depreciates equipment over 3 to 15 years, but Tootsie Roll depreciates them over 5 to 20 years. Such differences markedly impact financial statements.

Depreciation Methods

Depreciation methods are used to allocate a plant asset's cost over the accounting periods in its useful life. The most frequently used method of depreciation is the straight-line method. Another common depreciation method is the units-of-production method. We explain both of these methods in this section. This section also describes accelerated depreciation methods, with a focus on the declining-balance method.

The computations in this section use information about a machine that inspects athletic shoes before packaging. Manufacturers such as **Converse**, **Reebok**, **Adidas**, and **Fila** use this machine. Data for this machine are in Exhibit 10.5.

EXHIBIT 10.5

Data for Athletic Shoe-Inspecting Machine

Cost	$10,000
Salvage value	1,000
Depreciable cost	$ 9,000
Useful life	
Accounting periods	5 years
Units inspected	36,000 shoes

P2 Compute and record depreciation using the straight-line, units-of-production, and declining-balance methods.

Straight-Line Method   **Straight-line depreciation** charges the same amount of expense to each period of the asset's useful life. A two-step process is used. We first compute the *depreciable cost* of the asset, also called the *cost to be depreciated*. It is computed by subtracting the asset's salvage value from its total cost. Second, depreciable cost is divided by the number of accounting periods in the asset's useful life. The formula for straight-line depreciation, along with its computation for the inspection machine just described, is shown in Exhibit 10.6.

EXHIBIT 10.6

Straight-Line Depreciation Formula and Example

$$\frac{\textbf{Cost} - \textbf{Salvage value}}{\textbf{Useful life in periods}} = \frac{\$10,000 - \$1,000}{5 \text{ years}} = \$1,800 \text{ per year}$$

If this machine is purchased on December 31, 2008, and used throughout its predicted useful life of five years, the straight-line method allocates an equal amount of depreciation to each of the years 2009 through 2013. We make the following adjusting entry at the end of each of the five years to record straight-line depreciation of this machine.

Assets = Liabilities + Equity
−1,800   −1,800

Dec. 31	Depreciation Expense.......................	1,800	
	Accumulated Depreciation—Machinery		1,800
	To record annual depreciation.		

Example: If the salvage value of the machine is $2,500, what is the annual depreciation? *Answer:* ($10,000 − $2,500)/5 years = $1,500

The $1,800 Depreciation Expense is reported on the income statement among operating expenses. The $1,800 Accumulated Depreciation is a contra asset account to the Machinery account in the balance sheet. The graph on the left in Exhibit 10.7 shows the $1,800 per year expenses reported in each of the five years. The graph on the right shows the amounts reported on each of the six December 31 balance sheets.

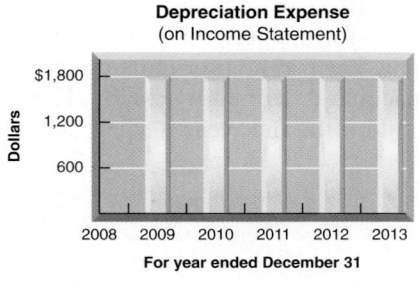
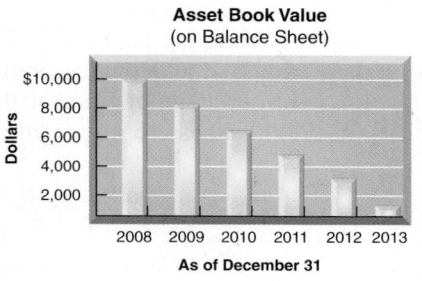

EXHIBIT 10.7

Financial Statement Effects of Straight-Line Depreciation

The net balance sheet amount is the **asset book value,** or simply *book value,* and is computed as the asset's total cost less its accumulated depreciation. For example, at the end of year 2 (December 31, 2010), its book value is $6,400 and is reported in the balance sheet as follows:

Machinery	$10,000	
Less accumulated depreciation	3,600	$6,400

The book value of this machine declines by $1,800 each year due to depreciation. From the graphs in Exhibit 10.7 we can see why this method is called straight-line.

We also can compute the *straight-line depreciation rate,* defined as 100% divided by the number of periods in the asset's useful life. For the inspection machine, this rate is 20% (100% ÷ 5 years, or 1/5 per period). We use this rate, along with other information, to compute the machine's *straight-line depreciation schedule* shown in Exhibit 10.8. Note three points in this exhibit. First, depreciation expense is the same each period. Second, accumulated depreciation is the sum of current and prior periods' depreciation expense. Third, book value declines each period until it equals salvage value at the end of the machine's useful life.

Point: Depreciation requires estimates for salvage value and useful life. Ethics are relevant when managers might be tempted to choose estimates to achieve desired results on financial statements.

Annual Period	Depreciation for the Period			End of Period	
	Depreciable Cost*	Depreciation Rate	Depreciation Expense	Accumulated Depreciation	Book Value†
2008	—	—	—	—	$10,000
2009	$9,000	20%	$1,800	$1,800	8,200
2010	9,000	20	1,800	3,600	6,400
2011	9,000	20	1,800	5,400	4,600
2012	9,000	20	1,800	7,200	2,800
2013	9,000	20	1,800	9,000	1,000

* $10,000 − $1,000.   † Book value is total cost minus accumulated depreciation.

EXHIBIT 10.8

Straight-Line Depreciation Schedule

Units-of-Production Method   The straight-line method charges an equal share of an asset's cost to each period. If plant assets are used up in about equal amounts each accounting period, this method produces a reasonable matching of expenses with revenues. However, the use of some plant assets varies greatly from one period to the next. A builder, for instance, might use a piece of construction equipment for a month and then not use it again for several months. When equipment use varies from period to period, the units-of-production depreciation method can better match expenses with revenues. **Units-of-production depreciation** charges a varying amount to expense for each period of an asset's useful life depending on its usage.

A two-step process is used to compute units-of-production depreciation. We first compute *depreciation per unit* by subtracting the asset's salvage value from its total cost and then dividing by the total number of units expected to be produced during its useful life. Units of production can be expressed in product or other units such as hours used or miles driven. The second step is to compute depreciation expense for the period by multiplying the units produced in the period by the depreciation per unit. The formula for units-of-production depreciation, along with its computation for the machine described in Exhibit 10.5, is shown in Exhibit 10.9. (7,000 shoes are inspected and sold in its first year.)

EXHIBIT 10.9

Units-of-Production Depreciation Formula and Example

Step 1

$$\text{Depreciation per unit} = \frac{\text{Cost} - \text{Salvage value}}{\text{Total units of production}} = \frac{\$10,000 - \$1,000}{36,000 \text{ shoes}} = \$0.25 \text{ per shoe}$$

Step 2

$$\text{Depreciation expense} = \text{Depreciation per unit} \times \text{Units produced in period}$$
$$\$0.25 \text{ per shoe} \times 7,000 \text{ shoes} = \$1,750$$

Using data on the number of shoes inspected by the machine, we can compute the *units-of-production depreciation schedule* shown in Exhibit 10.10. For example, depreciation for the first year is $1,750 (7,000 shoes at $0.25 per shoe). Depreciation for the second year is $2,000 (8,000 shoes at $0.25 per shoe). Other years are similarly computed. Exhibit 10.10 shows that (1) depreciation expense depends on unit output, (2) accumulated depreciation is the sum of current and prior periods' depreciation expense, and (3) book value declines each period until it equals salvage value at the end of the asset's useful life. **Boise Cascade** is one of many companies using the units-of-production depreciation method. It reports that most of its "**paper and wood products manufacturing facilities determine depreciation by a units-of-production method.**" **Kimberly-Clark** also reports that much of its "**depreciable property is depreciated on the . . . units-of-production method.**"

Example: Refer to Exhibit 10.10. If the number of shoes inspected in 2013 is 5,500, what is depreciation for 2013? *Answer:* $1,250 (never depreciate below salvage value)

EXHIBIT 10.10

Units-of-Production Depreciation Schedule

Annual Period	Depreciation for the Period			End of Period	
	Number of Units	Depreciation per Unit	Depreciation Expense	Accumulated Depreciation	Book Value
2008	—	—	—	—	$10,000
2009	7,000	$0.25	$1,750	$1,750	8,250
2010	8,000	0.25	2,000	3,750	6,250
2011	9,000	0.25	2,250	6,000	4,000
2012	7,000	0.25	1,750	7,750	2,250
2013	5,000	0.25	1,250	9,000	1,000

Declining-Balance Method   An **accelerated depreciation method** yields larger depreciation expenses in the early years of an asset's life and less depreciation in later years. The most common accelerated method is the **declining-balance method** of depreciation, which uses a depreciation rate that is a multiple of the straight-line rate and applies it to the asset's beginning-of-period book value. The amount of depreciation declines each period because book value declines each period.

A common depreciation rate for the declining-balance method is double the straight-line rate. This is called the *double-declining-balance* (*DDB*) method. This method is applied in three steps: (1) compute the asset's straight-line depreciation rate, (2) double the straight-line rate, and (3) compute depreciation expense by multiplying this rate by the asset's beginning-of-period book value. To illustrate, let's return to the machine in Exhibit 10.5 and apply the double-declining-balance method to compute depreciation expense. Exhibit 10.11 shows the first-year depreciation computation for the machine. The three-step process is to (1) divide

Point: In the DDB method, *double* refers to the rate and *declining balance* refers to book value. The rate is applied to beginning book value each period.

100% by five years to determine the straight-line rate of 20%, or 1/5, per year, (2) double this 20% rate to get the declining-balance rate of 40%, or 2/5, per year, and (3) compute depreciation expense as 40%, or 2/5, multiplied by the beginning-of-period book value.

EXHIBIT 10.11

Double-Declining-Balance Depreciation Formula*

Step 1

   Straight-line rate = 100% ÷ Useful life = 100% ÷ 5 years = 20%

Step 2

   Double-declining-balance rate = 2 × Straight-line rate = 2 × 20% = 40%

Step 3

   Depreciation expense = Double-declining-balance rate × Beginning-period book value
   $$40\% \times \$10,000 = \$4,000 \text{ (for 2009)}$$

* To simplify: DDB depreciation = (2 × Beginning-period book value)/Useful life.

The *double-declining-balance depreciation schedule* is shown in Exhibit 10.12. The schedule follows the formula except for year 2013, when depreciation expense is $296. This $296 is not equal to 40% × $1,296, or $518.40. If we had used the $518.40 for depreciation expense in 2013, the ending book value would equal $777.60, which is less than the $1,000 salvage value. Instead, the $296 is computed by subtracting the $1,000 salvage value from the $1,296 book value at the beginning of the fifth year (the year when DDB depreciation cuts into salvage value).

Example: What is the DDB depreciation expense in year 2012 if the salvage value is $2,000? *Answer:* $2,160 − $2,000 = $160

EXHIBIT 10.12

Double-Declining-Balance Depreciation Schedule

	Depreciation for the Period			End of Period	
Annual Period	Beginning of Period Book Value	Depreciation Rate	Depreciation Expense	Accumulated Depreciation	Book Value
2008	—	—	—	—	$10,000
2009	$10,000	40%	$4,000	$4,000	6,000
2010	6,000	40	2,400	6,400	3,600
2011	3,600	40	1,440	7,840	2,160
2012	2,160	40	864	8,704	1,296
2013	1,296	40	296*	9,000	**1,000**

* Year 2013 depreciation is $1,296 − $1,000 = $296 (never depreciate book value below salvage value).

Comparing Depreciation Methods   Exhibit 10.13 shows depreciation expense for each year of the machine's useful life under each of the three depreciation methods. While depreciation expense per period differs for different methods, total depreciation expense of $9,000 is the same over the machine's useful life.

A1 Compare and analyze alternative depreciation methods.

EXHIBIT 10.13

Depreciation Expense for the Different Methods

	Period	Straight-Line	Units-of-Production	Double-Declining-Balance
1	Period	Straight-Line	Units-of-Production	Double-Declining-Balance
2	2009	$1,800	$1,750	$4,000
3	2010	1,800	2,000	2,400
4	2011	1,800	2,250	1,440
5	2012	1,800	1,750	864
6	2013	1,800	1,250	296
7	Totals	$9,000	$9,000	$9,000

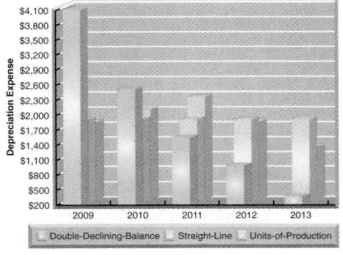

Each method starts with a total cost of $10,000 and ends with a salvage value of $1,000. The difference is the pattern in depreciation expense over the useful life. The book value of the asset when using straight-line is always greater than the book value from using double-declining-balance, except at the beginning and end of the asset's useful life, when it is the same.

Also, the straight-line method yields a steady pattern of depreciation expense while the units-of-production depreciation depends on the number of units produced. Each of these methods is acceptable because it allocates cost in a systematic and rational manner.

Decision Insight

In Vogue   About 85% of companies use straight-line depreciation for plant assets, 4% use units-of-production, and 4% use declining-balance. Another 7% use an unspecified accelerated method—most likely declining-balance.

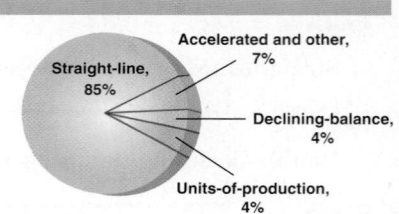

Depreciation for Tax Reporting   The records a company keeps for financial accounting purposes are usually separate from the records it keeps for tax accounting purposes. This is so because financial accounting aims to report useful information on financial performance and position, whereas tax accounting reflects government objectives in raising revenues. Differences between these two accounting systems are normal and expected. Depreciation is a common example of how the records differ. For example, many companies use accelerated depreciation in computing taxable income. Reporting higher depreciation expense in the early years of an asset's life reduces the company's taxable income in those years and increases it in later years, when the depreciation expense is lower. The company's goal here is to *postpone* its tax payments.

The U.S. federal income tax law has rules for depreciating assets. These rules include the **Modified Accelerated Cost Recovery System (MACRS),** which allows straight-line depreciation for some assets but requires accelerated depreciation for most kinds of assets. MACRS separates depreciable assets into different classes and defines the depreciable life and rate for each class. MACRS is *not* acceptable for financial reporting because it often allocates costs over an arbitrary period that is less than the asset's useful life and it fails to estimate salvage value. Details of MACRS are covered in tax accounting courses.

Partial-Year Depreciation

Plant assets are purchased and disposed of at various times. When an asset is purchased (or disposed of) at a time other than the beginning or end of an accounting period, depreciation is recorded for part of a year. This is done so that the year of purchase or the year of disposal is charged with its share of the asset's depreciation.

To illustrate, assume that the machine in Exhibit 10.5 is purchased and placed in service on October 8, 2008, and the annual accounting period ends on December 31. Since this machine is purchased and used for nearly three months in 2008, the calendar-year income statement should report depreciation expense on the machine for that part of the year. Normally, depreciation assumes that the asset is purchased on the first day of the month nearest the actual date of purchase. In this case, since the purchase occurred on October 8, we assume an October 1 purchase date. This means that three months' depreciation is recorded in 2008. Using straight-line depreciation, we compute three months' depreciation of $450 as follows.

$$\frac{\$10,000 - \$1,000}{5 \text{ years}} \times \frac{3}{12} = \$450$$

A similar computation is necessary when an asset disposal occurs during a period. To illustrate, assume that the machine is sold on June 24, 2013. Depreciation is recorded for the period January 1 through June 24 when it is disposed of. This partial year's depreciation, computed to the nearest whole month, is

$$\frac{\$10,000 - \$1,000}{5 \text{ years}} \times \frac{6}{12} = \$900$$

Change in Estimates for Depreciation

Depreciation is based on estimates of salvage value and useful life. During the useful life of an asset, new information may indicate that these estimates are inaccurate. If our estimate of an asset's useful life and/or salvage value changes, what should we do? The answer is to use the new estimate to compute depreciation for current and future periods. This means that we revise the depreciation expense computation by spreading the cost yet to be depreciated over the remaining useful life. This approach is used for all depreciation methods.

Point: Remaining depreciable cost equals book value less revised salvage value at the point of revision.

Let's return to the machine described in Exhibit 10.8 using straight-line depreciation. At the beginning of this asset's third year, its book value is $6,400, computed as $10,000 minus $3,600. Assume that at the beginning of its third year, the estimated number of years remaining in its useful life changes from three to four years *and* its estimate of salvage value changes from $1,000 to $400. Straight-line depreciation for each of the four remaining years is computed as shown in Exhibit 10.14.

Point: Income is overstated (and depreciation understated) when useful life is too high; when useful life is too low, the opposite results.

$$\frac{\text{Book value} - \text{Revised salvage value}}{\text{Revised remaining useful life}} = \frac{\$6,400 - \$400}{4 \text{ years}} = \$1,500 \text{ per year}$$

EXHIBIT 10.14

Computing Revised Straight-Line Depreciation

Thus, $1,500 of depreciation expense is recorded for the machine at the end of the third through sixth years—each year of its remaining useful life. Since this asset was depreciated at $1,800 per year for the first two years, it is tempting to conclude that depreciation expense was overstated in the first two years. However, these expenses reflected the best information available at that time. We do not go back and restate prior years' financial statements for this type of new information. Instead, we adjust the current and future periods' statements to reflect this new information. Revising an estimate of the useful life or salvage value of a plant asset is referred to as a **change in an accounting estimate** and is reflected in current and future financial statements, not in prior statements.

Example: If at the beginning of its second year the machine's remaining useful life changes from four to three years and salvage value from $1,000 to $400, how much straight-line depreciation is recorded in remaining years? *Answer:* Revised depreciation = ($8,200 − $400)/3 = $2,600.

Reporting Depreciation

Both the cost and accumulated depreciation of plant assets are reported on the balance sheet or in its notes. **Dale Jarrett Racing Adventure**, for instance, reports the following.

Office furniture and equipment	$ 45,386
Shop and track equipment	123,378
Race vehicles and other	775,363
Property and equipment, gross	944,127
Less accumulated depreciation	715,435
Property and equipment, net	$228,692

Many companies also show plant assets on one line with the net amount of cost less accumulated depreciation. When this is done, the amount of accumulated depreciation is disclosed in a note. **Circuit City** reports only the net amount of its property and equipment in its balance sheet in Appendix A. To satisfy the full-disclosure principle, Circuit City describes its depreciation methods in its Note 2 and the amounts comprising plant assets in its Note 6—see its 10-K at **www.SEC.gov**.

Point: A company usually keeps records for each asset showing its cost and depreciation to date. The combined records for individual assets are a type of *plant asset subsidiary ledger*.

Reporting both the cost and accumulated depreciation of plant assets helps users compare the assets of different companies. For example, a company holding assets costing $50,000 and accumulated depreciation of $40,000 is likely in a situation different from a company with new assets costing $10,000. While the net undepreciated cost of $10,000 is the same in both cases, the first company may have more productive capacity available but likely is facing the need to replace older assets. These insights are not provided if the two balance sheets report only the $10,000 book values.

Users must remember that plant assets are reported on a balance sheet at their undepreciated costs (book value), not at market values. This emphasis on costs rather than market values is based on the *going-concern assumption* described in Chapter 1. This assumption states that, unless there is evidence to the contrary, we assume that a company continues in business.

This implies that plant assets are held and used long enough to recover their cost through the sale of products and services. Since plant assets are not for sale, their market values are not reported. An exception is when there is a *permanent decline* in the market value of an asset relative to its book value, called an asset **impairment.** In this case the company writes the asset down to this market value (details for write-downs are in advanced courses).

Accumulated Depreciation is a contra asset account with a normal credit balance. It does *not* reflect funds accumulated to buy new assets when the assets currently owned are replaced. If a company has funds available to buy assets, the funds are shown on the balance sheet among liquid assets such as Cash or Investments.

Decision Ethics

Controller   You are the controller for a struggling company. Its operations require regular investments in equipment, and depreciation is its largest expense. Its competitors frequently replace equipment—often depreciated over three years. The company president instructs you to revise useful lives of equipment from three to six years and to use a six-year life on all new equipment. What actions do you take? [Answer—p. 416]

Quick Check   Answers—p. 416

4. On January 1, 2009, a company pays $77,000 to purchase office furniture with a zero salvage value. The furniture's useful life is somewhere between 7 and 10 years. What is the year 2009 straight-line depreciation on the furniture using (*a*) a 7-year useful life and (*b*) a 10-year useful life?

5. What does the term *depreciation* mean in accounting?

6. A company purchases a machine for $96,000 on January 1, 2009. Its useful life is five years or 100,000 units of product, and its salvage value is $8,000. During 2009, 10,000 units of product are produced. Compute the book value of this machine on December 31, 2009, assuming (*a*) straight-line depreciation and (*b*) units-of-production depreciation.

7. In early January 2009, a company acquires equipment for $3,800. The company estimates this equipment to have a useful life of three years and a salvage value of $200. Early in 2011, the company changes its estimates to a total four-year useful life and zero salvage value. Using the straight-line method, what is depreciation for the year ended 2011?

Additional Expenditures

P3 Distinguish between revenue and capital expenditures, and account for them.

After a company acquires a plant asset and puts it into service, it often makes additional expenditures for that asset's operation, maintenance, repair, and improvement. In recording these expenditures, it must decide whether to capitalize or expense them (to capitalize an expenditure is to debit the asset account). The issue is whether these expenditures are reported as current period expenses or added to the plant asset's cost and depreciated over its remaining useful life.

Revenue expenditures, also called *income statement expenditures,* are additional costs of plant assets that do not materially increase the asset's life or productive capabilities. They are recorded as expenses and deducted from revenues in the current period's income statement. Examples of revenue expenditures are cleaning, repainting, adjustments, and lubricants. **Capital expenditures,** also called *balance sheet expenditures,* are additional costs of plant assets that provide benefits extending beyond the current period. They are debited to asset accounts and reported on the balance sheet. Capital expenditures increase or improve the type or amount of service an asset provides. Examples are roofing replacement, plant expansion, and major overhauls of machinery and equipment.

Financial statements are affected for several years by the accounting choice of recording costs as either revenue expenditures or capital expenditures. This decision is based on whether the expenditures are identified as ordinary repairs or as betterments and extraordinary repairs.

Financial Statement Effect		
	Accounting	**Expense Timing**
Revenue expenditure	Income stmt. account debited	Expensed currently
Capital expenditure	Balance sheet account debited	Expensed in future

Ordinary Repairs

Ordinary repairs are expenditures to keep an asset in normal, good operating condition. They are necessary if an asset is to perform to expectations over its useful life. Ordinary repairs do not extend an asset's useful life beyond its original estimate or increase its productivity beyond original expectations. Examples are normal costs of cleaning, lubricating, adjusting, and replacing small parts of a machine. Ordinary repairs are treated as *revenue expenditures*. This means their costs are reported as expenses on the current period income statement. Following this rule, **Brunswick** reports that "maintenance and repair costs are expensed as incurred." If Brunswick's current year repair costs are $9,500, it makes the following entry.

Point: Many companies apply the *materiality constraint* to treat *low-cost plant assets* (say, less than $500) as revenue expenditures.

Dec. 31	Repairs Expense............................	9,500	
	Cash		9,500
	To record ordinary repairs of equipment.		

Assets = Liabilities + Equity
−9,500   −9,500

Betterments and Extraordinary Repairs

Accounting for betterments and extraordinary repairs is similar—both are treated as *capital expenditures*.

Video 10.1

Betterments (Improvements)   **Betterments,** also called *improvements,* are expenditures that make a plant asset more efficient or productive. A betterment often involves adding a component to an asset or replacing one of its old components with a better one, and does not always increase an asset's useful life. An example is replacing manual controls on a machine with automatic controls. One special type of betterment is an *addition,* such as adding a new wing or dock to a warehouse. Since a betterment benefits future periods, it is debited to the asset account as a capital expenditure. The new book value (less salvage value) is then depreciated over the asset's remaining useful life. To illustrate, suppose a company pays $8,000 for a machine with an eight-year useful life and no salvage value. After three years and $3,000 of depreciation, it adds an automated control system to the machine at a cost of $1,800. This results in reduced labor costs in future periods. The cost of the betterment is added to the Machinery account with this entry.

Example: Assume a firm owns a Web server. Identify each cost as a revenue or capital expenditure: (1) purchase price, (2) necessary wiring, (3) platform for operation, (4) circuits to increase capacity, (5) cleaning after each month of use, (6) repair of a faulty switch, and (7) replaced a worn fan. *Answer:* Capital expenditures: 1, 2, 3, 4; revenue expenditures: 5, 6, 7.

Jan. 2	Machinery	1,800	
	Cash		1,800
	To record installation of automated system.		

Assets = Liabilities + Equity
+1,800
−1,800

After the betterment is recorded, the remaining cost to be depreciated is $6,800, computed as $8,000 − $3,000 + $1,800. Depreciation expense for the remaining five years is $1,360 per year, computed as $6,800/5 years.

Point: Both extraordinary repairs and betterments require revising future depreciation.

Extraordinary Repairs (Replacements)   **Extraordinary repairs** are expenditures extending the asset's useful life beyond its original estimate. Extraordinary repairs are *capital expenditures* because they benefit future periods. Their costs are debited to the asset account (or to accumulated depreciation). For example, **America West Airlines** reports, "cost of major scheduled airframe, engine and certain component overhauls are capitalized (and expensed) ... over the periods benefited."

Decision Maker

Entrepreneur   Your start-up Internet services company needs cash, and you are preparing financial statements to apply for a short-term loan. A friend suggests that you treat as many expenses as possible as capital expenditures. What are the impacts on financial statements of this suggestion? What do you think is the aim of this suggestion? [Answer—p. 416]

Disposals of Plant Assets

Plant assets are disposed of for several reasons. Some are discarded because they wear out or become obsolete. Others are sold because of changing business plans. Regardless of the reason, disposals of plant assets occur in one of three basic ways: discarding, sale, or exchange. The general steps in accounting for a disposal of plant assets are described in Exhibit 10.15.

EXHIBIT 10.15

Accounting for Disposals of Plant Assets

1. Record depreciation up to the date of disposal—this also updates Accumulated Depreciation.
2. Record the removal of the disposed asset's account balances—including its Accumulated Depreciation.
3. Record any cash (and/or other assets) received or paid in the disposal.
4. Record any gain or loss—computed by comparing the disposed asset's book value with the market value of any assets received.*

* An exception to step 4 is the case of an exchange that lacks *commercial substance*—see Appendix 10A.

Discarding Plant Assets

P4 Account for asset disposal through discarding or selling an asset.

A plant asset is *discarded* when it is no longer useful to the company and it has no market value. To illustrate, assume that a machine costing $9,000 with accumulated depreciation of $9,000 is discarded. When accumulated depreciation equals the asset's cost, it is said to be *fully depreciated* (zero book value). The entry to record the discarding of this asset is

Assets = Liabilities + Equity
+9,000
−9,000

June 5	Accumulated Depreciation—Machinery...........	9,000	
	Machinery.............................		9,000
	To discard fully depreciated machinery.		

This entry reflects all four steps of Exhibit 10.15. Step 1 is unnecessary since the machine is fully depreciated. Step 2 is reflected in the debit to Accumulated Depreciation and credit to Machinery. Since no other asset is involved, step 3 is irrelevant. Finally, since book value is zero and no other asset is involved, no gain or loss is recorded in step 4.

How do we account for discarding an asset that is not fully depreciated or one whose depreciation is not up-to-date? To answer this, consider equipment costing $8,000 with accumulated depreciation of $6,000 on December 31 of the prior fiscal year-end. This equipment is being depreciated using the straight-line method over eight years with zero salvage. On July 1 of the current year it is discarded. Step 1 is to bring depreciation up-to-date.

Point: Recording depreciation expense up-to-date gives an up-to-date book value for determining gain or loss.

Assets = Liabilities + Equity
−500   −500

July 1	Depreciation Expense........................	500	
	Accumulated Depreciation—Equipment		500
	To record 6 months' depreciation ($1,000 × 6/12).		

Steps 2 through 4 of Exhibit 10.15 are reflected in the second (and final) entry.

Assets = Liabilities + Equity
+6,500   −1,500
−8,000

July 1	Accumulated Depreciation—Equipment...........	6,500	
	Loss on Disposal of Equipment.................	1,500	
	Equipment		8,000
	To discard equipment with a $1,500 book value.		

Point: Gain or loss is determined by comparing "value given" (book value) to "value received."

This loss is computed by comparing the equipment's $1,500 book value ($8,000 − $6,000 − $500) with the zero net cash proceeds. The loss is reported in the Other Expenses and Losses section of the income statement. Discarding an asset can sometimes require a cash payment that would increase the loss.

Selling Plant Assets

Companies often sell plant assets when they restructure or downsize operations. To illustrate the accounting for selling plant assets, we consider BTO's March 31 sale of equipment that cost $16,000 and has accumulated depreciation of $12,000 at December 31 of the prior calendar year-end. Annual depreciation on this equipment is $4,000 computed using straight-line depreciation. Step 1 of this sale is to record depreciation expense and update accumulated depreciation to March 31 of the current year.

March 31	Depreciation Expense.........................	1,000	
	Accumulated Depreciation—Equipment		1,000
	To record 3 months' depreciation ($4,000 × 3/12).		

Assets = Liabilities + Equity
−1,000   −1,000

Steps 2 through 4 of Exhibit 10.15 can be reflected in one final entry that depends on the amount received from the asset's sale. We consider three different possibilities.

Sale at Book Value   If BTO receives $3,000 cash, an amount equal to the equipment's book value as of March 31 (book value = $16,000 − $12,000 − $1,000), no gain or loss occurs on disposal. The entry is

March 31	Cash.....................................	3,000	
	Accumulated Depreciation—Equipment..........	13,000	
	Equipment		16,000
	To record sale of equipment for no gain or loss.		

Assets = Liabilities + Equity
+3,000
+13,000
−16,000

Sale above Book Value   If BTO receives $7,000, an amount that is $4,000 above the equipment's $3,000 book value as of March 31, a gain on disposal occurs. The entry is

March 31	Cash.....................................	7,000	
	Accumulated Depreciation—Equipment..........	13,000	
	Gain on Disposal of Equipment		4,000
	Equipment		16,000
	To record sale of equipment for a $4,000 gain.		

Assets = Liabilities + Equity
+7,000   +4,000
+13,000
−16,000

Sale below Book Value   If BTO receives $2,500, an amount that is $500 below the equipment's $3,000 book value as of March 31, a loss on disposal occurs. The entry is

March 31	Cash.....................................	2,500	
	Loss on Disposal of Equipment.................	500	
	Accumulated Depreciation—Equipment..........	13,000	
	Equipment		16,000
	To record sale of equipment for a $500 loss.		

Assets = Liabilities + Equity
+2,500   −500
+13,000
−16,000

Decision Insight

IFRSs   Unlike U.S. GAAP, IFRSs require an annual review of useful life and salvage value estimates. IFRSs also permit revaluation of plant assets to market value if market value is reliably determined.

Quick Check
Answers—p. 416

8. Early in the fifth year of a machine's six-year useful life, it is overhauled, and its useful life is extended to nine years. This machine originally cost $108,000 and the overhaul cost is $12,000. Prepare the entry to record the overhaul cost.

9. Explain the difference between revenue expenditures and capital expenditures and how both are recorded.

10. What is a betterment? How is a betterment recorded?

11. A company acquires equipment on January 10, 2009, at a cost of $42,000. Straight-line depreciation is used with a five-year life and $7,000 salvage value. On June 27, 2010, the company sells this equipment for $32,000. Prepare the entry(ies) for June 27, 2010.

Section 2—Natural Resources

P5	Account for natural resource assets and their depletion.

Natural resources are assets that are physically consumed when used. Examples are standing timber, mineral deposits, and oil and gas fields. Since they are consumed when used, they are often called *wasting assets*. These assets represent soon-to-be inventories of raw materials that will be converted into one or more products by cutting, mining, or pumping. Until that conversion takes place, they are noncurrent assets and are shown in a balance sheet using titles such as timberlands, mineral deposits, or oil reserves. Natural resources are reported under either plant assets or their own separate category. **Alcoa**, for instance, reports its natural resources under the balance sheet title *Properties, plants and equipment.* In a note to its financial statements, Alcoa reports a separate amount for *Land and land rights, including mines.* **Weyerhaeuser**, on the other hand, reports its timber holdings in a separate balance sheet category titled *Timber and timberlands.*

Cost Determination and Depletion

Natural resources are recorded at cost, which includes all expenditures necessary to acquire the resource and prepare it for its intended use. **Depletion** is the process of allocating the cost of a natural resource to the period when it is consumed. Natural resources are reported on the balance sheet at cost less *accumulated depletion.* The depletion expense per period is usually based on units extracted from cutting, mining, or pumping. This is similar to units-of-production depreciation. **Exxon Mobil** uses this approach to amortize the costs of discovering and operating its oil wells.

To illustrate depletion of natural resources, let's consider a mineral deposit with an estimated 250,000 tons of available ore. It is purchased for $500,000, and we expect zero salvage value. The depletion charge per ton of ore mined is $2, computed as $500,000 ÷ 250,000 tons. If 85,000 tons are mined and sold in the first year, the depletion charge for that year is $170,000. These computations are detailed in Exhibit 10.16.

EXHIBIT 10.16

Depletion Formula and Example

Step 1

$$\text{Depletion per unit} = \frac{\text{Cost} - \text{Salvage value}}{\text{Total units of capacity}} = \frac{\$500{,}000 - \$0}{250{,}000 \text{ tons}} = \$2 \text{ per ton}$$

Step 2

$$\text{Depletion expense} = \text{Depletion per unit} \times \text{Units extracted and sold in period}$$
$$= \$2 \times 85{,}000 = \$170{,}000$$

Depletion expense for the first year is recorded as follows.

Assets	= Liabilities +	Equity
−170,000		−170,000

Dec. 31	Depletion Expense—Mineral Deposit	170,000	
	Accumulated Depletion—Mineral Deposit		170,000
	To record depletion of the mineral deposit.		

The period-end balance sheet reports the mineral deposit as shown in Exhibit 10.17.

EXHIBIT 10.17

Balance Sheet Presentation of Natural Resources

Mineral deposit	$500,000	
Less accumulated depletion	**170,000**	$330,000

Since all 85,000 tons of the mined ore are sold during the year, the entire $170,000 of depletion is reported on the income statement. If some of the ore remains unsold at year-end, however, the depletion related to the unsold ore is carried forward on the balance sheet and reported as Ore Inventory, a current asset. To illustrate, and continuing with our example, assume that 40,000 tons are mined in the second year, but only 34,000 tons are sold. We record depletion of $68,000 (34,000 tons $\times$ $2 depletion per unit) and the remaining Ore Inventory of $12,000 (6,000 tons $\times$ $2 depletion per unit) as follows.

Dec. 31	Depletion Expense—Mineral Deposit	68,000	
	Ore Inventory	12,000	
	Accumulated Depletion—Mineral Deposit		80,000
	To record depletion and inventory of mineral deposit.		

Assets = Liabilities + Equity
−80,000   −68,000
+12,000

Plant Assets Used in Extracting

Video10.1

The conversion of natural resources by mining, cutting, or pumping usually requires machinery, equipment, and buildings. When the usefulness of these plant assets is directly related to the depletion of a natural resource, their costs are depreciated using the units-of-production method in proportion to the depletion of the natural resource. For example, if a machine is permanently installed in a mine and 10% of the ore is mined and sold in the period, then 10% of the machine's cost (less any salvage value) is allocated to depreciation expense. The same procedure is used when a machine is abandoned once resources have been extracted. If, however, a machine will be moved to and used at another site when extraction is complete, the machine is depreciated over its own useful life.

Section 3—Intangible Assets

Intangible assets are nonphysical assets (used in operations) that confer on their owners long-term rights, privileges, or competitive advantages. Examples are patents, copyrights, licenses, leaseholds, franchises, goodwill, and trademarks. Lack of physical substance does not necessarily imply an intangible asset. Notes and accounts receivable, for instance, lack physical substance, but they are not intangibles. This section identifies the more common types of intangible assets and explains the accounting for them.

P6 Account for intangible assets.

Cost Determination and Amortization

An intangible asset is recorded at cost when purchased. Intangibles are then separated into those with limited lives or indefinite lives. If an intangible has a **limited life,** its cost is systematically allocated to expense over its estimated useful life through the process of **amortization.** If an intangible asset has an **indefinite life**—meaning that no legal, regulatory, contractual, competitive, economic, or other factors limit its useful life—it should not be amortized. (If an intangible with an indefinite life is later judged to have a limited life, it is amortized over that limited life.) Amortization of intangible assets is similar to depreciation of plant assets and the depletion of natural resources in that it is a process of cost allocation. However, only the straight-line method is used for amortizing intangibles *unless* the company can show that another method is preferred. The effects of amortization are recorded in a contra account (Accumulated Amortization). The gross acquisition cost of intangible assets is disclosed in the balance sheet along with their accumulated amortization (these disclosures are new). The eventual disposal of an intangible asset involves removing its book value, recording any other asset(s) received or given up, and recognizing any gain or loss for the difference.

Many intangibles have limited lives due to laws, contracts, or other asset characteristics. Examples are patents, copyrights, and leaseholds. Other intangibles such as goodwill, trademarks, and trade names have lives that cannot be easily determined. The cost of intangible assets is amortized over the periods expected to benefit by their use, but in no case can this period be longer than the asset's legal existence. The values of some intangible assets such as goodwill continue indefinitely into the future and are not amortized. (An intangible asset that is not amortized is tested annually for **impairment**—if necessary, an impairment loss is recorded. Details for this test are in advanced courses.)

Point: The cost to acquire a Website address is an intangible asset.

Point: Goodwill is not amortized; instead, it is annually tested for impairment.

Intangible assets are often shown in a separate section of the balance sheet immediately after plant assets. Callaway Golf, for instance, follows this approach in reporting nearly $150 million of intangible assets in its balance sheet. Companies usually disclose their amortization periods for intangibles. The remainder of our discussion focuses on accounting for specific types of intangible assets.

Types of Intangibles

Patents The federal government grants patents to encourage the invention of new technology, mechanical devices, and production processes. A **patent** is an exclusive right granted to its owner to manufacture and sell a patented item or to use a process for 20 years. When patent rights are purchased, the cost to acquire the rights is debited to an account called Patents. If the owner engages in lawsuits to successfully defend a patent, the cost of lawsuits is debited to the Patents account. However, the costs of research and development leading to a new patent are expensed when incurred.

A patent's cost is amortized over its estimated useful life (not to exceed 20 years). If we purchase a patent costing $25,000 with a useful life of 10 years, we make the following adjusting entry at the end of each of the 10 years to amortize one-tenth of its cost.

Assets = Liabilities + Equity
−2,500   −2,500

Dec. 31	Amortization Expense—Patents	2,500	
	Accumulated Amortization—Patents		2,500
	To amortize patent costs over its useful life.		

The $2,500 debit to Amortization Expense appears on the income statement as a cost of the product or service provided under protection of the patent. The Accumulated Amortization—Patents account is a contra asset account to Patents.

Decision Insight

Mention "drug war" and most people think of illegal drug trade. But another drug war is under way: Brand-name drugmakers are fighting to stop generic copies of their products from hitting the market once patents expire. Delaying a generic rival can yield millions in extra sales.

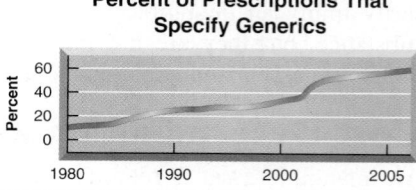

Percent of Prescriptions That Specify Generics

Copyrights A **copyright** gives its owner the exclusive right to publish and sell a musical, literary, or artistic work during the life of the creator plus 70 years, although the useful life of most copyrights is much shorter. The costs of a copyright are amortized over its useful life. The only identifiable cost of many copyrights is the fee paid to the Copyright Office of the federal government or international agency granting the copyright. If this fee is immaterial, it is charged directly to an expense account; but if the identifiable costs of a copyright are material, they are capitalized (recorded in an asset account) and periodically amortized by debiting an account called Amortization Expense—Copyrights.

Franchises and Licenses **Franchises** and **licenses** are rights that a company or government grants an entity to deliver a product or service under specified conditions. Many organizations grant franchise and license rights—McDonald's, Pizza Hut, and Major League Baseball are just a few examples. The costs of franchises and licenses are debited to a Franchises and Licenses asset account and are amortized over the lives of the agreements. If an agreement is for an indefinite or perpetual period, those costs are not amortized.

Trademarks and Trade Names Companies often adopt unique symbols or select unique names and brands in marketing their products. A **trademark** or **trade (brand) name** is a symbol, name, phrase, or jingle identified with a company, product, or service. Examples are Nike swoosh, Marlboro Man, Big Mac, Coca-Cola, and Corvette. Ownership and exclusive right to use a trademark or trade name is often established by showing that one company used it before another. Ownership is best established by registering a trademark or trade name with the government's Patent Office. The cost of developing, maintaining, or enhancing the value of a trademark or trade name (such as advertising) is charged to expense when incurred. If a trademark or trade name is purchased, however, its cost is debited to an asset account and then amortized over its expected life. If the company plans to renew indefinitely its right to the trademark or trade name, the cost is not amortized.

Point: McDonald's "golden arches" are one of the world's most valuable trademarks, yet this asset is not shown on McDonald's balance sheet.

Goodwill   **Goodwill** has a specific meaning in accounting. Goodwill is the amount by which a company's value exceeds the value of its individual assets and liabilities. This usually implies that the company as a whole has certain valuable attributes not measured among its individual assets and liabilities. These can include superior management, skilled workforce, good supplier or customer relations, quality products or services, good location, or other competitive advantages.

To keep accounting information from being too subjective, goodwill is not recorded unless an entire company or business segment is purchased. Purchased goodwill is measured by taking the purchase price of the company and subtracting the market value of its individual net assets (excluding goodwill). For instance, Yahoo! paid nearly $3.0 billion to acquire GeoCities; about $2.8 of the $3.0 billion was for goodwill and other intangibles.

Goodwill is measured as the excess of the cost of an acquired entity over the value of the acquired net assets. Goodwill is recorded as an asset, and it is *not* amortized. Instead, goodwill is annually tested for impairment. If the book value of goodwill does not exceed its fair (market) value, goodwill is not impaired. However, if the book value of goodwill does exceed its fair value, an impairment loss is recorded equal to that excess. (Details of this test are in advanced courses.)

Point: Amortization of goodwill is different for financial accounting and tax accounting. The IRS requires the amortization of goodwill over 15 years.

Leaseholds   Property is rented under a contract called a **lease.** The property's owner, called the **lessor,** grants the lease. The one who secures the right to possess and use the property is called the **lessee.** A **leasehold** refers to the rights the lessor grants to the lessee under the terms of the lease. A leasehold is an intangible asset for the lessee.

Certain leases require no advance payment from the lessee but require monthly rent payments. In this case, we do not set up a Leasehold account. Instead, the monthly payments are debited to a Rent Expense account. If a long-term lease requires the lessee to pay the final period's rent in advance when the lease is signed, the lessee records this advance payment with a debit to the Leasehold account. Since the advance payment is not used until the final period, the Leasehold account balance remains intact until that final period when its balance is transferred to Rent Expense. (Some long-term leases give the lessee essentially the same rights as a purchaser. This results in a tangible asset and a liability reported by the lessee. Chapter 14 describes these so-called *capital leases.*)

A long-term lease can increase in value when current rental rates for similar property rise while the required payments under the lease remain constant. This increase in value of a lease is not reported on the lessee's balance sheet. However, if the property is subleased and the new tenant makes a cash payment to the original lessee for the rights under the old lease, the new tenant debits this payment to a Leasehold account, which is amortized to Rent Expense over the remaining life of the lease.

Point: A leasehold account implies existence of future benefits that the lessee controls because of a prepayment. It also meets the definition of an asset.

Leasehold Improvements   A lessee sometimes pays for alterations or improvements to the leased property such as partitions, painting, and storefronts. These alterations and improvements are called **leasehold improvements,** and the lessee debits these costs to a Leasehold Improvements account. Since leasehold improvements become part of the property and revert to the lessor at the end of the lease, the lessee amortizes these costs over the life of the lease or the life of the improvements, whichever is shorter. The amortization entry debits Amortization Expense—Leasehold Improvements and credits Accumulated Amortization—Leasehold Improvements.

Other Intangibles   There are other types of intangible assets such as *software, noncompete covenants, customer lists,* and so forth. Our accounting for them is the same. First, we record the intangible asset's costs. Second, we determine whether the asset has a limited or indefinite life. If limited, we allocate its costs over that period. If indefinite, its costs are not amortized.

Quick Check

Answers—p. 416

12. Give an example of a natural resource and of an intangible asset.

13. A company pays $650,000 for an ore deposit. The deposit is estimated to have 325,000 tons of ore that will be mined over the next 10 years. During the first year, it mined, processed, and sold 91,000 tons. What is that year's depletion expense?

14. On January 6, 2009, a company pays $120,000 for a patent with a remaining 17-year legal life to produce a toy expected to be marketable for three years. Prepare entries to record its acquisition and the December 31, 2009, amortization entry.

Decision Analysis   Total Asset Turnover

A2 Compute total asset turnover and apply it to analyze a company's use of assets.

A company's assets are important in determining its ability to generate sales and earn income. Managers devote much attention to deciding what assets a company acquires, how much it invests in assets, and how to use assets most efficiently and effectively. One important measure of a company's ability to use its assets is **total asset turnover,** defined in Exhibit 10.18.

EXHIBIT 10.18

Total Asset Turnover

$$\text{Total asset turnover} = \frac{\text{Net sales}}{\text{Average total assets}}$$

The numerator reflects the net amounts earned from the sale of products and services. The denominator reflects the average total resources devoted to operating the company and generating sales.

To illustrate, let's look at total asset turnover in Exhibit 10.19 for two competing companies: Molson Coors and Anheuser-Busch.

EXHIBIT 10.19

Analysis Using Total Asset Turnover

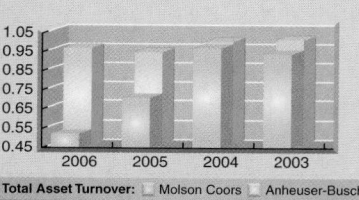

Total Asset Turnover: Molson Coors, Anheuser-Busch

Company	Figure ($ millions)	2006	2005	2004	2003
Molson Coors	Net sales	$ 5,845	$ 5,507	$ 4,306	$ 4,000
	Average total assets	$11,701	$ 8,228	$ 4,551	$ 4,392
	Total asset turnover	0.50	0.67	0.95	0.91
Anheuser-Busch	Net sales	$15,717	$15,036	$14,934	$14,147
	Average total assets	$16,466	$16,362	$15,431	$14,405
	Total asset turnover	0.95	0.92	0.97	0.98

Point: An estimate of **plant asset useful life** equals the plant asset cost divided by depreciation expense.

Point: The **plant asset age** is estimated by dividing accumulated depreciation by depreciation expense. Older plant assets can signal needed asset replacements; they may also signal less efficient assets.

To show how we use total asset turnover, let's look at Molson Coors. We express Molson Coors's use of assets in generating net sales by saying "it turned its assets over 0.50 times during 2006." This means that each $1.00 of assets produced $0.50 of net sales. Is a total asset turnover of 0.50 good or bad? It is safe to say that all companies desire a high total asset turnover. Like many ratio analyses, however, a company's total asset turnover must be interpreted in comparison with those of prior years and of its competitors. Interpreting the total asset turnover also requires an understanding of the company's operations. Some operations are capital intensive, meaning that a relatively large amount is invested in assets to generate sales. This suggests a relatively lower total asset turnover. Other companies' operations are labor intensive, meaning that they generate sales more by the efforts of people than the use of assets. In that case, we expect a higher total asset turnover. Companies with low total asset turnover require higher profit margins (examples are hotels and real estate); companies with high total asset turnover can succeed with lower profit margins (examples are food stores and toy merchandisers). Molson Coors's turnover recently declined and is now much lower than that for Anheuser-Busch. Total asset turnover for Molson Coors's competitors, available in industry publications such as Dun & Bradstreet, is generally in the range of 0.7 to 1.0 over this same period. Overall, Molson Coors must improve relative to its competitors on total asset turnover.

Decision Maker

Environmentalist   A paper manufacturer claims it cannot afford more environmental controls. It points to its low total asset turnover of 1.9 and argues that it cannot compete with companies whose total asset turnover is much higher. Examples cited are food stores (5.5) and auto dealers (3.8). How do you respond? [Answer—p. 416]

Demonstration Problem

On July 14, 2009, Tulsa Company pays $600,000 to acquire a fully equipped factory. The purchase involves the following assets and information.

DP10

Asset	Appraised Value	Salvage Value	Useful Life	Depreciation Method
Land	$160,000			Not depreciated
Land improvements	80,000	$ 0	10 years	Straight-line
Building	320,000	100,000	10 years	Double-declining-balance
Machinery	240,000	20,000	10,000 units	Units-of-production*
Total	$800,000			

* The machinery is used to produce 700 units in 2009 and 1,800 units in 2010.

Required

1. Allocate the total $600,000 purchase cost among the separate assets.
2. Compute the 2009 (six months) and 2010 depreciation expense for each asset, and compute the company's total depreciation expense for both years.
3. On the last day of calendar year 2011, Tulsa discarded machinery that had been on its books for five years. The machinery's original cost was $12,000 (estimated life of five years) and its salvage value was $2,000. No depreciation had been recorded for the fifth year when the disposal occurred. Journalize the fifth year of depreciation (straight-line method) and the asset's disposal.
4. At the beginning of year 2011, Tulsa purchased a patent for $100,000 cash. The company estimated the patent's useful life to be 10 years. Journalize the patent acquisition and its amortization for the year 2011.
5. Late in the year 2011, Tulsa acquired an ore deposit for $600,000 cash. It added roads and built mine shafts for an additional cost of $80,000. Salvage value of the mine is estimated to be $20,000. The company estimated 330,000 tons of available ore. In year 2011, Tulsa mined and sold 10,000 tons of ore. Journalize the mine's acquisition and its first year's depletion.
6.^AOn the first day of 2011, Tulsa exchanged machinery that was acquired on July 14, 2009, and $5,000 cash for machinery with a $210,000 market value. Journalize the exchange of these assets assuming the exchange lacked commercial substance.

Planning the Solution

- Complete a three-column table showing the following amounts for each asset: appraised value, percent of total value, and apportioned cost.
- Using allocated costs, compute depreciation for 2009 (only one-half year) and 2010 (full year) for each asset. Summarize those computations in a table showing total depreciation for each year.
- Remember that depreciation must be recorded up-to-date before discarding an asset. Calculate and record depreciation expense for the fifth year using the straight-line method. Since salvage value is not received at the end of a discarded asset's life, the amount of any salvage value becomes a loss on disposal. Record the loss on the disposal as well as the removal of the discarded asset and its related accumulated depreciation.
- Record the patent (an intangible asset) at its purchase price. Use straight-line amortization over its useful life to calculate amortization expense.
- Record the ore deposit (a natural resource asset) at its cost, including any added costs to ready the mine for use. Calculate depletion per ton using the depletion formula. Multiply the depletion per ton by the amount of tons mined and sold to calculate depletion expense for the year.
- Remember that gains and losses on asset exchanges that lack commercial substance are not recognized. Make a journal entry to add the acquired machinery to the books and to remove the old machinery, along with its accumulated depreciation, and to record the cash given in the exchange.

Solution to Demonstration Problem

1. Allocation of the total cost of $600,000 among the separate assets.

Asset	Appraised Value	Percent of Total Value	Apportioned Cost
Land	$160,000	20%	$120,000 ($600,000 × 20%)
Land improvements	80,000	10	60,000 ($600,000 × 10%)
Building	320,000	40	240,000 ($600,000 × 40%)
Machinery	240,000	30	180,000 ($600,000 × 30%)
Total	$800,000	100%	$ 600,000

2. Depreciation for each asset. (Land is not depreciated.)

Land Improvements

Cost	$ 60,000
Salvage value	0
Depreciable cost	$ 60,000
Useful life	10 years
Annual depreciation expense ($60,000/10 years)	$ 6,000
2009 depreciation ($6,000 × 6/12)	$ 3,000
2010 depreciation	$ 6,000

Building

Straight-line rate = 100%/10 years = 10%
Double-declining-balance rate = 10% × 2 = 20%

2009 depreciation ($240,000 × 20% × 6/12)	$ 24,000
2010 depreciation [($240,000 − $24,000) × 20%]	$ 43,200

Machinery

Cost	$180,000
Salvage value	20,000
Depreciable cost	$160,000
Total expected units of production	10,000 units
Depreciation per unit ($160,000/10,000 units)	$ 16
2009 depreciation ($16 × 700 units)	$ 11,200
2010 depreciation ($16 × 1,800 units)	$ 28,800

Total depreciation expense for each year:

	2009	2010
Land improvements	$ 3,000	$ 6,000
Building	24,000	43,200
Machinery	11,200	28,800
Total	$38,200	$78,000

3. Record the depreciation up-to-date on the discarded asset.

Depreciation Expense—Machinery	2,000	
Accumulated Depreciation—Machinery		2,000
To record depreciation on date of disposal: ($12,000 − $2,000)/5		

Record the removal of the discarded asset and its loss on disposal.

Accumulated Depreciation—Machinery	10,000	
Loss on Disposal of Machinery	2,000	
Machinery		12,000
To record the discarding of machinery with a $2,000 book value.		

4.

Patent	100,000	
Cash		100,000
To record patent acquisition.		

Amortization Expense—Patent	10,000	
Accumulated Amortization—Patent		10,000
To record amortization expense: $100,000/10 years = $10,000.		

5.

Ore Deposit	680,000	
Cash		680,000
To record ore deposit acquisition and its related costs.		

Depletion Expense—Ore Deposit	20,000	
Accumulated Depletion—Ore Deposit		20,000
To record depletion expense: ($680,000 − $20,000)/330,000 tons =		
$2 per ton. 10,000 tons mined and sold × $2 = $20,000 depletion.		

6. Record the asset exchange: The book value on the exchange date is $180,000 (cost) − $40,000 (accumulated depreciation). The book value of the machinery given up in the exchange ($140,000) plus the $5,000 cash paid is less than the $210,000 value of the machine acquired. The entry to record this exchange of assets that lacks commercial substance does not recognize the $65,000 "gain."

Machinery (new)	145,000*	
Accumulated Depreciation—Machinery (old)	40,000	
Machinery (old)		180,000
Cash		5,000
To record asset exchange that lacks commercial substance.		

* Market value of the acquired asset of $210,000 minus $65,000 "gain."

Exchanging Plant Assets

10A

P7A Account for asset exchanges.

Many plant assets such as machinery, automobiles, and office equipment are disposed of by exchanging them for newer assets. In a typical exchange of plant assets, a *trade-in allowance* is received on the old asset and the balance is paid in cash. Accounting for the exchange of assets depends on whether the transaction has *commercial substance* (per *SFAS 153,* commercial substance implies that it alters the company's future cash flows). If an asset exchange has commercial substance, a gain or loss is recorded based on the difference between the book value of the asset(s) given up and the market value of the asset(s) received. If an asset exchange lacks commercial substance, no gain or loss is recorded, and the asset(s) received is recorded based on the book value of the asset(s) given up. An exchange has commercial substance if the company's future cash flows change as a result of the transaction. This section describes the accounting for the exchange of assets.

Exchange with Commercial Substance: A Loss A company acquires $42,000 in new equipment. In exchange, the company pays $33,000 cash and trades in old equipment. The old equipment originally cost $36,000 and has accumulated depreciation of $20,000, which implies a $16,000 book value at the time of exchange. We are told this exchange has commercial substance and that the old equipment has a trade-in allowance of $9,000. This exchange yields a loss as computed in the middle (Loss) columns of Exhibit 10A.1; the loss is computed as Asset received − Assets given = $42,000 − $49,000 = $(7,000). We can also compute the loss as Trade-in allowance − Book value of asset given = $9,000 − $16,000 = $(7,000).

EXHIBIT 10A.1

Computing Gain or Loss on
Asset Exchange with Commercial
Substance

Asset Exchange Has Commercial Substance	Loss		Gain	
Market value of asset received		$42,000		$52,000
Book value of assets given:				
Equipment ($36,000 − $20,000)	$16,000		$16,000	
Cash	33,000	49,000	33,000	49,000
Gain (loss) on exchange		$(7,000)		$ 3,000

The entry to record this asset exchange is

Assets = Liabilities + Equity
+42,000   −7,000
+20,000
−36,000
−33,000

Jan. 3	Equipment (**new**)	42,000	
	Loss on Exchange of Assets	7,000	
	Accumulated Depreciation—Equipment (**old**)	20,000	
	Equipment (**old**)		36,000
	Cash		33,000
	To record exchange (with commercial substance) of		
	old equipment and cash for new equipment.		

Point: Parenthetical notes to "new"
and "old" equipment are for illustration
only. Both the debit and credit are to
the same Equipment account.

Exchange with Commercial Substance: A Gain

Let's assume the same facts as in the preceding asset exchange *except* that the new equipment received has a market value of $52,000 instead of $42,000. We are told that this exchange has commercial substance and that the old equipment has a trade-in allowance of $19,000. This exchange yields a gain as computed in the right-most (Gain) columns of Exhibit 10A.1; the gain is computed as Asset received − Assets given = $52,000 − $49,000 = $3,000. We can also compute the gain as Trade-in allowance − Book value of asset given = $19,000 − $16,000 = $3,000. The entry to record this asset exchange is

Assets = Liabilities + Equity
+52,000   +3,000
+20,000
−36,000
−33,000

Jan. 3	Equipment (**new**)	52,000	
	Accumulated Depreciation—Equipment (**old**)	20,000	
	Equipment (**old**)		36,000
	Cash		33,000
	Gain on Exchange of Assets		3,000
	To record exchange (with commercial substance)		
	of old equipment and cash for new equipment.		

Exchanges without Commercial Substance

Let's assume the same facts as in the preceding asset exchange involving new equipment received with a market value of $52,000, but let's instead assume the transaction *lacks commercial substance*. The entry to record this asset exchange is

Assets = Liabilities + Equity
+49,000
+20,000
−36,000
−33,000

Jan. 3	Equipment (**new**)	49,000	
	Accumulated Depreciation—Equipment (**old**)	20,000	
	Equipment (**old**)		36,000
	Cash		33,000
	To record exchange (without commercial substance)		
	of old equipment and cash for new equipment.		

Point: No gain or loss is recorded for
exchanges *without* commercial substance.

The $3,000 gain recorded when the transaction has commercial substance is *not* recognized in this entry because of the rule prohibiting recording a gain or loss on asset exchanges without commercial substance. The $49,000 recorded for the new equipment equals its cash price ($52,000) less the unrecognized gain ($3,000) on the exchange. The $49,000 cost recorded is called the *cost basis* of the new machine. This cost basis is the amount we use to compute depreciation and its book value. The cost basis of the new asset also can be computed by summing the book values of the assets given up as shown in Exhibit 10A.2. The same analysis and approach are taken for a loss on an asset exchange without commercial substance.

EXHIBIT 10A.2

Cost Basis of New Asset When
Gain Not Recorded on Asset
Exchange without Commercial
Substance

Cost of old equipment	$ 36,000
Less accumulated depreciation	20,000
Book value of old equipment	16,000
Cash paid in the exchange	33,000
Cost recorded for new	
equipment	$49,000

Quick Check

Answer—p. 416

15. A company trades an old Web server for a new one. The cost of the old server is $30,000, and its accumulated depreciation at the time of the trade is $23,400. The new server has a cash price of $45,000. Prepare entries to record the trade under two different assumptions where the company receives a trade-in allowance of (*a*) $3,000 and the exchange has commercial substance, and (*b*) $7,000 and the exchange lacks commercial substance.

Summary

C1 **Describe plant assets and issues in accounting for them.** Plant assets are tangible assets used in the operations of a company and have a useful life of more than one accounting period. Plant assets are set apart from other tangible assets by two important features: use in operations and useful lives longer than one period. The four main accounting issues with plant assets are (1) computing their costs, (2) allocating their costs to the periods they benefit, (3) accounting for subsequent expenditures, and (4) recording their disposal.

C2 **Explain depreciation and the factors affecting its computation.** *Depreciation* is the process of allocating to expense the cost of a plant asset over the accounting periods that benefit from its use. Depreciation does not measure the decline in a plant asset's market value or its physical deterioration. Three factors determine depreciation: cost, salvage value, and useful life. Salvage value is an estimate of the asset's value at the end of its benefit period. Useful (service) life is the length of time an asset is productively used.

C3 **Explain depreciation for partial years and changes in estimates.** Partial-year depreciation is often required because assets are bought and sold throughout the year. Depreciation is revised when changes in estimates such as salvage value and useful life occur. If the useful life of a plant asset changes, for instance, the remaining cost to be depreciated is spread over the remaining (revised) useful life of the asset.

A1 **Compare and analyze alternative depreciation methods.** The amount of depreciation expense per period is usually different for different methods, yet total depreciation expense over an asset's life is the same for all methods. Each method starts with the same total cost and ends with the same salvage value. The difference is in the pattern of depreciation expense over the asset's life. Common methods are straight-line, double-declining-balance, and units-of-production.

A2 **Compute total asset turnover and apply it to analyze a company's use of assets.** Total asset turnover measures a company's ability to use its assets to generate sales. It is defined as net sales divided by average total assets. While all companies desire a high total asset turnover, it must be interpreted in comparison with those for prior years and its competitors.

P1 **Apply the cost principle to compute the cost of plant assets.** Plant assets are recorded at cost when purchased. Cost includes all normal and reasonable expenditures necessary to get the asset in place and ready for its intended use. The cost of a lump-sum purchase is allocated among its individual assets.

P2 **Compute and record depreciation using the straight-line, units-of-production, and declining-balance methods.** The straight-line method divides cost less salvage value by the asset's useful life to determine depreciation expense per period. The units-of-production method divides cost less salvage value by the estimated number of units the asset will produce over its life to determine depreciation per unit. The declining-balance method multiplies the asset's beginning-of-period book value by a factor that is often double the straight-line rate.

P3 **Distinguish between revenue and capital expenditures, and account for them.** Revenue expenditures expire in the current period and are debited to expense accounts and matched with current revenues. Ordinary repairs are an example of revenue expenditures. Capital expenditures benefit future periods and are debited to asset accounts. Examples of capital expenditures are extraordinary repairs and betterments.

P4 **Account for asset disposal through discarding or selling an asset.** When a plant asset is discarded or sold, its cost and accumulated depreciation are removed from the accounts. Any cash proceeds from discarding or selling an asset are recorded and compared to the asset's book value to determine gain or loss.

P5 **Account for natural resource assets and their depletion.** The cost of a natural resource is recorded in a noncurrent asset account. Depletion of a natural resource is recorded by allocating its cost to depletion expense using the units-of-production method. Depletion is credited to an Accumulated Depletion account.

P6 **Account for intangible assets.** An intangible asset is recorded at the cost incurred to purchase it. The cost of an intangible asset with a definite useful life is allocated to expense using the straight-line method, and is called *amortization*. Goodwill and intangible assets with an indefinite useful life are not amortized—they are annually tested for impairment. Intangible assets include patents, copyrights, leaseholds, goodwill, and trademarks.

P7ᴬ **Account for asset exchanges.** For an asset exchange with commercial substance, a gain or loss is recorded based on the difference between the book value of the asset given up and the market value of the asset received. For an asset exchange without commercial substance, no gain or loss is recorded, and the asset received is recorded based on the book value of the asset given up.

Guidance Answers to **Decision Maker** and **Decision Ethics**

Controller   The president's instructions may reflect an honest and reasonable prediction of the future. Since the company is struggling financially, the president may have concluded that the normal pattern of replacing assets every three years cannot continue. Perhaps the strategy is to avoid costs of frequent replacements and stretch use of equipment a few years longer until financial conditions improve. However, if you believe the president's decision is unprincipled, you might confront the president with your opinion that it is unethical to change the estimate to increase income. Another possibility is to wait and see whether the auditor will prohibit this change in estimate. In either case, you should insist that the statements be based on reasonable estimates.

Entrepreneur   Treating an expense as a capital expenditure means that reported expenses will be lower and income higher in the short run. This is so because a capital expenditure is not expensed imme-

diately but is spread over the asset's useful life. Treating an expense as a capital expenditure also means that asset and equity totals are reported at larger amounts in the short run. This continues until the asset is fully depreciated. Your friend is probably trying to help, but the suggestion is misguided. Only an expenditure benefiting future periods is a capital expenditure.

Environmentalist   The paper manufacturer's comparison of its total asset turnover with food stores and auto dealers is misdirected. These other industries' turnovers are higher because their profit margins are lower (about 2%). Profit margins for the paper industry are usually 3% to 3.5%. You need to collect data from competitors in the paper industry to show that a 1.9 total asset turnover is about the norm for this industry. You might also want to collect data on this company's revenues and expenses, along with compensation data for its high-ranking officers and employees.

Guidance Answers to **Quick Checks**

1. **a.** Supplies—current assets
   b. Office equipment—plant assets
   c. Inventory—current assets
   d. Land for future expansion—long-term investments
   e. Trucks used in operations—plant assets

2. a. Land   **b.** Land Improvements

3. $700,000 + $49,000 − $21,000 + $3,500
   + $3,000 + $2,500 = $737,000

4. a. Straight-line with 7-year life: ($77,000/7) = $11,000
   b. Straight-line with 10-year life: ($77,000/10) = $7,700

5. Depreciation is a process of allocating the cost of plant assets to the accounting periods that benefit from the assets' use.

6. a. Book value using straight-line depreciation:
   $96,000 − [($96,000 − $8,000)/5] = $78,400
   b. Book value using units of production:
   $96,000 − [($96,000 − $8,000) × (10,000/100,000)]
   = $87,200

7. ($3,800 − $200)/3 = $1,200 (original depreciation per year)
   $1,200 × 2 = $2,400 (accumulated depreciation)
   ($3,800 − $2,400)/2 = $700 (revised depreciation)

8.

Machinery	12,000	
Cash.		12,000

9. A revenue expenditure benefits only the current period and should be charged to expense in the current period. A capital expenditure yields benefits that extend beyond the end of the current period and should be charged to an asset.

10. A betterment involves modifying an existing plant asset to make it more efficient, usually by replacing part of the asset with an improved or superior part. The cost of a betterment is debited to the asset account.

11.

Depreciation Expense	3,500	
Accumulated Depreciation.		3,500
Cash.	32,000	
Accumulated Depreciation	10,500	
Gain on Sale of Equipment		500
Equipment		42,000

12. Examples of natural resources are timberlands, mineral deposits, and oil reserves. Examples of intangible assets are patents, copyrights, leaseholds, leasehold improvements, goodwill, trademarks, and licenses.

13. ($650,000/325,000 tons) × 91,000 tons = $182,000

14.

Jan. 6	Patents		120,000	
	Cash			120,000
Dec. 31	Amortization Expense		40,000*	
	Accumulated			
	Amortization—Patents			40,000

* $120,000/3 years = $40,000.

15.

(a) Equipment (new)	45,000	
Loss on Exchange of Assets	3,600	
Accumulated Depreciation—Equipment (old). .	23,400	
Equipment (old)		30,000
Cash ($45,000 − $3,000)		42,000

(b) Equipment (new)*	44,600	
Accumulated Depreciation—Equipment (old) .	23,400	
Equipment (old)		30,000
Cash ($45,000 − $7,000)		38,000

* Includes $400 unrecognized gain.

Key Terms

Key Terms are available at the book's Website for learning and testing in an online Flashcard Format.

Accelerated depreciation method (p. 398)
Amortization (p. 407)
Asset book value (p. 397)
Betterments (p. 403)
Capital expenditures (p. 402)
Change in an accounting estimate (p. 401)
Copyright (p. 408)
Cost (p. 393, 395)
Declining-balance method (p. 398)
Depletion (p. 406)
Depreciation (p. 395)
Extraordinary repairs (p. 403)
Franchises (p. 408)
Goodwill (p. 409)
Impairment (p. 402, 407)

Inadequacy (p. 395)
Indefinite life (p. 407)
Intangible assets (p. 407)
Land improvements (p. 394)
Lease (p. 409)
Leasehold (p. 409)
Leasehold improvements (p. 409)
Lessee (p. 409)
Lessor (p. 409)
Licenses (p. 408)
Limited life (p. 407)
Modified Accelerated Cost Recovery System (MACRS) (p. 400)
Natural resources (p. 406)

Obsolescence (p. 395)
Ordinary repairs (p. 402)
Patent (p. 408)
Plant asset age (p. 410)
Plant assets (p. 392)
Plant asset useful life (p. 410)
Revenue expenditures (p. 402)
Salvage value (p. 395)
Straight-line depreciation (p. 396)
Total asset turnover (p. 410)
Trademark or trade (brand) name (p. 408)
Units-of-production depreciation (p. 397)
Useful life (p. 395)

Multiple Choice Quiz

Answers on p. 431

Additional Quiz Questions are available at the book's Website.

1. A company paid $326,000 for property that included land, land improvements, and a building. The land was appraised at $175,000, the land improvements were appraised at $70,000, and the building was appraised at $105,000. What is the allocation of property costs to the three assets purchased?
  a. Land, $150,000; Land Improvements, $60,000; Building, $90,000
  b. Land, $163,000; Land Improvements, $65,200; Building, $97,800
  c. Land, $150,000; Land Improvements, $61,600; Building, $92,400
  d. Land, $159,000; Land Improvements, $65,200; Building, $95,400
  e. Land, $175,000; Land Improvements, $70,000; Building, $105,000

2. A company purchased a truck for $35,000 on January 1, 2009. The truck is estimated to have a useful life of four years and an estimated salvage value of $1,000. Assuming that the company uses straight-line depreciation, what is the depreciation expense on the truck for the year ended December 31, 2010?
  a. $8,750
  b. $17,500
  c. $8,500
  d. $17,000
  e. $25,500

3. A company purchased machinery for $10,800,000 on January 1, 2009. The machinery has a useful life of 10 years and an esti-

mated salvage value of $800,000. What is the depreciation expense on the machinery for the year ended December 31, 2010, assuming that the double-declining-balance method is used?
  a. $2,160,000
  b. $3,888,000
  c. $1,728,000
  d. $2,000,000
  e. $1,600,000

Quiz10

4. A company sold a machine that originally cost $250,000 for $120,000 when accumulated depreciation on the machine was $100,000. The gain or loss recorded on the sale of this machine is
  a. $0 gain or loss.
  b. $120,000 gain.
  c. $30,000 loss.
  d. $30,000 gain.
  e. $150,000 loss.

5. A company had average total assets of $500,000, gross sales of $575,000, and net sales of $550,000. The company's total asset turnover is
  a. 1.15
  b. 1.10
  c. 0.91
  d. 0.87
  e. 1.05

Superscript letter ^A denotes assignments based on Appendix 10A.

Discussion Questions

1. ♟ What characteristics of a plant asset make it different from other assets?

2. What is the general rule for costs' inclusion for plant assets?

3. What is different between land and land improvements?

4. Why is the cost of a lump-sum purchase allocated to the individual assets acquired?

5. ♟ Does the balance in the Accumulated Depreciation—Machinery account represent funds to replace the machinery when it wears out? If not, what does it represent?

6. Why is the Modified Accelerated Cost Recovery System not generally accepted for financial accounting purposes?

7. ♟ What accounting concept justifies charging low-cost plant asset purchases immediately to an expense account?

8. What is the difference between ordinary repairs and extraordinary repairs? How should each be recorded?

9. ♟ Identify events that might lead to disposal of a plant asset.

10. What is the process of allocating the cost of natural resources to expense as they are used?

11. Is the declining-balance method an acceptable way to compute depletion of natural resources? Explain.

12. What are the characteristics of an intangible asset?

13. What general procedures are applied in accounting for the acquisition and potential cost allocation of intangible assets?

14. ♟ When do we know that a company has goodwill? When can goodwill appear in a company's balance sheet?

15. ♟ Assume that a company buys another business and pays for its goodwill. If the company plans to incur costs each year to maintain the value of the goodwill, must it also amortize this goodwill?

16. ♟ How is total asset turnover computed? Why would a financial statement user be interested in total asset turnover?

17. Refer to **Best Buy**'s balance sheet in Appendix A. What plant and equipment assets does Best Buy list on its balance sheet? What is the book value of its total plant and equipment assets at March 3, 2007?

18. ♟ Refer to **Circuit City**'s balance sheet in Appendix A. What does it title its plant assets? What is the book value of its plant assets at February 28, 2007?

19. **RadioShack** lists its plant assets as "Property, plant, and equipment, net." What does "net" mean in this title? ® **RadioShack.**

20. Refer to the September 30, 2006, balance sheet of **Apple** in Appendix A. What long-term assets discussed in this chapter are reported by the company?

♟ *Denotes Discussion Questions that involve decision making.*

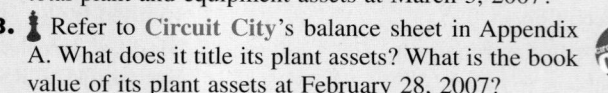
Available with McGraw-Hill's Homework Manager

QUICK STUDY

QS 10-1

Cost of plant assets

P1 ♟

Marlin Bowling installs automatic scorekeeping equipment with an invoice cost of $350,000. The electrical work required for the installation costs $10,000. Additional costs are $4,000 for delivery and $21,000 for sales tax. During the installation, a component of the equipment is carelessly left on a lane and hit by the automatic lane-cleaning machine. The cost of repairing the component is $4,200. What is the total recorded cost of the automatic scorekeeping equipment?

QS 10-2

Defining assets

C1 ♟

Identify the main difference between (1) plant assets and current assets, (2) plant assets and inventory, and (3) plant assets and long-term investments.

QS 10-3

Straight-line depreciation

P2

On January 2, 2009, the Deadra Band acquires sound equipment for concert performances at a cost of $32,500. The band estimates it will use this equipment for four years, during which time it anticipates performing about 200 concerts. It estimates that after four years it can sell the equipment for $2,500. During year 2009, the band performs 47 concerts. Compute the year 2009 depreciation using the straight-line method.

QS 10-4

Units-of-production depreciation

P2

Refer to the information in QS 10-3. Compute the year 2009 depreciation using the units-of-production method.

Refer to the facts in QS 10-3. Assume that the Deadra Band uses straight-line depreciation but realizes at the start of the second year that due to concert bookings beyond expectations, this equipment will last only a total of three years. The salvage value remains unchanged. Compute the revised depreciation for both the second and third years.

QS 10-5
Computing revised depreciation
C3

A fleet of refrigerated delivery trucks is acquired on January 5, 2009, at a cost of $1,200,000 with an estimated useful life of eight years and an estimated salvage value of $100,000. Compute the depreciation expense for the first three years using the double-declining-balance method.

QS 10-6
Double-declining-balance method
P2

1. Classify the following as either revenue or capital expenditures.
   a. Paid $40,000 cash to replace a compressor on a refrigeration system that extends its useful life by four years.
   b. Paid $200 cash per truck for the cost of their annual tune-ups.
   c. Paid $175 for the monthly cost of replacement filters on an air-conditioning system.
   d. Completed an addition to an office building for $225,000 cash.
2. Prepare the journal entries to record transactions *a* and *d* of part 1.

QS 10-7
Revenue and capital expenditures
P3 ♟

Tresler Co. owns equipment that cost $92,500, with accumulated depreciation of $54,000. Tresler sells the equipment for cash. Record the sale of the equipment assuming Tresler sells the equipment for (1) $42,000 cash, (2) $38,500 cash, and (3) $31,000 cash.

QS 10-8
Disposal of assets
P4

Crandon Company acquires an ore mine at a cost of $6,300,000. It incurs additional costs of $500,000 to access the mine, which is estimated to hold 1,000,000 tons of ore. The estimated value of the land after the ore is removed is $900,000.
1. Prepare the entry(ies) to record the cost of the ore mine.
2. Prepare the year-end adjusting entry if 125,000 tons of ore are mined and sold the first year.

QS 10-9
Natural resources and depletion
P5

Which of the following assets are reported on the balance sheet as intangible assets? Which are reported as natural resources? (*a*) Oil well, (*b*) trademark, (*c*) leasehold, (*d*) gold mine, (*e*) building, (*f*) copyright, (*g*) franchise, (*h*) timberland.

QS 10-10
Classify assets
P5   P6 ♟

On January 4 of this year, Brasen Boutique incurs a $275,000 cost to modernize its store. Improvements include new floors, ceilings, wiring, and wall coverings. These improvements are estimated to yield benefits for 10 years. Brasen leases its store and has eight years remaining on the lease. Prepare the entry to record (1) the cost of modernization and (2) amortization at the end of this current year.

QS 10-11
Intangible assets and amortization
P6

Camden Company reports the following ($ 000s): net sales of $14,880 for 2009 and $13,990 for 2008; end-of-year total assets of $15,869 for 2009 and $17,819 for 2008. Compute its total asset turnover for 2009, and assess its level if competitors average a total asset turnover of 2.0 times.

QS 10-12
Computing total asset turnover
A2 ♟

Gamma Co. owns a machine that costs $84,800 with accumulated depreciation of $36,800. Gamma exchanges the machine for a newer model that has a market value of $104,000. (1) Record the exchange assuming Gamma paid $60,000 cash and the exchange has commercial substance. (2) Record the exchange assuming Gamma pays $44,000 cash and the exchange lacks commercial substance.

QS 10-13[A]
Asset exchange
P7

McGraw-Hill's
HOMEWORK
MANAGER®   Available with McGraw-Hill's Homework Manager

EXERCISES

Kruz Co. purchases a machine for $10,400, terms 1/10, n/60, FOB shipping point. The seller prepaid the $235 freight charges, adding the amount to the invoice and bringing its total to $10,635. The machine requires special steel mounting and power connections costing $719. Another $339 is paid to assemble the machine and get it into operation. In moving the machine to its steel mounting, $250 in damages occurred. Materials costing $40 are used in adjusting the machine to produce a satisfactory product. The adjustments are normal for this machine and are not the result of the damages. Compute the cost recorded for this machine. (Kruz pays for this machine within the cash discount period.)

Exercise 10-1
Cost of plant assets
P1 ♟

Exercise 10-2
Recording costs of assets
C1 P1

Fisk Manufacturing purchases a large lot on which an old building is located as part of its plans to build a new plant. The negotiated purchase price is $209,000 for the lot plus $104,000 for the old building. The company pays $40,400 to tear down the old building and $59,722 to fill and level the lot. It also pays a total of $1,663,150 in construction costs—this amount consists of $1,564,400 for the new building and $98,750 for lighting and paving a parking area next to the building. Prepare a single journal entry to record these costs incurred by Fisk, all of which are paid in cash.

Exercise 10-3
Lump-sum purchase
of plant assets   C1

Dillon Company pays $404,000 for real estate plus $21,500 in closing costs. The real estate consists of land appraised at $217,140; land improvements appraised at $83,160; and a building appraised at $161,700. Allocate the total cost among the three purchased assets and prepare the journal entry to record the purchase.

Exercise 10-4
Straight-line depreciation
P2

In early January 2009, Sanchez Builders purchases equipment for $102,000 to use in operating activities for the next five years. It estimates the equipment's salvage value at $21,000. Prepare a table showing depreciation and book value for each of the five years assuming straight-line depreciation.

Exercise 10-5
Double-declining-balance
depreciation   P2

Refer to the information in Exercise 10-4. Prepare a table showing depreciation and book value for each of the five years assuming double-declining-balance depreciation.

Exercise 10-6
Straight-line depreciation
P2

Sarita Company installs a computerized manufacturing machine in its factory at the beginning of the year at a cost of $67,000. The machine's useful life is estimated at 10 years, or 420,000 units of product, with a $4,000 salvage value. During its second year, the machine produces 29,900 units of product. Determine the machine's second-year depreciation under the straight-line method.

Exercise 10-7
Units-of-production depreciation
P2

Refer to the information in Exercise 10-6. Determine the machine's second-year depreciation using the units-of-production method.

Exercise 10-8
Double-declining-balance
depreciation   P2

Refer to the information in Exercise 10-6. Determine the machine's second-year depreciation using the double-declining-balance method.

Exercise 10-9
Straight-line, partial-year
depreciation   C3

On April 1, 2008, Bricen Backhoe Co. purchases a trencher for $253,000. The machine is expected to last five years and have a salvage value of $25,300. Compute depreciation expense for year 2009 assuming the company uses the straight-line method.

Exercise 10-10
Double-declining-balance,
partial-year depreciation   C3

Refer to the information in Exercise 10-9. Compute depreciation expense for year 2009 assuming the company uses the double-declining-balance method.

Exercise 10-11
Revising depreciation
C3

Check   (2) $4,200

Siness Fitness Club uses straight-line depreciation for a machine costing $26,400, with an estimated four-year life and a $2,900 salvage value. At the beginning of the third year, Siness determines that the machine has three more years of remaining useful life, after which it will have an estimated $2,050 salvage value. Compute (1) the machine's book value at the end of its second year and (2) the amount of depreciation for each of the final three years given the revised estimates.

Exercise 10-12
Straight-line depreciation and
income effects

A1 ♟

Echo Enterprises pays $274,900 for equipment that will last five years and have a $41,000 salvage value. By using the equipment in its operations for five years, the company expects to earn $86,800 annually, after deducting all expenses except depreciation. Prepare a table showing income before depreciation, depreciation expense, and net (pretax) income for each year and for the total five-year period, assuming straight-line depreciation.

Refer to the information in Exercise 10-12. Prepare a table showing income before depreciation, depreciation expense, and net (pretax) income for each year and for the total five-year period, assuming double-declining-balance depreciation is used.

Exercise 10-13
Double-declining-balance
depreciation   A1

Check   Year 3 NI, $47,214

Horizon Company owns a building that appears on its prior year-end balance sheet at its original $620,000 cost less $496,000 accumulated depreciation. The building is depreciated on a straight-line basis assuming a 20-year life and no salvage value. During the first week in January of the current calendar year, major structural repairs are completed on the building at a $74,000 cost. The repairs extend its useful life for 7 years beyond the 20 years originally estimated.
1. Determine the building's age (plant asset age) as of the prior year-end balance sheet date.
2. Prepare the entry to record the cost of the structural repairs that are paid in cash.
3. Determine the book value of the building immediately after the repairs are recorded.
4. Prepare the entry to record the current calendar year's depreciation.

Exercise 10-14
Extraordinary repairs;
plant asset age
P3

Check   (3) $198,000

Bera Company pays $264,900 for equipment expected to last four years and have a $30,000 salvage value. Prepare journal entries to record the following costs related to the equipment.
1. During the second year of the equipment's life, $29,500 cash is paid for a new component expected to increase the equipment's productivity by 10% a year.
2. During the third year, $7,375 cash is paid for normal repairs necessary to keep the equipment in good working order.
3. During the fourth year, $22,450 is paid for repairs expected to increase the useful life of the equipment from four to five years.

Exercise 10-15
Ordinary repairs, extraordinary
repairs and betterments
P3

Sydney Company owns a milling machine that cost $250,000 and has accumulated depreciation of $182,000. Prepare the entry to record the disposal of the milling machine on January 3 under each of the following independent situations.
1. The machine needed extensive repairs, and it was not worth repairing. Sydney disposed of the machine, receiving nothing in return.
2. Sydney sold the machine for $35,000 cash.
3. Sydney sold the machine for $68,000 cash.
4. Sydney sold the machine for $80,000 cash.

Exercise 10-16
Disposal of assets
P4

Rayya Co. purchases and installs a machine on January 1, 2009, at a total cost of $94,000. Straight-line depreciation is taken each year for four years assuming an eight-year life and no salvage value. The machine is disposed of on July 1, 2013, during its fifth year of service. Prepare entries to record the partial year's depreciation on July 1, 2013, and to record the disposal under the following separate assumptions: (1) the machine is sold for $43,593 cash and (2) Rayya receives an insurance settlement of $39,480 resulting from the total destruction of the machine in a fire.

Exercise 10-17
Partial-year depreciation; disposal
of plant asset
P4

On April 2, 2009, Mitzu Mining Co. pays $3,920,000 for an ore deposit containing 1,400,000 tons. The company installs machinery in the mine costing $210,000, with an estimated seven-year life and no salvage value. The machinery will be abandoned when the ore is completely mined. Mitzu begins mining on May 1, 2009, and mines and sells 178,200 tons of ore during the remaining eight months of 2009. Prepare the December 31, 2009, entries to record both the ore deposit depletion and the mining machinery depreciation. Mining machinery depreciation should be in proportion to the mine's depletion.

Exercise 10-18
Depletion of natural resources
P2 P5

Galvano Gallery purchases the copyright on an oil painting for $432,000 on January 1, 2009. The copyright legally protects its owner for 19 more years. However, the company plans to market and sell prints of the original for only 15 years. Prepare entries to record the purchase of the copyright on January 1, 2009, and its annual amortization on December 31, 2009.

Exercise 10-19
Amortization of intangible assets
P6

Exercise 10-20
Goodwill

P6

On January 1, 2009, Jeffrey Company purchased Perrow Company at a price of $2,500,000. The fair market value of the net assets purchased equals $1,800,000.

1. What is the amount of goodwill that Jeffrey records at the purchase date?

2. Explain how Jeffrey would determine the amount of goodwill amortization for the year ended December 31, 2009.

3. Jeffrey Company believes that its employees provide superior customer service, and through their efforts, Jeffrey Company believes it has created $900,000 of goodwill. How would Jeffrey Company record this goodwill?

Exercise 10-21
Cash flows related to assets

C1

Refer to the statement of cash flows for Circuit City in Appendix A for the fiscal year ended February 28, 2007, to answer the following.

1. What amount of cash is used to purchase property and equipment?

2. How much depreciation and amortization are recorded?

3. What total amount of net cash is used in investing activities?

Exercise 10-22
Evaluating efficient use of assets

A2

Teridan Co. reports net sales of $4,796,000 for 2008 and $8,758,000 for 2009. End-of-year balances for total assets are 2007, $1,578,000; 2008, $1,824,000; and 2009, $1,946,000. (a) Compute Teridan's total asset turnover for 2008 and 2009. (b) Comment on Teridan's efficiency in using its assets if its competitors average a total asset turnover of 3.0.

Exercise 10-23ᴬ
Exchanging assets

P7

Corin Construction trades in an old tractor for a new tractor, receiving a $24,500 trade-in allowance and paying the remaining $71,750 in cash. The old tractor had cost $83,000, and straight-line accumulated depreciation of $45,000 had been recorded to date under the assumption that it would last eight years and have an $11,000 salvage value. Answer the following questions assuming the exchange has commercial substance.

1. What is the book value of the old tractor at the time of exchange?

Check (2) $13,500

2. What is the loss on this asset exchange?

3. What amount should be recorded (debited) in the asset account for the new tractor?

Exercise 10-24ᴬ
Recording plant asset disposals

P4 P7

Check (2) Dr. Machinery (new), $68,120

On January 2, 2009, Bering Co. disposes of a machine costing $52,400 with accumulated depreciation of $28,227. Prepare the entries to record the disposal under each of the following separate assumptions.

1. The machine is sold for $20,274 cash.

2. The machine is traded in for a newer machine having a $68,900 cash price. A $24,953 trade-in allowance is received, and the balance is paid in cash. Assume the asset exchange lacks commercial substance.

3. The machine is traded in for a newer machine having a $68,900 cash price. An $18,714 trade-in allowance is received, and the balance is paid in cash. Assume the asset exchange has commercial substance.

Available with McGraw-Hill's Homework Manager

PROBLEM SET A

Problem 10-1A
Plant asset costs; depreciation methods

C1 C2 A1 P1 P2

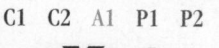

mhhe.com/wildFAP19e

Check (2) $31,000
          (3) $25,200

Teness Construction negotiates a lump-sum purchase of several assets from a company that is going out of business. The purchase is completed on January 1, 2009, at a total cash price of $900,000 for a building, land, land improvements, and four vehicles. The estimated market values of the assets are building, $514,250; land, $271,150; land improvements, $65,450; and four vehicles, $84,150. The company's fiscal year ends on December 31.

Required

1. Prepare a table to allocate the lump-sum purchase price to the separate assets purchased. Prepare the journal entry to record the purchase.

2. Compute the depreciation expense for year 2009 on the building using the straight-line method, assuming a 15-year life and a $30,000 salvage value.

3. Compute the depreciation expense for year 2009 on the land improvements assuming a five-year life and double-declining-balance depreciation.

Analysis Component

4. Defend or refute this statement: Accelerated depreciation results in payment of less taxes over the asset's life.

In January 2009, Solaris Co. pays $2,650,000 for a tract of land with two buildings on it. It plans to de-molish Building 1 and build a new store in its place. Building 2 will be a company office; it is appraised at $692,530, with a useful life of 20 years and an $85,000 salvage value. A lighted parking lot near Building 1 has improvements (Land Improvements 1) valued at $451,650 that are expected to last an-other 12 years with no salvage value. Without the buildings and improvements, the tract of land is val-ued at $1,866,820. Solaris also incurs the following additional costs:

Cost to demolish Building 1	$ 342,400
Cost of additional land grading	193,400
Cost to construct new building (Building 3), having a useful life of 25 years and a $400,000 salvage value	2,282,000
Cost of new land improvements (Land Improvements 2) near Building 2 having a 20-year useful life and no salvage value	168,000

Required

1. Prepare a table with the following column headings: Land, Building 2, Building 3, Land Improve-ments 1, and Land Improvements 2. Allocate the costs incurred by Solaris to the appropriate columns and total each column.

2. Prepare a single journal entry to record all the incurred costs assuming they are paid in cash on January 1, 2009.

3. Using the straight-line method, prepare the December 31 adjusting entries to record depreciation for the 12 months of 2009 when these assets were in use.

Maxil Contractors completed the following transactions and events involving the purchase and operation of equipment in its business.

2008

Jan. 1   Paid $293,660 cash plus $11,740 in sales tax and $1,500 in transportation (FOB shipping point) for a new loader. The loader is estimated to have a four-year life and a $36,000 salvage value. Loader costs are recorded in the Equipment account.

Jan. 3   Paid $5,100 to enclose the cab and install air conditioning in the loader to enable operations under harsher conditions. This increased the estimated salvage value of the loader by another $1,000.

Dec. 31   Recorded annual straight-line depreciation on the loader.

2009

Jan. 1   Paid $4,500 to overhaul the loader's engine, which increased the loader's estimated useful life by two years.

Feb. 17   Paid $1,125 to repair the loader after the operator backed it into a tree.

Dec. 31   Recorded annual straight-line depreciation on the loader.

Required

Prepare journal entries to record these transactions and events.

Dakota Company completed the following transactions and events involving its delivery trucks.

2008

Jan. 1   Paid $25,015 cash plus $1,485 in sales tax for a new delivery truck estimated to have a five-year life and a $2,000 salvage value. Delivery truck costs are recorded in the Trucks account.

Dec. 31   Recorded annual straight-line depreciation on the truck.

2009

Dec. 31   Due to new information obtained earlier in the year, the truck's estimated useful life was changed from five to four years, and the estimated salvage value was increased to $2,700. Recorded annual straight-line depreciation on the truck.

2010

Dec. 31, 2010, Dr. Loss on
Disposal of Trucks, $3,400

Dec. 31   Recorded annual straight-line depreciation on the truck.
Dec. 31   Sold the truck for $5,600 cash.

Required

Prepare journal entries to record these transactions and events.

Problem 10-5A
Depreciation methods

A1   P2

A machine costing $320,000 with a four-year life and an estimated $33,000 salvage value is installed in Luther Company's factory on January 1. The factory manager estimates the machine will produce 512,500 units of product during its life. It actually produces the following units: year 1, 127,500; year 2, 129,000; year 3, 128,500; and year 4, 127,900. The total number of units produced by the end of year 4 exceeds the original estimate—this difference was not predicted. (The machine must not be depreciated below its estimated salvage value.)

Required

Prepare a table with the following column headings and compute depreciation for each year (and total depreciation of all years combined) for the machine under each depreciation method.

Check   Year 4: units-of-production
depreciation, $71,400; DDB
depreciation, $7,000

Year	Straight-Line	Units-of-Production	Double-Declining-Balance

---

Problem 10-6A
Disposal of plant assets

P1   P2   P4

Platero Co. purchases a used machine for $198,750 cash on January 2 and readies it for use the next day at an $11,000 cost. On January 3, it is installed on a required operating platform costing $3,410, and it is further readied for operations. The company predicts the machine will be used for six years and have a $16,960 salvage value. Depreciation is to be charged on a straight-line basis. On December 31, at the end of its fifth year in operations, it is disposed of.

Required

1. Prepare journal entries to record the machine's purchase and the costs to ready and install it. Cash is paid for all costs incurred.

Check   (2b) Depr. Exp., $32,700

2. Prepare journal entries to record depreciation of the machine at December 31 of (a) its first year in operations and (b) the year of its disposal.

(3c) Dr. Loss from Fire,
$18,160

3. Prepare journal entries to record the machine's disposal under each of the following separate assumptions: (a) it is sold for $21,000 cash; (b) it is sold for $73,500 cash; and (c) it is destroyed in a fire and the insurance company pays $31,500 cash to settle the loss claim.

Problem 10-7A
Natural resources

P5

On July 23 of the current year, Serena Mining Co. pays $4,612,500 for land estimated to contain 5,125,000 tons of recoverable ore. It installs machinery costing $512,500 that has a 10-year life and no salvage value and is capable of mining the ore deposit in eight years. The machinery is paid for on July 25, seven days before mining operations begin. The company removes and sells 490,000 tons of ore during its first five months of operations ending on December 31. Depreciation of the machinery is in proportion to the mine's depletion as the machinery will be abandoned after the ore is mined.

Required

Check   (c) Depletion, $441,000
            (d) Depreciation, $49,000

Prepare entries to record (a) the purchase of the land, (b) the cost and installation of machinery, (c) the first five months' depletion assuming the land has a net salvage value of zero after the ore is mined, and (d) the first five months' depreciation on the machinery.

Analysis Component

Describe both the similarities and differences in amortization, depletion, and depreciation.

On July 1, 2004, Harper Company signed a contract to lease space in a building for 15 years. The lease contract calls for annual (prepaid) rental payments of $80,000 on each July 1 throughout the life of the lease and for the lessee to pay for all additions and improvements to the leased property. On June 25, 2009, Harper decides to sublease the space to Bosio & Associates for the remaining 10 years of the lease—Bosio pays $260,000 to Harper for the right to sublease and it agrees to assume the obligation to pay the $80,000 annual rent to the building owner beginning July 1, 2009. After taking possession of the leased space, Bosio pays for improving the office portion of the leased space at a $160,000 cost. The improvements are paid for by Bosio on July 5, 2009, and are estimated to have a useful life equal to the 16 years remaining in the life of the building.

Problem 10-8A
Intangible assets
P6

Required

1. Prepare entries for Bosio to record (*a*) its payment to Harper for the right to sublease the building space, (*b*) its payment of the 2009 annual rent to the building owner, and (*c*) its payment for the office improvements.

2. Prepare Bosio's year-end adjusting entries required at December 31, 2009, to (*a*) amortize the $260,000 cost of the sublease, (*b*) amortize the office improvements, and (*c*) record rent expense.

Check   Dr. Rent Expense for (2*a*) $13,000, (2*c*) $40,000

Clinton Company negotiates a lump-sum purchase of several assets from a contractor who is relocating. The purchase is completed on January 1, 2009, at a total cash price of $930,000 for a building, land, land improvements, and four trucks. The estimated market values of the assets are building, $469,200; land, $303,600; land improvements, $36,800; and four trucks, $110,400. The company's fiscal year ends on December 31.

PROBLEM SET B

Problem 10-1B
Plant asset costs; depreciation methods
C1 C2 A1 P1 P2

Required

1. Prepare a table to allocate the lump-sum purchase price to the separate assets purchased. Prepare the journal entry to record the purchase.

2. Compute the depreciation expense for year 2009 on the building using the straight-line method, assuming a 15-year life and a $30,000 salvage value.

3. Compute the depreciation expense for year 2009 on the land improvements assuming a five-year life and double-declining-balance depreciation.

Check   (2) $29,620

(3) $14,880

Analysis Component

4. Defend or refute this statement: Accelerated depreciation results in payment of more taxes over the asset's life.

In January 2009, Boulware Co. pays $2,750,000 for a tract of land with two buildings. It plans to demolish Building A and build a new shop in its place. Building B will be a company office; it is appraised at $687,700, with a useful life of 20 years and an $85,000 salvage value. A lighted parking lot near Building B has improvements (Land Improvements B) valued at $478,400 that are expected to last another 10 years with no salvage value. Without the buildings and improvements, the tract of land is valued at $1,823,900. Boulware also incurs the following additional costs.

Problem 10-2B
Asset cost allocation; straight-line depreciation
C1 C2 P1 P2

Cost to demolish Building A	$ 345,400
Cost of additional land grading	185,400
Cost to construct new building (Building C), having a useful life of 25 years and a $400,000 salvage value	2,282,000
Cost of new land improvements (Land Improvements C) near Building C, having a 20-year useful life and no salvage value	173,000

Required

1. Prepare a table with the following column headings: Land, Building B, Building C, Land Improvements B, and Land Improvements C. Allocate the costs incurred by Boulware to the appropriate columns and total each column.

2. Prepare a single journal entry to record all incurred costs assuming they are paid in cash on January 1, 2009.

3. Using the straight-line method, prepare the December 31 adjusting entries to record depreciation for the 12 months of 2009 when these assets were in use.

Check   (1) Land costs, $2,208,300; Building B costs, $632,500

(3) Depr.—Land Improv. B and C, $44,000 and $8,650

Problem 10-3B

Computing and revising depreciation; revenue and capital expenditures

C3 P1 P3

Zander Delivery Service completed the following transactions and events involving the purchase and operation of equipment for its business.

2008

Jan. 1 Paid $58,000 cash plus $4,000 in sales tax for a new delivery van that was estimated to have a four-year life and a $3,000 salvage value. Van costs are recorded in the Equipment account.

Jan. 3 Paid $2,900 to install sorting racks in the van for more accurate and quicker delivery of packages. This increases the estimated salvage value of the van by another $200.

Dec. 31 Recorded annual straight-line depreciation on the van.

2009

Jan. 1 Paid $4,300 to overhaul the van's engine, which increased the van's estimated useful life by two years.

May 10 Paid $1,075 to repair the van after the driver backed it into a loading dock.

Dec. 31 Record annual straight-line depreciation on the van. (Round to the nearest dollar.)

Required

Prepare journal entries to record these transactions and events.

Problem 10-4B

Computing and revising depreciation; selling plant assets

C3 P2 P4

Walsh Instruments completed the following transactions and events involving its machinery.

2008

Jan. 1 Paid $20,515 cash plus $1,485 in sales tax for a new machine. The machine is estimated to have a five-year life and a $2,000 salvage value.

Dec. 31 Recorded annual straight-line depreciation on the machinery.

2009

Dec. 31 Due to new information obtained earlier in the year, the machine's estimated useful life was changed from five to four years, and the estimated salvage value was increased to $2,550. Recorded annual straight-line depreciation on the machinery.

2010

Dec. 31 Recorded annual straight-line depreciation on the machinery.

Dec. 31 Sold the machine for $5,600 cash.

Required

Prepare journal entries to record these transactions and events.

Problem 10-5B

Depreciation methods

A1 P2

On January 2, Gillette Co. purchases and installs a new machine costing $360,000 with a five-year life and an estimated $33,000 salvage value. Management estimates the machine will produce 2,180,000 units of product during its life. Actual production of units is as follows: year 1, 425,000; year 2, 452,000; year 3, 445,000; year 4, 438,000; and year 5, 441,000. The total number of units produced by the end of year 5 exceeds the original estimate—this difference was not predicted. (The machine must not be depreciated below its estimated salvage value.)

Required

Prepare a table with the following column headings and compute depreciation for each year (and total depreciation of all years combined) for the machine under each depreciation method.

Year	Straight-Line	Units-of-Production	Double-Declining-Balance

On January 1, Ammons purchases a used machine for $238,500 and readies it for use the next day at a cost of $11,000. On January 4, it is mounted on a required operating platform costing $3,600, and it is further readied for operations. Management estimates the machine will be used for six years and have a $22,100 salvage value. Depreciation is to be charged on a straight-line basis. On December 31, at the end of its fifth year of use, the machine is disposed of.

Problem 10-6B
Disposal of plant assets
P1 P2 P4

Required

1. Prepare journal entries to record the machine's purchase and the costs to ready and install it. Cash is paid for all costs incurred.

2. Prepare journal entries to record depreciation of the machine at December 31 of (*a*) its first year in operations and (*b*) the year of its disposal.

Check   (2*b*) Depr. Exp., $38,500

3. Prepare journal entries to record the machine's disposal under each of the following separate assumptions: (*a*) it is sold for $20,500 cash; (*b*) it is sold for $71,750 cash; and (*c*) it is destroyed in a fire and the insurance company pays $31,000 cash to settle the loss claim.

(3*c*) Dr. Loss from Fire, $29,600

On February 19 of the current year, Javier Co. pays $6,000,000 for land estimated to contain 4 million tons of recoverable ore. It installs machinery costing $480,000 that has a 16-year life and no salvage value and is capable of mining the ore deposit in 12 years. The machinery is paid for on March 21, seven days before mining operations begin. The company removes and sells 380,000 tons of ore during its first nine months of operations ending on December 31. Depreciation of the machinery is in proportion to the mine's depletion as the machinery will be abandoned after the ore is mined.

Problem 10-7B
Natural resources
P5

Required

Prepare entries to record (*a*) the purchase of the land, (*b*) the cost and installation of the machinery, (*c*) the first nine months' depletion assuming the land has a net salvage value of zero after the ore is mined, and (*d*) the first nine months' depreciation on the machinery.

Check   (*c*) Depletion, $570,000;
(*d*) Depreciation, $45,600

Analysis Component

Describe both the similarities and differences in amortization, depletion, and depreciation.

On January 1, 2002, Palos Co. entered into a 12-year lease on a building. The lease contract requires (1) annual (prepaid) rental payments of $90,000 each January 1 throughout the life of the lease and (2) for the lessee to pay for all additions and improvements to the leased property. On January 1, 2009, Palos decides to sublease the space to Callahan Co. for the remaining five years of the lease—Callahan pays $200,000 to Palos for the right to sublease and agrees to assume the obligation to pay the $90,000 annual rent to the building owner beginning January 1, 2009. After taking possession of the leased space, Callahan pays for improving the office portion of the leased space at a $150,000 cost. The improvements are paid for by Callahan on January 3, 2009, and are estimated to have a useful life equal to the 13 years remaining in the life of the building.

Problem 10-8B
Intangible assets
P6

Required

1. Prepare entries for Callahan to record (*a*) its payment to Palos for the right to sublease the building space, (*b*) its payment of the 2009 annual rent to the building owner, and (*c*) its payment for the office improvements.

2. Prepare Callahan's year-end adjusting entries required on December 31, 2009, to (*a*) amortize the $200,000 cost of the sublease, (*b*) amortize the office improvements, and (*c*) record rent expense.

Check   Dr. Rent Expense: (2*a*) $40,000,
(2*c*) $90,000

SERIAL PROBLEM

Success Systems

(This serial problem began in Chapter 1 and continues through most of the book. If previous chapter segments were not completed, the serial problem can begin at this point. It is helpful, but not necessary, to use the Working Papers that accompany the book.)

SP 10   Selected ledger account balances for Success Systems follow.

	For Three Months Ended December 31, 2009	For Three Months Ended March 31, 2010
Office equipment	$ 8,000	$ 8,000
Accumulated depreciation— . . . . Office equipment	400	800
Computer equipment	20,000	20,000
Accumulated depreciation— . . . . Computer equipment	1,250	2,500
Total revenue	31,284	43,853
Total assets	93,248	129,909

Required

1. Assume that Success Systems does not acquire additional office equipment or computer equipment in 2010. Compute the amounts for the year ended December 31, 2010, for Depreciation Expense—Office Equipment and for Depreciation Expense—Computer Equipment (assume use of the straight-line method).
2. Given the assumptions in part 1, what is the book value of both the office equipment and the computer equipment as of December 31, 2010?

Check   (3) Three-month (annual) turnover = 0.39 (1.56)

3. Compute the three-month total asset turnover for Success Systems as of March 31, 2010. Use total revenue for the numerator and average the December 31, 2009, total assets and the March 31, 2010, total assets for the denominator. Interpret its total asset turnover if competitors average 2.5 for annual periods.

BEYOND THE NUMBERS

REPORTING IN ACTION

A1   A2

BTN 10-1   Refer to the financial statements of Best Buy in Appendix A to answer the following.

1. What percent of the original cost of Best Buy's property and equipment remain to be depreciated as of March 3, 2007, and at February 25, 2006? Assume these assets have no salvage value.
2. Over what length(s) of time is Best Buy amortizing its intangible assets?
3. What is the change in total property and equipment (before accumulated depreciation) for the year ended March 3, 2007? What is the amount of cash provided (used) by investing activities for property and equipment for the year ended March 3, 2007? What is one possible explanation for the difference between these two amounts?
4. Compute its total asset turnover for the year ended March 3, 2007, and the year ended February 25, 2006. Assume total assets at February 26, 2005, are $10,294 ($ millions).

Fast Forward

5. Access Best Buy's financial statements for the fiscal years ending after March 3, 2007, at its Website (BestBuy.com) or the SEC's EDGAR database (www.SEC.gov). Recompute Best Buy's total asset turnover for the additional years' data you collect. Comment on any differences relative to the turnover computed in part 4.

COMPARATIVE ANALYSIS

A2

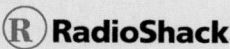

BTN 10-2   Comparative figures for Best Buy, Circuit City, and RadioShack follow.

($ millions)	Best Buy			Circuit City			RadioShack		
	Current Year	One Year Prior	Two Years Prior	Current Year	One Year Prior	Two Years Prior	Current Year	One Year Prior	Two Years Prior
Total assets	$13,570	$11,864	$10,294	$ 4,007	$ 4,069	$ 3,840	$2,070	$2,205	$2,517
Net sales	35,934	30,848	27,433	12,430	11,514	10,414	4,778	5,082	4,841

Required

1. Compute the total asset turnover for the most recent two years for Best Buy, Circuit City, and RadioShack using the data shown.

2. Which company is more efficient in generating net sales given the total assets it employs? Assume an industry average of 2.6.

BTN 10-3 Carmel Choi owns a small business and manages its accounting. Her company just finished a year in which a large amount of borrowed funds was invested in a new building addition as well as in equipment and fixture additions. Choi's banker requires her to submit semiannual financial statements so he can monitor the financial health of her business. He has warned her that if profit margins erode, he might raise the interest rate on the borrowed funds to reflect the increased loan risk from the bank's point of view. Choi knows profit margin is likely to decline this year. As she prepares year-end adjusting entries, she decides to apply the following depreciation rule: All asset additions are considered to be in use on the first day of the following month. (The previous rule assumed assets are in use on the first day of the month nearest to the purchase date.)

ETHICS CHALLENGE
C1 C2

Required

1. Identify decisions that managers like Choi must make in applying depreciation methods.

2. Is Choi's rule an ethical violation, or is it a legitimate decision in computing depreciation?

3. How will Choi's new depreciation rule affect the profit margin of her business?

BTN 10-4 Teams are to select an industry, and each team member is to select a different company in that industry. Each team member is to acquire the financial statements (Form 10-K) of the company selected—see the company's Website or the SEC's EDGAR database (www.sec.gov). Use the financial statements to compute total asset turnover. Communicate with teammates via a meeting, e-mail, or telephone to discuss the meaning of this ratio, how different companies compare to each other, and the industry norm. The team must prepare a one-page report that describes the ratios for each company and identifies the conclusions reached during the team's discussion.

COMMUNICATING IN PRACTICE
A2

BTN 10-5 Access the Yahoo! (ticker: YHOO) 10-K report for the year ended December 31, 2006, filed on February 23, 2007, at www.sec.gov.

TAKING IT TO THE NET
C1 P6

Required

1. What amount of goodwill is reported on Yahoo!'s balance sheet? What percentage of total assets does its goodwill represent? Is goodwill a major asset for Yahoo!? Explain.

2. Locate Note 5 to its financial statements. Identify the change in goodwill from December 31, 2005, to December 31, 2006. Comment on the change in goodwill over this period.

3. Locate Note 6 to its financial statements. What are the three categories of intangible assets that Yahoo! reports at December 31, 2006? What proportion of total assets do the intangibles represent?

4. What does Yahoo! indicate is the life of "Trademark, trade name, and domain name" according to its Note 6? Comment on the difference between the estimated economic life and the legal life of Yahoo!'s trademark.

BTN 10-6 Each team member is to become an expert on one depreciation method to facilitate teammates' understanding of that method. Follow these procedures:

a. Each team member is to select an area for expertise from one of the following depreciation methods: straight-line, units-of-production, or double-declining-balance.

b. Expert teams are to be formed from those who have selected the same area of expertise. The instructor will identify the location where each expert team meets.

c. Using the following data, expert teams are to collaborate and develop a presentation answering the requirements. Expert team members must write the presentation in a format they can show to their learning teams.

Data and Requirements On January 8, 2007, Whitewater Riders purchases a van to transport rafters back to the point of departure at the conclusion of the rafting adventures they operate. The cost of the van is $44,000. It has an estimated salvage value of $2,000 and is expected to be used for four years and

TEAMWORK IN ACTION
C2 A1 P2

Point: This activity can follow an overview of each method. Step 1 allows for three areas of expertise. Larger teams will have some duplication of areas, but the straight-line choice should not be duplicated. Expert teams can use the book and consult with the instructor.

driven 60,000 miles. The van is driven 12,000 miles in 2007, 18,000 miles in 2008, 21,000 in 2009, and 10,000 in 2010.

    1. Compute the annual depreciation expense for each year of the van's estimated useful life.

    2. Explain when and how annual depreciation is recorded.

    3. Explain the impact on income of this depreciation method versus others over the van's life.

    4. Identify the van's book value for each year of its life and illustrate the reporting of this amount for any one year.

  d. Re-form original learning teams. In rotation, experts are to present to their teams the results from part *c*. Experts are to encourage and respond to questions.

ENTREPRENEURIAL DECISION

A2

BTN 10-7   Review the chapter's opening feature involving Sambazon. Assume that the company currently has net sales of $8,000,000, and that it is planning an expansion that will increase net sales by $4,000,000. To accomplish this expansion, Sambazon must increase its average total assets from $2,500,000 to $3,000,000.

Required

1. Compute the company's total asset turnover under (*a*) current conditions and (*b*) proposed conditions.

2. Evaluate and comment on the merits of the proposal given your analysis in part 1. Identify any concerns you would express about the proposal.

HITTING THE ROAD

C1 P5 P6

BTN 10-8   Team up with one or more classmates for this activity. Identify companies in your community or area that must account for at least one of the following assets: natural resource; patent; lease; leasehold improvement; copyright; trademark; or goodwill. You might find a company having more than one type of asset. Once you identify a company with a specific asset, describe the accounting this company uses to allocate the cost of that asset to the periods benefited from its use.

GLOBAL DECISION

A2

BTN 10-9   DSG international, Best Buy, Circuit City, and RadioShack are all competitors in the global marketplace. Comparative figures for these companies' recent annual accounting periods follow.

(in millions)	DSG (£ millions) Current Year	DSG Prior Year	DSG Two Years Prior	Best Buy Current Year	Best Buy Prior Year	Circuit City Current Year	Circuit City Prior Year	RadioShack Current Year	RadioShack Prior Year
Total assets ..	£3,977	£4,120	£4,104	$13,570	$11,864	$ 4,007	$ 4,069	$2,070	$2,205
Net sales	7,930	6,984	6,983	35,934	30,848	12,430	11,514	4,778	5,082
Total asset turnover ...	?	?	—	2.83	2.78	3.08	2.91	2.24	2.15

Required

1. Compute the total asset turnover for the most recent two years for DSG using the data shown.

2. Which company is most efficient in generating net sales given the total assets it employs?

ANSWERS TO MULTIPLE CHOICE QUIZ

1. b;

	Appraisal Value	%	Total Cost	Allocated
Land	$175,000	50%	$326,000	$163,000
Land improvements	70,000	20	326,000	65,200
Building	105,000	30	326,000	97,800
Totals	$350,000			$326,000

2. c; ($35,000 − $1,000)/4 years = $8,500 per year.

3. c; 2009: $10,800,000 × (2 × 10%) = $2,160,000
    2010: ($10,800,000 − $2,160,000) × (2 × 10%) = $1,728,000

4. c;

Cost of machine	$250,000
Accumulated depreciation	100,000
Book value	150,000
Cash received	120,000
Loss on sale	$ 30,000

5. b; $550,000/$500,000 = 1.10

A Look Back

Chapter 10 focused on long-term assets including plant assets, natural resources, and intangibles. We showed how to account for and analyze those assets.

A Look at This Chapter

This chapter explains how to identify, compute, record, and report current liabilities in financial statements. We also analyze and interpret these liabilities, including those related to employee costs.

A Look Ahead

Chapter 12 explains the partnership form of organization. It also describes the accounting concepts and procedures for partnership transactions.

Current Liabilities and Payroll Accounting

Chapter

Learning Objectives

CAP

Conceptual

C1 Describe current and long-term liabilities and their characteristics. *(p. 434)*

C2 Identify and describe known current liabilities. *(p. 436)*

C3 Explain how to account for contingent liabilities. *(p. 445)*

Analytical

A1 Compute the times interest earned ratio and use it to analyze liabilities. *(p. 447)*

Procedural

P1 Prepare entries to account for short-term notes payable. *(p. 437)*

P2 Compute and record *employee* payroll deductions and liabilities. *(p. 439)*

P3 Compute and record *employer* payroll expenses and liabilities. *(p. 441)*

P4 Account for estimated liabilities, including warranties and bonuses. *(p. 443)*

P5 *Appendix 11A*—Identify and describe the details of payroll reports, records, and procedures. *(p. 450)*

LP11

Granola Gurus

"Get a clear vision and stick to it"—Jason Osborn

NEW YORK—Jason Osborn never planned to be an entrepreneur. "It was sort of an accident," explains Osborn. "I was looking for a healthy snack food as an alternative to cookies and brownies." Osborn starting cooking with granola and his concoctions caught on. After sharing it with his buddy, Jason Wright, the two decided to launch **Feed Granola Company (FeedGranola.com),** a provider of granola snacks made with organic multi-grains.

"We started peddling it . . . to a few different coffee shops and one natural health food store," recalls Osborn. "That created a small demand and we realized we had a viable product." Adds Wright, "I had no idea that I would have a granola company one day!" Their commitment to healthy food carries over to the financial side. The two especially focus on the important task of managing liabilities for payroll, supplies, employee benefits, vacations, training, and taxes. Both insist that effective management of liabilities, especially payroll and employee benefits, is crucial to success. They stress that monitoring and controlling liabilities are a must.

To help control liabilities, Osborn describes how they began by trading their granola products for kitchen space. "We partnered with a meal delivery service and bartered to use their kitchen space," explains Osborn. "We'd bake our granola during the night when they weren't using it and we paid for the usage in granola. That's how we paid rent." Creative payment of liabilities can mean success or failure.

The two continue to monitor liabilities and their payment patterns. "Trying to balance receivables versus payables is always a big challenge," explains Wright. "When you are a small, growing company, cash flow is always a problem." The two insist that accounting for and monitoring liabilities are key to a successful startup. Their company now generates sufficient income to pay for liabilities and produces revenue growth for expansion. "We want to expand our product line," says Osborn. "[Soon] we'll be available in almost every region of the country."

[Sources: *Feed Granola Website,* January 2009; *BusinessWeek,* September 2007; *Inc.com,* July and October 2007; *The Wall Street Journal,* May 2008]

Previous chapters introduced liabilities such as accounts payable, notes payable, wages payable, and unearned revenues. This chapter further explains these liabilities and additional ones such as warranties, taxes, payroll, vacation pay, and bonuses. It also describes contingent liabilities and introduces long-term liabilities. The focus is on how to define, classify, measure, report, and analyze these liabilities so that this information is useful to business decision makers.

Current Liabilities and Payroll Accounting

Liability Characteristics	Known Liabilities	Estimated Liabilities	Contingent Liabilities
• Definition • Classification • Uncertainty	• Accounts payable • Sales taxes payable • Unearned revenues • Short-term notes • Payroll liabilities	• Health and pension benefits • Vacation benefits • Bonus plans • Warranty liabilities	• Accounting for contingencies • Reasonably possible contingencies

Characteristics of Liabilities

This section discusses important characteristics of liabilities and how liabilities are classified and reported.

Defining Liabilities

C1 Describe current and long-term liabilities and their characteristics.

A *liability* is a probable future payment of assets or services that a company is presently obligated to make as a result of past transactions or events. This definition includes three crucial factors:

1. A past transaction or event.
2. A present obligation.
3. A future payment of assets or services.

These three important elements are portrayed visually in Exhibit 11.1. Liabilities reported in financial statements exhibit those characteristics. No liability is reported when one or more of those characteristics is absent. For example, most companies expect to pay wages to their employees in upcoming months and years, but these future payments are *not* liabilities because no past event such as employee work resulted in a present obligation. Instead, such liabilities arise when employees perform their work and earn the wages.

EXHIBIT 11.1

Characteristics of a Liability

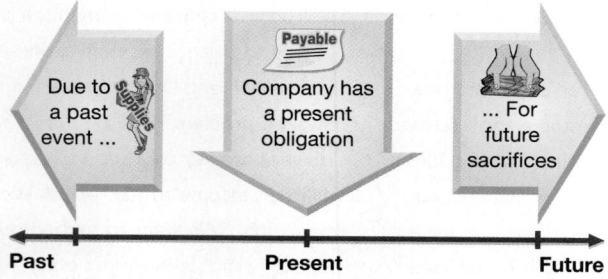

Due to a past event ...   Company has a present obligation   ... For future sacrifices

Past   Present   Future

Classifying Liabilities

Video 11.1

Information about liabilities is more useful when the balance sheet identifies them as either current or long term. Decision makers need to know when obligations are due so they can plan for them and take appropriate action.

Current Liabilities   **Current liabilities,** also called *short-term liabilities,* are obligations due within one year or the company's operating cycle, whichever is longer. They are expected to be paid using current assets or by creating other current liabilities. Common examples of current liabilities are accounts payable, short-term notes payable, wages payable, warranty liabilities, lease liabilities, taxes payable, and unearned revenues.

Point: Improper classification of liabilities can distort ratios used in financial statement analysis and business decisions.

Current liabilities differ across companies because they depend on the type of company operations. **Univision Communications,** for instance, included the following current liabilities related to its Spanish-language media operations ($000s):

Music copyright and artist royalties	$53,054
Program rights obligations	15,658

Harley-Davidson reports a much different set of current liabilities. It discloses current liabilities made up of items such as warranty, recall, and dealer incentive liabilities.

Long-Term Liabilities   A company's obligations not expected to be paid within the longer of one year or the company's operating cycle are reported as **long-term liabilities.** They can include long-term notes payable, warranty liabilities, lease liabilities, and bonds payable. They are sometimes reported on the balance sheet in a single long-term liabilities total or in multiple categories. **Domino's Pizza,** for instance, reports long-term liabilities of $982 million. They are reported after current liabilities. A single liability also can be divided between the current and noncurrent sections if a company expects to make payments toward it in both the short and long term. Domino's reports ($ millions) long-term debt, $789.9; and current portion of long-term debt, $1.5. The second item is reported in current liabilities. We sometimes see liabilities that do not have a fixed due date but instead are payable on the creditor's demand. These are reported as current liabilities because of the possibility of payment in the near term. Exhibit 11.2 shows amounts of current liabilities and as a percent of total liabilities for selected companies.

Point: The current ratio is overstated if a company fails to classify any portion of long-term debt due next period as a current liability.

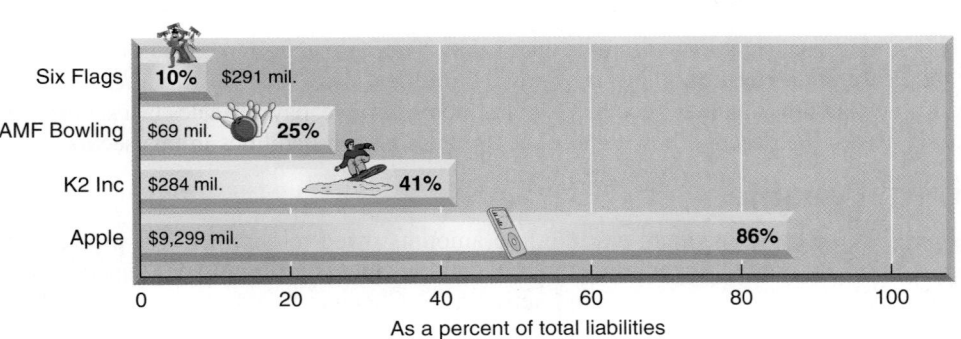

EXHIBIT 11.2

Current Liabilities of Selected Companies

Uncertainty in Liabilities

Accounting for liabilities involves addressing three important questions: Whom to pay? When to pay? How much to pay? Answers to these questions are often decided when a liability is incurred. For example, if a company has a $100 account payable to a specific individual, payable on March 15, the answers are clear. The company knows whom to pay, when to pay, and how much to pay. However, the answers to one or more of these questions are uncertain for some liabilities.

Uncertainty in Whom to Pay   Liabilities can involve uncertainty in whom to pay. For instance, a company can create a liability with a known amount when issuing a note that is payable to its holder. In this case, a specific amount is payable to the note's holder at a specified date, but the company does not know who the holder is until that date. Despite this uncertainty, the company reports this liability on its balance sheet.

Point: An *accrued expense* is an unpaid expense, and is also called an *accrued liability.*

Uncertainty in When to Pay A company can have an obligation of a known amount to a known creditor but not know when it must be paid. For example, a legal services firm can accept fees in advance from a client who plans to use the firm's services in the future. This means that the firm has a liability that it settles by providing services at an unknown future date. Although this uncertainty exists, the legal firm's balance sheet must report this liability. These types of obligations are reported as current liabilities because they are likely to be settled in the short term.

Uncertainty in How Much to Pay A company can be aware of an obligation but not know how much will be required to settle it. For example, a company using electrical power is billed only after the meter has been read. This cost is incurred and the liability created before a bill is received. A liability to the power company is reported as an estimated amount if the balance sheet is prepared before a bill arrives.

Decision Insight

IFRSs IFRSs record a contingent liability when an obligation exists from a past event if there is a 'probable' outflow of resources *and* the amount can be estimated reliably. However, IFRSs define probable as 'more likely than not' while U.S. GAAP defines it as 'likely to occur.'

Known Liabilities

Video11.1

Most liabilities arise from situations with little uncertainty. They are set by agreements, contracts, or laws and are measurable. These liabilities are **known liabilities,** also called *definitely determinable liabilities.* Known liabilities include accounts payable, notes payable, payroll, sales taxes, unearned revenues, and leases. We describe how to account for these known liabilities in this section.

Accounts Payable

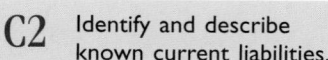

C2 Identify and describe known current liabilities.

Accounts payable, or trade accounts payable, are amounts owed to suppliers for products or services purchased on credit. Accounting for accounts payable is primarily explained and illustrated in our discussion of merchandising activities in Chapters 5 and 6.

Sales Taxes Payable

Nearly all states and many cities levy taxes on retail sales. Sales taxes are stated as a percent of selling prices. The seller collects sales taxes from customers when sales occur and remits these collections (often monthly) to the proper government agency. Since sellers currently owe these collections to the government, this amount is a current liability. **Home Depot**, for instance, reports sales taxes payable of $475 million in its recent annual report. To illustrate, if Home Depot sells materials on August 31 for $6,000 cash that are subject to a 5% sales tax, the revenue portion of this transaction is recorded as follows:

Assets = Liabilities + Equity
+6,300   +300   +6,000

Aug. 31	Cash..	6,300	
	Sales..		6,000
	Sales Taxes Payable ($6,000 × 0.05)..........		300
	To record cash sales and 5% sales tax.		

Sales Taxes Payable is debited and Cash credited when it remits these collections to the government. Sales Taxes Payable is not an expense. It arises because laws require sellers to collect this cash from customers for the government.[1]

Unearned Revenues

Unearned revenues (also called *deferred revenues, collections in advance,* and *prepayments*) are amounts received in advance from customers for future products or services. Advance ticket sales for sporting events or music concerts are examples. **Bon Jovi**, for instance, has "deferred revenues" from advance ticket sales. To illustrate, assume that Bon Jovi sells $5 million in tickets for eight concerts; the entry is

Point: To *defer* a revenue means to postpone recognition of a revenue collected in advance until it is earned. Sport teams must defer recognition of ticket sales until games are played.

June 30	Cash	5,000,000	
	Unearned Ticket Revenue		5,000,000
	To record sale of concert tickets.		

Assets = Liabilities + Equity
+5,000,000   +5,000,000

When a concert is played, Bon Jovi would record revenue for the portion earned.

Oct. 31	Unearned Ticket Revenue	625,000	
	Ticket Revenue		625,000
	To record concert ticket revenues earned.		

Assets = Liabilities + Equity
        −625,000   +625,000

Unearned Ticket Revenue is an unearned revenue account and is reported as a current liability. Unearned revenues also arise with airline ticket sales, magazine subscriptions, construction projects, hotel reservations, and custom orders.

Decision Insight

Reward Programs Gift card sales now exceed $100 billion annually, and reward (also called loyalty) programs are growing. There are no exact rules for how retailers account for rewards. When **Best Buy** launched its "Reward Zone," shoppers earned $5 on each $125 spent and had 90 days to spend it. Retailers make assumptions about how many reward program dollars will be spent and how to report it. Best Buy sets up a liability and reduces revenue by the same amount. **Talbots** does not reduce revenue but instead increases selling expense. **Men's Wearhouse** records rewards in cost of goods sold, whereas **Neiman Marcus** subtracts them from revenue. The FASB is reviewing reward programs.

Short-Term Notes Payable

A **short-term note payable** is a written promise to pay a specified amount on a definite future date within one year or the company's operating cycle, whichever is longer. These promissory notes are negotiable (as are checks), meaning they can be transferred from party to party by endorsement. The written documentation provided by notes is helpful in resolving disputes and for pursuing legal actions involving these liabilities. Most notes payable bear interest to compensate for use of the money until payment is made. Short-term notes payable can arise from many transactions. A company that purchases merchandise on credit can sometimes extend the credit period by signing a note to replace an account payable. Such notes also can arise when money is borrowed from a bank. We describe both of these cases.

P1 Prepare entries to account for short-term notes payable.

Point: Required characteristics for negotiability of a note: (1) unconditional promise, (2) in writing, (3) specific amount, and (4) definite due date.

---

[1] Sales taxes can be computed from total sales receipts when sales taxes are not separately identified on the register. To illustrate, assume a 5% sales tax and $420 in total sales receipts (which includes sales taxes). Sales are computed as follows:

$$\text{Sales} = \text{Total sales receipts}/(1 + \text{Sales tax percentage}) = \$420/1.05 = \$400$$

Thus, the sales tax amount equals total sales receipts minus sales, or $420 − $400 = $20.

Note Given to Extend Credit Period   A company can replace an account payable with a note payable. A common example is a creditor that requires the substitution of an interest-bearing note for an overdue account payable that does not bear interest. A less common situation occurs when a debtor's weak financial condition motivates the creditor to accept a note, sometimes for a lesser amount, and to close the account to ensure that this customer makes no additional credit purchases.

To illustrate, let's assume that on August 23, Brady Company asks to extend its past-due $600 account payable to McGraw. After some negotiations, McGraw agrees to accept $100 cash and a 60-day, 12%, $500 note payable to replace the account payable. Brady records the transaction with this entry:

Assets = Liabilities + Equity
−100   −600
          +500

Aug. 23	Accounts Payable—McGraw	600	
	Cash		100
	Notes Payable—McGraw		500
	Gave $100 cash and a 60-day, 12% note for payment on account.		

Point: Accounts payable are detailed in a subsidiary ledger, but notes payable are sometimes not. A file with copies of notes can serve as a subsidiary ledger.

Signing the note does not resolve Brady's debt. Instead, the form of debt is changed from an account payable to a note payable. McGraw prefers the note payable over the account payable because it earns interest and it is written documentation of the debt's existence, term, and amount. When the note comes due, Brady pays the note and interest by giving McGraw a check for $510. Brady records that payment with this entry:

Assets = Liabilities + Equity
−510   −500   −10

Oct. 22	Notes Payable—McGraw	500	
	Interest Expense	10	
	Cash		510
	Paid note with interest ($500 × 12% × 60/360).		

Point: Commercial companies commonly compute interest using a 360-day year. This is known as the *banker's rule.*

Interest expense is computed by multiplying the principal of the note ($500) by the annual interest rate (12%) for the fraction of the year the note is outstanding (60 days/360 days).

Note Given to Borrow from Bank   A bank nearly always requires a borrower to sign a promissory note when making a loan. When the note matures, the borrower repays the note with an amount larger than the amount borrowed. The difference between the amount borrowed and the amount repaid is *interest*. This section considers a type of note whose signer promises to pay *principal* (the amount borrowed) plus interest. In this case, the *face value* of the note equals principal. Face value is the value shown on the face (front) of the note. To illustrate, assume that a company needs $2,000 for a project and borrows this money from a bank at 12% annual interest. The loan is made on September 30, 2009, and is due in 60 days. Specifically, the borrowing company signs a note with a face value equal to the amount borrowed. The note includes a statement similar to this: *"I promise to pay $2,000 plus interest at 12% within 60 days after September 30."* This simple note is shown in Exhibit 11.3.

Point: When money is borrowed from a bank, the loan is reported as an asset (receivable) on the bank's balance sheet.

EXHIBIT 11.3

Note with Face Value Equal to Amount Borrowed

Promissory Note

$2,000   Sept. 30, 2009
Face Value   Date

Sixty days after date, ____I____ promise to pay to the order of
National Bank
Boston, MA
Two thousand and no/100 -------------------------- Dollars

plus interest at the annual rate of 12%.

Janet Lee

The borrower records its receipt of cash and the new liability with this entry:

Sept. 30	Cash	2,000	
	Notes Payable.........................		2,000
	Borrowed $2,000 cash with a 60-day, 12%, $2,000 note.		

Assets = Liabilities + Equity
+2,000   +2,000

When principal and interest are paid, the borrower records payment with this entry:

Nov. 29	Notes Payable	2,000	
	Interest Expense	40	
	Cash		2,040
	Paid note with interest ($2,000 × 12% × 60/360).		

Assets = Liabilities + Equity
−2,040   −2,000   −40

End-of-period interest adjustment.   When the end of an accounting period occurs between the signing of a note payable and its maturity date, the *matching principle* requires us to record the accrued but unpaid interest on the note. To illustrate, let's return to the note in Exhibit 11.3, but assume that the company borrows $2,000 cash on December 16, 2009, instead of September 30. This 60-day note matures on February 14, 2010, and the company's fiscal year ends on December 31. Thus, we need to record interest expense for the final 15 days in December. This means that one-fourth (15 days/60 days) of the $40 total interest is an expense of year 2009. The borrower records this expense with the following adjusting entry:

2009			
Dec. 31	Interest Expense	10	
	Interest Payable		10
	To record accrued interest on note ($2,000 ×		
	12% × 15/360).		

Assets = Liabilities + Equity
              +10   −10

When this note matures on February 14, the borrower must recognize 45 days of interest expense for year 2010 and remove the balances of the two liability accounts:

Example: If this note is dated Dec. 1 instead of Dec. 16, how much expense is recorded on Dec. 31? *Answer:* $2,000 × 12% × 30/360 = $20

2010			
Feb. 14	Interest Expense*...........................	30	
	Interest Payable	10	
	Notes Payable	2,000	
	Cash		2,040
	*Paid note with interest. *($2,000 × 12% × 45/360)*		

Assets = Liabilities + Equity
−2,040   −10   −30
                −2,000

Decision Insight

Many franchisors such as **Geeks on Call**, **Techs in a Sec**, and **Nerds on Site**, use notes to help entrepreneurs acquire their own franchises, including using notes to pay for the franchise fee and any equipment. Payments on these notes are usually collected monthly and often are secured by the franchisees' assets.

Payroll Liabilities

An employer incurs several expenses and liabilities from having employees. These expenses and liabilities are often large and arise from salaries and wages earned, from employee benefits, and from payroll taxes levied on the employer. **Anheuser-Busch**, for instance, reports payroll-related current liabilities of more than $342.8 million from "accrued salaries, wages and benefits." We discuss payroll liabilities and related accounts in this section. The appendix to this chapter describes details about payroll reports, records, and procedures.

P2   Compute and record *employee* payroll deductions and liabilities.

Employee Payroll Deductions   **Gross pay** is the total compensation an employee earns including wages, salaries, commissions, bonuses, and any compensation earned before deductions such as taxes. (*Wages* usually refer to payments to employees at an hourly rate. *Salaries* usually refer to payments to employees at a monthly or yearly rate.) **Net pay,** also called *take-home pay,* is gross pay less all deductions. **Payroll deductions,** commonly called *withholdings,* are amounts withheld from an employee's gross pay, either required or voluntary. Required deductions result from laws and include income taxes and Social Security taxes. Voluntary deductions, at an employee's option, include pension and health contributions, union dues, and charitable giving. Exhibit 11.4 shows the typical payroll deductions of an employee. The employer withholds payroll deductions from employees' pay and is obligated to transmit this money to the designated organization. The employer records payroll deductions as current liabilities until these amounts are transmitted. This section discusses the major payroll deductions.

EXHIBIT 11.4

Payroll Deductions

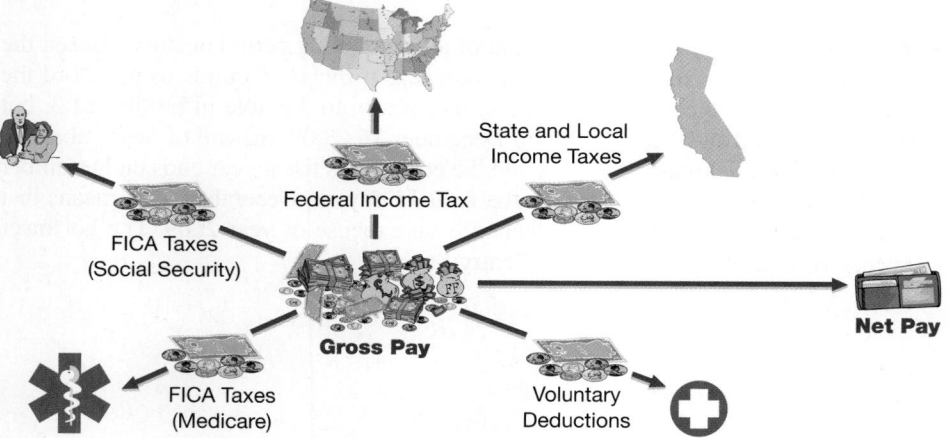

Employee FICA taxes.   The federal Social Security system provides retirement, disability, survivorship, and medical benefits to qualified workers. Laws *require* employers to withhold **Federal Insurance Contributions Act (FICA) taxes** from employees' pay to cover costs of the system. Employers usually separate FICA taxes into two groups: (1) retirement, disability, and survivorship and (2) medical. For the first group, the Social Security system provides monthly cash payments to qualified retired workers for the rest of their lives. These payments are often called *Social Security benefits.* Taxes related to this group are often called *Social Security taxes.* For the second group, the system provides monthly payments to deceased workers' surviving families and to disabled workers who qualify for assistance. These payments are commonly called *Medicare benefits;* like those in the first group, they are paid with *Medicare taxes* (part of FICA taxes).

Law requires employers to withhold FICA taxes from each employee's salary or wages on each payday. The taxes for Social Security and Medicare are computed separately. For example, for the year 2008, the amount withheld from each employee's pay for Social Security tax was 6.2% of the first $102,000 the employee earns in the calendar year, or a maximum of $6,324. The Medicare tax was 1.45% of *all* amounts the employee earns; there is no maximum limit to Medicare tax.

Employers must pay withheld taxes to the Internal Revenue Service (IRS) on specific filing dates during the year. Employers who fail to send the withheld taxes to the IRS on time can be assessed substantial penalties. Until all the taxes are sent to the IRS, they are included in employers' current liabilities. For any changes in rates or with the maximum earnings level, check the IRS Website at www.IRS.gov or the SSA Website at www.SSA.gov.

Employee income tax.   Most employers are required to withhold federal income tax from each employee's paycheck. The amount withheld is computed using tables published by the IRS. The amount depends on the employee's annual earnings rate and the number of *withholding allowances* the employee claims. Allowances reduce the amount of taxes one owes the government. The more allowances one claims, the less tax the employer will withhold. Employees can claim allowances for themselves and their dependents. They also can claim additional allowances if they expect major declines in their taxable income for medical expenses. (An employee who claims more allowances than appropriate is subject to a fine.) Most states and many local governments require employers to withhold income taxes from employees' pay and to remit them promptly to the proper government agency. Until they are paid, withholdings are reported as a current liability on the employer's balance sheet.

Employee voluntary deductions.   Beyond Social Security, Medicare, and income taxes, employers often withhold other amounts from employees' earnings. These withholdings arise from employee requests, contracts, unions, or other agreements. They can include amounts for charitable giving, medical insurance premiums, pension contributions, and union dues. Until they are paid, such withholdings are reported as part of employers' current liabilities.

Recording employee payroll deductions.   Employers must accrue payroll expenses and liabilities at the end of each pay period. To illustrate, assume that an employee earns a salary of $2,000 per month. At the end of January, the employer's entry to accrue payroll expenses and liabilities for this employee is

Jan. 31	Salaries Expense............................	2,000	
	FICA—Social Security Taxes Payable (6.2%)		124
	FICA—Medicare Taxes Payable (1.45%)		29
	Employee Federal Income Taxes Payable*		213
	Employee Medical Insurance Payable*		85
	Employee Union Dues Payable*		25
	Salaries Payable............................		1,524
	To record accrued payroll for January.		

Assets = Liabilities + Equity
        +124   −2,000
        +29
        +213
        +85
        +25
        +1,524

* Amounts taken from employer's accounting records.

Salaries Expense (debit) shows that the employee earns a gross salary of $2,000. The first five payables (credits) show the liabilities the employer owes on behalf of this employee to cover FICA taxes, income taxes, medical insurance, and union dues. The Salaries Payable account (credit) records the $1,524 net pay the employee receives from the $2,000 gross pay earned. When the employee is paid, another entry (or a series of entries) is required to record the check written and distributed (or funds transferred). The entry to record cash payment to this employee is to debit Salaries Payable and credit Cash for $1,524.

Decision Insight

A company's delay or failure to pay withholding taxes to the government has severe consequences. For example, a 100% penalty can be levied, with interest, on the unpaid balance. The government can even close a company, take its assets, and pursue legal actions against those involved.

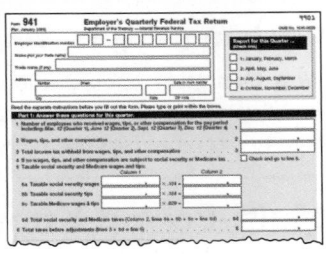

Employer Payroll Taxes   Employers must pay payroll taxes in addition to those required of employees. Employer taxes include FICA and unemployment taxes.

P3   Compute and record *employer* payroll expenses and liabilities.

Employer FICA tax.   Employers must pay FICA taxes *equal in amount to* the FICA taxes withheld from their employees. An employer's tax is credited to the same FICA Taxes Payable accounts used to record the Social Security and Medicare taxes withheld from employees. (A self-employed person must pay both the employee and employer FICA taxes.)

Federal and state unemployment taxes.   The federal government participates with states in a joint federal and state unemployment insurance program. Each state administers its program. These programs provide unemployment benefits to qualified workers. The federal government approves state programs and pays a portion of their administrative expenses.

Federal Unemployment Taxes (FUTA). Employers are subject to a federal unemployment tax on wages and salaries paid to their employees. For the year 2008, employers were required to pay FUTA taxes of as much as 6.2% of the first $7,000 earned by each employee. This federal tax can be reduced by a credit of up to 5.4% for taxes paid to a state program. As a result, the net federal unemployment tax is often only 0.8%.

State Unemployment Taxes (SUTA). All states support their unemployment insurance programs by placing a payroll tax on employers. (A few states require employees to make a contribution. In the book's assignments, we assume that this tax is only on the employer.) In most states, the base rate for SUTA taxes is 5.4% of the first $7,000 paid each employee. This base rate is adjusted according to an employer's merit rating. The state assigns a **merit rating** that reflects a company's stability or instability in employing workers. A good rating reflects stability in employment and means an employer can pay less than the 5.4% base rate. A low rating reflects high turnover or seasonal hirings and layoffs. To illustrate, an employer with 50 employees each of whom earns $7,000 or more per year saves $15,400 annually if it has a merit rating of 1.0% versus 5.4%. This is computed by comparing taxes of $18,900 at the 5.4% rate to only $3,500 at the 1.0% rate.

Recording employer payroll taxes. Employer payroll taxes are an added expense beyond the wages and salaries earned by employees. These taxes are often recorded in an entry separate from the one recording payroll expenses and deductions. To illustrate, assume that the $2,000 recorded salaries expense from the previous example is earned by an employee whose earnings have not yet reached $5,000 for the year. This means the entire salaries expense for this period is subject to tax because year-to-date pay is under $7,000. Also assume that the federal unemployment tax rate is 0.8% and the state unemployment tax rate is 5.4%. Consequently, the FICA portion of the employer's tax is $153, computed by multiplying both the 6.2% and 1.45% by the $2,000 gross pay. Moreover, state unemployment (SUTA) taxes are $108 (5.4% of the $2,000 gross pay), and federal unemployment (FUTA) taxes are $16 (0.8% of $2,000). The entry to record the employer's payroll tax expense and related liabilities is

Example: If the employer's merit rating in this example reduces its SUTA rate to 2.9%, what is its SUTA liability? *Answer:* SUTA payable = $2,000 × 2.9% = $58

Assets = Liabilities + Equity
+124   −277
+29
+108
+16

Jan. 31	Payroll Taxes Expense.....................	277	
	FICA—Social Security Taxes Payable (6.2%)		124
	FICA—Medicare Taxes Payable (1.45%)		29
	State Unemployment Taxes Payable		108
	Federal Unemployment Taxes Payable.........		16
	To record employer payroll taxes.		

Decision Ethics

Web Designer You take a summer job working for a family friend who runs a small IT service. On your first payday, the owner slaps you on the back, gives you full payment in cash, winks, and adds: "No need to pay those high taxes, eh." What action, if any, do you take? [Answer—p. 458]

Multi-Period Known Liabilities

Many known liabilities extend over multiple periods. These often include unearned revenues and notes payable. For example, if **Sports Illustrated** sells a four-year magazine subscription, it records amounts received for this subscription in an Unearned Subscription Revenues account. Amounts in this account are liabilities, but are they current or long term? They are *both*. The portion of the Unearned Subscription Revenues account that will be fulfilled in the next year is reported as a current liability. The remaining portion is reported as a long-term liability.

The same analysis applies to notes payable. For example, a borrower reports a three-year note payable as a long-term liability in the first two years it is outstanding. In the third year, the borrower reclassifies this note as a current liability since it is due within one year or the operating cycle, whichever is longer. The **current portion of long-term debt** refers to that part of long-term debt due within one year or the operating cycle, whichever is longer. Long-term debt is reported under long-term liabilities, but the *current portion due* is reported under current liabilities. To illustrate, assume that a $7,500 debt is paid in installments of $1,500 per year for five years. The $1,500 due within the year is reported as a current liability. No journal entry is necessary for this reclassification. Instead, we simply classify the amounts for debt as either current or long term when the balance sheet is prepared.

Some known liabilities are rarely reported in long-term liabilities. These include accounts payable, sales taxes, and wages and salaries.

Point: Alternatively, some accounting systems do make an entry to transfer the current amount due out of Long-Term Debt and into the Current Portion of Long-Term Debt.

Decision Insight

Liability Limits Probably the greatest number of frauds involve payroll. Companies must safeguard payroll activities. Controls include proper approvals and processes for employee additions, deletions, and pay rate changes. A common fraud is a manager adding a fictitious employee to the payroll and then cashing the fictitious employee's check.

Quick Check   Answers—p. 458

4. Why does a creditor prefer a note payable to a past-due account payable?

5. A company pays its one employee $3,000 per month. This company's FUTA rate is 0.8% on the first $7,000 earned; its SUTA rate is 4.0% on the first $7,000; its Social Security tax rate is 6.2% of the first $102,000; and its Medicare tax rate is 1.45% of all amounts earned. The entry to record this company's March payroll includes what amount for total payroll taxes expense?

6. Identify whether the employer or employee or both incurs each of the following: (a) FICA taxes, (b) FUTA taxes, (c) SUTA taxes, and (d) withheld income taxes.

Estimated Liabilities

An **estimated liability** is a known obligation that is of an uncertain amount but that can be reasonably estimated. Common examples are employee benefits such as pensions, health care and vacation pay, and warranties offered by a seller. We discuss each of these in this section. Other examples of estimated liabilities include property taxes and certain contracts to provide future services.

P4 Account for estimated liabilities, including warranties and bonuses.

Health and Pension Benefits

Many companies provide **employee benefits** beyond salaries and wages. An employer often pays all or part of medical, dental, life, and disability insurance. Many employers also contribute to *pension plans,* which are agreements by employers to provide benefits (payments) to employees after retirement. Many companies also provide medical care and insurance benefits to their retirees. When payroll taxes and charges for employee benefits are totaled, payroll cost often exceeds employees' gross earnings by 25% or more.

To illustrate, assume that an employer agrees to (1) pay an amount for medical insurance equal to $8,000 and (2) contribute an additional 10% of the employees' $120,000 gross salary to a retirement program. The entry to record these accrued benefits is

Dec. 31	Employee Benefits Expense	20,000	
	Employee Medical Insurance Payable		8,000
	Employee Retirement Program Payable		12,000
	To record costs of employee benefits.		

Assets = Liabilities + Equity
          +8,000   −20,000
          +12,000

Decision Insight

Postgame Spoils Baseball was the first pro sport to set up a pension, originally up to $100 per month depending on years played. Many former players now take home six-figure pensions. Cal Ripken Jr.'s pension when he reaches 62 is estimated at $160,000 per year (he played 21 seasons). The requirement is only 43 games for a full pension and just one game for full medical benefits.

Vacation Benefits

Many employers offer paid vacation benefits, also called *paid absences*. To illustrate, assume that salaried employees earn 2 weeks' vacation per year. This benefit increases employers' payroll expenses because employees are paid for 52 weeks but work for only 50 weeks. Total annual salary is the same, but the cost per week worked is greater than the amount paid per week. For example, if an employee is paid $20,800 for 52 weeks but works only 50 weeks, the total weekly expense to the employer is $416 ($20,800/50 weeks) instead of the $400 cash paid weekly to the employee ($20,800/52 weeks). The $16 difference between these two amounts is recorded weekly as follows:

Assets = Liabilities + Equity
         +16   −16

Vacation Benefits Expense.....................	16	
Vacation Benefits Payable..................		16
To record vacation benefits accrued.		

Vacation Benefits Expense is an operating expense, and Vacation Benefits Payable is a current liability. When the employee takes a vacation, the employer reduces (debits) the Vacation Benefits Payable and credits Cash (no additional expense is recorded).

Bonus Plans

Many companies offer bonuses to employees, and many of the bonuses depend on net income. To illustrate, assume that an employer offers a bonus to its employees equal to 5% of the company's annual net income (to be equally shared by all). The company's expected annual net income is $210,000. The year-end adjusting entry to record this benefit is

Assets = Liabilities + Equity
         +10,000   −10,000

Dec. 31			
	Employee Bonus Expense*....................	10,000	
	Bonus Payable.........................		10,000
	To record expected bonus costs.		

* Bonus Expense (B) equals 5% of net income, which equals $210,000 minus the bonus; this is computed as:

$$B = 0.05 (\$210,000 - B)$$
$$B = \$10,500 - 0.05B$$
$$1.05B = \$10,500$$
$$\mathbf{B = \$10,500/1.05 = \$10,000}$$

When the bonus is paid, Bonus Payable is debited and Cash is credited for $10,000.

Warranty Liabilities

A **warranty** is a seller's obligation to replace or correct a product (or service) that fails to perform as expected within a specified period. Most new cars, for instance, are sold with a warranty covering parts for a specified period of time. **Ford Motor Company** reported more than $21.9 billion in "dealer and customer allowances and claims" in its annual report. To comply with the *full disclosure* and *matching principles,* the seller reports the expected warranty expense in the period when revenue from the sale of the product or service is reported. The seller reports this warranty obligation as a liability, although the existence, amount, payee, and date of future sacrifices are uncertain. This is because such warranty costs are probable and the amount can be estimated using, for instance, past experience with warranties.

To illustrate, a dealer sells a used car for $16,000 on December 1, 2009, with a maximum one-year or 12,000-mile warranty covering parts. This dealer's experience shows that warranty expense averages about 4% of a car's selling price, or $640 in this case ($16,000 × 4%). The dealer records the estimated expense and liability related to this sale with this entry:

Assets = Liabilities + Equity
         +640   −640

2009			
Dec. 1			
	Warranty Expense	640	
	Estimated Warranty Liability...............		640
	To record estimated warranty expense.		

This entry alternatively could be made as part of end-of-period adjustments. Either way, the estimated warranty expense is reported on the 2009 income statement and the warranty liability on the 2009 balance sheet. To further extend this example, suppose the customer returns the car for warranty repairs on January 9, 2010. The dealer performs this work by replacing parts costing $200. The entry to record partial settlement of the estimated warranty liability is

Point: Recognition of warranty liabilities is necessary to comply with the matching and full disclosure principles.

2010			
Jan. 9	Estimated Warranty Liability	200	
	Auto Parts Inventory		200
	To record costs of warranty repairs.		

Assets = Liabilities + Equity
−200   −200

This entry reduces the balance of the estimated warranty liability. Warranty expense was previously recorded in 2009, the year the car was sold with the warranty. Finally, what happens if total warranty expenses are more or less than the estimated 4%, or $640? The answer is that management should monitor actual warranty expenses to see whether the 4% rate is accurate. If experience reveals a large difference from the estimate, the rate for current and future sales should be changed. Differences are expected, but they should be small.

Decision Insight

Guaranteed Profits   **Best Buy** and **Circuit City** profit from sales of extended-warranty contracts with their electronics [*BusinessWeek,* 2004].

	Best Buy	Circuit City
Warranty contracts as a percentage of sales	4.0%	3.3%
Warranty contracts as a percentage of operating profit	45	100
Profit margin on warranty contracts	60	50

Multi-Period Estimated Liabilities

Estimated liabilities can be both current and long term. For example, pension liabilities to employees are long term to workers who will not retire within the next period. For employees who are retired or will retire within the next period, a portion of pension liabilities is current. Other examples include employee health benefits and warranties. Specifically, many warranties are for 30 or 60 days in length. Estimated costs under these warranties are properly reported in current liabilities. Many other automobile warranties are for three years or 36,000 miles. A portion of these warranties is reported as long term.

Quick Check   Answers—p. 458

7. Estimated liabilities involve an obligation to pay which of these? (*a*) An uncertain but reasonably estimated amount owed on a known obligation or (*b*) A known amount to a specific entity on an uncertain due date.

8. A car is sold for $15,000 on June 1, 2009, with a one-year warranty on parts. Warranty expense is estimated at 1.5% of selling price at each calendar year-end. On March 1, 2010, the car is returned for warranty repairs costing $135. The amount recorded as warranty expense on March 1 is (*a*) $0; (*b*) $60; (*c*) $75; (*d*) $135; (*e*) $225.

Contingent Liabilities

A **contingent liability** is a potential obligation that depends on a future event arising from a past transaction or event. An example is a pending lawsuit. Here, a past transaction or event leads to a lawsuit whose result depends on the outcome of the suit. Future payment of a contingent liability depends on whether an uncertain future event occurs.

C3   Explain how to account for contingent liabilities.

Accounting for Contingent Liabilities

Accounting for contingent liabilities depends on the likelihood that a future event will occur and the ability to estimate the future amount owed if this event occurs. Three different possibilities are identified in the following chart: record liability, disclose in notes, or no disclosure.

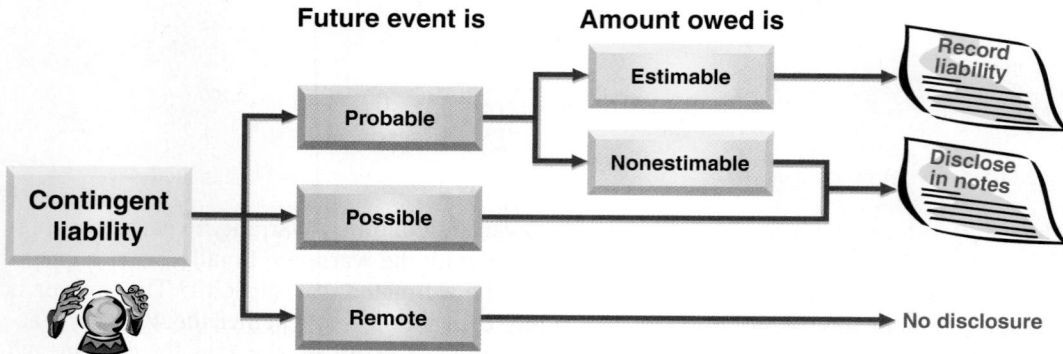

The conditions that determine each of these three possibilities follow:

1. The future event is *probable* (likely) and the amount owed can be *reasonably estimated*. We then record this amount as a liability. Examples are the estimated liabilities described earlier such as warranties, vacation pay, and income taxes.
2. The future event is *reasonably possible* (could occur). We disclose information about this type of contingent liability in notes to the financial statements.
3. The future event is *remote* (unlikely). We do not record or disclose information on remote contingent liabilities.

Reasonably Possible Contingent Liabilities

This section identifies and discusses contingent liabilities that commonly fall in the second category—when the future event is reasonably possible. Disclosing information about contingencies in this category is motivated by the *full-disclosure principle,* which requires information relevant to decision makers be reported and not ignored.

Potential Legal Claims   Many companies are sued or at risk of being sued. The accounting issue is whether the defendant should recognize a liability on its balance sheet or disclose a contingent liability in its notes while a lawsuit is outstanding and not yet settled. The answer is that a potential claim is recorded in the accounts *only* if payment for damages is probable and the amount can be reasonably estimated. If the potential claim cannot be reasonably estimated or is less than probable but reasonably possible, it is disclosed. **Ford Motor Company**, for example, includes the following note in its annual report: "Various legal actions, governmental investigations and proceedings and claims are pending . . . arising out of alleged defects in our products."

Debt Guarantees   Sometimes a company guarantees the payment of debt owed by a supplier, customer, or another company. The guarantor usually discloses the guarantee in its financial statement notes as a contingent liability. If it is probable that the debtor will default, the guarantor needs to record and report the guarantee in its financial statements as a liability. The **Boston Celtics** report a unique guarantee when it comes to coaches and players: "Certain of the contracts provide for guaranteed payments which must be paid even if the employee [player] is injured or terminated."

Other Contingencies   Other examples of contingencies include environmental damages, possible tax assessments, insurance losses, and government investigations. **Sunoco**, for instance, reports that "federal, state and local laws . . . result in liabilities and loss contingencies. Sunoco accrues . . . cleanup costs [that] are probable and reasonably estimable. Management believes it is reasonably possible (i.e., less than probable but greater than remote) that additional . . . losses will be incurred." Many of Sunoco's contingencies are revealed only in notes.

Decision Insight

Pricing Priceless   What's it worth to see from one side of the Grand Canyon to the other? What's the cost when beaches are closed due to pollution? A method to measure environmental liabilities is *contingent valuation,* by which people answer such questions. Regulators use their answers to levy fines and assess punitive damages.

Uncertainties That Are Not Contingencies

All organizations face uncertainties from future events such as natural disasters and the development of new competing products or services. These uncertainties are not contingent liabilities because they are future events *not* arising from past transactions. Accordingly, they are not disclosed.

Quick Check

Answers—p. 458

9. A future payment is reported as a liability on the balance sheet if payment is contingent on a future event that (*a*) is reasonably possible but the payment cannot be reasonably estimated; (*b*) is probable and the payment can be reasonably estimated; or (*c*) is not probable but the payment is known.

10. Under what circumstances is a future payment reported in the notes to the financial statements as a contingent liability?

Times Interest Earned Ratio

Decision Analysis

A company incurs interest expense on many of its current and long-term liabilities. Examples extend from its short-term notes and the current portion of long-term liabilities to its long-term notes and bonds. Interest expense is often viewed as a *fixed expense* because the amount of these liabilities is likely to remain in one form or another for a substantial period of time. This means that the amount of interest is unlikely to vary due to changes in sales or other operating activities. While fixed expenses can be advantageous when a company is growing, they create risk. This risk stems from the possibility that a company might be unable to pay fixed expenses if sales decline. To illustrate, consider Diego Co.'s results for 2009 and two possible outcomes for year 2010 in Exhibit 11.5.

A1   Compute the times interest earned ratio and use it to analyze liabilities.

		2010 Projections	
(\$ thousands)	2009	Sales Increase	Sales Decrease
Sales	\$600	\$900	\$300
Expenses (75% of sales)	450	675	225
Income before interest	150	225	75
Interest expense (fixed)	60	60	60
Net income	\$ 90	\$165	\$ 15

EXHIBIT 11.5

Actual and Projected Results

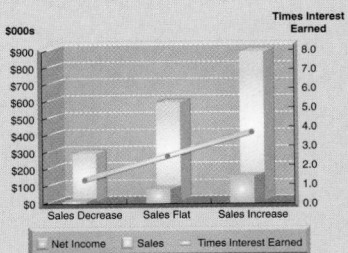

Expenses excluding interest are at, and expected to remain at, 75% of sales. Expenses such as these that change with sales volume are called *variable expenses.* However, interest expense is at, and expected to remain at, \$60,000 per year due to its fixed nature.

The middle numerical column of Exhibit 11.5 shows that Diego's income increases by 83% to \$165,000 if sales increase by 50% to \$900,000. In contrast, the far right column shows that income decreases by 83% if sales decline by 50%. These results reveal that the amount of fixed interest expense affects a company's risk of its ability to pay interest, which is numerically reflected in the **times interest earned** ratio in Exhibit 11.6.

$$\text{Times interest earned} = \frac{\text{Income before interest expense and income taxes}}{\text{Interest expense}}$$

EXHIBIT 11.6

Times Interest Earned

For 2009, Diego's times interest earned is computed as \$150,000/\$60,000, or 2.5 times. This ratio suggests that Diego faces low to moderate risk because its sales must decline sharply before it would be unable to cover its interest expenses. (Diego is an LLC and does not pay income taxes.)

Experience shows that when times interest earned falls below 1.5 to 2.0 and remains at that level or lower for several periods, the default rate on liabilities increases sharply. This reflects increased risk for companies and their creditors. We also must interpret the times interest earned ratio in light of information about the variability of a company's income before interest. If income is stable from year to year or if it is growing, the company can afford to take on added risk by borrowing. If its income greatly varies from year to year, fixed interest expense can increase the risk that it will not earn enough income to pay interest.

 Decision Maker

Entrepreneur   You wish to invest in a franchise for either one of two national chains. Each franchise has an expected annual net income *after* interest and taxes of \$100,000. Net income for the first franchise includes a regular fixed interest charge of \$200,000. The fixed interest charge for the second franchise is \$40,000. Which franchise is riskier to you if sales forecasts are not met? Does your decision change if the first franchise has more variability in its income stream? [Answer—p. 458]

Demonstration Problem

DP11

The following transactions and events took place at Kern Company during its recent calendar-year reporting period (Kern does not use reversing entries).

a. In September 2009, Kern sold \$140,000 of merchandise covered by a 180-day warranty. Prior experience shows that costs of the warranty equal 5% of sales. Compute September's warranty expense and prepare the adjusting journal entry for the warranty liability as recorded at September 30. Also prepare the journal entry on October 8 to record a \$300 cash expenditure to provide warranty service on an item sold in September.

b. On October 12, 2009, Kern arranged with a supplier to replace Kern's overdue \$10,000 account payable by paying \$2,500 cash and signing a note for the remainder. The note matures in 90 days and has a 12% interest rate. Prepare the entries recorded on October 12, December 31, and January 10, 2010, related to this transaction.

c. In late December, Kern learns it is facing a product liability suit filed by an unhappy customer. Kern's lawyer advises that although it will probably suffer a loss from the lawsuit, it is not possible to estimate the amount of damages at this time.

d. Sally Bline works for Kern. For the pay period ended November 30, her gross earnings are \$3,000. Bline has \$800 deducted for federal income taxes and \$200 for state income taxes from each paycheck. Additionally, a \$35 premium for her health care insurance and a \$10 donation for the United Way are deducted. Bline pays FICA Social Security taxes at a rate of 6.2% and FICA Medicare taxes at a rate of 1.45%. She has not earned enough this year to be exempt from any FICA taxes. Journalize the accrual of salaries expense of Bline's wages by Kern.

e. On November 1, Kern borrows \$5,000 cash from a bank in return for a 60-day, 12%, \$5,000 note. Record the note's issuance on November 1 and its repayment with interest on December 31.

f.[B] Kern has estimated and recorded its quarterly income tax payments. In reviewing its year-end tax adjustments, it identifies an additional \$5,000 of income tax expense that should be recorded. A portion of this additional expense, \$1,000, is deferrable to future years. Record this year-end income taxes expense adjusting entry.

g. For this calendar-year, Kern's net income is \$1,000,000, its interest expense is \$275,000, and its income taxes expense is \$225,000. Calculate Kern's times interest earned ratio.

Planning the Solution

- For *a,* compute the warranty expense for September and record it with an estimated liability. Record the October expenditure as a decrease in the liability.
- For *b,* eliminate the liability for the account payable and create the liability for the note payable. Compute interest expense for the 80 days that the note is outstanding in 2009 and record it as an additional liability. Record the payment of the note, being sure to include the interest for the 10 days in 2010.

- For *c*, decide whether the company's contingent liability needs to be disclosed or accrued (recorded) according to the two necessary criteria: probable loss and reasonably estimable.
- For *d*, set up payable accounts for all items in Bline's paycheck that require deductions. After deducting all necessary items, credit the remaining amount to Salaries Payable.
- For *e*, record the issuance of the note. Calculate 60 days' interest due using the 360-day convention in the interest formula.
- For *f*, determine how much of the income taxes expense is payable in the current year and how much needs to be deferred.
- For *g*, apply and compute times interest earned.

Solution to Demonstration Problem

a. Warranty expense = 5% × $140,000 = $7,000

Sept. 30	Warranty Expense	7,000	
	Estimated Warranty Liability.		7,000
	To record warranty expense for the month.		
Oct. 8	Estimated Warranty Liability	300	
	Cash		300
	To record the cost of the warranty service.		

b. Interest expense for 2009 = 12% × $7,500 × 80/360 = $200

Interest expense for 2010 = 12% × $7,500 × 10/360 = $25

Oct. 12	Accounts Payable.	10,000	
	Notes Payable.		7,500
	Cash		2,500
	Paid $2,500 cash and gave a 90-day, 12% note to extend the due date on the account.		
Dec. 31	Interest Expense	200	
	Interest Payable.		200
	To accrue interest on note payable.		
Jan. 10	Interest Expense	25	
	Interest Payable	200	
	Notes Payable	7,500	
	Cash		7,725
	Paid note with interest, including the accrued interest payable.		

c. Disclose the pending lawsuit in the financial statement notes. Although the loss is probable, no liability can be accrued since the loss cannot be reasonably estimated.

d.

Nov. 30	Salaries Expense.	3,000.00	
	FICA—Social Security Taxes Payable (6.2%)		186.00
	FICA—Medicare Taxes Payable (1.45%)		43.50
	Employee Federal Income Taxes Payable		800.00
	Employee State Income Taxes Payable.		200.00
	Employee Medical Insurance Payable.		35.00
	Employee United Way Payable		10.00
	Salaries Payable.		1,725.50
	To record Bline's accrued payroll.		

e.

Nov. 1	Cash.	5,000	
	Notes Payable.		5,000
	Borrowed cash with a 60-day, 12% note.		

When the note and interest are paid 60 days later, Kern Company records this entry:

Dec. 31	Notes Payable	5,000	
	Interest Expense	100	
	Cash		5,100
	Paid note with interest ($5,000 × 12% × 60/360).		

f.

Dec. 31	Income Taxes Expense	5,000	
	Income Taxes Payable		4,000
	Deferred Income Tax Liability		1,000
	To record added income taxes expense and the deferred tax liability.		

g. Times interest earned $= \dfrac{\$1,000,000 + \$275,000 + \$225,000}{\$275,000} = \underline{\underline{5.45 \text{ times}}}$

11A Payroll Reports, Records, and Procedures

Understanding payroll procedures and keeping adequate payroll reports and records are essential to a company's success. This appendix focuses on payroll accounting and its reports, records, and procedures.

Payroll Reports

P5 Identify and describe the details of payroll reports, records, and procedures.

Most employees and employers are required to pay local, state, and federal payroll taxes. Payroll expenses involve liabilities to individual employees, to federal and state governments, and to other organizations such as insurance companies. Beyond paying these liabilities, employers are required to prepare and submit reports explaining how they computed these payments.

Reporting FICA Taxes and Income Taxes   The Federal Insurance Contributions Act (FICA) requires each employer to file an Internal Revenue Service (IRS) **Form 941,** the *Employer's Quarterly Federal Tax Return,* within one month after the end of each calendar quarter. A sample Form 941 is shown in Exhibit 11A.1 for Phoenix Sales & Service, a landscape design company. Accounting information and software are helpful in tracking payroll transactions and reporting the accumulated information on Form 941. Specifically, the employer reports total wages subject to income tax withholding on line 2 of Form 941. (For simplicity, this appendix uses *wages* to refer to both wages and salaries.) The income tax withheld is reported on line 3. The combined amount of employee and employer FICA (Social Security) taxes for Phoenix Sales & Service is reported on line 5a (taxable Social Security wages, $36,599 × 12.4% = $4,538.28). The 12.4% is the sum of the Social Security tax withheld, computed as 6.2% tax withheld from the employee wages for the quarter plus the 6.2% tax levied on the employer. The combined amount of employee Medicare wages is reported on line 5c. The 2.9% is the sum of 1.45% withheld from employee wages for the quarter plus 1.45% tax levied on the employer. Total FICA taxes are reported on line 5d and are added to the total income taxes withheld of $3,056.47 to yield a total of $8,656.12. For this year, assume that income up to $102,000 is subject to Social Security tax. There is

Form **941**

Employer's QUARTERLY Federal Tax Return

Department of the Treasury — Internal Revenue Service

(EIN)
Employer identification number   8 6 – 3 2 1 4 5 8 7

Name (not your trade name)   Phoenix Sales & Service

Trade name (if any)

Address   1214   Mill Road

Number	Street		Suite or room number

Phoenix   AZ   85621

City		State	ZIP code

Report for this Quarter ...
(Check one.)

☐ **1:** January, February, March

☐ **2:** April, May, June

☐ **3:** July, August, September

☒ **4:** October, November, December

Part 1: Answer these questions for this quarter.

1 Number of employees who received wages, tips, or other compensation for the pay period including: *Mar. 12* (Quarter 1), *June 12* (Quarter 2), *Sept. 12* (Quarter 3), *Dec. 12* (Quarter 4) . . . . . **1** | 1

2 Wages, tips, and other compensation . . . . **2** | 36,599.00

3 Total income tax withheld from wages, tips, and other compensation . . . . . **3** | 3,056.47

4 If no wages, tips, and other compensation are subject to social security or Medicare tax . ☐ Check and go to line 6.

5 Taxable social security and Medicare wages and tips:

	Column 1		Column 2
5a Taxable social security wages . .	36,599.00	× .124 =	4,538.28
5b Taxable social security tips . .	.	× .124 =	
5c Taxable Medicare wages & tips . .	36,599.00	× .029 =	1,061.37

5d Total social security and Medicare taxes (*Column 2*, lines 5a + 5b + 5c = line 5d) . **5d** | 5,599.65

6 Total taxes before adjustments (lines 3 + 5d = line 6) . . . . **6** | 8,656.12

7 TAX ADJUSTMENTS (Read the instructions for line 7 before completing lines 7a through 7h.):

7a Current quarter's fractions of cents . . . . | .

7b Current quarter's sick pay . . . . | .

7c Current quarter's adjustments for tips and group-term life insurance | .

7d Current year's income tax withholding (attach Form 941c) . . | .

7e Prior quarters' social security and Medicare taxes (attach Form 941c) | .

7f Special additions to federal income tax (attach Form 941c) . . | .

7g Special additions to social security and Medicare (attach Form 941c) | .

7h TOTAL ADJUSTMENTS (Combine all amounts: lines 7a through 7g.) . . . . . **7h** | 0.00

8 Total taxes after adjustments (Combine lines 6 and 7h.) . . . . **8** | 8,656.12

9 Advance earned income credit (EIC) payments made to employees . . . . . **9** | .

10 Total taxes after adjustment for advance EIC (lines 8 – line 9 = line 10) . . . . **10** | 8,656.12

11 Total deposits for this quarter, including overpayment applied from a prior quarter . **11** | 8,656.12

12 Balance due (If line 10 is more than line 11, write the difference here.) . . . . **12** | 0.00
Make checks payable to *United States Treasury.*

13 Overpayment (If line 11 is more than line 10, write the difference here.) | 0.00 Check one ☐ Apply to next return.
☐ Send a refund.

Part 2: Tell us about your deposit schedule and tax liability for this quarter.

If you are unsure about whether you are a monthly schedule depositor or a semiweekly schedule depositor, see *Pub. 15 (Circular E)*, section 11.

14 A Z   Write the state abbreviation for the state where you made your deposits OR write "MU" if you made your deposits in *multiple* states.

15 Check one: ☐ Line 10 is less than $2,500. Go to Part 3.

☒ You were a monthly schedule depositor for the entire quarter. Fill out your tax liability for each month. Then go to Part 3.

Tax liability:	Month 1	3,079.11
	Month 2	2,049.77
	Month 3	3,527.24
	Total liability for quarter	8,656.12	Total must equal line 10.

☐ You were a semiweekly schedule depositor for any part of this quarter. Fill out *Schedule B (Form 941): Report of Tax Liability for Semiweekly Schedule Depositors*, and attach it to this form.

Part 3: Tell us about your business. If a question does NOT apply to your business, leave it blank.

16 If your business has closed or you stopped paying wages . . . . ☐ Check here, and

enter the final date you paid wages   /   /

17 If you are a seasonal employer and you do not have to file a return for every quarter of the year . ☐ Check here.

Part 4: May we speak with your third-party designee?

Do you want to allow an employee, a paid tax preparer, or another person to discuss this return with the IRS? See the instructions for details.

☐ Yes. Designee's name

Phone ( ) –   Personal Identification Number (PIN) ☐ ☐ ☐ ☐ ☐

☒ No.

Part 5: Sign here. You MUST fill out both sides of this form and SIGN it.

Under penalties of perjury, I declare that I have examined this return, including accompanying schedules and statements, and to the best of my knowledge and belief, it is true, correct, and complete.

✗ Sign your name here

Print name and title

Date   /   /   Phone ( ) –

no income limit on amounts subject to Medicare tax. Congress sets annual limits on the amount owed for Social Security tax.

Federal depository banks are authorized to accept deposits of amounts payable to the federal government. Deposit requirements depend on the amount of tax owed. For example, when the sum of FICA taxes plus the employee income taxes is less than $2,500 for a quarter, the taxes can be paid when Form 941 is filed. Companies with large payrolls are often required to pay monthly or even semiweekly.

Reporting FUTA Taxes and SUTA Taxes   An employer's federal unemployment taxes (FUTA) are reported on an annual basis by filing an *Annual Federal Unemployment Tax Return,* IRS **Form 940.** It must be mailed on or before January 31 following the end of each tax year. Ten more days are allowed if all required tax deposits are filed on a timely basis and the full amount of tax is paid on or before January 31. FUTA payments are made quarterly to a federal depository bank if the total amount due exceeds $500. If $500 or less is due, the taxes are remitted annually. Requirements for paying and reporting state unemployment taxes (SUTA) vary depending on the laws of each state. Most states require quarterly payments and reports.

Reporting Wages and Salaries   Employers are required to give each employee an annual report of his or her wages subject to FICA and federal income taxes along with the amounts of these taxes withheld. This report is called a *Wage and Tax Statement,* or **Form W-2.** It must be given to employees before January 31 following the year covered by the report. Exhibit 11A.2 shows Form W-2 for one of the employees at Phoenix Sales & Service. Copies of the W-2 Form must be sent to the Social Security Administration, where the amount of the employee's wages subject to FICA taxes and FICA taxes withheld are posted to each employee's Social Security account. These posted amounts become the basis for determining an employee's retirement and survivors' benefits. The Social Security Administration also transmits to the IRS the amount of each employee's wages subject to federal income taxes and the amount of taxes withheld.

Payroll Records

Employers must keep payroll records in addition to reporting and paying taxes. These records usually include a payroll register and an individual earnings report for each employee.

Payroll Register   A **payroll register** usually shows the pay period dates, hours worked, gross pay, deductions, and net pay of each employee for each pay period. Exhibit 11A.3 shows a payroll register for Phoenix Sales & Service. It is organized into nine columns:

Col. 1   Employee identification (ID); Employee name; Social Security number (SS No.); Reference (check number); and Date (date check issued)
Col. 2   Pay Type (regular and overtime)
Col. 3   Pay Hours (number of hours worked as regular and overtime)
Col. 4   Gross Pay (amount of gross pay)[2]
Col. 5   FIT (federal income taxes withheld); FUTA (federal unemployment taxes)
Col. 6   SIT (state income taxes withheld); SUTA (state unemployment taxes)
Col. 7   FICA-SS_EE (social security taxes withheld, employee); FICA-SS_ER (social security taxes, employer)
Col. 8   FICA-Med_EE (medicare tax withheld, employee); FICA-Med_ER (medicare tax, employer)
Col. 9   Net pay (Gross pay less amounts withheld from employees)

Net pay for each employee is computed as gross pay minus the items on the first line of columns 5–8. The employer's payroll tax for each employee is computed as the sum of items on the third line of columns 5–8. A payroll register includes all data necessary to record payroll. In some software programs the entries to record payroll are made in a special *payroll journal.*

---

[2] The Gross Pay column shows regular hours worked on the first line multiplied by the regular pay rate—this equals regular pay. Overtime hours multiplied by the overtime premium rate equals overtime premium pay reported on the second line. If employers are engaged in interstate commerce, federal law sets a minimum overtime rate of pay to employees. For this company, workers earn 150% of their regular rate for hours in excess of 40 per week.

EXHIBIT 11A.2

Form W-2

Form W-2 Wage and Tax Statement
Copy 1–For State, City, or Local Tax Department

Department of Treasury—Internal Revenue Service

a Control number	AR101
	22222 — OMB No. 1545-0006
b Employer identification number (EIN)	86-3214587
c Employer's name, address and ZIP code	Phoenix Sales & Service / 1214 Mill Road / Phoenix, AZ 85621
1 Wages, tips, other compensation	4,910.00
2 Federal income tax withheld	333.37
3 Social security wages	4,910.00
4 Social security tax withheld	304.42
5 Medicare wages and tips	4,910.00
6 Medicare tax withheld	71.20
d Employee's social security number	333-22-9999
e Employee's first name and initial	Robert J. — Last name: Austin
f Employee's address and ZIP code	18 Roosevelt Blvd., Apt. C / Tempe, AZ 86322

15 State	Employer's state ID number	16 State wages, tips, etc.	17 State income tax
AZ	13-902319	4,910.00	26.68

EXHIBIT 11A.3

Payroll Register

Phoenix Sales & Service
Payroll Register
For Week Ended Oct. 8, 2009

Employee ID / Employee / SS No. / Refer., Date	Pay Type	Pay Hours	Gross Pay	FIT / FUTA	SIT / SUTA	FICA-SS_EE / FICA-SS_ER	FICA-Med_EE / FICA-Med_ER	Net Pay
AR101 Robert Austin 333-22-9999 9001, 10/8/09	Regular	40.00	400.00	−28.99	−2.32	−24.80	−5.80	338.09
	Overtime	0.00	0.00					
			400.00	−3.20	−10.80	−24.80	−5.80	
CJ102 Judy Cross 299-11-9201 9002, 10/8/09	Regular	40.00	560.00	−52.97	−4.24	−36.02	−8.42	479.35
	Overtime	1.00	21.00					
			581.00	−4.65	−15.69	−36.02	−8.42	
DJ103 John Diaz 444-11-9090 9003, 10/8/09	Regular	40.00	560.00	−48.33	−3.87	−37.32	−8.73	503.75
	Overtime	2.00	42.00					
			602.00	−4.82	−16.25	−37.32	−8.73	
KK104 Kay Keife 909-11-3344 9004, 10/8/09	Regular	40.00	560.00	−68.57	−5.49	−34.72	−8.12	443.10
	Overtime	0.00	0.00					
			560.00	−4.48	−15.12	−34.72	−8.12	
ML105 Lee Miller 444-56-3211 9005, 10/8/09	Regular	40.00	560.00	−34.24	−2.74	−34.72	−8.12	480.18
	Overtime	0.00	0.00					
			560.00	−4.48	−15.12	−34.72	−8.12	
SD106 Dale Sears 909-33-1234 9006, 10/8/09	Regular	40.00	560.00	−68.57	−5.49	−34.72	−8.12	443.10
	Overtime	0.00	0.00					
			560.00	−4.48	−15.12	−34.72	−8.12	
Totals	Regular	240.00	3,200.00	−301.67	−24.15	−202.30	−47.31	2,687.57
	Overtime	3.00	63.00					
			3,263.00	−26.11	−88.10	−202.30	−47.31	

Payroll Check   Payment of payroll is usually done by check or electronic funds transfer. Exhibit 11A.4 shows a *payroll check* for a Phoenix employee. This check is accompanied with a detachable *statement of earnings* (at top) showing gross pay, deductions, and net pay.

EXHIBIT 11A.4

Check and Statement of Earnings

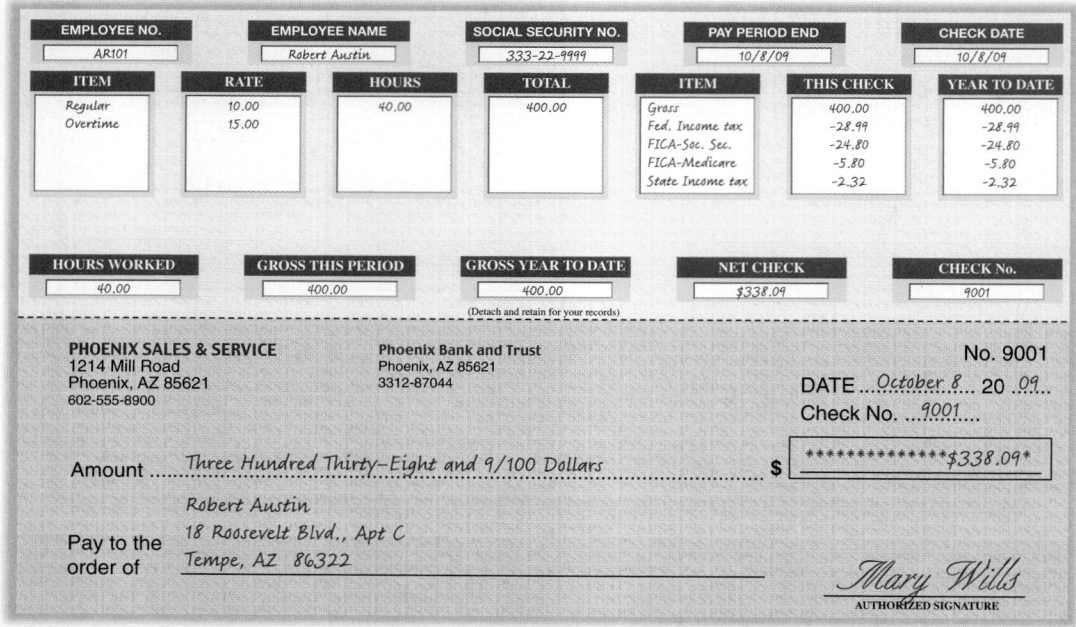

Employee Earnings Report   An **employee earnings report** is a cumulative record of an employee's hours worked, gross earnings, deductions, and net pay. Payroll information on this report is taken from the payroll register. The employee earnings report for R. Austin at Phoenix Sales & Service is shown in Exhibit 11A.5. An employee earnings report accumulates information that can show when an employee's earnings reach the tax-exempt points for FICA, FUTA, and SUTA taxes. It also gives data an employer needs to prepare Form W-2.

Payroll Procedures

Employers must be able to compute federal income tax for payroll purposes. This section explains how we compute this tax and how to use a payroll bank account.

Computing Federal Income Taxes   To compute the amount of taxes withheld from each employee's wages, we need to determine both the employee's wages earned and the employee's number of *withholding allowances*. Each employee records the number of withholding allowances claimed on a withholding allowance certificate, **Form W-4,** filed with the employer. When the number of withholding allowances increases, the amount of income taxes withheld decreases.

Employers often use a **wage bracket withholding table** similar to the one shown in Exhibit 11A.6 to compute the federal income taxes withheld from each employee's gross pay. The table in Exhibit 11A.6 is for a single employee paid weekly. Tables are also provided for married employees and for biweekly, semimonthly, and monthly pay periods (most payroll software includes these tables). When using a wage bracket withholding table to compute federal income tax withheld from an employee's gross wages, we need to locate an employee's wage bracket within the first two columns. We then find the amount withheld by looking in the withholding allowance column for that employee.

Payroll Bank Account   Companies with few employees often pay them with checks drawn on the company's regular bank account. Companies with many employees often use a special **payroll bank account** to pay employees. When this account is used, a company either (1) draws one check for total payroll on the regular bank account and deposits it in the payroll bank account or (2) executes an *electronic funds transfer* to the payroll bank account. Individual payroll checks are then drawn on this payroll bank account. Since only one check for the total payroll is drawn on the regular bank account each payday, use of a special payroll bank account helps with internal control. It also helps in reconciling the

EXHIBIT 11A.5

Employee Earnings Report

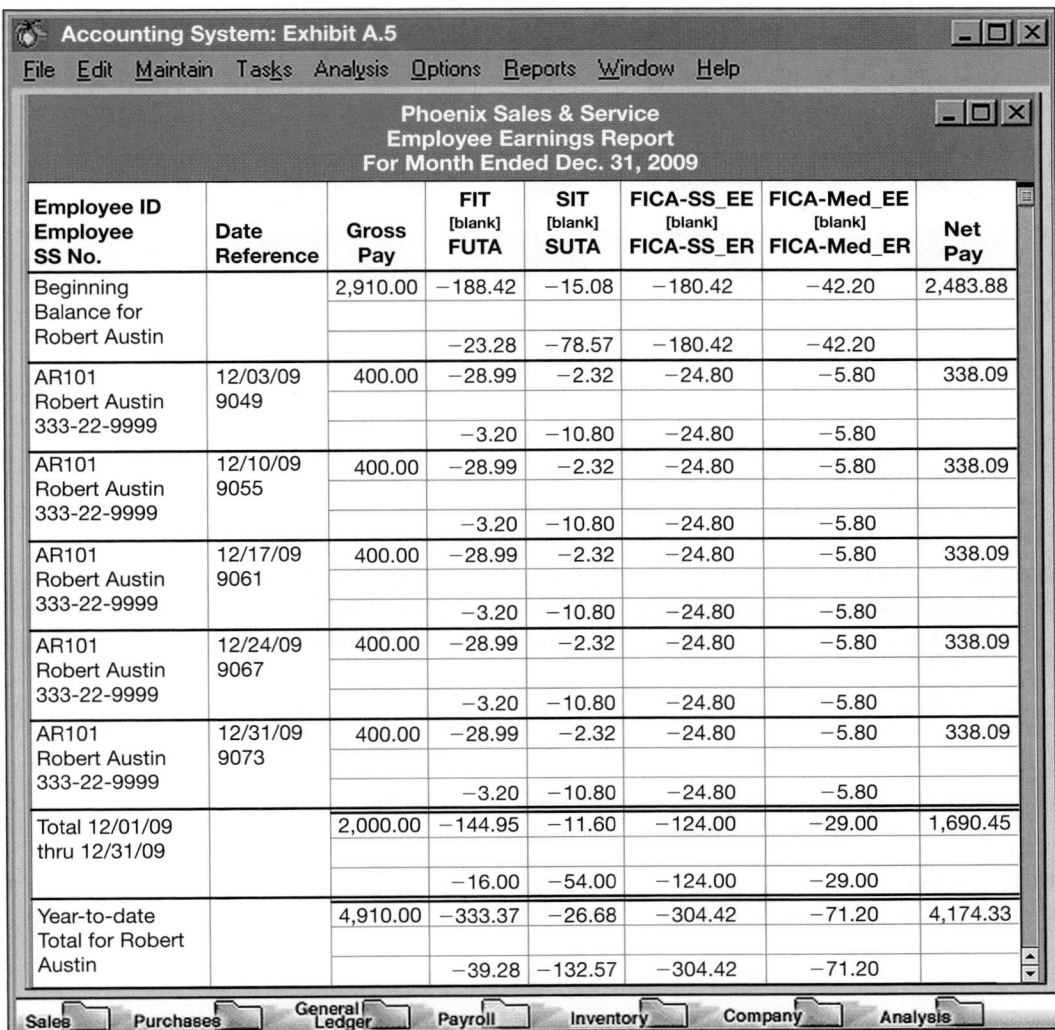

```
Accounting System: Exhibit A.5                                    _ □ ✕
File  Edit  Maintain  Tasks  Analysis  Options  Reports  Window  Help
```

Phoenix Sales & Service
Employee Earnings Report
For Month Ended Dec. 31, 2009

Employee ID Employee SS No.	Date Reference	Gross Pay	FIT [blank] FUTA	SIT [blank] SUTA	FICA-SS_EE [blank] FICA-SS_ER	FICA-Med_EE [blank] FICA-Med_ER	Net Pay
Beginning Balance for Robert Austin		2,910.00	−188.42	−15.08	−180.42	−42.20	2,483.88
			−23.28	−78.57	−180.42	−42.20	
AR101 Robert Austin 333-22-9999	12/03/09 9049	400.00	−28.99	−2.32	−24.80	−5.80	338.09
			−3.20	−10.80	−24.80	−5.80	
AR101 Robert Austin 333-22-9999	12/10/09 9055	400.00	−28.99	−2.32	−24.80	−5.80	338.09
			−3.20	−10.80	−24.80	−5.80	
AR101 Robert Austin 333-22-9999	12/17/09 9061	400.00	−28.99	−2.32	−24.80	−5.80	338.09
			−3.20	−10.80	−24.80	−5.80	
AR101 Robert Austin 333-22-9999	12/24/09 9067	400.00	−28.99	−2.32	−24.80	−5.80	338.09
			−3.20	−10.80	−24.80	−5.80	
AR101 Robert Austin 333-22-9999	12/31/09 9073	400.00	−28.99	−2.32	−24.80	−5.80	338.09
			−3.20	−10.80	−24.80	−5.80	
Total 12/01/09 thru 12/31/09		2,000.00	−144.95	−11.60	−124.00	−29.00	1,690.45
			−16.00	−54.00	−124.00	−29.00	
Year-to-date Total for Robert Austin		4,910.00	−333.37	−26.68	−304.42	−71.20	4,174.33
			−39.28	−132.57	−304.42	−71.20	

```
Sales    Purchases    General Ledger    Payroll    Inventory    Company    Analysis
```

EXHIBIT 11A.6

Wage Bracket Withholding Table

SINGLE Persons—**WEEKLY** Payroll Period

If the wages are—		And the number of withholding allowances claimed is—										
At least	But less than	0	1	2	3	4	5	6	7	8	9	10
		The amount of income tax to be withheld is—										
$600	$610	$76	$67	$58	$49	$39	$30	$21	$12	$6	$0	$0
610	620	79	69	59	50	41	32	22	13	7	1	0
620	630	81	70	61	52	42	33	24	15	8	2	0
630	640	84	72	62	53	44	35	25	16	9	3	0
640	650	86	73	64	55	45	36	27	18	10	4	0
650	660	89	75	65	56	47	38	28	19	11	5	0
660	670	91	76	67	58	48	39	30	21	12	6	0
670	680	94	78	68	59	50	41	31	22	13	7	1
680	690	96	81	70	61	51	42	33	24	14	8	2
690	700	99	83	71	62	53	44	34	25	16	9	3
700	710	101	86	73	64	54	45	35	27	17	10	4
710	720	104	88	74	65	56	47	37	28	19	11	5
720	730	106	91	76	67	57	48	39	30	20	12	6
730	740	109	93	78	68	59	50	40	31	22	13	7
740	750	111	96	80	70	60	51	42	33	23	14	8

regular bank account. When companies use a payroll bank account, they usually include check numbers in the payroll register. The payroll register in Exhibit 11A.3 shows check numbers in column 1. For instance, Check No. 9001 is issued to Robert Austin. With this information, the payroll register serves as a supplementary record of wages earned by and paid to employees.

Who Pays What Payroll Taxes and Benefits

We conclude this appendix with the following table identifying who pays which payroll taxes and which common employee benefits such as medical, disability, pension, charitable, and union costs. Who pays which employee benefits, and what portion, is subject to agreements between companies and their workers. Also, self-employed workers must pay both the employer and employee FICA taxes for Social Security and Medicare.

Employer Payroll Taxes and Costs	Employee Payroll Deductions
• FICA—Social Security Taxes	• FICA—Social Security taxes
• FICA—Medicare Taxes	• FICA—Medicare taxes
• FUTA (Federal Unemployment Taxes)	• Federal Income taxes
• SUTA (State Unemployment Taxes)	• State and local income taxes
• Share of medical coverage, if any	• Share of medical coverage, if any
• Share of pension coverage, if any	• Share of pension coverage, if any
• Share of other benefits, if any	• Share of other benefits, if any

Quick Check   Answers—p. 458

11. What two items determine the amount deducted from an employee's wages for federal income taxes?

12. What amount of income tax is withheld from the salary of an employee who is single with three withholding allowances and earnings of $675 in a week? (*Hint:* Use the wage bracket withholding table in Exhibit 11A.6.)

13. Which of the following steps are executed when a company draws one check for total payroll and deposits it in a special payroll bank account? (*a*) Write a check to the payroll bank account for the total payroll and record it with a debit to Salaries Payable and a credit to Cash. (*b*) Deposit a check (or transfer funds) for the total payroll in the payroll bank account. (*c*) Issue individual payroll checks drawn on the payroll bank account. (*d*) All of the above.

APPENDIX

11B   Corporate Income Taxes

This appendix explains current liabilities involving income taxes for corporations.

Income Tax Liabilities   Corporations are subject to income taxes and must estimate their income tax liability when preparing financial statements. Since income tax expense is created by earning income, a liability is incurred when income is earned. This tax must be paid quarterly under federal regulations. To illustrate, consider a corporation that prepares monthly financial statements. Based on its income in January 2009, this corporation estimates that it owes income taxes of $12,100. The following adjusting entry records this estimate:

Assets = Liabilities + Equity
       +12,100   −12,100

Jan. 31	Income Taxes Expense	12,100	
	Income Taxes Payable.................		12,100
	To accrue January income taxes.		

The tax liability is recorded each month until the first quarterly payment is made. If the company's estimated taxes for this first quarter total $30,000, the entry to record its payment is

Apr. 10	Income Taxes Payable....................	30,000	
	Cash...................................		30,000
	Paid estimated quarterly income taxes based on first quarter income.		

Assets = Liabilities + Equity
−30,000   −30,000

This process of accruing and then paying estimated income taxes continues through the year. When annual financial statements are prepared at year-end, the corporation knows its actual total income and the actual amount of income taxes it must pay. This information allows it to properly record income taxes expense for the fourth quarter so that the total of the four quarters' expense amounts equals the actual taxes paid to the government.

Deferred Income Tax Liabilities   An income tax liability for corporations can arise when the amount of income before taxes that the corporation reports on its income statement is not the same as the amount of income reported on its income tax return. This difference occurs because income tax laws and GAAP measure income differently. (Differences between tax laws and GAAP arise because Congress uses tax laws to generate receipts, stimulate the economy, and influence behavior, whereas GAAP are intended to provide financial information useful for business decisions. Also, tax accounting often follows the cash basis, whereas GAAP follows the accrual basis.)

Some differences between tax laws and GAAP are temporary. *Temporary differences* arise when the tax return and the income statement report a revenue or expense in different years. As an example, companies are often able to deduct higher amounts of depreciation in the early years of an asset's life and smaller amounts in later years for tax reporting in comparison to GAAP. This means that in the early years, depreciation for tax reporting is often more than depreciation on the income statement. In later years, depreciation for tax reporting is often less than depreciation on the income statement. When temporary differences exist between taxable income on the tax return and the income before taxes on the income statement, corporations compute income taxes expense based on the income reported on the income statement. The result is that income taxes expense reported in the income statement is often different from the amount of income taxes payable to the government. This difference is the **deferred income tax liability.**

To illustrate, assume that in recording its usual quarterly income tax payments, a corporation computes $25,000 of income taxes expense. It also determines that only $21,000 is currently due and $4,000 is deferred to future years (a timing difference). The entry to record this end-of-period adjustment is

Dec. 31	Income Taxes Expense......................	25,000	
	Income Taxes Payable....................		21,000
	Deferred Income Tax Liability.............		4,000
	To record tax expense and deferred tax liability.		

Assets = Liabilities + Equity
          +21,000   −25,000
          +4,000

The credit to Income Taxes Payable reflects the amount currently due to be paid. The credit to Deferred Income Tax Liability reflects tax payments deferred until future years when the temporary difference reverses.

Temporary differences also can cause a company to pay income taxes *before* they are reported on the income statement as expense. If so, the company reports a *Deferred Income Tax Asset* on its balance sheet.

Summary

C1 Describe current and long-term liabilities and their characteristics. Liabilities are probable future payments of assets or services that past transactions or events obligate an entity to make. Current liabilities are due within one year or the operating cycle, whichever is longer. All other liabilities are long term.

C2 Identify and describe known current liabilities. Known (determinable) current liabilities are set by agreements or laws and are measurable with little uncertainty. They include accounts payable, sales taxes payable, unearned revenues, notes payable, payroll liabilities, and the current portion of long-term debt.

C3 Explain how to account for contingent liabilities. If an uncertain future payment depends on a probable future event and the amount can be reasonably estimated, the payment is recorded as a liability. The uncertain future payment is reported as a contingent liability (in the notes) if (*a*) the future event is reasonably possible but not probable or (*b*) the event is probable but the payment amount cannot be reasonably estimated.

A1 Compute the times interest earned ratio and use it to analyze liabilities. Times interest earned is computed by dividing a company's net income before interest expense and income taxes by the amount of interest expense. The times interest earned ratio reflects a company's ability to pay interest obligations.

P1 Prepare entries to account for short-term notes payable. Short-term notes payable are current liabilities; most bear interest. When a short-term note's face value equals the amount borrowed, it identifies a rate of interest to be paid at maturity.

P2 Compute and record *employee* payroll deductions and liabilities. Employee payroll deductions include FICA taxes, income taxes, and voluntary deductions such as for pensions and charities. They make up the difference between gross and net pay.

P3 Compute and record *employer* payroll expenses and liabilities. An employer's payroll expenses include employees' gross earnings, any employee benefits, and the payroll taxes levied on the employer. Payroll liabilities include employees' net pay amounts, withholdings from employee wages, any employer-promised benefits, and the employer's payroll taxes.

P4 Account for estimated liabilities, including warranties and bonuses. Liabilities for health and pension benefits, warranties, and bonuses are recorded with estimated amounts. These items are recognized as expenses when incurred and matched with revenues generated.

P5ᴬ Identify and describe the details of payroll reports, records, and procedures. Employers report FICA taxes and federal income tax withholdings using Form 941. FUTA taxes are reported on Form 940. Earnings and deductions are reported to each employee and the federal government on Form W-2. An employer's payroll records often include a payroll register for each pay period, payroll checks and statements of earnings, and individual employee earnings reports.

Guidance Answers to **Decision Maker** and **Decision Ethics**

Web Designer You need to be concerned about being an accomplice to unlawful payroll activities. Not paying federal and state taxes on wages earned is illegal and unethical. Such payments also will not provide the employee with Social Security and some Medicare credits. The best course of action is to request payment by check. If this fails to change the owner's payment practices, you must consider quitting this job.

Entrepreneur Risk is partly reflected by the times interest earned ratio. This ratio for the first franchise is 1.5 [($100,000 + $200,000)/$200,000], whereas the ratio for the second franchise is 3.5 [($100,000 + $40,000)/$40,000]. This analysis shows that the first franchise is more at risk of incurring a loss if its sales decline. The second question asks about variability of income. If income greatly varies, this increases the risk an owner will not earn sufficient income to cover interest. Since the first franchise has the greater variability, it is a riskier investment.

Guidance Answers to **Quick Checks**

1. A liability involves a probable future payment of assets or services that an entity is presently obligated to make as a result of past transactions or events.

2. No, an expected future payment is not a liability unless an existing obligation was created by a past event or transaction.

3. In most cases, a liability due in 15 months is classified as long term. It is classified as a current liability if the company's operating cycle is 15 months or longer.

4. A creditor prefers a note payable instead of a past-due account payable so as to (a) charge interest and/or (b) have evidence of the debt and its terms for potential litigation or disputes.

5. $1,000* × (.008) + $1,000* × (.04) + $3,000 × (.062) + $3,000 × (.0145) = $277.50

* $1,000 of the $3,000 March pay is subject to FUTA and SUTA—the entire $6,000 pay from January and February was subject to them.

6. (a) FICA taxes are incurred by both employee and employer.
   (b) FUTA taxes are incurred by the employer.
   (c) SUTA taxes are incurred by the employer.
   (d) Withheld income taxes are incurred by the employee.

7. (a)

8. (a) Warranty expense was previously estimated and recorded.

9. (b)

10. A future payment is reported in the notes as a contingent liability if (a) the uncertain future event is probable but the amount of payment cannot be reasonably estimated or (b) the uncertain future event is not probable but has a reasonable possibility of occurring.

11. An employee's marital status, gross earnings and number of withholding allowances determine the deduction for federal income taxes.

12. $59

13. (d)

Key Terms   mhhe.com/wildFAP19e

Key Terms are available at the book's Website for learning and testing in an online Flashcard Format.

Contingent liability (p. 445)
Current liabilities (p. 435)
Current portion of long-term debt (p. 442)

Deferred income tax liability (p. 457)
Employee benefits (p. 443)
Employee earnings report (p. 454)

Estimated liability (p. 443)
Federal depository bank (p. 452)
Federal Insurance Contributions Act (FICA) Taxes (p. 440)

Federal Unemployment Taxes
 (FUTA) (p. 442)
Form 940 (p. 452)
Form 941 (p. 450)
Form W-2 (p. 452)
Form W-4 (p. 454)
Gross pay (p. 440)

Known liabilities (p. 436)
Long-term liabilities (p. 435)
Merit rating (p. 442)
Net pay (p. 440)
Payroll bank account (p. 454)
Payroll deductions (p. 440)
Payroll register (p. 452)

Short-term note payable (p. 437)
State Unemployment Taxes
 (SUTA) (p. 442)
Times interest earned (p. 447)
Wage bracket withholding table (p. 454)
Warranty (p. 444)

Multiple Choice Quiz   Answers on p. 475   mhhe.com/wildFAP19e

Additional Quiz Questions are available at the book's Website.

1. On December 1, a company signed a $6,000, 90-day, 5% note payable, with principal plus interest due on March 1 of the following year. What amount of interest expense should be accrued at December 31 on the note?
 a. $300
 b. $25
 c. $100
 d. $75
 e. $0

2. An employee earned $50,000 during the year. FICA tax for social security is 6.2% and FICA tax for Medicare is 1.45%. The employer's share of FICA taxes is
 a. Zero, since the employee's pay exceeds the FICA limit.
 b. Zero, since FICA is not an employer tax.
 c. $3,100
 d. $725
 e. $3,825

3. Assume the FUTA tax rate is 0.8% and the SUTA tax rate is 5.4%. Both taxes are applied to the first $7,000 of an employee's pay. What is the total unemployment tax an employer must pay on an employee's annual wages of $40,000?
 a. $2,480
 b. $434
 c. $56
 d. $378
 e. Zero; the employee's wages exceed the $7,000 maximum.

4. A company sells big screen televisions for $3,000 each. Each television has a two-year warranty that covers the replacement of defective parts. It is estimated that 1% of all televisions sold will be returned under warranty at an average cost of $250 each. During July, the company sold 10,000 big screen televisions, and 80 were serviced under the warranty during July at a total cost of $18,000. The credit balance in the Estimated Warranty Liability account at July 1 was $26,000. What is the company's warranty expense for the month of July?
 a. $51,000
 b. $1,000
 c. $25,000
 d. $33,000
 e. $18,000

5. Employees earn vacation pay at the rate of 1 day per month. During October, 150 employees qualify for one vacation day each. Their average daily wage is $175 per day. What is the amount of vacation benefit expense for October?
 a. $26,250
 b. $175
 c. $2,100
 d. $63,875
 e. $150

Superscript letter ^{A} $(^B)$ *denotes assignments based on Appendix 11A (11B).*

Discussion Questions

1. ♟ What are the three important questions concerning the uncertainty of liabilities?

2. ♟ What is the difference between a current and a long-term liability?

3. What is an estimated liability?

4. If $988 is the total of a sale that includes its sales tax of 4%, what is the selling price of the item only?

5. What is the combined amount (in percent) of the employee and employer Social Security tax rate?

6. What is the current Medicare tax rate? This rate is applied to what maximum level of salary and wages?

7. What determines the amount deducted from an employee's wages for federal income taxes?

8. Which payroll taxes are the employee's responsibility and which are the employer's responsibility?

9. What is an employer's unemployment merit rating? How are these ratings assigned to employers?

10. ♟ Why are warranty liabilities usually recognized on the balance sheet as liabilities even when they are uncertain?

11. ♟ Suppose that a company has a facility located where disastrous weather conditions often occur. Should it report a probable loss from a future disaster as a liability on its balance sheet? Explain.

12. What is a wage bracket withholding table?

13.^A What amount of income tax is withheld from the salary of an employee who is single with two withholding allowances and earning $725 per week? What if the employee earned $625 and has no withholding allowances? (Use Exhibit 11A.6.)

14. Refer to **Best Buy**'s balance sheet in Appendix A. What payroll-related liability does Best Buy report at March 3, 2007?

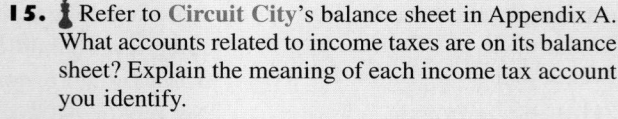

15. Refer to **Circuit City**'s balance sheet in Appendix A. What accounts related to income taxes are on its balance sheet? Explain the meaning of each income tax account you identify.

16. Refer to **RadioShack**'s balance sheet in Appendix A. What is the amount of RadioShack's accounts payable as of December 31, 2006?

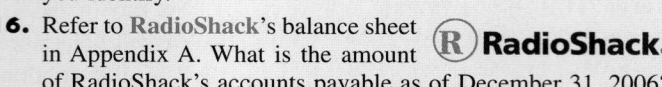

17. Refer to **Apple**'s balance sheet in Appendix A. List Apple's current liabilities as of September 30, 2006.

Denotes Discussion Questions that involve decision making.

Available with McGraw-Hill's Homework Manager

QUICK STUDY

QS 11-1
Classifying liabilities C1

Which of the following items are normally classified as a current liability for a company that has a 15-month operating cycle?

1. Note payable due in 18 months.
2. Note payable maturing in 2 years.
3. Portion of long-term note due in 15 months.
4. Salaries payable.
5. FICA taxes payable.
6. Note payable due in 11 months.

QS 11-2
Unearned revenue C2

Tickets, Inc., receives $7,500,000 cash in advance ticket sales for a five-date tour of Bruce Springsteen. Record the advance ticket sales on October 31. Record the revenue earned for the first concert date of November 5, assuming it represents one-fifth of the advance ticket sales.

QS 11-3
Accounting for sales taxes
C2

Wheeling Computing sells merchandise for $12,000 cash on September 30 (cost of merchandise is $7,800). The sales tax law requires Wheeling to collect 6% sales tax on every dollar of merchandise sold. Record the entry for the $12,000 sale and its applicable sales tax. Also record the entry that shows the remittance of the 6% tax on this sale to the state government on October 15.

QS 11-4
Interest-bearing note transactions
P1

On November 7, 2009, Stockmann Company borrows $80,000 cash by signing a 90-day, 8% note payable with a face value of $80,000. (1) Compute the accrued interest payable on December 31, 2009, (2) prepare the journal entry to record the accrued interest expense at December 31, 2009, and (3) prepare the journal entry to record payment of the note at maturity.

QS 11-5
Record employer payroll taxes
P2 P3

DeNise Co. has five employees, each of whom earns $3,000 per month and has been employed since January 1. FICA Social Security taxes are 6.2% of the first $102,000 paid to each employee, and FICA Medicare taxes are 1.45% of gross pay. FUTA taxes are 0.8% and SUTA taxes are 5.4% of the first $7,000 paid to each employee. Prepare the March 31 journal entry to record the March payroll taxes expense.

QS 11-6
Accounting for vacations
P4

Chavez Co.'s salaried employees earn four weeks vacation per year. It pays $156,000 in total employee salaries for 52 weeks but its employees work only 48 weeks. This means Chavez's total weekly expense is $3,250 ($156,000/48 weeks) instead of the $3,000 cash paid weekly to the employees ($156,000/52 weeks). Record Chavez's weekly vacation benefits expense.

QS 11-7
Accounting for bonuses P4

Erik Company offers an annual bonus to employees if the company meets certain net income goals. Prepare the journal entry to record a $15,000 bonus owed to its workers (to be shared equally) at calendar year-end.

QS 11-8
Recording warranty repairs
P4

On September 11, 2008, Lawn Outfitters sells a mower for $750 with a one-year warranty that covers parts. Warranty expense is estimated at 3% of sales. On July 24, 2009, the mower is brought in for repairs covered under the warranty requiring $55 in materials taken from the Repair Parts Inventory. Prepare the July 24, 2009, entry to record the warranty repairs.

QS 11-9
Accounting for contingent liabilities
C3

The following legal claims exist for VanBeek Co. Identify the accounting treatment for each claim as either (*a*) a liability that is recorded or (*b*) an item described in notes to its financial statements.

1. VanBeek (defendant) estimates that a pending lawsuit could result in damages of $250,000; it is reasonably possible that the plaintiff will win the case.
2. VanBeek faces a probable loss on a pending lawsuit; the amount is not reasonably estimable.
3. VanBeek estimates damages in a case at $1,500,000 with a high probability of losing the case.

QS 11-10
Times interest earned
A1

Compute the times interest earned for Zelma Company, which reports income before interest expense and income taxes of $1,044,000, and interest expense of $145,000. Interpret its times interest earned (assume that its competitors average a times interest earned of 4.0).

QS 11-11B
Record deferred income tax liability
P4

Eastwood Corporation has made and recorded its quarterly income tax payments. After a final review of taxes for the year, the company identifies an additional $40,000 of income tax expense that should be recorded. A portion of this additional expense, $6,000, is deferred for payment in future years. Record Eastwood's year-end adjusting entry for income tax expense.

McGraw-Hill's HOMEWORK MANAGER® Available with McGraw-Hill's Homework Manager

EXERCISES

Exercise 11-1
Classifying liabilities
C1

The following items appear on the balance sheet of a company with a two-month operating cycle. Identify the proper classification of each item as follows: *C* if it is a current liability, *L* if it is a long-term liability, or *N* if it is not a liability.

_____ 1. Notes payable (due in 120 days).
_____ 2. Notes payable (due in 6 to 12 months).
_____ 3. Notes payable (due in 13 to 24 months).
_____ 4. Accounts receivable.
_____ 5. FUTA taxes payable.
_____ 6. Notes payable (mature in five years).
_____ 7. Current portion of long-term debt.
_____ 8. Sales taxes payable.
_____ 9. Wages payable.
_____ 10. Salaries payable.

Exercise 11-2
Adjusting entries for liabilities
C2 C3 P4

Prepare any necessary adjusting entries at December 31, 2009, for Madison Company's year-end financial statements for each of the following separate transactions and events.

1. During December, Madison Company sold 4,100 units of a product that carries a 60-day warranty. December sales for this product total $164,000. The company expects 6% of the units to need warranty repairs, and it estimates the average repair cost per unit will be $14.
2. A disgruntled employee is suing Madison Company. Legal advisers believe that the company will probably need to pay damages, but the amount cannot be reasonably estimated.
3. Employees earn vacation pay at a rate of one day per month. During December, 28 employees qualify for one vacation day each. Their average daily wage is $105 per employee.
4. Madison Company guarantees the $13,000 debt of a supplier. The supplier will probably not default on the debt.
5. Madison Company records an adjusting entry for $520,000 of previously unrecorded cash sales (costing $260,000) and its sales taxes at a rate of 7%.
6. The company earned $104,000 of $260,000 previously received in advance for services.

Exercise 11-3
Computing and recording bonuses C2

For the year ended December 31, 2009, Kava Company has implemented an employee bonus program equal to 4% of Kava's net income, which employees will share equally. Kava's net income (prebonus) is expected to be $1,300,000, and bonus expense is deducted in computing net income.

1. Compute the amount of the bonus payable to the employees at year-end (use the method described in the chapter and round to the nearest dollar).
2. Prepare the journal entry at December 31, 2009, to record the bonus due the employees.
3. Prepare the journal entry at January 19, 2010, to record payment of the bonus to employees.

Check (1) $50,000

Exercise 11-4

Accounting for note payable

P1

Check (2b) Interest expense, $6,165

Motora Systems borrows $137,000 cash on May 15, 2009, by signing a 180-day, 9% note.

1. On what date does this note mature?

2. Suppose the face value of the note equals $137,000, the principal of the loan. Prepare the journal entries to record (*a*) issuance of the note and (*b*) payment of the note at maturity.

Exercise 11-5

Interest-bearing notes payable with year-end adjustments

P1

Check (2) $4,000
(3) $8,000

Keshena Co. borrows $240,000 cash on November 1, 2009, by signing a 180-day, 10% note with a face value of $240,000.

1. On what date does this note mature? (February of 2009 has 28 days.)

2. How much interest expense results from this note in 2009? (Assume a 360-day year.)

3. How much interest expense results from this note in 2010? (Assume a 360-day year.)

4. Prepare journal entries to record (*a*) issuance of the note, (*b*) accrual of interest at the end of 2009, and (*c*) payment of the note at maturity.

Exercise 11-6

Computing payroll taxes

P2 P3

RNG Co. has one employee, and the company is subject to the following taxes.

Tax	Rate	Applied To
FICA—Social Security	6.20%	First $102,000
FICA—Medicare	1.45	All gross pay
FUTA	0.80	First $7,000
SUTA	2.90	First $7,000

Compute RNG's amounts for each of these four taxes as applied to the employee's gross earnings for September under each of three separate situations (*a*), (*b*), and (*c*).

	Gross Pay through August	Gross Pay for September
a.	$ 5,900	$2,100
b.	17,700	2,500
c.	95,700	7,400

Check (*a*) FUTA, $8.80; SUTA, $31.90

Exercise 11-7

Payroll-related journal entries

P2 P3

Using the data in situation *a* of Exercise 11-6, prepare the employer's September 30 journal entries to record (1) salary expense and its related payroll liabilities for this employee and (2) the employer's payroll taxes expense and its related liabilities. The employee's federal income taxes withheld by the employer are $250 for this pay period.

Exercise 11-8

Warranty expense and liability computations and entries

P4

Check (1) $282

(4) $157

Lee Co. sold a copier costing $6,500 with a two-year parts warranty to a customer on August 16, 2009, for $9,400 cash. Lee uses the perpetual inventory system. On November 22, 2010, the copier requires on-site repairs that are completed the same day. The repairs cost $125 for materials taken from the Repair Parts Inventory. These are the only repairs required in 2010 for this copier. Based on experience, Lee expects to incur warranty costs equal to 3% of dollar sales. It records warranty expense with an adjusting entry at the end of each year.

1. How much warranty expense does the company report in 2009 for this copier?

2. How much is the estimated warranty liability for this copier as of December 31, 2009?

3. How much warranty expense does the company report in 2010 for this copier?

4. How much is the estimated warranty liability for this copier as of December 31, 2010?

5. Prepare journal entries to record (*a*) the copier's sale; (*b*) the adjustment on December 31, 2009, to recognize the warranty expense; and (*c*) the repairs that occur in November 2010.

Use the following information from separate companies *a* through *f* to compute times interest earned. Which company indicates the strongest ability to pay interest expense as it comes due?

	Net Income (Loss)	Interest Expense	Income Taxes
a.	$122,000	$36,600	$30,500
b.	116,600	11,660	41,976
c.	125,100	7,506	60,048
d.	103,700	31,110	43,554
e.	79,300	9,516	30,134
f.	(34,160)	74,469	0

Exercise 11-9
Computing and interpreting times interest earned

A1

Check (b) 14.60

The payroll records of Simplex Software show the following information about Ken LeShon, an employee, for the weekly pay period ending September 30, 2009. LeShon is single and claims one allowance. Compute his Social Security tax (6.2%), Medicare tax (1.45%), federal income tax withholding, state income tax (0.5%), and net pay for the current pay period. The state income tax is 0.5 percent on the first $9,000 earned. (Use the withholding table in Exhibit 11A.6 and round tax amounts to the nearest cent.)

Total (gross) earnings for current pay period .... $ 735
Cumulative earnings of previous pay periods 9,500

Exercise 11-10^A

Exercise 11-10ᴬ
Net pay and tax computations

P5

Check Net pay, $585.77

Tad Newbern, an unmarried employee, works 47 hours in the week ended January 12. His pay rate is $12 per hour, and his wages are subject to no deductions other than FICA—Social Security, FICA—Medicare, and federal income taxes. He claims two withholding allowances. Compute his regular pay, overtime pay (overtime premium is 50% of the regular rate for hours in excess of 40 per week), and gross pay. Then compute his FICA tax deduction (use 6.2% for the Social Security portion and 1.45% for the Medicare portion), income tax deduction (use the wage bracket withholding table of Exhibit 11A.6), total deductions, and net pay. (Round tax amounts to the nearest cent.)

Exercise 11-11ᴬ
Gross and net pay computation

P5

Check Net pay, $501.64

Florita Corporation prepares financial statements for each month-end. As part of its accounting process, estimated income taxes are accrued each month for 34% of the current month's net income. The income taxes are paid in the first month of each quarter for the amount accrued for the prior quarter. The following information is available for the fourth quarter of year 2009. When tax computations are completed on January 20, 2010, Florita determines that the quarter's Income Taxes Payable account balance should be $46,693 on December 31, 2009 (its unadjusted balance is $42,364).

October 2009 net income $45,200
November 2009 net income 29,400
December 2009 net income 50,000

Exercise 11-12ᴮ
Accounting for income taxes

P4

1. Determine the amount of the accounting adjustment (dated as of December 31, 2009) to produce the proper ending balance in the Income Taxes Payable account.
2. Prepare journal entries to record (*a*) the December 31, 2009, adjustment to the Income Taxes Payable account and (*b*) the January 20, 2010, payment of the fourth-quarter taxes.

Check (1) $4,329

Montag Co. entered into the following transactions involving short-term liabilities in 2008 and 2009.

PROBLEM SET A

2008

Apr. 20   Purchased $48,250 of merchandise on credit from Locust, terms are 1/10, n/30. Montag uses the perpetual inventory system.

May 19   Replaced the April 20 account payable to Locust with a 120-day, $39,000 note bearing 9% annual interest along with paying $9,250 in cash.

Problem 11-1A
Short-term notes payable transactions and entries

P1

July   8   Borrowed $120,000 cash from National Bank by signing a 120-day, 8.5% interest-bearing note with a face value of $100,000.

_____?_____   Paid the amount due on the note to Locust at the maturity date.

_____?_____   Paid the amount due on the note to National Bank at the maturity date.

Nov. 28   Borrowed $60,000 cash from Fargo Bank by signing a 60-day, 8% interest-bearing note with a face value of $60,000.

Dec. 31   Recorded an adjusting entry for accrued interest on the note to Fargo Bank.

2009

_____?_____   Paid the amount due on the note to Fargo Bank at the maturity date.

Required

1. Determine the maturity date for each of the three notes described.

2. Determine the interest due at maturity for each of the three notes. (Assume a 360-day year.)

3. Determine the interest expense to be recorded in the adjusting entry at the end of 2008.

4. Determine the interest expense to be recorded in 2009.

5. Prepare journal entries for all the preceding transactions and events for years 2008 and 2009.

Check   (2) Locust, $1,170
    (3) $440
    (4) $360

Problem 11-2A
Warranty expense and liability estimation

P4

On October 29, 2008, Bram Co. began operations by purchasing razors for resale. Bram uses the perpetual inventory method. The razors have a 90-day warranty that requires the company to replace any nonworking razor. When a razor is returned, the company discards it and mails a new one from Merchandise Inventory to the customer. The company's cost per new razor is $16 and its retail selling price is $60 in both 2008 and 2009. The manufacturer has advised the company to expect warranty costs to equal 7% of dollar sales. The following transactions and events occurred.

2008

Nov. 11   Sold 75 razors for $4,500 cash.
     30   Recognized warranty expense related to November sales with an adjusting entry.
Dec. 9   Replaced 15 razors that were returned under the warranty.
     16   Sold 210 razors for $12,600 cash.
     29   Replaced 30 razors that were returned under the warranty.
     31   Recognized warranty expense related to December sales with an adjusting entry.

2009

Jan. 5   Sold 130 razors for $7,800 cash.
     17   Replaced 35 razors that were returned under the warranty.
     31   Recognized warranty expense related to January sales with an adjusting entry.

Required

1. Prepare journal entries to record these transactions and adjustments for 2008 and 2009.

2. How much warranty expense is reported for November 2008 and for December 2008?

3. How much warranty expense is reported for January 2009?

4. What is the balance of the Estimated Warranty Liability account as of December 31, 2008?

5. What is the balance of the Estimated Warranty Liability account as of January 31, 2009?

Check   (3) $546
    (4) $477 Cr.
    (5) $463 Cr.

Problem 11-3A
Computing and analyzing times interest earned

A1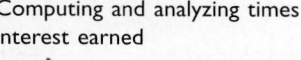

Shown here are condensed income statements for two different companies (both are organized as LLCs and pay no income taxes).

Milo Company	
Sales	$1,450,000
Variable expenses (80%)	1,160,000
Income before interest	290,000
Interest expense (fixed)	60,000
Net income	$ 230,000

Warner Company	
Sales	$1,450,000
Variable expenses (60%)	870,000
Income before interest	580,000
Interest expense (fixed)	350,000
Net income	$ 230,000

Required

1. Compute times interest earned for Milo Company.

2. Compute times interest earned for Warner Company.

3. What happens to each company's net income if sales increase by 40%?

4. What happens to each company's net income if sales increase by 50%?

5. What happens to each company's net income if sales increase by 80%?

6. What happens to each company's net income if sales decrease by 20%?

7. What happens to each company's net income if sales decrease by 30%?

8. What happens to each company's net income if sales decrease by 40%?

Check (4) Milo net income,
$375,000 (63% increase)

(6) Warner net income,
$114,000 (50% decrease)

Analysis Component

9. Comment on the results from parts 3 through 8 in relation to the fixed-cost strategies of the two companies and the ratio values you computed in parts 1 and 2.

Pardee Co. pays its employees each week. Its employees' gross pay is subject to these taxes.

Tax	Rate	Applied To
FICA—Social Security	6.20%	First $102,000
FICA—Medicare	1.45	All gross pay
FUTA	0.80	First $7,000
SUTA	2.15	First $7,000

Problem 11-4A
Payroll expenses, withholdings, and taxes

P2 P3

mhhe.com/wildFAP19e

The company is preparing its payroll calculations for the week ended August 25. Payroll records show the following information for the company's four employees.

	File Edit View Insert Format Tools Data Accounting Window Help		
1		**Gross Pay**	**Current Week**
2	**Name**	**through 8/18**	**Gross Pay**	**Income Tax Withholding**
3	Dahlia	$100,500	$3,600	$450
4	Trey	31,850	1,275	140
5	Kiesha	6,260	1,440	173
6	Chee	1,000	400	36
7				

In addition to gross pay, the company must pay one-half of the $22 per employee weekly health insurance; each employee pays the remaining one-half. The company also contributes an extra 8% of each employee's gross pay (at no cost to employees) to a pension fund.

Required

Compute the following for the week ended August 25 (round amounts to the nearest cent):

1. Each employee's FICA withholdings for Social Security.

2. Each employee's FICA withholdings for Medicare.

3. Employer's FICA taxes for Social Security.

4. Employer's FICA taxes for Medicare.

5. Employer's FUTA taxes.

6. Employer's SUTA taxes.

7. Each employee's net (take-home) pay.

8. Employer's total payroll-related expense for each employee.

Check (3) $286.13
(4) $97.37
(5) $9.12

(7) Total net pay, $5,488.50

Problem 11-5A

Entries for payroll transactions

P2   P3

On January 8, the end of the first weekly pay period of the year, Regal Company's payroll register showed that its employees earned $27,760 of office salaries and $70,240 of sales salaries. Withholdings from the employees' salaries include FICA Social Security taxes at the rate of 6.2%, FICA Medicare taxes at the rate of 1.45%, $13,360 of federal income taxes, $1,350 of medical insurance deductions, and $840 of union dues. No employee earned more than $7,000 in this first period.

Required

Check   (1) Cr. Salaries Payable, $74,953.00

(2) Dr. Payroll Taxes Expense, $13,181.00

1. Calculate FICA Social Security taxes payable and FICA Medicare taxes payable. Prepare the journal entry to record Regal Company's January 8 (employee) payroll expenses and liabilities.
2. Prepare the journal entry to record Regal's (employer) payroll taxes resulting from the January 8 payroll. Regal's merit rating reduces its state unemployment tax rate to 5% of the first $7,000 paid each employee. The federal unemployment tax rate is 0.8%.

Problem 11-6A[A]

Entries for payroll transactions

P2   P3   P5

Franco Company has 20 employees, each of whom earns $3,000 per month and is paid on the last day of each month. All 20 have been employed continuously at this amount since January 1. Franco uses a payroll bank account and special payroll checks to pay its employees. On March 1, the following accounts and balances exist in its general ledger:

a. FICA—Social Security Taxes Payable, $7,440; FICA—Medicare Taxes Payable, $1,740. (The balances of these accounts represent total liabilities for *both* the employer's and employees' FICA taxes for the February payroll only.)

b. Employees' Federal Income Taxes Payable, $5,250 (liability for February only).

c. Federal Unemployment Taxes Payable, $960 (liability for January and February together).

d. State Unemployment Taxes Payable, $4,800 (liability for January and February together).

During March and April, the company had the following payroll transactions.

Mar. 15   Issued check payable to Swift Bank, a federal depository bank authorized to accept employers' payments of FICA taxes and employee income tax withholdings. The $14,430 check is in payment of the February FICA and employee income taxes.

Check   March 31: Cr. Salaries Payable, $50,160

31   Recorded the March payroll and transferred funds from the regular bank account to the payroll bank account. Issued checks payable to each employee in payment of the March payroll. The payroll register shows the following summary totals for the March pay period.

Salaries and Wages					
Office Salaries	Shop Wages	Gross Pay	FICA Taxes*	Federal Income Taxes	Net Pay
$24,000	$36,000	$60,000	$3,720	$5,250	$50,160
			$ 870		

* FICA taxes are Social Security and Medicare, respectively.

March 31: Dr. Payroll Taxes Expenses, $5,550

April 15: Cr. Cash, $14,430 (Swift Bank)

31   Recorded the employer's payroll taxes resulting from the March payroll. The company has a merit rating that reduces its state unemployment tax rate to 4.0% of the first $7,000 paid each employee. The federal rate is 0.8%.

Apr. 15   Issued check to Swift Bank in payment of the March FICA and employee income taxes.

15   Issued check to the State Tax Commission for the January, February, and March state unemployment taxes. Mailed the check and the first quarter tax return to the Commission.

30   Issued check payable to Swift Bank in payment of the employer's FUTA taxes for the first quarter of the year.

30   Mailed Form 941 to the IRS, reporting the FICA taxes and the employees' federal income tax withholdings for the first quarter.

Required

Prepare journal entries to record the transactions and events for both March and April.

Nix Co. entered into the following transactions involving short-term liabilities in 2008 and 2009.

2008

Problem 11-1B
Short-term notes payable
transactions and entries
P1

Apr. 22   Purchased $6,000 of merchandise on credit from Wolf Products, terms are 1/10, n/30. Nix
          uses the perpetual inventory system.

May 23   Replaced the April 22 account payable to Wolf Products with a 60-day, $5,400 note bearing
         8% annual interest along with paying $600 in cash.

July 15   Borrowed $8,500 cash from Autumn Bank by signing a 90-day, 8% interest-bearing note with
          a face value of $8,500.

___?___   Paid the amount due on the note to Wolf Products at maturity.

___?___   Paid the amount due on the note to Autumn Bank at maturity.

Dec. 6   Borrowed $9,600 cash from City Bank by signing a 90-day, 6% interest-bearing note with a
          face value of $9,600.

      31 Recorded an adjusting entry for accrued interest on the note to City Bank.

2009

___?___   Paid the amount due on the note to City Bank at maturity. (February of 2009 has 28 days.)

Required

1. Determine the maturity date for each of the three notes described.

2. Determine the interest due at maturity for each of the three notes. (Assume a 360-day year.)

3. Determine the interest expense to be recorded in the adjusting entry at the end of 2008.

4. Determine the interest expense to be recorded in 2009.

5. Prepare journal entries for all the preceding transactions and events for years 2008 and 2009.

On November 10, 2009, Lorna Co. began operations by purchasing coffee grinders for resale. Lorna uses
the perpetual inventory method. The grinders have a 90-day warranty that requires the company to replace any nonworking grinder. When a grinder is returned, the company discards it and mails a new one
from Merchandise Inventory to the customer. The company's cost per new grinder is $15 and its retail
selling price is $85 in both 2009 and 2010. The manufacturer has advised the company to expect war-
ranty costs to equal 8% of dollar sales. The following transactions and events occurred.

2009

Nov. 16   Sold 50 grinders for $4,250 cash.
      30 Recognized warranty expense related to November sales with an adjusting entry.

Dec. 12   Replaced 11 grinders that were returned under the warranty.
      18 Sold 160 grinders for $13,600 cash.
      28 Replaced 22 grinders that were returned under the warranty.
      31 Recognized warranty expense related to December sales with an adjusting entry.

2010

Jan. 7   Sold 95 grinders for $8,075 cash.
      21 Replaced 45 grinders that were returned under the warranty.
      31 Recognized warranty expense related to January sales with an adjusting entry.

Required

1. Prepare journal entries to record these transactions and adjustments for 2009 and 2010.

2. How much warranty expense is reported for November 2009 and for December 2009?

3. How much warranty expense is reported for January 2010?

4. What is the balance of the Estimated Warranty Liability account as of December 31, 2009?

5. What is the balance of the Estimated Warranty Liability account as of January 31, 2010?

Problem 11-3B
Computing and analyzing times interest earned

A1

Shown here are condensed income statements for two different companies (both are organized as LLCs and pay no income taxes).

Ellis Company	
Sales	$250,000
Variable expenses (50%)	125,000
Income before interest	125,000
Interest expense (fixed)	75,000
Net income	$ 50,000

Seidel Company	
Sales	$250,000
Variable expenses (75%)	187,500
Income before interest	62,500
Interest expense (fixed)	12,500
Net income	$ 50,000

Required
1. Compute times interest earned for Ellis Company.
2. Compute times interest earned for Seidel Company.

Check   (3) Ellis net income, $100,000 (100% increase)

(6) Seidel net income, $37,500 (25% decrease)

3. What happens to each company's net income if sales increase by 40%?
4. What happens to each company's net income if sales increase by 50%?
5. What happens to each company's net income if sales increase by 80%?
6. What happens to each company's net income if sales decrease by 20%?
7. What happens to each company's net income if sales decrease by 30%?
8. What happens to each company's net income if sales decrease by 40%?

Analysis Component
9. Comment on the results from parts 3 through 8 in relation to the fixed-cost strategies of the two companies and the ratio values you computed in parts 1 and 2.

Problem 11-4B
Payroll expenses, withholdings, and taxes

P2   P3

Fishing Guides Co. pays its employees each week. Employees' gross pay is subject to these taxes.

Tax	Rate	Applied To
FICA—Social Security	6.20%	First $102,000
FICA—Medicare	1.45	All gross pay
FUTA	0.80	First $7,000
SUTA	1.75	First $7,000

The company is preparing its payroll calculations for the week ended September 30. Payroll records show the following information for the company's four employees.

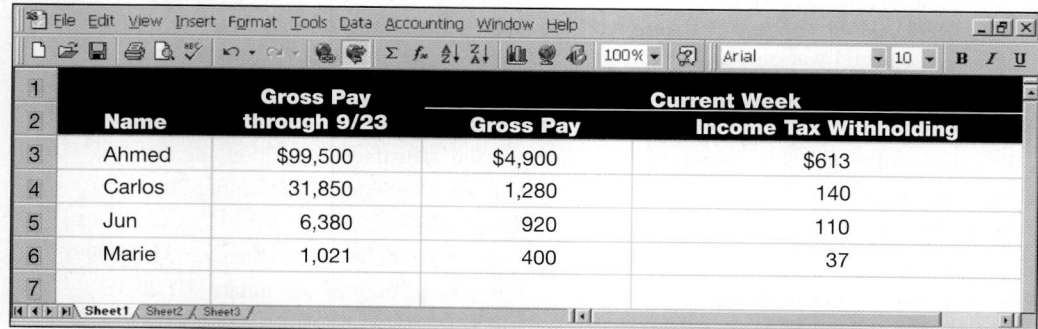

		Gross Pay	Current Week	
	Name	through 9/23	Gross Pay	Income Tax Withholding
3	Ahmed	$99,500	$4,900	$613
4	Carlos	31,850	1,280	140
5	Jun	6,380	920	110
6	Marie	1,021	400	37

In addition to gross pay, the company must pay one-half of the $20 per employee weekly health insurance; each employee pays the remaining one-half. The company also contributes an extra 8% of each employee's gross pay (at no cost to employees) to a pension fund.

Required

Compute the following for the week ended September 30 (round amounts to the nearest cent):

1. Each employee's FICA withholdings for Social Security.

2. Each employee's FICA withholdings for Medicare.

3. Employer's FICA taxes for Social Security.

4. Employer's FICA taxes for Medicare.

5. Employer's FUTA taxes.

6. Employer's SUTA taxes.

7. Each employee's net (take-home) pay.

8. Employer's total payroll-related expense for each employee.

Check (3) $316.20
(4) $108.75
(5) $8.16

(7) Total net pay, $6,135.05

Ravello Company's first weekly pay period of the year ends on January 8. On that date, the column totals in Ravello's payroll register indicate its sales employees earned $20,160, its office employees earned $70,840, and its delivery employees earned $3,000. The employees are to have withheld from their wages FICA Social Security taxes at the rate of 6.2%, FICA Medicare taxes at the rate of 1.45%, $12,760 of federal income taxes, $1,350 of medical insurance deductions, and $820 of union dues. No employee earned more than $7,000 in the first pay period.

Problem 11-5B
Entries for payroll transactions
P2   P3

Required

1. Calculate FICA Social Security taxes payable and FICA Medicare taxes payable. Prepare the journal entry to record Ravello Company's January 8 (employee) payroll expenses and liabilities.

2. Prepare the journal entry to record Ravello's (employer) payroll taxes resulting from the January 8 payroll. Ravello's merit rating reduces its state unemployment tax rate to 2% of the first $7,000 paid each employee. The federal unemployment tax rate is 0.8%.

Check (1) Cr. Salaries Payable,
$71,879.00
(2) Dr. Payroll Taxes
Expense, $9,823.00

JLS Company has 12 employees, each of whom earns $3,000 per month and is paid on the last day of each month. All 12 have been employed continuously at this amount since January 1. JLS uses a payroll bank account and special payroll checks to pay its employees. On March 1, the following accounts and balances exist in its general ledger:

Problem 11-6B[A]
Entries for payroll transactions
P2   P3   P5

a. FICA—Social Security Taxes Payable, $4,464; FICA—Medicare Taxes Payable, $1,044. (The balances of these accounts represent total liabilities for *both* the employer's and employees' FICA taxes for the February payroll only.)

b. Employees' Federal Income Taxes Payable, $4,050 (liability for February only).

c. Federal Unemployment Taxes Payable, $576 (liability for January and February together).

d. State Unemployment Taxes Payable, $3,600 (liability for January and February together).

During March and April, the company had the following payroll transactions.

March 15   Issued check payable to Security Bank, a federal depository bank authorized to accept employers' payments of FICA taxes and employee income tax withholdings. The $9,558 check is in payment of the February FICA and employee income taxes.

31   Recorded the March payroll and transferred funds from the regular bank account to the payroll bank account. Issued checks payable to each employee in payment of the March payroll. The payroll register shows the following summary totals for the March pay period.

Check   Mar. 31: Cr. Salaries
Payable, $29,196

| Salaries and Wages | | | | Federal | |
Office Salaries	Shop Wages	Gross Pay	FICA Taxes*	Income Taxes	Net Pay
$21,000	$15,000	$36,000	$2,232	$4,050	$29,196
			$ 522		

* FICA taxes are Social Security and Medicare, respectively.

31   Recorded the employer's payroll taxes resulting from the March payroll. The company has a merit rating that reduces its state unemployment tax rate to 5.0% of the first $7,000 paid each employee. The federal rate is 0.8%.

April 15   Issued check payable to Security Bank in payment of the March FICA and employee income taxes.

15   Issued check to the State Tax Commission for the January, February, and March state unemployment taxes. Mailed the check and the second quarter tax return to the State Tax Commission.

30   Issued check payable to Security Bank in payment of the employer's FUTA taxes for the first quarter of the year.

30   Mailed Form 941 to the IRS, reporting the FICA taxes and the employees' federal income tax withholdings for the first quarter.

Required

Prepare journal entries to record the transactions and events for both March and April.

SERIAL PROBLEM

Success Systems

(This serial problem began in Chapter 1 and continues through most of the book. If previous chapter segments were not completed, the serial problem can begin at this point. It is helpful, but not necessary, to use the Working Papers that accompany the book.)

SP 11   Review the February 26 and March 25 transactions for Success Systems (SP 5) from Chapter 5.

Required

1. Assume that Lyn Addie is an unmarried employee. Her $1,000 of wages are subject to no deductions other than FICA Social Security taxes, FICA Medicare taxes, and federal income taxes. Her federal income taxes for this pay period total $159. Compute her net pay for the eight days' work paid on February 26. (Round amounts to the nearest cent.)

2. Record the journal entry to reflect the payroll payment to Lyn Addie as computed in part 1.

3. Record the journal entry to reflect the (employer) payroll tax expenses for the February 26 payroll payment. Assume Lyn Addie has not met earnings limits for FUTA and SUTA—the FUTA rate is 0.8% and the SUTA rate is 4% for Success Systems. (Round amounts to the nearest cent.)

4. Record the entry(ies) for the merchandise sold on March 25 if a 4% sales tax rate applies.

COMPREHENSIVE PROBLEM

Bug-Off Exterminators
(Review of Chapters 1–11)

CP 11   Bug-Off Exterminators provides pest control services and sells extermination products manufactured by other companies. The following six-column table contains the company's unadjusted trial balance as of December 31, 2009.

BUG-OFF EXTERMINATORS December 31, 2009					
	Unadjusted Trial Balance		Adjustments	Adjusted Trial Balance	
Cash	$ 17,000				
Accounts receivable	4,000				
Allowance for doubtful accounts		$ 828			
Merchandise inventory	11,700				
Trucks	32,000				
Accum. depreciation—Trucks		0			
Equipment	45,000				
Accum. depreciation—Equipment		12,200			
Accounts payable		5,000			
Estimated warranty liability		1,400			

[continued on next page]

[continued from previous page]

Unearned services revenue		0
Interest payable		0
Long-term notes payable		15,000
D. Buggs, Capital		59,700
D. Buggs, Withdrawals	10,000	
Extermination services revenue		60,000
Interest revenue		872
Sales (of merchandise)		71,026
Cost of goods sold	46,300	
Depreciation expense—Trucks	0	
Depreciation expense—Equipment	0	
Wages expense	35,000	
Interest expense	0	
Rent expense	9,000	
Bad debts expense	0	
Miscellaneous expense	1,226	
Repairs expense	8,000	
Utilities expense	6,800	
Warranty expense	0	
Totals	$226,026	$226,026

The following information in *a* through *h* applies to the company at the end of the current year.

a. The bank reconciliation as of December 31, 2009, includes the following facts.

Cash balance per bank	$15,100
Cash balance per books	17,000
Outstanding checks	1,800
Deposit in transit	2,450
Interest earned (on bank account)	52
Bank service charges (miscellaneous expense)	15

Reported on the bank statement is a canceled check that the company failed to record. (Information from the bank reconciliation allows you to determine the amount of this check, which is a payment on an account payable.)

b. An examination of customers' accounts shows that accounts totaling $679 should be written off as uncollectible. Using an aging of receivables, the company determines that the ending balance of the Allowance for Doubtful Accounts should be $700.

c. A truck is purchased and placed in service on January 1, 2009. Its cost is being depreciated with the straight-line method using the following facts and estimates.

Original cost	$32,000
Expected salvage value	8,000
Useful life (years)	4

d. Two items of equipment (a sprayer and an injector) were purchased and put into service in early January 2007. They are being depreciated with the straight-line method using these facts and estimates.

	Sprayer	Injector
Original cost	$27,000	$18,000
Expected salvage value	3,000	2,500
Useful life (years)	8	5

e. On August 1, 2009, the company is paid $3,840 cash in advance to provide monthly service for an apartment complex for one year. The company began providing the services in August. When the cash was received, the full amount was credited to the Extermination Services Revenue account.

f. The company offers a warranty for the services it sells. The expected cost of providing warranty service is 2.5% of the extermination services revenue of $57,760 for 2009. No warranty expense has been recorded for 2009. All costs of servicing warranties in 2009 were properly debited to the Estimated Warranty Liability account.

g. The $15,000 long-term note is an 8%, five-year, interest-bearing note with interest payable annually on December 31. The note was signed with First National Bank on December 31, 2009.

h. The ending inventory of merchandise is counted and determined to have a cost of $11,700. Bug-Off uses a perpetual inventory system.

Required

1. Use the preceding information to determine amounts for the following items.

   a. Correct (reconciled) ending balance of Cash, and the amount of the omitted check.

   b. Adjustment needed to obtain the correct ending balance of the Allowance for Doubtful Accounts.

   c. Depreciation expense for the truck used during year 2009.

   d. Depreciation expense for the two items of equipment used during year 2009.

   e. The adjusted 2009 ending balances of the Extermination Services Revenue and Unearned Services Revenue accounts.

   f. The adjusted 2009 ending balances of the accounts for Warranty Expense and Estimated Warranty Liability.

   g. The adjusted 2009 ending balances of the accounts for Interest Expense and Interest Payable. (Round amounts to nearest whole dollar.)

2. Use the results of part 1 to complete the six-column table by first entering the appropriate adjustments for items *a* through *g* and then completing the adjusted trial balance columns. (*Hint:* Item *b* requires two adjustments.)

3. Prepare journal entries to record the adjustments entered on the six-column table. Assume Bug-Off's adjusted balance for Merchandise Inventory matches the year-end physical count.

4. Prepare a single-step income statement, a statement of owner's equity (cash withdrawals during 2009 were $10,000), and a classified balance sheet.

Check (1*a*) Cash bal. $15,750
(1*b*) $551 credit

(1*f*) Estim. warranty liability, $2,844 Cr.

(2) Adjusted trial balance totals, $238,207

(4) Net income, $9,274; Total assets, $82,771

BEYOND THE NUMBERS

REPORTING IN ACTION

A1 P4

BTN 11-1   Refer to the financial statements of **Best Buy** in Appendix A to answer the following.

1. Compute times interest earned for the fiscal years ended 2007, 2006, and 2005. Comment on Best Buy's ability to cover its interest expense for this period. Assume an industry average of 28.1.

2. Best Buy's current liabilities include "Unredeemed gift card liabilities." Explain how this liability is created and how Best Buy satisfies this liability.

3. Does Best Buy have any commitments or contingencies? Briefly explain them.

Fast Forward

4. Access Best Buy's financial statements for fiscal years ending after March 3, 2007, at its Website (BestBuy.com) or the SEC's EDGAR database (www.sec.gov). Compute its times interest earned for years ending after March 3, 2007, and compare your results to those in part 1.

COMPARATIVE ANALYSIS

A1

BTN 11-2   Key figures for **Best Buy**, **Circuit City**, and **RadioShack** follow.

($ millions)	Best Buy Current Year	One Year Prior	Two Years Prior	Circuit City Current Year	One Year Prior	Two Years Prior	RadioShack Current Year	One Year Prior	Two Years Prior
Net income	$1,377	$1,140	$984	$(8)	$140	$62	$73	$267	$337
Income taxes	752	581	509	31	86	36	38	52	205
Interest expense	31	30	44	2	3	4	44	45	30

Required

1. Compute times interest earned for the three years' data shown for each company.
2. Comment on which company appears stronger in its ability to pay interest obligations if income should decline. Assume an industry average of 28.1.

BTN 11-3 Connor Bly is a sales manager for an automobile dealership. He earns a bonus each year based on revenue from the number of autos sold in the year less related warranty expenses. Actual warranty expenses have varied over the prior 10 years from a low of 3% of an automobile's selling price to a high of 10%. In the past, Bly has tended to estimate warranty expenses on the high end to be conservative. He must work with the dealership's accountant at year-end to arrive at the warranty expense accrual for cars sold each year.

1. Does the warranty accrual decision create any ethical dilemma for Bly?
2. Since warranty expenses vary, what percent do you think Bly should choose for the current year? Justify your response.

ETHICS CHALLENGE

P4

BTN 11-4 Dustin Clemens is the accounting and finance manager for a manufacturer. At year-end, he must determine how to account for the company's contingencies. His manager, Madeline Pretti, objects to Clemens's proposal to recognize an expense and a liability for warranty service on units of a new product introduced in the fourth quarter. Pretti comments, "There's no way we can estimate this warranty cost. We don't owe anyone anything until a product fails and it is returned. Let's report an expense if and when we do any warranty work."

COMMUNICATING IN PRACTICE

C3

Required

Prepare a one-page memorandum for Clemens to send to Pretti defending his proposal.

BTN 11-5 Access the February 26, 2007, filing of the December 31, 2006, annual 10-K report of **McDonald's Corporation** (Ticker: MCD), which is available from www.SEC.gov.

TAKING IT TO THE NET

C1 A1

Required

1. Identify the current liabilities on McDonald's balance sheet as of December 31, 2006.
2. What portion (in percent) of McDonald's long-term debt matures within the next 12 months?
3. Use the consolidated statement of income for the year ended December 31, 2006, to compute McDonald's times interest earned ratio. Comment on the result. Assume an industry average of 7.9.

BTN 11-6 Assume that your team is in business and you must borrow $6,000 cash for short-term needs. You have been shopping banks for a loan, and you have the following two options.

A. Sign a $6,000, 90-day, 10% interest-bearing note dated June 1.
B. Sign a $6,000, 120-day, 8% interest-bearing note dated June 1.

TEAMWORK IN ACTION

C2 P1

Required

1. Discuss these two options and determine the best choice. Ensure that all teammates concur with the decision and understand the rationale.
2. Each member of the team is to prepare *one* of the following journal entries.
   a. Option A—at date of issuance.
   b. Option B—at date of issuance.
   c. Option A—at maturity date.
   d. Option B—at maturity date.
3. In rotation, each member is to explain the entry he or she prepared in part 2 to the team. Ensure that all team members concur with and understand the entries.

4. Assume that the funds are borrowed on December 1 (instead of June 1) and your business operates on a calendar-year reporting period. Each member of the team is to prepare *one* of the following entries.

   a. Option A—the year-end adjustment.

   b. Option B—the year-end adjustment.

   c. Option A—at maturity date.

   d. Option B—at maturity date.

5. In rotation, each member is to explain the entry he or she prepared in part 4 to the team. Ensure that all team members concur with and understand the entries.

ENTREPRENEURIAL DECISION

A1

BTN 11-7   Review the chapter's opening feature about Jason Osborn and Jason Wright, and their start-up company, **Feed Granola Company**. Assume that these young entrepreneurs are considering expanding their business to open an outlet in Europe. Assume their current income statement is as follows.

FEED GRANOLA COMPANY Income Statement For Year Ended December 31, 2009	
Sales	$1,000,000
Cost of goods sold (30%)	300,000
Gross profit	700,000
Operating expenses (25%)	250,000
Net income	$ 450,000

Feed Granola Company currently has no interest-bearing debt. If it expands to open a European location, it will require a $300,000 loan. Feed Granola Company has found a bank that will loan it the money on a 7% note payable. The company believes that, at least for the first few years, sales at its European location will be $250,000, and that all expenses (including cost of goods sold) will follow the same patterns as its current locations.

Required

1. Prepare an income statement (separately for current operations, European, and total) for Feed Granola Company assuming that it borrows the funds and expands to Europe. Annual revenues for current operations are expected to remain at $1,000,000.

2. Compute Feed Granola Company's times interest earned under the expansion assumptions in part 1.

3. Assume sales at its European location are $400,000. Prepare an income statement (separately for current operations, European, and total) for the company and compute times interest earned.

4. Assume sales at its European location are $100,000. Prepare an income statement (separately for current operations, European, and total) for the company and compute times interest earned.

5. Comment on your results from parts 1 through 4.

HITTING THE ROAD

P2

BTN 11-8   Check your phone book or the Social Security Administration Website (www.ssa.gov) to locate the Social Security office near you. Visit the office to request a personal earnings and estimate form. Fill out the form and mail according to the instructions. You will receive a statement from the Social Security Administration regarding your earnings history and future Social Security benefits you can receive. (Formerly the request could be made online. The online service has been discontinued and is now under review by the Social Security Administration due to security concerns.) It is good to request an earnings and benefit statement every 5 to 10 years to make sure you have received credit for all wages earned and for which you and your employer have paid taxes into the system.

BTN 11-9   DSG international, Best Buy, Circuit City, and RadioShack are all competitors in the global marketplace. Comparative figures for DSG (DSGiplc.com), along with selected figures from Best Buy, Circuit City, and RadioShack follow.

GLOBAL DECISION

A1

Key Figures	DSG (£ millions) Current Year	DSG (£ millions) Prior Year	Best Buy Current Year	Best Buy Prior Year	Circuit City Current Year	Circuit City Prior Year	RadioShack Current Year	RadioShack Prior Year
Net income	207	222	—	—	—	—	—	—
Income taxes	89	89	—	—	—	—	—	—
Interest expense*	73	65	—	—	—	—	—	—
Times interest earned . . .	?	?	69.7	58.4	12.5	76.3	3.5	8.1

* Titled Finance costs for DSG.

Required

1. Compute the times interest earned ratio for the most recent two years for DSG using the data shown.

2. Which company of the four presented provides the best coverage of interest expense? Explain.

ANSWERS TO MULTIPLE CHOICE QUIZ

1. b; $6,000 × 0.05 × 30/360 = $25

2. e; $50,000 × (.062 + .0145) = $3,825

3. b; $7,000 × (.008 + .054) = $434

4. c; 10,000 television sets × .01 × $250 = $25,000

5. a; 150 employees × $175 per day × 1 vacation day earned = $26,250

A Look Back

Chapter 11 focused on how current liabilities are identified, computed, recorded, and reported. Attention was directed at notes, payroll, sales taxes, warranties, employee benefits, and contingencies.

A Look at This Chapter

This chapter explains the partnership form of organization. Important partnership characteristics are described along with the accounting concepts and procedures for its most fundamental transactions.

A Look Ahead

Chapter 13 extends our discussion to the corporate form of organization. We describe the accounting and reporting for stock issuances, dividends, and other equity transactions.

Accounting for Partnerships

Chapter

Learning Objectives

CAP

Conceptual

C1 Identify characteristics of partnerships and similar organizations. *(p. 478)*

Analytical

A1 Compute partner return on equity and use it to evaluate partnership performance. *(p. 490)*

LP12

Procedural

P1 Prepare entries for partnership formation. *(p. 481)*

P2 Allocate and record income and loss among partners. *(p. 481)*

P3 Account for the admission and withdrawal of partners. *(p. 484)*

P4 Prepare entries for partnership liquidation. *(p. 488)*

In addition to gross pay, the company must pay one-half of the $20 per employee weekly health insurance; each employee pays the remaining one-half. The company also contributes an extra 8% of each employee's gross pay (at no cost to employees) to a pension fund.

Required

Compute the following for the week ended September 30 (round amounts to the nearest cent):

1. Each employee's FICA withholdings for Social Security.
2. Each employee's FICA withholdings for Medicare.
3. Employer's FICA taxes for Social Security.
4. Employer's FICA taxes for Medicare.
5. Employer's FUTA taxes.
6. Employer's SUTA taxes.
7. Each employee's net (take-home) pay.
8. Employer's total payroll-related expense for each employee.

Check (3) $316.20
(4) $108.75
(5) $8.16

(7) Total net pay, $6,135.05

Ravello Company's first weekly pay period of the year ends on January 8. On that date, the column totals in Ravello's payroll register indicate its sales employees earned $20,160, its office employees earned $70,840, and its delivery employees earned $3,000. The employees are to have withheld from their wages FICA Social Security taxes at the rate of 6.2%, FICA Medicare taxes at the rate of 1.45%, $12,760 of federal income taxes, $1,350 of medical insurance deductions, and $820 of union dues. No employee earned more than $7,000 in the first pay period.

Problem 11-5B
Entries for payroll transactions
P2   P3

Required

1. Calculate FICA Social Security taxes payable and FICA Medicare taxes payable. Prepare the journal entry to record Ravello Company's January 8 (employee) payroll expenses and liabilities.
2. Prepare the journal entry to record Ravello's (employer) payroll taxes resulting from the January 8 payroll. Ravello's merit rating reduces its state unemployment tax rate to 2% of the first $7,000 paid each employee. The federal unemployment tax rate is 0.8%.

Check (1) Cr. Salaries Payable,
$71,879.00
(2) Dr. Payroll Taxes
Expense, $9,823.00

JLS Company has 12 employees, each of whom earns $3,000 per month and is paid on the last day of each month. All 12 have been employed continuously at this amount since January 1. JLS uses a payroll bank account and special payroll checks to pay its employees. On March 1, the following accounts and balances exist in its general ledger:

Problem 11-6B[A]
Entries for payroll transactions
P2   P3   P5

a. FICA—Social Security Taxes Payable, $4,464; FICA—Medicare Taxes Payable, $1,044. (The balances of these accounts represent total liabilities for *both* the employer's and employees' FICA taxes for the February payroll only.)
b. Employees' Federal Income Taxes Payable, $4,050 (liability for February only).
c. Federal Unemployment Taxes Payable, $576 (liability for January and February together).
d. State Unemployment Taxes Payable, $3,600 (liability for January and February together).

During March and April, the company had the following payroll transactions.

March 15   Issued check payable to Security Bank, a federal depository bank authorized to accept employers' payments of FICA taxes and employee income tax withholdings. The $9,558 check is in payment of the February FICA and employee income taxes.

31   Recorded the March payroll and transferred funds from the regular bank account to the payroll bank account. Issued checks payable to each employee in payment of the March payroll. The payroll register shows the following summary totals for the March pay period.

Check Mar. 31: Cr. Salaries
Payable, $29,196

Salaries and Wages		Gross Pay	FICA Taxes*	Federal Income Taxes	Net Pay
Office Salaries	Shop Wages				
$21,000	$15,000	$36,000	$2,232	$4,050	$29,196
			$ 522		

* FICA taxes are Social Security and Medicare, respectively.

31   Recorded the employer's payroll taxes resulting from the March payroll. The company has a merit rating that reduces its state unemployment tax rate to 5.0% of the first $7,000 paid each employee. The federal rate is 0.8%.

April 15   Issued check payable to Security Bank in payment of the March FICA and employee income taxes.

15   Issued check to the State Tax Commission for the January, February, and March state unemployment taxes. Mailed the check and the second quarter tax return to the State Tax Commission.

30   Issued check payable to Security Bank in payment of the employer's FUTA taxes for the first quarter of the year.

30   Mailed Form 941 to the IRS, reporting the FICA taxes and the employees' federal income tax withholdings for the first quarter.

Required

Prepare journal entries to record the transactions and events for both March and April.

SERIAL PROBLEM

Success Systems

(This serial problem began in Chapter 1 and continues through most of the book. If previous chapter segments were not completed, the serial problem can begin at this point. It is helpful, but not necessary, to use the Working Papers that accompany the book.)

SP 11   Review the February 26 and March 25 transactions for Success Systems (SP 5) from Chapter 5.

Required

1. Assume that Lyn Addie is an unmarried employee. Her $1,000 of wages are subject to no deductions other than FICA Social Security taxes, FICA Medicare taxes, and federal income taxes. Her federal income taxes for this pay period total $159. Compute her net pay for the eight days' work paid on February 26. (Round amounts to the nearest cent.)

2. Record the journal entry to reflect the payroll payment to Lyn Addie as computed in part 1.

3. Record the journal entry to reflect the (employer) payroll tax expenses for the February 26 payroll payment. Assume Lyn Addie has not met earnings limits for FUTA and SUTA—the FUTA rate is 0.8% and the SUTA rate is 4% for Success Systems. (Round amounts to the nearest cent.)

4. Record the entry(ies) for the merchandise sold on March 25 if a 4% sales tax rate applies.

COMPREHENSIVE PROBLEM

Bug-Off Exterminators
(Review of Chapters 1–11)

CP 11   Bug-Off Exterminators provides pest control services and sells extermination products manufactured by other companies. The following six-column table contains the company's unadjusted trial balance as of December 31, 2009.

BUG-OFF EXTERMINATORS December 31, 2009					
	Unadjusted Trial Balance		Adjustments	Adjusted Trial Balance	
Cash	$ 17,000				
Accounts receivable	4,000				
Allowance for doubtful accounts		$ 828			
Merchandise inventory	11,700				
Trucks	32,000				
Accum. depreciation—Trucks		0			
Equipment	45,000				
Accum. depreciation—Equipment		12,200			
Accounts payable		5,000			
Estimated warranty liability		1,400			

[continued on next page]

[continued from previous page]

Unearned services revenue		0
Interest payable		0
Long-term notes payable		15,000
D. Buggs, Capital		59,700
D. Buggs, Withdrawals	10,000	
Extermination services revenue		60,000
Interest revenue		872
Sales (of merchandise)		71,026
Cost of goods sold	46,300	
Depreciation expense—Trucks	0	
Depreciation expense—Equipment	0	
Wages expense	35,000	
Interest expense	0	
Rent expense	9,000	
Bad debts expense	0	
Miscellaneous expense	1,226	
Repairs expense	8,000	
Utilities expense	6,800	
Warranty expense	0	
Totals	$226,026	$226,026

The following information in *a* through *h* applies to the company at the end of the current year.

a. The bank reconciliation as of December 31, 2009, includes the following facts.

Cash balance per bank	$15,100
Cash balance per books	17,000
Outstanding checks	1,800
Deposit in transit	2,450
Interest earned (on bank account)	52
Bank service charges (miscellaneous expense)	15

Reported on the bank statement is a canceled check that the company failed to record. (Information from the bank reconciliation allows you to determine the amount of this check, which is a payment on an account payable.)

b. An examination of customers' accounts shows that accounts totaling $679 should be written off as uncollectible. Using an aging of receivables, the company determines that the ending balance of the Allowance for Doubtful Accounts should be $700.

c. A truck is purchased and placed in service on January 1, 2009. Its cost is being depreciated with the straight-line method using the following facts and estimates.

Original cost	$32,000
Expected salvage value	8,000
Useful life (years)	4

d. Two items of equipment (a sprayer and an injector) were purchased and put into service in early January 2007. They are being depreciated with the straight-line method using these facts and estimates.

	Sprayer	Injector
Original cost	$27,000	$18,000
Expected salvage value	3,000	2,500
Useful life (years)	8	5

e. On August 1, 2009, the company is paid $3,840 cash in advance to provide monthly service for an apartment complex for one year. The company began providing the services in August. When the cash was received, the full amount was credited to the Extermination Services Revenue account.

f. The company offers a warranty for the services it sells. The expected cost of providing warranty service is 2.5% of the extermination services revenue of $57,760 for 2009. No warranty expense has been recorded for 2009. All costs of servicing warranties in 2009 were properly debited to the Estimated Warranty Liability account.

g. The $15,000 long-term note is an 8%, five-year, interest-bearing note with interest payable annually on December 31. The note was signed with First National Bank on December 31, 2009.

h. The ending inventory of merchandise is counted and determined to have a cost of $11,700. Bug-Off uses a perpetual inventory system.

Required

1. Use the preceding information to determine amounts for the following items.

   a. Correct (reconciled) ending balance of Cash, and the amount of the omitted check.

   b. Adjustment needed to obtain the correct ending balance of the Allowance for Doubtful Accounts.

   c. Depreciation expense for the truck used during year 2009.

   d. Depreciation expense for the two items of equipment used during year 2009.

   e. The adjusted 2009 ending balances of the Extermination Services Revenue and Unearned Services Revenue accounts.

   f. The adjusted 2009 ending balances of the accounts for Warranty Expense and Estimated Warranty Liability.

   g. The adjusted 2009 ending balances of the accounts for Interest Expense and Interest Payable. (Round amounts to nearest whole dollar.)

2. Use the results of part 1 to complete the six-column table by first entering the appropriate adjustments for items *a* through *g* and then completing the adjusted trial balance columns. (*Hint:* Item *b* requires two adjustments.)

3. Prepare journal entries to record the adjustments entered on the six-column table. Assume Bug-Off's adjusted balance for Merchandise Inventory matches the year-end physical count.

4. Prepare a single-step income statement, a statement of owner's equity (cash withdrawals during 2009 were $10,000), and a classified balance sheet.

Check (1*a*) Cash bal. $15,750
(1*b*) $551 credit

(1*f*) Estim. warranty liability, $2,844 Cr.

(2) Adjusted trial balance totals, $238,207

(4) Net income, $9,274; Total assets, $82,771

BEYOND THE NUMBERS

REPORTING IN ACTION

A1 P4

BTN 11-1   Refer to the financial statements of **Best Buy** in Appendix A to answer the following.

1. Compute times interest earned for the fiscal years ended 2007, 2006, and 2005. Comment on Best Buy's ability to cover its interest expense for this period. Assume an industry average of 28.1.

2. Best Buy's current liabilities include "Unredeemed gift card liabilities." Explain how this liability is created and how Best Buy satisfies this liability.

3. Does Best Buy have any commitments or contingencies? Briefly explain them.

Fast Forward

4. Access Best Buy's financial statements for fiscal years ending after March 3, 2007, at its Website (BestBuy.com) or the SEC's EDGAR database (www.sec.gov). Compute its times interest earned for years ending after March 3, 2007, and compare your results to those in part 1.

COMPARATIVE ANALYSIS

A1

BTN 11-2   Key figures for **Best Buy**, **Circuit City**, and **RadioShack** follow.

($ millions)	Best Buy			Circuit City			RadioShack		
	Current Year	One Year Prior	Two Years Prior	Current Year	One Year Prior	Two Years Prior	Current Year	One Year Prior	Two Years Prior
Net income	$1,377	$1,140	$984	$(8)	$140	$62	$73	$267	$337
Income taxes	752	581	509	31	86	36	38	52	205
Interest expense	31	30	44	2	3	4	44	45	30

Required

1. Compute times interest earned for the three years' data shown for each company.
2. Comment on which company appears stronger in its ability to pay interest obligations if income should decline. Assume an industry average of 28.1.

BTN 11-3 Connor Bly is a sales manager for an automobile dealership. He earns a bonus each year based on revenue from the number of autos sold in the year less related warranty expenses. Actual warranty expenses have varied over the prior 10 years from a low of 3% of an automobile's selling price to a high of 10%. In the past, Bly has tended to estimate warranty expenses on the high end to be conservative. He must work with the dealership's accountant at year-end to arrive at the warranty expense accrual for cars sold each year.

1. Does the warranty accrual decision create any ethical dilemma for Bly?
2. Since warranty expenses vary, what percent do you think Bly should choose for the current year? Justify your response.

ETHICS CHALLENGE
P4

BTN 11-4 Dustin Clemens is the accounting and finance manager for a manufacturer. At year-end, he must determine how to account for the company's contingencies. His manager, Madeline Pretti, objects to Clemens's proposal to recognize an expense and a liability for warranty service on units of a new product introduced in the fourth quarter. Pretti comments, "There's no way we can estimate this warranty cost. We don't owe anyone anything until a product fails and it is returned. Let's report an expense if and when we do any warranty work."

COMMUNICATING IN PRACTICE
C3

Required

Prepare a one-page memorandum for Clemens to send to Pretti defending his proposal.

BTN 11-5 Access the February 26, 2007, filing of the December 31, 2006, annual 10-K report of McDonald's Corporation (Ticker: MCD), which is available from www.sec.gov.

TAKING IT TO THE NET
C1 A1

Required

1. Identify the current liabilities on McDonald's balance sheet as of December 31, 2006.
2. What portion (in percent) of McDonald's long-term debt matures within the next 12 months?
3. Use the consolidated statement of income for the year ended December 31, 2006, to compute McDonald's times interest earned ratio. Comment on the result. Assume an industry average of 7.9.

BTN 11-6 Assume that your team is in business and you must borrow $6,000 cash for short-term needs. You been shopping banks for a loan, and you have the following two options.
A. Sign a $6,000, 90-day, 10% interest-bearing note dated June 1.
B. Sign a $6,000, 120-day, 8% interest-bearing note dated June 1.

TEAMWORK IN ACTION
C2 P1

Required

1. Discuss these two options and determine the best choice. Ensure that all teammates concur with the decision and understand the rationale.
2. Each member of the team is to prepare *one* of the following journal entries.
   a. Option A—at date of issuance.
   b. Option B—at date of issuance.
   c. Option A—at maturity date.
   d. Option B—at maturity date.
3. In rotation, each member is to explain the entry he or she prepared in part 2 to the team. Ensure that all team members concur with and understand the entries.

4. Assume that the funds are borrowed on December 1 (instead of June 1) and your business operates on a calendar-year reporting period. Each member of the team is to prepare *one* of the following entries.

    a. Option A—the year-end adjustment.

    b. Option B—the year-end adjustment.

    c. Option A—at maturity date.

    d. Option B—at maturity date.

5. In rotation, each member is to explain the entry he or she prepared in part 4 to the team. Ensure that all team members concur with and understand the entries.

ENTREPRENEURIAL DECISION

A1

BTN 11-7 Review the chapter's opening feature about Jason Osborn and Jason Wright, and their start-up company, **Feed Granola Company**. Assume that these young entrepreneurs are considering expanding their business to open an outlet in Europe. Assume their current income statement is as follows.

FEED GRANOLA COMPANY
Income Statement
For Year Ended December 31, 2009

Sales	$1,000,000
Cost of goods sold (30%)	300,000
Gross profit	700,000
Operating expenses (25%)	250,000
Net income	$ 450,000

Feed Granola Company currently has no interest-bearing debt. If it expands to open a European location, it will require a $300,000 loan. Feed Granola Company has found a bank that will loan it the money on a 7% note payable. The company believes that, at least for the first few years, sales at its European location will be $250,000, and that all expenses (including cost of goods sold) will follow the same patterns as its current locations.

Required

1. Prepare an income statement (separately for current operations, European, and total) for Feed Granola Company assuming that it borrows the funds and expands to Europe. Annual revenues for current operations are expected to remain at $1,000,000.

2. Compute Feed Granola Company's times interest earned under the expansion assumptions in part 1.

3. Assume sales at its European location are $400,000. Prepare an income statement (separately for current operations, European, and total) for the company and compute times interest earned.

4. Assume sales at its European location are $100,000. Prepare an income statement (separately for current operations, European, and total) for the company and compute times interest earned.

5. Comment on your results from parts 1 through 4.

HITTING THE ROAD

P2

BTN 11-8 Check your phone book or the Social Security Administration Website (www.ssa.gov) to locate the Social Security office near you. Visit the office to request a personal earnings and estimate form. Fill out the form and mail according to the instructions. You will receive a statement from the Social Security Administration regarding your earnings history and future Social Security benefits you can receive. (Formerly the request could be made online. The online service has been discontinued and is now under review by the Social Security Administration due to security concerns.) It is good to request an earnings and benefit statement every 5 to 10 years to make sure you have received credit for all wages earned and for which you and your employer have paid taxes into the system.

BTN 11-9   **DSG international**, **Best Buy**, **Circuit City**, and **RadioShack** are all competitors in the global marketplace. Comparative figures for DSG (DSGiplc.com), along with selected figures from Best Buy, Circuit City, and RadioShack follow.

Key Figures	DSG (£ millions) Current Year	DSG (£ millions) Prior Year	Best Buy Current Year	Best Buy Prior Year	Circuit City Current Year	Circuit City Prior Year	RadioShack Current Year	RadioShack Prior Year
Net income	207	222	—	—	—	—	—	—
Income taxes	89	89	—	—	—	—	—	—
Interest expense*	73	65	—	—	—	—	—	—
Times interest earned . . .	?	?	69.7	58.4	12.5	76.3	3.5	8.1

* Titled Finance costs for DSG.

Required

1. Compute the times interest earned ratio for the most recent two years for DSG using the data shown.

2. Which company of the four presented provides the best coverage of interest expense? Explain.

ANSWERS TO MULTIPLE CHOICE QUIZ

1. b; $6,000 × 0.05 × 30/360 = $25
2. e; $50,000 × (.062 + .0145) = $3,825
3. b; $7,000 × (.008 + .054) = $434

4. c; 10,000 television sets × .01 × $250 = $25,000
5. a; 150 employees × $175 per day × 1 vacation day earned = $26,250

A Look Back

Chapter 11 focused on how current liabilities are identified, computed, recorded, and reported. Attention was directed at notes, payroll, sales taxes, warranties, employee benefits, and contingencies.

A Look at This Chapter

This chapter explains the partnership form of organization. Important partnership characteristics are described along with the accounting concepts and procedures for its most fundamental transactions.

A Look Ahead

Chapter 13 extends our discussion to the corporate form of organization. We describe the accounting and reporting for stock issuances, dividends, and other equity transactions.

Accounting for Partnerships

Chapter

Learning Objectives

CAP

Conceptual

C1 Identify characteristics of partnerships and similar organizations. (p. 478)

Analytical

A1 Compute partner return on equity and use it to evaluate partnership performance. (p. 490)

LP12

Procedural

P1 Prepare entries for partnership formation. (p. 481)

P2 Allocate and record income and loss among partners. (p. 481)

P3 Account for the admission and withdrawal of partners. (p. 484)

P4 Prepare entries for partnership liquidation. (p. 488)

Decision Feature

A Fitting Pair

"Be your best, make a difference, and live with passion"—Samanta and Kelvin Joseph

 NEW YORK—Business recipe: Take one information systems graduate, mix a bit of international flair, add an accountant, and stir. The result is **Samanta Shoes** (**SamantaShoes.com**), a start-up shoe manufacturer. Founded by Samanta and Kelvin Joseph, their partnership is aimed at providing "stylish, comfortable, and affordable" shoes, explains Samanta. "I design every shoe, and nothing less than the best material is used."

Kelvin's focus is on the accounting and financial side of Samanta Shoes. "The knowledge gained from my years at Ernst & Young LLP [a major accounting firm]," explains Kelvin, "has enabled me to be more helpful." Kelvin's knowledge of partnerships and their financial implications are important to Samanta's success. Both partners stress the importance of attending to partnership formation, partnership agreements, and financial reports to stay afloat. They refer to the partners' return on equity and the organizational form as key inputs to partnership success.

Success is causing their partnership to evolve, but the partners adhere to a quality first mentality. "It's all in the design," insists Samanta.

"[A quality design] allows for more comfort and support." But quality also extends to style and uniqueness. "Women don't like other women having their shoe," explains Samanta. "We don't want to dilute our brand by being too mass market." Kelvin explains that the smallest manufacturing run they can have is 18 pairs of a special line. In a world of 6 billion people, that is unique.

The partners also continue to apply strict accounting fundamentals. "The partnership cannot survive," says Kelvin, "unless our business is profitable." They regularly review the accounting results and assess the partnership's costs and revenues. Although he adds, "money does not equal happiness." Samanta explains, "Live your dreams . . . make a difference . . . give back to your community"—advice that we can all live by. "If you're not enjoying it," continues Samanta, "there's no point to doing it."

[Sources: *Samanta Shoes Website,* January 2009; *New York Resident,* August 2004; *Caribbean Vibe,* August 2004; *Black Enterprise,* June 2006; *Regine Magazine,* Spring 2004; *Inc.com,* July 2007]

The three basic types of business organizations are proprietorships, partnerships, and corporations. Partnerships are similar to proprietorships, except they have more than one owner. This chapter explains partnerships and looks at several variations of them such as limited partnerships, limited liability partnerships, S corporations, and limited liability companies. Understanding the advantages and disadvantages of the partnership form of business organization is important for making informed business decisions.

Accounting for Partnerships

Partnership Organization	Basic Partnership Accounting	Partner Admission and Withdrawal	Partnership Liquidation
• Characteristics • Organizations with partnership characteristics • Choice of business form	• Organizing a partnership • Dividing income or loss • Partnership financial statements	• Admission of partner • Withdrawal of partner • Death of partner	• No capital deficiency • Capital deficiency

Partnership Form of Organization

C1 Identify characteristics of partnerships and similar organizations.

A **partnership** is an unincorporated association of two or more people to pursue a business for profit as co-owners. Many businesses are organized as partnerships. They are especially common in small retail and service businesses. Many professional practitioners, including physicians, lawyers, investors, and accountants, also organize their practices as partnerships.

Characteristics of Partnerships

Partnerships are an important type of organization because they offer certain advantages with their unique characteristics. We describe these characteristics in this section.

Voluntary Association   A partnership is a voluntary association between partners. Joining a partnership increases the risk to one's personal financial position. Some courts have ruled that partnerships are created by the actions of individuals even when there is no *express agreement* to form one.

Partnership Agreement   Forming a partnership requires that two or more legally competent people (who are of age and of sound mental capacity) agree to be partners. Their agreement becomes a **partnership contract,** also called *articles of copartnership.* Although it should be in writing, the contract is binding even if it is only expressed verbally. Partnership agreements normally include details of the partners' (1) names and contributions, (2) rights and duties, (3) sharing of income and losses, (4) withdrawal arrangement, (5) dispute procedures, (6) admission and withdrawal of partners, and (7) rights and duties in the event a partner dies.

Point: When a new partner is admitted, all parties usually must agree to the admission.

Limited Life   The life of a partnership is limited. Death, bankruptcy, or any event taking away the ability of a partner to enter into or fulfill a contract ends a partnership. Any one of the partners can also terminate a partnership at will.

Point: The end of a partnership is referred to as its *dissolution.*

Taxation   A partnership is not subject to taxes on its income. The income or loss of a partnership is allocated to the partners according to the partnership agreement, and it is included in determining the taxable income for each partner's tax return. Partnership income or loss is allocated each year whether or not cash is distributed to partners.

Point: Partners are taxed on their share of partnership income, not on their withdrawals.

Mutual Agency   **Mutual agency** implies that each partner is a fully authorized agent of the partnership. As its agent, a partner can commit or bind the partnership to any contract within the

scope of the partnership business. For instance, a partner in a merchandising business can sign contracts binding the partnership to buy merchandise, lease a store building, borrow money, or hire employees. These activities are all within the scope of a merchandising firm. A partner in a law firm, acting alone, however, cannot bind the other partners to a contract to buy snowboards for resale or rent an apartment for parties. These actions are outside the normal scope of a law firm's business. Partners also can agree to limit the power of any one or more of the partners to negotiate contracts for the partnership. This agreement is binding on the partners and on outsiders who know it exists. It is not binding on outsiders who do not know it exists. Outsiders unaware of the agreement have the right to assume each partner has normal agency powers for the partnership. Mutual agency exposes partners to the risk of unwise actions by any one partner.

Point: The majority of states adhere to the Uniform Partnership Act for the basic rules of partnership formation, operation, and dissolution.

Unlimited Liability   **Unlimited liability** implies that each partner can be called on to pay a partnership's debts. When a partnership cannot pay its debts, creditors usually can apply their claims to partners' *personal* assets. If a partner does not have enough assets to meet his or her share of the partnership debt, the creditors can apply their claims to the assets of the other partners. A partnership in which all partners have *mutual agency* and *unlimited liability* is called a **general partnership.** Mutual agency and unlimited liability are two main reasons that most general partnerships have only a few members.

Point: Limited life, mutual agency, and unlimited liability are disadvantages of a partnership.

Co-Ownership of Property   Partnership assets are owned jointly by all partners. Any investment by a partner becomes the joint property of all partners. Partners have a claim on partnership assets based on their capital account and the partnership contract.

Organizations with Partnership Characteristics

Organizations exist that combine certain characteristics of partnerships with other forms of organizations. We discuss several of these forms in this section.

Limited Partnerships   Some individuals who want to invest in a partnership are unwilling to accept the risk of unlimited liability. Their needs can be met with a **limited partnership.** This type of organization is identified in its name with the words "Limited Partnership" or "Ltd." or "LP." A limited partnership has two classes of partners, general and limited. At least one partner must be a **general partner,** who assumes management duties and unlimited liability for the debts of the partnership. The **limited partners** have no personal liability beyond the amounts they invest in the partnership. Limited partners have no active role except as specified in the partnership agreement. A limited partnership agreement often specifies unique procedures for allocating income and losses between general and limited partners. The accounting procedures are similar for both limited and general partnerships.

Decision Insight

Nutty Partners   The Hawaii-based **ML Macadamia Orchards LP** is one of the world's largest growers of macadamia nuts. It reported the following partners' capital balances ($ 000s) in its balance sheet:

General Partner	$ 81
Limited Partners	$43,297

Limited Liability Partnerships   Most states allow individuals to form a **limited liability partnership.** This is identified in its name with the words "Limited Liability Partnership" or by "LLP." This type of partnership is designed to protect innocent partners from malpractice or negligence claims resulting from the acts of another partner. When a partner provides service resulting in a malpractice claim, that partner has personal liability for the claim. The remaining partners who were not responsible for the actions resulting in the claim are not personally liable for it. However, most states hold all partners personally liable for other partnership debts. Accounting for a limited liability partnership is the same as for a general partnership.

Point: Many accounting services firms are set up as LLPs.

S Corporations   Certain corporations with 75 or fewer stockholders can elect to be treated as a partnership for income tax purposes. These corporations are called *Sub-Chapter S* or simply **S corporations.** This distinguishes them from other corporations, called *Sub-Chapter C* or simply **C corporations.** S corporations provide stockholders the same limited liability feature that C corporations do. The advantage of an S corporation is that it does not pay income taxes. If stockholders work for an S corporation, their salaries are treated as expenses of the corporation. The remaining income or loss of the corporation is allocated to stockholders for inclusion on their personal tax returns. Except for C corporations having to account for income tax expenses and liabilities, the accounting procedures are the same for both S and C corporations.

Point: The majority of proprietorships and partnerships that are organized today are set up as LLCs.

Limited Liability Companies   A relatively new form of business organization is the **limited liability company.** The names of these businesses usually include the words "Limited Liability Company" or an abbreviation such as "LLC" or "LC." This form of business has certain features similar to a corporation and others similar to a limited partnership. The owners, who are called *members,* are protected with the same limited liability feature as owners of corporations. While limited partners cannot actively participate in the management of a limited partnership, the members of a limited liability company can assume an active management role. A limited liability company usually has a limited life. For income tax purposes, a limited liability company is typically treated as a partnership. This treatment depends on factors such as whether the members' equity interests are freely transferable and whether the company has continuity of life. A limited liability company's accounting system is designed to help management comply with the dictates of the articles of organization and company regulations adopted by its members. The accounting system also must provide information to support the company's compliance with state and federal laws, including taxation.

Point: Accounting for LLCs is similar to that for partnerships (and proprietorships). One difference is that Owner (Partner), Capital is usually called *Members, Capital* for LLCs.

Choosing a Business Form

Choosing the proper business form is crucial. Many factors should be considered, including taxes, liability risk, tax and fiscal year-end, ownership structure, estate planning, business risks, and earnings and property distributions. The following table summarizes several important characteristics of business organizations:

	Proprietorship	Partnership	LLP	LLC	S Corp.	Corporation
Business entity	Yes	Yes	Yes	Yes	Yes	Yes
Legal entity	No	No	No	Yes	Yes	Yes
Limited liability	No	No	Limited*	Yes	Yes	Yes
Business taxed	No	No	No	No	No	Yes
One owner allowed	Yes	No	No	Yes	Yes	Yes

* A partner's personal liability for LLP debts is limited. Most LLPs carry insurance to protect against malpractice.

Point: The Small Business Administration provides suggestions and information on setting up the proper form for your organization—see **SBA.gov**.

We must remember that this table is a summary, not a detailed list. Many details underlie each of these business forms, and several details differ across states. Also, state and federal laws change, and a body of law is still developing around LLCs. Business owners should look at these details and consider unique business arrangements such as organizing various parts of their businesses in different forms.

Quick Check

Answers—p. 493

1. A partnership is terminated in the event (*a*) a partnership agreement is not in writing, (*b*) a partner dies, (*c*) a partner exercises mutual agency.
2. What does the term *unlimited liability* mean when applied to a general partnership?
3. Which of the following forms of organization do not provide limited liability to *all* of its owners? (*a*) S corporation, (*b*) limited liability company, (*c*) limited partnership.

Basic Partnership Accounting

Since ownership rights in a partnership are divided among partners, partnership accounting

- Uses a capital account for each partner.
- Uses a withdrawals account for each partner.
- Allocates net income or loss to partners according to the partnership agreement.

This section describes partnership accounting for organizing a partnership, distributing income and loss, and preparing financial statements.

Organizing a Partnership

When partners invest in a partnership, their capital accounts are credited for the invested amounts. Partners can invest both assets and liabilities. Each partner's investment is recorded at an agreed-on value, normally the market values of the contributed assets and liabilities at the date of contribution. To illustrate, Kayla Zayn and Hector Perez organize a partnership on January 11 called BOARDS that offers year-round facilities for skateboarding and snowboarding. Zayn's initial net investment in BOARDS is $30,000, made up of cash ($7,000), boarding facilities ($33,000), and a note payable reflecting a bank loan for the new business ($10,000). Perez's initial investment is cash of $10,000. These amounts are the values agreed on by both partners. The entries to record these investments follow.

P1	Prepare entries for partnership formation.

Zayn's Investment

Jan. 11	Cash	7,000	
	Boarding facilities	33,000	
	Note payable		10,000
	K. Zayn, Capital		30,000
	To record the investment of Zayn.		

Assets = Liabilities + Equity
+7,000   +10,000   +30,000
+33,000

Perez's Investment

Jan. 11	Cash	10,000	
	H. Perez, Capital		10,000
	To record the investment of Perez.		

Assets = Liabilities + Equity
+10,000   +10,000

In accounting for a partnership, the following additional relations hold true: (1) Partners' withdrawals are debited to their own separate withdrawals accounts. (2) Partners' capital accounts are credited (or debited) for their shares of net income (or net loss) when closing the accounts at the end of a period. (3) Each partner's withdrawals account is closed to that partner's capital account. Separate capital and withdrawals accounts are kept for each partner.

Point: Both equity and cash are reduced when a partner withdraws cash from a partnership.

Decision Insight

Broadway Partners **Big River Productions** is a partnership that owns the rights to the play *Big River*. The play is performed on tour and periodically on Broadway. For 2006, its Partners' Capital was $288,640, and it was distributed in its entirety to the partners.

Dividing Income or Loss

Partners are not employees of the partnership but are its owners. If partners devote their time and services to their partnership, they are understood to do so for profit, not for salary. This means there are no salaries to partners that are reported as expenses on the partnership income statement. However, when net income or loss of a partnership is allocated among partners, the partners can agree to allocate "salary allowances" reflecting the relative value of services

P2	Allocate and record income and loss among partners.

provided. Partners also can agree to allocate "interest allowances" based on the amount invested. For instance, since Zayn contributes three times the investment of Perez, it is only fair that this be considered when allocating income between them. Like salary allowances, these interest allowances are not expenses on the income statement.

Partners can agree to any method of dividing income or loss. In the absence of an agreement, the law says that the partners share income or loss of a partnership equally. If partners agree on how to share income but say nothing about losses, they share losses the same way they share income. Three common methods to divide income or loss use (1) a stated ratio basis, (2) the ratio of capital balances, or (3) salary and interest allowances and any remainder according to a fixed ratio. We explain each of these methods in this section.

Allocation on Stated Ratios   The *stated ratio* (also called the *income-and-loss-sharing ratio,* the *profit and loss ratio,* or the *P&L ratio*) method of allocating partnership income or loss gives each partner a fraction of the total. Partners must agree on the fractional share each receives. To illustrate, assume the partnership agreement of K. Zayn and H. Perez says Zayn receives two-thirds and Perez one-third of partnership income and loss. If their partnership's net income is $60,000, it is allocated to the partners when the Income Summary account is closed as follows.

Dec. 31	Income Summary	60,000	
	K. Zayn, Capital		40,000
	H. Perez, Capital		20,000
	To allocate income and close Income Summary.		

Allocation on Capital Balances   The *capital balances* method of allocating partnership income or loss assigns an amount based on the ratio of each partner's relative capital balance. If Zayn and Perez agree to share income and loss on the ratio of their beginning capital balances—Zayn's $30,000 and Perez's $10,000—Zayn receives three-fourths of any income or loss ($30,000/$40,000) and Perez receives one-fourth ($10,000/$40,000). The journal entry follows the same format as that using stated ratios (see the preceding entries).

Allocation on Services, Capital, and Stated Ratios   The *services, capital, and stated ratio* method of allocating partnership income or loss recognizes that service and capital contributions of partners often are not equal. Salary allowances can make up for differences in service contributions. Interest allowances can make up for unequal capital contributions. Also, the allocation of income and loss can include *both* salary and interest allowances. To illustrate, assume that the partnership agreement of K. Zayn and H. Perez reflects differences in service and capital contributions as follows: (1) annual salary allowances of $36,000 to Zayn and $24,000 to Perez, (2) annual interest allowances of 10% of a partner's beginning-year capital balance, and (3) equal share of any remaining balance of income or loss. These salaries and interest allowances are *not* reported as expenses on the income statement. They are simply a means of dividing partnership income or loss. The remainder of this section provides two illustrations using this three-point allocation agreement.

Illustration when income exceeds allowance.   If BOARDS has first-year net income of $70,000, and Zayn and Perez apply the three-point partnership agreement described in the prior paragraph, income is allocated as shown in Exhibit 12.1. Zayn gets $42,000 and Perez gets $28,000 of the $70,000 total.

Illustration when allowances exceed income.   The sharing agreement between Zayn and Perez must be followed even if net income is less than the total of the allowances. For example, if BOARDS' first-year net income is $50,000 instead of $70,000, it is allocated to the partners as shown in Exhibit 12.2. Computations for salaries and interest are identical to those in Exhibit 12.1. However, when we apply the total allowances against income, the balance of income is negative. This $(14,000) negative balance is allocated equally to the partners per their sharing agreement. This means that a negative $(7,000) is allocated to each partner. In this case, Zayn ends up with $32,000 and Perez with $18,000. If BOARDS had experienced a net loss, Zayn and Perez would share it in the same manner as the $50,000 income. The only difference is that they would have begun with a negative amount because of the loss. Specifically, the partners

	Zayn	Perez	Total
Net income			**$70,000**
Salary allowances			
Zayn	$ 36,000		
Perez		$ 24,000	
Interest allowances			
Zayn (10% × $30,000)	3,000		
Perez (10% × $10,000)		1,000	
Total salaries and interest	39,000	25,000	64,000
Balance of income			┌ 6,000
Balance allocated equally			
Zayn	3,000 ←		
Perez		3,000 ←	
Total allocated			6,000
Balance of income			$ 0
Income of each partner	**$42,000**	**$28,000**	

EXHIBIT 12.1

Dividing Income When Income Exceeds Allowances

	Zayn	Perez	Total
Net income			**$50,000**
Salary allowances			
Zayn	$ 36,000		
Perez		$ 24,000	
Interest allowances			
Zayn (10% × $30,000)	3,000		
Perez (10% × $10,000)		1,000	
Total salaries and interest	39,000	25,000	64,000
Balance of income			┌(14,000)
Balance allocated equally			
Zayn	(7,000) ←		
Perez		(7,000) ←	
Total allocated			(14,000)
Balance of income			$ 0
Income of each partner	**$32,000**	**$18,000**	

EXHIBIT 12.2

Dividing Income When Allowances Exceed Income

would still have been allocated their salary and interest allowances, further adding to the negative balance of the loss. This *total* negative balance *after* salary and interest allowances would have been allocated equally between the partners. These allocations would have been applied against the positive numbers from any allowances to determine each partner's share of the loss.

Point: When a loss occurs, it is possible for a specific partner's capital to increase (when closing income summary) if that partner's allowance is in excess of his or her share of the negative balance. This implies that decreases to the capital balances of other partners exceed the partnership's loss amount.

Quick Check
Answers—p. 493

4. Denzel and Shantell form a partnership by contributing $70,000 and $35,000, respectively. They agree to an interest allowance equal to 10% of each partner's capital balance at the beginning of the year, with the remaining income shared equally. Allocate first-year income of $40,000 to each partner.

Partnership Financial Statements

Partnership financial statements are similar to those of other organizations. The **statement of partners' equity,** also called *statement of partners' capital,* is one exception. It shows *each* partner's beginning capital balance, additional investments, allocated income or loss, withdrawals, and ending capital balance. To illustrate, Exhibit 12.3 shows the statement of partners' equity for BOARDS prepared using the sharing agreement of Exhibit 12.1. Recall that BOARDS' income was $70,000; also, assume that Zayn withdrew $20,000 and Perez $12,000 at year-end.

EXHIBIT 12.3

Statement of Partners' Equity

	Zayn		Perez		Total
		BOARDS			
		Statement of Partners' Equity			
		For Year Ended December 31, 2009			
Beginning capital balances	$ 0		$ 0		$ 0
Plus					
Investments by owners	30,000		10,000		40,000
Net income					
Salary allowances	$36,000		$24,000		
Interest allowances	3,000		1,000		
Balance allocated	3,000		3,000		
Total net income		42,000		28,000	70,000
		72,000		38,000	110,000
Less partners' withdrawals		(20,000)		(12,000)	(32,000)
Ending capital balances		**$52,000**		**$26,000**	**$78,000**

The equity section of the balance sheet of a partnership usually shows the separate capital account balance of each partner. In the case of BOARDS, both K. Zayn, Capital, and H. Perez, Capital, are listed in the equity section along with their balances of $52,000 and $26,000, respectively.

Decision Insight

Gambling Partners Trump Entertainment Resorts LP and subsidiaries operate three casino hotel properties in Atlantic City: Trump Taj Mahal Casino Resort ("Trump Taj Mahal"), Trump Plaza Hotel and Casino ("Trump Plaza"), and Trump Marina Hotel Casino ("Trump Marina"). Its recent statement of partners' equity reports $979,000 in partners' withdrawals, leaving $594,230,000 in partners' capital balances.

Admission and Withdrawal of Partners

P3 Account for the admission and withdrawal of partners.

A partnership is based on a contract between individuals. When a partner is admitted or withdraws, the present partnership ends. Still, the business can continue to operate as a new partnership consisting of the remaining partners. This section considers how to account for the admission and withdrawal of partners.

Admission of a Partner

A new partner is admitted in one of two ways: by purchasing an interest from one or more current partners or by investing cash or other assets in the partnership.

Purchase of Partnership Interest The purchase of partnership interest is a *personal transaction between one or more current partners and the new partner.* To become a partner, the current partners must accept the purchaser. Accounting for the purchase of partnership interest involves reallocating current partners' capital to reflect the transaction. To illustrate, at the end of BOARDS' first year, H. Perez sells one-half of his partnership interest to Tyrell Rasheed for $18,000. This means that Perez gives up a $13,000 recorded interest ($26,000 × 1/2) in the partnership (see the ending capital balance in Exhibit 12.3). The partnership records this January 4 transaction as follows.

Assets = Liabilities + Equity
−13,000
+13,000

Jan. 4	H. Perez, Capital...........................	13,000	
	T. Rasheed, Capital......................		13,000
	To record admission of Rasheed by purchase.		

After this entry is posted, BOARDS' equity shows K. Zayn, Capital; H. Perez, Capital; and T. Rasheed, Capital, and their respective balances of $52,000, $13,000, and $13,000.

Two aspects of this transaction are important. First, the partnership does *not* record the $18,000 Rasheed paid Perez. The partnership's assets, liabilities, and *total equity* are unaffected by this transaction among partners. Second, Zayn and Perez must agree that Rasheed is to become a partner. If they agree to accept Rasheed, a new partnership is formed and a new contract with a new income-and-loss-sharing agreement is prepared. If Zayn or Perez refuses to accept Rasheed as a partner, then (under the Uniform Partnership Act) Rasheed gets Perez's sold share of partnership income and loss. If the partnership is liquidated, Rasheed gets Perez's sold share of partnership assets. Rasheed gets no voice in managing the company unless Rasheed is admitted as a partner.

Point: Partners' withdrawals are not constrained by the partnership's annual income or loss.

Investing Assets in a Partnership   Admitting a partner by accepting assets is a *transaction between the new partner and the partnership*. The invested assets become partnership property. To illustrate, if Zayn (with a $52,000 interest) and Perez (with a $26,000 interest) agree to accept Rasheed as a partner in BOARDS after an investment of $22,000 cash, this is recorded as follows.

Jan. 4	Cash.....................................	22,000	
	T. Rasheed, Capital......................		22,000
	To record admission of Rasheed by investment.		

Assets = Liabilities + Equity
+22,000   +22,000

After this entry is posted, both assets (cash) and equity (T. Rasheed, Capital) increase by $22,000. Rasheed now has a 22% equity in the assets of the business, computed as $22,000 divided by the entire partnership equity ($52,000 + $26,000 + $22,000). Rasheed does not necessarily have a right to 22% of income. Dividing income and loss is a separate matter on which partners must agree.

Bonus to old partners.   When the current value of a partnership is greater than the recorded amounts of equity, the partners usually require a new partner to pay a bonus for the privilege of joining. To illustrate, assume that Zayn and Perez agree to accept Rasheed as a partner with a 25% interest in BOARDS if Rasheed invests $42,000. Recall that the partnership's accounting records show that Zayn's recorded equity in the business is $52,000 and Perez's recorded equity is $26,000 (see Exhibit 12.3). Rasheed's equity is determined as follows.

Equities of existing partners ($52,000 + $26,000)	$ 78,000
Investment of new partner	42,000
Total partnership equity	$120,000
Equity of Rasheed (25% × $120,000)	$ 30,000

Although Rasheed invests $42,000, the equity attributed to Rasheed in the new partnership is only $30,000. The $12,000 difference is called a *bonus* and is allocated to existing partners (Zayn and Perez) according to their income-and-loss-sharing agreement. A bonus is shared in this way because it is viewed as reflecting a higher value of the partnership that is not yet reflected in income. The entry to record this transaction follows.

Jan. 4	Cash.....................................	42,000	
	T. Rasheed, Capital......................		30,000
	K. Zayn, Capital ($12,000 × ½)............		6,000
	H. Perez, Capital ($12,000 × ½)............		6,000
	To record admission of Rasheed and bonus.		

Assets = Liabilities + Equity
+42,000   +30,000
                     +6,000
                     +6,000

Bonus to new partner.   Alternatively, existing partners can grant a bonus to a new partner. This usually occurs when they need additional cash or the new partner has exceptional talents. The bonus to the new partner is in the form of a larger share of equity than the amount invested. To illustrate, assume that Zayn and Perez agree to accept Rasheed as a partner with a 25%

interest in the partnership, but they require Rasheed to invest only $18,000. Rasheed's equity is determined as follows.

Equities of existing partners ($52,000 + $26,000)	$78,000
Investment of new partner	18,000
Total partnership equity	$96,000
Equity of Rasheed (25% × $96,000)	$24,000

The old partners contribute the $6,000 bonus (computed as $24,000 minus $18,000) to Rasheed according to their income-and-loss-sharing ratio. Moreover, Rasheed's 25% equity does not necessarily entitle Rasheed to 25% of future income or loss. This is a separate matter for agreement by the partners. The entry to record the admission and investment of Rasheed is

Assets = Liabilities + Equity
+18,000   −3,000
                     −3,000
                     +24,000

Jan. 4	Cash	18,000	
	K. Zayn, Capital ($6,000 × ½)	3,000	
	H. Perez, Capital ($6,000 × ½)	3,000	
	T. Rasheed, Capital.		24,000
	To record Rasheed's admission and bonus.		

Withdrawal of a Partner

A partner generally withdraws from a partnership in one of two ways. (1) First, the withdrawing partner can sell his or her interest to another person who pays for it in cash or other assets. For this, we need only debit the withdrawing partner's capital account and credit the new partner's capital account. (2) The second case is when cash or other assets of the partnership are distributed to the withdrawing partner in settlement of his or her interest. To illustrate these cases, assume that Perez withdraws from the partnership of BOARDS in some future period. The partnership shows the following capital balances at the date of Perez's withdrawal: K. Zayn, $84,000; H. Perez, $38,000; and T. Rasheed, $38,000. The partners (Zayn, Perez, and Rasheed) share income and loss equally. Accounting for Perez's withdrawal depends on whether a bonus is paid. We describe three possibilities.

No Bonus   If Perez withdraws and takes cash equal to Perez's capital balance, the entry is

Assets = Liabilities + Equity
−38,000   −38,000

Oct. 31	H. Perez, Capital.	38,000	
	Cash		38,000
	To record withdrawal of Perez from partnership		
	with no bonus.		

Perez can take any combination of assets to which the partners agree to settle Perez's equity. Perez's withdrawal creates a new partnership between the remaining partners. A new partnership contract and a new income-and-loss-sharing agreement are required.

Bonus to Remaining Partners   A withdrawing partner is sometimes willing to take less than the recorded value of his or her equity to get out of the partnership or because the recorded value is overstated. Whatever the reason, when this occurs, the withdrawing partner in effect gives the remaining partners a bonus equal to the equity left behind. The remaining partners share this unwithdrawn equity according to their income-and-loss-sharing ratio. To illustrate, if Perez withdraws and agrees to take $34,000 cash in settlement of Perez's capital balance, the entry is

Assets = Liabilities + Equity
−34,000   −38,000
                     +2,000
                     +2,000

Oct. 31	H. Perez, Capital.	38,000	
	Cash		34,000
	K. Zayn, Capital.		2,000
	T. Rasheed, Capital.		2,000
	To record withdrawal of Perez and bonus to		
	remaining partners.		

Perez withdrew $4,000 less than Perez's recorded equity of $38,000. This $4,000 is divided between Zayn and Rasheed according to their income-and-loss-sharing ratio.

Bonus to Withdrawing Partner   A withdrawing partner may be able to receive more than his or her recorded equity for at least two reasons. First, the recorded equity may be understated. Second, the remaining partners may agree to remove this partner by giving assets of greater value than this partner's recorded equity. In either case, the withdrawing partner receives a bonus. The remaining partners reduce their equity by the amount of this bonus according to their income-and-loss-sharing ratio. To illustrate, if Perez withdraws and receives $40,000 cash in settlement of Perez's capital balance, the entry is

Oct. 31	H. Perez, Capital...........................	38,000	
	K. Zayn, Capital...........................	1,000	
	T. Rasheed, Capital........................	1,000	
	Cash................................		40,000
	To record Perez's withdrawal from partnership with a bonus to Perez.		

Assets = Liabilities + Equity
−40,000   −38,000
                          −1,000
                          −1,000

Falcon Cable Communications LLC set up a partnership withdrawal agreement. Falcon owns and operates cable television systems and had two managing general partners. The partnership agreement stated that either partner "can offer to sell to the other partner the offering partner's entire partnership interest . . . for a negotiated price. If the partner receiving such an offer rejects it, the offering partner may elect to cause [the partnership] . . . to be liquidated and dissolved."

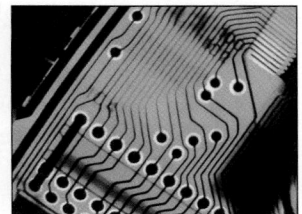

Death of a Partner

A partner's death dissolves a partnership. A deceased partner's estate is entitled to receive his or her equity. The partnership contract should contain provisions for settlement in this case. These provisions usually require (1) closing the books to determine income or loss since the end of the previous period and (2) determining and recording current market values for both assets and liabilities. The remaining partners and the deceased partner's estate then must agree to a settlement of the deceased partner's equity. This can involve selling the equity to remaining partners or to an outsider, or it can involve withdrawing assets.

Decision Ethics

Financial Planner   You are hired by the two remaining partners of a three-member partnership after the third partner's death. The partnership agreement states that a deceased partner's estate is entitled to a "share of partnership assets equal to the partner's relative equity balance" (partners' equity balances are equal). The estate argues that it is entitled to one-third of the current value of partnership assets. The remaining partners say the distribution should use asset book values, which are 75% of current value. They also point to partnership liabilities, which equal 40% of total asset book value and 30% of current value. How would you resolve this situation? [Answer—p. 493]

Liquidation of a Partnership

When a partnership is liquidated, its business ends and four concluding steps are required.

1. Record the sale of noncash assets for cash and any gain or loss from their liquidation.
2. Allocate any gain or loss from liquidation of the assets in step 1 to the partners using their income-and-loss-sharing ratio.

3. Pay or settle all partner liabilities.

4. Distribute any remaining cash to partners based on their capital balances.

Partnership liquidation usually falls into one of two cases, as described in this section.

No Capital Deficiency

P4 — Prepare entries for partnership liquidation.

No capital deficiency means that all partners have a zero or credit balance in their capital accounts for final distribution of cash. To illustrate, assume that Zayn, Perez, and Rasheed operate their partnership in BOARDS for several years, sharing income and loss equally. The partners then decide to liquidate. On the liquidation date, the current period's income or loss is transferred to the partners' capital accounts according to the sharing agreement. After that transfer, assume the partners' recorded equity balances (immediately prior to liquidation) are Zayn, $70,000; Perez, $66,000; and Rasheed, $62,000.

Next, assume that BOARDS sells its noncash assets for a net gain of $6,000. In a liquidation, gains or losses usually result from the sale of noncash assets, which are called *losses and gains from liquidation.* Partners share losses and gains from liquidation according to their income-and-loss-sharing agreement (equal for these partners) yielding the partners' revised equity balances of Zayn, $72,000; Perez, $68,000; and Rasheed, $64,000.[1] Then, after partnership assets are sold and any gain or loss is allocated, the liabilities must be paid. After creditors are paid, any remaining cash is divided among the partners according to their capital account balances. BOARDS' only liability at liquidation is $20,000 in accounts payable. The entries to record the payment to creditors and the final distribution of cash to partners follow.

Assets = Liabilities + Equity
−20,000   −20,000

Jan. 15	Accounts Payable	20,000	
	Cash		20,000
	To pay claims of creditors.		

Assets = Liabilities + Equity
−204,000   −72,000
                        −68,000
                        −64,000

Jan. 15	K. Zayn, Capital	72,000	
	H. Perez, Capital.	68,000	
	T. Rasheed, Capital	64,000	
	Cash		204,000
	To distribute remaining cash to partners.		

It is important to remember that the final cash payment is distributed to partners according to their capital account balances, whereas gains and losses from liquidation are allocated according to the income-and-loss-sharing ratio.

---

[1] The concepts behind these entries are not new. For example, assume that BOARDS has two noncash assets recorded as boarding facilities, $15,000, and land, $25,000. The entry to sell these assets for $46,000 is

Jan. 15	Cash	46,000	
	Boarding facilities		15,000
	Land		25,000
	Gain from liquidation		6,000
	Sold noncash assets at a gain.		

We then record the allocation of any loss or gain (a gain in this case) from liquidation according to the partners' income-and-loss-sharing agreement as follows.

Jan. 15	Gain from liquidation.	6,000	
	K. Zayn, Capital		2,000
	H. Perez, Capital		2,000
	T. Rasheed, Capital		2,000
	To allocate liquidation gain to partners.		

Capital Deficiency

Capital deficiency means that at least one partner has a debit balance in his or her capital account at the point of final cash distribution. This can arise from liquidation losses, excessive withdrawals before liquidation, or recurring losses in prior periods. A partner with a capital deficiency must, if possible, cover the deficit by paying cash into the partnership.

To illustrate, assume that Zayn, Perez, and Rasheed operate their partnership in BOARDS for several years, sharing income and losses equally. The partners then decide to liquidate. Immediately prior to the final distribution of cash, the partners' recorded capital balances are Zayn, $19,000; Perez, $8,000; and Rasheed, $(3,000). Rasheed's capital deficiency means that Rasheed owes the partnership $3,000. Both Zayn and Perez have a legal claim against Rasheed's personal assets. The final distribution of cash in this case depends on how this capital deficiency is handled. Two possibilities exist.

Partner Pays Deficiency   Rasheed is obligated to pay $3,000 into the partnership to cover the deficiency. If Rasheed is willing and able to pay, the entry to record receipt of payment from Rasheed follows.

Jan. 15	Cash.	3,000	
	T. Rasheed, Capital.		3,000
	To record payment of deficiency by Rasheed.		

Assets = Liabilities + Equity
+3,000   +3,000

After the $3,000 payment, the partners' capital balances are Zayn, $19,000; Perez, $8,000; and Rasheed, $0. The entry to record the final cash distributions to partners is

Jan. 15	K. Zayn, Capital	19,000	
	H. Perez, Capital.	8,000	
	Cash		27,000
	To distribute remaining cash to partners.		

Assets = Liabilities + Equity
−27,000   −19,000
                 −8,000

Partner Cannot Pay Deficiency   The remaining partners with credit balances absorb any partner's unpaid deficiency according to their income-and-loss-sharing ratio. To illustrate, if Rasheed is unable to pay the $3,000 deficiency, Zayn and Perez absorb it. Since they share income and loss equally, Zayn and Perez each absorb $1,500 of the deficiency. This is recorded as follows.

Jan. 15	K. Zayn, Capital	1,500	
	H. Perez, Capital.	1,500	
	T. Rasheed, Capital.		3,000
	To transfer Rasheed deficiency to Zayn and Perez.		

Assets = Liabilities + Equity
                 −1,500
                 −1,500
                 +3,000

After Zayn and Perez absorb Rasheed's deficiency, the capital accounts of the partners are Zayn, $17,500; Perez, $6,500; and Rasheed, $0. The entry to record the final cash distribution to the partners is

Jan. 15	K. Zayn, Capital	17,500	
	H. Perez, Capital.	6,500	
	Cash		24,000
	To distribute remaining cash to partners.		

Assets = Liabilities + Equity
−24,000   −17,500
                 −6,500

Rasheed's inability to cover this deficiency does not relieve Rasheed of the liability. If Rasheed becomes able to pay at a future date, Zayn and Perez can each collect $1,500 from Rasheed.

Decision Analysis | Partner Return on Equity

A1   Compute partner return on equity and use it to evaluate partnership performance.

An important role of partnership financial statements is to aid current and potential partners in evaluating partnership success compared with other opportunities. One measure of this success is the **partner return on equity** ratio:

$$\text{Partner return on equity} = \frac{\text{Partner net income}}{\text{Average partner equity}}$$

This measure is separately computed for each partner. To illustrate, Exhibit 12.4 reports selected data from the Boston Celtics LP. The return on equity for the *total* partnership is computed as $216/[($84 + $252)/2] = 128.6\%$. However, return on equity is quite different across the partners. For example, the Boston Celtics LP I partner return on equity is computed as $44/[($122 + $166)/2] = 30.6\%$, whereas the Celtics LP partner return on equity is computed as $111/[($270 + $333)/2] = 36.8\%$. Partner return on equity provides *each* partner an assessment of its return on its equity invested in the partnership. A specific partner often uses this return to decide whether additional investment or withdrawal of resources is best for that partner. Exhibit 12.4 reveals that the year shown produced good returns for all partners (the Boston Celtics LP II return is not computed because its average equity is negative due to an unusual and large distribution in the prior year).

EXHIBIT 12.4

Selected Data from Boston Celtics LP

($ thousands)	Total*	Boston Celtics LP I	Boston Celtics LP II	Celtics LP
Beginning-year balance	$ 84	$122	$(307)	$270
Net income (loss) for year	216	44	61	111
Cash distribution	(48)	—	—	(48)
Ending-year balance	$252	$166	$(246)	$333
Partner return on equity	128.6%	30.6%	n.a.	36.8%

* Totals may not add up due to rounding.

Demonstration Problem

DP12

The following transactions and events affect the partners' capital accounts in several successive partnerships. Prepare a table with six columns, one for each of the five partners along with a total column to show the effects of the following events on the five partners' capital accounts.

Part I

4/13/2007   Ries and Bax create R&B Company. Each invests $10,000, and they agree to share income and losses equally.

12/31/2007   R&B Co. earns $15,000 in income for its first year. Ries withdraws $4,000 from the partnership, and Bax withdraws $7,000.

1/1/2008   Royce is made a partner in RB&R Company after contributing $12,000 cash. The partners agree that a 10% interest allowance will be given on each partner's beginning-year capital balance. In addition, Bax and Royce are to receive $5,000 salary allowances. The remainder of the income or loss is to be divided evenly.

12/31/2008   The partnership's income for the year is $40,000, and withdrawals at year-end are Ries, $5,000; Bax, $12,500; and Royce, $11,000.

1/1/2009   Ries sells her interest for $20,000 to Murdock, whom Bax and Royce accept as a partner in the new BR&M Co. Income or loss is to be shared equally after Bax and Royce receive $25,000 salary allowances.

12/31/2009   The partnership's income for the year is $35,000, and year-end withdrawals are Bax, $2,500, and Royce, $2,000.

1/1/2010   Elway is admitted as a partner after investing $60,000 cash in the new Elway & Associates partnership. He is given a 50% interest in capital after the other partners transfer $3,000 to his account from each of theirs. A 20% interest allowance (on the beginning-year capital balances) will be used in sharing any income or loss, there will be no salary allowances, and Elway will receive 40% of the remaining balance—the other three partners will each get 20%.

12/31/2010 Elway & Associates earns $127,600 in income for the year, and year-end withdrawals are Bax, $25,000; Royce, $27,000; Murdock, $15,000; and Elway, $40,000.

1/1/2011 Elway buys out Bax and Royce for the balances of their capital accounts after a revaluation of the partnership assets. The revaluation gain is $50,000, which is divided in using a 1:1:1:2 ratio (Bax:Royce:Murdock:Elway). Elway pays the others from personal funds. Murdock and Elway will share income on a 1:9 ratio.

2/28/2011 The partnership earns $10,000 of income since the beginning of the year. Murdock retires and receives partnership cash equal to her capital balance. Elway takes possession of the partnership assets in his own name, and the partnership is dissolved.

Part 2

Journalize the events affecting the partnership for the year ended December 31, 2008.

Planning the Solution

- Evaluate each transaction's effects on the capital accounts of the partners.
- Each time a new partner is admitted or a partner withdraws, allocate any bonus based on the income-or-loss-sharing agreement.
- Each time a new partner is admitted or a partner withdraws, allocate subsequent net income or loss in accordance with the new partnership agreement.
- Prepare entries to (1) record Royce's initial investment; (2) record the allocation of interest, salaries, and remainder; (3) show the cash withdrawals from the partnership; and (4) close the withdrawal accounts on December 31, 2008.

Solution to Demonstration Problem

Part 1

Event	Ries	Bax	Royce	Murdock	Elway	Total
4/13/2007						
Initial investment	$10,000	$10,000				$ 20,000
12/31/2007						
Income (equal)	7,500	7,500				15,000
Withdrawals	(4,000)	(7,000)				(11,000)
Ending balance	$13,500	$10,500				$ 24,000
1/1/2008						
New investment			$12,000			$ 12,000
12/31/2008						
10% interest	1,350	1,050	1,200			3,600
Salaries		5,000	5,000			10,000
Remainder (equal)	8,800	8,800	8,800			26,400
Withdrawals	(5,000)	(12,500)	(11,000)			(28,500)
Ending balance	$18,650	$12,850	$16,000			$ 47,500
1/1/2009						
Transfer interest	(18,650)			$18,650		$ 0
12/31/2009						
Salaries		25,000	25,000			50,000
Remainder (equal)		(5,000)	(5,000)	(5,000)		(15,000)
Withdrawals		(2,500)	(2,000)			(4,500)
Ending balance	$ 0	$30,350	$34,000	$13,650		$ 78,000
1/1/2010						
New investment					$ 60,000	60,000
Bonuses to Elway		(3,000)	(3,000)	(3,000)	9,000	0
Adjusted balance		$27,350	$31,000	$10,650	$ 69,000	$138,000

[continued on next page]

[continued from previous page]

Event	Ries	Bax	Royce	Murdock	Elway	Total
12/31/2010						
20% interest		5,470	6,200	2,130	13,800	27,600
Remainder (1:1:1:2)		20,000	20,000	20,000	40,000	100,000
Withdrawals		(25,000)	(27,000)	(15,000)	(40,000)	(107,000)
Ending balance		$27,820	$30,200	$17,780	$ 82,800	$158,600
1/1/2011						
Gain (1:1:1:2)		10,000	10,000	10,000	20,000	50,000
Adjusted balance		$37,820	$40,200	$27,780	$102,800	$208,600
Transfer interests		(37,820)	(40,200)		78,020	0
Adjusted balance		$ 0	$ 0	$27,780	$180,820	$208,600
2/28/2011						
Income (1:9)				1,000	9,000	10,000
Adjusted balance				$28,780	$189,820	$218,600
Settlements				(28,780)	(189,820)	(218,600)
Final balance				$ 0	$ 0	$ 0

Part 2

2008			
Jan. 1	Cash	12,000	
	Royce, Capital		12,000
	To record investment of Royce.		
Dec. 31	Income Summary	40,000	
	Ries, Capital		10,150
	Bax, Capital		14,850
	Royce, Capital		15,000
	To allocate interest, salaries, and remainders.		
Dec. 31	Ries, Withdrawals	5,000	
	Bax, Withdrawals	12,500	
	Royce, Withdrawals	11,000	
	Cash		28,500
	To record cash withdrawals by partners.		
Dec. 31	Ries, Capital	5,000	
	Bax, Capital	12,500	
	Royce, Capital	11,000	
	Ries, Withdrawals		5,000
	Bax, Withdrawals		12,500
	Royce, Withdrawals		11,000
	To close withdrawal accounts.		

Summary

C1 **Identify characteristics of partnerships and similar organizations.** Partnerships are voluntary associations, involve partnership agreements, have limited life, are not subject to income tax, include mutual agency, and have unlimited liability. Organizations that combine selected characteristics of partnerships and corporations include limited partnerships, limited liability partnerships, S corporations, and limited liability companies.

A1 **Compute partner return on equity and use it to evaluate partnership performance.** Partner return on equity provides each partner an assessment of his or her return on equity invested in the partnership.

P1 **Prepare entries for partnership formation.** A partner's initial investment is recorded at the market value of the assets contributed to the partnership.

P2 **Allocate and record income and loss among partners.** A partnership agreement should specify how to allocate partnership income or loss among partners. Allocation can be based on a stated ratio, capital balances, or salary and interest allowances to compensate partners for differences in their service and capital contributions.

P3 **Account for the admission and withdrawal of partners.** When a new partner buys a partnership interest directly from one or more existing partners, the amount of cash paid from one partner to another does not affect the partnership total recorded equity. When a new partner purchases equity by investing additional assets in the partnership, the new partner's investment can yield a bonus either to existing partners or to the new partner. The entry to record a withdrawal can involve payment from either (1) the existing partners' personal assets or (2) partnership assets. The latter can yield a bonus to either the withdrawing or remaining partners.

P4 **Prepare entries for partnership liquidation.** When a partnership is liquidated, losses and gains from selling partnership assets are allocated to the partners according to their income-and-loss-sharing ratio. If a partner's capital account has a deficiency that the partner cannot pay, the other partners share the deficit according to their relative income-and-loss-sharing ratio.

Guidance Answers to **Decision Ethics**

Financial Planner The partnership agreement apparently fails to mention liabilities or use the term *net assets*. To give the estate one-third of total assets is not fair to the remaining partners because if the partner had lived and the partners had decided to liquidate, the liabilities would need to be paid out of assets before any liquidation. Also, a settlement based on the deceased partner's recorded equity would fail to recognize excess of current value over book value. This value increase would be realized if the partnership were liquidated. A fair settlement would seem to be a payment to the estate for the balance of the deceased partner's equity based on the *current value of net assets.*

Guidance Answers to **Quick Checks**

1. (*b*)

2. *Unlimited liability* means that the creditors of a partnership require each partner to be personally responsible for all partnership debts.

3. (*c*)

4.

	Denzel	Shantell	Total
Net income			$40,000
Interest allowance (10%)	$ 7,000	$ 3,500	10,500
Balance of income			$29,500
Balance allocated equally	14,750	14,750	29,500
Balance of income			$ 0
Income of partners	$21,750	$18,250	

Key Terms   mhhe.com/wildFAP19e

Key Terms are available at the book's Website for learning and testing in an online Flashcard Format.

C corporation (p. 480)
General partner (p. 479)
General partnership (p. 479)
Limited liability company (LLC) (p. 480)
Limited liability partnership (p. 479)

Limited partners (p. 479)
Limited partnership (p. 479)
Mutual agency (p. 478)
Partner return on equity (p. 490)
Partnership (p. 478)

Partnership contract (p. 478)
Partnership liquidation (p. 488)
S corporation (p. 480)
Statement of partners' equity (p. 483)
Unlimited liability (p. 479)

Multiple Choice Quiz   Answers on p. 503   mhhe.com/wildFAP19e

Additional Quiz Questions are available at the book's Website.

1. Stokely and Leder are forming a partnership. Stokely invests a building that has a market value of $250,000; and the partnership assumes responsibility for a $50,000 note secured by a mortgage on that building. Leder invests $100,000 cash. For the partnership, the amounts recorded for the building and for Stokely's Capital account are these:

   a. Building, $250,000; Stokely, Capital, $250,000.
   b. Building, $200,000; Stokely, Capital, $200,000.
   c. Building, $200,000; Stokely, Capital, $100,000.
   d. Building, $200,000; Stokely, Capital, $250,000.
   e. Building, $250,000; Stokely, Capital, $200,000.

2. Katherine, Alliah, and Paulina form a partnership. Katherine contributes $150,000, Alliah contributes $150,000, and Paulina contributes $100,000. Their partnership agreement calls for the income or loss division to be based on the ratio of capital invested. If the partnership reports income of $90,000 for its first year of operations, what amount of income is credited to Paulina's capital account?
   a. $22,500
   b. $25,000
   c. $45,000
   d. $30,000
   e. $90,000

3. Jamison and Blue form a partnership with capital contributions of $600,000 and $800,000, respectively. Their partnership agreement calls for Jamison to receive $120,000 per year in salary. Also, each partner is to receive an interest allowance equal to 10% of the partner's beginning capital contributions, with any remaining income or loss divided equally. If net income for its initial year is $270,000, then Jamison's and Blue's respective shares are
   a. $135,000; $135,000.
   b. $154,286; $115,714.
   c. $120,000; $150,000.
   d. $185,000; $85,000.
   e. $85,000; $185,000.

4. Hansen and Fleming are partners and share equally in income or loss. Hansen's current capital balance in the partnership is $125,000 and Fleming's is $124,000. Hansen and Fleming agree to accept Black with a 20% interest. Black invests $75,000 in the partnership. The bonus granted to Hansen and Fleming equals
   a. $13,000 each.
   b. $5,100 each.
   c. $4,000 each.
   d. $5,285 to Hansen; $4,915 to Fleming.
   e. $0; Hansen and Fleming grant a bonus to Black.

5. Mee Su is a partner in Hartford Partners, LLC. Her partnership capital balance at the beginning of the current year was $110,000, and her ending balance was $124,000. Her share of the partnership income is $10,500. What is her partner return on equity?
   a. 8.97%
   b. 1060.00%
   c. 9.54%
   d. 1047.00%
   e. 8.47%

Discussion Questions

1. If a partnership contract does not state the period of time the partnership is to exist, when does the partnership end?

2. What does the term *mutual agency* mean when applied to a partnership?

3. Can partners limit the right of a partner to commit their partnership to contracts? Would such an agreement be binding (*a*) on the partners and (*b*) on outsiders?

4. Assume that Amey and Lacey are partners. Lacey dies, and her son claims the right to take his mother's place in the partnership. Does he have this right? Why or why not?

5. Assume that the Barnes and Ardmore partnership agreement provides for a two-third/one-third sharing of income but says nothing about losses. The first year of partnership operation resulted in a loss, and Barnes argues that the loss should be shared equally because the partnership agreement said nothing about sharing losses. Is Barnes correct? Explain.

6. Allocation of partnership income among the partners appears on what financial statement?

7. What does the term *unlimited liability* mean when it is applied to partnership members?

8. How does a general partnership differ from a limited partnership?

9. George, Burton, and Dillman have been partners for three years. The partnership is being dissolved. George is leaving the firm, but Burton and Dillman plan to carry on the business. In the final settlement, George places a $75,000 salary claim against the partnership. He contends that he has a claim for a salary of $25,000 for each year because he devoted all of his time for three years to the affairs of the partnership. Is his claim valid? Why or why not?

10. Kay, Kat, and Kim are partners. In a liquidation, Kay's share of partnership losses exceeds her capital account balance. Moreover, she is unable to meet the deficit from her personal assets, and her partners shared the excess losses. Does this relieve Kay of liability?

11. After all partnership assets have been converted to cash and all liabilities paid, the remaining cash should equal the sum of the balances of the partners' capital accounts. Why?

12. Assume a partner withdraws from a partnership and receives assets of greater value than the book value of his equity. Should the remaining partners share the resulting reduction in their equities in the ratio of their relative capital balances or according to their income-and-loss-sharing ratio?

Denotes Discussion Questions that involve decision making.

Otis and Hunan are partners in operating a store. Without consulting Otis, Hunan enters into a contract to purchase merchandise for the store. Otis contends that he did not authorize the order and refuses to pay for it. The vendor sues the partners for the contract price of the merchandise. (*a*) Must the partnership pay for the merchandise? Why? (*b*) Does your answer differ if Otis and Hunan are partners in a public accounting firm? Explain.

QUICK STUDY

QS 12-1
Partnership liability
C1

Ramona Stolton and Jerry Bright are partners in a business they started two years ago. The partnership agreement states that Stolton should receive a salary allowance of $30,000 and that Bright should receive a $40,000 salary allowance. Any remaining income or loss is to be shared equally. Determine each partner's share of the current year's net income of $104,000.

QS 12-2
Partnership income allocation
P2

Hiram and Tyrone are partners who agree that Hiram will receive a $50,000 salary allowance and that any remaining income or loss will be shared equally. If Tyrone's capital account is credited for $1,000 as her share of the net income in a given period, how much net income did the partnership earn in that period?

QS 12-3
Partnership income allocation
P2

Vernon organized a limited partnership and is the only general partner. Xavier invested $40,000 in the partnership and was admitted as a limited partner with the understanding that he would receive 10% of the profits. After two unprofitable years, the partnership ceased doing business. At that point, partnership liabilities were $170,000 larger than partnership assets. How much money can the partnership's creditors obtain from Xavier's personal assets to satisfy the unpaid partnership debts?

QS 12-4
Liability in limited partnerships
P1

Dresden agrees to pay Choi and Amal $20,000 each for a one-third (33⅓%) interest in the Choi and Amal partnership. Immediately prior to Dresden's admission, each partner had a $60,000 capital balance. Make the journal entry to record Dresden's purchase of the partners' interest.

QS 12-5
Partner admission
through purchase of interest   P3

Neal and Vanier are partners, each with $80,000 in their partnership capital accounts. Brantford is admitted to the partnership by investing $80,000 cash. Make the entry to show Brantford's admission to the partnership.

QS 12-6
Admission of a partner   P3

Paulson and Fleming's company is organized as a partnership. At the prior year-end, partnership equity totaled $300,000 ($200,000 from Paulson and $100,000 from Fleming). For the current year, partnership net income is $49,000 ($38,400 allocated to Paulson and $10,600 allocated to Fleming), and year-end total partnership equity is $400,000 ($280,000 from Paulson and $120,000 from Fleming). Compute the total partnership return on equity *and* the individual partner return on equity ratios.

QS 12-7
Partner return on equity
A1

Next to the following list of eight characteristics of business organizations, enter a brief description of how each characteristic applies to general partnerships.

EXERCISES

Exercise 12-1
Characteristics of partnerships
C1

Characteristic	Application to General Partnerships
1. Life	
2. Owners' liability	
3. Legal status	
4. Tax status of income	
5. Owners' authority	
6. Ease of formation	
7. Transferability of ownership	
8. Ability to raise large amounts of capital	

Exercise 12-2

Forms of organization

C1

For each of the following separate cases, recommend a form of business organization. With each recommendation, explain how business income would be taxed if the owners adopt the form of organization recommended. Also list several advantages that the owners will enjoy from the form of business organization that you recommend.

a. Sharif, Henry, and Saanen are recent college graduates in computer science. They want to start a Website development company. They all have college debts and currently do not own any substantial computer equipment needed to get the company started.

b. Dr. LeBlanc and Dr. Liu are recent graduates from medical residency programs. Both are family practice physicians and would like to open a clinic in an underserved rural area. Although neither has any funds to bring to the new venture, a banker has expressed interest in making a loan to provide start-up funds for their practice.

c. Novato has been out of school for about five years and has become quite knowledgeable about the commercial real estate market. He would like to organize a company that buys and sells real estate. Novato believes he has the expertise to manage the company but needs funds to invest in commercial property.

Exercise 12-3

Journalizing partnership transactions

P2

On March 1, 2009, Eckert and Kelley formed a partnership. Eckert contributed $83,000 cash and Kelley contributed land valued at $66,400 and a building valued at $96,400. The partnership also assumed responsibility for Kelley's $77,800 long-term note payable associated with the land and building. The partners agreed to share income as follows: Eckert is to receive an annual salary allowance of $30,500, both are to receive an annual interest allowance of 11% of their beginning-year capital investment, and any remaining income or loss is to be shared equally. On October 20, 2009, Eckert withdrew $32,000 cash and Kelley withdrew $25,000 cash. After the adjusting and closing entries are made to the revenue and expense accounts at December 31, 2009, the Income Summary account had a credit balance of $86,000.

1. Prepare journal entries to record (*a*) the partners' initial capital investments, (*b*) their cash withdrawals, and (*c*) the December 31 closing of both the Withdrawals and Income Summary accounts.

Check (2) Kelley, $87,860

2. Determine the balances of the partners' capital accounts as of December 31, 2009.

Exercise 12-4

Income allocation in a partnership

P2

Daria and Farrah began a partnership by investing $64,000 and $58,000, respectively. During its first year, the partnership earned $175,000. Prepare calculations showing how the $175,000 income should be allocated to the partners under each of the following three separate plans for sharing income and loss: (1) the partners failed to agree on a method to share income; (2) the partners agreed to share income and loss in proportion to their initial investments (round amounts to the nearest dollar); and (3) the partners agreed to share income by granting a $52,000 per year salary allowance to Daria, a $42,000 per year salary allowance to Farrah, 8% interest on their initial capital investments, and the remaining balance shared equally.

Check Plan 3, Daria, $92,740

Exercise 12-5

Income allocation in a partnership

P2

Check (2) Daria, $(3,160)

Assume that the partners of Exercise 12-4 agreed to share net income and loss by granting annual salary allowances of $52,000 to Daria and $42,000 to Farrah, 8% interest allowances on their investments, and any remaining balance shared equally.

1. Determine the partners' shares of Daria and Farrah given a first-year net income of $98,800.

2. Determine the partners' shares of Daria and Farrah given a first-year net loss of $16,800.

Exercise 12-6

Sale of partnership interest   P3

The partners in the Biz Partnership have agreed that partner Estella may sell her $111,000 equity in the partnership to Sean, for which Sean will pay Estella $88,800. Present the partnership's journal entry to record the sale of Estella's interest to Sean on September 30.

Exercise 12-7

Admission of new partner

P3

The Josetti Partnership has total partners' equity of $558,000, which is made up of Dopke, Capital, $392,000, and Hughes, Capital, $166,000. The partners share net income and loss in a ratio of 85% to Dopke and 15% to Hughes. On November 1, Nillsen is admitted to the partnership and given a 10% interest in equity and a 10% share in any income and loss. Prepare the journal entry to record the admission of Nillsen under each of the following separate assumptions: Nillsen invests cash of (1) $62,000; (2) $97,000; and (3) $32,000.

Edison, Delray, and West have been partners while sharing net income and loss in a 5:4:1 ratio. On January 31, the date West retires from the partnership, the equities of the partners are Edison, $330,000; Delray, $231,000; and West, $165,000. Present journal entries to record West's retirement under each of the following separate assumptions: West is paid for her equity using partnership cash of (1) $165,000; (2) $192,000; and (3) $129,000.

Exercise 12-8
Retirement of partner
P3

The Red, White & Blue partnership was begun with investments by the partners as follows: Red, $153,000; White, $183,000; and Blue, $180,000. The operations did not go well, and the partners eventually decided to liquidate the partnership, sharing all losses equally. On August 31, after all assets were converted to cash and all creditors were paid, only $39,000 in partnership cash remained.

Exercise 12-9
Liquidation of partnership
P4

1. Compute the capital account balance of each partner after the liquidation of assets and the payment of creditors.

Check (1) Red, $(6,000)

2. Assume that any partner with a deficit agrees to pay cash to the partnership to cover the deficit. Present the journal entries on August 31 to record (*a*) the cash receipt from the deficient partner(s) and (*b*) the final disbursement of cash to the partners.

3. Assume that any partner with a deficit is not able to reimburse the partnership. Present journal entries (*a*) to transfer the deficit of any deficient partners to the other partners and (*b*) to record the final disbursement of cash to the partners.

Brewster, Conway, and Ogden are partners who share income and loss in a 1:5:4 ratio. After lengthy disagreements among the partners and several unprofitable periods, the partners decide to liquidate the partnership. Immediately before liquidation, the partnership balance sheet shows total assets, $117,000; total liabilities, $87,750; Brewster, Capital, $1,600; Conway, Capital, $11,600; and Ogden, Capital, $16,050. The cash proceeds from selling the assets were sufficient to repay all but $20,500 to the creditors. (*a*) Calculate the loss from selling the assets. (*b*) Allocate the loss to the partners. (*c*) Determine how much of the remaining liability should be paid by each partner.

Exercise 12-10
Liquidation of partnership   P4

Check (b) Ogden, Capital after allocation, $(3,850)

Assume that the Brewster, Conway, and Ogden partnership of Exercise 12-10 is a limited partnership. Brewster and Conway are general partners and Ogden is a limited partner. How much of the remaining $20,500 liability should be paid by each partner? (Round amounts to the nearest dollar.)

Exercise 12-11
Liquidation of limited partnership
P4

Hunt Sports Enterprises LP is organized as a limited partnership consisting of two individual partners: Soccer LP and Football LP. Both partners separately operate a minor league soccer team and a semipro football team. Compute partner return on equity for each limited partnership (and the total) for the year ended June 30, 2009, using the following selected data on partner capital balances from Hunt Sports Enterprises LP.

Exercise 12-12
Partner return on equity
A1

	Soccer LP	Football LP	Total
Balance at 6/30/2008	$331,000	$1,357,100	$1,688,100
Annual net income	35,405	725,803	761,208
Cash distribution	—	(65,000)	(65,000)
Balance at 6/30/2009	$366,405	$2,017,903	$2,384,308

Alex Jeffers, Jo Ford, and Rose Verne invested $32,500, $45,500, and $52,000, respectively, in a partnership. During its first calendar year, the firm earned $391,200.

PROBLEM SET A

Problem 12-1A
Allocating partnership income
P2

Check (3) Verne, Capital, $136,760

Required

Prepare the entry to close the firm's Income Summary account as of its December 31 year-end and to allocate the $391,200 net income to the partners under each of the following separate assumptions: The partners (1) have no agreement on the method of sharing income and loss; (2) agreed to share income and loss in the ratio of their beginning capital investments; and (3) agreed to share income and loss by providing annual salary allowances of $40,000 to Jeffers, $35,000 to Ford, and $46,000 to Verne; granting 8% interest on the partners' beginning capital investments; and sharing the remainder equally.

Problem 12-2A

Allocating partnership income
and loss; sequential years

P2

mhhe.com/wildFAP19e

Jasmine Watts and Liz Thomas are forming a partnership to which Watts will devote one-half time and Thomas will devote full time. They have discussed the following alternative plans for sharing income and loss: (*a*) in the ratio of their initial capital investments, which they have agreed will be $30,000 for Watts and $45,000 for Thomas; (*b*) in proportion to the time devoted to the business; (*c*) a salary allowance of $3,000 per month to Thomas and the balance in accordance with the ratio of their initial capital investments; or (*d*) a salary allowance of $3,000 per month to Thomas, 10% interest on their initial capital investments, and the balance shared equally. The partners expect the business to perform as follows: year 1, $18,000 net loss; year 2, $45,000 net income; and year 3, $75,000 net income.

Required

Prepare three tables with the following column headings.

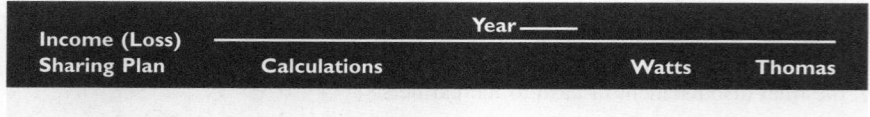

Income (Loss) Sharing Plan	Calculations	Year ———		
			Watts	Thomas

Check Plan d, year 1, Thomas's share, $9,750

Complete the tables, one for each of the first three years, by showing how to allocate partnership income or loss to the partners under each of the four plans being considered. (Round answers to the nearest whole dollar.)

Problem 12-3A

Partnership income allocation,
statement of partners' equity,
and closing entries

P2

mhhe.com/wildFAP19e

Will Beck, Trevor Beck, and Barb Beck formed the BBB Partnership by making capital contributions of $142,500, $118,750, and $213,750, respectively. They predict annual partnership net income of $210,000 and are considering the following alternative plans of sharing income and loss: (*a*) equally; (*b*) in the ratio of their initial capital investments; or (*c*) salary allowances of $38,000 to Will, $28,000 to Trevor, and $43,000 to Barb; interest allowances of 10% on their initial capital investments; and the balance shared equally.

Required

1. Prepare a table with the following column headings.

Income (Loss) Sharing Plan	Calculations	Will	Trevor	Barb	Total

Check (2) Barb, Ending Capital, $221,125

Use the table to show how to distribute net income of $210,000 for the calendar year under each of the alternative plans being considered. (Round answers to the nearest whole dollar.)

2. Prepare a statement of partners' equity showing the allocation of income to the partners assuming they agree to use plan (*c*), that income earned is $87,500, and that Will, Trevor, and Barb withdraw $18,000, $25,000, and $34,000, respectively, at year-end.

3. Prepare the December 31 journal entry to close Income Summary assuming they agree to use plan (*c*) and that net income is $87,500. Also close the withdrawals accounts.

Problem 12-4A

Partner withdrawal
and admission

P3

Check (1e) Cr. Ross, Capital, $93,500

Part 1. Meir, Zarcus, and Ross are partners and share income and loss in a 1:4:5 ratio. The partnership's capital balances are as follows: Meir, $43,000; Zarcus, $179,000; and Ross, $228,000. Zarcus decides to withdraw from the partnership, and the partners agree to not have the assets revalued upon Zarcus's retirement. Prepare journal entries to record Zarcus's February 1 withdrawal from the partnership under each of the following separate assumptions: Zarcus (*a*) sells her interest to Garcia for $160,000 after Meir and Ross approve the entry of Garcia as a partner; (*b*) gives her interest to a son-in-law, Fields, and thereafter Meir and Ross accept Fields as a partner; (*c*) is paid $179,000 in partnership cash for her equity; (*d*) is paid $215,000 in partnership cash for her equity; and (*e*) is paid $20,000 in partnership cash plus equipment recorded on the partnership books at $70,000 less its accumulated depreciation of $23,200.

Part 2. Assume that Zarcus does not retire from the partnership described in Part 1. Instead, Potter is admitted to the partnership on February 1 with a 25% equity. Prepare journal entries to record Potter's entry into the partnership under each of the following separate assumptions: Potter invests (*a*) $150,000; (*b*) $110,000; and (*c*) $196,000.

(2c) Cr. Zarcus, Capital, $13,800

Kendra, Cogley, and Mei share income and loss in a 3:2:1 ratio. The partners have decided to liquidate their partnership. On the day of liquidation their balance sheet appears as follows.

Problem 12-5A
Liquidation of a partnership
P4

KENDRA, COGLEY, AND MEI Balance Sheet May 31			
Assets		**Liabilities and Equity**	
Cash	$199,100	Accounts payable	$258,000
Inventory	548,400	Kendra, Capital	97,900
		Cogley, Capital	220,275
		Mei, Capital	171,325
Total assets	$747,500	Total liabilities and equity	$747,500

Required

Prepare journal entries for (*a*) the sale of inventory, (*b*) the allocation of its gain or loss, (*c*) the payment of liabilities at book value, and (*d*) the distribution of cash in each of the following separate cases: Inventory is sold for (1) $625,200; (2) $452,400; (3) $321,000 and any partners with capital deficits pay in the amount of their deficits; and (4) $249,000 and the partners have no assets other than those invested in the partnership. (Round to the nearest dollar.)

Check (4) Cash distribution: Mei, $104,158

Erin Rock, Sal Arthur, and Chloe Binder invested $47,840, $64,400, and $71,760, respectively, in a partnership. During its first calendar year, the firm earned $361,800.

PROBLEM SET B

Problem 12-1B
Allocating partnership income
P2

Required

Prepare the entry to close the firm's Income Summary account as of its December 31 year-end and to allocate the $361,800 net income to the partners under each of the following separate assumptions. (Round answers to whole dollars.) The partners (1) have no agreement on the method of sharing income and loss; (2) agreed to share income and loss in the ratio of their beginning capital investments; and (3) agreed to share income and loss by providing annual salary allowances of $33,000 to Rock, $28,000 to Arthur, and $40,000 to Binder; granting 10% interest on the partners' beginning capital investments; and sharing the remainder equally.

Check (3) Binder, Capital, $127,976

Maria Selk and David Green are forming a partnership to which Selk will devote one-third time and Green will devote full time. They have discussed the following alternative plans for sharing income and loss: (*a*) in the ratio of their initial capital investments, which they have agreed will be $208,000 for Selk and $312,000 for Green; (*b*) in proportion to the time devoted to the business; (*c*) a salary allowance of $8,000 per month to Green and the balance in accordance with the ratio of their initial capital investments; or (*d*) a salary allowance of $8,000 per month to Green, 10% interest on their initial capital investments, and the balance shared equally. The partners expect the business to perform as follows: year 1, $72,000 net loss; year 2, $152,000 net income; and year 3, $376,000 net income.

Problem 12-2B
Allocating partnership income and loss; sequential years
P2

Required

Prepare three tables with the following column headings.

Income (Loss) Sharing Plan	Year____		
	Calculations	Selk	Green

Complete the tables, one for each of the first three years, by showing how to allocate partnership income or loss to the partners under each of the four plans being considered. (Round answers to the nearest whole dollar.)

Problem 12-3B
Partnership income allocation, statement of partners' equity, and closing entries

P2

Sally Cook, Lin Xi, and Sami Bruce formed the CXB Partnership by making capital contributions of $169,750, $121,250, and $194,000, respectively. They predict annual partnership net income of $270,000 and are considering the following alternative plans of sharing income and loss: (a) equally; (b) in the ratio of their initial capital investments; or (c) salary allowances of $40,000 to Cook, $29,000 to Xi, and $42,000 to Bruce; interest allowances of 12% on their initial capital investments; and the balance shared equally.

Required

1. Prepare a table with the following column headings.

Income (Loss) Sharing Plan	Calculations	Cook	Xi	Bruce	Total

Use the table to show how to distribute net income of $270,000 for the calendar year under each of the alternative plans being considered. (Round answers to the nearest whole dollar.)

2. Prepare a statement of partners' equity showing the allocation of income to the partners assuming they agree to use plan (c), that income earned is $124,500, and that Cook, Xi, and Bruce withdraw $19,000, $26,000, and $36,000, respectively, at year-end.

3. Prepare the December 31 journal entry to close Income Summary assuming they agree to use plan (c) and that net income is $124,500. Also close the withdrawals accounts.

Problem 12-4B
Partner withdrawal and admission

P3

Part 1. Davis, Brown, and Nell are partners and share income and loss in a 5:1:4 ratio. The partnership's capital balances are as follows: Davis, $303,000; Brown, $74,000; and Nell, $223,000. Davis decides to withdraw from the partnership, and the partners agree not to have the assets revalued upon Davis's retirement. Prepare journal entries to record Davis's April 30 withdrawal from the partnership under each of the following separate assumptions: Davis (a) sells her interest to Leer for $125,000 after Brown and Nell approve the entry of Leer as a partner; (b) gives her interest to a daughter-in-law, Gibson, and thereafter Brown and Nell accept Gibson as a partner; (c) is paid $303,000 in partnership cash for her equity; (d) is paid $175,000 in partnership cash for her equity; and (e) is paid $100,000 in partnership cash plus manufacturing equipment recorded on the partnership books at $269,000 less its accumulated depreciation of $168,000.

Check (1e) Cr. Nell, Capital, $81,600

Part 2. Assume that Davis does not retire from the partnership described in Part 1. Instead, McCann is admitted to the partnership on April 30 with a 20% equity. Prepare journal entries to record the entry of McCann under each of the following separate assumptions: McCann invests (a) $150,000; (b) $98,000; and (c) $213,000.

Check (2c) Cr. Brown, Capital, $5,040

Problem 12-5B
Liquidation of a partnership

P4

London, Ramirez, and Toney, who share income and loss in a 3:2:1 ratio, plan to liquidate their partnership. At liquidation, their balance sheet appears as follows.

LONDON, RAMIREZ, AND TONEY
Balance Sheet
January 18

Assets		Liabilities and Equity	
Cash	$179,500	Accounts payable	$241,500
Equipment	552,000	London, Capital	98,000
		Ramirez, Capital	220,500
		Toney, Capital	171,500
Total assets	$731,500	Total liabilities and equity	$731,500

Required

Prepare journal entries for (*a*) the sale of equipment, (*b*) the allocation of its gain or loss, (*c*) the payment of liabilities at book value, and (*d*) the distribution of cash in each of the following separate cases: Equipment is sold for (1) $605,400; (2) $474,000; (3) $301,200 and any partners with capital deficits pay in the amount of their deficits; and (4) $271,200 and the partners have no assets other than those invested in the partnership. (Round amounts to the nearest dollar.)

Check (4) Cash distribution: Ramirez, $98,633

SERIAL PROBLEM

Success Systems

(This serial problem began in Chapter 1 and continues through most of the book. If previous chapter segments were not completed, the serial problem can begin at this point. It is helpful, but not necessary, to use the Working Papers that accompany the book.)

SP 12   At the start of 2010, Adriana Lopez is considering adding a partner to her business. She envisions the new partner taking the lead in generating sales of both services and merchandise for Success Systems. Lopez's equity in Success Systems as of January 1, 2010, is reflected in the following capital balance.

A. Lopez, Capital $90,148

Required

1. Lopez is evaluating whether the prospective partner should be an equal partner with respect to capital investment and profit sharing (1:1) or whether the agreement should be 4:1 with Lopez retaining four-fifths interest with rights to four-fifths of the net income or loss. What factors should she consider in deciding which partnership agreement to offer?

2. Prepare the January 1, 2010, journal entry(ies) necessary to admit a new partner to Success Systems through the purchase of a partnership interest for each of the following two separate cases: (*a*) 1:1 sharing agreement and (*b*) 4:1 sharing agreement.

3. Prepare the January 1, 2010, journal entry(ies) required to admit a new partner if the new partner invests cash of $22,537.

4. After posting the entry in part 3, what would be the new partner's equity percentage?

BEYOND THE NUMBERS

REPORTING IN ACTION

C1

BTN 12-1   Take a step back in time and imagine **Best Buy** in its infancy as a company. The year is 1966.

Required

1. Read the history of Best Buy at **BestBuymedia.tekgroup.com**. Can you determine from the history whether Best Buy was originally organized as a sole proprietorship, partnership, or corporation?

2. Assume that Best Buy was originally organized as a partnership. Best Buy's income statement in Appendix A varies in several key ways from what it would look like for a partnership. Identify at least two ways in which a corporate income statement differs from a partnership income statement.

3. Compare the Best Buy balance sheet in Appendix A to what a partnership balance sheet would have shown. Identify and explain any account differences you would anticipate.

COMPARATIVE ANALYSIS

C1

BTN 12-2   Over the years **Best Buy** and **Circuit City** have evolved into large corporations. Today it is difficult to imagine them as fledgling start-ups. Research each company's history online.

Required

1. Which company is older?
2. Which company started as a partnership?
3. In what years did each company first achieve $1,000,000 in sales?
4. In what years did each company have its first public offering of stock?

**ETHICS
CHALLENGE**

P2

BTN 12-3 Doctors Maben, Orlando, and Clark have been in a group practice for several years. Maben and Orlando are family practice physicians, and Clark is a general surgeon. Clark receives many referrals for surgery from his family practice partners. Upon the partnership's original formation, the three doctors agreed to a two-part formula to share income. Every month each doctor receives a salary allowance of $3,000. Additional income is divided according to a percent of patient charges the doctors generate for the month. In the current month, Maben generated 10% of the billings, Orlando 30%, and Clark 60%. The group's income for this month is $50,000. Clark has expressed dissatisfaction with the income-sharing formula and asks that income be split entirely on patient charge percents.

Required

1. Compute the income allocation for the current month using the original agreement.

2. Compute the income allocation for the current month using Clark's proposed agreement.

3. Identify the ethical components of this partnership decision for the doctors.

**COMMUNICATING
IN PRACTICE**

C1

BTN 12-4 Assume that you are studying for an upcoming accounting exam with a good friend. Your friend says that she has a solid understanding of general partnerships but is less sure that she understands organizations that combine certain characteristics of partnerships with other forms of business organization. You offer to make some study notes for your friend to help her learn about limited partnerships, limited liability partnerships, S corporations, and limited liability companies. Prepare a one-page set of well-organized, complete study notes on these four forms of business organization.

**TAKING IT TO
THE NET**

P1   P2

BTN 12-5 Access the March 6, 2007, filing of the December 31, 2006, 10-K of **America First Tax Exempt Investors LP**. This company deals with tax-exempt mortgage revenue bonds that, among other things, finance student housing properties.

1. Locate its December 31, 2006, balance sheet and list the account titles reported in the equity section of the balance sheet.

2. Locate its statement of partners' capital and comprehensive income (loss). How many units of limited partnership (known as "beneficial unit certificate holders") are outstanding at December 31, 2006?

3. What is the partnership's largest asset and its amount at December 31, 2006?

**TEAMWORK IN
ACTION**

P2

BTN 12-6 This activity requires teamwork to reinforce understanding of accounting for partnerships.

Required

1. Assume that Baker, Warner, and Rice form the BWR Partnership by making capital contributions of $200,000, $300,000, and $500,000, respectively. BWR predicts annual partnership net income of $600,000. The partners are considering various plans for sharing income and loss. Assign a different team member to compute how the projected $600,000 income would be shared under each of the following separate plans:

a. Shared equally.

b. In the ratio of the partners' initial capital investments.

c. Salary allowances of $50,000 to Baker, $60,000 to Warner, and $70,000 to Rice, with the remaining balance shared equally.

d. Interest allowances of 10% on the partners' initial capital investments, with the remaining balance shared equally.

2. In sequence, each member is to present his or her income-sharing calculations with the team.

3. As a team, identify and discuss at least one other possible way that income could be shared.

BTN 12-7 Recall the chapter's opening feature involving Samanta and Kelvin Joseph, and their company, **Samanta Shoes**. Assume that Samanta and Kelvin, partners in Samanta Shoes, decide to expand their business with the help of general partners.

ENTREPRENEURIAL DECISION

C1

Required

1. What details should Samanta, Kelvin, and their future partners specify in the general partnership agreements?
2. What advantages should Samanta, Kelvin, and their future partners be aware of with respect to organizing as a general partnership?
3. What disadvantages should Samanta, Kelvin, and their future partners be aware of with respect to organizing as a general partnership?

BTN 12-8 Access **DSG international**'s Website (www.DSGiplc.com) and research the company's history.

GLOBAL DECISION

C1

DSG

1. When was the company founded, and what was its original form of ownership?
2. Why did the company change its name from Dixons to DSG international?
3. What are some of the companies that are part of DSG international?

ANSWERS TO MULTIPLE CHOICE QUIZ

1. e; Capital = $250,000 − $50,000
2. a; $90,000 × [$100,000/($150,000 + $150,000 + $100,000)] = $22,500
3. d;

	Jamison	Blue	Total
Net income			$ 270,000
Salary allowance	$120,000		(120,000)
Interest allowance	60,000	$80,000	(140,000)
Balance of income			10,000
Balance divided equally	5,000	5,000	(10,000)
Totals	$185,000	$85,000	$ 0

4. b; Total partnership equity = $125,000 + $124,000 + $75,000 = $324,000
   Equity of Black = $324,000 × 20% = $64,800
   Bonus to old partners = $75,000 − $64,800 = $10,200, split equally
5. a; $10,500/[($110,000 + $124,000)/2] = 8.97%

 **A Look Back**

Chapter 12 focused on the partnership form of organization. We described crucial characteristics of partnerships and the accounting and reporting of their important transactions.

 A Look at This Chapter

This chapter emphasizes details of the corporate form of organization. The accounting concepts and procedures for equity transactions are explained. We also describe how to report and analyze income, earnings per share, and retained earnings.

A Look Ahead

Chapter 14 focuses on long-term liabilities. We explain how to value, record, amortize, and report these liabilities in financial statements.

Accounting for Corporations

Chapter

Learning Objectives

CAP

Conceptual

C1 Identify characteristics of corporations and their organization. (p. 506)

C2 Describe the components of stockholders' equity. (p. 509)

C3 Explain characteristics of common and preferred stock. (p. 517)

C4 Explain the items reported in retained earnings. (p. 522)

Analytical

A1 Compute earnings per share and describe its use. (p. 524)

A2 Compute price-earnings ratio and describe its use in analysis. (p. 525)

A3 Compute dividend yield and explain its use in analysis. (p. 525)

A4 Compute book value and explain its use in analysis. (p. 526)

Procedural

P1 Record the issuance of corporate stock. (p. 510)

P2 Record transactions involving cash dividends. (p. 513)

P3 Account for stock dividends and stock splits. (p. 514)

P4 Distribute dividends between common stock and preferred stock. (p. 517)

P5 Record purchases and sales of treasury stock and the retirement of stock. (p. 520)

LP13

Decision Feature

Breathing New Life

"*We weren't planning on starting a company*"
—Ali Perry

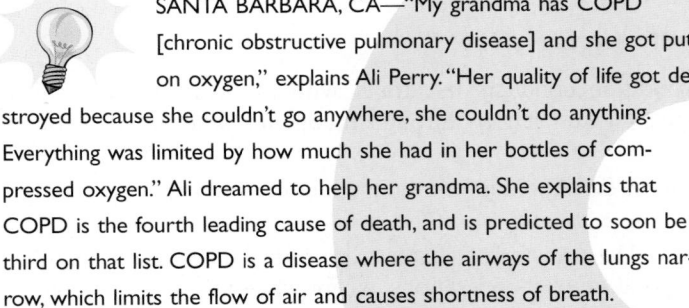 SANTA BARBARA, CA—"My grandma has COPD [chronic obstructive pulmonary disease] and she got put on oxygen," explains Ali Perry. "Her quality of life got destroyed because she couldn't go anywhere, she couldn't do anything. Everything was limited by how much she had in her bottles of compressed oxygen." Ali dreamed to help her grandma. She explains that COPD is the fourth leading cause of death, and is predicted to soon be third on that list. COPD is a disease where the airways of the lungs narrow, which limits the flow of air and causes shortness of breath.

To make her dream a reality, Ali enlisted the aid of two college classmates, Byron Myers and Brenton Taylor. The three of them designed a portable oxygen system, wrote a business plan, and set off to secure financing. Their company, named **Inogen**, which is a combination of the words innovation and oxygen (**Inogen.net),** soon had a portable oxygen supply unit whose sales exceed 10,000 units to date. "We worked really hard at the technology," explains Ali. "We saw the value of the company was in creating technology that was thought impossible in the marketplace."

The three founders insist that proper financing was a key to their success. To make it happen, says Ali, they needed equity (stock) financing. With their business plan and prototype, the three raised a whopping $4 million from a venture capital firm. Still, explains Ali, the focus is on helping folks, including her grandma. Adds Byron, "Oxygen users can now take off on a moment's notice, without having to watch the clock or guess at how long their oxygen will last."

Their equity financing "brings both opportunities and challenges," explains Byron. "New patients do not know anything about oxygen therapy. All they know is that their life has changed and they now need to have a supply of oxygen with them whenever and wherever." Inogen answers that call. Their focus on people continues to reap rewards as they recently secured another $22 million in equity financing. As Byron put it: "[Inogen] makes old ways of thinking and operating inadequate."

[Sources: *Inogen Website,* January 2009; *HME Business,* January 2006; *Daily Nexus,* January 2004; *Goleta Valley Voice,* December 2003; *Inc.com,* July 2007]

This chapter focuses on equity transactions. The first part of the chapter describes the basics of the corporate form of organization and explains the accounting for common and preferred stock. We then focus on several special financing transactions, including cash and stock dividends, stock splits, and treasury stock. The final section considers accounting for retained earnings, including prior period adjustments, retained earnings restrictions, and reporting guidelines.

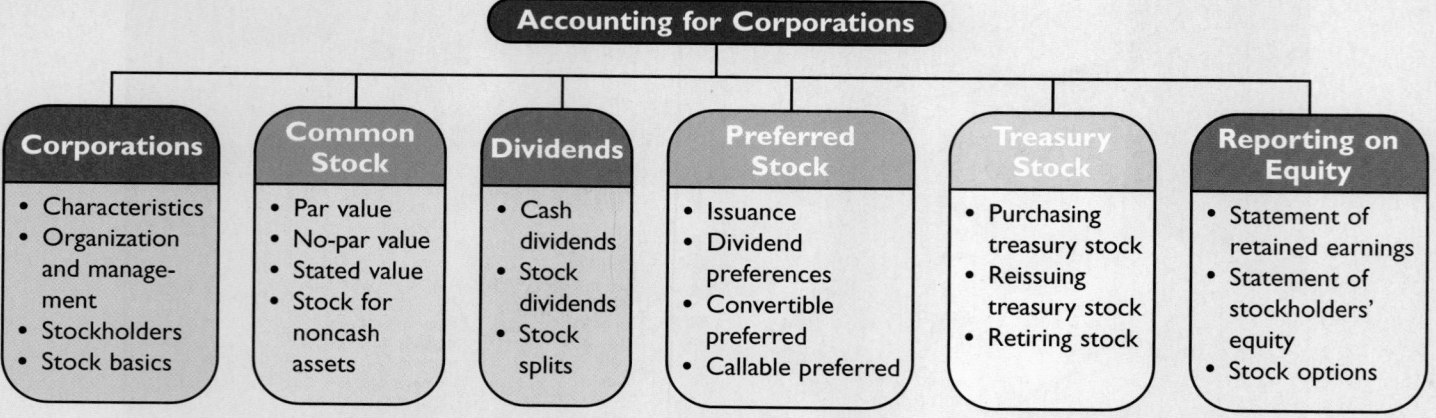

Accounting for Corporations

Corporations	Common Stock	Dividends	Preferred Stock	Treasury Stock	Reporting on Equity
• Characteristics • Organization and management • Stockholders • Stock basics	• Par value • No-par value • Stated value • Stock for noncash assets	• Cash dividends • Stock dividends • Stock splits	• Issuance • Dividend preferences • Convertible preferred • Callable preferred	• Purchasing treasury stock • Reissuing treasury stock • Retiring stock	• Statement of retained earnings • Statement of stockholders' equity • Stock options

Corporate Form of Organization

Video 13.1

A **corporation** is an entity created by law that is separate from its owners. It has most of the rights and privileges granted to individuals. Owners of corporations are called *stockholders* or *shareholders*. Corporations can be separated into two types. A *privately held* (or *closely held*) corporation does not offer its stock for public sale and usually has few stockholders. A *publicly held* corporation offers its stock for public sale and can have thousands of stockholders. *Public sale* usually refers to issuance and trading on an organized stock market.

Characteristics of Corporations

C1 Identify characteristics of corporations and their organization.

Corporations represent an important type of organization. Their unique characteristics offer advantages and disadvantages.

Advantages of Corporate Characteristics

■ **Separate legal entity:** A corporation conducts its affairs with the same rights, duties, and responsibilities of a person. It takes actions through its agents, who are its officers and managers.

■ **Limited liability of stockholders:** Stockholders are neither liable for corporate acts nor corporate debt.

Point: The *business entity assumption* requires a corporation to be accounted for separately from its owners (shareholders).

Global: U.S., U.K., and Canadian corporations finance much of their operations with stock issuances, but companies in countries such as France, Germany, and Japan finance mainly with note and bond issuances.

■ **Transferable ownership rights:** The transfer of shares from one stockholder to another usually has no effect on the corporation or its operations except when this causes a change in the directors who control or manage the corporation.

■ **Continuous life:** A corporation's life continues indefinitely because it is not tied to the physical lives of its owners.

■ **Lack of mutual agency for stockholders:** A corporation acts through its agents, who are its officers and managers. Stockholders, who are not its officers and managers, do not have the power to bind the corporation to contracts—referred to as *lack of mutual agency*.

■ **Ease of capital accumulation:** Buying stock is attractive to investors because (1) stockholders are not liable for the corporation's acts and debts, (2) stocks usually are transferred easily, (3) the life of the corporation is unlimited, and (4) stockholders are not corporate agents. These advantages enable corporations to accumulate large amounts of capital from the combined investments of many stockholders.

Disadvantages of Corporate Characteristics

■ **Government regulation:** A corporation must meet requirements of a state's incorporation laws, which subject the corporation to state regulation and control. Proprietorships and partnerships avoid many of these regulations and governmental reports.

■ **Corporate taxation:** Corporations are subject to the same property and payroll taxes as proprietorships and partnerships plus *additional* taxes. The most burdensome of these are federal and state income taxes that together can take 40% or more of corporate pretax income. Moreover, corporate income is usually taxed a second time as part of stockholders' personal income when they receive cash distributed as dividends. This is called *double taxation.* (The usual dividend tax is 15%; however, it is less than 15% for lower income taxpayers, and in some cases zero.)

Decision Insight

Stock Financing Marc Andreessen cofounded Netscape at age 22, only four months after earning his degree. One year later, he and friends issued Netscape shares to the public. The stock soared, making Andreessen a multimillionaire.

Corporate Organization and Management

This section describes the incorporation, costs, and management of corporate organizations.

Incorporation A corporation is created by obtaining a charter from a state government. A charter application usually must be signed by the prospective stockholders called *incorporators* or *promoters* and then filed with the proper state official. When the application process is complete and fees paid, the charter is issued and the corporation is formed. Investors then purchase the corporation's stock, meet as stockholders, and elect a board of directors. Directors oversee a corporation's affairs.

Organization Expenses **Organization expenses** (also called *organization costs*) are the costs to organize a corporation; they include legal fees, promoters' fees, and amounts paid to obtain a charter. The corporation records (debits) these costs to an expense account called *Organization Expenses.* Organization costs are expensed as incurred because it is difficult to determine the amount and timing of their future benefits.

Management of a Corporation The ultimate control of a corporation rests with stockholders who control a corporation by electing its *board of directors,* or simply, *directors.* Each stockholder usually has one vote for each share of stock owned. This control relation is shown in Exhibit 13.1. Directors are responsible for and have final authority for managing corporate activities. A board can act only as a collective body and usually limits its actions to setting general policy.

A corporation usually holds a stockholder meeting at least once a year to elect directors and transact business as its bylaws require. A group of stockholders owning or controlling votes of more than a 50% share of a corporation's stock can elect the board and control the corporation. Stockholders who do not attend stockholders' meetings must have an opportunity to delegate their voting rights to an agent by signing a **proxy,** a document that gives a designated agent the right to vote the stock.

Day-to-day direction of corporate business is delegated to executive officers appointed by the board. A corporation's chief executive officer (CEO) is often its president. Several vice

Point: A corporation is not required to have an office in its state of incorporation.

EXHIBIT 13.1
Corporate Structure

Point: *Bylaws* are guidelines that govern the behavior of individuals employed by and managing the corporation.

Global: Some corporate labels are:

Country	Label
United States	Inc.
France	SA
United Kingdom	
Public	PLC
Private	LTD
Germany	
Public	AG
Private	GmbH
Sweden	AB
Italy	SpA

presidents, who report to the president, are commonly assigned specific areas of management responsibility such as finance, production, and marketing. One person often has the dual role of chairperson of the board of directors and CEO. In this case, the president is usually designated the chief operating officer (COO).

Decision Insight

Seed Money   Sources for start-up money include (1) "angel" investors such as family, friends, or anyone who believes in a company, (2) employees, investors, and even suppliers who can be paid with stock, and (3) venture capitalists (investors) who have a record of entrepreneurial success. See the National Venture Capital Association (**NVCA.org**) for information.

Stockholders of Corporations

This section explains stockholder rights, stock purchases and sales, and the role of registrar and transfer agents.

Rights of Stockholders   When investors buy stock, they acquire all *specific* rights the corporation's charter grants to stockholders. They also acquire *general* rights granted stockholders by the laws of the state in which the company is incorporated. When a corporation has only one class of stock, it is identified as **common stock.** State laws vary, but common stockholders usually have the general right to

1. Vote at stockholders' meetings.
2. Sell or otherwise dispose of their stock.
3. Purchase their proportional share of any common stock later issued by the corporation. This **preemptive right** protects stockholders' proportionate interest in the corporation. For example, a stockholder who owns 25% of a corporation's common stock has the first opportunity to buy 25% of any new common stock issued.
4. Receive the same dividend, if any, on each common share of the corporation.
5. Share in any assets remaining after creditors and preferred stockholders are paid when, and if, the corporation is liquidated. Each common share receives the same amount.

Stockholders also have the right to receive timely financial reports.

Stock Certificates and Transfer   Investors who buy a corporation's stock, sometimes receive a *stock certificate* as proof of share ownership. Many corporations issue only one certificate for each block of stock purchased. A certificate can be for any number of shares. Exhibit 13.2 shows a stock certificate of the **Green Bay Packers**. A certificate shows the company name, stockholder name, number of shares, and other crucial information. Issuance of certificates is becoming less common. Instead, many stockholders maintain accounts with the corporation or their stockbrokers and never receive actual certificates.

EXHIBIT 13.2

Stock Certificate

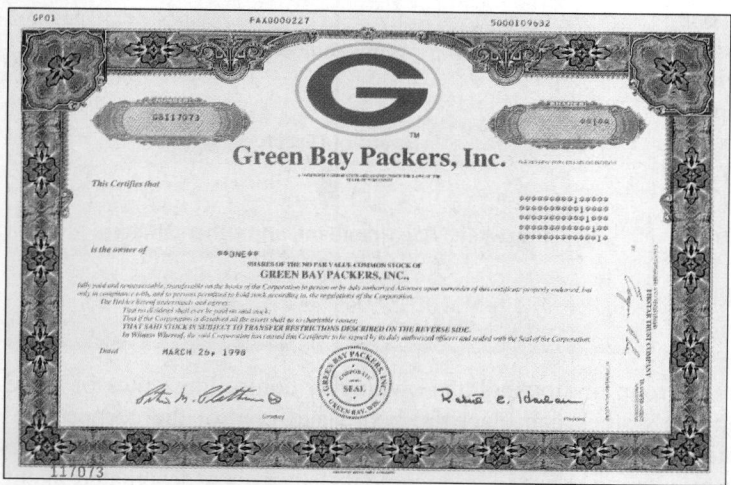

Registrar and Transfer Agents   If a corporation's stock is traded on a major stock exchange, the corporation must have a registrar and a transfer agent. A *registrar* keeps stockholder records and prepares official lists of stockholders for stockholder meetings and dividend payments. A *transfer agent* assists with purchases and sales of shares by receiving and issuing certificates as necessary. Registrars and transfer agents are usually large banks or trust companies with computer facilities and staff to do this work.

Decision Insight

Pricing Stock A prospectus accompanies a stock's initial public offering (IPO), giving financial information about the company issuing the stock. A prospectus should help answer these questions to price an IPO: (1) Is the underwriter reliable? (2) Is there growth in revenues, profits, and cash flows? (3) What is management's view of operations? (4) Are current owners selling? (5) What are the risks?

Basics of Capital Stock

Capital stock is a general term that refers to any shares issued to obtain capital (owner financing). This section introduces terminology and accounting for capital stock.

 C2 Describe the components of stockholders' equity.

Authorized Stock **Authorized stock** is the number of shares that a corporation's charter allows it to sell. The number of authorized shares usually exceeds the number of shares issued (and outstanding), often by a large amount. (*Outstanding stock* refers to issued stock held by stockholders.) No formal journal entry is required for stock authorization. A corporation must apply to the state for a change in its charter if it wishes to issue more shares than previously authorized. A corporation discloses the number of shares authorized in the equity section of its balance sheet or notes. **Best Buy**'s balance sheet in Appendix A reports 1 billion shares authorized as of the start of its 2008 fiscal year.

Subcategories of Authorized Stock

Selling (Issuing) Stock A corporation can sell stock directly or indirectly. To *sell directly,* it advertises its stock issuance to potential buyers. This type of issuance is most common with privately held corporations. To *sell indirectly,* a corporation pays a brokerage house (investment banker) to issue its stock. Some brokerage houses *underwrite* an indirect issuance of stock; that is, they buy the stock from the corporation and take all gains or losses from its resale.

Market Value of Stock **Market value per share** is the price at which a stock is bought and sold. Expected future earnings, dividends, growth, and other company and economic factors influence market value. Traded stocks' market values are available daily in newspapers such as *The Wall Street Journal* and online. The current market value of previously issued shares (for example, the price of stock in trades between investors) does not impact the issuing corporation's stockholders' equity.

Classes of Stock When all authorized shares have the same rights and characteristics, the stock is called *common stock.* A corporation is sometimes authorized to issue more than one class of stock, including preferred stock and different classes of common stock. **American Greetings**, for instance, has two types of common stock: Class A stock has 1 vote per share and Class B stock has 10 votes per share.

Par Value Stock **Par value stock** is stock that is assigned a **par value,** which is an amount assigned per share by the corporation in its charter. For example, Best Buy's common stock has a par value of $0.10. Other commonly assigned par values are $10, $5, $1 and $0.01. There is no restriction on the assigned par value. In many states, the par value of a stock establishes **minimum legal capital,** which refers to the least amount that the buyers of stock must contribute to the corporation or be subject to paying at a future date. For example, if a corporation issues 1,000 shares of $10 par value stock, the corporation's minimum legal capital in these states would be $10,000. Minimum legal capital is intended to protect a corporation's creditors. Since creditors cannot demand payment from stockholders' personal assets, their claims are limited to the corporation's assets and any minimum legal capital. At liquidation, creditor claims are paid before any amounts are distributed to stockholders.

No-Par Value Stock **No-par value stock,** or simply *no-par stock,* is stock *not* assigned a value per share by the corporate charter. Its advantage is that it can be issued at any price without the possibility of a minimum legal capital deficiency.

Point: Managers are motivated to set a low par value when minimum legal capital or state issuance taxes are based on par value.

Point: Minimum legal capital was intended to protect creditors by requiring a minimum level of net assets.

Point: Par, no-par, and stated value do *not* set the stock's market value.

EXHIBIT 13.3

Equity Composition

Point: Paid-in capital comes from stock-related transactions, whereas retained earnings comes from operations.

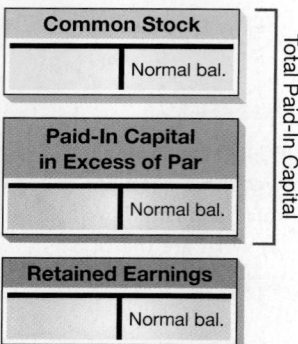

Corporation

Common Stock
Normal bal.

Paid-In Capital in Excess of Par
Normal bal.

Total Paid-In Capital

Retained Earnings
Normal bal.

Stated Value Stock   Stated value stock is no-par stock to which the directors assign a "stated" value per share. Stated value per share becomes the minimum legal capital per share in this case.

Stockholders' Equity   A corporation's equity is known as **stockholders' equity,** also called *shareholders' equity* or *corporate capital.* Stockholders' equity consists of (1) paid-in (or contributed) capital and (2) retained earnings; see Exhibit 13.3. **Paid-in capital** is the total amount of cash and other assets the corporation receives from its stockholders in exchange for its stock. **Retained earnings** is the cumulative net income (and loss) not distributed as dividends to its stockholders.

Decision Insight

Stock Quote   The **Best Buy** stock quote is interpreted as (left to right): **Hi,** highest price in past 52 weeks; **Lo,** lowest

52 Weeks				Yld		Vol				Net
Hi	Lo	Sym	Div	%	PE	mil.	Hi	Lo	Close	Chg
54.15	41.85	BBY	0.13	0.98	19	7.2	53.14	52.36	52.91	+0.20

price in past 52 weeks; **Sym,** company exchange symbol; **Div,** dividends paid per share in past year; **Yld %,** dividend divided by closing price; **PE,** stock price per share divided by earnings per share; **Vol mil.,** number (in millions) of shares traded; **Hi,** highest price for the day; **Lo,** lowest price for the day; **Close,** closing price for the day; **Net Chg,** change in closing price from prior day.

Quick Check   Answers—p. 531

1. Which of the following is *not* a characteristic of the corporate form of business? (*a*) Ease of capital accumulation, (*b*) Stockholder responsibility for corporate debts, (*c*) Ease in transferability of ownership rights, or (*d*) Double taxation.
2. Why is a corporation's income said to be taxed twice?
3. What is a proxy?

Common Stock

P1   Record the issuance of corporate stock.

Video 13.2

Accounting for the issuance of common stock affects only paid-in (contributed) capital accounts; no retained earnings accounts are affected.

Issuing Par Value Stock

Par value stock can be issued at par, at a premium (above par), or at a discount (below par). In each case, stock can be exchanged for either cash or noncash assets.

Issuing Par Value Stock at Par   When common stock is issued at par value, we record amounts for both the asset(s) received and the par value stock issued. To illustrate, the entry to record Dillon Snowboards' issuance of 30,000 shares of $10 par value stock for $300,000 cash on June 5, 2009, follows.

Assets = Liabilities + Equity
+300,000   +300,000

June 5	Cash	300,000	
	Common Stock, $10 Par Value		300,000
	Issued 30,000 shares of $10 par value common stock at par.		

Exhibit 13.4 shows the stockholders' equity of Dillon Snowboards at year-end 2009 (its first year of operations) after income of $65,000 and no dividend payments.

EXHIBIT 13.4

Stockholders' Equity for Stock Issued at Par

Stockholders' Equity

Common Stock—$10 par value; 50,000 shares authorized; 30,000 shares issued and outstanding	$300,000
Retained earnings	65,000
Total stockholders' equity	$365,000

Issuing Par Value Stock at a Premium A **premium on stock** occurs when a corporation sells its stock for more than par (or stated) value. To illustrate, if Dillon Snowboards issues its $10 par value common stock at $12 per share, its stock is sold at a $2 per share premium. The premium, known as **paid-in capital in excess of par value,** is reported as part of equity; it is not revenue and is not listed on the income statement. The entry to record Dillon Snowboards' issuance of 30,000 shares of $10 par value stock for $12 per share on June 5, 2009, follows

Point: A *premium* is the amount by which issue price exceeds par (or stated) value. It is recorded in the "Paid-In Capital in Excess of Par Value, Common Stock" account; also called "Additional Paid-In Capital, Common Stock."

June 5	Cash.	360,000	
	Common Stock, $10 Par Value.		300,000
	Paid-In Capital in Excess of Par Value, Common Stock		60,000
	Sold and issued 30,000 shares of $10 par value common stock at $12 per share.		

Assets	= Liabilities +	Equity
+360,000		+300,000
		+60,000

The Paid-In Capital in Excess of Par Value account is added to the par value of the stock in the equity section of the balance sheet as shown in Exhibit 13.5.

Point: The *Paid-In Capital* terminology is interchangeable with *Contributed Capital.*

EXHIBIT 13.5

Stockholders' Equity for Stock Issued at a Premium

Stockholders' Equity

Common Stock—$10 par value; 50,000 shares authorized; 30,000 shares issued and outstanding	$300,000
Paid-in capital in excess of par value, common stock	60,000
Retained earnings	65,000
Total stockholders' equity	$425,000

Issuing Par Value Stock at a Discount A **discount on stock** occurs when a corporation sells its stock for less than par (or stated) value. Most states prohibit the issuance of stock at a discount. In states that allow stock to be issued at a discount, its buyers usually become contingently liable to creditors for the discount. If stock is issued at a discount, the amount by which issue price is less than par is debited to a *Discount on Common Stock* account, a contra to the common stock account, and its balance is subtracted from the par value of stock in the equity section of the balance sheet. This discount is not an expense and does not appear on the income statement.

Point: Retained earnings can be negative, reflecting accumulated losses. Amazon.com had an accumulated deficit of $1.8 billion at the start of 2007.

Issuing No-Par Value Stock

When no-par stock is issued and is not assigned a stated value, the amount the corporation receives becomes legal capital and is recorded as Common Stock. This means that the entire proceeds are credited to a no-par stock account. To illustrate, a corporation records its October 20 issuance of 1,000 shares of no-par stock for $40 cash per share as follows.

Oct. 20	Cash	40,000	
	Common Stock, No-Par Value		40,000
	Issued 1,000 shares of no-par value common stock at $40 per share.		

Assets	= Liabilities +	Equity
+40,000		+40,000

Frequency of Stock Types

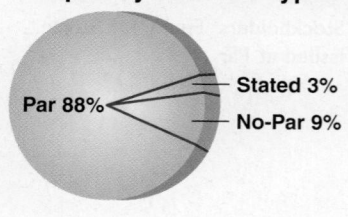

Par 88%

Stated 3%

No-Par 9%

Issuing Stated Value Stock

When no-par stock is issued and assigned a stated value, its stated value becomes legal capital and is credited to a stated value stock account. Assuming that stated value stock is issued at an amount in excess of stated value (the usual case), the excess is credited to Paid-In Capital in Excess of Stated Value, Common Stock, which is reported in the stockholders' equity section. To illustrate, a corporation that issues 1,000 shares of no-par common stock having a stated value of $40 per share in return for $50 cash per share records this as follows.

Assets = Liabilities + Equity
+50,000   +40,000
        +10,000

Oct. 20	Cash	50,000	
	Common Stock, $40 Stated Value		40,000
	Paid-In Capital in Excess of Stated		
	Value, Common Stock		10,000
	Issued 1,000 shares of $40 per share stated		
	value stock at $50 per share.		

Issuing Stock for Noncash Assets

Point: Stock issued for noncash assets should be recorded at the market value of either the stock or the noncash asset, whichever is more clearly determinable.

A corporation can receive assets other than cash in exchange for its stock. (It can also assume liabilities on the assets received such as a mortgage on property received.) The corporation records the assets received at their market values as of the date of the transaction. The stock given in exchange is recorded at its par (or stated) value with any excess recorded in the Paid-In Capital in Excess of Par (or Stated) Value account. (If no-par stock is issued, the stock is recorded at the assets' market value.) To illustrate, the entry to record receipt of land valued at $105,000 in return for issuance of 4,000 shares of $20 par value common stock on June 10 is

Assets = Liabilities + Equity
+105,000   +80,000
        +25,000

June 10	Land	105,000	
	Common Stock, $20 Par Value		80,000
	Paid-In Capital in Excess of Par Value,		
	Common Stock		25,000
	Exchanged 4,000 shares of $20 par value		
	common stock for land.		

Point: Any type of stock can be issued for noncash assets.

A corporation sometimes gives shares of its stock to promoters in exchange for their services in organizing the corporation, which the corporation records as **Organization Expenses.** The entry to record receipt of services valued at $12,000 in organizing the corporation in return for 600 shares of $15 par value common stock on June 5 is

Assets = Liabilities + Equity
       −12,000
       +9,000
       +3,000

June 5	Organization Expenses	12,000	
	Common Stock, $15 Par Value		9,000
	Paid-In Capital in Excess of Par Value,		
	Common Stock		3,000
	Gave promoters 600 shares of $15 par value		
	common stock in exchange for their services.		

Quick Check

Answers—p. 531

4. A company issues 7,000 shares of its $10 par value common stock in exchange for equipment valued at $105,000. The entry to record this transaction includes a credit to (*a*) Paid-In Capital in Excess of Par Value, Common Stock, for $35,000. (*b*) Retained Earnings for $35,000. (*c*) Common Stock, $10 Par Value, for $105,000.

5. What is a premium on stock issuance?

6. Who is intended to be protected by minimum legal capital?

Dividends

This section describes both cash and stock dividend transactions.

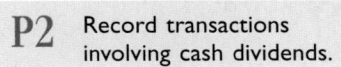

P2 Record transactions involving cash dividends.

Cash Dividends

The decision to pay cash dividends rests with the board of directors and involves more than evaluating the amounts of retained earnings and cash. The directors, for instance, may decide to keep the cash to invest in the corporation's growth, to meet emergencies, to take advantage of unexpected opportunities, or to pay off debt. Alternatively, many corporations pay cash dividends to their stockholders at regular dates. These cash flows provide a return to investors and almost always affect the stock's market value.

Video13.2

Accounting for Cash Dividends   Dividend payment involves three important dates: declaration, record, and payment. **Date of declaration** is the date the directors vote to declare and pay a dividend. This creates a legal liability of the corporation to its stockholders. **Date of record** is the future date specified by the directors for identifying those stockholders listed in the corporation's records to receive dividends. The date of record usually follows the date of declaration by at least two weeks. Persons who own stock on the date of record receive dividends. **Date of payment** is the date when the corporation makes payment; it follows the date of record by enough time to allow the corporation to arrange checks, money transfers, or other means to pay dividends.

Percent of Corporations Paying Dividends

Cash Dividend to Common   75%

Cash Dividend to Preferred   22%

0%   20%   40%   60%   80%   100%

To illustrate, the entry to record a January 9 declaration of a $1 per share cash dividend by the directors of Z-Tech, Inc., with 5,000 outstanding shares is

Date of Declaration

Jan. 9	Retained Earnings..........................	5,000	
	Common Dividend Payable		5,000
	Declared $1 per common share cash dividend.[1]		

Assets = Liabilities + Equity
      +5,000   −5,000

Common Dividend Payable is a current liability. The date of record for the Z-Tech dividend is January 22. *No formal journal entry is needed on the date of record.* The February 1 date of payment requires an entry to record both the settlement of the liability and the reduction of the cash balance, as follows:

Date of Payment

Feb. 1	Common Dividend Payable..................	5,000	
	Cash		5,000
	Paid $1 per common share cash dividend.		

Assets = Liabilities + Equity
−5,000   −5,000

Deficits and Cash Dividends   A corporation with a debit (abnormal) balance for retained earnings is said to have a **retained earnings deficit,** which arises when a company incurs cumulative losses and/or pays more dividends than total earnings from current and prior years. A deficit is reported as a deduction on the balance sheet, as shown in Exhibit 13.6. Most states prohibit a corporation with a deficit from paying a cash dividend to its stockholders. This legal restriction is designed to protect creditors by preventing distribution of assets to stockholders when the company may be in financial difficulty.

Point: It is often said a dividend is a distribution of retained earnings, but it is more precise to describe a dividend as a distribution of assets to satisfy stockholder claims.

Point: The Retained Earnings Deficit account is also called *Accumulated Deficit.*

---

[1] An alternative entry is to debit Dividends instead of Retained Earnings. The balance in Dividends is then closed to Retained Earnings at the end of the reporting period. The effect is the same: Retained Earnings is decreased and a Dividend Payable is increased. For simplicity, all assignments in this chapter use the Retained Earnings account to record dividend declarations.

EXHIBIT 13.6

Stockholders' Equity
with a Deficit

Common stock—$10 par value, 5,000 shares authorized, issued, and outstanding	$50,000
Retained earnings deficit	(6,000)
Total stockholders' equity	$44,000

Point: Amazon.com has never declared a cash dividend.

Some state laws allow cash dividends to be paid by returning a portion of the capital contributed by stockholders. This type of dividend is called a **liquidating cash dividend,** or simply *liquidating dividend,* because it returns a part of the original investment back to the stockholders. This requires a debit entry to one of the contributed capital accounts instead of Retained Earnings at the declaration date.

Quick Check   Answers—p. 531

7. What type of an account is the Common Dividend Payable account?
8. What three crucial dates are involved in the process of paying a cash dividend?
9. When does a dividend become a company's legal obligation?

Stock Dividends

P3 Account for stock dividends and stock splits.

A **stock dividend,** declared by a corporation's directors, is a distribution of additional shares of the corporation's own stock to its stockholders without the receipt of any payment in return. Stock dividends and cash dividends are different. A stock dividend does not reduce assets and equity but instead transfers a portion of equity from retained earnings to contributed capital.

Reasons for Stock Dividends Stock dividends exist for at least two reasons. First, directors are said to use stock dividends to keep the market price of the stock affordable. For example, if a corporation continues to earn income but does not issue cash dividends, the price of its common stock likely increases. The price of such a stock may become so high that it discourages some investors from buying the stock (especially in lots of 100 and 1,000). When a corporation has a stock dividend, it increases the number of outstanding shares and lowers the per share stock price. Another reason for a stock dividend is to provide evidence of management's confidence that the company is doing well and will continue to do well.

Accounting for Stock Dividends A stock dividend affects the components of equity by transferring part of retained earnings to contributed capital accounts, sometimes described as *capitalizing* retained earnings. Accounting for a stock dividend depends on whether it is a small or large stock dividend. A **small stock dividend** is a distribution of 25% or less of previously outstanding shares. It is recorded by capitalizing retained earnings for an amount equal to the market value of the shares to be distributed. A **large stock dividend** is a distribution of more than 25% of previously outstanding shares. A large stock dividend is recorded by capitalizing retained earnings for the minimum amount required by state law governing the corporation. Most states require capitalizing retained earnings equal to the par or stated value of the stock.

To illustrate stock dividends, we use the equity section of Quest's balance sheet shown in Exhibit 13.7 just *before* its declaration of a stock dividend on December 31.

EXHIBIT 13.7

Stockholders' Equity *before*
Declaring a Stock Dividend

Stockholders' Equity (before dividend)	
Common stock—$10 par value, 15,000 shares authorized, 10,000 shares issued and outstanding	$100,000
Paid-in capital in excess of par value, common stock	8,000
Retained earnings	35,000
Total stockholders' equity	$143,000

Recording a small stock dividend.   Assume that Quest's directors declare a 10% stock dividend on December 31. This stock dividend of 1,000 shares, computed as 10% of its 10,000 issued and outstanding shares, is to be distributed on January 20 to the stockholders of record on January 15. Since the market price of Quest's stock on December 31 is $15 per share, this small stock dividend declaration is recorded as follows:

Point: Small stock dividends are recorded at market value.

Date of Declaration

Dec. 31	Retained Earnings......................	15,000	
	Common Stock Dividend Distributable........		10,000
	Paid-In Capital in Excess of Par Value,		
	Common Stock......................		5,000
	Declared a 1,000-share (10%) stock dividend.		

Assets = Liabilities + Equity
−15,000
+10,000
+5,000

The $10,000 credit in the declaration entry equals the par value of the shares and is recorded in *Common Stock Dividend Distributable,* an equity account. Its balance exists only until the shares are issued. The $5,000 credit equals the amount by which market value exceeds par value. This amount increases the Paid-In Capital in Excess of Par Value account in anticipation of the issuance of shares. In general, the balance sheet changes in three ways when a stock dividend is declared. First, the amount of equity attributed to common stock increases; for Quest, from $100,000 to $110,000 for 1,000 additional declared shares. Second, paid-in capital in excess of par increases by the excess of market value over par value for the declared shares. Third, retained earnings decreases, reflecting the transfer of amounts to both common stock and paid-in capital in excess of par. The stockholders' equity of Quest is shown in Exhibit 13.8 *after* its 10% stock dividend is declared on December 31—the items impacted are in bold.

Point: The term *Distributable* (not *Payable*) is used for stock dividends. A stock dividend is never a liability because it never reduces assets.

Point: The credit to Paid-In Capital in Excess of Par Value is recorded when the stock dividend is declared. This account is not affected when stock is later distributed.

EXHIBIT 13.8

Stockholders' Equity *after* Declaring a Stock Dividend

Stockholders' Equity (after dividend)	
Common stock—$10 par value, 15,000 shares authorized, 10,000 shares issued and outstanding	$100,000
Common stock dividend distributable—1,000 shares	**10,000**
Paid-in capital in excess of par value, common stock	**13,000**
Retained earnings	**20,000**
Total stockholders' equity	$143,000

No entry is made on the date of record for a stock dividend. On January 20, the date of payment, Quest distributes the new shares to stockholders and records this entry:

Date of Payment

Jan. 20	Common Stock Dividend Distributable	10,000	
	Common Stock, $10 Par Value		10,000
	To record issuance of common stock dividend.		

Assets = Liabilities + Equity
−10,000
+10,000

The combined effect of these stock dividend entries is to transfer (or capitalize) $15,000 of retained earnings to paid-in capital accounts. The amount of capitalized retained earnings equals the market value of the 1,000 issued shares ($15 × 1,000 shares). A stock dividend has no effect on the ownership percent of individual stockholders.

Point: A stock dividend does not affect assets.

Recording a large stock dividend.   A corporation capitalizes retained earnings equal to the minimum amount required by state law for a large stock dividend. For most states, this amount is the par or stated value of the newly issued shares. To illustrate, suppose Quest's board declares a stock dividend of 30% instead of 10% on December 31. Since this dividend is more

Point: Large stock dividends are recorded at par or stated value.

than 25%, it is treated as a large stock dividend. Thus, the par value of the 3,000 dividend shares is capitalized at the date of declaration with this entry:

Date of Declaration

Assets = Liabilities + Equity
−30,000
+30,000

Dec. 31	Retained Earnings............................	30,000	
	Common Stock Dividend Distributable........		30,000
	Declared a 3,000-share (30%) stock dividend.		

This transaction decreases retained earnings and increases contributed capital by $30,000. On the date of payment the company debits Common Stock Dividend Distributable and credits Common Stock for $30,000. The effects from a large stock dividend on balance sheet accounts are similar to those for a small stock dividend except for the absence of any effect on paid-in capital in excess of par.

Stock Splits

A **stock split** is the distribution of additional shares to stockholders according to their percent ownership. When a stock split occurs, the corporation "calls in" its outstanding shares and issues more than one new share in exchange for each old share. Splits can be done in any ratio, including 2-for-1, 3-for-1, or higher. Stock splits reduce the par or stated value per share. The reasons for stock splits are similar to those for stock dividends.

To illustrate, CompTec has 100,000 outstanding shares of $20 par value common stock with a current market value of $88 per share. A 2-for-1 stock split cuts par value in half as it replaces 100,000 shares of $20 par value stock with 200,000 shares of $10 par value stock. Market value is reduced from $88 per share to about $44 per share. The split does not affect any equity amounts reported on the balance sheet or any individual stockholder's percent ownership. Both the Paid-In Capital and Retained Earnings accounts are unchanged by a split, and *no journal entry is made*. The only effect on the accounts is a change in the stock account description. CompTec's 2-for-1 split on its $20 par value stock means that after the split, it changes its stock account title to Common Stock, $10 Par Value. This stock's description on the balance sheet also changes to reflect the additional authorized, issued, and outstanding shares and the new par value.

The difference between stock splits and large stock dividends is often blurred. Many companies report stock splits in their financial statements without calling in the original shares by simply changing their par value. This type of "split" is really a large stock dividend and results in additional shares issued to stockholders by capitalizing retained earnings or transferring other paid-in capital to Common Stock. This approach avoids administrative costs of splitting the stock. **Harley-Davidson** recently declared a 2-for-1 stock split executed in the form of a 100% stock dividend.

Before 5:1 Split: 1 share, $50 par

After 5:1 Split: 5 shares, $10 par

Point: Berkshire Hathaway has resisted a stock split. Its recent stock price was $150,000 per share.

Point: A **reverse stock split** is the opposite of a stock split. It increases both the market value per share and the par or stated value per share with a split ratio less than 1-for-1, such as 1-for-2. A reverse split results in fewer shares.

Decision Maker

Entrepreneur   A company you cofounded and own stock in announces a 50% stock dividend. Has the value of your stock investment increased, decreased, or remained the same? Would it make a difference if it was a 3-for-2 stock split executed in the form of a dividend? [Answer—p. 531]

Quick Check

Answers—p. 531

10. How does a stock dividend impact assets and retained earnings?
11. What distinguishes a large stock dividend from a small stock dividend?
12. What amount of retained earnings is capitalized for a small stock dividend?

Preferred Stock

A corporation can issue two basic kinds of stock, common and preferred. **Preferred stock** has special rights that give it priority (or senior status) over common stock in one or more areas. Special rights typically include a preference for receiving dividends and for the distribution of assets if the corporation is liquidated. Preferred stock carries all rights of common stock unless the corporate charter nullifies them. Most preferred stock, for instance, does not confer the right to vote. Exhibit 13.9 shows that preferred stock is issued by about one-fourth of large corporations. All corporations issue common stock.

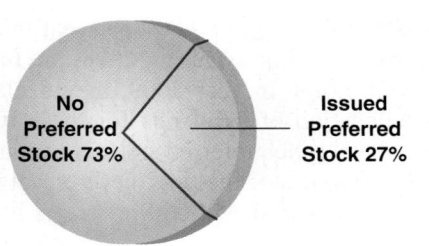

EXHIBIT 13.9

Corporations and
Preferred Stock

Issuance of Preferred Stock

Preferred stock usually has a par value. Like common stock, it can be sold at a price different from par. Preferred stock is recorded in its own separate capital accounts. To illustrate, if Dillon Snowboards issues 50 shares of $100 par value preferred stock for $6,000 cash on July 1, 2009, the entry is

C3	Explain characteristics of common and preferred stock.

July 1	Cash	6,000	
	Preferred Stock, $100 Par Value		5,000
	Paid-In Capital in Excess of Par Value,		
	Preferred Stock		1,000
	Issued preferred stock for cash.		

Assets = Liabilities + Equity
+6,000   +5,000
                          +1,000

The equity section of the year-end balance sheet for Dillon Snowboards, including preferred stock, is shown in Exhibit 13.10. (This exhibit assumes that common stock was issued at par.) Issuing no-par preferred stock is similar to issuing no-par common stock. Also, the entries for issuing preferred stock for noncash assets are similar to those for common stock.

Stockholders' Equity

Common stock—$10 par value; 50,000 shares authorized;	
30,000 shares issued and outstanding	$300,000
Preferred stock—$100 par value; 1,000 shares authorized;	
50 shares issued and outstanding	5,000
Paid-in capital in excess of par value, preferred stock	1,000
Retained earnings	65,000
Total stockholders' equity	$371,000

EXHIBIT 13.10

Stockholders' Equity with
Common and Preferred Stock

Dividend Preference of Preferred Stock

Preferred stock usually carries a preference for dividends, meaning that preferred stockholders are allocated their dividends before any dividends are allocated to common stockholders. The dividends allocated to preferred stockholders are usually expressed as a dollar amount per share or a percent applied to par value. A preference for dividends does *not* ensure dividends. If the directors do not declare a dividend, neither the preferred nor the common stockholders receive one.

P4	Distribute dividends between common stock and preferred stock.

Cumulative or Noncumulative Dividend Most preferred stocks carry a cumulative dividend right. **Cumulative preferred stock** has a right to be paid both the current and all prior periods' unpaid dividends before any dividend is paid to common stockholders. When preferred stock is cumulative and the directors either do not declare a dividend to preferred stockholders or declare one that does not cover the total amount of cumulative dividend, the unpaid dividend amount is called **dividend in arrears.** Accumulation of dividends in arrears on cumulative preferred stock does not guarantee they will be paid. **Noncumulative preferred stock** confers no right to prior periods' unpaid dividends if they were not declared in those prior periods.

To illustrate the difference between cumulative and noncumulative preferred stock, assume that a corporation's outstanding stock includes (1) 1,000 shares of $100 par, 9% preferred

Point: Dividend preference does not imply that preferred stockholders receive more dividends than common stockholders, nor does it guarantee a dividend.

Video13.2

stock—yielding $9,000 per year in potential dividends, and (2) 4,000 shares of $50 par value common stock. During 2008, the first year of operations, the directors declare cash dividends of $5,000. In year 2009, they declare cash dividends of $42,000. See Exhibit 13.11 for the allocation of dividends for these two years. Allocation of year 2009 dividends depends on whether the preferred stock is noncumulative or cumulative. With noncumulative preferred, the preferred stockholders never receive the $4,000 skipped in 2008. If the preferred stock is cumulative, the $4,000 in arrears is paid in 2009 before any other dividends are paid.

EXHIBIT 13.11

Allocation of Dividends (noncumulative vs. cumulative preferred stock)

Example: What dividends do cumulative preferred stockholders receive in 2009 if the corporation paid only $2,000 of dividends in 2008? How does this affect dividends to common stockholders in 2009? *Answers:* $16,000 ($7,000 dividends in arrears, plus $9,000 current preferred dividends). Dividends to common stockholders decrease to $26,000.

	Preferred	Common
Preferred Stock Is Noncumulative		
Year 2008	$ 5,000	$ 0
Year 2009		
Step 1: Current year's preferred dividend	$ 9,000	
Step 2: Remainder to common		$33,000
Preferred Stock Is Cumulative		
Year 2008	$ 5,000	$ 0
Year 2009		
Step 1: Dividend in arrears	$ 4,000	
Step 2: Current year's preferred dividend	9,000	
Step 3: Remainder to common		$29,000
Totals for year 2009	$13,000	$29,000

A liability for a dividend does not exist until the directors declare a dividend. If a preferred dividend date passes and the corporation's board fails to declare the dividend on its cumulative preferred stock, the dividend in arrears is not a liability. The *full-disclosure principle* requires a corporation to report (usually in a note) the amount of preferred dividends in arrears as of the balance sheet date.

Participating or Nonparticipating Dividend   **Nonparticipating preferred stock** has a feature that limits dividends to a maximum amount each year. This maximum is often stated as a percent of the stock's par value or as a specific dollar amount per share. Once preferred stockholders receive this amount, the common stockholders receive any and all additional dividends. **Participating preferred stock** has a feature allowing preferred stockholders to share with common stockholders in any dividends paid in excess of the percent or dollar amount stated on the preferred stock. This participation feature does not apply until common stockholders receive dividends equal to the preferred stock's dividend percent. Many corporations are authorized to issue participating preferred stock but rarely do, and most managers never expect to issue it.[2]

Convertible Preferred Stock

Preferred stock is more attractive to investors if it carries a right to exchange preferred shares for a fixed number of common shares. **Convertible preferred stock** gives holders the option to

---

[2] Participating preferred stock is usually authorized as a defense against a possible corporate *takeover* by an "unfriendly" investor (or a group of investors) who intends to buy enough voting common stock to gain control. Taking a term from spy novels, the financial world refers to this type of plan as a *poison pill* that a company swallows if enemy investors threaten its capture. A poison pill usually works as follows: A corporation's common stockholders on a given date are granted the right to purchase a large amount of participating preferred stock at a very low price. This right to purchase preferred shares is *not* transferable. If an unfriendly investor buys a large block of common shares (whose right to purchase participating preferred shares does *not* transfer to this buyer), the board can issue preferred shares at a low price to the remaining common shareholders who retained the right to purchase. Future dividends are then divided between the newly issued participating preferred shares and the common shares. This usually transfers value from common shares to preferred shares, causing the unfriendly investor's common stock to lose much of its value and reduces the potential benefit of a hostile takeover.

exchange their preferred shares for common shares at a specified rate. When a company prospers and its common stock increases in value, convertible preferred stockholders can share in this success by converting their preferred stock into more valuable common stock.

Callable Preferred Stock

Callable preferred stock gives the issuing corporation the right to purchase (retire) this stock from its holders at specified future prices and dates. The amount paid to call and retire a preferred share is its **call price,** or *redemption value,* and is set when the stock is issued. The call price normally includes the stock's par value plus a premium giving holders additional return on their investment. When the issuing corporation calls and retires a preferred stock, the terms of the agreement often require it to pay the call price *and* any dividends in arrears.

Point: The issuing corporation has the right, or option, to retire its callable preferred stock.

Decision Insight

IFRSs   Like U.S. GAAP, IFRSs require that preferred stock be classified as debt or equity based on analysis of the stock's contractual terms. However, IFRSs use different criteria for such classification.

Reasons for Issuing Preferred Stock

Corporations issue preferred stock for several reasons. One is to raise capital without sacrificing control. For example, suppose a company's organizers have $100,000 cash to invest and organize a corporation that needs $200,000 of capital to start. If they sell $200,000 worth of common stock (with $100,000 to the organizers), they would have only 50% control and would need to negotiate extensively with other stockholders in making policy. However, if they issue $100,000 worth of common stock to themselves and sell outsiders $100,000 of 8%, cumulative preferred stock with no voting rights, they retain control.

A second reason to issue preferred stock is to boost the return earned by common stockholders. To illustrate, suppose a corporation's organizers expect to earn an annual after-tax income of $24,000 on an investment of $200,000. If they sell and issue $200,000 worth of common stock, the $24,000 income produces a 12% return on the $200,000 of common stockholders' equity. However, if they issue $100,000 of 8% preferred stock to outsiders and $100,000 of common stock to themselves, their own return increases to 16% per year, as shown in Exhibit 13.12.

Net (after-tax) income	$24,000
Less preferred dividends at 8%	(8,000)
Balance to common stockholders	$16,000
Return to common stockholders ($16,000/$100,000)	16%

EXHIBIT 13.12

Return to Common Stockholders When Preferred Stock Is Issued

Common stockholders earn 16% instead of 12% because assets contributed by preferred stockholders are invested to earn $12,000 while the preferred dividend is only $8,000. Use of preferred stock to increase return to common stockholders is an example of **financial leverage** (also called *trading on the equity*). As a general rule, when the dividend rate on preferred stock is less than the rate the corporation earns on its assets, the effect of issuing preferred stock is to increase (or *lever*) the rate earned by common stockholders.

Point: Financial leverage also occurs when debt is issued and the interest rate paid on it is less than the rate earned from using the assets the creditors lend the company.

Other reasons for issuing preferred stock include its appeal to some investors who believe that the corporation's common stock is too risky or that the expected return on common stock is too low.

Decision Maker

Concert Organizer   Assume that you alter your business strategy from organizing concerts targeted at under 1,000 people to those targeted at between 5,000 to 20,000 people. You also incorporate because of increased risk of lawsuits and a desire to issue stock for financing. It is important that you control the company for decisions on whom to schedule. What types of stock do you offer? [Answer—p. 531]

Treasury Stock

P5 Record purchases and sales of treasury stock and the retirement of stock.

Corporations acquire shares of their own stock for several reasons: (1) to use their shares to acquire another corporation, (2) to purchase shares to avoid a hostile takeover of the company, (3) to reissue them to employees as compensation, and (4) to maintain a strong market for their stock or to show management confidence in the current price.

A corporation's reacquired shares are called **treasury stock,** which is similar to unissued stock in several ways: (1) neither treasury stock nor unissued stock is an asset, (2) neither receives cash dividends or stock dividends, and (3) neither allows the exercise of voting rights. However, treasury stock does differ from unissued stock in one major way: The corporation can resell treasury stock at less than par without having the buyers incur a liability, provided it was originally issued at par value or higher. Treasury stock purchases also require management to exercise ethical sensitivity because funds are being paid to specific stockholders instead of all stockholders. Managers must be sure the purchase is in the best interest of all stockholders. These concerns cause companies to fully disclose treasury stock transactions.

Corporations and Treasury Stock

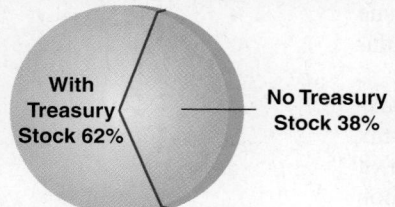

With Treasury Stock 62%   No Treasury Stock 38%

Purchasing Treasury Stock

Purchasing treasury stock reduces the corporation's assets and equity by equal amounts. (We describe the *cost method* of accounting for treasury stock, which is the most widely used method. The *par value* method is another method explained in advanced courses.) To illustrate, Exhibit 13.13 shows Cyber Corporation's account balances *before* any treasury stock purchase (Cyber has no liabilities).

EXHIBIT 13.13

Account Balances *before* Purchasing Treasury Stock

Assets		Stockholders' Equity	
Cash	$ 30,000	Common stock—$10 par; 10,000 shares	
Other assets	95,000	authorized, issued, and outstanding	$100,000
		Retained earnings	25,000
Total assets	$125,000	Total stockholders' equity	$125,000

Cyber then purchases 1,000 of its own shares for $11,500 on May 1, which is recorded as follows.

Assets = Liabilities + Equity
−11,500   −11,500

May 1	Treasury Stock, Common	11,500	
	Cash		11,500
	Purchased 1,000 treasury shares at $11.50 per share.		

This entry reduces equity through the debit to the Treasury Stock account, which is a contra equity account. Exhibit 13.14 shows account balances *after* this transaction.

Assets		Stockholders' Equity	
Cash	$ 18,500	Common stock—$10 par; 10,000 shares authorized and issued; 1,000 shares in treasury	$100,000
Other assets	95,000	Retained earnings, $11,500 restricted by treasury stock purchase	25,000
		Less cost of treasury stock	(11,500)
Total assets	$113,500	Total stockholders' equity	$113,500

EXHIBIT 13.14

Account Balances *after* Purchasing Treasury Stock

The treasury stock purchase reduces Cyber's cash, total assets, and total equity by $11,500 but does not reduce the balance of either the Common Stock or the Retained Earnings account. The equity reduction is reported by deducting the cost of treasury stock in the equity section. Also, two disclosures are evident. First, the stock description reveals that 1,000 issued shares are in treasury, leaving only 9,000 shares still outstanding. Second, the description for retained earnings reveals that it is partly restricted.

Point: The Treasury Stock account is *not* an asset. Treasury stock does not carry voting or dividend rights.

Point: A treasury stock purchase is also called a *stock buyback*.

Reissuing Treasury Stock

Treasury stock can be reissued by selling it at cost, above cost, or below cost.

Selling Treasury Stock at Cost If treasury stock is reissued at cost, the entry is the reverse of the one made to record the purchase. For instance, if on May 21 Cyber reissues 100 of the treasury shares purchased on May 1 at the same $11.50 per share cost, the entry is

May 21	Cash.	1,150	
	Treasury Stock, Common.		1,150
	Received $11.50 per share for 100 treasury shares costing $11.50 per share.		

Assets = Liabilities + Equity
+1,150   +1,150

Selling Treasury Stock *above* Cost If treasury stock is sold for more than cost, the amount received in excess of cost is credited to the Paid-In Capital, Treasury Stock account. This account is reported as a separate item in the stockholders' equity section. No gain is ever reported from the sale of treasury stock. To illustrate, if Cyber receives $12 cash per share for 400 treasury shares costing $11.50 per share on June 3, the entry is

Point: Treasury stock does not represent ownership. A company cannot own a part of itself.

June 3	Cash	4,800	
	Treasury Stock, Common.		4,600
	Paid-In Capital, Treasury Stock.		**200**
	Received $12 per share for 400 treasury shares costing $11.50 per share.		

Assets = Liabilities + Equity
+4,800   +4,600
                +200

Selling Treasury Stock *below* Cost When treasury stock is sold below cost, the entry to record the sale depends on whether the Paid-In Capital, Treasury Stock account has a credit balance. If it has a zero balance, the excess of cost over the sales price is debited to Retained Earnings. If the Paid-In Capital, Treasury Stock account has a credit balance, it is debited for the excess of the cost over the selling price but not to exceed the balance in this account. When the credit balance in this paid-in capital account is eliminated, any remaining difference between the cost and selling price is debited to Retained Earnings. To illustrate, if Cyber sells its remaining 500 shares of treasury stock at $10 per share on July 10,

Point: The phrase *treasury stock* is believed to arise from the fact that reacquired stock is held in a corporation's treasury.

Point: The Paid-In Capital, Treasury Stock account can have a zero or credit balance but never a debit balance.

equity is reduced by $750 (500 shares × $1.50 per share excess of cost over selling price), as shown in this entry:

Assets = Liabilities + Equity
+5,000
−200
−550
+5,750

July 10	Cash	5,000	
	Paid-In Capital, Treasury Stock	**200**	
	Retained Earnings	**550**	
	Treasury Stock, Common.		5,750
	Received $10 per share for 500 treasury shares costing $11.50 per share.		

This entry eliminates the $200 credit balance in the paid-in capital account created on June 3 and then reduces the Retained Earnings balance by the remaining $550 excess of cost over selling price. A company never reports a loss (or gain) from the sale of treasury stock.

Retiring Stock

A corporation can purchase its own stock and retire it. Retiring stock reduces the number of issued shares. Retired stock is the same as authorized and unissued shares. Purchases and retirements of stock are permissible under state law only if they do not jeopardize the interests of creditors and stockholders. When stock is purchased for retirement, we remove all capital amounts related to the retired shares. If the purchase price exceeds the net amount removed, this excess is debited to Retained Earnings. If the net amount removed from all capital accounts exceeds the purchase price, this excess is credited to the Paid-In Capital from Retirement of Stock account. A company's assets and equity are always reduced by the amount paid for the retiring stock.

Point: Recording stock retirement results in canceling the equity from the original issuance of the shares.

Quick Check   Answers—p. 531

16. Purchase of treasury stock (*a*) has no effect on assets; (*b*) reduces total assets and total equity by equal amounts; or (*c*) is recorded with a debit to Retained Earnings.

17. Southern Co. purchases shares of Northern Corp. Should either company classify these shares as treasury stock?

18. How does treasury stock affect the authorized, issued, and outstanding shares?

19. When a company purchases treasury stock, (*a*) retained earnings are restricted by the amount paid; (*b*) Retained Earnings is credited; or (*c*) it is retired.

Reporting of Equity

Statement of Retained Earnings

C4 Explain the items reported in retained earnings.

Retained earnings generally consist of a company's cumulative net income less any net losses and dividends declared since its inception. Retained earnings are part of stockholders' claims on the company's net assets, but this does *not* imply that a certain amount of cash or other assets is available to pay stockholders. For example, Circuit City has $1,336 million in retained earnings, but only $141 million in cash. This section describes events and transactions affecting retained earnings and how retained earnings are reported.

Video13.1

Restrictions and Appropriations The term **restricted retained earnings** refers to both statutory and contractual restrictions. A common *statutory* (or *legal*) *restriction* is to limit treasury stock purchases to the amount of retained earnings. The balance sheet in Exhibit 13.14 provides an example. A common *contractual restriction* involves loan agreements that restrict paying dividends beyond a specified amount or percent of retained earnings. Restrictions are usually described in the notes. The term **appropriated retained earnings** refers to a voluntary transfer of amounts from the Retained Earnings account to the Appropriated Retained Earnings account to inform users of special activities that require funds.

Prior Period Adjustments   **Prior period adjustments** are corrections of material errors in prior period financial statements. These errors include arithmetic mistakes, unacceptable accounting, and missed facts. Prior period adjustments are reported in the *statement of retained earnings* (or the statement of stockholders' equity), net of any income tax effects. Prior period adjustments result in changing the beginning balance of retained earnings for events occurring prior to the earliest period reported in the current set of financial statements. To illustrate, assume that ComUS makes an error in a 2007 journal entry for the purchase of land by incorrectly debiting an expense account. When this is discovered in 2009, the statement of retained earnings includes a prior period adjustment, as shown in Exhibit 13.15. This exhibit also shows the usual format of the statement of retained earnings.

Point: If a year 2007 error is discovered in 2008, the company records the adjustment in 2008. But if the financial statements include 2007 and 2008 figures, the statements report the correct amounts for 2007, and a note describes the correction.

EXHIBIT 13.15

Statement of Retained Earnings with a Prior Period Adjustment

ComUS Statement of Retained Earnings For Year Ended December 31, 2009	
Retained earnings, Dec. 31, 2008, as previously reported	$4,745,000
Prior period adjustment	
Cost of land incorrectly expensed (net of $63,000 income taxes)	147,000
Retained earnings, Dec. 31, 2008, as adjusted	4,892,000
Plus net income	1,224,300
Less cash dividends declared	(301,800)
Retained earnings, Dec. 31, 2009	$5,814,500

Many items reported in financial statements are based on estimates. Future events are certain to reveal that some of these estimates were inaccurate even when based on the best data available at the time. These inaccuracies are *not* considered errors and are *not* reported as prior period adjustments. Instead, they are identified as **changes in accounting estimates** and are accounted for in current and future periods. To illustrate, we know that depreciation is based on estimated useful lives and salvage values. As time passes and new information becomes available, managers may need to change these estimates and the resulting depreciation expense for current and future periods.

Point: Accounting for changes in estimates is sometimes criticized as two wrongs to make a right. Consider a change in an asset's life. Depreciation neither before nor after the change is the amount computed if the revised estimate were originally selected. Regulators chose this approach to avoid restating prior period numbers.

Closing Process   The closing process was explained earlier in the book as: (1) Close credit balances in revenue accounts to Income Summary, (2) Close debit balances in expense accounts to Income Summary, and (3) Close Income Summary to Retained Earnings. If dividends are recorded in a Dividends account, and not as an immediate reduction to Retained Earnings (as shown in this chapter), a fourth step is necessary to close the Dividends account to Retained Earnings.

Statement of Stockholders' Equity

Instead of a separate statement of retained earnings, companies commonly report a statement of stockholders' equity that includes changes in retained earnings. A **statement of stockholders' equity** lists the beginning and ending balances of key equity accounts and describes the changes that occur during the period. The companies in Appendix A report such a statement. The usual format is to provide a column for each component of equity and use the rows to describe events occurring in the period. Exhibit 13.16 shows a condensed statement for Apple.

Reporting Stock Options

The majority of corporations whose shares are publicly traded issue **stock options,** which are rights to purchase common stock at a fixed price over a specified period. As the stock's price rises, the option's value increases. Starbucks and Home Depot offer stock options to both full- and part-time employees. Stock options are said to motivate managers and employees to (1) focus on company performance, (2) take a long-run perspective, and (3) remain with

EXHIBIT 13.16

Statement of Stockholders' Equity

APPLE Statement of Stockholders' Equity					
($ millions, shares in thousands)	Common Stock Shares	Common Stock Amount	Retained Earnings	Other	Total Equity
Balance, Sept. 30, 2006	855,263	$4,355	$5,607	$22	$9,984
Net income	—	—	3,496	—	3,496
Issuance of Common Stock	17,066	364	(2)	—	362
Other	—	649	—	41	690
Cash Dividends ($0.00 per share)	—	—	—	—	—
Balance, Sept. 29, 2007	872,329	$5,368	$9,101	$63	$14,532

Video13.1

the company. A stock option is like having an investment with no risk ("a carrot with no stick").

To illustrate, Quantum grants each of its employees the option to purchase 100 shares of its $1 par value common stock at its current market price of $50 per share anytime within the next 10 years. If the stock price rises to $70 per share, an employee can exercise the option at a gain of $20 per share (acquire a $70 stock at the $50 option price). With 100 shares, a single employee would have a total gain of $2,000, computed as $20 × 100 shares. Companies report the cost of stock options in the income statement. Measurement of this cost is explained in advanced courses.

Decision Analysis

Earnings per Share, Price-Earnings Ratio, Dividend Yield, and Book Value per Share

Earnings per Share

A1 Compute earnings per share and describe its use.

The income statement reports **earnings per share,** also called *EPS* or *net income per share,* which is the amount of income earned per each share of a company's outstanding common stock. The **basic earnings per share** formula is shown in Exhibit 13.17. When a company has no preferred stock, then preferred dividends are zero. The weighted-average common shares outstanding is measured over the income reporting period; its computation is explained in advanced courses.

EXHIBIT 13.17

Basic Earnings per Share

$$\text{Basic earnings per share} = \frac{\text{Net income} - \text{Preferred dividends}}{\text{Weighted-average common shares outstanding}}$$

To illustrate, assume that Quantum Co. earns $40,000 net income in 2009 and declares dividends of $7,500 on its noncumulative preferred stock. (If preferred stock is *non*cumulative, the income available [numerator] is the current period net income less any preferred dividends *declared* in that same period. If preferred stock is cumulative, the income available [numerator] is the current period net income less the preferred dividends whether declared or not.) Quantum has 5,000 weighted-average common shares outstanding during 2009. Its basic EPS[3] is

$$\text{Basic earnings per share} = \frac{\$40,000 - \$7,500}{5,000 \text{ shares}} = \$6.50$$

---

[3] A corporation can be classified as having either a simple or complex capital structure. The term **simple capital structure** refers to a company with only common stock and nonconvertible preferred stock outstanding. The term **complex capital structure** refers to companies with dilutive securities. **Dilutive securities** include options, rights to purchase common stock, and any bonds or preferred stock that are convertible into common stock. A company with a complex capital structure must often report two EPS figures: basic and diluted. **Diluted earnings per share** is computed by adding all dilutive securities to the denominator of the basic EPS computation. It reflects the decrease in basic EPS *assuming* that all dilutive securities are converted into common shares.

Price-Earnings Ratio

A stock's market value is determined by its *expected* future cash flows. A comparison of a company's EPS and its market value per share reveals information about market expectations. This comparison is traditionally made using a **price-earnings** (or **PE) ratio,** expressed also as *price earnings, price to earnings,* or *PE.* Some analysts interpret this ratio as what price the market is willing to pay for a company's current earnings stream. Price-earnings ratios can differ across companies that have similar earnings because of either higher or lower expectations of future earnings. The price-earnings ratio is defined in Exhibit 13.18.

$$\text{Price-earnings ratio} = \frac{\text{Market value (price) per share}}{\text{Earnings per share}}$$

This ratio is often computed using EPS from the most recent period (for Amazon, its PE is 31; for Altria, its PE is 13). However, many users compute this ratio using *expected* EPS for the next period.

Some analysts view stocks with high PE ratios (higher than 20 to 25) as more likely to be overpriced and stocks with low PE ratios (less than 5 to 8) as more likely to be underpriced. These investors prefer to sell or avoid buying stocks with high PE ratios and to buy or hold stocks with low PE ratios. However, investment decision making is rarely so simple as to rely on a single ratio. For instance, a stock with a high PE ratio can prove to be a good investment if its earnings continue to increase beyond current expectations. Similarly, a stock with a low PE ratio can prove to be a poor investment if its earnings decline below expectations.

Decision Maker

Money Manager   You plan to invest in one of two companies identified as having identical future prospects. One has a PE of 19 and the other a PE of 25. Which do you invest in? Does it matter if your *estimate* of PE for these two companies is 29 as opposed to 22? [Answer—p. 531]

Dividend Yield

Investors buy shares of a company's stock in anticipation of receiving a return from either or both cash dividends and stock price increases. Stocks that pay large dividends on a regular basis, called *income stocks,* are attractive to investors who want recurring cash flows from their investments. In contrast, some stocks pay little or no dividends but are still attractive to investors because of their expected stock price increases. The stocks of companies that distribute little or no cash but use their cash to finance expansion are called *growth stocks.* One way to help identify whether a stock is an income stock or a growth stock is to analyze its dividend yield. **Dividend yield,** defined in Exhibit 13.19, shows the annual amount of cash dividends distributed to common shares relative to their market value.

$$\text{Dividend yield} = \frac{\text{Annual cash dividends per share}}{\text{Market value per share}}$$

Dividend yield can be computed for current and prior periods using actual dividends and stock prices and for future periods using expected values. Exhibit 13.20 shows recent dividend and stock price data for **Amazon** and **Altria Group** to compute dividend yield.

Company	Cash Dividends per Share	Market Value per Share	Dividend Yield
Amazon	$0.00	$90	0.0%
Altria Group	3.32	70	4.7

Dividend yield is zero for Amazon, implying it is a growth stock. An investor in Amazon would look for increases in stock prices (and eventual cash from the sale of stock). Altria has a dividend yield of 4.7%, implying it is an income stock for which dividends are important in assessing its value.

A2   Compute price-earnings ratio and describe its use in analysis.

Point: The average PE ratio of stocks in the 1950–2008 period is about 14.

EXHIBIT 13.18
Price-Earnings Ratio

Point: Average PE ratios for U.S. stocks increased over the past two decades. Some analysts interpret this as a signal the market is overpriced. But higher ratios can at least partly reflect accounting changes that have reduced reported earnings.

A3   Compute dividend yield and explain its use in analysis.

EXHIBIT 13.19
Dividend Yield

EXHIBIT 13.20
Dividend and Stock Price Information

Point: The *payout ratio* equals cash dividends declared on common stock divided by net income. A low payout ratio suggests that a company is retaining earnings for future growth.

Book Value per Share

A4   Compute book value and explain its use in analysis.

Case 1: Common Stock (Only) Outstanding. **Book value per common share,** defined in Exhibit 13.21, reflects the amount of equity applicable to *common* shares on a per share basis. To illustrate, we use Dillon Snowboards' data from Exhibit 13.4. Dillon has 30,000 outstanding common shares, and the stockholders' equity applicable to common shares is $365,000. Dillon's book value per common share is $12.17, computed as $365,000 divided by 30,000 shares.

EXHIBIT 13.21

Book Value per Common Share

$$\text{Book value per common share} = \frac{\text{Stockholders' equity applicable to common shares}}{\text{Number of common shares outstanding}}$$

Point: Book value per share is also referred to as *stockholders' claim to assets on a per share basis.*

Case 2: Common and Preferred Stock Outstanding. To compute book value when both common and preferred shares are outstanding, we allocate total equity between the two types of shares. The **book value per preferred share** is computed first; its computation is shown in Exhibit 13.22.

EXHIBIT 13.22

Book Value per Preferred Share

$$\text{Book value per preferred share} = \frac{\text{Stockholders' equity applicable to preferred shares}}{\text{Number of preferred shares outstanding}}$$

The equity applicable to preferred shares equals the preferred share's call price (or par value if the preferred is not callable) plus any cumulative dividends in arrears. The remaining equity is the portion applicable to common shares. To illustrate, consider LTD's equity in Exhibit 13.23. Its preferred stock is callable at $108 per share, and two years of cumulative preferred dividends are in arrears.

EXHIBIT 13.23

Stockholders' Equity with Preferred and Common Stock

Stockholders' Equity	
Preferred stock—$100 par value, 7% cumulative, 2,000 shares authorized, 1,000 shares issued and outstanding	$100,000
Common stock—$25 par value, 12,000 shares authorized, 10,000 shares issued and outstanding	250,000
Paid-in capital in excess of par value, common stock	15,000
Retained earnings	82,000
Total stockholders' equity	$447,000

The book value computations are in Exhibit 13.24. Equity is first allocated to preferred shares before the book value of common shares is computed.

EXHIBIT 13.24

Computing Book Value per Preferred and Common Share

Total stockholders' equity		$447,000
Less equity applicable to preferred shares		
Call price (1,000 shares × $108)	$108,000	
Dividends in arrears ($100,000 × 7% × 2 years)	14,000	(122,000)
Equity applicable to common shares		$325,000
Book value per preferred share ($122,000/1,000 shares)		**$ 122.00**
Book value per common share ($325,000/10,000 shares)		**$ 32.50**

Book value per share reflects the value per share if a company is liquidated at balance sheet amounts. Book value is also the starting point in many stock valuation models, merger negotiations, price setting for public utilities, and loan contracts. The main limitation in using book value is the potential difference between recorded value and market value for assets and liabilities. Investors often adjust their analysis for estimates of these differences.

 Decision Maker

Investor   You are considering investing in **BMX**, whose book value per common share is $4 and price per common share on the stock exchange is $7. From this information, are BMX's net assets priced higher or lower than its recorded values? [Answer—p. 531]

Demonstration Problem 1

Barton Corporation began operations on January 1, 2008. The following transactions relating to stockholders' equity occurred in the first two years of the company's operations.

DP13

2008

Jan. 1   Authorized the issuance of 2 million shares of $5 par value common stock and 100,000 shares of $100 par value, 10% cumulative, preferred stock.
Jan. 2   Issued 200,000 shares of common stock for $12 cash per share.
Jan. 3   Issued 100,000 shares of common stock in exchange for a building valued at $820,000 and merchandise inventory valued at $380,000.
Jan. 4   Paid $10,000 cash to the company's founders for organization activities.
Jan. 5   Issued 12,000 shares of preferred stock for $110 cash per share.

2009

June 4   Issued 100,000 shares of common stock for $15 cash per share.

Required

1. Prepare journal entries to record these transactions.

2. Prepare the stockholders' equity section of the balance sheet as of December 31, 2008, and December 31, 2009, based on these transactions.

3. Prepare a table showing dividend allocations and dividends per share for 2008 and 2009 assuming Barton declares the following cash dividends: 2008, $50,000, and 2009, $300,000.

4. Prepare the January 2, 2008, journal entry for Barton's issuance of 200,000 shares of common stock for $12 cash per share assuming

a. Common stock is no-par stock without a stated value.

b. Common stock is no-par stock with a stated value of $10 per share.

Planning the Solution

- Record journal entries for the transactions for 2008 and 2009.
- Determine the balances for the 2008 and 2009 equity accounts for the balance sheet.
- Prepare the contributed capital portion of the 2008 and 2009 balance sheets.
- Prepare a table similar to Exhibit 13.11 showing dividend allocations for 2008 and 2009.
- Record the issuance of common stock under both specifications of no-par stock.

Solution to Demonstration Problem 1

1. Journal entries.

2008			
Jan. 2	Cash	2,400,000	
	Common Stock, $5 Par Value		1,000,000
	Paid-In Capital in Excess of Par Value, Common Stock		1,400,000
	Issued 200,000 shares of common stock.		
Jan. 3	Building	820,000	
	Merchandise Inventory	380,000	
	Common Stock, $5 Par Value		500,000
	Paid-In Capital in Excess of Par Value, Common Stock		700,000
	Issued 100,000 shares of common stock.		
Jan. 4	Organization Expenses	10,000	
	Cash		10,000
	Paid founders for organization costs.		

[continued on next page]

[continued from previous page]

Jan. 5	Cash	1,320,000	
	Preferred Stock, $100 Par Value		1,200,000
	Paid-In Capital in Excess of Par Value, Preferred Stock		120,000
	Issued 12,000 shares of preferred stock.		
2009			
June 4	Cash	1,500,000	
	Common Stock, $5 Par Value		500,000
	Paid-In Capital in Excess of Par Value, Common Stock		1,000,000
	Issued 100,000 shares of common stock.		

2. Balance sheet presentations (at December 31 year-end).

	2009	2008
Stockholders' Equity		
Preferred stock—$100 par value, 10% cumulative, 100,000 shares authorized, 12,000 shares issued and outstanding	$1,200,000	$1,200,000
Paid-in capital in excess of par value, preferred stock	120,000	120,000
Total paid-in capital by preferred stockholders	1,320,000	1,320,000
Common stock—$5 par value, 2,000,000 shares authorized, 300,000 shares issued and outstanding in 2008, and 400,000 shares issued and outstanding in 2009	2,000,000	1,500,000
Paid-in capital in excess of par value, common stock	3,100,000	2,100,000
Total paid-in capital by common stockholders	5,100,000	3,600,000
Total paid-in capital	$6,420,000	$4,920,000

3. Dividend allocation table.

	Common	Preferred
2008 ($50,000)		
Preferred—current year (12,000 shares × $10 = $120,000)	$ 0	$ 50,000
Common—remainder (300,000 shares outstanding)	0	0
Total for the year	$ 0	$ 50,000
2009 ($300,000)		
Preferred—dividend in arrears from 2008 ($120,000 − $50,000)	$ 0	$ 70,000
Preferred—current year	0	120,000
Common—remainder (400,000 shares outstanding)	110,000	0
Total for the year	$110,000	$190,000
Dividends per share		
2008	$ 0.00	$ 4.17
2009	$ 0.28	$ 15.83

4. Journal entries.

a. For 2008 (no-par stock without a stated value):

Jan. 2	Cash	2,400,000	
	Common Stock, No-Par Value		2,400,000
	Issued 200,000 shares of no-par common stock at $12 per share.		

b. For 2008 (no-par stock with a stated value):

Jan. 2	Cash......................................	2,400,000	
	Common Stock, $10 Stated Value............		2,000,000
	Paid-In Capital in Excess of		
	Stated Value, Common Stock		400,000
	Issued 200,000 shares of $10 stated value		
	common stock at $12 per share.		

Demonstration Problem 2

Precision Company began year 2008 with the following balances in its stockholders' equity accounts.

Common stock—$10 par, 500,000 shares authorized,	
200,000 shares issued and outstanding	$2,000,000
Paid-in capital in excess of par, common stock	1,000,000
Retained earnings	5,000,000
Total	$8,000,000

All outstanding common stock was issued for $15 per share when the company was created. Prepare journal entries to account for the following transactions during year 2008.

Jan. 10   The board declared a $0.10 cash dividend per share to shareholders of record Jan. 28.
Feb. 15   Paid the cash dividend declared on January 10.
Mar. 31   Declared a 20% stock dividend. The market value of the stock is $18 per share.
May   1   Distributed the stock dividend declared on March 31.
July 1   Purchased 30,000 shares of treasury stock at $20 per share.
Sept. 1   Sold 20,000 treasury shares at $26 cash per share.
Dec. 1   Sold the remaining 10,000 shares of treasury stock at $7 cash per share.

Planning the Solution

- Calculate the total cash dividend to record by multiplying the cash dividend declared by the number of shares as of the date of record.
- Decide whether the stock dividend is a small or large dividend. Then analyze each event to determine the accounts affected and the appropriate amounts to be recorded.

Solution to Demonstration Problem 2

Jan. 10	Retained Earnings............................	20,000	
	Common Dividend Payable		20,000
	Declared a $0.10 per share cash dividend.		
Feb. 15	Common Dividend Payable....................	20,000	
	Cash		20,000
	Paid $0.10 per share cash dividend.		
Mar. 31	Retained Earnings............................	720,000	
	Common Stock Dividend Distributable........		400,000
	Paid-In Capital in Excess of		
	Par Value, Common Stock		320,000
	Declared a small stock dividend of 20% or		
	40,000 shares; market value is $18 per share.		

[continued on next page]

[continued from previous page]

May 1	Common Stock Dividend Distributable	400,000	
	Common Stock.		400,000
	Distributed 40,000 shares of common stock.		
July 1	Treasury Stock, Common	600,000	
	Cash		600,000
	Purchased 30,000 common shares at $20 per share.		
Sept. 1	Cash	520,000	
	Treasury Stock, Common.		400,000
	Paid-In Capital, Treasury Stock		120,000
	Sold 20,000 treasury shares at $26 per share.		
Dec. 1	Cash	70,000	
	Paid-In Capital, Treasury Stock.	120,000	
	Retained Earnings.	10,000	
	Treasury Stock, Common.		200,000
	Sold 10,000 treasury shares at $7 per share.		

Summary

C1 Identify characteristics of corporations and their organization. Corporations are legal entities whose stockholders are not liable for its debts. Stock is easily transferred, and the life of a corporation does not end with the incapacity of a stock holder. A corporation acts through its agents, who are its officers and managers. Corporations are regulated and subject to income taxes.

C2 Describe the components of stockholders' equity. Authorized stock is the stock that a corporation's charter authorizes it to sell. Issued stock is the portion of authorized shares sold. Par value stock is a value per share assigned by the charter. No-par value stock is stock *not* assigned a value per share by the charter. Stated value stock is no-par stock to which the directors assign a value per share. Stockholders' equity is made up of (1) paid-in capital and (2) retained earnings. Paid-in capital consists of funds raised by stock issuances. Retained earnings consists of cumulative net income (losses) not distributed.

C3 Explain characteristics of common and preferred stock. Preferred stock has a priority (or senior status) relative to common stock in one or more areas, usually (1) dividends and (2) assets in case of liquidation. Preferred stock usually does not carry voting rights and can be convertible or callable. Convertibility permits the holder to convert preferred to common. Callability permits the issuer to buy back preferred stock under specified conditions.

C4 Explain the items reported in retained earnings. Many companies face statutory and contractual restrictions on retained earnings. Corporations can voluntarily appropriate retained earnings to inform others about their disposition. Prior period adjustments are corrections of errors in prior financial statements.

A1 Compute earnings per share and describe its use. A company with a simple capital structure computes basic EPS by dividing net income less any preferred dividends by the weighted-average number of outstanding common shares. A company with a complex capital structure must usually report both basic and diluted EPS.

A2 Compute price-earnings ratio and describe its use in analysis. A common stock's price-earnings (PE) ratio is computed by dividing the stock's market value (price) per share by its EPS. A stock's PE is based on expectations that can prove to be better or worse than eventual performance.

A3 Compute dividend yield and explain its use in analysis. Dividend yield is the ratio of a stock's annual cash dividends per share to its market value (price) per share. Dividend yield can be compared with the yield of other companies to determine whether the stock is expected to be an income or growth stock.

A4 Compute book value and explain its use in analysis. Book value per common share is equity applicable to common shares divided by the number of outstanding common shares. Book value per preferred share is equity applicable to preferred shares divided by the number of outstanding preferred shares.

P1 Record the issuance of corporate stock. When stock is issued, its par or stated value is credited to the stock account and any excess is credited to a separate contributed capital account. If a stock has neither par nor stated value, the entire proceeds are credited to the stock account. Stockholders must contribute assets equal to minimum legal capital or be potentially liable for the deficiency.

P2 Record transactions involving cash dividends. Cash dividends involve three events. On the date of declaration, the directors bind the company to pay the dividend. A dividend declaration reduces retained earnings and creates a current liability. On the date of record, recipients of the dividend are identified. On the date of payment, cash is paid to stockholders and the current liability is removed.

P3 Account for stock dividends and stock splits. Neither a stock dividend nor a stock split alters the value of the company. However, the value of each share is less due to the distribution of additional shares. The distribution of additional shares is according to individual stockholders' ownership percent. Small stock dividends (≤25%) are recorded by capitalizing retained earnings equal to the market value of distributed shares. Large stock dividends (>25%) are recorded by capitalizing retained earnings equal to the par or stated value of distributed shares. Stock splits do not yield journal entries but do yield changes in the description of stock.

P4 **Distribute dividends between common stock and preferred stock.** Preferred stockholders usually hold the right to dividend distributions before common stockholders. When preferred stock is cumulative and in arrears, the amount in arrears must be distributed to preferred before any dividends are distributed to common.

P5 **Record purchases and sales of treasury stock and the retirement of stock.** When a corporation purchases its own previously issued stock, it debits the cost of these shares to Treasury Stock. Treasury stock is subtracted from equity in the balance sheet. If treasury stock is reissued, any proceeds in excess of cost are credited to Paid-In Capital, Treasury Stock. If the proceeds are less than cost, they are debited to Paid-In Capital, Treasury Stock to the extent a credit balance exists. Any remaining amount is debited to Retained Earnings. When stock is retired, all accounts related to the stock are removed.

Guidance Answers to **Decision Maker** and **Decision Ethics**

Entrepreneur The 50% stock dividend provides you no direct income. A stock dividend often reveals management's optimistic expectations about the future and can improve a stock's marketability by making it affordable to more investors. Accordingly, a stock dividend usually reveals "good news" and because of this, it likely increases (slightly) the market value for your stock. The same conclusions apply to the 3-for-2 stock split.

Concert Organizer You have two basic options: (1) different classes of common stock or (2) common and preferred stock. Your objective is to issue to yourself stock that has all or a majority of the voting power. The other class of stock would carry limited or no voting rights. In this way, you maintain control and are able to raise the necessary funds.

Money Manager Since one company requires a payment of $19 for each $1 of earnings, and the other requires $25, you would pre-

fer the stock with the PE of 19; it is a better deal given identical prospects. You should make sure these companies' earnings computations are roughly the same, for example, no extraordinary items, unusual events, and so forth. Also, your PE estimates for these companies do matter. If you are willing to pay $29 for each $1 of earnings for these companies, you obviously expect both to exceed current market expectations.

Investor Book value reflects recorded values. BMX's book value is $4 per common share. Stock price reflects the market's expectation of net asset value (both tangible and intangible items). BMX's market value is $7 per common share. Comparing these figures suggests BMX's market value of net assets is higher than its recorded values (by an amount of $7 versus $4 per share).

Guidance Answers to **Quick Checks**

1. (*b*)

2. A corporation pays taxes on its income, and its stockholders normally pay personal income taxes (at the 15% rate or lower) on any cash dividends received from the corporation.

3. A proxy is a legal document used to transfer a stockholder's right to vote to another person.

4. (*a*)

5. A stock premium is an amount in excess of par (or stated) value paid by purchasers of newly issued stock.

6. Minimum legal capital intends to protect creditors of a corporation by obligating stockholders to some minimum level of equity financing and by constraining a corporation from excessive payments to stockholders.

7. Common Dividend Payable is a current liability account.

8. The date of declaration, date of record, and date of payment.

9. A dividend is a legal liability at the date of declaration, on which date it is recorded as a liability.

10. A stock dividend does not transfer assets to stockholders, but it does require an amount of retained earnings to be transferred to a contributed capital account(s).

11. A small stock dividend is 25% or less of the previous outstanding shares. A large stock dividend is more than 25%.

12. Retained earnings equal to the distributable shares' market value should be capitalized for a small stock dividend.

13. Typically, preferred stock has a preference in receipt of dividends and in distribution of assets.

14. (*a*)

15. (*b*)

Total cash dividend	$288,000
To preferred shareholders	135,000*
Remainder to common shareholders	$153,000

* 9,000 × $50 × 10% × 3 years = $135,000.

16. (*b*)

17. No. The shares are an investment for Southern Co. and are issued and outstanding shares for Northern Corp.

18. Treasury stock does not affect the number of authorized or issued shares, but it reduces the outstanding shares.

19. (*a*)

Key Terms

mhhe.com/wildFAP19e

Key Terms are available at the book's Website for learning and testing in an online Flashcard Format.

Appropriated retained earnings (p. 523)	Discount on stock (p. 511)	Preemptive right (p. 508)
Authorized stock (p. 509)	Dividend in arrears (p. 517)	Preferred stock (p. 516)
Basic earnings per share (p. 524)	Dividend yield (p. 525)	Premium on stock (p. 511)
Book value per common share (p. 526)	Earnings per share (EPS) (p. 524)	Price-earnings (PE) ratio (p. 525)
Book value per preferred share (p. 526)	Financial leverage (p. 519)	Prior period adjustments (p. 523)
Call price (p. 519)	Large stock dividend (p. 514)	Proxy (p. 507)
Callable preferred stock (p. 519)	Liquidating cash dividend (p. 514)	Restricted retained earnings (p. 522)
Capital stock (p. 509)	Market value per share (p. 509)	Retained earnings (p. 510)
Changes in accounting estimates (p. 523)	Minimum legal capital (p. 509)	Retained earnings deficit (p. 513)
Common stock (p. 508)	Noncumulative preferred stock (p. 517)	Reverse stock split (p. 516)
Complex capital structure (p. 524)	Nonparticipating preferred stock (p. 518)	Simple capital structure (p. 524)
Convertible preferred stock (p. 518)	No-par value stock (p. 509)	Small stock dividend (p. 514)
Corporation (p. 506)	Organization expenses (pp. 507, 512)	Stated value stock (p. 510)
Cumulative preferred stock (p. 517)	Paid-in capital (p. 510)	Statement of stockholders' equity (p. 523)
Date of declaration (p. 513)	Paid-in capital in excess of par value (p. 511)	Stock dividend (p. 514)
Date of payment (p. 513)		Stock options (p. 523)
Date of record (p. 513)	Participating preferred stock (p. 518)	Stock split (p. 516)
Diluted earnings per share (p. 524)	Par value (p. 509)	Stockholders' equity (p. 510)
Dilutive securities (p. 524)	Par value stock (p. 509)	Treasury stock (p. 520)

Multiple Choice Quiz

Answers on p. 547   mhhe.com/wildFAP19e

Additional Quiz Questions are available at the book's Website.

Quiz13

1. A corporation issues 6,000 shares of $5 par value common stock for $8 cash per share. The entry to record this transaction includes:
  a. A debit to Paid-In Capital in Excess of Par Value for $18,000.
  b. A credit to Common Stock for $48,000.
  c. A credit to Paid-In Capital in Excess of Par Value for $30,000.
  d. A credit to Cash for $48,000.
  e. A credit to Common Stock for $30,000.

2. A company reports net income of $75,000. Its weighted-average common shares outstanding is 19,000. It has no other stock outstanding. Its earnings per share is:
  a. $4.69
  b. $3.95
  c. $3.75
  d. $2.08
  e. $4.41

3. A company has 5,000 shares of $100 par preferred stock and 50,000 shares of $10 par common stock outstanding. Its total stockholders' equity is $2,000,000. Its book value per common share is:
  a. $100.00
  b. $ 10.00

  c. $ 40.00
  d. $ 30.00
  e. $ 36.36

4. A company paid cash dividends of $0.81 per share. Its earnings per share is $6.95 and its market price per share is $45.00. Its dividend yield is:
  a. 1.8%
  b. 11.7%
  c. 15.4%
  d. 55.6%
  e. 8.6%

5. A company's shares have a market value of $85 per share. Its net income is $3,500,000, and its weighted-average common shares outstanding is 700,000. Its price-earnings ratio is:
  a. 5.9
  b. 425.0
  c. 17.0
  d. 10.4
  e. 41.2

Discussion Questions

1. What are organization expenses? Provide examples.
2. How are organization expenses reported?
3. ♟ Who is responsible for directing a corporation's affairs?
4. What is the preemptive right of common stockholders?
5. List the general rights of common stockholders.
6. What is the difference between authorized shares and outstanding shares?
7. ♟ Why would an investor find convertible preferred stock attractive?
8. What is the difference between the market value per share and the par value per share?
9. What is the difference between the par value and the call price of a share of preferred stock?
10. Identify and explain the importance of the three dates relevant to corporate dividends.
11. Why is the term *liquidating dividend* used to describe cash dividends debited against paid-in capital accounts?
12. ♟ How does declaring a stock dividend affect the corporation's assets, liabilities, and total equity? What are the effects of the eventual distribution of that stock?
13. ♟ What is the difference between a stock dividend and a stock split?
14. ♟ Courts have ruled that a stock dividend is not taxable income to stockholders. What justifies this decision?

15. How does the purchase of treasury stock affect the purchaser's assets and total equity?
16. ♟ Why do laws place limits on treasury stock purchases?
17. How are EPS results computed for a corporation with a simple capital structure?
18. What is a stock option?
19. How is book value per share computed for a corporation with no preferred stock? What is the main limitation of using book value per share to value a corporation?
20. Review the balance sheet for **Best Buy** in Appendix A and list the classes of stock that it has issued.
21. ♟ Refer to the balance sheet for **Circuit City** in Appendix A. What is the par value per share of its common stock? Suggest a rationale for the amount of par value it assigned.
22. Refer to **RadioShack**'s balance sheet in Appendix A. How many shares of common stock are authorized? How many shares of common stock are issued?
23. ♟ Refer to the financial statements for **Apple** in Appendix A. What are its cash proceeds from issuance of common stock and its cash repurchases of common stock for the year ended September 30, 2006? Explain.

♟ *Denotes Discussion Questions that involve decision making.*

McGraw-Hill's HOMEWORK MANAGER® ■ ▼ ■ ▲ Available with McGraw-Hill's Homework Manager

Of the following statements, which are true for the corporate form of organization?
1. Capital is more easily accumulated than with most other forms of organization.
2. Corporate income that is distributed to shareholders is usually taxed twice.
3. Owners have unlimited liability for corporate debts.
4. Ownership rights cannot be easily transferred.
5. Owners are not agents of the corporation.
6. It is a separate legal entity.
7. It has a limited life.

QUICK STUDY

QS 13-1
Characteristics of corporations

C1

Prepare the journal entry to record Miltone Company's issuance of 50,000 shares of $1 par value common stock assuming the shares sell for:
a. $1 cash per share.
b. $3 cash per share.

QS 13-2
Issuance of common stock

P1

Prepare the journal entry to record Katrick Company's issuance of 75,000 shares of its common stock assuming the shares have a:
a. $5 par value and sell for $12 cash per share.
b. $5 stated value and sell for $12 cash per share.

QS 13-3
Issuance of par and stated value common stock

P1

QS 13-4

Issuance of no-par common stock

P1

Prepare the journal entry to record Gaylord Company's issuance of 52,000 shares of no-par value common stock assuming the shares:

a. Sell for $30 cash per share.

b. Are exchanged for land valued at $1,560,000.

QS 13-5

Issuance of common stock

P1

Prepare the issuer's journal entry for each separate transaction. (*a*) On March 1, Atlantic Co. issues 37,500 shares of $5 par value common stock for $300,000 cash. (*b*) On April 1, BP Co. issues no-par value common stock for $90,000 cash. (*c*) On April 6, MPG issues 3,500 shares of $10 par value common stock for $20,000 of inventory, $130,000 of machinery, and acceptance of a $75,000 note payable.

QS 13-6

Issuance of preferred stock

C3

a. Prepare the journal entry to record Tamar Company's issuance of 6,000 shares of $100 par value 6% cumulative preferred stock for $102 cash per share.

b. Assuming the facts in part 1, if Tamar declares a year-end cash dividend, what is the amount of dividend paid to preferred shareholders? (Assume no dividends in arrears.)

QS 13-7

Accounting for cash dividends

P2

Prepare journal entries to record the following transactions for Forrest Corporation.

May 15   Declared a $32,000 cash dividend payable to common stockholders.
June 30   Paid the dividend declared on May 15.

QS 13-8

Accounting for small stock dividend

C2 P3

The stockholders' equity section of Atari Company's balance sheet as of April 1 follows. On April 2, Atari declares and distributes a 10% stock dividend. The stock's per share market value on April 2 is $18 (prior to the dividend). Prepare the stockholders' equity section immediately after the stock dividend.

Common stock—$5 par value, 375,000 shares authorized, 200,000 shares issued and outstanding	$1,000,000
Paid-in capital in excess of par value, common stock	600,000
Retained earnings	833,000
Total stockholders' equity	$2,433,000

QS 13-9

Dividend allocation between classes of shareholders

P4

Stockholders' equity of Marwick Company consists of 10,000 shares of $20 par value, 8% cumulative preferred stock and 400,000 shares of $1 par value common stock. Both classes of stock have been outstanding since the company's inception. Marwick did not declare any dividends in the prior year, but it now declares and pays a $92,000 cash dividend at the current year-end. Determine the amount distributed to each class of stockholders for this two-year-old company.

QS 13-10

Purchase and sale of treasury stock   P5

On May 3, Winmac Corporation purchased 3,000 shares of its own stock for $45,000 cash; On November 4, Winmac reissued 850 shares of this treasury stock for $14,450. Prepare the May 3 and November 4 journal entries to record Winmac's purchase and reissuance of treasury stock.

QS 13-11

Accounting for changes in estimates; error adjustments

C4

Answer the following questions related to a company's activities for the current year:

1. A review of the notes payable files discovers that three years ago the company reported the entire amount of a payment (principal and interest) on an installment note payable as interest expense. This mistake had a material effect on the amount of income in that year. How should the correction be reported in the current year financial statements?

2. After using an expected useful life of seven years and no salvage value to depreciate its office equipment over the preceding three years, the company decided early this year that the equipment will last only two more years. How should the effects of this decision be reported in the current year financial statements?

Campbell Company reports net income of $840,000 for the year. It has no preferred stock, and its weighted-average common shares outstanding is 300,000 shares. Compute its basic earnings per share.

QS 13-12
Basic earnings per share A1

Epic Company earned net income of $950,000 this year. The number of common shares outstanding during the entire year was 400,000, and preferred shareholders received a $40,000 cash dividend. Compute Epic Company's basic earnings per share.

QS 13-13
Basic earnings per share A1

Compute Tripp Company's price-earnings ratio if its common stock has a market value of $31.50 per share and its EPS is $3.75. Would an analyst likely consider this stock potentially over- or underpriced? Explain.

QS 13-14
Price-earnings ratio A2

Payne Company expects to pay a $1.62 per share cash dividend this year on its common stock. The current market value of Payne stock is $22.50 per share. Compute the expected dividend yield on the Payne stock. Would you classify the Payne stock as a growth or an income stock? Explain.

QS 13-15
Dividend yield

A3

The stockholders' equity section of Klaus Company's balance sheet follows. The preferred stock's call price is $25. Determine the book value per share of the common stock.

QS 13-16
Book value per common share

A4

Preferred stock—5% cumulative, $10 par value, 20,000 shares authorized, issued and outstanding	$ 200,000
Common stock—$5 par value, 200,000 shares authorized, 150,000 shares issued and outstanding	750,000
Retained earnings	889,500
Total stockholders' equity	$1,839,500

McGraw-Hill's
HOMEWORK
MANAGER®   Available with McGraw-Hill's Homework Manager

Describe how each of the following characteristics of organizations applies to corporations.

EXERCISES

1. Owner authority and control
2. Ease of formation
3. Transferability of ownership
4. Ability to raise large capital amounts
5. Duration of life
6. Owner liability
7. Legal status
8. Tax status of income

Exercise 13-1
Characteristics of corporations

C1

Rodriguez Corporation issues 12,000 shares of its common stock for $182,700 cash on February 20. Prepare journal entries to record this event under each of the following separate situations.
1. The stock has neither par nor stated value.
2. The stock has a $12 par value.
3. The stock has a $6 stated value.

Exercise 13-2
Accounting for par, stated, and no-par stock issuances

P1

Prepare journal entries to record the following four separate issuances of stock.
1. A corporation issued 2,500 shares of no-par common stock to its promoters in exchange for their efforts, estimated to be worth $43,500. The stock has no stated value.
2. A corporation issued 2,500 shares of no-par common stock to its promoters in exchange for their efforts, estimated to be worth $43,500. The stock has a $2 per share stated value.
3. A corporation issued 5,000 shares of $30 par value common stock for $180,000 cash.
4. A corporation issued 1,250 shares of $100 par value preferred stock for $168,500 cash.

Exercise 13-3
Recording stock issuances

P1

Soku Company issues 12,000 shares of $9 par value common stock in exchange for land and a building. The land is valued at $75,000 and the building at $120,000. Prepare the journal entry to record issuance of the stock in exchange for the land and building.

Exercise 13-4
Stock issuance for noncash assets

P1

Exercise 13-5
Identifying characteristics of preferred stock

C2 C3

Match each description 1 through 6 with the characteristic of preferred stock that it best describes by writing the letter of that characteristic in the blank next to each description.

A. Convertible   **B.** Cumulative   **C.** Noncumulative

D. Nonparticipating   **E.** Participating   **F.** Callable

_____ **1.** Holders of the stock are entitled to receive current and all past dividends before common stockholders receive any dividends.

_____ **2.** The issuing corporation can retire the stock by paying a prespecified price.

_____ **3.** Holders of the stock can receive dividends exceeding the stated rate under certain conditions.

_____ **4.** Holders of the stock are not entitled to receive dividends in excess of the stated rate.

_____ **5.** Holders of this stock can exchange it for shares of common stock.

_____ **6.** Holders of the stock lose any dividends that are not declared in the current year.

Exercise 13-6
Stock dividends and splits

P3

On June 30, 2009, Samson Corporation's common stock is priced at $30.50 per share before any stock dividend or split, and the stockholders' equity section of its balance sheet appears as follows.

Common stock—$8 par value, 80,000 shares authorized, 32,000 shares issued and outstanding	$256,000
Paid-in capital in excess of par value, common stock	100,000
Retained earnings	356,000
Total stockholders' equity	$712,000

1. Assume that the company declares and immediately distributes a 100% stock dividend. This event is recorded by capitalizing retained earnings equal to the stock's par value. Answer these questions about stockholders' equity as it exists *after* issuing the new shares.

     a. What is the retained earnings balance?

     b. What is the amount of total stockholders' equity?

     c. How many shares are outstanding?

2. Assume that the company implements a 2-for-1 stock split instead of the stock dividend in part 1. Answer these questions about stockholders' equity as it exists *after* issuing the new shares.

     a. What is the retained earnings balance?

     b. What is the amount of total stockholders' equity?

     c. How many shares are outstanding?

3. Explain the difference, if any, to a stockholder from receiving new shares distributed under a large stock dividend versus a stock split.

Check (1b) $712,000

(2a) $356,000

Exercise 13-7
Stock dividends and per share book values

P3

The stockholders' equity of Tyron Company at the beginning of the day on February 5 follows.

Common stock—$25 par value, 150,000 shares authorized, 64,000 shares issued and outstanding	$1,600,000
Paid-in capital in excess of par value, common stock	525,000
Retained earnings	671,800
Total stockholders' equity	$2,796,800

On February 5, the directors declare a 15% stock dividend distributable on February 28 to the February 15 stockholders of record. The stock's market value is $50 per share on February 5 before the stock dividend. The stock's market value is $43.60 per share on February 28.

1. Prepare entries to record both the dividend declaration and its distribution.

2. One stockholder owned 900 shares on February 5 before the dividend. Compute the book value per share and total book value of this stockholder's shares immediately before *and* after the stock dividend of February 5.

3. Compute the total market value of the investor's shares in part 2 as of February 5 and February 28.

Check (2) Book value per share: before, $43.70; after, $38.00

Norton's outstanding stock consists of (*a*) 13,000 shares of noncumulative 8% preferred stock with a $10 par value and (*b*) 32,500 shares of common stock with a $1 par value. During its first four years of operation, the corporation declared and paid the following total cash dividends.

2009	$ 8,000
2010	24,000
2011	120,000
2012	197,000

Determine the amount of dividends paid each year to each of the two classes of stockholders. Also compute the total dividends paid to each class for the four years combined.

Exercise 13-8
Dividends on common and noncumulative preferred stock
P4

Check   Total paid to preferred, $39,200

Use the data in Exercise 13-8 to determine the amount of dividends paid each year to each of the two classes of stockholders assuming that the preferred stock is cumulative. Also determine the total dividends paid to each class for the four years combined.

Exercise 13-9
Dividends on common and cumulative preferred stock   P4

On October 10, the stockholders' equity of Syntax Systems appears as follows.

Common stock—$10 par value, 72,000 shares authorized, issued, and outstanding	$ 720,000
Paid-in capital in excess of par value, common stock	216,000
Retained earnings	864,000
Total stockholders' equity	$1,800,000

1. Prepare journal entries to record the following transactions for Syntax Systems.
   a. Purchased 5,000 shares of its own common stock at $22 per share on October 11.
   b. Sold 1,000 treasury shares on November 1 for $28 cash per share.
   c. Sold all remaining treasury shares on November 25 for $17 cash per share.
2. Explain how the company's equity section changes after the October 11 treasury stock purchase, and prepare the revised equity section of its balance sheet at that date.

Exercise 13-10
Recording and reporting treasury stock transactions
P5

Check   (1c) Dr. Retained Earnings, $14,000

The following information is available for Arturo Company for the year ended December 31, 2009.
a. Balance of retained earnings, December 31, 2008, prior to discovery of error, $1,375,000.
b. Cash dividends declared and paid during 2009, $43,000.
c. It neglected to record 2007 depreciation expense of $55,500, which is net of $4,500 in income taxes.
d. The company earned $126,000 in 2009 net income.
Prepare a 2009 statement of retained earnings for Arturo Company.

Exercise 13-11
Preparing a statement of retained earnings
C4

Grossmont Company reports $1,375,500 of net income for 2009 and declares $192,500 of cash dividends on its preferred stock for 2009. At the end of 2009, the company had 350,000 weighted-average shares of common stock.
1. What amount of net income is available to common stockholders for 2009?
2. What is the company's basic EPS for 2009?

Exercise 13-12
Earnings per share
A1

Check   (2) $3.38

Franklin Company reports $1,875,000 of net income for 2009 and declares $262,500 of cash dividends on its preferred stock for 2009. At the end of 2009, the company had 250,000 weighted-average shares of common stock.
1. What amount of net income is available to common stockholders for 2009?
2. What is the company's basic EPS for 2009?

Exercise 13-13
Earnings per share
A1

Check   (2) $6.45

Exercise 13-14
Price-earnings ratio computation and interpretation

A2

Compute the price-earnings ratio for each of these four separate companies. Which stock might an analyst likely investigate as being potentially undervalued by the market? Explain.

Company	Earnings per Share	Market Value per Share
1	$12.00	$145.20
2	11.00	116.60
3	7.80	74.10
4	43.20	60.48

Exercise 13-15
Dividend yield computation and interpretation

A3

Compute the dividend yield for each of these four separate companies. Which company's stock would probably *not* be classified as an income stock? Explain.

Company	Annual Cash Dividend per Share	Market Value per Share
1	$14.00	$229.51
2	11.00	110.00
3	5.52	60.00
4	1.90	118.75

Exercise 13-16
Book value per share

A4

The equity section of Westchester Corporation's balance sheet shows the following.

Preferred stock—6% cumulative, $30 par value, $35 call price, 10,000 shares issued and outstanding	$300,000
Common stock—$10 par value, 35,000 shares issued and outstanding	350,000
Retained earnings	267,500
Total stockholders' equity	$917,500

Check (1) Book value of common, $16.21

Determine the book value per share of the preferred and common stock under two separate situations.

1. No preferred dividends are in arrears.

2. Three years of preferred dividends are in arrears.

McGraw-Hill's
Available with McGraw-Hill's Homework Manager

PROBLEM SET A

Problem 13-1A
Stockholders' equity transactions and analysis

C2 C3 P1

Keshena Co. is incorporated at the beginning of this year and engages in a number of transactions. The following journal entries impacted its stockholders' equity during its first year of operations.

a.	Cash..	320,000	
	Common Stock, $25 Par Value..............		250,000
	Paid-In Capital in Excess of Par Value, Common Stock		70,000
b.	Organization Expenses	160,000	
	Common Stock, $25 Par Value..............		125,000
	Paid-In Capital in Excess of Par Value, Common Stock		35,000

[continued on next page]

[continued from previous page]

c.	Cash	45,500	
	Accounts Receivable.	16,000	
	Building	82,000	
	Notes Payable.		59,500
	Common Stock, $25 Par Value		50,000
	Paid-In Capital in Excess of		
	Par Value, Common Stock		34,000
d.	Cash	123,000	
	Common Stock, $25 Par Value		75,000
	Paid-In Capital in Excess of		
	Par Value, Common Stock		48,000

Required

1. Explain the transaction(s) underlying each journal entry (*a*) through (*d*).

2. How many shares of common stock are outstanding at year-end?

3. What is the amount of minimum legal capital (based on par value) at year-end?

4. What is the total paid-in capital at year-end?

5. What is the book value per share of the common stock at year-end if total paid-in capital plus retained earnings equals $785,000?

Check (2) 20,000 shares
(3) $500,000
(4) $687,000

Rocklin Corporation reports the following components of stockholders' equity on December 31, 2009.

Problem 13-2A
Cash dividends, treasury stock, and statement of retained earnings

C2   C4   P2   P5

Common stock—$25 par value, 100,000 shares authorized, 45,000 shares issued and outstanding	$1,125,000
Paid-in capital in excess of par value, common stock	60,000
Retained earnings	460,000
Total stockholders' equity	$1,645,000

In year 2010, the following transactions affected its stockholders' equity accounts.

Jan.	1	Purchased 4,500 shares of its own stock at $25 cash per share.
Jan.	5	Directors declared a $3 per share cash dividend payable on Feb. 28 to the Feb. 5 stockholders of record.
Feb.	28	Paid the dividend declared on January 5.
July	6	Sold 1,688 of its treasury shares at $29 cash per share.
Aug.	22	Sold 2,812 of its treasury shares at $22 cash per share.
Sept.	5	Directors declared a $3 per share cash dividend payable on October 28 to the September 25 stockholders of record.
Oct.	28	Paid the dividend declared on September 5.
Dec.	31	Closed the $388,000 credit balance (from net income) in the Income Summary account to Retained Earnings.

Required

1. Prepare journal entries to record each of these transactions for 2010.

2. Prepare a statement of retained earnings for the year ended December 31, 2010.

3. Prepare the stockholders' equity section of the company's balance sheet as of December 31, 2010.

Check   (2) Retained earnings, Dec. 31, 2010, $589,816.

At September 30, the end of Chan Company's third quarter, the following stockholders' equity accounts are reported.

Problem 13-3A
Equity analysis—journal entries and account balances

P2   P3

Common stock, $10 par value	$420,000
Paid-in capital in excess of par value, common stock	100,000
Retained earnings	400,000

In the fourth quarter, the following entries related to its equity are recorded.

Oct. 2	Retained Earnings............................	63,000	
	Common Dividend Payable		63,000
Oct. 25	Common Dividend Payable	63,000	
	Cash		63,000
Oct. 31	Retained Earnings	92,400	
	Common Stock Dividend Distributable		42,000
	Paid-In Capital in Excess of Par Value, Common Stock		50,400
Nov. 5	Common Stock Dividend Distributable	42,000	
	Common Stock, $10 Par Value		42,000
Dec. 1	Memo—Change the title of the common stock account to reflect the new par value of $5.		
Dec. 31	Income Summary	230,000	
	Retained Earnings		230,000

Required

1. Explain the transaction(s) underlying each journal entry.
2. Complete the following table showing the equity account balances at each indicated date (include the balances from September 30).

	Oct. 2	Oct. 25	Oct. 31	Nov. 5	Dec. 1	Dec. 31
Common stock	$____	$____	$____	$____	$____	$____
Common stock dividend distributable	____	____	____	____	____	____
Paid-in capital in excess of par, common stock	____	____	____	____	____	____
Retained earnings	____	____	____	____	____	____
Total equity	$____	$____	$____	$____	$____	$____

Check Total equity: Oct. 2, $857,000; Dec. 31, $1,087,000

Problem 13-4A
Analysis of changes in stockholders' equity accounts

C4 P2 P3 P5

The equity sections from Sierra Group's 2009 and 2010 year-end balance sheets follow.

Stockholders' Equity (December 31, 2009)

Common stock—$6 par value, 100,000 shares authorized, 45,000 shares issued and outstanding	$270,000
Paid-in capital in excess of par value, common stock	230,000
Retained earnings	340,000
Total stockholders' equity	$840,000

Stockholders' Equity (December 31, 2010)

Common stock—$6 par value, 100,000 shares authorized, 53,200 shares issued, 4,000 shares in treasury	$319,200
Paid-in capital in excess of par value, common stock	262,800
Retained earnings ($60,000 restricted by treasury stock)	400,000
	982,000
Less cost of treasury stock	(60,000)
Total stockholders' equity	$922,000

The following transactions and events affected its equity during year 2010.

Jan.   5   Declared a $0.50 per share cash dividend, date of record January 10.
Mar. 20   Purchased treasury stock for cash.
Apr.   5   Declared a $0.50 per share cash dividend, date of record April 10.
July   5   Declared a $0.50 per share cash dividend, date of record July 10.
July 31   Declared a 20% stock dividend when the stock's market value is $10 per share.

Aug. 14   Issued the stock dividend that was declared on July 31.
Oct.   5   Declared a $0.50 per share cash dividend, date of record October 10.

Required

1. How many common shares are outstanding on each cash dividend date?

2. What is the total dollar amount for each of the four cash dividends?

3. What is the amount of the capitalization of retained earnings for the stock dividend?

4. What is the per share cost of the treasury stock purchased?

5. How much net income did the company earn during year 2010?

Check   (3) $82,000

(4) $15

(5) $230,100

Folsom Corporation's common stock is currently selling on a stock exchange at $183 per share, and its current balance sheet shows the following stockholders' equity section.

Problem 13-5A
Computation of book values and dividend allocations

C3   A4   P4

Preferred stock—5% cumulative, $___ par value, 1,000 shares authorized, issued, and outstanding	$ 85,000
Common stock—$___ par value, 4,000 shares authorized, issued, and outstanding	200,000
Retained earnings	350,000
Total stockholders' equity	$635,000

Required

1. What is the current market value (price) of this corporation's common stock?

2. What are the par values of the corporation's preferred stock and its common stock?

3. If no dividends are in arrears, what are the book values per share of the preferred stock and the common stock?

4. If two years' preferred dividends are in arrears, what are the book values per share of the preferred stock and the common stock?

5. If two years' preferred dividends are in arrears and the preferred stock is callable at $95 per share, what are the book values per share of the preferred stock and the common stock?

6. If two years' preferred dividends are in arrears and the board of directors declares cash dividends of $24,750, what total amount will be paid to the preferred and to the common shareholders? What is the amount of dividends per share for the common stock?

Check   (4) Book value of common, $135.38

(5) Book value of common, $132.88

(6) Dividends per common share, $3.00

Analysis Component

7. What are some factors that can contribute to a difference between the book value of common stock and its market value (price)?

Mayport Company is incorporated at the beginning of this year and engages in a number of transactions. The following journal entries impacted its stockholders' equity during its first year of operations.

PROBLEM SET B

Problem 13-1B
Stockholders' equity transactions and analysis

C2   C3   P1

a.	Cash	60,000	
	Common Stock, $1 Par Value		1,500
	Paid-In Capital in Excess of Par Value, Common Stock		58,500
b.	Organization Expenses	20,000	
	Common Stock, $1 Par Value		500
	Paid-In Capital in Excess of Par Value, Common Stock		19,500
c.	Cash	6,650	
	Accounts Receivable	4,000	
	Building	18,500	
	Notes Payable		9,150
	Common Stock, $1 Par Value		400
	Paid-In Capital in Excess of Par Value, Common Stock		19,600

[continued on next page]

Page 542

Chapter 13 Accounting for Corporations

[continued from previous page]

d.	Cash	30,000	
	Common Stock, $1 Par Value		600
	Paid-In Capital in Excess of Par Value, Common Stock		29,400

Required

1. Explain the transaction(s) underlying each journal entry (a) through (d).
2. How many shares of common stock are outstanding at year-end?
3. What is the amount of minimum legal capital (based on par value) at year-end?
4. What is the total paid-in capital at year-end?
5. What is the book value per share of the common stock at year-end if total paid-in capital plus retained earnings equals $141,500?

Check (2) 3,000 shares
(3) $3,000
(4) $130,000

Problem 13-2B
Cash dividends, treasury stock, and statement of retained earnings
C2 C4 P2 P5

San Marco Corp. reports the following components of stockholders' equity on December 31, 2009.

Common stock—$1 par value, 160,000 shares authorized, 100,000 shares issued and outstanding	$ 100,000
Paid-in capital in excess of par value, common stock	700,000
Retained earnings	1,080,000
Total stockholders' equity	$1,880,000

It completed the following transactions related to stockholders' equity in year 2010.

Jan. 10 Purchased 20,000 shares of its own stock at $12 cash per share.
Mar. 2 Directors declared a $1.50 per share cash dividend payable on March 31 to the March 15 stockholders of record.
Mar. 31 Paid the dividend declared on March 2.
Nov. 11 Sold 12,000 of its treasury shares at $13 cash per share.
Nov. 25 Sold 8,000 of its treasury shares at $9.50 cash per share.
Dec. 1 Directors declared a $2.50 per share cash dividend payable on January 2 to the December 10 stockholders of record.
Dec. 31 Closed the $536,000 credit balance (from net income) in the Income Summary account to Retained Earnings.

Required

1. Prepare journal entries to record each of these transactions for 2010.
2. Prepare a statement of retained earnings for the year ended December 31, 2010.
3. Prepare the stockholders' equity section of the company's balance sheet as of December 31, 2010.

Check (2) Retained earnings, Dec. 31, 2010, $1,238,000

Problem 13-3B
Equity analysis—journal entries and account balances
P2 P3

At December 31, the end of Santee Communication's third quarter, the following stockholders' equity accounts are reported.

Common stock, $10 par value	$480,000
Paid-in capital in excess of par value, common stock	192,000
Retained earnings	800,000

In the fourth quarter, the following entries related to its equity are recorded.

Jan. 17	Retained Earnings	48,000	
	Common Dividend Payable		48,000
Feb. 5	Common Dividend Payable	48,000	
	Cash		48,000

[continued on next page]

[continued from previous page]

Feb. 28	Retained Earnings.............................	126,000	
	Common Stock Dividend Distributable........		60,000
	Paid-In Capital in Excess of Par Value, Common Stock		66,000
Mar. 14	Common Stock Dividend Distributable	60,000	
	Common Stock, $10 Par Value		60,000
Mar. 25	Memo—Change the title of the common stock account to reflect the new par value of $5.		
Mar. 31	Income Summary	360,000	
	Retained Earnings		360,000

Required

1. Explain the transaction(s) underlying each journal entry.

2. Complete the following table showing the equity account balances at each indicated date (include the balances from December 31).

	Jan. 17	Feb. 5	Feb. 28	Mar. 14	Mar. 25	Mar. 31
Common stock	$____	$____	$____	$____	$____	$____
Common stock dividend distributable	____	____	____	____	____	____
Paid-in capital in excess of par, common stock	____	____	____	____	____	____
Retained earnings	____	____	____	____	____	____
Total equity	$____	$____	$____	$____	$____	$____

Check Total equity: Jan. 17, $1,424,000; Mar. 31, $1,784,000

The equity sections from Kiwa Corporation's 2009 and 2010 balance sheets follow.

Problem 13-4B
Analysis of changes in stockholders' equity accounts

C4 P2 P3 P5

Stockholders' Equity (December 31, 2009)

Common stock—$20 par value, 15,000 shares authorized, 8,500 shares issued and outstanding	$170,000
Paid-in capital in excess of par value, common stock	30,000
Retained earnings	135,000
Total stockholders' equity	$335,000

Stockholders' Equity (December 31, 2010)

Common stock—$20 par value, 15,000 shares authorized, 9,500 shares issued, 500 shares in treasury	$190,000
Paid-in capital in excess of par value, common stock	52,000
Retained earnings ($20,000 restricted by treasury stock)	147,600
	389,600
Less cost of treasury stock	(20,000)
Total stockholders' equity	$369,600

The following transactions and events affected its equity during year 2010.

Feb. 15 Declared a $0.40 per share cash dividend, date of record five days later.
Mar. 2 Purchased treasury stock for cash.
May 15 Declared a $0.40 per share cash dividend, date of record five days later.
Aug. 15 Declared a $0.40 per share cash dividend, date of record five days later.
Oct. 4 Declared a 12.5% stock dividend when the stock's market value is $42 per share.
Oct. 20 Issued the stock dividend that was declared on October 4.
Nov. 15 Declared a $0.40 per share cash dividend, date of record five days later.

Required

1. How many common shares are outstanding on each cash dividend date?
2. What is the total dollar amount for each of the four cash dividends?
3. What is the amount of the capitalization of retained earnings for the stock dividend?
4. What is the per share cost of the treasury stock purchased?
5. How much net income did the company earn during year 2010?

Check (3) $42,000
       (4) $40
       (5) $68,000

Problem 13-5B
Computation of book values and dividend allocations

C3 A4 P4

Hansen Company's common stock is currently selling on a stock exchange at $90 per share, and its current balance sheet shows the following stockholders' equity section.

Preferred stock—8% cumulative, $___ par value, 1,500 shares authorized, issued, and outstanding	$ 187,500
Common stock—$___ par value, 18,000 shares authorized, issued, and outstanding	450,000
Retained earnings	562,500
Total stockholders' equity	$1,200,000

Required

1. What is the current market value (price) of this corporation's common stock?
2. What are the par values of the corporation's preferred stock and its common stock?
3. If no dividends are in arrears, what are the book values per share of the preferred stock and the common stock?
4. If two years' preferred dividends are in arrears, what are the book values per share of the preferred stock and the common stock?
5. If two years' preferred dividends are in arrears and the preferred stock is callable at $140 per share, what are the book values per share of the preferred stock and the common stock?
6. If two years' preferred dividends are in arrears and the board of directors declares cash dividends of $50,000, what total amount will be paid to the preferred and to the common shareholders? What is the amount of dividends per share for the common stock?

Check (4) Book value of common, $54.58
       (5) Book value of common, $53.33
       (6) Dividends per common share, $0.28

Analysis Component

7. Discuss why the book value of common stock is not always a good estimate of its market value.

SERIAL PROBLEM

Success Systems

(This serial problem began in Chapter 1 and continues through most of the book. If previous chapter segments were not completed, the serial problem can begin at this point. It is helpful, but not necessary, to use the Working Papers that accompany the book.)

SP 13 Adriana Lopez created Success Systems on October 1, 2009. The company has been successful, and Adriana plans to expand her business. She believes that an additional $86,000 is needed and is investigating three funding sources.

a. Adriana's sister Cicely is willing to invest $86,000 in the business as a common shareholder. Since Adriana currently has about $129,000 invested in the business, Cicely's investment will mean that Adriana will maintain about 60% ownership, and Cicely will have 40% ownership of Success Systems.

b. Adriana's uncle Marcello is willing to invest $86,000 in the business as a preferred shareholder. Marcello would purchase 860 shares of $100 par value, 7% preferred stock.

c. Adriana's banker is willing to lend her $86,000 on a 7%, 10-year note payable. Adriana would make monthly payments of $1,000 per month for 10 years.

Required

1. Prepare the journal entry to reflect the initial $86,000 investment under each of the options (a), (b), and (c).

2. Evaluate the three proposals for expansion, providing the pros and cons of each option.

3. Which option do you recommend Adriana adopt? Explain.

BEYOND THE NUMBERS

BTN 13-1   Refer to **Best Buy**'s financial statements in Appendix A to answer the following.

1. How many shares of common stock are issued and outstanding at March 3, 2007, and February 25, 2006? How do these numbers compare with the basic weighted-average common shares outstanding at March 3, 2007, and February 25, 2006?

2. What is the book value of its entire common stock at March 3, 2007?

3. What is the total amount of cash dividends paid to common stockholders for the years ended March 3, 2007, and February 25, 2006?

4. Identify and compare basic EPS amounts across fiscal years 2007, 2006, and 2005. Identify and comment on any marked changes.

5. Does Best Buy hold any treasury stock as of March 3, 2007? As of February 25, 2006?

Fast Forward

6. Access Best Buy's financial statements for fiscal years ending after March 3, 2007, from its Website (**BestBuy.com**) or the SEC's EDGAR database (**www.SEC.gov**). Has the number of common shares outstanding increased since March 3, 2007? Has Best Buy increased the total amount of cash dividends paid compared to the total amount for fiscal year 2007?

REPORTING IN ACTION

C2   C3   A1   A4

BTN 13-2   Key comparative figures for **Best Buy**, **Circuit City**, and **RadioShack** follow.

Key Figures	Best Buy	Circuit City	RadioShack
Net income (in millions)	$1,377	$ (8)	$ 73
Cash dividends declared per common share	$ 0.36	$ 0.12	$ 0.25
Common shares outstanding (in millions)	481	171	136
Weighted-average common shares outstanding (in mil.)	482	170	136
Market value (price) per share	$46.35	$19.00	$16.78
Equity applicable to common shares (in millions)	$6,201	$1,791	$ 654

COMPARATIVE ANALYSIS

A1   A2   A3   A4

Required

1. Compute the book value per common share for each company using these data.

2. Compute the basic EPS for each company using these data.

3. Compute the dividend yield for each company using these data. Does the dividend yield of any of the companies characterize it as an income or growth stock? Explain.

4. Compute, compare, and interpret the price-earnings ratio for each company using these data.

BTN 13-3   Brianna Moore is an accountant for New World Pharmaceuticals. Her duties include tracking research and development spending in the new product development division. Over the course of the past six months, Brianna notices that a great deal of funds have been spent on a particular project for a new drug. She hears "through the grapevine" that the company is about to patent the drug and expects it to be a major advance in antibiotics. Brianna believes that this new drug will greatly improve company performance and will cause the company's stock to increase in value. Brianna decides to purchase shares of New World in order to benefit from this expected increase.

ETHICS CHALLENGE

C4

Required

What are Brianna's ethical responsibilities, if any, with respect to the information she has learned through her duties as an accountant for New World Pharmaceuticals? What are the implications to her planned purchase of New World shares?

COMMUNICATING IN PRACTICE

A1 A2
,

Hint: Make a transparency of each team's memo for a class discussion.

BTN 13-4 Teams are to select an industry, and each team member is to select a different company in that industry. Each team member then is to acquire the selected company's financial statements (or Form 10-K) from the SEC EDGAR site (www.sec.gov). Use these data to identify basic EPS. Use the financial press (or finance.yahoo.com) to determine the market price of this stock, and then compute the price-earnings ratio. Communicate with teammates via a meeting, e-mail, or telephone to discuss the meaning of this ratio, how companies compare, and the industry norm. The team must prepare a single memorandum reporting the ratio for each company and identifying the team conclusions or consensus of opinion. The memorandum is to be duplicated and distributed to the instructor and teammates.

TAKING IT TO THE NET

C2

BTN 13-5 Access the February 26, 2007, filing of the 2006 calendar-year 10-K report of McDonald's, (ticker MCD) from www.sec.gov.

Required

1. Review McDonald's balance sheet and identify how many classes of stock it has issued.
2. What are the par values, number of authorized shares, and issued shares of the classes of stock you identified in part 1?
3. Review its statement of cash flows and identify what total amount of cash it paid in 2006 to purchase treasury stock.
4. What amount did McDonald's pay out in common stock cash dividends for 2006?

TEAMWORK IN ACTION

P5

Hint: Instructor should be sure each team accurately completes part 1 before proceeding.

BTN 13-6 This activity requires teamwork to reinforce understanding of accounting for treasury stock.

1. Write a brief team statement (*a*) generalizing what happens to a corporation's financial position when it engages in a stock "buyback" and (*b*) identifying reasons that a corporation would engage in this activity.
2. Assume that an entity acquires 100 shares of its $100 par value common stock at a cost of $134 cash per share. Discuss the entry to record this acquisition. Next, assign *each* team member to prepare *one* of the following entries (assume each entry applies to all shares):
   a. Reissue treasury shares at cost.
   b. Reissue treasury shares at $150 per share.
   c. Reissue treasury shares at $120 per share; assume the paid-in capital account from treasury shares has a $1,500 balance.
   d. Reissue treasury shares at $120 per share; assume the paid-in capital account from treasury shares has a $1,000 balance.
   e. Reissue treasury shares at $120 per share; assume the paid-in capital account from treasury shares has a zero balance.
3. In sequence, each member is to present his/her entry to the team and explain the *similarities* and *differences* between that entry and the previous entry.

ENTREPRENEURIAL DECISION

C2 C3 P2

BTN 13-7 Assume that Ali Perry, Byron Myers, and Brenton Taylor of Inogen decide to launch a new retail chain to market their portable oxygen systems. This chain, named O-to-Go, requires $500,000 of start-up capital. The three contribute $375,000 of personal assets in return for 15,000 shares of common stock, but they need to raise another $125,000 in cash. There are two alternative plans for raising the additional cash. Plan A is to sell 3,750 shares of common stock to one or more investors for $125,000 cash. Plan B is to sell 1,250 shares of cumulative preferred stock to one or more investors for $125,000 cash (this preferred stock would have a $100 par value, an annual 8% dividend rate, and be issued at par).

1. If the new business is expected to earn $72,000 of after-tax net income in the first year, what rate of return on beginning equity will the three (as a group) earn under each alternative? Which plan will provide the higher expected return to them?
2. If the new business is expected to earn $16,800 of after-tax net income in the first year, what rate of return on beginning equity will the three (as a group) earn under each alternative? Which plan will provide the higher expected return to them?
3. Analyze and interpret the differences between the results for parts 1 and 2.

BTN 13-8   Watch 30 to 60 minutes of financial news programming on television. Take notes on companies that are catching analysts' attention. You might hear reference to over- and undervaluation of firms and to reports about PE ratios, dividend yields, and earnings per share. Be prepared to give a brief description to the class of your observations.

HITTING THE ROAD

A1 A2 A3

BTN 13-9   Financial information for **DSG international plc** (www.DSGiplc.com) follows.

GLOBAL DECISION

A1 C4

DSG

Net income (in millions)	£ 207
Cash dividends declared per share	£ 0.07
Number of shares outstanding (in millions)*	1,843
Equity applicable to shares (in millions)	£1,304

* Assume that the year-end number of shares outstanding approximates the weighted-average shares outstanding.

Required

1. Compute book value per share for DSG.

2. Compute earnings per share (EPS) for DSG.

3. Compare DSG's dividends per share with its EPS. Is DSG paying out a large or small amount of its income as dividends? Explain.

ANSWERS TO MULTIPLE CHOICE QUIZ

1. e; Entry to record this stock issuance is:

Cash (6,000 × $8)	48,000	
Common Stock (6,000 × $5)		30,000
Paid-In Capital in Excess of Par Value, Common Stock		18,000

2. b; $75,000/19,000 shares = $3.95 per share

3. d; Preferred stock = 5,000 × $100 = $500,000
Book value per share = ($2,000,000 − $500,000)/50,000 shares = $30 per common share

4. a; $0.81/$45.00 = 1.8%

5. c; Earnings per share = $3,500,000/700,000 shares = $5 per share
PE ratio = $85/$5 = 17.0

A Look Back

Chapter 13 focused on corporate equity transactions, including stock issuances and dividends. We also explained how to report and analyze income, earnings per share, and retained earnings.

A Look at This Chapter

This chapter describes the accounting for and analysis of bonds and notes. We explain their characteristics, payment patterns, interest computations, retirement, and reporting requirements. An appendix to this chapter introduces leases and pensions.

A Look Ahead

Chapter 15 focuses on how to classify, account for, and report investments in both debt and equity securities. We also describe accounting for transactions listed in a foreign currency.

Chapter 14

Long-Term Liabilities

Learning Objectives

CAP

Conceptual

C1 Explain the types and payment patterns of notes. *(p. 560)*

C2 *Appendix 14A*—Explain and compute the present value of an amount(s) to be paid at a future date(s). *(p. 567)*

C3 *Appendix 14C*—Describe the accrual of bond interest when bond payments do not align with accounting periods. *(p. 571)*

C4 *Appendix 14D*—Describe accounting for leases and pensions. *(p. 573)*

Analytical

A1 Compare bond financing with stock financing. *(p. 550)*

A2 Assess debt features and their implications. *(p. 563)*

A3 Compute the debt-to-equity ratio and explain its use. *(p. 563)*

LP14

Procedural

P1 Prepare entries to record bond issuance and bond interest expense. *(p. 552)*

P2 Compute and record amortization of bond discount. *(p. 553)*

P3 Compute and record amortization of bond premium. *(p. 556)*

P4 Record the retirement of bonds. *(p. 559)*

P5 Prepare entries to account for notes. *(p. 562)*

Hip-Hop Financing

"I wanted to create a product that inner-city kids would relate to" — James Lindsay

PHILADELPHIA—James "Fly" Lindsay and his three sisters were raised by their mother in North Philadelphia. "We were poor," explains Lindsay, "but we were rich in the values that she [mother] set forth." One of those values was education—Lindsay was the first in his family to attend college—and another was the commitment to community. "You have everyone taking away, but you have to give back," insists Lindsay.

Lindsay decided to give back by launching his own business. "I wanted to have a chip company that kids from the hood could relate to," he explains. But Lindsay knew that success depended on securing financing and then planning for long-term liabilities. "Between family and friends," explains Lindsay, "we put our dollars together and made it happen." With $40,000 in financing, he launched **Rap Snacks [RapSnacks.com]**, a maker of snack foods with a twist: Lindsay would sell his snacks with rappers on the wrappers. The snacks would be targeted to urban youth immersed in hip-hop culture. The snack wrappers, importantly, would include positive messages to the kids such as "Stay in School," "Respect Yourself," and "Money equals Education." Lindsay hopes they instill a craving for success, commitment, and entrepreneurship.

Lindsay insists that urban youth need to learn about business and how it can help a community. Basic accounting principles and financing concepts such as bonds and notes are like another language to urban youth, he explains. Lindsay struggles to change that and more. "You can make money," says Lindsay, "but also have a social responsibility to where you came from." Actor and rapper Lil' Romeo has recently taken a lead in funding Rap Snacks.

Making investments in urban youth is a priority, says Lindsay. He continually works to convey knowledge of business financing, with the belief that urban youth can be successful. He manages his own company's long-term liabilities, interest payments, and collateral agreements, and is confident that urban youth can do the same. Understanding liabilities is not easy, says Lindsay, but the costs of not understanding are more severe—and more of the same—for the kids. "It feels good to make a difference," says Lindsay, "and set an example for the kids."

[Sources: *Rap Snacks Website,* January 2009; *Entrepreneur,* July 2003; *Philadelphia Inquirer,* October 2002; *Source Magazine,* June 2001; *Maxim,* March 2002; *Business Review,* September 2007; *PR Newswire,* September 2007]

Individuals, companies, and governments issue bonds to finance their activities. In return for financing, bonds promise to repay the lender with interest. This chapter explains the basics of bonds and the accounting for their issuance and retirement. The chapter also describes long-term notes as another financ-

ing source. We explain how present value concepts impact both the accounting for and reporting of bonds and notes. Appendixes to this chapter discuss present value concepts applicable to liabilities, effective interest amortization, and the accounting for leases and pensions.

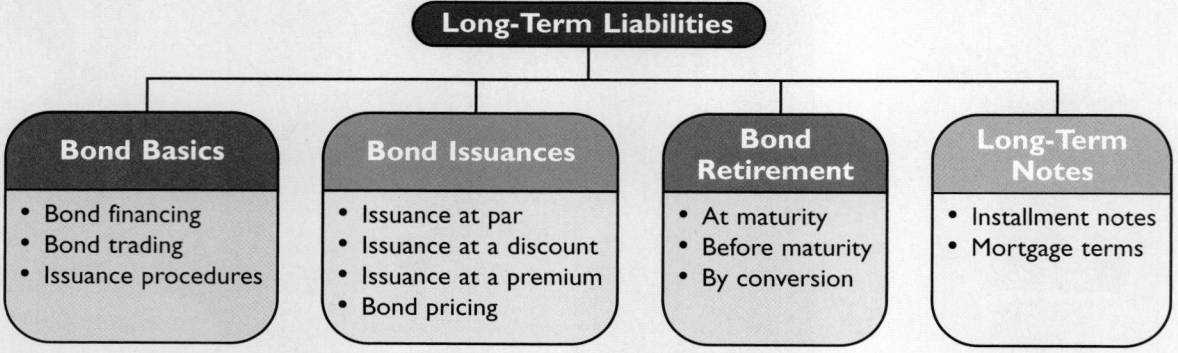

Long-Term Liabilities			
Bond Basics	**Bond Issuances**	**Bond Retirement**	**Long-Term Notes**
• Bond financing • Bond trading • Issuance procedures	• Issuance at par • Issuance at a discount • Issuance at a premium • Bond pricing	• At maturity • Before maturity • By conversion	• Installment notes • Mortgage terms

Basics of Bonds

Video 14.2

A1 Compare bond financing with stock financing.

This section explains the basics of bonds and a company's motivation for issuing them.

Bond Financing

Projects that demand large amounts of money often are funded from bond issuances. (Both for-profit and nonprofit companies, as well as governmental units, such as nations, states, cities, and school districts, issue bonds.) A **bond** is its issuer's written promise to pay an amount identified as the par value of the bond with interest. The **par value of a bond,** also called the *face amount* or *face value,* is paid at a specified future date known as the bond's *maturity date.* Most bonds also require the issuer to make semiannual interest payments. The amount of interest paid each period is determined by multiplying the par value of the bond by the bond's contract rate of interest. This section explains both advantages and disadvantages of bond financing.

Advantages of Bonds   There are three main advantages of bond financing:

1. *Bonds do not affect owner control.* Equity financing reflects ownership in a company, whereas bond financing does not. A person who contributes $1,000 of a company's $10,000 equity financing typically controls one-tenth of all owner decisions. A person who owns a $1,000, 11%, 20-year bond has no ownership right. This person, or bondholder, is to receive from the bond issuer 11% interest, or $110, each year the bond is outstanding and $1,000 when it matures in 20 years.

2. *Interest on bonds is tax deductible.* Bond interest payments are tax deductible for the issuer, but equity payments (distributions) to owners are not. To illustrate, assume that a corporation with no bond financing earns $15,000 in income *before* paying taxes at a 40% tax rate, which amounts to $6,000 ($15,000 × 40%) in taxes. If a portion of its financing is in bonds, however, the resulting bond interest is deducted in computing taxable income. That is, if bond interest expense is $10,000, the taxes owed would be $2,000 ([$15,000 − $10,000] × 40%), which is less than the $6,000 owed with no bond financing.

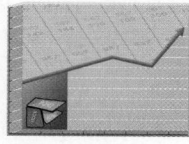

3. *Bonds can increase return on equity.* A company that earns a higher return with borrowed funds than it pays in interest on those funds increases its return on equity. This process is called *financial leverage* or *trading on the equity.*

Point: Financial leverage reflects issuance of bonds, notes, or preferred stock.

To illustrate the third point, consider Magnum Co., which has $1 million in equity and is planning a $500,000 expansion to meet increasing demand for its product. Magnum predicts the

$500,000 expansion will yield $125,000 in additional income before paying any interest. It currently earns $100,000 per year and has no interest expense. Magnum is considering three plans. Plan A is to not expand. Plan B is to expand and raise $500,000 from equity financing. Plan C is to expand and issue $500,000 of bonds that pay 10% annual interest ($50,000). Exhibit 14.1 shows how these three plans affect Magnum's net income, equity, and return on equity (net income/equity). The owner(s) will earn a higher return on equity if expansion occurs. Moreover, the preferred expansion plan is to issue bonds. Projected net income under Plan C ($175,000) is smaller than under Plan B ($225,000), but the return on equity is larger because of less equity investment. Plan C has another advantage if income is taxable. This illustration reflects a general rule: *Return on equity increases when the expected rate of return from the new assets is higher than the rate of interest expense on the debt financing.*

Example: Compute return on equity for all three plans if Magnum currently earns $150,000 instead of $100,000.
Answer ($ 000s):
Plan A = 15%   ($150/$1,000)
Plan B = 18.3%   ($275/$1,500)
Plan C = 22.5%   ($225/$1,000)

	Plan A: Do Not Expand	Plan B: Equity Financing	Plan C: Bond Financing
Income before interest expense	$ 100,000	$ 225,000	$ 225,000
Interest expense	—	—	(50,000)
Net income	$ 100,000	$ 225,000	$ 175,000
Equity	$1,000,000	$1,500,000	$1,000,000
Return on equity	10.0%	15.0%	17.5%

EXHIBIT 14.1

Financing with Bonds versus Equity

Disadvantages of Bonds   The two main disadvantages of bond financing are these:

1. *Bonds can decrease return on equity.* When a company earns a lower return with the borrowed funds than it pays in interest, it decreases its return on equity. This downside risk of financial leverage is more likely to arise when a company has periods of low income or net losses.

2. *Bonds require payment of both periodic interest and the par value at maturity.* Bond payments can be especially burdensome when income and cash flow are low. Equity financing, in contrast, does not require any payments because cash withdrawals (dividends) are paid at the discretion of the owner (or board).

Point: Debt financing is desirable when interest is tax deductible, when owner control is preferred, and when return on equity exceeds the debt's interest rate.

A company must weigh the risks and returns of the disadvantages and advantages of bond financing when deciding whether to issue bonds to finance operations.

Bond Trading

Bonds are securities that can be readily bought and sold. A large number of bonds trade on both the New York Exchange and the American Exchange. A bond *issue* consists of a number of bonds, usually in denominations of $1,000 or $5,000, and is sold to many different lenders. After bonds are issued, they often are bought and sold by investors, meaning that any particular bond probably has a number of owners before it matures. Since bonds are exchanged (bought and sold) in the market, they have a market value (price). For convenience, bond market values are expressed as a percent of their par (face) value. For example, a company's bonds might be trading at 103½, meaning they can be bought or sold for 103.5% of their par value. Bonds can also trade below par value. For instance, if a company's bonds are trading at 95, they can be bought or sold at 95% of their par value.

Decision Insight

Quotes   The **IBM** bond quote here is interpreted (left to right) as **Bonds,** issuer name; **Rate,** contract interest rate (7%); **Mat,** matures in year 2025 when

Bonds	Rate	Mat	Yld	Vol	Close	Chg
IBM	7	25	5.9	130	119¼	+1¼

principal is paid; **Yld,** yield rate (5.9%) of bond at current price; **Vol,** daily dollar worth ($130,000) of trades (in 1,000s); **Close,** closing price (119.25) for the day as percentage of par value; **Chg,** change (+1.25) in closing price from prior day's close.

Bond-Issuing Procedures

State and federal laws govern bond issuances. Bond issuers also want to ensure that they do not violate any of their existing contractual agreements when issuing bonds. Authorization of bond issuances includes the number of bonds authorized, their par value, and the contract interest rate.

EXHIBIT 14.2

Bond Certificate

Point: *Indenture* refers to a bond's legal contract; *debenture* refers to an unsecured bond.

The legal document identifying the rights and obligations of both the bondholders and the issuer is called the **bond indenture,** which is the legal contract between the issuer and the bondholders. A bondholder may also receive a bond certificate as evidence of the company's debt. A **bond certificate,** such as that shown in Exhibit 14.2, includes specifics such as the issuer's name, the par value, the contract interest rate, and the maturity date. Many companies reduce costs by not issuing paper certificates to bondholders.[1]

Bond Issuances

Video 14.2

This section explains accounting for bond issuances at par, below par (discount), and above par (premium). It also describes how to amortize a discount or premium and record bonds issued between interest payment dates.

Issuing Bonds at Par

P1 Prepare entries to record bond issuance and bond interest expense.

To illustrate an issuance of bonds at par value, suppose a company receives authorization to issue $800,000 of 9%, 20-year bonds dated January 1, 2009, that mature on December 31, 2028, and pay interest semiannually on each June 30 and December 31. After accepting the bond indenture on behalf of the bondholders, the trustee can sell all or a portion of the bonds to an underwriter. If all bonds are sold at par value, the issuer records the sale as follows.

Assets = Liabilities + Equity
+800,000   +800,000

	2009			
	Jan. 1	Cash	800,000	
		Bonds Payable		800,000
		Sold bonds at par.		

This entry reflects increases in the issuer's cash *and* long-term liabilities.
The issuer records the first semiannual interest payment as follows.

Assets = Liabilities + Equity
−36,000   −36,000

	2009			
	June 30	Bond Interest Expense	36,000	
		Cash		36,000
		Paid semiannual interest (9% × $800,000 × ½ year).		

Point: The *spread* between the dealer's cost and what buyers pay can be huge. Dealers earn more than $25 billion in annual spread revenue.

Global: In the United Kingdom, government bonds are called *gilts*— short for gilt-edged investments.

---

[1] The issuing company normally sells its bonds to an investment firm called an *underwriter,* which resells them to the public. An issuing company can also sell bonds directly to investors. When an underwriter sells bonds to a large number of investors, a *trustee* represents and protects the bondholders' interests. The trustee monitors the issuer to ensure that it complies with the obligations in the bond indenture. Most trustees are large banks or trust companies. The trustee writes and accepts the terms of a bond indenture before it is issued. When bonds are offered to the public, called *floating an issue,* they must be registered with the Securities and Exchange Commission (SEC). SEC registration requires the issuer to file certain financial information. Most company bonds are issued in par value units of $1,000 or $5,000. *A baby bond* has a par value of less than $1,000, such as $100.

The issuer pays and records its semiannual interest obligation every six months until the bonds mature. When they mature, the issuer records its payment of principal as follows.

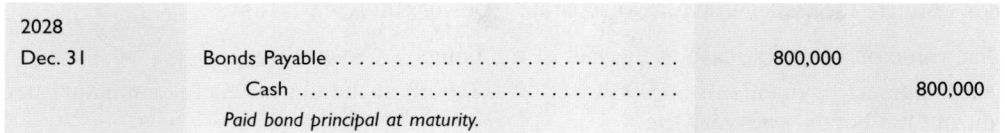

2028			
Dec. 31	Bonds Payable	800,000	
	Cash		800,000
	Paid bond principal at maturity.		

Assets	= Liabilities	+ Equity
−800,000	−800,000	

Bond Discount or Premium

The bond issuer pays the interest rate specified in the indenture, the **contract rate,** also referred to as the *coupon rate, stated rate,* or *nominal rate.* The annual interest paid is determined by multiplying the bond par value by the contract rate. The contract rate is usually stated on an annual basis, even if interest is paid semiannually. For example, if a company issues a $1,000, 8% bond paying interest semiannually, it pays annual interest of $80 (8% × $1,000) in two semiannual payments of $40 each.

The contract rate sets the amount of interest the issuer pays in *cash,* which is not necessarily the *bond interest expense* actually incurred by the issuer. Bond interest expense depends on the bond's market value at issuance, which is determined by market expectations of the risk of lending to the issuer. The bond's **market rate** of interest is the rate that borrowers are willing to pay and lenders are willing to accept for a particular bond and its risk level. As the risk level increases, the rate increases to compensate purchasers for the bonds' increased risk. Also, the market rate is generally higher when the time period until the bond matures is longer due to the risk of adverse events occurring over a longer time period.

Many bond issuers try to set a contract rate of interest equal to the market rate they expect as of the bond issuance date. When the contract rate and market rate are equal, a bond sells at par value, but when they are not equal, a bond does not sell at par value. Instead, it is sold at a *premium* above par value or at a *discount* below par value. Exhibit 14.3 shows the relation between the contract rate, market rate, and a bond's issue price.

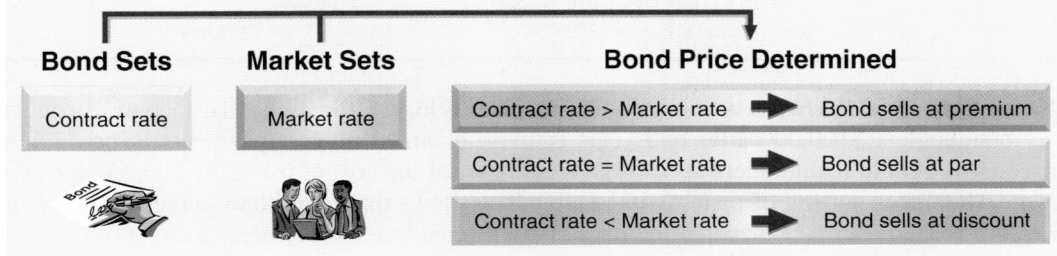

Bond Sets	Market Sets	Bond Price Determined	
Contract rate	Market rate	Contract rate > Market rate ➡	Bond sells at premium
		Contract rate = Market rate ➡	Bond sells at par
		Contract rate < Market rate ➡	Bond sells at discount

EXHIBIT 14.3

Relation between Bond Issue Price, Contract Rate, and Market Rate

Quick Check

Answers—p. 576

1. Unsecured bonds backed only by the issuer's general credit standing are called (a) serial bonds, (b) debentures, (c) registered bonds, or (d) convertible bonds.

2. How do you compute the amount of interest a bond issuer pays in cash each year?

3. When the contract rate is above the market rate, do bonds sell at a premium or a discount? Do purchasers pay more or less than the par value of the bonds?

Issuing Bonds at a Discount

A **discount on bonds payable** occurs when a company issues bonds with a contract rate less than the market rate. This means that the issue price is less than par value. To illustrate, assume that Fila announces an offer to issue bonds with a $100,000 par value, an 8% annual contract rate (paid semiannually), and a two-year life. Also assume that the market rate for Fila

P2 Compute and record amortization of bond discount.

Point: The difference between the contract rate and the market rate of interest on a new bond issue is usually a fraction of a percent. We use a difference of 2% to emphasize the effects.

bonds is 10%. These bonds then will sell at a discount since the contract rate is less than the market rate. The exact issue price for these bonds is stated as 96.454 (implying 96.454% of par value, or $96,454); we show how to compute this issue price later in the chapter. These bonds obligate the issuer to pay two separate types of future cash flows:

1. Par value of $100,000 cash at the end of the bonds' two-year life.
2. Cash interest payments of $4,000 (4% × $100,000) at the end of each semiannual period during the bonds' two-year life.

The exact pattern of cash flows for the Fila bonds is shown in Exhibit 14.4.

EXHIBIT 14.4

Cash Flows for Fila Bonds

				$100,000
	$4,000	$4,000	$4,000	$4,000
0	6 mo.	12 mo.	18 mo.	24 mo.

When Fila accepts $96,454 cash for its bonds on the issue date of December 31, 2009, it records the sale as follows:

Assets = Liabilities + Equity
+96,454 +100,000
            −3,546

Dec. 31	Cash......................................	96,454	
	Discount on Bonds Payable....................	3,546	
	Bonds Payable..........................		100,000
	Sold bonds at a discount on their issue date.		

Point: Book value at issuance always equals the issuer's cash borrowed.

These bonds are reported in the long-term liability section of the issuer's December 31, 2009, balance sheet as shown in Exhibit 14.5. A discount is deducted from the par value of bonds to yield the **carrying (book) value of bonds.** Discount on Bonds Payable is a contra liability account.

EXHIBIT 14.5

Balance Sheet Presentation of Bond Discount

Long-term liabilities		
Bonds payable, 8%, due December 31, 2011	$100,000	
Less discount on bonds payable	3,546	$96,454

Point: *Zero-coupon bonds* do not pay periodic interest (contract rate is zero). These bonds always sell at a discount because their 0% contract rate is always below the market rate.

Video14.2

Amortizing a Bond Discount   Fila receives $96,454 for its bonds; in return it must pay bondholders $100,000 after two years (plus semiannual interest payments). The $3,546 discount is paid to bondholders at maturity and is part of the cost of using the $96,454 for two years. The upper portion of panel A in Exhibit 14.6 shows that total bond interest expense of $19,546 is the difference between the total amount repaid to bondholders ($116,000) and the amount borrowed from bondholders ($96,454). Alternatively, we can compute total bond interest expense as the sum of the four interest payments and the bond discount. This alternative computation is shown in the lower portion of panel A.

The total $19,546 bond interest expense must be allocated across the four semiannual periods in the bonds' life, and the bonds' carrying value must be updated at each balance sheet date. This is accomplished using the straight-line method (or the effective interest method in Appendix 14B). Both methods systematically reduce the bond discount to zero over the two-year life. This process is called *amortizing a bond discount*.

Straight-Line Method   The **straight-line bond amortization** method allocates an equal portion of the total bond interest expense to each interest period. To apply the straight-line method to Fila's bonds, we divide the total bond interest expense of $19,546 by 4 (the number of semiannual periods in the bonds' life). This gives a bond interest expense of $4,887 per period, which is $4,886.5 rounded to the nearest dollar per period (all computations, including those for assignments, are rounded to the nearest whole dollar). Alternatively, we can find this number by first dividing the $3,546 discount by 4, which yields the $887 amount of discount to be amortized each interest period. When the $887 is added to the $4,000 cash payment, the

EXHIBIT 14.6

Interest Computation and Entry for Bonds Issued at a Discount

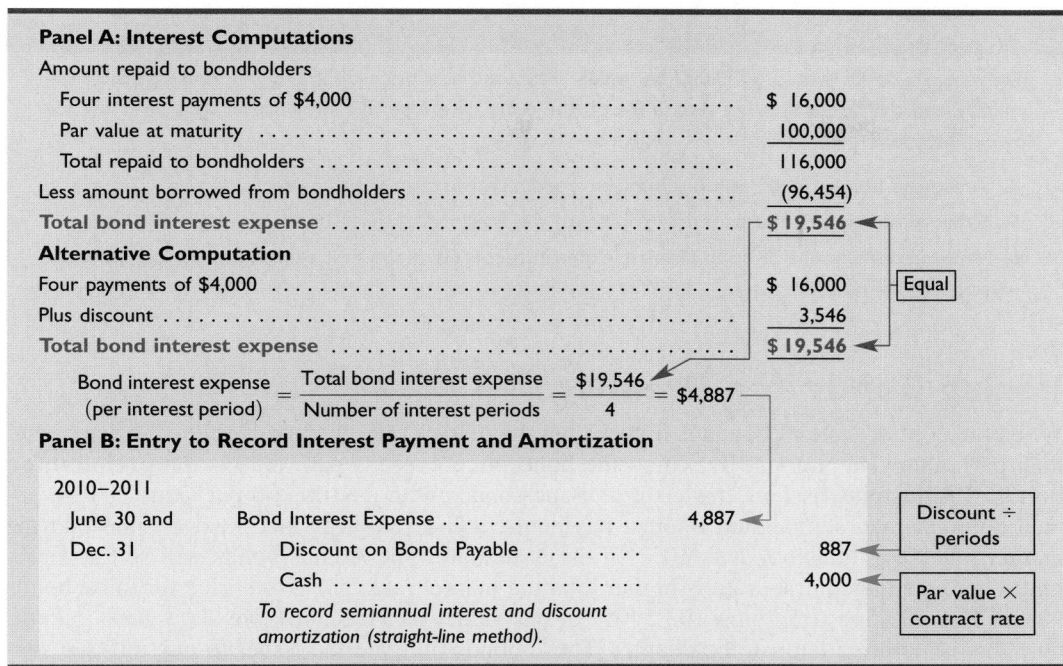

Panel A: Interest Computations

Amount repaid to bondholders

Four interest payments of $4,000	$ 16,000
Par value at maturity	100,000
Total repaid to bondholders	116,000
Less amount borrowed from bondholders	(96,454)
Total bond interest expense	**$ 19,546**

Alternative Computation

Four payments of $4,000	$ 16,000	Equal
Plus discount	3,546	
Total bond interest expense	**$ 19,546**	

$$\frac{\text{Bond interest expense}}{\text{(per interest period)}} = \frac{\text{Total bond interest expense}}{\text{Number of interest periods}} = \frac{\$19,546}{4} = \$4,887$$

Panel B: Entry to Record Interest Payment and Amortization

2010–2011

June 30 and	Bond Interest Expense	4,887	
Dec. 31	Discount on Bonds Payable		887
	Cash		4,000

To record semiannual interest and discount amortization (straight-line method).

Discount ÷ periods

Par value × contract rate

bond interest expense for each period is $4,887. Panel B of Exhibit 14.6 shows how the issuer records bond interest expense and updates the balance of the bond liability account at the end of *each* of the four semiannual interest periods (June 30, 2010, through December 31, 2011).

Exhibit 14.7 shows the pattern of decreases in the Discount on Bonds Payable account and the pattern of increases in the bonds' carrying value. The following points summarize the discount bonds' straight-line amortization:

1. At issuance, the $100,000 par value consists of the $96,454 cash received by the issuer plus the $3,546 discount.

2. During the bonds' life, the (unamortized) discount decreases each period by the $887 amortization ($3,546/4), and the carrying value (par value less unamortized discount) increases each period by $887.

3. At maturity, the unamortized discount equals zero, and the carrying value equals the $100,000 par value that the issuer pays the holder.

EXHIBIT 14.7

Straight-Line Amortization of Bond Discount

	Semiannual Period-End	Unamortized Discount*	Carrying Value†
(0)	12/31/2009	$3,546	$ 96,454
(1)	6/30/2010	2,659	97,341
(2)	12/31/2010	1,772	98,228
(3)	6/30/2011	885	99,115
(4)	12/31/2011	0‡	100,000

The two columns always sum to par value for a discount bond.

* Total bond discount (of $3,546) less accumulated periodic amortization ($887 per semiannual interest period).

† Bond par value (of $100,000) less unamortized discount.

‡ Adjusted for rounding.

We see that the issuer incurs a $4,887 bond interest expense each period but pays only $4,000 cash. The $887 unpaid portion of this expense is added to the bonds' carrying value. (The total $3,546 unamortized discount is "paid" when the bonds mature; $100,000 is paid at maturity but only $96,454 was received at issuance.)

Decision Insight

Ratings Game   Many bond buyers rely on rating services to assess bond risk. The best known are Standard & Poor's and Moody's. These services focus on the issuer's financial statements and other factors in setting ratings. Standard & Poor's ratings, from best quality to default, are AAA, AA, A, BBB, BB, B, CCC, CC, C, and D. Ratings can include a plus (+) or minus (−) to show relative standing within a category.

Issuing Bonds at a Premium

P3 Compute and record amortization of bond premium.

When the contract rate of bonds is higher than the market rate, the bonds sell at a price higher than par value. The amount by which the bond price exceeds par value is the **premium on bonds.** To illustrate, assume that Adidas issues bonds with a $100,000 par value, a 12% annual contract rate, semiannual interest payments, and a two-year life. Also assume that the market rate for Adidas bonds is 10% on the issue date. The Adidas bonds will sell at a premium because the contract rate is higher than the market rate. The issue price for these bonds is stated as 103.546 (implying 103.546% of par value, or $103,546); we show how to compute this issue price later in the chapter. These bonds obligate the issuer to pay out two separate future cash flows:

1. Par value of $100,000 cash at the end of the bonds' two-year life.
2. Cash interest payments of $6,000 (6% × $100,000) at the end of each semiannual period during the bonds' two-year life.

The exact pattern of cash flows for the Adidas bonds is shown in Exhibit 14.8.

EXHIBIT 14.8

Cash Flows for Adidas Bonds

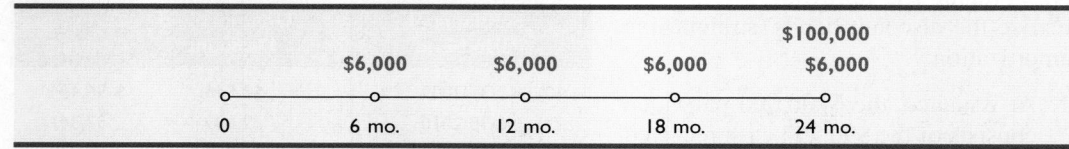

These bonds are reported in the long-term liability section of the issuer's December 31, 2009, balance sheet as shown in Exhibit 14.9. A premium is added to par value to yield the carrying (book) value of bonds. Premium on Bonds Payable is an adjunct (also called *accretion*) liability account.

When Adidas accepts $103,546 cash for its bonds on the issue date of December 31, 2009, it records this transaction as follows.

Assets = Liabilities + Equity
+103,546   +100,000
        +3,546

Dec. 31	Cash	103,546	
	Premium on Bonds Payable		3,546
	Bonds Payable.........................		100,000
	Sold bonds at a premium on their issue date.		

EXHIBIT 14.9

Balance Sheet Presentation of Bond Premium

Long-term liabilities		
Bonds payable, 12%, due December 31, 2011	$100,000	
Plus premium on bonds payable	3,546	$103,546

Amortizing a Bond Premium Adidas receives $103,546 for its bonds; in return, it pays bondholders $100,000 after two years (plus semiannual interest payments). The $3,546 premium not repaid to issuer's bondholders at maturity goes to reduce the issuer's expense of using the $103,546 for two years. The upper portion of panel A of Exhibit 14.10 shows that total bond interest expense of $20,454 is the difference between the total amount repaid to bondholders ($124,000) and the amount borrowed from bondholders ($103,546). Alternatively, we can compute

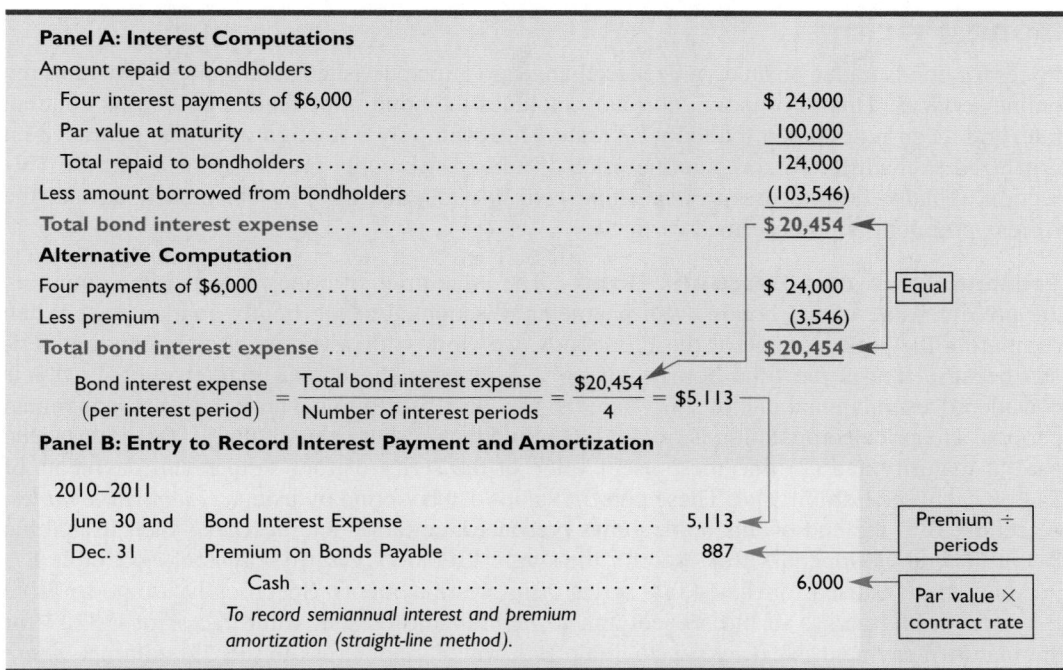

Panel A: Interest Computations

Amount repaid to bondholders

Four interest payments of $6,000	$ 24,000
Par value at maturity	100,000
Total repaid to bondholders	124,000
Less amount borrowed from bondholders	(103,546)
Total bond interest expense	**$ 20,454**

Alternative Computation

Four payments of $6,000	$ 24,000
Less premium	(3,546)
Total bond interest expense	**$ 20,454**

$$\text{Bond interest expense (per interest period)} = \frac{\text{Total bond interest expense}}{\text{Number of interest periods}} = \frac{\$20,454}{4} = \$5,113$$

Panel B: Entry to Record Interest Payment and Amortization

2010–2011

June 30 and	Bond Interest Expense	5,113	
Dec. 31	Premium on Bonds Payable	887	
	Cash		6,000

To record semiannual interest and premium amortization (straight-line method).

Premium ÷ periods

Par value × contract rate

EXHIBIT 14.10

Interest Computation and Entry for Bonds Issued at a Premium

total bond interest expense as the sum of the four interest payments less the bond premium. The premium is subtracted because it will not be paid to bondholders when the bonds mature; see the lower portion of panel A. Total bond interest expense must be allocated over the four semiannual periods using the straight-line method (or the effective interest method in Appendix 14B).

Straight-Line Method The straight-line method allocates an equal portion of total bond interest expense to each of the bonds' semiannual interest periods. To apply this method to Adidas bonds, we divide the two years' total bond interest expense of $20,454 by 4 (the number of semiannual periods in the bonds' life). This gives a total bond interest expense of $5,113 per period, which is $5,113.5 rounded down so that the journal entry balances and for simplicity in presentation (alternatively, one could carry cents). Panel B of Exhibit 14.10 shows how the issuer records bond interest expense and updates the balance of the bond liability account for *each* semiannual period (June 30, 2010, through December 31, 2011).

Exhibit 14.11 shows the pattern of decreases in the unamortized Premium on Bonds Payable account and in the bonds' carrying value. The following points summarize straight-line amortization of the premium bonds:

Semiannual Period-End	Unamortized Premium*	Carrying Value†
(0) 12/31/2009	$3,546	$103,546
(1) 6/30/2010	2,659	102,659
(2) 12/31/2010	1,772	101,772
(3) 6/30/2011	885	100,885
(4) 12/31/2011	0‡	100,000

* Total bond premium (of $3,546) less accumulated periodic amortization ($887 per semiannual interest period).

† Bond par value (of $100,000) plus unamortized premium.

‡ Adjusted for rounding.

EXHIBIT 14.11

Straight-Line Amortization of Bond Premium

During the bond life, carrying value is adjusted to par and the amortized premium to zero.

1. At issuance, the $100,000 par value plus the $3,546 premium equals the $103,546 cash received by the issuer.

2. During the bonds' life, the (unamortized) premium decreases each period by the $887 amortization ($3,546/4), and the carrying value decreases each period by the same $887.

3. At maturity, the unamortized premium equals zero, and the carrying value equals the $100,000 par value that the issuer pays the holder.

The next section describes bond pricing. An instructor can choose to cover bond pricing or not. Assignments requiring the next section are Quick Study 14-4, Exercises 14-9 & 14-10, and Problems 14-1A & 14-1B and 14-4A & 14-4B.

Bond Pricing

Prices for bonds traded on an organized exchange are often published in newspapers and through online services. This information normally includes the bond price (called *quote*), its contract rate, and its current market (called *yield*) rate. However, only a fraction of bonds are traded on organized exchanges. To compute the price of a bond, we apply present value concepts. This section explains how to use *present value concepts* to price the Fila discount bond and the Adidas premium bond described earlier.

Point: InvestingInBonds.com is a bond research and learning source.

Present Value of a Discount Bond The issue price of bonds is found by computing the present value of the bonds' cash payments, discounted at the bonds' market rate. When computing the present value of the Fila bonds, we work with *semiannual* compounding periods because this is the time between interest payments; the annual market rate of 10% is considered a semiannual rate of 5%. Also, the two-year bond life is viewed as four semiannual periods. The price computation is twofold: (1) Find the present value of the $100,000 par value paid at maturity and (2) find the present value of the series of four semiannual payments of $4,000 each; see Exhibit 14.4. These present values can be found by using *present value tables*. Appendix B at the end of this book shows present value tables and describes their use. Table B.1 at the end of Appendix B is used for the single $100,000 maturity payment, and Table B.3 in Appendix B is used for the $4,000 series of interest payments. Specifically, we go to Table B.1, row 4, and across to the 5% column to identify the present value factor of 0.8227 for the maturity payment. Next, we go to Table B.3, row 4, and across to the 5% column, where the present value factor is 3.5460 for the series of interest payments. We compute bond price by multiplying the cash flow payments by their corresponding present value factors and adding them together; see Exhibit 14.12.

Point: A bond's market value (price) at issuance equals the present value of its future cash payments, where the interest (discount) rate used is the bond's market rate.

Point: Many calculators have present value functions for computing bond prices.

EXHIBIT 14.12

Computing Issue Price for the Fila Discount Bonds

Cash Flow	Table	Present Value Factor		Amount		Present Value
$100,000 par (maturity) value	B.1	0.8227	×	$100,000	=	$ 82,270
$4,000 interest payments	B.3	3.5460	×	4,000	=	14,184
Price of bond						$96,454

Present Value of a Premium Bond We find the issue price of the Adidas bonds by using the market rate to compute the present value of the bonds' future cash flows. When computing the present value of these bonds, we again work with *semiannual* compounding periods because this is the time between interest payments. The annual 10% market rate is applied as a semiannual rate of 5%, and the two-year bond life is viewed as four semiannual periods. The computation is twofold: (1) Find the present value of the $100,000 par value paid at maturity and (2) find the present value of the series of four payments of $6,000 each; see Exhibit 14.8. These present values can be found by using present value tables. First, go to Table B.1, row 4, and across to the 5% column where the present value factor is 0.8227 for the maturity payment. Second, go to Table B.3, row 4, and across to the 5% column, where the present value factor is 3.5460 for the series of interest payments. The bonds' price is computed by multiplying the cash flow payments by their corresponding present value factors and adding them together; see Exhibit 14.13.

Point: There are nearly 5 million individual U.S. bond issues, ranging from huge treasuries to tiny municipalities. This compares to about 12,000 individual U.S. stocks that are traded.

EXHIBIT 14.13

Computing Issue Price for the Adidas Premium Bonds

Cash Flow	Table	Present Value Factor		Amount		Present Value
$100,000 par (maturity) value	B.1	0.8227	×	$100,000	=	$ 82,270
$6,000 interest payments	B.3	3.5460	×	6,000	=	21,276
Price of bond						$103,546

On December 31, 2008, a company issues 16%, 10-year bonds with a par value of $100,000. Interest is paid on June 30 and December 31. The bonds are sold to yield a 14% annual market rate at an issue price of $110,592. Use this information to answer questions 7 through 9:

7. Are these bonds issued at a discount or a premium? Explain your answer.

8. Using the straight-line method to allocate bond interest expense, the issuer records the second interest payment (on December 31, 2009) with a debit to Premium on Bonds Payable in the amount of (*a*) $7,470, (*b*) $530, (*c*) $8,000, or (*d*) $400.

9. How are these bonds reported in the long-term liability section of the issuer's balance sheet as of December 31, 2009?

Bond Retirement

This section describes the retirement of bonds (1) at maturity, (2) before maturity, and (3) by conversion to stock.

Bond Retirement at Maturity

The carrying value of bonds at maturity always equals par value. For example, both Exhibits 14.7 (a discount) and 14.11 (a premium) show that the carrying value of bonds at the end of their lives equals par value ($100,000). The retirement of these bonds at maturity, assuming interest is already paid and entered, is recorded as follows:

P4   Record the retirement of bonds.

2011			
Dec. 31	Bonds Payable	100,000	
	Cash		100,000
	To record retirement of bonds at maturity.		

Assets   = Liabilities + Equity
−100,000   −100,000

Bond Retirement before Maturity

Issuers sometimes wish to retire some or all of their bonds prior to maturity. For instance, if interest rates decline greatly, an issuer may wish to replace high-interest-paying bonds with new low-interest bonds. Two common ways to retire bonds before maturity are to (1) exercise a call option or (2) purchase them on the open market. In the first instance, an issuer can reserve the right to retire bonds early by issuing callable bonds. The bond indenture can give the issuer an option to *call* the bonds before they mature by paying the par value plus a *call premium* to bondholders. In the second case, the issuer retires bonds by repurchasing them on the open market at their current price. Whether bonds are called or repurchased, the issuer is unlikely to pay a price that exactly equals their carrying value. When a difference exists between the bonds' carrying value and the amount paid, the issuer records a gain or loss equal to the difference.

To illustrate the accounting for retiring callable bonds, assume that a company issued callable bonds with a par value of $100,000. The call option requires the issuer to pay a call premium of $3,000 to bondholders in addition to the par value. Next, assume that after the June 30, 2009, interest payment, the bonds have a carrying value of $104,500. Then on July 1, 2009, the issuer calls these bonds and pays $103,000 to bondholders. The issuer recognizes a $1,500 gain from the difference between the bonds' carrying value of $104,500 and the retirement price of $103,000. The issuer records this bond retirement as follows.

Point: Bond retirement is also referred to as *bond redemption.*

Point: Gains and losses from retiring bonds were *previously* reported as extraordinary items. New standards require that they now be judged by the "unusual and infrequent" criteria for reporting purposes.

July 1	Bonds Payable	100,000	
	Premium on Bonds Payable..................	4,500	
	Gain on Bond Retirement		1,500
	Cash		103,000
	To record retirement of bonds before maturity.		

Assets   = Liabilities + Equity
−103,000   −100,000   +1,500
           −4,500

An issuer usually must call all bonds when it exercises a call option. However, to retire as many or as few bonds as it desires, an issuer can purchase them on the open market. If it retires less than the entire class of bonds, it recognizes a gain or loss for the difference between the carrying value of those bonds retired and the amount paid to acquire them.

Bond Retirement by Conversion

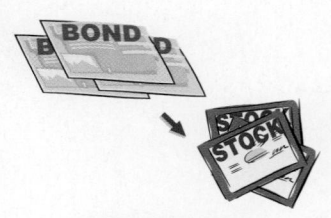

Convertible Bond

Assets = Liabilities + Equity
−100,000   +30,000
            +70,000

Holders of convertible bonds have the right to convert their bonds to stock. When conversion occurs, the bonds' carrying value is transferred to equity accounts and no gain or loss is recorded. (We further describe convertible bonds in the Decision Analysis section of this chapter.)

To illustrate, assume that on January 1 the $100,000 par value bonds of **Converse**, with a carrying value of $100,000, are converted to 15,000 shares of $2 par value common stock. The entry to record this conversion follows (the market prices of the bonds and stock are *not* relevant to this entry; the material in Chapter 13 is helpful in understanding this transaction):

Jan. 1	Bonds Payable	100,000	
	Common Stock		30,000
	Paid-In Capital in Excess of Par Value		70,000
	To record retirement of bonds by conversion.		

Decision Insight

Junk Bonds   Junk bonds are company bonds with low credit ratings due to a higher than average likelihood of default. On the upside, the high risk of junk bonds can yield high returns if the issuer survives and repays its debt.

Quick Check   Answer—p. 576

10. Six years ago, a company issued $500,000 of 6%, eight-year bonds at a price of 95. The current carrying value is $493,750. The company decides to retire 50% of these bonds by buying them on the open market at a price of 102½. What is the amount of gain or loss on the retirement of these bonds?

Long-Term Notes Payable

Video14.1

Like bonds, notes are issued to obtain assets such as cash. Unlike bonds, notes are typically transacted with a *single* lender such as a bank. An issuer initially records a note at its selling price—that is, the note's face value minus any discount or plus any premium. Over the note's life, the amount of interest expense allocated to each period is computed by multiplying the market rate (at issuance of the note) by the beginning-of-period note balance. The note's carrying (book) value at any time equals its face value minus any unamortized discount or plus any unamortized premium; carrying value is also computed as the present value of all remaining payments, discounted using the market rate at issuance.

Installment Notes

C1   Explain the types and payment patterns of notes.

An **installment note** is an obligation requiring a series of payments to the lender. Installment notes are common for franchises and other businesses when lenders and borrowers agree to spread payments over several periods. To illustrate, assume that Foghog borrows $60,000 from a bank to purchase equipment. It signs an 8% installment note requiring six annual payments of principal plus interest and it records the note's issuance at January 1, 2009, as follows.

Assets = Liabilities + Equity
+60,000   +60,000

Jan. 1	Cash	60,000	
	Notes Payable		60,000
	Borrowed $60,000 by signing an 8%, six-year installment note.		

Payments on an installment note normally include the accrued interest expense plus a portion of the amount borrowed (the *principal*). This section describes an installment note with equal payments.

The equal total payments pattern consists of changing amounts of both interest and principal. To illustrate, assume that Foghog borrows $60,000 by signing a $60,000 note that requires six *equal payments* of $12,979 at the end of each year. (The present value of an annuity of six annual payments of $12,979, discounted at 8%, equals $60,000; we show this computation in footnote 2 on the next page.) The $12,979 includes both interest and principal, the amounts of which change with each payment. Exhibit 14.14 shows the pattern of equal total payments and its two parts, interest and principal. Column A shows the note's beginning balance. Column B shows accrued interest for each year at 8% of the beginning note balance. Column C shows the impact on the note's principal, which equals the difference between the total payment in column D and the interest expense in column B. Column E shows the note's year-end balance.

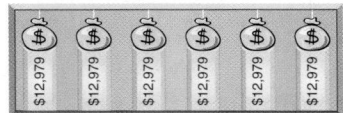

Years

2009 2010 2011 2012 2013 2014

Point: Most consumer notes are installment notes that require equal total payments.

EXHIBIT 14.14

Installment Note: Equal Total Payments

	(A)	(B) *Debit*		(C) *Debit*		(D) *Credit*	(E)
Period Ending Date	Beginning Balance	Interest Expense 8% × (A)	+	Notes Payable (D) − (B)	=	Cash (computed)	Ending Balance (A) − (C)
(1) 12/31/2009	$60,000	$ 4,800		$ 8,179		$12,979	$51,821
(2) 12/31/2010	51,821	4,146		8,833		12,979	42,988
(3) 12/31/2011	42,988	3,439		9,540		12,979	33,448
(4) 12/31/2012	33,448	2,676		10,303		12,979	23,145
(5) 12/31/2013	23,145	1,852		11,127		12,979	12,018
(6) 12/31/2014	12,018	961		12,018		12,979	0
		$17,874		$60,000		$77,874	

Interest Principal

Decreasing Accrued Interest ↓

Increasing Principal Component ↓

Equal Total Payments ↓

End of Year		
2009	$4,800	$8,179
2010	$4,146	$8,833
2011	$3,439	$9,540
2012	$2,676	$10,303
2013	$1,852	$11,127
2014	$961	$12,018

0   $2,500 $5,000 $7,500 $10,000 $12,500 $15,000

Cash Payment Pattern

Although the six cash payments are equal, accrued interest decreases each year because the principal balance of the note declines. As the amount of interest decreases each year, the portion of each payment applied to principal increases. This pattern is graphed in the lower part

Point: The Truth-in-Lending Act requires lenders to provide information about loan costs including finance charges and interest rate.

P5   Prepare entries to
account for notes.

of Exhibit 14.14. Foghog uses the amounts in Exhibit 14.14 to record its first two payments (for years 2009 and 2010) as follows:

Assets = Liabilities + Equity
−12,979   −8,179   −4,800

2009		
Dec. 31	Interest Expense 4,800	
	Notes Payable 8,179	
	Cash	12,979
	To record first installment payment.	

Assets = Liabilities + Equity
−12,979   −8,833   −4,146

2010		
Dec. 31	Interest Expense 4,146	
	Notes Payable 8,833	
	Cash	12,979
	To record second installment payment.	

Foghog records similar entries but with different amounts for each of the remaining four payments. After six years, the Notes Payable account balance is zero.[2]

Mortgage Notes and Bonds

A **mortgage** is a legal agreement that helps protect a lender if a borrower fails to make required payments on notes or bonds. A mortgage gives the lender a right to be paid from the cash proceeds of the sale of a borrower's assets identified in the mortgage. A legal document, called a *mortgage contract,* describes the mortgage terms.

Mortgage notes carry a mortgage contract pledging title to specific assets as security for the note. Mortgage notes are especially popular in the purchase of homes and the acquisition of plant assets. Less common *mortgage bonds* are backed by the issuer's assets. Accounting for mortgage notes and bonds is similar to that for unsecured notes and bonds, except that the mortgage agreement must be disclosed. For example, **Musicland** reports that its "mortgage note payable is collateralized by land, buildings and certain fixtures."

Decision Maker

Entrepreneur   You are an electronics retailer planning a holiday sale on a custom stereo system that requires no payments for two years. At the end of two years, buyers must pay the full amount. The system's suggested retail price is $4,100, but you are willing to sell it today for $3,000 cash. What is your holiday sale price if payment will not occur for two years and the market interest rate is 10%? [Answer—p. 576]

Quick Check

Answers—p. 576

11. Which of the following is true for an installment note requiring a series of equal total cash payments? (*a*) Payments consist of increasing interest and decreasing principal; (*b*) payments consist of changing amounts of principal but constant interest; or (*c*) payments consist of decreasing interest and increasing principal.

12. How is the interest portion of an installment note payment computed?

13. When a borrower records an interest payment on an installment note, how are the balance sheet and income statement affected?

---

[2] Table B.3 in Appendix B is used to compute the dollar amount of the six payments that equal the initial note balance of $60,000 at 8% interest. We go to Table B.3, row 6, and across to the 8% column, where the present value factor is 4.6229. The dollar amount is then computed by solving this relation:

Table	Present Value Factor	Dollar Amount	Present Value
B.3	4.6229	?	$60,000
	×	=	

The dollar amount is computed by dividing $60,000 by 4.6229, yielding $12,979.

| **Debt Features and the Debt-to-Equity Ratio** | **Decision Analysis** |

Collateral agreements can reduce the risk of loss for both bonds and notes. Unsecured bonds and notes are riskier because the issuer's obligation to pay interest and principal has the same priority as all other unsecured liabilities in the event of bankruptcy. If a company is unable to pay its debts in full, the unsecured creditors (including the holders of debentures) lose all or a portion of their balances. These types of legal agreements and other characteristics of long-term liabilities are crucial for effective business decisions. The first part of this section describes the different types of features sometimes included with bonds and notes. The second part explains and applies the debt-to-equity ratio.

Features of Bonds and Notes

This section describes common features of debt securities.

A2   Assess debt features and their implications.

Secured or Unsecured   **Secured bonds** (and notes) have specific assets of the issuer pledged (or *mortgaged*) as collateral. This arrangement gives holders added protection against the issuer's default. If the issuer fails to pay interest or par value, the secured holders can demand that the collateral be sold and the proceeds used to pay the obligation. **Unsecured bonds** (and notes), also called *debentures,* are backed by the issuer's general credit standing. Unsecured debt is riskier than secured debt. *Subordinated debentures* are liabilities that are not repaid until the claims of the more senior, unsecured (and secured) liabilities are settled.

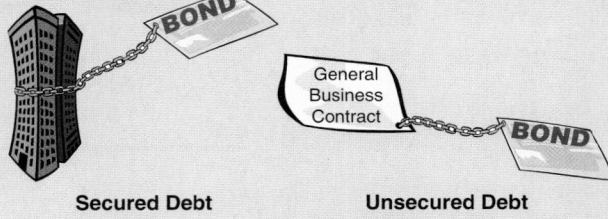

Secured Debt   **Unsecured Debt**

Term or Serial   **Term bonds** (and notes) are scheduled for maturity on one specified date. **Serial bonds** (and notes) mature at more than one date (often in series) and thus are usually repaid over a number of periods. For instance, $100,000 of serial bonds might mature at the rate of $10,000 each year from 6 to 15 years after they are issued. Many bonds are **sinking fund bonds,** which to reduce the holder's risk require the issuer to create a *sinking fund* of assets set aside at specified amounts and dates to repay the bonds.

Registered or Bearer   Bonds issued in the names and addresses of their holders are **registered bonds.** The issuer makes bond payments by sending checks (or cash transfers) to registered holders. A registered holder must notify the issuer of any ownership change. Registered bonds offer the issuer the practical advantage of not having to actually issue bond certificates. Bonds payable to whoever holds them (the *bearer*) are called **bearer bonds** or *unregistered bonds.* Sales or exchanges might not be recorded, so the holder of a bearer bond is presumed to be its rightful owner. As a result, lost bearer bonds are difficult to replace. Many bearer bonds are also **coupon bonds.** This term reflects interest coupons that are attached to the bonds. When each coupon matures, the holder presents it to a bank or broker for collection. At maturity, the holder follows the same process and presents the bond certificate for collection. Issuers of coupon bonds cannot deduct the related interest expense for taxable income. This is to prevent abuse by taxpayers who own coupon bonds but fail to report interest income on their tax returns.

Convertible and/or Callable   **Convertible bonds** (and notes) can be exchanged for a fixed number of shares of the issuing corporation's common stock. Convertible debt offers holders the potential to participate in future increases in stock price. Holders still receive periodic interest while the debt is held and the par value if they hold the debt to maturity. In most cases, the holders decide whether and when to convert debt to stock. **Callable bonds** (and notes) have an option exercisable by the issuer to retire them at a stated dollar amount before maturity.

Convertible Debt   **Callable Debt**

Decision Insight

Munis   More than a million municipal bonds, or "munis," exist, and many are tax exempt. Munis are issued by state, city, town, and county governments to pay for public projects including schools, libraries, roads, bridges, and stadiums.

Debt-to-Equity Ratio

Beyond assessing different characteristics of debt as just described, we want to know the level of debt, especially in relation to total equity. Such knowledge helps us assess the risk of a company's financing

A3   Compute the debt-to-equity ratio and explain its use.

structure. A company financed mainly with debt is more risky because liabilities must be repaid—usually with periodic interest—whereas equity financing does not. A measure to assess the risk of a company's financing structure is the **debt-to-equity ratio** (see Exhibit 14.15).

EXHIBIT 14.15

Debt-to-Equity Ratio

$$\text{Debt-to-equity} = \frac{\text{Total liabilities}}{\text{Total equity}}$$

The debt-to-equity ratio varies across companies and industries. Industries that are more variable tend to have lower ratios, while more stable industries are less risky and tend to have higher ratios. To apply the debt-to-equity ratio, let's look at this measure for Six Flags in Exhibit 14.16.

EXHIBIT 14.16

Six Flags' Debt-to-Equity Ratio

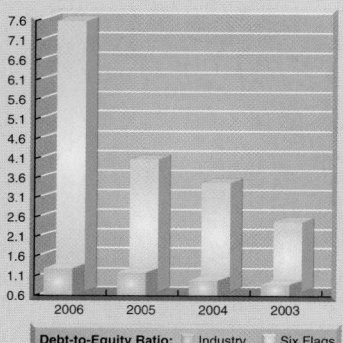

($ millions)	2006	2005	2004	2003
Total liabilities	$2,811	$2,799	$2,816	$3,321
Total equity	$ 376	$ 694	$ 826	$1,362
Debt-to-equity	7.5	4.0	3.4	2.4
Industry debt-to-equity	1.2	1.1	0.9	0.8

Six Flags' 2006 debt-to-equity ratio was 7.5, meaning that debtholders contributed $7.5 for each $1 contributed by equityholders. This implies a fairly risky financing structure for Six Flags. A similar concern is drawn from a comparison of Six Flags with its competitors, where the 2006 industry ratio was 1.2. Analysis across the years shows that Six Flags' financing structure has grown increasingly risky in recent years. Given its sluggish revenues and increasing operating expenses in recent years (see its annual report), Six Flags is increasingly at risk of financial distress.

Decision Maker

Bond Investor You plan to purchase debenture bonds from one of two companies in the same industry that are similar in size and performance. The first company has $350,000 in total liabilities, and $1,750,000 in equity. The second company has $1,200,000 in total liabilities, and $1,000,000 in equity. Which company's debenture bonds are less risky based on the debt-to-equity ratio? [Answer—p. 576]

Demonstration Problem

DP14

Water Sports Company (WSC) patented and successfully test-marketed a new product. To expand its ability to produce and market the new product, WSC needs to raise $800,000 of financing. On January 1, 2009, the company obtained the money in two ways:

a. WSC signed a $400,000, 10% installment note to be repaid with five equal annual installments to be made on December 31 of 2009 through 2013.

b. WSC issued five-year bonds with a par value of $400,000. The bonds have a 12% annual contract rate and pay interest on June 30 and December 31. The bonds' annual market rate is 10% as of January 1, 2009.

Required

1. For the installment note, (a) compute the size of each annual payment, (b) prepare an amortization table such as Exhibit 14.14, and (c) prepare the journal entry for the first payment.
2. For the bonds, (a) compute their issue price; (b) prepare the January 1, 2009, journal entry to record their issuance; (c) prepare an amortization table using the straight-line method; (d) prepare the June 30, 2009, journal entry to record the first interest payment; and (e) prepare a journal entry to record retiring the bonds at a $416,000 call price on January 1, 2011.
3.BRedo parts 2(c), 2(d), and 2(e) assuming the bonds are amortized using the effective interest method.

Planning the Solution

- For the installment note, divide the borrowed amount by the annuity factor (from Table B.3) using the 10% rate and five payments to compute the amount of each payment. Prepare a table similar to Exhibit 14.14 and use the numbers in the table's first line for the journal entry.
- Compute the bonds' issue price by using the market rate to find the present value of their cash flows (use tables found in Appendix B). Then use this result to record the bonds' issuance. Next, prepare an amortization table like Exhibit 14.11 (and Exhibit 14B.2) and use it to get the numbers needed for the journal entry. Also use the table to find the carrying value as of the date of the bonds' retirement that you need for the journal entry.

Solution to Demonstration Problem

Part 1: Installment Note

a. Annual payment = Note balance/Annuity factor = $400,000/3.7908 = $105,519 (The annuity factor is for five payments and a rate of 10%.)

b. An amortization table follows.

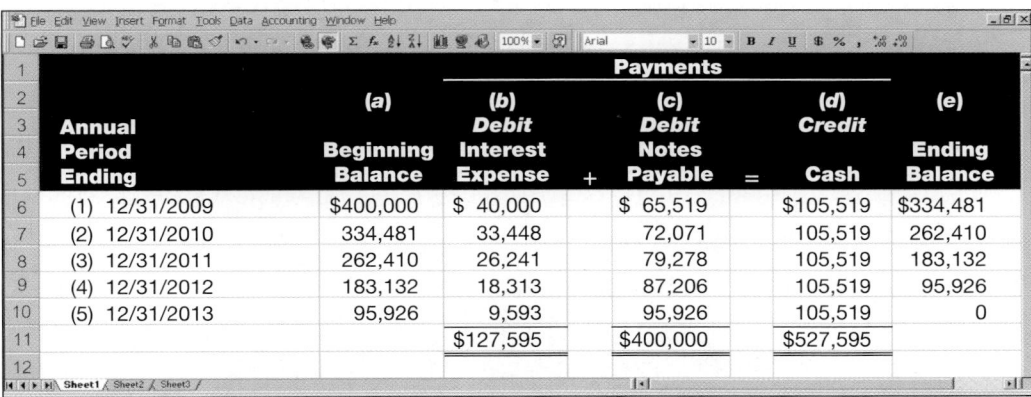

		Payments				
	(a)	(b)		(c)	(d)	(e)
Annual Period Ending	Beginning Balance	Debit Interest Expense	+	Debit Notes Payable =	Credit Cash	Ending Balance
(1) 12/31/2009	$400,000	$ 40,000		$ 65,519	$105,519	$334,481
(2) 12/31/2010	334,481	33,448		72,071	105,519	262,410
(3) 12/31/2011	262,410	26,241		79,278	105,519	183,132
(4) 12/31/2012	183,132	18,313		87,206	105,519	95,926
(5) 12/31/2013	95,926	9,593		95,926	105,519	0
		$127,595		$400,000	$527,595	

c. Journal entry for December 31, 2009, payment.

Dec. 31	Interest Expense	40,000	
	Notes Payable	65,519	
	Cash		105,519
	To record first installment payment.		

Part 2: Bonds (Straight-Line Amortization)

a. Compute the bonds' issue price.

Cash Flow	Table	Present Value Factor*	Amount	Present Value
Par (maturity) value	B.1 in App. B (PV of 1)	0.6139	× 400,000	= $245,560
Interest payments	B.3 in App. B (PV of annuity)	7.7217	× 24,000	= 185,321
Price of bond				$430,881

* Present value factors are for 10 payments using a semiannual market rate of 5%.

b. Journal entry for January 1, 2009, issuance.

Jan. 1	Cash	430,881	
	Premium on Bonds Payable		30,881
	Bonds Payable		400,000
	Sold bonds at a premium.		

c. Straight-line amortization table for premium bonds.

Semiannual Period-End	Unamortized Premium	Carrying Value
(0) 1/1/2009	$30,881	$430,881
(1) 6/30/2009	27,793	427,793
(2) 12/31/2009	24,705	424,705
(3) 6/30/2010	21,617	421,617
(4) 12/31/2010	18,529	418,529
(5) 6/30/2011	15,441	415,441
(6) 12/31/2011	12,353	412,353
(7) 6/30/2012	9,265	409,265
(8) 12/31/2012	6,177	406,177
(9) 6/30/2013	3,089	403,089
(10) 12/31/2013	0*	400,000

* Adjusted for rounding.

d. Journal entry for June 30, 2009, bond payment.

June 30	Bond Interest Expense	20,912	
	Premium on Bonds Payable	3,088	
	Cash		24,000
	Paid semiannual interest on bonds.		

e. Journal entry for January 1, 2011, bond retirement.

Jan. 1	Bonds Payable	400,000	
	Premium on Bonds Payable	18,529	
	Cash		416,000
	Gain on Retirement of Bonds		2,529
	To record bond retirement (carrying value as of Dec. 31, 2010).		

Part 3: Bonds (Effective Interest Amortization)[B]

c. The effective interest amortization table for premium bonds.

Semiannual Interest Period	(A) Cash Interest Paid 6% × $400,000	(B) Interest Expense 5% × Prior (E)	(C) Premium Amortization (A) − (B)	(D) Unamortized Premium Prior (D) − (C)	(E) Carrying Value $400,000 + (D)
(0) 1/1/2009				$30,881	$430,881
(1) 6/30/2009	$ 24,000	$ 21,544	$ 2,456	28,425	428,425
(2) 12/31/2009	24,000	21,421	2,579	25,846	425,846
(3) 6/30/2010	24,000	21,292	2,708	23,138	423,138
(4) 12/31/2010	24,000	21,157	2,843	20,295	420,295
(5) 6/30/2011	24,000	21,015	2,985	17,310	417,310
(6) 12/31/2011	24,000	20,866	3,134	14,176	414,176
(7) 6/30/2012	24,000	20,709	3,291	10,885	410,885
(8) 12/31/2012	24,000	20,544	3,456	7,429	407,429
(9) 6/30/2013	24,000	20,371	3,629	3,800	403,800
(10) 12/31/2013	24,000	20,200*	3,800	0	400,000
	$240,000	$209,119	$30,881		

* Adjusted for rounding

d. Journal entry for June 30, 2009, bond payment.

June 30	Bond Interest Expense	21,544	
	Premium on Bonds Payable.	2,456	
	Cash		24,000
	Paid semiannual interest on bonds.		

e. Journal entry for January 1, 2011, bond retirement.

Jan. 1	Bonds Payable	400,000	
	Premium on Bonds Payable.	20,295	
	Cash		416,000
	Gain on Retirement of Bonds		4,295
	To record bond retirement (carrying value *as of December 31, 2010).*		

APPENDIX

Present Values of Bonds and Notes

14A

This appendix explains how to apply present value techniques to measure a long-term liability when it is created and to assign interest expense to the periods until it is settled. Appendix B at the end of the book provides additional discussion of present value concepts.

Present Value Concepts

C2 Explain and compute the present value of an amount(s) to be paid at a future date(s).

The basic present value concept is that cash paid (or received) in the future has less value now than the same amount of cash paid (or received) today. To illustrate, if we must pay $1 one year from now, its present value is less than $1. To see this, assume that we borrow $0.9259 today that must be paid back in one year with 8% interest. Our interest expense for this loan is computed as $0.9259 × 8%, or $0.0741.

EXHIBIT 14A.1

Components of a One-Year Loan

When the $0.0741 interest is added to the $0.9259 borrowed, we get the $1 payment necessary to repay our loan with interest. This is formally computed in Exhibit 14A.1. The $0.9259 borrowed is the present value of the $1 future payment. More generally, an amount borrowed equals the present value of the

Amount borrowed	**$0.9259**
Interest for one year at 8%	0.0741
Amount owed after 1 year	$ 1.0000

future payment. (This same interpretation applies to an investment. If $0.9259 is invested at 8%, it yields $0.0741 in revenue after one year. This amounts to $1, made up of principal and interest.)

To extend this example, assume that we owe $1 two years from now instead of one year, and the 8% interest is compounded annually. *Compounded* means that interest during the second period is based on the total of the amount borrowed plus the interest accrued from the first period. The second period's interest is then computed as 8% multiplied by the sum of the amount borrowed plus interest earned in the first period. Exhibit 14A.2 shows how we compute the present value of $1 to be paid in two years. This amount is $0.8573. The first year's interest of $0.0686 is added to the principal so that the second year's interest is based on $0.9259. Total interest for this two-year period is $0.1427, computed as $0.0686 plus $0.0741.

Point: Benjamin Franklin is said to have described compounding as "the money, money makes, makes more money."

EXHIBIT 14A.2

Components of a Two-Year Loan

Amount borrowed	**$0.8573**
Interest for first year ($0.8573 × 8%)	0.0686
Amount owed after 1 year	0.9259
Interest for second year ($0.9259 × 8%)	0.0741
Amount owed after 2 years	$ 1.0000

Present Value Tables

The present value of $1 that we must repay at some future date can be computed by using this formula: $1/(1 + i)^n$. The symbol i is the interest rate per period and n is the number of periods until the future payment must be made. Applying this formula to our two-year loan, we get $\$1/(1.08)^2$, or $0.8573. This

EXHIBIT 14A.3

Present Value of 1

Periods	Rate		
	6%	8%	10%
1	0.9434	**0.9259**	0.9091
2	0.8900	**0.8573**	0.8264
3	0.8396	0.7938	0.7513
4	0.7921	0.7350	0.6830
5	0.7473	0.6806	0.6209
6	0.7050	0.6302	0.5645
7	0.6651	0.5835	0.5132
8	0.6274	0.5403	0.4665
9	0.5919	0.5002	0.4241
10	0.5584	0.4632	0.3855

is the same value shown in Exhibit 14A.2. We can use this formula to find any present value. However, a simpler method is to use a *present value table,* which lists present values computed with this formula for various interest rates and time periods. Many people find it helpful in learning present value concepts to first work with the table and then move to using a calculator.

Exhibit 14A.3 shows a present value table for a future payment of 1 for up to 10 periods at three different interest rates. Present values in this table are rounded to four decimal places. This table is drawn from the larger and more complete Table B.1 in Appendix B at the end of the book. Notice that the first value in the 8% column is 0.9259, the value we computed earlier for the present value of a $1 loan for one year at 8% (see Exhibit 14A.1). Go to

Example: Use Exhibit 14A.3 to find the present value of $1 discounted for 2 years at 6%. *Answer:* $0.8900

the second row in the same 8% column and find the present value of 1 discounted at 8% for two years, or 0.8573. This $0.8573 is the present value of our obligation to repay $1 after two periods at 8% interest (see Exhibit 14A.2).

Applying a Present Value Table

To illustrate how to measure a liability using a present value table, assume that a company plans to borrow cash and repay it as follows: $2,000 after one year, $3,000 after two years, and $5,000 after three

EXHIBIT 14A.4

Present Value of a Series of Unequal Payments

Periods	Payments	Present Value of 1 at 10%	Present Value of Payments
1	$2,000	0.9091	$ 1,818
2	3,000	0.8264	2,479
3	5,000	0.7513	3,757
Present value of all payments			**$8,054**

years. How much does this company receive today if the interest rate on this loan is 10%? To answer, we need to compute the present value of the three future payments, discounted at 10%. This computation is shown in Exhibit 14A.4 using present values from Exhibit 14A.3. The company can borrow $8,054 today at 10% interest in exchange for its promise to make these three payments at the scheduled dates.

Present Value of an Annuity

The $8,054 present value for the loan in Exhibit 14A.4 equals the sum of the present values of the three payments. When payments are not equal, their combined present value is best computed by adding the individual present values as shown in Exhibit 14A.4. Sometimes payments follow an **annuity,** which is a series of *equal* payments at equal time intervals. The present value of an annuity is readily computed.

To illustrate, assume that a company must repay a 6% loan with a $5,000 payment at each year-end for the next four years. This loan amount equals the present value of the four payments discounted at 6%. Exhibit

EXHIBIT 14A.5

Present Value of a Series of Equal Payments (Annuity) by Discounting Each Payment

Periods	Payments	Present Value of 1 at 6%	Present Value of Payments
1	$5,000	0.9434	$ 4,717
2	5,000	0.8900	4,450
3	5,000	0.8396	4,198
4	5,000	0.7921	3,961
Present value of all payments		**3.4651**	**$17,326**

14A.5 shows how to compute this loan's present value of $17,326 by multiplying each payment by its matching present value factor taken from Exhibit 14A.3.

However, the series of $5,000 payments is an annuity, so we can compute its present value with either of two shortcuts. First, the third column of Exhibit 14A.5 shows that the sum of the present values of 1 at 6% for periods 1 through 4 equals 3.4651. One shortcut is to multiply this total of 3.4651 by the $5,000 annual payment to get the combined present value of $17,326. It requires one multiplication instead of four.

The second shortcut uses an *annuity table* such as the one shown in Exhibit 14A.6, which is drawn from the more complete Table B.3 in Appendix B. We go directly to the annuity table to get the present value factor for a specific number of payments and interest rate. We then multiply this factor by the amount of the payment to find the present value of the annuity. Specifically, find the row for four periods and go across to the 6% column, where the factor is 3.4651. This factor equals the present value of an annuity with four payments of 1, discounted at 6%. We then multiply 3.4651 by $5,000 to get the $17,326 present value of the annuity.

Compounding Periods Shorter Than a Year

The present value examples all involved periods of one year. In many situations, however, interest is compounded over shorter periods. For example, the interest rate on bonds is usually stated as an annual rate but interest is often paid every six months (semiannually). This means that the present value of interest payments from such bonds must be computed using interest periods of six months.

Assume that a borrower wants to know the present value of a series of 10 *semiannual payments* of $4,000 made over five years at an *annual interest rate* of 12%. The interest rate is stated as an annual rate of 12%, but it is actually a rate of 6% per semiannual interest period. To compute the present value of this series of $4,000 payments, go to row 10 of Exhibit 14A.6 and across to the 6% column to find the factor 7.3601. The present value of this annuity is $29,440 (7.3601 × $4,000).

Appendix B further describes present value concepts and includes more complete present value tables and assignments.

EXHIBIT 14A.6
Present Value of an Annuity of 1

		Rate	
Periods	6%	8%	10%
1	0.9434	0.9259	0.9091
2	1.8334	1.7833	1.7355
3	2.6730	2.5771	2.4869
4	3.4651	3.3121	3.1699
5	4.2124	3.9927	3.7908
6	4.9173	4.6229	4.3553
7	5.5824	5.2064	4.8684
8	6.2098	5.7466	5.3349
9	6.8017	6.2469	5.7590
10	7.3601	6.7101	6.1446

Example: Use Exhibit 14A.6 to find the present value of an annuity of eight $15,000 payments with an 8% interest rate. *Answer:* $15,000 × 5.7466 = $86,199

Example: If this borrower makes five semiannual payments of $8,000, what is the present value of this annuity at a 12% rate? *Answer:* 4.2124 × $8,000 = $33,699

Quick Check
Answers—p. 576

14. A company enters into an agreement to make four annual year-end payments of $1,000 each, starting one year from now. The annual interest rate is 8%. The present value of these four payments is (a) $2,923, (b) $2,940, or (c) $3,312.

15. Suppose a company has an option to pay either (a) $10,000 after one year or (b) $5,000 after six months and another $5,000 after one year. Which choice has the lower present value?

APPENDIX

Effective Interest Amortization

14B

Effective Interest Amortization of a Discount Bond

The straight-line method yields changes in the bonds' carrying value while the amount for bond interest expense remains constant. This gives the impression of a changing interest rate when users divide a constant bond interest expense over a changing carrying value. As a result, accounting standards allow use of the straight-line method only when its results do not differ materially from those obtained using the effective interest method. The **effective interest method,** or simply *interest method,* allocates total bond interest expense over the bonds' life in a way that yields a constant rate of interest. This constant rate of interest is the market rate at the issue date. Thus, bond interest expense for a period equals the carrying value of the bond at the beginning of that period multiplied by the market rate when issued.

Point: The effective interest method computes bond interest expense using the market rate at issuance. This rate is applied to a changing carrying value.

Exhibit 14B.1 shows an effective interest amortization table for the Fila bonds (as described in Exhibit 14.4). The key difference between the effective interest and straight-line methods lies in computing bond interest expense. Instead of assigning an equal amount of bond interest expense to each period, the effective interest method assigns a bond interest expense amount that increases over the life of a discount bond. **Both methods allocate the *same* $19,546 of total bond interest expense to the bonds' life, but in different patterns.** Specifically, the amortization table in Exhibit 14B.1 shows that the balance of the discount (column D) is amortized until it reaches zero. Also, the bonds' carrying value (column E) changes each period until it equals par value at maturity. Compare columns D and E to the corresponding columns in Exhibit 14.7 to see the amortization patterns. Total bond interest expense is $19,546, consisting of $16,000 of semiannual cash payments and $3,546 of the original bond discount, the same for both methods.

EXHIBIT 14B.1

Effective Interest Amortization of Bond Discount

Bonds: $100,000 Par Value, Semiannual Interest Payments, Two-Year Life, 4% Semiannual Contract Rate, 5% Semiannual Market Rate					
	(A)	(B)	(C)	(D)	(E)
Semiannual Interest Period-End	Cash Interest Paid	Bond Interest Expense	Discount Amortization	Unamortized Discount	Carrying Value
(0) 12/31/2009				$3,546	$ 96,454
(1) 6/30/2010	$4,000	$4,823	$ 823	2,723	97,277
(2) 12/31/2010	4,000	4,864	864	1,859	98,141
(3) 6/30/2011	4,000	4,907	907	952	99,048
(4) 12/31/2011	4,000	4,952	952	0	100,000
	$16,000	$19,546	$3,546		

Column (A) is the par value ($100,000) multiplied by the semiannual contract rate (4%).
Column (B) is the prior period's carrying value multiplied by the semiannual market rate (5%).
Column (C) is the difference between interest paid and bond interest expense, or [(B) − (A)].
Column (D) is the prior period's unamortized discount less the current period's discount amortization.
Column (E) is the par value less unamortized discount, or [$100,000 − (D)].

Except for differences in amounts, journal entries recording the expense and updating the liability balance are the same under the effective interest method and the straight-line method. We can use the numbers in Exhibit 14B.1 to record each semiannual entry during the bonds' two-year life (June 30, 2010, through December 31, 2011). For instance, we record the interest payment at the end of the first semiannual period as follows:

Assets = Liabilities + Equity
−4,000   +823   −4,823

2010			
June 30	Bond Interest Expense	4,823	
	Discount on Bonds Payable		823
	Cash		4,000
	To record semiannual interest and discount amortization (effective interest method).		

Effective Interest Amortization of a Premium Bond

Exhibit 14B.2 shows the amortization table using the effective interest method for the Adidas bonds (as described in Exhibit 14.8). Column A lists the semiannual cash payments. Column B shows the amount of bond interest expense, computed as the 5% semiannual market rate at issuance multiplied by the beginning-of-period carrying value. The amount of cash paid in column A is larger than the bond interest expense because the cash payment is based on the higher 6% semiannual contract rate. The excess cash payment over the interest expense reduces the principal. These amounts are shown in column C. Column E

EXHIBIT 14B.2

Effective Interest Amortization of Bond Premium

```
File Edit View Insert Format Tools Data Accounting Window Help                    _|8|x|
D ⊟ ⊟ ⊕ ⊒ ⊽  % ⊑ ⊑ ⊘  ⋈ ⋈ ⋈  ⋈ ⋈ Σ ⨍ ⊋↓ ⊋↑ ⋈ ⊕ ⊕  100% ▾  ⊠  Arial  ▾ 10 ▾  B I U  $ % , ⋮⋮ ⋮⋮
```

	(A)	(B)	(C)	(D)	(E)
Bonds: $100,000 Par Value, Semiannual Interest Payments, Two-Year Life, 6% Semiannual Contract Rate, 5% Semiannual Market Rate					
Semiannual Interest Period-End	**Cash Interest Paid**	**Bond Interest Expense**	**Premium Amortization**	**Unamortized Premium**	**Carrying Value**
(0) 12/31/2009				$3,546	$103,546
(1) 6/30/2010	$6,000	$5,177	$ 823	2,723	102,723
(2) 12/31/2010	6,000	5,136	864	1,859	101,859
(3) 6/30/2011	6,000	5,093	907	952	100,952
(4) 12/31/2011	6,000	5,048	952	0	100,000
	$24,000	$20,454	$3,546		

`Sheet1  Sheet2  Sheet3  Sheet2  Sheet3`

Column (**A**) is the par value ($100,000) multiplied by the semiannual contract rate (6%).
Column (**B**) is the prior period's carrying value multiplied by the semiannual market rate (5%).
Column (**C**) is the difference between interest paid and bond interest expense, or [(A) − (B)].
Column (**D**) is the prior period's unamortized premium less the current period's premium amortization.
Column (**E**) is the par value plus unamortized premium, or [$100,000 + (D)].

shows the carrying value after deducting the amortized premium in column C from the prior period's carrying value. Column D shows the premium's reduction by periodic amortization. When the issuer makes the first semiannual interest payment, the effect of premium amortization on bond interest expense and bond liability is recorded as follows:

2010			
June 30	Bond Interest Expense	5,177	
	Premium on Bonds Payable	823	
	Cash		6,000
	To record semiannual interest and premium amortization (effective interest method).		

Assets = Liabilities + Equity
−6,000   −823   −5,177

Similar entries with different amounts are recorded at each payment date until the bond matures at the end of 2011. The effective interest method yields decreasing amounts of bond interest expense and increasing amounts of premium amortization over the bonds' life.

Decision Insight

IFRSs Unlike U.S. GAAP, IFRSs require that interest expense be computed using the effective interest method with *no exemptions*.

APPENDIX

Issuing Bonds between Interest Dates

14C

C3 Describe the accrual of bond interest when bond payments do not align with accounting periods.

An issuer can sell bonds at a date other than an interest payment date. When this occurs, the buyers normally pay the issuer the purchase price plus any interest accrued since the prior interest payment date. This accrued interest is then repaid to these buyers on the next interest payment date. To illustrate, suppose **Avia** sells $100,000 of its 9% bonds at par on March 1, 2009, 60 days after the stated issue date. The interest on Avia bonds is payable semiannually on each June 30 and December 31. Since 60 days have passed, the issuer collects accrued interest from the buyers at the time of issuance. This amount is $1,500 ($100,000 × 9% × $^{60}/_{360}$ year). This case is reflected in Exhibit 14C.1.

EXHIBIT 14C.1

Accruing Interest between Interest Payment Dates

Avia records the issuance of these bonds on March 1, 2009, as follows:

Assets	= Liabilities +	Equity
+101,500	+100,000	
	+1,500	

Mar. 1	Cash	101,500	
	Interest Payable.		1,500
	Bonds Payable.		100,000
	Sold bonds at par with accrued interest.		

Example: How much interest is collected from a buyer of $50,000 of Avia bonds sold at par 150 days after the contract issue date? *Answer:* $1,875 (computed as $50,000 × 9% × $^{150}/_{360}$ year)

Assets	= Liabilities +	Equity
−4,500	−1,500	−3,000

Liabilities for interest payable and bonds payable are recorded in separate accounts. When the June 30, 2009, semiannual interest date arrives, Avia pays the full semiannual interest of $4,500 ($100,000 × 9% × ½ year) to the bondholders. This payment includes the four months' interest of $3,000 earned by the bondholders from March 1 to June 30 *plus* the repayment of the 60 days' accrued interest collected by Avia when the bonds were sold. Avia records this first semiannual interest payment as follows:

June 30	Interest Payable	1,500	
	Bond Interest Expense	3,000	
	Cash		4,500
	Paid semiannual interest on the bonds.		

The practice of collecting and then repaying accrued interest with the next interest payment is to simplify the issuer's administrative efforts. To explain, suppose an issuer sells bonds on 15 or 20 different dates between the stated issue date and the first interest payment date. If the issuer does not collect accrued interest from buyers, it needs to pay different amounts of cash to each of them according to the time that passed after purchasing the bonds. The issuer needs to keep detailed records of buyers and the dates they bought bonds. Issuers avoid this recordkeeping by having each buyer pay accrued interest at purchase. Issuers then pay the full semiannual interest to all buyers, regardless of when they bought bonds.

Accruing Bond Interest Expense

If a bond's interest period does not coincide with the issuer's accounting period, an adjusting entry is needed to recognize bond interest expense accrued since the most recent interest payment. To illustrate, assume that the stated issue date for Adidas bonds described in Exhibit 14.10 is September 1, 2009, instead of December 31, 2009, and that the bonds are sold on September 1, 2009. As a result, four months' interest (and premium amortization) accrue before the end of the 2009 calendar year. Interest for this period equals $3,409, or ⅔ of the first six months' interest of $5,113. Also, the premium amortization is $591, or ⅔ of the first six months' amortization of $887. The sum of the bond interest expense and the amortization is $4,000 ($3,409 + $591), which equals ⅔ of the $6,000 cash payment due on February 28, 2010. Adidas records these effects with an adjusting entry at December 31, 2009.

Point: Computation of accrued bond interest may use months instead of days for simplicity purposes. For example, the accrued interest computation for the Adidas bonds is based on months.

Assets = Liabilities +	Equity
−591	−3,409
+4,000	

Dec. 31	Bond Interest Expense	3,409	
	Premium on Bonds Payable.	591	
	Interest Payable.		4,000
	To record four months' accrued interest and premium amortization.		

Similar entries are made on each December 31 throughout the bonds' two-year life. When the $6,000 cash payment occurs on each February 28 interest payment date, Adidas must recognize bond interest expense and amortization for January and February. It must also eliminate the interest payable liability created by the December 31 adjusting entry. For example, Adidas records its payment on February 28, 2010, as follows:

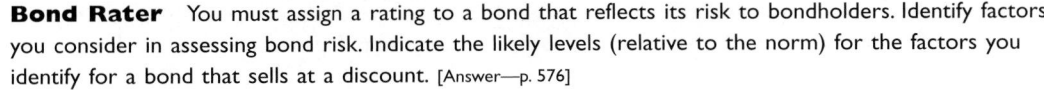

Feb. 28	Interest Payable	4,000	
	Bond Interest Expense ($5,113 × ⅔)	1,705	
	Premium on Bonds Payable ($887 × ⅔)	295*	
	Cash		6,000
	To record 2 months' interest and amortization, and eliminate accrued interest liability.		

Assets = Liabilities + Equity
−6,000   −4,000   −1,705
              −295

*Adjusted for rounding.

The interest payments made each August 31 are recorded as usual because the entire six-month interest period is included within this company's calendar-year reporting period.

Decision Maker

Bond Rater   You must assign a rating to a bond that reflects its risk to bondholders. Identify factors you consider in assessing bond risk. Indicate the likely levels (relative to the norm) for the factors you identify for a bond that sells at a discount. [Answer—p. 576]

Quick Check   Answer—p. 576

16. On May 1, a company sells 9% bonds with a $500,000 par value that pay semiannual interest on each January 1 and July 1. The bonds are sold at par plus interest accrued since January 1. The issuer records the first semiannual interest payment on July 1 with (*a*) a debit to Interest Payable for $15,000, (*b*) a debit to Bond Interest Expense for $22,500, or (*c*) a credit to Interest Payable for $7,500.

APPENDIX

Leases and Pensions

14D

This appendix briefly explains the accounting and analysis for both leases and pensions.

Lease Liabilities

A **lease** is a contractual agreement between a *lessor* (asset owner) and a *lessee* (asset renter or tenant) that grants the lessee the right to use the asset for a period of time in return for cash (rent) payments. Nearly one-fourth of all equipment purchases are financed with leases. The advantages of lease financing include the lack of an immediate large cash payment and the potential to deduct rental payments in computing taxable income. From an accounting perspective, leases can be classified as either operating or capital leases.

C4   Describe accounting for leases and pensions.

Operating Leases   **Operating leases** are short-term (or cancelable) leases in which the lessor retains the risks and rewards of ownership. Examples include most car and apartment rental agreements. The lessee records such lease payments as expenses; the lessor records them as revenue. The lessee does not report the leased item as an asset or a liability (it is the lessor's asset). To illustrate, if an employee of Amazon leases a car for $300 at an airport while on company business, Amazon (lessee) records this cost as follows:

Point: Home Depot reports that its rental expenses from operating leases total more than $900 million.

July 4	Rental Expense	300	
	Cash		300
	To record lease rental payment.		

Assets = Liabilities + Equity
−300   −300

Capital Leases **Capital leases** are long-term (or noncancelable) leases by which the lessor transfers substantially all risks and rewards of ownership to the lessee.[3] Examples include most leases of airplanes and department store buildings. The lessee records the leased item as its own asset along with a lease liability at the start of the lease term; the amount recorded equals the present value of all lease payments. To illustrate, assume that K2 Co. enters into a six-year lease of a building in which it will sell sporting equipment. The lease transfers all building ownership risks and rewards to K2 (the present value of its $12,979 annual lease payments is $60,000). K2 records this transaction as follows:

Assets = Liabilities + Equity
+60,000   +60,000

2009			
Jan. 1	Leased Asset—Building.......................	60,000	
	Lease Liability		60,000
	To record leased asset and lease liability.		

Point: Home Depot reports *"certain locations ... are leased under capital leases."* The net present value of this Lease Liability is about $400 million.

K2 reports the leased asset as a plant asset and the lease liability as a long-term liability. The portion of the lease liability expected to be paid in the next year is reported as a current liability.[4] At each year-end, K2 records depreciation on the leased asset (assume straight-line depreciation, six-year lease term, and no salvage value) as follows:

Assets = Liabilities + Equity
−10,000   −10,000

Dec. 31	Depreciation Expense—Building	10,000	
	Accumulated Depreciation—Building		10,000
	To record depreciation on leased asset.		

K2 also accrues interest on the lease liability at each year-end. Interest expense is computed by multiplying the remaining lease liability by the interest rate on the lease. Specifically, K2 records its annual interest expense as part of its annual lease payment ($12,979) as follows (for its first year):

Assets = Liabilities + Equity
−12,979   −8,179   −4,800

2009			
Dec. 31	Interest Expense	4,800	
	Lease Liability.............................	8,179	
	Cash		12,979
	*To record first annual lease payment.**		

* These numbers are computed from a *lease payment schedule.* For simplicity, we use the same numbers from Exhibit 14.14 for this lease payment schedule—with different headings as follows:

	Payments				
	(A)	(B) Debit	(C) Debit	(D) Credit	(E)
Period Ending Date	Beginning Balance of Lease Liability	Interest on Lease Liability 8% × (A)	+ Lease Liability (D) − (B)	= Cash Lease Payment	Ending Balance of Lease Liability (A) − (C)
12/31/2009	$60,000	$ 4,800	$ 8,179	$12,979	$51,821
12/31/2010	51,821	4,146	8,833	12,979	42,988
12/31/2011	42,988	3,439	9,540	12,979	33,448
12/31/2012	33,448	2,676	10,303	12,979	23,145
12/31/2013	23,145	1,852	11,127	12,979	12,018
12/31/2014	12,018	961	12,018	12,979	0
		$17,874	$60,000	$77,874	

[3] A *capital lease* meets any one or more of four criteria: (1) transfers title of leased asset to lessee, (2) contains a bargain purchase option, (3) has a lease term that is 75% or more of the leased asset's useful life, or (4) has a present value of lease payments that is 90% or more of the leased asset's market value.

[4] Most lessees try to keep leased assets and lease liabilities off their balance sheets by failing to meet any one of the four criteria of a capital lease. This is because a lease liability increases a company's total liabilities, making it more difficult to obtain additional financing. The acquisition of assets without reporting any related liabilities (or other asset outflows) on the balance sheet is called **off-balance-sheet financing.**

Pension Liabilities

A **pension plan** is a contractual agreement between an employer and its employees for the employer to provide benefits (payments) to employees after they retire. Most employers pay the full cost of the pension, but sometimes employees pay part of the cost. An employer records its payment into a pension plan with a debit to Pension Expense and a credit to Cash. A *plan administrator* receives payments from the employer, invests them in pension assets, and makes benefit payments to *pension recipients* (retired employees). Insurance and trust companies often serve as pension plan administrators.

Many pensions are known as *defined benefit plans* that define future benefits; the employer's contributions vary, depending on assumptions about future pension assets and liabilities. Several disclosures are necessary in this case. Specifically, a pension liability is reported when the accumulated benefit obligation is *more than* the plan assets, a so-called *underfunded plan*. The accumulated benefit obligation is the present value of promised future pension payments to retirees. *Plan assets* refer to the market value of assets the plan administrator holds. A pension asset is reported when the accumulated benefit obligation is *less than* the plan assets, a so-called *overfunded plan*. An employer reports pension expense when it receives the benefits from the employees' services, which is sometimes decades before it pays pension benefits to employees. (*Other Postretirement Benefits* refer to nonpension benefits such as health care and life insurance benefits. Similar to a pension, costs of these benefits are estimated and liabilities accrued when the employees earn them.)

Point: Fringe benefits are often 40% or more of salaries and wages, and pension benefits make up nearly 15% of fringe benefits.

Point: Two types of pension plans are (1) *defined benefit plan*—the retirement benefit is defined and the employer estimates the contribution necessary to pay these benefits—and (2) *defined contribution plan*—the pension contribution is defined and the employer and/or employee contributes amounts specified in the pension agreement.

Summary

C1 Explain the types and payment patterns of notes. Notes repaid over a period of time are called *installment notes* and usually follow one of two payment patterns: (1) decreasing payments of interest plus equal amounts of principal or (2) equal total payments. Mortgage notes also are common.

C2^A Explain and compute the present value of an amount(s) to be paid at a future date(s). The basic concept of present value is that an amount of cash to be paid or received in the future is worth less than the same amount of cash to be paid or received today. Another important present value concept is that interest is compounded, meaning interest is added to the balance and used to determine interest for succeeding periods. An annuity is a series of equal payments occurring at equal time intervals. An annuity's present value can be computed using the present value table for an annuity (or a calculator).

C3^C Describe the accrual of bond interest when bond payments do not align with accounting periods. Issuers and buyers of debt record the interest accrued when issue dates or accounting periods do not coincide with debt payment dates.

C4^D Describe accounting for leases and pensions. A lease is a rental agreement between the lessor and the lessee. When the lessor retains the risks and rewards of asset ownership (an *operating lease*), the lessee debits Rent Expense and credits Cash for its lease payments. When the lessor substantially transfers the risks and rewards of asset ownership to the lessee (a *capital lease*), the lessee capitalizes the leased asset and records a lease liability. Pension agreements can result in either pension assets or pension liabilities.

A1 Compare bond financing with stock financing. Bond financing is used to fund business activities. Advantages of bond financing versus stock include (1) no effect on owner control, (2) tax savings, and (3) increased earnings due to financial leverage. Disadvantages include (1) interest and principal payments and (2) amplification of poor performance.

A2 Assess debt features and their implications. Certain bonds are secured by the issuer's assets; other bonds, called *debentures,* are unsecured. Serial bonds mature at different points in time;

term bonds mature at one time. Registered bonds have each bondholder's name recorded by the issuer; bearer bonds are payable to the holder. Convertible bonds are exchangeable for shares of the issuer's stock. Callable bonds can be retired by the issuer at a set price. Debt features alter the risk of loss for creditors.

A3 Compute the debt-to-equity ratio and explain its use. Both creditors and equity holders are concerned about the relation between the amount of liabilities and the amount of equity. A company's financing structure is at less risk when the debt-to-equity ratio is lower, as liabilities must be paid and usually with periodic interest.

P1 Prepare entries to record bond issuance and bond interest expense. When bonds are issued at par, Cash is debited and Bonds Payable is credited for the bonds' par value. At bond interest payment dates (usually semiannual), Bond Interest Expense is debited and Cash credited—the latter for an amount equal to the bond par value multiplied by the bond contract rate.

P2 Compute and record amortization of bond discount. Bonds are issued at a discount when the contract rate is less than the market rate, making the issue (selling) price less than par. When this occurs, the issuer records a credit to Bonds Payable (at par) and debits both Discount on Bonds Payable and Cash. The amount of bond interest expense assigned to each period is computed using either the straight-line or effective interest method.

P3 Compute and record amortization of bond premium. Bonds are issued at a premium when the contract rate is higher than the market rate, making the issue (selling) price greater than par. When this occurs, the issuer records a debit to Cash and credits both Premium on Bonds Payable and Bonds Payable (at par). The amount of bond interest expense assigned to each period is computed using either the straight-line or effective interest method. The Premium on Bonds Payable is allocated to reduce bond interest expense over the life of the bonds.

P4 Record the retirement of bonds. Bonds are retired at maturity with a debit to Bonds Payable and a credit to Cash at par value. The issuer can retire the bonds early by exercising a call option or purchasing them in the market. Bondholders can also retire bonds early by exercising a conversion feature on convertible bonds. The issuer recognizes a gain or loss for the difference between the amount paid and the bond carrying value.

P5   Prepare entries to account for notes. Interest is allocated to each period in a note's life by multiplying its beginning-period carrying value by its market rate at issuance. If a note is repaid with equal payments, the payment amount is computed by dividing the borrowed amount by the present value of an annuity factor (taken from a present value table) using the market rate and the number of payments.

Guidance Answers to **Decision Maker**

Entrepreneur   This is a "present value" question. The market interest rate (10%) and present value ($3,000) are known, but the payment required two years later is unknown. This amount ($3,630) can be computed as $3,000 \times 1.10 \times 1.10$. Thus, the sale price is $3,630 when no payments are received for two years. The $3,630 received two years from today is equivalent to $3,000 cash today.

Bond Investor   The debt-to-equity ratio for the first company is 0.2 ($350,000/$1,750,000) and for the second company is 1.2 ($1,200,000/$1,000,000), suggesting that the financing structure of the second company is more risky than that of the first company. Consequently, as a buyer of unsecured debenture bonds, you prefer the first company (all else equal).

Bond Rater   Bonds with longer repayment periods (life) have higher risk. Also, bonds issued by companies in financial difficulties or facing higher than normal uncertainties have higher risk. Moreover, companies with higher than normal debt and large fluctuations in earnings are considered of higher risk. Discount bonds are more risky on one or more of these factors.

Guidance Answers to **Quick Checks**

1. (*b*)

2. Multiply the bond's par value by its contract rate of interest.

3. Bonds sell at a premium when the contract rate exceeds the market rate and the purchasers pay more than their par value.

4. The bonds are issued at a discount, meaning that issue price is less than par value. A discount occurs because the bond contract rate (6%) is less than the market rate (8%).

5.

Cash	91,893	
Discount on Bonds Payable	8,107	
Bonds Payable		100,000

6. $3,811 (total bond interest expense of $38,107 divided by 10 periods; or the $3,000 semiannual cash payment plus the $8,107 discount divided by 10 periods).

7. The bonds are issued at a premium, meaning issue price is higher than par value. A premium occurs because the bonds' contract rate (16%) is higher than the market rate (14%).

8. (*b*) For each semiannual period: $10,592/20 periods = $530 premium amortization.

9.

Bonds payable, 16%, due 12/31/2018	$100,000
Plus premium on bonds payable	9,532* $109,532

* Original premium balance of $10,592 less $530 and $530 amortized on 6/30/2009 and 12/31/2009, respectively.

10. $9,375 loss, computed as the difference between the repurchase price of $256,250 [50% of ($500,000 × 102.5%)] and the carrying value of $246,875 (50% of $493,750).

11. (*c*)

12. The interest portion of an installment payment equals the period's beginning loan balance multiplied by the market interest rate at the time of the note's issuance.

13. On the balance sheet, the account balances of the related liability (note payable) and asset (cash) accounts are decreased. On the income statement, interest expense is recorded.

14. (*c*), computed as 3.3121 × $1,000 = $3,312.

15. The option of paying $10,000 after one year has a lower present value. It postpones paying the first $5,000 by six months. More generally, the present value of a further delayed payment is always lower than a less delayed payment.

16. (*a*) Reflects payment of accrued interest recorded back on May 1; $500,000 × 9% × ⁴/₁₂ = $15,000.

Key Terms   mhhe.com/wildFAP19e

Key Terms are available at the book's Website for learning and testing in an online Flashcard Format.

Annuity (p. 568)
Bearer bonds (p. 563)
Bond (p. 550)
Bond certificate (p. 552)
Bond indenture (p. 552)
Callable bonds (p. 563)
Capital leases (p. 574)

Carrying (book) value of bonds (p. 554)
Contract rate (p. 553)
Convertible bonds (p. 563)
Coupon bonds (p. 563)
Debt-to-equity ratio (p. 564)
Discount on bonds payable (p. 553)
Effective interest method (p. 569)

Installment note (p. 560)
Lease (p. 573)
Market rate (p. 553)
Mortgage (p. 562)
Off-balance-sheet financing (p. 574)
Operating leases (p. 573)
Par value of a bond (p. 550)

Pension plan (p. 575)	**Secured bonds** (p. 563)	**Straight-line bond amortization** (p. 554)
Premium on bonds (p. 556)	**Serial bonds** (p. 563)	**Term bonds** (p. 563)
Registered bonds (p. 563)	**Sinking fund bonds** (p. 563)	**Unsecured bonds** (p. 563)

 **Multiple Choice Quiz**   Answers on p. 589   **mhhe.com/wildFAP19e**

Additional Quiz Questions are available at the book's Website.

Quiz14

1. A bond traded at 97½ means that
  a. The bond pays 97½% interest.
  b. The bond trades at $975 per $1,000 bond.
  c. The market rate of interest is below the contract rate of interest for the bond.
  d. The bonds can be retired at $975 each.
  e. The bond's interest rate is 2½%.

2. A bondholder that owns a $1,000, 6%, 15-year bond has
  a. The right to receive $1,000 at maturity.
  b. Ownership rights in the bond issuing entity.
  c. The right to receive $60 per month until maturity.
  d. The right to receive $1,900 at maturity.
  e. The right to receive $600 per year until maturity.

3. A company issues 8%, 20-year bonds with a par value of $500,000. The current market rate for the bonds is 8%. The amount of interest owed to the bondholders for each semiannual interest payment is
  a. $40,000.
  b. $0.
  c. $20,000.

  d. $800,000.
  e. $400,000.

4. A company issued 5-year, 5% bonds with a par value of $100,000. The company received $95,735 for the bonds. Using the straight-line method, the company's interest expense for the first semiannual interest period is
  a. $2,926.50.
  b. $5,853.00.
  c. $2,500.00.
  d. $5,000.00.
  e. $9,573.50.

5. A company issued 8-year, 5% bonds with a par value of $350,000. The company received proceeds of $373,745. Interest is payable semiannually. The amount of premium amortized for the first semiannual interest period, assuming straight-line bond amortization, is
  a. $2,698.
  b. $23,745.
  c. $8,750.
  d. $9,344.
  e. $1,484.

Superscript letter [B] *(*[C, D]*) denotes assignments based on Appendix 14B (14C, 14D).*

Discussion Questions

1. What is the main difference between a bond and a share of stock?
2. What is the main difference between notes payable and bonds payable?
3. ♟ What is the advantage of issuing bonds instead of obtaining financing from the company's owners?
4. What are the duties of a trustee for bondholders?
5. What is a bond indenture? What provisions are usually included in it?
6. What are the *contract* rate and the *market* rate for bonds?
7. ♟ What factors affect the market rates for bonds?
8.[B] ♟ Does the straight-line or effective interest method produce an interest expense allocation that yields a constant rate of interest over a bond's life? Explain.
9.[C] Why does a company that issues bonds between interest dates collect accrued interest from the bonds' purchasers?
10. ♟ If you know the par value of bonds, the contract rate, and the market rate, how do you compute the bonds' price?
11. What is the issue price of a $2,000 bond sold at 98¼? What is the issue price of a $6,000 bond sold at 101½?

12. Describe the debt-to-equity ratio and explain how creditors and owners would use this ratio to evaluate a company's risk.
13. ♟ What obligation does an entrepreneur (owner) have to investors that purchase bonds to finance the business?
14. Refer to **Best Buy**'s annual report in Appendix A. Is there any indication that Best Buy has issued bonds?
15. Refer to the statement of cash flows for **Circuit City** in Appendix A. For the year ended February 28, 2007, what was the amount of principal payments on long-term debt?
16. Did **RadioShack**'s long-term debt increase or decrease during 2006? **® RadioShack.**
17. Refer to the annual report for **Apple** in Appendix A. For the year ended September 30, 2006, did it raise more cash by issuing stock or debt?
18.[D] When can a lease create both an asset and a liability for the lessee?
19.[D] Compare and contrast an operating lease with a capital lease.
20.[D] Describe the two basic types of pension plans.

♟ *Denotes Discussion Questions that involve decision making.*

QUICK STUDY

Round dollar amounts to the nearest whole dollar.

QS 14-1
Bond computations—
straight-line   P1   P2

Randell Company issues 7%, 10-year bonds with a par value of $150,000 and semiannual interest payments. On the issue date, the annual market rate for these bonds is 8%, which implies a selling price of 93¼. The straight-line method is used to allocate interest expense.

1. What are the issuer's cash proceeds from issuance of these bonds?

2. What total amount of bond interest expense will be recognized over the life of these bonds?

3. What is the amount of bond interest expense recorded on the first interest payment date?

QS 14-2^B
Bond computations—
effective interest

P1   P3

Elton Company issues 7%, 15-year bonds with a par value of $350,000 and semiannual interest payments. On the issue date, the annual market rate for these bonds is 6%, which implies a selling price of 109¾. The effective interest method is used to allocate interest expense.

1. What are the issuer's cash proceeds from issuance of these bonds?

2. What total amount of bond interest expense will be recognized over the life of these bonds?

3. What amount of bond interest expense is recorded on the first interest payment date?

QS 14-3
Journalize bond issuance   P1

Prepare the journal entries for the issuance of the bonds in both QS 14-1 and QS 14-2. Assume that both bonds are issued for cash on January 1, 2009.

QS 14-4
Computing bond price   P2   P3

Using the bond details in both QS 14-1 and QS 14-2, confirm that the bonds' selling prices given in each problem are approximately correct. Use the present value tables B.1 and B.3 in Appendix B.

QS 14-5
Recording bond issuance and
discount amortization   P1   P2

Boulware Company issues 8%, five-year bonds, on December 31, 2008, with a par value of $100,000 and semiannual interest payments. Use the following straight-line bond amortization table and prepare journal entries to record (*a*) the issuance of bonds on December 31, 2008; (*b*) the first interest payment on June 30, 2009; and (*c*) the second interest payment on December 31, 2009.

Semiannual Period-End	Unamortized Discount	Carrying Value
(0) 12/31/2008	$7,723	$92,277
(1) 6/30/2009	6,951	93,049
(2) 12/31/2009	6,179	93,821

QS 14-6
Bond retirement by call option
P4

On July 1, 2009, Teller Company exercises a $4,000 call option (plus par value) on its outstanding bonds that have a carrying value of $208,000 and par value of $200,000. The company exercises the call option after the semiannual interest is paid on June 30, 2009. Record the entry to retire the bonds.

QS 14-7
Bond retirement by stock
conversion   P4

On January 1, 2009, the $1,000,000 par value bonds of Staten Company with a carrying value of $1,000,000 are converted to 500,000 shares of $1.00 par value common stock. Record the entry for the conversion of the bonds.

QS 14-8
Computing payments for
an installment note   C1

Jordyn Company borrows $600,000 cash from a bank and in return signs an installment note for five annual payments of equal amount, with the first payment due one year after the note is signed. Use Table B.3 in Appendix B to compute the amount of the annual payment for each of the following annual market rates: (*a*) 4%, (*b*) 6%, and (*c*) 8%.

QS 14-9
Bond features and terminology

A2

Enter the letter of the description A through H that best fits each term or phrase 1 through 8.

A. Records and tracks the bondholders' names.

B. Is unsecured; backed only by the issuer's credit standing.

C. Has varying maturity dates for amounts owed.

D. Identifies rights and responsibilities of the issuer and the bondholders.

E. Can be exchanged for shares of the issuer's stock.

F. Is unregistered; interest is paid to whoever possesses them.

G. Maintains a separate asset account from which bondholders are paid at maturity.

H. Pledges specific assets of the issuer as collateral.

1. _____ Convertible bond   **5.** _____ Registered bond
2. _____ Bond indenture   **6.** _____ Serial bond
3. _____ Sinking fund bond   **7.** _____ Secured bond
4. _____ Debenture   **8.** _____ Bearer bond

Compute the debt-to-equity ratio for each of the following companies. Which company appears to have a riskier financing structure? Explain.

	NLF Company	ABL Company
Total liabilities	$615,000	$ 480,000
Total equity	820,000	1,500,000

QS 14-10
Debt-to-equity ratio

A2

Knapp Company plans to issue 6% bonds on January 1, 2009, with a par value of $2,000,000. The company sells $1,800,000 of the bonds on January 1, 2009. The remaining $200,000 sells at par on March 1, 2009. The bonds pay interest semiannually as of June 30 and December 31. Record the entry for the March 1 cash sale of bonds.

QS 14-11^C
Issuing bonds between interest dates

P1

Lu Villena, an employee of ETrain.com, leases a car at O'Hare airport for a three-day business trip. The rental cost is $400. Prepare the entry by ETrain.com to record Lu Villena's short-term car lease cost.

QS 14-12^D
Recording operating leases   C4

Artel, Inc., signs a five-year lease for office equipment with Office Solutions. The present value of the lease payments is $13,500. Prepare the journal entry that Artel records at the inception of this capital lease.

QS 14-13^D
Recording capital leases   C4

McGraw-Hill's
HOMEWORK
MANAGER®   Available with McGraw-Hill's Homework Manager

Round dollar amounts to the nearest whole dollar. Assume no reversing entries are used.

EXERCISES

On January 1, 2009, Bartel Enterprises issues bonds that have a $3,650,000 par value, mature in 20 years, and pay 10% interest semiannually on June 30 and December 31. The bonds are sold at par.

1. How much interest will Bartel pay (in cash) to the bondholders every six months?
2. Prepare journal entries to record (a) the issuance of bonds on January 1, 2009; (b) the first interest payment on June 30, 2009; and (c) the second interest payment on December 31, 2009.
3. Prepare the journal entry for issuance assuming the bonds are issued at (a) 98 and (b) 105.

Exercise 14-1
Recording bond issuance and interest

P1

Sears issues bonds with a par value of $175,000 on January 1, 2009. The bonds' annual contract rate is 4%, and interest is paid semiannually on June 30 and December 31. The bonds mature in three years. The annual market rate at the date of issuance is 6%, and the bonds are sold for $165,523.

1. What is the amount of the discount on these bonds at issuance?
2. How much total bond interest expense will be recognized over the life of these bonds?
3. Prepare an amortization table like the one in Exhibit 14.7 for these bonds; use the straight-line method to amortize the discount.

Exercise 14-2
Straight-line amortization of bond discount

P2

Ritter issues bonds dated January 1, 2009, with a par value of $300,000. The bonds' annual contract rate is 9%, and interest is paid semiannually on June 30 and December 31. The bonds mature in three years. The annual market rate at the date of issuance is 12%, and the bonds are sold for $277,872.

1. What is the amount of the discount on these bonds at issuance?
2. How much total bond interest expense will be recognized over the life of these bonds?
3. Prepare an amortization table like the one in Exhibit 14B.1 for these bonds; use the effective interest method to amortize the discount.

Exercise 14-3^B
Effective interest amortization of bond discount

P2

Exercise 14-4

Straight-line amortization of bond premium   P3

Dell Co. issues bonds dated January 1, 2009, with a par value of $450,000. The bonds' annual contract rate is 9%, and interest is paid semiannually on June 30 and December 31. The bonds mature in three years. The annual market rate at the date of issuance is 8%, and the bonds are sold for $461,795.

1. What is the amount of the premium on these bonds at issuance?

2. How much total bond interest expense will be recognized over the life of these bonds?

3. Prepare an amortization table like the one in Exhibit 14.11 for these bonds; use the straight-line method to amortize the premium.

Exercise 14-5ᴮ

Effective interest amortization of bond premium   P3

Refer to the bond details in Exercise 14-4 and prepare an amortization table like the one in Exhibit 14B.2 for these bonds using the effective interest method to amortize the premium.

Exercise 14-6

Recording bond issuance and premium amortization

P1   P3

Anna Company issues 8%, five-year bonds, on December 31, 2008, with a par value of $100,000 and semiannual interest payments. Use the following straight-line bond amortization table and prepare journal entries to record (a) the issuance of bonds on December 31, 2008; (b) the first interest payment on June 30, 2009; and (c) the second interest payment on December 31, 2009.

Semiannual Period-End	Unamortized Premium	Carrying Value
(0) 12/31/2008	$7,720	$107,720
(1) 6/30/2009	6,948	106,948
(2) 12/31/2009	6,176	106,176

Exercise 14-7

Recording bond issuance and discount amortization

P1   P2

St. Charles Company issues 10%, four-year bonds, on December 31, 2009, with a par value of $100,000 and semiannual interest payments. Use the following straight-line bond amortization table and prepare journal entries to record (a) the issuance of bonds on December 31, 2009; (b) the first interest payment on June 30, 2010; and (c) the second interest payment on December 31, 2010.

Semiannual Period-End	Unamortized Discount	Carrying Value
(0) 12/31/2009	$8,000	$92,000
(1) 6/30/2010	7,000	93,000
(2) 12/31/2010	6,000	94,000

Exercise 14-8

Recording bond issuance and discount amortization

P1   P2

Zander Company issues 6%, two-year bonds, on December 31, 2009, with a par value of $100,000 and semiannual interest payments. Use the following straight-line bond amortization table and prepare journal entries to record (a) the issuance of bonds on December 31, 2009; (b) the first through fourth interest payments on each June 30 and December 31; and (c) the maturity of the bond on December 31, 2011.

Semiannual Period-End	Unamortized Discount	Carrying Value
(0) 12/31/2009	$4,000	$ 96,000
(1) 6/30/2010	3,000	97,000
(2) 12/31/2010	2,000	98,000
(3) 6/30/2011	1,000	99,000
(4) 12/31/2011	0	100,000

Exercise 14-9

Computing bond interest and price; recording bond issuance

P2

Target Company issues bonds with a par value of $950,000 on their stated issue date. The bonds mature in 15 years and pay 10% annual interest in semiannual payments. On the issue date, the annual market rate for the bonds is 12%.

1. What is the amount of each semiannual interest payment for these bonds?

2. How many semiannual interest payments will be made on these bonds over their life?

3. Use the interest rates given to determine whether the bonds are issued at par, at a discount, or at a premium.

Check   (4) $819,223

4. Compute the price of the bonds as of their issue date.

5. Prepare the journal entry to record the bonds' issuance.

Boston Company issues bonds with a par value of $160,000 on their stated issue date. The bonds mature in six years and pay 8% annual interest in semiannual payments. On the issue date, the annual market rate for the bonds is 6%.

1. What is the amount of each semiannual interest payment for these bonds?

2. How many semiannual interest payments will be made on these bonds over their life?

3. Use the interest rates given to determine whether the bonds are issued at par, at a discount, or at a premium.

4. Compute the price of the bonds as of their issue date.

5. Prepare the journal entry to record the bonds' issuance.

Exercise 14-10
Computing bond interest and price; recording bond issuance
P3

Check (4) $175,930

On January 1, 2009, Seldon issues $450,000 of 10%, 15-year bonds at a price of 93¼. Six years later, on January 1, 2015, Seldon retires 20% of these bonds by buying them on the open market at 109¾. All interest is accounted for and paid through December 31, 2014, the day before the purchase. The straight-line method is used to amortize any bond discount.

1. How much does the company receive when it issues the bonds on January 1, 2009?

2. What is the amount of the discount on the bonds at January 1, 2009?

3. How much amortization of the discount is recorded on the bonds for the entire period from January 1, 2009, through December 31, 2014?

4. What is the carrying (book) value of the bonds as of the close of business on December 31, 2014? What is the carrying value of the 20% soon-to-be-retired bonds on this same date?

5. How much did the company pay on January 1, 2015, to purchase the bonds that it retired?

6. What is the amount of the recorded gain or loss from retiring the bonds?

7. Prepare the journal entry to record the bond retirement at January 1, 2015.

Exercise 14-11
Bond computations, straight-line amortization, and bond retirement
P2 P4

Check (6) $12,420 loss

On May 1, 2009, Bradley Enterprises issues bonds dated January 1, 2009, that have a $1,950,000 par value, mature in 20 years, and pay 8% interest semiannually on June 30 and December 31. The bonds are sold at par plus four months' accrued interest.

1. How much accrued interest do the bond purchasers pay Bradley on May 1, 2009?

2. Prepare Bradley's journal entries to record (*a*) the issuance of bonds on May 1, 2009; (*b*) the first interest payment on June 30, 2009; and (*c*) the second interest payment on December 31, 2009.

Exercise 14-12^C
Recording bond issuance with accrued interest
C4 P1

Check (1) $52,000

Stockton Co. issues four-year bonds with a $50,000 par value on June 1, 2009, at a price of $47,850. The annual contract rate is 8%, and interest is paid semiannually on November 30 and May 31.

1. Prepare an amortization table like the one in Exhibit 14.7 for these bonds. Use the straight-line method of interest amortization.

2. Prepare journal entries to record the first two interest payments and to accrue interest as of December 31, 2009.

Exercise 14-13
Straight-line amortization and accrued bond interest expense
P1 P2

On January 1, 2009, American Eagle borrows $90,000 cash by signing a four-year, 5% installment note. The note requires four equal total payments of accrued interest and principal on December 31 of each year from 2009 through 2012.

1. Compute the amount of each of the four equal total payments.

2. Prepare an amortization table for this installment note like the one in Exhibit 14.14.

Exercise 14-14
Installment note with equal total payments C1 P5

Check (1) $25,381

Use the information in Exercise 14-14 to prepare the journal entries for American Eagle to record the loan on January 1, 2009, and the four payments from December 31, 2009, through December 31, 2012.

Exercise 14-15
Installment note entries P5

Motin Company is considering a project that will require a $250,000 loan. It presently has total liabilities of $110,000, and total assets of $310,000.

1. Compute Motin's (*a*) present debt-to-equity ratio and (*b*) the debt-to-equity ratio assuming it borrows $250,000 to fund the project.

2. Evaluate and discuss the level of risk involved if Motin borrows the funds to pursue the project.

Exercise 14-16
Applying debt-to-equity ratio
A3

Exercise 14-17^D

Identifying capital and operating leases

C4

Indicate whether the company in each separate case 1 through 3 has entered into an operating lease or a capital lease.

1. The lessor retains title to the asset, and the lease term is three years on an asset that has a five-year useful life.

2. The title is transferred to the lessee, the lessee can purchase the asset for $1 at the end of the lease, and the lease term is five years. The leased asset has an expected useful life of six years.

3. The present value of the lease payments is 95% of the leased asset's market value, and the lease term is 70% of the leased asset's useful life.

Exercise 14-18^D

Accounting for capital lease

C4

Hartel (lessee) signs a five-year capital lease for office equipment with a $21,000 annual lease payment. The present value of the five annual lease payments is $88,460, based on a 6% interest rate.

1. Prepare the journal entry Hartel will record at inception of the lease.

2. If the leased asset has a five-year useful life with no salvage value, prepare the journal entry Hartel will record each year to recognize depreciation expense related to the leased asset.

Exercise 14-19^D

Analyzing lease options

C2   C3   C4

General Motors advertised three alternatives for a 25-month lease on a new Blazer: (1) zero dollars down and a lease payment of $2,522 per month for 25 months, (2) $5,000 down and $2,240 per month for 25 months, or (3) $55,000 down and no payments for 25 months. Use the present value Table B.3 in Appendix B to determine which is the best alternative (assume you have enough cash to accept any alternative and the annual interest rate is 12% compounded monthly).

Available with McGraw-Hill's Homework Manager

McGraw-Hill's
HOMEWORK
MANAGER®

PROBLEM SET A

Round dollar amounts to the nearest whole dollar. Assume no reversing entries are used.

Problem 14-1A

Computing bond price and recording issuance

P1 P2 P3

Check (1) Premium, $4,760

(3) Discount, $4,223

Harvard Research issues bonds dated January 1, 2009, that pay interest semiannually on June 30 and December 31. The bonds have a $45,000 par value and an annual contract rate of 6%, and they mature in six years.

Required

For each of the following three separate situations, (*a*) determine the bonds' issue price on January 1, 2009, and (*b*) prepare the journal entry to record their issuance.

1. The market rate at the date of issuance is 4%.

2. The market rate at the date of issuance is 6%.

3. The market rate at the date of issuance is 8%.

Problem 14-2A

Straight-line amortization of bond discount and bond premium

P1 P2 P3

mhhe.com/wildFAP19e

Check (3) $4,676,000

(4) 12/31/2010 carrying value, $3,087,468

Braeburn issues $3,500,000 of 8%, 15-year bonds dated January 1, 2009, that pay interest semiannually on June 30 and December 31. The bonds are issued at a price of $3,024,000.

Required

1. Prepare the January 1, 2009, journal entry to record the bonds' issuance.

2. For each semiannual period, compute (*a*) the cash payment, (*b*) the straight-line discount amortization, and (*c*) the bond interest expense.

3. Determine the total bond interest expense to be recognized over the bonds' life.

4. Prepare the first two years of an amortization table like Exhibit 14.7 using the straight-line method.

5. Prepare the journal entries to record the first two interest payments.

6. Assume that the bonds are issued at a price of $4,284,000. Repeat parts 1 through 5.

Problem 14-3A

Straight-line amortization of bond premium

P1 P3

mhhe.com/wildFAP19e

Check (2) 6/30/2009 carrying value, $234,644

Jules issues 4.5%, five-year bonds dated January 1, 2009, with a $230,000 par value. The bonds pay interest on June 30 and December 31 and are issued at a price of $235,160. The annual market rate is 4% on the issue date.

Required

1. Calculate the total bond interest expense over the bonds' life.

2. Prepare a straight-line amortization table like Exhibit 14.11 for the bonds' life.

3. Prepare the journal entries to record the first two interest payments.

Refer to the bond details in Problem 14-3A.

Required

1. Compute the total bond interest expense over the bonds' life.

2. Prepare an effective interest amortization table like the one in Exhibit 14B.2 for the bonds' life.

3. Prepare the journal entries to record the first two interest payments.

4. Use the market rate at issuance to compute the present value of the remaining cash flows for these bonds as of December 31, 2011. Compare your answer with the amount shown on the amortization table as the balance for that date (from part 2) and explain your findings.

Problem 14-4A[B]
Effective interest amortization of bond premium; computing bond price   P1   P3

Check   (2) 6/30/2011 carrying value, $232,704

(4) $232,179

Legacy issues $345,000 of 5%, four-year bonds dated January 1, 2009, that pay interest semiannually on June 30 and December 31. They are issued at $332,888 and their market rate is 6% at the issue date.

Required

1. Prepare the January 1, 2009, journal entry to record the bonds' issuance.

2. Determine the total bond interest expense to be recognized over the bonds' life.

3. Prepare a straight-line amortization table like the one in Exhibit 14.7 for the bonds' first two years.

4. Prepare the journal entries to record the first two interest payments.

Analysis Component

5. Assume the market rate on January 1, 2009, is 4% instead of 6%. Without providing numbers, describe how this change affects the amounts reported on Legacy's financial statements.

Problem 14-5A
Straight-line amortization of bond discount

P1   P2

Check   (2) $81,112

(3) 12/31/2010 carrying value, $338,944

Refer to the bond details in Problem 14-5A.

Required

1. Prepare the January 1, 2009, journal entry to record the bonds' issuance.

2. Determine the total bond interest expense to be recognized over the bonds' life.

3. Prepare an effective interest amortization table like the one in Exhibit 14B.1 for the bonds' first two years.

4. Prepare the journal entries to record the first two interest payments.

Problem 14-6A[B]
Effective interest amortization of bond discount   P1   P2

Check   (2) $81,112

(3) 12/31/2010 carrying value, $338,586

eXcel
mhhe.com/wildFAP19e

Shopko issues $185,000 of 12%, three-year bonds dated January 1, 2009, that pay interest semiannually on June 30 and December 31. They are issued at $189,620. Their market rate is 11% at the issue date.

Required

1. Prepare the January 1, 2009, journal entry to record the bonds' issuance.

2. Determine the total bond interest expense to be recognized over the bonds' life.

3. Prepare an effective interest amortization table like Exhibit 14B.2 for the bonds' first two years.

4. Prepare the journal entries to record the first two interest payments.

5. Prepare the journal entry to record the bonds' retirement on January 1, 2011, at 97.

Analysis Component

6. Assume that the market rate on January 1, 2009, is 13% instead of 11%. Without presenting numbers, describe how this change affects the amounts reported on Shopko's financial statements.

Problem 14-7A[B]
Effective interest amortization of bond premium; retiring bonds

P1   P3   P4

Check   (3) 6/30/2010 carrying value, $187,494

(5) $7,256 gain

mhhe.com/wildFAP19e

On November 1, 2009, Norwood borrows $700,000 cash from a bank by signing a five-year installment note bearing 7% interest. The note requires equal total payments each year on October 31.

Required

1. Compute the total amount of each installment payment.

2. Complete an amortization table for this installment note similar to the one in Exhibit 14.14.

3. Prepare the journal entries in which Norwood records (*a*) accrued interest as of December 31, 2009 (the end of its annual reporting period), and (*b*) the first annual payment on the note.

Problem 14-8A
Installment notes

C1   P5

Check   (2) 10/31/2013 ending balance, $159,556

Problem 14-9A

Applying the debt-to-equity ratio

A3 ♟

At the end of the current year, the following information is available for both the Pulaski Company and the Scott Company.

	Pulaski Company	Scott Company
Total assets	$1,800,000	$900,000
Total liabilities	723,600	478,800
Total equity	1,080,000	420,000

Required

1. Compute the debt-to-equity ratios for both companies.
2. Comment on your results and discuss the riskiness of each company's financing structure.

Problem 14-10A[D]

Capital lease accounting

C4

Check (1) $55,898

(3) Year 3 ending balance, $24,966

Thomas Company signs a five-year capital lease with Universal Company for office equipment. The annual lease payment is $14,000, and the interest rate is 8%.

Required

1. Compute the present value of Thomas's five-year lease payments.
2. Prepare the journal entry to record Thomas's capital lease at its inception.
3. Complete a lease payment schedule for the five years of the lease with the following headings. Assume that the beginning balance of the lease liability (present value of lease payments) is $55,898. (*Hint:* To find the amount allocated to interest in year 1, multiply the interest rate by the beginning-of-year lease liability. The amount of the annual lease payment not allocated to interest is allocated to principal. Reduce the lease liability by the amount allocated to principal to update the lease liability at each year-end.)

Period Ending Date	Beginning Balance of Lease Liability	Interest on Lease Liability	Reduction of Lease Liability	Cash Lease Payment	Ending Balance of Lease Liability

4. Use straight-line depreciation and prepare the journal entry to depreciate the leased asset at the end of year 1. Assume zero salvage value and a five-year life for the office equipment.

PROBLEM SET B

Problem 14-1B

Computing bond price and recording issuance

P1 P2 P3

Check (1) Premium, $2,679

(3) Discount, $2,457

Round dollar amounts to the nearest whole dollar. Assume no reversing entries are used.

Fortune Systems issues bonds dated January 1, 2009, that pay interest semiannually on June 30 and December 31. The bonds have a $35,000 par value and an annual contract rate of 4%, and they mature in four years.

Required

For each of the following three separate situations, (*a*) determine the bonds' issue price on January 1, 2009, and (*b*) prepare the journal entry to record their issuance.

1. The market rate at the date of issuance is 2%.
2. The market rate at the date of issuance is 4%.
3. The market rate at the date of issuance is 6%.

Problem 14-2B

Straight-line amortization of bond discount and bond premium

P1 P2 P3

Check (3) $6,012,000

(4) 6/30/2010 carrying value, $3,949,200

Long Beach issues $4,500,000 of 8%, 15-year bonds dated January 1, 2009, that pay interest semiannually on June 30 and December 31. The bonds are issued at a price of $3,888,000.

Required

1. Prepare the January 1, 2009, journal entry to record the bonds' issuance.
2. For each semiannual period, compute (*a*) the cash payment, (*b*) the straight-line discount amortization, and (*c*) the bond interest expense.
3. Determine the total bond interest expense to be recognized over the bonds' life.
4. Prepare the first two years of an amortization table like Exhibit 14.7 using the straight-line method.
5. Prepare the journal entries to record the first two interest payments.
6. Assume that the bonds are issued at a price of $5,508,000. Repeat parts 1 through 5.

San Mateo Company issues 7%, five-year bonds dated January 1, 2009, with a $220,000 par value. The bonds pay interest on June 30 and December 31 and are issued at a price of $229,385. Their annual market rate is 6% on the issue date.

Problem 14-3B
Straight-line amortization of bond premium

P1   P3

Required

1. Calculate the total bond interest expense over the bonds' life.
2. Prepare a straight-line amortization table like Exhibit 14.11 for the bonds' life.
3. Prepare the journal entries to record the first two interest payments.

Check   (2) 12/31/2011 carrying
value, $223,751

Refer to the bond details in Problem 14-3B.

Problem 14-4B[B]
Effective interest amortization of bond premium; computing bond price   P1   P3

Required

1. Compute the total bond interest expense over the bonds' life.
2. Prepare an effective interest amortization table like the one in Exhibit 14B.2 for the bonds' life.
3. Prepare the journal entries to record the first two interest payments.
4. Use the market rate at issuance to compute the present value of the remaining cash flows for these bonds as of December 31, 2011. Compare your answer with the amount shown on the amortization table as the balance for that date (from part 2) and explain your findings.

Check   (2) 6/30/2011 carrying
value, $225,041

(4) $224,092

Kelly issues $315,000 of 4%, 15-year bonds dated January 1, 2009, that pay interest semiannually on June 30 and December 31. They are issued at $253,263, and their market rate is 6% at the issue date.

Problem 14-5B
Straight-line amortization of bond discount

P1   P2

Required

1. Prepare the January 1, 2009, journal entry to record the bonds' issuance.
2. Determine the total bond interest expense to be recognized over the life of the bonds.
3. Prepare a straight-line amortization table like the one in Exhibit 14.7 for the bonds' first two years.
4. Prepare the journal entries to record the first two interest payments.

Check   (2) $250,737

(3) 6/30/2010 carrying
value, $259,437

Refer to the bond details in Problem 14-5B.

Problem 14-6B[B]
Effective interest amortization of bond discount

P1   P2

Required

1. Prepare the January 1, 2009, journal entry to record the bonds' issuance.
2. Determine the total bond interest expense to be recognized over the bonds' life.
3. Prepare an effective interest amortization table like the one in Exhibit 14B.1 for the bonds' first two years.
4. Prepare the journal entries to record the first two interest payments.

Check   (2) $250,737;

(3) 6/30/2010 carrying
value, $257,275

Kendall issues $175,000 of 11%, three-year bonds dated January 1, 2009, that pay interest semiannually on June 30 and December 31. They are issued at $179,439, and their market rate is 10% at the issue date.

Problem 14-7B[B]
Effective interest amortization of bond premium; retiring bonds

P1   P3   P4

Required

1. Prepare the January 1, 2009, journal entry to record the bonds' issuance.
2. Determine the total bond interest expense to be recognized over the bonds' life.
3. Prepare an effective interest amortization table like the one in Exhibit 14B.2 for the bonds' first two years.
4. Prepare the journal entries to record the first two interest payments.
5. Prepare the journal entry to record the bonds' retirement on January 1, 2011, at 105.

Check   (3) 6/30/2010 carrying value,
$177,380

(5) $7,126 loss

Analysis Component

6. Assume that the market rate on January 1, 2009, is 12% instead of 10%. Without presenting numbers, describe how this change affects the amounts reported on Kendall's financial statements.

Problem 14-8B
Installment notes

C1   P5

On October 1, 2009, Miami Enterprises borrows $200,000 cash from a bank by signing a three-year installment note bearing 7% interest. The note requires equal total payments each year on September 30.

Required

1. Compute the total amount of each installment payment.
2. Complete an amortization table for this installment note similar to the one in Exhibit 14.14.
3. Prepare the journal entries to record (a) accrued interest as of December 31, 2009 (the end of its annual reporting period) and (b) the first annual payment on the note.

Problem 14-9B
Applying the debt-to-equity ratio

A3

At the end of the current year, the following information is available for both Caesar Company and Delta Company.

	Caesar Company	Delta Company
Total assets	$360,000	$1,500,000
Total liabilities	162,360	1,125,000
Total equity	198,000	375,000

Required

1. Compute the debt-to-equity ratios for both companies.
2. Comment on your results and discuss what they imply about the relative riskiness of these companies.

Problem 14-10B[D]
Capital lease accounting

C4

Allan Company signs a five-year capital lease with Vortal Company for office equipment. The annual lease payment is $13,000, and the interest rate is 8%.

Required

1. Compute the present value of Allan's lease payments.
2. Prepare the journal entry to record Allan's capital lease at its inception.
3. Complete a lease payment schedule for the five years of the lease with the following headings. Assume that the beginning balance of the lease liability (present value of lease payments) is $51,905. (*Hint:* To find the amount allocated to interest in year 1, multiply the interest rate by the beginning-of-year lease liability. The amount of the annual lease payment not allocated to interest is allocated to principal. Reduce the lease liability by the amount allocated to principal to update the lease liability at each year-end.)

Period Ending Date	Beginning Balance of Lease Liability	Interest on Lease Liability	Reduction of Lease Liability	Cash Lease Payment	Ending Balance of Lease Liability

4. Use straight-line depreciation and prepare the journal entry to depreciate the leased asset at the end of year 1. Assume zero salvage value and a five-year life for the office equipment.

SERIAL PROBLEM

Success Systems

(This serial problem began in Chapter 1 and continues through most of the book. If previous chapter segments were not completed, the serial problem can begin at this point. It is helpful, but not necessary, to use the Working Papers that accompany the book.)

SP 14   Adriana Lopez has consulted with her local banker and is considering financing an expansion of her business by obtaining a long-term bank loan. Selected account balances at March 31, 2010, for Success Systems follow.

Total assets .... $129,909   Total liabilities ...... $875   Total equity $129,034

Required

1. The bank has offered a long-term secured note to Success Systems. The bank's loan procedures require that a client's debt-to-equity ratio not exceed 0.8. As of March 31, 2010, what is the maximum amount that Success Systems could borrow from this bank (rounded to nearest dollar)?

Check (1) $102,352

2. If Success Systems borrows the maximum amount allowed from the bank, what percentage of assets would be financed (*a*) by debt and (*b*) by equity?

3. What are some factors Lopez should consider before borrowing the funds?

BEYOND THE NUMBERS

BTN 14-1 Refer to **Best Buy**'s financial statements in Appendix A to answer the following.

1. Identify the items that make up Best Buy's long-term debt at March 3, 2007. (*Hint:* See note 5.)

2. How much annual cash interest must Best Buy pay on its 2.25% convertible subordinated debt?

3. Did it have any additions to long-term debt that provided cash for the year ending March 3, 2007?

Fast Forward

4. Access Best Buy's financial statements for the years ending after March 3, 2007, from its Website (**BestBuy.com**) or the SEC's EDGAR database (**www.SEC.gov**). Has it issued additional long-term debt since the year-end March 3, 2007? If yes, identify the amount(s).

REPORTING IN ACTION

A1 A2

BTN 14-2 Key figures for **Best Buy**, **Circuit City**, and **RadioShack** follow.

($ millions)	Best Buy		Circuit City		RadioShack	
	Current Year	Prior Year	Current Year	Prior Year	Current Year	Prior Year
Total assets	$13,570	$11,864	$4,007	$4,069	$2,070	$2,205
Total liabilities	7,369	6,607	2,216	2,114	1,416	1,616
Total equity	6,201	5,257	1,791	1,955	654	589

COMPARATIVE ANALYSIS

A3

Required

1. Compute the debt-to-equity ratios for Best Buy, Circuit City, and RadioShack for both the current year and the prior year.

2. Use the ratios you computed in part 1 to determine which company's financing structure is least risky. Assume an industry average of 0.24 for debt-to-equity.

BTN 14-3 Brevard County needs a new county government building that would cost $24 million. The politicians feel that voters will not approve a municipal bond issue to fund the building since it would increase taxes. They opt to have a state bank issue $24 million of tax-exempt securities to pay for the building construction. The county then will make yearly lease payments (of principal and interest) to repay the obligation. Unlike conventional municipal bonds, the lease payments are not binding obligations on the county and, therefore, require no voter approval.

ETHICS CHALLENGE

C4 A1

Required

1. Do you think the actions of the politicians and the bankers in this situation are ethical?

2. How do the tax-exempt securities used to pay for the building compare in risk to a conventional municipal bond issued by Brevard County?

BTN 14-4 Your business associate mentions that she is considering investing in corporate bonds currently selling at a premium. She says that since the bonds are selling at a premium, they are highly valued and her investment will yield more than the going rate of return for the risk involved. Reply with a memorandum to confirm or correct your associate's interpretation of premium bonds.

COMMUNICATING IN PRACTICE

P3

**TAKING IT TO
THE NET**

A2

BTN 14-5   Access the March 29, 2007, filing of the 10-K report of **Home Depot** for the year ended January 28, 2007, from www.sec.gov (Ticker: HD). Refer to Home Depot's balance sheet, including its note 4 (on debt).

Required

1. Identify Home Depot's long-term liabilities and the amounts for those liabilities from Home Depot's balance sheet at January 28, 2007.
2. Review Home Depot's note 4. The note reports that it "issued $3.0 billion of 5.875% senior notes due December 16, 2036, at a discount of $42 million with interest payable semiannually on June 16 and December 16 each year."
   a. Why would Home Depot issue $3.0 billion of its notes for only $2.958 billion?
   b. How much cash interest must Home Depot pay each June 16 and December 16 on these notes?

**TEAMWORK IN
ACTION**

P2   P3

Hint: Rotate teams to report on parts 4 and 5. Consider requiring entries for issuance and interest payments.

BTN 14-6ᴮ   Break into teams and complete the following requirements related to effective interest amortization for a premium bond.

1. Each team member is to independently prepare a blank table with proper headings for amortization of a bond premium. When all have finished, compare tables and ensure that all are in agreement.

Parts 2 and 3 require use of these facts: On January 1, 2008, BC issues $100,000, 9%, five-year bonds at 104.1. The market rate at issuance is 8%. BC pays interest semiannually on June 30 and December 31.

2. In rotation, *each* team member must explain how to complete *one* line of the bond amortization table, including all computations for his or her line. (Round amounts to the nearest dollar.) All members are to fill in their tables during this process. You need not finish the table; stop after all members have explained a line.
3. In rotation, *each* team member is to identify a separate column of the table and indicate what the final number in that column will be and explain the reasoning.
4. Reach a team consensus as to what the total bond interest expense on this bond issue will be if the bond is not retired before maturity.
5. As a team, prepare a list of similarities and differences between the amortization table just prepared and the amortization table if the bond had been issued at a discount.

**ENTREPRENEURIAL
DECISION**

A1

BTN 14-7   James Lindsay is the founder of **Rap Snacks**. Assume that his company currently has $250,000 in equity, and he is considering a $100,000 expansion to meet increased demand. The $100,000 expansion would yield $16,000 in additional annual income before interest expense. Assume that the business currently earns $40,000 annual income before interest expense of $10,000, yielding a return on equity of 12% ($30,000/$250,000). To fund the expansion, he is considering the issuance of a 10-year, $100,000 note with annual interest payments (the principal due at the end of 10 years).

Required

1. Using return on equity as the decision criterion, show computations to support or reject the expansion if interest on the $100,000 note is (a) 10%, (b) 15%, (c) 16%, (d) 17%, and (e) 20%.
2. What general rule do the results in part 1 illustrate?

**HITTING THE
ROAD**

A1

BTN 14-8   Visit your city or county library. Ask the librarian to help you locate the recent financial records of your city or county government. Examine those records.

Required

1. Determine the amount of long-term bonds and notes currently outstanding.
2. Read the supporting information to your municipality's financial statements and record
   a. The market interest rate(s) when the bonds and/or notes were issued.
   b. The date(s) when the bonds and/or notes will mature.
   c. Any rating(s) on the bonds and/or notes received from **Moody's**, **Standard & Poor's**, or another rating agency.

BTN 14-9   DSG international plc (www.DSGiplc.com), Best Buy, Circuit City, and RadioShack are competitors in the global marketplace. Selected results from these companies follow.

Key Figures	DSG (£ millions)		Best Buy ($ millions)		Circuit City ($ millions)		RadioShack ($ millions)	
	Current Year	Prior Year	Current Year	Prior Year	Current Year	Prior Year	Current Year	Prior Year
Total assets	£3,977	£4,120	$13,570	$11,864	$4,007	$4,069	$2,070	$2,205
Total liabilities	2,673	2,696	7,369	6,607	2,216	2,114	1,416	1,616
Total equity	1,304	1,424	6,201	5,257	1,791	1,955	654	589
Debt-to-equity ratio	?	?	1.2	1.3	1.2	1.1	2.2	2.7

Required

1. Compute DSG's debt-to-equity ratios for the current year and the prior year.

2. Use the data provided and the ratios you computed in part 1 to determine which company's financing structure is least risky.

ANSWERS TO MULTIPLE CHOICE QUIZ

1. b

2. a

3. c; $500,000 × 0.08 × ½ year = $20,000

4. a; Cash interest paid = $100,000 × 5% × ½ year = $2,500
Discount amortization = ($100,000 − $95,735)/10 periods = $426.50
Interest expense = $2,500.00 + $426.50 = $2,926.50

5. e; ($373,745 − $350,000)/16 periods = $1,484

A Look Back

Chapter 14 focused on long-term liabilities—a main part of most companies' financing. We explained how to value, record, amortize, and report these liabilities in financial statements.

A Look at This Chapter

This chapter focuses on investments in securities. We explain how to identify, account for, and report investments in both debt and equity securities. We also explain accounting for transactions listed in a foreign currency.

A Look Ahead

Chapter 16 focuses on reporting and analyzing a company's cash flows. Special emphasis is directed at the statement of cash flows reported under the indirect method.

Chapter

Investments and International Operations

Learning Objectives

CAP

Conceptual

C1 Distinguish between debt and equity securities and between short-term and long-term investments. *(p. 592)*

C2 Identify and describe the different classes of investments in securities. *(p. 593)*

C3 Describe how to report equity securities with controlling influence. *(p. 599)*

C4 *Appendix 15A*—Explain foreign exchange rates between currencies. *(p. 605)*

Analytical

A1 Compute and analyze the components of return on total assets. *(p. 600)*

LP15

Procedural

P1 Account for trading securities. *(p. 595)*

P2 Account for held-to-maturity securities. *(p. 596)*

P3 Account for available-for-sale securities. *(p. 596)*

P4 Account for equity securities with significant influence. *(p. 598)*

P5 *Appendix 15A*—Record transactions listed in a foreign currency. *(p. 606)*

Designing Business

"It's a wonderful insanity"—Amy Smilovic

NEW YORK—Amy Smilovic loves business. But after a job transfer by her husband to Hong Kong, she quit her job and looked for her next inspiration. Within weeks, and inspired by the colorful and comfortable clothing she saw, Amy jumped into the designing business of clothes. Her company, **Tibi (Tibi.com),** experienced quick success. "I really kind of just did it," explains Amy. "I tried not to over-think it."

What Amy did was design a clothing line that appeals to the masses. "Just design for yourself, someone will identify with it," insists Amy. "You'll find a group of people who want to dress like you." Amy has been so successful that this group of people extends to many countries. She now has showrooms in Milan and London, and locations in Australia, Hong Kong, Indonesia, Japan, Korea, Malaysia, New Zealand, and Singapore.

This broad reach became what she calls her biggest challenge: investments and international operations. "I didn't know what custom regulations were," explains Amy. "I didn't know how to set up a U.S. base and distribute . . . I was buying books on customs and international shipping laws." Her investments in international operations require Amy to translate their performance into U.S. dollars for financial reports. It also requires conducting international transactions and doing currency translations. Those tasks require knowledge of accounting and reporting requirements for investments, including investments in securities of other companies.

Amy's continued success is sure to include more investments and further international operations. She views her business background and focus as key to that success. "People always ask me, 'How are you a designer without a design background,'" laughs Amy. "I always wonder, 'How are you a designer without a business background?' It's really a business at the end of the day."

[Sources: *Tibi Website,* January 2009, *Entrepreneur,* October 2007; *Fashion Week,* 2008; *Ladies Who Launch,* 2008; *New York Social Diary,* April 2007]

This chapter's main focus is investments in securities. Many companies have investments, and many of these are in the form of debt and equity securities issued by other companies. We describe investments in these securities and how to account for them. An increasing number of companies also invest in international operations. We explain how to account for and report international transactions listed in foreign currencies.

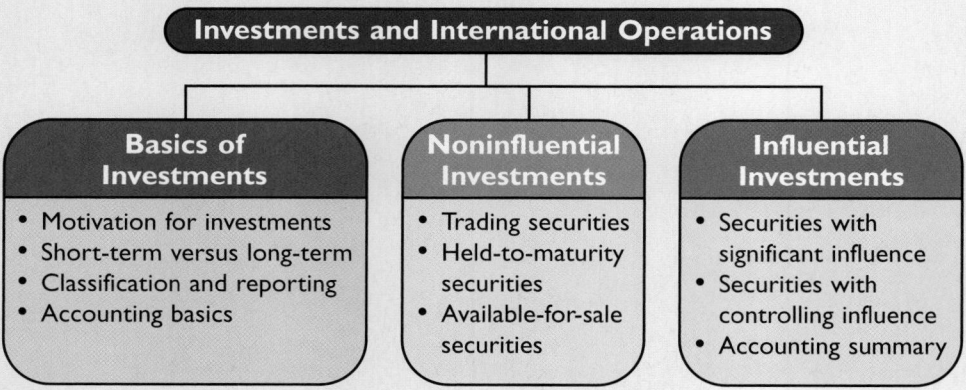

Investments and International Operations

Basics of Investments
- Motivation for investments
- Short-term versus long-term
- Classification and reporting
- Accounting basics

Noninfluential Investments
- Trading securities
- Held-to-maturity securities
- Available-for-sale securities

Influential Investments
- Securities with significant influence
- Securities with controlling influence
- Accounting summary

Basics of Investments

C1 | Distinguish between debt and equity securities and between short-term and long-term investments.

This section describes the motivation for investments, the distinction between short- and long-term investments, and the different classes of investments.

Motivation for Investments

Companies make investments for at least three reasons. First, companies transfer *excess cash* into investments to produce higher income. Second, some entities, such as mutual funds and pension funds, are set up to produce income from investments. Third, companies make investments for strategic reasons. Examples are investments in competitors, suppliers, and even customers. Exhibit 15.1 shows short-term (S-T) and long-term (L-T) investments as a percent of total assets for several companies.

EXHIBIT 15.1

Investments of Selected Companies

Pfizer	S-T 19% · · · · · · · · · L-T 4%
Gap	S-T 2% · L-T 1%
Starbucks	S-T 3% · L-T 5%
Coca-Cola	S-T 1% · · · · · · · · L-T 18%

0% — 25%
Percent of total assets

Short-Term versus Long-Term

Cash equivalents are investments that are both readily converted to known amounts of cash and mature within three months. Many investments, however, mature between 3 and 12 months. These investments are **short-term investments,** also called *temporary investments* and *marketable securities*. Specifically, short-term investments are securities that (1) management intends to convert to cash within one year or the operating cycle, whichever is longer, and (2) are readily convertible to cash. Short-term investments are reported under current assets and serve a purpose similar to cash equivalents.

Long-term investments in securities are defined as those securities that are not readily convertible to cash or are not intended to be converted into cash in the short term. Long-term investments can also include funds earmarked for a special purpose, such as bond sinking funds and investments in land or other assets not used in the company's operations. Long-term investments are reported in the noncurrent section of the balance sheet, often in its own separate line titled *Long-Term Investments*.

Investments in securities can include both debt and equity securities. *Debt securities* reflect a creditor relationship such as investments in notes, bonds, and certificates of deposit; they are issued by governments, companies, and individuals. *Equity securities* reflect an owner relationship such as shares of stock issued by companies.

Classification and Reporting

Accounting for investments in securities depends on three factors: (1) security type, either debt or equity, (2) the company's intent to hold the security either short term or long term, and (3) the company's (investor's) percent ownership in the other company's (investee's) equity securities. Exhibit 15.2 identifies five classes of securities using these three factors. It describes each of these five classes of securities and the standard reporting required under each class.

C2 Identify and describe the different classes of investments in securities.

EXHIBIT 15.2

Investments in Securities

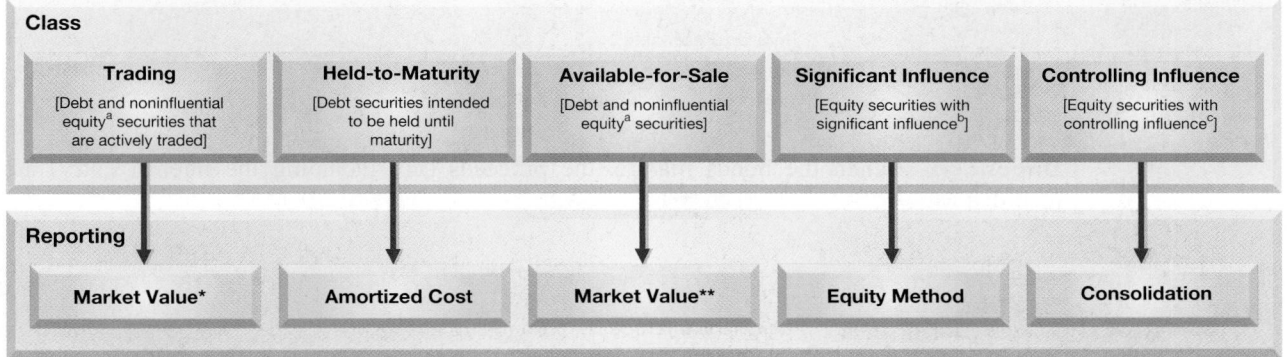

ª Holding less than 20% of voting stock (equity securities only).   ᵇ Holding 20% or more, but not more than 50%, of voting stock.
ᶜ Holding more than 50% of voting stock.
* Unrealized gains and losses reported on the income statement.
** Unrealized gains and losses reported in the equity section of the balance sheet and in comprehensive income.

Accounting Basics for <u>Debt Securities</u>

This section explains the accounting basics for *debt securities,* including that for acquisition, disposition, and any interest.

Acquisition.   Debt securities are recorded at cost when purchased. To illustrate, assume that Music City paid $29,500 plus a $500 brokerage fee on September 1, 2008, to buy Dell's 7%, two-year bonds payable with a $30,000 par value. The bonds pay interest semiannually on August 31 and February 28. Music City intends to hold the bonds until they mature on August 31, 2010; consequently, they are classified as held-to-maturity (HTM) securities. The entry to record this purchase follows. (If the maturity of the securities was short term, and management's intent was to hold them until they mature, then they would be classified as Short-Term Investments—HTM.)

2008			
Sept. 1	Long-Term Investments—HTM (Dell)	30,000	
	Cash		30,000
	Purchased bonds to be held to maturity.		

Assets = Liabilities + Equity
+30,000
−30,000

Interest earned.   Interest revenue for investments in debt securities is recorded when earned. To illustrate, on December 31, 2008, at the end of its accounting period, Music City accrues interest receivable as follows.

Dec. 31	Interest Receivable.	700	
	Interest Revenue.		700
	Accrued interest earned ($30,000 × 7% × ¹⁄₁₂).		

Assets = Liabilities + Equity
+700   +700

The $700 reflects 4/6 of the semiannual cash receipt of interest—the portion Music City earned as of December 31. Relevant sections of Music City's financial statements at December 31, 2008, are shown in Exhibit 15.3.

EXHIBIT 15.3

Financial Statement Presentation
of Debt Securities

On the income statement for year 2008:	
Interest revenue	**$ 700**
On the December 31, 2008, balance sheet:	
Long-term investments—Held-to-maturity securities (at amortized cost)	**$30,000**

On February 28, 2009, Music City records receipt of semiannual interest.

Assets = Liabilities + Equity
+1,050   +350
−700

Feb. 28	Cash	1,050	
	Interest Receivable		700
	Interest Revenue		350
	Received six months' interest on Dell bonds.		

Disposition.   When the bonds mature, the proceeds (not including the interest entry) are recorded as:

Assets = Liabilities + Equity
+30,000
−30,000

2010			
Aug. 31	Cash.....................................	30,000	
	Long-Term Investments—HTM (Dell)		30,000
	Received cash from matured bonds.		

Example: What is cost per share?
Answer: Cost per share is the total cost
of acquisition, including broker fees,
divided by number of shares acquired.

The cost of a debt security can be either higher or lower than its maturity value. When the investment is long term, the difference between cost and maturity value is amortized over the remaining life of the security. We assume for ease of computations that the cost of a long-term debt security equals its maturity value.

Accounting Basics for <u>Equity Securities</u>

This section explains the accounting basics for *equity securities,* including that for acquisition, dividends, and disposition.

Acquisition.   Equity securities are recorded at cost when acquired, including commissions or brokerage fees paid. To illustrate, assume that Music City purchases 1,000 shares of Intex common stock at par value for $86,000 on October 10, 2008. It records this purchase of available-for-sale (AFS) securities as follows.

Assets = Liabilities + Equity
+86,000
−86,000

Oct. 10	Long-Term Investments—AFS (Intex)	86,000	
	Cash		86,000
	Purchased 1,000 shares of Intex.		

Dividend earned.   Any cash dividends received are credited to Dividend Revenue and reported in the income statement. To illustrate, on November 2, Music City receives a $1,720 quarterly cash dividend on the Intex shares, which it records as:

Assets = Liabilities + Equity
+1,720   +1,720

Nov. 2	Cash	1,720	
	Dividend Revenue		1,720
	Received dividend of $1.72 per share.		

Disposition.   When the securities are sold, sale proceeds are compared with the cost, and any gain or loss is recorded. To illustrate, on December 20, Music City sells 500 of the Intex shares for $45,000 cash and records this sale as:

Assets = Liabilities + Equity
+45,000   +2,000
−43,000

Dec. 20	Cash.....................................	45,000	
	Long-Term Investments—AFS (Intex)		43,000
	Gain on Sale of Long-Term Investments		2,000
	Sold 500 Intex shares ($86,000 × 500/1,000).		

Reporting of *Non*influential Investments

Companies must value and report most noninfluential investments at *fair market value,* or simply *market value.* The exact reporting requirements depend on whether the investments are classified as (1) trading, (2) held-to-maturity, or (3) available-for-sale.

P1   Account for trading securities.

Trading Securities

Trading securities are *debt and equity securities* that the company intends to actively manage and trade for profit. Frequent purchases and sales are expected and are made to earn profits on short-term price changes. Trading securities are *always* reported as current assets.

Valuing and reporting trading securities.   The entire portfolio of trading securities is reported at its market value; this requires a "market adjustment" from the cost of the portfolio. The term *portfolio* refers to a group of securities. Any **unrealized gain (or loss)** from a change in the market value of the portfolio of trading securities is reported on the income statement. Most users believe accounting reports are more useful when changes in market value for trading securities are reported in income.

To illustrate, TechCom's portfolio of trading securities had a total cost of $11,500 and a market value of $13,000 on December 31, 2008, the first year it held trading securities. The difference between the $11,500 cost and the $13,000 market value reflects a $1,500 gain. It is an unrealized gain because it is not yet confirmed by actual sales. The market adjustment for trading securities is recorded with an adjusting entry at the end of each period to equal the difference between the portfolio's cost and its market value. TechCom records this gain as follows.

Point: *'Unrealized gain (or loss)'* refers to a change in market value that is not yet realized through actual sale.

Point: 'Market Adjustment—Trading' is a *permanent account,* shown as a deduction or addition to 'Short-Term Investments—Trading.'

Dec. 31	Market Adjustment—Trading.	1,500	
	Unrealized Gain—Income		1,500
	To reflect an unrealized gain in market values of trading securities.		

Assets = Liabilities + Equity
+1,500   +1,500

The Unrealized Gain (or Loss) is reported in the Other Revenues and Gains (or Expenses and Losses) section on the income statement. Unrealized Gain (or Loss)—Income is a *temporary* account that is closed to Income Summary at the end of each period. Market Adjustment—Trading is a *permanent* account, which adjusts the reported value of the trading securities portfolio from its prior period market value to the current period market value. The total cost of the trading securities portfolio is maintained in one account, and the market adjustment is recorded in a separate account. For example, TechCom's investment in trading securities is reported in the current assets section of its balance sheet as follows.

Example: If TechCom's trading securities have a cost of $14,800 and a market of $16,100 at Dec. 31, 2009, its adjusting entry is
Unrealized Loss—Income 200
  Market Adj.—Trading   200
This is computed as: $1,500 Beg. Dr. bal. + $200 Cr. = $1,300 End. Dr. bal.

Current Assets		
Short-term investments—Trading (at cost)	$11,500	
Market adjustment—Trading	1,500	
Short-term investments—Trading (at market)		$13,000
or simply		
Short-term investments—Trading (at market; cost is $11,500)		$13,000

Selling trading securities.   When individual trading securities are sold, the difference between the net proceeds (sale price less fees) and the cost of the individual trading securities that are sold is recognized as a gain or a loss. Any prior period market adjustment to the portfolio is *not* used to compute the gain or loss from sale of individual trading securities. For example, if TechCom sold some of its trading securities that had cost $1,000 for $1,200 cash on January 9, 2009, it would record the following.

Point: Reporting securities at market value is referred to as *mark-to-market* accounting.

Assets = Liabilities + Equity
+1,200   +200
−1,000

Jan. 9	Cash	1,200	
	Short-Term Investments—Trading		1,000
	Gain on Sale of Short-Term Investments		200
	Sold trading securities costing $1,000 for $1,200 cash.		

A gain is reported in the Other Revenues and Gains section on the income statement, whereas a loss is shown in Other Expenses and Losses. When the period-end market adjustment for the portfolio of trading securities is computed, it excludes the cost and market value of any securities sold.

Held-to-Maturity Securities

P2   Account for held-to-maturity securities.

Held-to-maturity (HTM) securities are *debt* securities a company intends and is able to hold until maturity. They are reported in current assets if their maturity dates are within one year or the operating cycle, whichever is longer. HTM securities are reported in long-term assets when the maturity dates extend beyond one year or the operating cycle, whichever is longer. All HTM securities are recorded at cost when purchased, and interest revenue is recorded when earned.

    The portfolio of HTM securities is usually reported at (amortized) cost, which is explained in advanced courses. There is no market adjustment to the portfolio of HTM securities—neither to the short-term nor long-term portfolios. The basics of accounting for HTM securities were described earlier in this chapter.

Point: Only debt securities can be classified as *held-to-maturity*; equity securities have no maturity date.

 ### Decision Maker

Money Manager You expect interest rates to sharply fall within a few weeks and remain at this lower rate. What is your strategy for holding investments in fixed-rate bonds and notes? [Answer—p. 608]

Available-for-Sale Securities

P3   Account for available-for-sale securities.

Available-for-sale (AFS) securities are *debt and equity securities* not classified as trading or held-to-maturity securities. AFS securities are purchased to yield interest, dividends, or increases in market value. They are not actively managed like trading securities. If the intent is to sell AFS securities within the longer of one year or operating cycle, they are classified as short-term investments. Otherwise, they are classified as long-term.

Valuing and reporting available-for-sale securities.   As with trading securities, companies adjust the cost of the portfolio of AFS securities to reflect changes in market value. This is done with a market adjustment to its total portfolio cost. However, any unrealized gain or loss for the portfolio of AFS securities is *not* reported on the income statement. Instead, it is reported in the equity section of the balance sheet (and is part of *comprehensive income,* explained later). To illustrate, assume that Music City had no prior period investments in available-for-sale securities other than those purchased in the current period. Exhibit 15.4 shows both the cost and market value of those investments on December 31, 2008, the end of its reporting period.

Example: If market value in Exhibit 15.4 is $70,000 (instead of $74,550), what entry is made? *Answer:*
Unreal. Loss—Equity . . . 3,000
   Market Adj.—AFS   3,000

EXHIBIT 15.4

Cost and Market Value of Available-for-Sale Securities

	Cost	Market Value	Unrealized Gain (Loss)
Improv bonds	$30,000	$29,050	$ (950)
Intex common stock, 500 shares	43,000	45,500	2,500
Total	$73,000	$74,550	$1,550

The year-end adjusting entry to record the market value of these investments follows.

Assets = Liabilities + Equity
+1,550   +1,550

Dec. 31	Market Adjustment—Available-for-Sale (LT)	1,550	
	Unrealized Gain—Equity		1,550
	To record adjustment to market value of		
	available-for-sale securities.		

Exhibit 15.5 shows the December 31, 2008, balance sheet presentation—it assumes these investments are long term, but they can also be short term. It is also common to combine the cost of investments with the balance in the Market Adjustment account and report the net as a single amount.

Point: 'Unrealized Loss—Equity' and 'Unrealized Gain—Equity' are *permanent* (balance sheet) equity *accounts.*

EXHIBIT 15.5

Balance Sheet Presentation of Available-for-Sale Securities

Reconciled		
Assets		
Long-term investments—Available-for-sale (at cost)	$73,000	
Market adjustment— Available-for-sale	1,550	
Long-term investments—Available-for-sale (at market)		$74,550
or simply		
Long-term investments—Available-for-sale (at market; cost is $73,000)		$74,550
Equity		
. . . consists of usual equity accounts . . .		
Add unrealized gain on available-for-sale securities*		$ 1,550

* Often included under the caption Accumulated Other Comprehensive Income.

Let's extend this illustration and assume that at the end of its next calendar year (December 31, 2009), Music City's portfolio of long-term AFS securities has an $81,000 cost and an $82,000 market value. It records the adjustment to market value as follows.

Point: Income can be window-dressed upward by selling AFS securities with unrealized gains; income is reduced by selling those with unrealized losses.

Dec. 31	Unrealized Gain—Equity.	550	
	Market Adjustment—Available-for-Sale (LT).		550
	To record adjustment to market value of available-for-sale securities.		

Assets = Liabilities + Equity
−550   −550

The effects of the 2008 and 2009 securities transactions are reflected in the following T-accounts.

Example: If cost is $83,000 and market is $82,000 at Dec. 31, 2009, it records the following adjustment:
Unreal. Gain—Equity . . . 1,550
Unreal. Loss—Equity . . . 1,000
  Mkt. Adj.—AFS   2,550

Unrealized Gain—Equity				
Adj. 12/31/09	550	Bal. 12/31/08	1,550	
		Bal. 12/31/09	1,000	

Market Adjustment—Available-for-Sale (LT)			
Bal. 12/31/08	1,550	Adj. 12/31/09	550
Bal. 12/31/09	1,000		

Amounts reconcile.

Selling available-for-sale securities.   Accounting for the sale of individual AFS securities is identical to that described for the sale of trading securities. When individual AFS securities are sold, the difference between the cost of the individual securities sold and the net proceeds (sale price less fees) is recognized as a gain or loss.

Point: 'Market Adjustment—Available-for-Sale' is a permanent account, shown as a deduction or addition to the Investment account.

Quick Check   Answers—p. 608

1. How are short-term held-to-maturity securities reported (valued) on the balance sheet?

2. How are trading securities reported (valued) on the balance sheet?

3. Where are unrealized gains and losses on available-for-sale securities reported?

4. Where are unrealized gains and losses on trading securities reported?

Alert   *The FASB released FAS 157 and FAS 159 that permit companies to use market value in reporting financial assets (referred to as the* fair value option).*This option allows companies to report any financial asset at fair market value and recognize value changes in income. This method was previously reserved only for trading securities, but would now be an option for available-for-sale and held-to-maturity securities (and other 'financial assets and liabilities' such as accounts and notes receivable, accounts and notes payable, and bonds).These standards also set a 3-level system to determine fair value:*
—Level 1: Use quoted market values
—Level 2: Use observable values from related assets or liabilities
—Level 3: Use unobservable values from estimates or assumptions
To date, a fairly small set of companies has chosen to broadly apply the fair value option—but, we continue to monitor its use...

Reporting of Influential Investments

Investment in Securities with Significant Influence

P4   Account for equity
securities with
significant influence.

A long-term investment classified as **equity securities with significant influence** implies that the investor can exert significant influence over the investee. An investor that owns 20% or more (but not more than 50%) of a company's voting stock is usually presumed to have a significant influence over the investee. In some cases, however, the 20% test of significant influence is overruled by other, more persuasive, evidence. This evidence can either lower the 20% requirement or increase it. The **equity method** of accounting and reporting is used for long-term investments in equity securities with significant influence, which is explained in this section.

Long-term investments in equity securities with significant influence are recorded at cost when acquired. To illustrate, Micron Co. records the purchase of 3,000 shares (30%) of Star Co. common stock at a total cost of $70,650 on January 1, 2008, as follows.

Assets = Liabilities + Equity
+70,650
−70,650

Jan. 1	Long-Term Investments—Star..................	70,650	
	Cash		70,650
	To record purchase of 3,000 Star shares.		

The investee's (Star) earnings increase both its net assets and the claim of the investor (Micron) on the investee's net assets. Thus, when the investee reports its earnings, the investor records its share of those earnings in its investment account. To illustrate, assume that Star reports net income of $20,000 for 2008. Micron then records its 30% share of those earnings as follows.

Assets = Liabilities + Equity
+6,000   +6,000

Dec. 31	Long-Term Investments—Star..................	6,000	
	Earnings from Long-Term Investment		6,000
	To record 30% equity in investee earnings.		

The debit reflects the increase in Micron's equity in Star. The credit reflects 30% of Star's net income. Earnings from Long-Term Investment is a *temporary* account (closed to Income Summary at each period-end) and is reported on the investor's (Micron's) income statement. If the investee incurs a net loss instead of a net income, the investor records its share of the loss and reduces (credits) its investment account. The investor closes this earnings or loss account to Income Summary.

The receipt of cash dividends is not revenue under the equity method because the investor has already recorded its share of the investee's earnings. Instead, cash dividends received by an investor from an investee are viewed as a conversion of one asset to another; that is, dividends reduce the balance of the investment account. To illustrate, Star declares and pays $10,000 in cash dividends on its common stock. Micron records its 30% share of these dividends received on January 9, 2009, as:

Assets = Liabilities + Equity
+3,000
−3,000

Jan. 9	Cash......................................	3,000	
	Long-Term Investments—Star..............		3,000
	To record share of dividend paid by Star.		

The book value of an investment under the equity method equals the cost of the investment plus (minus) the investor's equity in the *undistributed* (*distributed*) earnings of the investee. Once Micron records these transactions, its Long-Term Investments account appears as in Exhibit 15.6.

EXHIBIT 15.6

Investment in Star Common Stock (Ledger Account)

Date	Explanation	Debit	Credit	Balance
2008				
Jan. 1	Investment acquisition	70,650		70,650
Dec. 31	Share of earnings	6,000		76,650
2009				
Jan. 9	Share of dividend		3,000	73,650

Micron's account balance on January 9, 2009, for its investment in Star is $73,650. This is the investment's cost *plus* Micron's equity in Star's earnings since its purchase *less* Micron's equity in Star's cash dividends since its purchase. When an investment in equity securities is sold, the gain or loss is computed by comparing proceeds from the sale with the book value of the investment on the date of sale. If Micron sells its Star stock for $80,000 on January 10, 2009, it records the sale as:

Point: Security prices are sometimes listed in fractions. For example, a debt security with a price of $22\frac{1}{4}$ is the same as $22.25.

Jan. 10	Cash	80,000	
	Long-Term Investments—Star		73,650
	Gain on Sale of Investment		6,350
	Sold 3,000 shares of stock for $80,000.		

Assets = Liabilities + Equity
+80,000   +6,350
−73,650

Investment in Securities with Controlling Influence

A long-term investment classified as **equity securities with controlling influence** implies that the investor can exert a controlling influence over the investee. An investor who owns more than 50% of a company's voting stock has control over the investee. This investor can dominate all other shareholders in electing the corporation's board of directors and has control over the investee's management. In some cases, controlling influence can extend to situations of less than 50% ownership. Exhibit 15.7 summarizes the accounting for investments in equity securities based on an investor's ownership in the stock.

C3 Describe how to report equity securities with controlling influence.

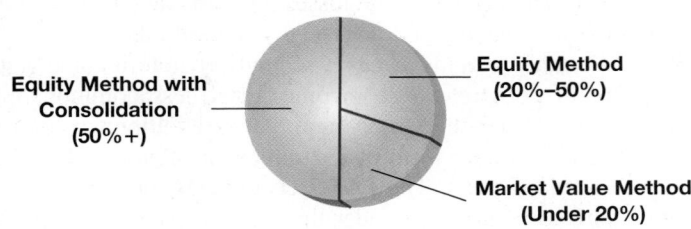

EXHIBIT 15.7

Accounting for Equity Investments by Percent of Ownership

The *equity method with consolidation* is used to account for long-term investments in equity securities with controlling influence. The investor reports *consolidated financial statements* when owning such securities. The controlling investor is called the **parent,** and the investee is called the **subsidiary.** Many companies are parents with subsidiaries. Examples are (1) **McGraw-Hill**, the parent of *BusinessWeek,* Standard & Poor's, and Compustat; (2) **Gap, Inc.**, the parent of Gap, Old Navy, and Banana Republic; and (3) **Brunswick**, the parent of Mercury Marine, Sea Ray, and U.S. Marine. A company owning all the outstanding stock of a subsidiary can, if it desires, take over the subsidiary's assets, retire the subsidiary's stock, and merge the subsidiary into the parent. However, there often are financial, legal, and tax advantages if a business operates as a parent controlling one or more subsidiaries. When a company operates as a parent with subsidiaries, each entity maintains separate accounting records. From a legal viewpoint, the parent and each subsidiary are separate entities with all rights, duties, and responsibilities of individual companies.

Consolidated financial statements show the financial position, results of operations, and cash flows of all entities under the parent's control, including all subsidiaries. These statements are prepared as if the business were organized as one entity. The parent uses the equity method in its accounts, but the investment account is *not* reported on the parent's financial statements. Instead, the individual assets and liabilities of the parent and its subsidiaries are combined on one balance sheet. Their revenues and expenses also are combined on one income statement, and their cash flows are combined on one statement of cash flows. The procedures for preparing consolidated financial statements are in advanced courses.

Decision Insight

IFRSs Unlike U.S. GAAP, IFRSs require uniform accounting policies be used throughout the group of consolidated subsidiaries. Also, unlike U.S. GAAP, IFRSs offer no detailed guidance on valuation procedures.

Accounting Summary for Investments in Securities

Exhibit 15.8 summarizes the standard accounting for investments in securities. Recall that many investment securities are classified as either short term or long term depending on management's

EXHIBIT 15.8

Accounting for Investments in Securities

Classification	Accounting
Short-Term Investment in Securities	
Held-to-maturity (debt) securities	Cost (without any discount or premium amortization)
Trading (debt and equity) securities	Market value (with market adjustment to income)
Available-for-sale (debt and equity) securities	Market value (with market adjustment to equity)
Long-Term Investment in Securities	
Held-to-maturity (debt) securities	Cost (with any discount or premium amortization)
Available-for-sale (debt and equity) securities	Market value (with market adjustment to equity)
Equity securities with significant influence	Equity method
Equity securities with controlling influence	Equity method (with consolidation)

intent and ability to convert them in the future. Understanding the accounting for these investments enables us to draw better conclusions from financial statements in making business decisions.

Comprehensive Income   The term **comprehensive income** refers to all changes in equity for a period except those due to investments and distributions to owners. This means that it includes (1) the revenues, gains, expenses, and losses reported in net income *and* (2) the gains and losses that bypass net income but affect equity. An example of an item that bypasses net income is unrealized gains and losses on available-for-sale securities. These items make up *other comprehensive income* and are usually reported as a part of the statement of stockholders' equity. (Two other options are as a second separate income statement or as a combined income statement of comprehensive income; these less common options are described in advanced courses.) Most often this simply requires one additional column for Other Comprehensive Income in the usual columnar form of the statement of stockholders' equity (the details of this are left for advanced courses). The FASB encourages, but does *not* require, other comprehensive income items to be grouped under the caption *Accumulated Other Comprehensive Income* in the equity section of the balance sheet, which would include unrealized gains and losses on available-for-sale securities. For instructional benefits, we use actual account titles for these items in the equity section instead of this general, less precise caption.

Point: Some users believe that since AFS securities are not actively traded, reporting market value changes in income would unnecessarily increase income variability and decrease usefulness.

Quick Check

5. Give at least two examples of assets classified as long-term investments.

6. What are the requirements for an equity security to be listed as a long-term investment?

7. Identify similarities and differences in accounting for long-term investments in debt securities that are held-to-maturity versus those available-for-sale.

8. What are the three possible classifications of long-term equity investments? Describe the criteria for each class and the method used to account for each.

Decision Analysis

Components of Return on Total Assets

A1 Compute and analyze the components of return on total assets.

A company's **return on total assets** (or simply *return on assets*) is important in assessing financial performance. The return on total assets can be separated into two components, profit margin and total asset turnover, for additional analyses. Exhibit 15.9 shows how these two components determine return on total assets.

EXHIBIT 15.9

Components of Return on Total Assets

$$\text{Return on total assets} = \text{Profit margin} \times \text{Total asset turnover}$$

$$\frac{\text{Net income}}{\text{Average total assets}} = \frac{\text{Net income}}{\text{Net sales}} \times \frac{\text{Net sales}}{\text{Average total assets}}$$

Profit margin reflects the percent of net income in each dollar of net sales. Total asset turnover reflects a company's ability to produce net sales from total assets. All companies desire a high return on total assets.

By considering these two components, we can often discover strengths and weaknesses not revealed by return on total assets alone. This improves our ability to assess future performance and company strategy.

To illustrate, consider return on total assets and its components for **Gap Inc.** in Exhibit 15.10.

Fiscal Year	Return on Total Assets	=	Profit Margin	×	Total Asset Turnover
2007	9.0%	=	4.9%	×	1.84
2006	11.8	=	6.9	×	1.70
2005	11.1	=	7.1	×	1.57

EXHIBIT 15.10

Gap's Components of Return on Total Assets

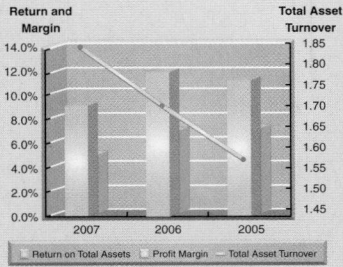

At least three findings emerge. First, Gap's return on total assets improved from 11.1% in 2005 to 11.8% in 2006, but then declined to 9.0% in 2007. Second, total asset turnover has markedly improved from 1.57 to 1.70 to 1.84 over this period. Third, Gap's profit margin steadily declined from 7.1% to 6.9%, and then to 4.9% over this period. These components reveal the dual role of profit margin and total asset turnover in determining return on total assets. They also reveal that the driver of Gap's recent decline is not total asset turnover but profit margin.

Generally, if a company is to maintain or improve its return on total assets, it must meet any decline in either profit margin or total asset turnover with an increase in the other. If not, return on assets will decline. Companies consider these components in planning strategies. A component analysis can also reveal where a company is weak and where changes are needed, especially in a competitor analysis. If asset turnover is lower than the industry norm, for instance, a company should focus on raising asset turnover at least to the norm. The same applies to profit margin.

Decision Maker

Retailer   You are an entrepreneur and owner of a retail sporting goods store. The store's recent annual performance reveals (industry norms in parentheses): return on total assets = 11% (11.2%); profit margin = 4.4% (3.5%); and total asset turnover = 2.5 (3.2). What does your analysis of these figures reveal?
[Answer—p. 608]

Demonstration Problem—1

Garden Company completes the following selected transactions related to its short-term investments during 2008.

DP15

May 8   Purchased 300 shares of FedEx stock as a short-term investment in available-for-sale securities at $40 per share plus $975 in broker fees.

Sept. 2   Sold 100 shares of its investment in FedEx stock at $47 per share and held the remaining 200 shares; broker's commission was $225.

Oct. 2   Purchased 400 shares of Ajay stock for $60 per share plus $1,600 in commissions. The stock is held as a short-term investment in available-for-sale securities.

Required

1. Prepare journal entries for the above transactions of Garden Company for 2008.

2. Prepare an adjusting journal entry as of December 31, 2008, if the market prices of the equity securities held by Garden Company are $48 per share for FedEx and $55 per share for Ajay. (Year 2008 is the first year Garden Company acquired short-term investments.)

Solution to Demonstration Problem—1

1.

May 8	Short-Term Investments—AFS (FedEx)	12,975	
	Cash		12,975
	Purchased 300 shares of FedEx stock		
	(300 × $40) + $975.		

[continued on next page]

[continued from previous page]

Sept. 2	Cash	4,475	
	Gain on Sale of Short-Term Investment		150
	Short-Term Investments—AFS (FedEx)		4,325
	Sold 100 shares of FedEx for $47 per share less		
	a $225 commission. The original cost is		
	($12,975 × 100/300).		
Oct. 2	Short-Term Investments—AFS (Ajay).............	25,600	
	Cash		25,600
	Purchased 400 shares of Ajay for $60 per share		
	plus $1,600 in commissions.		

2. Computation of unrealized gain or loss follows.

Short-Term Investments in Available-for-Sale Securities	Shares	Cost per Share	Total Cost	Market Value per Share	Total Market Value	Unrealized Gain (Loss)
FedEx	200	$43.25	$ 8,650	$48.00	$ 9,600	
Ajay	400	64.00	25,600	55.00	22,000	
Totals			$34,250		$31,600	$(2,650)

The adjusting entry follows.

Dec. 31	Unrealized Loss—Equity......................	2,650	
	Market Adjustment—Available-for-Sale (ST)		2,650
	To reflect an unrealized loss in market values		
	of available-for-sale securities.		

Demonstration Problem—2

The following transactions relate to Brown Company's long-term investments during 2008 and 2009. Brown did not own any long-term investments prior to 2008. Show (1) the appropriate journal entries and (2) the relevant portions of each year's balance sheet and income statement that reflect these transactions for both 2008 and 2009.

2008

Sept. 9   Purchased 1,000 shares of Packard, Inc., common stock for $80,000 cash. These shares represent 30% of Packard's outstanding shares.

Oct.   2   Purchased 2,000 shares of AT&T common stock for $60,000 cash. These shares represent less than a 1% ownership in AT&T.

17   Purchased as a long-term investment 1,000 shares of Apple Computer common stock for $40,000 cash. These shares are less than 1% of Apple's outstanding shares.

Nov. 1   Received $5,000 cash dividend from Packard.

30   Received $3,000 cash dividend from AT&T.

Dec. 15   Received $1,400 cash dividend from Apple.

31   Packard's net income for this year is $70,000.

31   Market values for the investments in equity securities are Packard, $84,000; AT&T, $48,000; and Apple Computer, $45,000.

31   For preparing financial statements, note the following post-closing account balances: Common Stock, $500,000, and Retained Earnings, $350,000.

2009

Jan.   1   Sold Packard, Inc., shares for $108,000 cash.

May 30   Received $3,100 cash dividend from AT&T.

June 15   Received $1,600 cash dividend from Apple.

Aug. 17   Sold the AT&T stock for $52,000 cash.

      19   Purchased 2,000 shares of Coca-Cola common stock for $50,000 cash as a long-term invest-ment. The stock represents less than a 5% ownership in Coca-Cola.

Dec. 15   Received $1,800 cash dividend from Apple.

      31   Market values of the investments in equity securities are Apple, $39,000, and Coca-Cola, $48,000.

      31   For preparing financial statements, note the following post-closing account balances: Common Stock, $500,000, and Retained Earnings, $410,000.

Planning the Solution

- Account for the investment in Packard under the equity method.
- Account for the investments in AT&T, Apple, and Coca-Cola as long-term investments in available-for-sale securities.
- Prepare the information for the two years' balance sheets by including the appropriate asset and equity accounts.

Solution to Demonstration Problem—2

1. Journal entries for 2008.

Sept. 9	Long-Term Investments—Packard	80,000	
	Cash		80,000
	Acquired 1,000 shares, representing a 30% equity in Packard.		
Oct. 2	Long-Term Investments—AFS (AT&T)	60,000	
	Cash		60,000
	Acquired 2,000 shares as a long-term investment in available-for-sale securities.		
Oct. 17	Long-Term Investments—AFS (Apple)	40,000	
	Cash		40,000
	Acquired 1,000 shares as a long-term investment in available-for-sale securities.		
Nov. 1	Cash	5,000	
	Long-Term Investments—Packard.		5,000
	Received dividend from Packard.		
Nov. 30	Cash	3,000	
	Dividend Revenue		3,000
	Received dividend from AT&T.		
Dec. 15	Cash	1,400	
	Dividend Revenue		1,400
	Received dividend from Apple.		
Dec. 31	Long-Term Investments—Packard	21,000	
	Earnings from Investment (Packard)		21,000
	To record 30% share of Packard's annual earnings of $70,000.		
Dec. 31	Unrealized Loss—Equity	7,000	
	Market Adjustment—Available-for-Sale (LT)*		7,000
	To record change in market value of long-term available-for-sale securities.		

* Market adjustment computations:

	Cost	Market Value	Unrealized Gain (Loss)
AT&T	$ 60,000	$48,000	$(12,000)
Apple	40,000	45,000	5,000
Total	$100,000	$93,000	$ (7,000)

Required balance of the Market
   Adjustment—Available-for-Sale
   (LT) account (credit) . . . . $(7,000)
Existing balance   0
Necessary adjustment (credit) . . . . . $(7,000)

2. The December 31, 2008, selected balance sheet items appear as follows.

Assets	
Long-term investments	
Available-for-sale securities (at market; cost is $100,000)	$ 93,000
Investment in equity securities	96,000
Total long-term investments	189,000
Stockholders' Equity	
Common stock	500,000
Retained earnings	350,000
Unrealized loss—Equity	(7,000)

The relevant income statement items for the year ended December 31, 2008, follow.

Dividend revenue	$ 4,400
Earnings from investment	21,000

1. Journal entries for 2009.

Jan. 1	Cash	108,000	
	Long-Term Investments—Packard.		96,000
	Gain on Sale of Long-Term Investments		12,000
	Sold 1,000 shares for cash.		
May 30	Cash	3,100	
	Dividend Revenue		3,100
	Received dividend from AT&T.		
June 15	Cash	1,600	
	Dividend Revenue		1,600
	Received dividend from Apple.		
Aug. 17	Cash	52,000	
	Loss on Sale of Long-Term Investments	8,000	
	Long-Term Investments—AFS (AT&T).		60,000
	Sold 2,000 shares for cash.		
Aug. 19	Long-Term Investments—AFS (Coca-Cola)	50,000	
	Cash		50,000
	Acquired 2,000 shares as a long-term investment in available-for-sale securities.		
Dec. 15	Cash	1,800	
	Dividend Revenue		1,800
	Received dividend from Apple.		
Dec. 31	Market Adjustment—Available-for-Sale (LT)*.	4,000	
	Unrealized Loss—Equity		4,000
	To record change in market value of long-term available-for-sale securities.		

* Market adjustment computations:

	Cost	Market Value	Unrealized Gain (Loss)
Apple	$40,000	$39,000	$(1,000)
Coca-Cola	50,000	48,000	(2,000)
Total	$90,000	$87,000	$(3,000)

Required balance of the Market Adjustment—Available-for-Sale (LT) account (credit)	$(3,000)
Existing balance (credit)	(7,000)
Necessary adjustment (debit)	$ 4,000

2. The December 31, 2009, balance sheet items appear as follows.

Assets	
Long-term investments	
Available-for-sale securities (at market; cost is $90,000)	$ 87,000
Stockholders' Equity	
Common stock	500,000
Retained earnings	410,000
Unrealized loss—Equity	(3,000)

The relevant income statement items for the year ended December 31, 2009, follow.

Dividend revenue	$ 6,500
Gain on sale of long-term investments	12,000
Loss on sale of long-term investments	(8,000)

APPENDIX

Investments in International Operations

15A

Many entities from small entrepreneurs to large corporations conduct business internationally. Some entities' operations occur in so many different countries that the companies are called **multinationals.** Many of us think of **Coca-Cola** and **McDonald's**, for example, as primarily U.S. companies, but most of their sales occur outside the United States. Exhibit 15A.1 shows the percent of international sales and income for selected U.S. companies. Managing and accounting for multinationals present challenges. This section describes some of these challenges and how to account for and report these activities.

EXHIBIT 15A.1

International Sales and Income as a Percent of Their Totals

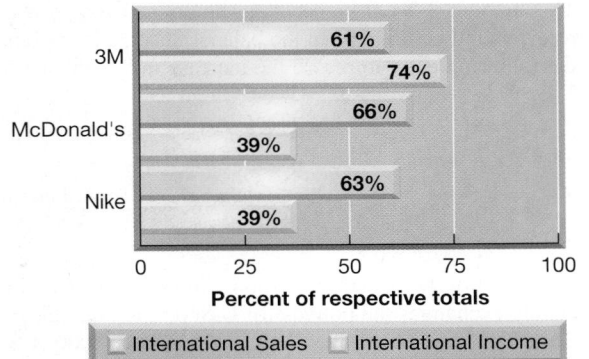

Two major accounting challenges that arise when companies have international operations relate to transactions that involve more than one currency. The first is to account for sales and purchases listed in a foreign currency. The second is to prepare consolidated financial statements with international subsidiaries. For ease in this discussion, we use companies with a U.S. base of operations and assume the need to prepare financial statements in U.S. dollars. This means the *reporting currency* of these companies is the U.S. dollar.

Point: Transactions *listed* or *stated* in a foreign currency are said to be *denominated* in that currency.

Exchange Rates between Currencies

Markets for the purchase and sale of foreign currencies exist all over the world. In these markets, U.S. dollars can be exchanged for Canadian dollars, British pounds, Japanese yen, Euros, or any other legal currencies. The price of one currency stated in terms of another currency is called a **foreign exchange rate.** Exhibit 15A.2 lists recent exchange rates for selected currencies. The exchange rate for British pounds and U.S. dollars is $1.8054, meaning 1 British pound could be purchased for $1.8054. On that same day, the exchange rate between Mexican pesos and U.S. dollars is $0.0925, or 1 Mexican peso can be purchased for $0.0925. Exchange rates fluctuate due to changing economic and political conditions, including the supply and demand for currencies and expectations about future events.

C4 Explain foreign exchange rates between currencies.

Point: To convert currency, see XE.com

Decision Insight

Rush to Russia   Investors are still eager to buy Russian equities even in the face of rampant crime, corruption, and slow economic growth. Why? Many argue Russia remains a bargain-priced, if risky, bet on future growth. Some analysts argue that natural-resource-rich Russia is one of the least expensive emerging markets.

EXHIBIT 15A.2

Foreign Exchange Rates for Selected Currencies*

Source (unit)	Price in $U.S.	Source (unit)	Price in $U.S.
Britain (pound)	$1.8980	Canada (dollar)	$0.9793
Mexico (peso)	0.0925	Japan (yen)	0.0090
Taiwan (dollar)	0.0305	Europe (Euro)	1.2920

* Rates will vary over time based on economic, political, and other changes.

Sales and Purchases Listed in a Foreign Currency

P5   Record transactions listed in a foreign currency.

When a U.S. company makes a credit sale to an international customer, accounting for the sale and the account receivable is straightforward if sales terms require the international customer's payment in U.S. dollars. If sale terms require (or allow) payment in a foreign currency, however, the U.S. company must account for the sale and the account receivable in a different manner.

Sales in a Foreign Currency   To illustrate, consider the case of the U.S.-based manufacturer Boston Company, which makes credit sales to London Outfitters, a British retail company. A sale occurs on December 12, 2008, for a price of £10,000 with payment due on February 10, 2009. Boston Company keeps its accounting records in U.S. dollars. To record the sale, Boston Company must translate the sales price from pounds to dollars. This is done using the exchange rate on the date of the sale. Assuming the exchange rate on December 12, 2008, is $1.80, Boston records this sale as follows.

Assets = Liabilities + Equity
+18,000   +18,000

Dec. 12	Accounts Receivable—London Outfitters	18,000	
	Sales*		18,000
	*To record a sale at £10,000, when the exchange rate equals $1.80. * (£10,000 × $1.80)*		

When Boston Company prepares its annual financial statements on December 31, 2008, the current exchange rate is $1.84. Thus, the current dollar value of Boston Company's receivable is $18,400 (10,000 × $1.84). This amount is $400 higher than the amount recorded on December 12. Accounting principles require a receivable to be reported in the balance sheet at its current dollar value. Thus, Boston Company must make the following entry to record the increase in the dollar value of this receivable at year-end.

Assets = Liabilities + Equity
+400   +400

Dec. 31	Accounts Receivable—London Outfitters	400	
	Foreign Exchange Gain		400
	To record the increased value of the British pound for the receivable.		

Point: Foreign exchange gains are credits, and foreign exchange losses are debits.

On February 10, 2009, Boston Company receives London Outfitters' payment of £10,000. It immediately exchanges the pounds for U.S. dollars. On this date, the exchange rate for pounds is $1.78. Thus, Boston Company receives only $17,800 (£10,000 × $1.78). It records the cash receipt and the loss associated with the decline in the exchange rate as follows.

Assets = Liabilities + Equity
+17,800   −600
−18,400

Feb. 10	Cash.....................................	17,800	
	Foreign Exchange Loss	600	
	Accounts Receivable—London Outfitters		18,400
	Received foreign currency payment of an account and converted it into dollars.		

Gains and losses from foreign exchange transactions are accumulated in the Foreign Exchange Gain (or Loss) account. After year-end adjustments, the balance in the Foreign Exchange Gain (or Loss) account is reported on the income statement and closed to the Income Summary account.

Purchases in a Foreign Currency   Accounting for credit purchases from an international seller is similar to the case of a credit sale to an international customer. In particular, if the U.S. company is required to make payment in a foreign currency, the account payable must be translated into dollars before the U.S. company can record it. If the exchange rate is different when preparing financial statements and when paying for the purchase, the U.S. company must recognize a foreign exchange gain or loss at those dates. To illustrate, assume NC Imports, a U.S. company, purchases products costing

Example: Assume that a U.S. company makes a credit purchase from a British company for £10,000 when the exchange rate is $1.62. At the balance sheet date, this rate is $1.72. Does this imply a gain or loss for the U.S. company? *Answer:* A loss.

€20,000 (euros) from Hamburg Brewing on January 15, when the exchange rate is $1.20 per euro. NC records this transaction as follows.

Jan. 15	Inventory....................................	24,000	
	Accounts Payable—Hamburg Brewing.........		24,000
	To record a €20,000 purchase when exchange rate is $1.20 (€20,000 × $1.20)		

Assets = Liabilities + Equity
+24,000   +24,000

NC Imports makes payment in full on February 14 when the exchange rate is $1.25 per euro, which is recorded as follows.

Feb. 14	Accounts Payable—Hamburg Brewing	24,000	
	Foreign Exchange Loss	1,000	
	Cash		25,000
	To record cash payment towards €20,000 account when exchange rate is $1.25 (€20.000 × $1.25).		

Assets = Liabilities + Equity
−25,000   −24,000   −1,000

Decision Insight

Global Greenback What do changes in foreign exchange rates mean? A decline in the price of the U.S. dollar against other currencies usually yields increased international sales for U.S. companies, without hiking prices or cutting costs, and puts them on a stronger competitive footing abroad. At home, they can raise prices without fear that foreign rivals will undercut them.

Consolidated Statements with International Subsidiaries

A second challenge in accounting for international operations involves preparing consolidated financial statements when the parent company has one or more international subsidiaries. Consider a U.S.-based company that owns a controlling interest in a French subsidiary. The reporting currency of the U.S. parent is the dollar. The French subsidiary maintains its financial records in euros. Before preparing consolidated statements, the parent must translate financial statements of the French company into U.S. dollars. After this translation is complete (including that for accounting differences), it prepares consolidated statements the same as for domestic subsidiaries. Procedures for translating an international subsidiary's account balances depend on the nature of the subsidiary's operations. The process requires the parent company to select appropriate foreign exchange rates and to apply those rates to the foreign subsidiary's account balances. This is described in advanced courses.

Global: A weaker U.S. dollar often increases global sales for U.S. companies.

Decision Maker

Entrepreneur You are a U.S. home builder that purchases lumber from mills in both the U.S. and Canada. The price of the Canadian dollar in terms of the U.S. dollar jumps from US$0.70 to US$0.80. Are you now more or less likely to buy lumber from Canadian or U.S. mills? [Answer—p. 608]

Summary

C1 Distinguish between debt and equity securities and between short-term and long-term investments. *Debt securities* reflect a creditor relationship and include investments in notes, bonds, and certificates of deposit. *Equity securities* reflect an owner relationship and include shares of stock issued by other companies. Short-term investments in securities are current assets that meet two criteria: (1) They are expected to be converted into cash within one year or the current operating cycle of the business, whichever is longer and (2) they are readily convertible to cash, or *marketable*. All other investments in securities are long-term. Long-term investments also include assets not used in operations and those held for special purposes, such as land for expansion.

C2 Identify and describe the different classes of investments in securities. Investments in securities are classified into one of five groups: (1) trading securities, which are always short-term, (2) debt securities held-to-maturity, (3) debt and equity securities available-for-sale, (4) equity securities in which an investor has a significant influence over the investee, and (5) equity securities in which an investor has a controlling influence over the investee.

C3 Describe how to report equity securities with controlling influence. If an investor owns more than 50% of another company's voting stock and controls the investee, the investor's financial reports are prepared on a consolidated basis. These reports are prepared as if the company were organized as one entity.

C4^A Explain foreign exchange rates between currencies. A foreign exchange rate is the price of one currency stated in terms of another. An entity with transactions in a foreign currency when the exchange rate changes between the transaction dates and their settlement will experience exchange gains or losses.

A1 Compute and analyze the components of return on total assets. Return on total assets has two components: profit margin and total asset turnover. A decline in one component must be met with an increase in another if return on assets is to be maintained. Component analysis is helpful in assessing company performance compared to that of competitors and its own past.

P1 Account for trading securities. Investments are initially recorded at cost, and any dividend or interest from these investments is recorded in the income statement. Investments classified as trading securities are reported at market value. Unrealized gains and losses on trading securities are reported in income. When investments are sold, the difference between the net proceeds from the sale and the cost of the securities is recognized as a gain or loss.

P2 Account for held-to-maturity securities. Debt securities held-to-maturity are reported at cost when purchased. Interest revenue is recorded as it accrues. The cost of long-term held-to-maturity securities is adjusted for the amortization of any difference between cost and maturity value.

P3 Account for available-for-sale securities. Debt and equity securities available-for-sale are recorded at cost when purchased. Available-for-sale securities are reported at their market values on the balance sheet with unrealized gains or losses shown in the equity section. Gains and losses realized on the sale of these investments are reported in the income statement.

P4 Account for equity securities with significant influence. The equity method is used when an investor has a significant influence over an investee. This usually exists when an investor owns 20% or more of the investee's voting stock but not more than 50%. The equity method means an investor records its share of investee earnings with a debit to the investment account and a credit to a revenue account. Dividends received reduce the investment account balance.

P5^A Record transactions listed in a foreign currency. When a company makes a credit sale to a foreign customer and sales terms call for payment in a foreign currency, the company must translate the foreign currency into dollars to record the receivable. If the exchange rate changes before payment is received, exchange gains or losses are recognized in the year they occur. The same treatment is used when a company makes a credit purchase from a foreign supplier and is required to make payment in a foreign currency.

Guidance Answers to **Decision Maker**

Money Manager If you have investments in fixed-rate bonds and notes when interest rates fall, the value of your investments increases. This is so because the bonds and notes you hold continue to pay the same (high) rate while the market is demanding a new lower interest rate. Your strategy is to continue holding your investments in bonds and notes, and, potentially, to increase these holdings through additional purchases.

Retailer Your store's return on assets is 11%, which is similar to the industry norm of 11.2%. However, disaggregation of return on assets reveals that your store's profit margin of 4.4% is much higher than the norm of 3.5%, but your total asset turnover of 2.5 is much lower than the norm of 3.2. These results suggest that, as compared with competitors, you are less efficient in using assets.

You need to focus on increasing sales or reducing assets. You might consider reducing prices to increase sales, provided such a strategy does not reduce your return on assets. For instance, you could reduce your profit margin to 4% to increase sales. If total asset turnover increases to more than 2.75 when profit margin is lowered to 4%, your overall return on assets is improved.

Entrepreneur You are now less likely to buy Canadian lumber because it takes more U.S. money to buy a Canadian dollar (and lumber). For instance, the purchase of lumber from a Canadian mill with a $1,000 (Canadian dollars) price would have cost the U.S. builder $700 (U.S. dollars, computed as C$1,000 × US$0.70) before the rate change, and $800 (US dollars, computed as C$1,000 × US$0.80) after the rate change.

Guidance Answers to **Quick Checks**

1. Short-term held-to-maturity securities are reported at cost.
2. Trading securities are reported at market value.
3. The equity section of the balance sheet (and in comprehensive income).
4. The income statement.
5. Long-term investments include (1) long-term funds earmarked for a special purpose, (2) debt and equity securities that do not meet current asset requirements, and (3) long-term assets not used in the regular operations of the business.
6. An equity investment is classified as long term if it is not marketable or, if marketable, it is not held as an available source of cash to meet the needs of current operations.
7. Debt securities held-to-maturity and debt securities available-for-sale are both recorded at cost. Also, interest on both is accrued as earned. However, only long-term securities held-to-maturity require amortization of the difference between cost and maturity value. In addition, only securities available-for-sale require a period-end adjustment to market value.
8. Long-term equity investments are placed in one of three categories and accounted for as follows: (a) **available-for-sale** (non-influential, less than 20% of outstanding stock)—market value; (b) **significant influence** (20% to 50% of outstanding stock)—equity method; and (c) **controlling influence** (holding more than 50% of outstanding stock)—equity method with consolidation.

Key Terms

mhhe.com/wildFAP19e

Key Terms are available at the book's Website for learning and testing in an online Flashcard Format.

Available-for-sale (AFS) securities (p. 596)
Comprehensive income (p. 600)
Consolidated financial statements (p. 599)
Equity method (p. 598)
Equity securities with controlling influence (p. 599)

Equity securities with significant influence (p. 598)
Foreign exchange rate (p. 605)
Held-to-maturity (HTM) securities (p. 596)
Long-term investments (p. 592)
Multinational (p. 605)
Parent (p. 599)

Return on total assets (p. 600)
Short-term investments (p. 592)
Subsidiary (p. 599)
Trading securities (p. 595)
Unrealized gain (loss) (p. 595)

Multiple Choice Quiz

Answers on p. 625

mhhe.com/wildFAP19e

Additional Quiz Questions are available at the book's Website.

1. A company purchased $30,000 of 5% bonds for investment purposes on May 1. The bonds pay interest on February 1 and August 1. The amount of interest revenue accrued at December 31 (the company's year-end) is:
  a. $1,500
  b. $1,375
  c. $1,000
  d. $625
  e. $300

2. Earlier this period, Amadeus Co. purchased its only available-for-sale investment in the stock of Bach Co. for $83,000. The period-end market value of this stock is $84,500. Amadeus records a:
  a. Credit to Unrealized Gain—Equity for $1,500
  b. Debit to Unrealized Loss—Equity for $1,500
  c. Debit to Investment Revenue for $1,500
  d. Credit to Market Adjustment—Available-for-Sale for $3,500
  e. Credit to Cash for $1,500

3. Mozart Co. owns 35% of Melody Inc. Melody pays $50,000 in cash dividends to its shareholders for the period. Mozart's entry to record the Melody dividend includes a:
  a. Credit to Investment Revenue for $50,000.
  b. Credit to Long-Term Investments for $17,500.

  c. Credit to Cash for $17,500.
  d. Debit to Long-Term Investments for $17,500.
  e. Debit to Cash for $50,000.

4. A company has net income of $300,000, net sales of $2,500,000, and total assets of $2,000,000. Its return on total assets equals:
  a. 6.7%
  b. 12.0%
  c. 8.3%
  d. 80.0%
  e. 15.0%

5. A company had net income of $80,000, net sales of $600,000, and total assets of $400,000. Its profit margin and total asset turnover are:

	Profit Margin	Total Asset Turnover
a.	1.5%	13.3
b.	13.3%	1.5
c.	13.3%	0.7
d.	7.0%	13.3
e.	10.0%	26.7

Superscript ᴬ denotes assignments based on Appendix 15A.

Discussion Questions

1. Under what two conditions should investments be classified as current assets?

2. 🖋 On a balance sheet, what valuation must be reported for short-term investments in trading securities?

3. If a short-term investment in available-for-sale securities costs $6,780 and is sold for $7,500, how should the difference between these two amounts be recorded?

4. Identify the three classes of noninfluential and two classes of influential investments in securities.

5. Under what conditions should investments be classified as current assets? As long-term assets?

6. If a company purchases its only long-term investments in available-for-sale debt securities this period and their market value is below cost at the balance sheet date, what entry is required to recognize this unrealized loss?

7. On a balance sheet, what valuation must be reported for debt securities classified as available-for-sale?

8. Under what circumstances are long-term investments in debt securities reported at cost and adjusted for amortization of any difference between cost and maturity value?

9. For investments in available-for-sale securities, how are unrealized (holding) gains and losses reported?

10. In accounting for investments in equity securities, when should the equity method be used?

11. Under what circumstances does a company prepare consolidated financial statements?

12.ᴬWhat are two major challenges in accounting for international operations?

13.ᴬAssume a U.S. company makes a credit sale to a foreign customer that is required to make payment in its foreign currency. In the current period, the exchange rate is $1.40 on the date of the sale and is $1.30 on the date the customer pays the receivable. Will the U.S. company record an exchange gain or loss?

14.ᴬ If a U.S. company makes a credit sale to a foreign customer required to make payment in U.S. dollars, can the U.S. company have an exchange gain or loss on this sale?

15. Refer to Best Buy's statement of changes in shareholders' equity in Appendix A. What is the amount of foreign currency translation adjustment for the year ended March 3, 2007? Is this adjustment an unrealized gain or an unrealized loss?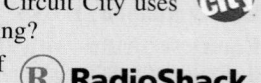

16. Refer to the balance sheet of Circuit City in Appendix A. How can you tell that Circuit City uses the consolidated method of accounting?

17. Refer to RadioShack's statement of stockholders' equity. What was the amount of its 2006 unrealized gain or loss on securities? (R) **RadioShack.**

18. Refer to the financial statements of Apple in Appendix A. Compute its return on total assets for the year ended September 30, 2006.

♟ **Denotes Discussion Questions that involve decision making.**

Available with McGraw-Hill's Homework Manager

McGraw-Hill's
HOMEWORK
MANAGER®

QUICK STUDY

QS 15-1
Short-term equity
investments   C2 P1

On April 18, Rollo Co. made a short-term investment in 600 common shares of TXT Co. The purchase price is $84 per share and the broker's fee is $500. The intent is to actively manage these shares for profit. On May 30, Rollo Co. receives $0.75 per share from TXT in dividends. Prepare the April 18 and May 30 journal entries to record these transactions.

QS 15-2
Available-for-sale securities
C2 P3

Malox Co. purchased short-term investments in available-for-sale securities at a cost of $100,000 on November 25, 2009. At December 31, 2009, these securities had a market value of $94,000. This is the first and only time the company has purchased such securities.

1. Prepare the December 31, 2009, year-end adjusting entry for the securities' portfolio.

2. For each account in the entry for part 1, explain how it is reported in financial statements.

3. Prepare the April 6, 2010, entry when Malox sells one-fourth of these securities for $27,000.

QS 15-3
Available-for-sale securities
C2 P3

Prepare Vikon Company's journal entries to reflect the following transactions for the current year.

May 7   Purchases 200 shares of Felton stock as a short-term investment in available-for-sale securities at a cost of $100 per share plus $400 in broker fees.

June 6   Sells 200 shares of its investment in Felton stock at $112 per share. The broker's commission on this sale is $250.

QS 15-4
Available-for-sale securities
C2 P3

Texar Company completes the following transactions during the current year.

May 9   Purchases 400 shares of Crayton stock as a short-term investment in available-for-sale securities at a cost of $30 per share plus $200 in broker fees.

June 2   Sells 200 shares of its investment in Crayton stock at $32 per share. The broker's commission on this sale is $120.

Dec. 31   The closing market price of the Crayton stock is $28 per share.

Prepare the May 9 and June 2 journal entries and the December 31 adjusting entry. This is the first and only time the company purchased such securities.

QS 15-5
Identifying long-term investments

C1

Which of the following statements are true of long-term investments?

a. They are held as an investment of cash available for current operations.

b. They can include funds earmarked for a special purpose, such as bond sinking funds.

c. They can include investments in trading securities.

d. They can include debt securities held-to-maturity.

e. They are always easily sold and therefore qualify as being marketable.

f. They can include debt and equity securities available-for-sale.

g. They can include bonds and stocks not intended to serve as a ready source of cash.

Complete the following descriptions by filling in the blanks.

1. Equity securities giving an investor significant influence are accounted for using the _____ _____.

2. Trading securities are classified as _____ assets.

3. Accrual of interest on bonds held as long-term investments requires a credit to _____ _____.

4. The controlling investor (more than 50% ownership) is called the _____, and the investee company is called the _____.

5. Available-for-sale debt securities are reported on the balance sheet at _____ _____.

QS 15-6
Describing investments in securities
C1 C2 C3

On February 1, 2009, Garzon purchased 6% bonds issued by Integal Utilities at a cost of $80,000, which is their par value. The bonds pay interest semiannually on July 31 and January 31. For 2009, prepare entries to record Garzon's July 31 receipt of interest and its December 31 year-end interest accrual.

QS 15-7
Debt securities transactions
C2 P2

On May 20, 2009, Chiu Co. paid $1,500,000 to acquire 25,000 common shares (10%) of BBE Corp. as a long-term investment. On August 5, 2010, Chiu sold one-half of these shares for $937,500. What valuation method should be used to account for this stock investment? Prepare entries to record both the acquisition and the sale of these shares.

QS 15-8
Recording equity securities
C2 P3

Assume the same facts as in QS 15-8 except that the stock acquired represents 40% of BBE Corp.'s outstanding stock. Also assume that BBE Corp. paid a $150,000 dividend on November 1, 2009, and reported a net income of $1,050,000 for 2009. Prepare the entries to record (*a*) the receipt of the dividend and (*b*) the December 31, 2009, year-end adjustment required for the investment account.

QS 15-9
Equity method transactions
C2 P4

During the current year, Marketplace Consulting Group acquired long-term available-for-sale securities at an $85,000 cost. At its December 31 year-end, these securities had a market value of $62,000. This is the first and only time the company purchased such securities.

1. Prepare the necessary year-end adjusting entry related to these securities.

2. Explain how each account used in part 1 is reported in the financial statements.

QS 15-10
Recording market adjustment for securities
P3

The return on total assets is the focus of analysts, creditors, and other users of financial statements.

1. How is the return on total assets computed?

2. What does this important ratio reflect?

QS 15-11
Return on total assets   A1

Return on total assets can be separated into two important components.

1. Write the formula to separate the return on total assets into its two basic components.

2. Explain how these components of the return on total assets are helpful to financial statement users for business decisions.

QS 15-12
Component return on total assets   A1

A U.S. company sells a product to a British company with the transaction listed in British pounds. On the date of the sale, the transaction total of $40,600 is billed as £20,000, reflecting an exchange rate of 2.03 (that is, $2.03 per pound). Prepare the entry to record (1) the sale and (2) the receipt of payment in pounds when the exchange rate is 1.95.

QS 15-13[A]
Foreign currency transactions
P5

On March 1, 2009, a U.S. company made a credit sale requiring payment in 30 days from a Malaysian company, Hamac Sdn. Bhd., in 20,000 Malaysian ringgits. Assuming the exchange rate between Malaysian ringgits and U.S. dollars is $0.2963 on March 1 and $0.3005 on March 31, prepare the entries to record the sale on March 1 and the cash receipt on March 31.

QS 15-14[A]
Foreign currency transactions
P5

EXERCISES

Exercise 15-1

Accounting for transactions in short-term securities

C2 P1 P2 P3

Check (c) Dr. Cash $173,400

(f) Dr. Cash $13,025

Prepare journal entries to record the following transactions involving the short-term securities investments of Bolton Co., all of which occurred during year 2009.

a. On February 15, paid $170,000 cash to purchase ACC's 90-day short-term debt securities ($170,000 principal), dated February 15, that pay 8% interest (categorized as held-to-maturity securities).

b. On March 22, purchased 850 shares of Ross Company stock at $21 per share plus a $100 brokerage fee. These shares are categorized as trading securities.

c. On May 16, received a check from ACC in payment of the principal and 90 days' interest on the debt securities purchased in transaction *a*.

d. On August 1, paid $70,000 cash to purchase Nita Co.'s 11% debt securities ($70,000 principal), dated July 30, 2009, and maturing January 30, 2010 (categorized as available-for-sale securities).

e. On September 1, received a $1.10 per share cash dividend on the Ross Company stock purchased in transaction *b*.

f. On October 8, sold 425 shares of Ross Co. stock for $31 per share, less a $150 brokerage fee.

g. On October 30, received a check from Nita Co. for 90 days' interest on the debt securities purchased in transaction *d*.

Exercise 15-2

Accounting for trading securities

C1 P1

Check (3) Gain, $2,250

Borchert Co. purchases various investments in trading securities at a cost of $76,000 on December 27, 2009. (This is its first and only purchase of such securities.) At December 31, 2009, these securities had a market value of $85,000.

1. Prepare the December 31, 2009, year-end adjusting entry for the trading securities' portfolio.

2. Explain how each account in the entry of part 1 is reported in financial statements.

3. Prepare the January 3, 2010, entry when Borchert sells a portion of its trading securities (that had originally cost $38,000) for $40,250.

Exercise 15-3

Adjusting available-for-sale securities to market

C2 P3

Check Unrealized loss, $392

On December 31, 2009, Tagert Company held the following short-term investments in its portfolio of available-for-sale securities. Tagert had no short-term investments in its prior accounting periods. Prepare the December 31, 2009, adjusting entry to report these investments at market value.

	Cost	Market Value
Verrizano Corporation bonds payable	$ 81,400	$92,000
Porter Corporation notes payable	54,900	47,928
Laverne Company common stock	100,500	96,480

Exercise 15-4

Transactions in short-term and long-term investments

C1 C2

Prepare journal entries to record the following transactions involving both the short-term and long-term investments of Corveau Corp., all of which occurred during calendar year 2009. Use the account Short-Term Investments for any transactions that you determine are short term.

a. On February 15, paid $100,000 cash to purchase Anthem's 90-day short-term notes at par, which are dated February 15 and pay 6% interest (classified as held-to-maturity).

b. On March 22, bought 600 shares of Frain Industries common stock at $43 cash per share plus a $140 brokerage fee (classified as long-term available-for-sale securities).

c. On May 15, received a check from Anthem in payment of the principal and 90 days' interest on the notes purchased in transaction *a*.

d. On July 30, paid $30,000 cash to purchase Moto Electronics' 5% notes at par, dated July 30, 2009, and maturing on January 30, 2010 (classified as trading securities).

e. On September 1, received a $0.40 per share cash dividend on the Frain Industries common stock purchased in transaction *b*.

f. On October 8, sold 300 shares of Frain Industries common stock for $49 cash per share, less a $120 brokerage fee.

g. On October 30, received a check from Moto Electronics for three months' interest on the notes purchased in transaction *d*.

On December 31, 2009, Loren Co. held the following short-term available-for-sale securities.

	Cost	Market Value
Nintendo Co. common stock	$64,500	$70,305
Unilever bonds payable	25,800	23,994
Kellogg Co. notes payable	46,440	43,654
McDonald's Corp. common stock	87,075	82,721

Loren had no short-term investments prior to the current period. Prepare the December 31, 2009, year-end adjusting entry to record the market adjustment for these securities.

Exercise 15-5
Market adjustment to available-for-sale securities
P3

Patica Co. began operations in 2008. The cost and market values for its long-term investments portfolio in available-for-sale securities are shown below. Prepare Patica's December 31, 2009, adjusting entry to reflect any necessary market adjustment for these investments.

	Cost	Market Value
December 31, 2008	$67,842	$61,736
December 31, 2009	73,479	77,888

Exercise 15-6
Market adjustment to available-for-sale securities
P3

Basil Services began operations in 2007 and maintains long-term investments in available-for-sale securities. The year-end cost and market values for its portfolio of these investments follow. Prepare journal entries to record each year-end market adjustment for these securities.

	Cost	Market Value
December 31, 2007	$392,900	$381,113
December 31, 2008	447,906	474,780
December 31, 2009	609,152	720,627
December 31, 2010	919,820	818,640

Exercise 15-7
Multi-year market adjustments to available-for-sale securities
P3

Information regarding Seaton Company's individual investments in securities during its calendar-year 2009, along with the December 31, 2009, market values, follows.

a. Investment in Beeman Company bonds: $443,150 cost, $481,704 market value. Seaton intends to hold these bonds until they mature in 2014.

b. Investment in Baybridge common stock: 29,500 shares; $352,304 cost; $382,954 market value. Seaton owns 32% of Baybridge's voting stock and has a significant influence over Baybridge.

c. Investment in Carroll common stock: 12,000 shares; $181,692 cost; $195,864 market value. This investment amounts to 3% of Carroll's outstanding shares, and Seaton's goal with this investment is to earn dividends over the next few years.

d. Investment in Newtech common stock: 3,500 shares; $101,038 cost; $99,320 market value. Seaton's goal with this investment is to reap an increase in market value of the stock over the next three to five years. Newtech has 30,000 common shares outstanding.

e. Investment in Flock common stock: 16,300 shares; $110,788 cost; $117,657 market value. This stock is marketable and is held as an investment of cash available for operations.

Required

1. Identify whether each investment should be classified as a short-term or long-term investment. For each long-term investment, indicate in which of the long-term investment classifications it should be placed.

2. Prepare a journal entry dated December 31, 2009, to record the market value adjustment of the long-term investments in available-for-sale securities. Seaton had no long-term investments prior to year 2009.

Exercise 15-8
Classifying investments in securities; recording market values
C1 C2 P2 P3 P4

Exercise 15-9
Securities transactions;
equity method

P4 C2

Prepare journal entries to record the following transactions and events of Kareen Company.

2009

Jan. 2 Purchased 55,000 shares of Altus Co. common stock for $374,000 cash plus a broker's fee of $2,650 cash. Altus has 137,500 shares of common stock outstanding and its policies will be significantly influenced by Kareen.
Sept. 1 Altus declared and paid a cash dividend of $3.05 per share.
Dec. 31 Altus announced that net income for the year is $1,106,900.

2010

June 1 Altus declared and paid a cash dividend of $3.30 per share.
Dec. 31 Altus announced that net income for the year is $1,240,900.
Dec. 31 Kareen sold 11,000 shares of Altus for $294,250 cash.

Exercise 15-10
Return on total assets

A1

The following information is available from the financial statements of Interstate Industries. Compute Interstate's return on total assets for 2009 and 2010. (Round returns to one-tenth of a percent.) Comment on the company's efficiency in using its assets in 2009 and 2010.

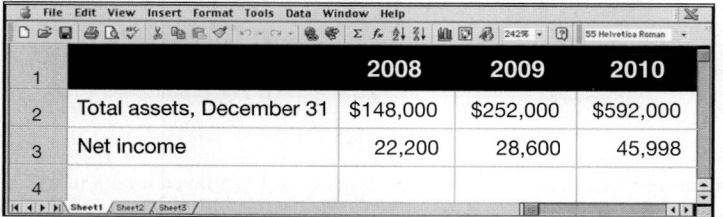

	2008	2009	2010
Total assets, December 31	$148,000	$252,000	$592,000
Net income	22,200	28,600	45,998

Exercise 15-11ᴬ
Foreign currency transactions

P5

Leigh of New York sells its products to customers in the United States and the United Kingdom. On December 16, 2009, Leigh sold merchandise on credit to Berton Ltd. of London at a price of 20,000 pounds. The exchange rate on that day for £1 was $2.0325. On December 31, 2009, when Leigh prepared its financial statements, the rate was £1 for $2.0292. Berton paid its bill in full on January 15, 2010, at which time the exchange rate was £1 for $2.0340. Leigh immediately exchanged the 20,000 pounds for U.S. dollars. Prepare Leigh's journal entries on December 16, December 31, and January 15 (round to the nearest dollar).

Exercise 15-12ᴬ
Computing foreign exchange
gains and losses on receivables

C4 P5

On May 8, 2009, Jett Company (a U.S. company) made a credit sale to Munoz (a Mexican company). The terms of the sale required Munoz to pay 850,000 pesos on February 10, 2010. Jett prepares quarterly financial statements on March 31, June 30, September 30, and December 31. The exchange rates for pesos during the time the receivable is outstanding follow.

May 8, 2009	$0.0932
June 30, 2009	0.0941
September 30, 2009	0.0952
December 31, 2009	0.0935
February 10, 2010	0.0974

Compute the foreign exchange gain or loss that Jett should report on each of its quarterly income statements for the last three quarters of 2009 and the first quarter of 2010. Also compute the amount reported on Jett's balance sheets at the end of each of its last three quarters of 2009.

Available with McGraw-Hill's Homework Manager

PROBLEM SET A

Problem 15-1A
Recording transactions and
market adjustments for
trading securities

C2 P1

Protom Company, which began operations in 2009, invests its idle cash in trading securities. The following transactions are from its short-term investments in its trading securities.

2009

Jan. 20 Purchased 800 shares of Ford Motor Co. at $26 per share plus a $120 commission.
Feb. 9 Purchased 2,600 shares of Lucent at $39 per share plus a $578 commission.
Oct. 12 Purchased 800 shares of Z-Seven at $7.50 per share plus a $200 commission.

2010

Apr. 15   Sold 800 shares of Ford Motor Co. at $30 per share less a $300 commission.
July   5   Sold 800 shares of Z-Seven at $11 per share less a $103 commission.
July 22   Purchased 2,000 shares of Hunt Corp. at $39 per share plus a $444 commission.
Aug. 19   Purchased 1,600 shares of Donna Karan at $19.50 per share plus a $290 commission.

2011

Feb. 27   Purchased 3,500 shares of HCA at $31 per share plus a $420 commission.
Mar. 3   Sold 2,000 shares of Hunt at $35 per share less a $250 commission.
June 21   Sold 2,600 shares of Lucent at $36.75 per share less a $420 commission.
June 30   Purchased 1,300 shares of Black & Decker at $47.50 per share plus a $595 commission.
Nov. 1   Sold 1,600 shares of Donna Karan at $19.50 per share less a $309 commission.

Required

1. Prepare journal entries to record these short-term investment activities for the years shown. (Ignore any year-end adjusting entries.)
2. On December 31, 2011, prepare the adjusting entry to record any necessary market adjustment for the portfolio of trading securities when HCA's share price is $33 and Black & Decker's share price is $43.50. (Assume the Market Adjustment—Trading account had an unadjusted balance of zero.)

Check (2) Dr. Market
Adjustment—Trading $785

Freema Company had no short-term investments prior to year 2009. It had the following transactions involving short-term investments in available-for-sale securities during 2009.

Apr. 16   Purchased 8,000 shares of Gem Co. stock at $29.75 per share plus a $440 brokerage fee.
May   1   Paid $125,000 to buy 90-day U.S. Treasury bills (debt securities): $125,000 principal amount, 4% interest, securities dated May 1.
July   7   Purchased 4,000 shares of PepsiCo stock at $47.75 per share plus a $410 brokerage fee.
      20   Purchased 2,000 shares of Xerox stock at $19.75 per share plus a $490 brokerage fee.
Aug. 3   Received a check for principal and accrued interest on the U.S. Treasury bills that matured on July 29.
      15   Received a $0.90 per share cash dividend on the Gem Co. stock.
      28   Sold 4,000 shares of Gem Co. stock at $36.50 per share less a $250 brokerage fee.
Oct.   1   Received a $1.75 per share cash dividend on the PepsiCo shares.
Dec. 15   Received a $1.05 per share cash dividend on the remaining Gem Co. shares.
      31   Received a $1.30 per share cash dividend on the PepsiCo shares.

Problem 15-2A
Recording, adjusting, and reporting short-term available-for-sale securities

C2 P3

Required

1. Prepare journal entries to record the preceding transactions and events.
2. Prepare a table to compare the year-end cost and market values of Freema's short-term investments in available-for-sale securities. The year-end market values per share are: Gem Co., $32.00; PepsiCo, $45.00; and Xerox, $16.75.
3. Prepare an adjusting entry, if necessary, to record the year-end market adjustment for the portfolio of short-term investments in available-for-sale securities.

Check (2) Cost = $350,620

(3) Dr. Unrealized Loss—
Equity $9,120

Analysis Component

4. Explain the balance sheet presentation of the market adjustment for Freema's short-term investments.
5. How do these short-term investments affect Freema's (a) income statement for year 2009 and (b) the equity section of its balance sheet at year-end 2009?

Tennant Security, which began operations in 2009, invests in long-term available-for-sale securities. Following is a series of transactions and events determining its long-term investment activity.

2009

Jan. 20   Purchased 1,200 shares of Johnson & Johnson at $20.50 per share plus a $240 commission.
Feb. 9   Purchased 1,000 shares of Sony at $46.20 per share plus a $220 commission.
June 12   Purchased 1,700 shares of Mattel at $28 per share plus a $195 commission.
Dec. 31   Per share market values for stocks in the portfolio are Johnson & Johnson, $21.50; Mattel, $26.50; Sony, $38.

Problem 15-3A
Recording, adjusting, and reporting long-term available-for-sale securities

C2 P3

2010

Apr. 15 Sold 1,200 shares of Johnson & Johnson at $23.50 per share less a $525 commission.
July 5 Sold 1,700 shares of Mattel at $26.50 per share less a $235 commission.
July 22 Purchased 500 shares of Sara Lee at $22.50 per share plus a $420 commission.
Aug. 19 Purchased 900 shares of Eastman Kodak at $14 per share plus a $198 commission.
Dec. 31 Per share market values for stocks in the portfolio are: Kodak, $16.25; Sara Lee, $20.00; Sony, $35.00.

2011

Feb. 27 Purchased 3,000 shares of Microsoft at $65 per share plus a $520 commission.
June 21 Sold 1,000 shares of Sony at $48.00 per share less an $880 commission.
June 30 Purchased 1,500 shares of Black & Decker at $38 per share plus a $435 commission.
Aug. 3 Sold 500 shares of Sara Lee at $16.25 per share less a $435 commission.
Nov. 1 Sold 900 shares of Eastman Kodak at $19.75 per share less a $625 commission.
Dec. 31 Per share market values for stocks in the portfolio are: Black & Decker, $41; Microsoft, $67.

Required

1. Prepare journal entries to record these transactions and events and any year-end market adjustments to the portfolio of long-term available-for-sale securities.

Check (2b) Market adjustment bal.: 12/31/09, $(10,205); 12/31/10; $(11,263)

2. Prepare a table that summarizes the (*a*) total cost, (*b*) total market adjustment, and (*c*) total market value of the portfolio of long-term available-for-sale securities at each year-end.

(3b) Unrealized Gain at 12/31/2011, $9,545

3. Prepare a table that summarizes (*a*) the realized gains and losses and (*b*) the unrealized gains or losses for the portfolio of long-term available-for-sale securities at each year-end.

Problem 15-4A
Long-term investment transactions; unrealized and realized gains and losses

C2 C3 P3 P4

Elevant Co.'s long-term available-for-sale portfolio at December 31, 2008, consists of the following.

Available-for-Sale Securities	Cost	Market Value
40,000 shares of Company A common stock	$535,300	$500,000
7,000 shares of Company B common stock	159,380	151,000
17,500 shares of Company C common stock	662,600	640,938

Elevant enters into the following long-term investment transactions during year 2009.

Jan. 29 Sold 3,500 shares of Company B common stock for $79,100 less a brokerage fee of $1,400.
Apr. 17 Purchased 9,900 shares of Company W common stock for $197,500 plus a brokerage fee of $2,300. The shares represent a 30% ownership in Company W.
July 6 Purchased 4,200 shares of Company X common stock for $118,125 plus a brokerage fee of $1,650. The shares represent a 10% ownership in Company X.
Aug. 22 Purchased 50,000 shares of Company Y common stock for $375,000 plus a brokerage fee of $1,100. The shares represent a 51% ownership in Company Y.
Nov. 13 Purchased 8,300 shares of Company Z common stock for $261,596 plus a brokerage fee of $2,350. The shares represent a 5% ownership in Company Z.
Dec. 9 Sold 40,000 shares of Company A common stock for $515,000 less a brokerage fee of $4,000.

The market values of its investments at December 31, 2009, are: B, $81,375; C, $610,312; W, $191,250; X, $110,250; Y, $531,250; and Z, $272,240.

Required

1. Determine the amount Elevant should report on its December 31, 2009, balance sheet for its long-term investments in available-for-sale securities.

Check (2) Cr. Unrealized Loss—Equity, $13,508

2. Prepare any necessary December 31, 2009, adjusting entry to record the market value adjustment for the long-term investments in available-for-sale securities.

3. What amount of gains or losses on transactions relating to long-term investments in available-for-sale securities should Elevant report on its December 31, 2009, income statement?

Selk Steel Co., which began operations on January 4, 2009, had the following subsequent transactions and events in its long-term investments.

2009

Jan.   5   Selk purchased 50,000 shares (20% of total) of Wulf's common stock for $1,567,000.
Oct. 23   Wulf declared and paid a cash dividend of $3.20 per share.
Dec. 31   Wulf's net income for 2009 is $1,164,000, and the market value of its stock at December 31 is $34 per share.

2010

Oct. 15   Wulf declared and paid a cash dividend of $2.50 per share.
Dec. 31   Wulf's net income for 2010 is $1,476,000, and the market value of its stock at December 31 is $36.00 per share.

2011

Jan.   2   Selk sold all of its investment in Wulf for $1,895,500 cash.

Part 1

Assume that Selk has a significant influence over Wulf with its 20% share of stock.

Required

1. Prepare journal entries to record these transactions and events for Selk.
2. Compute the carrying (book) value per share of Selk's investment in Wulf common stock as reflected in the investment account on January 1, 2011.
3. Compute the net increase or decrease in Selk's equity from January 5, 2009, through January 2, 2011, resulting from its investment in Wulf.

Part 2

Assume that although Selk owns 20% of Wulf's outstanding stock, circumstances indicate that it does not have a significant influence over the investee and that it is classified as an available-for-sale security investment.

Required

1. Prepare journal entries to record the preceding transactions and events for Selk. Also prepare an entry dated January 2, 2011, to remove any balance related to the market adjustment.
2. Compute the cost per share of Selk's investment in Wulf common stock as reflected in the investment account on January 1, 2011.
3. Compute the net increase or decrease in Selk's equity from January 5, 2009, through January 2, 2011, resulting from its investment in Wulf.

Problem 15-5A
Accounting for long-term investments in securities; with and without significant influence
C2 P3 P4

Check (2) Carrying value per share, $36.20

(1) 1/2/2011 Dr. Unrealized Gain—Equity $233,000

(3) Net increase, $613,500

Patriot Company, a U.S. corporation with customers in several foreign countries, had the following selected transactions for 2009 and 2010.

2009

Apr.   8   Sold merchandise to Salinas & Sons of Mexico for $27,456 cash. The exchange rate for pesos is $0.0932 on this day.
July 21   Sold merchandise on credit to Sumito Corp. in Japan. The price of 2.7 million yen is to be paid 120 days from the date of sale. The exchange rate for yen is $0.0082 on this day.
Oct. 14   Sold merchandise for 18,000 pounds to Smithers Ltd. of Great Britain, payment in full to be received in 90 days. The exchange rate for pounds is $2.0330 on this day.
Nov. 18   Received Sumito's payment in yen for its July 21 purchase and immediately exchanged the yen for dollars. The exchange rate for yen is $0.0079 on this day.
Dec. 20   Sold merchandise for 20,000 ringgits to Hamid Albar of Malaysia, payment in full to be received in 30 days. On this day, the exchange rate for ringgits is $0.2963.

Problem 15-6A[A]
Foreign currency transactions
C4 P5

Dec. 31   Recorded adjusting entries to recognize exchange gains or losses on Patriot's annual financial statements. Rates for exchanging foreign currencies on this day follow.

Pesos (Mexico)	$0.0937
Yen (Japan)	0.0075
Pounds (Britain)	2.0345
Ringgits (Malaysia)	0.2949

2010

Jan. 12   Received full payment in pounds from Smithers for the October 14 sale and immediately exchanged the pounds for dollars. The exchange rate for pounds is $2.0355 on this day.

Jan. 19   Received Hamid Albar's full payment in ringgits for the December 20 sale and immediately exchanged the ringgits for dollars. The exchange rate for ringgits is $0.2936 on this day.

Required

1. Prepare journal entries for the Patriot transactions and adjusting entries (round amounts to the nearest dollar).

2. Compute the foreign exchange gain or loss to be reported on Patriot's 2009 income statement.

Analysis Component

3. What actions might Patriot consider to reduce its risk of foreign exchange gains or losses?

Check   (2) 2009 total foreign exchange loss, $811

PROBLEM SET B

Problem 15-1B

Recording transactions and market adjustments for trading securities

C2 P1

Harter Company, which began operations in 2009, invests its idle cash in trading securities. The following transactions relate to its short-term investments in its trading securities.

2009

Mar. 10   Purchased 900 shares of Timex at $28.00 per share plus a $125 commission.
May   7   Purchased 2,500 shares of MTV at $37.00 per share plus a $578 commission.
Sept. 1   Purchased 780 shares of UPS at $7.00 per share plus a $200 commission.

2010

Apr. 26   Sold 2,500 shares of MTV at $35.50 per share less a $295 commission.
Apr. 27   Sold 780 shares of UPS at $10.50 per share less a $103 commission.
June   2   Purchased 1,600 shares of SPW at $34.00 per share plus a $444 commission.
June 14   Purchased 1,600 shares of Wal-Mart at $20.00 per share plus a $290 commission.

2011

Jan. 28   Purchased 3,400 shares of PepsiCo at $38.00 per share plus a $400 commission.
Jan. 31   Sold 1,600 shares of SPW at $29.00 per share less a $250 commission.
Aug. 22   Sold 900 shares of Timex at $26.25 per share less a $420 commission.
Sept. 3   Purchased 1,500 shares of Vodaphone at $47.50 per share plus a $600 commission.
Oct.   9   Sold 1,600 shares of Wal-Mart at $22.50 per share less a $309 commission.

Required

1. Prepare journal entries to record these short-term investment activities for the years shown. (Ignore any year-end adjusting entries.)

2. On December 31, 2011, prepare the adjusting entry to record any necessary market adjustment for the portfolio of trading securities when PepsiCo's share price is $36.00 and Vodaphone's share price is $44.00. (Assume the Market Adjustment—Trading account had an unadjusted balance of zero.)

Check   (2) Cr. Market Adjustment—Trading $13,050

SP Systems had no short-term investments prior to 2009. It had the following transactions involving short-term investments in available-for-sale securities during 2009.

Feb.   6   Purchased 6,000 shares of Nokia stock at $24.75 per share plus a $400 brokerage fee.
    15   Paid $250,000 to buy six-month U.S. Treasury bills (debt securities): $250,000 principal amount, 4% interest, securities dated February 15.
Apr.   7   Purchased 3,000 shares of Dell Co. stock at $49.25 per share plus a $370 brokerage fee.
June   2   Purchased 1,500 shares of Merck stock at $18.25 per share plus a $450 brokerage fee.
    30   Received a $0.19 per share cash dividend on the Nokia shares.
Aug. 11   Sold 1,500 shares of Nokia stock at $29.50 per share less a $490 brokerage fee.
    16   Received a check for principal and accrued interest on the U.S. Treasury bills purchased February 15.
    24   Received a $0.16 per share cash dividend on the Dell shares.
Nov.   9   Received a $0.20 per share cash dividend on the remaining Nokia shares.
Dec. 18   Received a $0.21 per share cash dividend on the Dell shares.

Required

1. Prepare journal entries to record the preceding transactions and events.

2. Prepare a table to compare the year-end cost and market values of the short-term investments in available-for-sale securities. The year-end market values per share are: Nokia, $23.50; Dell, $55.50; and Merck, $15.25.

3. Prepare an adjusting entry, if necessary, to record the year-end market adjustment for the portfolio of short-term investments in available-for-sale securities.

Analysis Component

4. Explain the balance sheet presentation of the market adjustment to SP's short-term investments.

5. How do these short-term investments affect (*a*) its income statement for year 2009 and (*b*) the equity section of its balance sheet at the 2009 year-end?

Problem 15-2B
Recording, adjusting, and reporting short-term available-for-sale securities

C2   P3

Check   (2) Cost = $287,620

(3) Cr. Unrealized Gain—Equity, $7,505

Bleeker Enterprises, which began operations in 2009, invests in long-term available-for-sale securities. Following is a series of transactions and events involving its long-term investment activity.

Problem 15-3B
Recording, adjusting, and reporting long-term available-for-sale securities

C2   P3

2009

Mar. 10   Purchased 1,000 shares of Apple at $23.00 per share plus $240 commission.
Apr.   7   Purchased 1,300 shares of Ford at $46.20 per share plus $225 commission.
Sept.   1   Purchased 1,500 shares of Polaroid at $25.00 per share plus $195 commission.
Dec. 31   Per share market values for stocks in the portfolio are: Apple, $24.00; Ford, $42.00; Polaroid, $27.00.

2010

Apr. 26   Sold 1,300 shares of Ford at $44.00 per share less a $250 commission.
June   2   Purchased 1,800 shares of Duracell at $19.25 per share plus a $235 commission.
June 14   Purchased 600 shares of Sears at $22.50 per share plus a $470 commission.
Nov. 27   Sold 1,500 shares of Polaroid at $29 per share less a $198 commission.
Dec. 31   Per share market values for stocks in the portfolio are: Apple, $26.00; Duracell, $18.00; Sears, $25.00.

2011

Jan. 28   Purchased 2,000 shares of Coca-Cola Co. at $69 per share plus a $530 commission.
Aug. 22   Sold 1,000 shares of Apple at $20.00 per share less a $280 commission.
Sept.   3   Purchased 2,000 shares of Motorola at $36 per share plus a $435 commission.
Oct.   9   Sold 600 shares of Sears at $26.25 per share less a $435 commission.
Oct. 31   Sold 1,800 shares of Duracell at $15.00 per share less a $425 commission.
Dec. 31   Per share market values for stocks in the portfolio are: Coca-Cola, $75.00; Motorola, $32.00.

Required

1. Prepare journal entries to record these transactions and events and any year-end market adjustments to the portfolio of long-term available-for-sale securities.

2. Prepare a table that summarizes the (*a*) total cost, (*b*) total market adjustment, and (*c*) total market value for the portfolio of long-term available-for-sale securities at each year-end.

3. Prepare a table that summarizes (*a*) the realized gains and losses and (*b*) the unrealized gains or losses for the portfolio of long-term available-for-sale securities at each year-end.

Problem 15-4B
Long-term investment transactions; unrealized and realized gains and losses

C2 C3 P3 P4

Chavez's long-term available-for-sale portfolio at December 31, 2008, consists of the following.

Available-for-Sale Securities	Cost	Market Value
55,000 shares of Company R common stock	$1,118,250	$1,198,000
17,000 shares of Company S common stock	600,600	586,500
22,000 shares of Company T common stock	294,590	303,600

Chavez enters into the following long-term investment transactions during year 2009.

Jan. 13 Sold 4,250 shares of Company S stock for $145,500 less a brokerage fee of $650.
Mar. 24 Purchased 31,000 shares of Company U common stock for $565,750 plus a brokerage fee of $1,980. The shares represent a 62% ownership interest in Company U.
Apr. 5 Purchased 85,000 shares of Company V common stock for $267,750 plus a brokerage fee of $1,125. The shares represent a 10% ownership in Company V.
Sept. 2 Sold 22,000 shares of Company T common stock for $313,500 less a brokerage fee of $2,700.
Sept. 27 Purchased 5,000 shares of Company W common stock for $101,000 plus a brokerage fee of $350. The shares represent a 25% ownership interest in Company W.
Oct. 30 Purchased 10,000 shares of Company X common stock for $97,500 plus a brokerage fee of $300. The shares represent a 13% ownership interest in Company X.

The market values of its investments at December 31, 2009, are: R, $1,136,250; S, $420,750; U, $545,600; V, $269,876; W, $109,378; and X, $91,250.

Required

1. Determine the amount Chavez should report on its December 31, 2009, balance sheet for its long-term investments in available-for-sale securities.

2. Prepare any necessary December 31, 2009, adjusting entry to record the market value adjustment of the long-term investments in available-for-sale securities.

3. What amount of gains or losses on transactions relating to long-term investments in available-for-sale securities should Chavez report on its December 31, 2009, income statement?

Problem 15-5B
Accounting for long-term investments in securities; with and without significant influence

C2 P3 P4

Devin Company, which began operations on January 3, 2009, had the following subsequent transactions and events in its long-term investments.

2009

Jan. 5 Devin purchased 25,000 shares (25% of total) of Bloch's common stock for $401,000.
Aug. 1 Bloch declared and paid a cash dividend of $1.10 per share.
Dec. 31 Bloch's net income for 2009 is $164,000, and the market value of its stock is $17.50 per share.

2010

Aug. 1 Bloch declared and paid a cash dividend of $1.30 per share.
Dec. 31 Bloch's net income for 2010 is $156,000, and the market value of its stock is $19.25 per share.

2011

Jan. 8 Devin sold all of its investment in Bloch for $550,000 cash.

Part 1

Assume that Devin has a significant influence over Bloch with its 25% share.

Required

1. Prepare journal entries to record these transactions and events for Devin.

2. Compute the carrying (book) value per share of Devin's investment in Bloch common stock as reflected in the investment account on January 7, 2011.

3. Compute the net increase or decrease in Devin's equity from January 5, 2009, through January 8, 2011, resulting from its investment in Bloch.

Check (2) Carrying value per share, $16.84

Part 2

Assume that although Devin owns 25% of Bloch's outstanding stock, circumstances indicate that it does not have a significant influence over the investee and that it is classified as an available-for-sale security investment.

Required

1. Prepare journal entries to record these transactions and events for Devin. Also prepare an entry dated January 8, 2011, to remove any balance related to the market adjustment.

2. Compute the cost per share of Devin's investment in Bloch common stock as reflected in the investment account on January 7, 2011.

3. Compute the net increase or decrease in Devin's equity from January 5, 2009, through January 8, 2011, resulting from its investment in Bloch.

(1) 1/8/2011 Dr. Unrealized Gain—Equity $80,250

(3) Net increase, $209,000

Kitna, a U.S. corporation with customers in several foreign countries, had the following selected transactions for 2009 and 2010.

Problem 15-6B[A]
Foreign currency transactions
C4 P5

2009

May 26 Sold merchandise for 5.5 million yen to Fuji Company of Japan, payment in full to be received in 60 days. On this day, the exchange rate for yen is $0.0088.

June 1 Sold merchandise to Fordham Ltd. of Great Britain for $73,500 cash. The exchange rate for pounds is $2.0331 on this day.

July 25 Received Fuji's payment in yen for its May 26 purchase and immediately exchanged the yen for dollars. The exchange rate for yen is $0.0087 on this day.

Oct. 15 Sold merchandise on credit to Martinez Brothers of Mexico. The price of 425,000 pesos is to be paid 90 days from the date of sale. On this day, the exchange rate for pesos is $0.0932.

Dec. 6 Sold merchandise for 300,000 yuans to Chi-Ying Company of China, payment in full to be received in 30 days. The exchange rate for yuans is $0.1335 on this day.

Dec. 31 Recorded adjusting entries to recognize exchange gains or losses on Kitna's annual financial statements. Rates of exchanging foreign currencies on this day follow.

Yen (Japan)	$0.0089
Pounds (Britain)	2.0402
Pesos (Mexico)	0.0994
Yuans (China)	0.1351

2010

Jan. 5 Received Chi-Ying's full payment in yuans for the December 6 sale and immediately exchanged the yuans for dollars. The exchange rate for yuans is $0.1372 on this day.

Jan. 13 Received full payment in pesos from Martinez for the October 15 sale and immediately exchanged the pesos for dollars. The exchange rate for pesos is $0.0960 on this day.

Required

1. Prepare journal entries for the Kitna transactions and adjusting entries.

2. Compute the foreign exchange gain or loss to be reported on Kitna's 2009 income statement.

Check 2009 total foreign exchange gain, $2,565

Analysis Component

3. What actions might Kitna consider to reduce its risk of foreign exchange gains or losses?

SERIAL PROBLEM

Success Systems

(This serial problem began in Chapter 1 and continues through most of the book. If previous chapter segments were not completed, the serial problem can begin at this point. It is helpful, but not necessary, to use the Working Papers that accompany the book.)

SP 15   While reviewing the March 31, 2010, balance sheet of Success Systems, Adriana Lopez notes that the business has built a large cash balance of $77,845. Its most recent bank money market statement shows that the funds are earning an annualized return of 0.75%. Lopez decides to make several investments with the desire to earn a higher return on the idle cash balance. Accordingly, in April 2010, Success Systems makes the following investments in trading securities:

April 16   Purchases 400 shares of Johnson & Johnson stock at $50 per share plus $300 commission.
April 30   Purchases 200 shares of Starbucks Corporation at $22 per share plus $250 commission.

On June 30, 2010, the per share market price of the Johnson & Johnson shares is $55 and the Starbucks shares is $19.

Required

1. Prepare journal entries to record the April purchases of trading securities by Success Systems.
2. On June 30, 2010, prepare the adjusting entry to record any necessary market adjustment to its portfolio of trading securities.

BEYOND THE NUMBERS

REPORTING IN ACTION

C3 C4 A1

BTN 15-1   Refer to Best Buy's financial statements in Appendix A to answer the following.
1. Are Best Buy's financial statements consolidated? How can you tell?
2. What is Best Buy's *comprehensive income* for the year ended March 3, 2007?
3. Does Best Buy have any foreign operations? How can you tell?
4. Compute Best Buy's return on total assets for the year ended March 3, 2007.

Fast Forward

5. Access Best Buy's annual report for a fiscal year ending after March 3, 2007, from either its Website (BestBuy.com) or the SEC's EDGAR database (www.sec.gov). Recompute Best Buy's return on total assets for the years subsequent to March 3, 2007.

COMPARATIVE ANALYSIS

A1

BTN 15-2   Key figures for Best Buy, Circuit City, and RadioShack follow.

($ millions)	Best Buy			Circuit City			RadioShack		
	Current Year	1 Year Prior	2 Years Prior	Current Year	1 Year Prior	2 Years Prior	Current Year	1 Year Prior	2 Years Prior
Net income	$ 1,377	$ 1,140	$ 984	$ (8)	$ 140	$ 62	$ 73	$ 267	$ 337
Net sales	35,934	30,848	27,433	12,430	11,514	10,414	4,778	5,082	4,841
Total assets	13,570	11,864	10,294	4,007	4,069	3,840	2,070	2,205	2,517

Required

1. Compute return on total assets for Best Buy, Circuit City, and RadioShack for the two most recent years.
2. Separate the return on total assets computed in part 1 into its components for all three companies and both years according to the formula in Exhibit 15.9.
3. Which company has the highest total return on assets? The highest profit margin? The highest total asset turnover? What does this comparative analysis reveal? (Assume an industry average of 8.2% for return on assets.)

BTN 15-3 Kaylee Wecker is the controller for Wildcat Company, which has numerous long-term investments in debt securities. Wildcat's investments are mainly in 10-year bonds. Wecker is preparing its year-end financial statements. In accounting for long-term debt securities, she knows that each long-term investment must be designated as a held-to-maturity or an available-for-sale security. Interest rates rose sharply this past year causing the portfolio's market value to substantially decline. The company does not intend to hold the bonds for the entire 10 years. Wecker also earns a bonus each year, which is computed as a percent of net income.

ETHICS CHALLENGE
C2 P2 P3

Required

1. Will Wecker's bonus depend in any way on the classification of the debt securities? Explain.

2. What criteria must Wecker use to classify the securities as held-to-maturity or available-for-sale?

3. Is there likely any company oversight of Wecker's classification of the securities? Explain.

BTN 15-4 Assume that you are Jackson Company's accountant. Company owner Abel Terrio has reviewed the 2009 financial statements you prepared and questions the $6,000 loss reported on the sale of its investment in Blackhawk Co. common stock. Jackson acquired 50,000 shares of Blackhawk's common stock on December 31, 2007, at a cost of $500,000. This stock purchase represented a 40% interest in Blackhawk. The 2008 income statement reported that earnings from all investments were $126,000. On January 3, 2009, Jackson Company sold the Blackhawk stock for $575,000. Blackhawk did not pay any dividends during 2008 but reported a net income of $202,500 for that year. Terrio believes that because the Blackhawk stock purchase price was $500,000 and was sold for $575,000, the 2009 income statement should report a $75,000 gain on the sale.

COMMUNICATING IN PRACTICE
C2 P4

Required

Draft a one-half page memorandum to Terrio explaining why the $6,000 loss on sale of Blackhawk stock is correctly reported.

BTN 15-5 Access the August 3, 2007, 10-K filing (for year-end June 30, 2007) of Microsoft (MSFT) at www.sec.gov. Review its note 3, "Investments."

TAKING IT TO THE NET
C1 C2

Required

1. How does the cost-basis total for its investments as of June 30, 2007, compare to the prior year-end amount?

2. Identify at least eight types of short-term investments held by Microsoft as of June 30, 2007.

3. What were Microsoft's unrealized gains and its unrealized losses from its investments for 2007?

4. Was the cost or market ("recorded") value of the investments higher as of June 30, 2007?

BTN 15-6 Each team member is to become an expert on a specific classification of long-term investments. This expertise will be used to facilitate other teammates' understanding of the concepts and procedures relevent to the classification chosen.

TEAMWORK IN ACTION
C1 C2 C3 P1 P2 P3 P4

1. Each team member must select an area for expertise by choosing one of the following classifications of long-term investments.

   a. Held-to-maturity debt securities

   b. Available-for-sale debt and equity securities

   c. Equity securities with significant influence

   d. Equity securities with controlling influence

2. Learning teams are to disburse and expert teams are to be formed. Expert teams are made up of those who select the same area of expertise. The instructor will identify the location where each expert team will meet.

3. Expert teams will collaborate to develop a presentation based on the following requirements. Students must write the presentation in a format they can show to their learning teams in part (4).

Required

1. Compute DSG's return on total assets for the most recent two years using the data provided.

2. Which of these four companies has the highest return on total assets? Highest profit margin? Highest total asset turnover?

ANSWERS TO MULTIPLE CHOICE QUIZ

1. d; $30,000 \times 5\% \times 5/12 = \$625$

2. a; Unrealized gain = $\$84{,}500 - \$83{,}000 = \$1{,}500$

3. b; $\$50{,}000 \times 35\% = \$17{,}500$

4. e; $\$300{,}000/\$2{,}000{,}000 = 15\%$

5. b; Profit margin = $\$80{,}000/\$600{,}000 = 13.3\%$
Total asset turnover = $\$600{,}000/\$400{,}000 = 1.5$

A Look Back

Chapter 15 focused on how to identify, account for, and report investments in securities. We also accounted for transactions listed in a foreign currency.

 A Look at This Chapter

This chapter focuses on reporting and analyzing cash inflows and cash outflows. We emphasize how to prepare and interpret the statement of cash flows.

A Look Ahead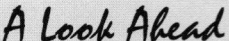

Chapter 17 focuses on tools to help us analyze financial statements. We also describe comparative analysis and the application of ratios for financial analysis.

Reporting the Statement of Cash Flows

Chapter

CAP

Conceptual

C1 Explain the purpose and importance of cash flow information. (p. 628)

C2 Distinguish between operating, investing, and financing activities. (p. 629)

C3 Identify and disclose noncash investing and financing activities. (p. 631)

C4 Describe the format of the statement of cash flows. (p. 631)

Analytical

A1 Analyze the statement of cash flows. (p. 645)

A2 Compute and apply the cash flow on total assets ratio. (p. 646)

Procedural

P1 Prepare a statement of cash flows. (p. 632)

P2 Compute cash flows from operating activities using the indirect method. (p. 635)

P3 Determine cash flows from both investing and financing activities. (p. 641)

P4 *Appendix 16A*—Illustrate use of a spreadsheet to prepare a statement of cash flows. (p. 649)

P5 *Appendix 16B*—Compute cash flows from operating activities using the direct method. (p. 652)

LP16

Wizard of Odd

"If you put enough energy into your dream, you can make anything happen" —Jim Bonaminio

FAIRFIELD, OH—Jim Bonaminio built his roadside produce stand while living in an abandoned gas station. "I would get up and leave at 4 in the morning to buy everything fresh [and] my wife opened the market at 8 a.m.," recalls Jim. "By 10 o'clock at night, we'd be sitting on the bed balancing the register receipts . . . we worked seven days a week." The fruit of those early efforts is **Jungle Jim's International Market (JungleJims.com).**

Jungle Jim's is no Wal-Mart wannabe, but it is arguably America's wackiest supermarket. Instead of trying to beat the big chains at the price-squeezing game, Jim's is a funhouse maze of a store. A seven-foot Elvis lion sings "Jailhouse Rock," an antique fire engine rests atop cases of hot sauce, port-a-potties lead to fancy restrooms, and Robin Hood greets customers with English food set within a 30-foot-tall Sherwood Forest. This is just a sampling.

"If you don't go out on a limb, then you're just like everybody else," insists Jim. "The stuff I've collected—all sorts of weird stuff—gets reused." Despite the wackiness, Jim is first and foremost a businessman. He learned firsthand about the importance of monitoring cash inflows and cash outflows. In the early days, recalls Jim, it was all about sales and profits. Then inventory and asset growth yielded negative cash flows, and Jim was in a pinch. That's when he realized that tracking cash flows was important, explains Jim.

Jim eventually learned how to monitor and control cash flows for each of his operating, investing, and financing activities. Today, says Jim, "I hire professional people to [help me monitor cash] . . . and to look for ways to make money." Yet Jim explains that he always reviews the statement of cash flows and the individual cash inflows and outflows.

Cash management has not curtailed Jim's fun-loving approach to business. "I'm trying to create something that has never been done," laughs Jim. "I just want to see if I can do it and have fun."

[Sources: *Jungle Jim's Website,* January 2009; *BusinessWeek,* April 2005; *Country Living,* November 2004; *Miamian,* Summer 2004; *Plain Dealer,* November 2004; *Supermarket News,* September 2006; *Cintas,* August 2007]

A company cannot achieve or maintain profits without carefully managing cash. Managers and other users of information pay attention to a company's cash position and the events and transactions affecting cash. This chapter explains how we prepare, analyze, and interpret a statement of cash flows. It also discusses the importance of cash flow information for predicting future performance and making managerial decisions. More generally, effectively using the statement of cash flows is crucial for managing and analyzing the operating, investing, and financing activities of businesses.

Reporting the Statement of Cash Flows

Basics of Cash Flow Reporting	Cash Flows from Operating	Cash Flows from Investing	Cash Flows from Financing
• Purpose • Importance • Measurement • Classification • Noncash activities • Format and preparation	• Indirect and direct methods of reporting • Application of indirect method of reporting • Summary of indirect method adjustments	• Three-stage process of analysis • Analysis of noncurrent assets • Analysis of other assets	• Three-stage process of analysis • Analysis of noncurrent liabilities • Analysis of equity

Basics of Cash Flow Reporting

This section describes the basics of cash flow reporting, including its purpose, measurement, classification, format, and preparation.

Purpose of the Statement of Cash Flows

C1 Explain the purpose and importance of cash flow information.

The purpose of the **statement of cash flows** is to report cash receipts (inflows) and cash payments (outflows) during a period. This includes separately identifying the cash flows related to operating, investing, and financing activities. The statement of cash flows does more than simply report changes in cash. It is the detailed disclosure of individual cash flows that makes this statement useful to users. Information in this statement helps users answer questions such as these:

■ How does a company obtain its cash?
■ Where does a company spend its cash?
■ What explains the change in the cash balance?

Point: Internal users rely on the statement of cash flows to make investing and financing decisions. External users rely on this statement to assess the amount and timing of a company's cash flows.

The statement of cash flows addresses important questions such as these by summarizing, classifying, and reporting a company's cash inflows and cash outflows for each period.

Importance of Cash Flows

Information about cash flows can influence decision makers in important ways. For instance, we look more favorably at a company that is financing its expenditures with cash from operations than one that does it by selling its assets. Information about cash flows helps users decide whether a company has enough cash to pay its existing debts as they mature. It is also relied upon to evaluate a company's ability to meet unexpected obligations and pursue unexpected opportunities. External information users especially want to assess a company's ability to take advantage of new business opportunities. Internal users such as managers use cash flow information to plan day-to-day operating activities and make long-term investment decisions.

Macy's striking turnaround is an example of how analysis and management of cash flows can lead to improved financial stability. Several years ago Macy's obtained temporary protection from bankruptcy, at which time it desperately needed to improve its cash flows. It did so by engaging in aggressive cost-cutting measures. As a result, Macy's annual cash flow rose to $210 million, up from a negative cash flow of $38.9 million in the prior year. Macy's eventually met its financial obligations and then successfully merged with Federated Department Stores.

The case of **W. T. Grant Co.** is a classic example of the importance of cash flow information in predicting a company's future performance and financial strength. Grant reported net income of more than $40 million per year for three consecutive years. At that same time, it was experiencing an alarming decrease in cash provided by operations. For instance, net cash outflow was more than $90 million by the end of that three-year period. Grant soon went bankrupt. Users who relied solely on Grant's income numbers were unpleasantly surprised. This reminds us that cash flows as well as income statement and balance sheet information are crucial in making business decisions.

Video16.1

Decision Insight

Cash Savvy "A lender must have a complete understanding of a borrower's cash flows to assess both the borrowing needs and repayment sources. This requires information about the major types of cash inflows and outflows. I have seen many companies, whose financial statements indicate good profitability, experience severe financial problems because the owners or managers lacked a good understanding of cash flows."—Mary E. Garza, **Bank of America**

Measurement of Cash Flows

Cash flows are defined to include both *cash* and *cash equivalents*. The statement of cash flows explains the difference between the beginning and ending balances of cash and cash equivalents. We continue to use the phrases *cash flows* and the *statement of cash flows,* but we must remember that both phrases refer to cash and cash equivalents. Recall that a cash equivalent must satisfy two criteria: (1) be readily convertible to a known amount of cash and (2) be sufficiently close to its maturity so its market value is unaffected by interest rate changes. In most cases, a debt security must be within three months of its maturity to satisfy these criteria. Companies must disclose and follow a clear policy for determining cash and cash equivalents and apply it consistently from period to period. **American Express**, for example, defines its cash equivalents as "time deposits and other highly liquid investments with original maturities of 90 days or less."

Classification of Cash Flows

Since cash and cash equivalents are combined, the statement of cash flows does not report transactions between cash and cash equivalents such as cash paid to purchase cash equivalents and cash received from selling cash equivalents. However, all other cash receipts and cash payments are classified and reported on the statement as operating, investing, or financing activities. Individual cash receipts and payments for each of these three categories are labeled to identify their originating transactions or events. A net cash inflow (source) occurs when the receipts in a category exceed the payments. A net cash outflow (use) occurs when the payments in a category exceed the receipts.

C2 Distinguish between operating, investing, and financing activities.

Operating Activities   **Operating activities** include those transactions and events that determine net income. Examples are the production and purchase of merchandise, the sale of goods and services to customers, and the expenditures to administer the business. Not all items in income, such as unusual gains and losses, are operating activities (we discuss these exceptions later in the chapter). Exhibit 16.1 lists the more common cash inflows and outflows from operating activities. (Although cash receipts and cash payments from buying and selling trading

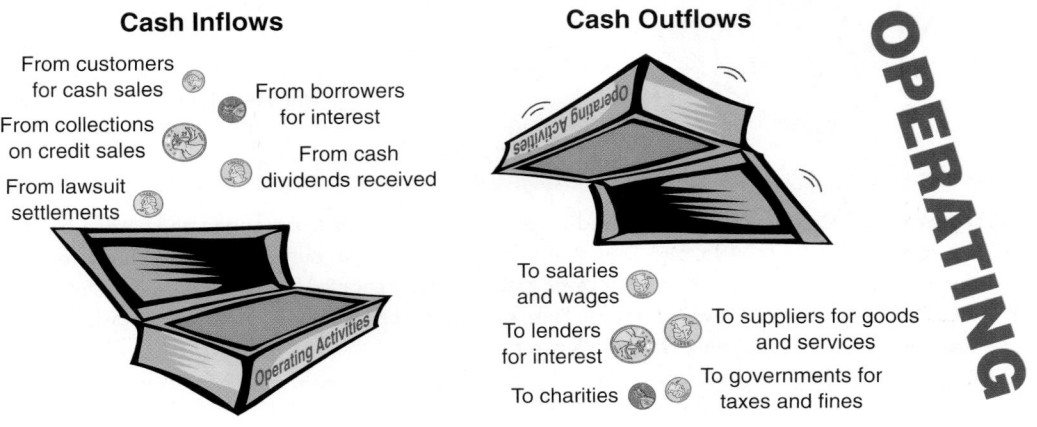

EXHIBIT 16.1

Cash Flows from Operating Activities

securities are often reported under operating activities, new standards require that these receipts and payments be classified based on the nature and purpose of those securities.)

Investing Activities   **Investing activities** generally include those transactions and events that affect long-term assets—namely, the purchase and sale of long-term assets. They also include (1) the purchase and sale of short-term investments in the securities of other entities, other than cash equivalents and trading securities and (2) lending and collecting money for notes receivable. Exhibit 16.2 lists examples of cash flows from investing activities. Proceeds from collecting the principal amounts of notes deserve special mention. If the note results from sales to customers, its cash receipts are classed as operating activities whether short-term or long-term. If the note results from a loan to another party apart from sales, however, the cash receipts from collecting the note principal are classed as an investing activity. The FASB requires that the collection of interest on loans be reported as an operating activity.

EXHIBIT 16.2

Cash Flows from
Investing Activities

Cash Inflows

From selling investments in securities

From collecting principal on loans

From selling (discounting) of notes

From selling long-term productive assets

Cash Outflows

To make loans to others

To purchase long-term productive assets

To purchase investments in securities

INVESTING

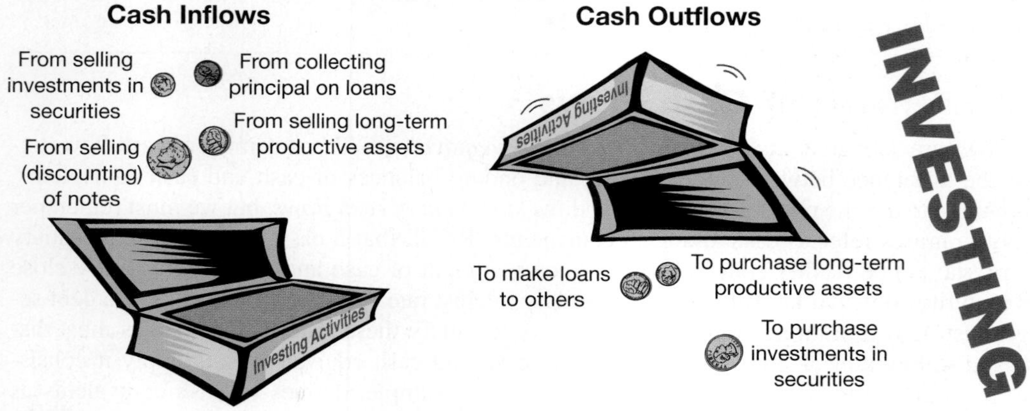

Financing Activities   **Financing activities** include those transactions and events that affect long-term liabilities and equity. Examples are (1) obtaining cash from issuing debt and repaying the amounts borrowed and (2) receiving cash from or distributing cash to owners. These activities involve transactions with a company's owners and creditors. They also often involve borrowing and repaying principal amounts relating to both short- and long-term debt. GAAP requires that payments of interest expense be classified as operating activities. Also, cash payments to settle credit purchases of merchandise, whether on account or by note, are operating activities. Exhibit 16.3 lists examples of cash flows from financing activities.

EXHIBIT 16.3

Cash Flows from
Financing Activities

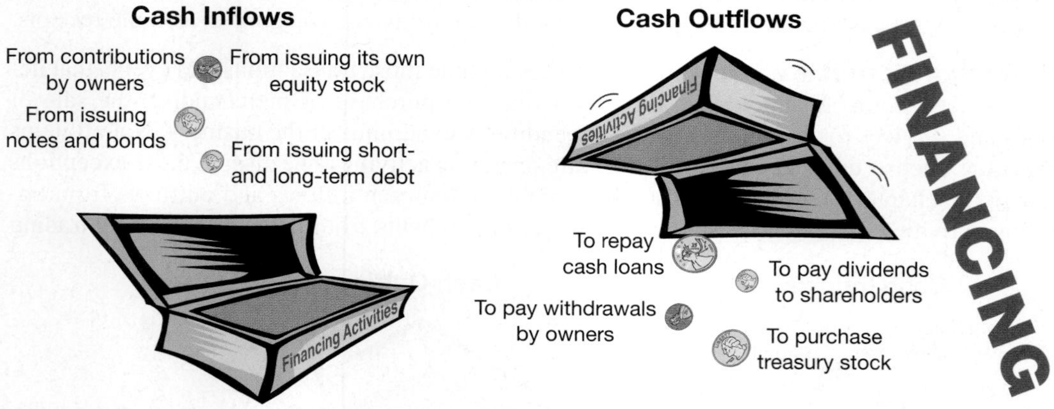

Cash Inflows

From contributions by owners

From issuing its own equity stock

From issuing notes and bonds

From issuing short- and long-term debt

Cash Outflows

To repay cash loans

To pay dividends to shareholders

To pay withdrawals by owners

To purchase treasury stock

FINANCING

Decision Insight

Cash Reporting   Cash flows can be delayed or accelerated at the end of a period to improve or reduce current period cash flows. Also, cash flows can be misclassified. Cash outflows reported under operations are interpreted as expense payments. However, cash outflows reported under investing activities are interpreted as a positive sign of growth potential. Thus, managers face incentives to misclassify cash flows. For these reasons, cash flow reporting warrants our scrutiny.

Noncash Investing and Financing

When important investing and financing activities do not affect cash receipts or payments, they are still disclosed at the bottom of the statement of cash flows or in a note to the statement because of their importance and the *full-disclosure principle*. One example of such a transaction is the purchase of long-term assets using a long-term note payable (loan). This transaction involves both investing and financing activities but does not affect any cash inflow or outflow and is not reported in any of the three sections of the statement of cash flows. This disclosure rule also extends to transactions with partial cash receipts or payments.

To illustrate, assume that Goorin purchases land for $12,000 by paying $5,000 cash and trading in used equipment worth $7,000. The investing section of the statement of cash flows reports only the $5,000 cash outflow for the land purchase. The $12,000 investing transaction is only partially described in the body of the statement of cash flows, yet this information is potentially important to users because it changes the makeup of assets. Goorin could either describe the transaction in a footnote or include information at the bottom of its statement that lists the $12,000 land purchase along with the cash financing of $5,000 and a $7,000 trade-in of equipment. As another example, Borg Co. acquired $900,000 of assets in exchange for $200,000 cash and a $700,000 long-term note, which should be reported as follows:

Fair value of assets acquired	$900,000
Less cash paid	200,000
Liabilities incurred or assumed	$700,000

Exhibit 16.4 lists transactions commonly disclosed as noncash investing and financing activities.

- Retirement of debt by issuing equity stock.
- Conversion of preferred stock to common stock.
- Lease of assets in a capital lease transaction.
- Purchase of long-term assets by issuing a note or bond.
- Exchange of noncash assets for other noncash assets.
- Purchase of noncash assets by issuing equity or debt.

C3 Identify and disclose noncash investing and financing activities.

Point: A stock dividend transaction involving a transfer from retained earnings to common stock or a credit to contributed capital is *not* considered a noncash investing and financing activity because the company receives no consideration for shares issued.

EXHIBIT 16.4

Examples of Noncash Investing and Financing Activities

Format of the Statement of Cash Flows

Accounting standards require companies to include a statement of cash flows in a complete set of financial statements. This statement must report information about a company's cash receipts and cash payments during the period. Exhibit 16.5 shows the usual format. A company must report cash flows from three activities: operating, investing, and financing. The statement explains how transactions and events impact the prior period-end cash (and cash equivalents) balance to produce its current period-end balance.

C4 Describe the format of the statement of cash flows.

EXHIBIT 16.5

Format of the Statement of Cash Flows

COMPANY NAME
Statement of Cash Flows
For period Ended date

Cash flows from operating activities		
[List of individual inflows and outflows]		
Net cash provided (used) by operating activities	$ #	
Cash flows from investing activities		
[List of individual inflows and outflows]		
Net cash provided (used) by investing activities	#	
Cash flows from financing activities		
[List of individual inflows and outflows]		
Net cash provided (used) by financing activities	#	
Net increase (decrease) in cash	$ #	
Cash (and equivalents) balance at prior period-end	#	
Cash (and equivalents) balance at current period-end	$ #	

Separate schedule or note disclosure of any "noncash investing and financing transactions" is required.

Decision Maker

Entrepreneur You are considering purchasing a start-up business that recently reported a $110,000 annual net loss and a $225,000 annual net cash inflow. How are these results possible? [Answer—p. 658]

Quick Check
Answers—p. 658

1. Does a statement of cash flows report the cash payments to purchase cash equivalents? Does it report the cash receipts from selling cash equivalents?

2. Identify the three categories of cash flows reported separately on the statement of cash flows.

3. Identify the cash activity category for each transaction: (*a*) purchase equipment for cash, (*b*) cash payment of wages, (*c*) sale of common stock for cash, (*d*) receipt of cash dividends from stock investment, (*e*) cash collection from customers, (*f*) notes issued for cash.

Preparing the Statement of Cash Flows

P1 Prepare a statement of cash flows.

Preparing a statement of cash flows involves five steps: (1) compute the net increase or decrease in cash; (2) compute and report the net cash provided or used by operating activities (using either the direct or indirect method; both are explained); (3) compute and report the net cash provided or used by investing activities; (4) compute and report the net cash provided or used by financing activities; and (5) compute the net cash flow by combining net cash provided or used by operating, investing, and financing activities and then *prove it* by adding it to the beginning cash balance to show that it equals the ending cash balance.

Step 1: Compute net increase or decrease in cash

Step 2: Compute net cash from operating activities

Step 3: Compute net cash from investing activities

Step 4: Compute net cash from financing activities

Step 5: Prove and report beginning and ending cash balances

Computing the net increase or net decrease in cash is a simple but crucial computation. It equals the current period's cash balance minus the prior period's cash balance. This is the *bottom-line* figure for the statement of cash flows and is a check on accuracy. The information we need to prepare a statement of cash flows comes from various sources including comparative balance sheets at the beginning and end of the period, and an income statement for the period. There are two alternative approaches to preparing the statement: (1) analyzing the Cash account and (2) analyzing noncash accounts.

Analyzing the Cash Account A company's cash receipts and cash payments are recorded in the Cash account in its general ledger. The Cash account is therefore a natural place to look for information about cash flows from operating, investing, and financing activities. To illustrate, review the summarized Cash T-account of Genesis, Inc., in Exhibit 16.6. Individual cash transactions are summarized in this Cash account according to the major types of cash receipts and cash payments. For instance, only the total of cash receipts from all customers is listed. Individual cash transactions underlying these totals can number in the thousands. Accounting software is available to provide summarized cash accounts.

Preparing a statement of cash flows from Exhibit 16.6 requires determining whether an individual cash inflow or outflow is an operating, investing, or financing activity, and then listing each by

EXHIBIT 16.6

```
Accounting System:                                                    _ □ ✕
File  Edit  Maintain  Tasks  Analysis  Options  Reports  Window  Help
                              Cash                                   _ □ ✕
Balance, Dec. 31, 2008 ...........   12,000
Receipts from customers ........  570,000 │ Payments for merchandise ...............................  319,000
Receipts from asset sales ........  12,000 │ Payments for wages and operating expenses .....  218,000
Receipts from stock issuance ..  15,000 │ Payments for interest ...........................................  8,000
                                         │ Payments for taxes .............................................  5,000
                                         │ Payments for assets ............................................  10,000
                                         │ Payments for notes retirement ...........................  18,000
                                         │ Payments for dividends .......................................  14,000
Balance, Dec. 31, 2009 ...........  17,000 │
Sales   Purchases   General   Payroll    Inventory    Company    Analysis
                    Ledger
```

activity. This yields the statement shown in Exhibit 16.7. However, preparing the statement of cash flows from an analysis of the summarized Cash account has two limitations. First, most companies have many individual cash receipts and payments, making it difficult to review them all. Accounting software minimizes this burden, but it is still a task requiring professional judgment for many transactions. Second, the Cash account does not usually carry an adequate description of each cash transaction, making assignment of all cash transactions according to activity difficult.

Point: View the change in cash as a *target* number that we will fully explain and prove in the statement of cash flows.

EXHIBIT 16.7

GENESIS		
Statement of Cash Flows		
For Year Ended December 31, 2009		
Cash flows from operating activities		
Cash received from customers	$570,000	
Cash paid for merchandise	(319,000)	
Cash paid for wages and other operating expenses	(218,000)	
Cash paid for interest	(8,000)	
Cash paid for taxes	(5,000)	
Net cash provided by operating activities		$20,000
Cash flows from investing activities		
Cash received from sale of plant assets	12,000	
Cash paid for purchase of plant assets	(10,000)	
Net cash provided by investing activities		2,000
Cash flows from financing activities		
Cash received from issuing stock	15,000	
Cash paid to retire notes	(18,000)	
Cash paid for dividends	(14,000)	
Net cash used in financing activities		(17,000)
Net increase in cash		$ 5,000
Cash balance at prior year-end		12,000
Cash balance at current year-end		$17,000

Analyzing Noncash Accounts   A second approach to preparing the statement of cash flows is analyzing noncash accounts. This approach uses the fact that when a company records cash inflows and outflows with debits and credits to the Cash account (see Exhibit 16.6), it also records credits and debits in noncash accounts (reflecting double-entry accounting). Many of these noncash accounts are balance sheet accounts—for instance, from the sale of land for cash. Others are revenue and expense accounts that are closed to equity. For instance, the sale of services for cash yields a credit to Services Revenue that is closed to Retained Earnings for a corporation. In sum, *all cash transactions eventually affect noncash balance sheet accounts*. Thus, we can determine cash inflows and outflows by analyzing changes in noncash balance sheet accounts.

Exhibit 16.8 uses the accounting equation to show the relation between the Cash account and the noncash balance sheet accounts. This exhibit starts with the accounting equation at the top. It is then expanded in line (2) to separate cash from noncash asset accounts. Line (3) moves noncash asset accounts to the right-hand side of the equality where they are subtracted. This shows that cash equals the sum of the liability and equity accounts *minus* the noncash asset accounts. Line (4) points

EXHIBIT 16.8

Relation between Cash and Noncash Accounts

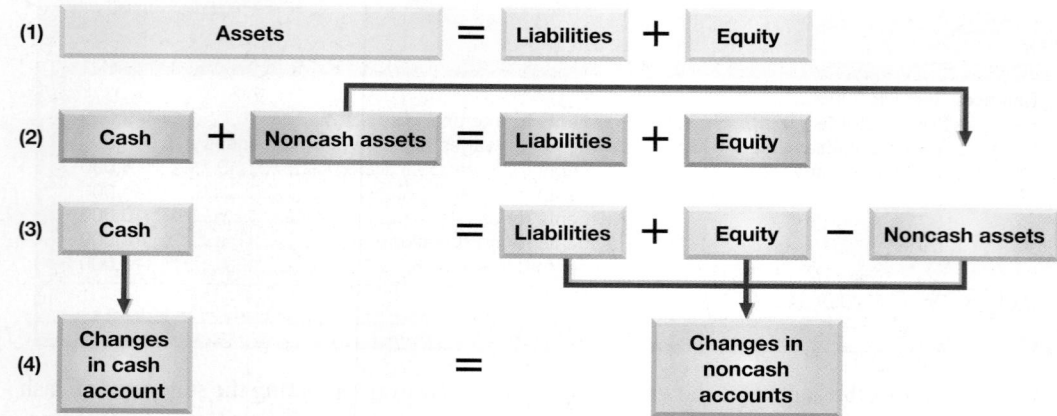

out that *changes* on one side of the accounting equation equal *changes* on the other side. It shows that we can explain changes in cash by analyzing changes in the noncash accounts consisting of liability accounts, equity accounts, and noncash asset accounts. By analyzing noncash balance sheet accounts and any related income statement accounts, we can prepare a statement of cash flows.

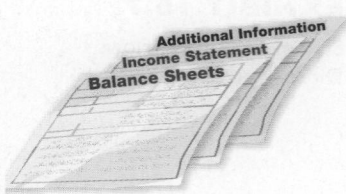

Information to Prepare the Statement   Information to prepare the statement of cash flows usually comes from three sources: (1) comparative balance sheets, (2) the current income statement, and (3) additional information. Comparative balance sheets are used to compute changes in noncash accounts from the beginning to the end of the period. The current income statement is used to help compute cash flows from operating activities. Additional information often includes details on transactions and events that help explain both the cash flows and noncash investing and financing activities.

Decision Insight

e-Cash   Every credit transaction on the Net leaves a trail that a hacker or a marketer can pick up. Enter e-cash—or digital money. The encryption of e-cash protects your money from snoops and thieves and cannot be traced, even by the issuing bank.

Cash Flows from Operating

Indirect and Direct Methods of Reporting

Cash flows provided (used) by operating activities are reported in one of two ways: the *direct method* or the *indirect method.* **These two different methods apply only to the operating activities section.**

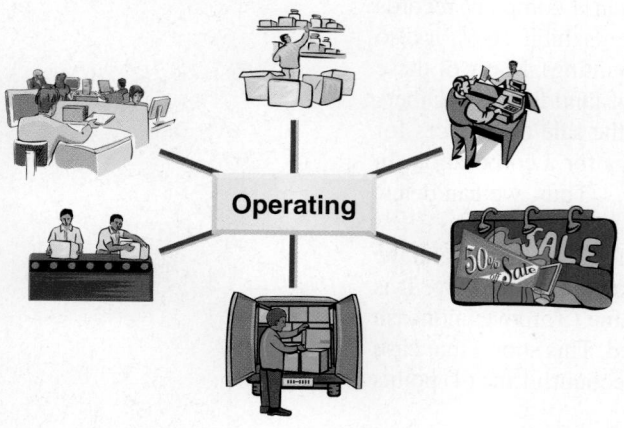

The **direct method** separately lists each major item of operating cash receipts (such as cash received from customers) and each major item of operating cash payments (such as cash paid for merchandise). The cash payments are subtracted from cash receipts to determine the net cash provided (used) by operating activities. The operating activities section of Exhibit 16.7 reflects the direct method of reporting operating cash flows.

The **indirect method** reports net income and then adjusts it for items necessary to obtain net cash provided or used by operating activities. It does *not* report individual items of cash inflows and cash outflows from operating activities. Instead, the indirect method reports the necessary adjustments to reconcile net income to net cash provided or used by operating activities. The operating activities section for Genesis prepared under the indirect method is shown in Exhibit 16.9.

Cash flows from operating activities		
Net income	$ 38,000	
Adjustments to reconcile net income to net cash provided by operating activities		
Increase in accounts receivable	(20,000)	
Increase in merchandise inventory	(14,000)	
Increase in prepaid expenses	(2,000)	
Decrease in accounts payable	(5,000)	
Decrease in interest payable	(1,000)	
Increase in income taxes payable	10,000	
Depreciation expense	24,000	
Loss on sale of plant assets	6,000	
Gain on retirement of notes	(16,000)	
Net cash provided by operating activities		**$20,000**

EXHIBIT 16.9

Operating Activities Section—
Indirect Method

The net cash amount provided by operating activities is *identical* under both the direct and indirect methods. This equality always exists. The difference in these methods is with the computation and presentation of this amount. The FASB recommends the direct method, but because it is not required and the indirect method is arguably easier to compute, nearly all companies report operating cash flows using the indirect method.

To illustrate, we prepare the operating activities section of the statement of cash flows for Genesis. Exhibit 16.10 shows the December 31, 2008 and 2009, balance sheets of Genesis along with its 2009 income statement. We use this information to prepare a statement of cash flows that explains the $5,000 increase in cash for 2009 as reflected in its balance sheets. This $5,000 is computed as Cash of $17,000 at the end of 2009 minus Cash of $12,000 at the end of 2008. Genesis discloses additional information on its 2009 transactions:

a. The accounts payable balances result from merchandise inventory purchases.

b. Purchased $70,000 in plant assets by paying $10,000 cash and issuing $60,000 of notes payable.

c. Sold plant assets with an original cost of $30,000 and accumulated depreciation of $12,000 for $12,000 cash, yielding a $6,000 loss.

d. Received $15,000 cash from issuing 3,000 shares of common stock.

e. Paid $18,000 cash to retire notes with a $34,000 book value, yielding a $16,000 gain.

f. Declared and paid cash dividends of $14,000.

Point: To better understand the direct and indirect methods of reporting operating cash flows, identify similarities and differences between Exhibits 16.7 and 16.11.

Video16.1

The next section describes the indirect method. Appendix 16B describes the direct method. An instructor can choose to cover either one or both methods. Neither section depends on the other.

Application of the Indirect Method of Reporting

Net income is computed using accrual accounting, which recognizes revenues when earned and expenses when incurred. Revenues and expenses do not necessarily reflect the receipt and payment of cash. The indirect method of computing and reporting net cash flows from operating activities involves adjusting the net income figure to obtain the net cash provided or used by operating activities. This includes subtracting noncash increases (credits) from net income and adding noncash charges (debits) back to net income.

To illustrate, the indirect method begins with Genesis's net income of $38,000 and adjusts it to obtain net cash provided by operating activities of $20,000. Exhibit 16.11 shows the results of the indirect method of reporting operating cash flows, which adjusts net income for three types of adjustments. There are adjustments ① to reflect changes in noncash current assets and current liabilities related to operating activities, ② to income statement items involving operating activities that do not affect cash inflows or outflows, and ③ to eliminate gains and losses resulting from investing and financing activities (not part of operating activities). This section describes each of these adjustments.

P2 Compute cash flows from operating activities using the indirect method.

Point: *Noncash credits* refer to *revenue* amounts reported on the income statement that are *not collected in cash* this period. *Noncash charges* refer to *expense* amounts reported on the income statement that are *not paid* this period.

EXHIBIT 16.10

Financial Statements

GENESIS Income Statement For Year Ended December 31, 2009		
Sales		$590,000
Cost of goods sold	$300,000	
Wages and other operating expenses . .	216,000	
Interest expense	7,000	
Depreciation expense	24,000	(547,000)
		43,000
Other gains (losses)		
Gain on retirement of notes	16,000	
Loss on sale of plant assets	(6,000)	10,000
Income before taxes		53,000
Income taxes expense		(15,000)
Net income		$ 38,000

GENESIS Balance Sheets December 31, 2009 and 2008		
	2009	2008
Assets		
Current assets		
Cash	$ 17,000	$ 12,000
Accounts receivable	60,000	40,000
Merchandise inventory	84,000	70,000
Prepaid expenses	6,000	4,000
Total current assets	167,000	126,000
Long-term assets		
Plant assets	250,000	210,000
Accumulated depreciation	(60,000)	(48,000)
Total assets	$357,000	$288,000
Liabilities		
Current liabilities		
Accounts payable	$ 35,000	$ 40,000
Interest payable	3,000	4,000
Income taxes payable	22,000	12,000
Total current liabilities	60,000	56,000
Long-term notes payable	90,000	64,000
Total liabilities	150,000	120,000
Equity		
Common stock, $5 par	95,000	80,000
Retained earnings	112,000	88,000
Total equity	207,000	168,000
Total liabilities and equity	$357,000	$288,000

① **Adjustments for Changes in Current Assets and Current Liabilities** This section describes adjustments for changes in noncash current assets and current liabilities.

Point: Operating activities are typically those that determine income, which are often reflected in changes in current assets and current liabilities.

Adjustments for changes in noncash current assets.   Changes in noncash current assets normally result from operating activities. Examples are sales affecting accounts receivable and building usage affecting prepaid rent. Decreases in noncash current assets yield the following adjustment:

Decreases in noncash current assets are added to net income.

To see the logic for this adjustment, consider that a decrease in a noncash current asset such as accounts receivable suggests more available cash at the end of the period compared to the beginning. This is so because a decrease in accounts receivable implies higher cash receipts than reflected in sales. We add these higher cash receipts (from decreases in noncash current assets) to net income when computing cash flow from operations.

In contrast, an increase in noncash current assets such as accounts receivable implies less cash receipts than reflected in sales. As another example, an increase in prepaid rent indicates that more cash is paid for rent than is deducted as rent expense. Increases in noncash current assets yield the following adjustment:

Increases in noncash current assets are subtracted from net income.

To illustrate, these adjustments are applied to the noncash current assets in Exhibit 16.10.

Accounts receivable. Accounts receivable *increase* $20,000, from a beginning balance of $40,000 to an ending balance of $60,000. This increase implies that Genesis collects less cash than is reported in sales. That is, some of these sales were in the form of accounts receivable and that amount increased during the period. To see this it is helpful to use *account analysis.* This usually involves setting up a T-account and reconstructing its major entries to compute cash receipts or payments. The following reconstructed Accounts Receivable T-account reveals that cash receipts are less than sales:

	Accounts Receivable		
Bal., Dec. 31, 2008	40,000		
Sales	590,000	**Cash receipts =**	**570,000**
Bal., Dec. 31, 2009	60,000		

> Numbers in black are taken from Exhibit 16.10. The red number is the computed (plug) figure.

We see that sales are $20,000 greater than cash receipts. This $20,000—as reflected in the $20,000 increase in Accounts Receivable—is subtracted from net income when computing cash provided by operating activities (see Exhibit 16.11).

Merchandise inventory. Merchandise inventory *increases* by $14,000, from a $70,000 beginning balance to an $84,000 ending balance. This increase implies that Genesis had greater cash purchases than cost of goods sold. This larger amount of cash purchases is in the form of inventory, as reflected in the following account analysis:

	Merchandise Inventory		
Bal., Dec. 31, 2008	70,000		
Purchases =	**314,000**	Cost of goods sold	300,000
Bal., Dec. 31, 2009	84,000		

GENESIS Statement of Cash Flows For Year Ended December 31, 2009		
Cash flows from operating activities		
Net income		$ 38,000
Adjustments to reconcile net income to net cash provided by operating activities		
① Increase in accounts receivable	(20,000)	
Increase in merchandise inventory	(14,000)	
Increase in prepaid expenses	(2,000)	
Decrease in accounts payable	(5,000)	
Decrease in interest payable	(1,000)	
Increase in income taxes payable	10,000	
② { Depreciation expense	24,000	
③ Loss on sale of plant assets	6,000	
Gain on retirement of notes	(16,000)	
Net cash provided by operating activities		$20,000
Cash flows from investing activities		
Cash received from sale of plant assets	12,000	
Cash paid for purchase of plant assets	(10,000)	
Net cash provided by investing activities		2,000
Cash flows from financing activities		
Cash received from issuing stock	15,000	
Cash paid to retire notes	(18,000)	
Cash paid for dividends	(14,000)	
Net cash used in financing activities		(17,000)
Net increase in cash		$ 5,000
Cash balance at prior year-end		12,000
Cash balance at current year-end		$17,000

EXHIBIT 16.11

Statement of Cash Flows—
Indirect Method

Point: Refer to Exhibit 16.10 and identify the $5,000 change in cash. This change is what the statement of cash flows explains; it serves as a check.

The amount by which purchases exceed cost of goods sold—as reflected in the $14,000 increase in inventory—is subtracted from net income when computing cash provided by operating activities (see Exhibit 16.11).

Prepaid expenses. Prepaid expenses *increase* $2,000, from a $4,000 beginning balance to a $6,000 ending balance, implying that Genesis's cash payments exceed its recorded prepaid expenses. These higher cash payments increase the amount of Prepaid Expenses, as reflected in its reconstructed T-account:

Prepaid Expenses			
Bal., Dec. 31, 2008	4,000		
Cash payments =	218,000	Wages and other operating exp.	216,000
Bal., Dec. 31, 2009	6,000		

The amount by which cash payments exceed the recorded operating expenses—as reflected in the $2,000 increase in Prepaid Expenses—is subtracted from net income when computing cash provided by operating activities (see Exhibit 16.11).

Adjustments for changes in current liabilities. Changes in current liabilities normally result from operating activities. An example is a purchase that affects accounts payable. Increases in current liabilities yield the following adjustment to net income when computing operating cash flows:

Increases in current liabilities are added to net income.

To see the logic for this adjustment, consider that an increase in the Accounts Payable account suggests that cash payments are less than the related (cost of goods sold) expense. As another example, an increase in wages payable implies that cash paid for wages is less than the recorded wages expense. Since the recorded expense is greater than the cash paid, we add the increase in wages payable to net income to compute net cash flow from operations.

Conversely, when current liabilities decrease, the following adjustment is required:

Decreases in current liabilities are subtracted from net income.

To illustrate, these adjustments are applied to the current liabilities in Exhibit 16.10.

Accounts payable. Accounts payable *decrease* $5,000, from a beginning balance of $40,000 to an ending balance of $35,000. This decrease implies that cash payments to suppliers exceed purchases by $5,000 for the period, which is reflected in the reconstructed Accounts Payable T-account:

Accounts Payable			
Cash payments =	319,000	Bal., Dec. 31, 2008	40,000
		Purchases	314,000
		Bal., Dec. 31, 2009	35,000

The amount by which cash payments exceed purchases—as reflected in the $5,000 decrease in Accounts Payable—is subtracted from net income when computing cash provided by operating activities (see Exhibit 16.11).

Interest payable. Interest payable *decreases* $1,000, from a $4,000 beginning balance to a $3,000 ending balance. This decrease indicates that cash paid for interest exceeds interest expense by $1,000, which is reflected in the Interest Payable T-account:

Interest Payable			
Cash paid for interest =	8,000	Bal., Dec. 31, 2008	4,000
		Interest expense	7,000
		Bal., Dec. 31, 2009	3,000

The amount by which cash paid exceeds recorded expense—as reflected in the $1,000 decrease in Interest Payable—is subtracted from net income (see Exhibit 16.11).

Income taxes payable. Income taxes payable *increase* $10,000, from a $12,000 beginning balance to a $22,000 ending balance. This increase implies that reported income taxes exceed the cash paid for taxes, which is reflected in the Income Taxes Payable T-account:

Income Taxes Payable			
		Bal., Dec. 31, 2008	12,000
Cash paid for taxes =	5,000	Income taxes expense	15,000
		Bal., Dec. 31, 2009	22,000

The amount by which cash paid falls short of the reported taxes expense—as reflected in the $10,000 increase in Income Taxes Payable—is added to net income when computing cash provided by operating activities (see Exhibit 16.11).

Summary Adjustments for Changes in Current Assets and Current Liabilities		
Account	**Increases**	**Decreases**
Noncash current assets	Deduct from NI	Add to NI
Current liabilities	Add to NI	Deduct from NI

② **Adjustments for Operating Items Not Providing or Using Cash**   The income statement usually includes some expenses that do not reflect cash outflows in the period. Examples are depreciation, amortization, depletion, and bad debts expense. The indirect method for reporting operating cash flows requires that

Expenses with no cash outflows are added back to net income.

To see the logic of this adjustment, recall that items such as depreciation, amortization, depletion, and bad debts originate from debits to expense accounts and credits to noncash accounts. These entries have *no* cash effect, and we add them back to net income when computing net cash flows from operations. Adding them back cancels their deductions.

Similarly, when net income includes revenues that do not reflect cash inflows in the period, the indirect method for reporting operating cash flows requires that

Revenues with no cash inflows are subtracted from net income.

We apply these adjustments to the Genesis operating items that do not provide or use cash.

Depreciation.   Depreciation expense is the only Genesis operating item that has no effect on cash flows in the period. We must add back the $24,000 depreciation expense to net income when computing cash provided by operating activities. (We later explain that any cash outflow to acquire a plant asset is reported as an investing activity.)

③ **Adjustments for Nonoperating Items**   Net income often includes losses that are not part of operating activities but are part of either investing or financing activities. Examples are a loss from the sale of a plant asset and a loss from retirement of notes payable. The indirect method for reporting operating cash flows requires that

Nonoperating losses are added back to net income.

To see the logic, consider that items such as a plant asset sale and a notes retirement are normally recorded by recognizing the cash, removing all plant asset or notes accounts, and recognizing any loss or gain. The cash received or paid is not part of operating activities but is part of either investing or financing activities. *No* operating cash flow effect occurs. However, because the nonoperating loss is a deduction in computing net income, we need to add it back to net income when computing cash flow from operations. Adding it back cancels the deduction.

Similarly, when net income includes gains not part of operating activities, the indirect method for reporting operating cash flows requires that

Nonoperating gains are subtracted from net income.

To illustrate these adjustments, we consider the nonoperating items of Genesis.

Point: An income statement reports revenues, gains, expenses, and losses on an accrual basis. The statement of cash flows reports cash received and cash paid for operating, financing, and investing activities.

Loss on sale of plant assets. Genesis reports a $6,000 loss on sale of plant assets as part of net income. This loss is a proper deduction in computing income, but it is *not part of operating activities*. Instead, a sale of plant assets is part of investing activities. Thus, the $6,000 non-operating loss is added back to net income (see Exhibit 16.11). Adding it back cancels the loss. We later explain how to report the cash inflow from the asset sale in investing activities.

Gain on retirement of debt. A $16,000 gain on retirement of debt is properly included in net income, but it is *not part of operating activities*. This means the $16,000 nonoperating gain must be subtracted from net income to obtain net cash provided by operating activities (see Exhibit 16.11). Subtracting it cancels the recorded gain. We later describe how to report the cash outflow to retire debt.

Summary of Adjustments for Indirect Method

Exhibit 16.12 summarizes the most common adjustments to net income when computing net cash provided or used by operating activities under the indirect method.

EXHIBIT 16.12

Summary of Selected
Adjustments for Indirect Method

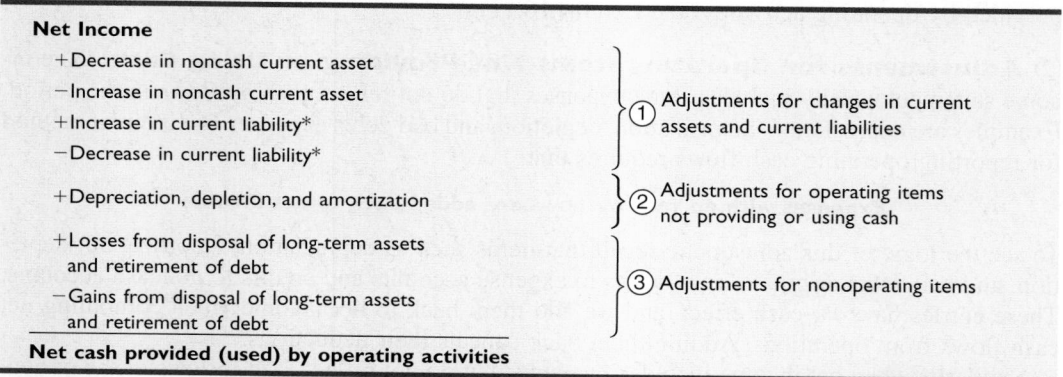

Net Income
   +Decrease in noncash current asset
   −Increase in noncash current asset   ⎫
   +Increase in current liability*   ⎬ ① Adjustments for changes in current
   −Decrease in current liability*   ⎭   assets and current liabilities

   +Depreciation, depletion, and amortization   ⎫ ② Adjustments for operating items
                                                 ⎭   not providing or using cash

   +Losses from disposal of long-term assets   ⎫
    and retirement of debt   ⎬ ③ Adjustments for nonoperating items
   −Gains from disposal of long-term assets   ⎭
    and retirement of debt
Net cash provided (used) by operating activities

* Excludes current portion of long-term debt and any (nonsales-related) short-term notes payable—both are financing activities.

The computations in determining cash provided or used by operating activities are different for the indirect and direct methods, but the result is identical. Both methods yield the same $20,000 figure for cash from operating activities for Genesis; see Exhibits 16.7 and 16.11.

Decision Insight

Cash or Income The difference between net income and operating cash flows can be large and sometimes reflects on the quality of earnings. This bar chart shows the net income and operating cash flows of three companies. Operating cash flows can be either higher or lower than net income.

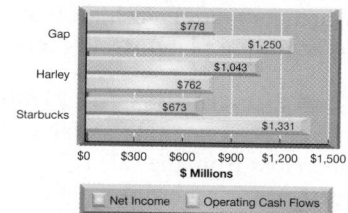

Quick Check
Answers—p. 658

4. Determine the net cash provided or used by operating activities using the following data: net income, $74,900; decrease in accounts receivable, $4,600; increase in inventory, $11,700; decrease in accounts payable, $1,000; loss on sale of equipment, $3,400; payment of cash dividends, $21,500.

5. Why are expenses such as depreciation and amortization added to net income when cash flow from operating activities is computed by the indirect method?

6. A company reports net income of $15,000 that includes a $3,000 gain on the sale of plant assets. Why is this gain subtracted from net income in computing cash flow from operating activities using the indirect method?

Cash Flows from Investing

The third major step in preparing the statement of cash flows is to compute and report cash flows from investing activities. We normally do this by identifying changes in (1) all noncurrent asset accounts and (2) the current accounts for both notes receivable and investments in securities (excluding trading securities). We then analyze changes in these accounts to determine their effect, if any, on cash and report the cash flow effects in the investing activities section of the statement of cash flows. **Reporting of investing activities is identical under the direct method and indirect method.**

Three-Stage Process of Analysis

Information to compute cash flows from investing activities is usually taken from beginning and ending balance sheets and the income statement. We use a three-stage process to determine cash provided or used by investing activities: (1) identify changes in investing-related accounts, (2) explain these changes using reconstruction analysis, and (3) report their cash flow effects.

Video16.1

Analysis of Noncurrent Assets

Information about the Genesis transactions provided earlier reveals that the company both purchased and sold plant assets during the period. Both transactions are investing activities and are analyzed for their cash flow effects in this section.

P3 Determine cash flows from both investing and financing activities.

Plant Asset Transactions   The first stage in analyzing the Plant Assets account and its related Accumulated Depreciation is to identify any changes in these accounts from comparative balance sheets in Exhibit 16.10. This analysis reveals a $40,000 increase in plant assets from $210,000 to $250,000 and a $12,000 increase in accumulated depreciation from $48,000 to $60,000.

Point: Investing activities include (1) purchasing and selling long-term assets, (2) lending and collecting on notes receivable, and (3) purchasing and selling short-term investments other than cash equivalents and trading securities.

The second stage is to explain these changes. Items *b* and *c* of the additional information for Genesis (page 635) are relevant in this case. Recall that the Plant Assets account is affected by both asset purchases and sales, while its Accumulated Depreciation account is normally increased from depreciation and decreased from the removal of accumulated depreciation in asset sales. To explain changes in these accounts and to identify their cash flow effects, we prepare *reconstructed entries* from prior transactions; *they are not the actual entries by the preparer.*

Point: Financing and investing info is available in ledger accounts to help explain changes in comparative balance sheets. Post references lead to relevant entries and explanations.

To illustrate, item *b* reports that Genesis purchased plant assets of $70,000 by issuing $60,000 in notes payable to the seller and paying $10,000 in cash. The reconstructed entry for analysis of item *b* follows:

Reconstruction	Plant Assets	70,000	
	Notes Payable		60,000
	Cash		**10,000**

This entry reveals a $10,000 cash outflow for plant assets and a $60,000 noncash investing and financing transaction involving notes exchanged for plant assets.

Next, item *c* reports that Genesis sold plant assets costing $30,000 (with $12,000 of accumulated depreciation) for $12,000 cash, resulting in a $6,000 loss. The reconstructed entry for analysis of item *c* follows:

Reconstruction	**Cash**	**12,000**	
	Accumulated Depreciation	12,000	
	Loss on Sale of Plant Assets	6,000	
	Plant Assets		30,000

This entry reveals a $12,000 cash inflow from assets sold. The $6,000 loss is computed by comparing the asset book value to the cash received and does not reflect any cash inflow or outflow. We also reconstruct the entry for Depreciation Expense using information from the income statement.

Reconstruction	Depreciation Expense	24,000	
	Accumulated Depreciation		24,000

This entry shows that Depreciation Expense results in no cash flow effect. These three reconstructed entries are reflected in the following plant asset and related T-accounts.

Plant Assets					Accumulated Depreciation—Plant Assets			
Bal., Dec. 31, 2008	210,000						Bal., Dec. 31, 2008	48,000
Purchase	**70,000**	Sale	30,000		Sale	12,000	**Depr. expense**	**24,000**
Bal., Dec. 31, 2009	250,000						Bal., Dec. 31, 2009	60,000

Example: If a plant asset costing $40,000 with $37,000 of accumulated depreciation is sold at a $1,000 loss, what is the cash flow? What is the cash flow if this asset is sold at a gain of $3,000? *Answers:* +$2,000; +$6,000.

This reconstruction analysis is complete in that the change in plant assets from $210,000 to $250,000 is fully explained by the $70,000 purchase and the $30,000 sale. Also, the change in accumulated depreciation from $48,000 to $60,000 is fully explained by depreciation expense of $24,000 and the removal of $12,000 in accumulated depreciation from an asset sale. (Preparers of the statement of cash flows have the entire ledger and additional information at their disposal, but for brevity reasons only the information needed for reconstructing accounts is given.)

The third stage looks at the reconstructed entries for identification of cash flows. The two identified cash flow effects are reported in the investing section of the statement as follows (also see Exhibit 16.7 or 16.11):

Cash flows from investing activities	
Cash received from sale of plant assets	$12,000
Cash paid for purchase of plant assets	(10,000)

The $60,000 portion of the purchase described in item *b* and financed by issuing notes is a noncash investing and financing activity. It is reported in a note or in a separate schedule to the statement as follows:

Noncash investing and financing activity	
Purchased plant assets with issuance of notes	$60,000

Analysis of Other Assets

Many other asset transactions (including those involving current notes receivable and investments in certain securities) are considered investing activities and can affect a company's cash flows. Since Genesis did not enter into other investing activities impacting assets, we do not need to extend our analysis to these other assets. If such transactions did exist, we would analyze them using the same three-stage process illustrated for plant assets.

Quick Check   Answer—p. 658

7. Equipment costing $80,000 with accumulated depreciation of $30,000 is sold at a loss of $10,000. What is the cash receipt from this sale? In what section of the statement of cash flows is this transaction reported?

Cash Flows from Financing

The fourth major step in preparing the statement of cash flows is to compute and report cash flows from financing activities. We normally do this by identifying changes in all noncurrent liability accounts (including the current portion of any notes and bonds) and the equity accounts. These accounts include long-term debt, notes payable, bonds payable, common stock, and retained earnings. Changes in these accounts are then analyzed using available information to determine their effect, if any, on cash. Results are reported in the financing activities section of the statement. **Reporting of financing activities is identical under the direct method and indirect method.**

Three-Stage Process of Analysis

We again use a three-stage process to determine cash provided or used by financing activities: (1) identify changes in financing-related accounts, (2) explain these changes using reconstruction analysis, and (3) report their cash flow effects.

Video 16.1

Analysis of Noncurrent Liabilities

Information about Genesis provided earlier reveals two transactions involving noncurrent liabilities. We analyzed one of those, the $60,000 issuance of notes payable to purchase plant assets. This transaction is reported as a significant noncash investing and financing activity in a footnote or a separate schedule to the statement of cash flows. The other remaining transaction involving noncurrent liabilities is the cash retirement of notes payable.

Point: Financing activities generally refer to changes in the noncurrent liability and the equity accounts. Examples are (1) receiving cash from issuing debt or repaying amounts borrowed and (2) receiving cash from or distributing cash to owners.

Notes Payable Transactions   The first stage in analysis of notes is to review the comparative balance sheets from Exhibit 16.10. This analysis reveals an increase in notes payable from $64,000 to $90,000.

The second stage explains this change. Item *e* of the additional information for Genesis (page 635) reports that notes with a carrying value of $34,000 are retired for $18,000 cash, resulting in a $16,000 gain. The reconstructed entry for analysis of item *e* follows:

Reconstruction	Notes Payable	34,000	
	Gain on retirement of debt		16,000
	Cash		**18,000**

This entry reveals an $18,000 cash outflow for retirement of notes and a $16,000 gain from comparing the notes payable carrying value to the cash received. This gain does not reflect any cash inflow or outflow. Also, item *b* of the additional information reports that Genesis purchased plant assets costing $70,000 by issuing $60,000 in notes payable to the seller and paying $10,000 in cash. We reconstructed this entry when analyzing investing activities: It showed a $60,000 increase to notes payable that is reported as a noncash investing and financing transaction. The Notes Payable account reflects (and is fully explained by) these reconstructed entries as follows:

Notes Payable			
		Bal., Dec. 31, 2008	64,000
Retired notes	34,000	Issued notes	60,000
		Bal., Dec. 31, 2009	90,000

The third stage is to report the cash flow effect of the notes retirement in the financing section of the statement as follows (also see Exhibit 16.7 or 16.11):

Cash flows from financing activities	
Cash paid to retire notes	$(18,000)

Analysis of Equity

The Genesis information reveals two transactions involving equity accounts. The first is the issuance of common stock for cash. The second is the declaration and payment of cash dividends. We analyze both.

Common Stock Transactions   The first stage in analyzing common stock is to review the comparative balance sheets from Exhibit 16.10, which reveals an increase in common stock from $80,000 to $95,000.

The second stage explains this change. Item *d* of the additional information (page 635) reports that 3,000 shares of common stock are issued at par for $5 per share. The reconstructed entry for analysis of item *d* follows:

Reconstruction   **Cash** 15,000
                  Common Stock 15,000

This entry reveals a $15,000 cash inflow from stock issuance and is reflected in (and explains) the Common Stock account as follows:

Common Stock	
Bal., Dec. 31, 2008	80,000
Issued stock	**15,000**
Bal., Dec. 31, 2009	95,000

The third stage discloses the cash flow effect from stock issuance in the financing section of the statement as follows (also see Exhibit 16.7 or 16.11):

Cash flows from financing activities
Cash received from issuing stock $15,000

Retained Earnings Transactions   The first stage in analyzing the Retained Earnings account is to review the comparative balance sheets from Exhibit 16.10. This reveals an increase in retained earnings from $88,000 to $112,000.

The second stage explains this change. Item *f* of the additional information (page 635) reports that cash dividends of $14,000 are paid. The reconstructed entry follows:

Reconstruction   Retained Earnings.......................... 14,000
                  Cash.................................. **14,000**

This entry reveals a $14,000 cash outflow for cash dividends. Also see that the Retained Earnings account is impacted by net income of $38,000. (Net income was analyzed under the operating section of the statement of cash flows.) The reconstructed Retained Earnings account follows:

Retained Earnings			
Cash dividend	**14,000**	Bal., Dec. 31, 2008	88,000
		Net income	**38,000**
		Bal., Dec. 31, 2009	112,000

The third stage reports the cash flow effect from the cash dividend in the financing section of the statement as follows (also see Exhibit 16.7 or 16.11):

Cash flows from financing activities
Cash paid for dividends .... $(14,000)

We now have identified and explained all of the Genesis cash inflows and cash outflows and one noncash investing and financing transaction. Specifically, our analysis has reconciled changes in all noncash balance sheet accounts.

Point: Financing activities not affecting cash flow include *declaration* of a cash dividend, *declaration* of a stock dividend, payment of a stock dividend, and a stock split.

Global: There are no requirements to separate domestic and international cash flows, leading some users to ask, "Where in the world is cash flow?"

Proving Cash Balances

The fifth and final step in preparing the statement is to report the beginning and ending cash balances and prove that the *net change in cash* is explained by operating, investing, and financing cash flows. This step is shown here for Genesis.

Net cash provided by operating activities	$20,000
Net cash provided by investing activities	2,000
Net cash used in financing activities	(17,000)
Net increase in cash	**$ 5,000**
Cash balance at 2008 year-end	12,000
Cash balance at 2009 year-end	$17,000

The preceding table shows that the $5,000 net increase in cash, from $12,000 at the beginning of the period to $17,000 at the end, is reconciled by net cash flows from operating ($20,000 inflow), investing ($2,000 inflow), and financing ($17,000 outflow) activities. This is formally reported at the bottom of the statement of cash flows as shown in both Exhibits 16.7 and 16.11.

Decision Maker

Reporter Management is in labor contract negotiations and grants you an interview. It highlights a recent $600,000 net loss that involves a $930,000 extraordinary loss and a total net cash outflow of $550,000 (which includes net cash outflows of $850,000 for investing activities and $350,000 for financing activities). What is your assessment of this company? [Answer—p. 658]

Cash Flow Analysis

Decision Analysis

Analyzing Cash Sources and Uses

Most managers stress the importance of understanding and predicting cash flows for business decisions. Creditors evaluate a company's ability to generate cash before deciding whether to lend money. Investors also assess cash inflows and outflows before buying and selling stock. Information in the statement of cash flows helps address these and other questions such as (1) How much cash is generated from or used in operations? (2) What expenditures are made with cash from operations? (3) What is the source of cash for debt payments? (4) What is the source of cash for distributions to owners? (5) How is the increase in investing activities financed? (6) What is the source of cash for new plant assets? (7) Why is cash flow from operations different from income? (8) How is cash from financing used?

 A1 Analyze the statement of cash flows.

To effectively answer these questions, it is important to separately analyze investing, financing, and operating activities. To illustrate, consider data from three different companies in Exhibit 16.13. These companies operate in the same industry and have been in business for several years.

($ thousands)	BMX	ATV	Trex
Cash provided (used) by operating activities	$90,000	$40,000	$(24,000)
Cash provided (used) by investing activities			
Proceeds from sale of plant assets			26,000
Purchase of plant assets	(48,000)	(25,000)	
Cash provided (used) by financing activities			
Proceeds from issuance of debt			13,000
Repayment of debt	(27,000)		
Net increase (decrease) in cash	$15,000	$15,000	$ 15,000

EXHIBIT 16.13

Cash Flows of Competing Companies

Each company generates an identical $15,000 net increase in cash, but its sources and uses of cash flows are very different. BMX's operating activities provide net cash flows of $90,000, allowing it to purchase plant assets of $48,000 and repay $27,000 of its debt. ATV's operating activities provide $40,000 of cash flows, limiting its purchase of plant assets to $25,000. Trex's $15,000 net cash increase is due to selling plant assets and incurring additional debt. Its operating activities yield a net cash outflow of $24,000.

Overall, analysis of these cash flows reveals that BMX is more capable of generating future cash flows than is ATV or Trex.

Free Cash Flows   Many investors use cash flows to value company stock. However, cash-based valuation models often yield different stock values due to differences in measurement of cash flows. Most models require cash flows that are "free" for distribution to shareholders. These *free cash flows* are defined as cash flows available to shareholders after operating asset reinvestments and debt payments. Knowledge of the statement of cash flows is key to proper computation of free cash flows. A company's growth and financial flexibility depend on adequate free cash flows.

Cash Flow on Total Assets

A2   Compute and apply the cash flow on total assets ratio.

Cash flow information has limitations, but it can help measure a company's ability to meet its obligations, pay dividends, expand operations, and obtain financing. Users often compute and analyze a cash-based ratio similar to return on total assets except that its numerator is net cash flows from operating activities. The **cash flow on total assets** ratio is in Exhibit 16.14.

EXHIBIT 16.14

Cash Flow on Total Assets

$$\text{Cash flow on total assets} = \frac{\text{Cash flow from operations}}{\text{Average total assets}}$$

This ratio reflects actual cash flows and is not affected by accounting income recognition and measurement. It can help business decision makers estimate the amount and timing of cash flows when planning and analyzing operating activities.

To illustrate, the 2007 cash flow on total assets ratio for Nike is 18.3%—see Exhibit 16.15. Is an 18.3% ratio good or bad? To answer this question, we compare this ratio with the ratios of prior years (we could also compare its ratio with those of its competitors and the market). Nike's cash flow on total assets ratio for several prior years is in the second column of Exhibit 16.15. Results show that its 18.3% return is the median of the prior years' returns.

EXHIBIT 16.15

Nike's Cash Flow on Total Assets

Year	Cash Flow on Total Assets	Return on Total Assets
2007	18.3%	14.5%
2006	17.9	14.9
2005	18.8	14.5
2004	20.6	12.8
2003	13.9	7.1

As an indicator of *earnings quality,* some analysts compare the cash flow on total assets ratio to the return on total assets ratio. Nike's return on total assets is provided in the third column of Exhibit 16.15. Nike's cash flow on total assets ratio exceeds its return on total assets in each of the five years, leading some analysts to infer that Nike's earnings quality is high for that period because more earnings are realized in the form of cash.

Cash Flow Ratios   Analysts use various other cash-based ratios, including the following two:

$$(1) \qquad \text{Cash coverage of growth} = \frac{\text{Operating cash flow}}{\text{Cash outflow for plant assets}}$$

where a low ratio (less than 1) implies cash inadequacy to meet asset growth, whereas a high ratio implies cash adequacy for asset growth.

Point: The following ratio helps assess whether operating cash flow is adequate to meet long-term obligations:
Cash coverage of debt = Cash flow from operations ÷ Noncurrent liabilities. A low ratio suggests a higher risk of insolvency; a high ratio suggests a greater ability to meet long-term obligations.

$$(2) \qquad \text{Operating cash flow to sales} = \frac{\text{Operating cash flow}}{\text{Net sales}}$$

When this ratio substantially and consistently differs from the operating income to net sales ratio, the risk of accounting improprieties increases.

Demonstration Problem

Umlauf's comparative balance sheets, income statement, and additional information follow.

DP16

UMLAUF COMPANY Balance Sheets December 31, 2009 and 2008		
	2009	**2008**
Assets		
Cash	$ 43,050	$ 23,925
Accounts receivable	34,125	39,825
Merchandise inventory	156,000	146,475
Prepaid expenses	3,600	1,650
Equipment	135,825	146,700
Accum. depreciation—Equipment	(61,950)	(47,550)
Total assets	$310,650	$311,025
Liabilities and Equity		
Accounts payable	$ 28,800	$ 33,750
Income taxes payable	5,100	4,425
Dividends payable	0	4,500
Bonds payable	0	37,500
Common stock, $10 par	168,750	168,750
Retained earnings	108,000	62,100
Total liabilities and equity	$310,650	$311,025

UMLAUF COMPANY Income Statement For Year Ended December 31, 2009		
Sales		$446,100
Cost of goods sold	$222,300	
Other operating expenses	120,300	
Depreciation expense	25,500	(368,100)
		78,000
Other gains (losses)		
Loss on sale of equipment	3,300	
Loss on retirement of bonds	825	(4,125)
Income before taxes		73,875
Income taxes expense		(13,725)
Net income		$ 60,150

Additional Information

a. Equipment costing $21,375 with accumulated depreciation of $11,100 is sold for cash.

b. Equipment purchases are for cash.

c. Accumulated Depreciation is affected by depreciation expense and the sale of equipment.

d. The balance of Retained Earnings is affected by dividend declarations and net income.

e. All sales are made on credit.

f. All merchandise inventory purchases are on credit.

g. Accounts Payable balances result from merchandise inventory purchases.

h. Prepaid expenses relate to "other operating expenses."

Required

1. Prepare a statement of cash flows using the indirect method for year 2009.

2.ᴮ Prepare a statement of cash flows using the direct method for year 2009.

Planning the Solution

- Prepare two blank statements of cash flows with sections for operating, investing, and financing activities using the (1) indirect method format and (2) direct method format.
- Compute the cash paid for equipment and the cash received from the sale of equipment using the additional information provided along with the amount for depreciation expense and the change in the balances of equipment and accumulated depreciation. Use T-accounts to help chart the effects of the sale and purchase of equipment on the balances of the Equipment account and the Accumulated Depreciation account.
- Compute the effect of net income on the change in the Retained Earnings account balance. Assign the difference between the change in retained earnings and the amount of net income to dividends declared. Adjust the dividends declared amount for the change in the Dividends Payable balance.
- Compute cash received from customers, cash paid for merchandise, cash paid for other operating expenses, and cash paid for taxes as illustrated in the chapter.
- Enter the cash effects of reconstruction entries to the appropriate section(s) of the statement.
- Total each section of the statement, determine the total net change in cash, and add it to the beginning balance to get the ending balance of cash.

Solution to Demonstration Problem

Supporting computations for cash receipts and cash payments.

(1)	*Cost of equipment sold	$ 21,375
	Accumulated depreciation of equipment sold	(11,100)
	Book value of equipment sold	10,275
	Loss on sale of equipment	(3,300)
	Cash received from sale of equipment	$ 6,975
	Cost of equipment sold	$ 21,375
	Less decrease in the equipment account balance	(10,875)
	Cash paid for new equipment	$ 10,500
(2)	Loss on retirement of bonds	$ 825
	Carrying value of bonds retired	37,500
	Cash paid to retire bonds	$ 38,325
(3)	Net income	$ 60,150
	Less increase in retained earnings	45,900
	Dividends declared	14,250
	Plus decrease in dividends payable	4,500
	Cash paid for dividends	$ 18,750
(4)B	Sales	$ 446,100
	Add decrease in accounts receivable	5,700
	Cash received from customers	$451,800
(5)B	Cost of goods sold	$ 222,300
	Plus increase in merchandise inventory	9,525
	Purchases	231,825
	Plus decrease in accounts payable	4,950
	Cash paid for merchandise	$236,775
(6)B	Other operating expenses	$ 120,300
	Plus increase in prepaid expenses	1,950
	Cash paid for other operating expenses	$122,250
(7)B	Income taxes expense	$ 13,725
	Less increase in income taxes payable	(675)
	Cash paid for income taxes	$ 13,050

* Supporting T-account analysis for part 1 follows:

Equipment				
Bal., Dec. 31, 2008	146,700			
Cash purchase	10,500	Sale		21,375
Bal., Dec. 31, 2009	135,825			

Accumulated Depreciation—Equipment				
			Bal., Dec. 31, 2008	47,550
Sale	11,100		Depr. expense	25,500
			Bal., Dec. 31, 2009	61,950

UMLAUF COMPANY
Statement of Cash Flows (Indirect Method)
For Year Ended December 31, 2009

Cash flows from operating activities		
Net income	$60,150	
Adjustments to reconcile net income to net cash provided by operating activities		
Decrease in accounts receivable	5,700	
Increase in merchandise inventory	(9,525)	
Increase in prepaid expenses	(1,950)	
Decrease in accounts payable	(4,950)	
Increase in income taxes payable	675	
Depreciation expense	25,500	
Loss on sale of plant assets	3,300	
Loss on retirement of bonds	825	
Net cash provided by operating activities		$79,725

[continued on next page]

[continued from previous page]

Cash flows from investing activities		
Cash received from sale of equipment	6,975	
Cash paid for equipment	(10,500)	
Net cash used in investing activities		(3,525)
Cash flows from financing activities		
Cash paid to retire bonds payable	(38,325)	
Cash paid for dividends	(18,750)	
Net cash used in financing activities		(57,075)
Net increase in cash		$19,125
Cash balance at prior year-end		23,925
Cash balance at current year-end		$43,050

UMLAUF COMPANY
Statement of Cash Flows (Direct Method)
For Year Ended December 31, 2009

Cash flows from operating activities		
Cash received from customers	$451,800	
Cash paid for merchandise	(236,775)	
Cash paid for other operating expenses	(122,250)	
Cash paid for income taxes	(13,050)	
Net cash provided by operating activities		$79,725
Cash flows from investing activities		
Cash received from sale of equipment	6,975	
Cash paid for equipment	(10,500)	
Net cash used in investing activities		(3,525)
Cash flows from financing activities		
Cash paid to retire bonds payable	(38,325)	
Cash paid for dividends	(18,750)	
Net cash used in financing activities		(57,075)
Net increase in cash		$19,125
Cash balance at prior year-end		23,925
Cash balance at current year-end		$43,050

APPENDIX

Spreadsheet Preparation of the Statement of Cash Flows

16A

This appendix explains how to use a spreadsheet to prepare the statement of cash flows under the indirect method.

Preparing the Indirect Method Spreadsheet

Analyzing noncash accounts can be challenging when a company has a large number of accounts and many operating, investing, and financing transactions. A *spreadsheet*, also called *work sheet* or *working paper*, can help us organize the information needed to prepare a statement of cash flows. A spreadsheet also makes it easier to check the accuracy of our work. To illustrate, we return to the comparative balance sheets and income statement shown in Exhibit 16.10. We use the following identifying letters *a* through *g* to code

P4 Illustrate use of a spreadsheet to prepare a statement of cash flows.

changes in accounts, and letters *h* through *m* for additional information, to prepare the statement of cash flows:

  a. Net income is $38,000.
  b. Accounts receivable increase by $20,000.
  c. Merchandise inventory increases by $14,000.
  d. Prepaid expenses increase by $2,000.
  e. Accounts payable decrease by $5,000.
  f. Interest payable decreases by $1,000.
  g. Income taxes payable increase by $10,000.
  h. Depreciation expense is $24,000.
  i. Plant assets costing $30,000 with accumulated depreciation of $12,000 are sold for $12,000 cash. This yields a loss on sale of assets of $6,000.
  j. Notes with a book value of $34,000 are retired with a cash payment of $18,000, yielding a $16,000 gain on retirement.
  k. Plant assets costing $70,000 are purchased with a cash payment of $10,000 and an issuance of notes payable for $60,000.
  l. Issued 3,000 shares of common stock for $15,000 cash.
  m. Paid cash dividends of $14,000.

Exhibit 16A.1 shows the indirect method spreadsheet for Genesis. We enter both beginning and ending balance sheet amounts on the spreadsheet. We also enter information in the Analysis of Changes columns (keyed to the additional information items *a* through *m*) to explain changes in the accounts and determine the cash flows for operating, investing, and financing activities. Information about noncash investing and financing activities is reported near the bottom.

Entering the Analysis of Changes on the Spreadsheet

The following sequence of procedures is used to complete the spreadsheet after the beginning and ending balances of the balance sheet accounts are entered:

① Enter net income as the first item in the Statement of Cash Flows section for computing operating cash inflow (debit) and as a credit to Retained Earnings.

② In the Statement of Cash Flows section, adjustments to net income are entered as debits if they increase cash flows and as credits if they decrease cash flows. Applying this same rule, adjust net income for the change in each noncash current asset and current liability account related to operating activities. For each adjustment to net income, the offsetting debit or credit must help reconcile the beginning and ending balances of a current asset or current liability account.

③ Enter adjustments to net income for income statement items not providing or using cash in the period. For each adjustment, the offsetting debit or credit must help reconcile a noncash balance sheet account.

④ Adjust net income to eliminate any gains or losses from investing and financing activities. Because the cash from a gain must be excluded from operating activities, the gain is entered as a credit in the operating activities section. Losses are entered as debits. For each adjustment, the related debit and/or credit must help reconcile balance sheet accounts and involve reconstructed entries to show the cash flow from investing or financing activities.

⑤ After reviewing any unreconciled balance sheet accounts and related information, enter the remaining reconciling entries for investing and financing activities. Examples are purchases of plant assets, issuances of long-term debt, stock issuances, and dividend payments. Some of these may require entries in the noncash investing and financing section of the spreadsheet (reconciled).

⑥ Check accuracy by totaling the Analysis of Changes columns and by determining that the change in each balance sheet account has been explained (reconciled).

We illustrate these steps in Exhibit 16A.1 for Genesis:

Point: Analysis of the changes on the spreadsheet are summarized here:

1. Cash flows from operating activities generally affect net income, current assets, and current liabilities.

2. Cash flows from investing activities generally affect noncurrent asset accounts.

3. Cash flows from financing activities generally affect noncurrent liability and equity accounts.

Step	Entries
①	(*a*)
②	(*b*) through (*g*)
③	(*h*)
④	(*i*) through (*j*)
⑤	(*k*) through (*m*)

EXHIBIT 16A.1

Spreadsheet for Preparing
Statement of Cash Flows—
Indirect Method

File Edit View Insert Format Tools Data Accounting Window Help

GENESIS
Spreadsheet for Statement of Cash Flows—Indirect Method
For Year Ended December 31, 2009

	Dec. 31, 2008		Analysis of Changes Debit		Credit	Dec. 31, 2009
Balance Sheet—Debits						
Cash	$ 12,000					$ 17,000
Accounts receivable	40,000	(b)	$ 20,000			60,000
Merchandise inventory	70,000	(c)	14,000			84,000
Prepaid expenses	4,000	(d)	2,000			6,000
Plant assets	210,000	(k1)	70,000	(i)	$ 30,000	250,000
	$336,000					$417,000
Balance Sheet—Credits						
Accumulated depreciation	$ 48,000	(i)	12,000	(h)	24,000	$ 60,000
Accounts payable	40,000	(e)	5,000			35,000
Interest payable	4,000	(f)	1,000			3,000
Income taxes payable	12,000			(g)	10,000	22,000
Notes payable	64,000	(j)	34,000	(k2)	60,000	90,000
Common stock, $5 par value	80,000			(l)	15,000	95,000
Retained earnings	88,000	(m)	14,000	(a)	38,000	112,000
	$336,000					$417,000
Statement of Cash Flows						
Operating activities						
Net income		(a)	38,000			
Increase in accounts receivable				(b)	20,000	
Increase in merchandise inventory				(c)	14,000	
Increase in prepaid expenses				(d)	2,000	
Decrease in accounts payable				(e)	5,000	
Decrease in interest payable				(f)	1,000	
Increase in income taxes payable		(g)	10,000			
Depreciation expense		(h)	24,000			
Loss on sale of plant assets		(i)	6,000			
Gain on retirement of notes				(j)	16,000	
Investing activities						
Receipts from sale of plant assets		(i)	12,000			
Payment for purchase of plant assets				(k1)	10,000	
Financing activities						
Payment to retire notes				(j)	18,000	
Receipts from issuing stock		(l)	15,000			
Payment of cash dividends				(m)	14,000	
Noncash Investing and Financing Activities						
Purchase of plant assets with notes		(k2)	60,000	(k1)	60,000	
			$337,000		$337,000	

Sheet1 / Sheet2 / Sheet3 /

Since adjustments *i, j,* and *k* are more challenging, we show them in the following debit and credit format.
These entries are for purposes of our understanding; they are *not* the entries actually made in the journals.
Changes in the Cash account are identified as sources or uses of cash.

i.	Loss from sale of plant assets	6,000	
	Accumulated depreciation	12,000	
	Receipt from sale of plant assets **(source of cash)**	12,000	
	Plant assets		30,000
	To describe sale of plant assets.		

[continued on next page]

[continued from previous page]

j.	Notes payable....................................		34,000	
	Payments to retire notes **(use of cash)**			18,000
	Gain on retirement of notes.........................			16,000
	To describe retirement of notes.			
k1.	Plant assets......................................		70,000	
	Payment to purchase plant assets **(use of cash)**			10,000
	Purchase of plant assets financed by notes...............			60,000
	To describe purchase of plant assets.			
k2.	Purchase of plant assets financed by notes		60,000	
	Notes payable			60,000
	To issue notes for purchase of assets.			

APPENDIX

16B Direct Method of Reporting Operating Cash Flows

P5   Compute cash flows from operating activities using the direct method.

We compute cash flows from operating activities under the direct method by adjusting accrual-based income statement items to the cash basis. The usual approach is to adjust income statement accounts related to operating activities for changes in their related balance sheet accounts as follows:

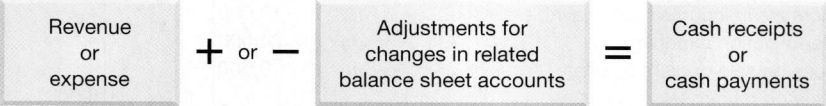

The framework for reporting cash receipts and cash payments for the operating section of the cash flow statement under the direct method is shown in Exhibit 16B.1. We consider cash receipts first and then cash payments.

EXHIBIT 16B.1

Major Classes of Operating Cash Flows

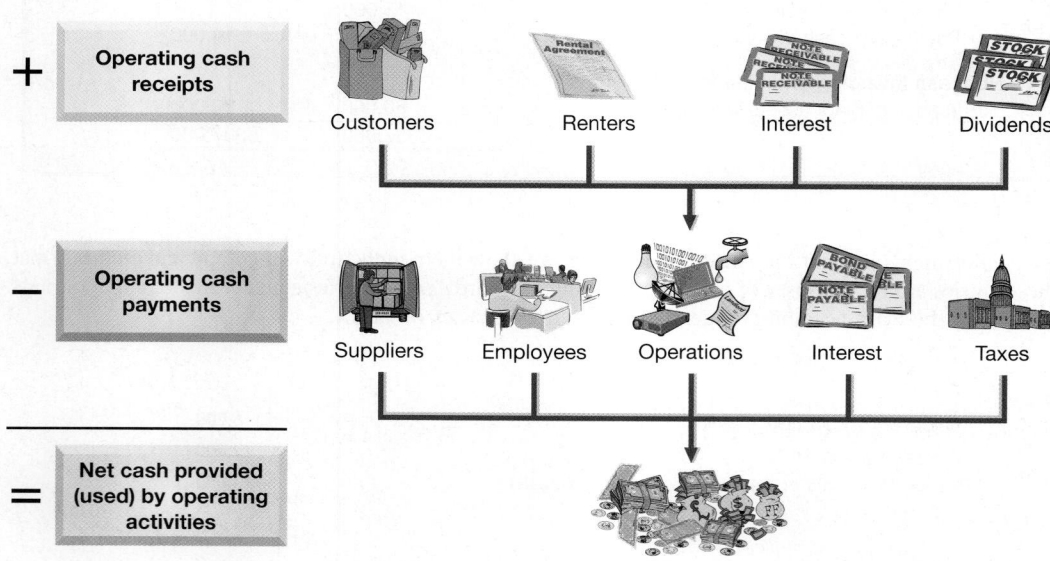

Operating Cash Receipts

A review of Exhibit 16.10 and the additional information reported by Genesis suggests only one potential cash receipt: sales to customers. This section, therefore, starts with sales to customers as reported on the income statement and then adjusts it as necessary to obtain cash received from customers to report on the statement of cash flows.

Cash Received from Customers If all sales are for cash, the amount received from customers equals the sales reported on the income statement. When some or all sales are on account, however, we must adjust the amount of sales for the change in Accounts Receivable. It is often helpful to use *account analysis* to do this. This usually involves setting up a T-account and reconstructing its major entries, with emphasis on cash receipts and payments. To illustrate, we use a T-account that includes accounts receivable balances for Genesis on December 31, 2008 and 2009. The beginning balance is $40,000 and the ending balance is $60,000. Next, the income statement shows sales of $590,000, which we enter on the debit side of this account. We now can reconstruct the Accounts Receivable account to determine the amount of cash received from customers as follows:

Point: An accounts receivable increase implies that cash received from customers is less than sales (the converse is also true).

Accounts Receivable			
Bal., Dec. 31, 2008	40,000		
Sales	590,000	Cash receipts =	570,000
Bal., Dec. 31, 2009	60,000		

This T-account shows that the Accounts Receivable balance begins at $40,000 and increases to $630,000 from sales of $590,000, yet its ending balance is only $60,000. This implies that cash receipts from customers are $570,000, computed as $40,000 + $590,000 − [?] = $60,000. This computation can be rearranged to express cash received as equal to sales of $590,000 minus a $20,000 increase in accounts receivable. This computation is summarized as a general rule in Exhibit 16B.2. The statement of cash flows in Exhibit 16.7 reports the $570,000 cash received from customers as a cash inflow from operating activities.

Example: If the ending balance of accounts receivable is $20,000 (instead of $60,000), what is cash received from customers? *Answer:* $610,000

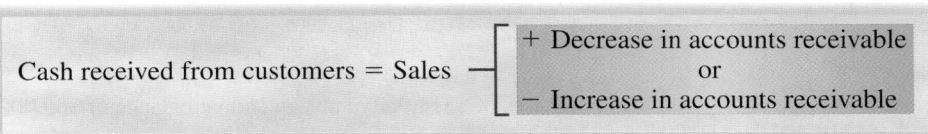

$$\text{Cash received from customers} = \text{Sales} - \left[\begin{array}{c} + \text{ Decrease in accounts receivable} \\ \text{or} \\ - \text{ Increase in accounts receivable} \end{array} \right.$$

EXHIBIT 16B.2

Formula to Compute Cash Received from Customers— Direct Method

Other Cash Receipts While Genesis's cash receipts are limited to collections from customers, we often see other types of cash receipts, most commonly cash receipts involving rent, interest, and dividends. We compute cash received from these items by subtracting an increase in their respective receivable or adding a decrease. For instance, if rent receivable increases in the period, cash received from renters is less than rent revenue reported on the income statement. If rent receivable decreases, cash received is more than reported rent revenue. The same logic applies to interest and dividends. The formulas for these computations are summarized later in this appendix.

Point: Net income is measured using accrual accounting. Cash flows from operations are measured using cash basis accounting.

Operating Cash Payments

A review of Exhibit 16.10 and the additional Genesis information shows four operating expenses: cost of goods sold; wages and other operating expenses; interest expense; and taxes expense. We analyze each expense to compute its cash amounts for the statement of cash flows. (We then examine depreciation and the other losses and gains.)

Cash Paid for Merchandise We compute cash paid for merchandise by analyzing both cost of goods sold and merchandise inventory. If all merchandise purchases are for cash and the ending balance of Merchandise Inventory is unchanged from the beginning balance, the amount of cash paid for merchandise equals cost of goods sold—an uncommon situation. Instead, there normally is some change in the Merchandise Inventory balance. Also, some or all merchandise purchases are often made on credit, and this yields changes in the Accounts Payable balance. When the balances of both Merchandise Inventory and Accounts Payable change, we must adjust the cost of goods sold for changes in both accounts to compute cash paid for merchandise. This is a two-step adjustment.

First, we use the change in the account balance of Merchandise Inventory, along with the cost of goods sold amount, to compute cost of purchases for the period. An increase in merchandise inventory implies that we bought more than we sold, and we add this inventory increase to cost of goods sold to compute cost of purchases. A decrease in merchandise inventory implies that we bought less than we sold, and we subtract the inventory decrease from cost of goods sold to compute purchases. We illustrate the *first step* by reconstructing the Merchandise Inventory account of Genesis:

Merchandise Inventory			
Bal., Dec. 31, 2008	70,000		
Purchases =	314,000	Cost of goods sold	300,000
Bal., Dec. 31, 2009	84,000		

The beginning balance is $70,000, and the ending balance is $84,000. The income statement shows that cost of goods sold is $300,000, which we enter on the credit side of this account. With this information, we determine the amount for cost of purchases to be $314,000. This computation can be rearranged to express cost of purchases as equal to cost of goods sold of $300,000 plus the $14,000 increase in inventory.

The second step uses the change in the balance of Accounts Payable, and the amount of cost of purchases, to compute cash paid for merchandise. A decrease in accounts payable implies that we paid for more goods than we acquired this period, and we would then add the accounts payable decrease to cost of purchases to compute cash paid for merchandise. An increase in accounts payable implies that we paid for less than the amount of goods acquired, and we would subtract the accounts payable increase from purchases to compute cash paid for merchandise. The *second step* is applied to Genesis by reconstructing its Accounts Payable account:

Accounts Payable			
		Bal., Dec. 31, 2008	40,000
Cash payments =	319,000	Purchases	314,000
		Bal., Dec. 31, 2009	35,000

Example: If the ending balances of Inventory and Accounts Payable are $60,000 and $50,000, respectively (instead of $84,000 and $35,000), what is cash paid for merchandise? *Answer:* $280,000

Its beginning balance of $40,000 plus purchases of $314,000 minus an ending balance of $35,000 yields cash paid of $319,000 (or $40,000 + $314,000 − [?] = $35,000). Alternatively, we can express cash paid for merchandise as equal to purchases of $314,000 plus the $5,000 decrease in accounts payable. The $319,000 cash paid for merchandise is reported on the statement of cash flows in Exhibit 16.7 as a cash outflow under operating activities.

We summarize this two-step adjustment to cost of goods sold to compute cash paid for merchandise inventory in Exhibit 16B.3.

EXHIBIT 16B.3

Two Steps to Compute Cash Paid for Merchandise—Direct Method

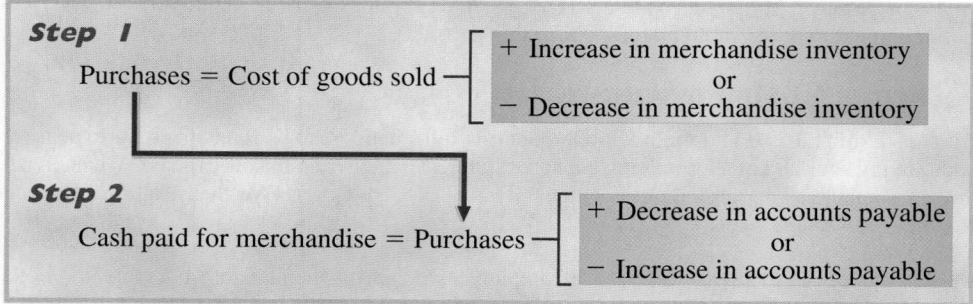

Cash Paid for Wages and Operating Expenses (Excluding Depreciation)
The income statement of Genesis shows wages and other operating expenses of $216,000 (see Exhibit 16.10). To compute cash paid for wages and other operating expenses, we adjust this amount for any changes in their related balance sheet accounts. We begin by looking for any prepaid expenses and accrued liabilities related to wages and other operating expenses in the balance sheets of Genesis in

Exhibit 16.10. The balance sheets show prepaid expenses but no accrued liabilities. Thus, the adjustment is limited to the change in prepaid expenses. The amount of adjustment is computed by assuming that all cash paid for wages and other operating expenses is initially debited to Prepaid Expenses. This assumption allows us to reconstruct the Prepaid Expenses account:

Prepaid Expenses			
Bal., Dec. 31, 2008	4,000		
Cash payments =	218,000	Wages and other operating exp.	216,000
Bal., Dec. 31, 2009	6,000		

Prepaid Expenses increase by $2,000 in the period, meaning that cash paid for wages and other operating expenses exceeds the reported expense by $2,000. Alternatively, we can express cash paid for wages and other operating expenses as equal to its reported expenses of $216,000 plus the $2,000 increase in prepaid expenses.[1]

Point: A decrease in prepaid expenses implies that reported expenses include an amount(s) that did not require a cash outflow in the period.

Exhibit 16B.4 summarizes the adjustments to wages (including salaries) and other operating expenses. The Genesis balance sheet did not report accrued liabilities, but we include them in the formula to explain the adjustment to cash when they do exist. A decrease in accrued liabilities implies that we paid cash for more goods or services than received this period, so we add the decrease in accrued liabilities to the expense amount to obtain cash paid for these goods or services. An increase in accrued liabilities implies that we paid cash for less than what was acquired, so we subtract this increase in accrued liabilities from the expense amount to get cash paid.

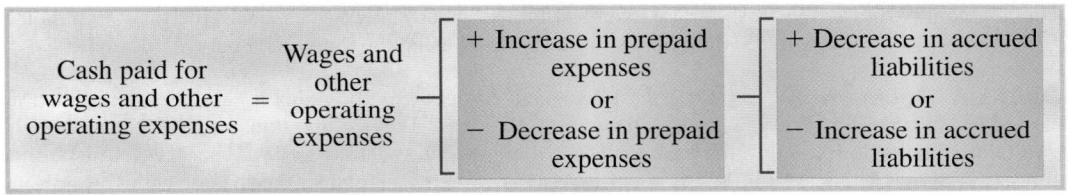

EXHIBIT 16B.4

Formula to Compute Cash Paid for Wages and Operating Expenses—Direct Method

Cash Paid for Interest and Income Taxes   Computing operating cash flows for interest and taxes is similar to that for operating expenses. Both require adjustments to their amounts reported on the income statement for changes in their related balance sheet accounts. We begin with the Genesis income statement showing interest expense of $7,000 and income taxes expense of $15,000. To compute the cash paid, we adjust interest expense for the change in interest payable and then the income taxes expense for the change in income taxes payable. These computations involve reconstructing both liability accounts:

Interest Payable			
		Bal., Dec. 31, 2008	4,000
Cash paid for interest =	8,000	Interest expense	7,000
		Bal., Dec. 31, 2009	3,000

Income Taxes Payable			
		Bal., Dec. 31, 2008	12,000
Cash paid for taxes =	5,000	Income taxes expense	15,000
		Bal., Dec. 31, 2009	22,000

These accounts reveal cash paid for interest of $8,000 and cash paid for income taxes of $5,000. The formulas to compute these amounts are in Exhibit 16B.5. Both of these cash payments are reported as operating cash outflows on the statement of cash flows in Exhibit 16.7.

---

[1] The assumption that all cash payments for wages and operating expenses are initially debited to Prepaid Expenses is not necessary for our analysis to hold. If cash payments are debited directly to the expense account, the total amount of cash paid for wages and other operating expenses still equals the $216,000 expense plus the $2,000 increase in Prepaid Expenses (which arise from end-of-period adjusting entries).

EXHIBIT 16B.5

Formulas to Compute Cash
Paid for Both Interest and
Taxes—Direct Method

$$\text{Cash paid for interest} = \text{Interest expense} \begin{cases} + \text{Decrease in interest payable} \\ \text{or} \\ - \text{Increase in interest payable} \end{cases}$$

$$\text{Cash paid for taxes} = \text{Income taxes expenses} \begin{cases} + \text{Decrease in income taxes payable} \\ \text{or} \\ - \text{Increase in income taxes payable} \end{cases}$$

Analysis of Additional Expenses, Gains, and Losses Genesis has three additional items reported on its income statement: depreciation, loss on sale of assets, and gain on retirement of debt. We must consider each for its potential cash effects.

Depreciation Expense Depreciation expense is $24,000. It is often called a *noncash expense* because depreciation has no cash flows. Depreciation expense is an allocation of an asset's depreciable cost. The cash outflow with a plant asset is reported as part of investing activities when it is paid for. Thus, depreciation expense is *never* reported on a statement of cash flows using the direct method; nor is depletion or amortization expense.

Loss on Sale of Assets Sales of assets frequently result in gains and losses reported as part of net income, but the amount of recorded gain or loss does *not* reflect any cash flows in these transactions. Asset sales result in cash inflow equal to the cash amount received, regardless of whether the asset was sold at a gain or a loss. This cash inflow is reported under investing activities. Thus, the loss or gain on a sale of assets is *never* reported on a statement of cash flows using the direct method.

Gain on Retirement of Debt Retirement of debt usually yields a gain or loss reported as part of net income, but that gain or loss does *not* reflect cash flow in this transaction. Debt retirement results in cash outflow equal to the cash paid to settle the debt, regardless of whether the debt is retired at a gain or loss. This cash outflow is reported under financing activities; the loss or gain from retirement of debt is *never* reported on a statement of cash flows using the direct method.

Summary of Adjustments for Direct Method

Exhibit 16B.6 summarizes common adjustments for net income to yield net cash provided (used) by operating activities under the direct method.

Point: The direct method is usually viewed as *user friendly* because less accounting knowledge is required to understand and use it.

EXHIBIT 16B.6

Summary of Selected
Adjustments for Direct Method

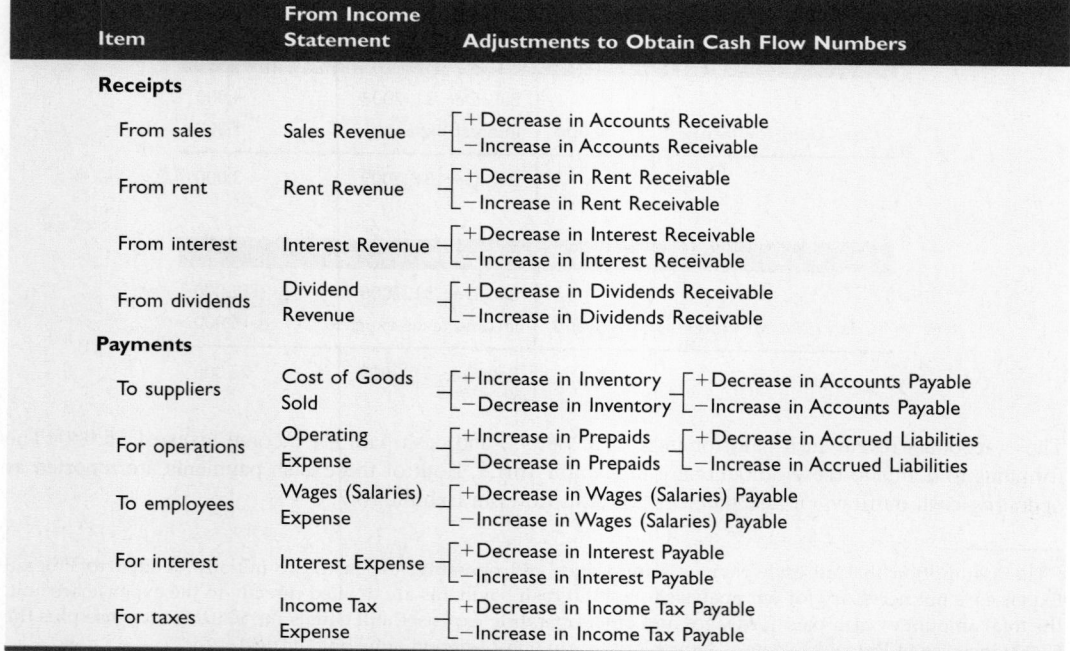

Item	From Income Statement	Adjustments to Obtain Cash Flow Numbers	
Receipts			
From sales	Sales Revenue	+Decrease in Accounts Receivable −Increase in Accounts Receivable	
From rent	Rent Revenue	+Decrease in Rent Receivable −Increase in Rent Receivable	
From interest	Interest Revenue	+Decrease in Interest Receivable −Increase in Interest Receivable	
From dividends	Dividend Revenue	+Decrease in Dividends Receivable −Increase in Dividends Receivable	
Payments			
To suppliers	Cost of Goods Sold	+Increase in Inventory −Decrease in Inventory	+Decrease in Accounts Payable −Increase in Accounts Payable
For operations	Operating Expense	+Increase in Prepaids −Decrease in Prepaids	+Decrease in Accrued Liabilities −Increase in Accrued Liabilities
To employees	Wages (Salaries) Expense	+Decrease in Wages (Salaries) Payable −Increase in Wages (Salaries) Payable	
For interest	Interest Expense	+Decrease in Interest Payable −Increase in Interest Payable	
For taxes	Income Tax Expense	+Decrease in Income Tax Payable −Increase in Income Tax Payable	

Direct Method Format of Operating Activities Section

Exhibit 16.7 shows the Genesis statement of cash flows using the direct method. Major items of cash inflows and cash outflows are listed separately in the operating activities section. The format requires that operating cash outflows be subtracted from operating cash inflows to get net cash provided (used) by operating activities. The FASB recommends that the operating activities section of the statement of cash flows be reported using the direct method, which is considered more useful to financial statement users. *However, the FASB requires a reconciliation of net income to net cash provided (used) by operating activities when the direct method is used* (which can be reported in the notes). This reconciliation is similar to preparation of the operating activities section of the statement of cash flows using the indirect method.

Point: Some preparers argue that it is easier to prepare a statement of cash flows using the indirect method. This likely explains its greater frequency in financial statements.

Decision Insight

IFRSs Like U.S. GAAP, IFRSs allow cash flows from operating activities to be reported using either the indirect method or the direct method.

Quick Check

Answers—p. 658

8. Net sales in a period are $590,000, beginning accounts receivable are $120,000, and ending accounts receivable are $90,000. What cash amount is collected from customers in the period?

9. The Merchandise Inventory account balance decreases in the period from a beginning balance of $32,000 to an ending balance of $28,000. Cost of goods sold for the period is $168,000. If the Accounts Payable balance increases $2,400 in the period, what is the cash amount paid for merchandise inventory?

10. This period's wages and other operating expenses total $112,000. Beginning-of-period prepaid expenses totaled $1,200, and its ending balance is $4,200. There were no beginning-of-period accrued liabilities, but end-of-period wages payable equal $5,600. How much cash is paid for wages and other operating expenses?

Summary

C1 Explain the purpose and importance of cash flow information. The main purpose of the statement of cash flows is to report the major cash receipts and cash payments for a period. This includes identifying cash flows as relating to operating, investing, or financing activities. Most business decisions involve evaluating activities that provide or use cash.

C2 Distinguish between operating, investing, and financing activities. Operating activities include transactions and events that determine net income. Investing activities include transactions and events that mainly affect long-term assets. Financing activities include transactions and events that mainly affect long-term liabilities and equity.

C3 Identify and disclose noncash investing and financing activities. Noncash investing and financing activities must be disclosed in either a note or a separate schedule to the statement of cash flows. Examples are the retirement of debt by issuing equity and the exchange of a note payable for plant assets.

C4 Describe the format of the statement of cash flows. The statement of cash flows separates cash receipts and cash payments into operating, investing, or financing activities.

A1 Analyze the statement of cash flows. To understand and predict cash flows, users stress identification of the sources and uses of cash flows by operating, investing, and financing activities. Emphasis is on operating cash flows since they derive from continuing operations.

A2 Compute and apply the cash flow on total assets ratio. The cash flow on total assets ratio is defined as operating cash flows divided by average total assets. Analysis of current and past values for this ratio can reflect a company's ability to yield regular and positive cash flows. It is also viewed as a measure of earnings quality.

P1 Prepare a statement of cash flows. Preparation of a statement of cash flows involves five steps: (1) Compute the net increase or decrease in cash; (2) compute net cash provided or used by operating activities (*using either the direct or indirect method*); (3) compute net cash provided or used by investing activities; (4) compute net cash provided or used by financing activities; and (5) report the beginning and ending cash balance and prove that it is explained by net cash flows. Noncash investing and financing activities are also disclosed.

P2 Compute cash flows from operating activities using the indirect method. The indirect method for reporting net cash provided or used by operating activities starts with net income and then adjusts it for three items: (1) changes in noncash current assets and current liabilities related to operating activities, (2) revenues and expenses not providing or using cash, and (3) gains and losses from investing and financing activities.

P3 Determine cash flows from both investing and financing activities. Cash flows from both investing and financing activities are determined by identifying the cash flow effects of transactions and events affecting each balance sheet account related to these activities. All cash flows from these activities are identified when we can explain changes in these accounts from the beginning to the end of the period.

P4^A Illustrate use of a spreadsheet to prepare a statement of cash flows. A spreadsheet is a useful tool in preparing a statement of cash flows. Six key steps (see Appendix 16A) are applied when using the spreadsheet to prepare the statement.

P5^B Compute cash flows from operating activities using the direct method. The direct method for reporting net cash provided or used by operating activities lists major operating cash inflows less cash outflows to yield net cash inflow or outflow from operations.

Guidance Answers to **Decision Maker**

Entrepreneur Several factors might explain an increase in net cash flows when a net loss is reported, including (1) early recognition of expenses relative to revenues generated (such as research and development), (2) cash advances on long-term sales contracts not yet recognized in income, (3) issuances of debt or equity for cash to finance expansion, (4) cash sale of assets, (5) delay of cash payments, and (6) cash prepayment on sales. Analysis needs to focus on the components of both the net loss and the net cash flows and their implications for future performance.

Reporter Your initial reaction based on the company's $600,000 loss with a $550,000 decrease in net cash flows is not positive. However, closer scrutiny reveals a more positive picture of this company's performance. Cash flow from operating activities is $650,000, computed as [?] − $850,000 − $350,000 = $(550,000). You also note that net income *before* the extraordinary loss is $330,000, computed as [?] − $930,000 = $(600,000).

Guidance Answers to **Quick Checks**

1. No to both. The statement of cash flows reports changes in the sum of cash plus cash equivalents. It does not report transfers between cash and cash equivalents.
2. The three categories of cash inflows and outflows are operating activities, investing activities, and financing activities.
3. **a.** Investing **c.** Financing **e.** Operating
   b. Operating **d.** Operating **f.** Financing
4. $74,900 + $4,600 − $11,700 − $1,000 + $3,400 = $70,200
5. Expenses such as depreciation and amortization do not require current cash outflows. Therefore, adding these expenses back to

net income eliminates these noncash items from the net income number, converting it to a cash basis.
6. A gain on the sale of plant assets is subtracted from net income because a sale of plant assets is not an operating activity; it is an investing activity for the amount of cash received from its sale. Also, such a gain yields no cash effects.
7. $80,000 − $30,000 − $10,000 = $40,000 cash receipt. The $40,000 cash receipt is reported as an investing activity.
8. $590,000 + ($120,000 − $90,000) = $620,000
9. $168,000 − ($32,000 − $28,000) − $2,400 = $161,600
10. $112,000 + ($4,200 − $1,200) − $5,600 = $109,400

Key Terms   mhhe.com/wildFAP19e

Key Terms are available at the book's Website for learning and testing in an online Flashcard Format.

Cash flow on total assets (p. 646)
Direct method (p. 634)
Financing activities (p. 630)
Indirect method (p. 634)
Investing activities (p. 630)
Operating activities (p. 629)
Statement of cash flows (p. 628)

Multiple Choice Quiz   Answers on p. 677   mhhe.com/wildFAP19e

Additional Quiz Questions are available at the book's Website.

1. A company uses the indirect method to determine its cash flows from operating activities. Use the following information to determine its net cash provided or used by operating activities.

Net income	$15,200
Depreciation expense	10,000
Cash payment on note payable	8,000
Gain on sale of land	3,000
Increase in inventory	1,500
Increase in accounts payable	2,850

Quiz16

a. $23,550 used by operating activities
b. $23,550 provided by operating activities
c. $15,550 provided by operating activities
d. $42,400 provided by operating activities
e. $20,850 provided by operating activities

2. A machine with a cost of $175,000 and accumulated depreciation of $94,000 is sold for $87,000 cash. The amount reported as a source of cash under cash flows from investing activities is
   a. $81,000.
   b. $6,000.
   c. $87,000.
   d. Zero; this is a financing activity.
   e. Zero; this is an operating activity.

3. A company settles a long-term note payable plus interest by paying $68,000 cash toward the principal amount and $5,440 cash for interest. The amount reported as a use of cash under cash flows from financing activities is
   a. Zero; this is an investing activity.
   b. Zero; this is an operating activity.
   c. $73,440.
   d. $68,000.
   e. $5,440.

4. The following information is available regarding a company's annual salaries and wages. What amount of cash is paid for salaries and wages?

Salaries and wages expense	$255,000
Salaries and wages payable, prior year-end	8,200
Salaries and wages payable, current year-end	10,900

a. $252,300
b. $257,700
c. $255,000
d. $274,100
e. $235,900

5. The following information is available for a company. What amount of cash is paid for merchandise for the current year?

Cost of goods sold	$545,000
Merchandise inventory, prior year-end	105,000
Merchandise inventory, current year-end	112,000
Accounts payable, prior year-end	98,500
Accounts payable, current year-end	101,300

a. $545,000
b. $554,800
c. $540,800
d. $535,200
e. $549,200

Superscript letter ^{A}(^{B}) denotes assignments based on Appendix 16A (16B).

Discussion Questions

1. What is the reporting purpose of the statement of cash flows? Identify at least two questions that this statement can answer.
2. Describe the direct method of reporting cash flows from operating activities.
3. When a statement of cash flows is prepared using the direct method, what are some of the operating cash flows?
4. Describe the indirect method of reporting cash flows from operating activities.
5. What are some investing activities reported on the statement of cash flows?
6. What are some financing activities reported on the statement of cash flows?
7. Where on the statement of cash flows is the payment of cash dividends reported?
8. ♟ Assume that a company purchases land for $100,000, paying $20,000 cash and borrowing the remainder with a long-term note payable. How should this transaction be reported on a statement of cash flows?
9. ♟ On June 3, a company borrows $50,000 cash by giving its bank a 160-day, interest-bearing note. On the statement of cash flows, where should this be reported?

10. ♟ If a company reports positive net income for the year, can it also show a net cash outflow from operating activities? Explain.
11. ♟ Is depreciation a source of cash flow?
12. ♟ Refer to **Best Buy**'s statement of cash flows in Appendix A. (a) Which method is used to compute its net cash provided by operating activities? (b) While its balance sheet shows an increase in receivables from fiscal years 2006 to 2007, why is this increase in receivables subtracted when computing net cash provided by operating activities for the year ended March 3, 2007?
13. ♟ Refer to **Circuit City**'s statement of cash flows in Appendix A. What are its cash flows from financing activities for the year ended February 28, 2007? List items and amounts.
14. ♟ Refer to **RadioShack**'s statement of cash flows in Appendix A. List its cash flows from operating activities, investing activities, and financing activities.
15. ♟ Refer to **Apple**'s statement of cash flows in Appendix A. What investing activities result in cash outflows for the year ended September 30, 2006? List items and amounts.

♟ *Denotes Discussion Questions that involve decision making.*

Available with McGraw-Hill's Homework Manager

McGraw-Hill's
HOMEWORK
MANAGER®

QUICK STUDY

QS 16-1
Statement of cash flows

C1 C2 C3

The statement of cash flows is one of the four primary financial statements.
1. Describe the content and layout of a statement of cash flows, including its three sections.
2. List at least three transactions classified as investing activities in a statement of cash flows.
3. List at least three transactions classified as financing activities in a statement of cash flows.
4. List at least three transactions classified as significant noncash financing and investing activities in the statement of cash flows.

QS 16-2
Transaction classification by activity

C2

Classify the following cash flows as operating, investing, or financing activities.
1. Sold long-term investments for cash.
2. Received cash payments from customers.
3. Paid cash for wages and salaries.
4. Purchased inventories for cash.
5. Paid cash dividends.
6. Issued common stock for cash.
7. Received cash interest on a note.
8. Paid cash interest on outstanding notes.
9. Received cash from sale of land at a loss.
10. Paid cash for property taxes on building.

QS 16-3
Computing cash from operations (indirect)

P2

Use the following information to determine this company's cash flows from operating activities using the indirect method.

LOLLAND COMPANY
Selected Balance Sheet Information
December 31, 2009 and 2008

	2009	2008
Current assets		
Cash	$169,300	$ 53,600
Accounts receivable	50,000	64,000
Inventory	120,000	108,200
Current liabilities		
Accounts payable	60,800	51,400
Income taxes payable	4,100	4,400

LOLLAND COMPANY
Income Statement
For Year Ended December 31, 2009

Sales		$1,030,000
Cost of goods sold		663,200
Gross profit		366,800
Operating expenses		
Depreciation expense	$ 72,000	
Other expenses	243,000	315,000
Income before taxes		51,800
Income taxes expense		15,400
Net income		$ 36,400

QS 16-4
Computing cash from asset sales

P3

The following selected information is from Manning Company's comparative balance sheets.

At December 31	2009	2008
Furniture	$ 264,000	$ 369,000
Accumulated depreciation—Furniture	(174,400)	(221,400)

The income statement reports depreciation expense for the year of $36,000. Also, furniture costing $105,000 was sold for its book value. Compute the cash received from the sale of furniture.

QS 16-5
Computing financing cash flows

P3

The following selected information is from the Tanner Company's comparative balance sheets.

At December 31	2009	2008
Common stock, $10 par value	$ 210,000	$200,000
Paid-in capital in excess of par	1,134,000	684,000
Retained earnings	627,000	575,000

The company's net income for the year ended December 31, 2009, was $96,000.
1. Compute the cash received from the sale of its common stock during 2009.
2. Compute the cash paid for dividends during 2009.

Use the following balance sheets and income statement to answer QS 16-6 through QS 16-11.

Use the indirect method to prepare the cash provided or used from operating activities section only of the statement of cash flows for this company.

QS 16-6
Computing cash from operations (indirect)   P2

AMMONS, INC.
Comparative Balance Sheets
December 31, 2009

	2009	2008
Assets		
Cash	$189,600	$ 48,000
Accounts receivable, net	82,000	102,000
Inventory	171,600	191,600
Prepaid expenses	10,800	8,400
Furniture	218,000	238,000
Accum. depreciation—Furniture	(34,000)	(18,000)
Total assets	$638,000	$570,000
Liabilities and Equity		
Accounts payable	$ 30,000	$ 42,000
Wages payable	18,000	10,000
Income taxes payable	2,800	5,200
Notes payable (long-term)	58,000	138,000
Common stock, $5 par value	458,000	358,000
Retained earnings	71,200	16,800
Total liabilities and equity	$638,000	$570,000

AMMONS, INC.
Income Statement
For Year Ended December 31, 2009

Sales		$976,000
Cost of goods sold		628,000
Gross profit		348,000
Operating expenses		
Depreciation expense	$ 75,200	
Other expenses	178,200	253,400
Income before taxes		94,600
Income taxes expense		34,600
Net income		$ 60,000

Refer to the data in QS 16-6.
Furniture costing $110,000 is sold at its book value in 2009. Acquisitions of furniture total $90,000 cash, on which no depreciation is necessary because it is acquired at year-end. What is the cash inflow related to the sale of furniture?

QS 16-7
Computing cash from asset sales   P3

Refer to the data in QS 16-6.
1. Assume that all common stock is issued for cash. What amount of cash dividends is paid during 2009?
2. Assume that no additional notes payable are issued in 2009. What cash amount is paid to reduce the notes payable balance in 2009?

QS 16-8
Computing financing cash outflows   P3

Refer to the data in QS 16-6.
1. How much cash is received from sales to customers for year 2009?
2. What is the net increase or decrease in cash for year 2009?

QS 16-9[B]
Computing cash received from customers   P5

Refer to the data in QS 16-6.
1. How much cash is paid to acquire merchandise inventory during year 2009?
2. How much cash is paid for operating expenses during year 2009?

QS 16-10[B]
Computing operating cash outflows   P5

Refer to the data in QS 16-6.
Use the direct method to prepare the cash provided or used from operating activities section only of the statement of cash flows for this company.

QS 16-11[B]
Computing cash from operations (direct)   P5

Financial data from three competitors in the same industry follow.
1. Which of the three competitors is in the strongest position as shown by its statement of cash flows?
2. Analyze and compare the strength of Peña's cash flow on total assets ratio to that of Garcia.

QS 16-12
Analyses of sources and uses of cash   A1   A2

	File Edit View Insert Format Tools Data Accounting Window Help			_|8|×

($ thousands)	Peña	Garcia	Piniella
Cash provided (used) by operating activities	$ 140,000	$ 120,000	$ (48,000)
Cash provided (used) by investing activities			
Proceeds from sale of operating assets			52,000
Purchase of operating assets	(56,000)	(68,000)	
Cash provided (used) by financing activities			
Proceeds from issuance of debt			46,000
Repayment of debt	(12,000)		
Net increase (decrease) in cash	$ 72,000	$ 52,000	$ 50,000
Average total assets	$ 1,580,000	$ 1,250,000	$ 600,000

QS 16-13^A
Noncash accounts
on a spreadsheet P4

When a spreadsheet for a statement of cash flows is prepared, all changes in noncash balance sheet accounts are fully explained on the spreadsheet. Explain how these noncash balance sheet accounts are used to fully account for cash flows on a spreadsheet.

QS 16-14
Computing cash flows from operations (indirect)

P2

For each of the following separate cases, compute cash flows from operations. The list includes all balance sheet accounts related to operating activities.

	Case A	Case B	Case C
Net income	$ 8,000	$200,000	$144,000
Depreciation expense	60,000	16,000	48,000
Accounts receivable increase (decrease)	80,000	40,000	(8,000)
Inventory increase (decrease)	(40,000)	(20,000)	21,000
Accounts payable increase (decrease)	48,000	(44,000)	28,000
Accrued liabilities increase (decrease)	(88,000)	24,000	(16,000)

QS 16-15
Computing cash flows from investing

P3

Compute cash flows from investing activities using the following company information.

Sale of short-term investments	$12,000
Cash collections from customers	32,000
Purchase of used equipment	10,000
Depreciation expense	4,000

QS 16-16
Computing cash flows from financing

P3

Compute cash flows from financing activities using the following company information.

Additional short-term borrowings	$40,000
Purchase of short-term investments	10,000
Cash dividends paid	32,000
Interest paid	16,000

Available with McGraw-Hill's Homework Manager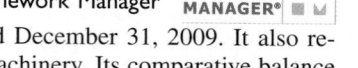

EXERCISES

Exercise 16-1
Cash flow from
operations (indirect)

P2

Hehman Company reports net income of $530,000 for the year ended December 31, 2009. It also reports $95,400 depreciation expense and a $4,000 gain on the sale of machinery. Its comparative balance sheets reveal a $42,400 increase in accounts receivable, $21,730 increase in accounts payable, $11,660 decrease in prepaid expenses, and $16,430 decrease in wages payable.

Required

Prepare only the operating activities section of the statement of cash flows for 2009 using the *indirect method.*

The following transactions and events occurred during the year. Assuming that this company uses the *indirect method* to report cash provided by operating activities, indicate where each item would appear on its statement of cash flows by placing an *x* in the appropriate column.

Exercise 16-2
Cash flow classification
(indirect) C2 C3 P2

	Statement of Cash Flows			Noncash Investing and Financing Activities	Not Reported on Statement or in Notes
	Operating Activities	Investing Activities	Financing Activities		
a. Paid cash to purchase inventory.	——	——	——	——	——
b. Purchased land by issuing common stock.	——	——	——	——	——
c. Accounts receivable decreased in the year.	——	——	——	——	——
d. Sold equipment for cash, yielding a loss.	——	——	——	——	——
e. Recorded depreciation expense.	——	——	——	——	——
f. Income taxes payable increased in the year.	——	——	——	——	——
g. Declared and paid a cash dividend.	——	——	——	——	——
h. Accounts payable decreased in the year	——	——	——	——	——
i. Paid cash to settle notes payable	——	——	——	——	——
j. Prepaid expenses increased in the year	——	——	——	——	——

The following transactions and events occurred during the year. Assuming that this company uses the *direct method* to report cash provided by operating activities, indicate where each item would appear on the statement of cash flows by placing an *x* in the appropriate column.

Exercise 16-3[B]
Cash flow classification
(direct) C2 C3 P5

	Statement of Cash Flows			Noncash Investing and Financing Activities	Not Reported on Statement or in Notes
	Operating Activities	Investing Activities	Financing Activities		
a. Retired long-term notes payable by issuing common stock	——	——	——	——	——
b. Recorded depreciation expense.	——	——	——	——	——
c. Paid cash dividend that was declared in a prior period.	——	——	——	——	——
d. Sold inventory for cash.	——	——	——	——	——
e. Borrowed cash from bank by signing a nine-month note payable.	——	——	——	——	——
f. Paid cash to purchase a patent.	——	——	——	——	——
g. Accepted six-month note receivable in exchange for plant assets.	——	——	——	——	——
h. Paid cash toward accounts payable.	——	——	——	——	——
i. Collected cash from sales.	——	——	——	——	——
j. Paid cash to acquire treasury stock.	——	——	——	——	——

Zander Company's calendar-year 2009 income statement shows the following: Net Income, $395,000; Depreciation Expense, $48,980; Amortization Expense, $9,875; Gain on Sale of Plant Assets, $4,900. An examination of the company's current assets and current liabilities reveals the following changes (all from operating activities): Accounts Receivable decrease, $7,600; Merchandise Inventory decrease, $22,040; Prepaid Expenses increase, $2,000; Accounts Payable decrease, $5,000; Other Payables increase, $760. Use the *indirect method* to compute cash flow from operating activities.

Exercise 16-4
Cash flows from operating activities (indirect)

P2

Exercise 16-5ᴮ
Computation of cash flows (direct)

P5

For each of the following three separate cases, use the information provided about the calendar-year 2010 operations of Kowa Company to compute the required cash flow information.

Case A: Compute cash received from customers:		
	Sales	$590,000
	Accounts receivable, December 31, 2009	38,000
	Accounts receivable, December 31, 2010	52,440
Case B: Compute cash paid for rent:		
	Rent expense	$117,400
	Rent payable, December 31, 2009	6,700
	Rent payable, December 31, 2010	5,561
Case C: Compute cash paid for merchandise:		
	Cost of goods sold	$651,000
	Merchandise inventory, December 31, 2009	201,810
	Accounts payable, December 31, 2009	84,760
	Merchandise inventory, December 31, 2010	165,484
	Accounts payable, December 31, 2010	105,102

Exercise 16-6
Cash flows from operating activities (indirect)

P2

Use the following income statement and information about changes in noncash current assets and current liabilities to prepare only the cash flows from operating activities section of the statement of cash flows using the *indirect* method.

SEYMOUR COMPANY
Income Statement
For Year Ended December 31, 2009

Sales		$2,175,000
Cost of goods sold		1,065,750
Gross profit		1,109,250
Operating expenses		
Salaries expense	$297,975	
Depreciation expense	52,200	
Rent expense	58,725	
Amortization expenses—Patents	6,525	
Utilities expense	23,925	439,350
		669,900
Gain on sale of equipment		8,700
Net income		$ 678,600

Changes in current asset and current liability accounts for the year that relate to operations follow.

Accounts receivable	$45,300 increase		Accounts payable	$10,075 decrease
Merchandise inventory	35,150 increase		Salaries payable	4,750 decrease

---

Exercise 16-7ᴮ
Cash flows from operating activities (direct)   P5

Refer to the information about Seymour Company in Exercise 16-6.
Use the *direct method* to prepare only the cash provided or used by operating activities section of the statement of cash flows for this company.

Use the following information to determine this company's cash flows from investing activities.

a. Equipment with a book value of $72,500 and an original cost of $158,000 was sold at a loss of $22,000.

b. Paid $95,000 cash for a new truck.

c. Sold land costing $315,000 for $400,000 cash, yielding a gain of $15,000.

d. Long-term investments in stock were sold for $94,700 cash, yielding a gain of $5,750.

Exercise 16-8
Cash flows from investing activities

P3

Use the following information to determine this company's cash flows from financing activities.

a. Net income was $53,000.

b. Issued common stock for $75,000 cash.

c. Paid cash dividend of $13,000.

d. Paid $90,000 cash to settle a note payable at its $90,000 maturity value.

e. Paid $18,000 cash to acquire its treasury stock.

f. Purchased equipment for $67,000 cash.

Exercise 16-9
Cash flows from financing activities

P3

Use the following financial statements and additional information to (1) prepare a statement of cash flows for the year ended June 30, 2009, using the *indirect method,* and (2) compute the company's cash flow on total assets ratio for its fiscal year 2009.

Exercise 16-10
Preparation of statement of cash flows (indirect)

C2   A2   P1   P2   P3

BOULWARE INC. Comparative Balance Sheets June 30, 2009 and 2008		
	2009	**2008**
Assets		
Cash	$ 84,663	$ 49,494
Accounts receivable, net	65,720	56,952
Inventory	62,620	106,107
Prepaid expenses	4,960	5,763
Equipment	118,387	131,532
Accum. depreciation—Equipment	(26,350)	(10,848)
Total assets	$310,000	$339,000
Liabilities and Equity		
Accounts payable	$ 24,490	$ 35,256
Wages payable	6,510	17,628
Income taxes payable	2,170	4,068
Notes payable (long term)	31,953	76,953
Common stock, $5 par value	208,000	158,000
Retained earnings	36,877	47,095
Total liabilities and equity	$310,000	$339,000

BOULWARE INC. Income Statement For Year Ended June 30, 2009		
Sales		$976,600
Cost of goods sold		625,024
Gross profit		351,576
Operating expenses		
Depreciation expense	$ 88,753	
Other expenses	101,879	
Total operating expenses		190,632
		160,944
Other gains (losses)		
Gain on sale of equipment		3,125
Income before taxes		164,069
Income taxes expense		56,604
Net income		$107,465

Additional Information

a. A $45,000 note payable is retired at its carrying (book) value in exchange for cash.

b. The only changes affecting retained earnings are net income and cash dividends paid.

c. New equipment is acquired for $85,000 cash.

d. Received cash for the sale of equipment that had cost $98,145, yielding a $3,125 gain.

e. Prepaid Expenses and Wages Payable relate to Other Expenses on the income statement.

f. All purchases and sales of merchandise inventory are on credit.

Refer to the data in Exercise 16-10.

Using the *direct method,* prepare the statement of cash flows for the year ended June 30, 2009.

Exercise 16-11[B]
Preparation of statement of cash flows (direct)   C2   P1   P3   P5

Exercise 16-12[B]

Preparation of statement of cash flows (direct) and supporting note

C2   C3   C4   P1

Use the following information about the cash flows of Valencia Company to prepare a complete statement of cash flows (*direct method*) for the year ended December 31, 2009. Use a note disclosure for any noncash investing and financing activities.

Cash and cash equivalents balance, December 31, 2008	$ 43,000
Cash and cash equivalents balance, December 31, 2009	120,916
Cash received as interest	4,300
Cash paid for salaries	124,700
Bonds payable retired by issuing common stock (no gain or loss on retirement)	180,000
Cash paid to retire long-term notes payable	215,000
Cash received from sale of equipment	105,350
Cash received in exchange for six-month note payable	43,000
Land purchased by issuing long-term note payable	104,400
Cash paid for store equipment	40,850
Cash dividends paid	25,800
Cash paid for other expenses	68,800
Cash received from customers	834,200
Cash paid for merchandise	433,784

Exercise 16-13[B]

Preparation of statement of cash flows (direct) from Cash T-account

C2   A1   P1   P3   P5

The following summarized Cash T-account reflects the total debits and total credits to the Cash account of Clarett Corporation for calendar year 2009.

(1) Use this information to prepare a complete statement of cash flows for year 2009. The cash provided or used by operating activities should be reported using the *direct method.*

(2) Refer to the statement of cash flows prepared for part 1 to answer the following questions *a* through *d*: (*a*) Which section—operating, investing, or financing—shows the largest cash (i) inflow and (ii) outflow? (*b*) What is the largest individual item among the investing cash outflows? (*c*) Are the cash proceeds larger from issuing notes or issuing stock? (*d*) Does the company have a net cash inflow or outflow from borrowing activities?

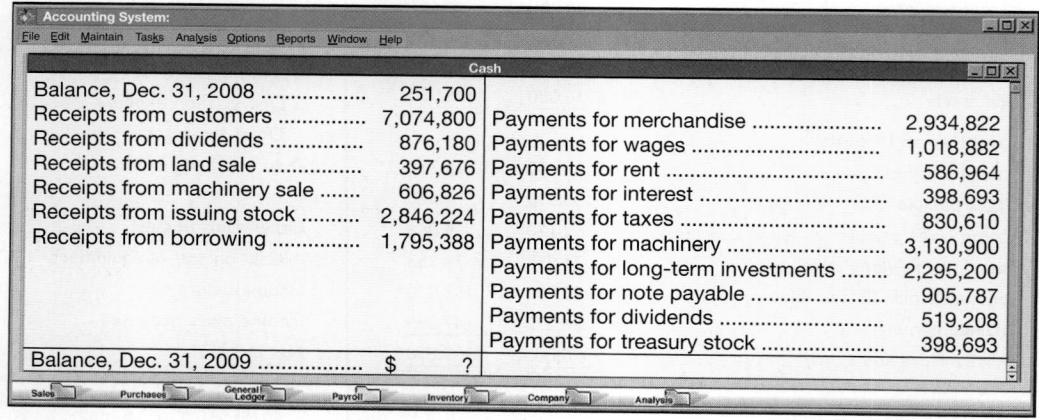

Exercise 16-14

Reporting cash flows from operations (indirect)

C4   P2

Woodlock Company reports the following information for its recent calendar year.

Sales		$80,000
Expenses		
Cost of goods sold		50,000
Salaries expense		12,000
Depreciation expense		6,000
Net income		$12,000
Accounts receivable increase		$ 5,000
Inventory decrease		8,000
Salaries payable increase		500

Required

Prepare the operating activities section of the statement of cash flows for Woodlock Company using the indirect method.

Portland Company disclosed the following information for its recent calendar year.

Exercise 16-15
Reporting and interpreting cash flows from operations (indirect)

C4 P2

Revenues	$200,000
Expenses	
Salaries expense	168,000
Utilities expense	28,000
Depreciation expense	29,200
Other expenses	6,800
Net loss	$ (32,000)
Accounts receivable decrease	$ 48,000
Purchased a machine	20,000
Salaries payable increase	36,000
Other accrued liabilities decrease	16,000

Required

1. Prepare the operating activities section of the statement of cash flows using the indirect method.
2. What were the major reasons that this company was able to report a net loss but positive cash flow from operations?
3. Of the potential causes of differences between cash flow from operations and net income, which are the most important to investors?

McGraw-Hill's
HOMEWORK
MANAGER® Available with McGraw-Hill's Homework Manager

Georgia Company, a merchandiser, recently completed its calendar-year 2009 operations. For the year, (1) all sales are credit sales, (2) all credits to Accounts Receivable reflect cash receipts from customers, (3) all purchases of inventory are on credit, (4) all debits to Accounts Payable reflect cash payments for inventory, and (5) Other Expenses are paid in advance and are initially debited to Prepaid Expenses. The company's balance sheets and income statement follow.

PROBLEM SET A

Problem 16-1A
Statement of cash flows (indirect method)

C2 C3 A1 P1 P2 P3

GEORGIA COMPANY
Comparative Balance Sheets
December 31, 2009 and 2008

	2009	2008
Assets		
Cash	$ 49,800	$ 73,500
Accounts receivable	65,840	56,000
Merchandise inventory	277,000	252,000
Prepaid expenses	1,000	1,500
Equipment	158,500	107,500
Accum. depreciation—Equipment	(43,000)	(52,000)
Total assets	$509,140	$438,500
Liabilities and Equity		
Accounts payable	$ 42,965	$113,000
Short-term notes payable	10,000	7,000
Long-term notes payable	70,000	48,000
Common stock, $5 par value	162,750	151,000
Paid-in capital in excess of par, common stock	35,250	0
Retained earnings	188,175	119,500
Total liabilities and equity	$509,140	$438,500

GEORGIA COMPANY
Income Statement
For Year Ended December 31, 2009

Sales		$584,500
Cost of goods sold		281,000
Gross profit		303,500
Operating expenses		
Depreciation expense	$ 20,000	
Other expenses	132,800	152,800
Other gains (losses)		
Loss on sale of equipment		5,875
Income before taxes		144,825
Income taxes expense		24,250
Net income		$120,575

Additional Information on Year 2009 Transactions

a. The loss on the cash sale of equipment was $5,875 (details in *b*).

b. Sold equipment costing $46,500, with accumulated depreciation of $29,000, for $11,625 cash.

c. Purchased equipment costing $97,500 by paying $35,000 cash and signing a long-term note payable for the balance.

d. Borrowed $3,000 cash by signing a short-term note payable.

e. Paid $40,500 cash to reduce the long-term notes payable.

f. Issued 2,350 shares of common stock for $20 cash per share.

g. Declared and paid cash dividends of $51,900.

Required

Check   Cash from operating activities, $42,075

1. Prepare a complete statement of cash flows; report its operating activities using the *indirect method.* Disclose any noncash investing and financing activities in a note.

Analysis Component

2. Analyze and discuss the statement of cash flows prepared in part 1, giving special attention to the wisdom of the cash dividend payment.

Problem 16-2A^A

Cash flows spreadsheet (indirect method)

P1   P2   P3   P4

Refer to the information reported about Georgia Company in Problem 16-1A.

Required

Prepare a complete statement of cash flows using a spreadsheet as in Exhibit 16A.1; report its operating activities using the indirect method. Identify the debits and credits in the Analysis of Changes columns with letters that correspond to the following list of transactions and events.

a. Net income was $120,575.

b. Accounts receivable increased.

c. Merchandise inventory increased.

d. Prepaid expenses decreased.

e. Accounts payable decreased.

f. Depreciation expense was $20,000.

g. Sold equipment costing $46,500, with accumulated depreciation of $29,000, for $11,625 cash. This yielded a loss of $5,875.

h. Purchased equipment costing $97,500 by paying $35,000 cash and **(i.)** by signing a long-term note payable for the balance.

j. Borrowed $3,000 cash by signing a short-term note payable.

k. Paid $40,500 cash to reduce the long-term notes payable.

Check   Analysis of Changes column totals, $594,850

l. Issued 2,350 shares of common stock for $20 cash per share.

m. Declared and paid cash dividends of $51,900.

Problem 16-3A^B

Statement of cash flows (direct method)   C3   P1   P3   P5

Check   Cash used in financing activities, $(42,400)

Refer to Georgia Company's financial statements and related information in Problem 16-1A.

Required

Prepare a complete statement of cash flows; report its operating activities according to the *direct method.* Disclose any noncash investing and financing activities in a note.

Problem 16-4A

Statement of cash flows (indirect method)   C3   P1   P2   P3

mhhe.com/wildFAP19e

Memphis Corp., a merchandiser, recently completed its 2009 operations. For the year, (1) all sales are credit sales, (2) all credits to Accounts Receivable reflect cash receipts from customers, (3) all purchases of inventory are on credit, (4) all debits to Accounts Payable reflect cash payments for inventory, (5) Other Expenses are all cash expenses, and (6) any change in Income Taxes Payable reflects the accrual and cash payment of taxes. The company's balance sheets and income statement follow.

MEMPHIS CORPORATION Comparative Balance Sheets December 31, 2009 and 2008		
	2009	**2008**
Assets		
Cash	$ 165,000	$137,000
Accounts receivable	82,000	74,000
Merchandise inventory	620,000	525,000
Equipment	345,000	240,000
Accum. depreciation—Equipment	(159,000)	(102,000)
Total assets	$1,053,000	$874,000
Liabilities and Equity		
Accounts payable	$ 160,000	$ 96,000
Income taxes payable	22,000	19,000
Common stock, $2 par value	588,000	560,000
Paid-in capital in excess of par value, common stock	201,000	159,000
Retained earnings	82,000	40,000
Total liabilities and equity	$1,053,000	$874,000

MEMPHIS CORPORATION Income Statement For Year Ended December 31, 2009		
Sales		$1,794,000
Cost of goods sold		1,088,000
Gross profit		706,000
Operating expenses		
Depreciation expense	$ 57,000	
Other expenses	500,000	557,000
Income before taxes		149,000
Income taxes expense		22,000
Net income		$ 127,000

Additional Information on Year 2009 Transactions

a. Purchased equipment for $105,000 cash.

b. Issued 14,000 shares of common stock for $5 cash per share.

c. Declared and paid $85,000 in cash dividends.

Required

Prepare a complete statement of cash flows; report its cash inflows and cash outflows from operating activities according to the *indirect method*.

Check Cash from operating activities, $148,000

Refer to the information reported about Memphis Corporation in Problem 16-4A.

Required

Prepare a complete statement of cash flows using a spreadsheet as in Exhibit 16A.1; report operating activities under the indirect method. Identify the debits and credits in the Analysis of Changes columns with letters that correspond to the following list of transactions and events.

a. Net income was $127,000.

b. Accounts receivable increased.

c. Merchandise inventory increased.

d. Accounts payable increased.

e. Income taxes payable increased.

f. Depreciation expense was $57,000.

g. Purchased equipment for $105,000 cash.

h. Issued 14,000 shares at $5 cash per share.

i. Declared and paid $85,000 of cash dividends.

Problem 16-5A[A]

Cash flows spreadsheet (indirect method)

P1 P2 P3 P4

mhhe.com/wildFAP19e

Check Analysis of Changes column totals, $614,000

Refer to Memphis Corporation's financial statements and related information in Problem 16-4A.

Required

Prepare a complete statement of cash flows; report its cash flows from operating activities according to the *direct method*.

Problem 16-6A[B]

Statement of cash flows (direct method)   P1 P3 P5

mhhe.com/wildFAP19e

Check Cash used in financing activities, $(15,000)

Problem 16-7A
Computing cash flows from operations (indirect)

C4 P2

Rawling Company's 2009 income statement and selected balance sheet data at December 31, 2008 and 2009, follow ($ thousands).

RAWLING COMPANY Selected Balance Sheet Accounts		
At December 31	**2009**	**2008**
Accounts receivable	$280	$290
Inventory	99	77
Accounts payable	220	230
Salaries payable	44	35
Utilities payable	11	8
Prepaid insurance	13	14
Prepaid rent	11	9

RAWLING COMPANY Income Statement	
Sales revenue	$48,600
Expenses	
Cost of goods sold	21,000
Depreciation expense	6,000
Salaries expense	9,000
Rent expense	4,500
Insurance expense	1,900
Interest expense	1,800
Utilities expense	1,400
Net income	$ 3,000

Required

Check Cash from operating activities, $8,989

Prepare the cash flows from operating activities section only of the company's 2009 statement of cash flows using the indirect method.

Problem 16-8A[B]
Computing cash flows from operations (direct)

C4 P5

Refer to the information in Problem 16-7A.

Required

Prepare the cash flows from operating activities section only of the company's 2009 statement of cash flows using the direct method.

PROBLEM SET B

Problem 16-1B
Statement of cash flows (indirect method)

C2 C3 A1 P1 P2 P3

Wilson Corporation, a merchandiser, recently completed its calendar-year 2009 operations. For the year, (1) all sales are credit sales, (2) all credits to Accounts Receivable reflect cash receipts from customers, (3) all purchases of inventory are on credit, (4) all debits to Accounts Payable reflect cash payments for inventory, and (5) Other Expenses are paid in advance and are initially debited to Prepaid Expenses. The company's balance sheets and income statement follow.

WILSON CORPORATION Income Statement For Year Ended December 31, 2009		
Sales		$585,000
Cost of goods sold		285,000
Gross profit		300,000
Operating expenses		
Depreciation expense	$ 20,000	
Other expenses	134,000	
Total operating expenses		154,000
		146,000
Other gains (losses)		
Loss on sale of equipment		5,625
Income before taxes		140,375
Income taxes expense		24,250
Net income		$116,125

WILSON CORPORATION Comparative Balance Sheets December 31, 2009 and 2008		
	2009	**2008**
Assets		
Cash	$ 49,400	$ 74,000
Accounts receivable	65,830	55,000
Merchandise inventory	277,000	252,000
Prepaid expenses	1,250	1,600
Equipment	158,500	107,500
Accum. depreciation—Equipment	(36,625)	(46,000)
Total assets	$515,355	$444,100
Liabilities and Equity		
Accounts payable	$ 55,380	$112,000
Short-term notes payable	9,000	7,000
Long-term notes payable	70,000	48,250
Common stock, $5 par	162,500	150,750
Paid-in capital in excess of par, common stock	35,250	0
Retained earnings	183,225	126,100
Total liabilities and equity	$515,355	$444,100

Additional Information on Year 2009 Transactions

a. The loss on the cash sale of equipment was $5,625 (details in *b*).

b. Sold equipment costing $46,500, with accumulated depreciation of $29,375, for $11,500 cash.

c. Purchased equipment costing $97,500 by paying $25,000 cash and signing a long-term note payable for the balance.

d. Borrowed $2,000 cash by signing a short-term note payable.

e. Paid $50,750 cash to reduce the long-term notes payable.

f. Issued 2,350 shares of common stock for $20 cash per share.

g. Declared and paid cash dividends of $59,000.

Required

1. Prepare a complete statement of cash flows; report its operating activities using the *indirect method.* Disclose any noncash investing and financing activities in a note.

Check Cash from operating activities, $49,650

Analysis Component

2. Analyze and discuss the statement of cash flows prepared in part 1, giving special attention to the wisdom of the cash dividend payment.

Refer to the information reported about Wilson Corporation in Problem 16-1B.

Required

Prepare a complete statement of cash flows using a spreadsheet as in Exhibit 16A.1; report its operating activities using the *indirect method.* Identify the debits and credits in the Analysis of Changes columns with letters that correspond to the following list of transactions and events.

a. Net income was $116,125.

b. Accounts receivable increased.

c. Merchandise inventory increased.

d. Prepaid expenses decreased.

e. Accounts payable decreased.

f. Depreciation expense was $20,000.

g. Sold equipment costing $46,500, with accumulated depreciation of $29,375, for $11,500 cash. This yielded a loss of $5,625.

h. Purchased equipment costing $97,500 by paying $25,000 cash and **(i.)** by signing a long-term note payable for the balance.

j. Borrowed $2,000 cash by signing a short-term note payable.

k. Paid $50,750 cash to reduce the long-term notes payable.

l. Issued 2,350 shares of common stock for $20 cash per share.

m. Declared and paid cash dividends of $59,000.

Problem 16-2B[A]
Cash flows spreadsheet (indirect method)

P1 P2 P3 P4

Check Analysis of Changes column totals, $604,175

Refer to Wilson Corporation's financial statements and related information in Problem 16-1B.

Required

Prepare a complete statement of cash flows; report its operating activities according to the *direct method.* Disclose any noncash investing and financing activities in a note.

Problem 16-3B[B]
Statement of cash flows (direct method) C3 P1 P3 P5

Check Cash used in financing activities, $(60,750)

Problem 16-4B
Statement of cash flows
(indirect method)

C3 P1 P2 P3

Prius Company, a merchandiser, recently completed its 2009 operations. For the year, (1) all sales are credit sales, (2) all credits to Accounts Receivable reflect cash receipts from customers, (3) all purchases of inventory are on credit, (4) all debits to Accounts Payable reflect cash payments for inventory, (5) Other Expenses are cash expenses, and (6) any change in Income Taxes Payable reflects the accrual and cash payment of taxes. The company's balance sheets and income statement follow.

PRIUS COMPANY
Comparative Balance Sheets
December 31, 2009 and 2008

	2009	2008
Assets		
Cash	$ 164,000	$ 131,000
Accounts receivable	82,000	70,000
Merchandise inventory	605,000	515,000
Equipment	350,000	276,000
Accum. depreciation—Equipment	(157,000)	(102,000)
Total assets	$1,044,000	$ 890,000
Liabilities and Equity		
Accounts payable	$ 173,000	$ 119,000
Income taxes payable	20,000	17,000
Common stock, $2 par value	580,000	560,000
Paid-in capital in excess of par, common stock	193,000	163,000
Retained earnings	78,000	31,000
Total liabilities and equity	$1,044,000	$ 890,000

PRIUS COMPANY
Income Statement
For Year Ended December 31, 2009

Sales		$1,792,000
Cost of goods sold		1,087,000
Gross profit		705,000
Operating expenses		
Depreciation expense	$ 55,000	
Other expenses	494,000	549,000
Income before taxes		156,000
Income taxes expense		24,000
Net income		$ 132,000

Additional Information on Year 2009 Transactions

a. Purchased equipment for $74,000 cash.

b. Issued 10,000 shares of common stock for $5 cash per share.

c. Declared and paid $85,000 of cash dividends.

Required

Check Cash from operating activities, $142,000

Prepare a complete statement of cash flows; report its cash inflows and cash outflows from operating activities according to the *indirect method*.

Problem 16-5B[A]
Cash flows spreadsheet
(indirect method)

P1 P2 P3 P4

Refer to the information reported about Prius Company in Problem 16-4B.

Required

Prepare a complete statement of cash flows using a spreadsheet as in Exhibit 16A.1; report operating activities under the *indirect method*. Identify the debits and credits in the Analysis of Changes columns with letters that correspond to the following list of transactions and events.

a. Net income was $132,000.

b. Accounts receivable increased.

c. Merchandise inventory increased.

d. Accounts payable increased.

e. Income taxes payable increased.

f. Depreciation expense was $55,000.

g. Purchased equipment for $74,000 cash.

Check Analysis of Changes column totals, $555,000

h. Issued 10,000 shares at $5 cash per share.

i. Declared and paid $85,000 of cash dividends.

Refer to Prius Company's financial statements and related information in Problem 16-4B.

Required

Prepare a complete statement of cash flows; report its cash flows from operating activities according to the *direct method.*

Problem 16-6B[B]
Statement of cash flows (direct method)   P1 P3 P5

Check   Cash used by financing activities, $(35,000)

Kodak Company's 2009 income statement and selected balance sheet data at December 31, 2008 and 2009, follow ($ thousands).

Problem 16-7B
Computing cash flows from operations (indirect)

C4 P2

KODAK COMPANY Income Statement	
Sales revenue	$312,000
Expenses	
Cost of goods sold	144,000
Depreciation expense	64,000
Salaries expense	40,000
Rent expense	10,000
Insurance expense	5,200
Interest expense	4,800
Utilities expense	4,000
Net income	$ 40,000

KODAK COMPANY Selected Balance Sheet Accounts		
At December 31	2009	2008
Accounts receivable	$720	$600
Inventory	172	196
Accounts payable	480	520
Salaries payable	180	120
Utilities payable	40	0
Prepaid insurance	28	36
Prepaid rent	20	40

Required

Prepare the cash flows from operating activities section only of the company's 2009 statement of cash flows using the indirect method.

Check   Cash from operating activities, $103,992

Refer to the information in Problem 16-7B.

Required

Prepare the cash flows from operating activities section only of the company's 2009 statement of cash flows using the direct method.

Problem 16-8B[B]
Computing cash flows from operations (direct)

C4 P5

(This serial problem began in Chapter 1 and continues through most of the book. If previous chapter segments were not completed, the serial problem can begin at this point. It is helpful, but not necessary, to use the Working Papers that accompany the book.)

SERIAL PROBLEM

Success Systems

SP 16   Adriana Lopez, owner of Success Systems, decides to prepare a statement of cash flows for her business. (Although the serial problem allowed for various ownership changes in earlier chapters, we will prepare the statement of cash flows using the following financial data.)

SUCCESS SYSTEMS Income Statement For Three Months Ended March 31, 2010		
Computer services revenue		$25,160
Net sales		18,693
Total revenue		43,853
Cost of goods sold	$14,052	
Depreciation expense— Office equipment	400	
Depreciation expense— Computer equipment	1,250	
Wages expense	3,250	
Insurance expense	555	
Rent expense	2,475	
Computer supplies expense	1,305	
Advertising expense	600	
Mileage expense	320	
Repairs expense—Computer	960	
Total expenses		25,167
Net income		$18,686

SUCCESS SYSTEMS Comparative Balance Sheets December 31, 2009, and March 31, 2010		
	2010	**2009**
Assets		
Cash	$ 77,845	$58,160
Accounts receivable	22,720	5,668
Merchandise inventory	704	0
Computer supplies	2,005	580
Prepaid insurance	1,110	1,665
Prepaid rent	825	825
Office equipment	8,000	8,000
Accumulated depreciation—Office equipment	(800)	(400)
Computer equipment	20,000	20,000
Accumulated depreciation— Computer equipment	(2,500)	(1,250)
Total assets	$129,909	$93,248
Liabilities and Equity		
Accounts payable	$ 0	$ 1,100
Wages payable	875	500
Unearned computer service revenue	0	1,500
Common stock	108,000	83,000
Retained earnings	21,034	7,148
Total liabilities and equity	$129,909	$93,248

Required

Check Cash flows used by operations: $(515)

Prepare a statement of cash flows for Success Systems using the *indirect method* for the three months ended March 31, 2010. Recall that the owner Adriana Lopez contributed $25,000 to the business in exchange for additional stock in the first quarter of 2010 and has received $4,800 in cash dividends.

BEYOND THE NUMBERS

REPORTING IN ACTION

C4 A1

BTN 16-1   Refer to Best Buy's financial statements in Appendix A to answer the following.

1. Is Best Buy's statement of cash flows prepared under the direct method or the indirect method? How do you know?
2. For each fiscal year 2007, 2006, and 2005, is the amount of cash provided by operating activities more or less than the cash paid for dividends?
3. What is the largest amount in reconciling the difference between net income and cash flow from operating activities in 2007? In 2006? In 2005?
4. Identify the largest cash flows for investing and for financing activities in 2007 and in 2006.

Fast Forward

5. Obtain Best Buy's financial statements for a fiscal year ending after March 3, 2007, from either its Website (BestBuy.com) or the SEC's EDGAR database (www.sec.gov). Since March 3, 2007, what are Best Buy's largest cash outflows and cash inflows in the investing and in the financing sections of its statement of cash flow?

BTN 16-2 Key figures for **Best Buy**, **Circuit City**, and **RadioShack** follow.

($ millions)	Best Buy			Circuit City			RadioShack		
	Current Year	1 Year Prior	2 Years Prior	Current Year	1 Year Prior	2 Years Prior	Current Year	1 Year Prior	2 Years Prior
Operating cash flows	$ 1,762	$ 1,740	$ 1,981	$ 316	$ 365	$ 389	$ 315	$ 363	$ 353
Total assets	13,570	11,864	10,294	4,007	4,069	3,840	2,070	2,205	2,517

Required

1. Compute the recent two years' cash flow on total assets ratios for Best Buy, Circuit City, and RadioShack.
2. What does the cash flow on total assets ratio measure?
3. Which company has the highest cash flow on total assets ratio for the periods shown?
4. Does the cash flow on total assets ratio reflect on the quality of earnings? Explain.

BTN 16-3 Kaelyn Gish is preparing for a meeting with her banker. Her business is finishing its fourth year of operations. In the first year, it had negative cash flows from operations. In the second and third years, cash flows from operations were positive. However, inventory costs rose significantly in year 4, and cash flows from operations will probably be down 25%. Gish wants to secure a line of credit from her banker as a financing buffer. From experience, she knows the banker will scrutinize operating cash flows for years 1 through 4 and will want a projected number for year 5. Gish knows that a steady progression upward in operating cash flows for years 1 through 4 will help her case. She decides to use her discretion as owner and considers several business actions that will turn her operating cash flow in year 4 from a decrease to an increase.

Required

1. Identify two business actions Gish might take to improve cash flows from operations.
2. Comment on the ethics and possible consequences of Gish's decision to pursue these actions.

BTN 16-4 Your friend, Hanna Willard, recently completed the second year of her business and just received annual financial statements from her accountant. Willard finds the income statement and balance sheet informative but does not understand the statement of cash flows. She says the first section is especially confusing because it contains a lot of additions and subtractions that do not make sense to her. Willard adds, "The income statement tells me the business is more profitable than last year and that's most important. If I want to know how cash changes, I can look at comparative balance sheets."

Required

Write a half-page memorandum to your friend explaining the purpose of the statement of cash flows. Speculate as to why the first section is so confusing and how it might be rectified.

BTN 16-5 Access the April 19, 2007, filing of the 10-K report (for fiscal year ending February 3, 2007) of **J. Crew Group, Inc.**, at www.SEC.gov.

Required

1. Does J. Crew use the direct or indirect method to construct its consolidated statement of cash flows?
2. For the fiscal year ended February 3, 2007, what is the largest item in reconciling the net income to net cash provided by operating activities?
3. In the recent three years, has the company been more successful in generating operating cash flows or in generating net income? Identify the figures to support the answer.
4. In the year ended February 3, 2007, what was the largest cash outflow for investing activities and for financing activities?
5. What item(s) does J. Crew report as supplementary cash flow information?
6. Does J. Crew report any noncash financing activities for fiscal year 2007? Identify them, if any.

TEAMWORK IN ACTION

C1 C4 A1 P2 P5

BTN 16-6   Team members are to coordinate and independently answer one question within each of the following three sections. Team members should then report to the team and confirm or correct team-mates' answers.

1. Answer *one* of the following questions about the statement of cash flows.
 a. What are this statement's reporting objectives?
 b. What two methods are used to prepare it? Identify similarities and differences between them.
 c. What steps are followed to prepare the statement?
 d. What types of analyses are often made from this statement's information?

2. Identify and explain the adjustment from net income to obtain cash flows from operating activities using the indirect method for *one* of the following items.
 a. Noncash operating revenues and expenses.
 b. Nonoperating gains and losses.
 c. Increases and decreases in noncash current assets.
 d. Increases and decreases in current liabilities.

3.ᴮIdentify and explain the formula for computing cash flows from operating activities using the direct method for *one* of the following items.
 a. Cash receipts from sales to customers.
 b. Cash paid for merchandise inventory.
 c. Cash paid for wages and operating expenses.
 d. Cash paid for interest and taxes.

Note: For teams of more than four, some pairing within teams is necessary. Use as an in-class activity or as an assignment. If used in class, specify a time limit on each part. Conclude with reports to the entire class, using team rotation. Each team can prepare responses on a transparency.

ENTREPRENEURIAL DECISION

C1 A1

BTN 16-7   Review the chapter's opener involving **Jungle Jim's International Market.**

Required

1. In a business such as Jungle Jim's, monitoring cash flow is always a priority. Even though Jungle Jim's now has thousands in annual sales and earns a positive net income, explain how cash flow can lag behind earnings.

2. Jungle Jim's is a closely held corporation. What are potential sources of financing for its future expansion?

C2 A1

BTN 16-8   Jenna and Matt Wilder are completing their second year operating Mountain High, a downhill ski area and resort. Mountain High reports a net loss of $(10,000) for its second year, which includes an $85,000 extraordinary loss from fire. This past year also involved major purchases of plant assets for renovation and expansion, yielding a year-end total asset amount of $800,000. Mountain High's net cash outflow for its second year is $(5,000); a summarized version of its statement of cash flows follows:

Net cash flow provided by operating activities	$295,000
Net cash flow used by investing activities	(310,000)
Net cash flow provided by financing activities	10,000

Required

Write a one-page memorandum to the Wilders evaluating Mountain High's current performance and assessing its future. Give special emphasis to cash flow data and their interpretation.

HITTING THE ROAD

C1

BTN 16-9   Visit **The Motley Fool**'s Website (**Fool.com**). Click on the sidebar link titled *Fool's School* (or *Fool.com/School*). Identify and select the link *How to Value Stocks.*

Required

1. Click on *Introduction to Valuation,* and then *Cash-Flow-Based Valuations.* How does the Fool's school define cash flow? What is the school's reasoning for this definition?

2. Per the school's instruction, why do analysts focus on earnings before interest and taxes (EBIT)?

3. Visit other links at this Website that interest you such as "How to Read a Balance Sheet," or find out what the "Fool's Ratio" is. Write a half-page report on what you find.

BTN 16-10   Key comparative information for **DSG international plc** (DSGiplc.com) follows.

GLOBAL DECISION

C1   C2   C4

DSG

 R RadioShack.

(£ millions)	Current Year	1 Year Prior	2 Years Prior
Operating cash flows	£ 207	£ 338	£ 375
Total assets	3,977	4,120	4,104

Required

1. Compute the recent two years' cash flow on total assets ratio for DSG.

2. How does DSG's ratio compare to Best Buy's, Circuit City's, and RadioShack's ratios from BTN 16-2?

ANSWERS TO MULTIPLE CHOICE QUIZ

1. b;

Net income	$15,200
Depreciation expense	10,000
Gain on sale of land	(3,000)
Increase in inventory	(1,500)
Increase in accounts payable	2,850
Net cash provided by operations	$23,550

2. c; cash received from sale of machine is reported as an investing activity.

3. d; FASB requires cash interest paid to be reported under operating.

4. a; Cash paid for salaries and wages = $255,000 + $8,200 − $10,900 = $252,300

5. e; Increase in inventory = $112,000 − $105,000 = $7,000
Increase in accounts payable = $101,300 − $98,500 = $2,800
Cash paid for merchandise = $545,000 + $7,000 − $2,800 = $549,200

A Look Back

Chapter 16 focused on reporting and analyzing cash inflows and cash outflows. We explained how to prepare, analyze, and interpret the statement of cash flows.

 A Look at This Chapter

This chapter emphasizes the analysis and interpretation of financial statement information. We learn to apply horizontal, vertical, and ratio analyses to better understand company performance and financial condition.

A Look Ahead

Chapter 18 introduces us to managerial accounting. We discuss its purposes, concepts, and roles in helping managers gather and organize information for decisions. We also explain basic management principles.

17

Chapter

Analysis of Financial Statements

Learning Objectives

CAP

Conceptual

C1 Explain the purpose of analysis. (p. 680)

C2 Identify the building blocks of analysis. (p. 681)

C3 Describe standards for comparisons in analysis. (p. 682)

C4 Identify the tools of analysis. (p. 682)

Analytical

A1 Summarize and report results of analysis. (p. 700)

A2 *Appendix 17A*—Explain the form and assess the content of a complete income statement. (p. 703)

LP17

Procedural

P1 Explain and apply methods of horizontal analysis. (p. 682)

P2 Describe and apply methods of vertical analysis. (p. 687)

P3 Define and apply ratio analysis. (p. 690)

Motley Fool

"What goes on at The Motley Fool . . . is similar to what goes on in a library"
—Tom Gardner (David Gardner on left)

ALEXANDRIA, VA—In Shakespeare's Elizabethan comedy *As You Like It*, only the fool could speak truthfully to the King without getting his head lopped off. Inspired by Shakespeare's stage character, Tom and David Gardner vowed to become modern-day fools who tell it like it is. With under $10,000 in start-up money, the brothers launched **The Motley Fool (Fool.com).** And befitting of a Shakespearean play, the two say they are "dedicated to educating, amusing, and enriching individuals in search of the truth."

The Gardners do not fear the wrath of any King, real or fictional. They are intent on exposing the truth, as they see it, "that the financial world preys on ignorance and fear." As Tom explains, "There is such a great need in the general populace for financial information." Who can argue, given their brilliant success through practically every medium; including their Website, radio shows, newspaper columns, online store, investment newsletters, and global expansion.

Despite the brothers' best efforts, however, ordinary people still do not fully use information contained in financial statements. For instance, discussions keep appearing on The Motley Fool's online bulletin board that can be easily resolved using reliable and available accounting data. So, it would seem that the Fools must continue their work of "educating and enriching" individuals.

Resembling The Motley Fools' objectives, this chapter introduces horizontal and vertical analyses—tools used to reveal crucial trends and insights from financial information. It also expands on ratio analysis, which gives insight into a company's financial condition and performance. By arming ourselves with the information contained in this chapter and the investment advice of The Motley Fool, we can be sure to not play the fool in today's financial world.

[Sources: *Motley Fool Website,* January 2009; *Entrepreneur,* July 1997; *What to Do with Your Money Now,* June 2002; *USA Weekend,* July 2004; *Washington Post,* November 2007; *Money after 40,* April 2007]

This chapter shows how we use financial statements to evaluate a company's financial performance and condition. We explain financial statement analysis, its basic building blocks, the information available, standards for comparisons, and tools of analysis. Three major analysis tools are presented: horizontal analysis, vertical analysis, and ratio analysis. We apply each of these tools using **Best Buy**'s financial statements, and we introduce comparative analysis using **Circuit City** and **RadioShack**. This chapter expands and organizes the ratio analyses introduced at the end of each chapter.

Analysis of Financial Statements

Basics of Analysis	Horizontal Analysis	Vertical Analysis	Ratio Analysis
• Purpose • Building blocks • Information • Standards for comparisons • Tools	• Comparative balance sheets • Comparative income statements • Trend analysis	• Common-size balance sheet • Common-size income statement • Common-size graphics	• Liquidity and efficiency • Solvency • Profitability • Market prospects • Ratio summary

Basics of Analysis

Video17.1

Financial statement analysis applies analytical tools to general-purpose financial statements and related data for making business decisions. It involves transforming accounting data into more useful information. Financial statement analysis reduces our reliance on hunches, guesses, and intuition as well as our uncertainty in decision making. It does not lessen the need for expert judgment; instead, it provides us an effective and systematic basis for making business decisions. This section describes the purpose of financial statement analysis, its information sources, the use of comparisons, and some issues in computations.

Purpose of Analysis

C1 Explain the purpose of analysis.

Internal users of accounting information are those involved in strategically managing and operating the company. They include managers, officers, internal auditors, consultants, budget directors, and market researchers. The purpose of financial statement analysis for these users is to provide strategic information to improve company efficiency and effectiveness in providing products and services.

Point: Financial statement analysis tools are also used for personal financial investment decisions.

External users of accounting information are *not* directly involved in running the company. They include shareholders, lenders, directors, customers, suppliers, regulators, lawyers, brokers, and the press. External users rely on financial statement analysis to make better and more informed decisions in pursuing their own goals.

Point: Financial statement analysis is a topic on the CPA, CMA, CIA, and CFA exams.

We can identify other uses of financial statement analysis. Shareholders and creditors assess company prospects to make investing and lending decisions. A board of directors analyzes financial statements in monitoring management's decisions. Employees and unions use financial statements in labor negotiations. Suppliers use financial statement information in establishing credit terms. Customers analyze financial statements in deciding whether to establish supply relationships. Public utilities set customer rates by analyzing financial statements. Auditors use financial statements in assessing the "fair presentation" of their clients' financial results. Analyst services such as **Dun & Bradstreet**, **Moody's**, and **Standard & Poor's** use financial statements in making buy-sell recommendations and in setting credit ratings. The common goal of these users is to evaluate company performance and financial condition. This includes evaluating (1) past and current performance, (2) current financial position, and (3) future performance and risk.

Building Blocks of Analysis

Financial statement analysis focuses on one or more elements of a company's financial condition or performance. Our analysis emphasizes four areas of inquiry—with varying degrees of importance. These four areas are described and illustrated in this chapter and are considered the *building blocks* of financial statement analysis:

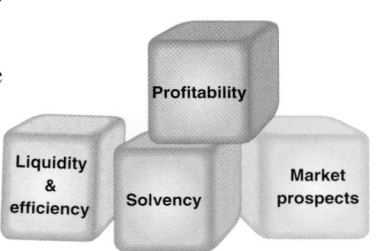

C2   Identify the building blocks of analysis.

- **Liquidity** and **efficiency**—ability to meet short-term obligations and to efficiently generate revenues.
- **Solvency**—ability to generate future revenues and meet long-term obligations.
- **Profitability**—ability to provide financial rewards sufficient to attract and retain financing.
- **Market prospects**—ability to generate positive market expectations.

Applying the building blocks of financial statement analysis involves determining (1) the objectives of analysis and (2) the relative emphasis among the building blocks. We distinguish among these four building blocks to emphasize the different aspects of a company's financial condition or performance, yet we must remember that these areas of analysis are interrelated. For instance, a company's operating performance is affected by the availability of financing and short-term liquidity conditions. Similarly, a company's credit standing is not limited to satisfactory short-term liquidity but depends also on its profitability and efficiency in using assets. Early in our analysis, we need to determine the relative emphasis of each building block. Emphasis and analysis can later change as a result of evidence collected.

Decision Insight

Chips and Brokers   The phrase *blue chips* refers to stock of big, profitable companies. The phrase comes from poker; where the most valuable chips are blue. The term *brokers* refers to those who execute orders to buy or sell stock. The term comes from wine retailers—individuals who broach (break) wine casks.

Information for Analysis

Some users, such as managers and regulatory authorities, are able to receive special financial reports prepared to meet their analysis needs. However, most users must rely on **general-purpose financial statements** that include the (1) income statement, (2) balance sheet, (3) statement of stockholders' equity (or statement of retained earnings), (4) statement of cash flows, and (5) notes to these statements.

    Financial reporting refers to the communication of financial information useful for making investment, credit, and other business decisions. Financial reporting includes not only general-purpose financial statements but also information from SEC 10-K or other filings, press releases, shareholders' meetings, forecasts, management letters, auditors' reports, and Webcasts.

    Management's Discussion and Analysis (MD&A) is one example of useful information outside traditional financial statements. **Best Buy**'s MD&A (available at BestBuy.com), for example, begins with an overview and strategic initiatives. It then discusses operating results followed by liquidity and capital resources—roughly equivalent to investing and financing. The final few parts discuss special financing arrangements, key accounting policies, interim results, and the next year's outlook. The MD&A is an excellent starting point in understanding a company's business activities.

Decision Insight

Analysis Online   Many Websites offer free access and screening of companies by key numbers such as earnings, sales, and book value. For instance, **Standard & Poor's** has information for more than 10,000 stocks (StandardPoor.com).

Standards for Comparisons

C3   Describe standards for comparisons in analysis.

When interpreting measures from financial statement analysis, we need to decide whether the measures indicate good, bad, or average performance. To make such judgments, we need standards (benchmarks) for comparisons that include the following:

- *Intracompany*—The company under analysis can provide standards for comparisons based on its own prior performance and relations between its financial items. **Best Buy**'s current net income, for instance, can be compared with its prior years' net income and in relation to its revenues or total assets.
- *Competitor*—One or more direct competitors of the company being analyzed can provide standards for comparisons. **Coca-Cola**'s profit margin, for instance, can be compared with **PepsiCo**'s profit margin.
- *Industry*—Industry statistics can provide standards of comparisons. Such statistics are available from services such as **Dun & Bradstreet**, **Standard & Poor's**, and **Moody's**.
- *Guidelines (rules of thumb)*—General standards of comparisons can develop from experience. Examples are the 2:1 level for the current ratio or 1:1 level for the acid-test ratio. Guidelines, or rules of thumb, must be carefully applied because context is crucial.

Point: Each chapter's *Reporting in Action* problems engage students in *intracompany* analysis, whereas *Comparative Analysis* problems require competitor analysis (Best Buy vs. Circuit City).

All of these comparison standards are useful when properly applied, yet measures taken from a selected competitor or group of competitors are often best. Intracompany and industry measures are also important. Guidelines or rules of thumb should be applied with care, and then only if they seem reasonable given past experience and industry norms.

Tools of Analysis

C4   Identify the tools of analysis.

Three of the most common tools of financial statement analysis are

1. **Horizontal analysis**—Comparison of a company's financial condition and performance across time.
2. **Vertical analysis**—Comparison of a company's financial condition and performance to a base amount.
3. **Ratio analysis**—Measurement of key relations between financial statement items.

The remainder of this chapter describes these analysis tools and how to apply them.

Quick Check   Answers—p. 706

1. Who are the intended users of general-purpose financial statements?
2. General-purpose financial statements consist of what information?
3. Which of the following is *least* useful as a basis for comparison when analyzing ratios? (*a*) Company results from a different economic setting. (*b*) Standards from past experience. (*c*) Rule-of-thumb standards. (*d*) Industry averages.
4. What is the preferred basis of comparison for ratio analysis?

Horizontal Analysis

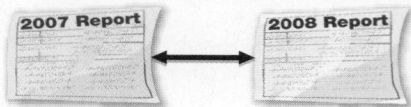

Analysis of any single financial number is of limited value. Instead, much of financial statement analysis involves identifying and describing relations between numbers, groups of numbers, and changes in those numbers. Horizontal analysis refers to examination of financial statement data *across time*. [The term *horizontal analysis* arises from the left-to-right (or right-to-left) movement of our eyes as we review comparative financial statements across time.]

Comparative Statements

P1   Explain and apply methods of horizontal analysis.

Comparing amounts for two or more successive periods often helps in analyzing financial statements. **Comparative financial statements** facilitate this comparison by showing financial amounts in side-by-side columns on a single statement, called a *comparative format*. Using figures from **Best Buy**'s financial statements, this section explains how to compute dollar changes and percent changes for comparative statements.

Computation of Dollar Changes and Percent Changes   Comparing financial statements over relatively short time periods—two to three years—is often done by analyzing changes in line items. A change analysis usually includes analyzing absolute dollar amount changes and percent changes. Both analyses are relevant because dollar changes can yield large percent changes inconsistent with their importance. For instance, a 50% change from a base figure of $100 is less important than the same percent change from a base amount of $100,000 in the same statement. Reference to dollar amounts is necessary to retain a proper perspective and to assess the importance of changes. We compute the *dollar change* for a financial statement item as follows:

$$\text{Dollar change} = \text{Analysis period amount} - \text{Base period amount}$$

Analysis period is the point or period of time for the financial statements under analysis, and *base period* is the point or period of time for the financial statements used for comparison purposes. The prior year is commonly used as a base period. We compute the *percent change* by dividing the dollar change by the base period amount and then multiplying this quantity by 100 as follows:

$$\text{Percent change (\%)} = \frac{\text{Analysis period amount} - \text{Base period amount}}{\text{Base period amount}} \times 100$$

We can always compute a dollar change, but we must be aware of a few rules in working with percent changes. To illustrate, look at four separate cases in this chart:

Case	Analysis Period	Base Period	Change Analysis	
			Dollar	Percent
A	$ 1,500	$(4,500)	$ 6,000	—
B	(1,000)	2,000	(3,000)	—
C	8,000	—	8,000	—
D	0	10,000	(10,000)	(100%)

When a negative amount appears in the base period and a positive amount in the analysis period (or vice versa), we cannot compute a meaningful percent change; see cases A and B. Also, when no value is in the base period, no percent change is computable; see case C. Finally, when an item has a value in the base period and zero in the analysis period, the decrease is 100 percent; see case D.

It is common when using horizontal analysis to compare amounts to either average or median values from prior periods (average and median values smooth out erratic or unusual fluctuations).[1] We also commonly round percents and ratios to one or two decimal places, but practice on this matter is not uniform. Computations are as detailed as necessary, which is judged by whether rounding potentially affects users' decisions. Computations should not be excessively detailed so that important relations are lost among a mountain of decimal points and digits.

Comparative Balance Sheets   Comparative balance sheets consist of balance sheet amounts from two or more balance sheet dates arranged side by side. Its usefulness is often improved by showing each item's dollar change and percent change to highlight large changes.

---

[1] *Median* is the middle value in a group of numbers. For instance, if five prior years' incomes are (in 000s) $15, $19, $18, $20, and $22, the median value is $19. When there are two middle numbers, we can take their average. For instance, if four prior years' sales are (in 000s) $84, $91, $96, and $93, the median is $92 (computed as the average of $91 and $93).

Analysis of comparative financial statements begins by focusing on items that show large dollar or percent changes. We then try to identify the reasons for these changes and, if possible, determine whether they are favorable or unfavorable. We also follow up on items with small changes when we expected the changes to be large.

Exhibit 17.1 shows comparative balance sheets for **Best Buy**. A few items stand out. Many asset categories substantially increase, which is probably not surprising because Best Buy is a growth company. Much of the increase in current assets is from the 20.7% increase in merchandise inventories. The long-term assets of property, equipment, and goodwill also increased. Of course, its sizeable total asset growth of 14.4% must be accompanied by future income to validate Best Buy's growth strategy.

We likewise see substantial increases on the financing side, the most notable ones being accounts payable and long-term debt totaling about $1,112 million. The increase in payables is related to the increase in cash levels, and the increase in debt is partly explained by the increase in long-term assets. Best Buy also reinvested much of its income as reflected in the $1,203 million increase in retained earnings. Again, we must monitor these increases in

EXHIBIT 17.1

Comparative Balance Sheets

BEST BUY Comparative Balance Sheets March 3, 2007, and February 25, 2006				
(in millions)	2007	2006	Dollar Change	Percent Change
Assets				
Cash and cash equivalents	$ 1,205	$ 748	$ 457	61.1%
Short-term investments	2,588	3,041	(453)	(14.9)
Receivables, net	548	449	99	22.0
Merchandise inventories	4,028	3,338	690	20.7
Other current assets	712	409	303	74.1
Total current assets	9,081	7,985	1,096	13.7
Property and equipment	4,904	4,836	68	1.4
Less accumulated depreciation	1,966	2,124	(158)	(7.4)
Net property and equipment	2,938	2,712	226	8.3
Goodwill	919	557	362	65.0
Tradenames	81	44	37	84.1
Long-term investments	318	218	100	45.9
Other long-term assets	233	348	(115)	(33.0)
Total assets	$13,570	$11,864	$1,706	14.4
Liabilities				
Accounts payable	$ 3,934	$ 3,234	$ 700	21.6%
Unredeemed gift card liabilities	496	469	27	5.8
Accrued compensation and related expenses	332	354	(22)	(6.2)
Accrued liabilities	990	878	112	12.8
Accrued income taxes	489	703	(214)	(30.4)
Short-term debt	41	0	41	—
Current portion of long-term debt	19	418	(399)	(95.5)
Total current liabilities	6,301	6,056	245	4.0
Long-term liabilities	443	373	70	18.8
Long-term debt	590	178	412	231.5
Minority interests	35	0	35	—
Stockholders' Equity				
Common stock	48	49	(1)	(2.0)
Additional paid-in capital	430	643	(213)	(33.1)
Retained earnings	5,507	4,304	1,203	28.0
Accumulated other comprehensive income	216	261	(45)	(17.2)
Total stockholders' equity	6,201	5,257	944	18.0
Total liabilities and stockholders' equity	$13,570	$11,864	$1,706	14.4

investing and financing activities to be sure they are reflected in increased operating performance.

Comparative Income Statements   Comparative income statements are prepared similarly to comparative balance sheets. Amounts for two or more periods are placed side by side, with additional columns for dollar and percent changes. Exhibit 17.2 shows Best Buy's comparative income statements.

BEST BUY Comparative Income Statements For Years Ended March 3, 2007, and February 25, 2006				
(in millions, except per share data)	2007	2006	Dollar Change	Percent Change
Revenues	$35,934	$30,848	$5,086	16.5%
Cost of goods sold	27,165	23,122	4,043	17.5
Gross profit	8,769	7,726	1,043	13.5
Selling, general, and administrative expenses	6,770	6,082	688	11.3
Operating income	1,999	1,644	355	21.6
Net interest income (expense)	111	77	34	44.2
Gain on investments	20	0	20	—
Earnings from continuing operations before income taxes	2,130	1,721	409	23.8
Income tax expense	752	581	171	29.4
Minority interest in earnings	1	0	1	—
Net earnings	$ 1,377	$ 1,140	$ 237	20.8
Basic earnings per share	$ 2.86	$ 2.33	$ 0.53	22.7
Diluted earnings per share	$ 2.79	$ 2.27	$ 0.52	22.9

EXHIBIT 17.2

Comparative Income Statements

   Best Buy has substantial revenue growth of 16.5% in 2007. This finding helps support management's growth strategy as reflected in the comparative balance sheets. Best Buy also reveals some ability to control cost of sales and general and administrative expenses, which increased 17.5% and 11.3%, respectively. Best Buy's net income growth of 20.8% on revenue growth of 16.5% is impressive.

Point: Percent change can also be computed by dividing the current period by the prior period and subtracting 1.0. For example, the 16.5% revenue increase of Exhibit 17.2 is computed as: ($35,934/$30,848) − 1.

Trend Analysis

Trend analysis, also called *trend percent analysis* or *index number trend analysis,* is a form of horizontal analysis that can reveal patterns in data across successive periods. It involves computing trend percents for a series of financial numbers and is a variation on the use of percent changes. The difference is that trend analysis does not subtract the base period amount in the numerator. To compute trend percents, we do the following:

1. Select a *base period* and assign each item in the base period a weight of 100%.
2. Express financial numbers as a percent of their base period number.

Specifically, a *trend percent,* also called an *index number,* is computed as follows:

$$\text{Trend percent } (\%) = \frac{\text{Analysis period amount}}{\text{Base period amount}} \times 100$$

Point: *Index* refers to the comparison of the analysis period to the base period. Percents determined for each period are called *index numbers.*

To illustrate trend analysis, we use the Best Buy data shown in Exhibit 17.3.

(in millions)	2007	2006	2005	2004	2003
Revenues	$35,934	$30,848	$27,433	$24,548	$20,943
Cost of goods sold	27,165	23,122	20,938	18,677	15,998
Selling, general & administrative expenses	6,770	6,082	5,053	4,567	3,935

EXHIBIT 17.3

Revenues and Expenses

These data are from Best Buy's *Selected Financial Data* section. The base period is 2003 and the trend percent is computed in each subsequent year by dividing that year's amount by its 2003 amount. For instance, the revenue trend percent for 2007 is 171.6%, computed as $35,934/$20,943. The trend percents—using the data from Exhibit 17.3—are shown in Exhibit 17.4.

EXHIBIT 17.4

Trend Percents for Revenues and Expenses

	2007	2006	2005	2004	2003
Revenues	171.6%	147.3%	131.0%	117.2%	100.0%
Cost of goods sold	169.8	144.5	130.9	116.7	100.0
Selling, general & administrative expenses	172.0	154.6	128.4	116.1	100.0

Point: Trend analysis expresses a percent of base, not a percent of change.

Graphical depictions often aid analysis of trend percents. Exhibit 17.5 shows the trend percents from Exhibit 17.4 in a *line graph,* which can help us identify trends and detect changes in direction or magnitude. It reveals that the trend line for revenues consistently exceeds that for cost of goods sold. Moreover, the magnitude of that difference has slightly grown. This result bodes well for Best Buy because its cost of goods sold are by far its largest cost, and the company shows an ability to control these expenses as it expands. The line graph also reveals a consistent increase in each of these accounts, which is typical of growth companies. The trend line for selling, general and administrative expenses is less encouraging because it exceeds the revenue trend line in 2006–2007. The good news is that nearly all of that upward shift in costs occured in one year (2006). In other years, management appears to have limited those costs to not exceed revenue growth.

EXHIBIT 17.5

Trend Percent Lines for Revenues and Expenses of Best Buy

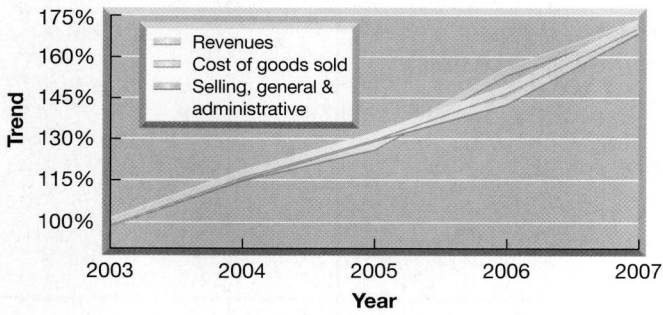

EXHIBIT 17.6

Trend Percent Lines—Best Buy, Circuit City, and RadioShack

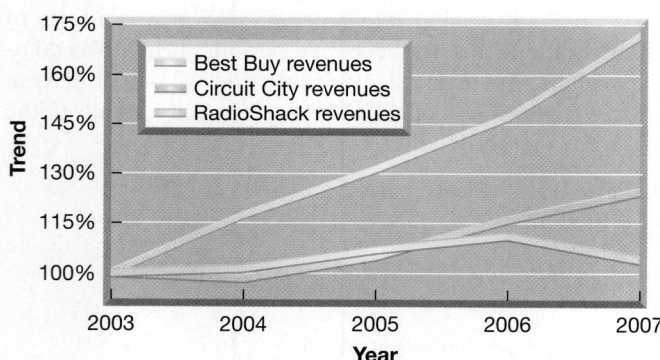

Exhibit 17.6 compares **Best Buy**'s revenue trend line to that of **Circuit City** and **RadioShack** for this same period. Best Buy's revenues sharply increased over this time period while those of Circuit City exhibited less growth, and those for RadioShack were flat. These data indicate that Best Buy's products and services have met with considerable consumer acceptance.

Trend analysis of financial statement items can include comparisons of relations between items on different financial statements. For instance, Exhibit 17.7 compares Best Buy's revenues and total assets. The rate of increase in total assets (176.4%) is greater than the increase in revenues (171.6%) since 2003. Is this result favorable or not? It suggests that Best Buy was slightly less efficient in using its assets in 2007. Management apparently is expecting future years' revenues to compensate for this asset growth.

Overall we must remember that an important role of financial statement analysis is identifying questions and areas of interest, which often direct us to important factors bearing

($ millions)	2007	2003	Trend Percent (2007 vs. 2003)
Revenues	$35,934	$20,943	171.6%
Total assets	13,570	7,694	176.4

EXHIBIT 17.7

Revenue and Asset Data for Best Buy

on a company's future. Accordingly, financial statement analysis should be seen as a continuous process of refining our understanding and expectations of company performance and financial condition.

Decision Maker

Auditor   Your tests reveal a 3% increase in sales from $200,000 to $206,000 and a 4% decrease in expenses from $190,000 to $182,400. Both changes are within your "reasonableness" criterion of ±5%, and thus you don't pursue additional tests. The audit partner in charge questions your lack of follow-up and mentions the *joint relation* between sales and expenses. To what is the partner referring? [Answer—p. 706]

Vertical Analysis

Vertical analysis is a tool to evaluate individual financial statement items or a group of items in terms of a specific base amount. We usually define a key aggregate figure as the base, which for an income statement is usually revenue and for a balance sheet is usually total assets. This section explains vertical analysis and applies it to Best Buy. [The term *vertical analysis* arises from the up-down (or down-up) movement of our eyes as we review common-size financial statements. Vertical analysis is also called *common-size analysis*.]

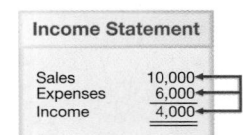

Common-Size Statements

The comparative statements in Exhibits 17.1 and 17.2 show the change in each item over time, but they do not emphasize the relative importance of each item. We use **common-size financial statements** to reveal changes in the relative importance of each financial statement item. All individual amounts in common-size statements are redefined in terms of common-size percents. A *common-size percent* is measured by dividing each individual financial statement amount under analysis by its base amount:

P2   Describe and apply methods of vertical analysis.

$$\text{Common-size percent (\%)} = \frac{\text{Analysis amount}}{\text{Base amount}} \times 100$$

Common-Size Balance Sheets   Common-size statements express each item as a percent of a *base amount,* which for a common-size balance sheet is usually total assets. The base amount is assigned a value of 100%. (This implies that the total amount of liabilities plus equity equals 100% since this amount equals total assets.) We then compute a common-size percent for each asset, liability, and equity item using total assets as the base amount. When we present a company's successive balance sheets in this way, changes in the mixture of assets, liabilities, and equity are apparent.

Exhibit 17.8 shows common-size comparative balance sheets for Best Buy. Some relations that stand out on both a magnitude and percentage basis include (1) a 41% increase in cash and equivalents, (2) a 6.5% decline in short-term investments as a percentage of assets, (3) a 1.2% decrease in net property and equipment as a percentage of assets, (4) a 1.7% increase in the percentage of accounts payable, (5) a 3.4% decline in the current portion of long-term debt, and (6) a marked increase in retained earnings. Most of these changes are characteristic of a successful growth/ stable company. The concern, if any, is whether Best Buy can continue to generate sufficient revenues and income to support its asset buildup within a very competitive industry.

Point: The *base* amount in common-size analysis is an *aggregate* amount from that period's financial statement.

Point: Common-size statements often are used to compare two or more companies in the same industry.

Point: Common-size statements are also useful in comparing firms that report in different currencies.

EXHIBIT 17.8

Common-Size Comparative
Balance Sheets

BEST BUY
Common-Size Comparative Balance Sheets
March 3, 2007, and February 25, 2006

(in millions)	2007	2006	Common-Size Percents* 2007	2006
Assets				
Cash and cash equivalents	$ 1,205	$ 748	8.9%	6.3%
Short-term investments	2,588	3,041	19.1	25.6
Receivables, net	548	449	4.0	3.8
Merchandise inventories	4,028	3,338	29.7	28.1
Other current assets	712	409	5.2	3.4
Total current assets	9,081	7,985	66.9	67.3
Property and equipment	4,904	4,836	36.1	40.8
Less accumulated depreciation	1,966	2,124	14.5	17.9
Net property and equipment	2,938	2,712	21.7	22.9
Goodwill	919	557	6.8	4.7
Tradenames	81	44	0.6	0.4
Long-term investments	318	218	2.3	1.8
Other long-term assets	233	348	1.7	2.9
Total assets	$13,570	$11,864	100.0%	100.0%
Liabilities				
Accounts payable	$ 3,934	$ 3,234	29.0%	27.3%
Unredeemed gift card liabilities	496	469	3.7	4.0
Accrued compensation and related expenses	332	354	2.4	3.0
Accrued liabilities	990	878	7.3	7.4
Accrued income taxes	489	703	3.6	5.9
Short-term debt	41	0	0.3	0.0
Current portion of long-term debt	19	418	0.1	3.5
Total current liabilities	6,301	6,056	46.4	51.0
Long-term liabilities	443	373	3.3	3.1
Long-term debt	590	178	4.3	1.5
Minority interests	35	0	0.3	0.0
Stockholders' Equity				
Common stock	48	49	0.4	0.4
Additional paid-in capital	430	643	3.2	5.4
Retained earnings	5,507	4,304	40.6	36.3
Accumulated other comprehensive income	216	261	1.6	2.2
Total stockholders' equity	6,201	5,257	45.7	44.3
Total liabilities and stockholders' equity	$13,570	$11,864	100.0%	100.0%

* Percents are rounded to tenths and thus may not exactly sum to totals and subtotals.

Common-Size Income Statements   Analysis also benefits from use of a common-size income statement. Revenues is usually the base amount, which is assigned a value of 100%. Each common-size income statement item appears as a percent of revenues. If we think of the 100% revenues amount as representing one sales dollar, the remaining items show how each revenue dollar is distributed among costs, expenses, and income.

Exhibit 17.9 shows common-size comparative income statements for each dollar of Best Buy's revenues. The past two years' common-size numbers are similar. The good news is that Best Buy has been able to squeeze an extra 0.1 cent in earnings per revenue dollar—evidenced by the 3.7% to 3.8% rise in earnings as a percentage of revenues. This implies that management is effectively controlling costs and/or the company is reaping growth benefits, so-called *economies of scale.* The bad news is that gross profit lost 0.6 cent per revenue dollar—evidenced by the 25.0% to 24.4% decline in gross profit as a percentage of revenues. This is a concern given the price-competitive

Global: International companies sometimes disclose "convenience" financial statements, which are statements translated in other languages and currencies. However, these statements rarely adjust for differences in accounting principles across countries.

EXHIBIT 17.9

Common-Size Comparative
Income Statements

BEST BUY Common-Size Comparative Income Statements For Years Ended March 3, 2007, and February 25, 2006			Common-Size Percents*	
($ millions)	2007	2006	2007	2006
Revenues	$35,934	$30,848	100.0%	100.0%
Cost of goods sold	27,165	23,122	75.6	75.0
Gross profit	8,769	7,726	24.4	25.0
Selling, general, and administrative expenses	6,770	6,082	18.8	19.7
Operating income	1,999	1,644	5.6	5.3
Net interest income (expense)	111	77	0.3	0.2
Gain on investments	20	0	0.1	0.0
Earnings from continuing operations before income taxes	2,130	1,721	5.9	5.6
Income tax expense	752	581	2.1	1.9
Minority interest in earnings	1	0	0.0	0.0
Net earnings	$ 1,377	$ 1,140	3.8%	3.7%

* Percents are rounded to tenths and thus may not exactly sum to totals and subtotals.

electronics market. Analysis here shows that common-size percents for successive income statements can uncover potentially important changes in a company's expenses. Evidence of no changes, especially when changes are expected, is also informative.

Common-Size Graphics

Two of the most common tools of common-size analysis are trend analysis of common-size statements and graphical analysis. The trend analysis of common-size statements is similar to that of comparative statements discussed under vertical analysis. It is not illustrated here because the only difference is the substitution of common-size percents for trend percents. Instead, this section discusses graphical analysis of common-size statements.

An income statement readily lends itself to common-size graphical analysis. This is so because revenues affect nearly every item in an income statement. Exhibit 17.10 shows **Best Buy**'s 2007 common-size income statement in graphical form. This pie chart highlights the contribution of each component of revenues for net earnings.

EXHIBIT 17.10

Common-Size Graphic of
Income Statement

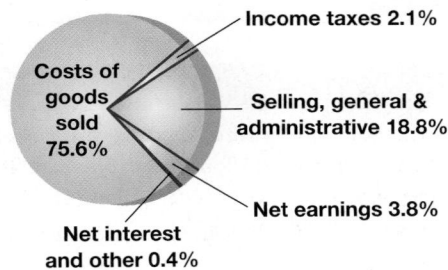

Exhibit 17.11 previews more complex graphical analyses available and the insights they provide. The data for this exhibit are taken from **Best Buy**'s *Segments* footnote. Best Buy has two reportable segments: domestic and international.

EXHIBIT 17.11

Revenue and Operating Income
Breakdown by Segment

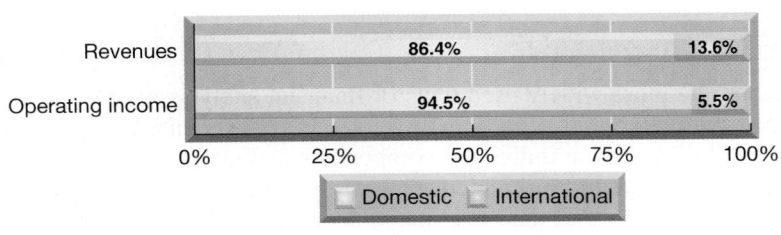

EXHIBIT 17.12

Common-Size Graphic of Asset Components

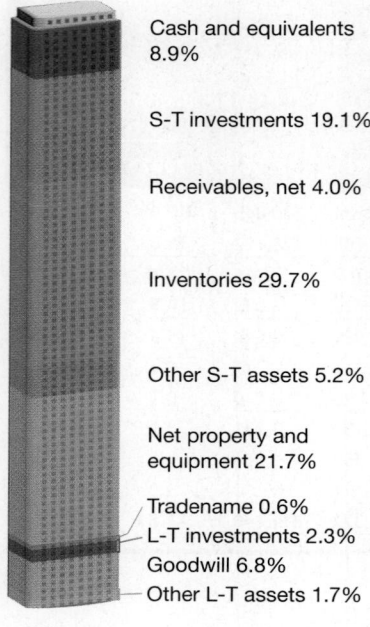

Cash and equivalents 8.9%

S-T investments 19.1%

Receivables, net 4.0%

Inventories 29.7%

Other S-T assets 5.2%

Net property and equipment 21.7%

Tradename 0.6%
L-T investments 2.3%
Goodwill 6.8%
Other L-T assets 1.7%

The upper bar in Exhibit 17.11 shows the percent of revenues from each segment. The major revenue source is Domestic (86.4%). The lower bar shows the percent of operating income from each segment. Although International provides 13.6% of revenues, it provides only 5.5% of operating income. This type of information can help users in determining strategic analyses and actions.

Graphical analysis is also useful in identifying (1) sources of financing including the distribution among current liabilities, noncurrent liabilities, and equity capital and (2) focuses of investing activities, including the distribution among current and noncurrent assets. As illustrative, Exhibit 17.12 shows a common-size graphical display of Best Buy's assets. Common-size balance sheet analysis can be extended to examine the composition of these subgroups. For instance, in assessing liquidity of current assets, knowing what proportion of current assets consists of inventories is usually important, and not simply what proportion inventories are of total assets.

Common-size financial statements are also useful in comparing different companies. Exhibit 17.13 shows common-size graphics of Best Buy, Circuit City, and RadioShack on financing sources. This graphic highlights the larger percent of equity financing for Best Buy and Circuit City than for RadioShack. It also highlights the much larger noncurrent (debt) financing of RadioShack. Comparison of a company's common-size statements with competitors' or industry common-size statistics alerts us to differences in the structure or distribution of its financial statements but not to their dollar magnitude.

EXHIBIT 17.13

Common-Size Graphic of Financing Sources— Competitor Analysis

	Best Buy	Circuit City	RadioShack
Current liabilities	46.4%	42.8%	47.5%
Noncurrent liabilities	7.9%	12.5%	20.9%
Equity	45.7%	44.7%	31.6%

Quick Check
Answers—p. 706

5. Which of the following is true for common-size comparative statements? (*a*) Each item is expressed as a percent of a base amount. (*b*) Total assets often are assigned a value of 100%. (*c*) Amounts from successive periods are placed side by side. (*d*) All are true. (*e*) None is true.

6. What is the difference between the percents shown on a comparative income statement and those shown on a common-size comparative income statement?

7. Trend percents are (*a*) shown on comparative income statements and balance sheets, (*b*) shown on common-size comparative statements, or (*c*) also called *index numbers*.

Ratio Analysis

P3 Define and apply ratio analysis.

Ratios are among the more widely used tools of financial analysis because they provide clues to and symptoms of underlying conditions. A ratio can help us uncover conditions and trends difficult to detect by inspecting individual components making up the ratio. Ratios, like other analysis tools, are usually future oriented; that is, they are often adjusted for their probable future trend and magnitude, and their usefulness depends on skillful interpretation.

A ratio expresses a mathematical relation between two quantities. It can be expressed as a percent, rate, or proportion. For instance, a change in an account balance from $100 to $250 can be expressed as (1) 150%, (2) 2.5 times, or (3) 2.5 to 1 (or 2.5:1). Computation of a ratio is a simple arithmetic operation, but its interpretation is not. To be meaningful, a ratio must refer to an economically important relation. For example, a direct and crucial relation exists between an item's sales price and its cost. Accordingly, the ratio of cost of goods sold to sales is meaningful. In contrast, no obvious relation exists between freight costs and the balance of long-term investments.

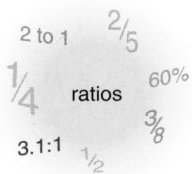

This section describes an important set of financial ratios and its application. The selected ratios are organized into the four building blocks of financial statement analysis: (1) liquidity and efficiency, (2) solvency, (3) profitability, and (4) market prospects. All of these ratios were explained at relevant points in prior chapters. The purpose here is to organize and apply them under a summary framework. We use four common standards, in varying degrees, for comparisons: intracompany, competitor, industry, and guidelines.

Point: Some sources for industry norms are *Annual Statement Studies* by Robert Morris Associates, *Industry Norms & Key Business Ratios* by Dun & Bradstreet, *Standard & Poor's Industry Surveys*, and Reuters.com/finance.

Liquidity and Efficiency

Liquidity refers to the availability of resources to meet short-term cash requirements. It is affected by the timing of cash inflows and outflows along with prospects for future performance. Analysis of liquidity is aimed at a company's funding requirements. *Efficiency* refers to how productive a company is in using its assets. Efficiency is usually measured relative to how much revenue is generated from a certain level of assets.

Both liquidity and efficiency are important and complementary. If a company fails to meet its current obligations, its continued existence is doubtful. Viewed in this light, all other measures of analysis are of secondary importance. Although accounting measurements assume the company's continued existence, our analysis must always assess the validity of this assumption using liquidity measures. Moreover, inefficient use of assets can cause liquidity problems. A lack of liquidity often precedes lower profitability and fewer opportunities. It can foretell a loss of owner control. To a company's creditors, lack of liquidity can yield delays in collecting interest and principal payments or the loss of amounts due them. A company's customers and suppliers of goods and services also are affected by short-term liquidity problems. Implications include a company's inability to execute contracts and potential damage to important customer and supplier relationships. This section describes and illustrates key ratios relevant to assessing liquidity and efficiency.

Working Capital and Current Ratio   The amount of current assets less current liabilities is called **working capital,** or *net working capital.* A company needs adequate working capital to meet current debts, to carry sufficient inventories, and to take advantage of cash discounts. A company that runs low on working capital is less likely to meet current obligations or to continue operating. When evaluating a company's working capital, we must not only look at the dollar amount of current assets less current liabilities, but also at their ratio. The *current ratio* is defined as follows (see Chapter 3 for additional explanation):

$$\text{Current ratio} = \frac{\text{Current assets}}{\text{Current liabilities}}$$

Drawing on information in Exhibit 17.1, **Best Buy**'s working capital and current ratio for both 2007 and 2006 are shown in Exhibit 17.14. **Circuit City** (1.68), **RadioShack** (1.63), and the Industry's current ratio of 1.6 is shown in the margin. Best Buy's 2007 ratio (1.44) is lower than any of the comparison ratios, but it does not appear in danger of defaulting on loan payments. A high current ratio suggests a strong liquidity position and an ability to meet current obligations. A company can, however, have a current ratio that is too high. An excessively high current ratio means that the company has invested too much in current assets compared to its current obligations. An

($ millions)	2007	2006
Current assets	$ 9,081	$ 7,985
Current liabilities	6,301	6,056
Working capital	$2,780	$1,929
Current ratio		
$9,081/$6,301	1.44 to 1	
$7,985/$6,056		1.32 to 1

EXHIBIT 17.14

Best Buy's Working Capital and Current Ratio

Current ratio
Circuit City = 1.68
RadioShack = 1.63
Industry = 1.6

excessive investment in current assets is not an efficient use of funds because current assets normally generate a low return on investment (compared with long-term assets).

Many users apply a guideline of 2:1 (or 1.5:1) for the current ratio in helping evaluate a company's debt-paying ability. A company with a 2:1 or higher current ratio is generally thought to be a good credit risk in the short run. Such a guideline or any analysis of the current ratio must recognize at least three additional factors: (1) type of business, (2) composition of current assets, and (3) turnover rate of current asset components.

Type of business. A service company that grants little or no credit and carries few inventories can probably operate on a current ratio of less than 1:1 if its revenues generate enough cash to pay its current liabilities. On the other hand, a company selling high-priced clothing or furniture requires a higher ratio because of difficulties in judging customer demand and cash receipts. For instance, if demand falls, inventory may not generate as much cash as expected. Accordingly, analysis of the current ratio should include a comparison with ratios from successful companies in the same industry and from prior periods. We must also recognize that a company's accounting methods, especially choice of inventory method, affect the current ratio. For instance, when costs are rising, a company using LIFO tends to report a smaller amount of current assets than when using FIFO.

Point: When a firm uses LIFO in a period of rising costs, the standard for an adequate current ratio usually is lower than if it used FIFO.

Composition of current assets. The composition of a company's current assets is important to an evaluation of short-term liquidity. For instance, cash, cash equivalents, and short-term investments are more liquid than accounts and notes receivable. Also, short-term receivables normally are more liquid than inventory. Cash, of course, can be used to immediately pay current debts. Items such as accounts receivable and inventory, however, normally must be converted into cash before payment is made. An excessive amount of receivables and inventory weakens a company's ability to pay current liabilities. The acid-test ratio (see below) can help with this assessment.

Turnover rate of assets. Asset turnover measures a company's efficiency in using its assets. One relevant measure of asset efficiency is the revenue generated. A measure of total asset turnover is revenues divided by total assets, but evaluation of turnover for individual assets is also useful. We discuss both receivables turnover and inventory turnover on the next page.

 Decision Maker

Banker   A company requests a one-year, $200,000 loan for expansion. This company's current ratio is 4:1, with current assets of $160,000. Key competitors carry a current ratio of about 1.9:1. Using this information, do you approve the loan application? Does your decision change if the application is for a 10-year loan?
[Answer—p. 706]

Acid-Test Ratio   Quick assets are cash, short-term investments, and current receivables. These are the most liquid types of current assets. The *acid-test ratio,* also called *quick ratio,* and introduced in Chapter 5, reflects on a company's short-term liquidity.

$$\text{Acid-test ratio} = \frac{\text{Cash + Short-term investments + Current receivables}}{\text{Current liabilities}}$$

Best Buy's acid-test ratio is computed in Exhibit 17.15. Best Buy's 2007 acid-test ratio (0.69) is between that for Circuit City (0.65) and RadioShack (0.73), and less than the 1:1 common

EXHIBIT 17.15

Acid-Test Ratio

Acid-test ratio
Circuit City = 0.65
RadioShack = 0.73
Industry = 0.7

($ millions)	2007	2006
Cash and equivalents	$1,205	$ 748
Short-term investments	2,588	3,041
Current receivables	548	449
Total quick assets	$4,341	$4,238
Current liabilities	$6,301	$6,056
Acid-test ratio		
$4,341/$6,301	0.69 to 1	
$4,238/$6,056		0.70 to 1

guideline for an acceptable acid-test ratio; each of these ratios is similar to the 0.7 industry ratio. As with analysis of the current ratio, we need to consider other factors. For instance, the frequency with which a company converts its current assets into cash affects its working capital requirements. This implies that analysis of short-term liquidity should also include an analysis of receivables and inventories, which we consider next.

Accounts Receivable Turnover   We can measure how frequently a company converts its receivables into cash by computing the *accounts receivable turnover*. This ratio is defined as follows (see Chapter 9 for additional explanation):

$$\text{Accounts receivable turnover} = \frac{\text{Net sales}}{\text{Average accounts receivable, net}}$$

Short-term receivables from customers are often included in the denominator along with accounts receivable. Also, accounts receivable turnover is more precise if credit sales are used for the numerator, but external users generally use net sales (or net revenues) because information about credit sales is typically not reported. Best Buy's 2007 accounts receivable turnover is computed as follows ($ millions).

$$\frac{\$35,934}{(\$548 + \$449)/2} = 72.1 \text{ times}$$

Best Buy's value of 72.1 is larger than Circuit City's 41.2 and RadioShack's 17.1. Accounts receivable turnover is high when accounts receivable are quickly collected. A high turnover is favorable because it means the company need not commit large amounts of funds to accounts receivable. However, an accounts receivable turnover can be too high; this can occur when credit terms are so restrictive that they negatively affect sales volume.

Inventory Turnover   How long a company holds inventory before selling it will affect working capital requirements. One measure of this effect is *inventory turnover*, also called *merchandise turnover* or *merchandise inventory turnover*, which is defined as follows (see Chapter 6 for additional explanation):

$$\text{Inventory turnover} = \frac{\text{Cost of goods sold}}{\text{Average inventory}}$$

Using Best Buy's cost of goods sold and inventories information, we compute its inventory turnover for 2007 as follows (if the beginning and ending inventories for the year do not represent the usual inventory amount, an average of quarterly or monthly inventories can be used).

$$\frac{\$27,165}{(\$4,028 + \$3,338)/2} = 7.38 \text{ times}$$

Best Buy's inventory turnover of 7.38 is higher than Circuit City's 5.70, RadioShack's 2.96, and the industry's 4.5. A company with a high turnover requires a smaller investment in inventory than one producing the same sales with a lower turnover. Inventory turnover can be too high, however, if the inventory a company keeps is so small that it restricts sales volume.

Days' Sales Uncollected   Accounts receivable turnover provides insight into how frequently a company collects its accounts. Days' sales uncollected is one measure of this activity, which is defined as follows (Chapter 8 provides additional explanation):

$$\text{Days' sales uncollected} = \frac{\text{Accounts receivable, net}}{\text{Net sales}} \times 365$$

Any short-term notes receivable from customers are normally included in the numerator.

Global: Ratio analysis helps overcome currency translation problems, but it does *not* overcome differences in accounting principles.

Point: Some users prefer using gross accounts receivable (before subtracting the allowance for doubtful accounts) to avoid the influence of a manager's bad debts estimate.

Accounts receivable turnover
Circuit City = 41.2
RadioShack = 17.1

Point: Ending accounts receivable can be substituted for the average balance in computing accounts receivable turnover if the difference between ending and average receivables is small.

Inventory turnover
Circuit City = 5.70
RadioShack = 2.96
Industry = 4.5

Best Buy's 2007 days' sales uncollected follows.

$$\frac{\$548}{\$35,934} \times 365 = 5.57 \text{ days}$$

Both Circuit City's days' sales uncollected of 11.23 days and RadioShack's 18.94 days are longer than the 5.57 days for Best Buy. Days' sales uncollected is more meaningful if we know company credit terms. A rough guideline states that days' sales uncollected should not exceed $1\frac{1}{3}$ times the days in its (1) credit period, *if* discounts are not offered or (2) discount period, *if* favorable discounts are offered.

Days' Sales in Inventory   *Days' sales in inventory* is a useful measure in evaluating inventory liquidity. Days' sales in inventory is linked to inventory in a way that days' sales uncollected is linked to receivables. We compute days' sales in inventory as follows (Chapter 6 provides additional explanation).

$$\textbf{Days' sales in inventory} = \frac{\textbf{Ending inventory}}{\textbf{Cost of goods sold}} \times \textbf{365}$$

Best Buy's days' sales in inventory for 2007 follows.

$$\frac{\$4,028}{\$27,165} \times 365 = 54.1 \text{ days}$$

If the products in Best Buy's inventory are in demand by customers, this formula estimates that its inventory will be converted into receivables (or cash) in 54.1 days. If all of Best Buy's sales were credit sales, the conversion of inventory to receivables in 54.1 days *plus* the conversion of receivables to cash in 5.57 days implies that inventory will be converted to cash in about 59.67 days (54.1 + 5.57).

Total Asset Turnover   *Total asset turnover* reflects a company's ability to use its assets to generate sales and is an important indication of operating efficiency. The definition of this ratio follows (Chapter 10 offers additional explanation).

$$\textbf{Total asset turnover} = \frac{\textbf{Net sales}}{\textbf{Average total assets}}$$

Best Buy's total asset turnover for 2007 follows and is less than Circuit City's, but greater than that for RadioShack.

$$\frac{\$35,934}{(\$13,570 + \$11,864)/2} = 2.83 \text{ times}$$

Quick Check

Answers—p. 706

8. Information from Paff Co. at Dec. 31, 2008, follows: cash, $820,000; accounts receivable, $240,000; inventories, $470,000; plant assets, $910,000; accounts payable, $350,000; and income taxes payable, $180,000. Compute its (a) current ratio and (b) acid-test ratio.

9. On Dec. 31, 2009, Paff Company (see question 8) had accounts receivable of $290,000 and inventories of $530,000. During 2009, net sales amounted to $2,500,000 and cost of goods sold was $750,000. Compute (a) accounts receivable turnover, (b) days' sales uncollected, (c) inventory turnover, and (d) days' sales in inventory.

Solvency

Solvency refers to a company's long-run financial viability and its ability to cover long-term obligations. All of a company's business activities—financing, investing, and operating—affect its solvency. Analysis of solvency is long term and uses less precise but more encompassing measures than liquidity. One of the most important components of solvency analysis is the composition of a company's capital structure. *Capital structure* refers to a company's financing sources. It ranges from relatively permanent equity financing to riskier or more temporary short-term financing. Assets represent security for financiers, ranging from loans secured by specific assets to the assets available as general security to unsecured creditors. This section describes the tools of solvency analysis. Our analysis focuses on a company's ability to both meet its obligations and provide security to its creditors *over the long run*. Indicators of this ability include *debt* and *equity* ratios, the relation between *pledged assets and secured liabilities,* and the company's capacity to earn sufficient income to *pay fixed interest charges.*

Debt and Equity Ratios One element of solvency analysis is to assess the portion of a company's assets contributed by its owners and the portion contributed by creditors. This relation is reflected in the debt ratio (also described in Chapter 2). The *debt ratio* expresses total liabilities as a percent of total assets. The **equity ratio** provides complementary information by expressing total equity as a percent of total assets. **Best Buy**'s debt and equity ratios follow.

> **Point:** For analysis purposes, Minority Interest is usually included in equity.

($ millions)	2007	Ratios	
Total liabilities	$ 7,369	54.3%	[Debt ratio]
Total equity	6,201	45.7	[Equity ratio]
Total liabilities and equity	$13,570	100.0%	

> **Debt ratio :: Equity ratio**
> Circuit City = 55.3% :: 44.7%
> RadioShack = 68.4% :: 31.6%

Best Buy's financial statements reveal more debt than equity. A company is considered less risky if its capital structure (equity and long-term debt) contains more equity. One risk factor is the required payment for interest and principal when debt is outstanding. Another factor is the greater the stockholder financing, the more losses a company can absorb through equity before the assets become inadequate to satisfy creditors' claims. From the stockholders' point of view, if a company earns a return on borrowed capital that is higher than the cost of borrowing, the difference represents increased income to stockholders. The inclusion of debt is described as *financial leverage* because debt can have the effect of increasing the return to stockholders. Companies are said to be highly leveraged if a large portion of their assets is financed by debt.

> **Point:** Bank examiners from the FDIC and other regulatory agencies use debt and equity ratios to monitor compliance with regulatory capital requirements imposed on banks and S&Ls.

Debt-to-Equity Ratio The ratio of total liabilities to equity is another measure of solvency. We compute the ratio as follows (Chapter 14 offers additional explanation).

$$\text{Debt-to-equity ratio} = \frac{\text{Total liabilities}}{\text{Total equity}}$$

Best Buy's debt-to-equity ratio for 2007 is

$$\$7,369/\$6,201 = 1.19$$

> **Debt-to-equity**
> Circuit City = 1.24
> RadioShack = 2.17
> Industry = 0.99

Best Buy's 1.19 debt-to-equity ratio is less than the 1.24 ratio for Circuit City and the 2.17 for RadioShack, but greater than the industry ratio of 0.99. Consistent with our inferences from the debt ratio, Best Buy's capital structure has more debt than equity, which increases risk. Recall that debt must be repaid with interest, while equity does not. These debt requirements can be burdensome when the industry and/or the economy experience a downturn. A larger debt-to-equity ratio also implies less opportunity to expand through use of debt financing.

Times Interest Earned The amount of income before deductions for interest expense and income taxes is the amount available to pay interest expense. The following

Point: The times interest earned ratio and the debt and equity ratios are of special interest to bank lending officers.

times interest earned ratio reflects the creditors' risk of loan repayments with interest (see Chapter 11 for additional explanation).

$$\text{Times interest earned} = \frac{\textbf{Income before interest expense and income taxes}}{\textbf{Interest expense}}$$

The larger this ratio, the less risky is the company for creditors. One guideline says that creditors are reasonably safe if the company earns its fixed interest expense two or more times each year. Best Buy's times interest earned ratio follows; its value suggests that its creditors have little risk of nonrepayment.

Times interest earned
Circuit City = 12.5
RadioShack = 3.5

$$\frac{\$1,377 + \$31 \text{ (see Best Buy note \#7)} + \$752}{\$31} = 69.7$$

Decision Insight

Bears and Bulls A *bear market* is a declining market. The phrase comes from bear-skin jobbers who often sold the skins before the bears were caught. The term *bear* was then used to describe investors who sold shares they did not own in anticipation of a price decline. A *bull market* is a rising market. This phrase comes from the once popular sport of bear and bull baiting. The term *bull* came to mean the opposite of *bear*.

Profitability

We are especially interested in a company's ability to use its assets efficiently to produce profits (and positive cash flows). *Profitability* refers to a company's ability to generate an adequate return on invested capital. Return is judged by assessing earnings relative to the level and sources of financing. Profitability is also relevant to solvency. This section describes key profitability measures and their importance to financial statement analysis.

Profit Margin A company's operating efficiency and profitability can be expressed by two components. The first is *profit margin,* which reflects a company's ability to earn net income from sales (Chapter 3 offers additional explanation). It is measured by expressing net income as a percent of sales (*sales* and *revenues* are similar terms). **Best Buy**'s profit margin follows.

Profit margin
Circuit City = −0.1%
RadioShack = 1.5%

$$\text{Profit margin} = \frac{\textbf{Net income}}{\textbf{Net sales}} = \frac{\$1,377}{\$35,934} = 3.8\%$$

To evaluate profit margin, we must consider the industry. For instance, an appliance company might require a profit margin between 10% and 15%; whereas a retail supermarket might require a profit margin of 1% or 2%. Both profit margin and *total asset turnover* make up the two basic components of operating efficiency. These ratios reflect on management because managers are ultimately responsible for operating efficiency. The next section explains how we use both measures to analyze return on total assets.

Return on Total Assets *Return on total assets* is defined as follows.

$$\text{Return on total assets} = \frac{\textbf{Net income}}{\textbf{Average total assets}}$$

Best Buy's 2007 return on total assets is

Return on total assets
Circuit City = −0.2%
RadioShack = 3.4%
Industry = 3.0

$$\frac{\$1,377}{(\$13,570 + \$11,864)/2} = 10.8\%$$

Best Buy's 10.8% return on total assets is lower than that for many businesses but is higher than RadioShack's return of 3.4% and the industry's 3.0% return. We also should evaluate any trend in the rate of return.

Point: Many analysts add back *Interest expense* × *(1 − Tax rate)* to net income in computing return on total assets.

The following equation shows the important relation between profit margin, total asset turnover, and return on total assets.

$$\text{Profit margin} \times \text{Total asset turnover} = \text{Return on total assets}$$

or

$$\frac{\text{Net income}}{\text{Net sales}} \times \frac{\text{Net sales}}{\text{Average total assets}} = \frac{\text{Net income}}{\text{Average total assets}}$$

Both profit margin and total asset turnover contribute to overall operating efficiency, as measured by return on total assets. If we apply this formula to Best Buy, we get

$$3.8\% \times 2.83 = 10.8\%$$

Circuit City: −0.1% × 3.08 = −0.2%
RadioShack: 1.5% × 2.24 =   3.4%
              (with rounding)

This analysis shows that Best Buy's superior return on assets versus that of Circuit City and RadioShack is driven mainly by its higher profit margin.

Return on Common Stockholders' Equity   Perhaps the most important goal in operating a company is to earn net income for its owner(s). *Return on common stockholders' equity* measures a company's success in reaching this goal and is defined as follows.

$$\text{Return on common stockholders' equity} = \frac{\text{Net income} - \text{Preferred dividends}}{\text{Average common stockholders' equity}}$$

Best Buy's 2007 return on common stockholders' equity is computed as follows:

$$\frac{\$1,377 - \$0}{(\$6,236 + \$5,257)/2} = 24.0\%$$

Return on common equity
Circuit City = −0.4%
RadioShack = 11.8%

The denominator in this computation is the book value of common equity (including minority interest). In the numerator, the dividends on cumulative preferred stock are subtracted whether they are declared or are in arrears. If preferred stock is noncumulative, its dividends are subtracted only if declared.

Decision Insight

Wall Street   *Wall Street* is synonymous with financial markets, but its name comes from the street location of the original New York Stock Exchange. The street's name derives from stockades built by early settlers to protect New York from pirate attacks.

Market Prospects

Market measures are useful for analyzing corporations with publicly traded stock. These market measures use stock price, which reflects the market's (public's) expectations for the company. This includes expectations of both company return and risk—as the market perceives it.

Price-Earnings Ratio   Computation of the *price-earnings ratio* follows (Chapter 13 provides additional explanation).

$$\text{Price-earnings ratio} = \frac{\text{Market price per common share}}{\text{Earnings per share}}$$

Predicted earnings per share for the next period is often used in the denominator of this computation. Reported earnings per share for the most recent period is also commonly used. In both cases, the ratio is used as an indicator of the future growth and risk of a company's earnings as perceived by the stock's buyers and sellers.

The market price of Best Buy's common stock at the start of fiscal year 2008 was $46.35. Using Best Buy's $2.86 basic earnings per share, we compute its price-earnings ratio as follows (some analysts compute this ratio using the median of the low and high stock price).

$$\frac{\$46.35}{\$2.86} = 16.2$$

Best Buy's price-earnings ratio is less than that for RadioShack, but is slightly higher than the norm. (Circuit City's ratio is negative due to its abnormally low earnings.) Best Buy's middle-of-the-pack ratio likely reflects investors' expectations of continued growth but normal earnings.

Dividend Yield   *Dividend yield* is used to compare the dividend-paying performance of different investment alternatives. We compute dividend yield as follows (Chapter 13 offers additional explanation).

$$\text{Dividend yield} = \frac{\textbf{Annual cash dividends per share}}{\textbf{Market price per share}}$$

Best Buy's dividend yield, based on its fiscal year-end market price per share of $46.35 and its policy of $0.36 cash dividends per share, is computed as follows.

$$\frac{\$0.36}{\$46.35} = 0.8\%$$

Some companies do not declare and pay dividends because they wish to reinvest the cash.

Summary of Ratios

Exhibit 17.16 summarizes the major financial statement analysis ratios illustrated in this chapter and throughout the book. This summary includes each ratio's title, its formula, and the purpose for which it is commonly used.

Decision Insight

Ticker Prices   *Ticker prices* refer to a band of moving data on a monitor carrying up-to-the-minute stock prices. The phrase comes from *ticker tape,* a 1-inch-wide strip of paper spewing stock prices from a printer that ticked as it ran. Most of today's investors have never seen actual ticker tape, but the phrase survives.

Quick Check

Answers—p. 706

10. Which ratio best reflects a company's ability to meet immediate interest payments? (*a*) Debt ratio. (*b*) Equity ratio. (*c*) Times interest earned.

11. Which ratio best measures a company's success in earning net income for its owner(s)?
(*a*) Profit margin. (*b*) Return on common stockholders' equity. (*c*) Price-earnings ratio.
(*d*) Dividend yield.

12. If a company has net sales of $8,500,000, net income of $945,000, and total asset turnover of 1.8 times, what is its return on total assets?

EXHIBIT 17.16

Financial Statement Analysis Ratios*

Ratio	Formula	Measure of
Liquidity and Efficiency		
Current ratio	$= \dfrac{\text{Current assets}}{\text{Current liabilities}}$	Short-term debt-paying ability
Acid-test ratio	$= \dfrac{\text{Cash + Short-term investments + Current receivables}}{\text{Current liabilities}}$	Immediate short-term debt-paying ability
Accounts receivable turnover	$= \dfrac{\text{Net sales}}{\text{Average accounts receivable, net}}$	Efficiency of collection
Inventory turnover	$= \dfrac{\text{Cost of goods sold}}{\text{Average inventory}}$	Efficiency of inventory management
Days' sales uncollected	$= \dfrac{\text{Accounts receivable, net}}{\text{Net sales}} \times 365$	Liquidity of receivables
Days' sales in inventory	$= \dfrac{\text{Ending inventory}}{\text{Cost of goods sold}} \times 365$	Liquidity of inventory
Total asset turnover	$= \dfrac{\text{Net sales}}{\text{Average total assets}}$	Efficiency of assets in producing sales
Solvency		
Debt ratio	$= \dfrac{\text{Total liabilities}}{\text{Total assets}}$	Creditor financing and leverage
Equity ratio	$= \dfrac{\text{Total equity}}{\text{Total assets}}$	Owner financing
Debt-to-equity ratio	$= \dfrac{\text{Total liabilities}}{\text{Total equity}}$	Debt versus equity financing
Times interest earned	$= \dfrac{\text{Income before interest expense and income taxes}}{\text{Interest expense}}$	Protection in meeting interest payments
Profitability		
Profit margin ratio	$= \dfrac{\text{Net income}}{\text{Net sales}}$	Net income in each sales dollar
Gross margin ratio	$= \dfrac{\text{Net sales} - \text{Cost of goods sold}}{\text{Net sales}}$	Gross margin in each sales dollar
Return on total assets	$= \dfrac{\text{Net income}}{\text{Average total assets}}$	Overall profitability of assets
Return on common stockholders' equity	$= \dfrac{\text{Net income} - \text{Preferred dividends}}{\text{Average common stockholders' equity}}$	Profitability of owner investment
Book value per common share	$= \dfrac{\text{Shareholders' equity applicable to common shares}}{\text{Number of common shares outstanding}}$	Liquidation at reported amounts
Basic earnings per share	$= \dfrac{\text{Net income} - \text{Preferred dividends}}{\text{Weighted-average common shares outstanding}}$	Net income per common share
Market Prospects		
Price-earnings ratio	$= \dfrac{\text{Market price per common share}}{\text{Earnings per share}}$	Market value relative to earnings
Dividend yield	$= \dfrac{\text{Annual cash dividends per share}}{\text{Market price per share}}$	Cash return per common share

* Additional ratios also examined in previous chapters included credit risk ratio; plant asset useful life; plant asset age; days' cash expense coverage; cash coverage of growth; cash coverage of debt; free cash flow; cash flow on total assets; and payout ratio.

Decision Analysis   Analysis Reporting

A1   Summarize and report results of analysis.

Understanding the purpose of financial statement analysis is crucial to the usefulness of any analysis. This understanding leads to efficiency of effort, effectiveness in application, and relevance in focus. The purpose of most financial statement analyses is to reduce uncertainty in business decisions through a rigorous and sound evaluation. A *financial statement analysis report* helps by directly addressing the building blocks of analysis and by identifying weaknesses in inference by requiring explanation: It forces us to organize our reasoning and to verify its flow and logic. A report also serves as a communication link with readers, and the writing process reinforces our judgments and vice versa. Finally, the report helps us (re)evaluate evidence and refine conclusions on key building blocks. A good analysis report usually consists of six sections:

1. **Executive summary**—brief focus on important analysis results and conclusions.
2. **Analysis overview**—background on the company, its industry, and its economic setting.
3. **Evidential matter**—financial statements and information used in the analysis, including ratios, trends, comparisons, statistics, and all analytical measures assembled; often organized under the building blocks of analysis.
4. **Assumptions**—identification of important assumptions regarding a company's industry and economic environment, and other important assumptions for estimates.
5. **Key factors**—list of important favorable and unfavorable factors, both quantitative and qualitative, for company performance; usually organized by areas of analysis.
6. **Inferences**—forecasts, estimates, interpretations, and conclusions drawing on all sections of the report.

We must remember that the user dictates relevance, meaning that the analysis report should include a brief table of contents to help readers focus on those areas most relevant to their decisions. All irrelevant matter must be eliminated. For example, decades-old details of obscure transactions and detailed miscues of the analysis are irrelevant. Ambiguities and qualifications to avoid responsibility or hedging inferences must be eliminated. Finally, writing is important. Mistakes in grammar and errors of fact compromise the report's credibility.

Decision Insight

Short Selling   *Short selling* refers to selling stock before you buy it. Here's an example: You borrow 100 shares of Nike stock, sell them at $40 each, and receive money from their sale. You then wait. You hope that Nike's stock price falls to, say, $35 each and you can replace the borrowed stock for less than you sold it for, reaping a profit of $5 each less any transaction costs.

Demonstration Problem

DP17

Use the following financial statements of Precision Co. to complete these requirements.

1. Prepare comparative income statements showing the percent increase or decrease for year 2009 in comparison to year 2008.
2. Prepare common-size comparative balance sheets for years 2009 and 2008.
3. Compute the following ratios as of December 31, 2009, or for the year ended December 31, 2009, and identify its building block category for financial statement analysis.

   a. Current ratio
   b. Acid-test ratio
   c. Accounts receivable turnover
   d. Days' sales uncollected
   e. Inventory turnover
   f. Debt ratio

   g. Debt-to-equity ratio
   h. Times interest earned
   i. Profit margin ratio
   j. Total asset turnover
   k. Return on total assets
   l. Return on common stockholders' equity

PRECISION COMPANY Comparative Balance Sheets December 31, 2009 and 2008		
	2009	**2008**
Assets		
Current assets		
Cash	$ 79,000	$ 42,000
Short-term investments	65,000	96,000
Accounts receivable, net	120,000	100,000
Merchandise inventory	250,000	265,000
Total current assets	514,000	503,000
Plant assets		
Store equipment, net	400,000	350,000
Office equipment, net	45,000	50,000
Buildings, net	625,000	675,000
Land	100,000	100,000
Total plant assets	1,170,000	1,175,000
Total assets	$1,684,000	$1,678,000
Liabilities		
Current liabilities		
Accounts payable	$ 164,000	$ 190,000
Short-term notes payable	75,000	90,000
Taxes payable	26,000	12,000
Total current liabilities	265,000	292,000
Long-term liabilities		
Notes payable (secured by		
mortgage on buildings)	400,000	420,000
Total liabilities	665,000	712,000
Stockholders' Equity		
Common stock, $5 par value	475,000	475,000
Retained earnings	544,000	491,000
Total stockholders' equity	1,019,000	966,000
Total liabilities and equity	$1,684,000	$1,678,000

PRECISION COMPANY Comparative Income Statements For Years Ended December 31, 2009 and 2008		
	2009	**2008**
Sales	$2,486,000	$2,075,000
Cost of goods sold	1,523,000	1,222,000
Gross profit	963,000	853,000
Operating expenses		
Advertising expense	145,000	100,000
Sales salaries expense	240,000	280,000
Office salaries expense	165,000	200,000
Insurance expense	100,000	45,000
Supplies expense	26,000	35,000
Depreciation expense	85,000	75,000
Miscellaneous expenses	17,000	15,000
Total operating expenses	778,000	750,000
Operating income	185,000	103,000
Interest expense	44,000	46,000
Income before taxes	141,000	57,000
Income taxes	47,000	19,000
Net income	$ 94,000	$ 38,000
Earnings per share	$ 0.99	$ 0.40

Planning the Solution

- Set up a four-column income statement; enter the 2009 and 2008 amounts in the first two columns and then enter the dollar change in the third column and the percent change from 2008 in the fourth column.
- Set up a four-column balance sheet; enter the 2009 and 2008 year-end amounts in the first two columns and then compute and enter the amount of each item as a percent of total assets.
- Compute the required ratios using the data provided. Use the average of beginning and ending amounts when appropriate (see Exhibit 17.16 for definitions).

Solution to Demonstration Problem

1.

PRECISION COMPANY Comparative Income Statements For Years Ended December 31, 2009 and 2008				
			Increase (Decrease) in 2009	
	2009	**2008**	**Amount**	**Percent**
Sales	$2,486,000	$2,075,000	$411,000	19.8%
Cost of goods sold	1,523,000	1,222,000	301,000	24.6
Gross profit	963,000	853,000	110,000	12.9
Operating expenses				
Advertising expense	145,000	100,000	45,000	45.0
Sales salaries expense	240,000	280,000	(40,000)	(14.3)
Office salaries expense	165,000	200,000	(35,000)	(17.5)

[continued on next page]

[continued from previous page]

Insurance expense	100,000	45,000	55,000	122.2
Supplies expense	26,000	35,000	(9,000)	(25.7)
Depreciation expense	85,000	75,000	10,000	13.3
Miscellaneous expenses	17,000	15,000	2,000	13.3
Total operating expenses	778,000	750,000	28,000	3.7
Operating income	185,000	103,000	82,000	79.6
Interest expense	44,000	46,000	(2,000)	(4.3)
Income before taxes	141,000	57,000	84,000	147.4
Income taxes	47,000	19,000	28,000	147.4
Net income	$ 94,000	$ 38,000	$ 56,000	147.4
Earnings per share	$ 0.99	$ 0.40	$ 0.59	147.5

2.

PRECISION COMPANY
Common-Size Comparative Balance Sheets
December 31, 2009 and 2008

	December 31		Common-Size Percents	
	2009	2008	2009*	2008*
Assets				
Current assets				
Cash	$ 79,000	$ 42,000	4.7%	2.5%
Short-term investments	65,000	96,000	3.9	5.7
Accounts receivable, net	120,000	100,000	7.1	6.0
Merchandise inventory	250,000	265,000	14.8	15.8
Total current assets	514,000	503,000	30.5	30.0
Plant Assets				
Store equipment, net	400,000	350,000	23.8	20.9
Office equipment, net	45,000	50,000	2.7	3.0
Buildings, net	625,000	675,000	37.1	40.2
Land	100,000	100,000	5.9	6.0
Total plant assets	1,170,000	1,175,000	69.5	70.0
Total assets	$1,684,000	$1,678,000	100.0	100.0
Liabilities				
Current liabilities				
Accounts payable	$ 164,000	$ 190,000	9.7%	11.3%
Short-term notes payable	75,000	90,000	4.5	5.4
Taxes payable	26,000	12,000	1.5	0.7
Total current liabilities	265,000	292,000	15.7	17.4
Long-term liabilities				
Notes payable (secured by				
mortgage on buildings)	400,000	420,000	23.8	25.0
Total liabilities	665,000	712,000	39.5	42.4
Stockholders' Equity				
Common stock, $5 par value	475,000	475,000	28.2	28.3
Retained earnings	544,000	491,000	32.3	29.3
Total stockholders' equity	1,019,000	966,000	60.5	57.6
Total liabilities and equity	$1,684,000	$1,678,000	100.0	100.0

* Columns do not always exactly add to 100 due to rounding.

3. **Ratios for 2009:**
   a. Current ratio: $514,000/$265,000 = 1.9:1 (liquidity and efficiency)
   b. Acid-test ratio: ($79,000 + $65,000 + $120,000)/$265,000 = 1.0:1 (liquidity and efficiency)
   c. Average receivables: ($120,000 + $100,000)/2 = $110,000
      Accounts receivable turnover: $2,486,000/$110,000 = 22.6 times (liquidity and efficiency)
   d. Days' sales uncollected: ($120,000/$2,486,000) × 365 = 17.6 days (liquidity and efficiency)
   e. Average inventory: ($250,000 + $265,000)/2 = $257,500
      Inventory turnover: $1,523,000/$257,500 = 5.9 times (liquidity and efficiency)

f. Debt ratio: $665,000/$1,684,000 = 39.5\%$ (solvency)

g. Debt-to-equity ratio: $665,000/$1,019,000 = 0.65$ (solvency)

h. Times interest earned: $185,000/$44,000 = 4.2$ times (solvency)

i. Profit margin ratio: $94,000/$2,486,000 = 3.8\%$ (profitability)

j. Average total assets: ($1,684,000 + $1,678,000)/2 = $1,681,000
   Total asset turnover: $2,486,000/$1,681,000 = 1.48$ times (liquidity and efficiency)

k. Return on total assets: $94,000/$1,681,000 = 5.6\%$ or $3.8\% \times 1.48 = 5.6\%$ (profitability)

l. Average total common equity: ($1,019,000 + $966,000)/2 = $992,500
   Return on common stockholders' equity: $94,000/$992,500 = 9.5\%$ (profitability)

Sustainable Income

17A

When a company's revenue and expense transactions are from normal, continuing operations, a simple income statement is usually adequate. When a company's activities include income-related events not part of its normal, continuing operations, it must disclose information to help users understand these events and predict future performance. To meet these objectives, companies separate the income statement into continuing operations, discontinued segments, extraordinary items, comprehensive income, and earnings per share. For illustration, Exhibit 17A.1 shows such an income statement for ComUS. These separate distinctions help us measure *sustainable income,* which is the income level most likely to continue into the future. Sustainable income is commonly used in PE ratios and other market-based measures of performance.

A2 Explain the form and assess the content of a complete income statement.

Continuing Operations

The first major section (①) shows the revenues, expenses, and income from continuing operations. Users especially rely on this information to predict future operations. Many users view this section as the most important. Earlier chapters explained the items comprising income from continuing operations.

Discontinued Segments

A **business segment** is a part of a company's operations that serves a particular line of business or class of customers. A segment has assets, liabilities, and financial results of operations that can be distinguished from those of other parts of the company. A company's gain or loss from selling or closing down a segment is separately reported. Section ② of Exhibit 17A.1 reports both (1) income from operating the discontinued segment for the current period prior to its disposal and (2) the loss from disposing of the segment's net assets. The income tax effects of each are reported separately from the income taxes expense in section ①.

Extraordinary Items

Section ③ reports **extraordinary gains and losses,** which are those that are *both unusual* and *infrequent.* An **unusual gain or loss** is abnormal or otherwise unrelated to the company's regular activities and environment. An **infrequent gain or loss** is not expected to recur given the company's operating environment. Reporting extraordinary items in a separate category helps users predict future performance, absent the effects of extraordinary items. Items usually considered extraordinary include (1) expropriation (taking away) of property by a foreign government, (2) condemning of property by a domestic government body, (3) prohibition against using an asset by a newly enacted law, and (4) losses and gains from an unusual and infrequent calamity ("act of God"). Items *not* considered extraordinary include (1) write-downs

EXHIBIT 17A.1

Income Statement (all-inclusive) for a Corporation

ComUS
Income Statement
For Year Ended December 31, 2009

Net sales			$8,478,000
Operating expenses			
	Cost of goods sold	$5,950,000		
	Depreciation expense	35,000		
	Other selling, general, and administrative expenses	515,000		
	Interest expense	20,000		
① { Total operating expenses			(6,520,000)
Other gains (losses)			
	Loss on plant relocation			(45,000)
	Gain on sale of surplus land			72,000
Income from continuing operations before taxes			1,985,000
Income taxes expense			(595,500)
Income from continuing operations			1,389,500
Discontinued segment			
② { Income from operating Division A (net of $180,000 taxes)		420,000	
	Loss on disposal of Division A (net of $66,000 tax benefit)		(154,000)	266,000
Income before extraordinary items			1,655,500
Extraordinary items			
③ { Gain on land expropriated by state (net of $85,200 taxes)		198,800	
	Loss from earthquake damage (net of $270,000 tax benefit)		(630,000)	(431,200)
Net income			$1,224,300
Earnings per common share (200,000 outstanding shares)			
	Income from continuing operations			$ 6.95
④ { Discontinued operations			1.33
	Income before extraordinary items			8.28
	Extraordinary items			(2.16)
	Net income (basic earnings per share)			$ 6.12

of inventories and write-offs of receivables, (2) gains and losses from disposing of segments, and (3) financial effects of labor strikes.

Gains and losses that are neither unusual nor infrequent are reported as part of continuing operations. Gains and losses that are *either* unusual *or* infrequent, but *not* both, are reported as part of continuing operations *but* after the normal revenues and expenses.

Decision Maker

Small Business Owner   You own an orange grove near Jacksonville, Florida. A bad frost destroys about one-half of your oranges. You are currently preparing an income statement for a bank loan. Can you claim the loss of oranges as extraordinary? [Answer—p. 706]

Earnings per Share

The final section ④ of the income statement in Exhibit 17A.1 reports earnings per share for each of the three subcategories of income (continuing operations, discontinued segments, and extraordinary items) when they exist. Earnings per share is discussed in Chapter 13.

Changes in Accounting Principles

The *consistency concept* directs a company to apply the same accounting principles across periods. Yet a company can change from one acceptable accounting principle (such as FIFO, LIFO, or weighted-average) to another as long as the change improves the usefulness of information in its financial statements. A footnote would describe the accounting change and why it is an improvement.

Point: Changes in principles are sometimes required when new accounting standards are issued.

Changes in accounting principles require retrospective application to prior periods' financial statements. *Retrospective application* involves applying a different accounting principle to prior periods as if that principle had always been used. Retrospective application enhances the consistency of financial information between periods, which improves the usefulness of information, especially with comparative analyses. (Prior to 2005, the cumulative effect of changes in accounting principles was recognized in net income in the period of the change.) Accounting standards also require that *a change in depreciation, amortization, or depletion method for long-term operating assets is accounted for as a change in accounting estimate*—that is, prospectively over current and future periods. This reflects the notion that an entity should change its depreciation, amortization, or depletion method only with changes in estimated asset benefits, the pattern of benefit usage, or information about those benefits.

Comprehensive Income

Comprehensive income is net income plus certain gains and losses that bypass the income statement. These items are recorded directly to equity. Specifically, comprehensive income equals the change in equity for the period, excluding investments from and distributions (dividends) to its stockholders. For **Best Buy**, it is computed as follows ($ millions):

Net income	$1,377
Accumulated other comprehensive income (loss)	(45)
Comprehensive income	$1,332

The most common items included in *accumulated other comprehensive income,* or *AOCI,* are unrealized gains and losses on available-for-sale securities and foreign currency translation adjustments. (Detailed computations for these items are in advanced courses.) Analysts disagree on how to treat these items. Some analysts believe that AOCI items should not be considered when predicting future performance, and some others believe AOCI items should be considered as they reflect on company and managerial performance. Whatever our position, we must be familiar with what AOCI items are as they are commonly reported in financial statements. Best Buy reports its comprehensive income in its statement of shareholders' equity (see Appendix A).

Quick Check
Answers—p. 706

13. Which of the following is an extraordinary item? (*a*) a settlement paid to a customer injured while using the company's product, (*b*) a loss to a plant from damages caused by a meteorite, or (*c*) a loss from selling old equipment.

14. Identify the four major sections of an income statement that are potentially reportable.

15. A company using FIFO for the past 15 years decides to switch to LIFO. The effect of this event on prior years' net income is (*a*) reported as if the new method had always been used; (*b*) ignored because it is a change in an accounting estimate; or (*c*) reported on the current year income statement.

Summary

C1 Explain the purpose of analysis. The purpose of financial statement analysis is to help users make better business decisions. Internal users want information to improve company efficiency and effectiveness in providing products and services. External users want information to make better and more informed decisions in pursuing their goals. The common goals of all users are to evaluate a company's (1) past and current performance, (2) current financial position, and (3) future performance and risk.

C2 Identify the building blocks of analysis. Financial statement analysis focuses on four "building blocks" of analysis: (1) liquidity and efficiency—ability to meet short-term obligations and efficiently generate revenues; (2) solvency—ability to generate future revenues and meet long-term obligations; (3) profitability—ability to provide financial rewards sufficient to attract and retain

financing; and (4) market prospects—ability to generate positive market expectations.

C3 Describe standards for comparisons in analysis. Standards for comparisons include (1) intracompany—prior performance and relations between financial items for the company under analysis; (2) competitor—one or more direct competitors of the company; (3) industry—industry statistics; and (4) guidelines (rules of thumb)—general standards developed from past experiences and personal judgments.

C4 Identify the tools of analysis. The three most common tools of financial statement analysis are (1) horizontal analysis—comparing a company's financial condition and performance across time; (2) vertical analysis—comparing a company's financial condition and performance to a base amount such as revenues or total assets; and (3) ratio analysis—using and quantifying key relations among financial statement items.

A1 Summarize and report results of analysis. A financial statement analysis report is often organized around the building blocks of analysis. A good report separates interpretations and conclusions of analysis from the information underlying them. An analysis report often consists of six sections: (1) executive summary, (2) analysis overview, (3) evidential matter, (4) assumptions, (5) key factors, and (6) inferences.

A2^A Explain the form and assess the content of a complete income statement. An income statement has four *potential* sections: (1) continuing operations, (2) discontinued segments, (3) extraordinary items, and (4) earnings per share.

P1 Explain and apply methods of horizontal analysis. Horizontal analysis is a tool to evaluate changes in data across time. Two important tools of horizontal analysis are comparative statements and trend analysis. Comparative statements show amounts for two or more successive periods, often with changes

disclosed in both absolute and percent terms. Trend analysis is used to reveal important changes occurring from one period to the next.

P2 Describe and apply methods of vertical analysis. Vertical analysis is a tool to evaluate each financial statement item or group of items in terms of a base amount. Two tools of vertical analysis are common-size statements and graphical analyses. Each item in common-size statements is expressed as a percent of a base amount. For the balance sheet, the base amount is usually total assets, and for the income statement, it is usually sales.

P3 Define and apply ratio analysis. Ratio analysis provides clues to and symptoms of underlying conditions. Ratios, properly interpreted, identify areas requiring further investigation. A ratio expresses a mathematical relation between two quantities such as a percent, rate, or proportion. Ratios can be organized into the building blocks of analysis: (1) liquidity and efficiency, (2) solvency, (3) profitability, and (4) market prospects.

Guidance Answers to **Decision Maker**

Auditor   The *joint relation* referred to is the combined increase in sales and the decrease in expenses yielding more than a 5% increase in income. Both *individual* accounts (sales and expenses) yield percent changes within the ±5% acceptable range. However, a joint analysis suggests a different picture. For example, consider a joint analysis using the profit margin ratio. The client's profit margin is 11.46% ($206,000 − $182,400/$206,000) for the current year compared with 5.0% ($200,000 − $190,000/$200,000) for the prior year—yielding a 129% increase in profit margin! This is what concerns the partner, and it suggests expanding audit tests to verify or refute the client's figures.

Banker   Your decision on the loan application is positive for at least two reasons. First, the current ratio suggests a strong ability to meet short-term obligations. Second, current assets of $160,000 and

a current ratio of 4:1 imply current liabilities of $40,000 (one-fourth of current assets) and a working capital excess of $120,000. This working capital excess is 60% of the loan amount. However, if the application is for a 10-year loan, our decision is less optimistic. The current ratio and working capital suggest a good safety margin, but indications of inefficiency in operations exist. In particular, a 4:1 current ratio is more than double its key competitors' ratio. This is characteristic of inefficient asset use.

Small Business Owner   The frost loss is probably not extraordinary. Jacksonville experiences enough recurring frost damage to make it difficult to argue this event is both unusual and infrequent. Still, you want to highlight the frost loss and hope the bank views this uncommon event separately from continuing operations.

Guidance Answers to **Quick Checks**

1. General-purpose financial statements are intended for a variety of users interested in a company's financial condition and performance—users without the power to require specialized financial reports to meet their specific needs.

2. General-purpose financial statements include the income statement, balance sheet, statement of stockholders' (owner's) equity, and statement of cash flows plus the notes related to these statements.

3. *a*

4. Data from one or more direct competitors are usually preferred for comparative purposes.

5. *d*

6. Percents on comparative income statements show the increase or decrease in each item from one period to the next. On common-size comparative income statements, each item is shown as a percent of net sales for that period.

7. *c*

8. (*a*) ($820,000 + $240,000 + $470,000)/
    ($350,000 + $180,000) = 2.9 to 1.

(*b*) ($820,000 + $240,000)/($350,000 + $180,000) = 2:1.

9. (*a*) $2,500,000/[($290,000 + $240,000)/2] = 9.43 times.
   (*b*) ($290,000/$2,500,000) × 365 = 42 days.
   (*c*) $750,000/[($530,000 + $470,000)/2] = 1.5 times.
   (*d*) ($530,000/$750,000) × 365 = 258 days.

10. *c*

11. *b*

12.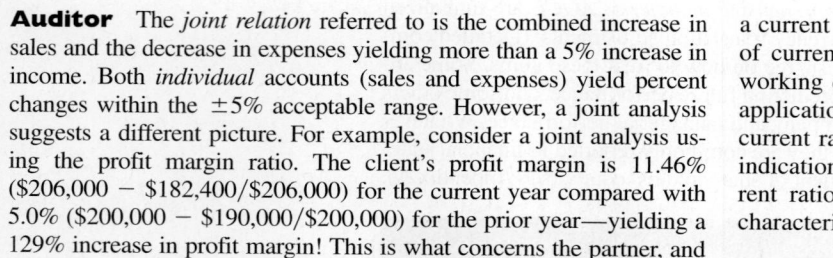

Profit margin × $\dfrac{\text{Total asset}}{\text{turnover}}$ = $\dfrac{\text{Return on}}{\text{total assets}}$

$\dfrac{\$945,000}{\$8,500,000}$ ×   1.8   =   20%

13. (*b*)

14. The four (potentially reportable) major sections are income from continuing operations, discontinued segments, extraordinary items, and earnings per share.

15. (*a*); known as retrospective application.

Key Terms   **mhhe.com/wildFAP19e**

Key Terms are available at the book's Website for learning and testing in an online Flashcard Format.

Business segment (p. 703)
Common-size financial statement (p. 687)
Comparative financial statements (p. 682)
Efficiency (p. 681)
Equity ratio (p. 695)
Extraordinary gains and losses (p. 703)
Financial reporting (p. 681)

Financial statement analysis (p. 680)
General-purpose financial statements (p. 681)
Horizontal analysis (p. 682)
Infrequent gain or loss (p. 703)
Liquidity (p. 681)
Market prospects (p. 681)

Profitability (p. 681)
Ratio analysis (p. 682)
Solvency (p. 681)
Unusual gain or loss (p. 703)
Vertical analysis (p. 682)
Working capital (p. 691)

Multiple Choice Quiz   Answers on p. 723   **mhhe.com/wildFAP19e**

Additional Quiz Questions are available at the book's Website.

Quiz17

1. A company's sales in 2008 were $300,000 and in 2009 were $351,000. Using 2008 as the base year, the sales trend percent for 2009 is:
  a. 17%
  b. 85%
  c. 100%
  d. 117%
  e. 48%

Use the following information for questions 2 through 5.

GALLOWAY COMPANY
Balance Sheet
December 31, 2009

Assets

Cash	$ 86,000
Accounts receivable	76,000
Merchandise inventory	122,000
Prepaid insurance	12,000
Long-term investments	98,000
Plant assets, net	436,000
Total assets	$830,000

Liabilities and Equity

Current liabilities	$124,000
Long-term liabilities	90,000
Common stock	300,000
Retained earnings	316,000
Total liabilities and equity	$830,000

2. What is Galloway Company's current ratio?
  a. 0.69
  b. 1.31
  c. 3.88
  d. 6.69
  e. 2.39

3. What is Galloway Company's acid-test ratio?
  a. 2.39
  b. 0.69
  c. 1.31
  d. 6.69
  e. 3.88

4. What is Galloway Company's debt ratio?
  a. 25.78%
  b. 100.00%
  c. 74.22%
  d. 137.78%
  e. 34.74%

5. What is Galloway Company's equity ratio?
  a. 25.78%
  b. 100.00%
  c. 34.74%
  d. 74.22%
  e. 137.78%

Superscript letter [A] *denotes assignments based on Appendix 17A.*

Discussion Questions

1. What is the difference between comparative financial statements and common-size comparative statements?

2. Which items are usually assigned a 100% value on (*a*) a common-size balance sheet and (*b*) a common-size income statement?

3. Explain the difference between financial reporting and financial statements.

4. What three factors would influence your evaluation as to whether a company's current ratio is good or bad?

5. ♟ Suggest several reasons why a 2:1 current ratio might not be adequate for a particular company.

6. ♟ Why is working capital given special attention in the process of analyzing balance sheets?

7. ♟ What does the number of days' sales uncollected indicate?

8. ♟ What does a relatively high accounts receivable turnover indicate about a company's short-term liquidity?

9. ♟ Why is a company's capital structure, as measured by debt and equity ratios, important to financial statement analysts?

10. ♟ How does inventory turnover provide information about a company's short-term liquidity?

11. ♟ What ratios would you compute to evaluate management performance?

12. ♟ Why would a company's return on total assets be different from its return on common stockholders' equity?

13. Where on the income statement does a company report an unusual gain not expected to occur more often than once every two years or so?

14. Use **Best Buy**'s financial statements in Appendix A to compute its return on total assets for the years ended March 3, 2007, and February 25, 2006. Total assets at February 26, 2005, were $10,294 (in millions).

15. Refer to **Circuit City**'s financial statements in Appendix A to compute its equity ratio as of February 28, 2007, and February 28, 2006.

16. Refer to **RadioShack**'s financial statements in Appendix A. Compute its debt ratio as of December 31, 2006, and December 31, 2005.

17. Refer to **Apple**'s financial statements in Appendix A. Compute its profit margin for the fiscal year ended September 30, 2006.

♟ **Denotes Discussion Questions that involve decision making.**

Available with McGraw-Hill's Homework Manager   McGraw-Hill's HOMEWORK MANAGER®

QUICK STUDY

QS 17-1
Financial reporting   C1

Which of the following items (1) through (9) are part of financial reporting but are *not* included as part of general-purpose financial statements? (1) stock price information and analysis, (2) statement of cash flows, (3) management discussion and analysis of financial performance, (4) income statement, (5) company news releases, (6) balance sheet, (7) financial statement notes, (8) statement of shareholders' equity, (9) prospectus.

QS 17-2
Standard of comparison   C3

What are four possible standards of comparison used to analyze financial statement ratios? Which of these is generally considered to be the most useful? Which one is least likely to provide a good basis for comparison?

QS 17-3
Common-size and trend percents
P1   P2

Use the following information for Owens Corporation to determine (1) the 2008 and 2009 common-size percents for cost of goods sold using net sales as the base and (2) the 2008 and 2009 trend percents for net sales using 2008 as the base year.

($ thousands)	2009	2008
Net sales	$101,400	$58,100
Cost of goods sold	55,300	30,700

QS 17-4
Horizontal analysis
P1

Compute the annual dollar changes and percent changes for each of the following accounts.

	2009	2008
Short-term investments	$110,000	$80,000
Accounts receivable	22,000	25,000
Notes payable	30,000	0

QS 17-5
Building blocks of analysis
C2   C4   P3

Match the ratio to the building block of financial statement analysis to which it best relates.

A. Liquidity and efficiency   **C.** Profitability
B. Solvency   **D.** Market prospects

1. _____ Gross margin ratio
2. _____ Acid-test ratio
3. _____ Equity ratio
4. _____ Return on total assets
5. _____ Dividend yield

6. _____ Book value per common share
7. _____ Days' sales in inventory
8. _____ Accounts receivable turnover
9. _____ Debt-to-equity
10. _____ Times interest earned

1. Which two short-term liquidity ratios measure how frequently a company collects its accounts?

2. What measure reflects the difference between current assets and current liabilities?

3. Which two ratios are key components in measuring a company's operating efficiency? Which ratio summarizes these two components?

QS 17-6
Identifying financial ratios
C4   P3

For each ratio listed, identify whether the change in ratio value from 2008 to 2009 is usually regarded as favorable or unfavorable.

QS 17-7
Ratio interpretation
P3

Ratio	2009	2008	Ratio	2009	2008
1. Profit margin	10%	9%	5. Accounts receivable turnover	6.7	5.5
2. Debt ratio	43%	39%	6. Basic earnings per share	$1.25	$1.10
3. Gross margin	32%	44%	7. Inventory turnover	3.4	3.6
4. Acid-test ratio	1.20	1.05	8. Dividend yield	4%	3.2%

A review of the notes payable files discovers that three years ago the company reported the entire amount of a payment (principal and interest) on an installment note payable as interest expense. This mistake had a material effect on the amount of income in that year. How should the correction be reported in the current year financial statements?

QS 17-8^A
Error adjustments
A2

McGraw-Hill's
HOMEWORK
MANAGER®   Available with McGraw-Hill's Homework Manager

Compute trend percents for the following accounts, using 2007 as the base year. State whether the situation as revealed by the trends appears to be favorable or unfavorable for each account.

EXERCISES

Exercise 17-1
Computation and analysis of trend percents
P1

	2011	2010	2009	2008	2007
Sales	$282,700	$270,700	$252,500	$234,460	$150,000
Cost of goods sold	128,100	121,980	115,180	106,340	67,000
Accounts receivable	18,000	17,200	16,300	15,100	9,000

Common-size and trend percents for Danian Company's sales, cost of goods sold, and expenses follow. Determine whether net income increased, decreased, or remained unchanged in this three-year period.

Exercise 17-2
Determination of income effects from common-size and trend percents
P1   P2

	Common-Size Percents			Trend Percents		
	2010	2009	2008	2010	2009	2008
Sales	100.0%	100.0%	100.0%	104.9%	103.7%	100.0%
Cost of goods sold	67.7	61.2	58.4	102.5	108.6	100.0
Total expenses	14.4	13.9	14.2	106.5	101.5	100.0

Express the following comparative income statements in common-size percents and assess whether or not this company's situation has improved in the most recent year.

Exercise 17-3
Common-size percent computation and interpretation
P2

MULAN CORPORATION		
Comparative Income Statements		
For Years Ended December 31, 2009 and 2008		
	2009	2008
Sales	$657,386	$488,400
Cost of goods sold	427,301	286,202
Gross profit	230,085	202,198
Operating expenses	138,051	94,750
Net income	$ 92,034	$107,448

Exercise 17-4
Analysis of short-term
financial condition

A1 P3

Team Project: Assume
that the two companies apply
for a one-year loan from the
team. Identify additional
information the companies
must provide before the
team can make a loan
decision.

The following information is available for Orkay Company and Lowes Company, similar firms operating in the same industry. Write a half-page report comparing Orkay and Lowes using the available information. Your discussion should include their ability to meet current obligations and to use current assets efficiently.

Microsoft Excel - Book1

File Edit View Insert Format Tools Data Accounting Window Help

100% ▾   Arial   ▾ 10 ▾   B I U $ % ,

	Orkay			Lowes		
	2010	**2009**	**2008**	**2010**	**2009**	**2008**
Current ratio	1.6	1.7	2.0	3.1	2.6	1.8
Acid-test ratio	0.9	1.0	1.1	2.7	2.4	1.5
Accounts receivable turnover	29.5	24.2	28.2	15.4	14.2	15.0
Merchandise inventory turnover	23.2	20.9	16.1	13.5	12.0	11.6
Working capital	$60,000	$48,000	$42,000	$121,000	$93,000	$68,000

Sheet1 Sheet2 Sheet3

Exercise 17-5
Analysis of efficiency and
financial leverage

A1 P3

Caren Company and Revlon Company are similar firms that operate in the same industry. Revlon began operations in 2009 and Caren in 2006. In 2011, both companies pay 7% interest on their debt to creditors. The following additional information is available.

	Caren Company			Revlon Company		
	2011	**2010**	**2009**	**2011**	**2010**	**2009**
Total asset turnover	3.0	2.7	2.9	1.6	1.4	1.1
Return on total assets	8.9%	9.5%	8.7%	5.8%	5.5%	5.2%
Profit margin ratio	2.3%	2.4%	2.2%	2.7%	2.9%	2.8%
Sales	$400,000	$370,000	$386,000	$200,000	$160,000	$100,000

Write a half-page report comparing Caren and Revlon using the available information. Your analysis should include their ability to use assets efficiently to produce profits. Also comment on their success in employing financial leverage in 2011.

Exercise 17-6
Common-size percents

P2

Nabisco Company's year-end balance sheets follow. Express the balance sheets in common-size percents. Round amounts to the nearest one-tenth of a percent. Analyze and comment on the results.

At December 31	2010	2009	2008
Assets			
Cash	$ 36,229	$ 42,780	$ 44,562
Accounts receivable, net	106,073	76,377	57,087
Merchandise inventory	137,408	98,929	62,038
Prepaid expenses	11,548	11,003	4,903
Plant assets, net	335,317	311,062	272,710
Total assets	$626,575	$540,151	$441,300
Liabilities and Equity			
Accounts payable	$157,577	$ 94,024	$ 57,087
Long-term notes payable secured by mortgages on plant assets	116,618	127,962	99,478
Common stock, $10 par value	163,500	163,500	163,500
Retained earnings	188,880	154,665	121,235
Total liabilities and equity	$626,575	$540,151	$441,300

Refer to Nabisco Company's balance sheets in Exercise 17-6. Analyze its year-end short-term liquidity position at the end of 2010, 2009, and 2008 by computing (1) the current ratio and (2) the acid-test ratio. Comment on the ratio results. (Round ratio amounts to two decimals.)

Exercise 17-7
Liquidity analysis

P3

Refer to the Nabisco Company information in Exercise 17-6. The company's income statements for the years ended December 31, 2010 and 2009, follow. Assume that all sales are on credit and then compute: (1) days' sales uncollected, (2) accounts receivable turnover, (3) inventory turnover, and (4) days' sales in inventory. Comment on the changes in the ratios from 2009 to 2010. (Round amounts to one decimal.)

Exercise 17-8
Liquidity analysis and interpretation

P3

For Year Ended December 31	2010		2009	
Sales		$685,000		$557,000
Cost of goods sold	$417,850		$356,265	
Other operating expenses	207,282		141,971	
Interest expense	8,175		8,960	
Income taxes	12,900		12,450	
Total costs and expenses		646,207		519,646
Net income		$ 38,793		$ 37,354
Earnings per share		$ 2.37		$ 2.28

Refer to the Nabisco Company information in Exercises 17-6 and 17-8. Compare the company's long-term risk and capital structure positions at the end of 2010 and 2009 by computing these ratios: (1) debt and equity ratios, (2) debt-to-equity ratio, and (3) times interest earned. Comment on these ratio results.

Exercise 17-9
Risk and capital structure analysis

P3

Refer to Nabisco Company's financial information in Exercises 17-6 and 17-8. Evaluate the company's efficiency and profitability by computing the following for 2010 and 2009: (1) profit margin ratio, (2) total asset turnover, and (3) return on total assets. Comment on these ratio results.

Exercise 17-10
Efficiency and
profitability analysis   P3

Refer to Nabisco Company's financial information in Exercises 17-6 and 17-8. Additional information about the company follows. To help evaluate the company's profitability, compute and interpret the following ratios for 2010 and 2009: (1) return on common stockholders' equity, (2) price-earnings ratio on December 31, and (3) dividend yield.

Exercise 17-11
Profitability analysis

P3

Common stock market price, December 31, 2010	$30.00
Common stock market price, December 31, 2009	28.00
Annual cash dividends per share in 2010	0.28
Annual cash dividends per share in 2009	0.24

In 2009, Simplon Merchandising, Inc., sold its interest in a chain of wholesale outlets, taking the company completely out of the wholesaling business. The company still operates its retail outlets. A listing of the major sections of an income statement follows:

A. Income (loss) from continuing operations
B. Income (loss) from operating, or gain (loss) from disposing, a discontinued segment
C. Extraordinary gain (loss)

Indicate where each of the following income-related items for this company appears on its 2009 income statement by writing the letter of the appropriate section in the blank beside each item.

Exercise 17-12ᴬ
Income statement categories

A2

Section	Item	Debit	Credit
_____	1. Net sales		$3,000,000
_____	2. Gain on state's condemnation of company property (net of tax)		330,000
_____	3. Cost of goods sold	$1,580,000	
_____	4. Income taxes expense	117,000	
_____	5. Depreciation expense	332,500	
_____	6. Gain on sale of wholesale business segment (net of tax)		875,000
_____	7. Loss from operating wholesale business segment (net of tax)	544,000	
_____	8. Salaries expense	740,000	

Exercise 17-13ᴬ
Income statement presentation
A2

Use the financial data for Simplon Merchandising, Inc., in Exercise 17-12 to prepare its income statement for calendar year 2009. (Ignore the earnings per share section.)

Available with McGraw-Hill's Homework Manager

McGraw-Hill's
HOMEWORK
MANAGER®

PROBLEM SET A

Selected comparative financial statements of Astalon Company follow.

Problem 17-1A
Ratios, common-size statements, and trend percents

P1 P2 P3 ♟

mhhe.com/wildFAP19e

ASTALON COMPANY Comparative Income Statements For Years Ended December 31, 2010, 2009, and 2008			
	2010	**2009**	**2008**
Sales	$526,304	$403,192	$279,800
Cost of goods sold	316,835	255,624	179,072
Gross profit	209,469	147,568	100,728
Selling expenses	74,735	55,640	36,934
Administrative expenses	47,367	35,481	23,223
Total expenses	122,102	91,121	60,157
Income before taxes	87,367	56,447	40,571
Income taxes	16,250	11,572	8,236
Net income	$ 71,117	$ 44,875	$ 32,335

ASTALON COMPANY Comparative Balance Sheets December 31, 2010, 2009, and 2008			
	2010	**2009**	**2008**
Assets			
Current assets	$ 48,242	$ 38,514	$ 51,484
Long-term investments	0	800	3,620
Plant assets, net	92,405	97,259	58,047
Total assets	$140,647	$136,573	$113,151
Liabilities and Equity			
Current liabilities	$ 20,534	$ 20,349	$ 19,801
Common stock	69,000	69,000	51,000
Other paid-in capital	8,625	8,625	5,667
Retained earnings	42,488	38,599	36,683
Total liabilities and equity	$140,647	$136,573	$113,151

Required

1. Compute each year's current ratio. (Round ratio amounts to one decimal.)

2. Express the income statement data in common-size percents. (Round percents to two decimals.)

3. Express the balance sheet data in trend percents with 2008 as the base year. (Round percents to two decimals.)

Check (3) 2010, Total assets trend, 124.30%

Analysis Component

4. Comment on any significant relations revealed by the ratios and percents computed.

Selected comparative financial statements of Adobe Company follow.

Problem 17-2A
Calculation and analysis of trend percents

A1 P1 ♟

ADOBE COMPANY Comparative Income Statements For Years Ended December 31, 2010–2004							
($ thousands)	2010	2009	2008	2007	2006	2005	2004
Sales	$2,431	$2,129	$1,937	$1,776	$1,657	$1,541	$1,263
Cost of goods sold	1,747	1,421	1,223	1,070	994	930	741
Gross profit	684	708	714	706	663	611	522
Operating expenses	521	407	374	276	239	236	196
Net income	$ 163	$ 301	$ 340	$ 430	$ 424	$ 375	$ 326

ADOBE COMPANY Comparative Balance Sheets December 31, 2010–2004							
($ thousands)	2010	2009	2008	2007	2006	2005	2004
Assets							
Cash	$ 163	$ 216	$ 224	$ 229	$ 238	$ 235	$ 242
Accounts receivable, net	1,173	1,232	1,115	855	753	714	503
Merchandise inventory	4,244	3,090	2,699	2,275	2,043	1,735	1,258
Other current assets	109	98	60	108	91	93	48
Long-term investments	0	0	0	334	334	334	334
Plant assets, net	5,192	5,172	4,526	2,553	2,639	2,345	2,015
Total assets	$10,881	$9,808	$8,624	$6,354	$6,098	$5,456	$4,400
Liabilities and Equity							
Current liabilities	$ 2,734	$2,299	$1,509	$1,255	$1,089	$1,030	$ 664
Long-term liabilities	2,924	2,547	2,478	1,151	1,176	1,273	955
Common stock	1,980	1,980	1,980	1,760	1,760	1,540	1,540
Other paid-in capital	495	495	495	440	440	385	385
Retained earnings	2,748	2,487	2,162	1,748	1,633	1,228	856
Total liabilities and equity	$10,881	$9,808	$8,624	$6,354	$6,098	$5,456	$4,400

Required

1. Compute trend percents for all components of both statements using 2004 as the base year. (Round percents to one decimal.)

Check (1) 2010, Total assets trend, 247.3%

Analysis Component

2. Analyze and comment on the financial statements and trend percents from part 1.

Page Corporation began the month of May with $884,000 of current assets, a current ratio of 2.6:1, and an acid-test ratio of 1.5:1. During the month, it completed the following transactions (the company uses a perpetual inventory system).

May 2 Purchased $70,000 of merchandise inventory on credit.
    8 Sold merchandise inventory that cost $60,000 for $130,000 cash.
  10 Collected $30,000 cash on an account receivable.
  15 Paid $31,000 cash to settle an account payable.

Problem 17-3A
Transactions, working capital, and liquidity ratios

P3

mhhe.com/wildFAP19e

17   Wrote off a $5,000 bad debt against the Allowance for Doubtful Accounts account.
22   Declared a $1 per share cash dividend on its 67,000 shares of outstanding common stock.
26   Paid the dividend declared on May 22.
27   Borrowed $85,000 cash by giving the bank a 30-day, 10% note.
28   Borrowed $100,000 cash by signing a long-term secured note.
29   Used the $185,000 cash proceeds from the notes to buy new machinery.

Required

Prepare a table showing Page's (1) current ratio, (2) acid-test ratio, and (3) working capital, after each transaction. Round ratios to two decimals.

Problem 17-4A
Calculation of financial
statement ratios

P3

mhhe.com/wildFAP19e

Selected year-end financial statements of Cadet Corporation follow. (All sales were on credit; selected balance sheet amounts at December 31, 2008, were inventory, $56,900; total assets, $219,400; common stock, $85,000; and retained earnings, $52,348.)

CADET CORPORATION Income Statement For Year Ended December 31, 2009	
Sales	$456,600
Cost of goods sold	297,450
Gross profit	159,150
Operating expenses	99,400
Interest expense	3,900
Income before taxes	55,850
Income taxes	22,499
Net income	$ 33,351

CADET CORPORATION Balance Sheet December 31, 2009			
Assets		**Liabilities and Equity**	
Cash	$ 20,000	Accounts payable	$ 21,500
Short-term investments	8,200	Accrued wages payable	4,400
Accounts receivable, net	29,400	Income taxes payable	3,700
Notes receivable (trade)*	7,000	Long-term note payable, secured	
Merchandise inventory	34,150	by mortgage on plant assets	67,400
Prepaid expenses	2,700	Common stock	85,000
Plant assets, net	147,300	Retained earnings	66,750
Total assets	$248,750	Total liabilities and equity	$248,750

* These are short-term notes receivable arising from customer (trade) sales.

Required

Compute the following: (1) current ratio, (2) acid-test ratio, (3) days' sales uncollected, (4) inventory turnover, (5) days' sales in inventory, (6) debt-to-equity ratio, (7) times interest earned, (8) profit margin ratio, (9) total asset turnover, (10) return on total assets, and (11) return on common stockholders' equity.

Problem 17-5A
Comparative ratio
analysis   A1   P3

Summary information from the financial statements of two companies competing in the same industry follows.

	Karto Company	Bryan Company			Karto Company	Bryan Company
Data from the current year-end balance sheets				**Data from the current year's income statement**		
Assets				Sales	$790,000	$897,200
Cash	$ 19,500	$ 36,000		Cost of goods sold	588,100	634,500
Accounts receivable, net	36,400	53,400		Interest expense	7,600	19,000
Current notes receivable (trade)	9,400	7,600		Income tax expense	15,185	24,769
Merchandise inventory	84,740	134,500		Net income	$179,115	$218,931
Prepaid expenses	6,200	7,250		Basic earnings per share	$ 4.71	$ 5.58
Plant assets, net	350,000	307,400				
Total assets	$506,240	$546,150				
				Beginning-of-year balance sheet data		
Liabilities and Equity				Accounts receivable, net	$ 26,800	$ 51,200
Current liabilities	$ 63,340	$ 73,819		Current notes receivable (trade)	0	0
Long-term notes payable	82,485	99,000		Merchandise inventory	55,600	107,400
Common stock, $5 par value	190,000	196,000		Total assets	408,000	422,500
Retained earnings	170,415	177,331		Common stock, $5 par value	190,000	196,000
Total liabilities and equity	$506,240	$546,150		Retained earnings	124,300	95,600

Required

1. For both companies compute the (*a*) current ratio, (*b*) acid-test ratio, (*c*) accounts (including notes) receivable turnover, (*d*) inventory turnover, (*e*) days' sales in inventory, and (*f*) days' sales uncollected. Identify the company you consider to be the better short-term credit risk and explain why.

2. For both companies compute the (*a*) profit margin ratio, (*b*) total asset turnover, (*c*) return on total assets, and (*d*) return on common stockholders' equity. Assuming that each company paid cash dividends of $3.50 per share and each company's stock can be purchased at $85 per share, compute their (*e*) price-earnings ratios and (*f*) dividend yields. Identify which company's stock you would recommend as the better investment and explain why.

Check (1) Bryan: Accounts receivable turnover, 16.0; Inventory turnover, 5.2

(2) Karto: Profit margin, 22.7%; PE, 18.0

Selected account balances from the adjusted trial balance for Lindo Corporation as of its calendar year-end December 31, 2009, follow.

Problem 17-6A[A]
Income statement computations and format

A2

	Debit	Credit
a. Interest revenue		$ 15,000
b. Depreciation expense—Equipment	$ 35,000	
c. Loss on sale of equipment	26,850	
d. Accounts payable		45,000
e. Other operating expenses	107,400	
f. Accumulated depreciation—Equipment		72,600
g. Gain from settlement of lawsuit		45,000
h. Accumulated depreciation—Buildings		175,500
i. Loss from operating a discontinued segment (pretax)	19,250	
j. Gain on insurance recovery of tornado damage (pretax and extraordinary)		30,120
k. Net sales		999,500
l. Depreciation expense—Buildings	53,000	
m. Correction of overstatement of prior year's sales (pretax)	17,000	
n. Gain on sale of discontinued segment's assets (pretax)		35,000
o. Loss from settlement of lawsuit	24,750	
p. Income taxes expense	?	
q. Cost of goods sold	483,500	

Required

Answer each of the following questions by providing supporting computations.

1. Assume that the company's income tax rate is 30% for all items. Identify the tax effects and after-tax amounts of the four items labeled pretax.
2. What is the amount of income from continuing operations before income taxes? What is the amount of the income taxes expense? What is the amount of income from continuing operations?
3. What is the total amount of after-tax income (loss) associated with the discontinued segment?
4. What is the amount of income (loss) before the extraordinary items?
5. What is the amount of net income for the year?

Check (3) $11,025
(4) $241,325
(5) $262,409

PROBLEM SET B

Problem 17-1B
Ratios, common-size statements, and trend percents

P1 P2 P3

Selected comparative financial statement information of Danno Corporation follows.

DANNO CORPORATION
Comparative Income Statements
For Years Ended December 31, 2010, 2009, and 2008

	2010	2009	2008
Sales	$392,000	$300,304	$208,400
Cost of goods sold	235,984	190,092	133,376
Gross profit	156,016	110,212	75,024
Selling expenses	55,664	41,442	27,509
Administrative expenses	35,280	26,427	17,297
Total expenses	90,944	67,869	44,806
Income before taxes	65,072	42,343	30,218
Income taxes	12,103	8,680	6,134
Net income	$ 52,969	$ 33,663	$ 24,084

DANNO CORPORATION
Comparative Balance Sheets
December 31, 2010, 2009, and 2008

	2010	2009	2008
Assets			
Current assets	$ 53,776	$ 42,494	$ 55,118
Long-term investments	0	400	4,110
Plant assets, net	99,871	106,303	64,382
Total assets	$153,647	$149,197	$123,610
Liabilities and Equity			
Current liabilities	$ 22,432	$ 22,230	$ 21,632
Common stock	70,000	70,000	52,000
Other paid-in capital	8,750	8,750	5,778
Retained earnings	52,465	48,217	44,200
Total liabilities and equity	$153,647	$149,197	$123,610

Required

1. Compute each year's current ratio. (Round ratio amounts to one decimal.)
2. Express the income statement data in common-size percents. (Round percents to two decimals.)
3. Express the balance sheet data in trend percents with 2008 as the base year. (Round percents to two decimals.)

Check (3) 2010, Total assets trend, 124.30%

Analysis Component

4. Comment on any significant relations revealed by the ratios and percents computed.

Selected comparative financial statements of Park Company follow.

Problem 17-2B
Calculation and analysis of trend percents

A1   P1

PARK COMPANY Comparative Income Statements For Years Ended December 31, 2010–2004							
($ thousands)	2010	2009	2008	2007	2006	2005	2004
Sales	$570	$620	$640	$690	$750	$780	$870
Cost of goods sold	286	300	304	324	350	360	390
Gross profit	284	320	336	366	400	420	480
Operating expenses	94	114	122	136	150	154	160
Net income	$190	$206	$214	$230	$250	$266	$320

PARK COMPANY Comparative Balance Sheets December 31, 2010–2004							
($ thousands)	2010	2009	2008	2007	2006	2005	2004
Assets							
Cash	$ 54	$ 56	$ 62	$ 64	$ 70	$ 72	$ 78
Accounts receivable, net	140	146	150	154	160	164	170
Merchandise inventory	176	182	188	190	196	200	218
Other current assets	44	44	46	48	48	50	50
Long-term investments	46	40	36	120	120	120	120
Plant assets, net	520	524	530	422	430	438	464
Total assets	$980	$992	$1,012	$998	$1,024	$1,044	$1,100
Liabilities and Equity							
Current liabilities	$158	$166	$ 196	$200	$ 220	$ 270	$ 290
Long-term liabilities	102	130	152	158	204	224	270
Common stock	180	180	180	180	180	180	180
Other paid-in capital	80	80	80	80	80	80	80
Retained earnings	460	436	404	380	340	290	280
Total liabilities and equity	$980	$992	$1,012	$998	$1,024	$1,044	$1,100

Required

1. Compute trend percents for all components of both statements using 2004 as the base year. (Round percents to one decimal.)

Check   (1) 2010, Total assets trend, 89.1%

Analysis Component

2. Analyze and comment on the financial statements and trend percents from part 1.

Menardo Corporation began the month of June with $600,000 of current assets, a current ratio of 2.5:1, and an acid-test ratio of 1.4:1. During the month, it completed the following transactions (the company uses a perpetual inventory system).

Problem 17-3B
Transactions, working capital, and liquidity ratios

P3

Check   June 3: Current ratio, 2.88; Acid-test ratio, 2.40

June 1   Sold merchandise inventory that cost $150,000 for $240,000 cash.
     3   Collected $176,000 cash on an account receivable.
     5   Purchased $300,000 of merchandise inventory on credit.
     7   Borrowed $200,000 cash by giving the bank a 60-day, 8% note.
    10   Borrowed $240,000 cash by signing a long-term secured note.
    12   Purchased machinery for $550,000 cash.
    15   Declared a $1 per share cash dividend on its 160,000 shares of outstanding common stock.
    19   Wrote off a $10,000 bad debt against the Allowance for Doubtful Accounts account.
    22   Paid $24,000 cash to settle an account payable.
    30   Paid the dividend declared on June 15.

June 30: Working capital, $(20,000); Current ratio, 0.97

Required

Prepare a table showing the company's (1) current ratio, (2) acid-test ratio, and (3) working capital after each transaction. Round ratios to two decimals.

Problem 17-4B
Calculation of financial
statement ratios

P3

Selected year-end financial statements of Steele Corporation follow. (All sales were on credit; selected balance sheet amounts at December 31, 2008, were inventory, $55,900; total assets, $249,400; common stock, $105,000; and retained earnings, $17,748.)

STEELE CORPORATION	
Income Statement	
For Year Ended December 31, 2009	
Sales	$447,600
Cost of goods sold	298,150
Gross profit	149,450
Operating expenses	98,500
Interest expense	4,600
Income before taxes	46,350
Income taxes	18,672
Net income	$ 27,678

STEELE CORPORATION			
Balance Sheet			
December 31, 2009			
Assets		**Liabilities and Equity**	
Cash	$ 8,000	Accounts payable	$ 25,500
Short-term investments	8,000	Accrued wages payable	3,000
Accounts receivable, net	28,800	Income taxes payable	4,000
Notes receivable (trade)*	8,000	Long-term note payable, secured	
Merchandise inventory	34,150	by mortgage on plant assets	63,400
Prepaid expenses	2,750	Common stock, $5 par value	105,000
Plant assets, net	150,300	Retained earnings	39,100
Total assets	$240,000	Total liabilities and equity	$240,000

* These are short-term notes receivable arising from customer (trade) sales.

Required

Check Acid-test ratio, 1.6 to 1;
Inventory turnover, 6.6

Compute the following: (1) current ratio, (2) acid-test ratio, (3) days' sales uncollected, (4) inventory turnover, (5) days' sales in inventory, (6) debt-to-equity ratio, (7) times interest earned, (8) profit margin ratio, (9) total asset turnover, (10) return on total assets, and (11) return on common stockholders' equity.

Problem 17-5B
Comparative
ratio analysis   A1   P3

Summary information from the financial statements of two companies competing in the same industry follows.

	Crisco Company	Silas Company		Crisco Company	Silas Company
Data from the current year-end balance sheets			**Data from the current year's income statement**		
Assets			Sales	$394,600	$668,500
Cash	$ 21,000	$ 37,500	Cost of goods sold	291,600	481,000
Accounts receivable, net	78,100	71,500	Interest expense	6,900	13,300
Current notes receivable (trade)	12,600	10,000	Income tax expense	6,700	14,300
Merchandise inventory	87,800	83,000	Net income	34,850	62,700
Prepaid expenses	10,700	11,100	Basic earnings per share	1.16	1.84
Plant assets, net	177,900	253,300			
Total assets	$388,100	$466,400			
			Beginning-of-year balance sheet data		
Liabilities and Equity			Accounts receivable, net	$ 73,200	$ 74,300
Current liabilities	$100,500	$ 98,000	Current notes receivable (trade)	0	0
Long-term notes payable	85,650	62,400	Merchandise inventory	106,100	81,500
Common stock, $5 par value	150,000	170,000	Total assets	384,400	444,000
Retained earnings	51,950	136,000	Common stock, $5 par value	150,000	170,000
Total liabilities and equity	$388,100	$466,400	Retained earnings	50,100	110,700

Required

1. For both companies compute the (*a*) current ratio, (*b*) acid-test ratio, (*c*) accounts (including notes) receivable turnover, (*d*) inventory turnover, (*e*) days' sales in inventory, and (*f*) days' sales uncollected. Identify the company you consider to be the better short-term credit risk and explain why.

2. For both companies compute the (*a*) profit margin ratio, (*b*) total asset turnover, (*c*) return on total assets, and (*d*) return on common stockholders' equity. Assuming that each company paid cash dividends of $1.10 per share and each company's stock can be purchased at $25 per share, compute their (*e*) price-earnings ratios and (*f*) dividend yields. Identify which company's stock you would recommend as the better investment and explain why.

Check (1) Crisco: Accounts receivable turnover, 4.8; Inventory turnover, 3.0

(2) Silas: Profit margin, 9.4%; PE, 13.6

Selected account balances from the adjusted trial balance for Harton Corp. as of its calendar year-end December 31, 2009, follow.

Problem 17-6B[A]
Income statement computations and format

A2

	Debit	Credit
a. Accumulated depreciation—Buildings		$ 410,000
b. Interest revenue		30,000
c. Net sales		2,650,000
d. Income taxes expense	$?	
e. Loss on hurricane damage (pretax and extraordinary)	74,000	
f. Accumulated depreciation—Equipment		230,000
g. Other operating expenses	338,000	
h. Depreciation expense—Equipment	110,000	
i. Loss from settlement of lawsuit	46,000	
j. Gain from settlement of lawsuit		78,000
k. Loss on sale of equipment	34,000	
l. Loss from operating a discontinued segment (pretax)	130,000	
m. Depreciation expense—Buildings	166,000	
n. Correction of overstatement of prior year's expense (pretax)		58,000
o. Cost of goods sold	1,050,000	
p. Loss on sale of discontinued segment's assets (pretax)	190,000	
q. Accounts payable		142,000

Required

Answer each of the following questions by providing supporting computations.

1. Assume that the company's income tax rate is 25% for all items. Identify the tax effects and after-tax amounts of the four items labeled pretax.

2. What is the amount of income from continuing operations before income taxes? What is the amount of income taxes expense? What is the amount of income from continuing operations?

3. What is the total amount of after-tax income (loss) associated with the discontinued segment?

4. What is the amount of income (loss) before the extraordinary items?

5. What is the amount of net income for the year?

Check (3) $(240,000)

(4) $520,500

(5) $465,000

(This serial problem began in Chapter 1 and continues through most of the book. If previous chapter segments were not completed, the serial problem can begin at this point. It is helpful, but not necessary, to use the Working Papers that accompany the book.)

SERIAL PROBLEM

Success Systems

SP 17 Use the following selected data from Success Systems' income statement for the three months ended March 31, 2010, and from its March 31, 2010, balance sheet to complete the requirements below: computer services revenue, $25,160; net sales (of goods), $18,693; total sales and revenue, $43,853; cost of goods sold, $14,052; net income, $18,686; quick assets, $100,205; current assets, $105,209; total assets, $129,909; current liabilities, $875; total liabilities, $875; and total equity, $129,034.

Required

1. Compute the gross margin ratio (both with and without services revenue) and net profit margin ratio.
2. Compute the current ratio and acid-test ratio.
3. Compute the debt ratio and equity ratio.
4. What percent of its assets are current? What percent are long term?

BEYOND THE NUMBERS

REPORTING IN ACTION

A1 P1 P2 ♟

BTN 17-1 Refer to Best Buy's financial statements in Appendix A to answer the following.

1. Using fiscal 2005 as the base year, compute trend percents for fiscal years 2005, 2006, and 2007 for revenues, cost of sales, selling general and administrative expenses, income taxes, and net income. (Round to the nearest whole percent.)
2. Compute common-size percents for fiscal years 2007 and 2006 for the following categories of assets: (a) total current assets, (b) property and equipment, net, and (c) intangible assets. (Round to the nearest tenth of a percent.)
3. Comment on any significant changes across the years for the income statement trends computed in part 1 and the balance sheet percents computed in part 2.

Fast Forward

4. Access Best Buy's financial statements for fiscal years ending after March 3, 2007, from Best Buy's Website (BestBuy.com) or the SEC database (www.sec.gov). Update your work for parts 1, 2, and 3 using the new information accessed.

COMPARATIVE ANALYSIS

C3 P2

BTN 17-2 Key figures for Best Buy, Circuit City, and RadioShack follow.

($ millions)	Best Buy	Circuit City	RadioShack
Cash and equivalents	$ 1,205	$ 141	$ 472
Accounts receivable, net	548	383	248
Inventories	4,028	1,637	752
Retained earnings	5,507	1,336	1,781
Cost of sales	27,165	9,501	2,544
Revenues	35,934	12,430	4,778
Total assets	13,570	4,007	2,070

Required

1. Compute common-size percents for each of the companies using the data provided. (Round percents to one decimal.)
2. Which company retains a higher portion of cumulative net income in the company?
3. Which company has a higher gross margin ratio on sales?
4. Which company holds a higher percent of its total assets as inventory?

ETHICS CHALLENGE

A1 ♟

BTN 17-3 As Beacon Company controller, you are responsible for informing the board of directors about its financial activities. At the board meeting, you present the following information.

	2009	2008	2007
Sales trend percent	147.0%	135.0%	100.0%
Selling expenses to sales	10.1%	14.0%	15.6%
Sales to plant assets ratio	3.8 to 1	3.6 to 1	3.3 to 1
Current ratio	2.9 to 1	2.7 to 1	2.4 to 1
Acid-test ratio	1.1 to 1	1.4 to 1	1.5 to 1
Inventory turnover	7.8 times	9.0 times	10.2 times
Accounts receivable turnover	7.0 times	7.7 times	8.5 times
Total asset turnover	2.9 times	2.9 times	3.3 times
Return on total assets	10.4%	11.0%	13.2%
Return on stockholders' equity	10.7%	11.5%	14.1%
Profit margin ratio	3.6%	3.8%	4.0%

After the meeting, the company's CEO holds a press conference with analysts in which she mentions the following ratios.

	2009	2008	2007
Sales trend percent	147.0%	135.0%	100.0%
Selling expenses to sales	10.1%	14.0%	15.6%
Sales to plant assets ratio	3.8 to 1	3.6 to 1	3.3 to 1
Current ratio	2.9 to 1	2.7 to 1	2.4 to 1

Required

1. Why do you think the CEO decided to report 4 ratios instead of the 11 prepared?

2. Comment on the possible consequences of the CEO's reporting of the ratios selected.

BTN 17-4   Each team is to select a different industry, and each team member is to select a different company in that industry and acquire its financial statements. Use those statements to analyze the company, including at least one ratio from each of the four building blocks of analysis. When necessary, use the financial press to determine the market price of its stock. Communicate with teammates via a meeting, e-mail, or telephone to discuss how different companies compare to each other and to industry norms. The team is to prepare a single one-page memorandum reporting on its analysis and the conclusions reached.

COMMUNICATING IN PRACTICE

C2 A1 P3

BTN 17-5   Access the February 23, 2007, filing of the 2006 10-K report of the **Hershey Foods Corporation** (ticker HSY) at www.sec.gov and complete the following requirements.

TAKING IT TO THE NET

C4 P3

Required

Compute or identify the following profitability ratios of Hershey for its years ending December 31, 2006, *and* December 31, 2005. Interpret its profitability using the results obtained for these two years.

1. Profit margin ratio.

2. Gross profit ratio.

3. Return on total assets. (Total assets in 2004 were $3,794,750,000.)

4. Return on common stockholders' equity. (Total shareholders' equity in 2004 was $1,137,103,000.)

5. Basic earnings per common share.

BTN 17-6   A team approach to learning financial statement analysis is often useful.

TEAMWORK IN ACTION

C2 P1 P2 P3

Required

1. Each team should write a description of horizontal and vertical analysis that all team members agree with and understand. Illustrate each description with an example.

2. *Each* member of the team is to select *one* of the following categories of ratio analysis. Explain what the ratios in that category measure. Choose one ratio from the category selected, present its formula, and explain what it measures.

    a. Liquidity and efficiency   **c.** Profitability

    b. Solvency   **d.** Market prospects

3. Each team member is to present his or her notes from part 2 to teammates. Team members are to confirm or correct other teammates' presentation.

Hint: Pairing within teams may be necessary for part 2. Use as an in-class activity or as an assignment. Consider presentations to the entire class using team rotation with transparencies.

**ENTREPRENEURIAL
DECISION**

A1 P1 P2 P3

BTN 17-7　Assume that David and Tom Gardner of The Motley Fool (Fool.com) have impressed you since you first heard of their rather improbable rise to prominence in financial circles. You learn of a staff opening at The Motley Fool and decide to apply for it. Your resume is successfully screened from the thousands received and you advance to the interview process. You learn that the interview consists of analyzing the following financial facts and answering analysis questions. (*Note:* The data are taken from a small merchandiser in outdoor recreational equipment.)

	2008	2007	2006
Sales trend percents	137.0%	125.0%	100.0%
Selling expenses to sales	9.8%	13.7%	15.3%
Sales to plant assets ratio	3.5 to 1	3.3 to 1	3.0 to 1
Current ratio	2.6 to 1	2.4 to 1	2.1 to 1
Acid-test ratio	0.8 to 1	1.1 to 1	1.2 to 1
Merchandise inventory turnover	7.5 times	8.7 times	9.9 times
Accounts receivable turnover	6.7 times	7.4 times	8.2 times
Total asset turnover	2.6 times	2.6 times	3.0 times
Return on total assets	8.8%	9.4%	11.1%
Return on equity	9.75%	11.50%	12.25%
Profit margin ratio	3.3%	3.5%	3.7%

Required

Use these data to answer each of the following questions with explanations.

1. Is it becoming easier for the company to meet its current liabilities on time and to take advantage of any available cash discounts? Explain.

2. Is the company collecting its accounts receivable more rapidly? Explain.

3. Is the company's investment in accounts receivable decreasing? Explain.

4. Is the company's investment in plant assets increasing? Explain.

5. Is the owner's investment becoming more profitable? Explain.

6. Did the dollar amount of selling expenses decrease during the three-year period? Explain.

**HITTING THE
ROAD**

C1 P3

BTN 17-8　You are to devise an investment strategy to enable you to accumulate $1,000,000 by age 65. Start by making some assumptions about your salary. Next compute the percent of your salary that you will be able to save each year. If you will receive any lump-sum monies, include those amounts in your calculations. Historically, stocks have delivered average annual returns of 10–11%. Given this history, you should probably not assume that you will earn above 10% on the money you invest. It is not necessary to specify exactly what types of assets you will buy for your investments; just assume a rate you expect to earn. Use the future value tables in Appendix B to calculate how your savings will grow. Experiment a bit with your figures to see how much less you have to save if you start at, for example, age 25 versus age 35 or 40. (For this assignment, do not include inflation in your calculations.)

GLOBAL DECISION

A1

BTN 17-9　DSG international plc (www.DSGiplc.com), Best Buy, Circuit City, and RadioShack are competitors in the global marketplace. Key figures for DSG follow (in millions).

Cash and equivalents	£ 441
Accounts receivable, net	393
Inventories	1,031
Retained earnings	1,490
Cost of sales	7,285
Revenues	7,930
Total assets	3,977

Required

1. Compute common-sized percents for DSG using the data provided. (Round percents to one decimal.)

2. Compare the results with Best Buy, Circuit City, and RadioShack from BTN 17-2.

ANSWERS TO MULTIPLE CHOICE QUIZ

1. d; ($351,000/$300,000) × 100 = 117%

2. e; ($86,000 + $76,000 + $122,000 + $12,000)/$124,000 = 2.39

3. c; ($86,000 + $76,000)/$124,000 = 1.31

4. a; ($124,000 + $90,000)/$830,000 = 25.78%

5. d; ($300,000 + $316,000)/$830,000 = 74.22%

A Look Back

Chapter 17 described the analysis and interpretation of financial statement information. We applied horizontal, vertical, and ratio analyses to better understand company performance and financial condition.

A Look at This Chapter

We begin our study of managerial accounting by explaining its purpose and describing its major characteristics. We also discuss cost concepts and describe how they help managers gather and organize information for making decisions. The reporting of manufacturing activities is also discussed.

A Look Ahead

The remaining chapters discuss the types of decisions managers must make and how managerial accounting helps with those decisions. The first of these chapters, Chapter 19, considers how we measure costs assigned to certain types of projects.

Managerial Accounting Concepts and Principles

Chapter

Learning Objectives

CAP

Conceptual

C1 Explain the purpose and nature of managerial accounting. (p. 726)

C2 Describe the lean business model. (p. 729)

C3 Describe fraud and the role of ethics in managerial accounting. (p. 731)

C4 Describe accounting concepts useful in classifying costs. (p. 732)

C5 Define product and period costs and explain how they impact financial statements. (p. 733)

C6 Explain how balance sheets and income statements for manufacturing and merchandising companies differ. (p. 735)

C7 Explain manufacturing activities and the flow of manufacturing costs. (p. 739)

Analytical

A1 Compute cycle time and cycle efficiency, and explain their importance to production management (p. 742)

Procedural

P1 Compute cost of goods sold for a manufacturer. (p. 737)

P2 Prepare a manufacturing statement and explain its purpose and links to financial statements. (p. 740)

LP18

No Naked Popcorn

"Find a niche and stay focused"—Brian Taylor

ELK GROVE VILLAGE, IL—As a hungry college student, Brian Taylor liked to eat popcorn. Lots of it. Bored with "naked popcorn," Brian began experimenting with seasonings such as nacho cheese, cajun, jalapeño, and apple cinnamon. After he shared his concoctions with friends, dorm mates, and others, the demand for Brian's seasonings ballooned. In less than two years, Brian had the number one shake-on popcorn seasoning in the market, **Kernel Season's** (**KernelSeasons.com**).

Brian launched Kernel Season's with $7,000 he earned from giving tennis lessons and selling knives. In the beginning, he gave away his popcorn seasonings to local theaters to build awareness. Just like his college friends, moviegoers loved the all-natural, low-calorie seasonings. Soon theaters across the country were asking for his seasonings, and Brian worked hard to meet demand. "I was the only employee," explains Brian. "I made sales and shipped orders. I was figuring it out as I went along."

Well, business is now popping. Fourteen varieties of Kernel Season's are available in over 14,000 movie theaters and 15,000 grocery stores. Annual sales now exceed $5 million, and Brian is on Inc.com's "30 under 30," a list of America's coolest young entrepreneurs.

Brian believes college is the best time to start a new business. "Risk is low, and banks understand young entrepreneurs are trying to get things going," explains Brian. But Brian emphasizes that understanding basic managerial principles, product and period costs, manufacturing statements, and cost flows is equally crucial. "[I was] dedicated to business classes," says Brian, including my "accounting class." Brian uses managerial accounting information from his production process to monitor and control costs and to assess new business opportunities, including Kernel Season's apparel. Brian further stresses that company success and growth require him to develop budgets, monitor product performance, and make quick decisions.

Brian believes entrepreneurs fill a void by creating a niche. However, financial success depends on monitoring and controlling operations to best meet customer needs. Brian cautions would-be entrepreneurs to "stay focused" because in the absence of applying managerial accounting principles and concepts, it's just naked popcorn.

[Sources: *Kernel Season's Website,* January 2009; *Lake County News Sun,* October 2003; *Female Entrepreneur,* July/August 2003; *Chicago Tonight* interview, August 2007; *StartupNation.com,* May 2007; *Inc.com Website,* May 2008]

Managerial accounting, like financial accounting, provides information to help users make better decisions. However, managerial accounting and financial accounting differ in important ways, which this chapter explains. This chapter also compares the accounting and reporting practices used by manufacturing and merchandising companies. A merchandising company sells products without changing their condition. A manufacturing company buys raw materials and turns them into finished products for sale to customers. A third type of company earns revenues by providing services rather than products. The skills, tools, and techniques developed for measuring a manufacturing company's activities apply to service companies as well. The chapter concludes by explaining the flow of manufacturing activities and preparing the manufacturing statement.

Managerial Accounting Concepts and Principles

Managerial Accounting Basics	Managerial Cost Concepts	Reporting Manufacturing Activities
• Purpose of managerial accounting • Nature of managerial accounting • Managerial decisions • Managerial accounting in business • Fraud and ethics in managerial accounting	• Types of cost classifications • Identification of cost classifications • Cost concepts for service companies	• Balance sheet • Income statement • Flow of activities • Manufacturing statement

Managerial Accounting Basics

Video18.1

Managerial accounting is an activity that provides financial and nonfinancial information to an organization's managers and other internal decision makers. This section explains the purpose of managerial accounting (also called *management accounting*) and compares it with financial accounting. The main purpose of the financial accounting system is to prepare general-purpose financial statements. That information is incomplete for internal decision makers who manage organizations.

Purpose of Managerial Accounting

C1 Explain the purpose and nature of managerial accounting.

The purpose of both managerial accounting and financial accounting is providing useful information to decision makers. They do this by collecting, managing, and reporting information in demand by their users. Both areas of accounting also share the common practice of reporting monetary information, although managerial accounting includes the reporting of nonmonetary information. They even report some of the same information. For instance, a company's financial statements contain information useful for both its managers (insiders) and other persons interested in the company (outsiders).

The remainder of this book looks carefully at managerial accounting information, how to gather it, and how managers use it. We consider the concepts and procedures used to determine the costs of products and services as well as topics such as budgeting, break-even analysis, product costing, profit planning, and cost analysis. Information about the costs of products and services is important for many decisions that managers make. These decisions include predicting the future costs of a product or service. Predicted costs are used in product pricing, profitability analysis, and in deciding whether to make or buy a product or component. More generally, much of managerial accounting involves gathering information about costs for planning and control decisions.

Planning is the process of setting goals and making plans to achieve them. Companies formulate long-term strategic plans that usually span a 5- to 10-year horizon and then refine them with medium-term and short-term plans. Strategic plans usually set a firm's long-term direction by developing a road map based on opportunities such as new products, new markets, and capital investments. A strategic plan's goals and objectives are broadly defined given its long-term

Point: Nonfinancial information, also called nonmonetary information, includes customer and employee satisfaction data, the percentage of on-time deliveries, and product defect rates.

Point: Costs are important to managers because they impact both the financial position and profitability of a business. Managerial accounting assists in analysis, planning, and control of costs.

orientation. Medium- and short-term plans are more operational in nature. They translate the strategic plan into actions. These plans are more concrete and consist of better defined objectives and goals. A short-term plan often covers a one-year period that, when translated in monetary terms, is known as a budget.

Control is the process of monitoring planning decisions and evaluating an organization's activities and employees. It includes the measurement and evaluation of actions, processes, and outcomes. Feedback provided by the control function allows managers to revise their plans. Measurement of actions and processes also allows managers to take corrective actions to avoid undesirable outcomes. For example, managers periodically compare actual results with planned results. Exhibit 18.1 portrays the important management functions of planning and control.

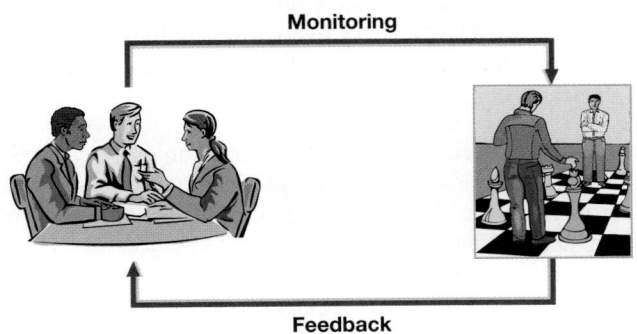

EXHIBIT 18.1

Planning and Control

Managers use information to plan and control business activities. In later chapters, we explain how managers also use this information to direct and improve business operations.

Nature of Managerial Accounting

Managerial accounting has its own special characteristics. To understand these characteristics, we compare managerial accounting to financial accounting; they differ in at least seven important ways. These differences are summarized in Exhibit 18.2. This section discusses each of these characteristics.

EXHIBIT 18.2

Key Differences between Managerial Accounting and Financial Accounting

	Financial Accounting	Managerial Accounting
1. Users and decision makers	Investors, creditors, and other users external to the organization	Managers, employees, and decision makers internal to the organization
2. Purpose of information	Assist external users in making investment, credit, and other decisions	Assist managers in making planning and control decisions
3. Flexibility of practice	Structured and often controlled by GAAP	Relatively flexible (no GAAP constraints)
4. Timeliness of information	Often available only after an audit is complete	Available quickly without the need to wait for an audit
5. Time dimension	Focus on historical information with some predictions	Many projections and estimates; historical information also presented
6. Focus of information	Emphasis on whole organization	Emphasis on an organization's projects, processes, and subdivisions
7. Nature of information	Monetary information	Mostly monetary; but also nonmonetary information

Users and Decision Makers   Companies accumulate, process, and report financial accounting and managerial accounting information for different groups of decision makers. Financial accounting information is provided primarily to external users including investors, creditors, analysts, and regulators. External users rarely have a major role in managing a company's daily activities. Managerial accounting information is provided primarily to internal users who are responsible for making and implementing decisions about a company's business activities.

Purpose of Information   Investors, creditors, and other external users of financial accounting information must often decide whether to invest in or lend to a company. If they have already done so, they must decide whether to continue owning the company or carrying the loan. Internal decision makers must plan a company's future. They seek to take advantage of opportunities or to overcome obstacles. They also try to control activities and ensure their effective and efficient implementation. Managerial accounting information helps these internal users make both planning and control decisions.

Flexibility of Practice   External users compare companies by using financial reports and need protection against false or misleading information. Accordingly, financial accounting relies on accepted principles that are enforced through an extensive set of rules and guidelines, or GAAP. Internal users need managerial accounting information for planning and controlling their company's activities rather than for external comparisons. They require different types of information depending on the activity. This makes standardizing managerial accounting systems across companies difficult. Instead, managerial accounting systems are flexible. The design of a company's managerial accounting system depends largely on the nature of the business and the arrangement of its internal operations. Managers can decide for themselves what information they want and how they want it reported. Even within a single company, different managers often design their own systems to meet their special needs. The important question a manager must ask is whether the information being collected and reported is useful for planning, decision making, and control purposes.

Timeliness of Information   Formal financial statements reporting past transactions and events are not immediately available to outside parties. Independent certified public accountants often must *audit* a company's financial statements before it provides them to external users. Thus, because audits often take several weeks to complete, financial reports to outsiders usually are not available until well after the period-end. However, managers can quickly obtain managerial accounting information. External auditors need not review it. Estimates and projections are acceptable. To get information quickly, managers often accept less precision in reports. As an example, an early internal report to management prepared right after the year-end could report net income for the year between $4.2 and $4.8 million. An audited income statement could later show net income for the year at $4.6 million. The internal report is not precise, but its information can be more useful because it is available earlier.

Internal auditing plays an important role in managerial accounting. Internal auditors evaluate the flow of information not only inside but also outside the company. Managers are responsible for preventing and detecting fraudulent activities in their companies.

Time Dimension   To protect external users from false expectations, financial reports deal primarily with results of both past activities and current conditions. While some predictions such as service lives and salvage values of plant assets are necessary, financial accounting avoids predictions whenever possible. Managerial accounting regularly includes predictions of conditions and events. As an example, one important managerial accounting report is a budget, which predicts revenues, expenses, and other items. If managerial accounting reports were restricted to the past and present, managers would be less able to plan activities and less effective in managing and evaluating current activities.

EXHIBIT 18.3

Focus of External Reports

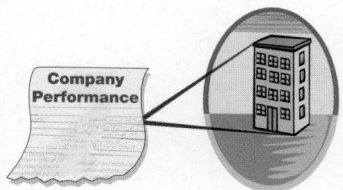

Focus of Information   Companies often organize into divisions and departments, but investors rarely can buy shares in one division or department. Nor do creditors lend money to a company's single division or department. Instead, they own shares in or make loans to the entire company. Financial accounting focuses primarily on a company as a whole as depicted in Exhibit 18.3.

The focus of managerial accounting is different. While top-level managers are responsible for managing the whole company, most other managers are responsible for much smaller sets of activities. These middle-level and lower-level managers need managerial accounting reports dealing with specific activities, projects, and subdivisions for which they are responsible. For instance, division sales managers are directly responsible only for the results achieved in their divisions. Accordingly, division sales managers need information about results achieved in their own divisions to improve their performance. This information includes the level of success achieved by each individual, product, or department in each division as depicted in Exhibit 18.4.

EXHIBIT 18.4

Focus of Internal Reports

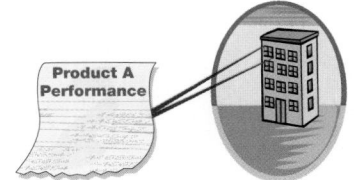

Nature of Information   Both financial and managerial accounting systems report monetary information. Managerial accounting systems also report considerable nonmonetary information. Monetary information is an important part of managerial decisions, and nonmonetary information plays a crucial role, especially when monetary effects are difficult to measure. Common examples of nonmonetary information are the quality and delivery criteria of purchasing decisions.

Decision Ethics

Production Manager   You invite three friends to a restaurant. When the dinner check arrives, David, a self-employed entrepreneur, picks it up saying, "Here, let me pay. I'll deduct it as a business expense on my tax return." Denise, a salesperson, takes the check from David's hand and says, "I'll put this on my company's credit card. It won't cost us anything." Derek, a factory manager for a company, laughs and says, "Neither of you understands. I'll put this on my company's credit card and call it overhead on a cost-plus contract my company has with a client." (*A cost-plus contract means the company receives its costs plus a percent of those costs.*) Adds Derek, "That way, my company pays for dinner *and* makes a profit." Who should pay the bill? Why? [Answer—p. 748]

Managerial Decision Making

The previous section emphasized differences between financial and managerial accounting, but they are not entirely separate. Similar information is useful to both external and internal users. For instance, information about costs of manufacturing products is useful to all users in making decisions. Also, both financial and managerial accounting affect peoples' actions. For example, **Trek**'s design of a sales compensation plan affects the behavior of its salesforce. It also must estimate the dual effects of promotion and sales compensation plans on buying patterns of customers. These estimates impact the equipment purchase decisions for manufacturing and can affect the supplier selection criteria established by purchasing. Thus, financial and managerial accounting systems do more than measure; they also affect people's decisions and actions.

Managerial Accounting in Business

We have explained the importance of managerial accounting for internal decision making. Although the analytical tools and techniques of managerial accounting have always been useful, their relevance and importance continue to increase. This is so because of changes in the business environment. This section describes some of these changes and their impact on managerial accounting.

C2   Describe the lean business model.

Lean Business Model   Two important factors have encouraged companies to be more effective and efficient in running their operations. First, there is an increased emphasis on *customers* as the most important constituent of a business. Customers expect to derive a certain value for the money they spend to buy products and services. Specifically, they expect that their suppliers will offer them the right service (or product) at the right time and the right price. This implies that companies accept the notion of **customer orientation**, which means that employees

understand the changing needs and wants of their customers and align their management and operating practices accordingly.

Second, our *global economy* expands competitive boundaries, thereby providing customers more choices. The global economy also produces changes in business activities. One notable case that reflects these changes in customer demand and global competition is auto manufacturing. The top three Japanese auto manufacturers (**Honda**, **Nissan**, and **Toyota**) once controlled more than 40% of the U.S. auto market. Customers perceived that Japanese auto manufacturers provided value not available from other manufacturers. Many European and North American auto manufacturers responded to this challenge and regained much of the lost market share.

Companies must be alert to these and other factors. Many companies have responded by adopting the **lean business model,** whose goal is to *eliminate waste* while "satisfying the customer" and "providing a positive return" to the company.

Lean Practices   **Continuous improvement** rejects the notions of "good enough" or "acceptable" and challenges employees and managers to continuously experiment with new and improved business practices. This has led companies to adopt practices such as total quality management (TQM) and just-in-time (JIT) manufacturing. The philosophy underlying both practices is continuous improvement; the difference is in the focus.

Point: Goals of a TQM process include reduced waste, better inventory control, fewer defects, and continuous improvement. Just-in-time concepts have similar goals.

Total quality management focuses on quality improvement and applies this standard to all aspects of business activities. In doing so, managers and employees seek to uncover waste in business activities including accounting activities such as payroll and disbursements. To encourage an emphasis on quality, the U.S. Congress established the Malcolm Baldrige National Quality Award (MBQNA). Entrants must conduct a thorough analysis and evaluation of their business using guidelines from the Baldrige committee. **Ritz Carlton Hotel** is a recipient of the Baldrige award in the service category. The company applies a core set of values, collectively called *The Gold Standards,* to improve customer service.

Point: The time between buying raw materials and selling finished goods is called *throughput time.*

Just-in-time manufacturing is a system that acquires inventory and produces only when needed. An important aspect of JIT is that companies manufacture products only after they receive an order (a *demand-pull* system) and then deliver the customer's requirements on time. This means that processes must be aligned to eliminate any delays and inefficiencies including inferior inputs and outputs. Companies must also establish good relations and communications with their suppliers. On the downside, JIT is more susceptible to disruption than traditional systems. As one example, several **General Motors** plants were temporarily shut down due to a strike at an assembly division; the plants supplied components *just in time* to the assembly division.

Decision Insight

Global Lean   **Toyota Motor Corporation** pioneered lean manufacturing, and it has since spread to other manufacturers throughout the world. The goals include improvements in quality, reliability, inventory turnover, productivity, exports, and—above all—sales and income.

Video18.3

Implications for Managerial Accounting   Adopting the lean business model can be challenging because to foster its implementation, all systems and procedures that a company follows must be realigned. Managerial accounting has an important role to play by providing accurate cost and performance information. Companies must understand the nature and sources of cost and must develop systems that capture costs accurately. Developing such a system is important to measuring the "value" provided to customers. The price that customers pay for acquiring goods and services is an important determinant of value. In turn, the costs a company incurs are key determinants of price. All else being equal, the better a company is at controlling its costs, the better its performance.

Decision Insight

Balanced Scorecard   The *balanced scorecard* aids continuous improvement by augmenting financial measures with information on the "drivers" (indicators) of future financial performance along four dimensions: (1) *financial*—profitability and risk, (2) *customer*—value creation and product and service differentiation, (3) *internal business processes*—business activities that create customer and owner satisfaction, and (4) *learning and growth*—organizational change, innovation, and growth.

Fraud and Ethics in Managerial Accounting

Fraud, and the role of ethics in reducing fraud, are important factors in running business operations. Fraud involves the use of one's job for personal gain through the deliberate misuse of the employer's assets. Examples include theft of the employer's cash or other assets, overstating reimbursable expenses, payroll schemes, and financial statement fraud. Fraud affects all business and it is costly: A 2006 *Report to the Nation* from the Association of Certified Fraud Examiners estimates the average U.S. business loses 5% of its annual revenues to fraud.

The most common type of fraud, where employees steal or misuse the employer's resources, results in an average loss of $150,000 per occurrence. For example, in a billing fraud, an employee sets up a bogus supplier. The employee then prepares bills from the supplier and pays these bills from the employer's checking account. The employee cashes the checks sent to the bogus supplier and uses them for his or her own personal benefit.

Although there are many types of fraud schemes, all fraud

- ■ Is done to provide direct or indirect benefit to the employee.
- ■ Violates the employee's duties to his employer.
- ■ Costs the employer money.
- ■ Is secret.

Implications for Managerial Accounting   Fraud increases a business's costs. Left undetected, these inflated costs can result in poor pricing decisions, an improper product mix, and faulty performance evaluations. Management can develop accounting systems to closely track costs and identify deviations from expected amounts. In addition, managers rely on an **internal control system** to monitor and control business activities. An internal control system is the policies and procedures managers use to

- ■ Urge adherence to company policies.
- ■ Promote efficient operations.
- ■ Ensure reliable accounting.
- ■ Protect assets.

Combating fraud and other dilemmas requires ethics in accounting. **Ethics** are beliefs that distinguish right from wrong. They are accepted standards of good and bad behavior. Identifying the ethical path can be difficult. The preferred path is a course of action that avoids casting doubt on one's decisions.

The **Institute of Management Accountants** (IMA), the professional association for management accountants, has issued a code of ethics to help accountants involved in solving ethical dilemmas. The IMA's Statement of Ethical Professional Practice requires that management accountants be competent, maintain confidentiality, act with integrity, and communicate information in a fair and credible manner.

The IMA provides a "road map" for resolving ethical conflicts. It suggests that an employee follow the company's policies on how to resolve such conflicts. If the conflict remains unresolved, an employee should contact the next level of management (such as the immediate supervisor) who is not involved in the ethical conflict.

C3   Describe fraud and the role of ethics in managerial accounting.

Point: The IMA also issues the Certified Management Accountant (CMA) and the Certified Financial Manager (CFM) certifications. Employees with the CMA or CFM certifications typically earn higher salaries than those without.

Point: The **Sarbanes-Oxley Act** requires each issuer of securities to disclose whether it has adopted a code of ethics for its senior officers and the content of that code.

Managerial Cost Concepts

C4 Describe accounting concepts useful in classifying costs.

An organization incurs many different types of costs that are classified differently, depending on management needs (different costs for different purposes). We can classify costs on the basis of their (1) behavior, (2) traceability, (3) controllability, (4) relevance, and (5) function. This section explains each concept for assigning costs to products and services.

Types of Cost Classifications

Video 18.2

Classification by Behavior   At a basic level, a cost can be classified as fixed or variable. A **fixed cost** does not change with changes in the volume of activity (within a range of activity known as an activity's *relevant range*). For example, straight-line depreciation on equipment is a fixed cost. A **variable cost** changes in proportion to changes in the volume of activity. Sales commissions computed as a percent of sales revenue are variable costs. Additional examples of fixed and variable costs for a bike manufacturer are provided in Exhibit 18.5. When cost items are combined, total cost can be fixed, variable, or mixed. *Mixed* refers to a combination of fixed and variable costs. Equipment rental often includes a fixed cost for some minimum amount and a variable cost based on amount of usage. Classification of costs by behavior is helpful in cost-volume-profit analyses and short-term decision making. We discuss these in Chapters 22 and 25.

EXHIBIT 18.5

Fixed and Variable Costs

Fixed Cost: Rent for Rocky Mountain Bikes' building is $22,000, and it doesn't change with the number of bikes produced.

Variable Cost: Cost of bicycle tires is variable with the number of bikes produced—this cost is $15 per pair.

Classification by Traceability   A cost is often traced to a **cost object,** which is a product, process, department, or customer to which costs are assigned. **Direct costs** are those traceable to a single cost object. For example, if a product is a cost object, its material and labor costs are usually directly traceable. **Indirect costs** are those that cannot be easily and cost–beneficially traced to a single cost object. An example of an indirect cost is a maintenance plan that benefits two or more departments. Exhibit 18.6 identifies examples of both direct and indirect costs for the maintenance department in a manufacturing plant. Thus, salaries of Rocky Mountain Bikes' maintenance department employees are considered indirect if the cost object is bicycles and direct if the cost object is the maintenance department. Classification of costs by traceability is useful for cost allocation. This is discussed in Chapter 21.

 Decision Maker ━━━━━━━━━━━━━━━━━━━━━━━

Entrepreneur   You wish to trace as many of your assembly department's direct costs as possible. You can trace 90% of them in an economical manner. To trace the other 10%, you need sophisticated and costly accounting software. Do you purchase this software? [Answer—p. 748]

EXHIBIT 18.6

Direct and Indirect Costs of a Maintenance Department

Direct Costs		Indirect Costs	
• Salaries of maintenance department employees • Equipment purchased by maintenance department	• Materials purchased by maintenance department • Maintenance department equipment depreciation	• Factory accounting • Factory administration • Factory rent • Factory managers' salary	• Factory light and heat • Factory internal audit • Factory intranet • Insurance on factory

Classification by Controllability A cost can be defined as **controllable** or **not controllable.** Whether a cost is controllable or not depends on the employee's responsibilities, as shown in Exhibit 18.7. This is referred to as *hierarchical levels* in management, or *pecking order.* For example, investments in machinery are controllable by upper-level managers but not lower-level managers. Many daily operating expenses such as overtime often are controllable by lower-level managers. Classification of costs by controllability is especially useful for assigning responsibility to and evaluating managers.

EXHIBIT 18.7

Controllability of Costs

Senior Manager
Controls costs of investments in land, buildings, and equipment.

Supervisor
Controls daily expenses such as supplies, maintenance, and overtime.

Classification by Relevance A cost can be classified by relevance by identifying it as either a sunk cost or an out-of-pocket cost. A **sunk cost** has already been incurred and cannot be avoided or changed. It is irrelevant to future decisions. One example is the cost of a company's office equipment previously purchased. An **out-of-pocket cost** requires a future outlay of cash and is relevant for decision making. Future purchases of equipment involve out-of-pocket costs. A discussion of relevant costs must also consider opportunity costs. An **opportunity cost** is the potential benefit lost by choosing a specific action from two or more alternatives. One example is a student giving up wages from a job to attend evening classes. Consideration of opportunity cost is important when, for example, an insurance company must decide whether to outsource its payroll function or maintain it internally. This is discussed in Chapter 25.

Point: Opportunity costs are not recorded by the accounting system.

Classification by Function Another cost classification (for manufacturers) is capitalization as inventory or to expense as incurred. Costs capitalized as inventory are called **product costs,** which refer to expenditures necessary and integral to finished products. They include direct materials, direct labor, and indirect manufacturing costs called *overhead costs.* Product costs pertain to activities carried out to manufacture the product. Costs expensed are called **period costs,** which refer to expenditures identified more with a time period than with finished products. They include selling and general administrative expenses. Period costs pertain to activities that are not part of the manufacturing process. A distinction between product and period costs is important because period costs are expensed in the income statement and product costs are assigned to inventory on the balance sheet until that inventory is sold. An ability to understand and identify product costs and period costs is crucial to using and interpreting a *manufacturing statement* described later in this chapter.

C5 Define product and period costs and explain how they impact financial statements.

Exhibit 18.8 shows the different effects of product and period costs. Period costs flow directly to the current income statement as expenses. They are not reported as assets. Product costs are first assigned to inventory. Their final treatment depends on when inventory is sold or disposed of. Product costs assigned to finished goods that are sold in year 2009 are reported on the 2009 income statement as part of cost of goods sold. Product costs assigned to unsold inventory are carried forward on the balance sheet at the end of year 2009. If this inventory is sold in year 2010, product costs assigned to it are reported as part of cost of goods sold in that year's income statement.

Point: Only costs of production and purchases are classed as product costs.

EXHIBIT 18.8

Period and Product Costs in
Financial Statements

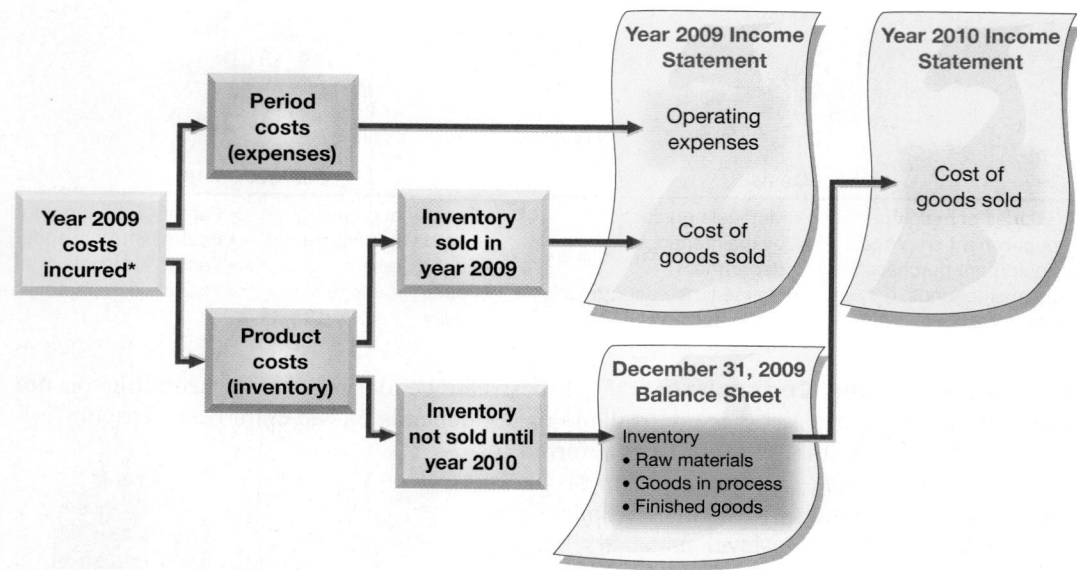

* This diagram excludes costs to acquire assets other than inventory.

Point: Product costs are either in the
income statement as part of cost of
goods sold or in the balance sheet as
inventory. Period costs appear only on
the income statement under operating
expenses. See Exhibit 18.8.

Point: For a team approach to identi-
fying period and product costs, see
Teamwork in Action in the *Beyond the
Numbers* section.

The difference between period and product costs explains why the year 2009 income statement does not report operating expenses related to either factory workers' wages or depreciation
on factory buildings and equipment. Instead, both costs are combined with the cost of raw materials to compute the product cost of finished goods. A portion of these manufacturing costs
(related to the goods sold) is reported in the year 2009 income statement as part of Cost of
Goods Sold. The other portion is reported on the balance sheet at the end of that year as part
of Inventory. The portion assigned to inventory could be included in any or all of raw materials, goods in process, or finished goods inventories.

 Decision Maker

Purchase Manager   You are evaluating two potential suppliers of seats for the manufacturing of
motorcycles. One supplier (A) quotes a $145 price per seat and ensures 100% quality standards and
on-time delivery. The second supplier (B) quotes a $115 price per seat but does not give any written
assurances on quality or delivery. You decide to contract with the second supplier (B), saving $30 per seat.
Does this decision have opportunity costs? [Answer—p. 749]

Identification of Cost Classifications

It is important to understand that a cost can be classified using any one (or combination) of
the five different means described here. To do this we must understand costs and operations.
Specifically, for the five classifications, we must be able to identify the *activity* for behavior,
cost object for traceability, *management hierarchical level* for controllability, *opportunity cost*
for relevance, and *benefit period* for function. Factory rent, for instance, can be classified as a
product cost; it is fixed with respect to number of units produced, it is indirect with respect to
the product, and it is not controllable by a production supervisor. Potential multiple classifications are shown in Exhibit 18.9 using different cost items incurred in manufacturing mountain bikes. The finished bike is the cost object. Proper allocation of these costs and the managerial decisions based on cost data depend on a correct cost classification.

Cost Concepts for Service Companies

Point: All expenses of service companies are period costs because these
companies do not have inventory.

The cost concepts described are generally applicable to service organizations. For example,
consider **Southwest Airlines**. Its cost of beverages for passengers is a variable cost based
on number of passengers. The cost of leasing an aircraft is fixed with respect to number of
passengers. We can also trace a flight crew's salary to a specific flight whereas we likely

Cost Item	By Behavior	By Traceability	By Function
Bicycle tires	Variable	Direct	Product
Wages of assembly worker*	Variable	Direct	Product
Advertising	Fixed	Indirect	Period
Production manager's salary	Fixed	Indirect	Product
Office depreciation	Fixed	Indirect	Period

EXHIBIT 18.9

Examples of Multiple Cost Classifications

* Although an assembly worker's wages are classified as variable costs, their actual behavior depends on how workers are paid and whether their wages are based on a union contract (such as piece rate or monthly wages).

cannot trace wages for the ground crew to a specific flight. Classification by function (such as product versus period costs) is not relevant to service companies because services are not inventoried. Instead, costs incurred by a service firm are expensed in the reporting period when incurred.

Managers in service companies must understand and apply cost concepts. They seek and rely on accurate cost estimates for many decisions. For example, an airline manager must often decide between canceling or rerouting flights. The manager must also be able to estimate costs saved by canceling a flight versus rerouting. Knowledge of fixed costs is equally important. We explain more about the cost requirements for these and other managerial decisions in Chapter 25.

Service Costs
• Beverages and snacks
• Cleaning fees
• Pilot and copilot salaries
• Attendant salaries
• Fuel and oil costs
• Travel agent fees
• Ground crew salaries

Quick Check   Answers—p. 749

5. Which type of cost behavior increases total costs when volume of activity increases?

6. How could traceability of costs improve managerial decisions?

Reporting Manufacturing Activities

Companies with manufacturing activities differ from both merchandising and service companies. The main difference between merchandising and manufacturing companies is that merchandisers buy goods ready for sale while manufacturers produce goods from materials and labor. **Payless** is an example of a merchandising company. It buys and sells shoes without physically changing them. **Adidas** is primarily a manufacturer of shoes, apparel, and accessories. It purchases materials such as leather, cloth, dye, plastic, rubber, glue, and laces and then uses employees' labor to convert these materials to products. **Southwest Airlines** is a service company that transports people and items.

Manufacturing activities differ from both selling merchandise and providing services. Also, the financial statements for manufacturing companies differ slightly. This section considers some of these differences and compares them to accounting for a merchandising company.

Manufacturer's Balance Sheet

Manufacturers carry several unique assets and usually have three inventories instead of the single inventory that merchandisers carry. Exhibit 18.10 shows three different inventories in the current asset section of the balance sheet for Rocky Mountain Bikes, a manufacturer. The three inventories are raw materials, goods in process, and finished goods.

C6 Explain how balance sheets and income statements for manufacturing and merchandising companies differ.

Point: Reducing the size of inventories saves storage costs and frees money for other uses.

Raw Materials Inventory **Raw materials inventory** refers to the goods a company acquires to use in making products. It uses raw materials in two ways: directly and indirectly. Most raw materials physically become part of a product and are identified with specific units or batches of a product. Raw materials used directly in a product are called *direct materials*. Other materials used to support production processes are sometimes not as clearly identified with specific units or batches of product. These materials are called **indirect materials** because they are not clearly identified with specific product units or batches. Items used as indirect materials often appear on a

EXHIBIT 18.10

Balance Sheet for a Manufacturer

ROCKY MOUNTAIN BIKES
Balance Sheet
December 31, 2009

Assets		Liabilities and Equity	
Current assets		Current liabilities	
Cash	$ 11,000	Accounts payable	$ 14,000
Accounts receivable, net	30,150	Wages payable	540
Raw materials inventory	9,000	Interest payable	2,000
Goods in process inventory	7,500	Income taxes payable	32,600
Finished goods inventory	10,300	Total current liabilities	49,140
Factory supplies	350	Long-term liabilities	
Prepaid insurance	300	Long-term notes payable	50,000
Total current assets	68,600	Total liabilities	99,140
Plant assets			
Small tools, net	1,100	Stockholders' equity	
Delivery equipment, net	5,000	Common stock, $1.2 par	24,000
Office equipment, net	1,300	Paid-in capital	76,000
Factory machinery, net	65,500	Retained earnings	49,760
Factory building, net	86,700	Total stockholders' equity	149,760
Land	9,500	Total liabilities and equity	$248,900
Total plant assets, net	169,100		
Intangible assets (patents), net	11,200		
Total assets	$248,900		

balance sheet as factory supplies or are included in raw materials. Some direct materials are classified as indirect materials when their costs are low (insignificant). Examples include screws and nuts used in assembling mountain bikes and staples and glue used in manufacturing shoes. Using the *materiality principle,* individually tracing the costs of each of these materials and classifying them separately as direct materials does not make much economic sense. For instance, keeping detailed records of the amount of glue used to manufacture one shoe is not cost beneficial.

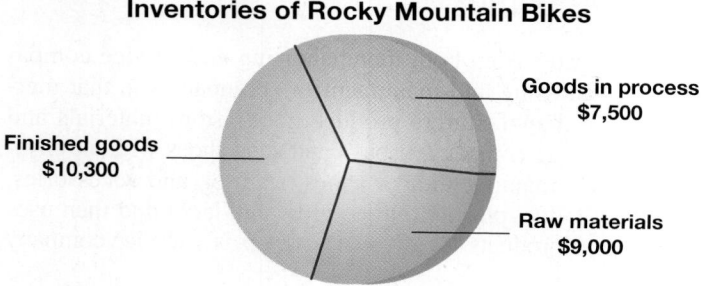

Inventories of Rocky Mountain Bikes

Goods in process $7,500

Finished goods $10,300

Raw materials $9,000

Goods in Process Inventory   Another inventory held by manufacturers is **goods in process inventory,** also called *work in process inventory.* It consists of products in the process of being manufactured but not yet complete. The amount of goods in process inventory depends on the type of production process. If the time required to produce a unit of product is short, the goods in process inventory is likely small; but if weeks or months are needed to produce a unit, the goods in process inventory is usually larger.

Finished Goods Inventory   A third inventory owned by a manufacturer is **finished goods inventory,** which consists of completed products ready for sale. This inventory is similar to merchandise inventory owned by a merchandising company. Manufacturers also often own unique plant assets such as small tools, factory buildings, factory equipment, and patents to manufacture products. The balance sheet in Exhibit 18.10 shows that Rocky Mountain Bikes owns all of these assets. Some manufacturers invest millions or even billions of dollars in production facilities and patents. **Briggs & Stratton's** recent balance sheet shows about $1 billion net investment in land, buildings, machinery and equipment, much of which involves production facilities. It manufactures more racing engines than any other company in the world.

Manufacturer's Income Statement

The main difference between the income statement of a manufacturer and that of a merchandiser involves the items making up cost of goods sold. Exhibit 18.11 compares the components of cost of goods sold for a manufacturer and a merchandiser. A merchandiser adds cost of goods purchased to beginning merchandise inventory and then subtracts ending merchandise inventory to get cost of goods sold. A manufacturer adds cost of goods manufactured to beginning finished goods inventory and then subtracts ending finished goods inventory to get cost of goods sold.

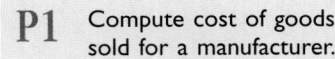

P1   Compute cost of goods sold for a manufacturer.

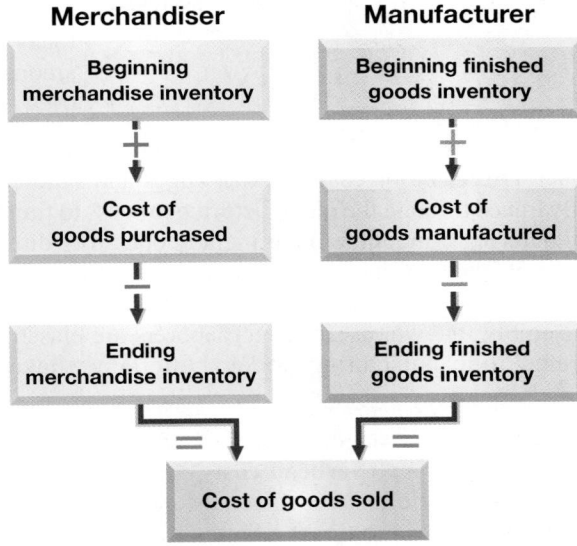

EXHIBIT 18.11

Cost of Goods Sold Computation

A merchandiser often uses the term *merchandise* inventory; a manufacturer often uses the term *finished goods* inventory. A manufacturer's inventories of raw materials and goods in process are not included in finished goods because they are not available for sale. A manufacturer also shows cost of goods *manufactured* instead of cost of goods *purchased*. This difference occurs because a manufacturer produces its goods instead of purchasing them ready for sale. We show later in this chapter how to derive cost of goods manufactured from the manufacturing statement.

The Cost of Goods Sold sections for both a merchandiser (Tele-Mart) and a manufacturer (Rocky Mountain Bikes) are shown in Exhibit 18.12 to highlight these differences. The remaining income statement sections are similar.

EXHIBIT 18.12

Cost of Goods Sold for a Merchandiser and Manufacturer

Merchandising (Tele-Mart) Company		Manufacturing (Rocky Mtn. Bikes) Company	
Cost of goods sold		Cost of goods sold	
Beginning *merchandise* inventory	$ 14,200	Beginning *finished goods* inventory	$ 11,200
Cost of merchandise *purchased*	234,150	Cost of goods *manufactured**	170,500
Goods available for sale	248,350	Goods available for sale	181,700
Less ending *merchandise* inventory	12,100	Less ending *finished goods* inventory	10,300
Cost of goods sold	$236,250	Cost of goods sold	$171,400

* Cost of goods manufactured is reported in the income statement of Exhibit 18.14.

Although the cost of goods sold computations are similar, the numbers in these computations reflect different activities. A merchandiser's cost of goods purchased is the cost of buying products to be sold. A manufacturer's cost of goods manufactured is the sum of direct materials, direct labor, and factory overhead costs incurred in producing products. The remainder of this section further explains these three manufacturing costs and describes prime and conversion costs.

Direct Materials **Direct materials** are tangible components of a finished product. **Direct material costs** are the expenditures for direct materials that are separately and readily traced through the manufacturing process to finished goods. Examples of direct materials in manufacturing a mountain bike include its tires, seat, frame, pedals, brakes, cables, gears, and handlebars. The chart in the margin shows that direct materials generally make up about 45% of manufacturing costs in today's products, but this amount varies across industries and companies.

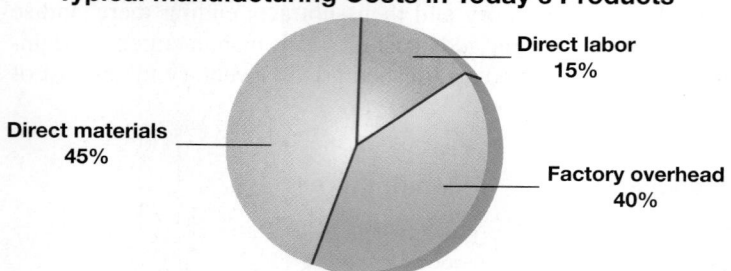

Typical Manufacturing Costs in Today's Products

Direct labor 15%
Direct materials 45%
Factory overhead 40%

Direct Labor **Direct labor** refers to the efforts of employees who physically convert materials to finished product. **Direct labor costs** are the wages and salaries for direct labor that are separately and readily traced through the manufacturing process to finished goods. Examples of direct labor in manufacturing a mountain bike include operators directly involved in converting raw materials into finished products (welding, painting, forming) and assembly workers who attach materials such as tires, seats, pedals, and brakes to the bike frames. Costs of other workers on the assembly line who assist direct laborers are classified as **indirect labor costs**. **Indirect labor** refers to manufacturing workers' efforts not linked to specific units or batches of the product.

Factory Overhead **Factory overhead** consists of all manufacturing costs that are not direct materials or direct labor. **Factory overhead costs** cannot be separately or readily traced to finished goods. These costs include indirect materials and indirect labor, costs not directly traceable to the product. Overtime paid to direct laborers is also included in overhead because overtime is due to delays, interruptions, or constraints not necessarily identifiable to a specific product or batches of product. Factory overhead costs also include maintenance of the mountain bike factory, supervision of its employees, repairing manufacturing equipment, factory utilities (water, gas, electricity), production manager's salary, factory rent, depreciation on factory buildings and equipment, factory insurance, property taxes on factory buildings and equipment, and factory accounting and legal services. Factory overhead does *not* include selling and administrative expenses because they are not incurred in manufacturing products. These expenses are called *period costs* and are recorded as expenses on the income statement when incurred.

EXHIBIT 18.13

Prime and Conversion Costs and Their Makeup

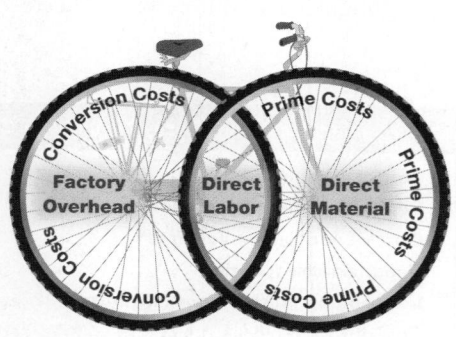

Prime and Conversion Costs Direct material costs and direct labor costs are also called **prime costs**—expenditures directly associated with the manufacture of finished goods. Direct labor costs and overhead costs are called **conversion costs**—expenditures incurred in the process of converting raw materials to finished goods. Direct labor costs are considered both prime costs and conversion costs. Exhibit 18.13 conveys the relation between prime and conversion costs and their components of direct material, direct labor, and factory overhead.

Reporting Performance Exhibit 18.14 shows the income statement for Rocky Mountain Bikes. Its operating expenses include sales salaries, office salaries, and depreciation of delivery and office equipment. Operating expenses do not include manufacturing costs such as factory workers' wages and depreciation of production equipment and the factory buildings. These manufacturing costs are reported as part of cost of goods manufactured and included in cost of goods sold. We explained why and how this is done in the section "Classification by Function."

EXHIBIT 18.14

Income Statement for a Manufacturer

ROCKY MOUNTAIN BIKES
Income Statement
For Year Ended December 31, 2009

Sales		$310,000
Cost of goods sold		
Finished goods inventory, Dec. 31, 2008	$ 11,200	
Cost of goods manufactured	170,500	
Goods available for sale	181,700	
Less finished goods inventory, Dec. 31, 2009	10,300	
Cost of goods sold		171,400
Gross profit		138,600
Operating expenses		
Selling expenses		
Sales salaries expense	18,000	
Advertising expense	5,500	
Delivery wages expense	12,000	
Shipping supplies expense	250	
Insurance expense—Delivery equipment	300	
Depreciation expense—Delivery equipment	2,100	
Total selling expenses		38,150
General and administrative expenses		
Office salaries expense	15,700	
Miscellaneous expense	200	
Bad debts expense	1,550	
Office supplies expense	100	
Depreciation expense—Office equipment	200	
Interest expense	4,000	
Total general and administrative expenses		21,750
Total operating expenses		59,900
Income before income taxes		78,700
Income taxes expense		32,600
Net income		$ 46,100
Net income per common share (20,000 shares)		$ 2.31

Quick Check

Answers—p. 749

7. What are the three types of inventory on a manufacturing company's balance sheet?

8. How does cost of goods sold differ for merchandising versus manufacturing companies?

Flow of Manufacturing Activities

To understand manufacturing and its reports, we must first understand the flow of manufacturing activities and costs. Exhibit 18.15 shows the flow of manufacturing activities for a manufacturer. This exhibit has three important sections: *materials activity, production activity,* and *sales activity.* We explain each activity in this section.

C7 Explain manufacturing activities and the flow of manufacturing costs.

Point: Knowledge of managerial accounting provides us a means of measuring manufacturing costs and is a sound foundation for studying advanced business topics.

Materials Activity   The far left side of Exhibit 18.15 shows the flow of raw materials. Manufacturers usually start a period with some beginning raw materials inventory carried over from the previous period. The company then acquires additional raw materials in the current period. Adding these purchases to beginning inventory gives total raw materials available for use in production. These raw materials are then either used in production in the current period or remain in inventory at the end of the period for use in future periods.

Production Activity   The middle section of Exhibit 18.15 describes production activity. Four factors come together in production: beginning goods in process inventory, direct materials,

EXHIBIT 18.15

Activities and Cost Flows in Manufacturing

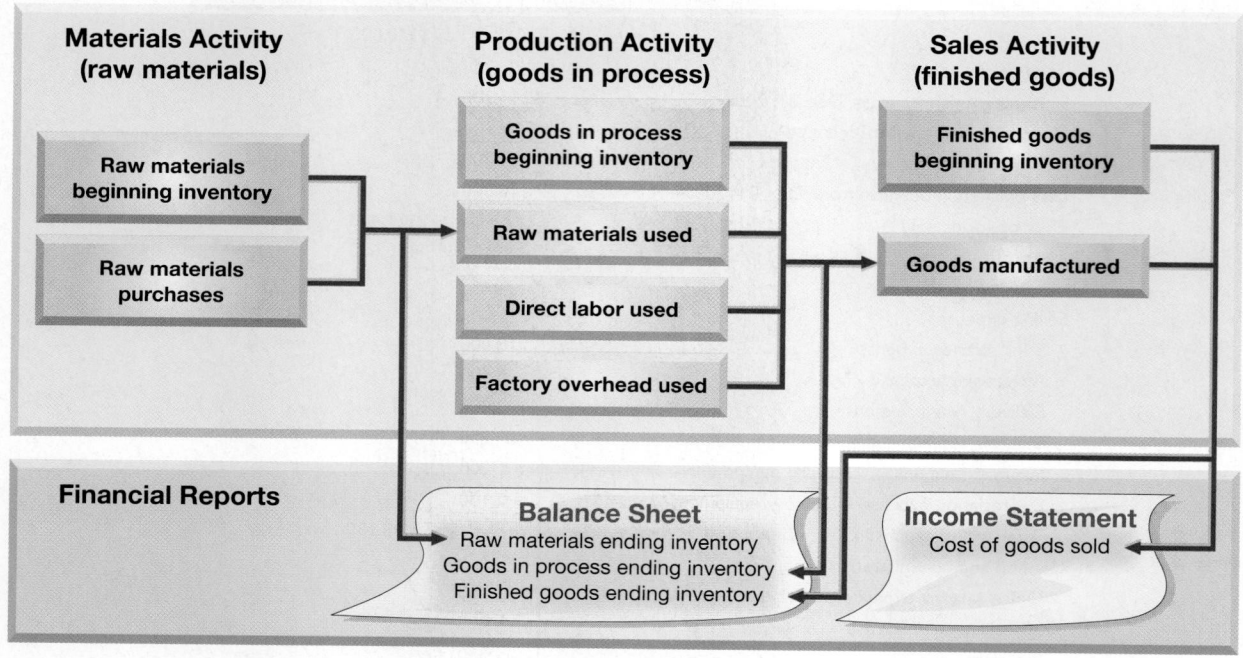

direct labor, and overhead. Beginning goods in process inventory consists of partly assembled products from the previous period. Production activity results in products that are either finished or remain unfinished. The cost of finished products makes up the cost of goods manufactured for the current period. Unfinished products are identified as ending goods in process inventory. The cost of unfinished products consists of direct materials, direct labor, and factory overhead, and is reported on the current period's balance sheet. The costs of both finished goods manufactured and goods in process are *product costs.*

Point: The series of activities that add value to a company's products or services is called a **value chain.**

Sales Activity   The company's sales activity is portrayed in the far right side of Exhibit 18.15. Newly completed units are combined with beginning finished goods inventory to make up total finished goods available for sale in the current period. The cost of finished products sold is reported on the income statement as cost of goods sold. The cost of products not sold is reported on the current period's balance sheet as ending finished goods inventory.

Manufacturing Statement

P2   Prepare a manufacturing statement and explain its purpose and links to financial statements.

A company's manufacturing activities are described in a **manufacturing statement,** also called the *schedule of manufacturing activities* or the *schedule of cost of goods manufactured.* The manufacturing statement summarizes the types and amounts of costs incurred in a company's manufacturing process. Exhibit 18.16 shows the manufacturing statement for Rocky Mountain Bikes. The statement is divided into four parts: *direct materials, direct labor, overhead,* and *computation of cost of goods manufactured.* We describe each of these parts in this section.

① The manufacturing statement begins by computing direct materials used. We start by adding beginning raw materials inventory of $8,000 to the current period's purchases of $86,500. This yields $94,500 of total raw materials available for use. A physical count of inventory shows $9,000 of ending raw materials inventory. This implies a total cost of raw materials used during the period of $85,500 ($94,500 total raw materials available for use − $9,000 ending inventory). (*Note:* All raw materials are direct materials for Rocky Mountain Bikes.)

EXHIBIT 18.16

Manufacturing Statement

ROCKY MOUNTAIN BIKES
Manufacturing Statement
For Year Ended December 31, 2009

Direct materials		
① Raw materials inventory, Dec. 31, 2008	$ 8,000	
Raw materials purchases	86,500	
Raw materials available for use	94,500	
Less raw materials inventory, Dec. 31, 2009	9,000	
Direct materials used		$ 85,500
② Direct labor		60,000
Factory overhead		
Indirect labor	9,000	
Factory supervision	6,000	
Factory utilities	2,600	
Repairs—Factory equipment	2,500	
Property taxes—Factory building	1,900	
③ Factory supplies used	600	
Factory insurance expired	1,100	
Depreciation expense—Small tools	200	
Depreciation expense—Factory equipment	3,500	
Depreciation expense—Factory building	1,800	
Amortization expense—Patents	800	
Total factory overhead		30,000
Total manufacturing costs		175,500
Add goods in process inventory, Dec. 31, 2008		2,500
④ Total cost of goods in process		178,000
Less goods in process inventory, Dec. 31, 2009		7,500
Cost of goods manufactured		$170,500

② The second part of the manufacturing statement reports direct labor costs. Rocky Mountain Bikes had total direct labor costs of $60,000 for the period. This amount includes payroll taxes and fringe benefits.

③ The third part of the manufacturing statement reports overhead costs. The statement lists each important factory overhead item and its cost. Total factory overhead cost for the period is $30,000. Some companies report only *total* factory overhead on the manufacturing statement and attach a separate schedule listing individual overhead costs.

④ The final section of the manufacturing statement computes and reports the *cost of goods manufactured.* (Total manufacturing costs for the period are $175,500 [$85,500 + $60,000 + $30,000], the sum of direct materials used and direct labor and overhead costs incurred.) This amount is first added to beginning goods in process inventory. This gives the total goods in process inventory of $178,000 ($175,500 + $2,500). We then compute the current period's cost of goods manufactured of $170,500 by taking the $178,000 total goods in process and subtracting the $7,500 cost of ending goods in process inventory that consists of direct materials, direct labor, and factory overhead. The cost of goods manufactured amount is also called *net cost of goods manufactured* or *cost of goods completed.* Exhibit 18.14 shows that this item and amount are listed in the Cost of Goods Sold section of Rocky Mountain Bikes' income statement and the balance sheet.

A managerial accounting system records costs and reports them in various reports that eventually determine financial statements. Exhibit 18.17 shows how overhead costs flow through the system: from an initial listing of specific costs, to a section of the manufacturing statement, to the reporting on the income statement and the balance sheet.

Point: Direct material and direct labor costs increase with increases in production volume and are called *variable costs.* Overhead can be both variable and fixed. When overhead costs vary with production, they are called *variable overhead.* When overhead costs don't vary with production, they are called *fixed overhead.*

Point: Manufacturers sometimes report variable and fixed overhead separately in the manufacturing statement to provide more information to managers about cost behavior.

"My boss wants us to appeal to a younger and hipper crowd. So, I'd like to get a tattoo that says-- 'Accounting rules!'"

EXHIBIT 18.17

Overhead Cost Flows across Accounting Reports

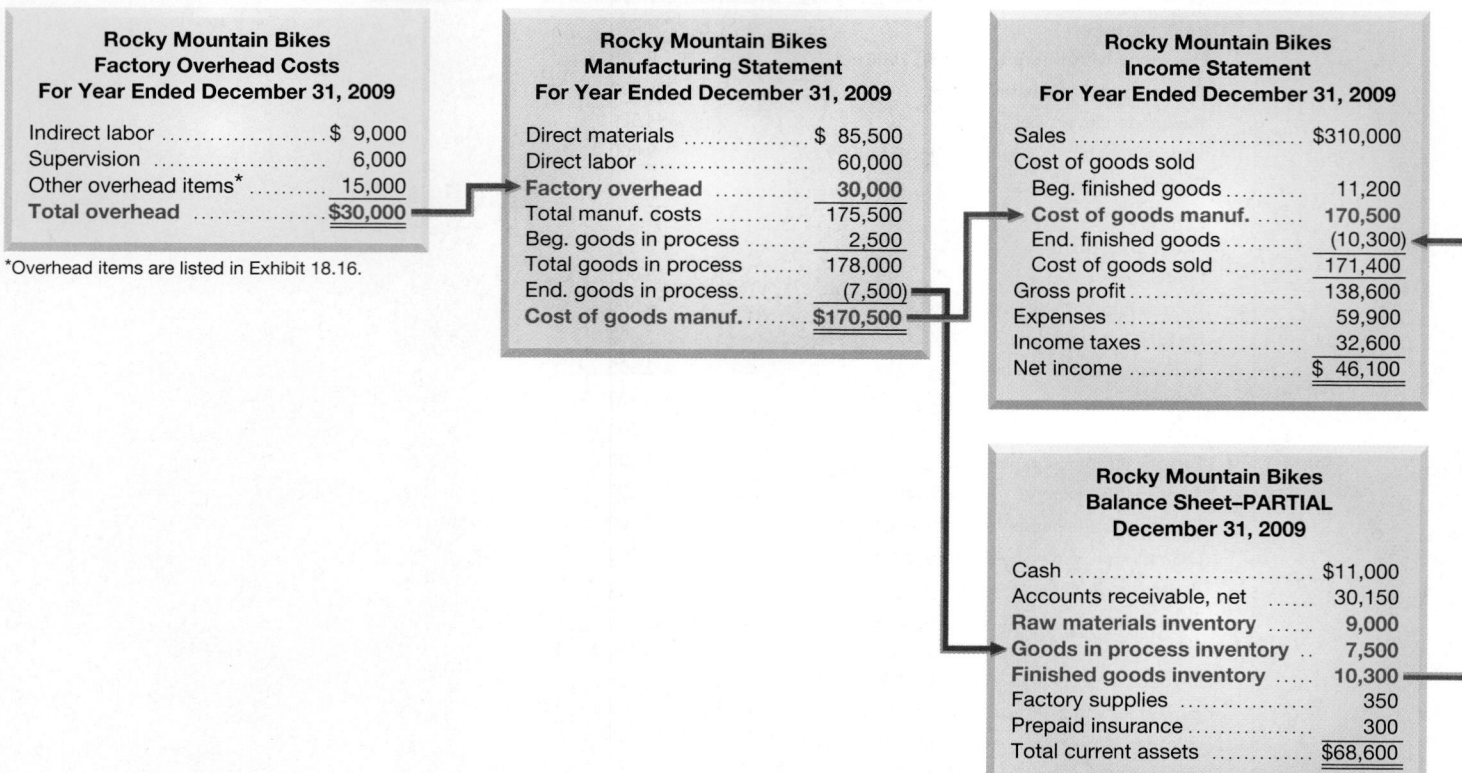

Rocky Mountain Bikes Factory Overhead Costs For Year Ended December 31, 2009	
Indirect labor	$ 9,000
Supervision	6,000
Other overhead items*	15,000
Total overhead	$30,000

*Overhead items are listed in Exhibit 18.16.

Rocky Mountain Bikes Manufacturing Statement For Year Ended December 31, 2009	
Direct materials	$ 85,500
Direct labor	60,000
Factory overhead	30,000
Total manuf. costs	175,500
Beg. goods in process	2,500
Total goods in process	178,000
End. goods in process	(7,500)
Cost of goods manuf.	$170,500

Rocky Mountain Bikes Income Statement For Year Ended December 31, 2009	
Sales	$310,000
Cost of goods sold	
Beg. finished goods	11,200
Cost of goods manuf.	170,500
End. finished goods	(10,300)
Cost of goods sold	171,400
Gross profit	138,600
Expenses	59,900
Income taxes	32,600
Net income	$ 46,100

Rocky Mountain Bikes Balance Sheet–PARTIAL December 31, 2009	
Cash	$11,000
Accounts receivable, net	30,150
Raw materials inventory	9,000
Goods in process inventory	7,500
Finished goods inventory	10,300
Factory supplies	350
Prepaid insurance	300
Total current assets	$68,600

Management uses information in the manufacturing statement to plan and control the company's manufacturing activities. To provide timely information for decision making, the statement is often prepared monthly, weekly, or even daily. In anticipation of release of its much-hyped iPhone, **Apple** grew its inventory of Flash-based memory chips, a critical component, and its finished goods inventory. The manufacturing statement contains information useful to external users but is not a general-purpose financial statement. Companies rarely publish the manufacturing statement because managers view this information as proprietary and potentially harmful to them if released to competitors.

Quick Check

Answers—p. 749

9. A manufacturing statement (a) computes cost of goods manufactured for the period, (b) computes cost of goods sold for the period, or (c) reports operating expenses incurred for the period.

10. Are companies required to report a manufacturing statement?

11. How are both beginning and ending goods in process inventories reported on a manufacturing statement?

Decision Analysis   Cycle Time and Cycle Efficiency

A1 Compute cycle time and cycle efficiency, and explain their importance to production management.

As lean manufacturing practices help companies move toward just-in-time manufacturing, it is important for these companies to reduce the time to manufacture their products and to improve manufacturing efficiency. One metric that measures that time element is **cycle time (CT).** A definition of cycle time is in Exhibit 18.18.

$$\boxed{\textbf{Cycle time = Process time + Inspection time + Move time + Wait time}}$$

EXHIBIT 18.18

Cycle Time

Process time is the time spent producing the product. *Inspection time* is the time spent inspecting (1) raw materials when received, (2) goods in process while in production, and (3) finished goods prior to shipment. *Move time* is the time spent moving (1) raw materials from storage to production and (2) goods in process from factory location to another factory location. *Wait time* is the time that an order or job sits with no production applied to it; this can be due to order delays, bottlenecks in production, and poor scheduling.

Process time is considered **value-added time** because it is the only activity in cycle time that adds value to the product from the customer's perspective. The other three time activities are considered **non-value-added time** because they add no value to the customer.

Companies strive to reduce non-value-added time to improve **cycle efficiency (CE).** Cycle efficiency is the ratio of value-added time to total cycle time—see Exhibit 18.19.

$$\text{Cycle efficiency} = \frac{\text{Value-added time}}{\text{Cycle time}}$$

EXHIBIT 18.19

Cycle Efficiency

To illustrate, assume that Rocky Mountain Bikes receives and produces an order for 500 Tracker® mountain bikes. Assume that the following times were measured during production of this order.

Process time... 1.8 days   **Inspection time... 0.5 days**   **Move time... 0.7 days**   **Wait time... 3.0 days**

In this case, cycle time is 6.0 days, computed as 1.8 days + 0.5 days + 0.7 days + 3.0 days. Also, cycle efficiency is 0.3, or 30%, computed as 1.8 days divided by 6.0 days. This means that Rocky Mountain Bikes spends 30% of its time working on the product (value-added time). The other 70% is spent on non-value-added activities.

If a company has a CE of 1, it means that its time is spent entirely on value-added activities. If the CE is low, the company should evaluate its production process to see if it can identify ways to reduce non-value-added activities. The 30% CE for Rocky Mountain Bikes is low and its management should look for ways to reduce non-value-added activities.

Demonstration Problem 1: Cost Behavior and Classification

Understanding the classification and assignment of costs is important. Consider a company that manufactures computer chips. It incurs the following costs in manufacturing chips and in operating the company.

DP18

1. Plastic board used to mount the chip, $3.50 each.
2. Assembly worker pay of $15 per hour to attach chips to plastic board.
3. Salary for factory maintenance workers who maintain factory equipment.
4. Factory supervisor pay of $55,000 per year to supervise employees.
5. Real estate taxes paid on the factory, $14,500.
6. Real estate taxes paid on the company office, $6,000.
7. Depreciation costs on machinery used by workers, $30,000.
8. Salary paid to the chief financial officer, $95,000.
9. Advertising costs of $7,800 paid to promote products.
10. Salespersons' commissions of $0.50 for each assembled chip sold.
11. Management has the option to rent the manufacturing plant to six local hospitals to store medical records instead of producing and assembling chips.

Classify each cost in the following table according to the categories listed in the table header. A cost can be classified under more than one category. For example, the plastic board used to mount chips is classified as a direct material product cost and as a direct unit cost.

Cost	Period Costs Selling and Administrative	Direct Material (Prime Cost)	Direct Labor (Prime and Conversion)	Factory Overhead (Conversion Cost)	Unit Cost Classification Direct	Indirect	Sunk Cost	Opportunity Cost
1. Plastic board used to mount the chip, $3.50 each		✔			✔			

Solution to Demonstration Problem 1

Cost*	Period Costs Selling and Administrative	Direct Material (Prime Cost)	Direct Labor (Prime and Conversion)	Factory Overhead (Conversion Cost)	Unit Cost Classification Direct	Indirect	Sunk Cost	Opportunity Cost
1.		✔			✔			
2.			✔		✔			
3.				✔		✔		
4.				✔		✔		
5.				✔		✔		
6.	✔							
7.				✔		✔	✔	
8.	✔							
9.	✔							
10.	✔							
11.								✔

* Costs 1 through 11 refer to the 11 cost items described at the beginning of the problem.

Demonstration Problem 2: Reporting for Manufacturers

A manufacturing company's balance sheet and income statement differ from those for a merchandising or service company.

Required

1. Fill in the [BLANK] descriptors on the partial balance sheets for both the manufacturing company and the merchandising company. Explain why a different presentation is required.

Manufacturing Company

ADIDAS GROUP Partial Balance Sheet December 31, 2009	
Current assets	
Cash	$10,000
[BLANK]	8,000
[BLANK]	5,000
[BLANK]	7,000
Supplies	500
Prepaid insurance	500
Total current assets	$31,000

Merchandising Company

PAYLESS SHOE OUTLET Partial Balance Sheet December 31, 2009	
Current assets	
Cash	$ 5,000
[BLANK]	12,000
Supplies	500
Prepaid insurance	500
Total current assets	$18,000

2. Fill in the [BLANK] descriptors on the income statements for the manufacturing company and the merchandising company. Explain why a different presentation is required.

Manufacturing Company

ADIDAS GROUP Partial Income Statement For Year Ended December 31, 2009	
Sales	$200,000
Cost of goods sold	
Finished goods inventory, Dec. 31, 2008	10,000
[BLANK]	120,000
Goods available for sale	130,000
Finished goods inventory, Dec. 31, 2009	(7,000)
Cost of goods sold	123,000
Gross profit	$ 77,000

Merchandising Company

PAYLESS SHOE OUTLET Partial Income Statement For Year Ended December 31, 2009	
Sales	$190,000
Cost of goods sold	
Merchandise inventory, Dec. 31, 2008	8,000
[BLANK]	108,000
Goods available for sale	116,000
Merchandise inventory, Dec. 31, 2009	(12,000)
Cost of goods sold	104,000
Gross profit	$ 86,000

3. The manufacturer's cost of goods manufactured is the sum of (a) _____, (b) _____, and (c) _____ costs incurred in producing the product.

Solution to Demonstration Problem 2

1. Inventories for a manufacturer and for a merchandiser.

Manufacturing Company

ADIDAS GROUP Partial Balance Sheet December 31, 2009	
Current assets	
Cash	$10,000
Raw materials inventory	8,000
Goods in process inventory	5,000
Finished goods inventory	7,000
Supplies	500
Prepaid insurance	500
Total current assets	$31,000

Merchandising Company

PAYLESS SHOE OUTLET Partial Balance Sheet December 31, 2009	
Current assets	
Cash	$ 5,000
Merchandise inventory	12,000
Supplies	500
Prepaid insurance	500
Total current assets	$18,000

Explanation: A manufacturing company must control and measure three types of inventories: raw materials, goods in process, and finished goods. In the sequence of making a product, the raw materials move into production—called *goods in process inventory*—and then to finished goods. All raw materials and goods in process inventory at the end of each accounting period are considered current assets. All unsold finished inventory is considered a current asset at the end of each accounting period. The merchandising company must control and measure only one type of inventory, purchased goods.

2. Cost of goods sold for a manufacturer and for a merchandiser.

Manufacturing Company		*Merchandising Company*	
ADIDAS GROUP Partial Income Statement For Year Ended December 31, 2009		**PAYLESS SHOE OUTLET** Partial Income Statement For Year Ended December 31, 2009	
Sales	$200,000	Sales	$190,000
Cost of goods sold		Cost of goods sold	
Finished goods inventory, Dec. 31, 2008	10,000	Merchandise inventory, Dec. 31, 2008	8,000
Cost of goods manufactured	120,000	Cost of purchases	108,000
Goods available for sale	130,000	Goods available for sale	116,000
Finished goods inventory, Dec. 31, 2009	(7,000)	Merchandise inventory, Dec. 31, 2009	(12,000)
Cost of goods sold	123,000	Cost of goods sold	104,000
Gross profit	$ 77,000	Gross profit	$ 86,000

Explanation: Manufacturing and merchandising companies use different reporting terms. In particular, the terms *finished goods* and *cost of goods manufactured* are used to reflect the production of goods, yet the concepts and techniques of reporting cost of goods sold for a manufacturing company and merchandising company are similar.

3. A manufacturer's cost of goods manufactured is the sum of (a) *direct material,* (b) *direct labor,* and (c) *factory overhead* costs incurred in producing the product.

Demonstration Problem 3: Manufacturing Statement

The following account balances and other information are from SUNN Corporation's accounting records for year-end December 31, 2009. Use this information to prepare (1) a table listing factory overhead costs, (2) a manufacturing statement (show only the total factory overhead cost), and (3) an income statement.

Advertising expense	$ 85,000	Goods in process inventory, Dec. 31, 2008	$ 8,000
Amortization expense—Factory Patents	16,000	Goods in process inventory, Dec. 31, 2009	9,000
Bad debts expense	28,000	Income taxes	53,400
Depreciation expense—Office equipment	37,000	Indirect labor	26,000
Depreciation expense—Factory building	133,000	Interest expense	25,000
Depreciation expense—Factory equipment	78,000	Miscellaneous expense	55,000
Direct labor	250,000	Property taxes on factory equipment	14,000
Factory insurance expired	62,000	Raw materials inventory, Dec. 31, 2008	60,000
Factory supervision	74,000	Raw materials inventory, Dec. 31, 2009	78,000
Factory supplies used	21,000	Raw materials purchases	313,000
Factory utilities	115,000	Repairs expense—Factory equipment	31,000
Finished goods inventory, Dec. 31, 2008	15,000	Salaries expense	150,000
Finished goods inventory, Dec. 31, 2009	12,500	Sales	1,630,000

Planning the Solution

- Analyze the account balances and select those that are part of factory overhead costs.
- Arrange these costs in a table that lists factory overhead costs for the year.
- Analyze the remaining costs and select those related to production activity for the year; selected costs should include the materials and goods in process inventories and direct labor.

- Prepare a manufacturing statement for the year showing the calculation of the cost of materials used in production, the cost of direct labor, and the total factory overhead cost. When presenting overhead cost on this statement, report only total overhead cost from the table of overhead costs for the year. Show the costs of beginning and ending goods in process inventory to determine cost of goods manufactured.
- Organize the remaining revenue and expense items into the income statement for the year. Combine cost of goods manufactured from the manufacturing statement with the finished goods inventory amounts to compute cost of goods sold for the year.

Solution to Demonstration Problem 3

SUNN CORPORATION
Factory Overhead Costs
For Year Ended December 31, 2009

Amortization expense—Factory patents	$ 16,000
Depreciation expense—Factory building	133,000
Depreciation expense—Factory equipment	78,000
Factory insurance expired	62,000
Factory supervision	74,000
Factory supplies used	21,000
Factory utilities	115,000
Indirect labor	26,000
Property taxes on factory equipment	14,000
Repairs expense—Factory equipment	31,000
Total factory overhead	$570,000

SUNN CORPORATION
Manufacturing Statement
For Year Ended December 31, 2009

Direct materials		
Raw materials inventory, Dec. 31, 2008	$ 60,000	
Raw materials purchase	313,000	
Raw materials available for use	373,000	
Less raw materials inventory, Dec. 31, 2009	78,000	
Direct materials used	295,000	
Direct labor	250,000	
Factory overhead	570,000	
Total manufacturing costs	1,115,000	
Goods in process inventory, Dec. 31, 2008	8,000	
Total cost of goods in process	1,123,000	
Less goods in process inventory, Dec. 31, 2009	9,000	
Cost of goods manufactured	$1,114,000	

SUNN CORPORATION
Income Statement
For Year Ended December 31, 2009

Sales		$1,630,000
Cost of goods sold		
Finished goods inventory, Dec. 31, 2008	$ 15,000	
Cost of goods manufactured	1,114,000	
Goods available for sale	1,129,000	
Less finished goods inventory, Dec. 31, 2009	12,500	
Cost of goods sold		1,116,500
Gross profit		513,500
Operating expenses		
Advertising expense	85,000	
Bad debts expense	28,000	
Depreciation expense—Office equipment	37,000	
Interest expense	25,000	
Miscellaneous expense	55,000	
Salaries expense	150,000	
Total operating expenses		380,000
Income before income taxes		133,500
Income taxes		53,400
Net income		$ 80,100

Summary

C1   **Explain the purpose and nature of managerial accounting.** The purpose of managerial accounting is to provide useful information to management and other internal decision makers. It does this by collecting, managing, and reporting both monetary and nonmonetary information in a manner useful to internal users. Major characteristics of managerial accounting include (1) focus on internal decision makers, (2) emphasis on planning and control, (3) flexibility, (4) timeliness, (5) reliance on forecasts and estimates, (6) focus on segments and projects, and (7) reporting both monetary and nonmonetary information.

C2   **Describe the lean business model.** The main purpose of the lean business model is the elimination of waste. Concepts such as total quality management and just-in-time production often aid in effective application of the model.

C3   **Describe fraud and the role of ethics in managerial accounting.** Fraud involves the use of one's job for personal gain through deliberate misuse of the employer's assets. All fraud is secret, violates the employee's job duties, provides financial benefits to the employee, and costs the employer money. A code of ethical beliefs can be used to resolve ethical conflicts.

C4   **Describe accounting concepts useful in classifying costs.** We can classify costs on the basis of their (1) behavior—fixed vs. variable, (2) traceability—direct vs. indirect, (3) controllability—controllable vs. uncontrollable, (4) relevance—sunk vs. out of pocket, and (5) function—product vs. period. A cost can be classified in more than one way, depending on the purpose for which the cost is being determined. These classifications help us understand cost patterns, analyze performance, and plan operations.

C5   **Define product and period costs and explain how they impact financial statements.** Costs that are capitalized because they are expected to have future value are called *product costs;* costs that are expensed are called *period costs.* This classification is important because it affects the amount of costs expensed in the income statement and the amount of costs assigned to inventory on the balance sheet. Product costs are commonly made up of direct materials, direct labor, and overhead. Period costs include selling and administrative expenses.

C6   **Explain how balance sheets and income statements for manufacturing and merchandising companies differ.** The main difference is that manufacturers usually carry three inventories

on their balance sheets—raw materials, goods in process, and finished goods—instead of one inventory that merchandisers carry. The main difference between income statements of manufacturers and merchandisers is the items making up cost of goods sold. A merchandiser adds beginning merchandise inventory to cost of goods purchased and then subtracts ending merchandise inventory to get cost of goods sold. A manufacturer adds beginning finished goods inventory to cost of goods manufactured and then subtracts ending finished goods inventory to get cost of goods sold.

C7   **Explain manufacturing activities and the flow of manufacturing costs.** Manufacturing activities consist of materials, production, and sales activities. The materials activity consists of the purchase and issuance of materials to production. The production activity consists of converting materials into finished goods. At this stage in the process, the materials, labor, and overhead costs have been incurred and the manufacturing statement is prepared. The sales activity consists of selling some or all of finished goods available for sale. At this stage, the cost of goods sold is determined.

A1   **Compute cycle time and cycle efficiency, and explain their importance to production management.** It is important for companies to reduce the time to produce their products and to improve manufacturing efficiency. One measure of that time is cycle time (CT), defined as Process time + Inspection time + Move time + Wait time. Process time is value-added time; the others are non-value-added time. Cycle efficiency (CE) is the ratio of value-added time to total cycle time. If CE is low, management should evaluate its production process to see if it can reduce non-value-added activities.

P1   **Compute cost of goods sold for a manufacturer.** A manufacturer adds beginning finished goods inventory to cost of goods manufactured and then subtracts ending finished goods inventory to get cost of goods sold.

P2   **Prepare a manufacturing statement and explain its purpose and links to financial statements.** The manufacturing statement reports computation of cost of goods manufactured for the period. It begins by showing the period's costs for direct materials, direct labor, and overhead and then adjusts these numbers for the beginning and ending inventories of the goods in process to yield cost of goods manufactured.

Guidance Answers to **Decision Maker** and **Decision Ethics**

Production Manager   It appears that all three friends want to pay the bill with someone else's money. David is using money belonging to the tax authorities, Denise is taking money from her company, and Derek is defrauding the client. To prevent such practices, companies have internal audit mechanisms. Many companies also adopt ethical codes of conduct to help guide employees. We must recognize that some entertainment expenses are justifiable and even encouraged. For example, the tax law allows certain deductions for entertainment that have a business purpose. Corporate policies also sometimes allow and encourage reimbursable spending for social activities, and contracts can include entertainment as allowable costs.

Nevertheless, without further details, payment for this bill should be made from personal accounts.

Entrepreneur   Tracing all costs directly to cost objects is always desirable, but you need to be able to do so in an economically feasible manner. In this case, you are able to trace 90% of the assembly department's direct costs. It may not be economical to spend more money on a new software to trace the final 10% of costs. You need to make a cost–benefit trade-off. If the software offers benefits beyond tracing the remaining 10% of the assembly department's costs, your decision should consider this.

Purchase Manager Opportunity costs relate to the potential quality and delivery benefits given up by not choosing supplier (A). Selecting supplier (B) might involve future costs of poor-quality seats (inspection, repairs, and returns). Also, potential delivery delays could interrupt work and increase manufacturing costs. Your company could also incur sales losses if the product quality of supplier (B) is low. As purchase manager, you are responsible for these costs and must consider them in making your decision.

Guidance Answers to **Quick Checks**

1. *d*

2. Financial accounting information is intended for users external to an organization such as investors, creditors, and government authorities. Managerial accounting focuses on providing information to managers, officers, and other decision makers within the organization.

3. No, GAAP do not control the practice of managerial accounting. Unlike external users, the internal users need managerial accounting information for planning and controlling business activities rather than for external comparison. Different types of information are required, depending on the activity. Therefore it is difficult to standardize managerial accounting.

4. Under TQM, all managers and employees should strive toward higher standards in their work and in the products and services they offer to customers.

5. Variable costs increase when volume of activity increases.

6. By being able to trace costs to cost objects (say, to products and departments), managers better understand the total costs associated with a cost object. This is useful when managers consider making changes to the cost object (such as when dropping the product or expanding the department).

7. Raw materials inventory, goods in process inventory, and finished goods inventory.

8. The cost of goods sold for merchandising companies includes all costs of acquiring the merchandise; the cost of goods sold for manufacturing companies includes the three costs of manufacturing: direct materials, direct labor, and overhead.

9. *a*

10. No; companies rarely report a manufacturing statement.

11. Beginning goods in process inventory is added to total manufacturing costs to yield total goods in process. Ending goods in process inventory is subtracted from total goods in process to yield cost of goods manufactured for the period.

Key Terms   mhhe.com/wildFAP19e

Key Terms are available at the book's Website for learning and testing in an online Flashcard Format.

Continuous improvement (p. 730)	**Factory overhead** (p. 738)	**Manufacturing statement** (p. 740)
Control (p. 727)	**Factory overhead costs** (p. 738)	**Non-value-added time** (p. 743)
Controllable or not controllable cost (p. 733)	**Finished goods inventory** (p. 736)	**Opportunity cost** (p. 733)
Conversion costs (p. 738)	**Fixed cost** (p. 732)	**Out-of-pocket cost** (p. 733)
Cost object (p. 732)	**Goods in process inventory** (p. 736)	**Period costs** (p. 733)
Customer orientation (p. 729)	**Indirect costs** (p. 732)	**Planning** (p. 726)
Cycle efficiency (CE) (p. 743)	**Indirect labor** (p. 738)	**Prime costs** (p. 738)
Cycle time (CT) (p. 742)	**Indirect labor costs** (p. 738)	**Product costs** (p. 733)
Direct costs (p. 732)	**Indirect material** (p. 735)	**Raw materials inventory** (p. 735)
Direct labor (p. 738)	**Institute of Management Accountants (IMA)** (p. 731)	**Sunk cost** (p. 733)
Direct labor costs (p. 738)	**Internal control system** (p. 731)	**Total quality management (TQM)** (p. 730)
Direct material (p. 738)	**Just-in-time (JIT) manufacturing** (p. 730)	**Value-added time** (p. 743)
Direct material costs (p. 738)	**Lean business model** (p. 730)	**Value chain** (p. 740)
Ethics (p. 731)	**Managerial accounting** (p. 726)	**Variable cost** (p. 732)

Multiple Choice Quiz   Answers on p. 767   mhhe.com/wildFAP19e

Additional Quiz Questions are available at the book's Website.

1. Continuous improvement
  a. Is used to reduce inventory levels.
  b. Is applicable only in service businesses.
  c. Rejects the notion of "good enough."
  d. Is used to reduce ordering costs.
  e. Is applicable only in manufacturing businesses.

Quiz18

2. A direct cost is one that is
   a. Variable with respect to the cost object.
   b. Traceable to the cost object.
   c. Fixed with respect to the cost object.
   d. Allocated to the cost object.
   e. A period cost.

3. Costs that are incurred as part of the manufacturing process, but are not clearly traceable to the specific unit of product or batches of product, are called
   a. Period costs.
   b. Factory overhead.
   c. Sunk costs.
   d. Opportunity costs.
   e. Fixed costs.

4. The three major cost components of manufacturing a product are
   a. Direct materials, direct labor, and factory overhead.
   b. Period costs, product costs, and sunk costs.

   c. Indirect labor, indirect materials, and fixed expenses.
   d. Variable costs, fixed costs, and period costs.
   e. Opportunity costs, sunk costs, and direct costs.

5. A company reports the following for the current year.

Finished goods inventory, beginning year	$6,000
Finished goods inventory, ending year	3,200
Cost of goods sold	7,500

Its cost of goods manufactured for the current year is
   a. $1,500.
   b. $1,700.
   c. $7,500.
   d. $2,800.
   e. $4,700.

Discussion Questions

1. Describe the managerial accountant's role in business planning, control, and decision making.

2. Distinguish between managerial and financial accounting on
   a. Users and decision makers.   **b.** Purpose of information.
   c. Flexibility of practice.   **d.** Time dimension.
   e. Focus of information.   **f.** Nature of information.

3. ♟ Identify the usual changes that a company must make when it adopts a customer orientation.

4. Distinguish between direct material and indirect material.

5. Distinguish between direct labor and indirect labor.

6. Distinguish between (a) factory overhead and (b) selling and administrative overhead.

7. What product cost is listed as both a prime cost and a conversion cost?

8. ♟ Assume that you tour Apple's factory where it makes its products. List three direct costs and three indirect costs that you are likely to see.

9. ♟ Should we evaluate a manager's performance on the basis of controllable or noncontrollable costs? Why?

10. ♟ Explain why knowledge of cost behavior is useful in product performance evaluation.

11. Explain why product costs are capitalized but period costs are expensed in the current accounting period.

12. ♟ Explain how business activities and inventories for a manufacturing company, a merchandising company, and a service company differ.

13. ♟ Why does managerial accounting often involve working with numerous predictions and estimates?

14. How do an income statement and a balance sheet for a manufacturing company and a merchandising company differ?

15. Besides inventories, what other assets often appear on manufacturers' balance sheets but not on merchandisers' balance sheets?

16. Why does a manufacturing company require three different inventory categories?

17. Manufacturing activities of a company are described in the _____. This statement summarizes the types and amounts of costs incurred in its manufacturing _____.

18. What are the three categories of manufacturing costs?

19. List several examples of factory overhead.

20. ♟ List the four components of a manufacturing statement and provide specific examples of each for Apple.

21. ♟ Prepare a proper title for the annual "manufacturing statement" of Apple. Does the date match the balance sheet or income statement? Why?

22. ♟ Describe the relations among the income statement, the manufacturing statement, and a detailed listing of factory overhead costs.

23. ♟ Define and describe *cycle time* and identify the components of cycle time.

24. ♟ Explain the difference between value-added time and non-value-added time.

25. Define and describe *cycle efficiency*.

26. ♟ Can management of a company such as Best Buy 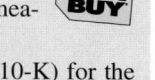 use cycle time and cycle efficiency as useful measures of performance? Explain.

27. Access Anheuser-Busch's 2006 annual report (10-K) for the fiscal year ended December 31, 2006, at the SEC's EDGAR database (SEC.gov) or its Website (Anheuser-Busch.com). From its financial statement notes, identify the titles and amounts of its inventory components.

♟ *Denotes Discussion Questions that involve decision making.*

McGraw-Hill's
HOMEWORK
MANAGER®   Available with McGraw-Hill's Homework Manager

Managerial accounting (choose one)

1. Provides information that is widely available to all interested parties.

2. Is directed at reporting aggregate data on the company as a whole.

3. Must follow generally accepted accounting principles.

4. Provides information to aid management in planning and controlling business activities.

QUICK STUDY

QS 18-1
Managerial accounting defined

C1

Identify whether each description most likely applies to managerial or financial accounting.

1. _____ It is directed at external users in making investment, credit, and other decisions.

2. _____ Its information is often available only after an audit is complete.

3. _____ Its primary focus is on the organization as a whole.

4. _____ Its principles and practices are very flexible.

5. _____ Its primary users are company managers.

QS 18-2
Managerial accounting versus financial accounting

C1

Match each lean business concept with its best description by entering its letter in the blank.

1. _____ Just-in-time manufacturing

2. _____ Continuous improvements

3. _____ Customer orientation

4. _____ Total quality management

A. Every manager and employee constantly looks for ways to improve company operations.

B. Focuses on quality throughout the production process.

C. Inventory is acquired or produced only as needed.

D. Flexible product designs can be modified to accommodate customer choices.

QS 18-3
Lean business concepts

C2

Which of these statements is true regarding fixed and variable costs?

1. Fixed costs increase and variable costs decrease in total as activity volume decreases.

2. Both fixed and variable costs stay the same in total as activity volume increases.

3. Both fixed and variable costs increase as activity volume increases.

4. Fixed costs stay the same and variable costs increase in total as activity volume increases.

QS 18-4
Fixed and variable costs

C4

Crosby Company produces sporting equipment, including footballs. Identify each of the following costs as direct or indirect if the cost object is a football produced by Crosby.

1. Depreciation on equipment used to produce footballs.

2. Salary of manager who supervises the entire plant.

3. Labor used on the football production line.

4. Electricity used in the production plant.

5. Materials used to produce footballs.

QS 18-5
Direct and indirect costs

C4

Which of these statements is true regarding product and period costs?

1. Factory maintenance is a product cost and sales commission is a period cost.

2. Sales commission is a product cost and factory rent is a period cost.

3. Factory wages are a product cost and direct material is a period cost.

4. Sales commission is a product cost and depreciation on factory equipment is a product cost.

QS 18-6
Product and period costs

C5

Three inventory categories are reported on a manufacturing company's balance sheet: (a) raw materials, (b) goods in process, and (c) finished goods. Identify the usual order in which these inventory items are reported on the balance sheet.

1. (b)(c)(a)   **2.** (c)(b)(a)   **3.** (a)(b)(c)   **4.** (b)(a)(c)

QS 18-7
Inventory reporting for manufacturers

C6

QS 18-8
Cost of goods sold   P1

A company has year-end cost of goods manufactured of $8,000, beginning finished goods inventory of $1,000, and ending finished goods inventory of $1,500. Its cost of goods sold is

1. $8,500   **2.** $8,000   **3.** $7,500   **4.** $7,800

QS 18-9
Manufacturing flows identified
C7

Identify the usual sequence of manufacturing activities by filling in the blank (with 1, 2, or 3) corresponding to its order: _____ Production activities; _____ sales activities; _____ materials activities.

QS 18-10
Cost of goods manufactured
P2

Prepare the 2009 manufacturing statement for Biron Company using the following information.

Direct materials	$381,000
Direct labor	126,300
Factory overhead costs	48,000
Goods in process, Dec. 31, 2008	315,200
Goods in process, Dec. 31, 2009	285,500

QS 18-11
Manufacturing cycle time and efficiency
A1

Compute and interpret (*a*) manufacturing cycle time and (*b*) manufacturing cycle efficiency using the following information from a manufacturing company.

Process time	7.5 hours
Inspection time	1.0 hours
Move time	3.2 hours
Wait time	18.3 hours

QS 18-12
Cost of goods sold
P1

Compute cost of goods sold for year 2009 using the following information.

Finished goods inventory, Dec. 31, 2008	$ 690,000
Goods in process inventory, Dec. 31, 2008	167,000
Goods in process inventory, Dec. 31, 2009	144,600
Cost of goods manufactured, year 2009	1,837,400
Finished goods inventory, Dec. 31, 2009	567,200

Available with McGraw-Hill's Homework Manager   McGraw-Hill's HOMEWORK MANAGER®

EXERCISES

Exercise 18-1
Sources of accounting information
C1

Both managerial accounting and financial accounting provide useful information to decision makers. Indicate in the following chart the most likely source of information for each business decision (a decision can require major input from both sources, in which case both can be marked).

	Primary Information Source	
Business Decision	**Managerial**	**Financial**
1. Determine amount of dividends to pay stockholders	_____	_____
2. Evaluate a purchasing department's performance	_____	_____
3. Report financial performance to board of directors	_____	_____
4. Estimate product cost for a new line of shoes	_____	_____
5. Plan the budget for next quarter	_____	_____
6. Measure profitability of all individual stores	_____	_____
7. Prepare financial reports according to GAAP	_____	_____
8. Determine location and size for a new plant	_____	_____

Complete the following statements by filling in the blanks.

1. _____ is the process of monitoring planning decisions and evaluating an organization's activities and employees.

2. _____ is the process of setting goals and making plans to achieve them.

3. _____ _____ usually covers a period of 5 to 10 years.

4. _____ _____ usually covers a period of one year.

Exercise 18-2
Planning and control descriptions
C1

In the following chart, compare financial accounting and managerial accounting by describing how each differs for the items listed. Be specific in your responses.

Exercise 18-3
Characteristics of financial accounting and managerial accounting
C1

	Financial Accounting	Managerial Accounting
1. Users and decision makers	_____	_____
2. Timeliness of information	_____	_____
3. Purpose of information	_____	_____
4. Nature of information	_____	_____
5. Flexibility of practice	_____	_____
6. Focus of information	_____	_____
7. Time dimension	_____	_____

Customer orientation means that a company's managers and employees respond to customers' changing wants and needs. A manufacturer of plastic fasteners has created a customer satisfaction survey that it asks each of its customers to complete. The survey asks about the following factors: (A) lead time; (B) delivery; (C) price; (D) product performance. Each factor is to be rated as unsatisfactory, marginal, average, satisfactory, or very satisfied.

Exercise 18-4
Customer orientation in practice
C2

a. Match the competitive forces 1 through 4 to the factors on the survey. A factor can be matched to more than one competitive force.

Survey Factor	Competitive Force
A. Lead time	_____ **1.** Cost
B. Delivery	_____ **2.** Time
C. Price	_____ **3.** Quality
D. Product performance	_____ **4.** Flexibility of service

b. How can managers of this company use the information from this customer satisfaction survey to better meet competitive forces and satisfy their customers?

Following are three separate events affecting the managerial accounting systems for different companies. Match the management concept(s) that the company is likely to adopt for the event identified. There is some overlap in the meaning of customer orientation and total quality management and, therefore, some responses can include more than one concept.

Exercise 18-5
Management concepts
C2

Event	Management Concept
_____ 1. The company starts reporting measures on customer complaints and product returns from customers.	a. Total quality management (TQM)
_____ 2. The company starts reporting measures such as the percent of defective products and the number of units scrapped.	b. Continuous improvement (CI) c. Customer orientation (CO)
_____ 3. The company starts measuring inventory turnover and discontinues elaborate inventory records. Its new focus is to pull inventory through the system.	d. Just-in-time (JIT) system

Exercise 18-6

Cost analysis and identification

C4 C5

Georgia Pacific, a manufacturer, incurs the following costs. (1) Classify each cost as either a product or a period cost. If a product cost, identify it as a prime and/or conversion cost. (2) Classify each product cost as either a direct cost or an indirect cost using the product as the cost object.

Cost	Product Cost		Period Cost	Direct Cost	Indirect Cost
	Prime	Conversion			
1. Amortization of patents on factory machine ...	___	___	___	___	___
2. Payroll taxes for production supervisor	___	___	___	___	___
3. Accident insurance on factory workers	___	___	___	___	___
4. Depreciation—Factory building	___	___	___	___	___
5. State and federal income taxes	___	___	___	___	___
6. Wages to assembly workers	___	___	___	___	___
7. Direct materials used	___	___	___	___	___
8. Office supplies used	___	___	___	___	___
9. Bad debts expense	___	___	___	___	___
10. Small tools used	___	___	___	___	___
11. Factory utilities	___	___	___	___	___
12. Advertising	___	___	___	___	___

Exercise 18-7

Cost classifications   C4

(1) Identify each of the five cost classifications discussed in the chapter. (2) List two purposes of identifying these separate cost classifications.

Exercise 18-8

Cost analysis and classification

C4

Listed here are product costs for the production of soccer balls. (1) Classify each cost (a) as either fixed or variable and (b) as either direct or indirect. (2) What pattern do you see regarding the relation between costs classified by behavior and costs classified by traceability?

Product Cost	Cost by Behavior		Cost by Traceability	
	Variable	Fixed	Direct	Indirect
1. Annual flat fee paid for office security	___	___	___	___
2. Leather covers for soccer balls	___	___	___	___
3. Lace to hold leather together	___	___	___	___
4. Wages of assembly workers	___	___	___	___
5. Coolants for machinery	___	___	___	___
6. Machinery depreciation	___	___	___	___
7. Taxes on factory	___	___	___	___

Exercise 18-9

Balance sheet identification and preparation

C6

Current assets for two different companies at calendar year-end 2009 are listed here. One is a manufacturer, Nordic Skis Mfg., and the other, Fresh Foods, is a grocery distribution company. (1) Identify which set of numbers relates to the manufacturer and which to the merchandiser. (2) Prepare the current asset section for each company from this information. Discuss why the current asset section for these two companies is different.

Account	Company 1	Company 2
Cash	$13,000	$11,000
Raw materials inventory	—	41,250
Merchandise inventory	44,250	—
Goods in process inventory	—	30,000
Finished goods inventory	—	50,000
Accounts receivable, net	62,000	81,000
Prepaid expenses	3,000	600

Compute cost of goods sold for each of these two companies for the year ended December 31, 2009.

Exercise 18-10
Cost of goods sold computation
C6 P1

	Computer Merchandising	Log Homes Manufacturing
3 Beginning inventory		
4 Merchandise	$301,000	
5 Finished goods		$602,000
6 Cost of purchases	580,000	
7 Cost of goods manufactured		790,000
8 Ending inventory		
9 Merchandise	201,000	
10 Finished goods		195,000

Check Computer Merchandising COGS, $680,000

Using the following data, compute (1) the cost of goods manufactured and (2) the cost of goods sold for both Jahmed Company and Kabiro Company.

Exercise 18-11
Cost of goods manufactured and cost of goods sold computation
P1 P2

	Jahmed Company	Kabiro Company
Beginning finished goods inventory	$15,000	$15,000
Beginning goods in process inventory	21,000	21,500
Beginning raw materials inventory	9,500	13,000
Rental cost on factory equipment	33,000	27,000
Direct labor	22,000	44,000
Ending finished goods inventory	19,500	12,000
Ending goods in process inventory	22,000	21,000
Ending raw materials inventory	10,500	9,400
Factory utilities	13,000	17,000
Factory supplies used	10,600	10,000
General and administrative expenses	22,000	54,000
Indirect labor	3,250	9,660
Repairs—Factory equipment	6,780	3,500
Raw materials purchases	24,000	47,000
Sales salaries	49,000	41,000

Check Jahmed COGS, $106,130

For each of the following account balances for a manufacturing company, place a ✔ in the appropriate column indicating that it appears on the balance sheet, the income statement, the manufacturing statement, and/or a detailed listing of factory overhead costs. Assume that the income statement shows the calculation of cost of goods sold and the manufacturing statement shows only the total amount of factory overhead. (An account balance can appear on more than one report.)

Exercise 18-12
Components of accounting reports
C7 P2

	Account	Balance Sheet	Income Statement	Manufacturing Statement	Overhead Report
3	Accounts receivable				
4	Computer supplies used in office				
5	Beginning finished goods inventory				
6	Beginning goods in process inventory				
7	Beginning raw materials inventory				
8	Cash				
9	Depreciation expense—Factory building				
10	Depreciation expense—Factory equipment				
11	Depreciation expense—Office building				
12	Depreciation expense—Office equipment				
13	Direct labor				
14	Ending finished goods inventory				
15	Ending goods in process inventory				
16	Ending raw materials inventory				
17	Factory maintenance wages				
18	Computer supplies used in factory				
19	Income taxes				
20	Insurance on factory building				
21	Rent cost on office building				
22	Office supplies used				
23	Property taxes on factory building				
24	Raw materials purchases				
25	Sales				

Exercise 18-13
Manufacturing statement preparation   P2

Given the following selected account balances of Spalding Company, prepare its manufacturing statement for the year ended on December 31, 2009. Include a listing of the individual overhead account balances in this statement.

Sales	$1,363,000
Raw materials inventory, Dec. 31, 2008	40,000
Goods in process inventory, Dec. 31, 2008	53,600
Finished goods inventory, Dec. 31, 2008	60,400
Raw materials purchases	181,900
Direct labor	243,000
Factory computer supplies used	15,700
Indirect labor	54,000
Repairs—Factory equipment	7,250
Rent cost of factory building	56,000
Advertising expense	92,000
General and administrative expenses	140,000
Raw materials inventory, Dec. 31, 2009	44,000
Goods in process inventory, Dec. 31, 2009	41,200
Finished goods inventory, Dec. 31, 2009	66,200

Check   Cost of goods manufactured, $566,250

Exercise 18-14
Income statement preparation   P2

Use the information in Exercise 18-13 to prepare an income statement for Spalding Company (a manufacturer). Assume that its cost of goods manufactured is $566,250.

Exercise 18-15
Cost flows in manufacturing

C7   P2

The following chart shows how costs flow through a business as a product is manufactured. Some boxes in the flowchart show cost amounts. Compute the cost amounts for the boxes that contain question marks.

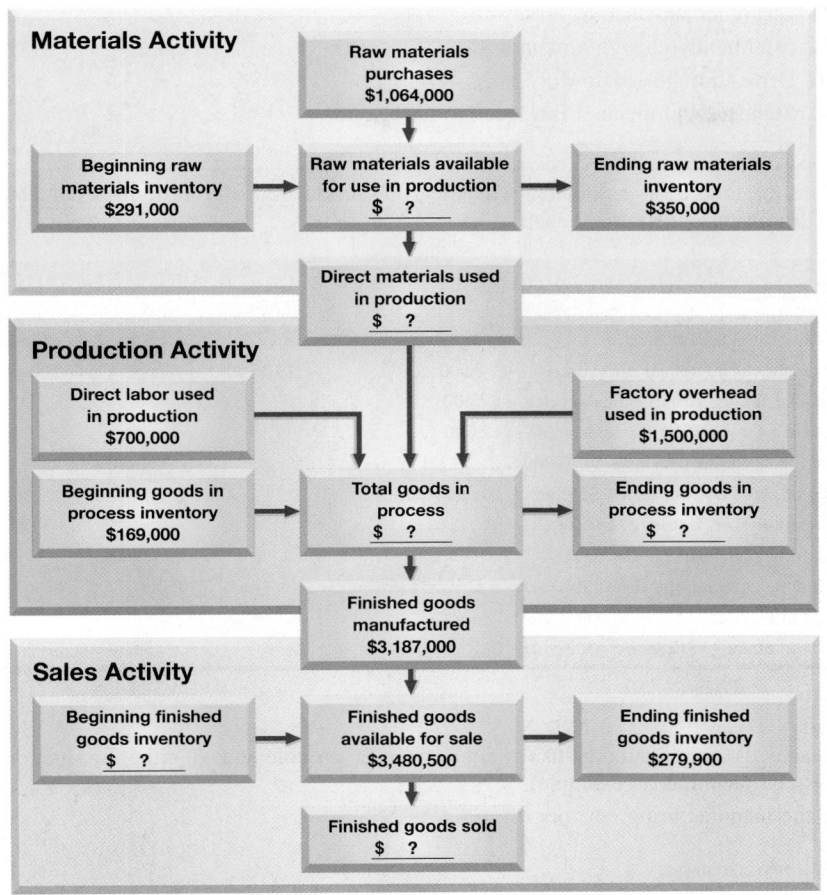

Fraud affects **Best Buy**. Refer to Best Buy's financial statements in Appendix A to answer the following:

1. Explain how inventory losses (such as theft) impact how Best Buy reports inventory on its balance sheet.

2. In what income statement account does Best Buy report inventory losses?

Exercise 18-16
C3

McGraw-Hill's
HOMEWORK
MANAGER® Available with McGraw-Hill's Homework Manager

This chapter explained the purpose of managerial accounting in the context of the current business environment. Review the *automobile* section of your local newspaper; the Sunday paper is often best. Review advertisements of sport-utility vehicles and identify the manufacturers that offer these products and the factors on which they compete.

Required

Discuss the potential contributions and responsibilities of the managerial accounting professional in helping an automobile manufacturer succeed. (*Hint:* Think about information and estimates that a managerial accountant might provide new entrants into the sport-utility market.)

PROBLEM SET A

Problem 18-1A
Managerial accounting role

C1 C2

Many fast-food restaurants compete on lean business concepts. Match each of the following activities at a fast-food restaurant with the lean business concept it strives to achieve. Some activities might relate to more than one lean business concept.

_____ **1.** Courteous employees
_____ **2.** Food produced to order
_____ **3.** New product development
_____ **4.** Clean tables and floors
_____ **5.** Orders filled within three minutes
_____ **6.** Standardized food making processes

a. Just-in-time (JIT)
b. Continuous improvement (CI)
c. Total quality management (TQM)

Problem 18-2A
Lean business concepts

C2

[continued on next page]

_____ **7.** Customer satisfaction surveys

_____ **8.** Continually changing menus

_____ **9.** Drive-through windows

_____ **10.** Standardized menus from location to location

Problem 18-3A

Cost computation, classification, and analysis

C4

Listed here are the total costs associated with the 2009 production of 700 drum sets manufactured by Roland. The drum sets sell for $600 each.

Costs	Cost by Behavior		Cost by Function	
	Variable	Fixed	Product	Period
1. Drum stands (700 stands outsourced)—$17,500	$17,500		$17,500	
2. Annual flat fee for maintenance service—$7,000				
3. Rent cost of equipment for sales staff—$12,000				
4. Upper management salaries—$170,000				
5. Wages of assembly workers—$59,500				
6. Property taxes on factory—$3,500				
7. Accounting staff salaries—$42,000				
8. Machinery depreciation—$28,000				
9. Sales commissions—$20 per unit				
10. Plastic for casing—$12,600				

Required

1. Classify each cost and its amount as (*a*) either fixed or variable and (*b*) either product or period (the last cost is completed as an example).

2. Compute the manufacturing cost per drum set.

Analysis Component

3. Assume that 1,000 drum sets are produced in the next month. What do you predict will be the total cost of plastic for the casings and the per unit cost of the plastic for the casings? Explain.

4. Assume that 1,000 drum sets are produced in the next month. What do you predict will be the total cost of property taxes and the per unit cost of the property taxes? Explain.

Check (1) Total variable
manufacturing cost, $89,600

Problem 18-4A

Cost classification and explanation

C4 C5

Assume that you must make a presentation to the marketing staff explaining the difference between product and period costs. Your supervisor tells you the marketing staff would also like clarification regarding prime and conversion costs and an explanation of how these terms fit with product and period cost. You are told that many on the staff are unable to classify costs in their merchandising activities.

Required

Prepare a one-page memorandum to your supervisor outlining your presentation to the marketing staff.

Problem 18-5A

Opportunity cost estimation and application

C1 C4

Refer to *Decision Maker,* **Purchase Manager,** in this chapter. Assume that you are the motorcycle manufacturer's managerial accountant. The purchasing manager asks you about preparing an estimate of the related costs for buying motorcycle seats from supplier (B). She tells you this estimate is needed because unless dollar estimates are attached to nonfinancial factors, such as lost production time, her supervisor will not give it full attention. The manager also shows you the following information.

• Production output is 1,000 motorcycles per year based on 250 production days a year.

• Production time per day is 8 hours at a cost of $2,000 per hour to run the production line.

• Lost production time due to poor quality is 1%.

• Satisfied customers purchase, on average, three motorcycles during a lifetime.

• Satisfied customers recommend the product, on average, to five other people.

• Marketing predicts that using seat (B) will result in five lost customers per year from repeat business and referrals.

• Average contribution margin per motorcycle is $3,000.

Required

Estimate the costs (including opportunity costs) of buying motorcycle seats from supplier (B). This problem requires that you think creatively and make reasonable estimates; thus there could be more than one correct answer. (*Hint:* Reread the answer to *Decision Maker* and compare the cost savings for buying from supplier [B] to the sum of lost customer revenue from repeat business and referrals and the cost of lost production time.)

Check Estimated cost of lost production time, $40,000

Laredo Boot Company makes specialty boots for the rodeo circuit. On December 31, 2008, the company had (*a*) 300 pairs of boots in finished goods inventory and (*b*) 1,400 heels at a cost of $16 each in raw materials inventory. During 2009, the company purchased 46,000 additional heels at $16 each and manufactured 16,800 pairs of boots.

Problem 18-6A
Ending inventory computation and evaluation

C2 C6 ♟

Required

1. Determine the unit and dollar amounts of raw materials inventory in heels at December 31, 2009.

Check (1) Ending (heel) inventory, 13,800 units; $220, 800

Analysis Component

2. Write a one-half page memorandum to the production manager explaining why a just-in-time inventory system for heels should be considered. Include the amount of working capital that can be reduced at December 31, 2009, if the ending heel raw material inventory is cut by 75%.

Shown here are annual financial data at December 31, 2009, taken from two different companies.

Problem 18-7A
Inventory computation and reporting

C4 C6 P1

mhhe.com/wildFAP19e

	Active Sports Retail	Sno-Board Manufacturing
Beginning inventory		
Merchandise	$145,000	
Finished goods		$340,000
Cost of purchases	240,000	
Cost of goods manufactured		582,000
Ending inventory		
Merchandise	110,000	
Finished goods		150,000

Required

1. Compute the cost of goods sold section of the income statement at December 31, 2009, for each company. Include the proper title and format in the solution.

Check (1) Sno-Board's cost of goods sold, $772,000

2. Write a half-page memorandum to your instructor (*a*) identifying the inventory accounts and (*b*) describing where each is reported on the income statement and balance sheet for both companies.

The following calendar year-end information is taken from the December 31, 2009, adjusted trial balance and other records of Gucci Company.

Problem 18-8A
Manufacturing and income statements; inventory analysis P2

Advertising expense	$ 26,600	Direct labor	680,400
Depreciation expense—Office equipment	11,500	Income taxes expense	291,500
Depreciation expense—Selling equipment	10,800	Indirect labor	58,800
Depreciation expense—Factory equipment	38,200	Miscellaneous production costs	9,800
Factory supervision	105,700	Office salaries expense	74,000
Factory supplies used	7,800	Raw materials purchases	965,000
Factory utilities	34,000	Rent expense—Office space	23,000
Inventories		Rent expense—Selling space	25,200
Raw materials, December 31, 2008	165,900	Rent expense—Factory building	81,600
Raw materials, December 31, 2009	187,000	Maintenance expense—Factory equipment	37,100
Goods in process, December 31, 2008	18,100	Sales	4,630,000
Goods in process, December 31, 2009	24,600	Sales discounts	63,600
Finished goods, December 31, 2008	164,100	Sales salaries expense	398,400
Finished goods, December 31, 2009	135,900		

Check (1) Cost of goods manufactured, $1,990,800

Required

1. Prepare the company's 2009 manufacturing statement.

2. Prepare the company's 2009 income statement that reports separate categories for (*a*) selling expenses and (*b*) general and administrative expenses.

Analysis Component

3. Compute the (*a*) inventory turnover, defined as cost of goods sold divided by average inventory, and (*b*) days' sales in inventory, defined as 365 times ending inventory divided by cost of goods sold, for both its raw materials inventory and its finished goods inventory. (To compute turnover and days' sales in inventory for raw materials, use raw materials used rather than cost of goods sold.) Discuss some possible reasons for differences between these ratios for the two types of inventories.

Problem 18-9A

Manufacturing cycle time and efficiency

A1

Mission Oak Company produces oak bookcases to customer order. It received an order from a customer to produce 5,000 bookcases. The following information is available for the production of the bookcases.

Process time	18.0 days
Inspection time	2.0 days
Move time	4.4 days
Wait time	20.6 days

Required

1. Compute the company's manufacturing cycle time.

2. Compute the company's manufacturing cycle efficiency. Interpret your answer.

Check (2) Manufacturing cycle efficiency, 0.40

Analysis Component

3. Assume that Mission Oak wishes to increase its manufacturing cycle efficiency to 0.75. What are some ways that it can accomplish this?

PROBLEM SET B

Problem 18-1B

Managerial accounting role

C1   C2

This chapter described the purpose of managerial accounting in the context of the current business environment. Review the *home electronics* section of your local newspaper; the Sunday paper is often best. Review advertisements of home electronics and identify the manufacturers that offer these products and the factors on which they compete.

Required

Discuss the potential contributions and responsibilities of the managerial accounting professional in helping a home electronics manufacturer succeed. (*Hint:* Think about information and estimates that a managerial accountant might provide new entrants into the home electronics market.)

Problem 18-2B

Lean business concepts

C2

Eastman-Kodak manufactures digital cameras and must compete on lean manufacturing concepts. Match each of the following activities that it engages in with the lean manufacturing concept it strives to achieve. (Some activities might relate to more than one lean manufacturing concept.)

_____ **1.** Lenses are received daily based on customer orders.

_____ **2.** Customers receive a satisfaction survey with each camera purchased.

_____ **3.** The manufacturing process is standardized and documented.

_____ **4.** Cameras are produced in small lots, and only to customer order.

_____ **5.** Manufacturing facilities are arranged to reduce move time and wait time.

_____ **6.** Kodak conducts focus groups to determine new features that customers want in digital cameras.

a. Just-in-time (JIT)

b. Continuous improvement (CI)

c. Total quality management (TQM)

[continued on next page]

_____ **7.** Orders received are filled within two business days.

_____ **8.** Kodak works with suppliers to reduce inspection time of incoming materials.

_____ **9.** Kodak monitors the market to determine what features its competitors are offering on digital cameras.

_____ **10.** Kodak asks production workers for ideas to improve production.

Listed here are the total costs associated with the production of 10,000 Blu-ray Discs (BDs) manufactured by New Age. The BDs sell for $15 each.

Costs	Cost by Behavior		Cost by Function	
	Variable	Fixed	Product	Period
1. Annual fixed fee for cleaning service—$3,000		$3,000		$3,000
2. Cost of office equipment rent—$700				
3. Upper management salaries—$100,000				
4. Labeling (10,000 outsourced)—$2,500				
5. Wages of assembly workers—$20,000				
6. Sales commissions—$0.50 per BD				
7. Machinery depreciation—$15,000				
8. Systems staff salaries—$10,000				
9. Cost of factory rent—$4,500				
10. Plastic for BDs—$1,000				

Problem 18-3B
Cost computation, classification, and analysis
C4

Required

1. Classify each cost and its amount as (a) either fixed or variable and (b) either product or period.
2. Compute the manufacturing cost per BD.

Analysis Component

3. Assume that 12,000 BDs are produced in the next month. What do you predict will be the total cost of plastic for the BDs and the per unit cost of the plastic for the BDs? Explain.
4. Assume that 12,000 BDs are produced in the next month. What do you predict will be the total cost of factory rent and the per unit cost of the factory rent? Explain.

Check (2) Total variable manufacturing cost, $23,500

Assume that you must make a presentation to a client explaining the difference between prime and conversion costs. The client makes and sells 200,000 cookies per week. The client tells you that her sales staff also would like a clarification regarding product and period costs. She tells you that most of the staff lack training in managerial accounting.

Problem 18-4B
Cost classification and explanation
C4 C5

Required

Prepare a one-page memorandum to your client outlining your planned presentation to her sales staff.

Refer to *Decision Maker,* **Purchase Manager,** in this chapter. Assume that you are the motorcycle manufacturer's managerial accountant. The purchasing manager asks you about preparing an estimate of the related costs for buying motorcycle seats from supplier (B). She tells you this estimate is needed because unless dollar estimates are attached to nonfinancial factors such as lost production time, her supervisor will not give it full attention. The manager also shows you the following information.

Problem 18-5B
Opportunity cost estimation and application
C1 C4

- Production output is 1,000 motorcycles per year based on 250 production days a year.
- Production time per day is 8 hours at a cost of $500 per hour to run the production line.
- Lost production time due to poor quality is 1%.
- Satisfied customers purchase, on average, three motorcycles during a lifetime.
- Satisfied customers recommend the product, on average, to four other people.
- Marketing predicts that using seat (B) will result in four lost customers per year from repeat business and referrals.
- Average contribution margin per motorcycle is $4,000.

Required

Check Cost of lost customer revenue, $16,000

Estimate the costs (including opportunity costs) of buying motorcycle seats from supplier (B). This problem requires that you think creatively and make reasonable estimates; thus there could be more than one correct answer. (*Hint:* Reread the answer to *Decision Maker,* and compare the cost savings for buying from supplier [B] to the sum of lost customer revenue from repeat business and referrals and the cost of lost production time.)

Problem 18-6B
Ending inventory computation and evaluation

C2   C6

CCMD Company makes specialty skates for the ice skating circuit. On December 31, 2008, the company had (*a*) 1,500 skates in finished goods inventory and (*b*) 2,500 blades at a cost of $15 each in raw materials inventory. During 2009, CCMD purchased 45,000 additional blades at $15 each and manufactured 20,000 pairs of skates.

Required

Check (1) Ending (blade) inventory, 7,500 units; $112,500

1. Determine the unit and dollar amounts of raw materials inventory in blades at December 31, 2009.

Analysis Component

2. Write a one-half page memorandum to the production manager explaining why a just-in-time inventory system for blades should be considered. Include the amount of working capital that can be reduced at December 31, 2009, if the ending blade raw material inventory is cut in half.

Problem 18-7B
Inventory computation and reporting

C4   C6   P1

Shown here are annual financial data at December 31, 2009, taken from two different companies.

	AAA Imports (Retail)	Marina Boats (Manufacturing)
Beginning inventory		
Merchandise	$ 50,000	
Finished goods		$200,000
Cost of purchases	350,000	
Cost of goods manufactured		686,000
Ending inventory		
Merchandise	25,000	
Finished goods		300,000

Required

Check (1) AAA Imports cost of goods sold, $375,000

1. Compute the cost of goods sold section of the income statement at December 31, 2009, for each company. Include the proper title and format in the solution.
2. Write a half-page memorandum to your instructor (*a*) identifying the inventory accounts and (*b*) identifying where each is reported on the income statement and balance sheet for both companies.

Problem 18-8B
Manufacturing and income statements; analysis of inventories

P2

The following calendar year-end information is taken from the December 31, 2009, adjusted trial balance and other records of Homestyle Furniture.

Advertising expense	$ 22,250		Direct labor	564,500
Depreciation expense—Office equipment	10,440		Income taxes expense	138,700
Depreciation expense—Selling equipment	12,125		Indirect labor	61,000
Depreciation expense—Factory equipment	37,400		Miscellaneous production costs	10,440
Factory supervision	123,500		Office salaries expense	72,875
Factory supplies used	8,060		Raw materials purchases	896,375
Factory utilities	39,500		Rent expense—Office space	25,625
Inventories			Rent expense—Selling space	29,000
Raw materials, December 31, 2008	42,375		Rent expense—Factory building	95,500
Raw materials, December 31, 2009	72,430		Maintenance expense—Factory equipment	32,375
Goods in process, December 31, 2008	14,500		Sales	5,002,000
Goods in process, December 31, 2009	16,100		Sales discounts	59,375
Finished goods, December 31, 2008	179,200		Sales salaries expense	297,300
Finished goods, December 31, 2009	143,750			

Required

1. Prepare the company's 2009 manufacturing statement.
2. Prepare the company's 2009 income statement that reports separate categories for (*a*) selling expenses and (*b*) general and administrative expenses.

Check (1) Cost of goods manufactured, $1,836,995

Analysis Component

3. Compute the (*a*) inventory turnover, defined as cost of goods sold divided by average inventory, and (*b*) days' sales in inventory, defined as 365 times ending inventory divided by cost of goods sold, for both its raw materials inventory and its finished goods inventory. (To compute turnover and days' sales in inventory for raw materials, use raw materials used rather than cost of goods sold.) Discuss some possible reasons for differences between these ratios for the two types of inventories.

Fast Ink produces ink-jet printers for personal computers. It received an order for 400 printers from a customer. The following information is available for this order.

Problem 18-9B
Manufacturing cycle time and efficiency

A1

Process time	8.0 hours
Inspection time	1.7 hours
Move time	4.5 hours
Wait time	10.8 hours

Required

1. Compute the company's manufacturing cycle time.
2. Compute the company's manufacturing cycle efficiency. Interpret your answer.

Analysis Component

3. Assume that Fast Ink wishes to increase its manufacturing cycle efficiency to 0.80. What are some ways that it can accomplish this?

(This serial problem begins in Chapter 1 and continues through most of the book. If previous chapter segments were not completed, the serial problem can begin at this point. It is helpful, but not necessary, to use the Working Papers that accompany the book.)

SERIAL PROBLEM

Success Systems

SP 18   Adriana Lopez, owner of Success Systems, decides to diversify her business by also manufacturing computer workstation furniture.

Required

1. Classify the following manufacturing costs of Success Systems by behavior and traceability.

	Cost by Behavior		Cost by Traceability	
Product Costs	**Variable**	**Fixed**	**Direct**	**Indirect**
1. Monthly flat fee to clean workshop	___	___	___	___
2. Laminate coverings for desktops	___	___	___	___
3. Taxes on assembly workshop	___	___	___	___
4. Glue to assemble workstation component parts	___	___	___	___
5. Wages of desk assembler	___	___	___	___
6. Electricity for workshop	___	___	___	___
7. Depreciation on tools	___	___	___	___

2. Prepare a manufacturing statement for Success Systems for the month ended January 31, 2010. Assume the following manufacturing costs:

Direct materials: $2,200

Factory overhead: $490

Direct labor: $900

Beginning goods in process: none (December 31, 2009)

Ending goods in process: $540 (January 31, 2010)

Beginning finished goods inventory: none (December 31, 2009)

Ending finished goods inventory: $350 (January 31, 2010)

Check (3) COGS, $2,700

3. Prepare the cost of goods sold section of a partial income statement for Success Systems for the month ended January 31, 2010.

BEYOND THE NUMBERS

REPORTING IN ACTION

C1 C2

BTN 18-1 Managerial accounting is more than recording, maintaining, and reporting financial results. Managerial accountants must provide managers with both financial and nonfinancial information including estimates, projections, and forecasts. There are many accounting estimates that management accountants must make, and **Best Buy** must notify shareholders of these estimates.

Required

1. Access and read Best Buy's "Critical Accounting Estimates" section (six pages), which is part of its *Management's Discussion and Analysis of Financial Condition and Results of Operations* section, from either its annual report or its 10-K for the year ended March 3, 2007 [BestBuy.com]. What are some of the accounting estimates that Best Buy made in preparing its financial statements? What are some of the effects if the actual results of Best Buy differ from its assumptions?

2. What is the management accountant's role in determining those estimates?

Fast Forward

3. Access **Best Buy**'s annual report for a fiscal year ending after March 3, 2007, from either its Website [BestBuy.com] or the SEC's EDGAR database [www.sec.gov]. Answer the questions in parts (1) and (2) after reading the current MD&A section. Identify any major changes.

COMPARATIVE ANALYSIS

C1 C2

BTN 18-2 **Best Buy** and **RadioShack** are both merchandisers that rely on customer satisfaction. Access and read (1) Best Buy's "Business Strategy and Core Philosophies" section (one page) and (2) RadioShack's "Financial Impact of Turnaround Program" section (one page). Both sections are located in the respective company's *Management Discussion and Analysis of Financial Condition and Results of Operations* section from the annual report or 10-K. The Best Buy report is for the year ended March 3, 2007, and the RadioShack report is for the year ended December 31, 2006.

Required

1. Identify the strategic initiatives that each company put forward in its desire to better compete and succeed in the marketplace.
2. For each of these strategic initiatives for both companies, explain how it reflects (or does not reflect) a customer satisfaction focus.

BTN 18-3   Assume that you are the managerial accountant at Infostore, a manufacturer of hard drives, CDs, and diskettes. Its reporting year-end is December 31. The chief financial officer is concerned about having enough cash to pay the expected income tax bill because of poor cash flow management. On November 15, the purchasing department purchased excess inventory of CD raw materials in anticipation of rapid growth of this product beginning in January. To decrease the company's tax liability, the chief financial officer tells you to record the purchase of this inventory as part of supplies and expense it in the current year; this would decrease the company's tax liability by increasing expenses.

ETHICS CHALLENGE

C3 C4 C5

Required

1. In which account should the purchase of CD raw materials be recorded?
2. How should you respond to this request by the chief financial officer?

BTN 18-4   Write a one-page memorandum to a prospective college student about salary expectations for graduates in business. Compare and contrast the expected salaries for accounting (including different subfields such as public, corporate, tax, audit, and so forth), marketing, management, and finance majors. Prepare a graph showing average starting salaries (and those for experienced professionals in those fields if available). To get this information, stop by your school's career services office; libraries also have this information. The Website JobStar.org (click on *Salary Info*) also can get you started.

COMMUNICATING IN PRACTICE

BTN 18-5   Managerial accounting professionals follow a code of ethics. As a member of the Institute of Management Accountants, the managerial accountant must comply with Standards of Ethical Conduct.

TAKING IT TO THE NET

C1 C3

Required

1. Identify, print, and read the *Statement of Ethical Professional Practice* posted at www.IMAnet.org. (Search using "ethical professional practice.")
2. What four overarching ethical principles underlie the IMA's statement?
3. Describe the courses of action the IMA recommends in resolving ethical conflicts.

TEAMWORK IN ACTION

C7   P2

BTN 18-6   The following calendar-year information is taken from the December 31, 2009, adjusted trial balance and other records of Dahlia Company.

Advertising expense	$ 19,125	Direct labor	650,750
Depreciation expense—Office equipment	8,750	Indirect labor	60,000
Depreciation expense—Selling equipment	10,000	Miscellaneous production costs	8,500
Depreciation expense—Factory equipment	32,500	Office salaries expense	100,875
Factory supervision	122,500	Raw materials purchases	872,500
Factory supplies used	15,750	Rent expense—Office space	21,125
Factory utilities	36,250	Rent expense—Selling space	25,750
Inventories		Rent expense—Factory building	79,750
Raw materials, December 31, 2008	177,500	Maintenance expense—Factory equipment	27,875
Raw materials, December 31, 2009	168,125	Sales	3,275,000
Goods in process, December 31, 2008	15,875	Sales discounts	57,500
Goods in process, December 31, 2009	14,000	Sales salaries expense	286,250
Finished goods, December 31, 2008	164,375		
Finished goods, December 31, 2009	129,000		

Required

1. *Each* team member is to be responsible for computing **one** of the following amounts. You are not to duplicate your teammates' work. Get any necessary amounts from teammates. Each member is to explain the computation to the team in preparation for reporting to class.

   a. Materials used.   **d.** Total cost of goods in process.
   b. Factory overhead.   **e.** Cost of goods manufactured.
   c. Total manufacturing costs.

2. Check your cost of goods manufactured with the instructor. If it is correct, proceed to part (3).

3. *Each* team member is to be responsible for computing **one** of the following amounts. You are not to duplicate your teammates' work. Get any necessary amounts from teammates. Each member is to explain the computation to the team in preparation for reporting to class.

   a. Net sales.   **d.** Total operating expenses.
   b. Cost of goods sold.   **e.** Net income or loss before taxes.
   c. Gross profit.

Point: Provide teams with transparencies and markers for presentation purposes.

ENTREPRENEURIAL DECISION

C1   C4

BTN 18-7   Brian Taylor of **Kernel Season's** must understand his manufacturing costs to effectively operate and succeed as a profitable and efficient company.

Required

1. What are the three main categories of manufacturing costs that Brian must monitor and control? Provide examples of each.

2. How can Brian make the Kernel Season's manufacturing process more cost-effective? Provide examples of two useful managerial measures of time and efficiency.

3. What are four goals of a total quality management process? How can Kernel Season's use TQM to improve its business activities?

HITTING THE ROAD

C1   C5

BTN 18-8   Visit your favorite fast-food restaurant. Observe its business operations.

Required

1. Describe all business activities from the time a customer arrives to the time that customer departs.

2. List all costs you can identify with the separate activities described in part 1.

3. Classify each cost from part 2 as fixed or variable, and explain your classification.

BTN 18-9   Access DSG's annual report for the year ended April 28, 2007 (www.DSGiplc.com). Read the section "Corporate Governance" dealing with the responsibilities of the board of directors.

Required

1. Identify the responsibilities (see the "schedule of matters reserved for the board") of DSG's board of directors.

2. How would management accountants be involved in assisting the board of directors in carrying out their responsibilities? Explain.

ANSWERS TO MULTIPLE CHOICE QUIZ

1. c
2. b
3. b
4. a
5. Beginning finished goods + Cost of goods manufactured (COGM) −
   Ending finished goods = Cost of goods sold
   $6,000 + COGM − $3,200 = $7,500
   COGM = <u>$4,700</u>

A Look Back

Chapter 18 introduced managerial accounting and explained basic cost concepts. We also described the lean business model and the reporting of manufacturing activities, including the manufacturing statement.

A Look at This Chapter

We begin this chapter by describing a cost accounting system. We then explain the procedures used to determine costs using a job order costing system. We conclude with a discussion of over- and underapplied overhead.

A Look Ahead

Chapter 20 focuses on measuring costs in process production companies. We explain process production, describe how to assign costs to processes, and compute and analyze cost per equivalent unit.

Job Order Cost Accounting

Chapter

Learning Objectives

CAP

Conceptual

C1 Explain the cost accounting system. *(p. 770)*

C2 Describe important features of job order production. *(p. 770)*

C3 Explain job cost sheets and how they are used in job order cost accounting. *(p. 772)*

Analytical

A1 Apply job order costing in pricing services. *(p. 782)*

Procedural

P1 Describe and record the flow of materials costs in job order cost accounting. *(p. 773)*

P2 Describe and record the flow of labor costs in job order cost accounting. *(p. 775)*

P3 Describe and record the flow of overhead costs in job order cost accounting. *(p. 776)*

P4 Determine adjustments for overapplied and underapplied factory overhead. *(p. 781)*

LP19

Working the Field

"Being successful is having a vision which you are excited to follow without the fear of failure"
—Hank Julicher

PHILADELPHIA, PA—One size fits all? Not when it comes to synthetic turf for athletic fields—this according to Hank Julicher, founder of **Sprinturf** (**Sprinturf.com**). "Not all fields are exactly alike, because no two owners have the same exact needs," insists Hank. "Many variables must be considered, including playing requirements, climate, and financial considerations." Designing, installing, and servicing synthetic turf systems are Sprinturf's mission.

"There is much more to a playing field than just the surface," explains Hank. "Many would argue that the base is the most important—it needs the strength to support athletes and vehicles, while still being able to drain over 20″ of rainfall per hour." For this, Sprinturf relies on its all-rubber infill system for its installations. Still, understanding customer needs is key. In extremely hot, arid climates, Sprinturf uses light-colored rubber infill to reduce the temperature of playing surfaces. In cold areas, Sprinturf offers solutions to reduce snow and ice buildup. Hank has put in fields from Utah State University to University of Montana to Long Beach City College. While a touchdown is worth 6 points on every Sprinturf field, each field is otherwise unique.

Manufacturers of custom products, such as that from Sprinturf, use state-of-the-art job order cost accounting to track costs. This includes tracking the cost of materials, labor and overhead, and managing those expenses. To help control costs and ensure product quality, Sprinturf does not outsource any part of the design or installation process. Controlling all aspects of the process enables it to better isolate costs and avoid the run-away costs often experienced by startups that fail to use costing techniques. Recruiting top-notch personnel and experienced supervisors also helps control labor costs. Reflecting the unique nature of each field, each installation is videotaped to ensure it is done exactly according to customer specifications.

Hank Julicher stresses cost control as vital to Sprinturf's success. "To take on two 800 pound gorillas in our industry, we had to be more creative, efficient, and cost-effective to win," explains Hank. "We just hung in there until the public recognized our quality and value." This winning formula has led to product growth that any team would envy.

[Sources: *Sprinturf Website,* January 2009; *Entrepreneur,* 2007; *PanStadia,* February and November 2005]

This chapter introduces a system for assigning costs to the flow of goods through a production process. We then describe the details of a *job order cost accounting system*. Job order costing is frequently used by manufacturers of custom products or providers of custom services. Manufacturers that use job order costing typically base it on a perpetual inventory system, which provides a continuous record of materials, goods in process, and finished goods inventories.

Job Order Cost Accounting

Job Order Cost Accounting
- Cost accounting system
- Job order manufacturing
- Events in job order costing
- Job cost sheet

Job Order Cost Flows and Reports
- Materials cost flows and documents
- Labor cost flows and documents
- Overhead cost flows and documents
- Summary of cost flows

Adjustment of Overapplied or Underapplied Overhead
- Underapplied overhead
- Overapplied overhead

Job Order Cost Accounting

This section describes a cost accounting system and job order production and costing.

Cost Accounting System

C1 Explain the cost accounting system.

An ever-increasing number of companies use a cost accounting system to generate timely and accurate inventory information. A **cost accounting system** records manufacturing activities using a *perpetual* inventory system, which continuously updates records for costs of materials, goods in process, and finished goods inventories. A cost accounting system also provides timely information about inventories and manufacturing costs per unit of product. This is especially helpful for managers' efforts to control costs and determine selling prices. (A **general accounting system** records manufacturing activities using a *periodic* inventory system. Some companies still use a general accounting system, but its use is declining as competitive forces and customer demands have increased pressures on companies to better manage inventories.)

Point: Cost accounting systems accumulate costs and then assign them to products and services.

The two basic types of cost accounting systems are *job order cost accounting* and *process cost accounting*. We describe job order cost accounting in this chapter. Process cost accounting is explained in the next chapter.

Job Order Production

C2 Describe important features of job order production.

Many companies produce products individually designed to meet the needs of a specific customer. Each customized product is manufactured separately and its production is called **job order production,** or *job order manufacturing* (also called *customized production,* which is the production of products in response to special orders). Examples of such products include synthetic football fields, special-order machines, a factory building, custom jewelry, wedding invitations, and artwork.

The production activities for a customized product represent a **job.** The principle of customization is equally applicable to both manufacturing *and* service companies. Most service companies meet customers' needs by performing a custom service for a specific customer. Examples of such services include an accountant auditing a client's financial statements, an interior designer remodeling an office, a wedding consultant planning and supervising a reception, and a lawyer defending a client. Whether the setting is manufacturing or services, job order operations involve meeting the needs of customers by producing or performing custom jobs.

Boeing's aerospace division is one example of a job order production system. Its primary business is twofold: (1) design, develop, and integrate space carriers and (2) provide systems engineering and integration of Department of Defense (DoD) systems. Many of its orders are customized and produced through job order operations.

When a job involves producing more than one unit of a custom product, it is often called a **job lot.** Products produced as job lots could include benches for a church, imprinted T-shirts for a 10K race or company picnic, or advertising signs for a chain of stores. Although these orders involve more than one unit, the volume of production is typically low, such as 50 benches, 200 T-shirts, or 100 signs. Another feature of job order production is the diversity, often called *heterogeneity,* of the products produced. Namely, each customer order is likely to differ from another in some important respect. These variations can be minor or major.

Point: Many professional examinations including the CPA and CMA exams require knowledge of job order and process cost accounting.

Decision Insight

Custom Design   Managers once saw companies as the center of a solar system orbited by suppliers and customers. Now the customer has become the center of the business universe. **Nike** allows custom orders over the Internet, enabling customers to select materials, colors, and to personalize their shoes with letters and numbers. Soon consumers may be able to personalize almost any product, from cellular phones to appliances to furniture.

Events in Job Order Costing

The initial event in a normal job order operation is the receipt of a customer order for a custom product. This causes the company to begin work on a job. A less common case occurs when management decides to begin work on a job before it has a signed contract. This is referred to as *jobs produced on speculation.*

Video19.1

The first step in both cases is to predict the cost to complete the job. This cost depends on the product design prepared by either the customer or the producer. The second step is to negotiate a sales price and decide whether to pursue the job. Other than for government or other cost-plus contracts, the selling price is determined by market factors. Producers evaluate the market price, compare it to cost, and determine whether the profit on the job is reasonable. If the profit is not reasonable, the producer would determine a desired **target cost.** The third step is for the producer to schedule production of the job to meet the customer's needs and to fit within its own production constraints. Preparation of this work schedule should consider workplace facilities including equipment, personnel, and supplies. Once this schedule is complete, the producer can place orders for raw materials. Production occurs as materials and labor are applied to the job.

Point: Some jobs are priced on a *cost-plus basis:* The customer pays the manufacturer for costs incurred on the job plus a negotiated amount or rate of profit.

An overview of job order production activity is shown in Exhibit 19.1. This exhibit shows the March production activity of Road Warriors, which manufactures security-equipped cars and trucks. The company converts any vehicle by giving it a diversity of security items such as alarms, reinforced exterior, bulletproof glass, and bomb detectors. The company began by catering to high-profile celebrities, but it now caters to anyone who desires added security in a vehicle.

Job order production for Road Warriors requires materials, labor, and overhead costs. Recall that direct materials are goods used in manufacturing that are clearly identified with a particular job. Similarly, direct labor is effort devoted to a particular job. Overhead costs support production of more than one job. Common overhead items are depreciation on factory buildings and equipment, factory supplies, supervision, maintenance, cleaning, and utilities.

Exhibit 19.1 shows that materials, labor, and overhead are added to Jobs B15, B16, B17, B18, and B19, which were started during March. Road Warriors completed Jobs B15, B16, and B17 in March and delivered Jobs B15 and B16 to customers. At the end of March, Jobs B18 and B19 remain in goods in process inventory and Job B17 is in finished goods inventory. Both labor and materials costs are also separated into their direct and indirect components. Their indirect amounts are added to overhead. Total overhead cost is then allocated to the various jobs.

Decision Insight

Target Costing   Many producers determine a target cost for their jobs. Target cost is determined as follows: Expected selling price − Desired profit = Target cost. If the projected target cost of the job as determined by job costing is too high, the producer can apply *value engineering,* which is a method of determining ways to reduce job cost until the target cost is met.

EXHIBIT 19.1

Job Order Production Activities

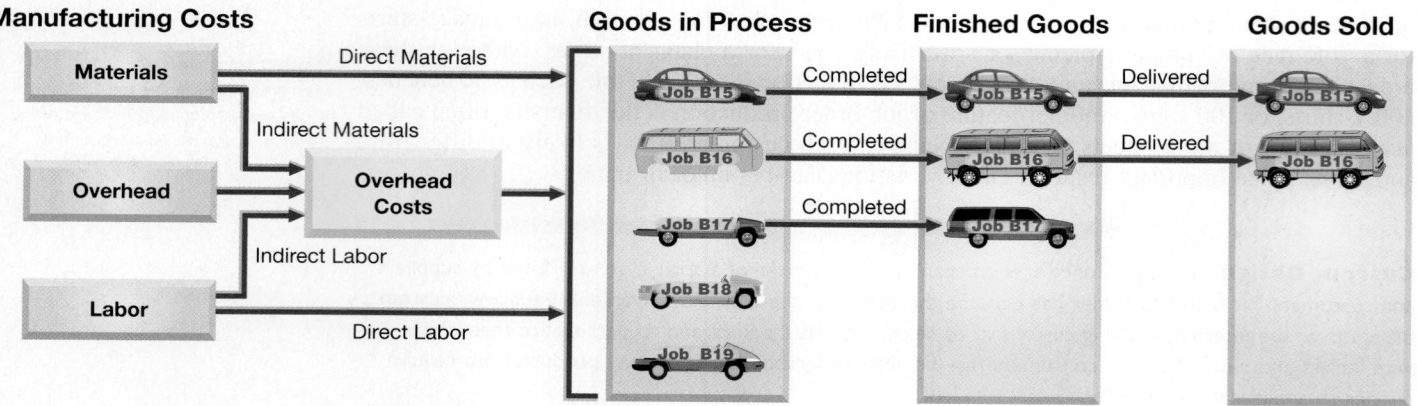

Job Cost Sheet

<table>
<tr><td>C3</td><td>Explain job cost sheets and how they are used in job order cost accounting.</td></tr>
</table>

General ledger accounts usually do not provide the accounting information that managers of job order cost operations need to plan and control production activities. This is so because the needed information often requires more detailed data. Such detailed data are usually stored in subsidiary records controlled by general ledger accounts. Subsidiary records store information about raw materials, overhead costs, jobs in process, finished goods, and other items. This section describes the use of these records.

A major aim of a **job order cost accounting system** is to determine the cost of producing each job or job lot. In the case of a job lot, the system also aims to compute the cost per unit. The accounting system must include separate records for each job to accomplish this, and it must capture information about costs incurred and charge these costs to each job.

A **job cost sheet** is a separate record maintained for each job. Exhibit 19.2 shows a job cost sheet for an alarm system that Road Warriors produced for a customer. This job cost sheet identifies the customer, the job number assigned, the product, and key dates. Costs incurred on the job are immediately recorded on this sheet. When each job is complete, the supervisor enters the date of completion, records any remarks, and signs the sheet. The job cost sheet in Exhibit 19.2 classifies costs as direct materials, direct labor, or overhead. It shows that a total of $600 in direct materials is added to Job B15 on four different dates. It also shows seven entries for direct labor costs that total $1,000. Road Warriors *allocates* (also termed *applies, assigns,* or *charges*) factory overhead costs of $1,600 to this job using an allocation rate of 160% of direct labor cost (160% × $1,000)—we discuss overhead allocation later in this chapter.

Point: Factory overhead consists of costs (other than direct materials and direct labor) that ensure the production activities are carried out.

While a job is being produced, its accumulated costs are kept in **Goods in Process Inventory.** The collection of job cost sheets for all jobs in process makes up a subsidiary ledger controlled by the Goods in Process Inventory account in the general ledger. Managers use job cost sheets to monitor costs incurred to date and to predict and control costs for each job.

Point: Documents (electronic and paper) are crucial in a job order system, and the job cost sheet is a cornerstone. Understanding it aids in grasping concepts of capitalizing product costs and product cost flow.

When a job is finished, its job cost sheet is completed and moved from the jobs in process file to the finished jobs file. This latter file acts as a subsidiary ledger controlled by the **Finished Goods Inventory** account. When a finished job is delivered to a customer, the job cost sheet is moved to a permanent file supporting the total cost of goods sold. This permanent file contains records from both current and prior periods.

♟ Decision Maker

Management Consultant   One of your tasks is to control and manage costs for a consulting company. At the end of a recent month, you find that three consulting jobs were completed and two are 60% complete. Each unfinished job is estimated to cost $10,000 and to earn a revenue of $12,000. You are unsure how to recognize goods in process inventory and record costs and revenues. Do you recognize any inventory? If so, how much? How much revenue is recorded for unfinished jobs this month?   [Answer—p. 786]

EXHIBIT 19.2

Job Cost Sheet

Accounting System: Exhibit 19-2   _ □ ☒

File   Edit   Maintain   Tasks   Analysis   Options   Reports   Window   Help

Road Warriors, Los Angeles, California   **JOB COST SHEET**

Customer's Name	Carroll Connor	**Job No.**	B15
Address	1542 High Point Dr.	**City & State**	Portland, Oregon
Job Description	Level 1 Alarm System on Ford Expedition		
Date promised	March 15 **Date started**	March 3 **Date completed**	March 11

Direct Materials			**Direct Labor**			**Overhead**		
Date	Requisition	Cost	Date	Time Ticket	Cost	Date	Rate	Cost
3/3/2009	R-4698	100.00	3/3/2009	L-3393	120.00	3/11/2009	160% of	1,600.00
3/7/2009	R-4705	225.00	3/4/2009	L-3422	150.00		Direct	
3/9/2009	R-4725	180.00	3/5/2009	L-3456	180.00		Labor	
3/10/2009	R-4777	95.00	3/8/2009	L-3479	60.00		Cost	
			3/9/2009	L-3501	90.00			
			3/10/2009	L-3535	240.00			
			3/11/2009	L-3559	160.00			
Total		600.00	**Total**		1,000.00	**Total**		1,600.00

REMARKS: Completed job on March 11, and shipped to customer on March 15. Met all specifications and requirements.

SUMMARY:

Materials	600.00
Labor	1,000.00
Overhead	1,600.00

Signed: *C. Luther, Supervisor*

Total cost	3,200.00

Quick Check

Answers—p. 787

1. Which of these products is likely to involve job order production? (*a*) inexpensive watches, (*b*) racing bikes, (*c*) bottled soft drinks, or (*d*) athletic socks.

2. What is the difference between a job and a job lot?

3. Which of these statements is correct? (*a*) The collection of job cost sheets for unfinished jobs makes up a subsidiary ledger controlled by the Goods in Process Inventory account, (*b*) Job cost sheets are financial statements provided to investors, or (*c*) A separate job cost sheet is maintained in the general ledger for each job in process.

4. What three costs are normally accumulated on job cost sheets?

Job Order Cost Flows and Reports

Materials Cost Flows and Documents

This section focuses on the flow of materials costs and the related documents in a job order cost accounting system. We begin analysis of the flow of materials costs by examining Exhibit 19.3. When materials are first received from suppliers, the employees count and inspect them and record the items' quantity and cost on a receiving report. The receiving report serves as the *source document* for recording materials received in both a materials ledger card and in the general ledger. In nearly all job order cost systems, **materials ledger cards** (or files) are perpetual records that are updated each time units are purchased and each time units are issued for use in production.

To illustrate the purchase of materials, Road Warriors acquired $450 of wiring and related materials on March 4, 2009. This purchase is recorded as follows.

Materials

Mar. 4	Raw Materials Inventory—M-347.	450	
	Accounts Payable		450
	To record purchase of materials for production.		

P1 Describe and record the flow of materials costs in job order cost accounting.

Point: Some companies certify certain suppliers based on the quality of their materials. Goods received from these suppliers are not always inspected by the purchaser to save costs.

Assets = Liabilities + Equity
+450   +450

EXHIBIT 19.3

Materials Cost Flows through
Subsidiary Records

Video19.1

Exhibit 19.3 shows that materials can be requisitioned for use either on a specific job (direct materials) or as overhead (indirect materials). Cost of direct materials flows from the materials ledger card to the job cost sheet. The cost of indirect materials flows from the materials ledger card to the Indirect Materials account in the factory overhead ledger, which is a subsidiary ledger controlled by the Factory Overhead account in the general ledger.

Exhibit 19.4 shows a materials ledger card for material received and issued by Road Warriors. The card identifies the item as alarm system wiring and shows the item's stock number, its location in the storeroom, information about the maximum and minimum quantities that should be available, and the reorder quantity. For example, alarm system wiring is issued and recorded on March 7, 2009. The job cost sheet in Exhibit 19.2 showed that Job B15 used this wiring.

EXHIBIT 19.4

Materials Ledger Card

MATERIALS LEDGER CARD

Road Warriors
Los Angeles, California

| Item | Alarm system wiring | Stock No. | M–347 | Location in Storeroom | Bin 137 |
| Maximum quantity | 5 units | Minimum quantity | 1 unit | Quantity to reorder | 2 units |

	Received				Issued				Balance		
Date	Receiving Report Number	Units	Unit Price	Total Price	Requisition Number	Units	Unit Price	Total Price	Units	Unit Price	Total Price
3/ 4/2009	C-7117	2	225.00	450.00					1	225.00	225.00
									3	225.00	675.00
3/ 7/2009					R–4705	1	225.00	225.00	2	225.00	450.00

When materials are needed in production, a production manager prepares a **materials requisition** and sends it to the materials manager. The requisition shows the job number, the type of material, the quantity needed, and the signature of the manager authorized to make the requisition. Exhibit 19.5 shows the materials requisition for alarm system wiring for Job B15. To see how this requisition ties to the flow of costs, compare the information on the requisition with the March 7, 2009, data in Exhibits 19.2 and 19.4.

Point: Requisitions are often accumulated and recorded in one entry. The frequency of entries depends on the job, the industry, and management procedures.

MATERIALS REQUISITION   No. R–4705

Road Warriors
Los Angeles, California

Job No. _____ B15	Date _____ 3/7/2009
Material Stock No. _____ M–347	Material Description _____ Alarm system wiring
Quantity Requested _____ 1	Requested By _____ *C. Luther*

Quantity Provided _____ 1	Date Provided _____ 3/7/2009
Filled By _____ *M. Bateman*	Material Received By _____ *C. Luther*
Remarks _____	

EXHIBIT 19.5

Materials Requisition

The use of alarm system wiring on Job B15 yields the following entry (locate this cost item in the job cost sheet shown in Exhibit 19.2).

Mar. 7	Goods in Process Inventory—Job B15.	225	
	Raw Materials Inventory—M-347		225
	To record use of material on Job B15.		

Assets = Liabilities + Equity
+225
−225

This entry is posted both to its general ledger accounts and to subsidiary records. Posting to subsidiary records includes a debit to a job cost sheet and a credit to a materials ledger card. (*Note:* An entry to record use of indirect materials is the same as that for direct materials *except* the debit is to Factory Overhead. In the subsidiary factory overhead ledger, this entry is posted to Indirect Materials.)

Labor Cost Flows and Documents

Exhibit 19.6 shows the flow of labor costs from clock cards and the Factory Payroll account to subsidiary records of the job order cost accounting system. Recall that costs in subsidiary records give detailed information needed to manage and control operations.

Labor

P2 Describe and record the flow of labor costs in job order cost accounting.

EXHIBIT 19.6

Labor Cost Flows through Subsidiary Records

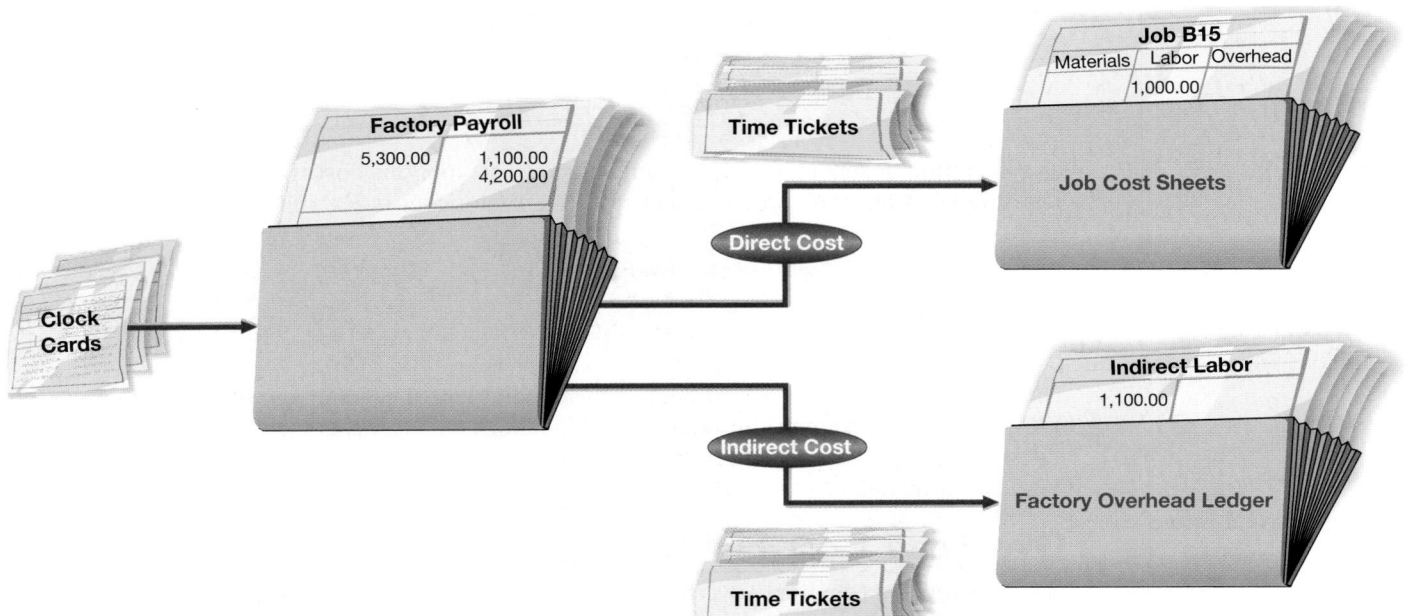

Point: Indirect materials are included in overhead on the job cost sheet. Assigning overhead costs to products is described in the next section.

Point: Many employee fraud schemes involve payroll, including overstated hours on clock cards.

The flow of costs in Exhibit 19.6 begins with **clock cards.** Employees commonly use these cards to record the number of hours worked, and they serve as source documents for entries to record labor costs. Clock card data on the number of hours worked is used at the end of each pay period to determine total labor cost. This amount is then debited to the Factory Payroll account, a temporary account containing the total payroll cost (both direct and indirect). Payroll cost is later allocated to both specific jobs and overhead.

According to clock card data, workers earned $1,500 for the week ended March 5. Illustrating the flow of labor costs, the accrual and payment of these wages are recorded as follows.

Assets = Liabilities + Equity
−1,500   −1,500

Mar. 6	Factory payroll............................	1,500	
	Cash		1,500
	To record the weekly payroll.		

"It's on Corporate Standard Time... It loses an hour of your pay every day."

To assign labor costs to specific jobs and to overhead, we must know how each employee's time is used and its costs. Source documents called **time tickets** usually capture these data. Employees regularly fill out time tickets to report how much time they spent on each job. An employee who works on several jobs during a day completes a separate time ticket for each job. Tickets are also prepared for time charged to overhead as indirect labor. A supervisor signs an employee's time ticket to confirm its accuracy.

Exhibit 19.7 shows a time ticket reporting the time a Road Warrior employee spent working on Job B15. The employee's supervisor signed the ticket to confirm its accuracy. The hourly rate and total labor cost are computed after the time ticket is turned in. To see the effect of this time ticket on the job cost sheet, look at the entry dated March 8, 2009, in Exhibit 19.2.

EXHIBIT 19.7

Time Ticket

ROAD WARRIORS **Road Warriors** Los Angeles, California	TIME TICKET		No. L–3479 Date March 8 20 09
	Employee Name	**Employee Number**	**Job No.**
	T. Zeller	3969	B15

TIME AND RATE INFORMATION:

Remarks	**Start Time**	**Finish Time**	**Elapsed Time**	**Hourly Rate**
	9:00	12:00	3.0	$20.00
	Approved By *C. Luther*		**Total Cost**	$60.00

Point: In the accounting equation, we treat accounts such as Factory Overhead and Factory Payroll as temporary accounts, which hold various expenses until they are allocated to balance sheet or income statement accounts.

Assets = Liabilities + Equity
+60   +60

When time tickets report labor used on a specific job, this cost is recorded as direct labor. The following entry records the data from the time ticket in Exhibit 19.7.

Mar. 8	Goods in Process Inventory—Job B15	60	
	Factory Payroll		60
	To record direct labor used on Job B15.		

The debit in this entry is posted both to the general ledger account and to the appropriate job cost sheet. (*Note:* An entry to record indirect labor is the same as for direct labor *except* that it debits Factory Overhead and credits Factory Payroll. In the subsidiary factory overhead ledger, the debit in this entry is posted to the Indirect Labor account.)

P3 Describe and record the flow of overhead costs in job order cost accounting.

Overhead Cost Flows and Documents

Factory overhead (or simply overhead) cost flows are shown in Exhibit 19.8. Factory overhead includes all production costs other than direct materials and direct labor. Two sources of

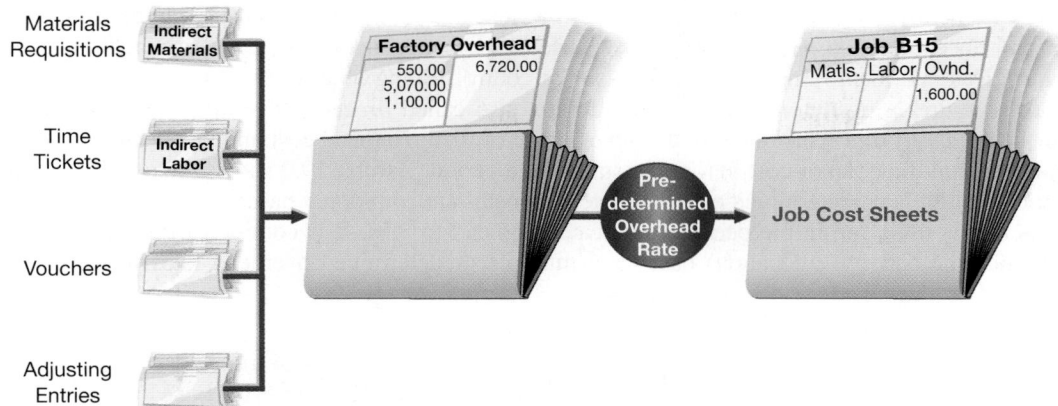

EXHIBIT 19.8

Overhead Cost Flows through Subsidiary Records

overhead costs are indirect materials and indirect labor. These costs are recorded from requisitions for indirect materials and time tickets for indirect labor. Two other sources of overhead are (1) vouchers authorizing payments for items such as supplies or utilities and (2) adjusting entries for costs such as depreciation on factory assets.

Overhead

Factory overhead usually includes many different costs and, thus, a separate account for each is often maintained in a subsidiary factory overhead ledger. This ledger is controlled by the Factory Overhead account in the general ledger. Factory Overhead is a temporary account that accumulates costs until they are allocated to jobs.

Recall that overhead costs are recorded with debits to the Factory Overhead account and with credits to other accounts such as Cash, Accounts Payable, and Accumulated Depreciation—Equipment. In the subsidiary factory overhead ledger, the debits are posted to their respective accounts such as Depreciation Expense—Equipment, Insurance Expense—Warehouse, or Amortization Expense—Patents.

To illustrate the recording of overhead, the following two entries reflect the depreciation of factory equipment and the accrual of utilities, respectively, for the week ended March 6.

Mar. 6	Factory Overhead	600		Assets = Liabilities + Equity
	Accumulated Depreciation—Equipment		600	−600 −600
	To record depreciation on factory equipment.			
Mar. 6	Factory Overhead	250		Assets = Liabilities + Equity
	Utilities Payable.		250	+250 −250
	To record the accrual of factory utilities.			

Exhibit 19.8 shows that overhead costs flow from the Factory Overhead account to job cost sheets. Because overhead is made up of costs not directly associated with specific jobs or job lots, we cannot determine the dollar amount incurred on a specific job. We know, however, that overhead costs represent a necessary part of business activities. If a job cost is to include all costs needed to complete the job, some amount of overhead must be included. Given the difficulty in determining the overhead amount for a specific job, however, we allocate overhead to individual jobs in some reasonable manner.

We generally allocate overhead by linking it to another factor used in production, such as direct labor or machine hours. The factor to which overhead costs are linked is known as the *allocation base*. A manager must think carefully about how many and which allocation bases to use. This managerial decision influences the accuracy with which overhead costs are allocated to individual jobs. In turn, the cost of individual jobs might impact a manager's decisions for pricing or performance evaluation. In Exhibit 19.2, overhead is expressed as 160% of direct labor. We then allocate overhead by multiplying 160% by the estimated amount of direct labor on the jobs.

We cannot wait until the end of a period to allocate overhead to jobs because perpetual inventory records are part of the job order costing system (demanding up-to-date costs). Instead, we

must predict overhead in advance and assign it to jobs so that a job's total costs can be estimated prior to its completion. This estimated cost is useful for managers in many decisions including setting prices and identifying costs that are out of control. Being able to estimate overhead in advance requires a **predetermined overhead rate,** also called *predetermined overhead allocation* (or *application*) *rate.* This rate requires an estimate of total overhead cost and an allocation factor such as total direct labor cost before the start of the period. Exhibit 19.9 shows the usual formula for computing a predetermined overhead rate (estimates are commonly based on annual amounts). This rate is used during the period to allocate overhead to jobs. It is common for companies to use multiple activity (allocation) bases and multiple predetermined overhead rates for different types of products and services.

EXHIBIT 19.9

Predetermined Overhead Allocation Rate Formula

$$\text{Predetermined overhead rate} = \frac{\text{Estimated overhead costs}}{\text{Estimated activity base}}$$

To illustrate, Road Warriors allocates overhead by linking it to direct labor. At the start of the current period, management predicts total direct labor costs of $125,000 and total overhead costs of $200,000. Using these estimates, management computes its predetermined overhead rate as 160% of direct labor cost ($200,000 ÷ $125,000). Specifically, reviewing the job order cost sheet in Exhibit 19.2, we see that $1,000 of direct labor went into Job B15. We then use the predetermined overhead rate of 160% to allocate $1,600 (equal to $1,000 × 1.60) of overhead to this job. The entry to record this allocation is

Mar. 11	Goods in Process Inventory—Job B15.	1,600	
	Factory Overhead		1,600
	To assign overhead to Job B15.		

Since the allocation rate for overhead is estimated at the start of a period, the total amount assigned to jobs during a period rarely equals the amount actually incurred. We explain how this difference is treated later in this chapter.

 Decision Ethics

Web Consultant You are working on seven client engagements. Two clients reimburse your firm for actual costs plus a 10% markup. The other five pay a fixed fee for services. Your firm's costs include overhead allocated at $47 per labor hour. The managing partner of your firm instructs you to record as many labor hours as possible to the two markup engagements by transferring labor hours from the other five. What do you do? [Answer—p. 786]

Summary of Cost Flows

We showed journal entries for charging Goods in Process Inventory (Job B15) with the cost of (1) direct materials requisitions, (2) direct labor time tickets, and (3) factory overhead. We made separate entries for each of these costs, but they are usually recorded in one entry. Specifically, materials requisitions are often collected for a day or a week and recorded with a single entry summarizing them. The same is done with labor time tickets. When summary entries are made, supporting schedules of the jobs charged and the types of materials used provide the basis for postings to subsidiary records.

To show all production cost flows for a period and their related entries, we again look at Road Warriors' activities. Exhibit 19.10 shows costs linked to all of Road Warriors' production activities for March. Road Warriors did not have any jobs in process at the beginning of March, but it did apply materials, labor, and overhead costs to five new jobs in March. Jobs B15 and B16 are completed and delivered to customers in March, Job B17 is completed but not delivered, and Jobs B18 and B19 are still in process. Exhibit 19.10 also shows purchases of raw materials for $2,750, labor costs incurred for $5,300, and overhead costs of $6,720.

The upper part of Exhibit 19.11 shows the flow of these costs through general ledger accounts and the end-of-month balances in key subsidiary records. Arrow lines are numbered

EXHIBIT 19.10

Job Order Costs of All Production Activities

| | | | Overhead | | Goods | | Cost of |
Explanation	**Materials**	**Labor**	**Incurred**	**Allocated**	**in Process**	**Finished Goods**	**Goods Sold**
ROAD WARRIORS — Job Order Manufacturing Costs — For Month Ended March 31, 2009							
Job B15	$ 600	$1,000		$1,600			$3,200
Job B16	300	800		1,280			2,380
Job B17	500	1,100		1,760		$3,360	
Job B18	150	700		1,120	$1,970		
Job B19	250	600		960	1,810		
Total job costs	1,800	4,200		$6,720	$3,780	$3,360	$5,580
Indirect materials	550		$ 550				
Indirect labor		1,100	1,100				
Other overhead			5,070				
Total costs used in production	2,350	$5,300	$6,720				
Ending materials inventory	1,400						
Materials available	3,750						
Less beginning materials inventory	(1,000)						
Materials purchased	$2,750						

EXHIBIT 19.11

Job Order Cost Flows and Ending Job Cost Sheets

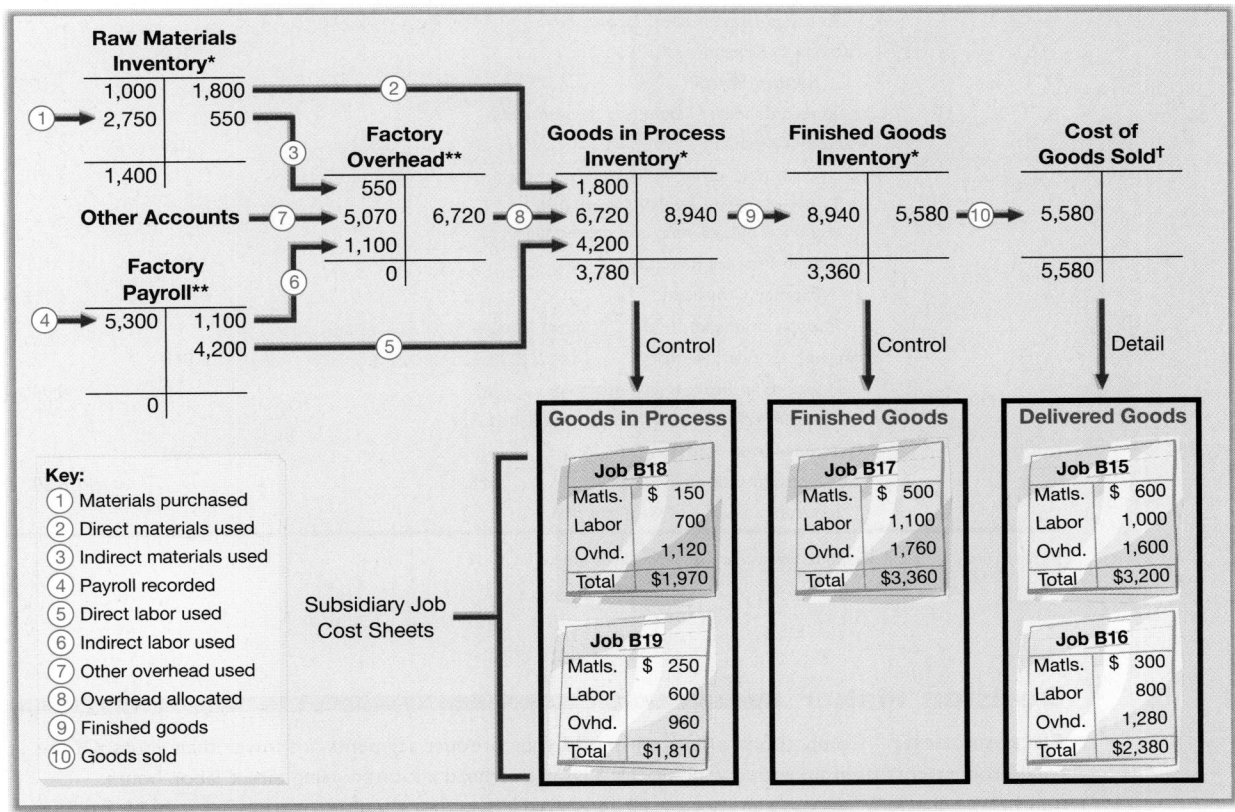

* The ending balances in the inventory accounts are carried to the balance sheet.

† The Cost of Goods Sold balance is carried to the income statement.

** Factory Payroll and Factory Overhead are considered temporary accounts; when these costs are allocated to jobs, the balances in these accounts are reduced.

to show the flows of costs for March. Each numbered cost flow reflects several entries made in March. The lower part of Exhibit 19.11 shows summarized job cost sheets and their status at the end of March. The sum of costs assigned to the jobs in process ($1,970 + $1,810) equals the $3,780 balance in Goods in Process Inventory shown in Exhibit 19.10. Also, costs assigned to Job B17 equal the $3,360 balance in Finished Goods Inventory. The sum of costs assigned to Jobs B15 and B16 ($3,200 + $2,380) equals the $5,580 balance in Cost of Goods Sold.

Exhibit 19.12 shows each cost flow with a single entry summarizing the actual individual entries made in March. Each entry is numbered to link with the arrow lines in Exhibit 19.11.

EXHIBIT 19.12

Entries for Job Order Production Costs*

①	Raw Materials Inventory	2,750	
	Accounts Payable		2,750
	Acquired materials on credit for factory use.		
②	Goods in Process Inventory	1,800	
	Raw Materials Inventory		1,800
	To assign costs of direct materials used.		
③	Factory Overhead	550	
	Raw Materials Inventory		550
	To record use of indirect materials.		
④	Factory Payroll	5,300	
	Cash (and other accounts)		5,300
	To record salaries and wages of factory workers (including various payroll liabilities).		
⑤	Goods in Process Inventory	4,200	
	Factory Payroll		4,200
	To assign costs of direct labor used.		
⑥	Factory Overhead	1,100	
	Factory Payroll		1,100
	To record indirect labor costs as overhead.		
⑦	Factory Overhead	5,070	
	Cash (and other accounts)		5,070
	To record factory overhead costs such as insurance, utilities, rent, and depreciation.		
⑧	Goods in Process Inventory	6,720	
	Factory Overhead		6,720
	To apply overhead at 160% of direct labor.		
⑨	Finished Goods Inventory	8,940	
	Goods in Process Inventory		8,940
	To record completion of Jobs B15, B16, and B17.		
⑩	Cost of Goods Sold	5,580	
	Finished Goods Inventory		5,580
	To record sale of Jobs B15 and B16.		

Point: *Actual* overhead is debited to Factory Overhead. *Allocated* overhead is credited to Factory Overhead.

* Transactions are numbered to be consistent with arrow lines in Exhibit 19.11.

 Decision Maker

Entrepreneur Competitors' prices on one of your product segments are lower than yours. Of the total product cost used in setting your prices, 53% is overhead allocated using direct labor hours. You believe that product costs are distorted and wonder whether there is a better way to allocate overhead and to set product price. What do you suggest? [Answer—p. 787]

Answers—p. 787

Quick Check

5. In job order cost accounting, which account is debited in recording a raw materials requisition? (*a*) Raw Materials Inventory, (*b*) Raw Materials Purchases, (*c*) Goods in Process Inventory if for a job, or (*d*) Goods in Process Inventory if they are indirect materials.

6. What are four sources of information for recording costs in the Factory Overhead account?

7. Why does job order cost accounting require a predetermined overhead rate?

8. What events result in a debit to Factory Payroll? What events result in a credit?

Adjustment of Overapplied or Underapplied Overhead

Refer to the debits in the Factory Overhead account in Exhibit 19.11 (or Exhibit 19.12). The total cost of factory overhead incurred during March is $6,720 ($550 + $5,070 + $1,100). The $6,720 exactly equals the amount assigned to goods in process inventory (see arrow line ⑧). Therefore, the overhead incurred equals the overhead applied in March. The amount of overhead incurred rarely equals the amount of overhead applied, however, because a job order cost accounting system uses a predetermined overhead rate in applying factory overhead costs to jobs. This rate is determined using estimated amounts before the period begins, and estimates rarely equal the exact amounts actually incurred. This section explains what we do when too much or too little overhead is applied to jobs.

Video19.1

Underapplied Overhead

When less overhead is applied than is actually incurred, the remaining debit balance in the Factory Overhead account at the end of the period is called **underapplied overhead.** To illustrate, assume that Road Warriors actually incurred *other overhead costs* of $5,550 instead of the $5,070 shown in Exhibit 19.11. This yields an actual total overhead cost of $7,200 in March. Since the amount of overhead applied was only $6,720, the Factory Overhead account is left with a $480 debit balance as shown in the ledger account in Exhibit 19.13.

P4 Determine adjustments for overapplied and underapplied factory overhead.

Factory Overhead				Acct. No. 540
Date	**Explanation**	**Debit**	**Credit**	**Balance**
Mar. 31	Indirect materials cost	550		550 Dr.
31	Indirect labor cost	1,100		1,650 Dr.
31	Other overhead cost	5,550		7,200 Dr.
31	Overhead costs applied to jobs		6,720	480 Dr.

EXHIBIT 19.13

Underapplied Overhead in the Factory Overhead Ledger Account

The $480 debit balance reflects manufacturing costs not assigned to jobs. This means that the balances in Goods in Process Inventory, Finished Goods Inventory, and Cost of Goods Sold do not include all production costs incurred. When the underapplied overhead amount is immaterial, it is allocated (closed) to the Cost of Goods Sold account with the following adjusting entry.

Example: If we do not adjust for underapplied overhead, will net income be overstated or understated? *Answer:* Overstated.

Mar. 31	Cost of Goods Sold	480	
	Factory Overhead		480
	To adjust for underapplied overhead costs.		

Assets = Liabilities + Equity

−480

+480

The $480 debit (increase) to Cost of Goods Sold reduces income by $480. (When the underapplied (or overapplied) overhead is material, the amount is normally allocated to the Cost of Goods Sold, Finished Goods Inventory, and Goods in Process Inventory accounts. This process is covered in advanced courses.)

Overapplied Overhead

When the overhead applied in a period exceeds the overhead incurred, the resulting credit balance in the Factory Overhead account is called **overapplied overhead.** We treat overapplied overhead at the end of the period in the same way we treat underapplied overhead, except that we debit Factory Overhead and credit Cost of Good Sold for the amount.

Decision Insight

Job Order Education   Many companies invest in their employees, and the demand for executive education is strong. Annual spending on training and education exceeds $20 billion. Annual revenues for providers of executive education continue to rise, with about 40% of revenues coming from custom programs designed for one or a select group of companies.

Quick Check

Answers—p. 787

9. In a job order cost accounting system, why does the Factory Overhead account usually have an overapplied or underapplied balance at period-end?

10. When the Factory Overhead account has a debit balance at period-end, does this reflect overapplied or underapplied overhead?

Decision Analysis	**Pricing for Services**

A1   Apply job order costing in pricing services.

The chapter described job order costing mainly using a manufacturing setting. However, these concepts and procedures are applicable to a service setting. Consider AdWorld, an advertising agency that develops Web-based ads for small firms. Each of its customers has unique requirements, so costs for each individual job must be tracked separately.

AdWorld uses two types of labor: Web designers ($65 per hour) and computer staff ($50 per hour). It also incurs overhead costs that it assigns using two different predetermined overhead allocation rates: $125 per designer hour and $96 per staff hour. For each job, AdWorld must estimate the number of designer and staff hours needed. Then total costs pertaining to each job are determined using the procedures in the chapter. (*Note:* Most service firms have neither the category of materials cost nor inventory.)

To illustrate, a manufacturer of golf balls requested a quote from AdWorld for an advertising engagement. AdWorld estimates that the job will require 43 designer hours and 61 staff hours, with the following total estimated cost for this job.

Direct Labor		
Designers (43 hours × $65)	$ 2,795	
Staff (61 hours × $50)	3,050	
Total direct labor		$ 5,845
Overhead		
Designer related (43 hours × $125)	5,375	
Staff related (61 hours × $96)	5,856	
Total overhead		11,231
Total estimated job cost		$17,076

AdWorld can use this cost information to help determine the price quote for the job (see *Decision Maker,* **Sales Manager,** scenario in this chapter).

Another source of information that AdWorld must consider is the market, that is, how much competitors will quote for this job. Competitor information is often unavailable; therefore, AdWorld's managers must use estimates based on their assessment of the competitive environment.

Decision Maker

Sales Manager   As AdWorld's sales manager, assume that you estimate costs pertaining to a proposed job as $17,076. Your normal pricing policy is to apply a markup of 18% from total costs. However, you learn that three other agencies are likely to bid for the same job, and that their quotes will range from $16,500 to $22,000. What price should you quote? What factors other than cost must you consider? [Answer—p. 787]

Demonstration Problem—Job Order Costing

The following information reflects Walczak Company's job order production activities for May.

DP19

Raw materials purchases	$16,000
Factory payroll cost	15,400
Overhead costs incurred	
Indirect materials	5,000
Indirect labor	3,500
Other factory overhead	9,500

Walczak's predetermined overhead rate is 150% of direct labor cost. Costs are allocated to the three jobs worked on during May as follows.

	Job 401	Job 402	Job 403
In-process balances on April 30			
Direct materials	$3,600		
Direct labor	1,700		
Applied overhead	2,550		
Costs during May			
Direct materials	3,550	$3,500	$1,400
Direct labor	5,100	6,000	800
Applied overhead	?	?	?
Status on May 31	Finished (sold)	Finished (unsold)	In process

Required

1. Determine the total cost of:
   a. The April 30 inventory of jobs in process.
   b. Materials used during May.
   c. Labor used during May.
   d. Factory overhead incurred and applied during May and the amount of any over- or underapplied overhead on May 31.
   e. Each job as of May 31, the May 31 inventories of both goods in process and finished goods, and the goods sold during May.

2. Prepare summarized journal entries for the month to record:
   a. Materials purchases (on credit), the factory payroll (paid with cash), indirect materials, indirect labor, and the other factory overhead (paid with cash).
   b. Assignment of direct materials, direct labor, and overhead costs to the Goods in Process Inventory account. (Use separate debit entries for each job.)
   c. Transfer of each completed job to the Finished Goods Inventory account.
   d. Cost of goods sold.
   e. Removal of any underapplied or overapplied overhead from the Factory Overhead account. (Assume the amount is not material.)

3. Prepare a manufacturing statement for May.

Planning the Solution

- Determine the cost of the April 30 goods in process inventory by totaling the materials, labor, and applied overhead costs for Job 401.

- Compute the cost of materials used and labor by totaling the amounts assigned to jobs and to overhead.
- Compute the total overhead incurred by summing the amounts for the three components. Compute the amount of applied overhead by multiplying the total direct labor cost by the predetermined overhead rate. Compute the underapplied or overapplied amount as the difference between the actual cost and the applied cost.
- Determine the total cost charged to each job by adding the costs incurred in April (if any) to the cost of materials, labor, and overhead applied during May.
- Group the costs of the jobs according to their completion status.
- Record the direct materials costs assigned to the three jobs, using a separate Goods in Process Inventory account for each job; do the same for the direct labor and the applied overhead.
- Transfer costs of Jobs 401 and 402 from Goods in Process Inventory to Finished Goods.
- Record the costs of Job 401 as cost of goods sold.
- Record the transfer of underapplied overhead from the Factory Overhead account to the Cost of Goods Sold account.
- On the manufacturing statement, remember to include the beginning and ending goods in process inventories and to deduct the underapplied overhead.

Solution to Demonstration Problem

1. Total cost of

a. April 30 inventory of jobs in process (Job 401).

Direct materials	$3,600
Direct labor	1,700
Applied overhead	2,550
Total cost	$7,850

b. Materials used during May.

Direct materials	
Job 401	$ 3,550
Job 402	3,500
Job 403	1,400
Total direct materials	8,450
Indirect materials	5,000
Total materials used	$13,450

c. Labor used during May.

Direct labor	
Job 401	$ 5,100
Job 402	6,000
Job 403	800
Total direct labor	11,900
Indirect labor	3,500
Total labor used	$15,400

d. Factory overhead incurred in May.

Actual overhead	
Indirect materials	$ 5,000
Indirect labor	3,500
Other factory overhead	9,500
Total actual overhead	18,000
Overhead applied (150% × $11,900)	17,850
Underapplied overhead	$ 150

e. Total cost of each job.

	401	402	403
In-process costs from April			
Direct materials	$ 3,600		
Direct labor	1,700		
Applied overhead*	2,550		
Cost incurred in May			
Direct materials	3,550	$ 3,500	$1,400
Direct labor	5,100	6,000	800
Applied overhead*	7,650	9,000	1,200
Total costs	$24,150	$18,500	$3,400

* Equals 150% of the direct labor cost.

Total cost of the May 31 inventory of goods in process (Job 403) = <u>$3,400</u>

Total cost of the May 31 inventory of finished goods (Job 402) = <u>$18,500</u>

Total cost of goods sold during May (Job 401) = <u>$24,150</u>

2. Journal entries.

a.

Raw Materials Inventory	16,000	
Accounts Payable		16,000
To record materials purchases.		
Factory Payroll	15,400	
Cash		15,400
To record factory payroll.		
Factory Overhead	5,000	
Raw Materials Inventory		5,000
To record indirect materials.		
Factory Overhead	3,500	
Factory Payroll		3,500
To record indirect labor.		
Factory Overhead	9,500	
Cash		9,500
To record other factory overhead.		

b. Assignment of costs to Goods in Process Inventory.

Goods in Process Inventory (Job 401)	3,550	
Goods in Process Inventory (Job 402)	3,500	
Goods in Process Inventory (Job 403)	1,400	
Raw Materials Inventory		8,450
To assign direct materials to jobs.		
Goods in Process Inventory (Job 401)	5,100	
Goods in Process Inventory (Job 402)	6,000	
Goods in Process Inventory (Job 403)	800	
Factory Payroll		11,900
To assign direct labor to jobs.		
Goods in Process Inventory (Job 401)	7,650	
Goods in Process Inventory (Job 402)	9,000	
Goods in Process Inventory (Job 403)	1,200	
Factory Overhead		17,850
To apply overhead to jobs.		

c. Transfer of completed jobs to Finished Goods Inventory.

Finished Goods Inventory	42,650	
Goods in Process Inventory (Job 401)		24,150
Goods in Process Inventory (Job 402)		18,500
To record completion of jobs.		

d.

Cost of Goods Sold	24,150	
Finished Goods Inventory		24,150
To record sale of Job 401.		

e.

Cost of Goods Sold	150	
Factory Overhead		150
To assign underapplied overhead.		

3.

WALCZAK COMPANY Manufacturing Statement For Month Ended May 31		
Direct materials		$ 8,450
Direct labor		11,900
Factory overhead		
Indirect materials	$5,000	
Indirect labor	3,500	
Other factory overhead	9,500	18,000
Total production costs		38,350
Add goods in process, April 30		7,850
Total cost of goods in process		46,200
Less goods in process, May 31		3,400
Less underapplied overhead		150
Cost of goods manufactured		$42,650

Note how underapplied overhead is reported. Overapplied overhead is similarly reported, but is added.

Summary

C1 **Explain the cost accounting system.** A cost accounting system records production activities using a perpetual inventory system, which continuously updates records for transactions and events that affect inventory costs.

C2 **Describe important features of job order production.**
Certain companies called *job order manufacturers* produce custom-made products for customers. These customized products are produced in response to a customer's orders. A job order manufacturer produces products that usually are different and, typically, produced in low volumes. The production systems of job order companies are flexible and are not highly standardized.

C3 **Explain job cost sheets and how they are used in job order cost accounting.** In a job order cost accounting system, the costs of producing each job are accumulated on a separate job cost sheet. Costs of direct materials, direct labor, and overhead are accumulated separately on the job cost sheet and then added to determine the total cost of a job. Job cost sheets for jobs in process, finished jobs, and jobs sold make up subsidiary records controlled by general ledger accounts.

A1 **Apply job order costing in pricing services.** Job order costing can usefully be applied to a service setting. The resulting job cost estimate can then be used to help determine a price for services.

P1 **Describe and record the flow of materials costs in job order cost accounting.** Costs of materials flow from receiving reports to materials ledger cards and then to either job cost sheets or the Indirect Materials account in the factory overhead ledger.

P2 **Describe and record the flow of labor costs in job order cost accounting.** Costs of labor flow from clock cards to the Factory Payroll account and then to either job cost sheets or the Indirect Labor account in the factory overhead ledger.

P3 **Describe and record the flow of overhead costs in job order cost accounting.** Overhead costs are accumulated in the Factory Overhead account that controls the subsidiary factory overhead ledger. Then, using a predetermined overhead rate, overhead costs are charged to jobs.

P4 **Determine adjustments for overapplied and underapplied factory overhead.** At the end of each period, the Factory Overhead account usually has a residual debit (underapplied overhead) or credit (overapplied overhead) balance. If the balance is not material, it is transferred to Cost of Goods Sold, but if it is material, it is allocated to Goods in Process Inventory, Finished Goods Inventory, and Cost of Goods Sold.

Guidance Answers to **Decision Maker** and **Decision Ethics**

Management Consultant Service companies (such as this consulting firm) do not recognize goods in process inventory or finished goods inventory—an important difference between service and manufacturing companies. For the two jobs that are 60% complete, you could recognize revenues and costs at 60% of the total expected amounts. This means you could recognize revenue of $7,200 (0.60 × $12,000) and costs of $6,000 (0.60 × $10,000), yielding net income of $1,200 from each job.

Web Consultant The partner has a monetary incentive to *manage* the numbers and assign more costs to the two cost-plus engagements. This also would reduce costs on the fixed-price engagements. To act in such a manner is unethical. As a professional and an honest person, it is your responsibility to engage in ethical behavior. You must not comply with the partner's instructions. If the partner insists you act in an unethical manner, you should report the matter to a higher authority in the organization.

Entrepreneur An inadequate cost system can distort product costs. You should review overhead costs in detail. Once you know the different cost elements in overhead, you can classify them into groups such as material related, labor related, or machine related. Other groups can also be formed (we discuss this in Chapter 21). Once you have classified overhead items into groups, you can better establish overhead allocation bases and use them to compute predetermined overhead rates. These multiple rates and bases can then be used to assign overhead costs to products. This will likely improve product pricing.

Sales Manager The price based on AdWorld's normal pricing policy is $20,150 ($17,076 × 1.18), which is within the price range offered by competitors. One option is to apply normal pricing policy and quote a price of $20,150. On the other hand, assessing the competition, particularly in terms of their service quality and other benefits they might offer, would be useful. Although price is an input customers use to select suppliers, factors such as quality and timeliness (responsiveness) of suppliers are important. Accordingly, your price can reflect such factors.

Guidance Answers to **Quick Checks**

1. *b*

2. A job is a special order for a custom product. A job lot consists of a quantity of identical, special-order items.

3. *a*

4. Three costs normally accumulated on a job cost sheet are direct materials, direct labor, and factory overhead.

5. *c*

6. Four sources of factory overhead are materials requisitions, time tickets, vouchers, and adjusting entries.

7. Since a job order cost accounting system uses perpetual inventory records, overhead costs must be assigned to jobs before the end of a period. This requires the use of a predetermined overhead rate.

8. Debits are recorded when wages and salaries of factory employees are paid or accrued. Credits are recorded when direct labor costs are assigned to jobs and when indirect labor costs are transferred to the Factory Overhead account.

9. Overapplied or underapplied overhead usually exists at the end of a period because application of overhead is based on estimates of overhead and another variable such as direct labor. Estimates rarely equal actual amounts incurred.

10. A debit balance reflects underapplied factory overhead.

Key Terms

mhhe.com/wildFAP19e

Key Terms are available at the book's Website for learning and testing in an online Flashcard Format.

Clock card (p. 776)
Cost accounting system (p. 770)
Finished Goods Inventory (p. 772)
General accounting system (p. 770)
Goods in Process Inventory (p. 772)
Job (p. 770)

Job cost sheet (p. 772)
Job lot (p. 771)
Job order cost accounting system (p. 772)
Job order production (p. 770)
Materials ledger card (p. 773)

Materials requisition (p. 774)
Overapplied overhead (p. 782)
Predetermined overhead rate (p. 778)
Target cost (p. 771)
Time ticket (p. 776)
Underapplied overhead (p. 781)

Multiple Choice Quiz

Answers on p. 805.   **mhhe.com/wildFAP19e**

Additional Quiz Questions are available at the book's Website.

Quiz19

1. A company's predetermined overhead allocation rate is 150% of its direct labor costs. How much overhead is applied to a job that requires total direct labor costs of $30,000?
  a. $15,000
  b. $30,000
  c. $45,000
  d. $60,000
  e. $75,000

2. A company's cost accounting system uses direct labor costs to apply overhead to goods in process and finished goods inventories. Its production costs for the period are: direct

materials, $45,000; direct labor, $35,000; and overhead applied, $38,500. What is its predetermined overhead allocation rate?
  a. 10%
  b. 110%
  c. 86%
  d. 91%
  e. 117%

3. A company's ending inventory of finished goods has a total cost of $10,000 and consists of 500 units. If the overhead applied to these goods is $4,000, and the predetermined overhead rate is 80% of direct labor costs, how much direct materials cost was incurred in producing these 500 units?

a. $10,000
b. $ 6,000
c. $ 4,000
d. $ 5,000
e. $ 1,000

4. A company's Goods in Process Inventory T-account follows.

Goods in Process Inventory			
Beginning balance	9,000		
Direct materials	94,200		
Direct labor	59,200	?	Finished goods
Overhead applied	31,600		
Ending balance	17,800		

The cost of units transferred to Finished Goods inventory is

a. $193,000
b. $211,800
c. $185,000
d. $144,600
e. $176,200

5. At the end of its current year, a company learned that its overhead was underapplied by $1,500 and that this amount is not considered material. Based on this information, the company should

a. Close the $1,500 to Finished Goods Inventory.
b. Close the $1,500 to Cost of Goods Sold.
c. Carry the $1,500 to the next period.
d. Do nothing about the $1,500 because it is not material and it is likely that overhead will be overapplied by the same amount next year.
e. Carry the $1,500 to the Income Statement as "Other Expense."

Discussion Questions

1. Why must a company estimate the amount of factory overhead assigned to individual jobs or job lots?

2. ♟ The chapter used a percent of labor cost to assign factory overhead to jobs. Identify another factor (or base) a company might reasonably use to assign overhead costs.

3. ♟ What information is recorded on a job cost sheet? How do management and employees use job cost sheets?

4. In a job order cost accounting system, what records serve as a subsidiary ledger for Goods in Process Inventory? For Finished Goods Inventory?

5. What journal entry is recorded when a materials manager receives a materials requisition and then issues materials (both direct and indirect) for use in the factory?

6. ♟ How does the materials requisition help safeguard a company's assets?

7. What is the difference between a clock card and a time ticket?

8. What events cause debits to be recorded in the Factory Overhead account? What events cause credits to be recorded in the Factory Overhead account?

9. What account(s) is(are) used to eliminate overapplied or underapplied overhead from the Factory Overhead account, assuming the amount is not material?

10. ♟ Assume that **Apple** produces a batch of 1,000 iPods. Does it account for this as 1,000 individual jobs or as a job lot? Explain (consider costs and benefits).

11. Why must a company prepare a predetermined overhead rate when using job order cost accounting?

12. ♟ How would a hospital apply job order costing? Explain.

13. ♟ **Harley-Davidson** manufactures 30 custom-made, luxury-model motorcycles. Does it account for these motorcycles as 30 individual jobs or as a job lot? Explain. **Harley-Davidson**

14. **Best Buy**'s GeekSquad performs computer and home theater installation and service, for an upfront flat price. How can Best Buy use a job order costing system?

♟ *Denotes Discussion Questions that involve decision making.*

Available with McGraw-Hill's Homework Manager   McGraw-Hill's HOMEWORK MANAGER®

QUICK STUDY

QS 19-1

Jobs and job lots

C2 ♟

Determine which products are most likely to be manufactured as a job and which as a job lot.

1. A custom-designed home.
2. Hats imprinted with company logo.
3. Little League trophies.
4. A hand-crafted table.
5. A 90-foot motor yacht.
6. Wedding dresses for a chain of stores.

The following information is from the materials requisitions and time tickets for Job 9-1005 completed by Franklin Boats. The requisitions are identified by code numbers starting with the letter Q and the time tickets start with W. At the start of the year, management estimated that overhead cost would equal 110% of direct labor cost for each job. Determine the total cost on the job cost sheet for Job 9-1005.

QS 19-2
Job cost computation
C3

Date	Document	Amount
7/1/2009	Q-4698	$2,500
7/1/2009	W-3393	1,200
7/5/2009	Q-4725	2,000
7/5/2009	W-3479	900
7/10/2009	W-3559	600

During the current month, a company that uses a job order cost accounting system purchases $25,000 in raw materials for cash. It then uses $6,000 of raw materials indirectly as factory supplies and uses $16,000 of raw materials as direct materials. Prepare entries to record these three transactions.

QS 19-3
Direct materials journal entries
P1

During the current month, a company that uses a job order cost accounting system incurred a monthly factory payroll of $75,000, paid in cash. Of this amount, $29,000 is classified as indirect labor and the remainder as direct. Prepare entries to record these transactions.

QS 19-4
Direct labor journal entries   P2

A company incurred the following manufacturing costs this period: direct labor, $234,000; direct materials, $292,000; and factory overhead, $58,500. Compute its overhead cost as a percent of (1) direct labor and (2) direct materials.

QS 19-5
Factory overhead rates   P3

During the current month, a company that uses a job order cost accounting system incurred a monthly factory payroll of $350,000, paid in cash. Of this amount, $90,000 is classified as indirect labor and the remainder as direct for the production of Job 65A. Factory overhead is applied at 90% of direct labor. Prepare the entry to apply factory overhead to this job lot.

QS 19-6
Factory overhead journal entries
P3

A company allocates overhead at a rate of 150% of direct labor cost. Actual overhead cost for the current period is $475,000, and direct labor cost is $300,000. Prepare the entry to close over- or underapplied overhead to cost of goods sold.

QS 19-7
Entry for over- or
underapplied overhead   P4

McGraw-Hill's
HOMEWORK
MANAGER®   Available with McGraw-Hill's Homework Manager

The left column lists the titles of documents and accounts used in job order cost accounting. The right column presents short descriptions of the purposes of the documents. Match each document in the left column to its numbered description in the right column.

EXERCISES

Exercise 19-1
Documents in job order
cost accounting

C2 C3 P1 P2 P3

A. Voucher
B. Materials requisition
C. Factory Overhead account
D. Clock card
E. Factory Payroll account
F. Materials ledger card
G. Time ticket

_____ **1.** Shows amount of time an employee works on a job.

_____ **2.** Temporarily accumulates incurred labor costs until they are assigned to specific jobs or to overhead.

_____ **3.** Shows only total time an employee works each day.

_____ **4.** Perpetual inventory record of raw materials received, used, and available for use.

_____ **5.** Shows amount approved for payment of an overhead or other cost.

_____ **6.** Temporarily accumulates the cost of incurred overhead until the cost is assigned to specific jobs.

_____ **7.** Communicates the need for materials to complete a job.

Exercise 19-2

Analysis of cost flows

C2 P1 P2 P3 ♟

As of the end of June, the job cost sheets at Tracer Wheels, Inc., show the following total costs accumulated on three custom jobs.

	Job 102	Job 103	Job 104
Direct materials	$25,000	$59,000	$56,000
Direct labor	14,000	26,700	40,000
Overhead	7,000	13,350	20,000

Job 102 was started in production in May and the following costs were assigned to it in May: direct materials, $13,000; direct labor, $3,600; and overhead, $1,600. Jobs 103 and 104 are started in June. Overhead cost is applied with a predetermined rate based on direct labor cost. Jobs 102 and 103 are finished in June, and Job 104 is expected to be finished in July. No raw materials are used indirectly in June. Using this information, answer the following questions. (Assume this company's predetermined overhead rate did not change across these months).

1. What is the cost of the raw materials requisitioned in June for each of the three jobs?

2. How much direct labor cost is incurred during June for each of the three jobs?

3. What predetermined overhead rate is used during June?

Check (4) $145,050

4. How much total cost is transferred to finished goods during June?

Exercise 19-3

Overhead rate; costs assigned to jobs

P3

Check (2) $23,450

In December 2008, Matsushi Electronics' management establishes the year 2009 predetermined overhead rate based on direct labor cost. The information used in setting this rate includes estimates that the company will incur $750,000 of overhead costs and $500,000 of direct labor cost in year 2009. During March 2009, Matsushi began and completed Job No. 13-56.

1. What is the predetermined overhead rate for year 2009?

2. Use the information on the following job cost sheet to determine the total cost of the job.

JOB COST SHEET

Customer's Name   ESPN Co. _____   Job No.   13-56

Job Description   ___ 5 plasma monitors—150 inch _____

Date	Direct Materials		Direct Labor		Overhead Costs Applied	
	Requisition No.	Amount	Time-Ticket No.	Amount	Rate	Amount
Mar. 8	4-129	$4,000	T-306	$ 680		
Mar. 11	4-142	7,450	T-432	1,280		
Mar. 18	4-167	3,800	T-456	1,320		_____
Totals		====		====		====

Exercise 19-4

Analysis of costs assigned to goods in process

P3

Wilson Company uses a job order cost accounting system that charges overhead to jobs on the basis of direct material cost. At year-end, the Goods in Process Inventory account shows the following.

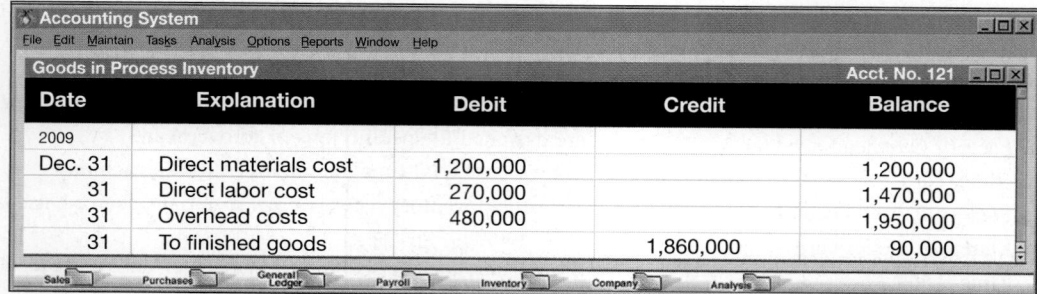

Date	Explanation	Debit	Credit	Balance
2009				
Dec. 31	Direct materials cost	1,200,000		1,200,000
31	Direct labor cost	270,000		1,470,000
31	Overhead costs	480,000		1,950,000
31	To finished goods		1,860,000	90,000

1. Determine the overhead rate used (based on direct material cost).

Check (2) Direct labor cost, $34,000

2. Only one job remained in the goods in process inventory at December 31, 2009. Its direct materials cost is $40,000. How much direct labor cost and overhead cost are assigned to it?

The following information is available for SafeLife Company, which produces special-order security products and uses a job order cost accounting system.

Exercise 19-5
Cost flows in a job order cost system
C3 P3

	April 30	May 31
Inventories		
Raw materials	$27,000	$ 41,000
Goods in process	9,000	20,600
Finished goods	70,000	33,000
Activities and information for May		
Raw materials purchases (paid with cash)		183,000
Factory payroll (paid with cash)		500,000
Factory overhead		
Indirect materials		6,000
Indirect labor		74,000
Other overhead costs		95,500
Sales (received in cash)		1,500,000
Predetermined overhead rate based on direct labor cost		55%

Compute the following amounts for the month of May.

1. Cost of direct materials used.   **4.** Cost of goods sold.*

2. Cost of direct labor used.   **5.** Gross profit.

3. Cost of goods manufactured.   **6.** Overapplied or underapplied overhead.

*Do not consider any underapplied or overapplied overhead.

Check (3) $811,700

Use information in Exercise 19-5 to prepare journal entries for the following events in May.

Exercise 19-6
Journal entries for a job order cost accounting system
P1 P2 P3 P4

1. Raw materials purchases for cash.

2. Direct materials usage.

3. Indirect materials usage.

4. Factory payroll costs in cash.

5. Direct labor usage.

6. Indirect labor usage.

7. Factory overhead excluding indirect materials and indirect labor (record credit to Other Accounts).

8. Application of overhead to goods in process.

9. Transfer of finished jobs to the finished goods inventory.

10. Sale and delivery of finished goods to customers for cash (record unadjusted cost of sales).

11. Allocation (closing) of overapplied or underapplied overhead to Cost of Goods Sold.

In December 2008, Dreamvision established its predetermined overhead rate for movies produced during year 2009 by using the following cost predictions: overhead costs, $1,700,000, and direct labor costs, $500,000. At year end 2009, the company's records show that actual overhead costs for the year are $1,710,000. Actual direct labor cost had been assigned to jobs as follows.

Exercise 19-7
Factory overhead computed, applied, and adjusted
P3 P4

Movies completed and released	$400,000
Movies still in production	90,000
Total actual direct labor cost	$490,000

1. Determine the predetermined overhead rate for year 2009.

2. Set up a T-account for overhead and enter the overhead costs incurred and the amounts applied to movies during the year using the predetermined overhead rate.

3. Determine whether overhead is overapplied or underapplied (and the amount) during the year.

Check (3) $44,000 underapplied

4. Prepare the adjusting entry to allocate any over- or underapplied overhead to Cost of Goods Sold.

Exercise 19-8
Factory overhead computed,
applied, and adjusted
P3   P4

In December 2008, Jens Company established its predetermined overhead rate for jobs produced during year 2009 by using the following cost predictions: overhead costs, $1,500,000, and direct labor costs, $1,250,000. At year end 2009, the company's records show that actual overhead costs for the year are $1,660,000. Actual direct labor cost had been assigned to jobs as follows.

Jobs completed and sold	$1,027,500
Jobs in finished goods inventory	205,500
Jobs in goods in process inventory	137,000
Total actual direct labor cost	$1,370,000

1. Determine the predetermined overhead rate for year 2009.

2. Set up a T-account for Factory Overhead and enter the overhead costs incurred and the amounts applied to jobs during the year using the predetermined overhead rate.

Check   (3) $16,000 underapplied

3. Determine whether overhead is overapplied or underapplied (and the amount) during the year.

4. Prepare the adjusting entry to allocate any over- or underapplied overhead to Cost of Goods Sold.

Exercise 19-9
Overhead rate calculation,
allocation, and analysis   P3

Campton Company applies factory overhead based on direct labor costs. The company incurred the following costs during 2009: direct materials costs, $635,500; direct labor costs, $2,000,000; and factory overhead costs applied, $1,200,000.

1. Determine the company's predetermined overhead rate for year 2009.

2. Assuming that the company's $54,000 ending Goods in Process Inventory account for year 2009 had $13,000 of direct labor costs, determine the inventory's direct materials costs.

Check   (3) $75,000 overhead costs

3. Assuming that the company's $337,435 ending Finished Goods Inventory account for year 2009 had $137,435 of direct materials costs, determine the inventory's direct labor costs and its overhead costs.

Exercise 19-10
Costs allocated to
ending inventories
P3

Santana Company's ending Goods in Process Inventory account consists of 10,000 units of partially completed product, and its Finished Goods Inventory account consists of 12,000 units of product. The factory manager determines that Goods in Process Inventory includes direct materials cost of $20 per unit and direct labor cost of $14 per unit. Finished goods are estimated to have $24 of direct materials cost per unit and $18 of direct labor cost per unit. The company established the predetermined overhead rate using the following predictions: estimated direct labor cost, $600,000, and estimated factory overhead, $750,000. The company allocates factory overhead to its goods in process and finished goods inventories based on direct labor cost. During the period, the company incurred these costs: direct materials, $1,070,000; direct labor, $580,000; and factory overhead applied, $725,000.

1. Determine the predetermined overhead rate.

2. Compute the total cost of the two ending inventories.

Check   (3) Cost of goods sold,
          $1,086,000

3. Compute cost of goods sold for the year (assume no beginning inventories and no underapplied or overapplied overhead).

Exercise 19-11
Cost-based pricing
A1

Clemente Corporation has requested bids from several architects to design its new corporate headquarters. Troy Architects is one of the firms bidding on the job. Troy estimates that the job will require the following direct labor.

	Labor	Estimated Hours	Hourly Rate
1			
2	Architects	300	$400
3	Staff	300	65
4	Clerical	600	20

Troy applies overhead to jobs at 160% of direct labor cost. Troy would like to earn at least $90,000 profit on the architectural job. Based on past experience and market research, it estimates that the competition will bid between $450,000 and $550,000 for the job.

1. What is Troy's estimated cost of the architectural job?

Check   (1) $393,900

2. What bid would you suggest that Troy submit?

McGraw-Hill's
HOMEWORK
MANAGER   Available with McGraw-Hill's Homework Manager

Lemmon Co.'s March 31 inventory of raw materials is $170,000. Raw materials purchases in April are $310,000, and factory payroll cost in April is $224,000. Overhead costs incurred in April are: indirect materials, $25,000; indirect labor, $19,000; factory rent, $25,000; factory utilities, $13,000; and factory equipment depreciation, $41,000. The predetermined overhead rate is 65% of direct labor cost. Job 306 is sold for $400,000 cash in April. Costs of the three jobs worked on in April follow.

PROBLEM SET A

Problem 19-1A
Production costs computed and recorded; reports prepared

C3 P1 P2 P3 P4

	Job 306	Job 307	Job 308
Balances on March 31			
Direct materials	$ 9,000	$ 17,000	
Direct labor	19,000	5,000	
Applied overhead	12,350	3,250	
Costs during April			
Direct materials	75,000	160,000	$ 65,000
Direct labor	31,000	74,000	100,000
Applied overhead	?	?	?
Status on April 30	Finished (sold)	Finished (unsold)	In process

Required

1. Determine the total of each production cost incurred for April (direct labor, direct materials, and applied overhead), and the total cost assigned to each job (including the balances from March 31).

2. Prepare journal entries for the month of April to record the following.

   a. Materials purchases (on credit), factory payroll (paid in cash), and actual overhead costs including indirect materials and indirect labor. (Factory rent and utilities are paid in cash.)

   b. Assignment of direct materials, direct labor, and applied overhead costs to the Goods in Process Inventory.

   c. Transfer of Jobs 306 and 307 to the Finished Goods Inventory.

   d. Cost of goods sold for Job 306.

   e. Revenue from the sale of Job 306.

   f. Assignment of any underapplied or overapplied overhead to the Cost of Goods Sold account. (The amount is not material.)

Check   (2f) $10,250 overapplied

3. Prepare a manufacturing statement for April (use a single line presentation for direct materials and show the details of overhead cost).

(3) Cost of goods manufactured, $473,850

4. Compute gross profit for April. Show how to present the inventories on the April 30 balance sheet.

Analysis Component

5. The over- or underapplied overhead is closed to Cost of Goods Sold. Discuss how this adjustment impacts business decision making regarding individual jobs or batches of jobs.

Mead Bay's computer system generated the following trial balance on December 31, 2009. The company's manager knows something is wrong with the trial balance because it does not show any balance for Goods in Process Inventory but does show balances for the Factory Payroll and Factory Overhead accounts.

Problem 19-2A
Source documents, journal entries, overhead, and financial reports

P1 P2 P3 P4

	Debit	Credit
Cash	$ 40,000	
Accounts receivable	34,000	
Raw materials inventory	22,000	

[continued on next page]

[continued from previous page]

Goods in process inventory	0	
Finished goods inventory	12,000	
Prepaid rent	4,000	
Accounts payable		$ 8,500
Notes payable		11,500
Common stock		40,000
Retained earnings		84,000
Sales		178,000
Cost of goods sold	112,000	
Factory payroll	18,000	
Factory overhead	26,000	
Operating expenses	54,000	
Totals	$322,000	$322,000

After examining various files, the manager identifies the following six source documents that need to be processed to bring the accounting records up to date.

Materials requisition 21-3010:	$4,100 direct materials to Job 402
Materials requisition 21-3011:	$7,100 direct materials to Job 404
Materials requisition 21-3012:	$2,400 indirect materials
Labor time ticket 6052:	$2,000 direct labor to Job 402
Labor time ticket 6053:	$15,000 direct labor to Job 404
Labor time ticket 6054:	$1,000 indirect labor

Jobs 402 and 404 are the only units in process at year-end. The predetermined overhead rate is 150% of direct labor cost.

Required

1. Use information on the six source documents to prepare journal entries to assign the following costs.
   a. Direct materials costs to Goods in Process Inventory.
   b. Direct labor costs to Goods in Process Inventory.
   c. Overhead costs to Goods in Process Inventory.
   d. Indirect materials costs to the Factory Overhead account.
   e. Indirect labor costs to the Factory Overhead account.

Check (2) $3,900 underapplied
overhead

2. Determine the revised balance of the Factory Overhead account after making the entries in part 1. Determine whether there is any under- or overapplied overhead for the year. Prepare the adjusting entry to allocate any over- or underapplied overhead to Cost of Goods Sold, assuming the amount is not material.

(3) T. B. totals, $322,000

(4) Net income, $8,100

3. Prepare a revised trial balance.
4. Prepare an income statement for year 2009 and a balance sheet as of December 31, 2009.

Analysis Component

5. Assume that the $2,400 on materials requisition 21-3012 should have been direct materials charged to Job 404. Without providing specific calculations, describe the impact of this error on the income statement for 2009 and the balance sheet at December 31, 2009.

Problem 19-3A
Source documents, journal entries, and accounts in job order cost accounting

P1 P2 P3

Challenger Watercraft's predetermined overhead rate for year 2009 is 200% of direct labor. Information on the company's production activities during May 2009 follows.
a. Purchased raw materials on credit, $200,000.
b. Paid $130,000 cash for factory wages.
c. Paid $16,000 cash to a computer consultant to reprogram factory equipment.
d. Materials requisitions record use of the following materials for the month.

Job 136	$ 50,000
Job 137	33,000
Job 138	19,800
Job 139	22,600
Job 140	6,800
Total direct materials	132,200
Indirect materials	20,000
Total materials used	$152,200

e. Time tickets record use of the following labor for the month.

Job 136	$ 12,100
Job 137	10,800
Job 138	37,500
Job 139	39,400
Job 140	3,200
Total direct labor	103,000
Indirect labor	27,000
Total	$130,000

f. Applied overhead to Jobs 136, 138, and 139.

g. Transferred Jobs 136, 138, and 139 to Finished Goods.

h. Sold Jobs 136 and 138 on credit at a total price of $550,000.

i. The company incurred the following overhead costs during the month (credit Prepaid Insurance for expired factory insurance).

Depreciation of factory building	$68,500
Depreciation of factory equipment	37,500
Expired factory insurance	11,000
Accrued property taxes payable	35,000

j. Applied overhead at month-end to the Goods in Process (Jobs 137 and 140) using the predetermined overhead rate of 200% of direct labor cost.

Required

1. Prepare a job cost sheet for each job worked on during the month. Use the following simplified form.

Job No. _____	
Materials	$ _____
Labor	_____
Overhead	_____
Total cost	$ _____

2. Prepare journal entries to record the events and transactions *a* through *j*.

3. Set up T-accounts for each of the following general ledger accounts, each of which started the month with a zero balance: Raw Materials Inventory; Goods in Process Inventory; Finished Goods Inventory; Factory Payroll; Factory Overhead; Cost of Goods Sold. Then post the journal entries to these T-accounts and determine the balance of each account.

4. Prepare a report showing the total cost of each job in process and prove that the sum of their costs equals the Goods in Process Inventory account balance. Prepare similar reports for Finished Goods Inventory and Cost of Goods Sold.

Check (2f) Cr. Factory Overhead, $178,000

Check (3) Finished Goods Inventory, $140,800

Problem 19-4A

Overhead allocation and adjustment using a predetermined overhead rate

C3 P3 P4

mhhe.com/wildFAP19e

In December 2008, Zander Company's manager estimated next year's total direct labor cost assuming 50 persons working an average of 2,000 hours each at an average wage rate of $30 per hour. The manager also estimated the following manufacturing overhead costs for year 2009.

Indirect labor	$ 339,200
Factory supervision	240,000
Rent on factory building	140,000
Factory utilities	318,000
Factory insurance expired	88,000
Depreciation—Factory equipment	480,000
Repairs expense—Factory equipment	60,000
Factory supplies used	88,800
Miscellaneous production costs	46,000
Total estimated overhead costs	$1,800,000

At the end of 2009, records show the company incurred $1,554,900 of actual overhead costs. It completed and sold five jobs with the following direct labor costs: Job 201, $604,000; Job 202, $573,000; Job 203, $318,000; Job 204, $726,000; and Job 205, $324,000. In addition, Job 206 is in process at the end of 2009 and had been charged $27,000 for direct labor. No jobs were in process at the end of 2008. The company's predetermined overhead rate is based on direct labor cost.

Required

1. Determine the following.

   a. Predetermined overhead rate for year 2009.

   b. Total overhead cost applied to each of the six jobs during year 2009.

   c. Over- or underapplied overhead at year-end 2009.

Check (1c) $11,700 underapplied

   (2) Cr. Factory Overhead $11,700

2. Assuming that any over- or underapplied overhead is not material, prepare the adjusting entry to allocate any over- or underapplied overhead to Cost of Goods Sold at the end of year 2009.

Problem 19-5A

Production transactions; subsidiary records; and source documents

P1 P2 P3 P4

If the working papers that accompany this book are unavailable, do not attempt to solve this problem.
Morton Company manufactures variations of its product, a technopress, in response to custom orders from its customers. On May 1, the company had no inventories of goods in process or finished goods but held the following raw materials.

Material M	200 units @ $125 =	$25,000
Material R	95 units @ 90 =	8,550
Paint	55 units @ 40 =	2,200
Total cost		$35,750

On May 4, the company began working on two technopresses: Job 102 for Global Company and Job 103 for Kaddo Company.

Required

Follow the instructions in this list of activities and complete the sheets provided in the working papers.

a. Purchased raw materials on credit and recorded the following information from receiving reports and invoices.

Receiving Report No. 426, Material M, 250 units at $125 each.
Receiving Report No. 427, Material R, 90 units at $90 each.

Instructions: Record these purchases with a single journal entry and post it to general ledger T-accounts, using the transaction letter *a* to identify the entry. Enter the receiving report information on the materials ledger cards.

b. Requisitioned the following raw materials for production.

> Requisition No. 35, for Job 102, 135 units of Material M.
> Requisition No. 36, for Job 102, 72 units of Material R.
> Requisition No. 37, for Job 103, 70 units of Material M.
> Requisition No. 38, for Job 103, 38 units of Material R.
> Requisition No. 39, for 15 units of paint.

Instructions: Enter amounts for direct materials requisitions on the materials ledger cards and the job cost sheets. Enter the indirect material amount on the materials ledger card and record a debit to the Indirect Materials account in the subsidiary factory overhead ledger. Do not record a journal entry at this time.

c. Received the following employee time tickets for work in May.

> Time tickets Nos. 1 to 10 for direct labor on Job 102, $45,000.
> Time tickets Nos. 11 to 30 for direct labor on Job 103, $32,500.
> Time tickets Nos. 31 to 36 for equipment repairs, $9,625.

Instructions: Record direct labor from the time tickets on the job cost sheets and then debit indirect labor to the Indirect Labor account in the subsidiary factory overhead ledger. Do not record a journal entry at this time.

d. Paid cash for the following items during the month: factory payroll, $87,125, and miscellaneous overhead items, $51,000.

Instructions: Record these payments with journal entries and then post them to the general ledger accounts. Also record a debit in the Miscellaneous Overhead account in the subsidiary factory overhead ledger.

e. Finished Job 102 and transferred it to the warehouse. The company assigns overhead to each job with a predetermined overhead rate equal to 80% of direct labor cost.

Instructions: Enter the allocated overhead on the cost sheet for Job 102, fill in the cost summary section of the cost sheet, and then mark the cost sheet "Finished." Prepare a journal entry to record the job's completion and its transfer to Finished Goods and then post it to the general ledger accounts.

f. Delivered Job 102 and accepted the customer's promise to pay $200,000 within 30 days.

Instructions: Prepare journal entries to record the sale of Job 102 and the cost of goods sold. Post them to the general ledger accounts.

g. Applied overhead to Job 103 based on the job's direct labor to date.

Instructions: Enter overhead on the job cost sheet but do not make a journal entry at this time.

h. Recorded the total direct and indirect materials costs as reported on all the requisitions for the month.

Instructions: Prepare a journal entry to record these costs and post it to general ledger accounts.

Check (h) Dr. Goods in Process Inventory, $35,525

i. Recorded the total direct and indirect labor costs as reported on all time tickets for the month.

Instructions: Prepare a journal entry to record these costs and post it to general ledger accounts.

j. Recorded the total overhead costs applied to jobs.

Instructions: Prepare a journal entry to record the allocation of these overhead costs and post it to general ledger accounts.

Check Balance in Factory Overhead, $775 Cr., overapplied

Grant Co.'s August 31 inventory of raw materials is $75,000. Raw materials purchases in September are $200,000, and factory payroll cost in September is $110,000. Overhead costs incurred in September are: indirect materials, $15,000; indirect labor, $7,000; factory rent, $10,000; factory utilities, $6,000; and factory equipment depreciation, $15,000. The predetermined overhead rate is 50% of direct labor cost. Job 114 is sold for $190,000 cash in September. Costs for the three jobs worked on in September follow.

PROBLEM SET B

Problem 19-1B
Production costs computed and recorded; reports prepared

C3 P1 P2 P3 P4

	Job 114	Job 115	Job 116
Balances on August 31			
Direct materials	$ 7,000	$ 9,000	
Direct labor	9,000	8,000	
Applied overhead	4,500	4,000	

[continued on next page]

[continued from previous page]

Costs during September			
Direct materials	50,000	85,000	$40,000
Direct labor	15,000	34,000	60,000
Applied overhead	?	?	?
Status on September 30	Finished (sold)	Finished (unsold)	In process

Required

1. Determine the total of each production cost incurred for September (direct labor, direct materials, and applied overhead), and the total cost assigned to each job (including the balances from August 31).

2. Prepare journal entries for the month of September to record the following.

   a. Materials purchases (on credit), factory payroll (paid in cash), and actual overhead costs including indirect materials and indirect labor. (Factory rent and utilities are paid in cash.)

   b. Assignment of direct materials, direct labor, and applied overhead costs to Goods in Process Inventory.

   c. Transfer of Jobs 114 and 115 to the Finished Goods Inventory.

   d. Cost of Job 114 in the Cost of Goods Sold account.

   e. Revenue from the sale of Job 114.

   f. Assignment of any underapplied or overapplied overhead to the Cost of Goods Sold account. (The amount is not material.)

3. Prepare a manufacturing statement for September (use a single line presentation for direct materials and show the details of overhead cost).

4. Compute gross profit for September. Show how to present the inventories on the September 30 balance sheet.

Analysis Component

5. The over- or underapplied overhead adjustment is closed to Cost of Goods Sold. Discuss how this adjustment impacts business decision making regarding individual jobs or batches of jobs.

Check (2f) $1,500 overapplied

(3) Cost of goods manufactured, $250,000

Problem 19-2B
Source documents, journal entries, overhead, and financial reports

P1 P2 P3 P4

Coleman Company's computer system generated the following trial balance on December 31, 2009. The company's manager knows that the trial balance is wrong because it does not show any balance for Goods in Process Inventory but does show balances for the Factory Payroll and Factory Overhead accounts.

	Debit	Credit
Cash	$ 96,000	
Accounts receivable	84,000	
Raw materials inventory	52,000	
Goods in process inventory	0	
Finished goods inventory	18,000	
Prepaid rent	6,000	
Accounts payable		$ 21,000
Notes payable		27,000
Common stock		60,000
Retained earnings		174,000
Sales		360,000
Cost of goods sold	210,000	
Factory payroll	32,000	
Factory overhead	54,000	
Operating expenses	90,000	
Totals	$642,000	$642,000

After examining various files, the manager identifies the following six source documents that need to be processed to bring the accounting records up to date.

Materials requisition 94-231:	$9,200 direct materials to Job 603
Materials requisition 94-232:	$15,200 direct materials to Job 604
Materials requisition 94-233:	$4,200 indirect materials
Labor time ticket 765:	$10,000 direct labor to Job 603
Labor time ticket 766:	$16,000 direct labor to Job 604
Labor time ticket 777:	$6,000 indirect labor

Jobs 603 and 604 are the only units in process at year-end. The predetermined overhead rate is 200% of direct labor cost.

Required

1. Use information on the six source documents to prepare journal entries to assign the following costs.
   a. Direct materials costs to Goods in Process Inventory.
   b. Direct labor costs to Goods in Process Inventory.
   c. Overhead costs to Goods in Process Inventory.
   d. Indirect materials costs to the Factory Overhead account.
   e. Indirect labor costs to the Factory Overhead account.

2. Determine the revised balance of the Factory Overhead account after making the entries in part 1. Determine whether there is under- or overapplied overhead for the year. Prepare the adjusting entry to allocate any over- or underapplied overhead to Cost of Goods Sold, assuming the amount is not material.

3. Prepare a revised trial balance.

4. Prepare an income statement for year 2009 and a balance sheet as of December 31, 2009.

Check (2) $12,200 underapplied overhead

(3) T. B. totals, $642,000
(4) Net income, $47,800

Analysis Component

5. Assume that the $4,200 indirect materials on materials requisition 94-233 should have been direct materials charged to Job 604. Without providing specific calculations, describe the impact of this error on the income statement for 2009 and the balance sheet at December 31, 2009.

Bradley Company's predetermined overhead rate is 200% of direct labor. Information on the company's production activities during September 2009 follows.
   a. Purchased raw materials on credit, $250,000.
   b. Paid $168,000 cash for factory wages.
   c. Paid $22,000 cash for miscellaneous factory overhead costs.
   d. Materials requisitions record use of the following materials for the month.

Problem 19-3B
Source documents, journal entries, and accounts in job order cost accounting

P1 P2 P3

Job 487	$60,000
Job 488	40,000
Job 489	24,000
Job 490	28,000
Job 491	8,000
Total direct materials	160,000
Indirect materials	24,000
Total materials used	$184,000

e. Time tickets record use of the following labor for the month.

Job 487	$ 16,000
Job 488	14,000
Job 489	50,000
Job 490	52,000
Job 491	4,000
Total direct labor	136,000
Indirect labor	32,000
Total	$168,000

f. Allocated overhead to Jobs 487, 489, and 490.

g. Transferred Jobs 487, 489, and 490 to Finished Goods.

h. Sold Jobs 487 and 489 on credit for a total price of $680,000.

i. The company incurred the following overhead costs during the month (credit Prepaid Insurance for expired factory insurance).

Depreciation of factory building	$74,000
Depreciation of factory equipment	42,000
Expired factory insurance	14,000
Accrued property taxes payable	62,000

j. Applied overhead at month-end to the Goods in Process (Jobs 488 and 491) using the predetermined overhead rate of 200% of direct labor cost.

Required

1. Prepare a job cost sheet for each job worked on in the month. Use the following simplified form.

Job No. _____
Materials . . . . $ _____
Labor . . . .   _____
Overhead . . . .   _____
Total cost . . . . $ _____

Check   (2f) Cr. Factory Overhead, $236,000

(3) Finished Goods Inventory, $184,000

2. Prepare journal entries to record the events and transactions *a* through *j*.

3. Set up T-accounts for each of the following general ledger accounts, each of which started the month with a zero balance: Raw Materials Inventory, Goods in Process Inventory, Finished Goods Inventory, Factory Payroll, Factory Overhead, Cost of Goods Sold. Then post the journal entries to these T-accounts and determine the balance of each account.

4. Prepare a report showing the total cost of each job in process and prove that the sum of their costs equals the Goods in Process Inventory account balance. Prepare similar reports for Finished Goods Inventory and Cost of Goods Sold.

Problem 19-4B
Overhead allocation and adjustment using a predetermined overhead rate

C3   P3   P4

In December 2008, Bigby Company's manager estimated next year's total direct labor cost assuming 100 persons working an average of 2,000 hours each at an average wage rate of $15 per hour. The manager also estimated the following manufacturing overhead costs for year 2009.

Indirect labor	$ 319,200
Factory supervision	240,000
Rent on factory building	140,000
Factory utilities	88,000
Factory insurance expired	68,000
Depreciation—Factory equipment	480,000
Repairs expense—Factory equipment	60,000
Factory supplies used	68,800
Miscellaneous production costs	36,000
Total estimated overhead costs	$1,500,000

At the end of 2009, records show the company incurred $1,450,000 of actual overhead costs. It completed and sold five jobs with the following direct labor costs: Job 625, $708,000; Job 626, $660,000; Job 627, $350,000; Job 628, $840,000; and Job 629, $368,000. In addition, Job 630 is in process at the end of 2009 and had been charged $20,000 for direct labor. No jobs were in process at the end of 2008. The company's predetermined overhead rate is based on direct labor cost.

Required

1. Determine the following.

   a. Predetermined overhead rate for year 2009.

   b. Total overhead cost applied to each of the six jobs during year 2009.

   c. Over- or underapplied overhead at year-end 2009.

2. Assuming that any over- or underapplied overhead is not material, prepare the adjusting entry to allocate any over- or underapplied overhead to Cost of Goods Sold at the end of year 2009.

Check   (1c) $23,000 overapplied

(2) Dr. Factory Overhead, $23,000

If the working papers that accompany this book are unavailable, do not attempt to solve this problem. Parador Company produces variations of its product, a megatron, in response to custom orders from its customers. On June 1, the company had no inventories of goods in process or finished goods but held the following raw materials.

Problem 19-5B
Production transactions; subsidiary records; and source documents

P1 P2 P3 P4

Material M	120 units @ $400 =	$48,000
Material R	80 units @ 320 =	25,600
Paint	44 units @ 144 =	6,336
Total cost		$79,936

On June 3, the company began working on two megatrons: Job 450 for Doso Company and Job 451 for Border, Inc.

Required

Follow instructions in this list of activities and complete the sheets provided in the working papers.

a. Purchased raw materials on credit and recorded the following information from receiving reports and invoices.

> Receiving Report No. 20, Material M, 150 units at $400 each.
> Receiving Report No. 21, Material R, 70 units at $320 each.

Instructions: Record these purchases with a single journal entry and post it to general ledger T-accounts, using the transaction letter *a* to identify the entry. Enter the receiving report information on the materials ledger cards.

b. Requisitioned the following raw materials for production.

> Requisition No. 223, for Job 450, 80 units of Material M.
> Requisition No. 224, for Job 450, 60 units of Material R.
> Requisition No. 225, for Job 451, 40 units of Material M.
> Requisition No. 226, for Job 451, 30 units of Material R.
> Requisition No. 227, for 12 units of paint.

Instructions: Enter amounts for direct materials requisitions on the materials ledger cards and the job cost sheets. Enter the indirect material amount on the materials ledger card and record a debit to the Indirect Materials account in the subsidiary factory overhead ledger. Do not record a journal entry at this time.

c. Received the following employee time tickets for work in June.

> Time tickets Nos. 1 to 10 for direct labor on Job 450, $80,000.
> Time tickets Nos. 11 to 20 for direct labor on Job 451, $64,000.
> Time tickets Nos. 21 to 24 for equipment repairs, $24,000.

Instructions: Record direct labor from the time tickets on the job cost sheets and then debit indirect labor to the Indirect Labor account in the subsidiary factory overhead ledger. Do not record a journal entry at this time.

d. Paid cash for the following items during the month: factory payroll, $168,000, and miscellaneous overhead items, $73,600.

Instructions: Record these payments with journal entries and post them to the general ledger accounts. Also record a debit in the Miscellaneous Overhead account in the subsidiary factory overhead ledger.

e. Finished Job 450 and transferred it to the warehouse. The company assigns overhead to each job with a predetermined overhead rate equal to 70% of direct labor cost.

Instructions: Enter the allocated overhead on the cost sheet for Job 450, fill in the cost summary section of the cost sheet, and then mark the cost sheet "Finished." Prepare a journal entry to record the job's completion and its transfer to Finished Goods and then post it to the general ledger accounts.

f. Delivered Job 450 and accepted the customer's promise to pay $580,000 within 30 days.

Instructions: Prepare journal entries to record the sale of Job 450 and the cost of goods sold. Post them to the general ledger accounts.

g. Applied overhead cost to Job 451 based on the job's direct labor used to date.

Instructions: Enter overhead on the job cost sheet but do not make a journal entry at this time.

Check (h) Dr. Goods in Process Inventory, $76,800

h. Recorded the total direct and indirect materials costs as reported on all the requisitions for the month.

Instructions: Prepare a journal entry to record these costs and post it to general ledger accounts.

i. Recorded the total direct and indirect labor costs as reported on all time tickets for the month.

Instructions: Prepare a journal entry to record these costs and post it to general ledger accounts.

j. Recorded the total overhead costs applied to jobs.

Check Balance in Factory Overhead, $1,472 Cr., overapplied

Instructions: Prepare a journal entry to record the allocation of these overhead costs and post it to general ledger accounts.

SERIAL PROBLEM

Success Systems

(This serial problem began in Chapter 1 and continues through most of the book. If previous chapter segments were not completed, the serial problem can begin at this point. It is helpful, but not necessary, to use the Working Papers that accompany the book.)

SP 19   The computer workstation furniture manufacturing that Adriana Lopez started in January is progressing well. As of the end of June, Success Systems' job cost sheets show the following total costs accumulated on three furniture jobs.

	Job 6.02	Job 6.03	Job 6.04
Direct materials	$1,500	$3,300	$2,700
Direct labor	800	1,420	2,100
Overhead	400	710	1,050

Job 6.02 was started in production in May, and these costs were assigned to it in May: direct materials, $600; direct labor, $180; and overhead, $90. Jobs 6.03 and 6.04 were started in June. Overhead cost is applied with a predetermined rate based on direct labor costs. Jobs 6.02 and 6.03 are finished in June, and Job 6.04 is expected to be finished in July. No raw materials are used indirectly in June. (Assume this company's predetermined overhead rate did not change over these months).

Required

Check (1) Total materials, $6,900

(3) 50%

1. What is the cost of the raw materials used in June for each of the three jobs and in total?

2. How much total direct labor cost is incurred in June?

3. What predetermined overhead rate is used in June?

4. How much cost is transferred to finished goods inventory in June?

BEYOND THE NUMBERS

REPORTING IN ACTION

C2

BTN 19-1   Best Buy's financial statements and notes in Appendix A provide evidence of growth potential in its domestic sales.

Required

1. Identify at least two types of costs that will predictably increase as a percent of sales with growth in domestic sales.

2. Explain why you believe the types of costs identified for part 1 will increase, and describe how you might assess Best Buy's success with these costs. (*Hint:* You might consider the gross margin ratio.)

Fast Forward

3. Access Best Buy's annual report for a fiscal year ending after March 3, 2007, from its Website [BestBuy.com] or the SEC's EDGAR database [www.sec.gov]. Review and report its growth in sales along with its cost and income levels (including its gross margin ratio).

BTN 19-2   Retailers as well as manufacturers can apply just-in-time (JIT) to their inventory management. Both **Best Buy** and **Circuit City** want to know the impact of a JIT inventory system for their operating cash flows. Review each company's statement of cash flows in Appendix A to answer the following.

COMPARATIVE ANALYSIS

C1

Required

1. Identify the impact on operating cash flows (increase or decrease) for changes in inventory levels (increase or decrease) for both companies for each of the three most recent years.

2. What impact would a JIT inventory system have on both Best Buy's and Circuit City's operating income? Link the answer to your response for part 1.

3. Would the move to a JIT system have a one-time or recurring impact on operating cash flow?

BTN 19-3   An accounting professional requires at least two skill sets. The first is to be technically competent. Knowing how to capture, manage, and report information is a necessary skill. Second, the ability to assess manager and employee actions and biases for accounting analysis is another skill. For instance, knowing how a person is compensated helps anticipate information biases. Draw on these skills and write a one-half page memo to the financial officer on the following practice of allocating overhead.

Background: Assume that your company sells portable housing to both general contractors and the government. It sells jobs to contractors on a bid basis. A contractor asks for three bids from different manufacturers. The combination of low bid and high quality wins the job. However, jobs sold to the government are bid on a cost-plus basis. This means price is determined by adding all costs plus a profit based on cost at a specified percent, such as 10%. You observe that the amount of overhead allocated to government jobs is higher than that allocated to contract jobs. These allocations concern you and motivate your memo.

ETHICS CHALLENGE

P3

Point: Students could compare responses and discuss differences in concerns with allocating overhead.

BTN 19-4   Assume that you are preparing for a second interview with a manufacturing company. The company is impressed with your credentials but has indicated that it has several qualified applicants. You anticipate that in this second interview, you must show what you offer over other candidates. You learn the company currently uses a periodic inventory system and is not satisfied with the timeliness of its information and its inventory management. The company manufactures custom-order holiday decorations and display items. To show your abilities, you plan to recommend that it use a cost accounting system.

COMMUNICATING IN PRACTICE

C2   C3

Required

In preparation for the interview, prepare notes outlining the following:

1. Your cost accounting system recommendation and why it is suitable for this company.

2. A general description of the documents that the proposed cost accounting system requires.

3. How the documents in part 2 facilitate the operation of the cost accounting system.

Point: Have students present a mock interview, one assuming the role of the president of the company and the other the applicant.

TAKING IT TO THE NET

C2

BTN 19-5　Many contractors work on custom jobs that require a job order costing system.

Required

Access the Website **AMSI.com** and click on *Construction Management Software,* and then on STARBUILDER. Prepare a one-page memorandum for the CEO of a construction company providing information about the job order costing software this company offers. Would you recommend that the company purchase this software?

TEAMWORK IN ACTION

C2

BTN 19-6　Consider the activities undertaken by a medical clinic in your area.

Required

1. Do you consider a job order cost accounting system appropriate for the clinic?
2. Identify as many factors as possible to lead you to conclude that it uses a job order system.

ENTREPRENEURIAL DECISION

C2

BTN 19-7　Refer to the chapter opener regarding Hank Julicher and his company, **Sprinturf**. All successful businesses track their costs, and it is especially important for startup businesses to monitor and control costs.

Required

1. Assume that Sprinturf uses a job order costing system. For the three basic cost categories of direct materials, direct labor, and overhead, identify at least two typical costs that would fall into each category for Sprinturf.
2. Assume a local high school expresses an interest in purchasing a synthetic field installation from Sprinturf. The high school's budget will allow them to pay no more than $600,000 for the field. How can Sprinturf use job cost information to assess whether to pursue this opportunity?

HITTING THE ROAD

C3　P2　P3　P4

BTN 19-8　Job order cost accounting is frequently used by home builders.

Required

1. You (or your team) are to prepare a job cost sheet for a single-family home under construction. List four items of both direct materials and direct labor. Explain how you think overhead should be applied.
2. Contact a builder and compare your job cost sheet to this builder's job cost sheet. If possible, speak to that company's accountant. Write your findings in a short report.

GLOBAL DECISION

C1

BTN 19-9　**DSG, Circuit City,** and **Best Buy** are competitors in the global marketplace. Access DSG's annual report (**www.DSGiplc.com**) for the year ended April 28, 2007. The following information is available for DSG.

(£ millions)	Current Year	One Year Prior	Two Years Prior
Inventories	£1,030	£873	£811

Required

1. Determine the change in DSG's inventories for the last two years. Then identify the impact on net resources generated by operating activities (increase or decrease) for changes in inventory levels (increase or decrease) for DSG for the last two years.

2. Would a move to a JIT system likely impact DSG more than it would Best Buy or Circuit City? Explain.

ANSWERS TO MULTIPLE CHOICE QUIZ

1. c; $30,000 \times 150\% = \$45,000$

2. b; $38,500/\$35,000 = \underline{110\%}$

3. e; Direct materials + Direct labor + Overhead = Total cost;
   Direct materials + ($4,000/.80) + \$4,000 = \$10,000$
   Direct materials = $\underline{\$1,000}$

4. e; $9,000 + \$94,200 + \$59,200 + \$31,600 -$ Finished goods $= \$17,800$
   Thus, finished goods = $\underline{\$176,200}$

5. b

A Look Back

Chapter 18 introduced managerial accounting and described cost concepts and the reporting of manufacturing activities. Chapter 19 explained job order costing—an important cost accounting system for customized products and services.

A Look at This Chapter

This chapter focuses on how to measure and account for costs in process operations. We explain process production, describe how to assign costs to processes, and compute cost per equivalent unit for a process.

A Look Ahead

Chapter 21 explains how to allocate factory overhead costs to different products and introduces the activity-based costing method of overhead allocation. It also explains responsibility accounting and measures of departmental performance.

20
Chapter

Process Cost Accounting

Learning Objectives

CAP

Conceptual

C1 Explain process operations and the way they differ from job order operations. (p. 808)

C2 Define equivalent units and explain their use in process cost accounting. (p. 815)

C3 Explain the four steps in accounting for production activity in a period. (p. 816)

C4 Define a process cost summary and describe its purposes. (p. 820)

C5 *Appendix 20A*—Explain and illustrate the four steps in accounting for production activity using FIFO. (p. 827)

Analytical

A1 Compare process cost accounting and job order cost accounting. (p. 809)

A2 Explain and illustrate a hybrid costing system. (p. 823)

Procedural

P1 Record the flow of direct materials costs in process cost accounting. (p. 812)

P2 Record the flow of direct labor costs in process cost accounting. (p. 813)

P3 Record the flow of factory overhead costs in process cost accounting. (p. 813)

P4 Compute equivalent units produced in a period. (p. 815)

P5 Prepare a process cost summary. (p. 820)

P6 Record the transfer of completed goods to Finished Goods Inventory and Cost of Goods Sold. (p. 821)

LP20

The Big Apple

"If we are willing to eat it, we're willing to squeeze it"
—David Ryan

HOOD RIVER, OR—After a few years of working in the family business of growing apples and making cider, David Ryan launched his own company, **Hood River Juice Company** [HRJCO.com], to focus on the processing stage of apple juice and cider. Like many entrepreneurs, David sought guidance from experienced mentors, in his case the Small Business Development Center located in the local community college. These mentors explained managerial accounting and the financial aspects of successful manufacturing.

Today, before an apple enters David's production process, it is inspected by his drivers when the apples are loaded from the field. A foreman then inspects the apples again when unloading them at his factory. David's factory employees then wash and hand select the best apples from those that survive the previous two inspections.

Apple quality is paramount. Explains David, "If we are willing to eat it, we're willing to squeeze it." From cutting apples into small pieces and squeezing those pieces into juice, through filtering the juice and packaging the finished product, David's production process is monitored and accounting reports are produced.

Entrepreneurs such as David are aided by process cost summaries that help them monitor and control the costs of material, labor, and overhead applied to production processes. For example, David tries to maintain regular full-time employees to better manage costs. Thus, he purchases and processes apples year-round as opposed to only seasonal production. David estimates this year-round process reduces his overhead costs by 40%. "Needless to say, every company has their own overhead they have to deal with," explains David. "If your total throughput is down by 35%, you must look elsewhere to get the margin to be sustainable. The only way to do that is to cut your overhead." Managerial accounting information aids in his decisions.

David's focus on cost management minimizes the risk of bad decisions, and his passion for quality control enables him to improve process operations. His overriding goal is customer satisfaction. That focus has led him to produce bulk apple juice for use in protein shakes and smoothies, and it has allowed his customers to select from over 50 varieties of apples for a custom-blended juice. Juice drinkers seem happy: From an initial investment of $36,000 in 2000, David's annual sales now exceed $14 million. Those are juicy numbers.

[Sources: *Hood River Juice Company Website,* January 2009; *Yakima-Herald.com,* March 2008; *Hood River News,* February 2006; *Entrepreneur,* April 2008]

The type of product or service a company offers determines its cost accounting system. Job order costing is used to account for custom products and services that meet the demands of a particular customer. Not all products are manufactured in this way; many carry standard designs so that one unit is no different than any other unit. Such a system often produces large numbers of units on a continuous basis, all of which pass through similar processes. This chapter describes how to use a process cost accounting system to account for these types of products. It also explains how costs are accumulated for each process and then assigned to units passing through those processes. This information helps us understand and estimate the cost of each process as well as find ways to reduce costs and improve processes.

Process Cost Accounting

Process Operations	Process Cost Accounting	Equivalent Units of Production (EUP)	Process Costing Illustration
• Comparing job order and process operations • Organization of process operations • GenX Company— an illustration	• Direct and indirect costs • Accounting for materials costs • Accounting for labor costs • Accounting for factory overhead	• Accounting for goods in process • Differences between EUP for materials, labor, and overhead	• Physical flow of units • EUP • Cost per EUP • Cost reconciliation • Process cost summary • Transfers to finished goods and to cost of goods sold

Process Operations

C1 Explain process operations and the way they differ from job order operations.

Process operations, also called *process manufacturing* or *process production,* is the mass production of products in a continuous flow of steps. This means that products pass through a series of sequential processes. Petroleum refining is a common example of process operations. Crude oil passes through a series of steps before it is processed into different grades of petroleum. **Exxon Mobil**'s oil activities reflect a process operation. An important characteristic of process operations is the high level of standardization necessary if the system is to produce large volumes of products. Process operations also extend to services. Examples include mail sorting in large post offices and order processing in large mail-order firms such as **L.L. Bean.** The common feature in these service organizations is that operations are performed in a sequential manner using a series of standardized processes. Other companies using process operations include **Kellogg** (cereals), **Pfizer** (drugs), **Procter & Gamble** (household products), **Xerox** (copiers), **Coca-Cola** (soft drinks), **Heinz** (ketchup), **Penn** (tennis balls), and **Hershey** (chocolate). For a virtual tour of tennis ball manufacturing, see pennracquet.com/factory.html.

Each of these examples of products and services involves operations having a series of *processes,* or steps. Each process involves a different set of activities. A production operation that processes chemicals, for instance, might include the four steps shown in Exhibit 20.1. Understanding such processes for companies with process operations is crucial for measuring their costs. Increasingly, process operations use machines and automation to control product quality and reduce manufacturing costs.

| Preparing the chemicals | → | Mixing the chemicals | → | Bottling the chemical mix | → | Packaging the bottles |

Comparing Job Order and Process Operations

Job order and process operations can be considered as two ends of a continuum. Important features of both systems are shown in Exhibit 20.2. We often describe job order and process operations with manufacturing examples, but both also apply to service companies. In a job order costing system, the measurement focus is on the individual job or batch. In a process costing system, the measurement focus is on the process itself and the standardized units produced.

| A1 | Compare process cost accounting and job order cost accounting. |

EXHIBIT 20.2

Comparing Job Order and Process Operations

Job Order Operations	Process Operations
• Custom orders	• Repetitive procedures
• Heterogeneous products and services	• Homogeneous products and services
• Low production volume	• High production volume
• High product flexibility	• Low product flexibility
• Low to medium standardization	• High standardization

Organization of Process Operations

In a process operation, each process is identified as a separate *production department, workstation,* or *work center.* With the exception of the first process or department, each receives the output from the prior department as a partially processed product. Depending on the nature of the process, a company applies direct labor, overhead, and, perhaps, additional direct materials to move the product toward completion. Only the final process or department in the series produces finished goods ready for sale to customers.

Tracking costs for several related departments can seem complex. Yet because process costing procedures are applied to the activity of each department or process separately, we need to consider only one process at a time. This simplifies the procedures.

When the output of one department becomes an input to another department, as is the case in sequential processing, we simply transfer the costs associated with those units from the first department into the next. We repeat these steps from department to department until the final process is complete. At that point the accumulated costs are transferred with the product from Goods in Process Inventory to Finished Goods Inventory. The next section illustrates a company with a single process, but the methods illustrated apply to a multiprocess scenario as each department's costs are handled separately for each department.

Decision Insight

Accounting for Health   Many service companies use process departments to perform specific tasks for consumers. Hospitals, for instance, have radiology and physical therapy facilities with special equipment and trained employees. When patients need services, they are processed through departments to receive prescribed care. Service companies need process cost accounting information as much as manufacturers to estimate costs of services, to plan future operations, to control costs, and to determine customer charges.

GenX Company— An Illustration

The GenX Company illustrates process operations. It produces Profen®, an over-the-counter pain reliever for athletes. GenX sells Profen to wholesale distributors, who in turn sell it to retailers. Profen is produced by mixing its active ingredient, Profelene, with flavorings and preservatives, molding it into Profen tablets, and packaging the tablets. Exhibit 20.3 shows a summary floor plan of the GenX factory, which has five areas.

1. *Storeroom*—materials are received and then distributed when requisitioned.
2. *Production support offices*—used by administrative and maintenance employees who support manufacturing operations.
3. *Locker rooms*—workers change from street clothes into sanitized uniforms before working in the factory.
4. *Production floor*—area where the powder is processed into tablets.
5. *Warehouse*—finished products are stored before being shipped to wholesalers.

Point: Electronic monitoring of operations is common in factories.

EXHIBIT 20.3

Floor Plan of GenX's Factory

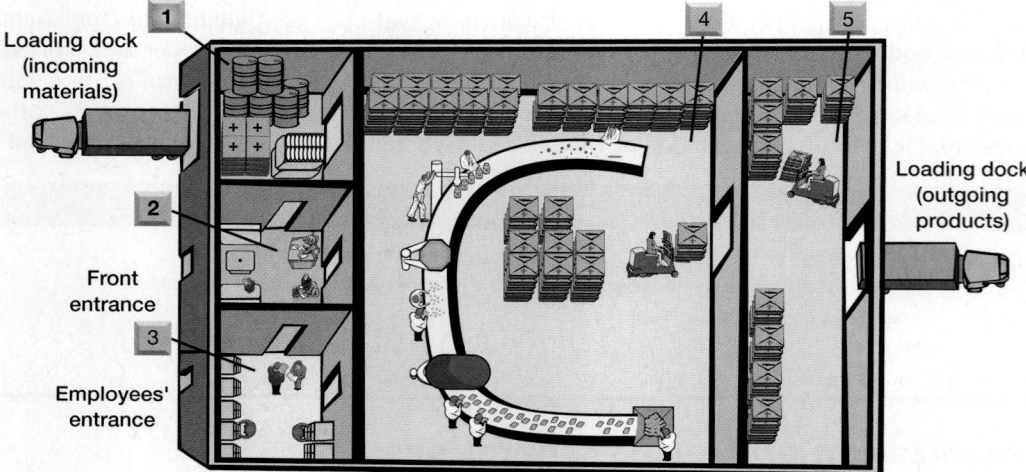

The first step in process manufacturing is to decide when to produce a product. Management determines the types and quantities of materials and labor needed and then schedules the work. Unlike a job order process, where production often begins only after receipt of a custom order, managers of companies with process operations often forecast the demand expected for their products. Based on these plans, production begins. The flowchart in Exhibit 20.4 shows the production steps for GenX. The following sections explain how GenX uses a process cost accounting system to compute these costs. Many of the explanations refer to this exhibit and its numbered cost flows ① through ⑩. (*Hint:* The amounts for the numbered cost flows in Exhibit 20.4 are summarized in Exhibit 20.21. Those amounts are explained in the following pages, but it can help to refer to Exhibit 20.21 as we proceed through the explanations.)

EXHIBIT 20.4

Process Operations and Costs: GenX

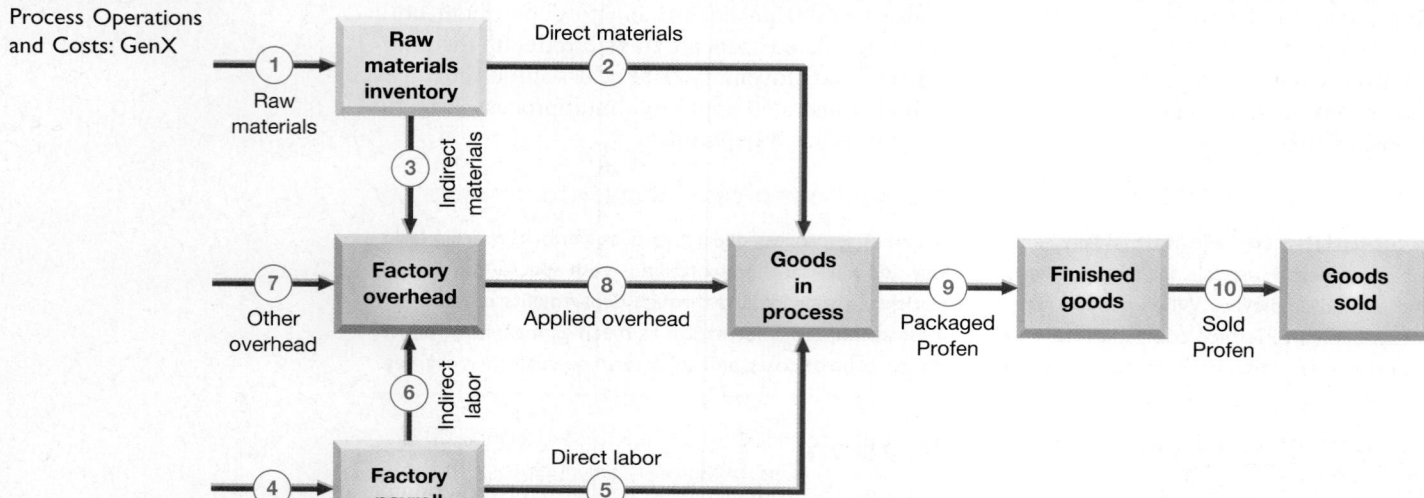

Process Cost Accounting

Process and job order operations are similar in that both combine materials, labor, and overhead in the process of producing products. They differ in how they are organized and managed. The measurement focus in a job order costing system is on the individual job or batch, whereas in a process costing system, it is on the individual process. Regardless of the measurement focus, we are ultimately interested in determining the cost per unit of product (or service) resulting from either system.

Specifically, the **job order cost accounting system** assigns direct materials, direct labor, and overhead to jobs. The total job cost is then divided by the number of units to compute a cost per unit for that job. The **process cost accounting system** assigns direct materials, direct labor, and overhead to specific processes (or departments). The total costs associated with each process are then divided by the number of units passing through that process to determine the cost per equivalent unit (defined later in the chapter) for that process. Differences in the way these two systems apply materials, labor, and overhead costs are highlighted in Exhibit 20.5.

Video20.1

Point: The cost object in a job order system is the specific job; the cost object in a process costing system is the process.

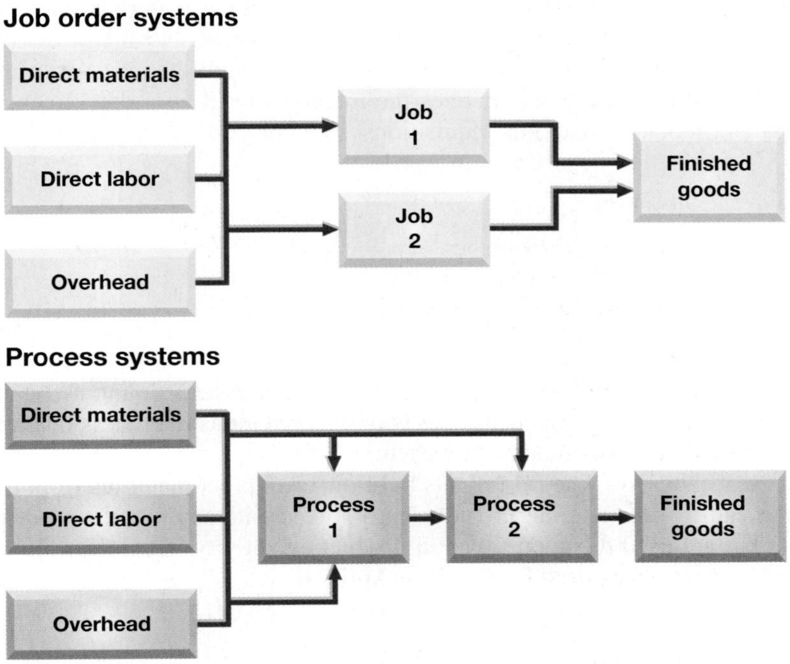

Job order systems

Direct materials → Job 1 → Finished goods
Direct labor → Job 2 → Finished goods
Overhead →

Process systems

Direct materials → Process 1 → Process 2 → Finished goods
Direct labor →
Overhead →

EXHIBIT 20.5

Comparing Job Order and Process Cost Accounting Systems

Direct and Indirect Costs

Like job order operations, process cost accounting systems use the concepts of direct and indirect costs. Materials and labor that can be traced to specific processes are assigned to those processes as direct costs. Materials and labor that cannot be traced to a specific process are indirect costs and are assigned to overhead. Some costs classified as overhead in a job order system may be classified as direct costs in process cost accounting. For example, depreciation of a machine used entirely by one process is a direct cost of that process.

Point: If a cost can be traced to the cost object, it is direct; if it cannot, it is indirect.

P1   Record the flow of direct materials costs in process cost accounting.

Accounting for Materials Costs

In Exhibit 20.4, arrow line ① reflects the arrival of materials at GenX's factory. These materials include Profelene, flavorings, preservatives, and packaging. They also include supplies for the production support office. GenX uses a perpetual inventory system and makes all purchases on credit. The summary entry for receipts of raw materials in April follows (dates in journal entries numbered ① through ⑩ are omitted because they are summary entries, often reflecting two or more transactions or events).

Assets = Liabilities + Equity
+11,095   +11,095

①	Raw Materials Inventory	11,095	
	Accounts Payable		11,095
	Acquired materials on credit for factory use.		

Arrow line ② in Exhibit 20.4 reflects the flow of direct materials to production, where they are used to produce Profen. Most direct materials are physically combined into the finished product; the remaining direct materials include those used and clearly linked with a specific process. The manager of a process usually obtains materials by submitting a *materials requisition* to the materials storeroom manager. In some situations, materials move continuously from raw materials inventory through the manufacturing process. **Pepsi Bottling**, for instance, uses a process in which inventory moves continuously through the system. In these cases, a **materials consumption report** summarizes the materials used by a department during a reporting period and replaces materials requisitions. The entry to record the use of direct materials by GenX's production department in April follows.

Assets = Liabilities + Equity
+9,900
−9,900

②	Goods in Process Inventory	9,900	
	Raw Materials Inventory		9,900
	To assign costs of direct materials used in production.		

This entry transfers costs from one asset account to another asset account. (When two or more production departments exist, a company uses two or more Goods in Process Inventory accounts to separately accumulate costs incurred by each.)

In Exhibit 20.4, the arrow line ③ reflects the flow of indirect materials from the storeroom to factory overhead. These materials are not clearly linked with any specific production process or department but are used to support overall production activity. The following entry records the cost of indirect materials used by GenX in April.

Example: What types of materials might the flow of arrow line ③ in Exhibit 20.4 reflect? *Answer:* Goggles, gloves, protective clothing, recordkeeping supplies, and cleaning supplies.

Assets = Liabilities + Equity
−1,195   −1,195

③	Factory Overhead	1,195	
	Raw Materials Inventory		1,195
	To record indirect materials used in April.		

After the entries for both direct and indirect materials are posted, the Raw Materials Inventory account appears as shown in Exhibit 20.6. The April 30 balance sheet reports the $4,000 Raw Materials Inventory account as a current asset.

EXHIBIT 20.6

Raw Materials Inventory

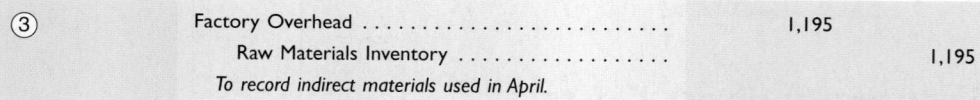

Raw Materials Inventory						Acct. No. 132
Date		Explanation		Debit	Credit	Balance
Mar.	31	Balance				4,000
Apr.	30	Materials purchases		11,095		15,095
	30	Direct materials usage			9,900	5,195
	30	Indirect materials usage			1,195	4,000

Accounting for Labor Costs

Exhibit 20.4 shows GenX factory payroll costs as reflected in arrow line ④. Total labor costs of $8,920 are paid in cash and are recorded in the Factory Payroll account.

④	Factory Payroll............................	8,920	
	Cash		8,920
	To record factory wages for April.		

> **P2** Record the flow of direct labor costs in process cost accounting.

Assets = Liabilities + Equity
−8,920   −8,920

Time reports from the production department and the production support office triggered this entry. (For simplicity, we do not separately identify withholdings and additional payroll taxes for employees.) In a process operation, the direct labor of a production department includes all labor used exclusively by that department. This is the case even if the labor is not applied to the product itself. If a production department in a process operation, for instance, has a full-time manager and a full-time maintenance worker, their salaries are direct labor costs of that process and are not factory overhead.

Arrow line ⑤ in Exhibit 20.4 shows GenX's use of direct labor in the production department. The following entry transfers April's direct labor costs from the Factory Payroll account to the Goods in Process Inventory account.

⑤	Goods in Process Inventory	5,700	
	Factory Payroll		5,700
	To assign costs of direct labor used in production.		

Assets = Liabilities + Equity
+5,700   +5,700

Arrow line ⑥ in Exhibit 20.4 reflects GenX's indirect labor costs. These employees provide clerical, maintenance, and other services that help produce Profen efficiently. For example, they order materials, deliver them to the factory floor, repair equipment, operate and program computers used in production, keep payroll and other production records, clean up, and move the finished goods to the warehouse. The following entry charges these indirect labor costs to factory overhead.

> **Point:** A department's indirect labor cost might include an allocated portion of the salary of a manager who supervises two or more departments. Allocation of costs between departments is discussed in a later chapter.

⑥	Factory Overhead	3,220	
	Factory Payroll		3,220
	To record indirect labor as overhead.		

Assets = Liabilities + Equity
                        −3,220
                        +3,220

After these entries for both direct and indirect labor are posted, the Factory Payroll account appears as shown in Exhibit 20.7. The temporary Factory Payroll account is now closed to another temporary account, Factory Overhead, and is ready to receive entries for May. Next we show how to apply overhead to production and close the temporary Factory Overhead account.

Factory Payroll			Acct. No. 530		
Date		Explanation	Debit	Credit	Balance
Mar.	31	Balance			0
Apr.	30	Total payroll for April	8,920		8,920
	30	Direct labor costs		5,700	3,220
	30	Indirect labor costs		3,220	0

EXHIBIT 20.7

Factory Payroll

Accounting for Factory Overhead

Overhead costs other than indirect materials and indirect labor are reflected by arrow line ⑦ in Exhibit 20.4. These overhead items include the costs of insuring production assets, renting the factory building, using factory utilities, and depreciating equipment not directly related to a specific process. The following entry records overhead costs for April.

> **P3** Record the flow of factory overhead costs in process cost accounting.

Assets = Liabilities + Equity
−180   +645   −2,425
−750
−850

⑦	Factory Overhead	2,425	
	Prepaid Insurance		180
	Utilities Payable		645
	Cash		750
	Accumulated Depreciation—Factory Equipment ..		850
	To record overhead items incurred in April.		

After this entry is posted, the Factory Overhead account balance is $6,840, comprising indirect materials of $1,195, indirect labor of $3,220, and $2,425 of other overhead.

Arrow line ⑧ in Exhibit 20.4 reflects the application of factory overhead to production. Factory overhead is applied to processes by relating overhead cost to another variable such as direct labor hours or machine hours used. With increasing automation, companies with process operations are more likely to use machine hours to allocate overhead. In some situations, a single allocation basis such as direct labor hours (or a single rate for the entire plant) fails to provide useful allocations. As a result, management can use different rates for different production departments. Based on an analysis of its operations, GenX applies its April overhead at a rate of 120% of direct labor cost, as shown in Exhibit 20.8.

Point: The time it takes to process (cycle) products through a process is sometimes used to allocate costs.

EXHIBIT 20.8

Applying Factory Overhead

	Direct Labor Cost	Predetermined Rate	Overhead Applied
Production Department	$5,700	120%	$6,840

GenX records its applied overhead with the following entry.

Assets = Liabilities + Equity
+6,840   +6,840

⑧	Goods in Process Inventory	6,840	
	Factory Overhead........................		6,840
	Allocated overhead costs to production at 120% of direct labor cost.		

After posting this entry, the Factory Overhead account appears as shown in Exhibit 20.9. For GenX, the amount of overhead applied equals the actual overhead incurred during April. In most cases, using a predetermined overhead rate leaves an overapplied or underapplied balance in the Factory Overhead account. At the end of the period, this overapplied or underapplied balance should be closed to the Cost of Goods Sold account, as described in the job order costing chapter.

EXHIBIT 20.9

Factory Overhead

Example: If applied overhead results in a $6,940 credit to the factory overhead account, does it yield an over- or underapplied overhead amount?
Answer: $100 overapplied overhead

	Factory Overhead			Acct. No. 540		
Date		Explanation	Debit	Credit	Balance
Mar.	31	Balance			0
Apr.	30	Indirect materials usage	1,195		1,195
	30	Indirect labor costs	3,220		4,415
	30	Other overhead costs	2,425		6,840
	30	Applied to production departments		6,840	0

Decision Ethics

Budget Officer   You are working to identify the direct and indirect costs of a new processing department that has several machines. This department's manager instructs you to classify a majority of the costs as indirect to take advantage of the direct labor-based overhead allocation method so it will be charged a lower amount of overhead (because of its small direct labor cost). This would penalize other departments with higher allocations. It also will cause the performance ratings of managers in these other departments to suffer. What action do you take? [Answer—p. 832]

Equivalent Units of Production

We explained how materials, labor, and overhead costs for a period are accumulated in the Goods in Process Inventory account, but we have not explained the arrow lines labeled ⑨ and ⑩ in Exhibit 20.4. These lines reflect the transfer of products from the production department to finished goods inventory, and from finished goods inventory to cost of goods sold. To determine the costs recorded for these flows, we must first determine the cost per unit of product and then apply this result to the number of units transferred.

C2 Define equivalent units and explain their use in process cost accounting.

Accounting for Goods in Process

If a process has *no beginning and no ending goods in process inventory,* the unit cost of goods transferred out of a process is computed as follows.

Video20.1

Total cost assigned to the process (direct materials, direct labor, and overhead)
Total number of units started and finished in the period

If a process has a beginning or ending inventory of partially processed units (or both), then the total cost assigned to the process must be allocated to all completed and incomplete units worked on during the period. Therefore, the denominator must measure the entire production activity of the process for the period, called **equivalent units of production** (or **EUP**), a phrase that refers to the number of units that could have been started *and* completed given the cost incurred during a period. This measure is then used to compute the cost per equivalent unit and to assign costs to finished goods and goods in process inventory.

To illustrate, assume that GenX adds (or introduces) 100 units into its process during a period. Suppose at the end of that period, the production supervisor determines that those 100 units are 60% of the way through the process. Therefore, equivalent units of production for that period total 60 EUP (100 units × 60%). This means that with the resources used to put 100 units 60% of the way through the process, GenX could have started and completed 60 whole units.

Point: For GenX, "units" might refer to individual Profen tablets. For a juice maker, units might refer to gallons.

Differences in Equivalent Units for Materials, Labor, and Overhead

In many processes, the equivalent units of production for direct materials are not the same with respect to direct labor and overhead. To illustrate, consider a five-step process operation shown in Exhibit 20.10.

P4 Compute equivalent units produced in a period.

EXHIBIT 20.10

An Illustrative Five-Step Process Operation

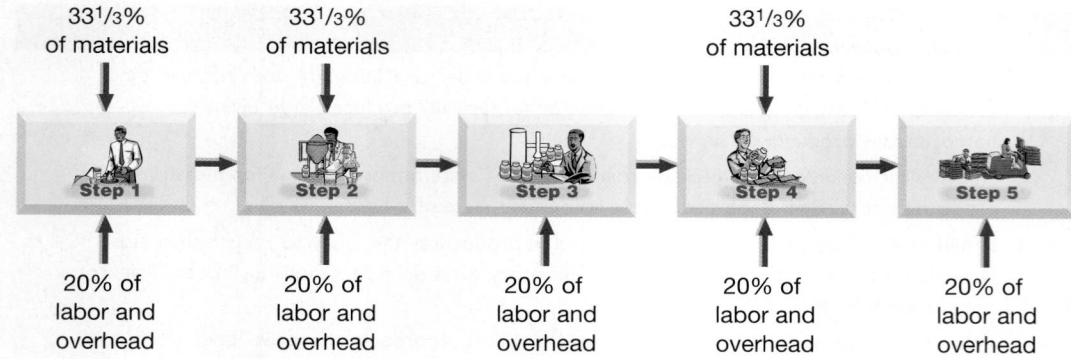

This exhibit shows that one-third of the direct material cost is added at each of three steps: 1, 2, and 4. One-fifth of the direct labor cost is added at each of the five steps. One-fifth of the overhead also is added at each step because overhead is applied as a percent of direct labor for this company.

When units finish step 1, they are one-third complete with respect to direct materials but only one-fifth complete with respect to direct labor and overhead. When they finish step 2, they are two-thirds complete with respect to direct materials but only two-fifths complete with respect to direct labor and overhead. When they finish step 3, they remain two-thirds complete with respect to materials but are now three-fifths complete with respect to labor and overhead. When they finish step 4, they are 100% complete with respect to materials (all direct materials have been added) but only four-fifths complete with respect to labor and overhead.

For example, if 300 units of product are started and processed through step 1 of Exhibit 20.10, they are said to be one-third complete *with respect to materials*. Expressed in terms of equivalent finished units, the processing of these 300 units is equal to finishing 100 EUP with respect to materials (300 units × 33⅓%). However, only one-fifth of direct labor and overhead has been applied to the 300 units at the end of step 1. This means that the equivalent units of production *with respect to labor and overhead* total 60 EUP (300 units × 20%).

Decision Insight

Process Services   Customer interaction software is a hot item in customer service processes. Whether in insurance, delivery, or technology services, companies are finding that this software can turn their customer service process into an asset. How does it work? For starters, it cuts time spent on service calls because a customer describes a problem only once. It also yields a database of customer questions and complaints that gives insights into needed improvements. It recognizes incoming phone numbers and accesses previous dealings.

Process Costing Illustration

C3 Explain the four steps in accounting for production activity in a period.

This section applies process costing concepts and procedures to GenX. **This illustration uses the weighted-average method for inventory costs. The FIFO method is illustrated in Appendix 20A.** (Assume a weighted-average cost flow for all computations and assignments in this chapter unless explicitly stated differently. When using a just-in-time inventory system, different inventory methods yield similar results because inventories are immaterial.)

Exhibit 20.11 shows selected information from the production department for the month of April. Accounting for a department's activity for a period includes four steps involving analysis of (1) physical flow, (2) equivalent units, (3) cost per equivalent unit, and (4) cost assignment and reconciliation. The next sections describe each step.

EXHIBIT 20.11

Production Data

Beginning goods in process inventory (March 31)	
Units of product	30,000
Percentage of completion—Direct materials	100%
Percentage of completion—Direct labor	65%
Direct materials costs	$ 3,300
Direct labor costs	$ 600
Factory overhead costs applied (120% of direct labor)	$ 720
Activities during the current period (April)	
Units started this period	90,000
Units transferred out (completed)	100,000
Direct materials costs	$ 9,900
Direct labor costs	$ 5,700
Factory overhead costs applied (120% of direct labor)	$ 6,840
Ending goods in process inventory (April 30)	
Units of product	20,000
Percentage of completion—Direct materials	100%
Percentage of completion—Direct labor	25%

Step 1: Determine the Physical Flow of Units

A *physical flow reconciliation* is a report that reconciles (1) the physical units started in a period with (2) the physical units completed in that period. A physical flow reconciliation for GenX is shown in Exhibit 20.12 for April.

Video20.1

EXHIBIT 20.12

Physical Flow Reconciliation

Units to Account For		Units Accounted For	
Beginning goods in process inventory	30,000 units	Units completed and transferred out	100,000 units
Units started this period	90,000 units	Ending goods in process inventory . . .	20,000 units
Total units to account for . . .	**120,000 units**	Total units accounted for	**120,000 units**

reconciled

The weighted-average method does not require us to separately track the units in beginning work in process from those units started this period. Instead, the units are treated as part of a large pool with an average cost per unit.

Step 2: Compute Equivalent Units of Production

The second step is to compute *equivalent units of production* for direct materials, direct labor, and factory overhead for April. Overhead is applied using direct labor as the allocation base for GenX. This also implies that equivalent units are the same for both labor and overhead.

GenX used its direct materials, direct labor, and overhead to make finished units of Profen and to begin processing some units that are not yet complete. We must convert the physical units measure to equivalent units based on how each input has been used. Equivalent units are computed by multiplying the number of physical units by the percentage of completion for each input—see Exhibit 20.13.

EXHIBIT 20.13

Equivalent Units of Production—
Weighted Average

Equivalent Units of Production	Direct Materials	Direct Labor	Factory Overhead
Equivalent units completed and transferred out (100,000 × 100%)	100,000 EUP	100,000 EUP	100,000 EUP
Equivalent units for ending goods in process			
Direct materials (20,000 × 100%)	20,000		
Direct labor (20,000 × 25%)		5,000	
Factory overhead (20,000 × 25%)			5,000
Equivalent units of production	120,000 EUP	105,000 EUP	105,000 EUP

The first row of Exhibit 20.13 reflects units transferred out in April. The production department entirely completed its work on the 100,000 units transferred out. These units have 100% of the materials, labor, and overhead required, or 100,000 equivalent units of each input (100,000 × 100%).

The second row references the ending goods in process, and rows three, four, and five break it down by materials, labor, and overhead. For direct materials, the units in ending goods in process inventory (20,000 physical units) include all materials required, so there are 20,000 equivalent units (20,000 × 100%) of materials in the unfinished physical units. Regarding labor, the units in ending goods in process inventory include 25% of the labor required, which implies 5,000 equivalent units of labor (20,000 × 25%). These units are only 25% complete and labor is used uniformly through the process. Overhead is applied on the basis of direct labor for GenX, so equivalent units for overhead are computed identically to labor (20,000 × 25%).

The final row reflects the whole units of product that could have been manufactured with the amount of inputs used to create some complete and some incomplete units. For GenX, the amount of inputs used to produce 100,000 complete units and to start 20,000 additional units is equivalent to the amount of direct materials in 120,000 whole units, the amount of direct labor in 105,000 whole units, and the amount of overhead in 105,000 whole units.

Step 3: Compute the Cost per Equivalent Unit

Equivalent units of production for each product (from step 2) is used to compute the average cost per equivalent unit. Under the **weighted-average method,** the computation of EUP does not separate the units in beginning inventory from those started this period; similarly, this method combines the costs of beginning goods in process inventory with the costs incurred in the current period. This process is illustrated in Exhibit 20.14.

EXHIBIT 20.14

Cost per Equivalent Unit of Production—Weighted Average

Cost per Equivalent Unit of Production	Direct Materials	Direct Labor	Factory Overhead
Costs of beginning goods in process inventory	$ 3,300	$ 600	$ 720
Costs incurred this period	9,900	5,700	6,840
Total costs	$13,200	$6,300	$7,560
÷ Equivalent units of production (from Step 2)	120,000 EUP	105,000 EUP	105,000 EUP
= Cost per equivalent unit of production	$0.11 per EUP*	$0.06 per EUP†	$0.072 per EUP‡

*$13,200 ÷ 120,000 EUP   †$6,300 ÷ 105,000 EUP   ‡$7,560 ÷ 105,000 EUP

For direct materials, the cost averages $0.11 per EUP, computed as the sum of direct materials cost from beginning goods in process inventory ($3,300) and the direct materials cost incurred in April ($9,900), and this sum ($13,200) is then divided by the 120,000 EUP for materials (from step 2). The costs per equivalent unit for labor and overhead are similarly computed. Specifically, direct labor cost averages $0.06 per EUP, computed as the sum of labor cost in beginning goods in process inventory ($600) and the labor costs incurred in April ($5,700), and this sum ($6,300) divided by 105,000 EUP for labor. Overhead costs averages $0.072 per EUP, computed as the sum of overhead cost in the beginning goods in process inventory ($720) and the overhead costs applied in April ($6,840), and this sum ($7,560) divided by 105,000 EUP for overhead.

Step 4: Assign and Reconcile Costs

The EUP from step 2 and the cost per EUP from step 3 are used in step 4 to assign costs to (a) units that production completed and transferred to finished goods and (b) units that remain in process. This is illustrated in Exhibit 20.15.

EXHIBIT 20.15

Report of Costs Accounted
For—Weighted Average

Cost of units completed and transferred out

Direct materials (100,000 EUP × $0.11 per EUP)	$11,000	
Direct labor (100,000 EUP × $0.06 per EUP)	6,000	
Factory overhead (100,000 EUP × $0.072 per EUP)	7,200	
Cost of units completed this period		$ 24,200

Cost of ending goods in process inventory

Direct materials (20,000 EUP × $0.11 per EUP)	2,200	
Direct labor (5,000 EUP × $0.06 per EUP)	300	
Factory overhead (5,000 EUP × $0.072 per EUP)	360	
Cost of ending goods in process inventory		2,860
Total costs accounted for		$27,060

Cost of Units Completed and Transferred The 100,000 units completed and transferred to finished goods inventory required 100,000 EUP of direct materials. Thus, we assign $11,000 (100,000 EUP × $0.11 per EUP) of direct materials cost to those units. Similarly, those units had received 100,000 EUP of direct labor and 100,000 EUP of factory overhead (recall Exhibit 20.13). Thus, we assign $6,000 (100,000 EUP × $0.06 per EUP) of direct labor and $7,200 (100,000 EUP × $0.072 per EUP) of overhead to those units. The total cost of the 100,000 completed and transferred units is $24,200 ($11,000 + $6,000 + $7,200) and their average cost per unit is $0.242 ($24,200 ÷ 100,000 units).

Cost of Units for Ending Goods in Process There are 20,000 incomplete units in goods in process inventory at period-end. For direct materials, those units have 20,000 EUP of material (from step 2) at a cost of $0.11 per EUP (from step 3), which yields the materials cost of goods in process inventory of $2,200 (20,000 EUP × $0.11 per EUP). For direct labor, the in-process units have 25% of the required labor, or 5,000 EUP (from step 2). Using the $0.06 labor cost per EUP (from step 3) we obtain the labor cost of goods in process inventory of $300 (5,000 EUP × $0.06 per EUP). For overhead, the in-process units reflect 5,000 EUP (from step 2). Using the $0.072 overhead cost per EUP (from step 3) we obtain overhead costs with in-process inventory of $360 (5,000 EUP × $0.072 per EUP). Total cost of goods in process inventory at period-end is $2,860 ($2,200 + $300 + $360).

As a check, management verifies that total costs assigned to those units completed and transferred plus the costs of those in process (from Exhibit 20.15) equal the costs incurred by production. Exhibit 20.16 shows the costs incurred by production this period. We then reconcile the *costs accounted for* in Exhibit 20.15 with the *costs to account for* in Exhibit 20.16.

EXHIBIT 20.16

Report of Costs to Account
For—Weighted Average

Cost of beginning goods in process inventory

Direct materials	$3,300	
Direct labor	600	
Factory overhead	720	$ 4,620

Cost incurred this period

Direct materials	9,900	
Direct labor	5,700	
Factory overhead	6,840	22,440
Total costs to account for		$27,060

At GenX, the production department manager is responsible for $27,060 in costs: $4,620 that is assigned to the goods in process at the start of the period plus $22,440 of materials, labor, and overhead incurred in the period. At period-end, that manager must show where these costs are assigned. The manager for GenX reports that $2,860 are assigned to units in process and $24,200 are assigned to units completed (per Exhibit 20.15). The sum of these amounts equals $27,060. Thus, the total *costs to account for* equal the total *costs accounted for* (minor differences can sometimes occur from rounding).

C4 Define a process cost summary and describe its purposes.

Point: Managers can examine changes in monthly costs per equivalent unit to help control the production process. When prices are set in a competitive market, managers can use process cost summary information to determine which costs should be cut to achieve a profit.

P5 Prepare a process cost summary.

EXHIBIT 20.17

Process Cost Summary

Process Cost Summary   An important managerial accounting report for a process cost accounting system is the **process cost summary** (also called *production report*), which is prepared separately for each process or production department. Three reasons for the summary are to (1) help department managers control and monitor their departments, (2) help factory managers evaluate department managers' performances, and (3) provide cost information for financial statements. A process cost summary achieves these purposes by describing the costs charged to each department, reporting the equivalent units of production achieved by each department, and determining the costs assigned to each department's output. For our purposes, it is prepared using a combination of Exhibits 20.13, 20.14, 20.15, and 20.16.

The process cost summary for GenX is shown in Exhibit 20.17. The report is divided into three sections. Section ① lists the total costs charged to the department, including direct materials, direct labor, and overhead costs incurred, as well as the cost of the beginning goods in process inventory. Section ② describes the equivalent units of production for the department. Equivalent units for materials, labor, and overhead are in separate columns. It also reports direct

GenX COMPANY
Process Cost Summary
For Month Ended April 30, 2009

① Costs Charged to Production

Costs of beginning goods in process
Direct materials ... $3,300
Direct labor ... 600
Factory overhead ... 720 $ 4,620

Costs incurred this period
Direct materials ... 9,900
Direct labor ... 5,700
Factory overhead ... 6,840   22,440

Total costs to account for ... **$27,060**

Unit Cost Information

Units to account for:
Beginning goods in process ... 30,000
Units started this period ... 90,000
Total units to account for ... 120,000

Units accounted for:
Completed and transferred out ... 100,000
Ending goods in process ... 20,000
Total units accounted for ... 120,000

Equivalent Units of Production (EUP)	Direct Materials	Direct Labor	Factory Overhead
Units completed and transferred out	100,000 EUP	100,000 EUP	100,000 EUP
Units of ending goods in process			
Direct materials (20,000 × 100%)	20,000		
Direct labor (20,000 × 25%)		5,000	
Factory overhead (20,000 × 25%)			5,000
Equivalent units of production	120,000 EUP	105,000 EUP	105,000 EUP

Cost per EUP	Direct Materials	Direct Labor	Factory Overhead
Costs of beginning goods in process	$ 3,300	$ 600	$ 720
Costs incurred this period	9,900	5,700	6,840
Total costs	$13,200	$6,300	$7,560
÷EUP	120,000 EUP	105,000 EUP	105,000 EUP
Cost per EUP	$0.11 per EUP	$0.06 per EUP	$0.072 per EUP

③ Cost Assignment and Reconciliation

Costs transferred out (cost of goods manufactured)
Direct materials (100,000 EUP × $0.11 per EUP) ... $11,000
Direct labor (100,000 EUP × $0.06 per EUP) ... 6,000
Factory overhead (100,000 EUP × $0.072 per EUP) ... 7,200 $ 24,200

Costs of ending goods in process
Direct materials (20,000 EUP × $0.11 per EUP) ... 2,200
Direct labor (5,000 EUP × $0.06 per EUP) ... 300
Factory overhead (5,000 EUP × $0.072 per EUP) ... 360   2,860

Total costs accounted for ... **$27,060**

(reconciled)

materials, direct labor, and overhead costs per equivalent unit. Section ③ allocates total costs among units worked on in the period. The $24,200 is the total cost of goods transferred out of the department, and the $2,860 is the cost of partially processed ending inventory units. The assigned costs are then added to show that the total $27,060 cost charged to the department in section ① is now assigned to the units in section ③.

Quick Check

6. Equivalent units are (a) a measure of a production department's productivity in using direct materials, direct labor, or overhead; (b) units of a product produced by a foreign competitor that are similar to units produced by a domestic company; or (c) generic units of a product similar to brand name units of a product.

7. Interpret the meaning of a department's equivalent units with respect to direct labor.

8. A department began the period with 8,000 units that were one-fourth complete with respect to direct labor. It completed 58,000 units, and ended with 6,000 units that were one-third complete with respect to direct labor. What were its direct labor equivalent units for the period using the weighted-average method?

9. A process cost summary for a department has three sections. What information is presented in each of them?

Transfers to Finished Goods Inventory and Cost of Goods Sold

P6 Record the transfer of completed goods to Finished Goods Inventory and Cost of Goods Sold.

Arrow line ⑨ in Exhibit 20.4 reflects the transfer of completed products from production to finished goods inventory. The process cost summary shows that the 100,000 units of finished Profen are assigned a cost of $24,200. The entry to record this transfer follows.

⑨	Finished Goods Inventory.....................	24,200	
	Goods in Process Inventory................		24,200
	To record transfer of completed units.		

Assets = Liabilities + Equity
+24,200
−24,200

The credit to Goods in Process Inventory reduces that asset balance to reflect that 100,000 units are no longer in production. The cost of these units has been transferred to Finished Goods Inventory, which is recognized as a $24,200 increase in this asset. After this entry is posted, there remains a balance of $2,860 in the Goods in Process Inventory account, which is the amount computed in Step 4 previously. The cost of units transferred from Goods in Process Inventory to Finished Goods Inventory is called the **cost of goods manufactured.** Exhibit 20.18 reveals the activities in the Goods in Process Inventory account for this period. The ending balance of this account equals the cost assigned to the partially completed units in section ③ of Exhibit 20.17.

Goods in Process Inventory			Acct. No. 134		
Date		Explanation	Debit	Credit	Balance
Mar.	31	Balance			4,620
Apr.	30	Direct materials usage	9,900		14,520
	30	Direct labor costs incurred	5,700		20,220
	30	Factory overhead applied	6,840		27,060
	30	Transfer completed product to warehouse		24,200	2,860

EXHIBIT 20.18

Goods in Process Inventory

Arrow line ⑩ in Exhibit 20.4 reflects the sale of finished goods. Assume that GenX sold 106,000 units of Profen this period, and that its beginning inventory of finished goods consisted of 26,000 units with a cost of $6,292. Also assume that its ending finished goods inventory consists of 20,000 units at a cost of $4,840. Using this information, we can compute its cost of goods sold for April as shown in Exhibit 20.19.

Point: We omit the journal entry for sales, but it totals the number of units sold times price per unit.

EXHIBIT 20.19

Cost of Goods Sold

Beginning finished goods inventory	$ 6,292
+ Cost of goods manufactured this period	24,200
= Cost of goods available for sale	$30,492
− Ending finished goods inventory	4,840
= Cost of goods sold	$25,652

The summary entry to record cost of goods sold for this period follows.

Assets = Liabilities + Equity
−25,652   −25,652

⑩	Cost of Goods Sold	25,652	
	Finished Goods Inventory		25,652
	To record cost of goods sold for April.		

The Finished Goods Inventory account now appears as shown in Exhibit 20.20.

EXHIBIT 20.20

Finished Goods Inventory

Finished Goods Inventory			Acct. No. 135		
Date		**Explanation**	**Debit**	**Credit**	**Balance**
Mar.	31	Balance			6,292
Apr.	30	Transfer in cost of goods manufactured	24,200		30,492
	30	Cost of goods sold		25,652	4,840

Summary of Cost Flows   Exhibit 20.21 shows GenX's manufacturing cost flows for April. Each of these cost flows and the entries to record them have been explained. The flow of costs through the accounts reflects the flow of production activities and products.

EXHIBIT 20.21*

Cost Flows through GenX

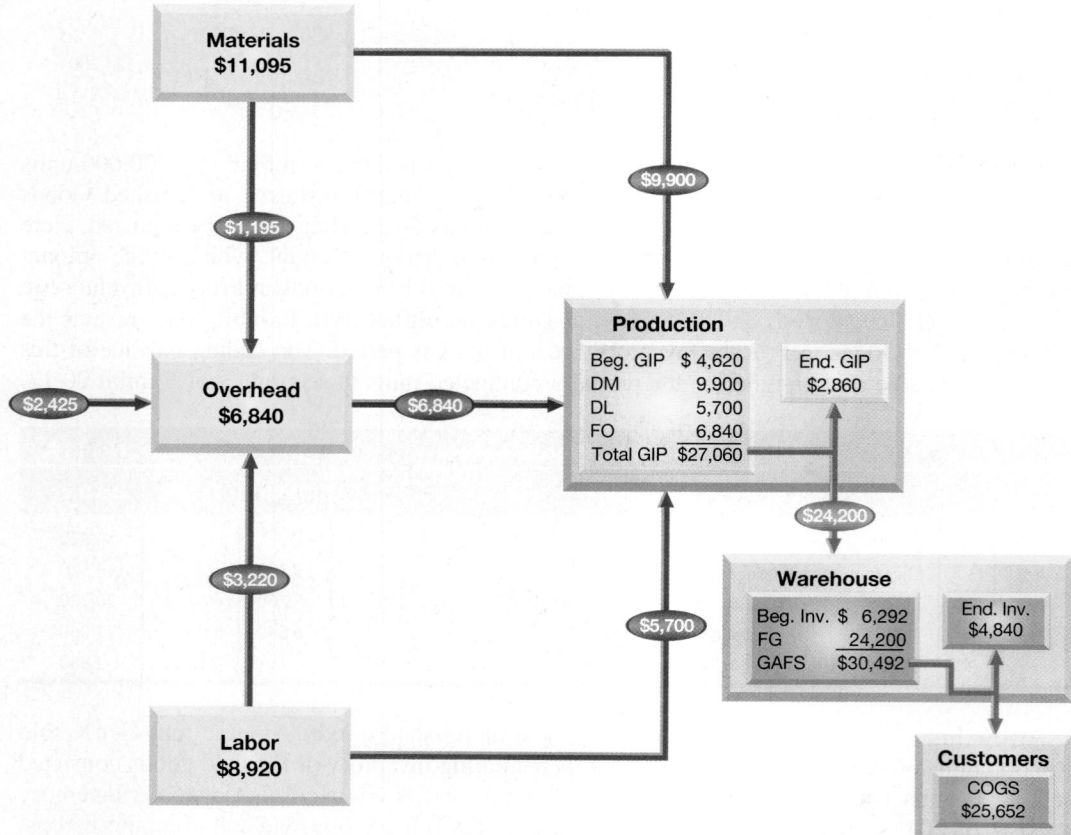

*Abbreviations: GIP (goods in process); DM (direct materials); DL (direct labor); FO (factory overhead); FG (finished goods); GAFS (goods available for sale); COGS (cost of goods sold).

Decision Insight

Best of Both   Customer orientation demands both flexibility and standardization. Flexibility allows companies to supply products or services to a customer's specifications as in a job order setting, and standardization helps achieve efficiencies and lower costs as in a process operation.

Effect of the Lean Business Model on Process Operations

Adopting lean business practices often yields changes in process operations. Management concerns with throughput and just-in-time manufacturing, for instance, cause boundary lines between departments to blur. In some cases, higher quality and better efficiency are obtained by entirely reorganizing production processes. For example, instead of producing different types of computers in a series of departments, a separate work center for each computer can be established in one department. When such a rearrangement occurs, the process cost accounting system is changed to account for each work center's costs.

To illustrate, when a company adopts a just-in-time inventory system, its inventories can be minimal. If raw materials are not ordered or received until needed, a Raw Materials Inventory account may be unnecessary. Instead, materials cost is immediately debited to the Goods in Process Inventory account. Similarly, a Finished Goods Inventory account may not be needed. Instead, cost of finished goods may be immediately debited to the Cost of Goods Sold account.

Decision Insight

Lean Machine   Attention to customer orientation has led to improved processes for companies. A manufacturer of control devices improved quality and reduced production time by forming teams to study processes and suggest improvements. Another company set up project groups to evaluate its production processes.

Hybrid Costing System	Decision Analysis

This chapter explained the process costing system and contrasted it with the job order costing system. Many organizations use a *hybrid system* that contains features of both process and job order operations. A recent survey of manufacturers revealed that a majority use hybrid systems.

A2   Explain and illustrate a hybrid costing system.

To illustrate, consider a car manufacturer's assembly line. On one hand, the line resembles a process operation in that the assembly steps for each car are nearly identical. On the other hand, the specifications of most cars have several important differences. At the Ford Mustang plant, each car assembled on a given day can be different from the previous car and the next car. This means that the costs of materials (subassemblies or components) for each car can differ. Accordingly, while the conversion costs (direct labor and overhead) can be accounted for using a process costing system, the component costs (direct materials) are accounted for using a job order system (separately for each car or type of car).

A hybrid system of processes requires a *hybrid costing system* to properly cost products or services. In the Ford plant, the assembly costs per car are readily determined using process costing. The costs of additional components can then be added to the assembly costs to determine each car's total cost (as in job order costing). To illustrate, consider the following information for a daily assembly process at Ford.

Assembly process costs	
Direct materials	$10,600,000
Direct labor	$5,800,000
Factory overhead	$6,200,000
Number of cars assembled	1,000
Costs of three different types of steering wheels	$240, $330, $480
Costs of three different types of seats	$620, $840, $1,360

The assembly process costs $22,600 per car. Depending on the type of steering wheel and seats the customer requests, the cost of a car can range from $23,460 to $24,440 (a $980 difference).

Today companies are increasingly trying to standardize processes while attempting to meet individual customer needs. To the extent that differences among individual customers' requests are large, understanding the costs to satisfy those requests is important. Thus, monitoring and controlling both process and job order costs are important.

 Decision Ethics

Entrepreneur   You operate a process production company making similar products for three different customers. One customer demands 100% quality inspection of products at your location before shipping. The added costs of that inspection are spread across all customers, not just the one demanding it. If you charge the added costs to that customer, you could lose that customer and experience a loss. Moreover, your other two customers have agreed to pay 110% of full costs. What actions (if any) do you take?
[Answer—pp. 832–833]

Demonstration Problem

Pennsylvania Company produces a product that passes through a single production process. Then completed products are transferred to finished goods in its warehouse. Information related to its manufacturing activities for July follows.

Raw Materials		Production Department	
Beginning inventory	$100,000	Beginning goods in process inventory (units)	5,000
Raw materials purchased on credit	211,400	Percentage completed—Materials	100%
Direct materials used	(190,000)	Percentage completed—Labor and overhead	60%
Indirect materials used	(51,400)	Beginning goods in process inventory (costs)	
Ending inventory	$ 70,000	Direct materials used	$ 20,000
		Direct labor incurred	9,600
Factory Payroll		Overhead applied (200% of direct labor)	19,200
Direct labor incurred	$ 55,500	Total costs of beginning goods in process	$ 48,800
Indirect labor incurred	50,625		
Total payroll (paid in cash)	$106,125	Units started this period	20,000
		Units completed this period	17,000
Factory Overhead			
Indirect materials used	$ 51,400	Ending goods in process inventory (units)	8,000
Indirect labor used	50,625	Percentage completed—Materials	100%
Other overhead costs	71,725	Percentage completed—Labor and overhead	20%
Total factory overhead incurred	$173,750		
		Finished Goods Inventory	
Factory Overhead Applied		Beginning finished goods inventory	$ 96,400
Overhead applied (200% of direct labor) . . .	$111,000	Cost transferred in from production	321,300
		Cost of goods sold	(345,050)
		Ending finished goods inventory	$ 72,650

DP20

Required

1. Prepare a physical flow reconciliation for July as illustrated in Exhibit 20.12.
2. Compute the equivalent units of production in July for direct materials, direct labor, and factory overhead.
3. Compute the costs per equivalent units of production in July for direct materials, direct labor, and factory overhead.
4. Prepare a report of costs accounted for and a report of costs to account for.

5. Prepare summary journal entries to record the transactions and events of July for (a) raw materials purchases, (b) direct materials usage, (c) indirect materials usage, (d) factory payroll costs, (e) direct labor usage, (f) indirect labor usage, (g) other overhead costs (credit Other Accounts), (h) application of overhead to production, (i) transfer of finished goods from production, and (j) the cost of goods sold.

Planning the Solution

- Track the physical flow to determine the number of units completed in July.
- Compute the equivalent unit of production for direct materials, direct labor, and factory overhead.
- Compute the costs per equivalent unit of production with respect to direct materials, direct labor, and overhead; and determine the cost per unit for each.
- Compute the total cost of the goods transferred to production by using the equivalent units and unit costs. Determine (a) the cost of the beginning in-process inventory, (b) the materials, labor, and over-head costs added to the beginning in-process inventory, and (c) the materials, labor, and overhead costs added to the units started and completed in the month.
- Determine the cost of goods sold using balances in finished goods and cost of units completed this period.
- Use the information to record the summary journal entries for July.

Solution to Demonstration Problem

I. Physical flow reconciliation.

Units to Account For		Units Accounted For	
Beginning goods in process inventory	5,000 units	Units completed and transferred out	17,000 units
Units started this period	20,000 units	Ending goods in process inventory	8,000 units
Total units to account for	**25,000 units**	Total units accounted for	**25,000 units**

reconciled

2. Equivalent units of production.

Equivalent Units of Production	Direct Materials	Direct Labor	Factory Overhead
Equivalent units completed and transferred out	17,000 EUP	17,000 EUP	17,000 EUP
Equivalent units in ending goods in process			
Direct materials (8,000 × 100%)	8,000		
Direct labor (8,000 × 20%)		1,600	
Factory overhead (8,000 × 20%)			1,600
Equivalent units of production	25,000 EUP	18,600 EUP	18,600 EUP

3. Costs per equivalent unit of production.

Costs per Equivalent Unit of Production	Direct Materials	Direct Labor	Factory Overhead
Costs of beginning goods in process	$ 20,000	$ 9,600	$ 19,200
Costs incurred this period	190,000	55,500	111,000**
Total costs	$210,000	$65,100	$130,200
÷ Equivalent units of production (from part 2) .	25,000 EUP	18,600 EUP	18,600 EUP
= Costs per equivalent unit of production	$8.40 per EUP	$3.50 per EUP	$7.00 per EUP

**Factory overhead applied

4. Reports of costs accounted for and of costs to account for

Report of Costs Accounted For		
Cost of units transferred out (cost of goods manufactured)		
Direct materials ($8.40 per EUP × 17,000 EUP)	$142,800	
Direct labor ($3.50 per EUP × 17,000 EUP)	59,500	
Factory overhead ($7.00 per EUP × 17,000 EUP)	119,000	
Cost of units completed this period		$ 321,300
Cost of ending goods in process inventory		
Direct materials ($8.40 per EUP × 8,000 EUP)	67,200	
Direct labor ($3.50 per EUP × 1,600 EUP)	5,600	
Factory overhead ($7.00 per EUP × 1,600 EUP)	11,200	
Cost of ending goods in process inventory		84,000
Total costs accounted for		**$405,300** ◄

Report of Costs to Account For		
Cost of beginning goods in process inventory		
Direct materials	$ 20,000	
Direct labor	9,600	
Factory overhead	19,200	$ 48,800
Cost incurred this period		
Direct materials	190,000	
Direct labor	55,500	
Factory overhead	111,000	356,500
Total costs to account for		**$405,300** ◄

reconciled

5. Summary journal entries for the transactions and events in July.

a.	Raw Materials Inventory	211,400	
	Accounts Payable		211,400
	To record raw materials purchases.		
b.	Goods in Process Inventory	190,000	
	Raw Materials Inventory		190,000
	To record direct materials usage.		
c.	Factory Overhead	51,400	
	Raw Materials Inventory		51,400
	To record indirect materials usage.		
d.	Factory Payroll	106,125	
	Cash		106,125
	To record factory payroll costs.		
e.	Goods in Process Inventory	55,500	
	Factory Payroll		55,500
	To record direct labor usage.		
f.	Factory Overhead	50,625	
	Factory Payroll		50,625
	To record indirect labor usage.		
g.	Factory Overhead	71,725	
	Other Accounts		71,725
	To record other overhead costs.		

[continued on next page]

[continued from previous page]

h.	Goods in Process Inventory	111,000	
	Factory Overhead		111,000
	To record application of overhead.		
i.	Finished Goods Inventory	321,300	
	Goods in Process Inventory		321,300
	To record transfer of finished goods		
	from production.		
j.	Cost of Goods Sold	345,050	
	Finished Goods Inventory		345,050
	To record cost of goods sold.		

APPENDIX

FIFO Method of Process Costing

20A

The **FIFO method** of process costing assigns costs to units assuming a first-in, first-out flow of product. The objectives, concepts, and journal entries (not amounts) are the same as for the weighted-average method, but computation of equivalent units of production and cost assignment are slightly different.

C5 Explain and illustrate the four steps in accounting for production activity using FIFO.

Exhibit 20A.1 shows selected information from GenX's production department for the month of April. Accounting for a department's activity for a period includes four steps: (1) determine physical flow, (2) compute equivalent units, (3) compute cost per equivalent unit, and (4) determine cost assignment and reconciliation. This appendix describes each of these steps using the FIFO method for process costing.

EXHIBIT 20A.1

Production Data

Beginning goods in process inventory (March 31)	
Units of product	30,000
Percentage of completion—Direct materials	100%
Percentage of completion—Direct labor	65%
Direct materials costs	$ 3,300
Direct labor costs	$ 600
Factory overhead costs applied (120% of direct labor)	$ 720
Activities during the current period (April)	
Units started this period	90,000
Units transferred out (completed)	100,000
Direct materials costs	$ 9,900
Direct labor costs	$ 5,700
Factory overhead costs applied (120% of direct labor)	$ 6,840
Ending goods in process inventory (April 30)	
Units of product	20,000
Percentage of completion—Direct materials	100%
Percentage of completion—Direct labor	25%

Step 1: Determine Physical Flow of Units

A *physical flow reconciliation* is a report that reconciles (1) the physical units started in a period with (2) the physical units completed in that period. The physical flow reconciliation for GenX is shown in Exhibit 20A.2 for April.

EXHIBIT 20A.2

Physical Flow Reconciliation

Units to Account For		Units Accounted For	
Beginning goods in process inventory	30,000 units	Units completed and transferred out	100,000 units
Units started this period	90,000 units	Ending goods in process inventory . . .	20,000 units
Total units to account for . . .	**120,000 units**	Total units accounted for	**120,000 units**

reconciled

FIFO assumes that the 100,000 units transferred to finished goods during April include the 30,000 units from the beginning goods in process inventory. The remaining 70,000 units transferred out are from units started in April. Of the total 90,000 units started in April, 70,000 were completed, leaving 20,000 units unfinished at period-end.

Step 2: Compute Equivalent Units of Production—FIFO

GenX used its direct materials, direct labor, and overhead both to make complete units of Profen and to start some units that are not yet complete. We need to convert the physical measure of units to equivalent units based on how much of each input has been used. We do this by multiplying the number of physical units by the percentage of processing applied to those units in the current period; this is done for each input (materials, labor, and overhead). The FIFO method accounts for cost flow in a sequential manner— earliest costs are the first to flow out. (This is different from the weighted-average method, which combines prior period costs—those in beginning Goods in Process Inventory—with costs incurred in the current period.)

Three distinct groups of units must be considered in determining the equivalent units of production under the FIFO method: (a) units in beginning Goods in Process Inventory that were completed this period, (b) units started *and* completed this period, and (c) units in ending Goods in Process Inventory. We must determine how much material, labor, and overhead are used for each of these unit groups. These computations are shown in Exhibit 20A.3. The remainder of this section explains these computations.

EXHIBIT 20A.3

Equivalent Units of Production—FIFO

Equivalent Units of Production	Direct Materials	Direct Labor	Factory Overhead
(a) Equivalent units to complete beginning goods in process			
Direct materials (30,000 × 0%)	0 EUP		
Direct labor (30,000 × 35%)		10,500 EUP	
Factory overhead (30,000 × 35%)			10,500 EUP
(b) Equivalent units started and completed*	70,000	70,000	70,000
(c) Equivalent units in ending goods in process			
Direct materials (20,000 × 100%)	20,000		
Direct labor (20,000 × 25%)		5,000	
Factory overhead (20,000 × 25%)			5,000
Equivalent units of production	**90,000 EUP**	**85,500 EUP**	**85,500 EUP**

*Units completed this period . . . . 100,000 units
Less units in beginning goods in process   30,000
Units started and completed this period . . . .   70,000 units

(a) Beginning Goods in Process Under FIFO, we assume that production first completes any units started in the prior period. There were 30,000 physical units in beginning goods in process inventory. Those units were 100% complete with respect to direct materials as of the end of the prior period. This means that no materials (0%) are needed in April to complete those 30,000 units. So the equivalent units of *materials* to complete beginning goods in process are zero (30,000 × 0%)—see first row under row "(a)" in Exhibit 20A.3. The units in process as of April 1 had already been through 65% of production prior to this period and need only go through the remaining 35% of production. The equivalent units of *labor* to complete the beginning goods in process are 10,500 (30,000 × 35%)—

see the second row under row "(a)." This implies that the amount of labor required this period to complete the 30,000 units started in the prior period is the amount of labor needed to make 10,500 units, start-to-finish. Finally, overhead is applied based on direct labor costs, so GenX computes equivalent units for overhead as it would for direct labor.

(b) Units Started and Completed This Period After completing any beginning goods in process, FIFO assumes that production begins on newly started units. GenX began work on 90,000 new units this period. Of those units, 20,000 remain incomplete at period-end. This means that 70,000 of the units started in April were completed in April. These complete units have received 100% of materials, labor, and overhead. Exhibit 20A.3 reflects this by including 70,000 equivalent units (70,000 × 100%) of materials, labor, and overhead in its equivalent units of production—see row "(b)."

(c) Ending Goods in Process The 20,000 units started in April that GenX was not able to complete by period-end consumed materials, labor, and overhead. Specifically, those 20,000 units received 100% of materials and, therefore, the equivalent units of materials in ending goods in process inventory are 20,000 (20,000 × 100%)—see the first row under row "(c)." For labor and overhead, the units in ending goods in process were 25% complete in production. This means the equivalent units of labor and overhead for those units are 5,000 (20,000 × 25%) as GenX incurs labor and overhead costs uniformly throughout its production process. Finally, for each input (direct materials, direct labor, and factory overhead), the equivalent units for each of the unit groups (a), (b), and (c) are added to determine the total equivalent units of production with respect to each—see the final row in Exhibit 20A.3.

Step 3: Compute Cost per Equivalent Unit—FIFO

To compute cost per equivalent unit, we take the product costs (for each of direct materials, direct labor, and factory overhead from Exhibit 20A.1) added in April and divide by the equivalent units of production from step 2. Exhibit 20A.4 illustrates these computations.

Cost per Equivalent Unit of Production	Direct Materials	Direct Labor	Factory Overhead
Costs incurred this period	$9,900	$5,700	$6,840
÷ Equivalent units of production (from Step 2)	90,000 EUP	85,500 EUP	85,500 EUP
Cost per equivalent unit of production	$0.11 per EUP	$0.067 per EUP	$0.08 per EUP

EXHIBIT 20A.4

Cost per Equivalent Unit of Production—FIFO

It is essential to compute costs per equivalent unit for *each* input because production inputs are added at different times in the process. The FIFO method computes the cost per equivalent unit based solely on this period's EUP and costs (unlike the weighted-average method, which adds in the costs of the beginning goods in process inventory).

Step 4: Assign and Reconcile Costs

The equivalent units determined in step 2 and the cost per equivalent unit computed in step 3 are both used to assign costs (1) to units that the production department completed and transferred to finished goods and (2) to units that remain in process at period-end.

In Exhibit 20A.5, under the section for cost of units transferred out, we see that the cost of units completed in April includes the $4,620 cost carried over from March for work already applied to the 30,000 units that make up beginning Goods in Process Inventory, plus the $1,544 incurred in April to complete those units. This section also includes the $17,990 of cost assigned to the 70,000 units started and completed this period. Thus, the total cost of goods manufactured in April is $24,154 ($4,620 + $1,544 + $17,990). The average cost per unit for goods completed in April is $0.242 ($24,154 ÷ 100,000 completed units).

The computation for cost of ending goods in process inventory is in the lower part of Exhibit 20A.5. The cost of units in process includes materials, labor, and overhead costs corresponding to the percentage of these resources applied to those incomplete units in April. That cost of $2,935 ($2,200 + $335 + $400) also is the ending balance for the Goods in Process Inventory account.

EXHIBIT 20A.5

Report of Costs Accounted
For—FIFO

Cost of units transferred out (cost of goods manufactured)			
Cost of beginning goods in process inventory			$ 4,620
Cost to complete beginning goods in process			
Direct materials ($0.11 per EUP × 0 EUP)		$ 0	
Direct labor ($0.067 per EUP × 10,500 EUP)		704	
Factory overhead ($0.08 per EUP × 10,500 EUP)		840	1,544
Cost of units started and completed this period			
Direct materials ($0.11 per EUP × 70,000 EUP)		7,700	
Direct labor ($0.067 per EUP × 70,000 EUP)		4,690	
Factory overhead ($0.08 per EUP × 70,000 EUP)		5,600	17,990
Total cost of units finished this period			24,154
Cost of ending goods in process inventory			
Direct materials ($0.11 per EUP × 20,000 EUP)		2,200	
Direct labor ($0.067 per EUP × 5,000 EUP)		335	
Factory overhead ($0.08 per EUP × 5,000 EUP)		400	
Total cost of ending goods in process inventory			2,935
Total costs accounted for			**$27,089**

Management verifies that the total costs assigned to units transferred out and units still in process equal the total costs incurred by production. We reconcile the costs accounted for (in Exhibit 20A.5) to the costs that production was charged for as shown in Exhibit 20A.6.

EXHIBIT 20A.6

Report of Costs to
Account For—FIFO

Cost of beginning goods in process inventory		
Direct materials	$3,300	
Direct labor	600	
Factory overhead	720	$ 4,620
Costs incurred this period		
Direct materials	9,900	
Direct labor	5,700	
Factory overhead	6,840	22,440
Total costs to account for		**$27,060**

The production manager is responsible for $27,060 in costs: $4,620 that had been assigned to the department's Goods in Process Inventory as of April 1 plus $22,440 of materials, labor, and overhead costs the department incurred in April. At period-end, the manager must identify where those costs were assigned. The production manager can report that $24,154 of cost was assigned to units completed in April and $2,935 was assigned to units still in process at period-end. The sum of these amounts is $29 different from the $27,060 total costs incurred by production due to rounding in step 3—rounding errors are common and not a concern.

The final report is the process cost summary, which summarizes key information from Exhibits 20A.3, 20A.4, 20A.5, and 20A.6. Reasons for the summary are to (1) help managers control and monitor costs, (2) help upper management assess department manager performance, and (3) provide cost information for financial reporting. The process cost summary, using FIFO, for GenX is in Exhibit 20A.7. Section ① lists the total costs charged to the department, including direct materials, direct labor, and overhead costs incurred, as well as the cost of the beginning goods in process inventory. Section ② describes the equivalent units of production for the department. Equivalent units for materials, labor, and overhead are in separate columns. It also reports direct materials, direct labor, and overhead costs per equivalent unit. Section ③ allocates total costs among units worked on in the period.

♟ **Decision Maker** ▬▬▬▬▬▬

Cost Manager   As cost manager for an electronics manufacturer, you apply a process costing system using FIFO. Your company plans to adopt a just-in-time system and eliminate inventories. What is the impact of the use of FIFO (versus the weighted-average method) given these plans? [Answer—p. 833]

GenX COMPANY
Process Cost Summary
For Month Ended April 30, 2009

Costs charged to production

Costs of beginning goods in process inventory

Direct materials	$3,300	
Direct labor	600	
Factory overhead	720	$ 4,620

① Costs incurred this period

Direct materials	9,900	
Direct labor	5,700	
Factory overhead	6,840	22,440
Total costs to account for		$27,060 ◄

Unit cost information

Units to account for		Units accounted for	
Beginning goods in process	30,000	Transferred out	100,000
Units started this period	90,000	Ending goods in process	20,000
Total units to account for	120,000	Total units accounted for	120,000

Equivalent units of production	Direct Materials	Direct Labor	Factory Overhead
Equivalent units to complete beginning goods in process			
Direct materials (30,000 × 0%)	0 EUP		
Direct labor (30,000 × 35%)		10,500 EUP	
Factory overhead (30,000 × 35%)			10,500 EUP
Equivalent units started and completed	70,000	70,000	70,000
Equivalent units in ending goods in process			
Direct materials (20,000 × 100%)	20,000		
Direct labor (20,000 × 25%)		5,000	
Factory overhead (20,000 × 25%)			5000
Equivalent units of production	90,000 EUP	85,500 EUP	85,500 EUP

Cost per equivalent unit of production	Direct Materials	Direct Labor	Factory Overhead
Costs incurred this period	$9,900	$5,700	$6,840
÷ Equivalent units of production	90,000 EUP	85,500 EUP	85,500 EUP
Cost per equivalent unit of production	$0.11 per EUP	$0.067 per EUP	$0.08 per EUP

Cost assignment and reconciliation

(cost of units completed and transferred out)

Cost of beginning goods in process		$ 4,620
Cost to complete beginning goods in process		
Direct materials ($0.11 per EUP × 0 EUP)	$ 0	
Direct labor ($0.067 per EUP × 10,500 EUP)	704	
Factory overhead ($0.08 per EUP × 10,500 EUP)	840	1,544
Cost of units started and completed this period		
Direct materials ($0.11 per EUP × 70,000 EUP)	7,700	
Direct labor ($0.067 per EUP × 70,000 EUP)	4,690	
Factory overhead ($0.08 per EUP × 70,000 EUP)	5,600	17,990
Total cost of units finished this period		24,154

Cost of ending goods in process

Direct materials ($0.11 per EUP × 20,000 EUP)	2,200	
Direct labor ($0.067 per EUP × 5,000 EUP)	335	
Factory overhead ($0.08 per EUP × 5,000 EUP)	400	
Total cost of ending goods in process		2,935
Total costs accounted for		$27,089* ◄

reconciled

*$29 difference due to rounding

Summary

C1 **Explain process operations and the way they differ from job order operations.** Process operations produce large quantities of similar products or services by passing them through a series of processes, or steps, in production. Like job order operations, they combine direct materials, direct labor, and overhead in the operations. Unlike job order operations that assign the responsibility for each job to a manager, process operations assign the responsibility for each *process* to a manager.

C2 **Define equivalent units and explain their use in process cost accounting.** Equivalent units of production measure the activity of a process as the number of units that would be completed in a period if all effort had been applied to units that were started and finished. This measure of production activity is used to compute the cost per equivalent unit and to assign costs to finished goods and goods in process inventory.

C3 **Explain the four steps in accounting for production activity in a period.** The four steps involved in accounting for production activity in a period are (1) recording the physical flow of units, (2) computing the equivalent units of production, (3) computing the cost per equivalent unit of production, and (4) reconciling costs. The last step involves assigning costs to finished goods and goods in process inventory for the period.

C4 **Define a process cost summary and describe its purposes.** A process cost summary reports on the activities of a production process or department for a period. It describes the costs charged to the department, the equivalent units of production for the department, and the costs assigned to the output. The report aims to (1) help managers control their departments, (2) help factory managers evaluate department managers' performances, and (3) provide cost information for financial statements.

C5 **Explain and illustrate the four steps in accounting for production activity using FIFO.** The FIFO method for process costing is applied and illustrated to (1) report the physical flow of units, (2) compute the equivalent units of production, (3) compute the cost per equivalent unit of production, and (4) assign and reconcile costs.

A1 **Compare process cost accounting and job order cost accounting.** Process and job order manufacturing operations are similar in that both combine materials, labor, and factory overhead to produce products or services. They differ in the way they are organized and managed. In job order operations, the job order cost accounting system assigns materials, labor, and overhead to specific jobs. In process operations, the process cost accounting system assigns materials, labor, and overhead to specific processes. The total costs associated with each process are then divided by the number of units passing through that process to get cost per

equivalent unit. The costs per equivalent unit for all processes are added to determine the total cost per unit of a product or service.

A2 **Explain and illustrate a hybrid costing system.** A hybrid costing system contains features of both job order and process costing systems. Generally, certain direct materials are accounted for by individual products as in job order costing, but direct labor and overhead costs are accounted for similar to process costing.

P1 **Record the flow of direct materials costs in process cost accounting.** Materials purchased are debited to a Raw Materials Inventory account. As direct materials are issued to processes, they are separately accumulated in a Goods in Process Inventory account for that process.

P2 **Record the flow of direct labor costs in process cost accounting.** Direct labor costs are initially debited to the Factory Payroll account. The total amount in it is then assigned to the Goods in Process Inventory account pertaining to each process.

P3 **Record the flow of factory overhead costs in process cost accounting.** The different factory overhead items are first accumulated in the Factory Overhead account and are then allocated, using a predetermined overhead rate, to the different processes. The allocated amount is debited to the Goods in Process Inventory account pertaining to each process.

P4 **Compute equivalent units produced in a period.** To compute equivalent units, determine the number of units that would have been finished if all materials (or labor or overhead) had been used to produce units that were started and completed during the period. The costs incurred by a process are divided by its equivalent units to yield cost per unit.

P5 **Prepare a process cost summary.** A process cost summary includes the physical flow of units, equivalent units of production, costs per equivalent unit, and a cost reconciliation. It reports the units and costs to account for during the period and how they were accounted for during the period. In terms of units, the summary includes the beginning goods in process inventory and the units started during the month. These units are accounted for in terms of the goods completed and transferred out, and the ending goods in process inventory. With respect to costs, the summary includes materials, labor, and overhead costs assigned to the process during the period. It shows how these costs are assigned to goods completed and transferred out, and to ending goods in process inventory.

P6 **Record the transfer of completed goods to Finished Goods Inventory and Cost of Goods Sold.** As units complete the final process and are eventually sold, their accumulated cost is transferred to Finished Goods Inventory and finally to Cost of Goods Sold.

Guidance Answers to **Decision Maker** and **Decision Ethics**

Budget Officer   By instructing you to classify a majority of costs as indirect, the manager is passing some of his department's costs to a common overhead pool that other departments will partially absorb. Since overhead costs are allocated on the basis of direct labor for this company and the new department has a relatively low direct labor cost, the new department will be assigned less overhead. Such action

suggests unethical behavior by this manager. You must object to such reclassification. If this manager refuses to comply, you must inform someone in a more senior position.

Entrepreneur   By spreading the added quality-related costs across three customers, the entrepreneur is probably trying to remain competitive with respect to the customer that demands the 100% quality inspection. Moreover, the entrepreneur is partly covering the added costs by recovering two-thirds of them from the other two customers who are paying 110% of total costs. This act likely breaches the trust placed by the two customers in this entrepreneur's application of its costing system. The costing system should be changed, and the entrepreneur should consider renegotiating the pricing and/or quality

test agreement with this one customer (at the risk of losing this currently loss-producing customer).

Cost Manager Differences between the FIFO and weighted-average methods are greatest when large work in process inventories exist and when costs fluctuate. The method used if inventories are eliminated does not matter; both produce identical costs.

Guidance Answers to **Quick Checks**

1. *c*

2. When a company produces large quantities of similar products/ services, a process cost system is often more suitable.

3. *b*

4. The costs are direct materials, direct labor, and overhead.

5. A goods in process inventory account is needed for *each* production department.

6. *a*

7. Equivalent units with respect to direct labor are the number of units that would have been produced if all labor had been used on units that were started and finished during the period.

8.

Units completed and transferred out	58,000 EUP
Units of ending goods in process	
Direct labor (6,000 × 1/3)	2,000 EUP
Units of production	60,000 EUP

9. The first section shows the costs charged to the department. The second section describes the equivalent units produced by the department. The third section shows the assignment of total costs to units worked on during the period.

Key Terms

mhhe.com/wildFAP19e

Key Terms are available at the book's Website for learning and testing in an online Flashcard Format.

Cost of goods manufactured (p. 821)
Equivalent units of production (EUP) (p. 815)
FIFO method (p. 827)

Job order cost accounting system (p. 811)
Materials consumption report (p. 812)
Process cost accounting system (p. 811)

Process cost summary (p. 820)
Process operations (p. 808)
Weighted-average method (p. 818)

Multiple Choice Quiz

Answers on p. 849

mhhe.com/wildFAP19e

Additional Quiz Questions are available at the book's Website.

1. Equivalent units of production are equal to
   a. Physical units that were completed this period from all effort being applied to them.
   b. The number of units introduced into the process this period.
   c. The number of finished units actually completed this period.
   d. The number of units that could have been started and completed given the cost incurred.
   e. The number of units in the process at the end of the period.

2. Recording the cost of raw materials purchased for use in a process costing system includes a
   a. Credit to Raw Materials Inventory.
   b. Debit to Goods in Process Inventory.
   c. Debit to Factory Overhead.
   d. Credit to Factory Overhead.
   e. Debit to Raw Materials Inventory.

3. The production department started the month with a beginning goods in process inventory of $20,000. During the month, it was assigned the following costs: direct materials, $152,000; direct labor, $45,000; overhead applied at the rate of 40% of direct labor cost. Inventory with a cost of $218,000 was transferred to finished goods. The ending balance of goods in process inventory is
   a. $330,000.
   b. $ 17,000.
   c. $220,000.
   d. $112,000.
   e. $118,000.

4. A company's beginning work in process inventory consists of 10,000 units that are 20% complete with respect to direct labor costs. A total of 40,000 units are completed this period. There

Quiz20

are 15,000 units in goods in process, one-third complete for direct labor, at period-end. The equivalent units of production (EUP) with respect to direct labor at period-end, assuming the weighted average method, are

  a. 45,000 EUP.
  b. 40,000 EUP.
  c. 5,000 EUP.
  d. 37,000 EUP.
  e. 43,000 EUP.

5. Assume the same information as in question 4. Also assume that beginning work in process had $6,000 in direct labor cost and that $84,000 in direct labor is added during this period. What is the cost per EUP for labor?

  a. $0.50 per EUP
  b. $1.87 per EUP
  c. $2.00 per EUP
  d. $2.10 per EUP
  e. $2.25 per EUP

Assume the weighted-average inventory method is used for all assignments unless stated differently.
Superscript letter ^{A} denotes assignments based on Appendix 20A.

Discussion Questions

1. ♟ Can services be delivered by means of process operations? Support your answer with an example.

2. ♟ What is the main factor for a company in choosing between the job order costing and process costing accounting systems? Give two likely applications of each system.

3. Identify the control document for materials flow when a materials requisition slip is not used.

4. The focus in a job order costing system is the job or batch. Identify the main focus in process costing.

5. Are the journal entries that match cost flows to product flows in process costing primarily the same or much different than those in job order costing? Explain.

6. ♟ Explain in simple terms the notion of equivalent units of production (EUP). Why is it necessary to use EUP in process costing?

7. ♟ What are the two main inventory methods used in process costing? What are the differences between these methods?

8. ♟ Why is it possible for direct labor in process operations to include the labor of employees who do not work directly on products or services?

9. Assume that a company produces a single product by processing it first through a single production department. Direct labor costs flow through what accounts in this company's process cost system?

10. After all labor costs for a period are allocated, what balance should remain in the Factory Payroll account?

11. ♟ Is it possible to have under- or overapplied overhead costs in a process cost accounting system? Explain.

12. Explain why equivalent units of production for both direct labor and overhead can be the same as, and why they can be different from, equivalent units for direct materials.

13. List the four steps in accounting for production activity in a reporting period (for process operations).

14. What purposes does a process cost summary serve?

15. ♟ Are there situations where **Best Buy** can use process costing? Identify at least one and explain it.

16. ♟ **Apple** produces iMacs with a multiple production line. Identify and list some of its production processing steps and departments.

♟ **Denotes Discussion Questions that involve decision making.**

Available with McGraw-Hill's Homework Manager

QUICK STUDY

QS 20-1
Matching of product to cost accounting system
C1

For each of the following products and services, indicate whether it is most likely produced in a process operation or in a job order operation.

  1. Door hinges
  2. Cut flower arrangements
  3. House paints
  4. Concrete swimming pools

  5. Custom tailored suits
  6. Grand pianos
  7. Wall clocks
  8. Sport shirts

  9. Bolts and nuts
  10. Folding chairs
  11. Headphones
  12. Designed boathouse

QS 20-2
Recording costs of direct materials
P1

Industrial Boxes makes cardboard shipping cartons in a single operation. This period, Industrial purchased $124,000 in raw materials. Its production department requisitioned $100,000 of those materials for use in producing cartons. Prepare journal entries to record its (1) purchase of raw materials and (2) requisition of direct materials.

QS 20-3
Recording costs of direct labor
P2

Refer to the information in QS 20-2. Industrial Boxes incurred $270,000 in factory payroll costs, of which $250,000 was direct labor. Prepare journal entries to record its (1) total factory payroll incurred and (2) direct labor used in production.

Refer to the information in QS 20-2 and QS 20-3. Industrial Boxes requisitioned $18,000 of indirect materials from its raw materials and used $20,000 of indirect labor in its production of boxes. Also, it incurred $312,000 of other factory overhead costs. It applies factory overhead at the rate of 135% of direct labor costs. Prepare journal entries to record its (1) indirect materials requisitioned, (2) indirect labor used in production, (3) other factory overhead costs incurred, and (4) application of overhead to production.

QS 20-4
Recording costs of factory overhead
P3

Refer to the information in QS 20-2, QS 20-3, and QS 20-4. Industrial Boxes completed 40,000 boxes costing $550,000 and transferred them to finished goods. Prepare its journal entry to record the transfer of the boxes from production to finished goods inventory.

QS 20-5
Recording transfer of costs to finished goods P6

The following refers to units processed in Sunflower Printing's binding department in March. Compute the total equivalent units of production with respect to labor for March using the weighted-average inventory method.

QS 20-6
Computing equivalent units of production

P4

	Units of Product	Percent of Labor Added
Beginning goods in process	75,000	85%
Goods started	155,000	100
Goods completed	170,000	100
Ending goods in process	60,000	25

The cost of beginning inventory plus the costs added during the period should equal the cost of units _____ plus the cost of _____.

QS 20-7
Computing EUP cost C4 P5

Explain a hybrid costing system. Identify a product or service operation that might well fit a hybrid costing system.

QS 20-8
Hybrid costing system A2

Refer to QS 20-6 and compute the total equivalent units of production with respect to labor for March using the FIFO inventory method.

QS 20-9^A
Computing equivalent units—FIFO C2 C5 P4

McGraw-Hill's
HOMEWORK MANAGER® Available with McGraw-Hill's Homework Manager

Match each of the following items A through G with the best numbered description of its purpose.

A. Raw Materials Inventory account
B. Materials requisition
C. Finished Goods Inventory account
D. Factory Overhead account
E. Process cost summary
F. Equivalent units of production
G. Goods in Process Inventory

EXERCISES

Exercise 20-1
Terminology in process cost accounting
C1 A1 P1 P2 P3

_____ **1.** Notifies the materials manager to send materials to a production department.
_____ **2.** Holds costs of indirect materials, indirect labor, and similar costs until assigned to production.
_____ **3.** Holds costs of direct materials, direct labor, and applied overhead until products are transferred from production to finished goods (or another department).
_____ **4.** Standardizes partially completed units into equivalent completed units.
_____ **5.** Holds costs of finished products until sold to customers.
_____ **6.** Describes the activity and output of a production department for a period.
_____ **7.** Holds costs of materials until they are used in production or as factory overhead.

Festive Toy Company manufactures toy trucks. Prepare journal entries to record its following production activities for January.

1. Purchased $40,000 of raw materials on credit.
2. Used $17,000 of direct materials in production.
3. Used $20,500 of indirect materials.

Exercise 20-2
Journal entries in process cost accounting
P1 P2 P3

4. Incurred total labor cost of $77,000, which is paid in cash.

5. Used $58,000 of direct labor in production.

6. Used $19,000 of indirect labor.

7. Incurred overhead costs of $22,000 (paid in cash).

8. Applied overhead at 90% of direct labor costs.

9. Transferred completed products with a cost of $137,000 to finished goods inventory.

10. Sold $450,000 of products on credit. Their cost is $150,000.

Exercise 20-3

Recording cost flows in a process
cost system

P1 P2 P3 P6

Seattle Lumber produces bagged bark for use in landscaping. Production involves packaging bark chips in plastic bags in a bagging department. The following information describes production operations for October.

	Bagging Department
File Edit View Insert Format Tools Data Window Help	
3 Direct materials used	$ 460,000
4 Direct labor used	$ 76,000
5 Predetermined overhead rate (based on direct labor)	180%
6 Goods transferred from bagging to finished goods	$(407,000)

The company's revenue for the month totaled $900,000 from credit sales, and its cost of goods sold for the month is $500,000. Prepare summary journal entries dated October 31 to record its October production activities for (1) direct material usage, (2) direct labor usage, (3) overhead allocation, (4) goods transfer from production to finished goods, and (5) sales.

Exercise 20-4

Interpretation of journal entries
in process cost accounting

P1 P2 P3 P6

The following journal entries are recorded in Lewis Co.'s process cost accounting system. Lewis produces apparel and accessories. Overhead is applied to production based on direct labor cost for the period. Prepare a brief explanation (including any overhead rates applied) for each journal entry *a* through *j*.

a.	Raw Materials Inventory	52,000	
	Accounts Payable		52,000
b.	Goods in Process Inventory	42,000	
	Raw Materials Inventory		42,000
c.	Goods in Process Inventory	26,000	
	Factory Payroll		26,000
d.	Factory Payroll	32,000	
	Cash		32,000
e.	Factory Overhead	10,000	
	Cash		10,000
f.	Factory Overhead	10,000	
	Raw Materials Inventory		10,000
g.	Factory Overhead	6,000	
	Factory Payroll		6,000
h.	Goods in Process Inventory	32,500	
	Factory Overhead		32,500
i.	Finished Goods Inventory	88,000	
	Goods in Process Inventory		88,000
j.	Accounts Receivable	250,000	
	Sales		250,000
	Cost of Goods Sold	100,000	
	Finished Goods Inventory		100,000

During April, the production department of a process manufacturing system completed a number of units of a product and transferred them to finished goods. Of these transferred units, 30,000 were in process in the production department at the beginning of April and 120,000 were started and completed in April. April's beginning inventory units were 60% complete with respect to materials and 40% complete with respect to labor. At the end of April, 41,000 additional units were in process in the production department and were 80% complete with respect to materials and 30% complete with respect to labor.

1. Compute the number of units transferred to finished goods.

2. Compute the number of equivalent units with respect to both materials used and labor used in the production department for April using the weighted-average method.

Exercise 20-5
Computing equivalent units of production—weighted average

C2   P4

Check   (2) EUP for materials, 182,800

The production department described in Exercise 20-5 had $425,184 of direct materials and $326,151 of direct labor cost charged to it during April. Also, its beginning inventory included $59,236 of direct materials cost and $22,794 of direct labor.

1. Compute the direct materials cost and the direct labor cost per equivalent unit for the department.

2. Using the weighted-average method, assign April's costs to the department's output—specifically, its units transferred to finished goods and its ending goods in process inventory.

Exercise 20-6
Costs assigned to output and inventories—weighted average

C3   P4   P5

Check   (2) Costs accounted for, $833,365

Refer to the information in Exercise 20-5 to compute the number of equivalent units with respect to both materials used and labor used in the production department for April using the FIFO method.

Exercise 20-7[A]
Computing equivalent units of production—FIFO

C5   P4

Refer to the information in Exercise 20-6 and complete its parts (1) and (2) using the FIFO method.

Exercise 20-8[A]
Costs assigned to output—FIFO

C5   P4   P5

The production department in a process manufacturing system completed 383,000 units of product and transferred them to finished goods during a recent period. Of these units, 63,000 were in process at the beginning of the period. The other 320,000 units were started and completed during the period. At period-end, 59,000 units were in process. Compute the department's equivalent units of production with respect to direct materials under each of three separate assumptions:

1. All direct materials are added to products when processing begins.

2. Direct materials are added to products evenly throughout the process. Beginning goods in process inventory was 40% complete, and ending goods in process inventory was 75% complete.

3. One-half of direct materials is added to products when the process begins and the other half is added when the process is 75% complete as to direct labor. Beginning goods in process inventory is 40% complete as to direct labor, and ending goods in process inventory is 60% complete as to direct labor.

Exercise 20-9
Equivalent units computed—weighted average

C2   P4   P5

Check   (3) EUP for materials, 412,500

Refer to the information in Exercise 20-9 and complete it for each of the three separate assumptions using the FIFO method for process costing.

Exercise 20-10[A]
Equivalent units computed—FIFO

C5   P4

Check   (3) EUP for materials, 381,000

The following flowchart shows the August production activity of the Jez Company. Use the amounts shown on the flowchart to compute the missing four numbers identified by blanks.

Exercise 20-11
Flowchart of costs for a process operation   P1   P2   P3   P6

Production

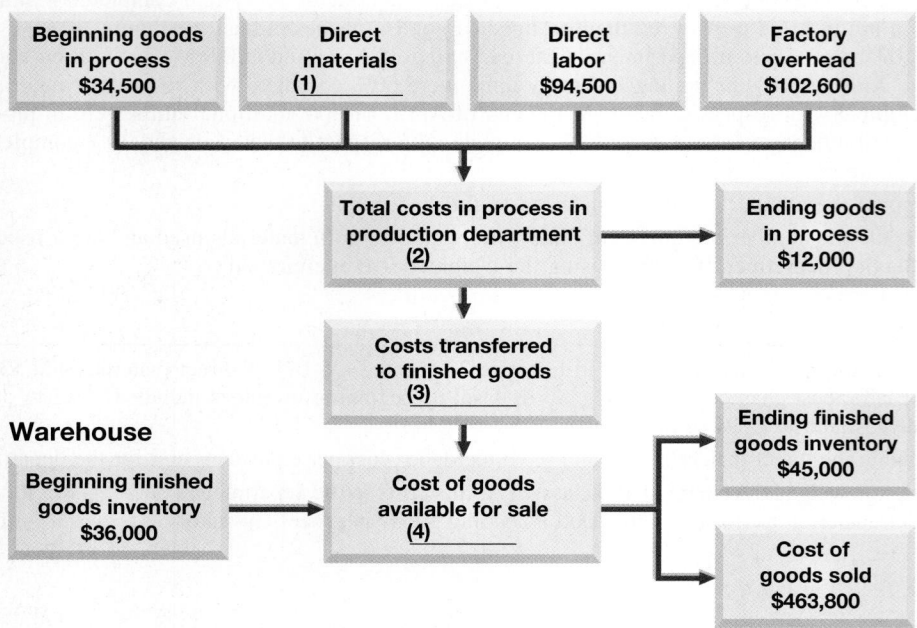

(1)

Exercise 20-12
Completing a process cost summary

P5 ♟

The following partially completed process cost summary describes the July production activities of Anton Company. Its production output is sent to its warehouse for shipping. Prepare its process cost summary using the weighted-average method.

Equivalent Units of Production	Direct Materials	Direct Labor	Factory Overhead
Units transferred out	64,000	64,000	64,000
Units of ending goods in process	5,000	3,000	3,000
Equivalent units of production	69,000	67,000	67,000

Costs per EUP	Direct Materials	Direct Labor	Factory Overhead
Costs of beginning goods in process	$ 37,100	$ 1,520	$ 3,040
Costs incurred this period	715,000	125,780	251,560
Total costs	$752,100	$127,300	$254,600

Units in beginning goods in process	4,000
Units started this period	65,000
Units completed and transferred out	64,000
Units in ending goods in process	5,000

Exercise 20-13
Process costing—weighted average

P1 P2 P6

Nu-Test Company uses the weighted-average method of process costing to assign production costs to its products. Information for September follows. Assume that all materials are added at the beginning of its production process, and that direct labor and factory overhead are added uniformly throughout the process.

Goods in process inventory, September 1 (4,000 units, 100% complete with respect to direct materials, 80% complete with respect to direct labor and overhead; includes $90,000 of direct material cost, $51,200 in direct labor cost, $61,440 overhead cost)	$202,640
Units started in September	56,000
Units completed and transferred to finished goods inventory	46,000
Goods in process inventory, September 30 (? units, 100% complete with respect to direct materials, 40% complete with respect to direct labor and overhead)	?

[continued on next page]

[continued from previous page]

Costs incurred in September	
Direct materials	$750,000
Direct labor	$310,000
Overhead applied at 120% of direct labor cost	?

Required

Fill in the blanks labeled *a* through *uu* in the following process cost summary.

NU-TEST COMPANY
Process Cost Summary
For Month Ended September 30

Costs Charged to Production

Costs of beginning goods in process		
Direct materials	$ 90,000	
Direct labor	51,200	
Factory overhead	61,440	$202,640
Costs incurred this period		
Direct materials	$750,000	
Direct labor	310,000	
Factory overhead	(a)_____	(b)_____
Total costs to account for		(c)_____

Check (c) $1,634,640

Unit Cost Information

Units to account for		Units accounted for	
Beginning goods in process	4,000	Completed and transferred out	46,000
Units started this period	56,000	Ending goods in process	(d)_____
Total units to account for	(e)_____	Total units accounted for	(f)_____

Equivalent Units of Production (EUP)			Direct Materials	Direct Labor	Factory Overhead
Units completed and transferred out			(g)_____EUP	(h)_____EUP	(i)_____EUP
Units of ending goods in process					
Materials	(j)_____	× 100%	(k)_____EUP		
Direct labor	(l)_____	× 40%		(m)_____EUP	
Factory overhead	(n)_____	× 40%			(o)_____EUP
Equivalent units of production (EUP)			(p)_____EUP	(q)_____EUP	(r)_____EUP

Cost per EUP	Direct Materials	Direct Labor	Factory Overhead
Costs of beginning goods in process	$ 90,000	$ 51,200	$61,440
Costs incurred this period	750,000	310,000	(s)_____
Total costs	$840,000	$361,200	(t)_____
÷ EUP	(u)_____	(v)_____	(w)_____
Cost per EUP	(x)_____	(y)_____	(z)_____

(z) $8.40 per EUP

Cost Assignment and Reconciliation

Costs transferred out	Cost/EUP	×	EUP		
Direct materials	(aa)_____	×	(bb)_____	(cc)_____	
Direct labor	(dd)_____	×	(ee)_____	(ff)_____	
Factory overhead	(gg)_____	×	(hh)_____	(ii)_____	
Costs of goods completed and transferred out					(jj)_____
Costs of ending goods in process					
Direct materials	(kk)_____	×	(ll)_____	(mm)_____	
Direct labor	(nn)_____	×	(oo)_____	(pp)_____	
Factory overhead	(qq)_____	×	(rr)_____	(ss)_____	
Costs of ending goods in process					(tt)_____
Total costs accounted for					(uu)_____

PROBLEM SET A

Problem 20-1A
Production cost flow and measurement; journal entries

P1 P2 P3 P6

Harvey Company manufactures woven blankets and accounts for product costs using process costing. The following information is available regarding its May inventories.

	Beginning Inventory	Ending Inventory
Raw materials inventory	$ 56,000	$ 51,000
Goods in process inventory	441,500	504,000
Finished goods inventory	638,000	554,000

The following additional information describes the company's production activities for May.

Raw materials purchases (on credit)	$ 270,000
Factory payroll cost (paid in cash)	1,583,000
Other overhead cost (Other Accounts credited)	86,000
Materials used	
Direct	$ 187,000
Indirect	62,000
Labor used	
Direct	$ 704,000
Indirect	879,000
Overhead rate as a percent of direct labor	110%
Sales (on credit)	$3,000,000

Required

Check   (1b) Cost of goods sold
$1,686,900

1. Compute the cost of (a) products transferred from production to finished goods, and (b) goods sold.

2. Prepare summary journal entries dated May 31 to record the following production activities during May: (a) raw materials purchases, (b) direct materials usage, (c) indirect materials usage, (d) payroll costs, (e) direct labor costs, (f) indirect labor costs, (g) other overhead costs, (h) overhead applied, (i) goods transferred from production to finished goods, and (j) sale of finished goods.

Problem 20-2A
Cost per equivalent unit; costs assigned to products

P4 P5

mhhe.com/wildFAP19e

Carmen Company uses weighted-average process costing to account for its production costs. Direct labor is added evenly throughout the process. Direct materials are added at the beginning of the process. During November, the company transferred 735,000 units of product to finished goods. At the end of November, the goods in process inventory consists of 207,000 units that are 90% complete with respect to labor. Beginning inventory had $244,920 of direct materials and $69,098 of direct labor cost. The direct labor cost added in November is $1,312,852, and the direct materials cost added is $1,639,080.

Required

Check   (2) Direct labor cost per
equivalent unit, $1.50

(3b) $693,450

1. Determine the equivalent units of production with respect to (a) direct labor and (b) direct materials.

2. Compute both the direct labor cost and the direct materials cost per equivalent unit.

3. Compute both direct labor cost and direct materials cost assigned to (a) units completed and transferred out, and (b) ending goods in process inventory.

Analysis Component

4. The company sells and ships all units to customers as soon as they are completed. Assume that an error is made in determining the percentage of completion for units in ending inventory. Instead of being 90% complete with respect to labor, they are actually 75% complete. Write a one-page memo to the plant manager describing how this error affects its November financial statements.

Crystal Company produces large quantities of a standardized product. The following information is available for its production activities for March.

Problem 20-3A
Journalizing in process costing; equivalent units and costs

P1 P2 P3 P4 P6

Raw materials		Factory overhead incurred	
Beginning inventory	$ 26,000	Indirect materials used	$ 81,500
Raw materials purchased (on credit)	255,000	Indirect labor used	50,000
Direct materials used	(172,000)	Other overhead costs	159,308
Indirect materials used	(81,500)	Total factory overhead incurred	$290,808
Ending inventory	$ 27,500		
		Factory overhead applied	
Factory payroll		**(140% of direct labor cost)**	
Direct labor used	$207,720	Total factory overhead applied	$290,808
Indirect labor used	50,000		
Total payroll cost (paid in cash)	$257,720		

Additional information about units and costs of production activities follows.

Units		Costs		
Beginning goods in process inventory	2,200	Beginning goods in process inventory		
Started	30,000	Direct materials	$3,500	
Ending goods in process inventory	5,900	Direct labor	3,225	
		Factory overhead	4,515	$ 11,240
Status of ending goods in process inventory		Direct materials added		172,000
Materials—Percent complete	50%	Direct labor added		207,720
Labor and overhead—Percent complete	65%	Overhead applied (140% of direct labor)		290,808
		Total costs		$681,768
		Ending goods in process inventory		$ 82,128

During March, 25,000 units of finished goods are sold for $85 cash each. Cost information regarding finished goods follows.

Beginning finished goods inventory	$155,000
Cost transferred in	599,640
Cost of goods sold	(612,500)
Ending finished goods inventory	$142,140

Required

1. Prepare journal entries dated March 31 to record the following March activities: (a) purchase of raw materials, (b) direct materials usage, (c) indirect materials usage, (d) factory payroll costs, (e) direct labor costs used in production, (f) indirect labor costs, (g) other overhead costs—credit Other Accounts, (h) overhead applied, (i) goods transferred to finished goods, and (j) sale of finished goods.

2. Prepare a process cost summary report for this company, showing costs charged to production, units cost information, equivalent units of production, cost per EUP, and its cost assignment and reconciliation.

Check (2) Cost per equivalent unit: materials, $6.00; labor, $7.00; overhead, $9.80

Analysis Component

3. The company provides incentives to its department managers by paying monthly bonuses based on their success in controlling costs per equivalent unit of production. Assume that the production department underestimates the percentage of completion for units in ending inventory with the result that its equivalent units of production in ending inventory for March are understated. What impact does this error have on the March bonuses paid to the production managers? What impact, if any, does this error have on April bonuses?

Problem 20-4A

Process cost summary; equivalent units

P4 P5 P6

mhhe.com/wildFAP19e

King Co. produces its product through a single processing department. Direct materials are added at the start of production, and direct labor and overhead are added evenly throughout the process. The company uses monthly reporting periods for its weighted-average process cost accounting system. Its Goods in Process Inventory account follows after entries for direct materials, direct labor, and overhead costs for October.

Goods in Process Inventory			Acct. No. 133	
Date	Explanation	Debit	Credit	Balance
Oct. 1	Balance			348,638
31	Direct materials	104,090		452,728
31	Direct labor	416,360		869,088
31	Applied overhead	244,920		1,114,008

Its beginning goods in process consisted of $60,830 of direct materials, $176,820 of direct labor, and $110,988 of factory overhead. During October, the company started 140,000 units and transferred 153,000 units to finished goods. At the end of the month, the goods in process inventory consisted of 20,600 units that were 80% complete with respect to direct labor and factory overhead.

Required

Check (1) Costs transferred to finished goods, $1,002,150

1. Prepare the company's process cost summary for October using the weighted-average method.

2. Prepare the journal entry dated October 31 to transfer the cost of the completed units to finished goods inventory.

Problem 20-5A

Process cost summary; equivalent units; cost estimates

P4 P5

Cisneros Co. manufactures a single product in one department. All direct materials are added at the beginning of the manufacturing process. Direct labor and overhead are added evenly throughout the process. The company uses monthly reporting periods for its weighted-average process cost accounting. During May, the company completed and transferred 11,100 units of product to finished goods inventory. Its 1,500 units of beginning goods in process consisted of $9,900 of direct materials, $61,650 of direct labor, and $49,320 of factory overhead. It has 1,200 units (100% complete with respect to direct materials and 80% complete with respect to direct labor and overhead) in process at month-end. After entries to record direct materials, direct labor, and overhead for May, the company's Goods in Process Inventory account follows.

Goods in Process Inventory			Acct. No. 133	
Date	Explanation	Debit	Credit	Balance
May 1	Balance			120,870
31	Direct materials	248,400		369,270
31	Direct labor	601,650		970,920
31	Applied overhead	481,320		1,452,240

Required

Check (1) EUP for labor and overhead, 12,060 EUP

(2) Cost transferred to finished goods, $1,332,000

1. Prepare the company's process cost summary for May.

2. Prepare the journal entry dated May 31 to transfer the cost of completed units to finished goods inventory.

Analysis Components

3. The cost accounting process depends on numerous estimates.

  a. Identify two major estimates that determine the cost per equivalent unit.

  b. In what direction might you anticipate a bias from management for each estimate in part 3a (assume that management compensation is based on maintaining low inventory amounts)? Explain your answer.

Problem 20-6A[A]

Process cost summary; equivalent units; cost estimates—FIFO

C5 P5 P6

Refer to the data in Problem 20-5A. Assume that Cisneros uses the FIFO method to account for its process costing system. The following additional information is available:

• Beginning goods in process consisted of 1,500 units that were 100% complete with respect to direct materials and 40% complete with respect to direct labor and overhead.

• Of the 11,100 units completed, 1,500 were from beginning goods in process. The remaining 9,600 were units started and completed during May.

Required

1. Prepare the company's process cost summary for May using FIFO.

2. Prepare the journal entry dated May 31 to transfer the cost of completed units to finished goods inventory.

Check (1) EUP for labor and overhead, 11,460 EUP

(2) Cost transferred to finished goods, $1,333,920

Select Toys Company manufactures video game consoles and accounts for product costs using process costing. The following information is available regarding its June inventories.

	Beginning Inventory	Ending Inventory
Raw materials inventory	$36,000	$ 55,000
Goods in process inventory	78,000	125,000
Finished goods inventory	80,000	99,000

The following additional information describes the company's production activities for June.

Raw materials purchases (on credit)	$100,000
Factory payroll cost (paid in cash)	200,000
Other overhead cost (Other Accounts credited)	85,250
Materials used	
Direct	$ 60,000
Indirect	21,000
Labor used	
Direct	$175,000
Indirect	25,000
Overhead rate as a percent of direct labor	75%
Sales (on credit)	$500,000

Required

1. Compute the cost of (a) products transferred from production to finished goods, and (b) goods sold.

2. Prepare journal entries dated June 30 to record the following production activities during June: (a) raw materials purchases, (b) direct materials usage, (c) indirect materials usage, (d) payroll costs, (e) direct labor costs, (f) indirect labor costs, (g) other overhead costs, (h) overhead applied, (i) goods transferred from production to finished goods, and (j) sale of finished goods.

PROBLEM SET B

Problem 20-1B
Production cost flow and measurement; journal entries

P1 P2 P3 P6

Check (1b) Cost of goods sold, $300,250

Maximus Company uses process costing to account for its production costs. Direct labor is added evenly throughout the process. Direct materials are added at the beginning of the process. During September, the production department transferred 40,000 units of product to finished goods. Beginning goods in process had $116,000 of direct materials and $172,800 of direct labor cost. At the end of September, the goods in process inventory consists of 4,000 units that are 25% complete with respect to labor. The direct materials cost added in September is $1,424,000, and direct labor cost added is $3,960,000.

Required

1. Determine the equivalent units of production with respect to (a) direct labor and (b) direct materials.

2. Compute both the direct labor cost and the direct materials cost per equivalent unit.

3. Compute both direct labor cost and direct materials cost assigned to (a) units completed and transferred out, and (b) ending goods in process inventory.

Analysis Component

4. The company sells and ships all units to customers as soon as they are completed. Assume that an error is made in determining the percentage of completion for units in ending inventory. Instead of being 25% complete with respect to labor, they are actually 75% complete. Write a one-page memo to the plant manager describing how this error affects its September financial statements.

Problem 20-2B
Cost per equivalent unit; costs assigned to products

P4 P5

Check (2) Direct labor cost per equivalent unit, $100.80

(3b) $240,800

Problem 20-3B
Journalizing in process costing;
equivalent units and costs

P1 P2 P3 P4 P6

Fantasia Company produces large quantities of a standardized product. The following information is available for its production activities for May.

Raw materials			Factory overhead incurred		
Beginning inventory	$ 16,000		Indirect materials used	$20,280	
Raw materials purchased (on credit)	110,560		Indirect labor used	18,160	
Direct materials used	(98,560)		Other overhead costs	17,216	
Indirect materials used	(20,280)		Total factory overhead incurred	$55,656	
Ending inventory	$ 7,720				
Factory payroll			**Factory overhead applied** **(90% of direct labor cost)**		
Direct labor used	$ 61,840		Total factory overhead applied	$55,656	
Indirect labor used	18,160				
Total payroll cost (paid in cash)	$ 80,000				

Additional information about units and costs of production activities follows.

Units		Costs		
Beginning goods in process inventory	8,000	Beginning goods in process inventory		
Started	24,000	Direct materials	$2,240	
Ending goods in process inventory	6,000	Direct labor	1,410	
		Factory overhead	1,269	$ 4,919
Status of ending goods in process inventory		Direct materials added		98,560
Materials—Percent complete	100%	Direct labor added		61,840
Labor and overhead—Percent complete	25%	Overhead applied (90% of direct labor)		55,656
		Total costs		$220,975
		Ending goods in process inventory		$ 25,455

During May, 30,000 units of finished goods are sold for $30 cash each. Cost information regarding finished goods follows.

Beginning finished goods inventory	$ 74,200	
Cost transferred in from production	195,520	
Cost of goods sold	(225,000)	
Ending finished goods inventory	$ 44,720	

Required

1. Prepare journal entries dated May 31 to record the following May activities: (a) purchase of raw materials, (b) direct materials usage, (c) indirect materials usage, (d) factory payroll costs, (e) direct labor costs used in production, (f) indirect labor costs, (g) other overhead costs—credit Other Accounts, (h) overhead applied, (i) goods transferred to finished goods, and (j) sale of finished goods.

Check (2) Cost per equivalent unit: materials, $3.15; labor, $2.30; overhead, $2.07

2. Prepare a process cost summary report for this company, showing costs charged to production, unit cost information, equivalent units of production, cost per EUP, and its cost assignment and reconciliation.

Analysis Component

3. This company provides incentives to its department managers by paying monthly bonuses based on their success in controlling costs per equivalent unit of production. Assume that production overestimates the percentage of completion for units in ending inventory with the result that its equivalent units of production in ending inventory for May are overstated. What impact does this error have on bonuses paid to the managers of the production department? What impact, if any, does this error have on these managers' June bonuses?

Paloma Company produces its product through a single processing department. Direct materials are added at the beginning of the process. Direct labor and overhead are added to the product evenly throughout the process. The company uses monthly reporting periods for its weighted-average process cost accounting. Its Goods in Process Inventory account follows after entries for direct materials, direct labor, and overhead costs for November.

Problem 20-4B
Process cost summary;
equivalent units
P4 P5 P6

Goods in Process Inventory				Acct. No. 133
Date	Explanation	Debit	Credit	Balance
Nov. 1	Balance			10,650
30	Direct materials	58,200		68,850
30	Direct labor	213,400		282,250
30	Applied overhead	320,100		602,350

The 3,750 units of beginning goods in process consisted of $3,400 of direct materials, $2,900 of direct labor, and $4,350 of factory overhead. During November, the company finished and transferred 50,000 units of its product to finished goods. At the end of the month, the goods in process inventory consisted of 6,000 units that were 100% complete with respect to direct materials and 25% complete with respect to direct labor and factory overhead.

Required

1. Prepare the company's process cost summary for November using the weighted-average method.
2. Prepare the journal entry dated November 30 to transfer the cost of the completed units to finished goods inventory.

Check (1) Cost transferred to finished goods, $580,000

Foster Co. manufactures a single product in one department. Direct labor and overhead are added evenly throughout the process. Direct materials are added as needed. The company uses monthly reporting periods for its weighted-average process cost accounting. During January, Foster completed and transferred 220,000 units of product to finished goods inventory. Its 10,000 units of beginning goods in process consisted of $8,400 of direct materials, $13,960 of direct labor, and $34,900 of factory overhead. 40,000 units (50% complete with respect to direct materials and 30% complete with respect to direct labor and overhead) are in process at month-end. After entries for direct materials, direct labor, and overhead for January, the company's Goods in Process Inventory account follows.

Problem 20-5B
Process cost summary;
equivalent units; cost estimates
P4 P5

Goods in Process Inventory				Acct. No. 133
Date	Explanation	Debit	Credit	Balance
Jan. 1	Balance			57,260
31	Direct materials	111,600		168,860
31	Direct labor	176,280		345,140
31	Applied overhead	440,700		785,840

Required

1. Prepare the company's process cost summary for January.
2. Prepare the journal entry dated January 31 to transfer the cost of completed units to finished goods inventory.

Check (1) EUP for labor and overhead, 232,000
(2) Cost transferred to finished goods, $741,400

Analysis Components

3. The cost accounting process depends on several estimates.
   a. Identify two major estimates that affect the cost per equivalent unit.
   b. In what direction might you anticipate a bias from management for each estimate in part 3a (assume that management compensation is based on maintaining low inventory amounts)? Explain your answer.

Problem 20-6B^A

Process cost summary; equivalent units; cost estimates—FIFO

C5 P5 P6

Refer to the information in Problem 20-5B. Assume that Foster uses the FIFO method to account for its process costing system. The following additional information is available.

- Beginning goods in process consists of 10,000 units that were 75% complete with respect to direct materials and 60% complete with respect to direct labor and overhead.
- Of the 220,000 units completed, 10,000 were from beginning goods in process; the remaining 210,000 were units started and completed during January.

Required

1. Prepare the company's process cost summary for January using FIFO. Round cost per EUP to one-tenth of a cent.
2. Prepare the journal entry dated January 31 to transfer the cost of completed units to finished goods inventory.

SERIAL PROBLEM

Success Systems

C1 A1

(This serial problem began in Chapter 1 and continues through most of the book. If previous chapter segments were not completed, the serial problem can begin at this point.)

SP 20 The computer workstation furniture manufacturing that Adriana Lopez started is progressing well. At this point, Adriana is using a job order costing system to account for the production costs of this product line. Adriana has heard about process costing and is wondering whether process costing might be a better method for her to keep track of and monitor her production costs.

Required

1. What are the features that distinguish job order costing from process costing?
2. Do you believe that Adriana should continue to use job order costing or switch to process costing for her workstation furniture manufacturing? Explain.

COMPREHENSIVE PROBLEM

Major League Bat Company

(Review of Chapters 2, 5, 18, 20)

CP 20 Major League Bat Company manufactures baseball bats. In addition to its goods in process inventories, the company maintains inventories of raw materials and finished goods. It uses raw materials as direct materials in production and as indirect materials. Its factory payroll costs include direct labor for production and indirect labor. All materials are added at the beginning of the process, and direct labor and factory overhead are applied uniformly throughout the production process.

Required

You are to maintain records and produce measures of inventories to reflect the July events of this company. Set up the following general ledger accounts and enter the June 30 balances: Raw Materials Inventory, $25,000; Goods in Process Inventory, $8,135 ($2,660 of direct materials, $3,650 of direct labor, and $1,825 of overhead); Finished Goods Inventory, $110,000; Sales, $0; Cost of Goods Sold, $0; Factory Payroll, $0; and Factory Overhead, $0.

1. Prepare journal entries to record the following July transactions and events.
   a. Purchased raw materials for $125,000 cash (the company uses a perpetual inventory system).
   b. Used raw materials as follows: direct materials, $52,440; and indirect materials, $10,000.
   c. Incurred factory payroll cost of $227,250 paid in cash (ignore taxes).
   d. Assigned factory payroll costs as follows: direct labor, $202,250; and indirect labor, $25,000.
   e. Incurred additional factory overhead costs of $80,000 paid in cash.
   f. Allocated factory overhead to production at 50% of direct labor costs.
2. Information about the July inventories follows. Use this information with that from part 1 to prepare a process cost summary, assuming the weighted-average method is used.

Units	
Beginning inventory	5,000 units
Started	14,000 units
Ending inventory	8,000 units
Beginning inventory	
Materials—Percent complete	100%
Labor and overhead—Percent complete	75%
Ending inventory	
Materials—Percent complete	100%
Labor and overhead—Percent complete	40%

3. Using the results from part 2 and the available information, make computations and prepare journal entries to record the following:

   a. Total costs transferred to finished goods for July (label this entry g).

   b. Sale of finished goods costing $265,700 for $625,000 in cash (label this entry h).

(3a) $271,150

4. Post entries from parts 1 and 3 to the ledger accounts set up at the beginning of the problem.

5. Compute the amount of gross profit from the sales in July. (*Note:* Add any underapplied overhead to, or deduct any overapplied overhead from, the cost of goods sold. Ignore the corresponding journal entry.)

BEYOND THE NUMBERS

BTN 20-1   Best Buy reports in notes to its financial statements that, in addition to its merchandise sold, it includes the following costs (among others) in cost of goods sold: freight expenses associated with moving inventories from vendors to distribution centers, costs of services provided, customer shipping and handling expenses, costs associated with operating its distribution network, and freight expenses associated with moving merchandise from distribution centers to retail stores.

REPORTING IN ACTION

C2

Required

1. Why do you believe Best Buy includes these costs in its cost of goods sold?

2. What effect does this cost accounting policy for its cost of goods sold have on Best Buy's financial statements and any analysis of these statements? Explain.

Fast Forward

3. Access Best Buy's financial statements for the fiscal years after March 3, 2007, from its Website (BestBuy.com) or the SEC's EDGAR Website (sec.gov). Review its footnote relating to Cost of Goods Sold and Selling, General, and Administrative Expense. Has Best Buy changed its policy with respect to what costs are included in the cost of goods sold? Explain.

BTN 20-2   Retailers such as Best Buy, Circuit City, and RadioShack usually work to maintain a high-quality and low-cost operation. One ratio routinely computed for this assessment is the cost of goods sold divided by total expenses. A decline in this ratio can mean that the company is spending too much on selling and administrative activities. An increase in this ratio beyond a reasonable level can mean that the company is not spending enough on selling activities. (Assume for this analysis that total expenses equal the cost of goods sold plus selling, general, and administrative expenses.)

COMPARATIVE ANALYSIS

C1

Required

1. For Best Buy, Circuit City, and RadioShack refer to Appendix A and compute the ratios of cost of goods sold to total expenses for their two most recent fiscal years.

2. Comment on the similarities or differences in the ratio results across both years among the companies.

**ETHICS
CHALLENGE**

C1 C3

BTN 20-3   Many accounting and accounting-related professionals are skilled in financial analysis, but most are not skilled in manufacturing. This is especially the case for process manufacturing environments (for example, a bottling plant or chemical factory). To provide professional accounting and financial services, one must understand the industry, product, and processes. We have an ethical responsibility to develop this understanding before offering services to clients in these areas.

Required

Write a one-page action plan, in memorandum format, discussing how you would obtain an understanding of key business processes of a company that hires you to provide financial services. The memorandum should specify an industry, a product, and one selected process and should draw on at least one reference, such as a professional journal or industry magazine.

**COMMUNICATING
IN PRACTICE**

A1 C1 P1 P2

BTN 20-4   You hire a new assistant production manager whose prior experience is with a company that produced goods to order. Your company engages in continuous production of homogeneous products that go through various production processes. Your new assistant e-mails you questioning some cost classifications on an internal report—specifically why the costs of some materials that do not actually become part of the finished product, including some labor costs not directly associated with producing the product, are classified as direct costs. Respond to this concern via memorandum.

**TAKING IT TO
THE NET**

C1 C3

BTN 20-5   Many companies acquire software to help them monitor and control their costs and as an aid to their accounting systems. One company that supplies such software is **proDacapo** (**prodacapo.com**). There are many other such vendors. Access proDacapo's Website, click on "Business Process Management," and review the information displayed.

Required

How is process management software helpful to businesses? Explain with reference to costs, efficiency, and examples, if possible.

**TEAMWORK IN
ACTION**

C1 P1 P2 P3 P6

BTN 20-6   The purpose of this team activity is to ensure that each team member understands process operations and the related accounting entries. Find the activities and flows identified in Exhibit 20.4 with numbers ①–⑩. Pick a member of the team to start by describing activity number ① in this exhibit, then verbalizing the related journal entry, and describing how the amounts in the entry are computed. The other members of the team are to agree or disagree; discussion is to continue until all members express understanding. Rotate to the next numbered activity and next team member until all activities and entries have been discussed. If at any point a team member is uncertain about an answer, the team member may pass and get back in the rotation when he or she can contribute to the team's discussion.

**ENTREPRENEURIAL
DECISION**

C4 A2

BTN 20-7   Read the chapter opener about **Hood River Juice Company**. David Ryan explained that purchasing apples year-round and processing them immediately reduces costs, and that his company blends juices to fit customer needs.

Required

1. How does not holding raw materials inventories (apples) reduce costs? If the items are not used in production, how can they affect profits? Explain.

2. Explain why Hood River Juice Company might use a hybrid costing system.

BTN 20-8   In process costing, the process is analyzed first and then a unit measure is computed in the form of equivalent units for direct materials, direct labor, overhead, and all three combined. The same analysis applies to both manufacturing and service processes.

HITTING THE ROAD

C3

Required

Visit your local **U.S. Mail** center. Look into the back room, and you will see several ongoing processes. Select one process, such as sorting, and list the costs associated with this process. Your list should include materials, labor, and overhead; be specific. Classify each cost as fixed or variable. At the bottom of your list, outline how overhead should be assigned to your identified process. The following format (with an example) is suggested.

Point: The class can compare and discuss the different processes studied and the answers provided.

Cost Description	Direct Material	Direct Labor	Overhead	Variable Cost	Fixed Cost
Manual sorting		X		X	
:					
Overhead allocation suggestions:					

BTN 20-9   **DSG international plc**, **Best Buy**, **Circuit City**, and **RadioShack** are competitors in the global marketplace. Selected data for DSG follow.

GLOBAL DECISION

C1

(millions of pounds)	Current Year	Prior Year
Cost of goods sold	£7,285	£6,369
General, selling, and administrative expenses	381	339
Total expenses	£7,666	£6,708

Required

1. Review the discussion of the importance of the cost of goods sold divided by total expenses ratio in BTN 20-2. Compute the cost of goods sold to total expenses ratio for DSG for the two years of data provided.

2. Comment on the similarities or differences in the ratio results calculated in part 1 and in BTN 20-2 across years and companies.

ANSWERS TO MULTIPLE CHOICE QUIZ

1. d

2. e

3. b; $20,000 + $152,000 + $45,000 + $18,000 − $218,000 = $17,000

4. a; 40,000 + (15,000 × 1/3) = 45,000 EUP

5. c; ($6,000 + $84,000) ÷ 45,000 EUP = $2 per EUP

A Look Back

Chapter 20 focused on how to measure and account for costs in process operations. It explained process production, described how to assign costs to processes, and computed cost per equivalent unit.

A Look at This Chapter

This chapter describes cost allocation and activity-based costing. It identifies managerial reports useful in directing a company's activities. It also describes responsibility accounting, measuring departmental performance, transfer pricing, and allocating common costs across departments.

A Look Ahead

Chapter 22 looks at cost behavior and explains how its identification is useful to managers in performing cost-volume-profit analyses. It also shows how to apply cost-volume-profit analysis for managerial decisions.

Chapter

Cost Allocation and Performance Measurement

Learning Objectives

CAP

Conceptual

C1 Explain departmentalization and the role of departmental accounting. *(p. 858)*

C2 Distinguish between direct and indirect expenses. *(p. 859)*

C3 Identify bases for allocating indirect expenses to departments. *(p. 860)*

C4 Explain controllable costs and responsibility accounting. *(p. 869)*

C5 *Appendix 21A*—Explain transfer pricing and methods to set transfer prices. *(p. 875)*

C6 *Appendix 21B*—Describe allocation of joint costs across products. *(p. 877)*

Analytical

A1 Analyze investment centers using return on assets, residual income, and balanced scorecard. *(p. 867)*

A2 Analyze investment centers using profit margin and investment turnover. *(p. 872)*

LP21

Procedural

P1 Assign overhead costs using two-stage cost allocation. *(p. 852)*

P2 Assign overhead costs using activity-based costing. *(p. 854)*

P3 Prepare departmental income statements. *(p. 861)*

P4 Prepare departmental contribution reports. *(p. 866)*

On The Green

"The more clicks we can get, the better our future"
—Todd Rath

ROCHESTER, NY—Brothers Tom and Todd Rath paid their college tuition by diving for lost golf balls and then reselling them. Today, their company RockBottomGolf.com applies a similar strategy of buying leftover products and reselling them. "Some of our critics refer to us as the 'graveyard of golf,'" explains Tom. "Oftentimes, we may be selling the last 3,000 drivers a manufacturer has ever made. If anyone can find a home for it, we can." The company boasts over 500,000 customers, affectionately referred to as "Rock Heads."

RockBottom's warehouse sports signs with "Scratch," the company's cartoonish, red-bearded caveman mascot. Scratch is surrounded with slogans such as: "A Clean Cave Is a Happy Cave" and "A Happy Rock Head Stays a Rock Head." Though Scratch is goofy, the company is all business. Offering a wide inventory of well-known brands of golf clubs, bags, balls, apparel, and accessories, the company buys in large lots and strives to keep overhead low. For example, they located their distribution center in Virginia—enabling them to ship to over 60% of the U.S. population within two days. Also, they pack items in small, uniformly sized boxes to lower costs and offer free shipping on certain orders.

Many other cost management procedures are applied. For example, they analyze "checkout flow," providing details on the point at which potential customers drop out of the checkout process and how many drop out. "If I had a 50% checkout success rate one day and 23% the next day, this lets me see that," explains Todd. This mix of financial and nonfinancial information helps Todd steer more customers through the checkout process. He also tracks customer approval ratings, currently above 99%, as a performance measure.

The diversity of its product offerings requires additional cost management. Company managers monitor direct, indirect, and controllable costs, and allocate them to departments and products. Understanding how it's product lines—such as clubs, bags, apparel—are performing and their contribution margins helps them plan for expansion. As Todd emphasizes, "We use tools to measure our ROI (return on investment). We will only expand as long as there are customers to win."

Their expansion plans do not stop with golf. RockBottomGolf wants to become RockBottomSports, with many other sporting goods products available. This increased departmentalization will require them to monitor contribution margins, return on investment, checkout flow, and customer approval. With its fast-paced growth and position as the top golf retailer on the Internet, RockBottomGolf is "on the green."

[Sources: *RockBottomGolf.com Website,* January 2009; *Internet Retailer,* July 2007; *Inside Business-Hampton Roads,* October 2006.]

This chapter describes how to allocate costs shared by more than one product across those different products and how to allocate indirect costs of shared items such as utilities, advertising, and rent. The chapter also describes activity-based costing and how it traces the costs of individual activities. This knowledge helps managers better understand how to assign costs and assess company performance. The chapter also introduces additional managerial accounting reports useful in managing a company's activities and explains how and why management divides companies into departments.

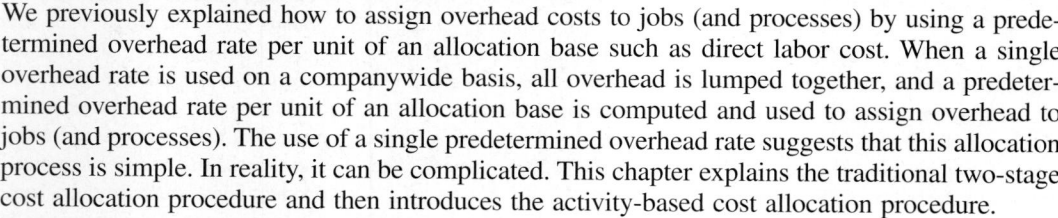

Cost Allocation and Performance Measurement

Overhead Cost Allocation Methods	Departmental Accounting	Departmental Expense Allocation	Investment Centers	Responsibility Accounting
• Two-stage cost allocation • Activity-based cost allocation • Comparison of allocation methods	• Motivation for departmentalization • Departmental evaluation • Departmental reporting and analysis	• Direct and indirect expenses • Allocation of indirect expenses • Departmental income statements • Departmental contribution to overhead	• Financial measures of performance • Nonfinancial measures of performance • Balanced scorecard	• Controllable versus direct costs • Responsibility accounting system • Transfer pricing

Section 1—Allocating Costs for Product Costing

Video21.1

This first of two sections in this chapter focuses on alternatives for allocation of costs to products and services. We explain and illustrate two basic methods: (1) traditional two-state cost allocation and (2) activity-based cost allocation. The second section describes and illustrates the allocation of costs for performance evaluation.

Overhead Cost Allocation Methods

P1 Assign overhead costs using two-stage cost allocation.

Point: Use of a single overhead allocation rate is known as using a *plantwide rate*.

We previously explained how to assign overhead costs to jobs (and processes) by using a predetermined overhead rate per unit of an allocation base such as direct labor cost. When a single overhead rate is used on a companywide basis, all overhead is lumped together, and a predetermined overhead rate per unit of an allocation base is computed and used to assign overhead to jobs (and processes). The use of a single predetermined overhead rate suggests that this allocation process is simple. In reality, it can be complicated. This chapter explains the traditional two-stage cost allocation procedure and then introduces the activity-based cost allocation procedure.

Two-Stage Cost Allocation

An organization incurs overhead costs in many activities. These activities can be identified with various departments, which can be broadly classified as either operating or service departments. *Operating departments* perform an organization's main functions. For example, an accounting firm's main functions usually include auditing, tax, and advisory services. Similarly, the production and selling departments of a manufacturing firm perform its main functions and serve as operating departments. *Service departments* provide support to an organization's operating departments. Examples of service departments are payroll, human resource management, accounting, and executive management. Service departments do not engage in activities that generate revenues, yet their support is crucial for the operating departments' success. In this section, we apply a two-stage cost allocation procedure to assign (1) service department costs to operating departments and (2) operating department costs, including those assigned from service departments, to the organization's output.

Illustration of Two-Stage Cost Allocation Exhibit 21.1 shows the two-stage cost allocation procedure. This exhibit uses data from **AutoGrand**, a custom automobile manufacturer. AutoGrand has five manufacturing-related departments: janitorial, maintenance, factory accounting, machining, and assembly. Expenses incurred by each of these departments are considered product costs. There are three service departments—janitorial, maintenance, and factory accounting; each incurs expenses of $10,000, $15,000 and $8,000, respectively. As shown in Exhibit 21.1, the first stage of the two-stage procedure involves allocating the costs of the three service departments to the two operating departments (machining and assembly). The two operating departments use the resources of these service departments.

EXHIBIT 21.1

Two-Stage Cost Allocation

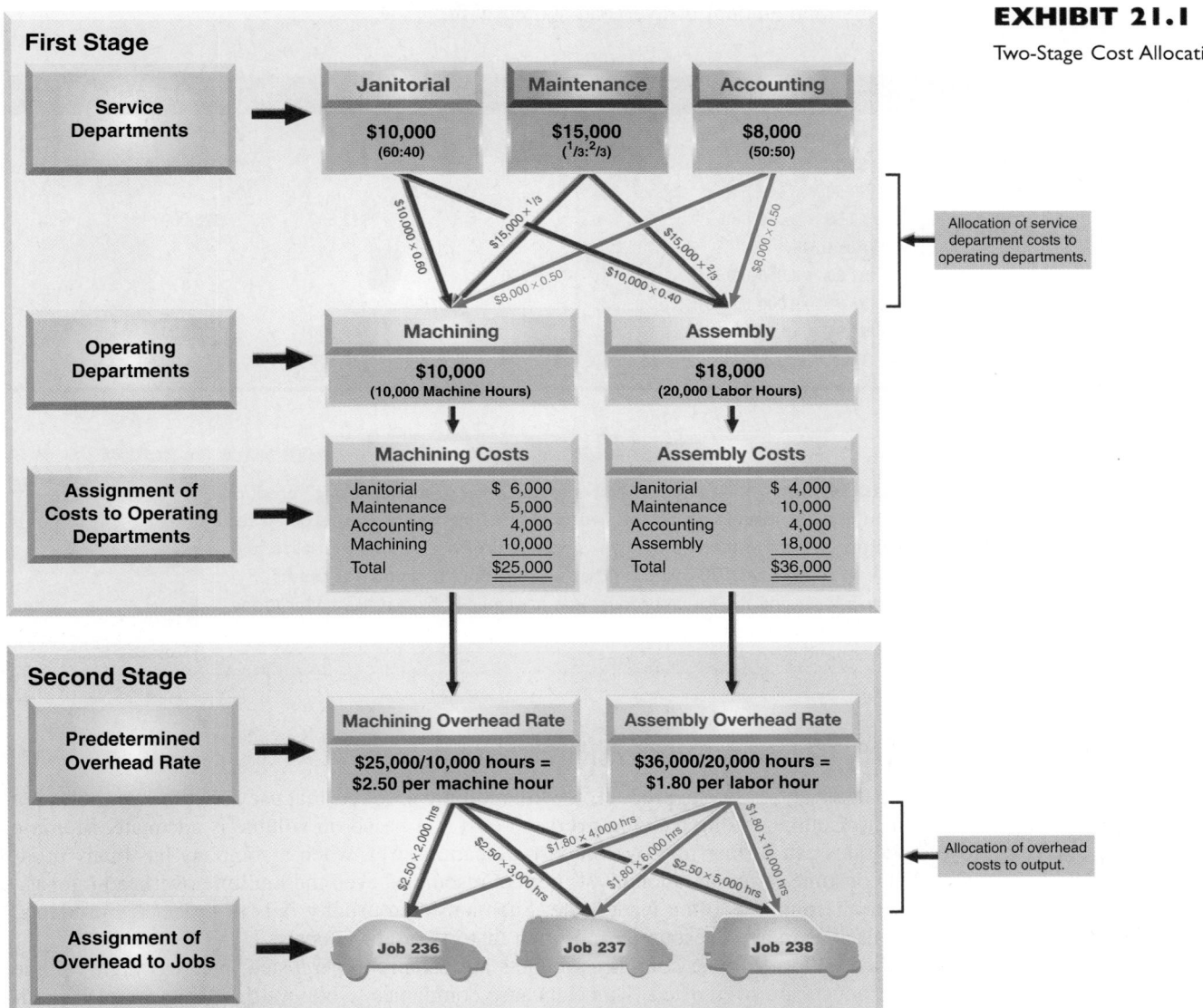

To illustrate the first stage of cost allocation, we use the janitorial department. Its costs are allocated to machining and assembly in the ratio 60 : 40. This means that 60%, or $6,000, of janitorial costs are assigned to the machining department and 40%, or $4,000, to the assembly department. The expenses incurred by the maintenance and factory accounting departments are similarly assigned to machining and assembly. We then add the expenses directly incurred by each operating department to these assigned costs to determine the total expenses for each operating department. This yields total costs of $25,000 for machining and $36,000 for assembly.

In the second stage, predetermined overhead rates are computed for each operating department. The allocation base is machine hours for machining and labor hours for assembly. The

Point: Use of a separate overhead allocation rate for each department is known as using *departmental rates.*

predetermined overhead rate is $2.50 per machine hour for the machining department and $1.80 per labor hour for the assembly department. These predetermined overhead rates are then used to assign overhead to output.

To illustrate this second stage, assume that three jobs were started and finished in a recent month. These jobs consumed resources as follows: Job 236—2,000 machine hours in machining and 4,000 labor hours in assembly; Job 237—3,000 machine hours and 6,000 labor hours; Job 238—5,000 machine hours and 10,000 labor hours. The overhead assigned to these three jobs is shown with the arrow lines in the bottom row of Exhibit 21.1.

Exhibit 21.2 summarizes these allocations. Total overhead allocated to Jobs 236, 237, and 238, is $12,200, $18,300, and $30,500, respectively. These allocated costs sum to $61,000, which is the total amount of overhead started with.

EXHIBIT 21.2

Assignment of Overhead Costs to Output

	Job 236	Job 237	Job 238	Department Totals
Machining				
$2.50 × 2,000 hours	$ 5,000			
$2.50 × 3,000 hours		$ 7,500		
$2.50 × 5,000 hours			$12,500	$25,000
Assembly				
$1.80 × 4,000 hours	7,200			
$1.80 × 6,000 hours		10,800		
$1.80 × 10,000 hours			18,000	36,000
Total overhead assigned	$12,200	$18,300	$30,500	$61,000

Decision Insight

Overhead Misled   **Futura Computer** outsourced a "money-losing" product to a Korean firm for manufacturing. Its own manufacturing facility was retooled to produce extra units of a "more profitable" product. Profits did not materialize, and losses grew to more than $20 million! What went wrong? It seems the better product was a loser and the losing product was a winner. Poor overhead allocations misled Futura's management.

Video21.2

P2   Assign overhead costs using activity-based costing.

Activity-Based Cost Allocation

For companies with only one product, or with multiple products that use about the same amount of indirect resources, using a single overhead cost rate based on volume is adequate. Multiple overhead rates can further improve on cost allocations. Yet, when a company has many products that consume different amounts of indirect resources, even the multiple overhead rate system based on volume is often inadequate. Such a system usually fails to reflect the products' different uses of indirect resources and often distorts products costs.

Specifically, low-volume complex products are usually undercosted, whereas high-volume simpler products are overcosted. This can cause companies to believe that their complex products are more profitable than they really are, which can lead those companies to focus on them to the detriment of high-volume simpler products. This creates a demand for a better cost allocation system for these indirect (overhead) costs.

Activity-based costing (ABC) attempts to better allocate costs to the proper users of overhead by focusing on *activities*. Costs are traced to individual activities and then allocated to cost objects. Exhibit 21.3 shows the (two-stage) activity-based cost allocation method. The first stage identifies the activities involved in processing Jobs 236, 237, and 238 and forms activity cost *pools* by combining those activities. The second stage involves computing predetermined overhead cost rates for each cost pool and then assigning costs to jobs.

We begin our explanation at the top of Exhibit 21.3. The first stage identifies individual activities, which are pooled in a logical manner into homogenous groups, or *cost pools*. A

Point: A survey found that most respondents believe that activity-based costing is worth the investment because of improved management decisions.

EXHIBIT 21.3

Activity-Based Cost Allocation

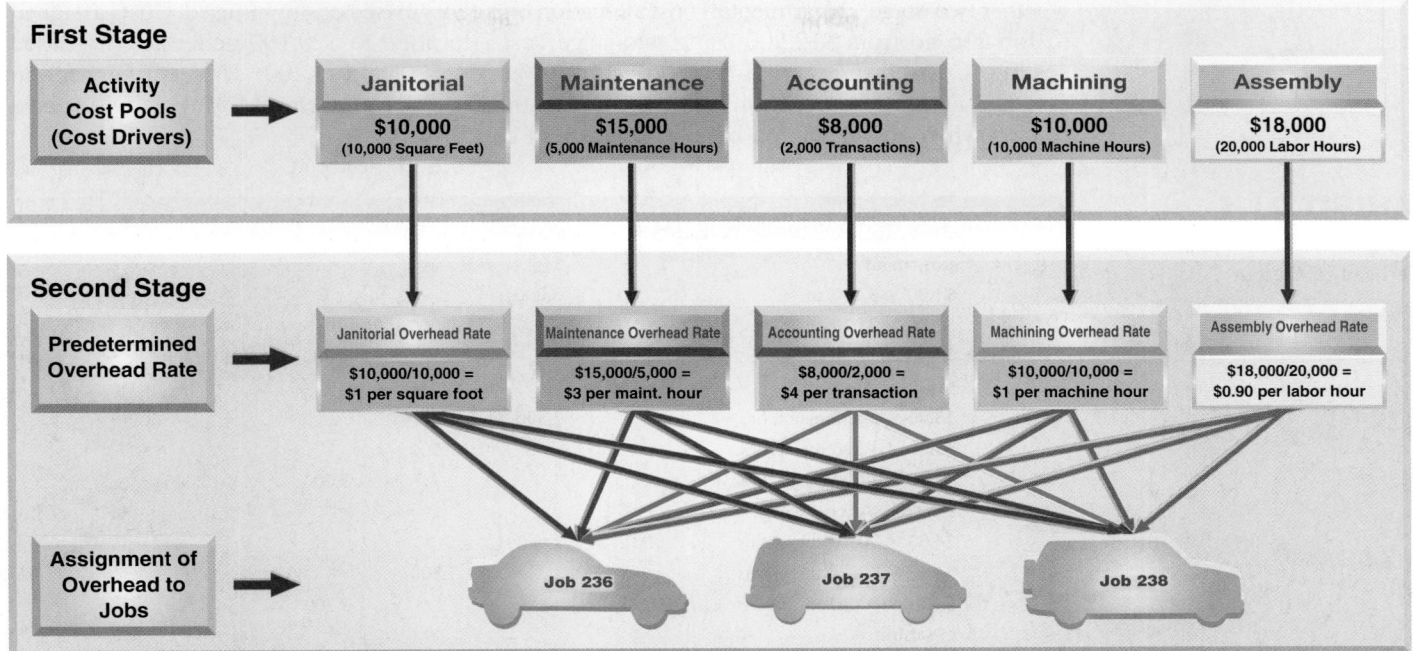

homogenous cost pool consists of activities that belong to the same process and/or are caused by the same cost driver. An **activity cost driver,** or simply *cost driver,* is a factor that causes the cost of an activity to go up or down. For example, preparing an invoice, checking it, and dispatching it are activities of the "invoicing" process and can therefore be grouped in a single cost pool. Moreover, the number of invoices processed likely drives the costs of these activities.

An **activity cost pool** is a temporary account accumulating the costs a company incurs to support an identified set of activities. Costs accumulated in an activity cost pool include the variable and fixed costs of the activities in the pool. Variable costs pertain to resources acquired as needed (such as materials); fixed costs pertain to resources acquired in advance (such as equipment). An activity cost pool account is handled like a factory overhead account.

In the second stage, after all activity costs are accumulated in an activity cost pool account, overhead rates are computed. Then, costs are allocated to cost objects (users) based on cost drivers (allocation bases).

> **Point:** A cost driver is different from an allocation base. An allocation base is used as a basis for assigning overhead but need not have a cause-effect relation with the costs assigned. However, a cost driver has a cause-effect relation with the cost assigned.

Decision Insight

Measuring Health   Activity-based costing is used in many settings. A study found that activity-based costing improves health care costing accuracy, enabling improved profitability analysis and decision making. However, identifying cost drivers in a health care setting is challenging.

Illustration of Activity-Based Costing   To illustrate, let's return to AutoGrand's three jobs. Assume that resources used to complete Jobs 236, 237, and 238 are shown in Exhibit 21.4.

Resources Used	Job 236	Job 237	Job 238
Square feet of space	5,000	3,000	2,000
Maintenance hours	2,500	1,500	1,000
Number of transactions	500	700	800
Machine hours	2,000	3,000	5,000
Direct labor hours	4,000	6,000	10,000

EXHIBIT 21.4

Activity Resource Use

The $61,000 of total costs are assigned to these three jobs using activity-based costing as shown in Exhibit 21.5 (rates are taken from the second stage of Exhibit 21.3). Comparing Exhibits 21.2 and 21.5, we see that the costs assigned to the three jobs vary markedly depending on whether two-stage (departmental) cost allocation or activity-based costing is used. Costs assigned to Job 236 go from $12,200 using two-stage cost allocation to $20,100 under activity-based costing. Costs assigned to Job 238 decline from $30,500 to $22,200. These differences in assigned amounts result from more accurately tracing costs to each job using activity-based costing where the allocation bases reflect actual cost drivers.

EXHIBIT 21.5

Activity-Based Assignment of Overhead to Output

	Job 236	Job 237	Job 238	Activity Totals
Janitorial				
$1.00 × 5,000 sq. ft.	$ 5,000			
$1.00 × 3,000 sq. ft.		$ 3,000		
$1.00 × 2,000 sq. ft.			$ 2,000	$10,000
Maintenance				
$3.00 × 2,500 maint. hrs.	7,500			
$3.00 × 1,500 maint. hrs.		4,500		
$3.00 × 1,000 maint. hrs.			3,000	15,000
Factory Accounting				
$4.00 × 500 transactions	2,000			
$4.00 × 700 transactions		2,800		
$4.00 × 800 transactions			3,200	8,000
Machining				
$1.00 × 2,000 machine hrs.	2,000			
$1.00 × 3,000 machine hrs.		3,000		
$1.00 × 5,000 machine hrs.			5,000	10,000
Assembly				
$0.90 × 4,000 labor hrs.	3,600			
$0.90 × 6,000 labor hrs.		5,400		
$0.90 × 10,000 labor hrs.			9,000	18,000
Total overhead assigned	$20,100	$18,700	$22,200	$61,000

Decision Maker

Director of Operations Two department managers at your ad agency complain to you that overhead costs assigned to them are too high. Overhead is assigned on the basis of labor hours for designers. These managers argue that overhead depends not only on designers' hours but on many activities unrelated to these hours. What is your response? [Answer—p. 879]

Comparison of Two-Stage and Activity-Based Cost Allocation

Traditional cost systems capture overhead costs by individual department (or function) and accumulate these costs in one or more overhead accounts. Companies then assign these overhead costs using a single allocation base such as direct labor or multiple volume-based allocation bases. Unfortunately, traditional cost systems have tended to use allocation bases that are often not closely related to the way these costs are actually incurred.

In contrast, activity-based cost systems capture costs by individual activity. These activities and their costs are then accumulated into activity cost pools. A company selects a cost driver (allocation base) for each activity pool. It uses this cost driver to assign the accumulated activity costs to cost objects (such as jobs or products) benefiting from the activity.

An activity-based costing system commonly consists of more allocation bases as compared to a traditional cost system. For example, a Chicago-based manufacturer currently uses nearly

Activity Cost Pool	Cost Driver
Materials purchasing	Number of purchase orders
Materials handling	Number of materials requisitions
Personnel processing	Number of employees hired or laid off
Equipment depreciation	Number of products produced or hours of use
Quality inspection	Number of units inspected
Indirect labor in setting up equipment	Number of setups required
Engineering costs for product modifications	Number of modifications (engineering change orders)

EXHIBIT 21.6

Cost Pools and Cost Drivers in Activity-Based Costing

20 different activity cost drivers to assign overhead costs to its products. Exhibit 21.6 lists common examples of overhead cost pools and their usual cost drivers.

Activity-based costing is especially effective when the same department or departments produce many different types of products. For instance, more complex products often require more help from service departments such as engineering, maintenance, and materials handling. If the same amount of direct labor is applied to the complex and simple products, a traditional overhead allocation system assigns the same overhead cost to both. With activity-based costing, however, the complex products are assigned a larger portion of overhead. The difference in overhead assigned can affect product pricing, make-or-buy, and other managerial decisions.

Activity-based costing encourages managers to focus on *activities* as well as the use of those activities. For instance, assume AutoGrand can reduce the number of transactions processed in Factory Accounting to 1,500 (375 transactions for Job 236, 525 transactions for Job 237, and 600 transactions for Job 238) and that through continuous improvement it can reduce costs of processing those transactions to $4,500. The resulting rate to process a transaction is $3 per transaction ($4,500/1,500 transactions—down from $4 per Exhibit 21.3). The cost of transaction processing is reduced for all jobs (Job 236, $1,125; Job 237, $1,575; Job 238, $1,800). However, if those accounting costs were grouped in a single overhead cost pool, it is more difficult to identify cost savings and understand their effects on product costs.

Activity-based costing requires managers to look at each item and encourages them to manage each cost to increase the benefit from each dollar spent. It also encourages managers to cooperate because it shows how their efforts are interrelated. This results in *activity-based management*.

Decision Ethics

Accounting Officer   Your company produces expensive garments, whose production involves many complex and specialized activities. Your general manager recently learned about activity-based costing (ABC) and asks your advice. However, your supervisor does not want to disturb the existing cost system and instructs you to prepare a report stating that "implementation of ABC is a complicated process involving too many steps and not worth the effort." You believe ABC will actually help the company identify sources of costs and control them. What action do you take? [Answer—p. 879]

Quick Check

Answers—p. 880

1. What is a cost driver?
2. When activity-based costing is used rather than traditional allocation methods, (*a*) managers must identify cost drivers for various items of overhead cost, (*b*) individual cost items in service departments are allocated directly to products or services, (*c*) managers can direct their attention to the activities that drive overhead cost, or (*d*) all of the above.

Section 2—Allocating Costs for Performance Evaluation

This second section of the chapter describes and illustrates allocation of costs for performance evaluation. We begin with departmental accounting and expense allocations and conclude with responsibility accounting.

Departmental Accounting

Video21.3

Companies are divided into *departments*, also called *subunits*, when they are too large to be managed effectively as a single unit. Managerial accounting for departments has two main goals. The first is to set up a **departmental accounting system** to provide information for managers to evaluate the profitability or cost effectiveness of each department's activities. The second goal is to set up a **responsibility accounting system** to control costs and expenses and evaluate managers' performances by assigning costs and expenses to the managers responsible for controlling them. Departmental and responsibility accounting systems are related and share much information.

Motivation for Departmentalization

C1 Explain departmentalization and the role of departmental accounting.

Many companies are so large and complex that they are broken into separate divisions for efficiency and/or effectiveness purposes. Divisions then are usually organized into separate departments. When a company is departmentalized, each department is often placed under the direction of a manager. As a company grows, management often divides departments into new departments so that responsibilities for a department's activities do not overwhelm the manager's ability to oversee and control them. A company also creates departments to take advantage of the skills of individual managers. Departments are broadly classified as either operating or service departments.

Departmental Evaluation

Point: To improve profitability, **Sears, Roebuck & Co.** eliminated several departments, including its catalog division.

When a company is divided into departments, managers need to know how each department is performing. The accounting system must supply information about resources used and outputs achieved by each department. This requires a system to measure and accumulate revenue and expense information for each department whenever possible.

Departmental information is rarely distributed publicly because of its potential usefulness to competitors. Information about departments is prepared for internal managers to help control operations, appraise performance, allocate resources, and plan strategy. If a department is highly profitable, management may decide to expand its operations, or if a department is performing poorly, information about revenues or expenses can suggest useful changes.

More companies are emphasizing customer satisfaction as a main responsibility of many departments. This has led to changes in the measures reported. Increasingly, financial measurements are being supplemented with quality and customer satisfaction indexes. **Motorola**, for instance, uses two key measures: the number of defective parts per million parts produced and the percent of orders delivered on time to customers. (Note that some departments have only "internal customers.")

Financial information used to evaluate a department depends on whether it is evaluated as a profit center, cost center, or investment center. A **profit center** incurs costs and generates revenues; selling departments are often evaluated as profit centers. A **cost center** incurs costs without directly generating revenues. An **investment center** incurs costs and generates revenues, and is responsible for effectively using center assets. The manufacturing departments of a manufacturer and its service departments such as accounting, advertising, and purchasing, are all cost centers.

Point: Selling departments are often treated as *revenue centers*; their managers are responsible for maximizing sales revenues.

Evaluating managers' performance depends on whether they are responsible for profit centers, cost centers, or investment centers. Profit center managers are judged on their abilities to generate revenues in excess of the department's costs. They are assumed to influence both revenue generation and cost incurrence. Cost center managers are judged on their abilities to control costs by keeping them within a satisfactory range under an assumption that only they influence costs. Investment center managers are evaluated on their use of center assets to generate income.

Decision Insight

Nonfinancial Measures   A majority of companies now report nonfinancial performance measures to management. Common measures are cycle time, defect rate, on-time deliveries, inventory turnover, customer satisfaction, and safety. When nonfinancial measures are used with financial measures, the performance measurement system resembles a *balanced scorecard.* Many of these companies also use activity-based management as part of their performance measurement system.

Departmental Reporting and Analysis

Companies use various measures (financial and nonfinancial) and reporting formats to evaluate their departments. The type and form of information depend on management's focus and philosophy. **Hewlett-Packard**'s statement of corporate objectives, for instance, indicates that its goal is to satisfy customer needs. Its challenge is to set up managerial accounting systems to provide relevant feedback for evaluating performance in terms of its stated objectives. Also, the means used to obtain information about departments depend on how extensively a company uses computer and information technology.

When accounts are not maintained separately in the general ledger by department, a company can create departmental information by using a *departmental spreadsheet analysis.* For example, after recording sales in its usual manner, a company can compute daily total sales by department and enter these totals on a sales spreadsheet. At period-end, column totals of the spreadsheet show sales by department. The combined total of all columns equals the balance of the Sales account. A merchandiser that uses a spreadsheet analysis of department sales often uses separate spreadsheets to accumulate sales, sales returns, purchases, and purchases returns by department. If each department keeps a count of its inventory, it can also compute its gross profit (assuming it's a profit center).

Point: Many retailers use a point-of-sales system capturing sales data and creating requests to release inventory from the warehouse and order more merchandise. **Wal-Mart**'s sales system not only collects data for internal use but also is used by **Procter & Gamble** to plan its production and product deliveries to **Wal-Mart**.

Point: Link Wood Products, a manufacturer of lawn and garden products, records each sale by department on a spreadsheet. Daily totals are accumulated in another spreadsheet to obtain monthly totals by department.

Quick Check

3. What is the difference between a departmental accounting system and a responsibility accounting system?
4. Service departments (a) manufacture products, (b) make sales directly to customers, (c) produce revenues, (d) assist operating departments.
5. Explain the difference between a cost center and a profit center. Cite an example of each.

Departmental Expense Allocation

When a company computes departmental profits, it confronts some accounting challenges that involve allocating its expenses across its operating departments.

Direct and Indirect Expenses

Direct expenses are costs readily traced to a department because they are incurred for that department's sole benefit. They require no allocation across departments. For example, the salary of an employee who works in only one department is a direct expense of that one department.

Indirect expenses are costs that are incurred for the joint benefit of more than one department and cannot be readily traced to only one department. For example, if two or more departments share a single building, all enjoy the benefits of the expenses for rent, heat, and light. Indirect expenses are allocated across departments benefiting from them when we need information about departmental profits. Ideally, we allocate indirect expenses by using a cause-effect

C2 Distinguish between direct and indirect expenses.

Point: Utility expense has elements of both direct and indirect expenses.

relation. When we cannot identify cause-effect relations, we allocate each indirect expense on a basis approximating the relative benefit each department receives. Measuring the benefit for each department from an indirect expense can be difficult.

Illustration of Indirect Expense Allocation   To illustrate how to allocate an indirect expense, we consider a retail store that purchases janitorial services from an outside company. Management allocates this cost across the store's three departments according to the floor space each occupies. Costs of janitorial services for a recent month are $300. Exhibit 21.7 shows the square feet of floor space each department occupies. The store computes the percent of total square feet allotted to each department and uses it to allocate the $300 cost.

EXHIBIT 21.7

Indirect Expense Allocation

Department	Square Feet	Percent of Total	Allocated Cost
Jewelry	2,400	60%	$180
Watch repair	600	15	45
China and silver	1,000	25	75
Totals	4,000	100%	$300

Specifically, because the jewelry department occupies 60% of the floor space, 60% of the total $300 cost is assigned to it. The same procedure is applied to the other departments. When the allocation process is complete, these and other allocated costs are deducted from the gross profit for each department to determine net income for each. One consideration in allocating costs is to motivate managers and employees to behave as desired. As a result, a cost incurred in one department might be best allocated to other departments when one of the other departments caused the cost.

Allocation of Indirect Expenses

C3 Identify bases for allocating indirect expenses to departments.

This section describes how to identify the bases used to allocate indirect expenses across departments. No standard rule identifies the best basis because expense allocation involves several factors, and the relative importance of these factors varies across departments and organizations. Judgment is required, and people do not always agree. In our discussion, note the parallels between activity-based costing and the departmental expense allocation procedures described here.

Point: Expense allocations cannot always avoid some arbitrariness.

Wages and Salaries   Employee wages and salaries can be either direct or indirect expenses. If their time is spent entirely in one department, their wages are direct expenses of that department. However, if employees work for the benefit of more than one department, their wages are indirect expenses and must be allocated across the departments benefited. An employee's contribution to a department usually depends on the number of hours worked in contributing to that department. Thus, a reasonable basis for allocating employee wages and salaries is the *relative amount of time spent in each department*. In the case of a supervisor who manages more than one department, recording the time spent in each department may not always be practical. Instead, a company can allocate the supervisor's salary to departments on the basis of the number of employees in each department—a reasonable basis if a supervisor's main task is managing people. Another basis of allocation is on sales across departments, also a reasonable basis if a supervisor's job reflects on departmental sales.

Point: Some companies ask supervisors to estimate time spent supervising specific departments for purposes of expense allocation.

Rent and Related Expenses   Rent expense for a building is reasonably allocated to a department on the basis of floor space it occupies. Location can often make some floor space more valuable than other space. Thus, the allocation method can charge departments that occupy more valuable space a higher expense per square foot. Ground floor retail space, for instance, is often more valuable than basement or upper-floor space because all customers pass departments near the entrance but fewer go beyond the first floor. When no precise measures of floor space values exist, basing allocations on data such as customer traffic and real estate assessments is helpful. When a company owns its building, its expenses for depreciation, taxes, insurance, and other related building expenses are allocated like rent expense.

Advertising Expenses   Effective advertising of a department's products increases its sales and customer traffic. Moreover, advertising products for some departments usually helps other departments' sales because customers also often buy unadvertised products. Thus, many stores treat advertising as an indirect expense allocated on the basis of each department's proportion of total sales. For example, a department with 10% of a store's total sales is assigned 10% of advertising expense. Another method is to analyze each advertisement to compute the Web/newspaper space or TV/radio time devoted to the products of a department and charge that department for the proportional costs of advertisements. Management must consider whether this more detailed and costly method is justified.

Equipment and Machinery Depreciation   Depreciation on equipment and machinery used only in one department is a direct expense of that department. Depreciation on equipment and machinery used by more than one department is an indirect expense to be allocated across departments. Accounting for each department's depreciation expense requires a company to keep records showing which departments use specific assets. The number of hours that a department uses equipment and machinery is a reasonable basis for allocating depreciation.

Point: Employee morale suffers when allocations are perceived as unfair. Thus, it is important to carefully design and explain the allocation of service department costs.

Utilities Expenses   Utilities expenses such as heating and lighting are usually allocated on the basis of floor space occupied by departments. This practice assumes their use is uniform across departments. When this is not so, a more involved allocation can be necessary, although there is often a trade-off between the usefulness of more precise allocations and the effort to compute them.

Point: Manufacturers often allocate electricity cost to departments on the basis of the horsepower of equipment located in each department.

Service Department Expenses   To generate revenues, operating departments require support services provided by departments such as personnel, payroll, advertising, and purchasing. Such service departments are typically evaluated as cost centers because they do not produce revenues. (Evaluating them as profit centers requires the use of a system that "charges" user departments a price that then serves as the "revenue" generated by service departments.) A departmental accounting system can accumulate and report costs incurred directly by each service department for this purpose. The system then allocates a service department's expenses to operating departments benefiting from them. This is often done, for example, using traditional two-stage cost allocation (see Exhibit 21.1). Exhibit 21.8 shows some commonly used bases for allocating service department expenses to operating departments.

Point: When a service department "charges" its user departments within a company, a *transfer pricing system* must be set up to determine the "revenue" from its services provided.

Service Department	Common Allocation Bases
Office expenses	Number of employees or sales in each department
Personnel expenses	Number of employees in each department
Payroll expenses	Number of employees in each department
Advertising expenses	Sales or amount of advertising charged directly to each department
Purchasing costs	Dollar amounts of purchases or number of purchase orders processed
Cleaning expenses	Square feet of floor space occupied
Maintenance expenses	Square feet of floor space occupied

EXHIBIT 21.8

Bases for Allocating Service Department Expenses

Departmental Income Statements

An income statement can be prepared for each operating department once expenses have been assigned to it. Its expenses include both direct expenses and its share of indirect expenses. For this purpose, compiling all expenses incurred in service departments before assigning them to operating departments is useful. We illustrate the steps to prepare departmental income statements using **A-1 Hardware** and its five departments. Two of them (office and purchasing) are

P3   Prepare departmental income statements.

service departments and the other three (hardware, housewares, and appliances) are operating (selling) departments. Allocating costs to operating departments and preparing departmental income statements involves four steps. (1) Accumulating direct expenses by department. (2) Allocating indirect expenses across departments. (3) Allocating service department expenses to operating department. (4) Preparing departmental income statements.

Step 1   Step 1 accumulates direct expenses for each service and operating department as shown in Exhibit 21.9. Direct expenses include salaries, wages, and other expenses that each department incurs but does not share with any other department. This information is accumulated in departmental expense accounts.

EXHIBIT 21.9

Step 1: Direct Expense Accumulation

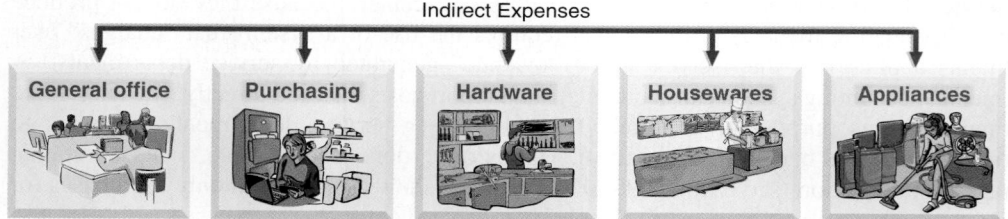

Point: We sometimes allocate service department costs across other service departments before allocating them to operating departments. This "step-wise" process is in advanced courses.

Step 2   Step 2 allocates indirect expenses across all departments as shown in Exhibit 21.10. Indirect expenses can include items such as depreciation, rent, advertising, and any other expenses that cannot be directly assigned to a department. Indirect expenses are recorded in company expense accounts, an allocation base is identified for each expense, and costs are allocated using a *departmental expense allocation spreadsheet* described in step 3.

EXHIBIT 21.10

Step 2: Indirect Expense Allocation

Indirect Expenses

General office | Purchasing | Hardware | Housewares | Appliances

Step 3   Step 3 allocates expenses of the service departments (office and purchasing) to the operating departments. Service department costs are not allocated to other service departments. Exhibit 21.11 reflects the allocation of service department expenses using the allocation base(s). All of the direct and indirect expenses of service departments are allocated to operating departments.[1]

EXHIBIT 21.11

Step 3: Service Department Expense Allocation to Operating Departments

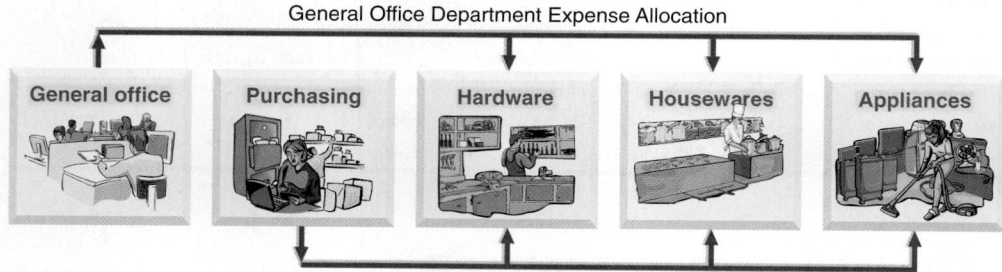

General Office Department Expense Allocation

Purchasing Department Expense Allocation

---

[1] In some cases we allocate a service department's expenses to other service departments when they use its services. For example, expenses of a payroll office benefit all service and operating departments and can be assigned to all departments. Nearly all examples and assignment materials in this book allocate service expenses only to operating departments for simplicity.

Computations for both steps 2 and 3 are commonly made using a departmental expense allocation spreadsheet as shown in Exhibit 21.12. The first two sections of this spreadsheet list direct expenses and indirect expenses by department. The third section lists the service department expenses and their allocations to operating departments. The allocation bases are identified in the second column, and total expense amounts are reported in the third column.

EXHIBIT 21.12

Departmental Expense Allocation Spreadsheet

File Edit View Insert Format Tools Data Window Help

A-1 HARDWARE
Departmental Expense Allocations
For Year Ended December 31, 2009

	Allocation Base	Expense Account Balance	General Office Dept.	Purchasing Dept.	Hardware Dept.	Housewares Dept.	Appliances Dept.
Direct expenses							
Salaries expense.....................	Payroll records........................	$51,900	$13,300	$8,200	$15,600	$ 7,000	$ 7,800
Depreciation—Equipment......	Depreciation records.............	1,500	500	300	400	100	200
Supplies expense...................	Requisitions............................	900	200	100	300	200	100
Indirect expenses							
Rent expense	Amount and value of space..	12,000	600	600	4,860	3,240	2,700
Utilities expense.....................	Floor space.............................	2,400	300	300	810	540	450
Advertising expense..............	Sales...	1,000			500	300	200
Insurance expense.................	Value of insured assets	2,500	400	200	900	600	400
Total department expenses......		72,200	15,300	9,700	23,370	11,980	11,850
Service department expenses							
General office department.....	Sales...		(15,300)		7,650	4,590	3,060
Purchasing department	Purchase orders.....................			(9,700)	3,880	2,630	3,190
Total expenses allocated to operating departments............		$72,200	$ 0	$ 0	$34,900	$19,200	$18,100

Sheet1 Sheet2 Sheet3

The departmental expense allocation spreadsheet is useful in implementing the first three steps. To illustrate, first (step 1) the three direct expenses of salaries, depreciation, and supplies are accumulated in each of the five departments.

Second (step 2), the four indirect expenses of rent, utilities, advertising, and insurance are allocated to all departments using the allocation bases identified. For example, consider rent allocation. Exhibit 21.13 lists the five departments' square footage of space occupied.

EXHIBIT 21.13

Departments' Allocation Bases

Department	Floor Space (Square Feet)	Value of Insured Assets ($)	Sales ($)	Number of Purchase Orders
General office	1,500	$ 38,000		—
Purchasing	1,500	19,000		—*
Hardware	4,050	85,500	$119,500	394
Housewares	2,700	57,000	71,700	267
Appliances	2,250	38,000	47,800	324
Total	12,000	$237,500	$239,000	985

* Purchasing department tracks purchase orders by department.

The two service departments (office and purchasing) occupy 25% of the total space (3,000 sq. feet/12,000 sq. feet). However, they are located near the back of the building, which is of lower value than space near the front that is occupied by operating departments. Management estimates that space near the back accounts for $1,200 of the total rent expense of $12,000. Exhibit 21.14 shows how we allocate the $1,200 rent expense between

EXHIBIT 21.14

Allocating Indirect (Rent) Expense to Service Departments

Department	Square Feet	Percent of Total	Allocated Cost
General office	1,500	50.0%	$ 600
Purchasing	1,500	50.0	600
Totals	3,000	100.0%	$1,200

these two service departments in proportion to their square footage. Exhibit 21.14 shows a simple rule for cost allocations: Allocated cost = Percentage of allocation base × Total cost. We then allocate the remaining $10,800 of rent expense to the three operating departments as shown in Exhibit 21.15. We continue step 2 by allocating the $2,400 of utilities expense to all departments based on the square footage occupied as shown in Exhibit 21.16.

EXHIBIT 21.15

Allocating Indirect (Rent) Expense to Operating Departments

Department	Square Feet	Percent of Total	Allocated Cost
Hardware	4,050	45.0%	$ 4,860
Housewares	2,700	30.0	3,240
Appliances	2,250	25.0	2,700
Totals	9,000	100.0%	$10,800

EXHIBIT 21.16

Allocating Indirect (Utilities) Expense to All Departments

Department	Square Feet	Percent of Total	Allocated Cost
General office	1,500	12.50%	$ 300
Purchasing	1,500	12.50	300
Hardware	4,050	33.75	810
Housewares	2,700	22.50	540
Appliances	2,250	18.75	450
Totals	12,000	100.00%	$2,400

Exhibit 21.17 shows the allocation of $1,000 of advertising expense to the three operating departments on the basis of sales dollars. We exclude service departments from this allocation because they do not generate sales.

EXHIBIT 21.17

Allocating Indirect (Advertising) Expense to Operating Departments

Department	Sales	Percent of Total	Allocated Cost
Hardware	$119,500	50.0%	$ 500
Housewares	71,700	30.0	300
Appliances	47,800	20.0	200
Totals	$239,000	100.0%	$1,000

To complete step 2 we allocate insurance expense to each service and operating department as shown in Exhibit 21.18.

EXHIBIT 21.18

Allocating Indirect (Insurance) Expense to All Departments

Department	Value of Insured Assets	Percent of Total	Allocated Cost
General Office	$ 38,000	16.0%	$ 400
Purchasing	19,000	8.0	200
Hardware	85,500	36.0	900
Housewares	57,000	24.0	600
Appliances	38,000	16.0	400
Total	$237,500	100.0%	$2,500

Third (step 3), total expenses of the two service departments are allocated to the three operating departments as shown in Exhibits 21.19 and 21.20.

EXHIBIT 21.19

Allocating Service Department (General Office) Expenses to Operating Departments

Department	Sales	Percent of Total	Allocated Cost
Hardware	$119,500	50.0%	$ 7,650
Housewares	71,700	30.0	4,590
Appliances	47,800	20.0	3,060
Total	$239,000	100.0%	$15,300

EXHIBIT 21.20

Allocating Service Department (Purchasing) Expenses to Operating Departments

Department	Number of Purchase Orders	Percent of Total	Allocated Cost
Hardware	394	40.00%	$3,880
Housewares	267	27.11	2,630
Appliances	324	32.89	3,190
Total	985	100.00%	$9,700

Step 4 The departmental expense allocation spreadsheet can now be used to prepare performance reports for the company's service and operating departments. The general office and purchasing departments are cost centers, and their managers will be evaluated on their control of costs. Actual amounts of service department expenses can be compared to budgeted amounts to help assess cost center manager performance.

Amounts in the operating department columns are used to prepare departmental income statements as shown in Exhibit 21.21. This exhibit uses the spreadsheet for its operating expenses; information on sales and cost of goods sold comes from departmental records.

Example: If the $15,300 general office expenses in Exhibit 21.12 are allocated equally across departments, what is net income for the hardware department and for the combined company? *Answer:* Hardware income, $13,350; combined income, $19,000.

EXHIBIT 21.21

Departmental Income Statements

A-1 HARDWARE
Departmental Income Statements
For Year Ended December 31, 2009

	Hardware Department	Housewares Department	Appliances Department	Combined
Sales	$119,500	$71,700	$47,800	$239,000
Cost of goods sold	73,800	43,800	30,200	147,800
Gross profit	45,700	27,900	17,600	91,200
Operating expenses				
Salaries expense	15,600	7,000	7,800	30,400
Depreciation expense—Equipment	400	100	200	700
Supplies expense	300	200	100	600
Rent expense	4,860	3,240	2,700	10,800
Utilities expense	810	540	450	1,800
Advertising expense	500	300	200	1,000
Insurance expense	900	600	400	1,900
Share of general office expenses	7,650	4,590	3,060	15,300
Share of purchasing expenses	3,880	2,630	3,190	9,700
Total operating expenses	34,900	19,200	18,100	72,200
Net income (loss)	$10,800	$8,700	$(500)	$19,000

Departmental Contribution to Overhead

Data from departmental income statements are not always best for evaluating each profit center's performance, especially when indirect expenses are a large portion of total expenses and when weaknesses in assumptions and decisions in allocating indirect expenses can markedly affect net income. In these and other cases, we might better evaluate profit center performance using the **departmental contribution to overhead,** which is a report of the amount of sales less *direct* expenses.[2] We can also examine cost center performance by focusing on control of direct expenses.

The upper half of Exhibit 21.22 shows a departmental (profit center) contribution to overhead as part of an expanded income statement. This format is common when reporting departmental contributions to overhead. Using the information in Exhibits 21.21 and 21.22, we can evaluate the profitability of the three profit centers. For instance, let's compare the performance of the appliances department as described in these two exhibits. Exhibit 21.21 shows a $500 net loss resulting from this department's operations, but Exhibit 21.22 shows a $9,500 positive contribution to overhead, which is 19.9% of the appliance department's sales. The contribution of the appliances department is not as large as that of the other selling departments, but a $9,500 contribution to overhead is better than a $500 loss. This tells us that the appliances department is not a money loser. On the contrary, it is contributing $9,500 toward defraying total indirect expenses of $40,500.

EXHIBIT 21.22

Departmental Contribution to Overhead

A-1 HARDWARE
Income Statement Showing Departmental Contribution to Overhead
For Year Ended December 31, 2009

	Hardware Department	Housewares Department	Appliances Department	Combined
Sales	$119,500	$ 71,700	$47,800	$239,000
Cost of goods sold	73,800	43,800	30,200	147,800
Gross profit	45,700	27,900	17,600	91,200
Direct expenses				
Salaries expense	15,600	7,000	7,800	30,400
Depreciation expense—Equipment	400	100	200	700
Supplies expense	300	200	100	600
Total direct expenses	16,300	7,300	8,100	31,700
Departmental contributions				
to overhead	$ 29,400	$20,600	$ 9,500	$ 59,500
Indirect expenses				
Rent expense				10,800
Utilities expense				1,800
Advertising expense				1,000
Insurance expense				1,900
General office department expense				15,300
Purchasing department expense				9,700
Total indirect expenses				40,500
Net income				$ 19,000
Contribution as percent of sales	24.6%	28.7%	19.9%	24.9%

---

[2] A department's contribution is said to be "to overhead" because of the practice of considering all indirect expenses as overhead. Thus, the excess of a department's sales over direct expenses is a contribution toward at least a portion of its total overhead.

6. If a company has two operating (selling) departments (shoes and hats) and two service departments (payroll and advertising), which of the following statements is correct? (a) Wages incurred in the payroll department are direct expenses of the shoe department, (b) Wages incurred in the payroll department are indirect expenses of the operating departments, or (c) Advertising department expenses are allocated to the other three departments.

7. Which of the following bases can be used to allocate supervisors' salaries across operating departments? (a) Hours spent in each department, (b) number of employees in each department, (c) sales achieved in each department, or (d) any of the above, depending on which information is most relevant and accessible.

8. What three steps are used to allocate expenses to operating departments?

9. An income statement showing departmental contribution to overhead, (a) subtracts indirect expenses from each department's revenues, (b) subtracts only direct expenses from each department's revenues, or (c) shows net income for each department.

Evaluating Investment Center Performance

This section introduces both financial and nonfinancial measures of investment center performance.

Financial Performance Evaluation Measures

Investment center managers are typically evaluated using performance measures that combine income and assets. Consider the following data for ZTel, a company which operates two divisions: LCD and S-Phone. The LCD division manufactures liquid crystal display (LCD) touch-screen monitors and sells them for use in computers, cellular phones, and other products. The S-Phone division sells smartphones, mobile phones that also function as personal computers, MP3 players, cameras, and global positioning satellite (GPS) systems. Exhibit 21.23 shows current year income and assets for those divisions.

A1 Analyze investment centers using return on assets, residual income, and balanced scorecard.

	LCD	S-Phone
Net income	$ 526,500	$ 417,600
Average invested assets	2,500,000	1,850,000

EXHIBIT 21.23

Investment Center Income and Assets

Investment Center Return on Total Assets   One measure to evaluate division performance is the **investment center return on total assets,** also called *return on investment* (ROI). This measure is computed as follows

$$\text{Return on investment} = \frac{\text{Investment center net income}}{\text{Investment center average invested assets}}$$

The return on investment for the LCD division is 21% (rounded), computed as $526,500/ $2,500,000. The S-Phone division's return on investment is 23% (rounded), computed as $417,600/$1,850,000. Though the LCD division earned more dollars of net income, it was less efficient in using its assets to generate income compared to the S-Phone division.

Investment Center Residual Income   Another way to evaluate division performance is to compute **investment center residual income,** which is computed as follows

$$\text{Residual income} = \frac{\text{Investment center}}{\text{net income}} - \frac{\text{Target investment center}}{\text{net income}}$$

Assume ZTel's top management sets target net income at 8% of divisional assets. For an investment center, this **hurdle rate** is typically the cost of obtaining financing. Applying this hurdle rate using the data from Exhibit 21.23 yields the residual income for ZTel's divisions in Exhibit 21.24:

EXHIBIT 21.24

Investment Center Residual Income

	LCD	S-Phone
Net income	$526,500	$417,600
Less: Target net income		
$2,500,000 × 8%	200,000	
$1,850,000 × 8%		148,000
Investment center residual income	$326,500	$269,600

Unlike return on assets, residual income is expressed in dollars. The LCD division outperformed the S-Phone division, on the basis of residual income. However, this result is due in part to the LCD division having a larger asset base than the S-Phone division.

Using residual income to evaluate division performance encourages division managers to accept all opportunities that return more than the target net income, thus increasing company value. For example, the S-Phone division might not want to accept a new customer that will provide a 15% return on investment, since that will reduce the S-Phone division's overall return on investment (23% as shown above). However, the S-Phone division should accept this opportunity because the new customer would increase residual income by providing net income above the target net income.

Point: Residual income is also called *economic value added* (EVA).

Nonfinancial Performance Evaluation Measures

Evaluating performance solely on financial measures such as return on investment or residual income has limitations. For example, some investment center managers might forgo profitable opportunities to keep their return on investment high. Also, residual income is less useful when comparing investment centers of different size. And, both return on investment and residual income can encourage managers to focus too heavily on short-term financial goals.

In response to these limitations, companies consider nonfinancial measures. For example, a delivery company such as **FedEx** might track the percentage of on-time deliveries. The percentage of defective tennis balls manufactured can be used to assess performance of **Penn**'s production managers. **Walmart**'s credit card screens commonly ask customers at check-out whether the cashier was friendly or the store was clean. This kind of information can help division managers run their divisions and help top management evaluate division manager performance.

Balanced Scorecard   The **balanced scorecard** is a system of performance measures, including nonfinancial measures, used to assess company and division manager performance. The balanced scorecard requires managers to think of their company from four perspectives:

1. *Customer:* What do customers think of us?
2. *Internal processes:* Which of our operations are critical to meeting customer needs?
3. *Innovation and learning:* How can we improve?
4. *Financial:* What do our owners think of us?

Point: One survey indicates that nearly 60% of global companies use some form of balanced scorecard.

The balanced scorecard collects information on several key performance indicators within each of the four perspectives. These key indicators vary across companies. Exhibit 21.25 lists common performance measures.

After selecting key performance indicators, companies collect data on each indicator and compare actual amounts to expected amounts to assess performance. For example, a company might have a goal of filling 98% of customer orders within two hours. Balanced scorecard reports are often presented in graphs or tables that can be updated frequently. Such timely information aids division managers in their decisions, and can be used by top management to evaluate division manager performance.

   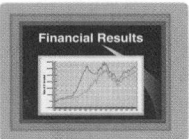

EXHIBIT 21.25

Balanced Scorecard Performance Indicators

Customer	Internal Process	Innovation/Learning	Financial
• Customer satisfaction rating • # of new customers acquired • % of on-time deliveries • % of sales from new products • Time to fill orders % of sales returned	• Defect rates • Cycle time • Product costs • Labor hours per order • Production days without an accident	• Employee satisfaction • Employee turnover • $ spent on training • # of new products • # of patents • $ spent on research	• Net income • ROI • Sales growth • Cash flow • Residual income • Stock price

Exhibit 21.26 is an example of balanced scorecard reporting on the customer perspective for an Internet retailer. This scorecard reports for example that the retailer is getting 62% of its potential customers successfully through the checkout process, and that 2.2% of all orders are returned. The *color* of the arrows in the right-most column reveals whether the company is exceeding its goal (green), barely meeting the goal (yellow), or not meeting the goal (red). The *direction* of the arrows reveals any trend in performance: an upward arrow indicates improvement, a downward arrow indicates declining performance, and an arrow pointing sideways indicates no change. A review of these arrows' color and direction suggests the retailer is meeting or exceeding its goals on checkout success, orders returned, and customer satisfaction. Further, checkout success and customer satisfaction are improving. The red arrow shows the company has received more customer complaints than was hoped for; however, the number of customer complaints is declining. A manager would combine this information with similar information on the internal process, innovation and learning, and financial perspectives to get an overall view of division performance.

EXHIBIT 21.26

Balanced Scorecard Reporting: Internet Retailer

Customer Perspective	Actual	Goal
Checkout success	62%	↑
Orders returned	2.20%	↔
Customer satisfaction rating	9.5	↑
Number of customer complaints	142	↓

Decision Maker

Center Manager   Your center's usual return on total assets is 19%. You are considering two new investments for your center. The first requires a $250,000 average investment and is expected to yield annual net income of $50,000. The second requires a $1 million average investment with an expected annual net income of $175,000. Do you pursue either? [Answer—pp. 879–880]

Responsibility Accounting

Departmental accounting reports often provide data used to evaluate a department's performance, but are they useful in assessing how well a department *manager* performs? Neither departmental income nor its contribution to overhead may be useful because many expenses can be outside a manager's control. Instead, we often evaluate a manager's performance using

C4   Explain controllable costs and responsibility accounting.

responsibility accounting reports that describe a department's activities in terms of **controllable costs.**[3] A cost is controllable if a manager has the power to determine or at least significantly affect the amount incurred. **Uncontrollable costs** are not within the manager's control or influence.

Controllable versus Direct Costs

Controllable costs are not always the same as direct costs. Direct costs are readily traced to a department, but the department manager might or might not control their amounts. For example, department managers often have little or no control over depreciation expense because they cannot affect the amount of equipment assigned to their departments. Also, department managers rarely control their own salaries. However, they can control or influence items such as the cost of supplies used in their department. When evaluating managers' performances, we should use data reflecting their departments' outputs along with their controllable costs and expenses.

Distinguishing between controllable and uncontrollable costs depends on the particular manager and time period under analysis. For example, the cost of property insurance is usually not controllable at the department manager's level but by the executive responsible for obtaining the company's insurance coverage. Likewise, this executive might not control costs resulting from insurance policies already in force. However, when a policy expires, this executive can renegotiate a replacement policy and then controls these costs. Therefore, all costs are controllable at some management level if the time period is sufficiently long. We must use good judgment in identifying controllable costs.

Responsibility Accounting System

A *responsibility accounting system* uses the concept of controllable costs to assign managers the responsibility for costs and expenses under their control. Prior to each reporting period, a company prepares plans that identify costs and expenses under each manager's control. These plans are called **responsibility accounting budgets.** To ensure the cooperation of managers and the reasonableness of budgets, managers should be involved in preparing their budgets.

A responsibility accounting system also involves performance reports. A **responsibility accounting performance report** accumulates and reports costs and expenses that a manager is responsible for and their budgeted amounts. Management's analysis of differences between budgeted amounts and actual costs and expenses often results in corrective or strategic managerial actions. Upper-level management uses performance reports to evaluate the effectiveness of lower-level managers in controlling costs and expenses and keeping them within budgeted amounts.

A responsibility accounting system recognizes that control over costs and expenses belongs to several levels of management. We illustrate this by considering the organization chart in Exhibit 21.27. The lines in this chart connecting the managerial positions reflect channels of authority. For example, the four department managers of this consulting firm (benchmarking, cost management, outsourcing, and service) are responsible for controllable costs and expenses incurred in their

EXHIBIT 21.27

Organizational Responsibility Chart

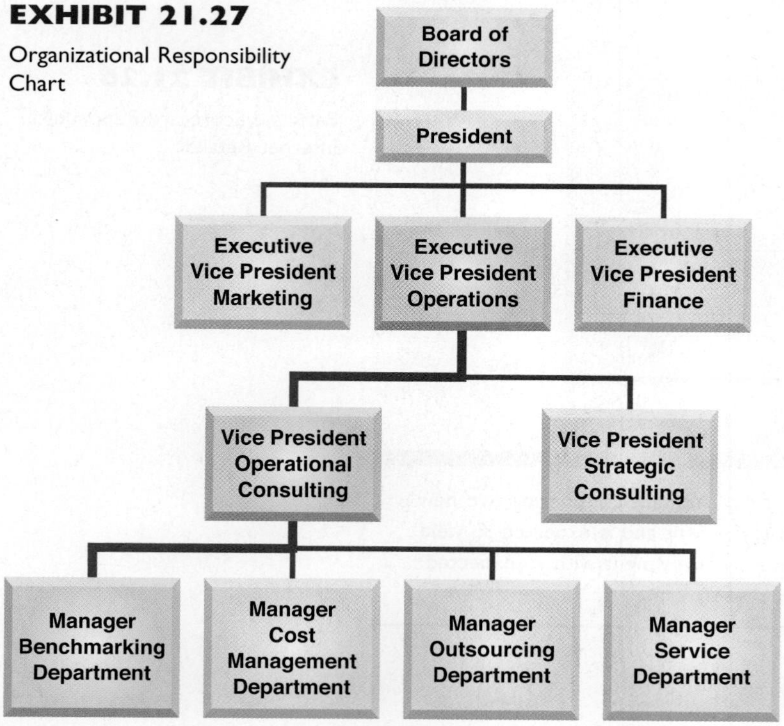

[3] The terms *cost* and *expense* are often used interchangeably in managerial accounting, but they are not necessarily the same. *Cost* often refers to the monetary outlay to acquire some resource that can have present and future benefit. *Expense* usually refers to an expired cost. That is, as the benefit of a resource expires, a portion of its cost is written off as an expense.

departments, but these same costs are subject to the overall control of the vice president (VP) for operational consulting. Similarly, this VP's costs are subject to the control of the executive vice president (EVP) for operations, the president, and, ultimately, the board of directors.

At lower levels, managers have limited responsibility and relatively little control over costs and expenses. Performance reports for low-level management typically cover few controllable costs. Responsibility and control broaden for higher-level managers; therefore, their reports span a wider range of costs. However, reports to higher-level managers seldom contain the details reported to their subordinates but are summarized for two reasons: (1) lower-level managers are often responsible for these detailed costs and (2) detailed reports can obscure broader, more important issues facing a company.

Point: Responsibility accounting does not place blame. Instead, responsibility accounting is used to identify opportunities for improving performance.

Exhibit 21.28 shows summarized performance reports for the three management levels identified in Exhibit 21.27. Exhibit 21.28 shows that costs under the control of the benchmarking department manager are totaled and included among controllable costs of the VP for operational consulting. Also, costs under the control of the VP are totaled and included among controllable costs of the EVP for operations. In this way, a responsibility accounting system provides relevant information for each management level.

EXHIBIT 21.28

Responsibility Accounting Performance Reports

Executive Vice President, Operations	For July		
Controllable Costs	**Budgeted Amount**	**Actual Amount**	**Over (Under) Budget**
Salaries, VPs	$ 80,000	$ 80,000	$ 0
Quality control costs	21,000	22,400	1,400
Office costs	29,500	28,800	(700)
Operational consulting	276,700	279,500	2,800
Strategic consulting	390,000	380,600	(9,400)
Totals	$ 797,200	$ 791,300	$ (5,900)

Vice President, Operational Consulting	For July		
Controllable Costs	**Budgeted Amount**	**Actual Amount**	**Over (Under) Budget**
Salaries, department managers	$ 75,000	$ 78,000	$ 3,000
Depreciation	10,600	10,600	0
Insurance	6,800	6,300	(500)
Benchmarking department	79,600	79,900	300
Cost management department	61,500	60,200	(1,300)
Outsourcing department	24,300	24,700	400
Service department	18,900	19,800	900
Totals	$276,700	$279,500	$2,800

Manager, Benchmarking Department	For July		
Controllable Costs	**Budgeted Amount**	**Actual Amount**	**Over (Under) Budget**
Salaries	$ 51,600	$ 52,500	$ 900
Supplies	8,000	7,800	(200)
Other controllable costs	20,000	19,600	(400)
Totals	$ 79,600	$ 79,900	$ 300

Technological advances increase our ability to produce vast amounts of information that often exceed our ability to use it. Good managers select relevant data for planning and controlling the areas under their responsibility. A good responsibility accounting system makes every effort to provide relevant information to the right person (the one who controls the cost) at the right time (before a cost is out of control).

Point: Responsibility accounting usually divides a company into subunits, or *responsibility centers*. A center manager is evaluated on how well the center performs, as reported in responsibility accounting reports.

10. Are the reports of departmental net income and the departmental contribution to overhead useful in assessing a department manager's performance? Explain.

11. Performance reports to evaluate managers should (*a*) include data about controllable expenses, (*b*) compare actual results with budgeted levels, or (*c*) both (*a*) and (*b*).

Decision Analysis | Investment Center Profit Margin and Investment Turnover

A2 Analyze investment centers using profit margin and investment turnover.

We can further examine investment center (division) performance by splitting return on investment into **profit margin** and **investment turnover** as follows

Return on investment	=	Profit margin	×	Investment turnover

$$\frac{\text{Investment center net income}}{\text{Investment center average assets}} = \frac{\text{Investment center net income}}{\text{Investment center sales}} \times \frac{\text{Investment center sales}}{\text{Investment center average assets}}$$

Profit margin measures the income earned per dollar of sales. **Investment turnover** measures how efficiently an investment center generates sales from its invested assets. Higher profit margin and higher investment turnover indicate better performance. To illustrate, consider Best Buy which reports in Exhibit 21.29 results for two divisions (segments): Domestic and International.

EXHIBIT 21.29

Best Buy Division Sales, Income, and Assets

($ millions)	Domestic	International
Sales	$24,616	$2,817
Net income	1,393	49
Average invested assets	8,372	1,922

Profit margin and investment turnover for its Domestic and International divisions are computed and shown in Exhibit 21.30:

EXHIBIT 21.30

Best Buy Division Profit Margin and Investment Turnover

($ millions)	Domestic	International
Profit Margin		
$1,393/$24,616	5.66%	
$49/$2,817		1.74%
Investment Turnover		
$24,616/$8,372	2.94	
$2,817/$1,922		1.47

Best Buy's Domestic division generates 5.66 cents of profit per $1 of sales, while its International division generates only 1.74 cents of profit per dollar of sales. Its Domestic division also uses its assets more efficiently; its investment turnover of 2.94 is twice that of its International division's 1.47. Top management can use profit margin and investment turnover to evaluate the performance of division managers. The measures can also aid management when considering further investment in its divisions.

 Decision Maker

Division Manager   You manage a division in a highly competitive industry. You will receive a cash bonus if your division achieves an ROI above 12%. Your division's profit margin is 7%, equal to the industry average, and your division's investment turnover is 1.5. What actions can you take to increase your chance of receiving the bonus? [Answer—p. 880]

Demonstration Problem

DP21

Management requests departmental income statements for Hacker's Haven, a computer store that has five departments. Three are operating departments (hardware, software, and repairs) and two are service departments (general office and purchasing).

	General Office	Purchasing	Hardware	Software	Repairs
Sales	—	—	$960,000	$600,000	$840,000
Cost of goods sold	—	—	500,000	300,000	200,000
Direct expenses					
Payroll	$60,000	$45,000	80,000	25,000	325,000
Depreciation	6,000	7,200	33,000	4,200	9,600
Supplies	15,000	10,000	10,000	2,000	25,000

The departments incur several indirect expenses. To prepare departmental income statements, the indirect expenses must be allocated across the five departments. Then the expenses of the two service departments must be allocated to the three operating departments. Total cost amounts and the allocation bases for each indirect expense follow.

Indirect Expense	Total Cost	Allocation Basis
Rent	$150,000	Square footage occupied
Utilities	50,000	Square footage occupied
Advertising	125,000	Dollars of sales
Insurance	30,000	Value of assets insured
Service departments		
General office	?	Number of employees
Purchasing	?	Dollars of cost of goods sold

The following additional information is needed for indirect expense allocations.

Department	Square Feet	Sales	Insured Assets	Employees	Cost of Goods Sold
General office	500		$ 60,000		
Purchasing	500		72,000		
Hardware	4,000	$ 960,000	330,000	5	$ 500,000
Software	3,000	600,000	42,000	5	300,000
Repairs	2,000	840,000	96,000	10	200,000
Totals	10,000	$2,400,000	$600,000	20	$1,000,000

Required

1. Prepare a departmental expense allocation spreadsheet for Hacker's Haven.
2. Prepare a departmental income statement reporting net income for each operating department and for all operating departments combined.

Planning the Solution

- Set up and complete four tables to allocate the indirect expenses—one each for rent, utilities, advertising, and insurance.
- Allocate the departments' indirect expenses using a spreadsheet like the one in Exhibit 21.12. Enter the given amounts of the direct expenses for each department. Then enter the allocated amounts of the indirect expenses that you computed.
- Complete two tables for allocating the general office and purchasing department costs to the three operating departments. Enter these amounts on the spreadsheet and determine the total expenses allocated to the three operating departments.
- Prepare departmental income statements like the one in Exhibit 21.17. Show sales, cost of goods sold, gross profit, individual expenses, and net income for each of the three operating departments and for the combined company.

Solution to Demonstration Problem

Allocations of the four indirect expenses across the five departments.

Rent	Square Feet	Percent of Total	Allocated Cost
General office	500	5.0%	$ 7,500
Purchasing	500	5.0	7,500
Hardware	4,000	40.0	60,000
Software	3,000	30.0	45,000
Repairs	2,000	20.0	30,000
Totals	10,000	100.0%	$150,000

Utilities	Square Feet	Percent of Total	Allocated Cost
General office	500	5.0%	$ 2,500
Purchasing	500	5.0	2,500
Hardware	4,000	40.0	20,000
Software	3,000	30.0	15,000
Repairs	2,000	20.0	10,000
Totals	10,000	100.0%	$50,000

Advertising	Sales Dollars	Percent of Total	Allocated Cost
Hardware	$ 960,000	40.0%	$ 50,000
Software	600,000	25.0	31,250
Repairs	840,000	35.0	43,750
Totals	$2,400,000	100.0%	$125,000

Insurance	Assets Insured	Percent of Total	Allocated Cost
General office	$ 60,000	10.0%	$ 3,000
Purchasing	72,000	12.0	3,600
Hardware	330,000	55.0	16,500
Software	42,000	7.0	2,100
Repairs	96,000	16.0	4,800
Totals	$600,000	100.0%	$30,000

I. Allocations of service department expenses to the three operating departments.

General Office Allocations to	Employees	Percent of Total	Allocated Cost
Hardware	5	25.0%	$23,500
Software	5	25.0	23,500
Repairs	10	50.0	47,000
Totals	20	100.0%	$94,000

Purchasing Allocations to	Cost of Goods Sold	Percent of Total	Allocated Cost
Hardware	$ 500,000	50.0%	$37,900
Software	300,000	30.0	22,740
Repairs	200,000	20.0	15,160
Totals	$1,000,000	100.0%	$75,800

HACKER'S HAVEN
Departmental Expense Allocations
For Year Ended December 31, 2009

	Allocation Base	Expense Account Balance	General Office Dept.	Purchasing Dept.	Hardware Dept.	Software Dept.	Repairs Dept.
Direct Expenses							
Payroll		$ 535,000	$ 60,000	$ 45,000	$ 80,000	$ 25,000	$ 325,000
Depreciation		60,000	6,000	7,200	33,000	4,200	9,600
Supplies		62,000	15,000	10,000	10,000	2,000	25,000
Indirect Expenses							
Rent	Square ft.	150,000	7,500	7,500	60,000	45,000	30,000
Utilities	Square ft.	50,000	2,500	2,500	20,000	15,000	10,000
Advertising	Sales	125,000	—	—	50,000	31,250	43,750
Insurance	Assets	30,000	3,000	3,600	16,500	2,100	4,800
Total expenses		1,012,000	94,000	75,800	269,500	124,550	448,150
Service Department Expenses							
General office	Employees		(94,000)		23,500	23,500	47,000
Purchasing	Goods sold			(75,800)	37,900	22,740	15,160
Total expenses allocated to operating departments		$1,012,000	$ 0	$ 0	$330,900	$170,790	$510,310

2. Departmental income statements for Hacker's Haven.

HACKER'S HAVEN Departmental Income Statements For Year Ended December 31, 2009	Hardware	Software	Repairs	Combined
Sales	$ 960,000	$ 600,000	$ 840,000	$2,400,000
Cost of goods sold	500,000	300,000	200,000	1,000,000
Gross profit	460,000	300,000	640,000	1,400,000
Expenses				
Payroll	80,000	25,000	325,000	430,000
Depreciation	33,000	4,200	9,600	46,800
Supplies	10,000	2,000	25,000	37,000
Rent	60,000	45,000	30,000	135,000
Utilities	20,000	15,000	10,000	45,000
Advertising	50,000	31,250	43,750	125,000
Insurance	16,500	2,100	4,800	23,400
Share of general office	23,500	23,500	47,000	94,000
Share of purchasing	37,900	22,740	15,160	75,800
Total expenses	330,900	170,790	510,310	1,012,000
Net income	$129,100	$129,210	$129,690	$ 388,000

Transfer Pricing

Divisions in decentralized companies sometimes do business with one another. For example, a separate division of **Harley-Davidson** manufactures its plastic and fiberglass parts used in the company's motorcycles. **Anheuser-Busch**'s metal container division makes cans and lids used in its brewing operations, and also sells cans and lids to soft-drink companies. A division of **Prince** produces strings used in tennis rackets made by **Prince** and other manufacturers.

Determining the price that should be used to record transfers between divisions in the same company is the focus of this appendix. Because these transactions are transfers within the same company, the price to record them is called the **transfer price.** In decentralized organizations, division managers have input on or decide those prices. Transfer prices can be used in cost, profit, and investment centers. Since these transfers are not with customers outside the company, the transfer price has no direct impact on the company's overall profits. However, transfer prices can impact performance evaluations and, if set incorrectly, lead to bad decisions.

C5 Explain transfer pricing and methods to set transfer prices.

Point: Transfer pricing can impact company profits when divisions are located in countries with different tax rates; this is covered in advanced courses.

Alternative Transfer Prices

Exhibit 21A.1 reports data on the LCD division of ZTel. LCD manufactures liquid crystal display (LCD) touch-screen monitors for use in ZTel's S-Phone division's smartphones, which sell for $400 each. The monitors can also be used in other products. So, LCD can sell its monitors to buyers other than S-Phone. Likewise, the S-Phone division can purchase monitors from suppliers other than LCD.

Exhibit 21A.1 reveals the range of transfer prices for transfers of monitors from LCD to S-Phone. The manager of LCD wants to report a division profit; thus, this manager will not accept a transfer price less than $40 (variable manufacturing cost per unit) because doing so would cause the division to lose

EXHIBIT 21A.1

LCD Division Manufacturing
Information—Monitors

Production capacity	100,000 units
Selling price per unit to outside customers	$80
Variable manufacturing costs per unit	$40
Fixed manufacturing costs	$2,000,000

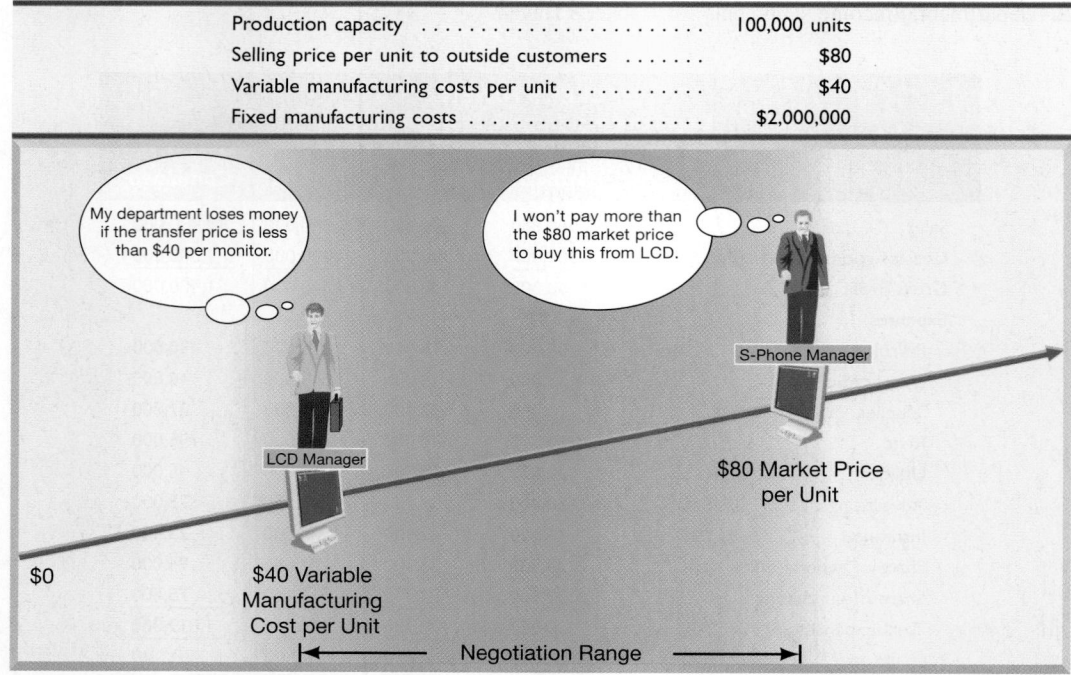

money on each monitor transferred. The LCD manager will only consider transfer prices of $40 or more. On the other hand, the S-Phone division manager also wants to report a division profit. Thus, this manager will not pay more than $80 per monitor because similar monitors can be bought from outside suppliers at that price. The S-Phone manager will only consider transfer prices of $80 or less. As any transfer price between $40 and $80 per monitor is possible, how does ZTel determine the transfer price? The answer depends in part on whether the LCD division has excess capacity to manufacture monitors.

No Excess Capacity   Assume the LCD division can sell every monitor it produces, and thus is producing 100,000 units. In that case, a **market-based transfer price** of $80 per monitor is preferred. At that price, the LCD division manager is willing to either transfer monitors to S-Phone or sell to outside customers. The S-Phone manager cannot buy monitors for less than $80 from outside suppliers, so the $80 price is acceptable. Further, with a transfer price of $80 per monitor, top management of ZTel is indifferent to S-Phone buying from LCD or buying similar-quality monitors from outside suppliers.

With no excess capacity, the LCD manager will not accept a transfer price less than $80 per monitor. For example, suppose the S-Phone manager suggests a transfer price of $70 per monitor. At that price the LCD manager incurs an unnecessary *opportunity cost* of $10 per monitor (computed as $80 market price minus $70 transfer price). This would lower the LCD division's income and hurt its performance evaluation.

Excess Capacity   Assume that the LCD division has excess capacity. For example, the LCD division might currently be producing only 80,000 units. Because LCD has $2,000,000 of fixed manufacturing costs, both LCD and the top management of ZTel prefer that S-Phone purchases its monitors from LCD. For example, if S-Phone purchases its monitors from an outside supplier at the market price of $80 each, LCD manufactures no units. Then, LCD reports a division loss equal to its fixed costs, and ZTel overall reports a lower net income as its costs are higher. Consequently, with excess capacity, LCD should accept any transfer price of $40 per unit or greater and S-Phone should purchase monitors from LCD. This will allow LCD to recover some (or all) of its fixed costs and increase ZTel's overall profits. For example, if a transfer price of $50 per monitor is used, the S-Phone manager is pleased to buy from LCD, since that price is below the market price of $80. For each monitor transferred from LCD to S-Phone at $50, the LCD division receives a *contribution margin* of $10 (computed as $50 transfer price less $40 variable cost) to contribute towards recovering its fixed costs. This form of transfer pricing is called **cost-based transfer pricing.** Under this approach the transfer price might be based on variable costs, total costs, or variable costs plus a markup. Determining the transfer price under excess capacity is complex and is covered in advanced courses.

Additional Issues in Transfer Pricing Several additional issues arise in determining transfer prices which include the following:

- **No market price exists.** Sometimes there is no market price for the product being transferred. The product might be a key component that requires additional conversion costs at the next stage and is not easily replicated by an outside company. For example, there is no market for a console for a **Nissan** Maxima and there is no substitute console **Nissan** can use in assembling a Maxima. In this case a market-based transfer price cannot be used.
- **Cost control.** To provide incentives for cost control, transfer prices might be based on standard, rather than actual costs. For example, if a transfer price of actual variable costs plus a markup of $20 per unit is used in the case above, LCD has no incentive to control its costs.
- **Division managers' negotiation.** With excess capacity, division managers will often negotiate a transfer price that lies between the variable cost per unit and the market price per unit. In this case, the **negotiated transfer price** and resulting departmental performance reports reflect, in part, the negotiating skills of the respective division managers. This might not be best for overall company performance.
- **Nonfinancial factors.** Factors such as quality control, reduced lead times, and impact on employee morale can be important factors in determining transfer prices.

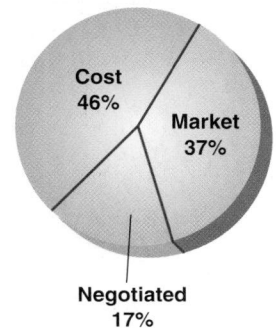

Transfer Pricing Approaches Used by Companies

Cost 46%
Market 37%
Negotiated 17%

APPENDIX

Joint Costs and Their Allocation

21B

Most manufacturing processes involve **joint costs,** which refer to costs incurred to produce or purchase two or more products at the same time. A joint cost is like an indirect expense in the sense that more than one cost object share it. For example, a sawmill company incurs a joint cost when it buys logs that it cuts into lumber as shown in Exhibit 21B.1. The joint cost includes the logs (raw material) and its cutting (conversion) into boards classified as Clear, Select, No. 1 Common, No. 2 Common, No. 3 Common, and other types of lumber and by-products.

C6 Describe allocation of joint costs across products.

When a joint cost is incurred, a question arises as to whether to allocate it to different products resulting from it. The answer is that when management wishes to estimate the costs of individual products, joint costs are included and must be allocated to these joint products. However, when management needs information to help decide whether to sell a product at a certain point in the production process or to process it further, the joint costs are ignored.

Joint Products

Joint Cost

Cutting of Logs

Clear
Select
No. 1 Common
No. 2 Common
No. 3 Common

Split-off Point

EXHIBIT 21B.1

Joint Products from Logs

Financial statements prepared according to GAAP must assign joint costs to products. To do this, management must decide how to allocate joint costs across products benefiting from these costs. If some products are sold and others remain in inventory, allocating joint costs involves assigning costs to both cost of goods sold and ending inventory.

The two usual methods to allocate joint costs are the (1) *physical basis* and (2) the *value basis.* The physical basis typically involves allocating joint cost using physical characteristics such as the ratio of pounds, cubic feet, or gallons of each joint product to the total pounds, cubic feet, or gallons of all joint products flowing from the cost. This method is not preferred because the resulting cost allocations do not reflect the relative market values the joint cost generates. The preferred approach is the value basis, which allocates joint cost in proportion to the sales value of the output produced by the process at the "split-off point"; see Exhibit 21B.1.

Physical Basis Allocation of Joint Cost   To illustrate the physical basis of allocating a joint cost, we consider a sawmill that bought logs for $30,000. When cut, these logs produce 100,000 board feet of lumber in the grades and amounts shown in Exhibit 21B.2. The logs produce 20,000 board feet of No. 3 Common lumber, which is 20% of the total. With physical allocation, the No. 3 Common lumber is assigned 20% of the $30,000 cost of the logs, or $6,000 ($30,000 × 20%). Because this low-grade lumber sells for $4,000, this allocation gives a $2,000 loss from its production and sale. The physical basis for allocating joint costs does not reflect the extra value flowing into some products or the inferior value flowing into others. That is, the portion of a log that produces Clear and Select grade lumber is worth more than the portion used to produce the three grades of common lumber, but the physical basis fails to reflect this.

EXHIBIT 21B.2

Allocating Joint Costs on a Physical Basis

Grade of Lumber	Board Feet Produced	Percent of Total	Allocated Cost	Sales Value	Gross Profit
Clear and Select	10,000	10.0%	$ 3,000	$12,000	$ 9,000
No. 1 Common	30,000	30.0	9,000	18,000	9,000
No. 2 Common	40,000	40.0	12,000	16,000	4,000
No. 3 Common	20,000	20.0	6,000	4,000	(2,000)
Totals	100,000	100.0%	$30,000	$50,000	$20,000

Value Basis Allocation of Joint Cost   Exhibit 21B.3 illustrates the value basis method of allocation. It determines the percents of the total costs allocated to each grade by the ratio of each grade's sales value to the total sales value of $50,000 (sales value is the unit selling price multiplied by the number of units produced). The Clear and Select lumber grades receive 24% of the total cost ($12,000/$50,000) instead of the 10% portion using a physical basis. The No. 3 Common lumber receives only 8% of the total cost, or $2,400, which is much less than the $6,000 assigned to it using the physical basis.

EXHIBIT 21B.3

Allocating Joint Costs on a Value Basis

Grade of Lumber	Sales Value	Percent of Total	Allocated Cost	Gross Profit
Clear and Select	$12,000	24.0%	$ 7,200	$ 4,800
No. 1 Common	18,000	36.0	10,800	7,200
No. 2 Common	16,000	32.0	9,600	6,400
No. 3 Common	4,000	8.0	2,400	1,600
Totals	$50,000	100.0%	$30,000	$20,000

Example: Refer to Exhibit 21B.3. If the sales value of Clear and Select lumber is changed to $10,000, what is the revised ratio of the market value of No. 1 Common to the total? *Answer:* $18,000/$48,000 = 37.5%

An outcome of value basis allocation is that *each* grade produces exactly the same 40% gross profit at the split-off point. This 40% rate equals the gross profit rate from selling all the lumber made from the $30,000 logs for a combined price of $50,000.

Quick Check   Answers—p. 880

12. A company produces three products, B1, B2, and B3. The joint cost incurred for the current month for these products is $180,000. The following data relate to this month's production:

Product	Units Produced	Unit Sales Value
B1	96,000	$3.00
B2	64,000	6.00
B3	32,000	9.00

The amount of joint cost allocated to product B3 using the value basis allocation is (a) $30,000, (b) $54,000, or (c) $90,000.

Summary

C1 Explain departmentalization and the role of departmental accounting. Companies are divided into departments when they are too large to be effectively managed as a single unit. Operating departments carry out an organization's main functions. Service departments support the activities of operating departments. Departmental accounting systems provide information for evaluating departmental performance.

C2 Distinguish between direct and indirect expenses. Direct expenses are traced to a specific department and are incurred for the sole benefit of that department. Indirect expenses benefit more than one department. Indirect expenses are allocated to departments when computing departmental net income.

C3 Identify bases for allocating indirect expenses to departments. Ideally, we allocate indirect expenses by using a cause-effect relation for the allocation base. When a cause-effect relation is not identifiable, each indirect expense is allocated on a basis reflecting the relative benefit received by each department.

C4 Explain controllable costs and responsibility accounting. A controllable cost is one that is influenced by a specific management level. The total expenses of operating a department often include some items a department manager does not control. Responsibility accounting systems provide information for evaluating the performance of department managers. A responsibility accounting system's performance reports for evaluating department managers should include only the expenses (and revenues) that each manager controls.

C5 Explain transfer pricing and methods to set transfer prices. Transfer prices are used to record transfers of items between divisions of the same company. Transfer prices can be based on costs or market prices, or can be negotiated by division managers.

C6 Describe allocation of joint costs across products. A joint cost refers to costs incurred to produce or purchase two or more products at the same time. When income statements are prepared, joint costs are usually allocated to the resulting joint products using either a physical or value basis.

A1 Analyze investment centers using return on assets, residual income, and balanced scorecard. A financial measure often used to evaluate an investment center manager is the *investment center return on total assets,* also called *return on investment.*

This measure is computed as the center's net income divided by the center's average total assets. Residual income, computed as investment center net income minus a target net income is an alternative financial measure of investment center performance. A balanced scorecard uses a combination of financial and non-financial measures to evaluate performance.

A2 Analyze investment centers using profit margin and investment turnover. Return on investment can also be computed as profit margin times investment turnover. Profit margin (equal to net income/sales) measures the income earned per dollar of sales and investment turnover (equal to sales/assets) measures how efficiently a division uses its assets.

P1 Assign overhead costs using two-stage cost allocation. In the traditional two-stage cost allocation procedure, service department costs are first assigned to operating departments. Then, in the second stage, a predetermined overhead allocation rate is computed for each operating department and is used to assign overhead to output.

P2 Assign overhead costs using activity-based costing. In activity-based costing, the costs of related activities are collected and then pooled in some logical manner into activity cost pools. After all activity costs have been accumulated in an activity cost pool account, users of the activity, termed *cost objects,* are assigned a portion of the total activity cost using a cost driver (allocation base).

P3 Prepare departmental income statements. Each profit center (department) is assigned its expenses to yield its own income statement. These costs include its direct expenses and its share of indirect expenses. The departmental income statement lists its revenues and costs of goods sold to determine gross profit. Its operating expenses (direct expenses and its indirect expenses allocated to the department) are deducted from gross profit to yield departmental net income.

P4 Prepare departmental contribution reports. The departmental contribution report is similar to the departmental income statement in terms of computing the gross profit for each department. Then the direct operating expenses for each department are deducted from gross profit to determine the contribution generated by each department. Indirect operating expenses are deducted *in total* from the company's combined contribution.

Guidance Answers to **Decision Maker** and **Decision Ethics**

Director of Operations You should collect details on overhead items and review them to see whether direct labor drives these costs. If it does not, overhead might be improperly assigned to departments. The situation also provides an opportunity to consider other overhead allocation bases, including use of activity-based costing.

Accounting Officer You should not author a report that you disagree with. You are responsible for ascertaining all the facts of ABC (implementation procedures, advantages and disadvantages, and costs). You should then approach your supervisor with these facts and suggest that you would like to modify the report to request, for

example, a pilot test. The pilot test will allow you to further assess the suitability of ABC. Your suggestion might be rejected, at which time you may wish to speak with a more senior-level manager.

Center Manager We must first realize that the two investment opportunities are not comparable on the basis of absolute dollars of income or on assets. For instance, the second investment provides a higher income in absolute dollars but requires a higher investment. Accordingly, we need to compute return on total assets for each alternative: (1) $50,000 ÷ $250,000 = 20%, and (2) $175,000 ÷ $1 million = 17.5%. Alternative 1 has the higher return and is preferred over alternative 2. Do you pursue one, both, or neither? Because alternative 1's return is higher than the center's usual return of 19%, it should be pursued, assuming its risks are acceptable. Also, since alternative 1 requires a small investment, top management is likely to be more agreeable to pursuing it. Alternative 2's return is lower than the usual 19% and is not likely to be acceptable.

Division Manager Your division's ROI without further action is 10.5% (equal to 7% × 1.5). In a highly competitive industry, it is

difficult to increase profit margins by raising prices. Your division might be better able to control its costs to increase its profit margin. In addition, you might engage in a marketing program to increase sales without increasing your division's invested assets. Investment turnover and thus ROI will increase if the marketing campaign attracts customers.

Guidance Answers to **Quick Checks**

1. Cost drivers are the factors that have a cause-effect relation with costs (or activities that pertain to costs).

2. *d*

3. A departmental accounting system provides information used to evaluate the performance of *departments*. A responsibility accounting system provides information used to evaluate the performance of *department managers*.

4. *d*

5. A cost center, such as a service department, incurs costs without directly generating revenues. A profit center, such as a product division, incurs costs but also generates revenues.

6. *b*

7. *d*

8. (1) Assign the direct expenses to each department. (2) Allocate indirect expenses to all departments. (3) Allocate the service department expenses to the operating departments.

9. *b*

10. No, because many expenses that enter into these calculations are beyond the manager's control, and managers should not be evaluated using costs they do not control.

11. *c*

12. *b*; $180,000 × ([32,000 × $9]/[96,000 × $3 + 64,000 × $6 + 32,000 × $9]) = $54,000.

Key Terms

mhhe.com/wildFAP19e

Key Terms are available at the book's Website for learning and testing in an online Flashcard Format.

Activity-based costing (ABC) (p. 854)	**Direct expenses** (p. 859)	**Market-based transfer price** (p. 876)
Activity cost driver (p. 855)	**Hurdle rate** (p. 868)	**Negotiated transfer price** (p. 877)
Activity cost pool (p. 855)	**Indirect expenses** (p. 859)	**Profit center** (p. 858)
Balanced scorecard (p. 868)	**Investment center** (p. 858)	**Profit margin** (p. 872)
Controllable costs (p. 870)	**Investment center residual income** (p. 867)	**Responsibility accounting budget** (p. 870)
Cost-based transfer pricing (p. 876)	**Investment center return on total assets** (p. 867)	**Responsibility accounting performance report** (p. 870)
Cost center (p. 858)		
Departmental accounting system (p. 858)	**Investment turnover** (p. 872)	**Responsibility accounting system** (p. 858)
Departmental contribution to overhead (p. 866)	**Joint cost** (p. 877)	**Transfer price** (p. 875)
		Uncontrollable costs (p. 870)

Multiple Choice Quiz   Answers on p. 899   mhhe.com/wildFAP19e

Additional Quiz Questions are available at the book's Website.

Quiz21

1. A retailer has three departments—housewares, appliances, and clothing—and buys advertising that benefits all departments. Advertising expense is $150,000 for the year, and departmental sales for the year follow: housewares, $356,250; appliances, $641,250; clothing, $427,500. How much advertising expense is allocated to appliances if allocation is based on departmental sales?

  a. $37,500
  b. $67,500
  c. $45,000
  d. $150,000
  e. $641,250

2. An activity-based costing system

  a. Does not require the level of detail that a traditional costing system requires.

  b. Does not enable the calculation of unit cost data.

  c. Allocates costs to products on the basis of activities performed on them.

d. Cannot be used by a service company.

e. Allocates costs to products based on the number of direct labor hours used.

3. A company produces two products, Grey and Red. The following information is available relating to those two products. Assume that the company's total setup cost is $162,000. Using activity-based costing, how much setup cost is allocated to each unit of Grey?

	Grey	Red
Units produced	500	40,000
Number of setups	50	100
Direct labor hours per unit	15	15

a. $1,080
b. $ 72
c. $ 162
d. $2,000
e. $ 108

4. A company operates three retail departments as profit centers, and the following information is available for each. Which department has the largest dollar amount of departmental contribution to overhead and what is the dollar amount contributed?

Department	Sales	Cost of Goods Sold	Direct Expenses	Allocated Indirect Expenses
X	$500,000	$350,000	$50,000	$40,000
Y	200,000	75,000	20,000	50,000
Z	350,000	150,000	75,000	10,000

a. Department Y, $ 55,000
b. Department Z, $125,000
c. Department X, $500,000
d. Department Z, $200,000
e. Department X, $ 60,000

5. Using the data in question 4, Department X's contribution to overhead as a percentage of sales is
a. 20%
b. 30%
c. 12%
d. 48%
e. 32%

Superscript letter $^A(^B)$ denotes assignments based on Appendix 21A (21B).

Discussion Questions

1. Why are many companies divided into departments?

2. Complete the following for a traditional two-stage allocation system: In the first stage, service department costs are assigned to _____ departments. In the second stage, a predetermined overhead rate is computed for each operating department and used to assign overhead to _____.

3. What is the difference between operating departments and service departments?

4. What is activity-based costing? What is its goal?

5. ♟ Identify at least four typical cost pools for activity-based costing in most organizations.

6. In activity-based costing, costs in a cost pool are allocated to _____ using predetermined overhead rates.

7. ♟ What company circumstances especially encourage use of activity-based costing?

8. ♟ What are two main goals in managerial accounting for reporting on and analyzing departments?

9. ♟ Is it possible to evaluate a cost center's profitability? Explain.

10. What is the difference between direct and indirect expenses?

11. ♟ Suggest a reasonable basis for allocating each of the following indirect expenses to departments: (a) salary of a supervisor who manages several departments, (b) rent, (c) heat, (d) electricity for lighting, (e) janitorial services, (f) advertising, (g) expired insurance on equipment, and (h) property taxes on equipment.

12. How is a department's contribution to overhead measured?

13. ♟ What are controllable costs?

14. Controllable and uncontrollable costs must be identified with a particular _____ and a definite _____ period.

15. ♟ Why should managers be closely involved in preparing their responsibility accounting budgets?

16. ♟ In responsibility accounting, who receives timely cost reports and specific cost information? Explain.

17.^{A}What is a transfer price? Under what conditions is a market-based transfer price most likely to be used?

18.^{B}What is a joint cost? How are joint costs usually allocated among the products produced from them?

19.^{B} ♟ Give two examples of products with joint costs.

20. ♟ Each retail store of **Best Buy** has several departments. Why is it useful for its management to (a) collect accounting information about each department and (b) treat each department as a profit center?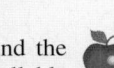

21. ♟ **Apple** delivers its products to locations around the world. List three controllable and three uncontrollable costs for its delivery department.

♟ *Denotes Discussion Questions that involve decision making.*

Available with McGraw-Hill's Homework Manager   McGraw-Hill's HOMEWORK MANAGER®

QUICK STUDY

QS 21-1

Allocation and measurement terms

C1 C2 C3 C4 A1

In each blank next to the following terms, place the identifying letter of its best description.

1. _____ Cost center
2. _____ Investment center
3. _____ Departmental accounting system
4. _____ Operating department
5. _____ Profit center
6. _____ Responsibility accounting system
7. _____ Service department

A. Engages directly in manufacturing or in making sales directly to customers.

B. Does not directly manufacture products but contributes to profitability of the entire company.

C. Incurs costs and also generates revenues.

D. Provides information used to evaluate the performance of a department.

E. Incurs costs without directly yielding revenues.

F. Provides information used to evaluate the performance of a department manager.

G. Holds manager responsible for revenues, costs, and investments.

QS 21-2

Basis for cost allocation

C3

For each of the following types of indirect expenses and service department expenses, identify one allocation basis that could be used to distribute it to the departments indicated.

1. Computer service expenses of production scheduling for operating departments.
2. General office department expenses of the operating departments.
3. Maintenance department expenses of the operating departments.
4. Electric utility expenses of all departments.

QS 21-3

Activity-based costing and overhead cost allocation

P2

The following is taken from Mortan Co.'s internal records of its factory with two operating departments. The cost driver for indirect labor and supplies is direct labor costs, and the cost driver for the remaining overhead items is number of hours of machine use. Compute the total amount of overhead cost allocated to Operating Department 1 using activity-based costing.

	Direct Labor	Machine Use Hours
Operating department 1	$18,800	2,000
Operating department 2	13,200	1,200
Totals	$32,000	3,200

Factory overhead costs	
Rent and utilities	$12,200
Indirect labor	5,400
General office expense	4,000
Depreciation—Equipment	3,000
Supplies	2,600
Total factory overhead	$27,200

Check Dept. 1 allocation, $16,700

QS 21-4

Departmental contribution to overhead

P4

Use the information in the following table to compute each department's contribution to overhead (both in dollars and as a percent). Which department contributes the largest dollar amount to total overhead? Which contributes the highest percent (as a percent of sales)?

	Dept. A	Dept. B	Dept. C
Sales	$106,000	$360,000	$168,000
Cost of goods sold	68,370	207,400	99,120
Gross profit	37,630	152,600	68,880
Total direct expenses	6,890	74,120	15,120
Contribution to overhead	$ _____	$ _____	$ _____
Contribution percent	_____ %	_____ %	_____ %

Compute return on assets for each of these **Best Buy** divisions (each is an investment center). Comment on the relative performance of each investment center.

Investment Center	Net Income	Average Assets	Return on Assets
Cameras and camcorders	$4,500,000	$20,000,000	_____
Phones and communications	1,500,000	12,500,000	_____
Computers and accessories	800,000	10,000,000	_____

Refer to information in QS 21-5. Assume a target income of 12% of average invested assets. Compute residual income for each of Best Buy's divisions.

A company's shipping division (an investment center) has sales of $2,700,000, net income of $216,000, and average invested assets of $2,000,000. Compute the division's return on invested assets, profit margin, and investment turnover.

Fill in the blanks in the schedule below for two separate investment centers A and B.

	Investment Center	
	A	**B**
Sales	$_____	$3,200,000
Net income	$126,000	$_____
Average invested assets	$700,000	_____
Profit margin	6%	_____%
Investment turnover	_____	1.6
Return on assets	_____%	10%

Classify each of the performance measures below into the most likely balanced scorecard perspective it relates to. Label your answers using C (customer), P (internal process), I (innovation and growth), or F (financial).

1. Change in market share   _____
2. Employee training sessions attended   _____
3. Number of days of employee absences   _____
4. Customer wait time   _____
5. Number of new products introduced   _____
6. Length of time raw materials are in inventory   _____
7. Profit margin   _____
8. Customer satisfaction index   _____

Walt Disney reports the following information for its two Parks and Resorts divisions.

	East Coast		West Coast	
	Current year	**Prior year**	**Current year**	**Prior year**
Hotel occupancy rates	89%	86%	92%	93%

Assume **Walt Disney** uses a balanced scorecard and sets a target of 90% occupancy in its resorts. Using Exhibit 21.26 as a guide, show how the company's performance on hotel occupancy would appear on a balanced scorecard report.

QS 21-11ᴬ
Determining transfer prices
without excess capacity
C5

The Windshield division of Chee Cycles makes windshields for use in Chee's Assembly division. The Windshield division incurs variable costs of $175 per windshield and has capacity to make 50,000 windshields per year. The market price is $300 per windshield. The Windshield division incurs total fixed costs of $1,500,000 per year. If the Windshield division is operating at full capacity, what transfer price should be used on transfers between the Windshield and Assembly divisions? Explain.

QS 21-12ᴬ
Determining transfer prices with
excess capacity
C5

Refer to information in QS 21-11. If the Windshield division has excess capacity, what is the range of possible transfer prices that could be used on transfers between the Windshield and Assembly divisions? Explain.

QS 21-13ᴮ
Joint cost allocation
C6

A company purchases a 10,020 square foot commercial building for $500,000 and spends an additional $50,000 to divide the space into two separate rental units and prepare it for rent. Unit A, which has the desirable location on the corner and contains 3,340 square feet, will be rented for $2.00 per square foot. Unit B contains 6,680 square feet and will be rented for $1.50 per square foot. How much of the joint cost should be assigned to Unit B using the value basis of allocation?

Available with McGraw-Hill's Homework Manager

EXERCISES

Exercise 21-1
Departmental expense allocations
P1　C3

Firefly Co. has four departments: materials, personnel, manufacturing, and packaging. In a recent month, the four departments incurred three shared indirect expenses. The amounts of these indirect expenses and the bases used to allocate them follow.

Indirect Expense	Cost	Allocation Base
Supervision	$ 80,000	Number of employees
Utilities	61,000	Square feet occupied
Insurance	16,700	Value of assets in use
Total	$157,700	

Departmental data for the company's recent reporting period follow.

Department	Employees	Square Feet	Asset Values
Materials	40	27,000	$ 60,000
Personnel	22	5,000	1,200
Manufacturing	104	45,000	42,000
Packaging	34	23,000	16,800
Total	200	100,000	$120,000

Check (2) Total of $40,820 assigned to Materials Dept.

(1) Use this information to allocate each of the three indirect expenses across the four departments. (2) Prepare a summary table that reports the indirect expenses assigned to each of the four departments.

Exercise 21-2
Activity-based costing
of overhead
P2

Northwest Company produces two types of glass shelving, rounded edge and squared edge, on the same production line. For the current period, the company reports the following data.

	Rounded Edge	Squared Edge	Total
Direct materials	$19,000	$ 43,200	$ 62,200
Direct labor	12,200	23,800	36,000
Overhead (300% of direct labor cost)	36,600	71,400	108,000
Total cost	$67,800	$138,400	$206,200
Quantity produced	10,500 ft.	14,100 ft.	
Average cost per ft.	$ 6.46	$ 9.82	

Northwest's controller wishes to apply activity-based costing (ABC) to allocate the $108,000 of overhead costs incurred by the two product lines to see whether cost per foot would change markedly from that reported above. She has collected the following information.

Overhead Cost Category (Activity Cost Pool)	Cost
Supervision	$ 5,400
Depreciation of machinery	56,600
Assembly line preparation	46,000
Total overhead	$108,000

She has also collected the following information about the cost drivers for each category (cost pool) and the amount of each driver used by the two product lines.

Overhead Cost Category (Activity Cost Pool)	Driver	Usage		
		Rounded Edge	Squared Edge	Total
Supervision	Direct labor cost($)	$12,200	$23,800	$36,000
Depreciation of machinery	Machine hours	500 hours	1,500 hours	2,000 hours
Assembly line preparation	Setups (number)	40 times	210 times	250 times

Use this information to (1) assign these three overhead cost pools to each of the two products using ABC, (2) determine average cost per foot for each of the two products using ABC, and (3) compare the average cost per foot under ABC with the average cost per foot under the current method for each product. For part 3, explain why a difference between the two cost allocation methods exists.

Check (2) Rounded edge, $5.19; Squared edge, $10.76

Expert Garage pays $128,000 rent each year for its two-story building. The space in this building is occupied by five departments as specified here.

Paint department	1,200 square feet of first-floor space
Engine department	3,600 square feet of first-floor space
Window department	1,920 square feet of second-floor space
Electrical department	1,056 square feet of second-floor space
Accessory department	1,824 square feet of second-floor space

The company allocates 65% of total rent expense to the first floor and 35% to the second floor, and then allocates rent expense for each floor to the departments occupying that floor on the basis of space occupied. Determine the rent expense to be allocated to each department. (Round percents to the nearest one-tenth and dollar amounts to the nearest whole dollar.)

Exercise 21-3
Rent expense allocated to departments

P1 C3

Check Allocated to Paint Dept., $20,800

Off-Road Cycle Shop has two service departments (advertising and administration) and two operating departments (cycles and clothing). During 2009, the departments had the following direct expenses and occupied the following amount of floor space.

Department	Direct Expenses	Square Feet
Advertising	$ 21,000	1,820
Administrative	15,000	1,540
Cycles	102,000	6,440
Clothing	12,000	4,200

Exercise 21-4
Departmental expense allocation spreadsheet

C3 P1

The advertising department developed and distributed 100 advertisements during the year. Of these, 72 promoted cycles and 28 promoted clothing. The store sold $300,000 of merchandise during the year. Of this amount, $228,000 is from the cycles department, and $72,000 is from the clothing department. The utilities expense of $65,000 is an indirect expense to all departments. Prepare a departmental expense allocation spreadsheet for Off-Road Cycle Shop. The spreadsheet should assign (1) direct expenses to each of the four departments, (2) the $65,000 of utilities expense to the four departments on the basis of floor space occupied, (3) the advertising department's expenses to the two operating departments on the basis of the number of ads placed that promoted a department's products, and (4) the administrative department's expenses to the two operating departments based on the amount of sales. Provide supporting computations for the expense allocations.

Check Total expenses allocated to Cycles Dept., $169,938

Exercise 21-5
Service department expenses allocated to operating departments
P3

The following is a partially completed lower section of a departmental expense allocation spreadsheet for Haston Bookstore. It reports the total amounts of direct and indirect expenses allocated to its five departments. Complete the spreadsheet by allocating the expenses of the two service departments (advertising and purchasing) to the three operating departments.

	File Edit View Insert Format Tools Data Window Help						
			Allocation of Expenses to Departments				
		Expense Account Balance	Advertising Dept.	Purchasing Dept.	Books Dept.	Magazines Dept.	Newspapers Dept.
	Allocation Base						
5	Total department expenses..........	$653,000	$23,000	$30,000	$426,000	$85,000	$89,000
6	**Service department expenses**						
7	Advertising department.............Sales		?		?	?	?
8	Purchasing department.............Purch. orders			?	?	?	?
9	Total expenses allocated to						
10	operating departments.............	?	$ 0	$ 0	?	?	?

Sheet1 / Sheet2 / Sheet3 /

Advertising and purchasing department expenses are allocated to operating departments on the basis of dollar sales and purchase orders, respectively. Information about the allocation bases for the three operating departments follows.

Department	Sales	Purchase Orders
Books	$440,000	400
Magazines	160,000	250
Newspapers	200,000	350
Total	$800,000	1,000

Check Total expenses allocated to Books Dept., $450,650

Exercise 21-6
Indirect payroll expense allocated to departments
C3

Jaria Stevens works in both the jewelry department and the hosiery department of a retail store. Stevens assists customers in both departments and arranges and stocks merchandise in both departments. The store allocates Stevens' $35,000 annual wages between the two departments based on a sample of the time worked in the two departments. The sample is obtained from a diary of hours worked that Stevens kept in a randomly chosen two-week period. The diary showed the following hours and activities spent in the two departments. Allocate Stevens' annual wages between the two departments.

Selling in jewelry department	41 hours
Arranging and stocking merchandise in jewelry department	4 hours
Selling in hosiery department	24 hours
Arranging and stocking merchandise in hosiery department	6 hours
Idle time spent waiting for a customer to enter one of the selling departments	5 hours

Check Assign $14,000 to Hosiery

Rex Stanton manages an auto dealership's service department. The recent month's income statement for his department follows. (1) Analyze the items on the income statement and identify those that definitely should be included on a performance report used to evaluate Stanton's performance. List them and explain why you chose them. (2) List and explain the items that should definitely be excluded. (3) List the items that are not definitely included or excluded and explain why they fall into that category.

Exercise 21-7
Managerial performance evaluation

C4

Revenues		
Sales of parts	$ 72,000	
Sales of services	105,000	$177,000
Costs and expenses		
Cost of parts sold	30,000	
Building depreciation	9,300	
Income taxes allocated to department	8,700	
Interest on long-term debt	7,500	
Manager's salary	12,000	
Payroll taxes	8,100	
Supplies	15,900	
Utilities	4,400	
Wages (hourly)	16,000	
Total costs and expenses		111,900
Departmental net income		$ 65,100

You must prepare a return on investment analysis for the regional manager of Veggie Burgers. This growing chain is trying to decide which outlet of two alternatives to open. The first location (A) requires a $500,000 investment and is expected to yield annual net income of $85,000. The second location (B) requires a $200,000 investment and is expected to yield annual net income of $42,000. Compute the return on investment for each Veggie Burgers alternative and then make your recommendation in a one-half page memorandum to the regional manager. (The chain currently generates an 18% return on total assets.)

Exercise 21-8
Investment center analysis

A1

ZMart, a retailer of consumer goods, provides the following information on two of its departments (each considered an investment center).

Exercise 21-9
Computing performance measures

A1

Investment Center	Sales	Net Income	Average Invested Assets
Electronics	$10,000,000	$750,000	$3,750,000
Sporting goods	8,000,000	800,000	5,000,000

(1) Compute return on investment for each department. Using return on investment, which department is most efficient at using assets to generate returns for the company? (2) Assume a target income level of 12% of average invested assets. Compute residual income for each department. Which department generated the most residual income for the company? (3) Assume the Electronics department is presented with a new investment opportunity that will yield a 15% return on assets. Should the new investment opportunity be accepted? Explain.

Refer to information in Exercise 21-9. Compute profit margin and investment turnover for each department. Which department generates the most net income per dollar of sales? Which department is most efficient at generating sales from average invested assets?

Exercise 21-10
Computing performance measures A2

Exercise 21-11
Performance measures—balanced scorecard
A1

MidCoast Airlines uses the following performance measures. Classify each of the performance measures below into the most likely balanced scorecard perspective it relates to. Label your answers using C (customer), P (internal process), I (innovation and growth), or F (financial).

1. Percentage of ground crew trained ________
2. On-time flight percentage ________
3. Percentage of on-time departures ________
4. Market value ________
5. Flight attendant training sessions attended ________
6. Revenue per seat ________
7. Customer complaints ________
8. Time airplane is on ground between flights ________
9. Number of reports of mishandled or lost baggage ________
10. Cash flow from operations ________
11. Accidents or safety incidents per mile flown ________
12. Airplane miles per gallon of fuel ________
13. Return on investment ________
14. Cost of leasing airplanes ________

Exercise 21-12^A
Determining transfer prices
C5

The Trailer department of Sprint Bicycles makes bike trailers that attach to bicycles and can carry children or cargo. The trailers have a retail price of $100 each. Each trailer incurs $40 of variable manufacturing costs. The Trailer department has capacity for 20,000 trailers per year, and incurs fixed costs of $500,000 per year.

Required

1. Assume the Assembly division of Sprint Bicycles wants to buy 5,000 trailers per year from the Trailer division. If the Trailer division can sell all of the trailers it manufactures to outside customers, what price should be used on transfers between Sprint Bicycle's divisions? Explain.
2. Assume the Trailer division currently only sells 10,000 trailers to outside customers, and the Assembly division wants to buy 5,000 trailers per year from the Trailer division. What is the range of acceptable prices that could be used on transfers between Sprint Bicycle's divisions? Explain.
3. Assume transfer prices of either $40 per trailer or $70 per trailer are being considered. Comment on the preferred transfer prices from the perspectives of the Trailer division manager, the Assembly division manager, and the top management of Sprint Bicycles.

Exercise 21-13^B
Joint real estate costs assigned
C6

Check Total Canyon cost, $2,700,000

Mountain Home Properties is developing a subdivision that includes 300 home lots. The 225 lots in the Canyon section are below a ridge and do not have views of the neighboring canyons and hills; the 75 lots in the Hilltop section offer unobstructed views. The expected selling price for each Canyon lot is $50,000 and for each Hilltop lot is $100,000. The developer acquired the land for $2,500,000 and spent another $2,000,000 on street and utilities improvements. Assign the joint land and improvement costs to the lots using the value basis of allocation and determine the average cost per lot.

Exercise 21-14^B
Joint product costs assigned
C6

Ocean Seafood Company purchases lobsters and processes them into tails and flakes. It sells the lobster tails for $20 per pound and the flakes for $15 per pound. On average, 100 pounds of lobster are processed into 57 pounds of tails and 24 pounds of flakes, with 19 pounds of waste. Assume that the company purchased 3,000 pounds of lobster for $6.00 per pound and processed the lobsters with an additional labor cost of $1,800. No materials or labor costs are assigned to the waste. If 1,570 pounds of tails and 640 pounds of flakes are sold, what is (1) the allocated cost of the sold items and (2) the allocated cost of the ending inventory? The company allocates joint costs on a value basis. (Round the dollar cost per pound to the nearest thousandth.)

Check   (2) Inventory cost, $1,760

McGraw-Hill's
HOMEWORK
MANAGER®   Available with McGraw-Hill's Homework Manager

Citizens Bank has several departments that occupy both floors of a two-story building. The departmental accounting system has a single account, Building Occupancy Cost, in its ledger. The types and amounts of occupancy costs recorded in this account for the current period follow.

PROBLEM SET A

Problem 21-1A
Allocation of building occupancy costs to departments

C3   P1

mhhe.com/wildFAP19e

Depreciation—Building	$ 31,500
Interest—Building mortgage	47,000
Taxes—Building and land	14,000
Gas (heating) expense	4,425
Lighting expense	5,250
Maintenance expense	9,625
Total occupancy cost	$111,800

The building has 5,000 square feet on each floor. In prior periods, the accounting manager merely divided the $111,800 occupancy cost by 10,000 square feet to find an average cost of $11.18 per square foot and then charged each department a building occupancy cost equal to this rate times the number of square feet that it occupied.

Helen Lanya manages a first-floor department that occupies 1,000 square feet, and Jose Jimez manages a second-floor department that occupies 1,700 square feet of floor space. In discussing the departmental reports, the second-floor manager questions whether using the same rate per square foot for all departments makes sense because the first-floor space is more valuable. This manager also references a recent real estate study of average local rental costs for similar space that shows first-floor space worth $40 per square foot and second-floor space worth $10 per square foot (excluding costs for heating, lighting, and maintenance).

Required

1. Allocate occupancy costs to the Lanya and Jimez departments using the current allocation method.

2. Allocate the depreciation, interest, and taxes occupancy costs to the Lanya and Jimez departments in proportion to the relative market values of the floor space. Allocate the heating, lighting, and maintenance costs to the Lanya and Jimez departments in proportion to the square feet occupied (ignoring floor space market values).

Check   (1) Total allocated to Lanya and Jimez, $30,186 (2) Total occupancy cost to Lanya, $16,730

Analysis Component

3. Which allocation method would you prefer if you were a manager of a second-floor department? Explain.

Health Co-op is an outpatient surgical clinic that was profitable for many years, but Medicare has cut its reimbursements by as much as 40%. As a result, the clinic wants to better understand its costs. It decides to prepare an activity-based cost analysis, including an estimate of the average cost of both general surgery and orthopedic surgery. The clinic's three cost centers and their cost drivers follow.

Problem 21-2A
Activity-based costing

P2

Cost Center	Cost	Cost Driver	Driver Quantity
Professional salaries	$1,600,000	Professional hours	10,000
Patient services and supplies	27,000	Number of patients	600
Building cost	150,000	Square feet	1,500

The two main surgical units and their related data follow.

Service	Hours	Square Feet*	Patients
General surgery	2,500	600	400
Orthopedic surgery	7,500	900	200

* Orthopedic surgery requires more space for patients, supplies, and equipment.

Required

1. Compute the cost per cost driver for each of the three cost centers.

Check (2) Average cost of general (orthopedic) surgery, $1,195 ($6,495) per patient

2. Use the results from part 1 to allocate costs from each of the three cost centers to both the general surgery and the orthopedic surgery units. Compute total cost and average cost per patient for both the general surgery and the orthopedic surgery units.

Analysis Component

3. Without providing computations, would the average cost of general surgery be higher or lower if all center costs were allocated based on the number of patients? Explain.

Problem 21-3A
Departmental income statements; forecasts

P3 ♟

eXcel

mhhe.com/wildFAP19e

Warton Company began operations in January 2009 with two operating (selling) departments and one service (office) department. Its departmental income statements follow.

WARTON COMPANY Departmental Income Statements For Year Ended December 31, 2009			
	Clock	**Mirror**	**Combined**
Sales	$170,000	$95,000	$265,000
Cost of goods sold	83,300	58,900	142,200
Gross profit	86,700	36,100	122,800
Direct expenses			
Sales salaries	21,000	7,100	28,100
Advertising	2,100	700	2,800
Store supplies used	550	350	900
Depreciation—Equipment	2,300	900	3,200
Total direct expenses	25,950	9,050	35,000
Allocated expenses			
Rent expense	7,040	3,780	10,820
Utilities expense	2,800	1,600	4,400
Share of office department expenses	13,500	6,500	20,000
Total allocated expenses	23,340	11,880	35,220
Total expenses	49,290	20,930	70,220
Net income	$ 37,410	$15,170	$ 52,580

Warton plans to open a third department in January 2010 that will sell paintings. Management predicts that the new department will generate $50,000 in sales with a 45% gross profit margin and will require the following direct expenses: sales salaries, $8,500; advertising, $1,100; store supplies, $400; and equipment depreciation, $1,000. It will fit the new department into the current rented space by taking some square footage from the other two departments. When opened the new painting department will fill one-fifth of the space presently used by the clock department and one-fourth used by the mirror department. Management does not predict any increase in utilities costs, which are allocated to the departments in proportion to occupied space (or rent expense). The company allocates office department expenses to the operating departments in proportion to their sales. It expects the painting department to increase total office department expenses by $8,000. Since the painting department will bring new customers into the store, management expects sales in both the clock and mirror departments to increase by 8%. No changes for those departments' gross profit percents or their direct expenses are expected except for store supplies used, which will increase in proportion to sales.

Required

Prepare departmental income statements that show the company's predicted results of operations for calendar year 2010 for the three operating (selling) departments and their combined totals. (Round percents to the nearest one-tenth and dollar amounts to the nearest whole dollar.)

Check 2010 forecasted combined net income (sales), $65,832 ($336,200)

Billie Whitehorse, the plant manager of Travel Free's Ohio plant, is responsible for all of that plant's costs other than her own salary. The plant has two operating departments and one service department. The camper and trailer operating departments manufacture different products and have their own managers. The office department, which Whitehorse also manages, provides services equally to the two operating departments. A budget is prepared for each operating department and the office department. The company's responsibility accounting system must assemble information to present budgeted and actual costs in performance reports for each operating department manager and the plant manager. Each performance report includes only those costs that a particular operating department manager can control: raw materials, wages, supplies used, and equipment depreciation. The plant manager is responsible for the department managers' salaries, utilities, building rent, office salaries other than her own, and other office costs plus all costs controlled by the two operating department managers. The annual departmental budgets and actual costs for the two operating departments follow.

Problem 21-4A
Responsibility accounting performance reports; controllable and budgeted costs

C4 P4

	Budget			Actual		
	Campers	Trailers	Combined	Campers	Trailers	Combined
Raw materials	$195,900	$276,200	$ 472,100	$194,800	$273,600	$ 468,400
Employee wages	104,200	205,200	309,400	107,200	208,000	315,200
Dept. manager salary	44,000	53,000	97,000	44,800	53,900	98,700
Supplies used	34,000	92,200	126,200	32,900	91,300	124,200
Depreciation—Equip.	63,000	127,000	190,000	63,000	127,000	190,000
Utilities	3,600	5,200	8,800	4,500	4,700	9,200
Building rent	5,700	10,000	15,700	6,200	9,300	15,500
Office department costs	67,750	67,750	135,500	68,550	68,550	137,100
Totals	$518,150	$836,550	$1,354,700	$521,950	$836,350	$1,358,300

The office department's annual budget and its actual costs follow.

	Budget	Actual
Plant manager salary	$100,000	$ 84,000
Other office salaries	46,500	30,100
Other office costs	22,000	21,000
Totals	$168,500	$135,100

Required

1. Prepare responsibility accounting performance reports like those in Exhibit 21.28 that list costs controlled by the following:
   a. Manager of the camper department.
   b. Manager of the trailer department.
   c. Manager of the Ohio plant.

   In each report, include the budgeted and actual costs and show the amount that each actual cost is over or under the budgeted amount.

Check (1a) $800 total over budget

(1c) Ohio plant controllable costs, $15,400 total under budget

Analysis Component

2. Did the plant manager or the operating department managers better manage costs? Explain.

Problem 21-5A^B

Allocation of joint costs

C6

Florida Orchards produced a good crop of peaches this year. After preparing the following income statement, the company believes it should have given its No. 3 peaches to charity and saved its efforts.

FLORIDA ORCHARDS Income Statement For Year Ended December 31, 2009				
	No. 1	No. 2	No. 3	Combined
Sales (by grade)				
No. 1: 300,000 lbs. @ $1.50/lb	$450,000			
No. 2: 250,000 lbs. @ $0.75/lb		$187,500		
No. 3: 600,000 lbs. @ $0.50/lb			$300,000	
Total sales				$937,500
Costs				
Tree pruning and care @ $0.40/lb	120,000	100,000	240,000	460,000
Picking, sorting, and grading @ $0.10/lb	30,000	25,000	60,000	115,000
Delivery costs	15,000	15,000	37,500	67,500
Total costs	165,000	140,000	337,500	642,500
Net income (loss)	$285,000	$ 47,500	$ (37,500)	$295,000

In preparing this statement, the company allocated joint costs among the grades on a physical basis as an equal amount per pound. The company's delivery cost records show that $30,000 of the $67,500 relates to crating the No. 1 and No. 2 peaches and hauling them to the buyer. The remaining $37,500 of delivery costs is for crating the No. 3 peaches and hauling them to the cannery.

Required

1. Prepare reports showing cost allocations on a sales value basis to the three grades of peaches. Separate the delivery costs into the amounts directly identifiable with each grade. Then allocate any shared delivery costs on the basis of the relative sales value of each grade.

2. Using your answers to part 1, prepare an income statement using the joint costs allocated on a sales value basis.

Analysis Component

3. Do you think delivery costs fit the definition of a joint cost? Explain.

PROBLEM SET B

Problem 21-1B

Allocation of building occupancy costs to departments

C3 P1

Marshall's has several departments that occupy all floors of a two-story building that includes a basement floor. Marshall rented this building under a long-term lease negotiated when rental rates were low. The departmental accounting system has a single account, Building Occupancy Cost, in its ledger. The types and amounts of occupancy costs recorded in this account for the current period follow.

Building rent	$320,000
Lighting expense	20,000
Cleaning expense	32,000
Total occupancy cost	$372,000

The building has 7,500 square feet on each of the upper two floors but only 5,000 square feet in the basement. In prior periods, the accounting manager merely divided the $372,000 occupancy cost by 20,000 square feet to find an average cost of $18.60 per square foot and then charged each department a building occupancy cost equal to this rate times the number of square feet that it occupies.

Riley Miller manages a department that occupies 2,000 square feet of basement floor space. In discussing the departmental reports with other managers, she questions whether using the same rate per square foot for all departments makes sense because different floor space has different values. Miller checked a recent real estate report of average local rental costs for similar space that shows first-floor space worth $48 per square foot, second-floor space worth $24 per square foot, and basement space worth $12 per square foot (excluding costs for lighting and cleaning).

Required

1. Allocate occupancy costs to Miller's department using the current allocation method.
2. Allocate the building rent cost to Miller's department in proportion to the relative market value of the floor space. Allocate to Miller's department the lighting and heating costs in proportion to the square feet occupied (ignoring floor space market values). Then, compute the total occupancy cost allocated to Miller's department.

Check Total costs allocated to Miller's Dept., (1) $37,200; (2) $18,000

Analysis Component

3. Which allocation method would you prefer if you were a manager of a basement department?

Verdant Landscape Architects has enjoyed profits for many years, but new competition has cut service revenue by as much as 30%. As a result, the company wants to better understand its costs. It decides to prepare an activity-based cost analysis, including an estimate of the average cost of both general landscaping services and custom design landscaping services. The company's three cost centers and their cost drivers follow.

Problem 21-2B
Activity-based costing

P2

Cost Center	Cost	Cost Driver	Driver Quantity
Professional salaries	$900,000	Professional hours	15,000
Customer supplies	225,000	Number of customers	1,200
Building cost	360,000	Square feet	3,750

The two main landscaping units and their related data follow.

Service	Hours	Square Feet*	Customers
General landscaping	3,750	1,500	900
Custom design landscaping	11,250	2,250	300

* Custom design landscaping requires more space for equipment, supplies, and planning.

Required

1. Compute the cost per cost driver for each of the three cost centers.
2. Use the results from part 1 to allocate costs from each of the three cost centers to both the general landscaping and the custom design landscaping units. Compute total cost and average cost per customer for both the general landscaping and the custom design landscaping units.

Check (2) Average cost of general (custom) landscaping, $597.50 ($3,157.50) per customer

Analysis Component

3. Without providing computations, would the average cost of general landscaping be higher or lower if all center costs were allocated based on the number of customers? Explain.

Collosal Entertainment began operations in January 2009 with two operating (selling) departments and one service (office) department. Its departmental income statements follow.

Problem 21-3B
Departmental income statements; forecasts

P3

COLLOSAL ENTERTAINMENT Departmental Income Statements For Year Ended December 31, 2009			
	Movies	Video Games	Combined
Sales	$900,000	$300,000	$1,200,000
Cost of goods sold	630,000	231,000	861,000
Gross profit	270,000	69,000	339,000
Direct expenses			
Sales salaries	55,500	22,500	78,000
Advertising	18,750	9,000	27,750
Store supplies used	6,000	1,500	7,500
Depreciation—Equipment	6,750	4,500	11,250
Total direct expenses	87,000	37,500	124,500

[continued on next page]

[continued from previous page]

Allocated expenses			
Rent expense	61,500	13,500	75,000
Utilities expense	11,070	2,430	13,500
Share of office department expenses	84,375	28,125	112,500
Total allocated expenses	156,945	44,055	201,000
Total expenses	243,945	81,555	325,500
Net income (loss)	$ 26,055	$ (12,555)	$ 13,500

The company plans to open a third department in January 2010 that will sell compact discs. Management predicts that the new department will generate $450,000 in sales with a 35% gross profit margin and will require the following direct expenses: sales salaries, $27,000; advertising, $15,000; store supplies, $3,000; and equipment depreciation, $1,800. The company will fit the new department into the current rented space by taking some square footage from the other two departments. When opened, the new compact disc department will fill one-fourth of the space presently used by the movie department and one-third of the space used by the video game department. Management does not predict any increase in utilities costs, which are allocated to the departments in proportion to occupied space (or rent expense). The company allocates office department expenses to the operating departments in proportion to their sales. It expects the compact disc department to increase total office department expenses by $15,000. Since the compact disc department will bring new customers into the store, management expects sales in both the movie and video game departments to increase by 8%. No changes for those departments' gross profit percents or for their direct expenses are expected, except for store supplies used, which will increase in proportion to sales.

Required

Check 2010 forecasted movies net income (sales), $78,674 ($972,000)

Prepare departmental income statements that show the company's predicted results of operations for calendar year 2010 for the three operating (selling) departments and their combined totals. (Round percents to the nearest one-tenth and dollar amounts to the nearest whole dollar.)

Problem 21-4B
Responsibility accounting performance reports; controllable and budgeted costs

C4   P4

Warren Brown, the plant manager of LMN Co.'s San Diego plant, is responsible for all of that plant's costs other than his own salary. The plant has two operating departments and one service department. The refrigerator and dishwasher operating departments manufacture different products and have their own managers. The office department, which Brown also manages, provides services equally to the two operating departments. A monthly budget is prepared for each operating department and the office department. The company's responsibility accounting system must assemble information to present budgeted and actual costs in performance reports for each operating department manager and the plant manager. Each performance report includes only those costs that a particular operating department manager can control: raw materials, wages, supplies used, and equipment depreciation. The plant manager is responsible for the department managers' salaries, utilities, building rent, office salaries other than his own, and other office costs plus all costs controlled by the two operating department managers. The April departmental budgets and actual costs for the two operating departments follow.

	Budget			Actual		
	Refrigerators	**Dishwashers**	**Combined**	**Refrigerators**	**Dishwashers**	**Combined**
Raw materials	$ 480,000	$240,000	$ 720,000	$ 462,000	$242,400	$ 704,400
Employee wages	204,000	96,000	300,000	209,640	97,800	307,440
Dept. manager salary	66,000	58,800	124,800	66,000	55,800	121,800
Supplies used	18,000	10,800	28,800	16,800	11,640	28,440
Depreciation—Equip.	63,600	44,400	108,000	63,600	44,400	108,000
Utilities	36,000	21,600	57,600	41,400	24,840	66,240
Building rent	75,600	20,400	96,000	78,960	19,800	98,760
Office department costs	84,600	84,600	169,200	90,000	90,000	180,000
Totals	$1,027,800	$576,600	$1,604,400	$1,028,400	$586,680	$1,615,080

The office department's budget and its actual costs for April follow.

	Budget	Actual
Plant manager salary	$ 96,000	$102,000
Other office salaries	48,000	42,240
Other office costs	25,200	35,760
Totals	$169,200	$180,000

Required

1. Prepare responsibility accounting performance reports like those in Exhibit 21.28 that list costs controlled by the following:

   a. Manager of the refrigerator department.

   b. Manager of the dishwasher department.

   c. Manager of the San Diego plant.

In each report, include the budgeted and actual costs for the month and show the amount by which each actual cost is over or under the budgeted amount.

Check (1a) $13,560 total under budget

(1c) San Diego plant controllable costs, $4,680 total over budget

Analysis Component

2. Did the plant manager or the operating department managers better manage costs? Explain.

Rita and Rick Redding own and operate a tomato grove. After preparing the following income statement, Rita believes they should have offered the No. 3 tomatoes to the public for free and saved themselves time and money.

Problem 21-5B[B]
Allocation of joint costs

C6

RITA AND RICK REDDING
Income Statement
For Year Ended December 31, 2009

	No. 1	No. 2	No. 3	Combined
Sales (by grade)				
No. 1: 600,000 lbs. @ $1.80/lb	$1,080,000			
No. 2: 480,000 lbs. @ $1.25/lb		$600,000		
No. 3: 120,000 lbs. @ $0.40/lb			$ 48,000	
Total sales				$1,728,000
Costs				
Land preparation, seeding, and cultivating @ $0.70/lb	420,000	336,000	84,000	840,000
Harvesting, sorting, and grading @ $0.04/lb	24,000	19,200	4,800	48,000
Delivery costs	20,000	14,000	6,000	40,000
Total costs	464,000	369,200	94,800	928,000
Net income (loss)	$ 616,000	$230,800	$(46,800)	$ 800,000

In preparing this statement, Rita and Rick allocated joint costs among the grades on a physical basis as an equal amount per pound. Also, their delivery cost records show that $34,000 of the $40,000 relates to crating the No. 1 and No. 2 tomatoes and hauling them to the buyer. The remaining $6,000 of delivery costs is for crating the No. 3 tomatoes and hauling them to the cannery.

Required

1. Prepare reports showing cost allocations on a sales value basis to the three grades of tomatoes. Separate the delivery costs into the amounts directly identifiable with each grade. Then allocate any shared delivery costs on the basis of the relative sales value of each grade. (Round percents to the nearest one-tenth and dollar amounts to the nearest whole dollar.)

Check (1) $1,344 harvesting, sorting and grading costs allocated to No. 3

(2) Net income from No. 1 &
No. 2 tomatoes, $503,138 & $279,726

2. Using your answers to part 1, prepare an income statement using the joint costs allocated on a sales value basis.

Analysis Component

3. Do you think delivery costs fit the definition of a joint cost? Explain.

BEYOND THE NUMBERS

**REPORTING IN
ACTION**

C4

BTN 21-1   Review Best Buy's income statement in Appendix A and identify its revenues for the years ended March 3, 2007, February 25, 2006, and February 26, 2005. For the year ended March 3, 2007, Best Buy reports the following product revenue mix. (Assume that its product revenue mix is the same for each of the three years reported when answering the requirements.)

Home Office	Entertainment Software	Consumer Electronics	Appliances
33%	12%	45%	10%

Required

1. Compute the amount of revenue from each of its product lines for the years ended March 3, 2007, February 25, 2006, and February 26, 2005.

2. If Best Buy wishes to evaluate each of its product lines, how can it allocate its operating expenses to each of them to determine each product line's profitability?

Fast Forward

3. Access Best Buy's annual report for a fiscal year ending after March 3, 2007, from its Website (BestBuy.com) or the SEC's EDGAR database (sec.gov). Compute its revenues for its product lines for the most recent year(s). Compare those results to those from part 1. How has its product mix changed?

**COMPARATIVE
ANALYSIS**

P3

BTN 21-2   Best Buy, Circuit City, and RadioShack compete across the country in several markets. The most common competitive markets for these companies are by location.

Required

1. Design a three-tier responsibility accounting organizational chart assuming that you have available internal information for all three companies. Use Exhibit 21.19 as an example. The goal of this assignment is to design a reporting framework for the companies; numbers are not required. Limit your reporting framework to sales activity only.

2. Explain why it is important to have similar performance reports when comparing performance within a company (and across different companies). Be specific in your response.

**ETHICS
CHALLENGE**

P3

BTN 21-3   Senior Security Co. offers a range of security services for senior citizens. Each type of service is considered within a separate department. Mary Pincus, the overall manager, is compensated partly on the basis of departmental performance by staying within the quarterly cost budget. She often revises operations to make sure departments stay within budget. Says Pincus, "I will not go over budget even if it means slightly compromising the level and quality of service. These are minor compromises that don't significantly affect my clients, at least in the short term."

Required

1. Is there an ethical concern in this situation? If so, which parties are affected? Explain.

2. Can Mary Pincus take action to eliminate or reduce any ethical concerns? Explain.

3. What is Senior Security's ethical responsibility in offering professional services?

BTN 21-4 Home Station is a national home improvement chain with more than 100 stores throughout the country. The manager of each store receives a salary plus a bonus equal to a percent of the store's net income for the reporting period. The following net income calculation is on the Denver store manager's performance report for the recent monthly period.

COMMUNICATING IN PRACTICE
C4 C5 P3

Sales	$2,500,000
Cost of goods sold	800,000
Wages expense	500,000
Utilities expense	200,000
Home office expense	75,000
Net income	$925,000
Manager's bonus (0.5%)	$ 4,625

In previous periods, the bonus had also been 0.5%, but the performance report had not included any charges for the home office expense, which is now assigned to each store as a percent of its sales.

Required

Assume that you are the national office manager. Write a one-half page memorandum to your store managers explaining why home office expense is in the new performance report.

BTN 21-5 This chapter described and used spreadsheets to prepare various managerial reports (see Exhibit 21-12). You can download from Websites various tutorials showing how spreadsheets are used in managerial accounting and other business applications.

TAKING IT TO THE NET
A1

Required

1. Link to the Website Lacher.com. Scroll down past "Microsoft Excel Examples" and select "Business Solutions." Identify and list three tutorials for review.

2. Describe in a one-half page memorandum to your instructor how the applications described in each tutorial are helpful in business and managerial decision making.

BTN 21-6 Activity-based costing (ABC) is increasingly popular as a useful managerial tool to (1) measure the cost of resources consumed and (2) assign cost to products and services. This managerial tool has been available to accounting and business decision makers for more than 25 years.

TEAMWORK IN ACTION
C1 C2

Required

Break into teams and identify at least three likely reasons that activity-based costing has gained popularity in recent years. Be prepared to present your answers in a class discussion. (*Hint:* What changes have occurred in products and services over the past 25 years?)

ENTREPRENEURIAL DECISION

P3 ♟ 💡

BTN 21-7   **RockBottomGolf** is an Internet retailer and the focus of this chapter's opener. It sells discounted golf merchandise through departments such as clubs, bags, apparel, and accessories. The company plans to expand to include many other types of sporting goods.

Required

1. How can RockBottomGolf use departmental income statements to assist in understanding and controlling operations?
2. Are departmental income statements always the best measure of a department's performance? Explain.
3. Provide examples of nonfinancial performace indicators RockBottomGolf might use as part of a balanced scorecard system of performance evaluation.

HITTING THE ROAD

P3 ♟

BTN 21-8   Visit a local movie theater and check out both its concession area and its showing areas. The manager of a theater must confront questions such as:

- How much return do we earn on concessions?
- What types of movies generate the greatest sales?
- What types of movies generate the greatest net income?

Required

Assume that you are the new accounting manager for a 16-screen movie theater. You are to set up a responsibility accounting reporting framework for the theater.

1. Recommend how to segment the different departments of a movie theater for responsibility reporting.
2. Propose an expense allocation system for heat, rent, insurance, and maintenance costs of the theater.

GLOBAL DECISION

DSG

BTN 21-9   Selected product data from **DSG international plc** (www.DSGiplc.com) follow.

Product Segment for Year Ended (£ millions)	Net Sales		Operating Income	
	April 28, 2007	April 29, 2006	April 28, 2007	April 29, 2006
Computing	£2,198	£2,040	£97	£107
Electrical	5,281	4,912	193	198
e-commerce	451	26	1	0

Required

1. Compute the percentage growth in net sales for each product line from fiscal year 2006 to 2007.
2. Which product line's net sales grew the fastest?
3. Which segment was the most profitable?
4. How can DSG's managers use this information?

ANSWERS TO MULTIPLE CHOICE QUIZ

1. b; [$641,250/($356,250 + $641,250 + $427,500)] × $150,000 = $67,500

2. c;

3. e; $162,000 × 50/150 setups = $54,000; $54,000/500 units = $108 per
Grey unit. (Red is $2.70 per unit.)

4. b;

	Department X	Department Y	Department Z
Sales	$500,000	$200,000	$350,000
Cost of goods sold	350,000	75,000	150,000
Gross profit	150,000	125,000	200,000
Direct expenses	50,000	20,000	75,000
Departmental contribution	$100,000	$105,000	$125,000

5. a; $100,000/$500,000 = 20%

A Look Back

Chapter 21 focused on cost allocation, activity-based costing, and performance measurement. We identified ways to measure and analyze company activities, its departments, and its managers.

A Look at This Chapter

This chapter shows how information on both costs and sales behavior is useful to managers in performing cost-volume-profit analysis. This analysis is an important part of successful management and sound business decisions.

A Look Ahead

Chapter 23 introduces and describes the budgeting process and its importance to management. It also explains the master budget and its usefulness to the planning of future company activities.

Chapter

Cost-Volume-Profit Analysis

Learning Objectives

CAP

Conceptual

C1 Describe different types of cost behavior in relation to production and sales volume. *(p. 902)*

C2 Identify assumptions in cost-volume-profit analysis and explain their impact. *(p. 911)*

C3 Describe several applications of cost-volume-profit analysis. *(p. 913)*

Analytical

A1 Compare the scatter diagram, high-low, and regression methods of estimating costs. *(p. 907)*

A2 Compute the contribution margin and describe what it reveals about a company's cost structure. *(p. 908)*

A3 Analyze changes in sales using the degree of operating leverage. *(p. 918)*

Procedural

P1 Determine cost estimates using three different methods. *(p. 905)*

P2 Compute the break-even point for a single product company. *(p. 909)*

P3 Graph costs and sales for a single product company. *(p. 910)*

P4 Compute the break-even point for a multiproduct company. *(p. 915)*

LP22

Recipe for Growth

"Don't sit on the sidelines talking about your dream . . . get out and make it happen"—Martin Sprock

"Welcome to Moe's"! A chorus of welcomes greets each customer at **Moe's Southwest Grill** (**Moes.com**), a chain of quirky Tex-Mex restaurants, which is part of Raving Brands. The zaniness continues with menu items such as Art Vandalay, Joey Bag of Donuts, the Close Talker, and the Billy Barou. They play music from "dead rock stars" like the Beatles, Elvis Presley, and Jimi Hendrix because "Moe wanted to pay tribute to his heroes who have passed on and would never have a chance to taste his food."

Moe's founder Martin Sprock explains, "We make a point of having the happiest associates. You feel good visiting our stores, and that means something to me. I'd go so far as to say I'd actually be willing to take a date to them."

But there is more to Moe's than fun. Moe's features burritos, tacos, quesadillas, and salads. To appeal to health-conscious diners, Moe's does not use frozen ingredients or microwaves or cook with fat. This recipe has resulted in Moe's being one of the fastest-growing "fast casual" restaurants.

With such rapid growth, an understanding of cost behavior is critical. Identifying fixed and variable costs is key to understanding break-even points and maintaining the right mix of menu choices. Each Moe's manager earns a degree from "Moe's Training School," where the finer points of cost management are taught. Moe's online ordering and payment system is linked with its cash registers to enable managers to better determine which menu items are in demand. An understanding of how costs relate to sales volume and profits helps drive the menu options.

Martin Sprock's vision is to run a chain of restaurants that treats employees as well as they treat owners. This family-first mentality and service-oriented approach have spurred Moe's growth. Sprock, a former ski bum, encourages potential entrepreneurs to get out and make it happen. "I had no money when I started trying to fulfill my ambitions . . . I just did it."

[Sources: *Moe's Southwest Grill Website*, January 2009; *Go AirTran Airways Magazine*, 2005; *Atlanta Business Chronicle*, May 2008; *Pittsburgh Business Times*, March 2008.]

This chapter describes different types of costs and shows how changes in a company's operating volume affect these costs. The chapter also analyzes a company's costs and sales to explain how different operating strategies affect profit or loss.

Managers use this type of analysis to forecast what will happen if changes are made to costs, sales volume, selling prices, or product mix. They then use these forecasts to select the best business strategy for the company.

Cost-Volume-Profit Analysis

Identifying Cost Behavior
- Fixed costs
- Variable costs
- Mixed costs
- Step-wise costs
- Curvilinear costs

Measuring Cost Behavior
- Scatter diagrams
- High-low method
- Least-squares regression
- Comparison of cost estimation methods

Using Break-Even Analysis
- Computing contribution margin
- Computing break-even
- Preparing a cost-volume-profit chart
- Making assumptions in cost-volume-profit analysis

Applying Cost-Volume-Profit Analysis
- Computing income from sales and costs
- Computing sales for target income
- Computing margin of safety
- Using sensitivity analysis
- Computing multiproduct break-even

Identifying Cost Behavior

Video22.1

Point: *Profit* is another term for *income*.

Planning a company's future activities and events is a crucial phase in successful management. One of the first steps in planning is to predict the volume of activity, the costs to be incurred, sales to be made, and profit to be received. An important tool to help managers carry out this step is **cost-volume-profit (CVP) analysis,** which helps them predict how changes in costs and sales levels affect income. In its basic form, CVP analysis involves computing the sales level at which a company neither earns an income nor incurs a loss, called the *break-even point.* For this reason, this basic form of cost-volume-profit analysis is often called *break-even analysis.* Managers use variations of CVP analysis to answer questions such as these:

■ What sales volume is needed to earn a target income?
■ What is the change in income if selling prices decline and sales volume increases?
■ How much does income increase if we install a new machine to reduce labor costs?
■ What is the income effect if we change the sales mix of our products or services?

Consequently, cost-volume-profit analysis is useful in a wide range of business decisions.
    Conventional cost-volume-profit analysis requires management to classify all costs as either *fixed* or *variable* with respect to production or sales volume. The remainder of this section discusses the concepts of fixed and variable cost behavior as they relate to CVP analysis.

Decision Insight

No Free Lunch   Hardly a week goes by without a company advertising a free product with the purchase of another. Examples are a free printer with a digital camera purchase or a free monitor with a computer purchase. Can these companies break even, let alone earn profits? We are reminded of the *no-free-lunch* adage, meaning that companies expect profits from the companion or add-on purchase to make up for the free product.

C1 Describe different types of cost behavior in relation to production and sales volume.

Fixed Costs

A *fixed cost* remains unchanged in amount when the volume of activity varies from period to period within a relevant range. For example, $5,000 in monthly rent paid for a factory building remains the same whether the factory operates with a single eight-hour shift or around the clock with three shifts. This means that rent cost is the same each month at any level of output from zero to the plant's full productive capacity. Notice that while *total* fixed cost does not change as the level of production changes, the fixed cost *per unit* of output decreases as volume increases. For instance, if 20 units are produced when monthly rent is $5,000, the average rent cost per unit is $250 (computed as $5,000/20 units). When production increases to 100 units per month, the average cost per unit decreases to $50 (computed as $5,000/100 units). The average cost decreases to $10 per unit if production increases to 500 units per month. Common examples of fixed costs include depreciation, property taxes, office salaries, and many service department costs.

When production volume and costs are graphed, units of product are usually plotted on the *horizontal axis* and dollars of cost are plotted on the *vertical axis.* Fixed costs then are represented as a horizontal line because they remain constant at all levels of production. To illustrate, the graph in Exhibit 22.1 shows that fixed costs remain at $32,000 at all production levels up to the company's monthly capacity of 2,000 units of output. The *relevant range* for fixed costs in Exhibit 22.1 is 0 to 2,000 units. If the relevant range changes (that is, production capacity extends beyond this range), the amount of fixed costs will likely change.

Point: Fixed costs do not change when volume changes, but the per unit cost declines as volume increases.

Example: If the fixed cost line in Exhibit 22.1 is shifted upward, does the total cost line shift up, down, or remain in the same place? *Answer:* It shifts up by the same amount.

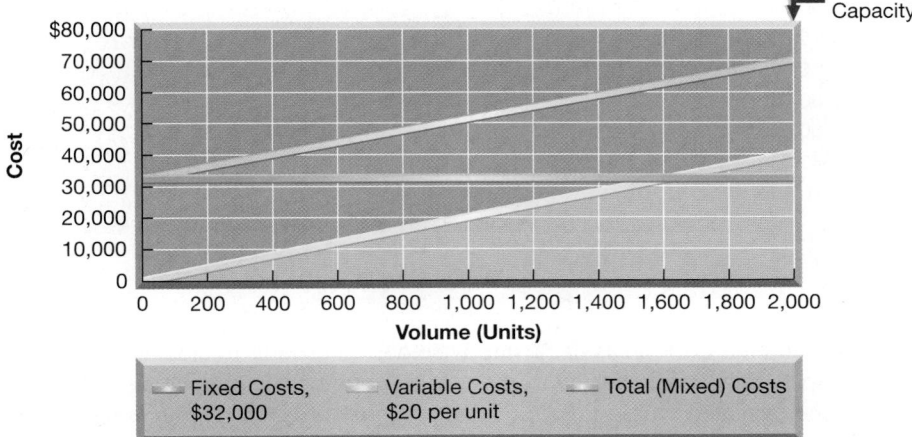

EXHIBIT 22.1

Relations of Fixed and Variable Costs to Volume

Example: If the level of fixed costs in Exhibit 22.1 changes, does the slope of the total cost line change? *Answer:* No, the slope doesn't change. The total cost line is simply shifted upward or downward.

Variable Costs

A *variable cost* changes in proportion to changes in volume of activity. The direct materials cost of a product is one example of a variable cost. If one unit of product requires materials costing $20, total materials costs are $200 when 10 units of product are manufactured, $400 for 20 units, $600 for 30 units, and so on. Notice that variable cost *per unit* remains constant but the *total* amount of variable cost changes with the level of production. In addition to direct materials, common variable costs include direct labor (if employees are paid per unit), sales commissions, shipping costs, and some overhead costs.

When variable costs are plotted on a graph of cost and volume, they appear as a straight line starting at the zero cost level. This straight line is upward (positive) sloping. The line rises as volume of activity increases. A variable cost line using a $20 per unit cost is graphed in Exhibit 22.1.

Point: Fixed costs are constant in total but vary (decline) per unit as more units are produced. Variable costs vary in total but are fixed per unit.

Mixed Costs

A **mixed cost** includes both fixed and variable cost components. For example, compensation for sales representatives often includes a fixed monthly salary and a variable commission based on sales. The total cost line in Exhibit 22.1 is a mixed cost. Like a fixed cost, it is greater than zero when volume is zero; but unlike a fixed cost, it increases steadily in proportion to increases in volume. The mixed cost line in Exhibit 22.1 starts on the vertical axis at the $32,000 fixed cost point. Thus, at the zero volume level, total cost equals the fixed costs. As the activity level increases, the mixed cost line increases at an amount equal to the variable cost per unit. This line is highest when volume of activity is at 2,000 units (the end point of the relevant range). In CVP analysis, mixed costs are often separated into fixed and variable components. The fixed component is added to other fixed costs, and the variable component is added to other variable costs.

Step-Wise Costs

A **step-wise cost** reflects a step pattern in costs. Salaries of production supervisors often behave in a step-wise manner in that their salaries are fixed within a *relevant range* of the current production volume. However, if production volume expands significantly (for example, with the addition of another shift), additional supervisors must be hired. This means that the total cost for supervisory salaries goes up by a lump-sum amount. Similarly, if volume takes another significant step up, supervisory salaries will increase by another lump sum. This behavior reflects a step-wise cost, also known as a *stair-step cost,* which is graphed in Exhibit 22.2. See how the step-wise cost line is flat within ranges (steps). Then, when volume significantly changes, it shifts to another level for that range (step).

EXHIBIT 22.2

Step-Wise and
Curvilinear Costs

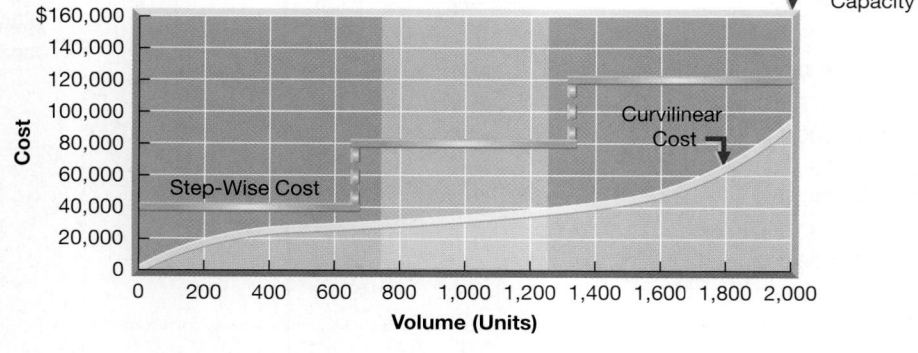

In a conventional CVP analysis, a step-wise cost is usually treated as either a fixed cost or a variable cost. This treatment involves manager judgment and depends on the width of the range and the expected volume. To illustrate, suppose after the production of every 25 snowboards, an operator lubricates the finishing machine. The cost of this lubricant reflects a step-wise pattern. Also, suppose that after the production of every 1,000 units, the snowboard cutting tool is replaced. Again, this is a step-wise cost. Note that the range of 25 snowboards is much narrower than the range of 1,000 snowboards. Some managers might treat the lubricant cost as a variable cost and the cutting tool cost as a fixed cost.

Curvilinear Costs

A variable cost, as explained, is a *linear* cost; that is, it increases at a constant rate as volume of activity increases. A **curvilinear cost,** also called a *nonlinear cost,* increases at a nonconstant rate as volume increases. When graphed, curvilinear costs appear as a curved line. Exhibit 22.2 shows a curvilinear cost beginning at zero when production is zero and then increasing at different rates.

An example of a curvilinear cost is total direct labor cost when workers are paid by the hour. At low to medium levels of production, adding more employees allows each of them to specialize by doing certain tasks repeatedly instead of doing several different tasks. This often yields additional units of output at lower costs. A point is eventually reached at which adding more employees creates inefficiencies. For instance, a large crew demands more time and effort in communicating and coordinating their efforts. While adding employees in this case increases output, the labor cost per unit increases, and the total labor cost goes up at a steeper slope. This pattern is seen in Exhibit 22.2 where the curvilinear cost curve starts at zero, rises, flattens out, and then increases at a faster rate as output nears the maximum.

Point: Computer spreadsheets are important and effective tools for CVP analysis and for analyzing alternative "what-if" strategies.

Point: Cost-volume-profit analysis helped Rod Canion, Jim Harris, and Bill Murto raise start-up capital of $20 million to launch **Compaq Computer.** They showed that break-even volumes were attainable within the first year.

Quick Check Answers—p. 922

1. Which of the following statements is typically true? (*a*) Variable cost per unit increases as volume increases, (*b*) fixed cost per unit decreases as volume increases, or (*c*) a curvilinear cost includes both fixed and variable elements.
2. Describe the behavior of a fixed cost.
3. If cost per unit of activity remains constant (fixed), why is it called a variable cost?

Measuring Cost Behavior

P1 Determine cost estimates using three different methods.

Identifying and measuring cost behavior requires careful analysis and judgment. An important part of this process is to identify costs that can be classified as either fixed or variable, which often requires analysis of past cost behavior. Three methods are commonly used to analyze past costs: scatter diagrams, high-low method, and least-squares regression. Each method is discussed in this section using the unit and cost data shown in Exhibit 22.3, which are taken from a start-up company that uses units produced as the activity base in estimating cost behavior.

EXHIBIT 22.3

Data for Estimating Cost Behavior

Month	Units Produced	Total Cost
January	17,500	$20,500
February	27,500	21,500
March	25,000	25,000
April	35,000	21,500
May	47,500	25,500
June	22,500	18,500
July	30,000	23,500
August	52,500	28,500
September	37,500	26,000
October	57,500	26,000
November	62,500	31,000
December	67,500	29,000

Scatter Diagrams

Scatter diagrams display past cost and unit data in graphical form. In preparing a scatter diagram, units are plotted on the horizontal axis and cost is plotted on the vertical axis. Each individual point on a scatter diagram reflects the cost and number of units for a prior period. In Exhibit 22.4, the prior 12 months' costs and numbers of units are graphed. Each point reflects total costs incurred and units produced for one of those months. For instance, the point labeled March had units produced of 25,000 and costs of $25,000.

EXHIBIT 22.4

Scatter Diagram

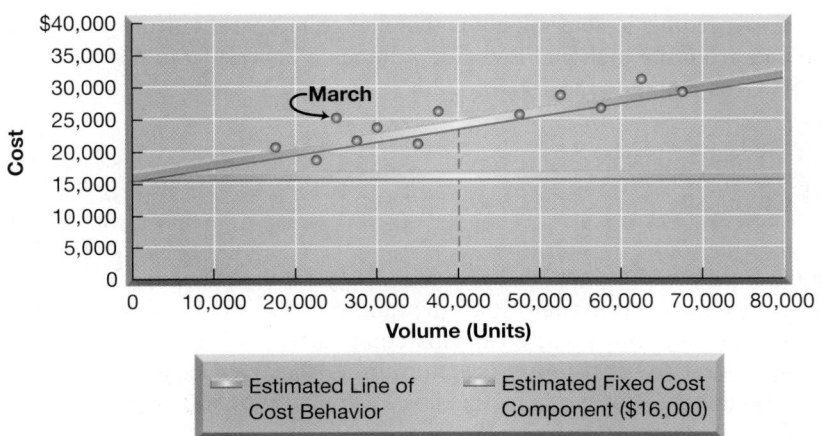

The **estimated line of cost behavior** is drawn on a scatter diagram to reflect the relation between cost and unit volume. This line best visually "fits" the points in a scatter diagram. Fitting this line demands judgment. The line drawn in Exhibit 22.4 intersects the vertical axis at approximately $16,000, which reflects fixed cost. To compute variable cost per unit, or the slope, we perform three steps. First, we select any two points on the horizontal axis (units), say 0 and 40,000. Second, we draw a vertical line from each of these points to intersect the estimated line of cost behavior. The point on the vertical axis (cost) corresponding to the 40,000 units point that intersects the estimated line is roughly $24,000. Similarly, the cost corresponding to zero units is $16,000 (the fixed cost point). Third, we compute the slope of the line, or variable cost, as the change in cost divided by the change in units. Exhibit 22.5 shows this computation.

EXHIBIT 22.5

Variable Cost per Unit
(Scatter Diagram)

$$\frac{\text{Change in cost}}{\text{Change in units}} = \frac{\$24{,}000 - \$16{,}000}{40{,}000 - 0} = \frac{\$8{,}000}{40{,}000} = \$0.20 \text{ per unit}$$

Example: In Exhibits 22.4 and 22.5, if units are projected at 30,000, what is the predicted cost? *Answer:* Approximately $22,000.

Variable cost is $0.20 per unit. Thus, the cost equation that management will use to estimate costs for different unit levels is **$16,000 plus $0.20 per unit.**

High-Low Method

The **high-low method** is a way to estimate the cost equation by graphically connecting the two cost amounts at the highest and lowest unit volumes. In our case, the lowest number of units is 17,500, and the highest is 67,500. The costs corresponding to these unit volumes are $20,500 and $29,000, respectively (see the data in Exhibit 22.3). The estimated line of cost behavior for the high-low method is then drawn by connecting these two points on the scatter diagram corresponding to the lowest and highest unit volumes as follows.

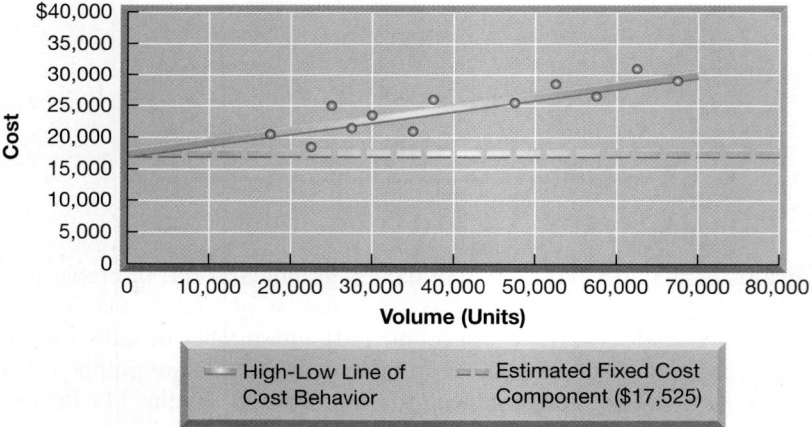

The variable cost per unit is determined as the change in cost divided by the change in units and uses the data from the high and low unit volumes. This results in a slope, or variable cost per unit, of $0.17 as computed in Exhibit 22.6.

Point: Note that the high-low method identifies the high and low points of the volume (activity) base, and the costs linked with those extremes—which may not be the highest and lowest costs.

EXHIBIT 22.6

Variable Cost per Unit
(High-Low Method)

$$\frac{\text{Change in cost}}{\text{Change in units}} = \frac{\$29{,}000 - \$20{,}500}{67{,}500 - 17{,}500} = \frac{\$8{,}500}{50{,}000} = \$0.17 \text{ per unit}$$

To estimate the fixed cost for the high-low method, we use the knowledge that total cost equals fixed cost plus variable cost per unit times the number of units. Then we pick either the high or low point to determine the fixed cost. This computation is shown in Exhibit 22.7—where we use the high point (67,500 units) in determining the fixed cost of $17,525. Use of the low point (17,500 units) yields the same fixed cost estimate: $20,500 = Fixed cost + ($0.17 per unit × 17,500), or Fixed cost = $17,525.

EXHIBIT 22.7

Fixed Cost (High-Low Method)

> **Total cost = Fixed cost + (Variable cost × Units)**
>
> $29,000 = Fixed cost + ($0.17 per unit × 67,500 units)
>
> Then, Fixed cost = $17,525

Thus, the cost equation used to estimate costs at different units is **$17,525 plus $0.17 per unit**. This cost equation differs slightly from that determined from the scatter diagram method. A deficiency of the high-low method is that it ignores all cost points except the highest and lowest. The result is less precision because the high-low method uses the most extreme points rather than the more usual conditions likely to recur.

Least-Squares Regression

Least-squares regression is a statistical method for identifying cost behavior. For our purposes, we use the cost equation estimated from this method but leave the computational details for more advanced courses. Such computations for least-squares regression are readily done using most spreadsheet programs or calculators. We illustrate this using Excel® in Appendix 22A.

The regression cost equation for the data presented in Exhibit 22.3 is **$16,947 plus $0.19 per unit**; that is, the fixed cost is estimated as $16,947 and the variable cost at $0.19 per unit. Both costs are reflected in the following graph.

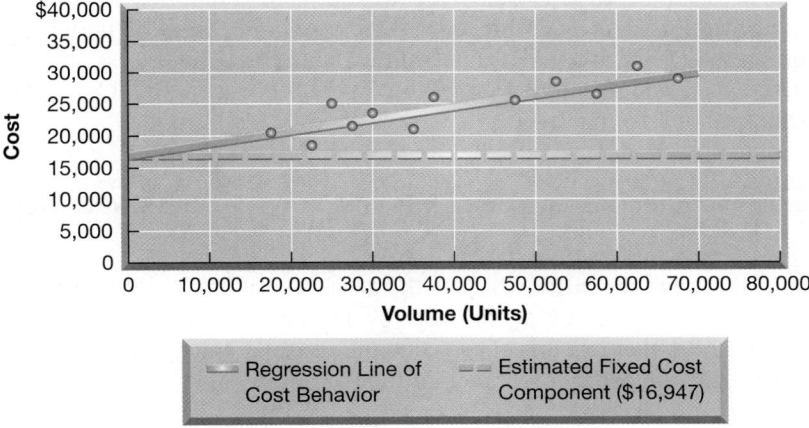

Comparison of Cost Estimation Methods

The three cost estimation methods result in slightly different estimates of fixed and variable costs as summarized in Exhibit 22.8. Estimates from the scatter diagram are based on a visual fit of the cost line and are subject to interpretation. Estimates from the high-low method use only two sets of values corresponding to the lowest and highest unit volumes. Estimates from least-squares regression use a statistical technique and all available data points.

A1 Compare the scatter diagram, high-low, and regression methods of estimating costs.

EXHIBIT 22.8

Comparison of Cost Estimation Methods

Estimation Method	Fixed Cost	Variable Cost
Scatter diagram	$16,000	$0.20 per unit
High-low method	17,525	0.17 per unit
Least-squares regression	16,947	0.19 per unit

We must remember that all three methods use *past data*. Thus, cost estimates resulting from these methods are only as good as the data used for estimation. Managers must establish that the data are reliable in deriving cost estimates for the future.

Quick Check Answers—p. 922

4. Which of the following methods is likely to yield the most precise estimated line of cost behavior? (*a*) High-low, (*b*) least-squares regression, or (*c*) scatter diagram.
5. What is the primary weakness of the high-low method?
6. Using conventional CVP analysis, a mixed cost should be (*a*) disregarded, (*b*) treated as a fixed cost, or (*c*) separated into fixed and variable components.

Using Break-Even Analysis

Video22.2

Break-even analysis is a special case of cost-volume-profit analysis. This section describes break-even analysis by computing the break-even point and preparing a CVP (or break-even) chart.

Contribution Margin and Its Measures

A2 Compute the contribution margin and describe what it reveals about a company's cost structure.

We explained how managers classify costs by behavior. This often refers to classifying costs as being fixed or variable with respect to volume of activity. In manufacturing companies, volume of activity usually refers to the number of units produced. We then classify a cost as either fixed or variable, depending on whether total cost changes as the number of units produced changes. Once we separate costs by behavior, we can then compute a product's contribution margin. **Contribution margin per unit,** or *unit contribution margin,* is the amount by which a product's unit selling price exceeds its total unit variable cost. This excess amount contributes to covering fixed costs and generating profits on a per unit basis. Exhibit 22.9 shows the contribution margin per unit formula.

EXHIBIT 22.9
Contribution Margin per Unit

Contribution margin per unit = Sales price per unit − Total variable cost per unit

The **contribution margin ratio,** which is the percent of a unit's selling price that exceeds total unit variable cost, is also useful for business decisions. It can be interpreted as the percent of each sales dollar that remains after deducting the total unit variable cost. Exhibit 22.10 shows the formula for the contribution margin ratio.

EXHIBIT 22.10
Contribution Margin Ratio

$$\text{Contribution margin ratio} = \frac{\text{Contribution margin per unit}}{\text{Sales price per unit}}$$

To illustrate the use of contribution margin, let's consider **Rydell,** which sells footballs for $100 per unit and incurs variable costs of $70 per unit sold. Its fixed costs are $24,000 per month with monthly capacity of 1,800 units (footballs). Rydell's contribution margin per unit is $30, which is computed as follows.

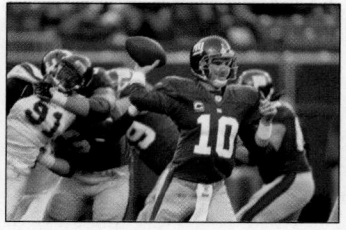

Selling price per unit	$100
Variable cost per unit	70
Contribution margin per unit	$ 30

Its contribution margin ratio is 30%, computed as $30/$100. This reveals that for each unit sold, Rydell has $30 that contributes to covering fixed cost and profit. If we consider sales in dollars, a contribution margin of 30% implies that for each $1 in sales, Rydell has $0.30 that contributes to fixed cost and profit.

Decision Maker

Sales Manager You are evaluating orders from two customers but can accept only one of the orders because of your company's limited capacity. The first order is for 100 units of a product with a contribution margin ratio of 60% and a selling price of $1,000. The second order is for 500 units of a product with a contribution margin ratio of 20% and a selling price of $800. The incremental fixed costs are the same for both orders. Which order do you accept? [Answer—p. 921]

Computing the Break-Even Point

The **break-even point** is the sales level at which a company neither earns a profit nor incurs a loss. The concept of break-even is applicable to nearly all organizations, activities, and events. One of the most important items of information when launching a project is whether it will break even—that is, whether sales will at least cover total costs. The break-even point can be expressed in either units or dollars of sales.

To illustrate the computation of break-even analysis, let's again look at Rydell, which sells footballs for $100 per unit and incurs $70 of variable costs per unit sold. Its fixed costs are $24,000 per month. Rydell breaks even for the month when it sells 800 footballs (sales volume of $80,000). We compute this break-even point using the formula in Exhibit 22.11. This formula uses the contribution margin per unit, which for Rydell is $30 ($100 − $70). From this we can compute the break-even sales volume as $24,000/$30, or 800 units per month.

$$\text{Break-even point in units} = \frac{\text{Fixed costs}}{\text{Contribution margin per unit}}$$

At a price of $100 per unit, monthly sales of 800 units yield sales dollars of $80,000 (called *break-even sales dollars*). This $80,000 break-even sales can be computed directly using the formula in Exhibit 22.12.

$$\text{Break-even point in dollars} = \frac{\text{Fixed costs}}{\text{Contribution margin ratio}}$$

Rydell's break-even point in dollars is computed as $24,000/0.30, or $80,000 of monthly sales. To verify that Rydell's break-even point equals $80,000 (or 800 units), we prepare a simplified income statement in Exhibit 22.13. It shows that the $80,000 revenue from sales of 800 units exactly equals the sum of variable and fixed costs.

RYDELL COMPANY	
Contribution Margin Income Statement (at Break-Even)	
For Month Ended January 31, 2009	
Sales (800 units at $100 each)	$80,000
Variable costs (800 units at $70 each)	56,000
Contribution margin	24,000
Fixed costs	24,000
Net income	$ 0

The statement in Exhibit 22.13 is called a *contribution margin income statement*. It differs in format from a conventional income statement in two ways. First, it separately classifies costs and expenses as variable or fixed. Second, it reports contribution margin (Sales − Variable costs). The contribution margin income statement format is used in this chapter's assignment materials because of its usefulness in CVP analysis.

P2 Compute the break-even point for a single product company.

EXHIBIT 22.11

Formula for Computing Break-Even Sales (in Units)

Point: The break-even point is where total expenses equal total sales and the profit is zero.

EXHIBIT 22.12

Formula for Computing Break-Even Sales (in Dollars)

Point: Even if a company operates at a level in excess of its break-even point, management may decide to stop operating because it is not earning a reasonable return on investment.

EXHIBIT 22.13

Contribution Margin Income Statement for Break-Even Sales

Point: A contribution margin income statement is also referred to as a *variable costing income statement.* This differs from the traditional **absorption costing** approach where all product costs are assigned to units sold and to units in ending inventory. Recall that variable costing expenses all fixed product costs. Thus, income for the two approaches differs depending on the level of finished goods inventory; the lower inventory is, the more similar the two approaches are.

Preparing a Cost-Volume-Profit Chart

P3 Graph costs and sales for a single product company.

Exhibit 22.14 is a graph of Rydell's cost-volume-profit relations. This graph is called a **cost-volume-profit (CVP) chart,** or a *break-even chart* or *break-even graph*. The horizontal axis is the number of units produced and sold and the vertical axis is dollars of sales and costs. The lines in the chart depict both sales and costs at different output levels.

EXHIBIT 22.14

Cost-Volume-Profit Chart

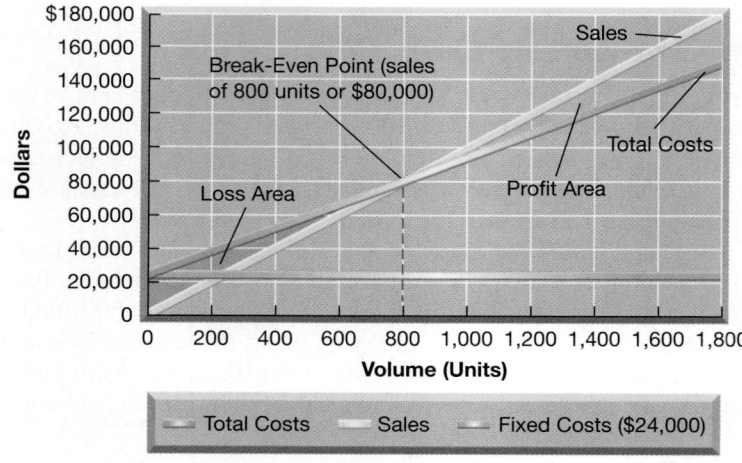

We follow three steps to prepare a CVP chart, which can also be drawn with computer programs that convert numeric data to graphs:

1. Plot fixed costs on the vertical axis ($24,000 for Rydell). Draw a horizontal line at this level to show that fixed costs remain unchanged regardless of output volume (drawing this fixed cost line is not essential to the chart).
2. Draw the total (variable plus fixed) costs line for a relevant range of volume levels. This line starts at the fixed costs level on the vertical axis because total costs equal fixed costs at zero volume. The slope of the total cost line equals the variable cost per unit ($70). To draw the line, compute the total costs for any volume level, and connect this point with the vertical axis intercept ($24,000). Do not draw this line beyond the productive capacity for the planning period (1,800 units for Rydell).
3. Draw the sales line. Start at the origin (zero units and zero dollars of sales) and make the slope of this line equal to the selling price per unit ($100). To sketch the line, compute dollar sales for any volume level and connect this point with the origin. Do not extend this line beyond the productive capacity. Total sales will be at the highest level at maximum capacity.

The total costs line and the sales line intersect at 800 units in Exhibit 22.14, which is the break-even point—the point where total dollar sales of $80,000 equals the sum of both fixed and variable costs ($80,000).

On either side of the break-even point, the vertical distance between the sales line and the total costs line at any specific volume reflects the profit or loss expected at that point. At volume levels to the left of the break-even point, this vertical distance is the amount of the expected loss because the total costs line is above the total sales line. At volume levels to the right of the break-even point, the vertical distance represents the expected profit because the total sales line is above the total costs line.

Example: In Exhibit 22.14, the sales line intersects the total cost line at 800 units. At what point would the two lines intersect if selling price is increased by 20% to $120 per unit? *Answer:* $24,000/ ($120 − $70) = 480 units

 Decision Maker ▬▬▬▬▬▬▬▬▬▬▬▬▬▬▬▬▬▬▬▬▬

Operations Manager   As a start-up manufacturer, you wish to identify the behavior of manufacturing costs to develop a production cost budget. You know three methods can be used to identify cost behavior from past data, but past data are unavailable because this is a start-up. What do you do? [Answer—p. 921]

Making Assumptions in Cost-Volume-Profit Analysis

Cost-volume-profit analysis assumes that relations can normally be expressed as simple lines similar to those in Exhibits 22.4 and 22.14. Such assumptions allow users to answer several important questions, but the usefulness of the answers depends on the validity of three assumptions: (1) constant selling price per unit, (2) constant variable costs per unit, and (3) constant total fixed costs. These assumptions are not always realistic, but they do not necessarily limit the usefulness of CVP analysis as a way to better understand costs and sales. This section discusses these assumptions and other issues for CVP analysis.

Working with Assumptions   The behavior of individual costs and sales often is not perfectly consistent with CVP assumptions. If the expected costs and sales behavior differ from the assumptions, the results of CVP analysis can be limited. Still, we can perform useful analyses in spite of limitations with these assumptions for several reasons.

Summing costs can offset individual deviations.   Deviations from assumptions with individual costs are often minor when these costs are summed. That is, individual variable cost items may not be perfectly variable, but when we sum these variable costs, their individual deviations can offset each other. This means the assumption of variable cost behavior can be proper for total variable costs. Similarly, an assumption that total fixed costs are constant can be proper even when individual fixed cost items are not exactly constant.

CVP is applied to a relevant range of operations.   Sales, variable costs, and fixed costs often are reasonably reflected in straight lines on a graph when the assumptions are applied over a relevant range. The **relevant range of operations** is the normal operating range for a business. Except for unusually difficult or prosperous times, management typically plans for operations within a range of volume neither close to zero nor at maximum capacity. The relevant range excludes extremely high and low operating levels that are unlikely to occur. The validity of assuming that a specific cost is fixed or variable is more acceptable when operations are within the relevant range. As shown in Exhibit 22.2, a curvilinear cost can be treated as variable and linear if the relevant range covers volumes where it has a nearly constant slope. If the normal range of activity changes, some costs might need reclassification.

CVP analysis yields estimates.   CVP analysis yields approximate answers to questions about costs, volumes, and profits. These answers do not have to be precise because the analysis makes rough estimates about the future. As long as managers understand that CVP analysis gives estimates, it can be a useful tool for starting the planning process. Other qualitative factors also must be considered.

Working with Output Measures   CVP analysis usually describes the level of activity in terms of *sales volume,* which can be expressed in terms of either units sold or dollar sales. However, other measures of output exist. For instance, a manufacturer can use the number of units produced as a measure of output. Also, to simplify analysis, we sometimes assume that the production level is the same as the sales level. That is, inventory levels do not change. This often is justified by arguing that CVP analysis provides only approximations.

C2 Identify assumptions in cost-volume-profit analysis and explain their impact.

Point: CVP analysis can be very useful for business decision making even when its assumptions are not strictly met.

Video22.2

Example: If the selling price declines, what happens to the break-even point? *Answer:* It increases.

Quick Check   Answers—p. 922

  7. Fixed cost divided by the contribution margin ratio yields the (*a*) break-even point in dollars, (*b*) contribution margin per unit, or (*c*) break-even point in units.

  8. A company sells a product for $90 per unit with variable costs of $54 per unit. What is the contribution margin ratio?

  9. Refer to Quick Check (8). If fixed costs for the period are $90,000, what is the break-even point in dollars?

 10. What three basic assumptions are used in CVP analysis?

Working with Changes in Estimates   Because CVP analysis uses estimates, knowing how changes in those estimates impact breakeven is useful. For example, a manager might form three estimates for each of the components of breakeven: optimistic, most likely, and pessimistic. Then ranges of break-even points in units can be computed using the formula in Exhibit 22.11.

To illustrate, assume Rydell's managers provide the set of estimates in Exhibit 22.15.

EXHIBIT 22.15

Alternative Estimates for
Break-Even Analysis

	Selling Price per Unit	Variable Cost per Unit	Total Fixed Costs
Optimistic	$105	$68	$21,000
Most likely	100	70	24,000
Pessimistic	95	72	27,000

If, for example, Rydell's managers believe they can raise the selling price of a football to $105, without any change in variable or fixed costs, then the revised contribution margin per football is $35, and the revised break-even in units follows in Exhibit 22.16.

EXHIBIT 22.16

Revised Break-Even in Units

$$\text{Revised break-even} \atop \text{point in units} = \frac{\$24,000}{\$35} = 686 \text{ units}$$

EXHIBIT 22.17

Scatter Diagrams—Break-Even
Points for Alternative Estimates

Repeating this calculation using each of the other eight separate estimates above, and graphing the results, yields the three scatter diagrams in Exhibit 22.17.

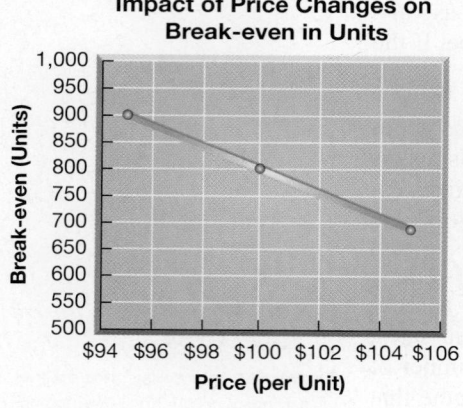

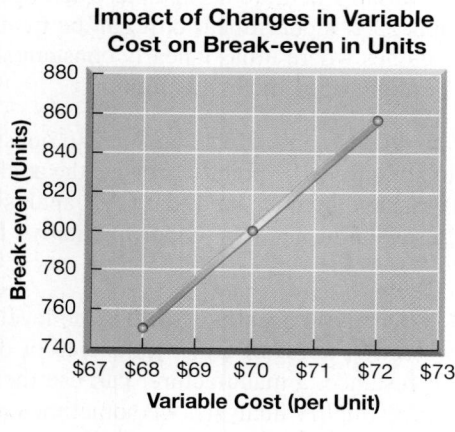

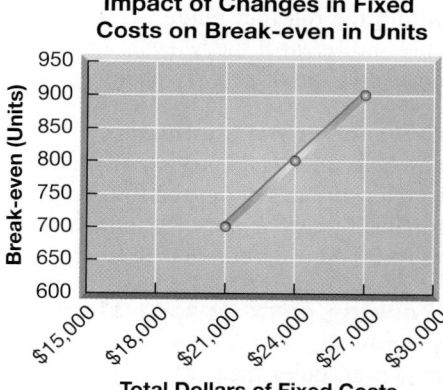

These scatter diagrams show how changes in selling prices, variable costs, and fixed costs impact break-even. When selling prices can be increased without impacting costs, break-even decreases. When competition drives selling prices down, and the company cannot reduce costs, break-even increases. Increases in either variable or fixed costs, if they cannot be passed on to customers via higher selling prices, will increase break-even. If costs can be reduced and selling prices held constant, the break-even decreases.

Point: This analysis changed only one estimate at a time; managers can examine how combinations of changes in estimates will impact break-even.

Applying Cost-Volume-Profit Analysis

Managers consider a variety of strategies in planning business operations. Cost-volume-profit analysis is useful in helping managers evaluate the likely effects of these strategies, which is the focus of this section.

Computing Income from Sales and Costs

An important question managers often need an answer to is "What is the predicted income from a predicted level of sales?" To answer this, we look at four variables in CVP analysis. These variables and their relations to income (pretax) are shown in Exhibit 22.18. We use these relations to compute expected income from predicted sales and cost levels.

Sales
− Variable costs
Contribution margin
− Fixed costs
Income (pretax)

C3 Describe several applications of cost-volume-profit analysis.

EXHIBIT 22.18

Income Relations in CVP Analysis

To illustrate, let's assume that Rydell's management expects to sell 1,500 units in January 2009. What is the amount of income if this sales level is achieved? Following Exhibit 22.18, we compute Rydell's expected income in Exhibit 22.19.

RYDELL COMPANY
Contribution Margin Income Statement
For Month Ended January 31, 2009

Sales (1,500 units at $100 each)	$150,000
Variable costs (1,500 units at $70 each)	105,000
Contribution margin	45,000
Fixed costs	24,000
Income (pretax)	$ 21,000

EXHIBIT 22.19

Computing Expected Pretax Income from Expected Sales

The $21,000 income is pretax. To find the amount of *after-tax* income from selling 1,500 units, management must apply the proper tax rate. Assume that the tax rate is 25%. Then we can prepare the after-tax income statement shown in Exhibit 22.20. We can also compute pretax income as after-tax income divided by (1 − tax rate); for Rydell, this is $15,750/(1 − 0.25), or $21,000.

RYDELL COMPANY
Contribution Margin Income Statement
For Month Ended January 31, 2009

Sales (1,500 units at $100 each)	$150,000
Variable costs (1,500 units at $70 each)	105,000
Contribution margin	45,000
Fixed costs	24,000
Pretax income	21,000
Income taxes (25%)	5,250
Net income (after tax)	$ 15,750

EXHIBIT 22.20

Computing Expected After-Tax Income from Expected Sales

Management then assesses whether this income is an adequate return on assets invested. Management should also consider whether sales and income can be increased by raising or lowering prices. CVP analysis is a good tool for addressing these kinds of "what-if" questions.

Computing Sales for a Target Income

Many companies' annual plans are based on certain income targets (sometimes called *budgets*). Rydell's income target for this year is to increase income by 10% over the prior year. When prior year income is known, Rydell easily computes its target income. CVP analysis helps to determine the sales level needed to achieve the target income. Computing this sales level is important because planning for the year is then based on this level. We use the formula shown in Exhibit 22.21 to compute sales for a target *after-tax* income.

"How many units must I sell to earn $50,000?"

EXHIBIT 22.21

Computing Sales (Dollars) for a Target After-Tax Income

$$\text{Dollar sales at target after-tax income} = \frac{\text{Fixed costs} + \text{Target pretax income}}{\text{Contribution margin ratio}}$$

To illustrate, Rydell has monthly fixed costs of $24,000 and a 30% contribution margin ratio. Assume that it sets a target monthly after-tax income of $9,000 when the tax rate is 25%. This means the pretax income is targeted at $12,000 [$9,000/(1 − 0.25)] with a tax expense of $3,000. Using the formula in Exhibit 22.21, we find that $120,000 of sales are needed to produce a $9,000 after-tax income as shown in Exhibit 22.22.

EXHIBIT 22.22

Rydell's Dollar Sales for a Target Income

$$\text{Dollar sales at target after-tax income} = \frac{\$24,000 + \$12,000}{30\%} = \$120,000$$

Point: Break-even is a special case of the formulas in Exhibits 22.21 and 22.23; simply set target pretax income to $0 and the formulas reduce to those in Exhibits 22.11 and 22.12.

We can alternatively compute *unit sales* instead of dollar sales. To do this, we substitute *contribution margin per unit* for the contribution margin ratio in the denominator. This gives the number of units to sell to reach the target after-tax income. Exhibit 22.23 illustrates this for Rydell. The two computations in Exhibits 22.22 and 22.23 are equivalent because sales of 1,200 units at $100 per unit equal $120,000 of sales.

EXHIBIT 22.23

Computing Sales (Units) for a Target After-Tax Income

$$\text{Unit sales at target after-tax income} = \frac{\text{Fixed costs} + \text{Target pretax income}}{\text{Contribution margin per unit}}$$
$$= \frac{\$24,000 + \$12,000}{\$30} = 1,200 \text{ units}$$

Computing the Margin of Safety

All companies wish to sell more than the break-even number of units. The excess of expected sales over the break-even sales level is called a company's **margin of safety,** the amount that sales can drop before the company incurs a loss. It can be expressed in units, dollars, or even as a percent of the predicted level of sales. To illustrate, if Rydell's expected sales are $100,000, the margin of safety is $20,000 above break-even sales of $80,000. As a percent, the margin of safety is 20% of expected sales as shown in Exhibit 22.24.

EXHIBIT 22.24

Computing Margin of Safety (in Percent)

$$\text{Margin of safety (in percent)} = \frac{\text{Expected sales} - \text{Break-even sales}}{\text{Expected sales}}$$
$$= \frac{\$100,000 - \$80,000}{\$100,000} = 20\%$$

Management must assess whether the margin of safety is adequate in light of factors such as sales variability, competition, consumer tastes, and economic conditions.

 Decision Ethics

Supervisor Your team is conducting a cost-volume-profit analysis for a new product. Different sales projections have different incomes. One member suggests picking numbers yielding favorable income because any estimate is "as good as any other." Another member points to a scatter diagram of 20 months' production on a comparable product and suggests dropping unfavorable data points for cost estimation. What do you do? [Answer—p. 921]

Using Sensitivity Analysis

Earlier we showed how changing one of the estimates in a CVP analysis impacts breakeven. We can also examine strategies that impact several estimates in the CVP analysis. For instance, we might want to know what happens to income if we automate a currently manual process. We can use CVP analysis to predict income if we can describe how these changes affect a company's fixed costs, variable costs, selling price, and volume.

To illustrate, assume that Rydell Company is looking into buying a new machine that would increase monthly fixed costs from $24,000 to $30,000 but decrease variable costs from $70 per unit to $60 per unit. The machine is used to produce output whose selling price will remain unchanged at $100. This results in increases in both the unit contribution margin and the contribution margin ratio. The revised contribution margin per unit is $40 ($100 − $60), and the revised contribution margin ratio is 40% of selling price ($40/$100). Using CVP analysis, Rydell's revised break-even point in dollars would be $75,000 as computed in Exhibit 22.25.

$$\frac{\text{Revised break-even}}{\text{point in dollars}} = \frac{\text{Revised fixed costs}}{\text{Revised contribution margin ratio}} = \frac{\$30,000}{40\%} = \$75,000$$

Example: If fixed costs decline, what happens to the break-even point? *Answer:* It decreases.

EXHIBIT 22.25

Revising Break-even When Changes Occur

The revised fixed costs and the revised contribution margin ratio can be used to address other issues including computation of (1) expected income for a given sales level and (2) the sales level needed to earn a target income. Once again, we can use sensitivity analysis to generate different sets of revenue and cost estimates that are *optimistic, pessimistic,* and *most likely.* Different CVP analyses based on these estimates provide different scenarios that management can analyze and use in planning business strategy.

Point: Price competition led paging companies to give business to resellers—companies that lease services at a discount and then resell to subscribers. **Paging Network** charged some resellers under $1 per month, less than a third of what was needed to break even. Its CEO now admits the low-price strategy was flawed.

Decision Insight

Eco-CVP   Ford Escape, Toyota Prius, and Honda Insight are hybrids. Many promise to save owners $1,000 or more a year in fuel costs relative to comparables, and they generate fewer greenhouse gases. Are these models economically feasible? Analysts estimate that **Ford** can break even with its Escape when a $3,000 premium is paid over comparable gas-based models.

Quick Check

Answers—p. 922

11. A company has fixed costs of $50,000 and a 25% contribution margin ratio. What dollar sales are necessary to achieve an after-tax net income of $120,000 if the tax rate is 20%? (a) $800,000, (b) $680,000, or (c) $600,000.

12. If a company's contribution margin ratio decreases from 50% to 25%, what can be said about the unit sales needed to achieve the same target income level?

13. What is a company's margin of safety?

Computing a Multiproduct Break-Even Point

To this point, we have looked only at cases where the company sells a single product or service. This was to keep the basic CVP analysis simple. However, many companies sell multiple products or services, and we can modify the CVP analysis for use in these cases. An important assumption in a multiproduct setting is that the sales mix of different products is known and remains constant during the planning period. **Sales mix** is the ratio (proportion) of the sales volumes for the various products. For instance, if a company normally sells 10,000 footballs, 5,000 softballs, and 4,000 basketballs per month, its sales mix can be expressed as 10:5:4 for footballs, softballs, and basketballs.

P4   Compute the break-even point for a multiproduct company.

To apply multiproduct CVP analysis, we can estimate the break-even point by using a **composite unit,** which consists of a specific number of units of each product in proportion to their expected sales mix. Multiproduct CVP analysis treats this composite unit as a single product. To illustrate, let's look at **Hair-Today,** a styling salon that offers three cuts: basic, ultra, and budget in the ratio of 4 basic units to 2 ultra units to 1 budget unit (expressed as 4:2:1). Management wants to estimate its break-even point for next year. Unit selling prices for these three cuts are basic, $20; ultra, $32; and budget, $16. Using the 4:2:1 sales mix, the selling price of a composite unit of the three products is computed as follows.

4 units of basic @ $20 per unit	$ 80
2 units of ultra @ $32 per unit	64
1 unit of budget @ $16 per unit	16
Selling price of a composite unit	$160

Point: Selling prices and variable costs are usually expressed in per unit amounts. Fixed costs are usually expressed in total amounts.

Hair-Today's fixed costs are $192,000 per year, and its variable costs of the three products are basic, $13; ultra, $18.00; and budget, $8.00. Variable costs for a composite unit of these products follow.

4 units of basic @ $13 per unit	$52
2 units of ultra @ $18 per unit	36
1 unit of budget @ $8 per unit	8
Variable costs of a composite unit	$96

Hair-Today's $64 contribution margin for a composite unit is computed by subtracting the variable costs of a composite unit ($96) from its selling price ($160). We then use the contribution margin to determine Hair-Today's break-even point in composite units in Exhibit 22.26.

EXHIBIT 22.26

Break-Even Point in
Composite Units

$$\text{Break-even point in composite units} = \frac{\text{Fixed costs}}{\text{Contribution margin per composite unit}}$$

$$= \frac{\$192,000}{\$64} = 3,000 \text{ composite units}$$

Point: The break-even point in dollars for Exhibit 22.26 is $192,000/($64/$160) = $480,000.

This computation implies that Hair-Today breaks even when it sells 3,000 composite units. To determine how many units of each product it must sell to break even, we multiply the number of units of each product in the composite by 3,000 as follows.

Basic:	4 × 3,000	. . . .	12,000 units
Ultra:	2 × 3,000	. . . .	6,000 units
Budget:	1 × 3,000	. . . .	3,000 units

Instead of computing contribution margin per composite unit, a company can compute a **weighted-average contribution margin.** Given the 4:2:1 product mix, basic cuts comprise 57.14% (computed as 4/7) of the company's haircuts, ultra makes up 14.29% of its business, and budget cuts comprise 28.57%. The weighted-average contribution margin follows in Exhibit 22.27.

EXHIBIT 22.27

Weighted-Average
Contribution Margin

	Unit contribution margin	× Percentage of sales mix	= Weighted unit contribution margin
Basic	$ 7	57.14%	$4.000
Ultra	14	28.57	4.000
Budget	8	14.29	1.143
Weighted-average contribution margin			$9.143

The company's break-even point in units is computed as follows:

$$\text{Break-even point in units} = \frac{\text{Fixed costs}}{\text{Weighted-average contribution margin}}$$

$$= \frac{\$192,000}{\$9.143} = 21,000 \text{ units}$$

EXHIBIT 22.28

Break-Even in Units using Weighted-Average Contribution Margin

We see that the weighted-average contribution margin method yields 21,000 whole units as the break-even amount, the same total as the composite unit approach.

Exhibit 22.29 verifies the results for composite units by showing Hair-Today's sales and costs at this break-even point using a contribution margin income statement.

EXHIBIT 22.29

Multiproduct Break-Even Income Statement

HAIR-TODAY Forecasted Contribution Margin Income Statement (at Breakeven)	Basic	Ultra	Budget	Totals
Sales				
Basic (12,000 @ $20)	$240,000			
Ultra (6,000 @ $32)		$192,000		
Budget (3,000 @ $16)			$48,000	
Total sales				$480,000
Variable costs				
Basic (12,000 @ $13)	156,000			
Ultra (6,000 @ $18)		108,000		
Budget (3,000 @ $8)			24,000	
Total variable costs				288,000
Contribution margin	$ 84,000	$ 84,000	$24,000	192,000
Fixed costs				192,000
Net income				$ 0

A CVP analysis using composite units can be used to answer a variety of planning questions. Once a product mix is set, all answers are based on the assumption that the mix remains constant at all relevant sales levels as other factors in the analysis do. We also can vary the sales mix to see what happens under alternative strategies.

Decision Maker

Entrepreneur   A CVP analysis indicates that your start-up, which markets electronic products, will break even with the current sales mix and price levels. You have a target income in mind. What analysis might you perform to assess the likelihood of achieving this income? [Answer—p. 921]

Quick Check   Answers—p. 922

14. The sales mix of a company's two products, X and Y, is 2:1. Unit variable costs for both products are $2, and unit sales prices are $5 for X and $4 for Y. What is the contribution margin per composite unit? (a) $5, (b) $10, or (c) $8.

15. What additional assumption about sales mix must be made in doing a conventional CVP analysis for a company that produces and sells more than one product?

Decision Analysis   Degree of Operating Leverage

A3   Analyze changes in sales using the degree of operating leverage.

CVP analysis is especially useful when management begins the planning process and wishes to predict outcomes of alternative strategies. These strategies can involve changes in selling prices, fixed costs, variable costs, sales volume, and product mix. Managers are interested in seeing the effects of changes in some or all of these factors.

One goal of all managers is to get maximum benefits from their fixed costs. Managers would like to use 100% of their output capacity so that fixed costs are spread over the largest number of units. This would decrease fixed cost per unit and increase income. The extent, or relative size, of fixed costs in the total cost structure is known as **operating leverage.** Companies having a higher proportion of fixed costs in their total cost structure are said to have higher operating leverage. An example of this is a company that chooses to automate its processes instead of using direct labor, increasing its fixed costs and lowering its variable costs. A useful managerial measure to help assess the effect of changes in the level of sales on income is the **degree of operating leverage (DOL)** defined in Exhibit 22.30.

EXHIBIT 22.30

Degree of Operating Leverage

DOL = Total contribution margin (in dollars)/Pretax income

To illustrate, let's return to Rydell Company. At a sales level of 1,200 units, Rydell's total contribution margin is $36,000 (1,200 units × $30 contribution margin per unit). Its pretax income, after subtracting fixed costs of $24,000, is $12,000 ($36,000 − $24,000). Rydell's degree of operating leverage at this sales level is 3.0, computed as contribution margin divided by pretax income ($36,000/$12,000). We then use DOL to measure the effect of changes in the level of sales on pretax income. For instance, suppose Rydell expects sales to increase by 10%. If this increase is within the relevant range of operations, we can expect this 10% increase in sales to result in a 30% increase in pretax income computed as DOL multiplied by the increase in sales (3.0 × 10%). Similar analyses can be done for expected decreases in sales.

Demonstration Problem

DP22

Sport Caps Co. manufactures and sells caps for different sporting events. The fixed costs of operating the company are $150,000 per month, and the variable costs for caps are $5 per unit. The caps are sold for $8 per unit. The fixed costs provide a production capacity of up to 100,000 caps per month.

Required

1. Use the formulas in the chapter to compute the following:
   a. Contribution margin per cap.
   b. Break-even point in terms of the number of caps produced and sold.
   c. Amount of net income at 30,000 caps sold per month (ignore taxes).
   d. Amount of net income at 85,000 caps sold per month (ignore taxes).
   e. Number of caps to be produced and sold to provide $45,000 of after-tax income, assuming an income tax rate of 25%.

2. Draw a CVP chart for the company, showing cap output on the horizontal axis. Identify (a) the break-even point and (b) the amount of pretax income when the level of cap production is 70,000. (Omit the fixed cost line.)

3. Use the formulas in the chapter to compute the
   a. Contribution margin ratio.
   b. Break-even point in terms of sales dollars.
   c. Amount of net income at $250,000 of sales per month (ignore taxes).
   d. Amount of net income at $600,000 of sales per month (ignore taxes).
   e. Dollars of sales needed to provide $45,000 of after-tax income, assuming an income tax rate of 25%.

Planning the Solution

- Identify the formulas in the chapter for the required items expressed in units and solve them using the data given in the problem.

- Draw a CVP chart that reflects the facts in the problem. The horizontal axis should plot the volume in units up to 100,000, and the vertical axis should plot the total dollars up to $800,000. Plot the total cost line as upward sloping, starting at the fixed cost level ($150,000) on the vertical axis and increasing until it reaches $650,000 at the maximum volume of 100,000 units. Verify that the break-even point (where the two lines cross) equals the amount you computed in part 1.
- Identify the formulas in the chapter for the required items expressed in dollars and solve them using the data given in the problem.

Solution to Demonstration Problem

1. a. Contribution margin per cap = Selling price per unit − Variable cost per unit
= $8 − $5 = $3

b. Break-even point in caps $= \dfrac{\text{Fixed costs}}{\text{Contribution margin per cap}} = \dfrac{\$150,000}{\$3} = \underline{\underline{50,000 \text{ caps}}}$

c. Net income at 30,000 caps sold = (Units × Contribution margin per unit) − Fixed costs
= (30,000 × $3) − $150,000 = $\underline{\$(60,000) \text{ loss}}$

d. Net income at 85,000 caps sold = (Units × Contribution margin per unit) − Fixed costs
= (85,000 × $3) − $150,000 = $\underline{\$105,000 \text{ profit}}$

e. Pretax income = $45,000/(1 − 0.25) = $60,000
Income taxes = $60,000 × 25% = $15,000

Units needed for $45,000 income $= \dfrac{\text{Fixed costs} + \text{Target pretax income}}{\text{Contribution margin per cap}}$
$= \dfrac{\$150,000 + \$60,000}{\$3} = \underline{\underline{70,000 \text{ caps}}}$

2. CVP chart.

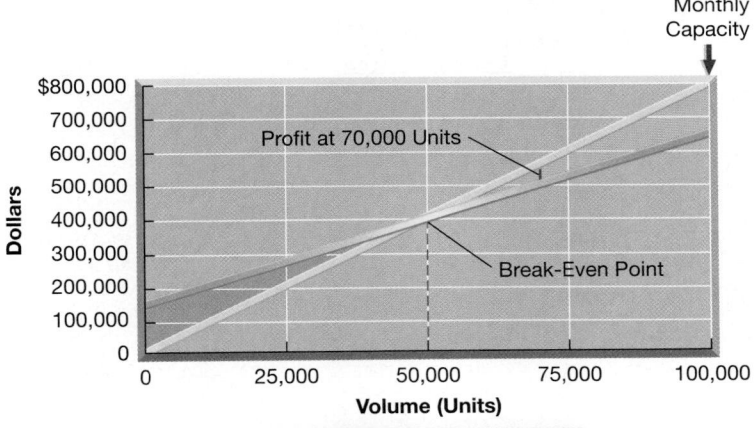

3. a. Contribution margin ratio $= \dfrac{\text{Contribution margin per unit}}{\text{Selling price per unit}} = \dfrac{\$3}{\$8} = \underline{0.375}, \text{ or } \underline{37.5\%}$

b. Break-even point in dollars $= \dfrac{\text{Fixed costs}}{\text{Contribution margin ratio}} = \dfrac{\$150,000}{37.5\%} = \underline{\underline{\$400,000}}$

c. Net income at sales of $250,000 = (Sales × Contribution margin ratio) − Fixed costs
= ($250,000 × 37.5%) − $150,000 = $\underline{\$(56,250) \text{ loss}}$

d. Net income at sales of $600,000 = (Sales × Contribution margin ratio) − Fixed costs
= ($600,000 × 37.5%) − $150,000 = $\underline{\$75,000 \text{ income}}$

e. Dollars of sales to yield $45,000 after-tax income $= \dfrac{\text{Fixed costs} + \text{Target pretax income}}{\text{Contribution margin ratio}}$
$= \dfrac{\$150,000 + \$60,000}{37.5\%} = \underline{\underline{\$560,000}}$

22A Using Excel to Estimate Least-Squares Regression

Microsoft Excel® 2007 and other spreadsheet software can be used to perform least-squares regressions to identify cost behavior. In Excel®, the INTERCEPT and SLOPE functions are used. The following screen shot reports the data from Exhibit 22.3 in cells Al through C13 and shows the cell contents to find the intercept (cell B16) and slope (cell B17). Cell B16 uses Excel® to find the intercept from a least-squares regression of total cost (shown as C2:C13 in cell B16) on units produced (shown as B2:B13 in cell B16). Spreadsheet software is useful in understanding cost behavior when many data points (such as monthly total costs and units produced) are available.

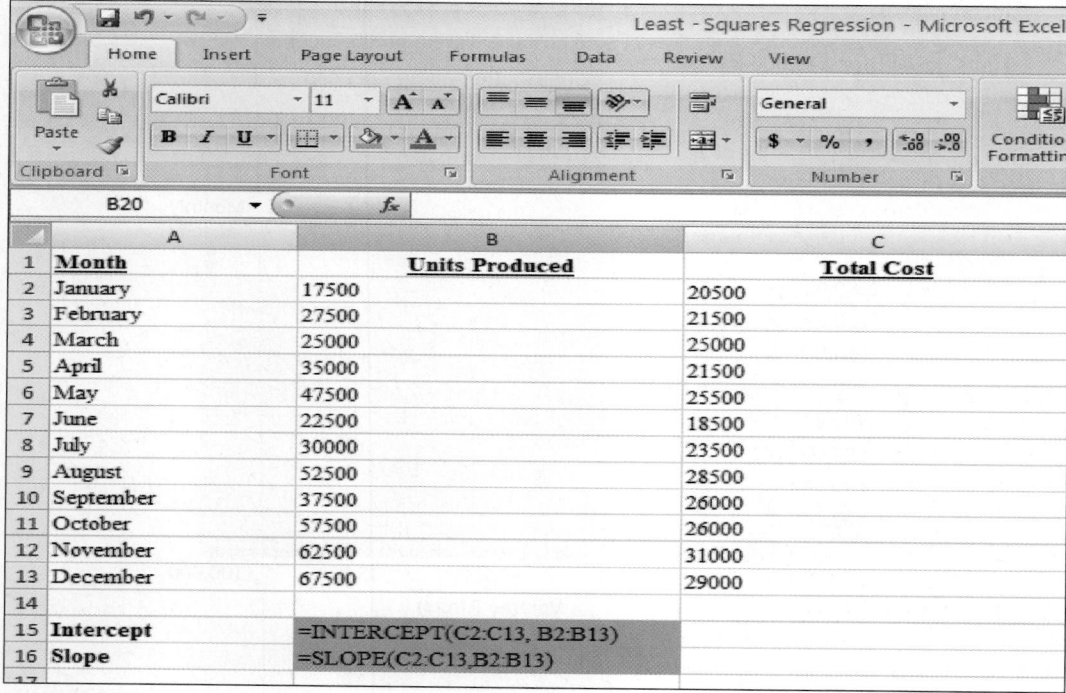

	A	B	C
1	**Month**	**Units Produced**	**Total Cost**
2	January	17500	20500
3	February	27500	21500
4	March	25000	25000
5	April	35000	21500
6	May	47500	25500
7	June	22500	18500
8	July	30000	23500
9	August	52500	28500
10	September	37500	26000
11	October	57500	26000
12	November	62500	31000
13	December	67500	29000
14			
15	**Intercept**	=INTERCEPT(C2:C13, B2:B13)	
16	**Slope**	=SLOPE(C2:C13,B2:B13)	

Excel® can also be used to create scatter diagrams such as that in Exhibit 22.4. In contrast to visually drawing a line that "fits" the data, Excel® more precisely fits the regression line. To draw a scatter diagram with a line of fit, follow these steps:

1. Highlight the data cells you wish to diagram; in this example, start from cell C13 and highlight through cell B2.

2. Then select "Insert" and "Scatter" from the drop-down menus. Selecting the chart type in the upper left corner of the choices under Scatter will produce a diagram that looks like that in Exhibit 22.4, without a line of fit.

3. To add a line of fit (also called trend line), select "Layout" and "Trendline" from the drop-down menus. Selecting "Linear Trendline" will produce a diagram that looks like that in Exhibit 22.4, including the line of fit.

Summary

C1 **Describe different types of cost behavior in relation to production and sales volume.** Cost behavior is described in terms of how its amount changes in relation to changes in volume of activity within a relevant range. Fixed costs remain constant to changes in volume. Total variable costs change in direct proportion to volume changes. Mixed costs display the effects of both fixed and variable components. Step-wise costs remain constant over a small volume range, then change by a lump sum and remain constant over another volume range, and so on. Curvilinear costs change in a nonlinear relation to volume changes.

C2 **Identify assumptions in cost-volume-profit analysis and explain their impact.** Conventional cost-volume-profit analysis is based on assumptions that the product's selling price remains constant and that variable and fixed costs behave in a manner consistent with their variable and fixed classifications.

C3 **Describe several applications of cost-volume-profit analysis.** Cost-volume-profit analysis can be used to predict what can happen under alternative strategies concerning sales volume, selling prices, variable costs, or fixed costs. Applications include "what-if" analysis, computing sales for a target income, and break-even analysis.

A1 **Compare the scatter diagram, high-low, and regression methods of estimating costs.** Cost estimates from a scatter diagram are based on a visual fit of the cost line. Estimates from the high-low method are based only on costs corresponding to the lowest and highest sales. The least-squares regression method is a statistical technique and uses all data points.

A2 **Compute the contribution margin and describe what it reveals about a company's cost structure.** Contribution margin per unit is a product's sales price less its total variable costs. Contribution margin ratio is a product's contribution margin per unit divided by its sales price. Unit contribution margin is the amount received from each sale that contributes to fixed costs and income.

The contribution margin ratio reveals what portion of each sales dollar is available as contribution to fixed costs and income.

A3 **Analyze changes in sales using the degree of operating leverage.** The extent, or relative size, of fixed costs in a company's total cost structure is known as *operating leverage.* One tool useful in assessing the effect of changes in sales on income is the degree of operating leverage, or DOL. DOL is the ratio of the contribution margin divided by pretax income. This ratio can be used to determine the expected percent change in income given a percent change in sales.

P1 **Determine cost estimates using three different methods.** Three different methods used to estimate costs are the scatter diagram, the high-low method, and least-squares regression. All three methods use past data to estimate costs.

P2 **Compute the break-even point for a single product company.** A company's break-even point for a period is the sales volume at which total revenues equal total costs. To compute a break-even point in terms of sales units, we divide total fixed costs by the contribution margin per unit. To compute a break-even point in terms of sales dollars, divide total fixed costs by the contribution margin ratio.

P3 **Graph costs and sales for a single product company.** The costs and sales for a company can be graphically illustrated using a CVP chart. In this chart, the horizontal axis represents the number of units sold and the vertical axis represents dollars of sales or costs. Straight lines are used to depict both costs and sales on the CVP chart.

P4 **Compute the break-even point for a multiproduct company.** CVP analysis can be applied to a multiproduct company by expressing sales volume in terms of composite units. A composite unit consists of a specific number of units of each product in proportion to their expected sales mix. Multiproduct CVP analysis treats this composite unit as a single product.

Guidance Answers to **Decision Maker** and **Decision Ethics**

Sales Manager The contribution margin per unit for the first order is $600 (60% of $1,000); the contribution margin per unit for the second order is $160 (20% of $800). You are likely tempted to accept the first order based on its high contribution margin per unit, but you must compute the total contribution margin based on the number of units sold for each order. Total contribution margin is $60,000 ($600 per unit × 100 units) and $80,000 ($160 per unit × 500 units) for the two orders, respectively. The second order provides the largest return in absolute dollars and is the order you would accept. Another factor to consider in your selection is the potential for a long-term relationship with these customers including repeat sales and growth.

Operations Manager Without the availability of past data, none of the three methods described in the chapter can be used to measure cost behavior. Instead, the manager must investigate whether data from similar manufacturers can be accessed. This is likely difficult due to the sensitive nature of such data. In the absence of data, the manager should develop a list of the different production inputs and identify input-output relations. This provides guidance to the manager in measuring cost behavior. After several months, actual cost data will be available for analysis.

Supervisor Your dilemma is whether to go along with the suggestions to "manage" the numbers to make the project look like it will achieve sufficient profits. You should not succumb to these suggestions. Many people will likely be affected negatively if you manage the predicted numbers and the project eventually is unprofitable. Moreover, if it does fail, an investigation would likely reveal that data in the proposal were "fixed" to make it look good. Probably the only benefit from managing the numbers is the short-term payoff of pleasing those who proposed the product. One way to deal with this dilemma is to prepare several analyses showing results under different assumptions and then let senior management make the decision.

Entrepreneur You must first compute the level of sales required to achieve the desired net income. Then you must conduct sensitivity analysis by varying the price, sales mix, and cost estimates. Results from the sensitivity analysis provide information you can use to assess the possibility of reaching the target sales level. For instance, you might have to pursue aggressive marketing strategies to push the high-margin products, or you might have to cut prices to increase sales and profits, or another strategy might emerge.

Guidance Answers to **Quick Checks**

1. *b*

2. A fixed cost remains unchanged in total amount regardless of output levels. However, fixed *cost per unit* declines with increased output.

3. Such a cost is considered variable because the *total* cost changes in proportion to volume changes.

4. *b*

5. The high-low method ignores all costs and sales (activity base) volume data points except the costs corresponding to the highest and lowest (most extreme) sales (activity base) volume.

6. *c*

7. *a*

8. ($90 − $54)/$90 = 40%

9. $90,000/40% = $225,000

10. Three basic CVP assumptions are that (1) selling price per unit is constant, (2) variable costs per unit are constant, and (3) total fixed costs are constant.

11. *a*; Two steps are required for explanation:
(1) Pretax income = $120,000/(1 − 0.20) = $150,000

(2) $\dfrac{\$50,000 + \$150,000}{25\%} = \$800,000$

12. If the contribution margin ratio decreases from 50% to 25%, unit sales would have to double.

13. A company's margin of safety is the excess of the predicted sales level over its break-even sales level.

14. *c*; Selling price of a composite unit:

2 units of X @ $5 per unit	$10
1 unit of Y @ $4 per unit	4
Selling price of a composite unit	$14

Variable costs of a composite unit:

2 units of X @ $2 per unit	$4
1 unit of Y @ $2 per unit	2
Variable costs of a composite unit	$6

Therefore, the contribution margin per composite unit is $8.

15. It must be assumed that the sales mix remains unchanged at all sales levels in the relevant range.

Key Terms

mhhe.com/wildFAP19e

Key Terms are available at the book's Website for learning and testing in an online Flashcard Format.

Break-even point (p. 909)
Composite unit (p. 916)
Contribution margin per unit (p. 908)
Contribution margin ratio (p. 908)
Cost-volume-profit (CVP) analysis (p. 902)
Cost-volume-profit (CVP) chart (p. 910)
Curvilinear cost (p. 904)

Degree of operating leverage (DOL) (p. 918)
Estimated line of cost behavior (p. 906)
High-low method (p. 906)
Least-squares regression (p. 907)
Margin of safety (p. 914)
Mixed cost (p. 903)

Operating leverage (p. 918)
Relevant range of operations (p. 911)
Sales mix (p. 915)
Scatter diagram (p. 905)
Step-wise cost (p. 904)
Weighted-average contribution margin (p. 916)

Multiple Choice Quiz

Answers on p. 937   **mhhe.com/wildFAP19e**

Additional Quiz Questions are available at the book's Website.

Quiz22

1. A company's only product sells for $150 per unit. Its variable costs per unit are $100, and its fixed costs total $75,000. What is its contribution margin per unit?
  a. $50
  b. $250
  c. $100
  d. $150
  e. $25

2. Using information from question 1, what is the company's contribution margin ratio?
  a. 66⅔%
  b. 100%
  c. 50%

  d. 0%
  e. 33⅓%

3. Using information from question 1, what is the company's break-even point in units?
  a. 500 units
  b. 750 units
  c. 1,500 units
  d. 3,000 units
  e. 1,000 units

4. A company's forecasted sales are $300,000 and its sales at break-even are $180,000. Its margin of safety in dollars is
  a. $180,000.
  b. $120,000.

c. $480,000.
d. $60,000.
e. $300,000.

5. A product sells for $400 per unit and its variable costs per unit are $260. The company's fixed costs are $840,000. If the company desires $70,000 pretax income, what is the required dollar sales?

a. $2,400,000
b. $200,000
c. $2,600,000
d. $2,275,000
e. $1,400,000

Superscript letter ᴬ *denotes assignments based on Appendix 22A.*

Discussion Questions

1. How is cost-volume-profit analysis useful?

2. What is a variable cost? Identify two variable costs.

3. When output volume increases, do variable costs per unit increase, decrease, or stay the same within the relevant range of activity? Explain.

4. When output volume increases, do fixed costs per unit increase, decrease, or stay the same within the relevant range of activity? Explain.

5. How do step-wise costs and curvilinear costs differ?

6. Define and describe *contribution margin* per unit.

7. Define and explain the *contribution margin ratio*.

8. Describe the contribution margin ratio in layperson's terms.

9. In performing CVP analysis for a manufacturing company, what simplifying assumption is usually made about the volume of production and the volume of sales?

10. What two arguments tend to justify classifying all costs as either fixed or variable even though individual costs might not behave exactly as classified?

11. How does assuming that operating activity occurs within a relevant range affect cost-volume-profit analysis?

12. List three methods to measure cost behavior.

13. How is a scatter diagram used to identify and measure the behavior of a company's costs?

14. In cost-volume-profit analysis, what is the estimated profit at the break-even point?

15. Assume that a straight line on a CVP chart intersects the vertical axis at the level of fixed costs and has a positive slope that rises with each additional unit of volume by the amount of the variable costs per unit. What does this line represent?

16. Why are fixed costs depicted as a horizontal line on a CVP chart?

17. Each of two similar companies has sales of $20,000 and total costs of $15,000 for a month. Company A's total costs include $10,000 of variable costs and $5,000 of fixed costs. If Company B's total costs include $4,000 of variable costs and $11,000 of fixed costs, which company will enjoy more profit if sales double?

18. _____ of _____ reflects expected sales in excess of the level of break-even sales.

19. Apple produces iPods for sale. Identify some of the variable and fixed product costs associated with that production. [*Hint:* Limit costs to product costs.]

20. Should Best Buy use single product or multiproduct break-even analysis? Explain.

21. Apple is thinking of expanding sales of its most popular Macintosh model by 65%. Do you expect its variable and fixed costs for this model to stay within the relevant range? Explain.

♟ *Denotes Discussion Questions that involve decision making.*

McGraw-Hill's
HOMEWORK
MANAGER®   Available with McGraw-Hill's Homework Manager

Determine whether each of the following is best described as a fixed, variable, or mixed cost with respect to product units.

1. Packaging expense.

2. Factory supervisor's salary.

3. Taxes on factory building.

4. Depreciation expense of warehouse.

5. Rubber used to manufacture athletic shoes.

6. Maintenance of factory machinery.

7. Wages of an assembly-line worker paid on the basis of acceptable units produced.

QUICK STUDY

QS 22-1
Cost behavior identification
C1

QS 22-2

Cost behavior identification

C1

Listed here are four series of separate costs measured at various volume levels. Examine each series and identify whether it is best described as a fixed, variable, step-wise, or curvilinear cost. (It can help to graph the cost series.)

Volume (Units)	Series 1	Series 2	Series 3	Series 4
0	$450	$ 0	$ 800	$100
100	450	800	800	105
200	450	1,600	800	120
300	450	2,400	1,600	145
400	450	3,200	1,600	190
500	450	4,000	2,400	250
600	450	4,800	2,400	320

QS 22-3

Cost behavior estimation

C1   P1

This scatter diagram reflects past maintenance hours and their corresponding maintenance costs.

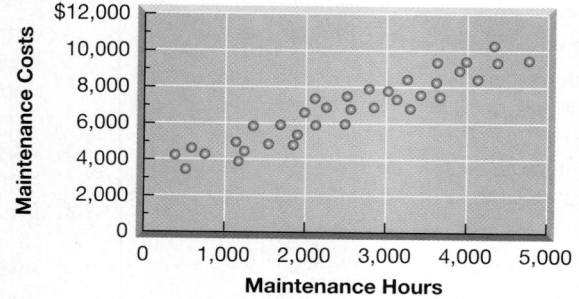

1. Draw an estimated line of cost behavior.
2. Estimate the fixed and variable components of maintenance costs.

QS 22-4

Cost behavior estimation—high-low method

C1   P1

The following information is available for a company's maintenance cost over the last seven months. Using the high-low method, estimate both the fixed and variable components of its maintenance cost.

Month	Maintenance Hours	Maintenance Cost
June	18	$5,450
July	36	6,900
August	24	5,100
September	30	6,000
October	42	6,900
November	48	8,100
December	12	3,600

QS 22-5

Contribution margin ratio

A2

Compute and interpret the contribution margin ratio using the following data: sales, $100,000; total variable cost, $60,000.

QS 22-6

Contribution margin per unit and break-even units

A2   P2

BSD Phone Company sells its cordless phone for $150 per unit. Fixed costs total $270,000, and variable costs are $60 per unit. Determine the (1) contribution margin per unit and (2) break-even point in units.

QS 22-7

Assumptions in CVP analysis

C2

Refer to the information from QS 22-6. How will the break-even point in units change in response to each of the following independent changes in selling price per unit, variable cost per unit, or total fixed costs? Use I for increase and D for decrease. (It is not necessary to compute new break-even points.)

Change	Breakeven in Units Will
1. Variable cost to $50 per unit	_____
2. Total fixed cost to $272,000	_____
3. Selling price per unit to $145	_____
4. Total fixed cost to $260,000	_____
5. Variable cost to $67 per unit	_____
6. Selling price per unit to $160	_____

Refer to QS 22-6. Determine the (1) contribution margin ratio and (2) break-even point in dollars.

QS 22-8
Contribution margin ratio and break-even dollars

P2

Refer to QS 22-6. Assume that BSD Phone Co. is subject to a 30% income tax rate. Compute the units of product that must be sold to earn after-tax income of $252,000.

QS 22-9
CVP analysis and target income

C3   P2

Which one of the following is an assumption that underlies cost-volume-profit analysis?

1. For costs classified as variable, the costs per unit of output must change constantly.

2. For costs classified as fixed, the costs per unit of output must remain constant.

3. All costs have approximately the same relevant range.

4. The selling price per unit must change in proportion to the number of units sold.

QS 22-10
CVP assumptions

C2

A high proportion of Company A's total costs are variable with respect to units sold; a high proportion of Company B's total costs are fixed with respect to units sold. Which company is likely to have a higher degree of operating leverage (DOL)? Explain.

QS 22-11
Operating leverage analysis

A3

Call Me Company manufactures and sells two products, green beepers and gold beepers, in the ratio of 5:3. Fixed costs are $66,500, and the contribution margin per composite unit is $95. What number of both green and gold beepers is sold at the break-even point?

QS 22-12
Multiproduct break-even

P4

McGraw-Hill's
HOMEWORK
MANAGER®   Available with McGraw-Hill's Homework Manager

A company reports the following information about its sales and its cost of sales. Each unit of its product sells for $1,000. Use these data to prepare a scatter diagram. Draw an estimated line of cost behavior and determine whether the cost appears to be variable, fixed, or mixed.

EXERCISES

Exercise 22-1
Measurement of cost behavior using a scatter diagram

P1

Period	Sales	Cost of Sales
1	$45,000	$30,300
2	34,500	22,500
3	31,500	21,000
4	22,500	16,500
5	27,000	18,000
6	37,500	28,500

Following are five graphs representing various cost behaviors. (1) Identify whether the cost behavior in each graph is mixed, step-wise, fixed, variable, or curvilinear. (2) Identify the graph (by number) that best illustrates each cost behavior: (a) Factory policy requires one supervisor for every 30 factory workers; (b) real estate taxes on factory; (c) electricity charge that includes the standard monthly charge plus a charge for each kilowatt hour; (d) commissions to salespersons; and (e) costs of hourly paid workers

Exercise 22-2
Cost behavior in graphs

C1

[continued on next page]

that provide substantial gains in efficiency when a few workers are added but gradually smaller gains in efficiency when more workers are added.

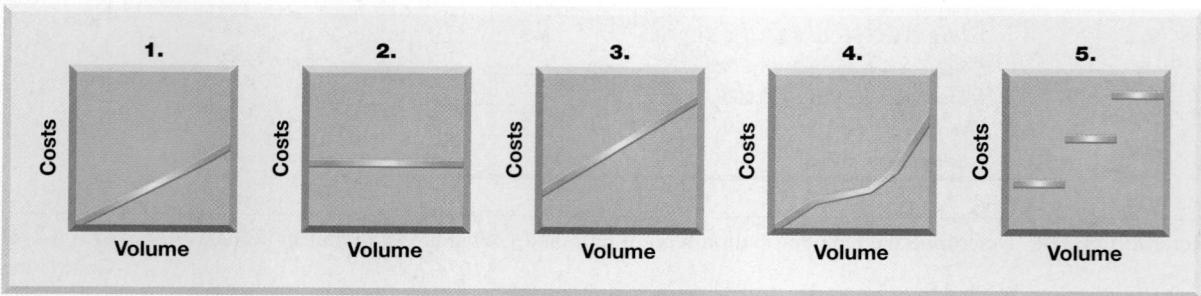

Exercise 22-3

Cost behavior defined

C1

The left column lists several cost classifications. The right column presents short definitions of those costs. In the blank space beside each of the numbers in the right column, write the letter of the cost best described by the definition.

A. Total cost

B. Variable cost

C. Fixed cost

D. Mixed cost

E. Curvilinear cost

F. Step-wise cost

_____ **1.** This cost is the combined amount of all the other costs.

_____ **2.** This cost remains constant over a limited range of volume; when it reaches the end of its limited range, it changes by a lump sum and remains at that level until it exceeds another limited range.

_____ **3.** This cost has a component that remains the same over all volume levels and another component that increases in direct proportion to increases in volume.

_____ **4.** This cost increases when volume increases, but the increase is not constant for each unit produced.

_____ **5.** This cost remains constant over all volume levels within the productive capacity for the planning period.

_____ **6.** This cost increases in direct proportion to increases in volume; its amount is constant for each unit produced.

Exercise 22-4

Cost behavior identification

C1

Following are five series of costs A through E measured at various volume levels. Examine each series and identify which is fixed, variable, mixed, step-wise, or curvilinear.

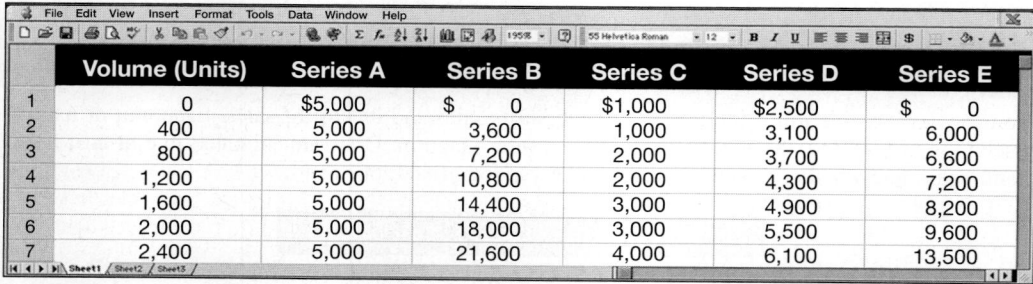

	Volume (Units)	Series A	Series B	Series C	Series D	Series E
1	0	$5,000	$ 0	$1,000	$2,500	$ 0
2	400	5,000	3,600	1,000	3,100	6,000
3	800	5,000	7,200	2,000	3,700	6,600
4	1,200	5,000	10,800	2,000	4,300	7,200
5	1,600	5,000	14,400	3,000	4,900	8,200
6	2,000	5,000	18,000	3,000	5,500	9,600
7	2,400	5,000	21,600	4,000	6,100	13,500

Exercise 22-5

Predicting sales and variable costs using contribution margin

C3

Stewart Company management predicts that it will incur fixed costs of $230,000 and earn pretax income of $350,000 in the next period. Its expected contribution margin ratio is 25%. Use this information to compute the amounts of (1) total dollar sales and (2) total variable costs.

Exercise 22-6

Scatter diagram and measurement of cost behavior

P1

Use the following information about sales and costs to prepare a scatter diagram. Draw a cost line that reflects the behavior displayed by this cost. Determine whether the cost is variable, step-wise, fixed, mixed, or curvilinear.

Period	Sales	Costs	Period	Sales	Costs
1	$1,520	$1,180	9	$1,160	$ 780
2	1,600	1,120	10	640	480
3	400	460	11	480	460
4	800	800	12	1,440	1,100
5	960	780	13	560	520
6	1,240	1,100	14	880	820
7	1,360	1,180	15	760	520
8	1,080	860			

A company reports the following information about its sales and cost of sales. Draw an estimated line of cost behavior using a scatter diagram, and compute fixed costs and variable costs per unit sold. Then use the high-low method to estimate the fixed and variable components of the cost of sales.

Exercise 22-7
Cost behavior estimation—scatter diagram and high-low

P1

Period	Units Sold	Cost of Sales	Period	Units Sold	Cost of Sales
1	0	$2,500	6	2,000	5,500
2	400	3,100	7	2,400	6,100
3	800	3,700	8	2,800	6,700
4	1,200	4,300	9	3,200	7,300
5	1,600	4,900	10	3,600	7,900

Refer to the information from Exercise 22-7. Use spreadsheet software to use ordinary least-squares regression to estimate the cost equation, including fixed and variable cost amounts.

Exercise 22-8^A
Measurement of cost behavior using regression

P1

Seton Company manufactures a single product that sells for $360 per unit and whose total variable costs are $270 per unit. The company's annual fixed costs are $1,125,000. (1) Use this information to compute the company's (a) contribution margin, (b) contribution margin ratio, (c) break-even point in units, and (d) break-even point in dollars of sales. (2) Draw a CVP chart for the company.

Exercise 22-9
Contribution margin, break-even, and CVP chart

P2 P3 A2

Refer to Exercise 22-9. (1) Prepare a contribution margin income statement for Seton Company showing sales, variable costs, and fixed costs at the break-even point. (2) If the company's fixed costs increase by $270,000, what amount of sales (in dollars) is needed to break even? Explain.

Exercise 22-10
Income reporting and break-even analysis

C3

Seton Company management (in Exercise 22-9) targets an annual after-tax income of $1,620,000. The company is subject to a 20% income tax rate. Assume that fixed costs remain at $1,125,000. Compute the (1) unit sales to earn the target after-tax net income and (2) dollar sales to earn the target after-tax net income.

Exercise 22-11
Computing sales to achieve target income

C3

Seton Company sales manager (in Exercise 22-9) predicts that annual sales of the company's product will soon reach 80,000 units and its price will increase to $400 per unit. According to the production manager, the variable costs are expected to increase to $280 per unit but fixed costs will remain at $1,125,000. The income tax rate is 20%. What amounts of pretax and after-tax income can the company expect to earn from these predicted changes? (*Hint:* Prepare a forecasted contribution margin income statement as in Exhibit 22.20.)

Exercise 22-12
Forecasted income statement

C3

Check Forecasted income, $6,780,000

Exercise 22-13
Predicting unit and dollar sales
C3

Maya Company management predicts $600,000 of variable costs, $700,000 of fixed costs, and a pretax income of $110,000 in the next period. Management also predicts that the contribution margin per unit will be $9. Use this information to compute the (1) total expected dollar sales for next period and (2) number of units expected to be sold next period.

Exercise 22-14
Computation of variable and fixed costs; CVP chart
P3

Corveau Company expects to sell 400,000 units of its product next year, which would generate total sales of $34 million. Management predicts that pretax net income for next year will be $2,500,000 and that the contribution margin per unit will be $50. (1) Use this information to compute next year's total expected (a) variable costs and (b) fixed costs. (2) Prepare a CVP chart from this information.

Exercise 22-15
CVP analysis using composite units   P4

Check (3) 1,500 units

Modern Home sells windows and doors in the ratio of 9:1 (windows:doors). The selling price of each window is $90 and of each door is $250. The variable cost of a window is $60 and of a door is $220. Fixed costs are $450,000. Use this information to determine the (1) selling price per composite unit, (2) variable costs per composite unit, (3) break-even point in composite units, and (4) number of units of each product that will be sold at the break-even point.

Exercise 22-16
CVP analysis using weighted-average contribution margin
P4

Refer to the information from Exercise 22-15. Use the information to determine the (1) weighted-average contribution margin, (2) break-even point in units, and (3) number of units of each product that will be sold at the break-even point.

Exercise 22-17
CVP analysis using composite units
P4

Precision Tax Service offers tax and consulting services to individuals and small businesses. Data for fees and costs of three types of tax returns follow. Precision provides services in the ratio of 5:3:2 (easy, moderate, business). Fixed costs total $18,000 for the tax season. Use this information to determine the (1) selling price per composite unit, (2) variable costs per composite unit, (3) break-even point in composite units, and (4) number of units of each product that will be sold at the break-even point.

Type of Return	Fee Charged	Variable Cost per Return
Easy (form 1040EZ)	$ 50	$ 30
Moderate (form 1040)	125	75
Business	275	100

Exercise 22-18
CVP analysis using weighted-average contribution margin
P4

Refer to the information from Exercise 22-17. Use the information to determine the (1) weighted-average contribution margin, (2) break-even point in units, and (3) number of units of each product that will be sold at the break-even point.

Exercise 22-19
Operating leverage computed and applied
A3

Company A is a manufacturer with current sales of $1,500,000 and a 60% contribution margin. Its fixed costs equal $650,000. Company B is a consulting firm with current service revenues of $1,500,000 and a 25% contribution margin. Its fixed costs equal $125,000. Compute the degree of operating leverage (DOL) for each company. Identify which company benefits more from a 20% increase in sales and explain why.

Available with McGraw-Hill's Homework Manager

The following costs result from the production and sale of 2,000 drum sets manufactured by Harris Drum Company for the year ended December 31, 2009. The drum sets sell for $500 each. The company has a 25% income tax rate.

Variable production costs	
Plastic for casing	$ 34,000
Wages of assembly workers	164,000
Drum stands	52,000
Variable selling costs	
Sales commissions	30,000
Fixed manufacturing costs	
Taxes on factory	10,000
Factory maintenance	20,000
Factory machinery depreciation	80,000
Fixed selling and administrative costs	
Lease of equipment for sales staff	20,000
Accounting staff salaries	70,000
Administrative management salaries	250,000

PROBLEM SET A

Problem 22-1A
Contribution margin income statement and contribution margin ratio

A2

Check (1) Net income, $202,500

Required

1. Prepare a contribution margin income statement for the company.

2. Compute its contribution margin per unit and its contribution margin ratio.

Analysis Component

3. Interpret the contribution margin and contribution margin ratio from part 2.

Extreme Equipment Co. manufactures and markets a number of rope products. Management is considering the future of Product HG, a special rope for hang gliding, that has not been as profitable as planned. Since Product HG is manufactured and marketed independently of the other products, its total costs can be precisely measured. Next year's plans call for a $200 selling price per 100 yards of HG rope. Its fixed costs for the year are expected to be $330,000, up to a maximum capacity of 20,000,000 yards of rope. Forecasted variable costs are $170 per 100 yards of HG rope.

Problem 22-2A
CVP analysis and charting

P2 P3

e**X**cel

mhhe.com/wildFAP19e

Required

1. Estimate Product HG's break-even point in terms of (a) sales units and (b) sales dollars.

2. Prepare a CVP chart for Product HG like that in Exhibit 22.14. Use 20,000,000 yards as the maximum number of sales units on the horizontal axis of the graph, and $4,000,000 as the maximum dollar amount on the vertical axis.

3. Prepare a contribution margin income statement showing sales, variable costs, and fixed costs for Product HG at the break-even point.

Check (1) Break-even sales, 11,000 units or $2,200,000

Alden Co.'s monthly sales and cost data for its operating activities of the past year follow. Management wants to use these data to predict future fixed and variable costs.

Problem 22-3A
Scatter diagram and cost behavior estimation

P1

Period	Sales	Total Cost	Period	Sales	Total Cost
1	$325,000	$162,500	7	$355,000	$242,000
2	170,000	106,250	8	275,000	156,750
3	270,000	210,600	9	75,000	60,000
4	210,000	105,000	10	155,000	135,625
5	295,000	206,500	11	99,000	99,000
6	195,000	117,000	12	105,000	76,650

Required

1. Prepare a scatter diagram for these data with sales volume (in $) plotted on the horizontal axis and total cost plotted on the vertical axis.

2. Estimate both the variable costs per sales dollar and the total monthly fixed costs using the high-low method. Draw the total costs line on the scatter diagram in part 1.

3. Use the estimated line of cost behavior and results from part 2 to predict future total costs when sales volume is (a) $210,000 and (b) $300,000.

Problem 22-4A

Break-even analysis; income targeting and forecasting

C3   P2

Teller Co. sold 20,000 units of its only product and incurred a $70,000 loss (ignoring taxes) for the current year as shown here. During a planning session for year 2010's activities, the production manager notes that variable costs can be reduced 50% by installing a machine that automates several operations. To obtain these savings, the company must increase its annual fixed costs by $210,000. The maximum output capacity of the company is 40,000 units per year.

TELLER COMPANY	
Contribution Margin Income Statement	
For Year Ended December 31, 2009	
Sales	$1,000,000
Variable costs	800,000
Contribution margin	200,000
Fixed costs	270,000
Net loss	$ (70,000)

Required

1. Compute the break-even point in dollar sales for year 2009.

2. Compute the predicted break-even point in dollar sales for year 2010 assuming the machine is installed and there is no change in the unit sales price.

3. Prepare a forecasted contribution margin income statement for 2010 that shows the expected results with the machine installed. Assume that the unit sales price and the number of units sold will not change, and no income taxes will be due.

4. Compute the sales level required in both dollars and units to earn $210,000 of after-tax income in 2010 with the machine installed and no change in the unit sales price. Assume that the income tax rate is 30%. (*Hint:* Use the procedures in Exhibits 22.21 and 22.23.)

5. Prepare a forecasted contribution margin income statement that shows the results at the sales level computed in part 4. Assume an income tax rate of 30%.

Problem 22-5A

Break-even analysis, different cost structures, and income calculations

C3

Shol Co. produces and sells two products, T and O. It manufactures these products in separate factories and markets them through different channels. They have no shared costs. This year, the company sold 51,000 units of each product. Sales and costs for each product follow.

	Product T	Product O
Sales	$2,040,000	$2,040,000
Variable costs	1,632,000	255,000
Contribution margin	408,000	1,785,000
Fixed costs	127,500	1,504,500
Income before taxes	280,500	280,500
Income taxes (34% rate)	95,370	95,370
Net income	$ 185,130	$ 185,130

Required

1. Compute the break-even point in dollar sales for each product.

2. Assume that the company expects sales of each product to decline to 40,000 units next year with no change in unit sales price. Prepare forecasted financial results for next year following the format of the contribution margin income statement as just shown with columns for each of the two products (assume a 34% tax rate). Also, assume that any loss before taxes yields a 34% tax savings.

3. Assume that the company expects sales of each product to increase to 65,000 units next year with no change in unit sales price. Prepare forecasted financial results for next year following the format of the contribution margin income statement shown with columns for each of the two products (assume a 34% tax rate).

Check (2) After-tax income: T, $127,050; O, $(68,970)

(3) After-tax income: T, $259,050; O, $508,530

Analysis Component

4. If sales greatly decrease, which product would experience a greater loss? Explain.

5. Describe some factors that might have created the different cost structures for these two products.

This year Calypso Company sold 60,000 units of its only product for $20 per unit. Manufacturing and selling the product required $97,500 of fixed manufacturing costs and $157,500 of fixed selling and administrative costs. Its per unit variable costs follow.

Material	$8.00
Direct labor (paid on the basis of completed units)	5.00
Variable overhead costs	1.60
Variable selling and administrative costs	0.40

Problem 22-6A

Analysis of price, cost, and volume changes for contribution margin and net income

C3 P2

mhhe.com/wildFAP19e

Next year the company will use new material, which will reduce material costs by 50% and direct labor costs by 60% and will not affect product quality or marketability. Management is considering an increase in the unit sales price to reduce the number of units sold because the factory's output is nearing its annual output capacity of 65,000 units. Two plans are being considered. Under plan 1, the company will keep the price at the current level and sell the same volume as last year. This plan will increase income because of the reduced costs from using the new material. Under plan 2, the company will increase price by 25%. This plan will decrease unit sales volume by 15%. Under both plans 1 and 2, the total fixed costs and the variable costs per unit for overhead and for selling and administrative costs will remain the same.

Required

1. Compute the break-even point in dollar sales for both (a) plan 1 and (b) plan 2.

2. Prepare a forecasted contribution margin income statement with two columns showing the expected results of plan 1 and plan 2. The statements should report sales, total variable costs, contribution margin, total fixed costs, income before taxes, income taxes (30% rate), and net income.

Check (1) Breakeven: Plan 1, $425,000; Plan 2, $375,000

(2) Net income: Plan 1, $325,500; Plan 2, $428,400

Patriot Co. manufactures and sells three products: red, white, and blue. Their unit sales prices are red, $74; white, $108; and blue, $99. The per unit variable costs to manufacture and sell these products are red, $48; white, $75; and blue, $90. Their sales mix is reflected in a ratio of 5:4:2 (red:white:blue). Annual fixed costs shared by all three products are $179,200. One type of raw material has been used to manufacture all three products. The company has developed a new material of equal quality for less cost. The new material would reduce variable costs per unit as follows: red, by $10; white, by $16; and blue, by $13. However, the new material requires new equipment, which will increase annual fixed costs by $22,400. (Round answers to whole composite units.)

Problem 22-7A

Break-even analysis with composite units

P4 C3 ♟

Required

1. If the company continues to use the old material, determine its break-even point in both sales units and sales dollars of each individual product.

2. If the company uses the new material, determine its new break-even point in both sales units and sales dollars of each individual product.

Check (1) Old plan breakeven, 640 composite units

(2) New plan breakeven, 480 composite units

Analysis Component

3. What insight does this analysis offer management for long-term planning?

PROBLEM SET B

Problem 22-1B
Contribution margin income statement and contribution margin ratio

A2

The following costs result from the production and sale of 240,000 CD sets manufactured by Jawan Company for the year ended December 31, 2009. The CD sets sell for $9 each. The company has a 25% income tax rate.

Variable manufacturing costs	
Plastic for CD sets	$ 21,600
Wages of assembly workers	300,000
Labeling	43,200
Variable selling costs	
Sales commissions	24,000
Fixed manufacturing costs	
Rent on factory	100,000
Factory cleaning service	75,000
Factory machinery depreciation	125,000
Fixed selling and administrative costs	
Lease of office equipment	120,000
Systems staff salaries	600,000
Administrative management salaries	300,000

Required

Check (1) Net income, $338,400

1. Prepare a contribution margin income statement for the company.
2. Compute its contribution margin per unit and its contribution margin ratio.

Analysis Component

3. Interpret the contribution margin and contribution margin ratio from part 2.

Problem 22-2B
CVP analysis and charting

P2 P3

Tip-Top Co. manufactures and markets several products. Management is considering the future of one product, electronic keyboards, that has not been as profitable as planned. Since this product is manufactured and marketed independently of the other products, its total costs can be precisely measured. Next year's plans call for a $175 selling price per unit. The fixed costs for the year are expected to be $420,000, up to a maximum capacity of 10,000 units. Forecasted variable costs are $105 per unit.

Required

Check (1) Break-even sales, 6,000 units or $1,050,000

1. Estimate the keyboards' break-even point in terms of (a) sales units and (b) sales dollars.
2. Prepare a CVP chart for keyboards like that in Exhibit 22.14. Use 10,000 keyboards as the maximum number of sales units on the horizontal axis of the graph, and $1,600,000 as the maximum dollar amount on the vertical axis.
3. Prepare a contribution margin income statement showing sales, variable costs, and fixed costs for keyboards at the break-even point.

Problem 22-3B
Scatter diagram and cost behavior estimation

P1

Merdam Co.'s monthly sales and costs data for its operating activities of the past year follow. Management wants to use these data to predict future fixed and variable costs.

Period	Sales	Total Cost	Period	Sales	Total Cost
1	$390	$194	7	$290	$186
2	250	174	8	370	210
3	210	146	9	270	170
4	310	178	10	170	116
5	190	162	11	350	190
6	430	220	12	230	158

Required

1. Prepare a scatter diagram for these data with sales volume (in $) plotted on the horizontal axis and total costs plotted on the vertical axis.

2. Estimate both the variable costs per sales dollar and the total monthly fixed costs using the high-low method. Draw the total costs line on the scatter diagram in part 1.

3. Use the estimated line of cost behavior and results from part 2 to predict future total costs when sales volume is (a) $200 and (b) $340.

Check   (2) Variable costs, $0.40 per sales dollar; fixed costs, $48

Noru Co. sold 30,000 units of its only product and incurred a $75,000 loss (ignoring taxes) for the current year as shown here. During a planning session for year 2010's activities, the production manager notes that variable costs can be reduced 40% by installing a machine that automates several operations. To obtain these savings, the company must increase its annual fixed costs by $220,000. The maximum output capacity of the company is 50,000 units per year.

Problem 22-4B
Break-even analysis; income targeting and forecasting
C3   P2

NORU COMPANY	
Contribution Margin Income Statement	
For Year Ended December 31, 2009	
Sales	$1,125,000
Variable costs	900,000
Contribution margin	225,000
Fixed costs	300,000
Net loss	$ (75,000)

Required

1. Compute the break-even point in dollar sales for year 2009.

2. Compute the predicted break-even point in dollar sales for year 2010 assuming the machine is installed and no change occurs in the unit sales price. (Round the change in variable costs to a whole number.)

3. Prepare a forecasted contribution margin income statement for 2010 that shows the expected results with the machine installed. Assume that the unit sales price and the number of units sold will not change, and no income taxes will be due.

Check   (3) Net income, $65,000

4. Compute the sales level required in both dollars and units to earn $104,000 of after-tax income in 2010 with the machine installed and no change in the unit sales price. Assume that the income tax rate is 20%. (*Hint:* Use the procedures in Exhibits 22.21 and 22.23.)

(4) Required sales, $1,250,000 or 33,334 units

5. Prepare a forecasted contribution margin income statement that shows the results at the sales level computed in part 4. Assume an income tax rate of 20%.

(5) Net income, $104,000 (rounded)

Best Co. produces and sells two products, BB and TT. It manufactures these products in separate factories and markets them through different channels. They have no shared costs. This year, the company sold 100,000 units of each product. Sales and costs for each product follow.

Problem 22-5B
Break-even analysis, different cost structures, and income calculations
C3

	Product BB	Product TT
Sales	$1,600,000	$1,600,000
Variable costs	1,120,000	200,000
Contribution margin	480,000	1,400,000
Fixed costs	200,000	1,120,000
Income before taxes	280,000	280,000
Income taxes (32% rate)	89,600	89,600
Net income	$ 190,400	$ 190,400

Required

1. Compute the break-even point in dollar sales for each product.

2. Assume that the company expects sales of each product to decline to 67,000 units next year with no change in the unit sales price. Prepare forecasted financial results for next year following the format of the contribution margin income statement as shown here with columns for each of the two products (assume a 32% tax rate, and that any loss before taxes yields a 32% tax savings).

Check   (2) After-tax income: BB, $82,688; TT, $(123,760)

3. Assume that the company expects sales of each product to increase to 125,000 units next year with no change in the unit sales prices. Prepare forecasted financial results for next year following the format of the contribution margin income statement as shown here with columns for each of the two products (assume a 32% tax rate).

(3) After-tax income: BB, $272,000; TT, $428,400

Analysis Component

4. If sales greatly increase, which product would experience a greater increase in profit? Explain.

5. Describe some factors that might have created the different cost structures for these two products.

Problem 22-6B
Analysis of price, cost, and volume changes for contribution margin and net income

C3   P2

This year Blanko Company earned a disappointing 3.85% after-tax return on sales (Net income/Sales) from marketing 50,000 units of its only product. The company buys its product in bulk and repackages it for resale at the price of $20 per unit. Blanko incurred the following costs this year.

Total variable unit costs	$400,000
Total variable packaging costs	50,000
Fixed costs	$495,000
Income tax rate	30%

The marketing manager claims that next year's results will be the same as this year's unless some changes are made. The manager predicts the company can increase the number of units sold by 60% if it reduces the selling price by 20% and upgrades the packaging. This change would increase variable packaging costs by 20%. Increased sales would allow the company to take advantage of a 25% quantity purchase discount on the cost of the bulk product. Neither the packaging change nor the volume discount would affect fixed costs, which provide an annual output capacity of 100,000 units.

Required

Check (1) Breakeven for new strategy, $900,000

(2) Net income: Existing strategy, $38,500; new strategy, $146,300

1. Compute the break-even point in dollar sales under the (a) existing business strategy and (b) new strategy that alters both unit sales price and variable costs.

2. Prepare a forecasted contribution margin income statement with two columns showing the expected results of (a) the existing strategy and (b) changing to the new strategy. The statements should report sales, total variable costs (unit and packaging), contribution margin, fixed costs, income before taxes, income taxes, and net income. Also determine the after-tax return on sales for these two strategies.

Problem 22-7B
Break-even analysis with composite units

P4   C3

Milagro Co. manufactures and sells three products: product 1, product 2, and product 3. Their unit sales prices are product 1, $200; product 2, $150; and product 3, $100. The per unit variable costs to manufacture and sell these products are product 1, $150; product 2, $75; and product 3, $40. Their sales mix is reflected in a ratio of 6:4:2. Annual fixed costs shared by all three products are $5,400,000. One type of raw material has been used to manufacture products 1 and 2. The company has developed a new material of equal quality for less cost. The new material would reduce variable costs per unit as follows: product 1 by $50, and product 2, by $25. However, the new material requires new equipment, which will increase annual fixed costs by $200,000.

Required

Check (1) Old plan breakeven, 7,500 composite units

(2) New plan breakeven, 5,000 composite units

1. If the company continues to use the old material, determine its break-even point in both sales units and sales dollars of each individual product.

2. If the company uses the new material, determine its new break-even point in both sales units and sales dollars of each individual product.

Analysis Component

3. What insight does this analysis offer management for long-term planning?

SERIAL PROBLEM

Success Systems

(This serial problem began in Chapter 1 and continues through most of the book. If previous chapter segments were not completed, the serial problem can begin at this point. It is helpful, but not necessary, to use the working papers that accompany the book.)

SP 22 Success Systems sells upscale modular desk units and office chairs in the ratio of 3:2 (desk unit:chair). The selling prices are $1,250 per desk unit and $500 per chair. The variable costs are $750 per desk unit and $250 per chair. Fixed costs are $120,000.

Required

1. Compute the selling price per composite unit.
2. Compute the variable costs per composite unit.
3. Compute the break-even point in composite units.
4. Compute the number of units of each product that would be sold at the break-even point.

Check   (3) 60 composite units

BEYOND THE NUMBERS

BTN 22-1   **Best Buy** offers services to customers that help them use products they purchase from Best Buy. One of these services is its Geek Squad, which is Best Buy's 24-hour computer support task force. As you complete the following requirements, assume that the Geek Squad uses many of Best Buy's existing resources such as its purchasing department and its buildings and equipment.

REPORTING IN ACTION

C1

Required

1. Identify several of the variable, mixed, and fixed costs that the Geek Squad is likely to incur in carrying out its services.
2. Assume that Geek Squad revenues are expected to grow by 25% in the next year. How do you expect the costs identified in part 1 to change, if at all?
3. How is your answer to part 2 different from many of the examples discussed in the chapter? (*Hint:* Consider how the contribution margin ratio changes as volume—sales or customers served—increases.)

BTN 22-2   Both **Best Buy** and **Circuit City** sell numerous consumer products, and each of these companies has a different product mix.

COMPARATIVE ANALYSIS

P2   C3   A2

Required

1. Assume the following data are available for both companies. Compute each company's break-even point in unit sales. (Each company sells many products at many different selling prices, and each has its own variable costs. This assignment assumes an *average* selling price per unit and an *average* cost per item.)

	Best Buy	Circuit City
Average selling price per item sold	$90	$40
Average variable cost per item sold	$64	$30
Total fixed costs	$5,980 million	$2,570 million

2. If unit sales were to decline, which company would experience the larger decline in operating profit? Explain.

BTN 22-3   Labor costs of an auto repair mechanic are seldom based on actual hours worked. Instead, the amount paid a mechanic is based on an industry average of time estimated to complete a repair job. The repair shop bills the customer for the industry average amount of time at the repair center's billable cost per hour. This means a customer can pay, for example, $120 for two hours of work on a car when the actual time worked was only one hour. Many experienced mechanics can complete repair jobs faster than the industry average. The average data are compiled by engineering studies and surveys conducted in the auto repair business. Assume that you are asked to complete such a survey for a repair center. The survey calls for objective input, and many questions require detailed cost data and analysis. The mechanics and owners know you have the survey and encourage you to complete it in a way that increases the average billable hours for repair work.

ETHICS CHALLENGE

C1

Required

Write a one-page memorandum to the mechanics and owners that describes the direct labor analysis you will undertake in completing this survey.

COMMUNICATING IN PRACTICE

C2

BTN 22-4   Several important assumptions underlie CVP analysis. Assumptions often help simplify and focus our analysis of sales and costs. A common application of CVP analysis is as a tool to forecast sales, costs, and income.

Required

Assume that you are actively searching for a job. Prepare a one-half page report identifying (1) three assumptions relating to your expected revenue (salary) and (2) three assumptions relating to your expected costs for the first year of your new job. Be prepared to discuss your assumptions in class.

TAKING IT TO THE NET

C1   C3

BTN 22-5   Access and review the entrepreneurial information at **Business Owner's Toolkit** [Toolkit.cch.com]. Access and review its *New Business Cash Needs Estimate* under the Business Tools/Business Finance menu bar or similar worksheets related to controls of cash and costs.

Required

Write a one-half page report that describes the information and resources available at the Business Owner's Toolkit to help the owner of a start-up business to control and monitor its costs.

TEAMWORK IN ACTION

C2

BTN 22-6   A local movie theater owner explains to you that ticket sales on weekends and evenings are strong, but attendance during the weekdays, Monday through Thursday, is poor. The owner proposes to offer a contract to the local grade school to show educational materials at the theater for a set charge per student during school hours. The owner asks your help to prepare a CVP analysis listing the cost and sales projections for the proposal. The owner must propose to the school's administration a charge per child. At a minimum, the charge per child needs to be sufficient for the theater to break even.

Required

Your team is to prepare two separate lists of questions that enable you to complete a reliable CVP analysis of this situation. One list is to be answered by the school's administration, the other by the owner of the movie theater.

ENTREPRENEURIAL DECISION

C1

BTN 22-7   Martin Sprock is a diligent businessman. He continually searches for new menu items to further increase the profitability of **Moe's Southwest Grill**.

Required

1. What information should Sprock search for to help him decide whether to add new menu items or other products to existing Moe's product lines?

2. What managerial tools are available to Sprock to help make the decisions in part 1?

HITTING THE ROAD

P4

BTN 22-8   Multiproduct break-even analysis is often viewed differently when actually applied in practice. You are to visit a local fast-food restaurant and count the number of items on the menu. To apply multiproduct break-even analysis to the restaurant, similar menu items must often be fit into groups. A reasonable approach is to classify menu items into approximately five groups. We then estimate average selling price and average variable cost to compute average contribution margin. (*Hint:* For fast-food restaurants, the highest contribution margin is with its beverages, at about 90%.)

Required

1. Prepare a one-year multiproduct break-even analysis for the restaurant you visit. Begin by establishing groups. Next, estimate each group's volume and contribution margin. These estimates are necessary to compute each group's contribution margin. Assume that annual fixed costs in total are $500,000 per year. (*Hint:* You must develop your own estimates on volume and contribution margin for each group to obtain the break-even point and sales.)

2. Prepare a one-page report on the results of your analysis. Comment on the volume of sales necessary to break even at a fast-food restaurant.

BTN 22-9   Access and review **DSG**'s Website (www.DSGiplc.com) to answer the following questions.

GLOBAL DECISION

1. Do you believe that DSG's managers use single product CVP analysis or multiproduct break-even point analysis? Explain.

C3

2. How does the addition of a new product line affect DSG's CVP analysis?

DSG

3. How does the addition of a new store affect DSG's CVP analysis?

ANSWERS TO MULTIPLE CHOICE QUIZ

1. a; $150 − $100 = $50
2. e; ($150 − $100)/$150 = 33⅓%
3. c; $75,000/$50 CM per unit = 1,500 units

4. b; $300,000 − $180,000 = $120,000
5. c; Contribution margin ratio = ($400 − $260)/$400 = 0.35
   Targeted sales = ($840,000 + $70,000)/0.35 = $2,600,000

A Look Back

Chapter 22 looked at cost behavior and its use by managers in performing cost-volume-profit analysis. It also illustrated the application of cost-volume-profit analysis.

A Look at This Chapter

This chapter explains the importance of budgeting and describes the master budget and its preparation. It also discusses the value of the master budget to the planning of future business activities.

A Look Ahead

Chapter 24 focuses on flexible budgets, standard costs, and variance reporting. It explains the usefulness of these procedures and reports for business decisions.

Chapter

Master Budgets and Planning

Learning Objectives

CAP

Conceptual

C1 Describe the importance and benefits of budgeting. *(p. 940)*

C2 Explain the process of budget administration. *(p. 942)*

C3 Describe a master budget and the process of preparing it. *(p. 944)*

Analytical

A1 Analyze expense planning using activity-based budgeting. *(p. 953)*

LP23

Procedural

P1 Prepare each component of a master budget and link each to the budgeting process. *(p. 946)*

P2 Link both operating and capital expenditures budgets to budgeted financial statements. *(p. 950)*

P3 *Appendix 23A*—Prepare production and manufacturing budgets. *(p. 959)*

Lucky Charms

"The Number One thing is you have got to take the chance"—Rich Schmelzer

BOULDER, CO—Each pair of **Crocs (Crocs.com)** shoes includes ventilation holes for breathability and to filter water out. Sheri Schmelzer and her kids thought it more fun to use clay and rhinestones to decorate the holes with fun charms. Sheri's husband Rich, an entrepreneur, immediately saw the profit potential—within 48 hours the Schmelzer's had filed patents for the design of **Jibbitz (Jibbitz.com),** which are small accessories made to fit in the holes of Crocs. Today, Jibbitz accessories come in various shapes and sizes, and include more than 1100 designs such as peace signs, flowers, musical notes, sports gear, and letters to spell out words.

Jibbitz started small, with an assembly line in the family's basement and a Website to process orders. Like many new businesses, Jibbitz began with few formal budgets or plans. "We didn't write a business plan" admits Sheri. Rich explains "We recalibrated our business every week depending on what we sold. We were very nimble." Soon, Jibbitz was processing hundreds of orders per day. "It turned from a very simple business to a very complex business," says Rich.

As business grew, master budgets and the budgeting process became more important. Budgets helped formalize business plans and goals, and helped direct employees—a team of staff designers and warehouse personnel in Boulder, and a manufacturing group in Asia. Realizing that a too-rapid sales growth could strain its capacity to meet customer expectations, Jibbitz avoids advertising and has turned down some large retailers' bids to carry its products. An understanding of sales budgets and their link to expense budgets was vital in making these decisions. Likewise, production and manufacturing budgets helped plan for use of materials, labor, and overhead.

Eventually, Rich and Sheri teamed up with Crocs. Now operating as a division within Crocs, budgeting remains important. If Jibbitz meets certain sales and income targets, Rich and Sheri will receive an additional payment from Crocs. Linking their budgeted data to budgeted income statements, and using that information to control costs, is key to that future payment. Still, both Sheri and Rich stress the importance of having fun and a passion for what they do as keys to success. "I'm having a blast," explains Sheri. "I don't want it to stop."

[Sources: *Jibbitz Website,* January 2009; *Crocs Website,* January 2009; *Crocs 2007 10-K report; Rocky Mountain News,* September 2007; *Ladies Who Launch Magazine,* March 2008; *Business 2.0,* November 2006; *Boulder Daily Camera,* August 2006; *Denverpost.com,* October 2006]

Management seeks to turn its strategies into action plans. These action plans include financial details that are compiled in a master budget. The budgeting process serves several purposes, including motivating employees and communicating with them. The budget process also helps coordinate a company's activities toward common goals and is useful in evaluating results and management performance. This chapter explains how to prepare a master budget and use it as a formal plan of a company's future activities. The ability to prepare this type of plan is of enormous help in starting and operating a company. Such planning gives managers a glimpse into the future, and it can help translate ideas into actions.

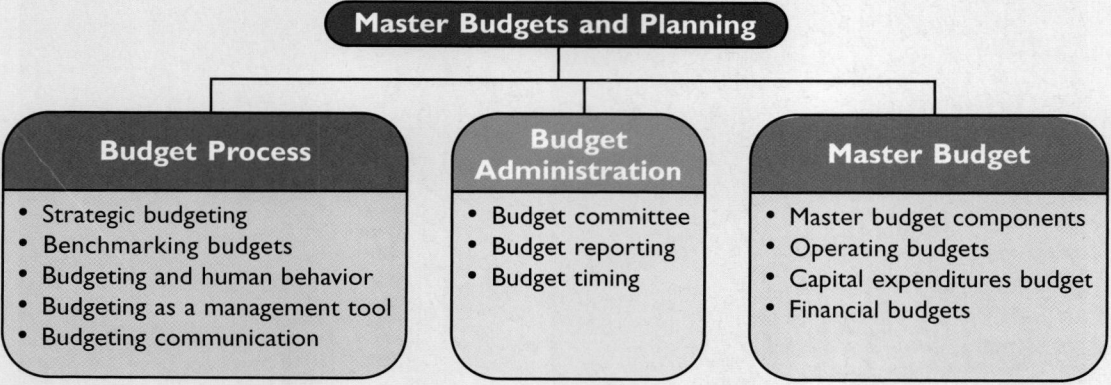

Budget Process

Strategic Budgeting

C1 Describe the importance and benefits of budgeting.

Most companies prepare long-term strategic plans spanning 5 to 10 years. They then fine-tune them in preparing medium-term and short-term plans. Strategic plans usually set a company's long-term direction. They provide a road map for the future about potential opportunities such as new products, markets, and investments. The strategic plan can be inexact, given its long-term focus. Medium- and short-term plans are more operational and translate strategic plans into actions. These action plans are fairly concrete and consist of defined objectives and goals.

Short-term financial plans are called *budgets* and typically cover a one-year period. A **budget** is a formal statement of a company's future plans. It is usually expressed in monetary terms because the economic or financial aspects of the business are the primary factors driving management's decisions. All managers should be involved in **budgeting,** the process of planning future business actions and expressing them as formal plans. Managers who plan carefully and formalize plans in a budgeting process increase the likelihood of both personal and company success. (Although most firms prepare annual budgets, it is not unusual for organizations to prepare three-year and five-year budgets that are revised at least annually.)

Companies Performing Annual Budgeting

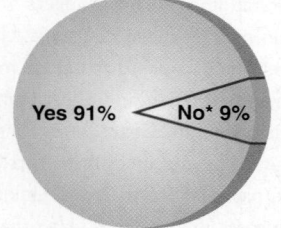

Yes 91%   No* 9%

*Most of the 9% have eliminated annual budgeting in favor of rolling or continual budgeting.

The relevant focus of a budgetary analysis is the future. Management must focus on future transactions and events and the opportunities available. A focus on the future is important because the pressures of daily operating problems often divert management's attention and take precedence over planning. A good budgeting system counteracts this tendency by formalizing the planning process and demanding relevant input. Budgeting makes planning an explicit management responsibility.

Benchmarking Budgets

The control function requires management to evaluate (benchmark) business operations against some norm. Evaluation involves comparing actual results against one of two usual alternatives: (1) past performance or (2) expected performance.

An evaluation assists management in identifying problems and taking corrective actions if necessary. Evaluation using expected, or budgeted, performance is potentially superior to using

Video23.1

past performance to decide whether actual results trigger a need for corrective actions. This is so because past performance fails to consider several changes that can affect current and future activities. Changes in economic conditions, shifts in competitive advantages within the industry, new product developments, increased or decreased advertising, and other factors reduce the usefulness of comparisons with past results. In hi-tech industries, for instance, increasing competition, technological advances, and other innovations often reduce the usefulness of performance comparisons across years.

Budgeted performance is computed after careful analysis and research that attempts to anticipate and adjust for changes in important company, industry, and economic factors. Therefore, budgets usually provide management an effective control and monitoring system.

Point: Managers can evaluate performance by preparing reports that compare actual results to budgeted plans.

Budgeting and Human Behavior

Budgeting provides standards for evaluating performance and can affect the attitudes of employees evaluated by them. It can be used to create a positive effect on employees' attitudes, but it can also create negative effects if not properly applied. Budgeted levels of performance, for instance, must be realistic to avoid discouraging employees. Personnel who will be evaluated should be consulted and involved in preparing the budget to increase their commitment to meeting it. Performance evaluations must allow the affected employees to explain the reasons for apparent performance deficiencies.

The budgeting process has three important guidelines: (1) Employees affected by a budget should be consulted when it is prepared (*participatory budgeting*), (2) goals reflected in a budget should be attainable, and (3) evaluations should be made carefully with opportunities to explain any failures. Budgeting can be a positive motivating force when these guidelines are followed. Budgeted performance levels can provide goals for employees to attain or even exceed as they carry out their responsibilities. This is especially important in organizations that consider the annual budget a "sacred" document.

Point: The practice of involving employees in the budgeting process is known as *participatory budgeting*.

Decision Insight

Budgets Exposed   When companies go public and trade their securities on an organized exchange, management usually develops specific future plans and budgets. For this purpose, companies often develop detailed six- to twelve-month budgets and less-detailed budgets spanning 2 to 5 years.

Budgeting as a Management Tool

An important management objective in large companies is to ensure that activities of all departments contribute to meeting the company's overall goals. This requires coordination. Budgeting provides a way to achieve this coordination.

We describe later in this chapter that a company's budget, or operating plan, is based on its objectives. This operating plan starts with the sales budget, which drives all other budgets including production, materials, labor, and overhead. The budgeting process coordinates the activities of these various departments to meet the company's overall goals.

Budgeting Communication

Managers of small companies can adequately explain business plans directly to employees through conversations and other informal communications. However, conversations can create uncertainty and confusion if not supported by clear documentation of the plans. A written budget is preferred and can inform employees in all types of organizations about management's plans. The budget can also communicate management's specific action plans for the employees in the budget period.

Decision Ethics

Budget Staffer   Your company's earnings for the current period will be far below the budgeted amount reported in the press. One of your superiors, who is aware of the upcoming earnings shortfall, has accepted a management position with a competitor. This superior is selling her shares of the company. What are your ethical concerns, if any? [Answer—p. 961]

Budget Administration

Budget Committee

C2 Explain the process of budget administration.

The task of preparing a budget should not be the sole responsibility of any one department. Similarly, the budget should not be simply handed down as top management's final word. Instead, budget figures and budget estimates developed through a *bottom-up* process usually are more useful. This includes, for instance, involving the sales department in preparing sales estimates. Likewise, the production department should have initial responsibility for preparing its own expense budget. Without active employee involvement in preparing budget figures, there is a risk these employees will feel that the numbers fail to reflect their special problems and needs.

Most budgets should be developed by a bottom-up process, but the budgeting system requires central guidance. This guidance is supplied by a budget committee of department heads and other executives responsible for seeing that budgeted amounts are realistic and coordinated. If a department submits initial budget figures not reflecting efficient performance, the budget committee should return them with explanatory comments on how to improve them. Then the originating department must either adjust its proposals or explain why they are acceptable. Communication between the originating department and the budget committee should continue as needed to ensure that both parties accept the budget as reasonable, attainable, and desirable.

Point: In a large company, developing a budget through a bottom-up process can involve hundreds of employees and take several weeks to finalize.

The concept of continuous improvement applies to budgeting as well as production. **BP**, one of the world's largest energy companies, streamlined its monthly budget report from a one-inch-thick stack of monthly control reports to a tidy, two-page flash report on monthly earnings and key production statistics. The key to this efficiency gain was the integration of new budgeting and cost allocation processes with its strategic planning process. BP's controller explained the new role of the finance department with respect to the budgetary control process as follows: "there's less of an attitude that finance's job is to control. People really have come to see that our job is to help attain business objectives."

Budget Reporting

The budget period usually coincides with the accounting period. Most companies prepare at least an annual budget, which reflects the objectives for the next year. To provide specific guidance, the annual budget usually is separated into quarterly or monthly budgets. These short-term budgets allow management to periodically evaluate performance and take needed corrective action.

Managers can compare actual results to budgeted amounts in a report such as that shown in Exhibit 23.1. This report shows actual amounts, budgeted amounts, and their differences. A difference is called a *variance*. Management examines variances to identify areas for improvement and corrective action.

Budget Timing

The time period required for the annual budgeting process can vary considerably. For example, budgeting for 2010 can begin as early as January 2009 or as late as December 2009. Large, complex organizations usually require a longer time to prepare their budgets than do smaller organizations. This is so because considerable effort is required to coordinate the different units (departments) within large organizations.

Companies Using Rolling Budgets

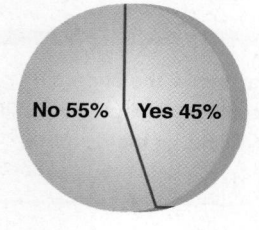

No 55%   Yes 45%

Many companies apply **continuous budgeting** by preparing **rolling budgets.** As each monthly or quarterly budget period goes by, these companies revise their entire set of budgets for the months or quarters remaining and add new monthly or quarterly budgets to replace the ones that have lapsed. At any point in time, monthly or quarterly budgets are available for the next

EXHIBIT 23.1

Comparing Actual Performance with Budgeted Performance

ECCENTRIC MUSIC
Income Statement with Variations from Budget
For Month Ended April 30, 2009

	Actual	Budget	Variance
Net sales	$60,500	$57,150	$+3,350
Cost of goods sold	41,350	39,100	+2,250
Gross profit	19,150	18,050	+1,100
Operating expenses			
Selling expenses			
Sales salaries	6,250	6,000	+250
Advertising	900	800	+100
Store supplies	550	500	+50
Depreciation—Store equipment	1,600	1,600	
Total selling expenses	9,300	8,900	+400
General and administrative expenses			
Office salaries	2,000	2,000	
Office supplies used	165	150	+15
Rent	1,100	1,100	
Insurance	200	200	
Depreciation—Office equipment	100	100	
Total general and administrative expenses	3,565	3,550	+15
Total operating expenses	12,865	12,450	+415
Net income	$ 6,285	$ 5,600	$ +685

Example: Assume that you must explain variances to top management. Which variances in Exhibit 23.1 would you research and why? *Answer:* Sales and cost of goods sold—due to their large variances.

12 months or four quarters. Exhibit 23.2 shows rolling budgets prepared at the end of five consecutive periods. The first set (at top) is prepared in December 2008 and covers the four calendar quarters of 2009. In March 2009, the company prepares another rolling budget for the next four quarters through March 2010. This same process is repeated every three months. As a result, management is continuously planning ahead.

EXHIBIT 23.2

Rolling Budgets

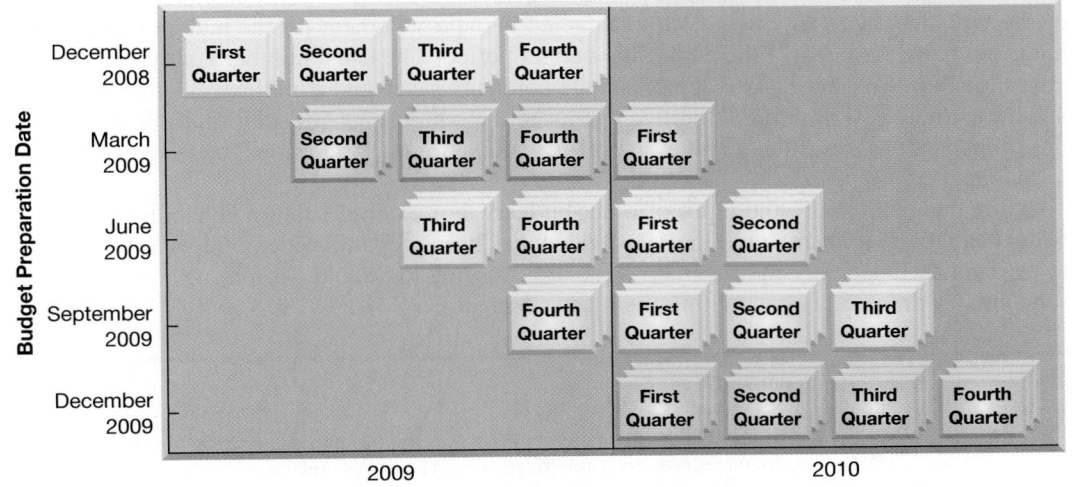

Exhibit 23.2 reflects an annual budget composed of four quarters prepared four times per year using the most recent information available. For example, the budget for the fourth quarter of 2009 is prepared in December 2008 and revised in March, June, and September of 2009. When continuous budgeting is not used, the fourth-quarter budget is nine months old and perhaps out of date when applied.

Decision Insight

Budget Calendar   Many companies use long-range operating budgets. For large companies, three groups usually determine or influence the budgets: creditors, directors, and management. All three are interested in the companies' future cash flows and earnings. The annual budget process often begins six months or more before the budget is due to the board of directors. A typical budget calendar, shown here, provides insight into the budget process during a typical calendar year.

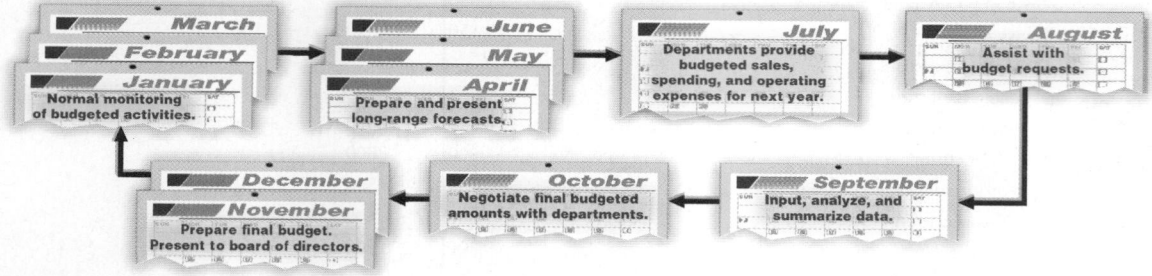

Quick Check

Answers—p. 961

1. What are the major benefits of budgeting?
2. What is the main responsibility of the budget committee?
3. What is the usual time period covered by a budget?
4. What are rolling budgets?

Master Budget

C3   Describe a master budget and the process of preparing it.

A **master budget** is a formal, comprehensive plan for a company's future. It contains several individual budgets that are linked with each other to form a coordinated plan.

Master Budget Components

The master budget typically includes individual budgets for sales, purchases, production, various expenses, capital expenditures, and cash. Managers often express the expected financial results of these planned activities with both a budgeted income statement for the budget period and a budgeted balance sheet for the end of the budget period. The usual number and types of budgets included in a master budget depend on the company's size and complexity. A master budget should include, at a minimum, the budgets listed in Exhibit 23.3. In addition to these individual budgets, managers often include supporting calculations and additional tables with the master budget.

Some budgets require the input of other budgets. For example, the merchandise purchases budget cannot be prepared until the sales budget has been prepared because the number of units to be purchased depends on how many units are expected to be sold. As a result, we often must sequentially prepare budgets within the master budget.

EXHIBIT 23.3

Basic Components of a Master Budget

Operating budgets
- *Sales budget*
- For merchandisers add: *Merchandise purchases budget* (units to be purchased)
- For manufacturers add: *Production budget* (units to be produced)
    Manufacturing budget (manufacturing costs)
- *Selling expense budget*
- *General and administrative expense budget*

Capital expenditures budget (expenditures for plant assets)

Financial budgets
- *Cash budget* (cash receipts and disbursements)
- *Budgeted income statement*
- *Budgeted balance sheet*

Decision Insight

Video23.1

Budgeting Targets   Budgeting is a crucial part of any acquisition. Analysis begins by projecting annual sales volume and prices. It then estimates cost of sales, expenses, and income for the next several years. Using the present value of this projected income stream, buyers determine an offer price.

A typical sequence for a quarterly budget consists of the five steps in Exhibit 23.4. Any stage in this budgeting process might reveal undesirable outcomes, so changes often must be made to prior budgets by repeating the previous steps. For instance, an early version of the cash budget could show an insufficient amount of cash unless cash outlays are reduced. This could yield a reduction in planned equipment purchases. A preliminary budgeted balance sheet could also reveal too much debt from an ambitious capital expenditures budget. Findings such as these often result in revised plans and budgets.

EXHIBIT 23.4

Master Budget Sequence

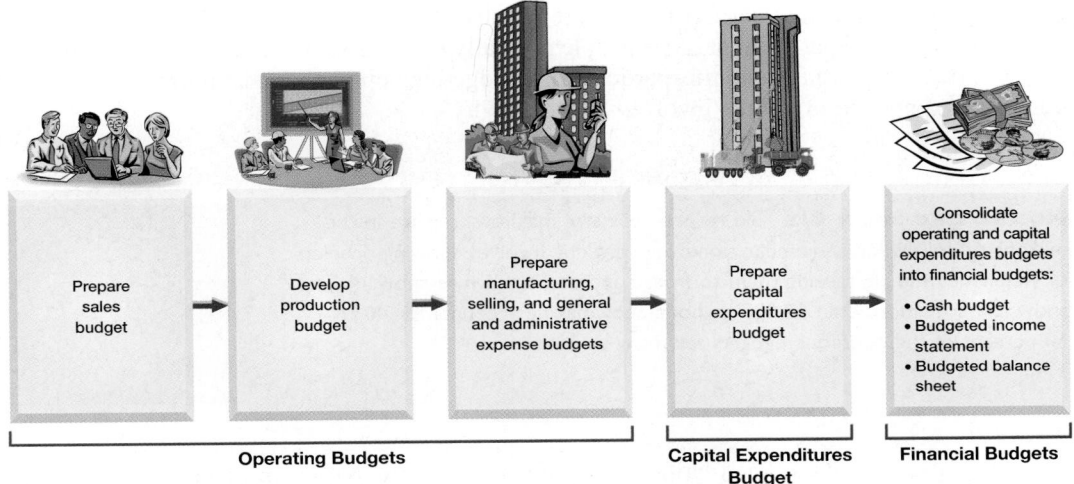

The remainder of this section explains how Hockey Den (HD), a retailer of youth hockey sticks, prepares its master budget. Its master budget includes operating, capital expenditures, and cash budgets for each month in each quarter. It also includes a budgeted income statement for each quarter and a budgeted balance sheet as of the last day of each quarter. We show how HD prepares budgets for October, November, and December 2009. Exhibit 23.5 presents HD's balance sheet at the start of this budgeting period, which we often refer to as we prepare the component budgets.

EXHIBIT 23.5

Balance Sheet Prior to the Budgeting Periods

HOCKEY DEN		
Balance Sheet		
September 30, 2009		
Assets		
Cash		$ 20,000
Accounts receivable		42,000
Inventory (900 units @ $60)		54,000
Equipment*	$200,000	
Less accumulated depreciation	36,000	164,000
Total assets		$280,000
Liabilities and Equity		
Liabilities		
Accounts payable	$ 58,200	
Income taxes payable (due 10/31/2009)	20,000	
Note payable to bank	10,000	$ 88,200
Stockholders' equity		
Common stock	150,000	
Retained earnings	41,800	191,800
Total liabilities and equity		$280,000

* Equipment is depreciated on a straight-line basis over 10 years (salvage value is $20,000).

Operating Budgets

| P1 | Prepare each component of a master budget and link each to the budgeting process. |

This section explains HD's preparation of operating budgets. Its operating budgets consist of the sales budget, merchandise purchases budget, selling expense budget, and general and administrative expense budget. HD does not prepare production and manufacturing budgets because it is a merchandiser. (The preparation of production budgets and manufacturing budgets is described in Appendix 23A.)

Sales Budget   The first step in preparing the master budget is planning the **sales budget,** which shows the planned sales units and the expected dollars from these sales. The sales budget is the starting point in the budgeting process because plans for most departments are linked to sales.

The sales budget should emerge from a careful analysis of forecasted economic and market conditions, business capacity, proposed selling expenses (such as advertising), and predictions of unit sales. A company's sales personnel are usually asked to develop predictions of sales for each territory and department because people normally feel a greater commitment to goals they help set. Another advantage to this participatory budgeting approach is that it draws on knowledge and experience of people involved in the activity.

Decision Insight

No Biz Like Snow Biz   Ski resorts' costs of making snow are in the millions of dollars for equipment alone. Snowmaking involves spraying droplets of water into the air, causing them to freeze and come down as snow. Making snow can cost more than $2,000 an hour. Snowmaking accounts for 40 to 50 percent of the operating budgets for many ski resorts.

Example: Assume a company's sales force receives a bonus when sales exceed the budgeted amount. How would this arrangement affect the bottom-up process of sales forecasts? *Answer:* Sales reps may understate their budgeted sales.

To illustrate, in September 2009, HD sold 700 hockey sticks at $100 per unit. After considering sales predictions and market conditions, HD prepares its sales budget for the next quarter (three months) plus one extra month (see Exhibit 23.6). The sales budget includes January 2010 because the purchasing department relies on estimated January sales to decide on December 2009 inventory purchases. The sales budget in Exhibit 23.6 includes forecasts of both unit sales and unit prices. Some sales budgets are expressed only in total sales dollars, but most are more detailed. Management finds it useful to know budgeted units and unit prices for many different products, regions, departments, and sales representatives.

EXHIBIT 23.6

Sales Budget for Planned Unit and Dollar Sales

HOCKEY DEN Monthly Sales Budget October 2009–January 2010			
	Budgeted Unit Sales	Budgeted Unit Price	Budgeted Total Sales
September 2009 (actual)	700	$100	$ 70,000
October 2009	1,000	$100	$100,000
November 2009	800	100	80,000
December 2009	1,400	100	140,000
Totals for the quarter	3,200	100	$320,000
January 2010	900	100	$ 90,000

 ## Decision Maker

Entrepreneur   You run a start-up that manufactures designer clothes. Business is seasonal, and fashions and designs quickly change. How do you prepare reliable annual sales budgets? [Answer—p. 961]

Merchandise Purchases Budget Companies use various methods to help managers make inventory purchasing decisions. These methods recognize that the number of units added to inventory depends on budgeted sales volume. Whether a company manufactures or purchases the product it sells, budgeted future sales volume is the primary factor in most inventory management decisions. A company must also consider its inventory system and other factors that we discuss next.

Just-in-time inventory systems. Managers of *just-in-time* (JIT) inventory systems use sales budgets for short periods (often as few as one or two days) to order just enough merchandise or materials to satisfy the immediate sales demand. This keeps the amount of inventory to a minimum (or zero in an ideal situation). A JIT system minimizes the costs of maintaining inventory, but it is practical only if customers are content to order in advance or if managers can accurately determine short-term sales demand. Suppliers also must be able and willing to ship small quantities regularly and promptly.

Point: Accurate estimates of future sales are crucial in a JIT system.

Safety stock inventory systems. Market conditions and manufacturing processes for some products do not allow use of a just-in-time system. Companies in these cases maintain sufficient inventory to reduce the risk and cost of running short. This practice requires enough purchases to satisfy the budgeted sales amounts and to maintain a **safety stock,** a quantity of inventory that provides protection against lost sales caused by unfulfilled demands from customers or delays in shipments from suppliers.

Merchandise purchases budget preparation. A merchandiser usually expresses a **merchandise purchases budget** in both units and dollars. Exhibit 23.7 shows the general layout for this budget in equation form. If this formula is expressed in units and only one product is involved, we can compute the number of dollars of inventory to be purchased for the budget by multiplying the units to be purchased by the cost per unit.

EXHIBIT 23.7

General Formula for a Merchandise Purchases Budget

To illustrate, after assessing the cost of keeping inventory along with the risk and cost of inventory shortages, HD decided that the number of units in its inventory at each month-end should equal 90% of next month's predicted sales. For example, inventory at the end of October should equal 90% of budgeted November sales, and the November ending inventory should equal 90% of budgeted December sales, and so on. Also, HD's suppliers expect the September 2009 per unit cost of $60 to remain unchanged through January 2010. This information along with knowledge of 900 units in inventory at September 30 (see Exhibit 23.5) allows the company to prepare the merchandise purchases budget shown in Exhibit 23.8.

Example: Assume Hockey Den adopts a JIT system in purchasing merchandise. How will its sales budget differ from its merchandise purchases budget? *Answer:* The two budgets will be similar because future inventory should be near zero.

EXHIBIT 23.8

Merchandise Purchases Budget

HOCKEY DEN Merchandise Purchases Budget October 2009–December 2009	October	November	December
Next month's budgeted sales (units)	800	1,400	900
Ratio of inventory to future sales	× 90%	× 90%	× 90%
Budgeted ending inventory (units)	720	1,260	810
Add budgeted sales (units)	1,000	800	1,400
Required units of available merchandise	1,720	2,060	2,210
Deduct beginning inventory (units)	900	720	1,260
Units to be purchased	820	1,340	950
Budgeted cost per unit	$ 60	$ 60	$ 60
Budgeted cost of merchandise purchases	$49,200	$80,400	$57,000

Example: If ending inventory in Exhibit 23.8 is required to equal 80% of next month's predicted sales, how many units must be purchased each month? *Answer:* Budgeted ending inventory: Oct. = 640 units; Nov. = 1,120 units; Dec. = 720 units. Required purchases: Oct. = 740 units; Nov. = 1,280 units; Dec. = 1,000 units.

The first three lines of HD's merchandise purchases budget determine the required ending inventories (in units). Budgeted unit sales are then added to the desired ending inventory to give the required units of available merchandise. We then subtract beginning inventory to determine the budgeted number of units to be purchased. The last line is the budgeted cost of the purchases, computed by multiplying the number of units to be purchased by the predicted cost per unit.

We already indicated that some budgeting systems describe only the total dollars of budgeted sales. Likewise, a system can express a merchandise purchases budget only in terms of the total cost of merchandise to be purchased, omitting the number of units to be purchased. This method assumes a constant relation between sales and cost of goods sold. HD, for instance, might assume the expected cost of goods sold to be 60% of sales, computed from the budgeted unit cost of $60 and the budgeted sales price of $100. However, it still must consider the effects of changes in beginning and ending inventories in determining the amounts to be purchased.

Selling Expense Budget   The **selling expense budget** is a plan listing the types and amounts of selling expenses expected during the budget period. Its initial responsibility usually rests with the vice president of marketing or an equivalent sales manager. The selling expense budget is normally created to provide sufficient selling expenses to meet sales goals reflected in the sales budget. Predicted selling expenses are based on both the sales budget and the experience of previous periods. After some or all of the master budget is prepared, management might decide that projected sales volume is inadequate. If so, subsequent adjustments in the sales budget can require corresponding adjustments in the selling expense budget.

To illustrate, HD's selling expense budget is in Exhibit 23.9. The firm's selling expenses consist of commissions paid to sales personnel and a $2,000 monthly salary paid to the sales manager. Sales commissions equal 10% of total sales and are paid in the month sales occur. Sales commissions are variable with respect to sales volume, but the sales manager's salary is fixed. No advertising expenses are budgeted for this particular quarter.

EXHIBIT 23.9

Selling Expense Budget

HOCKEY DEN Selling Expense Budget October 2009–December 2009				
	October	November	December	Totals
Budgeted sales	$100,000	$80,000	$140,000	$320,000
Sales commission percent	× 10%	× 10%	× 10%	× 10%
Sales commissions	10,000	8,000	14,000	32,000
Salary for sales manager	2,000	2,000	2,000	6,000
Total selling expenses	$ 12,000	$10,000	$ 16,000	$ 38,000

General and Administrative Expense Budget   The **general and administrative expense budget** plans the predicted operating expenses not included in the selling expenses budget. General and administrative expenses can be either variable or fixed with respect to sales volume. The office manager responsible for general administration often is responsible for preparing the initial general and administrative expense budget.

Interest expense and income tax expense are often classified as general and administrative expenses in published income statements, but normally cannot be planned at this stage of the budgeting process. The prediction of interest expense follows the preparation of the cash budget and the decisions regarding debt. The predicted income tax expense depends on the budgeted amount of pretax income. Both interest and income taxes are usually beyond the control of the office manager. As a result, they are not used in comparison to the budget to evaluate that person's performance.

Exhibit 23.10 shows HD's general and administrative expense budget. It includes salaries of $54,000 per year, or $4,500 per month (paid each month when they are earned). Using information in Exhibit 23.5, the depreciation on equipment is computed as $18,000 per year [($200,000 − $20,000)/10 years], or $1,500 per month ($18,000/12 months).

EXHIBIT 23.10

General and Administrative Expense Budget

HOCKEY DEN General and Administrative Expense Budget October 2009–December 2009				
	October	November	December	Totals
Administrative salaries	$4,500	$4,500	$4,500	$13,500
Depreciation of equipment	1,500	1,500	1,500	4,500
Total general and administrative expenses	$6,000	$6,000	$6,000	$18,000

Example: In Exhibit 23.10, how would a rental agreement of $5,000 per month plus 1% of sales affect the general and administrative expense budget? (Budgeted sales are in Exhibit 23.6.) *Answer: Rent expense:* Oct. = $6,000; Nov. = $5,800; Dec. = $6,400; Total = $18,200; *Revised total general and administrative expenses:* Oct. = $12,000; Nov. = $11,800; Dec. = $12,400; Total = $36,200.

Quick Check
Answers—p. 961

5. What is a master budget?

6. A master budget (a) always includes a manufacturing budget specifying the units to be produced; (b) is prepared with a process starting with the operating budgets and continues with the capital expenditures budget and then financial budgets; or (c) is prepared with a process ending with the sales budget.

7. What are the three primary categories of budgets in the master budget?

8. In preparing monthly budgets for the third quarter, a company budgeted sales of 120 units for July and 140 units for August. Management wants each month's ending inventory to be 60% of next month's sales. The June 30 inventory consists of 50 units. How many units of product for July acquisition should the merchandise purchases budget specify for the third quarter? (a) 84, (b) 120, (c) 154, or (d) 204.

9. How do the operating budgets for merchandisers and manufacturers differ?

10. How does a just-in-time inventory system differ from a safety stock system?

Capital Expenditures Budget

The **capital expenditures budget** lists dollar amounts to be both received from plant asset disposals and spent to purchase additional plant assets to carry out the budgeted business activities. It is usually prepared after the operating budgets. Since a company's plant assets determine its productive capacity, this budget is usually affected by long-range plans for the business. Yet the process of preparing a sales or purchases budget can reveal that the company requires more (or less) capacity, which implies more (or less) plant assets.

Capital budgeting is the process of evaluating and planning for capital (plant asset) expenditures. This is an important management task because these expenditures often involve long-run commitments of large amounts, affect predicted cash flows, and impact future debt and equity financing. This means that the capital expenditures budget is often linked with management's evaluation of the company's ability to take on more debt. We describe capital budgeting in Chapter 25.

Hockey Den does not anticipate disposal of any plant assets through December 2009, but it does plan to acquire additional equipment for $25,000 cash near the end of December 2009. This is the only budgeted capital expenditure from October 2009 through January 2010. Thus, no separate budget is shown. The cash budget in Exhibit 23.11 reflects this $25,000 planned expenditure.

Financial Budgets

After preparing its operating and capital expenditures budgets, a company uses information from these budgets to prepare at least three financial budgets: the cash budget, budgeted income statement, and budgeted balance sheet.

EXHIBIT 23.11

Cash Budget

HOCKEY DEN Cash Budget October 2009–December 2009			
	October	**November**	**December**
Beginning cash balance	$ 20,000	$ 20,000	$ 22,272
Cash receipts from customers (Exhibit 23.12)	82,000	92,000	104,000
Total cash available	102,000	112,000	126,272
Cash disbursements			
Payments for merchandise (Exhibit 23.13)	58,200	49,200	80,400
Sales commissions (Exhibit 23.9)	10,000	8,000	14,000
Salaries			
Sales (Exhibit 23.9)	2,000	2,000	2,000
Administrative (Exhibit 23.10)	4,500	4,500	4,500
Income taxes payable (Exhibit 23.5)	20,000		
Dividends ($150,000 × 2%)		3,000	
Interest on bank loan			
October ($10,000 × 1%)	100		
November ($22,800 × 1%)		228	
Purchase of equipment			25,000
Total cash disbursements	94,800	66,928	125,900
Preliminary cash balance	$ 7,200	$ 45,072	$ 372
Additional loan from bank	12,800		19,628
Repayment of loan to bank		22,800	
Ending cash balance	$ 20,000	$ 22,272	$ 20,000
Loan balance, end of month	$ 22,800	$ 0	$ 19,628

Example: If the minimum ending cash balance in Exhibit 23.11 is changed to $25,000 for each month, what is the projected loan balance at Dec. 31, 2009?

Answer:

Loan balance, Oct. 31	$27,800
November interest	278
November payment	25,022
Loan balance, Nov. 30	2,778
December interest	28
Additional loan in Dec.	21,928
Loan balance, Dec. 31	$24,706

P2	Link both operating and capital expenditures budgets to budgeted financial statements.

Cash Budget   After developing budgets for sales, merchandise purchases, expenses, and capital expenditures, the next step is to prepare the **cash budget,** which shows expected cash inflows and outflows during the budget period. It is especially important to maintain a cash balance necessary to meet ongoing obligations. By preparing a cash budget, management can prearrange loans to cover anticipated cash shortages before they are needed. A cash budget also helps management avoid a cash balance that is too large. Too much cash is undesirable because it earns a relatively low (if any) return.

When preparing a cash budget, we add expected cash receipts to the beginning cash balance and deduct expected cash disbursements. If the expected ending cash balance is inadequate, additional cash requirements appear in the budget as planned increases from short-term loans. If the expected ending cash balance exceeds the desired balance, the excess is used to repay loans or to acquire short-term investments. Information for preparing the cash budget is mainly taken from the operating and capital expenditures budgets.

To illustrate, Exhibit 23.11 presents HD's cash budget. The beginning cash balance for October is taken from the September 30, 2009, balance sheet in Exhibit 23.5. The remainder of this section describes the computations in the cash budget.

We begin with reference to HD's budgeted sales (Exhibit 23.6). Analysis of past sales indicates that 40% of the firm's sales are for cash. The remaining 60% are credit sales; these customers are expected to pay in full in the month following the sales. We now can compute the budgeted cash receipts from customers as shown in Exhibit 23.12. October's budgeted cash receipts consist of $40,000 from expected cash sales ($100,000 × 40%) plus the anticipated collection of $42,000 of accounts receivable from the end of September. Each month's cash receipts from customers are transferred to the second line of Exhibit 23.11.

Next, we see that HD's merchandise purchases are entirely on account. It makes full payment during the month following its purchases. Therefore, cash disbursements for

	September	October	November	December
Sales	$70,000	$100,000	$80,000	$140,000
Less ending accounts receivable (60%)	42,000	60,000	48,000	84,000
Cash receipts from				
Cash sales (40% of sales)		40,000	32,000	56,000
Collections of prior month's receivables		42,000	60,000	48,000
Total cash receipts		$ 82,000	$92,000	$104,000

EXHIBIT 23.12

Computing Budgeted
Cash Receipts

purchases can be computed from the September 30, 2009, balance sheet (Exhibit 23.5) and the merchandise purchases budget (Exhibit 23.8). This computation is shown in Exhibit 23.13.

October payments (September 30 balance)	$58,200
November payments (October purchases)	49,200
December payments (November purchases)	80,400

EXHIBIT 23.13

Computing Cash
Disbursements for Purchases

The monthly budgeted cash disbursements for sales commissions and salaries are taken from the selling expense budget (Exhibit 23.9) and the general and administrative expense budget (Exhibit 23.10). The cash budget is unaffected by depreciation as reported in the general and administrative expenses budget.

Income taxes are due and payable in October as shown in the September 30, 2009, balance sheet (Exhibit 23.5). The cash budget in Exhibit 23.11 shows this $20,000 expected payment in October. Predicted income tax expense for the quarter ending December 31 is 40% of net income and is due in January 2010. It is therefore not reported in the October–December 2009 cash budget but in the budgeted income statement as income tax expense and on the budgeted balance sheet as income tax liability.

Hockey Den also pays a cash dividend equal to 2% of the par value of common stock in the second month of each quarter. The cash budget in Exhibit 23.11 shows a November payment of $3,000 for this purpose (2% of $150,000; see Exhibit 23.5).

Hockey Den has an agreement with its bank that promises additional loans at each month-end, if necessary, to keep a minimum cash balance of $20,000. If the cash balance exceeds $20,000 at a month-end, HD uses the excess to repay loans. Interest is paid at each month-end at the rate of 1% of the beginning balance of these loans. For October, this payment is 1% of the $10,000 amount reported in the balance sheet of Exhibit 23.5. For November, HD expects to pay interest of $228, computed as 1% of the $22,800 expected loan balance at October 31. No interest is budgeted for December because the company expects to repay the loans in full at the end of November. Exhibit 23.11 shows that the October 31 cash balance declines to $7,200 (before any loan-related activity). This amount is less than the $20,000 minimum. Hockey Den will bring this balance up to the minimum by borrowing $12,800 with a short-term note. At the end of November, the budget shows an expected cash balance of $45,072 before any loan activity. This means that HD expects to repay $22,800 of debt. The equipment purchase budgeted for December reduces the expected cash balance to $372, far below the $20,000 minimum. The company expects to borrow $19,628 in that month to reach the minimum desired ending balance.

Example: Give one reason for maintaining a minimum cash balance when the budget shows extra cash is not needed. *Answer:* For unexpected events.

Decision Insight

Netting Cash   The **Hockey Company**—whose brands include CCM, JOFA, and KOHO—reported net cash outflows for investing activities of $32 million. Much of this amount was a prepayment to the NHL for a 10-year license agreement.

Budgeted Income Statement One of the final steps in preparing the master budget is to summarize the income effects. The **budgeted income statement** is a managerial accounting report showing predicted amounts of sales and expenses for the budget period. Information needed for preparing a budgeted income statement is primarily taken from already prepared budgets. The volume of information summarized in the budgeted income statement is so large for some companies that they often use spreadsheets to accumulate the budgeted transactions and classify them by their effects on income. We condense HD's budgeted income statement and show it in Exhibit 23.14. All information in this exhibit is taken from earlier budgets. Also, we now can predict the amount of income tax expense for the quarter, computed as 40% of the budgeted pretax income. This amount is included in the cash budget and/or the budgeted balance sheet as necessary.

EXHIBIT 23.14

Budgeted Income Statement

HOCKEY DEN		
Budgeted Income Statement		
For Three Months Ended December 31, 2009		
Sales (Exhibit 23.6, 3,200 units @ $100)		$320,000
Cost of goods sold (3,200 units @ $60)		192,000
Gross profit		128,000
Operating expenses		
Sales commissions (Exhibit 23.9)	$32,000	
Sales salaries (Exhibit 23.9)	6,000	
Administrative salaries (Exhibit 23.10)	13,500	
Depreciation on equipment (Exhibit 23.10)	4,500	
Interest expense (Exhibit 23.11)	328	56,328
Income before income taxes		71,672
Income tax expense ($71,672 × 40%)		28,669
Net income		$ 43,003

Budgeted Balance Sheet The final step in preparing the master budget is summarizing the company's financial position. The **budgeted balance sheet** shows predicted amounts for the company's assets, liabilities, and equity as of the end of the budget period. HD's budgeted balance sheet in Exhibit 23.15 is prepared using information from the other budgets. The sources of amounts are reported in the notes to the budgeted balance sheet.[1]

Decision Insight

Plan Ahead Most companies allocate dollars based on budgets submitted by department managers. These managers verify the numbers and monitor the budget. Managers must remember, however, that a budget is judged by its success in helping achieve the company's mission. One analogy is that a hiker must know the route to properly plan a hike and monitor hiking progress.

[1] An eight-column spreadsheet, or work sheet, can be used to prepare a budgeted balance sheet (and income statement). The first two columns show the ending balance sheet amounts from the period prior to the budget period. The budgeted transactions and adjustments are entered in the third and fourth columns in the same manner as adjustments are entered on an ordinary work sheet. After all budgeted transactions and adjustments have been entered, the amounts in the first two columns are combined with the budget amounts in the third and fourth columns and sorted to the proper Income Statement (fifth and sixth columns) and Balance Sheet columns (seventh and eighth columns). Amounts in these columns are used to prepare the budgeted income statement and balance sheet.

BIT 23.15**

Budgeted Balance Sheet

HOCKEY DEN
Budgeted Balance Sheet
December 31, 2009

Assets

Cash[a]		$ 20,000
Accounts receivable[b]		84,000
Inventory[c]		48,600
Equipment[d]	$225,000	
Less accumulated depreciation[e]	40,500	184,500
Total assets		$337,100

Liabilities and Equity

Liabilities		
Accounts payable[f]	$ 57,000	
Income taxes payable[g]	28,669	
Bank loan payable[h]	19,628	$105,297
Stockholders' equity		
Common stock[i]	150,000	
Retained earnings[j]	81,803	231,803
Total liabilities and equity		$337,100

[a] Ending balance for December from the cash budget in Exhibit 23.11.
[b] 60% of $140,000 sales budgeted for December from the sales budget in Exhibit 23.6.
[c] 810 units in budgeted December ending inventory at the budgeted cost of $60 per unit (from the purchases budget in Exhibit 23.8).
[d] September 30 balance of $200,000 from the beginning balance sheet in Exhibit 23.5 plus $25,000 cost of new equipment from the cash budget in Exhibit 23.11.
[e] September 30 balance of $36,000 from the beginning balance sheet in Exhibit 23.5 plus $4,500 expense from the general and administrative expense budget in Exhibit 23.10.
[f] Budgeted cost of purchases for December from the purchases budget in Exhibit 23.8.
[g] Income tax expense from the budgeted income statement for the fourth quarter in Exhibit 23.14.
[h] Budgeted December 31 balance from the cash budget in Exhibit 23.11.
[i] Unchanged from the beginning balance sheet in Exhibit 23.5.
[j] September 30 balance of $41,800 from the beginning balance sheet in Exhibit 23.5 plus budgeted net income of $43,003 from the budgeted income statement in Exhibit 23.14 minus budgeted cash dividends of $3,000 from the cash budget in Exhibit 23.11.

Quick Check
Answers—p. 961

11. In preparing a budgeted balance sheet, (a) plant assets are determined by analyzing the capital expenditures budget and the balance sheet from the beginning of the budget period, (b) liabilities are determined by analyzing the general and administrative expense budget, or (c) retained earnings are determined from information contained in the cash budget and the balance sheet from the beginning of the budget period.

12. What sequence is followed in preparing the budgets that constitute the master budget?

Activity-Based Budgeting
Decision Analysis

Activity-based budgeting (ABB) is a budget system based on expected activities. Knowledge of expected activities and their levels for the budget period enables management to plan for resources required to perform the activities. To illustrate, we consider the budget of a company's accounting department. Traditional budgeting systems list items such as salaries, supplies, equipment, and utilities. Such an itemized budget informs management of the use of the funds budgeted (for example, salaries), but management cannot assess the basis for increases or decreases in budgeted amounts as compared to prior periods. Accordingly, management often makes across-the-board cuts or increases. In contrast, ABB requires management to list activities performed by, say, the accounting department such as auditing, tax reporting, financial reporting, and cost accounting. Exhibit 23.16 contrasts a traditional budget with an activity-based budget for a company's accounting department. An understanding of the resources required to perform the activities, the costs associated with these resources,

A1 Analyze expense planning using activity-based budgeting.

EXHIBIT 23.16

Activity-Based Budgeting versus Traditional Budgeting (for an accounting department)

Activity-Based Budget		Traditional Budget	
Auditing	$ 58,000	Salaries	$152,000
Tax reporting	71,000	Supplies	22,000
Financial reporting	63,000	Depreciation	36,000
Cost accounting	32,000	Utilities	14,000
Total	$224,000	Total	$224,000

and the way resource use changes with changes in activity levels allows management to better assess how expenses will change to accommodate changes in activity levels. Moreover, by knowing the relation between activities and costs, management can attempt to reduce costs by eliminating nonvalue-added activities.

 Decision Maker

Environmental Manager You hold the new position of environmental control manager for a chemical company. You are asked to develop a budget for your job and identify job responsibilities. How do you proceed? [Answer—p. 961]

Demonstration Problem

DP23

Wild Wood Company's management asks you to prepare its master budget using the following information. The budget is to cover the months of April, May, and June of 2009.

WILD WOOD COMPANY
Balance Sheet
March 31, 2009

Assets		Liabilities and Equity	
Cash	$ 50,000	Accounts payable	$156,000
Accounts receivable	175,000	Short-term notes payable	12,000
Inventory	126,000	Total current liabilities	168,000
Total current assets	351,000	Long-term note payable	200,000
Equipment, gross	480,000	Total liabilities	368,000
Accumulated depreciation	(90,000)	Common stock	235,000
Equipment, net	390,000	Retained earnings	138,000
		Total stockholders' equity	373,000
Total assets	$741,000	Total liabilities and equity	$741,000

Additional Information

a. Sales for March total 10,000 units. Each month's sales are expected to exceed the prior month's results by 5%. The product's selling price is $25 per unit.

b. Company policy calls for a given month's ending inventory to equal 80% of the next month's expected unit sales. The March 31 inventory is 8,400 units, which complies with the policy. The purchase price is $15 per unit.

c. Sales representatives' commissions are 12.5% of sales and are paid in the month of the sales. The sales manager's monthly salary will be $3,500 in April and $4,000 per month thereafter.

d. Monthly general and administrative expenses include $8,000 administrative salaries, $5,000 depreciation, and 0.9% monthly interest on the long-term note payable.

e. The company expects 30% of sales to be for cash and the remaining 70% on credit. Receivables are collected in full in the month following the sale (none is collected in the month of the sale).

f. All merchandise purchases are on credit, and no payables arise from any other transactions. One month's purchases are fully paid in the next month.

g. The minimum ending cash balance for all months is $50,000. If necessary, the company borrows enough cash using a short-term note to reach the minimum. Short-term notes require an interest payment of 1% at each month-end (before any repayment). If the ending cash balance exceeds the minimum, the excess will be applied to repaying the short-term notes payable balance.

h. Dividends of $100,000 are to be declared and paid in May.

i. No cash payments for income taxes are to be made during the second calendar quarter. Income taxes will be assessed at 35% in the quarter.

j. Equipment purchases of $55,000 are scheduled for June.

Required

Prepare the following budgets and other financial information as required:

1. Sales budget, including budgeted sales for July.
2. Purchases budget, the budgeted cost of goods sold for each month and quarter, and the cost of the June 30 budgeted inventory.
3. Selling expense budget.
4. General and administrative expense budget.
5. Expected cash receipts from customers and the expected June 30 balance of accounts receivable.
6. Expected cash payments for purchases and the expected June 30 balance of accounts payable.
7. Cash budget.
8. Budgeted income statement.
9. Budgeted statement of retained earnings.
10. Budgeted balance sheet.

Planning the Solution

- The sales budget shows expected sales for each month in the quarter. Start by multiplying March sales by 105% and then do the same for the remaining months. July's sales are needed for the purchases budget. To complete the budget, multiply the expected unit sales by the selling price of $25 per unit.

- Use these results and the 80% inventory policy to budget the size of ending inventory for April, May, and June. Add the budgeted sales to these numbers and subtract the actual or expected beginning inventory for each month. The result is the number of units to be purchased each month. Multiply these numbers by the per unit cost of $15. Find the budgeted cost of goods sold by multiplying the unit sales in each month by the $15 cost per unit. Compute the cost of the June 30 ending inventory by multiplying the expected units available at that date by the $15 cost per unit.

- The selling expense budget has only two items. Find the amount of the sales representatives' commissions by multiplying the expected dollar sales in each month by the 12.5% commission rate. Then include the sales manager's salary of $3,500 in April and $4,000 in May and June.

- The general and administrative expense budget should show three items. Administrative salaries are fixed at $8,000 per month, and depreciation is $5,000 per month. Budget the monthly interest expense on the long-term note by multiplying its $200,000 balance by the 0.9% monthly interest rate.

- Determine the amounts of cash sales in each month by multiplying the budgeted sales by 30%. Add to this amount the credit sales of the prior month (computed as 70% of prior month's sales). April's cash receipts from collecting receivables equals the March 31 balance of $175,000. The expected June 30 accounts receivable balance equals 70% of June's total budgeted sales.

- Determine expected cash payments on accounts payable for each month by making them equal to the merchandise purchases in the prior month. The payments for April equal the March 31 balance of accounts payable shown on the beginning balance sheet. The June 30 balance of accounts payable equals merchandise purchases for June.

- Prepare the cash budget by combining the given information and the amounts of cash receipts and cash payments on account that you computed. Complete the cash budget for each month by either borrowing enough to raise the preliminary balance to the minimum or paying off short-term debt as much as the balance allows without falling below the minimum. Show the ending balance of the short-term note in the budget.

- Prepare the budgeted income statement by combining the budgeted items for all three months. Determine the income before income taxes and multiply it by the 35% rate to find the quarter's income tax expense.

- The budgeted statement of retained earnings should show the March 31 balance plus the quarter's net income minus the quarter's dividends.

- The budgeted balance sheet includes updated balances for all items that appear in the beginning balance sheet and an additional liability for unpaid income taxes. Amounts for all asset, liability, and equity accounts can be found either in the budgets, other calculations, or by adding amounts found there to the beginning balances.

Solution to Demonstration Problem

1. Sales budget

	April	May	June	July
Prior period's unit sales	10,000	10,500	11,025	11,576
Plus 5% growth	500	525	551	579
Projected unit sales	10,500	11,025	11,576	12,155

	April	May	June	Quarter
Projected unit sales	10,500	11,025	11,576	
Selling price per unit	× $25	× $25	× $25	
Projected sales	$262,500	$275,625	$289,400	$827,525

2. Purchases budget

	April	May	June	Quarter
Next period's unit sales (part 1)	11,025	11,576	12,155	
Ending inventory percent	× 80%	× 80%	× 80%	
Desired ending inventory	8,820	9,261	9,724	
Current period's unit sales (part 1)	10,500	11,025	11,576	
Units to be available	19,320	20,286	21,300	
Less beginning inventory	8,400	8,820	9,261	
Units to be purchased	10,920	11,466	12,039	
Budgeted cost per unit	× $15	× $15	× $15	
Projected purchases	$163,800	$171,990	$180,585	$516,375

Budgeted cost of goods sold

	April	May	June	Quarter
This period's unit sales (part 1)	10,500	11,025	11,576	
Budgeted cost per unit	× $15	× $15	× $15	
Projected cost of goods sold	$157,500	$165,375	$173,640	$496,515

Budgeted inventory for June 30

Units (part 2)	9,724
Cost per unit	× $15
Total	$145,860

3. Selling expense budget

	April	May	June	Quarter
Budgeted sales (part 1)	$262,500	$275,625	$289,400	$827,525
Commission percent	× 12.5%	× 12.5%	× 12.5%	× 12.5%
Sales commissions	32,813	34,453	36,175	103,441
Manager's salary	3,500	4,000	4,000	11,500
Projected selling expenses	$ 36,313	$ 38,453	$ 40,175	$114,941

4. General and administrative expense budget

	April	May	June	Quarter
Administrative salaries	$ 8,000	$ 8,000	$ 8,000	$24,000
Depreciation	5,000	5,000	5,000	15,000
Interest on long-term note payable (0.9% × $200,000)	1,800	1,800	1,800	5,400
Projected expenses	$14,800	$14,800	$14,800	$44,400

5. Expected cash receipts from customers

	April	May	June	Quarter
Budgeted sales (part 1)	$262,500	$275,625	$289,400	
Ending accounts receivable (70%)	$183,750	$192,938	$202,580	
Cash receipts				
Cash sales (30%)	$ 78,750	$ 82,687	$ 86,820	$248,257
Collections of prior period's receivables	175,000	183,750	192,938	551,688
Total cash to be collected	$253,750	$266,437	$279,758	$799,945

6. Expected cash payments to suppliers

	April	May	June	Quarter
Cash payments (equal to prior period's purchases)	$156,000	$163,800	$171,990	$491,790
Expected June 30 balance of accounts payable (June purchases)			$180,585	

7. Cash budget

	April	May	June
Beginning cash balance	$ 50,000	$ 89,517	$ 50,000
Cash receipts (part 5)	253,750	266,437	279,758
Total cash available	303,750	355,954	329,758
Cash payments			
Payments for merchandise (part 6)	156,000	163,800	171,990
Sales commissions (part 3)	32,813	34,453	36,175
Salaries			
Sales (part 3)	3,500	4,000	4,000
Administrative (part 4)	8,000	8,000	8,000
Interest on long-term note (part 4)	1,800	1,800	1,800
Dividends		100,000	
Equipment purchase			55,000
Interest on short-term notes			
April ($12,000 × 1.0%)	120		
June ($6,099 × 1.0%)			61
Total cash payments	202,233	312,053	277,026
Preliminary balance	101,517	43,901	52,732
Additional loan		6,099	
Loan repayment	(12,000)		(2,732)
Ending cash balance	$ 89,517	$ 50,000	$ 50,000
Ending short-term notes	$ 0	$ 6,099	$ 3,367

8.

WILD WOOD COMPANY
Budgeted Income Statement
For Quarter Ended June 30, 2009

Sales (part 1)		$ 827,525
Cost of goods sold (part 2)		496,515
Gross profit		331,010
Operating expenses		
Sales commissions (part 3)	$103,441	
Sales salaries (part 3)	11,500	
Administrative salaries (part 4)	24,000	
Depreciation (part 4)	15,000	
Interest on long-term note (part 4)	5,400	
Interest on short-term notes (part 7)	181	
Total operating expenses		159,522
Income before income taxes		171,488
Income taxes (35%)		60,021
Net income		$ 111,467

9.

WILD WOOD COMPANY
Budgeted Statement of Retained Earnings
For Quarter Ended June 30, 2009

Beginning retained earnings (given)	$138,000
Net income (part 8)	111,467
	249,467
Less cash dividends (given)	100,000
Ending retained earnings	$149,467

10.

WILD WOOD COMPANY
Budgeted Balance Sheet
June 30, 2009

Assets		
Cash (part 7)		$ 50,000
Accounts receivable (part 5)		202,580
Inventory (part 2)		145,860
Total current assets		398,440
Equipment (given plus purchase)	$535,000	
Less accumulated depreciation (given plus expense)	105,000	430,000
Total assets		$828,440
Liabilities and Equity		
Accounts payable (part 6)		$180,585
Short-term notes payable (part 7)		3,367
Income taxes payable (part 8)		60,021
Total current liabilities		243,973
Long-term note payable (given)		200,000
Total liabilities		443,973
Common stock (given)		235,000
Retained earnings (part 9)		149,467
Total stockholders' equity		384,467
Total liabilities and equity		$828,440

Production and Manufacturing Budgets

23A

Unlike a merchandising company, a manufacturer must prepare a **production budget** instead of a merchandise purchases budget. A production budget, which shows the number of units to be produced each month, is similar to merchandise purchases budgets except that the number of units to be purchased each month (as shown in Exhibit 23.8) is replaced by the number of units to be manufactured each month. A production budget does not show costs; it is *always expressed in units of product*. Exhibit 23A.1 shows the production budget for **Toronto Sticks Company (TSC),** a manufacturer of hockey sticks. TSC is an exclusive supplier of hockey sticks to Hockey Den, meaning that TSC uses HD's budgeted sales figures (Exhibit 23.6) to determine its production and manufacturing budgets.

P3 Prepare production and manufacturing budgets.

EXHIBIT 23A.1

Production Budget

TSC Production Budget October 2009–December 2009	October	November	December
Next period's budgeted sales (units)	800	1,400	900
Ratio of inventory to future sales	× 90%	× 90%	× 90%
Budgeted ending inventory (units)	720	1,260	810
Add budgeted sales for the period (units)	1,000	800	1,400
Required units of available production	1,720	2,060	2,210
Deduct beginning inventory (units)	(900)	(720)	(1,260)
Units to be produced	820	1,340	950

A **manufacturing budget** shows the budgeted costs for direct materials, direct labor, and overhead. It is based on the budgeted production volume from the production budget. The manufacturing budget for most companies consists of three individual budgets: direct materials budget, direct labor budget, and overhead budget. Exhibits 23A.2–23A.4 show these three manufacturing budgets for TSC. These budgets yield the total expected cost of goods to be manufactured in the budget period.

The *direct materials budget* is driven by the budgeted materials needed to satisfy each month's production requirement. To this we must add the desired ending inventory requirements. The desired ending inventory of direct materials as shown in Exhibit 23A.2 is 50% of next month's budgeted materials requirements of wood. For instance, in October 2009, an ending inventory of 335 units of material is desired (50% of November's 670 units). The desired ending inventory for December 2009 is 225 units,

EXHIBIT 23A.2

Direct Materials Budget

TSC Direct Materials Budget October 2009–December 2009	October	November	December
Budget production (units)	820	1,340	950
Materials requirements per unit	× 0.5	× 0.5	× 0.5
Materials needed for production (units)	410	670	475
Add budgeted ending inventory (units)	335	237.5	225
Total materials requirements (units)	745	907.5	700
Deduct beginning inventory (units)	(205)	(335)	(237.5)
Materials to be purchased (units)	540	572.5	462.5
Material price per unit	$ 20	$ 20	$ 20
Total cost of direct materials purchases	$10,800	$11,450	$9,250

computed from the direct material requirement of 450 units for a production level of 900 units in January 2010. The total materials requirements are computed by adding the desired ending inventory figures to that month's budgeted production material requirements. For October 2009, the total materials requirement is 745 units (335 + 410). From the total materials requirement, we then subtract the units of materials available in beginning inventory. For October 2009, the materials available from September 2009 are computed as 50% of October's materials requirements to satisfy production, or 205 units (50% of 410). Therefore, direct materials purchases in October 2009 are budgeted at 540 units (745 − 205). See Exhibit 23A.2.

TSC's *direct labor budget* is shown in Exhibit 23A.3. About 15 minutes of labor time is required to produce one unit. Labor is paid at the rate of $12 per hour. Budgeted labor hours are computed by multiplying the budgeted production level for each month by one-quarter (0.25) of an hour. Direct labor cost is then computed by multiplying budgeted labor hours by the labor rate of $12 per hour.

EXHIBIT 23A.3

Direct Labor Budget

TSC
Direct Labor Budget
October 2009–December 2009

	October	November	December
Budgeted production (units)	820	1,340	950
Labor requirements per unit (hours)	× 0.25	× 0.25	× 0.25
Total labor hours needed	205	335	237.5
Labor rate (per hour)	$ 12	$ 12	$ 12
Labor dollars	$2,460	$4,020	$2,850

TSC's *factory overhead budget* is shown in Exhibit 23A.4. The variable portion of overhead is assigned at the rate of $2.50 per unit of production. The fixed portion stays constant at $1,500 per month. The budget in Exhibit 23A.4 is in condensed form; most overhead budgets are more detailed, listing each overhead cost item.

EXHIBIT 23A.4

Factory Overhead Budget

TSC
Factory Overhead Budget
October 2009–December 2009

	October	November	December
Budgeted production (units)	820	1,340	950
Variable factory overhead rate	× $2.50	× $2.50	× $2.50
Budgeted variable overhead	2,050	3,350	2,375
Budgeted fixed overhead	1,500	1,500	1,500
Budgeted total overhead	$3,550	$4,850	$3,875

Summary

C1 Describe the importance and benefits of budgeting.
Planning is a management responsibility of critical importance to business success. Budgeting is the process management uses to formalize its plans. Budgeting promotes management analysis and focuses its attention on the future. Budgeting also provides a basis for evaluating performance, serves as a source of motivation, is a means of coordinating activities, and communicates management's plans and instructions to employees.

C2 Explain the process of budget administration. Budgeting is a detailed activity that requires administration. At least three aspects are important: budget committee, budget reporting, and budget timing. A budget committee oversees the budget preparation. The budget period pertains to the time period for which the budget is prepared such as a year or month.

C3 Describe a master budget and the process of preparing it.
A master budget is a formal overall plan for a company. It consists of plans for business operations and capital expenditures, plus the financial results of those activities. The budgeting process begins with a sales budget. Based on expected sales volume, companies can budget purchases, selling expenses, and administrative expenses. Next, the capital expenditures budget is prepared, followed by the cash budget and budgeted financial statements. Manufacturers also must budget production quantities, materials purchases, labor costs, and overhead.

A1 Analyze expense planning using activity-based budgeting.
Activity-based budgeting requires management to identify activities performed by departments, plan necessary activity levels, identify resources required to perform these activities, and budget the resources.

P1 **Prepare each component of a master budget and link each to the budgeting process.** The term *master budget* refers to a collection of individual component budgets. Each component budget is designed to guide persons responsible for activities covered by that component. A master budget must reflect the components of a company and their interaction in pursuit of company goals.

P2 **Link both operating and capital expenditures budgets to budgeted financial statements.** The operating budgets, capital expenditures budget, and cash budget contain much of the infor-

mation to prepare a budgeted income statement for the budget period and a budgeted balance sheet at the end of the budget period. Budgeted financial statements show the expected financial consequences of the planned activities described in the budgets.

P3 **Prepare production and manufacturing budgets.** A manufacturer must prepare a *production budget* instead of a purchases budget. A *manufacturing budget* shows the budgeted production costs for direct materials, direct labor, and overhead.

Guidance Answers to **Decision Maker** and **Decision Ethics**

Budget Staffer Your superior's actions appear unethical because she is using private information for personal gain. As a budget staffer, you are low in the company's hierarchical structure and probably unable to confront this superior directly. You should inform an individual with a position of authority within the organization about your concerns.

Entrepreneur You must deal with two issues. First, because fashions and designs frequently change, you cannot heavily rely on previous budgets. As a result, you must carefully analyze the market to understand what designs are in vogue. This will help you plan the product mix and estimate demand. The second issue is the

budgeting period. An annual sales budget may be unreliable because tastes can quickly change. Your best bet might be to prepare monthly and quarterly sales budgets that you continuously monitor and revise.

Environmental Manager You are unlikely to have data on this new position to use in preparing your budget. In this situation, you can use activity-based budgeting. This requires developing a list of activities to conduct, the resources required to perform these activities, and the expenses associated with these resources. You should challenge yourself to be absolutely certain that the listed activities are necessary and that the listed resources are required.

Guidance Answers to **Quick Checks**

1. Major benefits include promoting a focus on the future; providing a basis for evaluating performance; providing a source of motivation; coordinating the departments of a business; and communicating plans and instructions.

2. The budget committee's responsibility is to provide guidance to ensure that budget figures are realistic and coordinated.

3. Budget periods usually coincide with accounting periods and therefore cover a month, quarter, or a year. Budgets can also be prepared for longer time periods, such as five years.

4. Rolling budgets are budgets that are periodically revised in the ongoing process of continuous budgeting.

5. A master budget is a comprehensive or overall plan for the company that is generally expressed in monetary terms.

6. *b*

7. The master budget includes operating budgets, the capital expenditures budget, and financial budgets.

8. *c*; Computed as $(60\% \times 140) + 120 - 50 = 154$.

9. Merchandisers prepare merchandise purchases budgets; manufacturers prepare production and manufacturing budgets.

10. A just-in-time system keeps the level of inventory to a minimum and orders merchandise or materials to meet immediate sales demand. A safety stock system maintains an inventory that is large enough to meet sales demands plus an amount to satisfy unexpected sales demands and an amount to cover delayed shipments from suppliers.

11. *a*

12. (a) Operating budgets (such as sales, selling expense, and administrative budgets), (b) capital expenditures budget, (c) financial budgets: cash budget, budgeted income statement, and budgeted balance sheet.

 **Key Terms** **mhhe.com/wildFAP19e**

Key Terms are available at the book's Website for learning and testing in an online Flashcard Format.

Activity-based budgeting (ABB) (p. 953)
Budget (p. 940)
Budgeted balance sheet (p. 952)
Budgeted income statement (p. 952)
Budgeting (p. 940)
Capital expenditures budget (p. 949)

Cash budget (p. 950)
Continuous budgeting (p. 942)
General and administrative expense budget (p. 948)
Manufacturing budget (p. 959)
Master budget (p. 944)

Merchandise purchases budget (p. 947)
Production budget (p. 959)
Rolling budgets (p. 942)
Safety stock (p. 947)
Sales budget (p. 946)
Selling expense budget (p. 948)

Multiple Choice Quiz　　　Answers on p. 977　　　mhhe.com/wildFAP19e

Additional Quiz Questions are available at the book's Website.

Quiz23

1. A plan that reports the units or costs of merchandise to be purchased by a merchandising company during the budget period is called a
 a. Capital expenditures budget.
 b. Cash budget.
 c. Merchandise purchases budget.
 d. Selling expenses budget.
 e. Sales budget.

2. A hardware store has budgeted sales of $36,000 for its power tool department in July. Management wants to have $7,000 in power tool inventory at the end of July. Its beginning inventory of power tools is expected to be $6,000. What is the budgeted dollar amount of merchandise purchases?
 a. $36,000
 b. $43,000
 c. $42,000
 d. $35,000
 e. $37,000

3. A store has the following budgeted sales for the next five months.

May	$210,000
June	186,000
July	180,000
August	220,000
September	240,000

Cash sales are 25% of total sales and all credit sales are expected to be collected in the month following the sale. The total amount of cash expected to be received from customers in September is

 a. $240,000
 b. $225,000
 c. $ 60,000
 d. $165,000
 e. $220,000

4. A plan that shows the expected cash inflows and cash outflows during the budget period, including receipts from loans needed to maintain a minimum cash balance and repayments of such loans, is called
 a. A rolling budget.
 b. An income statement.
 c. A balance sheet.
 d. A cash budget.
 e. An operating budget.

5.[A] The following sales are predicted for a company's next four months.

	September	October	November	December
Unit sales . .	480	560	600	480

Each month's ending inventory of finished goods should be 30% of the next month's sales. At September 1, the finished goods inventory is 140 units. The budgeted production of units for October is
 a. 572 units.
 b. 560 units.
 c. 548 units.
 d. 600 units.
 e. 180 units.

Superscript letter [A] *denotes assignments based on Appendix 23A.*

Discussion Questions

1. ♟Identify at least three roles that budgeting plays in helping managers control and monitor a business.

2. What two common benchmarks can be used to evaluate actual performance? Which of the two is generally more useful?

3. ♟What is the benefit of continuous budgeting?

4. Identify three usual time horizons for short-term planning and budgets.

5. ♟Why should each department participate in preparing its own budget?

6. ♟How does budgeting help management coordinate and plan business activities?

7. ♟Why is the sales budget so important to the budgeting process?

8. What is a selling expense budget? What is a capital expenditures budget?

9. Budgeting promotes good decision making by requiring managers to conduct _____ and by focusing their attention on the _____.

10. What is a cash budget? Why must operating budgets and the capital expenditures budget be prepared before the cash budget?

11.[A] What is the difference between a production budget and a manufacturing budget?

12. ♟Would a manager of a **Best Buy** retail store participate more in budgeting than a manager at the corporate offices? Explain.

13. ♟Does the manager of a local **Circuit City** retail store participate in long-term budgeting? Explain.

14. ♟Assume that **Apple**'s iMac division is charged with preparing a master budget. Identify the participants— for example, the sales manager for the sales budget— and describe the information each person provides in preparing the master budget.

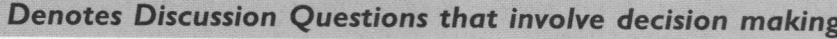

♟ **Denotes Discussion Questions that involve decision making.**

Which one of the following sets of items are all necessary components of the master budget?

1. Prior sales reports, capital expenditures budget, and financial budgets.

2. Sales budget, operating budgets, and historical financial budgets.

3. Operating budgets, financial budgets, and capital expenditures budget.

4. Operating budgets, historical income statement, and budgeted balance sheet.

QUICK STUDY

QS 23-1
Components of a master budget
C3

The motivation of employees is one goal of budgeting. Identify three guidelines that organizations should follow if budgeting is to serve effectively as a source of motivation for employees.

QS 23-2
Budget motivation C1

Brill Company's July sales budget calls for sales of $800,000. The store expects to begin July with $30,000 of inventory and to end the month with $35,000 of inventory. Gross margin is typically 40% of sales. Determine the budgeted cost of merchandise purchases for July.

QS 23-3
Purchases budget P1

Good management includes good budgeting. (1) Explain why the bottom-up approach to budgeting is considered a more successful management technique than a top-down approach. (2) Provide an example of implementation of the bottom-up approach to budgeting.

QS 23-4
Budgeting process C2 ♟

RedTop Company anticipates total sales for June and July of $540,000 and $472,000, respectively. Cash sales are normally 30% of total sales. Of the credit sales, 25% are collected in the same month as the sale, 70% are collected during the first month after the sale, and the remaining 5% are collected in the second month. Determine the amount of accounts receivable reported on the company's budgeted balance sheet as of July 31.

QS 23-5
Computing budgeted accounts receivable
P2

Use the following information to prepare a cash budget for the month ended on March 31 for Grant Company. The budget should show expected cash receipts and cash disbursements for the month of March and the balance expected on March 31.

a. Beginning cash balance on March 1, $75,000.

b. Cash receipts from sales, $315,000.

c. Budgeted cash disbursements for purchases, $204,000.

d. Budgeted cash disbursements for salaries, $90,000.

e. Other budgeted cash expenses, $30,000.

f. Cash repayment of bank loan, $25,000.

QS 23-6
Cash budget
P1 P2

Activity-based budgeting is a budget system based on *expected activities*. (1) Describe activity-based budgeting, and explain its preparation of budgets. (2) How does activity-based budgeting differ from traditional budgeting?

QS 23-7
Activity-based budgeting
A1 ♟

Luna Company manufactures watches and has a JIT policy that ending inventory must equal 8% of the next month's sales. It estimates that October's actual ending inventory will consist of 24,000 watches. November and December sales are estimated to be 300,000 and 250,000 watches, respectively. Compute the number of watches to be produced that would appear on the company's production budget for the month of November.

QS 23-8[A]
Production budget
P3

Refer to information from QS 23-8[A]. Luna Company assigns variable overhead at the rate of $1.75 per unit of production. Fixed overhead equals $5,000,000 per month. Prepare a factory overhead budget for November.

QS 23-9[A]
Factory overhead budget P3

Tech-Cam sells miniature digital cameras for $800 each. 450 units were sold in May, and it forecasts 2% growth in unit sales each month. Determine (a) the number of camera sales and (b) the dollar amount of camera sales for the month of June.

QS 23-10
Sales budget P1

QS 23-11
Selling expense budget   P1

Refer to information from QS 23-10. Tech-Cam pays a sales manager a monthly salary of $3,000 and a commission of 7.5% of camera sales (in dollars). Prepare a selling expense budget for the month of June.

QS 23-12
Cash budget   P1

Refer to information from QS 23-10. Assume 30% of Tech-Cam's sales are for cash. The remaining 70% are credit sales; these customers pay in the month following the sale. Compute the budgeted cash receipts for June.

QS 23-13
Budgeted financial statements
P2

Following are selected accounts for a company. For each account, indicate whether it will appear on a budgeted income statement (BIS) or a budgeted balance sheet (BBS). If an item will not appear on either budgeted financial statement, label it NA.

Sales . . . .   _____
Administrative salaries paid . . . .   _____
Accumulated depreciation . . . .   _____
Depreciation expense . . . .   _____
Interest paid on bank loan   . . . .   _____
Cash dividends paid . . . .   _____
Bank loan owed . . . .   _____

Available with McGraw-Hill's Homework Manager

EXERCISES

Exercise 23-1
Preparation of merchandise purchases budgets (for three periods)
C3 P1

Check July budgeted ending inventory, 64,000

Troy Company prepares monthly budgets. The current budget plans for a September ending inventory of 38,000 units. Company policy is to end each month with merchandise inventory equal to a specified percent of budgeted sales for the following month. Budgeted sales and merchandise purchases for the three most recent months follow. (1) Prepare the merchandise purchases budget for the months of July, August, and September. (2) Compute the ratio of ending inventory to the next month's sales for each budget prepared in part 1. (3) How many units are budgeted for sale in October?

	Sales (Units)	Purchases (Units)
July	170,000	200,000
August	320,000	312,000
September	280,000	262,000

Exercise 23-2
Preparation of cash budgets (for three periods)
C3 P2

Franke Co. budgeted the following cash receipts and cash disbursements for the first three months of next year.

	Cash Receipts	Cash Disbursements
January	$525,000	$484,000
February	411,000	350,000
March	456,000	520,000

Check January ending cash balance, $20,600

According to a credit agreement with the company's bank, Franke promises to have a minimum cash balance of $20,000 at each month-end. In return, the bank has agreed that the company can borrow up to $160,000 at an annual interest rate of 12%, paid on the last day of each month. The interest is computed based on the beginning balance of the loan for the month. The company has a cash balance of $20,000 and a loan balance of $40,000 at January 1. Prepare monthly cash budgets for each of the first three months of next year.

Exercise 23-3
Preparation of a cash budget
C3 P2

Use the following information to prepare the July cash budget for Anker Co. It should show expected cash receipts and cash disbursements for the month and the cash balance expected on July 31.

a. Beginning cash balance on July 1: $63,000.

b. Cash receipts from sales: 30% is collected in the month of sale, 50% in the next month, and 20% in the second month after sale (uncollectible accounts are negligible and can be ignored). Sales amounts are: May (actual), $1,700,000; June (actual), $1,200,000; and July (budgeted), $1,400,000.

c. Payments on merchandise purchases: 90% in the month of purchase and 10% in the month following purchase. Purchases amounts are: June (actual), $620,000; and July (budgeted), $790,000.

d. Budgeted cash disbursements for salaries in July: $220,000.

e. Budgeted depreciation expense for July: $11,000.

f. Other cash expenses budgeted for July: $230,000.

g. Accrued income taxes due in July: $50,000.

h. Bank loan interest due in July: $7,000.

Check   Ending cash balance, $143,000

Use the information in Exercise 23-3 and the following additional information to prepare a budgeted income statement for the month of July and a budgeted balance sheet for July 31.

a. Cost of goods sold is 60% of sales.

b. Inventory at the end of June is $80,000 and at the end of July is $30,000.

c. Salaries payable on June 30 are $50,000 and are expected to be $60,000 on July 31.

d. The equipment account balance is $1,600,000 on July 31. On June 30, the accumulated depreciation on equipment is $280,000.

e. The $7,000 cash payment of interest represents the 1% monthly expense on a bank loan of $700,000.

f. Income taxes payable on July 31 are $24,600, and the income tax rate applicable to the company is 30%.

g. The only other balance sheet accounts are: Common Stock, with a balance of $850,000 on June 30; and Retained Earnings, with a balance of $931,000 on June 30.

Exercise 23-4
Preparing a budgeted income statement and balance sheet

C3 P2

Check   Net income, $57,400; Total assets, $2,702,000

DeVon Company's cost of goods sold is consistently $30 per unit. The company plans to carry ending merchandise inventory for each month equal to 20% of the next month's budgeted unit sales; August beginning inventory is 2,000 units. All merchandise is purchased on credit, and 40% of the purchases made during a month is paid for in that month. Another 25% is paid for during the first month after purchase, and the remaining 35% is paid for during the second month after purchase. Expected unit sales are: August (actual), 10,000; September (actual), 9,500; October (estimated), 8,750; November (estimated), 8,250. Use this information to determine October's expected cash payments for purchases. (*Hint:* Use the layout of Exhibit 23.8, but revised for the facts given here.)

Exercise 23-5
Computing budgeted cash payments for purchases

C3 P2

Check   Budgeted purchases: August, $297,000; October, $259,500

Dollar Value Company purchases all merchandise on credit. It recently budgeted the following month-end accounts payable balances and merchandise inventory balances. Cash payments on accounts payable during each month are expected to be: May, $1,500,000; June, $1,530,000; July, $1,350,000; and August, $1,495,000. Use the available information to compute the budgeted amounts of (1) merchandise purchases for June, July, and August, and (2) cost of goods sold for June, July, and August.

Exercise 23-6
Computing budgeted purchases and costs of goods sold

C3 P1 P2

	Accounts Payable	Merchandise Inventory
May 31	$120,000	$250,000
June 30	170,000	200,000
July 31	300,000	250,000
August 31	150,000	350,000

Check   June purchases, $1,580,000; June cost of goods sold, $1,630,000

E-Sound, a merchandising company specializing in home computer speakers, budgets its monthly cost of goods sold to equal 50% of sales. Its inventory policy calls for ending inventory in each month to equal 40% of the next month's budgeted cost of goods sold. All purchases are on credit, and 40% of the purchases in a month is paid for in the same month. Another 40% is paid for during the first month after purchase, and the remaining 20% is paid for in the second month after purchase. The following sales budgets are set: July, $200,000; August, $140,000; September, $170,000; October, $125,000; and

Exercise 23-7
Computing budgeted accounts payable and purchases—sales forecast in dollars

P1 P2

November, $115,000. Compute the following: (1) budgeted merchandise purchases for July, August, September, and October; (2) budgeted payments on accounts payable for September and October; and (3) budgeted ending balances of accounts payable for September and October. (*Hint:* For part 1, refer to Exhibits 23.7 and 23.8 for guidance, but note that budgeted sales are in dollars for this assignment.)

Exercise 23-8ᴬ
Preparing production
budgets (for two periods) P3

Electro Company manufactures an innovative automobile transmission for electric cars. Management predicts that ending inventory for the first quarter will be 38,500 units. The following unit sales of the transmissions are expected during the rest of the year: second quarter, 221,000 units; third quarter, 497,000 units; and fourth quarter, 243,500 units. Company policy calls for the ending inventory of a quarter to equal 40% of the next quarter's budgeted sales. Prepare a production budget for both the second and third quarters that shows the number of transmissions to manufacture.

Exercise 23-9ᴬ
Direct materials budget P3

Refer to information from Exercise 23-8ᴬ. Electro Company reports direct materials requirements of 0.60 per unit. It also aims to end each quarter with an ending inventory of direct materials equal to 40% of next quarter's budgeted materials requirements. Direct materials cost $175 per unit. Prepare a direct materials budget for the second quarter.

Exercise 23-10ᴬ
Direct labor budget P3

Refer to information from Exercise 23-8ᴬ. Each transmission requires 2 direct labor hours, at a cost of $18 per hour. Prepare a direct labor budget for the second quarter.

Available with McGraw-Hill's Homework Manager   McGraw-Hill's
HOMEWORK
MANAGER®

PROBLEM SET A

Problem 23-1A
Preparation and analysis of
merchandise purchases budgets

C3 P1 ♟

mhhe.com/wildFAP19e

Herron Supply is a merchandiser of three different products. The company's February 28 inventories are footwear, 18,500 units; sports equipment, 80,000 units; and apparel, 50,000 units. Management believes that excessive inventories have accumulated for all three products. As a result, a new policy dictates that ending inventory in any month should equal 29% of the expected unit sales for the following month. Expected sales in units for March, April, May, and June follow.

	Budgeted Sales in Units			
	March	**April**	**May**	**June**
Footwear	15,000	26,500	31,500	35,000
Sports equipment	70,500	89,000	96,000	89,500
Apparel	40,000	38,000	34,000	23,000

Required

1. Prepare a merchandise purchases budget (in units) for each product for each of the months of March, April, and May.

Analysis Component

2. The purchases budgets in part 1 should reflect fewer purchases of all three products in March compared to those in April and May. What factor caused fewer purchases to be planned? Suggest business conditions that would cause this factor to both occur and impact the company in this way.

Problem 23-2A
Preparation of cash budgets
(for three periods) C3 P2

mhhe.com/wildFAP19e

During the last week of August, Muir Company's owner approaches the bank for a $100,000 loan to be made on September 2 and repaid on November 30 with annual interest of 12%, for an interest cost of $3,000. The owner plans to increase the store's inventory by $80,000 during September and needs the loan to pay for inventory acquisitions. The bank's loan officer needs more information about Muir's ability to repay the loan and asks the owner to forecast the store's November 30 cash position. On September 1, Muir is expected to have a $4,000 cash balance, $152,000 of accounts receivable, and $115,000 of accounts payable. Its budgeted sales, merchandise purchases, and various cash disbursements for the next three months follow.

	File Edit View Insert Format Tools Data Window Help			
1	**Budgeted Figures***	**September**	**October**	**November**
2	Sales	$350,000	$400,000	$425,000
3	Merchandise purchases	275,000	185,000	180,000
4	Cash disbursements			
5	Payroll	25,000	30,000	35,000
6	Rent	12,000	12,000	12,000
7	Other cash expenses	38,000	29,000	24,500
8	Repayment of bank loan			100,000
9	Interest on the bank loan			3,000
10				

* Operations began in August; August sales were $200,000 and purchases were $115,000.

The budgeted September merchandise purchases include the inventory increase. All sales are on account. The company predicts that 24% of credit sales is collected in the month of the sale, 44% in the month following the sale, 21% in the second month, 8% in the third, and the remainder is uncollectible. Applying these percents to the August credit sales, for example, shows that $88,000 of the $200,000 will be collected in September, $42,000 in October, and $16,000 in November. All merchandise is purchased on credit; 85% of the balance is paid in the month following a purchase, and the remaining 15% is paid in the second month. For example, of the $115,000 August purchases, $97,750 will be paid in September and $17,250 in October.

Required

Prepare a cash budget for September, October, and November for Muir Company. Show supporting calculations as needed.

Check   Budgeted cash balance: September, $103,250; October, $73,250; November, $67,750

Culver Company sells its product for $165 per unit. Its actual and projected sales follow.

Problem 23-3A
Preparation and analysis of cash budgets with supporting inventory and purchases budgets

C3   P2

	Units	**Dollars**
April (actual)	4,000	$ 660,000
May (actual)	2,200	363,000
June (budgeted)	5,000	825,000
July (budgeted)	6,500	1,072,500
August (budgeted)	3,700	610,500

All sales are on credit. Recent experience shows that 28% of credit sales is collected in the month of the sale, 42% in the month after the sale, 25% in the second month after the sale, and 5% proves to be uncollectible. The product's purchase price is $110 per unit. All purchases are payable within 10 days. Thus, 60% of purchases made in a month is paid in that month and the other 40% is paid in the next month. The company has a policy to maintain an ending monthly inventory of 19% of the next month's unit sales plus a safety stock of 135 units. The April 30 and May 31 actual inventory levels are consistent with this policy. Selling and administrative expenses for the year are $1,140,000 and are paid evenly throughout the year in cash. The company's minimum cash balance at month-end is $60,000. This minimum is maintained, if necessary, by borrowing cash from the bank. If the balance exceeds $60,000, the company repays as much of the loan as it can without going below the minimum. This type of loan carries an annual 12% interest rate. On May 31, the loan balance is $39,000, and the company's cash balance is $60,000.

Required

1. Prepare a table that shows the computation of cash collections of its credit sales (accounts receivable) in each of the months of June and July.

2. Prepare a table that shows the computation of budgeted ending inventories (in units) for April, May, June, and July.

3. Prepare the merchandise purchases budget for May, June, and July. Report calculations in units and then show the dollar amount of purchases for each month.

Check   (1) Cash collections: June, $548,460; July, $737,550

(3) Budgeted purchases: May, $300,520; June, $581,350

4. Prepare a table showing the computation of cash payments on product purchases for June and July.

5. Prepare a cash budget for June and July, including any loan activity and interest expense. Compute the loan balance at the end of each month.

(5) Budgeted ending loan balance: June, $54,948; July, $39,375

Analysis Component

6. Refer to your answer to part 5. Culver's cash budget indicates the company will need to borrow more than $15,000 in June and will be able to pay most of it back in July. Suggest some reasons that knowing this information in May would be helpful to management.

Problem 23-4A

Preparation and analysis of budgeted income statements

C3 P2

Poole, a one-product mail-order firm, buys its product for $75 per unit and sells it for $140 per unit. The sales staff receives a 10% commission on the sale of each unit. Its December income statement follows.

POOLE COMPANY Income Statement For Month Ended December 31, 2009	
Sales	$1,400,000
Cost of goods sold	750,000
Gross profit	650,000
Expenses	
Sales commissions (10%)	140,000
Advertising	215,000
Store rent	26,000
Administrative salaries	42,000
Depreciation	52,000
Other expenses	13,000
Total expenses	488,000
Net income	$ 162,000

Management expects December's results to be repeated in January, February, and March of 2010 without any changes in strategy. Management, however, has an alternative plan. It believes that unit sales will increase at a rate of 10% *each* month for the next three months (beginning with January) if the item's selling price is reduced to $125 per unit and advertising expenses are increased by 15% and remain at that level for all three months. The cost of its product will remain at $75 per unit, the sales staff will continue to earn a 10% commission, and the remaining expenses will stay the same.

Required

Check (1) Budgeted net income: January, $32,250; February, $73,500; March, $118,875

1. Prepare budgeted income statements for each of the months of January, February, and March that show the expected results from implementing the proposed changes. Use a three-column format, with one column for each month.

Analysis Component

2. Use the budgeted income statements from part 1 to recommend whether management should implement the proposed changes. Explain.

Problem 23-5A

Preparation of a complete master budget

C2 C3 P1 P2

Near the end of 2009, the management of Nygaard Sports Co., a merchandising company, prepared the following estimated balance sheet for December 31, 2009.

NYGAARD SPORTS COMPANY Estimated Balance Sheet December 31, 2009		
Assets		
Cash		$ 35,000
Accounts receivable		520,000
Inventory		142,500
Total current assets		697,500
Equipment	$540,000	
Less accumulated depreciation	67,500	472,500
Total assets		$1,170,000

[continued on next page]

[continued from previous page]

Liabilities and Equity		
Accounts payable	$345,000	
Bank loan payable	14,000	
Taxes payable (due 3/15/2010)	91,000	
Total liabilities		$ 450,000
Common stock	473,000	
Retained earnings	247,000	
Total stockholders' equity		720,000
Total liabilities and equity		$1,170,000

To prepare a master budget for January, February, and March of 2010, management gathers the following information.

a. Nygaard Sports' single product is purchased for $30 per unit and resold for $53 per unit. The expected inventory level of 4,750 units on December 31, 2009, is more than management's desired level for 2010, which is 20% of the next month's expected sales (in units). Expected sales are: January, 7,500 units; February, 9,250 units; March, 10,750 units; and April, 10,500 units.

b. Cash sales and credit sales represent 20% and 80%, respectively, of total sales. Of the credit sales, 57% is collected in the first month after the month of sale and 43% in the second month after the month of sale. For the December 31, 2009, accounts receivable balance, $130,000 is collected in January and the remaining $390,000 is collected in February.

c. Merchandise purchases are paid for as follows: 20% in the first month after the month of purchase and 80% in the second month after the month of purchase. For the December 31, 2009, accounts payable balance, $70,000 is paid in January and the remaining $275,000 is paid in February.

d. Sales commissions equal to 20% of sales are paid each month. Sales salaries (excluding commissions) are $72,000 per year.

e. General and administrative salaries are $156,000 per year. Maintenance expense equals $2,100 per month and is paid in cash.

f. Equipment reported in the December 31, 2009, balance sheet was purchased in January 2009. It is being depreciated over eight years under the straight-line method with no salvage value. The following amounts for new equipment purchases are planned in the coming quarter: January, $36,000; February, $96,000; and March, $28,800. This equipment will be depreciated under the straight-line method over eight years with no salvage value. A full month's depreciation is taken for the month in which equipment is purchased.

g. The company plans to acquire land at the end of March at a cost of $155,000, which will be paid with cash on the last day of the month.

h. Nygaard Sports has a working arrangement with its bank to obtain additional loans as needed. The interest rate is 12% per year, and interest is paid at each month-end based on the beginning balance. Partial or full payments on these loans can be made on the last day of the month. The company has agreed to maintain a minimum ending cash balance of $25,000 in each month.

i. The income tax rate for the company is 43%. Income taxes on the first quarter's income will not be paid until April 15.

Required

Prepare a master budget for each of the first three months of 2010; include the following component budgets (show supporting calculations as needed, and round amounts to the nearest dollar):

1. Monthly sales budgets (showing both budgeted unit sales and dollar sales).
2. Monthly merchandise purchases budgets.
3. Monthly selling expense budgets.
4. Monthly general and administrative expense budgets.
5. Monthly capital expenditures budgets.
6. Monthly cash budgets.
7. Budgeted income statement for the entire first quarter (not for each month).
8. Budgeted balance sheet as of March 31, 2010.

Check   (2) Budgeted purchases: January, $138,000; February, $286,500
   (3) Budgeted selling expenses: January, $85,500; February, $104,050

   (6) Ending cash bal.: January, $25,000; February, $175,308
   (8) Budgeted total assets at March 31, $1,527,448

Problem 23-6A^A
Preparing production and direct materials budgets

C3 P3

Black Diamond Company produces snow skis. Each ski requires 2 pounds of carbon fiber. The company's management predicts that 4,800 skis and 6,100 pounds of carbon fiber will be in inventory on June 30 of the current year and that 152,000 skis will be sold during the next (third) quarter. Management wants to end the third quarter with 3,700 skis and 4,200 pounds of carbon fiber in inventory. Carbon fiber can be purchased for $15 per pound.

Required

1. Prepare the third-quarter production budget for skis.

2. Prepare the third-quarter direct materials (carbon fiber) budget; include the dollar cost of purchases.

PROBLEM SET B

Problem 23-1B
Preparation and analysis of merchandise purchases budgets

C3 P1

Water Sports Corp. is a merchandiser of three different products. The company's March 31 inventories are water skis, 60,000 units; tow ropes, 45,000 units; and life jackets, 75,000 units. Management believes that excessive inventories have accumulated for all three products. As a result, a new policy dictates that ending inventory in any month should equal 10% of the expected unit sales for the following month. Expected sales in units for April, May, June, and July follow.

	Budgeted Sales in Units			
	April	May	June	July
Water skis	105,000	135,000	195,000	150,000
Tow ropes	50,000	45,000	55,000	50,000
Life jackets	80,000	95,000	100,000	60,000

Required

1. Prepare a merchandise purchases budget (in units) for each product for each of the months of April, May, and June.

Analysis Component

2. The purchases budgets in part 1 should reflect fewer purchases of all three products in April compared to those in May and June. What factor caused fewer purchases to be planned? Suggest business conditions that would cause this factor to both occur and affect the company as it has.

Problem 23-2B
Preparation of cash budgets (for three periods)

C3 P2

During the last week of March, Harlan Stereo's owner approaches the bank for an $80,000 loan to be made on April 1 and repaid on June 30 with annual interest of 12%, for an interest cost of $2,400. The owner plans to increase the store's inventory by $120,000 in April and needs the loan to pay for inventory acquisitions. The bank's loan officer needs more information about Harlan Stereo's ability to repay the loan and asks the owner to forecast the store's June 30 cash position. On April 1, Harlan Stereo is expected to have a $6,000 cash balance, $270,000 of accounts receivable, and $200,000 of accounts payable. Its budgeted sales, merchandise purchases, and various cash disbursements for the next three months follow.

Budgeted Figures*	April	May	June
Sales	$440,000	$600,000	$760,000
Merchandise purchases	420,000	360,000	440,000
Cash disbursements			
Payroll	32,000	34,000	36,000
Rent	12,000	12,000	12,000
Other cash expenses	128,000	16,000	14,000
Repayment of bank loan			80,000
Interest on the bank loan.........			2,400

* Operations began in March; March sales were $360,000 and purchases were $200,000.

The budgeted April merchandise purchases include the inventory increase. All sales are on account. The company predicts that 25% of credit sales is collected in the month of the sale, 45% in the month following the sale, 20% in the second month, 9% in the third, and the remainder is uncollectible. Applying these percents to the March credit sales, for example, shows that $162,000 of the $360,000 will be collected in April, $72,000 in May, and $32,400 in June. All merchandise is purchased on credit; 80% of the balance is paid in the month following a purchase and the remaining 20% is paid in the second month. For example, of the $200,000 March purchases, $160,000 will be paid in April and $40,000 in May.

Required

Prepare a cash budget for April, May, and June for Harlan Stereo. Show supporting calculations as needed.

Parador Company sells its product for $22 per unit. Its actual and projected sales follow.

	Units	Dollars
January (actual)	9,000	$198,000
February (actual)	11,250	247,500
March (budgeted)	9,500	209,000
April (budgeted)	9,375	206,250
May (budgeted)	10,500	231,000

All sales are on credit. Recent experience shows that 40% of credit sales is collected in the month of the sale, 35% in the month after the sale, 23% in the second month after the sale, and 2% proves to be uncollectible. The product's purchase price is $12 per unit. All purchases are payable within 21 days. Thus, 30% of purchases made in a month is paid in that month and the other 70% is paid in the next month. The company has a policy to maintain an ending monthly inventory of 20% of the next month's unit sales plus a safety stock of 100 units. The January 31 and February 28 actual inventory levels are consistent with this policy. Selling and administrative expenses for the year are $960,000 and are paid evenly throughout the year in cash. The company's minimum cash balance for month-end is $25,000. This minimum is maintained, if necessary, by borrowing cash from the bank. If the balance exceeds $25,000, the company repays as much of the loan as it can without going below the minimum. This type of loan carries an annual 12% interest rate. At February 28, the loan balance is $20,000, and the company's cash balance is $25,000.

Required

1. Prepare a table that shows the computation of cash collections of its credit sales (accounts receivable) in each of the months of March and April.

2. Prepare a table showing the computations of budgeted ending inventories (units) for January, February, March, and April.

3. Prepare the merchandise purchases budget for February, March, and April. Report calculations in units and then show the dollar amount of purchases for each month.

4. Prepare a table showing the computation of cash payments on product purchases for March and April.

5. Prepare a cash budget for March and April, including any loan activity and interest expense. Compute the loan balance at the end of each month.

Analysis Component

6. Refer to your answer to part 5. Parador's cash budget indicates whether the company must borrow additional funds at the end of March. Suggest some reasons that knowing the loan needs in advance would be helpful to management.

Tech-Media buys its product for $90 and sells it for $200 per unit. The sales staff receives a 12% commission on the sale of each unit. Its June income statement follows.

TECH-MEDIA COMPANY
Income Statement
For Month Ended June 30, 2009

Sales	$2,000,000
Cost of goods sold	900,000
Gross profit	1,100,000
Expenses	
Sales commissions (12%)	240,000
Advertising	225,000
Store rent	32,000
Administrative salaries	75,000
Depreciation	80,000
Other expenses	25,000
Total expenses	677,000
Net income	$ 423,000

Management expects June's results to be repeated in July, August, and September without any changes in strategy. Management, however, has another plan. It believes that unit sales will increase at a rate of 10% *each* month for the next three months (beginning with July) if the item's selling price is reduced to $180 per unit and advertising expenses are increased by 20% and remain at that level for all three months. The cost of its product will remain at $90 per unit, the sales staff will continue to earn a 12% commission, and the remaining expenses will stay the same.

Required

Check Budgeted net income: July, $270,400; August, $345,640; September, $428,404

1. Prepare budgeted income statements for each of the months of July, August, and September that show the expected results from implementing the proposed changes. Use a three-column format, with one column for each month.

Analysis Component

2. Use the budgeted income statements from part 1 to recommend whether management should implement the proposed plan. Explain.

Problem 23-5B
Preparation of a complete master budget

C2 C3 P1 P2

Near the end of 2009, the management of Pak Corp., a merchandising company, prepared the following estimated balance sheet for December 31, 2009.

PAK CORPORATION
Estimated Balance Sheet
December 31, 2009

Assets		
Cash		$ 36,000
Accounts receivable		470,000
Inventory		300,000
Total current assets		806,000
Equipment	$1,080,000	
Less accumulated depreciation	135,000	945,000
Total assets		$1,751,000
Liabilities and Equity		
Accounts payable	$395,000	
Bank loan payable	25,000	
Taxes payable (due 3/15/2010)	20,000	
Total liabilities		$ 440,000
Common stock	550,000	
Retained earnings	761,000	
Total stockholders' equity		1,311,000
Total liabilities and equity		$1,751,000

To prepare a master budget for January, February, and March of 2010, management gathers the following information.

a. Pak Corp.'s single product is purchased for $30 per unit and resold for $45 per unit. The expected inventory level of 10,000 units on December 31, 2009, is more than management's desired level for 2010, which is 25% of the next month's expected sales (in units). Expected sales are: January, 12,000 units; February, 16,000 units; March, 20,000 units; and April, 18,000 units.

b. Cash sales and credit sales represent 25% and 75%, respectively, of total sales. Of the credit sales, 60% is collected in the first month after the month of sale and 40% in the second month after the month of sale. For the $470,000 accounts receivable balance at December 31, 2009, $330,000 is collected in January 2010 and the remaining $140,000 is collected in February 2010.

c. Merchandise purchases are paid for as follows: 20% in the first month after the month of purchase and 80% in the second month after the month of purchase. For the $395,000 accounts payable balance at December 31, 2009, $207,000 is paid in January 2010 and the remaining $188,000 is paid in February 2010.

d. Sales commissions equal to 20% of sales are paid each month. Sales salaries (excluding commissions) are $180,000 per year.

e. General and administrative salaries are $540,000 per year. Maintenance expense equals $6,000 per month and is paid in cash.

f. Equipment reported in the December 31, 2009, balance sheet was purchased in January 2009. It is being depreciated over 8 years under the straight-line method with no salvage value. The following amounts for new equipment purchases are planned in the coming quarter: January, $72,000; February, $96,000; and March, $28,800. This equipment will be depreciated using the straight-line method over 8 years with no salvage value. A full month's depreciation is taken for the month in which equipment is purchased.

g. The company plans to acquire land at the end of March at a cost of $150,000, which will be paid with cash on the last day of the month.

h. Pak Corp. has a working arrangement with its bank to obtain additional loans as needed. The interest rate is 12% per year, and interest is paid at each month-end based on the beginning balance. Partial or full payments on these loans can be made on the last day of the month. Pak has agreed to maintain a minimum ending cash balance of $36,000 in each month.

i. The income tax rate for the company is 30%. Income taxes on the first quarter's income will not be paid until April 15.

Required

Prepare a master budget for each of the first three months of 2010; include the following component budgets (show supporting calculations as needed, and round amounts to the nearest dollar):

1. Monthly sales budgets (showing both budgeted unit sales and dollar sales).
2. Monthly merchandise purchases budgets.
3. Monthly selling expense budgets.
4. Monthly general and administrative expense budgets.
5. Monthly capital expenditures budgets.
6. Monthly cash budgets.
7. Budgeted income statement for the entire first quarter (not for each month).
8. Budgeted balance sheet as of March 31, 2010.

Check (2) Budgeted purchases: January, $180,000; February, $510,000; (3) Budgeted selling expenses: January, $123,000; February, $159,000

(6) Ending cash bal.: January, $36,000; February, $55,617 (8) Budgeted total assets at March 31, $2,355,317

Thorpe Company produces baseball bats. Each bat requires 3 pounds of aluminum alloy. Management predicts that 4,000 bats and 7,500 pounds of aluminum alloy will be in inventory on March 31 of the current year and that 125,000 bats will be sold during this year's second quarter. Management wants to end the second quarter with 3,000 finished bats and 6,000 pounds of aluminum alloy in inventory. Aluminum alloy can be purchased for $4 per pound.

Problem 23-6B[A]
Preparing production and direct materials budgets
C3 P3

Required

1. Prepare the second-quarter production budget for bats.
2. Prepare the second-quarter direct materials (aluminum alloy) budget; include the dollar cost of purchases.

Check (1) Units manuf., 124,000; (2) Cost of aluminum purchases, $1,482,000

SERIAL PROBLEM

Success Systems

(This serial problem began in Chapter 1 and continues through most of the book. If previous chapter segments were not completed, the serial problem can begin at this point. It is helpful, but not necessary, to use the Working Papers that accompany the book.)

SP 23   Adriana Lopez expects second quarter 2010 sales of her new line of computer furniture to be the same as the first quarter's sales (reported below) without any changes in strategy. Monthly sales averaged 40 desk units (sales price of $1,250) and 20 chairs (sales price of $500).

SUCCESS SYSTEMS	
Segment Income Statement*	
For Quarter Ended March 31, 2010	
Sales[†]	$180,000
Cost of goods sold[‡]	115,000
Gross profit	65,000
Expenses	
Sales commissions (10%)	18,000
Advertising expenses	9,000
Other fixed expenses	18,000
Total expenses	45,000
Net income	$ 20,000

* Reflects revenue and expense activity only related to the computer furniture segment.

[†] Revenue: (120 desks $\times$ $1,250) + (60 chairs $\times$ $500) = $150,000 + $30,000 = $180,000

[‡] Cost of goods sold: (120 desks $\times$ $750) + (60 chairs $\times$ $250) + $10,000 = $115,000

Lopez believes that sales will increase each month for the next three months (April, 48 desks, 32 chairs; May, 52 desks, 35 chairs; June, 56 desks, 38 chairs) *if* selling prices are reduced to $1,150 for desks and $450 for chairs, and advertising expenses are increased by 10% and remain at that level for all three months. The products' variable cost will remain at $750 for desks and $250 for chairs. The sales staff will continue to earn a 10% commission, the fixed manufacturing costs per month will remain at $10,000 and other fixed expenses will remain at $6,000 per month.

Required

Check (1) Budgeted income (loss):
April, $(660); May, $945

1. Prepare budgeted income statements for each of the months of April, May, and June that show the expected results from implementing the proposed changes. Use a three-column format, with one column for each month.

2. Use the budgeted income statements from part 1 to recommend whether Lopez should implement the proposed changes. Explain.

BEYOND THE NUMBERS

REPORTING IN ACTION

P2 C2 C3

BTN 23-1   Financial statements often serve as a starting point in formulating budgets. You are assigned to review **Best Buy**'s financial statements to determine its cash paid for dividends in the current year and the budgeted cash needed to pay its next year's dividend.

Required

1. Which financial statement(s) reports the amount of (a) cash dividends paid and (b) annual cash dividends declared? Explain where on the statement(s) this information is reported.

2. Indicate the amount of cash dividends (a) paid in the year ended March 3, 2007, and (b) to be paid (budgeted for) next year under the assumption that annual cash dividends equal 20% of the prior year's net income.

Fast Forward

3. Access Best Buy's financial statements for a fiscal year ending after March 3, 2007, from either its Website [BestBuy.com] or the SEC's EDGAR database [www.sec.gov]. Compare your answer for part 2 with actual cash dividends paid for that fiscal year. Compute the error, if any, in your estimate. Speculate as to why dividends were higher or lower than budgeted.

BTN 23-2   One source of cash savings for a company is improved management of inventory. To illustrate, assume that **Best Buy** and **Circuit City** both have $300,000 per month in sales in the Virginia area, and both forecast this level of sales per month for the next 24 months. Also assume that both Best Buy and Circuit City have a 20% contribution margin and equal fixed costs, and that cost of goods sold is the only variable cost. Assume that the main difference between Best Buy and Circuit City is the distribution system. Best Buy uses a just-in-time system and requires ending inventory of only 10% of next month's sales in inventory at each month-end. However, Circuit City is building an improved distribution system and currently requires 40% of next month's sales in inventory at each month-end.

COMPARATIVE ANALYSIS

P2

Required

1. Compute the amount by which Circuit City can reduce its inventory level if it can match Best Buy's system of maintaining an inventory equal to 10% of next month's sales. (*Hint:* Focus on the facts given and only on the Virginia area.)

2. Explain how the analysis in part 1 that shows ending inventory levels for both the 40% and 10% required inventory policies can help justify a just-in-time inventory system. You can assume a 15% interest cost for resources that are tied up in ending inventory.

BTN 23-3   Both the budget process and budgets themselves can impact management actions, both positively and negatively. For instance, a common practice among not-for-profit organizations and government agencies is for management to spend any amounts remaining in a budget at the end of the budget period, a practice often called "use it or lose it." The view is that if a department manager does not spend the budgeted amount, top management will reduce next year's budget by the amount not spent. To avoid losing budget dollars, department managers often spend all budgeted amounts regardless of the value added to products or services. All of us pay for the costs associated with this budget system.

ETHICS CHALLENGE

C1   C2

Required

Write a one-half page report to a local not-for-profit organization or government agency offering a solution to the "use it or lose it" budgeting problem.

BTN 23-4   The sales budget is usually the first and most crucial of the component budgets in a master budget because all other budgets usually rely on it for planning purposes.

COMMUNICATING IN PRACTICE

P1

Required

Assume that your company's sales staff provides information on expected sales and selling prices for items making up the sales budget. Prepare a one-page memorandum to your supervisor outlining concerns with the sales staff's input in the sales budget when its compensation is at least partly tied to these budgets. More generally, explain the importance of assessing any potential bias in information provided to the budget process.

TAKING IT TO THE NET

C2 P1 P2

BTN 23-5   Access information on e-budgets through The Manage Mentor:
http://www.themanagementor.com/kuniverse/kmailers_universe/finance_kmailers/cfa/budgeting2.htm
Read the information provided.

Required

1. Assume the role of a senior manager in a large, multidivision company. What are the benefits of using e-budgets?

2. As a senior manager, what concerns do you have with the concept and application of e-budgets?

TEAMWORK IN ACTION

A1

BTN 23-6   Your team is to prepare a budget report outlining the costs of attending college (full-time) for the next two semesters (30 hours) or three quarters (45 hours). This budget's focus is solely on attending college; do not include personal items in the team's budget. Your budget must include tuition, books, supplies, club fees, food, housing, and all costs associated with travel to and from college. This budgeting exercise is similar to the initial phase in activity-based budgeting. Include a list of any assumptions you use in completing the budget. Be prepared to present your budget in class.

ENTREPRENEURIAL DECISION

C1

BTN 23-7   **Jibbitz** produces charms to fit in the holes of **Crocs** shoes. Assume Jibbitz is considering expanding its product line to include necklaces that hold the charms. They plan on meeting with a financial institution for potential funding and have asked by its loan officers for their business plan.

Required

1. What should Jibbitz's business plan include?

2. How can budgeting help the owners efficiently develop and operate their business?

HITTING THE ROAD

C3 P1

BTN 23-8   To help understand the factors impacting a sales budget, you are to visit three businesses with the same ownership or franchise membership. Record the selling prices of two identical products at each location, such as regular and premium gas sold at **Chevron** stations. You are likely to find a difference in prices for at least one of the three locations you visit.

Required

1. Identify at least three external factors that must be considered when setting the sales budget. (*Note:* There is a difference between internal and external factors that impact the sales budget.)

2. What factors might explain any differences identified in the prices of the businesses you visited?

GLOBAL DECISION

DSG

BTN 23-9   Access **DSG**'s income statement (www.DSGiplc.com) for the year ended April 28, 2007.

Required

1. Is DSG's administrative expense budget likely to be an important budget in its master budgeting process? Explain. (*Hint:* Review its Note 3.)

2. Identify three types of expenses that would be reported as administrative expenses on DSG's income statement.

3. Who likely has the initial responsibility for DSG's administrative expense budget? Explain.

ANSWERS TO MULTIPLE CHOICE QUIZ

1. c

2. e; Budgeted purchases = $36,000 + $7,000 − $6,000 = $37,000

3. b; Cash collected = 25% of September sales + 75% of August sales =
(0.25 × $240,000) + (0.75 × $220,000) = $225,000

4. d

5. a; 560 units + (0.30 × 600 units) − (0.30 × 560 units) = 572 units

A Look Back
Chapter 23 explained the master budget and its component budgets as well as their usefulness for planning and monitoring company activities.

A Look at This Chapter
This chapter describes flexible budgets, variance analysis, and standard costs. It explains how each is used for purposes of better controlling and monitoring business activities.

A Look Ahead
Chapter 25 focuses on capital budgeting decisions. It also explains and illustrates several procedures used in evaluating short-term managerial decisions.

Chapter 24

Flexible Budgets and Standard Costs

Learning Objectives

CAP

Conceptual

C1 Define *standard costs* and explain their computation and uses. *(p. 985)*

C2 Describe variances and what they reveal about performance. *(p. 986)*

C3 Explain how standard cost information is useful for management by exception. *(p. 996)*

Analytical

A1 Compare fixed and flexible budgets. *(p. 982)*

A2 Analyze changes in sales from expected amounts. *(p. 998)*

LP24

Procedural

P1 Prepare a flexible budget and interpret a flexible budget performance report. *(p. 982)*

P2 Compute materials and labor variances. *(p. 988)*

P3 Compute overhead variances. *(p. 992)*

P4 Prepare journal entries for standard costs and account for price and quantity variances. *(p. 996)*

Good Vibrations

"Look at each part of the process and improve it"
—Chris Martin

NAZARETH, PA—Eric Clapton. Paul McCartney. Johnny Cash. Jimi Hendrix. What do these musical legends have in common? All played guitars manufactured by the **Martin Guitar Company** (**MartinGuitar.com**). Martin manufactures high-quality guitars and recently sold its millionth. This family-owned company, headed by Christian (Chris) F. Martin, has prospered by hurdling challenges facing all manufacturers—materials quality, product design, quality control, manufacturing methods, and new investment.

Chris' entrepreneurial spirit stimulated innovative product design and growth while adhering closely to product quality. Understanding cost analysis and variances, flexible and fixed budgets, and standard costs helps his company control its production process. Martin's "X" bracing system is a key part of the distinctive Martin guitar tone. The company also embraces continuous improvement. Recently it began a lean manufacturing project to improve production efficiency, work flow, and cycle time in one of its plants.

Martin Guitar adheres to tight standards variances. Vince Gentilcore, Martin's director of quality, classifies production problems into three types: materials, process, and employee. Developing managerial accounting systems to evaluate its performance on each of these dimensions is key. "[Defects] in wood affect yield, productivity, and costs of quality," explains Vince. "We have exacting specifications and controls in place to detect problems; we don't allow material to go into a guitar that doesn't satisfy our requirements." As for process, he closely monitors the company's computer-controlled machines to ensure excessive tool wear does not impair product quality. Another key to process control, explains Vince, is "the moisture content of the wood, which we track on a regular basis." Regarding employee costs, Chris Martin explains that "we have work quotas; we know how much labor costs and how long it takes."

Achieving high standards is the goal at Martin Guitar. "We're trying to make the best," proclaims Chris. "We are doing so much more volume today, even with all those competitors. [Our workers] hold the company to an extraordinarily high standard." With standards like these, Chris' company produces a pretty tune.

[Sources: *Martin Guitar Website,* January 2009; *Quality Digest,* November 2007; *Modern Guitars Magazine,* December and March 2005; For a virtual tour of Martin Guitars see MartinGuitar.com/visit/vtour.php]

Budgeting helps organize and formalize management's planning activities. This chapter extends the study of budgeting to look more closely at the use of budgets to evaluate performance. Evaluations are important for controlling and monitoring business activities. This chapter also describes and illustrates the use of standard costs and variance analyses. These managerial tools are useful for both evaluating and controlling organizations and for the planning of future activities.

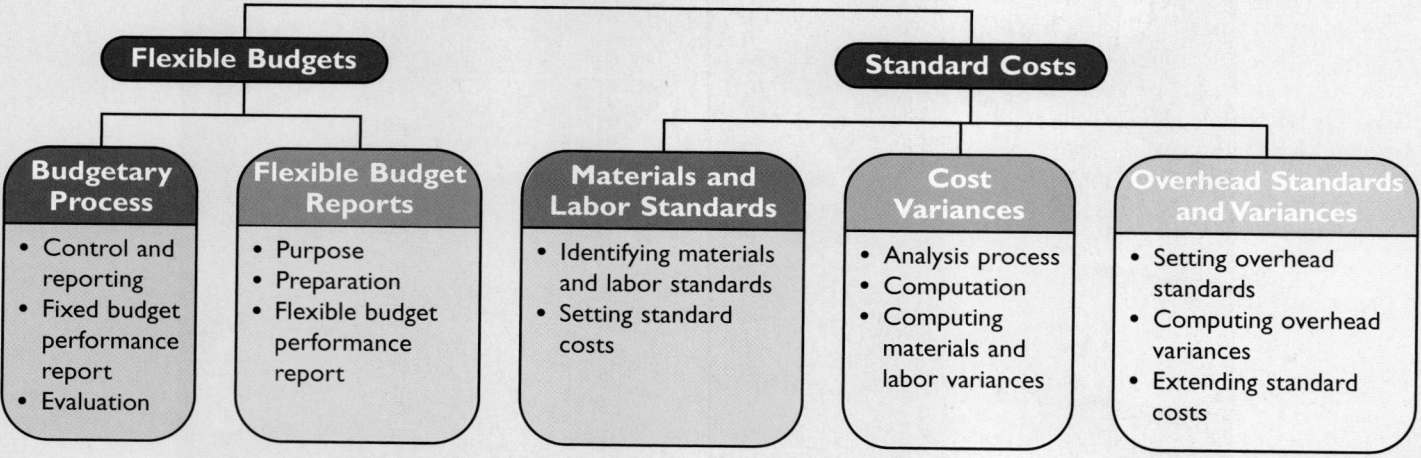

Flexible Budgets

Budgetary Process
- Control and reporting
- Fixed budget performance report
- Evaluation

Flexible Budget Reports
- Purpose
- Preparation
- Flexible budget performance report

Standard Costs

Materials and Labor Standards
- Identifying materials and labor standards
- Setting standard costs

Cost Variances
- Analysis process
- Computation
- Computing materials and labor variances

Overhead Standards and Variances
- Setting overhead standards
- Computing overhead variances
- Extending standard costs

Section 1—Flexible Budgets

This section introduces fixed budgets and fixed budget performance reports. It then introduces flexible budgets and flexible budget performance reports and illustrates their advantages.

Budgetary Process

Video24.2

A master budget reflects management's planned objectives for a future period. The preparation of a master budget is based on a predicted level of activity such as sales volume for the budget period. This section discusses the effects on the usefulness of budget reports when the actual level of activity differs from the predicted level.

Budgetary Control and Reporting

Budgetary control refers to management's use of budgets to monitor and control a company's operations. This includes using budgets to see that planned objectives are met. **Budget reports** contain relevant information that compares actual results to planned activities. This comparison is motivated by a need to both monitor performance and control activities. Budget reports are sometimes viewed as progress reports, or *report cards,* on management's performance in achieving planned objectives. These reports can be prepared at any time and for any period. Three common periods for a budget report are a month, quarter, and year.

Point: Budget reports are often used as a base to determine bonuses of managers.

The budgetary control process involves at least four steps: (1) develop the budget from planned objectives, (2) compare actual results to budgeted amounts and analyze any differences, (3) take corrective and strategic actions, and (4) establish new planned objectives and prepare a new budget. Exhibit 24.1 shows this continual process of budgetary control. Budget

EXHIBIT 24.1

Process of Budgetary Control

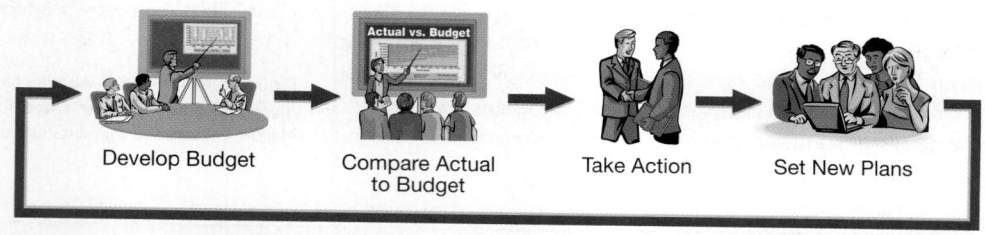

Develop Budget → Compare Actual to Budget → Take Action → Set New Plans

reports and related documents are effective tools for managers to obtain the greatest benefits from this budgetary process.

Fixed Budget Performance Report

In a fixed budgetary control system, the master budget is based on a single prediction for sales volume or other activity level. The budgeted amount for each cost essentially assumes that a specific (or *fixed*) amount of sales will occur. A **fixed budget,** also called a *static budget,* is based on a single predicted amount of sales or other measure of activity.

One benefit of a budget is its usefulness in comparing actual results with planned activities. Information useful for analysis is often presented for comparison in a performance report. As shown in Exhibit 24.2, a **fixed budget performance report** for **Optel** compares actual results for January 2009 with the results expected under its fixed budget that predicted 10,000 (composite) units of sales. Optel manufactures inexpensive eyeglasses, frames, contact lens, and related supplies. For this report, its production volume equals sales volume (its inventory level did not change).

EXHIBIT 24.2

Fixed Budget
Performance Report

OPTEL Fixed Budget Performance Report For Month Ended January 31, 2009	Fixed Budget	Actual Results	Variances*
Sales (in units)	10,000	12,000	
Sales (in dollars)	$100,000	$125,000	$25,000 F
Cost of goods sold			
Direct materials	10,000	13,000	3,000 U
Direct labor	15,000	20,000	5,000 U
Overhead			
Factory supplies	2,000	2,100	100 U
Utilities	3,000	4,000	1,000 U
Depreciation—machinery	8,000	8,000	0
Supervisory salaries	11,000	11,000	0
Selling expenses			
Sales commissions	9,000	10,800	1,800 U
Shipping expenses	4,000	4,300	300 U
General and administrative expenses			
Office supplies	5,000	5,200	200 U
Insurance expenses	1,000	1,200	200 U
Depreciation—office equipment	7,000	7,000	0
Administrative salaries	13,000	13,000	0
Total expenses	88,000	99,600	11,600 U
Income from operations	$ 12,000	$ 25,400	$13,400 F

* F = Favorable variance; U = Unfavorable variance.

This type of performance report designates differences between budgeted and actual results as variances. We see the letters *F* and *U* located beside the numbers in the third number column of this report. Their meanings are as follows:

F = **Favorable variance** When compared to budget, the actual cost or revenue contributes to a *higher* income. That is, actual revenue is higher than budgeted revenue, or actual cost is lower than budgeted cost.

U = **Unfavorable variance** When compared to budget, the actual cost or revenue contributes to a *lower* income; actual revenue is lower than budgeted revenue, or actual cost is higher than budgeted cost.

This convention is common in practice and is used throughout this chapter.

Example: How is it that the favorable sales variance in Exhibit 24.2 is linked with so many unfavorable cost and expense variances? *Answer:* Costs have increased with the increase in sales.

Budget Reports for Evaluation

A primary use of budget reports is as a tool for management to monitor and control operations. Evaluation by Optel management is likely to focus on a variety of questions that might include these:

■ Why is actual income from operations $13,400 higher than budgeted?
■ Are amounts paid for each expense item too high?
■ Is manufacturing using too much direct material?
■ Is manufacturing using too much direct labor?

The performance report in Exhibit 24.2 provides little help in answering these questions because actual sales volume is 2,000 units higher than budgeted. A manager does not know if this higher level of sales activity is the cause of variations in total dollar sales and expenses or if other factors have influenced these amounts. This inability of fixed budget reports to adjust for changes in activity levels is a major limitation of a fixed budget performance report. That is, it fails to show whether actual costs are out of line due to a change in actual sales volume or some other factor.

Decision Insight

Green Budget   Budget reporting and evaluation are used at the **Environmental Protection Agency (EPA)**. It regularly prepares performance plans and budget requests that describe performance goals, measure outcomes, and analyze variances.

Flexible Budget Reports

Purpose of Flexible Budgets

A1 Compare fixed and flexible budgets.

Video24.2

To help address limitations with the fixed budget performance report, particularly from the effects of changes in sales volume, management can use a flexible budget. A **flexible budget,** also called a *variable budget,* is a report based on predicted amounts of revenues and expenses corresponding to the actual level of output. Flexible budgets are useful both before and after the period's activities are complete.

A flexible budget prepared before the period is often based on several levels of activity. Budgets for those different levels can provide a "what-if" look at operations. The different levels often include both a best case and worst case scenario. This allows management to make adjustments to avoid or lessen the effects of the worst case scenario.

A flexible budget prepared after the period helps management evaluate past performance. It is especially useful for such an evaluation because it reflects budgeted revenues and costs based on the actual level of activity. Thus, comparisons of actual results with budgeted performance are more likely to identify the causes of any differences. This can help managers focus attention on real problem areas and implement corrective actions. This is in contrast to a fixed budget, whose primary purpose is to assist managers in planning future activities and whose numbers are based on a single predicted amount of budgeted sales or production.

Preparation of Flexible Budgets

P1 Prepare a flexible budget and interpret a flexible budget performance report.

A flexible budget is designed to reveal the effects of volume of activity on revenues and costs. To prepare a flexible budget, management relies on the distinctions between fixed and variable costs. Recall that the cost per unit of activity remains constant for variable costs so that the total amount of a variable cost changes in direct proportion to a change in activity level. The total amount of fixed cost remains unchanged regardless of changes in the level of activity within a relevant (normal) operating range. (Assume that costs can be reasonably classified as variable or fixed within a relevant range.)

When we create the numbers constituting a flexible budget, we express each variable cost as either a constant amount per unit of sales or as a percent of a sales dollar. In the case of a fixed cost, we express its budgeted amount as the total amount expected to occur at any sales volume within the relevant range.

Exhibit 24.3 shows a set of flexible budgets for Optel in January 2009. Seven of its expenses are classified as variable costs. Its remaining five expenses are fixed costs. These classifications result from management's investigation of each expense. Variable and fixed expense categories are *not* the same for every company, and we must avoid drawing conclusions from specific cases. For example, depending on the nature of a company's operations, office supplies expense can be either fixed or variable with respect to sales.

Point: The usefulness of a flexible budget depends on valid classification of variable and fixed costs. Some costs are mixed and must be analyzed to determine their variable and fixed portions.

EXHIBIT 24.3

Flexible Budgets

OPTEL
Flexible Budgets
For Month Ended January 31, 2009

	Flexible Budget Variable Amount per Unit	Flexible Budget Total Fixed Cost	Flexible Budget for Unit Sales of 10,000	Flexible Budget for Unit Sales of 12,000	Flexible Budget for Unit Sales of 14,000
Sales	$10.00		$100,000	$120,000	$140,000
Variable costs					
Direct materials	1.00		10,000	12,000	14,000
Direct labor	1.50		15,000	18,000	21,000
Factory supplies	0.20		2,000	2,400	2,800
Utilities	0.30		3,000	3,600	4,200
Sales commissions	0.90		9,000	10,800	12,600
Shipping expenses	0.40		4,000	4,800	5,600
Office supplies	0.50		5,000	6,000	7,000
Total variable costs	4.80		48,000	57,600	67,200
Contribution margin	$ 5.20		$ 52,000	$ 62,400	$ 72,800
Fixed costs					
Depreciation—machinery		$ 8,000	8,000	8,000	8,000
Supervisory salaries		11,000	11,000	11,000	11,000
Insurance expense		1,000	1,000	1,000	1,000
Depreciation—office equipment		7,000	7,000	7,000	7,000
Administrative salaries		13,000	13,000	13,000	13,000
Total fixed costs		$40,000	40,000	40,000	40,000
Income from operations			$ 12,000	$ 22,400	$ 32,800

The layout for the flexible budgets in Exhibit 24.3 follows a *contribution margin format*—beginning with sales followed by variable costs and then fixed costs. Both the expected individual and total variable costs are reported and then subtracted from sales. The difference between sales and variable costs equals contribution margin. The expected amounts of fixed costs are listed next, followed by the expected income from operations before taxes.

The first and second number columns of Exhibit 24.3 show the flexible budget amounts for variable costs per unit and each fixed cost for any volume of sales in the relevant range. The third, fourth, and fifth columns show the flexible budget amounts computed for three different sales volumes. For instance, the third column's flexible budget is based on 10,000 units. These numbers are the same as those in the fixed budget of Exhibit 24.2 because the expected volumes are the same for these two budgets.

Recall that Optel's actual sales volume for January is 12,000 units. This sales volume is 2,000 units more than the 10,000 units originally predicted in the master budget. When differences between actual and predicted volume arise, the usefulness of a flexible budget is apparent. For instance, compare the flexible budget for 10,000 units in the third column (which is the same as the fixed budget in Exhibit 24.2) with the flexible budget for 12,000 units in the

Example: Using Exhibit 24.3, what is the budgeted income from operations for unit sales of (a) 11,000 and (b) 13,000? *Answers:* $17,200 for unit sales of 11,000; $27,600 for unit sales of 13,000.

Point: Flexible budgeting allows a budget to be prepared at the *actual* output level. Performance reports are then prepared comparing the flexible budget to actual revenues and costs.

fourth column. The higher levels for both sales and variable costs reflect nothing more than the increase in sales activity. Any budget analysis comparing actual with planned results that ignores this information is less useful to management.

To illustrate, when we evaluate Optel's performance, we need to prepare a flexible budget showing actual and budgeted values at 12,000 units. As part of a complete profitability analysis, managers could compare the actual income of $25,400 (from Exhibit 24.2) with the $22,400 income expected at the actual sales volume of 12,000 units (from Exhibit 24.3). This results in a total favorable income variance of $3,000 to be explained and interpreted. This variance is markedly lower from the $13,400 favorable variance identified in Exhibit 24.2 using a fixed budget, but still suggests good performance. After receiving the flexible budget based on January's actual volume, management must determine what caused this $3,000 difference. The next section describes a flexible budget performance report that provides guidance in this analysis.

Decision Maker

Entrepreneur The heads of both the strategic consulting and tax consulting divisions of your financial services firm complain to you about the unfavorable variances on their performance reports. "We worked on more consulting assignments than planned. It's not surprising our costs are higher than expected. To top it off, this report characterizes our work as *poor!*" How do you respond? [Answer—p. 1004]

Flexible Budget Performance Report

A **flexible budget performance report** lists differences between actual performance and budgeted performance based on actual sales volume or other activity level. This report helps direct management's attention to those costs or revenues that differ substantially from budgeted amounts. Exhibit 24.4 shows Optel's flexible budget performance report for January. We prepare this report after the actual volume is known to be 12,000 units. This report shows a $5,000 favorable variance in total dollar sales. Because actual and budgeted volumes are both 12,000 units, the $5,000 sales variance must have resulted from a higher than expected selling price. Further analysis of the facts surrounding this $5,000 sales variance reveals a favorable sales variance per unit of nearly $0.42 as shown here:

Actual average price per unit (rounded to cents)	$125,000/12,000 = $10.42
Budgeted price per unit	$120,000/12,000 = 10.00
Favorable sales variance per unit	$5,000/12,000 = $ 0.42

The other variances in Exhibit 24.4 also direct management's attention to areas where corrective actions can help control Optel's operations. Each expense variance is analyzed as the sales variance was. We can think of each expense as the joint result of using a given number of units of input and paying a specific price per unit of input. Optel's expense variances total $2,000 unfavorable, suggesting poor control of some costs, particularly direct materials and direct labor.

Each variance in Exhibit 24.4 is due in part to a difference between *actual price* per unit of input and *budgeted price* per unit of input. This is a **price variance.** Each variance also can be due in part to a difference between *actual quantity* of input used and *budgeted quantity* of input. This is a **quantity variance.** We explain more about this breakdown, known as **variance analysis,** later in the standard costs section.

Quick Check
Answers—p. 1004

1. A flexible budget (a) shows fixed costs as constant amounts of cost per unit of activity, (b) shows variable costs as constant amounts of cost per unit of activity, or (c) is prepared based on one expected amount of budgeted sales or production.
2. What is the initial step in preparing a flexible budget?
3. What is the main difference between a fixed and a flexible budget?
4. What is the contribution margin?

OPTEL Flexible Budget Performance Report For Month Ended January 31, 2009	Flexible Budget	Actual Results	Variances*
Sales (12,000 units)	$120,000	$125,000	$5,000 F
Variable costs			
Direct materials	12,000	13,000	1,000 U
Direct labor	18,000	20,000	2,000 U
Factory supplies	2,400	2,100	300 F
Utilities	3,600	4,000	400 U
Sales commissions	10,800	10,800	0
Shipping expenses	4,800	4,300	500 F
Office supplies	6,000	5,200	800 F
Total variable costs	57,600	59,400	1,800 U
Contribution margin	62,400	65,600	3,200 F
Fixed costs			
Depreciation—machinery	8,000	8,000	0
Supervisory salaries	11,000	11,000	0
Insurance expense	1,000	1,200	200 U
Depreciation—office equipment	7,000	7,000	0
Administrative salaries	13,000	13,000	0
Total fixed costs	40,000	40,200	200 U
Income from operations	$ 22,400	$ 25,400	$3,000 F

EXHIBIT 24.4

Flexible Budget Performance Report

* F = Favorable variance; U = Unfavorable variance.

Section 2—Standard Costs

Standard costs are preset costs for delivering a product or service under normal conditions. These costs are established by personnel, engineering, and accounting studies using past experiences and data. Management uses these costs to assess the reasonableness of actual costs incurred for producing the product or service. When actual costs vary from standard costs, management follows up to identify potential problems and take corrective actions.

Standard costs are often used in preparing budgets because they are the anticipated costs incurred under normal conditions. Terms such as *standard materials cost, standard labor cost,* and *standard overhead cost* are often used to refer to amounts budgeted for direct materials, direct labor, and overhead.

C1 Define *standard costs* and explain their computation and uses.

Point: Since standard costs are often budgeted costs, they can be used to prepare both fixed budgets and flexible budgets.

Materials and Labor Standards

This section explains how to set materials and labor standards and how to prepare a standard cost card.

Identifying Standard Costs

Managerial accountants, engineers, personnel administrators, and other managers combine their efforts to set standard costs. To identify standards for direct labor costs, we can conduct time and motion studies for each labor operation in the process of providing a product or service. From these studies, management can learn the best way to perform the operation and then set the standard labor time required for the operation under normal conditions. Similarly, standards for materials are set by studying the quantity, grade, and cost of each material used. Standards for overhead costs are explained later in the chapter.

Regardless of the care used in setting standard costs and in revising them as conditions change, actual costs frequently differ from standard costs, often as a result of one or more factors. For instance, the actual quantity of material used can differ from the standard, or the price paid per unit of material can differ from the standard. Quantity and price differences from

Video24.1

Point: Business practice often uses the word *budget* when speaking of total amounts and *standard* when discussing per unit amounts.

Example: What factors might be considered when deciding whether to revise standard costs? *Answer:* Changes in the processes and/or resources needed to carry out the processes.

standard amounts can also occur for labor. That is, the actual labor time and actual labor rate can vary from what was expected. The same analysis applies to overhead costs.

Decision Insight

Cruis'n Standards The **Corvette** consists of hundreds of parts for which engineers set standards. Various types of labor are also involved in its production, including machining, assembly, painting, and welding, and standards are set for each. Actual results are periodically compared with standards to assess performance.

Setting Standard Costs

To illustrate the setting of a standard cost, we consider a professional league baseball bat manufactured by **ProBat.** Its engineers have determined that manufacturing one bat requires 0.90 kg. of high-grade wood. They also expect some loss of material as part of the process because of inefficiencies and waste. This results in adding an *allowance* of 0.10 kg., making the standard requirement 1.0 kg. of wood for each bat.

Point: Companies promoting continuous improvement strive to achieve ideal standards by eliminating inefficiencies and waste.

The 0.90 kg. portion is called an *ideal standard;* it is the quantity of material required if the process is 100% efficient without any loss or waste. Reality suggests that some loss of material usually occurs with any process. The standard of 1.0 kg. is known as the *practical standard,* the quantity of material required under normal application of the process.

High-grade wood can be purchased at a standard price of $25 per kg. The purchasing department sets this price as the expected price for the budget period. To determine this price, the purchasing department considers factors such as the quality of materials, future economic conditions, supply factors (shortages and excesses), and any available discounts. The engineers also decide that two hours of labor time (after including allowances) are required to manufacture a bat. The wage rate is $20 per hour (better than average skilled labor is required). ProBat assigns all overhead at the rate of $10 per labor hour. The standard costs of direct materials, direct labor, and overhead for one bat are shown in Exhibit 24.5 in what is called a *standard cost card.* These cost amounts are then used to prepare manufacturing budgets for a budgeted level of production.

EXHIBIT 24.5

Standard Cost Card

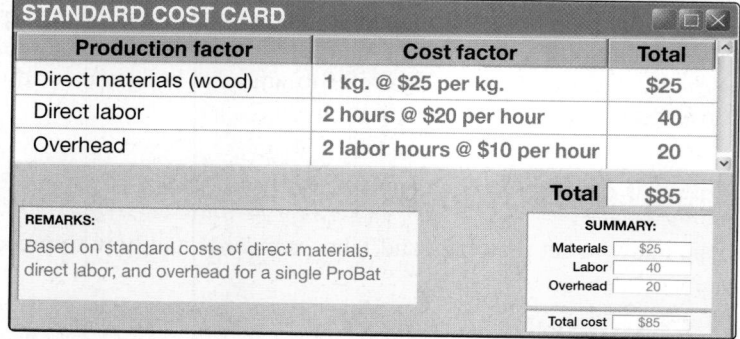

STANDARD COST CARD		
Production factor	**Cost factor**	**Total**
Direct materials (wood)	1 kg. @ $25 per kg.	$25
Direct labor	2 hours @ $20 per hour	40
Overhead	2 labor hours @ $10 per hour	20
	Total	**$85**

REMARKS:
Based on standard costs of direct materials, direct labor, and overhead for a single ProBat

SUMMARY:
Materials $25
Labor 40
Overhead 20
Total cost $85

Cost Variances

C2 Describe variances and what they reveal about performance.

A **cost variance,** also simply called a *variance,* is the difference between actual and standard costs. A cost variance can be favorable or unfavorable. A variance from standard cost is considered favorable if actual cost is less than standard cost. It is considered unfavorable if actual cost is more than standard cost.[1] This section discusses variance analysis.

---

[1] Short-term favorable variances can sometimes lead to long-term unfavorable variances. For instance, if management spends less than the budgeted amount on maintenance or insurance, the performance report would show a favorable variance. Cutting these expenses can lead to major losses in the long run if machinery wears out prematurely or insurance coverage proves inadequate.

Cost Variance Analysis

Variances are usually identified in performance reports. When a variance occurs, management wants to determine the factors causing it. This often involves analysis, evaluation, and explanation. The results of these efforts should enable management to assign responsibility for the variance and then to take actions to correct the situation.

To illustrate, ProBat's standard materials cost for producing 500 bats is $12,500. Assume, that its actual materials cost for those 500 bats proved to be $13,000. The $500 unfavorable variance raises questions that call for answers that, in turn, can lead to changes to correct the situation and eliminate this variance in the next period. A performance report often identifies the existence of a problem, but we must follow up with further investigation to see what can be done to improve future performance.

Exhibit 24.6 shows the flow of events in the effective management of variance analysis. It shows four steps: (1) preparing a standard cost performance report, (2) computing and analyzing variances, (3) identifying questions and their explanations, and (4) taking corrective and strategic actions. These variance analysis steps are interrelated and are frequently applied in good organizations.

Video24.1

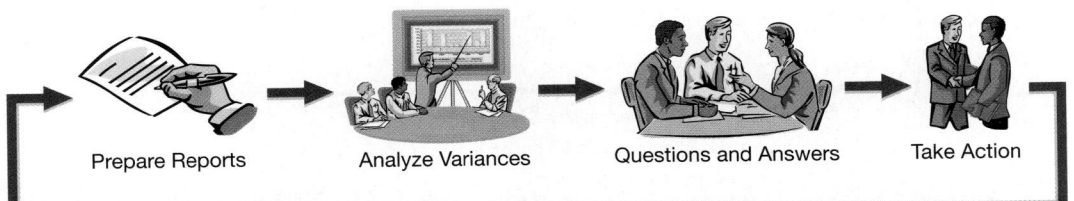

Prepare Reports   Analyze Variances   Questions and Answers   Take Action

EXHIBIT 24.6

Variance Analysis

Cost Variance Computation

Management needs information about the factors causing a cost variance, but first it must properly compute the variance. In its most simple form, a cost variance (CV) is computed as the difference between actual cost (AC) and standard cost (SC) as shown in Exhibit 24.7.

> **Cost Variance** (CV) = **Actual Cost** (AC) − **Standard Cost** (SC)
>
> where:
>
> **Actual Cost** (AC) = **Actual Quantity** (AQ) × **Actual Price** (AP)
> **Standard Cost** (SC) = **Standard Quantity** (SQ) × **Standard Price** (SP)

EXHIBIT 24.7

Cost Variance Formulas

A cost variance is further defined by its components. Actual quantity (AQ) is the input (material or labor) used to manufacture the quantity of output. Standard quantity (SQ) is the expected input for the quantity of output. Actual price (AP) is the amount paid to acquire the input (material or labor), and standard price (SP) is the expected price.

Two main factors cause a cost variance: (1) the difference between actual price and standard price results in a *price* (or rate) *variance* and (2) the difference between actual quantity and standard quantity results in a *quantity* (or usage or efficiency) *variance*. To assess the impacts of these two factors in a cost variance, we use the formulas in Exhibit 24.8.

Point: Price and quantity variances for direct labor are nearly always referred to as *rate* and *efficiency variances*, respectively.

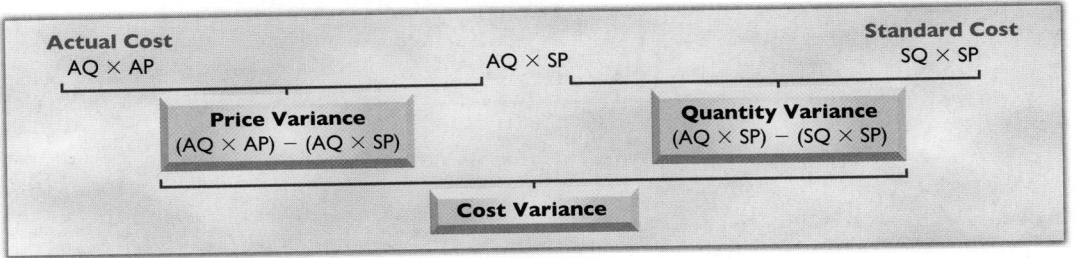

EXHIBIT 24.8

Price Variance and Quantity Variance Formulas

In computing a price variance, the quantity (actual) is held constant. In computing a quantity variance, the price (standard) is held constant. The cost variance, or total variance, is the sum of the price and quantity variances. These formulas identify the sources of the cost variance. Managers sometimes find it useful to apply an alternative (but equivalent) computation for the price and quantity variances as shown in Exhibit 24.9.

EXHIBIT 24.9

Alternative Price Variance and Quantity Variance Formulas

> **Price Variance (PV) = [Actual Price (AP) − Standard Price (SP)] × Actual Quantity (AQ)**
>
> **Quantity Variance (QV) = [Actual Quantity (AQ) − Standard Quantity (SQ)] × Standard Price (SP)**

The results from applying the formulas in Exhibits 24.8 and 24.9 are identical.

Computing Materials and Labor Variances

P2   Compute materials and labor variances.

We illustrate the computation of the materials and labor cost variances using data from **G-Max,** a company that makes specialty golf equipment and accessories for individual customers. This company has set the following standard quantities and costs for materials and labor per unit for one of its hand-crafted golf clubheads:

Direct materials (1 lb. per unit at $1 per lb.)	$1.00
Direct labor (1 hr. per unit at $8 per hr.)	8.00
Total standard direct cost per unit	$9.00

Materials Cost Variances   During May 2009, G-Max budgeted to produce 4,000 clubheads (units). It actually produced only 3,500 units. It used 3,600 pounds of direct materials (titanium) costing $1.05 per pound, meaning its total materials cost was $3,780. This information allows us to compute both actual and standard direct materials costs for G-Max's 3,500 units and its direct materials cost variance as follows:

Actual cost	3,600 lbs. @ $1.05 per lb.	= $3,780
Standard cost	3,500 lbs. @ $1.00 per lb.	= 3,500
Direct materials cost variance (unfavorable)		= $ 280

To better isolate the causes of this $280 unfavorable total direct materials cost variance, the materials price and quantity variances for these G-Max clubheads are computed and shown in Exhibit 24.10.

EXHIBIT 24.10

Materials Price and Quantity Variances

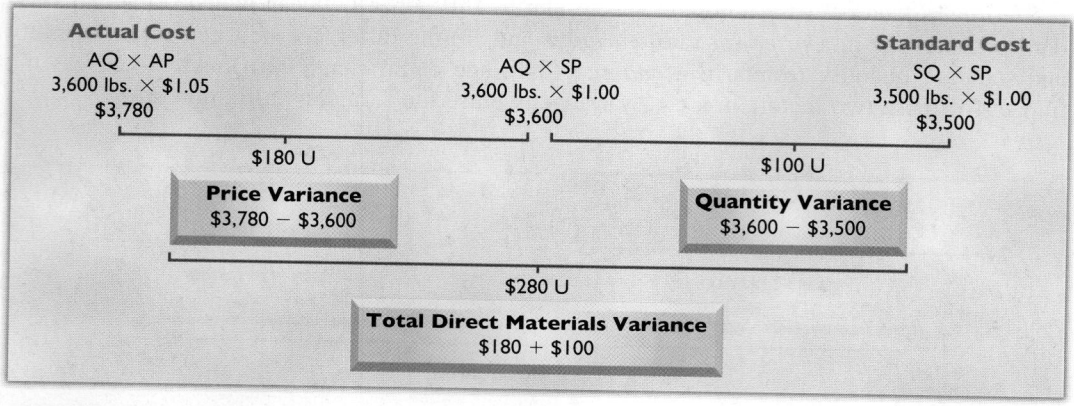

The $180 unfavorable price variance results from paying 5 cents more per unit than the standard price, computed as 3,600 lbs. × $0.05. The $100 unfavorable quantity variance is due to using 100 lbs. more materials than the standard quantity, computed as 100 lbs. × $1. The total direct materials variance is $280 and it is unfavorable. This information allows management to ask the responsible individuals for explanations and corrective actions.

The purchasing department is usually responsible for the price paid for materials. Responsibility for explaining the price variance in this case rests with the purchasing manager if a price higher than standard caused the variance. The production department is usually responsible for the amount of material used and in this case is responsible for explaining why the process used more than the standard amount of materials.

Variance analysis presents challenges. For instance, the production department could have used more than the standard amount of material because its quality did not meet specifications and led to excessive waste. In this case, the purchasing manager is responsible for explaining why inferior materials were acquired. However, the production manager is responsible for explaining what happened if analysis shows that waste was due to inefficiencies, not poor quality material.

In evaluating price variances, managers must recognize that a favorable price variance can indicate a problem with poor product quality. **Redhook Ale**, a micro brewery in the Pacific Northwest, can probably save 10% to 15% in material prices by buying six-row barley malt instead of the better two-row from Washington's Yakima valley. Attention to quality, however, has helped Redhook Ale become the first craft brewer to be kosher certified. Redhook's purchasing activities are judged on both the quality of the materials and the purchase price variance.

Example: Identify at least two factors that might have caused the $100 unfavorable quantity variance and the $180 unfavorable price variance in Exhibit 24.10. *Answer:* Poor quality materials or untrained workers for the former; poor price negotiation or higher-quality materials for the latter.

Labor Cost Variances Labor cost for a specific product or service depends on the number of hours worked (quantity) and the wage rate paid to employees (price). When actual amounts for a task differ from standard, the labor cost variance can be divided into a rate (price) variance and an efficiency (quantity) variance.

To illustrate, G-Max's direct labor standard for 3,500 units of its hand-crafted clubheads is one hour per unit, or 3,500 hours at $8 per hour. Since only 3,400 hours at $8.30 per hour were actually used to complete the units, the actual and standard labor costs are

Actual cost	3,400 hrs. @ $8.30 per hr.	= $28,220
Standard cost	3,500 hrs. @ $8.00 per hr.	= 28,000
Direct labor cost variance (unfavorable)		= $ 220

This analysis shows that actual cost is merely $220 over the standard and suggests no immediate concern. Computing both the labor rate and efficiency variances reveals a different picture, however, as shown in Exhibit 24.11.

EXHIBIT 24.11

Labor Rate and Efficiency Variances*

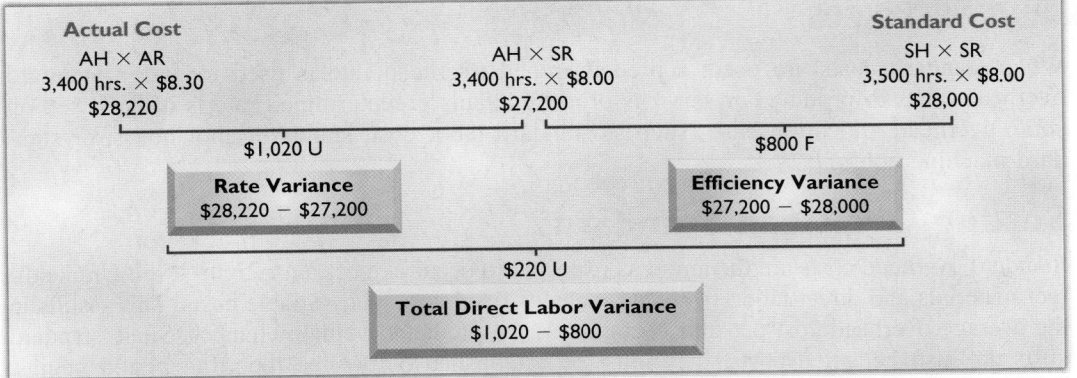

* AH is actual direct labor hours; AR is actual wage rate; SH is standard direct labor hours allowed for actual output; SR is standard wage rate.

The analysis in Exhibit 24.11 shows that an $800 favorable efficiency variance results from using 100 fewer direct labor hours than standard for the units produced, but this favorable variance is more than offset by a wage rate that is $0.30 per hour higher than standard. The personnel administrator or the production manager needs to explain why the wage rate is higher than expected. The production manager should also explain how the labor hours were reduced. If this experience can be repeated and transferred to other departments, more savings are possible.

One possible explanation of these labor rate and efficiency variances is the use of workers with different skill levels. If this is the reason, senior management must discuss the implications with the production manager who has the responsibility to assign workers to tasks with the appropriate skill level. In this case, an investigation might show that higher-skilled workers were used to produce 3,500 units of hand-crafted clubheads. As a result, fewer labor hours might be required for the work, but the wage rate paid these workers is higher than standard because of their greater skills. The effect of this strategy is a higher than standard total cost, which would require actions to remedy the situation or adjust the standard.

 Decision Maker ▬▬▬▬▬▬▬▬▬▬▬▬▬▬▬▬▬

Human Resource Manager   You receive the manufacturing variance report for June and discover a large unfavorable labor efficiency (quantity) variance. What factors do you investigate to identify its possible causes? [Answer—p. 1004]

Quick Check   Answers—pp. 1004–1005

5. A standard cost (*a*) changes in direct proportion to changes in the level of activity, (*b*) is an amount incurred at the actual level of production for the period, or (*c*) is an amount incurred under normal conditions to provide a product or service.

6. What is a cost variance?

7. The following information is available for York Company.

Actual direct labor hours per unit	2.5 hours
Standard direct labor hours per unit	2.0 hours
Actual production (units)	2,500 units
Budgeted production (units)	3,000 units
Actual rate per hour	$3.10
Standard rate per hour	$3.00

The labor efficiency variance is (*a*) $3,750 U, (*b*) $3,750 F, or (*c*) $3,875 U.

8. Refer to Quick Check 7; the labor rate variance is (*a*) $625 F or (*b*) $625 U.

9. If a materials quantity variance is favorable and a materials price variance is unfavorable, can the total materials cost variance be favorable?

Overhead Standards and Variances

Video24.1&24.3

When standard costs are used, a predetermined overhead rate is used to assign standard overhead costs to products or services produced. This predetermined rate is often based on some overhead allocation base (such as standard labor cost, standard labor hours, or standard machine hours).

Setting Overhead Standards

Standard overhead costs are the amounts expected to occur at a certain activity level. Unlike direct materials and direct labor, overhead includes fixed costs and variable costs. This results in the average overhead cost per unit changing as the predicted volume changes. Since standard costs are also budgeted costs, they must be established before the reporting period begins. Standard overhead costs are therefore average per unit costs based on the predicted activity level.

To establish the standard overhead cost rate, management uses the same cost structure it used to construct a flexible budget at the end of a period. This cost structure identifies the different overhead cost components and classifies them as variable or fixed. To get the standard overhead rate, management selects a level of activity (volume) and predicts total overhead cost. It then divides this total by the allocation base to get the standard rate. Standard direct labor hours expected to be used to produce the predicted volume is a common allocation base and is used in this section.

To illustrate, Exhibit 24.12 shows the overhead cost structure used to develop G-Max's flexible overhead budgets for May 2009. The predetermined standard overhead rate for May is set before the month begins. The first two number columns list the per unit amounts of variable costs and the monthly amounts of fixed costs. The four right-most columns show the costs expected to occur at four different levels of production activity. The predetermined overhead rate per labor hour is smaller as volume of activity increases because total fixed costs remain constant.

G-Max managers predicted an 80% activity level for May, or a production volume of 4,000 clubheads. At this volume, they budget $8,000 as the May total overhead. This choice implies a $2 per unit (labor hour) average overhead cost ($8,000/4,000 units). Since G-Max has a standard of one direct labor hour per unit, the predetermined standard overhead rate for May is $2 per standard direct labor hour. The variable overhead rate remains constant at $1 per direct labor hour regardless of the budgeted production level. The fixed overhead rate changes according to the budgeted production volume. For instance, for the predicted level of 4,000 units of production, the fixed rate is $1 per hour ($4,000 fixed costs/4,000 units). For a production level of 5,000 units, however, the fixed rate is $0.80 per hour ($4,000 fixed costs/5,000 units).

When choosing the predicted activity level, management considers many factors. The level can be set as high as 100% of capacity, but this is rare. Factors causing the activity level to

Point: Managers consider the types of overhead costs when choosing the basis for assigning overhead costs to products.

Point: With increased automation, machine hours are frequently used in applying overhead instead of labor hours.

Point: Variable costs per unit remain constant, but fixed costs per unit decline with increases in volume. This means the average total overhead cost per unit declines with increases in volume.

EXHIBIT 24.12

Flexible Overhead Budgets

G-MAX Flexible Overhead Budgets For Month Ended May 31, 2009						
	Flexible Budget					
	Variable Amount per Unit	Total Fixed Cost	Flexible Budget at 70% Capacity	Flexible Budget at 80% Capacity	Flexible Budget at 90% Capacity	Flexible Budget at 100% Capacity
Production (in units)	1 unit		3,500	4,000	4,500	5,000
Factory overhead						
Variable costs						
Indirect labor	$0.40/unit		$1,400	$1,600	$1,800	$2,000
Indirect materials	0.30/unit		1,050	1,200	1,350	1,500
Power and lights	0.20/unit		700	800	900	1,000
Maintenance	0.10/unit		350	400	450	500
Total variable overhead costs . . .	$1.00/unit		3,500	4,000	4,500	5,000
Fixed costs (per month)						
Building rent		$1,000	1,000	1,000	1,000	1,000
Depreciation—machinery		1,200	1,200	1,200	1,200	1,200
Supervisory salaries		1,800	1,800	1,800	1,800	1,800
Total fixed overhead costs		$4,000	4,000	4,000	4,000	4,000
Total factory overhead			$7,500	$8,000	$8,500	$9,000
Standard direct labor hours 1 hr./unit			3,500 hrs.	4,000 hrs.	4,500 hrs.	5,000 hrs.
Predetermined overhead rate per standard direct labor hour			$ 2.14	$ 2.00	$ 1.89	$ 1.80

be less than full capacity include difficulties in scheduling work, equipment under repair or maintenance, and insufficient product demand. Good long-run management practices often call for some plant capacity in excess of current operating needs to allow for special opportunities and demand changes.

Decision Insight

Measuring Up   In the spirit of continuous improvement, competitors compare their processes and performance standards against benchmarks established by industry leaders. Those that use **benchmarking** include Precision Lube, Jiffy Lube, All Tune and Lube, and Speedee Oil Change and Tune-Up.

Computing Overhead Cost Variances

When standard costs are used, the cost accounting system applies overhead to the good units produced using the predetermined standard overhead rate. At period-end, the difference between the total overhead cost applied to products and the total overhead cost actually incurred is called an **overhead cost variance** (total overhead variance), which is defined in Exhibit 24.13.

EXHIBIT 24.13

Overhead Cost Variance

> **Overhead cost variance (OCV) = Actual overhead incurred (AOI) − Standard overhead applied (SOA)**

EXHIBIT 24.14

Framework for Understanding Total Overhead Variance

```
          Total
    Overhead Variance
          |
   ---------------
   |             |
 Variable       Fixed
 Overhead      Overhead
 Variance      Variance
```

To help identify factors causing the overhead cost variance, managers analyze this variance separately for variable and fixed overhead, as illustrated in Exhibit 24.14. The results provide information useful for taking strategic actions to improve company performance.

Computing Variable and Fixed Overhead Cost Variances   To illustrate the computation of overhead cost variances, we return to the G-Max data. We know that G-Max produced 3,500 units when 4,000 units were budgeted. Additional data from cost reports show that the actual overhead cost incurred is $7,650 (the variable portion of $3,650 and the fixed portion of $4,000). Recall from Exhibit 24.12 that each unit requires 1 hour of direct labor, that variable overhead is applied at a rate of $1.00 per direct labor hour, and that the predetermined fixed overhead rate is $1.00 per direct labor hour. Using this information, we can compute overhead variances for both variable and fixed overhead as follows:

P3	Compute overhead variances.

Actual variable overhead (given)	$3,650
Applied variable overhead (3,500 × $1.00)	3,500
Unfavorable variable overhead variance	$ 150

Actual fixed overhead (given)	$4,000
Applied fixed overhead (3,500 × $1.00)	3,500
Unfavorable fixed overhead variance	$ 500

"Well, according to the books, you've got too much overhead."

Management should seek to determine the causes of these unfavorable variances and take corrective action. To help better isolate the causes of these variances, more detailed overhead variances can be used, as shown in the next section.

Computing Controllable Overhead Variances and Volume Variances
The total overhead variance for G-Max is $650 unfavorable, consisting of $150 unfavorable variable overhead variance and $500 unfavorable fixed overhead variance.

Similar to analysis of direct materials and direct labor, both the variable and fixed overhead variances can be separately analyzed. Exhibit 24.15 shows an expanded framework for understanding these component overhead variances. A **spending variance** occurs when management pays an amount different than the standard price to acquire an item. For instance, the actual wage rate paid to indirect labor might be higher than the standard rate. Similarly, actual supervisory salaries might be different than expected. Spending variances such as these cause management to investigate the reasons that the amount paid differs from the standard. Both variable and fixed overhead costs can yield their own spending variances. Analyzing variable overhead includes computing an **efficiency variance,** which occurs when standard direct labor hours (the allocation base) expected for actual production differ from the actual direct labor hours used. This efficiency variance reflects on the cost-effectiveness in using the overhead allocation base (such as direct labor).

A **volume variance** occurs when a difference occurs between the actual volume of production and the standard volume of production. The budgeted fixed overhead amount is the same regardless of the volume of production (within the relevant range). This budgeted amount is computed based on the standard direct labor hours that the budgeted production volume allows. The applied overhead is based, however, on the standard direct labor hours allowed for the actual volume of production. A difference between budgeted and actual production volumes results in a difference in the standard direct labor hours allowed for these two production levels. This situation yields a volume variance different from zero.

We can combine the variable overhead spending variance, the fixed overhead spending variance, and the variable overhead efficiency variance to get **controllable variance.** The controllable variance is so named because it refers to activities usually under management control. Exhibit 24.16

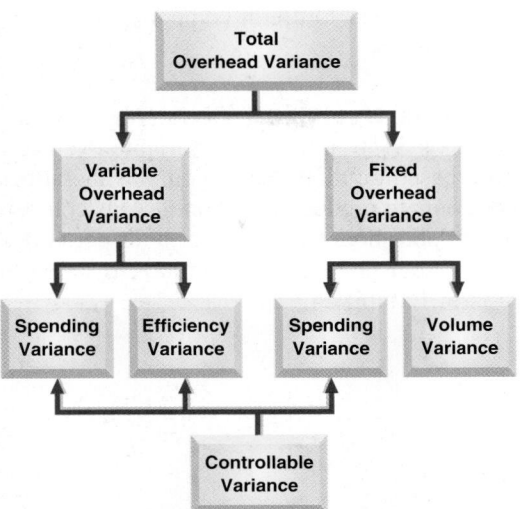

EXHIBIT 24.15

Expanded Framework for Total Overhead Variance

Example: Does an unfavorable volume variance indicate poor management performance? *Answer.* No, it only indicates production volume was less than expected. This can be due to many factors, such as falling demand for company products, that are usually viewed outside a manager's control.

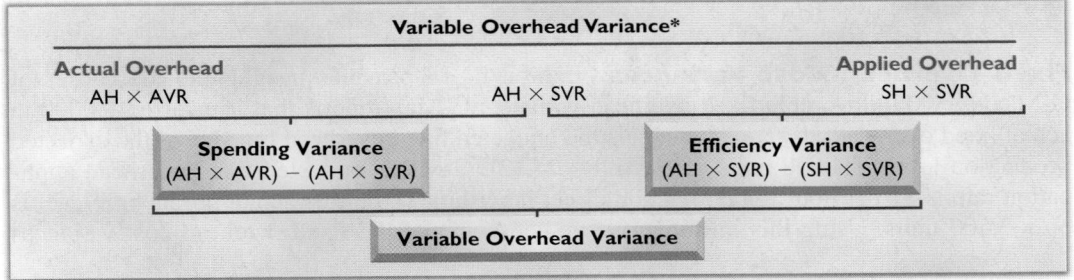

* AH = actual direct labor hours; AVR = actual variable overhead rate; SH = standard direct labor hours; SVR = standard variable overhead rate.

EXHIBIT 24.16

Variable and Fixed Overhead Variances

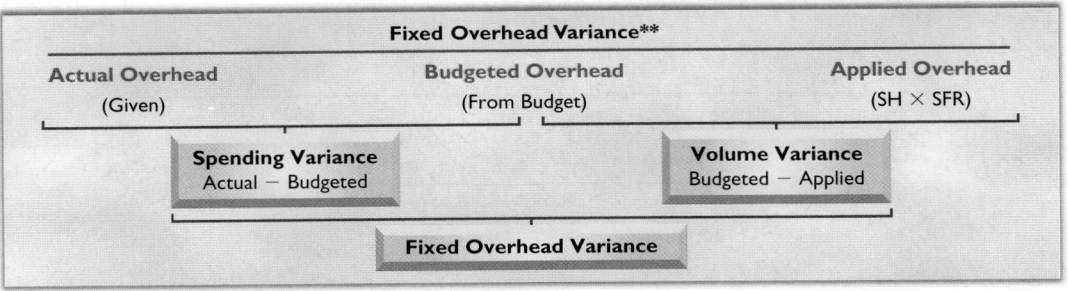

** SH = standard direct labor hours; SFR = standard fixed overhead rate.

shows formulas to use in computing detailed overhead variances that can better identify reasons for variances.

Variable Overhead Cost Variances   Exhibit 24.17 offers insight into the causes of G-Max's $150 unfavorable variable overhead cost variance. Recall that G-Max applies overhead based on direct labor hours as the allocation base. We know that it used 3,400 direct labor hours to produce 3,500 units. This compares favorably to the standard requirement of 3,500 direct labor hours at one labor hour per unit. At a standard variable overhead rate of $1.00 per direct labor hour, this should have resulted in variable overhead costs of $3,400 (middle column of Exhibit 24.17).

EXHIBIT 24.17

Computing Variable Overhead Cost Variances

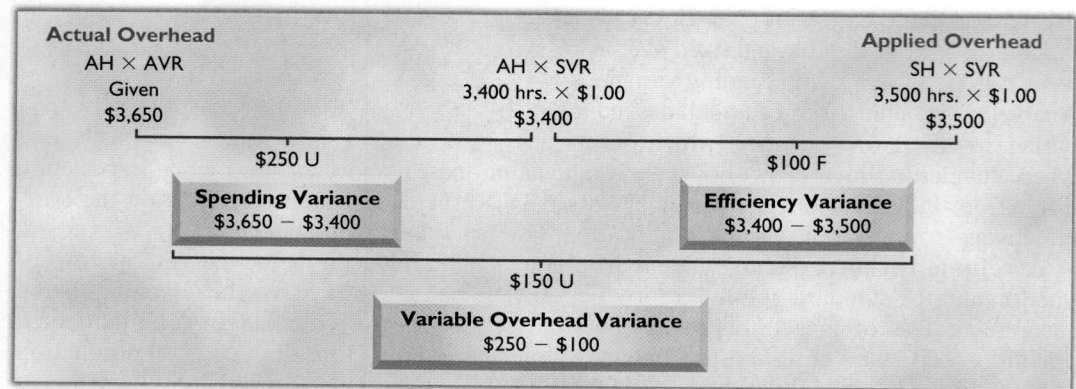

G-Max's cost records, however, report actual variable overhead of $3,650, or $250 higher than expected. This means G-Max has an unfavorable variable overhead spending variance of $250 ($3,650 − $3,400). On the other hand, G-Max used 100 fewer labor hours than expected to make 3,500 units, and its actual variable overhead is lower than its applied variable overhead. Thus, G-Max has a favorable variable overhead efficiency variance of $100 ($3,400 − $3,500).

Fixed Overhead Cost Variances   Exhibit 24.18 provides insight into the causes of G-Max's $500 unfavorable fixed overhead variance. G-Max reports that it incurred $4,000 in actual fixed overhead; this amount equals the budgeted fixed overhead for May at the expected production level of 4,000 units (see Exhibit 24.12). G-Max's budgeted fixed overhead application rate is $1 per hour ($4,000/4,000 direct labor hours), but the actual production level is only 3,500 units. Using this information, we can compute the fixed overhead cost variances

EXHIBIT 24.18

Computing Fixed Overhead Cost Variances

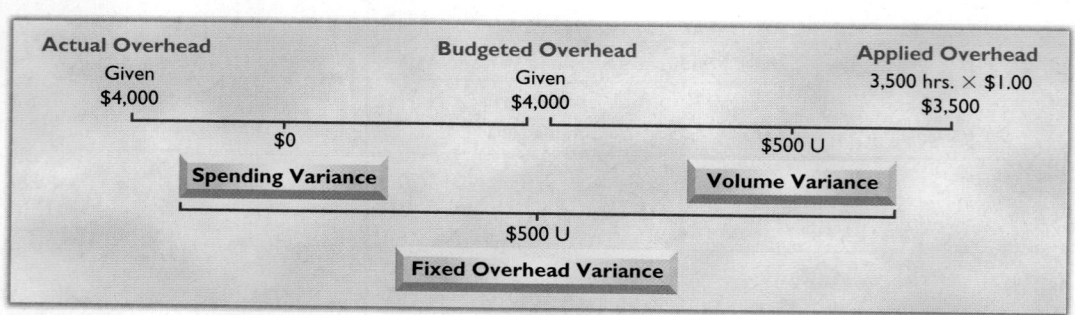

shown in Exhibit 24.18. The applied fixed overhead is computed by multiplying 3,500 standard hours allowed for the actual production by the $1 fixed overhead allocation rate. Exhibit 24.18 reveals that the fixed overhead spending variance is zero, suggesting good control of fixed overhead costs. The volume variance of $500 occurs because 500 fewer units are produced than budgeted; namely, 80% of the manufacturing capacity is budgeted but only 70% is used.

An unfavorable volume variance implies that the company did not reach its predicted operating level. Management needs to know why the actual level of performance differs from the expected level. The main purpose of the volume variance is to identify what portion of the total variance is caused by failing to meet the expected volume level. This information permits management to focus on the controllable variance.

Overhead Variance Reports   Using the information from Exhibits 24.17 and 24.18, we compute the total controllable overhead variance as $150 unfavorable ($250 U + $100 F + $0). To help management isolate the reasons for this controllable variance, an *overhead variance report* can be prepared.

A complete overhead variance report provides managers information about specific overhead costs and how they differ from budgeted amounts. Exhibit 24.19 shows G-Max's overhead variance report for May. It reveals that (1) fixed costs and maintenance cost were incurred as expected, (2) costs for indirect labor and power and lights were higher than expected, and (3) indirect materials cost was less than expected.

The total controllable variance amount is also readily available from Exhibit 24.19. The overhead variance report shows the total volume variance as $500 unfavorable (shown at the top) and the $150 unfavorable controllable variance (reported at the bottom right). The sum of the controllable variance and the volume variance equals the total (fixed and variable) overhead variance of $650 unfavorable.

EXHIBIT 24.19

Overhead Variance Report

G-MAX
Overhead Variance Report
For Month Ended May 31, 2009

Volume Variance

Expected production level	80% of capacity
Production level achieved	70% of capacity
Volume variance	$500 (unfavorable)

Controllable Variance	Flexible Budget	Actual Results	Variances*
Variable overhead costs			
Indirect labor	$1,400	$1,525	$125 U
Indirect materials	1,050	1,025	25 F
Power and lights	700	750	50 U
Maintenance	350	350	0
Total variable overhead costs	3,500	3,650	150 U[†]
Fixed overhead costs			
Building rent	1,000	1,000	0
Depreciation—machinery	1,200	1,200	0
Supervisory salaries	1,800	1,800	0
Total fixed overhead costs	4,000	4,000	0[‡]
Total overhead costs	$7,500	$7,650	$150 U

* F = Favorable variance; U = Unfavorable variance.

[†] Total variable overhead (spending and efficiency) variance.

[‡] Fixed overhead spending variance.

Extensions of Standard Costs

This section extends the application of standard costs for control purposes, for service companies, and for accounting systems.

Standard Costs for Control

C3 Explain how standard cost information is useful for management by exception.

To control business activities, top management must be able to affect the actions of lower-level managers responsible for the company's revenues and costs. After preparing a budget and establishing standard costs, management should take actions to gain control when actual costs differ from standard or budgeted amounts.

Reports such as the ones illustrated in this chapter call management's attention to variances from business plans and other standards. When managers use these reports to focus on problem areas, the budgeting process contributes to the control function. In using budgeted performance reports, practice of management by exception is often useful. **Management by exception** means that managers focus attention on the most significant variances and give less attention to areas where performance is reasonably close to the standard. This practice leads management to concentrate on the exceptional or irregular situations. Management by exception is especially useful when directed at controllable items.

♟ Decision Ethics ▮▮▮▮▮▮▮▮

Internal Auditor   You discover a manager who always spends exactly what is budgeted. About 30% of her budget is spent just before the period-end. She admits to spending what is budgeted, whether or not it is needed. She offers three reasons: (1) she doesn't want her budget cut, (2) "management by exception" focuses on budget deviations; and (3) she believes the money is budgeted to be spent. What action do you take? [Answer—p. 1004]

Standard Costs for Services

Many managers use standard costs and variance analysis to investigate manufacturing costs. Many managers also recognize that standard costs and variances can help them control *nonmanufacturing* costs. Companies providing services instead of products can benefit from the use of standard costs. Application of standard costs and variances can be readily adapted to nonmanufacturing situations. To illustrate, many service providers use standard costs to help control expenses. First, they use standard costs as a basis for budgeting all services. Second, they use periodic performance reports to compare actual results to standards. Third, they use these reports to identify significant variances within specific areas of responsibility. Fourth, they implement the appropriate control procedures.

Decision Insight ▮▮▮▮▮▮▮▮

Health Budget   Medical professionals continue to struggle with business realities. Quality medical service is paramount, but efficiency in providing that service also is important. The use of budgeting and standard costing is touted as an effective means to control and monitor medical costs, especially overhead.

Standard Cost Accounting System

P4 Prepare journal entries for standard costs and account for price and quantity variances.

We have shown how companies use standard costs in management reports. Most standard cost systems also record these costs and variances in accounts. This practice simplifies record-keeping and helps in preparing reports. Although we do not need knowledge of standard cost accounting practices to understand standard costs and their use, we must know how to interpret the accounts in which standard costs and variances are recorded. The entries in this section briefly illustrate the important aspects of this process for G-Max's standard costs and variances for May.

The first of these entries records standard materials cost incurred in May in the Goods in Process Inventory account. This part of the entry is similar to the usual accounting entry, but the amount of the debit equals the standard cost ($3,500) instead of the actual cost ($3,780).

This entry credits Raw Materials Inventory for actual cost. The difference between standard and actual direct materials costs is recorded with debits to two separate materials variance accounts (recall Exhibit 21.10). Both the materials price and quantity variances are recorded as debits because they reflect additional costs higher than the standard cost (if actual costs were less than the standard, they are recorded as credits). This treatment (debit) reflects their unfavorable effect because they represent higher costs and lower income.

May 31	Goods in Process Inventory	3,500	
	Direct Materials Price Variance*	180	
	Direct Materials Quantity Variance	100	
	Raw Materials Inventory		3,780
	To charge production for standard quantity of materials used (3,500 lbs.) at the standard price ($1 per lb.), and to record material price and material quantity variances.		

Assets = Liabilities + Equity
+3,500   −100
−3,780   −180

* Many companies record the materials price variance when materials are purchased. For simplicity, we record both the materials price and quantity variances when materials are issued to production.

The second entry debits Goods in Process Inventory for the standard labor cost of the goods manufactured during May ($28,000). Actual labor cost ($28,220) is recorded with a credit to the Factory Payroll account. The difference between standard and actual labor costs is explained by two variances (see Exhibit 21.11). The direct labor rate variance is unfavorable and is debited to that account. The direct labor efficiency variance is favorable and that account is credited. The direct labor efficiency variance is favorable because it represents a lower cost and a higher net income.

May 31	Goods in Process Inventory	28,000	
	Direct Labor Rate Variance	1,020	
	Direct Labor Efficiency Variance		800
	Factory Payroll		28,220
	To charge production with 3,500 standard hours of direct labor at the standard $8 per hour rate, and to record the labor rate and efficiency variances.		

Assets = Liabilities + Equity
+28,000   +28,220
                           − 1,020
                           +   800

The entry to assign standard predetermined overhead to the cost of goods manufactured must debit the $7,000 predetermined amount to the Goods in Process Inventory account. Actual overhead costs of $7,650 were debited to Factory Overhead during the period (entries not shown here). Thus, when Factory Overhead is applied to Goods in Process Inventory, the actual amount is credited to the Factory Overhead account. To account for the difference between actual and standard overhead costs, the entry includes a $250 debit to the Variable Overhead Spending Variance, a $100 credit to the Variable Overhead Efficiency Variance, and a $500 debit to the Volume Variance (recall Exhibits 21.17 and 21.18). An alternative (simpler) approach is to record the difference with a $150 debit to the Controllable Variance account and a $500 debit to the Volume Variance account (recall from Exhibit 21.15 that controllable variance is the sum of both variable overhead variances and the fixed overhead spending variance).

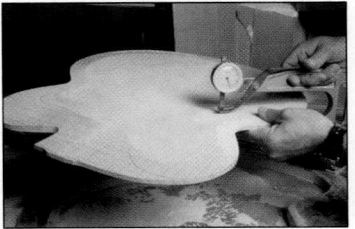

May 31	Goods in Process Inventory	7,000	
	Volume Variance	500	
	Variable Overhead Spending Variance	250	
	Variable Overhead Efficiency Variance		100
	Factory Overhead		7,650
	To apply overhead at the standard rate of $2 per standard direct labor hour (3,500 hours), and to record overhead variances.		

Assets = Liabilities + Equity
+7,000   +7,650
                           − 250
                           − 500
                           + 100

The balances of these different variance accounts accumulate until the end of the accounting period. As a result, the unfavorable variances of some months can offset the favorable variances of other months.

These ending variance account balances, which reflect results of the period's various transactions and events, are closed at period-end. If the amounts are *immaterial,* they are added to or subtracted from the balance of the Cost of Goods Sold account. This process is similar to that shown in the job order costing chapter for eliminating an underapplied or overapplied balance in the Factory Overhead account. (*Note:* These variance balances, which represent differences between actual and standard costs, must be added to or subtracted from the materials, labor, and overhead costs recorded. In this way, the recorded costs equal the actual costs incurred in the period; a company must use actual costs in external financial statements prepared in accordance with generally accepted accounting principles.)

Point: If variances are material they can be allocated between Goods in Process Inventory, Finished Goods Inventory, and Cost of Goods Sold. This closing process is explained in advanced courses.

Quick Check
Answers—p. 1005

10. Under what conditions is an overhead volume variance considered favorable?
11. To use management by exception with standard costs, a company (*a*) must record standard costs in its accounting, (*b*) should compute variances from flexible budget amounts to allow management to focus its attention on significant differences between actual and budgeted results, or (*c*) should analyze only variances for direct materials and direct labor.
12. A company uses a standard cost accounting system. Prepare the journal entry to record these direct materials variances:

Direct materials cost actually incurred	$73,200
Direct materials quantity variance (favorable)	3,800
Direct materials price variance (unfavorable)	1,300

13. If standard costs are recorded in the manufacturing accounts, how are recorded variances treated at the end of an accounting period?

Decision Analysis — Sales Variances

A2 Analyze changes in sales from expected amounts.

This chapter explained the computation and analysis of cost variances. A similar variance analysis can be applied to sales. To illustrate, consider the following sales data from G-Max for two of its golf products, Excel golf balls and Big Bert® drivers.

	Budgeted	Actual
Sales of Excel golf balls (units)	1,000 units	1,100 units
Sales price per Excel golf ball	$10	$10.50
Sales of Big Bert® drivers (units)	150 units	140 units
Sales price per Big Bert® driver	$200	$190

Using this information, we compute both the *sales price variance* and the *sales volume variance* as shown in Exhibit 24.20. The total sales price variance is $850 unfavorable, and the total sales volume variance is $1,000 unfavorable. Neither variance implies anything positive about these two products. However, further analysis of these total sales variances reveals that both the sales price and sales volume variances for Excel golf balls are favorable, meaning that both the unfavorable total sales price variance and the unfavorable total sales volume variance are due to the Big Bert driver.

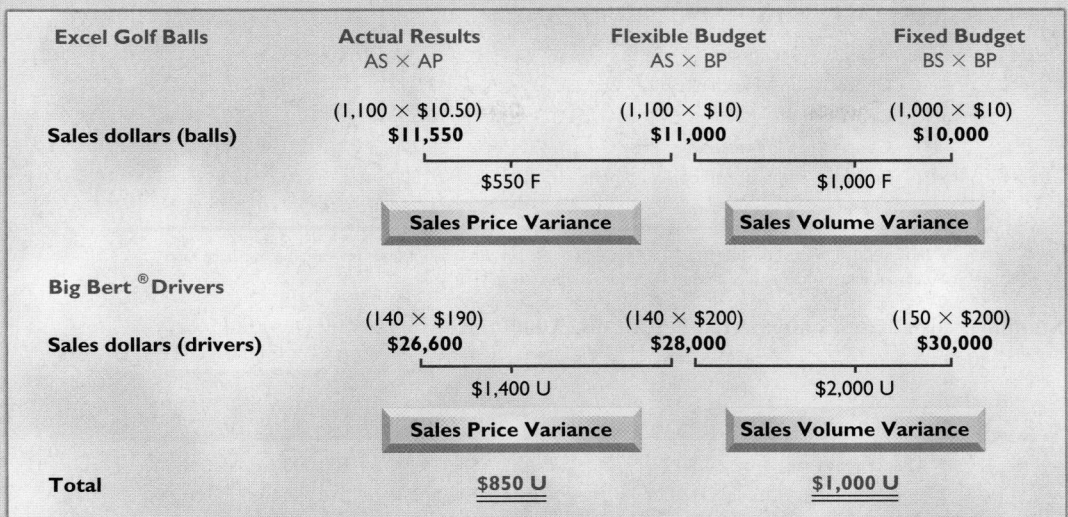

EXHIBIT 24.20

Computing Sales Variances*

Excel Golf Balls	Actual Results AS × AP	Flexible Budget AS × BP	Fixed Budget BS × BP
Sales dollars (balls)	(1,100 × $10.50) **$11,550**	(1,100 × $10) **$11,000**	(1,000 × $10) **$10,000**
	$550 F		**$1,000 F**
	Sales Price Variance		**Sales Volume Variance**
Big Bert ®Drivers			
Sales dollars (drivers)	(140 × $190) **$26,600**	(140 × $200) **$28,000**	(150 × $200) **$30,000**
	$1,400 U		**$2,000 U**
	Sales Price Variance		**Sales Volume Variance**
Total	**$850 U**		**$1,000 U**

* AS = actual sales units; AP = actual sales price; BP = budgeted sales price; BS = budgeted sales units (fixed budget).

Managers use sales variances for planning and control purposes. The sales variance information is used to plan future actions to avoid unfavorable variances. G-Max sold 90 total combined units (both balls and drivers) more than planned, but these 90 units were not sold in the proportion budgeted. G-Max sold fewer than the budgeted quantity of the higher-priced driver, which contributed to the unfavorable total sales variances. Managers use such detail to question what caused the company to sell more golf balls and fewer drivers. Managers also use this information to evaluate and even reward their salespeople. Extra compensation is paid to salespeople who contribute to a higher profit margin. Finally, with multiple products, the sales volume variance can be separated into a *sales mix variance* and a *sales quantity variance*. The sales mix variance is the difference between the actual and budgeted sales mix of the products. The sales quantity variance is the difference between the total actual and total budgeted quantity of units sold.

Decision Maker

Sales Manager The current performance report reveals a large favorable sales volume variance but an unfavorable sales price variance. You did not expect to see a large increase in sales volume. What steps do you take to analyze this situation? [Answer—p. 1004]

Demonstration Problem

Pacific Company provides the following information about its budgeted and actual results for June 2009. Although the expected June volume was 25,000 units produced and sold, the company actually produced and sold 27,000 units as detailed here:

DP24

	Budget (25,000 units)	Actual (27,000 units)
Selling price	$5.00 per unit	$5.23 per unit
Variable costs (per unit)		
Direct materials	1.24 per unit	1.12 per unit
Direct labor	1.50 per unit	1.40 per unit
Factory supplies*	0.25 per unit	0.37 per unit
Utilities*	0.50 per unit	0.60 per unit
Selling costs	0.40 per unit	0.34 per unit

[continued on next page]

[continued from previous page]

Fixed costs (per month)		
Depreciation—machinery*	$3,750	$3,710
Depreciation—building*	2,500	2,500
General liability insurance	1,200	1,250
Property taxes on office equipment	500	485
Other administrative expense	750	900

* Indicates factory overhead item; $0.75 per unit or $3 per direct labor hour for variable overhead, and
$0.25 per unit or $1 per direct labor hour for fixed overhead.

Standard costs based on expected output of 25,000 units

	Per Unit of Output	Quantity to Be Used	Total Cost
Direct materials, 4 oz. @ $0.31/oz.	$1.24/unit	100,000 oz.	$31,000
Direct labor, 0.25 hrs. @ $6.00/hr.	1.50/unit	6,250 hrs.	37,500
Overhead	1.00/unit		25,000

Actual costs incurred to produce 27,000 units

	Per Unit of Output	Quantity Used	Total Cost
Direct materials, 4 oz. @ $0.28/oz.	$1.12/unit	108,000 oz.	$30,240
Direct labor, 0.20 hrs. @ $7.00/hr.	1.40/unit	5,400 hrs.	37,800
Overhead	1.20/unit		32,400

Standard costs based on expected output of 27,000 units

	Per Unit of Output	Quantity to Be Used	Total Cost
Direct materials, 4 oz. @ $0.31/oz.	$1.24/unit	108,000 oz.	$33,480
Direct labor, 0.25 hrs. @ $6.00/hr.	1.50/unit	6,750 hrs.	40,500
Overhead			26,500

Required

1. Prepare June flexible budgets showing expected sales, costs, and net income assuming 20,000, 25,000, and 30,000 units of output produced and sold.

2. Prepare a flexible budget performance report that compares actual results with the amounts budgeted if the actual volume had been expected.

3. Apply variance analysis for direct materials, for direct labor, and for overhead.

4. Prepare journal entries to record standard costs, and price and quantity variances, for direct materials, direct labor, and factory overhead.

Planning the Solution

- Prepare a table showing the expected results at the three specified levels of output. Compute the variable costs by multiplying the per unit variable costs by the expected volumes. Include fixed costs at the given amounts. Combine the amounts in the table to show total variable costs, contribution margin, total fixed costs, and income from operations.

- Prepare a table showing the actual results and the amounts that should be incurred at 27,000 units. Show any differences in the third column and label them with an *F* for favorable if they increase income or a *U* for unfavorable if they decrease income.

- Using the chapter's format, compute these total variances and the individual variances requested:
  - Total materials variance (including the direct materials quantity variance and the direct materials price variance).

- Total direct labor variance (including the direct labor efficiency variance and rate variance).
- Total overhead variance (including both variable and fixed overhead variances and their component variances).

Solution to Demonstration Problem

1.

PACIFIC COMPANY
Flexible Budgets
For Month Ended June 30, 2009

	Flexible Budget — Variable Amount per Unit	Flexible Budget — Total Fixed Cost	Flexible Budget for Unit Sales of 20,000	Flexible Budget for Unit Sales of 25,000	Flexible Budget for Unit Sales of 30,000
Sales	$5.00		$100,000	$125,000	$150,000
Variable costs					
Direct materials	1.24		24,800	31,000	37,200
Direct labor	1.50		30,000	37,500	45,000
Factory supplies	0.25		5,000	6,250	7,500
Utilities	0.50		10,000	12,500	15,000
Selling costs	0.40		8,000	10,000	12,000
Total variable costs	3.89		77,800	97,250	116,700
Contribution margin	$1.11		22,200	27,750	33,300
Fixed costs					
Depreciation—machinery		$3,750	3,750	3,750	3,750
Depreciation—building		2,500	2,500	2,500	2,500
General liability insurance		1,200	1,200	1,200	1,200
Property taxes on office equipment		500	500	500	500
Other administrative expense		750	750	750	750
Total fixed costs		$8,700	8,700	8,700	8,700
Income from operations			$ 13,500	$ 19,050	$ 24,600

2.

PACIFIC COMPANY
Flexible Budget Performance Report
For Month Ended June 30, 2009

	Flexible Budget	Actual Results	Variance*
Sales (27,000 units)	$135,000	$141,210	$6,210 F
Variable costs			
Direct materials	33,480	30,240	3,240 F
Direct labor	40,500	37,800	2,700 F
Factory supplies	6,750	9,990	3,240 U
Utilities	13,500	16,200	2,700 U
Selling costs	10,800	9,180	1,620 F
Total variable costs	105,030	103,410	1,620 F
Contribution margin	29,970	37,800	7,830 F
Fixed costs			
Depreciation—machinery	3,750	3,710	40 F
Depreciation—building	2,500	2,500	0
General liability insurance	1,200	1,250	50 U
Property taxes on office equipment	500	485	15 F
Other administrative expense	750	900	150 U
Total fixed costs	8,700	8,845	145 U
Income from operations	$ 21,270	$ 28,955	$7,685 F

* F = Favorable variance; U = Unfavorable variance.

3. Variance analysis of materials, labor, and overhead costs.

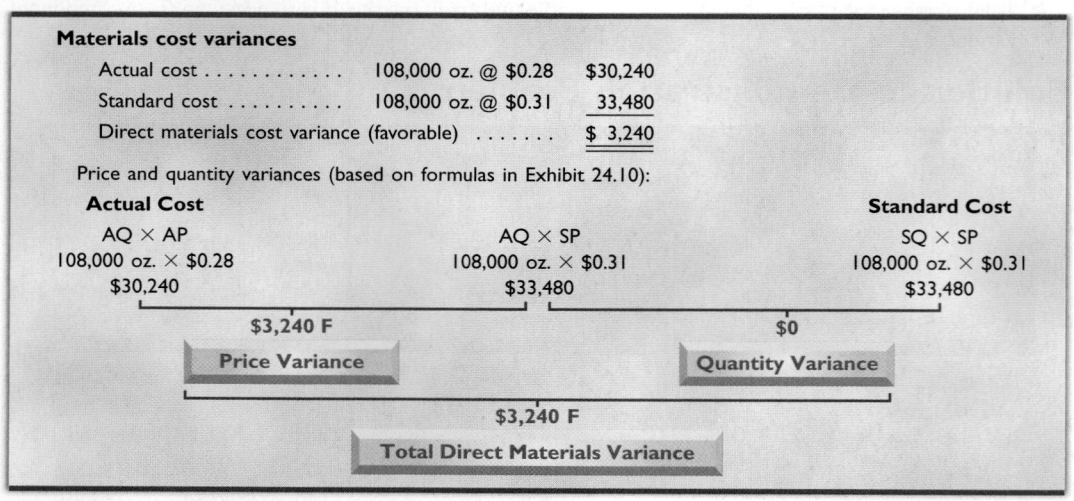

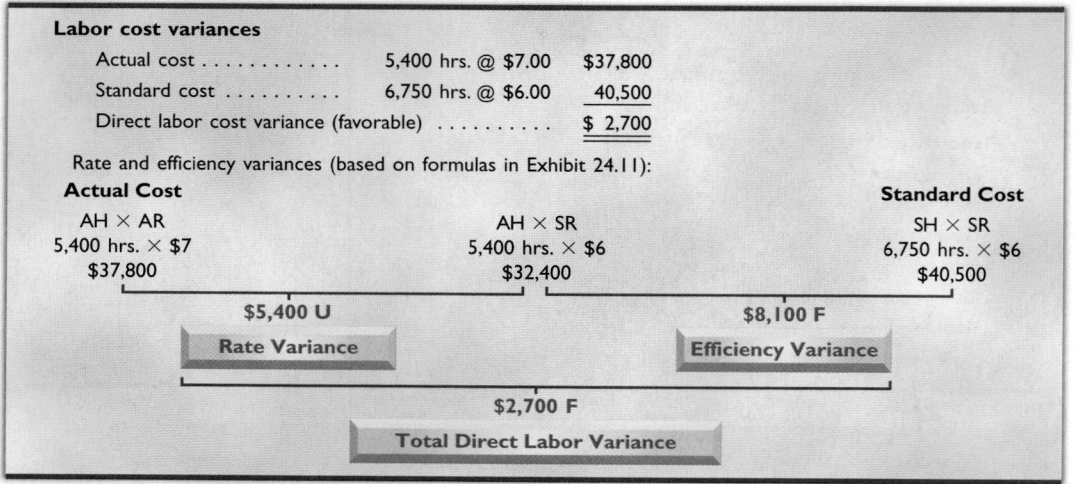

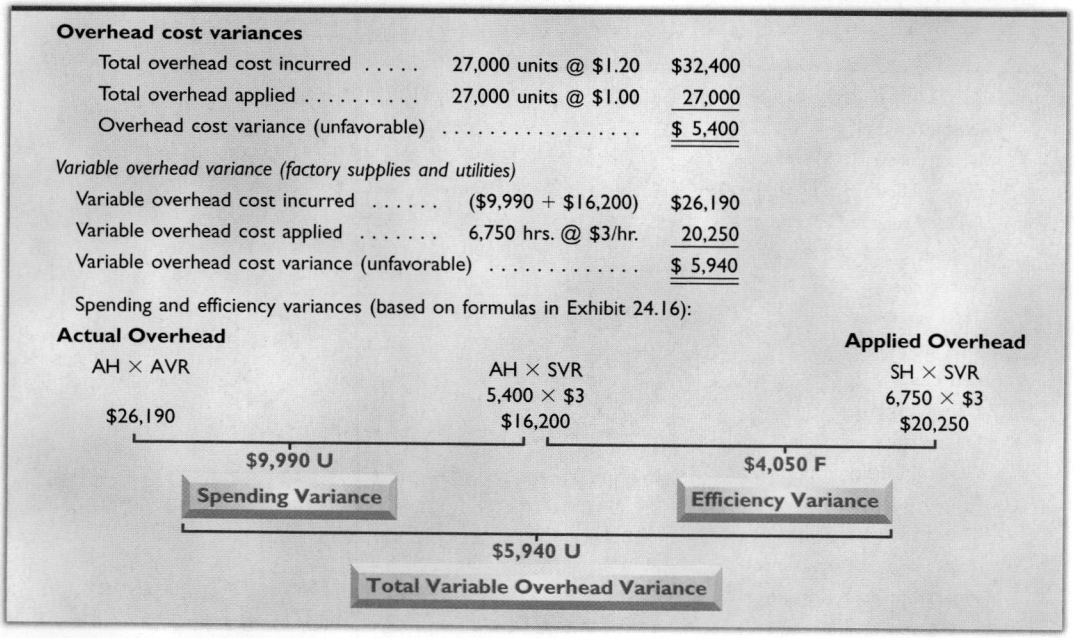

[continued on next page]

[continued from previous page]

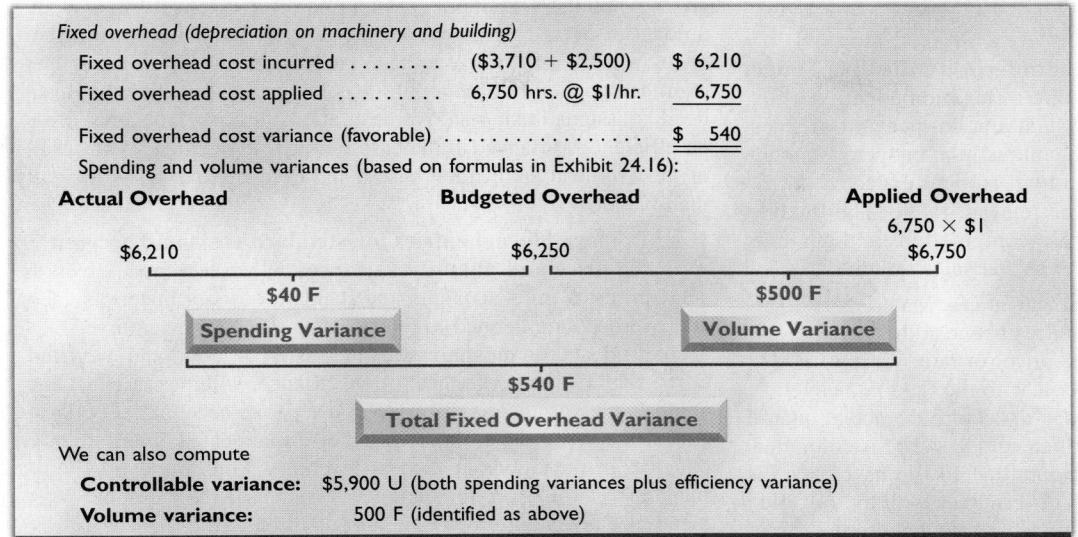

Fixed overhead (depreciation on machinery and building)

Fixed overhead cost incurred . . . . ($3,710 + $2,500) $ 6,210

Fixed overhead cost applied . . . . 6,750 hrs. @ $1/hr. 6,750

Fixed overhead cost variance (favorable) . . . . $ 540

Spending and volume variances (based on formulas in Exhibit 24.16):

Actual Overhead	**Budgeted Overhead**	**Applied Overhead**
		6,750 × $1
$6,210	$6,250	$6,750

$40 F — **Spending Variance**

$500 F — **Volume Variance**

$540 F — **Total Fixed Overhead Variance**

We can also compute

Controllable variance: $5,900 U (both spending variances plus efficiency variance)

Volume variance: 500 F (identified as above)

4.

Goods in Process Inventory	33,480	
Direct Materials Price Variance		3,240
Raw Materials Inventory		30,240
Goods in Process Inventory	40,500	
Direct Labor Rate Variance	5,400	
Direct Labor Efficiency Variance		8,100
Factory Payroll		37,800
Goods in Process Inventory*	27,000	
Variable Overhead Spending Variance	9,990	
Variable Overhead Efficiency Variance		4,050
Fixed Overhead Spending Variance		40
Fixed Overhead Volume Variance		500
Factory Overhead**		32,400

* $20,250 + $6,750   **$26,190 + $6,210

Summary

C1 **Define *standard costs* and explain their computation and uses.** Standard costs are the normal costs that should be incurred to produce a product or perform a service. They should be based on a careful examination of the processes used to produce a product or perform a service as well as the quantities and prices that should be incurred in carrying out those processes. On a performance report, standard costs (which are flexible budget amounts) are compared to actual costs, and the differences are presented as variances.

C2 **Describe variances and what they reveal about performance.** Management can use variances to monitor and control activities. Total cost variances can be broken into price and quantity variances to direct management's attention to those responsible for quantities used and prices paid.

C3 **Explain how standard cost information is useful for management by exception.** Standard cost accounting provides management information about costs that differ from budgeted (expected) amounts. Performance reports disclose the costs or areas of operations that have significant variances from budgeted amounts. This allows managers to focus attention on the exceptions and less attention on areas proceeding normally.

A1 **Compare fixed and flexible budgets.** A fixed budget shows the revenues and costs expected to occur at a specified volume level. If actual volume is at some other level, the amounts in the fixed budget do not provide a reasonable basis for evaluating actual performance. A flexible budget expresses variable costs in per unit terms so that it can be used to develop budgeted amounts for any volume level within the relevant range. Thus, managers compute budgeted amounts for evaluation after a period for the volume that actually occurred.

A2 **Analyze changes in sales from expected amounts.** Actual sales can differ from budgeted sales, and managers can investigate this difference by computing both the sales price and sales volume variances. The *sales price variance* refers to that portion of total variance resulting from a difference between actual and budgeted selling prices. The *sales volume variance* refers to that portion of total variance resulting from a difference between actual and budgeted sales quantities.

P1   **Prepare a flexible budget and interpret a flexible budget performance report.** To prepare a flexible budget, we express each variable cost as a constant amount per unit of sales (or as a percent of sales dollars). In contrast, the budgeted amount of each fixed cost is expressed as a total amount expected to occur at any sales volume within the relevant range. The flexible budget is then determined using these computations and amounts for fixed and variable costs at the expected sales volume.

P2   **Compute materials and labor variances.** Materials and labor variances are due to differences between the actual costs incurred and the budgeted costs. The price (or rate) variance is computed by comparing the actual cost with the flexible budget amount that should have been incurred to acquire the actual quantity of resources. The quantity (or efficiency) variance is computed by comparing the flexible budget amount that should have been incurred to acquire the actual quantity of resources with the flexible budget amount that should have been incurred to acquire the standard quantity of resources.

P3   **Compute overhead variances.** Overhead variances are due to differences between the actual overhead costs incurred and

the overhead applied to production. An overhead spending variance arises when the actual amount incurred differs from the budgeted amount of overhead. An overhead efficiency (or volume) variance arises when the flexible overhead budget amount differs from the overhead applied to production. It is important to realize that overhead is assigned using an overhead allocation base, meaning that an efficiency variance (in the case of variable overhead) is a result of the overhead application base being used more or less efficiently than planned.

P4   **Prepare journal entries for standard costs and account for price and quantity variances.** When a company records standard costs in its accounts, the standard costs of materials, labor, and overhead are debited to the Goods in Process Inventory account. Based on an analysis of the material, labor, and overhead costs, each quantity variance, price variance, volume variance, and controllable variance is recorded in a separate account. At period-end, if the variances are material, they are allocated among the balances of the Goods in Process Inventory, Finished Goods Inventory, and Cost of Goods Sold accounts. If they are not material, they are simply debited or credited to the Cost of Goods Sold account.

Guidance Answers to **Decision Maker** and **Decision Ethics**

Entrepreneur   From the complaints, this performance report appears to compare actual results with a fixed budget. This comparison is useful in determining whether the amount of work actually performed was more or less than planned, but it is not useful in determining whether the divisions were more or less efficient than planned. If the two consulting divisions worked on more assignments than expected, some costs will certainly increase. Therefore, you should prepare a flexible budget using the actual number of consulting assignments and then compare actual performance to the flexible budget.

Human Resource Manager   As HR manager, you should investigate the causes for any labor-related variances although you may not be responsible for them. An unfavorable labor efficiency variance occurs because more labor hours than standard were used during the period. There are at least three possible reasons for this: (1) materials quality could be poor, resulting in more labor consumption due to rework; (2) unplanned interruptions (strike, breakdowns, accidents) could have occurred during the period; and (3) the production manager could have used a different labor mix to expedite orders. This new labor mix could have consisted of a larger proportion of untrained labor, which resulted in more labor hours.

Internal Auditor   Although the manager's actions might not be unethical, this action is undesirable. The internal auditor should report this behavior, possibly recommending that for the purchase of such discretionary items, the manager must provide budgetary requests using an activity-based budgeting process. The internal auditor would then be given full authority to verify this budget request.

Sales Manager   The unfavorable sales price variance suggests that actual prices were lower than budgeted prices. As the sales manager, you want to know the reasons for a lower than expected price. Perhaps your salespeople lowered the price of certain products by offering quantity discounts. You then might want to know what prompted them to offer the quantity discounts (perhaps competitors were offering discounts). You want to break the sales volume variance into both the sales mix and sales quantity variances. You could find that although the sales quantity variance is favorable, the sales mix variance is not. Then you need to investigate why the actual sales mix differs from the budgeted sales mix.

Guidance Answers to **Quick Checks**

1. *b*

2. The first step is classifying each cost as variable or fixed.

3. A fixed budget is prepared using an expected volume of sales or production. A flexible budget is prepared using the actual volume of activity.

4. The contribution margin equals sales less variable costs.

5. *c*

6. It is the difference between actual cost and standard cost.

7. *a*; Total actual hours: 2,500 × 2.5 = 6,250

Total standard hours: 2,500 × 2.0 = 5,000

Efficiency variance = (6,250 − 5,000) × $3.00
= $3,750 U

8. *b*; Rate variance = ($3.10 − $3.00) × 6,250 = $625 U

9. Yes, this will occur when the materials quantity variance is more than the materials price variance.

10. The overhead volume variance is favorable when the actual operating level is higher than the expected level.

11. *b*

12.

Goods in Process Inventory	75,700	
Direct Materials Price Variance	1,300	
Direct Materials Quantity Variance		3,800
Raw Materials Inventory		73,200

13. If the variances are material, they should be prorated among the Goods in Process Inventory, Finished Goods Inventory, and Cost of Goods Sold accounts. If they are not material, they can be closed to Cost of Goods Sold.

Key Terms   mhhe.com/wildFAP19e

Key Terms are available at the book's Website for learning and testing in an online Flashcard Format.

Budgetary control (p. 980)
Budget report (p. 980)
Controllable variance (p. 993)
Cost variance (p. 986)
Efficiency variance (p. 993)
Favorable variance (p. 981)
Fixed budget (p. 981)

Fixed budget performance report (p. 981)
Flexible budget (p. 982)
Flexible budget performance report (p. 984)
Management by exception (p. 996)
Overhead cost variance (p. 992)
Price variance (p. 984)

Quantity variance (p. 984)
Spending variance (p. 993)
Standard costs (p. 985)
Unfavorable variance (p. 981)
Variance analysis (p. 984)
Volume variance (p. 993)

Multiple Choice Quiz   Answers on p. 1021   mhhe.com/wildFAP19e

Additional Quiz Questions are available at the book's Website.

Quiz24

1. A company predicts its production and sales will be 24,000 units. At that level of activity, its fixed costs are budgeted at $300,000, and its variable costs are budgeted at $246,000. If its activity level declines to 20,000 units, what will be its fixed costs and its variable costs?
  a. Fixed, $300,000; variable, $246,000
  b. Fixed, $250,000; variable, $205,000
  c. Fixed, $300,000; variable, $205,000
  d. Fixed, $250,000; variable, $246,000
  e. Fixed, $300,000; variable, $300,000

2. Using the following information about a single product company, compute its total actual cost of direct materials used.
  • Direct materials standard cost: 5 lbs. × $2 per lb. = $10.
  • Total direct materials cost variance: $15,000 unfavorable.
  • Actual direct materials used: 300,000 lbs.
  • Actual units produced: 60,000 units.
  a. $585,000
  b. $600,000
  c. $300,000
  d. $315,000
  e. $615,000

3. A company uses four hours of direct labor to produce a product unit. The standard direct labor cost is $20 per hour. This period the company produced 20,000 units and used 84,160 hours of direct labor at a total cost of $1,599,040. What is its labor rate variance for the period?
  a. $83,200 F
  b. $84,160 U
  c. $84,160 F
  d. $83,200 U
  e. $ 960 F

4. A company's standard for a unit of its single product is $6 per unit in variable overhead (4 hours × $1.50 per hour). Actual data for the period show variable overhead costs of $150,000 and production of 24,000 units. Its total variable overhead cost variance is
  a. $ 6,000 F.
  b. $ 6,000 U.
  c. $114,000 U.
  d. $114,000 F.
  e. $ 0.

5. A company's standard for a unit of its single product is $4 per unit in fixed overhead ($24,000 total/6,000 units budgeted). Actual data for the period show total actual fixed overhead of $24,100 and production of 4,800 units. Its volume variance is
  a. $4,800 U.
  b. $4,800 F.
  c. $ 100 U.
  d. $ 100 F.
  e. $4,900 U.

Discussion Questions

1. ♟ What limits the usefulness to managers of fixed budget performance reports?
2. ♟ Identify the main purpose of a flexible budget for managers.
3. Prepare a flexible budget performance report title (in proper form) for Spalding Company for the calendar year 2009. Why is a proper title important for this or any report?
4. ♟ What type of analysis does a flexible budget performance report help management perform?
5. In what sense can a variable cost be considered constant?
6. ♟ What department is usually responsible for a direct labor rate variance? What department is usually responsible for a direct labor efficiency variance? Explain.
7. What is a price variance? What is a quantity variance?
8. ♟ What is the purpose of using standard costs?
9. In an analysis of fixed overhead cost variances, what is the volume variance?
10. What is the predetermined standard overhead rate? How is it computed?

11. In general, variance analysis is said to provide information about _____ and _____ variances.
12. ♟ In an analysis of overhead cost variances, what is the controllable variance and what causes it?
13. What are the relations among standard costs, flexible budgets, variance analysis, and management by exception?
14. ♟ How can the manager of a music department of a Best Buy retail store use flexible budgets to enhance performance?
15. ♟ Is it possible for a retail store such as Circuit City to use variances in analyzing its operating performance? Explain.
16. ♟ Assume that Apple is budgeted to operate at 80% of capacity but actually operates at 75% of capacity. What effect will the 5% deviation have on its controllable variance? Its volume variance?

♟ *Denotes Discussion Questions that involve decision making.*

Available with McGraw-Hill's Homework Manager   McGraw-Hill's HOMEWORK MANAGER®

QUICK STUDY

QS 24-1

Flexible budget performance report

P1

Quail Company reports the following selected financial results for May. For the level of production achieved in May, the budgeted amounts would be sales, $650,000; variable costs, $375,000; and fixed costs, $150,000. Prepare a flexible budget performance report for May.

Sales (100,000 units)	$637,500
Variable costs	356,250
Fixed costs	150,000

QS 24-2

Labor cost variances

C2 P2

Martin Company's output for the current period results in a $10,000 unfavorable direct labor rate variance and a $5,000 unfavorable direct labor efficiency variance. Production for the current period was assigned a $200,000 standard direct labor cost. What is the actual total direct labor cost for the current period?

QS 24-3

Materials cost variances

C2 P2

Blanda Company's output for the current period was assigned a $300,000 standard direct materials cost. The direct materials variances included a $24,000 favorable price variance and a $4,000 favorable quantity variance. What is the actual total direct materials cost for the current period?

QS 24-4

Materials cost variances

C2 P2

For the current period, Roja Company's manufacturing operations yield an $8,000 unfavorable price variance on its direct materials usage. The actual price per pound of material is $156; the standard price is $154. How many pounds of material are used in the current period?

QS 24-5

Management by exception

C3 ♟

Managers use *management by exception* for control purposes. (1) Describe the concept of management by exception. (2) Explain how standard costs help managers apply this concept to monitor and control costs.

QS 24-6

Overhead cost variances   P3

Gohan Company's output for the current period yields a $12,000 favorable overhead volume variance and a $21,500 unfavorable overhead controllable variance. Standard overhead charged to production for the period is $410,000. What is the actual total overhead cost incurred for the period?

Refer to the information in QS 24-6. Gohan records standard costs in its accounts. Prepare the journal entry to charge overhead costs to the Goods in Process Inventory account and to record any variances.

QS 24-7
Preparing overhead entries   P4

Wills Company specializes in selling used trucks. During the first six months of 2009, the dealership sold 50 trucks at an average price of $18,000 each. The budget for the first six months of 2009 was to sell 45 trucks at an average price of $19,000 each. Compute the dealership's sales price variance and sales volume variance for the first six months of 2009.

QS 24-8
Computing sales price and volume variances

A2

Harp Company applies overhead using machine hours and reports the following information. Compute the total variable overhead cost variance.

QS 24-9
Overhead cost variances

P3

Actual machine hours used	4,950 hours
Standard machine hours	5,000 hours
Actual variable overhead rate per hour	$2.10
Standard variable overhead rate per hour	$2.00

Refer to the information from QS 24-9. Compute the variable overhead spending variance and the variable overhead efficiency variance.

QS 24-10
Overhead spending and efficiency variances   P3

McGraw-Hill's
HOMEWORK
MANAGER®   **Available with McGraw-Hill's Homework Manager**

Tryon Company's fixed budget for the first quarter of calendar year 2009 reveals the following. Prepare flexible budgets following the format of Exhibit 24.3 that show variable costs per unit, fixed costs, and three different flexible budgets for sales volumes of 14,500, 15,000, and 15,500 units.

EXERCISES

Exercise 24-1
Preparation of flexible budgets

P1

Sales (15,000 units)		$3,030,000
Cost of goods sold		
Direct materials	$345,000	
Direct labor	705,000	
Production supplies	405,000	
Plant manager salary	90,000	1,545,000
Gross profit		1,485,000
Selling expenses		
Sales commissions	150,000	
Packaging	240,000	
Advertising	100,000	490,000
Administrative expenses		
Administrative salaries	110,000	
Depreciation—office equip.	60,000	
Insurance	48,000	
Office rent	54,000	272,000
Income from operations		$ 723,000

Check   Income (at 14,500 units), $683,500

RTEX Company manufactures and sells mountain bikes. It normally operates eight hours a day, five days a week. Using this information, classify each of the following costs as fixed or variable. If additional information would affect your decision, describe the information.

Exercise 24-2
Classification of costs as fixed or variable

P1

a. Management salaries
b. Incoming shipping expenses
c. Office supplies
d. Taxes on property

e. Gas used for heating
f. Direct labor
g. Repair expense for tools
h. Depreciation on tools

i. Pension cost
j. Bike frames
k. Screws for assembly

Exercise 24-3
Preparation of a flexible budget performance report

A1

Check Income variance, $13,950 F

Hall Company's fixed budget performance report for June follows. The $660,000 budgeted expenses include $450,000 variable expenses and $210,000 fixed expenses. Actual expenses include $200,000 fixed expenses. Prepare a flexible budget performance report that shows any variances between budgeted results and actual results. List fixed and variable expenses separately.

	Fixed Budget	Actual Results	Variances
Sales (in units)	9,000	7,900	
Sales (in dollars)	$720,000	$647,800	$72,200 U
Total expenses	660,000	606,850	53,150 F
Income from operations	$ 60,000	$ 40,950	$19,050 U

Exercise 24-4
Preparation of a flexible budget performance report

A1

Check Income variance, $34,200 F

Burton Company's fixed budget performance report for July follows. The $675,000 budgeted expenses include $634,500 variable expenses and $40,500 fixed expenses. Actual expenses include $52,500 fixed expenses. Prepare a flexible budget performance report showing any variances between budgeted and actual results. List fixed and variable expenses separately.

	Fixed Budget	Actual Results	Variances
Sales (in units)	9,000	11,400	
Sales (in dollars)	$900,000	$1,140,000	$240,000 F
Total expenses	675,000	810,000	135,000 U
Income from operations	$225,000	$ 330,000	$105,000 F

Exercise 24-5
Computation and interpretation of labor variances   C2   P2

Check October rate variance, $14,880 F

After evaluating Pima Company's manufacturing process, management decides to establish standards of 1.4 hours of direct labor per unit of product and $15 per hour for the labor rate. During October, the company uses 3,720 hours of direct labor at a $40,920 total cost to produce 4,000 units of product. In November, the company uses 4,560 hours of direct labor at a $54,720 total cost to produce 3,500 units of product. (1) Compute the rate variance, the efficiency variance, and the total direct labor cost variance for each of these two months. (2) Interpret the October direct labor variances.

Exercise 24-6
Computation and interpretation of total variable and fixed overhead variances

C2   P3

Venture Company set the following standard costs for one unit of its product for 2009.

Direct material (20 lbs. @ $5.00 per lb.)	$100.00
Direct labor (10 hrs. @ $16.00 per hr.)	160.00
Factory variable overhead (10 hrs. @ $8.00 per hr.)	80.00
Factory fixed overhead (10 hrs. @ $3.20 per hr.)	32.00
Standard cost	$372.00

The $11.20 ($8.00 + $3.20) total overhead rate per direct labor hour is based on an expected operating level equal to 75% of the factory's capacity of 50,000 units per month. The following monthly flexible budget information is also available.

	Operating Levels (% of capacity)		
	70%	75%	80%
Budgeted output (units)	35,000	37,500	40,000
Budgeted labor (standard hours)	350,000	375,000	400,000
Budgeted overhead (dollars)			
Variable overhead	$2,800,000	$3,000,000	$3,200,000
Fixed overhead	1,200,000	1,200,000	1,200,000
Total overhead	$4,000,000	$4,200,000	$4,400,000

During the current month, the company operated at 70% of capacity, employees worked 340,000 hours, and the following actual overhead costs were incurred.

Variable overhead costs	$2,750,000
Fixed overhead costs	1,257,200
Total overhead costs	$4,007,200

(1) Show how the company computed its predetermined overhead application rate per hour for total overhead, variable overhead, and fixed overhead. (2) Compute the variable and fixed overhead variances.

Check (2) Variable overhead cost variance, $50,000 F

Refer to the information from Exercise 24-6. Compute and interpret the following.

1. Variable overhead spending and efficiency variances.

2. Fixed overhead spending and volume variances.

3. Controllable variance.

Exercise 24-7
Computation and interpretation of overhead spending, efficiency, and volume variances P3

Check (2) Variable overhead: Spending, $30,000 U; efficiency, $80,000 F

Listor Company made 3,800 bookshelves using 23,200 board feet of wood costing $290,000. The company's direct materials standards for one bookshelf are 8 board feet of wood at $12 per board foot. (1) Compute the direct materials variances incurred in manufacturing these bookshelves. (2) Interpret the direct materials variances.

Exercise 24-8
Computation and interpretation of materials variances

C2 P2

Check Price variance, $11,600 U

Refer to Exercise 24-8. Listor Company records standard costs in its accounts and its material variances in separate accounts when it assigns materials costs to the Goods in Process Inventory account. (1) Show the journal entry that both charges the direct materials costs to the Goods in Process Inventory account and records the materials variances in their proper accounts. (2) Assume that Listor's material variances are the only variances accumulated in the accounting period and that they are immaterial. Prepare the adjusting journal entry to close the variance accounts at period-end. (3) Identify the variance that should be investigated according to the management by exception concept. Explain.

Exercise 24-9
Materials variances recorded and closed

C3 P4

Check (2) Cr. to cost of goods sold, $74,800

Integra Company expects to operate at 80% of its productive capacity of 52,000 units per month. At this planned level, the company expects to use 26,000 standard hours of direct labor. Overhead is allocated to products using a predetermined standard rate based on direct labor hours. At the 80% capacity level, the total budgeted cost includes $57,200 fixed overhead cost and $280,800 variable overhead cost. In the current month, the company incurred $320,000 actual overhead and 23,000 actual labor hours while producing 37,000 units. (1) Compute its overhead application rate for total overhead, variable overhead, and fixed overhead. (2) Compute its total overhead variance.

Exercise 24-10
Computation of total variable and fixed overhead variances

P3

Check (1) Variable overhead rate, $10.80 per hour

Refer to the information from Exercise 24-10. Compute the (1) overhead volume variance and (2) overhead controllable variance.

Exercise 24-11
Computation of volume and controllable overhead variances P3

Check (2) $13,050 U

Wiz Electronics sells computers. During May 2009, it sold 500 computers at a $1,000 average price each. The May 2009 fixed budget included sales of 550 computers at an average price of $950 each. (1) Compute the sales price variance and the sales volume variance for May 2009. (2) Interpret the findings.

Exercise 24-12
Computing and interpreting sales variances A2

McGraw-Hill's
HOMEWORK
MANAGER® Available with McGraw-Hill's Homework Manager

Beck Company set the following standard unit costs for its single product.

Direct materials (26 lbs. @ $4 per lb.)	$104.00
Direct labor (8 hrs. @ $8 per hr.)	64.00
Factory overhead—variable (8 hrs. @ $5 per hr.)	40.00
Factory overhead—fixed (8 hrs. @ $7 per hr.)	56.00
Total standard cost	$264.00

PROBLEM SET A

Problem 24-1A
Computation of materials, labor, and overhead variances

C2 P2 P3

The predetermined overhead rate is based on a planned operating volume of 70% of the productive capacity of 50,000 units per quarter. The following flexible budget information is available.

	Operating Levels		
	60%	70%	80%
Production in units	30,000	35,000	40,000
Standard direct labor hours	240,000	280,000	320,000
Budgeted overhead			
Fixed factory overhead	$1,960,000	$1,960,000	$1,960,000
Variable factory overhead	$1,200,000	$1,400,000	$1,600,000

During the current quarter, the company operated at 80% of capacity and produced 40,000 units of product; actual direct labor totaled 178,600 hours. Units produced were assigned the following standard costs:

Direct materials (1,040,000 lbs. @ $4 per lb.)	$ 4,160,000
Direct labor (320,000 hrs. @ $8 per hr.)	2,560,000
Factory overhead (320,000 hrs. @ $12 per hr.)	3,840,000
Total standard cost	$10,560,000

Actual costs incurred during the current quarter follow:

Direct materials (1,035,000 lbs. @ $4.10)	$ 4,243,500
Direct labor (327,000 hrs. @ $7.75)	2,534,250
Fixed factory overhead costs	1,875,000
Variable factory overhead costs	1,482,717
Total actual costs	$10,135,467

Required

1. Compute the direct materials cost variance, including its price and quantity variances.

2. Compute the direct labor variance, including its rate and efficiency variances.

3. Compute the total variable overhead and total fixed overhead variances.

4. Compute these variances: (a) variable overhead spending and efficiency, (b) fixed overhead spending and volume, and (c) total overhead controllable.

Problem 24-2A
Preparation and analysis
of a flexible budget

P1 A1

Major Company's 2009 master budget included the following fixed budget report. It is based on an expected production and sales volume of 15,000 units.

MAJOR COMPANY		
Fixed Budget Report		
For Year Ended December 31, 2009		
Sales		$3,300,000
Cost of goods sold		
Direct materials	$960,000	
Direct labor	240,000	
Machinery repairs (variable cost)	60,000	
Depreciation—plant equipment	300,000	
Utilities ($60,000 is variable)	180,000	
Plant management salaries	210,000	1,950,000
Gross profit		1,350,000
Selling expenses		
Packaging	75,000	
Shipping	105,000	
Sales salary (fixed annual amount)	235,000	415,000
General and administrative expenses		
Advertising expense	100,000	
Salaries	241,000	
Entertainment expense	85,000	426,000
Income from operations		$ 509,000

Required

1. Classify all items listed in the fixed budget as variable or fixed. Also determine their amounts per unit or their amounts for the year, as appropriate.

2. Prepare flexible budgets (see Exhibit 24.3) for the company at sales volumes of 14,000 and 16,000 units.

3. The company's business conditions are improving. One possible result is a sales volume of approximately 18,000 units. The company president is confident that this volume is within the relevant range of existing capacity. How much would operating income increase over the 2009 budgeted amount of $509,000 if this level is reached without increasing capacity?

4. An unfavorable change in business is remotely possible; in this case, production and sales volume for 2009 could fall to 12,000 units. How much income (or loss) from operations would occur if sales volume falls to this level?

Check (2) Budgeted income at 16,000 units, $629,000

(4) Potential operating income, $149,000

Refer to the information in Problem 24-2A. Major Company's actual income statement for 2009 follows.

Problem 24-3A
Preparation and analysis of a flexible budget performance report

P1   A2

mhhe.com/wildFAP19e

MAJOR COMPANY Statement of Income from Operations For Year Ended December 31, 2009		
Sales (18,000 units)		$3,948,000
Cost of goods sold		
Direct materials	$1,160,000	
Direct labor	293,000	
Machinery repairs (variable cost)	63,000	
Depreciation—plant equipment	300,000	
Utilities (fixed cost is $147,500)	215,500	
Plant management salaries	220,000	2,251,500
Gross profit		1,696,500
Selling expenses		
Packaging	87,500	
Shipping	118,500	
Sales salary (annual)	253,000	459,000
General and administrative expenses		
Advertising expense	107,000	
Salaries	241,000	
Entertainment expense	88,500	436,500
Income from operations		$ 801,000

Required

1. Prepare a flexible budget performance report for 2009.

Analysis Component

2. Analyze and interpret both the (a) sales variance and (b) direct materials variance.

Check (1) Variances: Fixed costs, $66,000 U; income, $68,000 U

Silver Company set the following standard costs for one unit of its product.

Problem 24-4A
Flexible budget preparation; computation of materials, labor, and overhead variances; and overhead variance report

P1 P2 P3 C2

Direct materials (5 lbs. @ $6 per lb.)	$30.00
Direct labor (2 hrs. @ $12 per hr.)	24.00
Overhead (2 hrs. @ $16.65 per hr.)	33.30
Total standard cost	$87.30

The predetermined overhead rate ($16.65 per direct labor hour) is based on an expected volume of 75% of the factory's capacity of 20,000 units per month. Following are the company's budgeted overhead costs per month at the 75% level.

Overhead Budget (75% Capacity)		
Variable overhead costs		
Indirect materials	$ 21,000	
Indirect labor	96,000	
Power	22,500	
Repairs and maintenance	57,000	
Total variable overhead costs		$196,500
Fixed overhead costs		
Depreciation—building	23,000	
Depreciation—machinery	71,000	
Taxes and insurance	18,000	
Supervision	191,000	
Total fixed overhead costs		303,000
Total overhead costs		$499,500

The company incurred the following actual costs when it operated at 75% of capacity in October.

Direct materials (75,500 lbs. @ $6.10 per lb.)		$ 460,550
Direct labor (29,000 hrs. @ $12.20 per hr.)		353,800
Overhead costs		
Indirect materials	$ 22,500	
Indirect labor	88,800	
Power	21,500	
Repairs and maintenance	60,250	
Depreciation—building	23,000	
Depreciation—machinery	65,000	
Taxes and insurance	18,100	
Supervision	185,000	484,150
Total costs		$1,298,500

Required

Check (2) Budgeted total overhead at 13,000 units, $473,300.

(3) Materials variances: Price, $7,550 U; quantity, $3,000 U

(4) Labor variances: Rate, $5,800 U; efficiency, $12,000 F

1. Examine the monthly overhead budget to (a) determine the costs per unit for each variable overhead item and its total per unit costs, and (b) identify the total fixed costs per month.

2. Prepare flexible overhead budgets (as in Exhibit 24.12) for October showing the amounts of each variable and fixed cost at the 65%, 75%, and 85% capacity levels.

3. Compute the direct materials cost variance, including its price and quantity variances.

4. Compute the direct labor cost variance, including its rate and efficiency variances.

5. Compute the (a) variable overhead spending and efficiency variances, (b) fixed overhead spending and volume variances, and (c) total overhead controllable variance.

6. Prepare a detailed overhead variance report (as in Exhibit 24.19) that shows the variances for individual items of overhead.

Problem 24-5A

Materials, labor, and overhead variances; and overhead variance report

C2 P2 P3

Green Company has set the following standard costs per unit for the product it manufactures.

Direct materials (15 lbs. @ $3.90 per lb.)	$ 58.50
Direct labor (4 hrs. @ $18 per hr.)	72.00
Overhead (4 hrs. @ $4.20 per hr.)	16.80
Total standard cost	$147.30

The predetermined overhead rate is based on a planned operating volume of 80% of the productive capacity of 10,000 units per month. The following flexible budget information is available.

	Operating Levels		
	70%	80%	90%
Production in units	7,000	8,000	9,000
Standard direct labor hours	28,000	32,000	36,000
Budgeted overhead			
Variable overhead costs			
Indirect materials	$ 14,000	$ 16,000	$ 18,000
Indirect labor	20,300	23,200	26,100
Power	5,600	6,400	7,200
Maintenance	38,500	44,000	49,500
Total variable costs	78,400	89,600	100,800
Fixed overhead costs			
Rent of factory building	15,000	15,000	15,000
Depreciation—machinery	10,000	10,000	10,000
Supervisory salaries	19,800	19,800	19,800
Total fixed costs	44,800	44,800	44,800
Total overhead costs	$123,200	$134,400	$145,600

During May, the company operated at 90% of capacity and produced 9,000 units, incurring the following actual costs.

Direct materials (139,000 lbs. @ $3.80 per lb.)		$ 528,200
Direct labor (33,000 hrs. @ $18.50 per hr.)		610,500
Overhead costs		
Indirect materials	$16,000	
Indirect labor	27,500	
Power	7,200	
Maintenance	42,000	
Rent of factory building	15,000	
Depreciation—machinery	10,000	
Supervisory salaries	24,000	141,700
Total costs		$1,280,400

Required

1. Compute the direct materials variance, including its price and quantity variances.
2. Compute the direct labor variance, including its rate and efficiency variances.
3. Compute these variances: (a) variable overhead spending and efficiency, (b) fixed overhead spending and volume, and (c) total overhead controllable.
4. Prepare a detailed overhead variance report (as in Exhibit 24.19) that shows the variances for individual items of overhead.

Check (1) Materials variances: Price, $13,900 F; quantity, $15,600 U (2) Labor variances: Rate, $16,500 U; efficiency, $54,000 F

Brose Company's standard cost accounting system recorded this information from its December operations.

Problem 24-6A
Materials, labor, and overhead variances recorded and analyzed

C3 P4

Standard direct materials cost	$104,000
Direct materials quantity variance (unfavorable)	3,000
Direct materials price variance (favorable)	550
Actual direct labor cost	90,000
Direct labor efficiency variance (favorable)	6,850
Direct labor rate variance (unfavorable)	1,200
Actual overhead cost	375,000
Volume variance (unfavorable)	13,000
Controllable variance (unfavorable)	9,000

Required

1. Prepare December 31 journal entries to record the company's costs and variances for the month. (Do not prepare the journal entry to close the variances.)

Analysis Component

2. Identify the areas that would attract the attention of a manager who uses management by exception. Explain what action(s) the manager should consider.

PROBLEM SET B

Problem 24-1B
Computation of materials, labor, and overhead variances

C2 P2 P3

Krug Company set the following standard unit costs for its single product.

Direct materials (5 lbs. @ $2 per lb.)	$10.00
Direct labor (0.3 hrs. @ $15 per hr.)	4.50
Factory overhead—variable (0.3 hrs. @ $10 per hr.)	3.00
Factory overhead—fixed (0.3 hrs. @ $14 per hr.)	4.20
Total standard cost	$21.70

The predetermined overhead rate is based on a planned operating volume of 80% of the productive capacity of 600,000 units per quarter. The following flexible budget information is available.

	Operating Levels		
	70%	**80%**	**90%**
Production in units	420,000	480,000	540,000
Standard direct labor hours	126,000	144,000	162,000
Budgeted overhead			
Fixed factory overhead	$2,016,000	$2,016,000	$2,016,000
Variable factory overhead	1,260,000	1,440,000	1,620,000

During the current quarter, the company operated at 70% of capacity and produced 420,000 units of product; direct labor hours worked were 125,000. Units produced were assigned the following standard costs:

Direct materials (2,100,000 lbs. @ $2 per lb.)	$4,200,000
Direct labor (126,000 hrs. @ $15 per hr.)	1,890,000
Factory overhead (126,000 hrs. @ $24 per hr.)	3,024,000
Total standard cost	$9,114,000

Actual costs incurred during the current quarter follow:

Direct materials (2,000,000 lbs. @ $2.15)	$4,300,000
Direct labor (125,000 hrs. @ $15.50)	1,937,500
Fixed factory overhead costs	1,960,000
Variable factory overhead costs	1,200,000
Total actual costs	$9,397,500

Required

1. Compute the direct materials cost variance, including its price and quantity variances.
2. Compute the direct labor variance, including its rate and efficiency variances.
3. Compute the total variable overhead and total fixed overhead variances.
4. Compute these variances: (a) variable overhead spending and efficiency, (b) fixed overhead spending and volume, and (c) total overhead controllable.

Problem 24-2B
Preparation and analysis of a flexible budget P1 A1

Toronto Company's 2009 master budget included the following fixed budget report. It is based on an expected production and sales volume of 10,000 units.

TORONTO COMPANY
Fixed Budget Report
For Year Ended December 31, 2009

Sales		$1,500,000
Cost of goods sold		
Direct materials	$600,000	
Direct labor	130,000	
Machinery repairs (variable cost)	28,500	
Depreciation—machinery	125,000	
Utilities (25% is variable cost)	100,000	
Plant manager salaries	70,000	1,053,500
Gross profit		446,500
Selling expenses		
Packaging	40,000	
Shipping	58,000	
Sales salary (fixed annual amount)	80,000	178,000
General and administrative expenses		
Advertising	40,500	
Salaries	120,500	
Entertainment expense	45,000	206,000
Income from operations		$ 62,500

Required

1. Classify all items listed in the fixed budget as variable or fixed. Also determine their amounts per unit or their amounts for the year, as appropriate.

2. Prepare flexible budgets (see Exhibit 24.3) for the company at sales volumes of 9,500 and 10,500 units.

3. The company's business conditions are improving. One possible result is a sales volume of approximately 12,000 units. The company president is confident that this volume is within the relevant range of existing capacity. How much would operating income increase over the 2009 budgeted amount of $62,500 if this level is reached without increasing capacity?

4. An unfavorable change in business is remotely possible; in this case, production and sales volume for 2009 could fall to 8,000 units. How much income (or loss) from operations would occur if sales volume falls to this level?

Check (2) Budgeted income at 10,500 units, $93,425

(4) Potential operating loss, $(61,200)

Refer to the information in Problem 24-2B. Toronto Company's actual income statement for 2009 follows.

Problem 24-3B
Preparation and analysis of a flexible budget performance report

P1 A2

TORONTO COMPANY
Statement of Income from Operations
For Year Ended December 31, 2009

Sales (10,500 units)		$1,596,000
Cost of goods sold		
Direct materials	$612,500	
Direct labor	157,500	
Machinery repairs (variable cost)	26,250	
Depreciation—machinery	125,000	
Utilities (variable cost, $28,000)	105,000	
Plant manager salaries	77,500	1,103,750
Gross profit		492,250
Selling expenses		
Packaging	39,375	
Shipping	54,250	
Sales salary (annual)	81,000	174,625
General and administrative expenses		
Advertising expense	52,000	
Salaries	116,000	
Entertainment expense	50,000	218,000
Income from operations		$ 99,625

Required

1. Prepare a flexible budget performance report for 2009.

Analysis Component

2. Analyze and interpret both the (a) sales variance and (b) direct materials variance.

Problem 24-4B

Flexible budget preparation; computation of materials, labor, and overhead variances; and overhead variance report

P1 P2 P3 C2

Stevens Company set the following standard costs for one unit of its product.

Direct materials (9 lb. @ $6 per lb.)	$ 54.00
Direct labor (3 hrs. @ $16 per hr.)	48.00
Overhead (3 hrs. @ $11.75 per hr.)	35.25
Total standard cost	137.25

The predetermined overhead rate ($11.75 per direct labor hour) is based on an expected volume of 75% of the factory's capacity of 20,000 units per month. Following are the company's budgeted overhead costs per month at the 75% level.

Overhead Budget (75% Capacity)		
Variable overhead costs		
Indirect materials	$ 33,750	
Indirect labor	135,000	
Power	22,500	
Repairs and maintenance	67,500	
Total variable overhead costs		$258,750
Fixed overhead costs		
Depreciation—building	36,000	
Depreciation—machinery	108,000	
Taxes and insurance	27,000	
Supervision	99,000	
Total fixed overhead costs		270,000
Total overhead costs		$528,750

The company incurred the following actual costs when it operated at 75% of capacity in December.

Direct materials (139,000 lbs. @ $6.10)		$ 847,900
Direct labor (43,500 hrs. @ $16.30)		709,050
Overhead costs		
Indirect materials	$ 31,600	
Indirect labor	133,400	
Power	23,500	
Repairs and maintenance	69,700	
Depreciation—building	36,000	
Depreciation—machinery	110,000	
Taxes and insurance	24,500	
Supervision	99,000	527,700
Total costs		$2,084,650

Required

1. Examine the monthly overhead budget to (a) determine the costs per unit for each variable overhead item and its total per unit costs, and (b) identify the total fixed costs per month.

2. Prepare flexible overhead budgets (as in Exhibit 24.12) for December showing the amounts of each variable and fixed cost at the 65%, 75%, and 85% capacity levels.

3. Compute the direct materials cost variance, including its price and quantity variances.

4. Compute the direct labor cost variance, including its rate and efficiency variances.

5. Compute the (a) variable overhead spending and efficiency variances, (b) fixed overhead spending and volume variances, and (c) total overhead controllable variance.

6. Prepare a detailed overhead variance report (as in Exhibit 24.19) that shows the variances for individual items of overhead.

(4) Labor variances: Rate, $13,050 U; efficiency, $24,000 F

Harris Company has set the following standard costs per unit for the product it manufactures.

Problem 24-5B
Materials, labor, and overhead variances; and overhead variance report

C2   P2   P3

Direct materials (5 lbs. @ $3.00 per lb.)	$15
Direct labor (2 hr. @ $20 per hr.)	40
Overhead (2 hr. @ $10 per hr.)	20
Total standard cost	$75

The predetermined overhead rate is based on a planned operating volume of 80% of the productive capacity of 10,000 units per month. The following flexible budget information is available.

	Operating Levels		
	70%	**80%**	**90%**
Production in units	7,000	8,000	9,000
Standard direct labor hours	14,000	16,000	18,000
Budgeted overhead			
Variable overhead costs			
Indirect materials	$ 17,500	$ 20,000	$22,500
Indirect labor	28,000	32,000	36,000
Power	7,000	8,000	9,000
Maintenance	3,500	4,000	4,500
Total variable costs	56,000	64,000	72,000
Fixed overhead costs			
Rent of factory building	24,000	24,000	24,000
Depreciation—machinery	40,000	40,000	40,000
Taxes and insurance	4,800	4,800	4,800
Supervisory salaries	27,200	27,200	27,200
Total fixed costs	96,000	96,000	96,000
Total overhead costs	$152,000	$160,000	$168,000

During March, the company operated at 90% of capacity and produced 9,000 units, incurring the following actual costs.

Direct materials (46,000 lbs. @ $2.95 per lb.)		$ 135,700
Direct labor (18,800 hrs. @ $20.10 per hr.)		377,880
Overhead costs		
Indirect materials	$22,000	
Indirect labor	32,000	
Power	9,600	
Maintenance	4,750	
Rent of factory building	24,000	
Depreciation—machinery	39,400	
Taxes and insurance	5,200	
Supervisory salaries	28,000	164,950
Total costs		$678,530

Required

1. Compute the direct materials cost variance, including its price and quantity variances.
2. Compute the direct labor variance, including its rate and efficiency variances.
3. Compute these variances: (a) variable overhead spending and efficiency, (b) fixed overhead spending and volume, and (c) total overhead controllable.
4. Prepare a detailed overhead variance report (as in Exhibit 24.19) that shows the variances for individual items of overhead.

Problem 24-6B
Materials, labor, and overhead
variances recorded and analyzed

C3   P4

Del Company's standard cost accounting system recorded this information from its June operations.

Standard direct materials cost	$260,000
Direct materials quantity variance (favorable)	10,000
Direct materials price variance (favorable)	3,000
Actual direct labor cost	130,000
Direct labor efficiency variance (favorable)	6,000
Direct labor rate variance (unfavorable)	1,000
Actual overhead cost	500,000
Volume variance (unfavorable)	24,000
Controllable variance (unfavorable)	16,000

Required

1. Prepare journal entries dated June 30 to record the company's costs and variances for the month. (Do not prepare the journal entry to close the variances.)

Analysis Component

2. Identify the areas that would attract the attention of a manager who uses management by exception. Describe what action(s) the manager should consider.

SERIAL PROBLEM

Success Systems

(This serial problem began in Chapter 1 and continues through most of the book. If previous chapter segments were not completed, the serial problem can begin at this point. It is helpful, but not necessary, to use the working papers that accompany the book.)

SP 24   Success Systems' second quarter 2010 fixed budget performance report for its computer furniture operations follows. The $156,000 budgeted expenses include $108,000 in variable expenses for desks and $18,000 in variable expenses for chairs, as well as $30,000 fixed expenses. The actual expenses include $31,000 fixed expenses. Prepare a flexible budget performance report that shows any variances between budgeted results and actual results. List fixed and variable expenses separately.

	Fixed Budget	Actual Results	Variances
Desk sales (in units)	144	150	
Chair sales (in units)	72	80	
Desk sales (in dollars)	$180,000	$186,000	$6,000 F
Chair sales (in dollars)	$ 36,000	$ 41,200	$5,200 F
Total expenses	$156,000	$163,880	$7,880 U
Income from operations	$ 60,000	$ 63,320	$3,320 F

BEYOND THE NUMBERS

**REPORTING IN
ACTION**

C1

BTN 24-1   Analysis of flexible budgets and standard costs emphasizes the importance of a similar unit of measure for meaningful comparisons and evaluations. When Best Buy compiles its financial reports in compliance with GAAP, it applies the same unit of measurement, U.S. dollars, for most measures of business operations. One issue for Best Buy is how best to adjust account values for its subsidiaries that compile financial reports in currencies other than the U.S. dollar.

Required

1. Read Best Buy's Note 1 in Appendix A and identify the financial statement where it reports the annual adjustment for foreign currency translation.

2. Record the annual amount of its foreign currency translation adjustment for the fiscal years 2005 through 2007.

Fast Forward

3. Access Best Buy's financial statements for a fiscal year ending after March 3, 2007, from either its Website [BestBuy.com] or the SEC's EDGAR database [www.sec.gov]. (a) Identify its foreign currency translation adjustment. (b) Does this adjustment increase or decrease net income? Explain.

BTN 24-2   The usefulness of budgets, variances, and related analyses often depends on the accuracy of management's estimates of future sales activity.

COMPARATIVE ANALYSIS

A2

Required

1. Identify and record the prior three years' sales (in dollars) for both Best Buy, Circuit City, and RadioShack using their financial statements in Appendix A.

2. Using the data in part 1, predict all three companies' sales activity for the next two to three years. (If possible, compare your predictions to actual sales figures for these years.)

BTN 24-3   Setting materials, labor, and overhead standards is challenging. If standards are set too low, companies might purchase inferior products and employees might not work to their full potential. If standards are set too high, companies could be unable to offer a quality product at a profitable rate and employees could be overworked. The ethical challenge is to set a high but reasonable standard. Assume that as a manager, you are asked to set the standard materials price and quantity for the new 1,000 CKB Mega-Max chip, a technically advanced product. To properly set the price and quantity standards, you assemble a team of specialists to provide input.

ETHICS CHALLENGE

C1

Required

Identify four types of specialists that you would assemble to provide information to help set the materials price and quantity standards. Briefly explain why you chose each individual.

BTN 24-4   The reason we use the words *favorable* and *unfavorable* when evaluating variances is made clear when we look at the closing of accounts. To see this, consider that (1) all variance accounts are closed at the end of each period (temporary accounts), (2) a favorable variance is always a credit balance, and (3) an unfavorable variance is always a debit balance. Write a one-half page memorandum to your instructor with three parts that answer the three following requirements. (Assume that variance accounts are closed to Cost of Goods Sold.)

COMMUNICATING IN PRACTICE

P4 C2

Required

1. Does Cost of Goods Sold increase or decrease when closing a favorable variance? Does gross margin increase or decrease when a favorable variance is closed to Cost of Goods Sold? Explain.

2. Does Cost of Goods Sold increase or decrease when closing an unfavorable variance? Does gross margin increase or decrease when an unfavorable variance is closed to Cost of Goods Sold? Explain.

3. Explain the meaning of a favorable variance and an unfavorable variance.

TAKING IT TO THE NET

C1

BTN 24-5 Access iSixSigma's Website (**iSixSigma.com**) to search for and read information about *benchmarking* to complete the following requirements.

Required

1. Write a one-paragraph explanation (in layperson's terms) of benchmarking.

2. How does standard costing relate to benchmarking?

TEAMWORK IN ACTION

C2

BTN 24-6 Many service industries link labor rate and time (quantity) standards with their processes. One example is the standard time to board an aircraft. The reason time plays such an important role in the service industry is that it is viewed as a competitive advantage: best service in the shortest amount of time. Although the labor rate component is difficult to observe, the time component of a service delivery standard is often readily apparent—for example, "Lunch will be served in less than five minutes, or it is free."

Required

Break into teams and select two service industries for your analysis. Identify and describe all the time elements each industry uses to create a competitive advantage.

ENTREPRENEURIAL DECISION

C1 C2

BTN 24-7 Entrepreneur Chris Martin of **Martin Guitar Company** (see Chapter opener) uses a costing system with standard costs for direct materials, direct labor, and overhead costs. Two comments frequently are mentioned in relation to standard costing and variance analysis: "Variances are not explanations" and "Management's goal is not to minimize variances."

Required

Write Chris Martin a short memo (no more than 1 page) interpreting these two comments.

HITTING THE ROAD

C1

BTN 24-8 Training employees to use standard amounts of materials in production is common. Typically large companies invest in this training but small organizations do not. One can observe these different practices in a trip to two different pizza businesses. Visit both a local pizza business and a national pizza chain business and then complete the following.

Required

1. Observe and record the number of raw material items used to make a typical cheese pizza. Also observe how the person making the pizza applies each item when preparing the pizza.

2. Record any differences in how items are applied between the two businesses.

3. Estimate which business is more profitable from your observations. Explain.

GLOBAL DECISION

BTN 24-9 Access the annual report of **DSG** (at www.DSGiplc.com) for the year ended April 28, 2007. The usefulness of its budgets, variances, and related analyses depends on the accuracy of management's estimates of future sales activity.

Required

1. Identify and record the prior two years' sales (in pounds) for DSG from its income statement.

2. Using the data in part 1, predict sales activity for DSG for the next two years. Explain your prediction process.

ANSWERS TO MULTIPLE CHOICE QUIZ

1. c; Fixed costs remain at $300,000; Variable costs = ($246,000/24,000 units) × 20,000 units = $205,000.

2. e; Budgeted direct materials + Unfavorable variance = Actual cost of direct materials used; or, 60,000 units × $10 per unit = $600,000 + $15,000 U = $615,000.

3. c; (AH × AR) − (AH × SR) = $1,599,040 − (84,160 hours × $20 per hour) = $84,160 F.

4. b; Actual variable overhead − Variable overhead applied to production = Variable overhead cost variance; or $150,000 − (96,000 hours × $1.50 per hour) = $6,000 U.

5. a; Budgeted fixed overhead − Fixed overhead applied to production = Volume variance; or $24,000 − (4,800 units × $4 per unit) = $4,800 U.

A Look Back

Chapter 24 discussed flexible budgets, variance analysis, and standard costs. It explained how management uses each to control and monitor business activities.

A Look at This Chapter

This chapter focuses on evaluating capital budgeting decisions. It also explains several tools and procedures used in making and evaluating short-term managerial decisions.

Chapter **25**

Capital Budgeting and Managerial Decisions

Learning Objectives

CAP

Conceptual

C1 Explain the importance of capital budgeting. (p. 1024)

C2 Describe the selection of a hurdle rate for an investment. (p. 1033)

C3 Describe the importance of relevant costs for short-term decisions. (p. 1035)

Analytical

A1 Evaluate short-term managerial decisions using relevant costs. (p. 1035)

A2 Analyze a capital investment project using break-even time. (p. 1043)

LP25

Procedural

P1 Compute payback period and describe its use. (p. 1025)

P2 Compute accounting rate of return and explain its use. (p. 1027)

P3 Compute net present value and describe its use. (p. 1029)

P4 Compute internal rate of return and explain its use. (p. 1031)

Batter Up

"Now batting, a 34-ounce Prairie Sticks double-dipped black maple bat!"—PA Announcer

RED DEER, CANADA—Jared Greenberg, of the Red Deer Riggers, and Dan Zinger of the Red Deer Stags, dream to make it to the major leagues . . . not as players, but as makers of baseball bats. Their start-up company, **Prairie Sticks Bat Company (PrairieSticks.com),** started in Jared's workshop with a hand lathe and a piece of wood when local amateur players had trouble getting maple bats from manufacturers. Jared says he began producing bats for his teammates and friends "just like you would do in your middle school shop class."

Prairie Sticks' bats are made from four different types of wood, each with different prices (the company also makes fungo bats and training bats). Jared and Dan use product contribution margins in determining their best sales mix. This is especially important given their constraints on machine hours and labor—they have only one hydraulic tracing lathe and no other employees that make bats.

This past year they sold 1,500 bats. With production growth comes new business questions. Do we take a one-time deal with a buyer? Do we scrap or rework unacceptable inventory? Do we make or buy certain raw materials? These questions need answers. Jared and Dan focus on relevant costs and incremental revenues for insight into answering those questions. If a customer wants a bat in a color Prairie Sticks does not stock, the company charges a higher price to cover the incremental cost of the new color. The company makes novelty bats, unusable for play but fine for gifts and awards, out of inferior wood. These novelty bats sell at reduced prices, but enable the company to avoid costly rework and processing costs. They also sell apparel and hats, made by outside manufacturers.

Prairie Sticks now makes bats for big leaguers. It uses the same wood as the major batmakers; and $100,000 worth of equipment, including the hydraulic lathe, can turn out an unfinished bat in less than two minutes. Soon, they hope to step to the plate to accept additional business. Jared and Dan apply capital budgeting methods to help assess payback periods, rates of return, present values, and break-even points to their equipment and other expenditures. This aids them in decisions on what, and when, to buy.

A recent news release reported that a minor league player had been traded for "10 Prairie Sticks double-dipped maple bats, black," which led to major publicity and a surge in orders. "It's been crazy," says Jared. "[Since] this story has broken . . . we're on the verge of picking up our Major League vendor's license," explains Dan. That would be a tape-measure home run.

[Sources: *Prairie Sticks Bat Company Website,* January 2009; *AlbertaLocalNews.com,* May 2008; *Fox Sports on MSN.com,* May 2008; *Edmonton CityTV.com* interview, May 2008]

Making business decisions involves choosing between alternative courses of action. Many factors affect business decisions, yet analysis typically focuses on finding the alternative that offers the highest return on investment or the greatest reduction in costs. Some decisions are based on little more than an intuitive understanding of the situation because available information is too limited to allow a more systematic analysis. In other cases, intangible factors such as convenience, prestige, and environmental considerations are more important than strictly quantitative factors. In all situations, managers can reach a sounder decision if they identify the consequences of alternative choices in financial terms. This chapter explains several methods of analysis that can help managers make those business decisions.

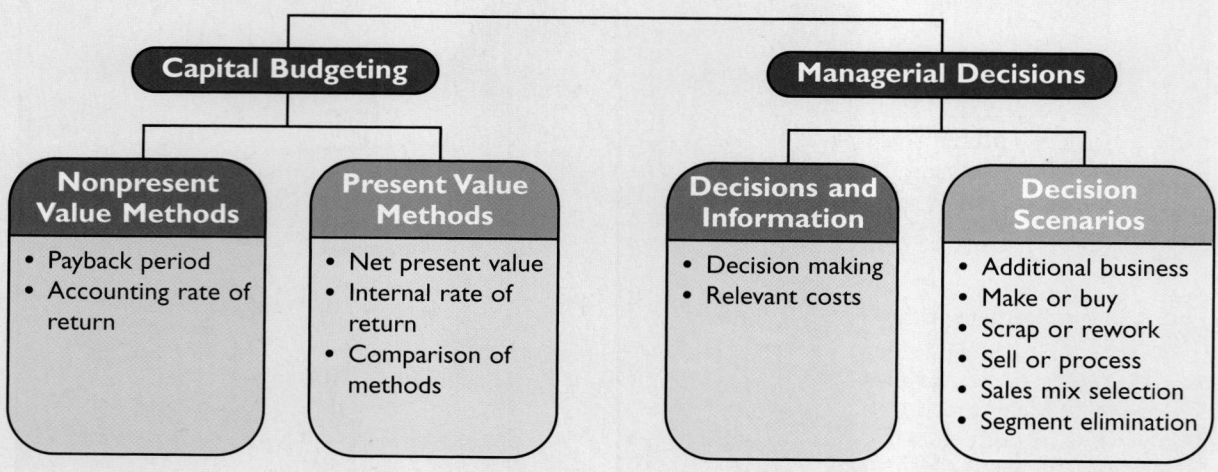

Capital Budgeting		Managerial Decisions	
Nonpresent Value Methods	**Present Value Methods**	**Decisions and Information**	**Decision Scenarios**
• Payback period • Accounting rate of return	• Net present value • Internal rate of return • Comparison of methods	• Decision making • Relevant costs	• Additional business • Make or buy • Scrap or rework • Sell or process • Sales mix selection • Segment elimination

Section 1—Capital Budgeting

C1 Explain the importance of capital budgeting.

Video25.2

Point: The nature of capital spending has changed with the business environment. Budgets for information technology have increased from about 25% of corporate capital spending 20 years ago to an estimated 35% today.

The capital expenditures budget is management's plan for acquiring and selling plant assets. **Capital budgeting** is the process of analyzing alternative long-term investments and deciding which assets to acquire or sell. These decisions can involve developing a new product or process, buying a new machine or a new building, or acquiring an entire company. An objective for these decisions is to earn a satisfactory return on investment.

Capital budgeting decisions require careful analysis because they are usually the most difficult and risky decisions that managers make. These decisions are difficult because they require predicting events that will not occur until well into the future. Many of these predictions are tentative and potentially unreliable. Specifically, a capital budgeting decision is risky because (1) the outcome is uncertain, (2) large amounts of money are usually involved, (3) the investment involves a long-term commitment, and (4) the decision could be difficult or impossible to reverse, no matter how poor it turns out to be. Risk is especially high for investments in technology due to innovations and uncertainty.

Managers use several methods to evaluate capital budgeting decisions. Nearly all of these methods involve predicting cash inflows and cash outflows of proposed investments, assessing the risk of and returns on those flows, and then choosing the investments to make. Management often restates future cash flows in terms of their present value. This approach applies the time value of money: A dollar today is worth more than a dollar tomorrow. Similarly, a dollar tomorrow is worth less than a dollar today. The process of restating future cash flows in terms of their present value is called *discounting*. The time value of money is important when evaluating capital investments, but managers sometimes apply evaluation methods that ignore present value. This section describes four methods for comparing alternative investments.

Methods Not Using Time Value of Money

All investments, whether they involve the purchase of a machine or another long-term asset, are expected to produce net cash flows. *Net cash flow* is cash inflows minus cash outflows. Sometimes managers perform simple analyses of the financial feasibility of an investment's net cash flow without using the time value of money. This section explains two of the most common methods in this category: (1) payback period and (2) accounting rate of return.

Payback Period

An investment's **payback period (PBP)** is the expected time period to recover the initial investment amount. Managers prefer investing in assets with shorter payback periods to reduce the risk of an unprofitable investment over the long run. Acquiring assets with short payback periods reduces a company's risk from potentially inaccurate long-term predictions of future cash flows.

P1 Compute payback period and describe its use.

Computing Payback Period with Even Cash Flows To illustrate use of the payback period for an investment with even cash flows, we look at data from FasTrac, a manufacturer of exercise equipment and supplies. (*Even cash flows* are cash flows that are the same each and every year; *uneven cash flows* are cash flows that are not all equal in amount.) FasTrac is considering several different capital investments, one of which is to purchase a machine to use in manufacturing a new product. This machine costs $16,000 and is expected to have an eight-year life with no salvage value. Management predicts this machine will produce 1,000 units of product each year and that the new product will be sold for $30 per unit. Exhibit 25.1 shows the expected annual net cash flows for this asset over its life as well as the expected annual revenues and expenses (including depreciation and income taxes) from investing in the machine.

EXHIBIT 25.1

Cash Flow Analysis

FASTRAC Cash Flow Analysis—Machinery Investment January 15, 2009	Expected Accrual Figures	Expected Net Cash Flows
Annual sales of new product	$30,000	$30,000
Deduct annual expenses		
Cost of materials, labor, and overhead (except depreciation)	15,500	15,500
Depreciation—Machinery	2,000	
Additional selling and administrative expenses	9,500	9,500
Annual pretax accrual income	3,000	
Income taxes (30%)	900	900
Annual net income	$ 2,100	
Annual net cash flow		$ 4,100

The amount of net cash flow from the machinery is computed by subtracting expected cash outflows from expected cash inflows. The cash flows column of Exhibit 25.1 excludes all noncash revenues and expenses. Depreciation is FasTrac's only noncash item. Alternatively, managers can adjust the projected net income for revenue and expense items that do not affect cash flows. For FasTrac, this means taking the $2,100 net income and adding back the $2,000 depreciation.

The formula for computing the payback period of an investment that yields even net cash flows is in Exhibit 25.2.

Point: Annual net cash flow in Exhibit 25.1 equals net income plus depreciation (a noncash expense).

$$\text{Payback period} = \frac{\text{Cost of investment}}{\text{Annual net cash flow}}$$

EXHIBIT 25.2

Payback Period Formula with Even Cash Flows

The payback period reflects the amount of time for the investment to generate enough net cash flow to return (or pay back) the cash initially invested to purchase it. FasTrac's payback period for this machine is just under four years:

$$\text{Payback period} = \frac{\$16,000}{\$4,100} = 3.9 \text{ years}$$

Example: If an alternative machine (with different technology) yields a payback period of 3.5 years, which one does a manager choose? Answer: The alternative (3.5 is less than 3.9).

The initial investment is fully recovered in 3.9 years, or just before reaching the halfway point of this machine's useful life of eight years.

Decision Insight

Payback Phones Profits of telecoms have declined as too much capital investment chased too little revenue. Telecom success depends on new technology, and communications gear is evolving at a dizzying rate. Consequently, managers of telecoms often demand short payback periods and large expected net cash flows to compensate for the investment risk.

Computing Payback Period with Uneven Cash Flows   Computing the payback period in the prior section assumed even net cash flows. What happens if the net cash flows are uneven? In this case, the payback period is computed using the *cumulative total of net cash flows*. The word *cumulative* refers to the addition of each period's net cash flows as we progress through time. To illustrate, consider data for another investment that FasTrac is considering. This machine is predicted to generate uneven net cash flows over the next eight years. The relevant data and payback period computation are shown in Exhibit 25.3.

EXHIBIT 25.3

Payback Period Calculation with Uneven Cash Flows

Period*	Expected Net Cash Flows	Cumulative Net Cash Flows
Year 0	$(16,000)	$(16,000)
Year 1	3,000	(13,000)
Year 2	4,000	(9,000)
Year 3	4,000	(5,000)
Year 4	4,000	(1,000)
Year 5	5,000	4,000
Year 6	3,000	7,000
Year 7	2,000	9,000
Year 8	2,000	11,000
		Payback period = 4.2 years

* All cash inflows and outflows occur uniformly during the year.

Example: Find the payback period in Exhibit 25.3 if net cash flows for the first 4 years are:
Year 1 = $6,000; Year 2 = $5,000; Year 3 = $4,000; Year 4 = $3,000. *Answer:* 3.33 years

Year 0 refers to the period of initial investment in which the $16,000 cash outflow occurs at the end of year 0 to acquire the machinery. By the end of year 1, the cumulative net cash flow is reduced to $(13,000), computed as the $(16,000) initial cash outflow plus year 1's $3,000 cash inflow. This process continues throughout the asset's life. The cumulative net cash flow amount changes from negative to positive in year 5. Specifically, at the end of year 4, the cumulative net cash flow is $(1,000). As soon as FasTrac receives net cash inflow of $1,000 during the fifth year, it has fully recovered the investment. If we assume that cash flows are received uniformly *within* each year, receipt of the $1,000 occurs about one-fifth of the way through the year. This is computed as $1,000 divided by year 5's total net cash flow of $5,000, or 0.20. This yields a payback period of 4.2 years, computed as 4 years plus 0.20 of year 5.

Using the Payback Period   Companies desire a short payback period to increase return and reduce risk. The more quickly a company receives cash, the sooner it is available for other uses and the less time it is at risk of loss. A shorter payback period also improves the company's ability to respond to unanticipated changes and lowers its risk of having to keep an unprofitable investment.

Payback period should never be the only consideration in evaluating investments. This is so because it ignores at least two important factors. First, it fails to reflect differences in the timing of net cash flows within the payback period. In Exhibit 25.3, FasTrac's net cash flows in the first five years were $3,000, $4,000, $4,000, $4,000, and $5,000. If another investment had predicted cash flows of $9,000, $3,000, $2,000, $1,800, and $1,000 in these five years, its payback period would also be 4.2 years, but this second alternative could be more desirable because it provides cash more quickly. The second important factor is that the payback period ignores *all* cash flows after the point where its costs are fully recovered. For example, one investment might pay back its cost in 3 years but stop producing cash after 4 years. A second investment might require 5 years to pay back its cost yet continue to produce net cash flows for another 15 years. A focus on only the payback period would mistakenly lead management to choose the first investment over the second.

"So what if I underestimated costs and overestimated revenues? It all averages out in the end."

Quick Check
Answers—p. 1049

1. Capital budgeting is (a) concerned with analyzing alternative sources of capital, including debt and equity, (b) an important activity for companies when considering what assets to acquire or sell, or (c) best done by intuitive assessments of the value of assets and their usefulness.
2. Why are capital budgeting decisions often difficult?
3. A company is considering purchasing equipment costing $75,000. Future annual net cash flows from this equipment are $30,000, $25,000, $15,000, $10,000, and $5,000. The payback period is (a) 4 years, (b) 3.5 years, or (c) 3 years.
4. If depreciation is an expense, why is it added back to an investment's net income to compute the net cash flow from that investment?
5. If two investments have the same payback period, are they equally desirable? Explain.

Accounting Rate of Return

The **accounting rate of return,** also called *return on average investment,* is computed by dividing a project's after-tax net income by the average amount invested in it. To illustrate, we return to FasTrac's $16,000 machinery investment described in Exhibit 25.1. We first compute (1) the after-tax net income and (2) the average amount invested. The $2,100 after-tax net income is already available from Exhibit 25.1. To compute the average amount invested, we assume that net cash flows are received evenly throughout each year. Thus, the average investment for each year is computed as the average of its beginning and ending book values. If FasTrac's $16,000 machine is depreciated $2,000 each year, the average amount invested in the machine for each year is computed as shown in Exhibit 25.4. The average for any year is the average of the beginning and ending book values.

P2 Compute accounting rate of return and explain its use.

EXHIBIT 25.4

Computing Average Amount Invested

	Beginning Book Value	Annual Depreciation	Ending Book Value	Average Book Value
Year 1	$16,000	$2,000	$14,000	$15,000
Year 2	14,000	2,000	12,000	13,000
Year 3	12,000	2,000	10,000	11,000
Year 4	10,000	2,000	8,000	9,000
Year 5	8,000	2,000	6,000	7,000
Year 6	6,000	2,000	4,000	5,000
Year 7	4,000	2,000	2,000	3,000
Year 8	2,000	2,000	0	1,000
All years				**$ 8,000**

Next we need the average book value for the asset's entire life. This amount is computed by taking the average of the individual yearly averages. This average equals $8,000, computed as $64,000 (the sum of the individual years' averages) divided by eight years (see last column of Exhibit 25.4). If a company uses straight-line depreciation, we can find the average amount invested by using the formula in Exhibit 25.5. Because FasTrac uses straight-line depreciation, its average

Point: General formula for *annual average investment* is the sum of individual years' average book values divided by the number of years of the planned investment.

amount invested for the eight years equals the sum of the book value at the beginning of the asset's investment period and the book value at the end of its investment period, divided by 2, as shown in Exhibit 25.5.

EXHIBIT 25.5

Computing Average Amount Invested under Straight-Line Depreciation

$$\text{Annual average investment} = \frac{\text{Beginning book value} + \text{Ending book value}}{2}$$

(straight-line case only)

$$= \frac{\$16,000 + \$0}{2} = \$8,000$$

If an investment has a salvage value, the average amount invested when using straight-line depreciation is computed as (Beginning book value + Salvage value)/2.

Once we determine the after-tax net income and the average amount invested, the accounting rate of return on the investment can be computed from the annual after-tax net income divided by the average amount invested, as shown in Exhibit 25.6.

EXHIBIT 25.6

Accounting Rate of Return Formula

$$\text{Accounting rate of return} = \frac{\text{Annual after-tax net income}}{\text{Annual average investment}}$$

This yields an accounting rate of return of 26.25% ($2,100/$8,000). FasTrac management must decide whether a 26.25% accounting rate of return is satisfactory. To make this decision, we must factor in the investment's risk. For instance, we cannot say an investment with a 26.25% return is preferred over one with a lower return unless we recognize any differences in risk. Thus, an investment's return is satisfactory or unsatisfactory only when it is related to returns from other investments with similar lives and risk.

When accounting rate of return is used to choose among capital investments, the one with the least risk, the shortest payback period, and the highest return for the longest time period is often identified as the best. However, use of accounting rate of return to evaluate investment opportunities is limited because it bases the amount invested on book values (not predicted market values) in future periods. Accounting rate of return is also limited when an asset's net incomes are expected to vary from year to year. This requires computing the rate using *average* annual net incomes, yet this accounting rate of return fails to distinguish between two investments with the same average annual net income but different amounts of income in early years versus later years or different levels of income variability.

Quick Check   Answers—p. 1049

6. The following data relate to a company's decision on whether to purchase a machine:

Cost	$180,000
Salvage value	15,000
Annual after-tax net income	40,000

The machine's accounting rate of return, assuming the even receipt of its net cash flows during the year and use of straight-line depreciation, is (a) 22%, (b) 41%, or (c) 21%.

7. Is a 15% accounting rate of return for a machine a good rate?

Methods Using Time Value of Money

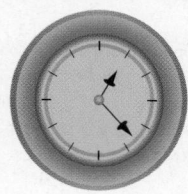

This section describes two methods that help managers with capital budgeting decisions and that use the time value of money: (1) net present value and (2) internal rate of return. *(To apply these methods, you need a basic understanding of the concept of present value. An expanded explanation of present value concepts is in Appendix B near the end of the book. You can use the present value tables at the end of Appendix B to solve many of this chapter's assignments that use the time value of money.)*

Net Present Value

Net present value analysis applies the time value of money to future cash inflows and cash out-flows so management can evaluate a project's benefits and costs at one point in time. Specifically, **net present value (NPV)** is computed by discounting the future net cash flows from the investment at the project's required rate of return and then subtracting the initial amount invested. A company's required return, often called its **hurdle rate**, is typically its **cost of capital,** which is the rate the company must pay to its long-term creditors and shareholders.

To illustrate, let's return to FasTrac's proposed machinery purchase described in Exhibit 25.1. Does this machine provide a satisfactory return while recovering the amount invested? Recall that the machine requires a $16,000 investment and is expected to provide $4,100 annual net cash inflows for the next eight years. If we assume that net cash flows from this machine are received at each year-end and that FasTrac requires a 12% annual return, net present value can be computed as in Exhibit 25.7.

P3   Compute net present value and describe its use.

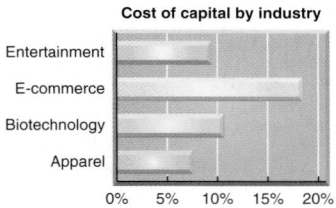

Cost of capital by industry

Net Cash Flows*	Present Value of 1 at 12%†	Present Value of Net Cash Flows
Year 1 .... $ 4,100	0.8929	$ 3,661
Year 2 4,100	0.7972	3,269
Year 3 4,100	0.7118	2,918
Year 4 4,100	0.6355	2,606
Year 5 4,100	0.5674	2,326
Year 6 4,100	0.5066	2,077
Year 7 4,100	0.4523	1,854
Year 8 4,100	0.4039	1,656
Totals $32,800		$20,367
Amount invested		(16,000)
Net present value		$ 4,367

EXHIBIT 25.7

Net Present Value Calculation with Equal Cash Flows

* Cash flows occur at the end of each year.

† Present value of 1 factors are taken from Table B.1 in Appendix B.

The first number column of Exhibit 25.7 shows the annual net cash flows. Present value of 1 factors, also called *discount factors,* are shown in the second column. Taken from Table B.1 in Appendix B, they assume that net cash flows are received at each year-end. *(To simplify present value computations and for assignment material at the end of this chapter, we assume that net cash flows are received at each year-end.)* Annual net cash flows from the first column of Exhibit 25.7 are multiplied by the discount factors in the second column to give present values shown in the third column. The last three lines of this exhibit show the final NPV computations. The asset's $16,000 initial cost is deducted from the $20,367 total present value of all future net cash flows to give this asset's NPV of $4,367. The machine is thus expected to (1) recover its cost, (2) provide a 12% compounded return, and (3) generate $4,367 above cost. We summarize this analysis by saying the present value of this machine's future net cash flows to FasTrac exceeds the $16,000 investment by $4,367.

Point: The assumption of end-of-year cash flows simplifies computations and is common in practice.

Point: The amount invested includes all costs that must be incurred to get the asset in its proper location and ready for use.

Example: What is the net present value in Exhibit 25.7 if a 10% return is applied? *Answer:* $5,873

Net Present Value Decision Rule   The decision rule in applying NPV is as follows: When an asset's expected cash flows are discounted at the required rate and yield a *positive* net present value, the asset should be acquired. This decision rule is reflected in the graphic below. When comparing several investment opportunities of about the same cost and same risk, we prefer the one with the highest positive net present value.

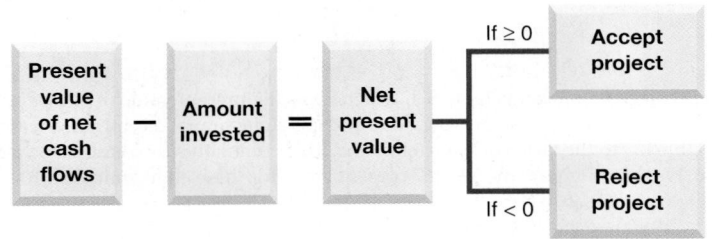

Simplifying Computations The computations in Exhibit 25.7 use separate present value of 1 factors for each of the eight years. Each year's net cash flow is multiplied by its present value of 1 factor to determine its present value. The individual present values for each of the eight net cash flows are added to give the asset's total present value. This computation can be simplified in two ways if annual net cash flows are equal in amount. One way is to add the eight annual present value of 1 factors for a total of 4.9676 and multiply this amount by the annual $4,100 net cash flow to get the $20,367 total present value of net cash flows.[1] A second simplification is to use a calculator with compound interest functions or a spreadsheet program. We show how to use Excel functions to compute net present value in this chapter's Appendix. Whatever procedure you use, it is important to understand the concepts behind these computations.

 Decision Ethics

Systems Manager Top management adopts a policy requiring purchases in excess of $5,000 to be submitted with cash flow projections to the cost analyst for capital budget approval. As systems manager, you want to upgrade your computers at a $25,000 cost. You consider submitting several orders all under $5,000 to avoid the approval process. You believe the computers will increase profits and wish to avoid a delay. What do you do? [Answer—p. 1048]

Uneven Cash Flows Net present value analysis can also be applied when net cash flows are uneven (unequal). To illustrate, assume that FasTrac can choose only one capital investment from among projects A, B, and C. Each project requires the same $12,000 initial investment. Future net cash flows for each project are shown in the first three number columns of Exhibit 25.8.

EXHIBIT 25.8

Net Present Value Calculation with Uneven Cash Flows

	Net Cash Flows			Present Value of 1 at 10%	Present Value of Net Cash Flows		
	A	B	C		A	B	C
Year 1	$ 5,000	$ 8,000	$ 1,000	0.9091	$ 4,546	$ 7,273	$ 909
Year 2	5,000	5,000	5,000	0.8264	4,132	4,132	4,132
Year 3	5,000	2,000	9,000	0.7513	3,757	1,503	6,762
Totals	$15,000	$15,000	$15,000		12,435	12,908	11,803
Amount invested					(12,000)	(12,000)	(12,000)
Net present value ...					$ 435	$ 908	$ (197)

The three projects in Exhibit 25.8 have the same expected total net cash flows of $15,000. Project A is expected to produce equal amounts of $5,000 each year. Project B is expected to produce a larger amount in the first year. Project C is expected to produce a larger amount in the third year. The fourth column of Exhibit 25.8 shows the present value of 1 factors from Table B.1 assuming 10% required return.

Computations in the right-most columns show that Project A has a $435 positive NPV. Project B has the largest NPV of $908 because it brings in cash more quickly. Project C has a $(197) *negative* NPV because its larger cash inflows are delayed. If FasTrac requires a 10% return, it should reject Project C because its NPV implies a return *under* 10%. If only one project can be accepted, project B appears best because it yields the highest NPV.

Example: Why does the net present value of an investment increase when a lower discount rate is used? *Answer:* The present value of net cash flows increases.

Example: If 12% is the required return in Exhibit 25.8, which project is preferred? *Answer:* Project B. Net present values are: A = $10; B = $553; C = $(715).

Example: Will the rankings of Projects A, B, and C change with the use of different discount rates, assuming the same rate is used for all projects? *Answer:* No; only the NPV amounts will change.

---

[1] We can simplify this computation using Table B.3, which gives the present value of 1 to be received periodically for a number of periods. To determine the present value of these eight annual receipts discounted at 12%, go down the 12% column of Table B.3 to the factor on the eighth line. This cumulative discount factor, also known as an *annuity* factor, is 4.9676. We then compute the $20,367 present value for these eight annual $4,100 receipts, computed as 4.9676 × $4,100.

Salvage Value and Accelerated Depreciation   FasTrac predicted the $16,000 machine to have zero salvage value at the end of its useful life (recall Exhibit 25.1). In many cases, assets are expected to have salvage values. If so, this amount is an additional net cash inflow received at the end of the final year of the asset's life. All other computations remain the same.

Depreciation computations also affect net present value analysis. FasTrac computes depreciation using the straight-line method. Accelerated depreciation is also commonly used, especially for income tax reports. Accelerated depreciation produces larger depreciation deductions in the early years of an asset's life and smaller deductions in later years. This pattern results in smaller income tax payments in early years and larger payments in later years. Accelerated depreciation does not change the basics of a present value analysis, but it can change the result. Using accelerated depreciation for tax reporting affects the NPV of an asset's cash flows because it produces larger net cash inflows in the early years of the asset's life and smaller ones in later years. Being able to use accelerated depreciation for tax reporting always makes an investment more desirable because early cash flows are more valuable than later ones.

Use of Net Present Value   In deciding whether to proceed with a capital investment project, we approve the proposal if the NPV is positive but reject it if the NPV is negative. When considering several projects of similar investment amounts and risk levels, we can compare the different projects' NPVs and rank them on the basis of their NPVs. However, if the amount invested differs substantially across projects, the NPV is of limited value for comparison purposes. One means to compare projects, especially when a company cannot fund all positive net present value projects, is to use the **profitability index,** which is computed as:

$$\text{Profitability index} = \frac{\text{Net present value of cash flows}}{\text{Investment}}$$

A higher profitability index suggests a more desirable project. To illustrate, suppose that Project X requires a $1 million investment and provides a $100,000 NPV. Project Y requires an investment of only $100,000 and returns a $75,000 NPV. Ranking on the basis of NPV puts Project X ahead of Y, yet X's profitability index is only 0.10 ($100,000/$1,000,000) whereas Y's profitability index is 0.75. We must also remember that when reviewing projects with different risks, we computed the NPV of individual projects using different discount rates. The higher the risk, the higher the discount rate.

Inflation   Large price-level increases should be considered in NPV analyses. Hurdle rates already include investor's inflation forecasts. Net cash flows can be adjusted for inflation by using *future value* computations. For example, if the expected net cash inflow in year 1 is $4,100 and 5% inflation is expected, then the expected net cash inflow in year 2 is $4,305, computed as $4,100 × 1.05 (1.05 is the future value of $1 (Table B.2) for 1 period with a 5% rate).

Internal Rate of Return

Another means to evaluate capital investments is to use the **internal rate of return (IRR),** which equals the rate that yields an NPV of zero for an investment. This means that if we compute the total present value of a project's net cash flows using the IRR as the discount rate and then subtract the initial investment from this total present value, we get a zero NPV.

To illustrate, we use the data for FasTrac's Project A from Exhibit 25.8 to compute its IRR. Exhibit 25.9 shows the two-step process in computing IRR.

Point: Projects with higher cash flows in earlier years generally yield higher net present values.

Example: When is it appropriate to use different discount rates for different projects? *Answer:* When risk levels are different.

Point: Tax savings from depreciation is called: **depreciation tax shield.**

P4 Compute internal rate of return and explain its use.

EXHIBIT 25.9

Computing Internal Rate of
Return (with even cash flows)

Step 1: Compute the present value factor for the investment project.

$$\text{Present value factor} = \frac{\text{Amount invested}}{\text{Net cash flows}} = \frac{\$12,000}{\$5,000} = 2.4000$$

Step 2: Identify the discount rate (IRR) yielding the present value factor

Search Table B.3 for a present value factor of 2.4000 in the three-year row (equaling the 3-year project duration). The 12% discount rate yields a present value factor of 2.4018. This implies that the IRR is approximately 12%.*

* Since the present value factor of 2.4000 is not exactly equal to the 12% factor of 2.4018, we can more precisely estimate the IRR as follows:

Discount rate	Present Value Factor from Table B.3
12%	2.4018
15%	2.2832
	0.1186 = difference

Then, IRR $= 12\% + \left[(15\% - 12\%) \times \dfrac{2.4018 - 2.4000}{0.1186} \right] = \underline{\underline{12.05\%}}$

When cash flows are equal, as with Project A, we compute the present value factor (as shown in Exhibit 25.9) by dividing the initial investment by its annual net cash flows. We then use an annuity table to determine the discount rate equal to this present value factor. For FasTrac's Project A, we look across the three-period row of Table B.3 and find that the discount rate corresponding to the present value factor of 2.4000 roughly equals the 2.4018 value for the 12% rate. This row is reproduced here:

Present Value of an Annuity of 1 for Three Periods

	Discount Rate				
Periods	**1%**	**5%**	**10%**	**12%**	**15%**
3	2.9410	2.7232	2.4869	2.4018	2.2832

The 12% rate is the Project's IRR. A more precise IRR estimate can be computed following the procedure shown in the note to Exhibit 25.9. Spreadsheet software and calculators can also compute this IRR. We show how to use an Excel function to compute IRR in this chapter's Appendix.

Uneven Cash Flows   If net cash flows are uneven, we must use trial and error to compute the IRR. We do this by selecting any reasonable discount rate and computing the NPV. If the amount is positive (negative), we recompute the NPV using a higher (lower) discount rate. We continue these steps until we reach a point where two consecutive computations result in NPVs having different signs (positive and negative). Because the NPV is zero using IRR, we know that the IRR lies between these two discount rates. We can then estimate its value. Spreadsheet programs and calculators can do these computations for us.

Decision Insight

Fun-IRR   Many theme parks use both financial and nonfinancial criteria to evaluate their investments in new rides and activities. The use of IRR is a major part of this evaluation. This requires good estimates of future cash inflows and outflows. It also requires risk assessments of the uncertainty of the future cash flows.

Use of Internal Rate of Return   When we use the IRR to evaluate a project, we compare it to a predetermined **hurdle rate,** which is a minimum acceptable rate of return and is applied as follows.

C2 Describe the selection of a hurdle rate for an investment.

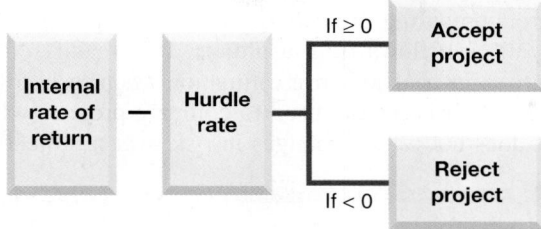

Top management selects the hurdle rate to use in evaluating capital investments. Financial formulas aid in this selection, but the choice of a minimum rate is subjective and left to management. For projects financed from borrowed funds, the hurdle rate must exceed the interest rate paid on these funds. The return on an investment must cover its interest and provide an additional profit to reward the company for its risk. For instance, if money is borrowed at 10%, an average risk investment often requires an after-tax return of 15% (or 5% above the borrowing rate). Remember that lower-risk investments require a lower rate of return compared with higher-risk investments.

Example: How can management evaluate the risk of an investment? *Answer:* It must assess the uncertainty of future cash flows.

Point: A survey reports that 41% of top managers would reject a project with an internal rate of return *above* the cost of capital, *if* the project would cause the firm to miss its earnings forecast. The roles of benchmarks and manager compensation plans must be considered in capital budgeting decisions.

If the project is internally financed, the hurdle rate is often based on actual returns from comparable projects. If the IRR is higher than the hurdle rate, the project is accepted. Multiple projects are often ranked by the extent to which their IRR exceeds the hurdle rate. The hurdle rate for individual projects is often different, depending on the risk involved. IRR is not subject to the limitations of NPV when comparing projects with different amounts invested because the IRR is expressed as a percent rather than as an absolute dollar value in NPV.

Decision Maker

Entrepreneur   You are developing a new product and you use a 12% discount rate to compute its NPV. Your banker, from whom you hope to obtain a loan, expresses concern that your discount rate is too low. How do you respond? [Answer—p. 1048]

Comparison of Capital Budgeting Methods

We explained four methods that managers use to evaluate capital investment projects. How do these methods compare with each other? Exhibit 25.10 addresses that question. Neither the payback period nor the accounting rate of return considers the time value of money. On the other hand, both the net present value and the internal rate of return do.

EXHIBIT 25.10

Comparing Capital Budgeting Methods

	Payback Period	Accounting Rate of Return	Net Present Value	Internal Rate of Return
Measurement basis	■ Cash flows	■ Accrual income	■ Cash flows ■ Profitability	■ Cash flows ■ Profitability
Measurement unit	■ Years	■ Percent	■ Dollars	■ Percent
Strengths	■ Easy to understand	■ Easy to understand	■ Reflects time value of money	■ Reflects time value of money
	■ Allows comparison of projects	■ Allows comparison of projects	■ Reflects varying risks over project's life	■ Allows comparisons of dissimilar projects
Limitations	■ Ignores time value of money	■ Ignores time value of money	■ Difficult to compare dissimilar projects	■ Ignores varying risks over life of project
	■ Ignores cash flows after payback period	■ Ignores annual rates over life of project		

The payback period is probably the simplest method. It gives managers an estimate of how soon they will recover their initial investment. Managers sometimes use this method when they have limited cash to invest and a number of projects to choose from. The accounting rate of return yields a percent measure computed using accrual income instead of cash flows. The accounting rate of return is an average rate for the entire investment period. Net present value considers all estimated net cash flows for the project's expected life. It can be applied to even and uneven cash flows and can reflect changes in the level of risk over a project's life. Since it yields a dollar measure, comparing projects of unequal sizes is more difficult. The internal rate of return considers all cash flows from a project. It is readily computed when the cash flows are even but requires some trial and error estimation when cash flows are uneven. Because the IRR is a percent measure, it is readily used to compare projects with different investment amounts. However, IRR does not reflect changes in risk over a project's life.

Decision Insight

And the Winner Is . . . How do we choose among the methods for evaluating capital investments? Management surveys consistently show the internal rate of return (IRR) as the most popular method followed by the payback period and net present value (NPV). Few companies use the accounting rate of return (ARR), but nearly all use more than one method.

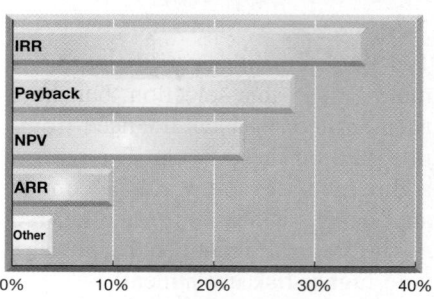

Company Usage for Capital Budgeting Methods

Quick Check

Answers—p. 1049

8. A company can invest in only one of two projects, A or B. Each project requires a $20,000 investment and is expected to generate end-of-period, annual cash flows as follows:

	Year 1	Year 2	Year 3	Total
Project A	$12,000	$8,500	$4,000	$24,500
Project B	4,500	8,500	13,000	26,000

Assuming a discount rate of 10%, which project has the higher net present value?

9. Two investment alternatives are expected to generate annual cash flows with the same net present value (assuming the same discount rate applied to each). Using this information, can you conclude that the two alternatives are equally desirable?

10. When two investment alternatives have the same total expected cash flows but differ in the timing of those flows, which method of evaluating those investments is superior, (a) accounting rate of return or (b) net present value?

Section 2—Managerial Decisions

This section focuses on methods that use accounting information to make several important managerial decisions. Most of these involve short-term decisions. This differs from methods used for longer-term managerial decisions that are described in the first section of this chapter and in several other chapters of this book.

Decisions and Information

Video25.1

This section explains how managers make decisions and the information relevant to those decisions.

Decision Making

Managerial decision making involves five steps: (1) define the decision task, (2) identify alternative courses of action, (3) collect relevant information and evaluate each alternative,

(4) select the preferred course of action, and (5) analyze and assess decisions made. These five steps are illustrated in Exhibit 25.11.

| Define Task and Goal | Identify Alternative Actions | Collect Relevant Information | Select Course of Action | Analyze and Assess Decision |

EXHIBIT 25.11

Managerial Decision Making

Both managerial and financial accounting information play an important role in most management decisions. The accounting system is expected to provide primarily *financial* information such as performance reports and budget analyses for decision making. *Nonfinancial* information is also relevant, however; it includes information on environmental effects, political sensitivities, and social responsibility.

Relevant Costs

Most financial measures of revenues and costs from accounting systems are based on historical costs. Although historical costs are important and useful for many tasks such as product pricing and the control and monitoring of business activities, we sometimes find that an analysis of *relevant costs,* or *avoidable costs,* is especially useful. Three types of costs are pertinent to our discussion of relevant costs: sunk costs, out-of-pocket costs, and opportunity costs.

A *sunk cost* arises from a past decision and cannot be avoided or changed; it is irrelevant to future decisions. An example is the cost of computer equipment previously purchased by a company. Most of a company's allocated costs, including fixed overhead items such as depreciation and administrative expenses, are sunk costs.

An *out-of-pocket cost* requires a future outlay of cash and is relevant for current and future decision making. These costs are usually the direct result of management's decisions. For instance, future purchases of computer equipment involve out-of-pocket costs.

An *opportunity cost* is the potential benefit lost by taking a specific action when two or more alternative choices are available. An example is a student giving up wages from a job to attend summer school. Companies continually must choose from alternative courses of action. For instance, a company making standardized products might be approached by a customer to supply a special (nonstandard) product. A decision to accept or reject the special order must consider not only the profit to be made from the special order but also the profit given up by devoting time and resources to this order instead of pursuing an alternative project. The profit given up is an opportunity cost. Consideration of opportunity costs is important. The implications extend to internal resource allocation decisions. For instance, a computer manufacturer must decide between internally manufacturing a chip versus buying it externally. In another case, management of a multidivisional company must decide whether to continue operating or close a particular division.

Besides relevant costs, management must also consider the relevant benefits associated with a decision. **Relevant benefits** refer to the additional or *incremental* revenue generated by selecting a particular course of action over another. For instance, a student must decide the relevant benefits of taking one course over another. In sum, both relevant costs and relevant benefits are crucial to managerial decision making.

C3 Describe the importance of relevant costs for short-term decisions.

Example: Depreciation and amortization are allocations of the original cost of plant and intangible assets. Are they out-of-pocket costs? *Answer:* No; they are sunk costs.

Point: Opportunity costs are not entered in accounting records. This does not reduce their relevance for managerial decisions.

Managerial Decision Scenarios

Managers experience many different scenarios that require analyzing alternative actions and making a decision. We describe several different types of decision scenarios in this section. We set these tasks in the context of FasTrac, an exercise supplies and equipment manufacturer introduced earlier. *We treat each of these decision tasks as separate from each other.*

A1 Evaluate short-term managerial decisions using relevant costs.

Video25.1

Additional Business

FasTrac is operating at its normal level of 80% of full capacity. At this level, it produces and sells approximately 100,000 units of product annually. Its per unit and annual total costs are shown in Exhibit 25.12.

EXHIBIT 25.12

Selected Operating Income Data

	Per Unit	Annual Total
Sales (100,000 units)	$10.00	$1,000,000
Direct materials	(3.50)	(350,000)
Direct labor	(2.20)	(220,000)
Overhead	(1.10)	(110,000)
Selling expenses	(1.40)	(140,000)
Administrative expenses	(0.80)	(80,000)
Total costs and expenses	(9.00)	(900,000)
Operating income	$ 1.00	$ 100,000

A current buyer of FasTrac's products wants to purchase additional units of its product and export them to another country. This buyer offers to buy 10,000 units of the product at $8.50 per unit, or $1.50 less than the current price. The offer price is low, but FasTrac is considering the proposal because this sale would be several times larger than any single previous sale and it would use idle capacity. Also, the units will be exported, so this new business will not affect current sales.

To determine whether to accept or reject this order, management needs to know whether accepting the offer will increase net income. The analysis in Exhibit 25.13 shows that if management relies on per unit historical costs, it would reject the sale because it yields a loss. However, historical costs are *not* relevant to this decision. Instead, the relevant costs are the additional costs, called **incremental costs.** These costs, also called *differential costs,* are the additional costs incurred if a company pursues a certain course of action. FasTrac's incremental costs are those related to the added volume that this new order would bring.

EXHIBIT 25.13

Analysis of Additional Business Using Historical Costs

	Per Unit	Total
Sales (10,000 additional units)	$ 8.50	$ 85,000
Direct materials	(3.50)	(35,000)
Direct labor	(2.20)	(22,000)
Overhead	(1.10)	(11,000)
Selling expenses	(1.40)	(14,000)
Administrative expenses	(0.80)	(8,000)
Total costs and expenses	(9.00)	(90,000)
Operating loss	$(0.50)	$ (5,000)

To make its decision, FasTrac must analyze the costs of this new business in a different manner. The following information regarding the order is available:

- Manufacturing 10,000 additional units requires direct materials of $3.50 per unit and direct labor of $2.20 per unit (same as for all other units).
- Manufacturing 10,000 additional units adds $5,000 of incremental overhead costs for power, packaging, and indirect labor (all variable costs).
- Incremental commissions and selling expenses from this sale of 10,000 additional units would be $2,000 (all variable costs).
- Incremental administrative expenses of $1,000 for clerical efforts are needed (all fixed costs) with the sale of 10,000 additional units.

We use this information, as shown in Exhibit 25.14, to assess how accepting this new business will affect FasTrac's income.

	Current Business	Additional Business	Combined
Sales	$1,000,000	$ 85,000	$1,085,000
Direct materials	(350,000)	(35,000)	(385,000)
Direct labor	(220,000)	(22,000)	(242,000)
Overhead	(110,000)	(5,000)	(115,000)
Selling expenses	(140,000)	(2,000)	(142,000)
Administrative expense	(80,000)	(1,000)	(81,000)
Total costs and expenses	(900,000)	(65,000)	(965,000)
Operating income	$ 100,000	$ 20,000	$ 120,000

EXHIBIT 25.14

Analysis of Additional Business Using Relevant Costs

The analysis of relevant costs in Exhibit 25.14 suggests that the additional business be accepted. It would provide $85,000 of added revenue while incurring only $65,000 of added costs. This would yield $20,000 of additional pretax income, or a pretax profit margin of 23.5%. More generally, FasTrac would increase its income with any price that exceeded $6.50 per unit ($65,000 incremental cost/10,000 additional units).

An analysis of the incremental costs pertaining to the additional volume is always relevant for this type of decision. We must proceed cautiously, however, when the additional volume approaches or exceeds the factory's existing available capacity. If the additional volume requires the company to expand its capacity by obtaining more equipment, more space, or more personnel, the incremental costs could quickly exceed the incremental revenue. Another cautionary note is the effect on existing sales. All new units of the extra business will be sold outside FasTrac's normal domestic sales channels. If accepting additional business would cause existing sales to decline, this information must be included in our analysis. The contribution margin lost from a decline in sales is an opportunity cost. If future cash flows over several time periods are affected, their net present value also must be computed and used in this analysis.

The key point is that *management must not blindly use historical costs, especially allocated overhead costs.* Instead, the accounting system needs to provide information about the incremental costs to be incurred if the additional business is accepted.

Example: Exhibit 25.14 uses quantitative information. Suggest some qualitative factors to be considered when deciding whether to accept this project. *Answer:* (1) Impact on relationships with other customers and (2) Improved relationship with customer buying additional units.

Decision Maker

Partner   You are a partner in a small accounting firm that specializes in keeping the books and preparing taxes for clients. A local restaurant is interested in obtaining these services from your firm. Identify factors that are relevant in deciding whether to accept the engagement. [Answer—p. 1048]

Make or Buy

The managerial decision to make or buy a component for one of its current products is commonplace and depends on incremental costs. To illustrate, FasTrac has excess productive capacity it can use to manufacture Part 417, a component of the main product it sells. The part is currently purchased and delivered to the plant at a cost of $1.20 per unit. FasTrac estimates that making Part 417 would cost $0.45 for direct materials, $0.50 for direct labor, and an undetermined amount for overhead. The task is to determine how much overhead to add to these costs so we can decide whether to make or buy Part 417. If FasTrac's normal predetermined overhead application rate is 100% of direct labor cost, we might be tempted to conclude that overhead cost is $0.50 per unit, computed as 100% of the $0.50 direct labor cost. We would then mistakenly conclude that total cost is $1.45 ($0.45 of materials + $0.50 of labor + $0.50 of overhead). A wrong decision in this case would be to conclude that the company is better off buying the part at $1.20 each than making it for $1.45 each.

Instead, as we explained earlier, only incremental overhead costs are relevant in this situation. Thus, we must compute an *incremental overhead rate.* Incremental overhead costs might include, for example, additional power for operating machines, extra supplies, added cleanup costs, materials handling, and quality control. We can prepare a per unit analysis in this case as shown in Exhibit 25.15.

EXHIBIT 25.15

Make or Buy Analysis

	Make	Buy
Direct materials	$0.45	—
Direct labor	0.50	—
Overhead costs	[?]	—
Purchase price	—	$ 1.20
Total incremental costs	$0.95 + [?]	$1.20

Point: Managers must consider nonfinancial factors when making decisions.

We can see that if incremental overhead costs are less than $0.25 per unit, the total cost of making the component is less than the purchase price of $1.20 and FasTrac should make the part. FasTrac's decision rule in this case is that any amount of overhead less than $0.25 per unit yields a total cost for Part 417 that is less than the $1.20 purchase price. FasTrac must consider several nonfinancial factors in the make or buy decision, including product quality, timeliness of delivery (especially in a just-in-time setting), reactions of customers and suppliers, and other intangibles such as employee morale and workload. It must also consider whether making the part requires incremental fixed costs to expand plant capacity. When these added factors are considered, small cost differences may not matter.

Decision Insight

Make or Buy Services   Companies apply make or buy decisions to their services. Many now outsource their payroll activities to a payroll service provider. It is argued that the prices paid for such services are close to what it costs them to do it, and without the headaches.

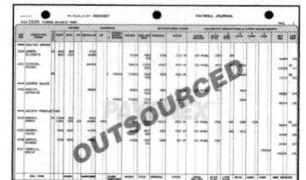

Scrap or Rework

Managers often must make a decision on whether to scrap or rework products in process. Remember that costs already incurred in manufacturing the units of a product that do not meet quality standards are sunk costs that have been incurred and cannot be changed. Sunk costs are irrelevant in any decision on whether to sell the substandard units as scrap or to rework them to meet quality standards.

To illustrate, assume that FasTrac has 10,000 defective units of a product that have already cost $1 per unit to manufacture. These units can be sold as is (as scrap) for $0.40 each, or they can be reworked for $0.80 per unit and then sold for their full price of $1.50 each. Should FasTrac sell the units as scrap or rework them?

To make this decision, management must recognize that the already incurred manufacturing costs of $1 per unit are sunk (unavoidable). These costs are *entirely irrelevant* to the decision. In addition, we must be certain that all costs of reworking defects, including interfering with normal operations, are accounted for in our analysis. For instance, reworking the defects means that FasTrac is unable to manufacture 10,000 *new* units with an incremental cost of $1 per unit and a selling price of $1.50 per unit, meaning it incurs an opportunity cost equal to the lost $5,000 net return from making and selling 10,000 new units. This opportunity cost is the difference between the $15,000 revenue (10,000 units × $1.50) from selling these new units and their $10,000 manufacturing costs (10,000 units × $1). Our analysis is reflected in Exhibit 25.16.

EXHIBIT 25.16

Scrap or Rework Analysis

	Scrap	Rework
Sale of scrapped/reworked units	$ 4,000	$ 15,000
Less costs to rework defects		(8,000)
Less opportunity cost of not making new units		**(5,000)**
Incremental net income	$4,000	$ 2,000

The analysis yields a $2,000 difference in favor of scrapping the defects, yielding a total incremental net income of $4,000. If we had failed to include the opportunity costs of $5,000, the rework option would have shown an income of $7,000 instead of $2,000, mistakenly making the reworking appear more favorable than scrapping.

Quick Check

Answers—p. 1049

11. A company receives a special order for 200 units that requires stamping the buyer's name on each unit, yielding an additional fixed cost of $400 to its normal costs. Without the order, the company is operating at 75% of capacity and produces 7,500 units of product at the following costs:

Direct materials	$37,500
Direct labor	60,000
Overhead (30% variable)	20,000
Selling expenses (60% variable)	25,000

The special order will not affect normal unit sales and will not increase fixed overhead and selling expenses. Variable selling expenses on the special order are reduced to one-half the normal amount. The price per unit necessary to earn $1,000 on this order is (*a*) $14.80, (*b*) $15.80, (*c*) $19.80, (*d*) $20.80, or (*e*) $21.80.

12. What are the incremental costs of accepting additional business?

Sell or Process

The managerial decision to sell partially completed products as is or to process them further for sale depends significantly on relevant costs. To illustrate, suppose that FasTrac has 40,000 units of partially finished Product Q. It has already spent $0.75 per unit to manufacture these 40,000 units at a $30,000 total cost. FasTrac can sell the 40,000 units to another manufacturer as raw material for $50,000. Alternatively, it can process them further and produce finished products X, Y, and Z at an incremental cost of $2 per unit. The added processing yields the products and revenues shown in Exhibit 25.17. FasTrac must decide whether the added revenues from selling finished products X, Y, and Z exceed the costs of finishing them.

EXHIBIT 25.17

Revenues from Processing Further

Product	Price	Units	Revenues
Product X	$4.00	10,000	$ 40,000
Product Y	6.00	22,000	132,000
Product Z	8.00	6,000	48,000
Spoilage	—	2,000	0
Totals		40,000	$220,000

Exhibit 25.18 shows the two-step analysis for this decision. First, FasTrac computes its incremental revenue from further processing Q into products X, Y, and Z. This amount is the difference between the $220,000 revenue from the further processed products and the $50,000 FasTrac will give up by not selling Q as is (a $50,000 opportunity cost). Second, FasTrac computes its incremental costs from further processing Q into X, Y, and Z. This amount is $80,000 (40,000 units × $2 incremental cost). The analysis shows that FasTrac can earn incremental net income of $90,000 from a decision to further process Q. (Notice that the earlier incurred $30,000 manufacturing cost for the 40,000 units of Product Q does not appear in Exhibit 25.18 because it is a sunk cost and as such is irrelevant to the decision.)

Example: Does the decision change if incremental costs in Exhibit 25.18 increase to $4 per unit and the opportunity cost increases to $95,000? *Answer:* Yes. There is now an incremental net loss of $35,000.

EXHIBIT 25.18

Sell or Process Analysis

Revenue if processed	$220,000
Revenue if sold as is	(50,000)
Incremental revenue	170,000
Cost to process	(80,000)
Incremental net income	**$ 90,000**

13. A company has already incurred a $1,000 cost in partially producing its four products. Their selling prices when partially and fully processed follow with additional costs necessary to finish these partially processed units:

Product	Unfinished Selling Price	Finished Selling Price	Further Processing Costs
Alpha	$300	$600	$150
Beta	450	900	300
Gamma	275	425	125
Delta	150	210	75

Which product(s) should *not* be processed further, (a) Alpha, (b) Beta, (c) Gamma, or (d) Delta?

14. Under what conditions is a sunk cost relevant to decision making?

Sales Mix Selection

Point: A method called *linear programming* is useful for finding the optimal sales mix for several products subject to many market and production constraints. This method is described in advanced courses.

When a company sells a mix of products, some are likely to be more profitable than others. Management is often wise to concentrate sales efforts on more profitable products. If production facilities or other factors are limited, an increase in the production and sale of one product usually requires reducing the production and sale of others. In this case, management must identify the most profitable combination, or *sales mix* of products. To identify the best sales mix, management must know the contribution margin of each product, the facilities required to produce each product, any constraints on these facilities, and its markets.

To illustrate, assume that FasTrac makes and sells two products, A and B. The same machines are used to produce both products. A and B have the following selling prices and variable costs per unit:

	Product A	Product B
Selling price per unit	$5.00	$7.50
Variable costs per unit	3.50	5.50
Contribution margin per unit	$1.50	$2.00

The variable costs are included in the analysis because they are the incremental costs of producing these products within the existing capacity of 100,000 machine hours per month. We consider three separate cases.

Case 1: Assume that (1) each product requires 1 machine hour per unit for production and (2) the markets for these products are unlimited. Under these conditions, FasTrac should produce as much of Product B as it can because of its larger contribution margin of $2 per unit. At full capacity, FasTrac would produce $200,000 of total contribution margin per month, computed as $2 per unit times 100,000 machine hours.

Case 2: Assume that (1) Product A requires 1 machine hour per unit, (2) Product B requires 2 machine hours per unit, and (3) the markets for these products are unlimited. Under these conditions, FasTrac should produce as much of Product A as it can because it has a contribution margin of $1.50 per machine hour compared with only $1 per machine hour for Product B. Exhibit 25.19 shows the relevant analysis.

	Product A	Product B
Selling price per unit	$ 5.00	$ 7.50
Variable costs per unit	3.50	5.50
Contribution margin per unit	$ 1.50	$ 2.00
Machine hours per unit	1.0	2.0
Contribution margin per machine hour	**$1.50**	**$1.00**

EXHIBIT 25.19

Sales Mix Analysis

At its full capacity of 100,000 machine hours, FasTrac would produce 100,000 units of Product A, yielding $150,000 of total contribution margin per month. In contrast, if it uses all 100,000 hours to produce Product B, only 50,000 units would be produced yielding a contribution margin of $100,000. These results suggest that when a company faces excess demand and limited capacity, only the most profitable product per input should be manufactured.

Case 3: The need for a mix of different products arises when market demand is not sufficient to allow a company to sell all that it produces. For instance, assume that (1) Product A requires 1 machine hour per unit, (2) Product B requires 2 machine hours per unit, and (3) the market for Product A is limited to 80,000 units. Under these conditions, FasTrac should produce no more than 80,000 units of Product A. This would leave another 20,000 machine hours of capacity for making Product B. FasTrac should use this spare capacity to produce 10,000 units of Product B. This sales mix would maximize FasTrac's total contribution margin per month at an amount of $140,000.

Example: For Case 2, if Product B's variable costs per unit increase to $6, Product A's variable costs per unit decrease to $3, and the same machine hours per unit are used, which product should FasTrac produce? *Answer:* Product A. Its contribution margin of $2 per machine hour is higher than B's $.75 per machine hour.

Decision Insight

Companies such as **Gap, Abercrombie & Fitch,** and **American Eagle** must continuously monitor and manage the sales mix of their product lists. Selling their products in hundreds of countries and territories further complicates their decision process. The contribution margin of each product is crucial to their product mix strategies.

Segment Elimination

When a segment such as a department or division is performing poorly, management must consider eliminating it. Segment information on either net income (loss) or its contribution to overhead is not sufficient for this decision. Instead, we must look at the segment's avoidable expenses and unavoidable expenses. **Avoidable expenses,** also called *escapable expenses,* are amounts the company would not incur if it eliminated the segment. **Unavoidable expenses,** also called *inescapable expenses,* are amounts that would continue even if the segment is eliminated.

To illustrate, FasTrac considers eliminating its treadmill division because its $48,300 total expenses are higher than its $47,800 sales. Classification of this division's operating expenses into avoidable or unavoidable expenses is shown in Exhibit 25.20.

Point: FasTrac might consider buying another machine to reduce the constraint on production. A strategy designed to reduce the impact of constraints or bottlenecks, on production, is called the *theory of constraints.*

EXHIBIT 25.20

Classification of Segment
Operating Expenses for Analysis

	Total	Avoidable Expenses	Unavoidable Expenses
Cost of goods sold	$ 30,000	$ 30,000	—
Direct expenses			
Salaries expense	7,900	7,900	—
Depreciation expense—Equipment	200	—	$ 200
Indirect expenses			
Rent and utilities expense	3,150	—	3,150
Advertising expense	400	400	—
Insurance expense	400	300	100
Service department costs			
Share of office department expenses	3,060	2,200	860
Share of purchasing expenses	3,190	1,000	2,190
Total	$48,300	$41,800	$6,500

FasTrac's analysis shows that it can avoid $41,800 expenses if it eliminates the treadmill division. Because this division's sales are $47,800, eliminating it will cause FasTrac to lose $6,000 of income. *Our decision rule is that a segment is a candidate for elimination if its revenues are less than its avoidable expenses.* Avoidable expenses can be viewed as the costs to generate this segment's revenues.

When considering elimination of a segment, we must assess its impact on other segments. A segment could be unprofitable on its own, but it might still contribute to other segments' revenues and profits. It is possible then to continue a segment even when its revenues are less than its avoidable expenses. Similarly, a profitable segment might be discontinued if its space, assets, or staff can be more profitably used by expanding existing segments or by creating new ones. Our decision to keep or eliminate a segment requires a more complex analysis than simply looking at a segment's performance report. Such reports provide useful information, but they do not provide all the information necessary for this decision.

Qualitative Decision Factors

Managers must consider qualitative factors in making managerial decisions. Consider a decision on whether to buy a component from an outside supplier or continue to make it. Several qualitative decision factors must be considered. For example, the quality, delivery, and reputation of the proposed supplier are important. The effects from deciding not to make the component can include potential layoffs and impaired worker morale. Consider another situation in which a company is considering a one-time sale to a new customer at a special low price. Qualitative factors to consider in this situation include the effects of a low price on the company's image and the threat that regular customers might demand a similar price. The company must also consider whether this customer is really a one-time customer. If not, can it continue to offer this low price in the long run? Clearly, management cannot rely solely on financial data to make such decisions.

| Break-Even Time | Decision Analysis |

The first section of this chapter explained several methods to evaluate capital investments. Break-even time of an investment project is a variation of the payback period method that overcomes the limitation of not using the time value of money. **Break-even time (BET)** is a time-based measure used to evaluate a capital investment's acceptability. Its computation yields a measure of expected time, reflecting the time period until the *present value* of the net cash flows from an investment equals the initial cost of the investment. In basic terms, break-even time is computed by restating future cash flows in terms of present values and then determining the payback period using these present values.

A2   Analyze a capital investment project using break-even time.

To illustrate, we return to the FasTrac case described in Exhibit 25.1 involving a $16,000 investment in machinery. The annual net cash flows from this investment are projected at $4,100 for eight years. Exhibit 25.21 shows the computation of break-even time for this investment decision.

EXHIBIT 25.21

Break-Even Time Analysis*

Year	Cash Flows	Present Value of 1 at 10%	Present Value of Cash Flows	Cumulative Present Value of Cash Flows
0	$(16,000)	1.0000	$(16,000)	$(16,000)
1	4,100	0.9091	3,727	(12,273)
2	4,100	0.8264	3,388	(8,885)
3	4,100	0.7513	3,080	(5,805)
4	4,100	0.6830	2,800	(3,005)
5	4,100	0.6209	2,546	(459)
6	4,100	0.5645	2,314	1,855
7	4,100	0.5132	2,104	3,959
8	4,100	0.4665	1,913	5,872

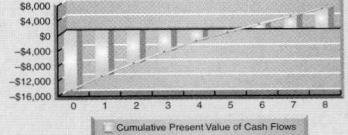

* The time of analysis is the start of year 1 (same as end of year 0). All cash flows occur at the end of each year.

The right-most column of this exhibit shows that break-even time is between 5 and 6 years, or about 5.2 years—also see margin graph (where the line crosses the zero point). This is the time the project takes to break even after considering the time value of money (recall that the payback period computed without considering the time value of money was 3.9 years). We interpret this as cash flows earned after 5.2 years contribute to a positive net present value that, in this case, eventually amounts to $5,872.

Break-even time is a useful measure for managers because it identifies the point in time when they can expect the cash flows to begin to yield net positive returns. Managers expect a positive net present value from an investment if break-even time is less than the investment's estimated life. The method allows managers to compare and rank alternative investments, giving the project with the shortest break-even time the highest rank.

Decision Maker

Investment Manager Management asks you, the investment manager, to evaluate three alternative investments. Investment recovery time is crucial because cash is scarce. The time value of money is also important. Which capital budgeting method(s) do you use to assess the investments? [Answer—p. 1048]

Demonstration Problem

Determine the appropriate action in each of the following managerial decision situations.

1. Packer Company is operating at 80% of its manufacturing capacity of 100,000 product units per year. A chain store has offered to buy an additional 10,000 units at $22 each and sell them to customers so as not to compete with Packer Company. The following data are available.

DP25

Costs at 80% Capacity	Per Unit	Total
Direct materials	$ 8.00	$ 640,000
Direct labor	7.00	560,000
Overhead (fixed and variable)	12.50	1,000,000
Totals	$27.50	$2,200,000

In producing 10,000 additional units, fixed overhead costs would remain at their current level but incremental variable overhead costs of $3 per unit would be incurred. Should the company accept or reject this order?

2. Green Company uses Part JR3 in manufacturing its products. It has always purchased this part from a supplier for $40 each. It recently upgraded its own manufacturing capabilities and has enough excess capacity (including trained workers) to begin manufacturing Part JR3 instead of buying it. The company prepares the following cost projections of making the part, assuming that overhead is allocated to the part at the normal predetermined rate of 200% of direct labor cost.

Direct materials	$11
Direct labor	15
Overhead (fixed and variable) (200% of direct labor)	30
Total	$56

The required volume of output to produce the part will not require any incremental fixed overhead. Incremental variable overhead cost will be $17 per unit. Should the company make or buy this part?

3. Gold Company's manufacturing process causes a relatively large number of defective parts to be produced. The defective parts can be (a) sold for scrap, (b) melted to recover the recycled metal for reuse, or (c) reworked to be good units. Reworking defective parts reduces the output of other good units because no excess capacity exists. Each unit reworked means that one new unit cannot be produced. The following information reflects 500 defective parts currently available.

Proceeds of selling as scrap	$2,500
Additional cost of melting down defective parts	400
Cost of purchases avoided by using recycled metal from defects	4,800
Cost to rework 500 defective parts	
Direct materials	0
Direct labor	1,500
Incremental overhead	1,750
Cost to produce 500 new parts	
Direct materials	6,000
Direct labor	5,000
Incremental overhead	3,200
Selling price per good unit	40

Should the company melt the parts, sell them as scrap, or rework them?

4. White Company can invest in one of two projects, TD1 or TD2. Each project requires an initial investment of $100,000 and produces the year-end cash inflows shown in the following table. Use net present values to determine which project, if any, should be chosen. Assume that the company requires a 10% return from its investments.

	Net Cash Flows	
	TD1	TD2
Year 1	$ 20,000	$ 40,000
Year 2	30,000	40,000
Year 3	70,000	40,000
Totals	$120,000	$120,000

Planning the Solution

- Determine whether Packer Company should accept the additional business by finding the incremental costs of materials, labor, and overhead that will be incurred if the order is accepted. Omit fixed costs that the order will not increase. If the incremental revenue exceeds the incremental cost, accept the order.
- Determine whether Green Company should make or buy the component by finding the incremental cost of making each unit. If the incremental cost exceeds the purchase price, the component should be purchased. If the incremental cost is less than the purchase price, make the component.
- Determine whether Gold Company should sell the defective parts, melt them down and recycle the metal, or rework them. To compare the three choices, examine all costs incurred and benefits received from the alternatives in working with the 500 defective units versus the production of 500 new units. For the scrapping alternative, include the costs of producing 500 new units and subtract the $2,500 proceeds from selling the old ones. For the melting alternative, include the costs of melting the defective units, add the net cost of new materials in excess over those obtained from recycling, and add the direct labor and overhead costs. For the reworking alternative, add the costs of direct labor and incremental overhead. Select the alternative that has the lowest cost. The cost assigned to the 500 defective units is sunk and not relevant in choosing among the three alternatives.
- Compute White Company's net present value of each investment using a 10% discount rate.

Solution to Demonstration Problem

1. This decision involves accepting additional business. Since current unit costs are $27.50, it appears initially as if the offer to sell for $22 should be rejected, but the $27.50 cost includes fixed costs. When the analysis includes only *incremental* costs, the per unit cost is as shown in the following table. The offer should be accepted because it will produce $4 of additional profit per unit (computed as $22 price less $18 incremental cost), which yields a total profit of $40,000 for the 10,000 additional units.

Direct materials	$ 8.00
Direct labor	7.00
Variable overhead (given)	3.00
Total incremental cost	$18.00

2. For this make or buy decision, the analysis must not include the $13 nonincremental overhead per unit ($30 − $17). When only the $17 incremental overhead is included, the relevant unit cost of manufacturing the part is shown in the following table. It would be better to continue buying the part for $40 instead of making it for $43.

Direct materials	$11.00
Direct labor	15.00
Variable overhead	17.00
Total incremental cost	$43.00

3. The goal of this scrap or rework decision is to identify the alternative that produces the greatest net benefit to the company. To compare the alternatives, we determine the net cost of obtaining 500 marketable units as follows:

Incremental Cost to Produce 500 Marketable Units	Sell as Is	Melt and Recycle	Rework Units
Direct materials			
New materials	$ 6,000	$6,000	
Recycled metal materials		(4,800)	
Net materials cost		1,200	
Melting costs		400	
Total direct materials cost	6,000	1,600	
Direct labor	5,000	5,000	$1,500
Incremental overhead	3,200	3,200	1,750
Cost to produce 500 marketable units	14,200	9,800	3,250
Less proceeds of selling defects as scrap	(2,500)		
Opportunity costs*			5,800
Net cost	$11,700	$9,800	$9,050

* The $5,800 opportunity cost is the lost contribution margin from not being able to produce and sell 500 units because of reworking, computed as ($40 − [$14,200/500 units]) × 500 units.

The incremental cost of 500 marketable parts is smallest if the defects are reworked.

4. TD1:

	Net Cash Flows	Present Value of 1 at 10%	Present Value of Net Cash Flows
Year 1	$ 20,000	0.9091	$ 18,182
Year 2	30,000	0.8264	24,792
Year 3	70,000	0.7513	52,591
Totals	$120,000		95,565
Amount invested			(100,000)
Net present value			$ (4,435)

TD2:

	Net Cash Flows	Present Value of 1 at 10%	Present Value of Net Cash Flows
Year 1	$ 40,000	0.9091	$ 36,364
Year 2	40,000	0.8264	33,056
Year 3	40,000	0.7513	30,052
Totals	$120,000		99,472
Amount invested			(100,000)
Net present value			$ (528)

White Company should not invest in either project. Both are expected to yield a negative net present value, and it should invest only in positive net present value projects.

Using Excel to Compute Net Present Value and Internal Rate of Return

25A

Computing present values and internal rates of return for projects with uneven cash flows is tedious and error prone. These calculations can be performed simply and accurately by using functions built into Excel. Many calculators and other types of spreadsheet software can perform them too. To illustrate, consider Fastrac, a company that is considering investing in a new machine with the expected cash flows shown in the following spreadsheet. Cash outflows are entered as negative numbers, and cash inflows are entered as positive numbers. Assume Fastrac requires a 12% annual return, entered as 0.12 in cell C1.

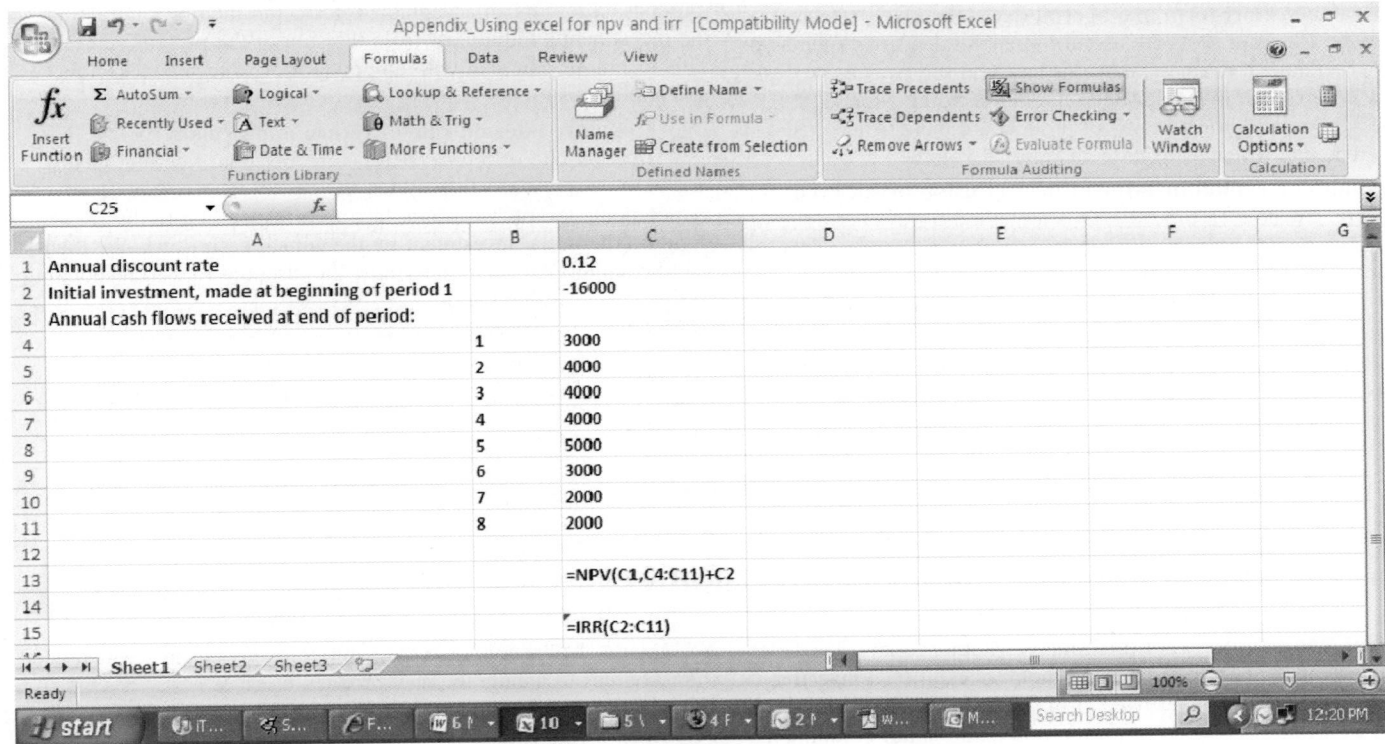

To compute the net present value of this project, the following is entered into cell C13:

$$=NPV(C1,C4:C11)+C2.$$

This instructs Excel to use its NPV function to compute the present value of the cash flows in cells C4 through C11, using the discount rate in cell C1, and then add the amount of the (negative) initial investment. For this stream of cash flows and a discount rate of 12%, the net present value is $1,326.03.

To compute the internal rate of return for this project, the following is entered into cell C15:

$$=IRR(C2:C11).$$

This instructs Excel to use its IRR function to compute the internal rate of return of the cash flows in cells C2 through C11. By default, Excel starts with a guess of 10%, and then uses trial and error to find the IRR. The IRR equals 14% for this project.

Summary

C1 **Explain the importance of capital budgeting.** Capital budgeting is the process of analyzing alternative investments and deciding which assets to acquire or sell. It involves predicting the cash flows to be received from the alternatives, evaluating their merits, and then choosing which ones to pursue.

C2 **Describe the selection of a hurdle rate for an investment.** Top management should select the hurdle (discount) rate to use in evaluating capital investments. The required hurdle rate should be at least higher than the interest rate on money borrowed because the return on an investment must cover the interest and provide an additional profit to reward the company for risk.

C3 **Describe the importance of relevant costs for short-term decisions.** A company must rely on relevant costs pertaining to alternative courses of action rather than historical costs. Out-of-pocket expenses and opportunity costs are relevant because these are avoidable; sunk costs are irrelevant because they result from past decisions and are therefore unavoidable. Managers must also consider the relevant benefits associated with alternative decisions.

A1 **Evaluate short-term managerial decisions using relevant costs.** Relevant costs are useful in making decisions such as to accept additional business, make or buy, and sell as is or process further. For example, the relevant factors in deciding whether to produce and sell additional units of product are incremental costs and incremental revenues from the additional volume.

A2 **Analyze a capital investment project using break-even time.** Break-even time (BET) is a method for evaluating capital investments by restating future cash flows in terms of their present values (discounting the cash flows) and then calculating the payback period using these present values of cash flows.

P1 **Compute payback period and describe its use.** One way to compare potential investments is to compute and compare their payback periods. The payback period is an estimate of the expected time before the cumulative net cash inflow from the investment equals its initial cost. A payback period analysis fails to reflect risk of the cash flows, differences in the timing of cash flows within the payback period, and cash flows that occur after the payback period.

P2 **Compute accounting rate of return and explain its use.** A project's accounting rate of return is computed by dividing the expected annual after-tax net income by the average amount of investment in the project. When the net cash flows are received evenly throughout each period and straight-line depreciation is used, the average investment is computed as the average of the investment's initial book value and its salvage value.

P3 **Compute net present value and describe its use.** An investment's net present value is determined by predicting the future cash flows it is expected to generate, discounting them at a rate that represents an acceptable return, and then by subtracting the investment's initial cost from the sum of the present values. This technique can deal with any pattern of expected cash flows and applies a superior concept of return on investment.

P4 **Compute internal rate of return and explain its use.** The internal rate of return (IRR) is the discount rate that results in a zero net present value. When the cash flows are equal, we can compute the present value factor corresponding to the IRR by dividing the initial investment by the annual cash flows. We then use the annuity tables to determine the discount rate corresponding to this present value factor.

Guidance Answers to **Decision Maker** and **Decision Ethics**

Systems Manager   Your dilemma is whether to abide by rules designed to prevent abuse or to bend them to acquire an investment that you believe will benefit the firm. You should not pursue the latter action because breaking up the order into small components is dishonest and there are consequences of being caught at a later stage. Develop a proposal for the entire package and then do all you can to expedite its processing, particularly by pointing out its benefits. When faced with controls that are not working, there is rarely a reason to overcome its shortcomings by dishonesty. A direct assault on those limitations is more sensible and ethical.

Entrepreneur   The banker is probably concerned because new products are risky and should therefore be evaluated using a higher rate of return. You should conduct a thorough technical analysis and obtain detailed market data and information about any similar products available in the market. These factors might provide sufficient information to support the use of a lower return. You must convince yourself that the risk level is consistent with the discount rate used.

You should also be confident that your company has the capacity and the resources to handle the new product.

Partner   You should identify the differences between existing clients and this potential client. A key difference is that the restaurant business has additional inventory components (groceries, vegetables, meats, etc.) and is likely to have a higher proportion of depreciable assets. These differences imply that the partner must spend more hours auditing the records and understanding the business, regulations, and standards that pertain to the restaurant business. Such differences suggest that the partner must use a different "formula" for quoting a price to this potential client vis-à-vis current clients.

Investment Manager   You should probably focus on either the payback period or break-even time because both the time value of money and recovery time are important. Break-even time method is superior because it accounts for the time value of money, which is an important consideration in this decision.

Guidance Answers to **Quick Checks**

1. *b*

2. A capital budgeting decision is difficult because (1) the outcome is uncertain, (2) large amounts of money are usually involved, (3) a long-term commitment is required, and (4) the decision could be difficult or impossible to reverse.

3. *b*

4. Depreciation expense is subtracted from revenues in computing net income but does not use cash and should be added back to net income to compute net cash flows.

5. Not necessarily. One investment can continue to generate cash flows beyond the payback period for a longer time period than the other. The timing of their cash flows within the payback period also can differ.

6. *b*; Annual average investment = ($180,000 + $15,000)/2
= $97,500

Accounting rate of return = $40,000/$97,500 = 41%

7. For this determination, we need to compare it to the returns expected from alternative investments with similar risk.

8. Project A has the higher net present value as follows:

		Project A		Project B	
Year	Present Value of 1 at 10%	Net Cash Flows	Present Value of Net Cash Flows	Net Cash Flows	Present Value of Net Cash Flows
1	0.9091	$12,000	$10,909	$ 4,500	$ 4,091
2	0.8264	8,500	7,024	8,500	7,024
3	0.7513	4,000	3,005	13,000	9,767
Totals		$24,500	$20,938	$26,000	$20,882
Amount invested			(20,000)		(20,000)
Net present value			**$ 938**		**$ 882**

9. No, the information is too limited to draw that conclusion. For example, one investment could be riskier than the other, or one could require a substantially larger initial investment.

10. *b*

11. *e*; Variable costs per unit for this order of 200 units follow:

Direct materials ($37,500/7,500)	$ 5.00
Direct labor ($60,000/7,500)	8.00
Variable overhead [(0.30 × $20,000)/7,500]	0.80
Variable selling expenses [(0.60 × $25,000 × 0.5)/7,500]	1.00
Total variable costs per unit	$14.80

Cost to produce special order: (200 × $14.80) + $400
= $3,360.

Price per unit to earn $1,000: ($3,360 + $1,000)/200 = 21.80.

12. They are the additional (new) costs of accepting new business.

13. *d*;

	Incremental benefits		Incremental costs
Alpha	$300 ($600 − $300)	>	$150 (given)
Beta	$450 ($900 − $450)	>	$300 (given)
Gamma	$150 ($425 − $275)	>	$125 (given)
Delta	$ 60 ($210 − $150)	<	$ 75 (given)

14. A sunk cost is *never* relevant because it results from a past decision and is already incurred.

15. Avoidable expenses are ones a company will not incur by eliminating a segment; unavoidable expenses will continue even after a segment is eliminated.

16. *a*

Key Terms

mhhe.com/wildFAP19e

Key Terms are available at the book's Website for learning and testing in an online Flashcard Format.

Accounting rate of return (p. 1027)
Avoidable expense (p. 1041)
Break-even time (BET) (p. 1043)
Capital budgeting (p. 1024)
Cost of capital (p. 1029)

Hurdle rate (p. 1033)
Incremental cost (p. 1036)
Internal rate of return (IRR) (p. 1031)
Net present value (NPV) (p. 1029)
Payback period (PBP) (p. 1025)

Profitability index (p. 1031)
Relevant benefits (p. 1035)
Unavoidable expense (p. 1041)

Multiple Choice Quiz

Answers on p. 1064   **mhhe.com/wildFAP19e**

Additional Quiz Questions are available at the book's Website.

1. A company inadvertently produced 3,000 defective MP3 players. The players cost $12 each to produce. A recycler offers to purchase the defective players as they are for $8 each. The production manager reports that the defects can be corrected for $10 each, enabling them to be sold at their regular market price of $19 each. The company should:

a. Correct the defect and sell them at the regular price.

b. Sell the players to the recycler for $8 each.

c. Sell 2,000 to the recycler and repair the rest.

d. Sell 1,000 to the recycler and repair the rest.

e. Throw the players away.

Quiz25

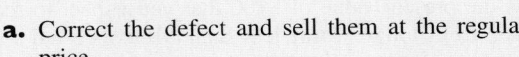

2. A company's productive capacity is limited to 480,000 machine hours. Product X requires 10 machine hours to produce; and Product Y requires 2 machine hours to produce. Product X sells for $32 per unit and has variable costs of $12 per unit; Product Y sells for $24 per unit and has variable costs of $10 per unit. Assuming that the company can sell as many of either product as it produces, it should:
a. Produce X and Y in the ratio of 57% and 43%.
b. Produce X and Y in the ratio of 83% X and 17% Y.
c. Produce equal amounts of Product X and Product Y.
d. Produce only Product X.
e. Produce only Product Y.

3. A company receives a special one-time order for 3,000 units of its product at $15 per unit. The company has excess capacity and it currently produces and sells the units at $20 each to its regular customers. Production costs are $13.50 per unit, which includes $9 of variable costs. To produce the special order, the company must incur additional fixed costs of $5,000. Should the company accept the special order?
a. Yes, because incremental revenue exceeds incremental costs.
b. No, because incremental costs exceed incremental revenue.
c. No, because the units are being sold for $5 less than the regular price.

d. Yes, because incremental costs exceed incremental revenue.
e. No, because incremental cost exceeds $15 per unit when total costs are considered.

4. A company is considering the purchase of equipment for $270,000. Projected annual cash inflow from this equipment is $61,200 per year. The payback period is:
a. 0.2 years
b. 5.0 years
c. 4.4 years
d. 2.3 years
e. 3.9 years

5. A company buys a machine for $180,000 that has an expected life of nine years and no salvage value. The company expects an annual net income (after taxes of 30%) of $8,550. What is the accounting rate of return?
a. 4.75%
b. 42.75%
c. 2.85%
d. 9.50%
e. 6.65%

Discussion Questions

1. What is capital budgeting?

2. ♟ Identify four reasons that capital budgeting decisions by managers are risky.

3. Capital budgeting decisions require careful analysis because they are generally the _____ _____ and _____ decisions that management faces.

4. Identify two disadvantages of using the payback period for comparing investments.

5. ♟ Why is an investment more attractive to management if it has a shorter payback period?

6. What is the average amount invested in a machine during its predicted five-year life if it costs $200,000 and has a $20,000 salvage value? Assume that net income is received evenly throughout each year and straight-line depreciation is used.

7. If the present value of the expected net cash flows from a machine, discounted at 10%, exceeds the amount to be invested, what can you say about the investment's expected rate of return? What can you say about the expected rate of return if the present value of the net cash flows, discounted at 10%, is less than the investment amount?

8. Why is the present value of $100 that you expect to receive one year from today worth less than $100 received today? What is the present value of $100 that you expect to receive one year from today, discounted at 12%?

9. ♟ Why should managers set the required rate of return higher than the rate at which money can be borrowed when making a typical capital budgeting decision?

10. ♟ Why does the use of the accelerated depreciation method (instead of straight line) for income tax reporting increase an investment's value?

11. What is an out-of-pocket cost? What is an opportunity cost? Are opportunity costs recorded in the accounting records?

12. ♟ Why are sunk costs irrelevant in deciding whether to sell a product in its present condition or to make it into a new product through additional processing?

13. ♟ Identify the incremental costs incurred by **Best Buy** for shipping one additional iPod from a warehouse to a retail store along with the store's normal order of 75 iPods.

14. ♟ **Circuit City** is considering expanding a store. Identify three methods management can use to evaluate whether to expand.

15. ♟ Assume that **Apple** manufactures and sells 500,000 units of a product at $30 per unit in domestic markets. It costs $20 per unit to manufacture ($13 variable cost per unit, $7 fixed cost per unit). Can you describe a situation under which the company is willing to sell an additional 25,000 units of the product in an international market at $15 per unit?

♟ *Denotes Discussion Questions that involve decision making.*

Trek Company is considering two alternative investments. The payback period is 2.5 years for Investment A and 3 years for Investment B. (1) If management relies on the payback period, which investment is preferred? (2) Why might Trek's analysis of these two alternatives lead to the selection of B over A?

QUICK STUDY

QS 25-1
Analyzing payback periods   P1

Foster Company is considering an investment that requires immediate payment of $360,000 and provides expected cash inflows of $120,000 annually for four years. What is the investment's payback period?

QS 25-2
Payback period   P1

If Kimball Company invests $100,000 today, it can expect to receive $20,000 at the end of each year for the next seven years plus an extra $12,000 at the end of the seventh year. What is the net present value of this investment assuming a required 8% return on investments?

QS 25-3
Computation of
net present value   P3

Camino Company is considering an investment expected to generate an average net income after taxes of $3,825 for three years. The investment costs $90,000 and has an estimated $12,000 salvage value. Compute the accounting rate of return for this investment; assume the company uses straight-line depreciation. Hint: Use the formula in Exhibit 25.5 when computing the average annual investment.

QS 25-4
Computation of
accounting rate of return   P2

Flash Memory Company can sell all units of computer memory X and Y that it can produce, but it has limited production capacity. It can produce four units of X per hour *or* six units of Y per hour, and it has 16,000 production hours available. Contribution margin is $10 for Product X and $8 for Product Y. What is the most profitable sales mix for this company?

QS 25-5
Selection of sales mix

C3 A1

Falcon Company incurs a $18 per unit cost for Product A, which it currently manufactures and sells for $27 per unit. Instead of manufacturing and selling this product, the company can purchase Product B for $10 per unit and sell it for $24 per unit. If it does so, unit sales would remain unchanged and $10 of the $18 per unit costs assigned to Product A would be eliminated. Should the company continue to manufacture Product A or purchase Product B for resale?

QS 25-6
Analysis of incremental costs

C3 A1

Fast Feet, a shoe manufacturer, is evaluating the costs and benefits of new equipment that would custom fit each pair of athletic shoes. The customer would have his or her foot scanned by digital computer equipment; this information would be used to cut the raw materials to provide the customer a perfect fit. The new equipment costs $300,000 and is expected to generate an additional $105,000 in cash flows for five years. A bank will make a $300,000 loan to the company at a 8% interest rate for this equipment's purchase. Use the following table to determine the break-even time for this equipment. (Round the present value of cash flows to the nearest dollar.)

QS 25-7
Computation of break-even time

A2

Year	Cash Flows*	Present Value of 1 at 8%	Present Value of Cash Flows	Cumulative Present Value of Cash Flows
0	$(300,000)	1.0000		
1	105,000	0.9259		
2	105,000	0.8573		
3	105,000	0.7938		
4	105,000	0.7350		
5	105,000	0.6806		

* All cash flows occur at year-end.

Jemak Company is considering two alternative projects. Project 1 requires an initial investment of $800,000 and has a net present value of cash flows of $1,600,000. Project 2 requires an initial investment of $4,000,000 and has a net present value of cash flows of $2,000,000. Compute the profitability index for each project. Based on the profitability index, which project should the company prefer? Explain.

QS 25-8
Profitability index

P3

EXERCISES

Exercise 25-1
Payback period computation; even cash flows
P1

Compute the payback period for each of these two separate investments (round the payback period to two decimals):

a. A new operating system for an existing machine is expected to cost $250,000 and have a useful life of four years. The system yields an incremental after-tax income of $72,000 each year after deducting its straight-line depreciation. The predicted salvage value of the system is $10,000.

b. A machine costs $180,000, has a $12,000 salvage value, is expected to last eight years, and will generate an after-tax income of $39,000 per year after straight-line depreciation.

Exercise 25-2
Payback period computation; uneven cash flows
P1

Walker Company is considering the purchase of an asset for $90,000. It is expected to produce the following net cash flows. The cash flows occur evenly throughout each year. Compute the payback period for this investment.

Check 2.5 years

	Year I	Year 2	Year 3	Year 4	Year 5	Total
Net cash flows	$40,000	$30,000	$40,000	$70,000	$29,000	$209,000

Exercise 25-3
Payback period computation; declining-balance depreciation
P1

A machine can be purchased for $600,000 and used for 5 years, yielding the following net incomes. In projecting net incomes, double-declining balance depreciation is applied, using a 5-year life and a zero salvage value. Compute the machine's payback period (ignore taxes). (Round the payback period to two decimals.)

Check 2.27 years

	Year I	Year 2	Year 3	Year 4	Year 5
Net incomes	$40,000	$100,000	$200,000	$150,000	$400,000

Exercise 25-4
Accounting rate of return   P2

A machine costs $200,000 and is expected to yield an after-tax net income of $5,040 each year. Management predicts this machine has a 12-year service life and a $40,000 salvage value, and it uses straight-line depreciation. Compute this machine's accounting rate of return.

Exercise 25-5
Payback period and accounting rate of return on investment
P1 P2

MLM Co. is considering the purchase of equipment that would allow the company to add a new product to its line. The equipment is expected to cost $324,000 with a 12-year life and no salvage value. It will be depreciated on a straight-line basis. The company expects to sell 128,000 units of the equipment's product each year. The expected annual income related to this equipment follows. Compute the (1) payback period and (2) accounting rate of return for this equipment.

Sales	$200,000
Costs	
Materials, labor, and overhead (except depreciation)	107,000
Depreciation on new equipment	27,000
Selling and administrative expenses	20,000
Total costs and expenses	154,000
Pretax income	46,000
Income taxes (30%)	13,800
Net income	$ 32,200

Check (1) 5.47 years (2) 19.88%

Exercise 25-6
Computing net present value   P3

After evaluating the risk of the investment described in Exercise 25-5, MLM Co. concludes that it must earn at least a 10% return on this investment. Compute the net present value of this investment. (Round the net present value to the nearest dollar.)

Cerritos Company can invest in each of three cheese-making projects: C1, C2, and C3. Each project requires an initial investment of $438,374 and would yield the following annual cash flows.

	CI	C2	C3
Year 1	$ 24,000	$192,000	$360,000
Year 2	216,000	192,000	120,000
Year 3	336,000	192,000	96,000
Totals	$576,000	$576,000	$576,000

(1) Assuming that the company requires a 12% return from its investments, use net present value to determine which projects, if any, should be acquired. (2) Using the answer from part 1, explain whether the internal rate of return is higher or lower than 12% for project C2. (3) Compute the internal rate of return for project C2.

Exercise 25-7
Computation and interpretation of net present value and internal rate of return

P3   P4

Check   (3) IRR = 15%

Following is information on two alternative investments being considered by Jakem Company. The company requires a 10% return from its investments.

	Project A	Project B
Initial investment	$(180,325)	$(150,960)
Expected net cash flows in year:		
1	45,000	35,000
2	50,000	52,000
3	82,295	58,000
4	86,400	75,000
5	64,000	29,000

For each alternative project compute the (a) net present value, and (b) profitability index. If the company can only select one project, which should it choose? Explain.

Exercise 25-8
NPV and profitability index

P3

Refer to the information in Exercise 25-8. Create an Excel spreadsheet to compute the internal rate of return for each of the projects. Round the percentage return to two decimals.

Exercise 25-9^A
Using Excel to compute IRR

P4

Harlan Co. expects to sell 300,000 units of its product in the next period with the following results.

Sales (300,000 units)	$4,500,000
Costs and expenses	
Direct materials	600,000
Direct labor	1,200,000
Overhead	300,000
Selling expenses	450,000
Administrative expenses	771,000
Total costs and expenses	3,321,000
Net income	$1,179,000

Exercise 25-10
Decision to accept additional business or not

C3   A1

The company has an opportunity to sell 30,000 additional units at $13 per unit. The additional sales would not affect its current expected sales. Direct materials and labor costs per unit would be the same for the additional units as they are for the regular units. However, the additional volume would create the following incremental costs: (1) total overhead would increase by 16% and (2) administrative expenses would increase by $129,000. Prepare an analysis to determine whether the company should accept or reject the offer to sell additional units at the reduced price of $13 per unit.

Check   Income increase, $33,000

Exercise 25-11
Make or buy decision

C3 A1

Check $1,600 increased costs to make

Simons Company currently manufactures one of its crucial parts at a cost of $2.72 per unit. This cost is based on a normal production rate of 40,000 units per year. Variable costs are $1.20 per unit, fixed costs related to making this part are $40,000 per year, and allocated fixed costs are $50,000 per year. Allocated fixed costs are unavoidable whether the company makes or buys the part. Simons is considering buying the part from a supplier for a quoted price of $2.16 per unit guaranteed for a three-year period. Should the company continue to manufacture the part, or should it buy the part from the outside supplier? Support your answer with analyses.

Exercise 25-12
Sell or process decision

C3 A1

Starr Company has already manufactured 50,000 units of Product A at a cost of $50 per unit. The 50,000 units can be sold at this stage for $1,250,000. Alternatively, it can be further processed at a $750,000 total additional cost and be converted into 10,000 units of Product B and 20,000 units of Product C. Per unit selling price for Product B is $75 and for Product C is $50. Prepare an analysis that shows whether the 50,000 units of Product A should be processed further or not.

Exercise 25-13
Analysis of income effects from eliminating departments

C3 A1

Johns Co. expects its five departments to yield the following income for next year.

	Dept. M	Dept. N	Dept. O	Dept. P	Dept. T
Sales	$34,000	$23,500	$33,000	$27,500	$ 10,500
Expenses					
Avoidable	4,700	18,900	15,800	8,000	14,900
Unavoidable	20,000	5,100	2,900	15,000	5,900
Total expenses	24,700	24,000	18,700	23,000	20,800
Net income (loss)	$ 9,300	$ (500)	$14,300	$ 4,500	$(10,300)

Check Total income (2) $17,100, (3) $21,700

Recompute and prepare the departmental income statements (including a combined total column) for the company under each of the following separate scenarios: Management (1) does not eliminate any department, (2) eliminates departments with expected net losses, and (3) eliminates departments with sales dollars that are less than avoidable expenses. Explain your answers to parts 2 and 3.

Exercise 25-14
Sales mix determination and analysis

C3 A1

Jersey Company owns a machine that can produce two specialized products. Production time for Product TLX is two units per hour and for Product MTV is five units per hour. The machine's capacity is 2,200 hours per year. Both products are sold to a single customer who has agreed to buy all of the company's output up to a maximum of 3,740 units of Product TLX and 2,090 units of Product MTV. Selling prices and variable costs per unit to produce the products follow. Determine (1) the company's most profitable sales mix and (2) the contribution margin that results from that sales mix.

	Product TLX	Product MTV
Selling price per unit	$11.50	$6.90
Variable costs per unit	3.45	4.14

Check (2) $34,661

Exercise 25-15
Comparison of payback and BET

P1 A2

This chapter explained two methods to evaluate investments using recovery time, the payback period and break-even time (BET). Refer to QS 25-7 and (1) compute the recovery time for both the payback period and break-even time, (2) discuss the advantage(s) of break-even time over the payback period, and (3) list two conditions under which payback period and break-even time are similar.

Burtle Company is planning to add a new product to its line. To manufacture this product, the company needs to buy a new machine at a $488,000 cost with an expected four-year life and a $15,200 salvage value. All sales are for cash, and all costs are out of pocket except for depreciation on the new machine. Additional information includes the following.

Expected annual sales of new product	$1,870,000
Expected annual costs of new product	
Direct materials	465,000
Direct labor	680,000
Overhead excluding straight-line depreciation on new machine	335,000
Selling and administrative expenses	158,000
Income taxes	40%

Required

1. Compute straight-line depreciation for each year of this new machine's life. (Round depreciation amounts to the nearest dollar.)
2. Determine expected net income and net cash flow for each year of this machine's life. (Round answers to the nearest dollar.)
3. Compute this machine's payback period, assuming that cash flows occur evenly throughout each year. (Round the payback period to two decimals.)
4. Compute this machine's accounting rate of return, assuming that income is earned evenly throughout each year. (Round the percentage return to two decimals.)
5. Compute the net present value for this machine using a discount rate of 8% and assuming that cash flows occur at each year-end. (*Hint:* Salvage value is a cash inflow at the end of the asset's life. Round the net present value to the nearest dollar.)

Jackson Company has an opportunity to invest in one of two new projects. Project Y requires a $360,000 investment for new machinery with a four-year life and no salvage value. Project Z requires a $360,000 investment for new machinery with a three-year life and no salvage value. The two projects yield the following predicted annual results. The company uses straight-line depreciation, and cash flows occur evenly throughout each year.

	Project Y	Project Z
Sales	$355,000	$265,000
Expenses		
Direct materials	49,700	30,125
Direct labor	71,000	36,750
Overhead including depreciation	127,800	129,250
Selling and administrative expenses	25,000	20,000
Total expenses	273,500	216,125
Pretax income	81,500	48,875
Income taxes (30%)	24,450	14,663
Net income	$ 57,050	$ 34,212

Required

1. Compute each project's annual expected net cash flows. (Round the net cash flows to the nearest dollar.)
2. Determine each project's payback period. (Round the payback period to two decimals.)
3. Compute each project's accounting rate of return. (Round the percentage return to one decimal.)
4. Determine each project's net present value using 6% as the discount rate. For part 4 only, assume that cash flows occur at each year-end. (Round the net present value to the nearest dollar.)

Analysis Component

5. Identify the project you would recommend to management and explain your choice.

PROBLEM SET A

Problem 25-1A
Computation of payback period, accounting rate of return, and net present value

P1 P2 P3

mhhe.com/wildFAP19e

Check (4) 27.14%

(5) $140,794

Problem 25-2A
Analysis and computation of payback period, accounting rate of return, and net present value

P1 P2 P3

Check For Project Y: (2) 2.45 years, (3) 31.7%, (4) $149,543

Problem 25-3A
Computation of cash flows and net present values with alternative depreciation methods

P3

Deandra Corporation is considering a new project requiring a $97,500 investment in test equipment with no salvage value. The project would produce $71,000 of pretax income before depreciation at the end of each of the next six years. The company's income tax rate is 32%. In compiling its tax return and computing its income tax payments, the company can choose between the two alternative depreciation schedules shown in the table.

	Straight-Line Depreciation	MACRS Depreciation*
Year 1	$ 9,750	$19,500
Year 2	19,500	31,200
Year 3	19,500	18,720
Year 4	19,500	11,232
Year 5	19,500	11,232
Year 6	9,750	5,616
Totals	$97,500	$97,500

* The modified accelerated cost recovery system (MACRS) for depreciation is discussed in Chapter 10.

Required

1. Prepare a five-column table that reports amounts (assuming use of straight-line depreciation) for each of the following for each of the six years: (a) pretax income before depreciation, (b) straight-line depreciation expense, (c) taxable income, (d) income taxes, and (e) net cash flow. Net cash flow equals the amount of income before depreciation minus the income taxes. (Round answers to the nearest dollar.)
2. Prepare a five-column table that reports amounts (assuming use of MACRS depreciation) for each of the following for each of the six years: (a) pretax income before depreciation, (b) MACRS depreciation expense, (c) taxable income, (d) income taxes, and (e) net cash flow. Net cash flow equals the income amount before depreciation minus the income taxes. (Round answers to the nearest dollar.)

Check Net present value:
(3) $135,347, (4) $136,893

3. Compute the net present value of the investment if straight-line depreciation is used. Use 10% as the discount rate. (Round the net present value to the nearest dollar.)
4. Compute the net present value of the investment if MACRS depreciation is used. Use 10% as the discount rate. (Round the net present value to the nearest dollar.)

Analysis Component

5. Explain why the MACRS depreciation method increases this project's net present value.

Problem 25-4A
Analysis of income effects of additional business

C3 A1

mhhe.com/wildFAP19e

Ingraham Products manufactures and sells to wholesalers approximately 200,000 packages per year of underwater markers at $4 per package. Annual costs for the production and sale of this quantity are shown in the table.

Direct materials	$256,000
Direct labor	64,000
Overhead	192,000
Selling expenses	80,000
Administrative expenses	53,000
Total costs and expenses	$645,000

A new wholesaler has offered to buy 33,000 packages for $3.44 each. These markers would be marketed under the wholesaler's name and would not affect Ingraham Products' sales through its normal channels. A study of the costs of this additional business reveals the following:

• Direct materials costs are 100% variable.
• Per unit direct labor costs for the additional units would be 50% higher than normal because their production would require overtime pay at one-and-one-half times the usual labor rate.
• 35% of the normal annual overhead costs are fixed at any production level from 150,000 to 300,000 units. The remaining 65% of the annual overhead cost is variable with volume.

- Accepting the new business would involve no additional selling expenses.
- Accepting the new business would increase administrative expenses by a $5,000 fixed amount.

Required

Prepare a three-column comparative income statement that shows the following:

1. Annual operating income without the special order (column 1).
2. Annual operating income received from the new business only (column 2).
3. Combined annual operating income from normal business and the new business (column 3).

Check Operating income:
(1) $155,000, (2) $29,848

Virginia Company is able to produce two products, G and B, with the same machine in its factory. The following information is available.

Problem 25-5A
Analysis of sales mix strategies

C3 A1 ♟

	Product G	Product B
Selling price per unit	$280	$240
Variable costs per unit	130	60
Contribution margin per unit	$150	$180
Machine hours to produce 1 unit	0.2 hours	2.0 hours
Maximum unit sales per month	1,200 units	200 units

The company presently operates the machine for a single eight-hour shift for 22 working days each month. Management is thinking about operating the machine for two shifts, which will increase its productivity by another eight hours per day for 22 days per month. This change would require $63,000 additional fixed costs per month.

Required

1. Determine the contribution margin per machine hour that each product generates.
2. How many units of Product G and Product B should the company produce if it continues to operate with only one shift? How much total contribution margin does this mix produce each month?
3. If the company adds another shift, how many units of Product G and Product B should it produce? How much total contribution margin would this mix produce each month? Should the company add the new shift? Explain.
4. Suppose that the company determines that it can increase Product G's maximum sales to 1,400 units per month by spending $24,000 per month in marketing efforts. Should the company pursue this strategy and the double shift? Explain.

Check Units of Product G: (2) 880,
(3) 1,200, (4) 1,400

Eclectic Decor Company's management is trying to decide whether to eliminate Department 200, which has produced losses or low profits for several years. The company's 2009 departmental income statement shows the following.

Problem 25-6A
Analysis of possible elimination of a department

C3 A1 ♟

ECLECTIC DECOR COMPANY Departmental Income Statements For Year Ended December 31, 2009			
	Dept. 100	Dept. 200	Combined
Sales	$437,000	$280,000	$717,000
Cost of goods sold	263,000	207,000	470,000
Gross profit	174,000	73,000	247,000
Operating expenses			
Direct expenses			
Advertising	17,500	13,500	31,000
Store supplies used	5,000	4,600	9,600
Depreciation—Store equipment	4,200	3,000	7,200
Total direct expenses	26,700	21,100	47,800

[continued on next page]

[continued from previous page]

Allocated expenses			
Sales salaries	52,000	31,200	83,200
Rent expense	9,500	4,750	14,250
Bad debts expense	9,500	7,400	16,900
Office salary	15,600	10,400	26,000
Insurance expense	1,900	1,000	2,900
Miscellaneous office expenses	2,500	1,700	4,200
Total allocated expenses	91,000	56,450	147,450
Total expenses	117,700	77,550	195,250
Net income (loss)	$ 56,300	$ (4,550)	$ 51,750

In analyzing whether to eliminate Department 200, management considers the following:

a. The company has one office worker who earns $500 per week, or $26,000 per year, and four sales-clerks who each earn $400 per week, or $20,800 per year.

b. The full salaries of two salesclerks are charged to Department 100. The full salary of one sales clerk is charged to Department 200. The salary of the fourth clerk, who works half-time in both departments, is divided evenly between the two departments.

c. Eliminating Department 200 would avoid the sales salaries and the office salary currently allocated to it. However, management prefers another plan. Two salesclerks have indicated that they will be quitting soon. Management believes that their work can be done by the other two clerks if the one office worker works in sales half-time. Eliminating Department 200 will allow this shift of duties. If this change is implemented, half the office worker's salary would be reported as sales salaries and half would be reported as office salary.

d. The store building is rented under a long-term lease that cannot be changed. Therefore, Department 100 will use the space and equipment currently used by Department 200.

e. Closing Department 200 will eliminate its expenses for advertising, bad debts, and store supplies; 70% of the insurance expense allocated to it to cover its merchandise inventory; and 25% of the miscellaneous office expenses presently allocated to it.

Required

Check (1) Total expenses:
(a) $665,250, (b) $275,225

(2) Forecasted net income without Department 200, $46,975

1. Prepare a three-column report that lists items and amounts for (a) the company's total expenses (including cost of goods sold)—in column 1, (b) the expenses that would be eliminated by closing Department 200—in column 2, and (c) the expenses that will continue—in column 3.

2. Prepare a forecasted annual income statement for the company reflecting the elimination of Department 200 assuming that it will not affect Department 100's sales and gross profit. The statement should reflect the reassignment of the office worker to one-half time as a salesclerk.

Analysis Component

3. Reconcile the company's combined net income with the forecasted net income assuming that Department 200 is eliminated (list both items and amounts). Analyze the reconciliation and explain why you think the department should or should not be eliminated.

PROBLEM SET B

Problem 25-1B
Computation of payback period, accounting rate of return, and net present value

P1 P2 P3

Sorbo Company is planning to add a new product to its line. To manufacture this product, the company needs to buy a new machine at a $600,000 cost with an expected four-year life and a $20,000 salvage value. All sales are for cash and all costs are out of pocket, except for depreciation on the new machine. Additional information includes the following.

Expected annual sales of new product	$2,300,000
Expected annual costs of new product	
Direct materials	600,000
Direct labor	840,000
Overhead excluding straight-line depreciation on new machine	420,000
Selling and administrative expenses	200,000
Income taxes	30%

Required

1. Compute straight-line depreciation for each year of this new machine's life. (Round depreciation amounts to the nearest dollar.)

2. Determine expected net income and net cash flow for each year of this machine's life. (Round answers to the nearest dollar.)

3. Compute this machine's payback period, assuming that cash flows occur evenly throughout each year. (Round the payback period to two decimals.)

4. Compute this machine's accounting rate of return, assuming that income is earned evenly throughout each year. (Round the percentage return to two decimals.)

5. Compute the net present value for this machine using a discount rate of 7% and assuming that cash flows occur at each year-end. (*Hint:* Salvage value is a cash inflow at the end of the asset's life.)

Check (4) 21.45%

(5) $131,650

Morris Company has an opportunity to invest in one of two projects. Project A requires a $480,000 investment for new machinery with a four-year life and no salvage value. Project B also requires a $480,000 investment for new machinery with a three-year life and no salvage value. The two projects yield the following predicted annual results. The company uses straight-line depreciation, and cash flows occur evenly throughout each year.

Problem 25-2B
Analysis and computation of payback period, accounting rate of return, and net present value

P1 P2 P3

	Project A	Project B
Sales	$500,000	$400,000
Expenses		
Direct materials	70,000	50,000
Direct labor	100,000	60,000
Overhead including depreciation	180,000	180,000
Selling and administrative expenses	36,000	36,000
Total expenses	386,000	326,000
Pretax income	114,000	74,000
Income taxes (30%)	34,200	22,200
Net income	$ 79,800	$ 51,800

Required

1. Compute each project's annual expected net cash flows. (Round net cash flows to the nearest dollar.)

2. Determine each project's payback period. (Round the payback period to two decimals.)

3. Compute each project's accounting rate of return. (Round the percentage return to one decimal.)

4. Determine each project's net present value using 8% as the discount rate. For part 4 only, assume that cash flows occur at each year-end. (Round net present values to the nearest dollar.)

Check For Project A: (2) 2.4 years, (3) 33.3%, (4) $181,758

Analysis Component

5. Identify the project you would recommend to management and explain your choice.

Lee Corporation is considering a new project requiring a $300,000 investment in an asset having no salvage value. The project would produce $125,000 of pretax income before depreciation at the end of each of the next six years. The company's income tax rate is 35%. In compiling its tax return and computing its income tax payments, the company can choose between two alternative depreciation schedules as shown in the table.

Problem 25-3B
Computation of cash flows and net present values with alternative depreciation methods

P3

	Straight-Line Depreciation	MACRS Depreciation*
Year 1	$ 30,000	$ 60,000
Year 2	60,000	96,000
Year 3	60,000	57,600
Year 4	60,000	34,560
Year 5	60,000	34,560
Year 6	30,000	17,280
Totals	$300,000	$300,000

* The modified accelerated cost recovery system (MACRS) for depreciation is discussed in Chapter 10.

Required

1. Prepare a five-column table that reports amounts (assuming use of straight-line depreciation) for each of the following items for each of the six years: (a) pretax income before depreciation, (b) straight-line depreciation expense, (c) taxable income, (d) income taxes, and (e) net cash flow. Net cash flow equals the amount of income before depreciation minus the income taxes. (Round answers to the nearest dollar.)

2. Prepare a five-column table that reports amounts (assuming use of MACRS depreciation) for each of the following items for each of the six years: (a) income before depreciation, (b) MACRS depreciation expense, (c) taxable income, (d) income taxes, and (e) net cash flow. Net cash flow equals the amount of income before depreciation minus the income taxes. (Round answers to the nearest dollar.)

Check   Net present value:
(3) $129,846, (4) $135,050

3. Compute the net present value of the investment if straight-line depreciation is used. Use 10% as the discount rate. (Round the net present value to the nearest dollar.)

4. Compute the net present value of the investment if MACRS depreciation is used. Use 10% as the discount rate. (Round the net present value to the nearest dollar.)

Analysis Component

5. Explain why the MACRS depreciation method increases the net present value of this project.

Problem 25-4B
Analysis of income effects of additional business

C3 A1

Wyn Company manufactures and sells to local wholesalers approximately 150,000 units per month at a sales price of $4 per unit. Monthly costs for the production and sale of this quantity follow.

Direct materials	$192,000
Direct labor	48,000
Overhead	144,000
Selling expenses	60,000
Administrative expenses	40,000
Total costs and expenses	$484,000

A new out-of-state distributor has offered to buy 25,000 units next month for $3.44 each. These units would be marketed in other states and would not affect Wyn's sales through its normal channels. A study of the costs of this new business reveals the following:

- Direct materials costs are 100% variable.
- Per unit direct labor costs for the additional units would be 50% higher than normal because their production would require time-and-a-half overtime pay to meet the distributor's deadline.
- Twenty-five percent of the normal annual overhead costs are fixed at any production level from 125,000 to 200,000 units. The remaining 75% is variable with volume.
- Accepting the new business would involve no additional selling expenses.
- Accepting the new business would increase administrative expenses by a $2,000 fixed amount.

Required

Prepare a three-column comparative income statement that shows the following:

Check   Operating income:
(1) $116,000, (2) $22,000

1. Monthly operating income without the special order (column 1).
2. Monthly operating income received from the new business only (column 2).
3. Combined monthly operating income from normal business and the new business (column 3).

Problem 25-5B
Analysis of sales mix strategies

C3 A1

Verto Company is able to produce two products, R and T, with the same machine in its factory. The following information is available.

	Product R	Product T
Selling price per unit	$ 120	$160
Variable costs per unit	65	90
Contribution margin per unit	$ 55	$ 70
Machine hours to produce 1 unit	0.2 hours	0.5 hours
Maximum unit sales per month	1,100 units	350 units

The company presently operates the machine for a single eight-hour shift for 22 working days each month. Management is thinking about operating the machine for two shifts, which will increase its productivity by another eight hours per day for 22 days per month. This change would require $30,000 additional fixed costs per month.

Required

1. Determine the contribution margin per machine hour that each product generates.

2. How many units of Product R and Product T should the company produce if it continues to operate with only one shift? How much total contribution margin does this mix produce each month?

3. If the company adds another shift, how many units of Product R and Product T should it produce? How much total contribution margin would this mix produce each month? Should the company add the new shift? Explain.

4. Suppose that the company determines that it can increase Product R's maximum sales to 1,350 units per month by spending $9,000 per month in marketing efforts. Should the company pursue this strategy and the double shift? Explain.

Check   Units of Product R: (2) 880, (3) 1,100, (4) 1,350

Kumar Company's management is trying to decide whether to eliminate Department Z, which has produced low profits or losses for several years. The company's 2009 departmental income statement shows the following.

Problem 25-6B
Analysis of possible elimination of a department

C3 A1

KUMAR COMPANY Departmental Income Statements For Year Ended December 31, 2009			
	Dept. A	Dept. Z	Combined
Sales	$1,050,000	$262,500	$1,312,500
Cost of goods sold	691,950	187,650	879,600
Gross profit	358,050	74,850	432,900
Operating expenses			
Direct expenses			
Advertising	40,500	4,500	45,000
Store supplies used	8,400	2,100	10,500
Depreciation—Store equipment	21,000	10,500	31,500
Total direct expenses	69,900	17,100	87,000
Allocated expenses			
Sales salaries	105,300	35,100	140,400
Rent expense	33,120	8,280	41,400
Bad debts expense	31,500	6,000	37,500
Office salary	31,200	7,800	39,000
Insurance expense	6,300	2,100	8,400
Miscellaneous office expenses	2,550	3,750	6,300
Total allocated expenses	209,970	63,030	273,000
Total expenses	279,870	80,130	360,000
Net income (loss)	$ 78,180	$ (5,280)	$ 72,900

In analyzing whether to eliminate Department Z, management considers the following items:

a. The company has one office worker who earns $750 per week or $39,000 per year and four sales-clerks who each earn $675 per week or $35,100 per year.

b. The full salaries of three salesclerks are charged to Department A. The full salary of one salesclerk is charged to Department Z.

c. Eliminating Department Z would avoid the sales salaries and the office salary currently allocated to it. However, management prefers another plan. Two salesclerks have indicated that they will be quitting soon. Management believes that their work can be done by the two remaining clerks if the one office worker works in sales half time. Eliminating Department Z will allow this shift of duties. If this change is implemented, half the office worker's salary would be reported as sales salaries and half would be reported as office salary.

d. The store building is rented under a long-term lease that cannot be changed. Therefore, Department A will use the space and equipment currently used by Department Z.

e. Closing Department Z will eliminate its expenses for advertising, bad debts, and store supplies; 65% of the insurance expense allocated to it to cover its merchandise inventory; and 30% of the miscellaneous office expenses presently allocated to it.

Required

1. Prepare a three-column report that lists items and amounts for (a) the company's total expenses (including cost of goods sold)—in column 1, (b) the expenses that would be eliminated by closing Department Z—in column 2, and (c) the expenses that will continue—in column 3.

2. Prepare a forecasted annual income statement for the company reflecting the elimination of Department Z assuming that it will not affect Department A's sales and gross profit. The statement should reflect the reassignment of the office worker to one-half time as a salesclerk.

Analysis Component

3. Reconcile the company's combined net income with the forecasted net income assuming that Department Z is eliminated (list both items and amounts). Analyze the reconciliation and explain why you think the department should or should not be eliminated.

SERIAL PROBLEM

Success Systems

(This serial problem began in Chapter 1 and continues through most of the book. If previous chapter segments were not completed, the serial problem can begin at this point. It is helpful, but not necessary, to use the Working Papers that accompany the book.)

SP 25 Adriana Lopez is considering the purchase of equipment for Success Systems that would allow the company to add a new product to its computer furniture line. The equipment is expected to cost $300,000 and to have a six-year life and no salvage value. It will be depreciated on a straight-line basis. Success Systems expects to sell 100 units of the equipment's product each year. The expected annual income related to this equipment follows.

Sales	$375,000
Costs	
Materials, labor, and overhead (except depreciation)	200,000
Depreciation on new equipment	50,000
Selling and administrative expenses	37,500
Total costs and expenses	287,500
Pretax income	87,500
Income taxes (30%)	26,250
Net income	$ 61,250

Required

Compute the (1) payback period and (2) accounting rate of return for this equipment.

BEYOND THE NUMBERS

REPORTING IN ACTION

C1 A1 P3

BTN 25-1 In fiscal 2007, **Best Buy** invested $251 million in store-related projects that included store remodels, relocations, expansions, and various merchandising projects. Assume that these projects have a seven-year life, and that Best Buy requires a 12% internal rate of return on these projects.

Required

1. What is the amount of annual cash flows that Best Buy must earn from these projects to have a 12% internal rate of return? (*Hint:* Identify the seven-period, 12% factor from the present value of an annuity table, and then divide $251 million by this factor to get the annual cash flows necessary.)

Fast Forward

2. Access Best Buy's financial statements for fiscal years ended after March 3, 2007, from its Website (BestBuy.com) or the SEC's Website (SEC.gov).

  a. Determine the amount that Best Buy invested in similar store-related projects for the most recent year.

  b. Assume a seven-year life and a 12% internal rate of return. What is the amount of cash flows that Best Buy must earn on these new projects?

BTN 25-2 **Best Buy**, **Circuit City**, and **RadioShack** sell several different products; most are profitable but some are not. Teams of employees in each company make advertising, investment, and product mix decisions. A certain portion of advertising for both companies is on a local basis to a target audience.

Required

1. Find one major advertisement of a product or group of products for each company in your local newspaper. Contact the newspaper and ask the approximate cost of this ad space (for example, cost of one page or one-half page of advertising).

2. Estimate how many products this advertisement must sell to justify its cost. Begin by taking the product's sales price advertised for each company and assume a 20% contribution margin.

3. Prepare a one-half page memorandum explaining the importance of effective advertising when making a product mix decision. Be prepared to present your ideas in class.

COMPARATIVE ANALYSIS

C3

BTN 25-3 A consultant commented that "too often the numbers look good but feel bad." This comment often stems from estimation error common to capital budgeting proposals that relate to future cash flows. Three reasons for this error often exist. First, reliably predicting cash flows several years into the future is very difficult. Second, the present value of cash flows many years into the future (say, beyond 10 years) is often very small. Third, it is difficult for personal biases and expectations not to unduly influence present value computations.

Required

1. Compute the present value of $100 to be received in 10 years assuming a 12% discount rate.

2. Why is understanding the three reasons mentioned for estimation errors important when evaluating investment projects? Link this response to your answer for part 1.

ETHICS CHALLENGE

P3

BTN 25-4 Payback period, accounting rate of return, net present value, and internal rate of return are common methods to evaluate capital investment opportunities. Assume that your manager asks you to identify the type of measurement basis and unit that each method offers and to list the advantages and disadvantages of each. Present your response in memorandum format of less than one page.

COMMUNICATING IN PRACTICE

P1 P2 P3 P4

BTN 25-5 Many companies must determine whether to internally produce their component parts or to outsource them. Further, some companies now outsource key components or business processes to international providers. Access the Website BizBrim.com and review the available information on outsourcing—especially as it relates to both the advantages and the negative effects of outsourcing.

Required

1. What does Bizbrim identify as the major advantages and the major disadvantages of outsourcing?

2. Does it seem that Bizbrim is generally in favor of or opposed to outsourcing? Explain.

TAKING IT TO THE NET

A1

BTN 25-6 Break into teams and identify four reasons that an international airline such as **Southwest**, **Northwest**, or **American** would invest in a project when its direct analysis using both payback period and net present value indicate it to be a poor investment. (*Hint:* Think about qualitative factors.) Provide an example of an investment project supporting your answer.

TEAMWORK IN ACTION

P1 P3

ENTREPRENEURIAL DECISION

A1

BTN 25-7 Jared Greenberg and Dan Zinger of **Prairie Sticks Bat Company** make baseball bats. They must decide on the best sales mix. Assume their company has a capacity of 80 hours of lathe/processing time available each month and it makes two types of bats, Deluxe and Premium. Information on these bats follows.

	Deluxe	Premium
Selling price per bat	$70	$90
Variable costs per bat	$40	$50
Lathe/processing minutes per bat	6 minutes	12 minutes

Required

1. Assume the markets for both models of bats are unlimited. How many Deluxe bats and how many Premium bats should the company make each month? Explain. How much total contribution margin does this mix produce each month?

2. Assume the market for Deluxe bats is limited to 600 bats per month, with no market limit for Premium bats. How many Deluxe bats and how many Premium bats should the company make each month? Explain. How much total contribution margin does this mix produce each month?

HITTING THE ROAD

C1 P3

BTN 25-8 Visit or call a local auto dealership and inquire about leasing a car. Ask about the down payment and the required monthly payments. You will likely find the salesperson does not discuss the cost to purchase this car but focuses on the affordability of the monthly payments. This chapter gives you the tools to compute the cost of this car using the lease payment schedule in present dollars and to estimate the profit from leasing for an auto dealership.

Required

1. Compare the cost of leasing the car to buying it in present dollars using the information from the dealership you contact. (Assume you will make a final payment at the end of the lease and then own the car.)

2. Is it more costly to lease or buy the car? Support your answer with computations.

GLOBAL DECISION

C1

DSG

BTN 25-9 Access **DSG**'s 2006 annual report dated April 29, 2006, from its Website **www.DSGiplc.com**. Identify its report on corporate responsibility.

Required

Dixons reports that it recycled 25,607 tons of waste. Efforts such as these can be costly to a company. Why would a company like DSG pursue these costly efforts?

ANSWERS TO MULTIPLE CHOICE QUIZ

1. a; Reworking provides incremental revenue of $11 per unit ($19 − $8); and, it costs $10 to rework them. The company is better off by $1 per unit when it reworks these products and sells them at the regular price.

2. e; Product X has a $2 contribution margin per machine hour [($32 − $12)/10 MH]; Product Y has a $7 contribution margin per machine hour [($24 − $10)/2 MH]. It should produce as much of Product Y as possible.

3. a; Total revenue from the special order = 3,000 units × $15 per unit = $45,000; and, Total costs for the special order = (3,000 units × $9 per unit) + $5,000 = $32,000. Net income from the special order = $45,000 − $32,000 = $13,000. Thus, yes, it should accept the order.

4. c; Payback = $270,000/$61,200 per year = 4.4 years.

5. d; Accounting rate of return = $8,550/[($180,000 + $0)/2] = 9.5%.

A Financial Statement Information

This appendix includes financial information for (1) **Best Buy**, (2) **Circuit City**, (3) **RadioShack**, and (4) **Apple**. This information is taken from their annual 10-K reports filed with the SEC. An **annual report** is a summary of a company's financial results for the year along with its current financial condition and future plans. This report is directed to external users of financial information, but it also affects the actions and decisions of internal users.

A company uses an annual report to showcase itself and its products. Many annual reports include attractive photos, diagrams, and illustrations related to the company. The primary objective of annual reports, however, is the *financial section,* which communicates much information about a company, with most data drawn from the accounting information system. The layout of an annual report's financial section is fairly established and typically includes the following:

- ■ Letter to Shareholders
- ■ Financial History and Highlights
- ■ Management Discussion and Analysis
- ■ Management's Report on Financial Statements and on Internal Controls
- ■ Report of Independent Accountants (Auditor's Report) and on Internal Controls
- ■ Financial Statements
- ■ Notes to Financial Statements
- ■ List of Directors and Officers

This appendix provides the financial statements for Best Buy (plus selected notes), Circuit City, RadioShack, and Apple. The appendix is organized as follows:

- ■ **Best Buy A-2** through **A-18**
- ■ **Circuit City A-19** through **A-23**
- ■ RadioShack **A-24** through **A-28**
- ■ **Apple Computer A-29** through **A-33**

Many assignments at the end of each chapter refer to information in this appendix. We encourage readers to spend time with these assignments; they are especially useful in showing the relevance and diversity of financial accounting and reporting.

Special note: The SEC maintains the EDGAR (**E**lectronic **D**ata **G**athering, **A**nalysis, and **R**etrieval) database at www.sec.gov. The **Form 10-K** is the annual report form for most companies. It provides electronically accessible information. The **Form 10-KSB** is the annual report form filed by small businesses. It requires slightly less information than the Form 10-K. One of these forms must be filed within 90 days after the company's fiscal year-end. (Forms 10-K405, 10-KT, 10-KT405, and 10-KSB405 are slight variations of the usual form due to certain regulations or rules.)

Financial Report

Selected Financial Data

The following table presents our selected financial data. In fiscal 2004, we sold our interest in Musicland. All fiscal years presented reflect the classification of Musicland's financial results as discontinued operations.

Five-Year Financial Highlights

$ in millions, except per share amounts

Fiscal Year	2007[1]	2006	2005	2004	2003
Consolidated Statements of Earnings Data					
Revenue	$35,934	$30,848	$27,433	$24,548	$20,943
Operating income	1,999	1,644	1,442	1,304	1,010
Earnings from continuing operations	1,377	1,140	934	800	622
Loss from discontinued operations, net of tax	—	—	—	(29)	(441)
Gain (loss) on disposal of discontinued operations, net of tax	—	—	50	(66)	—
Cumulative effect of change in accounting principles, net of tax	—	—	—	—	(82)
Net earnings	1,377	1,140	984	705	99
Per Share Data					
Continuing operations	$ 2.79	$ 2.27	$ 1.86	$ 1.61	$ 1.27
Discontinued operations	—	—	—	(0.06)	(0.89)
Gain (loss) on disposal of discontinued operations	—	—	0.10	(0.13)	—
Cumulative effect of accounting changes	—	—	—	—	(0.16)
Net earnings	2.79	2.27	1.96	1.42	0.20
Cash dividends declared and paid	0.36	0.31	0.28	0.27	—
Common stock price:					
High	59.50	56.00	41.47	41.80	35.83
Low	43.51	31.93	29.25	17.03	11.33
Operating Statistics					
Comparable store sales gain	5.0%	4.9%	4.3%	7.1%	2.4%
Gross profit rate	24.4%	25.0%	23.7%	23.9%	23.6%
Selling, general and administrative expenses rate	18.8%	19.7%	18.4%	18.6%	18.8%
Operating income rate	5.6%	5.3%	5.3%	5.3%	4.8%
Year-End Data					
Current ratio	1.4	1.3	1.4	1.3	1.3
Total assets	$13,570	$11,864	$10,294	$ 8,652	$ 7,694
Debt, including current portion	650	596	600	850	834
Total shareholders' equity	6,201	5,257	4,449	3,422	2,730
Number of stores					
Domestic	868	774	694	631	567
International	304	167	144	127	112
Total	1,172	941	838	758	679
Retail square footage (000s)					
Domestic	33,959	30,826	28,465	26,640	24,432
International	7,926	3,564	3,139	2,800	2,375
Total	41,885	34,390	31,604	29,440	26,807

[1] Fiscal 2007 included 53 weeks. All other periods presented included 52 weeks.

Consolidated Balance Sheets

$ in millions, except per share amounts

	March 3, 2007	February 25, 2006
Assets		
Current Assets		
Cash and cash equivalents	$ 1,205	$ 748
Short-term investments	2,588	3,041
Receivables	548	449
Merchandise inventories	4,028	3,338
Other current assets	712	409
Total current assets	9,081	7,985
Property and Equipment		
Land and buildings	705	580
Leasehold improvements	1,540	1,325
Fixtures and equipment	2,627	2,898
Property under capital lease	32	33
	4,904	4,836
Less accumulated depreciation	1,966	2,124
Net property and equipment	2,938	2,712
Goodwill	919	557
Tradenames	81	44
Long-Term Investments	318	218
Other Assets	233	348
Total Assets	$13,570	$11,864
Liabilities and Shareholders' Equity		
Current Liabilities		
Accounts payable	$ 3,934	$ 3,234
Unredeemed gift card liabilities	496	469
Accrued compensation and related expenses	332	354
Accrued liabilities	990	878
Accrued income taxes	489	703
Short-term debt	41	—
Current portion of long-term debt	19	418
Total current liabilities	6,301	6,056
Long-Term Liabilities	443	373
Long-Term Debt	590	178
Minority Interests	35	—
Shareholders' Equity		
Preferred stock, $1.00 par value: Authorized — 400,000 shares; Issued and outstanding — none	—	—
Common stock, $.10 par value: Authorized — 1 billion shares; Issued and outstanding — 480,655,000 and 485,098,000 shares, respectively	48	49
Additional paid-in capital	430	643
Retained earnings	5,507	4,304
Accumulated other comprehensive income	216	261
Total shareholders' equity	6,201	5,257
Total Liabilities and Shareholders' Equity	$13,570	$11,864

Consolidated Statements of Earnings

$ in millions, except per share amounts

Fiscal Years Ended	March 3, 2007	February 25, 2006	February 26, 2005
Revenue	$35,934	$30,848	$27,433
Cost of goods sold	27,165	23,122	20,938
Gross profit	8,769	7,726	6,495
Selling, general and administrative expenses	6,770	6,082	5,053
Operating income	1,999	1,644	1,442
Net interest income	111	77	1
Gain on investments	20	—	—
Earnings from continuing operations before income tax expense	2,130	1,721	1,443
Income tax expense	752	581	509
Minority interest in earnings	1	—	—
Earnings from continuing operations	1,377	1,140	934
Gain on disposal of discontinued operations, net of tax	—	—	50
Net earnings	$ 1,377	$ 1,140	$ 984
Basic earnings per share:			
Continuing operations	$ 2.86	$ 2.33	$ 1.91
Gain on disposal of discontinued operations	—	—	0.10
Basic earnings per share	$ 2.86	$ 2.33	$ 2.01
Diluted earnings per share:			
Continuing operations	$ 2.79	$ 2.27	$ 1.86
Gain on disposal of discontinued operations	—	—	0.10
Diluted earnings per share	$ 2.79	$ 2.27	$ 1.96
Basic weighted-average common shares outstanding (in millions)	482.1	490.3	488.9
Diluted weighted-average common shares outstanding (in millions)	496.2	504.8	505.0

BEST BUY

BEST BUY

Consolidated Statements of Changes in Shareholders' Equity
$ and shares in millions

	Common Shares	Common Stock	Additional Paid-In Capital	Retained Earnings	Accumulated Other Comprehensive Income	Total
Balances at February 28, 2004	**487**	**$49**	**$819**	**$ 2,468**	**$ 86**	**$3,422**
Net earnings	—	—	—	984	—	984
Other comprehensive income, net of tax:						
Foreign currency translation adjustments	—	—	—	—	59	59
Other	—	—	—	—	4	4
Total comprehensive income						1,047
Stock options exercised	10	1	219	—	—	220
Tax benefit from stock options exercised and employee stock purchase plan	—	—	60	—	—	60
Issuance of common stock under employee stock purchase plan	2	—	36	—	—	36
Vesting of restricted stock awards	—	—	1	—	—	1
Common stock dividends, $0.28 per share	—	—	—	(137)	—	(137)
Repurchase of common stock	(6)	(1)	(199)	—	—	(200)
Balances at February 26, 2005	**493**	**49**	**936**	**3,315**	**149**	**4,449**
Net earnings	—	—	—	1,140	—	1,140
Other comprehensive income, net of tax:						
Foreign currency translation adjustments	—	—	—	—	101	101
Other	—	—	—	—	11	11
Total comprehensive income						1,252
Stock options exercised	9	1	256	—	—	257
Tax benefit from stock options exercised and employee stock purchase plan	—	—	55	—	—	55
Issuance of common stock under employee stock purchase plan	1	—	35	—	—	35
Stock-based compensation	—	—	132	—	—	132
Common stock dividends, $0.31 per share	—	—	—	(151)	—	(151)
Repurchase of common stock	(18)	(1)	(771)	—	—	(772)
Balances at February 25, 2006	**485**	**49**	**643**	**4,304**	**261**	**5,257**
Net earnings	—	—	—	1,377	—	1,377
Other comprehensive loss, net of tax:						
Foreign currency translation adjustments	—	—	—	—	(33)	(33)
Other	—	—	—	—	(12)	(12)
Total comprehensive income						1,332
Stock options exercised	7	1	167	—	—	168
Tax benefit from stock options exercised and employee stock purchase plan	—	—	47	—	—	47
Issuance of common stock under employee stock purchase plan	1	—	49	—	—	49
Stock-based compensation	—	—	121	—	—	121
Common stock dividends, $0.36 per share	—	—	—	(174)	—	(174)
Repurchase of common stock	(12)	(2)	(597)	—	—	(599)
Balances at March 3, 2007	**481**	**$48**	**$430**	**$5,507**	**$216**	**$6,201**

Consolidated Statements of Cash Flows
$ in millions

Fiscal Years Ended	March 3, 2007	February 25, 2006	February 26, 2005
Operating Activities			
Net earnings	$1,377	$1,140	$ 984
Gain from disposal of discontinued operations, net of tax	—	—	(50)
Earnings from continuing operations	1,377	1,140	934
Adjustments to reconcile earnings from continuing operations to total cash provided by operating activities from continuing operations:			
Depreciation	509	456	459
Asset impairment charges	32	4	22
Stock-based compensation	121	132	(1)
Deferred income taxes	82	(151)	(28)
Excess tax benefits from stock-based compensation	(50)	(55)	—
Other, net	(11)	(3)	24
Changes in operating assets and liabilities, net of acquired assets and liabilities:			
Receivables	(70)	(43)	(30)
Merchandise inventories	(550)	(457)	(240)
Other assets	(47)	(11)	(50)
Accounts payable	320	385	347
Other liabilities	185	165	243
Accrued income taxes	(136)	178	301
Total cash provided by operating activities from continuing operations	1,762	1,740	1,981
Investing Activities			
Additions to property and equipment, net of $75 and $117 noncash capital expenditures in fiscal 2006 and 2005, respectively	(733)	(648)	(502)
Purchases of available-for-sale securities	(4,541)	(4,319)	(8,517)
Sales of available-for-sale securities	4,886	4,187	7,730
Acquisitions of businesses, net of cash acquired	(421)	—	—
Proceeds from disposition of investments	24	—	—
Change in restricted assets	—	(20)	(140)
Other, net	5	46	7
Total cash used in investing activities from continuing operations	(780)	(754)	(1,422)
Financing Activities			
Repurchase of common stock	(599)	(772)	(200)
Issuance of common stock under employee stock purchase plan and for the exercise of stock options	217	292	256
Dividends paid	(174)	(151)	(137)
Repayments of debt	(84)	(69)	(371)
Proceeds from issuance of debt	96	36	—
Excess tax benefits from stock-based compensation	50	55	—
Other, net	(19)	(10)	(7)
Total cash used in financing activities from continuing operations	(513)	(619)	(459)
Effect of Exchange Rate Changes on Cash	(12)	27	9
Increase in Cash and Cash Equivalents	457	394	109
Cash and Cash Equivalents at Beginning of Year	748	354	245
Cash and Cash Equivalents at End of Year	$1,205	$ 748	$ 354
Supplemental Disclosure of Cash Flow Information			
Income taxes paid	$ 804	$ 547	$ 241
Interest paid	14	16	35

BEST BUY

SELECTED Notes to Consolidated Financial Statements

$ in millions, except per share amounts

1. Summary of Significant Accounting Policies

Description of Business

Best Buy Co., Inc. is a specialty retailer of consumer electronics, home-office products, entertainment software, appliances and related services, with fiscal 2007 revenue from continuing operations of $35.9 billion.

We operate two reportable segments: Domestic and International. The Domestic segment is comprised of all U.S. store and online operations of Best Buy, Geek Squad, Magnolia Audio Video and Pacific Sales Kitchen and Bath Centers, Inc. ("Pacific Sales"). We acquired Pacific Sales on March 7, 2006. U.S. Best Buy stores offer a wide variety of consumer electronics, home-office products, entertainment software, appliances and related services through 822 stores at the end of fiscal 2007. Geek Squad provides residential and commercial computer repair, support and installation services in all U.S. Best Buy stores and at 12 stand-alone stores at the end of fiscal 2007. Magnolia Audio Video stores offer high-end audio and video products and related services through 20 stores at the end of fiscal 2007. Pacific Sales stores offer high-end home-improvement products, appliances and related services through 14 stores at the end of fiscal 2007.

Fiscal Year

Our fiscal year ends on the Saturday nearest the end of February. Fiscal 2007 included 53 weeks and fiscal 2006 and 2005 each included 52 weeks.

Cash and Cash Equivalents

Cash primarily consists of cash on hand and bank deposits. Cash equivalents primarily consist of money market accounts and other highly liquid investments with an original maturity of three months or less when purchased. We carry these investments at cost, which approximates market value. The amounts of cash equivalents at March 3, 2007, and February 25, 2006,

were $695 and $350, respectively, and the weighted-average interest rates were 4.8% and 3.3%, respectively.

Outstanding checks in excess of funds on deposit ("book overdrafts") totaled $183 and $230 at March 3, 2007, and February 25, 2006, respectively, and are reflected as current liabilities in our consolidated balance sheets.

Merchandise Inventories

Merchandise inventories are recorded at the lower of average cost or market. In-bound freight-related costs from our vendors are included as part of the net cost of merchandise inventories. Also included in the cost of inventory are certain vendor allowances that are not a reimbursement of specific, incremental and identifiable costs to promote a vendor's products. Other costs associated with acquiring, storing and transporting merchandise inventories to our retail stores are expensed as incurred and included in cost of goods sold.

Our inventory loss reserve represents anticipated physical inventory losses (e.g., theft) that have occurred since the last physical inventory date. Independent physical inventory counts are taken on a regular basis to ensure that the inventory reported in our consolidated financial statements is properly stated. During the interim period between physical inventory counts, we reserve for anticipated physical inventory losses on a location-by-location basis.

Property and Equipment

Property and equipment are recorded at cost. We compute depreciation using the straight-line method over the estimated useful lives of the assets. Leasehold improvements are depreciated over the shorter of their estimated useful lives or the period from the date the assets are placed in service to the end of the initial lease term. Leasehold improvements made significantly after the initial lease term are depreciated over the shorter of their estimated useful lives or the remaining lease term, including renewal periods, if reasonably assured.

$ in millions, except per share amounts

Accelerated depreciation methods are generally used for income tax purposes.

When property is fully depreciated, retired or otherwise disposed of, the cost and accumulated depreciation are removed from the accounts and any resulting gain or loss is reflected in the consolidated statement of earnings.

Repairs and maintenance costs are charged directly to expense as incurred. Major renewals or replacements that substantially extend the useful life of an asset are capitalized and depreciated.

Estimated useful lives by major asset category are as follows:

Asset	Life (in years)
Buildings	30–40
Leasehold improvements	3–25
Fixtures and equipment	3–20
Property under capital lease	3–20

Impairment of Long-Lived Assets

We account for the impairment or disposal of long-lived assets in accordance with SFAS No. 144, *Accounting for the Impairment* or *Disposal of Long-Lived Assets,* which requires long-lived assets, such as property and equipment, to be evaluated for impairment whenever events or changes in circumstances indicate the carrying value of an asset may not be recoverable. Factors considered important that could result in an impairment review include, but are not limited to, significant underperformance relative to historical or planned operating results, significant changes in the manner of use of the assets or significant changes in our business strategies. An impairment loss is recognized when the estimated undiscounted cash flows expected to result from the use of the asset plus net proceeds expected from disposition of the asset (if any) are less than the carrying value of the asset. When an impairment loss is recognized, the carrying amount of the asset is reduced to its estimated fair value based on quoted market prices or other valuation techniques.

Leases

We conduct the majority of our retail and distribution operations from leased locations. The leases require payment of real estate taxes, insurance and common area maintenance, in addition to rent. The terms of our lease agreements generally range from 10 to 20 years. Most of the leases contain renewal options and escalation clauses, and certain store leases require contingent rents based on factors such as specified percentages of revenue or the consumer price index. Other leases contain covenants related to the maintenance of financial ratios.

Goodwill and Intangible Assets

Goodwill

Goodwill is the excess of the purchase price over the fair value of identifiable net assets acquired in business combinations accounted for under the purchase method. We do not amortize goodwill but test it for impairment annually, or when indications of potential impairment exist, utilizing a fair value approach at the reporting unit level. A reporting unit is the operating segment, or a business unit one level below that operating segment, for which discrete financial information is prepared and regularly reviewed by segment management.

Tradenames

We have an indefinite-lived intangible asset related to our Pacific Sales tradename which is included in the Domestic segment. We also have indefinite-lived intangible assets related to our Future Shop and Five Star tradenames which are included in the International segment.

We determine fair values utilizing widely accepted valuation techniques, including discounted cash flows and market multiple analyses. During the fourth quarter of fiscal 2007, we completed our annual impairment testing of our goodwill and tradenames, using the valuation techniques as described above, and determined there was no impairment.

Lease Rights

Lease rights represent costs incurred to acquire the lease of a specific commercial property. Lease rights are recorded at cost and are amortized to rent expense over the remaining lease term, including renewal periods, if reasonably assured. Amortization periods range up to 16 years, beginning with the date we take possession of the property.

BEST BUY

$ in millions, except per share amounts

Investments

Short-term and long-term investments are comprised of municipal and United States government debt securities as well as auction-rate securities and variable-rate demand notes. In accordance with SFAS No. 115, *Accounting for Certain Investments in Debt and Equity Securities,* and based on our ability to market and sell these instruments, we classify auction-rate securities, variable-rate demand notes and other investments in debt securities as available-for-sale and carry them at amortized cost, which approximates fair value. Auction-rate securities and variable-rate demand notes are similar to short-term debt instruments because their interest rates are reset periodically. Investments in these securities can be sold for cash on the auction date. We classify auction-rate securities and variable-rate demand notes as short-term or long-term investments based on the reset dates.

We also hold investments in marketable equity securities and classify them as available-for-sale. Investments in marketable equity securities are included in other assets in our consolidated balance sheets. Investments in marketable equity securities are reported at fair value, based on quoted market prices when available. All unrealized holding gains or losses are reflected net of tax in accumulated other comprehensive income in shareholders' equity.

We review the key characteristics of our debt and marketable equity securities portfolio and their classification in accordance with GAAP on an annual basis, or when indications of potential impairment exist. If a decline in the fair value of a security is deemed by management to be other than temporary, the cost basis of the investment is written down to fair value, and the amount of the write-down is included in the determination of net earnings.

Income Taxes

We account for income taxes under the liability method. Under this method, deferred tax assets and liabilities are recognized for the estimated future tax consequences attributable to differences between the financial statement carrying amounts of existing assets and liabilities and their respective tax bases, and operating loss and tax credit carryforwards. Deferred tax assets and liabilities are measured using enacted income tax rates in effect for the year in which those temporary differences are expected to be recovered or settled. The effect on deferred tax assets and liabilities of a change in income tax rates is recognized in our consolidated statement of earnings in the period that includes the enactment date. A valuation allowance is recorded to reduce the carrying amounts of deferred tax assets if it is more likely than not that such assets will not be realized.

Long-Term Liabilities

The major components of long-term liabilities at March 3, 2007, and February 25, 2006, included long-term rent-related liabilities, deferred compensation plan liabilities, self-insurance reserves and advances received under vendor alliance programs.

Foreign Currency

Foreign currency denominated assets and liabilities are translated into U.S. dollars using the exchange rates in effect at our consolidated balance sheet date. Results of operations and cash flows are translated using the average exchange rates throughout the period. The effect of exchange rate fluctuations on translation of assets and liabilities is included as a component of shareholders' equity in accumulated other comprehensive income. Gains and losses from foreign currency transactions, which are included in SG&A, have not been significant.

Revenue Recognition

We recognize revenue when the sales price is fixed or determinable, collectibility is reasonably assured and the customer takes possession of the merchandise, or in the case of services, at the time the service is provided.

$ in millions, except per share amounts

Amounts billed to customers for shipping and handling are included in revenue. Revenue is reported net of estimated sales returns and excludes sales taxes.

We estimate our sales returns reserve based on historical return rates. We initially established our sales returns reserve in the fourth quarter of fiscal 2005. Our sales returns reserve was $104 and $78, at March 3, 2007, and February 25, 2006, respectively.

We sell extended service contracts on behalf of an unrelated third party. In jurisdictions where we are not deemed to be the obligor on the contract, commissions are recognized in revenue at the time of sale. In jurisdictions where we are deemed to be the obligor on the contract, commissions are recognized in revenue ratably over the term of the service contract. Commissions represented 2.2%, 2.5% and 2.6% of revenues in fiscal 2007, 2006 and 2005, respectively.

For revenue transactions that involve multiple deliverables, we defer the revenue associated with any undelivered elements. The amount of revenue deferred in connection with the undelivered elements is determined using the relative fair value of each element, which is generally based on each element's relative retail price. See additional information regarding our customer loyalty program in *Sales Incentives* below.

Gift Cards

We sell gift cards to our customers in our retail stores, through our Web sites, and through selected third parties. We do not charge administrative fees on unused gift cards and our gift cards do not have an expiration date. We recognize income from gift cards when: (i) the gift card is redeemed by the customer; or (ii) the likelihood of the gift card being redeemed by the customer is remote ("gift card breakage") and we determine that we do not have a legal obligation to remit the value of unredeemed gift cards to the relevant jurisdictions. We determine our gift card breakage rate based upon historical redemption patterns. Based on our historical information, the

likelihood of a gift card remaining unredeemed can be determined 24 months after the gift card is issued. At that time, we recognize breakage income for those cards for which the likelihood of redemption is deemed remote and we do not have a legal obligation to remit the value of such unredeemed gift cards to the relevant jurisdictions. Gift card breakage income is included in revenue in our consolidated statements of earnings.

We began recognizing gift card breakage income during the third quarter of fiscal 2006. Gift card breakage income was as follows in fiscal 2007, 2006 and 2005:

	2007[1]	2006[1]	2005
Gift card breakage income	$46	$43	$ —

[1] Due to the resolution of certain legal matters associated with gift card liabilities, we recognized $19 and $27 of gift card breakage income in fiscal 2007 and 2006, respectively, that related to prior fiscal years.

Sales Incentives

We frequently offer sales incentives that entitle our customers to receive a reduction in the price of a product or service. Sales incentives include discounts, coupons and other offers that entitle a customer to receive a reduction in the price of a product or service by submitting a claim for a refund or rebate. For sales incentives issued to a customer in conjunction with a sale of merchandise or services, for which we are the obligor, the reduction in revenue is recognized at the time of sale, based on the retail value of the incentive expected to be redeemed.

Customer Loyalty Program

We have a customer loyalty program which allows members to earn points for each qualifying purchase. Points earned enable members to receive a certificate that may be redeemed on future purchases at U.S. Best Buy stores.

$ in millions, except per share amounts

Cost of Goods Sold and Selling, General and Administrative Expenses

The following table illustrates the primary costs classified in each major expense category:

Cost of Goods Sold	SG&A
• Total cost of products sold including: —Freight expenses associated with moving merchandise inventories from our vendors to our distribution centers; —Vendor allowances that are not a reimbursement of specific, incremental and identifiable costs to promote a vendor's products; and —Cash discounts on payments to vendors; • Cost of services provided including: —Payroll and benefits costs for services employees; and —Cost of replacement parts and related freight expenses; • Physical inventory losses; • Markdowns; • Customer shipping and handling expenses; • Costs associated with operating our distribution network, including payroll and benefit costs, occupancy costs, and depreciation; • Freight expenses associated with moving merchandise inventories from our distribution centers to our retail stores; and • Promotional financing costs.	• Payroll and benefit costs for retail and corporate employees; • Occupancy costs of retail, services and corporate facilities; • Depreciation related to retail, services and corporate assets; • Advertising; • Vendor allowances that are a reimbursement of specific, incremental and identifiable costs to promote a vendor's products; • Charitable contributions; • Outside service fees; • Long-lived asset impairment charges; and • Other administrative costs, such as credit card service fees, supplies, and travel and lodging.

Advertising Costs

Advertising costs, which are included in SG&A, are expensed the first time the advertisement runs. Advertising costs consist primarily of print and television advertisements as well as promotional events. Net advertising expenses were $692, $644 and $597 in fiscal 2007, 2006 and 2005, respectively. Allowances received from vendors for advertising of $140, $123 and $115, in fiscal 2007, 2006 and 2005, respectively, were classified as reductions of advertising expenses.

$ in millions, except per share amounts

4. Investments

Short-Term and Long-Term Investments

The following table presents the amortized principal amounts, related weighted-average interest rates, maturities and major security types for our investments:

	March 3, 2007		Feb. 25, 2006	
	Amortized Principal Amount	Weighted-Average Interest Rate	Amortized Principal Amount	Weighted-Average Interest Rate
Short-term investments (less than one year)	$2,588	5.68%	$3,041	4.76%
Long-term investments (one to three years)	318	5.68%	218	4.95%
Total	$2,906		$3,259	
Municipal debt securities	$2,840		$3,155	
Auction-rate and asset-backed securities	66		97	
Debt securities issued by U.S. Treasury and other U.S. government entities	—		7	
Total	$2,906		$3,259	

The carrying value of our investments approximated fair value at March 3, 2007, and February 25, 2006, due to the rapid turnover of our portfolio and the highly liquid nature of these investments. Therefore, there were no significant realized or unrealized gains or losses.

Marketable Equity Securities

The carrying values of our investments in marketable equity securities at March 3, 2007, and February 25, 2006, were $4 and $28, respectively. Net unrealized (loss)/gain, net of tax, included in accumulated other comprehensive income was ($1) and $12 at March 3, 2007, and February 25, 2006, respectively.

$ in millions, except per share amounts

5.   Debt

Short-term debt consisted of the following:

	March 3, 2007	Feb. 25, 2006
Notes payable to banks, secured, interest rates ranging from 3.5% to 6.7%	$ 21	$ —
Revolving credit facility, secured, variable interest rate of 5.6% at March 3, 2007	20	—
Total short-term debt	$ 41	$ —
Weighted-average interest rate	5.3%	—

Long-term debt consisted of the following:

	March 3, 2007	Feb. 25, 2006
Convertible subordinated debentures, unsecured, due 2022, interest rate 2.25%	$402	$ 402
Financing lease obligations, due 2009 to 2023, interest rates ranging from 3.0% to 6.5%	171	157
Capital lease obligations, due 2008 to 2026, interest rates ranging from 1.8% to 8.0%	24	27
Other debt, due 2010, interest rate 8.8%	12	10
Total debt	609	596
Less: current portion[1]	(19)	(418)
Total long-term debt	$590	$ 178

[1] Since holders of our debentures due in 2022 could have required us to purchase all or a portion of their debentures on January 15, 2007, we classified our debentures in the current portion of long-term debt at February 25, 2006. However, no holders of our debentures exercised this put option on January 15, 2007. The next time the holders of our debentures could require us to purchase all or a portion of their debentures is January 15, 2012. Therefore, we classified our debentures as long-term debt at March 3, 2007.

Certain debt is secured by property and equipment with a net book value of $80 and $41 at March 3, 2007, and February 25, 2006, respectively.

Convertible Debentures

In January 2002, we sold convertible subordinated debentures having an aggregate principal amount of $402. The proceeds from the offering, net of $6 in offering expenses, were $396. The debentures mature in 2022 and are callable at par, at our option, for cash on or after January 15, 2007.

Holders may require us to purchase all or a portion of their debentures on January 15, 2012, and January 15, 2017, at a purchase price equal to 100% of the principal amount of the debentures plus accrued and unpaid interest up to but not including the date of purchase. We have the option to settle the purchase price in cash, stock, or a combination of cash and stock.

$ in millions, except per share amounts

Other

The fair value of debt approximated $683 and $693 at March 3, 2007, and February 25, 2006, respectively, based on the ask prices quoted from external sources, compared with carrying values of $650 and $596, respectively.

At March 3, 2007, the future maturities of long-term debt, including capitalized leases, consisted of the following:

Fiscal Year	
2008	$ 19
2009	18
2010	27
2011	18
2012	420
Thereafter	107
	$609

Earnings per Share

Our basic earnings per share calculation is computed based on the weighted-average number of common shares outstanding. Our diluted earnings per share calculation is computed based on the weighted-average number of common shares outstanding adjusted by the number of additional shares that would have been outstanding had the potentially dilutive common shares been issued. Potentially dilutive shares of common stock include stock options, nonvested share awards and shares issuable under our ESPP, as well as common shares that would have resulted from the assumed conversion of our convertible debentures. Since the potentially dilutive shares related to the convertible debentures are included in the calculation, the related interest expense, net of tax, is added back to earnings from continuing operations, as the interest would not have been paid if the convertible debentures had been converted to common stock. Nonvested market-based share awards and nonvested performance-based share awards are included in the average diluted shares outstanding each period if established market or performance criteria have been met at the end of the respective periods.

The following table presents a reconciliation of the numerators and denominators of basic and diluted earnings per share from continuing operations in fiscal 2007, 2006 and 2005:

	2007	2006	2005
Numerator:			
Earnings from continuing operations, basic	$1,377	$1,140	$ 934
Adjustment for assumed dilution:			
Interest on convertible debentures due in 2022, net of tax	7	7	7
Earnings from continuing operations, diluted	$1,384	$1,147	$ 941
Denominator (in millions):			
Weighted-average common shares outstanding	482.1	490.3	488.9
Effect of potentially dilutive securities:			
Shares from assumed conversion of convertible debentures	8.8	8.8	8.8
Stock options and other	5.3	5.7	7.3
Weighted-average common shares outstanding, assuming dilution	496.2	504.8	505.0
Basic earnings per share — continuing operations	$ 2.86	$ 2.33	$ 1.91
Diluted earnings per share — continuing operations	$ 2.79	$ 2.27	$ 1.86

A-16 Appendix A Financial Statement Information

$ in millions, except per share amounts

Comprehensive Income

Comprehensive income is computed as net earnings plus certain other items that are recorded directly to shareholders' equity. In addition to net earnings, the significant components of comprehensive income include foreign currency translation adjustments and unrealized gains and losses, net of tax, on available-for-sale marketable equity securities. Foreign currency translation adjustments do not include a provision for income tax expense when earnings from foreign operations are considered to be indefinitely reinvested outside the United States. Comprehensive income was $1,332, $1,252 and $1,047 in fiscal 2007, 2006 and 2005, respectively.

7. Net Interest Income

Net interest income was comprised of the following in fiscal 2007, 2006 and 2005:

	2007	2006	2005
Interest income	$142	$103	$ 45
Interest expense	(31)	(30)	(44)
Dividend income	—	4	—
Net interest income	$111	$ 77	$ 1

8. Leases

The composition of net rent expense for all operating leases, including leases of property and equipment, was as follows in fiscal 2007, 2006 and 2005:

	2007	2006	2005
Minimum rentals	$679	$569	$516
Contingent rentals	1	1	1
Total rent expense	680	570	517
Less: sublease income	(20)	(18)	(16)
Net rent expense	$660	$552	$501

$ in millions, except per share amounts

The future minimum lease payments under our capital, financing and operating leases by fiscal year (not including contingent rentals) at March 3, 2007, were as follows:

Fiscal Year	Capital Leases	Financing Leases	Operating Leases
2008	$ 6	$ 23	$ 741
2009	4	23	715
2010	4	23	672
2011	3	23	632
2012	1	23	592
Thereafter	17	112	3,316
Subtotal	35	227	$6,668
Less: imputed interest	(11)	(56)	
Present value of lease obligations	$24	$171	

Total minimum lease payments have not been reduced by minimum sublease rent income of approximately $119 due under future noncancelable subleases.

10. Income Taxes

The following is a reconciliation of the federal statutory income tax rate to income tax expense from continuing operations in fiscal 2007, 2006 and 2005:

	2007	2006	2005
Federal income tax at the statutory rate	$ 747	$ 603	$ 505
State income taxes, net of federal benefit	38	34	29
Benefit from foreign operations	(36)	(37)	(7)
Non-taxable interest income	(34)	(28)	(22)
Other	37	9	4
Income tax expense	$ 752	$ 581	$ 509
Effective income tax rate	35.3%	33.7%	35.3%

Income tax expense was comprised of the following in fiscal 2007, 2006 and 2005:

	2007	2006	2005
Current:			
Federal	$609	$640	$502
State	45	78	36
Foreign	16	14	(1)
	670	732	537
Deferred:			
Federal	51	(131)	(4)
State	19	(14)	(20)
Foreign	12	(6)	(4)
	82	(151)	(28)
Income tax expense	$752	$581	$509

Deferred taxes are the result of differences between the bases of assets and liabilities for financial reporting and income tax purposes.

$ in millions, except per share amounts

11. Segment and Geographic Information

Segment Information

We operate two reportable segments: Domestic and International. The Domestic segment is comprised of U.S. store and online operations, including Best Buy, Geek Squad, Magnolia Audio Video and Pacific Sales. The International segment is comprised of all Canada store and online operations, including Best Buy, Future Shop and Geek Squad, as well as our Five Star and Best Buy retail and online operations in China.

The following tables present our business segment information for continuing operations in fiscal 2007, 2006 and 2005:

	2007	2006	2005
Revenue			
Domestic	$31,031	$27,380	$24,616
International	4,903	3,468	2,817
Total revenue	$35,934	$30,848	$27,433
Operating Income			
Domestic	$ 1,889	$ 1,588	$ 1,393
International	110	56	49
Total operating income	1,999	1,644	1,442
Net interest income	111	77	1
Gain on investments	20	—	—
Earnings from continuing operations before income tax expense	$ 2,130	$ 1,721	$ 1,443
Assets			
Domestic	$10,614	$ 9,722	$ 8,372
International	2,956	2,142	1,922
Total assets	$13,570	$11,864	$10,294

12. Contingencies and Commitments

Contingencies

On December 8, 2005, a purported class action lawsuit captioned, *Jasmen Holloway, et cl. v. Best Buy Co., Inc.,* was filed in the U.S. District Court for the Northern District of California alleging we discriminate against women and minority individuals on the basis of gender, race, color and/or national origin with respect to our employment policies and practices. The action seeks an end to discriminatory policies and practices, an award of back and front pay, punitive damages and injunctive relief, including rightful place relief for all class members. As of March 3, 2007, no accrual had been established as it was not possible to estimate the possible loss or range of loss because this matter had not advanced to a stage where we could make any such estimate. We believe the allegations are without merit and intend to defend this action vigorously.

We are involved in various other legal proceedings arising in the normal course of conducting business. We believe the amounts provided in our consolidated financial statements, as prescribed by GAAP, are adequate in light of the probable and estimable liabilities. The resolution of those other proceedings is not expected to have a material impact on our results of operations or financial condition.

Commitments

We engage Accenture LLP ("Accenture") to assist us with improving our operational capabilities and reducing our costs in the information systems, procurement and human resources areas. Our future contractual obligations to Accenture are expected to range from $76 to $334 per year through 2012, the end of the contract period. Prior to our engagement of Accenture, a significant portion of these costs were incurred as part of normal operations.

We had outstanding letters of credit for purchase obligations with a fair value of $85 at March 3, 2007.

At March 3, 2007, we had commitments for the purchase and construction of facilities valued at approximately $69. Also, at March 3, 2007, we had entered into lease commitments for land and buildings for 115 future locations. These lease commitments with real estate developers provide for minimum rentals ranging from seven to 20 years, which if consummated based on current cost estimates, will approximate $84 annually over the initial lease terms. These minimum rentals have been included in the future minimum lease payments included in Note 8, Leases.

Financial Reports

CIRCUIT CITY STORES, INC.

Circuit City Stores, Inc.
CONSOLIDATED BALANCE SHEETS

(Amounts in thousands except share data)	At February 28 2007	2006
ASSETS		
CURRENT ASSETS:		
Cash and cash equivalents	$ 141,141	$ 315,970
Short-term investments	598,341	521,992
Accounts receivable, net of allowance for doubtful accounts	382,555	220,869
Merchandise inventory	1,636,507	1,698,026
Deferred income taxes	34,868	29,598
Income tax receivable	42,722	5,571
Prepaid expenses and other current assets	47,378	41,315
TOTAL CURRENT ASSETS	2,883,512	2,833,341
Property and equipment, net of accumulated depreciation	921,027	839,356
Deferred income taxes	31,910	97,889
Goodwill	121,774	223,999
Other intangible assets, net of accumulated amortization	19,285	30,372
Other assets	29,775	44,087
TOTAL ASSETS	$4,007,283	$4,069,044
LIABILITIES AND STOCKHOLDERS' EQUITY		
CURRENT LIABILITIES:		
Merchandise payable	$ 922,205	$ 850,359
Expenses payable	281,709	202,300
Accrued expenses and other current liabilities	404,444	379,768
Accrued compensation	98,509	84,743
Accrued income taxes	–	75,909
Short-term debt	–	22,003
Current installments of long-term debt	7,162	7,248
TOTAL CURRENT LIABILITIES	1,714,029	1,622,330
Long-term debt, excluding current installments	50,487	51,985
Accrued straight-line rent and deferred rent credits	277,636	256,120
Accrued lease termination costs	76,326	79,091
Other liabilities	97,561	104,885
TOTAL LIABILITIES	2,216,039	2,114,411
Commitments and contingent liabilities		
STOCKHOLDERS' EQUITY:		
Common stock, $0.50 par value; 525,000,000 shares authorized; 170,689,406 shares issued and outstanding (174,789,390 in 2006)	85,345	87,395
Additional paid-in capital	344,144	458,211
Retained earnings	1,336,317	1,364,740
Accumulated other comprehensive income	25,438	44,287
TOTAL STOCKHOLDERS' EQUITY	1,791,244	1,954,633
TOTAL LIABILITIES AND STOCKHOLDERS' EQUITY	$4,007,283	$4,069,044

Circuit City Stores, Inc.
CONSOLIDATED STATEMENTS OF OPERATIONS

	Years Ended February 28					
(Amounts in thousands except per share data)	**2007**	**%**	2006	%	2005	%
NET SALES	**$12,429,754**	100.0	$11,514,151	100.0	$10,413,524	100.0
Cost of sales, buying and warehousing	**9,501,438**	76.4	8,703,683	75.6	7,861,364	75.5
GROSS PROFIT	**2,928,316**	23.6	2,810,468	24.4	2,552,160	24.5
Selling, general and administrative expenses	**2,841,619**	22.9	2,595,706	22.5	2,470,712	23.7
Impairment of goodwill	**92,000**	0.7	–	–	–	–
Finance income	–	–	–	–	5,564	0.1
OPERATING (LOSS) INCOME	**(5,303)**	–	214,762	1.9	87,012	0.8
Interest income	**27,150**	0.2	21,826	0.2	14,404	0.1
Interest expense	**1,519**	–	3,143	–	4,451	–
Earnings from continuing operations before income taxes	**20,328**	0.2	233,445	2.0	96,965	0.9
Income tax expense	**30,510**	0.2	85,996	0.7	36,396	0.3
NET (LOSS) EARNINGS FROM CONTINUING OPERATIONS	**(10,182)**	(0.1)	147,449	1.3	60,569	0.6
EARNINGS (LOSS) FROM DISCONTINUED OPERATIONS, NET OF TAX	**128**	–	(5,350)	–	1,089	–
CUMULATIVE EFFECT OF CHANGE IN ACCOUNTING PRINCIPLES, NET OF TAX	**1,773**	–	(2,353)	–	–	–
NET (LOSS) EARNINGS	**$ (8,281)**	(0.1)	$ 139,746	1.2	$ 61,658	0.6

Weighted average common shares:

Basic	**170,448**		177,456		193,466
Diluted	**170,448**		180,653		196,227

(LOSS) EARNINGS PER SHARE:

Basic:

Continuing operations	$	**(0.06)**	$ 0.83	$ 0.31
Discontinued operations	$	**–**	$ (0.03)	$ 0.01
Cumulative effect of change in accounting principles	$	**0.01**	$ (0.01)	$ –
Basic (loss) earnings per share	$	**(0.05)**	$ 0.79	$ 0.32

Diluted:

Continuing operations	$	**(0.06)**	$ 0.82	$ 0.31
Discontinued operations	$	**–**	$ (0.03)	$ 0.01
Cumulative effect of change in accounting principles	$	**0.01**	$ (0.01)	$ –
Diluted (loss) earnings per share	$	**(0.05)**	$ 0.77	$ 0.31

CIRCUIT CITY

CIRCUIT CITY

Circuit City Stores, Inc.

CONSOLIDATED STATEMENTS OF STOCKHOLDERS' EQUITY AND COMPREHENSIVE INCOME

(Amounts in thousands except per share data)	Common Stock Shares	Common Stock Amount	Additional Paid-in Capital	Retained Earnings	Accumulated Other Comprehensive Income	Total
BALANCE AT FEBRUARY 29, 2004	203,899	$101,950	$922,600	$1,191,904	$ –	$2,216,454
Comprehensive income:						
Net earnings	–	–	–	61,658	–	61,658
Other comprehensive income, net of taxes:						
Foreign currency translation adjustment						
(net of deferred taxes of $13,707)	–	–	–	–	25,100	25,100
Comprehensive income						86,758
Repurchases of common stock	(19,163)	(9,582)	(250,250)	–	–	(259,832)
Compensation for stock awards	–	–	18,305	–	–	18,305
Exercise of common stock options	3,489	1,745	26,761	–	–	28,506
Shares issued under stock-based incentive plans,						
net of cancellations, and other	(75)	(38)	(1,312)	–	–	(1,350)
Tax effect from stock issued	–	–	(1,564)	–	–	(1,564)
Shares issued in acquisition of InterTAN, Inc.	–	–	6,498	–	–	6,498
Dividends – common stock ($0.07 per share)	–	–	–	(13,848)	–	(13,848)
BALANCE AT FEBRUARY 28, 2005	188,150	94,075	721,038	1,239,714	25,100	2,079,927
Comprehensive income:						
Net earnings	–	–	–	139,746	–	139,746
Other comprehensive income (loss), net of taxes:						
Foreign currency translation adjustment						
(net of deferred taxes of $11,316)	–	–	–	–	19,500	19,500
Minimum pension liability adjustment						
(net of deferred taxes of $182)	–	–	–	–	(313)	(313)
Comprehensive income						158,933
Repurchases of common stock	(19,396)	(9,698)	(328,778)	–	–	(338,476)
Compensation for stock awards	–	–	24,386	–	–	24,386
Exercise of common stock options	3,830	1,915	36,752	–	–	38,667
Shares issued under stock-based incentive plans,						
net of cancellations, and other	2,205	1,103	(2,160)	–	–	(1,057)
Tax effect from stock issued	–	–	6,973	–	–	6,973
Redemption of preferred share purchase rights	–	–	–	(1,876)	–	(1,876)
Dividends – common stock ($0.07 per share)	–	–	–	(12,844)	–	(12,844)
BALANCE AT FEBRUARY 28, 2006	174,789	87,395	458,211	1,364,740	44,287	1,954,633
Comprehensive loss:						
Net loss	–	–	–	(8,281)	–	(8,281)
Other comprehensive (loss) income, net of taxes:						
Foreign currency translation adjustment						
(net of deferred taxes of $3,630)	–	–	–	–	(7,793)	(7,793)
Unrealized gain on available-for-sale						
securities (net of deferred taxes of $219)	–	–	–	–	377	377
Minimum pension liability adjustment						
(net of deferred taxes of $136)	–	–	–	–	(229)	(229)
Comprehensive loss						(15,926)
Adjustment to initially apply SFAS No. 158 (net of						
deferred taxes of $6,628)	–	–	–	–	(11,204)	(11,204)
Repurchases of common stock	(10,032)	(5,016)	(232,187)	–	–	(237,203)
Compensation for stock awards	–	–	26,727	–	–	26,727
Adjustment to initially apply SFAS No. 123(R)	–	–	(2,370)	–	–	(2,370)
Exercise of common stock options, net	5,767	2,883	86,228	–	–	89,111
Shares issued under stock-based incentive plans,						
net of cancellations, and other	165	83	(1,027)	–	–	(944)
Tax effect from stock issued	–	–	8,562	–	–	8,562
Dividends – common stock ($0.115 per share)	–	–	–	(20,142)	–	(20,142)
BALANCE AT FEBRUARY 28, 2007	170,689	$85,345	$344,144	$1,336,317	$25,438	$1,791,244

Circuit City Stores, Inc.
CONSOLIDATED STATEMENTS OF CASH FLOWS

(Amounts in thousands)	Years Ended February 28		
	2007	2006	2005[a]
OPERATING ACTIVITIES:			
Net (loss) earnings	$ (8,281)	$ 139,746	$ 61,658
Adjustments to reconcile net (loss) earnings to net cash provided by operating activities of continuing operations:			
Net (earnings) loss from discontinued operations	(128)	5,350	(1,089)
Depreciation expense	177,828	160,608	151,597
Amortization expense	3,645	2,618	1,851
Impairment of goodwill	92,000	–	–
Stock-based compensation expense	26,727	24,386	18,305
(Gain) loss on dispositions of property and equipment	(1,439)	2,370	(206)
Provision for deferred income taxes	72,717	(14,252)	(116,300)
Cumulative effect of change in accounting principles	(1,773)	2,353	–
Other	1,689	(1,726)	–
Changes in operating assets and liabilities:			
Accounts receivable, net	(133,152)	16,552	(58,738)
Retained interests in securitized receivables	–	–	32,867
Merchandise inventory	49,352	(231,114)	160,037
Prepaid expenses and other current assets	(9,580)	(17,341)	7,207
Other assets	535	(3,061)	3,816
Merchandise payable	73,317	211,362	28,199
Expenses payable	55,722	40,921	(17,372)
Accrued expenses and other current liabilities, and accrued income taxes	(81,364)	43,202	54,021
Other long-term liabilities	(1,474)	(17,032)	63,494
NET CASH PROVIDED BY OPERATING ACTIVITIES OF CONTINUING OPERATIONS	316,341	364,942	389,347
INVESTING ACTIVITIES:			
Purchases of property and equipment	(285,725)	(254,451)	(261,461)
Proceeds from sales of property and equipment	38,620	55,421	106,369
Purchases of investment securities	(2,002,123)	(1,409,760)	(125,325)
Sales and maturities of investment securities	1,926,086	1,014,910	–
Other investing activities	(11,567)	–	–
Proceeds from the sale of the private-label finance operation	–	–	475,857
Acquisitions, net of cash acquired of $30,615	–	–	(262,320)
NET CASH USED IN INVESTING ACTIVITIES OF CONTINUING OPERATIONS	(334,709)	(593,880)	(66,880)
FINANCING ACTIVITIES:			
Proceeds from short-term borrowings	35,657	73,954	12,329
Principal payments on short-term borrowings	(56,912)	(53,893)	(13,458)
Proceeds from long-term debt	1,216	1,032	–
Principal payments on long-term debt	(6,724)	(1,829)	(28,008)
Changes in overdraft balances	19,347	(22,540)	36,329
Repurchases of common stock	(237,203)	(338,476)	(259,832)
Issuances of common stock	89,662	38,038	27,156
Dividends paid	(20,126)	(12,844)	(13,848)
Excess tax benefit from stock-based payments	15,729	–	–
Redemption of preferred share purchase rights	–	(1,876)	–
Other financing activities	(1,424)	–	–
NET CASH USED IN FINANCING ACTIVITIES OF CONTINUING OPERATIONS	(160,778)	(318,434)	(239,332)
DISCONTINUED OPERATIONS:			
Operating cash flows	3,310	(9,884)	(7,193)
Investing cash flows	2,958	(8,089)	(6,615)
Financing cash flows	(592)	–	(724)
NET CASH PROVIDED BY (USED IN) DISCONTINUED OPERATIONS	5,676	(17,973)	(14,532)
EFFECT OF EXCHANGE RATE CHANGES ON CASH	(1,359)	1,655	2,016
(Decrease) increase in cash and cash equivalents	(174,829)	(563,690)	70,619
Cash and cash equivalents at beginning of year	315,970	879,660	809,041
CASH AND CASH EQUIVALENTS AT END OF YEAR	$ 141,141	$ 315,970	$879,660

RADIOSHACK

Alabama Albertville, Alexander City, Andalusia, Arab, Ardmore, Athens, Atmore, Attalla, Bay Minette, Bayou La Batre, Bessemer, Birmingham, Butler, Calera, Camden, Center Point, Centre, Childersburg, Clanton, Cullm
Daphne, Decatur, Demopolis, Dothan, Enterprise, Fairfield, Fairhope, Florence, Foley, Fort Payne, Gadsden, Gardendale, Gulf Shores, Guntersville, Haleyville, Hamilton, Hartselle, Hoover, Huntsville, Jackson, Jasper, Lee
Linden, Luverne, Madison, Marion, Mobile, Montgomery, Moulton, Northport, Opelika, Opp, Oxford, Pelham, Pell City, Phenix City, Piedmont, Prattville, Robertsdale, Rogersville, Russellville, Saraland, Scottsboro, Sel
Sumiton, Sylacauga, Tallassee, Thomasville, Troy, Tuscaloosa *Alaska* Anchorage, Bethel, Cordova, Craig, Eagle River, Fairbanks, Glennallen, Haines, Homer, Juneau, Kenai, Ketchikan, Kodiak, Petersburg, Seward, Si
Skagway, Soldotna, Valdez, Wasilla *Arizona* Ajo, Apache Junction, Avondale, Benson, Bullhead City, Camp Verde, Casa Grande, Chandler, Chino Valley, Colorado City, Coolidge, Cottonwood, Douglas, Flagstaff, Floren
Fort Mohave, Fountain Hills, Gilbert, Glendale, Greenvalley, Heber, Holbrook, Kayenta, Kingman, Lake Havasu, Lakeside, Maricopa, Mesa, Miami, Morenci, New River, Nogales, Oro Valley, Parker, Payson, Peoria, Phoe
Prescott, Prescott Valley, Quartzsite, Safford, San Manuel, Scottsdale, Sedona, Show Low, Sierra Vista, Springerville, St. Johns, Sun City, Surprise, Taylor, Tempe, Thatcher, Tuba City, Tucson, Wickenburg, Willcox, Yu
Arkansas Arkadelphia, Ash Flat, Batesville, Beebe, Benton, Bentonville, Berryville, Brinkley, Bryant, Cabot, Camden, Cave City, Clarksville, Clinton, Conway, Danville, De Queen, De Witt, Dumas, El Dorado, Fayetteville, Flip
Forrest City, Fort Smith, Glenwood, Harrison, Heber Springs, Hope, Hot Springs, Jacksonville, Jasper, Jonesboro, Little Rock, Magnolia, Malvern, Mammoth Springs, Marshall, Melbourne, Mena, Mountain Home, Moun
View, North Little Rock, Nashville, Newport, Paragould, Paris, Pine Bluff, Prescott, Rogers, Russellville, Salem, Searcy, Sheridan, Siloam Springs, Springdale, Star City, Stuttgart, Van Buren, West Helena, West Memp
Wynne *California* Agoura, Alameda, Albany, Alhambra, Alta Loma, Alturas, American Canyon, Anaheim, Anaheim Hills, Anderson, Angels Camp, Antioch, Apple Valley, Arcadia, Arcata, Arnold, Arroyo Grande, Atascade
Atwater, Auburn, Avalon, Azusa, Bakersfield, Baldwin Park, Barstow, Beaumont, Bell, Belmont, Benicia, Berkeley, Beverly Hills, Big Bear Lake, Bishop, Blue Jay, Blythe, Brawley, Brea, Buellton, Buena Park, Burba
Burlingame, Calexico, California City, Camarillo, Canoga Park, Canyon Country, Capitola, Carlsbad, Carmichael, Carpinteria, Carson, Castro Valley, Cathedral City, Cerritos, Chatsworth, Chico, Chino, Chino Hills, Chula Vi
Citrus Heights, City of Industry, Clearlake, Cloverdale, Clovis, Coachella, Coalinga, Colton, Colusa, Compton, Concord, Corcoran, Corning, Corona, Corte Madera, Costa Mesa, Covina, Crescent City, Crestline, Culver C
Cupertino, Cypress, Daly City, Dana Point, Danville, Davis, Del Mar, Delano, Desert Hot Springs, Diamond Bar, Dinuba, Downey, Duarte, Dublin, E Los Angeles, El Cajon, El Centro, El Cerrito, El Monte, Elk Grove, Emeryv
Encinitas, Encino, Escondido, Eureka, Fairfield, Fall River Mills, Fallbrook, Folsom, Fontana, Foothill Ranch, Fortuna, Foster City, Fountain Valley, Freedom, Fremont, Fresno, Fort Bragg, Fullerton, Garberville, Garden Gro
Gardena, Gilroy, Glendale, Glendora, Goleta, Gonzales, Granada Hills, Grass Valley, Greenfield, Grover Beach, Hanford, Harbor City, Hawthorne, Hayward, Hemet, Hercules, Hesperia, Highland, Hollister, Hollywo
Huntington Beach, Huntington Park, Indio, Inglewood, Irvine, Jackson, King City, La Habra, La Jolla, La Mesa, La Mirada, La Puente, La Quinta, La Verne, Lafayette, Laguna Hills, Laguna Niguel, Lake Elsinore, Lake Isabe
Lakeport, Lakewood, Lancaster, Lawndale, Lemoore, Lincoln Heights, Livermore, Lodi, Lompoc, Long Beach, Los Alamitos, Los Angeles, Los Banos, Los Gatos, Los Osos, Lynwood, Madera, Malibu, Mammoth Lak
Manhattan Beach, Manteca, Marina Del Rey, Martinez, Marysville, Maywood, Merced, Milpitas, Mission Hills, Modesto, Mojave, Monrovia, Montclair, Montebello, Monterey, Monterey Park, Montrose, Moorpark, Mor
Valley, Morgan Hill, Morro Bay, Mountain View, Mount Shasta, Murrieta, Napa, National City, Newbury Park, Newhall, Newport Beach, North Highlands, North Hollywood, Northridge, Norwalk, Novato, Oakdale, Oakhu
Oakland, Oakley, Oceanside, Ojai, Ontario, Orange, Orangevale, Orland, Oroville, Oxnard, Pacifica, Palm Desert, Palm Springs, Palmdale, Palo Alto, Panorama City, Paradise, Paramount, Pasadena, Paso Robles, Patters
Perris, Petaluma, Phelan, Pico Rivera, Pinole, Pittsburg, Placentia, Placerville, Pleasant Hill, Pleasanton, Pollock Pines, Pomona, Porterville, Poway, Quincy, Ramona, Rancho Cordova, Rancho Cucamonga, Rancho Sa
Margarita, Red Bluff, Redding, Redlands, Redondo Beach, Redwood City, Reedley, Rialto, Ridgecrest, Rio Vista, Riverbank, Riverside, Rocklin, Rohnert Park, Rolling Hills, Rosamond, Rosemead, Roseville, Rowland Heigh
Sacramento, Salinas, San Bernardino, San Bruno, San Clemente, San Diego, San Dimas, San Francisco, San Jose, San Leandro, San Luis Obispo, San Marcos, San Mateo, San Pablo, San Pedro, San Rafael, San Ram
Sanger, Santa Ana, Santa Barbara, Santa Clara, Santa Cruz, Santa Maria, Santa Monica, Santa Paula, Santa Rosa, Santee, Saugus, Scotts Valley, Seal Beach, Seaside, Sebastopol, Selma, Sherman Oaks, Signal Hill, Si
San Juan Capistrano, Soledad, Sonoma, Sonora, South Gate, South Lake Tahoe, South Pasadena, South San Francisco, Spring Valley, Stockton, Studio City, Sun Valley, Sunnyvale, Susanville, Sylmar, Taft, Tehacha
Temecula, Temple City, Thousand Oaks, Torrance, Tracy, Truckee, Tujunga, Tulare, Turlock, Tustin, Twentynine Palms, Ukiah, Union City, Upland, Vacaville, Valencia, Vallejo, Valley Springs, Van Nuys, Venice, Ventu
Victorville, Visalia, Vista, Walnut Creek, Wasco, Watsonville, Weaverville, West Covina, West Hollywood, West Los Angeles, West Sacramento, Westchester, Westminster, Whittier, Willits, Willows, Wilmington, Winds
Woodland, Woodland Hills, Yorba Linda, Yreka, Yuba City, Yucaipa, Yucca Valley *Colorado* Alamosa, Arvada, Aspen, Aurora, Avon, Bayfield, Bennett, Boulder, Brighton, Broomfield, Buena Vista, Burlington, Canon City, Cas
Rock, Castle Rock, Centennial, Center, Colorado Springs, Conifer, Cortez, Craig, Crested Butte, Denver, Durango, Elizabeth, Englewood, Estes Park, Evergreen, Flagler, Fort Collins, Fountain, Fraser, Frisco, Glenwood Spri
Golden, Grand Junction, Greeley, Greenwood Village, Gunnison, Highlands Ranch, Holyoke, Idaho Springs, La Junta, Lafayette, Lakewood, Lamar, Limon, Littleton, Longmont, Loveland, Meeker, Monte Vista, Montro
Monument, Northglenn, Pagosa Springs, Paonia, Parachute, Parker, Pueblo, Rifle, Salida, Springfield, Steamboat Springs, Sterling, Thornton, Westminster, Woodland Park, Wray, Yuma *Connecticut* Avon, Barkhamst
Bloomfield, Branford, Bridgeport, Bristol, Canaan, Cheshire, Clinton, Cos Cob, Cromwell, Danbury, Derby, East Haven, Enfield, Fairfield, Farmington, Glastonbury, Groton, Guilford, Hamden, Hartford, Manchester, Merid
Middletown, Milford, Naugatuck, New Britain, New Canaan, New Haven, New London, New Milford, Newington, Newtown, North Haven, Norwalk, Norwich, Old Saybrook, Orange, Plainfield, Putnam, Ridgefield, Riversi
Southbury, Southington, Stamford, Torrington, Trumbull, Vernon, Wallingford, Waterbury, Waterford, Watertown, West Hartford, Westport, Wethersfield, Willimantic, Wilton, Windsor, *D.C.* Washington *Delaware* Be
Claymont, Dover, Georgetown, Middletown, Milford, New Castle, Newark, Rehoboth Beach, Seaford, Smyrna, Wilmington *Florida* Alachua, Altamonte, Altamonte Springs, Apopka, Arcadia, Atlantic Beach, Auburndale, Av
Park, Bartow, Bayonet Point, Belle Glade, Belleview, Big Pine Key, Boca Raton, Bonita Springs, Boynton Beach, Bradenton, Brandon, Branford, Brooksville, Callaway, Cape Coral, Casselberry, Century, Chiefland, Chip
Clearwater, Clermont, Clewiston, Cocoa, Cocoa Beach, Cooper City, Coral Gables, Coral Springs, Crawfordville, Crestview, Crystal River, Davie, Daytona Beach, Deerfield, Deerfield Beach, Defuniak Springs, Deland, Del
Beach, Deltona, Destin, Dunnellon, Englewood, Fernandina Beach, Florida City, Fort Lauderdale, Fort Myers, Fort Pierce, Fort Walton Beach, Gainesville, Greenacres, Gulf Breeze, Haines City, Hialeah, Hilliard, Holid
Hollywood, Homestead, Homosassa, Immokalee, Indiantown, Inverness, Jacksonville, Jensen Beach, Jupiter, Key Largo, Key West, Keystone Heights, Kissimmee, Lady Lake, Lake City, Lake Mary, Lake Placid, Lake Wal
Lake Worth, Lakeland, Lantana, Largo, Lauderdale Lakes, Lauderhill, Leesburg, Lehigh Acres, Live Oak, Longwood, Lutz, Macclenny, Madison, Marathon, Marco Island, Margate, Marianna, Mary Esther, Melbourne, Mer
Island, Miami, Miami Beach, Milton, Miramar, Monticello, Mount Dora, North Fort Myers, North Miami Beach, Naples, Navarre, New Port Richey, New Smyrna Beach, Niceville, Oakland Park, Ocala, Ocoee, Okeechob
Orange City, Orange Park, Orlando, Ormond Beach, Oviedo, Palatka, Palm Bay, Palm Beach Garden, Palm Coast, Palm Harbor, Panama City, Pembroke Pines, Pensacola, Perry, Plant City, Plantation, Pompano Beach, P
Charlotte, Port Orange, Port Richey, Port St. Joe, Port St. Lucie, Punta Gorda, Riverview, Royal Palm Beach, Ruskin, Sanford, Santa Rosa Beach, Sarasota, Satellite Beach, Sebastian, Sebring, Seffner, Seminole, So
Daytona, Spring Hill, St. Augustine, St. Cloud, St. Petersburg, Starke, Stuart, Sunrise, Tallahassee, Tampa, Tarpon Springs, Temple Terrace, Tequesta, Titusville, Venice, Vero Beach, Wauchula, Wellington, West Palm Bea
Weston, Wildwood, Wilton Manors, Winter Haven, Winter Park, Winter Springs, Zephyrhills *Georgia* Adel, Albany, Alpharetta, Americus, Athens, Atlanta, Augusta, Austell, Bainbridge, Barnesville, Baxley, Blairsville, Blake
Blue Ridge, Brunswick, Buford, Cairo, Calhoun, Canton, Carrollton, Cartersville, Cedartown, Centerville, Chamblee, Chatsworth, Clayton, Cleveland, Columbus, Commerce, Conyers, Cordele, Cornelia, Covington, Cummi
Cuthbert, Dahlonega, Dalton, Dawson, Dawsonville, Decatur, Donalsonville, Douglas, Douglasville, Dublin, Duluth, East Ellijay, Elberton, Fayetteville, Fitzgerald, Folkston, Forest Park, Forsyth, Fort Gaines, Fort Oglethor
Fort Valley, Gainesville, Griffin, Hampton, Hartwell, Hazlehurst, Hiawassee, Hinesville, Hiram, Homerville, Jackson, Jasper, Jesup, Kennesaw, Lafayette, Lagrange, Lawrenceville, Lilburn, Lincolnton, Lithonia, Mac
Madison, Marietta, Martinez, Mc Rae, McDonough, Metter, Milledgeville, Monroe, Monticello, Morrow, Moultrie, Nashville, Newnan, Norcross, Oakwood, Peachtree City, Perry, Quitman, Richmond Hill, Riverdale, Rockma
Rome, Roswell, Royston, Savannah, Smyrna, Snellville, St. Marys, St. Simons Island, Statesboro, Stockbridge, Stone Mountain, Summerville, Suwanee, Sylvania, Sylvester, Thomaston, Thomasville, Thomson, Tifton, Tocc
Trenton, Union City, Valdosta, Vidalia, Villa Rica, Warner Robins, Washington, Waycross, Winder, Woodbury, Woodstock *Hawaii* Aiea, Ewa Beach, Haleiwa, Hilo, Honolulu, Kahului, Kailua, Kailua-Kona, Kamuela, Kaneoh
Kapolei, Kihei, Lahaina, Lihue, Mililani, Wahiawa, Waianae, Waipahu *Idaho* American Falls, Blackfoot, Boise, Bonners Ferry, Buhl, Burley, Caldwell, Chubbuck, Coeur d'Alene, Cottonwood, Driggs, Emmett, Grangeville, Hail
Idaho Falls, Lewiston, McCall, Meridian, Montpelier, Moscow, Mountain Home, Nampa, Orofino, Pocatello, Post Falls, Rexburg, Rigby, Salmon, Sandpoint, Twin Falls, Wendell *Illinois* Aledo, Alton, Anna, Antioch, Arco
Arlington Heights, Arthur, Aurora, Bartlett, Batavia, Belleville, Belvidere, Bensenville, Benton, Berwyn, Bloomingdale, Bloomington, Blue Island, Bolingbrook, Bourbonnais, Burbank, Calumet City, Canton, Carbonda
Carlinville, Carmi, Centralia, Champaign, Channahon, Chester, Chicago, Chicago Heights, Cicero, Collinsville, Crystal Lake, Danville, Decatur, Des Plaines, Dixon, Dolton, Downers Grove, Du Quoin, Dwight, East Peoria, Ea
St Louis, Effingham, El Paso, Elgin, Elk Grove Village, Eureka, Evanston, Fairbury, Fairfield, Fairview Heights, Flora, Fox Lake, Frankfort, Freeport, Galesburg, Geneseo, Gibson City, Glen Carbon, Glen Ellyn, Glencoe, Glenvie
Granite City, Greenville, Gurnee, Harrisburg, Havana, Highland, Highland Park, Hoffman Estates, Homer Glen, Homewood, Hoopeston, Jacksonville, Jerseyville, Joliet, Kankakee, Kewanee, La Grange, Lake Zurich, Lansin
Lemont, Lincoln, Litchfield, Lake in the Hills, Lombard, Machesney Park, Macomb, Marengo, Marion, Markham, Mascoutah, Matteson, Mattoon, McHenry, Melrose Park, Mendota, Midlothian, Moline, Montgomery, Morr
Mount Vernon, Mundelein, Naperville, Nashville, Niles, Norridge, North Riverside, Oak Lawn, Oak Park, Olney, Ottawa, Palatine, Palos Heights, Paris, Pekin, Peoria, Peru, Petersburg, Pontiac, Princeton, Quincy, Robinso
Rochelle, Rockford, Round Lake Beach, Salem, Sandwich, Savanna, Savoy, Schaumburg, Seneca, Shiloh, Skokie, South Elgin, South Holland, Sparta, Springfield, St. Charles, Staunton, Sterling, Streator, Sullivan, Sycamo
Tinley Park, Tuscola, Urbana, Vernon Hills, Villa Park, Virden, Waterloo, Watseka, Waukegan, West Dundee, Wheaton, Wheeling, Willowbrook, Wilmington, Wood River, Yorkville, Zion *Indiana* Anderson, Angola, Arge
Auburn, Aurora, Avon, Batesville, Bedford, Berne, Bicknell, Bloomington, Bluffton, Brazil, Bremen, Brook, Brookville, Brownsburg, Brownstown, Cannelton, Carmel, Clarksville, Columbia City, Columbus, Corydon, Covingto
Crawfordsville, Crown Point, Decatur, Demotte, Elkhart, Elwood, Evansville, Fishers, Fort Wayne, Fowler, Frankfort, Franklin, Gary, Goshen, Greencastle, Greenfield, Greensburg, Greenwood, Griffith, Hammond, Hoba
Huntington, Indianapolis, Jasper, Kendallville, Knox, Kokomo, La Porte, Lafayette, Lagrange, Lebanon, Ligonier, Linton, Madison, Marion, Martinsville, Merrillville, Michigan City, Mishawaka, Monticello, Mooresville, Munc
Munster, Nappanee, New Albany, New Carlisle, New Castle, New Haven, Noblesville, North Manchester, North Vernon, Paoli, Peru, Petersburg, Plainfield, Plymouth, Portage, Portland, Princeton, Rensselaer, Richmon
Rising Sun, Rochester, Rockport, Rockville, Rushville, Schererville, Seymour, Shelbyville, South Bend, Syracuse, Terre Haute, Tipton, Valparaiso, Vincennes, W Lafayette, Wabash, Warsaw, Washington, Winamac, Winches
Iowa Adel, Altoona, Ames, Ankeny, Atlantic, Belle Plaine, Boone, Carroll, Cedar Falls, Cedar Rapids, Chariton, Charles City, Cherokee, Clarinda, Clinton, Coralville, Council Bluffs, Cresco, Creston, Davenport, Decora
Denison, Des Moines, Dubuque, Dyersville, Eagle Grove, Estherville, Fairfield, Fort Dodge, Fort Madison, Garner, Glenwood, Greenfield, Grinnell, Hampton, Harlan, Humboldt, Independence, Iowa City, Iowa Falls, Jefferso
Keokuk, Knoxville, Le Mars, Logan, Manchester, Maquoketa, Marengo, Marshalltown, Mason City, Mount Pleasant, Muscatine, New Hampton, Newton, Orange City, Osage, Osceola, Ottumwa, Pella, Perry, Pocahontas, R
Oak, Rock Valley, Sac City, Sheldon, Sioux Center, Sioux City, Spencer, Spirit Lake, Stuart, Vinton, Washington, Waterloo, Webster City, West Burlington, West Des Moines, West Union, Winterset *Kansas* Abilene, Anthor
Arkansas City, Atchison, Atwood, Bonner Springs, Burlington, Chanute, Clay Center, Colby, Columbus, Concordia, Derby, Dodge City, El Dorado, Ellsworth, Emporia, Fort Scott, Garden City, Garnett, Girard, Goodland, Gre
Bend, Hays, Hillsboro, Horton, Hutchinson, Independence, Iola, Junction City, Kansas City, Lawrence ... Lenexa, Liberal, Manhattan, McPherson, Mission, Newton, Oakley, Olathe, Osage City, Osawatom
Ottawa, Overland Park, Parsons, Pittsburg, Pratt, Salina, Scott City, Seneca, Shawnee Mission ... Wellington, Wichita, Winfield *Kentucky* Alexandria, Ashland, Barbourville, Bardstown, Bardwe
Beaver Dam, Berea, Bowling Green, Brandenburg, Cadiz, Campbellsville, Campton, Carrollt ... City, Columbia, ... Danville, Dry Ridge, Elizabethtown, Erlanger, Falmouth, Flemingsburg, Florence, Frankfo
Franklin, Georgetown, Glasgow, Grayson, Hazard, Henderson, Hopkinsville, Jackson, ... La Grange, Latonia, Leba... exington, London, Louisville, Madisonville, Mayfield, Maysville, Middlesboro, Monticell
Morehead, Morgantown, Mount Sterling, Mount Vernon, Murray, Newport, Nichol... Owensboro, Paducah, Paris, Pike... Pineville, Prestonsburg, Princeton, Radcliff, Richmond, Russell Springs, Russellvil
Salyersville, Scottsville, Shelbyville, Somerset, South Williamson, Stanton, Taylorsvil... arsaw, West Liberty, Whitley City, Williams... Winchester *Louisiana* Abbeville, Alexandria, Bastrop, Baton Rouge, Bogalusa, Bossi
City, Boutte, Crowley, Cut Off, Denham Springs, Deridder, Eunice, Franklinton, G... Hammond, Harahan, Harvey, Houma, Jea... Jena, Jennings, Kenner, Kentwood, La Place, Lafayette, Lake Charles, Leesvil
Mandeville, Mansfield, Many, Metairie, Minden, Monroe, Morgan City, Natchi... New Iberia, New Orleans, New Roads, Oakdal... elousas, Pineville, Plaquemine, Rayne, Ruston, Shreveport, Slidell, Springhill, S
Francisville, Sulphur, Thibodaux, Ville Platte, West Monroe, Westwego, Winfiel... innsboro, Zachary *Maine* Auburn, Augusta, Bangor, B... arbor, Belfast, Biddeford, Boothbay Harbor, Brunswick, Bucksport, Damariscott
Dover-Foxcroft, Ellsworth, Falmouth, Farmington, Fort Kent, Lewiston, Ma... Madawaska, Mexico, Millinocket, Oxford, Portland, ... Isle, Rockland, Sanford, Skowhegan, South Portland, Standish, Topshar
Waterville, Wells, Windham *Maryland* Aberdeen, Annapolis, Baltimore, Bel... Beltsville, Bethesda, Bowie, Burtonsville, Cambridge, Cator... le, Charlotte Hall, Chestertown, Clinton, Cockeysville, College Park, Columbi
Denton, Derwood, Dunkirk, Easton, Edgewood, Eldersburg, Elkton, Ellicott... rederick, Gaithersburg, Gan... ls, Germantown, Glen Burnie, Greenbelt, Hagerstown, Hampstead, Hanove
Hyattsville, Kensington, La Plata, La Vale, Largo, Laurel, Leonardtown, Lexi... on Park, M... ights, M... Mount Airy, Oakland, Ocea... y, Odenton, Olney, Owings Mills, Oxon Hill, Oxon Hill, Pasadena, Pocomol
City, Potomac, Prince Fredrick, Randallstown, Reisterstown, Rockville, S... bury, Seat... Severna... er Spring, Stevensville, ... oma Park, Towson, Waldorf, Westminster, Wheaton *Massachusetts* Acto
Andover, Ashland, Athol, Auburn, Bedford, Beverly, Billerica, Boston, Bra... ee, Bridge... ckton, Br... rlington, Cambridge, Che... sford, Chicopee, Danvers, Dedham, Dorchester, East Boston, East Walpol
East Wareham, Fairhaven, Fall River, Falmouth, Fitchburg, Foxboro, Fra... Gardner, ... r, Greenfi... Barrington, Hadley, Hano... Haverhill, Holyoke, Hyannis, Kingston, Lanesborough, Lenox, Leominste
Lowell, Lynn, Malden, Marlborough, Marshfield, Medford, Milford, Nan... ket, Natick, ... ford, New... Newton, North Adams, N... Attleboro, North Dartmouth, Northampton, Orleans, Peabody, Pittsfiel
Plymouth, Quincy, Raynham, Revere, Roslindale, Saugus, South Attle... o, South Bo... uth Denni... Easton, South Lawrence, ... th Yarmouth, Southbridge, Springfield, Stoneham, Stoughton, Sudbur
Swampscott, Swansea, Taunton, Vineyard Haven, Waltham, Watertow... Webster, We... field, We... gn, Westfield, Westford, Whi... sville, Wilmington, Woburn, Worcester *Michigan* Adrian, Albion, Allega
Alpena, Ann Arbor, Auburn Hills, Bad Axe, Battle Creek, Bay City, Bellaire... elleville, Ben... Big Rapids, Birmingham, Bloomfie... Boyne City, Brighton, Brooklyn, Brown City, Burton, Byron Center, Cadilla
Canton, Caro, Carson City, Cass City, Center Line, Charlevoix, Cheboyga... esaning, Cl... n Township, Clio, Coldwater, Co... erce, Davison, Dearborn, Dearborn Heights, Detroit, Dowagiac, Eastpoint
Eaton Rapids, Escanaba, Evart, Farmington Hills, Farmington, Fenton, F... Flint, F... t, Fran... Fremont, Gaylord, Grand Bla... Grand Haven, Grand Rapids, Grayling, Greenville, Grosse Pointe, Hasting
Hemlock, Highland Park, Holland, Houghton Lake, Howell, Imlay City, Ion... ron Mount... ood, Ish... Jackson, Jenison, Jonesville ... lamazoo, Kalkaska, Kentwood, Lake Orion, L'Anse, Lansing, Lapeer, Linco
Park, Livonia, Ludington, Madison Heights, Manistee, Manistique, Marin... ty, Marqu... hall, Mi... ord, Monroe, Mount Pleas... Munising, Muskegon, Newberry, Niles, Novi, Oak Park, Okemos, Oscod
Owosso, Petoskey, Pinconning, Plainwell, Pontiac, Port Huron, Portage, Re... d, Reed C... ond, Roc... s, Rogers City, Roseville, ... al Oak, Saginaw, Sandusky, Sault St. Marie, Shelby, South Haven, Southfiel
Southgate, St. Ignace, St. Johns, Standish, Stanton, Sturgis, Suttons Bay, ... as City, ... ee Oaks, ... rs, Traverse City, Troy, ... a, Vassar, Washington Township, Waterford, Wayne, Westland, White Clou
White Pigeon, Whitehall, Woodhaven, Wyoming, Ypsilanti *Minnesota* Ada, ... n, Alba... Lea, Alex... ple Valley, Austin, Bau... te, Baxter, Bemidji, Benson, Blaine, Bloomington, Brooklyn Center, Burnsvill
Cambridge, Chanhassen, Coon Rapids, Cottage Grove, Crystal, Detroit Lakes, ... uth, Du... gan, Eden ... na, Elk River, Erskine ... irmont, Faribault, Fergus Falls, Forest Lake, Golden Valley, Grand Marais, Gran
Rapids, Hibbing, Hilltop, Hutchinson, International Falls, Jackson, Lake City, L... ueur ... Little Fall... airie, Mankato, Ma... Grove, Marshall, Minneapolis, Minnetonka, Montevideo, Monticello, Moorhea
Moose Lake, Mora, Morris, New Ulm, North Branch, Ortonville, Owatonna, Pa... pids, Ph... eton, Red W... Redwood Falls, Richfield, Rochester, Roseau, Roseville, Saint Cloud, Saint Pau
Savage, Shakopee, Sleepy Eye, St. Cloud, St. James, St. Louis Park, St. Paul, S... ter, Stillwater, Thief River Falls, Vadnais Height... rginia, Walker, Warroad, Waseca, Wayzata, Willmar, Windom, Winona, Woodbur
Worthington, Young America *Mississippi* Amory, Batesville, Biloxi, Booneville, Bro... ven, Canton, Carthage, Clarksdale, Clevel... linton, Columbia, Columbus, Corinth, Crystal Springs, D'Iberville, Flora, Greenvill
Greenwood, Grenada, Gulfport, Hattiesburg, Houston, Jackson, Laurel, Lucedale, Mag... McComb, Mendenhall, Meridian, Monti... Morton, Natchez, New Albany, Ocean Springs, Olive Branch, Oxford, Pascagoula, Pear
Philadelphia, Picayune, Pontotoc, Poplarville, Prentiss, Purvis, Quitman, Ridgeland, Se... Southaven, Starkville, Tupel... rtown, Vicksburg, Waynesboro, West Point, Wiggins, Yazoo City *Missouri* Alton, Arnol

RadioShack.

RadioShack Corporation | **Financial Reports**

CONSOLIDATED BALANCE SHEETS
RadioShack Corporation and Subsidiaries

(In millions, except for share amounts)	December 31, 2006	December 31, 2005
Assets		
Current assets:		
Cash and cash equivalents	$ 472.0	$ 224.0
Accounts and notes receivable, net	247.9	309.4
Inventories	752.1	964.9
Other current assets	127.6	129.0
Total current assets	1,599.6	1,627.3
Property, plant and equipment, net	386.3	476.2
Other assets, net	84.1	101.6
Total assets	$ 2,070.0	$ 2,205.1
Liabilities and Stockholders' Equity		
Current liabilities:		
Short-term debt, including current maturities of long-term debt	$ 194.9	$ 40.9
Accounts payable	254.5	490.9
Accrued expenses and other current liabilities	442.2	379.5
Income taxes payable	92.6	75.0
Total current liabilities	984.2	986.3
Long-term debt, excluding current maturities	345.8	494.9
Other non-current liabilities	86.2	135.1
Total liabilities	1,416.2	1,616.3
Commitments and contingent liabilities		
Stockholders' equity:		
Preferred stock, no par value, 1,000,000 shares authorized:		
Series A junior participating, 300,000 shares designated and none issued	—	—
Common stock, $1 par value, 650,000,000 shares authorized; 191,033,000 shares issued	191.0	191.0
Additional paid-in capital	92.6	87.7
Retained earnings	1,780.9	1,741.4
Treasury stock, at cost; 55,196,000 and 56,071,000 shares, respectively	(1,409.1)	(1,431.6)
Accumulated other comprehensive (loss) income	(1.6)	0.3
Total stockholders' equity	653.8	588.8
Total liabilities and stockholders' equity	$ 2,070.0	$ 2,205.1

RADIOSHACK

CONSOLIDATED STATEMENTS OF INCOME
RadioShack Corporation and Subsidiaries

| | Year Ended December 31, | | | | | |
| | 2006 | | 2005 | | 2004 | |
(In millions, except per share amounts)	Dollars	% of Revenues	Dollars	% of Revenues	Dollars	% of Revenues
Net sales and operating revenues	$ 4,777.5	100.0%	$ 5,081.7	100.0%	$ 4,841.2	100.0%
Cost of products sold	2,544.4	53.3	2,706.3	53.3	2,406.7	49.7
Gross profit	2,233.1	46.7	2,375.4	46.7	2,434.5	50.3
Operating expenses:						
Selling, general and administrative	1,903.7	39.8	1,901.7	37.4	1,774.8	36.7
Depreciation and amortization	128.2	2.7	123.8	2.4	101.4	2.1
Impairment of long-lived assets and other charges	44.3	0.9	—	—	—	—
Total operating expenses	2,076.2	43.4	2,025.5	39.8	1,876.2	38.8
Operating income	156.9	3.3	349.9	6.9	558.3	11.5
Interest income	7.4	0.1	5.9	0.1	11.4	0.2
Interest expense	(44.3)	(0.9)	(44.5)	(0.8)	(29.6)	(0.5)
Other (loss) income	(8.6)	(0.2)	10.2	0.2	2.0	—
Income before income taxes	111.4	2.3	321.5	6.4	542.1	11.2
Income tax provision	38.0	0.8	51.6	1.0	204.9	4.2
Income before cumulative effect of change in accounting principle	73.4	1.5	269.9	5.4	337.2	7.0
Cumulative effect of change in accounting principle, net of $1.8 million tax benefit in 2005	—	—	(2.9)	(0.1)	—	—
Net income	$ 73.4	1.5%	$ 267.0	5.3%	$ 337.2	7.0%

Net income per share

Basic:

Income before cumulative effect of change in accounting principle	$ 0.54		$ 1.82		$ 2.09	
Cumulative effect of change in accounting principle, net of taxes	—		(0.02)		—	
Basic income per share	$ 0.54		$ 1.80		$ 2.09	

Assuming dilution:

Income before cumulative effect of change in accounting principle	$ 0.54		$ 1.81		$ 2.08	
Cumulative effect of change in accounting principle, net of taxes	—		(0.02)		—	
Diluted income per share	$ 0.54		$ 1.79		$ 2.08	

Shares used in computing income per share:

Basic	136.2		148.1		161.0	
Diluted	136.2		148.8		162.5	

RADIOSHACK

CONSOLIDATED STATEMENTS OF STOCKHOLDERS' EQUITY AND COMPREHENSIVE INCOME
RadioShack Corporation and Subsidiaries

(In millions)	Shares at December 31,			Dollars at December 31,		
	2006	2005	2004	2006	2005	2004
Common stock						
Beginning and end of year	191.0	191.0	191.0	$ 191.0	$ 191.0	$ 191.0
Treasury stock						
Beginning of year	(56.0)	(32.8)	(28.5)	$ (1,431.6)	$ (859.4)	$ (707.2)
Purchase of treasury stock	—	(25.3)	(8.0)	—	(625.8)	(246.9)
Issuance of common stock	0.6	1.2	1.3	18.6	31.8	33.8
Exercise of stock options and grant of stock awards	0.2	0.9	2.4	3.9	21.8	60.9
End of year	(55.2)	(56.0)	(32.8)	$ (1,409.1)	$ (1,431.6)	$ (859.4)
Additional paid-in capital						
Beginning of year				$ 87.7	$ 82.7	$ 75.2
Issuance of common stock				(5.7)	3.5	5.7
Exercise of stock options and grant of stock awards				(1.7)	(5.0)	(9.5)
Stock option compensation				12.0	—	—
Stock option income tax benefits				0.3	6.5	11.3
End of year				$ 92.6	$ 87.7	$ 82.7
Retained earnings						
Beginning of year				$ 1,741.4	$ 1,508.1	$ 1,210.6
Net income				73.4	267.0	337.2
Common stock cash dividends declared				(33.9)	(33.7)	(39.7)
End of year				$ 1,780.9	$ 1,741.4	$ 1,508.1
Accumulated other comprehensive (loss) income						
Beginning of year				$ 0.3	$ (0.3)	$ (0.3)
Pension adjustments, net of tax				(1.0)	—	—
Other comprehensive (loss) income				(0.9)	0.6	—
End of year				$ (1.6)	$ 0.3	$ (0.3)
Total stockholders' equity				$ 653.8	$ 588.8	$ 922.1
Comprehensive income						
Net income				$ 73.4	$ 267.0	$ 337.2
Other comprehensive income, net of tax:						
Foreign currency translation adjustments				0.3	(0.4)	0.1
Amortization of gain on cash flow hedge				(0.1)	(0.1)	(0.1)
Unrealized (loss) gain on securities				(1.1)	1.1	—
Other comprehensive (loss) income				(0.9)	0.6	—
Comprehensive income				$ 72.5	$ 267.6	$ 337.2

RADIOSHACK

CONSOLIDATED STATEMENTS OF CASH FLOWS
RadioShack Corporation and Subsidiaries

(In millions)	2006	2005	2004
Cash flows from operating activities:			
Net income	$ 73.4	$ 267.0	$ 337.2
Adjustments to reconcile net income to net cash provided by operating activities:			
Depreciation and amortization	128.2	123.8	101.4
Cumulative effect of change in accounting principle	—	4.7	—
Impairment of long-lived assets and other charges	44.3	—	—
Stock option compensation	12.0	—	—
Deferred income taxes and other items	(27.6)	(76.9)	50.2
Provision for credit losses and bad debts	0.4	0.1	(0.3)
Changes in operating assets and liabilities, excluding acquisitions:			
Accounts and notes receivable	61.8	(68.2)	(53.0)
Inventories	212.8	38.8	(234.2)
Other current assets	2.5	28.5	(7.5)
Accounts payable, accrued expenses, income taxes payable and other	(193.0)	45.1	158.7
Net cash provided by operating activities	314.8	362.9	352.5
Cash flows from investing activities:			
Additions to property, plant and equipment	(91.0)	(170.7)	(229.4)
Proceeds from sale of property, plant and equipment	11.1	226.0	2.5
Purchase of kiosk business	—	—	(59.1)
Other investing activities	0.6	(16.0)	(4.2)
Net cash (used in) provided by investing activities	(79.3)	39.3	(290.2)
Cash flows from financing activities:			
Purchases of treasury stock	—	(625.8)	(251.1)
Sale of treasury stock to employee benefit plans	10.5	30.1	35.4
Proceeds from exercise of stock options	1.7	17.4	50.4
Payments of dividends	(33.9)	(33.7)	(39.7)
Changes in short-term borrowings and outstanding checks in excess of cash balances, net	42.2	(4.0)	(14.0)
Reductions of long-term borrowings	(8.0)	(0.1)	(40.1)
Net cash provided by (used in) financing activities	12.5	(616.1)	(259.1)
Net increase (decrease) in cash and cash equivalents	248.0	(213.9)	(196.8)
Cash and cash equivalents, beginning of period	224.0	437.9	634.7
Cash and cash equivalents, end of period	$ 472.0	$ 224.0	$ 437.9
Supplemental cash flow information:			
Interest paid	$ 44.0	$ 43.4	$ 29.3
Income taxes paid	52.9	158.5	182.7

Apple Financial Report

CONSOLIDATED BALANCE SHEETS

(In millions, except share amounts)

	September 30, 2006	September 24, 2005
ASSETS		
Current assets:		
Cash and cash equivalents	$ 6,392	$ 3,491
Short-term investments	3,718	4,770
Accounts receivable, less allowances of $52 and $46, respectively	1,252	895
Inventories	270	165
Deferred tax assets	607	331
Other current assets	2,270	648
Total current assets	14,509	10,300
Property, plant, and equipment, net	1,281	817
Goodwill	38	69
Acquired intangible assets, net	139	27
Other assets	1,238	303
Total assets	$17,205	$11,516
LIABILITIES AND SHAREHOLDERS' EQUITY		
Current liabilities:		
Accounts payable	$ 3,390	$ 1,779
Accrued expenses	3,081	1,708
Total current liabilities	6,471	3,487
Noncurrent liabilities	750	601
Total liabilities	7,221	4,088
Commitments and contingencies		
Shareholders' equity:		
Common stock, no par value; 1,800,000,000 shares authorized; 855,262,568 and 835,019,364 shares issued and outstanding, respectively	4,355	3,564
Deferred stock compensation	—	(61)
Retained earnings	5,607	3,925
Accumulated other comprehensive income	22	—
Total shareholders' equity	9,984	7,428
Total liabilities and shareholders' equity	$17,205	$11,516

CONSOLIDATED STATEMENTS OF OPERATIONS

(In millions, except share and per share amounts)

Three fiscal years ended September 30, 2006	2006	2005	2004
Net sales.	$ 19,315	$ 13,931	$ 8,279
Cost of sales.	13,717	9,889	6,022
Gross margin.	5,598	4,042	2,257
Operating expenses:			
Research and development.	712	535	491
Selling, general, and administrative.	2,433	1,864	1,430
Restructuring costs	—	—	23
Total operating expenses	3,145	2,399	1,944
Operating income.	2,453	1,643	313
Other income and expense.	365	165	57
Income before provision for income taxes.	2,818	1,808	370
Provision for income taxes	829	480	104
Net income	$ 1,989	$ 1,328	$ 266
Earnings per common share:			
Basic.	$ 2.36	$ 1.64	$ 0.36
Diluted.	$ 2.27	$ 1.55	$ 0.34
Shares used in computing earnings per share (in thousands):			
Basic.	844,058	808,439	743,180
Diluted.	877,526	856,878	774,776

APPLE

CONSOLIDATED STATEMENTS OF SHAREHOLDERS' EQUITY
(In millions, except share amounts which are in thousands)

	Common Stock		Deferred Stock Compensation	Retained Earnings	Accumulated Other Comprehensive Income (Loss)	Total Shareholders' Equity
	Shares	Amount				
Balances as of September 27, 2003 as previously reported	733,454	$1,926	$ (62)	$2,394	$(35)	$4,223
Adjustments to opening shareholders' equity	—	85	(22)	(63)	—	—
Balance as of September 27, 2003 as restated	733,454	$2,011	$ (84)	$2,331	$(35)	$4,223
Components of comprehensive income:						
Net income	—	—	—	266	—	266
Change in foreign currency translation	—	—	—	—	13	13
Change in unrealized gain on available-for-sale securities, net of tax	—	—	—	—	(5)	(5)
Change in unrealized loss on derivative investments, net of tax	—	—	—	—	12	12
Total comprehensive income						286
Issuance of stock-based compensation awards	—	63	(63)	—	—	—
Adjustment to common stock related to a prior year acquisition	(159)	(2)	—	—	—	(2)
Stock-based compensation	—	—	46	—	—	46
Common stock issued under stock plans	49,592	427	—	—	—	427
Tax benefit related to stock options	—	83	—	—	—	83
Balances as of September 25, 2004	782,887	$2,582	$(101)	$2,597	$(15)	$5,063
Components of comprehensive income:						
Net income	—	—	—	1,328	—	1,328
Change in foreign currency translation	—	—	—	—	7	7
Change in unrealized gain on derivative investments, net of tax	—	—	—	—	8	8
Total comprehensive income						1,343
Issuance of stock-based compensation awards	—	7	(7)	—	—	—
Stock-based compensation	—	—	47	—	—	47
Common stock issued under stock plans	52,132	547	—	—	—	547
Tax benefit related to stock options	—	428	—	—	—	428
Balances as of September 24, 2005	835,019	$3,564	$ (61)	$3,925	$ —	$7,428
Components of comprehensive income:						
Net income	—	—	—	1,989	—	1,989
Change in foreign currency translation	—	—	—	—	19	19
Change in unrealized gain on available-for-sale securities, net of tax	—	—	—	—	4	4
Change in unrealized loss on derivative investments, net of tax	—	—	—	—	(1)	(1)
Total comprehensive income						2,011
Common stock repurchased	(4,574)	(48)	—	(307)	—	(355)
Stock-based compensation	—	163	—	—	—	163
Deferred compensation	—	(61)	61	—	—	—
Common stock issued under stock plans	24,818	318	—	—	—	318
Tax benefit related to stock-based compensation	—	419	—	—	—	419
Balances as of September 30, 2006	855,263	$4,355	$ —	$5,607	$ 22	$9,984

CONSOLIDATED STATEMENTS OF CASH FLOWS

(In millions)

Three fiscal years ended September 30, 2006	2006	2005	2004
Cash and cash equivalents, beginning of the year	$ 3,491	$ 2,969	$ 3,396
Operating Activities:			
Net income	1,989	1,328	266
Adjustments to reconcile net income to cash generated by operating activities:			
Depreciation, amortization and accretion	225	179	150
Stock-based compensation expense	163	49	46
Provision for deferred income taxes	53	50	19
Excess tax benefits from stock options	—	428	83
Gain on sale of PowerSchool net assets	(4)	—	—
Loss on disposition of property, plant, and equipment	15	9	7
Gains on sales of investments, net	—	—	(5)
Changes in operating assets and liabilities:			
Accounts receivable	(357)	(121)	(8)
Inventories	(105)	(64)	(45)
Other current assets	(1,626)	(150)	(176)
Other assets	(1,040)	(35)	(25)
Accounts payable	1,611	328	297
Other liabilities	1,296	534	325
Cash generated by operating activities	2,220	2,535	934
Investing Activities:			
Purchases of short-term investments	(7,255)	(11,470)	(3,270)
Proceeds from maturities of short-term investments	7,226	8,609	1,141
Proceeds from sales of investments	1,086	586	806
Purchases of long-term investments	(25)	—	—
Proceeds from sale of PowerSchool net assets	40	—	—
Purchases of property, plant, and equipment	(657)	(260)	(176)
Other	(58)	(21)	11
Cash generated by (used for) investing activities	357	(2,556)	(1,488)
Financing Activities:			
Payment of long-term debt	—	—	(300)
Proceeds from issuance of common stock	318	543	427
Excess tax benefits from stock-based compensation	361	—	—
Repurchases of common stock	(355)	—	—
Cash generated by financing activities	324	543	127
Increase (decrease) in cash and cash equivalents	2,901	522	(427)
Cash and cash equivalents, end of the year	$ 6,392	$ 3,491	$ 2,969
Supplemental cash flow disclosures:			
Cash paid during the year for interest	$ —	$ —	$ 10
Cash paid (received) for income taxes, net	$ 194	$ 17	$ (7)

APPLE

B Time Value of Money

Learning Objectives

CAP

Conceptual

C1 Describe the earning of interest and the concepts of present and future values. *(p. B-1)*

Procedural

P1 Apply present value concepts to a single amount by using interest tables. *(p. B-3)*

P2 Apply future value concepts to a single amount by using interest tables. *(p. B-4)*

P3 Apply present value concepts to an annuity by using interest tables. *(p. B-5)*

P4 Apply future value concepts to an annuity by using interest tables. *(p. B-6)*

The concepts of present and future values are important to modern business, including the preparation and analysis of financial statements. The purpose of this appendix is to explain, illustrate, and compute present and future values. This appendix applies these concepts with reference to both business and everyday activities.

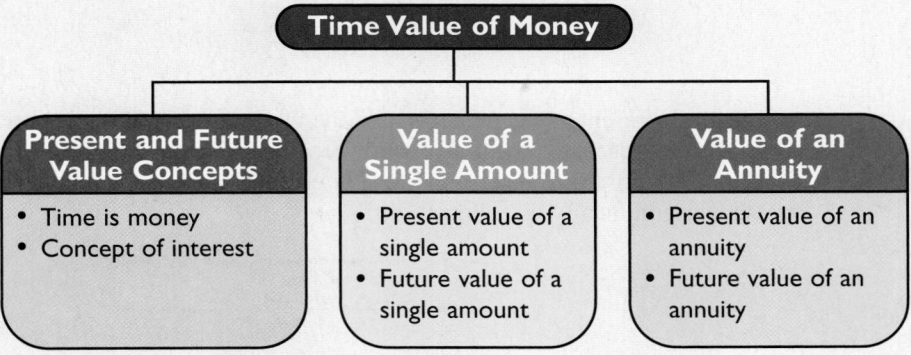

Time Value of Money

Present and Future Value Concepts	Value of a Single Amount	Value of an Annuity
• Time is money • Concept of interest	• Present value of a single amount • Future value of a single amount	• Present value of an annuity • Future value of an annuity

Present and Future Value Concepts

The old saying "Time is money" reflects the notion that as time passes, the values of our assets and liabilities change. This change is due to *interest*, which is a borrower's payment to the owner of an asset for its use. The most common example of interest is a savings account asset. As we keep a balance of cash in the account, it earns interest that the financial institution pays us. An example of a liability is a car loan. As we carry the balance of the loan, we accumulate interest costs on it. We must ultimately repay this loan with interest.

Present and future value computations enable us to measure or estimate the interest component of holding assets or liabilities over time. The present value computation is important when we want to know the value of future-day assets *today*. The future value computation is important when we want to know the value of present-day assets *at a future date*. The first section focuses on the present value of a single amount. The second section focuses on the future value of a single amount. Then both the present and future values of a series of amounts (called an *annuity*) are defined and explained.

C1 Describe the earning of interest and the concepts of present and future values.

Decision Insight

Keep That Job   Lottery winners often never work again. Kenny Dukes, a recent Georgia lottery winner, doesn't have that option. He is serving parole for burglary charges, and Georgia requires its parolees to be employed (or in school). For his lottery winnings, Dukes had to choose between $31 million in 30 annual payments or $16 million in one lump sum ($10.6 million after-tax); he chose the latter.

Present Value of a Single Amount

We graphically express the present value, called p, of a single future amount, called f, that is received or paid at a future date in Exhibit B.1.

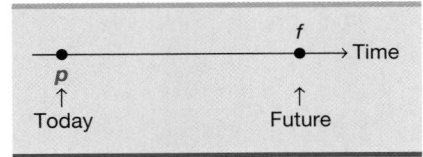

EXHIBIT B.1

Present Value of a Single Amount Diagram

The formula to compute the present value of a single amount is shown in Exhibit B.2, where p = present value; f = future value; i = rate of interest per period; and n = number of periods. (Interest is also called the *discount,* and an interest rate is also called the *discount rate.*)

EXHIBIT B.2

Present Value of a Single
Amount Formula

$$p = \frac{f}{(1 + i)^n}$$

To illustrate present value concepts, assume that we need $220 one period from today. We want to know how much we must invest now, for one period, at an interest rate of 10% to provide for this $220. For this illustration, the p, or present value, is the unknown amount—the specifics are shown graphically as follows:

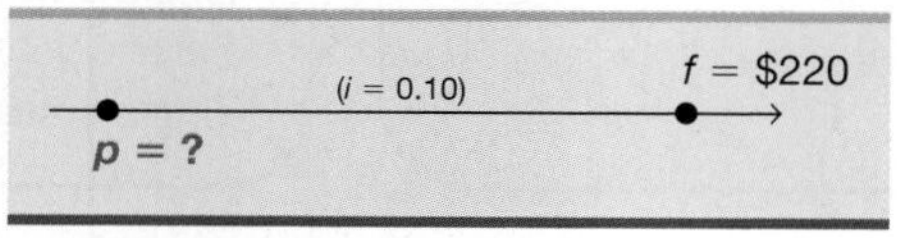

$(i = 0.10)$ $f = \$220$

$p = ?$

Conceptually, we know p must be less than $220. This is obvious from the answer to this question: Would we rather have $220 today or $220 at some future date? If we had $220 today, we could invest it and see it grow to something more than $220 in the future. Therefore, we would prefer the $220 today. This means that if we were promised $220 in the future, we would take less than $220 today. But how much less? To answer that question, we compute an estimate of the present value of the $220 to be received one period from now using the formula in Exhibit B.2 as follows:

$$p = \frac{f}{(1 + i)^n} = \frac{\$220}{(1 + 0.10)^1} = \$200$$

We interpret this result to say that given an interest rate of 10%, we are indifferent between $200 today or $220 at the end of one period.

We can also use this formula to compute the present value for *any number of periods.* To illustrate, consider a payment of $242 at the end of two periods at 10% interest. The present value of this $242 to be received two periods from now is computed as follows:

$$p = \frac{f}{(1 + i)^n} = \frac{\$242}{(1 + 0.10)^2} = \$200$$

Together, these results tell us we are indifferent between $200 today, or $220 one period from today, or $242 two periods from today given a 10% interest rate per period.

The number of periods (n) in the present value formula does not have to be expressed in years. Any period of time such as a day, a month, a quarter, or a year can be used. Whatever period is used, the interest rate (i) must be compounded for the same period. This means that if a situation expresses n in months and i equals 12% per year, then i is transformed into interest earned per month (or 1%). In this case, interest is said to be *compounded monthly.*

A present value table helps us with present value computations. It gives us present values (factors) for a variety of both interest rates (i) and periods (n). Each present value in a present value table assumes that the future value (f) equals 1. When the future value (f) is different from 1, we simply multiply the present value (p) from the table by that future value to give us the estimate. The formula used to construct a table of present values for a single future amount of 1 is shown in Exhibit B.3.

I will pay your allowance at the end of the month. Do you want to wait or receive its present value today?

EXHIBIT B.3

Present Value of 1 Formula

$$p = \frac{1}{(1 + i)^n}$$

This formula is identical to that in Exhibit B.2 except that f equals 1. Table B.1 at the end of this appendix is such a present value table. It is often called a **present value of 1 table**. A present value table involves three factors: p, i, and n. Knowing two of these three factors allows us to compute the third. (A fourth is f, but as already explained, we need only multiply the 1 used in the formula by f.) To illustrate the use of a present value table, consider three cases.

> **P1** Apply present value concepts to a single amount by using interest tables.

Case 1 (solve for p when knowing i and n). To show how we use a present value table, let's look again at how we estimate the present value of $220 (the f value) at the end of one period ($n = 1$) where the interest rate (i) is 10%. To solve this case, we go to the present value table (Table B.1) and look in the row for 1 period and in the column for 10% interest. Here we find a present value (p) of 0.9091 based on a future value of 1. This means, for instance, that $1 to be received one period from today at 10% interest is worth $0.9091 today. Since the future value in this case is not $1 but $220, we multiply the 0.9091 by $220 to get an answer of $200.

Case 2 (solve for n when knowing p and i). To illustrate, assume a $100,000 future value ($f$) that is worth $13,000 today ($p$) using an interest rate of 12% (i) but where n is unknown. In particular, we want to know how many periods (n) there are between the present value and the future value. To put this in context, it would fit a situation in which we want to retire with $100,000 but currently have only $13,000 that is earning a 12% return and we will be unable to save any additional money. How long will it be before we can retire? To answer this, we go to Table B.1 and look in the 12% interest column. Here we find a column of present values (p) based on a future value of 1. To use the present value table for this solution, we must divide $13,000 ($p$) by $100,000 ($f$), which equals 0.1300. This is necessary because *a present value table defines* f *equal to 1, and* p *as a fraction of 1*. We look for a value nearest to 0.1300 (p), which we find in the row for 18 periods (n). This means that the present value of $100,000 at the end of 18 periods at 12% interest is $13,000; alternatively stated, we must work 18 more years.

Case 3 (solve for i when knowing p and n). In this case, we have, say, a $120,000 future value ($f$) worth $60,000 today ($p$) when there are nine periods (n) between the present and future values, but the interest rate is unknown. As an example, suppose we want to retire with $120,000, but we have only $60,000 and we will be unable to save any additional money, yet we hope to retire in nine years. What interest rate must we earn to retire with $120,000 in nine years? To answer this, we go to the present value table (Table B.1) and look in the row for nine periods. To use the present value table, we must divide $60,000 ($p$) by $120,000 ($f$), which equals 0.5000. Recall that this step is necessary because a present value table defines f equal to 1 and p as a fraction of 1. We look for a value in the row for nine periods that is nearest to 0.5000 (p), which we find in the column for 8% interest (i). This means that the present value of $120,000 at the end of nine periods at 8% interest is $60,000 or, in our example, we must earn 8% annual interest to retire in nine years.

Quick Check   Answer—p. B-7

1. A company is considering an investment expected to yield $70,000 after six years. If this company demands an 8% return, how much is it willing to pay for this investment?

Future Value of a Single Amount

We must modify the formula for the present value of a single amount to obtain the formula for the future value of a single amount. In particular, we multiply both sides of the equation in Exhibit B.2 by $(1 + i)^n$ to get the result shown in Exhibit B.4.

$$f = p \times (1 + i)^n$$

EXHIBIT B.4

Future Value of a Single Amount Formula

The future value (f) is defined in terms of p, i, and n. We can use this formula to determine that $200 ($p$) invested for 1 ($n$) period at an interest rate of 10% (i) yields a future value of

$220 as follows:

$$f = p \times (1 + i)^n$$
$$= \$200 \times (1 + 0.10)^1$$
$$= \$220$$

P2	Apply future value concepts to a single amount by using interest tables.

This formula can also be used to compute the future value of an amount for *any number of periods* into the future. To illustrate, assume that $200 is invested for three periods at 10%. The future value of this $200 is $266.20, computed as follows:

$$f = p \times (1 + i)^n$$
$$= \$200 \times (1 + 0.10)^3$$
$$= \$266.20$$

A future value table makes it easier for us to compute future values (f) for many different combinations of interest rates (i) and time periods (n). Each future value in a future value table assumes the present value (p) is 1. As with a present value table, if the future amount is something other than 1, we simply multiply our answer by that amount. The formula used to construct a table of future values (factors) for a single amount of 1 is in Exhibit B.5.

EXHIBIT B.5

Future Value of 1 Formula

$$f = (1 + i)^n$$

Table B.2 at the end of this appendix shows a table of future values for a current amount of 1. This type of table is called a **future value of 1 table**.

There are some important relations between Tables B.1 and B.2. In Table B.2, for the row where $n = 0$, the future value is 1 for each interest rate. This is so because no interest is earned when time does not pass. We also see that Tables B.1 and B.2 report the same information but in a different manner. In particular, one table is simply the *inverse* of the other. To illustrate this inverse relation, let's say we invest $100 for a period of five years at 12% per year. How much do we expect to have after five years? We can answer this question using Table B.2 by finding the future value (f) of 1, for five periods from now, compounded at 12%. From that table we find $f = 1.7623$. If we start with $100, the amount it accumulates to after five years is $176.23 ($100 × 1.7623). We can alternatively use Table B.1. Here we find that the present value (p) of 1, discounted five periods at 12%, is 0.5674. Recall the inverse relation between present value and future value. This means that $p = 1/f$ (or equivalently, $f = 1/p$). We can compute the future value of $100 invested for five periods at 12% as follows: $f = \$100 \times (1/0.5674) = \$176.24$ (which equals the $176.23 just computed, except for a 1 cent rounding difference).

A future value table involves three factors: f, i, and n. Knowing two of these three factors allows us to compute the third. To illustrate, consider these three possible cases.

Case 1   (solve for f when knowing i and n). Our preceding example fits this case. We found that $100 invested for five periods at 12% interest accumulates to $176.24.

Case 2   (solve for n when knowing f and i). In this case, we have, say, $2,000 ($p$) and we want to know how many periods (n) it will take to accumulate to $3,000 ($f$) at 7% ($i$) interest. To answer this, we go to the future value table (Table B.2) and look in the 7% interest column. Here we find a column of future values (f) based on a present value of 1. To use a future value table, we must divide $3,000 ($f$) by $2,000 ($p$), which equals 1.500. This is necessary because *a future value table defines* p *equal to 1, and* f *as a multiple of 1.* We look for a value nearest to 1.50 (f), which we find in the row for six periods (n). This means that $2,000 invested for six periods at 7% interest accumulates to $3,000.

Case 3   (solve for i when knowing f and n). In this case, we have, say, $2,001 ($p$), and in nine years ($n$) we want to have $4,000 ($f$). What rate of interest must we earn to accomplish this? To answer that, we go to Table B.2 and search in the row for nine periods. To use a future value table, we must divide $4,000 ($f$) by $2,001 ($p$), which equals 1.9990. Recall that this is necessary because a future value table defines p equal to 1 and f as a multiple of 1. We look for a value nearest to 1.9990 (f), which we find in the column for 8% interest (i). This means that $2,001 invested for nine periods at 8% interest accumulates to $4,000.

Quick Check
Answer—p. B-7

2. Assume that you win a $150,000 cash sweepstakes. You decide to deposit this cash in an account earning 8% annual interest, and you plan to quit your job when the account equals $555,000. How many years will it be before you can quit working?

Present Value of an Annuity

An *annuity* is a series of equal payments occurring at equal intervals. One example is a series of three annual payments of $100 each. An *ordinary annuity* is defined as equal end-of-period payments at equal intervals. An ordinary annuity of $100 for three periods and its present value (p) are illustrated in Exhibit B.6.

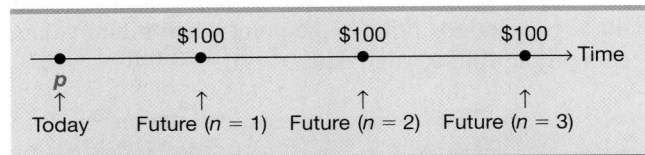

EXHIBIT B.6

Present Value of an Ordinary Annuity Diagram

One way to compute the present value of an ordinary annuity is to find the present value of each payment using our present value formula from Exhibit B.3. We then add each of the three present values. To illustrate, let's look at three $100 payments at the end of each of the next three periods with an interest rate of 15%. Our present value computations are

P3 Apply present value concepts to an annuity by using interest tables.

$$p = \frac{\$100}{(1 + 0.15)^1} + \frac{\$100}{(1 + 0.15)^2} + \frac{\$100}{(1 + 0.15)^3} = \$228.32$$

This computation is identical to computing the present value of each payment (from Table B.1) and taking their sum or, alternatively, adding the values from Table B.1 for each of the three payments and multiplying their sum by the $100 annuity payment.

A more direct way is to use a present value of annuity table. Table B.3 at the end of this appendix is one such table. This table is called a **present value of an annuity of 1 table**. If we look at Table B.3 where $n = 3$ and $i = 15\%$, we see the present value is 2.2832. This means that the present value of an annuity of 1 for three periods, with a 15% interest rate, equals 2.2832.

A present value of an annuity formula is used to construct Table B.3. It can also be constructed by adding the amounts in a present value of 1 table. To illustrate, we use Tables B.1 and B.3 to confirm this relation for the prior example:

From Table B.1		From Table B.3	
$i = 15\%, n = 1$	0.8696		
$i = 15\%, n = 2$	0.7561		
$i = 15\%, n = 3$	0.6575		
Total	2.2832	$i = 15\%, n = 3$	2.2832

We can also use business calculators or spreadsheet programs to find the present value of an annuity.

Decision Insight

Better Lucky Than Good "I don't have good luck—I'm blessed," proclaimed Andrew "Jack" Whittaker, 55, a sewage treatment contractor, after winning the largest ever undivided jackpot in a U.S. lottery. Whittaker had to choose between $315 million in 30 annual installments or $170 million in one lump sum ($112 million after-tax).

Answer—p. B-7

Quick Check

3. A company is considering an investment paying $10,000 every six months for three years. The first payment would be received in six months. If this company requires an 8% annual return, what is the maximum amount it is willing to pay for this investment?

Future Value of an Annuity

The future value of an *ordinary annuity* is the accumulated value of each annuity payment with interest as of the date of the final payment. To illustrate, let's consider the earlier annuity of three annual payments of $100. Exhibit B.7 shows the point in time for the future value (f). The first payment is made two periods prior to the point when future value is determined, and the final payment occurs on the future value date.

EXHIBIT B.7

Future Value of an Ordinary
Annuity Diagram

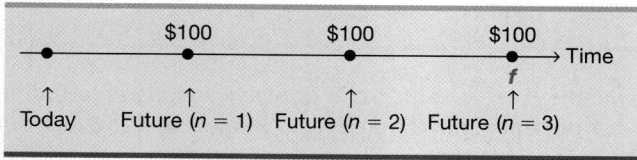

One way to compute the future value of an annuity is to use the formula to find the future value of *each* payment and add them. If we assume an interest rate of 15%, our calculation is

$$f = \$100 \times (1 + 0.15)^2 + \$100 \times (1 + 0.15)^1 + \$100 \times (1 + 0.15)^0 = \$347.25$$

This is identical to using Table B.2 and summing the future values of each payment, or adding the future values of the three payments of 1 and multiplying the sum by $100.

P4 Apply future value concepts to an annuity by using interest tables.

A more direct way is to use a table showing future values of annuities. Such a table is called a **future value of an annuity of 1 table**. Table B.4 at the end of this appendix is one such table. Note that in Table B.4 when $n = 1$, the future values equal 1 $(f = 1)$ for all rates of interest. This is so because such an annuity consists of only one payment and the future value is determined on the date of that payment—no time passes between the payment and its future value. The future value of an annuity formula is used to construct Table B.4. We can also construct it by adding the amounts from a future value of 1 table. To illustrate, we use Tables B.2 and B.4 to confirm this relation for the prior example:

From Table B.2		From Table B.4	
$i = 15\%, n = 0$	1.0000		
$i = 15\%, n = 1$	1.1500		
$i = 15\%, n = 2$	1.3225		
Total	3.4725	$i = 15\%, n = 3$	3.4725

Note that the future value in Table B.2 is 1.0000 when $n = 0$, but the future value in Table B.4 is 1.0000 when $n = 1$. Is this a contradiction? No. When $n = 0$ in Table B.2, the future value is determined on the date when a single payment occurs. This means that no interest is earned because no time has passed, and the future value equals the payment. Table B.4 describes annuities with equal payments occurring at the end of each period. When $n = 1$, the annuity has one payment, and its future value equals 1 on the date of its final and only payment. Again, no time passes between the payment and its future value date.

Quick Check   Answer—p. B-7

4. A company invests $45,000 per year for five years at 12% annual interest. Compute the value of this annuity investment at the end of five years.

Summary

C1 Describe the earning of interest and the concepts of present and future values. Interest is payment by a borrower to the owner of an asset for its use. Present and future value computations are a way for us to estimate the interest component of holding assets or liabilities over a period of time.

P1 Apply present value concepts to a single amount by using interest tables. The present value of a single amount received at a future date is the amount that can be invested now at the specified interest rate to yield that future value.

P2 Apply future value concepts to a single amount by using interest tables. The future value of a single amount

invested at a specified rate of interest is the amount that would accumulate by the future date.

P3 Apply present value concepts to an annuity by using interest tables. The present value of an annuity is the amount that can be invested now at the specified interest rate to yield that series of equal periodic payments.

P4 Apply future value concepts to an annuity by using interest tables. The future value of an annuity invested at a specific rate of interest is the amount that would accumulate by the date of the final payment.

Guidance Answers to Quick Checks

1. $70,000 × 0.6302 = $44,114 (use Table B.1, $i = 8\%$, $n = 6$).
2. $555,000/$150,000 = 3.7000; Table B.2 shows this value is not achieved until after 17 years at 8% interest.
3. $10,000 × 5.2421 = $52,421 (use Table B.3, $i = 4\%$, $n = 6$).
4. $45,000 × 6.3528 = $285,876 (use Table B.4, $i = 12\%$, $n = 5$).

McGraw-Hill's
HOMEWORK
MANAGER®   **Available with McGraw-Hill's Homework Manager**

Assume that you must make future value estimates using the *future value of 1 table* (Table B.2). Which interest rate column do you use when working with the following rates?

1. 8% compounded quarterly
2. 12% compounded annually
3. 6% compounded semiannually
4. 12% compounded monthly

QUICK STUDY

QS B-1
Identifying interest rates in tables
C1

Ken Francis is offered the possibility of investing $2,745 today and in return to receive $10,000 after 15 years. What is the annual rate of interest for this investment? (Use Table B.1.)

QS B-2
Interest rate on an investment   P1

Megan Brink is offered the possibility of investing $6,651 today at 6% interest per year in a desire to accumulate $10,000. How many years must Brink wait to accumulate $10,000? (Use Table B.1.)

QS B-3
Number of periods of an investment   P1

Flaherty is considering an investment that, if paid for immediately, is expected to return $140,000 five years from now. If Flaherty demands a 9% return, how much is she willing to pay for this investment?

QS B-4
Present value of an amount   P1

CII, Inc., invests $630,000 in a project expected to earn a 12% annual rate of return. The earnings will be reinvested in the project each year until the entire investment is liquidated 10 years later. What will the cash proceeds be when the project is liquidated?

QS B-5
Future value of an amount   P2

QS B-6 Present value of an annuity P3	Beene Distributing is considering a project that will return $150,000 annually at the end of each year for six years. If Beene demands an annual return of 7% and pays for the project immediately, how much is it willing to pay for the project?
QS B-7 Future value of an annuity P4	Claire Fitch is planning to begin an individual retirement program in which she will invest $1,500 at the end of each year. Fitch plans to retire after making 30 annual investments in the program earning a return of 10%. What is the value of the program on the date of the last payment?

Available with McGraw-Hill's Homework Manager

McGraw-Hill's
HOMEWORK
MANAGER®

EXERCISES

Exercise B-1 Number of periods of an investment P2	Bill Thompson expects to invest $10,000 at 12% and, at the end of a certain period, receive $96,463. How many years will it be before Thompson receives the payment? (Use Table B.2.)
Exercise B-2 Interest rate on an investment P2	Ed Summers expects to invest $10,000 for 25 years, after which he wants to receive $108,347. What rate of interest must Summers earn? (Use Table B.2.)
Exercise B-3 Interest rate on an investment P3	Jones expects an immediate investment of $57,466 to return $10,000 annually for eight years, with the first payment to be received one year from now. What rate of interest must Jones earn? (Use Table B.3.)
Exercise B-4 Number of periods of an investment P3	Keith Riggins expects an investment of $82,014 to return $10,000 annually for several years. If Riggins earns a return of 10%, how many annual payments will he receive? (Use Table B.3.)
Exercise B-5 Interest rate on an investment P4	Algoe expects to invest $1,000 annually for 40 years to yield an accumulated value of $154,762 on the date of the last investment. For this to occur, what rate of interest must Algoe earn? (Use Table B.4.)
Exercise B-6 Number of periods of an investment P4	Kate Beckwith expects to invest $10,000 annually that will earn 8%. How many annual investments must Beckwith make to accumulate $303,243 on the date of the last investment? (Use Table B.4.)
Exercise B-7 Present value of an annuity P3	Sam Weber finances a new automobile by paying $6,500 cash and agreeing to make 40 monthly payments of $500 each, the first payment to be made one month after the purchase. The loan bears interest at an annual rate of 12%. What is the cost of the automobile?
Exercise B-8 Present value of bonds P1 P3	Spiller Corp. plans to issue 10%, 15-year, $500,000 par value bonds payable that pay interest semiannually on June 30 and December 31. The bonds are dated December 31, 2008, and are issued on that date. If the market rate of interest for the bonds is 8% on the date of issue, what will be the total cash proceeds from the bond issue?
Exercise B-9 Present value of an amount P1	McAdams Company expects to earn 10% per year on an investment that will pay $606,773 six years from now. Use Table B.1 to compute the present value of this investment. (Round the amount to the nearest dollar.)
Exercise B-10 Present value of an amount and of an annuity P1 P3	Compute the amount that can be borrowed under each of the following circumstances: **1.** A promise to repay $90,000 seven years from now at an interest rate of 6%. **2.** An agreement made on February 1, 2008, to make three separate payments of $20,000 on February 1 of 2009, 2010, and 2011. The annual interest rate is 10%.
Exercise B-11 Present value of an amount P1	On January 1, 2008, a company agrees to pay $20,000 in three years. If the annual interest rate is 10%, determine how much cash the company can borrow with this agreement.

Find the amount of money that can be borrowed today with each of the following separate debt agreements *a* through *f*. (Round amounts to the nearest dollar.)

Exercise B-12
Present value
of an amount   P1

Case	Single Future Payment	Number of Periods	Interest Rate
a.	$40,000	3	4%
b.	75,000	7	8
c.	52,000	9	10
d.	18,000	2	4
e.	63,000	8	6
f.	89,000	5	2

C&H Ski Club recently borrowed money and agrees to pay it back with a series of six annual payments of $5,000 each. C&H subsequently borrows more money and agrees to pay it back with a series of four annual payments of $7,500 each. The annual interest rate for both loans is 6%.

Exercise B-13
Present values of annuities

P3

1. Use Table B.1 to find the present value of these two separate annuities. (Round amounts to the nearest dollar.)

2. Use Table B.3 to find the present value of these two separate annuities. (Round amounts to the nearest dollar.)

Otto Co. borrows money on April 30, 2008, by promising to make four payments of $13,000 each on November 1, 2008; May 1, 2009; November 1, 2009; and May 1, 2010.

Exercise B-14
Present value with semiannual compounding

C1   P3

1. How much money is Otto able to borrow if the interest rate is 8%, compounded semiannually?

2. How much money is Otto able to borrow if the interest rate is 12%, compounded semiannually?

3. How much money is Otto able to borrow if the interest rate is 16%, compounded semiannually?

Mark Welsch deposits $7,200 in an account that earns interest at an annual rate of 8%, compounded quarterly. The $7,200 plus earned interest must remain in the account 10 years before it can be withdrawn. How much money will be in the account at the end of 10 years?

Exercise B-15
Future value
of an amount   P2

Kelly Malone plans to have $50 withheld from her monthly paycheck and deposited in a savings account that earns 12% annually, compounded monthly. If Malone continues with her plan for two and one-half years, how much will be accumulated in the account on the date of the last deposit?

Exercise B-16
Future value
of an annuity   P4

Starr Company decides to establish a fund that it will use 10 years from now to replace an aging production facility. The company will make a $100,000 initial contribution to the fund and plans to make quarterly contributions of $50,000 beginning in three months. The fund earns 12%, compounded quarterly. What will be the value of the fund 10 years from now?

Exercise B-17
Future value of
an amount plus
an annuity   P2   P4

Catten, Inc., invests $163,170 today earning 7% per year for nine years. Use Table B.2 to compute the future value of the investment nine years from now. (Round the amount to the nearest dollar.)

Exercise B-18
Future value of
an amount   P2

For each of the following situations, identify (1) the case as either (*a*) a present or a future value and (*b*) a single amount or an annuity, (2) the table you would use in your computations (but do not solve the problem), and (3) the interest rate and time periods you would use.

Exercise B-19
Using present and future value tables

C1   P1   P2   P3   P4

a. You need to accumulate $10,000 for a trip you wish to take in four years. You are able to earn 8% compounded semiannually on your savings. You plan to make only one deposit and let the money accumulate for four years. How would you determine the amount of the one-time deposit?

b. Assume the same facts as in part (*a*) except that you will make semiannual deposits to your savings account.

c. You want to retire after working 40 years with savings in excess of $1,000,000. You expect to save $4,000 a year for 40 years and earn an annual rate of interest of 8%. Will you be able to retire with more than $1,000,000 in 40 years? Explain.

d. A sweepstakes agency names you a grand prize winner. You can take $225,000 immediately or elect to receive annual installments of $30,000 for 20 years. You can earn 10% annually on any investments you make. Which prize do you choose to receive?

TABLE B.1

Present Value of 1

$$p = 1/(1 + i)^n$$

Periods	|Rate 1%	2%	3%	4%	5%	6%	7%	8%	9%	10%	12%	15%
1	0.9901	0.9804	0.9709	0.9615	0.9524	0.9434	0.9346	0.9259	0.9174	0.9091	0.8929	0.8696
2	0.9803	0.9612	0.9426	0.9246	0.9070	0.8900	0.8734	0.8573	0.8417	0.8264	0.7972	0.7561
3	0.9706	0.9423	0.9151	0.8890	0.8638	0.8396	0.8163	0.7938	0.7722	0.7513	0.7118	0.6575
4	0.9610	0.9238	0.8885	0.8548	0.8227	0.7921	0.7629	0.7350	0.7084	0.6830	0.6355	0.5718
5	0.9515	0.9057	0.8626	0.8219	0.7835	0.7473	0.7130	0.6806	0.6499	0.6209	0.5674	0.4972
6	0.9420	0.8880	0.8375	0.7903	0.7462	0.7050	0.6663	0.6302	0.5963	0.5645	0.5066	0.4323
7	0.9327	0.8706	0.8131	0.7599	0.7107	0.6651	0.6227	0.5835	0.5470	0.5132	0.4523	0.3759
8	0.9235	0.8535	0.7894	0.7307	0.6768	0.6274	0.5820	0.5403	0.5019	0.4665	0.4039	0.3269
9	0.9143	0.8368	0.7664	0.7026	0.6446	0.5919	0.5439	0.5002	0.4604	0.4241	0.3606	0.2843
10	0.9053	0.8203	0.7441	0.6756	0.6139	0.5584	0.5083	0.4632	0.4224	0.3855	0.3220	0.2472
11	0.8963	0.8043	0.7224	0.6496	0.5847	0.5268	0.4751	0.4289	0.3875	0.3505	0.2875	0.2149
12	0.8874	0.7885	0.7014	0.6246	0.5568	0.4970	0.4440	0.3971	0.3555	0.3186	0.2567	0.1869
13	0.8787	0.7730	0.6810	0.6006	0.5303	0.4688	0.4150	0.3677	0.3262	0.2897	0.2292	0.1625
14	0.8700	0.7579	0.6611	0.5775	0.5051	0.4423	0.3878	0.3405	0.2992	0.2633	0.2046	0.1413
15	0.8613	0.7430	0.6419	0.5553	0.4810	0.4173	0.3624	0.3152	0.2745	0.2394	0.1827	0.1229
16	0.8528	0.7284	0.6232	0.5339	0.4581	0.3936	0.3387	0.2919	0.2519	0.2176	0.1631	0.1069
17	0.8444	0.7142	0.6050	0.5134	0.4363	0.3714	0.3166	0.2703	0.2311	0.1978	0.1456	0.0929
18	0.8360	0.7002	0.5874	0.4936	0.4155	0.3503	0.2959	0.2502	0.2120	0.1799	0.1300	0.0808
19	0.8277	0.6864	0.5703	0.4746	0.3957	0.3305	0.2765	0.2317	0.1945	0.1635	0.1161	0.0703
20	0.8195	0.6730	0.5537	0.4564	0.3769	0.3118	0.2584	0.2145	0.1784	0.1486	0.1037	0.0611
25	0.7798	0.6095	0.4776	0.3751	0.2953	0.2330	0.1842	0.1460	0.1160	0.0923	0.0588	0.0304
30	0.7419	0.5521	0.4120	0.3083	0.2314	0.1741	0.1314	0.0994	0.0754	0.0573	0.0334	0.0151
35	0.7059	0.5000	0.3554	0.2534	0.1813	0.1301	0.0937	0.0676	0.0490	0.0356	0.0189	0.0075
40	0.6717	0.4529	0.3066	0.2083	0.1420	0.0972	0.0668	0.0460	0.0318	0.0221	0.0107	0.0037

TABLE B.2

Future Value of 1

$$f = (1 + i)^n$$

Periods	|Rate 1%	2%	3%	4%	5%	6%	7%	8%	9%	10%	12%	15%
0	1.0000	1.0000	1.0000	1.0000	1.0000	1.0000	1.0000	1.0000	1.0000	1.0000	1.0000	1.0000
1	1.0100	1.0200	1.0300	1.0400	1.0500	1.0600	1.0700	1.0800	1.0900	1.1000	1.1200	1.1500
2	1.0201	1.0404	1.0609	1.0816	1.1025	1.1236	1.1449	1.1664	1.1881	1.2100	1.2544	1.3225
3	1.0303	1.0612	1.0927	1.1249	1.1576	1.1910	1.2250	1.2597	1.2950	1.3310	1.4049	1.5209
4	1.0406	1.0824	1.1255	1.1699	1.2155	1.2625	1.3108	1.3605	1.4116	1.4641	1.5735	1.7490
5	1.0510	1.1041	1.1593	1.2167	1.2763	1.3382	1.4026	1.4693	1.5386	1.6105	1.7623	2.0114
6	1.0615	1.1262	1.1941	1.2653	1.3401	1.4185	1.5007	1.5869	1.6771	1.7716	1.9738	2.3131
7	1.0721	1.1487	1.2299	1.3159	1.4071	1.5036	1.6058	1.7138	1.8280	1.9487	2.2107	2.6600
8	1.0829	1.1717	1.2668	1.3686	1.4775	1.5938	1.7182	1.8509	1.9926	2.1436	2.4760	3.0590
9	1.0937	1.1951	1.3048	1.4233	1.5513	1.6895	1.8385	1.9990	2.1719	2.3579	2.7731	3.5179
10	1.1046	1.2190	1.3439	1.4802	1.6289	1.7908	1.9672	2.1589	2.3674	2.5937	3.1058	4.0456
11	1.1157	1.2434	1.3842	1.5395	1.7103	1.8983	2.1049	2.3316	2.5804	2.8531	3.4785	4.6524
12	1.1268	1.2682	1.4258	1.6010	1.7959	2.0122	2.2522	2.5182	2.8127	3.1384	3.8960	5.3503
13	1.1381	1.2936	1.4685	1.6651	1.8856	2.1329	2.4098	2.7196	3.0658	3.4523	4.3635	6.1528
14	1.1495	1.3195	1.5126	1.7317	1.9799	2.2609	2.5785	2.9372	3.3417	3.7975	4.8871	7.0757
15	1.1610	1.3459	1.5580	1.8009	2.0789	2.3966	2.7590	3.1722	3.6425	4.1772	5.4736	8.1371
16	1.1726	1.3728	1.6047	1.8730	2.1829	2.5404	2.9522	3.4259	3.9703	4.5950	6.1304	9.3576
17	1.1843	1.4002	1.6528	1.9479	2.2920	2.6928	3.1588	3.7000	4.3276	5.0545	6.8660	10.7613
18	1.1961	1.4282	1.7024	2.0258	2.4066	2.8543	3.3799	3.9960	4.7171	5.5599	7.6900	12.3755
19	1.2081	1.4568	1.7535	2.1068	2.5270	3.0256	3.6165	4.3157	5.1417	6.1159	8.6128	14.2318
20	1.2202	1.4859	1.8061	2.1911	2.6533	3.2071	3.8697	4.6610	5.6044	6.7275	9.6463	16.3665
25	1.2824	1.6406	2.0938	2.6658	3.3864	4.2919	5.4274	6.8485	8.6231	10.8347	17.0001	32.9190
30	1.3478	1.8114	2.4273	3.2434	4.3219	5.7435	7.6123	10.0627	13.2677	17.4494	29.9599	66.2118
35	1.4166	1.9999	2.8139	3.9461	5.5160	7.6861	10.6766	14.7853	20.4140	28.1024	52.7996	133.1755
40	1.4889	2.2080	3.2620	4.8010	7.0400	10.2857	14.9745	21.7245	31.4094	45.2593	93.0510	267.8635

$$p = \left[1 - \frac{1}{(1 + i)^n}\right]/i$$

TABLE B.3

Present Value of an Annuity of 1

	Rate											
Periods	1%	2%	3%	4%	5%	6%	7%	8%	9%	10%	12%	15%
1	0.9901	0.9804	0.9709	0.9615	0.9524	0.9434	0.9346	0.9259	0.9174	0.9091	0.8929	0.8696
2	1.9704	1.9416	1.9135	1.8861	1.8594	1.8334	1.8080	1.7833	1.7591	1.7355	1.6901	1.6257
3	2.9410	2.8839	2.8286	2.7751	2.7232	2.6730	2.6243	2.5771	2.5313	2.4869	2.4018	2.2832
4	3.9020	3.8077	3.7171	3.6299	3.5460	3.4651	3.3872	3.3121	3.2397	3.1699	3.0373	2.8550
5	4.8534	4.7135	4.5797	4.4518	4.3295	4.2124	4.1002	3.9927	3.8897	3.7908	3.6048	3.3522
6	5.7955	5.6014	5.4172	5.2421	5.0757	4.9173	4.7665	4.6229	4.4859	4.3553	4.1114	3.7845
7	6.7282	6.4720	6.2303	6.0021	5.7864	5.5824	5.3893	5.2064	5.0330	4.8684	4.5638	4.1604
8	7.6517	7.3255	7.0197	6.7327	6.4632	6.2098	5.9713	5.7466	5.5348	5.3349	4.9676	4.4873
9	8.5660	8.1622	7.7861	7.4353	7.1078	6.8017	6.5152	6.2469	5.9952	5.7590	5.3282	4.7716
10	9.4713	8.9826	8.5302	8.1109	7.7217	7.3601	7.0236	6.7101	6.4177	6.1446	5.6502	5.0188
11	10.3676	9.7868	9.2526	8.7605	8.3064	7.8869	7.4987	7.1390	6.8052	6.4951	5.9377	5.2337
12	11.2551	10.5753	9.9540	9.3851	8.8633	8.3838	7.9427	7.5361	7.1607	6.8137	6.1944	5.4206
13	12.1337	11.3484	10.6350	9.9856	9.3936	8.8527	8.3577	7.9038	7.4869	7.1034	6.4235	5.5831
14	13.0037	12.1062	11.2961	10.5631	9.8986	9.2950	8.7455	8.2442	7.7862	7.3667	6.6282	5.7245
15	13.8651	12.8493	11.9379	11.1184	10.3797	9.7122	9.1079	8.5595	8.0607	7.6061	6.8109	5.8474
16	14.7179	13.5777	12.5611	11.6523	10.8378	10.1059	9.4466	8.8514	8.3126	7.8237	6.9740	5.9542
17	15.5623	14.2919	13.1661	12.1657	11.2741	10.4773	9.7632	9.1216	8.5436	8.0216	7.1196	6.0472
18	16.3983	14.9920	13.7535	12.6593	11.6896	10.8276	10.0591	9.3719	8.7556	8.2014	7.2497	6.1280
19	17.2260	15.6785	14.3238	13.1339	12.0853	11.1581	10.3356	9.6036	8.9501	8.3649	7.3658	6.1982
20	18.0456	16.3514	14.8775	13.5903	12.4622	11.4699	10.5940	9.8181	9.1285	8.5136	7.4694	6.2593
25	22.0232	19.5235	17.4131	15.6221	14.0939	12.7834	11.6536	10.6748	9.8226	9.0770	7.8431	6.4641
30	25.8077	22.3965	19.6004	17.2920	15.3725	13.7648	12.4090	11.2578	10.2737	9.4269	8.0552	6.5660
35	29.4086	24.9986	21.4872	18.6646	16.3742	14.4982	12.9477	11.6546	10.5668	9.6442	8.1755	6.6166
40	32.8347	27.3555	23.1148	19.7928	17.1591	15.0463	13.3317	11.9246	10.7574	9.7791	8.2438	6.6418

$$f = [(1 + i)^n - 1]/i$$

TABLE B.4

Future Value of an Annuity of 1

	Rate											
Periods	1%	2%	3%	4%	5%	6%	7%	8%	9%	10%	12%	15%
1	1.0000	1.0000	1.0000	1.0000	1.0000	1.0000	1.0000	1.0000	1.0000	1.0000	1.0000	1.0000
2	2.0100	2.0200	2.0300	2.0400	2.0500	2.0600	2.0700	2.0800	2.0900	2.1000	2.1200	2.1500
3	3.0301	3.0604	3.0909	3.1216	3.1525	3.1836	3.2149	3.2464	3.2781	3.3100	3.3744	3.4725
4	4.0604	4.1216	4.1836	4.2465	4.3101	4.3746	4.4399	4.5061	4.5731	4.6410	4.7793	4.9934
5	5.1010	5.2040	5.3091	5.4163	5.5256	5.6371	5.7507	5.8666	5.9847	6.1051	6.3528	6.7424
6	6.1520	6.3081	6.4684	6.6330	6.8019	6.9753	7.1533	7.3359	7.5233	7.7156	8.1152	8.7537
7	7.2135	7.4343	7.6625	7.8983	8.1420	8.3938	8.6540	8.9228	9.2004	9.4872	10.0890	11.0668
8	8.2857	8.5830	8.8923	9.2142	9.5491	9.8975	10.2598	10.6366	11.0285	11.4359	12.2997	13.7268
9	9.3685	9.7546	10.1591	10.5828	11.0266	11.4913	11.9780	12.4876	13.0210	13.5795	14.7757	16.7858
10	10.4622	10.9497	11.4639	12.0061	12.5779	13.1808	13.8164	14.4866	15.1929	15.9374	17.5487	20.3037
11	11.5668	12.1687	12.8078	13.4864	14.2068	14.9716	15.7836	16.6455	17.5603	18.5312	20.6546	24.3493
12	12.6825	13.4121	14.1920	15.0258	15.9171	16.8699	17.8885	18.9771	20.1407	21.3843	24.1331	29.0017
13	13.8093	14.6803	15.6178	16.6268	17.7130	18.8821	20.1406	21.4953	22.9534	24.5227	28.0291	34.3519
14	14.9474	15.9739	17.0863	18.2919	19.5986	21.0151	22.5505	24.2149	26.0192	27.9750	32.3926	40.5047
15	16.0969	17.2934	18.5989	20.0236	21.5786	23.2760	25.1290	27.1521	29.3609	31.7725	37.2797	47.5804
16	17.2579	18.6393	20.1569	21.8245	23.6575	25.6725	27.8881	30.3243	33.0034	35.9497	42.7533	55.7175
17	18.4304	20.0121	21.7616	23.6975	25.8404	28.2129	30.8402	33.7502	36.9737	40.5447	48.8837	65.0751
18	19.6147	21.4123	23.4144	25.6454	28.1324	30.9057	33.9990	37.4502	41.3013	45.5992	55.7497	75.8364
19	20.8109	22.8406	25.1169	27.6712	30.5390	33.7600	37.3790	41.4463	46.0185	51.1591	63.4397	88.2118
20	22.0190	24.2974	26.8704	29.7781	33.0660	36.7856	40.9955	45.7620	51.1601	57.2750	72.0524	102.4436
25	28.2432	32.0303	36.4593	41.6459	47.7271	54.8645	63.2490	73.1059	84.7009	98.3471	133.3339	212.7930
30	34.7849	40.5681	47.5754	56.0849	66.4388	79.0582	94.4608	113.2832	136.3075	164.4940	241.3327	434.7451
35	41.6603	49.9945	60.4621	73.6522	90.3203	111.4348	138.2369	172.3168	215.7108	271.0244	431.6635	881.1702
40	48.8864	60.4020	75.4013	95.0255	120.7998	154.7620	199.6351	259.0565	337.8824	442.5926	767.0914	1,779.0903

Glossary

Absorption costing Costing method that assigns both variable and fixed costs to products.

Accelerated depreciation method Method that produces larger depreciation charges in the early years of an asset's life and smaller charges in its later years. *(p. 398)*

Account Record within an accounting system in which increases and decreases are entered and stored in a specific asset, liability, equity, revenue, or expense. *(p. 49)*

Account balance Difference between total debits and total credits (including the beginning balance) for an account. *(p. 53)*

Account form balance sheet Balance sheet that lists assets on the left side and liabilities and equity on the right. *(p. 18)*

Account payable Liability created by buying goods or services on credit; backed by the buyer's general credit standing. *(p. 50)*

Accounting Information and measurement system that identifies, records, and communicates relevant information about a company's business activities. *(p. 4)*

Accounting cycle Recurring steps performed each accounting period, starting with analyzing transactions and continuing through the post-closing trial balance (or reversing entries). *(p. 144)*

Accounting equation Equality involving a company's assets, liabilities, and equity; Assets = Liabilities + Equity; also called *balance sheet equation*. *(p. 12)*

Accounting information system People, records, and methods that collect and process data from transactions and events, organize them in useful forms, and communicate results to decision makers. *(p. 268)*

Accounting period Length of time covered by financial statements; also called *reporting period*. *(p. 92)*

Accounting rate of return Rate used to evaluate the acceptability of an investment; equals the after-tax periodic income from a project divided by the average investment in the asset; also called *rate of return on average investment*. *(p. 1027)*

Accounts payable ledger Subsidiary ledger listing individual creditor (supplier) accounts. *(p. 273)*

Accounts receivable Amounts due from customers for credit sales; backed by the customer's general credit standing. *(p. 358)*

Accounts receivable ledger Subsidiary ledger listing individual customer accounts. *(p. 273)*

Accounts receivable turnover Measure of both the quality and liquidity of accounts receivable; indicates how often receivables are received and collected during the period; computed by dividing net sales by average accounts receivable. *(p. 372)*

Accrual basis accounting Accounting system that recognizes revenues when earned and expenses when incurred; the basis for GAAP. *(p. 93)*

Accrued expenses Costs incurred in a period that are both unpaid and unrecorded; adjusting entries for recording accrued expenses involve increasing expenses and increasing liabilities. *(p. 99)*

Accrued revenues Revenues earned in a period that are both unrecorded and not yet received in cash (or other assets); adjusting entries for recording accrued revenues involve increasing assets and increasing revenues. *(p. 101)*

Accumulated depreciation Cumulative sum of all depreciation expense recorded for an asset. *(p. 97)*

Acid-test ratio Ratio used to assess a company's ability to settle its current debts with its most liquid assets; defined as quick assets (cash, short-term investments, and current receivables) divided by current liabilities. *(p. 193)*

Activity-based budgeting (ABB) Budget system based on expected activities. *(p. 953)*

Activity-based costing (ABC) Cost allocation method that focuses on activities performed; traces costs to activities and then assigns them to cost objects. *(p. 854)*

Activity cost driver Variable that causes an activity's cost to go up or down; a causal factor. *(p. 855)*

Activity cost pool Temporary account that accumulates costs a company incurs to support an activity. *(p. 855)*

Adjusted trial balance List of accounts and balances prepared after period-end adjustments are recorded and posted. *(p. 104)*

Adjusting entry Journal entry at the end of an accounting period to bring an asset or liability account to its proper amount and update the related expense or revenue account. *(p. 94)*

Aging of accounts receivable Process of classifying accounts receivable by how long they are past due for purposes of estimating uncollectible accounts. *(p. 366)*

Allowance for Doubtful Accounts Contra asset account with a balance approximating uncollectible accounts receivable; also called *Allowance for Uncollectible Accounts*. *(p. 363)*

Allowance method Procedure that (a) estimates and matches bad debts expense with its sales for the period and/or (b) reports accounts receivable at estimated realizable value. *(p. 362)*

Amortization Process of allocating the cost of an intangible asset to expense over its estimated useful life. *(p. 407)*

Annual financial statements Financial statements covering a one-year period; often based on a calendar year, but any consecutive 12-month (or 52-week) period is acceptable. *(p. 92)*

Annual report Summary of a company's financial results for the year with its current financial condition and future plans; directed to external users of financial information. *(p. A-1)*

Annuity Series of equal payments at equal intervals. *(p. 568)*

Appropriated retained earnings Retained earnings separately reported to inform stockholders of funding needs. *(p. 523)*

Asset book value (See *book value.*)

Assets Resources a business owns or controls that are expected to provide current and future benefits to the business. *(p. 13)*

Audit Analysis and report of an organization's accounting system, its records, and its reports using various tests. *(p. 11)*

Auditors Individuals hired to review financial reports and information systems. *Internal auditors* of a company are employed to assess and evaluate its system of internal controls, including the resulting reports. *External auditors* are independent of a company and are hired to assess and evaluate the "fairness" of financial statements (or to perform other contracted financial services) *(p. 11).*

Authorized stock Total amount of stock that a corporation's charter authorizes it to issue. *(p. 509)*

Available-for-sale (AFS) securities Investments in debt and equity securities that are not classified as trading securities or held-to-maturity securities. *(p. 596)*

Average cost See *weighted average. (p. 230)*

Avoidable expense Expense (or cost) that is relevant for decision making; expense that is not incurred if a department, product, or service is eliminated. *(p. 1041)*

Bad debts Accounts of customers who do not pay what they have promised to pay; an expense of selling on credit; also called *uncollectible accounts. (p. 361)*

Balance column account Account with debit and credit columns for recording entries and another column for showing the balance of the account after each entry. *(p. 56)*

Balance sheet Financial statement that lists types and dollar amounts of assets, liabilities, and equity at a specific date. *(p. 18)*

Balance sheet equation (See *accounting equation.*)

Bank reconciliation Report that explains the difference between the book (company) balance of cash and the cash balance reported on the bank statement. *(p. 329)*

Bank statement Bank report on the depositor's beginning and ending cash balances, and a listing of its changes, for a period. *(p. 327)*

Basic earnings per share Net income less any preferred dividends and then divided by weighted-average common shares outstanding. *(p. 524)*

Batch processing Accumulating source documents for a period of time and then processing them all at once such as once a day, week, or month. *(p. 282)*

Bearer bonds Bonds made payable to whoever holds them (the *bearer*); also called *unregistered bonds. (p. 563)*

Benchmarking Practice of comparing and analyzing company financial performance or position with other companies or standards.

Betterments Expenditures to make a plant asset more efficient or productive; also called *improvements. (p. 403)*

Bond Written promise to pay the bond's par (or face) value and interest at a stated contract rate; often issued in denominations of $1,000. *(p. 550)*

Bond certificate Document containing bond specifics such as issuer's name, bond par value, contract interest rate, and maturity date. *(p. 552)*

Bond indenture Contract between the bond issuer and the bondholders; identifies the parties' rights and obligations. *(p. 552)*

Book value Asset's acquisition costs less its accumulated depreciation (or depletion, or amortization); also sometimes used synonymously as the *carrying value* of an account. *(p. 98)*

Book value per common share Recorded amount of equity applicable to common shares divided by the number of common shares outstanding. *(p. 526)*

Book value per preferred share Equity applicable to preferred shares (equals its call price [or par value if it is not callable] plus any cumulative dividends in arrears) divided by the number of preferred shares outstanding. *(p. 526)*

Bookkeeping (See *recordkeeping.*)

Break-even point Output level at which sales equals fixed plus variable costs; where income equals zero. *(p. 909)*

Break-even time (BET) Time-based measurement used to evaluate the acceptability of an investment; equals the time expected to pass before the present value of the net cash flows from an investment equals its initial cost. *(p. 1043)*

Budget Formal statement of future plans, usually expressed in monetary terms. *(p. 940)*

Budget report Report comparing actual results to planned objectives; sometimes used as a progress report. *(p. 980)*

Budgetary control Management use of budgets to monitor and control company operations. *(p. 980)*

Budgeted balance sheet Accounting report that presents predicted amounts of the company's assets, liabilities, and equity balances as of the end of the budget period. *(p. 952)*

Budgeted income statement Accounting report that presents predicted amounts of the company's revenues and expenses for the budget period. *(p. 952)*

Budgeting Process of planning future business actions and expressing them as formal plans. *(p. 940)*

Business An organization of one or more individuals selling products and/or services for profit. *(p. 10)*

Business entity assumption Principle that requires a business to be accounted for separately from its owner(s) and from any other entity. *(p. 10)*

Business segment Part of a company that can be separately identified by the products or services that it provides or by the geographic markets that it serves; also called *segment. (p. 703)*

C corporation Corporation that does not qualify for nor elect to be treated as a proprietorship or partnership for income tax purposes and therefore is subject to income taxes; also called *C corp. (p. 480)*

Call price Amount that must be paid to call and retire a callable preferred stock or a callable bond. *(p. 519)*

Callable bonds Bonds that give the issuer the option to retire them at a stated amount prior to maturity. *(p. 563)*

Callable preferred stock Preferred stock that the issuing corporation, at its option, may retire by paying the call price plus any dividends in arrears. *(p. 519)*

Canceled checks Checks that the bank has paid and deducted from the depositor's account. *(p. 328)*

Capital budgeting Process of analyzing alternative investments and deciding which assets to acquire or sell. *(p. 1024)*

Capital expenditures Additional costs of plant assets that provide material benefits extending beyond the current period; also called *balance sheet expenditures*. *(p. 402)*

Capital expenditures budget Plan that lists dollar amounts to be both received from disposal of plant assets and spent to purchase plant assets. *(p. 949)*

Capital leases Long-term leases in which the lessor transfers substantially all risk and rewards of ownership to the lessee. *(p. 574)*

Capital stock General term referring to a corporation's stock used in obtaining capital (owner financing). *(p. 509)*

Capitalize Record the cost as part of a permanent account and allocate it over later periods. *(p. 402)*

Carrying (book) value of bonds Net amount at which bonds are reported on the balance sheet; equals the par value of the bonds less any unamortized discount or plus any unamortized premium; also called *carrying amount* or *book value*. *(p. 554)*

Cash Includes currency, coins, and amounts on deposit in bank checking or savings accounts. *(p. 319)*

Cash basis accounting Accounting system that recognizes revenues when cash is received and records expenses when cash is paid. *(p. 93)*

Cash budget Plan that shows expected cash inflows and outflows during the budget period, including receipts from loans needed to maintain a minimum cash balance and repayments of such loans. *(p. 950)*

Cash disbursements journal Special journal normally used to record all payments of cash; also called *cash payments journal*. *(p. 280)*

Cash discount Reduction in the price of merchandise granted by a seller to a buyer when payment is made within the discount period. *(p. 181)*

Cash equivalents Short-term, investment assets that are readily convertible to a known cash amount or sufficiently close to their maturity date (usually within 90 days) so that market value is not sensitive to interest rate changes. *(p. 319)*

Cash flow on total assets Ratio of operating cash flows to average total assets; not sensitive to income recognition and measurement; partly reflects earnings quality. *(p. 646)*

Cash Over and Short Income statement account used to record cash overages and cash shortages arising from errors in cash receipts or payments. *(p. 321)*

Cash receipts journal Special journal normally used to record all receipts of cash. *(p. 277)*

Change in an accounting estimate Change in an accounting estimate that results from new information, subsequent developments, or improved judgment that impacts current and future periods. *(pp. 401 & 523)*

Chart of accounts List of accounts used by a company; includes an identification number for each account. *(p. 52)*

Check Document signed by a depositor instructing the bank to pay a specified amount to a designated recipient. *(p. 326)*

Check register Another name for a cash disbursements journal when the journal has a column for check numbers. *(pp. 280 & 337)*

Classified balance sheet Balance sheet that presents assets and liabilities in relevant subgroups, including current and noncurrent classifications. *(p. 145)*

Clock card Source document used to record the number of hours an employee works and to determine the total labor cost for each pay period. *(p. 776)*

Closing entries Entries recorded at the end of each accounting period to transfer end-of-period balances in revenue, gain, expense, loss, and withdrawal (dividend for a corporation) accounts to the capital account (to retained earnings for a corporation). *(p. 141)*

Closing process Necessary end-of-period steps to prepare the accounts for recording the transactions of the next period. *(p. 140)*

Columnar journal Journal with more than one column. *(p. 274)*

Common stock Corporation's basic ownership share; also generically called *capital stock*. *(pp. 11 & 508)*

Common-size financial statement Statement that expresses each amount as a percent of a base amount. In the balance sheet, total assets is usually the base and is expressed as 100%. In the income statement, net sales is usually the base. *(p. 687)*

Comparative financial statement Statement with data for two or more successive periods placed in side-by-side columns, often with changes shown in dollar amounts and percents. *(p. 682)*

Compatibility principle Information system principle that prescribes an accounting system to conform with a company's activities, personnel, and structure. *(p. 269)*

Complex capital structure Capital structure that includes outstanding rights or options to purchase common stock, or securities that are convertible into common stock. *(p. 524)*

Components of accounting systems Five basic components of accounting systems are source documents, input devices, information processors, information storage, and output devices. *(p. 269)*

Composite unit Generic unit consisting of a specific number of units of each product; unit comprised in proportion to the expected sales mix of its products. *(p. 916)*

Compound journal entry Journal entry that affects at least three accounts. *(p. 61)*

Comprehensive income Net change in equity for a period, excluding owner investments and distributions. *(p. 600)*

Computer hardware Physical equipment in a computerized accounting information system.

Computer network Linkage giving different users and different computers access to common databases and programs. *(p. 283)*

Computer software Programs that direct operations of computer hardware.

Conservatism constraint Principle that prescribes the less optimistic estimate when two estimates are about equally likely. *(p. 234)*

Consignee Receiver of goods owned by another who holds them for purposes of selling them for the owner. *(p. 224)*

Consignor Owner of goods who ships them to another party who will sell them for the owner. *(p. 224)*

Consistency concept Principle that prescribes use of the same accounting method(s) over time so that financial statements are comparable across periods. *(p. 233)*

Consolidated financial statements Financial statements that show all (combined) activities under the parent's control, including those of any subsidiaries. *(p. 599)*

Contingent liability Obligation to make a future payment if, and only if, an uncertain future event occurs. *(p. 445)*

Continuous budgeting Practice of preparing budgets for a selected number of future periods and revising those budgets as each period is completed. *(p. 942)*

Continuous improvement Concept requiring every manager and employee continually to look to improve operations. *(p. 730)*

Contra account Account linked with another account and having an opposite normal balance; reported as a subtraction from the other account's balance. *(p. 97)*

Contract rate Interest rate specified in a bond indenture (or note); multiplied by the par value to determine the interest paid each period; also called *coupon rate, stated rate,* or *nominal rate. (p. 553)*

Contributed capital Total amount of cash and other assets received from stockholders in exchange for stock; also called *paid-in capital. (p. 13)*

Contributed capital in excess of par value Difference between the par value of stock and its issue price when issued at a price above par.

Contribution margin Sales revenue less total variable costs.

Contribution margin income statement Income statement that separates variable and fixed costs; highlights the contribution margin, which is sales less variable expenses.

Contribution margin per unit Amount that the sale of one unit contributes toward recovering fixed costs and earning profit; defined as sales price per unit minus variable expense per unit. *(p. 908)*

Contribution margin ratio Product's contribution margin divided by its sale price. *(p. 908)*

Control Process of monitoring planning decisions and evaluating the organization's activities and employees. *(p. 727)*

Control principle Information system principle that prescribes an accounting system to aid managers in controlling and monitoring business activities. *(p. 268)*

Controllable costs Costs that a manager has the power to control or at least strongly influence. *(pp. 733 & 870)*

Controllable variance Combination of both overhead spending variances (variable and fixed) and the variable overhead efficiency variance. *(p. 993)*

Controlling account General ledger account, the balance of which (after posting) equals the sum of the balances in its related subsidiary ledger. *(p. 273)*

Conversion costs Expenditures incurred in converting raw materials to finished goods; includes direct labor costs and overhead costs. *(p. 738)*

Convertible bonds Bonds that bondholders can exchange for a set number of the issuer's shares. *(p. 563)*

Convertible preferred stock Preferred stock with an option to exchange it for common stock at a specified rate. *(p. 518)*

Copyright Right giving the owner the exclusive privilege to publish and sell musical, literary, or artistic work during the creator's life plus 70 years. *(p. 408)*

Corporation Business that is a separate legal entity under state or federal laws with owners called *shareholders* or *stockholders. (pp. 11 & 506)*

Cost All normal and reasonable expenditures necessary to get an asset in place and ready for its intended use. *(p. 393)*

Cost accounting system Accounting system for manufacturing activities based on the perpetual inventory system. *(p. 770)*

Cost-benefit principle Information system principle that prescribes the benefits from an activity in an accounting system to outweigh the costs of that activity. *(p. 269)*

Cost center Department that incurs costs but generates no revenues; common example is the accounting or legal department. *(p. 858)*

Cost object Product, process, department, or customer to which costs are assigned. *(p. 732)*

Cost of goods available for sale Consists of beginning inventory plus net purchases of a period.

Cost of goods manufactured Total manufacturing costs (direct materials, direct labor, and factory overhead) for the period plus beginning goods in process less ending goods in process; also called *net cost of goods manufactured* and *cost of goods completed. (p. 821)*

Cost of goods sold Cost of inventory sold to customers during a period; also called *cost of sales. (p. 178)*

Cost principle Accounting principle that prescribes financial statement information to be based on actual costs incurred in business transactions. *(p. 9)*

Cost variance Difference between the actual incurred cost and the standard cost. *(p. 986)*

Cost-volume-profit (CVP) analysis Planning method that includes predicting the volume of activity, the costs incurred, sales earned, and profits received. *(p. 902)*

Cost-volume-profit (CVP) chart Graphic representation of cost-volume-profit relations. *(p. 910)*

Coupon bonds Bonds with interest coupons attached to their certificates; bondholders detach coupons when they mature and present them to a bank or broker for collection. *(p. 563)*

Credit Recorded on the right side; an entry that decreases asset and expense accounts, and increases liability, revenue, and most equity accounts; abbreviated Cr. *(p. 53)*

Credit memorandum Notification that the sender has credited the recipient's account in the sender's records. *(p. 187)*

Credit period Time period that can pass before a customer's payment is due. *(p. 181)*

Credit terms Description of the amounts and timing of payments that a buyer (debtor) agrees to make in the future. *(p. 181)*

Creditors Individuals or organizations entitled to receive payments. *(p. 50)*

Cumulative preferred stock Preferred stock on which undeclared dividends accumulate until paid; common stockholders cannot receive dividends until cumulative dividends are paid. *(p. 517)*

Current assets Cash and other assets expected to be sold, collected, or used within one year or the company's operating cycle, whichever is longer. *(p. 146)*

Current liabilities Obligations due to be paid or settled within one year or the company's operating cycle, whichever is longer. *(pp. 147 & 435)*

Current portion of long-term debt Portion of long-term debt due within one year or the operating cycle, whichever is longer; reported under current liabilities. *(p. 442)*

Current ratio Ratio used to evaluate a company's ability to pay its short-term obligations, calculated by dividing current assets by current liabilities. *(p. 147)*

Curvilinear cost Cost that changes with volume but not at a constant rate. *(p. 904)*

Customer orientation Company position that its managers and employees be in tune with the changing wants and needs of consumers. *(p. 729)*

Cycle efficiency (CE) A measure of production efficiency, which is defined as value-added (process) time divided by total cycle time. *(p. 743)*

Cycle time (CT) A measure of the time to produce a product or service, which is the sum of process time, inspection time, move time, and wait time; also called *throughput time. (p. 742)*

Date of declaration Date the directors vote to pay a dividend. *(p. 513)*

Date of payment Date the corporation makes the dividend payment. *(p. 513)*

Date of record Date directors specify for identifying stockholders to receive dividends. *(p. 513)*

Days' sales in inventory Estimate of number of days needed to convert inventory into receivables or cash; equals ending inventory divided by cost of goods sold and then multiplied by 365; also called *days' stock on hand. (p. 237)*

Days' sales uncollected Measure of the liquidity of receivables computed by dividing the current balance of receivables by the annual credit (or net) sales and then multiplying by 365; also called *days' sales in receivables. (p. 332)*

Debit Recorded on the left side; an entry that increases asset and expense accounts, and decreases liability, revenue, and most equity accounts; abbreviated Dr. *(p. 53)*

Debit memorandum Notification that the sender has debited the recipient's account in the sender's records. *(p. 182)*

Debt ratio Ratio of total liabilities to total assets; used to reflect risk associated with a company's debts. *(p. 67)*

Debt-to-equity ratio Defined as total liabilities divided by total equity; shows the proportion of a company financed by non-owners (creditors) in comparison with that financed by owners. *(p. 564)*

Debtors Individuals or organizations that owe money. *(p. 49)*

Declining-balance method Method that determines depreciation charge for the period by multiplying a depreciation rate (often twice the straight-line rate) by the asset's beginning-period book value. *(p. 398)*

Deferred income tax liability Corporation income taxes that are deferred until future years because of temporary differences between GAAP and tax rules. *(p. 457)*

Degree of operating leverage (DOL) Ratio of contribution margin divided by pretax income; used to assess the effect on income of changes in sales. *(p. 918)*

Departmental accounting system Accounting system that provides information useful in evaluating the profitability or cost effectiveness of a department. *(p. 858)*

Departmental contribution to overhead Amount by which a department's revenues exceed its direct expenses. *(p. 866)*

Depletion Process of allocating the cost of natural resources to periods when they are consumed and sold. *(p. 406)*

Deposit ticket Lists items such as currency, coins, and checks deposited and their corresponding dollar amounts. *(p. 326)*

Deposits in transit Deposits recorded by the company but not yet recorded by its bank. *(p. 329)*

Depreciable cost Cost of a plant asset less its salvage value.

Depreciation Expense created by allocating the cost of plant and equipment to periods in which they are used; represents the expense of using the asset. *(pp. 97 & 395)*

Diluted earnings per share Earnings per share calculation that requires dilutive securities be added to the denominator of the basic EPS calculation. *(p. 524)*

Dilutive securities Securities having the potential to increase common shares outstanding; examples are options, rights, convertible bonds, and convertible preferred stock. *(p. 524)*

Direct costs Costs incurred for the benefit of one specific cost object. *(p. 732)*

Direct expenses Expenses traced to a specific department (object) that are incurred for the sole benefit of that department. *(p. 859)*

Direct labor Efforts of employees who physically convert materials to finished product. *(p. 738)*

Direct labor costs Wages and salaries for direct labor that are separately and readily traced through the production process to finished goods. *(p. 738)*

Direct material Raw material that physically becomes part of the product and is clearly identified with specific products or batches of product. *(p. 738)*

Direct material costs Expenditures for direct material that are separately and readily traced through the production process to finished goods. *(p. 738)*

Direct method Presentation of net cash from operating activities for the statement of cash flows that lists major operating cash receipts less major operating cash payments. *(p. 634)*

Direct write-off method Method that records the loss from an uncollectible account receivable at the time it is determined to be uncollectible; no attempt is made to estimate bad debts. *(p. 361)*

Discount on bonds payable Difference between a bond's par value and its lower issue price or carrying value; occurs when the contract rate is less than the market rate. *(p. 553)*

Discount on note payable Difference between the face value of a note payable and the (lesser) amount borrowed; reflects the added interest to be paid on the note over its life.

Discount on stock Difference between the par value of stock and its issue price when issued at a price below par value. *(p. 511)*

Discount period Time period in which a cash discount is available and the buyer can make a reduced payment. *(p. 181)*

Discount rate Expected rate of return on investments; also called *cost of capital, hurdle rate,* or *required rate of return. (p. B-2)*

Discounts lost Expenses resulting from not taking advantage of cash discounts on purchases. *(p. 338)*

Dividend in arrears Unpaid dividend on cumulative preferred stock; must be paid before any regular dividends on preferred stock and before any dividends on common stock. *(p. 517)*

Dividend yield Ratio of the annual amount of cash dividends distributed to common shareholders relative to the common stock's market value (price). *(p. 525)*

Dividends Corporation's distributions of assets to its owners.

Double-declining-balance (DDB) depreciation Depreciation equals beginning book value multiplied by 2 times the straight-line rate.

Double-entry accounting Accounting system in which each transaction affects at least two accounts and has at least one debit and one credit. *(p. 53)*

Double taxation Corporate income is taxed and then its later distribution through dividends is normally taxed again for shareholders. *(p. 11)*

Earnings (See *net income.*)

Earnings per share (EPS) Amount of income earned by each share of a company's outstanding common stock; also called *net income per share. (p. 524)*

Effective interest method Allocates interest expense over the bond life to yield a constant rate of interest; interest expense for a period is found by multiplying the balance of the liability at the beginning of the period by the bond market rate at issuance; also called *interest method. (p. 569)*

Efficiency Company's productivity in using its assets; usually measured relative to how much revenue a certain level of assets generates. *(p. 681)*

Efficiency variance Difference between the actual quantity of an input and the standard quantity of that input. *(p. 993)*

Electronic funds transfer (EFT) Use of electronic communication to transfer cash from one party to another. *(p. 327)*

Employee benefits Additional compensation paid to or on behalf of employees, such as premiums for medical, dental, life, and disability insurance, and contributions to pension plans. *(p. 443)*

Employee earnings report Record of an employee's net pay, gross pay, deductions, and year-to-date payroll information. *(p. 454)*

Enterprise resource planning (ERP) software Programs that manage a company's vital operations, which range from order taking to production to accounting. *(p. 283)*

Entity Organization that, for accounting purposes, is separate from other organizations and individuals. *(p. 10)*

EOM Abbreviation for *end of month;* used to describe credit terms for credit transactions. *(p. 181)*

Equity Owner's claim on the assets of a business; equals the residual interest in an entity's assets after deducting liabilities; also called *net assets. (p. 13)*

Equity method Accounting method used for long-term investments when the investor has "significant influence" over the investee. *(p. 598)*

Equity ratio Portion of total assets provided by equity, computed as total equity divided by total assets. *(p. 695)*

Equity securities with controlling influence Long-term investment when the investor is able to exert controlling influence over the investee; investors owning 50% or more of voting stock are presumed to exert controlling influence. *(p. 599)*

Equity securities with significant influence Long-term investment when the investor is able to exert significant influence over the investee; investors owning 20 percent or more (but less than 50 percent) of voting stock are presumed to exert significant influence. *(p. 598)*

Equivalent units of production (EUP) Number of units that would be completed if all effort during a period had been applied to units that were started and finished. *(p. 815)*

Estimated liability Obligation of an uncertain amount that can be reasonably estimated. *(p. 443)*

Estimated line of cost behavior Line drawn on a graph to visually fit the relation between cost and sales. *(p. 906)*

Ethics Codes of conduct by which actions are judged as right or wrong, fair or unfair, honest or dishonest. *(pp. 8, 731)*

Events Happenings that both affect an organization's financial position and can be reliably measured. *(p. 14)*

Expanded accounting equation Assets = Liabilities + Equity; Equity equals [Owner capital − Owner withdrawals + Revenues − Expenses] for a noncorporation; Equity equals [Contributed capital + Retained earnings + Revenues − Expenses] for a corporation where dividends are subtracted from retained earnings. *(p. 13)*

Expenses Outflows or using up of assets as part of operations of a business to generate sales. *(p. 13)*

External transactions Exchanges of economic value between one entity and another entity. *(p. 13)*

External users Persons using accounting information who are not directly involved in running the organization. *(p. 5)*

Extraordinary gains or losses Gains or losses reported separately from continuing operations because they are both unusual and infrequent. *(p. 703)*

Extraordinary repairs Major repairs that extend the useful life of a plant asset beyond prior expectations; treated as a capital expenditure. *(p. 403)*

Factory overhead Factory activities supporting the production process that are not direct material or direct labor; also called *overhead* and *manufacturing overhead. (p. 738)*

Factory overhead costs Expenditures for factory overhead that cannot be separately or readily traced to finished goods; also called *overhead costs.* *(p. 738)*

Favorable variance Difference in actual revenues or expenses from the budgeted amount that contributes to a higher income. *(p. 981)*

Federal depository bank Bank authorized to accept deposits of amounts payable to the federal government. *(p. 452)*

Federal Insurance Contributions Act (FICA) Taxes Taxes assessed on both employers and employees; for Social Security and Medicare programs. *(p. 440)*

Federal Unemployment Taxes (FUTA) Payroll taxes on employers assessed by the federal government to support its unemployment insurance program. *(p. 442)*

FIFO method (See *first-in, first-out.*)

Financial accounting Area of accounting mainly aimed at serving external users. *(p. 5)*

Financial Accounting Standards Board (FASB) Independent group of full-time members responsible for setting accounting rules. *(p. 9)*

Financial leverage Earning a higher return on equity by paying dividends on preferred stock or interest on debt at a rate lower than the return earned with the assets from issuing preferred stock or debt; also called *trading on the equity.* *(p. 519)*

Financial reporting Process of communicating information relevant to investors, creditors, and others in making investment, credit, and business decisions. *(p. 681)*

Financial statement analysis Application of analytical tools to general-purpose financial statements and related data for making business decisions. *(p. 680)*

Financial statements Includes the balance sheet, income statement, statement of owner's (or stockholders') equity, and statement of cash flows. *(p. 17)*

Financing activities Transactions with owners and creditors that include obtaining cash from issuing debt, repaying amounts borrowed, and obtaining cash from or distributing cash to owners. *(p. 630)*

Finished goods inventory Account that controls the finished goods files, which acts as a subsidiary ledger (of the Inventory account) in which the costs of finished goods that are ready for sale are recorded. *(pp. 736 & 772)*

First-in, first-out (FIFO) Method to assign cost to inventory that assumes items are sold in the order acquired; earliest items purchased are the first sold. *(pp. 229, 827)*

Fiscal year Consecutive 12-month (or 52-week) period chosen as the organization's annual accounting period. *(p. 93)*

Fixed budget Planning budget based on a single predicted amount of volume; unsuitable for evaluations if the actual volume differs from predicted volume. *(p. 981)*

Fixed budget performance report Report that compares actual revenues and costs with fixed budgeted amounts and identifies the differences as favorable or unfavorable variances. *(p. 981)*

Fixed cost Cost that does not change with changes in the volume of activity. *(p. 732)*

Flexibility principle Information system principle that prescribes an accounting system be able to adapt to changes in the company, its operations, and needs of decision makers. *(p. 269)*

Flexible budget Budget prepared (using actual volume) once a period is complete that helps managers evaluate past performance; uses fixed and variable costs in determining total costs. *(p. 982)*

Flexible budget performance report Report that compares actual revenues and costs with their variable budgeted amounts based on actual sales volume (or other level of activity) and identifies the differences as variances. *(p. 958)*

FOB Abbreviation for *free on board;* the point when ownership of goods passes to the buyer; *FOB shipping point* (or *factory*) means the buyer pays shipping costs and accepts ownership of goods when the seller transfers goods to carrier; *FOB destination* means the seller pays shipping costs and buyer accepts ownership of goods at the buyer's place of business. *(p. 183)*

Foreign exchange rate Price of one currency stated in terms of another currency. *(p. 605)*

Form 940 IRS form used to report an employer's federal unemployment taxes (FUTA) on an annual filing basis. *(p. 452)*

Form 941 IRS form filed to report FICA taxes owed and remitted. *(p. 450)*

Form 10-K (or 10-KSB) Annual report form filed with SEC by businesses (small businesses) with publicly traded securities. *(p. A-1)*

Form W-2 Annual report by an employer to each employee showing the employee's wages subject to FICA and federal income taxes along with amounts withheld. *(p. 452)*

Form W-4 Withholding allowance certificate, filed with the employer, identifying the number of withholding allowances claimed. *(p. 454)*

Franchises Privileges granted by a company or government to sell a product or service under specified conditions. *(p. 408)*

Full disclosure principle Principle that prescribes financial statements (including notes) to report all relevant information about an entity's operations and financial condition. *(p. 10)*

GAAP (See *generally accepted accounting principles.*)

General accounting system Accounting system for manufacturing activities based on the *periodic* inventory system. *(p. 770)*

General and administrative expenses Expenses that support the operating activities of a business. *(p. 191)*

General and administrative expense budget Plan that shows predicted operating expenses not included in the selling expenses budget. *(p. 948)*

General journal All-purpose journal for recording the debits and credits of transactions and events. *(pp. 54 & 272)*

General ledger (See *ledger.*)

General partner Partner who assumes unlimited liability for the debts of the partnership; responsible for partnership management. *(p. 479)*

General partnership Partnership in which all partners have mutual agency and unlimited liability for partnership debts. *(p. 479)*

Generally accepted accounting principles (GAAP) Rules that specify acceptable accounting practices. *(p. 8)*

Generally accepted auditing standards (GAAS) Rules that specify acceptable auditing practices.

General-purpose financial statements Statements published periodically for use by a variety of interested parties; includes the income statement, balance sheet, statement of owner's equity (or statement of retained earnings for a corporation), statement of cash flows, and notes to these statements. *(p. 681)*

Going-concern assumption Principle that prescribes financial statements to reflect the assumption that the business will continue operating. *(p. 10)*

Goods in process inventory Account in which costs are accumulated for products that are in the process of being produced but are not yet complete; also called *work in process inventory*. *(pp. 736 & 772)*

Goodwill Amount by which a company's (or a segment's) value exceeds the value of its individual assets less its liabilities. *(p. 409)*

Gross margin (See *gross profit*.)

Gross margin ratio Gross margin (net sales minus cost of goods sold) divided by net sales; also called *gross profit ratio*. *(p. 193)*

Gross method Method of recording purchases at the full invoice price without deducting any cash discounts. *(p. 338)*

Gross pay Total compensation earned by an employee. *(p. 440)*

Gross profit Net sales minus cost of goods sold; also called *gross margin*. *(p. 178)*

Gross profit method Procedure to estimate inventory when the past gross profit rate is used to estimate cost of goods sold, which is then subtracted from the cost of goods available for sale. *(p. 248)*

Held-to-maturity (HTM) securities Debt securities that a company has the intent and ability to hold until they mature. *(p. 596)*

High-low method Procedure that yields an estimated line of cost behavior by graphically connecting costs associated with the highest and lowest sales volume. *(p. 906)*

Horizontal analysis Comparison of a company's financial condition and performance across time. *(p. 682)*

Hurdle rate Minimum acceptable rate of return (set by management) for an investment. *(pp. 868 & 1033)*

Impairment Diminishment of an asset value. *(pp. 402 & 407)*

Imprest system Method to account for petty cash; maintains a constant balance in the fund, which equals cash plus petty cash receipts.

Inadequacy Condition in which the capacity of plant assets is too small to meet the company's production demands. *(p. 395)*

Income (See *net income*.)

Income statement Financial statement that subtracts expenses from revenues to yield a net income or loss over a specified period of time; also includes any gains or losses. *(p. 17)*

Income Summary Temporary account used only in the closing process to which the balances of revenue and expense accounts (including any gains or losses) are transferred; its balance is transferred to the capital account (or retained earnings for a corporation). *(p. 141)*

Incremental cost Additional cost incurred only if a company pursues a specific course of action. *(p. 1036)*

Indefinite life Asset life that is not limited by legal, regulatory, contractual, competitive, economic, or other factors. *(p. 407)*

Indirect costs Costs incurred for the benefit of more than one cost object. *(p. 732)*

Indirect expenses Expenses incurred for the joint benefit of more than one department (or cost object). *(p. 859)*

Indirect labor Efforts of production employees who do not work specifically on converting direct materials into finished products and who are not clearly identified with specific units or batches of product. *(p. 738)*

Indirect labor costs Labor costs that cannot be physically traced to production of a product or service; included as part of overhead. *(p. 738)*

Indirect material Material used to support the production process but not clearly identified with products or batches of product. *(p. 735)*

Indirect method Presentation that reports net income and then adjusts it by adding and subtracting items to yield net cash from operating activities on the statement of cash flows. *(p. 634)*

Information processor Component of an accounting system that interprets, transforms, and summarizes information for use in analysis and reporting. *(p. 270)*

Information storage Component of an accounting system that keeps data in a form accessible to information processors. *(p. 270)*

Infrequent gain or loss Gain or loss not expected to recur given the operating environment of the business. *(p. 703)*

Input device Means of capturing information from source documents that enables its transfer to information processors. *(p. 270)*

Installment note Liability requiring a series of periodic payments to the lender. *(p. 560)*

Institute of Management Accountants (IMA) A professional association of management accountants. *(p. 731)*

Intangible assets Long-term assets (resources) used to produce or sell products or services; usually lack physical form and have uncertain benefits. *(pp. 147 & 407)*

Interest Charge for using money (or other assets) loaned from one entity to another. *(p. 368)*

Interim financial statements Financial statements covering periods of less than one year; usually based on one-, three-, or six-month periods. *(pp. 92 & 247)*

Internal controls or **Internal control system** All policies and procedures used to protect assets, ensure reliable accounting, promote efficient operations, and urge adherence to company policies. *(pp. 268 & 314)*

Internal rate of return (IRR) Rate used to evaluate the acceptability of an investment; equals the rate that yields a net present value of zero for an investment. *(p. 1031)*

Internal transactions Activities within an organization that can affect the accounting equation. *(p. 13)*

Internal users Persons using accounting information who are directly involved in managing the organization. *(p. 6)*

International Accounting Standards Board (IASB) Group that identifies preferred accounting practices and encourages global acceptance; issues International Financial Reporting Standards (IFRS). *(p. 9)*

Inventory Goods a company owns and expects to sell in its normal operations. *(p. 179)*

Inventory turnover Number of times a company's average inventory is sold during a period; computed by dividing cost of goods sold by average inventory; also called *merchandise turnover*. *(p. 236)*

Investing activities Transactions that involve purchasing and selling of long-term assets, includes making and collecting notes receivable and investments in other than cash equivalents. *(p. 630)*

Investment center Center of which a manager is responsible for revenues, costs, and asset investments. *(p. 858)*

Investment center residual income The net income an investment center earns above a target return on average invested assets. *(p. 867)*

Investment center return on total assets Center net income divided by average total assets for the center. *(p. 867)*

Investment turnover The efficiency with which a company generates sales from its available assets; computed as sales divided by average invested assets. *(p. 872)*

Invoice Itemized record of goods prepared by the vendor that lists the customer's name, items sold, sales prices, and terms of sale. *(p. 335)*

Invoice approval Document containing a checklist of steps necessary for approving the recording and payment of an invoice; also called *check authorization*. *(p. 336)*

Job Production of a customized product or service. *(p. 770)*

Job cost sheet Separate record maintained for each job. *(p. 772)*

Job lot Production of more than one unit of a customized product or service. *(p. 771)*

Job order cost accounting system Cost accounting system to determine the cost of producing each job or job lot. *(pp. 772 & 811)*

Job order production Production of special-order products; also called *customized production*. *(p. 770)*

Joint cost Cost incurred to produce or purchase two or more products at the same time. *(p. 877)*

Journal Record in which transactions are entered before they are posted to ledger accounts; also called *book of original entry*. *(p. 54)*

Journalizing Process of recording transactions in a journal. *(p. 54)*

Just-in-time (JIT) manufacturing Process of acquiring or producing inventory only when needed. *(p. 730)*

Known liabilities Obligations of a company with little uncertainty; set by agreements, contracts, or laws; also called *definitely determinable liabilities*. *(p. 436)*

Land improvements Assets that increase the benefits of land, have a limited useful life, and are depreciated. *(p. 394)*

Large stock dividend Stock dividend that is more than 25% of the previously outstanding shares. *(p. 514)*

Last-in, first-out (LIFO) Method to assign cost to inventory that assumes costs for the most recent items purchased are sold first and charged to cost of goods sold. *(p. 229)*

Lean business model Practice of eliminating waste while meeting customer needs and yielding positive company returns. *(p. 730)*

Lease Contract specifying the rental of property. *(pp. 409 & 573)*

Leasehold Rights the lessor grants to the lessee under the terms of a lease. *(p. 409)*

Leasehold improvements Alterations or improvements to leased property such as partitions and storefronts. *(p. 409)*

Least-squares regression Statistical method for deriving an estimated line of cost behavior that is more precise than the high-low method and the scatter diagram. *(p. 907)*

Ledger Record containing all accounts (with amounts) for a business; also called *general ledger*. *(p. 49)*

Lessee Party to a lease who secures the right to possess and use the property from another party (the lessor). *(p. 409)*

Lessor Party to a lease who grants another party (the lessee) the right to possess and use its property. *(p. 409)*

Liabilities Creditors' claims on an organization's assets; involves a probable future payment of assets, products, or services that a company is obligated to make due to past transactions or events. *(p. 12)*

Licenses (See *franchises*.) *(p. 408)*

Limited liability Owner can lose no more than the amount invested. *(p. 11)*

Limited liability company Organization form that combines select features of a corporation and a limited partnership; provides limited liability to its members (owners), is free of business tax, and allows members to actively participate in management. *(p. 480)*

Limited liability partnership Partnership in which a partner is not personally liable for malpractice or negligence unless that partner is responsible for providing the service that resulted in the claim. *(p. 479)*

Limited life (See *useful life*.)

Limited partners Partners who have no personal liability for partnership debts beyond the amounts they invested in the partnership. *(p. 479)*

Limited partnership Partnership that has two classes of partners, limited partners and general partners. *(p. 479)*

Liquid assets Resources such as cash that are easily converted into other assets or used to pay for goods, services, or liabilities. *(p. 319)*

Liquidating cash dividend Distribution of assets that returns part of the original investment to stockholders; deducted from contributed capital accounts. *(p. 514)*

Liquidation Process of going out of business; involves selling assets, paying liabilities, and distributing remainder to owners.

Liquidity Availability of resources to meet short-term cash requirements. *(pp. 319 & 681)*

List price Catalog (full) price of an item before any trade discount is deducted. *(p. 180)*

Long-term investments Long-term assets not used in operating activities such as notes receivable and investments in stocks and bonds. *(pp. 147 & 592)*

Long-term liabilities Obligations not due to be paid within one year or the operating cycle, whichever is longer. *(pp. 147 & 435)*

Lower of cost or market (LCM) Required method to report inventory at market replacement cost when that market cost is lower than recorded cost. *(p. 233)*

Maker of the note Entity who signs a note and promises to pay it at maturity. *(p. 368)*

Management by exception Management process to focus on significant variances and give less attention to areas where performance is close to the standard. *(p. 996)*

Managerial accounting Area of accounting mainly aimed at serving the decision-making needs of internal users; also called *management accounting*. *(pp. 6 & 726)*

Manufacturer Company that uses labor and operating assets to convert raw materials to finished goods. *(p. 13)*

Manufacturing budget Plan that shows the predicted costs for direct materials, direct labor, and overhead to be incurred in manufacturing units in the production budget. *(p. 959)*

Manufacturing statement Report that summarizes the types and amounts of costs incurred in a company's production process for a period; also called *cost of goods manufacturing statement*. *(p. 740)*

Margin of safety Excess of expected sales over the level of break-even sales. *(p. 914)*

Market prospects Expectations (both good and bad) about a company's future performance as assessed by users and other interested parties. *(p. 681)*

Market rate Interest rate that borrowers are willing to pay and lenders are willing to accept for a specific lending agreement given the borrowers' risk level. *(p. 553)*

Market value per share Price at which stock is bought or sold. *(p. 509)*

Master budget Comprehensive business plan that includes specific plans for expected sales, product units to be produced, merchandise (or materials) to be purchased, expenses to be incurred, plant assets to be purchased, and amounts of cash to be borrowed or loans to be repaid, as well as a budgeted income statement and balance sheet. *(p. 944)*

Matching principle Prescribes expenses to be reported in the same period as the revenues that were earned as a result of the expenses. *(pp. 10 & 362)*

Materiality constraint Prescribes that accounting for items that significantly impact financial statement and any inferences from them adhere strictly to GAAP. *(p. 362)*

Materials consumption report Document that summarizes the materials a department uses during a reporting period; replaces materials requisitions. *(p. 812)*

Materials ledger card Perpetual record updated each time units are purchased or issued for production use. *(p. 773)*

Materials requisition Source document production managers use to request materials for production; used to assign materials costs to specific jobs or overhead. *(p. 774)*

Maturity date of a note Date when a note's principal and interest are due. *(p. 368)*

Merchandise (See *merchandise inventory*.)

Merchandise inventory Goods that a company owns and expects to sell to customers; also called *merchandise* or *inventory*. *(p. 179)*

Merchandise purchases budget Plan that shows the units or costs of merchandise to be purchased by a merchandising company during the budget period. *(p. 947)*

Merchandiser Entity that earns net income by buying and selling merchandise. *(p. 178)*

Merit rating Rating assigned to an employer by a state based on the employer's record of employment. *(p. 442)*

Minimum legal capital Amount of assets defined by law that stockholders must (potentially) invest in a corporation; usually defined as par value of the stock; intended to protect creditors. *(p. 509)*

Mixed cost Cost that behaves like a combination of fixed and variable costs. *(p. 903)*

Modified Accelerated Cost Recovery System (MACRS) Depreciation system required by federal income tax law. *(p. 400)*

Monetary unit assumption Principle that assumes transactions and events can be expressed in money units. *(p. 10)*

Mortgage Legal loan agreement that protects a lender by giving the lender the right to be paid from the cash proceeds from the sale of a borrower's assets identified in the mortgage. *(p. 562)*

Multinational Company that operates in several countries. *(p. 605)*

Multiple-step income statement Income statement format that shows subtotals between sales and net income, categorizes expenses, and often reports the details of net sales and expenses. *(p. 191)*

Mutual agency Legal relationship among partners whereby each partner is an agent of the partnership and is able to bind the partnership to contracts within the scope of the partnership's business. *(p. 478)*

Natural business year Twelve-month period that ends when a company's sales activities are at their lowest point. *(p. 93)*

Natural resources Assets physically consumed when used; examples are timber, mineral deposits, and oil and gas fields; also called *wasting assets*. *(p. 406)*

Net assets (See *equity*.)

Net income Amount earned after subtracting all expenses necessary for and matched with sales for a period; also called *income, profit*, or *earnings*. *(p. 13)*

Net loss Excess of expenses over revenues for a period. *(p. 18)*

Net method Method of recording purchases at the full invoice price less any cash discounts. *(p. 338)*

Net pay Gross pay less all deductions; also called *take-home pay*. *(p. 440)*

Net present value (NPV) Dollar estimate of an asset's value that is used to evaluate the acceptability of an investment; computed by discounting future cash flows from the investment at a satisfactory rate and then subtracting the initial cost of the investment. *(p. 1029)*

Net realizable value Expected selling price (value) of an item minus the cost of making the sale. *(p. 224)*

Noncumulative preferred stock Preferred stock on which the right to receive dividends is lost for any period when dividends are not declared. *(p. 517)*

Noninterest-bearing note Note with no stated (contract) rate of interest; interest is implicitly included in the note's face value.

Nonparticipating preferred stock Preferred stock on which dividends are limited to a maximum amount each year. *(p. 518)*

No-par value stock Stock class that has not been assigned a par (or stated) value by the corporate charter. *(p. 509)*

Nonsufficient funds (NSF) check Maker's bank account has insufficient money to pay the check; also called *hot check*.

Non-value-added time The portion of cycle time that is not directed at producing a product or service; equals the sum of inspection time, move time, and wait time. *(p. 743)*

Not controllable costs Costs that a manager does not have the power to control or strongly influence. *(p. 733)*

Note (See promissory note.)

Note payable Liability expressed by a written promise to pay a definite sum of money on demand or on a specific future date(s).

Note receivable Asset consisting of a written promise to receive a definite sum of money on demand or on a specific future date(s).

Objectivity principle Principle that prescribes independent, unbiased evidence to support financial statement information. *(p. 9)*

Obsolescence Condition in which, because of new inventions and improvements, a plant asset can no longer be used to produce goods or services with a competitive advantage. *(p. 395)*

Off-balance-sheet financing Acquisition of assets by agreeing to liabilities not reported on the balance sheet. *(p. 574)*

Online processing Approach to inputting data from source documents as soon as the information is available. *(p. 282)*

Operating activities Activities that involve the production or purchase of merchandise and the sale of goods or services to customers, including expenditures related to administering the business. *(p. 629)*

Operating cycle Normal time between paying cash for merchandise or employee services and receiving cash from customers. *(p. 145)*

Operating leases Short-term (or cancelable) leases in which the lessor retains risks and rewards of ownership. *(p. 573)*

Operating leverage Extent, or relative size, of fixed costs in the total cost structure. *(p. 918)*

Opportunity cost Potential benefit lost by choosing a specific action from two or more alternatives. *(p. 733)*

Ordinary repairs Repairs to keep a plant asset in normal, good operating condition; treated as a revenue expenditure and immediately expensed. *(p. 402)*

Organization expenses (costs) Costs such as legal fees and promoter fees to bring an entity into existence. *(pp. 507 & 512)*

Out-of-pocket cost Cost incurred or avoided as a result of management's decisions. *(p. 733)*

Output devices Means by which information is taken out of the accounting system and made available for use. *(p. 271)*

Outsourcing Manager decision to buy a product or service from another entity; part of a *make-or-buy* decision; also called *make or buy*.

Outstanding checks Checks written and recorded by the depositor but not yet paid by the bank at the bank statement date. *(p. 329)*

Outstanding stock Corporation's stock held by its shareholders.

Overapplied overhead Amount by which the overhead applied to production in a period using the predetermined overhead rate exceeds the actual overhead incurred in a period. *(p. 782)*

Overhead cost variance Difference between the total overhead cost applied to products and the total overhead cost actually incurred. *(p. 992)*

Owner, Capital Account showing the owner's claim on company assets; equals owner investments plus net income (or less net losses) minus owner withdrawals since the company's inception; also referred to as *equity*. *(p. 13)*

Owner investment Assets put into the business by the owner. *(p. 13)*

Owner's equity (See *equity*.)

Owner, Withdrawals Account used to record asset distributions to the owner. (See also *withdrawals*.) *(pp. 13 & 51)*

Paid-in capital (See *contributed capital*.) *(p. 510)*

Paid-in capital in excess of par value Amount received from issuance of stock that is in excess of the stock's par value. *(p. 511)*

Par value Value assigned a share of stock by the corporate charter when the stock is authorized. *(p. 509)*

Par value of a bond Amount the bond issuer agrees to pay at maturity and the amount on which cash interest payments are based; also called *face amount* or *face value* of a bond. *(p. 550)*

Par value stock Class of stock assigned a par value by the corporate charter. *(p. 509)*

Parent Company that owns a controlling interest in a corporation (requires more than 50% of voting stock). *(p. 599)*

Participating preferred stock Preferred stock that shares with common stockholders any dividends paid in excess of the percent stated on preferred stock. *(p. 518)*

Partner return on equity Partner net income divided by average partner equity for the period. *(p. 490)*

Partnership Unincorporated association of two or more persons to pursue a business for profit as co-owners. *(pp. 10 & 478)*

Partnership contract Agreement among partners that sets terms under which the affairs of the partnership are conducted; also called *articles of partnership*. *(p. 478)*

Partnership liquidation Dissolution of a partnership by (1) selling noncash assets and allocating any gain or loss according to partners' income-and-loss ratio, (2) paying liabilities, and (3) distributing any remaining cash according to partners' capital balances. *(p. 488)*

Patent Exclusive right granted to its owner to produce and sell an item or to use a process for 17 years. *(p. 408)*

Payback period (PBP) Time-based measurement used to evaluate the acceptability of an investment; equals the time expected to pass before an investment's net cash flows equal its initial cost. *(p. 1025)*

Payee of the note Entity to whom a note is made payable. *(p. 368)*

Payroll bank account Bank account used solely for paying employees; each pay period an amount equal to the total employees' net pay is deposited in it and the payroll checks are drawn on it. *(p. 454)*

Payroll deductions Amounts withheld from an employee's gross pay; also called *withholdings. (p. 440)*

Payroll register Record for a pay period that shows the pay period dates, regular and overtime hours worked, gross pay, net pay, and deductions. *(p. 452)*

Pension plan Contractual agreement between an employer and its employees for the employer to provide benefits to employees after they retire; expensed when incurred. *(p. 575)*

Period costs Expenditures identified more with a time period than with finished products costs; includes selling and general administrative expenses. *(p. 733)*

Periodic inventory system Method that records the cost of inventory purchased but does not continuously track the quantity available or sold to customers; records are updated at the end of each period to reflect the physical count and costs of goods available. *(p. 180)*

Permanent accounts Accounts that reflect activities related to one or more future periods; balance sheet accounts whose balances are not closed; also called *real accounts. (p. 140)*

Perpetual inventory system Method that maintains continuous records of the cost of inventory available and the cost of goods sold. *(p. 180)*

Petty cash Small amount of cash in a fund to pay minor expenses; accounted for using an imprest system. *(p. 323)*

Planning Process of setting goals and preparing to achieve them. *(p. 726)*

Plant assets Tangible long-lived assets used to produce or sell products and services; also called *property, plant and equipment (PP&E)* or *fixed assets. (p. 403)*

Pledged assets to secured liabilities Ratio of the book value of a company's pledged assets to the book value of its secured liabilities.

Post-closing trial balance List of permanent accounts and their balances from the ledger after all closing entries are journalized and posted. *(p. 144)*

Posting Process of transferring journal entry information to the ledger; computerized systems automate this process. *(p. 54)*

Posting reference (PR) column A column in journals in which individual ledger account numbers are entered when entries are posted to those ledger accounts. *(p. 56)*

Predetermined overhead rate Rate established prior to the beginning of a period that relates estimated overhead to another variable, such as estimated direct labor, and is used to assign overhead cost to production. *(p. 778)*

Preemptive right Stockholders' right to maintain their proportionate interest in a corporation with any additional shares issued. *(p. 508)*

Preferred stock Stock with a priority status over common stockholders in one or more ways, such as paying dividends or distributing assets. *(p. 516)*

Premium on bonds Difference between a bond's par value and its higher carrying value; occurs when the contract rate is higher than the market rate; also called *bond premium. (p. 556)*

Premium on stock (See *contributed capital in excess of par value.) (p. 511)*

Prepaid expenses Items paid for in advance of receiving their benefits; classified as assets. *(p. 95)*

Price-earnings (PE) ratio Ratio of a company's current market value per share to its earnings per share; also called *price-to-earnings. (p. 525)*

Price variance Difference between actual and budgeted revenue or cost caused by the difference between the actual price per unit and the budgeted price per unit. *(p. 984)*

Prime costs Expenditures directly identified with the production of finished goods; include direct materials costs and direct labor costs. *(p. 738)*

Principal of a note Amount that the signer of a note agrees to pay back when it matures, not including interest. *(p. 368)*

Principles of internal control Principles prescribing management to establish responsibility, maintain records, insure assets, separate recordkeeping from custody of assets, divide responsibility for related transactions, apply technological controls, and perform reviews. *(p. 315)*

Prior period adjustment Correction of an error in a prior year that is reported in the statement of retained earnings (or statement of stockholders' equity) net of any income tax effects. *(p. 523)*

Pro forma financial statements Statements that show the effects of proposed transactions and events as if they had occurred. *(p. 140)*

Process cost accounting system System of assigning direct materials, direct labor, and overhead to specific processes; total costs associated with each process are then divided by the number of units passing through that process to determine the cost per equivalent unit. *(p. 811)*

Process cost summary Report of costs charged to a department, its equivalent units of production achieved, and the costs assigned to its output. *(p. 820)*

Process operations Processing of products in a continuous (sequential) flow of steps; also called *process manufacturing* or *process production. (p. 808)*

Product costs Costs that are capitalized as inventory because they produce benefits expected to have future value; include direct materials, direct labor, and overhead. *(p. 733)*

Production budget Plan that shows the units to be produced each period. *(p. 959)*

Profit (See *net income.*)

Profit center Business unit that incurs costs and generates revenues. *(p. 858)*

Profit margin Ratio of a company's net income to its net sales; the percent of income in each dollar of revenue; also called *net profit margin. (pp. 106 & 872)*

Profitability Company's ability to generate an adequate return on invested capital. *(p. 681)*

Profitability index A measure of the relation between the expected benefits of a project and its investment, computed as the present value of expected future cash flows from the investment divided by the cost of the investment; a higher value indicates a more desirable investment, and a value below 1 indicates an unacceptable project. *(p. 1031)*

Promissory note (or **note**) Written promise to pay a specified amount either on demand or at a definite future date; is a *note receivable* for the lender but a *note payable* for the lendee. *(p. 368)*

Proprietorship (See *sole proprietorship.*)

Proxy Legal document giving a stockholder's agent the power to exercise the stockholder's voting rights. *(p. 507)*

Purchase discount Term used by a purchaser to describe a cash discount granted to the purchaser for paying within the discount period. *(p. 181)*

Purchase order Document used by the purchasing department to place an order with a seller (vendor). *(p. 335)*

Purchase requisition Document listing merchandise needed by a department and requesting it be purchased. *(p. 335)*

Purchases journal Journal normally used to record all purchases on credit. *(p. 279)*

Quantity variance Difference between actual and budgeted revenue or cost caused by the difference between the actual number of units and the budgeted number of units. *(p. 984)*

Ratio analysis Determination of key relations between financial statement items as reflected in numerical measures. *(p. 682)*

Raw materials inventory Goods a company acquires to use in making products. *(p. 735)*

Realizable value Expected proceeds from converting an asset into cash. *(p. 363)*

Receiving report Form used to report that ordered goods are received and to describe their quantity and condition. *(p. 336)*

Recordkeeping Part of accounting that involves recording transactions and events, either manually or electronically; also called *bookkeeping*. *(p. 4)*

Registered bonds Bonds owned by investors whose names and addresses are recorded by the issuer; interest payments are made to the registered owners. *(p. 563)*

Relevance principle Information system principle prescribing that its reports be useful, understandable, timely, and pertinent for decision making. *(p. 268)*

Relevant benefits Additional or incremental revenue generated by selecting a particular course of action over another. *(p. 1035)*

Relevant range of operations Company's normal operating range; excludes extremely high and low volumes not likely to occur. *(p. 911)*

Report form balance sheet Balance sheet that lists accounts vertically in the order of assets, liabilities, and equity. *(p. 18)*

Responsibility accounting budget Report of expected costs and expenses under a manager's control. *(p. 870)*

Responsibility accounting performance report Responsibility report that compares actual costs and expenses for a department with budgeted amounts. *(p. 870)*

Responsibility accounting system System that provides information that management can use to evaluate the performance of a department's manager. *(p. 858)*

Restricted retained earnings Retained earnings not available for dividends because of legal or contractual limitations. *(p. 510)*

Retail inventory method Method to estimate ending inventory based on the ratio of the amount of goods for sale at cost to the amount of goods for sale at retail. *(p. 247)*

Retailer Intermediary that buys products from manufacturers or wholesalers and sells them to consumers. *(p. 178)*

Retained earnings Cumulative income less cumulative losses and dividends. *(p. 510)*

Retained earnings deficit Debit (abnormal) balance in Retained Earnings; occurs when cumulative losses and dividends exceed cumulative income; also called *accumulated deficit*. *(p. 513)*

Return Monies received from an investment; often in percent form. *(p. 23)*

Return on assets (See *return on total assets*) *(p. 20)*

Return on equity Ratio of net income to average equity for the period.

Return on total assets Ratio reflecting operating efficiency; defined as net income divided by average total assets for the period; also called *return on assets* or *return on investment*. *(p. 600)*

Revenue expenditures Expenditures reported on the current income statement as an expense because they do not provide benefits in future periods. *(p. 402)*

Revenue recognition principle The principle prescribing that revenue is recognized when earned. *(p. 10)*

Revenues Gross increase in equity from a company's business activities that earn income; also called *sales*. *(p. 13)*

Reverse stock split Occurs when a corporation calls in its stock and replaces each share with less than one new share; increases both market value per share and any par or stated value per share. *(p. 516)*

Reversing entries Optional entries recorded at the beginning of a period that prepare the accounts for the usual journal entries as if adjusting entries had not occurred in the prior period. *(p. 151)*

Risk Uncertainty about an expected return. *(p. 24)*

Rolling budget New set of budgets a firm adds for the next period (with revisions) to replace the ones that have lapsed. *(p. 942)*

S corporation Corporation that meets special tax qualifications so as to be treated like a partnership for income tax purposes. *(p. 480)*

Safety stock Quantity of inventory or materials over the minimum needed to satisfy budgeted demand. *(p. 947)*

Sales (See *revenues*.)

Sales budget Plan showing the units of goods to be sold or services to be provided; the starting point in the budgeting process for most departments. *(p. 946)*

Sales discount Term used by a seller to describe a cash discount granted to buyers who pay within the discount period. *(p. 181)*

Sales journal Journal normally used to record sales of goods on credit. *(p. 274)*

Sales mix Ratio of sales volumes for the various products sold by a company. *(p. 915)*

Salvage value Estimate of amount to be recovered at the end of an asset's useful life; also called *residual value* or *scrap value*. *(p. 395)*

Sarbanes-Oxley Act (SOX) Created the Public *Company Accounting Oversight Board*, regulates analyst conflicts, imposes corporate governance requirements, enhances accounting and control disclosures, impacts insider transactions and executive loans, establishes new types of criminal conduct, and expands penalties for violations of federal securities laws. *(pp. 11 & 314)*

Scatter diagram Graph used to display data about past cost behavior and sales as points on a diagram. *(p. 905)*

Schedule of accounts payable List of the balances of all accounts in the accounts payable ledger and their total. *(p. 280)*

Schedule of accounts receivable List of the balances for all accounts in the accounts receivable ledger and their total. *(p. 275)*

Secured bonds Bonds that have specific assets of the issuer pledged as collateral. *(p. 563)*

Securities and Exchange Commission (SEC) Federal agency Congress has charged to set reporting rules for organizations that sell ownership shares to the public. *(p. 9)*

Segment return on assets Segment operating income divided by segment average (identifiable) assets for the period. *(p. 284)*

Selling expense budget Plan that lists the types and amounts of selling expenses expected in the budget period. *(p. 948)*

Selling expenses Expenses of promoting sales, such as displaying and advertising merchandise, making sales, and delivering goods to customers. *(p. 191)*

Serial bonds Bonds consisting of separate amounts that mature at different dates. *(p. 563)*

Service company Organization that provides services instead of tangible products.

Shareholders Owners of a corporation; also called *stockholders*. *(p. 11)*

Shares Equity of a corporation divided into ownership units; also called *stock. (p. 11)*

Short-term investments Debt and equity securities that management expects to convert to cash within the next 3 to 12 months (or the operating cycle if longer); also called *temporary investments* or *marketable securities. (p. 592)*

Short-term note payable Current obligation in the form of a written promissory note. *(p. 437)*

Shrinkage Inventory losses that occur as a result of theft or deterioration. *(p. 188)*

Signature card Includes the signatures of each person authorized to sign checks on the bank account. *(p. 326)*

Simple capital structure Capital structure that consists of only common stock and nonconvertible preferred stock; consists of no dilutive securities. *(p. 524)*

Single-step income statement Income statement format that includes cost of goods sold as an expense and shows only one subtotal for total expenses. *(p. 192)*

Sinking fund bonds Bonds that require the issuer to make deposits to a separate account; bondholders are repaid at maturity from that account. *(p. 563)*

Small stock dividend Stock dividend that is 25% or less of a corporation's previously outstanding shares. *(p. 514)*

Social responsibility Being accountable for the impact that one's actions might have on society. *(p. 8)*

Sole proprietorship Business owned by one person that is not organized as a corporation; also called *proprietorship. (p. 10)*

Solvency Company's long-run financial viability and its ability to cover long-term obligations. *(p. 681)*

Source documents Source of information for accounting entries that can be in either paper or electronic form; also called *business papers. (p. 49)*

Special journal Any journal used for recording and posting transactions of a similar type. *(p. 272)*

Specific identification Method to assign cost to inventory when the purchase cost of each item in inventory is identified and used to compute cost of inventory. *(p. 227)*

Spending variance Difference between the actual price of an item and its standard price. *(p. 993)*

Spreadsheet Computer program that organizes data by means of formulas and format; also called *electronic work sheet.*

Standard costs Costs that should be incurred under normal conditions to produce a product or component or to perform a service. *(p. 985)*

State Unemployment Taxes (SUTA) State payroll taxes on employers to support its unemployment programs. *(p. 442)*

Stated value stock No-par stock assigned a stated value per share; this amount is recorded in the stock account when the stock is issued. *(p. 510)*

Statement of cash flows A financial statement that lists cash inflows (receipts) and cash outflows (payments) during a period; arranged by operating, investing, and financing. *(p. 628)*

Statement of owner's equity Report of changes in equity over a period; adjusted for increases (owner investment and net income) and for decreases (withdrawals and net loss). *(p. 17)*

Statement of partners' equity Financial statement that shows total capital balances at the beginning of the period, any additional investment by partners, the income or loss of the period, the partners' withdrawals, and the partners' ending capital balances; also called *statement of partners' capital. (p. 483)*

Statement of retained earnings Report of changes in retained earnings over a period; adjusted for increases (net income), for decreases (dividends and net loss), and for any prior period adjustment. *(p. 7)*

Statement of stockholders' equity Financial statement that lists the beginning and ending balances of each major equity account and describes all changes in those accounts. *(p. 523)*

Statements of Financial Accounting Standards (SFAS) FASB publications that establish U.S. GAAP. *(p. 9)*

Step-wise cost Cost that remains fixed over limited ranges of volumes but changes by a lump sum when volume changes occur outside these limited ranges. *(p. 904).*

Stock (See *shares.*)

Stock dividend Corporation's distribution of its own stock to its stockholders without the receipt of any payment. *(p. 514)*

Stock options Rights to purchase common stock at a fixed price over a specified period of time. *(p. 523)*

Stock split Occurs when a corporation calls in its stock and replaces each share with more than one new share; decreases both the market value per share and any par or stated value per share. *(p. 516)*

Stock subscription Investor's contractual commitment to purchase unissued shares at future dates and prices.

Stockholders (See *shareholders.*) *(p. 11)*

Stockholders' equity A corporation's equity; also called *shareholders' equity* or *corporate capital*. *(p. 510)*

Straight-line depreciation Method that allocates an equal portion of the depreciable cost of plant asset (cost minus salvage) to each accounting period in its useful life. *(pp. 97 & 396)*

Straight-line bond amortization Method allocating an equal amount of bond interest expense to each period of the bond life. *(p. 554)*

Subsidiary Entity controlled by another entity (parent) in which the parent owns more than 50% of the subsidiary's voting stock. *(p. 599)*

Subsidiary ledger List of individual sub-accounts and amounts with a common characteristic; linked to a controlling account in the general ledger. *(p. 272)*

Sunk cost Cost already incurred and cannot be avoided or changed. *(p. 733)*

Supplementary records Information outside the usual accounting records; also called *supplemental records*. *(p. 184)*

Supply chain Linkages of services or goods extending from suppliers, to the company itself, and on to customers.

T-account Tool used to show the effects of transactions and events on individual accounts. *(p. 53)*

Target cost Maximum allowable cost for a product or service; defined as expected selling price less the desired profit. *(p. 771)*

Temporary accounts Accounts used to record revenues, expenses, and withdrawals (dividends for a corporation); they are closed at the end of each period; also called *nominal accounts*. *(p. 140)*

Term bonds Bonds scheduled for payment (maturity) at a single specified date. *(p. 563)*

Throughput time (See *cycle time.*)

Time period assumption Assumption that an organization's activities can be divided into specific time periods such as months, quarters, or years. *(p. 92)*

Time ticket Source document used to report the time an employee spent working on a job or on overhead activities and then to determine the amount of direct labor to charge to the job or the amount of indirect labor to charge to overhead. *(p. 776)*

Times interest earned Ratio of income before interest expense (and any income taxes) divided by interest expense; reflects risk of covering interest commitments when income varies. *(p. 447)*

Total asset turnover Measure of a company's ability to use its assets to generate sales; computed by dividing net sales by average total assets. *(p. 410)*

Total quality management (TQM) Concept calling for all managers and employees at all stages of operations to strive toward higher standards and reduce number of defects. *(p. 730)*

Trade discount Reduction from a list or catalog price that can vary for wholesalers, retailers, and consumers. *(p. 180)*

Trademark or **Trade (Brand) name** Symbol, name, phrase, or jingle identified with a company, product, or service. *(p. 408)*

Trading on the equity (See *financial leverage.*)

Trading securities Investments in debt and equity securities that the company intends to actively trade for profit. *(p. 595)*

Transaction Exchange of economic consideration affecting an entity's financial position that can be reliably measured. *(p. 13)*

Treasury stock Corporation's own stock that it reacquired and still holds. *(p. 520)*

Trial balance List of accounts and their balances at a point in time; total debit balances equal total credit balances. *(p. 63)*

Unadjusted trial balance List of accounts and balances prepared before accounting adjustments are recorded and posted. *(p. 104)*

Unavoidable expense Expense (or cost) that is not relevant for business decisions; an expense that would continue even if a department, product, or service is eliminated. *(p. 1041)*

Unclassified balance sheet Balance sheet that broadly groups assets, liabilities, and equity accounts. *(p. 145)*

Uncontrollable costs Costs that a manager does not have the power to determine or strongly influence. *(p. 870)*

Underapplied overhead Amount by which overhead incurred in a period exceeds the overhead applied to that period's production using the predetermined overhead rate. *(p. 781)*

Unearned revenue Liability created when customers pay in advance for products or services; earned when the products or services are later delivered. *(pp. 50 & 98)*

Unfavorable variance Difference in revenues or costs, when the actual amount is compared to the budgeted amount, that contributes to a lower income. *(p. 981)*

Unit contribution margin Amount a product's unit selling price exceeds its total unit variable cost.

Units-of-production depreciation Method that charges a varying amount to depreciation expense for each period of an asset's useful life depending on its usage. *(p. 397)*

Unlimited liability Legal relationship among general partners that makes each of them responsible for partnership debts if the other partners are unable to pay their shares. *(p. 479)*

Unrealized gain (loss) Gain (loss) not yet realized by an actual transaction or event such as a sale. *(p. 595)*

Unsecured bonds Bonds backed only by the issuer's credit standing; almost always riskier than secured bonds; also called *debentures*. *(p. 563)*

Unusual gain or loss Gain or loss that is abnormal or unrelated to the company's ordinary activities and environment. *(p. 703)*

Useful life Length of time an asset will be productively used in the operations of a business; also called *service life* or *limited life*. *(p. 395)*

Value-added time The portion of cycle time that is directed at producing a product or service; equals process time. *(p. 743)*

Value chain Sequential activities that add value to an entity's products or services; includes design, production, marketing, distribution, and service. *(p. 740)*

Variable cost Cost that changes in proportion to changes in the activity output volume. *(p. 732)*

Variance analysis Process of examining differences between actual and budgeted revenues or costs and describing them in terms of price and quantity differences. *(p. 984)*

Vendee Buyer of goods or services. *(p. 335)*

Vendor Seller of goods or services. *(p. 335)*

Vertical analysis Evaluation of each financial statement item or group of items in terms of a specific base amount. *(p. 682)*

Volume variance Difference between two dollar amounts of fixed overhead cost; one amount is the total budgeted overhead cost, and the other is the overhead cost allocated to products using the predetermined fixed overhead rate. *(p. 993)*

Voucher Internal file used to store documents and information to control cash disbursements and to ensure that a transaction is properly authorized and recorded. *(p. 322)*

Voucher register Journal (referred to as *book of original entry*) in which all vouchers are recorded after they have been approved. *(p. 337)*

Voucher system Procedures and approvals designed to control cash disbursements and acceptance of obligations. *(p. 322)*

Wage bracket withholding table Table of the amounts of income tax withheld from employees' wages. *(p. 454)*

Warranty Agreement that obligates the seller to correct or replace a product or service when it fails to perform properly within a specified period. *(p. 444)*

Weighted average Method to assign inventory cost to sales; the cost of available-for-sale units is divided by the number of units available to determine per unit cost prior to each sale that is then multiplied by the units sold to yield the cost of that sale. *(pp. 230, 245 & 818)*

Weighted-average method (See *weighted average*.)

Wholesaler Intermediary that buys products from manufacturers or other wholesalers and sells them to retailers or other wholesalers. *(p. 178)*

Withdrawals Payment of cash or other assets from a proprietorship or partnership to its owner or owners. *(p. 13)*

Work sheet Spreadsheet used to draft an unadjusted trial balance, adjusting entries, adjusted trial balance, and financial statements. *(p. 136)*

Working capital Current assets minus current liabilities at a point in time. *(p. 691)*

Working papers Analyses and other informal reports prepared by accountants and managers when organizing information for formal reports and financial statements. *(p. 136)*

Credits

Index

Note: Page numbers followed by *n* indicate material in footnotes.

Chart of Accounts

Following is a typical chart of accounts. Each company has its own unique accounts and numbering system.

Assets

Current Assets

101 Cash
102 Petty cash
103 Cash equivalents
104 Short-term investments
105 Market adjustment, _____ securities (S-T)
106 Accounts receivable
107 Allowance for doubtful accounts
108 Legal fees receivable
109 Interest receivable
110 Rent receivable
111 Notes receivable
119 Merchandise inventory
120 _____ inventory
121 _____ inventory
124 Office supplies
125 Store supplies
126 _____ supplies
128 Prepaid insurance
129 Prepaid interest
131 Prepaid rent
132 Raw materials inventory
133 Goods in process inventory, _____
134 Goods in process inventory, _____
135 Finished goods inventory

Long-Term Investments

141 Long-term investments
142 Market adjustment, _____ securities (L-T)
144 Investment in _____
145 Bond sinking fund

Plant Assets

151 Automobiles
152 Accumulated depreciation—Automobiles
153 Trucks
154 Accumulated depreciation—Trucks
155 Boats
156 Accumulated depreciation—Boats
157 Professional library
158 Accumulated depreciation—Professional
    library
159 Law library
160 Accumulated depreciation—Law library
161 Furniture
162 Accumulated depreciation—Furniture
163 Office equipment
164 Accumulated depreciation—Office equipment
165 Store equipment
166 Accumulated depreciation—Store equipment
167 _____ equipment

168 Accumulated depreciation—_____
    equipment
169 Machinery
170 Accumulated depreciation—Machinery
173 Building _____
174 Accumulated depreciation—Building _____
175 Building _____
176 Accumulated depreciation—Building _____
179 Land improvements _____
180 Accumulated depreciation—Land
    improvements _____
181 Land improvements _____
182 Accumulated depreciation—Land
    improvements _____
183 Land

Natural Resources

185 Mineral deposit
186 Accumulated depletion—Mineral deposit

Intangible Assets

191 Patents
192 Leasehold
193 Franchise
194 Copyrights
195 Leasehold improvements
196 Licenses
197 Accumulated amortization—_____

Liabilities

Current Liabilities

201 Accounts payable
202 Insurance payable
203 Interest payable
204 Legal fees payable
207 Office salaries payable
208 Rent payable
209 Salaries payable
210 Wages payable
211 Accrued payroll payable
214 Estimated warranty liability
215 Income taxes payable
216 Common dividend payable
217 Preferred dividend payable
218 State unemployment taxes payable
219 Employee federal income taxes payable
221 Employee medical insurance payable
222 Employee retirement program payable
223 Employee union dues payable
224 Federal unemployment taxes payable
225 FICA taxes payable
226 Estimated vacation pay liability

Unearned Revenues

230 Unearned consulting fees
231 Unearned legal fees
232 Unearned property management fees
233 Unearned _____ fees
234 Unearned _____ fees
235 Unearned janitorial revenue
236 Unearned _____ revenue
238 Unearned rent

Notes Payable

240 Short-term notes payable
241 Discount on short-term notes payable
245 Notes payable
251 Long-term notes payable
252 Discount on long-term notes payable

Long-Term Liabilities

253 Long-term lease liability
255 Bonds payable
256 Discount on bonds payable
257 Premium on bonds payable
258 Deferred income tax liability

Equity

Owner's Equity

301 _____, Capital
302 _____, Withdrawals
303 _____, Capital
304 _____, Withdrawals
305 _____, Capital
306 _____, Withdrawals

Paid-In Capital

307 Common stock, $ _____ par value
308 Common stock, no-par value
309 Common stock, $ _____ stated value
310 Common stock dividend distributable
311 Paid-in capital in excess of par value,
    Common stock
312 Paid-in capital in excess of stated value,
    No-par common stock
313 Paid-in capital from retirement of common
    stock
314 Paid-in capital, Treasury stock
315 Preferred stock
316 Paid-in capital in excess of par value,
    Preferred stock

Retained Earnings

318 Retained earnings
319 Cash dividends (or Dividends)
320 Stock dividends

Other Equity Accounts

321 Treasury stock, Common
322 Unrealized gain—Equity
323 Unrealized loss—Equity

Revenues

401 _____ fees earned
402 _____ fees earned
403 _____ services revenue
404 _____ services revenue
405 Commissions earned
406 Rent revenue (or Rent earned)
407 Dividends revenue (or Dividend earned)
408 Earnings from investment in _____
409 Interest revenue (or Interest earned)
410 Sinking fund earnings
413 Sales
414 Sales returns and allowances
415 Sales discounts

Cost of Sales

Cost of Goods Sold

502 Cost of goods sold
505 Purchases
506 Purchases returns and allowances
507 Purchases discounts
508 Transportation-in

Manufacturing

520 Raw materials purchases
521 Freight-in on raw materials
530 Factory payroll
531 Direct labor
540 Factory overhead
541 Indirect materials
542 Indirect labor
543 Factory insurance expired
544 Factory supervision
545 Factory supplies used
546 Factory utilities
547 Miscellaneous production costs
548 Property taxes on factory building
549 Property taxes on factory equipment
550 Rent on factory building
551 Repairs, factory equipment
552 Small tools written off
560 Depreciation of factory equipment
561 Depreciation of factory building

Standard Cost Variance

580 Direct material quantity variance
581 Direct material price variance
582 Direct labor quantity variance
583 Direct labor price variance
584 Factory overhead volume variance
585 Factory overhead controllable variance

Expenses

Amortization, Depletion, and Depreciation

601 Amortization expense—_____
602 Amortization expense—_____
603 Depletion expense—_____
604 Depreciation expense—Boats
605 Depreciation expense—Automobiles
606 Depreciation expense—Building _____
607 Depreciation expense—Building _____
608 Depreciation expense—Land improvements _____
609 Depreciation expense—Land improvements _____
610 Depreciation expense—Law library
611 Depreciation expense—Trucks
612 Depreciation expense—_____ equipment
613 Depreciation expense—_____ equipment
614 Depreciation expense—_____
615 Depreciation expense—_____

Employee-Related Expenses

620 Office salaries expense
621 Sales salaries expense
622 Salaries expense
623 _____ wages expense
624 Employees' benefits expense
625 Payroll taxes expense

Financial Expenses

630 Cash over and short
631 Discounts lost
632 Factoring fee expense
633 Interest expense

Insurance Expenses

635 Insurance expense—Delivery equipment
636 Insurance expense—Office equipment
637 Insurance expense—_____

Rental Expenses

640 Rent expense
641 Rent expense—Office space
642 Rent expense—Selling space
643 Press rental expense
644 Truck rental expense
645 _____ rental expense

Supplies Expenses

650 Office supplies expense
651 Store supplies expense
652 _____ supplies expense
653 _____ supplies expense

Miscellaneous Expenses

655 Advertising expense
656 Bad debts expense
657 Blueprinting expense
658 Boat expense
659 Collection expense
661 Concessions expense
662 Credit card expense
663 Delivery expense
664 Dumping expense
667 Equipment expense
668 Food and drinks expense
671 Gas and oil expense
672 General and administrative expense
673 Janitorial expense
674 Legal fees expense
676 Mileage expense
677 Miscellaneous expenses
678 Mower and tools expense
679 Operating expense
680 Organization expense
681 Permits expense
682 Postage expense
683 Property taxes expense
684 Repairs expense—_____
685 Repairs expense—_____
687 Selling expense
688 Telephone expense
689 Travel and entertainment expense
690 Utilities expense
691 Warranty expense
695 Income taxes expense

Gains and Losses

701 Gain on retirement of bonds
702 Gain on sale of machinery
703 Gain on sale of investments
704 Gain on sale of trucks
705 Gain on _____
706 Foreign exchange gain or loss
801 Loss on disposal of machinery
802 Loss on exchange of equipment
803 Loss on exchange of _____
804 Loss on sale of notes
805 Loss on retirement of bonds
806 Loss on sale of investments
807 Loss on sale of machinery
808 Loss on _____
809 Unrealized gain—Income
810 Unrealized loss—Income

Clearing Accounts

901 Income summary
902 Manufacturing summary

A Rose by Any Other Name

The same financial statement sometimes receives different titles. Following are some of the more common aliases.*

Balance Sheet	Statement of Financial Position
	Statement of Financial Condition
Income Statement	Statement of Income
	Operating Statement
	Statement of Operations
	Statement of Operating Activity
	Earnings Statement
	Statement of Earnings
	Profit and Loss (P&L) Statement
Statement of Cash Flows	Statement of Cash Flow
	Cash Flows Statement
	Statement of Changes in Cash Position
	Statement of Changes in Financial Position
Statement of Owner's Equity	Statement of Changes in Owner's Equity
	Statement of Changes in Owner's Capital
	Statement of Shareholders' Equity[†]
	Statement of Changes in Shareholders' Equity[†]
	Statement of Stockholders' Equity and Comprehensive Income[†]
	Statement of Changes in Capital Accounts[†]

* The term **Consolidated** often precedes or follows these statement titles to reflect the combination of different entities, such as a parent company and its subsidiaries.
[†] Corporation only.

We thank Dr. Louella Moore from Arkansas State University for suggesting this listing.

MANAGERIAL ANALYSES AND REPORTS

① Cost Types

Variable costs: Total cost changes in proportion to volume of activity
Fixed costs: Total cost does not change in proportion to volume of activity
Mixed costs: Cost consists of both a variable and a fixed element

② Cost Sources

Direct materials: Raw materials costs directly linked to finished product
Direct labor: Employee costs directly linked to finished product
Overhead: Costs indirectly linked to finished product

③ Costing Systems

Job order costing: Costs assigned to each unique unit or batch of units
Process costing: Costs assigned to similar products that are mass-produced in a continuous manner

④ Costing Ratios

Contribution margin ratio = (Net sales − Variable costs)/Net sales
Predetermined overhead rate = Estimated overhead costs/Estimated activity base
Break-even point in units = Total fixed costs/Contribution margin per unit

⑤ Planning and Control Metrics

Cost variance = Actual cost − Standard (budgeted) cost
Sales (revenue) variance = Actual sales − Standard (budgeted) sales

⑥ Capital Budgeting

Payback period = Time expected to recover investment cost
Accounting rate of return = Expected annual net income/Average annual investment
Net present value (NPV) = Present value of future cash flows − Investment cost
NPV rule: 1. Compute net present value (NPV in $)
2. If NPV ≥ 0, then accept project; If NPV < 0, then reject project
Internal rate 1. Compute internal rate of return (IRR in %)
of return rule: 2. If IRR ≥ hurdle rate, accept project; If IRR < hurdle rate, reject project

⑦ Costing Terminology

Relevant range: Organization's normal range of operating activity.
Direct cost: Cost incurred for the benefit of one cost object.
Indirect cost: Cost incurred for the benefit of more than one cost object.
Product cost: Cost that is necessary and integral to finished products.
Period cost: Cost identified more with a time period than with finished products.
Overhead cost: Cost not separately or directly traceable to a cost object.
Relevant cost: Cost that is pertinent to a decision.
Opportunity cost: Benefit lost by choosing an action from two or more alternatives.
Sunk cost: Cost already incurred that cannot be avoided or changed.
Standard cost: Cost computed using standard price and standard quantity.
Cost variance: Difference between actual cost and budgeted (standard) cost.
Budget: Formal statement of an organization's future plans.
Break-even point: Sales level at which an organization earns zero profit.
Incremental cost: Cost incurred only if the organization undertakes certain action.
Transfer price: Price on transactions between divisions within a company.

⑧ Standard Cost Variances

$$\text{Total materials variance} = \text{Materials price variance} + \text{Materials quantity variance}$$

$$\text{Total labor variance} = \text{Labor (rate) variance} + \text{Labor efficiency (quantity) variance}$$

$$\text{Total overhead variance} = \text{Overhead controllable variance} + \text{Fixed overhead volume variance}$$

$$\text{Variable overhead variance} = \text{Variable overhead spending variance} + \text{Variable overhead efficiency variance}$$

$$\text{Fixed overhead variance} = \text{Fixed overhead spending variance} + \text{Fixed overhead volume variance}$$

} = Total overhead variance

$$\text{Overhead controllable variance} = \text{Variable overhead spending variance} + \text{Variable overhead efficiency variance} + \text{Fixed overhead spending variance}$$

$$\text{Materials price variance} = [AQ \times AP] - [AQ \times SP]$$

$$\text{Materials quantity variance} = [AQ \times SP] - [SQ \times SP]$$

$$\text{Labor (rate) variance} = [AH \times AR] - [AH \times SR]$$

$$\text{Labor efficiency (quantity) variance} = [AH \times SR] - [SH \times SR]$$

$$\text{Variable overhead spending variance} = [AH \times AVR] - [AH \times SVR]$$

$$\text{Variable overhead efficiency variance} = [AH \times SVR] - [SH \times SVR]$$

$$\text{Fixed overhead spending variance} = \text{Actual overhead} - \text{Budgeted overhead}$$

$$\text{Fixed overhead volume variance} = \text{Budgeted overhead} - \text{Applied overhead}$$

where
AQ is actual quantity of materials; AP is actual price of materials; AH is actual hours of labor; AR is actual rate of wages; AVR is actual variable rate of overhead; SQ is standard quantity of materials; SP is standard price of materials; SH is standard hours of labor; SR is standard rate of wages; SVR is standard variable rate of overhead.

Manufacturing Statement
For _period_ Ended _date_

Direct materials		
Raw materials inventory, Beginning	$	#
Raw materials purchases		#
Raw materials available for use		#
Raw materials inventory, Ending		(#)
Direct materials used		#
Direct labor		#
Overhead costs		
Total overhead costs		#
Total manufacturing costs		#
Add goods in process inventory, Beginning		#
Total cost of goods in process		#
Deduct goods in process inventory, Ending		(#)
Cost of goods manufactured	$	#

Contribution Margin Income Statement
For _period_ Ended _date_

Net sales (revenues)	$	#
Total variable costs		#
Contribution margin		#
Total fixed costs		#
Net income	$	#

Flexible Budget
For _period_ Ended _date_

	Flexible Budget — Variable Amount per Unit	Flexible Budget — Fixed Cost	Flexible Budget for Unit Sales of #
Sales (revenues)	$ #		$ #
Variable costs			
Examples: Direct materials, Direct labor,			
Other variable costs	#		#
Total variable costs	#		#
Contribution margin	$ #		#
Fixed costs			
Examples: Depreciation, Manager		$ #	#
salaries, Administrative salaries		#	#
Total fixed costs		$ #	#
Income from operations			$ #

Fixed Budget Performance Report
For _period_ Ended _date_

	Fixed Budget	Actual Performance	Variances[†]
Sales: In units	#	#	
In dollars	$ #	$ #	$ # F or U
Cost of sales			
Direct costs	#	#	# F or U
Indirect costs	#	#	# F or U
Selling expenses			
Examples: Commissions,	#	#	# F or U
Shipping expenses	#	#	# F or U
General and administrative expenses			
Examples: Administrative salaries	#	#	# F or U
Total expenses	$ #	$ #	$ # F or U
Income from operations	$ #	$ #	$ # F or U

[†]F = Favorable variance; U = Unfavorable variance.

Master Budget Sequence

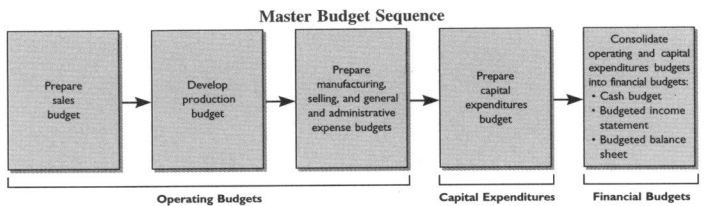

Prepare sales budget → Develop production budget → Prepare manufacturing, selling, and general and administrative expense budgets → Prepare capital expenditures budget → Consolidate operating and capital expenditures budgets into financial budgets: • Cash budget • Budgeted income statement • Budgeted balance sheet

Operating Budgets | Capital Expenditures Budget | Financial Budgets

FUNDAMENTALS

① Accounting Equation

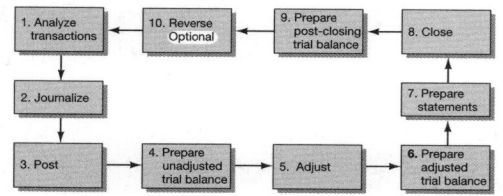

Assets		=	Liabilities		+	Equity	
↑	↓		↓	↑		↓	↑
Debit for increases	Credit for decreases		Debit for decreases	Credit for increases		Debit for decreases	Credit for increases

Owner's Capital*		−	Owner's Withdrawals*		+	Revenues		−	Expenses	
↓	↑		↓	↑		↓	↑		↑	↓
Dr. for decreases	Cr. for increases		Dr. for increases	Cr. for decreases		Dr. for decreases	Cr. for increases		Dr. for increases	Cr. for decreases

Indicates normal balance.

*Comparable corporate accounts are Common Stock (Paid-In Capital) and Dividends.

② Accounting Cycle

1. Analyze transactions
2. Journalize
3. Post
4. Prepare unadjusted trial balance
5. Adjust
6. Prepare adjusted trial balance
7. Prepare statements
8. Close
9. Prepare post-closing trial balance
10. Reverse Optional

③ Adjustments and Entries

Type	Adjusting Entry	
Prepaid Expenses	Dr. Expense	Cr. Asset*
Unearned Revenues	Dr. Liability	Cr. Revenue
Accrued Expenses	Dr. Expense	Cr. Liability
Accrued Revenues	Dr. Asset	Cr. Revenue

*For depreciation, credit Accumulated Depreciation (contra asset).

④ 4-Step Closing Process

1. Transfer revenue and gain account balances to Income Summary.
2. Transfer expense and loss account balances to Income Summary.
3. Transfer Income Summary balance to Owner's Capital.
4. Transfer Withdrawals balance to Owner's Capital.

⑤ Accounting Concepts

Characteristics	Assumptions	Principles	Constraints
Relevance	Business entity	Historical cost	Cost-benefit
Reliability	Going concern	Revenue recognition	Materiality
Comparability	Monetary unit	Matching	Industry practice
Consistency	Periodicity	Full disclosure	Conservatism

⑥ Ownership of Inventory

	Ownership Transfers When Goods Passed To	Transportation Costs Paid By
FOB Shipping Point	Carrier	Buyer
FOB Destination	Buyer	Seller

⑦ Inventory Costing Methods

Specific Identification
First-In, First-Out (FIFO)

Weighted-Average
Last-In, First-Out (LIFO)

⑧ Depreciation and Depletion

Straight-Line: $\dfrac{\text{Cost} - \text{Salvage value}}{\text{Useful life in periods}} \times \text{Periods expired}$

Units-of-Production: $\dfrac{\text{Cost} - \text{Salvage value}}{\text{Useful life in units}} \times \text{Units produced}$

Declining-Balance: $\text{Rate*} \times \text{Beginning-of-period book value}$
*Rate is often double the straight-line rate, or $2 \times (1/\text{Useful life})$

Depletion: $\dfrac{\text{Cost} - \text{Salvage value}}{\text{Total capacity in units}} \times \text{Units extracted}$

⑨ Interest Computation

$\text{Interest} = \text{Principal (face)} \times \text{Rate} \times \text{Time}$

⑩ Accounting for Investment Securities

Trading (debt and equity) securities .... Market value (with market adjustment to income)

Held-to-maturity (debt) securities*
  Short-term .... Cost (without any discount or premium amortization)
  Long-term .... Cost (with any discount or premium amortization)

Available-for-sale (debt and equity) securities* .. Market value (with market adjustment to equity)

Equity securities with significant influence ..... Equity method

*A *fair value option* allows companies to report these securities much like trading securities.

ANALYSES

① Liquidity and Efficiency

Current ratio $= \dfrac{\text{Current assets}}{\text{Current liabilities}}$ — p. 148

Working capital $= \text{Current assets} - \text{Current liabilities}$ — p. 691

Acid-test ratio $= \dfrac{\text{Cash} + \text{Short-term investments} + \text{Current receivables}}{\text{Current liabilities}}$ — p. 193

Accounts receivable turnover $= \dfrac{\text{Net sales}}{\text{Average accounts receivable, net}}$ — p. 372

Credit risk ratio $= \dfrac{\text{Allowance for doubtful accounts}}{\text{Accounts receivable, net}}$ — p. 372

Inventory turnover $= \dfrac{\text{Cost of goods sold}}{\text{Average inventory}}$ — p. 236

Days' sales uncollected $= \dfrac{\text{Accounts receivable, net}}{\text{Net sales}} \times 365\text{*}$ — p. 332

Days' sales in inventory $= \dfrac{\text{Ending inventory}}{\text{Cost of goods sold}} \times 365\text{*}$ — p. 237

Total asset turnover $= \dfrac{\text{Net sales}}{\text{Average total assets}}$ — p. 410

Plant asset useful life $= \dfrac{\text{Plant asset cost}}{\text{Depreciation expense}}$ — p. 410

Plant asset age $= \dfrac{\text{Accumulated depreciation}}{\text{Depreciation expense}}$ — p. 410

Days' cash expense coverage $= \dfrac{\text{Cash and cash equivalents}}{\text{Average daily cash expenses}}$ — p. 320

*360 days is also commonly used.

② Solvency

Debt ratio $= \dfrac{\text{Total liabilities}}{\text{Total assets}}$ Equity ratio $= \dfrac{\text{Total equity}}{\text{Total assets}}$ — pp. 67 & 695

Debt-to-equity $= \dfrac{\text{Total liabilities}}{\text{Total equity}}$ — p. 564

Times interest earned $= \dfrac{\text{Income before interest expense and income taxes}}{\text{Interest expense}}$ — p. 447

Cash coverage of growth $= \dfrac{\text{Cash flow from operations}}{\text{Cash outflow for plant assets}}$ — p. 646

Cash coverage of debt $= \dfrac{\text{Cash flow from operations}}{\text{Total noncurrent liabilities}}$ — p. 646

③ Profitability

Profit margin ratio $= \dfrac{\text{Net income}}{\text{Net sales}}$ — p. 106

Gross margin ratio $= \dfrac{\text{Net sales} - \text{Cost of goods sold}}{\text{Net sales}}$ — p. 193

Return on total assets $= \dfrac{\text{Net income}}{\text{Average total assets}}$ — p. 20

$= \text{Profit margin ratio} \times \text{Total asset turnover}$ — p. 697

Return on common stockholders' equity $= \dfrac{\text{Net income} - \text{Preferred dividends}}{\text{Average common stockholders' equity}}$ — p. 697

Book value per common share $= \dfrac{\text{Stockholders' equity applicable to common shares}}{\text{Number of common shares outstanding}}$ — p. 526

Basic earnings per share $= \dfrac{\text{Net income} - \text{Preferred dividends}}{\text{Weighted-average common shares outstanding}}$ — p. 524

Cash flow on total assets $= \dfrac{\text{Cash flow from operations}}{\text{Average total assets}}$ — p. 646

Payout ratio $= \dfrac{\text{Cash dividends declared on common stock}}{\text{Net income}}$ — p. 525

④ Market

Price-earnings ratio $= \dfrac{\text{Market value (price) per share}}{\text{Earnings per share}}$ — p. 525

Dividend yield $= \dfrac{\text{Annual cash dividends per share}}{\text{Market price per share}}$ — p. 525

Residual income $= \text{Net income} - \text{Target net income}$